Royal Air Force
BOMBER COMMAND LOSSES

Volume 9
Roll of Honour
Advanced Air Striking Force
Air Component of the British Expeditionary Force
(18 and 57 Squadron)
Bomber Command
1939 - 1947

'When I look around to see how we can win the war I see that there is only one sure path. We have no continental army which can defeat the German military power. The blockade is broken and Hitler has Asia and probably Africa to draw from. Should he be repulsed here or not try invasion, he will recoil eastward, and we have nothing to stop him. But there is one thing that will bring him back and bring him down, and that is an absolutely devastating, exterminating attack by very heavy bombers from this country upon the Nazi homeland.'

Winston Churchill, 8th July 1940.

MIDLAND
An imprint of
Ian Allan Publishing

Royal Air Force
BOMBER COMMAND LOSSES
Volume 9

ROLL OF HONOUR
1939-1947

W R CHORLEY

First published 2007

ISBN (10) 1 85780 195 4
ISBN (13) 978 1 85780 195 8

All rights reserved. No part of this book may be reproduced or transmitted in any form or by any means, electronic or mechanical, including photocopying, recording or by any information storage and retrieval system, without permission from the Publisher in writing.

© W R Chorley 2007

Published by Midland Publishing
an imprint of Ian Allan Publishing Ltd, Hersham, Surrey
KT12 4RG

Printed in England by Ian Allan Printing Ltd, Hersham, Surrey KT12 4RG

Visit the Ian Allan Publishing website at:
www.ianallanpublishing.com

Code: 0712/B2

The illustration above:
The Berlin 1939-1945 War Cemetery where nearly 3,000 Allied airmen now rest. Most lost their lives in the gruelling winter of 1943-1944, a period now recognised as ranking with the hardest in Bomber Command's history. Martin Grädler

On the half-title page:
The Cross of Sacrifice at the Berlin 1939-1945 War Cemetery. Martin Grädler

The Royal Air Force Bomber Command badge featured on the front cover and title page is acknowledged as a Crown copyright / RAF photograph.

Contents

	A Table of Units and Dates 3rd September 1939 to 31st December 1947	6
	Introduction	7
Part 1	Advanced Air Striking Force Roll of Honour	9
Part 2	Air Component of the British Expeditionary Force (18 and 57 Squadron) Roll of Honour	14
Part 3	Bomber Command Roll of Honour 3rd September to 31st December 1939	16
Part 4	Bomber Command Roll of Honour – 1940	21
Part 5	Bomber Command Roll of Honour – 1941	44
Part 6	Bomber Command Roll of Honour – 1942	91
Part 7	Bomber Command Roll of Honour – 1943	168
Part 8	Bomber Command Roll of Honour – 1944	295
Part 9	Bomber Command Roll of Honour – 1945	438
Part 10	Bomber Command Roll of Honour – 1946	478
Part 11	Bomber Command Roll of Honour – 1947	480
Appendix 1	A Table of Casualty Statistics	483
Appendix 2	A Table of Personnel Statistics	485
Appendix 3	Airmen Who Died in Captivity	487
	Sources & Bibliography	494

Royal Air Force – Bomber Command
3rd September 1939 to 31st December 1947

A table of dates for operational squadrons and No.1409 Flight, followed by the Operational Training Units, Heavy Conversion Units, No.1655 Mosquito Training Unit and Lancaster Finishing Schools, whose fallen are eligible for inclusion in the Roll of Honour. Omitted from the table, but whose members are commemorated in the Roll, are the myriad of flights and various miscellaneous units formed to assist in the training and development of Bomber Command operations.

Unit	From		To	Unit	From		To	Unit	From		To	Unit	From		To
7 Sqn	3-09-39	to	31-12-47	139 Sqn	3-09-39	to	1-12-41	408 Sqn	24-06-41	to	14-06-45	14 OTU	8-04-40	to	24-06-45
9 Sqn	3-09-40	to	31-12-47		8-06-42	to	31-12-47	415 Sqn	12-07-44	to	15-05-45	15 OTU	8-04-40	to	15-03-44
10 Sqn	3-09-39	to	7-05-45	141 Sqn	4-12-43	to	2-09-45	419 Sqn	15-12-41	to	4-06-45	16 OTU	8-04-40	to	15-03-47
12 Sqn	3-09-39	to	31-12-47	142 Sqn	3-09-39	to	27-01-43	420 Sqn	19-12-42	to	12-06-45	17 OTU	8-04-40	to	15-03-47
15 Sqn	3-09-39	to	31-12-47		25-10-44	to	28-09-45	424 Sqn	15-10-42	to	15-10-45	18 OTU	15-06-40	to	30-01-45
18 Sqn	3-09-39	to	11-11-42	144 Sqn	3-09-39	to	22-04-42	425 Sqn	25-06-42	to	13-06-45	19 OTU	27-05-40	to	26-06-45
21 Sqn	3-09-39	to	1-06-43	148 Sqn	3-09-39	to	23-05-40	426 Sqn	15-10-42	to	25-05-45	20 OTU	27-05-40	to	17-07-45
23 Sqn	1-06-44	to	25-09-45		4-11-46	to	31-12-47	427 Sqn	7-11-42	to	31-05-46	21 OTU	21-01-41	to	15-03-47
35 Sqn	3-09-39	to	31-12-47	149 Sqn	3-09-39	to	31-12-47	428 Sqn	7-11-42	to	31-05-45	22 OTU	14-04-41	to	24-07-45
37 Sqn	3-09-39	to	30-11-40	150 Sqn	3-09-39	to	27-01-43	429 Sqn	7-11-42	to	31-05-46	23 OTU	1-04-41	to	15-03-44
38 Sqn	3-09-39	to	22-11-40		1-11-44	to	7-11-45	431 Sqn	11-11-42	to	12-06-45	24 OTU	15-03-42	to	27-07-45
40 Sqn	3-09-39	to	31-10-41	153 Sqn	7-10-44	to	28-09-45	432 Sqn	1-05-43	to	15-05-45	25 OTU	1-03-41	to	1-02-43
44 Sqn	3-09-39	to	31-12-47	156 Sqn	14-02-42	to	25-09-45	433 Sqn	25-09-43	to	15-10-45	26 OTU	15-01-42	to	4-03-46
49 Sqn	3-09-39	to	31-12-47	157 Sqn	7-05-44	to	16-08-45	434 Sqn	13-06-43	to	15-06-45	27 OTU	23-04-41	to	22-06-45
50 Sqn	3-09-39	to	31-12-47	158 Sqn	14-02-42	to	7-05-45	455 Sqn	6-06-41	to	27-04-42	28 OTU	16-05-42	to	15-10-44
51 Sqn	3-09-39	to	7-05-45	161 Sqn	15-02-42	to	9-03-45	458 Sqn	25-08-41	to	20-03-42	29 OTU	21-04-42	to	27-05-45
52 Sqn	3-09-39	to	8-04-40	162 Sqn	18-12-44	to	10-07-45	460 Sqn	15-11-41	to	10-10-45	30 OTU	28-06-42	to	12-06-45
57 Sqn	3-09-39	to	31-12-47	163 Sqn	25-01-45	to	10-08-45	462 Sqn	12-08-44	to	24-09-45	81 OTU	10-07-42	to	1-01-44
58 Sqn	3-09-39	to	7-04-42	166 Sqn	3-09-39	to	18-11-45	463 Sqn	25-11-43	to	25-09-45	82 OTU	1-06-43	to	9-01-45
61 Sqn	3-09-39	to	31-12-47	169 Sqn	8-12-43	to	10-08-45	464 Sqn	1-09-42	to	1-06-43	83 OTU	1-08-43	to	28-10-44
63 Sqn	3-09-39	to	8-04-40	170 Sqn	15-10-44	to	14-11-45	466 Sqn	15-10-42	to	7-05-45	84 OTU	1-09-43	to	14-06-45
75 Sqn	3-09-39	to	15-10-45	171 Sqn	8-09-44	to	27-07-45	467 Sqn	7-11-42	to	30-09-45				
76 Sqn	3-09-39	to	7-05-45	180 Sqn	13-09-42	to	1-06-43	487 Sqn	15-08-42	to	1-06-43	1651 HCU	2-01-42	to	13-07-45
77 Sqn	3-09-39	to	7-05-45	185 Sqn	3-09-39	to	17-05-40	514 Sqn	1-09-43	to	22-08-45	1652 HCU	2-01-42	to	25-06-45
78 Sqn	3-09-39	to	7-05-45	186 Sqn	5-10-44	to	17-07-45	515 Sqn	15-12-43	to	10-06-45	1653 HCU	9-01-42	to	15-03-47
82 Sqn	3-09-39	to	21-03-42	189 Sqn	15-10-44	to	20-11-45	550 Sqn	25-11-43	to	31-10-45	1654 HCU	19-05-42	to	1-09-45
83 Sqn	3-09-39	to	31-12-47	192 Sqn	4-01-43	to	22-08-45	571 Sqn	7-04-44	to	20-09-45	1656 HCU	10-10-42	to	10-11-45
85 Sqn	1-05-44	to	27-06-45	195 Sqn	14-10-44	to	25-10-45	576 Sqn	25-11-43	to	13-09-45	1657 HCU	2-10-42	to	15-12-44
88 Sqn	3-09-39	to	23-06-40	196 Sqn	7-11-42	to	18-11-43	578 Sqn	14-01-44	to	15-04-45	1658 HCU	7-10-42	to	13-04-45
	8-07-41	to	1-06-43	199 Sqn	7-11-42	to	29-07-45	582 Sqn	1-04-44	to	10-09-45	1659 HCU	7-10-42	to	10-09-45
90 Sqn	3-09-39	to	31-12-47	207 Sqn	3-09-39	to	31-12-47	608 Sqn	1-08-44	to	28-08-45	1660 HCU	22-10-42	to	11-11-46
97 Sqn	3-09-39	to	31-12-47	214 Sqn	3-09-39	to	27-07-45	617 Sqn	21-03-43	to	31-12-47	1661 HCU	9-11-42	to	24-08-45
98 Sqn	3-09-39	to	27-07-40		4-11-46	to	31-12-47	619 Sqn	18-04-43	to	18-07-45	1662 HCU	26-01-43	to	6-04-45
	12-09-42	to	1-06-43	215 Sqn	3-09-39	to	12-02-42	620 Sqn	17-06-43	to	13-11-43	1663 HCU	2-03-43	to	28-05-45
99 Sqn	3-09-39	to	1-01-42	218 Sqn	3-09-39	to	10-08-45	622 Sqn	10-08-43	to	15-08-45	1664 HCU	10-05-43	to	6-04-45
100 Sqn	15-12-42	to	31-12-47	223 Sqn	23-08-44	to	29-07-45	623 Sqn	10-08-43	to	6-12-43	1665 HCU	23-04-43	to	23-01-44
101 Sqn	3-09-39	to	31-12-47	226 Sqn	3-09-39	to	27-06-40	625 Sqn	1-10-43	to	7-10-45	1666 HCU	5-06-43	to	3-08-45
102 Sqn	3-09-39	to	7-05-45		26-05-41	to	1-06-43	626 Sqn	7-11-43	to	14-10-45	1667 HCU	1-06-43	to	9-11-45
103 Sqn	3-09-39	to	26-11-45	227 Sqn	7-10-44	to	5-09-45	627 Sqn	12-11-43	to	1-10-45	1668 HCU	15-08-43	to	7-03-46
104 Sqn	3-09-39	to	14-02-42	239 Sqn	9-12-43	to	1-07-45	630 Sqn	15-11-43	to	18-07-45	1669 HCU	15-08-44	to	16-03-45
105 Sqn	3-09-39	to	1-02-46	300 Sqn	1-07-40	to	11-10-46	635 Sqn	20-03-44	to	1-09-45	1678 HCU	18-05-43	to	12-06-44
106 Sqn	3-09-39	to	18-02-46	301 Sqn	22-07-40	to	7-04-43	640 Sqn	7-01-44	to	7-05-44	1679 HCU	18-05-43	to	27-01-44
107 Sqn	3-09-39	to	1-06-43	304 Sqn	22-08-40	to	7-05-42	692 Sqn	1-01-44	to	20-09-44				
108 Sqn	3-09-39	to	8-04-40	305 Sqn	29-08-40	to	5-09-43					1655 MTU	30-08-42	to	31-12-44
109 Sqn	10-12-40	to	31-12-47	311 Sqn	29-07-40	to	28-04-42	1409 Flight	1-04-43	to	10-10-44				
110 Sqn	3-09-39	to	17-03-42	320 Sqn	15-03-43	to	1-06-43					1 LFS	21-11-43	to	25-11-44
114 Sqn	3-09-39	to	15-11-42	342 Sqn	7-04-43	to	1-06-43	10 OTU	8-04-40	to	10-09-46	3 LFS	21-11-43	to	31-01-45
115 Sqn	3-09-39	to	31-12-47	346 Sqn	16-05-44	to	20-10-45	11 OTU	8-04-40	to	18-09-45	5 LFS	21-11-43	to	1-04-45
128 Sqn	15-09-44	to	20-09-45	347 Sqn	20-06-44	to	20-10-45	12 OTU	8-04-40	to	22-06-45				
138 Sqn	25-08-41	to	31-12-47	405 Sqn	23-04-41	to	16-06-45	13 OTU	8-04-40	to	1-06-43				

Introduction

'The service being ended the Commander-in-Chief, Bomber Command* led the congregation in procession past the Memorial, where relatives placed their floral tributes and silently filed out of the great Cathedral into the dusk of a November evening.'
*(Air Marshall Sir George H. Mills KCB DFC)

These solemn words ended the report of a ceremony that took place over fifty years ago during the afternoon of the 6th November, 1955, in the proceedings of which the Memorial Books of Nos. 2, 3, 8 and 100 Groups were laid in a special cabinet in Ely Cathedral. Six years previous, a similar service of dedication had been held in Lincoln Cathedral where, in the Airmen's Chapel of St. Michael, the Memorial books of Nos. 1 and 5 Bomber Groups were deposited.

These two ceremonies collectively commemorate the names of 40,000 airmen and airwomen, since when Books of Remembrance for those who died in the service of Nos. 4, 6 and 7 Groups have been laid up in York Minster.

No other Command in the rich history of the Royal Air Force witnessed such a sacrifice of lives. Each time that I read the opening lines of my first paragraph, I think of those aircrew who walked out *'into the dusk'* never to see such a spectacle again. Since the publication in 1992, of the first volume in this series of books it has been my intention to set down in much fuller detail their names and those of the not insignificant numbers of ground staff without whose unstinting support final Victory in the bombing campaign would not have been possible. The first appendix to this volume will explain in detail the breakdown of the Command's casualties and, therefore, for the purpose of this introduction it is suffice to say that the pages that follow commemorate the names of well over 57,000 service personnel and the few civilians whose occupation brought them into the fold of the Command's duties.

An explanation of the manner in which the Roll is being presented and the appropriate, and very necessary acknowledgements is most important, particularly in respect of my fellow researchers who have without exception been so generous in allowing me to use material from their published works. Concerning the layout, it was my intention to append against each entry and where appropriate the serial number of the aircraft in which they were flying along with some form of abbreviated reference as to their place of burial, plus the page number in the volume relevant to their place in the Roll. For a multitude of reasons, this approach proved impossible and, therefore, a decision was made to confine each entry to service number, rank, surname, decorations (if any), Christian names, date of death and unit. This much simplified presentation allows for a double column of names on each page and a less than fussy appearance overall. I must draw attention to the fact that there are discrepancies between official documents, most commonly in the reporting of dates of death where variances of 24-hours are rife and the interpretation of common Christian names; 'Alan/Allan' being a prime example. I have attempted to reconcile these differences but I am certain that in doing so there are instances where I have strayed in the wrong direction.

It was also agreed that the Roll should be broken down into a series of parts, each part commencing with an introduction and ending (where thought necessary) with a postscript. Heading the names within each part are those who fell while serving with the Royal Air Force and, as the war progressed and the Commonwealth and Dominion and other Allied air forces became involved, headings in the order of the Royal Australian Air Force, Royal Canadian Air Force *et al* with a final section for Attached personnel. As will be seen, I have added notes to some of the sections and I particularly wish to apologise in advance for any omissions that some readers may consider to have been important for me to comment upon. May I assure everyone that I intend no slight, for I am forever mindful of the anguish and pain that remains to this day amongst the families and friends who lost their loved ones in those terrible years of conflict.

I now come to the important task of identifying my sources, first and foremost of which are the cemetery registers published by the Commonwealth War Graves Commission, supported by their quite indispensable website and on the occasions when I have found it necessary to speak direct to their Maidenhead office, an ever approachable and very professional staff.

Of equal importance has been the unqualified access allowed me by the Air Historical Branch to look at the Casualty Returns which have been invaluable in providing me with details in respect of the Free French Air Force and, to a limited degree, the United States Army Air Force, information that is not readily available from the Commonwealth War Graves Commission. Where Polish Air Force casualties are concerned, I pay the most generous tribute to Betty Clements who, since the outset of writing these nine volumes, has been instrumental in checking my data and I know that Betty would wish me to give *blanket* acknowledgement and thanks to the many individuals and institutions, particularly the Polish Institute and Sikorski Museum and its Keeper of Archives, Dr. Andrzey Suchcitz F.R.Hist.S, with whom she has corresponded with over the years in building up her own database dedicated to those gallant Polish airmen who arrived upon our shores in the early years of the war to carry on the fight to free their country of Nazi domination. Their sacrifice has been particularly poignant in that when Victory at last came, their homeland was left in the grip of a regime that was nearly equal to that of their previous oppressors.

I am also indebted to the Australian War Memorial Roll of Honour website (which is one of the many links available off the Commonwealth War Graves Commission's website) which has enabled me to identify more than a few Royal Australian Air Force personnel that lost their lives while posted to Bomber Command units, but whose death occurred in non-flying circumstances.

Likewise, Les Allison's and Harry Hayward's magnificent tribute to the Royal Canadian Air Force, published under the title *They Shall Grow Not Old* has been consulted constantly in respect of Canadian deaths and I freely acknowledge that the notes appended at the end of the Royal Canadian Air Force sections would not have been possible without the information provided by the authors concerned in recording a biography for over 18,000 airmen whose names appear between the covers of their work. In the same vein it has been my good fortune to have in my library copies of *For Your Tomorrow*, Errol Martyn's two volume dedication to the New Zealanders who have died in their country's air force and other Allied air services twixt 1915 and 1998. His many observations (like those of Allison and Hayward) have provided me with much additional material to add to the lists of names that appear under the heading, 'Royal New Zealand Air Force'. I also acknowledge the meticulous research of Oliver Clutton-Brock which culminated in 2003 with the publication of his treatise on Bomber Command's 10,999 prisoners of war. Thus, any reference to deaths occurring in captivity has as its source Oliver's titled work *Footprints On The Sands Of Time*. These three publications are essential reading for any student of air force history.

A secondary source, though no less important, are the Rolls of Honour alluded to in my opening paragraph. A bound copy, the property of the late Bill Baguley (whose name will be familiar to readers of my work) was kindly presented to me by Moira Baguley in the knowledge that when the time came to preparing the Roll, I would make full use of its content. Prepared in the late 1940s and early 1950s, these Rolls are similar in presentation to the layout of this volume, except for service numbers that have been omitted from five of the six Rolls, the exception being No.5 Group where such data is included at the expense of any unit detail! Nevertheless, I have been able to identify the names of numerous ground staff that otherwise would have escaped my attention.

I also wish to thank the many individuals who have lent their support to the series as a whole and who have produced booklets or longer treatises from which I have been allowed to draw notes. Principal of those coming within this area of assistance are Peter and Maureen Wilson who produced a Roll of Honour commemorating those who died in service of 149 Squadron and 622 Squadron; Roy Walker's similar work in respect of 77 Squadron; the Roll of Honour prepared by Frank Slack and Raymond Glynne-Owen for the two Royal Australian Air Force Lancasters squadrons '467' and '463' and in acknowledging Raymond Glynne-Owen I add a very special *'thank you'* for giving his time to read through and amend where necessary the 207 Squadron entries reported in the pages that follow this introduction.

Hugh Cawdron has not only written two detailed accounts of 578 Squadron in which the names of those who fell are recorded in full, but has worked tirelessly since in editing the squadron's newsletter *The LK Times*. Similarly, Frank Haslam has for many years edited the *207 Squadron Royal Air Force Association* newsletter and, in more recent times, the squadron's excellent website. Both produce letters of the highest standard, the '207' missive often carrying commemorative features in respect of memorials to their wartime colleagues who failed to return.

Three authors deserve a special salute for the fact they have produced books that concentrate not on the bomber squadrons but on airfields that were primarily concerned with the vital training formations without which the front-line units could not have functioned effectively. Eric Kaye and Brian Kedward turned their attention to those airfields that, in the main, principally supported Operational Training Units, Brian's contribution being a detailed account of the airfields at Honeybourne and Long Marston, the former base being home twixt March 1942 and its disbandment in July 1945, for No.24 Operational Training Unit. Eric, meanwhile, has made a major contribution to Royal Air Force history in his telling of the story of Royal Air Force Edgehill, better known to the villagers who lived within the airfield circuit as Shenington Aerodrome. Satellite at various times to both Nos. 12 and 21 Operational Training Units, Edgehill provided a key role in the training of embryo bomber crews. Brian Mennell took the history of Rufforth airfield as his subject and in doing so has commemorated well the activities of No.1663 Heavy Conversion Unit. A fourth author is also worthy of mention in the context of this subject matter; A. A. B. Todd, a chartered architect by profession who in the early 1990s published the history of Royal Air Force Croft which from 1941 onwards hosted operational squadrons that were assigned firstly to No.4 Group and secondly to No.6 (RCAF) Group interspersed (May to December 1943) with a training formation before reverting back to hosting two Royal Canadian Air Force operational bomber squadrons. All four books contain reference to aircrew and ground staff casualties and from which I have been able to enhance the value of my Roll. Also, it would be remiss of me not to acknowledge past help provided by Peter Cunliffe, Chris Pointon, Gerry V. Tyack MBE and Graham Warner.

Eric E. Rowley and Colin Lees' Roll of Honour 1939-1945 for Sparkhill Commercial School and Don Morgan's work *Lest We Forget* have been drawn upon and I also acknowledge the help and support of John Whitehouse who has done so much over several decades to ensure that those who died while flying from Stradishall are never forgotten. In the same vein, Peter Walker has done much to perpetuate the names of those who laid down their lives in the service of 214 Squadron, while the late Keith Ford will be forever remembered for his meticulous account of 51 Squadron.

The photographs used in this volume have come from a number of helpers and in respect of private archive material I thank Brian Walker whose enthusiasm and willing help in all things historical are legion, Andrew Chorley for his coverage of Boldre cemetery and Martin Grädler of Berlin for his selection of images taken at the city's 1939-1945 War Cemetery. The selection of photographs illustrating some of the major concentration cemeteries and the back cover view showing The Runnymede Memorial have been reproduced through the kind permission of the Commonwealth War Graves Commission.

I also pay a most deserved tribute to my publishers who have provided me with unqualified support throughout the span of this series, particularly remembering Chris Salter and Neil Lewis at the Hinckley facility and now both enjoying retirement; Russ Strong, who has been instrumental in pulling my exported files into shape and helping to allay my concerns over various matters concerning final presentation, an area in which my very technically minded son, Andrew, has been able to provide on the spot help and calming assurance when I have become frustrated in my limited knowledge of computer workings. I also thank Peter Waller and his successor Nick Grant, my principal and ever-helpful contacts at Ian Allan's Hersham office. Our discussions have always been concluded in mutual agreement on the way forward throughout the production of this ninth volume.

Finally, and bearing in mind the solemnity of the subject matter that follows I conclude with the third verse of Henry H. Milman's inspirational Palm Sunday hymn:

Ride on, ride on in majesty!

The winged squadrons of the sky

Look down with sad and wondering eyes

To see the approaching Sacrifice.

Bill Chorley, September 2007.

Part 1

Advanced Air Striking Force Roll of Honour

On the 24th of August, 1939, No.1 Group, Bomber Command, was redesignated Headquarters Advanced Air Striking Force (AASF) and, thus, on the eve of war its ten squadrons of Fairey Battle light bombers left their bases in the United Kingdom and headed for France. It is not within the remit of this volume to report, in detail, an exact account of what happened to these squadrons but it is worth recording that the limitations of the Battle as an effective vehicle to carry out daylight reconnaissance (low-level bombing did not feature until the *Blitzkrieg* of May, 1940) operations was cruelly exposed within a few weeks of their arrival on French soil. Perhaps, somewhat fortuitously, a combination of circumstances not least being the prevarication of the French when discussing operational policy, restricted the Battle squadrons from being overly used and it is the cataclysmic events of May, 1940 for which the sacrificial bravery of the Fairey Battle crews is best remembered. As the following pages show most died in the five weeks or so that it took the Germans to inflict a humiliating defeat on the British and French armies, culminating in the evacuation from the beaches around Dunkirk of the British Expeditionary Force, and for the proud nation of France, the beginning of an uncertain future under the heel of Nazi domination. In closing this brief summary mention must be made of the two Blenheim squadrons that joined the Advanced Air Striking Force, and the loss to enemy bombing of the 16,243 ton HMT *Lancastria* lying in Charpentier Roads off St. Nazaire during the afternoon of the 17th of June. The two Blenheim squadrons, namely 114 Squadron and 139 Squadron, had replaced two Battle squadrons during the winter of 1939-1940 and, I surmise, had the so called *Phoney War* lasted a few months longer further replacements by Blenheim squadrons may well have taken place. However, of the former (114 Squadron), its participation in the ensuing debacle of air operations was practically non-existent for most of its Blenheims were destroyed on the ground within 24 hours of the *Blitzkrieg* commencing, while the latter suffered the most appalling casualties on the 12th and 14th of May while carrying out low-level attacks on German columns (it was on the 12th, and while attempting to stem enemy spearhead attacks near the Dutch city of Maastricht that F/O McPherson, famed for his part in leading the Second World War's first operational sortie, lost his life and it was the day, too, that F/O Garland and Sgt Gray, pilot and observer respectively of a 12 Squadron Battle, each won their country's highest honour, the Victoria Cross). The tragedy of the *Lancastria* is mentioned because the sinking claimed the lives of between 4,500 and 5,000* servicemen and civilians, which included nearly one hundred airmen, primarily ground staff, from 98 Squadron, a Battle formation that had joined the AASF in a training capacity in mid-April, 1940. Ironically, therefore, it was a non-operational unit that sustained the most casualties under AASF control. Most are commemorated on the Runnymede Memorial, as is AC1 Richardson, whose details appear in this section, but with a date of presumed death given as the 25th of June, 1940.

* News of the disaster did not break until the 26th of July, 1940, on which date the first reports of what had befallen the *Lancastria* appeared in newspapers published in New York. Until then Winston Churchill had placed a strict embargo on any hint of what had occurred and the sensitivity of this the worst British maritime loss (eclipsing the loss of life from the *Titanic* by a substantial margin) will not be fully debated by historians until 2040 with the release into the National Archives of the courts of enquiry findings. Thus, the figures shown above are only an estimate as the precise recording of numbers boarding the vessel was abandoned after, it is thought, 4,000 had been ferried out from the quayside and with many more still to come. Amongst those who had been waiting to board was the author's brother, Aircraftman Edwin Chorley and it was only a last-minute demand being put on his ambulance unit that saved him from being a potential victim.

ROYAL AIR FORCE,
AUXILIARY AIR FORCE and
ROYAL AIR FORCE (VOLUNTEER RESERVE)
personnel

563017	Sgt	ABBOTT Frank Bernard	14-05-40	105 Sqn
551745	Sgt	AINSWORTH Ronald Theodore	14-05-40	12 Sqn
563545	Sgt	ALDERSON Kenneth	14-05-40	12 Sqn
40350	P/O	ANDERSON Colin Cecil Robert	26-05-40	88 Sqn
525720	Sgt	ANNING William John	12-05-40	105 Sqn
906916	AC2	APPLIN Edward Charles Sydney	17-06-40	98 Sqn
581488	Sgt	ARDERN Walter	17-06-40	98 Sqn
907022	AC2	ASHARD Ernest Francis	17-06-40	98 Sqn
751819	Sgt	ATKINS Jack Frederick	7-06-40	150 Sqn
580557	Sgt	ATKINSON Gordon	14-05-40	105 Sqn
529181	LAC	BAGULEY Herbert	10-05-40	218 Sqn
552069	AC1	BAILEY Albert	20-04-40	218 Sqn
533587	LAC	BAKER Harold Reginald	14-05-40	139 Sqn
581492	Sgt	BAKER Leslie George	17-06-40	98 Sqn
580936	Sgt	BALLANTYNE John	12-06-40	88 Sqn
563835	F/S	BARKER George Thomas	14-05-40	150 Sqn
580937	Sgt	BARKER Thomas Roy	12-05-40	150 Sqn
566573	Sgt	BARNWELL Harold James	11-05-40	105 Sqn
547360	LAC	BARRIE George Wellesley	17-06-40	98 Sqn
535546	LAC	BATEMAN George	17-06-40	98 Sqn
70790	P/O	BAZALGETTE Frederick Sidney	12-05-40	218 Sqn
44679	P/O	BEALE Roy Cuthbert	13-06-40	150 Sqn
522176	Sgt	BEAMES Frank Ennis	14-05-40	88 Sqn
580477	Sgt	BELCHER Edward Joseph	19-05-40	12 Sqn
947377	AC2	BELLAMY Charles Victor	17-06-40	98 Sqn
563098	Sgt	BEVAN Herbert Cyril Claude	7-06-40	12 Sqn
631221	AC1	BIRD Raymond	20-05-40	142 Sqn
954766	AC2	BLACKETT George	17-06-40	98 Sqn
935698	LAC	BLACKWELL Frank James	17-06-40	98 Sqn
541182	Sgt	BLIGH Peter Ivo	10-06-40	103 Sqn
77782	P/O	BLOWFIELD Philip Harvey	14-05-40	12 Sqn
523009	Sgt	BODDINGTON John Percy	8-06-40	12 Sqn
751838	Sgt	BONIFACE Ronald John	17-06-40	98 Sqn

Number	Rank	Name	Date	Sqn
40597	P/O	BOON John	14-05-40	150 Sqn
913271	AC2	BOTT Kenneth Victor	17-06-40	98 Sqn
581262	Sgt	BOWEN Donald Joseph	14-05-40	150 Sqn
618097	LAC	BOYLE William Donald	19-05-40	142 Sqn
564122	Sgt	BRANTON John Royal	7-04-40	226 Sqn
560537	Sgt	BROOKES MiD James	14-05-40	142 Sqn
627081	AC2	BROWN Douglas	17-06-40	98 Sqn
943513	AC2	BROWN George Oswald	17-06-40	98 Sqn
534385	LAC	BROWN Thomas Wilfred	14-05-40	114 Sqn
946579	AC2	BRUNTON John	17-06-40	98 Sqn
973456	AC2	BURROWS Harry	17-06-40	98 Sqn
542020	LAC	BURT Charles Sydney	8-06-40	12 Sqn
520538	Sgt	BUTLER Richard William [Canada]	26-05-40	88 Sqn
70894	P/O	BUTTERY Robert Thomas Lothian	14-05-40	218 Sqn
580434	Sgt	CALDWELL Robert Charles	11-06-40	88 Sqn
565694	Sgt	CALLAGHAN James Benedict	13-06-40	226 Sqn
39491	P/O	CALVERT James Lionel	20-09-39	150 Sqn
39455	F/O	CAMERON Douglas Alexander [Australia]	10-05-40	226 Sqn
40603	P/O	CAMPBELL-IRONS Ian	12-05-40	150 Sqn
534454	Sgt	CARTER Douglas Barfield	13-06-40	150 Sqn
580604	Sgt	CARTWRIGHT Geoffrey Andrew	14-05-40	105 Sqn
510279	Cpl	CARTWRIGHT James	17-06-40	98 Sqn
580408	Sgt	CHAPMAN Ernest Walter James	29-05-40	88 Sqn
541344	LAC	CHILD Charles Colby [Canada]	12-05-40	139 Sqn
906929	AC2	CHILDS Thomas Harry	17-06-40	98 Sqn
537378	Cpl	CLARK Robert Stanley	14-05-40	226 Sqn
640028	AC1	CLARKE Donald Basil	17-06-40	98 Sqn
518910	LAC	CLARKE Sydney	17-06-40	98 Sqn
533480	Sgt	CLAWLEY George William	7-06-40	150 Sqn
366072	Sgt	COLE William Frederick Lessey 'Willie'	30-09-39	150 Sqn
532979	Cpl	COOK Albert Charles	17-06-40	98 Sqn
633627	AC1	COOPER James William	17-06-40	98 Sqn
32190	F/O	CORELLI Fernald Michael Clifford	30-09-39	150 Sqn
580948	Sgt	COTTERELL Norman Clifford	13-06-40	12 Sqn
533672	Cpl	COUGHTREY Frank	31-03-40	105 Sqn
39858	F/O	CRANE John Frederick Ryder	14-05-40	218 Sqn
900352	LAC	CROSS Reginald Alfred Richard	17-06-40	98 Sqn
36212	P/O	CUNNINGHAM Vernon Allan [New Zealand]	14-05-40	103 Sqn
39861	F/O	CURTIS Christopher Douglas	1-01-40	114 Sqn
564067	Sgt	CURTIS Ernest Frank Wilton	13-06-40	142 Sqn
568835	Cpl	DANIEL Henry	17-06-40	98 Sqn
537015	LAC	DAVIES Leslie Douglas	12-05-40	218 Sqn
540572	LAC	DAVIES Percy Kenyon	7-04-40	226 Sqn
580509	Sgt	DAVIS Thomas William	12-05-40	139 Sqn
563790	Sgt	DAVISON Edward	20-04-40	218 Sqn
509566	Sgt	DENTON Thomas Frederick	17-06-40	98 Sqn
39228	P/O	DEVOTO David [Eire]	31-03-40	150 Sqn
522984	Sgt	DEWAR Frank	1-03-40	218 Sqn
33185	F/O	de MONTMORENCY Reymond Hervey	14-05-40	139 Sqn
41679	P/O	DE SOUZA Kenneth Mitchell Alves	16-05-40	139 Sqn
619976	AC2	DIGNAN George Alfred	17-06-40	98 Sqn
563473	Sgt	DOCKRILL Charles James Ernest	11-05-40	218 Sqn
41525	P/O	DODGSON Harold	27-02-40	114 Sqn
563966	Sgt	DORMER Percival Frank	11-05-40	218 Sqn
751081	LAC	DOWDING John Henry	17-06-40	98 Sqn
580365	Sgt	DOWLING Albert Nelson	15-06-40	103 Sqn
40610	P/O	DRABBLE Kenneth John	10-05-40	103 Sqn
563086	F/S	DUNN William Alfred	14-05-40	226 Sqn
41270	P/O	EDGAR Allan Matheson [Australia]	26-03-40	105 Sqn
550864	AC1	EDWARDS Clement Allan	29-05-40	88 Sqn
563772	Sgt	EGGINGTON Alfred William	20-09-39	88 Sqn
580950	Sgt	EMERY Gerald Henry	14-06-40	12 Sqn
563100	Sgt	EVERETT William Stanley	20-09-39	88 Sqn
40216	F/O	EVITT Henry George	29-05-40	88 Sqn
39866	F/O	FARRELL Patrick Arthur Ludlow	7-04-40	142 Sqn
41388	P/O	FARROW Robert William [Australia]	3-03-40	114 Sqn
535052	Sgt	FIELD Frederick James	7-06-40	12 Sqn
565318	Sgt	FINDLAY Duncan Cameron	26-03-40	103 Sqn
551310	LAC	FISHER Harry	17-06-40	98 Sqn
629004	AC1	FitzPATRICK Thomas	17-06-40	98 Sqn
564186	Sgt	FLISHER Leonard Charles	12-05-40	218 Sqn
580423	Sgt	FOOTNER Kenneth Douglas	12-05-40	12 Sqn
521800	Sgt	FORTUNE Thomas	14-05-40	150 Sqn
581049	Sgt	FRASER Jack Nairn	11-06-40	142 Sqn
533153	LAC	GARBETT Harold Tebbutt	12-05-40	139 Sqn
40105	F/O	GARLAND VC Donald Edward	12-05-40	12 Sqn
978500	AC2	GARSIDE Cyril	17-06-40	98 Sqn
637128	AC1	GAVIN Patrick	17-06-40	98 Sqn
551690	AC1	GAY Kenneth Vear	30-09-39	150 Sqn
551672	LAC	GEGG John Howard Keith	14-05-40	88 Sqn
564658	Sgt	GIDDINGS Norman Frederick Fiddler	6-05-40	88 Sqn
40690	P/O	GILLAM John Douglas Walker	11-06-40	88 Sqn
551885	LAC	GODDARD Cyril James	6-05-40	88 Sqn
525013	LAC	GODFRAY Roy Percival	15-06-40	12 Sqn
511338	Cpl	GORDON Francis Lowson	17-06-40	98 Sqn
749442	Sgt	GRANT David Laing	14-06-40	12 Sqn
536339	LAC	GRANT Leonard Ogilvie	8-06-40	150 Sqn
580511	Sgt	GRAY Phillip Cole	12-05-40	139 Sqn
563627	Sgt	GRAY VC Thomas	12-05-40	12 Sqn
977406	AC2	GREENMAN Wilfred James	17-06-40	98 Sqn
580512	Sgt	GREGORY Francis Wynell	12-05-40	139 Sqn
551303	AC1	GREGORY Kenneth George	11-05-40	218 Sqn
636117	AC2	GRIFFIN Kenneth Willoughby	17-06-40	98 Sqn
627989	AC2	GRIFFITHS Daniel Myrddin	17-06-40	98 Sqn
569713	AC1	GROVES George Edward	17-06-40	98 Sqn
33385	P/O	GULLEY Alfred Richard	14-06-40	150 Sqn
624110	LAC	GUYMER Hugh Percy Francis	17-06-40	98 Sqn
623494	AC1	HARPHAM Wilfred	17-06-40	98 Sqn
751759	Sgt	HARRIS Stanley Louis	17-06-40	98 Sqn
580203	Sgt	HARRISON Tom Charles Raymond	12-05-40	139 Sqn
531631	AC1	HATTON Harold	14-05-40	105 Sqn
564673	Sgt	HAYWARD Eric George	26-05-40	103 Sqn
580956	Sgt	HERRIOT Norman Basil	14-05-40	218 Sqn
564714	Sgt	HIBBERD Stanley Dennis	14-05-40	226 Sqn
564863	Sgt	HIBBERT Edward	23-05-40	88 Sqn
908668	AC2	HILL Albert Dennis	17-06-40	98 Sqn
631209	Sgt	HILLS George Gresham Stanley [Canada]	17-06-40	98 Sqn
551612	LAC	HINDER Reginald Henry	12-05-40	150 Sqn
40592	P/O	HINTON Ian Percival	26-03-40	103 Sqn
751593	F/S	HISLOP John	14-05-40	12 Sqn
908944	AC2	HODGETTS Albert Henry James	17-06-40	98 Sqn
580159	F/S	HORNER John Bland	12-05-40	218 Sqn
759330	Sgt	HOSKINS Ernest Daniel Charles	17-06-40	98 Sqn
653766	AC1	HOW Victor Hugh	17-06-40	98 Sqn
620073	Sgt	HUBBARD William Frank	26-05-40	103 Sqn
551679	LAC	HUGHES Raymond Douglas	14-05-40	105 Sqn
70860	P/O	HULSE Cecil Laing	4-06-40	12 Sqn
33388	P/O	HURST Tom	12-05-40	105 Sqn
524532	Sgt	HUTCHINSON Olaf Arthur	10-05-40	103 Sqn
39987	F/O	ING John	14-05-40	150 Sqn
521686	LAC	INGRAHAM Ian	17-06-40	98 Sqn
580456	Sgt	IRVINE George Boyle	10-05-40	142 Sqn
519291	Cpl	JACOBS Gordon William Egbert	31-05-40	226 Sqn
974666	AC2	JARVIS Patrick Joseph (served as KIRK William Henry)	17-06-40	98 Sqn
548328	AC1	JENKINS Leonard	20-05-40	142 Sqn
580427	Sgt	JENNINGS Cedric Maurice	11-05-40	218 Sqn
531085	AC1	JOHN David Joshua	20-09-39	88 Sqn
563884	Sgt	JOHNSON Arthur Geoffrey	14-05-40	12 Sqn
617968	AC1	JOHNSON Joseph	14-05-40	103 Sqn
531577	Cpl	JONES Alexander Egerton	26-03-40	105 Sqn
536553	Sgt	JONES Charles Phillips	17-06-40	98 Sqn

Service No	Rank	Name	Date	Sqn
533484	LAC	JONES Douglas Walter	17-06-40	98 Sqn
580417	Sgt	JONES Norman Spencer Denver	12-05-40	139 Sqn
528052	Cpl	JONES Tegwyn Davies	17-06-40	98 Sqn
561183	Sgt	JONES Tom	19-05-40	142 Sqn
39991	P/O	JORDAN Charles Bromley	14-05-40	114 Sqn
580581	Sgt	KEEGAN Joseph Belk	12-05-40	139 Sqn
39199	F/L	KERRIDGE Brian Rutter	15-05-40	226 Sqn
551137	Sgt	KETTLEWELL George Hammond	13-06-40	142 Sqn
564874	Cpl	KING George Roland	17-06-40	98 Sqn
518693	Sgt	KIRBY Ronald Alfred Percival	11-05-40	88 Sqn
900320	AC2	KNOWLTON Daniel	23-05-40	142 Sqn
550831	LAC	LAMBLE Phillip James	10-05-40	103 Sqn
615807	AC1	LANGTON Leon Meredith	10-05-40	142 Sqn
571314	LAC	LATTER Gordon Albert	17-06-40	98 Sqn
41431	P/O	LAWS Frederick Stanley	10-05-40	142 Sqn
615842	Sgt	LEDSON James Henshall	11-06-40	142 Sqn
37323	F/L	LEE Andrew Wynyard	12-05-40	139 Sqn
550668	Sgt	LEWIS Cecil Thomas	7-06-40	88 Sqn
530918	Cpl	LITTLE Herbert Francis	14-05-40	226 Sqn
562187	Sgt	LIVINGSTON Alexander	22-05-40	226 Sqn
909562	AC2	LUNT Harold	17-06-40	98 Sqn
751949	Sgt	MacKRELL John Frederick Walter	7-06-40	12 Sqn
39467	F/O	MACE Cecil Raymond [Australia]	31-03-40	105 Sqn
642192	LAC	MACPHERSON William	17-06-40	98 Sqn
551172	LAC	MADDOX Stanley Archibald	14-05-40	139 Sqn
621178	AC1	MALTBY Eric Wright	11-05-40	88 Sqn
514450	Sgt	MARLAND Fred	12-05-40	12 Sqn
522870	Sgt	MARROWS Ernest	11-06-40	226 Sqn
551571	AC1	MARSH John Leonard	20-09-39	150 Sqn
40127	F/L	MARTIN Arthur Douglas Joseph	13-06-40	142 Sqn
550964	AC1	MARTIN Sydney	14-05-40	150 Sqn
913127	AC2	MARTIN William Walter	17-06-40	98 Sqn
625295	AC2	McCARTHY William John	16-05-40	139 Sqn
40630	P/O	McELLIGOTT James Joseph 'Jimmy' [Eire]	19-05-40	12 Sqn
545595	LAC	McFADDEN William Allan	12-05-40	139 Sqn
975628	AC2	McFARLANE James	17-06-40	98 Sqn
297701	AC1	McGRATH John	20-05-40	142 Sqn
761198	Sgt	McKELVIE John	17-06-40	98 Sqn
613055	AC1	McLEOD Henry George	17-06-40	98 Sqn
580205	Sgt	McLOUGHLIN Gerald Patrick	11-06-40	226 Sqn
749340	LAC	McNAUGHTON Norman	17-06-40	98 Sqn
39200	F/O	McPHERSON DFC Andrew	12-05-40	139 Sqn
616790	AC2	MILLAR Michael Benedict [Eire]	14-05-40	226 Sqn
521994	Sgt	MILLER Robert Finlayson	10-05-40	142 Sqn
563340	Sgt	MORGAN Arthur Charles	14-05-40	105 Sqn
40131	F/O	MORGAN-DEAN George Barry [Canada]	12-05-40	103 Sqn
40635	P/O	MORTON Edgar Elliot [New Zealand]	12-05-40	103 Sqn
580085	Sgt	MOSELEY Victor Harry	14-05-40	226 Sqn
568184	LAC	MOULT Harold Thompson	27-02-40	114 Sqn
613363	AC1	NOLAN William Joseph [Eire]	14-05-40	150 Sqn
537353	LAC	NUGENT Ronald Harold	14-05-40	142 Sqn
551634	LAC	OVER Hubert Frank	12-05-40	139 Sqn
562673	F/S	PAGE Douglas Aubrey [India]	20-09-39	88 Sqn
526717	Cpl	PARK Albert	17-06-40	98 Sqn
39111	F/L	PARKER Eric [Canada]	10-05-40	150 Sqn
625250	AC1	PARKER Walter	14-05-40	139 Sqn
612745	AC1	PARSONS William Leonard	11-05-40	88 Sqn
627956	Cpl	PASSEY Wilfred	20-05-40	142 Sqn
947539	AC2	PEARSON Harry Vincent	17-06-40	98 Sqn
562846	Sgt	PERCIVAL Frederick John	14-05-40	226 Sqn
537397	LAC	PERRIN John Lawrence	12-05-40	12 Sqn
561615	Sgt	PERRY DFM Charles David	14-05-40	103 Sqn
900985	AC2	PETERS John Edward	17-06-40	98 Sqn
580495	Sgt	PETTIT Hugh Edward	26-03-40	105 Sqn
580454	Sgt	PIKE Richard Cecil Luscombe	13-11-39	218 Sqn
39007	F/L	PITFIELD DFC Alan Leonard [Australia]	12-06-40	88 Sqn
580624	Sgt	PITTAR William David Parke	8-06-40	150 Sqn
615972	AC1	PLUMB Eric George	17-06-40	98 Sqn
580416	Sgt	POOLE Christopher John Stafford	10-05-40	103 Sqn
41319	P/O	POSSELT Arthur Francis [Swaziland]	14-05-40	150 Sqn
610963	AC1	POTTER James	14-05-40	105 Sqn
40850	P/O	POWER James O'Brien	14-05-40	139 Sqn
565189	Sgt	PRICE Norman James	14-03-40	139 Sqn
542863	AC1	PUGH William	17-06-40	98 Sqn
534283	AC1	RADFORD Edward Arthur William	20-09-39	88 Sqn
618627	AC1	RADFORD William Edward	17-06-40	98 Sqn
621890	AC2	RANSON Morrison Wilfred Joseph	17-06-40	98 Sqn
516071	Sgt	RAPER Leslie Alfred	7-04-40	142 Sqn
40260	F/O	REA Kenneth Noel [New Zealand]	14-06-40	226 Sqn
908528	AC2	READING George	17-06-40	98 Sqn
644120	AC2	REDFERN Leslie	17-06-40	98 Sqn
642662	AC2	REEVES Eric Charles	17-06-40	98 Sqn
550860	LAC	REYNOLDS Lawrence Royston	12-05-40	12 Sqn
550743	AC1	RICHARDSON Douglas Henry	25-06-40	98 Sqn
550941	AC1	RICHARDSON Vivian William Liddle	13-11-39	218 Sqn
615860	LAC	RIDDELL Robert	17-06-40	98 Sqn
41208	P/O	RIDLEY Frederick Heward	14-05-40	105 Sqn
532880	Cpl	RIGBY Geoffrey Arthur	17-06-40	98 Sqn
625691	AC1	ROBINSON Herbert	17-06-40	98 Sqn
633727	AC1	ROBINSON William	14-05-40	218 Sqn
591650	AC1	ROGERS John	17-06-40	98 Sqn
39473	F/L	ROGERS Kenneth Russell [Australia]	14-05-40	142 Sqn
544996	LAC	ROONEY John	12-05-40	139 Sqn
613676	AC1	ROSS Alexander Strachan	12-05-40	103 Sqn
516232	Sgt	ROSS William Guthrie	14-05-40	88 Sqn
937857	Cpl	ROXBOROUGH James Henry	17-06-40	98 Sqn
907056	AC2	RUCK Gordon	17-06-40	98 Sqn
618567	F/S	RUSSELL Jack Alfred	11-06-40	226 Sqn
37901	F/L	SAMMELS Harold Courtenay	14-05-40	105 Sqn
620465	AC2	SANDERS Arthur William Bates	3-03-40	114 Sqn
40145	P/O	SAUNDERS John Richard	30-09-39	150 Sqn
34225	S/L	SCOTT William Ian	12-05-40	139 Sqn
628742	AC2	SCOTT-KIDDIE Andrew John	17-06-40	98 Sqn
523566	Sgt	SEDGWICK Arthur Francis	14-05-40	226 Sqn
531362	AC1	SEWELL Horace Basil	12-05-40	103 Sqn
617513	AC2	SHARPE John Alexander [Eire]	26-03-40	103 Sqn
563688	Sgt	SHELTON-JONES Christopher	14-05-40	12 Sqn
702682	AC2	SIBBORN Joseph Alan	17-06-40	98 Sqn
40644	P/O	SKIDMORE Bruce Ian Muddiman	11-05-40	88 Sqn
631548	AC1	SLATER Clarence Frederick	17-06-40	98 Sqn
612896	AC1	SMALL Walter Lochrie	17-06-40	98 Sqn
626102	AC2	SMITH Frederick Horatio	17-06-40	98 Sqn
580500	Sgt	SMITH Thomas Daw	10-05-40	103 Sqn
580531	Sgt	SOUTHWOOD Paul McKelvie	14-05-40	114 Sqn
580570	Sgt	STANLEY MiD Roy Joseph	14-03-40	139 Sqn
935588	LAC	STOCKER Frank	17-06-40	98 Sqn
740503	Sgt	STOKES Lawrence Jesse	17-06-40	98 Sqn
628640	AC1	STONES Dennis	17-06-40	98 Sqn
580593	Sgt	STUART-HARRIS Douglas Trevor	14-05-40	139 Sqn
628702	AC1	SYMMONDS Albert Leslie	17-06-40	98 Sqn
614845	LAC	TAWS Stanley	17-06-40	98 Sqn
540413	LAC	TAYLOR Alfred James	14-05-40	218 Sqn
530913	Sgt	TAYLOR Cyril	12-05-40	139 Sqn
545991	AC1	TAYLOR William Fraser [Eire]	31-03-40	150 Sqn
41963	P/O	THOMAS Cecil Vernon	10-06-40	103 Sqn
545990	AC1	THOMAS Donald Leighton	30-09-39	150 Sqn
613420	AC1	THOMSON James Samuel	14-05-40	105 Sqn
40650	P/O	THYNNE Robert	13-11-39	218 Sqn
573560	AC2	TIMMS Cyril	17-06-40	98 Sqn
539637	Cpl	TODD Henry	14-05-40	142 Sqn
581008	Sgt	TOUGH Edmund Winchester	16-06-40	139 Sqn
563511	Sgt	TRESCOTHIC Herbert Frank	14-05-40	142 Sqn
564992	LAC	TURNER John Daniel	14-05-40	150 Sqn
751657	Sgt	TURNER Leslie	13-06-40	226 Sqn

506095	Sgt	TUTT Harold James Frank	13-06-40	150 Sqn
630788	AC2	VANO Norman Victor	14-05-40	150 Sqn
37838	F/O	VAUGHAN Eric Richard Dennis	14-05-40	12 Sqn
36145	F/O	VERNON DFC James Edward [New Zealand]	7-06-40	150 Sqn
516606	Sgt	VICKERS Medaille Militaire John Henry	5-10-39	103 Sqn
524140	LAC	WAITE James Albert	17-06-40	98 Sqn
580439	Sgt	WALL Clifford	31-03-40	150 Sqn
37839	F/O	WALL Richard Nap	14-05-40	105 Sqn
580532	Sgt	WALLIS Howard Beckett	14-05-40	139 Sqn
510142	LAC	WASS Rae Stuart	15-05-40	12 Sqn
630224	AC1	WATERSTON William Coates	14-05-40	218 Sqn
625205	LAC	WATKIN Francis William	17-06-40	98 Sqn
620691	AC1	WATSON Albert	17-06-40	98 Sqn
37534	F/L	WEEKS Reginald Alleyne	8-06-40	150 Sqn
551357	LAC	WELLS Clifford Ronald	12-05-40	105 Sqn
630351	AC2	WHELAN Matthew [Canada]	23-05-40	88 Sqn
581009	Sgt	WHITE Edward Frederick	14-05-40	12 Sqn
528627	Sgt	WHITE Howard Percival	2-08-40	226 Sqn
40787	P/O	WHITE Hugh Edgar	14-05-40	105 Sqn
742095	LAC	WHITMARSH Kenneth Ronald	17-06-40	98 Sqn
563211	Sgt	WHITTLE Eward James Mortimer	11-05-40	88 Sqn
36200	P/O	WICKHAM Albert Edgar [New Zealand]	23-05-40	88 Sqn
534269	Cpl	WILBURN Clifford Edgar	7-04-40	142 Sqn
537423	Sgt	WILKS Edmund	26-05-40	88 Sqn
590740	Sgt	WILLCOX Ronald John	14-06-40	12 Sqn
562632	Sgt	WILLIAMS James Douglas Frederick	14-05-40	150 Sqn
532511	LAC	WILLIAMSON William John	17-06-40	98 Sqn
636044	AC1	WILSON Frederick James	17-06-40	98 Sqn
550694	AC1	WILTSHIRE Robert Francis James	1-03-40	218 Sqn
562366	Sgt	WOODMASON Thomas Baker	20-09-39	150 Sqn
908737	AC2	WRIGHT John Noble	17-06-40	98 Sqn
538668	AC2	WRIGHT Wilfred	4-01-40	103 Sqn
640245	AC2	WYATT Kenneth Leslie	17-06-40	98 Sqn

Note

For the parents of P/O Blowfield, news of his death came as a double tragedy for as recently as the 28th of February, 1940, they had been notified of the death of his brother, Bernard John, while on active service with 176 Heavy Regiment RA. He is buried in Twickenham Cemetery, while Philip rests in France at Les Minieres Communal Cemetery. AC1 How, one of the many lost from 98 Squadron when the *Lancastria* sunk, lost his younger brother in the first full year of peace, AC2 Charles Kenneth How dying on the 16th of January, 1946. Devonian F/L Victor Fernley Baker Pike DFC and P/O William George Jack Woodmason DFC, brothers respectively to Sgt Pike and Sgt Woodmason commemorated in this section, both served in Bomber Command and died during the course of the war. The former perished on the 9th of April, 1941 while flying Stirlings with 7 Squadron (see Volume 2 page 39 for details of his demise) while P/O Woodmason's death is presumed to have occurred on the 25th of April, 1942, while serving with RAF Ferry Command and he is commemorated on Canada's Ottawa Memorial.

P/O Calvert's father, 2Lt Lionel Calvert of the 175th Tunnelling Company RE was killed in action on the Somme on the 30th of January, 1917. Both father and son are buried in France.

Sgt Butler is reported as hailing from Westmount, Quebec, though his entry in the Commonwealth War Graves Commission register for Haraucourt Churchyard shows his parents as living in Sussex at St. Leonards-on-Sea. Similarly, the parents of LAC Child are given as living in Stanford Bridge, Worcestershire and those of AC2 Whelan as being domicile in Liverpool though Canadian records indicate their sons as coming respectively from Vancouver in British Columbia and Saskatoon, Saskatchewan. Of the Australians mentioned in this section, F/O Mace of Heidelberg, Victoria, had qualified as a Pharmaceutical Chemist.

Other points of interest; Sgt Chapman's unit is incorrectly reported as 86 Squadron and Cranwell graduate P/O Hurst was the recipient of the King's Gold Medal in 1938.

Postscript

Of the 331 officers and airmen from the AASF here commemorated, only nine had been decorated for valour at the time of their deaths. As reported in my introduction, two, F/O Garland and Sgt Gray, received their country's highest accolade, the Victoria Cross (albeit posthumously); three, F/O McPherson, F/L Pitfield and F/O Vernon, had been awarded the Distinguished Flying Cross (DFC), one, Sgt Perry, had gained a Distinguished Flying Medal (DFM), two, Sgt Brookes and Sgt Stanley had been mentioned in despatches, while Sgt Vickers had been honoured by the French with the Medaille Militaire* as he lay dying from his wounds in a French hospital, following a reconnaissance sortie on the 27th of September, 1939.

The citation for the two Victoria Crosses appeared in the *Supplement to The London Gazette* on the 11th of June, 1940; 'Flying Officer Garland was the pilot and Sergeant Gray the observer of the leading aircraft of a formation of five aircraft that attacked a bridge over the Albert Canal which had not been destroyed and was allowing the enemy to advance into Belgium. All the air crews of the squadron concerned volunteered for the operation and, after five crews had been selected by drawing lots, the attack was delivered at low altitude against this vital target. Orders were issued that this bridge was to be destroyed at all costs. As had been anticipated, exceptionally intense machine gun fire and anti-aircraft fire was encountered, and the bridge area was heavily protected by enemy fighters. In spite of this the formation successfully delivered a dive bombing attack from the lowest practicable altitude and British fighters in the vicinity reported that the target was obscured by the bombs bursting on it and in its vicinity. Only one aircraft returned from this mission out of the five concerned. The pilot of this aircraft reports that in addition to the extremely heavy anti-aircraft fire, through which our aircraft dived to attack the objective, they were also attacked by a large number of enemy fighters after they had released their bombs on the target. Much of the success of this vital operation must be attributed to the formation leader; Flying Officer Garland, and to the coolness and resource of Sergeant Gray, who navigated Flying Officer Garland's aircraft under most difficult conditions in such a manner that the whole formation was able successfully to attack the target in spite of subsequent heavy losses. Flying Officer Garland and Sergeant Gray unfortunately failed to return from the mission.'

For reasons that can only be known to the authorities responsible for recommending F/O Garland and Sgt Gray for their very deserved conspicuous gallantry awards, the name of the aircraft's wireless operator/air gunner, LAC Reynolds, was not put forward for any award whatsoever.

The war was to prove particularly cruel to the Garlands for as the weary months of conflict slipped by so they received the dread news that Desmond was missing from a mining operation (see page 118 of Volume 3 for further details) while serving with 50 Squadron; then came the death of John soon after being invalided out of the air force where he had been serving as a Medical Officer and then on New Year's Day 1945, Patrick, an experienced photo reconnaissance pilot of 2 Squadron based at Gilze-Rijen in Holland, died in a flying accident. From what had been a family of five, only their daughter was alive to provide them with some solace.

In respect of the three officers decorated with the DFC, that awarded to F/O McPherson was *Gazetted* ahead of his arrival in France and, therefore, the due recognition of his gallantry was not specific to his actions with the AASF. Published on the 10th of October, 1939, the citation reads, 'This officer carried out reconnaissance flights early in September, 1939. On one occasion he was forced by extremely bad weather conditions to fly close to the enemy coast at very low *altitudes. These flights made possible a successful raid on enemy naval forces.'*

His father, Captain Andrew McPherson, had been decorated with the DSO, probably for gallantry during the Great War though, as yet, I have not been able to trace the citation for his award.

F/L Pitfield and F/O Vernon appear to have received non-immediate awards, these being *Gazetted* within a batch of seven named recipients on the 16th of July, 1940. Both officers (and F/O McPherson) had joined the Royal Air Force on short service commissions in the late 1930s, Pitfield hailing from Hobart in Tasmania and Vernon from New Zealand's south island.

Details of Sgt Perry's DFM appeared in the *Supplement to The London Gazette* issue of the 11th of June, 1940, *'In May, 1940, during a low flying attack against the enemy, Sergeant Perry was seriously wounded in the thigh and stomach by two bullets. He showed great courage and stamina in piloting his aircraft to the vicinity of his base and then finding himself about to faint, he made a forced landing.'* Mere words cannot describe fully the agony that this young airman must have experienced as he limped towards Betheniville in the early hours of daylight on the 14th of May. Evacuated to England, he died three days after the official notification of his award and was buried in the extension to Benson (St. Helen) Churchyard.

One death was reported after the disbandment of the AASF (No.1 Group was reformed on the 14th of June, 1940), namely that of Sgt White of 226 Squadron who is buried in France at Doullens Communal Cemetery. It is presumed his death, in captivity, was as a result of wounds, or injuries, received while on active service and, therefore, it is logical that he should be commemorated within this section, rather than being placed in Section 4 (1940).

To close this postscript, I draw attention to the entries concerning AC2 Knowlton, AC2 Sibborn and Sgts Atkins and MacKrell; Knowlton was the first war enlisted volunteer reserve airman to lose his life while serving with a squadron (142 Squadron) which had an affinity with Bomber Command; AC2 Sibborn had been called up in July, 1939, under the terms of the Military Training Act, while Atkins and MacKrell were pre-war volunteer reserve wireless operator/air gunners.

* The Medaille Militaire, which dates from 1852, is one of the rarest decorations for bravery that France can bestow on a foreign serviceman. Its issue is generally restricted to non-commissioned officers and recipients so honoured are recognised for their outstanding leadership and courage in the face of the enemy. Many regard the award as being more coveted than the Croix de Guerre.

Part 2

Air Component of the British Expeditionary Force (18 and 57 Squadron), Roll of Honour

In addition to the ten squadrons of Fairey Battles sent to France in late August, 1939, to form the AASF (see Section 1), two squadrons of Bristol Blenheim Mk. 1 bombers from No.6 Group were assigned to the Air Component of the British Expeditionary Force (AC BEF). Thus, on the 24th of September, 1939, 57 Squadron commenced moving from Upper Heyford in Oxfordshire to Roye/Amy, followed six days later by their sister unit at Upper Heyford, 18 Squadron, which took up temporary residence at Beauvraignes before continuing to Meharicourt in mid-October, 1939 (57 Squadron, meanwhile, settled at Rosieres-en-Santerre). In total four squadrons of Blenheims, five squadrons of Lysanders and six fighter squadrons came under the umbrella of the AC BEF but in keeping with the parameters governing the content of this *Roll of Honour* the names of those who died in service with the AC BEF are limited to the two squadrons identified in the title of this section.

The role of the Blenheim squadrons was to fly strategic reconnaissance missions with the aim of providing the commanders on the ground with a degree of intelligence regarding German military intent. It was an undertaking that on many occasions proved to be extremely costly, particularly in respect of operations that found the Blenheim crews operating deep into enemy territory. 18 Squadron flew its first sorties on the 16th of October, 1939, with two aircraft carrying out a strategic reconnaissance of the Siegfried Line, while two more Blenheims were tasked for a photographic reconnaissance sweep over north-west Germany. Meanwhile, three days previous, the commanding officer of 57 Squadron, W/C H. M. A. Day, operating from a forward base at Metz, had taken off at 11.40 hours, instructed to reconnoitre road and rail traffic in the Hamm-Hannover-Soest areas. It was to be his first and last sortie of the war for during the operation his Blenheim was intercepted and shot down by Uffz Stephan Lutjens, piloting a Me 109 from ll./JG53. W/C Day survived the encounter to become a prisoner of war but his crew were less fortunate and 57 Squadron had sustained its first casualties of the Second World War.

An hour after Day's departure, F/O C. T. Norman, also operating from Metz, carried out a deep penetration reconnaissance of the Munster-Bremen regions, on completion of which he continued to fly over Germany (Belgium and Holland were still neutral and their airspace was sacrosanct) before crossing the North Sea and heading for the United Kingdom. As reported on page 18 of the first volume in this series of books devoted to Bomber Command losses, he encountered dreadful weather and his mission ended in a crash-landing in Hertfordshire, Norman and his crew escaping serious hurt.

And so the business of war continued with both squadrons suffering the consequences of such hazardous work. With the *Blitzkrieg* of May, 1940, opening up an entirely new vista for the Allies in the mode of offensive operations, bombs were carried on the majority of reconnaissance operations flown by the hard-pressed crews before they were ordered back to the United Kingdom. On their return (circa the 20th and 21st May), both squadrons, now fully equipped with Mk.IV Blenheims, joined No.2 Group and, as the saying goes, *'they had jumped from the frying pan into the fire'*.

ROYAL AIR FORCE,
AUXILIARY AIR FORCE and
ROYAL AIR FORCE (VOLUNTEER RESERVE)
personnel

39838	F/O	ADAM William Ward [Jamaica]	15-03-40	57 Sqn
552443	AC2	BEAUMONT Owen Ralph	14-05-40	57 Sqn
39847	F/O	BELLIS Charlie	12-05-40	18 Sqn
580596	Sgt	BENDALL Douglas James	25-01-40	57 Sqn
563613	Sgt	BORTHWICK David	16-05-40	18 Sqn
362800	F/S	BOWDEN Frederick Samuel	15-11-39	57 Sqn
161373	Cpl	BRADSHAW Albert Richardson	10-05-40	18 Sqn
539683	AC1	BURROWS John Stanley	30-10-39	18 Sqn
564599	Cpl	CATMORE George Edward	27-03-40	57 Sqn
565544	Sgt	COUZENS George Frederick	12-05-40	57 Sqn
564130	Sgt	CRELLIN Ewart Harrison	30-10-39	18 Sqn
563071	Sgt	CREW Kenneth Burton	30-10-39	18 Sqn
539392	LAC	DAVIES Ronald David	11-05-40	18 Sqn
37525	F/L	DILNOT Alan Arthur	30-10-39	18 Sqn
42111	P/O	DIXON Leonard Thomas	10-05-40	18 Sqn
580537	Sgt	DUMBRECK Oliver William	21-03-40	18 Sqn
291424	AC2	EADES Edward Victor	1-10-39	18 Sqn
39075	F/O	ELLIOT Denis Frederick [Canada]	30-10-39	18 Sqn
563653	Sgt	FARMER Stanley John	15-11-39	57 Sqn
537306	AC1	GARRICK John Arthur	30-10-39	18 Sqn
39516	F/O	GRAHAM-HOGG Horace Gaulterus	14-04-40	57 Sqn
33438	P/O	HARDING Geoffrey Fawconer	11-05-40	18 Sqn
537545	AC1	HARRIS Peter Bothamley	3-01-40	18 Sqn
580542	Sgt	HARVEY Victor	27-12-39	18 Sqn
580543	Sgt	HILLIER Eric Bernard	13-10-39	57 Sqn
33428	P/O	HULTON Henry Stephen Penton	21-03-40	18 Sqn
40394	P/O	HUME Oliver Carlisle [South Africa]	23-11-39	57 Sqn
625656	AC2	HUNTER John Raymond	25-01-40	57 Sqn
614259	LAC	JAMES Horace Gwyn	16-05-40	18 Sqn
567602	LAC	JOB Jasen	27-12-39	18 Sqn
624246	LAC	JORDAN Leslie Frederick [Canada]	10-05-40	57 Sqn
625870	AC1	LINDSAY George	11-04-40	57 Sqn
621138	LAC	MANTLE Frederick John	15-03-40	57 Sqn
540304	AC1	MARTIN William S.	27-12-39	18 Sqn
548626	AC2	MOLLER Frederick George	13-10-39	57 Sqn
581237	Sgt	MONGEY Thomas John [Eire]	16-05-40	18 Sqn
39890	P/O	MORTON Alexander Donald	6-11-39	57 Sqn
42474	P/O	O'REILLY-BLACKWOOD John Noel	25-01-40	57 Sqn
550953	LAC	PARRY Kenneth	12-05-40	18 Sqn
545847	LAC	PARTLOW Ivor Robert William	15-11-39	57 Sqn
581241	Sgt	PEACH Thomas Arthur	10-05-40	18 Sqn
562838	Sgt	POTTER John Abraham Humphries	25-02-40	18 Sqn
515376	Sgt	PROCTOR John Rose	14-04-40	57 Sqn
580175	Sgt	SABIN Leonard James	27-12-39	18 Sqn

516530	Sgt	SHROSBREE Kenneth Norman	11-05-40	18 Sqn
626490	AC1	SHUTTLEWORTH James	14-04-40	57 Sqn
514006	Sgt	STORR Geoffrey	6-11-39	57 Sqn
70654	F/O	STUART Arnold James	16-05-40	18 Sqn
41332	P/O	THOMAS Alban	10-05-40	57 Sqn
562935	Sgt	THOMAS Alfred William Swinburne	18-05-40	18 Sqn
563934	Sgt	THOMAS Peter Llewelyn	10-05-40	57 Sqn
552526	AC1	TOWNSLEY John	10-05-40	18 Sqn
543541	AC1	TWINNING Frederick Albert	6-11-39	57 Sqn
565950	Sgt	WELCH Horace David	12-05-40	18 Sqn

Note

It is believed that each of the 54 airman mentioned in this section was a regular and the service numbers for three of those named deserve some comment. Two, Cpl Bradshaw (161373) and AC2 Eades (291424) appear to have been veterans of the Great War (1914 to 1918), Bradshaw's number coming within a block issued during April and May, 1918, to a mixture of civilian entrants and transfers from the other services and, similarly, Eades, too, has a number from a block issued to both civilian and other service transfers covering the period, July to October, 1918. F/S Bowden (362800), the last of our trio, entered the Royal Air Force as a Boy Entrant twixt July, 1922 and January, 1924.

Further observations of interest are made in respect of Sgt Crellin from Ramsey on the Isle of Man who won The King's 100 at the Bisley rifle shoot in 1938, and F/O Elliot who, according to Canadian air force records came from Vancouver in British Columbia but whose entry in the Commonwealth War Graves Commission register for burials in Cologne's southern cemetery indicate a Dorsetshire connection as his parents are shown as living in the coastal resort of Lyme Regis.

Postscript

Two airmen from the squadrons here commemorated died whilst in captivity and both are recorded in Part 8 (1944). However, the circumstances in which they met their death is worthy of comment within this section as both were murdered by the Gestapo. F/L Michael James Casey of 57 Squadron had been captured as early as the 16th of October, 1939 (see Volume 1 page 19) and in March 1944 he was a successful participant in the mass escape of Allied officers from Sagan only to become one of the fifty to be shot by the Gestapo following their recapture. The execution of W/O Roland Brainerd Herbert Townsend-Coles (his capture is reported on page 46 of Volume 1) is clouded in mystery, though Oliver Clutton-Brock's masterpiece on Bomber Command's prisoners of war* goes some way to explaining his final days of freedom. In essence, following his *departure* from Heydekrug in early April 1944, Townsend-Coles got as far as the Baltic Sea port of Danzig only to be picked up as he attempted to board a Swedish vessel. From that point onwards his movements cannot be verified though he is believed to have been put to death on the 15th of July, 1944. In recognition of what he achieved he, along with other officers and non-commissioned officers, was mentioned in despatches in the *Supplement to The London Gazette* issued on the 13th of June, 1946.

* *Footprints on the Sands of Time – RAF Bomber Command Prisoners of War in Germany 1939-1945* published by Grub Street (2003) and with particular reference to pages 43 and 103 to 105.

Part 3

Bomber Command, Roll of Honour
3rd September to 31st December 1939

A phrase often used by those with a vested interest in the promotion of air power in the 1930s was, *'The bomber will always get through'*. It was an expression that was not restricted to the advocates of air power; the *'popular press'*, and in particular the editors of the widely-read aviation magazines of the day regaled their readers with portents of vast air fleets, flying in close formation, their crews adequately protected against defensive fighter attack by the guns fitted to their aircraft. These visions of an as yet unproven concept caught the publics imagination and the so called *'Bomber Barons'* of the day must have felt well pleased as the number of bomber squadrons increased steadily throughout the expansionist years of the late '30s.

Charged with overseeing this huge increase in material were the air officers commanding-in-chief of Bomber Command, the first appointee being Air Chief Marshal Sir John Steel, whose appointment was announced with the formation of headquarters Bomber Command on the 14th of July, 1936. By the end of the year Steel had 44 squadrons, spread amongst the four bomber groups that had been formed under the overall umbrella of Bomber Command. Although '44 *squadrons*' was, for the time, a reasonably impressive number, the performance of the aircraft that equipped the embryo bomber squadrons was far from satisfactory. All were biplanes* (the most advanced being the two-seat Hawker Hind then in service with 17 Squadrons) and the types that equipped the 14 squadrons administered by No.3 Group were, in the main, more suited to the Great War of 1914 to 1918 than for any conflict that might erupt in the immediate future.

Over the three years of peace remaining numerous changes took place within the structure of Bomber Command. The auxiliary air force units that formed No.6 (Auxiliary) Group were released to other commands, group headquarters being retained and retitled No.6 (Bomber) Group on the 1st of January, 1939. Meanwhile, in June and September of 1937, respectively, No.4 Group and No.5 Group came into existence while in respect of aircraft types, Battles, Blenheims, Hampdens, Wellingtons and Whitleys had been produced in sufficient numbers to replace the antiquated biplanes that had been the backbone of the 1936 force. For the most part these changes had been overseen by Air Chief Marshal Sir Edgar Ludlow-Hewitt who had replaced Steel as air officer commanding in chief on the 12th of September, 1937.

Running in parallel with the changes in equipment came the expansion in bomber bases, particularly on the eastern side of the United Kingdom from East Anglia northwards. Well constructed, many of these airfields exist to the present day, though some in recent years have passed into the hands of the army while of the remainder only a handful retain an offensive capability.

Thus, we arrive at that fateful first weekend of September, 1939. With the departure of the ten Battle squadrons to France on the Saturday, Ludlow-Hewitt's command was left with 45 squadrons (two, 18 Squadron and 57 Squadron (see Section 2) would transfer to France under the aegis of the Air Component of the British Expeditionary Force later in the month), of which 23 were deemed to be ready to commence operational duties. On paper, at least, this would appear adequate to start the bombing campaign, though with his front line squadrons lacking any advanced radio and navigational aids Hewitt could not have been overly confident. But, to his relief and that of his group commanders, there was to be no major bombing offensive! With the German invasion of Poland barely underway the American President, Franklin D. Roosevelt, cabled the three major protagonists requesting that they refrain from unleashing their bomber arms against undefended towns, or against any military targets where there was a risk of civilian casualties being incurred. Britain and France agreed immediately to defer to Roosevelt's plea and on the 18th of September, with victory now assured over Poland, Adolf Hitler let it be known that the Luftwaffe would not be used in an indiscriminate manner.

Despite these limitations in the use of air power Ludlow-Hewitt was permitted to use his bombers against any German naval units detected on the high seas and, provided that vessels were not tied up alongside wharfs, any ships at anchor in a harbour were considered to be legitimate targets. Also allowed were night reconnaissance flights over the German mainland, a task that was pursued with much vigour from the very start of the war by the Whitley squadrons of No.4 Group.

And so it came about that the daylight offensive mounted by Bomber Command in the first four months of war was aimed towards units of the German fleet. This involved the squadrons from Nos. 2, 3 and 5 Groups in many hours of tedious searching, often without any sightings of their adversaries. However, as events were to prove, such forays over the North Sea could be fraught with extreme danger as proved to be the case on the 29th of September, 1939, when eleven Hampdens from 144 Squadron, split into two sections, explored the seas of the Heligoland Bight, flying to within sight of the German mainland. The section led by the squadron commander, W/C J. C. Cunningham, had the misfortune to run into a swarm of Me 109s, operating out of Jever, and in the running battle that followed all five Hampdens were clinically despatched into the sea. Of the 20 airmen involved, four, shocked by their close encounter with death, were plucked from the water and taken into captivity; Cunningham was not amongst them.

Two months later it was the turn of 99 Squadron to receive a drubbing while over the North Sea hunting for enemy shipping. Having successfully located a convoy in the Schillig Roads, north of Wilhelmshaven, the Wellington crews were thwarted by a combination of low cloud and poor visibility and it was not long before the Luftwaffe arrived on the scene. Theoretically, the Wellingtons should have been better equipped to deal with the fighters than the luckless Hampden crews, but the outcome of the running engagements that followed makes depressing reading. Two Wellingtons collided as they tried to evade the attention of the Me 109s and Me 110s; two others were last seen spiralling down into the gloom and a fifth is believed to have fallen to gunfire from the convoy. From these five aircraft not one airman survived and when a sixth Wellington crashed as it tried to land at Newmarket, the rescue services faced the grim task of extricating three dead bodies from the wreckage.

Four days later, on the 18th of December, 1939, three squadrons of Wellingtons set out in close formation to attack shipping reported in the port of Wilhelmshaven. Two bombers from the 24 despatched returned early with technical problems, but the remainder pressed on in weather conditions that some describe as *gin clear* with barely a cloud in sight. Nearing their objective and flying, as ordered, above 10,000 feet, the bomber force had for sometime been the focal point of the German radar operators and with the ground controller ordering the fighters to close on the formation the fate of the bomber crews was all but sealed. It was around this time that the Wellingtons ran into a heavy concentration of flak which succeeded in breaking up the tight defensive boxes, after which the converging fighters had little difficulty in picking off their targets. In total ten Wellingtons were shot down in the main engagement area while two others were so badly crippled that they were obliged to ditch long before reaching the safety of the East Anglia coast. This raid, aligned to the memories of the debacle of the first bombing raid of the war launched on the 4th of September, 1939, and which witnessed the destruction of five Blenheims and two Wellingtons, destroyed the illusion that *'the bomber will always get through'* and forced upon the air staff a complete reappraisal of future bombing operations.

* A handful of Fairey Hendon twin-engine monoplane bombers were delivered to 38 Squadron at Mildenhall late in 1936.

**ROYAL AIR FORCE,
AUXILIARY AIR FORCE and
ROYAL AIR FORCE (VOLUNTEER RESERVE)
personnel**

70769	F/O	ALLISON Douglas Bellamy	18-12-39	9 Sqn
580857	Sgt	ALLON Ross	14-12-39	99 Sqn
39452	F/L	ALLSOP John William [Australia]	2-10-39	10 Sqn
41647	P/O	ANDERSON John Ross [Canada]	18-10-39	52 Sqn
580390	Sgt	ANDERSON William	27-12-39	107 Sqn
564245	Sgt	ANTELL William Fishwick	14-12-39	99 Sqn
534149	AC1	ANTHONY John	29-09-39	144 Sqn
34227	F/L	APPLEBY Thomas Gaufrey Wearmouth	18-12-39	37 Sqn
580817	Sgt	ATKINS William James	14-12-39	99 Sqn
39656	F/O	ATKINSON John Edgar	18-12-39	9 Sqn
39924	F/L	BAILEY Donald Charles Ephraim	18-12-39	9 Sqn
569331	AC1	BAILEY John Clarence	5-11-39	38 Sqn
548036	AC2	BARKER David William	11-11-39	114 Sqn
516752	Sgt	BARRINGTON-TAYLOR Maurice William	18-12-39	37 Sqn
550716	LAC	BARSTOW John Arundel	18-12-39	37 Sqn
34213	F/L	BARTON William Frank	4-09-39	107 Sqn
41817	P/O	BARWELL George Francis Astley	3-11-39	63 Sqn
533911	AC1	BATESON John	28-09-39	110 Sqn
516285	LAC	BEAUMONT Howard Eric	14-12-39	99 Sqn
37923	F/O	BECK Norman Croxen	29-09-39	144 Sqn
40334	P/O	BEERE Ian St. John [New Zealand]	8-11-39	97 Sqn
29158	S/L	BEGG James Aldo Bartlett	11-11-39	77 Sqn
550003	AC1	BELL John Rogerson	2-10-39	10 Sqn
580320	Sgt	BIGGER Reginald Austin	24-10-39	77 Sqn
567249	Cpl	BLACK Reginald Thomas	18-12-39	9 Sqn
580708	Sgt	BORAM Brian Thomas	14-12-39	99 Sqn
365199	F/S	BORLEY Ian Edward Maitland	4-09-39	9 Sqn
40882	P/O	BOURNE Alistair Hugh Richmond	18-12-39	9 Sqn
563894	Sgt	BRACE Richard Henry James	14-12-39	99 Sqn
39706	F/O	BRIDEN Michael Franklin	18-12-39	149 Sqn
580848	Sgt	BRISTER John Archibald	18-12-39	9 Sqn
547193	AC2	BRITTON Ronald Victor	1-10-39	139 Sqn
546065	AC1	BROCKING George Thomas	4-09-39	9 Sqn
365778	Sgt	BROWN Henry Edward	23-09-39	207 Sqn
562022	Sgt	BROWN William	1-10-39	139 Sqn
70794	P/O	BROWN William Stanley Francis	18-12-39	149 Sqn
590534	Sgt	BRYANT Cyril Arthur	30-10-39	9 Sqn
580939	Sgt	BRYANT Frederick George	10-10-39	108 Sqn
619734	AC2	BUCKLAND James Crompton	1-12-39	63 Sqn
620416	AC1	BULL Leslie Reginald	9-12-39	98 Sqn
612813	AC1	BURGE Joseph Frank	31-10-39	50 Sqn
510603	Sgt	BURRELL George Jonathan	24-10-39	77 Sqn
549796	AC1	BUTLER George Henry	10-09-39	82 Sqn
564505	Sgt	CALDWELL Charles Denis [New Zealand]	14-12-39	99 Sqn
41900	P/O	CAMERON Angus [Canada]	1-12-39	63 Sqn
40987	P/O	CAMERON Colin Charles [New Zealand]	30-10-39	215 Sqn
24225	W/C	CAMERON Ivan McLeod [Australia]	28-09-39	110 Sqn
534563	LAC	CARR Robert Taylor	14-12-39	99 Sqn
39041	F/O	CHALLES John Thomas Irvine [Canada]	18-12-39	9 Sqn
39221	F/O	CHANDLER John Frank	30-10-39	9 Sqn
620138	AC2	CHAPMAN Walter James	30-10-39	9 Sqn
567489	AC1	CLARK John Baker	18-10-39	102 Sqn
36170	P/O	CLIFFORD-JONES Bruce Innes [New Zealand]	8-09-39	9 Sqn
40366	P/O	CODY James Doan [Canada]	31-10-39	108 Sqn
565860	Sgt	COE Albert	18-12-39	97 Sqn
42473	P/O	COLMER William Leonard	13-12-39	214 Sqn
615297	AC2	CONNOR Bernard	29-10-39	35 Sqn
39065	F/O	COOPER John Arkell Harding	14-12-39	9 Sqn
565161	Sgt	CORDLE Ralph Sunei Wallace	30-10-39	50 Sqn
521647	Cpl	CORRY Edward	14-12-39	99 Sqn
40606	P/O	COVENTRY Charles Robey [Australia]	1-12-39	63 Sqn
566740	LAC	COX Gurth Ernest	18-12-39	9 Sqn
41670	P/O	COX Robert Ernest [Australia]	31-10-39	108 Sqn
523342	AC1	CUMMING James White	29-09-39	144 Sqn
16219	W/C	CUNNINGHAM James Charles	29-09-39	144 Sqn
528576	AC1	DAVIES Robert George	25-09-39	144 Sqn
549741	AC2	DAY Kenneth George	4-09-39	9 Sqn
566708	LAC	DICKIE Alex Morrison	18-12-39	9 Sqn
613687	AC2	DICKS Leonard George	30-10-39	9 Sqn
534038	Cpl	DODDS Thomas Doddridge	14-12-39	99 Sqn
562505	Sgt	DOODEY Frederick William	11-11-39	114 Sqn
531093	LAC	DORE Harry	4-09-39	9 Sqn
561103	F/S	DOWNEY William Howarth	14-12-39	99 Sqn
40374	P/O	DRAWWATER Matthew Infield	18-12-39	37 Sqn
552565	AC2	DUFF Ernest	8-11-39	97 Sqn
622509	AC2	DYE William Henry	5-11-39	38 Sqn
626364	AC2	EDWARDS Roy Henry	16-12-39	52 Sqn
628712	AC2	ELLIS William James	18-12-39	149 Sqn
526415	LAC	ELLISON Fred	2-10-39	10 Sqn
36138	F/O	EMDEN Henry Lovell	4-09-39	110 Sqn
620231	AC2	EMERY William James	9-10-39	7 Sqn
524025	Sgt	ENGLISH Thomas Henry	18-12-39	9 Sqn
542335	AC1	ENTWISTLE Ronald	14-12-39	99 Sqn
537187	AC1	EVANS Ralph	4-09-39	110 Sqn
563436	F/S	FEARNSIDE Alfred Kitto	18-12-39	9 Sqn
520361	LAC	FORSYTH Robert	14-12-39	99 Sqn

Service No.	Rank	Name	Date	Unit
621741	AC2	FOSTER Alan Gordon	18-12-39	149 Sqn
522192	AC1	FULLERTON Thomas	28-09-39	110 Sqn
562936	Sgt	GAUT Herbert John	18-10-39	102 Sqn
539328	AC1	GEDDES George Warne	19-12-39	37 Sqn
525139	LAC	GEORGE David	5-11-39	38 Sqn
550960	LAC	GIBBIN Terrance	21-12-39	44 Sqn
581212	Sgt	GIBSON Alvin Gordon	1-12-39	63 Sqn
533107	LAC	GOODENOUGH Albert George	18-12-39	9 Sqn
564696	Sgt	GOODWIN Frederic George	14-12-39	99 Sqn
543996	AC2	GORMLAY Hugh Oliver Wilson	1-12-39	63 Sqn
531937	AC1	GRANT Edward	30-10-39	9 Sqn
33189	F/O	GREEN Dennis Richard Dale	31-10-39	108 Sqn
565535	Sgt	GRIFFITHS Frank Hugo	19-09-39	51 Sqn
563464	Sgt	GUNN William McKenzie	28-09-39	110 Sqn
34155	S/L	GUTHRIE Archibald John [Canada]	18-12-39	9 Sqn
41402	P/O	HABGOOD George John	30-09-39	15 Sqn
580734	Sgt	HAMMOND Richard Robin	18-12-39	149 Sqn
562535	Sgt	HAMMOND Thomas Cecil [Eire]	28-09-39	110 Sqn
628360	AC2	HARDMAN Alan	5-11-39	38 Sqn
40620	P/O	HARKER Brian Leslie Gordon [New Zealand]	4-10-39	49 Sqn
580491	Sgt	HARRISON Ronald Leslie	7-11-39	98 Sqn
41709	P/O	HARVEY JACOBS Kenneth Charles	16-11-39	108 Sqn
518104	LAC	HAWKINS Stanley	30-10-39	9 Sqn
562536	F/S	HEALEY James Ernest Kirby	14-12-39	99 Sqn
740112	Sgt	HEMSLEY Phillip Geoffrey Vezey	10-10-39	108 Sqn
565893	Cpl	HENDERSON Archibald McDonald	23-11-39	50 Sqn
618765	AC2	HENDERSON Robert	4-09-39	9 Sqn
564710	Sgt	HERD Ronald Ernest	29-09-39	144 Sqn
566050	Sgt	HESLOP Alexander Oliver	5-09-39	9 Sqn
39026	F/L	HETHERINGTON Eugene John [New Zealand]	14-12-39	99 Sqn
523569	AC1	HEYWOOD Rolf	14-12-39	99 Sqn
544752	AC1	HILL Alexander Maxwell	18-12-39	37 Sqn
545939	AC1	HILL Alfred Francis	2-10-39	10 Sqn
616753	AC2	HILSDON William Charles	8-09-39	215 Sqn
296603	Sgt	HINSON Frederick	9-12-39	98 Sqn
531390	LAC	HODGE David Graham	14-12-39	99 Sqn
515110	Sgt	HOLLEY Thomas William	18-12-39	37 Sqn
547172	AC1	HOOKER Frederick George	14-12-39	99 Sqn
32173	S/L	HOPE Nigel	30-11-39	185 Sqn
546818	AC2	HOULDSWORTH Hughie	14-12-39	99 Sqn
39526	F/O	HOWARD John Gaskell	18-12-39	97 Sqn
564670	Sgt	HOWELLS Owen Lobb Dunkirk	4-09-39	107 Sqn
29210	S/L	HUE-WILLIAMS Ian Victor	18-12-39	37 Sqn
36206	P/O	HULL James Edward [New Zealand]	19-09-39	207 Sqn
580342	Sgt	HULME Harvey	14-12-39	99 Sqn
529268	AC1	HUMPHRY Edward Henry	21-12-39	49 Sqn
523436	Cpl	HUNTER Thomas	14-12-39	99 Sqn
621052	AC2	ISHERWOOD Stanley	29-09-39	144 Sqn
565602	Sgt	JARVIS Donald Edward	4-09-39	9 Sqn
552464	AC2	JOHNSON Frank James	14-12-39	99 Sqn
519664	AC1	JOHNSON Gilbert John	11-11-39	114 Sqn
540554	AC1	JONES Peter Thomas	18-12-39	37 Sqn
563978	Sgt	JONES Thomas Edwin	14-12-39	99 Sqn
348825	Cpl	KEATING Thomas Alexander	23-11-39	49 Sqn
620024	LAC	KELLY Walter Gerald	23-11-39	49 Sqn
569519	AC1	KEOGH Robert Allan Walker	18-12-39	52 Sqn
520262	LAC	KEY Josias Melville Fletcher	18-12-39	9 Sqn
563852	Sgt	KIRKUS Nigel Miller	29-09-39	144 Sqn
348684	Sgt	LACEY Henry	9-11-39	West Raynham
741579	Sgt	LAMB Dennis Charles	19-10-39	108 Sqn
29171	S/L	LAMB Lennox Stanley [New Zealand]	30-10-39	9 Sqn
619132	LAC	LANDING George Thomas	23-11-39	Waddington
541531	LAC	LANE Alfred William Walter	18-12-39	37 Sqn
70389	P/O	LAXTON Keith	27-12-39	107 Sqn
525796	AC1	LAYBOURNE Harry	11-11-39	77 Sqn
547262	AC2	LEIGHTON Isaac Davidson	18-12-39	149 Sqn
40399	P/O	LEWIS Norman Leonard	14-12-39	99 Sqn
40054	F/O	LEWIS Oliver John Trevor [Australia]	18-12-39	37 Sqn
531954	LAC	LEWIS Truscott Victor	27-12-39	107 Sqn
37884	F/O	LIGHTOLLER Herbert Brian	4-09-39	107 Sqn
538024	LAC	LILLEY Walter	18-12-39	9 Sqn
36224	P/O	LINES Eric Francis	18-12-39	9 Sqn
70892	P/O	LINES Fred Norman	18-12-39	149 Sqn
70866	P/O	LINGWOOD John	6-11-39	214 Sqn
770908	AC2	LOCKWOOD Robert George	10-09-39	Mildenhall
551250	AC1	LOOKER Ewart Wynne	29-10-39	35 Sqn
540706	LAC	LOWE Ernest	18-12-39	37 Sqn
39744	P/O	LUCKMAN Reginald Arthur Morton	18-10-39	102 Sqn
621435	AC2	LUMSDEN Alexander	13-10-39	114 Sqn
546679	AC1	LYON Ernest William	4-09-39	110 Sqn
551388	AC1	MacDONALD Alexander Bernard Bogle	24-10-39	77 Sqn
551644	AC2	MALCOLM Robert	19-09-39	207 Sqn
550205	LAC	MARLIN Thomas Leo	18-12-39	9 Sqn
580786	Sgt	MARTIN Gordon Ernest Francis	14-12-39	99 Sqn
40733	P/O	MARTYR Boyd Alan	11-11-39	114 Sqn
564032	Sgt	MARWOOD George Walton	13-10-39	114 Sqn
580718	Sgt	MASON Frank Michael	18-12-39	9 Sqn
534864	AC1	MATTHEWS Arthur	6-11-39	214 Sqn
36157	P/O	McCRACKEN William George [Australia]	30-10-39	139 Sqn
535916	AC1	McGARVIE Leslie	23-11-39	49 Sqn
541603	AC1	McGREEVY Hugh Hamilton	8-09-39	9 Sqn
546733	AC2	McGURK Francis Leo	4-10-39	49 Sqn
580160	F/S	MILLER George	4-09-39	9 Sqn
37605	F/L	MILLS Ronald Edward	11-11-39	114 Sqn
580376	Sgt	MITCHELL Stanley Robert	30-10-39	139 Sqn
753619	AC2	MONTGOMERY Robert Eckford	13-10-39	Bicester
517390	Cpl	MOORES Francis James Wilson	15-11-39	139 Sqn
580738	Sgt	MORGAN Elvies Bowen	14-12-39	99 Sqn
518032	Sgt	MOSS Thomas Robert	28-11-39	75 Sqn
563337	Sgt	MULLIN Bernard	19-09-39	51 Sqn
39748	P/O	MURPHY William Joseph [Eire]	4-09-39	107 Sqn
41197	P/O	MUSGRAVE John	30-11-39	185 Sqn
569513	LAC	NAYLOR Ernest John	13-12-39	149 Sqn
753277	AC2	NEWMAN George Henry Charles	5-11-39	38 Sqn
580831	Sgt	NORRIS Alister Raymond	18-12-39	37 Sqn
509143	Sgt	OTTY Stanley George McKenna	4-09-39	110 Sqn
632442	AC2	OVERALL Frederick Challenger	28-11-39	148 Sqn
624786	AC2	O'REGAN Daniel John	30-11-39	185 Sqn
524855	Cpl	PARK George William	4-09-39	9 Sqn
548974	AC2	PATEMAN Edward	4-09-39	110 Sqn
620054	AC1	PATERSON Charles	18-10-39	102 Sqn
41732	P/O	PEELER Trevor Anthony	16-11-39	90 Sqn
624358	AC2	PENTENY Leonard James	31-10-39	50 Sqn
580809	Sgt	PICKESS Bertie Joseph	18-12-39	9 Sqn
39679	P/O	PLAYFAIR Anthony Richard [Canada]	5-09-39	7 Sqn
551731	AC1	POLHILL Edward Malcolm George	18-12-39	9 Sqn
567777	LAC	PONTEY Richard	10-09-39	7 Sqn
580464	Sgt	POTTS Samuel Hainey	21-12-39	49 Sqn
618060	AC2	POUNTAIN Wilfred Henry	14-12-39	99 Sqn
366390	Sgt	POVEY Albert Edward Charles	29-09-39	144 Sqn
516867	Sgt	PRATT James (served as McLAUGHLIN)	10-09-39	82 Sqn
512105	LAC	PRICE Frederick Thomas	8-09-39	Honington
580195	Sgt	PRINCE Albert Stanley [Canada]	4-09-39	107 Sqn
545624	AC1	PURDIE Thomas	8-09-39	9 Sqn
41063	P/O	RADCLIFFE Michael	18-12-39	37 Sqn
41463	P/O	RALPH Joe	30-09-39	40 Sqn
41322	P/O	RHIND Geoffrey Arthur Cyril	29-10-39	35 Sqn
564063	Sgt	RICHARDSON Valentine Henry Garner	18-12-39	149 Sqn
519859	Cpl	RICKETTS James Leslie	4-09-39	107 Sqn

70578	P/O	ROBERTSON Donald Kerr	7-11-39	207 Sqn
75171	P/O	ROBINSON Clair Neil	18-12-39	97 Sqn
535440	Cpl	ROBINSON Wilson	18-12-39	37 Sqn
40022	P/O	ROSOFSKY Harold	8-09-39	9 Sqn
41070	P/O	ROSS Roderick Menzie [Canada]	18-12-39	37 Sqn
41743	P/O	RUSSELL-FORBES Rex Alan	13-12-39	214 Sqn
40061	F/O	SADLER John Tulloch Burrill [Australia]	29-09-39	144 Sqn
40321	P/O	SALMON Alan Gordon	2-10-39	10 Sqn
522788	Cpl	SHARP Andrew	14-12-39	99 Sqn
625176	AC2	SHEARER James	10-10-39	108 Sqn
580702	Sgt	SHEPPARD Leslie Alfred	18-12-39	37 Sqn
517970	LAC	SINTON John Humble	18-12-39	149 Sqn
590640	Sgt	SKELTON Kenneth Olford	26-11-39	Waddington
520179	LAC	SMITH Ivor James Travers	16-12-39	149 Sqn
526371	AC1	SMITH Robert Boaler	30-10-39	139 Sqn
39801	F/O	SPEIRS James Heggie Cumming	18-12-39	149 Sqn
580679	Sgt	SPROSTON Percy Edmund Boyce	29-09-39	144 Sqn
580680	Sgt	STEPHENS William Henry	29-09-39	144 Sqn
42273	P/O	STEVENS Charles Douiglas [Canada]	11-12-39	76 Sqn
520962	LAC	STOCK Leonard Arthur	18-12-39	37 Sqn
39179	F/O	STOREY Thomas William	28-11-39	148 Sqn
39580	F/O	STRACHAN Donald Arthur	28-09-39	110 Sqn
522075	Sgt	STRONG Arnold Vernon	8-11-39	97 Sqn
509103	Sgt	SUMMERS AFM Edward Thomas	5-11-39	38 Sqn
551857	AC2	TALBOT Frank Leslie	23-11-39	49 Sqn
580855	Sgt	TALBOT Gerald Roland Cecil	28-11-39	148 Sqn
533806	Cpl	TAYLOR Frederick James	18-12-39	37 Sqn
565020	Sgt	TAYLOR Gerald Harold Boutall	11-11-39	114 Sqn
537970	AC1	TAYLOR Harry	11-11-39	77 Sqn
552191	AC1	TAYLOR Stanley	23-11-39	49 Sqn
531938	AC1	TELFER Alexander	18-12-39	9 Sqn
580682	Sgt	THOM Lindsay	30-11-39	185 Sqn
550369	Sgt	THOMAS Charles	11-11-39	77 Sqn
39353	F/O	THOMPSON Arthur Telford	18-12-39	37 Sqn
40445	P/O	THOMPSON Kenneth George Sheldon	13-10-39	114 Sqn
621153	AC2	THOMSON Thomas	4-09-39	149 Sqn
580398	Sgt	THORNE Victor Brunsden	13-11-39	110 Sqn
513966	Sgt	TILLEY Alfred John	18-12-39	37 Sqn
551613	AC1	TOPHAM James Alfred	24-10-39	77 Sqn
37726	F/O	TORKINGTON-LEECH Peter Edward [South Africa]	30-10-39	9 Sqn
39622	F/O	TREWBY John Preston	14-12-39	99 Sqn
521968	Sgt	TURNBULL Joseph Buglast Adamson	18-12-39	9 Sqn
561939	F/S	TURNER Albion John	4-09-39	9 Sqn
508292	Sgt	TURNER Herbert Harold	29-09-39	144 Sqn
70689	P/O	TURNER Roger [Canada]	29-09-39	144 Sqn
516328	Sgt	TYRRELL Harold Walter	18-12-39	9 Sqn
33293	F/O	VAUGHAN WILLIAMS Arthur Richard	18-12-39	37 Sqn
627354	AC2	WALKER Clifford	18-12-39	9 Sqn
70706	P/O	WALKER Philip Edwin William	24-10-39	77 Sqn
564425	Sgt	WALSH Richard	11-11-39	77 Sqn
550292	Sgt	WALTON Bertie Greville	4-09-39	9 Sqn
564477	Sgt	WARD Leslie Robert	4-09-39	107 Sqn
547949	AC1	WARREN Peter John	18-12-39	149 Sqn
615941	LAC	WARRINER John Thomas	13-12-39	214 Sqn
567346	AC1	WATSON Charles	14-12-39	99 Sqn
618630	AC1	WATSON William	5-11-39	38 Sqn
16257	S/L	WATT Peter McGregor	23-11-39	49 Sqn
528158	Cpl	WHITEHOUSE Henry David	14-12-39	99 Sqn
537645	AC1	WHITTAKER Arthur John	28-11-39	148 Sqn
618247	AC2	WILKES Francis Joseph	7-11-39	97 Sqn
580687	Sgt	WILLIAMS Charles George	29-09-39	144 Sqn
37141	F/L	WILLIAMS Roland	15-10-39	77 Sqn
366471	F/S	WILLIAMS Siriol	29-09-39	144 Sqn
41512	P/O	WILLIAMS Thomas Ross [Canada]	28-11-39	207 Sqn
569344	LAC	WILLIS Richard Hampton	20-12-39	99 Sqn
551660	Sgt	WILSON Alan	29-09-39	144 Sqn
617452	AC2	WILSON Herbert	6-12-39	7 Sqn

Note

Although named on the Runnymede Memorial as belonging to 9 Squadron, Sgt Heslop lost his life when the 206 Squadron Anson in which he was flying was shot down during the course of a prolonged dogfight with a Heinkel He 115 (see Ross McNeill's first volume of *Royal Air Force Coastal Command Losses of the Second World War* (Midland Publishing, 2003). It can only be assumed that he had been detached to Bircham Newton where 206 Squadron was based or his details have been wrongly reported to the Commonwealth War Graves Commission. Such mistakes are rare, though in the context of this section the entries for P/O Beere and Sgt Strong are incorrectly recorded as '77 Sqn', though bearing in mind that 97 Squadron was at this stage of the war a Whitley training unit it is conceivable that the two airmen had been officially earmarked for posting to 77 Squadron and their service documents marked accordingly. LAC Lowe, who died on the 18th of December 1939, is recorded as missing on the 20th of December.

Probably at the request of Frank and Elsie Barton of Ferring in West Sussex, their son's entry in the Commonwealth War Graves Commission register for Sage War Cemetery is annotated, 'One of the first battle casualties of the Second World War.' It is also observed that the three officers with the surname 'Cameron' who lost their lives in 1939 all hailed from the Commonwealth.

At least three of those here commemorated belonged to families with an air force connection; AC1 Alexander Hill's father rose to the rank of squadron leader while serving with the volunteer reserve while F/O Howard's and P/O Lingwood's fathers were regular officers attaining the ranks of wing commander and squadron leader respectively. Tragically, in the case of the latter, he was to suffer the loss of a second son, F/O David Lingwood, whose 220 Squadron Hudson came down in the North Sea on the 4th of December, 1940 (see page 82 of *Royal Air Force Coastal Command Losses of the Second World War*, Volume 1 by Ross McNeill and published by Midland Publishing 2003).

This section (and in the eight parts that follow) show the names of a handful of officers and airmen that died on Bomber Command stations whose unit details are not reported but who, at the time of their death, seem to have been on the nominal roll of the station named.

Attached personnel

516460	Sgt	GROSSEY Raymond Charles	4-09-39	42 Sqn
39340	F/O	ROSS John Frederick	4-09-39	48 Sqn

Note

Both airmen belonged to Coastal Command squadrons but had been attached to 110 Squadron and 107 Squadron respectively for the raid on shipping in Wilhelmshaven harbour (see Volume 1, pages 14 and 15 for further information).

Postscript

Excluding the casualties sustained by the AASF and AC BEF, in the first four months of war Bomber Command lost 282* officers and airmen. Of these Sgt Summers had been awarded the Air Force Medal though I have not been able to trace the relevant *London Gazette* entry (his service number (509103) indicates that he joined the service in the 1920s). It will be observed that a considerable number of airmen aircrew are identified in this section and it may be helpful to remind readers that the more or less universal rank of 'Sgt' for qualified aircrew of non-officer status did not come into existence until the summer of 1940.

AC2 Lockwood (770908) is identified as having joined the volunteer reserve in or around October 1938, for operations room staff duties. Amongst the early casualties are a number of ex-Boy Entrants whose service commenced between July 1922 and January 1924; F/S Borley (365199), who was killed in action during the first bombing raid of the war being one example, while Sgt Hinson (296603) was a Great War veteran, his number indicating he was either a transfer from another of the armed services, or a direct civilian entrant twixt July 1918 and October of the same year. Sgt Hemsley (740112) was first of the pre-war volunteer reserve trained pilots to lose his life in Bomber Command service.

In conclusion, the names of P/O Habgood and P/O Ralph have been included in this section, even though their squadron identities suggest they were part of the AASF. However, neither died in France and the circumstances of their demise has been reported as follows. On the 30th of September, 1939, both were authorised to fly in Hind K5373 belonging to Abingdon's station flight, their duty being a cross-country exercise to the armament practice camp at Catfoss in Yorkshire, land and then return to Abingdon. It is not clear if the pair reached Catfoss, but at some point during the sortie and, it is thought, while *'hedge-hopping'* their aircraft flew into the ground roughly 2 miles north of the Royal Air Force College at Cranwell, Lincolnshire and burst into flames. Although assigned to station flight this particular Hind was intended for use by Oxford University Air Squadron.

* Including Sgt Heslop (see footnote on page 19).

Part 4

Bomber Command
Roll of Honour – 1940

The reappraisal of bomber operations, referred to in the closing paragraph of the introduction to Part 3, requires little explanation. In essence, Bomber Command shelved its pre-war concept of daylight operations and began to train for a night bombing campaign. It will be recalled, however, that in the first four months of 1940, any night incursions over Germany had to be restricted to reconnaissance and the frequent dropping of propaganda leaflets, popularly referred to as *'Nickels'*, a task that since the first night of the war had been carried out by the Whitley squadrons of No.4 Group. Now, the Wellington crews of No.3 Group and the Hampden boys of No.5 Group would begin an extensive period of night flying training, leaving the gallant Blenheim airmen that staffed the squadrons of No.2 Group to bear the brunt of any daylight offensive.

It will be more appropriate to comment in the form of a postscript the outcome of operations in 1940, and to confine this introduction to the more mundane, but no less important, matters that affected Bomber Command. In January, 1940, Air Chief Marshal Sir Edgar Ludlow-Hewitt, had 43 squadrons under his command, precisely the same number that he had at the end of September, 1939. But, as reported in the last section, only 23 were operationally proficient, the remainder being restricted to the vitally important role of training. The situation of maintaining 20 squadrons as either training formations, reserve squadrons or group pool units, was unsatisfactory and so it came to pass, early in April, 1940, that the majority of the 15 squadrons administered by No.6 Group were merged, along with their station headquarters, to form Operational Training Units (OTUs). In time the majority of the squadrons affected by this seed change in direction would re-form, as operational formations, in Bomber Command, but in the case of 52 Squadron and 63 Squadron, both merging with station headquarters at Benson to become 12 OTU, 108 Squadron, 148 Squadron and 185 Squadron, their role of duty under Bomber Command control was over, at least for the duration of the present hostilities.

On the 3rd of April, 1940, having set in train the procedures that would lead to the establishment of the OTUs, Ludlow-Hewitt vacated his chair at High Wycombe and took up the post of Inspector-General of the Royal Air Force, a position he was to hold for the remainder of the Second World War. His successor was Air Marshal Sir Charles Frederick Algernon Portal, a man of immense talent and who was already marked down for higher office. In fact, his tenure of command was relatively brief for on the 5th of October, 1940, he handed over command to Air Marshal Sir Richard E. C. Peirse, late Vice-Chief of the Air Staff. Portal, meanwhile, became Chief of the Air Staff, remaining as such for the duration of the war.

Thus, the command that Peirse inherited was little changed from that handed over by Ludlow-Hewitt, six months previous. During his time spent as Vice-Chief of the Air Staff, Peirse had been closely involved with bombing policy and his appointment to succeed Portal would have been regarded as a logical progression. Unfortunately, his direction of Bomber Command was less than successful, though in fairness to Peirse, many of the problems that manifested themselves during the 15 months of his command were not entirely of his own making. By the end of 1940, three new bombers were about to enter service and due to the extremities of the hour, all three were introduced to front-line usage before all their faults could be fully ironed out. In respect of the Manchester, no amount of effort could fully eradicate the problems experienced with its twin Vulture engines, and the early production Stirlings and Halifaxes fared little better, though, in time, both types were developed to acceptable standards. Time, however, was a luxury that Bomber Command could ill afford. When Peirse arrived at High Wycombe, the *'Battle of Britain'* had peaked and the Luftwaffe had turned its attention to conducting a night blitz on the major cities of the United Kingdom with London, in particular, suffering raids of a most devastating nature. The desire of the public at large to feel that Bomber Command was responding in kind was natural, but though it was not for the want of trying, the plain truth is that very little material damage was being inflicted on Germany's major industrial towns.

However, firm evidence as to the paucity of pain being inflicted on Germany's resources, at the close of 1940, was, as yet, not forthcoming. And, at least, a very gradual expansion of Bomber Command was underway. 7 Squadron, whose *'number plate'* had been placed in abeyance with the formation of the OTUs in April, was resurrected for the issue of the first Stirlings into squadron service; likewise, 35 Squadron had re-formed for the purpose of introducing the Halifax, while the task of getting the Manchester into operational service had been given to 207 Squadron, whose re-emergence as a bomber squadron had taken place at Waddington on the 1st of November. The embryo re-equipment programme for three of the four main night bombing groups had been set in train.

Meanwhile, Wellington production was sufficient for the type to begin replacing the less satisfactory aircraft in Bomber Command's inventory, and by the end of the year, the four Polish Air Force (PAF) squadrons, formed within No.1 Group*, had exchanged their Battles for the stalwart Wellington Ic. Noteworthy, too, was the formation of the sole Czechoslovakian bomber squadron to operate in Bomber Command, 311 Squadron, which came into being at Honington on the 29th of July, 1940, administration of the new unit coming under the aegis of No.3 Group. And, by the end of the year, a gradual expansion of the command's training units had resulted in the formation of a second training group, namely No.7 Group, while the initial establishment of 8 OTUs had grown to 11. A very solid foundation stone had been laid.

As the material strength of Bomber Command increased, so did its manpower. In 1934, the all regular air force operated with 30,000 men; then, with the expansion programmes of the late 1930s set in train and the introduction of the volunteer reserve scheme that offered enthusiastic young men the opportunity to undergo weekend training, either as pilots, navigators or wireless operators, the foundations for continued expansion of the air force was on a firm footing. By mid-1940, the first fruits of the volunteer reserve scheme, along with a small trickle of auxiliary air force personnel, were blending with the regulars in that cosmopolitan mix that was now a feature of all the air force's operational squadrons. At first, the many Commonwealth and Dominion airmen that had arrived on British shores in the last years of peace were taken in by the professional air force, a high percentage signing up for short service commissions. However, by the end of 1940, airmen of the Royal New Zealand Air Force were operating alongside the regulars and volunteer reserve of the Royal Air Force and, as will be seen from this section, laying down their lives in the fight for freedom. And, it would not be long before they were joined by their colleagues from the Royal Australian Air Force and the Royal Canadian Air Force.

As indicated above, observations on progress made with the night bombing campaign, along with an appraisal of the outstanding bravery of the Blenheim crews of No.2 Group, are reserved for the postscript. To close this introduction it is worth mentioning that during 1913 and 1914, Richard Pierse, the Command's new commander-in-chief, had been one of several flying instructors tasked with teaching Winston Churchill to fly.

* After disbanding at Abingdon in late August, 1939, No.1 Group commenced re-forming at Benson with effect from the 12th of September, 1939, but disbanded ten days later. Now, with the fall of France and the return of what remained of the Battle squadrons, re-formation of a group headquarters was set in train on the 22nd of June, 1940, at Hucknall, Nottinghamshire.

ROYAL AIR FORCE,
AUXILIARY AIR FORCE and
ROYAL AIR FORCE (VOLUNTEER RESERVE)
personnel

590429	F/S	ABBOTT Ronald	30-04-40	110 Sqn
549202	Sgt	ABEL Richard	12-08-40	83 Sqn
904333	Sgt	ABERY Edward Stanley	19-07-40	18 Sqn
626935	AC2	ABLETT Henry George	7-04-40	115 Sqn
580418	Sgt	ABRAHAMS Frederick Joseph	29-10-40	102 Sqn
630069	AC2	ADAMS James Campbell	30-05-40	38 Sqn
551554	Sgt	ADAMS DFM Peter David	1-11-40	144 Sqn
525865	Sgt	ADAMS Peter Edward Frederick	23-06-40	107 Sqn
936634	AC2	ADAMS Trevor George	16-09-40	57 Sqn
41646	P/O	ADDIE Peter Aubrey Forrester	17-03-40	50 Sqn
745662	Sgt	ADLAM Leonard Frank Percy	21-10-40	58 Sqn
581196	Sgt	ADLAM Richard Perry	10-10-40	107 Sqn
625621	AC2	AHERNE Patrick [Eire]	14-05-40	110 Sqn
42177	P/O	AINSWORTH Kenneth Richard Baverstock	8-04-40	10 OTU
563022	Sgt	AITCHISON James Dougal	12-04-40	9 Sqn
513170	Sgt	AITKEN Alexander	7-07-40	37 Sqn
751854	LAC	AITKEN Robert Stuart	27-05-40	16 OTU
787410	Sgt	ALBRECHT Josef [Czechoslovakia]	16-10-40	311 Sqn
953906	AC1	ALCOCK John Charles	12-11-40	21 Sqn
622419	Sgt	ALDOM Douglas Ronald	13-08-40	61 Sqn
562397	Sgt	ALEXANDER Jack Leslie	25-04-40	40 Sqn
970031	Sgt	ALGAR Alan	5-10-40	61 Sqn
540542	LAC	ALLAM DFM Frederick John	11-05-40	110 Sqn
748744	Sgt	ALLARDICE Kenneth Gordon	15-12-40	102 Sqn
929984	Sgt	ALLCOCK Frank Thomas	14-12-40	78 Sqn
648865	Sgt	ALLEN Arthur Grenfell	9-08-40	10 OTU
649497	Sgt	ALLEN Dudley Brooking	26-09-40	77 Sqn
740664	Sgt	ALLEN John Wollaston Keith	4-09-40	18 Sqn
70009	F/O	ALLEN Richard Guy	11-09-40	38 Sqn
550539	Sgt	ALVES Dennis Frank	7-08-40	16 OTU
532047	Sgt	ANDERSON William Flight	28-06-40	61 Sqn
746706	Sgt	ANDREW John Gordon	9-07-40	57 Sqn
36252	P/O	ANDREW Neville Halsey [New Zealand]	1-10-40	78 Sqn
745535	Sgt	ANDREWS Edgar James	15-10-40	50 Sqn
41648	P/O	ANDREWS John Frederick Edward [Canada]	13-06-40	144 Sqn
26196	S/L	ANDREWS Lionel Vincent	9-09-40	149 Sqn
641627	Sgt	ANDREWS Robert Ernest	11-11-40	82 Sqn
754951	Sgt	ANGELL Dennis	14-12-40	78 Sqn
751690	Sgt	ANGUS John Henry	17-09-40	44 Sqn
581136	Sgt	ANKERS George Cyril	13-08-40	105 Sqn
751929	Sgt	ANSTEY Philip James	16-12-40	77 Sqn
940153	Sgt	ANTCLIFFE Gordon Ellis	8-10-40	13 OTU
580923	Sgt	APPERSON Eric Thomas	4-07-40	44 Sqn
543847	LAC	ARMSTRONG Daniel	7-04-40	115 Sqn
78736	P/O	ARNOLD Philip	14-11-40	83 Sqn
521409	Sgt	ARROWSMITH Vincent	24-09-40	139 Sqn
74658	P/O	ARUP Peter Dahl	5-08-40	15 OTU
944309	LAC	ASH Bertram	15-08-40	102 Sqn
43278	P/O	ASH Ronald George [Australia]	12-12-40	50 Sqn
40198	F/O	ASHFIELD Leslie James	15-05-40	44 Sqn
740908	Sgt	ASHFORTH Lewis Ernest	1-09-40	106 Sqn
742042	Sgt	ASHLEY Nigel Clifford	23-12-40	139 Sqn
751950	Sgt	ASHURST Thomas Eldon	16-11-40	105 Sqn
561992	Sgt	ASHLEY Cecil Henry	24-09-40	19 OTU
906102	Sgt	ASHMAN Arthur Charles	7-12-40	214 Sqn
581077	Sgt	ASHTON David Allan	14-05-40	110 Sqn
630781	Sgt	ASTBURY Ronald Charles	11-06-40	77 Sqn
631239	Sgt	ATACK Dallas	1-06-40	37 Sqn
580497	Sgt	ATCHISON Thomas Todd	12-05-40	77 Sqn
41360	P/O	ATKIN-BERRY Harold Leslie	10-07-40	107 Sqn
652440	Sgt	ATKINSON Alfred Stanley	11-12-40	50 Sqn
42329	P/O	ATKINSON George Andrew [Eire]	13-06-40	61 Sqn
515180	Sgt	ATKINSON James	15-04-40	61 Sqn
745008	Sgt	ATTFIELD Reginald Albert	8-12-40	61 Sqn
643865	Sgt	ATTWOOD Cecil Alfred Victor	24-08-40	11 OTU
812291	Sgt	AUSTEN Douglas William	18-09-40	58 Sqn
77130	P/O	AUSTIN Guy Paul Wentworth [South Africa]	15-10-40	9 Sqn
615205	LAC	AUSTIN Ronald William	24-05-40	15 Sqn
566960	Sgt	AVENT Douglas John	12-05-40	15 Sqn
39479	F/O	AYRES Vivian Howard	17-03-40	50 Sqn
751665	LAC	BACKSHALL Eric Owen	6-05-40	16 OTU
640031	Sgt	BAGHURST Reginald James	14-06-40	38 Sqn
642862	Sgt	BAGULEY John	18-09-40	77 Sqn
44463	P/O	BAILEY Geoffrey Donald	14-11-40	77 Sqn
552072	Sgt	BAILEY Percy Fallows	4-07-40	144 Sqn
581258	Sgt	BAILEY Robert James	1-01-40	7 Sqn
581078	Sgt	BAINBRIDGE George Henry	30-08-40	214 Sqn
639105	Sgt	BAIRD Arthur	4-07-40	44 Sqn
745904	LAC	BAIRD Thomas	27-05-40	16 OTU
751839	Sgt	BAKER John	25-08-40	49 Sqn
645894	Sgt	BAKER Sydney Nevil	1-08-40	16 OTU
625671	Sgt	BALDWIN DFM Jack	14-10-40	44 Sqn
524840	LAC	BALL John Brayfield	6-04-40	21 Sqn
745177	Sgt	BALL Leslie	21-11-40	49 Sqn
42585	P/O	BALL Ralph Alan Anthony	7-07-40	37 Sqn
580780	Sgt	BALLANTYNE Robert	2-01-40	149 Sqn
42688	P/O	BALLAS-ANDERSEN Konstantine	28-10-40	49 Sqn
745574	Sgt	BALMER John Hawes	26-08-40	101 Sqn
564120	Sgt	BALMER William Lockie	12-04-40	9 Sqn
42375	P/O	BAMBER Hugh Christopher Morris	7-07-40	15 Sqn

Number	Rank	Name	Date	Squadron
562429	Sgt	BANCROFT Leslie	15-04-40	110 Sqn
36223	P/O	BARBER Frederick Edward	12-04-40	115 Sqn
647990	Sgt	BARBER Peter William	2-09-40	37 Sqn
42043	P/O	BARKER David Conquest	24-05-40	44 Sqn
580732	Sgt	BARKER Ernest Arthur	1-11-40	144 Sqn
15181	W/C	BARLOW Ernest Cecil	15-05-40	40 Sqn
36235	P/O	BARNETT Michael Edward Fulton [New Zealand]	8-04-40	12 OTU
36163	F/L	BARNWELL Richard Antony	29-10-40	102 Sqn
638908	AC1	BARON Thomas Joseph	30-08-40	12 Sqn
550995	Cpl	BARRASS Alexander Scougal Gibson	12-04-40	50 Sqn
580865	Sgt	BARRETT Duncan Henry James	20-05-40	102 Sqn
905832	Sgt	BARRETT Warren Seymour	2-08-40	18 Sqn
580566	Sgt	BARRETT DFM William John	23-06-40	107 Sqn
542271	Sgt	BARROW Victor St. George	1-08-40	114 Sqn
624718	Sgt	BARTLETT Charles Alfred	12-06-40	107 Sqn
78994	P/O	BARTLETT John Edward	15-10-40	9 Sqn
37537	F/L	BASKERVILLE John Edward [Canada]	20-03-40	51 Sqn
580902	Sgt	BASS Frederick John	1-05-40	102 Sqn
40781	F/O	BASSETT Thomas George [New Zealand]	12-05-40	15 Sqn
1183781	AC2	BATCHELOR Albert Edward	27-10-40	149 Sqn
563051	Sgt	BATCHELOR Frederick William	14-04-40	50 Sqn
580629	Sgt	BATHO Reginald Frank	6-08-40	49 Sqn
39055	S/L	BATT DFC Robert Hector	9-07-40	40 Sqn
523469	Sgt	BATTLE Edward Hulme	28-12-40	50 Sqn
516469	Sgt	BATTRICK Reginald Henry John	30-04-40	110 Sqn
581137	Sgt	BAUM Alfred James	11-08-40	49 Sqn
524225	Sgt	BAXTER William	18-05-40	15 Sqn
551819	Cpl	BAYBUTT Thomas	26-05-40	144 Sqn
44057	P/O	BAYLISS Gilbert Louis	26-08-40	40 Sqn
42479	P/O	BAYNES Roy	30-05-40	38 Sqn
755028	Sgt	BAZELEY Douglas Stanley	30-10-40	106 Sqn
741185	Sgt	BEALE Frederick Allen	17-08-40	51 Sqn
742726	Sgt	BEALES Rex	2-08-40	83 Sqn
39367	S/L	BEAMAN DFC Robert Carleton	31-12-40	139 Sqn
581138	Sgt	BEARD Harold Norman	4-08-40	15 Sqn
526936	Sgt	BEARDWOOD George	10-05-40	40 Sqn
619827	Sgt	BEATTIE John Milton	10-08-40	50 Sqn
910397	Sgt	BEATTIE John Stainton	29-12-40	115 Sqn
745372	Sgt	BEATTIE Joseph	15-12-40	77 Sqn
631456	Sgt	BEAVERS William Robert Noel	28-12-40	106 Sqn
563045	Sgt	BEAVIS Frank James Robert	30-04-40	110 Sqn
33106	S/L	BECK Hugh Denis	7-12-40	16 OTU
524300	Sgt	BECK Oswald	6-05-40	14 OTU
653372	AC2	BECKER Leslie Alderman Edward	1-06-40	110 Sqn
550969	LAC	BEDFORD Michael Frederick	12-04-40	38 Sqn
629952	Sgt	BEEBY DFM Augustus Spencer	13-08-40	82 Sqn
40663	P/O	BELL Brian Stallard [Canada]	1-08-40	50 Sqn
624554	Sgt	BELL William	6-09-40	44 Sqn
581261	Sgt	BELTON DFM Spencer Lewis Smith	10-08-40	144 Sqn
926823	Sgt	BENBOW Frederick Charles	4-12-40	82 Sqn
649294	Sgt	BENNETT Benjamin Michael	11-07-40	58 Sqn
742843	Sgt	BENNETT Denis	22-07-40	9 Sqn
549557	Sgt	BENNETT Harry	5-10-40	144 Sqn
620296	AC1	BENNETT Hubert Bapaume	10-06-40	13 OTU
40664	P/O	BENNETT John Keith	26-05-40	49 Sqn
16216	W/C	BENNETT Leslie Clive [New Zealand]	9-07-40	21 Sqn
41656	P/O	BENNETT MiD Richard Henry Montague [Canada]	30-06-40	107 Sqn
926312	AC2	BENNETT Robert William	20-07-40	Scampton
969978	Sgt	BENNETT Russell Gordon	21-10-40	44 Sqn
43131	P/O	BENSON Arthur Herbert	25-04-40	49 Sqn
552444	Sgt	BENTHAM Henry	30-08-40	107 Sqn
627034	AC2	BERRIDGE Leslie Askham	12-05-40	107 Sqn
34206	F/L	BERRILL Edward Reginald	8-03-40	9 Sqn
39959	F/O	BERRY Ernest Reginald	30-08-40	107 Sqn
626342	Sgt	BEST Herbert Henry	30-08-40	50 Sqn
580598	Sgt	BESTICK Frank Frederick [Canada]	12-04-40	38 Sqn
701775	AC1	BETTS John Herbert	11-11-40	110 Sqn
651939	Sgt	BEVERLEY Victor	18-09-40	99 Sqn
759127	Sgt	BEWS Stanley	4-09-40	107 Sqn
523511	LAC	BEYNON MiD Elvie	5-04-40	51 Sqn
650625	Sgt	BICHARD Frederick James William	28-10-40	49 Sqn
563033	Sgt	BIGG Frederick John Raymond	17-02-40	110 Sqn
936831	Sgt	BILTON John Norman	18-08-40	218 Sqn
943809	Sgt	BINKS George Arnold	7-12-40	16 OTU
40984	F/O	BIRCH DFC Colin Granville	28-11-40	20 OTU
540261	LAC	BIRCH Frank	16-02-40	21 Sqn
39430	F/O	BIRCH James Ronald	23-04-40	51 Sqn
538032	Sgt	BIRKHEAD George Thomas	30-10-40	Wattisham
759123	Sgt	BIRT Allan Maurice	10-12-40	82 Sqn
754664	Sgt	BISHOP John	19-08-40	14 OTU
653306	Sgt	BISHOP Robert Charles	23-11-40	214 Sqn
751016	Sgt	BISSETT DFM William Slater	14-09-40	61 Sqn
37373	S/L	BLACK George Roderick Hartwell	15-10-40	77 Sqn
536996	Sgt	BLACK James McDonald	11-06-40	10 Sqn
754538	Sgt	BLAIR David Jack	17-09-40	14 OTU
39196	F/O	BLAKE John Christopher Howell	27-02-40	82 Sqn
41248	P/O	BLANCKENSEE Lewis Mervyn	13-06-40	21 Sqn
746887	Sgt	BLAZIER John Kenneth	10-08-40	82 Sqn
42186	P/O	BLIGH Orley Whitney [Canada]	10-02-40	97 Sqn
40041	F/L	BLOM DFC Walter Michael	27-07-40	150 Sqn
580567	Sgt	BLOOMER Peter	25-05-40	15 Sqn
633207	Sgt	BLOOR Gordon Elijah	19-07-40	101 Sqn
907481	AC1	BLYTH Charles Frederick	9-10-40	110 Sqn
43020	P/O	BOAK Andrew Stenhouse	5-10-40	50 Sqn
749598	Sgt	BOAST William Edwin Herbert	18-12-40	99 Sqn
73028	P/O	BODY John	12-08-40	149 Sqn
751147	Sgt	BOGUE James Joseph Aloysius	27-09-40	106 Sqn
631257	Sgt	BOLAND Alfred Edward	13-08-40	82 Sqn
37712	F/O	BOMFORD Charles Powell [Eire]	9-06-40	107 Sqn
630373	AC1	BOOTH John	18-04-40	99 Sqn
747801	Sgt	BOOTH Philip Watson	25-09-40	101 Sqn
550339	Sgt	BOOTH Stanley Keable	8-09-40	101 Sqn
742082	Sgt	BOTT Norman Kelvin	29-08-40	102 Sqn
741844	Sgt	BOULTER Hugh Herman	13-08-40	11 OTU
936282	Sgt	BOULTON Gordon	9-12-40	114 Sqn
636888	AC2	BOULTON Sidney	12-06-40	17 OTU
748589	Sgt	BOWDEN Rupert James	18-12-40	99 Sqn
562025	Sgt	BOWEN Charles Ronald	12-04-40	9 Sqn
515101	Sgt	BOWEN James Thomas	1-05-40	37 Sqn
743077	Sgt	BOWERS Henry	15-08-40	15 Sqn
568528	LAC	BOWES James Weston	16-06-40	50 Sqn
745179	Sgt	BOWLER James Arthur	25-11-40	99 Sqn
580170	Sgt	BOWLES Cyril	18-09-40	105 Sqn
580756	Sgt	BOWMAN Robert Anthony	9-06-40	107 Sqn
580692	Sgt	BOWMER Harry Alexander	2-08-40	83 Sqn
805458	Sgt	BOWTELL Richard Thomas	8-10-40	16 OTU
619108	AC1	BOYD James	5-04-40	51 Sqn
33019	S/L	BRADFORD Ridley Lewkenor	1-05-40	37 Sqn
581140	Sgt	BRADING Ronald James	10-09-40	44 Sqn
72463	P/O	BRAHAM David Frederick	11-06-40	10 Sqn
700497	Sgt	BRAMS Gerald Charlesbeth	3-08-40	103 Sqn
580637	Sgt	BRATTON Harry	12-04-40	50 Sqn
42390	P/O	BRAUN Michael Ryves	20-09-40	75 Sqn
42187	P/O	BRAYNE Ronald Percy	18-09-40	77 Sqn
755007	Sgt	BREEZE Lionel Bradley	6-11-40	58 Sqn
549506	Sgt	BRENNAN Kevin Barry	19-06-40	9 Sqn
355933	F/S	BRENT John William Lewis Goldie	1-05-40	99 Sqn
971032	Sgt	BRETT Walter James	8-10-40	13 OTU
546678	LAC	BREWSTER William Edward	30-04-40	37 Sqn
620409	Sgt	BRIDGE James	1-06-40	37 Sqn
539332	LAC	BRIDSON Harold	10-05-40	40 Sqn
754172	Sgt	BRITNOR Stanley	19-08-40	14 OTU

Number	Rank	Name	Date	Sqn
565447	F/S	BROADHURST Rodolphe Burford	2-09-40	40 Sqn
581316	Sgt	BROOK Harold Wignell	23-11-40	214 Sqn
745993	Sgt	BROOKE John	14-08-40	15 OTU
41251	P/O	BROOKE-TAYLOR Keith [New Zealand]	7-04-40	83 Sqn
742459	Sgt	BROOKER Alec Albert	13-09-40	61 Sqn
742131	Sgt	BROOKER Francis John	5-10-40	50 Sqn
937552	Sgt	BROOKER Kenneth Angus	10-10-40	107 Sqn
751046	Sgt	BROOKER Sydney George	28-09-40	9 Sqn
745413	Sgt	BROOKES Birt	16-11-40	50 Sqn
742109	Sgt	BROOKS Leonard John	28-05-40	77 Sqn
551008	LAC	BROWN Aldewin Arthur	2-01-40	149 Sqn
41550	F/O	BROWN Ernest Henry	21-10-40	58 Sqn
970851	Sgt	BROWN George Warden	17-09-40	14 OTU
566550	Sgt	BROWN George William	9-10-40	77 Sqn
613213	Cpl	BROWN Harold Dennis	12-04-40	44 Sqn
968371	Sgt	BROWN Jack Leonard	8-09-40	149 Sqn
970119	Sgt	BROWN James	17-10-40	49 Sqn
565062	Sgt	BROWN James Francis	31-05-40	37 Sqn
741269	Sgt	BROWN John Barnet Mathieson	9-07-40	21 Sqn
937342	Sgt	BROWN John Edward	31-12-40	114 Sqn
742961	Sgt	BROWN John Herbert	17-10-40	144 Sqn
745568	Sgt	BROWN John Raymond	30-10-40	51 Sqn
518807	Sgt	BROWN DFM Norman Wilson	26-07-40	75 Sqn
532583	Cpl	BROWN William John	2-10-40	Hemswell
537351	Sgt	BROWNING John Raymond	13-06-40	107 Sqn
524136	Sgt	BRUCE Robert George	5-04-40	51 Sqn
77036	P/O	BRUNDISH George William	12-04-40	38 Sqn
76003	P/O	BRYAN-SMITH Anthony	15-04-40	49 Sqn
755318	Sgt	BRYANT Kenneth Roy	2-08-40	18 Sqn
524310	Cpl	BRYSON Robert Strang	18-04-40	99 Sqn
758023	Sgt	BUCKINGHAM Francis Thomas	7-12-40	214 Sqn
638746	Sgt	BUCKLE Francis Arthur	8-12-40	50 Sqn
744989	Sgt	BUCKLEY Alexander	17-11-40	21 Sqn
987980	Sgt	BUCKLEY Ronald John	13-08-40	83 Sqn
742529	Sgt	BUCKNELL Ronald	15-11-40	83 Sqn
742113	Sgt	BUDDEN Philip Henry James	11-06-40	77 Sqn
74328	P/O	BUFTON John Raymond	28-10-40	49 Sqn
42690	P/O	BUIST Clement Neville [Australia]	19-06-40	58 Sqn
40599	P/O	BULL John Bartlett [Australia]	12-04-40	50 Sqn
904181	Sgt	BULL Nugent Joseph [Australia]	9-09-40	149 Sqn
76004	P/O	BULL Peter Edward Tucker	12-04-40	115 Sqn
75682	F/L	BULL William Sharman	4-07-40	44 Sqn
39372	F/O	BULLARD-DAVIES Royston Henry	20-03-40	144 Sqn
42391	P/O	BULLER Alexander John Stuart	6-06-40	101 Sqn
37788	F/O	BULLOCH Hugh Laromor McLearn	2-01-40	149 Sqn
74665	F/O	BULMER Alan	11-11-40	49 Sqn
580601	Sgt	BUNDOCK Frank Vyvyan	3-10-40	105 Sqn
745279	Sgt	BUNKER Anthony St. John	16-07-40	18 Sqn
563432	Sgt	BURGE Ronald William	14-06-40	40 Sqn
544110	LAC	BURGESS Arthur Christopher Bradfield	12-03-40	21 Sqn
551687	AC1	BURKE Harry Squire	12-03-40	61 Sqn
26100	S/L	BURKE Wilfred Ivanhoe Harris	8-06-40	15 Sqn
613517	LAC	BURNETT Eric William	1-05-40	37 Sqn
619744	Sgt	BURNETT Ralph	30-06-40	61 Sqn
640669	Sgt	BURNS Angus John	2-09-40	40 Sqn
968516	Sgt	BURNS Robert	26-11-40	15 OTU
551796	AC1	BURNSIDE David	17-04-40	144 Sqn
580941	Sgt	BURRELL Peter Arthur Merrick	23-05-40	40 Sqn
551597	Sgt	BURROW John	15-08-40	77 Sqn
751659	Sgt	BURT Brian William	8-06-40	82 Sqn
629928	Sgt	BURT Christopher James	9-07-40	21 Sqn
971328	Sgt	BURT Eric	30-09-40	106 Sqn
566634	Sgt	BURT Leonard John	14-10-40	44 Sqn
627969	AC2	BURTON John	24-05-40	149 Sqn
580867	Sgt	BURTON Noel Huckman	22-07-40	78 Sqn
751221	Sgt	BUSHELL Edwin James	1-11-40	144 Sqn
80805	P/O	BUSHNELL Patrick William Michael	19-09-40	50 Sqn
627874	Sgt	BUTLER Benjamin	28-11-40	20 OTU
745989	Sgt	BUTLER Charles Herbert	28-05-40	77 Sqn
76576	P/O	BUTLER Francis Charles Joseph	19-06-40	9 Sqn
33182	F/O	BUTLER Peter Saumarez	25-05-40	49 Sqn
650521	AC1	BUTTERY Harold	1-05-40	102 Sqn
627950	Sgt	BYATT John	8-06-40	82 Sqn
755885	Sgt	BYRNE Thomas Patrick Joseph	15-08-40	18 Sqn
83243	P/P	BYWATER Maurice	10-10-40	107 Sqn
746944	Sgt	CAMERON Alexander Douglas	1-10-40	115 Sqn
902597	Sgt	CAMERON Alexander Lindsay	19-09-40	20 OTU
36237	P/O	CAMERON Edward Colin Joseph [New Zealand]	20-07-40	75 Sqn
33458	P/O	CAMERON John Stewart [Cuba]	26-05-40	37 Sqn
40669	F/O	CAMPBELL Alan Andrew	24-11-40	107 Sqn
78450	P/O	CAMPBELL Colin	9-06-40	107 Sqn
937405	Sgt	CAMPBELL John Erik	15-12-40	77 Sqn
755497	Sgt	CAMPBELL Lewis Duthie	27-08-40	101 Sqn
742698	Sgt	CAMPION Alfred Norman	14-08-40	10 Sqn
533257	Sgt	CANDLISH James Wilson	23-07-40	58 Sqn
638518	LAC	CANN Walter Ypres	27-07-40	150 Sqn
751769	Sgt	CANNING Cornelius Daniel McColgan	6-11-40	99 Sqn
746801	Sgt	CANNON William Arthur	5-10-40	61 Sqn
581320	Sgt	CANTWELL Nicholas William [Eire]	20-09-40	12 OTU
751903	Sgt	CAPELING Robert	1-09-40	106 Sqn
581270	Sgt	CARLILE Neville William	13-06-40	82 Sqn
77350	P/O	CARNEGIE David Stuart	20-07-40	61 Sqn
75687	P/O	CARRELL Ronald Mark	14-10-40	44 Sqn
942329	Sgt	CARROLL John Adrian	23-12-40	11 OTU
42693	P/O	CARSON Arthur Frederick Copithorne [Canada]	16-09-40	21 Sqn
74667	P/O	CARSON Illtyd Thomas Holden	13-08-40	114 Sqn
568628	LAC	CARTER George Walter Dennis	14-04-40	115 Sqn
628721	Sgt	CARTER Hughie William	27-08-40	10 Sqn
72448	P/O	CARTER John Nemours	3-03-40	99 Sqn
740975	Sgt	CARTER Johnathan Wallace	6-09-40	144 Sqn
563527	Sgt	CARTER Robert Frederick	17-04-40	144 Sqn
742681	Sgt	CARTHEW Eric Frank	25-11-40	50 Sqn
741674	Sgt	CARTWRIGHT Norman Byng	4-12-40	82 Sqn
902238	Sgt	CARYLL-TILKIN Marcel Cuthbert	21-10-40	58 Sqn
553120	Sgt	CASEY Arthur Joseph Patrick	17-12-40	49 Sqn
515481	F/S	CASON Frederick George William	1-11-40	Wattisham
614511	Sgt	CASSELLS MiD William Hogg	8-09-40	82 Sqn
581374	Sgt	CASWELL James John	14-10-40	10 Sqn
745724	Sgt	CATLEY Frederick Norman Colin	29-09-40	49 Sqn
758161	Sgt	CATTO Patrick Tawse	10-10-40	149 Sqn
581499	Sgt	CATTON Anthony Charles	8-04-40	13 OTU
542287	LAC	CAVANAGH William Timothy	12-05-40	15 Sqn
43700	P/O	CAVE Jack Milton [New Zealand]	30-10-40	101 Sqn
751648	Sgt	CAVE William	10-11-40	50 Sqn
72328	P/O	CAZALET Alexander Brise Travers	9-09-40	107 Sqn
651713	Sgt	CHAMBERLAIN John William	23-12-40	58 Sqn
33305	F/L	CHALMERS Alan	10-06-40	13 OTU
619757	AC1	CHALMERS Peter William Simpson	12-04-40	77 Sqn
740907	Sgt	CHAMBERS David William Arlidge	12-04-40	50 Sqn
632993	Sgt	CHAMBERS Hunter	22-08-40	144 Sqn
759176	Sgt	CHAMBERS Sydney	8-10-40	13 OTU
745628	Sgt	CHAMBERS William	28-12-40	106 Sqn
70124	F/O	CHAMPNESS John Alec	14-11-40	58 Sqn
534704	LAC	CHAPMAN Arthur Rex	21-02-40	38 Sqn
43280	P/O	CHAPMAN Colin Deans	14-11-40	61 Sqn
580942	Sgt	CHAPMAN George	8-04-40	82 Sqn
37718	F/L	CHAPMAN Paul Geoffrey	18-05-40	15 Sqn
74349	P/O	CHARLES Derek Elliott Stafford	17-08-40	149 Sqn
628854	AC1	CHARLTON Robert	11-05-40	21 Sqn
512011	Sgt	CHARNOCK Leonard	9-07-40	107 Sqn
630838	Sgt	CHATFIELD Kenneth Charles	28-05-40	77 Sqn

Number	Rank	Name	Date	Unit
580605	Sgt	CHECKLEY Francis	10-05-40	40 Sqn
751223	Sgt	CHEESMAN Alfred Jack	3-10-40	58 Sqn
581170	Sgt	CHENERY Leslie Charles	18-01-40	148 Sqn
28214	S/L	CHESTER Hurll Fontayne	2-07-40	82 Sqn
742972	Sgt	CHESTER Stanley Charles	23-11-40	214 Sqn
76006	P/O	CHESTER-MASTER Julian Paul	7-04-40	115 Sqn
966961	Sgt	CHETTER Alan Ernest	3-10-40	58 Sqn
39183	F/L	CHIVERS Eugene George Frederick	24-10-40	38 Sqn
741732	Sgt	CHIVERS Peter	19-04-40	107 Sqn
76458	P/O	CHRISTENSEN Severin	17-05-40	82 Sqn
81686	P/O	CHRISTOPHER Henry Morton	8-09-40	82 Sqn
530058	Sgt	CLAPPERTON Robert White	18-08-40	218 Sqn
749331	Sgt	CLARK Andrew Milne	27-06-40	82 Sqn
1163223	AC2	CLARK Charles Edward	21-07-40	Finningley
616627	Sgt	CLARK Eric Godfrey	2-10-40	144 Sqn
618202	AC2	CLARK Robert Michael Godfrey	14-04-40	38 Sqn
39968	F/O	CLARK Ronald Belmore Gower Edward	11-06-40	15 Sqn
759347	Sgt	CLARK Scott	26-11-40	61 Sqn
535562	Cpl	CLARK Temple Frederick Sinclair	10-05-40	40 Sqn
744846	Sgt	CLARKE Alfred Robert	23-12-40	139 Sqn
745257	Sgt	CLARKE Charles Owen	6-09-40	144 Sqn
580485	Sgt	CLARKE Edward	15-05-40	40 Sqn
624944	Sgt	CLARKE Edward John	2-08-40	83 Sqn
39375	F/O	CLARKE Edward Joseph Taylor	1-05-40	115 Sqn
759120	Sgt	CLARKE Edwin Jack	25-08-40	77 Sqn
564585	Sgt	CLARKE Ernest Reginald	15-04-40	83 Sqn
754445	Sgt	CLARKE Henry James	16-12-40	101 Sqn
743056	Sgt	CLARKE James Cunningham	25-08-40	49 Sqn
580869	Sgt	CLARKE Roy Desmond Edward	17-08-40	51 Sqn
754914	Sgt	CLAYTON Cyril Marsden	19-06-40	102 Sqn
741533	Sgt	CLAYTON Gerald Lawrence [Eire]	8-09-40	218 Sqn
77961	P/O	CLEAK Frederick Bernard	24-10-40	75 Sqn
548680	LAC	CLEAVER Donald Vincent	25-05-40	21 Sqn
81027	P/O	CLEMERSON William Herbert	17-10-40	61 Sqn
751589	Sgt	CLEMETT John Alfred	15-12-40	102 Sqn
39855	F/O	CLINKARD Derek Charles Gray [New Zealand]	8-03-40	61 Sqn
548536	LAC	CLOSE Leslie	20-03-40	51 Sqn
566061	Sgt	COAD DFM Alan James	7-12-40	16 OTU
616989	LAC	COALTER Richards	12-04-40	149 Sqn
644895	Sgt	COATES Jack	31-12-40	114 Sqn
72479	F/O	COBBE Alexander William Locke	8-09-40	82 Sqn
580946	Sgt	COBURN Alfred Robert	2-09-40	40 Sqn
638760	Sgt	COCKBURN Andrew McNab	20-07-40	61 Sqn
70850	P/O	COCKERELL Kenneth Andre	19-06-40	50 Sqn
642593	Sgt	COCKS Ronald Joseph	12-08-40	149 Sqn
39274	F/O	COGMAN William Curwin Gavine	28-05-40	102 Sqn
581203	Sgt	COISH Frederick Charles	8-09-40	218 Sqn
580435	Sgt	COLBOURN Cecil Ernest	18-05-40	15 Sqn
755025	Sgt	COLE Douglas Owen	6-11-40	50 Sqn
627020	AC2	COLEBOURNE William Arnold	18-01-40	149 Sqn
742031	Sgt	COLEMAN George Alfred	20-09-40	9 Sqn
34232	S/L	COLLETT Wilfred Ira [New Zealand]	4-08-40	75 Sqn
745240	Sgt	COLLIER Ralph	28-11-40	102 Sqn
580571	Sgt	COLLING Arthur	11-05-40	110 Sqn
742237	Sgt	COLLINGE Harry Kenneth	26-11-40	21 Sqn
564603	Sgt	COLLINGHAM John Raymond	24-05-40	106 Sqn
517528	Sgt	COLLINS Harold George	24-05-40	44 Sqn
565482	Sgt	COMPTON Lionel Arthur	23-04-40	51 Sqn
580724	Sgt	COND Leslie Charles	21-02-40	38 Sqn
580913	Sgt	CONNELL Samuel Patrick [Eire]	4-06-40	44 Sqn
40892	F/O	CONNOR DFC Clare Arthur [Canada]	4-11-40	83 Sqn
748780	Sgt	COOK Charles Owen	30-09-40	106 Sqn
620895	Sgt	COOK Matthew	6-07-40	106 Sqn
580997	Sgt	COOK Robert Donaldson	10-07-40	82 Sqn
563427	Sgt	COOKE Charles William	8-09-40	101 Sqn
523013	Sgt	COOKE Louis Charles	10-08-40	110 Sqn
76007	F/O	COOMBES Wilfred Francis Ernest	11-09-40	44 Sqn
84954	P/O	COOMBS Herbert Martin	24-10-40	20 OTU
81678	P/O	COONEY Kenneth	14-10-40	10 Sqn
539921	LAC	COOPER Ernest William Laurie	12-05-40	15 Sqn
34001	F/L	COOPER Frederick Edgar Howard	20-12-40	61 Sqn
971470	Sgt	COOPER John Douglas Laing	17-09-40	14 OTU
580606	Sgt	COOPER Joseph Herbert	8-06-40	82 Sqn
550541	Sgt	COOPER Kenneth	26-06-40	110 Sqn
80556	P/O	COOPER Walter Arthur	9-09-40	103 Sqn
84720	P/O	COPLESTONE Anthony Drake [Channel Islands]	22-09-40	17 OTU
618707	Sgt	CORBETT Frank	16-10-40	49 Sqn
741719	Sgt	CORE Frederick Albert	16-11-40	115 Sqn
751198	Sgt	CORKER William John Cheshire	26-08-40	101 Sqn
580050	Sgt	CORNISH Herbert	24-09-40	58 Sqn
549742	AC1	CORVAN Peter William	3-03-40	99 Sqn
39456	F/L	COSGROVE Robert James [Australia]	14-04-40	50 Sqn
629330	Sgt	COSGROVE William 'Bill' [Eire]	24-10-40	38 Sqn
546959	LAC	COSTELLO Maurice Henry	8-04-40	10 OTU
562567	Sgt	COTTERELL Maurice Charles	23-03-40	90 Sqn
637463	Sgt	COTTHAM Cleveland	9-10-40	77 Sqn
552518	AC2	COULL Angus William Adams	24-05-40	12 OTU
37794	F/L	COUTTS-WOOD DFC Stewart Farquharson	8-10-40	13 OTU
580764	Sgt	COVENEY Walter Richard	30-04-40	51 Sqn
33023	F/L	COVENTRY Robert George [Canada]	23-09-40	17 OTU
565574	Sgt	COWAN DFM George Edward	17-12-40	61 Sqn
628277	Sgt	COWELL Walter Robert	20-07-40	9 Sqn
580643	Sgt	COWLEY Robert Hurst	2-09-40	57 Sqn
580883	Sgt	COWLEY Victor Charles	19-09-40	77 Sqn
39502	F/L	COX Anthony Howard Caldicott	29-09-40	9 Sqn
80848	P/O	COX David Spencer	18-09-40	149 Sqn
580645	Sgt	COX Ronald	25-11-40	101 Sqn
358376	Sgt	CRAIG Arthur Ernest	21-05-40	18 Sqn
743022	Sgt	CRAIG John William	12-07-40	149 Sqn
39066	F/O	CRAIG-HALKETT Lionel Montague	30-08-40	214 Sqn
42947	P/O	CRANIDGE Thomas Johnson	13-08-40	82 Sqn
751938	Sgt	CRANSTON Thomas George James	26-08-40	101 Sqn
581207	Sgt	CRAVEN Derek Joseph	11-06-40	12 OTU
542430	Sgt	CRAVEN Henry Eric Archibald [New Zealand]	2-07-40	58 Sqn
620421	Sgt	CRAWFORD Frank	19-09-40	77 Sqn
759149	Sgt	CRAWFORD Peter	4-12-40	82 Sqn
41380	P/O	CRAWLEY Charles Douglas [Australia]	15-05-40	44 Sqn
580572	Sgt	CRAWLEY Joseph Kenneth	17-05-40	82 Sqn
937069	Sgt	CRESWELL DFM Albert Edward	7-12-40	51 Sqn
32155	W/C	CROCKART Norman David	27-06-40	50 Sqn
635759	Sgt	CROFT Jack Millen	3-08-40	115 Sqn
532528	Cpl	CROOK William	24-05-40	44 Sqn
751554	Sgt	CROOKS William Wilson	8-09-40	149 Sqn
40679	P/O	CROSBY George Lesley	14-04-40	38 Sqn
742933	Sgt	CROSS John Davies	7-10-40	9 Sqn
629121	AC1	CROSS Norman James	16-12-40	149 Sqn
581037	Sgt	CROSS Raymond Wilfred	26-03-40	44 Sqn
532141	Sgt	CROSSLAND Albert Alfred Ellis	18-09-40	58 Sqn
580508	Sgt	CROUCH Arthur George Bernard	17-05-40	82 Sqn
746758	Sgt	CRUISE Arthur	22-12-40	17 OTU
754166	Sgt	CRYER Edward Francis	3-10-40	19 OTU
743076	Sgt	CUMMING Gordon Murray	20-07-40	75 Sqn
537830	Cpl	CUMMINS Thomas Henry	17-05-40	82 Sqn
40680	P/O	CUNDILL Thomas Cedric	13-08-40	61 Sqn
580784	Sgt	CUNNINGHAM Peter Chris	1-05-40	99 Sqn
41560	P/O	CUNYNGHAME Wilfred Bertram Stuart	30-08-40	214 Sqn
570163	LAC	CURRIE Philip Raymond	19-09-40	50 Sqn
754790	Sgt	CURROR Ian Munro	14-12-40	17 OTU
573507	Sgt	CURRY Patrick Joseph [Eire]	6-07-40	106 Sqn

37006	F/L	CURRY Stephen Edward Frederick	20-07-40	51 Sqn		79372	P/O	DICKINSON Robert James	15-10-40	10 Sqn
516395	Sgt	CUTHBERT William	17-04-40	144 Sqn		33164	F/L	DICKSON Frederick Oscar	5-04-40	51 Sqn
649644	Sgt	CUTLER Joseph	1-11-40	144 Sqn		626161	Sgt	DICKSON George Middleton	26-08-40	40 Sqn
40367	F/O	DADSWELL David Allan	7-12-40	214 Sqn		759323	Sgt	DICKSON MiD John Campbell	28-11-40	20 OTU
651852	Sgt	DALE Sidney	15-11-40	83 Sqn		72148	F/O	DINGLE Arthur Collins	29-09-40	37 Sqn
85015	P/O	DALES Jack Haverfield	22-12-40	17 OTU		581277	Sgt	DINGLE Bryan Norman [Canada]	21-07-40	144 Sqn
742697	Sgt	DALGRESS Arthur Stuart	7-08-40	106 Sqn		652610	Sgt	DISMORE William Alfred	23-10-40	13 OTU
749342	Sgt	DALL James Mitchell	26-10-40	83 Sqn		550777	Cpl	DITMAS Patrick Harold Devereux	1-05-40	58 Sqn
42592	P/O	DALLY Paul Spencer [Rhodesia]	3-10-40	58 Sqn		745629	Sgt	DOBB Kenneth Herbert	19-08-40	114 Sqn
581504	Sgt	DALY Kenneth Lavery	5-09-40	21 Sqn		568823	LAC	DOBSON John Fisher	22-04-40	16 OTU
566178	Sgt	DANCER Elton Arthur	3-10-40	19 OTU		938826	Sgt	DOCKER John	22-12-40	9 Sqn
900593	Sgt	DANDRIDGE Alfred Clarence	19-09-40	20 OTU		746988	Sgt	DODD Edward Laurence	19-07-40	101 Sqn
748206	Sgt	DANKS Harry Edward	29-10-40	102 Sqn		627157	AC1	DOHERTY Edmund Brian	12-04-40	149 Sqn
751654	Sgt	DARBISHIRE Peter O'Neill	16-12-40	77 Sqn		1102926	AC2	DOKE William	19-08-40	Watton
745785	Sgt	DARDS Monty Richard	7-12-40	16 OTU		902515	Sgt	DOLAN John	30-05-40	38 Sqn
653259	Sgt	DAVENPORT-JONES Garton Vincent				631053	AC2	DOLAN Michael David	20-05-40	102 Sqn
			7-12-40	49 Sqn		977404	AC2	DONALD John	8-09-40	Wyton
553939	Sgt	DAVEY Derrick Joseph	21-12-40	106 Sqn		542646	Sgt	DONALDSON Robert	11-06-40	149 Sqn
751113	Sgt	DAVIDSON Alan Johnston	29-06-40	77 Sqn		632880	LAC	DONKIN Harold	23-10-40	77 Sqn
966854	Sgt	DAVIDSON Kenneth McNab	10-10-40	149 Sqn		521006	Sgt	DONLON James Frederick	11-12-40	105 Sqn
580364	Sgt	DAVIDSON Percival Matthew	24-09-40	139 Sqn		535553	Cpl	DORAN James	14-04-40	50 Sqn
		[Canada]				900499	Sgt	DORRINGTON Jack Brereton	9-07-40	21 Sqn
743094	Sgt	DAVIES Alfred Ridley	7-09-40	77 Sqn		749549	Sgt	DORRIS David Lawson	12-06-40	40 Sqn
42203	P/O	DAVIES Arthur Howell [South Africa]	15-10-40	50 Sqn		551342	LAC	DOUGHTY Dennis Gordon	20-03-40	144 Sqn
553877	Sgt	DAVIES Edward	14-10-40	10 Sqn		571664	LAC	DOUGLAS David East	23-08-40	61 Sqn
552076	Sgt	DAVIES Gordon	13-08-40	82 Sqn		510876	LAC	DOUGLAS Shane	6-03-40	Wyton
903408	Sgt	DAVIES Gwyn	26-11-40	17 OTU		43040	P/O	DOUGLAS Walter Morrison [Canada]	18-09-40	77 Sqn
632374	Sgt	DAVIES Harold	15-08-40	77 Sqn		37964	F/O	DOUGLAS-COOPER John Stainforth		
523102	Sgt	DAVIES Henry Carlton	10-06-40	61 Sqn					11-06-40	149 Sqn
742518	Sgt	DAVIES John Harold	2-08-40	18 Sqn		39933	F/O	DOUGLASS Peter Norman	12-05-40	15 Sqn
40994	P/O	DAVIES John Milton	8-04-40	10 OTU		355626	W/O	DOW Douglas Cameron	2-03-40	Feltwell
630694	Sgt	DAVIES Malcolm Haydn	7-12-40	49 Sqn		632780	Sgt	DOWDS John	26-07-40	75 Sqn
74669	P/O	DAVIES William Michael Arlingham	13-05-40	15 OTU		514307	Sgt	DOWLE Alfred Albert Gilbert	16-02-40	44 Sqn
745882	Sgt	DAVIS Francis William	24-10-40	38 Sqn		580712	Sgt	DOWNHAM Edward Alan	1-06-40	37 Sqn
751270	LAC	DAVISON George	6-06-40	101 Sqn		650716	Sgt	DOWSETT Colin	1-10-40	115 Sqn
1258580	AC2	DAVISON Reginald Alvan	11-11-40	110 Sqn		76599	P/O	DRAKE-CARNELL Francis John	6-09-40	144 Sqn
752795	AC1	DAWS Arthur Sydney	15-08-40	77 Sqn		751327	Sgt	DRAPER Kenneth Raymond	30-10-40	115 Sqn
745180	Sgt	DAWSON Anthony Kyle	15-08-40	51 Sqn		580431	Sgt	DREW George Thomas	10-07-40	107 Sqn
580767	Sgt	DAWSON Donald William	19-06-40	102 Sqn		77202	P/O	DREWRY John Richard	12-09-40	144 Sqn
41384	F/O	DAWSON DFC Eric Henry [Australia]	10-11-40	114 Sqn		541979	Sgt	DRINKWATER Fred	9-09-40	103 Sqn
42205	P/O	DAWSON Michael Benedict	11-06-40	149 Sqn		906313	AC1	DRIVER Richard Henry	18-11-40	110 Sqn
637484	Sgt	DAWSON Raymond Carter	19-09-40	77 Sqn		625339	AC2	DRURY Douglas James	2-01-40	149 Sqn
42339	P/O	DAWSON Thomas	1-11-40	144 Sqn		76164	P/O	DRYBURGH Neil George	27-05-40	16 OTU
37741	F/O	DAWSON JONES Francis Desmond	18-05-40	15 Sqn		551700	Sgt	DUCK Gerald Ernest	9-07-40	21 Sqn
903467	Sgt	DAY Cyril James	8-09-40	101 Sqn		71091	F/O	DUCKER Francis Edward Robert	19-07-40	101 Sqn
742008	Sgt	DAY Harold	1-10-40	44 Sqn		1182877	AC2	DUDLEY George William Leslie	19-08-40	9 Sqn
742004	Sgt	DAY Oswald George	1-08-40	16 OTU		610539	LAC	DUFF Jack Holman	20-09-40	50 Sqn
754574	Sgt	DEAN Edgar Albert	15-11-40	115 Sqn		525887	Sgt	DUFFY Phillip Paul	4-08-40	142 Sqn
971483	Sgt	DEEHAN Owen	8-12-40	61 Sqn		42820	P/O	DUFTON Charles Theodore	11-09-40	38 Sqn
640266	Sgt	DEMPSEY James	3-08-40	115 Sqn		631247	AC2	DUGGAN Douglas	21-05-40	115 Sqn
42487	P/O	DENCH Francis George Hurleston	13-08-40	15 Sqn		619755	Sgt	DUNBAR Hugh	3-10-40	105 Sqn
42206	P/O	DENISON Arthur Cecil [Canada]	2-09-40	57 Sqn		564609	Sgt	DUNCAN Alexander	1-09-40	106 Sqn
552584	Sgt	DENISON Holman Thomas	30-06-40	107 Sqn		581442	Sgt	DUNCAN Harry Horatio	1-09-40	105 Sqn
652740	Sgt	DENNING Randolph Frederick	13-10-40	99 Sqn		521723	Sgt	DUNCAN Thomas Samuel	23-08-40	142 Sqn
755456	Sgt	DENNIS David Wesley	18-08-40	218 Sqn		40215	F/O	DUNFORD-WOOD Hugh Diarmid Sherbrooke		
518112	Sgt	DENNIS Thomas Owen	1-01-40	7 Sqn					8-06-40	21 Sqn
974127	Sgt	DENNIS Walter Frederick	15-12-40	102 Sqn		42822	P/O	DUNKELS Cedric Owen	29-08-40	44 Sqn
755832	Sgt	DENT Christopher Joseph	10-07-40	15 OTU		618345	Sgt	DUNLEAVY Alfred Scott	2-12-40	101 Sqn
524057	Sgt	DENT Malcolm Llewellyn	19-06-40	58 Sqn		41685	P/O	DUNN DFC Andrew Woodrow	26-09-40	77 Sqn
755390	Sgt	DEVLIN George James	1-10-40	44 Sqn		74671	F/O	DUNN Derek John	7-12-40	51 Sqn
580488	Sgt	DEWHURST Joseph Langley	13-08-40	83 Sqn		517894	Sgt	DUPE Reginald Frederick Cyril	10-02-40	97 Sqn
79235	P/O	de BRESSEY Bernard Albert Zadock	14-11-40	83 Sqn		580510	Sgt	DURIE George Christopher	24-04-40	107 Sqn
41990	P/O	de LABOUCHERE-STARLING Francis Albert Gabriel Fernand Joseph	21-05-40	75 Sqn		547594	Sgt	DUTTON Ronald Leslie James	27-06-40	49 Sqn
						39073	F/O	DYER DFC John Phillip [Canada]	22-05-40	99 Sqn
966256	Sgt	DICK William Rattray Allan	25-11-40	115 Sqn		40162	P/O	D'ARCY-WRIGHT Gerald [Canada] (served as WRIGHT)	6-10-40	61 Sqn
34149	S/L	DICKINS Charles John Scott	19-12-40	99 Sqn						
523204	Sgt	DICKINSON Harry	17-08-40	144 Sqn		33473	P/O	EADIE John [Canada]	8-07-40	61 Sqn
525760	Sgt	DICKINSON DFM Richard Cuthbert	13-09-40	61 Sqn		550790	Sgt	EADIE Robert	6-06-40	83 Sqn

Number	Rank	Name	Date	Unit
41770	P/O	EARL Raymond Patrick [Australia]	26-09-40	61 Sqn
44631	P/O	EAST DFM Louis Frank	11-10-40	10 OTU
524673	Sgt	EASTMENT Richard Samuel	11-10-40	214 RFlt
754751	Sgt	EASTOE Eric Richard	24-08-40	11 OTU
755173	Sgt	EASTON James Harley	9-09-40	107 Sqn
640007	Sgt	EASTON John Kerr	23-07-40	58 Sqn
619088	Sgt	EATON William Moss	28-12-40	106 Sqn
524172	Sgt	EDDLESTON Walter	30-04-40	37 Sqn
940397	Sgt	EDDOWES Frank	7-12-40	51 Sqn
751841	Sgt	EDMEADS Anthony Charles Henry	2-09-40	144 Sqn
75997	P/O	EDMUNDS Charles Evelyn Walter Roy Neethorpe Van-Notten-Pole	14-04-40	38 Sqn
513935	P/O	EDMUNDS AFM David William	17-04-40	107 Sqn
39784	F/L	EDWARDS David Harold [Canada]	21-07-40	144 Sqn
751003	LAC	EDWARDS Ernest Nepture	14-05-40	110 Sqn
741487	Sgt	EDWARDS Frank Richard	13-06-40	9 Sqn
36151	F/O	EDWARDS John Ernest [New Zealand]	15-05-40	40 Sqn
540912	LAC	EDWARDS John Hendrie	15-04-40	83 Sqn
85285	P/O	EDWARDS Kenneth William	29-12-40	17 OTU
42937	P/O	EDWARDS William George	23-05-40	40 Sqn
742166	Sgt	EDWIN Edward Francis	14-11-40	61 Sqn
41912	P/O	ELDRIDGE Peter Ernest	19-09-40	77 Sqn
552585	Sgt	ELLICOTT Reginald John Spurway	5-07-40	114 Sqn
626895	AC2	ELLIOT Angus Whitson	22-05-40	82 Sqn
740509	Sgt	ELLIOTT Raymond Graham	19-06-40	9 Sqn
935731	Sgt	ELLIOTT Stanley Frederick	20-11-40	44 Sqn
966874	Sgt	ELLIOTT Thomas Douglas	21-11-40	102 Sqn
755784	Sgt	ELLIOTT William Ernest	30-10-40	115 Sqn
523372	Sgt	ELLIS Hylton Daniel	9-12-40	115 Sqn
512499	Sgt	ELLWOOD George Edward	29-10-40	114 Sqn
533022	LAC	ELLWOOD John	30-04-40	102 Sqn
754825	Sgt	ELTON Francis Raymond	6-11-40	58 Sqn
563099	Sgt	EMANUEL Victor	15-04-40	61 Sqn
905343	Sgt	EMM Kenneth	6-11-40	50 Sqn
642716	Sgt	EMMERSON Norman	11-07-40	58 Sqn
742163	Sgt	ENGLISH Denis Duncan	16-11-40	115 Sqn
70896	P/O	ENNIS Alexander Campbell	30-06-40	61 Sqn
40292	F/O	ESPLEY William Charles [Canada]	3-10-40	58 Sqn
40376	P/O	ESSON Stephen George	23-06-40	107 Sqn
565877	Sgt	ETHERIDGE Ronald	15-04-40	61 Sqn
78460	P/O	ETHERINGTON Arthur Frederick	25-09-40	107 Sqn
551709	LAC	ETTERSHANK Peter Raymond Victor	17-05-40	82 Sqn
552163	Sgt	EVANS Arfon	13-07-40	82 Sqn
617444	Sgt	EVANS Christopher Douglas	1-08-40	50 Sqn
629150	Sgt	EVANS DFM Edward Joseph	28-11-40	218 Sqn
40377	F/O	EVANS Herbert Prestyl	16-05-40	115 Sqn
532819	Cpl	EVANS John Henry	12-04-40	44 Sqn
967877	Sgt	EVANS Owen Prys	3-08-40	139 Sqn
654511	Sgt	EVANS Sidney	20-12-40	61 Sqn
566421	Cpl	EVANS William Henry Glyndwr	12-04-40	44 Sqn
78439	P/O	EVANS William Rupert	30-08-40	40 Sqn
580714	Sgt	EVERATT Gordon William	14-04-40	50 Sqn
643045	Sgt	EVEREST Albert Ernest George	13-11-40	77 Sqn
654354	Sgt	EVERITT Maurice Vivian	24-07-40	12 OTU
540232	LAC	FAGG Ernest John	18-05-40	15 Sqn
518379	Cpl	FALLOWS Reginald Frederick	16-05-40	115 Sqn
39311	F/O	FANSHAWE Basil Verney	19-03-40	115 Sqn
565737	Sgt	FARMER Edward Deryck	1-08-40	44 Sqn
580368	Sgt	FARMES Ernest Thomas	2-12-40	101 Sqn
623895	Cpl	FAWCETT George [Eire]	12-04-40	50 Sqn
41005	P/O	FAWCETT Nicoll Brian [New Zealand]	25-08-40	49 Sqn
580369	Sgt	FEARNLEY Frank	17-05-40	82 Sqn
40293	P/O	FENNELL Emery Orville [Canada]	20-03-40	51 Sqn
747822	Sgt	FENSOME John Stanley	31-12-40	20 OTU
638788	Sgt	FENWICK Eric Parker	26-11-40	61 Sqn
645352	Sgt	FERGUSON John Adam	17-10-40	144 Sqn
745363	Sgt	FERGUSON Andrew	10-12-40	17 OTU
32099	W/C	FERGUSON Kenneth Francis	14-11-40	10 Sqn
748733	Sgt	FETHERSTON Alan James	6-08-40	16 OTU
1157195	AC1	FEW William Edward Ronald	14-11-40	Honington
26158	S/L	FIELD Denys Brian Douglas	6-06-40	83 Sqn
37346	F/O	FIELD Leo Reginald	2-03-40	149 Sqn
80837	P/O	FIELDER Derrick John	28-12-40	83 Sqn
43257	P/O	FIELDS Antony Henry 'Tony'	4-06-40	10 Sqn
749540	Sgt	FINDLAY Alexander	11-06-40	77 Sqn
36268	P/O	FINLAYSON William David [New Zealand]	24-05-40	12 OTU
615843	AC1	FIRTH Sydney Ewbank	24-05-40	106 Sqn
43702	P/O	FISHER Arthur Vivian [New Zealand]	6-08-40	12 OTU
618704	Sgt	FISHER Edward	30-10-40	115 Sqn
936320	Sgt	FISHER Eric George	11-12-40	114 Sqn
508027	F/S	FISHER William	30-10-40	Wattisham
41916	P/O	FISK Kenneth Frederick	7-03-40	108 Sqn
532927	Sgt	FLANAGAN Dominick	17-10-40	61 Sqn
903094	Sgt	FLANAGAN Peter	17-10-40	49 Sqn
552105	AC1	FLANIGAN Gerard Edward	21-05-40	115 Sqn
743005	Sgt	FLEMING Donald Bannerman	2-10-40	9 Sqn
581173	Sgt	FLEMING Geoffrey Bernard	11-06-40	149 Sqn
42828	P/O	FLETCHER Alexander William	29-08-40	102 Sqn
42494	P/O	FLETCHER Frederick Alan Smith	12-06-40	101 Sqn
48924	AC1	FLETCHER Frederick Samuel Randolph	19-07-40	107 Sqn
548378	Sgt	FLETCHER John	11-10-40	10 OTU
935733	Sgt	FLETCHER Ronald Samuel	8-09-40	82 Sqn
42703	P/O	FLEWELLING Ross Leslie [Canada]	22-12-40	10 Sqn
548610	AC2	FLYNN Dennis	11-04-40	15 OTU
628401	P/O	FLYNN Gerald [Eire]	12-04-40	38 Sqn
630269	LAC	FLYNN Henry	18-09-40	150 Sqn
758162	Sgt	FOLEY Norman Reginald	24-09-40	19 OTU
79542	P/O	FORD Eric	18-09-40	58 Sqn
79236	P/O	FORD George Reginald Michael	18-09-40	149 Sqn
562682	Sgt	FORD Gordon James	18-06-40	58 Sqn
524766	LAC	FORSTER James Crawford	3-03-40	99 Sqn
581328	Sgt	FOSTER Brian Holmes	17-08-40	144 Sqn
552135	AC1	FOSTER James	6-05-40	14 OTU
630009	AC2	FOSTER Leonard Frederick	5-04-40	149 Sqn
980807	AC1	FOSTER Thomas	11-11-40	110 Sqn
971467	Sgt	FOX Alfred Russell	15-12-40	77 Sqn
37797	F/L	FOX Charles Douglas	2-10-40	9 Sqn
535872	Cpl	FOX Donald	1-11-40	110 Sqn
580739	Sgt	FRANCE Eric Basil Hartley	11-07-40	144 Sqn
40616	P/O	FRANKISH Claude Randolph [New Zealand]	12-05-40	15 Sqn
522061	Sgt	FRANKLIN BEM William Henry James	27-07-40	150 Sqn
965774	Sgt	FRASER James	6-11-40	99 Sqn
552209	Sgt	FRASER John	10-06-40	61 Sqn
551601	Sgt	FRASER John McLean	19-09-40	106 Sqn
747914	Sgt	FRASER Walter	14-11-40	10 Sqn
40818	P/O	FRIEND Jack Ernest Anthony	1-05-40	61 Sqn
747724	Sgt	FRIEND Kenneth Charles	16-10-40	49 Sqn
42342	P/O	FROST Cecil Denis	23-06-40	144 Sqn
580650	Sgt	FROST Charles	1-05-40	61 Sqn
42497	P/O	FROST Rupert Chatham	27-05-40	16 OTU
44409	P/O	FRY Frederick Philip	8-11-40	109 Sqn
626227	Sgt	FRYER Arthur	28-05-40	77 Sqn
759334	Sgt	FRYER Gordon Russell	16-11-40	115 Sqn
741624	Sgt	FULTON Basil Terence Macy	21-11-40	49 Sqn
537429	Sgt	FURBY Willie	6-06-40	40 Sqn
74673	P/O	FURNESS Roy Giffard	10-10-40	149 Sqn
748526	Sgt	FURZE Luke James	15-09-40	78 Sqn
641321	Sgt	FUTCHER John Vernon	12-07-40	149 Sqn
24208	S/L	FYFE DFC John Bernard	11-08-40	107 Sqn
580575	Sgt	GAINSFORD Gerald Patterson	26-06-40	110 Sqn
643194	Sgt	GALLAGHER Sam Patrick	7-11-40	19 OTU

Number	Rank	Name	Date	Sqn
637611	Sgt	GALLEWSKI Michael Montague	4-09-40	57 Sqn
552107	Sgt	GANDER Owen Sandford	2-07-40	83 Sqn
745876	Sgt	GAPP James Frederick 'Jimmy'	22-12-40	9 Sqn
580425	Sgt	GARCKA John Edward	6-06-40	40 Sqn
41840	P/O	GARD Peter Joseph	29-06-40	77 Sqn
78461	P/O	GARDENER Donald Edwin	13-08-40	61 Sqn
72558	P/O	GARDNER Edwin Charles	17-10-40	61 Sqn
741796	Sgt	GARVEY Peter Kevin	15-08-40	15 Sqn
646822	Sgt	GASKELL Norman	28-11-40	20 OTU
643900	Sgt	GATES Frank Arthur Edwin	24-08-40	11 OTU
84029	P/O	GAULDIE Clarence Carnegie Milne	8-10-40	13 OTU
78748	P/O	GAUNTLETT Maurice Lowden	7-11-40	99 Sqn
580393	Sgt	GAVIN Charles Dennis	15-11-40	105 Sqn
40295	P/O	GAYFORD Roy Allen [Canada]	7-04-40	115 Sqn
749520	Sgt	GAYWOOD Hugh Dowling	7-11-40	19 OTU
33311	F/O	GEACH Trevor James	28-05-40	77 Sqn
744982	Sgt	GEEN Henry Ernest	28-11-40	101 Sqn
626245	Sgt	GEORGE John Henry	20-08-40	101 Sqn
41013	P/O	GERRY Reginald Torrance [Canada]	3-08-40	115 Sqn
745221	Sgt	GIBBONS Derek Albert	26-09-40	77 Sqn
755158	Sgt	GIBBS David Allen	7-08-40	17 OTU
625697	Sgt	GIBBS DFM Jack	24-10-40	75 Sqn
81657	P/O	GIBBS John Vicary Frank	30-10-40	106 Sqn
523945	Sgt	GIBLIN Harold Albert Francis	19-06-40	102 Sqn
751217	Sgt	GIBSON Alexander	26-08-40	57 Sqn
653464	Sgt	GIBSON James William Chesterton	4-11-40	83 Sqn
905664	Sgt	GIBSON Kenneth Victor	25-07-40	101 Sqn
549511	Sgt	GIFFORD Vivian Charles	11-12-40	105 Sqn
581092	Sgt	GILES Alexander Joseph	21-07-40	144 Sqn
41842	P/O	GILLING Jack Humphrey	4-07-40	144 Sqn
79180	P/O	GILLINGHAM Maurice Hardy	13-08-40	82 Sqn
623761	AC2	GILLOTT Harry	12-04-40	149 Sqn
41690	P/O	GILMER John Martin [New Zealand]	2-05-40	51 Sqn
40382	P/O	GILMORE Robert Gerald Maxwell	14-05-40	21 Sqn
743017	Sgt	GILMOUR William John	16-11-40	105 Sqn
552188	Sgt	GIRVAN Thomas Eckford	13-08-40	82 Sqn
918556	AC2	GITTINS Cyril William	7-11-40	Wyton
745498	Sgt	GLADWIN Kenneth Bruce	28-09-40	9 Sqn
580651	Sgt	GLASSON Ronald Philips	8-03-40	61 Sqn
614892	Sgt	GLEDHILL Herbert Gresford	8-09-40	149 Sqn
37558	S/L	GLEED Gerald William Chevallier	14-06-40	40 Sqn
629156	Sgt	GLEN Alexander	7-07-40	37 Sqn
26230	S/L	GLENCROSS Arthur Roger	28-05-40	37 Sqn
742263	Sgt	GLENN Thomas William	22-10-40	106 Sqn
39659	F/O	GLOVER Charles William [Canada]	1-05-40	61 Sqn
563876	Sgt	GOAD Geoffrey Edmund	12-04-40	149 Sqn
1157569	AC2	GODWIN Alfred John	22-07-40	Wyton
551547	LAC	GOFFE Dennis	25-05-40	40 Sqn
39312	F/O	GOFTON Alexander Moresby [New Guinea]	17-05-40	82 Sqn
522805	LAC	GOLDER Anthony James Patrick	17-04-40	107 Sqn
745606	Sgt	GOLDIE Leonard George	1-10-40	115 Sqn
631889	Sgt	GOLDIE Thomas	7-12-40	49 Sqn
516472	Sgt	GOLDING Sydney John	13-06-40	61 Sqn
43135	P/O	GOLDSMITH George Edward	9-11-40	109 Sqn
745580	Sgt	GOLDSMITH Peter Dickens	13-11-40	10 Sqn
648512	Sgt	GOLDSMITH William Claude	7-08-40	106 Sqn
40691	P/O	GOODE John Douglas	1-08-40	114 Sqn
80829	P/O	GOODE Richard Gordon	17-09-40	44 Sqn
751954	Sgt	GOODERICK Clifford John	30-10-40	101 Sqn
620440	Sgt	GOODWILL William	11-09-40	44 Sqn
740682	Sgt	GORDON David Bruce	22-10-40	10 Sqn
39080	F/O	GORDON Gerald Victor	30-04-40	37 Sqn
43157	P/O	GORDON James Hamilton	25-05-40	15 Sqn
943151	LAC	GORDON Robert Henry	18-09-40	9 Sqn
550891	Sgt	GORWOOD DFM John Ernest	24-09-40	83 Sqn
903566	Sgt	GOSTICK Thomas Walter	16-11-40	115 Sqn
522865	Sgt	GOTT Merle	20-07-40	9 Sqn
524674	Sgt	GOULD Albert Edward Frank	28-07-40	150 Sqn
33312	F/O	GOULD Dermot Evelyn	5-04-40	51 Sqn
978247	AC2	GOULDING Albert Edward	23-12-40	35 Sqn
742021	Sgt	GOW John Gray	30-09-40	106 Sqn
40693	P/O	GOWER Richard Francis	11-08-40	49 Sqn
755642	Sgt	GOWING-SCOPES Alistair	23-12-40	58 Sqn
742817	Sgt	GOWLAND Kenyon Stafford	6-11-40	50 Sqn
581508	Sgt	GRAHAM Fred	8-04-40	13 OTU
970896	Sgt	GRAHAM Granville	6-11-40	58 Sqn
551827	AC1	GRAHAM Peter Gladstone	15-04-40	61 Sqn
972571	AC2	GRAHAM Thomas	28-11-40	20 OTU
971771	AC2	GRAHAM Thomas Wilfred	22-06-40	Dishforth
26011	S/L	GRANNUM Clifton Winnington	28-10-40	105 Sqn
742551	Sgt	GRANT Alexander McGilvray	30-12-40	61 Sqn
651489	Sgt	GRANT John	9-08-40	14 OTU
751434	Sgt	GRANT Stanley Charles	8-09-40	149 Sqn
37501	F/L	GRANT-CRAWFORD Ian Douglas	24-05-40	149 Sqn
39728	F/O	GRATTAN Gordon Reginald [Canada]	11-05-40	110 Sqn
969384	Sgt	GRATTON Gordon Hughes	19-09-40	20 OTU
581175	Sgt	GRAY Angus Nigel	13-08-40	15 Sqn
641045	Sgt	GRAY John	24-11-40	77 Sqn
40342	F/O	GRAY DFC MC [Czechoslovakia] Kenneth Neil [New Zealand]	1-05-40	102 Sqn
751313	Sgt	GRAY Thomas	7-12-40	51 Sqn
43166	P/O	GRAY AFM William Alfred	9-06-40	37 Sqn
741824	Sgt	GREEN Alfred Joseph	20-09-40	75 Sqn
747715	Sgt	GREEN Cyril Sidney Garrick	23-10-40	58 Sqn
742028	Sgt	GREEN Herbert Frederick	7-10-40	38 Sqn
639031	Sgt	GREEN John Henry	3-11-40	83 Sqn
551605	Sgt	GREEN Joseph Donald	15-11-40	44 Sqn
965313	Sgt	GREEN Rendle	9-09-40	105 Sqn
547006	AC1	GREENALL John Bell	1-05-40	61 Sqn
749874	AC2	GREENHEAD William Ernest George	1-11-40	110 Sqn
41284	P/O	GREENWELL Charles Eric	4-06-40	83 Sqn
532939	Sgt	GREENWOOD James Edward	28-10-40	105 Sqn
580696	Sgt	GREET John	12-04-40	50 Sqn
740008	Sgt	GREEVES Stuart Gordon	7-12-40	49 Sqn
641163	AC2	GREGGANS Henry	19-04-40	107 Sqn
548517	Sgt	GREIG James Walter	30-06-40	61 Sqn
966648	Sgt	GREIG John Cresswell	15-09-40	78 Sqn
532679	LAC	GREIG DFM Walter	2-01-40	149 Sqn
44976	P/O	GRIERSON James Joseph [Canada]	17-05-40	82 Sqn
755893	LAC	GRIFFIN Harold George	21-05-40	115 Sqn
563663	Sgt	GRIFFIN Norman John	17-04-40	107 Sqn
581384	Sgt	GRIFFITHS Arthur James	10-08-40	144 Sqn
1250935	AC2	GRIFFITHS Frederick Percy	3-12-40	Linton on Ouse
581509	Sgt	GROCOTT Joseph Alan	7-12-40	9 Sqn
26032	W/C	GROOM Samuel Robert	21-11-40	102 Sqn
629162	AC2	GROVE Denis Harry	2-01-40	149 Sqn
626540	Sgt	GUEST DFM Jack	13-06-40	21 Sqn
905255	Sgt	GUEST Richard Bernard	16-11-40	115 Sqn
580613	Sgt	GUNNING Frank Vivian	12-06-40	15 Sqn
33314	F/O	GUTHRIE James Reed	10-06-40	61 Sqn
616922	Sgt	HADFIELD Thomas	7-12-40	16 OTU
79511	P/O	HADLEY Ronald Arnold [New Zealand]	9-10-40	58 Sqn
626994	Sgt	HAGGETT Harry	17-08-40	51 Sqn
581095	Sgt	HAIGH Arthur Cooper	18-02-40	90 Sqn
567057	Cpl	HAIRE Oscar	12-04-40	77 Sqn
524167	Sgt	HAITHWAITE MiD Norman	26-04-40	102 Sqn
551723	Sgt	HALDANE Sydney John	30-08-40	214 Sqn
42219	P/O	HALE Earl Robert [Canada]	13-08-40	82 Sqn
43704	P/O	HALKETT Charles de Vic [New Zealand]	9-10-40	107 Sqn
740183	Sgt	HALL Alfred Ernest	8-04-40	13 OTU
619068	LAC	HALL George Arthur	27-07-40	150 Sqn

Service No	Rank	Name	Date	Sqn
900575	Sgt	HALL George Edgar	9-10-40	58 Sqn
37350	S/L	HALL George Freeman	22-05-40	110 Sqn
564340	Sgt	HALL Hubert Ronald	12-05-40	15 Sqn
740620	Sgt	HALL John Robert	28-09-40	214 Sqn
43151	P/O	HALL Ronald	18-04-40	77 Sqn
635364	AC2	HALL Stanley	31-08-40	49 Sqn
566919	Sgt	HALLAM Walter Thomas	29-09-40	149 Sqn
564194	Sgt	HALLETT Cyril Richard	8-07-40	83 Sqn
78684	P/O	HALLOWS Eric Stewart Isaacson	30-10-40	99 Sqn
632830	Sgt	HALLS Reginald	10-09-40	50 Sqn
970093	Sgt	HAM Michael Gervase	29-11-40	13 OTU
581214	Sgt	HAMILTON Claude	10-08-40	82 Sqn
581097	Sgt	HAMILTON Richard Stephen Edward	6-11-40	61 Sqn
581386	Sgt	HAMLYN William Arthur	9-07-40	21 Sqn
551348	AC1	HAMMAN Anthony Creighton	26-03-40	44 Sqn
628296	Sgt	HANLON Charlie	19-06-40	102 Sqn
755457	Sgt	HANLON Thomas	14-11-40	58 Sqn
580541	Sgt	HANN Cecil John	27-12-40	21 Sqn
741853	Sgt	HANNA Robert	29-07-40	12 OTU
42123	F/L	HANNAH Kenneth Thomas	15-12-40	102 Sqn
629054	Sgt	HANNAN Hugh	10-07-40	15 OTU
564212	Sgt	HANNE John Henry	10-01-40	110 Sqn
581333	Sgt	HARBOUR Ronald Jesse	23-03-40	90 Sqn
627887	Sgt	HARDCASTLE Jack	28-10-40	105 Sqn
550526	Cpl	HARDING Benjamin Morgan	25-05-40	18 Sqn
749521	Sgt	HARDING Edgar George	6-11-40	10 Sqn
580426	Sgt	HARDING Walter Cecil	27-06-40	50 Sqn
624501	Sgt	HARDY Frederick Donald	13-06-40	9 Sqn
522533	Sgt	HARDY Leonard William	28-09-40	9 Sqn
648104	AC1	HARE Bernard Francis	14-11-40	44 Sqn
580775	Sgt	HARGRAVE DFM Ronald Charles	6-06-40	9 Sqn
77035	P/O	HARGREAVES John Denton	4-04-40	214 Sqn
07128	W/C	HARGROVES Joseph Henry	5-07-40	101 Sqn
39520	F/O	HARRIES Glyn	1-04-40	82 Sqn
41846	P/O	HARRIMAN Douglas Sidney Reeve	25-05-40	15 Sqn
534211	Sgt	HARRIS Aubrey John	20-07-40	51 Sqn
77934	P/O	HARRIS Edwin Arthur	11-08-40	49 Sqn
39231	F/L	HARRIS Francis Beach	30-08-40	20 OTU
530943	Sgt	HARRIS DFM Kenneth Henry	13-06-40	82 Sqn
581152	Sgt	HARRIS Peter Raymond	16-07-40	18 Sqn
33256	F/L	HARRIS Wilfred Arthur	7-12-40	214 Sqn
747970	Sgt	HARRISON Charles William Cavey Fleming	29-08-40	102 Sqn
527017	Sgt	HARRISON Denis Store	30-06-40	107 Sqn
538889	Sgt	HARRISON Henry Herbert	18-09-40	149 Sqn
580653	Sgt	HARRISON John	26-05-40	49 Sqn
911733	AC1	HARRISON Robert Hawley	18-08-40	218 Sqn
741615	Sgt	HARRISON Robert Norman	22-12-40	9 Sqn
632176	AC1	HART Alfred William Henry	1-05-40	102 Sqn
631366	AC2	HART Frank	3-03-40	99 Sqn
740678	Sgt	HARTFIELD John William	22-05-40	82 Sqn
745206	Sgt	HARTLAND Geoffrey William	12-12-40	115 Sqn
580655	Sgt	HARTLEY John Douglas	12-03-40	61 Sqn
581153	Sgt	HARTLEY Willoughby	9-07-40	21 Sqn
568749	Sgt	HARTNELL Richard Sidney	24-08-40	11 OTU
741985	Sgt	HARTOP Charles William	21-10-40	44 Sqn
936441	Sgt	HARVEY Bernard	27-09-40	106 Sqn
625809	AC1	HARWOOD Frederick	17-04-40	107 Sqn
42470	P/O	HARWOOD-SMITH Norman Henry	10-08-40	82 Sqn
550065	Sgt	HASTE Harry Scott	15-11-40	83 Sqn
905660	Sgt	HASTIE Bertram Victor	29-09-40	49 Sqn
33028	S/L	HASTINGS Mark	29-06-40	77 Sqn
903079	Sgt	HATCH John Frederick	16-07-40	18 Sqn
87045	P/O	HAVILAND David Reginald Ferrers	23-12-40	11 OTU
510166	Sgt	HAWKINS DFM George	21-05-40	21 Sqn
745962	Sgt	HAWTHORNE Noel Raymond Allenby	28-06-40	13 OTU
39735	F/O	HAWXBY Noel	21-02-40	38 Sqn
638754	Sgt	HAWXBY Thomas William	15-11-40	44 Sqn
519077	Sgt	HAY Andrew William	5-11-40	214 Sqn
965765	Sgt	HAY Colin	15-10-40	9 Sqn
906233	Sgt	HAY Ian De Sailly Errol	24-09-40	19 OTU
39663	F/O	HAYDON Francis John	4-06-40	83 Sqn
580893	Sgt	HAYES John Francis	26-04-40	102 Sqn
755394	Sgt	HAYES Ronald Leslie	1-11-40	144 Sqn
610705	LAC	HAYNES Francis Albert Skuce	18-09-40	99 Sqn
628965	Sgt	HAYWOOD Walter Frank	17-08-40	102 Sqn
970881	Sgt	HEANEY Michael Joseph Oliver [Eire]	16-12-40	101 Sqn
647632	Sgt	HEARD Douglas Thom	18-09-40	99 Sqn
42344	P/O	HEATH-BROWN John Alastair	9-07-40	21 Sqn
562741	F/S	HEAYES Cecil Robert	1-05-40	58 Sqn
40390	P/O	HEBELER MiD Christopher Rendel	12-04-40	77 Sqn
935937	Sgt	HELLEWELL Clifford	11-10-40	214 RFlt
649426	Sgt	HEMINGWAY Marchant	28-12-40	50 Sqn
901353	Sgt	HENDERSON Cyril Clifford	20-09-40	12 OTU
76460	F/O	HENDERSON Duncan	24-05-40	15 Sqn
581453	Sgt	HENDERSON James	4-12-40	82 Sqn
1379801	AC2	HENDERSON James Ian	16-12-40	149 Sqn
565332	Sgt	HENDERSON Thomas Valentine	17-09-40	44 Sqn
37805	S/L	HENDRY Maxwell Frederick	24-09-40	139 Sqn
82688	P/O	HENOCQ Geoffrey	13-11-40	77 Sqn
551737	Sgt	HENRY Bert Llewellyn	14-10-40	10 Sqn
630142	AC2	HENRY James	12-04-40	149 Sqn
620438	AC1	HEPBURN Angus	4-05-40	51 Sqn
632182	Sgt	HERDMAN George	11-11-40	49 Sqn
517823	Sgt	HERMELS Alphonse Roger	12-03-40	35 Sqn
42708	P/O	HERMON William Duncan [South Africa]	26-09-40	61 Sqn
631890	AC2	HERON William	18-01-40	148 Sqn
645617	Sgt	HETTLE Robert McGregor	29-07-40	142 Sqn
86424	P/O	HEWER Reginald Thomas	29-12-40	115 Sqn
41178	P/O	HEWETT Eric Iver	12-03-40	61 Sqn
39878	F/O	HEWETT Jack Patrick Majendie	4-04-40	149 Sqn
547085	AC1	HEWITT Edgar Sydney	24-05-40	149 Sqn
521236	Sgt	HEWITT Robert	13-06-40	9 Sqn
622581	Sgt	HEWITT William Hutchinson [Eire]	17-10-40	61 Sqn
972662	AC2	HEYES John	1-11-40	110 Sqn
742062	Sgt	HEYWARD Clifford Charles	24-07-40	110 Sqn
580871	Sgt	HEYWORTH Ronald Macaulay	15-09-40	78 Sqn
42408	P/O	HIDE Kenneth John	20-11-40	149 Sqn
580577	Sgt	HIGGINS Francis Charles	13-06-40	107 Sqn
649099	AC2	HIGGS Granville John	6-07-40	106 Sqn
70305	F/O	HIGSON Kenneth Hesketh	16-08-40	10 Sqn
590559	F/S	HILL Anthony	21-02-40	38 Sqn
550068	Sgt	HILL Christopher Grimwade	22-07-40	78 Sqn
633167	Sgt	HILL Eric	23-07-40	58 Sqn
42226	P/O	HILL Eric Arthur Charles	1-01-40	185 Sqn
72024	F/O	HILL James Jewill	30-10-40	106 Sqn
567598	Sgt	HILL Matthew	31-08-40	58 Sqn
741410	Sgt	HILL Stanley Denys	12-08-40	83 Sqn
745287	Sgt	HILLELSON Leslie Henry	21-10-40	13 OTU
566066	Sgt	HILLS John Edwin	24-09-40	61 Sqn
581219	Sgt	HILTON Ronald	7-09-40	10 Sqn
610120	AC2	HINCHLIFFE Aubrey	2-01-40	149 Sqn
36014	S/L	HINKS John Olding	15-10-40	9 Sqn
40592	P/O	HINTON Ian Percival	26-03-40	103 Sqn
755307	Sgt	HINTON Stanley Edward	10-07-40	107 Sqn
76582	P/O	HISSEY Peter Bouch	29-10-40	114 Sqn
510387	Sgt	HISTON Herbert	2-07-40	82 Sqn
937501	Sgt	HITCHEN John Gregson	30-10-40	101 Sqn
653978	Sgt	HITCHMOUGH William Grice	24-10-40	75 Sqn
740516	Sgt	HOBBS Charles Carlile	8-03-40	61 Sqn
562149	Sgt	HOBBS Victor Knowle	26-11-40	17 OTU
551722	Sgt	HOBSON Alan Gordon	29-09-40	50 Sqn
643610	Sgt	HOBSON George John	11-09-40	44 Sqn

635433	LAC	HODGE Edward	2-10-40	144 Sqn		519997	Sgt	HUTTON Frank	7-07-40	82 Sqn
636770	Sgt	HODGSON Albert William	28-12-40	214 Sqn		901860	Sgt	HUXTABLE John Francis	28-12-40	214 Sqn
566166	Sgt	HODSON Dennis Derrick Raymond	9-09-40	105 Sqn		749403	Sgt	HYAM Alfred	23-11-40	214 Sqn
524701	Sgt	HOGARTH Leslie	21-11-40	102 Sqn		580658	Sgt	HYLAND Robert Cecil	10-11-40	50 Sqn
543524	LAC	HOGARTH Thomas	25-04-40	49 Sqn		580861	Sgt	IBBOTSON John Raleigh	12-04-40	77 Sqn
42752	P/O	HOHNEN Michael	4-08-40	15 Sqn		748039	Sgt	IMBER Dennis Sydney	16-10-40	49 Sqn
41703	P/O	HOLBROOK Dennis Frederick Stanford				580958	Sgt	INGRAM Allen John Dennis	27-06-40	50 Sqn
			20-05-40	102 Sqn		759238	Sgt	INGRAMS William Desmond	8-12-40	214 Sqn
1173749	AC2	HOLDAWAY Frank Alan Crawford	19-08-40	9 Sqn		40227	F/O	INNES DFC Herome Alexander	4-04-40	214 Sqn
749458	Sgt	HOLDSWORTH John	7-07-40	15 Sqn		39988	P/O	IRVINE James Melville Dundas	24-05-40	106 Sqn
942207	AC2	HOLDSWORTH Joseph	17-08-40	50 Sqn		550470	Sgt	ISHERWOOD Leonard	11-07-40	58 SQN
968318	Sgt	HOLKER Maurice	22-12-40	9 Sqn		745438	Sgt	ISMAY Geoffrey Lucien	1-10-40	10 Sqn
745631	Sgt	HOLLAND Charles Julius	23-07-40	107 Sqn		580659	Sgt	ISON William John	12-04-40	44 Sqn
516539	Sgt	HOLLAND Leonard Edward	23-12-40	139 Sqn		741530	Sgt	IVATT Richard Spencer Castle	22-11-40	61 Sqn
569978	Cpl	HOLLAND Oliver Henry Selby	26-10-40	21 Sqn		747985	Sgt	IVE Charles Jason Arthur	14-08-40	15 OTU
936348	Sgt	HOLLIDAY George	7-10-40	38 Sqn		904303	Sgt	IVES Hubert Geoffrey	24-08-40	11 OTU
966474	Sgt	HOLLINGSHEAD Ronald Emes	14-09-40	15 Sqn		755494	Sgt	JACKSON Arthur Raymond	24-05-40	17 OTU
561153	Sgt	HOLLISTER William Frederick George	20-06-40	144 Sqn		43018	P/O	JACKSON Frances Stanley	17-05-40	82 Sqn
581222	Sgt	HOLMES Arthur Noel	24-05-40	15 Sqn		40851	P/O	JACKSON George Hauteville	2-09-40	37 Sqn
570723	LAC	HOLT Robert	22-04-40	16 OTU		528709	Sgt	JACKSON Harrison	23-04-40	51 Sqn
42710	P/O	HOLYOKE George Royal [Canada]	4-09-40	57 Sqn		746821	Sgt	JACKSON James Joseph	17-10-40	144 Sqn
746840	Sgt	HOOD Claude Lionel Geoffrey	15-08-40	77 Sqn		651960	Sgt	JACKSON John Angus	19-08-40	14 OTU
812340	Sgt	HOOKER Donald	26-09-40	114 Sqn		532409	Cpl	JACKSON Roy	8-03-40	9 Sqn
700445	Sgt	HOOPER Alfred Harold	21-05-40	115 Sqn		755443	Sgt	JACOBS Alec Victor	9-09-40	107 Sqn
755311	Sgt	HOOPER Cyril John	2-09-40	37 Sqn		745515	Sgt	JAGGS Walter Vincent	30-10-40	115 Sqn
741881	Sgt	HOPES Denis Beach	11-07-40	58 Sqn		580961	Sgt	JAMES Arthur Francis	25-04-40	49 Sqn
531180	Sgt	HOPKINS John	26-11-40	61 Sqn		77464	P/O	JAMES Blake Bamford	6-06-40	40 Sqn
561177	Sgt	HOPKINS Reginald George	18-05-40	15 Sqn		581513	Sgt	JAMES Eric	11-09-40	38 Sqn
70324	F/O	HOPKINSON Richard Adrian	9-07-40	57 Sqn		751999	LAC	JAMES Geoffrey Halstead	8-04-40	13 OTU
518878	Sgt	HOPPER John Hamilton	1-05-40	102 Sqn		637282	Sgt	JAMES Raymond Wallace	24-10-40	38 Sqn
41418	P/O	HORDERN Alfred Peter Burdett	25-04-40	49 Sqn		972478	Sgt	JAMES William Henry	7-12-40	214 Sqn
551285	LAC	HORNSBY Norman	26-04-40	49 Sqn		787545	Sgt	JANOUSEK Jiri [Czechoslovakia]	16-12-40	311 Sqn
39525	F/O	HORRIGAN MiD Owen Gerard	26-04-40	102 Sqn		937239	Sgt	JARMAN Theos Geoffrey Scott	9-09-40	40 Sqn
580957	Sgt	HORSFALL Alan Albert	30-08-40	50 Sqn		82605	P/O	JAROSEK Hubert Z. [Czechoslovakia]	16-10-40	311 Sqn
543161	Sgt	HORTON Leslie John	26-07-40	15 Sqn		42841	P/O	JARVIS Peter Guy Vargas	19-09-40	20 OTU
33568	P/O	HOSSACK Ian Milne	11-07-40	144 Sqn		564866	Sgt	JEFFREY William	12-06-40	44 Sqn
581100	Sgt	HOUGHTON-BROWN Roland	22-06-40	61 Sqn		81649	P/O	JEFFREYS Albert Frederick	8-10-40	16 OTU
32197	S/L	HOUSE Charles Constantine	23-08-40	218 Sqn		78762	P/O	JELLEY Edward Arthur	30-09-40	75 Sqn
77936	P/O	HOUSEMAN Ridley Elgood	12-08-40	149 Sqn		751725	Sgt	JELLEY Percy William Norman	11-08-40	49 Sqn
37806	F/L	HOW DFC Douglas James	13-09-40	61 Sqn		748696	Sgt	JENKINS Edward Bertram Douglas	28-12-40	214 Sqn
566374	Sgt	HOWARD Harold Herbert George	27-08-40	10 Sqn		580289	Sgt	JENKINS Stanley William	23-05-40	83 Sqn
552504	Sgt	HOWARD Leonard	8-07-40	83 Sqn		759191	Sgt	JENNER Donald Alfred	1-11-40	144 Sqn
566350	Sgt	HOWARD Sidney John	16-10-40	14 OTU		565910	Sgt	JENNINGS DFM Robert James	6-08-40	49 Sqn
966313	Sgt	HOWARD Stanley Gordon	9-12-40	115 Sqn		524198	Sgt	JERMOND Sidney George	17-08-40	102 Sqn
1009174	AC2	HOWARTH Albert	23-12-40	Oakington		740889	Sgt	JERRITT Robert Anderson	8-09-40	149 Sqn
644790	Sgt	HOWE George Lawson	30-10-40	106 Sqn		936651	Sgt	JERVIS Frederick Roy	17-11-40	115 Sqn
567595	Cpl	HOWELLS Emyrs George	1-11-40	110 Sqn		551360	Sgt	JERVIS Terrence James	9-07-40	57 Sqn
562745	Sgt	HOWELLS William Trevor	25-04-40	110 Sqn		787141	Sgt	JIRSAK Otto [Czechoslovakia]	16-10-40	311 Sqn
77937	P/O	HOWIE Charles William	12-07-40	149 Sqn		573409	LAC	JOHNS Denys William Gordon	28-07-40	15 OTU
83259	P/O	HUBBARD Michael	21-12-40	106 Sqn		37290	S/L	JOHNSON Charles Edward	24-05-40	44 Sqn
581225	Sgt	HUDSON George Howard	3-06-40	12 OTU		968136	Sgt	JOHNSON Douglas George	28-11-40	20 OTU
653137	Sgt	HUGHES Alan Joseph	24-10-40	38 Sqn		938783	Sgt	JOHNSON Irwin Geoffrey	23-12-40	58 Sqn
937392	Sgt	HUGHES Dennis Victor	18-09-40	77 Sqn		39533	F/O	JOHNSON Neville	15-05-40	83 Sqn
39084	F/L	HUGHES Francis Noel	19-07-40	15 OTU		550384	Sgt	JOHNSON Percival Eric	9-07-40	40 Sqn
581182	Sgt	HUGHES Kenneth William	21-05-40	115 Sqn		40833	P/O	JOHNSON Peter Richard	12-03-40	166 Sqn
81069	P/O	HUGHES Philip Leslie Norgrove	14-09-40	15 Sqn		541085	LAC	JOHNSON Stanley	15-05-40	40 Sqn
563882	Sgt	HUGHES William Arthur	16-08-40	144 Sqn		937626	Sgt	JOHNSON Sydney Wallace	14-06-40	40 Sqn
621199	AC2	HUGHSON Laurence Bruce	2-03-40	149 Sqn		538052	LAC	JOHNSON Thomas Frederick	21-02-40	38 Sqn
638879	Sgt	HULL Norman William	22-11-40	106 Sqn		935192	Sgt	JOHNSON Thomas Kenneth	26-09-40	114 Sqn
741337	Sgt	HUMPHREY Keith Reginald	26-10-40	61 Sqn		635088	Sgt	JOHNSON William Aubrey	10-09-40	50 Sqn
553383	Sgt	HUNT James Douglas	28-12-40	83 Sqn		580546	Sgt	JOHNSTON Norman Reid	27-08-40	10 Sqn
77208	P/O	HUNTER Harry Blakeway	12-03-40	166 Sqn		552521	Sgt	JOHNSTONE James Ward	11-09-40	38 Sqn
745670	Sgt	HURST Arthur	16-10-40	14 OTU		40619	P/O	JOHNSTONE Kenneth John Alan	12-04-40	44 Sqn
525267	Sgt	HURST Percy Joseph	26-04-40	49 Sqn				[Fiji]		
77938	P/O	HUTCHINS David	17-08-40	144 Sqn		523203	Sgt	JOLLY DFM Ronald	13-06-40	144 Sqn
581390	Sgt	HUTCHINSON Herbert	13-11-40	77 Sqn		566191	Sgt	JONES Albert Richard	26-03-40	44 Sqn
755639	Sgt	HUTCHINSON Joseph Dick	29-11-40	107 Sqn		531577	Cpl	JONES Alexander Egerton	26-03-40	105 Sqn
975183	Sgt	HUTSON Frank	24-10-40	20 OTU		42843	P/O	JONES Anthony Leonard	6-11-40	10 Sqn

Service No	Rank	Name	Date	Sqn
42679	P/O	JONES Arthur Bevan	19-07-40	18 Sqn
70805	P/O	JONES Cecil John Trevelyan	2-07-40	58 Sqn
970183	Sgt	JONES David Lloyd	13-08-40	11 OTU
566209	Sgt	JONES Edwin	8-06-40	21 Sqn
654469	AC2	JONES Ernest Alfred Llewellyn	14-04-40	77 Sqn
44074	P/O	JONES Francis Herbert	30-07-40	15 Sqn
567277	LAC	JONES Frederick Glyn	21-02-40	38 Sqn
590727	Sgt	JONES Geoffrey Wyatt	26-07-40	83 Sqn
638275	Sgt	JONES Hywel	26-10-40	21 Sqn
565170	Sgt	JONES Jack Bramwell	23-07-40	58 Sqn
638740	Sgt	JONES John	6-08-40	49 Sqn
581185	Sgt	JONES Maurice Guy	11-06-40	15 Sqn
741975	Sgt	JONES Maurice Herbert	5-09-40	51 Sqn
518847	Sgt	JONES Ninian Lewis	26-04-40	49 Sqn
33061	S/L	JONES Norman Clifford	13-08-40	82 Sqn
905466	Sgt	JONES Ralph Henderson Goff	31-08-40	18 Sqn
1171578	AC2	JONES Richard Glynne	19-08-40	Honington
70351	F/L	JONES Ronald Watcyn	7-11-40	99 Sqn
624943	AC2	JONES Tudno	12-05-40	77 Sqn
965067	Sgt	JONES William Henry	11-09-40	44 Sqn
966020	Sgt	JONES William Llewellyn	23-12-40	11 OTU
580580	Sgt	JONES-ROBERTS Eric	18-06-40	58 Sqn
754758	Sgt	JOORIS Raymond Albert	12-09-40	12 OTU
550598	Sgt	JOPLING John Robert	12-04-40	50 Sqn
359518	Sgt	JOSSE Peter William	23-05-40	83 Sqn
580962	Sgt	JOYCE Dennis Arthur	11-09-40	44 Sqn
514904	Sgt	JUBY Geoffrey William James	12-04-40	115 Sqn
742168	Sgt	KAY Robert Frederick	6-06-40	214 Sqn
564740	Sgt	KEAST Leslie Arthur	11-06-40	10 Sqn
528054	Sgt	KEATES Arthur Knightley Roland	25-05-40	21 Sqn
745998	Sgt	KEATS Sidney Bertie	19-09-40	106 Sqn
41711	P/O	KEEBLE Eric James	25-06-40	82 Sqn
41427	P/O	KEEDWELL Osborne Harvey [New Zealand]	12-05-40	107 Sqn
638360	Sgt	KEELING Ralph Alexander Walter [Canada]	8-10-40	16 OTU
745306	Sgt	KEIGHLEY Edgar Arthur James	21-09-40	20 OTU
363152	Sgt	KEILLER Colin	2-01-40	104 Sqn
41296	F/O	KELLER William Edmund Norman [Canada]	13-10-40	99 Sqn
561573	Sgt	KELLEWAY Herbert Henry	1-04-40	82 Sqn
935752	Sgt	KELLY James [Eire]	15-09-40	78 Sqn
581155	Sgt	KELSO Alexander Dean	27-06-40	40 Sqn
629791	AC2	KEMPTON John William	8-04-40	82 Sqn
70358	F/O	KENDALL Colin Frankland	11-11-40	83 Sqn
624417	Sgt	KENDREW Albert Gross	4-06-40	44 Sqn
562829	Sgt	KENMURE Colin	19-09-40	106 Sqn
983513	AC2	KENNEDY James	21-08-40	3 Group
632947	AC2	KENNEDY Thomas	21-05-40	115 Sqn
968455	Sgt	KENNY Edward [Canada]	5-11-40	214 Sqn
581396	Sgt	KENYON Harold	23-06-40	110 Sqn
79182	P/O	KERR Archie Ronald	20-11-40	44 Sqn
748075	Sgt	KERR James Francis Ferguson	21-10-40	13 OTU
581286	Sgt	KERR Lachlan Livingstone	6-06-40	83 Sqn
976712	AC2	KERR Samuel John	26-11-40	Honington
70863	P/O	KERR Talbot	30-04-40	37 Sqn
611349	LAC	KERSHAW Stanley	12-04-40	50 Sqn
758211	Sgt	KESTING Hugh Morrison	14-11-40	58 Sqn
633978	LAC	KEY Harry	10-10-40	107 Sqn
563851	Sgt	KIDD William Henry Cecil	2-01-40	149 Sqn
966804	Sgt	KILGOUR William Hutchison	19-09-40	107 Sqn
925805	AC1	KING Ronald Walter	10-11-40	49 Sqn
81356	P/O	KING William Euerby	19-08-40	14 OTU
631666	AC1	KINGDOM Henry Norman	12-09-40	10 OTU
523885	Sgt	KINTON Bssil	8-07-40	83 Sqn
515103	Sgt	KIRCHER Cecil Bertram	13-06-40	9 Sqn
36254	P/O	KIRDY Matthew John Alexander [New Zealand]	29-07-40	142 Sqn
566117	Sgt	KIRKBRIDE Sydney Chapman	15-07-40	37 Sqn
580599	Sgt	KIRKHAM Thomas Russell [Canada]	16-05-40	115 Sqn
565269	Sgt	KIRKNESS Donald James	2-01-40	149 Sqn
787547	Sgt	KLIMT Karl [Czechoslovakia]	16-10-40	311 Sqn
651393	Sgt	KNIGHT Charles Henry George	1-09-40	106 Sqn
746916	Sgt	KNIGHT Charles John	6-09-40	61 Sqn
581515	Sgt	KNIGHT John	30-05-40	38 Sqn
82736	P/O	KNIGHT Norman Arthur	28-10-40	105 Sqn
530226	Sgt	KNOWLES Albert Vernon	17-05-40	82 Sqn
580790	Sgt	KNOWLES Basil Elles Sharp	1-05-40	37 Sqn
787615	Sgt	KOUKOL Frantisek [Czechoslovakia]	1-10-40	311 Sqn
787209	Sgt	KRIVDA Jan [Czechoslovakia]	16-12-40	311 Sqn
787252	Sgt	KUNKA Karel [Czechoslovakia]	25-09-40	311 Sqn
568800	Cpl	LACEY Frank Arthur	27-10-40	149 Sqn
523679	Sgt	LACEY Herbert George	10-09-40	44 Sqn
620363	Sgt	LACKENBY Abraham	18-09-40	105 Sqn
581017	Sgt	LAMB DFM John Robert Graham	10-11-40	114 Sqn
536874	LAC	LAMB Ralph John	12-04-40	9 Sqn
39635	F/O	LAMBART Frederick Arthur Henry [Canada]	13-08-40	11 OTU
631468	LAC	LAMBE William Robert [Eire]	1-11-40	110 Sqn
552634	AC1	LAMONT Robert Ritchie	24-05-40	12 OTU
40121	F/O	LANCASTER Eric Bell [South Africa]	4-07-40	144 Sqn
905836	Sgt	LAND Victor Robert Thomas	8-08-40	18 Sqn
82557	P/O	LANDA Bohumil [Czechoslovakia]	16-10-40	311 Sqn
76916	P/O	LANE Tom Hwfa Nixon	13-09-40	61 Sqn
523561	F/S	LANG DFM Geoffrey Edward	27-05-40	107 Sqn
787416	Sgt	LANG Karel [Czechoslovakia]	17-10-40	311 Sqn
70381	F/L	LANGDON George Ellis	26-11-40	15 OTU
42848	P/O	LANGFORD John Graham	14-11-40	61 Sqn
581238	Sgt	LANGFORD Albert Bernard	30-06-40	107 Sqn
906240	AC2	LARKIN Frederick Leonard	19-08-40	9 Sqn
742991	Sgt	LARKMAN Donald Ewart	16-11-40	115 Sqn
05102	W/C	LART DSO Edward Collis De Virac	13-08-40	82 Sqn
41715	P/O	LAUNDERS Oliver Harry	8-07-40	83 Sqn
37549	S/L	LAWRENCE Hector Yeates	18-05-40	15 Sqn
37409	S/L	LAWRENCE DFC Leslie Scott	10-06-40	61 Sqn
581399	Sgt	LAWRENCE Ronald William	12-06-40	107 Sqn
580791	Sgt	LAWRENSON John Heaton	22-05-40	99 Sqn
77944	P/O	LEACH Philip Allen	21-07-40	38 Sqn
569067	Sgt	LEAMY Edward Dennis	11-07-40	144 Sqn
566470	Sgt	LEE Cyril	2-07-40	83 Sqn
969132	Sgt	LEE Edward Cooper	7-12-40	214 Sqn
43162	P/O	LEE Terence Edward	2-11-40	102 Sqn
41716	P/O	LEEDS John Leeming [Canada]	8-09-40	149 Sqn
565583	Sgt	LEES David John	17-05-40	82 Sqn
78545	P/O	LEES Harold Frederic Archdale	20-07-40	9 Sqn
516225	Sgt	LEFEVRE Percy Thomas	23-08-40	218 Sqn
902217	Sgt	LEGG Alan Thomas	19-06-40	9 Sqn
742686	Sgt	LEGGE Frank Sidney	7-11-40	19 OTU
751309	Sgt	LEISHMAN David	2-07-40	58 Sqn
634058	AC2	LENNON James	13-06-40	16 OTU
620407	Sgt	LEONARD Denis Leonard	3-06-40	12 OTU
42851	P/O	LESTER Eric John	5-08-40	15 Sqn
631973	Sgt	LEWIS Frederick William	7-11-40	19 OTU
580549	Sgt	LEWIS Gwyn	11-06-40	21 Sqn
644842	AC2	LEWIS James Frederick Byng [Canada]	14-04-40	40 Sqn
547112	LAC	LEWIS Percival Arthur	11-06-40	12 OTU
70399	F/L	LEWIS Peter Humphrey	13-07-40	82 Sqn
636576	Sgt	LEWIS Ronald Norman	20-07-40	51 Sqn
40234	F/O	LIDDELL Eric Beck 'Squibs'	11-12-40	50 Sqn
33479	P/O	LIGHT Cyril	21-05-40	18 Sqn
631565	AC1	LILLEY Donald	1-05-40	99 Sqn
42134	P/O	LINDEN Michael Cunningham Andrews	18-09-40	99 Sqn
751189	Sgt	LINDSAY Alfred Burrows	16-11-40	115 Sqn
39018	F/O	LINDSAY Douglas Weatherall	7-07-40	37 Sqn

Service #	Rank	Name	Date	Sqn
638486	Sgt	LINDSAY James Fenton	6-08-40	49 Sqn
81036	P/O	LINSDELL Arthur Peter	18-09-40	83 Sqn
938842	Sgt	LISTER John Menzies	1-11-40	110 Sqn
754795	Sgt	LISTER Raylton Barclay	14-11-40	58 Sqn
751534	Sgt	LITTLE Frank	30-08-40	40 Sqn
547515	Sgt	LITTLE George Elliott	2-07-40	83 Sqn
641310	AC1	LITTLE Herbert William	16-12-40	149 Sqn
642775	Sgt	LITTLE Kenneth William Arthur	14-11-40	58 Sqn
79207	P/O	LITTLEJOHN John	29-09-40	37 Sqn
550254	Sgt	LIVERMORE Robert Mark	5-07-40	101 Sqn
524173	Sgt	LIVESEY Walter	28-11-40	102 Sqn
80831	P/O	LLEWELLYN Charles Gordon	4-08-40	16 OTU
26060	W/C	LLEWELYN John Griffith	23-05-40	40 Sqn
1108516	AC2	LLOYD Emlyn	27-10-40	West Raynham
742839	Sgt	LLOYD Richard Seaton Whittington	16-12-40	149 Sqn
740660	Sgt	LOADSMAN Horace Cecil	26-10-40	61 Sqn
941709	AC1	LOCK Owen Reginald	23-10-40	77 Sqn
41718	P/O	LOCKHEAD Clifford Molyneux	19-09-40	49 Sqn
751506	Sgt	LOFTHOUSE William Arthur	22-10-40	10 Sqn
580616	Sgt	LONG MiD Brian Conway	1-08-40	12 Sqn
906098	Sgt	LONG Harold Edward Minifie	12-09-40	12 OTU
747748	Sgt	LONGCLUSE Norman	29-07-40	142 Sqn
517486	Sgt	LORD Kenneth	3-10-40	105 Sqn
741604	Sgt	LORRIMAR Francis Raines	25-09-40	101 Sqn
971490	Sgt	LOUIS Victor Henry	14-11-40	77 Sqn
518071	LAC	LOVEJOY Charles Robin Archibald	22-05-40	99 Sqn
566553	Sgt	LOVELUCK James Gwyn	26-10-40	83 Sqn
581516	Sgt	LOWE Francis Alfred George	21-05-40	115 Sqn
42373	P/O	LOWE John Edgecombe	27-09-40	44 Sqn
649386	Sgt	LOWRY Laurence Mortimer	23-08-40	142 Sqn
551706	Sgt	LUCAS DFM Philip Henry	24-09-40	19 OTU
75169	P/O	LUMB Raymond Fletcher	29-06-40	77 Sqn
86372	P/O	LUPTON Cyril Peter	16-11-40	115 Sqn
82667	P/O	LUPTON John Sheppard Hewitt	27-09-40	14 OTU
751633	Sgt	LUSTY William Edward	29-11-40	18 Sqn
40628	P/O	LUXMOORE Anthony Seton [New Zealand]	26-06-40	50 Sqn
28112	W/C	LUXMOORE Arthur Noble	12-05-40	144 Sqn
644738	AC1	LYNCH Desmond Hugh	20-03-40	115 Sqn
70415	P/O	MacALISTER John Edmund Seaton	13-06-40	16 OTU
755134	Sgt	MacDONALD Norman	20-09-40	75 Sqn
41856	F/O	MacGREGOR Robert Butler 'Bobbie' [Kenya]	15-08-40	77 Sqn
37753	F/O	MacINNES John Thomson [Canada]	19-06-40	58 Sqn
551045	Sgt	MacKAY Duncan	10-08-40	144 Sqn
551673	Sgt	MacLEAN Donald Robert Charles	8-06-40	21 Sqn
755502	Sgt	MacNAIR James George Campbell	1-10-40	115 Sqn
615194	Sgt	MacPHERSON Keith Dalroy	29-07-40	82 Sqn
936778	Sgt	MACASKIE John Cunningham	7-12-40	214 Sqn
580877	Sgt	MACDONALD William Livingstone	7-04-40	115 Sqn
41855	P/O	MACGREGOR Horace Miers	1-01-40	7 Sqn
36015	S/L	MACINTYRE James Galt	29-07-40	44 Sqn
550348	Sgt	MACKAY DFM William Ian	6-09-40	144 Sqn
621783	AC1	MACKENZIE Leonard Leopold James	8-03-40	9 Sqn
580459	Sgt	MACKENZIE Robert Ian Leonard	25-04-40	49 Sqn
79167	P/O	MACLEAN Donald	1-10-40	38 Sqn
42415	P/O	MACLEY William Duncan	9-07-40	21 Sqn
755622	Sgt	MACMILLAN Alan	6-06-40	101 Sqn
751459	Sgt	MACMORLAND William Goodall	9-10-40	77 Sqn
968485	Sgt	MACNAB Alistair	25-11-40	99 Sqn
39089	F/O	MACRAE DFC William John [Canada]	8-03-40	9 Sqn
624822	AC2	MAHON William	26-02-40	98 Sqn
548565	Sgt	MAHONEY John	27-05-40	107 Sqn
632772	AC2	MAIN George	25-05-40	107 Sqn
965079	Sgt	MAIR Matthew Coutts	25-11-40	106 Sqn
905031	Sgt	MALCOLM Charles	16-12-40	142 Sqn
564260	Sgt	MALLARD James William	5-08-40	103 Sqn
629358	Sgt	MALONEY Terence Joseph William	9-07-40	15 Sqn
564042	Sgt	MALPASS David Vincent	13-07-40	218 Sqn
41600	P/O	MANATON Albert Charles [Canada]	12-03-40	61 Sqn
581517	Sgt	MANSER Norman Cyril	16-09-40	21 Sqn
521552	LAC	MANTLE Albert John	2-01-40	149 Sqn
550436	Sgt	MAPPLETHORPE Christopher Parker	22-10-40	10 Sqn
42860	P/O	MARCH David Michael	27-07-40	16 OTU
749307	Sgt	MARSDEN Arthur	2-09-40	40 Sqn
86420	P/O	MARSDEN Robert George Gordon Malben	25-11-40	99 Sqn
580966	Sgt	MARSH Alan	23-05-40	83 Sqn
580884	Sgt	MARSHALL Charles Frederick	18-09-40	58 Sqn
817326	Sgt	MARSHALL James Douglas	5-10-40	50 Sqn
77039	P/O	MARSHMAN John	1-05-40	115 Sqn
746983	Sgt	MARTIN Alfred Charles	8-09-40	149 Sqn
740246	Sgt	MASHAM Stanley Edwin	19-06-40	102 Sqn
42624	P/O	MASLIN Thomas William	10-07-40	107 Sqn
612668	Sgt	MASTERS Harold Emmanuel	4-08-40	142 Sqn
42249	P/O	MASTERS James Graham	23-05-40	15 Sqn
41722	P/O	MATHESON Colin	20-06-40	61 Sqn
82524	P/O	MATOUSEK Jaroslav A. [Czechoslovakia]	16-10-40	311 Sqn
581164	Sgt	MATSON George Enos [Canada]	1-10-40	78 Sqn
552074	Sgt	MATTHEWS Charles Ernest	11-09-40	38 Sqn
755027	Sgt	MATTHEWS Christopher George	16-12-40	149 Sqn
567678	Cpl	MATTHEWS Eric Samuel	28-10-40	105 Sqn
581518	Sgt	MATTHEWS Lloyd Albert Winston	12-06-40	101 Sqn
580787	Sgt	MATTICK Arthur Reginald	13-10-40	99 Sqn
42568	P/O	MAUDE-ROXBY John Leycester [Canada]	1-11-40	9 Sqn
580968	Sgt	MAWDSLEY Alfred Ellis	7-03-40	101 Sqn
33325	F/O	MAYBURY Donald Conrad	12-04-40	38 Sqn
580719	Sgt	MAYBURY John Gordon William	15-11-40	44 Sqn
538737	Sgt	MAYDON George Edwin	4-07-40	18 Sqn
643912	AC2	MAYOR DFM John Richard	12-05-40	107 Sqn
749508	Sgt	McALISTER William Gordon	9-09-40	51 Sqn
627936	Sgt	McALLISTER Robert James	2-07-40	82 Sqn
755640	Sgt	McCARTHY Charles Gordon	18-09-40	83 Sqn
41637	F/O	McCARTNEY Thomas James	4-12-40	82 Sqn
564908	Sgt	McCAULEY John Francis	15-07-40	37 Sqn
80827	P/O	McCAUSLAND James Maxwell	8-09-40	82 Sqn
621224	AC1	McCLENAGHAN Thomas	17-05-40	13 OTU
40241	P/O	McCOMB William Ralph [New Zealand]	26-01-40	102 Sqn
580972	Sgt	McCONNEL John Bretland	24-10-40	38 Sqn
755215	Sgt	McCONNELL Eric	11-12-40	50 Sqn
580801	Sgt	McCORMICK Joseph Edward	20-09-40	75 Sqn
580666	Sgt	McCROAY George Hugh	5-08-40	61 Sqn
615278	Sgt	McCRORIE William	22-07-40	78 Sqn
745703	Sgt	McCULLOCH Charles	5-11-40	214 Sqn
901582	Sgt	McCULLOCH Ian Maywood	19-06-40	58 Sqn
936241	Sgt	McDONALD Francis George Rae	10-10-40	149 Sqn
981977	AC2	McDONALD William John	28-10-40	40 Sqn
538044	LAC	McDONNELL Patrick Joseph	12-05-40	15 Sqn
624157	AC1	McEWAN William	18-02-40	90 Sqn
42413	P/O	McFARLAND Grenville James [New Zealand]	10-05-40	17 OTU
39545	F/O	McFARLANE Laurence Herbert [New Zealand]	2-07-40	58 Sqn
644316	Sgt	McGEOCH George	8-11-40	99 Sqn
971662	Sgt	McINNES Thomas Ireland	14-11-40	58 Sqn
522777	Cpl	McINTYRE James Cheyne	23-04-40	51 Sqn
549190	Sgt	McKAY Cornelius Francis	19-06-40	58 Sqn
755598	Sgt	McKEE James	8-09-40	101 Sqn
911283	Sgt	McKEE Patrick Percy	11-10-40	10 OTU
516750	Sgt	McKENZIE Charles William	9-08-40	10 OTU

Service No	Rank	Name	Date	Unit
581187	Sgt	McKINLAY Francis Wallace	15-05-40	44 Sqn
77985	P/O	McLAGGAN Alexander Livingstone	26-07-40	15 Sqn
35151	F/L	McLAREN MiD Ian Ledoux [Canada]	24-05-40	58 Sqn
42245	P/O	McLEAN James Archibald Dunlop	18-02-40	90 Sqn
523836	Sgt	McLEAN John	1-06-40	37 Sqn
967910	Sgt	McLEOD Lloyd Haig Beatty	27-09-40	106 Sqn
581290	Sgt	McLOUGHLIN Patrick Henry [Eire]	15-11-40	83 Sqn
85277	P/O	McMURRAY Frederick William	10-12-40	82 Sqn
563207	Sgt	McNICOL Andrew	7-04-40	83 Sqn
39640	F/O	McSHERRY Lewslie Andrew [Canada]	8-04-40	10 OTU
938736	Sgt	MEIKLE Robert	26-11-40	105 Sqn
638466	Sgt	MEIN Cuthbert	5-09-40	21 Sqn
580586	Sgt	MELLERSHIP Kenneth	12-05-40	107 Sqn
755040	Sgt	MELLON Tom Henry	21-11-40	49 Sqn
546929	LAC	MERCER Richard Henry	15-04-40	110 Sqn
639880	Sgt	MERCER Roy	10-07-40	107 Sqn
41860	P/O	MEREWETHER Arthur Guy Wyndham [New Zealand]	14-04-40	38 Sqn
520314	Sgt	MERRETT Jack Edwin	30-09-40	107 Sqn
746888	Sgt	MERRETT Sydney Richard	11-11-40	82 Sqn
755031	Sgt	MERRICK Peter Anthony	29-09-40	50 Sqn
523851	Sgt	MERRITT Albert Edward	13-06-40	82 Sqn
563345	Sgt	MERRITT Leonard John	12-05-40	107 Sqn
936580	Sgt	MERRY Allan Roger	7-11-40	139 Sqn
547673	Sgt	MERRYWEATHER George Edward	30-08-40	214 Sqn
39100	S/L	MERTENS John Albert Fraser	7-11-40	139 Sqn
41723	F/O	MICHIE Kenneth William	7-12-40	49 Sqn
580461	Sgt	MIDDLEMASS Neville Craig	12-05-40	15 Sqn
39105	F/L	MIDDLETON Douglas Davidson [Canada]	20-07-40	9 Sqn
521578	Sgt	MIDDLETON George Leslie	26-10-40	83 Sqn
611040	AC1	MIDDLETON Samuel Newton	27-02-40	82 Sqn
613210	AC2	MIDDLETON William Eric	29-05-40	9 Sqn
652446	Sgt	MILBOURNE Richard Lindsley	21-10-40	44 Sqn
751326	Sgt	MILES George Alfred	9-07-40	57 Sqn
74682	P/O	MILLAR Kenneth Leslie	14-11-40	44 Sqn
615087	LAC	MILLARD Albert Ernest	15-05-40	40 Sqn
632538	Sgt	MILLARD Ernest Stanley	24-09-40	19 OTU
364705	Sgt	MILLER DFM Frank	25-05-40	18 Sqn
515573	Sgt	MILLER Frederick Stanley	17-05-40	82 Sqn
580921	Sgt	MILLER James Emerson [Canada]	28-03-40	77 Sqn
42865	P/O	MILLER John Garland	12-08-40	149 Sqn
551536	Sgt	MILLER Reginald Talbot	20-07-40	44 Sqn
742485	Sgt	MILLER William Elliott	1-08-40	50 Sqn
748521	Sgt	MILLS David	9-12-40	115 Sqn
525767	Sgt	MILLS David Kinnaird	7-08-40	144 Sqn
740119	Sgt	MILLS Frank George	9-07-40	57 Sqn
967453	Sgt	MILSOM Edward John	28-09-40	9 Sqn
568093	Sgt	MINIHANE William Hubner	1-11-40	110 Sqn
641683	Sgt	MITCHELL Anthony John 'Tony'	20-11-40	149 Sqn
41862	P/O	MITCHELL Jeffrey Guy	22-06-40	61 Sqn
751395	Sgt	MITCHELL Leslie George	12-09-40	12 OTU
641364	Sgt	MOBBERLEY David Vivian	23-07-40	21 Sqn
967526	Sgt	MOFFAT George Gordon	29-11-40	21 Sqn
77921	P/O	MOFFAT Robert	8-06-40	15 Sqn
32109	F/L	MONCRIEFF Alexander	14-11-40	61 Sqn
580343	Sgt	MONKHOUSE Victor Clarence	22-07-40	78 Sqn
41863	P/O	MONTAGU DFC Charles James Drogo	25-08-40	77 Sqn
29098	S/L	MONYPENNY John Blackwell Sinclair	20-07-40	9 Sqn
702054	Sgt	MOORE Albert	26-11-40	21 Sqn
748765	Sgt	MOORE Frederick Leslie	24-11-40	77 Sqn
510601	F/S	MOORE George Percy	13-08-40	82 Sqn
638683	AC2	MOORE Gordon	20-03-40	Hemswell
522730	Sgt	MOORE Robert John	7-04-40	115 Sqn
563572	F/S	MOORES Leonard George	21-05-40	115 Sqn
653917	Sgt	MOORES Leslie Edwin	13-08-40	114 Sqn
1053259	AC2	MORAN Thomas Gardner	1-11-40	Wattisham
651574	Sgt	MORGAN Aneurin	14-08-40	15 OTU
80553	P/O	MORGAN Gilbert	1-11-40	144 Sqn
43708	P/O	MORGAN Harry Wright [New Zealand]	1-10-40	78 Sqn
580290	Sgt	MORRICE John	2-01-40	149 Sqn
41048	P/O	MORRIS Douglas William West [Canada]	21-05-40	115 Sqn
741203	Sgt	MORRIS Lionel Austin	14-06-40	38 Sqn
37866	F/L	MORRIS Mervyn Lascelles	15-04-40	110 Sqn
551580	LAC	MORRIS Raymonde	17-05-40	82 Sqn
965279	Sgt	MORRISON Archibald Finlayson	13-08-40	82 Sqn
41096	P/O	MORRISON James Douglas [Canada]	1-05-40	37 Sqn
653323	Sgt	MORRISON Robert McCrindle	13-08-40	61 Sqn
580414	Sgt	MORRISSY Donald Patrick [Eire]	13-08-40	114 Sqn
39446	F/O	MORSE Edward Barham	26-11-40	17 OTU
37521	F/L	MORTIMER Edward Patrick	7-08-40	17 OTU
629523	AC1	MORTON Edward	22-05-40	99 Sqn
751980	Sgt	MORTON Frederick Charles	12-12-40	115 Sqn
642718	Sgt	MORTON James	9-07-40	21 Sqn
741362	Sgt	MORTON James Litster	27-06-40	40 Sqn
1379786	AC2	MORTON Neil	16-12-40	149 Sqn
552152	AC2	MOSS Anthony Foreman	11-06-40	149 Sqn
72027	F/O	MOSS Brian Elwyn	1-08-40	12 Sqn
629737	AC1	MOSS John	7-04-40	115 Sqn
745478	Sgt	MOSS John Edward	5-09-40	21 Sqn
937153	Sgt	MOTT Malcolm Brian	16-11-40	115 Sqn
36164	F/O	MOTTRAM Standish Cecil	7-03-40	101 Sqn
643193	Sgt	MOYES James Inglis	8-11-40	61 Sqn
965758	AC1	MUIR Archibald	25-11-40	14 OTU
42632	P/O	MUIRHEAD George Hamilton	21-07-40	37 Sqn
580583	Sgt	MULLALLY William Michael [Eire]	19-04-40	107 Sqn
39558	F/O	MULLER Herbert Gage	1-05-40	99 Sqn
41864	F/O	MULLIGAN Robert Trevor [New Zealand]	8-12-40	50 Sqn
610830	AC1	MULLINEUX Alec	12-03-40	61 Sqn
40636	P/O	MULLOY DFC William Arthur Coote	26-07-40	50 Sqn
40637	F/O	MUNDAY Wynton Scott [Australia]	17-10-40	15 OTU
580698	Sgt	MUNN James	9-02-40	44 Sqn
967455	Sgt	MURCHISON George Ross	23-06-40	107 Sqn
580576	Sgt	MURDOCH Ian	8-04-40	82 Sqn
580799	Sgt	MURDOCH James Chalmers	2-03-40	149 Sqn
42759	P/O	MURFITT Thomas Russell [New Zealand]	24-10-40	102 Sqn
519962	Sgt	MURGATROYD Robert Beattie	6-07-40	9 Sqn
580800	Sgt	MURPHY Cornelius Thomas [Eire]	8-03-40	9 Sqn
36177	P/O	MURPHY John Dawson [New Zealand]	24-04-40	107 Sqn
631909	Sgt	MURPHY John Edgar	8-11-40	109 Sqn
624178	Sgt	MURPHY Michael [Eire]	11-06-40	149 Sqn
580735	Sgt	MURPHY Michael Francis [Eire]	7-04-40	115 Sqn
532831	Sgt	MURPHY Patrick [Eire]	30-07-40	15 Sqn
759321	Sgt	MURRAY Alastair Gordon	11-06-40	21 Sqn
553919	Sgt	MURRAY Cyril	16-10-40	14 OTU
41050	F/L	MURRAY DFC Dennis	15-11-40	105 Sqn
39559	F/L	MURRAY John David William [New Zealand]	9-07-40	21 Sqn
580910	Sgt	MYERS John Jacob	11-06-40	10 Sqn
748705	Sgt	MYERS Julian Gilbert Keydell	9-12-40	115 Sqn
77613	P/O	MYLAND Douglas Eric Charles	4-09-40	15 Sqn
759229	Sgt	NANSON John James Coulsham	7-12-40	9 Sqn
581407	Sgt	NAYLOR Charles	19-06-40	9 Sqn
1158708	AC2	NEAL Sidney Thomas	21-10-40	Marham
745300	Sgt	NEALE Robert John	5-10-40	144 Sqn
651567	Sgt	NEAVERSON Kenneth Walter	13-08-40	82 Sqn
751416	Sgt	NEED Walter Edward	16-12-40	101 Sqn
976437	Sgt	NEILL David	14-10-40	139 Sqn
580853	Sgt	NELSON Robert Melville	4-04-40	214 Sqn
808425	Sgt	NELSON William	9-08-40	13 OTU

Service #	Rank	Name	Date	Sqn
631165	Sgt	NEVILL William Eric	26-07-40	75 Sqn
901772	Sgt	NEVILLE Brian Walter	7-09-40	10 Sqn
901776	Sgt	NEVILLE Leslie Peter	15-10-40	10 Sqn
742656	Sgt	NEVILLE Maurice William	11-10-40	61 Sqn
580494	Sgt	NEVINSON William Stuart	12-04-40	50 Sqn
567295	LAC	NEW Kenneth Eric	15-08-40	77 Sqn
580271	Sgt	NEWBATT Reginald Edward	17-05-40	82 Sqn
626884	Sgt	NEWBERRY James	13-07-40	82 Sqn
549885	LAC	NEWBERRY Reginald John	20-05-40	102 Sqn
702680	AC2	NEWCOMBE Leslie Timothy	19-05-40	149 Sqn
746922	Sgt	NEWCOMBE Sydney James	9-07-40	57 Sqn
755404	Sgt	NEWSON Frederick Henry	26-08-40	40 Sqn
536600	Sgt	NEWTON Alec William	22-11-40	106 Sqn
37824	F/L	NEWTON George Edward	18-08-40	218 Sqn
39943	F/O	NEWTON Terence	13-07-40	218 Sqn
551758	LAC	NEWTON William George	20-03-40	51 Sqn
33492	P/O	NEWTON-CLARE John Edward	6-09-40	144 Sqn
653942	Sgt	NICHOLAS Frank Joseph Leslie	2-09-40	57 Sqn
561600	Sgt	NICHOLS David William Gibb	27-03-40	107 Sqn
624403	Sgt	NICHOLS Gerald	27-06-40	50 Sqn
902486	Sgt	NICHOLS Leslie William	22-12-40	9 Sqn
42635	P/O	NICHOLS Michael Ivor	29-09-40	9 Sqn
70501	P/O	NICHOLSON John Freeman	6-06-40	214 Sqn
543932	Sgt	NICOL Andrew Isaac John	4-07-40	144 Sqn
742765	Sgt	NICOL William	29-09-40	49 Sqn
740335	Sgt	NICOL William Frederick	7-04-40	115 Sqn
968346	Sgt	NIELD Eric	15-10-40	9 Sqn
551747	Sgt	NINEHAM Leslie Donald	13-06-40	82 Sqn
580671	Sgt	NIXON Percy Dryden	20-07-40	44 Sqn
42518	P/O	NIXON Thomas Arthur	27-05-40	16 OTU
902559	Sgt	NOAKES Frederick Walter	11-09-40	38 Sqn
41727	P/O	NOLAN George Grant Kingsmill	10-08-40	50 Sqn
37114	S/L	NOLAN Maurice	12-04-40	38 Sqn
904840	Sgt	NORMAN Adolphus Wilfred	2-11-40	101 Sqn
70871	P/O	NORMAN Graham Louis	28-03-40	77 Sqn
751289	Sgt	NORRIS Ronald	4-11-40	83 Sqn
938877	Sgt	NOVEMBER John	22-09-40	17 OTU
624643	LAC	NUTTALL Raymond Robin Henry [New Zealand]	11-06-40	10 Sqn
36132	F/O	OAKLEY Albert Edward [Australia]	12-05-40	15 Sqn
787369	Sgt	ODSTRCILEK Otakar [Czechoslovakia]	30-09-40	12 OTU
948296	AC2	OFFORD Eric	15-08-40	77 Sqn
70507	F/L	OGILVIE Glencairn Sholto	18-12-40	99 Sqn
632492	AC1	OGILVIE Stanley Carter	22-05-40	99 Sqn
754920	Sgt	OGILVY Allister Smith	14-10-40	139 Sqn
32182	S/L	OLDFIELD John Humphrey Ridding	6-11-40	61 Sqn
581525	Sgt	OLIVER Ralston George	13-08-40	82 Sqn
633791	Sgt	OMBLER Edward	11-06-40	77 Sqn
551751	LAC	OPENSHAW John Derek	25-04-40	49 Sqn
540249	AC1	ORCHARD Jack	17-02-40	110 Sqn
43644	P/O	OSBORN Edward Read [New Zealand]	28-11-40	102 Sqn
581526	Sgt	OSBORNE Douglas George	26-11-40	21 Sqn
528798	Sgt	OTTAWAY Jack Leonard Frederick	20-11-40	44 Sqn
42873	P/O	OTTERWAY Francis James	4-09-40	107 Sqn
565200	Sgt	OUTHWAITE John James	11-06-40	21 Sqn
39332	F/L	OWEN David William Hew	20-05-40	102 Sqn
565435	Sgt	OWENS Thomas	26-02-40	98 Sqn
748693	Sgt	OWLES Aubrey Ernest	31-08-40	18 Sqn
550762	Sgt	O'BRIEN John Barrie	15-08-40	51 Sqn
580123	Sgt	O'DRISCOLL Augustine Daniel Flurence	6-06-40	214 Sqn
643564	Sgt	O'HENEY William Patrick	23-07-40	107 Sqn
747713	Sgt	O'REGAN Francis Patrick	7-10-40	38 Sqn
621221	AC1	O'SULLIVAN Michael John [Eire]	1-05-40	99 Sqn
621150	AC1	PACKER John Thomas	21-05-40	115 Sqn
40745	F/O	PAINTER DFC John Frederick	7-11-40	19 Sqn
645628	Sgt	PAINTER Kenneth	7-10-40	9 Sqn
511862	Sgt	PAISH William Charles Henry	27-05-40	107 Sqn
649968	Sgt	PALLETT Denis Isiah	26-10-40	61 Sqn
581351	Sgt	PALMER Douglas Gerald	4-09-40	57 Sqn
743071	Sgt	PALMER Edward Bartle	9-09-40	105 Sqn
37981	F/L	PALMER Esmond John	8-09-40	101 Sqn
1252718	AC2	PALMER George Edward	24-09-40	Hemswell
748570	Sgt	PALMER Gordon	2-12-40	101 Sqn
551629	LAC	PALMER William Edward	12-05-40	107 Sqn
42875	P/O	PARFITT Douglas Alfred John	13-08-40	82 Sqn
818132	Sgt	PARISH Edward Francis	7-12-40	49 Sqn
917250	LAC	PARISH John Edward	19-08-40	3 Group
904426	Sgt	PARKER Charles William Ian	15-11-40	50 Sqn
84981	P/O	PARKER David Langley	19-09-40	20 OTU
74687	F/O	PARKER Richard Cecil	17-10-40	49 Sqn
754182	Sgt	PARKER Robert Coates	7-12-40	9 Sqn
580804	Sgt	PARKER William Claude	12-04-40	149 Sqn
580833	Sgt	PARKHOUSE Raymond Cranmer	26-05-40	37 Sqn
748411	Sgt	PARKINSON Jack	25-07-40	101 Sqn
39112	F/O	PARROTT Thomas Hayward	12-05-40	77 Sqn
43370	P/O	PARSONS DFC Ernest Ian [New Zealand]	14-08-40	10 Sqn
547309	LAC	PARSONS George Rene Joseph	26-05-40	49 Sqn
748208	Sgt	PARTON Frank Albert	24-11-40	77 Sqn
581118	Sgt	PARVIN Frederick Finkill	8-08-40	18 Sqn
33441	P/O	PARVIN John Hugh Keith	27-08-40	10 Sqn
40746	P/O	PASCOE Alfred George [Australia]	30-06-40	61 Sqn
526360	Sgt	PASCOE Terence George Jackson [South Africa]	28-06-40	13 OTU
581296	Sgt	PATCHETT Arthur Homer	13-08-40	82 Sqn
79171	P/O	PATE DFC Alexander John Roberts	30-10-40	115 Sqn
740369	Sgt	PATRICK William Ian Struan	9-09-40	40 Sqn
631112	Sgt	PATTERSON James	17-08-40	102 Sqn
626953	AC2	PATTERSON John Hedley	17-05-40	82 Sqn
565282	Sgt	PAUL Eric Howard	6-06-40	83 Sqn
581002	Sgt	PAUL Joseph William	17-05-40	82 Sqn
42877	P/O	PAY John Sydney	18-09-40	149 Sqn
902467	Sgt	PAYNE Donald Mayston	8-08-40	149 Sqn
33067	S/L	PEACOCK DFC George Ernest	6-06-40	9 Sqn
740307	Sgt	PEACOCK Roy Leslie	14-08-40	15 OTU
580805	Sgt	PEARCE Alan Sydney	12-04-40	115 Sqn
742651	Sgt	PEARCE Edward Albert	23-08-40	142 Sqn
560875	Sgt	PEARCE Harold	2-07-40	44 Sqn
564385	Sgt	PEARCE Thomas Robert Arthur Dalton	14-05-40	21 Sqn
84012	P/O	PEARS Edward Robert Matheson	23-11-40	214 Sqn
527531	Sgt	PEEL Harvey Alderson	1-05-40	58 Sqn
629076	AC2	PEEL Robert Charles	7-04-40	115 Sqn
612685	Sgt	PEGLER Victor William	9-09-40	40 Sqn
632154	Sgt	PEGRAM Thomas Henry	29-10-40	102 Sqn
741416	Sgt	PELHAM Rowland	22-11-40	61 Sqn
749447	LAC	PELLING Maurice	6-06-40	214 Sqn
748397	Sgt	PENMAN George Wright	10-12-40	17 OTU
581410	Sgt	PENNINGTON Alan Jervis	1-10-40	115 Sqn
751121	Sgt	PENNY Ronald Trevor	25-08-40	77 Sqn
87353	P/O	PENNYMORE Arthur Frederick	23-12-40	11 OTU
42640	P/O	PERCY Ralph Arthur	27-06-40	82 Sqn
590585	Sgt	PERKINS Kenneth Walsingham Boyd	21-12-40	106 Sqn
41201	F/O	PERKINS Reginald Derek [Canada]	15-11-40	44 Sqn
581058	Sgt	PERRIN Edward Reuben	12-05-40	15 Sqn
581005	Sgt	PERRY George Cyril [Canada]	15-04-40	83 Sqn
581034	Sgt	PERRY Jack Lenton	4-06-40	83 Sqn
629841	Sgt	PETRIE Peter John	4-09-40	15 Sqn
614230	Sgt	PEULEVE David Hilary	12-06-40	15 Sqn
970469	Sgt	PEWSEY Douglas	14-11-40	44 Sqn
78663	P/O	PHILIPPE Henri	2-09-40	37 Sqn
580524	Sgt	PHILLIPS Alfred Norman	17-05-40	82 Sqn
39153	F/L	PHILLIPS DFC Allan Smith	22-10-40	10 Sqn

Number	Rank	Name	Date	Unit
567099	Sgt	PHILLIPS Frank Herbert Edward	21-07-40	37 Sqn
1054826	AC2	PHILLIPS Harold	16-08-40	Wyton
79756	P/O	PHILLIPS Richard Arthur	9-10-40	58 Sqn
563677	Sgt	PHILLIPS Frederick	22-05-40	82 Sqn
581159	Sgt	PHIPP John Charles	9-06-40	82 Sqn
971265	Sgt	PHOENIX Frederick Douglas	11-10-40	10 OTU
539009	LAC	PICKARD John George	15-05-40	83 Sqn
742976	Sgt	PICKERING Charles William	7-07-40	82 Sqn
1150578	AC2	PIGGOTT Thomas Christopher [Eire]	21-10-40	11 OTU
40848	P/O	PILCHER Alonzo Derek	12-04-40	50 Sqn
531692	Cpl	PILGRIM Roger Colin John	16-05-40	115 Sqn
751549	Sgt	PILLANS Alexander Morrison	19-08-40	114 Sqn
29178	S/L	PILLING AFC Herbert	30-06-40	107 Sqn
759021	Sgt	PINCHARD John	14-12-40	17 OTU
626070	AC1	PIRIE George Rosse	22-05-40	57 Sqn
33201	S/L	PITCAIRN HILL DSO DFC James Anderson	18-09-40	83 Sqn
70545	F/O	PITMAN Charles Derek	17-10-40	49 Sqn
906866	AC1	PITT Ernest Neville	16-08-40	15 OTU
43141	P/O	PLUMB Edward Walter [New Zealand]	16-06-40	38 Sqn
551624	LAC	POAD Terrence	12-05-40	77 Sqn
742311	Sgt	POLLARD Maurice William James	17-08-40	102 Sqn
39115	F/O	POLTOCK Trevor Victor	17-04-40	107 Sqn
967876	Sgt	PONTIN William Humphrey	7-12-40	9 Sqn
42722	P/O	POOLE Frank Twain [New Zealand]	26-07-40	75 Sqn
76015	P/O	POOLE Gerard Arthur Hugh	1-05-40	99 Sqn
966654	Sgt	POPE William Ray	18-09-40	149 Sqn
39619	F/O	PORTER John Douglas Victor	4-04-40	107 Sqn
747830	Sgt	POTTER Jack Harold	16-11-40	115 Sqn
643788	Sgt	POTTER Robert	17-10-40	49 Sqn
1055450	AC2	POUND George Edward	7-10-40	9 Sqn
651514	Sgt	POWELL Raymond William	25-11-40	99 Sqn
614266	Sgt	POWELL Rex Spurway	20-06-40	61 Sqn
42643	P/O	POWELL Trevor Jack	23-07-40	21 Sqn
902976	Sgt	POWELL William Henry	25-09-40	107 Sqn
641379	Sgt	POWELL William Leslie	6-09-40	144 Sqn
75988	P/O	POWER Bruce Andrew [Canada]	25-07-40	99 Sqn
742000	Sgt	POWERS Kenneth Sidney	6-10-40	106 Sqn
627228	Sgt	POWIS George Owen	1-10-40	311 Sqn
745352	Sgt	POWRIE Charles Duncan	7-12-40	214 Sqn
581411	Sgt	POWYS-JONES Hugh Arthur	4-09-40	15 Sqn
43292	P/O	PREECE Malcolm James [Australia]	8-12-40	50 Sqn
85227	P/O	PRESCOTT Thomas Clare	23-06-40	110 Sqn
81070	P/O	PRESTON Cyril	19-09-40	107 Sqn
551160	Cpl	PRESTON Frank	15-05-40	44 Sqn
41060	P/O	PRICE John Frederic Sydney Pritchard	21-08-40	110 Sqn
638145	Sgt	PRICE Thomas Oliver	11-08-40	107 Sqn
564931	Sgt	PRIESTLEY Wilbert	25-04-40	110 Sqn
37299	F/O	PRINGLE DFC Alec Edward	16-05-40	115 Sqn
562834	Sgt	PRIOR Albert George Henry	13-04-40	15 Sqn
546726	LAC	PRIOR Ernest Harry	2-03-40	149 Sqn
751821	Sgt	PRITCHARD Harold William	1-10-40	115 Sqn
41950	P/O	PROSSER Ian	28-10-40	105 Sqn
745400	Sgt	PROUDFOOT David Scott	24-09-40	19 OTU
741959	Sgt	PRYKE Peter Berry Fairweather	13-08-40	11 OTU
42723	P/O	PRYOR Ronald William	3-08-40	115 Sqn
742203	AC2	PULFREY Albert Norman	13-05-40	15 OTU
516705	Sgt	PURSGLOVE Fred	30-06-40	61 Sqn
755485	Sgt	PUZEY Arthur Burnham	30-08-40	214 Sqn
580810	Sgt	QUARRINGTON Kenneth Frederick	22-05-40	110 Sqn
755038	Sgt	QUILL Philip	21-09-40	106 Sqn
611465	Sgt	QUINN Edward Stanislaws	10-08-40	50 Sqn
580445	Sgt	RADFORD Victor	18-09-40	105 Sqn
646336	Sgt	RADLEY Thomas James	1-08-40	12 Sqn
41203	F/O	RAFTER Charles William Arthur Haughton	11-10-40	214 RFlt
971156	Sgt	RAGGENBASS John	30-11-40	214 RFlt
564383	Sgt	RALLS Harry Leonard	12-12-40	115 Sqn
523261	Sgt	RAMSAY James Munro	9-10-40	58 Sqn
40430	P/O	RAMSAY Kenneth Allan	6-05-40	14 OTU
748785	Sgt	RANDS Edward Anthony Gaston	17-10-40	144 Sqn
36180	P/O	RANKIN David Alexander [New Zealand]	12-04-40	115 Sqn
548176	Sgt	RAPER Bernard	6-06-40	214 Sqn
751803	Sgt	RAPER John Alan	18-09-40	77 Sqn
970885	Sgt	RATCLIFFE Jack	4-12-40	82 Sqn
72451	F/L	RATHBONE John Rankin	10-12-40	82 Sqn
580595	Sgt	RAWSON William Lloyd	9-07-40	21 Sqn
751840	Sgt	RAYMENT Walter Benedict	5-10-40	61 Sqn
42647	P/O	REA John	28-09-40	214 Sqn
580828	Sgt	READ Charles Edward	15-07-40	37 Sqn
628775	AC1	READ James	15-04-40	3 Group
626591	AC1	REAY Gordon	25-08-40	49 Sqn
37421	S/L	REBBECK Peter Henry	17-08-40	144 Sqn
740422	Sgt	REDGROVE Basil Edward	3-11-40	83 Sqn
41206	P/O	REDMAYNE Douglas [Canada]	2-07-40	83 Sqn
226215	LAC	REED Davis Hewson	21-06-40	13 OTU
552567	LAC	REED Kenneth Gordon	17-05-40	82 Sqn
40059	F/L	REED Robert James [Australia]	10-09-40	50 Sqn
39158	F/L	REES John Llewelyn	5-08-40	15 OTU
78280	P/O	REEVE Edwin	17-12-40	61 Sqn
42438	P/O	REID Bruce Douglas George Houstoun	12-06-40	107 Sqn
746818	Sgt	REID George	7-07-40	15 Sqn
77040	P/O	RENDELL Victor Arthur	19-09-40	83 Sqn
1307761	AC2	RENNIE Robert	10-11-40	Scampton
514831	Sgt	REVELL Ernest Albert	6-06-40	214 Sqn
747880	Sgt	REYNOLDS Marcus Pete	10-10-40	149 Sqn
996999	AC2	RHODES George William	1-08-40	16 OTU
551007	Cpl	RICHARDS DFM Allen Glyndwr	17-05-40	82 Sqn
529564	Sgt	RICHARDSON Colin	16-11-40	50 Sqn
526112	Sgt	RICHARDSON Harrnet Richard	17-12-40	61 Sqn
581413	Sgt	RICHARDSON Horace William	13-07-40	82 Sqn
565331	F/S	RICHARDSON Patrick Ranby	11-12-40	105 Sqn
740461	Sgt	RICHARDSON Royston Thomas	24-08-40	11 OTU
639639	Sgt	RICHMOND Philip Hall	1-10-40	78 Sqn
540110	AC1	RICKETTS Percy Frank	12-04-40	9 Sqn
39127	F/L	RIEPENHAUSEN James Eric	11-10-40	10 OTU
741996	Sgt	RILEY Charles Peace	26-08-40	40 Sqn
550943	Sgt	RILEY Eddie Andreas Hals	26-08-40	57 Sqn
966315	Sgt	RILEY William	22-12-40	9 Sqn
624959	Sgt	RIMES Edwin Samuel	17-12-40	49 Sqn
580587	Sgt	RIMMER George	5-07-40	114 Sqn
628511	Sgt	ROBB William	29-07-40	12 OTU
590338	Sgt	ROBERTON Alfred John	10-05-40	40 Sqn
818025	Sgt	ROBERTS Denziel Sydney	16-12-40	149 Sqn
563483	Sgt	ROBERTS Edwin George	12-05-40	15 Sqn
541978	LAC	ROBERTS Jack Brian	27-03-40	107 Sqn
749756	Sgt	ROBERTS James	10-12-40	17 OTU
540263	LAC	ROBERTS Robert Arthur	25-04-40	110 Sqn
566679	Sgt	ROBERTS Roly Frederick	31-08-40	49 Sqn
40319	P/O	ROBERTS Wilfred [Australia]	7-04-40	83 Sqn
746740	Sgt	ROBERTSON Andrew	6-11-40	61 Sqn
633753	AC1	ROBERTSON David	1-05-40	58 Sqn
644958	Sgt	ROBERTSON John Devine	2-10-40	9 Sqn
758182	Sgt	ROBERTSON John St. Clair	10-12-40	110 Sqn
751021	Sgt	ROBERTSON Robert Forrest	28-10-40	49 Sqn
631370	AC2	ROBINSON Allen	21-05-40	115 Sqn
749454	Sgt	ROBINSON Arthur	26-11-40	17 OTU
70873	P/O	ROBINSON Charles Henry	26-07-40	15 Sqn
562272	Sgt	ROBINSON Fred	4-07-40	50 Sqn
939568	Sgt	ROBINSON Sims	13-08-40	11 OTU
756719	AC1	ROBINSON Thomas	31-08-40	49 Sqn
41471	P/O	ROBSON DFC Angus [Australia]	22-08-40	144 Sqn
41323	P/O	ROBSON Clarence Sydney [Canada]	15-09-40	78 Sqn

Number	Rank	Name	Date	Unit
39759	F/O	ROBSON Harry Wood	12-04-40	44 Sqn
509364	Sgt	ROBSON DFM Henry	31-12-40	139 Sqn
939777	Sgt	ROBSON Thomas	15-11-40	105 Sqn
632049	Sgt	RODGER Robert	16-11-40	115 Sqn
751935	Sgt	RODGERS Ronald Mackintosh	23-12-40	139 Sqn
965303	Sgt	ROGERS Anthony Arthur	7-12-40	9 Sqn
741897	Sgt	ROGERS Charles Stanley	14-11-40	10 Sqn
39174	F/L	ROGERS Douglas John	10-09-40	44 Sqn
900084	Sgt	ROGERS John Aidan	7-07-40	82 Sqn
40432	P/O	ROGERS Mark Hubbard	17-08-40	102 Sqn
748198	Sgt	ROLISON Ronald Edward	7-11-40	19 OTU
615888	Sgt	ROLLS Henry	15-08-40	15 Sqn
87344	P/O	ROMBACH Charles Sutherland	22-12-40	17 OTU
39955	F/L	ROONEY Louis John [South Africa]	28-12-40	83 Sqn
36202	P/O	ROOTS Reginald William [New Zealand]	4-06-40	44 Sqn
633114	Sgt	ROSCOE Arthur	1-10-40	78 Sqn
631369	Sgt	ROSE Clarence	11-07-40	144 Sqn
39901	F/O	ROSE Frank Charles	18-05-40	51 Sqn
630965	AC2	ROSE George Thomas	19-03-40	115 Sqn
42887	P/O	ROSE John Alexander	12-07-40	149 Sqn
900030	Sgt	ROSE Maurice	29-10-40	102 Sqn
740263	Sgt	ROSE Robert Frederick	16-10-40	49 Sqn
41473	P/O	ROSE Stephen Gregory [Canada]	14-05-40	110 Sqn
533258	LAC	ROSEMOND Joseph	30-04-40	110 Sqn
40021	F/O	ROSEWARNE Vivian Allen William	30-05-40	38 Sqn
40060	F/O	ROSS DFC Ellis Henry [Australia]	13-08-40	83 Sqn
741786	Sgt	ROSS Reginald Douglas	16-12-40	77 Sqn
740049	Sgt	ROSS Thomas David Weston	19-09-40	107 Sqn
513919	Sgt	ROUTLEDGE Joseph Newton	13-07-40	218 Sqn
580737	Sgt	ROUTLEDGE Leonard Wingate	13-06-40	9 Sqn
36133	F/O	ROWAN Percival John Hamilton	10-05-40	40 Sqn
39173	F/O	ROWAN-ROBINSON Derrick Paul Woodrow	25-04-40	49 Sqn
631427	Sgt	ROWCLIFFE William Stanley	20-06-40	61 Sqn
626639	AC2	ROWE Peter John Hanley	8-01-40	101 Sqn
745268	Sgt	ROWE Philip	16-12-40	77 Sqn
742816	Sgt	ROWE Thomas Edward	25-09-40	38 Sqn
936289	Sgt	ROWLANDS James	23-12-40	58 Sqn
1108295	AC2	ROWLANDS Robert Rankin McHarry	3-11-40	83 Sqn
972006	Sgt	ROWLEY Dennis	28-11-40	102 Sqn
514444	Sgt	ROWLING George Albert	17-03-40	50 Sqn
42889	P/O	ROYLANCE Peter William	10-09-40	50 Sqn
359517	F/S	RUFFELL-HAZELL DFM Richard James	3-08-40	115 Sqn
770830	AC1	RULE Alfred James	23-01-40	2 Group
968588	Sgt	RUSSELL Clarence Edward	14-11-40	61 Sqn
41744	P/O	RYAN Leonard Terence Jervis [New Zealand]	26-11-40	105 Sqn
741765	Sgt	SABIN Harold William	14-08-40	15 Sqn
37945	F/O	SADDINGTON MiD MC [Czechoslovakia] George Edgar	12-08-40	77 Sqn
633936	Sgt	SALISBURY Robert Edward	18-09-40	58 Sqn
551589	Sgt	SALMON Peter Duncan	17-08-40	51 Sqn
41071	P/O	SALMON Peter Gordon Hedley	29-12-40	115 Sqn
33476	P/O	SALMOND John Geoffrey Carr	18-04-40	99 Sqn
935979	Sgt	SAMBROOK Harry Edward	30-09-40	214 Sqn
540079	Sgt	SAMMELLS Alen Frederick William	14-06-40	40 Sqn
516159	Sgt	SANDALL Jack Francis	12-06-40	44 Sqn
42727	P/O	SANDERSON Rex Martyn [New Zealand]	24-10-40	75 Sqn
746826	Sgt	SANDERSON Samuel	9-08-40	13 OTU
902416	Sgt	SANSUM Thomas Henry	5-11-40	214 Sqn
702278	AC2	SAUNDERS Edward John	16-08-40	15 OTU
70602	Sgt	SAUNDERS Roi Leonard	22-05-40	57 Sqn
40756	P/O	SAUNDERS William Anthony	14-06-40	21 Sqn
511350	Cpl	SAVAGE Alfred	9-12-40	Topcliffe
581475	Sgt	SAVILL DFM Bernard Leonard	25-09-40	77 Sqn
745096	Sgt	SAVILLE Jack Herbert	8-08-40	18 Sqn
744976	Sgt	SAXBY Herbert Edward	23-12-40	139 Sqn
581022	Sgt	SAXON Arthur Kenneth	3-03-40	99 Sqn
548614	Sgt	SAYER DFM Kenneth Anthony	13-08-40	83 Sqn
70608	F/L	SCOLTOCK Anthony Terence Nicholas	17-12-40	49 Sqn
755254	Sgt	SCOTT John James	12-08-40	149 Sqn
37484	F/L	SCOTT John Stanley	17-08-40	51 Sqn
754733	Sgt	SCOTT Laurence William	12-12-40	115 Sqn
615919	Sgt	SCRASE Edgar Enoch	13-08-40	15 Sqn
552947	Sgt	SCULFER John Matthew	11-06-40	21 Sqn
42962	P/O	SEARLE Frederick Maurice Norman	30-04-40	110 Sqn
79000	P/O	SEARLES Walter George	9-09-40	149 Sqn
621033	Sgt	SEDGLEY Alan	15-12-40	102 Sqn
42443	P/O	SEDGLEY Edgar Albert Ernest [New Zealand]	13-06-40	16 OTU
540186	Sgt	SEED Harold Victor	7-09-40	10 Sqn
40264	F/O	SELBY Anthony Marmaduke Langdale	21-11-40	102 Sqn
743306	Sgt	SELLWOOD Kenneth Reginald	25-07-40	99 Sqn
39575	F/O	SELWYN Harold Morrey	3-07-40	51 Sqn
624835	AC1	SETTLE Frederick Gordon	7-05-40	9 Sqn
755373	Sgt	SEXTON Gerald Francis	6-07-40	99 Sqn
629671	AC1	SEYMOUR William Aubrey	30-04-40	37 Sqn
43711	P/O	SHANN Winton Selwood	25-09-40	107 Sqn
746954	Sgt	SHAPLAND Edward Arthur	6-11-40	58 Sqn
619842	Cpl	SHARP Dennis Harold	27-07-40	150 Sqn
72284	F/O	SHARP Patrick Duart	8-10-40	13 OTU
541437	LAC	SHARPE Denis William	7-04-40	83 Sqn
751718	LAC	SHARPE Hugh	27-05-40	16 OTU
741808	Sgt	SHEILS Joseph Desmond	8-10-40	16 OTU
42155	P/O	SHELDON Harry Christie [Canada]	13-08-40	61 Sqn
639947	Sgt	SHELDRICK Bertie	29-12-40	115 Sqn
742908	Sgt	SHELFER Eric Henry William	27-09-40	106 Sqn
625253	Sgt	SHEPHERD David George	27-12-40	21 Sqn
910413	Sgt	SHEPPARD Benjamin Quinney	23-12-40	11 OTU
561926	Sgt	SHEPPERSON Bertram David	20-03-40	51 Sqn
536431	Sgt	SHERWOOD Charles Alfred	5-10-40	83 Sqn
550468	Sgt	SHEWRY Cyril Joseph	22-05-40	144 Sqn
759263	Sgt	SHILDRICK Derek Arthur	9-12-40	114 Sqn
741468	Sgt	SHILLING Joseph Donald	7-12-40	50 Sqn
749466	Sgt	SHIMELLS Kenneth	10-10-40	149 Sqn
581534	Sgt	SHOOK Frederick Charles	10-08-40	50 Sqn
42770	P/O	SHORT Rupert Edward [New Zealand]	25-07-40	101 Sqn
562875	Sgt	SHORTLAND Wilfred Owen	12-05-40	15 Sqn
627701	Sgt	SHUTTLEWORTH Bernard	13-10-40	99 Sqn
76022	P/O	SHUTTLEWORTH Richard Ormonde	2-08-40	12 OTU
740141	Sgt	SIDEBOTHAM Charles Edward Richard	28-12-40	106 Sqn
36276	P/O	SIGLEY Peter Knox [New Zealand]	24-05-40	12 OTU
640098	Sgt	SILLETT Ernest Robert	1-10-40	44 Sqn
39344	F/O	SIMMONS Robert Collin	1-06-40	37 Sqn
564409	Sgt	SIMMONS Samuel Frank	22-05-40	57 Sqn
905662	Sgt	SIMMS Donald Brill	25-09-40	101 Sqn
42444	P/O	SIMPSON Basil	2-06-40	16 OTU
526079	Sgt	SIMPSON James	12-06-40	44 Sqn
521263	LAC	SIMS Alfred George	17-05-40	82 Sqn
744969	Sgt	SINCLAIR Donald	26-09-40	61 Sqn
755604	Sgt	SINCLAIR Robert	14-11-40	61 Sqn
742236	Sgt	SKIDMORE Albert Edgar	15-10-40	9 Sqn
743057	Sgt	SKINNER Eric William Joseph	30-08-40	50 Sqn
742219	Sgt	SKIPWORTH William	16-12-40	101 Sqn
82529	P/O	SKUTIL Jaroslav V. [Czechoslovakia]	1-10-40	311 Sqn
82637	P/O	SLABY Jaroslav [Czechoslovakia]	16-10-40	311 Sqn
749586	Sgt	SLADE Stanley Walter	26-10-40	105 Sqn
77920	P/O	SLATER Peter Henderson	26-10-40	21 Sqn

Number	Rank	Name	Date	Unit
82638	P/O	SLOVAK Josef [Czechoslovakia]	1-10-40	311 Sqn
754430	Sgt	SMALL William Raymond	11-10-40	10 OTU
747711	Sgt	SMART Harold Edgar	18-09-40	99 Sqn
41877	P/O	SMETTEM Kenneth Richard Killey	30-08-40	50 Sqn
580591	Sgt	SMEWIN Charles John	23-07-40	21 Sqn
39346	F/O	SMITH Abraham Frederick [South Africa]	18-04-40	99 Sqn
40187	P/O	SMITH Albert Stanley	20-06-40	61 Sqn
550966	Sgt	SMITH Arthur Harry	27-06-40	50 Sqn
618641	AC1	SMITH Benjamin Brian Charles	10-06-40	13 OTU
903160	Sgt	SMITH Cyril Arthur	9-08-40	13 OTU
612904	Sgt	SMITH Cyril James	8-12-40	50 Sqn
648240	Sgt	SMITH David William	21-12-40	106 Sqn
366413	Sgt	SMITH Ewart William	5-07-40	101 Sqn
580384	Sgt	SMITH Frederick Leece	15-08-40	18 Sqn
518492	Sgt	SMITH Frederick Trevor Martin	18-01-40	75 Sqn
615035	Sgt	SMITH George Gray	28-12-40	50 Sqn
39692	F/O	SMITH Henry Vernon	20-06-40	10 Sqn
755623	Sgt	SMITH James Scott	26-08-40	40 Sqn
741944	Sgt	SMITH John Anthony	3-10-40	19 OTU
42901	P/O	SMITH John Digby	23-07-40	58 Sqn
905353	Sgt	SMITH Norman Sidney	14-11-40	58 Sqn
754103	Sgt	SMITH Phillip Trevor Harding	6-11-40	10 Sqn
646729	Sgt	SMITH Robert Daniel	27-11-40	13 OTU
626998	AC2	SMITH Thomas Edgeley	2-03-40	149 Sqn
900116	Sgt	SMITH William Leslie	18-08-40	218 Sqn
565748	Sgt	SMYTH John Alexander	26-05-40	144 Sqn
647592	AC1	SMYTH Peter	3-12-40	83 Sqn
43143	F/L	SMYTHE DFC Thomas Laidlaw Scott	11-09-40	44 Sqn
535929	LAC	SNELL Thomas Arthur	27-10-40	9 Sqn
745231	Sgt	SNELL Victor	1-10-40	10 Sqn
42366	P/O	SNOOKE Dudley Delacourtte	28-09-40	83 Sqn
624710	AC1	SNOWDEN George William	31-08-40	49 Sqn
580330	Sgt	SONGEST Norman Martin	11-06-40	77 Sqn
643394	AC2	SOUTH Roy	24-05-40	17 OTU
514566	F/S	SOUTHEY William Thomas Joseph	27-06-40	50 Sqn
42083	P/O	SOWTER Basil York	17-09-40	14 OTU
580466	Sgt	SPENCER DFM Alan	9-07-40	40 Sqn
755611	Sgt	SPENCER Dennis Douglas George	30-05-40	38 Sqn
580627	Sgt	SPENCER Douglas Frederick	3-08-40	139 Sqn
939190	Sgt	SPENCER Robert Nettleton	8-09-40	101 Sqn
627782	Sgt	SPENCER Ronald	11-06-40	15 Sqn
516666	Sgt	SPICKETT William Alfred	27-06-40	49 Sqn
521985	Sgt	SPILLER Reginald William	7-11-40	139 Sqn
561257	Sgt	SPURR Victor	10-05-40	40 Sqn
86724	P/O	SQUIRE Lawrence Francis	22-12-40	17 OTU
654662	Sgt	STACEY Richard Francis	7-12-40	214 Sqn
33336	F/L	STANLEY Desmond Geoffrey [Eire]	7-12-40	9 Sqn
581359	Sgt	STANLEY Jesse George	4-07-40	18 Sqn
40438	P/O	STAPLEDON Ian	6-04-40	21 Sqn
741963	Sgt	STARNS William Reginald	29-11-40	21 Sqn
36263	P/O	STEDMAN Michael Lomax [New Zealand]	14-10-40	78 Sqn
550484	Sgt	STEEL Alan	29-08-40	102 Sqn
742995	Sgt	STEEL John Clement	14-11-40	77 Sqn
759143	Sgt	STEELL Douglas George Buchan	21-11-40	49 Sqn
748214	Sgt	STEIN John Drummond	6-04-40	35 Sqn
39904	F/O	STENHOUSE William Alan	15-08-40	77 Sqn
967065	Sgt	STEPHENS Evan John	24-08-40	11 OTU
580772	Sgt	STEPHENS George Maxwell	24-05-40	12 OTU
32024	S/L	STEPHENS John Frank	20-07-40	110 Sqn
749413	Sgt	STEPHENS Reginald	7-10-40	38 Sqn
743026	Sgt	STEPHENSON Donald	16-12-40	101 Sqn
550132	Sgt	STEPHENSON Joseph William	27-08-40	10 Sqn
77981	P/O	STERLING Robert Carnac	23-07-40	149 Sqn
74967	F/O	STEVENS Alwyn Oswald Laurence	7-11-40	99 Sqn
33415	P/O	STEVENS Barry Osborne Cornelius	18-01-40	75 Sqn
581538	Sgt	STEVENS Claude Donald	9-07-40	21 Sqn
81060	P/O	STEVENS Dennis Joseph Arthur	7-09-40	10 Sqn
74568	F/O	STEVENS Edward Denys	21-11-40	102 Sqn
41330	P/O	STEWART Alan	5-07-40	114 Sqn
70819	P/O	STEWART Alexander	3-03-40	99 Sqn
624161	Sgt	STEWART Angus Lamont	26-07-40	50 Sqn
42683	P/O	STEWART Donald Eglington [Canada]	11-09-40	44 Sqn
638353	AC1	STEWART Frederick	27-07-40	150 Sqn
42448	P/O	STIDSTON Arthur Frank	13-06-40	107 Sqn
580407	Sgt	STILES George Herbert [Canada]	27-03-40	107 Sqn
639949	Sgt	STILES Royston Charles Edward	26-08-40	57 Sqn
749309	Sgt	STILWELL Raymond Brooks	29-11-40	21 Sqn
906289	Sgt	STOCKMAN Clifton	14-11-40	58 Sqn
538833	Sgt	STOREY Harold Alfred	29-06-40	77 Sqn
44486	P/O	STORROW Arthur Raymond	10-08-40	110 Sqn
42905	P/O	STOTHARD Harry Reed	19-09-40	20 OTU
751322	Sgt	STUBBERFIELD Laurence Paul	15-08-40	51 Sqn
581045	Sgt	STUBBINGS Geoffrey Harry	4-11-40	83 Sqn
745425	Sgt	STUBBS Cecil Vernon	21-10-40	44 Sqn
640962	Sgt	STURT Edwin Horatio	5-11-40	21 Sqn
536657	Sgt	SUGDEN James	17-09-40	44 Sqn
644680	Sgt	SUGGETT Charles	12-07-40	149 Sqn
969335	Sgt	SULLIVAN Vincent Gerald	24-11-40	77 Sqn
581542	Sgt	SULLY Alfred Peter	30-08-40	107 Sqn
617486	Sgt	SULTER James Anthony	22-07-40	78 Sqn
563808	Sgt	SUMMERS Albert Thomas	9-07-40	21 Sqn
748246	Sgt	SUMNER Stanley Robert	16-10-40	14 OTU
564422	F/S	SUMPSTER Cyril Leslie	12-06-40	44 Sqn
903630	AC2	SUMPTER Stanley Thomas	6-06-40	Upwood
72508	F/O	SUTHERLAND Ian Welsh	4-08-40	15 Sqn
43049	P/O	SVENSON Neil Anzac [New Zealand]	15-12-40	77 Sqn
653807	Sgt	SWAIN Jack	12-12-40	115 Sqn
540806	Sgt	SWALLOW Vincent Joseph	23-06-40	110 Sqn
515500	F/S	SWATTON MiD Frank	25-11-40	99 Sqn
903248	Sgt	SWEET Reginald Philip	2-10-40	9 Sqn
40328	F/O	SWENSEN Stanley Powell [Canada]	15-08-40	51 Sqn
644387	Sgt	SWIFT James Henry	12-08-40	149 Sqn
77213	P/O	SWIFT John Rupert	11-06-40	149 Sqn
39907	F/O	SYLVESTER Kenneth Richard Hugh	15-04-40	83 Sqn
42541	P/O	TAGG Maurice Roy	20-07-40	61 Sqn
526290	Sgt	TAILFORD Donald	1-08-40	50 Sqn
751664	Sgt	TAIT Richard Albert William [Canada]	15-08-40	51 Sqn
42368	P/O	TAKIDELI Alexander	12-06-40	15 Sqn
581480	Sgt	TANNER Melville	3-09-40	17 OTU
633130	Sgt	TANSLEY John	20-07-40	51 Sqn
906563	Sgt	TAYLOR Albert Edward	23-11-40	214 Sqn
40443	P/O	TAYLOR Brian Anthony	23-06-40	144 Sqn
651358	Sgt	TAYLOR Edward	14-11-40	83 Sqn
644896	Sgt	TAYLOR George Henry	29-09-40	37 Sqn
965631	Sgt	TAYLOR Gordon	8-09-40	218 Sqn
34115	S/L	TAYLOR John Cornelius [Eire]	29-09-40	50 Sqn
581192	Sgt	TAYLOR Leslie Hambleton	24-09-40	58 Sqn
581362	Sgt	TAYLOR Philip Bernard	11-08-40	107 Sqn
22092	S/L	TAYLOR Rex Oliver Oxley	7-10-40	38 Sqn
77205	P/O	TAYLOR Thomas Monka	26-07-40	50 Sqn
652777	Sgt	TAYLOR William Barrie	13-08-40	61 Sqn
40155	F/O	TAYLOR William George	12-04-40	44 Sqn
70666	F/O	TEDDER Arthur Richard Brian	15-08-40	139 Sqn
39767	F/O	TEMPLEMAN Philip Francis [Canada]	31-03-40	37 Sqn
70668	F/P	THEVENARD George Holland	1-08-40	16 OTU
802490	Sgt	THIRD Hugh William	20-11-40	149 Sqn
619032	Sgt	THOMAS David Reginald Ivan	4-06-40	83 Sqn
37332	S/L	THOMAS Frank George Ralph	26-08-40	40 Sqn
580177	Sgt	THOMAS Ivor Llewellyn	10-05-40	40 Sqn
40648	P/O	THOMAS Mervyn [Australia]	12-04-40	50 Sqn
41222	F/O	THOMAS Roy Haydn	7-09-40	10 Sqn
561946	Sgt	THOMAS Thomas	10-11-40	50 Sqn
18081	S/L	THOMPSON Chester William McKinley	16-09-40	19 OTU

551783	Sgt	THOMPSON Clifford William	23-05-40	15 Sqn		530080	Sgt	VICKERY Roy Fox	12-04-40	149 Sqn
755298	Sgt	THOMPSON Edward Francis	9-09-40	107 Sqn		747717	Sgt	VINCE Norman Eric	20-11-40	149 Sqn
755768	Sgt	THOMPSON George	8-06-40	15 Sqn		03092	S/L	WADHAM Nicholas Wyndham	6-08-40	3 Group
745185	Sgt	THOMPSON Neville William Gordon	1-10-40	115 Sqn		564478	Sgt	WADMORE John Howard	16-02-40	21 Sqn
745851	Sgt	THOMPSON Ronald Edwin	2-10-40	9 Sqn		971677	Sgt	WAKE Kenneth Henry	16-12-40	77 Sqn
36264	P/O	THOMSON Basil Percy [New Zealand]	11-06-40	12 OTU		580685	Sgt	WAKE Robert Leslie	16-08-40	144 Sqn
624332	Sgt	THOMSON John	27-08-40	101 Sqn		82681	P/O	WAKEFORD Donald William	11-11-40	49 Sqn
647064	Sgt	THOMSON John	7-12-40	Finningley		563597	Sgt	WAKEHAM Harry Richard Bennett	2-01-40	149 Sqn
759316	Sgt	THOMSON Robert Champney	29-07-40	12 OTU		740420	Sgt	WAKELING Laurie Charles	12-04-40	149 Sqn
637347	Sgt	THOMSON William	6-09-40	144 Sqn		551324	AC2	WAKELY Leslie James	18-01-40	148 Sqn
743029	Sgt	THORN Robert Leonard	26-11-40	17 OTU		615619	Sgt	WALKER Albert Eric	2-09-40	144 Sqn
41497	P/O	THORNTON Stanley George [Australia]	12-05-40	107 Sqn		581250	Sgt	WALKER Bernard	14-10-40	139 Sqn
						41759	P/O	WALKER Colin James Ray	6-11-40	50 Sqn
625669	AC1	THORNTON Willie	23-05-40	83 Sqn		755305	Sgt	WALKER Leslie Alfred Nevison	24-07-40	110 Sqn
746949	Sgt	THREFALL James Clifton	14-11-40	83 Sqn		935524	Sgt	WALKER Walter Llewellyn Thomas	6-11-40	10 Sqn
580889	Sgt	THRIFT Kenneth Victor	20-05-40	102 Sqn		76457	P/O	WALKER Wilfred	19-07-40	44 Sqn
751512	Sgt	THROWER Charles Edward	13-08-40	61 Sqn		550802	LAC	WALLACE Allan Vincent	17-03-40	50 Sqn
37134	S/L	THWAITES AFC Evelyn Harry Toller	17-08-40	149 Sqn		905336	Sgt	WALLACE David Ernest	9-12-40	115 Sqn
507671	Sgt	TICE George Hedley	16-02-40	21 Sqn		743867	AC1	WALLWORK Fred	6-05-40	102 Sqn
755441	Sgt	TIEDEMAN James Henry	17-12-40	49 Sqn		581126	Sgt	WALSH Edmond Ernest Raymond [Eire]	4-09-40	18 Sqn
43294	P/O	TINDALL Albert [Australia]	9-12-40	115 Sqn						
42162	P/O	TODD Desmond Arthur [New Zealand]	4-07-40	44 Sqn		635501	Sgt	WALTER Frank Douglas	26-10-40	61 Sqn
640677	Sgt	TODD Thomas Huntley	16-10-40	14 OTU		902245	Sgt	WALTER James Le Blond Robert	1-10-40	115 Sqn
581125	Sgt	TOMLINSON John	1-10-40	44 Sqn		626198	Sgt	WALTERS Sidney	30-09-40	107 Sqn
580338	Sgt	TOMLINSON Leonard Frank	1-05-40	58 Sqn		633350	Sgt	WALTHO Frederick Stanley	20-07-40	61 Sqn
564502	Sgt	TONKISS Joseph Raybould	12-04-40	44 Sqn		748446	Sgt	WALTON John Carse	16-11-40	115 Sqn
550284	Sgt	TOOMEY Richard William	14-11-40	77 Sqn		41760	P/O	WANKLYN Peter Roderick Bawtree	22-07-40	9 Sqn
625665	AC2	TOOTLE Frederick	12-04-40	149 Sqn		81340	Sgt	WARD Edward Noel	20-12-40	61 Sqn
42732	P/O	TORGALSON Joseph Simon [Canada]	12-07-40	149 Sqn		741435	Sgt	WARD James Walter	25-08-40	77 Sqn
759298	LAC	TORRANCE Charles Scott	22-05-40	110 Sqn		742466	Sgt	WARD John Montague	22-11-40	106 Sqn
787237	Sgt	TOSOVSKY Oldrich [Czechoslovakia]	17-10-40	311 Sqn		641509	Sgt	WARD Maurice [Australia]	28-11-40	20 OTU
82642	P/O	TOUL Jaromir [Czechoslovakia]	16-12-40	311 Sqn		358641	F/S	WARD Wilfred	13-08-40	61 Sqn
580075	Sgt	TOWNSEND Douglas George John	26-07-40	83 Sqn		742468	Sgt	WARDEL KNIGHT Eric Cecil	21-09-40	142 Sqn
77983	P/O	TOZER James Johnstone	23-06-40	107 Sqn		40157	P/O	WARDLAW David Herbert	7-04-40	115 Sqn
510762	Sgt	TREMEER Frederick Jethro	4-08-40	142 Sqn		938888	Sgt	WARDMAN Joseph Reginald	9-10-40	77 Sqn
619035	Sgt	TRIGWELL Douglas	31-12-40	139 Sqn		580275	Sgt	WARMAN Harry	27-05-40	107 Sqn
581482	Sgt	TRUSCOTT Granville Thomas	10-07-40	107 Sqn		37898	F/L	WARNE Peter Ellis	17-04-40	107 Sqn
581420	F/S	TUCKER Eugene	23-05-40	15 Sqn		516040	Sgt	WATCHOUS Kenneth Harrison	29-09-40	50 Sqn
41224	P/O	TUDHOPE DFC William Frank [Canada]	10-08-40	144 Sqn		631726	Sgt	WATERFALL DFM John Henry	7-07-40	37 Sqn
						553302	Sgt	WATERS Jack Arthur	8-12-40	61 Sqn
581592	Sgt	TUNE Harold Arthur	31-08-40	110 Sqn		755869	Sgt	WATERS James Percy	11-06-40	21 Sqn
81339	P/O	TUPPEN Donald Ralph	18-09-40	149 Sqn		43130	P/O	WATKIN Eric Thomas	19-09-40	106 Sqn
741188	Sgt	TURNER Edward Gordon	24-08-40	11 OTU		551877	Sgt	WATSON Alexander	14-11-40	10 Sqn
755019	Sgt	TURNER Edward Victor	13-08-40	82 Sqn		39249	F/L	WATSON Arthur David [New Zealand]	12-05-40	21 Sqn
903333	Sgt	TURNER Eric Howard McKenzie	27-06-40	50 Sqn						
614601	Sgt	TURNER Gerald Percy	29-09-40	37 Sqn		42945	P/O	WATSON DFC Francis Joseph	24-09-40	83 Sqn
79576	P/O	TURNER Gilbert Ernest	5-11-40	214 Sqn		580743	Sgt	WATSON Fred	20-07-40	9 Sqn
745245	Sgt	TURNER John Wynne	3-09-40	17 OTU		37218	F/L	WATSON George William Campbell	17-05-40	82 Sqn
745271	Sgt	TURNER Kenneth Victor	13-08-40	82 Sqn		754082	Sgt	WATSON Keith Leonard	23-12-40	58 Sqn
937492	Sgt	TURNER William	29-10-40	114 Sqn		74345	P/O	WATSON Peter George Anthony	23-07-40	107 Sqn
650773	Sgt	TWAMLEY Arnold Edward Desmond [Eire]	28-05-40	21 Sqn		77026	F/O	WATSON MiD Samuel Miles Mackenzie [New Zealand]	20-07-40	75 Sqn
580573	Sgt									
40767	P/O	TWEDDELL DFC William Oliver Digby [Canada]	26-07-40	83 Sqn		965301	Sgt	WATSON Thomas	18-09-40	99 Sqn
						79577	P/O	WATSON Thomas Colvin	10-07-40	15 OTU
741308	Sgt	TYLDESEY Harold Edward	15-08-40	18 Sqn		630423	Sgt	WATSON William	4-08-40	15 Sqn
541348	LAC	TYLER Philip Andrew	1-05-40	37 Sqn		41503	F/O	WATSON William Ross [New Zealand]	9-12-40	114 Sqn
755019	Sgt	TYSON Norman	11-11-40	83 Sqn		630207	Sgt	WATT David Walter	11-11-40	49 Sqn
626850	Sgt	UNDERWOOD Arthur James	10-08-40	110 Sqn		516242	Sgt	WATT George Thomas	17-10-40	15 OTU
70825	P/O	VAGG Edward Alan	15-05-40	83 Sqn		522273	Sgt	WATT Gordon Reeves	26-07-40	50 Sqn
787244	Sgt	VALOSEK Oskar [Czechoslovakia]	1-10-40	311 Sqn		647062	Sgt	WATT James Beasley	6-11-40	10 Sqn
580261	Sgt	VART Stanley Vernon	12-04-40	50 Sqn		755255	Sgt	WATT John Archibald	30-08-40	40 Sqn
40579	F/L	VAUX Richard Bowyer	12-03-40	166 Sqn		41638	P/O	WATTERSON Arnold Irwin [Canada]	24-09-40	58 Sqn
82533	P/O	VEJRAZKA Miloslav E. [Czechoslovakia]	17-10-40	311 Sqn		759089	Sgt	WATTS Cecil James	24-11-40	107 Sqn
						569073	LAC	WATTS Cyril Grace	18-05-40	15 Sqn
85279	P/O	VERITY Richard Lawrence	29-11-40	13 OTU		650383	Sgt	WATTS Henry Victor	23-08-40	115 Sqn
82582	S/L	VESELY Jan [Czechoslovakia]	16-10-40	311 Sqn		32152	W/C	WATTS DSO Joseph John	13-06-40	144 Sqn
87653	P/O	VEVERS Robert	28-11-40	20 OTU		41504	F/O	WAUGH Stanley Alfred [Canada]	25-11-40	101 Sqn
540323	AC1	VICK Edwin	10-01-40	110 Sqn		564469	Sgt	WEBB Alan Lawrence Fortescue	12-05-40	21 Sqn

Number	Rank	Name	Date	Sqn
755836	Sgt	WEBB Llewellyn Frank	1-11-40	110 Sqn
647419	Sgt	WEBBER Arthur Frank	25-08-40	77 Sqn
631464	Sgt	WEBSTER Charles Norman [Eire]	22-06-40	61 Sqn
740738	Sgt	WEBSTER Goulden Oliver	20-11-40	149 Sqn
749541	Sgt	WEBSTER Kenneth Oswald	19-07-40	18 Sqn
40494	P/O	WEEKS Courtenay Arthur	25-04-40	49 Sqn
550893	LAC	WEEKS Edward Lewis	24-04-40	107 Sqn
564455	Sgt	WEIGHTMAN Thomas Sinclair	27-02-40	82 Sqn
42289	P/O	WERNER Raymond Henry	11-06-40	15 Sqn
742634	Sgt	WESSELS Cyril	1-10-40	115 Sqn
620494	Sgt	WEST George Edward	28-11-40	102 Sqn
533941	Sgt	WEST DFM James Victor	20-07-40	110 Sqn
1153852	AC2	WEST Kenneth Aubrey	27-10-40	Honington
750452	AC1	WEST Victor	27-10-40	Honington
515582	Sgt	WESTBROOK Walter Joseph James	16-11-40	Binbrook
545537	LAC	WESTCOTT Lionel Allen	12-04-40	115 Sqn
629457	Sgt	WESTHORP Bernard Newman	10-09-40	44 Sqn
650218	AC1	WESTLEY Herbert Charles	6-11-40	99 Sqn
903273	Sgt	WESTON Kenneth Frederick	14-11-40	10 Sqn
805525	Sgt	WESTWOOD Douglas Eric	1-10-40	115 Sqn
580533	Sgt	WETTON Walter Jonathan	6-04-40	21 Sqn
632938	Sgt	WHALEN Henry Bernard	28-12-40	83 Sqn
180860	Cpl	WHEATLEY Frederick	1-11-40	Wattisham
742136	Sgt	WHEELER Frank Albert Roberts	26-09-40	114 Sqn
621799	LAC	WHEELER Kenneth George	7-10-40	9 Sqn
747805	Sgt	WHEELER William Hubert	12-06-40	17 OTU
41763	P/O	WHEELWRIGHT William Brian [Canada]	18-08-40	218 Sqn
562377	Sgt	WHELLER Horace James	12-04-40	149 Sqn
751267	Sgt	WHELPTON Harry	7-10-40	38 Sqn
540565	Sgt	WHITE Alfred	1-10-40	10 OTU
580429	Sgt	WHITE Charles Thomas	15-05-40	40 Sqn
39090	F/O	WHITE David	26-04-40	49 Sqn
626213	Sgt	WHITE DFM Lewis Alan	20-09-40	75 Sqn
956165	Sgt	WHITE Phillip James	7-12-40	214 Sqn
755956	Sgt	WHITE Reginald William Bryant	24-10-40	75 Sqn
625991	Sgt	WHITE DFM William	10-11-40	114 Sqn
525569	Sgt	WHITFIELD Charles	16-11-40	105 Sqn
632190	AC2	WHITLEY Cyril Cecil	26-04-40	102 Sqn
533685	Sgt	WHITTLE Leonard	19-06-40	58 Sqn
611596	LAC	WHITTLE Peter Rex	23-05-40	40 Sqn
936540	Sgt	WHITWORTH Harry	20-11-40	149 Sqn
745909	LAC	WHYTE James	27-05-40	16 OTU
41088	P/O	WICKENCAMP MBE Estelles Arthur [Canada]	7-04-40	115 Sqn
571765	LAC	WIFFEN Edward	23-10-40	77 Sqn
580312	Sgt	WIFFEN Maurice	2-03-40	149 Sqn
580852	Sgt	WIGHAM Ernest	24-05-40	12 OTU
79536	P/O	WIGLEY Clive Warrington	13-08-40	82 Sqn
580291	Sgt	WILD Gerald Marsden	12-04-40	50 Sqn
76931	P/O	WILDE Sidney John Scott	3-08-40	115 Sqn
76932	P/O	WILK Jack	17-08-40	149 Sqn
534598	LAC	WILKIN John Lenton	12-04-40	9 Sqn
580929	Sgt	WILL Ernest Alexander	1-08-40	114 Sqn
755151	Sgt	WILLCOX George Matheson	16-12-40	101 Sqn
580502	Sgt	WILLIAMS Albert	12-06-40	21 Sqn
646080	Sgt	WILLIAMS Arthur	10-07-40	15 OTU
818161	Sgt	WILLIAMS Cyril	15-12-40	77 Sqn
1171590	AC2	WILLIAMS Cyril Pearson	19-08-40	Honington
580927	Sgt	WILLIAMS Edward Howard	18-04-40	99 Sqn
638726	Sgt	WILLIAMS Emyr	9-07-40	21 Sqn
566298	Sgt	WILLIAMS Francis	21-05-40	115 Sqn
524733	Sgt	WILLIAMS George Llewelyn	10-01-40	110 Sqn
642147	Sgt	WILLIAMS James Clough	26-09-40	61 Sqn
40450	F/O	WILLIAMS Leonard	9-08-40	10 OTU
745324	Sgt	WILLIAMS Leslie Arthur	31-08-40	18 Sqn
39091	F/O	WILLIAMS Owen Lloyd	22-05-40	99 Sqn
580191	Sgt	WILLIAMS Stephen Alfred	26-03-40	44 Sqn
968020	Sgt	WILLIAMSON Donald	28-11-40	20 OTU
751575	Sgt	WILLIAMSON Frederick George	26-11-40	61 Sqn
969167	Sgt	WILLS Ian George	22-10-40	10 Sqn
580722	Sgt	WILLS Ronald Henry	14-04-40	38 Sqn
751064	Sgt	WILMOT Arthur Alexander	22-08-40	144 Sqn
971171	Sgt	WILSON Alexander Duff	13-11-40	77 Sqn
538054	AC1	WILSON Alfred George	14-05-40	21 Sqn
624190	Sgt	WILSON Angus Stewart	2-11-40	102 Sqn
75684	P/O	WILSON Sir Arnold Talbot KCIE CSI CMG DSO	31-05-40	37 Sqn
566477	Sgt	WILSON Douglas Warren	24-03-40	37 Sqn
742942	Sgt	WILSON Edward Frank	15-12-40	77 Sqn
808414	Sgt	WILSON George Robert	11-11-40	83 Sqn
745159	Sgt	WILSON Hubert Henry	22-09-40	17 OTU
755653	Sgt	WILSON Roy Fleming	7-08-40	106 Sqn
908795	Sgt	WILSON-NORTH Bruce	26-11-40	17 OTU
633996	AC1	WILTSHIRE John Stanley	19-08-40	44 Sqn
755989	Sgt	WINBERG Israel	24-07-40	110 Sqn
640278	Sgt	WINCH Frederick John Baulch	21-07-40	37 Sqn
752773	AC1	WINDLE John William Morgan	15-08-40	77 Sqn
580294	Sgt	WINDSOR James	17-04-40	144 Sqn
33470	P/O	WINGATE David Leslie	22-08-40	144 Sqn
617595	Sgt	WINSTANLEY Alexander	13-06-40	144 Sqn
935571	Sgt	WINSTON Joseph Charles	27-06-40	40 Sqn
651791	Sgt	WINTERBOTTOM Robert	12-12-40	115 Sqn
624045	AC2	WINTERTON Kenneth Charles	23-03-40	90 Sqn
505501	Sgt	WISE Charles Harold	5-10-40	50 Sqn
741551	Sgt	WISE Peter Clarkson	18-11-40	21 Sqn
79554	P/O	WISE Stanley Cuthbert	11-09-40	44 Sqn
580446	Sgt	WOLSTENHOLME Douglas	15-05-40	83 Sqn
544700	LAC	WOLVERSON Eric Lionel	1-04-40	82 Sqn
817163	Sgt	WOOD Alexander Milne	17-12-40	49 Sqn
638499	Sgt	WOOD Cyril Edward Thomas	1-08-40	44 Sqn
755876	Sgt	WOOD Eric Purdy	24-07-40	12 OTU
580689	Sgt	WOOD George	5-10-40	144 Sqn
754548	Sgt	WOOD Maurice Ernest Langton	18-09-40	99 Sqn
751655	Sgt	WOOD Sidney Metcalf	10-07-40	107 Sqn
550803	LAC	WOOD Winston Kitchener	8-03-40	61 Sqn
759297	Sgt	WOODBURN Andrew	11-11-40	83 Sqn
564824	Sgt	WOODCOCK Frederick Albert	12-04-40	149 Sqn
526291	Sgt	WOODHOUSE Colin	26-05-40	144 Sqn
745040	Sgt	WOODING Alan Asquith	7-12-40	214 Sqn
551556	LAC	WOODS Denis Victor	12-05-40	15 Sqn
940148	Sgt	WOODS Jack	28-09-40	9 Sqn
580401	Sgt	WOODS William Barnard	17-02-40	110 Sqn
580688	Sgt	WOODWARD Alan Henry	20-03-40	144 Sqn
748483	Sgt	WOODWARD Harold	26-11-40	15 OTU
581025	Sgt	WOOTTEN Francis Charles	17-05-40	82 Sqn
41516	P/O	WORBOYS Cyril Ray	26-06-40	110 Sqn
754549	Sgt	WORDSWORTH Dennis Wilfred	8-10-40	13 OTU
758099	Sgt	WORMALD Stanley Allan	5-11-40	214 Sqn
25062	F/L	WORTHINGTON-WILMER Ivor Chudleigh Bethune	4-07-40	18 Sqn
42174	P/O	WRAY Eric Aubrey	10-07-40	107 Sqn
746763	Sgt	WRIGHT Albert	13-10-40	99 Sqn
740280	Sgt	WRIGHT Charles Austin	9-10-40	58 Sqn
741930	Sgt	WRIGHT Dennis Raymond	14-10-40	10 Sqn
1165055	AC2	WRIGHT Frederick	1-11-40	110 Sqn
40453	F/O	WYATT George Michael	30-06-40	61 Sqn
997621	AC2	WYATT John	27-10-40	Mildenhall
84973	P/O	WYLAM-WALKER Norman	7-12-40	51 Sqn
541172	Sgt	WYLIE William	21-07-40	144 Sqn
754799	Sgt	YARD Clifford Ernest Rich	29-12-40	115 Sqn
755730	Sgt	YARWOOD Reginald William	29-12-40	115 Sqn
741086	Sgt	YEOMANS Oswald Morris	14-09-40	15 Sqn
532375	F/S	YORATH Philip Herbert	5-10-40	144 Sqn
517288	Sgt	YOUNG Frederick	11-07-40	58 Sqn
41094	P/O	YOUNG James Cameron	30-05-40	99 Sqn

751187	Sgt	YOUNG Kenneth Ernest	26-10-40	83 Sqn
751115	Sgt	YOUNG Leslie	7-12-40	49 Sqn
742982	Sgt	YOUNG Leslie Alfred	31-12-40	114 Sqn
627971	AC1	YOUNG Nairn Alexander	23-04-40	51 Sqn
650682	Sgt	YOUNG Peter Archibald	29-09-40	37 Sqn
580690	Sgt	YOUNG Robert Gilmour	17-10-40	144 Sqn
580905	Sgt	YOUNGS Leslie Reginald	13-08-40	82 Sqn
632041	Sgt	YOUNGSON Selwyn Frederick	13-06-40	9 Sqn
749523	Sgt	ZAMEK Ian Alexander	3-10-40	58 Sqn
787242	Sgt	ZAPLETAL Frant [Czechoslovakia]	16-10-40	311 Sqn

Note

At the age of 56, P/O Sir Arnold Talbot Wilson was probably the oldest Bomber Command officer to lose his life on bombing operations in the Second World War. He was something of a controversial figure in that despite receiving numerous honours, as will be noted from his entry on page 71 of Volume 1, his opinionated style of debate aroused feelings of hostility towards him, particularly at the time when he represented the people of Hitchin (1933-1940) in the House of Westminster when sections of the press labelled him as an apologist for the likes of Hitler and Mussolini. Nevertheless, when war came his sense of patriotism led him to volunteer his services and his appointment as a pilot officer in the volunteer reserve came, I believe, through the commissioned air gunner scheme. His meritorious service in the Great War, throughout which he was in the political department of the Indian Army, was first noted by his appointment to the Companion of the Distinguished Service Order, details of this being promulgated in the *Supplement to the London Gazette* of the 17th of April, 1916. Further honours followed but his time as the British civil commissioner in Baghdad (1918-1920) terminated amidst scenes of revolt by the local populace inflamed by his dictatorial style of administration. Nevertheless, he gained a senior position with the Anglo-Persian Oil Company, serving as their residential director in the Gulf twixt 1920 and 1932, when he left the company and returned to England. Finally, it is recorded that two years after joining Anglo-Persian he married Rose Caroline Carver, widow of Lt Robin Creswell Carver who died on the 17th of July, 1918, while serving with the Royal Air Force. At the age of 41, Lt Carver could be regarded as senior in years to have been on active service.

Meanwhile, LAC David Hewson Reed is a contender for one of the oldest ground staff members to die in Bomber Command service, his death at the age of 53 being reported on the 21st of June, 1940, at which time he was on the strength of 13 OTU Bicester. As in all cases his service number provides a wealth of detail concerning his past service for he was just one of thousands of Royal Naval Air Service personnel who, in April 1918, were transferred to the fledgling Royal Air Force. Blocks of numbers, commencing at 200001 and finishing at 260000 were issued. The first block, ending at 202902, took care of the 1914 entrants and the final issues, starting at 244711 were set aside for those who enlisted in 1918. Reed's number indicates he was a 1917 entrant, but I am not able to say whether his air force service from the date of transfer to his death was continuous. Buried on the west side of Bicester airfield in Caversfield (St. Laurence) Churchyard, his entry indicates that he was married and hailed from Ilford in Essex.

As far as I can be certain, the two airmen with the surname West and who both died on the same day at Honington were not related, though by coincidence their mothers shared the same first Christian name, Edith. The former hailed from Grove in Berkshire, while the latter came from Luton, Bedfordshire.

In respect of F/S McLeod of 106 Squadron, I believe his Christian names, Lloyd Haig Beatty, were given to commemorate three outstanding leaders of the Great War; Lloyd George, Douglas Haig and David Beatty.

Lastly, I think it appropriate that I draw attention to the death of F/O Arthur Richard Brian Tedder. Known to his friends as 'Dick' his father was Marshal of the Royal Air Force Sir Arthur Tedder (later 1st Baron Tedder) who gained many plaudits for his direction of air operations in the Middle East before becoming General Dwight D. Eisenhower's deputy in the planning for D-Day and beyond; in fact, it was Tedder who signed the surrender documents on behalf of Eisenhower in May 1945.

ROYAL NEW ZEALAND AIR FORCE
personnel

NZ391321	Sgt	ANDERSON Lindsay Douglas	20-09-40	75 Sqn
A36139	F/S	ANDERSON Ronald Alexander John	20-07-40	75 Sqn
A391377	Sgt	ANNAN William Donald Francis	26-07-40	75 Sqn
NZ401220	Sgt	BAIN Claude Horace	30-11-40	214 RFlt
NZ40185	Sgt	BLATCH Alfred Frederick	24-09-40	83 Sqn
NZ40199	Sgt	BRACEGIRDLE James	6-09-40	44 Sqn
NZ40913	Sgt	BROWN Reginald	9-12-40	115 Sqn
NZ40201	Sgt	BROWNE Thomas Chamberlain Molineux	2-09-40	37 Sqn
NZ391341	Sgt	CLIFFORD Robert Henry	23-08-40	15 OTU
NZ2526	F/O	COLEMAN DFC William Harcourt	26-07-40	75 Sqn
NZ2513	F/O	COLLINS John Noel	21-05-40	75 Sqn
NZ39964	Sgt	DALLAS Arthur Fraser	28-10-40	105 Sqn
NZ391346	Sgt	DOUGLAS Charles Harold	13-10-40	99 Sqn
NZ39911	P/O	FINLAYSON William John	24-10-40	75 Sqn
A39913	Sgt	FULLER John Edward	14-08-40	15 OTU
NZ39919	P/O	HOADLEY Henry Michael	28-08-40	17 OTU
NZ39922	Sgt	HUNT George William	11-10-40	214 RFlt
A37156	Cpl	LANGRIDGE Jack Harry	12-04-40	149 Sqn
A39929	Sgt	MILLER Henry Algernon Gascoyne	13-08-40	13 OTU
NZ40726	Sgt	NEWBERY Charles Hugh Le Blanc	2-10-40	9 Sqn
A391332	Sgt	OWEN John Lewis	20-07-40	75 Sqn
NZ401519	Sgt	PETERS Errol James	23-12-40	11 OTU
NZ39971	Sgt	PHILPOTT John Bernard	8-09-40	82 Sqn
NZ391365	P/O	PRITCHARD Arthur Partnell	18-12-40	99 Sqn
NZ39936	Sgt	PROUT Reginald Wilfred	6-11-40	58 Sqn
A391869	Sgt	REWA Douglas Oswald	13-08-40	11 OTU
NZ40742	P/O	REYNOLDS Vernon Sinclair	29-12-40	17 OTU
NZ40207	Sgt	RITCHIE Alfred Henry	22-12-40	75 Sqn
NZ391870	Sgt	SCOULAR Ian Cowie	24-10-40	102 Sqn
NZ40743	Sgt	SECKER Alfred James Victor	14-12-40	17 OTU
NZ39942	Sgt	SMITH Stronach Vivian	23-12-40	58 Sqn

Note

Cpl Langridge (as reported by Errol Martyn) arrived in the United Kingdom in January 1939 in the company of five fellow wireless operators, their mission to assist in the delivery of Wellington bombers to New Zealand. Subsequently posted to 149 Squadron, he became the first airman from the Royal New Zealand Air Force to lose his life on overseas service. Prior to September 1939, officers were not assigned personal numbers; consequently, in respect of F/Os Coleman and Collins their allocations were made posthumously.

POLISH AIR FORCE
personnel

P.782081	LAC	ANDRZEJEWSKI Edward	18-12-40	304 Sqn
P.793314	Sgt	BLYSKAL Franciszek	26-11-40	12 OTU
P.782092	LAC	BROS Wladyslaw	18-12-40	304 Sqn
P.780251	Sgt	EGIERSKI Tadeusz	13-10-40	300 Sqn
P.76694	F/O	FENGLER Dominik	8-08-40	301 Sqn
P.76828	F/O	FIRLEJ-BIELANSKI Stanislaw	29-10-40	300 Sqn
P.76605	F/O	GEBICKI Jan	13-10-40	300 Sqn
P.780040	Sgt	GOEBEL Gerhard	29-10-40	300 Sqn
P.0071	P/O	IGNASZAK Antoni	26-11-40	12 OTU
P.76611	F/L	KRYNSKI Stefan	28-12-40	300 Sqn
P.76677	P/O	KULINSKI Jozef Stanislaw	25-09-40	301 Sqn
P.0063	P/O	MAKAREWICZ Wladyslaw	26-11-40	12 OTU
P.780113	Sgt	MORAWA Edward	13-10-40	300 Sqn
P.780495	Sgt	PALIWODA Karol	25-09-40	301 Sqn
P.793003	Sgt	ROZEWICKI Boleslaw Dobieslaw	18-11-40	301 Sqn
P.780609	LAC	ROZMIAREK Edmund	23-09-40	18 OTU

P.1368	P/O	SOKOLOWSKI de JENKO Jerzy Marian Ryszard		1-10-40	12 OTU
P.780068	Sgt	SZMAJDROWICZ Tadeusz Jerzy		29-10-40	300 Sqn
P.76683	P/O	WARONSKI Jozef		25-09-40	301 Sqn
P.781192	Sgt	WEGRZYN Henryk		29-12-40	300 Sqn

Note

Although in my introduction I acknowledged the generous help of Mrs Betty Clements who, in turn, has spent countless hours in correspondence with Polish authors and officials, I cannot emphasise too strongly Betty's influence on the entries pertaining to the Polish Air Force throughout this Roll of Honour. Thus, all subsequent notes footing the Polish Air Force sections will, unless stated to the contrary, carry the stamp of her authority on what is reported.

Attached personnel

FLEET AIR ARM

- S/Lt DE SANDOVAL-SIEVIER Robert Adrian
  (detached from HMS *Daedalus*) 9-09-40
- S/Lt FRANKLIN Lionel Cooper 14-04-40
  (detached from HMS *Sparrowhawk*)
- Mid HADINGHAM David Arthur Charles 9-10-40
  (detached from HMS *Daedalus*)
- Mid MORTIMER Charles George 24-07-40
  (detached from HMS *Daedalus*)
- S/Lt NEAL Thomas Alfred 14-11-40
  (detached from HMS *Daedalus*)
- S/Lt WEBB Ivan Rhys 14-11-40
  (detached from HMS *Daedalus*)
- S/Lt WILLIAMS Peter Owen 18-09-40
  (detached from HMS *Daedalus*)

Note

Please refer to the appropriate dates in volumes 1 and 7 for details of the circumstances which claimed the lives of those listed above. It is also observed from entries in my books and other publications that 15 officers and airmen were taken prisoner in 1940, only to be killed or die beyond the year here described. Thus, their details will appear under the appropriate part of the Roll.

Postscript

It is difficult to adequately report the sacrifice made by the airmen of Bomber Command in 1940. In the first five months of the year, during which time squadrons were obliged to conduct their operations within the limits imposed by the War Cabinet in 1939, at least 337 airmen perished. Added to the 281 officers and men who lost their lives between the outbreak of war and December, 1939, Bomber Command's casualties stood at 619, as at the 9th of May, 1940. And, this not insignificant figure excludes those who died in this same period while serving in France with the AASF, and with the two squadrons attached to the AC BEF.

Training accidents accounted for a high proportion of the 619 deaths, but the harsh lessons learnt in the first winter of the war had resulted in many telegrams being sent to next of kin, and more were to follow in the wake of the German invasion of Denmark and Norway as Bomber Command attempted, with only marginal success, to deny the enemy the use of airfields in these recently captured countries. The contempt held by the Nazi regime for the concept of neutrality was, by now, crystal clear and with the entrance to the Baltic Sea firmly under German control, the ultimate fate of the Netherlands was almost a foregone conclusion. The Soviets, too, who had shared in the spoils of the defeated Poland must have viewed Adolf Hitler's latest conquest with alarm, though another year would pass before their pre-war non-aggression pact with Germany would prove not to be worth the paper it was written on.

And still Bomber Command continued to be held in check until, at last, the hammer blow fell in the west with German armour and infantry, closely supported by an umbrella of dive-bombers and fighters, sweeping almost unchecked through Luxembourg, Belgium and into Holland. The outstanding bravery of the airmen serving with the two air components sent to France in 1939 has been touched upon in parts 1 and 2, and detailed comment on bomber operations prior to the thunderclap that sounded on that awful first morning is beyond the remit of this work. In the time it took for the BEF to be ignominiously expelled from France and the crumbling of the last vestiges of French resistance, Bomber Command was catapulted into a campaign of trying to stem the tidal wave of progress on the ground and at the same time commence the task of attacking communications and those parts of Germany's industrial base identified as crucial to the support of her armies in the field. The stemming of the tide fell, in respect of the United Kingdom based squadrons, mainly to No.2 Group and the exploits of the Blenheim crews* during the summer of 1940 have, rightly, passed into history as being an unsurpassed record of sacrifice. On practically a daily basis, the Blenheim squadrons were sent into action against hotly defended targets from which they suffered the most appalling casualties. Two days, in particular, stand out as beacons to their unselfish bravery; at first light on the 17th of May, a dozen crews from 82 Squadron set forth from Watton with orders to bomb enemy columns that had forced a gap in the Allied lines near the Belgian town of Gembloux. At the hurried briefing, the formation leader had been advised that Tangmere would provide an escort of Hurricanes, but this never materialised and, flying at 8,000 feet, the Blenheims pressed on across the Channel to enter France near Le Touquet. It was still barely breakfast time as the formation hurried through the skies, passing close to Lille and then into Belgian airspace. And then, with just moments to go before the grim business of the day would commence, accurate and fierce enemy ground fire caused the tightly packed formation to split apart and as each bomber was loosened from the protective fire-power of its nearest neighbour, so the waiting Messerschmitts pounced. In the minutes that followed, 11 Blenheims were shot from the sky leaving one badly damaged survivor to limp back to base and their report the terrible news of what had befallen the rest of the squadron. From the 36 airmen that had set out with such purpose mere hours ago, 22 were dead, three were prisoners of war and the rest were either safe in Allied hands or on the run from their would be captors.

Within hours of these awful events, 82 Squadron was undergoing the process of rebuilding, a process that the squadron would repeat on the 13th of August, 1940, in the aftermath of a quite disastrous attempt to bomb, by day, Aalborg airfield in Denmark. Again, 12 crews set out, one returned with technical problems and the rest were shot down in the target area. This time 20 died, including their commanding officer, while the rest were obliged to view the remainder of the war from *behind the wire* of various prisoner of war camps.

At the time of the Aalborg raid, the *'Battle of Britain'* was in full cry, while Bomber Command continued to pit its available strength against a multitude of targets and tasks which now included the industrial towns of northern Italy, for with the fall of France, Mussolini concluded that there were many rich spoils for the taking and he was now more than anxious to become a committed player in the grand scheme of Nazi ambitions. However, within a few months of throwing his hat into the ring the seemingly unstoppable might of the German military machine had been forced to abandon its planned invasion of Britain, thwarted by the squadrons of Fighter Command that had denied the Luftwaffe dominance over the Channel.

As recounted in the introduction to this section, the outcome of this first victory was a reversion by the Luftwaffe to a quite ferocious night bombing campaign and towns and cities across the United Kingdom were soon bearing the brunt of this change in direction and, naturally, the British public was turning their attention to the newspaper reports of Bomber Command's response. London had suffered its first serious night raid on the 24th/25th of August, and within 24 hours this action galvanised the War Cabinet (now led by Winston Churchill) to sanction a retaliatory attack on Germany's capital city, Berlin. It is necessary to mention that the first incursion over Berlin had taken place on the 1st/2nd of October, 1939, when three Whitley crews from 10 Squadron deposited a sizeable number of *'Nickels'* for the populace to read. Now, the Whitleys were returning, along with Hampdens and Wellingtons, to unleash a far more deadly cargo. The results of this first operation, deep into the heart of Germany, are inconclusive. Thick cloud over Berlin prevented the majority of crews from sighting their targets (the Whitley crews of 51 Squadron were assigned to one of Siemens electrical plants) thus reducing the night's work to a series of alternative attacks or, in many cases, crews being obliged to jettison their bomb loads into the sea. The Hampden crews of No.5 Group, in particular, had a torrid time. Flying at the limits of their aircraft's endurance, the return flights became hazardous affairs as it became apparent that very strong head winds were slowing their progress and causing precious fuel reserves to dwindle. Three crews are known to have ditched, all surviving; another crew crashed while trying to land at Usworth and two others failed to return, though in time news came through that one crew had survived, albeit as prisoners of war.

With the year wearing on more raids to Berlin took place, but it was the attack on Mannheim, executed on the night of 16th/17th of December, 1940, that signalled the start of what in a few years time would become the norm for Bomber Command's night bombing campaign when a general attack on the city centre was authorised. Until now, all operations were carried out against clearly identified targets; oil refining plant, rail marshalling yards, port facilities, the Krupp factory complex at Essen to quote a few examples. And, more often than not, when Berlin was the focus of attention individual buildings or specially selected service facilities were earmarked, a prime example being the Charlottenburg gasworks which was chosen as an aiming point for the raid carried out on the 23rd/24th of September. But, to return to the Mannheim operation, authorised by the War Cabinet in retaliation for the recent heavy raids by the Luftwaffe on Coventry and Southampton, a force, considerable for the time, of 200 bombers of all types were prepared. As the day progressed a less than satisfactory weather forecast was issued and this resulted in a reduced effort of 134 aircraft setting forth.

Many hopes were pinned on this operation and, initially, it was thought that considerable damage had been inflicted but in truth Mannheim had escaped relatively lightly. Upwards of 80 crews claim to have identified Mannheim, and a postwar analysis based on records kept in the city archives show that 1,266 citizens were left homeless, while the hospitals dealt with over 80 persons injured and the mortuary attendants processed the remains of the 34 dead. Bomber Command's fatalities for the night totalled 17, six of this number coming from two Blenheims missing from 101 Squadron.

Thus, Bomber Command's first full year operations drew to a close. It is now generally accepted that a good deal of effort had been expended for relatively few returns, but it had not been all doom and gloom. Particularly worthy of note was the success achieved earlier in the year with the near nightly security patrols flown, mainly by the Whitley crews of No.4 Group, off the German Frisian islands from where the Luftwaffe had based seaplanes with a mine-laying capability. With any illumination of their flare paths likely to attract a stick of bombs, operations that had achieved considerable success in the first three months of war were curtailed and our east coast shipping losses decreased accordingly. Mine-laying, or *'Gardening'* as it was popularly referred to, was not a prerogative of the Germans and in April, 1940, Hampdens from No.5 Group flew the first of what would be many thousands of sorties of this nature. But of the night bombing campaign proper, success came only in small measure as group commanders continued to plough their own furrow with the result that the strength of the command was too thinly spread to be effective. Nonetheless, useful lessons were being learned and the quality of leadership within the bomber squadrons was of the highest order. As early as the 17th/18th of May, the benefits to be gained from the use of target marking had been identified and reports published in the Operations Record Book (ORB) for 10 Squadron suggest that a quite successful raid had been made against oil refining plant at Bremen. A force of 24 Whitley bombers, drawn from 10, 51 and 58 Squadrons participated from which 22 crews claim to have identified the target and released their bombs accordingly (Sgt A. Dixon of 58 Squadron reached Bremen but was thwarted from making his attack due to a fault in the bomb release mechanism). The principal architect in this bright gem of delight was W/C W. E. Staton, a holder of the Military Cross and a veteran of the Great War, who from the outset of hostilities being declared inspired everyone who served under him in 10 Squadron.

Although such gems were few and far between, the fact that Bomber Command was the only effective force that could take the war into the heart of Germany was already gaining reward in that the German High Command was being obliged to retain a considerable force of both men and material in homeland defence.

Appropriately, however, the grim statistic of close on 3,000 personnel killed from the Command brings this postscript to near conclusion. In addition, a number of airmen from other commands of the service, along with civilians, had lost their lives in circumstances pertaining to Bomber Command matters and their details are reported as an appendix to this volume.

Less than a hundred from those whose lives were taken in 1940 had been decorated for acts of gallantry, and I trust I will be forgiven for illustrating only a few of the reports published in *The London Gazette* during the year in question. Thus, from the few copies at my immediate disposal I offer the DFC citation for F/L Walter Michael Blom, killed by a bomb exploding on the 27th of July, 1940, as his 150 Squadron Battle was being prepared for operations. The actions quoted in the citation, which appeared in the *Supplement to The London Gazette, 31st May, 1940,* are in recognition of his gallantry while serving in France with the AASF. *'During May, 1940, this officer was detailed to lead a half section of aircraft in a low level bombing attack against an enemy motorised column of all arms advancing on a road in Luxemburg. Before reaching his objective a petrol tank was pierced by machine-gun fire and, although unable to locate his allotted target through being drenched and almost blinded by the escaping petrol, he pressed home his attack on another enemy column with considerable success. During this time the aircraft was subjected to very heavy fire from the ground and was repeatedly hit, receiving such damage as to render it beyond repair, but this did not prevent Flying Officer Blom from flying back to base, a distance of 90 miles. He displayed outstanding courage and tenacity.'*

Next, an immediate DFM citation regarding Cpl Ronald Jolly, who died when his 144 Squadron aircraft collided with a balloon cable near Ipswich during the night of 12th/13th of June, 1940. It was published in the same *Supplement* as the DFC confirred on F/L Blom; *'This airman was the wireless operator and air gunner of an aircraft engaged in an attack on a target at Gladbach-Rheydt on a night in May, 1940. The aircraft was severely damaged by anti-aircraft fire, which stopped one engine and shot away the rudder controls, but Corporal Jolly maintained wireless communication and obtained positions to assist the pilot and navigator. On reaching friendly territory after a flight of over 100 miles, the pilot gave an order to abandon the aircraft, and Corporal Jolly then destroyed the aircraft's papers, locked the wireless telegraph key, and leaving the transmitter switched on, jumped from the aircraft at a very low altitude. His coolness and efficiency throughout materially assisted in preventing the aircraft from falling in the hands of the enemy.'*

Of those who were decorated, only a handful gained more than a single honour and it is the citation reporting S/L James Anderson Pitcairn Hill's DSO that ends this trio of accounts. It appeared in the *Supplement* issued on the 27th of August, 1940; *'One night in August, 1940, Flight Lieutenant Pitcairn Hill (DFC) led a formation of aircraft, one of which was piloted by Pilot Officer Matthews, in a low-flying attack on the Dortmund-Ems Canal. In spite of intense enemy opposition over the target area, in which all aircraft were seriously damaged and two were shot down, these officers carried out a successful attack from 150 feet precisely at zero hour. The timing of this difficult operation was dependent on the skill, judgement and personal resolution of Flight Lieutenant Pitcairn Hill who has at all times displayed outstanding gallantry, skill and devotion to duty. Pilot Officer Matthews, by his courage, determination and skill has at all times set an excellent example.'* P/O Matthews gained an immediate DFC for his part in the attack; he was destined to be killed on the 13th of March, 1941, when his 207 Squadron Manchester was shot down by an enemy intruder as it took off from Waddington for operations against Hamburg.

* In order to gain a more complete picture of the terrible losses sustained by the Blenheim squadrons of No.2 Group, I recommend a study of the writings of Michael Bowyer whose history of No.2 Group was first published in 1974, and for a more general view of Blenheim operations, in all theatres of the Second World War, I suggest Graham Warner's *magnum opus,* published in 2002 under the apt title, *The Bristol Blenheim: A Complete History.*

Part 5

Bomber Command Roll of Honour – 1941

1941; the immediate threat of German invasion had been lifted though the potential for such an event to happen remained real. Hitler's dominance of Western Europe was almost total with his armed forces firmly in control of all territory from Norway in the north to the Pyrenees mountain range in the south. Only Spain, now controlled by the Fascist dictator, Franco, and neutral Portugal remained outside the sphere of direct Nazi influence though, let it not be forgotten, the Rock of Gibraltar still stood as a silent sentinel guarding our interests to the all-important gateway into the Mediterranean sea, now very much an area of strategic importance since Italy's decision to join the conflict on the side of Germany.

This was the scenario which Sir Richard Peirse and his staff at High Wycombe had to contend with and, thereby, plan the most effective way in which to execute the bombing campaign. As recounted in the previous section the strength of Bomber Command was increasing, both in terms of equipment and manpower. Taking the latter resource first the next twelve months would witness the burgeoning impact of Australia and Canada's contribution in providing trained air crew for the expanding bomber squadrons which at the beginning of the year stood at 43 front line squadrons (in November 1940, 37 Squadron and 38 Squadron had been given up to the Middle East theatre in order to bolster our forces now embroiled in the Desert Campaign). Additional to the Australians, Canadians and New Zealanders joining the ranks of Bomber Command sizeable numbers of airmen of Rhodesian and South African stock were in evidence at the training units and, for a while at least, there were sufficient numbers of Polish airmen available to man the four PAF squadrons assigned to No.1 Group. True, the equipment of these squadrons was little different from that which Peirse inherited three months earlier, but an exciting change was in the air as, gradually, the pace of bomber aircraft production increased and the challenge of operating the four-engined *heavies* advanced towards the stage when they would be ready to make their operational debut.

Initially, however, the tempo of operations was very low-key and for the most part the night raiding in the first six weeks of 1941 can only be best described as being of a nuisance value. It has to be remembered that Peirse was still required to direct his forces within the restraints of the directives handed down from the Air Ministry and area bombing, which could only be sanctioned by the War Cabinet, was still very much in the future. The raid on Mannheim in mid-December 1940 (see the postscript to Part 4) was very much a one-off affair and though it was totally unrealistic to assume that every operation attempted would be so finely executed that only the immediate target area would be affected, nevertheless every effort was made to try and ensure that collateral damage was kept to a minimum. This was particularly important when attacks were carried out on targets in the Occupied Countries where ports and other facilities identified with the war effort could not be ignored, now that they were under German control.

Operations by day continued to be the prerogative of No.2 Group and despite the terrible drubbing inflicted on the Blenheim boys in 1940, no bright horizon in the way of improved aircraft was yet in the offing. And the year had barely got underway before a new task was thrust upon their bowed, but still willing shoulders. Code-named *Circus*, this called for a small number of Blenheims, operating beneath a protective umbrella of fighters, to cross the Channel and strike at selected targets, mainly in the Pas de Calais region of northern France. It is unlikely that the planners envisaged that the Blenheims would cause any extensive damage to the facilities being attacked, their numbers being deliberately kept to little more than a dozen, or even less, on any one occasion but it was hoped that the Luftwaffe would be forced into joining battle with the escorting fighters and with the recent success of the *'Battle of Britain'* fresh in mind further useful attrition rates of the enemy fighter stock might be realised.

Prior to the introduction of *Circus* operations three squadrons, 40, 57 and 218, left No.2 Group in favour of No.3 Group where they were joined six months later by 101 Squadron, all four units being re-equipped with Wellingtons and fully absorbed into the night bombing campaign. Their departure from No.2 Group was partially offset by the arrival of 88 Squadron and 226 Squadron, ex-AASF and a lengthy period of re-building in Northern Ireland. Before the year was out the former of these two squadrons would have the honour of introducing the American-built twin-engined Douglas Boston to bomber operations. Sturdily built, the Boston quickly became a firm favourite of the crews who were fortunate enough to make its acquaintance. However, it would be in the Middle East that the type would stamp its mark and in the event only three of No.2 Group's squadrons received Bostons. Thus for the majority of airmen serving with the group, 1941 would be another year of Blenheim operations, a year in which the squadrons found themselves operating out of Malta (rolling detachments from 21, 82, 105, 107, 110 and 139 Squadrons were the principal units involved, their detachments taking place from May 1941 onwards) in a deadly game of low-level anti-shipping operations and equally hazardous, though less frequent, incursions against enemy land targets. And it was not only over the Mediterranean theatre that so many crews flew to their doom but similar strikes over the North Sea, sometimes while attached for brief periods to Coastal Command, took their toll as the following extract illustrates. It is taken from a letter, written on the 12th of May, 1941, to the parents of Sgt Arthur Barron, a pre-war regular airman who had qualified as a wireless operator/air gunner and served with 21 Squadron based at Watton in Norfolk; *'Your son's aircraft was detailed to perform an operational sweep (6th of May, 1941) for enemy shipping off the Dutch coast and proceeded, in company with another aircraft, to carry out the task set. The crew of the accompanying aircraft have related that two ships were sighted and attacked, each pilot choosing a vessel. Just after its bombs had been dropped from your son's aircraft, a flash of flame was seen in the port wing of the aircraft which seemed to indicate to the other crew that a hostile shell had found its mark on the petrol tank carried in that wing. Crippled in one wing, the machine fell away quickly to sea level, striking the water a very little distance ahead of the vessel which had just been attacked. The accompanying aircraft could not see whether any survivors managed to extricate themselves before the wrecked machine sank a few moments later, but it would be wholly pessimistic to take the view that they could not have done so. If they escaped it is most likely that they were picked up by the ship's crew and are now prisoners of war. It is well known that the Germans treat R.A.F. prisoners well, and it is not unreasonable to hope that your son may be both alive and well.*

'It would be a wholly unkind and false charity to pretend that we are very hopeful that your son escaped, but in the absence of proof that all were killed I do think you have good grounds for hope.'

The author of the letter, P/O J. G. B. Draper, Adjutant of 21 Squadron, underlined 'do' as if to emphasise the optimism of the second part of the last sentence but, sadly, Sgt Barron's mother and father would never receive word of his survival and along with over 20,000 airmen from the Royal Air Force, Commonwealth and Dominion air forces his name is now commemorated in perpetuity on the panels of the Runnymede Memorial sited on Cooper's Hill overlooking the Thames as silent tribute to all those airmen who lost their lives while serving in the United Kingdom (including Northern Ireland), Iceland, the Faroe Islands, The Azores and from bases on the Continent of Europe and who have no known grave. It is a sombre fact that a very high percentage of the '20,000' served with Bomber Command.

Before closing this broad assessment of No.2 Group brief reference must be made of the group's fleeting involvement with the Boeing B-17, a number of which were issued to the re-formed 90 Squadron in the spring of 1941. Although improved versions of the Fortress would become a byword for American bombing operations over Europe these early examples allocated to 90 Squadron proved quite unsuited and their operational use was confined to 52 sorties, attempted between the 8th of July and the 25th of September, during which two were lost to enemy action and several others were written off in training accidents.

Mention has already been made of the Manchester, Stirling and Halifax, now waiting in the wings, their crews anxious to prove their worth in offensive operations. Of this trio of new types, the Stirlings of 7 Squadron were the first to see action when on the 10th/11th of February, 1941, three aircraft were included in a force of 43 bombers attacking oil-storage tanks at Rotterdam. Then, during the night of 24th/25th February, half-a-dozen Manchesters from 207 Squadron featured in the contingent of 57 aircraft raiding Brest, while on the 10th/11th of March, 35 Squadron despatched six Halifaxes to accompany a handful of Blenheims assigned to targets at Le Havre. In respect of these operations all three Stirlings returned safely but one of 207 Squadron's precious Manchesters was badly damaged after being obliged to land with its starboard undercarriage leg jammed in the retracted position (it was repaired and returned to service, hence its exclusion from the second volume in this series). The outcome of the first Halifax sorties, however, ended in tragedy when S/L P. A. Gilchrist's aircraft was intercepted by one of our own night fighters and in a case of mistaken identity shot down over Surrey with the loss of four of its crew, only Gilchrist and Sgt R. G. Aedy managing to parachute from the stricken bomber.

Over the next few weeks all three types were used in smallish numbers and the raid by 88 aircraft on the Blohm & Voss U-boat yards at Hamburg on the 12th/13th of March included both the Manchester and the Halifax, but it would be the middle of the month before a single Stirling joined in an attack on a German target, namely Bremen. Not surprisingly, considering the complexities of these advanced bombers, technical snags resulted in a series of frustrating groundings and by the end of 1941, of the 13 first-line squadrons equipping No.3 Group only three had been able to exchange their Wellingtons for Stirlings. Within No.4 Group the picture was no better. Of the 10 active squadrons only two were fully operational with the Halifax with 10 Squadron in the process of conversion training.

The unfortunate saga surrounding the Manchester is all too well known and, therefore, suffice it to say that it was left to the Hampden squadrons to bear the brunt of No.5 Group's operations throughout the year, a year that ended with the issue of the first of Avro's Manchester replacement, the Lancaster.

But how, in general, did the bombing campaign fare in 1941? I have mentioned that Sir Richard Peirse had received various directives from the Air Ministry, the first of which arrived within a few weeks of his appointment as Air Officer Commanding-in-Chief. Heading the list of targets to be attacked were the oil producing plants while industry and marshalling yards were included along with minelaying and sundry other military objectives. With only limited resources at hand Peirse protested that he would not be able to afford the concentration necessary to attack the oil centres and at the same time pay sufficient attention to the other areas identified in the directive. To his undoubted relief a missive arrived at High Wycombe instructing him to concentrate on oil and attend to the other targets as and when the opportunity presented itself. Unfortunately, the reality of the situation that Peirse found himself in was that he would be hard pressed to deliver on any of the aims cited in the directive, even in its revised format. Early in 1941 the Air Ministry again stressed the importance of destroying Germany's synthetic-oil industry, but within a matter of weeks, this time on direct orders from Winston Churchill, Peirse was ordered to change tack and concentrate on shipbuilding centres, particularly those involved in the production of U-boats. Also, the French ports that were now host to the battle-cruisers *Scharnhorst* and *Gneisenau* were to be bombed whenever these dangerous adversaries were known to be present and, as if this were not enough, resources had to be found to attack the Focke-Wulf Condor airfields as far apart as Stavanger in Norway and their French base at Merignac. Where the Luftwaffe had failed in 1940, the German Navy, through the dual medium of surface raiders and U-boats, was coming perilously close to starving the United Kingdom base of the raw ingredients necessary for the continued prosecution of the war. For close on four months the main emphasis of attack had to be directed in support of naval and air operations by Coastal Command as the *'Battle of the Atlantic'* gathered momentum. Little wonder then that Peirse felt more than a degree of frustration, but any misgivings on his part found no support from his predecessor, Portal, now Chief of the Air Staff.

And as the last weeks of winter gave way to spring and the direction of the bombing swung into line with Churchill's demands, some positive results were achieved, particularly against the shipbuilding centres of Hamburg and Kiel. Operations against the French ports were, perhaps, less successful, but sufficient damage was caused to the two surface raiders that their forays into the Atlantic were held in check. On reflection, therefore, the period between mid-March and early July 1941 can be regarded as the most productive of Sir Richard's command, for with the easing of the situation at sea and the release of his forces to resume their assault on mainland Germany, oil was no longer on the agenda! Beyond the confines of the planning rooms at High Wycombe and in the more exalted corridors of power at the Air Ministry, those responsible for analysing the bombing reports and matching their content against data obtained from other sources; photographic reconnaissance and intelligence gleaned from agents, to quote but two, were coming to the opinion that Bomber Command was failing in its task, particularly in its ability to seriously reduce Germany's oil supply. These seeds of doubt in the minds of the Air Staff were soon to be supported by the conclusions reached with the release in August 1941 of the Butt Report, the statistics of which made for most unhappy digestion at command and group headquarters.

As autumn set in, an air of considerable gloom pervaded, and in the face of rising losses the future prospects of the Air Officer Commanding-in-Chief hung in the balance. By the onset of winter and with no marked improvement in performance, Sir Richard's fate was finally sealed and following a meeting at Chequers with Winston Churchill, instigated in the wake of a costly raid on Berlin (see Volume 2, pages 173 to 178), his continued tenure at High Wycombe was now in the hands of the Prime Minister. Thus, it came to pass that Pierse was informed on the 13th of November that operations were to be pared to the bone while the future of his command was debated by the War Cabinet.

In conclusion, perhaps the only chinks of light in this most dark of years was that Hitler had committed Germany to a war on two fronts, the invasion of Russia having taken place in the summer, and with Japan's entry into the war the industrial and manpower potential of the United States of America was now firmly in the Allied camp.

ROYAL AIR FORCE,
AUXILIARY AIR FORCE and
ROYAL AIR FORCE (VOLUNTEER RESERVE)
personnel

903090	Sgt	ABBOTT Bernard Thomas	4-02-41	18 OTU
1274161	AC2	ABDEE Norman John	12-12-41	15 OTU
1164848	Sgt	ABERNETHY Robert Francis	20-09-41	144 Sqn
69490	P/O	ABREY Cyril William	21-09-41	214 Sqn
1250963	Sgt	ACRES Leonard	17-08-41	106 Sqn
638744	Sgt	ACTON Eric Phillips	26-04-41	21 Sqn
550042	Cpl	ACTON George Alfred	18-05-41	139 Sqn
980197	Sgt	ADAIR Robert Simpson	24-06-41	76 Sqn
749453	Sgt	ADAIR Singleton Wilson	20-03-41	82 Sqn
1378155	Sgt	ADAMS Archibald William	29-06-41	76 Sqn
86722	P/O	ADAMS George Redvers Newton	10-05-41	149 Sqn
742983	F/S	ADAMS DFM Linford Herbert	18-11-41	25 OTU
901172	Sgt	ADAMS Peter Alexander	31-03-41	21 Sqn
754726	Sgt	ADAMSON Ronald William	23-07-41	18 Sqn
106142	P/O	ADCOCK Reginald	7-12-41	61 Sqn
26195	W/C	ADDENBROOKE Derek	3-04-41	101 Sqn
945079	Sgt	ADEY Ivan John	16-05-41	40 Sqn
101139	P/O	ADKINS Arthur Edward Charles	29-08-41	35 Sqn
755932	Sgt	ADKINS Irvine Horace	17-02-41	114 Sqn
87069	P/O	ADSHEAD Patrick James Neil	31-07-41	61 Sqn
41240	F/O	AGAR George Brian Shelton	25-04-41	218 Sqn
1164647	Sgt	AIKEN Ronald Lurring	21-10-41	15 Sqn
632038	Sgt	AIKENHEAD George Swinton	15-06-41	115 Sqn
916333	Sgt	AINSCOUGH Hugh Thomas Martland	11-07-41	9 Sqn
967756	Sgt	AINSLIE Tom Dale	26-02-41	75 Sqn
968113	F/S	AIRD Robert Inglis Hugh	6-07-41	10 Sqn
62298	P/O	AIRES Ernest Keith	11-06-41	18 Sqn
953705	Sgt	AITKEN John	21-09-41	214 Sqn
747920	Sgt	AITKEN William Cutherbertson	21-03-41	207 Sqn
937390	Sgt	AKRIGG Ben	31-08-41	207 Sqn
63437	P/O	ALBRECHT Vannio Max	1-11-41	102 Sqn
978333	Sgt	ALCOCK Graham Aeron	1-07-41	10 Sqn
954525	Sgt	ALDER John Norman	3-08-41	7 Sqn
45234	P/O	ALDERSON DFM Peter	30-07-41	20 OTU
1261389	AC1	ALDERTON Eric George Henry	20-09-41	Swanton Morley
77687	F/O	ALDERTON Stanley Victor	14-06-41	102 Sqn
1254695	Sgt	ALDOUS Robert Frederick	28-12-41	57 Sqn
950520	Sgt	ALDRIDGE Horace	6-07-41	49 Sqn
70836	F/L	ALDRIDGE DFC Richard Sydney Edward	18-04-41	61 Sqn
85014	P/O	ALERS-HANKEY Nigel Clinton [Canada]	11-06-41	82 Sqn
44267	F/O	ALEXANDER James Okeden [Canada]	28-08-41	88 Sqn
904039	Sgt	ALLAN David Henry	15-08-41	115 Sqn
969943	Sgt	ALLAN Ian	27-12-41	58 Sqn
951386	Sgt	ALLAN Robert	8-09-41	90 Sqn
755584	Sgt	ALLAN William Brian	8-12-41	18 Sqn
549662	F/S	ALLANSON George	4-04-41	106 Sqn
106364	P/O	ALLCHIN James Cecil Alcuin	8-11-41	102 Sqn
84861	F/O	ALLEN Alastair Gordon	21-06-41	99 Sqn
05233	S/L	ALLEN Arthur Henry	18-03-41	21 Sqn
960514	Sgt	ALLEN Claude William	2-09-41	83 Sqn
1274127	AC2	ALLEN Harry	27-11-41	106 Sqn
974030	Sgt	ALLEN James	13-08-41	207 Sqn
106109	F/O	ALLEN James Eric	7-12-41	22 OTU
1150195	Sgt	ALLEN Keith Ruthven	7-04-41	3 GTrgFlt
751997	Sgt	ALLEN Norman Oswald	13-01-41	114 Sqn
759220	Sgt	ALLEWAY Frederick William	6-08-41	103 Sqn
968171	Sgt	ALLISON William	12-06-41	25 OTU
909911	Sgt	ALLNATT Edward Ernest	18-04-41	149 Sqn
1167409	Sgt	ALLPORT Richard Butt	20-10-41	99 Sqn
1325280	Sgt	ALLSOP John Shaw	12-05-41	58 Sqn
1375217	Sgt	ALMOND Charles William	17-10-41	15 OTU
911565	Sgt	ALSTON Thomas Reid	21-03-41	21 Sqn
927508	Sgt	ALSTROM Francis Norman	24-04-41	11 OTU
1165311	Sgt	ALTON William	20-10-41	106 Sqn
1053017	Sgt	ALWAY Cecil George	15-08-41	115 Sqn
1154190	Sgt	AMBROSE Denis George	3-06-41	11 OTU
646435	F/S	AMBROSE Sidney	16-08-41	90 Sqn
995955	Sgt	AMOS Edward Roy	3-08-41	7 Sqn
1199695	Sgt	AMOTT Jack	29-09-41	16 OTU
902859	F/S	AMY Kenneth Charles [Channel Islands]	7-07-41	12 Sqn
909949	Sgt	ANDERSON Alexander Ian Pryce	15-08-41	218 Sqn
1006358	Sgt	ANDERSON Charles Thomas Roderick	30-11-41	102 Sqn
1372860	Sgt	ANDERSON James Deane	27-12-41	101 Sqn
969380	Sgt	ANDERSON John	10-05-41	115 Sqn
751818	Sgt	ANDERSON John Albert	12-08-41	226 Sqn
974017	Sgt	ANDERSON Joseph	9-04-41	9 Sqn
88023	P/O	ANDERSON Peter Gordon	24-07-41	144 Sqn
997631	Sgt	ANDERSON William Hamilton	8-09-41	104 Sqn
550043	F/S	ANDERTON James Matthew	13-04-41	18 Sqn
563158	F/S	ANDREWS Clifford William	25-04-41	218 Sqn
745533	F/S	ANDREWS Cyril George	19-08-41	11 OTU
1380771	Sgt	ANDREWS Edward Whybrow	26-10-41	88 Sqn
69451	P/O	ANDREWS DFM Sydney Rupert	26-06-41	99 Sqn
924774	Sgt	ANGELL Jeffcote Louvain	17-06-41	405 Sqn
905394	Sgt	ANNESLEY-COOKE Edward	12-06-41	10 Sqn
922597	Sgt	ANNETTS William Harvey Kenneth	23-06-41	13 OTU
1154272	Sgt	ANSON Reginald Kenneth	7-12-41	104 Sqn
1177724	Sgt	ANSTEY Thomas Eric	27-12-41	110 Sqn
1187860	Sgt	ANSTEY William John	14-10-41	114 Sqn

Number	Rank	Name	Date	Unit
1251722	Sgt	APPLEBY Frederick William	18-08-41	14 OTU
930962	Sgt	APPLEBY John	26-08-41	40 Sqn
551671	F/S	APPLEBY Michael Barton	18-04-41	114 Sqn
751242	Sgt	APPLEBY Norman Walter	20-06-41	105 Sqn
548102	F/S	APPLETON DFM George Edward	27-07-41	49 Sqn
1065666	F/S	APPLEYARD George Henry	12-08-41	139 Sqn
751902	Sgt	ARCHER DFM Frank	24-03-41	82 Sqn
747939	Sgt	ARCHER Harold Thorpe	30-06-41	7 Sqn
1005718	Sgt	ARCHER Jack	29-08-41	61 Sqn
1181824	Sgt	ARCHER Reginald Frederick	21-09-41	77 Sqn
1181737	Sgt	ARCHER Ronald George	21-11-41	7 Sqn
961388	Sgt	ARCHER William Frederick	16-07-41	57 Sqn
745517	Sgt	ARKWRIGHT David William	13-03-41	77 Sqn
1375391	Sgt	ARMER Edward William	15-12-41	50 Sqn
988954	Sgt	ARMES Henry Ivison Shipley	22-10-41	150 Sqn
648415	LAC	ARMISHAW Joseph Edward [Canada]	6-07-41	76 Sqn
988483	Sgt	ARMITAGE Frank	23-11-41	10 Sqn
1039943	AC1	ARMITAGE Harry	18-09-41	405 Sqn
966934	Sgt	ARMSTRONG George Russel	27-02-41	78 Sqn
965766	Sgt	ARMSTRONG James Gerard	3-06-41	7 Sqn
1167158	Sgt	ARMSTRONG John Gordon	17-08-41	44 Sqn
637491	Sgt	ARMSTRONG Thomas	19-08-41	9 Sqn
922743	Sgt	ARNOLD Albert Charles	15-11-41	11 OTU
647324	Sgt	ARNOLD Arthur Joseph	12-06-41	99 Sqn
77908	P/O	ARNOLD Edward Rolfe	10-03-41	35 Sqn
1181408	Sgt	ARNOLD Ronald Ernest	17-10-41	15 OTU
29198	W/C	ARNOLD MiD Roy George Claringbould	9-06-41	9 Sqn
748376	F/S	ARNOTT John Woodrow	20-07-41	207 Sqn
1378785	Sgt	ARTHUR John Leslie Louvain	11-11-41	115 Sqn
86705	P/O	ARTHURS Kenneth Norman [Canada]	24-02-41	115 Sqn
755393	Sgt	ASBREY George Frederick	10-03-41	144 Sqn
62316	P/O	ASHBY Philip Bernard	23-07-41	21 Sqn
916414	Sgt	ASHCROFT Cyril Clifford Gordon	2-06-41	18 Sqn
966017	Sgt	ASHER Colin Dingwall	27-06-41	57 Sqn
908768	Sgt	ASHLEY John Richard	12-10-41	75 Sqn
67051	P/O	ASHTON John Frederick	1-09-41	101 Sqn
966591	Sgt	ASHURST Frederick	8-04-41	44 Sqn
1109200	Sgt	ASHURST John James	12-10-41	82 Sqn
925021	Sgt	ASHWOOD Albert Henry	27-09-41	27 OTU
904070	Sgt	ASHWOOD Eric William	4-06-41	21 Sqn
759036	Sgt	ASHWORTH Victor Edwin	25-04-41	218 Sqn
939723	Sgt	ASTLE Arthur William	9-01-41	76 Sqn
63426	P/O	ATCHISON Ian Alexander Nigel	30-09-41	58 Sqn
1378489	Sgt	ATKIN James Henry	8-11-41	58 Sqn
28124	S/L	ATKINS John Croft	12-09-41	40 Sqn
1164953	Sgt	ATKINS Lloyd James	8-11-41	150 Sqn
984792	Sgt	ATKINSON Cyril Taylor	26-03-41	15 OTU
650052	F/S	ATKINSON Ernest Charles	28-12-41	49 Sqn
1006920	Sgt	ATKINSON Richard Alfred Palmer Vincent	13-12-41	144 Sqn
46325	P/O	ATKINSON Robert	8-02-41	12 Sqn
1213421	AC2	ATKINSON Robert Johnson	25-02-41	11 OTU
988994	Sgt	ATKINSON Ronald Henry	24-10-41	44 Sqn
920450	Sgt	ATKINSON Wilfred Venus	30-08-41	102 Sqn
1236756	AC1	ATTER Wilfred Leslie	16-11-41	19 OTU
1252618	Sgt	ATTEW Kenneth Victor	12-08-41	21 Sqn
550042	Sgt	AUSTEN-JOHNSON Joseph Eckersley	13-05-41	82 Sqn
565799	Sgt	AUSTIN Cecil	13-08-41	76 Sqn
1262243	Sgt	AUSTIN Francis Edward	12-10-41	75 Sqn
754933	Sgt	AUSTIN James	16-07-41	50 Sqn
908623	Sgt	AUSTIN Ronald Joseph	27-05-41	82 Sqn
910543	Sgt	AUSTIN Walter Edward	21-10-41	44 Sqn
926777	Sgt	AVORY George Alfred	3-07-41	78 Sqn
787148	Sgt	BABACEK Pavel [Czechoslovakia]	19-07-41	311 Sqn
770790	Sgt	BABER Alfred Thomas	17-12-41	5 Group
787505	Sgt	BABICEK Zdenek [Czechoslovakia]	15-09-41	311 Sqn
1253305	Sgt	BACKHOUSE Edward Ronald	11-10-41	57 Sqn
748320	Sgt	BACON Leslie William	18-04-41	21 Sqn
68803	P/O	BAERLEIN Anthony	22-10-41	51 Sqn
754080	Sgt	BAGLEY John Lawrence	13-03-41	214 Sqn
805437	F/S	BAGNALL Ronald Stanley	4-07-41	106 Sqn
955016	Sgt	BAGSHAW George Edward	15-08-41	51 Sqn
1375120	Sgt	BAILEY Allan Edward	6-12-41	110 Sqn
942807	Sgt	BAILEY Harry	16-06-41	78 Sqn
971793	Sgt	BAILEY Herbert Eric	9-05-41	78 Sqn
86371	F/L	BAILEY DFC Jack Alexander James	30-06-41	115 Sqn
44598	F/L	BAILEY Raymond Arthur	4-07-41	107 Sqn
87386	P/O	BAILEY Stanley Leonard	16-05-41	144 Sqn
88443	P/O	BAILIE John	8-07-41	7 Sqn
1113021	Sgt	BAINBRIDGE Ernest	12-08-41	82 Sqn
63826	P/O	BAINBRIDGE George Bewick	13-06-41	15 OTU
942468	Sgt	BAINBRIDGE Jack	19-08-41	101 Sqn
37031	S/L	BAIRD Andrew George Gordon	7-07-41	102 Sqn
962502	Sgt	BAIRD Ronald Ernest	9-07-41	110 Sqn
551811	Sgt	BAIRD William John	21-06-41	218 Sqn
968147	Sgt	BAKER Ernest George	25-04-41	18 Sqn
754085	Sgt	BAKER Frank Weldon	18-04-41	9 Sqn
60559	F/O	BAKER Murray Richard Frederick	30-06-41	106 Sqn
911948	Sgt	BAKER Peter Dorsan	23-07-41	18 Sqn
745721	Sgt	BAKER Victor Edward	9-08-41	61 Sqn
778405	Sgt	BALDACHIN Sydney Douglas [Rhodesia]	16-08-41	25 OTU
1163598	Sgt	BALDOCK Frederick Edward	16-12-41	102 Sqn
1433982	AC2	BALDRY Ernest James	7-11-41	Swanton Morley
744950	Sgt	BALDWIN Conrad Thomas Frederick	14-06-41	102 Sqn
935264	Sgt	BALDWIN Frank Henry	14-03-41	10 OTU
969301	Cpl	BALKIN Morris Ernest	18-06-41	50 Sqn
953924	Sgt	BALL Alec	2-06-41	139 Sqn
39925	F/L	BALL MiD Kenneth Rhodes	12-08-41	9 Sqn
994358	Sgt	BALL Wilfrid Langdon	26-11-41	106 Sqn
636996	LAC	BALLANCE Samuel	23-08-41	40 Sqn
643070	LAC	BALLARD Robert Christopher	20-06-41	105 Sqn
952991	Sgt	BALLS William Ronald	8-09-41	9 Sqn
544600	Sgt	BALMFORTH George	12-05-41	58 Sqn
34065	W/C	BALSDON Denys Finlay	18-12-41	97 Sqn
751616	Sgt	BANHAM Douglas Walter	20-06-41	10 Sqn
909983	Sgt	BANKS Douglas Norman	28-05-41	82 Sqn
1165223	Sgt	BANKS Reginald George	15-10-41	226 Sqn
1163961	Sgt	BANKS Reginald John	12-10-41	82 Sqn
1100940	Sgt	BANKS Robert Arthur	8-09-41	9 Sqn
33298	F/L	BARBER Anthony Louis Henry	22-03-41	57 Sqn
754425	Sgt	BARCLAY Douglas McLeod	27-03-41	14 OTU
111329	P/O	BARCLAY James Arthur	8-12-41	18 Sqn
748707	Sgt	BARCLAY John Bell	15-02-41	50 Sqn
944985	Sgt	BARCROFT Richard Neilson	6-08-41	104 Sqn
102076	P/O	BARFORD Alan Hedges	29-11-41	214 Sqn
70043	F/L	BARKER DFC Desmond Wallace Ferguson [New Zealand]	12-02-41	83 Sqn
937271	F/S	BARKER Frank	24-07-41	103 Sqn
1379176	Sgt	BARKER Leslie	28-12-41	15 OTU
1006907	Sgt	BARKER Richard Charlwood	15-10-41	75 Sqn
39052	S/L	BARKER Robert Bramston	7-05-41	18 Sqn
649528	F/S	BARKER Thomas Anthony	9-09-41	50 Sqn
1378561	Sgt	BARKER William John	6-09-41	75 Sqn
1186621	Sgt	BARKER-BENFIELD George Francis	19-09-41	10 OTU
1381373	Sgt	BARLOW Owen Hugh	30-08-41	101 Sqn
939872	F/S	BARNARD George Henry	24-06-41	76 Sqn
981748	Sgt	BARNES Geoffrey	8-12-41	144 Sqn
511912	Sgt	BARNES AFM Thomas Edward	15-02-41	114 Sqn
565063	F/S	BARNETT Leonard Martin	22-09-41	105 Sqn
84726	P/O	BARNETT Stewart Sidney	4-04-41	115 Sqn
902522	F/S	BARNFIELD Kenneth William	30-11-41	142 Sqn

Number	Rank	Name	Date	Sqn
758054	Sgt	BARON DFM Norman	20-07-41	139 Sqn
759105	Sgt	BARR Hubert William John	12-05-41	214 Sqn
1108927	Sgt	BARR Robert	6-12-41	17 OTU
999073	LAC	BARRAT Douglas Harry Montague	21-02-41	16 OTU
755776	Sgt	BARRATT Eric	4-05-41	7 Sqn
1152714	Sgt	BARRETT Albert Edward	8-09-41	51 Sqn
901205	Sgt	BARRETT Duncan Henry [South Africa]	29-08-41	49 Sqn
1281815	Sgt	BARRETT Frank George	8-09-41	104 Sqn
754552	Sgt	BARRETT Henry Thomas	9-07-41	9 Sqn
60820	P/O	BARRETT John	1-07-41	10 Sqn
06204	G/C	BARRETT DSO* DFC John Francis Tufnell	3-09-41	North Luffenham
540328	F/S	BARRETT William Edward	13-08-41	15 Sqn
553534	Sgt	BARRON Arthur	6-05-41	21 Sqn
944140	Sgt	BARRON Hugh Forster	13-08-41	9 Sqn
936554	Sgt	BARRON John Aitken	11-06-41	99 Sqn
526491	F/S	BARRY Joseph	16-09-41	44 Sqn
84318	F/L	BARSBY Eric Arthur	31-10-41	51 Sqn
922271	F/S	BARTLETT Donald Harry	12-09-41	14 OTU
32071	W/C	BARTLETT DFC George Arthur	26-04-41	21 Sqn
1250704	LAC	BARTON Harry	18-06-41	50 Sqn
1377210	Sgt	BARTON Henry Harvey Molyneux	15-08-41	150 Sqn
615896	Sgt	BARTON Herbert Ronald	24-07-41	218 Sqn
930289	Sgt	BARTON Samuel	23-10-41	50 Sqn
926354	Sgt	BARTRIP Douglas Arthur	17-09-41	82 Sqn
87459	P/O	BASER Wylie	4-06-41	139 Sqn
923222	Sgt	BASEVI Bernard Athelstan	10-12-41	83 Sqn
87356	P/O	BASHAM John Angus	2-05-41	77 Sqn
983207	Sgt	BASS Dudley Cecil	8-09-41	51 Sqn
909973	Sgt	BASS George Keech	9-06-41	18 Sqn
37493	F/L	BASSETT David John	10-09-41	25 OTU
909151	Sgt	BASTIN Stuart George	26-08-41	105 Sqn
754477	Sgt	BASTON Thomas James	17-06-41	51 Sqn
581494	Sgt	BATCH Alexander Richard	2-07-41	226 Sqn
951764	Sgt	BATCHELLOR Cecil Ridge	29-06-41	15 Sqn
65498	P/O	BATEMAN Cyril McCulloch	27-06-41	61 Sqn
1104340	Sgt	BATEMAN George Frederick	13-10-41	40 Sqn
755299	Sgt	BATES Bernard William Frederick	5-07-41	114 Sqn
751214	F/S	BATES Reginald Arthur	26-07-41	35 Sqn
923430	Sgt	BATES Roger Edward	15-10-41	40 Sqn
580419	F/S	BATES Thomas Arthur	21-11-41	109 Sqn
86711	P/O	BATES William Albert	1-01-41	78 Sqn
100045	P/O	BATTER Raymond Herbert	27-10-41	114 Sqn
619060	F/S	BATTY DFM Arthur Henry Dennis	27-07-41	226 Sqn
525889	Sgt	BATTY James John Castleman	8-02-41	12 Sqn
1251280	Sgt	BAUMBER Robert Charles	8-09-41	12 Sqn
787186	Sgt	BAUMRUK Bohumil [Czechoslovakia]	16-01-41	311 Sqn
921668	Sgt	BAWDEN Reginald Vernon	15-11-41	149 Sqn
742962	F/S	BAXTER DFM Ronald William Hazard	18-11-41	25 OTU
39213	F/L	BAXTER William Bethune	2-07-41	12 Sqn
1053331	Sgt	BAYLEY Edward	8-08-41	10 Sqn
1153744	Sgt	BAYLISS Frank Raymond	27-10-41	17 OTU
974237	Sgt	BAYLY George Lee Morris	18-05-41	218 Sqn
1182064	Sgt	BEACHAM Derrick Oliver	20-06-41	105 Sqn
1152341	Sgt	BEADMAN Edric Arthur Bernel	3-06-41	40 Sqn
745653	Sgt	BEAL Donald Newbegin	12-02-41	99 Sqn
1161382	Sgt	BEALE Ronald	13-10-41	139 Sqn
89340	P/O	BEANEY Victor Douglas	1-11-41	49 Sqn
567064	Sgt	BEARD Edward John	26-10-41	40 Sqn
918433	Sgt	BEARDMORE John Clifford	17-08-41	78 Sqn
939008	Sgt	BEARDSLEY Bruce	19-04-41	114 Sqn
976174	Sgt	BEARNE Wilfred	6-09-41	75 Sqn
67663	P/O	BEATSON Walter Gordon Clement	27-10-41	114 Sqn
964587	Sgt	BEATTIE Evan Bruce [New Zealand]	16-06-41	15 OTU
966004	Sgt	BEATTIE John	11-06-41	99 Sqn
527756	Sgt	BEATTIE Robert Henry	8-09-41	90 Sqn
561696	F/S	BEATTIE DFM Thomas	13-08-41	207 Sqn
974076	Sgt	BEATTIE Tudor	21-05-41	110 Sqn
976102	Sgt	BEAUMONT Leonard	16-06-41	103 Sqn
1257957	Sgt	BEAUMONT Sidney Victor	6-09-41	25 OTU
902554	F/S	BECKETT Percy Herbert	12-05-41	40 Sqn
948443	Sgt	BECKWITH Edward Peter	15-08-41	150 Sqn
923724	Sgt	BECKWITH George Joseph	24-07-41	103 Sqn
563055	Sgt	BEDDALL Harold	21-03-41	150 Sqn
748747	Sgt	BEDDOW Douglas Corbett	2-03-41	51 Sqn
937912	Sgt	BEEVER George Francis	22-04-41	18 Sqn
100594	P/O	BEGBIE Ian Mouland	21-06-41	14 OTU
626736	Sgt	BEHAN Thomas Fraser	3-01-41	102 Sqn
1291838	Sgt	BELDAM Ian Robert	23-12-41	14 OTU
937637	F/S	BELL Albert Henry	24-07-41	21 OTU
931536	Sgt	BELL Alfred Ronald	15-08-41	218 Sqn
621608	Sgt	BELL Derek	27-12-41	50 Sqn
581312	F/S	BELL Ian Redmayne	11-12-41	35 Sqn
89081	P/O	BELL Jack	30-07-41	82 Sqn
1378980	Sgt	BELL James Bulman	21-09-41	103 Sqn
1100845	Sgt	BELL James Logan	27-12-41	110 Sqn
754397	Sgt	BELL John William	8-11-41	78 Sqn
777798	Sgt	BELL Peter Hastings [Rhodesia]	24-10-41	44 Sqn
567353	F/S	BELL Robert Ronald	8-08-41	97 Sqn
1064095	Sgt	BELL Tom	13-08-41	104 Sqn
33533	F/O	BELOE Charles Edward	5-12-41	15 OTU
971753	Sgt	BELTON Kenyon Charles	12-5-41	17 OTU
745763	F/S	BENDALL Jack	17-09-41	105 Sqn
1258097	Sgt	BENDON John Hartley	12-09-41	16 OTU
960078	Sgt	BENEY David Levick	15-10-41	75 Sqn
942393	Sgt	BENFIELD Norman	8-04-41	40 Sqn
905356	Sgt	BENINGFIELD Anthony Stephen	6-07-41	49 Sqn
1113757	Sgt	BENNETT George Henry Sydney	5-11-41	144 Sqn
902292	Sgt	BENNETT Norman Oliver	30-04-41	99 Sqn
926721	Sgt	BENNETT Peter Maxwell	10-09-41	103 Sqn
968187	Sgt	BENNETT Richard Edward	19-08-41	51 Sqn
754408	Sgt	BENNETT Robert	7-04-41	139 Sqn
62299	P/O	BENNETT Robert Francis	7-09-41	226 Sqn
908791	Sgt	BENNETT Robert John	9-05-41	214 Sqn
975748	Sgt	BENNETT William	21-06-41	99 Sqn
759219	Sgt	BENNETTS Geoffrey Andrews	9-05-41	99 Sqn
1001940	Sgt	BENSLEY George Gilbert	31-08-41	83 Sqn
963269	Sgt	BENT James Walter	7-07-41	115 Sqn
564087	Sgt	BENTE John Francis	18-12-41	15 Sqn
956443	Sgt	BENTLEY George Leslie	24-06-41	57 Sqn
67590	P/O	BENTLEY Harry Roderick	19-08-41	114 Sqn
568024	Sgt	BENTLEY Sidney	13-10-41	15 Sqn
954085	Sgt	BENTON George	12-08-41	139 Sqn
751802	F/S	BERESFORD Charles Stanley	24-07-41	40 Sqn
785019	Sgt	BERG Norman William [Far East]	18-08-41	110 Sqn
1166613	Sgt	BERRY John James	13-08-41	76 Sqn
961524	Sgt	BERRY Montague Victor	7-06-41	107 Sqn
940846	Sgt	BERRY Nathaniel	6-05-41	21 Sqn
754402	Sgt	BERRY Richard Alan	7-11-41	101 Sqn
745915	F/S	BERWICK Robert Charles	19-06-41	78 Sqn
1195191	AC1	BEST Arthur Ernest	6-04-41	Marham
942555	Sgt	BESTWICK John	12-06-41	61 Sqn
43713	P/O	BETHRIDGE-TOPP Edward [New Zealand]	16-07-41	150 Sqn
37648	S/L	BETTS John Carleton	10-10-41	25 OTU
641035	F/S	BETTS Kenneth George	8-07-41	44 Sqn
755892	F/S	BEVAN Cyril John	8-07-41	10 Sqn
89373	P/O	BEVAN MiD George Norman	31-07-41	99 Sqn
1164941	Sgt	BEVAN James Eric Singleton	16-06-41	21 Sqn
741680	Sgt	BEVANS John Henry	30-06-41	106 Sqn
748353	F/S	BEVERIDGE Alan Reid	1-07-41	10 Sqn
532403	Sgt	BEVERLEY Albert Edward Rathbone	14-10-41	15 OTU
1150773	Sgt	BEVERLEY Douglas Bernard	26-07-41	10 Sqn
1377919	Sgt	BEYNON Arthur Winston	8-10-41	15 OTU

Number	Rank	Name	Date	Sqn
35462	S/L	BICKFORD DFC Richard	30-08-41	76 Sqn
1167450	Sgt	BICKNELL Donald Trevor	19-09-41	10 OTU
918823	Sgt	BIDLAKE Victor Marcel	27-03-41	16 OTU
1051615	Sgt	BILLETT James Ford	26-12-41	18 Sqn
967253	F/S	BILLING Gordon	9-06-41	78 Sqn
1305795	Sgt	BILLS James William	29-08-41	78 Sqn
1050632	Sgt	BILSBOROUGH Peter William	27-11-41	9 Sqn
970880	Sgt	BIMSON John	1-03-41	105 Sqn
62697	P/O	BINGHAM-HALL Donald Vincent	28-06-41	10 Sqn
746790	Sgt	BINGLEY Leslie George John	28-06-41	106 Sqn
34101	W/C	BIRCH Arthur Montague Aubrey	18-04-41	107 Sqn
745792	Sgt	BIRCH Norman	21-03-41	207 Sqn
910508	Sgt	BIRD Arthur	8-07-41	58 Sqn
33301	F/L	BIRD DFC Gerald Oscar Ladler	15-05-41	97 Sqn
60817	P/O	BIRD Peter Reginald Stephenson	11-05-41	15 Sqn
1163345	Sgt	BIRD Robert Walters	30-09-41	78 Sqn
635899	Sgt	BIRD Samuel Edward	30-06-41	40 Sqn
938323	Sgt	BIRDSELL George Benjamin Holt	3-04-41	101 Sqn
955477	Sgt	BIRKHEAD Robert Neville 'Bob'	29-04-41	10 OTU
624302	F/S	BIRT DFM George Robert	13-08-41	207 Sqn
747971	Sgt	BISHOP George Henry	10-04-41	12 Sqn
1181628	Sgt	BISSELL Alfred William	17-10-41	15 OTU
39778	S/L	BISSET DFC* MM [Czechoslovakia] Robert Clare [Canadian]	30-11-41	405 Sqn
1377719	Sgt	BLACK Charles Thomas	7-11-41	75 Sqn
979716	Sgt	BLACK Duncan Rodger	18-06-41	58 Sqn
983869	Sgt	BLACK Foster Wilson	8-07-41	44 Sqn
923087	Sgt	BLACK Harris [Canada]	8-07-41	10 Sqn
915945	Sgt	BLACK Horace Philip	22-06-41	90 Sqn
42739	F/L	BLACK DFC Hugh James Waller	24-03-41	82 Sqn
955681	Sgt	BLACK John Charles Eric	24-06-41	214 Sqn
948150	Sgt	BLACK Lionel	3-09-41	214 Sqn
553849	Sgt	BLACKBURN Clement Peter	16-07-41	57 Sqn
1069571	Sgt	BLACKBURN Thomas	17-10-41	10 Sqn
1006363	Sgt	BLACKBURN William Alan	27-12-41	77 Sqn
16236	W/C	BLACKDEN Vyvian Quentery	10-04-41	12 Sqn
100610	P/O	BLACKWELL Leonard Richard	21-07-41	76 Sqn
1052240	Sgt	BLACKWOOD James Blair	6-11-41	144 Sqn
78743	P/O	BLAIR Charles Edward	25-04-41	218 Sqn
955468	Sgt	BLAIR Lawrence	30-11-41	76 Sqn
1153348	Sgt	BLAKE Desmond	21-09-41	103 Sqn
915475	Sgt	BLAKE Gordon Eric	13-06-41	25 OTU
936547	Sgt	BLAKEY John William	29-08-41	7 Sqn
1164368	Sgt	BLAMEY Richard Cubitt	23-10-41	50 Sqn
645312	Sgt	BLANDON Cyril George	8-07-41	9 Sqn
83740	P/O	BLANDY Robert Henry Pettiplace [South Africa]	15-03-41	3 GTrgFlt
633564	Sgt	BLATCHFORD Robert Charles Henry	9-05-41	83 Sqn
82734	P/O	BLEAKEY Austen	27-06-41	102 Sqn
944792	Sgt	BLENCOE John Kenneth	4-02-41	20 OTU
745912	Sgt	BLOMELEY Eric Edwin	3-04-41	101 Sqn
45553	F/O	BLOODWORTH Charles Oscar	9-10-41	107 Sqn
945219	Sgt	BLOOMFIELD Mendel Gilbert	7-11-41	50 Sqn
928425	Sgt	BLUNDELL John Mortimer	30-07-41	139 Sqn
87343	F/O	BLUNDEN Kenneth Oswald	25-08-41	7 Sqn
1167740	Sgt	BLUNT Charles John Harvey	30-11-41	455 Sqn
565854	Sgt	BOARDMAN Terrance King	19-06-41	44 Sqn
908934	Sgt	BODY Raymond William	3-06-41	40 Sqn
905397	Sgt	BOGGIS John William Rolfe	21-07-41	76 Sqn
1054956	Sgt	BOLAND John Robert	30-11-41	214 Sqn
787583	Sgt	BOLFIK Rudolf	16-01-41	311 Sqn
63435	P/O	BOLSTER Richard Vary Campbell	28-06-41	10 Sqn
903615	Sgt	BOLTON John Randolph	16-06-41	15 OTU
987466	Sgt	BOLTON Joseph Hagan	7-08-41	150 Sqn
944667	Sgt	BOLTON Peter George	24-07-41	35 Sqn
45619	P/O	BOLTON Thomas Everest	1-07-41	7 Sqn
85271	P/O	BOND John Crewdson Ashton	10-04-41	12 Sqn
903298	Sgt	BOND William David Gordon	24-02-41	13 OTU
751183	Sgt	BONNETT Alan Chester	18-04-41	21 Sqn
1066482	Sgt	BONNETT Hubert	26-08-41	82 Sqn
580480	Sgt	BONNEY Edwin Jones	22-01-41	139 Sqn
1007432	Sgt	BONSER Clifford Winfield	30-07-41	20 OTU
755544	Sgt	BOOLS John Stafford	18-04-41	77 Sqn
67591	P/O	BOON Ronald Owen	12-07-41	17 OTU
78995	P/O	BOON William Lawton	18-04-41	77 Sqn
27219	W/C	BOOTH Arthur Frank Calvert	12-07-41	107 Sqn
61042	P/O	BOREHAM Peter Frederick Joseph	7-11-41	50 Sqn
1055841	Sgt	BORROWS Norman	25-11-41	142 Sqn
80134	P/O	BOSCH Johannes Carolus [Rhodesia]	31-08-41	16 OTU
622252	Sgt	BOSWELL Roy Gerald	19-08-41	218 Sqn
912744	F/S	BOTSFORD Kenneth Charles James	7-07-41	97 Sqn
929256	Sgt	BOTTERMAN Leslie Charles	23-06-41	13 OTU
943398	Sgt	BOTTOMLEY Jack Wilson	7-08-41	75 Sqn
759315	Sgt	BOUCHER Raymond	8-11-41	78 Sqn
755542	Sgt	BOUGIN John Montague Charles	14-04-41	21 Sqn
983202	Sgt	BOUNDS William Charles Kenneth	23-07-41	18 Sqn
971237	Sgt	BOUSFIELD Edward Ronald	19-07-41	50 Sqn
68167	P/O	BOWDEN David Roy	27-10-41	106 Sqn
1287232	Sgt	BOWDEN Geoffrey Bernard Denzil	15-11-41	15 OTU
61262	P/O	BOWDEN Wilfrid Edgar [Canada]	21-04-41	99 Sqn
754579	F/S	BOWERING MiD Norman Edward	4-07-41	106 Sqn
947062	Sgt	BOWES John	27-02-41	51 Sqn
989280	Sgt	BOWES Michael Reginald [Eire]	30-08-41	102 Sqn
89371	P/O	BOWES-CAVANAGH Brian Derek	13-10-41	207 Sqn
64934	P/O	BOWKER John Nesbitt [Canada]	17-07-41	14 OTU
1133886	AC2	BOWKER William Arthur	15-06-41	4 Flt
945312	Sgt	BOWLES Harold Douglas	17-04-41	77 Sqn
564563	W/O	BOWLES MiD Thomas William	26-04-41	51 Sqn
1500548	Sgt	BOWMAN Eric Ritchie	24-12-41	26 CFlt
580568	F/S	BOX DFM Alfred Joseph	1-09-41	144 Sqn
922969	Sgt	BOX Leslie Bowen	9-06-41	18 Sqn
613172	Sgt	BOX Wallace Howell	14-10-41	15 OTU
1154278	Sgt	BOXALL George Edward	1-09-41	99 Sqn
1259364	AC1	BOXALL James David	8-02-41	12 Sqn
742786	Sgt	BOYALL John Fred Reginald	10-04-41	106 Sqn
984710	AC1	BOYD Reginald	15-09-41	207 Sqn
903054	P/O	BOYLE Neil Colin [New Zealand]	8-02-41	12 Sqn
976903	P/O	BOYLE Thomas Charles	1-09-41	102 Sqn
1381931	Sgt	BRACE Elwyn Harry	9-10-41	19 OTU
62294	P/O	BRADBURN Leonard Sinclair	29-04-41	10 OTU
748093	Sgt	BRADBURY Gordon Stephenson	6-08-41	44 Sqn
937480	Sgt	BRADBURY Roy	1-03-41	78 Sqn
903762	Sgt	BRADFORD William Rowland	19-06-41	10 Sqn
959020	Sgt	BRADLEY George Edwin	29-10-41	106 Sqn
922544	Sgt	BRADLEY George Hosford	28-08-41	14 OTU
1255817	Sgt	BRADLEY James Wilson	27-10-41	114 Sqn
113428	P/O	BRADLEY John Whitfield	15-10-41	139 Sqn
742284	F/S	BRADLEY Reginald Gilbert	28-07-41	90 Sqn
1182378	Sgt	BRADSHAW Arthur Leslie	22-10-41	150 Sqn
1355770	Sgt	BRADSHAW John	12-06-41	51 Sqn
921388	Sgt	BRADY Patrick John	19-08-41	9 Sqn
755275	Sgt	BRAMES Ronald	21-03-41	49 Sqn
747958	Sgt	BRAMHALL Joseph Dennis	6-05-41	110 Sqn
1053576	Sgt	BRAMHALL Ronald	15-11-41	149 Sqn
1150208	Sgt	BRAMLEY Ronald Arthur	8-11-41	150 Sqn
649171	Sgt	BRAND David	17-01-41	83 Sqn
1357702	Sgt	BRANSBY Stanley Bertram	25-05-41	139 Sqn
72436	P/O	BRANSON John Peter Leslie	11-04-41	40 Sqn
60834	P/O	BRANT Harry	6-08-41	104 Sqn
81655	P/O	BRANT DFC Kenneth Douglas	26-06-41	19 OTU
911179	Sgt	BRATLEY Peter Henry Hay	12-06-41	99 Sqn
1249520	AC2	BRAY Percival Blewitt	12-08-41	311 Sqn
1257106	Sgt	BRAY Ronald Thomas	18-12-41	97 Sqn
32187	W/C	BRAYE DFC Igor William	1-05-41	139 Sqn
1177594	Sgt	BREARLEY Elias Cyril	7-09-41	17 OTU
1306090	Sgt	BREARLEY Reginald	10-07-41	77 Sqn

Number	Rank	Name	Date	Sqn
811144	Sgt	BRECKELL Ralph Hollesley	26-11-41	106 Sqn
614088	F/S	BREENE Patrick Joseph	12-06-41	61 Sqn
540886	Cpl	BREEZE Robert	23-11-41	311 Sqn
1162052	Sgt	BRELSFORD Harold	29-08-41	35 Sqn
1168185	Sgt	BRETT Collan Michael Anthony Bawden	25-11-41	142 Sqn
641766	Sgt	BRETT David Thompson	6-07-41	107 Sqn
1123272	AC1	BRETT Thomas Edwin	6-09-41	Wyton
1169141	Sgt	BRIAN Raymond Frank	28-08-41	21 Sqn
1262175	Sgt	BRICKETT Reginald Hermon	24-10-41	16 OTU
945177	F/S	BRIDEWELL Terence Alfred Evelyn	4-08-41	218 Sqn
742924	Sgt	BRIDGART Reginald Albert	5-01-41	16 OTU
945594	Sgt	BRIDGES Sidney	10-07-41	7 Sqn
911575	Sgt	BRIDGMAN Francis Harley	25-04-41	105 Sqn
36123	P/O	BRIDSON DFC Allan [New Zealand]	14-03-41	10 OTU
651910	Sgt	BRIGGS Eric Sydney	27-12-41	58 Sqn
533717	Sgt	BRIGGS John Lionel	28-08-41	88 Sqn
938689	Sgt	BRINDLEY William Norman	3-04-41	51 Sqn
88418	P/O	BRISTOW Charles Wilfred Symons	8-06-41	11 OTU
552121	F/S	BRITTAIN George	28-08-41	21 Sqn
63438	P/O	BROADHURST John Charles	24-07-41	104 Sqn
550817	Sgt	BROADHURST Stanley	10-03-41	35 Sqn
989687	Sgt	BROADWAY John Alexander Collingridge	15-07-41	110 Sqn
1166466	Sgt	BROCKETT Leonard Reginald	27-12-41	50 Sqn
758014	Sgt	BROCKWAY Ronald Charles	3-03-41	115 Sqn
957178	AC1	BROMAGE Leslie Alfred	12-06-41	4 Flt
89598	P/O	BROMHAM John William Thomas	7-09-41	49 Sqn
1017894	Sgt	BROOK George Henry	2-09-41	139 Sqn
741669	F/S	BROOK Hubert Charles Gerard	28-07-41	90 Sqn
919146	Sgt	BROOKER Maurice Dudley	21-06-41	21 Sqn
1166497	Sgt	BROOKES Alan Fincher	21-07-41	455 Sqn
974126	Sgt	BROOKMAN Leonard Peter	16-01-41	10 Sqn
925829	Sgt	BROOKS Bernard Frank	17-09-41	107 Sqn
1380784	Sgt	BROOKS Edward Owen	8-11-41	7 Sqn
956167	F/S	BROOKS John Alexander	7-09-41	57 Sqn
1057985	Sgt	BROOKS John Charles	1-11-41	102 Sqn
581201	Sgt	BROOKS Wilfred Stanley	31-07-41	142 Sqn
925823	Sgt	BROOKS William Albert	11-10-41	83 Sqn
956849	Sgt	BROTHERTON Norman Frederick	13-08-41	76 Sqn
82722	F/O	BROUGHTON John Du Vernet [Australia]	10-04-41	12 Sqn
754853	Sgt	BROWELL William Herbert	9-05-41	214 Sqn
60782	P/O	BROWN Alastair Boyd	17-06-41	115 Sqn
552771	F/S	BROWN Alexander	17-09-41	105 Sqn
941387	F/S	BROWN Arthur	17-08-41	78 Sqn
83303	P/O	BROWN Charles Desmond	3-05-41	101 Sqn
83727	P/O	BROWN DFC Charles Raymond	19-03-41	101 Sqn
902211	F/S	BROWN Charles Walter Dryburgh	30-06-41	7 Sqn
67705	P/O	BROWN Clifford Harris	25-07-41	11 OTU
64288	P/O	BROWN Douglas Edwin William	8-11-41	58 Sqn
985200	Sgt	BROWN Douglas George	29-06-41	15 Sqn
106530	P/O	BROWN Eric Ernest	7-11-41	57 Sqn
634099	Sgt	BROWN Gordon Wilfred	9-04-41	99 Sqn
108027	P/O	BROWN Harold Stanley	15-09-41	35 Sqn
983315	Sgt	BROWN Henry	17-06-41	115 Sqn
627077	F/S	BROWN DFM John	18-04-41	107 Sqn
759281	Sgt	BROWN John	8-09-41	90 Sqn
970094	Sgt	BROWN John Donald	10-04-41	218 Sqn
567245	Sgt	BROWN Maurice George	30-06-41	7 Sqn
64324	P/O	BROWN Peter	30-07-41	139 Sqn
1158274	Sgt	BROWN Peter	21-06-41	21 Sqn
88403	P/O	BROWN Peter Robert Duncan [Australia]	3-06-41	50 Sqn
936406	F/S	BROWN Reginald	4-10-41	18 OTU
944326	Sgt	BROWN Richard	9-04-41	214 Sqn
952523	Sgt	BROWN Robert	5-08-41	76 Sqn
1100635	Sgt	BROWN Robert	8-11-41	102 Sqn
60071	P/O	BROWN Victor King	14-07-41	214 Sqn
86350	P/O	BROWN Walter	4-04-41	106 Sqn
514578	F/S	BROWN DFM William	22-06-41	207 Sqn
86634	P/O	BROWN William Adam	16-05-41	97 Sqn
995904	Sgt	BROWNBILL Albert Edward	5-07-41	106 Sqn
912105	Sgt	BROWNE Henry Gallaugher	10-05-41	51 Sqn
550701	F/S	BROWNE Michael Vincent	22-06-41	207 Sqn
618322	Sgt	BROYD Stanley Henry	8-08-41	15 Sqn
88444	P/O	BRUCE Alistair Ferguson	7-08-41	150 Sqn
1001163	Sgt	BRUCE Donald Macdonald	22-07-41	44 Sqn
929001	Sgt	BRUCE George Robert	24-11-41	115 Sqn
975045	Sgt	BRUCE James Harold	18-04-41	21 Sqn
1053027	Sgt	BRUCKSHAW James	1-07-41	102 Sqn
903379	Sgt	BRUNDISH Eric Norman	17-04-41	44 Sqn
745639	F/S	BRUTEY Ronald Charles	9-07-41	83 Sqn
87049	P/O	BRYANT Francis Egerton [Australia]	29-06-41	218 Sqn
1151896	Sgt	BRYANT Keith	11-11-41	49 Sqn
976876	Sgt	BRYANT Peter Williams	6-09-41	10 Sqn
973936	Sgt	BUCHAN Wilfred	7-11-41	101 Sqn
1254035	Sgt	BUCK Douglas William	19-11-41	18 Sqn
1156870	Sgt	BUCKBY Peter	30-11-41	75 Sqn
755267	Sgt	BUCKINGHAM Edward Graham	8-06-41	11 OTU
1256279	Sgt	BUCKLE Cuthbert Jermy Stuart [Canada]	17-10-41	15 OTU
80085	P/O	BUCKLEY David Greville Litt [South Africa]	11-07-41	16 OTU
104512	P/O	BUCKLEY Herbert Donald	11-12-41	35 Sqn
1179983	Sgt	BUCKLEY Thomas Ronald	8-11-41	18 Sqn
745402	Sgt	BUCKNOLE John Stanley	24-07-41	103 Sqn
69422	P/O	BUDD William Hayward	21-10-41	44 Sqn
1254040	Sgt	BULL Alec John George	14-08-41	25 OTU
60794	P/O	BULL George William	30-09-41	142 Sqn
1198667	Sgt	BULL Thomas William	29-09-41	115 Sqn
745781	F/S	BULLIVANT Ian Arthur	9-06-41	18 Sqn
42392	F/O	BUNCE Gordon	18-12-41	15 Sqn
906190	Sgt	BUNCE Ronald Seward	9-06-41	9 Sqn
60830	F/L	BUNDEY Gordon Frederick	24-10-41	101 Sqn
903957	Sgt	BUNDOCK Leonard Ernest Eric	8-04-41	40 Sqn
540692	F/S	BUNKER Alfred Alan	27-06-41	12 Sqn
748368	Sgt	BUNN Stanley Victor	3-03-41	58 Sqn
951997	Sgt	BURBRIDGE Albert George	13-06-41	103 Sqn
60078	P/O	BURBRIDGE George Frederick	1-07-41	149 Sqn
754234	F/S	BURCH Cyril Robertson	9-05-41	149 Sqn
919091	Sgt	BURCHER Leslie James	4-12-41	107 Sqn
957747	Sgt	BURDON Stanley	26-08-41	226 Sqn
953783	Sgt	BURGESS Hector George [Channel Islands]	27-06-41	150 Sqn
951888	Sgt	BURGESS Samuel	1-11-41	51 Sqn
551290	F/S	BURGESS DFM Thomas Oakley	7-07-41	12 Sqn
60072	P/O	BURKE Ian Campbell	20-09-41	142 Sqn
995760	Sgt	BURKE James Edward Stanley	19-07-41	50 Sqn
1152213	Sgt	BURLEY Peter Richard Kenneth	12-5-41	214 Sqn
754658	Sgt	BURLEY Stanley Hudson	9-01-41	78 Sqn
1053569	Sgt	BURNETT Robert Gordon	7-08-41	214 Sqn
538670	Sgt	BURNSIDE John Stanley	8-07-41	9 Sqn
917065	Sgt	BURR Ronald Henry	21-06-41	218 Sqn
638941	Sgt	BURRELL Frank	17-09-41	107 Sqn
755937	Sgt	BURRELL William Ezra	21-04-41	106 Sqn
751057	Sgt	BURROWS Albert Edward	29-09-41	7 Sqn
1255395	Sgt	BURROWS Leonard Robert	3-08-41	7 Sqn
748672	Sgt	BURROWS Peter Ian	3-04-41	101 Sqn
69423	P/O	BURROWS William Brandwood	28-07-41	50 Sqn
74652	W/C	BURT DFC Kenyon Oswald	2-08-41	82 Sqn
967093	Sgt	BURTON James	11-01-41	82 Sqn
61045	F/L	BURTON William Westbrooke [South Africa]	20-08-41	104 Sqn
751354	Sgt	BUSBY William Gordon	29-04-41	82 Sqn
65532	P/O	BUSE Geoffrey Burridge	15-10-41	40 Sqn

633380	F/S	BUSH Arthur	26-06-41	22 OTU	935349	Sgt	CARTER George Henry	2-03-41	51 Sqn
928579	Sgt	BUSH Derrick John McKenzie	21-08-41	102 Sqn	39711	F/L	CARTER MiD John Edward	22-07-41	10 OTU
1375816	Sgt	BUSH Edward John	2-11-41	17 OTU	1164195	Sgt	CARTER Keith	22-10-41	150 Sqn
67608	P/O	BUSHELL DFM Jack Reginald	19-07-41	15 Sqn	962609	LAC	CARTER Leslie Wilfred	15-09-41	207 Sqn
915960	Sgt	BUSHFORD Charles Edward	17-05-41	149 Sqn	968383	Sgt	CARTER Nicholas Cecil James	1-09-41	102 Sqn
88867	P/O	BUSSY Geoffrey Moir	4-04-41	77 Sqn	942764	Sgt	CARTLEDGE Eric Kenneth	7-09-41	58 Sqn
581496	Sgt	BUTCHER Leslie Charles	25-02-41	103 Sqn	968781	Sgt	CASE John Henry	27-03-41	14 OTU
962421	Sgt	BUTCHER Rodney Victor	8-07-41	10 Sqn	916895	Sgt	CASH Eric Laurence	20-08-41	82 Sqn
759258	Sgt	BUTLER Eric James	10-04-41	106 Sqn	642096	Sgt	CASSELLS Andrew Stanley	4-08-41	57 Sqn
991500	Sgt	BUTLER James Wilfred	1-11-41	83 Sqn	980330	Sgt	CASSELS James King	12-06-41	99 Sqn
761002	Sgt	BUTLER John Ronald	27-05-41	49 Sqn	747984	Sgt	CASSEY Sidney Reginald	10-04-41	50 Sqn
1051918	Sgt	BUTLER Leslie Booker [Eire]	16-06-41	15 OTU	301755	W/O	CASSEY Tom	18-02-41	Lindholme
751411	Sgt	BUTLER Percival Ernest	1-04-41	149 Sqn	102975	P/O	CATHLES Noel Alfred Campbell	23-07-41	110 Sqn
645433	Sgt	BUTLER Wilfred Leonard	31-07-41	61 Sqn	1282905	Sgt	CATTERSON Charles Edgar	9-09-41	21 OTU
932611	Sgt	BUTT Henry Wright	1-09-41	16 OTU	84035	P/O	CAUNTER-JACKSON Frederick Arthur		
930644	Sgt	BUTT Raymond George	12-10-41	75 Sqn				12-06-41	61 Sqn
917346	Sgt	BUTTELL Harold Bernard	30-09-41	78 Sqn	754964	Sgt	CAUSON John Albert	7-07-41	139 Sqn
1378565	Sgt	BUTTERWORTH Jesse	30-11-41	142 Sqn	615262	F/S	CAVE Arthur Ernest	31-07-41	142 Sqn
747859	Sgt	BUTTERWORTH John	11-02-41	49 Sqn	754710	Sgt	CAWTHORNE Colin	28-07-41	10 OTU
1069853	Sgt	BUTTERWORTH John Maurice	1-11-41	16 OTU	1109519	Sgt	CHADWICK John Edwin	8-11-41	7 Sqn
640781	F/S	BYRES Neil Erskine	23-06-41	83 Sqn	88454	P/O	CHADWICK John Messiter	13-05-41	82 Sqn
1377672	Sgt	BYRNE Louis	9-07-41	78 Sqn	1163174	Sgt	CHALLIS Harold	30-06-41	107 Sqn
1309261	Sgt	BYRNE Matthew Joseph	10-09-41	25 OTU	633576	Sgt	CHAMBERLAIN Eric Frank	12-09-41	14 OTU
949386	Sgt	CADDICK John Edward	9-04-41	57 Sqn	777660	Sgt	CHAMBERLAIN Herbert Edward [Rhodesia]	12-10-41	144 Sqn
1181561	Sgt	CAESAR Gerald Coodon	16-07-41	57 Sqn					
638553	Sgt	CAIN Ronald	8-01-41	214 Sqn	33229	S/L	CHAMBERLAIN Paul Burton	12-10-41	75 Sqn
1378313	Sgt	CAINE William Michael	9-07-41	58 Sqn	65566	F/L	CHAMBERLAIN DFC Richard John	13-10-41	139 Sqn
778424	Sgt	CALCUTT Frank Kert [Rhodesia]	8-12-41	144 Sqn	922688	Sgt	CHAMBERLAIN Stanley David	7-09-41	149 Sqn
755498	Sgt	CALDWELL David Alexander	11-02-41	49 Sqn	751740	Sgt	CHAMBERLAIN Thomas Henry	6-01-41	49 Sqn
84689	F/O	CALDWELL James Andrew	28-11-41	408 Sqn	549631	Sgt	CHAMBERLAIN William James	12-03-41	218 Sqn
629173	Sgt	CALVERT Cecil	4-04-41	51 Sqn	640019	Sgt	CHAMBERS William	31-07-41	61 Sqn
902229	Sgt	CAMBRAY John Percival Basil	15-10-41	40 Sqn	913929	Sgt	CHAMPION Philip Arthur	2-11-41	102 Sqn
985637	Sgt	CAMERON Donald	8-11-41	78 Sqn	1261560	Sgt	CHANCELLOR Peter Rees	7-12-41	22 OTU
969956	Sgt	CAMERON John	13-03-41	50 Sqn	112733	P/O	CHANCELLOR Roland Niall	18-12-41	15 Sqn
976415	Sgt	CAMERON John Glen	10-04-41	82 Sqn	755118	Sgt	CHANDLER Cyril Harry	12-08-41	9 Sqn
32072	W/C	CAMERON Waverley Edward	6-04-41	107 Sqn	950324	Sgt	CHANDOS Ronald George	18-09-41	405 Sqn
909525	Sgt	CAMMAERTS Pieter Emile Gerard	30-03-41	101 Sqn	754943	Sgt	CHANIN Robert Arthur	10-02-41	61 Sqn
974217	Sgt	CAMPBELL Alexander	18-06-41	50 Sqn	902268	Sgt	CHANNER Richard William	27-04-41	15 Sqn
60835	F/L	CAMPBELL James Reith	2-11-41	78 Sqn	1250594	Sgt	CHANT Dennis Vivien	14-10-41	207 Sqn
971123	Sgt	CAMPBELL John James [Eire]	10-04-41	50 Sqn	632414	Sgt	CHANT William Gordon	27-09-41	20 OTU
974031	Sgt	CAMPBELL Kenneth Patrick	16-07-41	115 Sqn	63432	P/O	CHAPMAN Geoffrey Bertrand	14-03-41	10 OTU
942304	Sgt	CAMPBELL Kenneth Stevenson	8-04-41	44 Sqn	522572	Sgt	CHAPMAN Harold	18-03-41	149 Sqn
916042	Sgt	CAMPBELL Ronald William	25-10-41	21 OTU	1377590	Sgt	CHAPMAN Henry Raymond Gordon		
529658	Sgt	CAMPBELL William Archibald	17-05-41	106 Sqn				12-10-41	40 Sqn
1164961	Sgt	CAMPBELL William Sidney	30-07-41	139 Sqn	1055284	Sgt	CHAPMAN John	15-10-41	40 Sqn
78357	F/O	CAMPBELL-MARTIN MC Peter Clifford			1151802	Sgt	CHAPMAN John	13-06-41	102 Sqn
			17-10-41	40 Sqn	929858	Sgt	CHAPMAN Leonard Tyne	8-09-41	214 Sqn
939106	Sgt	CANNELL Dudley Roy Cluett	17-01-41	40 Sqn	906790	Sgt	CHAPPELL Denis	11-05-41	40 Sqn
1286496	AC2	CANTON Victor Edwin	13-08-41	11 OTU	67611	P/O	CHAPPELL Peter Clarence	28-07-41	10 OTU
759110	Sgt	CAPEL Douglas John [Canada]	18-03-41	149 Sqn	755822	F/S	CHAPPELL William Edwin	24-07-41	104 Sqn
1365016	Sgt	CARBERRY Stephen John	11-11-41	16 OTU	902225	F/S	CHAPPLE Douglas William Ernest	28-06-41	7 Sqn
581143	F/S	CARDELL Nevill Southwell	12-08-41	226 Sqn	904176	Sgt	CHARD Humphrey Yule	4-04-41	115 Sqn
816208	F/S	CARLILE Samuel Shannon	27-06-41	102 Sqn	949785	Sgt	CHARLES Frederick William Rodney	4-07-41	105 Sqn
950217	Sgt	CARLING Rodney Patrick	24-07-41	75 Sqn	910759	Sgt	CHARLTON Stanley	24-02-41	115 Sqn
743067	F/S	CARN Leslie Albert	10-04-41	50 Sqn	101503	S/L	CHARNEY DFC Frederick Richard Howard		
984207	Sgt	CARPENTER Arthur Vincent	8-11-41	51 Sqn				12-09-41	105 Sqn
1168332	Sgt	CARR John Herbert	7-09-41	226 Sqn	647420	Sgt	CHATFIELD Ronald Arthur	8-04-41	214 Sqn
87026	P/O	CARRAPIETT Ronald McCoy	8-04-41	58 Sqn	740630	Sgt	CHATTAWAY Albert	11-02-41	21 Sqn
1053141	Sgt	CARRIE William Gordon	10-11-41	144 Sqn	742195	Sgt	CHEESMAN Ronald Frank	5-04-41	50 Sqn
82665	P/O	CARROLL Wilfrid Patrick	21-09-41	144 Sqn	1162808	Sgt	CHEESMAN William Rowland	28-12-41	144 Sqn
635295	Sgt	CARSON Arthur Stewart	28-06-41	10 Sqn	951748	Sgt	CHEETHAM George Thomas	3-06-41	50 Sqn
1062319	Sgt	CARSON Robert Samuel	27-11-41	14 OTU	46090	P/O	CHEETHAM William Harris	1-11-41	49 Sqn
1056065	Sgt	CARSTAIRS Alexander	20-09-41	142 Sqn	751489	Sgt	CHELL John Francis	3-05-41	101 Sqn
68170	P/O	CARTER Anthony	21-12-41	106 Sqn	808036	F/S	CHESMAN George Hall	8-11-41	7 Sqn
1161981	Sgt	CARTER Anthony Joseph	13-10-41	207 Sqn	911216	Sgt	CHILD Bertram John	23-07-41	110 Sqn
650974	Sgt	CARTER Edward Frederick 'Ted' [Canada]	8-02-41	12 Sqn	631792	Sgt	CHILD Frank Cecil [Canada]	29-08-41	7 Sqn
					60569	P/O	CHILDS Brian Austin	15-04-41	102 Sqn
1375286	Sgt	CARTER Edwin Rowland	11-12-41	57 Sqn	104444	P/O	CHILVERS John Ernest	29-08-41	7 Sqn

Service No	Rank	Name	Date	Squadron
939762	Sgt	CHINN Edward James	24-03-41	21 Sqn
921063	Sgt	CHIPPERFIELD Charles Townsend	30-06-41	50 Sqn
87021	P/O	CHIPPERFIELD Gordon Frederick	8-04-41	61 Sqn
104513	P/O	CHISHOLM John Norman [Australia]	27-12-41	77 Sqn
79509	F/O	CHISHOLM Robert Stanley [New Zealand]	13-06-41	103 Sqn
970071	Sgt	CHORLTON Hugh Gartside	28-06-41	77 Sqn
982230	Sgt	CHRISP Robert Brown	31-07-41	144 Sqn
29160	W/C	CHRISTIAN Twice MiD Arnold Louis	8-05-41	105 Sqn
1100680	Sgt	CHRISTIE Ernest Tastard	15-10-41	57 Sqn
971579	F/S	CHRISTIE George	25-07-41	10 Sqn
921144	Sgt	CHRISTIE John	25-08-41	144 Sqn
908072	Sgt	CHRISTOPHER Kenneth William Marshall	8-07-41	77 Sqn
1257675	Sgt	CHRISTY Charles Gordon Alexander	28-07-41	21 OTU
940378	Sgt	CHURCH Frederick William	17-10-41	15 OTU
748425	Sgt	CHURCH Philip Johnson	18-04-41	77 Sqn
37036	S/L	CHURCHILL Arthur John Frank	21-09-41	7 Flt
930774	Sgt	CLABBURN-DETREZ Dennis Arthur	15-08-41	115 Sqn
104485	P/O	CLAMP Ronald Richards	6-11-41	22 OTU
33160	S/L	CLARK Anthony William John	17-05-41	149 Sqn
990778	AC1	CLARK Arthur Douglas	1-08-41	44 Sqn
538094	Sgt	CLARK Donald Grant	3-06-41	7 Sqn
947880	Sgt	CLARK George Dixon	19-08-41	83 Sqn
69469	P/O	CLARK Hugh Maxwell	12-08-41	82 Sqn
1061082	Sgt	CLARK John Alexander Dallas	31-08-41	83 Sqn
748437	Sgt	CLARK Kenneth Lynch	17-04-41	16 OTU
947450	Sgt	CLARK Kenneth William Charlton	16-09-41	57 Sqn
101050	P/O	CLARK Patrick Hourston Moar	5-11-41	18 Sqn
209448	F/S	CLARK Percy Ernest	17-12-41	138 Sqn
918535	Sgt	CLARK Philip George	27-12-41	77 Sqn
755818	Sgt	CLARK Raymond	1-03-41	78 Sqn
1208623	Sgt	CLARK Reginald John	24-12-41	26 CFlt
956053	Sgt	CLARK Ronald Thornton	6-08-41	144 Sqn
755398	Sgt	CLARKE Arthur George	29-08-41	61 Sqn
744913	Sgt	CLARKE Charles John	30-04-41	11 OTU
1162832	Sgt	CLARKE Edward John	25-08-41	83 Sqn
936598	Sgt	CLARKE Ernest	3-06-41	7 Sqn
100064	P/O	CLARKE Herbert Mitchell	15-10-41	139 Sqn
639565	Sgt	CLARKE John Butterworth	24-03-41	7 Sqn
1166161	Sgt	CLARKE Reginald Kenneth	19-08-41	114 Sqn
745499	Sgt	CLARKE Richard William Tudor	2-03-41	61 Sqn
1165625	Sgt	CLARKE Terence Vincent Gerard	11-08-41	25 OTU
800570	Sgt	CLARKE William Charles	8-11-41	102 Sqn
630870	Sgt	CLARKE William James	27-06-41	102 Sqn
1376787	Sgt	CLARKSON Henry Paul [Chile]	14-07-41	75 Sqn
1258554	Sgt	CLAY Antony Dennis Warden	18-08-41	14 OTU
951057	Sgt	CLAYTON John	7-07-41	139 Sqn
745519	Sgt	CLAYTON Leslie Ernest	4-02-41	16 OTU
61217	P/O	CLAYTON Leslie Sheridon	7-06-41	105 Sqn
911382	Sgt	CLEBURNE Patrick Brian Neil	28-06-41	142 Sqn
754863	Sgt	CLEGG John Verdun	8-07-41	58 Sqn
643076	LAC	CLEMENTS Colin Harvey John [Australia]	29-09-41	10 Sqn
701654	F/S	CLIFFORD-READE Alfred Pearsall	15-04-41	102 Sqn
521403	Sgt	CLIFTON Reginald Jack	10-07-41	7 Sqn
906677	Sgt	CLIFTON Talbot Charles Cyril	17-04-41	149 Sqn
616589	F/S	CLINCH DFM John Joseph	27-06-41	97 Sqn
968041	Sgt	CLINTON William Robert	24-03-41	21 Sqn
746799	Sgt	CLOUGH Alan Raymond	12-02-41	99 Sqn
959158	Sgt	CLOVER Jack Samuel	27-06-41	40 Sqn
970463	Sgt	CLOW David John [Canada]	9-07-41	78 Sqn
629430	Sgt	COAKES Albert Edward	13-08-41	207 Sqn
907743	Sgt	COATES Alfred [Canada]	2-03-41	10 Sqn
745552	Sgt	COATES Kenneth Wilson	18-05-41	218 Sqn
953084	Sgt	COATESWORTH Norman	27-12-41	110 Sqn
754447	Sgt	COBB Victor Albert	14-04-41	21 Sqn
88025	P/O	COCHRANE William Ernest [Eire]	8-04-41	14 OTU
614827	F/S	COCKBURN William	23-07-41	15 Sqn
1062466	Sgt	COCKING Francis	12-10-41	21 Sqn
1066470	Sgt	COCKRAM Leslie Gordon	17-10-41	15 OTU
84690	P/O	COLBORNE Cyril George	29-06-41	61 Sqn
1282764	Sgt	COLBOURNE Hugh Anthony	26-06-41	19 OTU
45444	P/O	COLBOURNE Victor Charles Henry	13-10-41	15 Sqn
908710	Sgt	COLE Arthur Thomas	28-06-41	7 Sqn
26101	W/C	COLE Francis Charles	8-04-41	102 Sqn
755513	F/S	COLE George Arthur	5-05-41	21 Sqn
1163918	Sgt	COLE Ronald Leslie	3-09-41	44 Sqn
932991	Sgt	COLE Wallace Howard	26-08-41	40 Sqn
1107286	Sgt	COLEMAN Noel Eric Henry	9-07-41	35 Sqn
1100623	Sgt	COLLIER Alfred	28-12-41	144 Sqn
1261192	Sgt	COLLIER Samuel Stephen John	22-09-41	114 Sqn
581204	F/S	COLLINGE MiD Robert Victor	26-07-41	35 Sqn
82972	F/O	COLLINS Albert Henry	28-08-41	21 Sqn
1254914	Sgt	COLLINS Charles Lloyd Allan	16-11-41	218 Sqn
905359	F/S	COLLINS John	30-11-41	35 Sqn
40082	F/L	COLLINS John Kenneth	28-06-41	7 Sqn
952836	Sgt	COLLINS Ronald Howard George	15-10-41	40 Sqn
617140	Sgt	COLLINS Walter Norman	25-08-41	35 Sqn
87034	P/O	COLLIS DFM Gordon	19-03-41	101 Sqn
745249	Sgt	COLLIS Paul Fraser	12-10-41	40 Sqn
566133	Sgt	COLLOPY John Henry	12-03-41	218 Sqn
748379	F/S	COLLYER Walter Robert Laidlow	13-06-41	25 OTU
1187047	Sgt	COLMER James Cecil Valentine	20-09-41	226 Sqn
553425	Sgt	COLSON Frederick Arnold	4-02-41	106 Sqn
82973	P/O	COMBER-HIGGS Edward Dmitri	30-11-41	58 Sqn
1251975	Sgt	COMINS Thomas Edward	22-07-41	10 OTU
1379298	Sgt	COMPTON Lewis John	14-10-41	207 Sqn
968155	Sgt	CONDIE Andrew Young	20-10-41	458 Sqn
755735	F/S	CONEY Kenneth	6-07-41	49 Sqn
932380	Sgt	CONIBEAR David Henry	17-07-41	75 Sqn
939928	F/S	CONLON Patrick	7-07-41	105 Sqn
989237	Sgt	CONN John Robert	18-12-41	97 Sqn
971904	Sgt	CONN William Alford	14-08-41	15 Sqn
1105549	Sgt	CONNELL Robert Alexander Crawford	19-06-41	16 OTU
1060539	Sgt	CONNELL William	16-09-41	103 Sqn
974039	Sgt	CONNOLLY James Aloysius	22-07-41	44 Sqn
1017550	Sgt	COOGAN Laurence Dominick	15-07-41	104 Sqn
748179	Sgt	COOK Anthony Leonard Roger	13-03-41	102 Sqn
648600	Sgt	COOK Clifford Fletcher	19-06-41	78 Sqn
87387	P/O	COOK Frank Henry	21-04-41	99 Sqn
746999	Sgt	COOK Geoffrey Ernest	16-04-41	13 OTU
988368	Sgt	COOK George Alfred	8-09-41	115 Sqn
1051933	Sgt	COOK James Roland	6-08-41	144 Sqn
740487	F/S	COOK Neil Caldwell	16-07-41	115 Sqn
60811	P/O	COOK Peter Trevor-Roper	22-04-41	18 Sqn
754743	Sgt	COOKE Albert	29-05-41	78 Sqn
61277	P/O	COOKE Arthur Allen	18-06-41	14 OTU
967092	Sgt	COOKE Evan Roy	18-03-41	149 Sqn
106879	P/O	COOKE John Charles	10-12-41	15 OTU
968394	Sgt	COOKE Ronald Llewellyn	15-11-41	99 Sqn
742792	Sgt	COOKE Thomas Henry	24-03-41	82 Sqn
944245	Sgt	COOPER Albert Bertram	24-07-41	144 Sqn
77963	F/O	COOPER Albert Edward	10-03-41	35 Sqn
1167421	Sgt	COOPER Alfred Richard	30-09-41	115 Sqn
1254701	Sgt	COOPER Arthur William	11-10-41	58 Sqn
87050	P/O	COOPER Ernest Ronald Peter Shackle	26-07-41	35 Sqn
932086	Sgt	COOPER Harold James	26-11-41	214 Sqn
551283	F/S	COOPER John Stewart	21-10-41	207 Sqn
749383	Sgt	COOPER Kenneth John	2-03-41	51 Sqn
61279	P/O	COOPER Kenneth Tyrrell	23-10-41	50 Sqn
740693	Sgt	COOPER Kingsley Gerard	2-03-41	61 Sqn

64325	P/O	COOPER Nicholas Aitken	4-07-41	82 Sqn	1379167	Sgt	CRAWFORD James	7-12-41	61 Sqn
1154317	Sgt	COPE John Anthony Stephens	7-06-41	10 Sqn	745258	Sgt	CRAWFORD John Geoffrey	15-03-41	3 GTrgFlt
956081	Sgt	COPELAND Reginald	4-07-41	105 Sqn	1006701	Sgt	CRAWLEY Roland	28-11-41	408 Sqn
903447	Sgt	COPLEY Alfred Thomas	29-05-41	78 Sqn	944322	Sgt	CRAWSHAW Luther	18-05-41	218 Sqn
1356487	AC1	COPNEIGH James	5-08-41	Oakington	61989	P/O	CRICHTON Cecil Ernest [Canada]	17-06-41	51 Sqn
955476	Sgt	COPSEY Tom	8-11-41	44 Sqn	997005	Sgt	CRICHTON David George	17-05-41	25 OTU
1163172	Sgt	CORBETT Guy Trevor	12-06-41	25 OTU	551030	F/S	CRICHTON William McLaren	13-07-41	50 Sqn
977033	Sgt	CORBETT John Turner	8-08-41	15 Sqn	1453008	AC2	CRISP Bearnard Douglas	12-12-41	50 Sqn
910665	Sgt	CORBETT Peter Barnard	8-09-41	90 Sqn	619801	F/S	CRITCHLEY Ronald	24-07-41	103 Sqn
82974	P/O	CORBETT William Howard	19-06-41	16 OTU	978005	Sgt	CRITCHLOW Alfred	13-08-41	76 Sqn
1282595	Sgt	CORDY Peter Morton	5-09-41	12 OTU	747874	F/S	CROCKER Bryan	2-07-41	12 Sqn
65533	P/O	CORFIELD James Wilmot	12-08-41	21 Sqn	911566	Sgt	CROCKER Frank Wilson	11-12-41	35 Sqn
754931	Sgt	CORLETT DFM Fred	22-07-41	10 OTU	1164935	Sgt	CROCOMBE John	15-09-41	21 Sqn
1101047	Sgt	CORMACK Alexander Adam	29-08-41	40 Sqn	1057218	Sgt	CROMPTON George Arthur [Canada]	7-07-41	19 OTU
624289	F/S	CORNFORTH James William	21-11-41	109 Sqn	969953	Sgt	CRONE Thomas William Archibald	17-05-41	77 Sqn
1008479	Sgt	CORNISH George Herbert	27-11-41	144 Sqn	101049	P/O	CROOK Frank	25-07-41	11 OTU
749328	F/S	CORNWALL George Simpson	18-04-41	110 Sqn	909112	Sgt	CROOK Lynford Colin	6-07-41	144 Sqn
580641	Sgt	CORRIGAN Eugene Patrick [Eire]	2-03-41	61 Sqn	636137	Sgt	CROOKS Arthur	8-02-41	12 Sqn
1166447	Sgt	COSGRAVE Robert Gerald	13-06-41	15 OTU	923910	Sgt	CROSBIE Percy George	24-11-41	115 Sqn
968259	Sgt	COSGROVE Alfred Edward	11-10-41	12 Sqn	1216273	AC2	CROSS Michael Fraser	21-05-41	83 Sqn
545351	Sgt	COSTER Alfred George	9-04-41	149 Sqn	747741	Sgt	CROSS Peter James	16-04-41	13 OTU
1181894	Sgt	COSTER Frederick George	10-09-41	25 OTU	993388	Sgt	CROSS Walter	3-07-41	144 Sqn
741754	F/S	COTTERELL Anthony Robert	13-08-41	207 Sqn	41154	F/O	CROSSE William Peter	12-03-41	218 Sqn
1162559	Sgt	COTTERELL Norman Ivor	6-11-41	83 Sqn	1182834	Sgt	CROSSLEY Edwin	24-12-41	107 Sqn
930649	Sgt	COTTINGHAM James Charles	15-08-41	218 Sqn	925452	Sgt	CROSSLEY Francis Kenneth	3-09-41	57 Sqn
945560	Sgt	COTTON Godfrey Allenby Douglas	24-06-41	214 Sqn	903426	Sgt	CROSSWELL William Arthur	25-03-41	20 OTU
60546	P/O	COTTON Graham Hardy	17-05-41	149 Sqn	755399	Sgt	CROUCH David Arthur Donald	4-03-41	106 Sqn
1164422	Sgt	COUCH Arthur Frederick Conroy	31-10-41	77 Sqn	63106	P/O	CROUCHER John Rhodes	7-09-41	102 Sqn
929219	Sgt	COULBY Frank Gerald	1-07-41	102 Sqn	759081	Sgt	CROWE Edgar	6-11-41	144 Sqn
538866	Sgt	COULT Ernest Joseph	12-03-41	218 Sqn	986890	Sgt	CROWSLEY William John Vincent	7-08-41	214 Sqn
1162807	Sgt	COUNTER Michael John	12-10-41	21 Sqn	1206005	Sgt	CROZIER Charles Chilton	11-11-41	13 OTU
640819	Sgt	COURTMAN Thomas Samuel	2-03-41	21 Sqn	749336	Sgt	CRUICKSHANK David Alexander	11-02-41	49 Sqn
965050	Sgt	COUSER DFM Robert James	15-01-41	58 Sqn	87357	F/O	CRUICKSHANK David James Williamson	21-11-41	109 Sqn
88405	P/O	COUSINS Herbert Leslie	24-07-41	144 Sqn	1051632	Sgt	CRUICKSHANK John Milne Rigg	26-07-41	35 Sqn
543971	F/S	COUSINS James	9-06-41	51 Sqn	33364	F/L	CRUICKSHANK DFC* Raymond Alfred	3-05-41	7 Sqn
988256	Sgt	COUSINS Oliver	18-02-41	19 OTU	34191	W/C	CRUICKSHANKS DFC Grahame Lawrence [South Africa]	8-09-41	214 Sqn
41667	F/O	COUTTS Desmond Christian Frederick	3-01-41	102 Sqn	82666	F/O	CRUMP Ernest Edwin Gordon [South Africa]	15-09-41	207 Sqn
751961	Sgt	COVEY William Walter	7-12-41	104 Sqn	43027	P/O	CRUSH Richard Hope [New Zealand]	27-04-41	83 Sqn
743097	Sgt	COWAN Alfred Julius	11-04-41	1419 Flt	1061578	Sgt	CRYER Noel Desmond	5-08-41	20 OTU
923093	Sgt	COWELL George Albert	18-08-41	50 Sqn	787433	Sgt	CTVRTLIK Jan [Czechoslovakia]	19-07-41	311 Sqn
1068173	Sgt	COWELL Wilfred John	30-08-41	115 Sqn	968654	Sgt	CUBBON William Henry	21-10-41	207 Sqn
1062575	Sgt	COWIN Norman Richard	29-08-41	7 Sqn	72480	F/O	CUBITT Eaton Geoffrey	13-03-41	102 Sqn
87384	P/O	COWINGS George Hendry	22-03-41	18 Sqn	1002371	Sgt	CULLEN Aidan Francis	12-10-41	18 Sqn
754176	Sgt	COX Alfred Douglas	2-03-41	61 Sqn	995688	Sgt	CULLEN Edward	12-08-41	9 Sqn
623823	Sgt	COX Eddy Stewart	7-09-41	44 Sqn	553001	Sgt	CULLERNE Mervyn Wyndham	7-11-41	57 Sqn
939111	Sgt	COX Gerald	13-08-41	104 Sqn	947158	Sgt	CULLEY William John	7-08-41	150 Sqn
648868	F/S	COX John Alfred Arthur	14-08-41	35 Sqn	748640	Sgt	CULLUM Jack Leonard	24-06-41	76 Sqn
921698	Sgt	COX John James	24-07-41	103 Sqn	1182529	Sgt	CUMING William John	8-12-41	107 Sqn
923770	Sgt	COX Leslie Roy	16-09-41	44 Sqn	988003	Sgt	CUNDILL William Bernard	7-07-41	139 Sqn
64874	P/O	COX Reginald	2-08-41	405 Sqn	61502	P/O	CUNNING James Erskine	8-08-41	83 Sqn
751616	F/S	COX Robert Louis	14-06-41	110 Sqn	970664	Sgt	CUNNINGHAM Andrew Hannay 'Drew'	4-02-41	16 OTU
68752	P/O	COX Roy le Masurier	8-09-41	115 Sqn	88868	P/O	CUNNINGHAM John Charles	30-05-41	50 Sqn
1101054	Sgt	COYLE Douglas Edward	29-09-41	7 Sqn	906143	Sgt	CUNNINGHAM Walbey John	8-04-41	14 OTU
82975	P/O	CRABB George James Leonard	3-08-41	218 Sqn	87051	P/O	CURL John Smethurst	30-06-41	14 OTU
540277	F/S	CRAIG MiD Albert Douglas Foch	8-09-41	104 Sqn	82171	P/O	CURLEY Joseph George	8-04-41	44 Sqn
974166	Sgt	CRAIG David Carnegie	14-03-41	10 OTU	755911	F/S	CURR DFM Angus Douglas Willis	2-08-41	82 Sqn
903947	F/S	CRAIG Douglas John Robert	21-05-41	107 Sqn	974050	Sgt	CURRIE MiD Hugh	17-08-41	97 Sqn
41832	F/L	CRAIG MiD Frederick Henry [New Zealand]	24-07-41	101 Sqn	88199	F/O	CURRIE Lorne	29-05-41	11 OTU
947814	Sgt	CRAIG Robert Samuel Carson	24-07-41	75 Sqn	63085	P/O	CURTIS Bernard Castle	31-07-41	99 Sqn
87648	P/O	CRAIGMILE Harry George	4-02-41	20 OTU	912441	AC1	CURTIS Harry John	11-04-41	Stradishall
1181874	Sgt	CRANE Gerald	17-08-41	99 Sqn	961776	F/S	CURTIS Ronald William	13-10-41	50 Sqn
945868	Sgt	CRANE John Stewart	8-04-41	40 Sqn	88456	P/O	CUSHION John Peter Boston	3-09-41	35 Sqn
1154434	Sgt	CRANSTON David Charles	29-10-41	106 Sqn					
968368	Sgt	CRAVEN Terence	9-08-41	61 Sqn					
966524	F/S	CRAVEN Walter Edward	8-04-41	102 Sqn					
984906	Sgt	CRAWFORD Harry	15-05-41	16 OTU					

745758	Sgt	CUSWORTH John Philip	9-04-41	214 Sqn	903312	Sgt	DEAN Kenneth Albert	6-08-41	51 Sqn
941260	Sgt	CUTLER Albert Charles	12-08-41	18 Sqn	964554	Sgt	DEAN Raymond	7-11-41	99 Sqn
43028	P/O	CUTMORE Jack [Canada]	21-04-41	106 Sqn	933354	Sgt	DEAN Tom	16-06-41	18 Sqn
926352	Sgt	CUTMORE John Henry Howard	6-08-41	144 Sqn	968587	Sgt	DEANE Clarence Hubert	3-05-41	101 Sqn
754997	Sgt	DACEY Frank	31-08-41	83 Sqn	550318	Cpl	DEARDEN Arnold Delday	9-05-41	Waddington
1206638	AC2	DALE Arthur	15-05-41	35 Sqn	1110712	Sgt	DEARDEN Frederick Harry Ewart	14-10-41	115 Sqn
26050	W/C	DALE Herbert Reginald	11-05-41	15 Sqn	1020220	Sgt	DEARNLEY Hubert	25-07-41	405 Sqn
751528	F/S	DALE James Ronald	30-06-41	7 Sqn	1113660	Sgt	DEGES Carl	5-08-41	103 Sqn
87044	P/O	DALGLIESH William Ian	4-03-41	7 Sqn	939302	Sgt	DENNING James Albert	22-12-41	28 CFlt
980425	Sgt	DALLEY George William Neill	15-11-41	15 OTU	922218	Sgt	DENNIS-SMITHER Derek Godfrey	30-07-41	139 Sqn
754100	Sgt	DALTON Kenneth	26-02-41	82 Sqn	990446	Sgt	DENT Leslie	18-06-41	14 OTU
100550	P/O	DAMES Geoffrey Laurence	5-09-41	12 OTU	580768	F/S	DERBYSHIRE John	8-04-41	102 Sqn
1154126	Sgt	DANCE Harry Edward	20-10-41	99 Sqn	961536	Sgt	DEW Brian Ernest	11-11-41	115 Sqn
1255075	Sgt	DANE Stanley William	8-11-41	149 Sqn	745497	Sgt	DEWIN Ronald George James	7-07-41	105 Sqn
1377216	Sgt	DANGERFIELD Peter Edward Hay	12-08-41	149 Sqn	903468	Sgt	DEWING Maurice Stafford	30-04-41	21 Sqn
618264	Sgt	DANIEL George Cedric	13-03-41	214 Sqn	1283306	Sgt	DEXTER Amos Richard Albert	8-11-41	97 Sqn
1160552	Sgt	DANIELS Albert Frederick	5-11-41	18 Sqn	778294	Sgt	de BRATH Dennis Napier Neville [Rhodesia]	3-09-41	44 Sqn
68738	P/O	DANIELS Harry Joseph	26-07-41	10 Sqn					
1053117	Sgt	DARBYSHIRE John	29-09-41	99 Sqn	905830	Sgt	DE ROECK Leo Frank	25-02-41	11 OTU
998985	Sgt	DARCY Desmond Philip	22-12-41	107 Sqn	1173902	Sgt	DICK Alexander Ronald James	26-08-41	82 Sqn
82976	P/O	DARE Edgar Alan	5-08-41	20 OTU	33238	S/L	DICKENSON Peter George Scott	8-11-41	51 Sqn
759296	Sgt	DARNELL Frederick Edward	1-03-41	144 Sqn	43029	P/O	DICKIE David Gray [New Zealand]	16-06-41	106 Sqn
629252	Cpl	DARRAH Norman Graham	12-10-41	19 OTU	79538	F/L	DICKINSON DFC John	13-03-41	110 Sqn
917066	Sgt	DARTNALL George Herbert	9-11-41	9 Sqn	1191423	Sgt	DICKINSON William Alexander Caleb		
906184	Sgt	DAUNCEY William George Hugh	9-05-41	149 Sqn				17-10-41	15 OTU
1163587	Sgt	DAVEY Peter John	15-08-41	104 Sqn	639545	Sgt	DICKSON John George Thomson	14-06-41	44 Sqn
1253258	Sgt	DAVEY William Richard	2-08-41	101 Sqn	1304338	Sgt	DIGGORY John	3-07-41	106 Sqn
88683	P/O	DAVID Mervyn James	1-03-41	78 Sqn	1375644	Sgt	DIMOND Leonard Gordon Charles	30-11-41	101 Sqn
937250	F/S	DAVID Raymond John	6-08-41	104 Sqn	87616	P/O	DITTRICH Frantisek K. [Czechoslovakia]		
70160	F/O	DAVIDSON John Peter Archibald	4-01-41	99 Sqn				23-10-41	311 Sqn
971260	Sgt	DAVIDSON Rudolf Dey	27-06-41	102 Sqn	936940	Sgt	DIX Jack	24-11-41	115 Sqn
620056	Sgt	DAVIE Alexander James	30-06-41	35 Sqn	1106166	Sgt	DIXON Colin James	13-07-41	15 OTU
626848	Sgt	DAVIES Alan	5-08-41	50 Sqn	62269	P/O	DIXON-SPAIN Peter	18-05-41	25 OTU
537136	F/S	DAVIES Basil Douglas	26-08-41	88 Sqn	946585	Sgt	DOBINSON Laurence	28-06-41	77 Sqn
1251345	Sgt	DAVIES David Emrys	18-08-41	16 OTU	84883	P/O	DOBSON John Maxwell	23-08-41	114 Sqn
1375288	Sgt	DAVIES Evan Aneurin	12-08-41	17 OTU	1104391	Sgt	DODD Frank Craighton	4-08-41	218 Sqn
1376829	Sgt	DAVIES George Clarence	30-11-41	58 Sqn	527613	Cpl	DODD John Desmond	14-05-41	57 Sqn
924555	Sgt	DAVIES George Devereux	17-07-41	13 OTU	940286	F/S	DODD Victor Stuart	12-05-41	58 Sqn
916408	Cpl	DAVIES George Ian Frederick	26-10-41	40 Sqn	62022	P/O	DODDS-FORREST John	25-06-41	214 Sqn
748617	Sgt	DAVIES Gordon Ewart	10-07-41	40 Sqn	347541	W/O	DOE Walter	5-07-41	49 Sqn
1254976	Sgt	DAVIES Howard Stanley	28-08-41	14 OTU	42207	F/O	DOGGETT Charles William	17-01-41	10 OTU
977311	Sgt	DAVIES John William Thomas	29-08-41	405 Sqn	787820	Sgt	DOLEJS Adolf [Czechoslovakia]	2-07-41	311 Sqn
568241	Sgt	DAVIES Kenneth Godfrey Howard	18-07-41	15 Sqn	1257597	Sgt	DONALD John Abbott	21-06-41	218 Sqn
103505	P/O	DAVIES Kenneth William	29-08-41	78 Sqn	1279832	AC2	DONCICH Joseph	12-11-41	5 Group
652999	F/S	DAVIES Norman Hinton	8-09-41	90 Sqn	653474	Sgt	DONNELLY John Gordon	8-04-41	61 Sqn
1251274	Sgt	DAVIES Peter Arnold	19-08-41	114 Sqn	643184	F/S	DONNELLY John Todd	2-06-41	50 Sqn
751130	Sgt	DAVIES Ronald	6-09-41	75 Sqn	1151173	Sgt	DONOGHUE Stephen Philip	15-08-41	51 Sqn
580453	F/S	DAVIES DFM Thomas Clifford	4-07-41	226 Sqn	951120	Sgt	DONOVAN Joseph Arthur	21-05-41	110 Sqn
990743	Sgt	DAVIES Trevor Vaughan	13-07-41	15 OTU	1195390	AC1	DONOVAN William Edward	17-09-41	115 Sqn
74467	S/L	DAVIES William	8-09-41	214 Sqn	91199	F/O	DOORLY Patrick Braund	7-08-41	20 OTU
924914	Sgt	DAVIS Albert Charles Arthur	8-11-41	149 Sqn	101480	P/O	DOTCHIN Norman	17-08-41	99 Sqn
742310	Sgt	DAVIS Alan	16-11-41	19 OTU	1113679	Sgt	DOTT William	6-11-41	16 OTU
60122	P/O	DAVIS Ernest Rene	14-08-41	83 Sqn	1378433	Sgt	DOUGLAS Benjamin	25-08-41	78 Sqn
800559	Sgt	DAVIS Frank Edward	29-04-41	82 Sqn	89060	P/O	DOVE Cyril Bertie	15-02-41	15 Sqn
1181613	Sgt	DAVIS Kenneth Aubrey	27-12-41	114 Sqn	777809	AC2	DOWLE Edward James [Rhodesia]	27-08-41	44 Sqn
927362	Sgt	DAVIS William Albert James	21-06-41	218 Sqn	754022	Sgt	DOWLING Harold Joseph	4-04-41	77 Sqn
951301	Sgt	DAWE Mark Seymour	12-09-41	19 OTU	549726	Sgt	DOWLING Rupert Oscar	30-11-41	142 Sqn
41262	F/L	DAWES Edward	20-12-41	15 OTU	911266	Sgt	DOWNES Henry Thomas Herbert	28-04-41	101 Sqn
926208	Sgt	DAWSON Edward Kerfoot	18-05-41	25 OTU	749418	F/S	DOWSE Ernest Edward	3-09-41	61 Sqn
84729	P/O	DAWSON Norman Frederick	28-04-41	114 Sqn	1261133	Sgt	DRAKE Francis Ernest [New Zealand]	16-06-41	15 OTU
87361	P/O	DAWSON Raymond Woodrow	13-06-41	102 Sqn	40214	S/L	DRAKES David Baron	1-11-41	49 Sqn
102116	P/O	DAY Arthur Edward	26-10-41	88 Sqn	755119	Sgt	DRANE Albert Patrick	30-06-41	50 Sqn
1154357	AC1	DAY Charles	11-08-41	Oakington	46121	P/O	DREW Edgar Frederick	25-08-41	7 Sqn
758035	Sgt	DAY Donald	9-04-41	57 Sqn	45356	P/O	DREW William Edward	13-04-41	19 OTU
1161141	Sgt	DAY Frederick Ernest Victor	12-10-41	82 Sqn	100033	P/O	DREWSEN Jeffrey	15-08-41	104 Sqn
1375181	Sgt	DAY Maurice Ronald	13-10-41	75 Sqn	1258153	Sgt	DROBIG Eric Geoffrey Raymond	15-09-41	21 Sqn
1014105	Sgt	DEADMAN Kenneth David	16-11-41	218 Sqn	954514	Sgt	DRUMMOND Simon Fullard	7-07-41	10 OTU
926810	Sgt	DEAN Alan Walter	9-05-41	214 Sqn	639718	Sgt	DRURY Arthur	18-04-41	61 Sqn

Number	Rank	Name	Date	Unit
968019	Sgt	DRURY Jack Burton	16-11-41	218 Sqn
25055	W/C	DRYSDALE DSO James Kenneth Montague	15-09-41	305 Sqn
999577	Sgt	DRYSDALE Thomas Andrew Hillock	30-06-41	107 Sqn
967901	Sgt	DUCKERS Glyn George	5-07-41	51 Sqn
904067	Sgt	DUCKMANTON George William	30-08-41	76 Sqn
77116	F/O	DUCKWORTH Lawrence	3-09-41	61 Sqn
745531	F/S	DUFFIELD Henry William	15-11-41	458 Sqn
745565	Sgt	DUFFUS George Morton	25-05-41	18 Sqn
553936	Sgt	DUFFY Patrick James	7-09-41	49 Sqn
86635	P/O	DUFTY Robert James	21-02-41	16 OTU
84034	P/O	DUGDALE Cyril Peter	22-03-41	105 Sqn
1376520	Sgt	DUGGAN Rennie Frank	2-11-41	78 Sqn
982155	Sgt	DUGUID Duncan Coutts	1-11-41	102 Sqn
1015615	Sgt	DUKE Ronald Walter	15-08-41	115 Sqn
641010	Sgt	DUNCAN Robert Fortune Jamieson [Canada]	15-01-41	58 Sqn
948043	Sgt	DUNDAS Gordon Bannerman	27-12-41	104 Sqn
986084	Sgt	DUNDAS Richard	8-11-41	75 Sqn
995903	Sgt	DUNDON Richard Anthony	12-10-41	40 Sqn
952912	Sgt	DUNKLEY Ronald William	30-09-41	77 Sqn
1005738	Sgt	DUNLOP Derek Frederick	12-09-41	75 Sqn
44816	P/O	DUNN George Bannatyne	26-08-41	88 Sqn
86391	P/O	DUNN John Robert Leslie	4-07-41	99 Sqn
1109715	Sgt	DUNN Robert	30-06-41	35 Sqn
987476	Sgt	DUNN William	10-12-41	13 OTU
978199	Sgt	DUNNE Desmond Colbert Kent	3-07-41	106 Sqn
754532	Sgt	DUNNING John	18-04-41	21 Sqn
959420	Sgt	DUPREE David Arthur	4-07-41	107 Sqn
950610	Sgt	DURHAM Eric Victor	7-09-41	49 Sqn
64280	P/O	DURHAM Victor Digby	13-08-41	76 Sqn
650617	F/S	DURTNALL DFM Rex Ronald Boyce	31-07-41	61 Sqn
787825	Sgt	DUSEK Frantisek [Czechoslovakia]	25-05-41	311 Sqn
1052828	Sgt	DUTHIE John Davidson	26-08-41	40 Sqn
921363	Sgt	DUTTON Gordon David Hankinson	11-11-41	115 Sqn
905200	Sgt	DU PLESSIS Stephen Arnold [South Africa]	18-04-41	114 Sqn
1187087	Sgt	DU PRE Phillip Peter Francis	22-10-41	150 Sqn
905235	Sgt	DVORJETZ George Arthur	16-07-41	18 Sqn
1160202	Sgt	DYER DFM Eric	2-09-41	44 Sqn
62253	P/O	DYER DFM MiD Hedley James Allen	16-09-41	15 Sqn
552130	Sgt	DYER Lawrence Stanley	13-06-41	77 Sqn
934408	Sgt	DYMOTT Basil Christie	14-10-41	40 Sqn
1288762	Sgt	D'ARCY James Marcus	8-11-41	49 Sqn
747876	Sgt	DE'ATH Ernest William	2-02-41	101 Sqn
754504	Sgt	EADES John Henry 'Jack'	23-02-41	115 Sqn
959010	Sgt	EAKIN John Andrew	10-09-41	19 OTU
626196	F/S	EAMES DFM Peter Kershaw	26-04-41	21 Sqn
970686	Sgt	EARLEY Joseph Gerald	1-03-41	78 Sqn
904166	Sgt	EARLY Fergus Francis	12-02-41	149 Sqn
631813	AC1	EARNSHAW Denis	18-04-41	214 Sqn
957727	Sgt	EARP Alfred William	25-07-41	10 Sqn
1252258	Sgt	EASTMAN Charles Reginald	24-10-41	40 Sqn
45069	P/O	EASTWOOD John Hastings	30-07-41	19 OTU
958669	Sgt	EATON Frederick	30-12-41	76 Sqn
1199104	Sgt	EATON William Arthur	15-11-41	114 Sqn
977347	Sgt	EAVES Albert	10-07-41	77 Sqn
937441	Sgt	EBRILL Thomas Frederick	24-07-41	104 Sqn
1257328	Sgt	EBSWORTH Ronald William	30-11-41	214 Sqn
63486	P/O	ECCLES Gordon Scott	1-09-41	99 Sqn
39377	S/L	EDDISON DFC Frank Leslie Herbert	9-05-41	214 Sqn
906009	Sgt	EDEN Leslie Ralph	4-04-41	83 Sqn
1152264	Sgt	EDGE Walter Donald	25-08-41	78 Sqn
1030367	AC2	EDGECOMBE John	7-08-41	20 OTU
942975	LAC	EDGINTON Stanley	15-06-41	Wyton
37087	S/L	EDINGER Peter Francis	8-09-41	12 Sqn
1253211	Sgt	EDIS Kenneth George	15-10-41	40 Sqn
969492	Sgt	EDMOND David Smith	27-12-41	101 Sqn
1163120	Sgt	EDMONDS James Oswald	30-11-41	142 Sqn
1163977	Sgt	EDWARDS Allan Clifford	11-10-41	75 Sqn
937838	Sgt	EDWARDS Norman Victor	6-07-41	144 Sqn
63840	P/O	EDWARDS Peter Bernard Gill [Australia]	10-07-41	40 Sqn
979039	Sgt	EDWARDS Ray Berysford	28-06-41	77 Sqn
1160972	Sgt	EDWARDS Stanley Thomas Frank	30-06-41	107 Sqn
909506	Sgt	EDWARDS Sydney Cyril	17-08-41	44 Sqn
44819	P/O	EDWARDS Tudor Gwynn	28-08-41	88 Sqn
636523	Sgt	EGAR Edward	22-05-41	44 Sqn
914938	AC1	EGGLETON Gordon Idris	12-05-41	58 Sqn
754780	Sgt	ELDER Alexander Grahame	13-03-41	214 Sqn
84884	P/O	ELDER Esmond Clive	30-07-41	139 Sqn
978048	Sgt	ELDER Hugh Miller	7-09-41	57 Sqn
650805	F/S	ELKINGTON James	27-06-41	97 Sqn
41159	F/O	ELLIOT Charles Hamerton	21-03-41	150 Sqn
754431	Sgt	ELLIOTT Alexander Charles	13-03-41	102 Sqn
937772	Sgt	ELLIOTT George Liddell	3-03-41	115 Sqn
1005747	Sgt	ELLIOTT Harry Redfern	31-10-41	77 Sqn
581379	Sgt	ELLIOTT Richard Booth	10-01-41	75 Sqn
743064	Sgt	ELLIOTT Victor Godfrey	17-04-41	144 Sqn
1251685	Sgt	ELLIS Frederick Shirley	7-08-41	149 Sqn
1253992	Sgt	ELLIS Henry Turnell	24-07-41	40 Sqn
921460	Sgt	ELLIS Leonard Harold	30-09-41	115 Sqn
742693	Sgt	ELLIS Richard Leonard Ashburton [South Africa]	21-03-41	49 Sqn
46122	P/O	ELLIS DFM William [Eire]	18-08-41	14 OTU
937599	Sgt	ELLIS DFM William Thomas	2-08-41	82 Sqn
89596	P/O	ELLNER Ernest Edward	29-06-41	218 Sqn
943709	Sgt	ELLSLEY Wilfred	25-07-41	50 Sqn
1190612	Sgt	ELMES Eric Selwyn	14-08-41	110 Sqn
641574	F/S	ELMS Robert	10-09-41	25 OTU
755881	Sgt	ELSE Joseph Shield	14-07-41	214 Sqn
26133	W/C	ELSMIE DFC George Reginald Alexander	18-08-41	114 Sqn
976995	Sgt	EMERY Jack	13-04-41	19 OTU
936208	Sgt	EMMERSON Leslie	27-02-41	83 Sqn
909056	Sgt	EMMETT Peter William Reynolds	9-05-41	78 Sqn
1180457	Sgt	ENDERBY Arthur Richard	1-11-41	16 OTU
980443	Sgt	ENGLAND Reginald Charles	29-10-41	218 Sqn
911094	Sgt	ENNIS Patrick Joseph William	4-07-41	102 Sqn
956616	Sgt	ENTWISTLE George Frederick	4-07-41	105 Sqn
553897	Sgt	ERDWIN Frederick Henry	17-04-41	44 Sqn
929408	Sgt	ESNOUF Greville Gascoyne	24-07-41	35 Sqn
82979	F/O	ESPLEN William	8-09-41	214 Sqn
755112	Sgt	ESSEX Victor Thomas	4-03-41	106 Sqn
40613	F/L	EUSTACE DFC Francis Edwin [New Zealand]	27-06-41	97 Sqn
529463	Cpl	EVA Charles Percy	21-06-41	99 Sqn
648973	Sgt	EVANS Albert Charles	28-04-41	50 Sqn
89303	P/O	EVANS Amery Yeo	17-06-41	115 Sqn
1106238	Sgt	EVANS Arthur	7-07-41	214 Sqn
947286	Sgt	EVANS Arthur Walford	16-07-41	57 Sqn
908598	Sgt	EVANS Brindley Morgan	21-04-41	99 Sqn
923988	Sgt	EVANS Charles Max	6-09-41	77 Sqn
641531	F/S	EVANS Clifford George	21-05-41	82 Sqn
67606	P/O	EVANS David Ivor	20-09-41	101 Sqn
929691	Sgt	EVANS David Morgan	7-07-41	40 Sqn
516135	F/S	EVANS Evan David	4-07-41	57 Sqn
1162520	Sgt	EVANS Hywell	8-11-41	150 Sqn
918268	Sgt	EVANS Ivor Llewellyn	13-10-41	15 Sqn
974425	Sgt	EVANS James Leonard	17-06-41	51 Sqn
967743	Sgt	EVANS John	20-07-41	139 Sqn
61954	P/O	EVANS John Emrys	8-08-41	10 Sqn
939688	Sgt	EVANS John Thomas	15-09-41	51 Sqn
61048	F/O	EVANS Kenneth Guy	30-04-41	11 OTU
82981	P/O	EVANS Leonard Frederick	23-07-41	18 Sqn
42702	P/O	EVANS Leslie Richard	4-04-41	83 Sqn

65534	P/O	EVANS Llewellyn Newton	5-11-41	144 Sqn		1056135	Sgt	FIELDSMAN Eric	27-12-41	77 Sqn
649215	Sgt	EVANS Robert	24-07-41	50 Sqn		977754	Sgt	FILLINGHAM William Vernon	15-05-41	21 Sqn
552737	F/S	EVANS Thomas Eric	15-04-41	149 Sqn		975594	Sgt	FILLMORE Kenneth Marcel	31-07-41	61 Sqn
1152551	Sgt	EVANS William Leslie	30-11-41	405 Sqn		907613	Sgt	FINCH Raymond Edward	22-04-41	218 Sqn
929643	Sgt	EVANS William Myrddin	24-11-41	115 Sqn		930735	Sgt	FINDON Eric Charles	25-08-41	78 Sqn
623045	Sgt	EVE Percy Henry	19-07-41	15 Sqn		62265	P/O	FIRTH Desmond Charles	8-11-41	106 Sqn
967757	Sgt	EVERED Lionel Lewis	17-04-41	105 Sqn		991152	AC1	FIRTH George Allan	11-04-41	17 OTU
952521	Sgt	EVEREST William	15-07-41	104 Sqn		740123	F/S	FISHER Ian Malcolm Temple	6-07-41	49 Sqn
918270	Sgt	EVERITT Cecil Thomas	19-08-41	9 Sqn		549997	F/S	FISHER Jack Stanley	29-09-41	18 OTU
1166619	Sgt	EVERSON William Herbert Arthur	11-10-41	106 Sqn		88230	P/O	FISHER John Norman	9-04-41	9 Sqn
925745	Sgt	EVETTS Leslie Arthur	19-08-41	51 Sqn		1152463	Sgt	FISHER Michael Oakley	15-08-41	50 Sqn
102082	P/O	EVILL William Allen Strathern	19-08-41	10 Sqn		935316	Sgt	FISHER Richard James	25-08-41	50 Sqn
624596	F/S	EXELBY MiD Raymond	18-12-41	15 Sqn		1153832	Sgt	FISHER William	26-08-41	40 Sqn
1152143	Sgt	EXLEY Harry Morton	25-11-41	142 Sqn		1250538	Sgt	FISHER William Royston	19-08-41	101 Sqn
1152524	Sgt	EYRE Harold Frederick	13-10-41	40 Sqn		949960	Sgt	FISHWICK Fred	30-11-41	142 Sqn
1165193	Sgt	EYRE Philip Colmer	7-09-41	102 Sqn		65581	P/O	FITCH Arthur Robert	3-09-41	40 Sqn
89791	P/O	FAINT Douglas William Drummond	11-10-41	12 Sqn		944058	Sgt	FITCH John Dennis	6-07-41	49 Sqn
1375034	Sgt	FAIRBAIRN Allan Ian Wilson [Gibraltar]	24-10-41	17 OTU		1164381	Sgt	FITSELL Richard Louis	12-09-41	10 Sqn
						906661	Sgt	FitzGERALD Kenneth Brian	6-05-41	21 Sqn
86394	F/L	FAIRBAIRN Garnet Mackenzie	27-05-41	82 Sqn		1293508	Sgt	FITZGERALD Joseph Gerald	25-09-41	21 OTU
100608	P/O	FAIRFAX DFM John Edward Anthony Harrington	4-10-41	21 OTU		1375074	Sgt	FITZGERALD Michael Joseph	30-11-41	214 Sqn
						976088	Sgt	FLANDERS Denis Bernard	3-03-41	77 Sqn
85673	P/O	FAIRHURST Thomas	9-04-41	99 Sqn		759151	F/S	FLANNIGAN James	31-10-41	76 Sqn
945584	Sgt	FAIRLAMB Robert Whyman	7-04-41	3 GTrgFlt		1380918	Sgt	FLEMING Gordon James Walter	30-11-41	214 Sqn
995061	Sgt	FAIRWEATHER Richard George Glasby	29-06-41	82 Sqn		1284768	Sgt	FLEMING William	9-10-41	19 OTU
						565697	W/O	FLETCHER Alexander	30-09-41	7 Sqn
84730	F/L	FALCONER DFC Keith James	8-09-41	214 Sqn		952276	Sgt	FLETCHER Arthur Charles	14-06-41	102 Sqn
43317	F/L	FANNING MBE John	16-06-41	Stradishall		1165250	Sgt	FLETCHER Charles Harold	18-09-41	405 Sqn
917595	Sgt	FARBROTHER Gerald	7-07-41	10 OTU		902403	Sgt	FLETCHER Deryck	12-05-41	40 Sqn
1179323	Sgt	FARLEY Dennis Henry	17-09-41	17 OTU		1008482	Sgt	FLETCHER Gordon	23-08-41	10 Sqn
1252028	Sgt	FARMAN Sidney George Thomas	8-11-41	150 Sqn		05218	W/C	FLETCHER John Lionel Howe	4-08-41	218 Sqn
621070	Sgt	FARMER Daniel Gilfillan [Canada]	4-04-41	51 Sqn		957191	Sgt	FLETCHER William Frederick George	27-12-41	114 Sqn
1053520	Sgt	FARMER James Thompson	7-08-41	149 Sqn						
1111562	Sgt	FARMERY George Albert	15-11-41	99 Sqn		1163046	Sgt	FLINT Alfred	5-12-41	20 OTU
785036	Sgt	FARNAN Marven Ernest [Far East]	26-09-41	115 Sqn		945734	Sgt	FLINT John	17-08-41	44 Sqn
107977	P/O	FARNES Kenneth	20-10-41	12 OTU		906004	Sgt	FLINT Leonard William	17-04-41	77 Sqn
754014	Sgt	FARNS Albert Victor Message	4-04-41	82 Sqn		85016	P/O	FLORIGNY Alan Addison	2-03-41	10 Sqn
929616	Sgt	FARROW Victor Gordon	19-07-41	105 Sqn		34235	S/L	FLORIGNY Clive Eugene Erwin	2-03-41	102 Sqn
88661	P/O	FARVIS Cecil Harry	3-05-41	101 Sqn		1166146	Sgt	FLOWER Ian Arthur	30-11-41	214 Sqn
754442	Sgt	FASS Leonard	19-04-41	114 Sqn		945047	Sgt	FLYNNE Vincent	15-09-41	51 Sqn
755949	Sgt	FAWCETT Derek Richard	15-09-41	75 Sqn		966522	F/S	FORBES David George	31-08-41	44 Sqn
102969	P/O	FAWKES David Kimber	20-10-41	458 Sqn		88662	P/O	FORD Alan Arthur	2-04-41	82 Sqn
819035	Sgt	FAWKES John Albert	24-07-41	405 Sqn		60785	P/O	FORD Frank Stewart Heathcote	25-03-41	20 OTU
1002245	Sgt	FAZAKERLEY James Stanley	18-08-41	110 Sqn		1050822	LAC	FORD George Alexander	15-09-41	103 Sqn
628378	Sgt	FEATHERSTONE Edwin	27-02-41	12 OTU		956103	Sgt	FORD Morgan	30-06-41	106 Sqn
641560	Sgt	FELL George Gardiner	18-12-41	97 Sqn		903256	Sgt	FORDHAM Harry Frederick	7-06-41	107 Sqn
974515	F/S	FELMAN Sidney	10-04-41	57 Sqn		1101878	Sgt	FORD-HUTCHINSON Roger Francis Stuart	24-07-41	76 Sqn
909100	Sgt	FELTON Alan William	24-07-41	12 Sqn						
631695	Sgt	FENSON Sidney John	8-11-41	7 Sqn		1060749	Sgt	FORREST James	21-10-41	142 Sqn
1001597	Sgt	FENTON George William	7-09-41	149 Sqn		562549	F/S	FORSE Alfred	30-08-41	115 Sqn
745797	Sgt	FENTON Ian Harrington	27-02-41	51 Sqn		44806	P/O	FORSTER Michael	28-07-41	21 Sqn
952943	Sgt	FENTON Norman	8-11-41	58 Sqn		700529	Sgt	FORSTER DFM Peter Charles Thomas	17-04-41	16 OTU
646171	Sgt	FENTON Richard Ernest	7-02-41	16 OTU						
85286	P/O	FENTON William Johnston [Canada]	3-04-41	101 Sqn		982883	Sgt	FORSTER William	9-07-41	78 Sqn
939539	Sgt	FENWICK Edward	3-03-41	115 Sqn		740756	Sgt	FORSYTH George Alexander	27-02-41	78 Sqn
550178	Sgt	FEREBEE Philip Ivan	2-07-41	12 Sqn		564607	F/S	FORSYTH Ian Newton	10-08-41	226 Sqn
745113	Sgt	FERGUSON Andrew Blair	2-03-41	21 Sqn		1001203	Sgt	FORSYTH James Alexander Gordon	3-07-41	139 Sqn
1051609	Sgt	FERGUSON Brown	15-11-41	149 Sqn		759292	Sgt	FORSYTHE Alan	1-08-41	44 Sqn
803507	Sgt	FERGUSON David	18-12-41	15 Sqn		960594	Sgt	FORTY Laurence Arthur	27-05-41	106 Sqn
921752	Sgt	FERGUSON Douglas Arthur	15-12-41	50 Sqn		927159	Sgt	FORTY Mowbray Ronald	22-10-41	12 Sqn
77931	F/L	FERRIS John Outerson William Kenneth	30-09-41	142 Sqn		944444	Sgt	FOSTER Cedric Arthur	21-09-41	77 Sqn
						945066	Sgt	FOSTER Edward Ryder	3-07-41	144 Sqn
614026	Sgt	FEW Jesse	24-11-41	97 Sqn		999277	Sgt	FOSTER Ernest David	17-04-41	25 OTU
1050516	Sgt	FEWKES Herbert Walter	7-11-41	50 Sqn		951266	Sgt	FOSTER Jack Edward	3-07-41	83 Sqn
1404289	AC2	FIDELL Ernest Alfred	23-07-41	Oakington		68739	P/O	FOSTER Leslie John Percival	30-12-41	35 Sqn
1378155	Sgt	FIELDHOUSE Edward	29-09-41	99 Sqn		36210	F/O	FOSTER William Alan [New Zealand]	8-06-41	11 OTU
1001686	Sgt	FIELDING Robert Bamber	9-11-41	9 Sqn		971160	Sgt	FOSTER William Anthony	6-04-41	83 Sqn
1375183	Sgt	FIELDMAN John Donald	7-09-41	226 Sqn		901845	Sgt	FOTHERGILL Dennis Gold	5-08-41	50 Sqn

Service No	Rank	Name	Date	Unit
909428	Sgt	FOULKES John Gifford	15-09-41	75 Sqn
85242	P/O	FOURNIER Bernard Maurice	29-08-41	49 Sqn
1164028	Sgt	FOWLER Frederick Douglas	5-08-41	149 Sqn
957199	Sgt	FOX Ernest	14-07-41	75 Sqn
956797	Cpl	FOX James Crosby	24-11-41	115 Sqn
1014018	Sgt	FOX Matthew Francis	7-09-41	17 OTU
973020	Sgt	FOX William Watson	4-04-41	82 Sqn
65504	F/O	FRAAS Ronald John	8-07-41	405 Sqn
42210	F/O	FRAMPTON DFC Allan Douglas	27-07-41	10 OTU
751138	F/S	FRANCE Joseph Robert	24-10-41	101 Sqn
755849	Sgt	FRANCIS Harry Walter	9-05-41	83 Sqn
943397	LAC	FRANCKS Donald George	11-04-41	17 OTU
652586	Sgt	FRANCO Jack Lewis	4-02-41	106 Sqn
1254939	Sgt	FRANK Robert Lionel	5-11-41	144 Sqn
67592	P/O	FRANKLIN Ronald Thomas	22-07-41	17 OTU
42212	F/O	FRASER DFC Cecil Victor [Canada]	10-07-41	7 Sqn
88869	P/O	FRASER Douglas Stewart	3-09-41	35 Sqn
649384	Sgt	FRASER Ivor Roderick	8-09-41	144 Sqn
632616	Sgt	FRASER James Robert	14-06-41	102 Sqn
10091	S/L	FREDERICK William Bernard	2-03-41	HQBC
742673	Sgt	FREEMAN Richard Harry	17-01-41	10 OTU
759027	F/S	FREESTONE Ronald Albert	6-05-41	110 Sqn
745264	Sgt	FRENCH Herbert Arnold	29-08-41	104 Sqn
63087	P/O	FREW Garth Campbell	11-10-41	12 Sqn
104518	P/O	FREW Robert Alexander Fisher	30-12-41	35 Sqn
549040	Sgt	FRIEND George Thomas	23-09-41	15 Sqn
1150550	F/S	FRITH John Edward	28-12-41	15 OTU
968496	F/S	FRODSHAM John	15-04-41	21 Sqn
642523	Sgt	FROST Anthony Cecil	24-06-41	57 Sqn
1375651	Sgt	FROST Arthur Walter Dudley	18-07-41	15 Sqn
910014	Sgt	FROST Charles Henry Dennis	27-03-41	16 OTU
747744	F/S	FROST Colin George Charles	17-08-41	12 Sqn
101588	P/O	FROST Walter John	8-11-41	44 Sqn
72543	F/L	FRUTIGER Walter Eric	10-02-41	61 Sqn
755511	Sgt	FRY Charles Williams	13-03-41	110 Sqn
741738	F/S	FRY DFM Edward Frank	28-02-41	12 OTU
107930	P/O	FUDGE Gordon Dyson	10-12-41	15 Sqn
618116	Sgt	FULBECK Charles Waghorn	29-09-41	7 Sqn
1236035	AC2	FULCHER Walter Henry	11-11-41	49 Sqn
754070	Sgt	FULFORD Frank	18-04-41	11 OTU
969220	Sgt	FULFORD John Michael	8-05-41	150 Sqn
1377934	Sgt	FULLARD Frank	16-07-41	115 Sqn
101526	P/O	FULLER Henry John	23-08-41	114 Sqn
987503	Sgt	FULLER Jack	25-08-41	35 Sqn
87416	P/O	FULLERTON William	17-01-41	10 OTU
927831	Sgt	FURLEY Kenneth Sidney	20-10-41	50 Sqn
61994	P/O	FYLES Thomas Raymond	26-08-41	40 Sqn
80115	P/O	FYNN Castle Blunden Stapleton 'Chum' [Rhodesia]	1-09-41	16 OTU
1252534	Sgt	FYVIE Kenneth	25-08-41	50 Sqn
85017	P/O	GADSBY John Wilfred	10-04-41	82 Sqn
958561	Sgt	GAILEY Charles Edward [Canada]	11-12-41	144 Sqn
950922	Sgt	GALBRAITH Robert Alfred	16-07-41	150 Sqn
798515	Sgt	GALLANT Thomas Cyril [Newfoundland]	7-08-41	20 OTU
580539	F/S	GALLERY Samuel Douglas	9-06-41	18 Sqn
903639	Sgt	GALLYON John Newman	3-03-41	13 OTU
88231	P/O	GALT Robert Brownlie	14-07-41	139 Sqn
754608	Sgt	GAMBLE Thomas	8-04-41	40 Sqn
919090	Sgt	GAMMON Peter Crowhurst [South Africa]	27-07-41	44 Sqn
938047	Sgt	GANE George Leslie	28-06-41	10 Sqn
938067	Sgt	GANSLER Cyril Edward	17-04-41	77 Sqn
701878	F/S	GAPP Robert Alfred	10-02-41	61 Sqn
993802	Sgt	GARDE Fred	11-10-41	75 Sqn
968317	Sgt	GARDINER Michael Edward	28-05-41	150 Sqn
37807	F/L	GARDINER Walter Ronald	15-09-41	305 Sqn
960979	Sgt	GARDNER Herbert Charles	21-10-41	207 Sqn
1002281	Sgt	GARFIN Michael Terence	18-12-41	139 Sqn
759206	F/S	GARLISH Reginald James	16-05-41	78 Sqn
919092	Sgt	GARN Douglas Grant	2-05-41	77 Sqn
1168520	Sgt	GARNER Michael Gerard	15-08-41	35 Sqn
	G/C	GARRAWAY OBE Frederick Frank	12-05-41	Linton on Ouse
920499	Sgt	GARROD Ernest Henry	21-06-41	11 OTU
910169	Sgt	GARROD Robert John	6-09-41	10 Sqn
60818	P/O	GARROULD John Aubrey Trevor	16-05-41	78 Sqn
701916	F/S	GARWOOD George James	22-06-41	90 Sqn
85287	P/O	GATES Donald Henry	27-02-41	78 Sqn
631151	Sgt	GATES Ronald William	18-02-41	19 OTU
751359	F/S	GEAR DFM Stanley Robert	9-05-41	304 Sqn
1167730	Sgt	GEARING John Stanley	30-11-41	58 Sqn
581090	F/S	GEATER Roy John West	31-07-41	61 Sqn
1157216	Sgt	GEE Arthur Henry	30-11-41	455 Sqn
903398	Sgt	GEER Norman Augustus	4-04-41	82 Sqn
68769	P/O	GENTH Anthony William	11-08-41	25 OTU
61999	P/O	GEORGE Courtney Claude Orwin	12-08-41	139 Sqn
759205	F/S	GEORGE Henry Richards	19-06-41	78 Sqn
104430	F/O	GIBB DFM Eric Arthur Fawns	22-12-41	28 CFlt
624127	Sgt	GIBB George	18-04-41	9 Sqn
1284320	Sgt	GIBBINS Peter	18-07-41	149 Sqn
755569	Sgt	GIBBS Frederick	23-03-41	105 Sqn
1376985	Sgt	GIBBS Henry John	6-08-41	77 Sqn
1174298	Sgt	GIBBS John Adrian	8-08-41	139 Sqn
910804	Sgt	GIBLETT Peter Thomas	31-07-41	144 Sqn
746891	Sgt	GIBLIN DFM Norman Joseph	23-07-41	21 Sqn
82982	P/O	GIBSON Andrew Hamilton Clark	4-02-41	20 OTU
749389	Sgt	GIBSON Arnold Walker	12-05-41	214 Sqn
1056826	Sgt	GIBSON Cyril Charles	15-12-41	408 Sqn
927583	Sgt	GIBSON Donald Fraser	4-07-41	102 Sqn
39938	F/L	GIBSON Donovan	17-04-41	77 Sqn
987889	Sgt	GIBSON John	8-11-41	107 Sqn
642202	Sgt	GIBSON John Murray	25-04-41	51 Sqn
42833	F/O	GILBERT DFC Harry Trevor	3-08-41	25 OTU
1252428	Sgt	GILBERT Reginald Aubrey	5-07-41	106 Sqn
939525	Sgt	GILBY Fred	9-07-41	9 Sqn
89587	P/O	GILL Alexander George	7-08-41	20 OTU
1377118	Sgt	GILL Edward Felix Gwynne	15-10-41	139 Sqn
954678	Sgt	GILL Edward Jack	12-10-41	21 Sqn
935706	Sgt	GILL Francis	15-08-41	51 Sqn
43034	P/O	GILL Frederick Kennett [New Zealand]	8-05-41	83 Sqn
759007	Sgt	GILL James Vivian	2-07-41	115 Sqn
60343	P/O	GILL Julian	24-05-41	110 Sqn
551736	Sgt	GILLAM Leonard George	15-04-41	149 Sqn
944800	LAC	GILLEARD Fred	2-08-41	40 Sqn
971685	Sgt	GILLESPIE Charles	15-03-41	3 GTrgFlt
1378490	Sgt	GILLIATT Fred	8-07-41	11 OTU
1100647	Sgt	GILLIES Donald Watson	7-09-41	77 Sqn
989975	Sgt	GILMAN John Leonard 'Jack' [Canada]	19-08-41	51 Sqn
68817	P/O	GILMORE Charles George	7-11-41	99 Sqn
818024	Sgt	GILMORE Daniel	19-03-41	75 Sqn
1060748	Sgt	GILMOUR Alexander	30-11-41	142 Sqn
997911	Sgt	GIOVETTI Peitro Alfredo [Portugal]	21-09-41	144 Sqn
937720	Sgt	GITTINS James Edward	12-06-41	51 Sqn
1172525	Sgt	GLADEN Robert Alfred	26-10-41	106 Sqn
745778	Sgt	GLASS Derek Keith	5-05-41	21 Sqn
904034	Sgt	GLASSBOROW Kenneth Percy	14-06-41	102 Sqn
973039	Sgt	GLAVES Albert Leslie	15-06-41	106 Sqn
88446	P/O	GLENN Keith Fereday	16-07-41	150 Sqn
74674	F/O	GLENNIE Donald Gordon	8-04-41	61 Sqn
1021175	F/S	GLENNY Robert Edmund	16-11-41	218 Sqn
62023	P/O	GLOCK Kenneth Frederick	27-06-41	40 Sqn
948672	Sgt	GLOVER Albert	16-07-41	218 Sqn
1169260	Sgt	GLOVER Jeffrey	1-11-41	102 Sqn
67037	P/O	GLOVER Laurence Trevor	27-06-41	61 Sqn

Number	Rank	Name	Date	Sqn
1001141	Sgt	GODDARD James Walter	22-08-41	106 Sqn
929534	Sgt	GODFREY Robert Kenneth	24-07-41	12 Sqn
748691	Sgt	GODFREY William Edgar	3-04-41	77 Sqn
84024	P/O	GODSMARK Bernard Albert	24-05-41	114 Sqn
745859	F/S	GODWIN Clarence Arthur	24-07-41	35 Sqn
1064090	Sgt	GOFF Ralph	6-11-41	16 OTU
1257745	Sgt	GOLDING James	27-04-41	15 Sqn
777611	Sgt	GOLDMAN Joseph Jessie [South Africa]	19-06-41	16 OTU
39459	S/L	GOOD DFC Duncan Charles Frederick	28-04-41	50 Sqn
758181	Sgt	GOOD Kenneth	4-03-41	106 Sqn
935854	Sgt	GOODALL Ernest Hugh	13-03-41	102 Sqn
1058533	Sgt	GOODBRAND Jack	30-11-41	106 Sqn
751480	F/S	GOODE Lewis Victor	17-06-41	405 Sqn
905643	Sgt	GOODENOUGH Nigel Rodney Patrick	21-06-41	218 Sqn
939708	F/S	GOODFELLOW Colin Gordon	12-07-41	107 Sqn
1162826	Sgt	GOODWIN Frederick James	27-09-41	5 Group
1164411	Sgt	GOODWIN John Clayton	28-06-41	77 Sqn
901329	Sgt	GOODWIN Peter William	8-07-41	58 Sqn
914176	Sgt	GORDON Donald Kenneth 'Ken' [Canada]	28-12-41	405 Sqn
80138	P/O	GORDON George Arthur Ormond [Rhodesia]	11-10-41	106 Sqn
1160229	Sgt	GORDON George Russell Stewart	28-12-41	138 Sqn
747861	Sgt	GORDON Harold	3-03-41	58 Sqn
1052297	Sgt	GORDON Ian Patrick McHaffie	8-09-41	115 Sqn
1354337	Sgt	GORDON Peter Ronie	18-05-41	139 Sqn
993200	Sgt	GORDON Ramsay	22-10-41	16 OTU
742058	F/S	GOSS Harold Sidney Douglas	5-12-41	20 OTU
653281	Sgt	GOUGH Maurice	2-03-41	61 Sqn
42599	F/O	GOUGH Peter Beckford	11-05-41	10 Sqn
87061	P/O	GOULD James Dugald	20-08-41	83 Sqn
85265	P/O	GOULDING Robert	6-07-41	10 Sqn
68754	P/O	GOULSTON Sydney	21-09-41	77 Sqn
88221	P/O	GOURLAY William Leslie	31-03-41	21 Sqn
748724	Sgt	GOVE Ronald Gordon	29-09-41	9 Sqn
570309	Sgt	GOVETT William Roy	16-04-41	50 Sqn
728424	Sgt	GOW Iain Fraser	25-05-41	18 Sqn
955046	Sgt	GOWAN Thomas Francis	30-11-41	106 Sqn
777668	Sgt	GRAAF Stafford [Rhodesia]	12-09-41	16 OTU
1241702	AC2	GRACE James William	15-09-41	207 Sqn
1062114	Sgt	GRACIE Ronald Davidson	13-12-41	107 Sqn
89603	P/O	GRAHAM John Malcolm	28-07-41	50 Sqn
974360	Sgt	GRAHAM Joseph Douglas	10-04-41	17 OTU
34005	W/C	GRAHAM William Monteith	9-05-41	304 Sqn
965679	F/S	GRAIL Frank	4-08-41	218 Sqn
758212	Sgt	GRAINGER Robert Little	13-03-41	50 Sqn
45950	P/O	GRANEY James	7-07-41	10 OTU
570227	Sgt	GRANT Adam	21-11-41	7 Sqn
100206	P/O	GRANT James	17-08-41	106 Sqn
974494	Sgt	GRASSOM John	29-08-41	103 Sqn
537006	F/S	GRAY DFM Brian	22-09-41	105 Sqn
1382320	Sgt	GRAY George Dixon	17-05-41	149 Sqn
1054132	Sgt	GRAY George William	9-10-41	19 OTU
742207	Sgt	GRAY Kenneth	17-05-41	77 Sqn
751951	Sgt	GRAY DFM Norman	15-08-41	50 Sqn
808255	F/S	GRAY DFM Raymond Marshall	30-06-41	115 Sqn
553874	F/S	GRAY Reginald Wilfred	31-08-41	207 Sqn
902902	Sgt	GRAY Ronald Henry	23-02-41	115 Sqn
1053321	Sgt	GRAY Sidney Dennis Colley	7-11-41	57 Sqn
930741	AC2	GRAY William	18-03-41	Binbrook
971158	Sgt	GREAVES William James	18-03-41	149 Sqn
745784	Sgt	GREEN Frederick Louis	25-07-41	57 Sqn
969371	Sgt	GREEN George Eric	25-05-41	105 Sqn
939533	Sgt	GREEN Herbert Walter	3-03-41	115 Sqn
1154443	Sgt	GREEN Ivan John	21-09-41	214 Sqn
755095	F/S	GREEN Leslie Cyril	7-11-41	75 Sqn
530614	Sgt	GREEN Philip	24-03-41	7 Sqn
547790	F/S	GREEN DFM Reginald William John	4-07-41	226 Sqn
964420	Sgt	GREEN Ronald Stanley	29-06-41	78 Sqn
1256366	Sgt	GREEN Stanley William	6-11-41	16 OTU
63088	P/O	GREEN Wallace Geoffrey	27-06-41	40 Sqn
932940	Sgt	GREEN William Cleary	29-12-41	10 Sqn
553190	Sgt	GREENAWAY Anthony Maurice	17-06-41	14 OTU
650863	F/S	GREENAWAY Robert	14-06-41	44 Sqn
68772	P/O	GREENFIELD John Charles	12-09-41	10 Sqn
87385	P/O	GREENHALGH George Frederick Edward	5-07-41	106 Sqn
751037	Sgt	GREENHALGH Reginald Ernest	29-09-41	49 Sqn
42377	F/O	GREENHILL Ronald Arthur	11-10-41	107 Sqn
1053685	Sgt	GREENOUGH Reginald James	26-08-41	82 Sqn
755086	F/S	GREENSIDES Alan	13-06-41	103 Sqn
1176111	Sgt	GREENWOOD Arthur Henry	29-09-41	57 Sqn
570897	Sgt	GREENWOOD Arthur Stanley	30-12-41	35 Sqn
1051500	Sgt	GREENWOOD Keith Douglas	29-09-41	16 OTU
904243	Sgt	GREEY Denis Maxwell	5-08-41	103 Sqn
1250820	Sgt	GREGO Eric Ivor Llewellyn	7-11-41	57 Sqn
975990	Sgt	GREGORY Alfred	29-05-41	78 Sqn
1183942	AC2	GREGORY Denis Walters	19-01-41	Feltwell
908385	Sgt	GREIG Charles Forrest	19-06-41	44 Sqn
62000	P/O	GRENON Theodore Buckland	7-06-41	107 Sqn
568042	Sgt	GRENYER Alfred James	21-07-41	76 Sqn
1285564	Sgt	GRESHAM Edwin Frederick	8-11-41	58 Sqn
552727	Sgt	GRESTY Kenneth Gaston	17-04-41	105 Sqn
652883	Sgt	GRETTON Harry	16-06-41	139 Sqn
651970	F/S	GRIEVE William John	27-06-41	150 Sqn
67698	P/O	GRIFFIN Harold William	5-08-41	20 OTU
611935	Sgt	GRIFFIN John	18-04-41	40 Sqn
645408	Sgt	GRIFFIN Patrick Michael [Eire]	7-07-41	106 Sqn
950620	Sgt	GRIFFIN Peter Ryland	15-08-41	51 Sqn
947898	Sgt	GRIFFIN Robert Grattan Gurney [Eire]	5-08-41	103 Sqn
37734	S/L	GRIFFITH-JONES DFC John Martin	3-03-41	7 Sqn
755687	Sgt	GRIFFITHS David William	19-06-41	10 Sqn
1199265	Sgt	GRIFFITHS Henry	30-11-41	106 Sqn
650725	F/S	GRIFFITHS John Walter Ronald	11-09-41	102 Sqn
81939	P/O	GRIFFITHS Melville Percy	15-01-41	58 Sqn
922776	Sgt	GRIFFITHS Norman Joffre	27-11-41	14 OTU
1150627	Sgt	GRIFFITHS Peter Grosvenor	20-06-41	105 Sqn
1282592	Sgt	GRIFFITHS Thomas Douglas	29-09-41	115 Sqn
1165305	Sgt	GRIGG Gerald Leonard	11-12-41	35 Sqn
903403	Sgt	GRINDLEY Alfred Richard	13-01-41	114 Sqn
654640	Sgt	GRISWOLD William Edward	8-01-41	214 Sqn
581015	F/S	GROCOCK Bernard William	30-06-41	7 Sqn
931741	Sgt	GROOM Henry John	28-12-41	51 Sqn
964955	Sgt	GROOM John Alfred	30-11-41	102 Sqn
653716	F/S	GROSVENOR Terence Alfred	13-06-41	25 OTU
929402	Sgt	GROVE Frank	28-08-41	14 OTU
916275	Sgt	GROVE-PALMER Basil Leonard	15-12-41	11 OTU
910392	Sgt	GRUBB James Henry	23-06-41	51 Sqn
1166485	Sgt	GRUER Lawrence Harold	30-07-41	139 Sqn
955332	Sgt	GRUNDY Alan Peter James	26-08-41	106 Sqn
752233	Sgt	GRUNSELL MiD Ernest Alfred Francis	27-03-41	78 Sqn
745814	F/S	GUESFORD Arthur Edwin	15-06-41	110 Sqn
525488	F/S	GUEST BEM Jack	12-07-41	50 Sqn
541646	AC2	GUEST Jack	9-12-41	50 Sqn
938872	Sgt	GUEST Ronald	1-02-41	61 Sqn
62273	P/O	GUILD Edward John Douglas	16-09-41	15 Sqn
63809	P/O	GUNNIS Stanley Frederick Maude	28-08-41	21 Sqn
1375232	Sgt	GUTTRIDGE Ronald Frederick	19-08-41	11 OTU
913013	Sgt	HADAWAY Gordon Alfred	27-05-41	49 Sqn
967535	Sgt	HADFIELD James	25-08-41	78 Sqn
1375622	Sgt	HAFNER Edgar Antoine	12-10-41	17 OTU
63828	F/L	HAGGITT Clarence Edward Charles [Canada]	9-09-41	226 Sqn

Service No	Rank	Name	Date	Sqn
950824	Sgt	HAINES George	7-08-41	51 Sqn
550956	F/S	HAINES George Charles Pecival	21-10-41	82 Sqn
937447	Sgt	HALBERT Billy	18-05-41	25 OTU
755386	Sgt	HALBERT Robert Lang Riddet	18-05-41	139 Sqn
82983	P/O	HALE Eric Sidney	30-07-41	82 Sqn
923928	Sgt	HALE Victor John	26-10-41	40 Sqn
948309	Sgt	HALESTRAP Ernest	29-08-41	214 Sqn
1002012	Sgt	HALEY Rowland	30-07-41	139 Sqn
549626	F/S	HALFPENNY DFM Arthur	13-08-41	207 Sqn
758066	Sgt	HALL Bernard Preston	11-03-41	9 Sqn
944123	Sgt	HALL Charles William	9-04-41	99 Sqn
1108004	Sgt	HALL Dennis Edward	15-11-41	99 Sqn
749477	Sgt	HALL Edward Ralph	15-06-41	106 Sqn
1186787	Sgt	HALL Ernest William	12-08-41	149 Sqn
902311	Sgt	HALL George	2-03-41	61 Sqn
960499	Sgt	HALL George Leonard	26-11-41	214 Sqn
903968	Sgt	HALL Gilbert Townsend	27-04-41	83 Sqn
552714	Sgt	HALL James	13-06-41	102 Sqn
988980	Sgt	HALL John	7-05-41	75 Sqn
743002	Sgt	HALL John Napier	13-01-41	35 Sqn
778193	Sgt	HALL Kenneth Esler [Rhodesia]	17-12-41	44 Sqn
751473	Sgt	HALL Owen	4-07-41	82 Sqn
364803	F/S	HALL MiD Ronald Edward	13-09-41	21 Sqn
552215	Sht	HALL Wilfred	30-05-41	50 Sqn
553968	Sgt	HALLAS Vincent	13-03-41	102 Sqn
63440	P/O	HALLEY William Alexander Munro	4-05-41	10 OTU
936497	Sgt	HALSALL Edward Sinclair Cameron	2-03-41	51 Sqn
936240	Sgt	HALWARD Oliver	27-10-41	106 Sqn
955336	Sgt	HAMBLETON Clifford	3-09-41	214 Sqn
106871	P/O	HAMBURGER Samuel George Arthur	10-12-41	15 OTU
995713	Sgt	HAMILTON Ian	8-11-41	107 Sqn
912835	Sgt	HAMILTON Peter John Maxwell [Australia]	20-10-41	458 Sqn
85676	P/O	HAMILTON Robert James	10-04-41	144 Sqn
977049		HAMILTON Ronald [Channel Islands]	26-08-41	21 Sqn
1051939	Sgt	HAMILTON Thomas Alexander Walter	11-10-41	58 Sqn
746975	Sgt	HAMILTON William Clark	9-05-41	304 Sqn
106365	P/O	HAMMERSLEY Frederick Denis	30-11-41	58 Sqn
581056	F/S	HAMMERSLEY Seymour Robert Edward	18-09-41	88 Sqn
535641	F/S	HAMMOND Albert Edward	9-07-41	35 Sqn
1200763	AC2	HAMMOND Albert Stanley	29-01-41	Watton
944304	Sgt	HAMMOND John William	11-03-41	9 Sqn
902472	Sgt	HAMMOND Percy Albert	6-08-41	144 Sqn
946762	Sgt	HAMPSON Arthur Noel	13-08-41	149 Sqn
909505	Sgt	HANCOCK Charles William	26-06-41	49 Sqn
580443	F/S	HANCOCK Harold Frederick	8-05-41	105 Sqn
1057059	Sgt	HANCOCK Harry	9-10-41	19 OTU
648598	Cpl	HANCOCK James Anthony	22-12-41	28 CFlt
969382	Sgt	HANCOCK John Bernard	26-06-41	99 Sqn
977649	Sgt	HANCOCK Laurence	30-06-41	35 Sqn
755236	Sgt	HANDLEY Arthur William	23-07-41	21 Sqn
1280935	Sgt	HANEY James	19-08-41	104 Sqn
908785	Sgt	HANKINS Frank Albert Lancelot	27-03-41	14 OTU
928426	Sgt	HANLIN Josiah George	11-10-41	57 Sqn
754908	F/S	HANMER Robert Beaumont	21-04-41	83 Sqn
1006118	Sgt	HANNAM Robert Neville	16-11-41	218 Sqn
748787	F/S	HANNAN Walter Anthony	22-07-41	11 OTU
754380	F/S	HANNAY DFM Herbert	12-06-41	51 Sqn
39611	S/L	HANNIGAN Alexander John	6-09-41	77 Sqn
551808	Sgt	HANNIGAN Wallace Patrick	15-05-41	97 Sqn
754929	Sgt	HANSON Reginald Greenhow	29-04-41	82 Sqn
966859	F/S	HANSON Robert	23-04-41	18 OTU
82603	P/O	HAPALA Richard [Czechoslovakia]	2-07-41	311 Sqn
89393	P/O	HARDCASTLE Arthur Vernon John	13-06-41	103 Sqn
983863	Sgt	HARDIE Hugh Wright	16-07-41	57 Sqn
525327	Sgt	HARDIE William	28-06-41	7 Sqn
64312	P/O	HARDIE William Dave Clayton	7-11-41	101 Sqn
746787	F/S	HARDIMAN Frederick James	24-07-41	12 Sqn
751347	Sgt	HARDING James	9-05-41	99 Sqn
1059179	Sgt	HARDING Lynn	11-12-41	408 Sqn
922058	Sgt	HARDING Norman Laurence	23-07-41	18 Sqn
910064	Sgt	HARDING Norman Walter	7-07-41	9 Sqn
1100069	Sgt	HARDISTY Thomas Hollas	8-12-41	49 Sqn
1062691	Sgt	HARDMAN Eric Henry Charles	16-10-41	25 OTU
580954	F/S	HARDY Alexander James	28-08-41	88 Sqn
903792	Sgt	HARE William George Nelson	8-06-41	11 OTU
1113461	Sgt	HARES Richard Norman	30-06-41	35 Sqn
617355	LAC	HARKNESS John Arthur Martin	28-11-41	138 Sqn
964594	Sgt	HARLEY Roy	21-07-41	10 OTU
987367	Sgt	HARMAN Alfred Henry	17-10-41	40 Sqn
904079	Sgt	HARMER Frederick Alfred	15-07-41	104 Sqn
61970	P/O	HARPER Courteney John [Argentina]	17-09-41	82 Sqn
916770		HARPER Gerald Thomas [New Zealand]	29-08-41	78 Sqn
929132	Sgt	HARPUR Bernard Caldwell Culy	29-06-41	77 Sqn
39439	F/L	HARRINGTON James [Eire]	4-04-41	51 Sqn
100046	P/O	HARRIS Henry Gordon	27-12-41	110 Sqn
976160	Sgt	HARRIS John Albion	11-05-41	40 Sqn
746915	F/S	HARRIS John Hubert	19-06-41	78 Sqn
909974	Sgt	HARRIS Leonard Frank	8-05-41	150 Sqn
1162926	Sgt	HARRIS Leslie Wilfred	30-07-41	19 OTU
1177011	Sgt	HARRIS Percival Wilfred	10-10-41	16 OTU
751285	F/S	HARRIS Reuben John	9-05-41	5 Group
551662	F/S	HARRIS Wilfred Marshall	4-07-41	107 Sqn
39732	F/L	HARRISON DSO Alan Bruce	3-09-41	61 Sqn
641056	Sgt	HARRISON Alfred Edward	9-01-41	139 Sqn
812347	F/S	HARRISON Anthony Robert James	2-07-41	149 Sqn
748703	Sgt	HARRISON Christopher Basil	30-03-41	83 Sqn
975057	Sgt	HARRISON Dennis Higham	21-06-41	218 Sqn
952921	Sgt	HARRISON Jeffrey Frederick	21-05-41	17 OTU
621937	LAC	HARRISON John Thomas	9-06-41	150 Sqn
1051557	Sgt	HARRISON Kenneth	15-08-41	12 Sqn
1062366	Sgt	HARRISON Leslie James	17-07-41	40 Sqn
755521	F/S	HARRISON William	3-08-41	25 OTU
628840	Sgt	HARROP Albert Charles Frank	7-11-41	99 Sqn
755701	F/S	HARROWER Thomas Henderson	30-09-41	142 Sqn
923042	Sgt	HARRY Edwin Alfred	28-11-41	408 Sqn
102970	P/O	HART Frank Gordon	8-09-41	90 Sqn
818222	Sgt	HART John Lewis	8-05-41	150 Sqn
1252027	Sgt	HART Sydney Albert	8-11-41	142 Sqn
70839	W/C	HARTE DFC Frazer Apsley [South Africa]	9-10-41	107 Sqn
950571	Sgt	HARTLETT Gordon John Poole	1-09-41	144 Sqn
87064	F/O	HARTLEY Stanley	6-11-41	83 Sqn
44570	P/O	HARTWRIGHT DFM Valentine Ronald	30-06-41	7 Sqn
745752	Sgt	HARVEY Gordon	31-07-41	144 Sqn
924777	Sgt	HARVEY John Richard Gell	18-08-41	110 Sqn
553279	F/S	HARVEY Maurice Charles	8-08-41	97 Sqn
621634	Sgt	HARVEY Sidney Norman	17-06-41	405 Sqn
778343	Sgt	HARVEY Stafford Arthur [Rhodesia]	1-09-41	44 Sqn
65986	P/O	HARVEY Stuart James	17-05-41	106 Sqn
740429	Sgt	HARWOOD DFM Frank Briant	21-03-41	207 Sqn
40824	F/O	HARWOOD DFC Michael James Carr	26-08-41	106 Sqn
918371	Sgt	HARWOOD-SMITH Kenneth	8-11-41	102 Sqn
990447	Sgt	HASSALL Bernard	17-07-41	40 Sqn
1160085	Sgt	HASTE Eric	26-10-41	106 Sqn
978923	Sgt	HASTINGS Herbert	12-07-41	82 Sqn
1254713	Sgt	HASTINGS Max Emanuel Gerald	11-10-41	57 Sqn
1254392	F/O	HASWELL Joseph Arthur	31-07-41	150 Sqn
990190	Sgt	HATHAWAY Thomas Stanley	31-07-41	142 Sqn
932189	Sgt	HATHERILL Reginald Ernest	6-11-41	16 OTU

944238	Sgt	HATTEMORE Wilfred Norman	13-12-41	14 OTU		1293627	Sgt	HESKETH Raymond Denis	16-07-41	40 Sqn
930965	Sgt	HATTON Edward Christopher	7-09-41	149 Sqn		549514	Sgt	HESLOP Douglas Alfred Thomas	2-03-41	9 Sqn
936274	Sgt	HATTON Fred Anthony 'Tony'	18-06-41	58 Sqn		85018	P/O	HESLOP Geoffrey Vivian	13-06-41	77 Sqn
64916	P/O	HAVELOCK Charles Acton Chaplin	27-12-41	77 Sqn		1379096	Sgt	HEWISON George	17-08-41	21 OTU
969726	Sgt	HAVERY Ronald Sebastian	3-05-41	7 Sqn		968361	Sgt	HEWITSON Frank	30-04-41	99 Sqn
929404	Sgt	HAWKES David Preston	21-09-41	103 Sqn		87418	P/O	HEWITSON Leslie Barker	18-04-41	107 Sqn
1356738	Sgt	HAWKES Denis Farmbrough	17-08-41	78 Sqn		1378390	Sgt	HEWITT Edward Walter	24-10-41	40 Sqn
917381	Sgt	HAWKES Ronald Charles	27-12-41	110 Sqn		1169514	Sgt	HEWITT Peter Wilson	30-11-41	77 Sqn
81030	P/O	HAWKES Ronald James	29-04-41	18 OTU		977450	Sgt	HEWLETT Raymond Allen	24-05-41	110 Sqn
44803	P/O	HAWKINS David Edward Somerville	3-06-41	226 Sqn		1153276	Sgt	HIBBERT Reginald Ernest	22-07-41	11 OTU
1375393	Sgt	HAWKINS Edgar Walter	12-10-41	144 Sqn		905964	F/S	HIBBIN Arthur Edward	11-06-41	99 Sqn
1263188	Sgt	HAWKINS John Edward	15-10-41	40 Sqn		545913	F/S	HIBBS DFM Harold Robert	25-05-41	114 Sqn
42002	F/O	HAWLEY John Charles Michael	22-06-41	90 Sqn		740338	F/S	HICKINGBOTHAM Jack	18-04-41	107 Sqn
742914	Sgt	HAWLEY Leslie Richard	14-03-41	149 Sqn		952662	Sgt	HICKMAN Gordon Wilfred	28-04-41	101 Sqn
973032	Sgt	HAWTHORNE James Thomas	1-02-41	144 Sqn		1162408	Sgt	HICKMOTT Richard Samuel Keith	17-05-41	25 OTU
748459	Sgt	HAY Ian Colin	21-08-41	102 Sqn		742738	Sgt	HICKS Thomas Ivor	31-07-41	99 Sqn
942288	Sgt	HAYCOCK Richard Edward	3-07-41	75 Sqn		919879	Sgt	HIGGINS Howard Daniel	14-08-41	110 Sqn
611997	Sgt	HAYDEN Robert	30-09-41	58 Sqn		564652	F/S	HIGGINSON Harry	26-10-41	40 Sqn
108017	P/O	HAYES Cecil Harry	21-10-41	12 OTU		1163235	Sgt	HIGGS Albert Henry	16-09-41	18 Sqn
986083	Sgt	HAYES Joseph	18-02-41	19 OTU		1378328	Sgt	HIGHFIELD George Albert	11-10-41	101 Sqn
1254653	Sgt	HAYES Kenneth	28-08-41	21 Sqn		645598	F/S	HIGHTON DFM Thomas	10-09-41	25 OTU
1001204	Sgt	HAYES Richard Kellett	1-09-41	44 Sqn		1186752	Sgt	HILDEBRANT Alfred	14-10-41	22 OTU
923871	Sgt	HAYNES Derek Cecil	13-07-41	15 OTU		751924	F/S	HILL Alfred Frederick	25-07-41	61 Sqn
936340	Sgt	HAYNES William Clifford	2-04-41	82 Sqn		924564	Sgt	HILL Arthur Edward	30-11-41	106 Sqn
917812	Sgt	HAYTER Alfred Charles	24-10-41	101 Sqn		1154518	Sgt	HILL Charles Herbert	17-09-41	105 Sqn
923694	Sgt	HAYWARD Dennis Claude	29-08-41	104 Sqn		25030	W/C	HILL DFC Christopher Grant	15-04-41	18 Sqn
522167	Sgt	HAYWARD Thomas	21-12-41	7 Sqn		939863	Sgt	HILL Ernest Philip	6-05-41	77 Sqn
1177043	Sgt	HAZELL Richard Henry	19-08-41	11 OTU		902598	Sgt	HILL Frederick William	29-08-41	35 Sqn
755948	Sgt	HEADLAND Bertram Arthur	15-05-41	20 OTU		82677	F/O	HILL Henry Thomas	24-11-41	97 Sqn
754418	F/S	HEALD Harold	24-07-41	12 Sqn		778463	Sgt	HILL James Cornelius [Rhodesia]	24-10-41	16 OTU
642544	Sgt	HEALING Frank Douglas	2-03-41	61 Sqn		935567	Sgt	HILL John Edward	10-02-41	61 Sqn
978873	Sgt	HEALY Walter Brendan	26-08-41	105 Sqn		83253	P/O	HILL John Kenneth	17-04-41	50 Sqn
979954	Sgt	HEANEY William Thomas	23-04-41	105 Sqn		979240	Sgt	HILL Lawrence	2-08-41	101 Sqn
40389	F/L	HEATHCOTE MiD Gilbert Gresley	18-12-41	15 Sqn		742464	F/S	HILL Lewis Albert	18-10-41	27 OTU
905779	Sgt	HEATHER Edward James Henry	29-09-41	18 OTU		1256667	AC2	HILL Lionel Peter	30-08-41	218 Sqn
83997	P/O	HEAVENS Richard John	23-06-41	83 Sqn		1006747	Sgt	HILL Richard George	8-09-41	12 Sqn
754459	Sgt	HEAYSMAN Gordon Ernest	18-04-41	9 Sqn		40300	F/L	HILL DFC Robert James	14-03-41	13 OTU
1001649	Sgt	HEDIN DFM Sigurd Edgar	11-12-41	18 Sqn		1167921	Sgt	HILL Rowland Bertram Dunstan	8-09-41	115 Sqn
1117288	Sgt	HEDLEY John Alexander	27-10-41	17 OTU		65762	P/O	HILL Rowland Mytton	25-07-41	11 OTU
967663	Sgt	HEGGIE Alistair Alexander Stobie	25-08-41	35 Sqn		551932	F/S	HILL Roy William Joseph	24-07-41	76 Sqn
745475	Sgt	HEIGHTON Hubert Richard	8-07-41	10 Sqn		967754	Sgt	HILL Stanley Godfrey	14-04-41	139 Sqn
787204	F/S	HEJNA Jan [Czechoslovakia]	2-06-41	311 Sqn		581454	Sgt	HILL Victor Clarence	4-02-41	18 OTU
552112	F/S	HELLER DFM Albert James	26-07-41	35 Sqn		1403363	AC1	HILTON George Sanders	13-08-41	11 OTU
650057	Sgt	HELLIER Harry Thomas [Canada]	21-02-41	75 Sqn		41179	F/L	HILTON Horace Colvill	7-07-41	139 Sqn
787190	Sgt	HELMA Oldrich [Czechoslovakia]	2-07-41	311 Sqn		61296	P/O	HINCHLIFFE Walter Edmund	13-10-41	50 Sqn
82724	F/O	HELMORE Henry Victor Thomas	27-06-41	12 Sqn		948679	Sgt	HIND Michael Christopher	26-08-41	82 Sqn
547503	Sgt	HEMINGWAY Harry Walker	13-03-41	207 Sqn		648984	F/S	HIND Robert Frederick	9-06-41	18 Sqn
935682	Sgt	HEMMINGS Bernard	7-09-41	144 Sqn		926469	Sgt	HINDE Lawrence Rex	18-06-41	50 Sqn
628516	F/S	HEMSLEY George William	7-08-41	20 OTU		569132	Sgt	HINTON Roger [South Africa]	3-03-41	7 Sqn
82170	F/O	HENDERSON Andrew James	6-07-41	49 Sqn		81687	P/O	HIPPS Arnold	19-07-41	15 Sqn
978536	Sgt	HENDERSON David Francis	10-04-41	218 Sqn		936364	F/S	HIRD Leonard	28-06-41	10 Sqn
1054954	Sgt	HENDERSON John George	17-12-41	44 Sqn		964851	Sgt	HIRONS Richard Eric	8-12-41	144 Sqn
33406	F/O	HENDERSON Ian Stuart	21-02-41	149 Sqn		754017	Sgt	HIRSCHFIELD Sidney Owen	5-08-41	50 Sqn
918442	Sgt	HENDERSON Ivor Howard Arthur	16-08-41	104 Sqn		1261971	Sgt	HISCOCK John Robert	15-10-41	40 Sqn
83932	F/L	HENDERSON Roger Arnold	23-11-41	13 OTU		920537	Sgt	HISCOCK Wilfred Leonard	12-07-41	82 Sqn
982890	Sgt	HENDERSON Robert	28-07-41	90 Sqn		904310	Sgt	HITCHCOCK Cornelius Matthew Flinders		
1253157	Sgt	HENLEY Roy Frederick Joseph	22-12-41	107 Sqn					9-04-41	214 Sqn
43631	F/S	HENNESSEY Brendan Patrick	21-11-41	109 Sqn		625698	Sgt	HIVES Samuel Arthur	3-05-41	7 Sqn
628890	F/S	HENNIGAN DFM Patrick Leo	17-10-41	40 Sqn		1280511	Sgt	HOAD Harry George	26-03-41	15 OTU
909599	Sgt	HENNING William Charles	17-05-41	20 OTU		745891	Sgt	HOARE Alfred Charles	2-03-41	10 Sqn
39876	F/L	HENRY DFC Michael Thomas Gibson				956948	Sgt	HOARE David Allen Downer	15-08-41	105 Sqn
			13-01-41	35 Sqn		622339	Sgt	HOBAN James	24-07-41	40 Sqn
88474	P/O	HERBERT Christopher Reginald	27-06-41	150 Sqn		944085	Sgt	HOBBS Hubert	15-09-41	455 Sqn
60137	F/L	HERD DFC Thomas Brodie	8-11-41	106 Sqn		645979	Sgt	HOBBS Raymond John	22-10-41	458 Sqn
940628	Sgt	HERMAN William Peter	19-06-41	78 Sqn		64915	P/O	HODGE Andrew Charles Lang	20-10-41	149 Sqn
536989	Sgt	HERRING Robert Stephen	15-08-41	104 Sqn		1152494	Sgt	HODGE David Gall	3-08-41	104 Sqn
940147	F/S	HERRINGTON Tom	13-08-41	104 Sqn		1104390	Sgt	HODGE Donald Hartley	1-09-41	99 Sqn
1154057	Sgt	HERROD William Grenville	31-07-41	99 Sqn		80091	P/O	HODGE Donald Kinnear	8-11-41	97 Sqn

1179658	Sgt	HODGE Samuel Carter	15-10-41	40 Sqn
964968	Sgt	HODGES Eric Frank Elkanah	27-12-41	58 Sqn
912102	Sgt	HODGES John Edward	11-05-41	40 Sqn
1266648	AC1	HODGES Wilson Aubrey	24-10-41	40 Sqn
83725	P/O	HODGSON Phillip Booth	3-06-41	50 Sqn
89066	P/O	HODGSON Thomas Riley	17-05-41	17 OTU
746845	Sgt	HODKINSON Charles	29-08-41	49 Sqn
1158544	Sgt	HODNETT Leslie Owen	19-06-41	12 OTU
944266	Sgt	HODSON Will Frank	11-05-41	7 Sqn
940001	Sgt	HOGAN Edward Peter	13-08-41	76 Sqn
45523	P/O	HOGAN DFC Frederick James	8-09-41	90 Sqn
1057325	Sgt	HOGDEN John Denis	27-09-41	20 OTU
625425	Sgt	HOGG Bennett	21-03-41	207 Sqn
748344	Sgt	HOLBOROW Robert John	8-04-41	14 OTU
45096	P/O	HOLDEN Frederick William [Canada]	18-04-41	61 Sqn
968028	Sgt	HOLDEN Thomas Arthur	5-07-41	61 Sqn
992165	Sgt	HOLDEN Willie	9-11-41	25 OTU
745890	Sgt	HOLDER Kenneth Ernest	31-03-41	14 OTU
1223122	AC2	HOLDSTOCK Frederick Benjamin	25-02-41	11 OTU
749461	Sgt	HOLDSWORTH Jack Nicholson	3-03-41	7 Sqn
560790	F/S	HOLE Alfred George	2-09-41	139 Sqn
751976	Sgt	HOLLAND DFM Ernest John	13-04-41	149 Sqn
1183850	Sgt	HOLLAND Stanley Keith	22-10-41	16 OTU
1190121	Sgt	HOLLEY Douglas Cecil	12-10-41	75 Sqn
553797	Sgt	HOLLINGSHEAD Marcus Anthony	6-04-41	83 Sqn
968358	Sgt	HOLLINGWORTH John French	3-07-41	78 Sqn
912623	Cpl	HOLLIS Harold Edward	29-04-41	82 Sqn
1251619	Sgt	HOLLOBONE Roy James	29-08-41	405 Sqn
947424	Sgt	HOLLOWAY John Lemuel	8-11-41	51 Sqn
84890	F/O	HOLLOWAY Royston Charles	15-10-41	139 Sqn
966883	Sgt	HOLMAN Edward John	4-04-41	106 Sqn
966817	Sgt	HOLME Herbert Thomas	24-07-41	50 Sqn
968372	Sgt	HOLMES Anthony Russell	26-07-41	102 Sqn
78276	F/O	HOLMES Frank	30-04-41	18 Sqn
1152495	Sgt	HOLMES Kenneth Amory	24-10-41	44 Sqn
993614	Sgt	HOLROYD Howgate Ian	3-06-41	11 OTU
1007372	Sgt	HOLT Fred	24-11-41	97 Sqn
749319	Sgt	HOLT John	9-05-41	214 Sqn
755357	Sgt	HOLT Stanley John	30-04-41	99 Sqn
907357	Sgt	HOLYMAN Rodney Charles	13-08-41	104 Sqn
1376306	Sgt	HOMES Alan Christopher	15-11-41	115 Sqn
1150620	Sgt	HONEY Walter George	8-09-41	90 Sqn
923077	Sgt	HOOD Kenneth Frederick	20-09-41	226 Sqn
754749	Sgt	HOOK Leslie Herbert	5-09-41	12 OTU
759193	Sgt	HOPE Peter	18-04-41	21 Sqn
1280952	Sgt	HOPKINS Michael John	15-05-41	16 OTU
111240	P/O	HOPKINS Reginald John [South Africa]	23-12-41	21 OTU
910292	Sgt	HOPKINSON Kenneth William	20-07-41	139 Sqn
1007199	Sgt	HORABIN John	26-09-41	115 Sqn
580697	F/S	HORN Arthur Anthony	5-07-41	61 Sqn
960947	Sgt	HORNE Joseph Edwin	30-09-41	58 Sqn
560615	F/S	HORNER Charles Henry	24-07-41	76 Sqn
759240	F/S	HORNIMAN John Knob Emslie	13-06-41	103 Sqn
74653	P/O	HORROCKS David Wilson	27-06-41	40 Sqn
998711	Sgt	HORROCKS James Wilfred	20-10-41	149 Sqn
88864	P/O	HORSFIELD John Ellis	1-07-41	149 Sqn
751373	Sgt	HORSHAM John Frederick	11-04-41	18 Sqn
1177136	Sgt	HORSLEY John Miller	15-11-41	115 Sqn
943238	Sgt	HORTON Eric	7-09-41	144 Sqn
1209438	Sgt	HOSKIN Eric Charles	12-12-41	10 Sqn
1251656	Sgt	HOSKINS William Joseph Harry	4-07-41	57 Sqn
1062428	Sgt	HOUGH Ronald Foxley	25-11-41	49 Sqn
906068	Sgt	HOUGHTON George	16-06-41	103 Sqn
748793	Sgt	HOUSE Donald Vaughan	17-04-41	83 Sqn
959988	Sgt	HOW Reginald Burchell	9-11-41	9 Sqn
755223	Sgt	HOWARD George Herbert	31-03-41	21 Sqn
916066	Sgt	HOWE David Hinton	6-08-41	44 Sqn
922431	Sgt	HOWE Jack Kenneth	29-09-41	16 OTU
631240	Sgt	HOWELL Harry	13-03-41	50 Sqn
552601	Sgt	HOWELL DFM Jack	10-04-41	144 Sqn
67709	P/O	HOWELL James Clarence	19-09-41	58 Sqn
551850	Sgt	HOWELLS Brinley	15-12-41	408 Sqn
920805	Sgt	HOWES Albert John	21-07-41	76 Sqn
62300	P/O	HOWES Peter Ronald Greville	14-06-41	110 Sqn
745810	Sgt	HOWETT John	7-11-41	50 Sqn
550180	Sgt	HOWLETT William John	6-04-41	107 Sqn
961341	Sgt	HUBANK Francis Everard	17-04-41	16 OTU
1256349	Sgt	HUBBARD Frederick Charles	8-12-41	82 Sqn
551931	Sgt	HUBBARD James William	7-12-41	21 OTU
960339	Sgt	HUCKETT Richard Henry	15-11-41	115 Sqn
938919	Sgt	HUDDLESTONE John Nevil	2-03-41	9 Sqn
82604	F/O	HUDEC Josef [Czechoslovakia]	16-01-41	311 Sqn
964546	Sgt	HUDGELL Kenneth Napier	21-07-41	76 Sqn
620414	Sgt	HUDSON George	29-09-41	57 Sqn
88226	P/O	HUDSON Gordon David Gerald	9-05-41	83 Sqn
564248	F/S	HUDSON DFM Philip	7-07-41	97 Sqn
591141	Sgt	HUDSON Ronald Edward Cornwall	13-08-41	104 Sqn
632878	Sgt	HUFFINLEY Jack	13-03-41	218 Sqn
745281	Sgt	HUGGETT Vernon Douglas	28-05-41	150 Sqn
988137	Sgt	HUGHES Arthur William	18-04-41	20 OTU
1165297	Sgt	HUGHES Dennis Walter	4-07-41	82 Sqn
541349	F/S	HUGHES Edward	15-05-41	20 OTU
751491	Sgt	HUGHES Eric	2-03-41	51 Sqn
1153459	Sgt	HUGHES George Percival	30-11-41	142 Sqn
1053682	Sgt	HUGHES Harry	25-10-41	25 OTU
1153798	Sgt	HUGHES James	1-09-41	83 Sqn
965678	Sgt	HUGHES James Finlay	2-05-41	77 Sqn
987753	Sgt	HUGHES John	16-07-41	18 Sqn
929395	Sgt	HUGHES Michael Joseph	21-10-41	44 Sqn
759019	Sgt	HUGHES Vernon	7-05-41	18 Sqn
754151	Sgt	HUGHES DFM Wilfred Douglas	30-06-41	50 Sqn
41182	S/L	HUGHES MiD William	20-07-41	18 Sqn
912001	Sgt	HULL Ronald Douglas	14-07-41	214 Sqn
1110718	Sgt	HULLS Arthur Robert	29-09-41	115 Sqn
939951	Sgt	HUMBLE MiD Cyril Gerrard	12-06-41	51 Sqn
39317	F/L	HUMPHERSON DFC John Bernard William	22-06-41	90 Sqn
553851	Sgt	HUMPHREY David Alfred	9-06-41	9 Sqn
06251	G/C	HUMPHREYS Dudley d'Herbez	15-03-41	3 Group
922019	Sgt	HUMPHRIES Albert William	15-10-41	139 Sqn
653209	Sgt	HUMPHRIES Arthur George	15-04-41	149 Sqn
937273	Sgt	HUMPHRIES Joseph	28-06-41	77 Sqn
755673	Sgt	HUNT Claude Samuel	30-04-41	3 GTrgFlt
944629	Sgt	HUNT George Thomas	23-06-41	214 Sqn
923092	Sgt	HUNT Nigel Frederick	20-10-41	97 Sqn
1060924	Sgt	HUNT Reginald Lewis	22-10-41	150 Sqn
37356	W/C	HUNT DFC Theodore Moseley	18-07-41	110 Sqn
1376651	AC1	HUNT Walter Francis	28-08-41	11 OTU
754134	Sgt	HUNTER Ivor Peter	14-06-41	102 Sqn
992581	Sgt	HUNTER Joseph	20-07-41	18 Sqn
755013	Sgt	HUNTER Thomas Seymour Henley	4-02-41	3 GTrgFlt
945410	Sgt	HUNTER William	12-05-41	17 OTU
580011	F/S	HUNTLEY Denis Arthur	2-07-41	226 Sqn
620452	Sgt	HUNTLEY Kenneth	1-07-41	7 Sqn
37288	W/C	HURST Ralph George	4-07-41	226 Sqn
543293	Sgt	HURT Harry Franklin	18-04-41	9 Sqn
550811	F/S	HURT John Ronald	17-06-41	115 Sqn
787557	Sgt	HURT Karel [Czechoslovakia]	23-10-41	311 Sqn
751601	Sgt	HURWORTH George Fenwick	15-02-41	15 Sqn
745934	Sgt	HUSTON Reginald Vere	2-03-41	51 Sqn
104449	P/O	HUTCHIN Ronald Edward	14-09-41	76 Sqn
944317	Sgt	HUTCHINSON Cyril	2-05-41	77 Sqn
938149	Sgt	HUTCHINSON Harry	21-06-41	218 Sqn
961049	Sgt	HUTCHINSON Kenneth	17-08-41	104 Sqn
942328	Sgt	HUTCHINSON Ronald	13-04-41	149 Sqn

538150	Sgt	HUTCHISON John	1-05-41	139 Sqn	904430	Sgt	JARRETT Frank Maitland	9-04-41	149 Sqn
755666	Sgt	HUTSON Gerald George	5-07-41	106 Sqn	923216	Sgt	JARRETT Peter William	14-10-41	115 Sqn
523734	F/S	HUTT Kenneth John [Canada]	15-05-41	97 Sqn	759159	Sgt	JARVIS Peter	28-05-41	150 Sqn
1161691	Sgt	HUTT Robert Keith	7-09-41	57 Sqn	758013	Sgt	JEEVES Dennis Herbert	19-07-41	15 Sqn
580579	Sgt	HYDE Thomas Eric	3-06-41	139 Sqn	88034	P/O	JEFF John Ernest Philip	3-05-41	44 Sqn
921902	Sgt	HYNAM Charles Colin	8-11-41	405 Sqn	79240	F/O	JEFFCOAT Henry Jeffrey	13-12-41	44 Sqn
646891	Sgt	HYSLOP William Morgan	10-01-41	51 Sqn	911827	AC1	JEFFCOTE Thomas Bernard	1-08-41	44 Sqn
1193119	Sgt	ILLINGWORTH George Stuart	30-11-41	10 Sqn	759325	Sgt	JEFFERIES James Farrar	10-05-41	144 Sqn
1162800	Sgt	ILSLEY Ivan Walter Robert	20-08-41	83 Sqn	902482	F/S	JEFFERIS Douglas John	17-06-41	51 Sqn
994392	Sgt	IMISON Gerald Percy	8-08-41	97 Sqn	1176659	Sgt	JEFFERY William Frederick	17-09-41	17 OTU
78739	F/O	INDERWICK Alan Gerard	7-09-41	58 Sqn	1165680	Sgt	JEFFREYS Kenneth Ainslie	18-12-41	15 Sqn
526092	Sgt	INGHAM Percy	30-06-41	35 Sqn	1259260	Sgt	JEFFRIES Arthur William	12-10-41	57 Sqn
919910	Sgt	INGRAM Edward Robert	29-06-41	78 Sqn	129267	P/O	JENKINS Frederick	13-10-41	40 Sqn
1286290	Sgt	INGRAM Peter Arthur	8-11-41	106 Sqn	64315	P/O	JENKINS John Charles	15-07-41	214 Sqn
571077	Cpl	INKPEN William	25-08-41	83 Sqn	1255580	Sgt	JENKINS Maurice Albert	7-11-41	455 Sqn
748460	Sgt	INMAN Edwin Bentall	27-05-41	82 Sqn	968179	Sgt	JENKINS William Kenneth	5-07-41	114 Sqn
43036	P/O	INNISS George Harold Frederick [Barbados]	4-02-41	106 Sqn	76584	F/O	JENKYNS Reginald Maurice Peter	7-07-41	214 Sqn
					511537	F/S	JENNINGS DFM Clifford	18-04-41	114 Sqn
902411	Sgt	IRELAND Eric William	11-10-41	218 Sqn	748740	Sgt	JENNINGS David Walter	15-10-41	57 Sqn
755021	Sgt	IRESON Frank Lewis Thomas	25-07-41	83 Sqn	509138	Sgt	JENNINGS Herbert Frederick	3-03-41	58 Sqn
934541	Sgt	IRISH Cyril Vivian	18-10-41	27 OTU	976358	Sgt	JEPSON Albert	3-07-41	78 Sqn
88407	P/O	IRVING Desmond	1-07-41	83 Sqn	77965	F/L	JEREMY DFC Ithel David	15-09-41	305 Sqn
754792	Sgt	IRVING Henry	12-01-41	49 Sqn	961532	Sgt	JERRARD John Edward	29-08-41	214 Sqn
741216	F/S	IRVING John Maurice	10-04-41	82 Sqn	635446	Sgt	JESS Samuel Hugh Albert	13-03-41	102 Sqn
951459	Sgt	IRWIN John Cecil Brandon	4-07-41	57 Sqn	633777	Sgt	JESSE DFM William Charles Browne [Eire]	13-01-41	35 Sqn
1259257	Sgt	ISAAC Peter Frederick	28-12-41	408 Sqn					
60344	F/O	IVENS Douglas Hickling	6-12-41	110 Sqn	950861	Sgt	JESSOP Fred Senior	31-03-41	14 OTU
916104	Sgt	IVORY Herbert Thomas	16-06-41	78 Sqn	911895	Sgt	JESSUP Alexander Anthony	8-09-41	51 Sqn
1283378	Sgt	IXER John Howard	20-09-41	16 OTU	923700	Sgt	JEWELL Frederick Lancelot Charles	13-10-41	139 Sqn
994357	Sgt	JACKETS Allan	17-08-41	21 OTU	788021	Sgt	JINDRA Miroslav [Czechoslovakia]	19-07-41	311 Sqn
61942	P/O	JACKSON DFM Anthony Eyre	6-04-41	83 Sqn	745105	Sgt	JINKS William Pryce	21-02-41	149 Sqn
939087	F/S	JACKSON Arthur	10-05-41	51 Sqn	1288650	Sgt	JOHNSON Alan Hewitt Abbott	25-07-41	17 OTU
44194	P/O	JACKSON Eric	21-05-41	Oakington	1166116	Sgt	JOHNSON Bramwell Frederick Thomas	17-07-41	40 Sqn
927080	Sgt	JACKSON Garrick David	28-06-41	102 Sqn					
1253256	Sgt	JACKSON George William Turner	15-10-41	57 Sqn	989623	LAC	JOHNSON Clifford Ambrose	28-08-41	114 Sqn
1250304	Sgt	JACKSON John Ernest	13-06-41	25 OTU	553988	Sgt	JOHNSON Douglas Alfred	5-07-41	61 Sqn
974097	Sgt	JACKSON Leonard	12-01-41	49 Sqn	942099	Sgt	JOHNSON Harry Ellse	20-08-41	104 Sqn
745522	Sgt	JACKSON Maurice George	21-05-41	110 Sqn	66519	P/O	JOHNSON James Edward	6-09-41	75 Sqn
972564	Sgt	JACKSON Norman Frederick	16-04-41	10 Sqn	751266	Sgt	JOHNSON John Ernest	18-04-41	9 Sqn
39016	S/L	JACKSON Philip Howard	9-05-41	99 Sqn	646573	Sgt	JOHNSON Norman Frank	13-03-41	77 Sqn
1251073	Sgt	JACKSON Robert	24-10-41	40 Sqn	652268	Sgt	JOHNSON Reginald Alfred	27-12-41	58 Sqn
1062368	Sgt	JACKSON Stanley Heelis	11-12-41	57 Sqn	958966	Sgt	JOHNSON Stanley	27-12-41	101 Sqn
1182826	Sgt	JACKSON Stuart William	16-07-41	57 Sqn	591395	Sgt	JOHNSTON Arthur Gerald	5-12-41	15 OTU
995859	Sgt	JACKSON Thomas	20-10-41	458 Sqn	39319	F/L	JOHNSTON Donald Thurston	13-03-41	50 Sqn
1158295	Sgt	JACOBOVITCH Israel (served as JACKSON)	12-07-41	50 Sqn	913313	Sgt	JOHNSTON Henry Bruce Stirling	19-08-41	9 Sqn
					913608	Sgt	JOHNSTON John St. George	20-10-41	149 Sqn
112160	P/O	JACOBS Derek	11-12-41	83 Sqn	776002	Sgt	JOHNSTON Peter Simpson Dickson [Middle East]	6-09-41	75 Sqn
1285616	Sgt	JACOBS Henry Emanuel	25-10-41	25 OTU					
912736	Sgt	JACOBS John Henry Scott	24-02-41	115 Sqn	1052109	Sgt	JOHNSTONE Peter	8-11-41	7 Sqn
963442	Sgt	JACOBS Michael Stanley	8-11-41	7 Sqn	552490	F/S	JOLIN Cyril John	28-07-41	50 Sqn
79375	F/O	JACOBY Maurice	30-09-41	142 Sqn	748009	Sgt	JONES Arthur Edwin	16-01-41	40 Sqn
751860	Sgt	JAGGER Harry	2-04-41	21 Sqn	88684	P/O	JONES Benedict Warren Melvill	6-08-41	104 Sqn
927337	Sgt	JAGGERS Alexander Frederick	3-09-41	102 Sqn	1061957	Sgt	JONES Brynmor Samuel	15-10-41	57 Sqn
904013	Sgt	JAGO John Barker Churchill	9-04-41	149 Sqn	84892	P/O	JONES Cecil Ernest Benton	25-07-41	11 OTU
933166	Sgt	JAKINS Cyril	25-11-41	142 Sqn	89361	P/O	JONES Cecil Frank [Rhodesia]	8-04-41	58 Sqn
748461	Sgt	JAMES Alick Michael	22-06-41	207 Sqn	1253004	Sgt	JONES Dan Davies	30-11-41	106 Sqn
751375	Sgt	JAMES Cyril Douglas	8-09-41	90 Sqn	1071392	AC2	JONES David Stephen	15-03-41	214 Sqn
1252091	Sgt	JAMES Edwin Ralph	20-10-41	50 Sqn	947825	Sgt	JONES Edward Stanley	29-08-41	104 Sqn
943703	Sgt	JAMES Harry	7-02-41	16 OTU	580925	F/S	JONES Edward Thomas William	19-08-41	114 Sqn
917059	Sgt	JAMES Ronald	28-12-41	405 Sqn	947989	Sgt	JONES Godfrey Tegid	25-06-41	214 Sqn
42062	F/O	JAMES DFC Ross	3-09-41	35 Sqn	977479	Sgt	JONES Harold	3-07-41	75 Sqn
541997	Sgt	JAMES Thomas Webley	12-05-41	214 Sqn	63068	P/O	JONES Harold Peter Griffith	11-04-41	18 Sqn
911034	Sgt	JAMES Williams Phillips	30-04-41	99 Sqn	100047	P/O	JONES Haydn	27-10-41	114 Sqn
1002131	Sgt	JAMIESON John Alexander Barrie	19-08-41	51 Sqn	916706	LAC	JONES Henry	18-11-41	15 OTU
928276	Sgt	JAMIESON Samuel	11-12-41	408 Sqn	973995	Sgt	JONES Henry	12-03-41	40 Sqn
787846	Sgt	JANUJ Otakar [Czechoslovakia]	23-10-41	311 Sqn	1059799	Sgt	JONES John Emrys	4-09-41	107 Sqn
988504	Sgt	JAQUES Ernest Henry	15-11-41	11 OTU	573164	Cpl	JONES John Eric	23-07-41	21 OTU
787394	Sgt	JARNOT Alois [Czechoslovakia]	15-09-41	311 Sqn	975754	Sgt	JONES John Graham	20-09-41	142 Sqn

Number	Rank	Name	Date	Unit
39441	P/O	JONES John Reginald Arthur	26-08-41	88 Sqn
982910	Sgt	JONES Kenneth Ivor	29-06-41	78 Sqn
905337	F/S	JONES DFM Leslie William	18-12-41	97 Sqn
88866	P/O	JONES Morray Nigel Feltham	27-06-41	102 Sqn
348270	Cpl	JONES Norman Grenville	12-03-41	12 OTU
553850	Sgt	JONES Raymond James Stanley	1-03-41	144 Sqn
777678	Sgt	JONES Robert Charles Dillon [Rhodesia]	24-10-41	16 OTU
974122	F/S	JONES Ronald Gibson	28-06-41	10 Sqn
1150676	Sgt	JONES Sidney James Holroyd	8-11-41	106 Sqn
1053361	Sgt	JONES Stanley	9-10-41	107 Sqn
968353	Sgt	JONES Sylvester	1-03-41	105 Sqn
611218	Sgt	JONES Thomas	24-06-41	57 Sqn
1006271	Sgt	JONES Thomas Gronwy	20-10-41	106 Sqn
902910	Sgt	JONES Trevor Henry Barton	16-09-41	15 Sqn
529825	F/S	JOPLING Robert	17-08-41	78 Sqn
754881	Sgt	JORDAN Arthur	26-04-41	21 Sqn
949055	Sgt	JORDAN John Johnstone	29-06-41	218 Sqn
1253067	Sgt	JORDAN Roy Harold	6-07-41	10 Sqn
67086	P/O	JUDD Kenneth Charles	26-08-41	82 Sqn
998283	Sgt	JUDGE Horace Hill	11-10-41	218 Sqn
581459	F/S	JUPP Anthony Charles	9-04-41	7 Sqn
941669	Sgt	KABY Norman	27-12-41	110 Sqn
1019003	AC2	KANE Thomas	17-05-41	106 Sqn
80117	P/O	KASCHULA Therald Lionel [Rhodesia]	17-12-41	44 Sqn
984058	Sgt	KAY Donald Stephen	30-11-41	58 Sqn
983616	Sgt	KAY Harold	2-09-41	83 Sqn
1052113	Sgt	KAY Harold	15-08-41	104 Sqn
647782	Sgt	KAY John	12-05-41	58 Sqn
1164457	Sgt	KAY John Hampson	22-10-41	99 Sqn
1377632	Sgt	KAY Philip	20-10-41	99 Sqn
919902	Sgt	KAYE Gordon Allan	7-06-41	107 Sqn
748708	F/S	KEANE David Graham	25-05-41	18 Sqn
650014	Sgt	KEARNEY Francis Theodore	1-07-41	149 Sqn
924343	Sgt	KEARSLEY Bernard Thomas	29-08-41	40 Sqn
940033	Sgt	KEATES John Alfred	9-05-41	149 Sqn
915015	Sgt	KEDDIE John Maitland	4-01-41	99 Sqn
927368	Sgt	KEEBLE Jock Gordon Clement	30-09-41	115 Sqn
747727	Sgt	KEEN James Henry	15-08-41	150 Sqn
937434	Sgt	KEETLEY Eric	4-04-41	115 Sqn
551825	Sgt	KEHOE John Edward [Eire]	8-11-41	49 Sqn
1058822	Sgt	KEIGHLEY Ralph	13-08-41	115 Sqn
86324	P/O	KEIGHLEY Richard Francis	21-09-41	7 Flt
89067	P/O	KEIGHTLEY-SMITH Thomas	25-04-41	105 Sqn
944883	Sgt	KELLINGTON Clifford	21-09-41	144 Sqn
751745	Sgt	KELLY Charles	28-06-41	7 Sqn
33207	S/L	KELLY Three times MiD Dermot Daly Aloysius	16-06-41	103 Sqn
1375470	Sgt	KELLY George Eugene	21-09-41	20 OTU
1004519	Sgt	KELLY Howard Gordon	23-12-41	21 OTU
971259	Sgt	KELLY Hugh Alphonsus	29-08-41	103 Sqn
970149	Sgt	KELLY John Desmond Lamb	4-01-41	51 Sqn
903258	Sgt	KELLY John Henderson	20-03-41	82 Sqn
746454	Sgt	KELLY Thomas	11-10-41	57 Sqn
945217	F/S	KELLY William	19-06-41	10 Sqn
943287	Sgt	KEMP Clifford Roy	17-01-41	10 OTU
37882	S/L	KEMP Cyril Sydney	23-02-41	107 Sqn
961558	Sgt	KEMP Derek George	7-09-41	77 Sqn
755825	Sgt	KEMP Edwin Howard Whitley	12-05-41	58 Sqn
1141845	AC2	KEMP Percy Charles	18-06-41	50 Sqn
646706	Sgt	KEMP Stanley William	27-05-41	82 Sqn
755195	Sgt	KENDALL Norman Ernest Thomas	18-04-41	110 Sqn
942317	Sgt	KENNARD Kenneth [Canada]	23-02-41	115 Sqn
743053	F/S	KENNARD Leslie John	16-05-41	40 Sqn
552595	Sgt	KENNEDY Alan Leigh	3-04-41	77 Sqn
919756	Sgt	KENNEDY Eric Douglas	27-10-41	114 Sqn
66527	P/O	KENNEDY Gerald Moore	3-07-41	78 Sqn
974128	Sgt	KENNEDY James	3-01-41	102 Sqn
1360281	Sgt	KENNEDY John Wilson	26-12-41	13 OTU
551620	F/S	KENNY Thomas Brendon	13-04-41	19 OTU
1350617	AC2	KENT Arthur	13-02-41	Waterbeach
745050	Sgt	KENT Robert	2-08-41	214 Sqn
559083	Sgt	KENT Robert William George	11-12-41	35 Sqn
1193600	Sgt	KENVIN Robert Herbert	12-09-41	149 Sqn
974196	Sgt	KENYON Jeffrey Clifford	17-06-41	10 OTU
983129	Sgt	KERR Frank Young Downie	18-12-41	97 Sqn
87062	F/O	KERR George Donald	30-10-41	14 OTU
81041	P/O	KERR Noel James [Eire]	10-04-41	144 Sqn
43295	P/O	KERR MiD Robert Ernest [Australia]	5-07-41	51 Sqn
912844	Sgt	KERRIDGE Cyril Walter	16-04-41	13 OTU
1255195	Sgt	KERRISON Jack William	14-10-41	114 Sqn
966033	Sgt	KERRUISH Robert William Ronald	7-07-41	115 Sqn
1153499	Sgt	KETTERINGHAM Laurence William	11-12-41	35 Sqn
1050133	Sgt	KETTLEWELL Arthur	7-09-41	49 Sqn
948441	Sgt	KEYMER Robert Sydney Langston	16-05-41	78 Sqn
904428	Sgt	KEYMER John Gilbert	10-05-41	149 Sqn
1157291	Sgt	KIDBY Robert George	4-12-41	107 Sqn
88029	P/O	KIDD Frederick Lawrence	6-11-41	144 Sqn
60813	P/O	KIDD Gordon Herbert	25-04-41	51 Sqn
745006	Sgt	KIDDLE Leslie Ernest	30-03-41	101 Sqn
751525	Sgt	KILLEN John	21-03-41	150 Sqn
1383050	Sgt	KILSBY William George	10-09-41	25 OTU
904527	Sgt	KING Cecil Hubert	23-03-41	105 Sqn
751304	Sgt	KING Douglas Stevenson Hutcheon	24-04-41	107 Sqn
918289	Sgt	KING Edward Henry	7-07-41	214 Sqn
27107	S/L	KING George Stephen	13-05-41	82 Sqn
998504	Sgt	KING Harold	15-05-41	20 OTU
1288638	Sgt	KING Harold Christopher	24-10-41	21 OTU
625416	Sgt	KING James Ernest	16-11-41	149 Sqn
63820	P/O	KING John Edward	29-08-41	40 Sqn
944474	Sgt	KING John Rennie	21-02-41	16 OTU
966959	Sgt	KING Kenneth Albert	5-07-41	51 Sqn
1104414	Sgt	KING Walter	8-11-41	106 Sqn
995249	AC2	KINLOCH John	2-01-41	106 Sqn
1105563	Sgt	KINNEAR Alexander Greig	7-11-41	58 Sqn
754444	Sgt	KIPLING Bernard	10-05-41	51 Sqn
614312	Sgt	KIPLING Matthew George	30-12-41	35 Sqn
905800	Sgt	KIRBY Arthur William	14-08-41	110 Sqn
327242	LAC	KIRBY George William Alfred	28-07-41	Mildenhall
745805	Sgt	KIRBY Henry	17-04-41	144 Sqn
759233	Sgt	KIRBY Reginald Denis	12-05-41	58 Sqn
755374	Sgt	KIRK Lewis John	21-03-41	150 Sqn
921911	Sgt	KIRK Victor Frank Douglas	8-11-41	51 Sqn
1169259	Sgt	KISSACK Laurence Douglas	21-09-41	214 Sqn
34198	S/L	KITCHING Grenville Arthur	27-06-41	12 Sqn
945736	LAC	KITE Cuthbert Ernest	1-07-41	15 Sqn
740629	F/S	KITELY Frank Christopher Nugent	27-09-41	20 OTU
1257373	Sgt	KITLEY John Edward	27-12-41	114 Sqn
625948	F/S	KITSON DFM Herbert James Hawkins	27-09-41	20 OTU
580055	F/S	KITSON DFM Walter Stanley	29-08-41	9 Sqn
915976	Sgt	KLUSKY Gerald	29-08-41	214 Sqn
918540	Sgt	KNAPE Alan Harwood	28-06-41	10 Sqn
1161364	Sgt	KNIGHT Gordon	26-08-41	40 Sqn
65538	P/O	KNIGHT Harold	30-11-41	58 Sqn
918519	Sgt	KNIGHT Jack Harris	31-10-41	51 Sqn
745273	Sgt	KNIGHTON Thomas Halford	4-04-41	51 Sqn
929872	Sgt	KNIGHTON Victor George	8-11-41	150 Sqn
1259857	Sgt	KNOTT Reginald Cooper	11-11-41	115 Sqn
45123	P/O	KNOWLES John Samuel	30-11-41	10 Sqn
948920	Sgt	KNOX Francis Samuel Burnside	7-06-41	107 Sqn
929438	Sgt	KOLAR Charles Ceasar	20-10-41	97 Sqn
80119	P/O	KOLITZ Louis Phillip [Rhodesia]	24-07-41	218 Sqn
82608	P/O	KONSTACKY Vilem [Czechoslovakia]	23-06-41	311 Sqn
920227	Sgt	KORANSKY Michael	4-09-41	18 Sqn

Service No	Rank	Name	Date	Sqn
936531	F/S	KOSSICK Arnold	13-06-41	44 Sqn
82609	P/O	KOSULIC Vaclav J. J. [Czechoslovakia]	17-04-41	311 Sqn
787244	Sgt	KRACMER Frantisek [Czechoslovakia]	17-04-41	311 Sqn
82612	P/O	KRAL Jaromir Oldrich [Czechoslovakia]	16-01-41	311 Sqn
82613	P/O	KUBICEK Vladimir [Czechoslovakia]	17-04-41	311 Sqn
82556	F/O	KUBIZNAK Antonin [Czechoslovakia]	16-01-41	311 Sqn
914495	Sgt	KYBIRD Stanley George	24-07-41	40 Sqn
37505	S/L	KYDD DSO DFC Charles John French	23-06-41	207 Sqn
1117204	Sgt	KYLE James	15-08-41	12 Sqn
742023	Sgt	KYLE Kenneth George William	3-04-41	77 Sqn
755076	Sgt	LABAN Ernest William	7-04-41	139 Sqn
1155594	LAC	LACKEY Harold	12-05-41	58 Sqn
921758	Sgt	LAGER Eric Harry	17-08-41	10 Sqn
88408	P/O	LAIDLAW William	20-10-41	50 Sqn
625929	Sgt	LAING Alexander Edwards	25-02-41	103 Sqn
778163	Sgt	LAING Alexander Turner [Rhodesia]	24-10-41	44 Sqn
627416	Sgt	LAING David	10-03-41	144 Sqn
41590	F/O	LAIRD Kenneth Malcolm [Canada]	16-06-41	139 Sqn
60535	P/O	LAKE Dennys Savage Walton	16-06-41	78 Sqn
1164974	Sgt	LAKE Noel John	7-09-41	57 Sqn
755874	Sgt	LAKE Wilfred	26-02-41	82 Sqn
43039	P/O	LAKIN Ronald Maurice Alexander	21-04-41	61 Sqn
1163552	Sgt	LALLY Patrick [Eire]	19-06-41	16 OTU
39994	S/L	LALOR MiD Joseph Oswald [Eire]	30-08-41	102 Sqn
42614	F/O	LAMB DFC Douglas Ferguson	9-06-41	9 Sqn
1171689	Sgt	LAMB Frederick Alexander	13-10-41	15 Sqn
1261295	Sgt	LAMB John Alan	17-10-41	40 Sqn
754628	Sgt	LAMB John Thompson	17-04-41	50 Sqn
69444	P/O	LAMBERT Arthur Wilfred	7-08-41	150 Sqn
1113728	Sgt	LAMBERT Frank	23-12-41	14 OTU
42132	F/O	LAMBERT Michael Montgomery	4-07-41	105 Sqn
759287	F/S	LAMBOURNE Robert George Lester	1-04-41	144 Sqn
924902	Sgt	LAMIN Francis Roland	29-10-41	106 Sqn
787859	Sgt	LANCIK Jaroslav [Czechoslovakia]	2-07-41	311 Sqn
70379	S/L	LANDALE DFC Peter Wellwood Fortune	25-07-41	10 Sqn
905186	Sgt	LANDER Henry Frederick	17-01-41	40 Sqn
610879	F/S	LANDON Cecil George	27-06-41	12 Sqn
61996	P/O	LANDRETH Cowan	7-08-41	150 Sqn
1152881	Sgt	LANE Ernest Raymond Verdun	1-09-41	101 Sqn
919901	Sgt	LANE Frederick Valentine Francis	12-10-41	82 Sqn
945263	Sgt	LANE Norman Leslie	27-02-41	78 Sqn
627829	Sgt	LANE Sydney David	16-07-41	57 Sqn
39420	S/L	LANGEBEAR Richard	9-05-41	18 Sqn
959792	AC1	LANGFORD William Daniel	27-09-41	88 Sqn
1056726	Sgt	LANGHORNE Willis	28-12-41	405 Sqn
33512	F/L	LANGLEY DFC Ralph Reginald	16-06-41	139 Sqn
741461	Sgt	LANGRISH Victor Horace	6-12-41	110 Sqn
551820	Sgt	LAPSLEY MiD William Hamilton	4-07-41	106 Sqn
1263483	Sgt	LARGE George Frederick	10-09-41	25 OTU
40398	W/C	LASCELLES DFC Francis Alfred George	26-08-41	82 Sqn
68720	P/O	LAURIE-DIXON John Forbes	6-09-41	10 Sqn
913861	AC1	LAVER George Francis	8-03-41	13 OTU
87065	P/O	LAVERACK Edward Townley	8-04-41	44 Sqn
977534	Sgt	LAW Albert Edward	24-02-41	115 Sqn
87053	P/O	LAW Andrew Allison	3-09-41	58 Sqn
61297	P/O	LAW Henry [Canada]	18-08-41	50 Sqn
88021	P/O	LAW William Edgar	24-09-41	107 Sqn
954205	Sgt	LAWLEY Edward	28-06-41	10 Sqn
1378013	Sgt	LAWRENCE Ernest Alfred	24-11-41	115 Sqn
32228	S/L	LAWRENCE Phillip Cutliffe	8-02-41	12 Sqn
1260997	Sgt	LAWS Douglas Charles	12-10-41	18 Sqn
535558	Sgt	LAWSON Cyril Webster Fitzmaurice [Canada]	26-07-41	10 Sqn
40307	F/O	LAWSON Hugh Gavin Lydford	2-03-41	9 Sqn
981601	Sgt	LAWSON Lawrence	22-10-41	18 Sqn
627244	Sgt	LAWSON Neil Rolf	13-10-41	50 Sqn
801445	Cpl	LAXTON Joshua	4-10-41	21 OTU
919442	Sgt	LEACH Arthur Frederick	21-06-41	14 OTU
62295	P/O	LEACOCK John Trelawney	14-07-41	75 Sqn
942407	Sgt	LEADLEY Geoffrey Norman	24-10-41	10 OTU
910873	Sgt	LEAGAS Robert	20-09-41	16 Sqn
647891	F/S	LEAHY Michael John	16-08-41	90 Sqn
552078	Sgt	LEAPER Ronald John	2-05-41	44 Sqn
999653	Sgt	LEASON John William	13-10-41	207 Sqn
745760	F/S	LEAVERS DFM Evered Arthur Reginald Rex	16-06-41	21 Sqn
759309	Sgt	LEE Albert	2-04-41	82 Sqn
759278	Sgt	LEE Eric Arthur	22-03-41	18 Sqn
952170	Sgt	LEE Geoffrey Goddard	30-07-41	82 Sqn
921732	Sgt	LEE Harold Benjamin	8-12-41	18 Sqn
908627	Sgt	LEE Herbert Conroy	13-10-41	58 Sqn
936277	Sgt	LEE James Henry	17-01-41	40 Sqn
638198	Sgt	LEE James Williamson	29-09-41	9 Sqn
904884	Sgt	LEE John Roland	18-08-41	14 OTU
545781	Sgt	LEE Walter John	30-10-41	138 Sqn
994068	AC1	LEEHANE Patrick P.	19-07-41	99 Sqn
1196622	Sgt	LEEMAN Patrick Ian	8-11-41	149 Sqn
62274	P/O	LEES Ian Alister	4-06-41	139 Sqn
701647	Sgt	LEGG Harry Richard	13-10-41	40 Sqn
567417	Sgt	LEGGE John Stephen	3-03-41	7 Sqn
989819	Sgt	LEGGETT DFM Leonard Dalton	13-12-41	44 Sqn
552119	Sgt	LEIGHTON Francis Xavier	23-03-41	13 OTU
1304325	Sgt	LEITCH James Terris	6-07-41	144 Sqn
741611	Sgt	LEITCH Terence Denis	10-03-41	144 Sqn
1150760	Sgt	LENG Vernon Hardcastle	16-07-41	40 Sqn
743003	Sgt	LENNARD John Archdale	13-08-41	9 Sqn
1183441	Sgt	LENNON Ernest George Birch	21-09-41	103 Sqn
82617	P/O	LESKAUER Jindrich [Czechoslovakia]	15-01-41	311 Sqn
969273	F/S	LESLIE James Guthrie	28-05-41	49 Sqn
46305	P/O	LETCHFORD Frederick Arthur	28-08-41	88 Sqn
971231	Sgt	LEVACK Sidney Joesph Lawrence	22-10-41	75 Sqn
979838	Sgt	LEVER Thomas Leonard	30-04-41	11 OTU
906354	F/S	LEVITT Charles Eric	24-10-41	10 OTU
742554	Sgt	LEWERY Neville John	15-10-41	57 Sqn
84304	F/L	LEWIN Austin Ellerker	24-07-41	76 Sqn
991335	Sgt	LEWIN Eric	13-08-41	9 Sqn
62254	P/O	LEWIN GC Raymond Mayhew	21-11-41	109 Sqn
1154594	Sgt	LEWIS Claude Mortimer Spratt	22-07-41	11 OTU
805396	F/S	LEWIS George Bertram	8-07-41	10 Sqn
44668	F/L	LEWIS Gwilym Ivor	12-08-41	226 Sqn
1183310	Sgt	LEWIS John David Henry	22-10-41	99 Sqn
625523	F/S	LEWIS Keith Francis	15-08-41	218 Sqn
917969	Sgt	LEWIS Paul James [New Zealand]	31-08-41	12 Sqn
955758	Sgt	LEWIS Peter James	9-05-41	78 Sqn
749416	Sgt	LEWIS Victor Alfred	11-06-41	107 Sqn
957920	Sgt	LEWIS William Frank Whittington	24-10-41	101 Sqn
967100	F/S	LEWIS William George	14-07-41	214 Sqn
936821	Sgt	LEWIS William Henry	21-06-41	99 Sqn
1163279	Sgt	LEWIS William Joseph	30-11-41	142 Sqn
778260	Sgt	LE BLANC SMITH Godfrey Michael [Rhodesia]	1-08-41	44 Sqn
924197	Sgt	LE POIDEVIN Alfred John	24-07-41	103 Sqn
1052299	Sgt	LICKLEY Geoffrey	7-08-41	149 Sqn
787284	AC2	LIEBOLD Jindrich [Czechoslovakia]	5-01-41	311 Sqn
787533	Sgt	LIFCIC Rudolf [Czechoslovakia]	17-04-41	311 Sqn
916185	Sgt	LIFE John Douglas	21-10-41	21 Sqn
1163420	Sgt	LIFFORD Raymond George	26-09-41	9 Sqn
987760	Sgt	LIGHTLEY George	9-07-41	77 Sqn
63489	P/O	LIND Harold Andrew Thomas	7-08-41	107 Sqn
103560	P/O	LINDSAY John	8-11-41	44 Sqn
905091	F/S	LINDSAY Louis Edward David	15-08-41	102 Sqn
40235	S/L	LINDSAYE Hugh John Norman	30-04-41	18 Sqn
632655	F/S	LINES Eddie Renown	22-07-41	10 OTU
33344	F/L	LINGS DFC George Oldfield	26-04-41	110 Sqn

81616	F/O	LINIEWSKI Michael [Poland]	9-08-41	301 Sqn
787395	Sgt	LINKA Stanislav [Czechoslovakia]	16-11-41	311 Sqn
522558	Sgt	LINLEY Henry Frederick	18-03-41	21 Sqn
956846	Sgt	LINLEY Sidney	5-07-41	106 Sqn
1359517	Sgt	LINTOTT Harold George	21-09-41	10 OTU
100618	P/O	LISLE Ronald	15-08-41	35 Sqn
754209	Sgt	LISTER Alan Henderson	23-04-41	105 Sqn
1115844	Sgt	LISTER Granville Fallows	6-08-41	104 Sqn
1009143	AC2	LISTER Jack	15-09-41	207 Sqn
628033	F/S	LISTER Joseph Nowill	30-06-41	40 Sqn
1202558	Sgt	LISTER Peter Norman	15-12-41	11 OTU
914307	Sgt	LISTER Trevor Gordon	20-09-41	142 Sqn
654626	Sgt	LITTLE Geoffrey John	4-02-41	3 GTrgFlt
522543	Sgt	LITTLE Thomas William	10-03-41	144 Sqn
909736	Sgt	LITTLEFIELD Jack Richard	12-08-41	149 Sqn
26159	W/C	LITTLER Charles Eric	30-03-41	103 Sqn
87649	P/O	LITTLEWOOD Maurice [Canada]	8-08-41	10 Sqn
970744	Sgt	LIVESEY Albert	12-05-41	214 Sqn
759055	Sgt	LLOYD Alan	23-02-41	107 Sqn
67070	P/O	LLOYD Arthur Edward	1-11-41	83 Sqn
946978	Sgt	LLOYD Eric Allan	25-05-41	18 Sqn
742802	Sgt	LLOYD Malcolm Francis	24-02-41	115 Sqn
64266	P/O	LLOYD Roger Llewellyn	13-10-41	77 Sqn
1378120	Sgt	LLOYD Victor Lawrence	8-12-41	99 Sqn
944768	Sgt	LLOYD Victor Marshall Raymond	22-04-41	218 Sqn
1377212	Sgt	LOADER Herbert Samuel	5-12-41	15 OTU
617644	Sgt	LOATES Henry George [Canada]	2-03-41	61 Sqn
1153101	Sgt	LOBO Joseph Oswald Maurice [Ceylon]	15-11-41	99 Sqn
100631	P/O	LODGE Alan	26-10-41	40 Sqn
993224	Sgt	LODGE Bernard Joseph	17-04-41	16 OTU
640442	Sgt	LODINGTON Geoffrey Stewart	8-08-41	61 Sqn
921574	Sgt	LOMAS-SMITH Robei Harold	8-07-41	7 Sqn
69454	P/O	LOMAX Robert Arthur	28-06-41	142 Sqn
36190	F/L	LONG DFC Frank Hugh [New Zealand]	13-03-41	102 Sqn
42374	F/O	LONG John George Keith	28-04-41	114 Sqn
1161938	Sgt	LONGMORE John Leonard Frederick	12-09-41	144 Sqn
921757	Sgt	LORD Kenneth John	12-07-41	50 Sqn
634506	Sgt	LOUGHLIN DFM Godric	19-03-41	101 Sqn
901226	F/S	LOVE Cyril	14-12-41	83 Sqn
936561	Sgt	LOVE Donald	24-07-41	101 Sqn
1378203	Sgt	LOVEDAY Herbert Leon	30-11-41	214 Sqn
1168643	Sgt	LOVEDAY Sidney Arthur	17-08-41	10 Sqn
1026738	AC2	LOWE John Edward	31-01-41	Wattisham
1283270	Sgt	LOWE Philip Arthur Layen	3-06-41	11 OTU
516598	F/S	LOWE Walter Basil	8-09-41	9 Sqn
61222	P/O	LOWE Walter Hugh	9-07-41	110 Sqn
1186854	Sgt	LOWE William	31-10-41	77 Sqn
911887	Sgt	LOWN Ernest Arthur	18-03-41	149 Sqn
1051796	Sgt	LOWREY Frank	24-07-41	40 Sqn
41306	F/L	LOWSON DFC Donald Urquhart	7-07-41	10 OTU
754883	Sgt	LOWSON William Harry	12-02-41	83 Sqn
42798	P/O	LOWTHER-CLARKE David	13-01-41	114 Sqn
651870	F/S	LUCAS Owen Roderick	8-07-41	10 Sqn
741992	Sgt	LUCAS Reginald	10-03-41	35 Sqn
522251	F/S	LUCKHURST Albert	7-07-41	405 Sqn
1254971	Sgt	LUCKING John Harold	30-11-41	142 Sqn
1153878	Sgt	LUKE Henry Gordon	24-12-41	107 Sqn
914263	Sgt	LUMMUS Harold	9-07-41	110 Sqn
1169553	Sgt	LUNN Kenneth	21-07-41	10 OTU
742043	Sgt	LUSCOMBE Frederick Tom	11-05-41	40 Sqn
581401	F/S	LUSHER Noel	26-08-41	106 Sqn
89063	P/O	LYMBERY Brian Edward	18-05-41	218 Sqn
550334	F/S	LYNCH Arthur Edward Walter	5-07-41	10 OTU
927545	Sgt	LYNCH Cyril Duncan	25-07-41	57 Sqn
551822	Sgt	LYNCH Gerard	16-04-41	10 Sqn
1064697	Sgt	LYNCH Harry Ponsonby	25-07-41	57 Sqn
914965	Sgt	LYNCH Peter Joseph	22-07-41	44 Sqn
42066	F/O	LYNES DFC Gavin John	9-05-41	304 Sqn
89386	P/O	LYNN John Christian	18-08-41	149 Sqn
974218	Sgt	LYON Charles John	21-03-41	49 Sqn
37975	F/L	LYON Horace John	17-06-41	West Raynham
619200	F/S	LYTLE Samuel John	8-07-41	44 Sqn
1173610	AC2	MABBOTT Robin	5-02-41	Mildenhall
60081	P/O	MacALISTER Peter Donald (served as FARRAGUT)	2-07-41	12 Sqn
1117205	Sgt	MacALPINE Donald Macmaster	7-12-41	21 OTU
45200	P/O	MacCOUBREY DFM James Grant	18-02-41	19 OTU
938105	Sgt	MacGREGOR William Florence	17-06-41	405 Sqn
755844	Sgt	MacILWRAITH John Gardner	10-04-41	82 Sqn
88694	P/O	MacIVER Norman Crichton	22-03-41	57 Sqn
1105997	Sgt	MacKENZIE Archie	9-10-41	19 OTU
1001681	Sgt	MacKINNON Ian Donald	25-08-41	49 Sqn
527591	Sgt	MacKINNON Roderick	2-03-41	61 Sqn
41191	F/O	MacLAREN Phillip Frederick	15-01-41	218 Sqn
1002066	Sgt	MacLEAN Hector John	6-08-41	77 Sqn
995759	Sgt	MacLEAY Kenneth George	7-07-41	115 Sqn
101552	P/O	MacLEOD John Bruce	27-12-41	110 Sqn
982696	Sgt	MacPHERSON Alexander	9-07-41	83 Sqn
1365180	Sgt	MACDONALD Alan Scotland	8-09-41	9 Sqn
1014028	AC1	MACDONALD John Mackay	8-07-41	9 Sqn
903519	Sgt	MACILWRAITH James Melven [Eire]	6-08-41	106 Sqn
67071	P/O	MACINTYRE Thomas George Matheson	25-08-41	83 Sqn
550208	F/S	MACKAN Dennis John	28-08-41	21 Sqn
44564	F/O	MACKAY Donald	11-05-41	7 Sqn
993210	Sgt	MACKAY John Douglas	8-08-41	114 Sqn
958556	Sgt	MACKAY William John	8-08-41	83 Sqn
1006455	Sgt	MACKENZIE Alexander	7-11-41	99 Sqn
742152	Sgt	MACKENZIE Archibald Peter Anthony	30-08-41	58 Sqn
1000335	Sgt	MACKENZIE Henry Douglas	8-07-41	44 Sqn
760775	Sgt	MACKEY Denis John	21-11-41	109 Sqn
1053612	Sgt	MACKILLOP William Angus	4-07-41	105 Sqn
580619	F/S	MACKINNON John	18-09-41	13 OTU
751713	Sgt	MACKINTOSH David John	20-09-41	142 Sqn
1253249	Sgt	MACKINTOSH Ian Robert [Brazil]	24-07-41	21 OTU
86640	P/O	MACLAREN Charles Peter Hope	24-04-41	107 Sqn
525672	Sgt	MACLEAN Douglas Alfred	18-06-41	142 Sqn
976194	Sgt	MACLEAN Gordon	16-05-41	103 Sqn
904361	Sgt	MACLEOD William Holland	21-02-41	149 Sqn
957267	Sgt	MACMILLAN Norman Robertson	12-05-41	17 OTU
1160249	Sgt	MACNAMARA George Horace	23-08-41	114 Sqn
63805	P/O	MACPHERSON Alasdair Charles	1-08-41	107 Sqn
43288	P/O	MACROSSAN Hugh Murtagh [Australia]	5-04-41	50 Sqn
78700	F/O	MADDEN DFC Herbert Joseph	19-08-41	114 Sqn
974094	Sgt	MADDISON Eric Dunn	24-05-41	114 Sqn
741793	Sgt	MADGWICK Bernard Keith	15-07-41	7 Sqn
911942	Sgt	MAFLIN Peter Clement Godwyn	30-12-41	35 Sqn
370460	W/O	MAGEE Samuel Joseph	4-07-41	107 Sqn
926955	Sgt	MAGRATH Ernest Robert Butson	13-10-41	40 Sqn
1378011	Sgt	MAGUIRE Sydney Arthur	18-08-41	218 Sqn
972925	Sgt	MAHER George	11-10-41	57 Sqn
76448	F/L	MAHON Denis William	9-06-41	103 Sqn
914182	Sgt	MAHON Theophilos Harry Cardew	22-10-41	99 Sqn
748205	F/S	MAIN Richard Kenneth	13-06-41	44 Sqn
650247	F/S	MAINEY Henry	5-07-41	61 Sqn
78277	P/O	MAIR John Olaf [Canada]	22-03-41	105 Sqn
80086	P/O	MAJOR Michael Wakeman [Rhodesia]	22-07-41	16 OTU
989146	Sgt	MALET-WARDEN John Hamish	17-08-41	78 Sqn
83279	P/O	MALIM Frederick George	13-03-41	102 Sqn
1210544	AC2	MALIN Frederick George	9-11-41	144 Sqn
937913	Sgt	MALLEN Spencer	28-08-41	44 Sqn

Service No	Rank	Name	Date	Sqn
921945	AC2	MALLETT Albert Walter Richard	11-02-41	12 OTU
914170	Sgt	MALLETT Douglas Richard	1-09-41	99 Sqn
643375	F/S	MALONE Allan	22-06-41	207 Sqn
745198	Sgt	MANCHIP Leonard	11-05-41	10 Sqn
910906	Sgt	MANGER William James	11-03-41	9 Sqn
60549	P/O	MANISON Ernest Edward	19-08-41	10 Sqn
923195	Sgt	MANN Horace	8-09-41	106 Sqn
900288	Sgt	MANN Ronald Roy	18-04-41	114 Sqn
632301	Sgt	MANNERS Frederick William	8-11-41	97 Sqn
961238	Sgt	MANNING Alfred James	29-08-41	35 Sqn
924208	Sgt	MANNING Leslie George	30-11-41	455 Sqn
561305	F/S	MANSEL Glyn Davies	2-07-41	12 Sqn
751041	Sgt	MANSFIELD Dennis John	9-06-41	9 Sqn
751557	Sgt	MANSFIELD Herbert Henry	30-09-41	7 Sqn
33121	F/L	MANSON Timothy Roderick	25-02-41	17 OTU
1153158	Sgt	MANWARING Ranulph Paul	11-12-41	57 Sqn
1380356	Sgt	MAPPIN Sir Charles Thomas Hewitt	8-11-41	75 Sqn
580428	F/S	MARAIS Stephanus Francois [South Africa]	16-06-41	103 Sqn
1360363	Sgt	MARCUS Derek Julius	5-12-41	15 OTU
787393	Sgt	MARES Jiri [Czechoslovakia]	17-07-41	311 Sqn
60124	P/O	MARES John	30-06-41	14 OTU
639154	Sgt	MARETT William George [Channel Islands]	14-03-41	149 Sqn
1167721	Sgt	MARKALL Douglas Victor	9-11-41	408 Sqn
902643	LAC	MARKE James Sylvester	29-06-41	218 Sqn
960989	Sgt	MARKHAM James Francis	13-06-41	25 OTU
100032	P/O	MARKHAM Vivian Maxwell	25-08-41	35 Sqn
72519	F/L	MARKS DFC Michael John Colvie	17-02-41	114 Sqn
748016	F/S	MARKS Victor Howes	19-06-41	78 Sqn
620923	Cpl	MARLOTH Kenneth Hamilton	12-05-41	35 Sqn
1153788	Sgt	MARLOW Thomas Harold	30-11-41	58 Sqn
988208	Sgt	MARQUISS Thomas Henry	9-07-41	144 Sqn
981749	Sgt	MARSDEN Edwin	25-07-41	83 Sqn
754463	Sgt	MARSDEN Joseph	13-03-41	207 Sqn
745742	F/S	MARSH Gordon Cedric	3-07-41	144 Sqn
88696	P/O	MARSH Kenneth Granville Anderson	23-05-41	82 Sqn
1377521	Sgt	MARSH William George	1-07-41	7 Sqn
992620	Sgt	MARSHALL Duncan Watt	15-10-41	139 Sqn
77376	F/O	MARSHALL Harold	10-04-41	12 Sqn
81049	P/O	MARSHALL Herbert Kitchener	18-04-41	21 Sqn
925012	Sgt	MARSHALL Jack Allan	3-10-41	7 Sqn
611372	F/S	MARSHALL Thomas Robson	29-06-41	218 Sqn
920238	Sgt	MARSHALL William Charles [Canada]	26-12-41	18 Sqn
32051	S/L	MARTIN Alan Cresswell	26-08-41	40 Sqn
528453	F/S	MARTIN Charles Ion [Eire]	26-04-41	110 Sqn
83298	P/O	MARTIN David	9-05-41	149 Sqn
1151998	Sgt	MARTIN Ernest George	30-07-41	82 Sqn
1198837	Sgt	MARTIN Francis Edward	24-11-41	97 Sqn
1375907	Sgt	MARTIN Frederick Victor	10-09-41	25 OTU
904487	Sgt	MARTIN Harold Raymond [Canada]	8-04-41	102 Sqn
950327	Sgt	MARTIN Henry	29-09-41	99 Sqn
539616	Sgt	MARTIN Kenneth Bowers	12-05-41	40 Sqn
1174896	Sgt	MARTIN Peter Richard	11-10-41	106 Sqn
758129	Sgt	MARTIN Robert Tuck	17-06-41	405 Sqn
1376762	Sgt	MASINI Peter John	17-10-41	15 OTU
1250143	Sgt	MASON Bernard Victor	25-08-41	83 Sqn
1191148	Sgt	MASON Eric Colebourne	4-10-41	18 OTU
'946342'	P/O	MASON Frank	14-10-41	207 Sqn
900472	AC1	MASON Fred	17-12-41	77 Sqn
1166636	Sgt	MASON Gordon	8-06-41	139 Sqn
937382	Sgt	MASON John Raymond	24-07-41	12 Sqn
1365268	Sgt	MASSEY William	8-11-41	75 Sqn
1179327	Sgt	MASTERS Albert Edward	30-08-41	102 Sqn
926095	Sgt	MASTERS Leslie Gordon	9-10-41	19 OTU
778235	Sgt	MATETICH John Anthony [Rhodesia]	15-10-41	75 Sqn
931086	Sgt	MATHESON Cyril Vincent	7-09-41	78 Sqn
552542	F/S	MATHIAS William Ronald	4-07-41	226 Sqn
82687	S/L	MATHIESON Alexander	8-09-41	90 Sqn
1058529	Sgt	MATHISON Norman Alan	15-09-41	207 Sqn
924222	Sgt	MATTHEWMAN Ellis Charles	8-08-41	83 Sqn
1154787	Sgt	MATTHEWS Alfred Albert	26-08-41	82 Sqn
62004	P/O	MATTHEWS Bernard Frederick West	12-08-41	18 Sqn
751430	Sgt	MATTHEWS Charles James	15-08-41	218 Sqn
1164085	Sgt	MATTHEWS Cyril Frank	8-06-41	139 Sqn
1285469	Sgt	MATTHEWS Edgar James	3-08-41	25 OTU
640340	Sgt	MATTHEWS Ernest Frederick	2-03-41	51 Sqn
100059	P/O	MATTHEWS George Joyce	17-08-41	21 OTU
33389	F/O	MATTHEWS DFC Hugh Vernon	13-03-41	207 Sqn
810051	Sgt	MATTHEWS John Henry	5-04-41	50 Sqn
921666	Sgt	MATTHEWS Malcolm Todd	8-07-41	83 Sqn
1167443	Sgt	MATTHEWS Reginald Charles	8-11-41	102 Sqn
1057674	Sgt	MATTINGLY James Henry	5-12-41	15 OTU
754677	Sgt	MAY Fred	21-02-41	149 Sqn
60822	F/L	MAY Reginald Hubert	3-09-41	214 Sqn
63072	P/O	MAYBURY Victor Charles Ormond Royd	25-08-41	83 Sqn
741929	Sgt	MAYERS Reginald Percival	15-05-41	21 Sqn
755992	Sgt	MAYES Stanley Charles	13-08-41	76 Sqn
976107	Sgt	MAYOR Gordon Hogarth	18-07-41	15 Sqn
1152989	Sgt	MAYOR Spencer Ronald	4-07-41	99 Sqn
908800	Sgt	MAYSTON DFM Stanley Robert	22-12-41	28 CFlt
67671	F/O	McALLISTER Samuel	16-10-41	107 Sqn
948560	Sgt	McALONAN John Marshall	28-06-41	10 Sqn
62291	P/O	McANALLY John	7-07-41	214 Sqn
43694	S/L	McARTHUR DFM William Condie	27-06-41	102 Sqn
778208	Sgt	McBARNET Edward William [Rhodesia]	18-08-41	16 OTU
1304399	Sgt	McBETH Walter	2-09-41	44 Sqn
967874	Sgt	McCALLUM James Dennison	23-03-41	13 OTU
61025	P/O	McCALLUM John Davis Walker	18-07-41	15 Sqn
1287876	Sgt	McCARTHY Ivor	30-09-41	78 Sqn
64291	P/O	McCARTHY Neil	7-07-41	10 OTU
749382	Sgt	McCARTHY Robert Lee [Eire]	4-03-41	7 Sqn
1073490	LAC	McCLUSKEY Martin	21-12-41	Oakington
104492	P/O	McCOMBE George Marshall	8-11-41	78 Sqn
551688	F/S	McCORMACK DFM Robert	7-07-41	97 Sqn
87352	P/O	McCOSH Hargrave	6-04-41	15 Sqn
1166019	Sgt	McCOY Anthony Richard [Canada]	5-12-41	20 OTU
652274	Sgt	McCRACKEN Robert Cameron [Canada]	7-04-41	3 GTrgFlt
1375023	Sgt	McCREADY Daniel	30-11-41	75 Sqn
70421	S/L	McCULLAGH Harold Featherstone	8-11-41	51 Sqn
521585	Sgt	McDONALD George William	8-11-41	102 Sqn
818092	F/S	McDONALD Ivor Joseph	15-10-41	40 Sqn
79513	P/O	McDONALD Leslie Joseph [New Zealand]	13-01-41	35 Sqn
974023	Sgt	McDONALD Walter Tomson	16-07-41	115 Sqn
987680	Sgt	McDONOUGH John Anthony	20-10-41	99 Sqn
751148	F/S	McDOUGALL Duncan	10-04-41	12 Sqn
625871	F/S	McDOUGALL William Henderson	9-07-41	110 Sqn
1153051	Sgt	McELDON Arthur Robert [Canada]	15-08-41	150 Sqn
985457	AC1	McFADZEAN George	20-06-41	105 Sqn
748349	Sgt	McFARLAND Donald Keith	13-06-41	77 Sqn
935691	Sgt	McGARROW Henry Brodie	7-12-41	104 Sqn
1379359	Sgt	McGARRY William Michael	14-10-41	15 OTU
969452	Sgt	McGARVEY George Albert	7-11-41	455 Sqn
1052301	Sgt	McGAW Francis James	30-08-41	115 Sqn
1365815	Sgt	McGILL Thomas	7-09-41	102 Sqn
926591	Sgt	McGINLEY William Albert [Canada]	26-07-41	102 Sqn
103491	P/O	McGLASHAN Robert Hubert	3-08-41	104 Sqn
922404	Sgt	McGOWAN John Hamilton	28-05-41	82 Sqn
990467	Sgt	McGREGOR William James Stephen	9-05-41	214 Sqn
64889	P/O	McGREGOR-CHEERS Jack	25-08-41	35 Sqn

Service #	Rank	Name	Date	Sqn
741064	Sgt	McHALE John	13-08-41	76 Sqn
936804	Sgt	McHALE Thomas Percival	25-08-41	35 Sqn
973376	Sgt	McHARDY Alexander John	9-04-41	218 Sqn
905333	Sgt	McINERY Geoffrey Louis	22-10-41	12 Sqn
1001428	Sgt	McINNES John Hutcheon	7-07-41	19 OTU
644566	Sgt	McINTOSH William	25-02-41	103 Sqn
534062	Sgt	McINTYRE Daniel	19-08-41	101 Sqn
755698	F/S	McINTYRE John	3-05-41	7 Sqn
990193	Sgt	McKAY William Fraser	3-07-41	106 Sqn
84935	P/O	McKENNA Joseph Francis Patrick John	24-07-41	76 Sqn
1116548	Sgt	McKENZIE Henry Bruce	2-08-41	405 Sqn
1067429	Sgt	McKILLOP Alan	8-11-41	57 Sqn
998292	Sgt	McKINNELL Robert Smith	19-08-41	218 Sqn
745365	Sgt	McLAFFERTY Neil	21-06-41	14 OTU
115139	P/O	McLAREN David	13-12-41	144 Sqn
920382	Sgt	McLEAN John Alfred	29-09-41	9 Sqn
988136	Sgt	McLEAN Peter John	10-07-41	77 Sqn
37413	S/L	McLEOD Donald Ian	3-10-41	7 Sqn
1179883	AC2	McLEOD George William	23-09-41	15 OTU
968141	Sgt	McMAHON Owen Bernard [New Zealand]	25-08-41	49 Sqn
1018010	AC2	McMAHON William	13-08-41	11 OTU
85679	P/O	McMASTER William Wilson	22-03-41	57 Sqn
948818	Sgt	McMULLAN Cecil Brian	30-09-41	58 Sqn
42856	P/O	McNAMARA Brian Patrick	10-01-41	75 Sqn
915420	Sgt	McNAMARE Ronald	14-10-41	22 OTU
1058392	Sgt	McNEILL Forbes	3-09-41	57 Sqn
543628	Sgt	McPHAIL Donald Hugh	14-08-41	207 Sqn
580969	F/S	McPHEE Charles Duthrie	15-04-41	21 Sqn
575079	Sgt	McQUIGG Edward Torrens	15-08-41	35 Sqn
995761	Sgt	McROBERT Robert Gordon	30-07-41	139 Sqn
1252094	Sgt	McVETY Maurice Wyndham Stuart	12-09-41	75 Sqn
61010	P/O	McVIE William Alexander	16-05-41	144 Sqn
950398	Sgt	McWALTER Thomas Ross	31-03-41	15 Sqn
971400	Sgt	McWILLIAM James McKenzie	24-05-41	114 Sqn
33197	F/L	MEAD Ian Alan	2-06-41	18 Sqn
924132	Sgt	MEADOWS Horace Edward	28-06-41	142 Sqn
924395	Sgt	MEADOWS Walter	20-09-41	18 Sqn
1109620	Sgt	MEAGHER Bryan Dominic	30-11-41	75 Sqn
917235	Sgt	MEAKER William Roy	4-06-41	21 Sqn
755671	Sgt	MEANWELL Norman Henry	7-05-41	18 Sqn
939016	Sgt	MEASON Harold Edward	15-03-41	Stradishall
654720	Sgt	MEDDEN Albert Edward	25-07-41	50 Sqn
1358010	Sgt	MEDDER Edwin Stephen John Toye	7-12-41	21 OTU
1281206	Sgt	MEDHURST Joseph Ernest	11-10-41	57 Sqn
910491	Sgt	MEECH Richmond	16-05-41	40 Sqn
925004	Sgt	MEES Bernard Joseph	21-06-41	218 Sqn
1258724	AC2	MEESON Hector Herbert	12-05-41	35 Sqn
919089	Sgt	MEGGINSON Lister Mowbray	24-07-41	50 Sqn
901032	Sgt	MEGRAN William James	2-07-41	149 Sqn
1073540	AC2	MELLING James Ronald	2-06-41	Waterbeach
1176808	Sgt	MELLON William Neill Kennedy	7-08-41	75 Sqn
87329	F/L	MELLOWS Harold Sidney	11-11-41	115 Sqn
992851	Sgt	MELVILLE Alexander	26-06-41	99 Sqn
82707	P/O	MELVILLE Andrew McDougall	27-02-41	83 Sqn
749441	Sgt	MELVILLE William Wotherspoon	26-06-41	99 Sqn
541524	F/S	MELVIN James Timothy	2-07-41	226 Sqn
518613	Sgt	MENAGE Thomas Nathan	10-05-41	149 Sqn
82988	P/O	MENDOZA Michael Isaac Archibald	18-08-41	149 Sqn
940550	Sgt	MENNIE Douglas James	26-07-41	35 Sqn
41604	F/L	MENZIES DFC Guy Jerrold [New Zealand]	22-01-41	139 Sqn
968118	Sgt	MERCER Cecil Harry Reuben	8-04-41	214 Sqn
741668	F/S	MERCER Colwyn Trevor Cottell	13-06-41	44 Sqn
1158395	Sgt	MERCER Desmond William [USA]	7-09-41	77 Sqn
34243	S/L	MERCER James	2-11-41	78 Sqn
85284	P/O	MERCER MiD Lewis Henry	9-05-41	99 Sqn
951583	Sgt	MEREDITH Charles	4-06-41	139 Sqn
702545	Sgt	MERRIFIELD Leslie	22-12-41	28 CFlt
915446	Sgt	MERTENS Peter Eric Montague	9-04-41	149 Sqn
1255268	Sgt	METAXA Anthony Michael	29-06-41	15 Sqn
1061866	AC2	METCALFE John	21-05-41	83 Sqn
649028	Sgt	MEW Ronald George	20-05-41	218 Sqn
758135	Sgt	MEYNELL Peter Robert Birch	15-04-41	149 Sqn
90371	S/L	MIDDLETON DFC Stuart Auldjo	30-12-41	35 Sqn
787339	Sgt	MIKLOSEK Jan [Czechoslovakia]	15-09-41	311 Sqn
516240	F/S	MILES Donald Lionel Henry	15-02-41	11 OTU
968313	Sgt	MILLAR James Keiller	22-10-41	12 Sqn
748196	Sgt	MILLAR William Alexander	21-03-41	83 Sqn
923982	Sgt	MILLARD-TUCKER Anthony John Rylands	17-08-41	78 Sqn
937781	Sgt	MILLER John Robert	14-06-41	44 Sqn
778058	AC2	MILLER Ray Bernadine [Rhodesia]	29-03-41	44 Sqn
1180027	Sgt	MILLER Samuel James	29-11-41	214 Sqn
966385	Sgt	MILLER William	8-11-41	102 Sqn
976204	Sgt	MILLIGAN Robert Murray	4-07-41	102 Sqn
742274	Sgt	MILLS Alan Kingsley	27-03-41	78 Sqn
41195	F/L	MILLS DFC Anthony John George	25-08-41	83 Sqn
924127	Sgt	MILLS Douglas Edgar	8-11-41	18 Sqn
79170	F/O	MILLS DFC Lionel Abel John	21-10-41	97 Sqn
924027	Sgt	MILLS Martin John	11-12-41	18 Sqn
1113963	Sgt	MILLS Norman Evans	7-08-41	214 Sqn
639593	Sgt	MILLS Stalford Keith	12-05-41	58 Sqn
105164	P/O	MILNE Andrew Gordon	21-09-41	103 Sqn
743035	F/S	MILROY David Drummond	15-06-41	105 Sqn
742851	Sgt	MILTON Edwin Joseph	23-02-41	115 Sqn
1168114	Sgt	MILTON Peter Alan	13-10-41	40 Sqn
911592	Sgt	MINASSIAN Ken Leon	12-01-41	51 Sqn
751355	Sgt	MINCHIN Robert Michael	6-09-41	75 Sqn
975773	Sgt	MINTY Kenneth Buck	23-07-41	21 Sqn
932393	Sgt	MISKIN Thomas George	5-11-41	144 Sqn
34050	W/C	MISSELBROOK DSO Sidney Trevor	13-12-41	44 Sqn
1164377	Sgt	MITCHELL Alan	26-08-41	106 Sqn
970184	Sgt	MITCHELL Anthony George Lendrum	24-07-41	405 Sqn
902876	Sgt	MITCHELL Arthur John	23-07-41	15 Sqn
43977	F/O	MITCHELL Arthur Page	15-08-41	218 Sqn
992122	Sgt	MITCHELL Charles McPherson	13-04-41	19 OTU
942752	Sgt	MITCHELL Jack	27-03-41	78 Sqn
36233	F/O	MITCHELL John	3-06-41	7 Sqn
1002064	Sgt	MITCHELL Kenneth Turner	19-06-41	12 OTU
748757	Sgt	MITCHELL Leslie	17-05-41	9 Sqn
759261	Sgt	MITCHELL Peter Anthony Otho Windsor	13-07-41	50 Sqn
1367288	AC1	MITCHELL Xela Cambria	2-09-41	Honington
995980	Sgt	MOCHAN John Alfred	4-05-41	10 OTU
82622	F/O	MOHR Josef [Czechoslovakia]	28-12-41	311 Sqn
101582	P/O	MOHR-BELL Harold	13-10-41	15 Sqn
1375799	Sgt	MOLE Herbert George	17-08-41	21 OTU
84936	P/O	MOLLER Peter Harry	22-01-41	82 Sqn
88697	P/O	MOLLOY Paul	9-06-41	18 Sqn
740943	Sgt	MOLONY John Bernard	23-04-41	18 OTU
938085	Sgt	MOLTENI Frederick Leonard	31-07-41	99 Sqn
985594	Sgt	MOLYNEAUX Geoffrey	22-04-41	218 Sqn
917421	Sgt	MONK Bernard John	8-11-41	58 Sqn
998943	Sgt	MONK Dennis Aloysius	31-07-41	150 Sqn
60771	P/O	MONKS John Thomas	15-07-41	104 Sqn
976080	Sgt	MONTAGUE James Leslie	22-03-41	57 Sqn
902248	Sgt	MONTGOMERY Charles George	25-07-41	50 Sqn
942525	Sgt	MONTGOMERY Harold Thomas Whitfield	18-04-41	107 Sqn
923174	AC1	MOODY Kenneth Harry	12-05-41	58 Sqn
82737	P/O	MOODY Peter	23-02-41	107 Sqn
67079	P/O	MOORE Anthony David	26-11-41	214 Sqn
778391	Sgt	MOORE Arthur John [Rhodesia]	30-11-41	106 Sqn

Service No	Rank	Name	Date	Unit
1252146	Sgt	MOORE John Francis [Eire]	17-08-41	21 OTU
88698	P/O	MOORE Leslie John	12-06-41	40 Sqn
903063	Sgt	MOORE William Ernest	16-05-41	40 Sqn
974190	Sgt	MOORE William Robert	9-04-41	99 Sqn
1304369	Sgt	MOORES Norman	9-08-41	10 Sqn
902874	Sgt	MORANT Norman Albert	16-04-41	10 Sqn
82963	P/O	MORGAN Alan Albert	27-06-41	97 Sqn
551004	Sgt	MORGAN Arthur John	3-05-41	101 Sqn
914113	Sgt	MORGAN Arthur William	13-08-41	115 Sqn
950393	Sgt	MORGAN Gordon Eric	1-09-41	144 Sqn
581292	F/S	MORGAN Ronald	6-07-41	226 Sqn
924905	Sgt	MORGAN Thomas	18-05-41	25 OTU
631925	Sgt	MORGAN William James	12-03-41	40 Sqn
86641	P/O	MORISON Ronald Rutherford	13-04-41	149 Sqn
67024	P/O	MORLEY Reginald David	8-07-41	7 Sqn
964723	Sgt	MORLEY Ronald George Lehmann	7-06-41	107 Sqn
1126340	AC1	MORLEY Walter	13-08-41	11 OTU
626050	F/S	MORLEY William Haggan	28-08-41	14 OTU
102989	P/O	MORRIS DFM Alexander Douglas	21-09-41	20 OTU
971521	Sgt	MORRIS Cyril Midford	12-10-41	144 Sqn
902415	Sgt	MORRIS Edward George	4-02-41	20 OTU
924152	Sgt	MORRIS Frank	11-10-41	106 Sqn
928516	Sgt	MORRIS Frank Ronald	26-12-41	13 OTU
1253782	Sgt	MORRIS Jack	15-11-41	99 Sqn
553926	F/S	MORRIS Keith	7-11-41	455 Sqn
985066	Sgt	MORRIS Kenneth	29-08-41	214 Sqn
628708	Sgt	MORRIS Lloyd George	11-04-41	1419 Flt
1001152	Sgt	MORRIS Peter Haselden	5-07-41	10 OTU
1261532	Sgt	MORRIS Reginald John	5-11-41	18 Sqn
1064705	Sgt	MORRIS Solomon	5-08-41	149 Sqn
1013749	Sgt	MORRIS Ticwyn	27-06-41	40 Sqn
779002	Sgt	MORRISON Duncan [Rhodesia]	6-07-41	10 Sqn
987765	Sgt	MORRISON Norman Begg	7-09-41	83 Sqn
946356	Sgt	MORRISON William Donald	21-02-41	75 Sqn
914193	Sgt	MORSE Stanley Carlton	5-07-41	106 Sqn
1002556	Sgt	MORTIMER Joseph Edward	12-09-41	107 Sqn
911889	Sgt	MORTIMER Wilfred Edward	13-10-41	77 Sqn
956949	Sgt	MOSELEY John Kenneth	10-04-41	149 Sqn
37113	S/L	MOSELEY Oswald Robert Compton	4-07-41	102 Sqn
1170249	Sgt	MOSS Anthony Cade	24-07-41	218 Sqn
1063794	Sgt	MOSS John Kenneth	15-11-41	149 Sqn
1168622	Sgt	MOSS Raymond John	11-08-41	25 OTU
961666	Sgt	MOSS Walter James	26-11-41	106 Sqn
922320	Sgt	MOTT Geoffrey Seaby Hayden	30-11-41	58 Sqn
621167	F/S	MOULDING Ernest	14-10-41	207 Sqn
959229	Sgt	MOULES Jack	6-08-41	103 Sqn
745708	Sgt	MOUNSER Wilfred Harold	25-06-41	18 Sqn
45061	P/O	MOUNSEY Eric Graham	7-11-41	58 Sqn
86428	P/O	MOUNTAIN Herbert Hutin	9-07-41	78 Sqn
925336	Sgt	MOUNTIER Russell Johnston [New Zealand]	8-09-41	104 Sqn
940764	Sgt	MOUNTNEY John Philip	26-03-41	15 OTU
755552	Sgt	MOWER Robert	13-03-41	110 Sqn
999279	Sgt	MOWFORTH Stanley Gordon	18-02-41	19 OTU
40413	F/O	MOXHAM DFC Swain	7-02-41	16 OTU
643697	F/S	MUIR Ronald Charles Andrew	28-07-41	90 Sqn
580522	F/S	MULFORD Frederick Bertie	9-07-41	110 Sqn
751617	Sgt	MULFORD John William	17-04-41	44 Sqn
1251152	Sgt	MULLENGER Stanley Gordon	8-11-41	49 Sqn
581112	F/S	MULLIGAN Eugene Michael [Eire]	11-05-41	40 Sqn
1019049	AC1	MUNDIE Alexander	16-08-41	Honington
998367	Sgt	MUNRO Gordon Alexander	15-08-41	218 Sqn
1310864	Sgt	MURCH Cyril	8-11-41	7 Sqn
63821	P/O	MURCHIE Ian	21-09-41	103 Sqn
919872	Sgt	MURCUTT Alfred Dennis Ford	5-07-41	82 Sqn
930728	Sgt	MURDOCH John Kemp	30-11-41	115 Sqn
68758	P/O	MURPHY Matthew	27-12-41	110 Sqn
106682	P/O	MURPHY Patrick Joseph	16-08-41	104 Sqn
755142	Sgt	MURPHY Robert Friar	23-03-41	105 Sqn
970316	Sgt	MURRAY Alan Mitchel	4-04-41	83 Sqn
976892	Sgt	MURRAY Hubert Stephen	25-03-41	20 OTU
988364	Sgt	MURRAY James Bartle	12-05-41	40 Sqn
968178	Sgt	MURRAY James Noel	2-03-41	9 Sqn
977615	Sgt	MURRAY Percy Brown	15-06-41	105 Sqn
1378898	Sgt	MYCOCK James	31-10-41	76 Sqn
83257	P/O	MYERS Peter	10-05-41	51 Sqn
1378482	Sgt	MYERS Richard	9-08-41	10 Sqn
39893	F/L	MYERS Thomas Herbert [Canada]	18-04-41	114 Sqn
1293271	AC2	MYLES Frank William John	31-01-41	Wattisham
1354733	Sgt	MYNOTT Leonard Richard	16-07-41	21 Sqn
64318	F/L	NAMIAS Mayer Henry Richard	20-09-41	226 Sqn
564733	F/S	NANCARROW Edward Horatio	17-08-41	12 Sqn
912737	Sgt	NAPIER Douglas Macdonald	3-07-41	144 Sqn
909971	Sgt	NATHAN Harry	30-04-41	21 Sqn
1380790	Sgt	NAYLOR Kenneth	30-11-41	101 Sqn
911409	Sgt	NEALE Richard Morley	26-03-41	15 OTU
1375564	Sgt	NEALE Ronald St. Clair	15-11-41	50 Sqn
1306694	Sgt	NEEDHAM Arthur	16-09-41	15 Sqn
101032	F/O	NEEDHAM Frank James	8-08-41	15 Sqn
60808	P/O	NEEDHAM Roland	25-04-41	105 Sqn
983086	Sgt	NEEDLE Harold	16-08-41	90 Sqn
920736	Sgt	NEEDLER George Stephenson	15-10-41	226 Sqn
1074968	Sgt	NESBITT Thomas Alexander	5-12-41	15 OTU
939319	Sgt	NETHERCLIFT Leslie	26-07-41	102 Sqn
920591	Sgt	NETHERCOTT Eric Gordon	4-07-41	105 Sqn
787211	Sgt	NETIK Vaclav [Czechoslovakia]	20-07-41	311 Sqn
650196	F/S	NEWBERY MiD Alec Kenneth	9-05-41	18 Sqn
1163009	Sgt	NEWBOLD Gilbert Arthur	14-08-41	83 Sqn
88700	P/O	NEWBOROUGH Sidney George	23-07-41	110 Sqn
798536	Sgt	NEWBURY Robert Owen [Canada]	11-11-41	115 Sqn
928443	Sgt	NEWCOMBE James Risdon	7-09-41	44 Sqn
943521	Sgt	NEWHOUSE Edgar	14-04-41	21 Sqn
42633	P/O	NEWHOUSE Hugh Francis Perceval	12-01-41	49 Sqn
999517	Sgt	NEWLANDS John Cruikshanks	1-07-41	102 Sqn
1375423	Sgt	NEWMAN George	10-09-41	25 OTU
915028	Sgt	NEWMAN Robert Hugh	15-02-41	11 OTU
1250836	Sgt	NEWNES Horace James William	30-08-41	102 Sqn
567204	Sgt	NEWSTEAD Conrad Howard	24-07-41	35 Sqn
983323	Sgt	NEWTON James Lyle	15-05-41	16 OTU
994648	Sgt	NEWTON John	24-11-41	97 Sqn
935382	Sgt	NEWTON Kenneth McIntosh	7-09-41	58 Sqn
973877	Sgt	NICHOLL John	13-07-41	144 Sqn
908683	Sgt	NICHOLLS Barrie Kendal	1-07-41	7 Sqn
1257909	Sgt	NICHOLLS Bruce Warren	24-10-41	40 Sqn
100623	P/O	NICHOLLS Maurice Sydney	24-07-41	104 Sqn
975787	Sgt	NICHOLS Frederick Robert	30-06-41	115 Sqn
985867	Sgt	NICHOLS James Alfred	19-08-41	101 Sqn
975306	Sgt	NICHOLS Ralph Edward	31-03-41	21 Sqn
942995	Sgt	NICHOLSON James Ernest	3-09-41	61 Sqn
37686	W/C	NICOL DSO James Lauder	19-08-41	114 Sqn
969415	Sgt	NICOLL Albert Philip	27-06-41	102 Sqn
529189	Sgt	NICOLSON George	25-08-41	7 Sqn
992922	Sgt	NIGHTINGALE Joseph	12-09-41	10 Sqn
755645	Sgt	NIGHTINGARL John William	18-04-41	9 Sqn
1325203	Sgt	NIVEN Alexander Thompson	13-08-41	76 Sqn
949798	Sgt	NOAKES Kenneth Thomas	23-06-41	107 Sqn
45723	P/O	NOBLE William Gershon	21-10-41	97 Sqn
910919	Sgt	NODDLE Kenneth	9-07-41	78 Sqn
918570	Sgt	NOLAN Desmond Joseph	13-08-41	115 Sqn
1068914	Sgt	NORCROSS Samuel	19-08-41	10 Sqn
653750	F/S	NORDON Aldwyn Anthony	11-11-41	12 Sqn
904624	Sgt	NORMAN Arthur John	22-01-41	82 Sqn
935299	Sgt	NORMAN Eric George	27-04-41	83 Sqn
996501	Sgt	NORMAN Frank	12-12-41	106 Sqn
755448	Sgt	NORMAN Lawrence Dudley	9-01-41	78 Sqn
947151	Sgt	NORMAN William Ronald	16-07-41	150 Sqn

Number	Rank	Name	Date	Sqn
908609	Sgt	NORMAN-ARTERTON Harry Walter Crouch 5-05-41		21 Sqn
755647	Sgt	NORRIS Alfred Henry	26-04-41	51 Sqn
741381	Sgt	NORRIS James Arthur	15-04-41	102 Sqn
956820	Sgt	NORTH Arthur Charles	16-05-41	105 Sqn
1167139	Sgt	NORTH Ronald	15-11-41	99 Sqn
1059632	Sgt	NORTHCOTE John Richard	31-10-41	218 Sqn
1194655	Sgt	NORTHCOTT Cyril	15-11-41	149 Sqn
755216	Sgt	NORTHWOOD Hilsby Reginald	30-03-41	83 Sqn
1280431	Sgt	NORTON Douglas Frederick William	9-11-41	408 Sqn
613822	Sgt	NOSWORTHY Albert Edward	15-11-41	99 Sqn
78549	P/O	NOTTIDGE John Jephson	13-08-41	207 Sqn
928472	Sgt	NOWLAN John Walter	17-08-41	104 Sqn
1375467	Sgt	NUBLEY John Greener	15-10-41	11 OTU
1252728	Sgt	NUNN Geoffrey Sidney	8-11-41	75 Sqn
101556	P/O	NUTT John Alfred	8-11-41	51 Sqn
639538	Sgt	NUTT Peter Norman	15-05-41	97 Sqn
977208	Sgt	NUTTALL Norman Howarth	11-05-41	15 Sqn
910572	Sgt	NYKERK Henry	28-06-41	142 Sqn
1284980	Sgt	NYMAN John Lionel	8-09-41	13 OTU
975986	Sgt	OAKES Edward	16-05-41	78 Sqn
546317	Sgt	OAKES William Bernard	13-07-41	15 OTU
751150	F/S	OASTLER MiD William Alexander	27-08-41	106 Sqn
939727	Sgt	OATEN Jack	5-07-41	82 Sqn
745949	Sgt	OATES Robert	4-02-41	20 OTU
1057912	Sgt	OATES William	15-12-41	408 Sqn
910417	Sgt	OCKENDEN Frederick Charles	10-05-41	149 Sqn
1308648	Sgt	ODDY Frank Morton	9-11-41	25 OTU
40133	F/L	OETTLE DFC Albert John	30-10-41	138 Sqn
973724	AC2	OGEN Colin	25-08-41	83 Sqn
87025	P/O	OGILVIE James Flockhart Thom	15-05-41	21 Sqn
89369	P/O	OGSTON Alexander William	6-08-41	77 Sqn
1002067	Sgt	OLDFIELD Stanley	21-06-41	11 OTU
931979	Sgt	OLDMAN Leonard Henry [Australia]	9-10-41	19 OTU
978156	Sgt	OLIVE John	10-01-41	75 Sqn
517536	Sgt	OLIVER Arthur George	7-07-41	40 Sqn
1375280	Sgt	OMAN Alex Stanley	26-08-41	21 Sqn
1176656	Sgt	ONIONS Clifford William	8-11-41	103 Sqn
964468	Sgt	ONIONS Donald	13-07-41	50 Sqn
1352331	AC2	ORBELL Eric Sydney	4-02-41	Waterbeach
570718	Sgt	ORCHARD Leslie Osborn	19-07-41	15 Sqn
41313	F/L	ORCHARD DFC Russell Ernest [New Zealand]	19-09-41	58 Sqn
529743	F/S	ORDWAY William John	26-08-41	82 Sqn
754090	Sgt	ORR James	14-03-41	10 OTU
964519	Sgt	ORTON John Albert	30-12-41	35 Sqn
62313	P/O	ORTON Ronald Henry	26-06-41	11 OTU
551839	F/S	ORWIN Peter Francis Barclay	18-08-41	50 Sqn
919874	Sgt	OSBORNE Thomas Charles	4-06-41	139 Sqn
904494	Sgt	OSMAN Patrick George	18-12-41	15 Sqn
644162	Sgt	OSTERFIELD William Edward	9-04-41	7 Sqn
903084	Sgt	OVERALL DFM Arthur Percy	12-09-41	14 OTU
1375509	Sgt	OVERALL Vincent Ernest	21-11-41	19 OTU
1250279	Sgt	OVERY Jack Henry	24-07-41	11 OTU
1163347	Sgt	OWEN Arthur Edward	24-07-41	103 Sqn
82990	F/O	OWEN Charles Duncan	12-09-41	107 Sqn
640901	Sgt	OWEN Denison	13-05-41	82 Sqn
778393	Sgt	OWEN Edgar [Rhodesia]	14-10-41	44 Sqn
610846	Sgt	OWEN Joseph Thomas	30-03-41	83 Sqn
61285	P/O	OWEN Patrick Richard	31-08-41	44 Sqn
84914	F/L	OWEN DFC Robert Fenwick	22-12-41	28 CFlt
926790	Sgt	OWEN Roy William	17-07-41	50 Sqn
754046	Sgt	OWENS Glyndwr	8-07-41	61 Sqn
88012	P/O	OWENS Henry Moncrieff	17-07-41	50 Sqn
759253	Sgt	OXLEY John Molesworth	13-05-41	102 Sqn
41053	F/L	O'BRIEN John Thompson	18-11-41	7 Sqn
977255	Sgt	O'DELL Cyril Patrick	19-08-41	10 Sqn
618583	Sgt	O'DONNELL James [Eire]	27-06-41	57 Sqn
960478	Sgt	O'GRADY John Mons	10-08-41	114 Sqn
1186872	Sgt	O'HARA Bernard William	21-07-41	115 Sqn
976138	Sgt	O'HARE Joseph Francis	28-04-41	50 Sqn
1325149	Sgt	O'MARA Sidney Timothy	29-06-41	15 Sqn
62292	P/O	O'REILLY Lawrence Beresford	10-07-41	7 Sqn
929820	Sgt	O'SHEA Henry Norman	24-11-41	115 Sqn
907690	Sgt	PACK Derek Gordon	8-11-41	7 Sqn
745411	F/S	PAGE Arthur John	24-10-41	101 Sqn
1376222	Sgt	PAGE Arthur Norman	8-09-41	214 Sqn
60780	P/O	PAGE Clifford Frederick	7-05-41	75 Sqn
1050934	Sgt	PAGE Edgar James	7-08-41	214 Sqn
908004	Sgt	PAGE Horace Cuthbert	28-04-41	50 Sqn
964964	Sgt	PAGE Leslie Charles	27-06-41	40 Sqn
776003	Sgt	PAGE Neville Hamilton [Middle East]	12-09-41	144 Sqn
1259273	Sgt	PAINE Derek Alfred John	20-09-41	16 OTU
1375140	Sgt	PAINE Edward William	21-10-41	82 Sqn
1258617	Sgt	PAINE James Douglas	24-10-41	40 Sqn
1111875	Sgt	PAINE Seymour Leslie Thomas	15-10-41	226 Sqn
1359501	Sgt	PAINTER Eric Henry James	30-11-41	75 Sqn
933248	Sgt	PALASTANGA Bernard William	7-11-41	408 Sqn
551743	F/S	PALMER Donald	10-08-41	226 Sqn
747878	Sgt	PALMER Ernest Richard	29-08-41	49 Sqn
957006	Sgt	PALMER John Richard	29-09-41	9 Sqn
922977	Sgt	PALMER Leonard Roy	22-07-41	17 OTU
1375568	Sgt	PALMER Richard	16-07-41	115 Sqn
975770	Sgt	PANES Elton Talbot	30-06-41	115 Sqn
1113234	Sgt	PANTING Thomas Leslie	29-10-41	106 Sqn
925050	Sgt	PAPLES Norman William	7-08-41	107 Sqn
1293168	Sgt	PARDY Ronald Victor	27-12-41	150 Sqn
62293	P/O	PARFITT Leslie William	16-07-41	218 Sqn
580553	F/S	PARK Alec John	21-10-41	82 Sqn
999479	Sgt	PARK James Reid	13-06-41	44 Sqn
1375834	Sgt	PARKER Eric Bramwell	20-09-41	144 Sqn
921837	Sgt	PARKER Robert Noel	11-10-41	107 Sqn
89314	P/O	PARKER The Hon. William Richard Christopher Boyle 14-12-41		83 Sqn
526677	Sgt	PARKES Thomas Arthur	9-07-41	35 Sqn
45232	P/O	PARKHURST Roland Clive	21-03-41	150 Sqn
989144	Sgt	PARKIN Donald	24-07-41	144 Sqn
630839	F/S	PARKIN John	30-09-41	142 Sqn
955962	Sgt	PARKINSON Thomas	26-08-41	21 Sqn
42876	F/L	PARNELL MiD Bernard	18-12-41	7 Sqn
82626	P/O	PAROLEK Jan Frantiser [Czechoslovakia]	16-11-41	311 Sqn
946264	Sgt	PARR Stanley	25-05-41	105 Sqn
908233	Sgt	PARRIS Cyril Bruce	9-04-41	9 Sqn
940374	Sgt	PARROTT Percival Harold Charles	31-07-41	150 Sqn
976645	Sgt	PARROTT Sydney George	5-12-41	15 OTU
1166710	Sgt	PARRY Gordon Stanley	28-07-41	21 OTU
1181625	Sgt	PARRY Herbert William	19-06-41	12 OTU
988362	Sgt	PARRY Leonard	8-06-41	11 OTU
954380	Sgt	PARRY Lewis Desmond	4-09-41	107 Sqn
42637	F/O	PARRY Maurice	24-07-41	61 Sqn
1252800	Sgt	PARSLOW Christopher Frederick James 14-07-41		139 Sqn
808419	Sgt	PARSONS Albert	18-03-41	21 Sqn
922946	Sgt	PARSONS George Newton	19-11-41	18 Sqn
1151990	Sgt	PARSONS Harold Frederick Dolland	22-12-41	107 Sqn
917000	Sgt	PARSONS William Frederick	8-11-41	150 Sqn
1180179	Sgt	PARTINGTON John Claude	9-06-41	9 Sqn
1057686	Sgt	PARTINGTON William	31-10-41	77 Sqn
927620	Sgt	PARTRIDGE Robert Douglas	22-10-41	99 Sqn
37574	W/C	PARTRIDGE DFC Thomas Noel	16-07-41	18 Sqn
82627	P/O	PARTYK Jaroslav [Czechoslovakia]	20-07-41	311 Sqn
1360214	Sgt	PASHLEY Harry	28-12-41	15 OTU
88020	P/O	PASKELL DFM Lionel Arthur	14-10-41	207 Sqn
921874	Sgt	PASSY Ian Harry Deare	13-10-41	207 Sqn
745953	Sgt	PATERSON Gordon Borden	11-05-41	150 Sqn

904673	Sgt	PATON Cyril	9-05-41	214 Sqn		755277	Sgt	PHILLIPS Ernest Stanley	21-04-41	83 Sqn
1019210	Sgt	PATRICK Arthur Russell	16-09-41	15 OTU		1076249	AC1	PHILLIPS Francis Gordon	13-08-41	11 OTU
903309	Sgt	PATTEN Henry William	15-04-41	149 Sqn		932831	Sgt	PHILLIPS Frank Kent	7-09-41	226 Sqn
550572	Sgt	PATTERSON DFM John Anderson	27-02-41	51 Sqn		976646	Sgt	PHILLIPS Gabriel	18-09-41	405 Sqn
65514	P/O	PATTERSON John Bridges	17-09-41	82 Sqn		617380	F/S	PHILLIPS John Ernest	1-09-41	44 Sqn
651853	Sgt	PATTINSON Harry Matthew	4-02-41	16 OTU		62301	P/O	PHILLIPS Victor Eric George	7-06-41	105 Sqn
1062768	Sgt	PATTISON James Muir	30-09-41	142 Sqn		984421	Sgt	PHILP Donald Macauley	27-06-41	102 Sqn
1112339	Sgt	PAUL Eric George	21-09-41	103 Sqn		997009	Sgt	PHILP Richard Thomas [Eire]	15-08-41	102 Sqn
102610	P/O	PAUL Isaac	24-12-41	107 Sqn		85709	P/O	PHILPOTT John Farmer	1-07-41	149 Sqn
1102556	AC2	PAUL John Graham	20-04-41	110 Sqn		84320	P/O	PICKERING Gordon Harold John	8-11-41	97 Sqn
996505	Sgt	PAUL John William	29-09-41	57 Sqn		530878	Sgt	PICKERING Herbert Andrew	28-12-41	138 Sqn
78452	F/O	PAXTON Thomas Roy	15-10-41	139 Sqn		751550	Sgt	PICKERING John Muirhead	27-06-41	12 Sqn
1051617	Sgt	PAXTON Wilson	1-10-41	99 Sqn		567731	Sgt	PICKERS Ronald Anthony	11-05-41	7 Sqn
103572	P/O	PAYNE Christopher Bradley	11-12-41	144 Sqn		997069	Sgt	PICKUP Jack	17-12-41	107 Sqn
906880	Sgt	PAYNE Frank Stubbington	21-07-41	115 Sqn		45647	P/O	PIERCE Eric Robert	7-04-41	139 Sqn
1154473	Sgt	PAYNE Reginald Cyril	15-04-41	149 Sqn		902481	Sgt	PIKE Geoffrey Rochfort	3-03-41	115 Sqn
86643	F/O	PAYNE Robert Frederick	12-06-41	40 Sqn		41868	F/L	PIKE DFC Victor Fernley Baker	9-04-41	7 Sqn
645583	F/S	PEACH Ronald Ivor	23-12-41	21 OTU		918421	Sgt	PILBEAM John Mitchell	24-07-41	76 Sqn
950411	Sgt	PEACOCK Ernest Ronald	17-05-41	20 OTU		917339	Sgt	PILKINGTON Arthur	11-10-41	12 Sqn
932162	Sgt	PEARCE Thomas John	13-12-41	144 Sqn		910886	Sgt	PILLEY DFM John Herbert	8-12-41	107 Sqn
64268	P/O	PEARSON Charles James	29-08-41	35 Sqn		552859	Sgt	PINGEL Douglas Howard John	13-06-41	77 Sqn
64269	P/O	PEARSON Henry Hetley	17-08-41	10 Sqn		1023027	Sgt	PINKERTON Robert	20-10-41	99 Sqn
1305075	Sgt	PEARSON John Edward	20-09-41	18 Sqn		748000	Sgt	PITT Bernard George	9-07-41	9 Sqn
42639	F/O	PEARSON Leslie Edward	17-04-41	77 Sqn		905166	F/S	PLAISTOWE Ralph Cuthbert	1-09-41	83 Sqn
740666	Sgt	PEART Peter Robert	8-01-41	214 Sqn		640058	Sgt	PLANT John	8-09-41	106 Sqn
910540	Sgt	PECK Raymond Stanley	26-06-41	99 Sqn		60781	P/O	PLATT Kenneth Ernest	17-04-41	149 Sqn
962565	Sgt	PEDLEY Alan Harry Keeling	30-09-41	77 Sqn		846567	Sgt	PLATTEN Ralph William	15-11-41	115 Sqn
580623	F/S	PEEK Kenneth Charles	1-05-41	139 Sqn		745848	Sgt	PLAYER Robert	4-02-41	3 GTrgFlt
1272896	Sgt	PEEL Jack	17-04-41	149 Sqn		102600	P/O	PLAYFAIR Orion George Sedgwick	1-09-41	16 OTU
88011	P/O	PEERS William Edgar	15-01-41	58 Sqn		1052823	Sgt	PLAYFORTH Herbert	30-10-41	14 OTU
758164	Sgt	PELL Norman Brook	17-05-41	77 Sqn		1151557	Sgt	PLEDGE Victor George	29-04-41	10 OTU
69461	P/O	PELMORE Gerald Kurt Kenneth Keston				787355	Sgt	PLOCEK Antonin [Czechoslavakia]	2-07-41	311 Sqn
			27-12-41	101 Sqn		567918	Sgt	PLOWMAN Francis Leslie	13-01-41	35 Sqn
742015	Sgt	PENBERTHY Charles Paull	27-06-41	97 Sqn		904038	Sgt	PLUMB Arthur George	10-04-41	218 Sqn
745807	F/S	PENDRILL DFM George Edward Alfred				908131	Sgt	PLUMB Stanley Philip	11-05-41	15 Sqn
			18-12-41	97 Sqn		944822	Sgt	PLUMMER Roylance Claude	8-04-41	214 Sqn
1378703	Sgt	PENGELLY John Charles	8-11-41	149 Sqn		76925	P/O	POCKNEY Ewart Duncan	19-08-41	218 Sqn
1056141	Sgt	PENMAN David Glass	18-12-41	15 Sqn		745235	Sgt	POCOCK Edgar Ian	18-04-41	77 Sqn
746729	F/S	PENN Alfred [Canada]	29-08-41	7 Sqn		922907	Sgt	POCOCK Fred Cecil	7-07-41	40 Sqn
550997	Sgt	PEPLAR Stephen George	26-04-41	110 Sqn		787593	Sgt	POLEDNIK Jaroslav [Czechoslovakia]	23-10-41	311 Sqn
652884	Sgt	PEPPER Alfred	17-05-41	149 Sqn		29146	W/C	POLGLASE MiD Patrick Julyan	4-04-41	106 Sqn
946888	Sgt	PEPPER Douglas Bertram	15-11-41	458 Sqn		632893	Sgt	POLKINGHORNE Eric Downing	16-01-41	10 Sqn
39335	W/C	PEPPER DFC Neville Ernest Wetherell	3-06-41	139 Sqn		571833	Cpl	POLLARD Gordon Wardley	22-09-41	7 Sqn
922185	Sgt	PEPPLER David George	15-10-41	114 Sqn		630476	F/S	POOLE DFM Dennis Howard Glyn	30-06-41	7 Sqn
975062	Sgt	PERCIVAL Desmond Fitzgerald	29-04-41	10 OTU		105197	P/O	POOLE Edward George	15-11-41	15 OTU
1251844	Sgt	PEREIRA Vernon Edward	28-05-41	150 Sqn		538193	Sgt	POOLE Kenneth Mossman	11-06-41	82 Sqn
1284018	Sgt	PERKS Henry Anthony	7-09-41	58 Sqn		1352297	AC2	POPE George William		3-02-41 Waterbeach
1165232	Sgt	PERRIN Harold Dennis	11-11-41	13 OTU		1101568	AC1	POPELEY Alec Charles	8-12-41	405 Sqn
961016	Sgt	PERRIN John Lyon	22-10-41	51 Sqn		984451	Sgt	PORTEOUS Sidney	12-09-41	105 Sqn
908796	Sgt	PERRY Hugh Raymond	3-04-41	101 Sqn		951752	Sgt	PORTEOUS Thomas	6-07-41	144 Sqn
957337	Sgt	PERRY-KEENE Anthony Peter	15-08-41	150 Sqn		542209	F/S	PORTER Edward Francis	2-07-41	12 Sqn
60562	P/O	PERTWEE James Raymond	9-06-41	51 Sqn		943625	Sgt	PORTER Kenneth William	23-04-41	105 Sqn
619397	F/S	PETERS Jack	18-12-41	15 Sqn		937567	Sgt	PORTHOUSE John	13-08-41	115 Sqn
1151181	Sgt	PETHERICK Anthony William	30-09-41	115 Sqn		60814	F/L	POTIER Michael Ernest	9-07-41	110 Sqn
72107	F/L	PETLEY Charles Robert McLeod	8-07-41	77 Sqn		88013	P/O	POTTS Richard John	19-08-41	83 Sqn
37418	W/C	PETLEY Lawrence Victor Elliott	4-07-41	107 Sqn		42642	P/O	POULSEN Alfred Harmon	11-01-41	82 Sqn
1102286	Sgt	PETRATOS William Henry	7-08-41	20 OTU		998507	Sgt	POULSTON Derek	15-10-41	226 Sqn
89794	P/O	PETRIE David Layton	10-09-41	103 Sqn		1375132	Sgt	POULTON James Samuel	19-11-41	18 Sqn
787873	Sgt	PETRUCHA Jaroslav [Czechoslavakia]	2-07-41	311 Sqn		1378026	Sgt	POULTON Walter James	28-12-41	57 Sqn
913197	Sgt	PETTER Robert Albert	17-05-41	149 Sqn		934286	Sgt	POUPARD Aubrey	6-09-41	10 Sqn
919705	Sgt	PHARE Denis Edgar	15-08-41	104 Sqn		1376081	Sgt	POUPARD Bernard	15-12-41	27 OTU
751054	Sgt	PHELPS Joseph William Howell	16-06-41	21 Sqn		1256952	Sgt	POWELL Cullen Eric	1-08-41	107 Sqn
87413	P/O	PHILLIPS Anthony Frank	7-04-41	83 Sqn		42880	P/O	POWELL David Evan Frank	10-04-41	50 Sqn
970558	Sgt	PHILLIPS Charles Douglas	23-07-41	21 Sqn		920529	Sgt	POWELL Gerald Keith [Canada]	15-08-41	102 Sqn
931747	Sgt	PHILLIPS David Frederick John	12-08-41	139 Sqn		936534	F/S	POWELL John Reginald	24-07-41	104 Sqn
63417	P/O	PHILLIPS Edgar Richard	1-05-41	139 Sqn		552157	F/S	POWELL William	13-06-41	15 OTU
751196	F/S	PHILLIPS Edwin Leslie	21-10-41	142 Sqn		1163881	Sgt	POWELL William	1-11-41	83 Sqn
911366	Sgt	PHILLIPS Ernest Eric Craddock	3-03-41	13 OTU		39600	F/L	POWLES DFC Frederick Charles	21-10-41	21 Sqn

975871	LAC	PRAHL Ronald Sydney	22-04-41	18 Sqn	939469	Sgt	RANSSON Jeffrey Leon	28-06-41	77 Sqn
808346	F/S	PRATT Arthur	27-06-41	102 Sqn	751176	F/S	RAPER Ernest John James	27-06-41	102 Sqn
1255739	Sgt	PRATT Cecil Mervyn	8-09-41	13 OTU	748174	Sgt	RAPLEY Eric John	11-05-41	7 Sqn
82991	P/O	PRATT Frank Edward	31-07-41	144 Sqn	81413	P/O	RASBARY Walter Charles	14-08-41	83 Sqn
969698	Sgt	PRATT John Royal Crossley	25-02-41	103 Sqn	748372	Sgt	RATCLIFFE John	10-04-41	50 Sqn
45376	P/O	PRATT Thomas Pinckney	29-08-41	49 Sqn	900862	Sgt	RAWKINS William George	4-04-41	77 Sqn
990739	Sgt	PRATT William Norman [Eire]	15-09-41	455 Sqn	1251662	Sgt	RAWLINGS Donald Reginald	7-11-41	455 Sqn
552603	F/S	PREECE Chris Redvers	24-07-41	12 Sqn	938396	Sgt	RAWLINGS Douglas Ray	9-07-41	9 Sqn
1375153	Sgt	PREECE Mervyn Stanley	14-10-41	115 Sqn	924494	Sgt	RAWLINSON Anthony Leonard Powell		
104499	P/O	PRENTICE Ian	19-09-41	10 OTU				22-08-41	106 Sqn
1408408	AC2	PREST Frank Burdett [Canada]	31-08-41	44 Sqn	968188	Sgt	RAY Charles Lawrence	26-08-41	49 Sqn
1051814	Sgt	PREST Frederick Thomas	6-08-41	144 Sqn	908502	LAC	RAYMENT Leonard Silvester Henry	25-08-41	83 Sqn
547805	F/S	PRESTON DFM Hubert Everard	21-04-41	106 Sqn	1152158	Sgt	READ Peter Verrall	8-05-41	150 Sqn
749386	Sgt	PRETTYMAN Edward Guy	14-03-41	149 Sqn	569447	F/S	READING Alfred George	30-06-41	7 Sqn
546681	F/S	PRICE DFM Alexander Philip	6-08-41	106 Sqn	967118	Sgt	REARDON Glyndwr	11-02-41	15 Sqn
41736	F/L	PRICE DFC Charles Peter Dovey	8-11-41	97 Sqn	43042	S/L	REARDON DFC John Damien [Canada]	11-09-41	102 Sqn
916138	Sgt	PRICE Denis Arthur	16-07-41	40 Sqn					
1073399	AC2	PRICE Evan James	11-12-41	Waterbeach	999621	Sgt	REAY Philip Herbert	4-07-41	57 Sqn
1355067	Sgt	PRICE Frederick Joseph Edward	14-07-41	75 Sqn	42766	F/O	REDFEARN-SMITH Maurice Viner	23-06-41	107 Sqn
64871	P/O	PRICE DFM Gordon Ernest	6-01-41	49 Sqn	778284	Sgt	REDFERN Leonard Frank [Rhodesia]	27-12-41	50 Sqn
1100588	Sgt	PRICE Kenneth Herbert	11-10-41	12 Sqn	743047	Sgt	REDGRAVE Henry Cecil	13-03-41	207 Sqn
981412	Sgt	PRICE Leslie Whitehouse	3-09-41	214 Sqn	975988	Sgt	REDMOND James Patrick	21-02-41	149 Sqn
902862	Sgt	PRICE Walter George	23-06-41	83 Sqn	1185406	Sgt	REDWOOD Arthur Francis George	21-10-41	97 Sqn
755352	Sgt	PRICE William Henry	24-07-41	101 Sqn	742647	F/S	REED Henry George Albert	17-06-41	14 OTU
979868	Sgt	PRIESTLEY Ronald Albert	28-12-41	51 Sqn	993639	AC1	REED Herbert Leslie	19-07-41	50 Sqn
63490	P/O	PRINGLE George	25-07-41	10 Sqn	994355	Sgt	REED John Moorby	2-08-41	405 Sqn
746741	Sgt	PRINGLE James	4-02-41	3 GTrgFlt	1377448	Sgt	REELS Edward Henry	15-08-41	104 Sqn
1060898	Sgt	PRITCHARD David Roe	8-11-41	102 Sqn	44176	P/O	REEMAN Edward Arthur	13-08-41	207 Sqn
44197	F/O	PRITCHARD Peter Harold Howard	11-06-41	61 Sqn	63845	P/O	REES William Larry	26-07-41	102 Sqn
1162796	Sgt	PROCTER John Gordon	30-08-41	50 Sqn	634988	Sgt	REEVE Eric Francis	6-08-41	144 Sqn
62675	P/O	PROSSER Garfield Arthur	8-06-41	139 Sqn	1168648	Sgt	REEVE Fred Charles	16-11-41	218 Sqn
994378	Sgt	PROSSER Peter	15-08-41	218 Sqn	978132	Sgt	REID Douglas John	12-09-41	107 Sqn
755713	Sgt	PROSSER Peter Charles	12-01-41	49 Sqn	997006	Sgt	REID James Henry	8-11-41	75 Sqn
42644	P/O	PROUDLOCK Michael Seymour	18-04-41	114 Sqn	920054	Sgt	REID Jeffrey Walter	29-12-41	75 Sqn
926529	Sgt	PUGH James Douglas	11-10-41	218 Sqn	974500	Sgt	REID John Adam Smith	11-06-41	99 Sqn
944287	Sgt	PUGH Philip Stanley	28-07-41	90 Sqn	1050106	Sgt	REID Joseph	21-10-41	19 OTU
904994	Sgt	PUGH Thomas Charles	10-05-41	149 Sqn	1269254	AC1	REID Robert Wilson	13-08-41	11 OTU
912307	Sgt	PULFORD John Henry Martin	18-12-41	7 Sqn	979560	Sgt	REIDMULLER Cecil Charles	2-07-41	149 Sqn
1256360	Sgt	PULHAM Ronald John	13-12-41	144 Sqn	1250438	Sgt	REIS Ian Leslie Toynton	4-07-41	106 Sqn
76016	F/O	PULLEN Arthur Leslie [Canada]	1-07-41	102 Sqn	513099	Sgt	RELF Percy Thomas	28-06-41	142 Sqn
62021	P/O	PULLEN Geoffrey Hiram Standeford	17-06-41	405 Sqn	87056	P/O	RENDALL Francis	21-06-41	99 Sqn
745547	Sgt	PURDON John Kirkwood	4-04-41	51 Sqn	549839	F/S	RENDEL Kenneth Charles	11-09-41	142 Sqn
564392	W/O	PURDY DFM Thomas	28-12-41	57 Sqn	87354	P/O	RENDLE Richard Cardew	9-04-41	9 Sqn
43965	P/O	PURVIS Robert Peter	12-09-41	10 Sqn	60567	P/O	RENSHAW Richard Christopher Sykes		
929723	Sgt	PUTTICK Wilfred	26-07-41	10 Sqn				29-06-41	15 Sqn
759117	Sgt	PYATT Reginald George	15-05-41	97 Sqn	905812	Sgt	RETTER Stanley Cyril	11-07-41	9 Sqn
1161595	Sgt	QUICK Kenneth	8-11-41	9 Sqn	1154916	Sgt	REX Anthony Hughenden	21-09-41	103 Sqn
745144	Sgt	QUINCEY James William	2-03-41	78 Sqn	84298	P/O	REYNOLDS Eric Walter	30-03-41	83 Sqn
927098	Sgt	QUINLAN Thomas Christopher	2-08-41	101 Sqn	1164659	Sgt	REYNOLDS John Alfred	8-09-41	51 Sqn
623852	Sgt	QUINN Thomas Albert	29-11-41	214 Sqn	67080	P/O	REYNOLDS Reginald Robert	26-08-41	40 Sqn
84901	P/O	RACE William Frederick	26-08-41	82 Sqn	908653	Sgt	REYNOLDS Russell John	15-07-41	104 Sqn
617104	F/S	RAE Edward Watt	12-04-41	110 Sqn	1100648	Sgt	RHODES Cecil	6-08-41	106 Sqn
623969	Sgt	RAE Robert Campbell	16-06-41	78 Sqn	1113460	Sgt	RHODES Leslie Mellor	27-09-41	104 Sqn
927081	Sgt	RAGG Percy Albert George	22-10-41	408 Sqn	986420	Sgt	RHODES Raymond Irwin	27-12-41	58 Sqn
993211	Sgt	RAINE Albert	29-09-41	49 Sqn	518719	Sgt	RICE Leonard Thomas	24-07-41	76 Sqn
33518	P/O	RALSTON John Kenneth Churchill	25-02-41	103 Sqn	945054	Sgt	RICE William James Pickering	1-07-41	10 Sqn
905139	Sgt	RAMPLEY Harry Footer	3-02-41	101 Sqn	741105	W/O	RICH DFM James Augustus	6-11-41	22 OTU
749503	Sgt	RAMPTON Robert Hooker	25-07-41	50 Sqn	923801	Sgt	RICHARDS Charles Frederick	30-07-41	20 OTU
92992	F/O	RAMSAY Charles Douglas	7-09-41	226 Sqn	745011	Sgt	RICHARDS Geoffrey Kempshall	25-06-41	18 Sqn
990194	Sgt	RAMSAY Gerrard Robert	14-10-41	44 Sqn	745715	Sgt	RICHARDS Leonard Thomas	2-03-41	50 Sqn
88659	P/O	RAMSEY Alastair Stewart	1-08-41	105 Sqn	60819	P/O	RICHARDS Richard Alban	16-05-41	105 Sqn
1168173	Sgt	RANCE Owen Ernest	27-12-41	101 Sqn	87665	P/O	RICHARDS Thomas Clarkson	19-06-41	78 Sqn
78754	F/O	RANDALL Charles Buckingham	8-11-41	106 Sqn	572635	Cpl	RICHARDS Walter John	3-03-41	7 Sqn
974663	Sgt	RANDALL John Victor	7-12-41	61 Sqn	751431	Sgt	RICHARDS William Frank	2-06-41	18 Sqn
567345	Sgt	RANDALL Peter Davies	30-12-41	76 Sqn	1150785	Sgt	RICHARDSON Barrie Arthur John	5-08-41	149 Sqn
751826	Sgt	RANDALL Thomas	3-03-41	13 OTU	1379034	Sgt	RICHARDSON David	29-09-41	99 Sqn
950534	Sgt	RANSON Charles Frederick	9-06-41	51 Sqn	751536	Sgt	RICHARDSON Edward	12-03-41	82 Sqn
61957	P/O	RANSON Jeffery Bohun	19-04-41	25 OTU	957246	Sgt	RICHARDSON Geoffrey William	7-09-41	57 Sqn

Number	Rank	Name	Date	Unit
45731	P/O	RICHARDSON James Harold	21-10-41	82 Sqn
1254013	Sgt	RICHARDSON Joseph George	19-08-41	101 Sqn
976613	Sgt	RICHARDSON Robert	11-05-41	10 Sqn
1059709	Sgt	RICHMOND Herbert	29-08-41	61 Sqn
88014	P/O	RICHMOND John Edward	31-03-41	14 OTU
977274	Sgt	RICKCORD Anthony George	28-06-41	10 Sqn
755658	Sgt	RIDDELL Thomas Percy Alexander	3-09-41	44 Sqn
925927	Sgt	RIDDIFORD Victor Ernest Thomas	27-09-41	104 Sqn
39567	F/L	RIDDLESWORTH DFC Allen Fairhurst	25-02-41	11 OTU
939009	Sgt	RIDGMAN-PARSONS Reginald	28-04-41	101 Sqn
574936	LAC	RIDING John Frederick	15-09-41	207 Sqn
924632	Sgt	RIDLER Frank Ernest	15-10-41	40 Sqn
635981	Sgt	RILEY Jack	1-04-41	144 Sqn
39620	S/L	RILEY John Lawrence	7-12-41	61 Sqn
45062	P/O	RIMMER Richard	26-06-41	19 OTU
918272	Sgt	RINTOUL Reginald Ormsby	19-06-41	10 Sqn
363472	W/O	RIPLEY Sidney	23-04-41	18 OTU
918984	Sgt	RISHWORTH Sidney Richard	16-07-41	57 Sqn
39684	F/L	RITCHIE John Frederic	25-03-41	20 OTU
631868	Sgt	RITCHIE Matthew Roy	10-01-41	75 Sqn
949712	Sgt	RITCHIE William McLean	12-06-41	99 Sqn
1375091	Sgt	RITTER Peter Ernest	13-09-41	21 Sqn
78690	F/L	ROACH Richard John	30-12-41	10 Sqn
83264	F/O	ROAKE Reginald John	7-09-41	144 Sqn
1070180	Sgt	ROBB David Gordon	13-10-41	77 Sqn
955007	Sgt	ROBBENS Bernard Walter	8-09-41	104 Sqn
754051	F/S	ROBBINS Alfred Ronald	11-10-41	58 Sqn
924860	Sgt	ROBBINS Geoffrey Alfred	12-10-41	82 Sqn
1254570	Sgt	ROBERTS Albert Lionel	30-09-41	115 Sqn
745524	Sgt	ROBERTS Antony John	24-03-41	7 Sqn
746816	Sgt	ROBERTS Archibald Sinclair	8-01-41	Stradishall
1256277	Sgt	ROBERTS Denis Herbert	27-12-41	50 Sqn
919569	Sgt	ROBERTS Frank Gordon Warwick [Rhodesia]	28-12-41	51 Sqn
1136561	AC1	ROBERTS George	9-11-41	144 Sqn
648863	F/S	ROBERTS George Henry	14-10-41	207 Sqn
651715	Sgt	ROBERTS Gerald Brinley	28-06-41	77 Sqn
1375133	Sgt	ROBERTS Harold Every	31-10-41	77 Sqn
918118	Sgt	ROBERTS Wynne	10-08-41	226 Sqn
745125	Sgt	ROBERTSON Eric Gilbert	17-01-41	40 Sqn
943039	F/S	ROBERTSON Eric Nigel Riddell	9-08-41	61 Sqn
565441	Sgt	ROBERTSON Ian James	29-09-41	99 Sqn
997198	Sgt	ROBERTSON James Cotland	1-07-41	149 Sqn
563380	F/S	ROBERTSON DFM John Stewart	1-07-41	21 Sqn
951819	Sgt	ROBERTSON Leslie Alexander	3-09-41	44 Sqn
1063077	Sgt	ROBERTSON Maxwell George [Canada]	9-05-41	214 Sqn
39259	S/L	ROBERTSON Stuart Alistair Frederick	24-03-41	7 Sqn
1004282	Sgt	ROBERTSON Thomas	3-09-41	40 Sqn
928400	Sgt	ROBERTSON-PRYOR Leslie Walter	21-05-41	17 OTU
32179	S/L	ROBINS Augustine Stuart Quallett	18-04-41	114 Sqn
1067681	Sgt	ROBINSON Eric	22-10-41	16 OTU
1052470	Sgt	ROBINSON Geoffrey	22-10-41	18 Sqn
1020772	Cpl	ROBINSON Jack Bracewell	24-10-41	40 Sqn
967533	F/S	ROBINSON Oswald Harry	19-07-41	105 Sqn
65572	P/O	ROBINSON Peter Edward Covell	17-09-41	107 Sqn
1112906	AC2	ROBINSON Terence	14-08-41	25 OTU
84938	F/O	ROBINSON Terence Myles	10-10-41	106 Sqn
42768	F/L	ROBISON Thomas Douglas Inglis [New Zealand]	30-06-41	35 Sqn
1133491	AC2	ROBSON Albert	15-05-41	16 OTU
991762	LAC	ROBSON Clifford	26-10-41	40 Sqn
23394	S/L	ROBSON MB CHB David Alan Hope	22-06-41	90 Sqn
1091810	AC1	ROBSON George	25-12-41	Oakington
956012	Sgt	ROBSON John Joseph	20-09-41	226 Sqn
992840	AC1	ROBSON J. McArthur	9-03-41	21 Sqn
1133491	AC2	ROBSON Robert	15-05-41	16 OTU
1371161	Sgt	ROBSON-SCOTT Thomas	12-12-41	106 Sqn
921751	Sgt	ROCH Thomas Reginald Frederick John	10-09-41	25 OTU
1325233	Sgt	RODGER Eric James	29-09-41	7 Sqn
42650	F/L	RODGER John Kennedy	4-09-41	13 OTU
67593	P/O	RODGERS Jack Hartley	16-09-41	18 Sqn
60563	P/O	RODWELL Benjamin Bernard Hunter	8-08-41	97 Sqn
922191	Sgt	RODWELL John Leslie	8-09-41	13 OTU
79153	F/O	ROE Hubert Jack	15-08-41	105 Sqn
1250397	Sgt	ROE Keith Vernon Dudley	12-09-41	75 Sqn
37830	S/L	ROGERS AFC Bernard John	20-06-41	99 Sqn
900955	Sgt	ROGERS Charles Barrie	14-03-41	149 Sqn
88235	P/O	ROGERS Denis Alan	31-03-41	21 Sqn
977272	Sgt	ROGERS Ernest Hildred	10-07-41	7 Sqn
1181900	Sgt	ROGERS Frank Denis	20-09-41	101 Sqn
966861	F/S	ROGERS John Johnston	15-08-41	35 Sqn
923086	Sgt	ROGERS Lawrence William	22-10-41	12 Sqn
955269	Sgt	ROGERS Thomas	8-11-41	102 Sqn
521372	Sgt	ROGERS William George	25-08-41	78 Sqn
787686	Sgt	ROLENC Jaroslav [Czechoslovakia]	23-10-41	311 Sqn
778218	Sgt	ROLFE Frank Edwin [Rhodesia]	30-11-41	106 Sqn
755505	Sgt	ROLFE Leslie Percy Charles	15-06-41	110 Sqn
67674	P/O	ROLLAND Graham Cooper	12-08-41	82 Sqn
103022	P/O	ROLLINSON Jack	26-10-41	88 Sqn
42265	F/O	ROMANS DFC David Albert Alton [Canada]	8-09-41	90 Sqn
976171	Sgt	RONNIE John Robert	21-04-41	83 Sqn
957053	Sgt	ROPER William Charles Goy	9-06-41	51 Sqn
986176	Sgt	ROSE Albert William	9-04-41	149 Sqn
746835	Sgt	ROSE Alfred William	29-08-41	35 Sqn
625936	Sgt	ROSE Cyril Douglas	28-07-41	50 Sqn
110127	P/O	ROSE Harry	26-10-41	23 OTU
1263633	Sgt	ROSE James Edward	18-11-41	7 Sqn
777696	Sgt	ROSE-INNES Cosmo Patrick Alastair Innes 'Pat' [Rhodesia]	10-10-41	16 OTU
92726	P/O	ROSS Alan George St. John	27-06-41	150 Sqn
543012	F/S	ROSS Douglas Frederick	28-04-41	50 Sqn
1351249	AC2	ROSS Peter	5-02-41	20 OTU
979551	F/S	ROSS Robert Alexander	8-08-41	15 Sqn
570966	Sgt	ROSS William	8-07-41	7 Sqn
65509	P/O	ROSSITER Alexander Charles	12-08-41	226 Sqn
1183356	Sgt	ROUTH Alfred Daryl Martin	11-10-41	107 Sqn
942668	Sgt	ROUTLEDGE Eric	2-03-41	9 Sqn
943478	Sgt	ROUTLEY Allan Ernest	4-07-41	107 Sqn
973925	Sgt	ROWAN Archibald Sinclair	30-06-41	40 Sqn
1104087	Sgt	ROWAN Arthur Wilson	2-09-41	83 Sqn
925497	Sgt	ROWE Geoffrey William	11-05-41	150 Sqn
1283048	Sgt	ROWE John William	17-07-41	14 OTU
755292	Sgt	ROWELL Norman	4-02-41	3 Group
910608	Sgt	ROWLAND Douglas Cyril	9-04-41	214 Sqn
1050936	Sgt	ROWLAND Eric	15-11-41	458 Sqn
903289	Sgt	ROWLANDS Bertram Charles	10-04-41	17 OTU
741334	Sgt	ROWLETT John Eustace	16-01-41	10 Sqn
748690	Sgt	ROWLEY Kenneth Leslie	8-08-41	15 Sqn
745434	Sgt	ROWLEY Raymond Eric	18-04-41	107 Sqn
1052303	Sgt	ROWLEY-BLAKE Douglas	8-11-41	58 Sqn
745849	Sgt	ROWNEY Ford	9-09-41	50 Sqn
61503	P/O	ROWSE William George	15-07-41	104 Sqn
102583	P/O	ROY Bruce Buchanan Percival	8-11-41	102 Sqn
652894	F/S	ROYAL Richard Albert	10-04-41	50 Sqn
787169	F/S	ROZUM Alois [Czechoslovakia]	22-06-41	311 Sqn
87024	P/O	RUCK-KEENE John Charles Lancelot	21-10-41	207 Sqn
959587	Sgt	RUDKIN John Alfred	23-06-41	107 Sqn
912084	Sgt	RUDLIN Reginald Thomas	24-07-41	35 Sqn
923101	Sgt	RUGG Raymond James	15-11-41	75 Sqn
67075	P/O	RUMBO Keith Howard Naughton [Brazil]	29-09-41	99 Sqn
1250471	Sgt	RUNCORN Kenneth Frederick	26-08-41	106 Sqn
1198669	Sgt	RUSCOE George Reginald	15-11-41	115 Sqn

60816	P/O	RUSHBROOKE George Eric Joseph	25-05-41	105 Sqn		904184	Sgt	SCOTT Ronald John	26-08-41	105 Sqn
904441	Sgt	RUSSELL Anthony Charles Henry Reid				1206630	AC1	SCOTT Sidney Albert	6-07-41	Honington
			13-01-41	35 Sqn		103534	P/O	SCOTT-MARTIN Anthony David	27-12-41	77 Sqn
646900	F/S	RUSSELL Douglas Edward	17-07-41	50 Sqn		45338	P/O	SCOTT-WORTHINGTON Russell	22-11-41	139 Sqn
1377293	Sgt	RUSSELL Ronald Benjamin	31-08-41	12 Sqn		973878	Sgt	SCOURFIELD Islwyn Davey	16-06-41	139 Sqn
949560	Sgt	RUSSELL Walter	7-05-41	75 Sqn		103031	P/O	SCROGGIE John Alexander Douglas	17-10-41	16 OTU
960415	Sgt	RUTT Christopher Keith	24-10-41	21 OTU		85289	P/O	SEAGER Kenneth Frank	27-03-41	78 Sqn
104353	P/O	RUTTER Raymond Mervyn Stephen	15-11-41	15 OTU		45689	S/L	SEALE Douglas Holland	9-07-41	110 Sqn
809200	F/S	RUTTERFORD Brian Arthur	27-06-41	12 Sqn		37694	S/L	SEALE William Terrance Chambers	30-06-41	7 Sqn
1137038	AC2	RYALL Edward Charles	4-10-41	21 OTU		1190805	Sgt	SEAMAN Kenneth John	30-07-41	20 OTU
987979	Sgt	RYE George Stevens	10-09-41	103 Sqn		906075	Sgt	SEDEN John Benjamin	2-05-41	77 Sqn
61509	P/O	SABINE Albert	22-04-41	13 OTU		82634	F/O	SEDLACEK Mojmir [Czechoslovakia]	15-09-41	311 Sqn
545514	Sgt	SADLER Thomas Samuel	28-12-41	15 OTU		81416	P/O	SEELEY Gerald Henry	23-07-41	21 Sqn
1253402	Sgt	SAICH DFM Jack Cyril	8-09-41	9 Sqn		751875	Sgt	SELBY George Arthur	10-05-41	51 Sqn
535826	Sgt	SAINSBURY Albert Edward	24-07-41	101 Sqn		1357695	Sgt	SELL DFM Horace	8-11-41	106 Sqn
956950	Sgt	SALE Bertram Edward	8-07-41	58 Sqn		932198	Sgt	SELLEY John Gordon	8-09-41	115 Sqn
520346	Sgt	SALES Sidney Ernest	17-10-41	15 OTU		755097	Sgt	SELLEY Robert Thomas	15-04-41	102 Sqn
947364	Sgt	SALT Horace Charles	25-03-41	20 OTU		749347	Sgt	SERVICE Arthur	15-10-41	75 Sqn
745138	Sgt	SALWAY Robert Victor	16-04-41	10 Sqn		939987	Sgt	SEVERN Archibald Roland	1-03-41	139 Sqn
87422	P/O	SAMMONS Reginald Gwynne	11-06-41	107 Sqn		986958	Sgt	SEVERN Stanley Richard Bowman	30-07-41	139 Sqn
552093	F/S	SAMWAYS Stuart Rex	15-08-41	105 Sqn		902550	Sgt	SEWARD Harold Samuel	15-02-41	114 Sqn
1251297	Sgt	SANDERS Cyril Raymond	16-06-41	15 OTU		751350	Sgt	SEWELL Kenneth Randolph	15-08-41	35 Sqn
1168621	Sgt	SANDERS Frederick Harold	7-11-41	99 Sqn		526601	Sgt	SEYMOUR Eric Victor	24-03-41	7 Sqn
942722	Sgt	SANDERS Kenneth Harold	23-06-41	107 Sqn		971308	Sgt	SHADBOLT Cecil John	30-06-41	14 OTU
959645	Sgt	SANDERSON George Charles Peter	5-07-41	10 OTU		916694	Sgt	SHADDICK Allan Arthur Cecil	28-08-41	21 Sqn
581191	Sgt	SANDLAND George Charles	16-01-41	10 Sqn		755009	Sgt	SHARKEY John	8-04-41	40 Sqn
939013	Sgt	SANDON William Stewart	14-04-41	106 Sqn		751062	F/S	SHARP Donald Ivor	25-08-41	83 Sqn
995851	Sgt	SANGSTER Robert	28-12-41	21 Sqn		84036	P/O	SHARP George Guy [South Africa]	9-04-41	9 Sqn
946695	Sgt	SANNE Albert Edward	17-05-41	20 OTU		40025	F/L	SHARP John Francis	3-07-41	106 Sqn
904435	Sgt	SARGENT Ernest Johnston	8-11-41	78 Sqn		86422	P/O	SHARVELL George Eltham	11-02-41	21 Sqn
		[South Africa]				1152490	Sgt	SHAW Francis Elliott	22-04-41	115 Sqn
748167	F/S	SARGENT Patrick Dickson	3-06-41	40 Sqn		82674	P/O	SHAW Gerald Frederick	10-01-41	51 Sqn
745120	F/S	SARGENT William Henry	22-07-41	110 Sqn		920449	Sgt	SHAW James Pierson [Canada]	8-08-41	139 Sqn
742026	Sgt	SARJEANT Ivor Griffiths	17-04-41	105 Sqn		908401	Sgt	SHAW John Stanley	28-06-41	10 Sqn
963441	Sgt	SAUL Edwin Kerrison	15-10-41	114 Sqn		80564	F/O	SHAW Reginald	24-07-41	103 Sqn
1257669	Sgt	SAUL Leslie Albert Harry	17-10-41	15 OTU		746878	Sgt	SHAYLER Douglas Gordon	29-04-41	82 Sqn
562617	W/O	SAUNDERS DFM Christopher Arthur	8-11-41	49 Sqn		1377747	Sgt	SHEA Edward Charles	26-08-41	40 Sqn
925661	Sgt	SAUNDERS Edwin Cyril	19-07-41	105 Sqn		982669	Sgt	SHEARER Gordon	14-10-41	44 Sqn
963858	Sgt	SAUNDERS John Stanley	30-11-41	142 Sqn		873227	Sgt	SHEARER Robert	18-12-41	15 Sqn
754479	F/S	SAUNDERS Leonard	31-07-41	142 Sqn		758034	Sgt	SHEARING Kenneth Charles	18-08-41	218 Sqn
924676	Sgt	SAUNDERS Richard Stanley	21-07-41	115 Sqn		1160566	Sgt	SHEARING Leonard Walter	21-10-41	142 Sqn
937785	Sgt	SAUNDERS Stanley Percival Charles	14-06-41	44 Sqn		935434	Sgt	SHEARN Clifford Frank	15-06-41	110 Sqn
948262	Sgt	SAUNDERS William Arthur	20-10-41	50 Sqn		581120	F/S	SHEPHERD William Charles	27-06-41	57 Sqn
40263	F/L	SAVAGE Frederick Henry	8-05-41	150 Sqn		942020	Sgt	SHERMAN John Stephen Christopher	4-04-41	115 Sqn
106545	P/O	SAVAGE Kenneth Edward Algar	18-09-41	75 Sqn		751878	Sgt	SHERRATT Frank	8-04-41	40 Sqn
975994	Sgt	SAVAGE Maurice Alfred John	21-04-41	99 Sqn		989157	Sgt	SHERRIFF John Hillhouse	21-09-41	57 Sqn
745970	Sgt	SAVAGE Paul Anthony	12-03-41	82 Sqn		1256759	Sgt	SHERWIN Alexander Valentine William		
651810	Sgt	SAVAGE Philip	17-05-41	17 OTU					27-12-41	50 Sqn
944281	Sgt	SAVAGE Walter James	14-03-41	10 OTU		1258472	Sgt	SHERWIN Derrick Robert	15-08-41	150 Sqn
569909	Sgt	SAVOY Gerland Harry	24-12-41	26 CFlt		563931	Sgt	SHERWOOD Eric Wilfrid	24-10-41	40 Sqn
1375274	Sgt	SAWDY Edward George	28-12-41	49 Sqn		65542	P/O	SHILLITOE Peter Gerald	30-07-41	139 Sqn
931753	Sgt	SAYER Ronald Ernest	22-10-41	51 Sqn		1050391	Sgt	SHIPLEY Eric	25-07-41	11 OTU
1203874	Sgt	SCANTLEBURY Leonard Eric	20-10-41	149 Sqn		742189	Sgt	SHIPLEY Howard Peter	15-01-41	58 Sqn
1378123	Sgt	SCHOFIELD Edward Reginald	7-11-41	99 Sqn		81054	P/O	SHIRLAW Ian Murray	22-03-41	105 Sqn
1304361	Sgt	SCHOLES Ronald	25-08-41	83 Sqn		978462	Sgt	SHIRLEY Glyn Thomas	19-08-41	83 Sqn
955766	Sgt	SCHOLEY Vernon	5-08-41	149 Sqn		804422	F/S	SHIRLEY Sidney Harry James	24-07-41	35 Sqn
43073	W/C	SCIVIER AFC Donald William	22-09-41	105 Sqn		1375139	Sgt	SHOREY Alexander Charles	20-11-41	455 Sqn
921994	Sgt	SCIVILLE Lionel Robert Eames	25-08-41	50 Sqn		567019	Sgt	SHORT MiD Ernest	26-07-41	35 Sqn
40643	S/L	SCOTT Anthony Aloysius McDonald	7-07-41	105 Sqn		567767	Sgt	SHORT Gilbert Maurice	24-03-41	7 Sqn
925659	Sgt	SCOTT Arnold	8-11-41	58 Sqn		751644	Sgt	SHUTT John Frederick	1-03-41	144 Sqn
87404	P/O	SCOTT Edward Alan	9-07-41	78 Sqn		65543	F/L	SHUTTLEWORTH Harold Raymond		
778351	Sgt	SCOTT George Murray [Rhodesia]	28-07-41	21 OTU				[Kenya]	26-08-41	82 Sqn
754816	Sgt	SCOTT Lawrence Armstrong	4-10-41	18 OTU		33548	S/L	SHUTTLEWORTH Richard Ashton	28-08-41	21 Sqn
60831	P/O	SCOTT Michael Andrew	24-05-41	110 Sqn		958722	Sgt	SHUTTLEWORTH Ronald	27-12-41	77 Sqn
997955	Sgt	SCOTT Norman	10-12-41	15 OTU		36155	F/L	SIEBERT DFC John Aloysius	28-03-41	207 Sqn
981198	Sgt	SCOTT Randal Archibald	27-12-41	58 Sqn				[Australia]		
995063	Sgt	SCOTT Robert Buist	1-09-41	83 Sqn		79514	P/O	SIEVERS DFC John Winston	27-06-41	150 Sqn
991861	Sgt	SCOTT Ronald Corsar	12-06-41	99 Sqn				[New Zealand]		

751881	Sgt	SILLS Donald	1-07-41	102 Sqn	926528	Sgt	SMITH Henry Toomer	11-10-41	57 Sqn
1150677	Sgt	SIMM Dennis Russell	9-06-41	78 Sqn	908525	Sgt	SMITH Herbert	5-08-41	50 Sqn
1359691	Sgt	SIMMONDS Oliver John	4-10-41	21 OTU	87038	P/O	SMITH Ian Ogg Mackenzie	9-05-41	99 Sqn
553454	Sgt	SIMMONDS Thomas Herbert Melvin			993461	Sgt	SMITH James Murray	16-07-41	57 Sqn
			23-02-41	115 Sqn	931770	Sgt	SMITH John	14-08-41	25 OTU
957726	Sgt	SIMPKIN Arthur Ernest	3-08-41	104 Sqn	1101859	Sgt	SMITH John Frederick	17-05-41	20 OTU
647593	Sgt	SIMPSON Alexander Urquhart	30-06-41	35 Sqn	748177	Sgt	SMITH John Leslie	9-05-41	214 Sqn
67082	F/O	SIMPSON Frank	31-10-41	77 Sqn	550971	F/S	SMITH DFM John Oscar Noel	16-07-41	18 Sqn
942030	Sgt	SIMPSON Grenville	15-02-41	15 Sqn	1174439	Sgt	SMITH Keith Ernest	15-08-41	218 Sqn
541087	F/S	SIMPSON John Hall	1-07-41	21 Sqn	745765	Sgt	SMITH Kenneth Harold	3-01-41	102 Sqn
940302	Sgt	SIMPSON Peter Douglas	24-07-41	104 Sqn	936263	Sgt	SMITH Laurence	11-05-41	7 Sqn
104414	P/O	SIMS Arthur Thomas	2-11-41	17 OTU	551183	F/S	SMITH Laurence Henry Wood	2-07-41	226 Sqn
81417	P/O	SINCLAIR Alexander Elder	19-06-41	16 OTU	1305460	Sgt	SMITH Leonard Arthur	21-09-41	144 Sqn
968514	Sgt	SINCLAIR Charles Grindlay	4-01-41	51 Sqn	630023	Sgt	SMITH Leslie Norman	8-07-41	Wyton
68133	P/O	SINGLETON Peter	26-06-41	77 Sqn	742581	Sgt	SMITH Paul Mackenzie	15-02-41	15 Sqn
82574	F/O	SIXTA Frank [Czechoslovakia]	17-04-41	311 Sqn	754563	F/S	SMITH Peter Bernard Eric	3-06-41	7 Sqn
934205	Sgt	SIZMUIR Douglas Victor	30-11-41	75 Sqn	553827	Sgt	SMITH Robert Cyril	8-04-41	102 Sqn
787283	Sgt	SKALICKY Rudolf [Czechoslovakia]	28-12-41	311 Sqn	758058	Sgt	SMITH Ronald	2-03-41	51 Sqn
817099	Sgt	SKENE Donald	10-04-41	106 Sqn	742572	Sgt	SMITH Ronald Cecil	30-06-41	15 Sqn
1326336	Sgt	SKINGSLEY John Frederick	28-12-41	144 Sqn	1057332	Sgt	SMITH Ronald James	12-07-41	17 OTU
903147	Sgt	SKINNER Norman Reginald	13-03-41	102 Sqn	751164	Sgt	SMITH Roy	28-07-41	90 Sqn
787888	Sgt	SKUTEK Pavel [Czechoslovakia]	16-11-41	311 Sqn	1006448	Sgt	SMITH Thomas Haydon	29-09-41	49 Sqn
41213	F/O	SKYRME Henry Beaucourt [Eire]	16-01-41	10 Sqn	983138	Sgt	SMITH William	18-02-41	19 OTU
915327	Sgt	SLADE Leonard Arthur	2-06-41	139 Sqn	945932	Sgt	SMITH William Leslie	11-03-41	9 Sqn
89316	P/O	SLADE Ralph Martin	16-07-41	21 Sqn	41216	F/O	SMITH DFC William Michael Ronald	13-08-41	207 Sqn
923998	Sgt	SLADE Victor Frederick William	15-10-41	114 Sqn	754932	Sgt	SMITHIES Donald Arthur	13-03-41	77 Sqn
755528	Sgt	SLATER Denis	3-09-41	35 Sqn	1378146	Sgt	SMITHSON Jack Gordon	26-06-41	22 OTU
552486	F/S	SLATER George Robert	27-07-41	44 Sqn	935541	F/S	SMITHSON William	9-11-41	9 Sqn
1326353	Sgt	SLATER Samuel	24-10-41	10 OTU	82639	P/O	SMRCEK Leonard [Czechoslovakia]	22-06-41	311 Sqn
102591	P/O	SLATER-EIGGERT Peter Henry	14-08-41	83 Sqn	816010	Sgt	SMYTH Joseph Hunter	7-09-41	58 Sqn
742142	F/S	SLEATH Herbert David Platten	8-09-41	90 Sqn	1053919	Sgt	SMYTH William Bennett Megarry	18-09-41	75 Sqn
929627	Sgt	SLOMAN Horace Gordon	15-09-41	75 Sqn			[Eire]		
1150612	Sgt	SMALE Ronald Walter	31-07-41	144 Sqn	755873	F/S	SNAPE Thomas David	21-11-41	109 Sqn
748545	Sgt	SMALE William Herbert Roland	30-04-41	21 Sqn	741369	Sgt	SNEESTON James Edward	17-04-41	44 Sqn
63445	P/O	SMALL Charles Nairn	4-05-41	10 OTU	1375169	Sgt	SNELL Thomas John	14-10-41	15 OTU
971258	Sgt	SMALL Cyril Alexander [Eire]	6-01-41	49 Sqn	89600	P/O	SNELLING Alfred Victor	9-06-41	78 Sqn
943824	Sgt	SMALLBONE Donald Charles	29-06-41	218 Sqn	977632	Sgt	SNODDON George Stewartson	10-04-41	218 Sqn
649465	Sgt	SMALLDON Ronald William John	15-08-41	115 Sqn	745108	Sgt	SNODDON Samuel Wesley	13-03-41	77 Sqn
925574	Sgt	SMITH Alan Mackenzie	11-10-41	107 Sqn	1174338	Sgt	SNOWDEN John Noel	24-07-41	21 OTU
653803	F/S	SMITH Alexander Plant	16-05-41	78 Sqn	1151905	Sgt	SNUGGS Kenneth	27-07-41	44 Sqn
1164124	AC2	SMITH Alfred	17-06-41	218 Sqn	751069	Sgt	SNUTCH Ernest Edmund Farrow	16-05-41	105 Sqn
913015	Sgt	SMITH Archibald Murdock	3-07-41	139 Sqn	964528	Sgt	SOAMES Martin Strahan	12-06-41	40 Sqn
84307	P/O	SMITH Arthur	4-02-41	16 OTU	748685	F/S	SOAR Harold	3-08-41	25 OTU
1097588	Sgt	SMITH Arthur	4-07-41	226 Sqn	1101599	Sgt	SODEN Denis William	22-10-41	99 Sqn
745479	F/S	SMITH Arthur Carriss	24-11-41	97 Sqn	754364	Sgt	SOFFE Harold George	10-01-41	51 Sqn
1165989	Sgt	SMITH Arthur Winston	25-10-41	144 Sqn	34090	S/L	SOLBE Edward Ulric Guerin	21-02-41	75 Sqn
742847	Sgt	SMITH Charles Arthur	9-01-41	78 Sqn	986567	Sgt	SOMERFIELD Raymond Jervis	28-08-41	21 Sqn
47808	P/O	SMITH DFM Charles Leslie	18-12-41	15 Sqn	550679	Sgt	SOMERS Peter	16-05-41	106 Sqn
1370935	Sgt	SMITH David	16-08-41	11 OTU	745354	Sgt	SOMERVILLE John Andrew Allan	25-08-41	83 Sqn
39347	S/L	SMITH David Arthur	28-05-41	49 Sqn	927551	Sgt	SOMERVILLE-WOODIWIS Adrian John		
1260826	Sgt	SMITH Donald George Kenneth	12-09-41	14 OTU				1-09-41	83 Sqn
936117	Sgt	SMITH Douglas Byrne	26-03-41	15 OTU	66535	P/O	SORENSEN Harold	15-08-41	105 Sqn
101035	P/O	SMITH Edgar Gordon	30-09-41	77 Sqn	787246	Sgt	SOUKUP Vilem [Czechoslovakia]	15-09-41	311 Sqn
778398	Sgt	SMITH Edward Boucher [Rhodesia]	27-10-41	106 Sqn	748346	Sgt	SOUTAR Leonard Albert	8-07-41	44 Sqn
580592	Sgt	SMITH Francis Joseph 'Joe' [Canada]	22-07-41	144 Sqn	959543	Sgt	SOUTHALL Arthur Dexter	29-11-41	214 Sqn
102606	P/O	SMITH Francis Leonard	8-11-41	44 Sqn	920870	Sgt	SOUTHWOOD Anthony James	14-10-41	114 Sqn
541957	Sgt	SMITH Frank Augustus Sidney	11-05-41	15 Sqn	635706	Sgt	SPARKES Robert Simeon	4-07-41	57 Sqn
581357	F/S	SMITH Geoffrey	11-05-41	150 Sqn	992848	Sgt	SPARKES Selwyn	19-07-41	105 Sqn
998266	Sgt	SMITH George Edward	30-06-41	106 Sqn	511016	F/S	SPATCHETT John Henry	6-04-41	107 Sqn
1033011	AC2	SMITH George Edward	15-10-41	Polebrook	1052466	Sgt	SPENCER James	29-08-41	61 Sqn
1151664	Sgt	SMITH George Edward	25-11-41	49 Sqn	745618	Sgt	SPENCER John	10-04-41	106 Sqn
944678	Sgt	SMITH George William	3-05-41	7 Sqn	973637	Sgt	SPENCER Roy	7-07-41	139 Sqn
649336	Sgt	SMITH Gilbert Vincent [Australia]	26-08-41	226 Sqn	1252576	Sgt	SPICER Ernest Alfred	28-12-41	51 Sqn
974757	Sgt	SMITH Gordon Alan	2-08-41	101 Sqn	959543	Sgt	SPICER William John	30-07-41	20 OTU
751485	Sgt	SMITH Gordon Charles	25-08-41	144 Sqn	903270	Sgt	SPICKETT George Herbesrt	29-08-41	104 Sqn
755541	F/S	SMITH Gordon Percy Carver	9-04-41	7 Sqn	88038	P/O	SPIERS John Reynolds	21-02-41	16 OTU
911524	Sgt	SMITH Henry Bruce Barcroft Teesdale			87666	P/O	SPIERS MiD William McNaughton	26-07-41	10 Sqn
			2-09-41	83 Sqn	43569	F/L	SPIKINS MiD Frank	25-12-41	12 Sqn

Number	Rank	Name	Date	Unit
41077	F/O	SPILLER Victor Gundred Distin	11-05-41	150 Sqn
1168686	Sgt	SPINDLER Douglas Frederick	1-11-41	83 Sqn
759054	Sgt	SPINDLER George Paul	13-10-41	207 Sqn
751927	F/S	SPONDER Eric William	23-06-41	83 Sqn
742601	Sgt	SPOUGE Cyril Francis	26-04-41	21 Sqn
1380461	Sgt	SPRAGGE John Charles	14-10-41	15 OTU
745815	Sgt	SPROSON Sidney Ernest	25-03-41	21 Sqn
1252680	Sgt	SQUIRRELL Kenneth William	9-12-41	15 OTU
526438	F/S	STABLES DFM Darrel Barry	27-10-41	106 Sqn
1300132	AC1	STACK Edward [Eire]	20-06-41	Oakington
26214	W/C	STAINTHORPE AFC William Waters	27-02-41	83 Sqn
89357	P/O	STANDFAST Peter Howard	15-08-41	105 Sqn
68760	P/O	STANES Alan Geoffrey	21-09-41	103 Sqn
1169092	Sgt	STANIER Arnold	27-10-41	110 Sqn
533826	F/S	STANLEY DFM Christopher	8-11-41	97 Sqn
102980	P/O	STANLEY Eric Lionel Victor	6-12-41	110 Sqn
745652	F/S	STANLEY James William	2-07-41	226 Sqn
652027	Sgt	STANLEY John Glynne	3-03-41	218 Sqn
90748	P/O	STANNARD Lionel Edward	13-03-41	50 Sqn
1357061	Sgt	STANSFIELD Edwin	15-08-41	405 Sqn
1055943	Sgt	STANSFIELD Robert Arthur	21-10-41	408 Sqn
920793	Sgt	STANTON Philip Henry	8-11-41	102 Sqn
755820	Sgt	STAPLES Denis Charles	12-04-41	110 Sqn
967475	Sgt	STARK Robert Donald Cowan	18-04-41	9 Sqn
88701	P/O	STARKEY Charles Frank	15-06-41	114 Sqn
755098	Sgt	START Ernest John	19-09-41	58 Sqn
970156	Sgt	STATTON Donald Allen Benjamin [Canada]	3-05-41	13 OTU
917200	Sgt	STAYTE William Edward	8-09-41	12 Sqn
977400	Sgt	STEAD John	12-08-41	114 Sqn
1250598	Sgt	STEADMAN Alfred William	10-12-41	13 OTU
40955	F/L	STEEL Edward Nation [New Zealand]	6-05-41	110 Sqn
922331	Sgt	STEELE Thomas Victor	12-10-41	82 Sqn
1051619	Sgt	STEELE William Reid	22-10-41	75 Sqn
755408	Sgt	STEGGALL Charles Oliver	4-09-41	58 Sqn
983447	Sgt	STEPHENS Frank	15-08-41	83 Sqn
923720	Sgt	STEPHENS Richard Thomas	14-07-41	139 Sqn
966808	Sgt	STEPHENSON Norman	3-01-41	102 Sqn
1377136	Sgt	STERLING Eric William	15-12-41	408 Sqn
787497	Sgt	STETKA Vaclav [Czechoslovakia]	17-04-41	311 Sqn
905233	Sgt	STEVENS Eric Charles	30-04-41	99 Sqn
751652	Sgt	STEVENS James	3-09-41	44 Sqn
972788	Sgt	STEVENS John Bernard [Canada]	9-06-41	78 Sqn
924333	Sgt	STEVENS Vernon Arkwright	18-08-41	18 Sqn
1111939	AC1	STEVENSON William Ronald	25-08-41	83 Sqn
755954	F/S	STEWARD Stanley Charles	17-08-41	104 Sqn
987915	Sgt	STEWART Frank Parker	14-10-41	115 Sqn
969410	Sgt	STEWART Frederick Gordon	11-05-41	10 Sqn
945565	Sgt	STEWART James	21-02-41	149 Sqn
801590	Sgt	STEWART John Campbell	21-06-41	99 Sqn
627588	F/S	STEWART Joseph	22-07-41	11 OTU
1254483	Sgt	STEWART Kenneth Ernest	27-12-41	58 Sqn
748297	Sgt	STEWART Lawrence	12-03-41	82 Sqn
42275	F/O	STEYN DFC James Henry [South Africa]	13-04-41	19 OTU
974773	Sgt	STICKLAND Donald Roy	29-05-41	78 Sqn
745430	Sgt	STICKLAND Victor John	16-04-41	10 Sqn
44808	P/O	STICKNEY Crichton MacKnight	5-07-41	226 Sqn
1152032	Sgt	STIDDARD Arthur James	7-06-41	105 Sqn
86396	P/O	STOBBS Walter Kell	24-06-41	76 Sqn
787890	Sgt	STOCEK Maxmilian [Czechoslovakia]	25-05-41	311 Sqn
43258	F/L	STOCK DFC Sidney George	3-10-41	7 Sqn
1055309	Sgt	STOCKDALE Neil	15-07-41	102 Sqn
1051502	Sgt	STOCKS Peter	30-07-41	82 Sqn
70820	F/L	STOKES John	16-07-41	218 Sqn
45278	F/O	STOKES Leslie	30-10-41	88 Sqn
60345	P/O	STOKES Neville George [Australia]	18-12-41	97 Sqn
581123	Sgt	STONE Albert Ernest	30-04-41	18 Sqn
45899	P/O	STONE DFM Harold Walter	24-07-41	35 Sqn
65515	P/O	STONE Jack Richard	9-05-41	18 Sqn
634726	Sgt	STONE William Connor	22-03-41	57 Sqn
975763	Sgt	STONES Frank	12-03-41	40 Sqn
755080	Sgt	STORER Charles James	7-09-41	78 Sqn
754355	Sgt	STOREY John Harold	16-07-41	218 Sqn
1108561	F/S	STORIE Richard Smith	30-06-41	15 Sqn
751053	Sgt	STOTT Joshua Ernest	15-08-41	405 Sqn
569717	Sgt	STRACHAN Robert Brown	13-08-41	15 Sqn
1381648	Sgt	STRATTON Maurice Albert	18-09-41	88 Sqn
65557	P/O	STRATTON Ronald Arthur	19-08-41	114 Sqn
948587	Sgt	STRAUGHAN Robert	24-06-41	57 Sqn
78701	P/O	STRICKLAND Walter Patrick	9-04-41	9 Sqn
748716	Sgt	STROMBERG Olaf Nicholas	21-05-41	83 Sqn
1380882	Sgt	STRONACH Donald Henry	8-11-41	7 Sqn
82714	P/O	STRONG Philip Joseph	17-01-41	83 Sqn
755999	Sgt	STROTHER Walter Irvine	18-09-41	405 Sqn
909968	Sgt	STROUD Arthur Henry	3-09-41	35 Sqn
87651	P/O	STRUTHERS Alastair Fulton	28-06-41	142 Sqn
1182408	Sgt	STRUTT Cecil William	28-08-41	13 OTU
754925	Sgt	STUART Robert Surfleet	13-10-41	207 Sqn
42449	S/L	STUBBS DFC Richard Thomas	15-10-41	139 Sqn
754904	F/S	STUBBS Gordon	9-06-41	51 Sqn
518225	F/S	STURGEON Eric Ernest	28-07-41	21 Sqn
551203	F/S	ST. JAMES-SMITH Ronald Godfrey	13-04-41	18 Sqn
1377232	Sgt	SUCKLING Alfred Frederick	8-09-41	12 Sqn
1294259	Sgt	SULLIVAN Dennis Alfred Gilbert 'Den'	15-12-41	15 OTU
532602	Sgt	SULLIVAN John Patrick	23-07-41	21 Sqn
967240	Sgt	SUMMERS George	24-07-41	76 Sqn
759043	Sgt	SUMMERS Harold	11-01-41	82 Sqn
1177035	Sgt	SUMMERS Oswald Colin	26-12-41	18 Sqn
759004	Sgt	SUMMERSGILL Stanley	4-02-41	20 OTU
1168373	Sgt	SUMMERTON Peter Cyril de Bank	15-11-41	15 OTU
742439	Sgt	SUMNER Clifford	9-04-41	7 Sqn
327457	F/S	SUMNER Frank	30-11-41	142 Sqn
1280696	AC2	SUMNER William Percy	27-02-41	Horsham St. Faith
42908	F/O	SUTCLIFFE Carmen Fletcher [Canada]	24-07-41	21 OTU
976127	Sgt	SUTHERLAND Leslie George	10-05-41	149 Sqn
976352	Sgt	SUTTON Philip Richard	4-06-41	21 Sqn
528254	Sgt	SUTTON Victor Ronald	31-07-41	142 Sqn
82578	P/O	SVIC Miloslav [Czechoslovakia]	4-06-41	311 Sqn
935828	Sgt	SWAFFIELD Charles Thomas	4-01-41	51 Sqn
107514	P/O	SWEENEY George Edward	8-11-41	7 Sqn
754947	Sgt	SYKES Fred Hugh	1-04-41	144 Sqn
991337	Sgt	SYKES Jack	7-07-41	139 Sqn
1100792	Sgt	SYKES Walter Bradbury	18-08-41	16 OTU
975686	Sgt	SYMES Lionel John	19-04-41	114 Sqn
106965	P/O	SYMES Ronald Clarke	26-10-41	23 OTU
1160231	Sgt	SYMONDSON Sidney Norman	19-07-41	15 Sqn
82966	P/O	TAFFENDER William Clifford	13-06-41	103 Sqn
1154074	Sgt	TAFT Stanley Eric	7-09-41	144 Sqn
968103	Sgt	TAGUE John	30-07-41	82 Sqn
755370	Sgt	TAIT Hugh	7-07-41	106 Sqn
984659	AC2	TAIT John Brown	10-04-41	17 OTU
85278	P/O	TAIT John Lawrence	2-04-41	82 Sqn
974125	Sgt	TAIT Kennedy	9-05-41	214 Sqn
970360	Sgt	TALBOT Gerald Joseph	9-05-41	99 Sqn
1010735	AC2	TALBOT Walter Joseph	13-08-41	11 OTU
84014	F/L	TALLIS DFC Ralph Eric	29-04-41	82 Sqn
1055982	Sgt	TANKARD Joseph	20-09-41	144 Sqn
1158394	Sgt	TANNER Herbert McGahey	15-11-41	15 OTU
84025	F/O	TAPP Ronald Frederick	13-04-41	18 Sqn
1375439	Sgt	TARRAN John Francis	26-11-41	106 Sqn
970710	Sgt	TARRANT Victor	9-01-41	78 Sqn
1381172	Sgt	TASKER Robert Holtby	22-10-41	75 Sqn
912606	Sgt	TATE John Nicholas Bailey	25-07-41	83 Sqn

Service No	Rank	Name	Date	Sqn/Unit
944250	Sgt	TATHAM Arthur Gordon	24-07-41	104 Sqn
1377918	Sgt	TATTERSFIELD Harold	17-10-41	15 OTU
1163487	Sgt	TATTON Cyril	24-07-41	405 Sqn
1355405	Sgt	TATTON Douglas	30-10-41	14 OTU
1168359	Sgt	TAYLOR Alfred Harry	13-12-41	144 Sqn
1100661	Sgt	TAYLOR Cyril	22-10-41	75 Sqn
102613	P/O	TAYLOR David Carl	23-11-41	139 Sqn
567000	Sgt	TAYLOR Frederick George	1-07-41	7 Sqn
755630	Sgt	TAYLOR Frederick Herbert Harry	22-01-41	82 Sqn
36134	S/L	TAYLOR DFC George Richard	13-08-41	207 Sqn
1169554	Sgt	TAYLOR Guy Trevor	13-08-41	15 Sqn
1377674	Sgt	TAYLOR Harold William	27-10-41	17 OTU
759305	Sgt	TAYLOR Jack	14-07-41	214 Sqn
1100675	Sgt	TAYLOR James Marron	13-06-41	25 OTU
701582	Sgt	TAYLOR Jesse	8-09-41	51 Sqn
998674	Sgt	TAYLOR John	19-08-41	51 Sqn
1355410	Sgt	TAYLOR John Arthur	15-10-41	11 OTU
936556	Sgt	TAYLOR John Melville	17-04-41	44 Sqn
937118	F/S	TAYLOR Keith Edward	25-04-41	51 Sqn
1180052	Sgt	TAYLOR Leslie Morley	25-06-41	13 OTU
755472	Sgt	TAYLOR Norman Frank	28-04-41	114 Sqn
1007315	Sgt	TAYLOR Percival Miles	24-11-41	115 Sqn
995861	Sgt	TAYLOR Philip Anthony	30-11-41	102 Sqn
957728	Sgt	TAYLOR Ronald	15-08-41	50 Sqn
942851	Sgt	TAYLOR Stanley Albert	11-05-41	144 Sqn
1162840	Sgt	TAYLOR Victor Arthur	4-10-41	21 OTU
967101	Sgt	TCHAOUSSOGLOU Constantinos Marios (served as THOMPSON)	4-04-41	115 Sqn
747731	Sgt	TEETON Horace	17-02-41	114 Sqn
61986	P/O	TEMPERLEY Roy Frederick Benson	25-08-41	50 Sqn
800532	Sgt	TEMPLE Herbert Edward	13-08-41	9 Sqn
–	G/C	TENNANT DSO MC John Edward	7-08-41	Lossiemouth
944262	Sgt	TERRY Solomon	10-04-41	57 Sqn
60757	P/O	TETLOW George Walter	30-06-41	115 Sqn
1265842	Sgt	THACKWELL Leslie Henry	24-10-41	21 OTU
1104565	Sgt	THAIN George McAra	8-11-41	75 Sqn
69436	P/O	THOMAS Alan Roderick	20-07-41	51 Sqn
1006925	Sgt	THOMAS Albert John	15-10-41	40 Sqn
984452	Sgt	THOMAS Allan Theophilus	29-06-41	82 Sqn
1051799	Sgt	THOMAS Bryan Robert	21-10-41	142 Sqn
748019	Sgt	THOMAS Charles Alfred Frederick	20-09-41	103 Sqn
818179	Sgt	THOMAS Claude Percival	8-04-41	61 Sqn
963046	Sgt	THOMAS Cyril David	8-11-41	51 Sqn
903395	Sgt	THOMAS David William Montague	23-02-41	115 Sqn
618140	Sgt	THOMAS Eric Rees	8-11-41	35 Sqn
1169719	Sgt	THOMAS Evan John	20-08-41	16 OTU
1253304	Sgt	THOMAS Frank Seeley	15-11-41	115 Sqn
91200	F/O	THOMAS Howard Stepney	15-05-41	20 OTU
967631	Sgt	THOMAS Percy	2-03-41	61 Sqn
755579	Sgt	THOMAS Ronald Henry	26-02-41	82 Sqn
971203	F/S	THOMAS Ronald Mason	2-08-41	405 Sqn
1182155	Sgt	THOMAS Thomas James Wade	13-09-41	21 Sqn
72251	F/O	THOMAS William Kelman Burr	4-02-41	106 Sqn
1379144	Sgt	THOMPSON Alan	23-08-41	20 OTU
925058	Sgt	THOMPSON Donald Roy	24-10-41	101 Sqn
60564	P/O	THOMPSON Edward Alan Wilfred	2-09-41	44 Sqn
748054	F/S	THOMPSON Edward Carson	8-08-41	101 Sqn
1113931	Sgt	THOMPSON Frank	19-11-41	18 Sqn
637513	Sgt	THOMPSON George Edward	16-12-41	102 Sqn
1052413	Sgt	THOMPSON Herbert	29-08-41	35 Sqn
1152206	Sgt	THOMPSON Jack Dennis	7-11-41	75 Sqn
1191611	AC2	THOMPSON John Edwin	23-05-41	Mildenhall
1168424	Sgt	THOMPSON Matthew	6-12-41	17 OTU
64270	P/O	THOMPSON Norman Frederick	23-08-41	114 Sqn
1181167	Sgt	THOMPSON Peter Desmond	24-10-41	17 OTU
74343	F/L	THOMPSON Reginald Perronet Campbell	4-04-41	83 Sqn
974372	Sgt	THOMPSON Robert Ferguson	8-11-41	35 Sqn
938712	F/S	THOMPSON Robert Henry	8-07-41	10 Sqn
918136	Sgt	THOMPSON Samuel George	27-12-41	77 Sqn
79575	F/O	THOMPSON William Henry John	30-09-41	7 Sqn
654088	Sgt	THOMPSON William Keith	27-04-41	83 Sqn
1281923	Sgt	THOMSON Arthur Anthony	8-11-41	57 Sqn
984788	Sgt	THOMSON Cyril Stuart	28-06-41	10 Sqn
912133	Sgt	THOMSON Eric Alexander Raven	5-08-41	149 Sqn
922720	Sgt	THOMSON Fairlie Hamilton	26-03-41	15 OTU
36094	S/L	THOMSON Hugh Frederick	1-08-41	107 Sqn
85703	P/O	THOMSON John Rauthmell	18-09-41	15 Sqn
974513	Sgt	THOMSON Samuel	8-11-41	102 Sqn
1152760	Sgt	THORLEY Thomas Henry	8-11-41	102 Sqn
920237	Sgt	THORNEYCROFT William George	25-05-41	139 Sqn
965427	F/S	THORNHILL Wilfred	25-04-41	218 Sqn
60565	P/O	THORPE Francis Bernard	7-09-41	78 Sqn
748308	Sgt	THORPE Lawrence	9-05-41	78 Sqn
905008	F/S	THORROWGOOD Leonard Samuel	14-08-41	83 Sqn
611006	F/S	THRIPP Frederick Samuel	18-07-41	110 Sqn
754791	Sgt	THURLBECK John Ford	1-02-41	144 Sqn
754631	Sgt	THURLING Thomas James	3-03-41	58 Sqn
909253	Sgt	THURSTON Stanley Edward	30-07-41	106 Sqn
952281	Sgt	TIDEY Wilfred John	11-07-41	9 Sqn
87667	P/O	TIDSWELL Ralph Edward	28-06-41	77 Sqn
1325220	Sgt	TIERNEY Christopher George	7-12-41	21 OTU
61034	P/O	TILLEY Michael William [South Africa]	6-08-41	51 Sqn
79164	P/O	TIMMINS Tom Eric	8-01-41	214 Sqn
580630	F/S	TIMMS John Douglas	15-08-41	105 Sqn
1153718	Sgt	TIMMS Ralph Thomas	8-08-41	10 Sqn
919073	Sgt	TINGLEY Frederick Ernest	25-06-41	115 Sqn
999616	Sgt	TINKER James	12-07-41	17 OTU
928888	Sgt	TIPPER Frederick Birkett	14-07-41	115 Sqn
964895	F/S	TITCOMB Francis Albert	22-10-41	408 Sqn
971149	F/S	TITTLEY James Hopkin	19-07-41	50 Sqn
79558	P/O	TODD Arthur Landon Thomas	4-02-41	3 GTrgFlt
742890	Sgt	TODD Ernest Frederick	16-01-41	40 Sqn
908659	Sgt	TODMAN Raymond Henry	11-10-41	12 Sqn
34033	W/C	TOLAND Gerald Thomas [Canada]	27-02-41	78 Sqn
1054292	Sgt	TOLLER Robert William	15-09-41	75 Sqn
924719	Sgt	TOLLETT Ralph	8-12-41	107 Sqn
1376875	Sgt	TOLLEY Francis Harry Patrick	26-10-41	23 OTU
787501	Sgt	TOMANEK Josef [Czechoslovakia]	28-12-41	311 Sqn
1258774	Sgt	TOMES Peter Beresford	14-10-41	15 OTU
701366	Sgt	TOMKINSON John La Bassee	13-03-41	214 Sqn
969697	Sgt	TOMKINSON John Staley	8-06-41	78 Sqn
69743	P/O	TOMLINSON Anthony Winslow	6-08-41	77 Sqn
1108182	Sgt	TOMLINSON Kenneth Aubyn	12-09-41	75 Sqn
550950	Sgt	TOMLINSON DFM Robert Tod [Eire]	8-02-41	12 Sqn
922929	Sgt	TOMPKINS Kenneth Mervyn	19-08-41	10 Sqn
931417	Sgt	TOMPSETT Harold Arthur	13-04-41	19 OTU
914760	Sgt	TOMPSETT Stanley Charles	15-06-41	75 Sqn
946159	Sgt	TOMPSON Gordon Leslie	12-06-41	40 Sqn
89606	P/O	TONGE Harry Clifford	29-08-41	49 Sqn
956044	Sgt	TONKS Harry Gilbert	31-08-41	83 Sqn
1114337	Sgt	TOOTHILL Kenneth Hutley	15-09-41	75 Sqn
61483	P/O	TOPLIS John Grahame	12-05-41	214 Sqn
1375624	Sgt	TOSKI Hubert John	30-12-41	76 Sqn
927548	Sgt	TOTHILL Frank Hugh Neville	11-10-41	12 Sqn
930343	Sgt	TOTTLE Stanley Charles	15-08-41	150 Sqn
1109112	Sgt	TOVEY Edward Donald	29-09-41	7 Sqn
1258909	Sgt	TOWERS Victor Edward	30-11-41	455 Sqn
1022750	Sgt	TOWNS John	18-12-41	7 Sqn
759109	Sgt	TOWNSEND Douglas William	18-04-41	107 Sqn
921516	Sgt	TOWNSEND Leonard Ronald	15-11-41	99 Sqn
1167363	Sgt	TRACEY Charles Henry	16-09-41	18 Sqn
746940	F/S	TRACEY Peter Frederick	22-10-41	12 Sqn
1166155	Sgt	TRAVISS John Thomas	11-07-41	16 OTU
85672	P/O	TREHERN Richard William	4-01-41	51 Sqn
1065995	Sgt	TREVOR Leslie	20-09-41	226 Sqn

614269	F/S	TREWHELLA Hugh Kingsley	11-05-41	150 Sqn	917610	Sgt	VERNON Aubrey Walter	10-09-41	103 Sqn
625678	Sgt	TRIBICK Roy	22-01-41	139 Sqn	1165333	Sgt	VERNON Hubert	21-07-41	115 Sqn
963497	AC1	TRICKETT Laurence Frederick Roy	11-04-41	17 OTU	43380	F/O	VERVER Peter Bernard	3-08-41	104 Sqn
973935	Sgt	TRIGGS Cyril Ernest	4-06-41	139 Sqn	652376	F/S	VICKERS Alan Edward	11-05-41	150 Sqn
91069	P/O	TRIPP Hugh Upton Howard	3-05-41	44 Sqn	918716	Sgt	VICKERS Harry	5-11-41	18 Sqn
1062958	Sgt	TROTT Eric	8-09-41	9 Sqn	981272	Sgt	VICKERY Percy James	24-07-41	76 Sqn
61969	P/O	TRUEMAN Ronald Victor	24-07-41	405 Sqn	740176	F/S	VIDLER Henry Alexander Vincent	31-07-41	142 Sqn
902080	Sgt	TRUSCOTT Gordon Jeoffre	29-08-41	7 Sqn	742189	Sgt	VIGAR Joseph Raymond	9-05-41	5 Group
550367	F/S	TRUSCOTT John Desmond	15-09-41	305 Sqn	63824	P/O	VINCENT Bernard Montague Jeffrey	17-08-41	12 Sqn
1252293	Sgt	TUCKER Howard	21-07-41	115 Sqn	89071	P/O	VIVIAN Edward Douglas [South Africa]	12-07-41	50 Sqn
636626	Sgt	TUCKER James	30-09-41	7 Sqn					
755162	Sgt	TUCKER Kenneth Charles	18-07-41	110 Sqn	37138	S/L	VIVIAN John [Eire]	8-08-41	15 Sqn
106543	P/O	TUCKEY Ernest James	13-09-41	21 Sqn	1250027	Sgt	VOSPER Roy Russell	30-09-41	78 Sqn
62307	P/O	TUCKFIELD Kenneth Monckton	8-11-41	58 Sqn	33401	S/L	WADDINGTON Martin Walter	10-08-41	226 Sqn
970471	F/S	TUCKWELL Harold Charles	12-05-41	40 Sqn	1375168	Sgt	WADE Edward	17-12-41	44 Sqn
1253671	Sgt	TUFF Herbert Roy	12-09-41	14 OTU	751442	Sgt	WADE George	8-05-41	105 Sqn
1288767	Sgt	TUGMAN John Richard	7-09-41	102 Sqn	1065792	Sgt	WADE Roy	2-11-41	15 OTU
778476	Sgt	TULLEY John Adney [Rhodesia]	27-11-41	14 OTU	89085	P/O	WADESON George Francis	5-07-41	106 Sqn
1252498	Sgt	TULLEY William Earley	15-09-41	21 Sqn	910016	Sgt	WAGON Charles Edward	10-09-41	103 Sqn
39911	S/L	TULLY Murray James	23-11-41	13 OTU	102551	P/O	WAITE Harold Ernest	7-08-41	20 OTU
981759	Sgt	TUNNAH John Matthew Bailey	13-06-41	102 Sqn	755534	Sgt	WAITE William Leslie	26-06-41	18 Sqn
79551	P/O	TUNSTAL Peter George	15-02-41	50 Sqn	67083	P/O	WAKEFIELD Ernest	15-08-41	218 Sqn
938890	F/S	TUNSTALL Lewis Benjamin	26-06-41	19 OTU	1215618	AC2	WAKEFIELD Gordon Sydney	24-11-41	115 Sqn
1460716	AC2	TUPPER Thomas John	31-10-41	816 Sqn	937804	Sgt	WAKEFIELD Leslie James Gordon	16-06-41	139 Sqn
742828	Sgt	TURNBULL John Grant	3-06-41	11 OTU	930342	Sgt	WAKEFIELD Peter Michael	12-09-41	149 Sqn
570035	Sgt	TURNER Alan	24-06-41	76 Sqn	1252727	Sgt	WAKEFORD Alan	15-08-41	12 Sqn
541403	Sgt	TURNER Alfred James	25-03-41	20 OTU	1152209	Sgt	WAKELING Maurice Victor	11-11-41	35 Sqn
921756	Sgt	TURNER Eric Charles William	21-09-41	144 Sqn	749378	Sgt	WALDER Philip James	30-07-41	139 Sqn
83003	P/O	TURNER Frank Wilfred	14-07-41	139 Sqn	41758	P/O	WALDERS Neville Whitford	9-10-41	107 Sqn
747850	F/S	TURNER Henry Benjamin	3-09-41	44 Sqn	1261477	Sgt	WALDRON Edward James 'Ted'	14-10-41	15 OTU
745663	F/S	TURNER Leonard Cyril	30-08-41	50 Sqn	1255722	Sgt	WALDRON Vernon Elliston	29-09-41	99 Sqn
1256781	Sgt	TURNER Raymond	7-12-41	104 Sqn	627395	Sgt	WALES Arthur Frederick	30-11-41	10 Sqn
1061032	Sgt	TURNER Raymond Burn	7-07-41	57 Sqn	62341	P/O	WALKDEN Malcolm Thomas Kershaw	12-08-41	18 Sqn
913804	Sgt	TURNER Reginald James	24-07-41	75 Sqn					
905119	F/S	TURNER Ronald Bertram	6-11-41	83 Sqn	983838	Sgt	WALKER Alan Lowther	28-05-41	82 Sqn
112730	P/O	TURNER DFM William Joseph	7-12-41	22 OTU	905129	Sgt	WALKER Alfred Cole	29-09-41	49 Sqn
970163	LAC	TURPIE David Liddell	31-03-41	19 OTU	78863	P/O	WALKER Charles Norman	8-01-41	38 Sqn
937811	Sgt	TURTON Frederick Peter	18-09-41	405 Sqn	902458	Sgt	WALKER Denzil Philip	28-06-41	10 Sqn
906290	Sgt	TWEED Alfred Francis	18-04-41	77 Sqn	85267	P/O	WALKER Donald Fezard	18-06-41	58 Sqn
522741	F/S	TWEEDALE Frank	28-08-41	88 Sqn	69466	P/O	WALKER Donald William Hirst	17-08-41	10 Sqn
745186	F/S	TYLER Eric Douglas	8-07-41	44 Sqn	1019154	Sgt	WALKER Frank Gordon	24-07-41	103 Sqn
1172555	Sgt	TYLER Eric William	12-06-41	40 Sqn	611566	Sgt	WALKER Hugh John	30-09-41	7 Sqn
903308	Sgt	TYLER William Archibald	17-04-41	144 Sqn	73012	S/L	WALKER James Godfrey	30-11-41	102 Sqn
958276	Sgt	TYRRELL James Abraham	12-06-41	25 OTU	543094	F/S	WALKER James Rankin	3-10-41	7 Sqn
1260229	Sgt	TYRRELL Robert Cecil	15-10-41	40 Sqn	903305	Sgt	WALKER Peter John	11-06-41	107 Sqn
759266	Sgt	ULLMER DFM Robert Walter	20-07-41	139 Sqn	552294	Sgt	WALKER Phillip	18-10-41	27 OTU
45306	P/O	UNSWORTH DFM Joseph	14-10-41	207 Sqn	1052257	Sgt	WALKER Roland Vivian Warren	19-11-41	18 Sqn
956821	Sgt	UNWIN Harry Nutt	3-09-41	44 Sqn	751990	F/S	WALKER Ronald Roderick	22-10-41	408 Sqn
1168118	Sgt	UPTON Gathorne Field	25-08-41	49 Sqn	630430	F/S	WALKER William	26-10-41	23 OTU
923863	Sgt	URPETH Robert Victor	30-08-41	50 Sqn	982279	Sgt	WALKER William Horace	2-08-41	101 Sqn
1256526	Sgt	URSELL Howard	19-06-41	12 OTU	903302	Sgt	WALKER William Waugh	17-04-41	16 OTU
787479	Sgt	VACLAVEK Arnost [Czechoslovakia]	16-11-41	311 Sqn	995698	Sgt	WALLACE Alexander Dempsey	15-09-41	15 Sqn
1178755	Sgt	VAISEY John Roland Maddison	30-09-41	58 Sqn	1253867	Sgt	WALLACE Walter Harry	4-09-41	107 Sqn
787551	F/S	VALACH Karel [Czechoslovakia]	22-06-41	311 Sqn	1168701	Sgt	WALLER Ernest	30-11-41	455 Sqn
05208	W/C	VALENTINE DSO George Engebret	3-09-41	61 Sqn	614456	Cpl	WALLETT William Harry	28-12-41	21 Sqn
787417	Sgt	VALES Vaclav [Czechoslovakia]	19-07-41	311 Sqn	80064	P/O	WALLIS-STOLZLE Ronald Walter	9-05-41	78 Sqn
778400	Sgt	van der MERWE Nichoolaas Petrus [Rhodesia]	20-09-41	16 OTU	1526894	AC2	WALLS Charles Leslie	11-12-41	5 Group
					88033	P/O	WALLS Joseph Henry	30-06-41	40 Sqn
777700	Sgt	VAN DEEMTER Cecil Broughton [South Africa]	10-10-41	16 OTU	551317	F/S	WALLS Roland Ernest	30-06-41	7 Sqn
					1100036	Sgt	WALLWORK Bernard	8-11-41	7 Sqn
903056	Sgt	VAN KLAVEREN William Edward	4-05-41	102 Sqn	40064	S/L	WALSH Kevin Harrold	2-09-41	139 Sqn
943468	Sgt	VARNSVERRY Albert Edwin	7-07-41	40 Sqn	751752	Sgt	WALSH Louis Staveacre	15-02-41	114 Sqn
969305	Sgt	VARDY Stanley	14-07-41	139 Sqn	749452	Sgt	WALSHE John O'Neill	19-06-41	44 Sqn
970952	Sgt	VAUGHAN Kenneth Herbert Aynge	15-03-41	Stradishall	930978	Sgt	WALTER Cyril David George	14-10-41	207 Sqn
78770	P/O	VAUGHAN Reginald Herbert	12-05-41	144 Sqn	67084	P/O	WALTER Harry	5-11-41	144 Sqn
976141	Sgt	VEITCH Stanley	22-06-41	207 Sqn	946880	Sgt	WALTERS Harry Spencer	17-04-41	149 Sqn
1061955	Sgt	VENN Alfred Gordon	21-06-41	218 Sqn	569348	Sgt	WALTON Cecil	8-11-41	7 Sqn
34185	S/L	VERDON-ROE Eric Alliott	26-07-41	102 Sqn	908698	Sgt	WALTON Joseph Frank	8-07-41	61 Sqn

Number	Rank	Name	Date	Unit
649374	F/S	WALTON Kennedy Charles	11-04-41	18 Sqn
1177185	Sgt	WALTON Robert Gordon Clifford	29-11-41	214 Sqn
84312	P/O	WAND Walter Edgar Anthony	12-08-41	17 OTU
988001	Sgt	WANSBROUGH Howard Vivian	9-04-41	99 Sqn
67021	F/L	WAPLES DFC Howard	23-07-41	21 Sqn
74344	F/O	WARBURTON David	4-02-41	18 OTU
978776	Sgt	WARBURTON Robert Lea	11-10-41	75 Sqn
748149	Sgt	WARCUP Allen	2-03-41	21 Sqn
754591	Sgt	WARD Albert John Wallace	4-03-41	106 Sqn
902192	F/S	WARD Anthony Edward	6-11-41	83 Sqn
640333	F/S	WARD Belph	30-09-41	78 Sqn
751296	Sgt	WARD Clifford Godfrey Harry	14-03-41	149 Sqn
999007	Sgt	WARD Hartley	24-06-41	57 Sqn
997361	Sgt	WARD John James Burchall	27-12-41	114 Sqn
1121014	AC1	WARD Keith Mervyn	31-08-41	Holme-in-Spalding Moor
80972	F/L	WARD William Charles	15-09-41	305 Sqn
22154	F/O	WARD William Francis [France]	7-07-41	12 Sqn
43987	F/O	WARDHAUGH Thomas	20-09-41	103 Sqn
958181	Sgt	WARDROP John	13-06-41	44 Sqn
1164194	Sgt	WAREHAM Bernard William	13-10-41	15 Sqn
102984	P/O	WARNER John Henry Eric	23-07-41	15 Sqn
754029	Sgt	WARREN Ronald	18-03-41	149 Sqn
41227	S/L	WARREN DFC Theophilus John Scott [South Africa]	24-09-41	107 Sqn
88022	F/O	WATERFALL John Terrence	24-09-41	107 Sqn
639743	Sgt	WATERS Alfred Ernest	2-03-41	9 Sqn
645635	LAC	WATERS Roland Henry	6-03-41	149 Sqn
572749	Sgt	WATKINS Raymond Charles	11-05-41	7 Sqn
77968	F/O	WATKINS Stanley Page	7-07-41	12 Sqn
45307	P/O	WATKINS DFM William Thomas	3-03-41	7 Sqn
755482	Sgt	WATKINSON George Derryck	3-05-41	101 Sqn
81421	P/O	WATSON Alexander Knox	27-06-41	10 Sqn
942231	Sgt	WATSON Dennis	29-08-41	49 Sqn
552237	Sgt	WATSON Desmond Frank Fitzwilliam	11-05-41	10 Sqn
1260187	Sgt	WATSON Donald Austin [Channel Islands]	11-12-41	57 Sqn
621058	F/S	WATSON DFM Harold	3-10-41	7 Sqn
62280	P/O	WATSON Ian William	16-06-41	18 Sqn
105199	P/O	WATSON Kenneth Wilfred	7-12-41	21 OTU
33337	S/L	WATSON Michael Litchfield	11-06-41	82 Sqn
754857	Sgt	WATSON Neville	19-03-41	10 Sqn
48277	P/O	WATSON Robert	27-12-41	50 Sqn
759157	Sgt	WATSON Robert Duncan	13-03-41	50 Sqn
755474	Sgt	WATSON William	7-11-41	101 Sqn
612507	F/S	WATSON William Anderson	1-11-41	49 Sqn
1104630	Sgt	WATSON Wilson	2-08-41	101 Sqn
778354	Sgt	WATT Archibald Allen [Rhodesia]	7-09-41	44 Sqn
777903	Sgt	WATT Archibald Campbell [Rhodesia]	28-12-41	49 Sqn
844595	Sgt	WATT David George	25-02-41	103 Sqn
1052238	Sgt	WATT John Sydney Ferguson	29-09-41	99 Sqn
1151053	Sgt	WATT William Martin	24-07-41	50 Sqn
912095	Sgt	WATTERS George Bow	30-09-41	58 Sqn
62020	F/O	WATTS Ernest Miller	29-08-41	405 Sqn
88016	P/O	WATTS Gordon Geoffrey	17-08-41	106 Sqn
41970	F/O	WATTS Peter Harris	15-06-41	105 Sqn
16258	S/L	WATTS-READ Archibald Martin	13-03-41	102 Sqn
1283647	Sgt	WEAVERS Mervyn Alfred	26-11-41	214 Sqn
755301	Sgt	WEAVING Douglas Vincent	27-02-41	83 Sqn
108140	P/O	WEBB Anthony Philip	13-12-41	14 OTU
1256737	Sgt	WEBB Charles Herbert	24-10-41	21 OTU
76020	F/O	WEBB Frank Stanley William	9-05-41	304 Sqn
924137	Sgt	WEBB Gilbert Terence	8-11-41	78 Sqn
42924	F/O	WEBB Kenneth Gordon	27-06-41	61 Sqn
751382	Sgt	WEBBER Frederick Kenneth	31-07-41	150 Sqn
88030	F/L	WEBBER Harold Dudley	12-12-41	106 Sqn
1005754	Sgt	WEBBER John	18-08-41	14 OTU
1356429	Sgt	WEBSTER Albert	7-07-41	115 Sqn
1101048	Sgt	WEBSTER Charles Alexander James	12-10-41	144 Sqn
1000903	AC2	WEBSTER Frederick Sager	9-08-41	Honington
1325222	Sgt	WEBSTER Leslie Arthur	11-07-41	16 OTU
1360045	Sgt	WEBSTER William	30-11-41	10 Sqn
24033	S/L	WEIGHILL Reginald George	16-07-41	40 Sqn
551626	F/S	WEIR Cecil Pollock	26-08-41	82 Sqn
926306	Sgt	WEIR Hugh	24-10-41	16 OTU
970663	Sgt	WEIR Norman Stewart	21-03-41	83 Sqn
967309	Sgt	WEIR William Douglas	12-05-41	58 Sqn
943567	Sgt	WELBOURNE Ernest	25-08-41	49 Sqn
747764	Sgt	WELCH Roy Desmond	13-03-41	207 Sqn
754071	Sgt	WELCH William Ruddock	26-06-41	99 Sqn
754906	Sgt	WELDON Ernest Edward	18-06-41	58 Sqn
920961	AC1	WELHAM Leslie William	15-08-41	51 Sqn
924396	Sgt	WELLER Cecil Norman	15-05-41	20 OTU
67689	P/O	WELLER Thomas Leonard	7-09-41	10 OTU
971654	F/S	WELLS Charles Robert	30-06-41	50 Sqn
615192	F/S	WELLS Charles William Albert	13-08-41	9 Sqn
918373	Sgt	WELLS Cyril Leslie	7-12-41	61 Sqn
85022	P/O	WELLS Harold Harry	4-07-41	102 Sqn
957427	Sgt	WELLS Sidney McLeod	10-04-41	17 OTU
1257327	Sgt	WELSH Edward Cameron [South Africa]	24-12-41	26 CFlt
980190	Sgt	WELSH John Ian	17-08-41	10 Sqn
924112	Sgt	WERNHAM Robert George	26-09-41	115 Sqn
66507	P/O	WEST Frederick Hornby Sutcliffe	28-02-41	12 OTU
517461	F/S	WEST DFM James Gardner Simpson	13-08-41	76 Sqn
983201	Sgt	WEST John Lenden	12-08-41	114 Sqn
88015	P/O	WEST Michael James	31-03-41	14 OTU
537995	Sgt	WEST Thomas Ian Arthur [Eire]	12-09-41	14 OTU
754746	Sgt	WESTLEY John Leo Guy	13-04-41	149 Sqn
60070	P/O	WESTON Denis Mark	29-05-41	11 OTU
83005	F/O	WEWAGE-SMITH Thomas	9-10-41	107 Sqn
919563	Sgt	WEYMOUTH Reginald Walter	30-11-41	77 Sqn
751097	Sgt	WHALLEY Thomas	19-08-41	9 Sqn
1052406	Sgt	WHEATLEY Douglas Joseph	12-08-41	114 Sqn
745900	F/S	WHEATLEY Ronald	18-12-41	7 Sqn
550389	F/S	WHEATLEY William Charles	15-09-41	305 Sqn
1196237	AC2	WHEELER Albert Ernest	13-08-41	11 OTU
742715	Sgt	WHEWELL Alan	30-11-41	58 Sqn
76930	F/O	WHIGHAM Robert George Murray	24-07-41	405 Sqn
45055	P/O	WHITAKER Gordon	8-11-41	35 Sqn
900226	Sgt	WHITBREAD James	17-05-41	20 OTU
900277	Sgt	WHITBY Alan James	9-04-41	7 Sqn
751366	Sgt	WHITCHER Arthur Ronald Norman	23-07-41	15 Sqn
903902	Sgt	WHITE Albert Walter	3-03-41	115 Sqn
745867	Sgt	WHITE Anthony John	8-04-41	58 Sqn
755211	Sgt	WHITE Arthur George Stafford	17-01-41	83 Sqn
538321	F/S	WHITE AFM Charles George	18-07-41	15 Sqn
60809	P/O	WHITE David	29-04-41	82 Sqn
618714	Sgt	WHITE Ernest	14-03-41	149 Sqn
1185985	Sgt	WHITE Ernest Montague	29-09-41	16 OTU
946158	Sgt	WHITE Frederick Alexander	15-12-41	50 Sqn
633512	Sgt	WHITE Frederick Ben [Australia]	30-03-41	7 Sqn
517683	Sgt	WHITE Harry William	26-09-41	9 Sqn
923509	Sgt	WHITE Henry William	12-06-41	25 OTU
1253786	Sgt	WHITE Hugh Peter Stuart	3-08-41	104 Sqn
1378118	Sgt	WHITE John Henry	15-10-41	40 Sqn
41888	F/O	WHITECROSS DFC James Alexander [Canada]	15-08-41	50 Sqn
916405	Sgt	WHITEHEAD Edward George	27-06-41	102 Sqn
745480	Sgt	WHITEHEAD Frank Archibald	21-04-41	83 Sqn
747027	Sgt	WHITEHEAD George William	7-05-41	5 Group
923812	Sgt	WHITFIELD Clarence Emerson	13-08-41	76 Sqn
945230	Sgt	WHITFIELD John Kenneth	29-09-41	99 Sqn
742674	Sgt	WHITING Donald Arthur	25-08-41	144 Sqn
751250	Sgt	WHITING Philip Edward	26-06-41	49 Sqn

Number	Rank	Name	Date	Unit
1107550	Sgt	WHITTAKER George	25-03-41	20 OTU
949600	Sgt	WHITTAKER Norman Horace	27-07-41	44 Sqn
85027	P/O	WHITTING Grahame Gordon	10-07-41	77 Sqn
1258599	Sgt	WHITTINGTON Richard Frederick	17-10-41	15 OTU
1528829	AC2	WHITTLE Joseph	25-12-41	21 Sqn
628887	Sgt	WHITTLE Laurence	30-06-41	7 Sqn
953719	Sgt	WHITTON Richard Frank	7-11-41	57 Sqn
88668	P/O	WHYTE Dixon Frederick Raeside	16-05-41	40 Sqn
909288	Sgt	WICKENS Arthur Ronald	10-04-41	144 Sqn
910019	Sgt	WICKS Phillip Charles Livesey	3-04-41	77 Sqn
1260386	Sgt	WIDDECOMBE Bernard Frederick	14-10-41	115 Sqn
1376554	Sgt	WIGGS George William Thomas	7-11-41	99 Sqn
625946	Sgt	WILCOX Ernest Burton	28-05-41	150 Sqn
945235	Sgt	WILCOX Windsor	10-07-41	7 Sqn
580836	F/S	WILDE DFM John Malcolm	8-10-41	15 OTU
1169109	Sgt	WILDGOOSE Frank Brian Harris	15-08-41	51 Sqn
991024	Sgt	WILDING Marshall	20-07-41	18 Sqn
63492	P/O	WILGAR-ROBINSON Hugh Vincent	9-11-41	9 Sqn
516847	Sgt	WILKIN Robert	8-09-41	90 Sqn
623678	Sgt	WILKINS Stanley Albert	22-03-41	57 Sqn
68728	P/O	WILKINSON Alexander Walter	16-07-41	40 Sqn
640883	Sgt	WILKINSON Charles	8-07-41	58 Sqn
42663	P/O	WILKINSON Einar Thor [Canada]	14-02-41	3 PRU
1062591	Sgt	WILKINSON Hugh Vernon	26-08-41	106 Sqn
755659	Sgt	WILKINSON Walter Hugh	13-04-41	149 Sqn
917136	Sgt	WILKINSON Walter Powney	25-03-41	20 OTU
40037	S/L	WILLCOX DFC Eric Peter 'Deado'	1-09-41	83 Sqn
1110530	Sgt	WILLCOX Walter Kenneth	11-08-41	25 OTU
934369	Sgt	WILLIAMS Albert Edward	21-07-41	10 OTU
65558	P/O	WILLIAMS Arthur Lionel Alfred	12-08-41	21 Sqn
909946	Sgt	WILLIAMS Arthur Norman	28-06-41	77 Sqn
970459	Sgt	WILLIAMS Daniel Pryce	13-03-41	77 Sqn
959135	Sgt	WILLIAMS Donald Ernest	30-11-41	101 Sqn
981262	Sgt	WILLIAMS Douglas Theodore	28-12-41	408 Sqn
966811	Sgt	WILLIAMS Frank	20-08-41	16 OTU
937303	Sgt	WILLIAMS Frederick Charles	28-06-41	7 Sqn
918480	Sgt	WILLIAMS Geoffrey Oliver	1-11-41	51 Sqn
969577	Sgt	WILLIAMS Herbert Llewellyn	7-04-41	3 GTrgFlt
927803	Sgt	WILLIAMS Ivor Morgan	30-10-41	14 OTU
924930	Sgt	WILLIAMS John Drax	27-12-41	50 Sqn
970005	F/S	WILLIAMS Leonard Charles	1-08-41	107 Sqn
84911	P/O	WILLIAMS Maurice Frederick	12-08-41	21 Sqn
1006119	Sgt	WILLIAMS Norman George	21-08-41	102 Sqn
1162621	Sgt	WILLIAMS Owen Lawrence Mitchell	6-08-41	51 Sqn
536363	F/S	WILLIAMS Peter	16-08-41	97 Sqn
746731	Sgt	WILLIAMS Peter Cedric	27-12-41	101 Sqn
967873	Sgt	WILLIAMS Reginald Ernest	18-04-41	114 Sqn
43077	S/L	WILLIAMS DFC AFM Reginald George	23-12-41	21 OTU
922895	Sgt	WILLIAMS Robert	21-02-41	16 OTU
87359	P/O	WILLIAMS Robert John Wyndham	15-04-41	102 Sqn
1251179	Sgt	WILLIAMS Roy Penry	24-07-41	103 Sqn
741780	Sgt	WILLIAMS Russell Arthur	8-04-41	214 Sqn
617504	F/S	WILLIAMS Simon James	21-10-41	21 Sqn
982517	F/S	WILLIAMS Wilfred Roy	15-12-41	408 Sqn
653373	F/S	WILLIAMS William George	8-07-41	7 Sqn
540821	Sgt	WILLIAMS William Gordon	13-03-41	50 Sqn
1001675	Sgt	WILLIAMSON James	27-12-41	114 Sqn
1057437	Sgt	WILLIAMSON John Henry	29-08-41	214 Sqn
922470	Sgt	WILLINGHAM Norman	3-09-41	35 Sqn
919875	Sgt	WILLIS Arthur Charles	29-08-41	49 Sqn
923043	Sgt	WILLIS David George	12-09-41	149 Sqn
88228	P/O	WILLIS John George Embleton	28-04-41	50 Sqn
44051	F/O	WILLIS Joshua Stephen	10-09-41	25 OTU
1007399	Sgt	WILLIS Robert	8-09-41	90 Sqn
946150	Sgt	WILLIS Roy	19-08-41	101 Sqn
1050344	Sgt	WILLIS Thomas Henry	30-08-41	50 Sqn
928906	Sgt	WILLISSON Derek Alan	30-11-41	101 Sqn
1183439	Sgt	WILLMER Bernard Kenneth George	27-09-41	104 Sqn
1306085	Sgt	WILLS Alan David	17-08-41	78 Sqn
67020	P/O	WILLSHER George Stephen	12-10-41	18 Sqn
970361	Sgt	WILSON Alfred William	8-07-41	44 Sqn
1105474	LAC	WILSON Andrew Garven	11-11-41	49 Sqn
935907	Sgt	WILSON Arnot Flaws	9-05-41	214 Sqn
1252828	Sgt	WILSON Dennis Arthur	12-08-41	139 Sqn
976170	Sgt	WILSON Douglas Anderson	17-08-41	78 Sqn
89362	P/O	WILSON Frank	8-07-41	10 Sqn
76021	P/O	WILSON Frank Selby	12-02-41	83 Sqn
64290	P/O	WILSON George Victor	21-05-41	17 OTU
1100861	Sgt	WILSON James Edward	28-12-41	17 OTU
747796	F/S	WILSON John	7-12-41	61 Sqn
741867	F/S	WILSON John Purdie	26-04-41	51 Sqn
959277	Sgt	WILSON Josiah Herbert	8-07-41	77 Sqn
572032	Sgt	WILSON Kenneth Frederick	3-05-41	7 Sqn
67691	P/O	WILSON Leslie Charles Ross	8-09-41	51 Sqn
918573	Sgt	WILSON Leslie Redvers	21-06-41	21 Sqn
917135	Sgt	WILSON Noel Sydney	12-06-41	40 Sqn
1164406	Sgt	WILSON Peter	16-07-41	57 Sqn
79546	P/O	WILSON The Hon. Robert David	22-03-41	49 Sqn
1065928	Sgt	WILSON Ronald	24-04-41	11 OTU
64904	P/O	WILSON Roy Stewart	14-07-41	139 Sqn
104525	P/O	WILSON Thomas McSkimming	8-12-41	82 Sqn
1020491	AC2	WILSON William Alexander	26-07-41	104 Sqn
87444	P/O	WILSON Winston Claude	15-08-41	218 Sqn
1164655	Sgt	WIMBUSH Adrian Durrant	7-09-41	44 Sqn
957879	Sgt	WINCHESTER Bernard	27-07-41	44 Sqn
1101847	Sgt	WINCOTT Gordon Louis	25-10-41	107 Sqn
82738	F/O	WINDER Arthur Frederick Stapley	26-04-41	21 Sqn
580868	Sgt	WINDLE Henry	2-03-41	61 Sqn
740610	Sgt	WINNING William Burton Cecil	6-01-41	49 Sqn
42932	F/L	WINDRAM Peter	14-06-41	110 Sqn
961048	Sgt	WINSTANLEY Douglas	4-10-41	21 OTU
1113182	LAC	WINTER Harold Francis	15-09-41	207 Sqn
977342	Sgt	WINTER Kenneth Ridd	13-06-41	102 Sqn
653507	Sgt	WINTER Stanley William	16-07-41	18 Sqn
1051879	Sgt	WINTERSGILL Sidney	12-08-41	9 Sqn
961110	Sgt	WISDOM Henry William	28-12-41	49 Sqn
46027	P/O	WISE DFM George Peter	24-07-41	61 Sqn
1109590	Sgt	WITHERINGTON Arthur John	16-09-41	57 Sqn
40491	F/O	WITHERS DFC John Douglas George	22-06-41	207 Sqn
975504	Sgt	WITHRINGTON Reginald Frederick George	19-07-41	105 Sqn
942477	Sgt	WITHYMAN Kenneth Pearson	7-09-41	102 Sqn
1057688	Sgt	WOLSTENHOLME William James Stanley	15-10-41	226 Sqn
917314	Sgt	WOOD Anthony Andre	4-05-41	149 Sqn
568343	Sgt	WOOD Charles Edward	31-10-41	76 Sqn
989818	Sgt	WOOD Edwin	5-07-41	51 Sqn
926082	Sgt	WOOD Frank	25-05-41	18 Sqn
975312	Sgt	WOOD Fred	16-07-41	218 Sqn
745625	F/S	WOOD Frederick John	8-08-41	83 Sqn
103525	P/O	WOOD James	7-09-41	58 Sqn
906925	Sgt	WOOD John	17-04-41	149 Sqn
785021	Sgt	WOOD John Patrick	8-09-41	51 Sqn
759352	Sgt	WOOD Kenneth Russell	10-07-41	7 Sqn
60568	P/O	WOOD Peter Guy Campbell	31-08-41	207 Sqn
535847	F/S	WOOD Thomas	19-09-41	58 Sqn
1105933	Sgt	WOOD Thomas Grahame	16-08-41	25 OTU
1261700	Sgt	WOOD William Christopher	12-10-41	57 Sqn
777708	Sgt	WOODALL Jack William [Rhodesia]	28-12-41	144 Sqn
745564	Sgt	WOODBRIDGE Philip Henry	2-03-41	10 Sqn
1003989	Sgt	WOODCOCK Frank	4-09-41	18 Sqn
1139637	Sgt	WOODFIELD Leslie Bernard	14-10-41	22 OTU
914532	Sgt	WOODHAMS John Kenneth	29-06-41	15 Sqn
1161131	Sgt	WOODHAMS Maurice Frederick	23-03-41	10 OTU
913008	Sgt	WOODHOUSE Thomas Peter	2-11-41	78 Sqn

Service No.	Rank	Name	Date	Unit
937800	F/S	WOODROFFE James William	30-11-41	77 Sqn
759317	F/S	WOODRUFF Frank	27-06-41	61 Sqn
652254	Sgt	WOODS Charles John	2-03-41	10 Sqn
751846	Sgt	WOODS Jack Cecil	12-08-41	226 Sqn
531299	F/S	WOODS William	13-08-41	76 Sqn
940837	Sgt	WOODWARD Derek Garth	12-06-41	99 Sqn
745911	F/S	WOODWARD John	27-06-41	61 Sqn
565236	F/S	WOOLDRIDGE DFM MiD Bertie Charles	18-09-41	139 Sqn
638150	F/S	WOOLDRIDGE Wilfred	18-12-41	15 Sqn
754953	Sgt	WOOLLEY John Gordon	19-06-41	78 Sqn
1202049	Sgt	WOOLMAN John Hedley	19-11-41	18 Sqn
628397	Sgt	WOOLSTON Robert Edward	27-07-41	10 OTU
61024	P/O	WOOTTON Thomas Edward	13-10-41	15 Sqn
969973	F/S	WORDSWORTH Raymond	8-07-41	61 Sqn
755764	Sgt	WORLLEDGE Frederick Harry	15-10-41	75 Sqn
654174	Sgt	WORTHINGTON Frederick Richard	5-04-41	50 Sqn
1056815	Sgt	WORTHINGTON Robert Muirhead Colin	21-10-41	97 Sqn
1051936	Sgt	WORTON John Stevens Meighan	14-09-41	97 Sqn
1275346	Sgt	WRAMPLING Brian James	7-11-41	101 Sqn
742730	Sgt	WRIGHT Anthony Denis	4-01-41	51 Sqn
1380378	Sgt	WRIGHT Harry	5-12-41	15 OTU
745187	Sgt	WRIGHT Harvey William	18-04-41	110 Sqn
751334	Sgt	WRIGHT John [South Africa]	7-07-41	97 Sqn
65591	P/O	WRIGHT John David	25-08-41	7 Sqn
817188	Sgt	WRIGHT John Thompson [Canada]	10-04-41	106 Sqn
975751	Sgt	WRIGHT Kenneth	3-03-41	58 Sqn
982911	Sgt	WRIGHT Louis Gerald	18-08-41	16 OTU
924550	Sgt	WRIGHT Matthew Ward	27-09-41	104 Sqn
61959	F/L	WRIGHT Robert Alan	18-12-41	97 Sqn
751744	Sgt	WRIGHT Stanley	17-04-41	44 Sqn
1006115	Sgt	WRIGHT Terence Patrick	18-12-41	7 Sqn
902905	F/S	WRIGHT Victor George	2-11-41	78 Sqn
77373	F/O	WRIGHT William	26-08-41	40 Sqn
1154295	Sgt	WRIGHT William Conyers	23-10-41	50 Sqn
580332	F/S	WRIGHTSON Leslie Howard	21-05-41	82 Sqn
1008485	Sgt	WRIGLEY Frederick	9-09-41	102 Sqn
904837	Sgt	WROATH Arthur Clifford	8-04-41	58 Sqn
745394	Sgt	WUNDERLICH Robert Edward Frederic	13-03-41	50 Sqn
1183616	Sgt	WYATT David John	12-09-41	149 Sqn
512841	Sgt	WYATT David William	18-07-41	21 Sqn
542890	F/S	WYATT Harold Kenneth Vincent	6-07-41	226 Sqn
905992	Sgt	WYATT William Henry	31-07-41	99 Sqn
519327	F/S	WYNNE Aidan Noel	3-06-41	7 Sqn
751486	Sgt	YARDLEY Harold	7-09-41	83 Sqn
72588	F/L	YARROW Gordon Percy	30-03-41	110 Sqn
639366	F/S	YEOMANS DFM Samuel David	6-08-41	44 Sqn
952493	Sgt	YORK Frederick Walter	17-08-41	99 Sqn
900216	Sgt	YOULDON Donald Frederick	26-08-41	40 Sqn
745128	Sgt	YOUNG Charles Frederick	12-08-41	149 Sqn
44820	F/L	YOUNG Hugh Stewart	12-08-41	226 Sqn
947403	Sgt	YOUNG John Kenneth	3-09-41	35 Sqn
1250140	Sgt	YOUNG Martin Anthony	3-08-41	7 Sqn
1059469	Sgt	YOUNG Michael Clive	11-10-41	57 Sqn
1258651	Sgt	YOUNG Reginald Frederick Arthur	18-10-41	16 OTU
979105	Sgt	YOUNG Thomas George	30-06-41	7 Sqn
778478	Sgt	YOUNG William John [Rhodesia]	15-12-41	50 Sqn
521590	Sgt	YOUNGER Leslie Shaw Bolton	8-09-41	51 Sqn
987165	Sgt	YOXALL Arthur	7-08-41	149 Sqn
82648	P/O	ZEINERT Stanislav [Czechoslovakia]	26-05-41	311 Sqn
82649	P/O	ZIMMER Antonin [Czechoslovakia]	15-09-41	311 Sqn

Note

F/O Peter Clifford Campbell-Martin had served in the Great War (1914-1918), initially with the Canadian Field Artillery. It is believed that he transferred to the Royal Flying Corps (date not known) and, subsequently became a prisoner of war. However, he escaped from captivity and for doing so was awarded the Military Cross, details of this being promulgated in The London Gazette on the 16th of December, 1919.

In the Second World War he joined the Volunteer Reserve as a commissioned air gunner and on completion of his training he joined 264 Squadron, then equipped with Defiants and operating in the night fighter role. At the time of his death, age 44, he was attached to 40 Squadron (see page 163 in the second volume of Bomber Command losses for further details).

Concerning the entry for AC2 Tupper who lost his life on the 31st of October, 1941, while serving with 816 Squadron of the Fleet Air Arm, it is believed he had been attached from a 3 Group unit, thus retaining his Bomber Command status. Similarly, AC2 Abdee from Cinderford in Gloucestershire and buried in Harwell Cemetery is shown in the cemetery register as belonging to 737 Squadron, while other documents indicate his unit to be that as recorded in this section.

Other interesting observations concern Sgt Farnan and Sgt Gailey. The former's service number (785036) indicates enlistment in the Far East circa July 1940, though his birthplace is recorded as Truro, Nova Scotia, while in respect of Sgt Gailey, he is reported as hailing from Vancouver, but I much suspect his roots were in the Irish Republic, for after his body was recovered from the sea, he was taken for burial in Dublin.

ROYAL AUSTRALIAN AIR FORCE
personnel

Service No.	Rank	Name	Date	Unit
404393	Sgt	AKES Vernon Charles	24-12-41	26 CFlt
400009	P/O	ARMSTRONG Donald Noel Robert	7-07-41	214 Sqn
404226	P/O	ASPREY John Lambert	17-08-41	78 Sqn
404229	Sgt	BALZER Christian Samuel	15-10-41	114 Sqn
400456	P/O	BARBER Bruce Bertram [United Kingdom]	21-10-41	82 Sqn
407071	Sgt	BARRETT Richard Lyndon	30-06-41	7 Sqn
407190	Sgt	BARTLETT Gordon Kenneth	20-09-41	226 Sqn
400074	Sgt	BARTON Allan Ernest Ross	29-06-41	218 Sqn
402497	Sgt	BELL Ronald Joshua	7-11-41	99 Sqn
400010	P/O	BELL-TOWERS Wadya Wellesley	15-08-41	102 Sqn
402217	Sgt	BENNETT Arthur Charles	15-11-41	7 Sqn
402103	P/O	BOLER Herbert Henry	18-04-41	11 OTU
402645	Sgt	BOURKE William	1-11-41	51 Sqn
402435	F/O	BOYD Thompson Neville Digby	26-10-41	21 OTU
402272	Sgt	BRENTON Edward Harry	16-10-41	107 Sqn
400139	Sgt	BROWN Vincent Leigh	8-11-41	102 Sqn
400407	Sgt	BROWNE Peter Leighton	14-10-41	115 Sqn
402725	Sgt	BRYANT Ronald Owen	8-11-41	102 Sqn
402768	Sgt	BUCKNELL Brian Wentworth	27-11-41	14 OTU
408069	Sgt	BUTLER Kenneth Herbert	15-11-41	11 OTU
400025	F/O	CAMPBELL Robert Balmain	23-07-41	15 Sqn
402457	Sgt	CHAPMAN Alfred William Musgrave	29-09-41	99 Sqn
402212	P/O	COHEN Geoffrey Landas	3-08-41	25 OTU
400696	Sgt	COOK Alan	16-11-41	218 Sqn
400580	Sgt	COOK Andrew Harry Theodore [New Zealand]	8-11-41	57 Sqn
402151	Sgt	CORMACK James Archer	3-07-41	139 Sqn
400460	Sgt	COX Alexander Lewis	15-10-41	458 Sqn
402567	P/O	CRANE William Henry	3-08-41	25 OTU
404089	P/O	CRICHTON David Lecky	1-09-41	101 Sqn
400410	Sgt	CRITTENDEN Philip George	20-10-41	458 Sqn
402230	Sgt	CURLEWIS Raymond Fullerton	11-10-41	75 Sqn
402323	Sgt	DENBY Warren Steen	6-08-41	104 Sqn
400014	Sgt	DENIER Desmond Ernest George	7-08-41	149 Sqn
402155	P/O	DIGGES DFC Charles Richardson	18-12-41	139 Sqn
407201	Sgt	DURDIN Reginald Wilton	9-11-41	25 OTU
404091	F/O	ELLERAY Desmond Barton	18-11-41	25 OTU
402649	Sgt	FAUNT Lindsay Gordon	20-10-41	99 Sqn
402650	P/O	FEILDEN Randle [Canada]	22-09-41	114 Sqn
406353	P/O	FISHER Osborne Kirkton	9-12-41	14 OTU

402651	F/S	FISHER Robert Wilson	27-12-41	114 Sqn
400190	Sgt	FLOWERS Sydney Thomas	1-07-41	15 OTU
404332	P/O	FUREY Ronald John	15-11-41	458 Sqn
400705	Sgt	GILLESPIE John Alexander	18-10-41	27 OTU
402654	Sgt	GILMOUR Charles Edward	28-12-41	15 OTU
400403	P/O	GOLDMAN William	15-11-41	458 Sqn
402656	Sgt	GOODEY James Henry	29-09-41	115 Sqn
402118	Sgt	GOURLEY William Henry James	24-07-41	76 Sqn
404461	P/O	GRANT Frederic Norman	13-09-41	21 Sqn
400222	P/O	GREENING Joseph Wesley	3-07-41	75 Sqn
404532	Sgt	GRIMES Harold Dawson	15-10-41	75 Sqn
402349	Sgt	GUAN Charles Allen	1-11-41	51 Sqn
404531	P/O	HAYNE William Keith	7-12-41	104 Sqn
400587	Sgt	HEARLE William Edward	11-10-41	57 Sqn
400277	Sgt	HIGGINS Eric Vincent Keiran	16-07-41	75 Sqn
400589	P/O	HISLOP Bruce Elwell	18-09-41	88 Sqn
402238	Sgt	HOLLIDAY Maurice Sydney	24-07-41	40 Sqn
406032	Sgt	HOPKINSON William Arthur	8-11-41	107 Sqn
402355	P/O	HORN John Read	2-08-41	405 Sqn
400471	Sgt	HOWARD Henry Clifford	9-11-41	25 OTU
400472	P/O	HUDSON Raymond Meredith	15-10-41	226 Sqn
402239	Sgt	HUTCHISON Lindsay Thomas	3-09-41	57 Sqn
407432	Sgt	HUTTON Ernest Charles	24-11-41	97 Sqn
404248	Sgt	JACK Douglas Gordon	16-12-41	102 Sqn
404104	Sgt	JAMES John Franklin	13-06-41	102 Sqn
402360	Sgt	JOHNSTON Robert	8-12-41	82 Sqn
404049	Sgt	JOHNSTON William Leo Newton	22-10-41	405 Sqn
404470	Sgt	KENT Malcolm Edward	5-12-41	20 OTU
402661	Sgt	KILLEN Richard Lyle	23-08-41	20 OTU
407077	F/O	KINNANE MiD John	1-07-41	7 Sqn
402368	Sgt	LEIGHTON Thomas Leo	24-10-41	12 OTU
402058	Sgt	LOGAN David Victor	7-09-41	78 Sqn
402448	F/O	LOPEZ James Albert	18-11-41	7 Sqn
402127	Sgt	LORD Clive Gordon	13-10-41	58 Sqn
402464	Sgt	LOWATER Ernest John	19-08-41	51 Sqn
400593	Sgt	MACDONALD Donald	11-10-41	57 Sqn
402060	F/O	MARSHALL Sydney Douglas	18-07-41	15 Sqn
407294	Sgt	McALLEN William Albert	15-11-41	99 Sqn
404410	Sgt	McALLISTER Robert Andrew	22-07-41	11 OTU
400283	Sgt	McKENZIE Duncan John	30-09-41	115 Sqn
404112	Sgt	McLEAN Oliver Wiley	9-07-41	78 Sqn
404007	P/O	McLEOD Eric William	25-03-41	20 OTU
408014	Sgt	McQUITTY William Morrison	9-07-41	78 Sqn
404348	Sgt	MILLER Keith John	15-10-41	57 Sqn
407091	Sgt	MILNE Angus	19-08-41	51 Sqn
402451	Sgt	MORGAN Henry Blanchard	12-10-41	17 OTU
407093	Sgt	MORPHETT Henry Leslie Benjamin	7-09-41	102 Sqn
400281	Sgt	MORRIS James William Cooper	8-11-41	7 Sqn
404636	Sgt	MYLES William Reginald	15-12-41	11 OTU
406024	F/O	NANGLE Patrick Claude [United Kingdom]	20-10-41	88 Sqn
400069	Sgt	NEAL John	22-07-41	10 OTU
402279	Sgt	NORTH Hunter Arthur Aubrey	30-09-41	57 Sqn
402169	Sgt	OSTENFELD Christian Conrad	28-07-41	21 OTU
400482	Sgt	PAUL Maxwell William Elliott	12-10-41	17 OTU
406044	Sgt	RICH Joseph Geoffrey	13-10-41	58 Sqn
402252	Sgt	RICHARDSON Frank	8-09-41	104 Sqn
404365	P/O	RITCHIE Douglas John	28-08-41	13 OTU
400310	Sgt	ROBERTS James	22-07-41	75 Sqn
404285	Sgt	ROBERTSON Kenneth Trewin	24-07-41	21 OTU
407019	Sgt	ROSS Maxwell Robert	27-06-41	57 Sqn
402170	Sgt	ROST Ronald James Brownee	16-07-41	18 Sqn
404263	Sgt	ROWLAND Henry Barrymore	24-12-41	26 CFlt
404626	P/O	RYDER Robert Leslie Owen	8-11-41	75 Sqn
404384	P/O	RYDER Robin Munro	12-09-41	40 Sqn
402578	P/O	SANDS Alan George	30-11-41	455 Sqn
402142	P/O	St. VINCENT WELCH Standish Locksley	2-07-41	149 Sqn
402763	F/O	SCARLETT Ronald Cave	27-12-41	57 Sqn
400492	Sgt	SCOTT Douglas Andrew	15-10-41	40 Sqn
404264	Sgt	SHANNON John	30-11-41	455 Sqn
400032	P/O	SHIRTCLIFFE William John [New Zealand]	25-02-41	11 OTU
404418	Sgt	STEPHENSON Robert Worrall	11-10-41	218 Sqn
407141	F/O	SUGG Eric John	12-10-41	40 Sqn
400359	Sgt	SULLIVAN Maurice Anthony	18-12-41	7 Sqn
404129	Sgt	SYMMONS William Mervyn	2-07-41	149 Sqn
400299	Sgt	THOMPSON Bruce Cathcart	22-07-41	11 OTU
402623	Sgt	THORNTON Kenneth Frederick	9-12-41	14 OTU
406018	Sgt	TURNER John Ernst	4-10-41	58 Sqn
402474	Sgt	TWEEDIE Norman	12-09-41	75 Sqn
402011	Sgt	UHRIG Robert James	10-04-41	149 Sqn
400360	Sgt	WALLWORK Ralph Stanley	24-07-41	142 Sqn
402581	P/O	WALSH Harry Maynard	25-09-41	15 OTU
404077	F/O	WELLS Geoffrey Lloyd	17-08-41	99 Sqn
400245	Sgt	WESTON Neville Jack	8-11-41	97 Sqn
402428	Sgt	WILLIAMS Gregory Percival	29-08-41	103 Sqn
404381	Sgt	WILLIAMS Thomas Gordon	1-11-41	16 OTU
400314	Sgt	WILSON Alexander Macgregor	18-08-41	218 Sqn
402081	Sgt	WILSON Stanley Maurice	30-12-41	76 Sqn
404274	Sgt	WOODHEAD Keith Moore	20-08-41	104 Sqn

Note

Before victory was secured over 4,000 Royal Australian Air Force personnel would lose their lives serving in units associated with Bomber Command and such was the scale of their sacrifice that more than one family in what was still a relatively sparsely inhabited land would experience the pain of losing more than one son or daughter. In my previous volumes I have attempted to draw attention to such tragedies and I beg forgiveness for any oversights of this nature.

Furthermore, it will be discovered from reading the Royal Air Force section (particularly in previous parts), and in scattered instances in other Commonwealth sections, a not insignificant number of Australians were killed flying with these air forces and not their own. Many had arrived in the United Kingdom in the late 1930s, the officers taking short service commissions. These observations are also mirrored in respect of Canadians and New Zealanders whose national air forces would contribute much to the effectiveness of Bomber Command.

ROYAL CANADIAN AIR FORCE
personnel

R/54373	Sgt	ADAMS Frederick Coulson	5-07-41	10 OTU
J/4782	P/O	AITCHISON Hugh Maclachlan [United Kingdom]	15-09-41	75 Sqn
R/69545	Sgt	ALDERSLEY Richard George Fane	13-08-41	115 Sqn
R/61302	Sgt	ALLAN William Everitt	25-08-41	7 Sqn
R/70612	Sgt	ALTERSON John	13-10-41	77 Sqn
J/4252	P/O	ANDERSON Edwin Graham Milton	1-09-41	102 Sqn
R/54021	Sgt	ANDERSON James Blain	25-08-41	35 Sqn
R/54533	F/S	ANDERSON Robert Edward Venning	10-04-41	218 Sqn
J/5679	P/O	ANDERSON Ronald Drury	27-09-41	20 OTU
R/61790	Sgt	ARMSTRONG Gerald Gordon	27-11-41	9 Sqn
J/4253	P/O	ARNOLD Victor Charles	5-05-41	20 OTU
J/4708	P/O	ARNOLD William Hilliard	27-07-41	10 OTU
J/6028	P/O	ATKIN James Welberne	25-10-41	25 OTU
R/52699	Sgt	BAKER Walter Merrill	18-12-41	7 Sqn
R/69651	F/S	BARCLAY William Scott	14-10-41	15 OTU
R/65416	Sgt	BARKHOUSE Donald Frederick	15-10-41	75 Sqn
R/60887	Sgt	BARTLEMAN William Archibald	5-07-41	10 OTU
R/64730	Sgt	BARTON Kenneth Judson	24-06-41	214 Sqn
R/78172	Sgt	BATCHEN Alexander George	12-09-41	19 OTU
R/75129	Sgt	BEARDALL Robert Haig	24-11-41	19 OTU
R/60728	Sgt	BEDARD Harry Hector	20-06-41	99 Sqn

ID	Rank	Name	Date	Sqn
J/3748	P/O	BEEMER Frederick Hill	12-08-41	149 Sqn
R/52850	F/S	BELL Charles Harold	8-11-41	405 Sqn
R/62744	F/S	BENNETT Donald Ward	12-09-41	149 Sqn
R/65349	Sgt	BENTLEY Logan Carmon	26-10-41	57 Sqn
R/57931	F/S	BERKEY Edward Roy	9-07-41	144 Sqn
R/59127	F/S	BERRY Wallace Llewellyn	15-08-41	35 Sqn
R/74903	Sgt	BISCHLAGER Harold	18-12-41	97 Sqn
R/59272	F/S	BLACKMORE George Ralph	10-09-41	103 Sqn
R/80013	Sgt	BLACKWELL Henry Westbrook	26-11-41	19 OTU
R/60725	Sgt	BLADES William Henry	30-08-41	115 Sqn
R/77398	Sgt	BOGGS William Fergsuon [USA]	26-12-41	13 OTU
R/67510	Sgt	BOROSKI Frank	2-06-41	139 Sqn
R/53935	Sgt	BOTT Stuart Frank Beeching	17-08-41	10 Sqn
J/4765	P/O	BOUCHER Thomas Gerald	11-08-41	25 OUT
R/78601	F/S	BOURGEAU Joseph Raymond Frederic	28-12-41	405 Sqn
J/5315	P/O	BOWEN Cyril Keith	28-08-41	13 OTU
R/65785	F/S	BOWEN Lawrence Milbert	3-09-41	102 Sqn
R/62091	F/S	BOYCE John William	1-09-41	115 Sqn
R/59286	F/S	BOYD Jack Marshall	31-10-41	77 Sqn
R/62712	F/S	BOZER Donald Machell	3-09-41	102 Sqn
R/54033	F/S	BRADLY Albert Thomas	1-11-41	51 Sqn
R/59582	Sgt	BRADSHAW James	27-10-41	114 Sqn
R/68117	Sgt	BRAKEMAN Jesse Clemence	3-09-41	214 Sqn
J/1447	P/O	BRANDER Huntley Donald	30-06-41	7 Sqn
R/65055	Sgt	BRISSENDEN Joseph	15-05-41	20 OTU
R/65658	Sgt	BRODRIBB Anthony Francis Bowyer	1-09-41	99 Sqn
R/74747	Sgt	BRONSON Clifford Robert [USA]	8-11-41	97 Sqn
J/15849	P/O	BROOKS Francis Conn	31-10-41	76 Sqn
J/5095	P/O	BROWN Fred Harvey	22-09-41	114 Sqn
R/64143	P/O	BROWN Lorne Edwin	13-08-41	76 Sqn
J/4785	P/O	BROWN William Raymond James	29-09-41	99 Sqn
J/5497	F/O	BRUBAKER Donald Warren	20-10-41	149 Sqn
R/62170	Sgt	BUCHANAN George Henderson Pepper	17-08-41	78 Sqn
R/59263	Sgt	BUCKINGHAM George Ellis	7-07-41	10 OTU
R/77029	Sgt	BUDDEN David Hastings	27-09-41	20 OTU
R/67110	F/S	BURCHELL Orval Henry	28-12-41	51 Sqn
J/5076	P/O	BURLINSON Robert Melville [USA]	18-09-41	88 Sqn
R/72647	F/S	BURNETT Niall Hope	8-07-41	11 OTU
R/64045	F/S	BURNS William Henry	13-10-41	58 Sqn
R/64717	Sgt	BURT Richard Percy [United Kingdom]	8-06-41	11 OTU
R/65505	Sgt	BURTIS Marvin Edson	9-07-41	9 Sqn
J/5768	P/O	BUSH Charles William [USA]	2-11-41	17 OTU
R/69632	Sgt	BYE George Allan	25-05-41	139 Sqn
R/68121	F/S	BYERS William Harold Stanley	12-10-41	57 Sqn
R/56255	Sgt	CADNEY William Morrant	31-08-41	207 Sqn
R/54294	Sgt	CALDERONE Dominico Guiseppe (served as CALDERONE Dominic Joseph)	17-07-41	13 OTU
R/64430	F/S	CALDERWOOD Jack Sidney Alexander	13-12-41	107 Sqn
R/68575	F/S	CALDWELL Wilson Gilmore	16-12-41	102 Sqn
J/3267	F/O	CAMERON Donald	16-06-41	15 OTU
R/65210	Sgt	CAMERON Donald Archibald	14-10-41	15 OTU
J/3274	P/O	CAMPBELL-ROGERS Leonard Herculese	27-06-41	15 OTU
R/65224	Sgt	CAPSTICK Francis Leo	20-10-41	149 Sqn
R/56171	F/S	CARMICHAEL Douglas John	26-10-41	106 Sqn
R/73253	Sgt	CARR Kenneth Claude	7-11-41	58 Sqn
R/54194	Sgt	CARREAU Paul Eugene	30-08-41	102 Sqn
R/71548	F/S	CARTY Arthur William	5-06-41	10 OTU
J/3270	P/O	CASEY William Aloysius	17-08-41	99 Sqn
R/61802	Sgt	CHAMBERS William Martin	8-11-41	51 Sqn
R/63908	Sgt	CHAPMAN Gordon Lindsay	29-09-41	57 Sqn
R/58292	Sgt	CHAPMAN Philip Pedrick	28-07-41	10 OTU
R/60713	F/S	CHATTELL David Gifford	20-09-41	101 Sqn
R/66045	Sgt	CHEVERS William John	28-07-41	21 OTU
R/68206	Sgt	CHILDS Alfred John	11-10-41	12 Sqn
J/5916	P/O	CHRISTIE David Darling	16-09-41	25 OTU
J/3601	P/O	CHRISTMAN Lorne Smith	5-07-41	106 Sqn
R/69860	Sgt	CLARK Howard Bevan	8-09-41	51 Sqn
R/68182	Sgt	CLARK William Brown	31-08-41	12 Sqn
R/68066	Sgt	CLARKE William Keith	15-05-41	16 OTU
J/5313	P/O	CLEMENTS John Russell	15-09-41	207 Sqn
J/15850	P/O	CLEVERDON Robert John Albert	31-10-41	77 Sqn
J/3272	P/O	COATES Grossett Keith	8-07-41	9 Sqn
J/6156	P/O	COLFE William Kenneth	29-09-41	115 Sqn
R/74329	Sgt	COLLINS Joseph Louis	12-09-41	19 OTU
R/74592	Sgt	COLLINS Maxwell Ritchie	14-07-41	214 Sqn
R/65640	F/S	COMROE Paul	18-11-41	7 Sqn
R/56147	Sgt	CONRY Edmund Joseph	19-06-41	10 Sqn
J/3603	P/O	COOK Herbert James	2-09-41	44 Sqn
J/15853	P/O	COOLING Charles David	26-11-41	214 Sqn
J/4110	P/O	COOPER Hugh James 'Jim'	7-07-41	19 OTU
R/54046	Sgt	COOPER James Hyndman	3-06-41	11 OTU
R/62788	Sgt	COUKELL Bruce Adams [USA]	7-09-41	17 OTU
J/3742	P/O	COUPER Thomas Mackintosh	18-04-41	12 OTU
R/69517	Sgt	COVER John Albert	29-06-41	82 Sqn
18074A	Sgt	CRAFTS Robert Harland	2-07-41	149 Sqn
R/53808	Sgt	CRAIG Malcolm James Courtland	17-05-41	20 OTU
R/69832	Sgt	CRAIG Robert Gerald	22-09-41	75 Sqn
R/61807	Sgt	CRICH Harvey Lewis	19-08-41	10 Sqn
R/64467	Sgt	CROSBY David Young Nurse	26-10-41	40 Sqn
J/15857	P/O	CROWE Herbert Roy	8-11-41	149 Sqn
R/61608	Sgt	CRUMP John Colvin	24-07-41	405 Sqn
R/56327	WO2	CUTHBERT Allan David Walker	8-12-41	12 OTU
R/71644	F/S	DARRELL Arthur Cyril	22-12-41	78 Sqn
J/15032	P/O	DAVIDSON William Howard	15-10-41	114 Sqn
R/65190	Sgt	DAVIS Charles William	19-06-41	16 OTU
R/73778	Sgt	DAWSON John Frederick Blair	15-08-41	405 Sqn
R/60129	Sgt	DAY Francis John	4-07-41	99 Sqn
R/68108	Sgt	DERMODY Bernard John	15-11-41	99 Sqn
J/3763	P/O	DETLOR Perry Byard	21-08-41	102 Sqn
R/58430	Sgt	DICKSON Alexander Fernie	14-10-41	207 Sqn
18077A	Sgt	DICKSON Harry George	13-08-41	15 Sqn
R/69039	Sgt	DIXON John Martin	7-09-41	149 Sqn
R/59295	Sgt	DOCKING Robert Owen	17-06-41	115 Sqn
R/62216	Sgt	DODDS Gilbert Derrick	1-08-41	44 Sqn
R/51644	Sgt	DODGE Lloyd Eldon	22-10-41	405 Sqn
R/65200	F/S	DONKIN Jack Cecil	28-12-41	405 Sqn
R/71909	Sgt	DONSON Hugh Holmes	13-10-41	58 Sqn
R/64114	Sgt	DOUGHERTY Leonard David	3-06-41	40 Sqn
R/60226	Sgt	DRAKE Richard Ellsworth	25-07-41	57 Sqn
R/67544	Sgt	DREW James Edward	11-07-41	9 Sqn
R/65046	Sgt	DRUHAN Kenneth Francis	30-07-41	20 OTU
R/68209	Sgt	DUFFY Donald Maclachlan	19-08-41	10 Sqn
R/76154	Sgt	DUGGAN John Frederick	4-10-41	21 OTU
R/60299	Sgt	DUNHAM William Matthie Gillam	23-07-41	18 Sqn
R/67572	F/S	DUNLOP James Lennox Scott [USA]	11-10-41	12 Sqn
J/15859	P/O	DUNN John Humphrey 'Bud'	11-12-41	144 Sqn
R/56412	Sgt	DUNN Stuart St. Helier Gwyllym	30-07-41	20 OTU
J/15038	P/O	DURBAN Nicholas Frederick	18-12-41	7 Sqn
R/55446	Sgt	DURNING Joseph Hermile	28-12-41	51 Sqn
R/59125	F/S	DUXBURY Thomas Lincoln	12-10-41	40 Sqn
R/71550	F/S	EARLY James Williard	15-11-41	11 OTU
R/56846	Sgt	EASTON Herbert Robinson	8-04-41	214 Sqn
R/65819	F/S	EDMONDSON Gerald Henry	14-10-41	44 Sqn
R/69694	Sgt	EDWARDS Charles Stanley Rutherford	7-07-41	115 Sqn
R/63542	Sgt	EDWORTHY John Duncan	25-08-41	7 Sqn
R/62406	Sgt	ELLIOTT Howard Lee	15-10-41	114 Sqn
J/4878	P/O	ELLIOTT James Gordon	1-07-41	7 Sqn
R/52050	F/S	ELLIOTT Thomas Edison	8-11-41	75 Sqn
J/3264	P/O	ERLY DFC James Paul	22-08-41	106 Sqn
R/78195	F/S	EVANS Walter Arthur [USA]	16-12-41	102 Sqn
R/58109	Sgt	EVELLE Jack Douglas	31-07-41	150 Sqn

Service No.	Rank	Name	Date	Unit
R/70522	Sgt	FAGAN William Henry	5-09-41	12 OTU
R/80157	Sgt	FALARDEAU William Leslie	14-10-41	22 OTU
R/69036	Sgt	FEAR Harold Edward	6-08-41	144 Sqn
R/60716	Sgt	FIGG Arthur Harry	29-08-41	103 Sqn
R/67682	Sgt	FINDLAY German Francis	21-09-41	103 Sqn
R/68111	Sgt	FISH Hilton William	4-07-41	102 Sqn
R/62981	Sgt	FISK Donald Sutherland	26-10-41	57 Sqn
J/4870	P/O	FLEMING George Howard	15-08-41	405 Sqn
R/54340	Sgt	FLEMING Gordon Edward	27-07-41	10 OTU
R/58084	Sgt	FOXLEE Edward Wilson	29-08-41	214 Sqn
J/5342	P/O	FREELAND John Roy	29-09-41	9 Sqn
J/7026	P/O	FRIESEN Victor Erwin	17-12-41	20 OTU
R/65032	F/S	FULLERTON Bernard	20-10-41	88 Sqn
R/59718	F/S	GATES William Ralph	30-12-41	76 Sqn
R/69514	F/S	GAULEY John Frederick	21-10-41	142 Sqn
R/78304	Sgt	GEDDES Archibald Grant	29-08-41	104 Sqn
R/69557	Sgt	GEORGE Lothian Julyan	18-08-41	218 Sqn
R/60227	Sgt	GIBB William Edgar	16-07-41	40 Sqn
R/60253	F/S	GIBSON Jack Lloyd	18-12-41	97 Sqn
J/6231	P/O	GIBSON Mark Fairweather	26-10-41	23 OTU
R/74283	Sgt	GITTINS Harold Bryan Livingstone [Argentina]	15-12-41	11 OTU
R/56903	F/S	GLOVER John	7-09-41	102 Sqn
R/77004	F/S	GOAT Frederick James	27-12-41	58 Sqn
R/1961	Sgt	GOODWIN George Joseph	13-10-41	15 Sqn
R/59662	Sgt	GORDON James	8-07-41	11 OTU
R/51664	F/S	GRAHAM Irwin Phillips	12-09-41	149 Sqn
J/3595	P/O	GRANT James Murray	24-07-41	44 Sqn
R/61931	Sgt	GRANT William Patrick	29-06-41	15 Sqn
R/77112	Sgt	GURD Philip Leslie	11-12-41	57 Sqn
R/65812	Sgt	HALE Howard	5-08-41	149 Sqn
R/74248	Sgt	HALL Cyril Roland	22-10-41	405 Sqn
R/54012	Sgt	HALL William Temple	31-10-41	77 Sqn
R/68193	Sgt	HALLAM John Norman	12-07-41	82 Sqn
R/52691	F/S	HALSEY Alan Leonard	7-09-41	102 Sqn
R/59540	Sgt	HALSTEAD Glen Elwyne	5-06-41	10 OTU
R/61805	Sgt	HAMBLY Ross Stewart	18-09-41	88 Sqn
R/54019	Sgt	HAMPSON Douglas Erle James	15-08-41	102 Sqn
R/61806	Sgt	HARBOTTLE Cecil Thornton	11-10-41	57 Sqn
R/71459	F/S	HARKNESS Alexander	26-09-41	115 Sqn
J/3268	P/O	HART Charles Francis	29-08-41	7 Sqn
R/56088	Sgt	HART Francis Joseph	27-06-41	150 Sqn
R/58086	Sgt	HARTRIDGE Henry Percival	23-07-41	21 Sqn
R/54186	Sgt	HARTRY William James Howard	16-07-41	115 Sqn
R/61068	F/S	HASSAN Alexander Lawrence Dennis	8-11-41	405 Sqn
4312A	Sgt	HATTON Arthur Thomas	12-08-41	9 Sqn
R/76013	Sgt	HEINISH Morton Ralph	18-12-41	97 Sqn
R/62015	Sgt	HENSON George Knowsley	13-08-41	15 Sqn
R/68075	F/S	HETTRICK Norman Gilbert	26-11-41	214 Sqn
J/4698	P/O	HEWSON Charles Dale	31-07-41	144 Sqn
R/52038	Sgt	HEYWOOD Wray William	8-05-41	150 Sqn
R/58819	Sgt	HICKS Allan Fenwick	3-06-41	40 Sqn
R/64424	F/S	HILLMER Charles Edward	30-10-41	405 Sqn
R/65468	Sgt	HILTZ John Clifton	30-09-41	77 Sqn
R/67520	Sgt	HINDLE William Hesketh	28-07-41	21 OTU
R/67911	Sgt	HOESE Bill Ingalls [USA]	14-10-41	22 OTU
R/58216	Sgt	HOLLINGWORTH Charles Raymond	1-11-41	16 OTU
R/64714	F/S	HOPKINS Talfryn Barton	12-09-41	75 Sqn
R/68200	Sgt	HOUSTON Frederick Slade	22-07-41	11 OTU
R/56214	Sgt	HUGHES Douglas Miller	29-08-41	405 Sqn
J/4790	P/O	HUGHES Orval Benjamin	20-11-41	109 Sqn
J/5918	P/O	HULL William Francis	11-12-41	408 Sqn
R/65191	Sgt	HUMPHREY John Weir	29-09-41	99 Sqn
R/51666	Sgt	HUMPHREY Morley Sidney	1-09-41	102 Sqn
R/69616	F/S	HUMPHREYS Francis Ridout	11-10-41	57 Sqn
R/62717	Sgt	HUNTING William Karl	9-10-41	107 Sqn
R/71753	Sgt	INGLEBY Harry	12-08-41	139 Sqn
R/76578	Sgt	INNES Stuart Laban	30-11-41	142 Sqn
R/65177	Sgt	IRVING Allister Nelson	26-10-41	40 Sqn
R/69540	Sgt	IRWIN Kenneth Albert	12-09-41	10 Sqn
R/60132	F/S	JACKSON Lawrence Herbert	22-10-41	405 Sqn
R/58300	Sgt	JACQUES John Allen [USA]	17-10-41	40 Sqn
R/53751	Sgt	JEFFREY George Wilbert	8-08-41	15 Sqn
J/15027	P/O	JENKINSON David Montgomery	27-12-41	110 Sqn
R/56089	Sgt	JOHNSON John Rudolph [Jamaica]	31-10-41	76 Sqn
R/75095	Sgt	JOHNSTON Howard Robert Franklin	19-08-41	51 Sqn
R/56091	Sgt	JOHNSTON Norman Lachlan	21-07-41	115 Sqn
R/62654	WO2	JOWETT William	27-12-41	77 Sqn
R/59288	Sgt	KAMEDISH John Benjamin	28-07-41	10 OTU
R/56146	F/S	KEATING John Gerald O'Hara	8-09-41	115 Sqn
R/62251	Sgt	KELLOUGH Howard John	28-06-41	23 OTU
J/15856	P/O	KELLY John Joseph [USA]	5-11-41	18 Sqn
R/78279	Sgt	KELLY Paul [USA]	9-10-41	19 OTU
R/56203	Sgt	KENNEDY Edward Richard	24-07-41	21 OTU
R/64768	Sgt	KESWICK Murray McLaren	7-09-41	149 Sqn
R/56344	Sgt	KIBBE Donald Kyle [USA]	30-09-41	102 Sqn
R/65229	Sgt	KILLIN Ronald Douglas	8-11-41	405 Sqn
J/4824	P/O	KING Douglas Stuart [Argentina]	30-12-41	76 Sqn
R/71720	Sgt	KIRK Thomas Lorne	26-06-41	22 OTU
R/71689	F/S	KNIGHT Alan John	30-11-41	405 Sqn
R/78169	Sgt	LACEY Patrick Earl 'Pat'	26-10-41	23 OTU
J/4777	P/O	LANE Carleton Thompson	8-11-41	58 Sqn
R/69575	Sgt	LAPPIN John Stephen	26-09-41	115 Sqn
R/69780	F/S	LAWRENCE Arthur Henry [Jamaica]	8-12-41	144 Sqn
R/58836	F/S	LAWSON Lloyd Theodore	3-09-41	57 Sqn
J/4764	P/O	LEARMONTH Andrew Owen	2-08-41	405 Sqn
R/54056	Sgt	LEFTLEY Emerson Master	8-11-41	102 Sqn
R/64722	F/S	LEGERE Frederick Maxwell	7-11-41	58 Sqn
R/67511	Sgt	LEOPOLD Herbert Arthur	15-11-41	11 OTU
R/58302	Sgt	LESLEY Arthur Bennet	15-08-41	405 Sqn
R/56912	Sgt	LEVERRIER Gabriel Charles	30-07-41	20 OTU
J/4255	P/O	LIEBECK Kenneth William	23-08-41	10 Sqn
R/56152	Sgt	LIVIS Mortimer	8-07-41	44 Sqn
R/69765	F/S	LIZOTTE Ray Leonidas Joseph	30-11-41	58 Sqn
R/58542	F/S	LOCKWOOD John Lawson	20-10-41	106 Sqn
J/3706	P/O	LONEY Wellington James	19-08-41	51 Sqn
R/69692	F/S	LOWE Gordon Albert	5-11-41	18 Sqn
R/52049	Sgt	LOWTHER Edward Arthur	20-11-41	109 Sqn
J/4707	P/O	LUGAR William Rand	20-09-41	101 Sqn
J/6170	P/O	LYNAS James	7-12-41	22 OTU
R/67234	F/S	LYNCH John Joseph [USA]	27-12-41	58 Sqn
R/64887	Sgt	MacAULAY Harold	19-11-41	18 Sqn
R/72503	Sgt	MacEACHERN John Andrew	21-09-41	20 OTU
R/2048A	Sgt	MacMILLAN James Forbes	24-07-41	21 Sqn
R/56111	Sgt	MacVICAR John Douglas	16-06-41	103 Sqn
J/5061	P/O	MACDONALD George Sinclair	21-10-41	207 Sqn
R/54025	Sgt	MACDONALD Ian Alistair	20-10-41	88 Sqn
R/60123	F/S	MACKENZIE Walter Cameron	16-09-41	15 Sqn
R/72266	Sgt	MALKEMUS William Risdon [USA]	7-09-41	149 Sqn
R/61354	Sgt	MANN Ronald Percy	30-11-41	405 Sqn
R/59283	Sgt	MANNING Percival Theodore	22-07-41	11 OTU
14040A	Sgt	MARR George Frederick	22-10-41	405 Sqn
R/57837	F/S	MARSHALL Douglas Crosbie	20-08-41	104 Sqn
R/60897	F/S	MARSHALL Hudson Eric	28-11-41	408 Sqn
R/64471	Sgt	MARTIN Clifford Mackenzie [United Kingdom]	9-07-41	78 Sqn
R/57938	Sgt	MARTIN Julian Lee Byron	24-07-41	405 Sqn
J/2830	F/O	MATHER Robert Addison	30-11-41	405 Sqn
R/62189	F/S	MATKIN Frederick Joseph	8-09-41	106 Sqn
R/53901	Sgt	MAVILLE John Allan	22-06-41	207 Sqn
R/56873	Sgt	MAVOR Grant John	18-04-41	9 Sqn
R/54040	Sgt	MAXON James Matthew [USA]	18-09-41	405 Sqn
J/3715	P/O	MAXWELL John Arthur	3-08-41	218 Sqn

Service No	Rank	Name	Date	Sqn
R/65593	Sgt	MAXWELL William	13-08-41	104 Sqn
R/56135	Sgt	McCOLM Harold Walton	30-09-41	77 Sqn
J/5093	P/O	McDONALD Donald Smith	11-10-41	58 Sqn
R/51806	Sgt	McGEAGLE Thomas Edward	12-08-41	9 Sqn
J/5681	P/O	McGOUN Kenneth Beverly	7-11-41	58 Sqn
R/60280	Sgt	McINNES Reginald James	13-08-41	76 Sqn
R/63936	F/S	McINTYRE John Jacob	15-09-41	106 Sqn
R/60111	F/S	McINTYRE Ronald Maitland	15-10-41	40 Sqn
J/3596	F/O	McIVER DFC Bruce Gordon	8-11-41	106 Sqn
R/10573	F/S	McKAY Duncan Gordon	30-11-41	58 Sqn
R/58824	F/S	McKAY James Patrick	3-09-41	214 Sqn
R/70767	F/S	McKENZIE John Mortimer	11-12-41	57 Sqn
R/64779	Sgt	McKIEL Donald Ivan	26-06-41	19 OTU
J/15023	P/O	McLACHLAN Roderick James	27-12-41	110 Sqn
R/70457	F/S	McLEAN Albert Perry	13-12-41	107 Sqn
R/66040	Sgt	McLEAN Donald	18-04-41	12 OTU
R/65208	Sgt	McLEOD Gerald Francis	11-10-41	107 Sqn
R/56648	Sgt	McLEOD Graham Alexander	8-11-41	405 Sqn
R/66076	Sgt	McMANUS Kenneth Allen	10-08-41	226 Sqn
R/67522	Sgt	McMILLAN Alexander Teryl	21-10-41	408 Sqn
R/65516	Sgt	McNEILL Stephen Thomas	13-07-41	15 OTU
R/69567	Sgt	McQUADE William Joseph	6-08-41	44 Sqn
R/59592	Sgt	MENISH George Raymond [USA]	30-07-41	139 Sqn
R/54891	Sgt	MERRILL Henry Marie Joseph Jacques Armand	8-09-41	90 Sqn
J/3600	P/O	MILLER Arthur Leonard	7-11-41	101 Sqn
J/4710	P/O	MITCHELL Robert George	1-07-41	50 Sqn
R/56234	F/S	MODELAND Seward Terry	3-09-41	102 Sqn
R/54911	Sgt	MOLLOY John Patrick	15-08-41	405 Sqn
J/4692	F/O	MONK Arthur John Benning	11-12-41	144 Sqn
R/70734	Sgt	MOORE Harold Edwin	11-09-41	102 Sqn
R/69579	F/S	MORLEY Charles Richard	17-08-41	44 Sqn
R/52871	Sgt	MORRIS Gerald	13-08-41	149 Sqn
R/69636	Sgt	MORROW Austin Wellington	26-06-41	19 OTU
R/56225	Sgt	MOULDS Stewart Ireland Collister	30-09-41	58 Sqn
R/64729	F/S	MUTTART Elmer Bagnell	13-10-41	76 Sqn
R/73011	Sgt	MYERS Ernest Charles Edward	6-09-41	77 Sqn
J/5331	P/O	MYERS Hilyard Lowell	12-10-41	57 Sqn
J/4781	P/O	NASH Philip Llewellyn	11-07-41	16 OTU
R/64890	Sgt	NEAL Donald Alexander	13-09-41	13 OTU
R/70069	F/S	NEWSOME Chester Douglas	19-11-41	18 Sqn
R/69892	F/S	NICKLESON John Murray	20-09-41	18 Sqn
J/4756	P/O	NIXON Jackson Corwin	3-09-41	102 Sqn
R/76040	Sgt	OLIVER Roy Tufts	21-10-41	19 OTU
R/66161	Sgt	OLSEN Gordon Leonard	17-08-41	78 Sqn
J/3739	P/O	ORME Frank Kerr	28-08-41	21 Sqn
R/68081	Sgt	OSBORNE John Maxwell	10-08-41	226 Sqn
R/58067	Sgt	OWEN William	24-07-41	75 Sqn
R/61122	F/S	OZMENT Donald Eric	27-12-41	77 Sqn
R/65254	F/S	O'BRIEN Charles Stuart	31-10-41	76 Sqn
J/3602	P/O	O'NEILL Gordon Campbell	22-10-41	150 Sqn
R/60975	F/S	O'NEILL William Henry	18-12-41	15 Sqn
R/64809	Sgt	PAINTER John Harry	7-09-41	77 Sqn
R/54368	Sgt	PARK James Gibson	15-08-41	115 Sqn
R/72165	Sgt	PARK Thomas Hill [USA]	19-08-41	10 Sqn
R/59119	F/S	PARKER Thomas Edward	21-10-41	142 Sqn
354A	Sgt	PAYTON Reginald Percy	17-08-41	405 Sqn
R/65821	Sgt	PEEL Henry Gerald	13-07-41	15 OTU
R/77119	Sgt	PEEVER Frederick	14-11-41	99 Sqn
R/54987	Sgt	PERRAS Roland Joseph Fidele	26-08-41	40 Sqn
R/60373	F/S	PETTS John Russell	28-12-41	138 Sqn
J/5086	P/O	PIBUS Henry Hodsmyth	21-10-41	82 Sqn
R/10286	Sgt	PITT Leonard Herbert	11-11-41	115 Sqn
R/51858	Sgt	PLATT Orville Insell	17-07-41	40 Sqn
R/52075	F/S	POSTANS Ronald George	29-09-41	57 Sqn
R/69896	Sgt	PROCTOR George Kenneth	21-09-41	103 Sqn
J/4823	F/L	PRYOR Gerald Cowes [Argentina]	8-11-41	18 Sqn
R/78136	Sgt	PULLAN Cyril	28-07-41	10 OTU
J/2832	P/O	PURSER John Henry	30-06-41	115 Sqn
J/4108	P/O	QUICK John Askey	6-08-41	77 Sqn
R/58012	Sgt	QUINLAN Vernon Beverley	7-08-41	149 Sqn
J/6154	P/O	RAY Howard Stanley	21-10-41	207 Sqn
R/65221	Sgt	REDDEN John Bernard	1-09-41	101 Sqn
R/69515	Sgt	REID Russell Addisson	3-07-41	106 Sqn
R/62627	Sgt	RELYEA William Robert Bain	22-07-41	44 Sqn
R/53944	Sgt	RHEAUME Joseph Arthur Donis	29-8-41	104 Sqn
R/54910	Sgt	ROBERTS Joseph Harold Campbell	16-07-41	75 Sqn
R/54107	Sgt	ROBERTSON John Donald	19-09-41	58 Sqn
J/15008	P/O	ROBERTSON John Ross	27-09-41	104 Sqn
R/57929	Sgt	ROBINSON Henry Edmund	16-07-41	57 Sqn
J/5684	P/O	ROBINSON Joseph Allan	12-10-41	75 Sqn
R/67035	Sgt	RODGERS Aubrey Addison	30-07-41	19 OTU
J/15013	P/O	ROGERS Jack Goode	20-08-41	104 Sqn
R/64728	Sgt	ROGERS James Graham	31-07-41	144 Sqn
J/5677	P/O	ROMILLY Esmond Mark David [USA]	30-11-41	58 Sqn
R/56850	Sgt	ROSE Thomas Herbert	12-03-41	40 Sqn
R/68123	Sgt	ROWED Samuel Edgar	29-08-41	78 Sqn
J/15002	P/O	RUSTON John Benjamin [USA]	21-09-41	214 Sqn
R/71664	Sgt	RUTHERFORD Douglas Alexander	14-10-41	15 OTU
R/72419	F/S	RUTHVEN James Lloyd	18-12-41	15 Sqn
R/52027	Sgt	SATURE Vincent [Poland]	31-10-41	51 Sqn
J/3714	P/O	SAUNDERS Arthur Mitchell	18-05-41	139 Sqn
J/5344	P/O	SAUNDERS Clyffurde George Randall	26-10-41	40 Sqn
J/5135	P/O	SAWYER John Patrick Anthony [United Kingdom]	15-09-41	207 Sqn
J/15031	P/O	SCHAFTEITLIN Donald	21-10-41	44 Sqn
R/65147	F/S	SCHRADER George Howard	10-12-41	13 OTU
J/3497	P/O	SCOTT Foster William Jack	12-08-41	149 Sqn
R/78122	Sgt	SELLERS William Francis Philip	7-11-41	57 Sqn
R/54577	Sgt	SEWELL Vernon Young Hodgson	17-08-41	10 Sqn
R/54366	F/S	SHAVER William Taylor	26-10-41	107 Sqn
J/4521	F/O	SHEA Edward Lees	5-11-41	144 Sqn
R/67559	Sgt	SHELNUTT Barney Walker [USA]	26-10-41	75 Sqn
R/69619	Sgt	SHERMAN Thomas Anthony [USA]	17-08-41	78 Sqn
J/5309	P/O	SIMPSON David Albert	8-11-41	51 Sqn
J/5321	P/O	SIMPSON William Egbert	14-10-41	207 Sqn
R/61222	Sgt	SINCLAIR Donald Alexander	25-08-41	78 Sqn
R/59542	Sgt	SINCLAIR Lloyd George	21-09-41	77 Sqn
R/54178	Sgt	SMITH George Barry 'Don'	13-08-41	9 Sqn
R/72387	F/S	SMITH James Gordon	3-11-41	15 OTU
R/62188	Sgt	SMITH Wilfred Bruce	29-05-41	78 Sqn
R/58848	Sgt	SNEAD Frederick Charles	16-09-41	15 Sqn
R/72462	Sgt	SNELL William Enoch	30-07-41	19 OTU
J/3732	P/O	SNYDER Paul Edward	12-06-41	51 Sqn
R/64339	Sgt	SOLES Donald Enright	3-09-41	57 Sqn
J/5984	P/O	SOLHEIM Merlin Kelmer	8-11-41	405 Sqn
R/59781	Sgt	STACK Arnold Harvey	11-11-41	16 OTU
J/3119	P/O	STACK Gerald Daniel Edward	7-08-41	214 Sqn
R/65417	Sgt	STEADMAN Hoyt Leslie	26-10-41	40 Sqn
R/64734	F/S	STEEVES James Allison	8-11-41	102 Sqn
R/64740	Sgt	STEEVES John Chesley	7-07-41	19 OTU
R/56106	Sgt	STEIN Isadore	8-11-41	102 Sqn
R/73201	Sgt	STENTIFORD Harold Frederick [USA]	8-11-41	58 Sqn
R/59262	F/S	STEPHENS Robert Francis	12-09-41	19 OTU
R/64431	Sgt	STEPHENSON Fred Chadwick	24-10-41	144 Sqn
R/52876	Sgt	STEPHENSON William Thomas Ross	17-08-41	104 Sqn
R/56257	Sgt	STEVENSON Benjamin Ross	8-10-41	15 OTU
R/59110	Sgt	STEVENSON Earle John	3-08-41	104 Sqn
R/65342	F/S	STEWART John Alvah	17-12-41	20 OTU
R/68173	Sgt	STOCK Leonard Albert	7-09-41	102 Sqn
R/64355	Sgt	STOLL John Harold	31-10-41	77 Sqn
R/64240	Sgt	STRACHAN William Alexander	7-07-41	115 Sqn
R/59586	Sgt	STRATTON Ronald Grant	5-07-41	10 OTU

Service No.	Rank	Name	Date	Unit
R/62632	Sgt	STUART James Francis Paul	17-08-41	21 OTU
R/60298	F/S	STUART William	7-09-41	10 Sqn
R/62186	Sgt	SUTHERLAND William Robertson	24-06-41	57 Sqn
R/69562	F/S	TAYLOR Cyril Garfield	13-10-41	77 Sqn
R/74275	Sgt	TAYLOR David Donald	21-10-41	207 Sqn
R/55406	Sgt	TAYLOR Harold Alvan	1-09-41	44 Sqn
R/68517	Sgt	TAYLOR John Philip	5-06-41	10 OTU
R/72296	Sgt	TAYLOR Johnston Playfair	6-08-41	103 Sqn
R/60125	Sgt	TESKEY Harold Rex	29-08-41	15 OTU
R/52824	Sgt	TETT George Hazen	27-06-41	57 Sqn
R/57928	Sgt	THOM William Paterson [United Kingdom]	15-10-41	139 Sqn
J/5094	P/O	THOMPSON John Baldwin	26-09-41	9 Sqn
R/58545	F/S	THOMPSON Ralph Lloyd	15-12-41	408 Sqn
R/78052	Sgt	TOMLIN John Charles	15-12-41	408 Sqn
R/10199	Sgt	TOPPING Charles Clinton	26-08-41	226 Sqn
R/65635	Sgt	TOWLSON William Frederick	27-06-41	57 Sqn
R/72506	Sgt	TREDENICK Ernest Ashton	14-10-41	15 OTU
R/69644	F/S	TREWIN Wallace Howard	4-09-41	58 Sqn
R/52883	F/S	TRIPP Warrington Wade	29-12-41	10 Sqn
R/60667	F/S	TURGEON Augustin Charles Joseph	3-09-41	57 Sqn
R/69132	Sgt	TURNER Frank Lees	16-07-41	13 OTU
R/69885	Sgt	VAUGHAN John Leslie	15-12-41	408 Sqn
J/3254	P/O	VAN BUSKIRK Douglas Byrd [USA]	8-11-41	7 Sqn
R/59770	Sgt	VENN Frank James	26-08-41	22 OTU
R/74102	Sgt	VOSE Reginald Bolles [USA]	30-11-41	77 Sqn
J/15858	P/O	WADE Frank William	26-10-41	57 Sqn
R/69633	Sgt	WAINWRIGHT Kenneth Rowland	13-06-41	77 Sqn
R/64120	Sgt	WALDRON Wilbur Lloyd	9-04-41	99 Sqn
R/78239	Sgt	WALKER Percy Thomas Walter	22-10-41	405 Sqn
R/56900	F/S	WARBURTON Eric	31-10-41	51 Sqn
R/56104	Sgt	WARD Robert Lawrence 'Larry' [USA]	4-09-41	58 Sqn
J/5041	P/O	WATSON John Archibald	27-10-41	57 Sqn
R/62250	Sgt	WEAVER Harold Douglas	20-09-41	144 Sqn
R/64119	Sgt	WEBB Gordon Thomas	28-06-41	7 Sqn
R/54909	Sgt	WEBBER Wilbur Frederick	18-05-41	218 Sqn
R/67523	Sgt	WEBSTER Howard Bate	28-07-41	21 OTU
R/69586	F/S	WEIR John Emerson	15-10-41	40 Sqn
R/64386	Sgt	WESTBROOK Stanley Gordon	22-10-41	99 Sqn
R/65205	Sgt	WHEELER Clarence Edmund	24-10-41	51 Sqn
R/62018	Sgt	WHIDDEN Charles Arthur	4-11-41	107 Sqn
J/5330	P/O	WHITE Charles Stewart	26-09-41	115 Sqn
R/56085	Sgt	WHITE David Roy	26-06-41	22 OTU
R/63731	F/S	WILBEE Bruce George	21-09-41	77 Sqn
R/53359	Sgt	WILLS Thomas James	22-06-41	90 Sqn
J/5224	P/O	WILSON John Cayley	9-11-41	408 Sqn
R/54036	Sgt	WILSON Matthew Gordon	30-07-41	20 OTU
R/54053	F/S	WILSON Robert Hector	6-09-41	10 Sqn
R/54207	F/S	WOLF Herbert Irwin	20-11-41	109 Sqn
R/53699	Sgt	WOLFF James Fitzgerald	31-08-41	12 Sqn
R/70062	Sgt	WOOD Thomas Hunter	1-09-41	102 Sqn
R/54201	F/S	WOODBURN DFM James Douglas	22-10-41	18 Sqn
J/4759	P/O	WOODWARD Norman [United Kingdom]	6-09-41	77 Sqn
J/6687	P/O	WOODWORTH Charles Herman	6-12-41	17 OTU
8164A	Sgt	WRIGHT Gordon	22-01-41	110 Sqn
R/59345	Sgt	YEO John Lenus	11-11-41	16 OTU
R/54983	F/S	YERBURY William Edmund Stuart	17-06-41	10 OTU
5509	F/S	YOUNGER Robert Laing Roy	12-09-41	19 OTU

Note

As the war progressed, the sacrifice of the Canadian men and women increased significantly so that by May 1945, in excess of 18,000 (the majority serving with the Royal Canadian Air Force) had laid down their lives and of this dreadful litany of death over 10,000 had been lost in the service of Bomber Command. From within this first section I have noted several double tragedies; for example, fifteen months after the death of P/O Hugh Cooper his brother, John Donald Cooper, was lost without trace while serving with 7 Squadron and in 1944, Sgt Figg's younger sibling died while flying with 12 Squadron. For the Leftley family of Ottawa, tragedy would strike twice within less than six months with their son Emerson missing from operations in November 1941, followed in April 1942 by the loss of Nelson, both having trained as observers. Similarly, the Rose brothers from Stoney Mountain in Manitoba trained as observers, though when Donald met his end over Berlin in January 1944, his status was that of air bomber. The younger of the Petts brothers trained as a pilot and lost his life with 138 (Special Duties) Squadron, while Henry, a navigator, was shot down over Holland in May 1943 while on Main Force operations with 100 Squadron.

Two unusual deaths concern the Littlewood brothers of Vermillion, Alberta. Both crossed over to the United Kingdom and joined the Royal Air Force, though Peter Littlewood was on the strength of a Canadian night fighter squadron when he was killed in July 1943.

There are many more instances of double tragedies where Commands other than Bomber are concerned and I can only recommend readers of this Roll to the outstanding work mentioned in my introduction, and at other appropriate junctures, of Les Allison and Harry Hayward.

An interesting entry in this section concerns that for P/O Sawyer. His details in the Commonwealth War Graves Commission register for Beaconsfield Cemetery suggest that he was English though his Canadian records report that he was from Nassau in the Bahamas. His father, too, Lt R. H. Sawyer Royal Air Force lost his life while on active service in the Great War and he rests in South Ealing Cemetery, but though his entry is devoid of next of kin or country of origin information, that for his son locates him as domicile in Beaconsfield.

Finally, readers will have noticed reference to the many Americans whose lives were lost while serving (in the main) with the Royal Canadian Air Force, more than a few dying before the events of Pearl Harbor which brought their country fully into the war. This sad state of affairs continued for the remainder of the war with a substantial number choosing to remain with the air force of their first choice, rather than transfer to the United States Army Air Force.

ROYAL NEW ZEALAND AIR FORCE
personnel

Service No.	Rank	Name	Date	Unit
NZ391335	Sgt	ALINGTON Richard Hugh	15-03-41	3 GTrgFlt
NZ403929	P/O	ANDERSON Alexander Cairns	7-08-41	150 Sqn
NZ402155	Sgt	ANDREWS Charles William	22-07-41	17 OTU
NZ403785	P/O	AUSTIN Richard Scott	7-09-41	10 Sqn
NZ391821	F/L	BAIRD Angus Bruce	30-06-41	40 Sqn
NZ41464	P/O	BARKER Richard Percival William	22-12-41	28 CFlt
NZ401720	Sgt	BATY Frederick Alphonsus	8-09-41	115 Sqn
NZ41301	P/O	BEATTIE William Stuart	22-12-41	28 CFlt
NZ402159	P/O	BEEDIE Stuart William Stott	6-08-41	144 Sqn
NZ402841	P/O	BELL Ronald Peter	12-08-41	17 OTU
NZ403936	F/S	BENTLEY Loch Lomond	23-12-41	75 Sqn
NZ401369	Sgt	BIRD Alan William Porteous	17-07-41	40 Sqn
NZ402976	Sgt	BISHOP Omer Wilbur John	26-08-41	82 Sqn
NZ402843	F/S	BLACK John William	8-11-41	75 Sqn
NZ402844	F/S	BLACK Stuart Corless	12-12-41	49 Sqn
NZ403118	F/L	BLEWETT Richard Trevor	27-12-41	110 Sqn
NZ401801	Sgt	BRADLEY Desmond George	21-10-41	408 Sqn
NZ403937	Sgt	BROADLEY John Duncan	29-09-41	99 Sqn
NZ391378	Sgt	BRODIE Andrew Moore	21-02-41	75 Sqn
NZ402241	P/O	BROOK Donald	31-07-41	144 Sqn
NZ40189	P/O	CAMPBELL David McLean	11-05-41	15 Sqn
NZ402979	Sgt	CARMAN Geoffrey	7-09-41	78 Sqn
NZ40932	Sgt	CATTELL James Clark	9-04-41	214 Sqn
NZ401371	Sgt	CLARK Bernard Allison	7-09-41	57 Sqn
NZ40754	P/O	CLAUSEN Basil Ivan	4-02-41	20 OTU
NZ437007	LAC	CONGREVE Robert Lance	16-04-41	15 OTU
NZ404531	Sgt	COOKE Percy Frederick Meadows	12-10-41	57 Sqn
NZ39901	P/O	COOPER Tancred Eric	18-09-41	88 Sqn

Service No.	Rank	Name	Date	Unit
NZ41471	Sgt	CREED Francis Howard	20-11-41	11 OTU
NZ404996	Sgt	CRONIN Maxwell Joseph	27-12-41	57 Sqn
NZ40755	Sgt	CROOKS Malcolm Bruce	22-04-41	218 Sqn
NZ402854	F/S	CROWHURST Samuel Victor	12-12-41	106 Sqn
NZ41313	Sgt	CROWTHER William Royal	24-10-41	10 OTU
NZ411978	P/O	CRUMP Sidney Arnold	23-12-41	21 OTU
NZ402106	Sgt	DABINETTE Tahu William	10-04-41	218 Sqn
NZ391327	Sgt	DACRE Desmond Aubrey	21-06-41	218 Sqn
NZ40747	P/O	DANIEL Robert	22-03-41	18 Sqn
NZ404480	P/O	DAVIS Robert Charles	27-12-41	110 Sqn
NZ405240	Sgt	DEMPSEY Dennis James	15-12-41	11 OTU
NZ401259	P/O	DIDSBURY Colin McDougall	7-08-41	214 Sqn
NZ403434	Sgt	DIL William Robert	21-09-41	101 Sqn
NZ40916	Sgt	DONEHUE Cyril Edgar	24-02-41	115 Sqn
NZ40758	Sgt	DYER Henry David Patrick	16-07-41	218 Sqn
NZ40101	Sgt	DYER Sydney Allan	16-07-41	75 Sqn
NZ40759	P/O	ECCLES Raymond Gordon	16-05-41	103 Sqn
NZ403312	F/L	EDMUNDS DFC Everest George	11-12-41	18 Sqn
NZ401804	Sgt	EVANS Bernard George	13-08-41	115 Sqn
NZ391832	Sgt	EVANS DFM Mervyn	24-07-41	40 Sqn
NZ39910	P/O	FALCONER Arthur James	21-02-41	75 Sqn
NZ401757	P/O	FIELD Ian Murray Vass	12-10-41	40 Sqn
NZ39923	Sgt	FINLAYSON Roderick William	12-05-41	40 Sqn
NZ40966	P/O	FOOKS Harry Gordon Compton	21-07-41	10 OTU
NZ402443	P/O	FOSTER Ralph Owen	8-11-41	75 Sqn
NZ391833	Sgt	FOTHERINGHAM Robert Ewen Ernest	16-07-41	75 Sqn
NZ40224	Sgt	FRASER Mason John	21-06-41	218 Sqn
NZ402110	Sgt	GANNAWAY Eric Francis	12-05-41	75 Sqn
NZ403041	Sgt	GENNON Peter	29-08-41	78 Sqn
NZ404352	Sgt	GIBSON John Cuthbert McKechnie	7-11-41	75 Sqn
NZ40621	Sgt	GLAZER Sol	13-03-41	214 Sqn
NZ39859	Sgt	GOSDEN Walter Lionel	4-02-41	18 OTU
NZ40764	Sgt	GOUGH Douglas William	12-03-41	40 Sqn
NZ401267	F/S	GOULDING Clarence Phillip	18-12-41	15 Sqn
NZ401268	Sgt	GRADY John Arthur	9-07-41	9 Sqn
NZ401207	P/O	GRAHAM John Alastair	9-04-41	149 Sqn
NZ41898	P/O	GRANT Ian Curtis	23-12-41	21 OTU
NZ403444	P/O	GRAY Peter Maxwell	21-07-41	10 OTU
NZ404356	Sgt	GRAY Trevor Hedley	8-11-41	75 Sqn
NZ405256	P/O	GRIERSON John Alexander	7-12-41	21 OTU
NZ34179	Sgt	GRIFFITHS Vincent Herbert	12-09-41	14 OTU
NZ402865	F/S	GUMBLEY Arthur Howard	13-12-41	44 Sqn
NZ401806	Sgt	HAMER Walter Duncan	3-09-41	61 Sqn
NZ40738	Sgt	HANNAH Anthony James	24-04-41	107 Sqn
NZ401227	Sgt	HARE Phillip Edgar	16-07-41	75 Sqn
NZ402183	F/S	HARRIS Alan Richard	16-07-41	150 Sqn
NZ403000	F/S	HARRISON Alfred Hubert	8-11-41	75 Sqn
NZ402184	F/S	HARRISON Lester Louis	21-10-41	97 Sqn
NZ403959	F/S	HARRISON-SMITH Francis Charles	30-11-41	75 Sqn
NN403777	F/S	HARROWBY Ian Gordon	7-11-41	99 Sqn
NZ402111	Sgt	HARTSTONE Roydon Horatio	3-07-41	75 Sqn
NZ403003	Sgt	HASELDEN Howard Clive McLeish	18-09-41	75 Sqn
NZ401807	P/O	HASLEMORE Francis Sydney	27-06-41	61 Sqn
NZ40971	Sgt	HAWKINS Anthony Henry Ryder	15-09-41	75 Sqn
NZ401763	F/L	HERBERT Alexander George	12-08-41	139 Sqn
NZ39635	Sgt	HIGGISON Alfred James	18-07-41	15 Sqn
NZ40284	Sgt	HINDRUP Frederick George	21-04-41	99 Sqn
NZ401274	Sgt	HOBDEN Frederick Simpson	18-04-41	20 OTU
NZ404464	P/O	HUNT Melville John Hyland	27-12-41	58 Sqn
NZ403549	Sgt	HUNTER Ian Hamish	16-11-41	7 Sqn
NZ401386	P/O	JAMIESON Douglas James	8-07-41	9 Sqn
NZ401388	Sgt	JESSON Wilfred George	8-07-41	9 Sqn
NZ40233	Sgt	JILLETT Gordon Grant	21-06-41	218 Sqn
NZ40648	P/O	JOLLY Morrison	24-07-41	218 Sqn
NZ401278	Sgt	JOYCE David Campbell	16-07-41	75 Sqn
NZ401768	Sgt	KENNEDY Brian Daniel James	1-07-41	149 Sqn
NZ391359	P/O	KIMBERLEY Gilbert Theodore	7-04-41	3 GTrgFlt
NZ401315	P/O	KIRKCALDIE Norman Mervyn Kebbell	9-05-41	214 Sqn
NZ402160	Sgt	KNOWLES William Leslie	6-08-41	106 Sqn
NZ40942	Sgt	LEIGH James Benjamin	7-12-41	61 Sqn
NZ40193	P/O	LEWIS Donald Alfred	23-07-41	15 Sqn
NZ402197	P/O	LLOYD Eric	8-11-41	75 Sqn
NZ40623	Sgt	LONG John David Campbell	12-05-41	40 Sqn
NZ391860	Sgt	LUCAS Eric Russell	11-05-41	15 Sqn
NZ40979	P/O	LUND Mervyn Sydney	24-07-41	103 Sqn
NZ40923	Sgt	MacKINNON Douglas Malcolm	16-07-41	75 Sqn
NZ402524	Sgt	MACDONALD Hugh McLennan	29-09-41	99 Sqn
NZ40654	Sgt	MANSON Kenneth	8-04-41	214 Sqn
NZ391842	Sgt	MATTHEWS Oswald Arthur	7-07-41	115 Sqn
NZ402199	P/O	McCRACKEN Roderick Urquhart	19-08-41	114 Sqn
NZ401439	Sgt	McDONALD Edward Campbell	24-07-41	103 Sqn
NZ401398	Sgt	McDONALD Lawrence Matthew George	25-10-41	25 OTU
NZ391665	Sgt	McGILL-NUTT Gordon James	15-10-41	11 OTU
NZ402201	P/O	McGRUER Allan Frederick	22-08-41	106 Sqn
NZ401811	Sgt	McKENZIE Cecil Keith	27-06-41	97 Sqn
NZ391862	Sgt	McLAREN DFM Peter Victor	27-06-41	97 Sqn
NZ403876	P/O	McLEAN Neil Frederick	31-10-41	76 Sqn
NZ40656	Sgt	MEE Alexander Coutts	7-05-41	75 Sqn
NZ401402	P/O	MILLER Brian William	10-10-41	16 OTU
NZ403015	P/O	MINNIS Richard John	7-09-41	77 Sqn
NZ401212	P/O	MORROW Rex Mulligan	21-04-41	99 Sqn
NZ40195	P/O	MUIR Anthony Vincent	21-02-41	75 Sqn
NZ40421	P/O	MURDOCH Bernard Norris	7-12-41	104 Sqn
NZ404037	Sgt	MURPHY Timothy Rowley	11-10-41	75 Sqn
NZ4095	Sgt	NATION John Ross	3-07-41	75 Sqn
NZ404400	P/O	NELSON Max Kiri	30-11-41	10 Sqn
NZ39930	Sgt	NOLA David Leo	7-05-41	75 Sqn
NZ401814	Sgt	NUTTALL Alfred Cecil	8-08-41	61 Sqn
NZ40985	Sgt	OSBORNE Gordon David	16-07-41	57 Sqn
NZ40727	P/O	OVERHEU DFM Ian	16-06-41	21 Sqn
NZ404492	Sgt	PARKER Anthony Joseph William	30-11-41	106 Sqn
NZ401287	F/S	PARRY Joseph Stewart	29-09-41	99 Sqn
NZ40206	Sgt	PASSMORE Ronald Ramsay	13-08-41	9 Sqn
NZ402891	F/S	PATTERSON Thomas Crawford Bentley	15-11-41	99 Sqn
NZ40242	P/O	REDSTONE Gilbert Peter Lewis	25-04-41	218 Sqn
NZ391846	Sgt	REID Ian Laurie	3-07-41	75 Sqn
NZ404556	Sgt	ROBERTSON Evan Bertram Te Makahi	9-11-41	408 Sqn
NZ404948	P/O	ROBERTSON Trevor Bernard	15-10-41	75 Sqn
NZ401290	Sgt	ROBSON Charles Hepburn	7-07-41	12 Sqn
NZ40947	Sgt	ROCHFORD DFM Hugh Francis	30-10-41	138 Sqn
NZ405322	Sgt	ROUGHTON Harry Gervase	21-10-41	19 OTU
NZ391367	P/O	RYAN Alexander James	10-01-41	75 Sqn
NZ41363	Sgt	SANDERSON Albert Leonard	15-12-41	11 OTU
NZ438024	LAC	SIMONSEN Horace Dean	17-04-41	75 Sqn
NZ40949	Sgt	SIMPSON Arthur William	4-06-41	139 Sqn
NZ402220	P/O	SMILEY Archibald Locksley	11-12-41	144 Sqn
NZ401415	P/O	SPARK Frederick Alexander	22-10-41	75 Sqn
NZ401417	P/O	STEEDS John Edwin MacKenzie	7-07-41	40 Sqn
NZ404424	P/O	STEEL Stanley David	31-10-41	51 Sqn
NZ401033	Sgt	STREETER Donald Frederick	24-07-41	75 Sqn
NZ403998	Sgt	STUART William Douglas	24-10-41	40 Sqn
NZ40665	Sgt	SWAIN William Henry	22-04-41	218 Sqn
NZ39786	Sgt	TAKRANGI Pine Tenga	6-09-41	10 Sqn
NZ404425	Sgt	TAYLOR Kenneth Roy	18-12-41	7 Sqn
NZ401790	Sgt	TAYLOR Ronald West	19-07-41	105 Sqn
NZ404557	F/S	THANE Desmond William	28-12-41	408 Sqn
NZ401447	Sgt	THOMAS Richard Raymond	30-04-41	99 Sqn
NZ404427	Sgt	THOMPSON Colin Maurice	11-10-41	75 Sqn

NZ402914	Sgt	THOMPSON Norman Watson	18-09-41	405 Sqn
NZ404575	F/S	TODD Duncan Luin	11-12-41	408 Sqn
NZ39288	Sgt	TOUT Albert Richard	30-06-41	14 OTU
NZ402230	P/O	WADDELL John Marshall	13-10-41	50 Sqn
NZ40668	Sgt	WALKER Daniel Munro	4-02-41	20 OTU
NZ401817	Sgt	WALKER Graham Stuart	24-07-41	75 Sqn
NZ401792	Sgt	WALL Jack Edward	12-09-41	14 OTU
NZ40669	Sgt	WALLACE John Trevor	13-08-41	115 Sqn
NZ401793	Sgt	WARD VC James Allen	15-09-41	75 Sqn
NZ401449	Sgt	WATTS Walter Alexander	7-04-41	3 GTrgFlt
NZ401818	Sgt	WAUGH Ivan Fenton	25-07-41	61 Sqn
NZ40670	Sgt	WEBB Thomas Geoffrey	12-03-41	40 Sqn
NZ391886	Sgt	WELLS George	15-07-41	10 Sqn
NZ391334	F/S	WELSH Neville Henry	15-10-41	75 Sqn
NZ402917	Sgt	WHITAKER Edward Boyce	28-12-41	144 Sqn
NZ39298	Sgt	WILLIAMS Edwin John	28-12-41	405 Sqn
NZ401296	Sgt	WILLIAMS Geoffrey Fraser	20-10-41	106 Sqn
NZ1068	F/L	WILLIAMS DFC Neville	11-05-41	7 Sqn
NZ404111	Sgt	WILSON Allan James	5-12-41	20 OTU
NZ40953	Sgt	WILSON Graham Robert	20-03-41	82 Sqn
NZ40746	Sgt	WILSON John Colin	21-05-41	107 Sqn
NZ402530	Sgt	WILSON John Stephen	8-11-41	75 Sqn
NZ404439	Sgt	WOOD Frederick Lionel Roy	15-10-41	75 Sqn
NZ404011	Sgt	WYLLIE Thomas Young	8-11-41	75 Sqn
NZ41390	P/O	YOUNIE Lewis Taylor	21-10-41	19 OTU

Note

Before the war was over, many New Zealand families would be dealt a double blow with news that a second (or even a third) son or daughter had died whilst on active service and in respect of this section the parents of Sgt Wilson (NZ40746) would be notified that John's younger brother, Arthur, had been killed (his details are recorded in Part 6 – 1942). F/L Baird's elder brother died in the South Pacific theatre of operations in January 1944, when the Ventura in which he was the navigator crashed into the sea, killing all 10 on board. On the 12th of March 1944, Sgt Reid's brother, serving with the Fleet Air Arm, was killed when he failed to recover his Seafire from a steep dive before plunging into the Irish Sea. Another 1944 casualty was F/O Ernest Berjen Fooks (see entry for P/O Fooks) who is buried near his brother in Brookwood Military Cemetery, having been killed when his 180 Squadron Mitchell collided in the air with a 98 Squadron machine near their Dunsfold base.

It was almost a year to the day following the death of P/O Lund that his parents received another telegram, this time informing them that a second son was missing from air operations (see Part 6 for his details) and by a terrible coincidence a similar missive was sent to George and Ada Wells that added to the grief they had suffered since the loss of George. For the Murdoch family of Upper Hutt, near Wellington, only a mere six months would elapse before the first indication of alarm would arrive with the news that Graham had failed to return from his 18th sortie.

Continuing in this same vein, Sgt Wallace's brother, Utrick, was killed in January 1943, when the Halifax he was piloting crashed in Spanish Morocco. Errol Martyn is not certain if Utrick had been detached from Bomber Command to Ferry Command for a one off flight to the Middle East, or whether he had been posted to this theatre of operations. In the same year, 1943, Sgt Bishop's brother disappeared without trace while serving with 207 Squadron (see Part 7), while 1944 claimed the life of Colin Thompson's brother, William, in a fatal Sunderland crash on the island of St. Kitts to the west of the Outer Hebrides, seven of the 10 crew being New Zealanders.

The deaths of John Black and Eric Lloyd on the 8th of November were the precursors for more family tragedies with both airmen losing brothers, Lloyd's in the Middle East on the 19th of April, 1942, while serving with 37 Squadron and Black's younger brother, Norman, during a tour of duty with 76 Squadron. By coincidence both boys died whilst operating against Berlin, Norman's Halifax being lost without trace on the 1st of March, 1943.

And, finally, in respect of this section reference to three who fell in 1944 and whose parents had been notified earlier of their brothers' loss; George Vincent Bentley Patterson, Robert Eric Leigh and Leslie Williams. The first two named are commemorated in Part 8, while P/O Williams died over Italy while flying Spitfires with 43 Squadron.

POLISH AIR FORCE
personnel

P.782122	Sgt	ADAMIK Wilhelm	21-10-41	304 Sqn
P.781252	Cpl	ANDRZEJCZUK Waclaw	11-06-41	301 Sqn
P.792784	Sgt	ASTRAMOWICZ Teofan	29-09-41	18 OTU
P.781177	Sgt	BANKOWSKI Piotr Ryszard	19-06-41	300 Sqn
P.781148	Sgt	BARACZ Eugeniusz Jerzy	23-12-41	305 Sqn
P.793337	Sgt	BERGER Antoni	15-04-41	304 Sqn
P.0734	F/O	BERNAS Kazimierz Tytus	19-06-41	301 Sqn
P.780723	Sgt	BIALEK Stanislaw	7-05-41	304 Sqn
P.0004	S/L	BLAZEJEWSKI Jan	17-12-41	304 Sqn
P.792786	LAC	BLUSZCZ Jerzy	29-07-41	Bramcote
P.782088	LAC	BOGUSZEWSKI Wladyslaw Sylvester	21-10-41	304 Sqn
P.780232	Sgt	BOJAKOWSKI Tadeusz	9-05-41	301 Sqn
P.780034	Sgt	BONKOWSKI Roman	19-06-41	301 Sqn
P.1543	P/O	BORZECKI Stanislaw Jozef	21-10-41	304 Sqn
P.0126	F/O	BRYK Antoni	17-10-41	305 Sqn
P.0238	F/O	BRZOZOWSKI Wladyslaw Franciszek	9-05-41	301 Sqn
P.784493	Sgt	BURAK Antoni	15-07-41	305 Sqn
P.780447	Sgt	BUSZKO Eugeniusz	27-09-41	305 Sqn
P.784720	Sgt	CEGLINSKI Kazimierz	18-08-41	300 Sqn
P.780821	Sgt	CHOWANSKI Zygmunt Jan	12-06-41	300 Sqn
P.0006	F/O	CHRISTMAN Rudolf	15-04-41	304 Sqn
P.76663	F/O	CHROSTOWSKI Tadeusz	7-08-41	300 Sqn
P.793330	Sgt	CHRZANOWSKI Bernard	21-03-41	301 Sqn
P.76667	F/L	CICHOWSKI Wladyslaw Henryk	7-08-41	300 Sqn
P.1445	F/O	CIOCH Stanislaw	9-08-41	301 Sqn
P.780970	Sgt	CUPRYK Stanislaw	29-09-41	18 OTU
P.782182	Sgt	CYMBORSKI Jan Adam	6-02-41	304 Sqn
P.793025	Sgt	CZERNIEJEWSKI Marian Jozef	18-07-41	304 Sqn
P.780554	Sgt	DOMANSKI Jozef	19-06-41	300 Sqn
P.780672	Sgt	DORMAN Jan Piotr	9-05-41	305 Sqn
P.780327	Sgt	DROZDZ Jozef	28-05-41	304 Sqn
P.0022	P/O	DUCHNICKI Stanislaw Feliks	7-05-41	304 Sqn
P.1346	F/O	DUDEK Ignacy Walenty	9-05-41	301 Sqn
P.1372	P/O	DZIUBINSKI Tadeusz Kazimierz	2-01-41	301 Sqn
P.76622	S/L	FLORYANOWICZ Stefan	1-01-41	301 Sqn
P.793315	Sgt	FRANASZCZUK Stanislaw	19-06-41	301 Sqn
P.780728	Sgt	GACHOWSKI Ludwik	1-01-41	301 Sqn
P.782652	Sgt	GAIK Zygmunt Pawel	29-04-41	18 OTU
P.781568	LAC	GAWAD Stanislaw	2-10-41	301 Sqn
P.0025	F/O	GISMAN Adam Edward	21-10-41	304 Sqn
P.793867	Sgt	GOLABEK Boguslaw	17-12-41	304 Sqn
P.1554	F/O	GOLACKI Czeslaw Stanislaw	23-12-41	305 Sqn
P.780323	Sgt	GOLEBIOWSKI Konstanty	9-05-41	301 Sqn
P.793336	Sgt	GUZOWSKI Adam Marian	1-01-41	301 Sqn
P.780156	Sgt	GWOZDZ Zdzislaw	9-05-41	305 Sqn
P.782237	Sgt	HAMPEL Leon	7-05-41	304 Sqn
P.783457	Sgt	HEJNOWSKI Jan	17-10-41	305 Sqn
P.780324	Sgt	HEJNOWSKI Jan Karol	1-01-41	301 Sqn
P.780041	Sgt	HERMAN Otton	4-07-41	300 Sqn
P.0767	F/O	HERMANOWSKI Stanislaw	4-10-41	18 OTU
P.780461	Sgt	HILDEBRANDT Stefan	17-10-41	305 Sqn
P.793746	Sgt	HORAK Andrzej	26-07-41	300 Sqn
P.780645	Sgt	JACHNA Ludwik	4-02-41	18 OTU
P.0483	F/O	JAKIMOWICZ Wladyslaw Zbigniew	26-07-41	300 Sqn
P.0061	F/O	JANOTA-BZOWSKI Jerzy	15-07-41	305 Sqn

P.782247	Sgt	JANUSZKIEWICZ Waclaw	25-06-41	305 Sqn		P.76671	F/O	REWKOWSKI Stanislaw	9-05-41	301 Sqn
P.0624	F/O	JASINSKI Stanislaw Konrad	7-08-41	300 Sqn		P.780346	Sgt	ROGOWSKI Henryk	19-06-41	305 Sqn
P.780326	Sgt	JEZIERSKI Feliks	7-08-41	300 Sqn		P.782473	Sgt	ROZPARA Henryk	23-12-41	305 Sqn
P.793311	Sgt	JONCZYK Jozef	6-02-41	304 Sqn		P.780347	Sgt	RUDLICKI Jerzy	23-04-41	18 OTU
P.0583	P/O	JOZEPAJT Jan	29-09-41	18 OTU		P.781201	Sgt	RUTKOWSKI Hubert	17-12-41	304 Sqn
P.0671	F/O	JURA Edmund	7-08-41	300 Sqn		P.782637	Sgt	RYBAK Waclaw	6-08-41	305 Sqn
P.780870	Sgt	KACZALSKI Czeslaw	15-07-41	305 Sqn		P.0114	F/O	RYSZKIEWICZ Mieczyslaw Jozef	3-05-41	305 Sqn
P.780732	Sgt	KARCZ Ludwik	9-05-41	305 Sqn		P.0764	F/O	RZEPA Stanislaw Wincenty	25-07-41	304 Sqn
P.0336	F/O	KARCZEWSKI Leszek Jerzy	25-07-41	304 Sqn		P.1438	P/O	SABLIK Oskar	23-04-41	18 OTU
P.781658	Sgt	KASIANOWSKI Gustaw	2-01-41	301 Sqn		P.1414	F/O	SADOWSKI Boleslaw	2-01-41	301 Sqn
P.76854	S/L	KIELICH Kazimierz Maciej	25-06-41	305 Sqn		P.0089	F/O	SAFERNA Mieczyslaw Julian	6-08-41	305 Sqn
P.0486	F/O	KLATT Bronislaw	18-07-41	304 Sqn		P.780617	Sgt	SALAMON Boleslaw	25-07-41	304 Sqn
P.780877	Sgt	KLIMIUK Ryszard	21-10-41	304 Sqn		P.780200	Sgt	SAWICZ Kazimierz	2-01-41	301 Sqn
P.0301	F/O	KOMLACZ Jan	17-12-41	304 Sqn		P.781405	Sgt	SIECZKA Walenty	19-06-41	300 Sqn
P.780577	Sgt	KORAB-BRZOZOWSKI Hubert	30-06-41	301 Sqn		P.780672	Sgt	SIKORSKI Henryk Franciszek	9-05-41	305 Sqn
P.780686	Sgt	KORCZYK Tadeusz	28-09-41	305 Sqn		P.1141	P/O	SIWIEC Jan	23-12-41	305 Sqn
P.76670	P/O	KORYCINSKI Jozef	21-03-41	301 Sqn		P.780434	Sgt	SLOMA Mieczyslaw	26-07-41	300 Sqn
P.0976	F/O	KOSOWSKI Marian Boleslaw	17-10-41	305 Sqn		P.0446	F/O	SMOLIK Zygmunt	26-10-41	18 OTU
P.0080	F/O	KOWALCZE Stanislaw	12-06-41	305 Sqn		P.0029	P/O	SOBIERALSKI Feliks	7-05-41	304 Sqn
P.782123	Sgt	KOZLOWSKI Edward	9-08-41	301 Sqn		P.1440	P/O	SOCHARSKI Maciej Wojciech	9-05-41	305 Sqn
P.76666	F/O	KRASSOWSKI Jerzy	19-06-41	301 Sqn		P.0331	F/O	SRZEDNICKI Tadeusz	26-07-41	300 Sqn
P.781563	Sgt	KRAWCZYK Jerzy	12-06-41	305 Sqn		P.76608	G/C	STACHON Boleslaw Feliks	4-07-41	Swinderby
P.792827	Sgt	KSIEZYC Jan	29-09-41	18 OTU		P.793182	Sgt	STANKIEWICZ Stanislaw	17-08-41	305 Sqn
P.76652	F/O	KULA Kazimierz	4-07-41	300 Sqn		P.0057	F/L	STEFANICKI Tadeusz Jan	12-06-41	305 Sqn
P.76626	F/O	KULBACKI Hieronim	1-01-41	301 Sqn		P.0885	F/O	STENOCKI Stefan Marian	27-10-41	304 Sqn
P.782286	Sgt	KUROPATWA Stanislaw	18-08-41	300 Sqn		P.0036	F/O	STEPIEN Zygfryd	29-09-41	18 OTU
P.781880	Sgt	KUROWSKI Zdzislaw	23-12-41	305 Sqn		P.0094	F/O	SUKIENNIK Jerzy Jan Stanislaw	6-08-41	305 Sqn
P.0009	F/O	KUSZCZYNSKI Bronislaw	28-05-41	304 Sqn		P.0110	F/O	SUKNIEWICZ Marian	5-09-41	18 OTU
P.0401	F/O	KUZIAN Boleslaw	18-07-41	304 Sqn		P.780356	Sgt	SUWALSKI Kazimierz	17-12-41	304 Sqn
P.783272	LAC	KWIATKOWSKI Henryk Rafal	4-02-41	18 OTU		P.793771	Sgt	SYLWESTROWICZ Jan	18-07-41	304 Sqn
P.784662	Sgt	LANG Tadeusz	17-10-41	305 Sqn		P.781233	LAC	SYCZ Kazimierz	10-03-41	18 OTU
P.782338	Sgt	LASKOS Zbigniew	26-10-41	18 OTU		P.0014	F/O	SYM Antoni	7-05-41	304 Sqn
P.780108	Sgt	LENCZOWSKI Kazimierz	21-03-41	301 Sqn		P.76740	F/O	SZCZODROWSKI Marian	17-12-41	304 Sqn
P.780482	Sgt	LEWONIEC Zbigniew Stanislaw	25-06-41	305 Sqn		P.781514	Sgt	SZCZUKOWSKI Czeslaw	7-08-41	300 Sqn
P.781385	Sgt	LEYCHE Jerzy Slawomir	27-09-41	305 Sqn		P.783508	Sgt	SZOSTAK Eugeniusz	29-04-41	18 OTU
P.781604	Sgt	LICHOTA Wojciech	6-02-41	304 Sqn		P.781654	Sgt	TEGOWSKI Czeslaw	23-06-41	301 Sqn
P.780336	Sgt	LIPECKI Antoni	9-05-41	301 Sqn		P.792778	Sgt	TEODORKO Jan	26-10-41	18 OTU
P.0097	F/O	LISINSKI Antoni Zenon	15-07-41	305 Sqn		P.782062	Sgt	TOFIN Stanislaw	6-02-41	304 Sqn
P.0077	F/O	LUCKI Jan	17-10-41	305 Sqn		P.783678	Sgt	TOMASZEWSKI Janusz	18-07-41	304 Sqn
P.781190	Sgt	LYDKA Mieczyslaw	26-10-41	18 OTU		P.780254	Sgt	URBANOWICZ Wladyslaw	4-07-41	300 Sqn
P.783042	Sgt	MAJEWSKI Edward	17-08-41	305 Sqn		P.780751	Sgt	WAGNER Andrzej Antoni	19-06-41	301 Sqn
P.0090	F/O	MALAK Waclaw Jozef	3-05-41	305 Sqn		P.792837	Sgt	WARDENSKI Feliks	17-08-41	305 Sqn
P.780085	Sgt	MANASIAK Marian	19-06-41	301 Sqn		P.0016	P/O	WAROCZEWSKI Jan Stanislaw	28-05-41	304 Sqn
P.76831	F/O	MIARCZYNSKI Roman Czeslaw	4-10-41	18 OTU		P.781021	Sgt	WASILENKO Wiktor	27-09-41	305 Sqn
P.780649	Sgt	MIECZKOWSKI Jan Roman	4-07-41	300 Sqn		P.0040	F/O	WIECZOREK Cezary	28-05-41	304 Sqn
P.1439	F/O	MINKIEWICZ Andrzej	4-02-41	18 OTU		P.0333	F/O	WISZNIEWSKI Jan Leonard Maria	9-08-41	301 Sqn
P.0776	F/O	MIONDLIKOWSKI Alfons	17-08-41	305 Sqn		P.792760	Sgt	WITCZAK Stanislaw	25-06-41	305 Sqn
P.780601	Sgt	MITKOWSKI Stanislaw Aleksander				P.780144	Sgt	WITKOWSKI Zygmunt	25-07-41	304 Sqn
			15-07-41	305 Sqn		P.781314	Sgt	WOJCIECHOWSKI Stefan Joachim	4-02-41	18 OTU
P.782362	Sgt	MRUK Kazimierz	12-06-41	305 Sqn		P.0076	F/O	WOJTOWICZ Marian Jan	12-06-41	305 Sqn
P.76678	P/O	MURAWSKI Boleslaw Roland	2-01-41	301 Sqn		P.780217	Sgt	ZEMMLER Feliks	26-07-41	300 Sqn
P.1374		MUSIAL Jan H. G.	25-07-41	304 Sqn		P.0356	F/O	ZEREBECKI Kazimierz	19-06-41	305 Sqn
P.0092	F/O	NOWAK Alfons Antoni Szymon	23-12-41	305 Sqn		P.0074	F/O	ZIRKWITZ Aleksander Aleksy	12-06-41	305 Sqn
P.0096	F/O	OKONSKI Brunon Pawel	10-07-41	305 Sqn		P.792950	Sgt	ZOLNOWSKI Wladyslaw	6-05-41	304 Sqn
P.76680	P/O	OLSZYNA Marian	1-01-41	301 Sqn		P.780720	Sgt	ZUWALA Zbigniew	25-07-41	304 Sqn
P.781172	Sgt	ORYNEK Jan Piotr	4-02-41	18 OTU		P.781199	Sgt	ZWOLSKI Jan	29-04-41	18 OTU
P.782309	Sgt	OSTROWSKI Jan	15-07-41	305 Sqn		P.782065	Sgt	ZYKOW Mikolaj	21-10-41	304 Sqn
P.780419	Sgt	PALENICZEK Wladyslaw	19-06-41	300 Sqn						
P.780498	Sgt	PERKOWSKI Zbigniew Jan	4-02-41	18 OTU						

Note

P.793339 Sgt PIETRUSZEWSKI Wieslaw Leszek 15-04-41 304 Sqn

LAC Bluszcz, who was on the photographic staff at Bramcote, was mortally injured after being struck by a propeller. He is buried in Nuneaton.

P.1379	P/O	PIETRUSZKA Stanislaw	23-06-41	301 Sqn	
P.781036	Sgt	PISARSKI Stanislaw	9-05-41	305 Sqn	
P.793615	Sgt	PLACHTA Jan	17-08-41	305 Sqn	
P.782026	Sgt	PLIS Henryk	21-10-41	304 Sqn	
P.781767	Sgt	PODZIEMSKI Jan	18-07-41	304 Sqn	
P.782061	Sgt	PRZECLAWSKI Stanislaw	17-08-41	305 Sqn	
P.1162	F/O	REBUSZYNSKI Wlodzimierz	25-07-41	301 Sqn	

FREE FRENCH AIR FORCE
personnel

–	Lt	LAURENT A. J. De V.	28-11-41	138 Sqn

ROYAL INDIAN AIR FORCE
personnel

–	P/O	CHAUDHURY Kali Prasad	18-06-41	10 OTU
–	P/O	DASTUR Rustom Nariman	31-08-41	12 Sqn
–	P/O	KHOSLA Chander Parkash	31-08-41	12 Sqn

Note
To the best of my knowledge, the three officers named above were the only Royal Indian Air Force personnel to lose their lives posted to Bomber Command.

WOMEN's AUXILIARY AIR FORCE
personnel

2020146	ACW2 HELEY Esme Joan	30-12-41	Dishforth

Note
Esme Joan Heley is believed to have been the first airwoman to die in the service of Bomber Command. Cremated at Harrogate Crematorium, her age and next of kin details are not known.

Attached personnel

FLEET AIR ARM

–	S/Lt HOAD MiD Peter John (detached from HMS *Daedalus*)	27-03-41	

Note
This officer had been attached to 78 Squadron and the circumstances of his death on bombing operations are explained in Volume 2, page 35.

UNITED STATES ARMY AIR FORCE

–	Lt	BRADLEY F.	22-06-41	90 Sqn
–	1Lt	HENDRICKS Laird W.	28-07-41	90 Sqn

Note
Notwithstanding America's neutrality, the two officers named lost their lives during 90 Squadron's brief flirtation with the Boeing Fortress. Both had arrived in the United Kingdom as members of the United States Army Air Corps and only two days had elapsed twixt the retitling of this force and Lt Bradley's death on air operations, the circumstances of which are reported on page 72 of Volume 2.

Postscript

1941, as written in the last paragraph of the introduction to this part, was a dark year in the annals of the Second World War and in respect of Bomber Command well in excess of 5,000 airmen had died in the pursance of thwarting Nazi ambitions. As will be observed, the four major air forces that were operating alongside the Royal Air Force in 1941 bore their share of grief. Included in the Royal Air Force section are the names of more than a few gallant Czechoslovakians, while a still-neutral America witnessed the deaths of two of their United States Army Air Force (USAAF) personnel. The threat of a sudden and violent end was never far from the minds of those now participating in the bombing campaign. Throughout the past twelve months the enemy had been strengthening its defences, particularly in Holland where the majority of the Luftwaffe's night-fighter units were based (the threat from day fighters had eased now that the Wehrmacht was advancing deep into Russia). Here, at the behest of General Josef Kammhuber, early warning radar stations had mushroomed along the coast, while numerous searchlight batteries were incorporated into the defensive chain. To reach Germany's heartland was fast becoming an extremely dangerous business and vigilance on the part of the bomber crews was a prerequisite for their survival. And, having pierced the first and second lines of defence, and then having entered the target area, the bomber crews invariably had to run the deadly gauntlet of more searchlights and accompanying anti-aircraft barrages.

Losses, inevitably, crept upwards so that by the end of 1941, few at squadron level would not have been concerned at their chances of survival. Being so fully aware of the inherent dangers that they faced each time their names appeared on the duty rosters it says much for the stoical qualities of these young men now streaming out of the training schools and into the maelstrom of operational life. Some had already survived heart-stopping moments in the course of their training, and yet so few faltered. Time and time again they would rise to the pinnacle of amazing acts of courage and self-sacrifice in the execution of their duties. Thus, it will be appropriate to end this brief postscript with a random selection of citations taken from the *Supplements to The London Gazette*. Pride of place goes to an extraordinarily brave New Zealander, Sgt James Allen Ward, who gained his pilot's wings on the 18th of January, 1941, and having arrived in the United Kingdom and finished off his training at 20 OTU at Lossiemouth reported to Feltwell, home of 75 Squadron, on the 13th of June. Like all new arrivals James Ward was assigned to an experienced captain, in his case S/L R. P. Widdowson, a Canadian, and it was with Widdowson that, on the 7th/8th of July, 1941, he found himself on the way to Munster. What happened during the course of this near fateful sortie is best told in the words of the official citation, which was published on the 5th of August, 1941, *'On the night of 7th July, 1941, Sergeant Ward was second pilot of a Wellington returning from an attack on Munster. When flying over the Zuider Zee at 13,000 feet, the aircraft was attacked from beneath by a Messerschmitt 110 which secured hits with cannon shell and incendiary bullets. The rear gunner was wounded in the foot but delivered a burst of fire which sent the enemy fighter down, apparently out of control.*

'Fire then broke out near the starboard engine and, fed by petrol from a split pipe, quickly gained an alarming hold and threatened to spread to the entire wing. The crew forced a hole in the fuselage and made strenuous efforts to reduce the fire with extinguishers and even the coffee in their vacuum flasks, but without success. They were then warned to be ready to abandon the aircraft.

'As a last resort, Sergeant Ward volunteered to make an attempt to smother the fire with an engine cover which happened to be in use as a cushion. At first he proposed to discard his parachute, to reduce wind resistance, but was finally persuaded to take it. A rope from the dinghy was tied to him, though this was of little help and might have become a danger had he been blown off the aircraft. With the help of the navigator, he then climbed through the narrow astro-hatch and put on his parachute. The bomber was flying at a reduced speed but the wind pressure must have been sufficient to render the operation one of extreme difficulty.

'Breaking the fabric to make hand and foot holds where necessary, and also taking advantage of existing holes in the fabric, Sergeant Ward succeeded in descending three feet to the wing and proceeding another three feet to a position behind the engine, despite the slipstream from the airscrew, which nearly blew him off the wing. Lying in this precarious position, he smothered the fire in the wing fabric and tried to push the cover into the hole in the wing and on to the leaking pipe from which the fire came. As soon as he removed his hand, however, the terrific wind blew the cover out and when he tried again it was lost. Tired as he was, he was able

with the navigator's assistance to make successfully the perilous journey back into the aircraft.

'There was now no danger of the fire spreading, as there was no fabric left nearby, and in due course it burnt itself out. When the aircraft was nearly home some petrol which had collected in the wing blazed up furiously but died down quite suddenly. A safe landing was then made despite the damage sustained by the aircraft. The flight home had been made possible by the gallant action of Sergeant Ward in extinguishing the fire on the wing in circumstances of the greatest difficulty and at the risk of his life.'

The aftermath of this operation resulted in a DFC for S/L Widdowson, a DFM for Sgt A. R. J. Box RNZAF, the wounded tail gunner, and for Sgt Ward the VC. Ward's was the 8th air VC of the Second World War, six of which had been gained by airmen from the bomber squadrons. Within weeks of gaining this most prestigious of honours Sgt James Allen Ward VC RNZAF was dead, shot down by flak over Hamburg on the night of 15th/16th September, 1941.

Next, a citation that appeared in the *Supplement* for the 28th of January, 1941, for DFMs awarded to Sgt Anthony Eyre Jackson and Sgt George Wannan Turner, both of 83 Squadron, and which describes their devotion to duty during a hazardous attack on an airfield in France during the previous December. Although the precise date of the action is not quoted, I suspect it may have been on the 8th/9th of the month when 90 aircraft, including Hampdens, raided airfields in Germany and in France, 'Sergeants Jackson and Turner were pilot and wireless operator air gunner respectively in an aircraft detailed to carry out an attack on an aerodrome near Bordeaux in the early morning of a day in December 1940. Owing to intense darkness, low cloud and uncertainty of position Sergeant Jackson considered there was insufficient time to reach this target and decided to attack the submarine base at Lorient. This target was identified from a height of 1,200 feet and the attack was successfully carried out. Anti-aircraft and searchlight opposition became intense and the aircraft was hit three or four times. One shell burst in the navigator's cockpit and seriously wounded the navigator and destroyed maps and charts. Sergeant Turner, however, succeeded in obtaining communication with a home station from which he received diversion instructions in consequence of fog at his own aerodrome. He then assisted the pilot to locate this aerodrome, sent messages requesting the attendance of an ambulance and medical aid for the wounded navigator. In spite of the damage done to his aircraft, Sergeant Jackson succeeded in making a safe landing. The courage and devotion to duty displayed by these airmen on this and other occasions have been of the highest order.'

On the 6th/7th of April, 1941, Jackson, now commissioned, failed to return from a minelaying sortie off Brest and, along with his crew, he is commemorated on the Runnymede Memorial. Sgt Turner, I am happy to report, survived the war, his place on that fateful April night having been taken by Sgt William Anthony Foster. By an odd quirk of coincidence the same *Supplement* carried another dual award where one of the recipients survived and the other, sadly, perished, 'Pilot Officer Dickinson and Sergeant Thompson were the pilot and air gunner respectively of an aircraft detailed to attack a target at Gelsenkirchen. Owing to adverse weather conditions they were unable to locate their primary objective but successfully bombed a factory near Recklinghausen as an alternative. After passing Eindhoven, on the return journey, an illuminated dummy flare path was observed. Pilot Officer Dickinson thereupon altered course for Gilze-Rijan (sic) aerodrome where two hostile aircraft, showing navigation lights, were seen flying in a westerly direction. Pursuing one of these for about 30 miles, Pilot Officer Dickinson skilfully manoeuvred his aircraft and enabled Sergeant Thompson to engage and eventually shoot down the enemy. Pilot Officer Dickinson and Sergeant Thompson showed great courage and initiative throughout the operation.'

Sergeant Thompson, the air gunner lived to see the end of the war but his resourceful skipper, now promoted to F/L, was killed when his 110 Squadron Blenheim was shot down over Holland (during operations against Hamburg) by Ofw Paul Gildner on the night of the 13th/14th of March, 1941.

Appropriately, in view of the tasks demanded of them and in recognition of their total dedication in trying to carry them out, I end this selection of citations with one taken from the *Supplement* issued on the 23rd of May, 1941. It concerns a Blenheim pilot from 82 Squadron, F/L Ralph Eric Tallis, 'In April, 1941, this officer was detailed to seek and attack enemy shipping off the Norwegian coast. Flying among the Norwegian islands, he observed a newly built runway on a small island and five Messerschmitts on the ground with their engines running; two others were flying round the aerodrome. Despite considerable anti-aircraft fire and the presence of the two fighters, Flight Lieutenant Tallis carried out a daring attack from a very low height. One of his bombs burst in the centre of the runway and another exploded beneath one of the enemy fighters as it was taking off, completely destroying it. The aircraft on the ground were also machine gunned. After the attack in company with another of our aircraft, he was engaged in resisting the attacks of three enemy fighters for about sixteen minutes. He has carried out numerous operational flights and has at all times displayed great courage and a keen determination to reach his objective under any conditions.'

F/L Tallis did not live to read this citation, or (I suspect) even to collect his well merited DFC for on the 29th of April, 1941, and while operating from Lossiemouth he failed to return from a shipping strike in Norwegian waters. In time his body was recovered and his grave is now located in the British plot at Sola Churchyard, some 13 kilometres south of Stavanger in Norway.

To conclude this postscript I quote from a letter received in the spring of 2005, from Neil Campbell who, with the rest of his 61 Squadron crew, survived their Hampden being shot down on the night of the 2nd/3rd of June, 1941, while raiding Dusseldorf. His description of what happened surely mirrors what befell so many bomber crews, not only in 1941, but throughout the long torturous years of the bombing campaign and well illustrates that slender thread that stood between survival and oblivion. It also sets the record straight in respect of my entry on page 61 of my second volume devoted to Bomber Command's losses, 'We approached Dusseldorf from the west in appalling weather, thick cloud lit up by many searchlights. We suddenly came into a clear area, and a lot of flak came up. Not being able to locate our position we decided to jettison our bombs and head for home.

'Shortly after some flak exploded under our tail which turned us on our backs and we started to dive vertically, soon to have the bomb aimers' Perspex panel blow in. We prepared to bail out, but regained control and decided to stay aboard. Light flak streamed up at us, now flying at about 1,500 feet. The port engine caught fire, was extinguished, but forced us to force land.

'I believe the time of landing must have been between 0100 and 0200, somewhere near Borken, north of Recklinghausen, where I spent six weeks in hospital.

'I heard later in POW camps that many crews turned for home that night because of the weather. Maybe that was the reason for the heavy and very accurate flak.'

Part 6

Bomber Command Roll of Honour – 1942

My introduction to the previous section finished with a hint that all was not well in respect of the conduct of the night bombing campaign. Following the most costly raid to the German capital in December 1941, Sir Richard Peirse had been ordered to attend the Prime Minister at Chequers for what must have been a most uncomfortable *tete-a-tete*, the outcome of which left his future career firmly at the whim of Churchill. For a few weeks, while a new policy was thrashed out by the War Cabinet and the high priests at the Air Ministry, Bomber Command's scope was severely restricted. Thus, perhaps, it came as no great surprise to the staff at High Wycombe when Sir Richard cleared his desk and departed early in the New Year for pastures new. His successor, Air-Vice Marshal Sir Arthur T. Harris, and his champion Portal, were in the United States of America when the Prime Minister (present, too, along with Beaverbrook and the Chiefs of Staff), on Portal's advice, confirmed his appointment, while in the interim period before he could occupy the vacant chair, Bomber Command's day-to-day business would be in the temporary, but capable, hands of the Air Officer Commanding No.3 Group, Air-Vice Marshal John Baldwin.

The arrival in mid-February 1942 of the new Air Officer Commanding-in-Chief marked the beginning of a new chapter in Bomber Command's history, which until now had been full of promise but short on delivery, though to be fair to the recently departed Peirse the circumstances in which he often found himself were not of his own making and within the limits of the material at his disposal he had achieved some success, particularly in the spring and summer of 1941, with attacks on port facilities in the Occupied Countries and in raids against centres of production in Germany concerned with submarine and ship building. It is, therefore, puzzling to envisage how the direction of Bomber Command could have been run more effectively, bearing in mind that whoever was at the helm, he would have had to conduct his operations within the guidelines of the directives agreed by the War Cabinet.

But now it was the turn of the new broom and within weeks of his arrival Harris was stamping his authority on everything that came under the umbrella of his control.

It is now important to say, at the outset of Harris's tenure of duty that he (Harris) was not the instigator of what, initially, had been identified as *area targets* and in course of time would become known as *area bombing*. Discussions at War Cabinet level as early as the summer of 1941, had agreed that trying to knock out individual targets, oil refining plant to take but one example, was a failing ambition and that by targeting an industrial *area* the general spread of bombing might improve the chance of success. Furthermore, it was mooted that German morale could well be effected by a more widespread approach to the night bombing campaign, though in truth the German citizen would prove to have as stout a heart as his British counterpart when tested to the limit from the spring of 1943 onwards. Thus, the new directive sanctioning a change in direction landed on Baldwin's desk two weeks in advance of Harris crossing the threshold of his latest post.

A clear message of intent came within months of Harris assuming command when the German High Command was stunned by three massive attacks, now commonly referred to as the '1,000 plan' series of operations directed against Cologne, Essen and Bremen (a precursor for these attacks can be traced back to the Palm Sunday raid by 234 aircraft, flying in three waves, on the Baltic port of Lubeck where a major factor had been the use of experienced crews making up the majority of the first wave and, for the time, a determined attempt to concentrate the bombers over the target into as short a timescale as possible). These three raids were a chilling portent of things to come and for the German population at large the writing was truly on the wall.

Raids on this scale would not be repeated for many a month, but Harris would call upon his OTUs (these establishments were major contributors in all three '1,000 plan' attacks) in the high summer of the year for operations against Hamburg and targets in the Ruhr and in the execution of eight attacks (including the visits to Cologne, Essen and Bremen) the training formations lost 128 aircraft, either directly to enemy action or in crashes within the United Kingdom.

But, to return to the beginning of 1942, with the Command seemingly drifting in purpose and with the squadrons of the five bomber groups still, in the main, equipped with aircraft that were totally unsuited for the tasks demanded from them, it was in this sphere that a sea change was about to take place. After a stuttering introduction to service of the Stirling and Halifax types, these two bombers were beginning to perform reasonably well, though in the case of the former scope for further development was limited. However, on Christmas Eve, 1941, the first Lancasters had arrived at Waddington for 44 Squadron and much to the delight of all concerned, this new addition to the ranks of Bomber Command's heavy bombers was proving to be a winner in all respects. And, still shrouded in secrecy, flight testing of De Havilland's twin-engine *wooden wonder*, the Mosquito had been in progress for just over a year (the prototype having made its debut flight in late November, 1940) and by the close of 1941, examples of the bomber version were coming off the production lines, though such were the demands from other commands Harris was unable to procure as many examples as he would have liked and only three squadrons could be formed during the year under review.

Nevertheless, well before the year was out the Command's Blenheims, Hampdens and Whitleys had been withdrawn from operational service and the disappointing Manchester was replaced within No.5 Group by its successor, the Lancaster. Two other types made their appearance in 1942; both twin-engine, both American in origin and both destined for No.2 Group. Of one, the Ventura, it cannot be said that it was a singular success, but the Mitchell was well received and alongside its sturdy counterpart, the Boston, provided the Group with a very useful medium bomber. It was, however, the last full year of participation by No.2 Group in Bomber Command affairs and though new squadrons were formed, others that had borne the brunt of the terrible losses inflicted during 1940 and 1941, were transferred to the Middle East and Far East theatres. Within the operational bomber groups, additional squadrons were added as the strength of the command increased and before the year was out the contribution from the Canadians had more than doubled with ten squadrons in existence serving, principally, with No.4 Group (405 Squadron being detached to Beaulieu late in the year for temporary duty with Coastal Command). Furthermore, a pattern of future establishment was in place; squadrons within No.1 Group and No.5 Group were destined to become all Lancaster equipped (the eleven squadrons that constituted the strength of No.5 Group in December, 1942 were already fully equipped with this type), while the Stirling and Halifax types would, in the main, be concentrated within No.3 Group and No.4 Group respectively.

Transfers between groups was also a feature of 1942, No.3 Group, in particular, witnessing many changes with no less than nine of its Wellington squadrons being assigned to other groups (in the majority of cases for immediate conversion to Lancasters) or overseas commands. Noteworthy of these transfers was the loss to Coastal Command of the sole Czechoslovakian unit in Bomber Command, 311 Squadron, which left East Wretham in late April for Aldergrove in Northern Ireland. In addition, 7 Squadron and its Stirlings was given up to the embryo Path Finder Force (PFF), which was established in mid-August 1942, thus depleting further the strength of the group which by December 1942, amounted to six squadrons equipped with Stirlings, one Wellington unit (115 Squadron) and two squadrons (138 Squadron and 161 Squadron) with a mixture of types, ranging from single-engine Lysanders to four-engine Halifaxes, assigned to *Special Duties*, though administered by Group headquarters. Of PFF, five squadrons formed the initial establishment and though its first forays as a target marking force were not an unqualified success, with the introduction of *Oboe* (six *Oboe* fitted Mosquitoes from 109 Squadron carried out the first bombing operation, with this device, during the night of 20th/21st of December, 1942) as a navigational and bombing radar aid, so the potential worth of PFF to the night bombing campaign was recognised. Although not specifically designed for PFF, *Gee* had been introduced earlier in the year (8th/9th of March, against Essen) and by the late summer this aid to navigation was coming into general usage.

Running in parallel with the increases in operational strength was the continued expansion of the OTUs, while the four-engine Conversion Units, few in number at the start of the year were, by December, on a firm footing and operating under the aegis of the main bomber groups, and with the title of Heavy Conversion Unit (HCU) applied to their formations. Sadly, of course, with this increase in units came a sharp rise in casualties as operational losses (particularly those now being inflicted on the squadrons by the scourge of the Luftwaffe's night-fighter units) and training accidents mounted against the background of war where much still needed to be done before victory could be assured. However, the year that had begun with the Axis forces of Germany, Italy and Japan seemingly in the ascendancy ended with many of their hopes dashed, particularly in the deserts of North Africa where Rommel's Afrika Korps was in full retreat and being squeezed by the newly arrived American forces in the east* and Montgomery's battle-hardened armies in the west. And, the once all conquering Wehrmacht that had swept into Russia in June 1941, had, at last, been brought to a stop amidst the bitter cold of winter with the Soviets successfully carrying the battle in their favour as an all-important victory for the Red armies at Stalingrad was about to be realised.

These few shafts of sunlight had not been gained without terrible sacrifice and though the outcome of land operations at the close of 1942, were beyond the influence of Bomber Command, the now near nightly attacks on Nazi Germany were contributing to the gradual grinding down of any lingering hope that the German High Command might have for outright victory.

* *Operation Torch* was launched in late October 1942, in the aftermath of which Bomber Command carried out a series of raids against industrial targets in northern Italy.

ROYAL AIR FORCE,
AUXILIARY AIR FORCE and
ROYAL AIR FORCE (VOLUNTEER RESERVE)
personnel

1199343	Sgt	ABBAS Philip Robert	5-05-42	103 Sqn
107179	P/O	ABBERTON John	11-08-42	218 Sqn
1326329	Sgt	ABBOTT Hezekiah	26-06-42	115 Sqn
120353	F/O	ABEL Jack Sydney	6-12-42	115 Sqn
978002	F/S	ABERCROMBIE Ronald Ross	11-11-42	57 Sqn
1177690	Sgt	ABRAHAM Arthur Leslie	21-12-42	57 Sqn
109094	P/O	ACKERNLEY Peter Rowland	18-12-42	1474 Flt
810144	Sgt	ACTON Norman	31-05-42	405 Sqn
965668	Sgt	ACTON Norman	24-07-42	149 Sqn
1234879	Sgt	ADAMS Alfred Joseph	11-09-42	10 OTU
1293087	Sgt	ADAMS Basil Andrew	15-01-42	104 Sqn
46084	F/L	ADAMS Dennis	29-08-42	88 Sqn
1377699	Sgt	ADAMS Desire Ernest Charles	27-06-42	150 Sqn
117416	P/O	ADAMS Francis James	16-09-42	12 OTU
932367	Sgt	ADAMS James Richard Branston	18-02-42	420 Sqn
657341	Sgt	ADAMS Kenneth Thomas John	8-11-42	9 Sqn
759300	F/S	ADAMS Reginald Thomas	30-06-42	405 Sqn
1381515	Sgt	ADAMS Wilfred Bertie	7-05-42	78 Sqn
960212	Sgt	ADAMS William Edward	20-12-42	76 Sqn
1167110	Sgt	ADAMSON James Alexander	13-08-42	7 Sqn
645659	F/S	ADAMSON DFM William	3-07-42	109 Sqn
544454	F/S	ADDERLY DFM Albert	24-05-42	1483 Flt
1208366	Sgt	ADDIS John Henry	25-03-42	75 Sqn
110134	P/O	ADDIS Ryland George	26-06-42	12 OTU
748538	F/S	ADDY DFM John Cedric	17-01-42	27 OTU
1332609	Sgt	ADEY Frank	24-10-42	50 Sqn
934201	Sgt	ADEY John Wilson	22-01-42	50 Sqn
1269014	Sgt	ADKINS Henry Charles	8-12-42	15 Sqn
655481	Sgt	ADLAM Alfred Ernest	13-02-42	21 OTU
922704	Sgt	ADNAMS Cyril George	8-12-42	102 Sqn
124742	P/O	AGAR John Robert	11-09-42	25 OTU
632884	Sgt	AGAR Wilfred	29-04-42	156 Sqn
118891	P/O	AINSLIE Robin Alexander	7-09-42	12 Sqn
634671	Sgt	AIREY Eric	20-12-42	103 Sqn
1377687	Sgt	AITCHISON Robert Smiles	19-01-42	9 Sqn
1551157	Sgt	AITKEN Charles	20-08-42	115 Sqn
655412	Sgt	AKERMAN Frederick Samuel	6-08-42	207 Sqn
125994	P/O	ALBERY Robert Lewis	6-10-42	115 Sqn
569046	Sgt	ALBRECHT John Martin Beart	3-12-42	102 Sqn
1204242	Sgt	ALBRIGHTON Edward Thomas	2-04-42	214 Sqn
568297	Sgt	ALDER George [Canada]	29-07-42	1651 CU
1056825	Sgt	ALDERDICE William Yarr	28-04-42	408 Sqn
1314643	Sgt	ALDRIDGE Alan	29-07-42	1651 CU
128049	P/O	ALDRIDGE Henry William	7-09-42	7 Sqn
75471	S/L	ALEXANDER George William	30-06-42	149 Sqn
1382705	Sgt	ALEXANDER Kenneth Joseph [Trinidad]	7-07-42	156 Sqn
1430574	Sgt	ALFORD Dennis	2-09-42	142 Sqn

1553931	Sgt	ALLAN James Calderwood	18-09-42	115 Sqn
1154268	Sgt	ALLAWAY Thomas George Richard	22-07-42	150 Sqn
1021545	Sgt	ALLEN Basil Derrik	16-11-42	149 Sqn
1259470	Sgt	ALLEN Edward Charles	28-08-42	44 Sqn
109054	P/O	ALLEN Eric George Henry	26-07-42	114 Sqn
118637	P/O	ALLEN Frank Edward	1-08-42	107 Sqn
514987	Sgt	ALLEN Frederick George	24-10-42	78 Sqn
1058478	Sgt	ALLEN Harold	20-08-42	61 Sqn
1261123	Sgt	ALLEN Ronald Gillam	29-03-42	75 Sqn
1355784	Sgt	ALLEN Thomas Harold	31-05-42	218 Sqn
1126560	F/S	ALLEN William Stansfield	29-08-42	115 Sqn
1145494	Sgt	ALLINSON Willie	3-09-42	11 OTU
550785	W/O	ALLISON William Royden	2-07-42	109 Sqn
1068457	Sgt	ALLSOPP Arthur	30-07-42	149 Sqn
1325072	Sgt	ALLWOOD Kenneth James	24-05-42	13 OTU
1259356	Sgt	ALLWORTH William Henry	10-10-42	150 Sqn
567429	Sgt	ALMOND James Stewart [Canada]	25-06-42	76 Sqn
126504	P/O	ALTER Leslie Israel	3-09-42	19 OTU
1063675	Sgt	AMBLER John Milroy [Canada]	16-02-42	82 Sqn
999543	Sgt	AMERY George Broughton	1-07-42	21 OTU
1377677	Sgt	AMOS Walter David	11-04-42	158 Sqn
910498	Sgt	AMPHLETT John	19-01-42	9 Sqn
101525	F/O	ANDERLE DFC Leo [Czechoslavakia]	10-12-42	138 Sqn
745577	W/O	ANDERSEN DFM Eliner Knud Alfred	20-08-42	75 Sqn
798500	Sgt	ANDERSON Alastair Macdonald [Newfoundland]	2-06-42	10 Sqn
938999	Sgt	ANDERSON Alfred	23-10-42	158 Sqn
1344036	Sgt	ANDERSON Archibald Watt	28-09-42	13 OTU
658255	Sgt	ANDERSON Charles Norman	10-09-42	75 Sqn
102294	F/O	ANDERSON Douglas [Brazil]	20-12-42	76 Sqn
657590	Sgt	ANDERSON George Stewart	20-07-42	106 Sqn
1083374	Sgt	ANDERSON James	21-05-42	21 OTU
591536	Sgt	ANDERSON James Falconer	5-07-42	13 OTU
68813	P/O	ANDERSON John Dalrymple	30-05-42	76 Sqn
1280773	Sgt	ANDERSON Reginald Stephen	24-02-42	106 Sqn
1126302	Sgt	ANDERSON Vincent	29-07-42	7 Sqn
650736	Sgt	ANDERSON William	3-09-42	75 Sqn
534829	F/S	ANDERTON Patrick James	15-10-42	419 Sqn
118718	P/O	ANDREW Robert William	22-09-42	226 Sqn
1190685	Sgt	ANDREWS Ewart John	6-05-42	18 Sqn
135019	P/O	ANDREWS DFM George Edward	9-11-42	57 Sqn
909841	F/S	ANDREWS Harold Clifford	3-06-42	57 Sqn
619953	Sgt	ANDREWS James Edward	16-02-42	458 Sqn
1251957	Sgt	ANDREWS Richard William	23-11-42	161 Sqn
931030	Sgt	ANDREWS Ronald Sydney	18-04-42	57 Sqn
64905	P/O	ANDREWS William Henry Thomson	10-03-42	49 Sqn
111564	P/O	ANGEL Alexander Alfred	12-07-42	101 Sqn
1181649	Sgt	ANGEL Leonard Arthur	14-01-42	50 Sqn
614800	Sgt	ANNABLE Eric	28-04-42	10 Sqn
1283858	Sgt	ANSELL Harry Edgar Wreyford	20-05-42	12 Sqn
1213401	Sgt	ANSELL Ronald Frank	27-06-42	405 Sqn
1017913	Sgt	ANSON George Albert	16-02-42	77 Sqn
1257553	Sgt	ANSON Harold Victor	3-08-42	51 Sqn
1314169	Sgt	ANSTEE Brian Robert	1-08-42	21 OTU
1376882	Sgt	ANSTRUTHER Jack De-La-War	17-11-42	158 Sqn
1313821	Sgt	ANTHONY Raymond Gwilym Gwyn	8-11-42	9 Sqn
108247	P/O	ANTOINE Joseph	25-08-42	7 Sqn
1259839	Sgt	ANYAN John Richard	28-01-42	106 Sqn
534437	Sgt	APPERSON Maxwell Warnock	24-07-42	405 Sqn
1262744	Sgt	APPI Stephen Renato	11-12-42	26 OTU
995056	Sgt	APPLEBY John Robinson	16-01-42	408 Sqn
106529	F/O	APPLETON David John	23-11-42	44 Sqn
536308	Sgt	APPLEY Samuel	8-02-42	21 OTU
1058273	F/S	APPLEYARD DFM Geoffrey	26-07-42	106 Sqn
637426	F/S	APPS Percy John	19-09-42	15 Sqn
1384432	Sgt	ARBUTT Leslie Arthur	10-12-42	11 OTU
1355706	Sgt	ARCHER George Walter Matthew	29-06-42	75 Sqn
917021	Sgt	ARCHER Ronald Albert	3-06-42	7 Sqn
924344	Sgt	ARCHER William	4-06-42	76 Sqn
656255	Sgt	ARCHER William Gordon	16-09-42	26 OTU
87451	F/O	ARCHIBALD Ronald Earle [Canada]	4-06-42	61 Sqn
533809	F/S	ARCHIBALD William Bruce	30-03-42	35 Sqn
118649	F/O	ARIS Jack Biddulph	11-12-42	158 Sqn
135457	P/O	ARMITAGE DFC James Lloyd	20-12-42	139 Sqn
571552	Sgt	ARMSTRONG Frederick	30-05-42	218 Sqn
998998	Sgt	ARMSTRONG John	28-06-42	218 Sqn
1287632	Sgt	ARMSTRONG Kenneth George	20-05-42	10 Sqn
1378839	Sgt	ARMSTRONG Richard	3-06-42	7 Sqn
1123091	Sgt	ARMSTRONG Robert Harvey	22-04-42	9 Sqn
574713	F/S	ARMSTRONG Thomas Rodham	23-11-42	83 Sqn
953171	Sgt	ARNETT Stanley	3-06-42	102 Sqn
1200938	Sgt	ARNOLD Douglas Gordon William	16-09-42	12 OTU
1280560	Sgt	ARNOLD William Harry	31-05-42	101 Sqn
74323	F/L	ARNOTT Hugh	6-12-42	7 Sqn
126850	P/O	ARNOTT Kenneth	16-07-42	15 Sqn
657780	Sgt	ARNOTT William McGowan	9-11-42	50 Sqn
931603	F/S	ARROWSMITH John Raymond St. George	5-05-42	103 Sqn
1108989	Sgt	ARTHAN Frederick Ralph	4-06-42	101 Sqn
534824	Sgt	ASH Maurice Samuel	31-05-42	49 Sqn
1171711	Sgt	ASH Richard Derrick	13-03-42	78 Sqn
778663	Sgt	ASHBY James William [Rhodesia]	5-06-42	1443 Flt
1284493	Sgt	ASHBY Robert Frederick	27-09-42	12 Sqn
1160840	Sgt	ASHFIELD Frederick William	12-02-42	420 Sqn
1148934	Sgt	ASHFORD Alan Richard	20-09-42	161 Sqn
46900	P/O	ASHFORD Frederick Herbert Ashton	17-04-42	107 Sqn
115690	S/L	ASHILL The Rev. Denis Edward Guy	29-12-42	15 Sqn
67649	P/O	ASHLEY Frederick Clifford	4-02-42	21 Sqn
1170676	Sgt	ASHPLANT William Leonard	17-02-42	460 Sqn
630344	Sgt	ASHTON Jack Glyn	22-11-42	57 Sqn
104333	P/O	ASHTON Thomas Reginald	22-07-42	408 Sqn
990550	Sgt	ASHUN William Philip	1-04-42	405 Sqn
553270	F/S	ASHURST Kenneth	16-02-42	61 Sqn
1214846	Sgt	ASHWELL Robert Hugh [Canada]	28-08-42	12 Sqn
1381000	Sgt	ASHWORTH Donald William	20-06-42	57 Sqn
76467	S/L	ASHWORTH DFC Harold John Vincent	20-06-42	218 Sqn
45094	F/O	ASPEY MiD Harold Edward	27-02-42	144 Sqn
1504396	LAC	ASPINALL Jack	9-11-42	180 Sqn
115981	P/O	ASTELL-BURT Henry	14-08-42	7 Sqn
1015608	Sgt	ASTON Arthur	25-06-42	76 Sqn
1379656	Sgt	ASTON John Walter	11-02-42	12 Sqn
1077710	Sgt	ATCHISON Cresswell	20-07-42	10 Sqn
1028991	Sgt	ATCHISON William John	29-07-42	16 OTU
1210043	Sgt	ATKINS George Thomas	6-01-42	49 Sqn
574300	Sgt	ATKINS William Anthony George	13-07-42	7 Sqn
1254703	Sgt	ATKINSON Charles	29-08-42	105 Sqn
62694	P/O	ATKINSON Denys Lowe	31-01-42	61 Sqn
1325633	Sgt	ATKINSON Douglas Bell	13-02-42	21 OTU
120721	F/L	ATKINSON DFM John Charles	18-12-42	50 Sqn
1105186	Sgt	ATKINSON John Wilfred	5-09-42	207 Sqn
810060	Sgt	ATKINSON Joseph	8-11-42	142 Sqn
39364	S/L	ATKINSON Matthew Richard	26-06-42	1481 Flt
104526	F/O	ATKINSON Rolf Edgar	27-09-42	78 Sqn
575448	Sgt	ATKINSON Sam Hawley	16-09-42	15 Sqn
621174	F/S	ATKINSON Thomas Donald	4-06-42	207 Sqn
1292935	Sgt	ATKINSON William Joseph	6-11-42	21 Sqn
1388679	Sgt	ATTRIDGE Thomas Philip	10-12-42	10 OTU
1264198	Sgt	ATTWATER Robin Aelred	7-07-42	156 Sqn
845508	Sgt	ATWELL William John	26-01-42	51 Sqn
113904	P/O	AUGUST Douglas Claude	31-05-42	26 OTU
1159702	Sgt	AUSTIN Albert Sydney	8-01-42	458 Sqn
120085	F/O	AUSTIN Francis Leslie	1-10-42	17 OTU
940606	F/S	AUSTIN John Henry	28-10-42	10 OTU
1283173	Sgt	AVENT Sydney Walter George	28-04-42	214 Sqn
1028776	Sgt	AVEYARD Colin	14-09-42	27 OTU

Number	Rank	Name	Date	Sqn
1181575	Sgt	AXFORD Norman Frank	27-07-42	420 Sqn
1181631	Sgt	AYRES Ronald Keith	29-04-42	9 Sqn
547973	Sgt	AYTON Edmund Sidney	27-02-42	77 Sqn
109106	P/O	BABER William Henry	27-07-42	102 Sqn
657185	Sgt	BACON Leslie	22-09-42	19 OTU
1375837	Sgt	BACON William Charles	18-08-42	76 Sqn
814205	F/S	BADDELEY Douglas Hiram	26-06-42	26 OTU
1378467	Sgt	BADDELEY Robert Ashton	14-01-42	50 Sqn
1109333	Sgt	BAGLEY Donald	26-07-42	460 Sqn
1315216	Sgt	BAGLEY William John	1-08-42	103 Sqn
1383102	Sgt	BAGSHAW Gerald	30-11-42	10 OTU
108241	P/O	BAILEY Derrick Bourchier	12-03-42	77 Sqn
1252567	Sgt	BAILEY Edgar Albert	27-03-42	115 Sqn
1114883	Sgt	BAILEY Harry	6-11-42	26 OTU
1293848	Sgt	BAILEY James Edwin	20-09-42	101 Sqn
546301	Sgt	BAILLIE James Henry	17-05-42	149 Sqn
559161	Sgt	BAILLIE John Ernest	9-05-42	15 Sqn
118058	F/L	BAIN Charles Guthrie Shields	17-12-42	9 Sqn
41243	F/L	BAIN David John [Canada]	10-08-42	405 Sqn
28259	W/C	BAIN Francis George Levett	8-12-42	207 Sqn
1006976	Sgt	BAINES Clifford	2-06-42	83 Sqn
746739	F/S	BAIRD Douglas Drennan	15-10-42	156 Sqn
1199377	Sgt	BAIRD Douglas Wilson	31-05-42	50 Sqn
1107265	Sgt	BAIRD Edmund Ronald	25-04-42	226 Sqn
64907	P/O	BAIRSTOW Edward Akeroyd	26-02-42	12 Sqn
48692	P/O	BAKE DFM Alfred George	2-06-42	106 Sqn
1182487	Sgt	BAKER Albert Wallace	25-03-42	61 Sqn
1330207	Sgt	BAKER Edward William	24-06-42	103 Sqn
1270911	Sgt	BAKER Frederick John	10-12-42	22 OTU
1390119	Sgt	BAKER Frederick Walter	5-09-42	142 Sqn
963611	Sgt	BAKER Frederick William	28-01-42	106 Sqn
115676	P/O	BAKER George Harman	20-05-42	10 Sqn
935848	Sgt	BAKER Gilbert	27-04-42	149 Sqn
116830	P/O	BAKER Gordon	17-04-42	50 Sqn
1169503	Sgt	BAKER Horace	18-02-42	420 Sqn
1175563	Sgt	BAKER Jack Hilton	21-12-42	9 Sqn
69491	P/O	BAKER Joseph Harold Andrews	2-04-42	214 Sqn
655271	Sgt	BAKER MiD Leonard Thomas	7-06-42	150 Sqn
616021	Sgt	BAKER Sydney Robert	7-01-42	18 Sqn
107286	F/O	BAKER Thomas Henry William	11-08-42	75 Sqn
1285545	Sgt	BAKER Victor Charles Rudkin	26-03-42	115 Sqn
1310106	Sgt	BAKER Victor Reginald	23-01-42	408 Sqn
1381154	Sgt	BAKES Wilfred	18-09-42	25 OTU
113352	P/O	BALES Leslie Percy	26-06-42	115 Sqn
656517	Sgt	BALFOUR Joseph Smillie	16-09-42	106 Sqn
1391203	Sgt	BALKWILL Henry John	5-09-42	142 Sqn
108148	P/O	BALL Brian Francis	26-06-42	218 Sqn
1062064	Sgt	BALL Frederick William Ewart	9-06-42	103 Sqn
1180226	Sgt	BALL Kenneth	19-04-42	14 OTU
113387	F/O	BALL DFM Peter Allen	5-08-42	44 Sqn
1166456	Sgt	BALL Richard	9-03-42	408 Sqn
523218	Sgt	BALL William Alfred Henry	7-11-42	207 Sqn
751937	F/S	BALLANTYNE Richard	25-04-42	9 Sqn
1258728	Sgt	BALLARD Philip Sidney	22-02-42	50 Sqn
1377131	Sgt	BALLARD William	28-03-42	115 Sqn
655642	Sgt	BALMFORTH Thomas Whiteley	30-10-42	105 Sqn
1586443	Sgt	BAMBURY Roy Henry	20-12-42	97 Sqn
787715	LAC	BAMBUSEK Ian [Czechoslovakia]	4-04-42	311 Sqn
748927	Sgt	BANCE Eric	8-12-42	15 Sqn
977386	Sgt	BANESS John Haycroft Henniker	12-02-42	144 Sqn
653184	Sgt	BANHAM Ulic Julian	14-08-42	19 OTU
917462	Sgt	BANKS John Charles Lyon	28-03-42	7 Sqn
1359899	Sgt	BANKS Thomas George	19-01-42	9 Sqn
1111864	F/S	BANNISTER Harry Ernest	11-09-42	15 Sqn
107988	P/O	BANTING John Albert Stokes	26-04-42	218 Sqn
1008486	Sgt	BARBER John Wallace	28-04-42	102 Sqn
1202956	Sgt	BARCLAY Owen Kidd	9-09-42	102 Sqn
1553993	Sgt	BARCLAY William Barrie	11-12-42	26 OTU
48726	F/O	BARFOD DFC Walter	7-11-42	107 Sqn
755880	F/S	BARHAM Wilfred	7-06-42	214 Sqn
118716	P/O	BARKER Frank Joseph	4-06-42	17 OTU
1049813	Sgt	BARKER Frederick	29-10-42	115 Sqn
613921	F/S	BARKER DFM Frederick Frank	31-05-42	26 OTU
1213488	Sgt	BARKER Herbert Hawley	11-12-42	25 OTU
646994	Sgt	BARKER Horace Sydney	25-06-42	214 Sqn
800585	Sgt	BARKER Kenneth William	15-04-42	158 Sqn
1310625	Sgt	BARKER Thomas	16-08-42	156 Sqn
106537	P/O	BARLOW Ronald William	13-04-42	115 Sqn
39845	S/L	BARNARD MiD Henry Walter	17-09-42	49 Sqn
1384144	Sgt	BARNARD Leslie William Arthur	7-08-42	218 Sqn
120665	F/O	BARNES Douglas Martin	12-12-42	139 Sqn
655006	Sgt	BARNES Frederick John Charles	5-09-42	207 Sqn
1233263	LAC	BARNES James Lewis Joseph	3-08-42	114 Sqn
1189038	Sgt	BARNES Owen Cicero Charles	22-04-42	9 Sqn
1377006	Sgt	BARNES Ronald Arthur	6-12-42	107 Sqn
67693	F/L	BARNES DFC William George	30-06-42	149 Sqn
1255348	Sgt	BARNETT Cecil Douglas	25-05-42	76 Sqn
1041484	LAC	BARNETT Frank Ernest	17-10-42	98 Sqn
1315315	Sgt	BARNETT Jack Henry	29-10-42	19 OTU
778270	Sgt	BARNETT George Andrew [Rhodesia]	24-02-42	144 Sqn
1105548	F/S	BARNICOTT Alfred Thomas James	14-09-42	12 Sqn
43627	F/L	BARR DFC* Leslie Ronald	11-09-42	7 Sqn
567143	Sgt	BARR Peter	27-07-42	76 Sqn
39482	S/L	BARR DFC Philip Rex	7-11-42	107 Sqn
1203767	Sgt	BARR Richard Eugene	30-06-42	149 Sqn
1062414	Sgt	BARR William Buntin	16-07-42	27 OTU
644523	Sgt	BARRACLOUGH Oswald	26-07-42	97 Sqn
1254392	Sgt	BARRETT Denis Robert	16-07-42	15 Sqn
29001	S/L	BARRETT Gerald Spencer	30-11-42	10 Sqn
568443	Sgt	BARRETT Maurice Alfred	30-07-42	102 Sqn
1254387	Sgt	BARRETT Percy Warren	26-06-42	83 Sqn
117443	P/O	BARRETT Thomas	1-08-42	12 Sqn
120409	F/O	BARRETT William Gustave	8-11-42	76 Sqn
977028	Sgt	BARRIE Charles Stewart	29-10-42	15 Sqn
524581	F/S	BARRIE Grahame Cowan	7-07-42	156 Sqn
967059	Sgt	BARRIE Ronald Harry Joseph	26-03-42	142 Sqn
49332	P/O	BARRITT John	14-09-42	156 Sqn
971341	F/S	BARROW Colin Hervey	21-08-42	218 Sqn
1287636	Sgt	BARROWS Albert Edwin	24-07-42	25 OTU
46708	P/O	BARTHEL Peter Vincent	9-03-42	35 Sqn
1585069	Sgt	BARTHOLOMEW Eric Edward	11-11-42	61 Sqn
1333014	Sgt	BARTLE Albert James Alfred	9-11-42	57 Sqn
120996	P/O	BARTLETT Alan	13-05-42	50 Sqn
622974	Sgt	BARTLETT Alexander McKenzie	16-09-42	26 OTU
118826	P/O	BARTLETT Denis Ross Crockford	27-09-42	10 OTU
1359903	Sgt	BARTON Albert Henry Dickebusch	2-04-42	150 Sqn
573423	Sgt	BARTON James Jeffrey	13-10-42	83 Sqn
1312006	F/S	BARTON-SMITH Hugh	28-08-42	15 Sqn
1376972	Sgt	BASHAM Reginald Walter William	18-07-42	10 OTU
655691	Sgt	BASSETT Robert George	20-09-42	150 Sqn
132605	P/O	BASSOM Richard Charles Edgar	24-09-42	102 Sqn
48081	P/O	BASSON Peter Henry	24-07-42	149 Sqn
1176636	Sgt	BASTOW Edward Henry	6-10-42	142 Sqn
1365683	Sgt	BATCHEN Ronald Tait [Canada]	11-05-42	115 Sqn
1195168	Sgt	BATE Harold [Australia]	21-12-42	207 Sqn
1031696	Sgt	BATE William George	16-08-42	156 Sqn
546137	Sgt	BATEMAN Arthur	11-12-42	25 OTU
1062580	Sgt	BATES Matthew	17-05-42	9 Sqn
1333842	Sgt	BATES Reginald Edward	6-11-42	7 Sqn
1323476	Sgt	BATH Percy Horace	27-09-42	78 Sqn
971129	Sgt	BATTERSBY John	4-06-42	76 Sqn
1006347	Sgt	BATTISON Gilbert George May	10-11-42	107 Sqn
986627	Sgt	BATTY Harry William	7-05-42	115 Sqn
1186666	Sgt	BATTEN WILKINS Bernard Henry	8-11-42	20 OTU
513278	W/O	BAXTER George Edward Albert	28-01-42	138 Sqn
1389143	Sgt	BAXTER Harold Albert	18-07-42	10 OTU
103529	P/O	BAXTER DFM John David	21-06-42	9 Sqn
1108776	Sgt	BAXTER John Frederick	22-06-42	218 Sqn

Service #	Rank	Name	Date	Unit	Service #	Rank	Name	Date	Unit
339004	Sgt	BAXTER Joseph Stevenson Thomson	16-12-42	15 OTU	546151	Sgt	BENNETT Alfred Thomas	9-03-42	35 Sqn
1375526	Sgt	BAXTER Victor	20-03-42	19 OTU	615915	Sgt	BENNETT Frederick	27-04-42	97 Sqn
113343	P/O	BAYLEY DFC George Corbett	29-07-42	1651 CU	998824	Sgt	BENNETT Geoffrey Harcourt	6-09-42	21 OTU
88024	F/O	BAYLEY George Reginald	9-01-42	207 Sqn	1381048	Sgt	BENNETT Jack William Augustus	16-09-42	142 Sqn
1210044	Sgt	BAYLEY Robert	15-10-42	12 Sqn	573729	Sgt	BENNETT John	24-09-42	102 Sqn
655073	Sgt	BAYLIS Anthony	22-05-42	19 OTU	1310784	Sgt	BENNETT John	28-03-42	13 OTU
567972	Sgt	BAYLISS John	9-01-42	15 OTU	1330697	Sgt	BENNETT Lionel Leslie	14-04-42	21 OTU
1330983	Sgt	BAYLY Frank Brenner Byron	11-09-42	10 OTU	1378737	F/S	BENNETT Thomas	20-12-42	103 Sqn
933068	Sgt	BEACH Alfred Ernest	16-11-42	101 Sqn	613080	Sgt	BENNETT William	26-06-42	1651 CU
617835	Sgt	BEADDIE Robert Lovie	26-07-42	106 Sqn	1552113	Sgt	BENNIE James	6-10-42	142 Sqn
129955	P/O	BEALE Edward	28-08-42	101 Sqn	100634	F/L	BENNITT DFC Neville Arthur	7-09-42	7 Sqn
1389654	Sgt	BEALE Frederick George	7-11-42	83 Sqn	1383049	Sgt	BENSTEAD Charles Edward	7-09-42	103 Sqn
752963	Sgt	BEALE Robert Noel	27-03-42	408 Sqn	995057	Sgt	BENTHAM Alan	9-06-42	109 Sqn
907416	Sgt	BEALES Deryck Bonney	10-11-42	7 Sqn	1057074	F/S	BENTHAM Thomas	21-12-42	7 Sqn
570398	Sgt	BEALES Robert Walter	24-08-42	218 Sqn	1310780	Sgt	BENTLEY Alan Frank	18-09-42	44 Sqn
1166172	Sgt	BEAMENT Thomas Hubert	16-04-42	101 Sqn	1020750	Sgt	BENTLEY Gordon Joseph	21-12-42	207 Sqn
1237250	Sgt	BEAMES George Norman	30-11-42	149 Sqn	936573	F/S	BENTLEY DFM Joseph Harold	5-08-42	44 Sqn
1198851	Sgt	BEARD Bernard Charles	6-12-42	14 OTU	633360	Sgt	BENTLEY Samuel Frederick	27-03-42	408 Sqn
1284966	Sgt	BEARE Walter Percy	30-06-42	405 Sqn	1004002	Sgt	BERNARD Alexander Russell	12-01-42	50 Sqn
139036	P/O	BEATON Derrick John Harry	12-08-42	150 Sqn	1257361	Sgt	BERGER David	22-07-42	142 Sqn
970834	F/S	BEATON James Alexander	24-09-42	9 Sqn	1181332	Sgt	BERRETT Eric Albert	28-08-42	49 Sqn
567281	Sgt	BEATTIE Albert John	20-07-42	10 Sqn	1061056	Sgt	BERRY Jack	17-09-42	61 Sqn
84878	F/L	BEATTIE George Liddell Carruthers	4-06-42	61 Sqn	128536	P/O	BERTRAM Robert	29-06-42	75 Sqn
655244	Sgt	BEATTIE John	18-09-42	44 Sqn	613995	Sgt	BESWICK Arthur	29-10-42	15 Sqn
987379	Sgt	BEATTIE Joseph Davidson	25-03-42	50 Sqn	1162656	Sgt	BESWICK Oliver Percy	3-06-42	61 Sqn
1386746	Sgt	BEATTIE Thomas	10-12-42	10 OTU	1138925	Sgt	BETTERIDGE Arthur Joseph	19-09-42	460 Sqn
1251658	Sgt	BEAUCHAMP John Samuel	26-03-42	114 Sqn	109064	P/O	BETTS Ivan Harold	14-09-42	1653 CU
1380675	Sgt	BEAUFOY Michael Henry	9-06-42	114 Sqn	81341	F/L	BEVAN Alwin Woodgate	20-06-42	7 Sqn
1710222	AC2	BEAUMONT John Ernest George	28-12-42	23 OTU	1317942	Sgt	BEVAN Thomas Ralph	24-09-42	61 Sqn
1002280	Sgt	BEAUMONT Samuel	22-07-42	114 Sqn	977143	Sgt	BEVERIDGE John	24-10-42	78 Sqn
37566	S/L	BEAVIS James	11-08-42	156 Sqn	657044	Sgt	BEYER Edwin Harry	3-09-42	75 Sqn
655832	Sgt	BEBBINGTON Richard John	3-09-42	15 Sqn	657342	Sgt	BICAT Victor Jack Foch	26-06-42	102 Sqn
1310501	Sgt	BECK Leonard	31-05-42	150 Sqn	1378704	Sgt	BICK Frederick George Albert	20-07-42	10 Sqn
622136	Sgt	BECKETT Geoffrey	17-12-42	44 Sqn	521924	Sgt	BICKERS Thomas	28-08-42	44 Sqn
120331	P/O	BECKETT DFM John Frank	17-04-42	44 Sqn	1496595	Sgt	BICKERTON Norman Victor	10-08-42	150 Sqn
1382013	F/S	BECKMAN Leslie John William	17-09-42	158 Sqn	1169946	Sgt	BIDDLECOMBE Robert William Antony		
121557	P/O	BEDFORD Ernest Lionel	25-06-42	24 OTU				28-01-42	106 Sqn
100577	F/O	BEDFORD Harold Ernest	5-06-42	78 Sqn	778574	Sgt	BIDDULPH Edward John [Rhodesia]	25-03-42	14 OTU
1331222	Sgt	BEDFORD Ronald Ernest Edward	30-07-42	142 Sqn	1255382	Sgt	BIDGOOD Harry Walter Trevor	9-03-42	15 Sqn
1180257	Sgt	BEE Alan Mowlem	30-05-42	50 Sqn	60569	F/O	BIGGANE DFC Denzil Francis Heriz	21-12-42	44 Sqn
1359941	Sgt	BEETON Wilfred Roy	17-01-42	27 OTU	754732	F/S	BIGGLESTONE George Milburn	3-01-42	22 OTU
1238972	Sgt	BEHN John Frederick Peter	6-10-42	405 Sqn	1390750	Sgt	BIGNELL Roy Arthur Frank	20-12-42	49 Sqn
1338412	Sgt	BELGROVE Derrick Morris	31-10-42	30 OTU	656623	Sgt	BILLINGS Lawrence Eric	7-09-42	10 Sqn
571310	Sgt	BELK Edward Leslie	26-03-42	7 Sqn	1317547	Sgt	BILLINGTON Arthur Reuben	8-11-42	9 Sqn
1295005	Sgt	BELL Alan Francis	5-08-42	1653 CU	1169761	Sgt	BILLINGTON Robert Anthony	6-02-42	455 Sqn
1072725	Sgt	BELL Arthur Ewart	15-10-42	158 Sqn	901690	F/S	BILTCLIFFE William Durham	9-03-42	83 Sqn
1117205	Sgt	BELL Clifford Allan	20-05-42	12 Sqn	787400	Sgt	BINDER Frantisek [Czechoslovakia]	4-03-42	311 Sqn
87412	S/L	BELL DFC David John	3-06-42	14 OTU	1163883	Sgt	BINGE Joseph Christopher	27-11-42	20 OTU
1002123	Sgt	BELL Donald	11-12-42	26 OTU	971062	F/S	BINGHAM James Henry Gordon	24-06-42	76 Sqn
657322	Sgt	BELL Ethelbert Oswald Peter	30-11-42	10 OTU	1365002	Sgt	BINGHAM John	28-08-42	115 Sqn
1527170	Sgt	BELL Harry	4-12-42	19 OTU	119177	P/O	BINGHAM Ronald Albert	28-08-42	103 Sqn
1123836	Sgt	BELL John	10-11-42	107 Sqn	39961	W/C	BINTLEY DSO AFC Sydney Bruce	24-10-42	102 Sqn
1164373	Sgt	BELL Lionel Horace	24-10-42	207 Sqn	1106187	Sgt	BIRCH Frank	2-09-42	218 Sqn
1110202	Sgt	BELL Richard	17-09-42	106 Sqn	1388177	Sgt	BIRCH George Herbert Arthur	9-09-42	207 Sqn
655176	Sgt	BELL Robert Curragh	14-03-42	78 Sqn	1056358	Sgt	BIRCH Kenneth Alan	14-04-42	420 Sqn
1056285	F/S	BELL Ronald Sample	5-05-42	150 Sqn	922333	Sgt	BIRCHER Richard Hubert	24-06-42	76 Sqn
953518	Sgt	BELL William	24-10-42	207 Sqn	1181384	Sgt	BIRD David Holley [Canada]	26-04-42	218 Sqn
1107284	Sgt	BELLAMY John Ernest	15-10-42	106 Sqn	927772	Sgt	BIRD Herman Albert Benjamin	27-03-42	408 Sqn
1221132	Sgt	BELLCHAMBERS Frederick George	1-10-42	61 Sqn	900012	F/S	BIRD Joseph Ronald	28-08-42	218 Sqn
1459372	Sgt	BELLERBY Douglas Arnold	30-11-42	10 Sqn	1281394	Sgt	BIRD Kenneth Maurice	28-01-42	114 Sqn
655304	F/S	BELLEW Reginald Victor Walker	16-12-42	23 OTU	1178733	F/S	BIRD Kenneth Sockling Hardwick	29-09-42	12 OTU
1285151	Sgt	BELLINGER James	27-08-42	142 Sqn	1006950	Sgt	BIRD Thomas Cunningham [Canada]	26-04-42	218 Sqn
1076769	Sgt	BELL-BERRY Raymond	6-08-42	207 Sqn	118723	P/O	BIRLEY Alan Fay	29-08-42	35 Sqn
80284	P/O	BELTON Frederick William	9-05-42	44 Sqn	1067279	Sgt	BISHOP John	14-09-42	12 Sqn
1381239	Sgt	BELTON Thomas William	1-06-42	20 OTU	1203303	Sgt	BISHOP Peter Derek	21-02-42	106 Sqn
1058416	Sgt	BELTON Wilfred Thomas	10-09-42	61 Sqn	619087	Sgt	BISHOP Ronald Frederick	15-01-42	115 Sqn
1500475	Sgt	BENDING Henry William	9-11-42	218 Sqn	1125069	Sgt	BLACK Charles	18-08-42	12 Sqn
90447	W/C	BENHAM Jack Elkin David	28-01-42	138 Sqn	748714	W/O	BLACK John Morton Burroughs	29-07-42	7 Sqn
701008	Sgt	BENN Reuben John	16-10-42	51 Sqn	755913	F/S	BLACK Robert Hammond	12-04-42	420 Sqn

985882	Sgt	BLACK William	31-01-42	144 Sqn
134028	P/O	BLACKADDER William Smith	24-07-42	18 Sqn
1051863	Sgt	BLACKBURN John Eric	22-02-42	150 Sqn
121555	P/O	BLACKFORD Harry William	26-06-42	24 OTU
967185	Sgt	BLACKLAW Edward	17-01-42	7 Sqn
917077	Sgt	BLACKMAN Alan	24-03-42	19 OTU
1585143	Sgt	BLACKMAN Stuart Edward	31-10-42	25 OTU
1195088	Sgt	BLACKMORE Hubert Waddy	27-02-42	77 Sqn
798552	Sgt	BLACKMORE Lester John [Newfoundland]	13-08-42	15 Sqn
1203414	Sgt	BLACKMORE Sidney Frederick Ogeley	24-07-42	57 Sqn
1386598	Sgt	BLACKSHIRE Alfred Stephen Edgar	6-11-42	13 OTU
79228	F/O	BLAIN Leonard Manley	9-05-42	9 Sqn
932614	Sgt	BLAKE Albert William	24-02-42	106 Sqn
1391561	Sgt	BLAKE Edward Albert	15-10-42	106 Sqn
1165296	F/S	BLAKE Peter James Widdell [Canada]	13-05-42	50 Sqn
1284072	Sgt	BLAKE Reginald Alfred	24-10-42	149 Sqn
1051834	Sgt	BLAND Eric	6-02-42	455 Sqn
1250196	Sgt	BLAND Peter Windermere	13-03-42	78 Sqn
1379420	Sgt	BLAND Reginald Alfred	27-02-42	144 Sqn
1024020	Sgt	BLAND Stanley	5-09-42	12 Sqn
1260143	Sgt	BLATCHLEY Ronald Bennet	7-04-42	142 Sqn
1068042	Sgt	BLATHERWICK George	24-07-42	149 Sqn
1258441	Sgt	BLENCOWE Arthur Frank	25-04-42	103 Sqn
777957	Sgt	BLIGNAUT Jochemus Johannes [Rhodesia]	8-12-42	15 Sqn
903489	F/S	BLOCK David	31-05-42	49 Sqn
1378566	Sgt	BLOCK Samuel	25-03-42	83 Sqn
910946	Sgt	BLOGG Archibald Charles	27-08-42	156 Sqn
1013747	Sgt	BLOOMFIELD John Alfred	6-06-42	44 Sqn
1381609	Sgt	BLOOR Harry	25-06-42	15 OTU
111785	P/O	BLOOR Richard	14-04-42	21 OTU
127285	P/O	BLUCK John	27-11-42	20 OTU
86728	P/O	BLUETT Peter Frederick Barlow	31-05-42	61 Sqn
751361	F/S	BLUNDALL Barriemore Smallwood	26-08-42	103 Sqn
1285751	Sgt	BLYTH Alfred Maurice 'Bob'	21-07-42	106 Sqn
1381018	Sgt	BLYTHE Thomas Francis	27-11-42	20 OTU
1310500	Sgt	BOAR Geoffrey Crisp 'Geoff'	14-09-42	1653 CU
610906	Sgt	BOARDMAN Roy	8-12-42	207 Sqn
1354324	Sgt	BOCOCK Arnold Geoffrey	7-02-42	50 Sqn
1378930	Sgt	BODDY David	3-06-42	102 Sqn
1185743	Sgt	BODE John William	22-05-42	75 Sqn
1382214	Sgt	BOGARD Joel	12-08-42	50 Sqn
1063352	Sgt	BOGGESS George William	2-05-42	13 OTU
923995	F/S	BOLDY David Adrian	11-07-42	207 Sqn
952598	Sgt	BOLTON George	31-05-42	78 Sqn
112308	P/O	BOLTON Warren Percy [USA]	12-06-42	12 OTU
628559	F/S	BOLUS Arthur Herbert	8-05-42	44 Sqn
1198862	Sgt	BOND Alan Denis	3-07-42	420 Sqn
1319092	Sgt	BOND Cecil Jacques	21-08-42	149 Sqn
971971	Sgt	BOND David Watson	26-03-42	57 Sqn
651275	Sgt	BOND Francis Charles	1-08-42	405 Sqn
1168700	Sgt	BOND Harold	9-06-42	12 Sqn
1207446	Sgt	BOND James Alfred	30-05-42	97 Sqn
1381416	Sgt	BOND William George	30-05-42	15 Sqn
1449150	AC1	BONE Edward John	31-10-42	88 Sqn
39059	S/L	BONNAR Kenneth Whyte	7-05-42	35 Sqn
959560	Sgt	BONNER George Henry	11-02-42	12 Sqn
1176413	Sgt	BONNER Bilbert Frederick Cummings	5-06-42	150 Sqn
45416	F/L	BONNETT DFC Dorian Dick	24-10-42	49 Sqn
656732	Sgt	BONORINO Carlos Frederick	5-12-42	1658 HCU
976336	Sgt	BONSER Alfred Kenneth	27-08-42	101 Sqn
992516	Sgt	BONSER Fred	11-04-42	214 Sqn
564555	W/O	BOOLS MiD Charles Ronald Kernick	9-04-42	105 Sqn
127112	P/O	BOOTH Allan	20-11-42	11 OTU
636621	Sgt	BOOTH Eric Foster William	8-06-42	149 Sqn
971036	F/S	BOOTH Croix de Guerre Fred	3-06-42	102 Sqn
519995	Sgt	BOOTH Hubert Allan	28-04-42	35 Sqn
1527423	AC2	BOOTH John	18-04-42	Tempsford
118627	P/O	BOOTH Lewis Alfred	26-06-42	1651 CU
953553	Sgt	BOOTH Maurice William	29-08-42	35 Sqn
81661	F/L	BOOTH Neville George Richardson	18-05-42	20 OTU
1376648	F/S	BOOTH Norman	13-11-42	105 Sqn
942419	Sgt	BOOTH Reginald	1-10-42	15 Sqn
1294878	Sgt	BOOTH William Henry Charles	5-08-42	1653 CU
1126805	Sgt	BOOTLE Joseph Frederick	24-12-42	10 OTU
617853	Sgt	BOOTY Eric Denis	17-09-42	149 Sqn
1377082	Sgt	BOREHAM Eric Herbert	17-10-42	98 Sqn
1310770	Sgt	BOREHAM Lawrence Frederick George	24-08-42	218 Sqn
1151361	F/S	BORROWDALE Joseph Lewthwaite	31-05-42	218 Sqn
1256937	F/S	BORSBERRY Ernest Richard	28-07-42	156 Sqn
1360092	Sgt	BOTTOMLEY Herbert	31-05-42	12 Sqn
1181181	Sgt	BOTTOMLEY John Edward	9-06-42	35 Sqn
106665	P/O	BOTTRILL Kenneth Hulbert	16-02-42	82 Sqn
1029681	Sgt	BOUFFLER Keith Arnold	17-09-42	49 Sqn
1376768	Sgt	BOUGHTWOOD Alan Gilbert	30-09-42	9 Sqn
1283854	Sgt	BOUMPHREY Eric Harold	24-07-42	149 Sqn
1269297	Sgt	BOUND Eric Guy	25-08-42	150 Sqn
625779	Sgt	BOURKE Cyril Wellesley	26-07-42	115 Sqn
572223	Sgt	BOURNE John Norman	5-10-42	102 Sqn
1167727	Sgt	BOW Lambert Philip	7-02-42	144 Sqn
107922	P/O	BOWACK Norman Hamilton	30-05-42	76 Sqn
1291430	Sgt	BOWDEN Douglas Joseph	24-10-42	149 Sqn
1187036	Sgt	BOWEN Alwyne Robert	26-07-42	115 Sqn
1265010	Sgt	BOWEN Richard Ivor	19-07-42	27 OTU
778625	Sgt	BOWER Kenneth Oswald [South Africa]	10-09-42	142 Sqn
977278	Sgt	BOWERS William Henry	9-03-42	9 Sqn
63827	F/O	BOWES Anthony John Lee	24-07-42	149 Sqn
1290940	Sgt	BOWES Cyril Alfred	30-07-42	50 Sqn
937978	Sgt	BOWES John William	8-11-42	9 Sqn
46894	P/O	BOWKER Ronald Arthur	20-05-42	7 Sqn
1339505	Sgt	BOWKETT Ronald Herbert George	8-11-42	76 Sqn
1381965	Sgt	BOWLER Reginald William	10-09-42	218 Sqn
110640	F/O	BOWLES Ronald Alfred	21-12-42	57 Sqn
1174321	Sgt	BOWREY James	14-09-42	1653 CU
535325	Sgt	BOWRING Bertie	17-01-42	51 Sqn
1311922	Sgt	BOX Frederick Ernest Arthur	8-12-42	102 Sqn
1291381	Sgt	BOXALL George Lascelles	24-08-42	218 Sqn
553845	Sgt	BOXWELL Noel Francis [Eire]	21-08-42	15 OTU
1559614	AC1	BOYCE William Gilchrist	24-05-42	138 Sqn
985883	Sgt	BOYD John	24-03-42	44 Sqn
126040	P/O	BOYES Roland Leslie	6-12-42	7 Sqn
996348	Sgt	BOYLE Alexander David	29-12-42	77 Sqn
1188342	Sgt	BOYLE Brian John Waldron	25-10-42	142 Sqn
631184	F/S	BOYLE MiD John George Ypres	24-05-42	1483 Flt
1109750	Sgt	BOYLE Malcolm	31-05-42	115 Sqn
969690	Sgt	BOYNE Alexander John	19-08-42	207 Sqn
798553	Sgt	BRACE Alexander Albert [Newfoundland]	9-07-42	101 Sqn
1053817	Sgt	BRACE Norman Edmund	19-07-42	150 Sqn
568805	Sgt	BRADBROOK Lawrence Harold	30-06-42	405 Sqn
122322	P/O	BRADBURY Leslie Elmer	14-07-42	158 Sqn
136336	P/O	BRADLEY Albert Gaston Thomas	24-09-42	78 Sqn
1065784	Sgt	BRADLEY Eric	1-11-42	88 Sqn
997206	Sgt	BRADLEY Ernest	26-07-42	106 Sqn
1058655	Sgt	BRADLEY James Calvert	15-01-42	10 Sqn
1199393	Sgt	BRADLEY John	9-11-42	142 Sqn
1238954	Sgt	BRADLEY John Dennett	4-12-42	19 OTU
990430	Sgt	BRADLEY Sidney	16-06-42	101 Sqn
1380983	Sgt	BRADSELL Bert James	28-10-42	10 OTU
1281428	Sgt	BRADSHAW Donald	9-07-42	15 OTU
119905	P/O	BRADSHAW Douglas James	8-11-42	142 Sqn
974193	Sgt	BRADSHAW John Charles	9-01-42	144 Sqn
1168179	Sgt	BRADSHAW Sydney Edward	23-06-42	61 Sqn

Service No	Rank	Name	Date	Squadron
627478	F/S	BRADY DFM Cecil Thomas Theobald	20-04-42	156 Sqn
45686	F/O	BRADY Noel Stuart	21-10-42	7 Sqn
535701	Sgt	BRAIN Philip Cecil John	7-08-42	7 Sqn
1379657	Sgt	BRAITHWAITE Robert Noel	22-12-42	21 OTU
1217973	AC2	BRAMHAM Harry	31-10-42	88 Sqn
84026	F/O	BRANCKER DFC* Henry Paul	27-03-42	114 Sqn
1113754	Sgt	BRAND William	27-03-42	21 OTU
1351987	Sgt	BRANDISH Russell Stanley	29-07-42	218 Sqn
656869	Sgt	BRANNON Walter Alan Frederick	20-09-42	142 Sqn
656327	Sgt	BRANS Sidney	15-10-42	97 Sqn
1238784	Sgt	BRANT Ronald Arthur	24-12-42	10 OTU
910235	Sgt	BRASH Robert Hugh	26-07-42	83 Sqn
1001423	Sgt	BRATT Eric Clement	9-04-42	158 Sqn
1188799	Sgt	BRAY Leonard Charles	12-08-42	57 Sqn
1204586	Sgt	BRAZENALL William Henry	27-10-42	1657 HCU
975641	Sgt	BRAZIER William Joseph	20-07-42	12 Sqn
110788	P/O	BRENER Henry	27-04-42	9 Sqn
930163	Sgt	BRETT Donald William	1-08-42	12 Sqn
798503	Sgt	BRETT John [Newfoundland]	30-05-42	12 Sqn
1187215	Sgt	BRETT Roy Harry	25-06-42	102 Sqn
637729	Sgt	BRETT Thomas Edward	1-10-42	10 Sqn
1382448	F/S	BRETTLE Lelies Robert	31-12-42	83 Sqn
1165987	F/S	BREWER Alfred	30-11-42	10 Sqn
1331144	Sgt	BREWER Robert Jack	4-06-42	1519 Flt
78926	P/O	BRIANT Edward Arthur Rutherford	28-08-42	103 Sqn
106371	F/O	BRIANT DFC Neville James	5-10-42	97 Sqn
1066008	Sgt	BRIDGE Ernest	28-07-42	101 Sqn
1051134	F/S	BRIDGE Silas Harry	19-02-42	107 Sqn
1431897	Sgt	BRIDGES Leslie Samuel	28-10-42	10 OTU
983068	Sgt	BRIERLEY Denison	20-12-42	76 Sqn
1005748	Sgt	BRIGGS Edgar Tong	11-09-42	20 OTU
1541522	Sgt	BRIGGS Frank	15-10-42	103 Sqn
967594	Sgt	BRIGGS Stanley	16-04-42	149 Sqn
137214	P/O	BRIMBLE William Stanley	20-12-42	76 Sqn
1288349	Sgt	BRIMFIELD Dennis George	1-08-42	21 OTU
1096831	Sgt	BRINDLE Alfred	3-12-42	27 OTU
42969	F/L	BRINDLEY Alfred	15-10-42	10 Sqn
917837	F/S	BRINKHURST DFM John Derrick	21-12-42	106 Sqn
1300474	Sgt	BRISCOE Benjamin	30-11-42	10 OTU
1275329	AC1	BRISTOW Arthur Ernest	1-07-42	12 Sqn
1337646	Sgt	BRISTOW Henry William Sydney	22-11-42	12 OTU
634328	F/S	BRITTAIN Allbutt	28-01-42	138 Sqn
749326	Sgt	BROAD Charles	9-03-42	83 Sqn
971256	F/S	BROADBENT DFM Harold Cyril Frederick	4-06-42	218 Sqn
1184497	Sgt	BROADBRIDGE Roland Percival	16-06-42	1651 CU
1001480	Sgt	BROADHEAD Harold Mayo Richard	17-09-42	61 Sqn
1579235	AC2	BROADHURST Granville	28-12-42	23 OTU
119833	P/O	BROADLEY Richard Henry	6-06-42	14 OTU
1395027	Sgt	BROCK Thomas William	23-11-42	44 Sqn
656934	Sgt	BROCKLEBANK Ernest	21-05-42	21 OTU
971199	Sgt	BROCKLEY Donald Charles	25-03-42	61 Sqn
115109	P/O	BRODERICK Kenneth James	9-07-42	106 Sqn
655081	Sgt	BRODIE William Craig	9-05-42	15 Sqn
1072884	Sgt	BROGAN James Anthony	29-07-42	115 Sqn
967977	Sgt	BROGDEN Fred William	17-09-42	158 Sqn
1207423	F/S	BROOK Frederick Victor	22-11-42	156 Sqn
656868	Sgt	BROOK Henry John	31-10-42	150 Sqn
942640	Sgt	BROOKE Francis Haydn	22-01-42	50 Sqn
103547	P/O	BROOKE Paul Rigby Sinclair	6-04-42	9 Sqn
1378129	Sgt	BROOKE Ronald	16-07-42	27 OTU
160029	P/O	BROOKE-NORRIS Sisson William [South Africa]	20-12-42	156 Sqn
922945	Sgt	BROOKER Ronald	15-10-42	103 Sqn
930979	Sgt	BROOKES Eric	30-10-42	49 Sqn
1198300	Sgt	BROOKES Ernest Albert	6-12-42	7 Sqn
1177718	Sgt	BROOKES Joseph Cecil	6-11-42	15 Sqn
1069578	Sgt	BROOKES Wilfred	2-06-42	78 Sqn
1177015	Sgt	BROOKS Albert James Jarvis	24-09-42	9 Sqn
638755	F/S	BROOKS DFM Alfred Bryan	17-09-42	49 Sqn
114155	P/O	BROOKS Alfred Victor	21-06-42	9 Sqn
1177569	Sgt	BROOKS Arthur Leslie	26-06-42	218 Sqn
1357673	Sgt	BROOKS Charles Harry Sidney	20-12-42	9 Sqn
947475	Sgt	BROOKS Douglas Percy	4-06-42	76 Sqn
616576	LAC	BROOKS E. J.	8-06-42	12 Sqn
924977	Sgt	BROOKS John	6-08-42	207 Sqn
1187214	F/S	BROOKS John Hooper	15-10-42	106 Sqn
1801977	Sgt	BROOKS Kenneth Alfred	31-12-42	16 OTU
1467383	Sgt	BROOM Frank Adrian	8-11-42	10 Sqn
1190407	Sgt	BROOME Sidney	9-11-42	102 Sqn
1231185	Sgt	BROOMHEAD Charles James	27-08-42	12 Sqn
1250057	Sgt	BROTHERS Peter Grenville	25-06-42	214 Sqn
1114334	Sgt	BROTHWELL George	24-09-42	9 Sqn
115672	P/O	BROUGH Harold Selwyn	29-03-42	106 Sqn
1311939	Sgt	BROUGHTON Geoffrey Eyre	9-10-42	1658 HCU
1027778	Sgt	BROWN Alfred Ernest	20-12-42	103 Sqn
1017124	Sgt	BROWN Arthur	23-10-42	218 Sqn
1108965	Sgt	BROWN Basil Sydney	3-06-42	7 Sqn
1281447	Sgt	BROWN Bernard Edward	6-02-42	455 Sqn
1356420	Sgt	BROWN Clifford	27-03-42	408 Sqn
1182504	Sgt	BROWN Desmond McCooey	9-06-42	109 Sqn
1263694	Sgt	BROWN Erlin Leslie Ross	3-12-42	102 Sqn
1320388	Sgt	BROWN Francis George	20-12-42	77 Sqn
944101	Sgt	BROWN Frederick George	30-05-42	156 Sqn
1335241	Sgt	BROWN George Alfred	29-11-42	15 OTU
535260	Sgt	BROWN George Kirtley	5-09-42	115 Sqn
1187004	Sgt	BROWN George William	17-06-42	35 Sqn
643275	Sgt	BROWN Hedley	15-02-42	9 Sqn
102098	F/O	BROWN Henry Ernest	24-07-42	9 Sqn
1167452	Sgt	BROWN Horace Stanley	15-04-42	49 Sqn
629164	Sgt	BROWN Jack	21-06-42	9 Sqn
956389	Sgt	BROWN Jack	4-07-42	61 Sqn
1378840	Sgt	BROWN James	31-05-42	12 Sqn
110820	P/O	BROWN James Watson	15-09-42	15 Sqn
981758	Sgt	BROWN John Downie	2-06-42	106 Sqn
531369	Sgt	BROWN John William	17-06-42	102 Sqn
925545	Sgt	BROWN Norman Francis Townshend	9-03-42	19 OTU
106502	P/O	BROWN Peter Gregory	31-03-42	35 Sqn
978265	Sgt	BROWN Richard Arnold	1-06-42	18 OTU
1053806	Sgt	BROWN Robert	21-01-42	408 Sqn
1006781	Sgt	BROWN Robert William Burdon	6-04-42	49 Sqn
104401	P/O	BROWN Stanley	30-05-42	218 Sqn
747994	F/S	BROWN Stanley James	9-03-42	101 Sqn
538671	Sgt	BROWN Thomas Beatty	19-09-42	15 Sqn
113391	P/O	BROWN Thomas Deathers	28-08-42	207 Sqn
1379120	Sgt	BROWN Walter	22-09-42	19 OTU
532296	Sgt	BROWN William	30-05-42	76 Sqn
1187000	F/S	BROWN William	21-08-42	218 Sqn
1385795	Sgt	BROWN William George	25-10-42	12 Sqn
1321471	Sgt	BROWN William James	9-11-42	12 OTU
643058	Sgt	BROWNE Anthony John	6-01-42	3 GTrgFlt
88436	F/O	BROWNE Douglas Jack	18-03-42	23 OTU
1378109	Sgt	BROWNE Joseph Ernest	16-01-42	15 OTU
987759	F/S	BROWNE William Alexander Coulson	15-04-42	144 Sqn
1048174	Sgt	BROWNHILL Stanley	6-12-42	102 Sqn
514188	W/O	BROWNING Cyril Mac	31-12-42	19 OTU
61917	P/O	BROZ Jaromir [Czechoslovakia]	17-01-42	311 Sqn
1051139	Sgt	BRUMMITT Charles Herbert	28-08-42	97 Sqn
927161	Sgt	BRUNSDON Peter Sydney	16-04-42	149 Sqn
553570	F/S	BRUNT Arthur Havelock	12-02-42	420 Sqn
1056497	Sgt	BRUNTON Andrew Turnbull	31-05-42	156 Sqn
927026	Sgt	BRYAN Douglas	9-01-42	144 Sqn
63479	F/L	BRYAN Jeffrey	5-09-42	76 Sqn
621027	Sgt	BRYAN Trevor	9-09-42	150 Sqn
565225	F/S	BRYANT Derek Arthur	28-04-42	Horsham St. Faith

Number	Rank	Name	Date	Unit
951974	F/S	BRYANT Francis Thomas James	11-12-42	27 OTU
580709	W/O	BRYCE Alexander Collingwood	2-05-42	106 Sqn
656407	Sgt	BRYDON John Lovat	29-07-42	115 Sqn
108564	P/O	BUCHAN Alastair William	25-03-42	61 Sqn
1355712	Sgt	BUCHAN Herbert	1-08-42	25 OTU
89769	F/L	BUCHAN DFC Robert Murray	25-08-42	83 Sqn
1375544	Sgt	BUCHANAN David	16-10-42	115 Sqn
572393	Sgt	BUCHANAN James	1-10-42	15 Sqn
1254247	Sgt	BUCHANAN Kenneth	6-06-42	156 Sqn
1330654	Sgt	BUCHWALTER Frederick David	7-12-42	102 Sqn
1030867	AC1	BUCKINGHAM Alfred Thomas	17-02-42	9 Sqn
1320255	Sgt	BUCKLAND George	9-10-42	1658 HCU
1233255	Sgt	BUCKLAND James	20-12-42	158 Sqn
614046	Sgt	BUCKLEY Arthur	20-06-42	214 Sqn
1312443	Sgt	BUCKLEY Howell James	20-11-42	27 OTU
1008481	Sgt	BUCKLEY Jack	26-03-42	61 Sqn
1080095	Sgt	BUCKLEY William	17-09-42	11 OTU
534220	Sgt	BUCKTON Eric John	30-07-42	149 Sqn
1262254	Sgt	BUDD William Charles	8-09-42	12 Sqn
1322367	Sgt	BUDGEN Cyril Frederick	11-12-42	10 Sqn
128029	F/O	BUGDEN Eric Theodore	17-12-42	115 Sqn
1422760	Sgt	BULL Glyn	17-12-42	97 Sqn
755397	F/S	BULL DFM Peter Ernest	13-07-42	420 Sqn
929396	Sgt	BULLEN Harry Bircham	25-04-42	103 Sqn
67650	F/O	BULLOCK Henry John	9-05-42	9 Sqn
570264	Sgt	BULLOCK Philip Harold	26-04-42	218 Sqn
553823	F/S	BULT Sidney Reginald	9-01-42	104 Sqn
101535	F/O	BUNBURY John Shirley	17-08-42	50 Sqn
657816	Sgt	BUNCLARK DFM Frank Charles	11-11-42	61 Sqn
521690	Sgt	BUNG Archibald Leslie	9-11-42	50 Sqn
1175562	Sgt	BUNN Cecil James	8-06-42	420 Sqn
932988	Sgt	BUNNING Geoffrey Charles	31-05-42	214 Sqn
580639	F/S	BUNTING James Arthur	16-01-42	408 Sqn
1392526	Sgt	BURBRIDGE Eric James	16-12-42	75 Sqn
1308006	Sgt	BURCHER John Edward	29-03-42	83 Sqn
78272	S/L	BURDETT Arthur Patrick	31-03-42	76 Sqn
778829	Sgt	BURFORD Unich Edward Thomas [Rhodesia]	20-09-42	44 Sqn
118601	P/O	BURGESS James Henry	22-08-42	10 OTU
1301588	Sgt	BURKE John	6-10-42	44 Sqn
900855	Sgt	BURKITT Albert Edward	20-08-42	218 Sqn
1159995	Sgt	BURLEY Roland Henry	19-07-42	408 Sqn
912226	Sgt	BURN Denis Riddel	13-04-42	9 Sqn
1259335	Sgt	BURNETT Basil Noran	16-04-42	101 Sqn
652923	Sgt	BURNETT Henry Brown	4-09-42	25 OTU
111958	P/O	BURNIE Andrew	31-03-42	13 OTU
995977	Sgt	BURNLEY John Douglas	27-04-42	149 Sqn
924900	Sgt	BURNS Alan	26-03-42	115 Sqn
1002252	Sgt	BURNS John	26-03-42	144 Sqn
1292223	Sgt	BURRELL Edmund Robert John	28-06-42	61 Sqn
804335	Sgt	BURRELL Edward Frederick	12-08-42	78 Sqn
1010359	Sgt	BURRELL George Alexander	20-06-42	15 Sqn
84274	S/L	BURROUGH DFC Thomas Noel Challoner	31-01-42	61 Sqn
1160932	Sgt	BURROWS Raymond Benjamin	25-03-42	106 Sqn
281307	Cpl	BURT Horace William	27-05-42	5 Group
1202457	F/S	BURTON Edward George	29-08-42	49 Sqn
1575141	Sgt	BURTON John Bernard	25-11-42	207 Sqn
1119750	Sgt	BURTT Marcus Heppell	27-08-42	15 Sqn
1172870	Sgt	BURTWELL Sydney [Canada]	2-04-42	214 Sqn
68815	F/L	BURY Ernest Martin	26-03-42	114 Sqn
121911	P/O	BUSBY Frank Rumsey	2-06-42	83 Sqn
576055	Sgt	BUSBY Peter	12-08-42	15 Sqn
902603	Sgt	BUSH Frank Henry Stuart	7-07-42	21 OTU
990047	Sgt	BUSH Graham Francis	28-08-42	35 Sqn
635036	Sgt	BUSH DFM Robert	27-07-42	142 Sqn
1057442	F/S	BUSHBY Joseph Bryan	31-05-42	35 Sqn
655155	Sgt	BUSHELL Brian Frederick	30-09-42	51 Sqn
1261880	Sgt	BUSHELL Herbert Randall	5-09-42	115 Sqn
1310132	Sgt	BUSHELL William James	27-08-42	214 Sqn
548783	Sgt	BUTCHER Philip Bertie Joseph	6-10-42	103 Sqn
1318591	Sgt	BUTCHER Sidney John	6-11-42	15 Sqn
1200354	Sgt	BUTCHER Reginald Alfred	6-01-42	3 GTrgFlt
1287068	Sgt	BUTLER Alfred Eric William	16-09-42	26 OTU
1154913	Sgt	BUTLER Cyril John Edmund	12-04-42	420 Sqn
1262460	Sgt	BUTLER Eric Davies	29-08-42	149 Sqn
1191385	Sgt	BUTLER Richard William	26-07-42	106 Sqn
102576	F/O	BUTLER Robert	23-09-42	218 Sqn
37465	W/C	BUTLER DFC Vernon Stanley	8-03-42	226 Sqn
567473	Sgt	BUTLER Victor John Arthur	25-08-42	97 Sqn
1061600	Sgt	BUTTERWORTH Douglas	9-01-42	12 Sqn
149856	F/O	BUTTERWORTH Ernest Rex	2-10-42	106 Sqn
1112329	Sgt	BUTTERWORTH Francis Norman	18-05-42	115 Sqn
928917	Sgt	BUTTERWORTH George William	28-04-42	102 Sqn
1307679	Sgt	BUTTERWORTH John Bernard	18-05-42	15 Sqn
856750	Sgt	BUTTERWORTH Thomas Arthur	31-01-42	61 Sqn
1332830	Sgt	BUTTON Frederick Oswald	11-11-42	57 Sqn
112527	F/O	BYRNE John Gordon	28-12-42	23 OTU
798555	Sgt	BYRNE Kenneth Edward [Newfoundland]	9-05-42	12 Sqn
1116631	Sgt	BYRNE Lawrence	17-09-42	158 Sqn
534732	Sgt	BYRNE Phillip Denis	26-07-42	15 Sqn
1100665	Sgt	BYROM Albert	2-09-42	97 Sqn
1330553	Sgt	BYGRAVE Ivor Pestell	17-11-42	11 OTU
1385190	Sgt	BYWATERS Thomas Bernard	15-10-42	149 Sqn
1111488	Sgt	CADDEN Andrew	20-06-42	7 Sqn
1016939	Sgt	CADMAN James Wilfred	14-01-42	207 Sqn
1165794	Sgt	CADMAN Ronald William	1-10-42	61 Sqn
1059121	Sgt	CAIE Andrew	31-05-42	78 Sqn
1165796	Sgt	CALCUTT Clarence Gilbert	16-09-42	26 OTU
1344659	Sgt	CALDER George Sinclair	15-10-42	21 OTU
992777	Sgt	CALDERHEAD Leslie Wilbur	9-03-42	101 Sqn
118607	P/O	CALDERWOOD Thomas McWhirter	10-08-42	405 Sqn
1116910	Sgt	CALDWELL James Clelland	30-09-42	51 Sqn
1166513	Sgt	CALDWELL Leslie James	10-03-42	158 Sqn
121509	P/O	CALDWELL DFM William Frazer	31-05-42	22 OTU
1381147	Sgt	CALE Ronald Philip	28-03-42	7 Sqn
1069247	Sgt	CALLAGHAN Matthew	8-05-42	21 OTU
1312476	Sgt	CALLAGHAN Richard Howell	1-08-42	21 OTU
981131	Sgt	CALLAGHAN William James	31-05-42	12 Sqn
567483	Sgt	CALLAN John Arthur	17-12-42	44 Sqn
45897	F/O	CALVERT Arthur James	23-09-42	218 Sqn
1191329	Sgt	CALVERT Cyril	20-12-42	156 Sqn
46910	P/O	CALVERT Eric Douglas	21-06-42	7 Sqn
903068	Sgt	CALVERT MiD Harrold Phillip [Canada]	20-05-42	10 Sqn
1311019	Sgt	CALVERT John William	14-07-42	150 Sqn
1002082	Sgt	CAMERON Alexander Henry	11-06-42	77 Sqn
747925	F/S	CAMERON James Douglas	9-05-42	9 Sqn
1365197	Sgt	CAMERON John McDonald	25-06-42	76 Sqn
1382014	Sgt	CAMFIELD Harold Reuben	5-06-42	150 Sqn
531455	Sgt	CAMLIN Brian Buchanan	31-05-42	26 OTU
798508	Sgt	CAMPBELL Colin David Evander [Newfoundland]	16-02-42	77 Sqn
997954	Sgt	CAMPBELL Colin Reynolds	29-04-42	78 Sqn
1373264	Sgt	CAMPBELL David	1-10-42	10 Sqn
1173814	Sgt	CAMPBELL Douglas Granville Joseph John	31-03-42	35 Sqn
1108043	F/S	CAMPBELL Duncan	12-04-42	103 Sqn
1335833	Sgt	CAMPBELL James Ross	1-08-42	25 OTU
1060537	Sgt	CAMPBELL John Bertram	12-06-42	114 Sqn
127017	P/O	CAMPBELL John Leslie Gordon	16-10-42	19 OTU
131110	P/O	CAMPBELL DFM Paul	11-11-42	61 Sqn
1111478	Sgt	CAMPBELL Thomas McCord	2-09-42	218 Sqn
102997	P/O	CAMPBELL DFC William Gordon	29-07-42	419 Sqn
137659	P/O	CAMPLIN Arthur Mussendine	21-12-42	106 Sqn
751643	F/S	CAMPS Kenneth William	11-06-42	44 Sqn
1071358	Sgt	CANAVAN John	12-02-42	144 Sqn

Number	Rank	Name	Date	Unit
77270	F/L	CANDLER MiD Peter Thorne	30-05-42	142 Sqn
100035	P/O	CANN Peter Norman	25-03-42	106 Sqn
652687	Sgt	CANNIFF James	25-06-42	106 Sqn
1376754	Sgt	CANNON Francis Thomas George	25-08-42	15 OTU
1383183	Sgt	CANSICK William	28-03-42	419 Sqn
1063357	Sgt	CANT George	2-04-42	20 OTU
1177846	Sgt	CANTELL Norman Walter Sydney	14-07-42	158 Sqn
1167818	Sgt	CANTERBURY Gerald Thomas	17-12-42	103 Sqn
798616	Sgt	CANTWELL Gerard Joseph Michael [Newfoundland]	7-08-42	78 Sqn
1377727	Sgt	CAPHAM Ronald George Peter	30-07-42	149 Sqn
1394911	AC1	CAPP John	24-05-42	138 Sqn
1192583	Sgt	CAREY William Frederick	6-09-42	21 OTU
1170430	F/S	CARLIN Mark Francis	8-11-42	158 Sqn
1252018	F/S	CARMICHAEL William	9-06-42	77 Sqn
1334417	Sgt	CARPENTER Anthony Thorpe	21-12-42	7 Sqn
1378971	F/S	CARR Clifford	7-12-42	102 Sqn
1058666	Sgt	CARR John Harrison	26-01-42	144 Sqn
1330310	Sgt	CARR Leslie George	28-08-42	115 Sqn
119716	P/O	CARR Philip William	10-08-42	150 Sqn
1220942	Sgt	CARRICK William Donald	10-09-42	16 OTU
630417	F/S	CARRILINE Victor	5-05-42	149 Sqn
124265	F/L	CARRINGTON Royston Denis William	5-10-42	35 Sqn
657211	Sgt	CARROLL Gerard	14-08-42	7 Sqn
994961	F/S	CARROLL Richard Francis [Eire]	26-06-42	218 Sqn
954000	F/S	CARRUTHERS Kenneth Edmondson	21-08-42	19 OTU
1063043	Sgt	CARRUTHERS William Alan	26-06-42	20 OTU
1033235	Sgt	CARSON Richard	6-10-42	103 Sqn
1253846	Sgt	CARTER Ambrose Thomas	30-11-42	149 Sqn
88404	F/O	CARTER Derek Guy [Rhodesia]	12-02-42	50 Sqn
1166938	Sgt	CARTER Francis Raymond	10-09-42	207 Sqn
1291956	Sgt	CARTER George Alfred	7-11-42	156 Sqn
128561	F/S	CARTER Gordon Kenneth	25-09-42	105 Sqn
926380	Sgt	CARTER Hedley Walter	3-11-42	1484 Flt
1381159	Sgt	CARTER Herbert	16-11-42	149 Sqn
1585838	Sgt	CARTER James Henry	9-12-42	24 OTU
571212	Sgt	CARTER John Alfred	25-06-42	10 Sqn
39220	S/L	CARTER John Noel Graydon	9-11-42	57 Sqn
637844	F/S	CARTER John Patrick	10-11-42	7 Sqn
126578	P/O	CARTER John Philip	31-05-42	49 Sqn
902810	Sgt	CARTER Stanley Arthur	12-08-42	106 Sqn
1577361	Sgt	CARTER Stanley Childs	1-10-42	10 Sqn
1271541	Sgt	CARTER Sydney Ernest Arthur	16-12-42	15 OTU
101529	P/O	CARTER Thomas Maughan	2-06-42	102 Sqn
1375377	Sgt	CARTER Tony Kevin	12-03-42	75 Sqn
1203179	Sgt	CARTER Victor George	7-05-42	22 OTU
655428	Sgt	CARTWRIGHT Edward Thomas Albert	13-02-42	21 OTU
1208967	Sgt	CARTWRIGHT Eric	24-07-42	207 Sqn
1304031	Sgt	CARTWRIGHT George	9-03-42	35 Sqn
1110531	Sgt	CARTWRIGHT James	9-03-42	9 Sqn
530247	Sgt	CARTWRIGHT Lancelot Cyril	11-09-42	50 Sqn
1467115	Sgt	CASBOLT Terence William Henry	20-11-42	76 Sqn
1270868	Sgt	CASELTON Kenneth	5-08-42	1653 CU
1348582	Sgt	CASEY James	29-12-42	77 Sqn
1058309	Sgt	CASH Noel	19-05-42	15 Sqn
1250185	Sgt	CASSAM Arthur Henry	2-04-42	144 Sqn
113273	P/O	CASSAVETTI Ian McKenzie	29-03-42	61 Sqn
104476	P/O	CASSIDY Eric Arthur	7-08-42	103 Sqn
778385	Sgt	CASSON William Harry [Rhodesia]	12-12-42	102 Sqn
48954	P/O	CASTELL Richard Albert	18-08-42	21 OTU
84005	F/L	CASTELLO DFC William Deryk	18-04-42	12 Sqn
1305765	Sgt	CATLEY Raymond	31-05-42	156 Sqn
1076033	Sgt	CATLIN Ernest West	10-09-42	61 Sqn
1320525	Sgt	CATLING George Walter	22-09-42	19 OTU
1261952	F/S	CATO Percy Charles	1-10-42	102 Sqn
1024370	Sgt	CATTO George Symon	2-09-42	15 OTU
1203557	Sgt	CAUSLEY Leonard	26-07-42	114 Sqn
1183330	Sgt	CAVANAGH George Clayton	7-08-42	218 Sqn
1332432	Sgt	CEENEY George Edmund Henry	28-11-42	150 Sqn
1185878	Sgt	CHADWICK Barton	20-06-42	57 Sqn
1006926	Sgt	CHADWICK Ernest	2-06-42	156 Sqn
77909	F/L	CHADWICK Roy Blackwell	8-06-42	35 Sqn
111553	P/O	CHADWICK George Kenneth	26-05-42	19 OTU
908544	Sgt	CHALDECOTT Eric William John	28-08-42	207 Sqn
1188863	Sgt	CHAMBERS George James	24-10-42	78 Sqn
778593	Sgt	CHALMERS Gerald Graham [Rhodesia]	11-09-42	106 Sqn
576578	Sgt	CHALMERS Kenneth Stuart	17-10-42	207 Sqn
1378042	F/S	CHAMBERLAIN John Alfred	9-03-42	115 Sqn
925519	Sgt	CHAMBERLIN Guy Hesketh	6-06-42	156 Sqn
1457097	Sgt	CHAMBERS John Claridge	14-09-42	150 Sqn
1305524	Sgt	CHAMBERS William Edmund	30-05-42	15 Sqn
1044874	Sgt	CHANCE Albert Donald	1-10-42	405 Sqn
1199671	Cpl	CHANDLER Roy Edward	10-12-42	138 Sqn
1186607	Sgt	CHANDLER William Thomas	11-12-42	27 OTU
73124	P/O	CHANT Cyril Dinham	24-06-42	23 OTU
1051972	Sgt	CHANTRELL Arthur Stuart	22-01-42	106 Sqn
1056809	Sgt	CHAPMAN Frank	19-05-42	106 Sqn
1378627	Sgt	CHAPMAN Henry Eric	20-05-42	10 Sqn
32097	W/C	CHAPMAN John Henry Abel	26-03-42	7 Sqn
1376923	Sgt	CHAPMAN Peter Lewis	20-01-42	101 Sqn
1046424	Sgt	CHAPMAN Ronald Arthur	26-06-42	23 OTU
925685	Sgt	CHAPMAN William Geoffrey	7-11-42	83 Sqn
934647	Sgt	CHAPMAN William John	13-07-42	420 Sqn
1000564	Sgt	CHAPMAN William Waddell	18-04-42	158 Sqn
928292	Sgt	CHAPPLE Peter Bernard	21-01-42	408 Sqn
1214346	Sgt	CHARLESWORTH George Elliott	16-09-42	11 OTU
987863	Sgt	CHARLESWORTH William Hustler	20-06-42	76 Sqn
743081	F/S	CHARLTON Alexander Nelson	24-08-42	149 Sqn
1077327	Sgt	CHARLTON Frank	28-12-42	10 OTU
103549	P/O	CHARLTON William Frederick Dixon	1-06-42	408 Sqn
1091736	Sgt	CHARLTON William Kenneth	22-12-42	26 OTU
33108	W/C	CHARLTON-JONES Cecil	29-08-42	149 Sqn
1053553	Sgt	CHARNOCK John Frederick	29-01-42	17 OTU
1181834	Sgt	CHASTON Thomas William	24-04-42	150 Sqn
127150	F/O	CHATTERTON Eric Frank	22-12-42	21 OTU
1016810	Sgt	CHEADLE Alfred Ronald	26-01-42	82 Sqn
121559	P/O	CHEESEMAN Sidney Arthur	26-06-42	24 OTU
103550	P/O	CHEETHAM Arnold Foster	5-05-42	15 Sqn
1138227	Sgt	CHEETHAM Ernest	29-10-42	10 OTU
615248	Sgt	CHEETHAM Herbert Thomas	22-11-42	102 Sqn
135485	P/O	CHELL David Graham	7-11-42	156 Sqn
1284528	Sgt	CHESSUN Laurent Harry	1-08-42	156 Sqn
1206770	Sgt	CHESTER Walter	5-10-42	35 Sqn
133052	P/O	CHIDDICK William Edward Ambrose	5-10-42	156 Sqn
116134	F/L	CHILD DFC Alan James	19-09-42	35 Sqn
116799	P/O	CHILDS Arthur Henry	11-09-42	16 OTU
1112050	Sgt	CHILVERS Harry	2-04-42	214 Sqn
1381629	Sgt	CHISHOLM Gordon Thomas Lister [Argentina]	22-11-42	57 Sqn
923913	Sgt	CHIVERS John	1-04-42	20 OTU
1280524	F/S	CHOTE Arthur Haydn Frederick	3-08-42	114 Sqn
1029516	Sgt	CHRISTIAN Roy James	29-11-42	15 OTU
1052883	F/S	CHRISTIE Frederick	2-10-42	78 Sqn
63779	F/L	CHRISTIE DSO DFM Templeton	12-12-42	7 Sqn
1264494	Sgt	CHUDLEIGH Frank Donald	28-08-42	101 Sqn
1376275	Sgt	CHURCH James Ernest	13-03-42	77 Sqn
1272476	Sgt	CHURCH Reginald Harry	22-11-42	12 OTU
1172507	Sgt	CHURCHER Leslie Alexander	10-01-42	408 Sqn
104514	P/O	CHURCHILL Cecil Stephen	29-03-42	61 Sqn
1189902	Sgt	CHURCHILL Ronald Frederick	6-08-42	419 Sqn
1185902	Sgt	CHURCHLEY George Harry	4-08-42	20 OTU
66491	P/O	CIBULKA Josef Frantisek [Czechoslovakia]	12-03-42	311 Sqn
78681	F/L	CLACK George Lionel	28-08-42	101 Sqn

1379459	F/S	CLADIS Lionel George	11-08-42	207 Sqn	1186919	Sgt	COCKAYNE Colin George	26-06-42	23 OTU
935675	F/S	CLAPHAM John Stanley	2-06-42	10 Sqn	952486	Sgt	COCKAYNE Ronald Cust	12-08-42	57 Sqn
1331580	Sgt	CLARIDGE Sidney Arthur	25-10-42	103 Sqn	1168673	Sgt	COCKBURN Donald Wilfred	14-01-42	50 Sqn
1395017	Sgt	CLARK Charles Frederick 'Bobby'	6-11-42	78 Sqn	1161773	Sgt	COCKBURN James William Bingham	5-06-42	1443 Flt
131772	P/O	CLARK Dennis Frederick Stephen	31-12-42	16 OTU	656606	Sgt	COCKIE Alastair Mackenzie	10-09-42	207 Sqn
1166730	Sgt	CLARK Harold Frederick Power	9-06-42	83 Sqn	1384870	Sgt	COCKS John Gilbert	31-10-42	150 Sqn
1104588	Sgt	CLARK Harold Moffat	2-10-42	78 Sqn	1312599	Sgt	COFFEY Brian Edward	30-07-42	419 Sqn
1015524	Sgt	CLARK Henry	14-02-42	20 OTU	1216731	Sgt	COFFIN Ronald Idris	26-06-42	15 OTU
1381121	F/S	CLARK Hugh Mackenzie	13-08-42	7 Sqn	1182229	F/S	COGGIN Stanley Alfred	19-05-42	218 Sqn
124634	P/O	CLARK Ian Patterson	26-06-42	24 OTU	840499	Sgt	COHEN Edward Charles	1-08-42	25 OTU
1166515	Sgt	CLARK John Calder	29-04-42	57 Sqn	39497	S/L	COHEN Lionel Rees	30-07-42	150 Sqn
1312585	Sgt	CLARK John Francis	1-07-42	21 OTU	655080	Sgt	COHEN Maurice	31-03-42	35 Sqn
657357	Sgt	CLARK Norman George	27-09-42	10 OTU	120429	F/O	COHEN Nathan	6-12-42	464 Sqn
102988	P/O	CLARK DFM Ralph Edward	3-06-42	61 Sqn	1265631	F/S	COLCLOUGH Maurice James	22-07-42	115 Sqn
1375655	Sgt	CLARK Sydney Frank	28-08-42	408 Sqn	570285	Sgt	COLDICOTT Cedric Nils	25-09-42	61 Sqn
903293	Sgt	CLARK William Graham	9-06-42	75 Sqn	1375124	F/S	COLE Ronald Sydney	1-10-42	61 Sqn
1026143	Sgt	CLARKE Albert Morriss	16-09-42	142 Sqn	1379680	Sgt	COLE William John	7-08-42	78 Sqn
115725	P/O	CLARKE Douglas Albert Edward	10-03-42	158 Sqn	101528	P/O	COLE William Joseph	25-06-42	76 Sqn
1025294	Sgt	CLARKE Eric	11-12-42	25 OTU	632891	F/S	COLEHAN Robert Arthur	27-08-42	214 Sqn
1187517	Sgt	CLARKE Frank Sidney	21-08-42	149 Sqn	1382363	Sgt	COLEMAN Christopher Leonard	16-11-42	101 Sqn
1333700	Sgt	CLARKE Frederick Charles	30-11-42	10 Sqn	1065788	Sgt	COLEMAN Eric	8-04-42	15 OTU
1183538	Sgt	CLARKE Harold Frank	24-07-42	207 Sqn	106074	P/O	COLEMAN John Eric	29-07-42	9 Sqn
1162625	Sgt	CLARKE Harry	1-04-42	1428 Flt	72585	S/L	COLEMAN DFC* Lloyd Watt [New Zealand]	11-03-42	149 Sqn
1575693	Sgt	CLARKE James Clifford	15-10-42	57 Sqn					
624831	Sgt	CLARKE James Joseph	21-01-42	51 Sqn	1254284	Sgt	COLEMAN Philip John	6-04-42	9 Sqn
121537	P/O	CLARKE John Peter Dixon	9-05-42	158 Sqn	45811	F/O	COLES DFC Francis Albert William	22-09-42	12 Sqn
943810	Sgt	CLARKE John William	6-08-42	78 Sqn	751410	F/S	COLES Ronald Alfred	25-05-42	25 OTU
748152	F/S	CLARKE Leslie	9-01-42	19 OTU	778240	F/S	COLEY Aubrey Wilson [Rhodesia]	7-11-42	83 Sqn
961663	Sgt	CLARKE Leslie Ernest	28-06-42	150 Sqn	1258650	Sgt	COLLEDGE Douglas Murton	28-03-42	77 Sqn
1166504	F/S	CLARKE Leslie Roland	3-09-42	150 Sqn	1027531	Sgt	COLLEY Douglas Sherwin	9-12-42	11 OTU
1151322	Sgt	CLARKE Stuart Robinson	16-11-42	101 Sqn	966512	Sgt	COLLIE John	8-05-42	57 Sqn
1058877	Sgt	CLARKE DFM Thomas	16-11-42	115 Sqn	37906	S/L	COLLIER Richard Theobold	13-09-42	156 Sqn
1022463	Sgt	CLARKSON Harold	22-11-42	102 Sqn	115183	F/O	COLLINGS Henry Philemon	31-10-42	107 Sqn
1112057	Sgt	CLAY Henry	28-08-42	115 Sqn	1600145	Sgt	COLLINGS Kenneth Victor George	14-11-42	97 Sqn
1376606	Sgt	CLAYTON Alan Harvey	15-11-42	150 Sqn	1006390	Sgt	COLLINGWOOD Eric	25-08-42	106 Sqn
1293639	Sgt	CLAYTON Michael James	16-09-42	26 OTU	1076726	Sgt	COLLINGWOOD Thomas	4-12-42	19 OTU
121334	P/O	CLAYTON Peter Levigne	6-06-42	149 Sqn	1381237	Sgt	COLLINS Arthur	18-08-42	76 Sqn
1254858	Sgt	CLAYTON William	9-06-42	12 Sqn	920126	Sgt	COLLINS Basil Osborn	26-07-42	158 Sqn
940025	Cpl	CLEAVER Donald Scott	29-10-42	15 Sqn	1180436	Sgt	COLLINS Edward Frank	6-04-42	9 Sqn
1495772	Sgt	CLEGG Herbert	27-08-42	15 Sqn	631179	Sgt	COLLINS Frederick Reginald	17-12-42	103 Sqn
1233498	LAC	CLEGG Richard	17-12-42	138 Sqn	999570	Sgt	COLLINS Maurice	10-08-42	150 Sqn
1112051	Sgt	CLELLAND Gordon	12-05-42	419 Sqn	1453186	Sgt	COLLINS Noel Briggs	8-11-42	142 Sqn
966275	F/S	CLELLAND John George	25-03-42	61 Sqn	39713	S/L	COLLINS DFC Raymond Noel	27-08-42	105 Sqn
104410	P/O	CLEMENT Donald Jack	4-02-42	21 Sqn	973486	Sgt	COLLINS William	17-05-42	149 Sqn
1264827	Sgt	CLEMSON Albert Thomas	25-09-42	10 OTU	903486	Sgt	COLLINS William Alfred	10-04-42	49 Sqn
919564	Sgt	CLEPHANE Donald Alexander	9-05-42	10 Sqn	1259856	Sgt	COLLINS William Edwin	18-08-42	57 Sqn
1365044	Sgt	CLEZY William [Australia]	12-03-42	75 Sqn	591325	Sgt	COLLINS William Stewart	3-09-42	49 Sqn
939658	Sgt	CLIFFE Jack	18-09-42	44 Sqn	930430	Sgt	COLLIS William Edward	20-06-42	57 Sqn
63650	Cpl	CLIFFORD Thomas Ashall	17-05-42	77 Sqn	1006104	Sgt	COLLOTON William	24-07-42	405 Sqn
1181870	Sgt	CLIFTON John James	5-06-42	150 Sqn	1284077	Sgt	COLLS Leslie John	26-03-42	88 Sqn
1016825	Sgt	CLIMIE Colin Black	29-04-42	12 Sqn	1186865	Sgt	COLLUMBELL John	17-09-42	149 Sqn
1314119	Sgt	CLIPSON Arthur Lascelles	9-03-42	21 OTU	80427	P/O	COLLYER Denis Ralph	11-12-42	158 Sqn
106562	P/O	CLOSE Peter Thrale	10-01-42	49 Sqn	1151281	Sgt	COLTMAN John	29-10-42	115 Sqn
646433	F/S	CLOUGH James Algernon	10-11-42	149 Sqn	1185189	Sgt	COLUMBINE Alfred Bernard	29-04-42	35 Sqn
106532	P/O	CLOUGH James Thomas Bartle	16-02-42	49 Sqn	567129	Sgt	COLVILLE James	6-08-42	102 Sqn
926499	Sgt	CLOUGH John Alfred	8-12-42	149 Sqn	1079649	Sgt	COLVIN Raymond	17-05-42	9 Sqn
923190	F/S	CLOUGH William Leonard	28-09-42	115 Sqn	1183362	Sgt	COLWILL Malcolm Charles	6-12-42	115 Sqn
1331382	Sgt	CLOUTING Albert	16-12-42	15 OTU	1254810	Sgt	COMBER Norman Seton	28-07-42	101 Sqn
1164937	Sgt	CLUFF Edward Burgess	24-03-42	44 Sqn	751280	F/S	COMERY Arthur	14-09-42	156 Sqn
1383996	Sgt	COAKER Frederic Peter	12-09-42	97 Sqn	1415871	AC2	COMMINS Oliver Frederick	20-05-42	420 Sqn
1268257	Sgt	COAKLEY DFM Cyril Hugh	11-11-42	61 Sqn	776150	Sgt	CONFAIT Armand Emile [Seychelles]	17-09-42	21 OTU
1104373	Sgt	COAKLEY Francis	21-01-42	17 OTU	929137	Sgt	CONISBEE Albert Allan	31-05-42	103 Sqn
1111952	Sgt	COATES Raymond	25-06-42	1651 CU	656483	Sgt	CONNELLY William	22-06-42	12 Sqn
655734	Sgt	COATES Raymond James	2-04-42	20 OTU	115777	P/O	CONNOLLY John Raymond	10-04-42	76 Sqn
46701	P/O	COBB Reginald Ernest	14-02-42	20 OTU	1211568	Sgt	CONNOR Thomas	20-11-42	11 OTU
1160567	Sgt	COBB Thomas Albert	9-11-42	50 Sqn	1077651	Sgt	CONSIDINE Anthony Talbot Percy [Eire]	10-04-42	49 Sqn
984803	F/S	COBDEN Gerald	27-06-42	150 Sqn					
568554	Sgt	COBELL Walter	13-04-42	15 Sqn	1101609	Sgt	CONSTANCE Dennis Winstone	16-09-42	9 Sqn
1330228	Sgt	COCHRANE Douglas Charles	28-07-42	103 Sqn	1104295	Sgt	CONWELL Edward Victor	19-06-42	408 Sqn

983702	Sgt	CONYBEAR Edward Arthur	9-06-42	12 Sqn	1283564	Sgt	COUNIHAN John Ernest	12-06-42	12 OTU
534642	Sgt	COOGAN Thomas Edward	16-03-42	19 OTU	622802	Sgt	COUPE Arthur Henry	26-01-42	12 Sqn
119536	P/O	COOK Alan Ramsey	22-08-42	10 OTU	77928	F/L	COURT Alexander William	31-07-42	27 OTU
1293852	Sgt	COOK Albert George	11-09-42	83 Sqn	1318105	Sgt	COURT Ronald	14-10-42	61 Sqn
68173	P/O	COOK Derek Alfred	17-03-42	49 Sqn	1383580	Sgt	COUZENS George Alfred Frederick	25-10-42	115 Sqn
1164424	F/S	COOK Geoffrey Robert	12-12-42	27 OTU	109510	P/O	COVENTRY Lawrence Andrew	29-04-42	18 Sqn
922612	Sgt	COOK John William	9-06-42	77 Sqn	1379636	Sgt	COWAN John Robert	28-04-42	150 Sqn
1577367	Sgt	COOK Richard	21-12-42	44 Sqn	1365284	Sgt	COWAN Thomas	15-01-42	10 Sqn
922125	Sgt	COOK Sidney George	31-10-42	25 OTU	1375898	Sgt	COWELL Lewis Wethey	7-05-42	21 OTU
540952	Sgt	COOK William James	23-04-42	218 Sqn	974577	Sgt	COWEN James	29-07-42	218 Sqn
655317	Sgt	COOKE Frank Oswald	5-06-42	114 Sqn	528664	Sgt	COWEN Leon	16-09-42	15 Sqn
1224802	Sgt	COOKE George Albert	5-08-42	10 OTU	132147	P/O	COWIN Robert	31-12-42	16 OTU
115185	P/O	COOKE Gerald Frank Russell	29-07-42	156 Sqn	1288359	Sgt	COWLEY Ronnie	18-04-42	101 Sqn
80346	F/L	COOKE DFC DFM Grimwood Choke [Rhodesia]	21-12-42	106 Sqn	1180183	Sgt	COX Arthur Meaker	17-04-42	97 Sqn
					127273	P/O	COX Geoffrey William	12-12-42	20 OTU
778541	Sgt	COOKE Harold [Rhodesia]	26-06-42	10 OTU	798636	Sgt	COX Horatio Leslie [Newfoundland]	1-08-42	16 OTU
1170027	Sgt	COOKE Maurice	19-07-42	27 OTU	1251520	Sgt	COX Ronald William	28-03-42	207 Sqn
913706	Sgt	COOKE Reginald	15-01-42	104 Sqn	869313	Sgt	COX Samuel	15-04-42	214 Sqn
1199261	Sgt	COOKE William Leslie	9-03-42	9 Sqn	1058314	Sgt	COX Stanley	2-06-42	18 Sqn
1377612	Sgt	COOMBES Geoffrey Cedric	28-08-42	150 Sqn	924154	Sgt	COX William Lawrence	29-03-42	83 Sqn
933684	Sgt	COOMBS Robert John	25-08-42	15 OTU	749430	F/S	COXON John Harry	6-06-42	103 Sqn
1334336	Sgt	COOMBS Victor Joseph	6-10-42	76 Sqn	528782	Sgt	COY James	29-07-42	1651 CU
1066273	Sgt	COOP Samuel	3-09-42	15 Sqn	1057448	Sgt	COYNE Joseph	7-09-42	12 Sqn
122937	P/O	COOPER Billie Bartusek	21-09-42	10 OTU	1175836	Sgt	CRABB Peter Henry	9-03-42	150 Sqn
1102279	Sgt	COOPER Edgar Frederick John	10-01-42	82 Sqn	1263387	Sgt	CRABTREE Norman Geoffrey	7-08-42	16 OTU
1223659	Sgt	COOPER Eric Harold	24-07-42	214 Sqn	1511232	AC1	CRADDOCK George	3-08-42	114 Sqn
1006147	F/S	COOPER Francis Weeks	7-04-42	15 Sqn	1066175	Sgt	CRAFT Charles	14-07-42	158 Sqn
1285428	Sgt	COOPER George Leslie	27-07-42	142 Sqn	526861	Sgt	CRAFT George William	27-04-42	7 Sqn
655307	F/S	COOPER John Stanley	4-09-42	97 Sqn	613300	Sgt	CRAIG Alexander Milne	16-08-42	207 Sqn
778188	Sgt	COOPER Joseph John [South Africa]	27-07-42	106 Sqn	540596	F/S	CRAIG David Leslie Thomas	25-08-42	150 Sqn
1164825	Sgt	COOPER Kenneth John	1-08-42	106 Sqn	1169555	Sgt	CRAIG Hugh Cuthbert	9-07-42	101 Sqn
1261844	Sgt	COOPER Kenneth John	1-10-42	218 Sqn	118685	P/O	CRAIG James Wilson	16-07-42	158 Sqn
60121	F/O	COOPER Robert Ward	9-03-42	83 Sqn	1051927	Sgt	CRAIG John David	28-08-42	103 Sqn
517109	F/S	COOPER Stanely	17-09-42	158 Sqn	996848	F/S	CRAIG William Neilson	25-06-42	214 Sqn
1186699	Sgt	COOPER Sydney	24-09-42	102 Sqn	69492	F/O	CRAIK Donald McLeod	24-03-42	1515 Flt
925750	Sgt	COOPER William Reuben	12-06-42	218 Sqn	988755	F/S	CRAMPTON MiD William Francis	31-05-42	115 Sqn
42804	F/O	COOTE MiD Michael Andean	24-05-42	1483 Flt	1067232	Sgt	CRANE Peter	26-05-42	19 OTU
1006396	Sgt	COPE Ellis Victor	29-08-42	97 Sqn	1201064	Sgt	CRANE William Maurice	7-08-42	103 Sqn
549229	Sgt	COPE James	7-11-42	83 Sqn	778309	Sgt	CRANE William McDonald [Rhodesia]	9-05-42	44 Sqn
113211	F/L	COPESTICK Arthur	2-10-42	Swanton Morley	129486	P/O	CRANSTOUN John Pugh	9-12-42	24 OTU
					1317502	Sgt	CRAPP Francis George	8-12-42	15 Sqn
1380366	Sgt	COPPING Albert John	3-01-42	99 Sqn	655397	Sgt	CRAVEN Alec Henry	5-05-42	22 OTU
1586180	Sgt	COPPLESTONE Alan Frank	17-12-42	218 Sqn	1185176	Sgt	CRAVEN Frank	8-12-42	149 Sqn
115161	P/O	CORAH Geoffrey Peter	1-08-42	107 Sqn	1245834	Sgt	CRAVEN Ronald	5-12-42	15 OTU
1312943	Sgt	CORBETT DFM Ernest Humphries	11-11-42	61 Sqn	1178840	Sgt	CRAWFORD George Bernard	18-07-42	18 Sqn
108833	P/O	CORDALL Robert Oswald	29-07-42	9 Sqn	655522	Sgt	CRAWFORD William Dunlope Cram	29-09-42	20 OTU
1255811	Sgt	CORDEROY Edwin Arthur	22-04-42	408 Sqn	990868	Sgt	CREED William Henry	3-09-42	15 Sqn
916421	Sgt	CORDEROY John James Stephen	8-07-42	19 OTU	104331	P/O	CRESSWELL Cyril	15-05-42	408 Sqn
906587	Sgt	CORDREY Ryall Edward	13-11-42	102 Sqn	751722	F/S	CRERAR Alexander	9-06-42	97 Sqn
128672	P/O	CORFIELD DFM Jack William	26-07-42	83 Sqn	1114086	Sgt	CREWE Kenneth Edward	6-10-42	419 Sqn
930297	Sgt	CORKE Kenneth Clarence Edward	13-03-42	77 Sqn	1162024	Sgt	CREWS Ralph Harry	13-04-42	158 Sqn
570419	Sgt	CORKER Alfred Willie	10-10-42	149 Sqn	1252143	Sgt	CRIDGE Robert John	12-02-42	49 Sqn
1270316	Sgt	CORKER Maurice Stanley Douglas	30-05-42	76 Sqn	1113251	Sgt	CRIGHTON Frederick Gordon	3-06-42	15 Sqn
1290672	Sgt	CORMACK Alexander McGee	25-09-42	61 Sqn	987558	Sgt	CRILLY Thomas	26-03-42	114 Sqn
985764	Sgt	CORMACK William George	4-06-42	101 Sqn	1315820	Sgt	CRISP Robert Philling	17-12-42	115 Sqn
1169609	Sgt	CORNES Gerald Geoffrey	6-01-42	3 GTrgFlt	100549	F/O	CRITCHISON Stanley Bryan	10-07-42	142 Sqn
553453	Sgt	CORNS Edward	26-06-42	83 Sqn	1389509	Sgt	CROCK Herbert Windsor	16-09-42	25 OTU
1379128	Sgt	CORNTHWAITE James William	9-04-42	158 Sqn	1380961	Sgt	CROFT Allan Blyth	6-06-42	44 Sqn
118634	P/O	CORR Rodney Ernest [Eire]	13-05-42	17 OTU	573453	Sgt	CROFT Morris William	20-12-42	405 Sqn
39500	S/L	CORR DFC William Duncan	17-10-42	61 Sqn	1001839	Sgt	CROFT William Alexander	24-02-42	144 Sqn
133527	P/O	CORRIE John Edwin	6-10-42	44 Sqn	1272132	Sgt	CROFTON Cecil Charles William	27-09-42	78 Sqn
1280615	Sgt	COSBY Bertie Harry	7-08-42	150 Sqn	1250335	F/S	CROFTON Richard Mervyn Echlin	28-09-42	88 Sqn
111551	P/O	COSHAM Brian Chester	22-05-42	19 OTU	68793	P/O	CROMBIE James Duncan	25-03-42	50 Sqn
1331982	Sgt	COULES Edwin Charles Alfred	3-09-42	405 Sqn	1377064	Sgt	CRONK Ernest Frank	25-08-42	150 Sqn
920313	Sgt	COULSON Frederick Ernest	15-02-42	9 Sqn	1351986	Sgt	CROOKS Raymond William John	11-12-42	10 Sqn
1063723	Sgt	COULSON Snowdon	1-08-42	156 Sqn	639771	F/S	CROSS Frank	25-06-42	21 OTU
1261820	Sgt	COULTER Barry Herbert	9-06-42	75 Sqn	913609	Sgt	CROSS Michael John Carlton	9-03-42	83 Sqn
569673	Sgt	COULTHARD John Charles	24-04-42	102 Sqn	917809	Sgt	CROSS Thomas Richard	29-03-42	75 Sqn
110823	P/O	COULTHARD Peter Cyprian	14-07-42	18 Sqn	1358624	Sgt	CROSSLEY Joe	8-02-42	21 OTU

571067	Sgt	CROSSLEY Lennox Ashton	17-09-42	106 Sqn	1384420	Sgt	DARCH Frank Edwin	10-12-42	11 OTU
624759	F/S	CROUCH Kenneth	9-03-42	12 Sqn	954705	Sgt	DARLEY Frederick Walter	16-09-42	142 Sqn
1169120	F/S	CROWE Mostyn Maurice	20-06-42	78 Sqn	628951	Sgt	DARNELL Reginald Clifden	25-04-42	226 Sqn
751521	F/S	CROWE William Smith	16-11-42	98 Sqn	925500	F/S	DARVILL DFM Montague	26-07-42	106 Sqn
129665	P/O	CROWFOOT DFC Thomas Bernard	15-10-42	106 Sqn	944533	Sgt	DARWIN Clifford Francis	26-02-42	10 Sqn
809173	Sgt	CROWTHER William Longster	3-06-42	102 Sqn	1162815	Sgt	DAUNCEY Harold	28-06-42	61 Sqn
107486	P/O	CROXTON William Leslie [Rhodesia]	26-06-42	115 Sqn	1262963	Sgt	DAUNCEY Phillip Bruce	24-04-42	101 Sqn
523187	Sgt	CRUISE Richard Sweet	31-05-42	214 Sqn	1585901	Sgt	DAVEY Cecil Albert	21-12-42	207 Sqn
1187096	Sgt	CRUZE Henry Eric	2-04-42	57 Sqn	1383321	Sgt	DAVEY Edward Victor	22-06-42	218 Sqn
550237	Sgt	CUBITT John Charles	26-06-42	11 OTU	1180118	Sgt	DAVEY Jack	20-12-42	76 Sqn
1063702	Sgt	CUDWORTH Thomas	2-06-42	156 Sqn	1186826	Sgt	DAVIDGE Shirley Vincent	23-04-42	218 Sqn
926722	Sgt	CULLEN Herbert Sidney George	12-03-42	75 Sqn	61280	F/O	DAVIDSON Allan Godfrey	8-03-42	50 Sqn
924150	F/S	CULLERNE Allan Percival	11-07-42	207 Sqn	1190622	Sgt	DAVIDSON DFM Frederick	13-04-42	9 Sqn
1186097	Sgt	CULLEY Jack	6-08-42	207 Sqn	527607	F/S	DAVIDSON John McNally	24-03-42	44 Sqn
1283606	Sgt	CULMER Stanley Wilson Charles	14-04-42	144 Sqn	1133451	Sgt	DAVIDSON John Thomson	29-07-42	218 Sqn
104516	P/O	CULMSEE William	13-04-42	76 Sqn	934262	F/S	DAVIDSON William Harry	24-09-42	102 Sqn
122943	F/O	CUMMING Robert Morison	3-12-42	103 Sqn	114159	P/O	DAVIDSON William Robert Norval	10-11-42	107 Sqn
1379896	Sgt	CUNNINGHAM Arthur Peter	31-10-42	30 OTU	752091	Sgt	DAVIE James Douglas	26-07-42	106 Sqn
1072712	Sgt	CUNNINGHAM Isaac Henry	17-02-42	11 OTU	1113655	Sgt	DAVIES Alfred Henry	24-07-42	57 Sqn
655503	Sgt	CUNNINGHAM Philip Edmund	25-09-42	10 OTU	1575222	Sgt	DAVIES Arnold Ernest	8-11-42	20 OTU
755113	F/S	CUNNINGHAM Raymond Leslie	13-05-42	50 Sqn	1052270	Sgt	DAVIES Cyril Caradoc	17-02-42	460 Sqn
526464	Sgt	CUNNINGHAM Robert	1-07-42	21 OTU	1058275	Sgt	DAVIES Edward Kenneth	20-06-42	78 Sqn
1110218	Sgt	CURD Nichol	8-11-42	9 Sqn	118141	P/O	DAVIES Frederick Randall Egerton	5-09-42	115 Sqn
1111814	Sgt	CURLE Joseph	11-10-42	218 Sqn	1359976	Sgt	DAVIES Goronwy Wynne	28-08-42	12 Sqn
610946	Sgt	CURLET William	13-03-42	17 OTU	1062332	Sgt	DAVIES Harold	25-01-42	408 Sqn
777661	Sgt	CURNICK Denis [South Africa]	28-01-42	78 Sqn	1163584	F/S	DAVIES Harold Lewis	2-06-42	97 Sqn
1387664	Sgt	CURRAN Kenneth Raymond	1-10-42	10 Sqn	655121	Sgt	DAVIES Hiley Rhys	20-08-42	218 Sqn
113935	P/O	CURRAN Robert Hugh	30-07-42	50 Sqn	108115	P/O	DAVIES Ivor Owen	25-03-42	50 Sqn
1113205	Sgt	CURRIE Alexander	29-03-42	106 Sqn	126537	F/O	DAVIES DFM John	21-12-42	7 Sqn
798557	Sgt	CURRIE Alfred James [Newfoundland]	18-04-42	12 Sqn	1379403	Sgt	DAVIES John Hywel	13-09-42	22 OTU
1060581	Sgt	CURRIE John	17-05-42	149 Sqn	952765	Sgt	DAVIES John Ivor Evans	15-03-42	78 Sqn
1071410	Sgt	CURRIE Roy Alexander	31-05-42	109 Sqn	1257750	Sgt	DAVIES John Osborn	2-04-42	144 Sqn
923436	Sgt	CURSETT-SUTHERLAND Anthony Frederick Phillip			1105685	Sgt	DAVIES John Richard	28-08-42	218 Sqn
			25-08-42	61 Sqn	1183683	Sgt	DAVIES Lawrence Albert	10-11-42	7 Sqn
537658	Sgt	CURSON Harold	6-08-42	207 Sqn	1289382	Sgt	DAVIES Leslie Hugh	9-09-42	25 OTU
1375137	Sgt	CURTIS Claude Francis	2-04-42	57 Sqn	1238468	Sgt	DAVIES Malcolm Charles	10-09-42	61 Sqn
107980	P/O	CURTIS Colin Hubert	20-01-42	101 Sqn	905368	Sgt	DAVIES Maurice John Morris	4-06-42	115 Sqn
921828	Sgt	CURTIS William Henry	8-07-42	106 Sqn	129659	P/O	DAVIES Percival Allan	17-12-42	10 OTU
922350	Sgt	CUSDEN Sydney Howard	18-09-42	14 OTU	921577	Sgt	DAVIES Richard George	2-05-42	106 Sqn
617704	Sgt	CUSDEN Victor Herbert	9-11-42	44 Sqn	1384224	Sgt	DAVIES Sidney Edward [Argentina]	6-06-42	35 Sqn
1285306	Sgt	CUSHWAY Arthur William	29-07-42	1651 CU	1381571	Sgt	DAVIES Stanley	14-09-42	21 OTU
1375218	Sgt	CUSHWAY Reginald Cecil	3-06-42	12 Sqn	977122	Sgt	DAVIES Thomas Anthony Frederick	12-04-42	158 Sqn
106075	P/O	CUSSEN Richard James	29-03-42	109 Sqn	116950	P/O	DAVIES Thomas Emlyn	12-04-42	226 Sqn
846953	Sgt	CUTTING Edward John	3-09-42	405 Sqn	1005931	Sgt	DAVIES Thomas Percy Willoughby	4-05-42	78 Sqn
1057233	Sgt	DABBS Alan	12-10-42	50 Sqn	109519	P/O	DAVIES William	31-05-42	214 Sqn
1325318	Sgt	DACEY Frederick Verdun	12-10-42	50 Sqn	915231	Sgt	DAVIES William Ernest	18-04-42	101 Sqn
1459273	AC2	DAGG Charles Canada Kirby	18-02-42	Driffield	1266757	Sgt	DAVIES William James	17-09-42	214 Sqn
614202	Sgt	DAINES Gwyn Barrington	10-03-42	149 Sqn	42204	S/L	DAVIES DFC William Twiston	30-07-42	138 Sqn
126790	P/O	DAINTITH Edward Terence	16-10-42	115 Sqn	125321	P/O	DAVIS Arthur Wilfrid	31-05-42	218 Sqn
1281400	Sgt	DAINTON John Samuel	15-01-42	103 Sqn	928365	F/S	DAVIS Benjamin John	25-08-42	61 Sqn
1310838	Sgt	DALBY George William	9-03-42	83 Sqn	81395	F/O	DAVIS Francis Montagu	9-05-42	10 Sqn
1285732	Sgt	DALE George Anthony	28-04-42	27 OTU	1254786	F/S	DAVIS Howard Leslie	8-06-42	149 Sqn
1434080	Sgt	DALE Harry	9-11-42	20 OTU	1375106	F/S	DAVIS James George Edward	10-09-42	158 Sqn
1001426	Sgt	DALE Joseph William	12-03-42	77 Sqn	642788	Sgt	DAVIS John William	30-05-42	218 Sqn
1005336	Sgt	DALGLIESH John Wilson	15-02-42	9 Sqn	755327	F/S	DAVIS Leonard Frank Rogers	13-03-42	83 Sqn
1383216	Sgt	DALTON John Charles	18-09-42	25 OTU	741375	F/S	DAVIS Leslie	7-04-42	49 Sqn
84882	F/L	DALTON Percy Arthur	30-05-42	156 Sqn	1006122	Sgt	DAVIS Stanley	31-03-42	76 Sqn
115408	P/O	DALY Arthur Timothy	22-02-42	455 Sqn	1165309	Sgt	DAVIS Sydney Bernard Thomas	29-08-42	75 Sqn
921754	Sgt	DALY Brian Ignatius Joseph	17-04-42	44 Sqn	1199530	Sgt	DAVIS Wilfred	16-09-42	142 Sqn
1065468	Sgt	DANBY Alan	27-06-42	405 Sqn	536101	Sgt	DAVISON Dennis Howard	10-11-42	7 Sqn
125677	P/O	DANDO Eric John	21-10-42	21 OTU	936543	F/S	DAVISON Gordon Hudson	13-04-42	83 Sqn
108834	P/O	DANDO Thomas McElligott	11-02-42	150 Sqn	1015616	Sgt	DAVISON Joseph	9-05-42	158 Sqn
1183536	Sgt	DANIEL Allan Wilfred	1-08-42	101 Sqn	1091396	Sgt	DAVISON Joseph	22-12-42	466 Sqn
1381051	Sgt	DANIEL William Kenneth	26-07-42	78 Sqn	1378875	Sgt	DAVISON Raymond	9-05-42	76 Sqn
62702	P/O	DANIELSEN Christopher Hugh	25-03-42	83 Sqn	1204001	F/S	DAVISON Ronald William	13-10-42	214 Sqn
787172	Sgt	DANIHELKA Karel [Czechoslovakia]	3-03-42	311 Sqn	107929	P/O	DAWKINS Glyndwr	13-08-42	77 Sqn
995945	Sgt	DANN Frank Arthur	6-04-42	16 OTU	928730	Sgt	DAWKINS Norman Wilfred	22-07-42	142 Sqn
929868	Sgt	DANN Leonard William	31-01-42	61 Sqn	1097030	Sgt	DAWSON Dan Oliver Richard	16-09-42	9 Sqn
1078711	Sgt	DARBYSHIRE George	1-10-42	17 OTU	1027697	Sgt	DAWSON Herbert	9-06-42	18 Sqn

61008	F/L	DAWSON DFC John	16-09-42	22 OTU	930296	Sgt	DICKERSON Alfred James	28-01-42	106 Sqn
1311085	Sgt	DAWSON John Robert	5-10-42	97 Sqn	1292128	Sgt	DICKESON Cyril Raymond	17-02-42	460 Sqn
941538	Sgt	DAWSON John William	1-10-42	218 Sqn	1551589	Sgt	DICKIE John Dundas	16-08-42	106 Sqn
110825	P/O	DAWSON Philip	12-08-42	57 Sqn	115687	P/O	DICKINSON DFM Harold	8-04-42	83 Sqn
938688	Sgt	DAWSON Raymond	29-03-42	61 Sqn	1121218	Sgt	DICKS Ronald	14-09-42	214 Sqn
102112	P/O	DAY Geoffrey Cyril	30-03-42	10 Sqn	1181845	Sgt	DIGBY Alexander Charles Frederick	16-04-42	156 Sqn
1319913	Sgt	DAY Gordon William	29-10-42	19 OTU	1377769	Sgt	DIGBY Francis Arthur	17-09-42	106 Sqn
1375479	F/L	DAY Norman Buckenham	12-06-42	114 Sqn	581147	W/O	DIGNAN Terence De Valera	9-03-42	9 Sqn
628069	Sgt	DAY Raymond	27-04-42	97 Sqn	1378506	Sgt	DILLON Patrick Joseph	10-07-42	158 Sqn
628063	Sgt	DAY Walter Harold	1-08-42	25 OTU	921126	F/S	DIMOND Edgar Robert	29-03-42	106 Sqn
80388	P/O	DAY William Herbert 'Bill' [Rhodesia]	20-09-42	44 Sqn	112742	P/O	DIMOND Sydney Stephen	31-05-42	214 Sqn
1058480	Sgt	DEAN Edward Hodgson	28-07-42	88 Sqn	655442	Sgt	DINSDALE Thomas William	1-08-42	103 Sqn
551023	F/S	DEAN George Henry Peter	4-09-42	97 Sqn	101658	P/O	DISLEY Ronald Max	9-03-42	15 Sqn
1318175	Sgt	DEAN George James	21-12-42	207 Sqn	1033162	Sgt	DITCHBURN Philip Wedgwood	8-12-42	149 Sqn
812230	Sgt	DEAN Joachim Charles	31-05-42	150 Sqn	637971	Sgt	DIXON Benjamin Robert	24-08-42	218 Sqn
110570	F/L	DEAN Josiah Arthur	29-07-42	57 Sqn	1169818	Sgt	DIXON Christopher Norman	7-05-42	460 Sqn
1306056	F/S	DEANS Robert James	3-09-42	150 Sqn	934409	Sgt	DIXON Eric	2-04-42	214 Sqn
1174036	Sgt	DEARLOVE Charles George Edwin	25-08-42	7 Sqn	996657	Sgt	DIXON John Harley	3-04-42	101 Sqn
1263525	Sgt	DEATON James Frederick	10-09-42	16 OTU	1059540	Sgt	DIXON John James	31-05-42	26 OTU
104388	P/O	DECK Harold Frederick	26-07-42	226 Sqn	631704	Sgt	DIXON John Joseph	21-12-42	7 Sqn
924734	Sgt	DECKMAN Harry Naughton	25-03-42	50 Sqn	32123	W/C	DIXON-WRIGHT DFC Frank William	27-07-42	115 Sqn
1047277	Sgt	DEED Sydney Victor	20-12-42	97 Sqn	639860	Cpl	DOAK Robert Victor	24-09-42	51 Sqn
1166185	Sgt	DEERE Aubrey Wilfred	21-01-42	106 Sqn	1575906	AC2	DOBELL Sidney	19-10-42	1656 HCU
1264627	F/S	DEETH Laurence Walter	20-10-42	105 Sqn	1000600	Sgt	DOBIE Leslie Arnold Jonathan	13-07-42	1654 CU
933277	Sgt	DEIGHTON Maurice	18-04-42	12 Sqn	539408	Sgt	DOBSON Denis Frank	24-07-42	214 Sqn
1111498	Sgt	DELANEY Thomas Alfred	10-01-42	12 Sqn	950135	Sgt	DOBSON James Robert	24-02-42	144 Sqn
798558	Sgt	DELANEY Thomas Joseph [Newfoundland]	12-04-42	107 Sqn	47287	F/O	DOBSON Leslie Noel William	29-04-42	156 Sqn
120328	P/O	DELLOW Cyril William	29-06-42	149 Sqn	536899	Sgt	DOBSON Ronald Welburn	28-01-42	78 Sqn
656838	Sgt	DELVE Richard James	17-10-42	61 Sqn	1283610	Sgt	DOCHERTY Colin Frank	12-04-42	107 Sqn
1164033	Sgt	DEMBREY Maurice John	27-07-42	106 Sqn	1101593	Sgt	DOCHERTY Edward	4-06-42	214 Sqn
1311761	F/S	DEMONT Marcel Auguste Henri	22-09-42	226 Sqn	570654	Sgt	DODD Edward Gerard	14-09-42	158 Sqn
938703	F/S	DENISON Maurice Hamilton	4-06-42	61 Sqn	1310824	Sgt	DODD Frederick Joseph	28-04-42	27 OTU
1501105	Sgt	DENNERLY Peter	9-12-42	11 OTU	923344	Sgt	DODD John Robert	29-03-42	103 Sqn
1160749	Sgt	DENNIS John Cecil	8-04-42	405 Sqn	591626	Sgt	DODDS Clifford	22-08-42	10 OTU
751783	F/S	DENNIS Ronald Victor George	24-04-42	101 Sqn	1002399	Sgt	DODDS Joseph	9-05-42	158 Sqn
948842	Sgt	DENNISON George	16-09-42	9 Sqn	118574	P/O	DODGE Stanley Wilbur [USA]	17-09-42	21 OTU
90993	F/L	DENNY Bernard Moreland	27-04-42	7 Sqn	551849	Sgt	DODSWORTH Joseph Dick	2-06-42	83 Sqn
1064390	Sgt	DENNY James	15-10-42	149 Sqn	970057	Sgt	DOLPHIN Edgar	13-07-42	7 Sqn
109483	P/O	DENT Harry	31-05-42	214 Sqn	110638	P/O	DOMAILLE William Edward George	10-09-42	158 Sqn
1379092	Sgt	DENT Lancelot	9-06-42	150 Sqn	778666	Sgt	DOMAN Gerald Anthony [Rhodesia]	29-08-42	35 Sqn
1166013	Sgt	DENTON Frank Henry	21-02-42	106 Sqn	1256326	Sgt	DOMAN Reginald Eric	4-06-42	17 OTU
1052819	Sgt	DENVILLE Dennis Charles Alfred Peter Roland	9-09-42	25 OTU	1176014	Sgt	DOMINY Ralph Henry	12-06-42	83 Sqn
					1345917	Sgt	DON Robert MacFarlane	9-11-42	20 OTU
575253	Cpl	DENYER Kenneth Ernest Victor	6-07-42	419 Sqn	1018492	Sgt	DONALD James	20-12-42	97 Sqn
1375654	Sgt	DESMOND Augustus Harold James George	5-10-42	97 Sqn	1219684	Sgt	DONALD Peter Laird	21-12-42	103 Sqn
					1378642	Sgt	DONELAN Peter John Henry	1-08-42	9 Sqn
1281123	Sgt	DETMOLD Percy George [Canada]	26-04-42	218 Sqn	657222	Sgt	DONLIN Edward Alan	14-09-42	419 Sqn
1059592	Sgt	DEVALLE Joshua Arnold	26-03-42	83 Sqn	932936	Sgt	DONNELLY Terence Eugene	24-09-42	9 Sqn
561527	F/S	DEVERSON Ernest Alfred	3-05-42	18 Sqn	528754	F/S	DONOHOE Martin Luke	6-08-42	20 OTU
931485	Sgt	DEWAR Alexander Shaw	17-08-42	214 Sqn	1580650	Sgt	DOORE Robert Sidney	17-12-42	57 Sqn
988654	Sgt	DEWAR Thomas Cuthbert	14-09-42	156 Sqn	932116	Sgt	DOPSON Ivor Bertie	26-03-42	7 Sqn
759000	F/S	DEWHURST William 'Billy'	9-09-42	78 Sqn	78438	F/L	DORE Maurice Ivan	4-11-42	464 Sqn
1255048	Sgt	de COURCY Robert Cecil William [Eire]	7-02-42	144 Sqn	944581	F/S	DORMAND Arthur William	1-06-42	12 OTU
					118547	P/O	DORMON Peter Wren	9-09-42	25 OTU
1282872	Sgt	de LISSER Louis Stanhope [Jamaica]	20-02-42	17 OTU	1437407	Sgt	DORN David	22-12-42	466 Sqn
1162262	Sgt	de VISSCHER Jean Jaques Gabriel [Holland] (served as HALL)	15-04-42	158 Sqn	1490734	AC2	DOUBLE Cyril William Stockwell	20-11-42	9 Sqn
					977761	Sgt	DOUGHTY Harry	30-05-42	15 Sqn
1325642	Sgt	DE LASPEE Harold Ralph Hutchinson	11-07-42	101 Sqn	1063795	Sgt	DOUGHTY Joseph	9-03-42	9 Sqn
					632776	Sgt	DOUGLAS Thomas	17-08-42	207 Sqn
41678	S/L	DE MESTRE DSO DFC Peter Morrice	7-06-42	49 Sqn	1172873	Sgt	DOUGLASS Albert	19-05-42	15 Sqn
117448	P/O	DE WALLENS Victor Pierre	25-06-42	16 OTU	570275	Sgt	DOUGLASS Edward Reed	26-06-42	218 Sqn
1252627	Sgt	DIBBEN Ronald Oswald	28-11-42	75 Sqn	960650	Sgt	DOVE Benjamin James	26-03-42	12 Sqn
1067547	Sgt	DICK Frederick	27-06-42	218 Sqn	120662	P/O	DOVE Edward	2-09-42	15 OTU
990410	Sgt	DICK Robert Ballantyne	11-02-42	150 Sqn	103490	P/O	DOWDELL Edwin Frederick	14-09-42	1654 CU
1288309	Sgt	DICKENS Charles William	17-12-42	9 Sqn	963176	Sgt	DOWDEN Norman Edwin	1-10-42	44 Sqn
934810	Sgt	DICKENSON George Kenneth [South Africa]	23-09-42	50 Sqn	1311793	Sgt	DOWLING Desmond Walter	8-04-42	23 OTU
					581376	Sgt	DOWLING John Alfred [Eire]	18-04-42	101 Sqn
1065732	Sgt	DICKENSON George Robert	21-12-42	7 Sqn	1312587	Sgt	DOWLING Lionel George	26-07-42	78 Sqn
					119719	P/O	DOWN Frederick Henry	1-08-42	12 Sqn

Service#	Rank	Name	Date	Unit
111550	P/O	DOWNER Desmond James	17-09-42	106 Sqn
1193593	Sgt	DOWNES Thomas Kenneth	12-02-42	49 Sqn
109923	P/O	DOWNIE Andrew	15-04-42	158 Sqn
1018813	Sgt	DOWNING Kenneth Dean	17-09-42	21 OTU
1270327	Sgt	DOWNING Stanley	18-08-42	76 Sqn
1377639	Sgt	DOWNING William Robert	7-11-42	156 Sqn
616823	Sgt	DOWNS Henry	2-04-42	214 Sqn
105178	P/O	DOWNWARD Arthur Cyril Read	23-06-42	103 Sqn
61287	F/O	DOYLE Francis Kingsley	30-05-42	15 Sqn
1112246	Sgt	DRACASS Hugh	29-03-42	61 Sqn
1394720	Sgt	DRAIN John Arthur	21-12-42	57 Sqn
1208628	Sgt	DRAKE Herbert Ernest	19-08-42	21 OTU
115107	F/O	DRAKE John Randal	1-10-42	218 Sqn
994507	Sgt	DRAKE Kenneth Noel	7-06-42	156 Sqn
1057464	Sgt	DRAPER Alfred Segar	30-05-42	12 Sqn
1331697	Sgt	DRAYTON Stanley Lawrence	28-11-42	30 OTU
924143	F/S	DRENNAN John Charles	8-05-42	44 Sqn
1208196	Sgt	DREW Dennis Waterman	4-05-42	78 Sqn
1255407	F/S	DREW Robert Henry [France]	6-11-42	15 Sqn
1180018	Sgt	DREW Sydney Trevor	10-03-42	49 Sqn
1219728	Sgt	DREW Vincent Thomas	8-12-42	21 OTU
968778	F/S	DRISCOLL Daniel	9-03-42	150 Sqn
1189757	Sgt	DRIVER Raymond Bertram Hamilton	6-01-42	12 Sqn
1107042	Sgt	DRONFIELD Harold	26-06-42	78 Sqn
1104362	Sgt	DRUMMOND William McFarlane	5-06-42	57 Sqn
1191572	Sgt	DRURY Charles	20-09-42	101 Sqn
43951	F/L	DRUSSEL Donald Patrickson	26-06-42	12 OTU
613297	Sgt	DRYDEN John Robert	23-06-42	61 Sqn
1005491	Sgt	DRYSDALE Adam Thomas	27-07-42	57 Sqn
1317232	Sgt	DUBBEN Arthur James	16-12-42	23 OTU
1154270	Sgt	DUCE Cyril Cubitt	7-02-42	144 Sqn
637517	Sgt	DUCKWORTH Harry Leslie	16-07-42	149 Sqn
979532	Sgt	DUCKWORTH Sidney	27-07-42	226 Sqn
1152502	F/S	DUDER Michael Sedgwick	9-03-42	12 Sqn
89378	F/L	DUFF DFC George Gordon [South Africa]	10-03-42	158 Sqn
613125	Sgt	DUFFIELD Ronald Alan	30-11-42	98 Sqn
525589	Sgt	DUFFUS Jack Duncan	3-09-42	1652 CU
798611	Sgt	DUFFY Thomas [Newfoundland]	2-10-42	218 Sqn
920226	F/S	DUFTON Victor Reginald	7-04-42	142 Sqn
1163246	F/S	DUKE George Henry	11-07-42	207 Sqn
1063676	Sgt	DUKE Gilbert Noel	14-02-42	12 OTU
66515	F/L	DUKES-SMITH Harold Frederick	14-01-42	21 Sqn
702735	Sgt	DUNBAR Harry Smith	4-08-42	20 OTU
986460	Sgt	DUNCAN Ian	17-06-42	102 Sqn
1346350	Sgt	DUNCAN John George	15-11-42	150 Sqn
1185949	Sgt	DUNCOMBE Walter	28-08-42	103 Sqn
938276	F/S	DUNDAS Lord Dundas of Orkney Bruce Thomas	24-02-42	144 Sqn
1167924	Sgt	DUNGEY Stanley Albert	28-01-42	106 Sqn
1281932	F/S	DUNKLING Leonard George	29-08-42	88 Sqn
1005984	Sgt	DUNKS Geoffrey Frederick	9-05-42	158 Sqn
119721	F/O	DUNLOP Andrew Peter Cathcart [Barbados]	10-12-42	10 OTU
1330863	Sgt	DUNLOP Duncan Darrock	4-06-42	12 OTU
547222	Sgt	DUNLOP James Black	31-03-42	35 Sqn
40685	F/L	DUNLOP-MACKENZIE Robert Jack	25-03-42	106 Sqn
1369631	Sgt	DUNN Alexander	16-07-42	158 Sqn
1081058	Sgt	DUNN Andrew Graham	6-12-42	115 Sqn
929387	Sgt	DUNN Donald Ian	28-03-42	7 Sqn
1284969	Sgt	DUNN Francis Ernest	21-01-42	101 Sqn
963723	Sgt	DUNN George Edward	28-08-42	78 Sqn
1310826	Sgt	DUNN John Clifford	2-04-42	214 Sqn
1001633	Sgt	DUNN Leslie Joseph	12-03-42	75 Sqn
126682	P/O	DUNN Maurice	31-08-42	21 OTU
1405922	LAC	DUNN Terence John	1-12-42	Tempsford
106041	P/O	DUNNE James Bernard	10-03-42	49 Sqn
777663	Sgt	DUPREEZ DFM Cornelious Johannes [Rhodesia]	7-09-42	7 Sqn
88416	F/O	DURO Hector	21-12-42	7 Sqn
1263757	Sgt	DURRANT Charles Henry	20-07-42	12 Sqn
1058876	Sgt	DUTHIE John	29-07-42	156 Sqn
1006728	Sgt	DUTTON Frederick	17-02-42	460 Sqn
34040	W/C	DUTTON Peter Hiley	6-12-42	107 Sqn
972095	Sgt	DUTTON Theodore Edward	27-03-42	21 OTU
902732	Sgt	DUVALL Stanley Valentine	25-06-42	10 Sqn
110826	F/L	DU TOIT Johannes Christiaan Frederick [South Africa]	1-10-42	218 Sqn
746829	F/S	DWYER DFM John Henry Patrick	9-11-42	57 Sqn
1283349	Sgt	DYE Leslie Richard	27-06-42	150 Sqn
111214	P/O	DYER Robert James	8-04-42	83 Sqn
1195067	Sgt	DYHOUSE James Ladas	20-09-42	101 Sqn
574454	Sgt	DYKE Hedley	3-12-42	103 Sqn
963881	Sgt	DYKES Bernard John	12-03-42	58 Sqn
1059428	Sgt	DYSON Edwin	25-09-42	61 Sqn
1283751	Sgt	DYSON Fred	9-11-42	57 Sqn
60506	F/O	d'URSEL Count Chevalier of the Order of Leopold, Croix de Guerre [Belgium] 1940 Jacques Marie Joseph Adrien [Belgium]	7-08-42	78 Sqn
749447	Sgt	EADES MiD Stanley Edward	17-04-42	97 Sqn
570100	Sgt	EAGLE Leonard Keil	28-03-42	7 Sqn
923470	Sgt	EAGLETON Irvine Leonard	2-04-42	214 Sqn
130102	P/O	EALES William Norman	20-12-42	97 Sqn
108243	P/O	EAMES Cyril William	29-07-42	57 Sqn
1182318	Sgt	EARDLEY William Mervyn Alastair	8-03-42	50 Sqn
1057318	Sgt	EARNSHAW Bryan	14-07-42	97 Sqn
926602	Sgt	EARNSHAW Sydney	10-01-42	50 Sqn
103574	F/O	EASLEY Gordon	11-08-42	207 Sqn
1124509	F/S	EASOM Ronald	9-11-42	44 Sqn
1311318	Sgt	EAST David John	25-04-42	15 Sqn
1180424	Sgt	EAST Oliver Raymond	16-04-42	156 Sqn
568667	Sgt	EASTING John	6-06-42	149 Sqn
1283710	Sgt	EASTON Alan James	20-12-42	44 Sqn
126451	P/O	EASTON Alexander	16-09-42	27 OTU
1175893	Sgt	EASTWOOD William Benjamin	30-03-42	10 Sqn
113398	P/O	EATON Arthur	19-08-42	61 Sqn
127142	P/O	EBSWORTH Ronald Edward Charles	1-07-42	21 OTU
998677	Sgt	ECKERSLEY Joseph Alban	26-01-42	82 Sqn
1577993	Sgt	EDEN Frederick John	6-12-42	102 Sqn
45985	P/O	EDGAR DFM Alexander Robertson	31-05-42	158 Sqn
621660	Sgt	EDGELEY William John	2-06-42	10 Sqn
901233	Sgt	EDGSON Reginald Edward	6-12-42	15 OTU
569765	Sgt	EDLINGTON Ronald	11-12-42	158 Sqn
905875	Sgt	EDMONDS Harold Vincent	19-05-42	15 Sqn
1288523	Sgt	EDMONDS Kenneth	2-06-42	26 OTU
1260393	F/S	EDMONDS Ronald Alfred	24-07-42	207 Sqn
1264540	Sgt	EDMONDS Robert Leslie James	9-01-42	19 OTU
1332823	Sgt	EDWARDS Alfred John Norman	30-10-42	10 OTU
570294	Sgt	EDWARDS Arthur William	20-12-42	78 Sqn
1180651	Sgt	EDWARDS Aubrey Harold	8-04-42	405 Sqn
1379351	Sgt	EDWARDS Emrys	31-05-42	115 Sqn
962190	Sgt	EDWARDS Ernest George	15-10-42	158 Sqn
1376134	Sgt	EDWARDS Frank Henry	28-08-42	13 OTU
533590	F/S	EDWARDS George Alfred	17-04-42	44 Sqn
905982	Sgt	EDWARDS Gilbert Murray	4-05-42	78 Sqn
1284631	Sgt	EDWARDS Gwilym Thomas	7-06-42	150 Sqn
648197	F/S	EDWARDS Henry Gordon	23-06-42	103 Sqn
1102285	Sgt	EDWARDS Iorwerth	28-04-42	102 Sqn
1168677	Sgt	EDWARDS Ivor	17-04-42	44 Sqn
42052	F/L	EDWARDS Jeffrey Hugh	28-03-42	7 Sqn
1253057	Sgt	EDWARDS John Arthur	6-05-42	7 Sqn
1052838	Sgt	EDWARDS John William	3-07-42	103 Sqn
137212	P/O	EDWARDS Kenneth Edward [Canada]	20-12-42	83 Sqn
50968	P/O	EDWARDS Kenneth Fraser	5-10-42	103 Sqn
1184050	Sgt	EDWARDS Leonard	6-11-42	83 Sqn
79510	F/L	EDWARDS Norman John [New Zealand]	4-06-42	101 Sqn

1293442	Sgt	EDWARDS Owen Glynne	17-10-42	61 Sqn	118100	P/O	EVANS David Christopher	26-06-42	15 OTU
106565	F/O	EDWARDS Peter Leslie	3-06-42	408 Sqn	1313491	Sgt	EVANS David Richard	22-09-42	103 Sqn
42113	F/L	EDWARDS Robert Howard	26-09-42	142 Sqn	1384041	Sgt	EVANS Derek Henry	21-09-42	115 Sqn
1429094	AC2	EDWARDS Thomas Arthur	19-05-42	15 Sqn	653677	Sgt	EVANS Edward Edwin Charles	8-06-42	35 Sqn
1312326	Sgt	EDWARDS Thomas Emlyn	9-11-42	57 Sqn	119172	P/O	EVANS Emrys	31-05-42	156 Sqn
1070497	Sgt	EGAN Joseph William	28-11-42	105 Sqn	1052467	Sgt	EVANS Frank Crawford	12-06-42	9 Sqn
1092735	Sgt	EGAN Vernon Ernest	16-04-42	214 Sqn	1051922	Sgt	EVANS Harry James	10-03-42	158 Sqn
656273	Sgt	EGERTON Robert	22-12-42	466 Sqn	943155	Sgt	EVANS Herbert Edmund	6-09-42	105 Sqn
1208948	Sgt	EGLINTON Eric Edwin	23-04-42	9 Sqn	1384070	Sgt	EVANS Hubert Richard	14-09-42	12 Sqn
1259439	Sgt	EIVERS Frank O'Kearney	25-04-42	103 Sqn	1048732	Sgt	EVANS James Harold	17-09-42	12 OTU
627523	Sgt	EKIN Harold	25-08-42	61 Sqn	1105192	Sgt	EVANS Kenneth	8-05-42	44 Sqn
118893	P/O	ELBY William George	7-09-42	12 Sqn	778831	Sgt	EVANS Kenneth Alexander Roderick [Rhodesia]	18-07-42	10 OTU
911677	Sgt	ELDRIDGE Gordon Frederick	19-09-42	15 Sqn					
122072	P/O	ELDRIDGE Roger Charles	29-07-42	218 Sqn	1166119	Sgt	EVANS Kenneth Archibald	9-05-42	15 Sqn
136941	P/O	ELGER Anthony Charles	20-12-42	44 Sqn	929941	Sgt	EVANS Leonard Edward	8-05-42	44 Sqn
922758	Sgt	ELKINS Kenneth McKerrow	26-03-42	88 Sqn	1105938	Sgt	EVANS Lloyd Francis	27-04-42	7 Sqn
1262787	Sgt	ELLINGHAM Frederick Thomas	8-04-42	23 OTU	920056	Sgt	EVANS Richard Arthur	22-07-42	142 Sqn
945426	Sgt	ELLIOTT George Henry	1-04-42	20 OTU	1286192	Sgt	EVANS Robert Edwin	16-09-42	15 Sqn
104529	P/O	ELLIOTT Graham Peter	13-04-42	158 Sqn	913939	Sgt	EVANS Thomas Alfred	31-01-42	61 Sqn
925929	Sgt	ELLIOTT Harold Reginald George Dennis	9-06-42	35 Sqn	1504712	AC2	EVANS Thomas Arthur	28-08-42	149 Sqn
					947420	Sgt	EVANS Thomas George	21-02-42	150 Sqn
1271235	Sgt	ELLIOTT John	29-06-42	11 OTU	1270758	Sgt	EVANS Thomas John Terence	30-11-42	81 OTU
954417	Sgt	ELLIOTT John Ridley	27-07-42	420 Sqn	526918	Sgt	EVANS William Charles	27-03-42	138 Sqn
103519	P/O	ELLIOTT Richard Frederick	12-10-42	49 Sqn	1360096	Sgt	EVANS William David	29-07-42	156 Sqn
1325341	Sgt	ELLIOTT Thomas Alfred	3-07-42	103 Sqn	1125799	Sgt	EVANSON Brian Ernest	4-06-42	1428 Flt
1058216	Sgt	ELLIOTT Thomas William	26-03-42	88 Sqn	970535	F/S	EVERARD Michael Gerrard [Eire]	11-11-42	57 Sqn
657672	Sgt	ELLIS Arthur Frank	29-08-42	115 Sqn	655036	Sgt	EVERATT George Hamilton	30-05-42	12 Sqn
915447	Sgt	ELLIS Arthur Stanley Charles	6-08-42	102 Sqn	979937	Sgt	EVERETT Andrew Paton	15-02-42	214 Sqn
129133	P/O	ELLIS Dudley	6-06-42	156 Sqn	920700	Sgt	EVERETT Harold William	12-04-42	144 Sqn
118619	P/O	ELLIS Frank Henry	18-09-42	115 Sqn	751919	F/S	EVERITT MM Cross of Merit [Poland] Geoffrey Charles	6-08-42	207 Sqn
149838	P/O	ELLIS George Thomas	17-01-42	51 Sqn					
929649	Sgt	ELLIS Horace Spencer Edward	22-01-42	106 Sqn	925834	Sgt	EVERITT Jack	20-05-42	10 Sqn
106978	P/O	ELLIS John Homfray	1-04-42	1428 Flt	922204	F/S	EVERSON Peter Michael	30-11-42	149 Sqn
1259306	Sgt	ELLIS Kenneth Custance	18-07-42	18 Sqn	929118	Sgt	EVES John Arthur	27-02-42	144 Sqn
1153272	Sgt	ELLIS Reginald	1-06-42	77 Sqn	1053464	Sgt	EVES Reginald Grenville	21-01-42	408 Sqn
1186850	Sgt	ELLIS Ronald	29-07-42	75 Sqn	1214198	Sgt	EVISON Ronald Granville	8-11-42	142 Sqn
902089	Sgt	ELLIS Victor Arthur Lionel	28-03-42	7 Sqn	89380	F/L	EWART MiD William John	2-06-42	23 OTU
1384878	Sgt	ELLIS William Howard [Canada]	8-12-42	207 Sqn	1180645	Sgt	EWINGS Eric	6-01-42	57 Sqn
1330124	Sgt	ELLIS-BUXTON Basil Lionel	1-08-42	106 Sqn	1323684	Sgt	EYERS John Alfred	2-07-42	109 Sqn
1263610	Sgt	ELLWOOD William Herbert	30-09-42	14 OTU	655819	Sgt	EYNON Ronald Owen	20-12-42	103 Sqn
1217079	Sgt	ELMES Stephen	10-04-42	9 Sqn	1288358	Sgt	FAGE Ronald Thomas	25-06-42	15 OTU
133051	P/O	ELSOM DFM Reginald Staynes	13-10-42	22 OTU	64935	P/O	FAIR Dennis Reginald	25-03-42	50 Sqn
986416	Sgt	ELTRINGHAM George	2-04-42	57 Sqn	1112526	Sgt	FAIRBANKS Philip Haig	10-09-42	61 Sqn
1378958	Sgt	ELVIN Leonard Roy	26-06-42	12 OTU	1311317	Sgt	FAIRCLOUGH Frederick Keith	8-04-42	15 OTU
48963	P/O	EMBELIN Raymond Cecil	12-08-42	156 Sqn	573362	Sgt	FAIRFIELD William Ross St. George	16-11-42	149 Sqn
128971	P/O	EMENEY John Frederick	9-12-42	11 OTU	1051595	Sgt	FAIRHURST Edward Ernest	12-04-42	103 Sqn
650193	F/S	EMENY Dick	10-09-42	218 Sqn	1057396	Sgt	FAIRHURST Richard	3-07-42	214 Sqn
1313486	AC2	EMERY Arnold Clifford	31-10-42	88 Sqn	657753	Sgt	FAIRLESS Alan	1-10-42	405 Sqn
922974	Sgt	EMERY Ronald Harry	6-04-42	75 Sqn	1262464	Sgt	FAIRWEATHER Robert James Godney	20-05-42	10 Sqn
1321172	Sgt	EMERY Trevor George	17-12-42	115 Sqn					
1120658	Sgt	EMMOTT Thomas William Burnett	24-06-42	103 Sqn	1377399	Sgt	FAITH Donald Hewett	15-01-42	115 Sqn
1376234	Sgt	EMMS Albert Frederick Mons	26-03-42	214 Sqn	1126920	Sgt	FALCONER George Campbell	1-06-42	20 OTU
930367	LAC	EMMS Graham Langley	25-05-42	25 OTU	798559	Sgt	FALK Frederick Harold [Newfoundland]	31-05-42	14 OTU
1352414	Sgt	EMMS Ronald Jack	15-10-42	106 Sqn					
1153736	Sgt	ENDLEY Harold John	28-08-42	97 Sqn	122380	P/O	FALKINDER Nicholas	25-08-42	15 OTU
1375251	Sgt	ENGLAND Kenneth William George	31-05-42	218 Sqn	117451	P/O	FALLAS Harry	27-08-42	12 Sqn
1359191	Sgt	ENGLAND Stanley Dennis	6-06-42	149 Sqn	1378748	Sgt	FALLON James Traynor	23-06-42	61 Sqn
1150934	Sgt	ENNION Maurice Adeney Ellis	11-06-42	77 Sqn	1101236	Sgt	FANNING John Black Fraser	24-06-42	76 Sqn
1250768	Sgt	ENNIS Alfred George	29-04-42	57 Sqn	87011	F/L	FANTA Frantisek [Czechoslovakia]	13-10-42	27 OTU
1199110	Sgt	ENNOR Rupert Vivian Pereira	26-02-42	12 Sqn	29089	W/C	FARLEY DFC Walter Ronald	21-04-42	138 Sqn
642811	Sgt	ENTWISTLE Jack	25-10-42	142 Sqn	754062	F/S	FARMBROUGH Brian Douglas	14-01-42	22 OTU
1287615	F/S	ERBY Edward Hamilton	1-04-42	214 Sqn	108074	P/O	FARQUHARSON Colin Macqueen	29-07-42	218 Sqn
1063724	Sgt	ERRINGTON Thomas Hunter	9-03-42	9 Sqn	1375165	Sgt	FARRELL Francis Harold John	9-09-42	102 Sqn
106076	P/O	ESLICK Joseph Norman	11-07-42	97 Sqn	917131	Sgt	FARRIMOND Clifford Alexander	18-12-42	97 Sqn
950909	F/S	ETHELL Frederick Colin	24-07-42	25 OTU	1114842	F/S	FARRIMOND John	21-08-42	218 Sqn
999910	Sgt	ETHERINGTON John Robert	9-05-42	12 Sqn	83803	P/O	FAULK Ivor George Arthur	21-12-42	103 Sqn
1155050	F/S	EVANS Austen Douglas	1-08-42	18 Sqn	637104	F/S	FAWKES Robert Gordon	31-05-42	61 Sqn
1033618	Sgt	EVANS Charles Denis	10-11-42	7 Sqn	1529983	Sgt	FAYE Francis John	3-11-42	408 Sqn
1313522	Sgt	EVANS David	3-07-42	12 Sqn	1384070	Sgt	FEAST Hubert Richard	14-09-42	12 Sqn

Service #	Rank	Name	Date	Unit
66498	P/O	FEGAN John Samuel Victor [Eire]	20-07-42	10 Sqn
106564	P/O	FEIRN John Rowland	13-03-42	83 Sqn
69443	F/L	FELCE Peter Gifford	16-09-42	27 OTU
571254	Sgt	FENTON Leonard Clinton	16-06-42	7 Sqn
1052485	Sgt	FENWICK James Roy	14-01-42	40 Sqn
998502	Sgt	FENWICK Maurice William	9-03-42	101 Sqn
139612	P/O	FENWICKE-CLENNELL Edward	21-12-42	9 Sqn
1322828	Sgt	FEORD John	22-12-42	26 OTU
1110578	Sgt	FERGUSON Anthony Alexander	2-04-42	214 Sqn
1370437	Sgt	FERGUSON Francis	15-11-42	150 Sqn
1550846	Sgt	FERGUSON Ian McNaughton	8-05-42	21 OTU
117356	P/O	FERGUSON Isiah Derry	16-09-42	15 Sqn
986430	Sgt	FERGUSON James	9-09-42	77 Sqn
1005492	Sgt	FERGUSON Robinson	3-06-42	12 Sqn
1022568	F/S	FERGUSON DFM Walter Colvin	6-11-42	26 OTU
1387312	Sgt	FERGUSON William John [New Zealand]	16-09-42	12 OTU
1277581	Sgt	FERN John St. Bernard	24-10-42	50 Sqn
111557	P/O	FERRER Robert Leslie William	31-05-42	12 OTU
106220	P/O	FERRIS Cecil Frank	14-03-42	78 Sqn
1381860	Sgt	FERRIS Joseph Gorman [Grenada]	15-10-42	214 Sqn
1314479	Sgt	FERRIS Wilfred John	24-10-42	218 Sqn
1066005	Sgt	FERRY George Lionel	29-07-42	9 Sqn
1293338	Sgt	FETHERSTON Hugh Henry	26-03-42	61 Sqn
1030626	Sgt	FEWTRELL Ronald George	14-07-42	158 Sqn
119347	P/O	FIELD Max Lightfoot	16-04-42	149 Sqn
655280	Sgt	FIELDING Ronald Smith	16-10-42	51 Sqn
938234	F/S	FILLINGHAM Geoffrey	21-08-42	19 OTU
787403	Sgt	FINA Jiri [Czechoslovakia]	12-03-42	311 Sqn
1270882	Sgt	FINCH Edward William	31-05-42	50 Sqn
1380468	Sgt	FINCH Harold Clifford	5-09-42	115 Sqn
1280951	Sgt	FINCH Patrick Austen Gwyer [Argentina]	26-03-42	115 Sqn
931408	F/S	FINCH Ronald John	4-06-42	214 Sqn
1220309	Sgt	FINNEY Alexander Edward	1-08-42	103 Sqn
109539	P/O	FIRMAN John Evans	9-06-42	103 Sqn
924722	Sgt	FIRMINGER Leslie Douglas	22-07-42	101 Sqn
1215307	Sgt	FIRTH Alan Watson	16-09-42	101 Sqn
986548	Sgt	FIRTH John Alexander George	7-05-42	35 Sqn
41165	F/L	FISCHER Sydney Adnil Pawle [South Africa]	9-01-42	90 Sqn
1061133	F/S	FISH Allan Kilshaw	28-08-42	142 Sqn
1383196	Sgt	FISH Frederick Stephen	3-09-42	150 Sqn
39814	S/L	FISHER Charles Gerald	29-10-42	15 Sqn
1265865	Sgt	FISHER Donald	14-09-42	26 OTU
577301	Sgt	FISHER Frank John	21-12-42	103 Sqn
103576	P/O	FISHER John	18-05-42	115 Sqn
778784	Sgt	FISHER Leslie Frank [South Africa]	7-05-42	23 OTU
1058488	Sgt	FISHER Ronald Willis	25-06-42	35 Sqn
927796	Sgt	FISKE Edward Lloyd	21-02-42	150 Sqn
926804	Sgt	FITCHETT Edward Augustine	8-04-42	83 Sqn
1113188	Sgt	FitzPATRICK Thomas	12-08-42	207 Sqn
121136	P/O	FITZGERALD Desmond Francis	16-10-42	115 Sqn
1152646	Sgt	FITZGERALD Thomas Merryweather	9-03-42	21 OTU
617112	Sgt	FITZSIMMONS Lawrence	25-10-42	103 Sqn
651415	F/S	FLANAGHAN Tom	2-04-42	214 Sqn
1254454	Sgt	FLANNERY Philip William Clement	25-04-42	9 Sqn
951190	Sgt	FLAVELL Howard	9-03-42	12 Sqn
532066	Sgt	FLECK George	5-09-42	207 Sqn
1254797	F/S	FLEETWOOD-MAY John	11-08-42	78 Sqn
1212046	Sgt	FLEMING Dennis Albert	9-03-42	15 OTU
1388513	Sgt	FLEMING James Arthur	15-10-42	103 Sqn
936912	F/S	FLEMING Joseph	9-06-42	405 Sqn
1252492	Sgt	FLETCHER Dennis Howard	31-05-42	26 OTU
49694	F/L	FLETCHER Edward Albert	22-11-42	156 Sqn
352613	F/S	FLETCHER Ernest Milo	6-07-42	Tempsford
652531	Sgt	FLETCHER John	17-08-42	44 Sqn
943590	Sgt	FLETCHER John Horace	22-07-42	115 Sqn
778412	Sgt	FLETCHER Martin Cargill [Rhodesia]	10-01-42	83 Sqn
1053905	Sgt	FLETCHER Ronald Desmond	6-02-42	21 Sqn
1169620	Sgt	FLINT Francis Edwin	20-05-42	35 Sqn
1319300	Sgt	FLINT Robert Bernard Lovett	30-09-42	149 Sqn
111936	P/O	FLINT Ronald Renshaw	24-03-42	19 OTU
755152	F/S	FLOCKHART John Spring	6-06-42	149 Sqn
1187916	Sgt	FLOWER Alan Frederick	30-11-42	10 Sqn
1381257	Sgt	FLOWER William Harold	24-03-42	44 Sqn
1264475	Sgt	FLOWERS Leslie William	31-05-42	103 Sqn
107521	P/O	FLOYD Philip Nevil	31-05-42	49 Sqn
646895	F/S	FLUX DFM Robert James	17-04-42	44 Sqn
1580257	Sgt	FLYNN Patrick Joseph	20-11-42	11 OTU
568446	Sgt	FOALE William Gordon	13-08-42	7 Sqn
104517	F/L	FOERS Geoffrey Charles	2-10-42	78 Sqn
1287626	Sgt	FOLLETT Eric Gordon	29-08-42	115 Sqn
1293633	Sgt	FOLLETT Ronald William Arthur	9-11-42	218 Sqn
48379	F/O	FOLLETT Thomas Henry	22-11-42	102 Sqn
1178923	Sgt	FOLLOWS Leslie Norman	8-03-42	50 Sqn
1004017	Sgt	FONE Alfred Thomas	26-04-42	115 Sqn
1407785	LAC	FOOT Henry George	17-06-42	24 OTU
1335996	Sgt	FOOT John Edward Thomas	30-06-42	405 Sqn
967145	Sgt	FORBES John	6-08-42	207 Sqn
1314891	Sgt	FORBES John	6-10-42	75 Sqn
1310041	Sgt	FORD Arthur Wilfred	10-02-42	11 OTU
906254	F/S	FORD DFM Edwin John	31-05-42	26 OTU
1291154	Sgt	FORD Harry George	20-12-42	9 Sqn
591286	F/S	FORDWYCH William Dundas	19-08-42	207 Sqn
653037	Sgt	FORGIE Robert	20-07-42	158 Sqn
649535	Sgt	FORMAN Ernest	1-08-42	44 Sqn
787826	Sgt	FORNUSEK Ladislav [Czechoslovakia]	10-03-42	138 Sqn
1375456	Sgt	FORRESTER Charles Oliver	9-03-42	150 Sqn
1109833	Sgt	FORSHAW Harold	27-08-42	218 Sqn
932391	Sgt	FORSTER Brian Henry	26-03-42	142 Sqn
1381349	Sgt	FORSTER George Peacock	9-06-42	83 Sqn
577519	LAC	FORSTER Herbert Roy	21-07-42	106 Sqn
130788	P/O	FORSTER Jack Edward	3-08-42	51 Sqn
985822	Sgt	FORSTER Kenneth	16-09-42	15 Sqn
39077	S/L	FORSYTH DFC Douglas Sinclair	3-09-42	61 Sqn
1007363	Sgt	FORSYTH John	11-07-42	97 Sqn
1195400	Sgt	FORSYTH John Dimmock	31-10-42	25 OTU
1217369	Sgt	FOSSEY Ronald	9-03-42	21 OTU
912925	Sgt	FOSSLEITNER BEM Louis Victor	10-11-42	149 Sqn
113415	P/O	FOSTER Alec Leonard	3-09-42	61 Sqn
1232596	Sgt	FOSTER Brian John	2-09-42	15 OTU
1074970	Sgt	FOSTER Frederick	21-12-42	107 Sqn
933501	Sgt	FOSTER Peter Hollowell	13-03-42	83 Sqn
1332676	Sgt	FOSTER Richard Henry	30-07-42	142 Sqn
1265480	Sgt	FOSTER Walter	29-07-42	12 Sqn
124804	P/O	FOULKES John Alfred	31-12-42	16 OTU
1062388	Sgt	FOUNTAIN Norman	7-07-42	156 Sqn
1211175	Sgt	FOWLER Edmund John Roberts	20-01-42	12 Sqn
81397	F/O	FOWLER Edward Graham	12-02-42	420 Sqn
1527505	Sgt	FOWLER Francis Joseph	11-12-42	19 OTU
39186	S/L	FOWLER John Anthony Lamond	24-05-42	21 Sqn
1450295	AC2	FOWLER Kenneth Frederick	31-10-42	88 Sqn
67666	F/L	FOX Edwin	29-01-42	21 Sqn
1204720	Sgt	FOX George Edward	26-02-42	12 Sqn
1382178	Sgt	FOX John Anthony	10-10-42	16 OTU
1255582	Sgt	FOX Leonard Armstrong	10-01-42	83 Sqn
1253600	F/S	FOX Leslie Henry	9-11-42	44 Sqn
102141	P/O	FOX Ronald Walter	19-04-42	156 Sqn
61467	S/L	FOX DFM Sidney Horace	25-10-42	103 Sqn
811126	Sgt	FOXLEY Albert Cecil	22-12-42	105 Sqn
1376982	Sgt	FRAME William Venn	26-03-42	88 Sqn
1315446	Sgt	FRANCIS Donald	31-10-42	97 Sqn
632346	Sgt	FRANCIS Douglas	30-03-42	35 Sqn
982893	Sgt	FRANCIS Roger Owen	10-04-42	9 Sqn
926593	Sgt	FRANKLAND Robert Kynnersley	19-06-42	78 Sqn
1168580	Sgt	FRANKLIN Brian	9-01-42	12 Sqn
124719	P/O	FRANKLIN Fred	11-12-42	10 OTU

744909	Sgt	FRANKLIN Leonard Sidney		30-07-42	138 Sqn	1288181	Sgt	GALLEY Arthur Frederick	7-07-42	156 Sqn
105182	P/O	FRANKLIN Robert William [Canada]		27-03-42	138 Sqn	632517	Sgt	GALLIMORE John James	25-11-42	207 Sqn
1504580	Sgt	FRANKLIN Ronald Eden		25-09-42	161 Sqn	1546101	Sgt	GALLOWAY Ernest Norman	18-08-42	218 Sqn
86720	S/L	FRANKS DFC John Henry		29-06-42	57 Sqn	121922	P/O	GALLOWAY-WILSON Bryan Geoffrey		
122327	F/O	FRANKS Robert		15-10-42	21 OTU				9-06-42	83 Sqn
951573	Sgt	FRASER Adam Brodie		25-08-42	150 Sqn	1051312	Sgt	GAMBLE Thomas Reginald	8-02-42	12 OTU
1108860	Sgt	FRASER Andrew Taylor		5-06-42	57 Sqn	1262786	F/S	GAME Henry Ernest	15-10-42	61 Sqn
996595	Sgt	FRASER Hugh Ian		29-03-42	103 Sqn	1264796	Sgt	GAME Ronald Walter	17-12-42	50 Sqn
974156	Sgt	FRASER James Alexander		25-06-42	102 Sqn	1320955	Sgt	GANDER Alfred	2-10-42	161 Sqn
987553	Sgt	FRASER Robin Jack		17-05-42	9 Sqn	1250546	Sgt	GANDER Charles Thomas	14-03-42	78 Sqn
903840	Sgt	FRASER Thomas James		17-09-42	15 OTU	951680	Sgt	GANDERTON Roy Buglar	2-06-42	61 Sqn
1117165	Sgt	FRATER Norman		17-12-42	103 Sqn	103553	P/O	GANDY Orrell	10-03-42	455 Sqn
1271712	Sgt	FRAYNE Frederick John		9-11-42	12 OTU	1375454	Sgt	GANE George Boyd	28-06-42	150 Sqn
118620	P/O	FRAZER John Wheelhouse		27-08-42	15 Sqn	1174904	Sgt	GANLY Conrad Charles William	9-03-42	35 Sqn
1257107	Sgt	FREAK Roy		26-03-42	115 Sqn	1377351	Sgt	GAPES Albert George Henry	15-12-42	405 Sqn
1376731	Sgt	FREE Colin William		28-08-42	13 OTU	624296	Sgt	GARBETT David Douglas	15-10-42	106 Sqn
1059256	Sgt	FREEAR Douglas Ronald		10-04-42	158 Sqn	1106543	Sgt	GARDINER Alfred Donald	17-04-42	107 Sqn
979399	F/S	FREELAND David Harrison		27-09-42	138 Sqn	625967	Sgt	GARDINER Edward Arthur	20-12-42	9 Sqn
988755	Sgt	FREEMAN Christopher Grant		26-03-42	57 Sqn	126870	P/O	GARDINER Frank Edward	25-08-42	35 Sqn
942986	Sgt	FREEMAN Diamond		26-07-42	106 Sqn	567298	Sgt	GARDINER Harold Phillip	7-08-42	218 Sqn
24252	S/L	FREEMAN Frederick Charles Gordon		11-07-42	101 Sqn	656465	Sgt	GARDINER James Victor	9-03-42	15 OTU
1334858	Sgt	FREEMAN Robert Walter		10-09-42	11 OTU	46917	P/O	GARDINER Peter	8-05-42	44 Sqn
1311904	Sgt	FREESTONE John Churley		14-09-42	1653 CU	1377610	Sgt	GARDNER Alan Francis	25-10-42	115 Sqn
1050023	Sgt	FREESTONE Thomas Harold		14-09-42	16 OTU	1375226	Sgt	GARDNER Albert Harry	3-01-42	106 Sqn
1381454	Sgt	FRENCH Leonard Percy James		8-12-42	149 Sqn	105175	P/O	GARDNER Anthony De Faye	31-05-42	101 Sqn
798590	Sgt	FRENCH Victor Raymond		11-09-42	405 Sqn	778828	Sgt	GARDNER Charles Norman	1-08-42	44 Sqn
		[Newfoundland]						[South Africa]		
657403	Sgt	FRICKER Alfred William		29-07-42	57 Sqn	1391822	Sgt	GARDNER Douglas Dean	9-11-42	408 Sqn
80090	F/O	FRIEND Arthur William [Rhodesia]		28-06-42	97 Sqn	1334803	Sgt	GARDNER George	22-12-42	26 OTU
63480	F/L	FRITH James Rothwell		28-08-42	103 Sqn	1264572	Sgt	GARDNER Jack Wilfred	11-09-42	26 OTU
1316854	Sgt	FRIZZELL Edward Charles James		9-11-42	50 Sqn	115223	P/O	GARLAND Desmond William	5-06-42	50 Sqn
1162831	Sgt	FROMINGS Aubrey John		14-07-42	158 Sqn	631134	Sgt	GARLAND John Henry	25-08-42	101 Sqn
106066	P/O	FROST Arthur John		18-05-42	149 Sqn	919969	Sgt	GARLAND William Charles	28-04-42	115 Sqn
114266	P/O	FROST DFM Christopher Ronald		9-03-42	83 Sqn	1290596	Sgt	GARNHAM Harry George Samuel	26-03-42	83 Sqn
1330615	Sgt	FROST Frank Arthur		6-08-42	102 Sqn	778783	Sgt	GAROS Alexander [Rhodesia]	20-06-42	49 Sqn
1347905	Sgt	FROST John Davidson		3-09-42	19 OTU	987428	F/S	GARRATT Reginald Henry Hobson	2-06-42	49 Sqn
1298071	Sgt	FROST Henry William		21-12-42	7 Sqn	651255	Sgt	GARRETT Sidney Charles	19-09-42	50 Sqn
1258080	Sgt	FROST Leonard John		4-02-42	21 Sqn	984752	Sgt	GARROWAY James	28-04-42	102 Sqn
798514	F/S	FROUDE Baxter [Newfoundland]		3-01-42	99 Sqn	106113	P/O	GARSCADDEN James	4-06-42	218 Sqn
905553	W/O	FRY David Wyndham		12-08-42	207 Sqn	569190	Sgt	GARSON James Gordon Bertie	2-06-42	10 Sqn
625746	Sgt	FRY Francis Alfred		29-03-42	106 Sqn	106967	P/O	GARSTIN Edward William Maitland	15-01-42	18 Sqn
909140	F/S	FRY Frederick George		25-06-42	16 OTU	1153383	Sgt	GARTELL Peter Edward	29-06-42	57 Sqn
1182272	Sgt	FRYER Douglas Henry		11-12-42	12 OTU	131659	P/O	GARTSIDE Charles Douglas Alan	11-10-42	139 Sqn
562690	W/O	FULBROOK DFC Reginald John		22-09-42	103 Sqn	123294	P/O	GASCOYNE DFM George	2-06-42	23 OTU
934063	Sgt	FULLER Robert Harry		16-09-42	25 OTU	807051	Sgt	GASKEN Robert	3-09-42	1652 CU
119188	P/O	FULLER William Alfred John		27-07-42	106 Sqn	119729	P/O	GASKIN Alfred Leslie	12-08-42	57 Sqn
103507	P/O	FULLERTON DFM William Arthur		30-05-42	22 OTU	1310825	Sgt	GASSON Arthur Cecil	25-06-42	76 Sqn
989159	Sgt	FULTON Andrew		7-02-42	144 Sqn	118603	P/O	GATIS Edward	20-09-42	158 Sqn
37095	W/C	FULTON DSO DFC AFC John 'Moose'		29-07-42	419 Sqn	982054	Sgt	GAULD Albert Alexander	10-03-42	49 Sqn
		[Canada]				1211952	Sgt	GAY Reginald Ernest	17-06-42	35 Sqn
534974	F/S	FUNNELL Archibald Stanley		6-09-42	150 Sqn	968122	F/S	GEDDIE William Norman	17-09-42	76 Sqn
942610	Sgt	FURBY Christopher George		25-03-42	61 Sqn	966815	W/O	GEE Donald Anthony	7-10-42	28 OTU
1386471	Sgt	FURLONG Cyril William		6-12-42	14 OTU	655012	Sgt	GEE George Muir	14-01-42	22 OTU
1311105	Sgt	FURNELL Robert Edwin		1-08-42	57 Sqn	1431988	AC2	GE Ronald	20-04-42	Molesworth
1379922	Sgt	FURNESS William Edward		3-07-42	18 Sqn	927418	Sgt	GEERS Alfred Edward	31-03-42	13 OTU
1575389	Sgt	FURNISS John William		11-12-42	158 Sqn	108248	P/O	GENT Reginald Philip	17-05-42	149 Sqn
1316055	Sgt	FUSSELL Marcel Alec		17-12-42	101 Sqn	915708	Sgt	GEORGE Cecil Spencer	6-01-42	19 OTU
1186829	Sgt	FUSSELL Phillip Goldham		28-04-42	150 Sqn	1070177	Sgt	GEORGE Charles Stuart	21-10-42	21 OTU
		[New Zealand]				1164451	Sgt	GEORGE Dennis Owen	2-04-42	214 Sqn
995951	Sgt	FUSSEY Leonard Arthur		2-06-42	114 Sqn	1317130	Sgt	GEORGE Henry Arthur	3-07-42	10 Sqn
83301	F/O	FYSON DFC Bertram John		29-03-42	103 Sqn	1167271	Sgt	GEORGE Thomas Alfred	6-06-42	149 Sqn
65556	F/O	GABE Thomas Albert		11-07-42	105 Sqn	567548	Sgt	GEORGE William Dennis Robert	14-04-42	76 Sqn
1054193	Sgt	GADSON Roy Baird		6-10-42	44 Sqn	1056639	Sgt	GERMAN Charles Kenneth	15-01-42	104 Sqn
1375303	Sgt	GALE Gerald Alan		14-01-42	50 Sqn	104535	P/O	GERRIE Alexander	17-04-42	44 Sqn
1166976	Sgt	GALE Paul Graham		17-01-42	405 Sqn	999003	Sgt	GETHING James Steele	3-06-42	420 Sqn
106042	F/O	GALES MiD Philip Frank Weller		23-09-42	218 Sqn	1507184	AC2	GIANNASI Frederick George	28-05-42	12 OTU
574930	Sgt	GALLAGHER Maurice Patrick [Eire]		17-08-42	50 Sqn	118662	P/O	GIBBS Edgar William Thomas	8-09-42	78 Sqn
1190214	Sgt	GALLAGHER Richard Thomas Patrick				551131	F/S	GIBBS Peter Anthony	9-01-42	90 Sqn
				29-06-42	149 Sqn	812346	F/S	GIBBY John Llewellyn	25-05-42	22 OTU

Service No	Rank	Name	Date	Unit
1360225	Sgt	GIBSON Alfred	7-02-42	144 Sqn
68175	F/O	GIBSON MiD Basil Douglas Gay	17-08-42	1652 CU
1340624	Sgt	GIBSON Robert Calder	6-11-42	18 Sqn
39458	S/L	GILBERT Colin Leslie	7-05-42	460 Sqn
115137	P/O	GILBY Joseph Norman	7-08-42	103 Sqn
616082	Sgt	GILDER Frederick	20-12-42	76 Sqn
1333184	Sgt	GILES Arthur Ernest Fuce	9-11-42	408 Sqn
1285035	Sgt	GILES Ernest Alfred	10-09-42	142 Sqn
115136	P/O	GILES Herbert Edward James	9-07-42	15 OTU
1186108	Sgt	GILES Wilfred	21-01-42	455 Sqn
116096	P/O	GILL Derek	28-08-42	57 Sqn
652637	Sgt	GILL Harold John [Canada]	3-07-42	10 Sqn
807146	F/S	GILL Henry Verdun	17-04-42	44 Sqn
938995	Sgt	GILL Kenneth John	19-05-42	106 Sqn
116091	P/O	GILL Norman Ingram	5-09-42	101 Sqn
1343515	Sgt	GILL Thomas	16-11-42	115 Sqn
1347529	Sgt	GILLAN Patrick Joseph	21-12-42	7 Sqn
1107618	Sgt	GILLARD Frank	21-08-42	15 OTU
115640	F/O	GILLELAND Harold	17-12-42	50 Sqn
1101025	Sgt	GILLESPIE Alexander John Shields	18-04-42	57 Sqn
43533	F/L	GILLESPIE Robert	12-04-42	103 Sqn
636033	Sgt	GILLIES Andrew Arthur	16-10-42	51 Sqn
741756	F/S	GILLIES John	18-08-42	76 Sqn
42214	F/L	GILMOUR DFC William	29-08-42	156 Sqn
1383594	Sgt	GIRDLESTONE Alfred Charles	13-10-42	10 Sqn
80237	P/O	GIRI Vincent Noel [Rhodesia]	20-12-42	44 Sqn
1113555	Sgt	GIRVIN Sidney Martin	4-09-42	97 Sqn
1260085	Sgt	GLANVILLE Gordon Arthur	10-01-42	408 Sqn
916282	Sgt	GLANVILLE William Arthur Ivor	26-02-42	10 Sqn
649748	Sgt	GLASSBROOK Gerald	3-06-42	61 Sqn
655483	Sgt	GLAVES John	9-09-42	150 Sqn
46019	F/O	GLAZEBROOK DFM Stanley	11-08-42	207 Sqn
1293167	Sgt	GLEADALL Keith Albert	5-08-42	10 OTU
1058280	Sgt	GLEDHILL Jack	15-04-42	144 Sqn
991158	Sgt	GLENDINNING John James	24-10-42	50 Sqn
552875	F/S	GLENWRIGHT DFM Edwin Campbell	29-07-42	1651 CU
612645	Sgt	GLOVER Derek Humphrey	12-08-42	106 Sqn
567204	Sgt	GLOVER Maurice Charles	24-06-42	76 Sqn
1086885	Sgt	GLOVER Stanley	10-08-42	150 Sqn
613280	F/S	GLYNN Michael Joseph	20-09-42	44 Sqn
108014	P/O	GOAD Leon Reginald	11-07-42	101 Sqn
1386536	F/S	GOALEN Laurence Walter	30-09-42	9 Sqn
629564	Sgt	GODDARD John Leslie	2-06-42	97 Sqn
1168510	F/S	GODFREY Douglas Charles	29-12-42	77 Sqn
1378233	Sgt	GODFREY Joseph Henry	12-03-42	75 Sqn
33251	W/C	GODFREY DFC Oliver	23-06-42	103 Sqn
1310251	Sgt	GODLY William John	23-09-42	142 Sqn
1257938	Sgt	GODSON Herbert Ernest	26-01-42	12 Sqn
1176030	Sgt	GOFF Alan Frank	10-11-42	107 Sqn
916785	Sgt	GOFF Stuart John	17-12-42	75 Sqn
1001635	F/S	GOLD David	28-01-42	138 Sqn
1187044	Sgt	GOLDIE Harry Edward	3-09-42	75 Sqn
33027	W/C	GOLDING DFC* Albert	26-03-42	12 Sqn
1331870	Sgt	GOLDING Geoffrey George	9-11-42	150 Sqn
657308	Sgt	GOLDRING Charles Edward	20-06-42	49 Sqn
1250808	Sgt	GOLDSACK Henry Edward	13-10-42	75 Sqn
1287042	Sgt	GOLDSMITH Benjamin Frederick	2-10-42	149 Sqn
80127	P/O	GOLDSMITH Norman Edward [Rhodesia]	17-12-42	50 Sqn
1266021	Sgt	GOLDSTEIN Mathias Aaron	8-11-42	158 Sqn
969407	F/S	GOLIGHTLY Frederick James	25-06-42	12 OTU
1289138	F/S	GOOBY Donald Paul	12-11-42	83 Sqn
120928	F/O	GOOD Michael Harvey	8-12-42	149 Sqn
1210053	Sgt	GOOD Walter Frank	8-04-42	15 OTU
977292	Sgt	GOOD Walter Henry	1-08-42	12 Sqn
1378584	Sgt	GOODE Cecil Francis	17-06-42	35 Sqn
653294	Sgt	GOODFELLOW William John	29-10-42	150 Sqn
1265668	Sgt	GOODHEW Stanley Victor	25-10-42	103 Sqn
81400	F/O	GOODMAN Donald	8-04-42	83 Sqn
954695	F/S	GOODRUM Lewis Edward	31-03-42	35 Sqn
905933	F/S	GOODRUM William Heriot	19-05-42	218 Sqn
120850	P/O	GOODWIN DFM Bernard Cuthbert	21-12-42	106 Sqn
954732	Sgt	GOODWIN Edmund Browne	2-06-42	97 Sqn
1499120	AC2	GOODWIN Frederick Stanley	14-04-42	1652 CU
124319	P/O	GOODWIN Ronald Stanley	16-12-42	23 OTU
818020	F/S	GOOLD Robert Wallace George	9-01-42	90 Sqn
1260360	Sgt	GORFUNKLE Norman	7-11-42	76 Sqn
908675	Sgt	GORMAN William	6-02-42	21 OTU
1120631	Sgt	GORMAN William	5-10-42	35 Sqn
627230	Sgt	GORTON Maurice Doughty	10-09-42	11 OTU
115163	P/O	GORTON William Howarth	31-05-42	14 OTU
1336609	Sgt	GOSDEN Douglas Charles	14-09-42	10 OTU
112424	P/O	GOSS Victor Emanuel George	9-05-42	158 Sqn
777667	Sgt	GOTTLIEB Abe Isadore [South Africa]	6-06-42	44 Sqn
1261768	Sgt	GOULD Edgar George Spencer	11-04-42	15 Sqn
1330116	Sgt	GOULDEN Eric	24-04-42	101 Sqn
798560	Sgt	GOVER Henry Patrick [Newfoundland]	10-08-42	405 Sqn
974840	Sgt	GOW George Anderson	28-06-42	218 Sqn
980327	Sgt	GOWER John Buxton	9-05-42	44 Sqn
1283120	Sgt	GRACE Maurice Edward John	29-11-42	29 OTU
31143	S/L	GRACEY Francis Joseph	17-01-42	20 OTU
622275	F/S	GRADY Lelie Thomas William	27-07-42	12 Sqn
751249	Sgt	GRAHAM Arthur Osborne	25-08-42	7 Sqn
1160000	Sgt	GRAHAM Donald Arthur	11-03-42	149 Sqn
1059997	Sgt	GRAHAM George Douglas	28-05-42	1443 Flt
1025508	AC1	GRAHAM Henry	26-09-42	88 Sqn
47909	P/O	GRAHAM DFM James	26-06-42	1651 CU
1059575	Sgt	GRAHAM James Stewart	14-08-42	19 OTU
46934	P/O	GRAHAM John Stuart	9-06-42	114 Sqn
778832	Sgt	GRAHAM John Luke [Rhodesia]	26-07-42	35 Sqn
968335	F/S	GRAHAM John Thompson	28-03-42	7 Sqn
120447	P/O	GRAHAM Laurence James Alexander	30-09-42	12 Sqn
912104	F/S	GRAHAM Wilfred	28-08-42	115 Sqn
1314324	Sgt	GRANSHAW Gerald Bamford	21-06-42	7 Sqn
127011	P/O	GRANT Alan George	14-09-42	19 OTU
116903	P/O	GRANT Clifford Harry	16-09-42	101 Sqn
1062255	Sgt	GRANT James	14-07-42	419 Sqn
44802	F/O	GRANT Malcolm Graeme	29-10-42	10 OTU
1337376	Sgt	GRANT Peter Anthony James	6-12-42	102 Sqn
1288356	Sgt	GRANT Ronald Frank Gordon	29-07-42	1651 CU
1066252	Sgt	GRAVES Leslie Douglas	18-08-42	12 Sqn
626019	F/S	GRAY DFM Charles Henry	27-03-42	114 Sqn
974897	Sgt	GRAY James	31-03-42	13 OTU
922567	Sgt	GRAY James William [South Africa]	29-08-42	149 Sqn
1253514	Sgt	GRAY Lawrence Aubrey Lytton	26-07-42	114 Sqn
1174107	Sgt	GRAY Leslie Charles	9-06-42	150 Sqn
1343177	Sgt	GRAY Thomas Main Gardner	31-10-42	25 OTU
970472	F/S	GRAY Trevor Morgan	30-07-42	138 Sqn
955478	Sgt	GRAY William	5-06-42	50 Sqn
963946	F/S	GRAY William Arthur 'Bill'	20-01-42	49 Sqn
1111477	Sgt	GRAY William Forbes	4-09-42	97 Sqn
51289	P/O	GRAYLAND George John	22-11-42	156 Sqn
123114	F/O	GRAYSON Ronald Leake	22-12-42	21 OTU
1485704	AC1	GREEN Albert Victor	29-12-42	77 Sqn
653953	Sgt	GREEN Arthur	5-10-42	218 Sqn
751257	Sgt	GREEN Cyril Wright	6-01-42	19 OTU
1006321	Sgt	GREEN David James	17-09-42	61 Sqn
778629	F/S	GREEN Dennis Arthur [South Africa]	4-09-42	25 OTU
1380982	Sgt	GREEN Edwin George	12-02-42	49 Sqn
618327	F/S	GREEN Frederick George	27-09-42	138 Sqn
571059	Sgt	GREEN George	5-10-42	103 Sqn
548497	Sgt	GREEN Henry Alfred Leslie	12-08-42	207 Sqn
45424	P/O	GREEN John Bryan	21-02-42	150 Sqn
1129517	Sgt	GREEN Joseph	26-05-42	19 OTU
1062799	Sgt	GREEN Norman Desmond	10-10-42	150 Sqn

Service No	Rank	Name	Date	Sqn
550338	W/O	GREEN Stanley Maurice	31-05-42	15 OTU
590953	Sgt	GREEN William	30-09-42	51 Sqn
1129659	Sgt	GREEN William	24-08-42	149 Sqn
1325719	Sgt	GREENAWAY Arthur John	1-08-42	420 Sqn
1161457	Sgt	GREENBECK Stanley	19-09-42	15 Sqn
1331747	Sgt	GREENE Stanley Howard	29-06-42	7 Sqn
533208	F/S	GREENING John Llewellyn	6-12-42	487 Sqn
45202	S/L	GREENSLADE DFC AFC MiD William Roy [Canada]	2-10-42	149 Sqn
962960	Sgt	GREENSMITH Richard Barton	17-11-42	158 Sqn
1257101	Sgt	GREENSTREET Irvine Stewart	12-02-42	49 Sqn
629695	Sgt	GREENWOOD Harry Stansfield	1-10-42	76 Sqn
1113288	Sgt	GREENWOOD John	10-09-42	7 Sqn
938264	Sgt	GREENWOOD Ronald	4-06-42	76 Sqn
1052205	Sgt	GREENWOOD Thomas Frederick	19-01-42	9 Sqn
543208	F/S	GREENWOOD Victor	21-12-42	106 Sqn
1497562	Sgt	GREET Dennis	25-08-42	15 OTU
902460	Sgt	GREGG Robert	13-10-42	10 Sqn
994457	F/S	GREGG William Humphreys	5-05-42	218 Sqn
1066775	Sgt	GREGORY John Kenneth	1-10-42	78 Sqn
923461	F/S	GREGORY Paul Walter [Canada]	28-06-42	61 Sqn
115239	P/O	GREGORY Walter Ewart	30-05-42	142 Sqn
961670	Sgt	GREGORY Walter Percy	6-12-42	21 Sqn
1005402	Sgt	GREGORY William Ronald	3-03-42	218 Sqn
1062058	Sgt	GREGSON Herbert	28-08-42	408 Sqn
569763	Sgt	GREGSON Norman Percy	11-08-42	149 Sqn
110831	P/O	GREIN Bernard Edward	12-08-42	106 Sqn
1377401	Sgt	GRELLIER DFM Richard William	9-11-42	57 Sqn
1495685	Sgt	GREY Thomas Allison	26-07-42	97 Sqn
1125948	Sgt	GRIEVE Bertram Wishaw	24-10-42	218 Sqn
987750	Sgt	GRIEVE Dreacus Callum	2-06-42	102 Sqn
101057	P/O	GRIEVE James Gavin Caldwell	6-02-42	21 Sqn
1308989	Sgt	GRIEVE James Small	26-04-42	115 Sqn
1101856	Sgt	GRIEVE Robert Elliot Pringle	6-06-42	103 Sqn
905561	Sgt	GRIFFIN Neville	8-04-42	23 OTU
120397	P/O	GRIFFIN DFC Walter William	9-11-42	57 Sqn
1306000	Sgt	GRIFFITHS Gerald Anthony	5-12-42	15 OTU
1283548	Sgt	GRIFFITHS Ivor Brinley	12-08-42	78 Sqn
1379390	Sgt	GRIFFITHS Maldwyn	2-10-42	218 Sqn
915076	Sgt	GRIFFITHS Myrddin	7-04-42	49 Sqn
1180830	Sgt	GRIFFITHS Richard Vivian	9-01-42	207 Sqn
1354014	Sgt	GRIFFITHS William Herbert	8-02-42	21 OTU
106136	P/O	GRILLS Francis Albert	17-04-42	107 Sqn
787831	Sgt	GRIMM Rudolf [Czechoslovakia]	6-04-42	1429 Flt
805349	Sgt	GRIMMETT James Frederick	28-03-42	7 Sqn
575319	Sgt	GRIMOLDBY Noel	14-04-42	102 Sqn
1379753	Sgt	GRIMSHAW Leslie Thomas	1-08-42	106 Sqn
1183176	Sgt	GRIMWOOD Eric Norman	26-07-42	97 Sqn
1053274	Sgt	GRISEDALE Thomas William	8-11-42	10 Sqn
1109846	Sgt	GROCOCK John	28-06-42	61 Sqn
126450	P/O	GROOM Robert Henry	17-09-42	11 OTU
1280705	Sgt	GROSSMITH Alan Thomas	11-07-42	97 Sqn
1262641	Sgt	GROUNSELL Arthur Edward	29-08-42	35 Sqn
657264	Sgt	GROVE Leslie James	5-06-42	1443 Flt
109063	P/O	GROVES DFM Alfred William	15-08-42	105 Sqn
1255452	Sgt	GROVES Donald Ivor	14-01-42	21 Sqn
1375174	Sgt	GROVES Eric Charles	25-03-42	142 Sqn
1388416	Sgt	GROVES George	4-12-42	14 OTU
112743	P/O	GROVES Maurice Walter	29-07-42	9 Sqn
31412	P/O	GROVES Stephen Eric	24-09-42	76 Sqn
120470	P/O	GRUBER John Anthony	28-08-42	218 Sqn
777669	Sgt	GRUBER Maurice [Rhodesia]	9-05-42	50 Sqn
777670	Sgt	GRUBER Rufus Isaacs [Rhodesia]	9-11-42	44 Sqn
798608	Sgt	GRUCHY Albert [Newfoundland]	16-05-42	9 Sqn
1057465	Sgt	GRUNDY Leonard	25-08-42	97 Sqn
1326330	Sgt	GRUNWELL Stanley	9-03-42	83 Sqn
1354001	Sgt	GUILFOYLE Hugh Patrick Anthony	12-02-42	110 Sqn
68189	P/O	GULLIVER Thomas George Hubert	9-03-42	9 Sqn
156458	F/S	GUMBLEY Robert George	26-06-42	35 Sqn
912780	Sgt	GUNN Thomas Gower	30-06-42	405 Sqn
1183183	Sgt	GUNNING James Walter	14-09-42	12 Sqn
1007367	Sgt	GUNTER Richard Ivor	20-12-42	44 Sqn
1378901	Sgt	GUNTRIP Ronald Joseph	31-05-42	218 Sqn
1184152	Sgt	GUPPY Frederick Richard	10-09-42	75 Sqn
527385	Sgt	GURNEY James Edward	14-02-42	1652 CU
129532	P/O	GURD Ronald Edward Eric	14-10-42	420 Sqn
568534	F/S	GURR Gordon Frederick	17-01-42	405 Sqn
37399	S/L	GUTHRIE Neil Drummond	9-05-42	10 Sqn
1286635	Sgt	GWYTHER John Frederick	6-06-42	149 Sqn
641680	Sgt	HACKER Raymond Albert Wilfred	12-10-42	50 Sqn
1199025	Sgt	HACKETT John Henry	17-04-42	44 Sqn
80218	F/O	HACKNEY DFC Thomas Gerald [Rhodesia]	7-11-42	83 Sqn
956676	Sgt	HADDOCK Donald	19-06-42	408 Sqn
932122	Sgt	HADGRAFT George William James	17-04-42	44 Sqn
1310499	Sgt	HADLEY Francis Norman	28-07-42	156 Sqn
568021	Sgt	HADWEN John Hornsby	24-09-42	78 Sqn
1109208	Sgt	HAGAN Charles Eric	2-09-42	142 Sqn
1261463	Sgt	HAGBORG Rex Valund	16-04-42	156 Sqn
119024	P/O	HAGE Robert Leo [USA]	14-09-42	26 OTU
820001	F/S	HAGGER Frank	24-08-42	44 Sqn
948242	Sgt	HAGUE Arnold	30-03-42	10 Sqn
84886	F/O	HAIG Rupert Alexander	19-08-42	61 Sqn
820044	Sgt	HAILSTONE Kenneth	27-03-42	138 Sqn
1335902	Sgt	HAINES Frederick Roger	29-11-42	29 OTU
104404	P/O	HAINS Gordon John	20-06-42	15 Sqn
1360695	Sgt	HAINSWORTH Edwin	6-04-42	75 Sqn
787484	Sgt	HAJEK Bohuml [Czechoslovakia]	10-12-42	138 Sqn
1578399	Sgt	HALE Joseph Edward William	20-09-42	158 Sqn
1378369	F/S	HALE Kenneth Graham Marcus	8-11-42	10 Sqn
755336	LAC	HALE Leonard	12-04-42	226 Sqn
117002	P/O	HALES Douglas Walter	9-05-42	10 Sqn
1270246	Sgt	HALEY John Simon Da-Silva	9-07-42	15 OTU
933625	Sgt	HALL Colin James Murray	4-06-42	207 Sqn
1266931	Sgt	HALL Dennis Shapley	16-04-42	156 Sqn
1477817	Sgt	HALL Edmund Arden	16-09-42	25 OTU
1200462	Sgt	HALL Eric Archibald	30-03-42	10 Sqn
1232357	Sgt	HALL Frederick Cecil	23-10-42	218 Sqn
104355	F/L	HALL George Raymond	9-05-42	18 Sqn
966952	Sgt	HALL James	16-09-42	9 Sqn
970800	Sgt	HALL James Herbert	8-09-42	16 OTU
41693	S/L	HALL DFC MiD John Charles	18-05-42	15 Sqn
1182395	F/S	HALL Philip Louis	5-10-42	218 Sqn
1381186	Sgt	HALL Ronald Rolfe	6-02-42	21 Sqn
1102753	Sgt	HALL William	30-03-42	10 Sqn
702828	Sgt	HALL William Anderson	2-06-42	83 Sqn
656384	Sgt	HALL William Thomas George	31-07-42	9 Sqn
1077240	Sgt	HALLAM Horace Ronald	31-05-42	103 Sqn
1160116	Sgt	HALLAM John William	20-01-42	49 Sqn
1360282	Sgt	HALLIDAY Douglas Stephen	6-06-42	49 Sqn
1126208	Sgt	HALLIDAY William Erick	10-12-42	22 OTU
758119	Sgt	HALLEWELL Arnold	1-11-42	138 Sqn
952897	Sgt	HALLIWELL Henry	9-06-42	103 Sqn
76009	F/L	HALLS DFC Leslie Oscar	6-06-42	44 Sqn
1066523	Sgt	HALLYBURTON William	29-07-42	115 Sqn
953502	AC2	HAMBLY William Henry	15-01-42	11 OTU
915400	Sgt	HAMER Frank	20-09-42	9 Sqn
1479880	Sgt	HAMILTON Alan Moffatt	3-12-42	103 Sqn
1153377	Sgt	HAMLYN Albert Joseph	30-07-42	7 Sqn
42501	F/L	HAMMAN DFC* Alwyn Crampton [South Africa]	31-05-42	22 OTU
113870	F/O	HAMMOND Francis Charles	13-11-42	107 Sqn
1381459	Sgt	HAMMOND John Bentley	12-08-42	15 Sqn
1331531	Sgt	HAMMOND Phillip Stevenson	14-09-42	156 Sqn
1173236	Sgt	HAMON Victor Arthur [Channel Islands]	28-08-42	97 Sqn
1014564	Sgt	HAMPSON Eric	1-06-42	77 Sqn
1191244	Sgt	HANCOCK Bernard Leslie	14-09-42	21 OTU

982853	Sgt	HANCOCK Frederick George	12-02-42	50 Sqn	126449	P/O	HARRISON Geoffrey William	12-12-42	27 OTU
1381377	Sgt	HANCOCK George	6-02-42	21 Sqn	1325787	Sgt	HARRISON Harold Richard	29-04-42	9 Sqn
1337937	Sgt	HANCOCK Henry William	11-09-42	25 OTU	1311960	Sgt	HARRISON Jackson Osbourne	11-08-42	78 Sqn
657174	Sgt	HANCOCK Owen Douglas	1-08-42	103 Sqn	47528	F/O	HARRISON DFM Kenneth Howard	5-10-42	97 Sqn
1314850	Sgt	HANCOCKS Harold	15-10-42	214 Sqn	1310830	Sgt	HARRISON Laurence Elgar	27-11-42	20 OTU
1256776	Sgt	HANCOX Alan Herbert	20-01-42	101 Sqn	564332	W/O	HARRISON MiD Leonard	17-04-42	97 Sqn
1183372	Sgt	HANDFORD Donald	27-04-42	226 Sqn	1142647	AC1	HARRISON Leslie	13-05-42	50 Sqn
1173935	Sgt	HANDLEY Albert Ernest William	9-11-42	7 Sqn	116554	F/L	HARRISON Norman	7-06-42	214 Sqn
1375359	F/S	HANISH Frederick Nelson	19-05-42	218 Sqn	1295509	Sgt	HARRISON Patrick	29-06-42	7 Sqn
1353269	Sgt	HANKINS John Phillips	26-06-42	102 Sqn	1025231	Sgt	HARRISON Philip Charles	15-10-42	150 Sqn
948764	Sgt	HANLOW Daniel	17-06-42	102 Sqn	118897	P/O	HARRISON Robert Walter	5-09-42	101 Sqn
1163556	Sgt	HANNAFORD Henry John	29-07-42	9 Sqn	1066469	Sgt	HARRISON Walter Gordon	5-05-42	103 Sqn
1057328	Sgt	HANNAH Harry	1-06-42	77 Sqn	1212100	Sgt	HARROLD John Christopher	26-07-42	114 Sqn
43035	F/L	HANNAN DFC Raymund Joseph [New Zealand]	25-11-42	207 Sqn	1325270	Sgt	HARROWELL Leslie Frederick	9-06-42	114 Sqn
					746920	F/S	HART Bernard Leslie	21-01-42	51 Sqn
649545	F/S	HANNATH Eric	12-07-42	15 OTU	104357	P/O	HART David Robert	28-03-42	7 Sqn
1199498	Sgt	HANRAHAN Edmond Patrick	12-03-42	77 Sqn	655066	F/S	HART Henry John	10-10-42	149 Sqn
117148	P/O	HANSON DFC Arthur Howard	10-09-42	158 Sqn	1154131	F/S	HART Kenneth Harry	11-07-42	207 Sqn
1210145	Sgt	HANSON Denis William Joseph	14-12-42	10 OTU	523663	Sgt	HART Robert	17-12-42	75 Sqn
1270444	Sgt	HANSON Frederick John Lawrence	3-06-42	61 Sqn	1312986	Sgt	HART Robert Isaac	2-06-42	106 Sqn
46968	F/O	HANSON DFM Joseph Edward	1-10-42	61 Sqn	915974	Sgt	HART Ronald Edward	31-05-42	101 Sqn
1025297	LAC	HANSON Willie	4-07-42	77 Sqn	1358088	Sgt	HARTE James Henry	4-06-42	76 Sqn
787491	Sgt	HANZL Vladimir [Czechoslovakia]	3-03-42	311 Sqn	106131	P/O	HARTELL Raymond Raynes	11-08-42	207 Sqn
610985	Sgt	HARBOARD Thomas John	10-09-42	16 OTU	989820	Sgt	HARTLEY John	23-04-42	218 Sqn
1160931	Sgt	HARBRIDGE Kenneth Thorpe	5-10-42	161 Sqn	1027319	Sgt	HARTLEY Leonard	21-08-42	218 Sqn
111259	P/O	HARCUS Leslie James	3-06-42	7 Sqn	935693	F/S	HARTLEY Norman Rhodes	3-06-42	61 Sqn
655306	Sgt	HARDIE James Graham	8-02-42	22 OTU	1375987	Sgt	HARVEY Alan Godfrey	15-04-42	405 Sqn
1060161	Sgt	HARDING Charles Stanley	7-06-42	156 Sqn	123115	F/O	HARVEY Alexander Albert	21-10-42	7 Sqn
117413	F/O	HARDING Donald Robert	31-10-42	25 OTU	88232	F/O	HARVEY Alexander Muir	20-01-42	49 Sqn
1286585	Sgt	HARDING Eric Roland	4-06-42	115 Sqn	954434	Sgt	HARVEY Kenneth Bertram	3-03-42	218 Sqn
1251250	Sgt	HARDING Sidney George	28-01-42	106 Sqn	1256530	Sgt	HARVEY Laurence George	8-09-42	76 Sqn
566866	F/S	HARDING Sydney Victor	3-06-42	7 Sqn	36112	S/L	HARVIE Guy de Laval [New Zealand]	2-04-42	57 Sqn
108016	P/O	HARDMAN Eric Arthur Lascelles	9-06-42	83 Sqn	1310053	Sgt	HASKINS Reginald Alfred	20-09-42	101 Sqn
1268636	Sgt	HARDY Harry	23-10-42	158 Sqn	1167689	Sgt	HASSALL John	26-09-42	24 OTU
1165162	Sgt	HARDY James	6-04-42	50 Sqn	120038	P/O	HASTINGS Adam Byers	5-09-42	207 Sqn
1067790	Sgt	HARFOOT William Charles Percival	27-07-42	7 Sqn	1061710	Sgt	HATCH Eric Geoffrey	8-02-42	12 OTU
754105	F/S	HARKER Alan	28-08-42	142 Sqn	1162515	Sgt	HATCH Ernest Samuel William	6-10-42	19 OTU
1076027	Sgt	HARKER Fred Victor	12-08-42	156 Sqn	1375458	Sgt	HATCH John	25-06-42	16 OTU
979397	Sgt	HARKNESS Archibald	14-07-42	158 Sqn	1260483	Sgt	HATCH Stewart Ernest Fenton	3-08-42	51 Sqn
121958	P/O	HARKNESS Charles	29-07-42	75 Sqn	1182470	Sgt	HATTON Alan Sydney	12-04-42	107 Sqn
41694	S/L	HARKNESS DFC Donald Joseph [New Zealand]	31-05-42	158 Sqn	1535749	Sgt	HATTON George William	10-12-42	21 Sqn
					1093768	Sgt	HATTON Jay Andrew John Duke	17-09-42	15 OTU
1280517	Sgt	HARLE Sidney Harold	25-04-42	103 Sqn	1062558	Sgt	HAVENHAND John Cooper	11-09-42	50 Sqn
1339030	Sgt	HARMSTON Colin	20-12-42	44 Sqn	1293324	Sgt	HAVER Thomas William	22-11-42	12 OTU
925454	Sgt	HARPER Eric Ronald	14-01-42	207 Sqn	1113420	Sgt	HAVILLE Edward	19-07-42	408 Sqn
1378742	Sgt	HARPER Leslie Henry	5-12-42	15 OTU	787521	Sgt	HAVLIK Oldrich [Czechoslovakia]	14-04-42	311 Sqn
1310507	Sgt	HARPER William Lusk	27-07-42	142 Sqn	111561	P/O	HAWARD Lewis Boyd	20-09-42	9 Sqn
112752	P/O	HARRAD John Henry	20-08-42	61 Sqn	127491	P/O	HAWES George Alan	1-10-42	61 Sqn
1304290	Sgt	HARRAN Michael Anthony	9-11-42	57 Sqn	1279523	Sgt	HAWKES Bernard George	5-12-42	15 OTU
1377756	Sgt	HARRIES David Harold	6-12-42	487 Sqn	128405	P/O	HAWKES Joseph Walter	9-09-42	77 Sqn
1258385	Sgt	HARRIES John Howard	29-04-42	115 Sqn	118647	P/O	HAWKINS Arthur Stuart	27-07-42	76 Sqn
1264074	Sgt	HARRINGTON Arthur Robert	27-02-42	77 Sqn	655684	Sgt	HAWKINS Gordon Thomas	21-12-42	103 Sqn
542756	F/S	HARRINGTON MiD David Walter	17-04-42	97 Sqn	1187280	Sgt	HAWKINS Leo Henry	5-10-42	218 Sqn
1056762	Sgt	HARRIS Albert	22-07-42	114 Sqn	635491	Sgt	HAWKINS Robert Arthur	16-07-42	149 Sqn
920869	Sgt	HARRIS Alexander Gordon	9-01-42	207 Sqn	104572	P/O	HAWKINS William George Francis	26-03-42	114 Sqn
1176650	Sgt	HARRIS Andrew Albert Sidney Frederick	29-03-42	103 Sqn	751184	F/S	HAWKINS William Stephen	30-05-42	22 OTU
					551586	F/S	HAWKSWORTH MiD Richard William Albert	13-04-42	76 Sqn
1360384	Sgt	HARRIS Bernard William	20-05-42	103 Sqn					
1182243	Sgt	HARRIS Dudley Howard	21-08-42	149 Sqn	545881	Sgt	HAWORTH Kenneth	29-07-42	218 Sqn
41406	S/L	HARRIS George Lawlor Bernays [New Zealand]	12-02-42	420 Sqn	625479	Sgt	HAWTHORN Kenneth	28-08-42	15 Sqn
					45428	P/O	HAY Robert Petrie	3-01-42	23 OTU
1166153	Sgt	HARRIS Leslie Desmond	22-07-42	12 Sqn	1160619	Sgt	HAYES Charles Errol	26-07-42	19 OTU
1283645	Sgt	HARRIS Leslie Godfrey	28-04-42	115 Sqn	1331642	Sgt	HAYES Cyril Clifford	23-12-42	138 Sqn
1168160	Sgt	HARRIS Ronald	9-06-42	97 Sqn	1360381	Sgt	HAYES Eric Edwards	3-06-42	15 Sqn
39662	S/L	HARRIS Roy Braham [Jamaica]	6-06-42	149 Sqn	641637	Sgt	HAYES Frank Arthur	14-08-42	7 Sqn
1201186	F/S	HARRIS Thomas Harold	8-12-42	149 Sqn	1377993	Sgt	HAYES George	19-09-42	15 Sqn
1208881	Sgt	HARRISON Albert Ernest	14-09-42	12 Sqn	1122536	Sgt	HAYES MiD Norman Craig	17-09-42	97 Sqn
1380678	Sgt	HARRISON Alfred James	17-04-42	44 Sqn	1260200	Sgt	HAYES Patrick	2-09-42	156 Sqn
1090941	Sgt	HARRISON Ernest	3-06-42	420 Sqn	69494	P/O	HAYES Raymond Lawrence	28-03-42	7 Sqn

69424	P/O	HAYES Ronald William Stanley	2-04-42	214 Sqn	566527	W/O	HERBERT MiD Edwin Henry	10-10-42	150 Sqn
1290931	F/S	HAYHOE Edmund George	27-09-42	138 Sqn	955014	Sgt	HERBERT Leonard Edward	20-12-42	76 Sqn
1330217	Sgt	HAYLOCK Basil Theodore	3-06-42	57 Sqn	959970	F/S	HERBERT Philip Richard	29-06-42	57 Sqn
1262068	Sgt	HAYMAN Richard Edwards	6-12-42	115 Sqn	644481	Sgt	HERBERT William	14-09-42	156 Sqn
1280307	Sgt	HAYNES George Charles	31-05-42	49 Sqn	1162357	F/S	HEREFORD Paul	1-10-42	44 Sqn
1263649	Sgt	HAYNES Malcolm Stevenson	21-08-42	15 OTU	1213839	Sgt	HERRING Jack	14-09-42	156 Sqn
102967	P/O	HAYNES Thomas Kenneth	26-03-42	7 Sqn	125688	P/O	HERRINGTON Jack	15-10-42	21 OTU
1113610	Sgt	HAYTON Cyril	22-05-42	75 Sqn	109016	P/O	HERSEY Alan George	5-05-42	12 Sqn
126810	P/O	HAYWARD Eric Lionel	24-07-42	207 Sqn	845742	Sgt	HESLOP James	9-03-42	9 Sqn
118659	P/O	HAYWARD Jeffrey	8-06-42	10 OTU	1375238	Sgt	HESLOP Stanley Harry	5-05-42	150 Sqn
590955	Sgt	HAYWARD Peter	7-11-42	83 Sqn	1112158	Sgt	HEWETSON Harold	19-07-42	150 Sqn
1283370	Sgt	HAZELGROVE John Cyril	14-07-42	142 Sqn	1180812	Sgt	HEWITSON John	4-05-42	78 Sqn
139323	P/O	HAZELL Leslie Charles	20-12-42	9 Sqn	900003	Sgt	HEWITT Harold	1-10-42	61 Sqn
903565	Sgt	HAZLEDINE John Toker Clough	26-01-42	102 Sqn	119746	P/O	HEWITT Philip Valters	7-09-42	12 Sqn
128445	P/O	HAZLETON Stanley Frank	25-06-42	35 Sqn	120120	F/O	HEWITT Samuel Tweedy	17-12-42	103 Sqn
1270197	Sgt	HEAD Peter David	29-10-42	15 Sqn	958780	Sgt	HEXTALL Stanley	18-04-42	158 Sqn
976825	F/S	HEALEY Reginald Paul	9-06-42	405 Sqn	655049	F/S	HEY John Alistair	23-11-42	161 Sqn
46921	P/O	HEAP Joseph Ogden	5-05-42	218 Sqn	1337470	Sgt	HEYCOCK David Melville	11-12-42	25 OTU
1283560	Sgt	HEAP Wilbert Dudley	24-05-42	13 OTU	529508	F/S	HEYCOCK Leslie	9-06-42	405 Sqn
1169558	Sgt	HEARD Kenneth William	12-02-42	49 Sqn	1358984	Sgt	HEYMAN John Frederick	5-08-42	20 OTU
925390	Sgt	HEATH John Kingston Lew	28-06-42	218 Sqn	1389460	Sgt	HEYWOOD Gilbert Charles James	29-10-42	10 OTU
37174	W/C	HEATH Peter George Roland	30-05-42	156 Sqn	103015	F/L	HEYWOOD DFC Peter	9-11-42	7 Sqn
1375414	Sgt	HEATH Philip Charles	25-10-42	103 Sqn	1384209	Sgt	HIBBEN Gilbert Edwin	17-06-42	24 OTU
1382823	Sgt	HEATHCOTE Roy Alan	19-09-42	15 Sqn	117003	P/O	HIBBERT Harry	21-07-42	35 Sqn
100065	P/O	HEATON Adrian Russel	18-04-42	12 Sqn	1630558	AC2	HIBBETT Alfred Eric	7-11-42	Foulsham
971029	Sgt	HEATON Frank Kenneth	8-06-42	10 OTU	1199910	Sgt	HIBBITT Albert	25-01-42	49 Sqn
60334	F/O	HEATON John Frankland	4-06-42	50 Sqn	1166737	Sgt	HICKLEY Philip Frank	29-06-42	149 Sqn
114168	F/S	HEBBLETHWAITE Edwin Charles Long 'Peter'			68134	S/L	HICKLING DFM Peter Frank	9-11-42	218 Sqn
			3-05-42	78 Sqn	1289238	Sgt	HICKMAN Herbert John	8-03-42	115 Sqn
657350	Sgt	HEBBLETHWAITE Gilbert	27-08-42	156 Sqn	1236171	Sgt	HICKMAN Tom	29-08-42	149 Sqn
1377994	F/S	HEBDON James George	18-12-42	97 Sqn	120655	P/O	HICKS Archibald Jack	3-08-42	114 Sqn
944060	Sgt	HEBRON Fred	20-07-42	76 Sqn	523113	W/O	HICKS Frank Edward Malcolm	20-10-42	105 Sqn
1117365	Sgt	HEDDLE John David Robert	7-07-42	156 Sqn	1381897	Sgt	HICKS George Walter	16-12-42	23 OTU
1033069	Sgt	HEFFERNAN Arthur Francis	24-10-42	57 Sqn	1026171	Sgt	HIGGINBOTTOM Frank Smith	14-12-42	10 OTU
129635	P/O	HEGAN Donald Stewart	31-10-42	30 OTU	567990	Sgt	HIGGINS Anthony John	6-05-42	7 Sqn
940014	Sgt	HELLIWELL William	20-05-42	7 Sqn	134511	P/O	HIGGINS Christopher William	8-12-42	149 Sqn
104573	P/O	HELLYER Denis	20-05-42	156 Sqn	48518	P/O	HIGGINS Clarence William [Canada]	11-09-42	15 Sqn
69429	F/O	HELME John Shirreff Milner	22-09-42	19 OTU	115557	P/O	HIGGINS DFM Herbert Reginald	28-06-42	76 Sqn
1154478	Sgt	HELYAR Roy	13-08-42	15 Sqn	568305	Sgt	HIGGINS Raymond Tom	21-08-42	218 Sqn
1221261	Sgt	HELYER Rodney Kenneth	29-07-42	218 Sqn	111787	P/O	HIGGS Kenneth Albert	29-08-42	35 Sqn
123945	P/O	HEMMING Douglas Leonard	15-10-42	150 Sqn	570376	Sgt	HIGHAM John Cornish	20-05-42	10 Sqn
1032155	Sgt	HEMMINGS James	10-12-42	20 OTU	1199531	Sgt	HIGHFIELD John Cyril	29-07-42	9 Sqn
104519	P/O	HEMY Claude Dominic	3-08-42	51 Sqn	1058150	Sgt	HIGSON Geoffrey William Ardern	24-09-42	9 Sqn
116744	P/O	HENDERSON Alan Macdonald	21-08-42	15 OTU	65996	F/O	HILL Arthur Raymond	29-08-42	156 Sqn
743055	F/S	HENDERSON Barry Martin Smythe	26-03-42	142 Sqn	81048	S/L	HILL DFC Charles Ernest	15-10-42	106 Sqn
1356436	Sgt	HENDERSON David	2-04-42	57 Sqn	937575	Sgt	HILL Cyril	10-11-42	149 Sqn
1457110	Sgt	HENDERSON Francis Robert William			1319144	Sgt	HILL Cyril Sydney Herbert	8-11-42	142 Sqn
			29-12-42	11 OTU	1151830	Sgt	HILL Eric	6-01-42	12 Sqn
542498	Sgt	HENDERSON George	20-12-42	97 Sqn	1553228	AC1	HILL Francis Alfred	3-06-42	14 OTU
625247	F/S	HENDERSON Ian John Argo	19-09-42	15 Sqn	120706	P/O	HILL Frank William Gosnell	28-04-42	35 Sqn
109515	P/O	HENDERSON James McKenzie	2-04-42	214 Sqn	1204717	F/S	HILL Frederic Winston	22-09-42	103 Sqn
1078358	Sgt	HENDERSON Norman	2-10-42	218 Sqn	819006	Sgt	HILL Gordon Anthony	10-09-42	61 Sqn
1185491	Sgt	HENDERSON Thomas	12-08-42	57 Sqn	1425545	Sgt	HILL Herbert Berkeley	2-09-42	142 Sqn
128966	P/O	HENDERSON William	28-06-42	156 Sqn	1326399	Sgt	HILL James	20-12-42	9 Sqn
117418	P/O	HENDLEY-CROSS Claud Christopher			1163247	Sgt	HILL John Valentine	26-03-42	57 Sqn
			17-09-42	21 OTU	1053799	Sgt	HILL Kimber	25-03-42	106 Sqn
981680	Sgt	HENDRIE Alexander Rae	12-10-42	49 Sqn	1174041	Sgt	HILL Norman Jack	24-09-42	76 Sqn
		[New Zealand]			104390	P/O	HILL Peter John	12-02-42	110 Sqn
1381919	Sgt	HENDRIKSEN Arnold Peter	5-09-42	26 OTU	656834	Sgt	HILL Richard Francis	8-11-42	142 Sqn
132073	P/O	HENLY Robert William	21-12-42	7 Sqn	121728	P/O	HILL Ronald Horace	16-09-42	101 Sqn
104360	P/O	HENNING Charles Masterman	4-07-42	226 Sqn	1410534	Sgt	HILLBERG Bernard	22-11-42	12 OTU
917785	Sgt	HENNING Douglas	30-05-42	405 Sqn	117681	F/O	HILLIER MiD William Charles	6-12-42	76 Sqn
48086	P/O	HENRY Gerard John Peter	28-04-42	35 Sqn	1281915	Sgt	HILLMAN Robert	7-01-42	18 Sqn
741544	F/S	HENSON DFM John Kenneth	9-01-42	90 Sqn	1258086	F/S	HILLS George Edward	8-12-42	149 Sqn
574386	F/S	HENSON Joseph Arthur	1-08-42	103 Sqn	1601304	Sgt	HILLYER Ronald George James	31-10-42	150 Sqn
990266	Sgt	HENVEY William Bradley	18-04-42	101 Sqn	986343	S/L	HILTON Edward	11-09-42	20 OTU
998624	Sgt	HEPPENSTALL Percy	16-04-42	214 Sqn	1101060	F/S	HILTON William James	9-09-42	77 Sqn
1378983	Sgt	HEPPLE Thomas	1-06-42	115 Sqn	657626	Sgt	HIND Peter Clinch	21-12-42	207 Sqn
1430680	Sgt	HEPWORTH Eric	29-08-42	115 Sqn	933418	Sgt	HINDE Dennis Findley James	19-08-42	88 Sqn

Service No	Rank	Name	Date	Squadron
620185	Sgt	HINDLE John Norman	7-05-42	35 Sqn
1106167	Sgt	HINDLE Thomas	28-04-42	408 Sqn
1182643	Sgt	HINE Paul William	11-02-42	150 Sqn
1021212	Sgt	HINGLEY Walter	8-12-42	207 Sqn
752964	Sgt	HINTON Fred	8-01-42	458 Sqn
1150584	Sgt	HINTON James William	29-03-42	75 Sqn
182913	Sgt	HIPWELL Frederick Roberts	4-05-42	78 Sqn
776076	Sgt	HIRST Reginald Frank William [Middle East]	21-02-42	106 Sqn
1310855	Sgt	HISCOCK Alfred Edward	19-09-42	106 Sqn
908307	Sgt	HISCOCK William Charles Henry	11-09-42	78 Sqn
548910	Sgt	HISLEY Maurice James	11-08-42	78 Sqn
1289983	Sgt	HOARE James George Arthur	7-08-42	78 Sqn
39523	S/L	HOBBS James	15-10-42	156 Sqn
338309	Sgt	HOBBS Kenneth Beresford	16-09-42	9 Sqn
912096	F/S	HOBSON Frank	10-09-42	61 Sqn
104531	P/O	HOCKADAY Dennis Richard	13-03-42	78 Sqn
655228	Sgt	HOCKENHULL James	6-10-42	115 Sqn
1394852	Sgt	HOCKLEY Charles Cornelius	9-11-42	57 Sqn
1334463	Sgt	HODGE Gordon	12-10-42	49 Sqn
1157240	AC1	HODGES Dennis William	19-10-42	1656 HCU
100638	F/L	HODGES Michael Ryland	31-05-42	9 Sqn
955322	Sgt	HODGKINSON Duncan Edward	28-01-42	106 Sqn
103577	P/O	HODGSON Robert Cyril	12-08-42	408 Sqn
524685	Sgt	HODGSON Thomas Ernest	2-06-42	106 Sqn
1286431	Sgt	HODGSON Wilfred	11-09-42	78 Sqn
1552074	Sgt	HOGG Adam	3-07-42	13 OTU
121776	F/O	HOGG Dennis Walter	22-12-42	21 OTU
969489	Sgt	HOLDEN Robert	26-06-42	11 OTU
1133022	Sgt	HOLDEN Robert Samuel	24-05-42	138 Sqn
1261903	Sgt	HOLDEN Stuart Cecil	28-08-42	156 Sqn
1376202	Sgt	HOLDER Albert Ernest 'Jim'	13-04-42	115 Sqn
1330817	Sgt	HOLDERNESS Joe	8-11-42	20 OTU
1105003	Sgt	HOLDING Albert Edward	5-10-42	76 Sqn
115722	P/O	HOLDSWORTH John Barry	7-06-42	214 Sqn
80116	P/O	HOLLAND Christopher Thomas [Rhodesia]	14-09-42	44 Sqn
616111	Sgt	HOLLAND Douglas Richard	19-04-42	156 Sqn
1051594	Sgt	HOLLAND Ellis Albert	27-07-42	35 Sqn
130725	P/O	HOLLAND Frank	19-09-42	105 Sqn
948335	Sgt	HOLLAND James	20-09-42	214 Sqn
1006787	Sgt	HOLLAND James Vincent	24-08-42	44 Sqn
528167	Sgt	HOLLAND John William Edward	6-08-42	207 Sqn
1167380	Sgt	HOLLAND Reginald Douglas	9-06-42	405 Sqn
1257890	Sgt	HOLLAND William	22-01-42	106 Sqn
1378766	Sgt	HOLLIER Francis Arthur Edward	28-03-42	13 OTU
115983	P/O	HOLLINGER Derrick Arnold	26-07-42	35 Sqn
1600384	Sgt	HOLLOWAY Derek Alfred James	16-11-42	101 Sqn
116417	P/O	HOLLOWAY Frederick Charles	29-07-42	218 Sqn
1332872	AC1	HOLLOWAY Leslie	16-09-42	22 OTU
547408	F/S	HOLLOWAY Reginald John	12-04-42	226 Sqn
1151744	Sgt	HOLLOWELL William Ernest	30-06-42	57 Sqn
1059419	Sgt	HOLLOWS Eric	9-05-42	158 Sqn
569420	Sgt	HOLMAN Alfred James Victor	27-04-42	149 Sqn
1317897	Sgt	HOLMAN Arthur William	16-04-42	101 Sqn
1377697	Sgt	HOLMAN Roland	8-05-42	44 Sqn
928689	Sgt	HOLMES Alan Robertson	29-04-42	12 Sqn
581425	W/O	HOLMES Cecil	31-05-42	14 OTU
1168170	Sgt	HOLMES Charles Albert	16-08-42	106 Sqn
1045921	Sgt	HOLMES Donald	11-12-42	25 OTU
1264339	Sgt	HOLMES Donald Richard George	12-02-42	103 Sqn
37502	S/L	HOLMES AFC Douglas Holbrook	25-04-42	9 Sqn
903163	Sgt	HOLMES Ernest Edward Charles	24-10-42	149 Sqn
1310316	Sgt	HOLMES Ernest Frank	1-08-42	106 Sqn
1252631	Sgt	HOLMES Frederick William [Canada]	27-07-42	158 Sqn
1119620	Sgt	HOLMES Harvey	12-06-42	9 Sqn
996754	Sgt	HOLMES Jack	15-10-42	214 Sqn
1181184	Sgt	HOLMES James Herbert	31-05-42	156 Sqn
1266936	Sgt	HOLMES John Edwin	14-09-42	19 OTU
629489	Sgt	HOLMES Ronald William Edward	12-08-42	207 Sqn
1154264	Sgt	HOLMES Rowland Geoffrey	8-02-42	12 OTU
1253462	Sgt	HOLMES William Thomas	31-01-42	61 Sqn
126879	P/O	HOLROYDE Kenneth Marshall	18-11-42	21 OTU
1271669	AC2	HONEKER Leonard Sydney	4-06-42	12 OTU
1168679	Sgt	HOOD Hugh Charles	6-06-42	49 Sqn
976069	Sgt	HOOD DFM Norman Henry	7-05-42	35 Sqn
65525	F/O	HOOEY DFC Gilbert Campbell [Canada]	25-08-42	97 Sqn
1319945	Sgt	HOOKER Eric Armstrong	28-08-42	13 OTU
798613	Sgt	HOOKEY Joseph Patrick [Newfoundland]	26-09-42	24 OTU
1030463	Sgt	HOOLEY Harold	30-05-42	12 Sqn
105179	P/O	HOOPER Edwin Morris	16-02-42	77 Sqn
522767	Sgt	HOOPER Ernest Henry	15-10-42	57 Sqn
1381953	Sgt	HOOTON Francis	29-11-42	405 Sqn
1384371	Sgt	HOPCRAFT William Robert	11-10-42	17 OTU
944653	Sgt	HOPE Frederick William	9-11-42	102 Sqn
111241	P/O	HOPKINS Percival Gerald	28-08-42	103 Sqn
636602	Sgt	HOPKINS William John	8-06-42	35 Sqn
610971	Sgt	HOPKINS William Richard	27-08-42	15 Sqn
1025619	F/S	HOPKINSON Stephen Holroyd	8-12-42	149 Sqn
778346	Sgt	HOPWOOD Verner James [Rhodesia]	13-02-42	455 Sqn
1095270	Sgt	HOPWOOD William Neville	8-12-42	102 Sqn
1360376	Sgt	HORDER Ronald Douglas	28-07-42	218 Sqn
80128	P/O	HORE Eric Vivian [Rhodesia]	14-01-42	50 Sqn
1181632	Sgt	HORGAN David	26-07-42	78 Sqn
787929	Sgt	HORINEK Jindrich [Czechoslovakia]	6-04-42	1429 Flt
924528	Sgt	HORLEY John Michael	14-01-42	50 Sqn
637223	F/S	HORLOCK Richard John	25-06-42	14 OTU
120123	F/O	HORNBY David Hulme	31-10-42	1655 MCU
911437	Sgt	HORNE Cecil Bruce	15-10-42	106 Sqn
104332	F/O	HORNE John William Beresford	12-10-42	49 Sqn
949946	Sgt	HORNE Ronald Guy	11-06-42	77 Sqn
1113335	Sgt	HORNER Geoffrey	2-06-42	26 OTU
101544	F/O	HORNER Reginald Dudley [South Africa]	19-10-42	1656 HCU
75544	S/L	HORSFALL Charles Michael	21-11-42	Hethel
1166451	Sgt	HORSFALL William Edward	27-07-42	460 Sqn
1061727	Sgt	HORTON George	1-04-42	1428 Flt
1264120	Sgt	HORTON Leonard Harlow	17-10-42	98 Sqn
1251169	Sgt	HOSKINS Bertie Frederick	16-06-42	76 Sqn
902193	Sgt	HOTHERSALL Harry Ernest	13-04-42	76 Sqn
1074122	Sgt	HOUGH Frank Bernard [Canada]	25-10-42	142 Sqn
777873	Sgt	HOUGH Gilbert Walter [Rhodesia]	9-05-42	44 Sqn
994140	Sgt	HOUGH James Eric	24-05-42	22 OTU
1166960	Sgt	HOUGHTON George	30-05-42	460 Sqn
44484	S/L	HOULSTON DFC AFC Jack Edward	20-12-42	139 Sqn
1165159	Cpl	HOUNSLOW Douglas Sidney	17-12-42	138 Sqn
120714	P/O	HOUSE Edwin Arthur [Canada]	18-04-42	101 Sqn
904338	F/S	HOUSE Frederick Clifford	26-06-42	10 OTU
1063716	Sgt	HOUSTON Matthew Cumming	4-02-42	21 Sqn
580998	W/O	HOWARD DFC Charles Anthony	23-12-42	138 Sqn
914083	Sgt	HOWARD Clifford Owen	14-09-42	12 Sqn
559204	Sgt	HOWARD Cyril Marrison	10-08-42	78 Sqn
102537	P/O	HOWARD DFM Donald Arthur	3-01-42	106 Sqn
1215278	Sgt	HOWARD Arthur Vincent	27-10-42	10 OTU
581154	F/S	HOWARTH DFM Kenneth Turner	1-08-42	57 Sqn
546918	Sgt	HOWARTH Robert Dudley	25-03-42	50 Sqn
1109278	Sgt	HOWAT Robert	28-08-42	142 Sqn
1311798	Sgt	HOWE Derek Leslie	25-08-42	83 Sqn
1194389	Sgt	HOWE John Thomas 'Jack'	14-01-42	207 Sqn
1375874	Sgt	HOWE Leonard John	4-06-42	115 Sqn
1284777	Sgt	HOWE Mervyn James	15-10-42	149 Sqn
1184247	Sgt	HOWE Vivian	9-11-42	218 Sqn
1380271	Sgt	HOWELL Alfred Thomas	14-04-42	1652 CU
70332	S/L	HOWELL Cecil Moreton	16-09-42	106 Sqn
944090	Sgt	HOWELL Robert Frederick	27-03-42	408 Sqn
117457	P/O	HOWELL Trevor	20-11-42	150 Sqn

1381796	Sgt	HOWELLS Ronald	1-08-42	21 OTU	1291752	F/S	HUNTING Eric Richmond	3-09-42	75 Sqn
1282831	Sgt	HOWES Denniss Vincent	26-06-42	218 Sqn	777675	Sgt	HUNTLEY DFM Donald Norman [Rhodesia]	14-09-42	44 Sqn
1168632	Sgt	HOWES George William	13-03-42	12 Sqn					
540188	Sgt	HOWES John Frederick	26-06-42	218 Sqn	1165241	Sgt	HUNTLEY Francis Geoffrey	7-04-42	142 Sqn
912524	Cpl	HOWES Kenneth John	28-02-42	75 Sqn	517556	Sgt	HUNTLEY Frank William	27-07-42	35 Sqn
1335400	Sgt	HOWES Ronald Vinson	28-10-42	10 OTU	777676	Sgt	HUNTLEY Frederick Hope [Rhodesia]	17-09-42	1654 CU
1378338	Sgt	HOWES Walter John	6-10-42	75 Sqn	549735	Sgt	HURLEY Cornelius Michael	8-12-42	207 Sqn
1153454	Sgt	HOWICK Victor Charles	20-05-42	10 Sqn	47905	P/O	HURLEY Frank Arthur	28-07-42	105 Sqn
1061582	Sgt	HOWISON Arnold	20-12-42	49 Sqn	1310344	Sgt	HURLEY William	5-06-42	1443 Flt
584590	LAC	HOWLETT Oliver Sidney	22-11-42	7 Sqn	1525184	Sgt	HURRELL William	9-11-42	150 Sqn
119296	P/O	HOWLETT Stanley	7-09-42	12 Sqn	921818	Sgt	HURST Henry Douglas	11-08-42	156 Sqn
1104350	Sgt	HOWSON Wilfred Joseph	4-02-42	21 OTU	630571	F/S	HUSSEY Anthony	14-01-42	21 Sqn
1281658	Sgt	HOYLE Peter John Lascelles	17-05-42	9 Sqn	89837	F/O	HUSTON John Clarke	17-01-42	12 OTU
787578	Sgt	HRADIL Bonuslav [Czechoslovakia]	3-03-42	311 Sqn	43481	S/L	HUTCHINGS DFC William Cyril	10-11-42	149 Sqn
788119	Sgt	HRALA Josef [Czechoslovakia]	13-10-42	27 OTU	1180254	Sgt	HUTCHINSON Aubrey George	28-04-42	150 Sqn
787310	Sgt	HRDINA Josef [Czechoslovakia]	11-04-42	311 Sqn	1499347	AC1	HUTCHINSON Harold Henry	10-12-42	138 Sqn
109513	P/O	HUBBARD John Ralph	25-03-42	61 Sqn	942809	Sgt	HUTCHINSON William	15-02-42	9 Sqn
1376005	Sgt	HUDD Richard Alfred	13-03-42	12 Sqn	951362	Sgt	HUTCHISON James Aitken	14-04-42	144 Sqn
1050628	Sgt	HUDDLESS Harold	7-08-42	158 Sqn	986794	Sgt	HUTSON Norman Charles [Eire]	16-04-42	149 Sqn
942732	Sgt	HUDSON Harold Hermon	26-06-42	24 OTU	1332295	Sgt	HUTT Maurice	10-12-42	20 OTU
935370	Sgt	HUDSON Jack	25-03-42	50 Sqn	576008	Sgt	HUTTON Grantley Charles George	16-12-42	15 Sqn
1060815	Sgt	HUDSON Kenneth	27-07-42	57 Sqn	121720	F/O	HUTTON John Scott [Argentina]	30-12-42	11 OTU
1165632	Sgt	HUDSON William Ernest	10-07-42	142 Sqn	939428	Sgt	HUXLEY William Lloyd	29-04-42	12 Sqn
1178083	LAC	HUGHES Alfred William	24-05-42	1483 Flt	1375119	Sgt	HYDE Allan John	28-04-42	214 Sqn
1360303	Sgt	HUGHES Douglas Llewellyn	29-04-42	18 Sqn	1114941	Sgt	HYDE Gilbert Cecil	10-09-42	142 Sqn
1080084	Sgt	HUGHES Frank	10-11-42	149 Sqn	1334211	Sgt	HYDE John William	4-12-42	14 OTU
628727	Sgt	HUGHES Frederick Leonard	2-10-42	149 Sqn	1088309	Sgt	HYDE Norbron Basil	24-07-42	25 OTU
1326549	Sgt	HUGHES Glyndwr	27-08-42	12 Sqn	988498	Sgt	IBBOTSON Ernest Claude	29-08-42	49 Sqn
133353	P/O	HUGHES Gordon Shotton	23-10-42	158 Sqn	1293218	AC1	IGGULDEN Henry	22-09-42	5 Group
1422214	AC2	HUGHES Herbert	5-02-42	West Raynham	971854	F/S	ILLINGWORTH Alfred Maurice	1-08-42	156 Sqn
					973013	Sgt	ILLINGWOTH John Lawson Main	16-09-42	11 OTU
984291	Sgt	HUGHES Idris	29-07-42	408 Sqn	1130483	LAC	IMBER George	30-11-42	98 Sqn
997105	Sgt	HUGHES James	7-12-42	101 Sqn	1019050	Sgt	IMRIE William	21-12-42	44 Sqn
1183354	F/S	HUGHES James Ernest	20-05-42	12 Sqn	656709	Sgt	INCH Thomas Henry	26-06-42	23 OTU
131806	P/O	HUGHES MiD James John	28-06-42	405 Sqn	104574	P/O	INGLIS Robert George	2-06-42	114 Sqn
1295212	Sgt	HUGHES John Alfred	10-08-42	150 Sqn	61471	F/L	INGS Gerald Antony	6-08-42	207 Sqn
119504	P/O	HUGHES Mervyn Frank	9-06-42	97 Sqn	1022097	Sgt	INMAN Howard	26-03-42	7 Sqn
60804	F/L	HUGHES DFC Patrick Frederick	12-02-42	214 Sqn	1108515	Sgt	INMAN Peter Frederick	3-07-42	214 Sqn
1071236	Sgt	HUGHES Stanley Howard	11-07-42	101 Sqn	1347937	Sgt	INNES Douglas Alexander Watt	11-09-42	218 Sqn
127205	Sgt	HUGHES William Frederick Gerrard	26-04-42	1443 Flt	1311661	Sgt	INNES Eric Moir	29-07-42	1651 CU
751551	F/S	HUGHES William Kilpatrick	16-09-42	22 OTU	100055	P/O	INSCH John Douglas	4-06-42	218 Sqn
1317463	Sgt	HUGHES William Robert	26-09-42	24 OTU	754690	F/S	IRONMONGER Ernest James	10-08-42	78 Sqn
570390	Sgt	HUGHES William Stanley	8-12-42	149 Sqn	640269	F/S	IRVINE Moffat Mannoch	29-04-42	156 Sqn
1022523	Sgt	HULL Maurice	16-09-42	9 Sqn	1293227	W/O	IRVINE Thomas Gardner	7-11-42	83 Sqn
121436	F/O	HULME Donald Kenneth	1-11-42	88 Sqn	1557616	Sgt	IRVING John Oswald	17-12-42	57 Sqn
46896	P/O	HULSE Thomas Mickle Fraser	30-07-42	149 Sqn	924231	Sgt	IRWIN Christopher John	28-01-42	214 Sqn
1153452	Sgt	HUME Donald Alastair Barham	29-03-42	61 Sqn	1190773	Sgt	ISAAC Alexander Howard	9-10-42	1658 HCU
1285720	Sgt	HUMM Harry	13-04-42	15 Sqn	1378292	Sgt	ISAAC Sidney James	6-12-42	487 Sqn
1131958	AC1	HUMPHREY Forrest Joseph	6-01-42	1 Group	106044	F/O	ISAACS Canon Frederick	24-08-42	106 Sqn
1265432	Sgt	HUMPHREY Jack Ward	10-09-42	218 Sqn	926326	Sgt	ISAACS Frederick Ralph	17-01-42	51 Sqn
1379770	Sgt	HUMPHREYS George Desmond Lloyd	10-08-42	78 Sqn	657163	Sgt	ISTED Ernest Charles	24-07-42	149 Sqn
527341	Sgt	HUMPHREYS John Edward	8-11-42	10 Sqn	910036	Sgt	IVES John Henry	25-03-42	12 Sqn
633303	F/S	HUNT Cyril Richard Douglas	8-05-42	44 Sqn	112553	P/O	IVORY Herbert John	6-07-42	150 Sqn
1184062	Sgt	HUNT Edward Samuel	14-07-42	142 Sqn	960182	Sgt	IZATT James	17-12-42	97 Sqn
109355	F/O	HUNT Edward Arthur Ronald	19-12-42	149 Sqn	552139	F/S	JACK John	29-08-42	156 Sqn
1027321	Sgt	HUNT George Arthur	26-06-42	10 OTU	747809	Sgt	JACKETT Philip Harry	27-07-42	12 Sqn
1058040	LAC	HUNT James Douglas	29-12-42	15 Sqn	1180364	Sgt	JACKMAN Eric Leslie	9-06-42	405 Sqn
1191011	Sgt	HUNT John Howard	16-04-42	101 Sqn	971671	Sgt	JACKSON Alexander	12-02-42	49 Sqn
1173925	Sgt	HUNT Richard William	10-03-42	149 Sqn	527848	Sgt	JACKSON Andrew Bradshaw	11-11-42	57 Sqn
924674	F/S	HUNT Robert	9-06-42	109 Sqn	1014696	Sgt	JACKSON Bernard Bernstein	4-05-42	76 Sqn
1136200	Sgt	HUNT William	16-09-42	9 Sqn	1576625	Sgt	JACKSON Edward	20-12-42	44 Sqn
520376	Sgt	HUNT William Richard	19-05-42	35 Sqn	976486	Sgt	JACKSON Ernest	17-06-42	102 Sqn
1069042	Sgt	HUNTER Brian	12-02-42	49 Sqn	618552	F/S	JACKSON Ernest William	19-04-42	49 Sqn
1006782	Sgt	HUNTER Edward	2-04-42	20 OTU	570642	Sgt	JACKSON DFM Francis Charles	29-12-42	15 Sqn
1569924	AC2	HUNTER George Penman	18-09-42	10 OTU	930818	Sgt	JACKSON George William	2-04-42	214 Sqn
646348	Sgt	HUNTER Jack Arthur	18-09-42	115 Sqn	1054492	Sgt	JACKSON George William	9-10-42	105 Sqn
529359	Sgt	HUNTER James	1-08-42	405 Sqn	89724	F/L	JACKSON Harold	21-06-42	10 Sqn
1205633	Sgt	HUNTER Leslie James	7-06-42	156 Sqn	960546	Sgt	JACKSON John Leslie	11-11-42	61 Sqn
					1292954	Sgt	JACKSON Lawrence Ernest Walter	6-12-42	158 Sqn

938013	Sgt	JACKSON Leonard	24-09-42	102 Sqn	80283	P/O	JOHNSON David Huntley [Rhodesia]	10-04-42	144 Sqn
62704	F/O	JACKSON Leslie John	22-07-42	114 Sqn	1334012	Sgt	JOHNSON Derrick	22-11-42	102 Sqn
1309939	Sgt	JACKSON Norman	29-07-42	218 Sqn	1062598	Sgt	JOHNSON Eric	13-03-42	17 OTU
1101252	F/S	JACKSON Samuel Harry	10-09-42	102 Sqn	108041	P/O	JOHNSON Eric Raymond	31-05-42	105 Sqn
1167723	Sgt	JACKSON William	7-06-42	150 Sqn	1042645	Sgt	JOHNSON George	17-11-42	158 Sqn
102605	P/O	JACOB Lawrence Mason	14-01-42	50 Sqn	1283052	Sgt	JOHNSON George Debbage	23-06-42	420 Sqn
67638	P/O	JACOBS Thomas Frederick	10-01-42	49 Sqn	120391	P/O	JOHNSON Horace	5-10-42	35 Sqn
1168909	Sgt	JACOBS Williams Frederick	5-08-42	10 OTU	1331397	Sgt	JOHNSON James Alexander	7-05-42	21 OTU
1265209	Sgt	JACQUES Ronald	6-04-42	9 Sqn	1066914	Sgt	JOHNSON John Lawton	29-07-42	218 Sqn
931904	Sgt	JAECKELS Arthur Edward	6-02-42	21 OTU	1150168	F/S	JOHNSON Keith Alan	15-04-42	420 Sqn
742695	F/S	JAGO Franci Derek	5-05-42	149 Sqn	956375	Sgt	JOHNSON Kenneth Joseph	28-03-42	13 OTU
1260203	Sgt	JAMES Alfred	30-07-42	150 Sqn	1029425	Sgt	JOHNSON Leonard	2-06-42	156 Sqn
914837	Sgt	JAMES Francis John	21-08-42	218 Sqn	1010577	F/S	JOHNSON Matthew Graham	19-07-42	226 Sqn
1191205	Sgt	JAMES Frank Leslie	28-08-42	13 OTU	1310164	Sgt	JOHNSON Norman Francis	25-08-42	106 Sqn
1204584	Sgt	JAMES Howard	12-08-42	106 Sqn	1102629	Sgt	JOHNSON Peter	9-09-42	77 Sqn
1381676	Sgt	JAMES Iestyn	27-06-42	150 Sqn	1331196	Sgt	JOHNSON Robert William	1-10-42	78 Sqn
1018969	Sgt	JAMES Joseph Sydney	1-10-42	102 Sqn	778348	F/S	JOHNSON Ronald [Rhodesia]	12-04-42	420 Sqn
37770	W/C	JAMES DFC Leslie Vidal	21-06-42	9 Sqn	580615	F/S	JOHNSTON Anthony Lionel Ely	16-02-42	61 Sqn
107495	P/O	JAMES Maxwell Hilton [Canada]	29-07-42	12 Sqn	798523	Sgt	JOHNSTON Clifton Hartman [Newfoundland]	27-04-42	149 Sqn
923885	Sgt	JAMES Melville	12-02-42	103 Sqn					
655258	F/S	JAMES Ronald Vincent	28-08-42	156 Sqn	1118841	Sgt	JOHNSTON George Frederick	11-04-42	144 Sqn
1285913	Sgt	JAMES William Edward	2-06-42	11 OTU	981988	LAC	JOHNSTON James Andrew	17-09-42	158 Sqn
1255166	Sgt	JAMES William Moreton	12-07-42	51 Sqn	1287332	Sgt	JOHNSTON Leo Richard [Eire]	29-11-42	29 OTU
778713	Sgt	JAMIESON Andrew Patton [Rhodesia]	11-09-42	106 Sqn	104532	P/O	JOHNSTONE Ian Alexander Bruce	12-3-42	58 Sqn
787845	Sgt	JANCA Frantisek [Czechoslovakia]	3-03-42	311 Sqn	998695	Sgt	JOHNSTONE John	15-04-42	408 Sqn
787577	Sgt	JANEK Jan [Czechoslovakia]	10-03-42	138 Sqn	655206	Sgt	JOHNSTONE William	24-09-42	102 Sqn
900161	Sgt	JARDINE Leonard Arthur	25-01-42	408 Sqn	1311129	Sgt	JONES Alfred	24-06-42	103 Sqn
1389491	Sgt	JARVIS Jack Stead	27-07-42	101 Sqn	1056876	Sgt	JONES Allen Hartwell	16-09-42	9 Sqn
1190623	Sgt	JARVIS Walter John	10-11-42	7 Sqn	1218575	Sgt	JONES Arthur Whiteley	24-09-42	78 Sqn
1297526	AC2	JASPER Trevor Norman	2-09-42	1474 Flt	612621	Sgt	JONES Arthur William	4-05-42	76 Sqn
1043669	Sgt	JAYE Alan Gordon	25-03-42	83 Sqn	102593	F/L	JONES Arthur Wyn Idwal	30-05-42	218 Sqn
798522	Sgt	JEANS Donald Templeman [Newfoundland]	13-08-42	15 Sqn	778684	Sgt	JONES Basil Everard Francis [Rhodesia]	11-06-42	25 OTU
126109	P/O	JEARY Geoffrey George	2-07-42	218 Sqn	37183	W/C	JONES DFC Christopher Hastie	1-08-42	18 Sqn
1163805	Sgt	JEFFERIES Clifford Stanley	9-05-42	408 Sqn	129218	P/O	JONES DFM David John	28-08-42	12 Sqn
85659	F/O	JEFFERY David Hamilton	2-04-42	20 OTU	63819	P/O	JONES David Morgan	14-03-42	18 OTU
576050	Sgt	JEFFERY James Ernest	29-11-42	149 Sqn	108245	P/O	JONES David Morgan Price	6-06-42	149 Sqn
1028004	Sgt	JEFFREY Cyril Edward	2-10-42	218 Sqn	549292	Sgt	JONES David Morris	3-07-42	10 Sqn
1062344	Sgt	JEFFREY John Haggan	11-08-42	218 Sqn	987879	Sgt	JONES Dewi Edmund	9-04-42	405 Sqn
1512110	Sgt	JEFFREYS Arthur	21-12-42	103 Sqn	1311541	Sgt	JONES Donald Haydn	9-05-42	10 OTU
118896	P/O	JEFFRIES Frank Gordon Roy	14-09-42	115 Sqn	127860	P/O	JONES Edward Hugh	10-12-42	10 OTU
569196	Sgt	JEFFRIES John Harold	26-02-42	10 Sqn	943461	Sgt	JONES Edwin Charles	11-12-42	26 OTU
1109614	Sgt	JEFFRIES Thomas Amwyl	3-09-42	61 Sqn	1430728	Sgt	JONES Edwin William Edgar	15-08-42	1651 CU
787713	Sgt	JELINEK Rudolf [Czechoslovakia]	13-10-42	27 OTU	1151000	F/S	JONES Emrys Evan	28-01-42	138 Sqn
61918	F/O	JELINEK Vaclav [Czechoslovakia]	10-03-42	138 Sqn	1062370	Sgt	JONES Eric Hampton	29-04-42	115 Sqn
1309716	Sgt	JELLY Alfred	26-03-42	142 Sqn	1053541	Sgt	JONES Francis Terence Pargeter	16-09-42	106 Sqn
1381351	Sgt	JELLYMAN Harry Champion	24-07-42	25 OTU	61672	F/L	JONES Frank Lewis	31-03-42	78 Sqn
1312853	Sgt	JENKINS George Francis	3-06-42	102 Sqn	1013672	Sgt	JONES Frederick Albert	22-11-42	57 Sqn
44555	F/O	JENKINS Gordon Ralph	16-02-42	49 Sqn	106525	P/O	JONES Frederick William	13-03-42	12 Sqn
1132754	Sgt	JENKINS Herbert Gregory	5-12-42	1658 HCU	611027	F/S	JONES DFM Geoffrey Patrick	21-06-42	10 Sqn
72517	W/C	JENKINS DSO DFC John Fraser Grant	27-03-42	114 Sqn	776041	Sgt	JONES George [Rhodesia]	12-06-42	218 Sqn
569903	Sgt	JENKINS Peter Edward James	21-08-42	149 Sqn	929936	Sgt	JONES George Edward	17-09-42	15 OTU
129669	P/O	JENKINS Richard Mowbray	9-04-42	20 OTU	1147366	Sgt	JONES Glyn	8-11-42	20 OTU
1385252	Sgt	JENNER Stanley George	15-10-42	158 Sqn	1395418	Sgt	JONES Gordon William	17-12-42	44 Sqn
1365432	F/S	JENNINGS Athol Herbert	28-08-42	408 Sqn	1169135	Sgt	JONES Gwilyn Mieron	27-07-42	102 Sqn
1171218	Sgt	JENNINGS Eric Maynard	10-03-42	455 Sqn	1378215	Sgt	JONES Handel	6-06-42	44 Sqn
994287	Sgt	JENNINGS Frank	24-03-42	19 OTU	965121	Sgt	JONES Harold	29-06-42	22 OTU
1179934	Sgt	JERMAN Allen Walter Crawford	8-07-42	21 OTU	1166141	Sgt	JONES Harry Raymond	18-04-42	12 Sqn
1256528	Sgt	JEWELL Harry Leonard	16-08-42	408 Sqn	1126073	Sgt	JONES Henry	7-12-42	102 Sqn
1166707	Sgt	JEWELL Walter James	28-04-42	27 OTU	1192997	Sgt	JONES Henry Edward	9-06-42	75 Sqn
902606	Sgt	JILLINGS Douglas George	20-07-42	158 Sqn	874526	Sgt	JONES Henry Leopold	31-05-42	9 Sqn
1054474	Sgt	JOBLING George Charlton	21-02-42	150 Sqn	1199275	Sgt	JONES Herbert Gwyn	10-08-42	150 Sqn
1287935	Sgt	JOBSON George Trueman	28-11-42	75 Sqn	1186654	Sgt	JONES Hubert Kilwa	3-01-42	23 OTU
1385838	Sgt	JOHN David Alan Vaughan	28-08-42	35 Sqn	47659	P/O	JONES John Charles	8-04-42	Abingdon
1112721	Sgt	JOHNSON Albert Edward	28-08-42	44 Sqn	551817	F/S	JONES DFM John Elias	9-01-42	207 Sqn
1313403	Sgt	JOHNSON Albert Henry	6-08-42	419 Sqn	1259649	Sgt	JONES John Elwyn	28-06-42	156 Sqn
741603	F/S	JOHNSON DFM Ben	24-03-42	1515 Flt	1059448	F/S	JONES John Grice	9-11-42	7 Sqn
748081	F/S	JOHNSON Bradley Winship	15-04-42	420 Sqn	656731	Sgt	JONES John Kenneth	9-06-42	18 Sqn
1164465	Sgt	JOHNSON Cyril Edmund	9-03-42	35 Sqn	112747	F/O	JONES John Leslie	1-10-42	10 Sqn

1023907	Sgt	JONES John Reginald	26-06-42	23 OTU	534180	LAC	KELLY Sidney Whitehill	5-01-42	144 Sqn
656040	Sgt	JONES John Richard Davies	10-12-42	21 Sqn	1000480	Sgt	KELLY William Leonard	13-02-42	455 Sqn
1167646	Sgt	JONES John Ryland	17-06-42	35 Sqn	916043	Sgt	KEMP Arthur John Bruce	9-05-42	10 OTU
657611	Sgt	JONES John Thomas	2-10-42	218 Sqn	1180388	Sgt	KEMP Ronald Victor	18-04-42	101 Sqn
1128890	Sgt	JONES Kenneth David	14-09-42	26 OTU	1380621	Sgt	KENDALL Alfred William	16-09-42	15 Sqn
1190815	Sgt	JONES Kenneth Islwyn	11-05-42	115 Sqn	1380281	Sgt	KENDALL Eric George	14-07-42	158 Sqn
965194	F/S	JONES Leslie	7-10-42	28 OTU	1060925	Sgt	KENDALL Richard Bigland	30-07-42	149 Sqn
934740	Sgt	JONES Leslie Frederick Walter	10-12-42	9 Sqn	1309012	Sgt	KENDALL William	3-06-42	460 Sqn
1380974	Sgt	JONES Leslie George	2-09-42	97 Sqn	1382039	Sgt	KENDRICK Harold James	30-09-42	12 Sqn
646858	Sgt	JONES Leslie Horace	22-09-42	460 Sqn	101549	P/O	KENNARD William Deryck	31-05-42	105 Sqn
924063	Sgt	JONES Lewis James	7-06-42	49 Sqn	632065	Sgt	KENNEDY John McRewin	26-06-42	15 OTU
1006968	Sgt	JONES Malcolm David	15-04-42	405 Sqn	749424	Sgt	KENNEDY Ronald John	18-01-42	142 Sqn
619483	Sgt	JONES Maurice	16-01-42	408 Sqn	550870	F/S	KENNEDY Tom Lumley	2-06-42	11 OTU
818076	F/S	JONES Norman John	12-02-42	408 Sqn	1060557	Sgt	KENNERLEY William Gordon	5-05-42	150 Sqn
923739	Sgt	JONES Oswald Austin	1-06-42	77 Sqn	47747	F/O	KENNY Alexander John [Eire]	25-06-42	1651 CU
651576	Sgt	JONES Percy Kenneth	14-09-42	1654 CU	1069235	Sgt	KENNY John	15-10-42	21 Sqn
741380	W/O	JONES DFM Peter Owen	8-05-42	44 Sqn	1121314	Sgt	KENNY Philip Reginald	12-08-42	207 Sqn
1052291	Sgt	JONES Philip Marsden	16-10-42	51 Sqn	1358378	Sgt	KENSETT Arthur Frederick Charles	10-09-42	207 Sqn
980188	Sgt	JONES Ronald	15-10-42	158 Sqn	1250215	Sgt	KENT Donavan Peter George	7-04-42	61 Sqn
645045	Sgt	JONES Ronald Sidney	31-01-42	61 Sqn	1384269	Sgt	KENT James Cyril	16-09-42	15 Sqn
1189783	Sgt	JONES Rowland Henry	8-05-42	44 Sqn	1182493	Sgt	KENT Stanley Arthur	24-02-42	106 Sqn
130138	P/O	JONES Rowland Thomas	28-08-42	12 Sqn	1384051	Sgt	KENT Thomas Donald	10-12-42	11 OTU
1169608	Sgt	JONES Russel James Gibson	9-03-42	35 Sqn	118888	P/O	KENWORTHY John Caleb	9-09-42	77 Sqn
630368	F/S	JONES Stanley	2-04-42	57 Sqn	1391871	Sgt	KENYON Robert Francis Hughes	3-12-42	102 Sqn
932085	Sgt	JONES Thomas Abel	22-07-42	57 Sqn	120396	P/O	KENYON Thomas Whiteside	24-07-42	57 Sqn
124260	P/O	JONES Thomas Henry	5-08-42	1653 CU	1109504	Sgt	KENZIE Cyril Raphael	23-11-42	161 Sqn
1196231	Sgt	JONES Trevor	9-11-42	50 Sqn	107056	F/L	KERR Alexander	20-10-42	5 Group
571733	Sgt	JONES William Henry	17-08-42	214 Sqn	959887	F/S	KERR Jack Vage	16-10-42	51 Sqn
1310250	Sgt	JONES William Kerr	31-05-42	103 Sqn	1118929	Sgt	KERR Stewart Gray	4-06-42	207 Sqn
1412377	Sgt	JONES William Lionel	30-11-42	7 Sqn	927015	Sgt	KERRY Edward Henry	30-07-42	138 Sqn
931605	Sgt	JORDAN Eric William	20-03-42	19 OTU	84325	S/L	KERRY DFC Jack Gordon	5-10-42	35 Sqn
1311122	Sgt	JORDAN George Herbert	24-03-42	150 Sqn	104567	P/O	KERRY Phadric Woodrow [Canada]	1-08-42	105 Sqn
1252615	Sgt	JORDAN Herbert Frederick	27-04-42	149 Sqn	936945	Sgt	KERRY Richard	18-08-42	214 Sqn
580372	F/S	JORDAN Hubert Hill	26-06-42	26 OTU	1360538	Sgt	KERSHAW Eric Gilbert	7-08-42	7 Sqn
1076959	Sgt	JORDAN Peter James	22-02-42	83 Sqn	1155502	Sgt	KETCHELL Brian John	8-12-42	102 Sqn
568237	Sgt	JORDAN Thomas Edward	10-03-42	149 Sqn	900301	Sgt	KETCHELL Ronald	26-06-42	7 Sqn
932941	Sgt	JORY Archibald Donald	22-01-42	50 Sqn	1219716	Sgt	KIDD Thomas Harold [Canada]	16-09-42	9 Sqn
87041	F/O	JOSHUA Frederick John	14-04-42	1652 CU	1150769	Sgt	KILLBY Kenneth Norman	2-06-42	23 OTU
131479	P/O	JOSLIN Peter Clement Vellacott	5-09-42	61 Sqn	1170643	Sgt	KILLELEA David Edmund	12-06-42	115 Sqn
1058855	Sgt	JOWETT Wilfred	3-01-42	17 OTU	1000270	Sgt	KILLHAM Edgar John Jex	9-05-42	408 Sqn
1238457	Sgt	JOY Terence Wong	26-06-42	23 OTU	967263	Sgt	KILLILEA James Francis	5-10-42	76 Sqn
927655	Sgt	JUKES Albert Charles	25-08-42	150 Sqn	1378401	Sgt	KILLINGBECK Matthew George	9-05-42	10 Sqn
1280784	Sgt	JUSTICE William James	18-08-42	101 Sqn	591195	Sgt	KILPATRICK George	11-12-42	10 Sqn
787177	Sgt	KALENSKY Josef [Czechoslovakia]	11-04-42	311 Sqn	45956	S/L	KIMBER Ronald Ernest	11-08-42	75 Sqn
1005750	F/S	KANE Samuel Forster	13-08-42	207 Sqn	47876	P/O	KING Brian Charles Henry	6-10-42	103 Sqn
1255416	Sgt	KAUFMAN John Hyman [Canada]	24-09-42	405 Sqn	1212441	AC2	KING Charles Lawley	8-03-42	101 Sqn
930699	Sgt	KAY Alfred Valentine	9-05-42	158 Sqn	1382135	Sgt	KING Donald James [New Zealand]	19-08-42	61 Sqn
788087	Sgt	KEDA Aldis [Czechoslovakia]	6-04-42	1429 Flt	1048821	AC1	KING Douglas Stewart	12-03-42	460 Sqn
656186	Sgt	KEARNS James Joseph	11-09-42	26 OTU	1272209	Sgt	KING Edward Arthur John	19-09-42	15 Sqn
937404	F/S	KEATLEY William Francis	14-09-42	12 Sqn	1271762	Sgt	KING Eric Charles	22-12-42	26 OTU
39535	S/L	KEDDY DFC Walter Bernard [Canada]	18-01-42	405 Sqn	1261989	Sgt	KING Eric Jesse	29-07-42	9 Sqn
1264506	Sgt	KEDGLEY Orme	26-07-42	142 Sqn	1127538	Sgt	KING Frederick	10-02-42	25 OTU
612229	Sgt	KEECH Terence Aloysius	8-11-42	76 Sqn	1330708	Sgt	KING Frederick Henry	20-09-42	149 Sqn
1381041	Sgt	KEELER Frederick John	18-04-42	158 Sqn	115277	P/O	KING Geoffrey Bernard Herbert	22-11-42	102 Sqn
929521	Sgt	KEEN Frederick John	20-06-42	101 Sqn	86730	F/O	KING Gerald Purdon	26-07-42	12 Sqn
844873	Sgt	KEEN Stanley Allan	21-07-42	35 Sqn	626528	Sgt	KING Jack	27-08-42	214 Sqn
1112884	Sgt	KEHOE Thomas James	2-06-42	156 Sqn	798525	Sgt	KING Robert Fowlow [Newfoundland]	27-03-42	14 OTU
1333962	AC1	KEIGHLEY Colin George Coltham	14-04-42	1652 CU	1013673	Sgt	KINGDON John Daniel	24-06-42	9 Sqn
1202833	Sgt	KEIGHTLEY John Cliff	26-09-42	26 OTU	616549	F/S	KINGHORN John	17-12-42	44 Sqn
568970	Sgt	KELLEHER Michael Joseph	6-06-42	149 Sqn	120041	P/O	KINGMAN Thomas Jack	9-11-42	50 Sqn
1006928	Sgt	KELLEHER William Henry Paul	17-12-42	97 Sqn	77393	F/O	KINGSTON Donald Arthur	12-08-42	78 Sqn
1378331	Sgt	KELLIE Stuart Alan Bain	26-04-42	218 Sqn	952527	Sgt	KINGSTON Harry George	13-04-42	15 Sqn
923177	Sgt	KELLOW William Laverson Field [Canada]	30-05-42	419 Sqn	70366	F/L	KINGSTON William John Wesley [Eire]	7-02-42	144 Sqn
535494	F/S	KELLY DFM Gerard	1-08-42	44 Sqn	67654	F/O	KINNIBURGH Alexander	6-06-42	156 Sqn
525449	Sgt	KELLY Leonard	11-08-42	78 Sqn	1072967	Sgt	KINSEY Edmund George	26-05-42	19 OTU
976635	Sgt	KELLY DFM Leonard Anthony	23-09-42	218 Sqn	969700	F/S	KINSEY Roylance	16-04-42	156 Sqn
1181766	Sgt	KELLY Ralph Andreae	24-09-42	78 Sqn	778046	Sgt	KIPPEN Cecil Roy [South Africa]	29-11-42	1446 Flt
570332	Sgt	KELLY Roland Hugh	30-06-42	7 Sqn	548297	Sgt	KIRK Eric Austin	16-04-42	149 Sqn

Service #	Rank	Name	Date	Sqn
107518	P/O	KIRK Joseph Henry	4-02-42	21 OTU
1270480	Sgt	KIRKPATRICK Ronald Herbert	11-09-42	26 OTU
127522	P/O	KIRKUS Colin Fletcher	14-09-42	156 Sqn
969453	F/S	KIRKWOOD James	30-07-42	102 Sqn
943904	Sgt	KITCHEN George Henry	21-12-42	103 Sqn
1021801	Sgt	KITCHEN Richard	10-04-42	76 Sqn
1360287	Sgt	KITCHER Eric	5-06-42	114 Sqn
39539	S/L	KITCHIN DFC Peter James Robert	12-03-42	75 Sqn
49684	P/O	KITE Joseph Alec Charles	2-10-42	161 Sqn
931029	Sgt	KITNEY Ralph	2-04-42	214 Sqn
1255391	Sgt	KNAPMAN Richard Mannering	20-01-42	49 Sqn
47850	F/O	KNAPP Henry	25-11-42	142 Sqn
1026154	Sgt	KNAPTON Maurice	4-12-42	14 OTU
1378284	Sgt	KNEESHAW John	30-05-42	218 Sqn
115281	P/O	KNELL Albert John	12-08-42	57 Sqn
655694	Sgt	KNIGHT Eric	4-07-42	61 Sqn
1171842	Sgt	KNIGHT Harold	17-04-42	50 Sqn
1001321	Sgt	KNIPE Humphrey Charles	9-05-42	15 Sqn
28043	W/C	KNOCKER Kenneth Duke	3-07-42	214 Sqn
1107655	Sgt	KNOWLES Arthur Cecil Peter	5-06-42	57 Sqn
80548	S/L	KNOWLES James Gerald Leslie	11-10-42	139 Sqn
1434075	Sgt	KNOWLES William Mark	30-11-42	10 OTU
122586	P/O	KNOWLING John Henry	31-05-42	14 OTU
575307	Sgt	KNOX John Albert	27-07-42	405 Sqn
787261	Sgt	KODES Karel [Czechoslovakia]	11-04-42	311 Sqn
116808	F/O	KOMISKI Robert Wallace	4-07-42	61 Sqn
787440	Sgt	KORMANOVIC Imrich [Czechoslovakia]	3-03-42	311 Sqn
1382212	Sgt	KORTRIGHT Nicholas Henry	6-06-42	149 Sqn
787532	Sgt	KOTRCH Jan [Czechoslovakia]	3-03-42	311 Sqn
787854	Sgt	KRAL Cenek [Czechoslovakia]	21-01-42	311 Sqn
87622	F/L	KRCHA Viktor [Czechoslovakia]	10-12-42	138 Sqn
82615	P/O	KULA Jaroslav [Czechoslovakia]	12-03-42	311 Sqn
1309292	Sgt	KUP Wilfrid Anthony	5-08-42	1653 CU
1190036	F/S	KYNASTON Maurice James	17-09-42	149 Sqn
1263271	Sgt	LACEY William Haylett	8-04-42	23 OTU
120035	P/O	LAIDLAW Francis Angus James	29-08-42	115 Sqn
517130	Sgt	LAING David Adamson	10-01-42	12 Sqn
44412	F/L	LAING Twice MiD Donald	3-09-42	150 Sqn
1003165	Sgt	LAING David Maxwell	7-04-42	142 Sqn
981143	Sgt	LAING Gerard Joseph	3-06-42	420 Sqn
518299	Sgt	LAKE Gordon	25-06-42	15 OTU
1307040	Sgt	LAKEMAN Graham	8-04-42	57 Sqn
1378670	Sgt	LAKER William James	2-06-42	10 Sqn
1320476	Sgt	LAMB Frederick Victor	20-12-42	106 Sqn
745650	W/O	LAMB DFM Neville Percy John	8-05-42	44 Sqn
906679	Sgt	LAMBERT William Lewis	2-06-42	106 Sqn
1255089	F/S	LAMBETH Hewart Joseph	10-04-42	76 Sqn
1376980	Sgt	LAMERTON Roy Charles	6-12-42	21 Sqn
1237647	Sgt	LAMPITT Edward Thomas William	28-10-42	10 OTU
611985	Sgt	LANCASTER Roland Wilfred	27-02-42	77 Sqn
122143	P/O	LANDAU Hyme	17-11-42	405 Sqn
1307388	F/S	LANE John Albert	25-08-42	150 Sqn
1376333	F/S	LANGAN Leslie Joseph	1-08-42	103 Sqn
752153	Sgt	LANGFORD David Charles	6-12-42	102 Sqn
1059609	F/S	LANGFORD Guy [Canada] (served as LANGFORD-PUDNEY)	12-08-42	405 Sqn
45429	F/L	LANGLEY John Charles Douglas	22-07-42	12 Sqn
1283289	Sgt	LANGSTON Arthur Richard	16-04-42	101 Sqn
927895	Sgt	LANGTON Alan George	13-10-42	10 Sqn
1286267	Sgt	LANSLEY Walter Alfred	5-08-42	10 OTU
121560	P/O	LAPHAM William George Webb	25-06-42	24 OTU
1050127	Sgt	LAPPING Gordon Thomas	9-09-42	150 Sqn
1177034	Sgt	LARGE Derek Stanley	16-07-42	27 OTU
1310060	Sgt	LARKIN Joseph Anthony	11-04-42	455 Sqn
122145	F/O	LARKINS Harry William	6-12-42	115 Sqn
921394	Sgt	LARMOUR George Yorke	1-04-42	105 Sqn
1270204	Sgt	LARTER Ronald	2-06-42	61 Sqn
1208560	Sgt	LASHLY Peter Alec	10-09-42	61 Sqn
932631	Sgt	LAUGHLIN William Alexander Benjamin	1-08-42	405 Sqn
137567	P/O	LAUNDON Alwyne Clarendon Redfern	21-12-42	7 Sqn
1062864	Sgt	LAURIE James Hunter	12-06-42	218 Sqn
530012	Sgt	LAVELLE Michael William	17-12-42	218 Sqn
1336386	Sgt	LAVERS Alan John Claude	17-12-42	218 Sqn
1290215	Sgt	LAVIS Leslie Harold	1-10-42	76 Sqn
934284	Sgt	LAW Francis Reginald	22-02-42	50 Sqn
1101018	Sgt	LAW James	4-09-42	75 Sqn
955416	Sgt	LAW John	3-12-42	102 Sqn
621400	F/S	LAW Leonard	17-04-42	44 Sqn
651685	F/S	LAWLER Leonard John	28-08-42	218 Sqn
954428	Sgt	LAWLOR Maurice Desmond	15-10-42	103 Sqn
1283153	Sgt	LAWRENCE Edward Bolton	28-03-42	115 Sqn
1376060	Sgt	LAWRENCE Ronald Frank [Canada]	9-03-42	101 Sqn
650253	F/S	LAWRENCE Victor George	28-08-42	15 Sqn
1109242	Sgt	LAWSON Frank Ebrey	29-07-42	7 Sqn
1558325	Sgt	LAWSON Laurence Cecil	30-11-42	81 OTU
804306	Sgt	LAWSON William Alfred	17-08-42	1652 CU
1060140	Sgt	LAWTON Donald	14-01-42	106 Sqn
643746	Sgt	LAWTON Thomas Henry	6-08-42	419 Sqn
741541	Sgt	LAX Arthur Lionel	16-01-42	214 Sqn
748097	F/S	LEA Laurence John	4-06-42	207 Sqn
916490	Sgt	LEA Walter Robinson	26-03-42	12 Sqn
113402	P/O	LEACH Francis	9-10-42	1658 HCU
1184443	Sgt	LEACH John Clifford	16-10-42	149 Sqn
982476	F/S	LEAHY John Michael	24-07-42	207 Sqn
130146	P/O	LEAKEY Kenneth William	23-10-42	158 Sqn
1167454	F/S	LEATHER George Thomas	29-10-42	142 Sqn
655486	Sgt	LEATHER James Stewart	25-06-42	15 OTU
36124	S/L	LEDGER Harry	29-07-42	9 Sqn
960555	Sgt	LEDLIE Robert James	9-01-42	15 OTU
926080	Sgt	LEE Clifford Lawson	12-02-42	49 Sqn
648957	Sgt	LEE John Charles	7-08-42	103 Sqn
1174918	F/S	LEE John Kennerleigh Barnett	26-11-42	207 Sqn
119904	P/O	LEE John Samuel	31-10-42	150 Sqn
1218848	Sgt	LEE Reginald George Arthur	29-08-42	75 Sqn
115352	P/O	LEE Robert Michael	11-07-42	101 Sqn
1310845	Sgt	LEE Thomas	1-06-42	460 Sqn
1395097	Sgt	LEE Vallantine Jack	9-11-42	44 Sqn
1263488	Sgt	LEEDHAM William Henry	7-07-42	156 Sqn
580297	W/O	LEEKE George Ernest	8-04-42	15 OTU
1119621	Sgt	LEES Douglas	5-04-42	20 OTU
1132278	Sgt	LEES Eric	10-09-42	75 Sqn
1154650	LAC	LEES Harry	7-03-42	50 Sqn
31160	P/O	LEES Malcolm George	12-07-42	14 OTU
132651	P/O	LEEWARDEN Jack	27-08-42	156 Sqn
1304727	Sgt	LEIGH Sydney William Francis	21-04-42	138 Sqn
40053	S/L	LEIGHTON Twice MiD John William Edward [Australia]	26-07-42	460 Sqn
571775	Sgt	LEITCH Cecil Gordon	14-07-42	97 Sqn
126897	P/O	LEITH-HAY-CLARK Richard Langton	19-09-42	35 Sqn
104588	P/O	LENEY Samuel Robert	30-03-42	10 Sqn
123286	P/O	LENNARD Douglas William	6-10-42	115 Sqn
1378346	F/S	LENNOCK Rowland	5-05-42	218 Sqn
1453057	Sgt	LENNOX James Mayson	6-11-42	26 OTU
1365293	Sgt	LEONARD John	30-05-42	114 Sqn
108541	P/O	LERWILL Norman Curtis	24-04-42	150 Sqn
1113762	Sgt	LESLIE Alexander	31-05-42	103 Sqn
1289840	Sgt	LESTER Harry George	16-10-42	142 Sqn
1378068	F/S	LESTER Sidney Carl	15-01-42	115 Sqn
745292	W/O	LEVENSON Stephen Austin	17-09-42	214 Sqn
125315	P/O	LEWIS Clifford	20-05-42	7 Sqn
526313	Sgt	LEWIS David Winston	19-05-42	15 Sqn
748323	F/S	LEWIS Edward George William	28-08-42	150 Sqn
1053802	Sgt	LEWIS Frederick William	13-09-42	27 OTU
1233715	Sgt	LEWIS George William	6-12-42	139 Sqn

566355	F/S	LEWIS Illtyd Gad Ivor	26-06-42	102 Sqn
1108878	Sgt	LEWIS Joseph	24-04-42	114 Sqn
129499	P/O	LEWIS Ronald George	3-09-42	49 Sqn
931608	Sgt	LEWIS Vivian Thomas	4-02-42	21 Sqn
1377097	Sgt	LEWRY Arthur Edward	18-04-42	101 Sqn
1311606	Sgt	LEYLAND Alfred George	26-06-42	15 OTU
1061093	Sgt	LEYLAND Ronald	20-03-42	19 OTU
650255	F/S	LEYSHON Claude Henry Rufus	6-10-42	44 Sqn
977837	Sgt	LEYSHON Kenneth	7-04-42	61 Sqn
911916	Sgt	LE BLANC Raymond George [France]	16-06-42	1651 CU
1181380	F/S	LE QUEUX Peter Lawrence Edward	1-02-42	144 Sqn
963007	Sgt	LE VACK Frank Harry	9-05-42	10 Sqn
1088070	Sgt	LIGHTOWLER Squire	1-08-42	103 Sqn
1271095	Sgt	LIND Richard	23-09-42	142 Sqn
614379	F/S	LINDEN Alexander James	18-08-42	20 OTU
120181	P/O	LINDLEY Arthur Alan Hewson	1-08-42	107 Sqn
1078148	Sgt	LINDSAY Graham Douglas	14-04-42	21 OTU
119793	P/O	LINDSAY John Semple	26-04-42	1443 Flt
1269884	Sgt	LINDSELL William Ernest	6-05-42	18 Sqn
1253866	Sgt	LINEGAR George James	31-01-42	144 Sqn
942146	Sgt	LINES Richard Leslie	12-12-42	102 Sqn
1310395	Sgt	LINEY John George	18-12-42	97 Sqn
656045	Sgt	LING John	29-10-42	15 Sqn
1059599	Sgt	LINGARD Norman Arthur	28-03-42	207 Sqn
777683	Sgt	LINTON Richard Henry [Rhodesia]	20-08-42	61 Sqn
1077330	Sgt	LISTER Frank	27-09-42	78 Sqn
117861	P/O	LITTLE Harvey Strong	31-05-42	14 OTU
115807	P/O	LITTLE DFM John Osmond	2-06-42	10 OTU
628631	F/S	LITTLE Raymond Edmund	26-06-42	7 Sqn
992167	Sgt	LITTLEWOOD DFM Leslie	11-11-42	61 Sqn
121572	P/O	LITZOW Arthur Ferdinand	29-07-42	16 OTU
72261	F/L	LIVERSIDGE Harold	30-06-42	405 Sqn
1257329	Sgt	LIVERSUCH Raymond John	3-07-42	109 Sqn
1122012	LAC	LIVESEY John	14-04-42	102 Sqn
66541	F/L	LIVINGSTON William Montgomery	26-06-42	1651 CU
1365877	Sgt	LIVINGSTONE Alexander	17-02-42	11 OTU
61282	F/O	LIVINGSTONE Ian Frederick	9-03-42	83 Sqn
1381320	Sgt	LLEWELYN John	21-08-42	19 OTU
106141	P/O	LLOYD Edward Frederick	17-06-42	102 Sqn
916338	Sgt	LLOYD Francis Joseph	17-01-42	7 Sqn
1256600	Sgt	LLOYD John Archibald	4-05-42	78 Sqn
111992	P/O	LLOYD Kenneth	14-04-42	214 Sqn
1256771	Sgt	LLOYD Kenneth Arthur	18-05-42	115 Sqn
1184530	Sgt	LLOYD Lawrence Stephen	30-05-42	149 Sqn
1126348	Sgt	LLOYD Norman Victor	5-06-42	1443 Flt
1259951	Sgt	LLOYD Richard Leslie	27-07-42	57 Sqn
932725	Sgt	LLOYD Sydney	28-08-42	97 Sqn
1265566	Sgt	LOBB Leonard	1-08-42	14 OTU
928200	Sgt	LOCK Alexander John	11-09-42	75 Sqn
929370	Sgt	LOCK Carrick Forbes	4-06-42	12 OTU
573786	Sgt	LOCK Gordon James Victor	18-05-42	149 Sqn
524132	F/S	LOCK Walter	25-04-42	9 Sqn
1168183	Sgt	LOCKE John Richard	18-09-42	44 Sqn
991121	Sgt	LOCKHART Henry James Ian	16-07-42	15 Sqn
108167	P/O	LOCKWOOD Arthur Eric	1-04-42	107 Sqn
1379704	Sgt	LODGE Ottiwell Francis	9-07-42	106 Sqn
1290876	Sgt	LOGAN Alan Frederick	2-04-42	57 Sqn
657262	Sgt	LOGAN Frank	14-09-42	12 Sqn
778687	Sgt	LOGAN John Innes Montgomery [Rhodesia]	3-09-42	12 Sqn
1108284	Sgt	LOGIE Alexander	6-06-42	49 Sqn
1076999	Sgt	LOMAX William McLafter	8-04-42	23 OTU
1028719	Sgt	LONG Charles Richard	8-12-42	149 Sqn
120559	P/O	LONG Henry William	16-06-42	106 Sqn
656328	Sgt	LONG Norman Alfred	1-08-42	16 OTU
101053	P/O	LONG William Leslie	9-05-42	76 Sqn
130067	P/O	LONGHURST John William	27-08-42	156 Sqn
1212686	Sgt	LONGSTAFF James Roy	6-12-42	12 OTU
656393	Sgt	LOOMBE Robert Cecil	6-10-42	115 Sqn
1117304	F/S	LORD Allan	20-12-42	77 Sqn
1169117	F/S	LORD Derek Rowland	13-08-42	1484 Flt
546170	Sgt	LORD Richard Samuel	25-10-42	12 Sqn
552531	F/S	LORIMER DFM David	4-06-42	61 Sqn
120039	P/O	LORKIN Joseph	8-07-42	19 OTU
624360	F/S	LOUCH DFM Brian Gordon	21-12-42	106 Sqn
120673	P/O	LOVE George Francis	29-07-42	1651 CU
1316650	Sgt	LOVEDAY Harold James	7-09-42	10 Sqn
109919	F/O	LOVEGROVE Charles Henry	14-09-42	44 Sqn
62324	F/O	LOVEGROVE Peter Anthony	12-11-42	83 Sqn
1376578	F/S	LOVEJOY William James	9-11-42	12 OTU
655547	Sgt	LOVELL Gordon William John	23-08-42	1651 CU
1376533	Sgt	LOVELL Robert James Tristrem	9-03-42	9 Sqn
1337502	Sgt	LOVELL Robert William	17-10-42	15 Sqn
45715	F/L	LOVETT Bernard James	31-05-42	158 Sqn
1379475	Sgt	LOVESEY Jack Horace	9-11-42	7 Sqn
106522	P/O	LOW Alan John	17-01-42	7 Sqn
82986	F/L	LOW David Septimus Stewart	27-07-42	57 Sqn
572143	Sgt	LOW Ronald Albert	17-09-42	1654 CU
1330594	Sgt	LOWDEN Noel Alexander	30-05-42	142 Sqn
1391379	Sgt	LOWERY Bernard	27-11-42	20 OTU
575843	Sgt	LOWRIE Robert Frederick	19-09-42	15 Sqn
1113437	Sgt	LOWTHER Ian David	27-07-42	142 Sqn
104490	P/O	LOWTHER Philip Henry	18-07-42	18 Sqn
519567	F/S	LOXTON Bertram	8-08-42	West Raynham
1435153	Sgt	LOYD Donald Robert	7-12-42	28 OTU
1312083	Sgt	LUCAS Charles	17-12-42	75 Sqn
656777	Sgt	LUCAS Robert Henry	22-08-42	10 OTU
562643	F/S	LUCK William Ernest Samuel	7-08-42	78 Sqn
1304714	Sgt	LUCKMAN Bernard Edwin Bentley	27-07-42	142 Sqn
1267163	Sgt	LUDGATE John Outram	28-08-42	15 Sqn
638777	F/S	LUDKIN Jack Robert	29-07-42	9 Sqn
100090	P/O	LUDWIG Charles	3-01-42	455 Sqn
1167425	Sgt	LUFF Frank Lewin	12-08-42	51 Sqn
115078	P/O	LUIN Cyril William	9-03-42	101 Sqn
61284	F/O	LUMB Theodore Arthur	29-03-42	83 Sqn
1282788	Sgt	LUMSDEN Eric Alexander Gordon	25-03-42	50 Sqn
1059215	Sgt	LUNEY William	1-04-42	1428 Flt
999230	Sgt	LUNN Brian Pearson	14-09-42	12 Sqn
49838	P/O	LUPTON Fred	16-09-42	27 OTU
1306388	Sgt	LUSH Arthur Sylwood	6-05-42	7 Sqn
561197	W/O	LUTWYCHE Charles Eade	24-07-42	25 OTU
1067838	Sgt	LYLE Alexander	27-07-42	101 Sqn
1379354	Sgt	LYLE Cyril	27-08-42	214 Sqn
70890	W/C	LYNCH-BLOSSE DFC Patrick Windsor	9-05-42	44 Sqn
118825	F/O	LYNES James William	20-12-42	9 Sqn
335281	Sgt	LYONS Joseph Edward Richard	2-06-42	78 Sqn
624994	F/S	LYONS Thomas Leo	31-05-42	15 OTU
926877	Sgt	LYONS Timothy John Joseph	19-04-42	156 Sqn
962415	Sgt	MAAS William John	14-07-42	158 Sqn
988987	Sgt	MABBETT William Ernest	21-01-42	455 Sqn
4620	S/L	MacCLANCY Michael Robert [Eire]	12-04-42	226 Sqn
1058534	Sgt	MacDONALD David	17-04-42	97 Sqn
1108340	Sgt	MacFARLANE Donald Malcolm [Canada]	15-04-42	405 Sqn
1062947	Sgt	MacFARLANE Thomas	26-04-42	218 Sqn
922684	Sgt	MacGILLIVRAY John David Robert	29-08-42	75 Sqn
552535	F/S	MacGREGOR DFM John Charles	22-02-42	83 Sqn
80094	F/O	MacKAY Donald George [Rhodesia]	9-05-42	44 Sqn
1189563	Sgt	MacKAY Ernest	7-11-42	83 Sqn
1253668	Sgt	MacKAY DFM Kenneth Oswald	5-10-42	97 Sqn
1341681	Sgt	MacKEAND Ian Currie	31-05-42	142 Sqn
924909	F/S	MacKENDER Hugh Laurence John	15-11-42	150 Sqn
1372522	Sgt	MacKENZIE George Cameron	29-10-42	10 OTU
1563387	Sgt	MacLACHLAN John Louis	29-08-42	103 Sqn
80118	F/O	MacLAGAN Gerald [Rhodesia]	9-05-42	44 Sqn
1006443	F/S	MacLEAN DFM Ian Dugald	8-11-42	20 OTU

117

1365878	Sgt	MacLELLAN Malcolm		20-12-42	49 Sqn	110870	P/O	MAPLE John Edward	26-07-42	35 Sqn
127119	P/O	MacLENNAN John		29-12-42	77 Sqn	1377000	Sgt	MARCHANT Edward Arthur	30-11-42	10 Sqn
1058806	Sgt	MacLEOD Kenneth Robert		17-12-42	44 Sqn	104575	P/O	MARCHINGTON John Mellor	9-01-42	15 OTU
901265	Sgt	MacMURDIE James		10-06-42	142 Sqn	114450	P/O	MARDON Cedric Hall	15-04-42	150 Sqn
1194240	Sgt	MacPHERSON Joseph Butler Alexander				591580	Sgt	MARGETTS Edward William	27-08-42	15 Sqn
				6-12-42	464 Sqn	778671	Sgt	MARILLIER Hugh Maxwell [South Africa]	7-05-42	21 OTU
1150278	Sgt	MacQUEEN John		9-06-42	103 Sqn					
115987	P/O	MACALLISTER Graham Watson		12-08-42	78 Sqn	1109413	Sgt	MARKHAM Young John	1-06-42	77 Sqn
1001911	F/S	MACAULAY John Crichton		5-12-42	1658 HCU	778497	Sgt	MARKIDES Paul [Rhodesia]	25-03-42	83 Sqn
1371493	Sgt	MACAULAY Robert		19-12-42	149 Sqn	1069580	Sgt	MARKLAND Geoffrey Sherwood	6-05-42	7 Sqn
1380294	Sgt	MACDONALD Robert George		10-10-42	16 OTU	1169564	Sgt	MARKS Gilbert	14-04-42	1652 CU
1381478	Sgt	MACINTYRE Roderick Hector		3-10-42	15 OTU	39670	W/C	MARLAND DSO* DFC James Hardy	19-09-42	35 Sqn
112493	P/O	MACKAY Phillip Stanley		11-06-42	83 Sqn	1101605	Sgt	MARLAND Alfred	2-06-42	408 Sqn
1108858	Sgt	MACKENZIE Charles		14-09-42	150 Sqn	104341	P/O	MARR John	28-03-42	7 Sqn
610731	Sgt	MACKENZIE Frederick Edward		28-06-42	97 Sqn	974024	Sgt	MARR Stanley Alexander [Canada]	5-06-42	156 Sqn
1309276	Sgt	MACKEY Vincent J		28-08-42	142 Sqn	1186031	F/S	MARRIOTT Jack Hubert Edward	16-09-42	142 Sqn
41042	DFC	MACKID DFC John Goodsir [Canada]		28-04-42	97 Sqn	1143666	AC2	MARRIOTT Robert Proctor	12-02-42	405 Sqn
994362	Sgt	MACKIE John William		29-11-42	149 Sqn	905358	W/O	MARROWS Basil	6-12-42	464 Sqn
106643	P/O	MACKINNON James George		1-04-42	405 Sqn	982777	Sgt	MARSDEN Douglas	25-01-42	408 Sqn
534400	F/S	MACKINTOSH MiD William Hogarth				1236807	Sgt	MARSDEN Edward	29-10-42	10 OTU
				30-11-42	10 OTU	1384344	Sgt	MARSH Dennis Charles	16-09-42	12 OTU
1161197	Sgt	MACKIRDY Ian Mactaggat		11-04-42	158 Sqn	1129033	Sgt	MARSH Ronald Herbert	20-03-42	19 OTU
1167372	Sgt	MACKRILL Albert Elvin		9-11-42	57 Sqn	1381070	Sgt	MARSH William George	28-04-42	150 Sqn
1022818	F/S	MACKS John Stewart		18-12-42	97 Sqn	921664	Sgt	MARSHALL Edward Colin	4-07-42	61 Sqn
1388402	Sgt	MACLEAN Henry		2-05-42	106 Sqn	1380346	Sgt	MARSHALL Geoffrey Herbert	1-01-42	61 Sqn
1001661	Sgt	MACLEOD Alexander		13-03-42	78 Sqn	1018213	Sgt	MARSHALL George Leonard	6-09-42	12 Sqn
978459	Sgt	MACLEOD Neil Alexander		30-11-42	149 Sqn	118459	P/O	MARSHALL George Paxton	5-08-42	44 Sqn
778645	Sgt	MACMAHON John Macintyre [Rhodesia]		1-08-42	44 Sqn	119338	F/O	MARSHALL Jack Walter	13-11-42	97 Sqn
						117005	P/O	MARSHALL John Edwin	6-08-42	158 Sqn
921364	Sgt	MACNAB Donald Norman		11-02-42	150 Sqn	1310853	Sgt	MARSHALL John Harold	3-01-42	23 OTU
117953	P/O	MACNAUGHTON Douglas Henry		28-08-42	12 Sqn	547242	Sgt	MARSHALL Kenneth	10-09-42	102 Sqn
135009	P/O	MACPHERSON James Forbes		13-12-42	57 Sqn	989009	Sgt	MARSHALL Robert	6-02-42	21 OTU
107992	P/O	MACTAGGART Alistair		10-04-42	9 Sqn	1311937	Sgt	MARSHALL Robert John	5-12-42	1658 HCU
923044	Sgt	MADDOCK Cyril Victor		6-04-42	9 Sqn	1113585	F/S	MARSHALL Thomas Robert	30-05-42	76 Sqn
81690	F/L	MAGEE Hugh Larmour		16-03-42	Feltwell	1375102	Sgt	MARSHALL William Keay Falconer	27-04-42	97 Sqn
637136	Sgt	MAGINN Henry Howard		11-09-42	15 Sqn	777687	Sgt	MARSTON Richard Alfred [Rhodesia]	24-03-42	44 Sqn
1430712	Sgt	MAGNESS Kenneth		28-11-42	150 Sqn	568524	Sgt	MARTIN Dennis Clifford	31-03-42	76 Sqn
1130814	Sgt	MAGSON Frank Raymond		24-06-42	1516 Flt	951050	Sgt	MARTIN Francis	18-12-42	50 Sqn
47152	F/L	MAGUIRE DFC James George Annesley				751921	F/S	MARTIN Joseph John Francis	3-07-42	10 Sqn
				6-12-42	226 Sqn	1499066	Sgt	MARTIN Joseph Potton	28-08-42	78 Sqn
1371443	AC1	MAHADY Thomas		14-04-42	1652 CU	1164450	F/S	MARTIN Raymond Gordon	13-08-42	77 Sqn
969454	Sgt	MAHAFFY William Matchett		13-04-42	158 Sqn	1381993	Sgt	MARTIN Robert Tom Charles	3-07-42	10 Sqn
37452	S/L	MAHLER DFC John Noel		17-01-42	7 Sqn	1315825	Sgt	MARTIN Ronald Claude	25-08-42	97 Sqn
1125296	Sgt	MAHONEY Alan		24-10-42	218 Sqn	1263897	F/S	MARTIN Ronald Frederick	16-11-42	78 Sqn
572972	Sgt	MAINWARING Jack		3-07-42	218 Sqn	967897	F/S	MARTIN Stanley	24-08-42	149 Sqn
81408	F/L	MAITLAND DFC Ian		28-08-42	408 Sqn	751681	W/O	MARTIN Thomas Henry	4-11-42	464 Sqn
111680	F/L	MAITLAND DFC Wilfred Ronald		30-05-42	156 Sqn	1269417	Sgt	MARTINS Gordon	30-07-42	149 Sqn
116416	P/O	MAJURY Alfred James		12-06-42	12 OTU	535222	F/S	MARVELL DFM Albert	1-06-42	20 OTU
1100613	Sgt	MAKIN William Stanley		26-03-42	12 Sqn	787865	Sgt	MASEK Rudolf [Czechoslovakia]	17-01-42	311 Sqn
1204858	Sgt	MALE David Tawelfryn		29-04-42	115 Sqn	575569	Sgt	MASON Alan Ernest	28-10-42	1651 HCU
953414	Sgt	MALE Harry		19-09-42	50 Sqn	1338138	Sgt	MASON Arthur William	18-11-42	21 OTU
1433012	AC2	MALIN George		1-05-42	49 Sqn	1167277	Sgt	MASON Eric	15-04-42	214 Sqn
1180129	Sgt	MALIN Peter Gordon Arthur		31-05-42	156 Sqn	747907	F/S	MASON DFM George Morton	18-04-42	101 Sqn
931919	Sgt	MALLETT Edward Walter		12-06-42	114 Sqn	1080462	AC1	MASON George William	22-09-42	Bury St. Edmunds
41939	F/L	MALLET Maurice Bradsury		17-09-42	12 OTU					
1029624	Sgt	MALLON Lawrence William		30-05-42	142 Sqn	1261842	Sgt	MASON John Charles	5-06-42	156 Sqn
526697	Sgt	MALLOTT Henry George		11-09-42	7 Sqn	1386307	Sgt	MASON Victor Stanley	1-08-42	25 OTU
110661	P/O	MANDER Michael D'Arcy		19-07-42	150 Sqn	1480500	Sgt	MASON West Stewart	15-10-42	103 Sqn
901548	Sgt	MANKELOW Walter James		17-01-42	7 Sqn	932392	Sgt	MASSEY Thomas Charles	28-03-42	207 Sqn
1208601	Sgt	MANLEY Frank		25-03-42	50 Sqn	1031306	Sgt	MASSEY William Chippindale	14-09-42	156 Sqn
951350	Sgt	MANLEY Kenneth James Arthur		31-05-42	158 Sqn	817211	F/S	MASSON Edward Savage	31-05-42	12 Sqn
1112428	Sgt	MANNING Dennis		14-04-42	144 Sqn	1058546	Sgt	MASSON Robert Macauley	3-01-42	17 OTU
581403	W/O	MANNING Terence Michael		28-08-42	78 Sqn	1050108	Sgt	MATE Thomas Henry	12-02-42	420 Sqn
951088	Sgt	MANSELL Roy Albert		26-07-42	142 Sqn	1002394	Sgt	MATHESON William	22-07-42	101 Sqn
1271941	Sgt	MANSER Dennis Rodney		6-08-42	207 Sqn	357970	F/S	MATHEWS Francis George	3-02-42	23 OTU
66542	F/O	MANSER VC Leslie Thomas		31-05-42	50 Sqn	785047	F/S	MATHEWS Richard [Far East]	1-10-42	102 Sqn
1210919	Sgt	MANSFIELD Sidney Pharies		11-09-42	15 Sqn	1324301	F/S	MATHEWS Richard Granville Douglas		
1388195	Sgt	MANTLE Herbert William		20-01-42	101 Sqn				6-09-42	51 Sqn
1311110	Sgt	MAPLE Frederick George		16-01-42	150 Sqn	1186687	Sgt	MATHIESON Douglas Wilfred	7-08-42	7 Sqn

Number	Rank	Name	Date	Unit
570019	Sgt	MATHIESON John Joseph	25-08-42	83 Sqn
628213	Sgt	MATHIESON Robert Muir	21-07-42	106 Sqn
941198	Sgt	MATTHEWMAN Cyril Thomas Raynes	26-06-42	11 OTU
615644	Sgt	MATTHEWS Albert David	6-01-42	3 GTrgFlt
1160730	F/S	MATTHEWS Cyril James	31-05-42	22 OTU
45522	P/O	MATTHEWS DFM Douglas Spencer	9-01-42	61 Sqn
778843	Sgt	MATTHEWS Keith Lash [Rhodesia]	25-08-42	150 Sqn
1027014	Sgt	MATTHEWS Leonard Horace	18-07-42	10 OTU
131591	P/O	MATTHEWS Norman	20-12-42	77 Sqn
109130	P/O	MATTHEWS Thomas Kirkham	28-07-42	88 Sqn
1056236	Sgt	MATTHIAS Llewelyn Clifford	6-06-42	10 Sqn
1269102	Sgt	MATTHISSEN Arthur Robert Vihelm	9-06-42	109 Sqn
48745	P/O	MAUNDERS Thomas Victor	14-07-42	142 Sqn
1215930	Sgt	MAW Cecil Albert	6-12-42	107 Sqn
132996	P/O	MAXFIELD Frederick	15-10-42	150 Sqn
114132	P/O	MAXWELL Andrew	16-08-42	106 Sqn
1257889	Sgt	MAXWELL Peter John	20-09-42	61 Sqn
1258209	Sgt	MAY Arthur Charles	18-04-42	158 Sqn
755631	F/S	MAY Edward Joseph	5-09-42	61 Sqn
1060142	Sgt	MAY James Stoddart	19-07-42	150 Sqn
1007103	Sgt	MAY Kenneth Coverdale	30-03-42	10 Sqn
1163935	Sgt	MAY Peter	26-01-42	102 Sqn
954180	Sgt	MAY Thomas Henry	26-06-42	102 Sqn
116969	P/O	MAY William	27-08-42	105 Sqn
1384147	Sgt	MAYCOCK Ronald	18-05-42	15 Sqn
1051991	F/S	MAYER Leonard Aspinall	5-05-42	218 Sqn
116790	F/O	MAYES Frank	13-11-42	97 Sqn
1254004	Sgt	MAYES John	17-01-42	51 Sqn
100639	P/O	MAYGOTHLING Gordon James	29-03-42	109 Sqn
1065233	Sgt	MAYNARD Arthur Stanley	12-02-42	114 Sqn
963891	F/S	MAYS George Henry	7-04-42	142 Sqn
104520	F/O	MAYS Herbert Gordon Badger	26-06-42	35 Sqn
1068223	Sgt	McALEESE Daniel Patrick	8-12-42	149 Sqn
995846	Sgt	McALLISTER Cecil Charles [South Africa]	26-04-42	1443 Flt
631875	Sgt	McALLISTER John Easton	22-02-42	150 Sqn
654274	F/S	McALWANE William Henry	7-09-42	12 Sqn
1118847	Sgt	McARTHUR John	16-08-42	207 Sqn
1128271	Sgt	McASH William Grant Stewart	20-11-42	76 Sqn
124267	P/O	McAULEY DFC George	20-08-42	218 Sqn
1006977	Sgt	McAULEY John Anthony	1-08-42	76 Sqn
1314722	Sgt	McAULIFFE Kevin William [Eire]	25-10-42	103 Sqn
785041	F/S	McAUSLAND Kenneth [Far East]	13-08-42	15 Sqn
1178919	Sgt	McBOYLE Gilbert Ingram	5-07-42	13 OTU
1118544	Sgt	McCALLUM Donald	9-03-42	15 Sqn
965300	Sgt	McCALLUMM Thomas	3-12-42	102 Sqn
656642	Sgt	McCANN Edmund James	10-08-42	150 Sqn
533268	Sgt	McCANN Patrick	12-08-42	78 Sqn
1355118	Sgt	McCARLEY James	17-01-42	7 Sqn
1359180	Sgt	McCARTHY Francis Robert Edwin	28-04-42	115 Sqn
49251	F/L	McCARTHY DFM Robert William	6-12-42	107 Sqn
149880	P/O	McCARTHY DFC William Ronald Berryman	27-08-42	218 Sqn
1326338	Sgt	McCARTEN John	26-07-42	83 Sqn
1354651	Sgt	McCARTNEY Herbert Sydney	28-08-42	35 Sqn
941607	Sgt	McCASKILL Kenneth William	3-02-42	61 Sqn
1126145	Sgt	McCLEARY John	25-08-42	61 Sqn
1066739	Sgt	McCLOUD Thomas James	6-11-42	18 Sqn
80251	F/L	McCLURE DFC Charles Surtis Cranmer [Rhodesia]	9-05-42	44 Sqn
1303065	Sgt	McCLUSKEY Francis Anthony	6-10-42	405 Sqn
1118849	Sgt	McCOLL Hugh Davison	13-03-42	78 Sqn
116737	P/O	McCOLL John Douglas Lamb	13-03-42	17 OTU
645923	Sgt	McCORMACK James	31-05-42	15 OTU
50661	P/O	McCORMACK John Bernard [Eire]	10-09-42	102 Sqn
1375172	Sgt	McCRAE Robert	6-06-42	156 Sqn
120561	P/O	McCREAVY Francis	20-08-42	150 Sqn
1088097	Sgt	McCREEDY Charles	13-11-42	107 Sqn
1024870	Sgt	McCRORY Robert Getgood	29-07-42	115 Sqn
1313020	Sgt	McCUTCHEON Denis Mervyn	14-08-42	19 OTU
990443	Sgt	McDERMOTT Eric	27-04-42	97 Sqn
964668	Sgt	McDONAGH Thomas	19-05-42	218 Sqn
655056	Sgt	McDONALD David Hugh	29-04-42	78 Sqn
1250197	Sgt	McDONALD John	15-10-42	10 OTU
1186278	Sgt	McDONALD Thomas Lindsay	1-08-42	103 Sqn
544774	Sgt	McDONALD William	24-07-42	25 OTU
619899	Sgt	McDONALD William Grant	25-03-42	106 Sqn
1553032	Sgt	McDONALD William Thomas [Chile]	25-10-42	50 Sqn
1375068	Sgt	McDONNELL William Albert	8-05-42	420 Sqn
1550625	Sgt	McDOUGALL Hugh Currie	20-09-42	10 Sqn
1076263	Sgt	McDOWELL John Ingram	28-05-42	1443 Flt
37476	W/C	McFADDEN DFC Richard Denis Barry	14-02-42	214 Sqn
1359519	F/S	McGANN John Claude	24-08-42	218 Sqn
1148266	Sgt	McGAUCHIE John	8-11-42	76 Sqn
1305505	Sgt	McGAVIN George McCulloch	5-05-42	103 Sqn
561820	F/S	McGAVIN Ian Malcolm James	18-11-42	90 Sqn
998735	Sgt	McGIBBON Robert	12-03-42	75 Sqn
41858	S/L	McGILLIVRAY DFC Thomas Campbell [New Zealand]	20-05-42	156 Sqn
1375485	Sgt	McGINN Bernard John	28-04-42	150 Sqn
571976	Sgt	McGLEN Ronald	2-06-42	78 Sqn
1001910	Sgt	McGOUGH Charles	20-09-42	44 Sqn
1118526	Sgt	McGOVERN John	20-06-42	15 Sqn
1081837	Sgt	McGRATH Patrick Gerald	31-05-42	214 Sqn
1057220	Sgt	McGRATH Terence Allen	4-06-42	115 Sqn
913353	Sgt	McGREGOR Keith Malcolm	27-07-42	101 Sqn
1100964	Sgt	McGREGOR Roderick	28-08-42	75 Sqn
1052525	Sgt	McGRENERY Thomas Hill	10-04-42	49 Sqn
60123	F/O	McGUFFIE Hugh Martin	23-03-42	49 Sqn
1367218	Sgt	McHARDY Alexander Joseph	19-05-42	106 Sqn
1053447	Sgt	McHARDY John Charles Donald	15-04-42	420 Sqn
1016740	Sgt	McHENRY Colin Shone	29-10-42	115 Sqn
118168	P/O	McHUGH Stanley	10-09-42	142 Sqn
1255402	Sgt	McHUTCHISON Hugh James	29-03-42	142 Sqn
633231	Sgt	McINTOSH Alexander Reid	29-10-42	15 Sqn
1108758	Sgt	McINTOSH Ronald Muirhead	2-06-42	114 Sqn
1112959	Sgt	McINTYRE Charles Stewart	9-06-42	12 Sqn
1197253	Sgt	McINTYRE George Andrew	1-10-42	102 Sqn
1061697	Sgt	McINTYRE James	24-04-42	114 Sqn
1552316	Sgt	McKEAN Robert Jack	7-07-42	21 OTU
1062986	Sgt	McKELLAR John Campbell	1-06-42	115 Sqn
971310	F/S	McKELVIE DFM Alastair Macnab	3-06-42	61 Sqn
1014114	Sgt	McKENNY Patrick	24-04-42	114 Sqn
915768	Sgt	McKENZIE Alfred Henry	16-08-42	207 Sqn
636348	F/S	McKENZIE DFM Kenneth	3-01-42	106 Sqn
973528	Sgt	McKENZIE Roderick George	11-06-42	77 Sqn
1114251	Sgt	McKENZIE Thomas Inglis	1-06-42	20 OTU
1378533	Sgt	McKINLAY Allan	22-11-42	57 Sqn
540450	AC1	McKINNEY Joseph	19-08-42	12 Sqn
1040701	Sgt	McKINSTRY John	8-06-42	35 Sqn
1055930	Sgt	McLACHLAN Ian	9-11-42	150 Sqn
993204	Sgt	McLAREN Archibald McCulloch	30-03-42	35 Sqn
109892	P/O	McLAREN Donald Gower	9-05-42	44 Sqn
1000530	Sgt	McLAREN Douglas Brian	14-01-42	21 Sqn
1001945	Sgt	McLAREN Ian	19-04-42	49 Sqn
1552169	Sgt	McLAREN James McIntosh [USA]	20-06-42	15 Sqn
999862	Sgt	McLARNON Paul	3-09-42	11 OTU
50586	P/O	McLELLAN Sidney Charles	18-12-42	1474 Flt
1368804	Sgt	McLENNAN Kenneth	30-07-42	142 Sqn
1006997	Sgt	McLEOD Stanley Ronald	24-02-42	106 Sqn
745477	Sgt	McLEOD William Arnott	31-05-42	115 Sqn
611555	Sgt	McLINDEN John Frederick	22-04-42	75 Sqn
1123740	Sgt	McMANUS Hugh	10-11-42	107 Sqn
1028939	Sgt	McMASTER Norman Tolson	5-10-42	103 Sqn
925439	Sgt	McMECHAN Alan George Julian	2-06-42	97 Sqn
1558953	AC2	McMILLAN Daniel	16-09-42	22 OTU

ID	Rank	Name	Date	Sqn
109159	F/L	McMILLAN James	31-12-42	83 Sqn
967661	F/S	McMILLAN William	28-12-42	23 OTU
551156	Sgt	McMORRINE Alexander Watson	3-12-42	75 Sqn
1184109	Sgt	McMULLIN Charles Alexander Brian	1-08-42	14 OTU
80193	F/O	McNAMARA Lawrence Gerard Lyons [Rhodesia]	17-12-42	44 Sqn
1066477	Sgt	McNAMEE David	29-08-42	149 Sqn
147829	W/O	McNAUGHTON William Smith	16-03-42	Holme-in-Spalding Moor
1329586	Sgt	McNEARY James	19-08-42	61 Sqn
540271	Sgt	McNEIL Alan	2-09-42	97 Sqn
1312485	Sgt	McNEIL Douglas Spencer [Tanganyika]	28-08-42	12 Sqn
43462	F/L	McNEILLY DFC William St. Clair	6-02-42	142 Sqn
986400	Sgt	McRAE George William	17-02-42	21 OTU
798530	Sgt	McRAE John Roderick [Newfoundland]	16-04-42	156 Sqn
1073860	Sgt	McSPARRON Ernest William	30-05-42	15 Sqn
655655	Sgt	McVICAR William Brodie [Australia]	16-08-42	207 Sqn
79101	F/L	McWILLIAM Ormiston Galloway Edgar	19-08-42	226 Sqn
620953	Sgt	MEADE Donald Frank	10-11-42	7 Sqn
920366	Sgt	MEADE Eric Talbot	31-03-42	35 Sqn
1381714	Sgt	MEADOWS Leslie Frank	15-10-42	214 Sqn
1254942	Sgt	MEAGER Leslie Ronald	13-03-42	12 Sqn
1359228	Sgt	MEAKIN Henry	2-06-42	114 Sqn
998262	Sgt	MEDD George Alfred	26-03-42	408 Sqn
1312588	Sgt	MEDHURST Gordon Francis	27-08-42	218 Sqn
'113468'	Sgt	MEDLEY Harold	9-03-42	15 OTU
122992	P/O	MEDUS DFC Richard William	22-06-42	218 Sqn
1380821	Sgt	MEECH Arthur Dennis	14-07-42	18 Sqn
118080	P/O	MEEK Reginald Thorley	26-07-42	19 OTU
1283406	Sgt	MEEKING Donald William	12-02-42	50 Sqn
939968	Sgt	MEIKLE David James	16-04-42	61 Sqn
1384447	Sgt	MELHADO Leslie Stanhope [Jamaica]	6-06-42	44 Sqn
913679	Sgt	MELHUISH John William	11-06-42	83 Sqn
1356712	Sgt	MELLINGS Robert Charles	18-01-42	142 Sqn
1008176	Sgt	MELLOR John George	28-08-42	78 Sqn
940704	Sgt	MELLORS Trevor	21-12-42	106 Sqn
1167148	Sgt	MELLOWES Kenneth Reginald	30-05-42	460 Sqn
1014741	Sgt	MELTON George Bullimore	17-09-42	214 Sqn
913638	Sgt	MELVILLE Douglas Archer	20-06-42	214 Sqn
973352	Sgt	MELVILLE George Anderson	19-08-42	61 Sqn
1037647	AC1	MENZIES Thomas	6-01-42	3 GTrgFlt
1263777	Sgt	MERCER Gordon Henry	9-06-42	97 Sqn
1063548	Sgt	MERCER Hill	31-05-42	158 Sqn
817193	F/S	MERCER Norman Alexander	25-10-42	103 Sqn
568070	Sgt	MEREDITH Elwyn	5-09-42	214 Sqn
937585	Sgt	MEREDITH Ronald H	31-03-42	35 Sqn
655376	Sgt	MERIFIELD John Wynne	5-09-42	115 Sqn
742016	W/O	MERRALLS DFC DFM Peter Ernest	1-08-42	106 Sqn
633309	Sgt	MERRICKS Cyril Leonard	17-04-42	44 Sqn
1330515	Sgt	MERRITT Dennis Edward Grahame	29-07-42	218 Sqn
1260396	Sgt	MERRONY Henry Arthur	29-10-42	115 Sqn
1365038	Sgt	MERRY James William McLean	13-10-42	10 OTU
648156	Sgt	MESSER Albert Ernest	24-10-42	78 Sqn
40057	S/L	MESSERVY DFC Norman Henry Edward [Australia]	19-09-42	105 Sqn
618362	Sgt	MESSHAM Sidney	2-10-42	405 Sqn
67621	F/L	METCALFE DFC Alan Herbert	25-03-42	455 Sqn
1010560	Sgt	METCALFE Charles Roland	4-06-42	76 Sqn
1375863	Sgt	METCALFE George Arthur	13-02-42	455 Sqn
1113285	Sgt	METCALFE Herbert	29-11-42	161 Sqn
967928	F/S	METHEVEN Douglas Haig	18-08-42	101 Sqn
787866	Sgt	MEZNIK Alois Wellington [Czechoslovakia]	12-03-42	311 Sqn
1263822	Sgt	MICHELIN Reginald Walter	16-09-42	11 OTU
990186	Sgt	MICKLETHWAITE Cecil Ward Chandos	6-02-42	142 Sqn
1127130	F/S	MIDDLETON Harry	11-12-42	158 Sqn
1391925	Sgt	MILBANK Ronald Leslie	1-10-42	102 Sqn
912519	Sgt	MILDON Thomas Ralph	13-04-42	9 Sqn
613827	Sgt	MILES Charles William	29-07-42	1651 CU
900970	Sgt	MILES John George Arscott	2-06-42	49 Sqn
116729	F/O	MILES John Thomas Norie	24-10-42	57 Sqn
1386192	Sgt	MILES Stanley Victor	16-09-42	9 Sqn
1376697	Sgt	MILLAR Alan John	9-05-42	12 Sqn
1066492	Sgt	MILLAR John Edward	26-07-42	19 OTU
1126135	Sgt	MILLAR John Martin Smith	14-04-42	21 OTU
1380205	Sgt	MILLAR Leonard George	30-07-42	61 Sqn
1380406	Sgt	MILLAR Robert George Gordon	9-01-42	90 Sqn
1179058	Sgt	MILLARD Graham George	11-09-42	83 Sqn
1380773	Sgt	MILLARD Norman Kenneth	6-12-42	28 OTU
815171	Sgt	MILLBAND Leonard	2-10-42	78 Sqn
1379181	Sgt	MILLER Bernard John	7-08-42	12 Sqn
36270	F/L	MILLER DFC Charles William [New Zealand]	11-07-42	97 Sqn
1051612	Sgt	MILLER David	31-05-42	109 Sqn
1181079	Sgt	MILLER David John	27-07-42	101 Sqn
1205877	Sgt	MILLER Francis Henry	2-04-42	57 Sqn
905995	Sgt	MILLER Joseph Henry	8-05-42	44 Sqn
130505	P/O	MILLER Raymond Herbert	14-12-42	22 OTU
1330953	Sgt	MILLER Robert George	31-07-42	9 Sqn
634701	Sgt	MILLER Stuart Alexander	13-10-42	214 Sqn
514426	Sgt	MILLER Thomas Henry	25-03-42	83 Sqn
624065	F/S	MILLER Thomas Henry	17-12-42	10 OTU
1025753	Sgt	MILLER William Thomas	20-12-42	9 Sqn
1252034	Sgt	MILLICHIP John	11-03-42	149 Sqn
130722	P/O	MILLIDGE Noel	27-08-42	156 Sqn
1310076	Sgt	MILLIGAN James McPherson	26-07-42	460 Sqn
1117073	Sgt	MILLIGAN Joseph	12-06-42	114 Sqn
1125315	Sgt	MILLINGTON Ernest	9-03-42	21 OTU
629942	F/S	MILLNS Jonathan Henry	29-08-42	88 Sqn
1377603	Sgt	MILLS Albert	28-08-42	12 Sqn
1169710	Sgt	MILLS Charles William	6-01-42	9 Sqn
567958	Sgt	MILLS Frederick Ross	3-05-42	78 Sqn
1333363	Sgt	MILLS Terence Alfred	12-08-42	15 Sqn
1179483	Sgt	MILLS Walter John	25-06-42	76 Sqn
998200	F/S	MILNE Angus McDonald	7-09-42	10 Sqn
100554	P/O	MILNE George Kildea Traynor	6-02-42	142 Sqn
49655	P/O	MILNE James Arthur Johnston	28-08-42	150 Sqn
124270	F/O	MILNE William Alexander	21-12-42	7 Sqn
1264477	Sgt	MILNER Jack	29-10-42	115 Sqn
1007366	Sgt	MILNES Percy	27-07-42	142 Sqn
512435	Sgt	MILTON Alan Sydney	12-08-42	1651 CU
1378025	Sgt	MILTON Arthur Thomas	6-12-42	21 Sqn
997221	Sgt	MILTON Peter Gray	28-01-42	214 Sqn
48226	P/O	MINCHIN Reginald Alfred	2-06-42	23 OTU
965937	F/S	MINER Douglas Albert	30-05-42	76 Sqn
903047	F/S	MINIKEN Frederick Thomas	6-01-42	3 GTrgFlt
938925	Sgt	MINNEY Alexander Richard	27-09-42	10 OTU
136346	P/O	MITCHELL Charles	9-11-42	7 Sqn
1282079	Sgt	MITCHELL Edwin	16-08-42	408 Sqn
1255790	Sgt	MITCHELL BEM Francis Beaumont	27-09-42	10 OTU
106363	P/O	MITCHELL Frank Alan	28-04-42	150 Sqn
959845	Sgt	MITCHELL Frederick Henry	6-06-42	20 OTU
1334834	Sgt	MITCHELL George William Arthur	30-09-42	12 Sqn
525420	Sgt	MITCHELL Hugh	1-04-42	214 Sqn
627659	Sgt	MITCHELL John	29-03-42	61 Sqn
655257	Sgt	MITCHELL John Leonard	2-06-42	114 Sqn
130145	P/O	MITCHELL Kenneth Ederic Michael	3-09-42	405 Sqn
1058531	Sgt	MITCHELL Stewart Robertson	17-08-42	50 Sqn
37755	W/C	MITCHELL DFC Victor	17-12-42	75 Sqn
102588	F/O	MITCHENER Charles	26-07-42	78 Sqn
1288036	Sgt	MIZEN Leslie George John	8-02-42	22 OTU
1168876	Sgt	MOCOCK Reginald Crosby	17-12-42	75 Sqn
755366	F/S	MOFFAT Alan	17-09-42	76 Sqn
128685	P/O	MOFFAT DFC John Alexander Wilson	21-12-42	9 Sqn

927587	Sgt	MOGFORD William Lionel	26-03-42	115 Sqn		117479	P/O	MORRIS-EDWARDS Denis Victor	19-08-42	207 Sqn
1180593	Sgt	MOGG Douglas George	27-07-42	158 Sqn		1061605	Sgt	MORRISON Falconer	1-11-42	138 Sqn
1059394	Sgt	MOGGACH Alexander Scott	2-04-42	20 OTU		656649	Sgt	MORRISON Leavis Wilson	25-09-42	61 Sqn
526468	Sgt	MOIR William Albert	9-11-42	102 Sqn		1365220	Sgt	MORRISON Roderick Urquhart	13-07-42	7 Sqn
1379764	Sgt	MOLLOY Laurence Clifford	3-12-42	102 Sqn		996502	Sgt	MORROW Allan Stott	8-05-42	44 Sqn
747753	F/S	MOLTON Frank Reginald	11-09-42	25 OTU		1354749	Sgt	MORTIMER Allen Frederick John	14-09-42	156 Sqn
1261115	Sgt	MONGER-GODFREY Stanley Edward				929523	Sgt	MORTON John Walter	4-07-42	61 Sqn
			29-09-42	20 OTU		1109114	Sgt	MORTON Robert Semple	16-09-42	9 Sqn
922739	Sgt	MONK Derrick John	11-06-42	83 Sqn		621322	Sgt	MORTON William Wilson	17-12-42	75 Sqn
634693	F/S	MONK Frank John	19-08-42	61 Sqn		1254452	Sgt	MOSELEY Cerris	12-04-42	103 Sqn
117142	P/O	MONTGOMERY Alexander Whyte Cassie				1161688	Sgt	MOSES Raymond Hill	27-07-42	57 Sqn
			7-08-42	7 Sqn		777646	Sgt	MOSS Brian Douglas [Rhodesia]	17-04-42	44 Sqn
1383719	Sgt	MOODY Charles Henry	1-08-42	25 OTU		937092	Sgt	MOSS Douglas Wallace	26-07-42	142 Sqn
117699	P/O	MOODY Donald Beverley [Canada]	17-09-42	49 Sqn		1161949	Sgt	MOSS John William	24-06-42	103 Sqn
1193594	Sgt	MOODY John Richard	21-02-42	455 Sqn		1338677	Sgt	MOSS Reginald Laurence	14-09-42	1654 CU
970388	Sgt	MOORCROFT Albert	3-06-42	15 Sqn		924139	F/S	MOSS Robert William	12-08-42	156 Sqn
1375598	Sgt	MOORE Antony Reginald	31-05-42	10 Sqn		1268307	Sgt	MOTH Albert	6-06-42	50 Sqn
1211456	Sgt	MOORE Ernest Leslie	2-10-42	149 Sqn		901709	Sgt	MOTT Douglas John Hayden	17-04-42	10 OTU
1114488	Sgt	MOORE Herbert Sydney	1-10-42	10 Sqn		1365131	Sgt	MOUAT James Hutchison	6-06-42	149 Sqn
990568	Sgt	MOORE John Bruce [USA]	1-06-42	460 Sqn		1181182	Sgt	MOUNT Alfred William	29-04-42	9 Sqn
1164946	Sgt	MOORE Reginald	10-09-42	102 Sqn		1069031	Sgt	MOUNTENEY Archibald	9-05-42	15 Sqn
959544	F/S	MOORE Stanley Raymond	9-06-42	83 Sqn		924847	Sgt	MOUNTSTEPHENS Victor Haig	6-01-42	57 Sqn
756552	LAC	MOORE Thomas	18-11-42	78 Sqn		1057893	Sgt	MOWAT James Thomas Heggie	9-03-42	83 Sqn
101555	P/O	MOOREHOUSE Harry Barker	9-05-42	76 Sqn		1038399	Sgt	MOWFORTH Eric Charles	6-12-42	487 Sqn
1053760	Sgt	MOORES Eric	16-07-42	149 Sqn		516218	W/O	MOWLAM Arthur Norman	31-01-42	144 Sqn
798533	Sgt	MOORES James [Newfoundland]	22-06-42	460 Sqn		121570	P/O	MOXEY Percy Leslie	7-08-42	16 OTU
917067	F/S	MOREY Paul Herrick	16-03-42	57 Sqn		913185	Sgt	MOXON Harry	23-11-42	161 Sqn
931913	Sgt	MORFFEW George Charles	22-07-42	101 Sqn		1310446	Sgt	MOYLAN William	9-09-42	150 Sqn
1270387	Sgt	MORGAN Arthur Richards	9-11-42	20 OTU		931774	Sgt	MOYNES Charles	16-04-42	149 Sqn
645324	Sgt	MORGAN Charles John	20-06-42	57 Sqn		127092	P/O	MUCHA Miroslav [Czechoslovakia]	13-10-42	27 OTU
1079178	Sgt	MORGAN Christopher Hubert	1-08-42	103 Sqn		1265929	Sgt	MUGFORD Gilbert James	25-06-42	214 Sqn
115393	P/O	MORGAN Denys William Evan	7-09-42	10 Sqn		100092	P/O	MUIRHEAD DFC John Patrick	20-07-42	12 Sqn
906071	F/S	MORGAN Donald Edward [Canada]	28-08-42	115 Sqn		647415	Sgt	MULES Ronald Morley	9-03-42	35 Sqn
1321184	Sgt	MORGAN Edward Douglas	25-09-42	10 OTU		119205	F/O	MULHOLLAND Alexander Eric	21-12-42	57 Sqn
1081231	Sgt	MORGAN Gerlad John	12-12-42	102 Sqn		552232	F/S	MULLINS David Lewis	28-02-42	110 Sqn
929383	Sgt	MORGAN John Willoughby	22-07-42	57 Sqn		655837	Sgt	MUMFORD Ronald John	16-09-42	15 Sqn
742728	Sgt	MORGAN Norman Anthony	26-02-42	158 Sqn		1375601	Sgt	MUNDAY John Henry	31-05-42	214 Sqn
1451853	Sgt	MORGAN Raymond	5-10-42	102 Sqn		120571	F/O	MUNNS Douglas Philip	15-10-42	103 Sqn
1056586	Sgt	MORGAN Rhedge Haydn Durham	26-03-42	420 Sqn		1186623	Sgt	MUNNS Walter Laurence	29-04-42	12 Sqn
1102280	Sgt	MORGAN Ronald William	20-06-42	78 Sqn		648623	Sgt	MUNRO Arthur William	29-04-42	57 Sqn
124630	P/O	MORGAN Stanley Edward Herbert	25-06-42	102 Sqn		1325058	Sgt	MUNRO John	19-04-42	156 Sqn
1313175	Sgt	MORGAN Stanley James	7-06-42	150 Sqn		1344207	Sgt	MUNRO John	1-08-42	103 Sqn
1253408	Sgt	MORGAN Thomas Gwynne	10-08-42	405 Sqn		1267233	Sgt	MUNRO John	22-07-42	115 Sqn
656079	Sgt	MORGAN Thomas Phillip	26-06-42	15 OTU		1151780	Sgt	MUNT Victor Frank	9-05-42	15 Sqn
1252574	Sgt	MORGAN Wilfred Frank	3-06-42	7 Sqn		1126541	Sgt	MURCHISON John	20-11-42	76 Sqn
522876	Sgt	MORGAN William Cecil	18-12-42	97 Sqn		1060255	Sgt	MURDO Henry Marshall	9-03-42	12 Sqn
120569	F/O	MORICE Peter James	20-11-42	76 Sqn		778282	Sgt	MURDOCH Alastair Fraser [Rhodesia]	24-03-42	44 Sqn
1310465	Sgt	MORISON Sydney Arthur	30-06-42	7 Sqn		116913	P/O	MURDOCH David Beveridge	15-10-42	103 Sqn
67046	P/O	MORPHETT Jack Heathcote	9-04-42	83 Sqn		1286633	Sgt	MURLIS Thomas Charles Robert	29-08-42	408 Sqn
938106	Sgt	MORRELL Fred	21-12-42	106 Sqn		631675	Sgt	MURPHY Frank Alfred	29-07-42	7 Sqn
1061512	Sgt	MORREY Charles Edward	9-01-42	12 Sqn		1382260	Sgt	MURPHY Gilbert Mansfield	26-06-42	10 OTU
655938	Sgt	MORRIS Arnold	16-11-42	115 Sqn		1165663	Sgt	MURPHY James	1-04-42	214 Sqn
1108551	Sgt	MORRIS Arthur	7-09-42	10 Sqn		641455	Sgt	MURPHY Paul Cameron [Canada]	14-09-42	44 Sqn
655223	Sgt	MORRIS David	24-07-42	149 Sqn		1250449	Sgt	MURRAY Cecil John	17-11-42	158 Sqn
48095	P/O	MORRIS David John	6-02-42	21 Sqn		778149	Sgt	MURRAY Donald Emslie	12-08-42	156 Sqn
297975	Sgt	MORRIS Edward James	20-05-42	35 Sqn				[South Africa]		
575984	Sgt	MORRIS Ernest William	16-06-42	1651 CU		1058530	Sgt	MURRAY Gerald Patrick	29-03-42	142 Sqn
535527	Sgt	MORRIS Frederick Arthur	30-05-42	15 Sqn		127523	P/O	MURRAY Hugh Douglas	6-10-42	26 OTU
561823	Sgt	MORRIS Frederick William	20-12-42	49 Sqn		104453	P/O	MURRAY James Walter	11-04-42	214 Sqn
1256392	Sgt	MORRIS John Ingram	22-07-42	115 Sqn		1238107	AC2	MURRAY John	17-06-42	24 OTU
617843	Sgt	MORRIS John Lewis	9-06-42	75 Sqn		536790	Sgt	MURRAY John Taylor	8-09-42	76 Sqn
1102284	Sgt	MORRIS Joseph	25-04-42	226 Sqn		968359	F/S	MURRAY Patrick Hatton	8-12-42	149 Sqn
1058833	Sgt	MORRIS Peter Cant	28-04-42	76 Sqn		1365896	Sgt	MURRAY Thomas Craik	21-07-42	35 Sqn
117480	P/O	MORRIS Philip	25-06-42	12 OTU		979137	Sgt	MURRAY Thomas Edward	30-05-42	218 Sqn
1230755	Sgt	MORRIS Robert Thomas	1-08-42	35 Sqn		570712	Sgt	MUSGRAVE Albert Edward	5-10-42	97 Sqn
1037412	Sgt	MORRIS Royston Delmare	22-11-42	115 Sqn		1161384	Sgt	MUSGROVE Dennis William	25-04-42	103 Sqn
915537	F/S	MORRIS Terence Albert George	2-06-42	10 Sqn		1166720	F/S	MUSITANO Grahame Leveson	4-06-42	207 Sqn
751295	Sgt	MORRIS William Douglas	9-03-42	408 Sqn		526121	F/S	MUSK David	9-01-42	90 Sqn
1430877	Sgt	MORRIS William Richard	12-08-42	156 Sqn		107994	F/O	MUSSELWHITE Leslie James	16-09-42	9 Sqn

619222	Sgt	MUSSELWHITE Vincent George	5-06-42	78 Sqn	525236	Sgt	NICHOLLS Robinson	16-07-42	15 Sqn
87421	F/O	MUTTER James Gordon	25-06-42	10 Sqn	49538	F/L	NICHOLLS DFC Walter	10-11-42	7 Sqn
818018	F/S	MUTTER DFM Leonard Harry	6-10-42	44 Sqn	1257377	Sgt	NICHOLS John Owen Henry	16-05-42	75 Sqn
1187659	F/S	MUTTON Fernleigh William	26-06-42	11 OTU	80278	P/O	NICHOLSON Denis Franklin [South Africa]	24-08-42	44 Sqn
754674	W/O	MYCOCK DFC Thomas James	17-04-42	97 Sqn					
1015522	F/S	MYERS James	29-08-42	156 Sqn	42074	F/L	NICHOLSON George William	9-03-42	15 Sqn
947280	Sgt	MYERS Joseph Barnby	16-01-42	214 Sqn	1333607	Sgt	NICHOLSON John	22-11-42	102 Sqn
107995	P/O	MYRING Norman Ernest	3-04-42	101 Sqn	1023368	F/S	NICHOLSON John Eric	8-09-42	76 Sqn
129073	P/O	M'ILVEEN James	11-09-42	26 OTU	1353479	Sgt	NICHOLSON Lawrence Henry	21-08-42	149 Sqn
111471	P/O	NADARAJA Gnani [Ceylon]	4-06-42	17 OTU	1066387	LAC	NICHOLSON Leslie Hamilton	28-12-42	23 OTU
124730	P/O	NADEN John Wilfred	26-07-42	12 Sqn	954208	F/S	NICHOLSON Robert	18-05-42	15 Sqn
641908	Sgt	NADIN Charles Henry	17-12-42	9 Sqn	1165282	Sgt	NICOL George	18-09-42	25 OTU
567168	Sgt	NAISH Thomas James	29-04-42	78 Sqn	966488	Sgt	NICOL James	30-05-42	76 Sqn
974768	F/S	NAPIER DFM John Kenneth	30-05-42	22 OTU	45683	F/L	NICOLL DFC David Andrew	8-12-42	207 Sqn
1378097	F/S	NASH John	2-04-42	214 Sqn	979889	Sgt	NICOLL William	28-04-42	102 Sqn
41310	F/L	NASH Kenneth Howell	10-01-42	82 Sqn	1057973	F/S	NICOLSON Samuel	15-10-42	10 OTU
1293064	Sgt	NASH Stanley Walter	31-10-42	107 Sqn	1182807	Sgt	NIGHTINGALE Alan	28-06-42	150 Sqn
925007	Sgt	NATION Ronald Edward George	14-04-42	144 Sqn	776067	Sgt	NIGHTINGALE DFM Ernest Ivo [Kenya]	12-02-42	144 Sqn
631267	Sgt	NAYLOR Arthur	6-04-42	9 Sqn					
916232	Sgt	NAYLOR Norman Joseph	8-04-42	57 Sqn	118449	P/O	NISBET William	12-08-42	57 Sqn
655072	Sgt	NEADE Reuben Howard	25-10-42	142 Sqn	1251529	Sgt	NISBETT Kenneth	24-04-42	101 Sqn
47176	P/O	NEAL Harry	1-04-42	107 Sqn	42257	S/L	NIXEY DSO Peter	20-06-42	214 Sqn
528927	Sgt	NEALE George Leonard Arthur	20-08-42	218 Sqn	1252858	Sgt	NIXON Bernard Stearman	23-12-42	138 Sqn
1376547	Sgt	NEARY John	8-04-42	83 Sqn	572665	Sgt	NIXON George	3-06-42	15 Sqn
1167643	Sgt	NEARY Leslie Eric	19-12-42	149 Sqn	1269069	Sgt	NOBBS Walter John	17-09-42	15 OTU
113760	F/L	NEATE Frederick George	30-07-42	149 Sqn	754635	F/S	NOBLE Eric William	7-04-42	61 Sqn
1380022	Sgt	NEATHWAY Ronald Edward	25-04-42	107 Sqn	1376567	Sgt	NOCKELS Leslie	24-10-42	218 Sqn
1153376	F/S	NEAVE Dennis Arthur	9-06-42	83 Sqn	1120097	Sgt	NORCROSS Horace Pilling	29-10-42	115 Sqn
117845	P/O	NEEDHAM Arthur Sidney [Australia]	5-09-42	12 Sqn	102559	P/O	NORFOLK Howard	20-06-42	76 Sqn
581522	W/O	NEESOM MiD Ernest	30-05-42	22 OTU	1385730	Sgt	NORGATE Kenneth	29-08-42	61 Sqn
632245	F/S	NEIL DFM Arthur Joseph	26-06-42	83 Sqn	548174	Sgt	NORMAN Arnold Bailey	26-06-42	83 Sqn
1368959	Sgt	NEILSON Clyde	22-11-42	57 Sqn	962166	Sgt	NORMAN Edward Vincent	25-08-42	83 Sqn
1152271	Sgt	NELMES Leslie John	30-03-42	35 Sqn	920538	Sgt	NORMINGTON Derek Harry	30-05-42	156 Sqn
1376868	Sgt	NELSON Arthur William Eaton	11-02-42	150 Sqn	1260261	Sgt	NORREGAARD Arne	1-10-42	10 Sqn
787353	Sgt	NEMECEK Ladislav [Czechoslovakia]	21-01-42	311 Sqn	1335250	Sgt	NORRIS Basil	12-12-42	102 Sqn
777691	Sgt	NESBITT Bertram Llewellyn [Rhodesia]	9-05-42	44 Sqn	926585	Sgt	NORRIS Louis Robert Martin	28-03-42	7 Sqn
1064494	Sgt	NESBITT James Festubert	16-04-42	101 Sqn	1375126	Sgt	NORRIS Ronald Leslie	6-06-42	14 OTU
994389	Sgt	NETTLETON Eric	20-08-42	218 Sqn	620700	F/S	NORTH James	25-04-42	9 Sqn
1452530	Sgt	NETTLETON Francis Peter	22-11-42	12 OTU	1381750	Sgt	NORTHCOTT Harry Arthur James	24-04-42	101 Sqn
118886	P/O	NEVE Cecil	22-08-42	10 OTU	1318802	Sgt	NORTHEY Douglas	20-09-42	150 Sqn
955436	Sgt	NEVE Desmond Roderick	9-05-42	76 Sqn	1388137	Sgt	NORTHFIELD Derryck Douglas	1-08-42	101 Sqn
798629	Sgt	NEVILLE Kevin Fenton [Newfoundland]	10-12-42	9 Sqn	1251246	Sgt	NORTHROP Kenneth Edward	25-01-42	49 Sqn
					1311697	Sgt	NORTON Alfred	28-08-42	12 Sqn
1308926	Sgt	NEWBOUND Fred	27-07-42	115 Sqn	798569	Sgt	NOSEWORTHY Bertram [Newfoundland]	25-03-42	14 OTU
759096	F/S	NEWBY Thomas Edgar	31-05-42	9 Sqn					
999799	F/S	NEWCOMB Stuart Spencer	17-09-42	214 Sqn	613267	Sgt	NUGENT Walter Crone	5-06-42	57 Sqn
1378361	Sgt	NEWELL Edmund George	2-06-42	102 Sqn	581294	W/O	NUTT James Arthur	1-06-42	18 OTU
115763	P/O	NEWELL Isaac Charles [Newfoundland]	21-08-42	218 Sqn	33209	W/C	OAKESHOTT DFC Alan Robertson	2-07-42	139 Sqn
					1186110	Sgt	OAKLEY Edward Richard Cyril	7-04-42	15 Sqn
1309490	Sgt	NEWEY Harold	9-06-42	83 Sqn	798702	Sgt	OAKLEY James Francis [Newfoundland]	16-09-42	25 OTU
958994	Sgt	NEWMAN Colin Alfred	24-09-42	78 Sqn					
1177845	Sgt	NEWMAN George Eric	1-04-42	214 Sqn	959151	Sgt	OATEN Percy	29-08-42	75 Sqn
1181418	Sgt	NEWMAN Gordon Kenneth Moyle	28-04-42	214 Sqn	1315757	Sgt	OATES Harold Alfred	30-07-42	142 Sqn
128436	P/O	NEWMAN Jack Godfrey	1-09-42	15 Sqn	646412	Sgt	OBARD Stanley	12-08-42	207 Sqn
116672	F/O	NEWMAN Laurence George	17-12-42	9 Sqn	1377693	Sgt	OBBARD Joseph	9-11-42	44 Sqn
1218863	AC2	NEWMAN Percy George	27-05-42	5 Group	111784	F/O	OBSIL Vaclav [Czechoslovakia]	13-10-42	27 OTU
108998	F/O	NEWPORT TINLEY DFC Gervase Francis Benton	23-12-42	138 Sqn	1264989	Sgt	ODDY Ernest Osmond	29-10-42	19 OTU
					1295480	Sgt	ODELL Harold Price	12-07-42	51 Sqn
1182450	F/S	NEWSON Edward Ranald	17-11-42	25 OTU	921915	Sgt	ODY Herbert John	5-05-42	12 Sqn
1376133	Sgt	NEWTON Eric Charles Percy	10-12-42	9 Sqn	1165262	Sgt	OERTEL Stanley James	27-07-42	142 Sqn
124001	P/O	NEWTON Leslie	30-05-42	156 Sqn	102584	P/O	OGIER Michael Owen	12-03-42	77 Sqn
1150596	Sgt	NEWTON Robert Eastwood	7-04-42	61 Sqn	1183624	F/S	OLIVER DFM Frank	30-09-42	51 Sqn
120242	F/O	NIAS Maurice Alfred	17-12-42	44 Sqn	1371746	Sgt	OLIVER John McKelvie Dunn	25-06-42	15 OTU
1376879	Sgt	NICE Francis Arnold Winter	28-08-42	13 OTU	1189941	Sgt	OLIVER Richard George	8-12-42	15 Sqn
1334237	Sgt	NICHOLAS Albert	11-09-42	20 OTU	120067	P/O	OLLAR DFM Alexander Johnston Stewart	27-07-42	115 Sqn
534052	Sgt	NICHOLAS David Stanley	9-03-42	9 Sqn					
951248	Sgt	NICHOLLS Gwilym	21-12-42	103 Sqn	777613	Sgt	OLVER Robert Duncan [Rhodesia]	9-05-42	44 Sqn
40560	S/L	NICHOLLS MiD John Paul Vipond	9-03-42	150 Sqn	1054935	F/S	ONIONS William	31-05-42	103 Sqn
1384306	Sgt	NICHOLLS Raymond George	14-09-42	16 OTU	935171	F/S	ORANGE William	2-10-42	149 Sqn

Service No	Rank	Name	Date	Unit
67039	F/L	ORDISH DFC Charles Brian	31-12-42	15 Sqn
630680	Sgt	ORFORD Stanley Arthur	15-01-42	115 Sqn
926978	Sgt	ORMAN William Harding	30-05-42	1502 Flt
1057349	Sgt	ORMEROD Frank Edwin	4-06-42	76 Sqn
1355088	Sgt	ORMSTON Charles Kay	11-04-42	455 Sqn
1145143	Sgt	ORR Albert Cyril	13-10-42	75 Sqn
655146	F/S	ORR John	29-12-42	77 Sqn
1332202	Sgt	ORR Thomas Clarence Field [South Africa]	16-09-42	15 Sqn
619496	Sgt	OSBALDESTON James Duckett	29-08-42	49 Sqn
73033	F/L	OSBORN DFC Andrew Francis Atterbury	28-08-42	75 Sqn
119245	P/O	OSBORN Thomas William	14-08-42	19 OTU
1333824	Sgt	OSBORN William	8-12-42	149 Sqn
64303	F/O	OSBORNE Derek Oscar	27-06-42	150 Sqn
1289551	Sgt	OSBORNE Douglas Lester	27-07-42	76 Sqn
1291071	Sgt	OSBORNE John Dennis	22-10-42	26 OTU
47685	F/O	OSMOND Charles Jack	2-10-42	106 Sqn
937288	F/S	OSSELTON William	19-08-42	226 Sqn
937889	Sgt	OSWIN Arthur Graham	28-08-42	15 Sqn
547288	Sgt	OTTAWAY Albert James	20-09-42	149 Sqn
656766	Sgt	OVENS John Roberts	28-10-42	150 Sqn
1126642	Sgt	OVEREND Jack	30-11-42	81 OTU
947971	Sgt	OVEREND William Ernest	3-09-42	15 Sqn
940865	Sgt	OVERTON DFM Douglas Leonard	9-06-42	97 Sqn
1031730	Sgt	OWEN Albert Edward	25-06-42	24 OTU
1253602	Sgt	OWEN Emrys	27-03-42	115 Sqn
1007568	Sgt	OWEN Groilyn Thomas	28-04-42	214 Sqn
1166741	F/S	OWEN MiD John	26-07-42	138 Sqn
1280353	Sgt	OWEN Norman Thomas	28-06-42	156 Sqn
994134	Sgt	OWEN Orthin Vaughan	12-08-42	57 Sqn
110644	P/O	OWEN Richard David	18-09-42	115 Sqn
47175	P/O	OWEN Richard Middleton	29-04-42	18 Sqn
528629	F/S	OWEN Thomas Idris Raglan	5-10-42	76 Sqn
1105210	Sgt	OWENS Hugh Ellis	4-05-42	76 Sqn
650947	Sgt	OXLEY Leslie Edward Caleb	26-07-42	226 Sqn
1127680	Sgt	OXLEY Richard	4-09-42	97 Sqn
45486	F/O	O'BRIEN Charles	2-06-42	16 OTU
1269969	Sgt	O'BRIEN John Fawell	1-08-42	405 Sqn
1312845	Sgt	O'BRIEN Michael	2-04-42	57 Sqn
650852	F/S	O'BRIEN Michael Thomas	20-01-42	142 Sqn
1117104	Sgt	O'BRIEN Patrick	21-08-42	15 OTU
547590	Sgt	O'CALLAGHAN Charles	2-10-42	218 Sqn
965660	Sgt	O'CONNELL Thomas Eric	5-10-42	102 Sqn
946944	Sgt	O'CONNELLEY Kenneth	14-04-42	102 Sqn
1378903	Sgt	O'CONNOR John Henry	14-01-42	22 OTU
1264157	Sgt	O'COY Terence Ernest Albert	17-04-42	10 OTU
1059607	Sgt	O'DAY Dennis Neill	11-06-42	83 Sqn
913527	Sgt	O'DONOGHUE Eugene Thomas John	2-12-42	12 OTU
1220416	Sgt	O'DWYER Francis Anthony [Eire]	21-12-42	7 Sqn
118202	P/O	O'GRADY James	4-02-42	21 Sqn
993457	F/S	O'HARA Laurence	9-06-42	83 Sqn
112290	P/O	O'HARA Leonard William [USA]	16-09-42	15 Sqn
798640	Sgt	O'KEEFE Ralph [Newfoundland]	29-06-42	14 OTU
48896	P/O	O'MEARA Patrick Edmund	29-06-42	57 Sqn
613758	Sgt	O'NEILL Charles	9-06-42	83 Sqn
119900	P/O	O'NEILL Robert Travers	17-06-42	17 OTU
1356185	Sgt	O'QUINN Arthur [Canada]	25-06-42	21 OTU
939114	Sgt	O'REILLY John Joseph	9-05-42	76 Sqn
984531	Sgt	O'ROURKE James	5-06-42	78 Sqn
1386634	Sgt	O'SHEA Patrick Francis	29-07-42	1651 CU
1330346	Sgt	O'SULLIVAN John Dennis	2-06-42	10 OTU
1403000	LAC	PACKARD Francis Frederick	31-10-42	88 Sqn
1041966	Sgt	PADDEN Gerald Thomas	17-12-42	75 Sqn
776139	Sgt	PADKIN Gordon Craig [Middle East]	1-08-42	25 OTU
41315	F/L	PAGE Harry Charles Shaw	31-01-42	61 Sqn
1376304	Sgt	PAGE Raymond Wyatt	28-03-42	7 Sqn
744324	F/S	PAGE Robert Gerald	24-08-42	44 Sqn
934237	Sgt	PAGE MiD Roderic Samuel	17-04-42	97 Sqn
1310464	Sgt	PAGE Walter Kenneth Drummond	23-11-42	44 Sqn
103051	F/O	PAGET Alfred Henry	27-08-42	142 Sqn
1261364	Sgt	PAIN Albert Ronald	9-06-42	109 Sqn
1253892	F/S	PAINE Peter John	26-03-42	57 Sqn
1600343	Sgt	PAINTING Herbert Philip	4-11-42	464 Sqn
1262810	Sgt	PAKENHAM-WALSH Henry Goodrich Le Barr	27-07-42	35 Sqn
1375473	Sgt	PALMER George Arthur	10-08-42	78 Sqn
47001	P/O	PALMER Henry Percival	6-05-42	18 Sqn
1155384	LAC	PALMER Horace Walter	17-06-42	83 Sqn
755739	F/S	PALMER John Frederick	4-11-42	464 Sqn
42020	F/L	PALMER John Harold Tearl	6-12-42	82 Sqn
1175892	Sgt	PALMER John Southey	2-04-42	57 Sqn
526215	Sgt	PALMER Samuel	30-03-42	35 Sqn
1212564	Sgt	PALMER Tristram Edward Leonard	3-07-42	214 Sqn
526543	F/S	PALMER Wilfred Thomas	5-10-42	35 Sqn
1105931	Sgt	PALMER William Dudley	15-05-42	408 Sqn
149097	P/O	PALMER-LETTINGTON DFM John William George	30-12-42	11 OTU
1377321	Sgt	PAMENTER George Arthur Francis	23-10-42	218 Sqn
1260384	Sgt	PANKHURST Charles Arthur	24-05-42	207 Sqn
84309	F/L	PARAMORE DFC Roger Edward Rawle	6-06-42	49 Sqn
622589	Sgt	PARISH John James	5-09-42	103 Sqn
1382096	Sgt	PARK Kenneth Hunton	3-12-42	27 OTU
909252	F/S	PARKER Albert Charles William	17-12-42	75 Sqn
1058722	Sgt	PARKER Colin Mellor	23-06-42	61 Sqn
68819	F/L	PARKER David Shirley	24-09-42	51 Sqn
1169228	Sgt	PARKER Eric Herbert	26-03-42	158 Sqn
36247	F/L	PARKER Graham Noel [New Zealand]	15-10-42	103 Sqn
985473	Sgt	PARKER James Monkman	12-03-42	77 Sqn
953678	Sgt	PARKER Robert	7-07-42	156 Sqn
655328	Sgt	PARKER Robert Peter Melton	19-05-42	218 Sqn
1172586	Sgt	PARKER Sidney Frank	10-04-42	76 Sqn
1330940	Sgt	PARKER Sydney Harold	12-10-42	50 Sqn
939160	Sgt	PARKER Thomas Henry	1-10-42	102 Sqn
915813	Sgt	PARKER William Fincham	3-08-42	51 Sqn
37982	S/L	PARKIN DFC Leslie Hugh William	27-02-42	77 Sqn
102961	F/L	PARKINS DFC Dennis Arthur	29-07-42	1651 CU
641949	F/S	PARKINSON James Douglas	28-08-42	57 Sqn
1254725	Sgt	PARNHAM John Frederick Massey	12-03-42	75 Sqn
1189810	Sgt	PARR Cyril George	16-10-42	115 Sqn
116479	P/O	PARR William Henry	16-05-42	16 OTU
1309980	Sgt	PARRIS Jack	6-06-42	149 Sqn
650499	Sgt	PARROTT Allan George	9-07-42	102 Sqn
1340641	Sgt	PARROTT John George James	28-07-42	156 Sqn
1379067	Sgt	PARRY Clwyd	9-03-42	101 Sqn
1381419	Sgt	PARRY David Ivan	26-06-42	10 OTU
1272284	Sgt	PARRY Percy Vinton	25-08-42	97 Sqn
1252836	Sgt	PARRY Ronald Robert	9-05-42	420 Sqn
1381589	Sgt	PARRY Thomas Wynford	9-10-42	5 Group
115326	P/O	PARRY Victor Henry	2-10-42	78 Sqn
111963	P/O	PARRY DFC Vivian Weston	5-09-42	150 Sqn
1067071	Sgt	PARRY William Charles	8-12-42	102 Sqn
111998	P/O	PARSLOW Kenneth Archibald	20-01-42	142 Sqn
1196149	Sgt	PARSONS Algernon	11-10-42	75 Sqn
110790	P/O	PARSONS Arthur Ernest	29-04-42	57 Sqn
88472	F/O	PARSONS John Robert Bruno	31-01-42	61 Sqn
1312836	Sgt	PARSONS Peter Richard	5-10-42	35 Sqn
962821	Sgt	PARSONS Robert Albert	30-07-42	61 Sqn
33462	S/L	PARSONS Robert James Sealer	28-09-42	115 Sqn
1198786	Sgt	PARTINGTON Rene Laughton [Argentina]	6-10-42	142 Sqn
1164030	F/S	PARTRIDGE Leslie James	2-06-42	61 Sqn
1308491	Sgt	PASCOE Tom	16-12-42	75 Sqn
1380051	Sgt	PASCOE William Allan	13-04-42	460 Sqn
1480175	F/S	PASSANT Fred Vincent	20-12-42	77 Sqn
106232	P/O	PASTERFIELD William Ernest Newton	25-04-42	226 Sqn

655399	Sgt	PATCH John	28-08-42	103 Sqn
1053543	Sgt	PATCHETT Edward Ernest	3-06-42	61 Sqn
656344	Sgt	PATE James Thomas	16-09-42	26 OTU
1177071	Sgt	PATEMAN Harry	20-09-42	161 Sqn
1378976	Sgt	PATERSON Andrew Picken	24-05-42	207 Sqn
36261	F/L	PATERSON Nathaniel [New Zealand]	6-05-42	115 Sqn
1002396	Sgt	PATERSON Ronald McLay	20-12-42	106 Sqn
37478	S/L	PATERSON DFC Victor Robertson	21-09-42	101 Sqn
1387395	Sgt	PATEY Ernest Albert	2-06-42	49 Sqn
1169975	F/S	PATON David Bruce	30-09-42	9 Sqn
106980	F/O	PATON DFM Norman James Alexander	6-12-42	226 Sqn
581409	W/O	PATTERSON Andrew Steel	31-07-42	27 OTU
1149385	Sgt	PATTERSON John	22-12-42	26 OTU
778001	Sgt	PATTISON Cecil Vivian [Rhodesia]	5-09-42	207 Sqn
1346524	Sgt	PATTON John	14-12-42	10 OTU
1378828	Sgt	PATTON Neville James	7-04-42	61 Sqn
996604	F/S	PAUL Harry [Canada]	9-09-42	20 OTU
1380822	Sgt	PAUL Jamie Kitchener Wendle	23-04-42	218 Sqn
84921	F/L	PAYNE DFC Anthony Bremner	31-05-42	12 Sqn
932935	Sgt	PAYNE Arthur Ernest	26-04-42	1443 Flt
1316406	Sgt	PAYNE Gerald Victor	28-08-42	15 Sqn
1375600	Sgt	PAYNE Harry Arthur	20-06-42	57 Sqn
984801	Sgt	PAYNE John Routledge	26-03-42	214 Sqn
747828	F/S	PAYNE Norman Frank	20-05-42	15 Sqn
1169097	Sgt	PAYNE Roland	19-09-42	106 Sqn
89609	F/O	PEACE David Brian	22-01-42	50 Sqn
45147	S/L	PEACE DFC Raymond Newport	20-12-42	76 Sqn
902440	Sgt	PEACEY Douglas William	9-03-42	9 Sqn
1286062	Sgt	PEACH Anthony John	31-03-42	35 Sqn
1087499	Sgt	PEACOCK William Spenseley	31-12-42	19 OTU
617057	Sgt	PEAKE Norman	8-06-42	149 Sqn
80067	P/O	PEALL Hurworth Anthony Paul [Rhodesia]	17-04-42	44 Sqn
1380700	Sgt	PEARCE Arthur George Edward	16-02-42	61 Sqn
1189938	F/S	PEARCE Donald Ivor	15-09-42	218 Sqn
111490	P/O	PEARCE Harold	19-07-42	408 Sqn
548246	Sgt	PEARL John Alister	12-08-42	156 Sqn
574729	Sgt	PEARMAN Frank Charles	26-06-42	83 Sqn
1067033	Sgt	PEARMAN Maurice Charles	21-12-42	57 Sqn
1109414	Sgt	PEARSON Denis	31-05-42	101 Sqn
1379640	Sgt	PEARSON Fred	11-01-42	40 Sqn
1152531	Sgt	PEARSON John Henry	25-03-42	50 Sqn
747858	W/O	PEARSON Reginald William	17-12-42	75 Sqn
568448	Sgt	PEARSON Wilfred Ernest	20-06-42	214 Sqn
1117168	Sgt	PEART John	12-08-42	78 Sqn
110304	F/L	PEBWORTH DFC Denis Arthur	24-08-42	149 Sqn
116952	P/O	PEEL Herbert Orlando	3-09-42	61 Sqn
115123	P/O	PEEL Jack Dempsey	24-07-42	214 Sqn
1053426	Sgt	PEEL Ronald	31-05-42	156 Sqn
132345	P/O	PEEL Stanley	1-10-42	405 Sqn
1376935	F/S	PELLOWE John Henry	7-11-42	83 Sqn
1264307	Sgt	PENDELPHO Charles Ronald	7-12-42	102 Sqn
994881	Sgt	PENLINGTON Edward Frederick	26-03-42	144 Sqn
1112514	Sgt	PENMAN Alan	27-04-42	7 Sqn
1309950	Sgt	PENMAN George	17-04-42	10 OTU
925051	Sgt	PENNY Cyril Walter	11-04-42	214 Sqn
1266840	Sgt	PENSTONE Norman Arthur	27-04-42	102 Sqn
565929	Sgt	PEPPER DFM Maurice Sidney	10-09-42	7 Sqn
787872	Sgt	PEPRNICEK Jan [Czechoslovakia]	11-04-42	311 Sqn
1334872	Sgt	PERCHARD Robert Charles [Channel Islands]	8-11-42	9 Sqn
111938	P/O	PERCIVAL Dennis	8-05-42	57 Sqn
1016944	Sgt	PERCIVAL Joseph Eric	28-07-42	107 Sqn
1312567	Sgt	PERCIVAL Robert George	20-12-42	21 OTU
1375503	Sgt	PERRETT Alwyn	31-08-42	21 OTU
1164775	Sgt	PERRETT Norman George Edmund	23-10-42	158 Sqn
1155037	Sgt	PERRIAM Ronald Charles	17-06-42	102 Sqn
1258979	F/S	PERRIN DFM Arthur John	7-11-42	207 Sqn
84646	F/L	PERRIN Walter Edwin [Australia]	12-02-42	455 Sqn
111943	F/O	PERRY Allan Ernest Kench	6-11-42	21 Sqn
1165304	Sgt	PERRY Charles Ronald Clive	25-03-42	50 Sqn
1252578	Sgt	PERRY Edward William	2-06-42	10 Sqn
1216130	Sgt	PERRY Harold Ernest	7-05-42	21 OTU
1261701	F/S	PERRY John James	15-11-42	150 Sqn
934086	Sgt	PERRY Lionel Frederick	14-07-42	150 Sqn
1174623	Sgt	PERRY Stanley	1-04-42	214 Sqn
1270404	Sgt	PETE Edmund John	25-10-42	75 Sqn
1281527	Sgt	PETERS Sydney Albert	21-01-42	50 Sqn
1375369	Sgt	PETERS Thomas Archie	28-01-42	114 Sqn
37207	W/C	PETERS-SMITH DFC Murray Vernon	27-07-42	57 Sqn
106152	P/O	PETHERBRIDGE Reginald Alfred	14-07-42	158 Sqn
1375988	Sgt	PETT Richard Lawrence	16-11-42	19 OTU
1375481	Sgt	PETTERSSON Philip Charles	14-01-42	50 Sqn
926764	Sgt	PETTICAN Reginald Stanley	1-10-42	10 Sqn
1183716	Sgt	PETTITT Frederick	3-09-42	21 OTU
108804	P/O	PETTY Alexander	29-01-42	17 OTU
1202557	Sgt	PEXMAN Kenneth Richard	31-05-42	9 Sqn
625456	Sgt	PHAROAH Kenneth William	10-12-42	57 Sqn
922248	Sgt	PHILLIPS Derek Howard	7-01-42	18 Sqn
1059982	Sgt	PHILLIPS Edward Walter	12-02-42	49 Sqn
112015	P/O	PHILLIPS Elias Alexander	8-06-42	149 Sqn
1335312	Sgt	PHILLIPS Eric Harold Cecil	30-09-42	149 Sqn
929901	Sgt	PHILLIPS Garfield James	28-08-42	35 Sqn
1380948	Sgt	PHILLIPS Gilbert Victor	16-04-42	149 Sqn
630457	Sgt	PHILLIPS Glyndwr	17-08-42	50 Sqn
655774	Sgt	PHILLIPS John Goodson	9-09-42	102 Sqn
1325179	Sgt	PHILLIPS Lloyd Lawson	6-02-42	142 Sqn
977631	Sgt	PHILLIPS Thomas James	13-04-42	115 Sqn
972384	F/S	PHILP BEM Charles Pearn	30-06-42	405 Sqn
133028	P/O	PHILP BEM John	8-12-42	149 Sqn
105196	P/O	PHILP John Adams	4-06-42	76 Sqn
137598	P/O	PHIPP Jack	20-12-42	83 Sqn
913952	Sgt	PHIPPEN William John	30-06-42	57 Sqn
1194506	Sgt	PICK Ben Michael	23-12-42	138 Sqn
574255	Sgt	PICKEN Valentine	15-09-42	218 Sqn
1166528	Sgt	PICKERING Francis Rex	31-10-42	88 Sqn
1529839	Sgt	PICKERING Maurice Alan	1-10-42	10 Sqn
987688	Cpl	PICKERSGILL Albert Edward	18-08-42	78 Sqn
1356057	Sgt	PICKERSGILL David Michael	6-02-42	455 Sqn
45434	P/O	PICKETT Astley Cleveland	18-01-42	142 Sqn
109972	P/O	PICKLES William Turner	18-12-42	1474 Flt
119352	P/O	PICKUP William Ewart	25-08-42	7 Sqn
1153786	Sgt	PICKWORTH Godfrey William	17-08-42	214 Sqn
1429229	Sgt	PIDDOCK Thomas Leonard Hill	15-10-42	106 Sqn
755786	W/O	PIERPOINT Morris Leslie	16-09-42	27 OTU
1237248	Sgt	PIERPOINT Robert	13-10-42	83 Sqn
1318724	Sgt	PIERSON Frederick George Edward	28-08-42	12 Sqn
1213919	Sgt	PIERSON Robert Thomas	30-06-42	14 OTU
120581	F/O	PIKE Donald Edward	3-12-42	102 Sqn
67717	F/O	PILKINGTON Charles Leslie	11-03-42	149 Sqn
65540	F/L	PILLING DFC Hector Garrick [New Zealand]	20-05-42	7 Sqn
100555	F/L	PINION Lawrence Jason	29-04-42	156 Sqn
116483	P/O	PINK Reginald Ernest Sidney	31-07-42	9 Sqn
906144	F/S	PINK Warnford Francis Victor	21-03-42	115 Sqn
934811	Sgt	PINKNEY John Thomas	7-12-42	102 Sqn
1319737	Sgt	PIPER Ernest Raymond Donald 'Roy'	25-11-42	207 Sqn
1153785	F/S	PITCHFORD Peter John	7-10-42	106 Sqn
650812	Sgt	PITCHFORTH Henry Lewis	15-10-42	103 Sqn
905958	F/S	PITHERS Ronald Ernest	2-07-42	218 Sqn
1291394	Sgt	PITTENDRIGH Wilfred Ernest	11-09-42	15 Sqn
1129411	Sgt	PLACE Edward	16-07-42	158 Sqn
1083915	Sgt	PLANT John Turner	4-06-42	115 Sqn
621106	Sgt	PLATT James Wilfrid	29-08-42	103 Sqn
939816	Sgt	PLATT Richard Arthur	1-04-42	214 Sqn

Service No	Rank	Name	Date	Unit
958563	F/S	PLATTEN Denis John	9-06-42	97 Sqn
1165993	Sgt	PLAYER Geoffrey Albert	19-04-42	420 Sqn
744631	Sgt	PLEASS Henry Norman	23-09-42	218 Sqn
787392	Sgt	PLECITY Miroslav [Czechoslovakia]	21-01-42	311 Sqn
1243415	Sgt	PLIMMER Cyril Geoffrey	13-11-42	97 Sqn
622703	Sgt	PLOWRIGHT Robert Stewart Chrichton	14-09-42	21 OTU
1376309	Sgt	PLUME Stanley James	24-07-42	25 OTU
1310474	Sgt	POCOCK Henry Arthur Douglas	5-10-42	218 Sqn
787589	Sgt	PODIVINSKY Adolf [Czechoslovakia]	3-03-42	311 Sqn
1066639	Sgt	PODMORE Norman	21-08-42	218 Sqn
1014112	Sgt	POGREL Arthur	19-08-42	21 OTU
787875	Sgt	POLITZER Josef [Czechoslovakia]	11-04-42	311 Sqn
787688	Sgt	POLITZER Maxmilian [Czechoslovakia]	10-03-42	138 Sqn
997213	F/S	POLLITT David Charles	12-02-42	49 Sqn
1006357	Sgt	POLLITT Harry	28-10-42	150 Sqn
976322	Sgt	POLLOCK John Howie	6-06-42	49 Sqn
1152526	Sgt	POMEROY Frederick Bertram	5-05-42	149 Sqn
1468057	Sgt	PONT Henry Clifford	21-12-42	44 Sqn
563370	Sgt	PONTING Roland George	29-10-42	15 Sqn
903242	F/S	POOK Stanley William	8-04-42	15 OTU
1268362	Sgt	POOLE Frederick Mac-coy	11-10-42	17 OTU
1281236	Sgt	POOLE Thomas Frederick Peter	19-02-42	107 Sqn
68736	F/L	POOLS Michael Reginald Mark	28-04-42	35 Sqn
1112416	Sgt	POPE Arthur	27-04-42	149 Sqn
1578663	Sgt	POPE Cyril John	3-12-42	102 Sqn
633257	F/S	POPPLE Douglas James	24-07-42	57 Sqn
655703	Sgt	PORT Edwin Thomas	16-10-42	115 Sqn
1109090	Sgt	PORTEOUS James Wallace	23-06-42	103 Sqn
917597	Sgt	PORTER Dennis Gerard	8-04-42	83 Sqn
1368484	Sgt	PORTER James	6-10-42	103 Sqn
82424	F/L	PORTER Robert King	5-07-42	207 Sqn
924331	Sgt	PORTER Roderick Merrington	26-03-42	88 Sqn
1078313	Sgt	POSNER Sydney	11-10-42	75 Sqn
628018	F/S	POTTER Dennis Kilvington	24-10-42	207 Sqn
1148933	Sgt	POTTER Duncan	30-11-42	28 OTU
1288649	Sgt	POTTER Jack	25-04-42	420 Sqn
1446712	AC2	POTTER Royal	27-04-42	150 Sqn
1109273	Sgt	POTTS Alan	5-09-42	76 Sqn
911454	F/S	POTTS Arthur Frederick	10-09-42	149 Sqn
1057542	Sgt	POTTS Arthur Owen	13-08-42	1484 Flt
1005766	Sgt	POTTS Frederick Wilberforce	28-04-42	150 Sqn
1054128	Sgt	POTTS John	28-04-42	76 Sqn
622342	LAC	POTTS John Heywood	22-02-42	19 OTU
1250821	F/S	POULSON Peter Ernest	20-12-42	103 Sqn
1214222	Sgt	POULTON Norman Frank	25-06-42	21 OTU
1333187	Sgt	POWELL Allan Sidney Herbert	3-10-42	15 OTU
533840	Sgt	POWELL Douglas Norman	20-04-42	83 Sqn
922976	Sgt	POWELL Geoffrey Noel Edward	31-03-42	35 Sqn
44355	S/L	POWELL DFM Gordon Allen	29-07-42	218 Sqn
1272598	Sgt	POWELL John Lawrence	20-07-42	20 OTU
1359999	Sgt	POWELL Leonard George	17-12-42	44 Sqn
1177614	Sgt	POWELL Patrick David	2-06-42	156 Sqn
45440	F/O	POWELL Ralph Hubert	2-04-42	150 Sqn
936328	Sgt	POWELL Walter [Canada]	16-02-42	77 Sqn
778440	Sgt	POWER Thomas Henry [Rhodesia]	16-04-42	106 Sqn
1043753	AC2	POWNALL Wilfred	28-02-42	75 Sqn
1375793	Sgt	POXON Douglas Guy Frank	12-02-42	49 Sqn
1069915	Sgt	PRATLEY Arthur James	12-03-42	77 Sqn
1160114	Sgt	PRATT Edwin Victor	10-04-42	12 Sqn
635526	Sgt	PRATT George Charles	26-06-42	102 Sqn
1254955	Sgt	PRATT Ian Frank	4-06-42	61 Sqn
1386122	Sgt	PRECEY William	22-12-42	26 OTU
569914	Sgt	PRECIOUS Sydney Walstead	3-06-42	7 Sqn
1168169	Sgt	PRESCOTT Maurice	8-05-42	57 Sqn
125629	P/O	PREST Cyril George	30-12-42	1443 Flt
633185	Sgt	PRESTON Jack	13-08-42	207 Sqn
1069569	Sgt	PRESTON Kenneth Stoddart	6-06-42	150 Sqn
540385	F/S	PRESTON Ronald John	29-07-42	218 Sqn
1256351	Sgt	PRESTON Shaun Craving	9-05-42	158 Sqn
778492	Sgt	PRICE Evan Moffat [South Africa]	26-03-42	83 Sqn
1280742	Sgt	PRICE Glyn	17-12-42	218 Sqn
1052836	Sgt	PRICE Harold	1-08-42	408 Sqn
70555	W/C	PRICE DFC Herbert Laurence	29-07-42	156 Sqn
1071870	Sgt	PRICE Herbert Leslie	26-03-42	142 Sqn
930432	Sgt	PRICE John Lewis Stanley	27-02-42	77 Sqn
1266398	Sgt	PRICE Peter Bertram Penton	10-09-42	7 Sqn
612719	LAC	PRICE Richard Dennis	3-06-42	14 OTU
1427176	Sgt	PRICE Stanley Victor	23-10-42	218 Sqn
960374	Sgt	PRIEST Alfred Frederick	2-09-42	97 Sqn
88037	F/L	PRIEST Thomas Findlay	10-01-42	408 Sqn
1064083	Sgt	PRIESTLEY Arthur	29-08-42	35 Sqn
916519	Sgt	PRIESTLEY John	14-01-42	40 Sqn
536221	Sgt	PRIME Norman Allan	11-09-42	15 Sqn
745378	W/O	PRIMROSE William Leonard	31-10-42	30 OTU
1166132	Sgt	PRINCE DFM Arthur	10-06-42	107 Sqn
1359922	Sgt	PRINGLE Joseph	8-02-42	21 OTU
591353	Sgt	PRIOR Robert Charles	1-10-42	10 Sqn
100606	F/O	PRITCHARD Donald Carr	28-08-42	150 Sqn
1377413	Sgt	PRITCHARD Jack	4-07-42	61 Sqn
642647	F/S	PROBERT Geoffrey Ernest	6-02-42	142 Sqn
1306729	Sgt	PROCTER Robert Dudley	9-06-42	150 Sqn
123455	P/O	PROCTOR Thurlow	21-10-42	21 OTU
950598	Sgt	PROSSER Richard Lionel	20-05-42	35 Sqn
44779	S/L	PROTHEROE Wilfred Morgan	13-04-42	158 Sqn
1382989	Sgt	PRYCE Herbert Howard Lloyd	14-09-42	12 Sqn
39564	S/L	PRYDE DFC David Douglas [Canada]	9-06-42	77 Sqn
624422	Sgt	PRYKE Arthur William	27-10-42	1657 HCU
1376031	Sgt	PUGH Thomas Noel	16-01-42	419 Sqn
920723	Sgt	PULLEN John Standeford [Australia]	12-02-42	114 Sqn
522426	F/S	PULLING Leonard Robert	28-07-42	7 Sqn
78688	F/O	PULTON James Ansford	21-04-42	138 Sqn
625225	Sgt	PYE James Marsden	19-09-42	15 Sqn
1181813	AC2	PYLE Robert Alfred Thomas	16-10-42	Wyton
1252457	Sgt	QUILTER John David	30-09-42	51 Sqn
1256373	Sgt	QUIN Joseph Guy	29-06-42	75 Sqn
924568	Sgt	QUINCEY Gilbert Lewis	6-04-42	50 Sqn
1095594	Sgt	QUINN Arthur	25-10-42	75 Sqn
1114417	Sgt	QUINN Bernard Francis	1-08-42	107 Sqn
112292	P/O	QUINN George Handy	3-09-42	15 Sqn
646803	Sgt	QUINN Brian	28-08-42	97 Sqn
553387	Sgt	QUINTRELL Harold Denzil	25-08-42	83 Sqn
934271	Sgt	RACINE Cedric	13-08-42	207 Sqn
1193558	Sgt	RACKSTRAW Gordon Frederick George	16-02-42	61 Sqn
122312	P/O	RADCLIFFE Hubert Alan	31-05-42	158 Sqn
123953	P/O	RAFFAN William Ferries	29-10-42	10 OTU
931128	Sgt	RAGAN Arthur Wilton	18-05-42	115 Sqn
1332125	Sgt	RAGGETT Cyril Edward	8-12-42	21 OTU
581030	W/O	RAILTON Kenneth	2-06-42	11 OTU
648020	Sgt	RAINE James Metcalfe	4-07-42	61 Sqn
1262263	Sgt	RAINES Reginald Stanley	29-01-42	13 OTU
42436	S/L	RAINFORD DFC* John Rawsthorn	22-02-42	83 Sqn
787876	Sgt	RAISKUP Frantisek [Czechoslovakia]	12-03-42	311 Sqn
1151893	Sgt	RAISWELL Kenneth John	13-04-42	115 Sqn
100580	P/O	RALSTON Ian	13-08-42	77 Sqn
108050	P/O	RAMPTON Albert John	9-03-42	15 Sqn
1365084	Sgt	RAMSAY John McFadyen	1-10-42	61 Sqn
1107764	Sgt	RAMSAY John	28-08-42	101 Sqn
1115867	Sgt	RAMSBOTTOM Norman	2-04-42	214 Sqn
1130777	Sgt	RAMSDEN Henry Thomas	24-09-42	9 Sqn
944122	Sgt	RAMSEY John Cook	31-05-42	49 Sqn
1182222	Sgt	RANDALL Basil Lyne	2-04-42	57 Sqn
116536	F/O	RANDALL Frank Kinder	24-10-42	149 Sqn
1170645	Sgt	RANDALL Graham Donald	16-04-42	156 Sqn
1334358	Sgt	RANDOLPH Charles Gordon	22-12-42	26 OTU

125

ID	Rank	Name	Date	Sqn
116488	P/O	RANSON Roger Mortlock	5-06-42	44 Sqn
617810	Sgt	RAPHAEL Donald Lindsay	24-08-42	149 Sqn
950595	Sgt	RARITY Donald Edgar	28-04-42	35 Sqn
636747	Sgt	RAULT Alfred Charles	17-09-42	149 Sqn
1199165	Sgt	RAVEN Walter Ernest	9-11-42	7 Sqn
814238	F/S	RAWCLIFFE Peter Welburn	1-08-42	156 Sqn
1237989	Sgt	RAWCLIFFE Richard	17-12-42	10 OTU
1306695	Sgt	RAWLINGS Eric Frank	22-02-42	150 Sqn
116058	F/O	RAWLINGS DFC Robert	29-10-42	115 Sqn
1234574	Sgt	RAWLINS Michael Howard	12-10-42	50 Sqn
572735	Sgt	RAWSON George Edward	20-11-42	76 Sqn
1288939	Sgt	RAY Cecil Robert	20-12-42	76 Sqn
1376053	Sgt	RAY Harold Reginald	9-03-42	83 Sqn
517749	F/S	RAY Norman Eric	1-08-42	10 OTU
47777	P/O	RAY Ronald Arthur	1-03-42	16 OTU
1258093	F/S	RAYMENT Thomas Watkins [Australia]	16-06-42	7 Sqn
43710	S/L	RAYMOND DFC Cuthbert [New Zealand]	23-09-42	218 Sqn
932197	Sgt	RAYMOND Donald Ernest	27-07-42	101 Sqn
934062	Sgt	RAYNES Dennis John	20-05-42	10 Sqn
1179230	Sgt	READ Ambrose Phillip	25-06-42	12 OTU
33076	W/C	READ Montagu Francis Baldwin [Canada]	1-10-42	218 Sqn
117644	F/O	REDBOURN Derrick Redvers	6-12-42	107 Sqn
1177700	Sgt	REDDISH Kenneth Harry	10-09-42	142 Sqn
940304	Sgt	REDHEAD George	1-08-42	16 OTU
1056192	Sgt	REDHEAD John Brewick	19-10-42	75 Sqn
1169796	Sgt	REDLER Douglas Arthur	20-07-42	158 Sqn
1011028	Sgt	REDSHAW James Victor	30-09-42	9 Sqn
1018355	Sgt	REES Alwyne Edward	28-08-42	142 Sqn
934390	Sgt	REES Arthur Edwin	2-04-42	214 Sqn
1251403	Sgt	REES Glyn	29-01-42	88 Sqn
70567	F/L	REES Patrick Elmore	20-05-42	103 Sqn
978350	Sgt	REES William Leslie Schlater	9-07-42	106 Sqn
1378098	Sgt	REEVE Frank Alfred	1-10-42	17 OTU
906270	W/O	REID Alan Johnstone	6-12-42	107 Sqn
1056078	F/S	REID Alexander John	9-05-42	158 Sqn
778673	Sgt	REID George Thompson [Rhodesia]	2-06-42	25 OTU
590717	F/S	REID Gordon Wemyss	14-01-42	5 Group
1271320	Sgt	REID John Girvan	14-07-42	12 Sqn
981682	Sgt	REID Thomas Allen	16-08-42	106 Sqn
702772	Sgt	REILLY John Mason	18-12-42	50 Sqn
121797	F/O	REILLY William Francis [USA]	4-12-42	14 OTU
1314399	Sgt	REINELT Norman Clapham	28-10-42	10 OTU
920320	F/S	RELPH Gordon Turnbull	27-08-42	107 Sqn
517630	Sgt	RENDALL William Stuart	15-10-42	97 Sqn
1305046	LAC	RENDELL Robert Frank	29-03-42	109 Sqn
918821	Sgt	RENDTORFF Donald Esmond Alan	26-03-42	7 Sqn
87414	F/L	RENNIE MC Basil John Allan [South Africa]	19-10-42	14 OTU
1057117	Sgt	RENNIE John Robertson	20-07-42	158 Sqn
86338	F/O	RENVOIZE Douglas James	8-04-42	83 Sqn
1552246	Sgt	RENWICK Andrew Scott	11-09-42	11 OTU
1380776	Sgt	REVELL Kenneth Sampson	22-07-42	12 Sqn
1186145	Sgt	REVITT Norman Arthur	15-10-42	10 OTU
911394	Sgt	REYNOLDS Edgar Cecil	12-03-42	77 Sqn
110136	P/O	REYNOLDS Harry Churchill	21-08-42	218 Sqn
1376649	Sgt	REYNOLDS John Gilbert	11-05-42	115 Sqn
1313246	Sgt	REYNOLDS Leonard Norman	26-06-42	10 OTU
658695	Sgt	REYNOLDS Michael	21-12-42	106 Sqn
932196	Sgt	REYNOLDS Peter Laurence	12-02-42	110 Sqn
1265583	Sgt	REYNOLDS Roy Frederick	14-09-42	214 Sqn
1190187	Sgt	REYNOLDS Walter Frank	29-04-42	115 Sqn
60795	F/L	RHODEN DFC Harold	24-10-42	78 Sqn
938642	Sgt	RHODES George Thomas	17-04-42	44 Sqn
1331658	Sgt	RHODES George William	6-10-42	75 Sqn
1380898	Sgt	RHYS William Leyson	31-10-42	1655 MCU
549992	Cpl	RICE John	7-09-42	10 Sqn
1305069	Sgt	RICE Joseph Albert	30-07-42	61 Sqn
1289891	Sgt	RICH Royston Dudlay	21-08-42	218 Sqn
755624	F/S	RICHARD George	8-05-42	57 Sqn
1162948	Sgt	RICHARDS Albert George	2-04-42	214 Sqn
121735	P/O	RICHARDS Arthur Gwyn	6-10-42	103 Sqn
66545	P/O	RICHARDS Brian Alfred Carter	30-06-42	7 Sqn
1055928	Sgt	RICHARDS Donald Arthur	21-01-42	51 Sqn
1162205	Sgt	RICHARDS Eric John	15-01-42	51 Sqn
1386264	Sgt	RICHARDS John Alan	19-09-42	15 Sqn
1313845	F/S	RICHARDS John Edward [USA]	29-08-42	61 Sqn
575840	Sgt	RICHARDS Reginald George Arthur	30-03-42	10 Sqn
1113440	Sgt	RICHARDS Ronald Geoffrey	8-04-42	57 Sqn
1261271	Sgt	RICHARDSON Arthur Edward	24-08-42	218 Sqn
521595	Sgt	RICHARDSON John	7-11-42	83 Sqn
751194	F/S	RICHARDSON John George	26-07-42	97 Sqn
918303	Sgt	RICHARDSON Lawrence Desmond	25-06-42	76 Sqn
568278	Sgt	RICHARDSON Peter	9-11-42	102 Sqn
1355073	Sgt	RICHARDSON Stanley George	25-04-42	107 Sqn
1202006	Sgt	RICHES Charles	6-12-42	115 Sqn
1066223	Sgt	RICHINGS Thomas Montague	6-12-42	487 Sqn
749388	F/S	RICHMOND William Burns	25-04-42	9 Sqn
574734	Sgt	RICKARD Godfrey Ernest	9-11-42	7 Sqn
133213	P/O	RICKARD Joseph Matthews	24-08-42	44 Sqn
1306083	Sgt	RIDDELL Michael Hardwick	27-08-42	15 OTU
979103	Sgt	RIDDELL Thomas Rodie	22-02-42	83 Sqn
1323687	Sgt	RIDDLE Milton Victor	9-11-42	102 Sqn
960489	Sgt	RIDER Arthur Henry	17-12-42	75 Sqn
995658	Sgt	RIDING Kenneth	29-01-42	13 OTU
121797	F/O	RIELLY William Francis [USA]	4-12-42	14 OTU
1271309	Sgt	RIETER Willem Joseph Gerard Paul [Holland]	23-04-42	218 Sqn
1386921	Sgt	RIGGS Albert Victor [Eire]	24-09-42	9 Sqn
82527	F/L	RIHA Ladislav [Czechoslovakia]	3-03-42	311 Sqn
1350151	Sgt	RILEY Dennis Robert	28-11-42	150 Sqn
1044347	AC2	RILEY Eric Arthur	9-01-42	15 OTU
995062	Sgt	RILEY John Bernard	19-01-42	20 OTU
658299	Sgt	RILEY William Ernest	10-12-42	20 OTU
1254402	Sgt	RILEY-HAWKINS Cyril John	13-04-42	9 Sqn
1068981	F/S	RIMMER John	21-09-42	101 Sqn
1394994	Sgt	RIMSCHA Walter Maurice	10-12-42	9 Sqn
1365387	Sgt	RITCHIE John Fisher Smith	16-09-42	12 OTU
817140	F/S	RITCHIE Robert Hendry	3-07-42	214 Sqn
1053550	F/S	RITCHIE Robert Leslie Sinclair	18-08-42	12 Sqn
778317	Sgt	RIX Peter [Rhodesia]	1-08-42	44 Sqn
818034	Sgt	RIXON William Percy	25-06-42	24 OTU
1331750	Sgt	ROAKE Herbert Charles	17-09-42	21 OTU
934278	Sgt	ROAN Peter Harding	16-02-42	77 Sqn
931136	Sgt	ROBBINS John James Henry	4-01-42	82 Sqn
1104522	Sgt	ROBERTS Albert	25-11-42	207 Sqn
1006798	Sgt	ROBERTS Arthur Ernest	7-11-42	156 Sqn
1375123	F/S	ROBERTS Brian Williams	20-08-42	218 Sqn
1379247	Sgt	ROBERTS Caradoc	20-05-42	12 Sqn
85141	F/L	ROBERTS Egerton James Ashurst	12-07-42	19 OTU
533593	Sgt	ROBERTS Frederick	10-09-42	149 Sqn
1381479	Sgt	ROBERTS George Christopher	31-05-42	103 Sqn
1336016	Sgt	ROBERTS Herbert Arthur	14-09-42	115 Sqn
1064638	Sgt	ROBERTS Ioan Henri	2-04-42	101 Sqn
977369	AC2	ROBERTS John	14-03-42	Swanton Morley
525683	Sgt	ROBERTS John Morton	16-02-42	82 Sqn
811009	Sgt	ROBERTS John Robert	16-09-42	106 Sqn
539749	AC1	ROBERTS Joseph	28-11-42	138 Sqn
1002346	Sgt	ROBERTS Leonard William	30-09-42	23 OTU
631867	F/S	ROBERTS Matthew Cameron	26-03-42	83 Sqn
1053676	Sgt	ROBERTS Robert Cecil	2-04-42	57 Sqn
932145	Sgt	ROBERTS Sidney Arthur	9-07-42	106 Sqn
924583	F/S	ROBERTS Sydney Douglas Gowshall	24-10-42	207 Sqn

Service No.	Rank	Name	Date	Unit
1176864	Sgt	ROBERTS William Arthur	26-03-42	61 Sqn
1113937	Sgt	ROBERTSON Alastair Charles	9-06-42	12 Sqn
1006965	Sgt	ROBERTSON Alexander William	14-04-42	419 Sqn
657056	Sgt	ROBERTSON Alexander Winton	22-11-42	115 Sqn
137579	P/O	ROBERTSON Bertram Samuel	15-10-42	97 Sqn
42264	S/L	ROBERTSON DFC Francis Harold [Rhodesia]	27-07-42	61 Sqn
129249	P/O	ROBERTSON Geoffrey Ernest	21-08-42	149 Sqn
1109416	Sgt	ROBERTSON George Crawford	21-02-42	16 OTU
1023142	Sgt	ROBERTSON John Beaton	21-08-42	19 OTU
652245	F/S	ROBERTSON Robert	14-09-42	1654 CU
1006888	Sgt	ROBERTSON Robert	16-04-42	106 Sqn
81415	F/O	ROBERTSON Weston James	26-03-42	226 Sqn
1059471	Sgt	ROBERTSON William Burns	10-01-42	49 Sqn
1284692	Sgt	ROBINS George Thomas Abel	12-06-42	114 Sqn
1333376	Sgt	ROBINSON Allan William Albert	10-12-42	9 Sqn
116211	F/O	ROBINSON Bryan Glendenen	5-10-42	76 Sqn
1117295	Sgt	ROBINSON David Barr	16-06-42	1651 CU
1018128	Sgt	ROBINSON Frederick James	1-10-42	102 Sqn
1169566	Sgt	ROBINSON George Marsh	28-01-42	214 Sqn
1057338	Sgt	ROBINSON Jack Machin	1-10-42	61 Sqn
119240	P/O	ROBINSON John Vernon	24-07-42	25 OTU
567796	Sgt	ROBINSON John Victor	20-08-42	15 Sqn
1128848	Sgt	ROBINSON Leslie	14-07-42	97 Sqn
108240	P/O	ROBINSON Patrick John Noble	25-06-42	102 Sqn
36274	S/L	ROBINSON DFC Peter Bettley [New Zealand]	10-09-42	158 Sqn
110612	P/O	ROBINSON DFC Ronald James	2-06-42	16 OTU
1380926	Sgt	ROBINSON Thomas Harry George	28-08-42	12 Sqn
568717	Sgt	ROBINSON Thomas Kenneth	28-04-42	102 Sqn
1065232	Sgt	ROBINSON Thomas Vaughan	3-09-42	19 OTU
66029	P/O	ROBLIN Howard Phillips	25-03-42	50 Sqn
123276	P/O	ROBSON Arnold	8-09-42	76 Sqn
996823	Sgt	ROBSON Arthur	11-02-42	10 OTU
562271	W/O	ROBSON DFM George	2-06-42	106 Sqn
1002130	Sgt	ROBSON George Allen	3-12-42	102 Sqn
68798	F/L	ROBSON James Alexander	26-02-42	405 Sqn
1218567	Sgt	ROBSON Peter Carlyle	29-07-42	1651 CU
954712	Sgt	ROBSON Robert	17-08-42	207 Sqn
1168914	F/S	ROCHFORD DFM Patrick George [France]	6-06-42	10 Sqn
649532	F/S	ROCK William George	26-07-42	138 Sqn
1160674	Sgt	ROCKS John George Smith	17-06-42	102 Sqn
1378871	Sgt	RODDAM Arthur	16-08-42	207 Sqn
927348	Sgt	RODERICK Keith	6-06-42	149 Sqn
1092742	AC1	RODHAM Robert Hunter Fraser	18-11-42	115 Sqn
956819	Sgt	RODWELL Ronald Leslie	7-08-42	7 Sqn
943217	F/S	ROE Frank	28-06-42	61 Sqn
1326327	Sgt	ROE Lawrence Joseph	6-01-42	57 Sqn
547371	Sgt	ROFF Leonard Arthur	17-12-42	75 Sqn
964849	Sgt	ROGERS Allen Charles Elliott	10-02-42	11 OTU
1386389	Sgt	ROGERS Brian Larcum	15-10-42	10 OTU
1170921	Sgt	ROGERS Charles Thomas	30-11-42	75 Sqn
118628	P/O	ROGERS Douglas	28-07-42	88 Sqn
49585	P/O	ROGERS Twice MiD Francis	3-09-42	218 Sqn
1365260	Sgt	ROGERS John Andrew	9-03-42	9 Sqn
614388	Sgt	ROGERS Joseph	9-05-42	44 Sqn
1166334	Sgt	ROGERS Kenneth George	25-06-42	218 Sqn
778781	Sgt	ROGERS Neville John [Rhodesia]	20-06-42	49 Sqn
122012	P/O	ROGERS Walter	23-10-42	218 Sqn
972624	Sgt	ROGERS William Frederick Douglas	7-12-42	149 Sqn
520277	Sgt	ROGERS William Henry	19-07-42	158 Sqn
1313869	Sgt	ROGERSON Michael Bruce	31-05-42	103 Sqn
1382426	Sgt	ROGERSON William Valentine	16-04-42	106 Sqn
982544	F/S	ROLESTON Frederick Livingston	2-10-42	218 Sqn
1311945	Sgt	ROLLINSON Irvine John	26-04-42	115 Sqn
39150	S/L	ROMANOFF Boris	10-03-42	138 Sqn
1310977	F/S	ROMIG Richard Leslie	20-12-42	83 Sqn
638340	Sgt	RONALDSON Sidney Bryan [Eire]	3-09-42	150 Sqn
1325076	Sgt	RONSON Ewart Gladstone	3-06-42	408 Sqn
1130712	Sgt	ROOKE Aubrey Francis	3-09-42	19 OTU
934159	Sgt	ROOKE Brian Edwin	11-06-42	25 OTU
1016994	Sgt	ROONEY Albert	29-07-42	1651 CU
1359687	Sgt	ROONEY James	29-03-42	83 Sqn
1311388	Sgt	ROONEY John	26-06-42	23 OTU
999574	F/S	ROONEY Thomas	28-08-42	142 Sqn
646652	Cpl	ROPER Bobbie Clarence	23-04-42	1515 Flt
1293105	Sgt	ROPER Geoffrey Charles	6-10-42	19 OTU
991771	F/S	ROPER Thomas	2-04-42	57 Sqn
530984	F/S	ROSE David	20-06-42	15 Sqn
954204	Sgt	ROSE Eric	13-03-42	83 Sqn
122095	P/O	ROSE Herbert Percy	3-06-42	57 Sqn
778285	F/S	ROSE DFM William James [Rhodesia]	7-11-42	207 Sqn
550591	W/O	ROSEKILLY Laurence	2-09-42	115 Sqn
109711	P/O	ROSENBERG Stanley	25-08-42	106 Sqn
125879	P/O	ROSS Finlay Farquharson	6-09-42	20 OTU
1310083	Sgt	ROSS Hamish	22-07-42	57 Sqn
90393	F/L	ROSS Henry Noel	14-04-42	102 Sqn
1068371	Sgt	ROSS John William Ernest	29-07-42	12 Sqn
1021381	Sgt	ROSS Thomas Stanley	3-07-42	18 Sqn
902896	Sgt	ROSS-HOFF Stanley Jack	2-06-42	83 Sqn
1058195	Sgt	ROTHERY Percy Vernon Edwin	12-02-42	420 Sqn
787878	Sgt	ROUS Stanislav [Czechoslovakia]	21-01-42	311 Sqn
1026535	F/S	ROUSSEAU Henry Edwin	17-12-42	75 Sqn
929946	Sgt	ROUTLEDGE Frank	11-07-42	207 Sqn
1184110	Sgt	ROW Findon Douglas Newton	10-04-42	12 Sqn
1111475	Sgt	ROWAN Thomas Edward	4-06-42	115 Sqn
1027453	Sgt	ROWBOTTOM Miles	28-08-42	44 Sqn
109942	P/O	ROWE Douglas William	18-08-42	12 Sqn
648115	F/S	ROWE Edwin John	21-09-42	101 Sqn
1176862	F/S	ROWE Herbert Reginald	1-10-42	44 Sqn
61306	F/O	ROWE John Laurence	9-06-42	83 Sqn
759221	F/S	ROWE Ronald Geoffrey	6-11-42	21 Sqn
116026	P/O	ROWE Rowland Richard Henry	2-06-42	10 OTU
1061453	Sgt	ROWELL Robert	7-02-42	144 Sqn
646781	F/S	ROWLAND Arthur	24-07-42	207 Sqn
819083	Sgt	ROWLAND Sidney Bertram	28-06-42	405 Sqn
1381269	Sgt	ROWLES Dan	28-08-42	101 Sqn
68759	P/O	ROWLEY James	6-02-42	21 Sqn
1264833	Sgt	ROWLING James William	11-09-42	26 OTU
569972	Sgt	ROWLINSON Cedric Reginald	2-06-42	102 Sqn
119475	P/O	ROWLINSON Leonard	17-06-42	24 OTU
798598	Sgt	ROWSELL Arthur Douglas [Newfoundland]	17-12-42	115 Sqn
798574	Sgt	ROWSELL Harry [Newfoundland]	12-02-42	419 Sqn
632784	Sgt	ROY Peter	14-07-42	158 Sqn
967125	Sgt	ROY Robert James	11-09-42	78 Sqn
82951	F/L	ROYAL Jack Douglas	18-05-42	20 OTU
79535	S/L	ROYLE DFC Norman Stanley	16-03-42	14 OTU
138677	P/O	ROZPRYM Miroslav [Czechoslovakia]	10-12-42	138 Sqn
971942	Sgt	RUDD Arthur Reginald	28-10-42	150 Sqn
1379252	Sgt	RUDDOCK John	29-01-42	13 OTU
1100638	Sgt	RUDGE Ernest Arnold	26-07-42	83 Sqn
938766	Sgt	RUDSTON Gerald Percival	24-07-42	35 Sqn
137209	P/O	RUMBOLL John Kitchener Plummer	21-12-42	7 Sqn
1319652	Sgt	RUMSEY Arthur Bernard Putnam	24-12-42	10 OTU
112446	P/O	RUNAGALL DFC Ronald Percy	9-03-42	115 Sqn
778696	Sgt	RUNDLE Cecil Richard [Rhodesia]	8-09-42	76 Sqn
118622	P/O	RUNNACLES Ernest Ronald Maurice [Argentina]	11-09-42	7 Sqn
1309498	Sgt	RUNNICLES Jack Ralph	17-09-42	76 Sqn
1053538	Sgt	RUSHTON Alan	7-05-42	78 Sqn
1432963	Sgt	RUSHTON Dennis John	11-09-42	218 Sqn
1164371	F/S	RUSHTON William Thomas	17-06-42	24 OTU
1379694	Sgt	RUSHWORTH Stanley	18-11-42	21 OTU
1002563	Sgt	RUSSELL Christopher Donaldson	14-01-42	40 Sqn

Service No	Rank	Name	Date	Sqn
1259848	Sgt	RUSSELL Cyril Frederick	28-04-42	35 Sqn
798654	Sgt	RUSSELL Gerald Aloysius [Newfoundland]	16-07-42	13 OTU
525328	Sgt	RUSSELL James	6-05-42	11 OTU
622505	Sgt	RUSSELL John	11-09-42	106 Sqn
1335518	Sgt	RUSSELL Ronald Alfred	17-09-42	149 Sqn
527236	F/S	RUSSELL-COLLINS Charles Robert	19-09-42	15 Sqn
966363	F/S	RUTHERFORD Isaac	7-08-42	103 Sqn
996598	Sgt	RUTHERFORD James	12-06-42	9 Sqn
935212	F/S	RUTHERFORD Kenneth	23-09-42	218 Sqn
1345498	LAC	RUTHERFORD Thomas	10-12-42	21 Sqn
942274	Sgt	RUTHERFORD William	20-01-42	12 Sqn
1384633	Sgt	RYAN George	8-06-42	10 OTU
1019207	Sgt	RYAN James	15-12-42	405 Sqn
621697	Sgt	RYAN Thomas	13-04-42	115 Sqn
985591	F/S	RYAN William Edward	21-12-42	103 Sqn
904055	F/S	RYAN William Patrick	25-08-42	35 Sqn
82632	F/O	RYCHNOVSKY Karel [Czechoslovakia]	11-04-42	311 Sqn
1267013	F/S	RYDER Richard Stanley	6-09-42	51 Sqn
537165	F/S	RYDER Stanley Norman	28-07-42	103 Sqn
67252	P/O	SADLER Basil Elgar Percy	28-03-42	109 Sqn
1381694	Sgt	SADLER George Henry	1-10-42	102 Sqn
1527312	Sgt	SAGAR John Sanderson	21-09-42	101 Sqn
798543	Sgt	SAINT Alexander Duncan [Newfoundland]	26-04-42	115 Sqn
62277	F/L	SALAZAR DFC, Count Tristan Edward	25-06-42	14 OTU
1184510	Sgt	SALE Arthur Gladstone	20-09-42	61 Sqn
746777	F/S	SALISBURY Joseph Leslie	21-06-42	10 Sqn
978882	Sgt	SALMON Japhet	12-04-42	420 Sqn
647009	F/S	SALTER Albert Henry	9-04-42	83 Sqn
45858	F/L	SALTER Harry Bishop	29-10-42	15 Sqn
654120	Sgt	SALTER William James	7-11-42	7 Sqn
749368	F/S	SALWAY Ernest	20-06-42	76 Sqn
537359	Sgt	SAMPSON George Kellock	29-04-42	9 Sqn
1380924	Sgt	SAMPSON Sidney	5-08-42	1653 CU
1369354	Sgt	SAMSON John	4-07-42	61 Sqn
121053	P/O	SAMUEL DFM William Charles	25-06-42	16 OTU
749547	Sgt	SAMUEL William McPhie	26-07-42	106 Sqn
1195426	Sgt	SAMWELL Phillip William Arthur	11-09-42	83 Sqn
1316262	Sgt	SANDERS John	25-11-42	207 Sqn
1380919	Sgt	SANDERS Patrick Gibbings	9-03-42	12 Sqn
904378	F/S	SANDERS Ronald Malcolm	30-05-42	22 OTU
627929	F/S	SANDERSON George	28-04-42	76 Sqn
42380	F/L	SANDFORD DFC Reginald Robert	17-09-42	44 Sqn
566157	Sgt	SANDISON Peter	17-09-42	7 Sqn
104477	P/O	SANDLAND Cyril Ian Andrew	2-06-42	408 Sqn
655186	Sgt	SANDLIN Douglas John	27-02-42	77 Sqn
116089	P/O	SANDON Anthony Henry Gauvain	16-09-42	142 Sqn
119523	P/O	SANKEY George Edmund	31-05-42	405 Sqn
1017157	Sgt	SANNHOLM David Martin	6-12-42	102 Sqn
1212654	Sgt	SANSOM Bernard William	31-05-42	103 Sqn
1053155	F/S	SARAVANOS Nicholas	16-11-42	98 Sqn
569773	Sgt	SARGAN George Arthur	21-06-42	10 Sqn
656315	Sgt	SARGEANT James DAouglas	6-09-42	51 Sqn
1431846	AC2	SARGENT John Pearce Henry	23-07-42	Stradishall
108002	P/O	SAUL Victor William	12-06-42	9 Sqn
130443	P/O	SAUNDERS Cyril Arthur	29-12-42	77 Sqn
1289637	Sgt	SAUNDERS Douglas Arnold Alexander	16-10-42	19 OTU
89814	F/O	SAUNDERS Frederick Paul	9-12-42	24 OTU
1263153	Sgt	SAUNDERS John Edwin Travers	30-04-42	158 Sqn
646213	Sgt	SAUNDERS Sidney Edgar	4-06-42	214 Sqn
1378823	Sgt	SAVAGE Arthur Wilson	17-01-42	27 OTU
962599	Sgt	SAVAGE George Douglas	11-02-42	150 Sqn
930778	F/S	SAVAGE Michael Gordon	27-08-42	156 Sqn
935745	Sgt	SAVAGE Terence James	27-04-42	7 Sqn
1251272	Sgt	SAVILLE George Robert	27-07-42	156 Sqn
980033	Sgt	SAVORY Allan Cyril	27-07-42	12 Sqn
39574	W/C	SAWREY-COOKSON DSO DFC Reginald	6-04-42	75 Sqn
563012	Sgt	SAWYER Ronald	7-09-42	7 Sqn
78861	F/O	SAYERS Basil Mervyn	8-03-42	226 Sqn
939971	F/S	SAYNER DFM AFM Arthur	15-10-42	156 Sqn
920390	Sgt	SCANLAN Alfred Brian	23-06-42	103 Sqn
106553	P/O	SCANLAN DFC Thomas Patrick	27-08-42	218 Sqn
656067	Sgt	SCARFF Robert James	20-03-42	19 OTU
567762	Sgt	SCARLETT Wilfred Charles	30-06-42	149 Sqn
106536	P/O	SCARLETT William George	15-01-42	82 Sqn
48459	P/O	SCATCHARD Charles	16-04-42	106 Sqn
1185940	Sgt	SCATTERGOOD Cyril Joseph	17-04-42	10 OTU
117134	P/O	SCHUMM Henry Alfred	23-04-42	9 Sqn
1166182	Sgt	SCHOFIELD Alfred	31-05-42	158 Sqn
1058797	Sgt	SCHOFIELD Derrick Rennie Wyn	10-09-42	102 Sqn
1113760	Sgt	SCORER James Henry	25-08-42	150 Sqn
835582	Sgt	SCOTLAND Francis Alfred	12-08-42	78 Sqn
1151101	Sgt	SCOTT Allan Frank	16-01-42	15 OTU
573717	Sgt	SCOTT Allan Randall	7-06-42	214 Sqn
1379715	Sgt	SCOTT Cecil John	30-04-42	50 Sqn
1002306	Sgt	SCOTT Donald Keith Newton	30-05-42	156 Sqn
992598	Sgt	SCOTT Ernest	20-02-42	17 OTU
1117206	Sgt	SCOTT George Gardener [Canada]	26-07-42	19 Sqn
1262777	Sgt	SCOTT George William [New Zealand]	7-08-42	78 Sqn
1388136	Sgt	SCOTT John Reginald Simpson	2-10-42	161 Sqn
116705	P/O	SCOTT John Walker	26-07-42	115 Sqn
987500	Sgt	SCOTT Miles William	16-01-42	15 OTU
934449	Sgt	SCOTT Russell Morris	9-06-42	83 Sqn
549357	Sgt	SCOTT Walter	24-10-42	50 Sqn
1325235	Sgt	SCOTT William Derek	5-08-42	44 Sqn
115802	P/O	SCRIVEN Reginald	2-06-42	23 OTU
918988	Sgt	SEAGOE Bryden Grange	17-04-42	44 Sqn
1325688	Sgt	SEAL Leon Harold	20-06-42	78 Sqn
1312054	Sgt	SEALEY John Charles William	24-06-42	1516 Flt
814230	Sgt	SEALS Frederick Kenneth Arthur	17-09-42	15 OTU
1179274	F/S	SEAMARK DFM Leslie Arthur	23-09-42	142 Sqn
67626	F/O	SEARBY Archibald Leonard	19-08-42	61 Sqn
752001	Sgt	SEARES Edward Henry	8-11-42	76 Sqn
753200	Sgt	SEARLE Albert Henry James	30-11-42	7 Sqn
1260920	Sgt	SEARS Frank John	14-09-42	115 Sqn
1052401	Sgt	SEATON Robert Harold	6-06-42	49 Sqn
29216	W/C	SEAVILL Francis Cecil [New Zealand]	6-12-42	487 Sqn
1377554	Sgt	SEAWARD Eric George	8-05-42	158 Sqn
1375679	Sgt	SECKERSON Philip Julian	9-06-42	12 Sqn
1311400	Sgt	SEDGWICK Norman Robert	15-10-42	103 Sqn
915124	Sgt	SEDIN Albert Edward	11-09-42	16 OTU
979577	Sgt	SEED William Carr	30-11-42	22 OTU
89084	F/O	SEELY KING Ronald	6-04-42	50 Sqn
553853	F/S	SEERY John	29-03-42	106 Sqn
126740	P/O	SEIGNE John Barter [Eire]	10-11-42	149 Sqn
1177286	Sgt	SELBY Arthur John	26-06-42	35 Sqn
1177132	Sgt	SELBY Harold	26-03-42	142 Sqn
101559	P/O	SELFE Robert Vincent	28-01-42	106 Sqn
37127	W/C	SELKIRK William Rattray	4-02-42	21 Sqn
1164554	Sgt	SELLARS Douglas Morton	9-05-42	10 OTU
122241	F/O	SELLARS George Leslie	22-12-42	466 Sqn
1376161	F/S	SELWAY Sidney Mervyn	5-09-42	103 Sqn
1169891	Sgt	SELWYN Guy Maurice	2-06-42	102 Sqn
107313	P/O	SENIOR Edward Ronald	21-06-42	10 Sqn
1127646	Sgt	SEPHTON Norman	6-09-42	51 Sqn
1330947	Sgt	SEWELL Horace Arthur William	28-06-42	214 Sqn
33042	S/L	SEYMOUR Paul De Grey Horatio	17-11-42	158 Sqn
1166511	Sgt	SEYMOUR Richard Henry Creed	20-07-42	158 Sqn
1101049	Sgt	SHACKLETON Gordon	8-03-42	50 Sqn
101560	P/O	SHACKLETON William Clifford	2-06-42	49 Sqn
1313191	Sgt	SHADDICK Raymond Fred	21-04-42	138 Sqn
902858	F/S	SHANKLAND Whitby	21-09-42	101 Sqn

Number	Rank	Name	Date	Unit
1291832	Sgt	SHANLEY Donald Patrick	30-09-42	9 Sqn
1272432	Sgt	SHAPCOTT John Tudor	26-06-42	12 OTU
108145	P/O	SHARMAN Edward [Canada]	11-02-42	12 Sqn
639164	Sgt	SHARMAN Gordon John	9-06-42	35 Sqn
1111468	Sgt	SHARMAN Peter Siegfried	28-08-42	15 Sqn
1190493	Sgt	SHARP Douglas Malcolm	3-06-42	57 Sqn
910003	Sgt	SHARP Frank Leslie	18-05-42	15 Sqn
542001	F/S	SHARP Gwladgwyn John	20-01-42	142 Sqn
1109186	Sgt	SHARP John Anthony	18-08-42	12 Sqn
1113588	Sgt	SHARP John Kay	2-04-42	57 Sqn
615021	Sgt	SHARP Reginald James	18-05-42	15 Sqn
527639	Sgt	SHARPE John Arthur	21-08-42	218 Sqn
798575	Sgt	SHARPE William John [Newfoundland]	28-08-42	115 Sqn
82995	F/O	SHARPLES Albert	26-06-42	16 OTU
1375039	F/S	SHARPLES Emrys Frederick	20-12-42	9 Sqn
1356710	Sgt	SHATTOCK Aubrey Harold	3-01-42	99 Sqn
102302	F/O	SHATTOCK Robert Mark	29-04-42	78 Sqn
1474780	AC2	SHAW Donald William John	14-05-42	Honington
748518	F/S	SHAW Edmund Verner	21-05-42	21 OTU
121375	P/O	SHAW Harold	7-08-42	12 Sqn
1283481	Sgt	SHAW Herbert Edward	6-11-42	18 Sqn
987871	AC1	SHAW Irwin	7-06-42	161 Sqn
968972	F/S	SHAW James Arthur	5-05-42	149 Sqn
1068083	F/S	SHAW James Douglas	1-10-42	51 Sqn
742749	Sgt	SHAW John Cecil	4-01-42	49 Sqn
120603	P/O	SHAW Joseph Simpson	17-09-42	15 OTU
1052795	Sgt	SHAW Robert Miller	15-01-42	115 Sqn
1166184	Sgt	SHAW Stanley Alfred George	16-05-42	75 Sqn
1375427	Sgt	SHAW Stanley Bernard	31-05-42	150 Sqn
567069	Sgt	SHEA Reginald Arthur	11-03-42	149 Sqn
645419	F/S	SHEAHAN Gordon John	25-03-42	12 Sqn
1061378	Sgt	SHEARER Leslie	30-06-42	149 Sqn
37587	W/C	SHEEHAN George Harcus	25-08-42	61 Sqn
120997	P/O	SHEEN Harold William	4-06-42	50 Sqn
119346	P/O	SHEFFIELD Joseph	16-04-42	156 Sqn
1112127	F/S	SHELDON William	24-09-42	405 Sqn
119896	F/O	SHELL Francis George	17-12-42	57 Sqn
1155843	F/S	SHELLEY Walter	17-04-42	97 Sqn
922210	Sgt	SHEPHERD Bernard	2-04-42	150 Sqn
1112237	Sgt	SHEPHERD Caleb Stanley Kenneth	6-08-42	207 Sqn
524942	Sgt	SHEPHERD Charles Duncan	6-10-42	44 Sqn
1127995	Sgt	SHEPHERD Charles Thomas	16-07-42	149 Sqn
629714	Sgt	SHEPHERD Frederick Valentine Herbert	27-08-42	156 Sqn
1053539	Sgt	SHEPHERD Henry Wright	12-08-42	106 Sqn
1430261	Sgt	SHEPHERD Laurence Arthur	14-09-42	115 Sqn
48980	F/L	SHEPHERD DFM Norman Henry	6-12-42	107 Sqn
114054	P/O	SHEPPARD Gordon Ernest	20-06-42	101 Sqn
744503	F/S	SHEPPARD William George	17-12-42	44 Sqn
778039	Sgt	SHEPPERSON Oswald Reynolds [South Africa]	9-11-42	44 Sqn
924232	Sgt	SHERRARD-SMITH Arthur Graham	24-09-42	102 Sqn
751629	Sgt	SHERRATT Cyril George	9-06-42	83 Sqn
954445	Sgt	SHERRATT William George	29-04-42	156 Sqn
1128034	Sgt	SHERRIFF Frank Henri	29-12-42	11 OTU
904509	Sgt	SHERRIFF Terence Joseph	10-03-42	149 Sqn
1392287	AC1	SHERRIN Edward Charles	20-03-42	Tempsford
1043275	Sgt	SHERWIN Robert White	6-09-42	20 OTU
115519	P/O	SHERWOOD Humphrey Gordon	1-09-42	76 Sqn
569100	Sgt	SHERWOOD Thomas Randall	5-05-42	218 Sqn
1163449	Sgt	SHEWARD Leslie Roland	1-10-42	405 Sqn
90191	W/C	SHEWELL John Morland	25-08-42	7 Sqn
946428	F/S	SHILAN John Meredith Farley	27-07-42	77 Sqn
646924	F/S	SHIP Charles Harry	8-05-42	44 Sqn
1375255	Sgt	SHIPMAN Peter Claude	5-12-42	21 OTU
1375957	F/S	SHIPTON Bernard Bruce	20-11-42	21 Sqn
922788	Sgt	SHIPTON Joseph Preston	15-04-42	420 Sqn
127160	P/O	SHIRLEY Kenneth James	11-07-42	207 Sqn
1330958	Sgt	SHIRLEY Robert Frederick	15-07-42	23 OTU
1189020	Sgt	SHOESMITH Terence	13-08-42	15 Sqn
564432	W/O	SHONE George Ernest	29-07-42	75 Sqn
574206	Sgt	SHORT MiD Arthur Goldsack	29-11-42	214 Sqn
552923	Sgt	SHORTHOUSE Robert Francis	14-07-42	12 Sqn
100558	P/O	SHORTT Harry Arthur	16-04-42	214 Sqn
930243	Sgt	SHOTTER Eric George Walter	1-04-42	214 Sqn
1183690	Sgt	SHRIMPTON Douglas Edward	25-06-42	214 Sqn
1263451	Sgt	SHULVER Percy Hugh	28-08-42	12 Sqn
1334367	Sgt	SIBLEY Norman Cyril Frederick	4-06-42	218 Sqn
130238	P/O	SIBLEY Norman Frank	9-12-42	24 OTU
100581	P/O	SIDES Bernard	21-01-42	51 Sqn
1056817	Sgt	SIDNEY-SMITH Desmond Edwin Sproule	28-03-42	7 Sqn
902414	F/S	SIEVE Leonard	14-01-42	207 Sqn
1293656	Sgt	SIGLER Benjamin	31-05-42	12 Sqn
1169281	Sgt	SILVER Leslie Raymond	29-04-42	9 Sqn
908638	F/S	SILVERMAN Philip	10-09-42	158 Sqn
1337030	Sgt	SILVESTER Arthur George	29-07-42	1651 CU
927095	Sgt	SIMKINS Frederick Henry George	20-07-42	158 Sqn
613714	Sgt	SIMMANS Albert Edward	26-04-42	115 Sqn
1013282	Sgt	SIMMONS Edward Hopkin	26-02-42	10 Sqn
1384563	Sgt	SIMMONS John William	6-12-42	7 Sqn
1378726	Sgt	SIMMONS Robert Louis Nathaniel	6-01-42	57 Sqn
1464445	Sgt	SIMMONS Ronald Charles	5-12-42	21 OTU
1014450	Sgt	SIMMS Norman Holland	24-10-42	218 Sqn
1381056	Sgt	SIMON Edward Leon	30-10-42	105 Sqn
116027	P/O	SIMON Horace Martin	28-06-42	218 Sqn
05144	W/C	SIMOND MiD Geoffrey Frederick	12-02-42	144 Sqn
117648	P/O	SIMONS Alexander	1-08-42	103 Sqn
1063602	Sgt	SIMONS William	3-06-42	61 Sqn
580847	W/O	SIMPKIN James George	25-06-42	21 OTU
571779	Sgt	SIMPSON Alexander	30-06-42	405 Sqn
1311743	Sgt	SIMPSON Dennis Roy	21-08-42	149 Sqn
1263891	Sgt	SIMPSON Douglas Thomson	21-09-42	115 Sqn
655086	Sgt	SIMPSON Gerald Anthony	28-04-42	76 Sqn
971578	F/S	SIMPSON DFM James	22-09-42	19 OTU
1310209	Sgt	SIMPSON James	2-06-42	10 Sqn
1383634	Sgt	SIMPSON John Richard	31-12-42	16 OTU
36147	S/L	SIMPSON MiD Joseph Cunningham [New Zealand]	23-10-42	105 Sqn
965570	Sgt	SIMPSON Peter	17-08-42	50 Sqn
656104	Sgt	SIMS Arthur Joseph	21-09-42	10 OTU
1117538	Sgt	SIMS Francis William	24-06-42	23 OTU
1388435	Sgt	SIMS Leonard Robert	10-08-42	149 Sqn
995657	Sgt	SINCLAIR Archibald	9-11-42	142 Sqn
125605	P/O	SINCLAIR John Malcolm	6-10-42	19 OTU
519693	Sgt	SINDEN John	6-06-42	20 OTU
1073899	Sgt	SINGER Ian Douglas	1-08-42	21 OTU
647330	Sgt	SINGERTON Albert Edward	9-03-42	9 Sqn
1135365	Sgt	SINNETT Thomas George	16-10-42	19 OTU
1055969	Sgt	SISTRON Andrew James	14-01-42	17 OTU
39800	S/L	SKEET Maurice	26-06-42	158 Sqn
1071281	Sgt	SKELLEY Frank	26-07-42	115 Sqn
108003	P/O	SKELLY Horace James	20-07-42	158 Sqn
1158660	Sgt	SKELTON Gerald Colin Stewart	6-04-42	50 Sqn
1001212	Sgt	SKELTON Harold	11-03-42	149 Sqn
1378783	Sgt	SKELTON John Charles	10-07-42	142 Sqn
954437	Sgt	SKELTON Robert	8-12-42	15 Sqn
45435	F/O	SKELTON Walter Allen	28-08-42	115 Sqn
1168891	Sgt	SKERMAN Peter Dennis	1-10-42	76 Sqn
747929	Sgt	SKINNER Arthur	16-09-42	23 OTU
611063	Sgt	SKINNER Frederick Newman	20-12-42	106 Sqn
1111867	Sgt	SKINNER Hugh Richard	28-07-42	156 Sqn
104502	P/O	SKINNER Thurstan Barns	10-06-42	107 Sqn
1182426	Sgt	SKINNER Walter Anthony	3-04-42	16 OTU
1014853	Sgt	SKIPSEY John	18-08-42	101 Sqn

Service No	Rank	Name	Date	Squadron
82194	F/O	SKIPWITH Grey D'Estotville Townsend	31-05-42	158 Sqn
68186	F/O	SKONE Alan Raymond	27-08-42	214 Sqn
82528	F/L	SKOREPA Zdenek [Czechoslovakia]	21-01-42	311 Sqn
120486	P/O	SKRENDER John Brooke	22-07-42	150 Sqn
1287890	Sgt	SLATER Geoffrey	6-10-42	75 Sqn
1536441	Sgt	SLATER Jack	25-11-42	207 Sqn
1183344	Sgt	SLATFORD Frederick Herbert	30-05-42	218 Sqn
1054129	Sgt	SLEEMAN Thomas	2-06-42	142 Sqn
1311806	Sgt	SLINGO Francis William	19-04-42	49 Sqn
1254845	Sgt	SLOWLY Brian Clifford	31-05-42	103 Sqn
109045	F/O	SMALE Peter David	15-10-42	106 Sqn
48111	P/O	SMARIDGE Richard Eric	6-02-42	88 Sqn
1006420	Sgt	SMART John Eric	26-03-42	61 Sqn
1282785	Sgt	SMART Shuthi Napoleon N. Leslie Oswald Banerjee	10-03-42	149 Sqn
1379256	Sgt	SMART Walter John Albert	26-04-42	1443 Flt
106538	P/O	SMETHURST Kenneth James Edward	4-02-42	21 Sqn
656871	Sgt	SMETHURST Norman Frederick	9-09-42	207 Sqn
933236	Sgt	SMITH Alan Frank	6-12-42	76 Sqn
656553	Sgt	SMITH Alexander Knox	14-09-42	26 OTU
1373320	Sgt	SMITH Alexander Munro	29-10-42	115 Sqn
1281992	Sgt	SMITH Alfred Henry	17-05-42	149 Sqn
1183165	Sgt	SMITH Archibald	8-02-42	12 OTU
651289	F/S	SMITH DFM Arnold George	1-08-42	106 Sqn
1252992	Sgt	SMITH Arthur Ronald George	3-01-42	99 Sqn
88729	P/O	SMITH Arthur Walter	24-06-42	23 OTU
143198	P/O	SMITH Aubrey Arthur	9-11-42	142 Sqn
1108685	Sgt	SMITH Austin	2-06-42	142 Sqn
569626	Sgt	SMITH Basil Ernest	5-05-42	149 Sqn
102134	F/O	SMITH Bernard George Harry [Brazil]	10-09-42	102 Sqn
1216295	Sgt	SMITH Bernard Murray	19-08-42	207 Sqn
925557	F/S	SMITH Bruce Ashby	31-08-42	21 OTU
987229	Sgt	SMITH Charles	30-11-42	149 Sqn
1209164	Sgt	SMITH Colin	21-08-42	218 Sqn
1181165	Sgt	SMITH Colin Clement	25-03-42	83 Sqn
350171	Sgt	SMITH BEM David	20-06-42	78 Sqn
1008971	F/S	SMITH David	31-12-42	83 Sqn
1308039	Sgt	SMITH David	11-04-42	214 Sqn
944264	Sgt	SMITH David Thomas	11-02-42	12 Sqn
751691	F/S	SMITH Dennis Goodwill	28-11-42	150 Sqn
127009	P/O	SMITH Derrick Vincent	30-11-42	10 OTU
975318	F/S	SMITH Donald Ernest Harvey	11-12-42	27 OTU
1387824	Sgt	SMITH Edward Albert	5-08-42	1653 CU
122022	P/O	SMITH Edward Anthony	11-06-42	77 Sqn
1213633	Sgt	SMITH Edward Jack	21-12-42	103 Sqn
1141673	LAC	SMITH Eric	28-03-42	78 Sqn
931910	Sgt	SMITH Eric Charles	3-05-42	78 Sqn
1294712	Sgt	SMITH Eric Norman	15-10-42	150 Sqn
1169531	Sgt	SMITH Eric Omar	27-06-42	405 Sqn
841279	Sgt	SMITH Eric William	10-12-42	10 OTU
1381724	Sgt	SMITH Ernest George	2-06-42	97 Sqn
114058	P/O	SMITH Francis Charles	16-09-42	106 Sqn
1291796	Sgt	SMITH Francis John	1-08-42	57 Sqn
543358	Sgt	SMITH Francis William	28-01-42	138 Sqn
994288	Sgt	SMITH Frank	5-09-42	12 Sqn
569386	Sgt	SMITH Geoffrey Archie	10-06-42	158 Sqn
1270159	AC1	SMITH George Edward	21-06-42	106 Sqn
1186096	Sgt	SMITH Harold Ryding	30-11-42	98 Sqn
625189	Sgt	SMITH Harry	17-06-42	102 Sqn
133038	P/O	SMITH Harry Bernard	17-12-42	103 Sqn
1264073	Sgt	SMITH Hector Leslie	31-05-42	26 OTU
798655	Sgt	SMITH Herbert Blatch [Newfoundland]	24-10-42	57 Sqn
622361	Sgt	SMITH Herbert Ralph	25-06-42	76 Sqn
1021190	Sgt	SMITH Jack Titterton	16-06-42	1651 CU
1331244	Sgt	SMITH James Thompson	13-04-42	49 Sqn
1108728	Sgt	SMITH John	31-05-42	49 Sqn
778676	Sgt	SMITH John Burton [Rhodesia]	26-06-42	102 Sqn
1110205	F/S	SMITH John Edward	20-12-42	83 Sqn
742471	W/O	SMITH John George	28-08-42	115 Sqn
1376601	Sgt	SMITH John James	16-04-42	156 Sqn
519241	W/O	SMITH John Lawrence	24-07-42	25 OTU
1314139	Sgt	SMITH Kenneth James	17-09-42	21 OTU
82499	F/L	SMITH Kenneth Samuel	6-12-42	21 Sqn
573395	Sgt	SMITH Kenneth William	29-03-42	142 Sqn
655493	Sgt	SMITH Leonard Frederick	2-06-42	83 Sqn
1027454	Sgt	SMITH Leonard Houghton	30-11-42	149 Sqn
616593	Sgt	SMITH Leonard James	4-06-42	218 Sqn
629603	F/S	SMITH Leonard Mervyn	24-05-42	207 Sqn
117026	F/O	SMITH Leslie George Oliver	6-11-42	21 Sqn
570749	Sgt	SMITH Marshal Kenneth	2-10-42	149 Sqn
967591	Sgt	SMITH Neil Shaw	13-03-42	77 Sqn
1305085	Sgt	SMITH Norman William	15-05-42	408 Sqn
123022	F/O	SMITH Peter Francis	25-10-42	51 Sqn
1027418	Sgt	SMITH Peter Horace	27-07-42	35 Sqn
778353	F/S	SMITH Reginald Newbald [Rhodesia]	7-02-42	50 Sqn
61009	F/L	SMITH DFC Richard Marcus	30-11-42	7 Sqn
1225704	Sgt	SMITH Roland Jack	20-07-42	158 Sqn
1065715	Sgt	SMITH Ronald Hayward	25-06-42	12 OTU
1252106	LAC	SMITH Ronald Leonard	7-08-42	16 OTU
1117198	Sgt	SMITH Roy	8-05-42	158 Sqn
1334598	Sgt	SMITH Thomas Charles	19-09-42	15 Sqn
954984	Sgt	SMITH Thomas Patrick	9-05-42	76 Sqn
106563	P/O	SMITH Trevor Hardy	22-02-42	83 Sqn
112306	P/O	SMITH Verle Marshall	29-07-42	1651 CU
1390006	Sgt	SMITH Victor Ralph	26-09-42	24 OTU
614191	Sgt	SMITH William	12-02-42	49 Sqn
1126014	Sgt	SMITH William	8-04-42	23 OTU
1382139	Sgt	SMITH William	27-07-42	405 Sqn
1325041	Sgt	SMITH William Anderson	9-11-42	12 OTU
1112639	Sgt	SMITH William Everard	6-02-42	13 OTU
997321	Sgt	SMITH William Gardiner	26-04-42	115 Sqn
1307055	Sgt	SMITH William Robert	24-07-42	207 Sqn
1060635	Sgt	SMITH William Thomson	23-06-42	57 Sqn
125723	P/O	SMITH DFC Wreford William George	22-10-42	161 Sqn
960672	Sgt	SMITHE Arthur Desmond St. Clare	11-01-42	40 Sqn
107932	P/O	SMITHERMAN Edward James	25-08-42	97 Sqn
1306692	Sgt	SMITHSON Alfred	31-05-42	114 Sqn
41075	F/L	SMYTH George Bruce [Canada]	15-10-42	97 Sqn
118650	P/O	SMYTH John Scott	17-09-42	158 Sqn
655106	Sgt	SMYTHSON Leslie	1-10-42	10 Sqn
1162390	Sgt	SNELLING Edward John	28-01-42	106 Sqn
109514	P/O	SNELLING Henry John	25-04-42	11 OTU
41076	S/L	SNOW Albert John Drake	3-05-42	78 Sqn
745286	F/S	SNOWBALL Robert Charles	26-03-42	83 Sqn
118096	P/O	SOAMES Geoffrey Gordon	26-03-42	115 Sqn
1289748	Sgt	SOFAER Edward Isaac	9-09-42	150 Sqn
571587	Sgt	SOGGEE Derick Arthur Dudley	30-11-42	10 Sqn
1177512	Sgt	SOLLARS Leslie Donald	28-03-42	7 Sqn
116152	P/O	SOMERVILLE John McFarlane Weir	9-05-42	44 Sqn
1268334	LAC	SONGEST Leslie Albert	1-09-42	57 Sqn
1263238	Sgt	SOPER Thomas Walter	30-05-42	15 Sqn
787489	Sgt	SOUKOP Oldrich [Czechoslovakia]	12-03-42	311 Sqn
908898	Sgt	SOUTER Edward George	30-09-42	149 Sqn
533687	Sgt	SOUTHERN Jack Joffre	25-06-42	102 Sqn
1335832	Sgt	SOUTGATE Stanley Terance	11-09-42	25 OTU
108144	P/O	SOUTHWELL Anthony Jeaffreson	17-08-42	207 Sqn
1376038	Sgt	SOUTHWELL Joseph Henry	21-09-42	10 OTU
1326356	Sgt	SPACKMAN Arthur Sidney	20-01-42	101 Sqn
104503	P/O	SPALDING James	12-03-42	77 Sqn
1264305	Sgt	SPALDING Noel	7-09-42	7 Sqn
1059680	Sgt	SPARK James Sydney	25-08-42	7 Sqn
128965	P/O	SPARK Norman	11-08-42	156 Sqn
108539	F/L	SPARKE Charles Lionel	11-12-42	158 Sqn
970251	F/S	SPARKS John Adam	20-08-42	218 Sqn

1053696	F/S	SPEAKMAN Charles Ronald	7-11-42	83 Sqn
1293315	Sgt	SPEED James	1-10-42	218 Sqn
1310195	Sgt	SPENCE Peter MacDougall	7-08-42	12 Sqn
636194	Sgt	SPENCELEY Frederick George	20-06-42	15 Sqn
115564	F/L	SPENCER DFM Arthur Charles	29-08-42	156 Sqn
903905	Sgt	SPENCER Ernest James	14-04-42	1652 CU
929737	Sgt	SPENCER George Reginald Stone	26-07-42	114 Sqn
1200412	Sgt	SPENCER Howard William	3-09-42	11 OTU
1433222	Sgt	SPENCER Ronald	20-09-42	149 Sqn
1310508	Sgt	SPENCER Stanley	16-08-42	207 Sqn
1282478	Sgt	SPERRING Reginald Philip Henry	15-01-42	104 Sqn
535526	Sgt	SPIBEY Dennis	17-12-42	138 Sqn
1181149	Sgt	SPICER Stanley Oswald	19-08-42	207 Sqn
787889	Sgt	SPINKA Dobromil Z. [Czechoslovakia]	3-03-42	311 Sqn
1310580	Sgt	SPINKS James Henry	4-06-42	214 Sqn
1323991	Sgt	SPINNER Henry	20-12-42	77 Sqn
1285153	F/S	SPIRES Leonard George	20-12-42	77 Sqn
1378900	Sgt	SPIRIT John Thompson	24-09-42	102 Sqn
1202111	Sgt	SPOONER Ivan Bernard Harry	31-05-42	101 Sqn
1479837	Sgt	SPOONER William Edleston	28-08-42	97 Sqn
547329	Sgt	SPOWART George William	1-10-42	10 Sqn
109943	P/O	SPRAKE Noel Geoffey	26-07-42	142 Sqn
1392772	Sgt	SPRATT Leonard Frederick Keith	7-11-42	10 OTU
1178776	Sgt	SPRAY Norman	29-04-42	12 Sqn
568054	Sgt	SPRIGGS Anthony	18-05-42	15 Sqn
751129	F/S	SPRIGGS William John Alton	6-12-42	107 Sqn
614665	Sgt	SPRINGHAM Samuel Knapper	29-04-42	78 Sqn
1177725	Sgt	SPROSTON Hubert	31-05-42	115 Sqn
929949	Sgt	SQUIRE Alfred Edward Charles	19-06-42	408 Sqn
545944	Sgt	SQUIRES Abson	23-04-42	218 Sqn
1132935	Sgt	SQUIRES Arthur	6-06-42	35 Sqn
1108725	Sgt	SQUIRES Frank	30-06-42	149 Sqn
1096448	Sgt	SQUIRES Peter	25-08-42	83 Sqn
759155	F/S	STABLES John	7-02-42	50 Sqn
126972	F/O	STABLES Robinson	22-12-42	21 OTU
1031421	Sgt	STAFF Arthur	21-12-42	7 Sqn
959971	Sgt	STAFF James Frederick	30-03-42	35 Sqn
1026227	Cpl	STAG William McGee	21-12-42	10 Sqn
1266055	Sgt	STAINFORTH Richard Frances	30-07-42	142 Sqn
954283	Sgt	STAINTON Charles	24-09-42	102 Sqn
959164	Sgt	STALEY Roy	9-04-42	158 Sqn
1310029	Sgt	STALKER Harold George	6-04-42	16 OTU
1323246	Sgt	STAMMERS John	29-11-42	214 Sqn
121573	P/O	STANAIR George Lawson	16-08-42	408 Sqn
910440	Sgt	STANDEN Leonard Alfred Charles	22-07-42	115 Sqn
927496	Sgt	STANDRING Gibbard Selkirk	23-06-42	57 Sqn
1388092	Sgt	STANGHAM Robert Horace	23-06-42	57 Sqn
76018	S/L	STANION DFC Vernon William Lamond	24-12-42	12 OTU
1176789	Sgt	STANLEY Eric Featherstonhaugh	20-08-42	115 Sqn
49057	P/O	STANLEY James Frederick	2-06-42	11 OTU
966184	Sgt	STANLEY Leonard Charles	26-03-42	12 Sqn
1280974	Sgt	STANLEY William Thomas	2-06-42	142 Sqn
1065713	Sgt	STANNERS David Thomson	25-06-42	15 OTU
787880	F/S	STANOVSKY Jan [Czechoslovakia]	6-04-42	1429 Flt
533901	Sgt	STANSFIELD Alfred	22-11-42	57 Sqn
1057672	Sgt	STANSFIELD Edward James [Canada]	28-08-42	408 Sqn
1005937	Sgt	STANSFIELD Joseph Ross	3-01-42	455 Sqn
1167685	Sgt	STANSFIELD Kenneth Richard	20-09-42	158 Sqn
1021906	Sgt	STANWORTH Joseph Thomas	7-05-42	35 Sqn
1325482	Sgt	STARBUCK Leonard	26-06-42	102 Sqn
1365782	Sgt	STARK George	1-10-42	15 Sqn
1378512	Sgt	STATON Derrick Frank	30-07-42	138 Sqn
1318706	Sgt	STAY Richard Francis	14-09-42	21 OTU
1525008	Sgt	STEAD George	20-08-42	75 Sqn
1378264	Sgt	STEAD Norman	26-01-42	51 Sqn
632284	Sgt	STEADMAN Dennis	20-09-42	158 Sqn
1188364	Sgt	STEEL Adam Innes	13-08-42	207 Sqn
126792	P/O	STEEL Bernard Reginald	27-09-42	10 OTU
1209183	Sgt	STEELE John Anthony	16-02-42	49 Sqn
1591275	Sgt	STEELE-NICHOLSON John Edwin Charles Averell	14-09-42	1653 CU
109916	P/O	STEEN John Ross	4-06-42	50 Sqn
931535	Sgt	STEER Ronald David	13-04-42	15 Sqn
100023	P/O	STEFEK Jan [Czechoslovakia]	6-06-42	1429 Flt
1051815	F/S	STELL John Walter	4-06-42	76 Sqn
1067562	Sgt	STEP George Edward	7-07-42	21 Sqn
1023143	Sgt	STEPHEN William	18-07-42	10 OTU
1284405	Sgt	STEPHENS Geoffrey Francis	29-07-42	12 Sqn
103510	F/O	STEPHENS DFC DFM James Douglas Vernon Stewart	1-10-42	44 Sqn
1315752	Sgt	STEPHENS John Brynmor	15-10-42	57 Sqn
75730	S/L	STEPHENS DFC Martin Tyringham	13-02-42	Stradishall
1119436	Sgt	STEPHENS Vincent Leslie	1-04-42	214 Sqn
528944	Sgt	STEPHENSON George	7-04-42	15 Sqn
653773	Sgt	STEPHENSON John Henry	19-05-42	218 Sqn
946087	Sgt	STEVENS Charles Corbett	20-05-42	156 Sqn
1377475	Sgt	STEVENS Eric George Andrew	16-04-42	156 Sqn
939982	Sgt	STEVENS Ernest Keith	2-04-42	214 Sqn
1177167	Sgt	STEVENS Kenneth William	29-04-42	9 Sqn
991511	Sgt	STEVENS Richard Quick	1-10-42	10 Sqn
577873	Sgt	STEVENS Ronald Ernest Leonard	18-09-42	10 OTU
1182379	F/S	STEVENS Ronald Leonard	8-09-42	76 Sqn
1270512	F/S	STEVENS Stanley Edgar	20-08-42	218 Sqn
931022	LAC	STEVENS William Stanley	13-05-42	50 Sqn
60772	F/L	STEVENS-FOX Aubrey Charles	30-03-42	10 Sqn
117686	P/O	STEVENSON Charles Joseph	11-09-42	78 Sqn
952944	Sgt	STEVENSON Sydney William	9-03-42	115 Sqn
922683	Sgt	STEWART Charles Duncan Stuart	25-01-42	49 Sqn
798545	Sgt	STEWART Charles Henry [Newfoundland]	9-07-42	101 Sqn
800061	F/S	STEWART Charles Noel Douglas	31-05-42	9 Sqn
78534	S/L	STEWART DFC Ian Adam	6-10-42	44 Sqn
949942	Sgt	STEWART Iain Menzies Robertson	5-09-42	214 Sqn
969988	Sgt	STEWART John Joseph	25-03-42	106 Sqn
777897	Sgt	STEWART John McWilliam [Rhodesia]	29-04-42	14 OTU
1260195	Sgt	STEWART Johnstone	11-08-42	156 Sqn
116891	P/O	STEWART Leonard Scott	19-07-42	226 Sqn
632138	F/S	STEWART Peter	16-09-42	23 OTU
1098537	Sgt	STEWART Philip James	3-08-42	114 Sqn
1060247	Sgt	STEWART Robert Watson	6-05-42	150 Sqn
1346251	Sgt	STEWART William	16-12-42	15 OTU
1182389	Sgt	STIBBS Kenneth Penwill	15-10-42	214 Sqn
655741	Sgt	STICKNEY Sidney Richard	19-05-42	35 Sqn
1208930	Sgt	STILL Leonard George	21-06-42	420 Sqn
115520	P/O	STILWELL Albert Wyndham	21-08-42	15 OTU
999188	Sgt	STIRK John Henry	17-09-42	15 OTU
997898	Sgt	STIRLING Edwin Ritchie	9-03-42	9 Sqn
1157823	Sgt	STOCK Donald Percival	6-04-42	75 Sqn
1254480	W/O	STOCK George John	7-11-42	83 Sqn
1381702	Sgt	STOCK Herbert Sidney	10-07-42	142 Sqn
101082	P/O	STOCK John Frederick	27-07-42	115 Sqn
1105479	Sgt	STOCKDALE Arthur	15-01-42	103 Sqn
940562	Sgt	STOCKER Neville Christian	9-05-42	158 Sqn
1314060	Sgt	STOCKFORD Stewart William	28-07-42	103 Sqn
551385	F/S	STOCKPORT DFM Wallace	12-06-42	83 Sqn
80217	P/O	STOFFER Harry Murdoch [Rhodesia]	24-04-42	106 Sqn
1055980	Sgt	STOKELL Charles Henry	26-01-42	51 Sqn
1377473	Sgt	STOKES Harold Burrows	20-12-42	9 Sqn
1397886	Sgt	STOKES Patrick James	6-12-42	487 Sqn
755061	F/S	STOLZ-PAGE Richard Grange [Luxembourg]	3-12-42	103 Sqn
121774	F/O	STONE Geoffrey William	16-12-42	15 OTU
1258969	Sgt	STONE George Henry	10-11-42	7 Sqn
49988	P/O	STONE MiD Gerald Cecil William	27-08-42	156 Sqn
1267726	Sgt	STONE Harold	2-09-42	405 Sqn

131

Service No.	Rank	Name	Date	Unit
966478	F/S	STONE John Knight	31-07-42	27 OTU
931488	Sgt	STONE Joseph Howard	9-03-42	83 Sqn
1332925	Sgt	STONE Ronald	16-11-42	19 OTU
931772	Sgt	STORER Donald Neale	16-04-42	106 Sqn
1072974	F/S	STOREY Harold Arthur	11-07-42	207 Sqn
925655	Sgt	STOREY James Henry	11-08-42	149 Sqn
937066	F/S	STOREY John	26-06-42	24 OTU
571845	Sgt	STOREY John Ralph	9-06-42	35 Sqn
617879	Sgt	STOREY Leonard Joseph	28-07-42	103 Sqn
1379962	Sgt	STOREY William	29-08-42	102 Sqn
1058698	Sgt	STOTT Herbert Harry	28-04-42	10 Sqn
1439951	Sgt	STOTT John Raymond	21-09-42	10 OTU
1290986	Sgt	STOWARD Cyril Robert	16-10-42	115 Sqn
1112228	Sgt	STRACHAN John George	14-07-42	12 Sqn
1348104	Sgt	STRACHAN John Lind	8-12-42	149 Sqn
580467	Sgt	STRACHAN Peter William Lindsey	27-02-42	77 Sqn
787569	Sgt	STRACHON Pribyslav [Czechoslovakia]	3-03-42	311 Sqn
995426	Sgt	STRAFFEN James Octon	27-07-42	142 Sqn
521347	Sgt	STRAIN Hugh Russell	8-05-42	158 Sqn
1357040	Sgt	STRAIN John Lawrence	1-06-42	115 Sqn
1378938	Sgt	STRANG James	2-06-42	78 Sqn
958284	Sgt	STRANG Thomas	15-04-42	158 Sqn
108827	P/O	STRASSER George Anthony	26-07-42	114 Sqn
1280887	Sgt	STREATER William Henry	11-08-42	149 Sqn
1100646	Sgt	STREET John Wilfred	14-08-42	7 Sqn
83000	F/O	STREET-PORTER Frederick Walter Ollis [Canada]	14-01-42	114 Sqn
550584	F/S	STRETCH Benjamin George	15-10-42	106 Sqn
904495	Sgt	STRICKLAND Algernon Guy	9-05-42	15 Sqn
964647	Sgt	STRINGER Clarence James	31-01-42	144 Sqn
1305057	Sgt	STROUD Herbert Frederick	9-05-42	408 Sqn
1165144	Sgt	STRUDWICK Percival George Henry	18-08-42	218 Sqn
1561497	Sgt	STRYDOM Stelmo Earl	30-11-42	22 OTU
751717	F/S	STUART David Robert	3-06-42	23 OTU
569233	Sgt	STUBBS Harry Gordon	21-08-42	218 Sqn
47188	F/O	STUDD AFC Reginald Arthur	23-10-42	218 Sqn
911756	Sgt	STUKINS John Richard	28-04-42	27 OTU
80132	P/O	STURGESS Hubert John Sand [Rhodesia]	9-05-42	44 Sqn
761201	F/S	STYLES Eric Leonard	1-08-42	24 OTU
1258955	Sgt	SUCKLING Herbert Lloyd	28-03-42	115 Sqn
1386506	Sgt	SUDBURY Richard Thomas	26-06-42	23 OTU
656437	Sgt	SULLIVAN Henry Edward	1-10-42	10 Sqn
1384304	Sgt	SULLIVAN James Timothy	7-11-42	156 Sqn
983200	Sgt	SULLIVAN John Elphege	30-07-42	61 Sqn
1281970	Sgt	SULLIVAN William John	17-01-42	51 Sqn
1168050	Sgt	SUMMERFIELD Edwin Clifford	30-06-42	78 Sqn
1172581	Sgt	SUMMERS Ronald	18-04-42	101 Sqn
1376704	Sgt	SURRIDGE Gordon Herbert	28-04-42	15 Sqn
1060163	Sgt	SUTCLIFFE Jack	24-03-42	19 OTU
1075478	Sgt	SUTHERLAND Leonard	27-08-42	15 OTU
1290835	F/S	SUTTON Anthony John	10-09-42	158 Sqn
918861	Sgt	SUTTON Kenneth Harold	14-04-42	102 Sqn
1098817	Sgt	SUTTON Philip Stanley	27-11-42	20 OTU
1250695	Sgt	SUTTON Ronald Marcus	27-04-42	150 Sqn
121511	F/O	SUTTON Terence William	16-09-42	23 OTU
118617	P/O	SUTTON William Charles	11-08-42	149 Sqn
787165	Sgt	SVOBODA Jindrich [Czechoslovakia]	17-01-42	311 Sqn
787881	Sgt	SVOBODA Josef [Czechoslovakia]	3-03-42	311 Sqn
1194408	Sgt	SWAFFIELD Brian William	12-06-42	114 Sqn
547856	Sgt	SWAIN Bernard Dudley [Canada]	25-10-42	103 Sqn
1168176	Sgt	SWAIN Murray Charles 'Fred'	10-04-42	76 Sqn
1378437	Sgt	SWAIN Stanley	17-09-42	11 OTU
1105999	Sgt	SWAINE Donald	29-03-42	106 Sqn
1378205	Sgt	SWAINSON Frank	31-10-42	226 Sqn
1138904	Sgt	SWALES Herbert	21-05-42	21 OTU
1378431	Sgt	SWALES Joseph	26-06-42	23 OTU
1272011	Sgt	SWALLOW Sydney Ernest	14-12-42	22 OTU
112365	P/O	SWATTON Edward William	19-07-42	408 Sqn
1113304	Sgt	SWEENEY James	11-09-42	10 OTU
1118157	Sgt	SWEENEY Michael	26-06-42	15 OTU
1387616	Sgt	SWIFT James Thomas	10-12-42	11 OTU
991501	Sgt	SWINBURN Frank	13-04-42	158 Sqn
1180160	Sgt	SWINGLER Edward Sextus	20-01-42	142 Sqn
1151672	Sgt	SWINNARD John Desmond David	10-08-42	150 Sqn
84698	F/L	SWORD DFC AFC John Arthur	7-05-42	115 Sqn
49281	P/O	SWORD Robert	17-12-42	10 OTU
744908	F/S	SYDES John Henry Ffolliott	18-08-42	76 Sqn
364767	W/O	SYKES James William Duley	2-04-42	150 Sqn
1014079	Sgt	SYKES John	20-12-42	9 Sqn
1285683	Sgt	SYKES John David Wilson [Canada]	14-07-42	150 Sqn
1175877	Sgt	SYMES Donald McGregor	12-02-42	50 Sqn
111586	P/O	SYMES Kenneth Peter	18-08-42	214 Sqn
932163	Sgt	SYMONDS Leslie John	9-07-42	101 Sqn
126506	P/O	SYMONDS Michael Robert	20-09-42	161 Sqn
84907	F/O	SYMONS Edward Graham De Twenebroke [Canada]	12-02-42	455 Sqn
1216892	Sgt	TAAFFE James John	8-11-42	9 Sqn
1254902	F/S	TACKLEY Sidney	28-06-42	76 Sqn
754021	F/S	TADMAN Reginald Seymour	6-08-42	102 Sqn
1365802	Sgt	TAIT James	29-06-42	7 Sqn
82967	F/O	TAIT Leonard James [Canada]	30-05-42	22 OTU
1312832	Sgt	TAIR Lionel Stanley Cross [Canada]	1-09-42	24 OTU
787892	Sgt	TALAB Josef [Czechoslovakia]	15-04-42	311 Sqn
1376849	F/S	TALBOT Edward Frederick	28-08-42	15 Sqn
927586	F/S	TALBOT Richard Kenneth Randolph	6-02-42	21 OTU
755804	F/S	TALES James	14-07-42	97 Sqn
1109766	Sgt	TALLENTIRE John Gilbert	27-02-42	16 OTU
1320265	Sgt	TALLEY Victor Frederick	14-09-42	1653 CU
48958	P/O	TALLIS DFM Dudley Arthur Ronald	31-05-42	22 OTU
1206121	Sgt	TANEY Alfred William	7-11-42	10 OTU
1254033	Sgt	TANNER Donald Charles	17-10-42	98 Sqn
1332536	Sgt	TANNER William John	1-08-42	57 Sqn
629978	F/S	TANSLEY MiD William Middleton	7-11-42	83 Sqn
656044	Sgt	TANSWELL Arnold	12-12-42	25 OTU
1525452	Sgt	TAPLEY Henry Maxwell	10-04-42	9 Sqn
915511	Sgt	TAPNER Edgar George	28-03-42	7 Sqn
114962	P/O	TARBITTEN DFC Harry Lionel	19-01-42	9 Sqn
1234537	Sgt	TARBUCK Robert Douglas	12-12-42	20 OTU
941653	F/S	TARRAN John Lauson	3-06-42	61 Sqn
123966	P/O	TART George Roland	15-10-42	10 OTU
575807	Sgt	TARVER Derek Hugh	1-10-42	102 Sqn
1450668	Sgt	TATE Frederick Cyril Graham	16-08-42	156 Sqn
46344	F/O	TATE John Edmond	1-10-42	44 Sqn
617977	Sgt	TATE Leslie	16-09-42	106 Sqn
1255945	Sgt	TATE Walter George	15-01-42	104 Sqn
1310893	Sgt	TATLEY Hubert Thomas	20-12-42	9 Sqn
968101	Sgt	TAXEIRA de MATTOS Ernest Ralph	26-06-42	102 Sqn
1061230	Sgt	TAYLERSON Wilfred Lloyd	9-01-42	15 OTU
908047	Sgt	TAYLOR Alfred	24-09-42	78 Sqn
549284	F/S	TAYLOR Arthur	18-12-42	1474 Flt
1383496	Sgt	TAYLOR Arthur Richard	25-10-42	142 Sqn
1457016	AC2	TAYLOR Aubrey George	28-12-42	97 Sqn
126549	P/O	TAYLOR Charles Frederick	12-08-42	156 Sqn
1285297	Sgt	TAYLOR Cyril Martin	17-12-42	218 Sqn
755137	F/S	TAYLOR David White	26-06-42	12 OTU
116420	P/O	TAYLOR Donald Martin Howard	21-12-42	7 Sqn
1170001	Sgt	TAYLOR Edward Manice	17-06-42	24 OTU
912911	Sgt	TAYLOR Eric Leonard	22-06-42	12 OTU
968984	Sgt	TAYLOR Frank	30-09-42	51 Sqn
643077	Sgt	TAYLOR George Ingate	12-02-42	214 Sqn
962315	Sgt	TAYLOR Gordon Peter	27-08-42	15 OTU
989480	Sgt	TAYLOR Harold	13-04-42	49 Sqn
990446	Sgt	TAYLOR Harry	28-04-42	115 Sqn
1260918	Sgt	TAYLOR Harry	27-03-42	115 Sqn
1805679	Sgt	TAYLOR Harry Stuart	19-12-42	149 Sqn

114965	P/O	TAYLOR Henry	27-03-42	115 Sqn	920520	Sgt	THOMPSON Hector Francis	22-02-42	50 Sqn
624640	F/S	TAYLOR Henry Charles	23-12-42	138 Sqn	524716	F/S	THOMPSON John	31-05-42	26 OTU
804258	Sgt	TAYLOR Herbert Kenneth	15-01-42	10 Sqn	1055985	Sgt	THOMPSON John	27-03-42	138 Sqn
1386118	Sgt	TAYLOR Hugh Cowan	28-08-42	207 Sqn	1130406	Sgt	THOMPSON John Morris	6-08-42	20 OTU
656277	F/S	TAYLOR Jack	13-10-42	156 Sqn	989028	Sgt	THOMPSON John Robert	2-06-42	76 Sqn
1379000	Sgt	TAYLOR James Arthur	28-10-42	150 Sqn	575861	Sgt	THOMPSON Peter John	25-11-42	207 Sqn
1061930	Sgt	TAYLOR Jess	12-08-42	150 Sqn	580501	W/O	THOMPSON Peter Richard	26-03-42	83 Sqn
1024292	Sgt	TAYLOR John Sharrock	10-02-42	11 OTU	1177179	Sgt	THOMPSON Ronald Edward	1-07-42	21 OTU
1390639	Sgt	TAYLOR John William	3-12-42	102 Sqn	999498	F/S	THOMPSON Ronald Norman	7-02-42	144 Sqn
1036176	Sgt	TAYLOR Joseph Gordon	24-10-42	57 Sqn	778361	Sgt	THOMPSON Roy Furnivall [Rhodesia]	7-02-42	144 Sqn
1105970	Sgt	TAYLOR Kenneth	7-04-42	15 Sqn	807161	Sgt	THOMPSON Thomas	20-09-42	61 Sqn
1034269	F/S	TAYLOR Kenneth Chadwick	31-12-42	83 Sqn	1062688	Sgt	THOMPSON Thomas Robinson	4-08-42	226 Sqn
1181905	Sgt	TAYLOR Lawrence Ernest	7-04-42	142 Sqn	1066764	Sgt	THOMPSON Walter	5-06-42	156 Sqn
116635	P/O	TAYLOR Raymond Charles	3-09-42	61 Sqn	581543	Sgt	THOMPSON William	2-06-42	78 Sqn
999390	Sgt	TAYLOR Robert Harold	22-02-42	83 Sqn	1024879	Sgt	THOMPSON William Arthur	14-09-42	12 Sqn
100051	P/O	TAYLOR Robert Edwin	29-01-42	21 Sqn	569528	Sgt	THOMPSON-HORAN Robert	7-04-42	15 Sqn
1383375	Sgt	TAYLOR Sidney Frederick	24-10-42	149 Sqn	1196328	Sgt	THOMSON Alan Copland	27-03-42	21 OTU
927153	Sgt	TAYLOR Walter John	26-07-42	78 Sqn	130164	P/O	THOMSON Gordon Temple	14-12-42	10 OTU
1154657	Sgt	TAYLOR Wilfred Lawson	9-05-42	158 Sqn	1380318	Sgt	THOMSON Wilfred George	30-05-42	156 Sqn
613131	Sgt	TAYLOR William Henry	17-12-42	57 Sqn	960871	Sgt	THORBURN Archibald John	23-04-42	218 Sqn
1211090	Sgt	TAYLOR William Paul	12-08-42	50 Sqn	1112970	Sgt	THORLEY Edward	5-08-42	1653 CU
127981	P/O	TAYLOR William Roderick	17-11-42	11 OTU	119173	P/O	THORNDYKE Ronald Henry James	7-06-42	49 Sqn
1381318	Sgt	TAYLOR William Swordy	16-03-42	57 Sqn	65508	F/L	THORNE Fred Martyn	24-07-42	18 Sqn
1262024	Sgt	TAYLOR William Thomas	8-12-42	149 Sqn	550874	Sgt	THORNE Frederick Arthur William	24-07-42	214 Sqn
1387361	Sgt	TAYLOR-THOMAS Arthur Kay	20-08-42	115 Sqn	652527	F/S	THORNLEY George Herbert	15-10-42	10 OTU
1191729	Sgt	TEALL Peter Granville	28-07-42	101 Sqn	111484	P/O	THORNLEY Robert Edward	2-09-42	115 Sqn
1385208	Sgt	TEASDALE Malcolm James Francis	31-12-42	19 OTU	1055021	Sgt	THORNTON Douglas	26-07-42	138 Sqn
1254448	Sgt	TEBBUT Ronald	31-10-42	107 Sqn	1181849	Sgt	THORNTON Frederick William	30-05-42	142 Sqn
902613	Sgt	TEESDALE-SMITH James Barcroft	2-06-42	102 Sqn	1378888	Sgt	THORNTON George Walker	18-05-42	20 OTU
1123156	Sgt	TEEVIN John	21-07-42	106 Sqn	112299	P/O	THORNTON John Riley	27-08-42	15 Sqn
655189	Sgt	TELFORD Donald Montgrove	25-04-42	11 OTU	1283342	Sgt	THOROGOOD Frederick Charles	19-07-42	226 Sqn
916899	Sgt	TELLING Robert Douglas	19-01-42	9 Sqn	1375386	Sgt	THOROGOOD Herbert John	24-04-42	150 Sqn
975654	Sgt	TEMPLE Ernest Walter	19-08-42	61 Sqn	1310941	Sgt	THORPE MiD Frederick Arnold	11-09-42	7 Sqn
138678	P/O	TESAR Josef [Czechoslovakia]	10-12-42	138 Sqn	1177709	Sgt	THORPE James	5-10-42	102 Sqn
545586	Sgt	TETLEY Leslie Mellor	28-08-42	142 Sqn	1378582	Sgt	THORPE Percival Gordon	26-03-42	12 Sqn
778286	F/S	TETLEY Norman [South Africa]	1-08-42	44 Sqn	1376043	Sgt	THORPE Wilfred	2-04-42	57 Sqn
1287689	Sgt	TEXTER John Ashburner	22-11-42	115 Sqn	1266088	Sgt	THURGAR Horace George	6-06-42	14 OTU
905398	F/S	THIRKELL DFM Patrick Herbert Harold	8-05-42	44 Sqn	1312235	Sgt	THURGOOD Peter Mitchell	21-07-42	35 Sqn
					936982	Cpl	THWAITE Donald Parr	1-04-42	107 Sqn
1375508	Sgt	THOM James Thomas	17-01-42	51 Sqn	1692614	AC2	THWAITES John	12-12-42	Syerston
1172599	Sgt	THOMAS Ambrose Bowen	15-01-42	103 Sqn	1256777	Sgt	TIBBATTS Kenneth Horace	2-04-42	214 Sqn
1162157	Sgt	THOMAS Arthur	25-08-42	150 Sqn	1315672	Sgt	TIDBALL Frederick Leonard	8-11-42	10 Sqn
1262993	Sgt	THOMAS Arthur Edgar	27-09-42	78 Sqn	1335965	Sgt	TIDMAN Brian Arthur	22-11-42	10 OTU
1318061	Sgt	THOMAS Bernard Haydn	6-12-42	487 Sqn	642450	Sgt	TIDMARSH Robert Frank	7-08-42	103 Sqn
1332256	Sgt	THOMAS Clifford James	28-05-42	1443 Flt	742642	W/O	TILEY Edwin Lyndon	28-03-42	1485 Flt
941095	Sgt	THOMAS Edward	29-03-42	83 Sqn	934087	Sgt	TILL Douglas Harold	11-04-42	158 Sqn
947742	Sgt	THOMAS Eric Albert	22-07-42	101 Sqn	115124	P/O	TILLARD John Nigel	26-03-42	142 Sqn
117131	P/O	THOMAS Eric Fielder	14-09-42	12 Sqn	1387083	Sgt	TILLETT Albert George	9-09-42	150 Sqn
1312704	Sgt	THOMAS Eugene Sydney	18-08-42	101 Sqn	1106850	Sgt	TILLEY Colin	24-05-42	21 Sqn
953589	F/S	THOMAS Frank Raymond	9-09-42	150 Sqn	1378541	Sgt	TILLEY George Albert	10-03-42	405 Sqn
1111152	F/S	THOMAS Frederick Edward	14-01-42	207 Sqn	1186959	Sgt	TILLIN Laurence Charles	17-09-42	214 Sqn
529207	Sgt	THOMAS Howell	6-06-42	35 Sqn	49679	F/O	TILLING George Edward	27-07-42	420 Sqn
545987	F/S	THOMAS John	12-07-42	51 Sqn	131807	P/O	TIMMIS John Harold 'Jack'	27-07-42	420 Sqn
1312854	Sgt	THOMAS John Hubert	2-09-42	15 OTU	997190	Sgt	TIMMONS Patrick Joseph	14-01-42	40 Sqn
117657	P/O	THOMAS Leonard Barclay	29-07-42	1651 CU	41333	F/L	TIPPETTS-AYLMER DFC Philip Hampden	8-09-42	78 Sqn
45490	F/O	THOMAS Owen Dixon	17-09-42	49 Sqn					
755868	Sgt	THOMAS Peter Anthony	24-02-42	144 Sqn	755837	F/S	TIPPLE Anthony Roland	7-08-42	150 Sqn
113370	P/O	THOMAS Raymond Bowen	3-01-42	99 Sqn	1291758	Sgt	TITCOMB William Arthur	29-07-42	75 Sqn
1282315	Sgt	THOMAS Stanley Henry	4-06-42	50 Sqn	1057551	Sgt	TITTERINGTON John	2-06-42	61 Sqn
1284757	Sgt	THOMAS Thomas Hugh	14-01-42	40 Sqn	931607	Sgt	TOBIN Joseph Arthur	7-02-42	144 Sqn
130101	F/O	THOMAS William Albert	10-09-42	158 Sqn	118588	F/O	TODD David Bryant [USA]	7-11-42	83 Sqn
1319646	Sgt	THOMAS William Earl	30-06-42	149 Sqn	641943	Cpl	TODD Harry	24-09-42	51 Sqn
1113658	F/S	THOMASSON Francis Neville	11-08-42	78 Sqn	1074252	F/S	TODD John William	28-08-42	408 Sqn
902444	W/O	THOMPSON Alfred Norman	8-09-42	76 Sqn	65555	F/O	TOFIELD Gordon Leslie	2-06-42	61 Sqn
119149	F/O	THOMPSON Allan	29-11-42	1446 Flt	612946	Sgt	TOGHILL Leslie Cyril	12-02-42	49 Sqn
1354657	Sgt	THOMPSON Fairfield	13-09-42	27 OTU	788183	Sgt	TOLAR Alois [Czechoslovakia]	3-03-42	311 Sqn
1198362	Sgt	THOMPSON Frederick Ralph [Canada]	22-11-42	102 Sqn	964792	Sgt	TOLLER Kenneth Richard	12-08-42	405 Sqn
109082	P/O	THOMPSON George David Ronald	9-11-42	142 Sqn	1287043	Sgt	TOLMIE John Lester	26-06-42	115 Sqn

120617	F/O	TOLMIE William Alexander		31-10-42	150 Sqn	47365	F/O	TURNHAM John Edward	1-11-42	138 Sqn
1376539	Sgt	TOMKINS Fred		20-05-42	7 Sqn	657241	Sgt	TURPITT Reginald Victor	9-09-42	25 OTU
1007437	Sgt	TOMLIN Norman		16-08-42	50 Sqn	1268038	Sgt	TURTILL Aubrey John Frank	29-01-42	15 OTU
37989	S/L	TOMLINSON DFC Dennis Brendon Geoffrey				40866	F/L	TURTLE DFC Reginald William Arthur	7-06-42	214 Sqn
				2-06-42	10 OTU	1167137	Sgt	TURTON Harry Victor	4-07-42	61 Sqn
1001269	Sgt	TOMLINSON James Brian		16-06-42	1651 CU	925966	Sgt	TURVEY Kenneth Tempest	2-10-42	115 Sqn
1253789	Sgt	TOMLINSON Ralph Edward		12-02-42	455 Sqn	1027511	Sgt	TUTTLE Meredith Edward [Eire]	24-06-42	13 OTU
1121000	Sgt	TOOLE Wilfred		29-08-42	61 Sqn	616062	Sgt	TWEEDALE Ernest Arthur	26-07-42	78 Sqn
1026790	Sgt	TOOTH Frank		1-10-42	102 Sqn	61481	F/L	TWEEDIE William Lang	1-06-42	18 OTU
1079014	Sgt	TOPHAM Stanley		16-08-42	106 Sqn	759034	F/S	TWELVES Eric	15-01-42	103 Sqn
915895	F/S	TOPPING Eric		1-10-42	76 Sqn	1061154	Sgt	TWIDALE Kenneth	27-02-42	16 OTU
103530	P/O	TOPPING DFM John Robert		12-02-42	420 Sqn	1210421	Sgt	TWINING Victor Henry	30-07-42	102 Sqn
1379180	Sgt	TORR Howard Yorke		10-11-42	107 Sqn	1265240	Sgt	TYAS Peter	11-02-42	21 Sqn
1365831	LAC	TORRANCE Archibald		31-10-42	88 Sqn	924164	Sgt	TYLER Gerald Osmond	20-08-42	115 Sqn
1053439	Sgt	TOUGH George		13-11-42	107 Sqn	990574	Sgt	TYNE Donald Hoyland	6-02-42	21 OTU
1126835	Sgt	TOWERS Joseph		10-12-42	20 OTU	1316919	Sgt	TYREMAN John William	20-12-42	9 Sqn
570416	Sgt	TOWLER Alec Ernest		9-05-42	10 Sqn	60076	F/L	TYRRELL Theodore Frank	16-09-42	23 OTU
1182234	Sgt	TOWLER David		26-03-42	144 Sqn	1180112	Sgt	TYTHERLEIGH Ernest Henry	1-10-42	78 Sqn
119476	F/O	TOWNER Jack		31-10-42	150 Sqn	131880	P/O	UNDERWOOD Charles Frederick Walter		
1182661	Sgt	TOWNS George		28-06-42	156 Sqn				3-09-42	61 Sqn
925413	Sgt	TOWNSEND Albert Eric		19-08-42	61 Sqn	122398	P/O	UNDERWOOD John Bennett	31-05-42	61 Sqn
1051659	Sgt	TOWNSEND Tom Gordon Prentis		3-06-42	460 Sqn	546445	Sgt	UNDERWOOD John William Caddick		
76019	F/L	TOZER Thomas Henry		2-04-42	57 Sqn				3-07-42	214 Sqn
1186404	Sgt	TRANTER Frederick James		22-06-42	12 OTU	104507	P/O	UNDERWOOD Ronald Benjamin	27-04-42	97 Sqn
976873	Sgt	TRAQUAIR William Lyall Edmond		6-06-42	103 Sqn	1057891	Sgt	UNSWORTH Donald	27-02-42	77 Sqn
		[Canada]				987978	Sgt	URQUHART Alexander Scouler	8-05-42	420 Sqn
1173842	Sgt	TRAWFORD Arthur Frederick		27-03-42	408 Sqn	522477	Sgt	UZZELL Edward Howard	16-10-42	149 Sqn
1378356	Sgt	TRAYLEN Lionel Denis		19-07-42	27 OTU	621311	Sgt	VALDER Claude William	3-04-42	101 Sqn
778839	Sgt	TREBLE Terence Bryce [South Africa]		9-09-42	142 Sqn	120171	P/O	VALENTINE Edward Francis	20-05-42	156 Sqn
934007	Sgt	TREDINNICK Francis Gerald		20-12-42	76 Sqn	997279	Sgt	VALLANCE Robert	10-09-42	218 Sqn
117991	P/O	TREE Basil Gordon		28-09-42	1507 Flt	102574	P/O	VALTERS Ronald Walter	19-05-42	35 Sqn
1260777	Sgt	TREE Raymond Douglas		12-08-42	15 Sqn	1377265	F/S	VANDERSTEEN Ronald	22-07-42	142 Sqn
104537	P/O	TREE Thomas Neville		27-04-42	97 Sqn	136560	P/O	VANICEK Frantisek [Czechoslovakia]	10-12-42	138 Sqn
104371	P/O	TREGEA James Richard [Argentina]		9-07-42	101 Sqn	787901	Sgt	VARJAN Pauel [Czechoslovakia]	14-04-42	311 Sqn
947664	Sgt	TREHEARN Philip Leonard Newell		14-04-42	102 Sqn	921823	F/S	VARLEY Peter Worthington Samuel	15-10-42	150 Sqn
44980	F/O	TREHERNE DFM Vernon Frank Evans		2-07-42	139 Sqn	1383563	Sgt	VASIL George Walter Albert Hamlet	19-09-42	15 Sqn
106547	P/O	TRENCH Richard Chenevix		9-03-42	21 OTU	1205010	Sgt	VAUGHAN DFM Bernard William	15-10-42	103 Sqn
108005	P/O	TREPPAS Leonard		7-06-42	214 Sqn	118660	P/O	VAUGHAN Robert Hilary	10-08-42	405 Sqn
113359	F/O	TRETHEWY John Hugh		17-08-42	1652 CU	117144	P/O	VAVASOUR Bede Joseph Stourton	12-06-42	12 OTU
755032	F/S	TREVILLIAN Ronald Anthony John		2-04-42	214 Sqn	778678	Sgt	van LELYVELD Peter [Rhodesia]	1-10-42	76 Sqn
1220162	Sgt	TREWIN Alfred		23-09-42	142 Sqn	1175399	Sgt	VEAL John Edward	1-06-42	77 Sqn
1258458	F/S	TRILLWOOD Harold Ernest		7-11-42	Wyton	123683	P/O	VENNEEAR Sidney Alfred	6-12-42	464 Sqn
1393247	Sgt	TRIMMER Frederick		21-12-42	103 Sqn	777701	Sgt	VENTER Peter Johannes [Rhodesia]	17-04-42	44 Sqn
1151434	Sgt	TRISCOTT John Adrian Rolt		18-08-42	76 Sqn	1263877	Sgt	VENTHAM Norman Frank	9-12-42	214 Sqn
1152528	Sgt	TROMANS William Thomas		21-01-42	50 Sqn	1331780	Sgt	VICK Edward John Florida	6-12-42	487 Sqn
959891	Sgt	TROTT Albert Edward		13-11-42	97 Sqn	1115126	F/S	VICKERS Charles Henry	29-08-42	75 Sqn
121213	P/O	TROTTER Thomas		7-11-42	107 Sqn	1375930	Sgt	VICKERY Stanley John	24-06-42	103 Sqn
547134	Sgt	TROTTIER William Henry		23-09-42	50 Sqn	1151773	Sgt	VIGERS Kenneth Hamilton	10-09-42	11 OTU
1204009	Sgt	TRUBSHAW Bertram Kenneth		9-12-42	24 OTU	978029	Sgt	VINCENT David Stanley Bonner	31-05-42	26 OTU
1168521	Sgt	TRUSCOTT Frank Godfrey [Canada]		28-01-42	214 Sqn	109373	P/O	VINCENT Harold Jesse	6-06-42	49 Sqn
1268146	Sgt	TRUSTRAM Richard Lattimore		17-04-42	44 Sqn	130210	P/O	VINCENT James Henry	1-10-42	15 Sqn
569400	Sgt	TUCK Douglas Francis Hooper		9-03-42	15 Sqn	1305770	Sgt	VINER Norman	21-01-42	51 Sqn
114979	F/O	TUCKER Richard Albert George		2-09-42	115 Sqn	1188483	Sgt	VINNICOMBE Vernon Frederick	17-09-42	12 OTU
909105	F/S	TUCKER-FELTHAM Patrick William		28-08-42	35 Sqn	915640	F/S	VINT Alexander Robert	2-04-42	214 Sqn
116028	P/O	TUDOR Gerald Leslie		21-08-42	218 Sqn	787584	Sgt	VOKURA Rudolf [Czechoslovakia]	6-04-42	1429 Flt
105185	F/L	TUDOR-JONES Robert		17-11-42	158 Sqn	1056269	Sgt	VOSPER Henry Ernest	15-04-42	420 Sqn
1061243	Sgt	TUNNACLIFFE John		6-09-42	51 Sqn	1315934	Sgt	VOWLES Samuel Richard	19-08-42	61 Sqn
102614	P/O	TUNNINGTON Eric		26-02-42	12 Sqn	133592	P/O	VOYZEY Percy James	4-07-42	226 Sqn
1107786	Sgt	TUPHOLME Eric		27-08-42	142 Sqn	985888	Sgt	WADDELL James	6-04-42	49 Sqn
787909	Sgt	TURKL Emil [Czechoslovakia]		13-10-42	27 OTU	108046	P/O	WADDELL James Douglas	17-01-42	7 Sqn
1261183	Sgt	TURLEY Raymond		3-09-42	15 Sqn	115918	F/O	WADDINGHAM DFC Cyril Douglas	9-03-42	9 Sqn
569548	Sgt	TURNBULL James Luther		2-06-42	405 Sqn	979926	Sgt	WADDINGTON John Noel	3-07-42	420 Sqn
917377	Sgt	TURNER Christopher William		28-04-42	150 Sqn	749351	F/S	WADE Henry James	23-09-42	50 Sqn
983303	Sgt	TURNER Fred Arnold		13-11-42	105 Sqn	121733	P/O	WAGSTAFF Ernest Adam	25-10-42	103 Sqn
1251531	Sgt	TURNER Geoffrey Malcolm Charles		16-01-42	214 Sqn	1309976	Sgt	WAGSTAFF William Richard	18-05-42	115 Sqn
109520	F/O	TURNER George Thomas		6-11-42	78 Sqn	1295715	Sgt	WAINWRIGHT George Albert	20-12-42	49 Sqn
645043	F/S	TURNER Harry Edward		31-01-42	61 Sqn	1167270	Sgt	WAIT Kenneth Albert	6-09-42	51 Sqn
126692	P/O	TURNER John Dayrell		15-10-42	97 Sqn	576297	Sgt	WAITE John Leslie Gordon	7-11-42	83 Sqn

135

1180917	Sgt	WAKEFIELD Frederick John	26-02-42	12 Sqn	902718	F/S	WANBON DFM Julian Robert	31-05-42	22 OTU
1165290	F/S	WAKEFIELD Kenneth	28-08-42	15 Sqn	1006452	Sgt	WANOSTROCHT Hugh Nicholas	17-05-42	9 Sqn
951404	Sgt	WAKEFIELD Thomas	22-07-42	57 Sqn	1215483	Sgt	WARBURTON Henry John	10-12-42	9 Sqn
650367	Sgt	WAKEFORD Herbert Reginald Frank	30-04-42	158 Sqn	553645	AC1	WARBURTON Herbert	7-07-42	161 Sqn
1389383	Sgt	WAKELIN Walter John	24-10-42	57 Sqn	110864	P/O	WARD Bertram Noel	26-07-42	142 Sqn
1458440	Sgt	WALDER Gerald	28-08-42	156 Sqn	1386499	Sgt	WARD Derek Charles	15-10-42	106 Sqn
1101233	Sgt	WALDIE Alexander Ashcroft	12-08-42	50 Sqn	1360009	Sgt	WARD Douglas Frederick James	8-02-42	21 OTU
1255786	Sgt	WALDMAN Sidney Solomon	1-10-42	78 Sqn	1261399	Sgt	WARD Eric	8-06-42	149 Sqn
1360573	Sgt	WALDRON Cyril	20-07-42	12 Sqn	84909	F/O	WARD George William	16-04-42	106 Sqn
1230768	Sgt	WALE Graham	2-05-42	106 Sqn	1064100	Sgt	WARD Jack	16-04-42	214 Sqn
1217287	Sgt	WALKER Alan Alfred	13-10-42	83 Sqn	66580	P/O	WARD John Edward	29-03-42	103 Sqn
1105816	Sgt	WALKER Anthony Gordon	26-01-42	12 Sqn	577760	LAC	WARD Kenneth	13-09-42	27 OTU
1116673	AC2	WALKER Arthur	11-09-42	102 Sqn	134027	P/O	WARD Lyn George Lloyd	14-07-42	18 Sqn
112738	P/O	WALKER Bryan Lister	16-09-42	15 Sqn	1377166	Sgt	WARD Maurice Victor	26-03-42	142 Sqn
641481	Sgt	WALKER Dermid McDermid Orrock	20-12-42	158 Sqn	755783	Sgt	WARD Peter Hallam [New Zealand]	19-05-42	218 Sqn
42285	F/L	WALKER Eric	31-07-42	27 OTU	1280557	Sgt	WARD Sidney Bertram	1-08-42	101 Sqn
1079155	Sgt	WALKER Eric Wilson	20-12-42	9 Sqn	905163	F/S	WARD Wesley Newell	6-05-42	13 OTU
1378434	Sgt	WALKER Fred	31-05-42	10 Sqn	1124718	Sgt	WARDLE James Stratton	8-07-42	19 OTU
1105111	Sgt	WALKER George Alec	14-09-42	1654 CU	1061454	Sgt	WARDLE Oscar	9-11-42	50 Sqn
936065	Sgt	WALKER George Henry	7-04-42	61 Sqn	1123342	Sgt	WARE Douglas John	30-07-42	50 Sqn
1059468	Sgt	WALKER Jack	10-04-42	9 Sqn	647870	Sgt	WARE Ronald George	17-09-42	15 OTU
1119267	Sgt	WALKER James Roy	21-12-42	207 Sqn	1013281	Sgt	WAREHAM William Elwyn Ronald	22-09-42	226 Sqn
118969	P/O	WALKER John Richard	6-06-42	20 OTU	1436077	Sgt	WARING Alan	5-10-42	76 Sqn
641700	Sgt	WALKER Maurice Robert	14-01-42	207 Sqn	995672	Sgt	WARKUP Robert Gymer	24-06-42	76 Sqn
120670	P/O	WALKER Philip	28-07-42	156 Sqn	1324368	Sgt	WARNE William Charles	15-10-42	158 Sqn
1147944	Sgt	WALKER Raymond	9-11-42	12 OTU	126982	P/O	WARNER Cecil	25-08-42	7 Sqn
1029511	Sgt	WALKER Robert Henry	29-10-42	115 Sqn	655996	Sgt	WARNER Derek Eaton	14-09-42	1653 CU
1061701	Sgt	WALKER Robert Hetherington	7-05-42	21 OTU	1392795	Sgt	WARNER Jack Edgar Novelli	20-12-42	76 Sqn
535972	F/S	WALKER Ronald Arthur	29-03-42	109 Sqn	1006895	Sgt	WARREN Bruce Bisset	11-09-42	78 Sqn
1232380	Sgt	WALKER Ronald James	17-11-42	11 OTU	115300	P/O	WARREN Eric Alfred	22-02-42	83 Sqn
1432657	Sgt	WALKER Warren	17-09-42	149 Sqn	1250053	Sgt	WARREN George Edward	9-03-42	12 Sqn
1237274	Sgt	WALKER William Spence	16-10-42	142 Sqn	1292464	Sgt	WARREN George John	17-12-42	101 Sqn
82715	S/L	WALKINGTON John Greet Gordon	3-12-42	102 Sqn	1060037	F/S	WARREN Jack Passmore	21-12-42	9 Sqn
565802	W/O	WALL William	4-06-42	214 Sqn	552592	Sgt	WARREN John	10-01-42	49 Sqn
591267	Sgt	WALLACE James McRobbie	10-09-42	149 Sqn	1184333	Sgt	WARREN John Robert	13-07-42	1654 CU
120810	F/O	WALLACE Reginald	3-12-42	103 Sqn	1199627	Sgt	WARREN Joseph	20-11-42	76 Sqn
963001	Sgt	WALLBRIDGE Jack Mayne	5-06-42	114 Sqn	968278	Sgt	WARREN Michael Switzer [Eire]	29-07-42	9 Sqn
1330646	Sgt	WALLER Albert William	28-08-42	142 Sqn	566874	Sgt	WARREN Phillip Alexander	11-12-42	10 Sqn
118654	P/O	WALLER Gordon John	21-06-42	10 Sqn	1318039	Sgt	WARREN William Thomas	7-12-42	101 Sqn
1313097	Sgt	WALLER William	26-06-42	1481 Flt	1104095	F/S	WARREN-SMITH Lyster [South Africa]	24-03-42	44 Sqn
1379352	Sgt	WALLER William Leonard	31-05-42	158 Sqn					
1152284	Sgt	WALLIS Donald Walter	28-08-42	97 Sqn	128420	P/O	WASHER Robert	20-12-42	405 Sqn
109941	F/O	WALLIS Frank Antony Stanley	15-10-42	57 Sqn	1030618	LAC	WASHINGTON John	22-06-42	Feltwell
928617	Sgt	WALLIS Jack Lewis	4-06-42	61 Sqn	656472	Sgt	WATCHAM Eric	25-10-42	142 Sqn
1184035	Sgt	WALLIS Malcolm Ronald	20-12-42	156 Sqn	1389548	Sgt	WATERMAN John Andrew	17-09-42	149 Sqn
1321236	Sgt	WALLIS Peter Thurston	6-12-42	158 Sqn	1286185	Sgt	WATERS George Robert	1-07-42	21 OTU
625132	Sgt	WALLIS Robert Joseph	24-10-42	49 Sqn	1193368	Sgt	WATERS Ralph	27-06-42	218 Sqn
1153790	Sgt	WALLITER Stanley William	27-07-42	142 Sqn	116706	P/O	WATERSON William Caufield	24-07-42	25 OTU
1061883	F/S	WALLS James David	20-09-42	161 Sqn	1022828	Sgt	WATERSTON Robert Reid	8-05-42	9 Sqn
120645	P/O	WALMSLEY Arthur Stanley	25-08-42	15 OTU	936068	Sgt	WATERWORTH Alfred	26-01-42	51 Sqn
1100114	Sgt	WALMSLEY Donald Parker	7-04-42	49 Sqn	564896	W/O	WATHEY Colin	4-06-42	207 Sqn
41634	F/L	WALMSLEY William Reginald Ivor	29-09-42	20 OTU	47586	F/O	WATHEY DFM Herbert	12-02-42	144 Sqn
574449	Sgt	WALPOLE Thomas Henry [Eire]	20-12-42	76 Sqn	570553	Sgt	WATKIN Charles Joseph Nicholas	28-03-42	7 Sqn
43421	W/C	WALSH DFC AFC Archibald Philip [Canada]	3-09-42	419 Sqn	1331702	Sgt	WATKINS Arthur Ernest	19-07-42	158 Sqn
					747879	F/S	WATKINS Arthur Reginald	26-06-42	26 OTU
126780	P/O	WALSH DFC* Maurice Edward	9-11-42	57 Sqn	650817	Sgt	WATKINS Jack	21-10-42	7 Sqn
1159245	Sgt	WALSH Michael William	29-07-42	156 Sqn	1309927	Sgt	WATKINSON James Herbert	27-03-42	115 Sqn
104427	P/O	WALSH Samuel Partington	2-06-42	61 Sqn	1134105	Sgt	WATSON Asa	30-11-42	22 OTU
1360278	Sgt	WALSH Wilfrid	14-02-42	12 OTU	1281960	Sgt	WATSON Denis John Whelan	20-06-42	460 Sqn
44227	F/L	WALTER Claud Bransby	23-10-42	105 Sqn	1073521	Sgt	WATSON Ernest	15-09-42	218 Sqn
1154055	Sgt	WALTERS Ernest Desmond	6-06-42	103 Sqn	1023590	Sgt	WATSON George Samuel	31-05-42	142 Sqn
1305405	Sgt	WALTERS Frederick	18-09-42	44 Sqn	633919	F/O	WATSON James John [Eire]	24-09-42	9 Sqn
1125354	Sgt	WALTERS Harry	2-12-42	12 OTU	1097953	Sgt	WATSON John Edwin	14-12-42	10 OTU
1154688	Sgt	WALTERS William Victor	12-02-42	144 Sqn	1101058	Sgt	WATSON John George	28-07-42	16 OTU
1197566	Sgt	WALTHO Dennis Stanley	26-12-42	26 OTU	546758	Sgt	WATSON John Wilfred	26-04-42	9 Sqn
1076366	Sgt	WALTON Eric	24-10-42	78 Sqn	574543	Sgt	WATSON Kenneth Storey	27-07-42	405 Sqn
1380196	Sgt	WALTON Stanley George	17-09-42	158 Sqn	541917	F/S	WATSON Louis Gilbert	15-12-42	405 Sqn
1104554	Sgt	WALTON William	14-07-42	158 Sqn	1172589	Sgt	WATSON Robert Walker	29-04-42	78 Sqn

Service No	Rank	Name	Date	Sqn/Unit
1133624	Sgt	WATSON Stanley	14-09-42	214 Sqn
1112566	Sgt	WATSON Walter McDonald	2-07-42	218 Sqn
1078071	Sgt	WATSON Willie	4-06-42	76 Sqn
571759	Sgt	WATT Alexander Clubb	17-12-42	138 Sqn
526911	Sgt	WATT Edwin James Duguid	20-12-42	106 Sqn
1349714	Sgt	WATT Fraser Hutchinson Kilpatrick	8-12-42	149 Sqn
1108788	Sgt	WATT William Rebecca	21-07-42	218 Sqn
610633	Sgt	WATTERS Ivor	1-08-42	405 Sqn
1258515	LAC	WATTS Claude	3-01-42	20 OTU
962662	Sgt	WATTS John Edwin	30-09-42	9 Sqn
1099956	Cpl	WATTS Thomas Albert	5-09-42	Wyton
107516	P/O	WAUGH Harry	4-02-42	21 OTU
116133	P/O	WAY Stanley William Alfred	12-02-42	49 Sqn
963167	Sgt	WAYLAN John Evan Francis	16-07-42	15 Sqn
1150946	Sgt	WAYLETT Kenneth Malcolm	1-08-42	18 Sqn
1032518	Sgt	WEARMOUTH Alan	25-06-42	76 Sqn
655156	Sgt	WEATHERSON Joseph	9-08-42	20 OTU
1063594	Sgt	WEAVER John Saunders	2-04-42	101 Sqn
47486	P/O	WEBB MiD Alfred Thomas	17-04-42	97 Sqn
920594	Sgt	WEBB Cultra Vallance	3-07-42	103 Sqn
644998	Sgt	WEBB Edward Frederick	5-05-42	12 Sqn
16212	G/C	WEBB Eric Bingham	2-04-42	Snaith
1260304	Sgt	WEBB Ernest Thomas	31-05-42	78 Sqn
1213917	Sgt	WEBB John Henry	21-08-42	218 Sqn
1320645	Sgt	WEBB Windsor Francis Richard	25-11-42	207 Sqn
1255058	Sgt	WEBBE Leslie William	15-04-42	49 Sqn
742913	F/S	WEBBER Harold Edward	1-10-42	15 Sqn
123861	P/O	WEBBER John Richard	4-06-42	218 Sqn
1021363	Sgt	WEBBER Leonard Edwin	22-11-42	57 Sqn
1154729	Sgt	WEBBER Norman Frederick	3-06-42	15 Sqn
1254246	Sgt	WEBLEY Raymond John	19-04-42	49 Sqn
1117211	Sgt	WEBSTER Eric	28-07-42	101 Sqn
1053681	Sgt	WEBSTER Ernest	25-08-42	83 Sqn
43127	S/L	WEBSTER DFC Frederick David	31-03-42	10 Sqn
778301	Sgt	WEBSTER Leonard Raymond [Rhodesia]	8-05-42	44 Sqn
531880	Sgt	WEBSTER Norman Harry	12-03-42	58 Sqn
989483	F/S	WEBSTER Peter Henry George	16-02-42	61 Sqn
1305420	Sgt	WEBSTER Samuel James	26-06-42	10 OTU
1214223	Sgt	WEBSTER Squire Arbuthnott	28-08-42	103 Sqn
1204039	Sgt	WEDGWOOD Samuel Cliff	17-09-42	12 OTU
46768	P/O	WEEKS Dennis Owens	28-01-42	138 Sqn
1102282	Sgt	WEEKS Thomas William	12-03-42	58 Sqn
114427	P/O	WEET John Derrick Forbes	9-05-42	158 Sqn
866405	Sgt	WEIGHTMAN William	26-06-42	102 Sqn
47895	P/O	WEIR John Davidson	3-06-42	15 Sqn
787519	W/O	WEISS Karel [Czechoslovakia]	21-01-42	311 Sqn
759335	Sgt	WELBY Harold Henry	17-09-42	12 OTU
122986	P/O	WELCH David Arthur	14-07-42	12 Sqn
926914	Sgt	WELCH Malcolm Hunter	17-01-42	27 OTU
751432	F/S	WELHAM Wilfred Deryck	25-03-42	106 Sqn
1333817	Sgt	WELLER Harold	7-08-42	150 Sqn
645684	F/S	WELSH Derek Shergold Drury	9-03-42	9 Sqn
930250	Sgt	WENTWORTH-HYDE Robert Charles	11-02-42	12 Sqn
930530	Sgt	WERREN Roy Ernest	8-11-42	9 Sqn
523056	F/S	WESCOMBE Basil Courtney	14-01-42	207 Sqn
649043	Sgt	WEST Donald Edwin	2-06-42	78 Sqn
1152156	Sgt	WEST Geoffrey Llewellyn	6-01-42	49 Sqn
1384504	Sgt	WEST George Walter	31-08-42	24 OTU
1256886	Sgt	WEST Leo	22-07-42	12 Sqn
40870	S/L	WEST DFC Peter Wynn Mason [New Zealand]	4-07-42	61 Sqn
657215	Sgt	WEST Thomas Anderson	16-11-42	149 Sqn
1110187	Sgt	WEST Thomas Ronald Augustus	2-06-42	76 Sqn
1337262	Sgt	WEST Walter Roy	5-06-42	50 Sqn
961733	Sgt	WESTBURY Claude Raymond	14-01-42	207 Sqn
922948	Sgt	WESTERN Albert James	24-04-42	405 Sqn
540813	Sgt	WESTGATE BEM John Herbert	16-08-42	156 Sqn
1100628	Sgt	WESTLAND John Joseph [Canada]	26-02-42	10 Sqn
1109648	Sgt	WESTON Cecil Stanley	26-07-42	115 Sqn
656324	Sgt	WESTON Dennis Hubert	12-08-42	12 OTU
41885	S/L	WESTON DFC George Ernest [New Zealand]	1-10-42	61 Sqn
111532	P/O	WESTON Robert	9-06-42	75 Sqn
1293607	Sgt	WESTON Robert	10-12-42	11 OTU
1379832	Sgt	WETHERED Ian Leslie	11-09-42	10 OTU
524640	Sgt	WEYMOUTH Charles Anthony	23-11-42	44 Sqn
952261	Sgt	WHALE Horace James	29-03-42	142 Sqn
751942	Sgt	WHALEN George Harvey	12-06-42	21 Sqn
1326440	Sgt	WHALLEY Charles James	29-08-42	57 Sqn
1072964	Sgt	WHALLEY James	26-07-42	138 Sqn
567426	Sgt	WHARFE Arthur Thomas	21-07-42	35 Sqn
1162294	Sgt	WHEATCROFT Montague Ernest	7-09-42	12 Sqn
567428	Sgt	WHEATLEY Harold Sydney	30-03-42	10 Sqn
120539	F/O	WHEATLEY Laurence	1-11-42	138 Sqn
110568	P/O	WHEATLEY DFM Robert Eric	24-03-42	19 OTU
933154	Sgt	WHEATON Vernon Philip Walrond	2-04-42	214 Sqn
127163	P/O	WHEBLE Ernest John Clifford	16-09-42	27 OTU
569291	Sgt	WHEELDON Philip Lawrence	13-04-42	76 Sqn
656880	Sgt	WHEELER Albert	3-06-42	13 OTU
923992	Sgt	WHEELER DFM Kenneth	5-05-42	218 Sqn
1577798	Sgt	WHEILDON Joseph William	30-11-42	7 Sqn
129281	P/O	WHELAN Kenneth Vincent	20-05-42	156 Sqn
656109	Sgt	WHELAN Patrick	7-11-42	21 Sqn
1253490	Sgt	WHELAN Thomas	5-06-42	156 Sqn
925047	Sgt	WHEWAY Harold Frank Vernon	28-04-42	214 Sqn
61037	F/O	WHISKEN DFC Kenneth Derek	26-06-42	1652 CU
1105947	Sgt	WHITAKER Arthur	24-04-42	77 Sqn
118618	P/O	WHITAKER Edgar	27-08-42	15 OTU
923920	Sgt	WHITBREAD Basil Edwin	10-04-42	158 Sqn
111523	P/O	WHITE Arthur Cyril	31-05-42	26 OTU
107315	P/O	WHITE Cyril Edwin	26-03-42	114 Sqn
1166180	Sgt	WHITE David John	25-03-42	142 Sqn
1257566	Sgt	WHITE Deric James	25-06-42	16 OTU
111485	P/O	WHITE Donald 'Don'	16-06-42	7 Sqn
647117	Sgt	WHITE Edwin James	31-05-42	218 Sqn
1388291	Sgt	WHITE Frederick George	8-11-42	10 Sqn
124628	P/O	WHITE MiD Frederick Sidney	27-07-42	158 Sqn
1163761	Sgt	WHITE Frank	12-04-42	103 Sqn
754076	Sgt	WHITE George	16-01-42	104 Sqn
1063335	Sgt	WHITE George Arthur	30-06-42	405 Sqn
615462	Sgt	WHITE Jack Herbert	29-07-42	7 Sqn
1123856	Sgt	WHITE John	13-05-42	17 OTU
1111871	Sgt	WHITE John Douglas	26-01-42	102 Sqn
624058	Sgt	WHITE Reginald James	15-01-42	51 Sqn
576796	Sgt	WHITE Robert Charles Montague	16-08-42	50 Sqn
1285421	Sgt	WHITE Stanley George	17-09-42	76 Sqn
1188851	Sgt	WHITE Sydney	1-11-42	138 Sqn
845279	Sgt	WHITE Sydney Thomas	13-08-42	77 Sqn
532269	Cpl	WHITE Victor Frederic	26-02-42	138 Sqn
969071	F/S	WHITEHEAD Christopher Derek Ainley	26-05-42	19 OTU
48895	P/O	WHITEHEAD DFM Harold Hopper	26-07-42	83 Sqn
1057167	Sgt	WHITEHEAD John Douglas	5-09-42	103 Sqn
1251376	F/S	WHITEHEAD Terence Raymond	4-09-42	97 Sqn
994746	Sgt	WHITEHEAD William Edwin	21-06-42	218 Sqn
121732	P/O	WHITELOCK Ralph	6-10-42	103 Sqn
41809	F/L	WHITEMAN Douglas Weston	29-04-42	7 Sqn
1166974	Sgt	WHITFIELD George Clive	6-06-42	49 Sqn
954271	Sgt	WHITFIELD John	2-06-42	10 Sqn
1115657	Sgt	WHITFIELD Norman	16-09-42	12 OTU
1175416	Sgt	WHITHAM Bryan	24-04-42	77 Sqn
1251357	Sgt	WHITING Donald Henry	13-08-42	207 Sqn
88680	F/O	WHITING William Robert Humphrey	31-05-42	26 OTU
1180652	Sgt	WHITING William Thomas	1-08-42	24 OTU
118892	P/O	WHITLEY Peter Percy	15-10-42	57 Sqn

48422	P/O	WHITTAKER DFM George	27-07-42	115 Sqn
1202337	Sgt	WHITTAKER Joseph Frank	30-07-42	150 Sqn
1286882	Sgt	WHITTEMORE Harold	6-06-42	49 Sqn
993807	Sgt	WHITTHAM Wilfred	27-02-42	77 Sqn
46402	F/O	WHITTINGHAM Clifford John	20-09-42	214 Sqn
102567	F/O	WHITTINGHAM John Arthur	26-06-42	78 Sqn
1310638	Sgt	WHITTLE Tom	8-06-42	149 Sqn
1202832	Sgt	WHITWORTH Charles Robert	25-05-42	22 OTU
120666	P/O	WHYTE Robert	5-10-42	218 Sqn
1108923	Sgt	WHYTE Thomas	5-05-42	218 Sqn
1338759	Sgt	WICK Sidney John	20-12-42	49 Sqn
1281297	Sgt	WICKS David John	8-11-42	9 Sqn
67703	P/O	WIDDUP Stanley	27-03-42	138 Sqn
1375081	F/S	WIELAND Ernest Victor Hallam	26-02-42	10 Sqn
946411	Sgt	WIGHAM Robert	26-06-42	218 Sqn
1284066	Sgt	WIGHT Charles Wilson	14-01-42	106 Sqn
982542	Sgt	WIGHTMAN Douglas	16-04-42	106 Sqn
1147930	Sgt	WIGLEY Horace	6-11-42	15 Sqn
1211499	Sgt	WILCOX Donald	9-01-42	90 Sqn
1208543	Sgt	WILCOX John Henry	25-10-42	12 Sqn
1057895	Sgt	WILD Jack	6-01-42	12 Sqn
1204241	Sgt	WILDE Edward	16-10-42	115 Sqn
1378164	Sgt	WILDE John William	6-11-42	26 OTU
1051977	Sgt	WILDE Reginald	24-04-42	77 Sqn
37437	W/C	WILDEY DFC Richard Kemp 'Dick'	15-10-42	10 Sqn
1257364	Sgt	WILDING Norman Seymour	28-08-42	57 Sqn
1116347	F/S	WILDING Vincent	17-04-42	97 Sqn
1209081	Sgt	WILDISH James Alfred David	29-10-42	115 Sqn
1150279	Sgt	WILKES Bernard	29-04-42	115 Sqn
569577	Sgt	WILKES John Bennett	28-08-42	218 Sqn
1335573	Sgt	WILKINS Kenneth Albert	21-10-42	7 Sqn
115993	P/O	WILKINSON Alfred	28-04-42	150 Sqn
103045	P/O	WILKINSON George	9-03-42	150 Sqn
1375311	Sgt	WILKINSON George Edmondson	21-01-42	455 Sqn
110571	P/O	WILKINSON George Winstone	27-04-42	7 Sqn
1319418	Sgt	WILKINSON Gordon Bowen	17-12-42	44 Sqn
907210	Sgt	WILKINSON Jack Edward	2-09-42	15 OTU
1050141	Sgt	WILKINSON John William	10-04-42	49 Sqn
943624	F/S	WILKINSON Joseph Cuthbert	28-08-42	97 Sqn
1254323	Sgt	WILKINSON Roland Marshall	11-07-42	101 Sqn
1125372	Sgt	WILKINSON Thomas Tweedy	3-12-42	103 Sqn
1378115	Sgt	WILLACY Herbert Richard	8-11-42	9 Sqn
1381545	Sgt	WILLANS Alec Gordon	15-10-42	12 Sqn
1309973	Sgt	WILLEY Henry Edward Arthur	24-06-42	103 Sqn
656396	Sgt	WILLEY Leonard Charles	1-11-42	88 Sqn
87802	F/O	WILLIAMS Absalom Samuel	21-06-42	10 Sqn
818241	F/S	WILLIAMS Albert Edward	5-08-42	44 Sqn
1122275	Sgt	WILLIAMS Alcwyn	17-09-42	106 Sqn
120626	P/O	WILLIAMS Alfred Cecil	17-08-42	15 OTU
358652	W/O	WILLIAMS Arthur Hamilton	4-06-42	13 OTU
982312	Sgt	WILLIAMS Bernard Wayne	16-09-42	106 Sqn
1312342	F/S	WILLIAMS Bryn	5-08-42	1653 CU
999235	Sgt	WILLIAMS Carl Vincent	13-04-42	9 Sqn
131637	P/O	WILLIAMS Charles Hanbury	6-10-42	44 Sqn
1255051	Sgt	WILLIAMS David	20-09-42	158 Sqn
106848	P/O	WILLIAMS David Llewelyn	29-01-42	78 Sqn
933496	Sgt	WILLIAMS Derek Bernard	29-07-42	18 Sqn
106560	P/O	WILLIAMS Donald George	12-06-42	83 Sqn
960375	Sgt	WILLIAMS Douglas Ernest	7-08-42	12 Sqn
118605	P/O	WILLIAMS Eric Llewellyn	15-06-42	19 OTU
1168354	Sgt	WILLIAMS Eric Humphrey	30-07-42	102 Sqn
1201671	Sgt	WILLIAMS Fernley Thomas	28-04-42	214 Sqn
1186280	Sgt	WILLIAMS George	27-03-42	115 Sqn
1205613	Sgt	WILLIAMS George William	19-12-42	149 Sqn
926466	Sgt	WILLIAMS Graham Colin	8-05-42	420 Sqn
917337	Sgt	WILLIAMS Gwyn Russell	10-03-42	149 Sqn
66508	F/L	WILLIAMS Harry Malcolm	14-04-42	102 Sqn
562624	Sgt	WILLIAMS Haydyn Taliesin	8-12-42	149 Sqn
657180	Sgt	WILLIAMS Henry Eric	11-09-42	15 Sqn
798632	Sgt	WILLIAMS Herbert Marmaduke [Newfoundland]	18-09-42	115 Sqn
572709	Sgt	WILLIAMS Jack Herbert	20-06-42	7 Sqn
1256892	F/S	WILLIAMS DFM James Eric	29-10-42	19 OTU
591301	Sgt	WILLIAMS James Roland	20-06-42	78 Sqn
1285053	Sgt	WILLIAMS James Warrell	20-06-42	101 Sqn
73459	F/O	WILLIAMS John	18-12-42	1474 Flt
550452	F/S	WILLIAMS John Arthur	16-08-42	106 Sqn
1253308	Sgt	WILLIAMS John Begby [Mauritius]	3-05-42	76 Sqn
575332	Sgt	WILLIAMS John Cyril	14-07-42	35 Sqn
573144	Sgt	WILLIAMS John Ellis	13-07-42	7 Sqn
983072	Sgt	WILLIAMS John Philpin	6-01-42	3 GTrgFlt
1062588	F/S	WILLIAMS Keith	16-11-42	98 Sqn
120074	P/O	WILLIAMS Kenneth James	26-07-42	97 Sqn
1377183	Sgt	WILLIAMS Leonard Chapple	10-01-42	50 Sqn
108831	P/O	WILLIAMS Leslie Howard	26-06-42	115 Sqn
44362	F/O	WILLIAMS Lyn Collis	1-06-42	115 Sqn
1379186	Sgt	WILLIAMS Owen Llewellyn	3-07-42	10 Sqn
1336529	Sgt	WILLIAMS Philip Seymour	12-08-42	1651 CU
547160	F/S	WILLIAMS Rees Davies	15-10-42	21 Sqn
923926	Sgt	WILLIAMS Reginald Stanley	9-04-42	83 Sqn
1238471	Sgt	WILLIAMS Richard Charles	31-05-42	26 OTU
1114018	F/S	WILLIAMS Robert	7-09-42	101 Sqn
778447	Sgt	WILLIAMS Robert Ernest [Rhodesia]	14-09-42	44 Sqn
1311511	Sgt	WILLIAMS Robert Henry	8-12-42	149 Sqn
1379360	Sgt	WILLIAMS Robert Oscar	3-07-42	420 Sqn
114099	F/O	WILLIAMS Ronald Ernest	5-10-42	102 Sqn
1381723	Sgt	WILLIAMS Samuel	21-01-42	455 Sqn
1184379	AC1	WILLIAMS Thomas Edward	10-05-42	50 Sqn
545642	F/S	WILLIAMS Thomas Glenville	8-12-42	149 Sqn
46839	P/O	WILLIAMS William Ogwyn	16-09-42	106 Sqn
1011696	Sgt	WILLIAMS William Owen Howard	17-12-42	115 Sqn
1160536	Sgt	WILLIAMSON Anthony	31-05-42	61 Sqn
817226	F/S	WILLIAMSON Douglas George	25-06-42	102 Sqn
1133614	Sgt	WILLIAMSON John Alwyn	6-10-42	19 OTU
656510	Sgt	WILLIAMSON DFM Reginald Claude	26-06-42	7 Sqn
989011	Sgt	WILLIAMSON Robert Emslie Wallace	1-10-42	44 Sqn
1325218	Sgt	WILLIG Herbert Thomas	4-07-42	226 Sqn
1281125	Sgt	WILLINGHAM Roy Charles Edgar	16-04-42	156 Sqn
1257268	Sgt	WILLIS Albert Edward	24-05-42	21 Sqn
1023440	Sgt	WILLIS Geoffrey Charles	15-10-42	12 Sqn
968437	F/S	WILLIS George John Anstey	17-10-42	61 Sqn
925267	Sgt	WILLIS Joseph Arthur	14-01-42	114 Sqn
1380070	F/S	WILLMOTT Edward John	30-11-42	10 Sqn
1383234	Sgt	WILLS Stanley Archibald	2-09-42	218 Sqn
574939	Sgt	WILLSHIRE Raymond Venables	10-08-42	102 Sqn
1001441	Sgt	WILMOT John	16-01-42	104 Sqn
741926	F/S	WILSHER George Herbert	21-05-42	21 OTU
748232	F/S	WILSON Alan Charles Russell	25-06-42	12 OTU
1152547	Sgt	WILSON Crawford Christie	19-02-42	107 Sqn
120352	P/O	WILSON David Maxwell	14-09-42	16 OTU
1074972	Sgt	WILSON Dennis	2-09-42	14 OTU
1062601	Sgt	WILSON Duncan Martin	17-12-42	50 Sqn
1280264	Sgt	WILSON Frank William Moles	2-06-42	49 Sqn
1378728	Sgt	WILSON Fred Hall	7-09-42	12 Sqn
1062775	Sgt	WILSON George Hunter	28-08-42	103 Sqn
971301	F/S	WILSON George Stevenson	25-03-42	455 Sqn
1379030	Sgt	WILSON John	22-07-42	158 Sqn
70884	F/L	WILSON AFC John Cyril Mason	29-07-42	156 Sqn
547737	Sgt	WILSON Joseph Greenwood	26-01-42	102 Sqn
70885	S/L	WILSON Matthew Drummond Henderson	11-04-42	15 Sqn
619929	Sgt	WILSON Patrick	28-03-42	115 Sqn
1059497	Sgt	WILSON Richard	15-10-42	103 Sqn
1108674	Sgt	WILSON Richard William	16-07-42	214 Sqn
995972	AC1	WILSON Robert Logan	28-06-42	11 OTU
135004	P/O	WILSON DFM Ronald Sydney	7-11-42	207 Sqn

Number	Rank	Name	Date	Unit
1026302	Sgt	WILSON Samuel James	19-07-42	27 OTU
620236	Sgt	WILSON Sidney	9-11-42	57 Sqn
1131727	Sgt	WILSON Stanley	9-11-42	57 Sqn
1375244	Sgt	WILSON Sydney Bell	24-02-42	144 Sqn
63816	P/O	WILSON Thomas Ivor Ravehill	9-01-42	61 Sqn
526503	Sgt	WILSON William 'Billy'	20-03-42	19 OTU
1113163	Sgt	WILSON William	8-04-42	15 OTU
1291584	Sgt	WILSON William Alexander	10-08-42	78 Sqn
1054130	Sgt	WILSTROP Allan	28-04-42	35 Sqn
1311452	Sgt	WILTCHER Norman Rigby	7-07-42	156 Sqn
562956	F/S	WILTSHIRE Leslie	30-06-42	149 Sqn
962373	Sgt	WINCH Herbert Vincent	28-08-42	44 Sqn
101084	F/L	WINCHESTER DFC Kenneth Frederick John	15-10-42	103 Sqn
1283559	Sgt	WINCOTT Arthur Henry	7-04-42	455 Sqn
999625	Sgt	WINDLE Harold	29-07-42	218 Sqn
971839	Sgt	WINDLE Norman	29-06-42	57 Sqn
1323417	Sgt	WING George Clive	20-12-42	9 Sqn
962167	Sgt	WING Robert Edward	17-04-42	44 Sqn
931850	Sgt	WINKLE Peter Fitzpatrick Vane	15-04-42	158 Sqn
989226	Sgt	WINTER George Norman	13-03-42	460 Sqn
933433	Sgt	WINTERTON Keith	26-02-42	158 Sqn
1112888	Sgt	WINTHROP William Alan	28-04-42	25 OTU
751991	Sgt	WISCHUSEN Benjamin Francis	4-06-42	115 Sqn
591613	Sgt	WISE Allan Frederick	11-08-42	156 Sqn
1264306	Sgt	WISE Jack	31-05-42	12 Sqn
921145	Sgt	WISE Stanley Howard	9-06-42	83 Sqn
1375338	Sgt	WISEMAN William Joseph Walter	25-06-42	10 Sqn
1376449	Sgt	WISHER John Henry	9-04-42	158 Sqn
1194265	Sgt	WITCHELL Samuel Arundall	17-09-42	76 Sqn
1117253	Sgt	WITCOMB Philip	16-09-42	106 Sqn
922083	F/S	WITHERS Arthur Henry	25-08-42	97 Sqn
924720	F/S	WITHERS Peter John	24-07-42	214 Sqn
114441	P/O	WITHY John Forster	16-07-42	158 Sqn
108009	P/O	WITTER Arthur Sidney	14-02-42	20 OTU
905332	F/S	WITTS Henry Herbert	31-05-42	109 Sqn
1237318	Sgt	WOLFENDEN Harold	11-10-42	75 Sqn
621032	F/S	WOLSTENCROFT Bertram Arthur	28-08-42	218 Sqn
545778	Sgt	WOLSTENHOLME Herbert	6-01-42	3 GTrgFlt
550298	F/S	WOMAR DFM Frederick John Ernest	2-06-42	408 Sqn
1208568	Sgt	WOOD Alfred Leonard	22-11-42	115 Sqn
1058548	Sgt	WOOD Cyril	27-07-42	405 Sqn
1065432	Sgt	WOOD Derek Anson [Uruguay]	28-03-42	207 Sqn
627322	Sgt	WOOD Douglas Arnold	5-08-42	1653 CU
1385934	Sgt	WOOD Douglas Jack	24-09-42	102 Sqn
918372	Sgt	WOOD Eric Ian Campbell	9-03-42	12 Sqn
120643	P/O	WOOD Fred Hall	24-06-42	103 Sqn
1215744	Sgt	WOOD Geoffrey Barrington	30-07-42	138 Sqn
1334807	Sgt	WOOD George Robert	27-03-42	138 Sqn
1383304	Sgt	WOOD Henry Frederick	25-10-42	103 Sqn
69426	P/O	WOOD James	14-02-42	214 Sqn
1269576	Sgt	WOOD Jerome Gordon [Brazil]	7-05-42	22 OTU
901160	Sgt	WOOD John Allen	31-03-42	35 Sqn
1437624	Sgt	WOOD Joseph	28-11-42	150 Sqn
1238480	Sgt	WOOD Joseph Clegg	17-12-42	115 Sqn
80659	F/L	WOOD MBE Leslie	20-01-42	105 Sqn
1310876	Sgt	WOOD Peter	2-04-42	214 Sqn
89608	F/O	WOOD DFC Stanley Le Vesconte	25-05-42	25 OTU
1127518	Sgt	WOOD Thomas	17-10-42	15 Sqn
940886	Sgt	WOOD Thomas Henry Forrest	12-02-42	49 Sqn
67642	F/O	WOOD Thomas Render Russell	3-06-42	115 Sqn
1105942	Sgt	WOOD Walter Page Laing	13-08-42	207 Sqn
1251279	Sgt	WOODBRIDGE Sydney Thomas	29-03-42	83 Sqn
654156	F/S	WOODCOCK Albert	25-03-42	83 Sqn
954449	Sgt	WOODFIELD Frank	11-04-42	144 Sqn
1459726	AC1	WOODFORD Lawrence Isaac	19-05-42	150 Sqn
108010	P/O	WOODFORD Thomas William Warwick	9-03-42	9 Sqn
933274	Sgt	WOODFORD William Leopold Llewellyn	26-03-42	144 Sqn
1377795	Sgt	WOODHAM Percy Benjamin Elliott	18-09-42	25 OTU
1165031	Sgt	WOODHEAD Oswald Wheatcroft	10-12-42	21 Sqn
1109752	Sgt	WOODHEAD Stuart	10-04-42	49 Sqn
1307063	Sgt	WOODHOUSE Thomas Charles	17-09-42	61 Sqn
1436485	Sgt	WOODHOUSE Walter George	24-10-42	207 Sqn
1189933	Sgt	WOODLAND Brian Thomas James	28-07-42	156 Sqn
1375573	Sgt	WOODLEY Bernard Jack	20-12-42	158 Sqn
1258982	Sgt	WOODMAN Stanley	1-08-42	405 Sqn
944244	Sgt	WOODROFFE John Arthur	16-02-42	49 Sqn
1359686	Sgt	WOODWARD Jack	13-03-42	460 Sqn
1379151	Sgt	WOOFF James William	7-06-42	156 Sqn
1390366	Sgt	WOOLGAR Albert Victor	9-11-42	57 Sqn
1376622	Sgt	WOOLLARD Edwin Cuthbert	25-10-42	142 Sqn
1381873	Sgt	WOOLLARD Reginald	29-06-42	7 Sqn
1575390	Sgt	WOOLLEY Carl Robert	12-12-42	102 Sqn
1148517	Sgt	WOOLLEY Samuel Herbert	17-06-42	35 Sqn
48586	P/O	WOOLNOUGH DFM Victor Ernest	31-05-42	14 OTU
1254886	F/S	WOOLSTON Peter Stanley	19-08-42	88 Sqn
107929	P/O	WOOTLEY Robert Leonard	6-05-42	7 Sqn
968034	F/S	WOOTTON James Michael	18-05-42	149 Sqn
1280312	Sgt	WORLING John Patterson Smith	13-04-42	15 Sqn
1162813	F/S	WORMLEIGHTON Donald	22-02-42	150 Sqn
568572	Sgt	WORSNOP Jack	17-12-42	101 Sqn
116145	P/O	WORSWICK DFC John Allan	2-06-42	106 Sqn
759163	Sgt	WORTHINGTON Denis Leonard	24-07-42	207 Sqn
535943	F/S	WORTHINGTON Hugh Arthur	19-05-42	218 Sqn
61231	F/O	WORTHY Reginald Percy	10-04-42	49 Sqn
126963	P/O	WOTTON Vivian James	17-12-42	10 OTU
1387626	Sgt	WRAIGHT Robert George	3-09-42	1652 CU
932296	Sgt	WRATTEN Alfred James	14-01-42	21 Sqn
1185788	Sgt	WREN George Ernest Smyth	21-08-42	218 Sqn
990757	Sgt	WRIGHT Albert Barclay	25-01-42	408 Sqn
33351	S/L	WRIGHT Claud Mandeville	16-10-42	115 Sqn
1265550	Sgt	WRIGHT Erskine Peter	29-03-42	103 Sqn
1287761	Sgt	WRIGHT Ewart	20-09-42	9 Sqn
544832	Sgt	WRIGHT Francis Noel	27-07-42	158 Sqn
1333771	Sgt	WRIGHT Harold	10-09-42	16 OTU
1311829	Sgt	WRIGHT John Alfred	22-07-42	57 Sqn
104511	P/O	WRIGHT John Frederick	26-01-42	51 Sqn
1057411	Sgt	WRIGHT John Ripley	11-04-42	455 Sqn
1325527	Sgt	WRIGHT Joseph	3-09-42	61 Sqn
42668	F/L	WRIGHT Kenneth Bernard	26-06-42	102 Sqn
1378917	F/S	WRIGHT Lawrence Ritelli	24-10-42	207 Sqn
981770	Sgt	WRIGHT Norman Duke	21-02-42	106 Sqn
960409	Sgt	WRIGHT Philip Thomas	30-07-42	138 Sqn
1293291	Sgt	WRIGHT Walter Ernest Ruskin	20-09-42	161 Sqn
1164158	Sgt	WRIGHT William	10-03-42	405 Sqn
1313271	Sgt	WRIGHTING Percy Walter	5-05-42	150 Sqn
1005381	Sgt	WRIGLEY Arthur Kenneth	18-09-42	44 Sqn
847519	Sgt	WYNNE George Henry	4-08-42	20 OTU
1157843	Sgt	WYNTON John Alfred	17-04-42	44 Sqn
1209309	Sgt	YATES Kenneth John	28-07-42	156 Sqn
1014573	F/S	YATES Robert	24-08-42	218 Sqn
1057877	Sgt	YEATES Lawrence John	31-05-42	49 Sqn
47550	P/O	YEO Arthur Thomas	22-07-42	158 Sqn
1326506	Sgt	YORK Desmond Albert	30-07-42	150 Sqn
999794	Sgt	YORK Maurice	21-01-42	17 OTU
1269029	Sgt	YOUNG Albert Joseph	12-6-42	114 Sqn
1109002	Sgt	YOUNG Harry	25-08-42	83 Sqn
1378544	Sgt	YOUNG Henry Edward	26-06-42	156 Sqn
1354828	Sgt	YOUNG James Henry	27-03-42	21 OTU
1140214	Sgt	YOUNG John Ernest	11-11-42	57 Sqn
1368840	Sgt	YOUNG Joseph Harvey	25-10-42	142 Sqn
1170647	Sgt	YOUNG Joseph Walter	6-01-42	12 Sqn
646548	Sgt	YOUNG Leonard Walter	26-07-42	106 Sqn
1162261	Sgt	YOUNG Peter Anthony	10-09-42	75 Sqn

1306078	Sgt	YOUNG Robert McKay	28-01-42	106 Sqn	
741708	W/O	YOUNG DFM Rodney Frederick Harling			
			25-08-42	106 Sqn	
1257537	Sgt	YOUNG Ronald John Craig	30-05-42	218 Sqn	
1310940	Sgt	YOUNG Stanley George	11-09-42	50 Sqn	
80194	P/O	YOUNG Stanley Ryder [Rhodesia]	23-11-42	44 Sqn	
1058075	F/S	YOUNG William Lewis Johnston	2-05-42	106 Sqn	
1344278	Sgt	YOUNG William Shirley	25-09-42	105 Sqn	
120631	F/O	YOUNGMAN Louis Rousseau	23-10-42	218 Sqn	
938506	Cpl	ZUCKER Ronald Moses Simon	13-09-42	27 OTU	

Note

Promulgation of the Cross of Merit [Poland] *(Krzyz Zaslugi)* awarded to Sgt Everitt had been *Gazetted* on the 15th of July, 1941, Everitt being one of four airmen so honoured. Conferred by the Polish Government (in exile), their names appear in the illustrious company of Air Chief Marshal Sir Charles Frederick Algernon Portal who, for a brief period in 1940, held the position of Air Officer Commanding-in-Chief Bomber Command and who was now permitted to wear the *Polonia Restuta – First Class*. Concerning the entry for Sgt Jerman, on some documents his Christian names are shown as Walter Crawford Allen. S/L Stephens had, according to his entry in the Commonwealth War Graves Commission register for Flushing (Vlissingen) Northern Cemetery, been attached from Station Headquarters Stradishall, though No.3 Group Roll of Honour published in 1955 and subsequently dedicated in Ely Cathedral on the 6th of November, 1955, shows his unit as 3 Group Training Flight. What is not in doubt is his age, 40, and that he joined the volunteer reserve under the terms of the commissioned air gunners scheme.

F/S Dundas, Lord Dundas of Orkney, who perished while serving with 144 Squadron, was the son of Lawrence John Lumley Dundas, 2nd Marquess of Zetland, who served with distinction as Secretary of State for India twixt 1935 and 1937, and then with the added responsibilities for Burma until 1940.

During a cross-referral of data, a discrepancy in the service number of Sgt Kenneth Bereford Hobbs has come to light. His entry on the Commonwealth War Graves Commission data base shows his number as '338309', thus indicating he was an army transfer to the air force circa November-December 1940. The No.5 Group Roll of Honour compiled in the late 1940s and published in 1950 indicates his number as '1338309' which falls within the block 1300001-1360800 that was issued to various United Kingdom enlistment centres and was extant between June 1940 and February 1941. For the purposes of this Roll I have decided to leave his number in the manner reported by the Commonwealth War Graves Commission.

Sgt Alastair Macdonald Anderson, who was killed on a raid to Essen early in June 1942, was the first of many locally enlisted Newfoundlanders joining the volunteer reserve, entering the service in early 1940. A close inspection of this section identifies a further 33 airmen from this sparsely populated island off Canada's Eastern seaboard.

New Zealander S/L Harkness arrived in the United Kingdom in November 1938, and was accepted for a short service commission. Prior to this, he had served as a clerk in the Royal New Zealand Air Force. Including Harkness, 17 officers and six airmen are identified in this section as hailing from New Zealand. Amongst the officers, many had by the time of their death accrued a considerable number of flying hours a high proportion of which were gained in operational flying. S/Ls Coleman, Raymond and West had each flown in excess of 50 sorties, the last two named logging at least 1,097 and 1,140 flying hours respectively, while others to exceed a thousand hours were F/L Miller, S/L Robinson and S/L Weston.

ROYAL AUSTRALIAN AIR FORCE
personnel

400451	F/L	ADAM Basil John	14-01-42	114 Sqn
407704	F/S	ADAMS Phillip Paul	16-07-42	13 OTU
404571	F/S	ADDISON Thomas William Sheridan	12-08-42	50 Sqn

403415	Sgt	AIRD Kenneth	30-05-42	150 Sqn
407886	Sgt	ALCORN James Alexander	16-07-42	27 OTU
403890	Sgt	ALLEN Colin Frederick	17-12-42	9 Sqn
401359	Sgt	ALLEN Keith	20-06-42	49 Sqn
400198	Sgt	ALLEN William Alexander McMeekin	11-04-42	144 Sqn
404370	Sgt	ALLISON John Leonard	30-06-42	14 OTU
411063	Sgt	ALLSOPP William Arthur	26-07-42	35 Sqn
402214	Sgt	ANDERSON Geoffrey Hamilton	24-02-42	144 Sqn
404823	Sgt	ANDREW Keith Alexander	12-03-42	455 Sqn
401408	Sgt	ANIVITTI Maurice Ermini	20-06-42	460 Sqn
402338	Sgt	AUSTIN Lewis Herbert	9-11-42	50 Sqn
405145	Sgt	BAILEY Edwin Alfred	5-06-42	1443 Flt
403491	Sgt	BAILEY Garnet James	26-07-42	106 Sqn
404614	P/O	BAILEY Lloyd Wilson	10-03-42	149 Sqn
400687	P/O	BAILEY Valden Leonard	28-04-42	150 Sqn
405670	Sgt	BAKER William John	20-11-42	27 OTU
407280	F/S	BALLEINE Bernard George Payn Lovelock		
			30-05-42	460 Sqn
411475	Sgt	BANNISTER Rupert Theodore	19-07-42	27 OTU
406341	F/S	BARKER John Norman	7-09-42	12 Sqn
401882	Sgt	BARLOW James Robert	20-11-42	27 OTU
400393	F/O	BARNFATHER Eliot Ralph	18-05-42	218 Sqn
406709	Sgt	BARRETT-LENNARD John Allen	5-12-42	1658 HCU
405341	Sgt	BARTON Druce Hawthorn	11-08-42	14 OTU
404600	Sgt	BASS Noel Gordon	27-08-42	460 Sqn
403088	Sgt	BATES Albert Henry Charles	29-07-42	7 Sqn
400689	F/S	BAXTER GM Robert Wilson	7-08-42	150 Sqn
403104	P/O	BEATTY Argyle Donald	10-06-42	50 Sqn
407888	Sgt	BEATTY Colin John	22-04-42	27 OTU
404165	F/S	BEDWELL Horace Kempton	30-04-42	158 Sqn
404631	F/S	BEESLEY Alec Henry	5-09-42	103 Sqn
403650	F/S	BEESTON Richard Denison [New Zealand]	26-07-42	150 Sqn
406136	F/S	BEINKE Dudley Raymond	2-06-42	460 Sqn
408140	F/O	BELBIN Sydney Frank	5-09-42	103 Sqn
404950	Sgt	BELFORD Thomas David	12-07-42	460 Sqn
406589	F/S	BELL Paton	12-08-42	150 Sqn
404881	Sgt	BENN John Walter	12-08-42	207 Sqn
407992	F/S	BENNETT Keith Campbell	14-09-42	460 Sqn
405066	Sgt	BICE Aubrey Archdale	26-07-42	460 Sqn
407282	F/S	BIGLANDS Reginald John	3-06-42	460 Sqn
406500	Sgt	BIRMINGHAM William John	28-07-42	103 Sqn
416113	Sgt	BISHOP Frank Elliott	19-09-42	460 Sqn
403495	Sgt	BLACKLEY Allan Neil	26-06-42	1481 Flt
403208	F/O	BLUNT Malcolm James Larke	7-06-42	150 Sqn
401412	Sgt	BOLTON George Frederick	31-05-42	23 OTU
402836	P/O	BOND Ralph	29-04-42	460 Sqn
407192	F/L	BOURKE Thomas Harrison	30-05-42	460 Sqn
404478	Sgt	BOWER Frank Graham	28-03-42	109 Sqn
404931	Sgt	BOYLE John	29-07-42	7 Sqn
411117	Sgt	BRADLEY Keith James	19-07-42	27 OTU
400502	Sgt	BRADY James Maxwell	16-01-42	15 OTU
403658	F/O	BRANDER Harry Sutton	19-08-42	460 Sqn
402585	F/S	BRANDT Augustus Ludwig [United Kingdom]	7-04-42	15 Sqn
404949	Sgt	BRASHER DFM Edward Keith Forbes	14-09-42	460 Sqn
403312	Sgt	BRATHWAITE Robert George Ashley	26-06-42	20 OTU
402848	F/S	BRAY John Terry	29-07-42	156 Sqn
403470	Sgt	BRAYBROOK Bertram Stanley	1-08-42	35 Sqn
404948	Sgt	BRAYNE Frederick Charles	12-07-42	460 Sqn
402760	F/O	BREEN Frederick James	27-07-42	460 Sqn
405388	Sgt	BRIGHOUSE Malcolm Stanley	29-08-42	408 Sqn
401229	Sgt	BRINDLEY Russell Walter	14-07-42	158 Sqn
402849	P/O	BROAD Edgar George	14-01-42	40 Sqn
400524	F/S	BRODIE Hugh Rowell	3-06-42	460 Sqn
405256	Sgt	BROODBANK Ronald Arthur	31-05-42	23 OTU
401587	Sgt	BROOK Robert	5-09-42	97 Sqn
403105	F/S	BROWN Albert Ernest	11-09-42	460 Sqn

Number	Rank	Name	Date	Unit
404867	P/O	BROWN Arthur Hugh Steyning	16-10-42	51 Sqn
400693	Sgt	BROWN John Raeburn	16-01-42	15 OTU
404932	F/O	BROWN Roye Wilmott	12-04-42	103 Sqn
402028	Sgt	BROWN Thomas Leslie	9-01-42	458 Sqn
404601	F/S	BRYDEN John Alexander	11-09-42	460 Sqn
400578	F/S	BUCKINGHAM Robert John	22-06-42	460 Sqn
406344	F/L	BURGESS Clifford Henry	26-07-42	460 Sqn
403183	Sgt	BURKE Mervyn Kevin	24-09-42	405 Sqn
400408	P/O	BURT Alan Gladstone	31-01-42	61 Sqn
407601	Sgt	BURT Rex Theodore	2-06-42	21 OTU
403856	Sgt	BURTON Ronald Garnet	7-06-42	50 Sqn
403314	Sgt	BUTCHER Charles Sydney	3-08-42	51 Sqn
406638	F/O	BUTCHER Raymond Edward Norton	21-09-42	101 Sqn
403717	Sgt	BUTTEL Albert Francois	7-06-42	49 Sqn
403685	Sgt	BYRNE Nial Thurlow	23-09-42	142 Sqn
404951	Sgt	CADDY Mervyn	4-07-42	61 Sqn
401366	Sgt	CALDER George Douglas	14-09-42	1653 CU
407358	Sgt	CALDER Robert Harvey Donald	26-06-42	83 Sqn
407637	Sgt	CALDWELL James Humphrey	27-07-42	7 Sqn
407890	F/O	CAMPBELL Alexander Craven	17-09-42	76 Sqn
402436	Sgt	CAMPBELL Coin Millis	9-06-42	460 Sqn
401298	Sgt	CANET David	19-08-42	61 Sqn
408045	Sgt	CANNING Frank Hill	11-0-42	455 Sqn
403040	P/O	CARMICHAEL David Norris	6-01-42	458 Sqn
403161	Sgt	CARNLEY James William	23-09-42	50 Sqn
404863	Sgt	CARPENDER John Francis	29-04-42	460 Sqn
404933	Sgt	CASSELLS Francis John	28-03-42	109 Sqn
412481	P/O	CHAPMAN Robert Herbert	25-10-42	460 Sqn
408046	Sgt	CHEESE William Desmond	20-07-42	460 Sqn
403652	F/O	CHICK Laurence Guy	28-04-42	27 OTU
404579	P/O	CHRISTIE Alec MacNaughton	3-01-42	455 Sqn
404277	Sgt	CHRISTSEN Walter Irvine	26-03-42	214 Sqn
402438	Sgt	CHURCH George Norman	28-01-42	114 Sqn
402310	F/O	CLARK Theodore Marcus	9-01-42	15 OTU
401300	F/O	CLARKE Harold George	1-08-42	14 OTU
400886	F/O	CLEGG William Alexander	13-08-42	460 Sqn
402565	Sgt	CLIFFORD Clive Edward Wigram	24-03-42	44 Sqn
404956	F/O	COATES John Edward	16-08-42	106 Sqn
408131	Sgt	CONDON William Harry	19-07-42	27 OTU
403041	Sgt	CONNELL Bernard Bradley	3-01-42	23 OTU
406548	P/O	COPELAND Gerald Ware	4-05-42	78 Sqn
402731	Sgt	CORNELL Colin Albert	10-03-42	158 Sqn
404452	F/O	CORSER Arthur Henry Cadell	9-01-42	15 OTU
404718	Sgt	CORSER Henry Graham Ronaldson	7-05-42	460 Sqn
408122	Sgt	COSGROVE John Percival	29-04-42	460 Sqn
404053	P/O	COUPER Frederick Andrew	18-12-42	1474 Flt
404092	F/O	COURTNEY James Geen	21-02-42	150 Sqn
405174	Sgt	COX Neville Holt	26-06-42	27 OTU
402589	F/S	COX Reginald George	22-09-42	460 Sqn
407927	F/O	CRANZ William August	28-10-42	150 Sqn
400581	P/O	CREED Eric William Cuthbert	26-03-42	214 Sqn
411996	F/S	CROAL Edward	17-12-42	44 Sqn
403393	Sgt	CROCKETT James Grant	5-09-42	103 Sqn
411007	Sgt	CROWTHER Allister Dalton	14-09-42	460 Sqn
402229	F/O	CROYDON Harold Leslie	9-04-42	158 Sqn
404779	F/S	CULLEN John Kennedy	12-10-42	49 Sqn
403644	Sgt	CUMBERLAND Russell Lloyd	24-10-42	50 Sqn
403848	Sgt	CUMMINS Francis Rodney	28-08-42	12 Sqn
402320	Sgt	DALTON James Edward	28-08-42	12 Sqn
411008	Sgt	DALZELL Henry Arnold	24-10-42	150 Sqn
403561	W/O	DAN Nicholas	10-08-42	460 Sqn
401272	F/S	DANGERFIELD DFM Richard Desmond	24-10-42	49 Sqn
404603	Sgt	DANIELS Raymond Vivien	25-03-42	14 OTU
404403	Sgt	DANKS-BROWN Keith John	11-09-42	460 Sqn
403237	Sgt	DARE George Francis	1-10-42	61 Sqn
401369	Sgt	DARE Keith Edward	9-07-42	106 Sqn
400751	Sgt	DAVEY John James	21-02-42	455 Sqn
404934	F/S	DAVIES Ernest Lewis	5-09-42	103 Sqn
401304	F/O	DAVIES Llewellyn Alfred	14-07-42	97 Sqn
407285	F/S	DAVIS Richard Paterson	30-05-42	460 Sqn
405576	F/S	DENING John Glen	17-12-42	44 Sqn
404634	Sgt	DICKSON Beaumont Churchill	19-01-42	20 OTU
401030	F/S	DICKSON Robert Walker	10-12-42	21 Sqn
401559	F/O	DILLON William	28-08-42	460 Sqn
404819	F/S	DIMMOCK Harold Edgar	3-06-42	12 Sqn
404992	F/S	DINNING John Hector	29-08-42	97 Sqn
403238	Sgt	DOBSON Reginald Patrick	28-08-42	49 Sqn
403132	Sgt	DONN-PATTERSON James	31-05-42	23 OTU
402591	Sgt	DONOHOE Frederick Max	25-03-42	455 Sqn
404174	F/O	DORWARD DFC Leslie Clement	5-10-42	97 Sqn
400463	F/O	DOWNE Geoffrey William	15-08-42	105 Sqn
407709	Sgt	DOWNING Darryl	3-07-42	460 Sqn
403565	Sgt	DOWNS Alexander Irvine Lewis	11-09-42	26 OTU
407844	Sgt	DREYER Leonard Charles Underwood	12-07-42	460 Sqn
404876		DUE Einar Ernest	25-03-42	12 Sqn
404927	F/S	DUNN Ian Clark	3-07-42	12 Sqn
404453	F/O	DURBRIDGE Robert Keep	10-03-42	405 Sqn
406351	Sgt	DYSON Dudley Harnett	25-02-42	27 OTU
402569	F/S	DYSON John Henry	26-02-42	405 Sqn
402223	P/O	ECHIN Henry Adolphus (served as CHINN)	30-06-42	405 Sqn
403508	F/O	EDMONDS Wilfrid Milton	17-08-42	207 Sqn
403570	Sgt	EDYE Bruce Henry	2-06-42	26 OTU
404887	Sgt	EKLUND Karl Hugo	24-02-42	144 Sqn
403663	F/O	ELRINGTON Richard Douglas	28-08-42	460 Sqn
404902	Sgt	ENGLAND Kenneth Hayne	12-06-42	83 Sqn
400952	F/L	FALKINER John Alexander	22-09-42	460 Sqn
400974	P/O	FERGUSON Keith McDowell	27-07-42	460 Sqn
408142	Sgt	FIELDING Tom Illenden	12-06-42	114 Sqn
405176	F/O	FINCH Ronald James	17-04-42	10 OTU
403175	F/S	FINLAY James Alexander	10-08-42	460 Sqn
403576	Sgt	FITZGERALD Maurice Michael	1-06-42	460 Sqn
402328	F/S	FLETCHER Colin Alais	10-04-42	12 Sqn
406476	Sgt	FLETCHER William John Percival	13-09-42	27 OTU
408143	F/S	FOLEY Max James	27-07-42	460 Sqn
407557	Sgt	FOOTE Arthur James	10-02-42	11 OTU
407639	Sgt	FORGAN William Wallace	8-01-42	458 Sqn
405580	F/O	FORRESTER Leonard	19-10-42	1656 HCU
401115	F/O	FRANKCOMB John Clarence	15-09-42	218 Sqn
14065	Sgt	FRASER Gilbert Gordon	24-10-42	57 Sqn
403327	Sgt	FRAZER Alan Richard	27-03-42	14 OTU
403047	Sgt	FROST Rae Rees	10-04-42	12 Sqn
405441	Sgt	GAFFNEY Thomas Stanislaus	26-06-42	14 OTU
400174	F/S	GAHAN Geoffrey Russell	6-05-42	7 Sqn
405020	Sgt	GAITER James Albert	3-06-42	460 Sqn
405205	Sgt	GALL Herbert Maurice	6-08-42	78 Sqn
404964	F/S	GALLOGLY Vincent John	23-06-42	103 Sqn
402829	Sgt	GAMMIE Colin	7-04-42	455 Sqn
404529	Sgt	GARROW James David	5-01-42	405 Sqn
407711	Sgt	GASKELL Henry Elliott	1-08-42	106 Sqn
406355	F/O	GEORGE Lloyd	23-01-42	21 OTU
405442	F/S	GIBSON James Maxwell	25-08-42	150 Sqn
407641	Sgt	GILCHRIST Donald Richard	17-09-42	1654 CU
411220	Sgt	GLAISTER Albert John	28-04-42	27 OTU
404913	Sgt	GLENTON-WRIGHT Michael Lotherington [United Kingdom]	31-05-42	23 OTU
406392	Sgt	GODFREY William Allen	26-02-42	27 OTU
407153	F/S	GOLDER Reginald William	7-04-42	15 Sqn
400344	Sgt	GOLDIE John Hunter	14-02-42	20 OTU
406450	Sgt	GOLDIE Peter Charles Herbert	9-01-42	207 Sqn
404865	F/O	GORDON Robert George	29-04-42	12 Sqn
400981	Sgt	GOTTS Rex Alfred	23-09-42	50 Sqn
402947	Sgt	GOWER Garth Richard	27-07-42	460 Sqn
401308	Sgt	GRABHAM Arthur James	8-06-42	420 Sqn

404963	F/S	GRACE Hilary Francis	14-09-42	150 Sqn	404404	Sgt	HYND Eric Leslie	26-06-42	7 Sqn
401623	F/O	GRAHAM Charles Andre	13-11-42	105 Sqn	400028	Sgt	INCE Ian Macpherson	21-01-42	455 Sqn
402948	P/O	GRAND Albert George	4-08-42	460 Sqn	402359	F/L	IRVING Donald Atherton	27-02-42	77 Sqn
402993	P/O	GRAY David	12-08-42	50 Sqn	403109	F/S	JAMES Lionel Heyman	20-06-42	460 Sqn
400707	P/O	GREEN Mervyn Richard Roberts	28-03-42	7 Sqn	411451	Sgt	JARRETT Warren Wallace	27-08-42	460 Sqn
404564	Sgt	GREEN Stirling Lindfield	2-04-42	57 Sqn	405154	F/S	JEFFERIES John Massey	21-12-42	103 Sqn
401064	Sgt	GREENFIELD Alastair Mackay	22-07-42	158 Sqn	411145	Sgt	JENNINGS Edward Douglas Reginald		
403170	Sgt	GREENWELL Robert Eric	25-03-42	12 Sqn				19-07-42	27 OTU
404476	Sgt	GREER Arthur William	28-04-42	27 OTU	412146	F/O	JOHANNESEN Jack	15-10-42	12 Sqn
404420	Sgt	GREGG Stanley Alfred	24-10-42	50 Sqn	400505	P/O	JOHN Gordon Lewis	7-09-42	7 Sqn
405244	Sgt	GREGORY-COLEMAN William Patrick Joseph			402710	Sgt	JOHNS Russell Archie	30-04-42	460 Sqn
			7-09-42	49 Sqn	400118	F/S	JOHNSON Allan Wilson	24-04-42	77 Sqn
403664	Sgt	GRIMWADE James William	26-07-42	106 Sqn	403139	Sgt	JOHNSON Douglas Westbury	14-09-42	460 Sqn
408144	Sgt	GROOM Rae	21-05-42	25 OTU	403813	Sgt	JOHNSON Edgar Griffits	26-08-42	50 Sqn
406649	F/O	GUTHRIE Robert Edmund	1-08-42	14 OTU	404784	Sgt	JOHNSTON Arthur Maxwell	3-07-42	460 Sqn
403809	Sgt	HAIN Noel Clive	6-08-42	102 Sqn	400716	Sgt	JOHNSTONE Victor William	8-01-42	458 Sqn
401213	Sgt	HALL Rex Victor	13-10-42	419 Sqn	403054	P/O	JONES Godfrey Rees	16-08-42	50 Sqn
400368	P/O	HANCOCK Leslie Pierson	29-07-42	1651 CU	403172	Sgt	JONES Norman Rex	1-10-42	78 Sqn
401237	Sgt	HANCOCKS Jack Douglas	3-07-42	460 Sqn	402967	F/O	JONES Russel Allen Pera	30-05-42	460 Sqn
407642	Sgt	HANNA Colin Leslie	20-09-42	214 Sqn	403179	F/S	JUDD Norman Keith	31-07-42	27 OTU
404584	Sgt	HANSON Allan Harold	8-03-42	14 OTU	407794	Sgt	KEATS Gilbert Carrington	7-08-42	12 Sqn
406178	Sgt	HANSON Leonard William	31-03-42	76 Sqn	400623	F/L	KECK Frederick Abbey	11-04-42	455 Sqn
411320	F/S	HARDEN Jack Bruce	26-09-42	12 Sqn	402742	F/O	KEENE John Walter	3-06-42	460 Sqn
407523	F/O	HARDING-BROWNE Richard	15-01-42	82 Sqn	404658	P/O	KELLY Charles Dermot	19-08-42	105 Sqn
404903	Sgt	HARDY Neil Malcolm	26-06-42	50 Sqn	404406	F/S	KENNEDY Cameron Duff	30-07-42	50 Sqn
401436	Sgt	HARE Eric Noel	28-08-42	460 Sqn	402362	F/O	KENNEDY William Joseph	7-05-42	460 Sqn
402302	Sgt	HARGRAVE Arthur Peter Roy	25-02-42	27 OTU	401220	Sgt	KEYS Frederick Raymond	19-09-42	460 Sqn
404790	F/O	HARLAND Charles Antony	11-04-42	455 Sqn	406359	F/L	KEYSER Vernon Frank	27-07-42	460 Sqn
402441	Sgt	HARPER Colin Raymond	13-04-42	158 Sqn	406980	Sgt	KING James Kevin	11-09-42	460 Sqn
406453	F/S	HARRIS Terence Claude	11-09-42	460 Sqn	400278	F/O	KINGSHOTT Melville John	3-01-42	17 OTU
400517	F/O	HARRISON George William Marshall			400805	W/O	KITCHEN David Gordon	20-06-42	460 Sqn
			19-09-42	50 Sqn	407695	F/S	KLEISDORFF Murray Ralph	27-06-42	405 Sqn
400413	Sgt	HART Ian Eric	13-03-42	460 Sqn	403428	Sgt	KROME Theodore Anton	29-06-42	14 OTU
404585	Sgt	HARTLEY Clement Alfred Victor	7-04-42	49 Sqn	400890	P/O	LAIDLAW Graeme Lonarch	12-10-42	49 Sqn
414026	Sgt	HASS Mervyn Lionel Vivian	6-12-42	464 Sqn	404344	Sgt	LAWER Ernest Joseph	3-07-42	10 Sqn
402504	F/S	HAWES William George	24-07-42	207 Sqn	403192	F/S	LAWRENCE Raymond George	24-10-42	49 Sqn
404433	Sgt	HAWKINS Hedley Maurice	21-09-42	101 Sqn	401069	F/O	LEIGO Douglas Percy	27-07-42	7 Sqn
22126	Cpl	HAZELTON William John Ronald	19-09-42	460 Sqn	402242	F/O	LESLIE Alan James	12-07-42	15 OTU
400708	F/O	HEARD Geoffrey Thomas	26-03-42	7 Sqn	402910	F/S	LEVITUS Solomon	3-06-42	460 Sqn
409114	F/O	HECK James William	10-12-42	20 OTU	400229	F/O	LIND Gordon Richard	26-06-42	24 OTU
400588	P/O	HEDGE Alfred William	4-05-42	78 Sqn	403194	Sgt	LINDSAY James William	26-06-42	50 Sqn
405075	F/S	HEHIR James Hassett	16-01-42	15 OTU	402821	P/O	LITTLE Archie Thomas	3-07-42	103 Sqn
408579	F/S	HEHIR Martin Randolph	8-11-42	142 Sqn	401070	F/S	LITTLEJOHN Gordon Breeny	7-09-42	12 Sqn
403406	Sgt	HENDERSON Edward Hamilton	16-09-42	106 Sqn	402798	F/S	LLOYD David Kilgour	13-04-42	405 Sqn
401573	Sgt	HENDERSON Valentine Stewart	7-05-42	23 OTU	404250	P/O	LLOYD-JONES Keith Francis	13-04-42	76 Sqn
403869	Sgt	HENNING James Darien	6-06-42	14 OTU	407868	Sgt	LODGE Wallace Eugene	9-12-42	207 Sqn
401819	Sgt	HENRY Ambrose James	7-09-42	10 Sqn	404550	Sgt	LONERGAN Robert Neville	10-03-42	405 Sqn
404820	Sgt	HERON Royal George	21-01-42	50 Sqn	416004	P/O	LONGBOTTOM Eric Harvey	19-07-42	27 OTU
402353	Sgt	HEWISH Arthur Leslie	9-01-42	458 Sqn	402293	Sgt	LONG-INNES George Selwyn	26-02-42	12 Sqn
404431	F/O	HICKEY Bernard Peter	8-01-42	458 Sqn	406694	Sgt	LOONEY Patrick Lawrence	16-09-42	26 OTU
404402	Sgt	HIESLER Francis James	16-03-42	14 OTU	414051	F/O	LOVE James	20-11-42	27 OTU
404484	F/S	HIGGINS Graham Henry David	11-08-42	78 Sqn	402243	F/O	LOVE Winston David	9-06-42	150 Sqn
403512	F/S	HIGSON William Frank	14-09-42	12 Sqn	408145	Sgt	LOVELL DFM John Henry	7-11-42	207 Sqn
403812	Sgt	HOBAN Walter John	17-09-42	49 Sqn	405277	Sgt	LOWIS Colin Roderick Donald	4-08-42	460 Sqn
404621	Sgt	HOBGEN John Edward	9-04-42	12 Sqn	406809	Sgt	LUEDEKE Clifford Douglas	1-08-42	460 Sqn
404313	Sgt	HOBGEN Thomas Cunnah	4-08-42	460 Sqn	403411	Sgt	LUTON John Campbell	5-09-42	207 Sqn
403189	Sgt	HOLDAWAY Neville Charles	25-08-42	150 Sqn	402526	P/O	LYNCH Walter Hugh	26-01-42	14 OTU
403092	F/S	HOLDEN Robert George Kenyon	31-05-42	12 Sqn	405315	P/O	LYONS Leon George	29-08-42	408 Sqn
405588	Sgt	HOLGATE Harold William	14-09-42	150 Sqn	404346	P/O	MacDONALD Edward John Norman	6-01-42	458 Sqn
405208	Sgt	HOLLAND Allen	13-08-42	460 Sqn	407178	Sgt	MacGREGOR-KING Thomas Freer	5-05-42	12 Sqn
404246	Sgt	HOLLINGWORTH Alexander	6-01-42	102 Sqn	402874	Sgt	MacPHEE William	17-09-42	61 Sqn
402354	Sgt	HOLT Mervyn Harry	12-02-42	49 Sqn	400476	F/O	MACDONALD Alexander Gordon	17-08-42	50 Sqn
401217	Sgt	HORE Samuel Leach	7-08-42	7 Sqn	405274	Sgt	MACLEOD Athole Douglas	4-08-42	460 Sqn
405273	F/O	HOWARD Albert William	4-08-42	460 Sqn	407946	Sgt	MADGE Raymond Corlett	25-02-42	27 OTU
404247	F/S	HOWSAN Moheddeen Abdul Ghias	1-04-42	405 Sqn	402517	F/O	MAHER James Brian	28-03-42	115 Sqn
406318	F/O	HUGALL Robert Leslie	26-06-42	50 Sqn	402376	P/O	MALONEY John Edward	2-04-42	455 Sqn
403743	F/O	HUNT Edmund Freeman	30-06-42	14 OTU	403142	F/O	MANNERS Seth Tilstone	11-04-42	455 Sqn
400504	Sgt	HUNTER Frederick D'Orsa	20-05-42	35 Sqn	407719	F/O	MANSELL Vincen William James	9-06-42	149 Sqn

Number	Rank	Name	Date	Sqn
402826	F/S	MANTELL John Martin	13-08-42	77 Sqn
400478	F/L	MARCHANT DFC Jack	20-12-42	83 Sqn
401575	F/S	MARSDEN Stanley	7-09-42	12 Sqn
400813	Sgt	MARSHALL John Alexander Brock	28-08-42	78 Sqn
400306	Sgt	MARSHALL Ronald	2-04-42	57 Sqn
407721	Sgt	MARSHMAN John Kenneth	21-07-42	106 Sqn
403479	Sgt	MARTIN Frederick Roy	22-06-42	460 Sqn
403060	F/S	MARTIN John Edward Freese	15-10-42	12 Sqn
402450	F/L	MARTIN DFC Wallace	6-12-42	21 Sqn
403940	Sgt	MATHERS James Bruce	26-06-42	27 OTU
400416	Sgt	MATTHAMS Ronald George	31-10-42	97 Sqn
401073	F/O	MAWDESLEY William James	2-06-42	23 OTU
403942	Sgt	MAYNE Reginald James	13-08-42	460 Sqn
402667	F/O	MAZENGARB Harris Lewington	11-09-42	83 Sqn
411343	Sgt	McALISTER Gilbert Norman	9-07-42	27 OTU
405452	F/S	McCAULEY Ronald Gerard	9-09-42	12 Sqn
403199	Sgt	McCLOY Geoffrey Browning	12-08-42	50 Sqn
406544	F/S	McCOLL Ian Fowler Stewart	9-11-42	408 Sqn
404109	F/O	McCONACHIE Donald	25-03-42	83 Sqn
413023	Sgt	McCOSKER Hector Gordon Roch	28-09-42	25 OTU
406444	Sgt	McCRAE Allan Edwin	3-07-42	460 Sqn
400352	Sgt	McDONALD Murray Alexander	12-03-42	75 Sqn
412070	Sgt	McGUIRE Laurie Arthur	7-12-42	21 OTU
400282	Sgt	McILRATH Kenneth William	7-04-42	455 Sqn
402600	Sgt	McILVEEN Trevor Hopetoun	29-04-42	460 Sqn
407603	Sgt	McINTOSH Douglas Howe	26-06-42	1481 Flt
401389	Sgt	McINTYRE Frank Lethbridge	29-07-42	7 Sqn
400353	Sgt	McKEAN Harold Gregory	21-02-42	150 Sqn
411031	Sgt	McKEE Charles Henry Robert	1-08-42	27 OTU
405162	Sgt	McKENNA Terence Francis Breen [New Guinea]	20-06-42	49 Sqn
403276	Sgt	McLEAN Donald Tennant	20-09-42	61 Sqn
403431	Sgt	McLEOD Finlay Donald	26-03-42	12 Sqn
404056	F/S	McMANUS Ian Frank	25-06-42	21 OTU
405360	Sgt	McMICHAEL Lewis Kershaw	13-08-42	460 Sqn
401244	Sgt	McPHERSON Ray Douglas	11-09-42	106 Sqn
403277	Sgt	McQUEEN William Stalker	22-06-42	460 Sqn
405094	Sgt	MEARS Ashleigh Thomas	17-08-42	50 Sqn
400637	P/O	MELVILLE Robert Lorraine	16-07-42	15 Sqn
402745	P/O	MIDDLETON VC Rawdon Hume	29-11-42	149 Sqn
14818	Sgt	MILLIGAN Douglas Arthur	8-12-42	101 Sqn
404637	Sgt	MILLIKEN Roy Alistair	19-01-42	20 OTU
401709	F/S	MILLIS Allan Squires	7-09-42	12 Sqn [United Kingdom]
407298	P/O	MILLS David Bruce	26-07-42	460 Sqn
408774	Sgt	MILNE James Gordon	13-09-42	27 OTU
406812	F/S	MITCHELL Phillip Rossiter	26-09-42	12 Sqn
401577	Sgt	MITCHELL Reginald Ernest	3-12-42	27 OTU
403197	Sgt	MONCKTON Francis Edward	3-09-42	12 Sqn
403793	Sgt	MONK William John Carr	14-09-42	460 Sqn
400931	F/S	MORANT Allan Ralph	19-09-42	460 Sqn
405450	Sgt	MORGAN Owen	1-08-42	27 OTU
404251	Sgt	MORRIS John Kilpatrick	14-04-42	102 Sqn
401242	F/S	MORTON Lindsey Herbert	7-11-42	83 Sqn
406574	F/S	MOSELEY Charles Henry Doyle	9-09-42	12 Sqn
407534	Sgt	MOYLE Alan Lipson	12-07-42	460 Sqn
400481	F/S	MUIR Clarence Henry	31-05-42	214 Sqn
411225	Sgt	MUIR John Brian	3-12-42	27 OTU
405216	Sgt	MUNRO Robert James	27-08-42	460 Sqn
404146	F/O	MURPHY Denis Michael	19-10-42	1656 HCU
401182	Sgt	MURPHY John Charles	19-08-42	207 Sqn
408194	Sgt	MURPHY John Howard	10-09-42	460 Sqn
404705	Sgt	MURPHY Reginald Henry	7-05-42	460 Sqn
403143	Sgt	MURPHY Rodger Bede	3-01-42	23 OTU
404353	F/O	MURPHY William Martin	30-05-42	460 Sqn
407094	F/S	MURRAY Geoffrey Hillam Gurr	30-03-42	35 Sqn
406149	Sgt	MUSTO Clifford William	11-08-42	207 Sqn
404869	Sgt	MUSTOE George Lawson	30-05-42	150 Sqn
404798	Sgt	MYERS DFM William Henry Ingham	24-10-42	49 Sqn
406576	F/O	NASH Arthur Frederick Richard	1-08-42	27 OTU
400330	F/S	NETTLE William Harrie	26-07-42	460 Sqn
407725	Sgt	NEWBERY Kent	29-08-42	49 Sqn
407726	Sgt	NICHOLLS William John	29-04-42	14 OTU
402698	Sgt	NICHOLSON Allan	9-05-42	12 Sqn
405135	Sgt	NIXON John Joseph	6-06-42	50 Sqn
406508	Sgt	NOONAN Vincent Ormerod	15-10-42	419 Sqn
406365	P/O	NORMAN Alexander	27-08-42	12 Sqn
400885	Sgt	NORTON William Wykes Robey	26-03-42	214 Sqn
407727	P/O	ODGERS Allan Howard	26-02-42	23 OTU
403599	Sgt	OGILVIE Creighton Carlyle	11-09-42	26 OTU
402670	Sgt	OGILVIE Robert William	6-06-42	50 Sqn
400731	F/L	OLDMEADOW Fenton Charles	20-12-42	83 Sqn
403173	F/S	OLIVER Claudius William Samuel	11-08-42	149 Sqn
400029	Sgt	ORBUCK Laurence David	10-04-42	9 Sqn
403292	Sgt	OWEN Robert Rupert Bisgrove	20-09-42	61 Sqn
403876	Sgt	O'BRIEN John Ormond	20-06-42	49 Sqn
402468	Sgt	O'CONNELL Edward	26-01-42	14 OTU
403991	Sgt	O'HALLORAN John Daniel	1-08-42	27 OTU
402604	Sgt	O'NEILL James Cornelius	18-12-42	50 Sqn
403432	Sgt	O'SULLIVAN John Gregory	26-06-42	1481 Flt
403171	Sgt	PANKHURST Alfred Joseph	16-08-42	50 Sqn
400288	F/O	PARKE Edwin Roy	21-01-42	17 OTU
402576	Sgt	PARSONS Alfred Charles Ringsley	19-01-42	104 Sqn
406579	F/O	PARSONS Frank Edward	27-08-42	460 Sqn
404598	Sgt	PARSONS Sidney John Rex	25-02-42	27 OTU
403117	Sgt	PARSONS Thomas Edward	26-03-42	12 Sqn
411102	F/O	PARTON Eric Cliffe	10-09-42	460 Sqn
404671	Sgt	PASCOE Vyvyan Roessler	25-05-42	22 OTU
400760	Sgt	PATON James Keith	20-07-42	158 Sqn
416228	F/S	PEARCE Kenneth Gard	8-11-42	142 Sqn
404941	F/S	PEARSON James Christopher	10-09-42	460 Sqn
405259	Sgt	PEIRCE William Dudley	28-08-42	49 Sqn
404661	Sgt	PERROUX William Walter	29-04-42	460 Sqn
403785	Sgt	PERRY Ronald John	12-07-42	460 Sqn
12419	Sgt	PETERS Jasper Stormond	26-06-42	50 Sqn
411374	F/O	PETTIFORD Keith	20-11-42	27 OTU
401079	Sgt	PEVERILL Roy George	30-05-42	150 Sqn
402537	P/O	PHILLIPS Clive Henry	6-08-42	158 Sqn
407873	Sgt	PHILLIPS Harold Arthur	23-09-42	50 Sqn
403532	Sgt	PHILPOT James Temple	24-10-42	50 Sqn
401589	Sgt	PICKUP James Dwight	10-11-42	149 Sqn
403878	F/O	PINFOLD Frederick Charles	27-08-42	460 Sqn
402538	Sgt	PODMORE Charles Robert	28-08-42	12 Sqn
401080	Sgt	PONTON Robert Allan	10-08-42	460 Sqn
404020	Sgt	POOLEY Charles William Lawrence	26-03-42	12 Sqn
403786	Sgt	POYNTING Kenneth Hastings	26-06-42	27 OTU
400761	Sgt	PRAAGST Geoffrey Clement	31-05-42	12 Sqn
402539	Sgt	PRICE Harrington Warren	20-06-42	49 Sqn
8063	Sgt	PROCTOR Farquharson	6-12-42	464 Sqn
416283	F/S	RATHJEN Frederick Herbert	25-08-42	15 OTU
402672	Sgt	REMFRY Maurice Ben	28-04-42	27 OTU
401462	F/O	RENFREE Eric Hurlstone	25-08-42	83 Sqn
400647	Sgt	REYNOLDS Charles Noel	10-04-42	76 Sqn
402979	Sgt	REYNOLDS Robert George	3-09-42	49 Sqn
402251	Sgt	RICE Clive William Pryer	28-01-42	21 OTU
403375	F/S	RICH Alwyn Charles	26-09-42	12 Sqn
416007	Sgt	RICHARDS Bruce William	16-07-42	27 OTU
404522	F/O	RICHARDSON DFC Norman Worsley	5-05-42	12 Sqn
411187	F/S	RIDING Edward Havelock	14-09-42	12 Sqn
408736	F/S	ROBB Robert Ian	21-12-42	103 Sqn
407833	Sgt	ROBERTS Rambler David	21-05-42	25 OTU
3200	P/O	ROBERTS Robert Charles	11-04-42	455 Sqn
400105	F/O	ROBERTS Trevor Emyln	7-04-42	455 Sqn
411052	Sgt	ROBSON Wallace Alan [Canada]	29-06-42	14 OTU
411053	Sgt	RODEN Jacob Henry	20-09-42	150 Sqn
400211	Sgt	ROGERSON Josephy Henry	17-01-42	27 OTU

Service #	Rank	Name	Date	Unit
400333	Sgt	ROGET Raymond George Marafu	22-06-42	460 Sqn
402755	Sgt	ROHRLACH Hermann Heinrich Julius	8-05-42	21 OTU
401249	F/L	ROSE DFC John Colin McIntosh	21-12-42	103 Sqn
404642	F/S	ROSS William Charles Henry	12-10-42	49 Sqn
407728	F/O	ROWLANDS Richard Gerald	5-09-42	207 Sqn
402611	Sgt	ROWLEY Horace Edward	2-04-42	455 Sqn
401287	F/O	ROWLING Percy William	18-12-42	50 Sqn
407834	Sgt	SAMS Laurence James	25-07-42	460 Sqn
402612	Sgt	SAMS Wallace Hugh	1-06-42	460 Sqn
404685	F/O	SANDERSON Owen James	21-08-42	218 Sqn
411530	Sgt	SANKEY Ronald Henry	3-12-42	27 OTU
411390	F/S	SAUTELLE Claude Bernard	8-11-42	142 Sqn
407951	F/O	SAWLEY Gordon Harold	14-08-42	19 OTU
404547	P/O	SAYER James Albert	25-03-42	455 Sqn
406153	Sgt	SCHOFIELD Albert Charles	9-06-42	35 Sqn
407990	Sgt	SCOTT Colin Robert	21-02-42	455 Sqn
407808	F/O	SEYMOUR William Rex	9-01-42	207 Sqn
406682	Sgt	SHADDICK DFM Bartlett Parker	25-10-42	142 Sqn
411406	Sgt	SHAILER Sidney Alan	1-08-42	14 OTU
400294	Sgt	SHANNON George Henry	2-10-42	405 Sqn
402551	Sgt	SHARKEY Raymond John Bruce	12-07-42	460 Sqn
403959	F/S	SHARPE Oswald Lloyd	1-08-42	25 OTU
400335	Sgt	SHEARER John Robert	7-05-42	460 Sqn
404994	F/O	SHEARER William Bruce	31-05-42	12 Sqn
402885	F/S	SHEPHARD Leslie Milton	29-04-42	460 Sqn
411265	Sgt	SHEPHERD Trevor Douglas	14-09-42	150 Sqn
403114	Sgt	SHERIDAN John Edward	31-05-42	14 OTU
403655	Sgt	SHOESMITH Kelvin Hewer	27-07-42	115 Sqn
405367	Sgt	SIMS Herbert Munro	17-12-42	57 Sqn
407461	Sgt	SKINNER Garfield Lloyd	10-03-42	455 Sqn
400604	Sgt	SLOGGATT William Rent	9-01-42	104 Sqn
407688	Sgt	SMITH Alfred Geoffrey	11-09-42	106 Sqn
411397	Sgt	SMITH Colin Hugh Mackenzie	27-08-42	460 Sqn
404622	P/O	SMITH DFM Henry William Joseph	18-12-42	50 Sqn
411413	Sgt	SMITH James Arthur	28-08-42	460 Sqn
402832	F/S	SMITH Kevin Argyle	10-08-42	460 Sqn
401251	Sgt	SMITH Norman Lindsay	11-07-42	97 Sqn
407209	Sgt	SMITH Peter Harold	9-01-42	458 Sqn
405194	Sgt	SMITH Ronald David	13-08-42	460 Sqn
403079	F/S	SOLOMONS Sidney Arthur	19-09-42	460 Sqn
401860	Sgt	SOMMERVILLE Leslie John	20-11-42	150 Sqn
402411	Sgt	SPENCE Harold Menzies	11-06-42	83 Sqn
14243	Sgt	SPONGBERG William Marcel	1-06-42	460 Sqn
404553	P/O	SPOONER DFM Douglas Wilberforce	3-07-42	103 Sqn
403451	Sgt	STALLARD Cyril John	30-07-42	50 Sqn
407303	F/S	STANDLEY Malcolm John	17-09-42	76 Sqn
404275	F/O	STANFIELD James Ernest Field [New Ireland]	21-01-42	455 Sqn
404856	Sgt	STEINBACH Kenneth Henry Charles	19-07-42	27 OTU
403098	Sgt	STEPHENS Arthur Hugh	30-06-42	14 OTU
406413	Sgt	STEPHENS Ernest Victor	2-06-42	21 OTU
401680	Sgt	STEPHENSON Leonard William	16-09-42	101 Sqn
400160	Sgt	STEVENS Geoffrey Lovell	20-06-42	460 Sqn
405028	Sgt	STEVENSON James Alexander	16-03-42	14 OTU
403965	Sgt	STOREY John	26-07-42	460 Sqn
21315	Sgt	STUBBS Cecil Raymond	21-12-42	57 Sqn
406374	Sgt	STUBBS John Henry	11-02-42	21 Sqn
403385	P/O	SULLIVAN Peter Richard Vincent	3-07-42	109 Sqn
403152	F/O	SUMMERS John Frederick	27-08-42	460 Sqn
404465	Sgt	SUMMERVILLE Kent Oswald Thompson	12-10-42	50 Sqn
404860	F/S	SUTTON James Thomas	19-09-42	460 Sqn
407354	Sgt	SWAN Gilbert Aitken	29-08-42	49 Sqn
400442	Sgt	SYNNOTT James Murray	26-06-42	27 OTU
402471	Sgt	TAYLOR Dudley George	9-01-42	458 Sqn
401469	F/O	TAYLOR Norman Allan	28-08-42	460 Sqn
403844	F/S	TAYLOR Ronald Ward	25-10-42	103 Sqn
402263	P/O	TAYLOR DFM Ronald Wilkins	17-01-42	7 Sqn
6201	Sgt	TAYLOR William George	25-07-42	460 Sqn
407775	Sgt	TAYLOR William James	2-07-42	460 Sqn
402282	Sgt	THOMAS Lloyd Watson	10-09-42	61 Sqn
403981	Sgt	THOMPSON Charles Herbert	28-08-42	408 Sqn
404367	Sgt	THOMPSON Evan Hamilton	21-01-42	455 Sqn
401864	F/S	THOMPSON Harold Classen	26-09-42	12 Sqn
402622	Sgt	THOMPSON Lawrence Chase	26-06-42	50 Sqn
411408	Sgt	THOMSON Craig Sloan	4-11-42	464 Sqn
405436	Sgt	THOMSON George Comrie	16-09-42	142 Sqn
401470	F/O	THOMSON Herbert James	9-09-42	12 Sqn
411409	Sgt	THORN Charles Maxwell	17-09-42	61 Sqn
400741	Sgt	TINKLER Archibald Edmond	26-07-42	460 Sqn
404786	Sgt	TOOHILL Noel Messines	9-01-42	207 Sqn
402894	Sgt	TRESIDDER Robert Litchfield	17-02-42	460 Sqn
402454	P/O	TROTTER James Arthur	24-08-42	149 Sqn
401865	Sgt	TULLOH Ivan Thomas	26-07-42	460 Sqn
411555	Sgt	TURNBULL Joseph Albert	13-09-42	27 OTU
403158	Sgt	TURNER Henry Thomas Augustus	27-08-42	460 Sqn
404688	Sgt	TURNOCK John Sivyer	13-03-42	460 Sqn
406335	Sgt	VEAL Colin Geoffrey	25-02-42	27 OTU
403153	F/S	VICKERS Edgar Henry	1-08-42	16 OTU
408139	F/S	VINEY Cyril Charles	27-08-42	460 Sqn
404270	P/O	VOLLER Peter Collin	6-01-42	12 Sqn
404793	Sgt	von der GROEBEN Richard Arthur	13-07-42	1654 CU
408133	P/O	WADDELL Alan Albert	31-05-42	12 Sqn
402699	P/O	WADDELL Hilton Graham	21-06-42	420 Sqn
400894	F/S	WALDON Ronald Frederick	3-06-42	460 Sqn
407956	F/O	WALKER Charles William	18-12-42	50 Sqn
401727	Sgt	WALKER Jack Lawton	14-04-42	14 OTU
404701	Sgt	WALSH John Francis	1-06-42	460 Sqn
411206	Sgt	WARBURTON George Ernest	19-07-42	27 OTU
402989	F/O	WARD Jack Stratford	26-09-42	12 Sqn
402897	Sgt	WARE James Henry	17-02-42	460 Sqn
402582	Sgt	WARR Herbert Cheval Archer	1-08-42	408 Sqn
404899	Sgt	WARREN Ralph Ernest	19-05-42	106 Sqn
411415	Sgt	WARREN William Howard	10-11-42	57 Sqn
407308	F/S	WATKINS Thomas Lincoln	2-06-42	460 Sqn
401258	F/O	WATSON Charles Francis	23-09-42	50 Sqn
403205	Sgt	WATSON Vivian John	20-08-42	61 Sqn
402210	P/O	WATTS Hector William Cuthbert	28-06-42	156 Sqn
406272	F/O	WEBB Albert Ernest William	3-07-42	460 Sqn
402767	Sgt	WEBB Evan Frederick	17-01-42	27 OTU
402176	F/O	WEEKES Frank Watson	28-07-42	105 Sqn
402990	Sgt	WEEKS Henry Charles	10-04-42	144 Sqn
405369	Sgt	WEIR Alexander Allan	2-06-42	14 OTU
400763	Sgt	WELCH Arnold Gregory	31-05-42	49 Sqn
404518	F/O	WELLER John Allan	28-03-42	115 Sqn
407565	Sgt	WHIBLEY Leonard Garth	13-02-42	82 Sqn
404742	P/O	WHITE Sydney Stanley	26-01-42	14 OTU
407022	F/S	WHITEHILL Maxwell Elliott	7-06-42	49 Sqn
407631	Sgt	WHITING Peter Robert Alfred Stewart	19-08-42	61 Sqn
404844	Sgt	WHITTICK Alexander Frederick	3-07-42	460 Sqn
402427	Sgt	WILLIAMS Alan Neal	28-01-42	78 Sqn
405459	Sgt	WILLIAMS Cecil Alfred	19-08-42	21 OTU
403206	Sgt	WILLIAMS David Alexander	30-04-42	50 Sqn
402687	Sgt	WILLIAMS Eric Douglas	26-06-42	10 OTU
404772	Sgt	WILLIAMS Frederick Ernest	17-01-42	27 OTU
405089	Sgt	WILLIAMS Herbert Noel	28-05-42	1443 Flt
402429	F/S	WILLIAMS Lindsay Ross	16-03-42	57 Sqn
407487	Sgt	WILLIAMS Walter Chantler	21-01-42	50 Sqn
401086	F/O	WILLIAMS William Kenneth	11-06-42	83 Sqn
401263	Sgt	WILLIAMS Willoughby Lloyd	8-05-42	21 OTU
400110	P/O	WILLOX John Lennox Siesel	3-01-42	455 Sqn
405140	F/S	WILSON John William Edward	3-12-42	103 Sqn
405008	Sgt	WILSON Ralph Alexander	26-07-42	83 Sqn
401728	Sgt	WISHART Harold Peter	22-12-42	27 OTU

401357	Sgt	WITHAM Ian Verdun	19-08-42	61 Sqn
408768	F/O	WOOD Roger Wyndham	19-10-42	1656 HCU
400301	Sgt	WOODBURN Calder Fenton	2-04-42	455 Sqn
400187	F/S	WOODFORD John Hamilton	11-09-42	78 Sqn
403846	F/S	WOODHOUSE Thomas	8-11-42	142 Sqn
408003	F/S	WOOLNOUGH Jack Stephen Richards	17-01-42	27 OTU
406378	F/O	WORKMAN Frederick John	6-02-42	21 Sqn
407659	Sgt	WORLEY Thomas Alfred	21-05-42	21 OTU
401333	Sgt	WOTHERSPOON Alexander	19-08-42	61 Sqn
401264	Sgt	WYLES Allan	30-07-42	50 Sqn
406670	Sgt	YEAMAN Alfred Neil	4-06-42	1519 Flt
402629	F/O	YOUNG Harry Neville	2-04-42	455 Sqn
405372	Sgt	ZISER Reginald	10-10-42	150 Sqn

ROYAL CANADIAN AIR FORCE
personnel

R/70976	F/S	ADAIR Arthur Dunham	21-06-42	9 Sqn
R/86603	Sgt	ADAMS John Joseph William	14-09-42	1654 CU
R/92747	F/S	ADSETT Frederick Charles	2-10-42	115 Sqn
R/68523	F/S	AILEY John Drew	27-06-42	405 Sqn
R/76714	F/S	ALBRIGHT Frederick Bruce	2-06-42	21 OTU
J/15590	P/O	ALBRIGHT Robert Baker	24-07-42	405 Sqn
R/56251	WO1	ALCAZAR William Etherington [Trinidad]	30-06-42	405 Sqn
R/101979	Sgt	ALCOCK Arthur Franklin	17-06-42	24 OTU
R/93188	F/S	ALLAN James McGregor	25-11-42	207 Sqn
R/78183	Sgt	ALLEN Donald George	21-02-42	16 OTU
R/87266	F/S	ALLEN Frank	12-12-42	102 Sqn
R/95975	Sgt	ALLENBY Thomas Peter 'Tom' [USA]	11-09-42	26 OTU
R/77970	F/S	AMLIN Arnold Herbert	28-08-42	142 Sqn
R/83648	F/S	ANDERSON Edward Allison	1-08-42	405 Sqn
J/6490	P/O	ANDERSON Henry Gordon	12-02-42	419 Sqn
R/84389	F/S	ANDERSON James	4-08-42	142 Sqn
R/92541	F/S	ANDERSON James	4-09-42	25 OTU
R/92560	Sgt	ANDERSON James Sangster	17-10-42	158 Sqn
J/8616	P/O	ANDERSON John Fraser	3-04-42	16 OTU
J/91833	F/S	ANDERSON Leonard Roy	7-12-42	101 Sqn
R/83108	Sgt	ANDERSON Richard Frank [USA]	6-02-42	21 OTU
R/77386	F/S	ANDERSON Richard John	2-07-42	218 Sqn
J/10415	F/O	ANDERSON Robert Fred Lindsay	13-11-42	105 Sqn
R/105561	F/S	ANDERSON William Oswald	10-09-42	14 OTU
R/72663	F/S	ANDREW Prentis Blair	28-07-42	16 OTU
R/92243	F/S	ANDREWS Walter Mowbray	11-09-42	106 Sqn
R/102644	Sgt	ARBUCKLE Irving	15-10-42	405 Sqn
J/9586	P/O	ARCHER Charles Douglas Haig	29-06-42	22 OTU
R/62668	F/S	ARMSTRONG Albert Winston	3-06-42	61 Sqn
J/15020	P/O	ARMSTRONG Gordon Kenneth	12-02-42	419 Sqn
R/88084	Sgt	ARMSTRONG John Marshall	5-10-42	425 Sqn
R/53363	F/S	ARMSTRONG Robert Alfred	30-05-42	22 OTU
R/77407	F/S	ARMSTRONG Thomas James	1-08-42	16 OTU
R/85348	F/S	ARONSON Kenneth Johannes	30-07-42	419 Sqn
R/117302	Sgt	ARPS Lysle Ralph	6-12-42	14 OTU
J/15708	P/O	ARTHUR Neil Greig	29-07-42	419 Sqn
R/105801	Sgt	ASH Norman Andrews	16-11-42	425 Sqn
R/101589	F/S	ATKINS Milton Wilbur	11-08-42	207 Sqn
R/66686	Sgt	ATKINSON Joseph Mackay	8-08-42	61 Sqn
J/8359	F/S	ATKINSON Merle William	1-10-42	76 Sqn
R/98159	F/S	AULD Charles W. [USA]	15-07-42	23 OTU
R/82683	F/S	AUSTIN Charles Wendell	5-10-42	156 Sqn
R/66434	Sgt	AVEDISIAN James Theodore	30-07-42	149 Sqn
R/79088	Sgt	AYERS Richard Butcher [USA]	28-07-42	22 OTU
J/7775	P/O	AYLES Russell James	1-10-42	405 Sqn
R/56438	Sgt	BACHELDER Allen Leland	7-08-42	218 Sqn
R/92595	F/S	BACKS William Henry	30-09-42	14 OTU
R/74696	F/S	BAILLIE John Robert	9-09-42	405 Sqn
R/99629	F/S	BAILLIE Thomas	17-09-42	23 OTU
J/6027	P/O	BAIN DFC John Douglas	31-05-42	156 Sqn
R/76305	F/S	BAIRD David Monroe	31-05-42	16 OTU
R/79439	F/S	BAITTLE Horace David	28-08-42	75 Sqn
J/5060	F/L	BAKER DFC Edward Donald	1-04-42	214 Sqn
R/69242	F/S	BAKER Joseph Kenneth	27-07-42	102 Sqn
R/87969	F/S	BALDOCK Richard Marlow	10-11-42	7 Sqn
R/55463	Sgt	BALL Norman Sargeant	28-08-42	150 Sqn
R/63745	F/S	BALLINGAL Donald Leslie	26-03-42	57 Sqn
R/129207	Sgt	BALLINGER Henry Clasper [USA]	27-11-42	20 OTU
J/15343	P/O	BALTZER Ross Lloyd	2-06-42	405 Sqn
J/5686	P/O	BARBER Herbert Boyd	26-07-42	83 Sqn
R/92306	Sgt	BARBER Richard Thomas	13-10-42	83 Sqn
22050A	F/S	BARBOUR Frank Douglas	14-04-42	419 Sqn
R/80160	F/S	BARCLAY Philip Grimshaw	31-05-42	22 OTU
R/117549	Sgt	BARNARD Leonard Joseph [USA]	24-10-42	149 Sqn
J/15520	P/O	BARR Charles Rae	17-06-42	102 Sqn
R/94714	F/S	BARRETT Eric Henry	2-11-42	1521 Flt
R/78791	F/S	BAUER Wilbert Francis	24-10-42	425 Sqn
R/77144	WO2	BEACH Carl Adrian [USA]	19-08-42	88 Sqn
R/102069	Sgt	BEALE Walter Stanley	9-11-42	420 Sqn
R/75332	F/S	BEATTY Harold Creighton	6-07-42	22 OTU
R/74134	Cpl	BEAUDRY Joseph Victor Raoul	29-11-42	405 Sqn
J/9205	P/O	BEAUMONT Leys Middleton	24-08-42	44 Sqn
R/55398	WO2	BEAUPRE John	7-08-42	103 Sqn
R/108447	Sgt	BEAUREGARD Joseph George	5-10-42	218 Sqn
R/55401	F/S	BECHARD Louis Joseph Raymond	8-02-42	22 OTU
J/16163	P/O	BECK John William [USA]	6-12-42	107 Sqn
R/77303	Sgt	BEDARD Joseph Phillipe	24-10-42	425 Sqn
R/98141	F/S	BEE Charles Robert	19-09-42	15 Sqn
J/9160	P/O	BEECH Gerald McKee	29-07-42	9 Sqn
R/61113	F/S	BEIRNES Donald Wood	4-01-42	82 Sqn
R/94770	Sgt	BELL Charles Herbert Leslie	10-09-42	22 OTU
J/10319	F/O	BELL Clarence Edgar	13-10-42	419 Sqn
R/64880	F/S	BELL James William	30-06-42	405 Sqn
J/17824	P/O	BELL DFM Ronald George	9-11-42	408 Sqn
R/61812	F/S	BELOUS Wesley Leonard	19-07-42	76 Sqn
R/90419	Sgt	BENNER David Stanley	1-10-42	102 Sqn
R/58098	Sgt	BENNETT Thomas Herbert	26-02-42	158 Sqn
R/137695	Sgt	BENNETT William John Bowles	6-10-42	22 OTU
J/15845	P/O	BENT DFM William Thomas [USA]	9-11-42	142 Sqn
R/87867	Sgt	BEN-HERTZ Maxwell	2-10-42	405 Sqn
J/7321	P/O	BERANEK Stanley Joseph	19-06-42	408 Sqn
R/95456	F/S	BERGQUIST Edwin Robert	13-10-42	83 Sqn
R/75831	F/S	BERTRAM Richard Edgar	11-09-42	25 OTU
J/7030	P/O	BEST Thomas	2-04-42	214 Sqn
R/84501	F/S	BICKERTON George Stanley	14-09-42	22 OTU
J/15780	P/O	BIDEN Byron Stanley	28-08-42	142 Sqn
R/100154	F/S	BIGGS James William	6-09-42	20 OTU
R/104923	Sgt	BIJUR Robert Duff [USA]	9-08-42	15 OTU
J/8610	P/O	BING Gerrard Roy	15-10-42	420 Sqn
J/15411	P/O	BIRCHALL Albert	19-09-42	15 Sqn
R/67791	F/S	BISSETT John Alexander	26-02-42	10 Sqn
R/91666	Sgt	BISSONNETTE Guy Andre Rene	26-07-42	78 Sqn
R/119121	F/S	BLACK Wendell Clifford	9-11-42	405 Sqn
R/85445	F/S	BLAIR John Lawrence	10-09-42	61 Sqn
R/79379	F/S	BLAIR Reginald George	15-10-42	149 Sqn
R/75117	F/S	BLAIR Timothy Clayton	24-07-42	207 Sqn
R/75090	Sgt	BLAKE Leonard Herbert	5-05-42	22 OTU
R/81457	F/S	BLOOMER George Taylor	1-08-42	14 OTU
R/54195	F/S	BLUE Donald Archibald	5-05-42	22 OTU
R/76229	F/S	BOATES Robert Melbourne	21-05-42	25 OTU
R/69637	F/S	BOISVERT Joseph Leonidas Rose Alphee	15-04-42	408 Sqn
J/6155	P/O	BOND Walter Frederick	12-02-42	419 Sqn
R/99122	Sgt	BOOMER Carl Stirling	9-11-42	22 OTU
R/67602	Sgt	BOOTH George Vincent [USA]	22-07-42	115 Sqn

Service No.	Rank	Name	Date	Unit
J/15775	P/O	BOOTSMA Donald Hill [USA]	11-06-42	77 Sqn
R/62974	Sgt	BOUDREAU Gerald Charles	14-01-42	22 OTU
R/62814	Sgt	BOUDREAULT Joseph Raoul Alphonse	22-09-42	425 Sqn
R/69426	F/S	BOURKE William Stanley	9-11-42	425 Sqn
J/6153	P/O	BOWMAN Lloyd Douglas	10-06-42	107 Sqn
J/5797	P/O	BOWSHER Norman Frederick	31-03-42	76 Sqn
R/67561	Sgt	BOYCE Norman George Wood	26-03-42	16 OTU
R/88736	F/S	BOYD Bruce Allan	9-11-42	57 Sqn
R/69361	F/S	BOYER Joseph Paul Albert	24-10-42	425 Sqn
J/16933	P/O	BOYES Harry Thomas	21-12-42	156 Sqn
R/102019	F/S	BRACEY Maurice John	30-09-42	23 OTU
R/61780	F/S	BRACKEN William Henry	20-05-42	7 Sqn
J/2501	P/O	BRADBURY John Leslie	1-04-42	20 OTU
J/15512	P/O	BRADBURY Richard Forrest	26-06-42	102 Sqn
J/18602	P/O	BRADLEY Allen Catto	29-11-42	405 Sqn
R/60627	F/S	BRADSHAW Robert Leonard	6-06-42	35 Sqn
R/10170	F/O	BRALEY Raymond Sydney	13-10-42	10 Sqn
R/67866	F/S	BRAMLEY Ennis Frederick	22-09-42	106 Sqn
R/86619	F/S	BRASNETT Raymond Gerard	15-10-42	214 Sqn
R/88827	F/S	BRAWLEY Paul Franklin [USA]	20-09-42	101 Sqn
R/78203	F/S	BRAY DFM Charles Lorne	25-04-42	103 Sqn
R/132533	Sgt	BREIVIS John [USA]	29-08-42	49 Sqn
R/74994	Sgt	BRENNAN Edmund Keith	30-06-42	405 Sqn
J/15860	P/O	BRICE Vincent Leslie	15-01-42	10 Sqn
R/71563	WO1	BRICHTA DFM Philip Sibbald Ogilvie	16-09-42	22 OTU
R/64409	Sgt	BRODDY James Morley	10-03-42	405 Sqn
R/78891	Sgt	BROOK Charles Cyril	9-11-42	102 Sqn
R/85929	F/S	BROOM Howard	5-10-42	419 Sqn
R/54171	F/S	BROPHY Allan Charles Vincent	6-05-42	419 Sqn
R/77127	WO2	BROPHY Bernard Anthony [United Kingdom]	13-08-42	207 Sqn
R/90611	P/O	BROVENDER Jack Lionel	4-09-42	25 OTU
R/64344	F/S	BROWN Charles Harold Latshaw	26-02-42	158 Sqn
R/61683	WO1	BROWN Clayton Penrose Lindon	7-07-42	419 Sqn
J/15685	P/O	BROWN Earl Herbert	18-08-42	101 Sqn
R/83258	Sgt	BROWN Eddie Hester [USA]	25-06-42	214 Sqn
R/67850	F/S	BROWN Harold Alexander	6-08-42	419 Sqn
J/5693	P/O	BROWN James Bernard Frederick	29-04-42	78 Sqn
R/110045	Sgt	BROWN Ray Edward	13-09-42	22 OTU
R/70880	Sgt	BROWN Thomas Lloyd	6-05-42	16 OTU
R/5227	F/L	BROWN William Beaumont	27-03-42	408 Sqn
R/78076	Sgt	BROWN William Elliott	22-07-42	115 Sqn
R/86420	Sgt	BROWNLEE David Ellis	28-08-42	14 OTU
J/15668	P/O	BRUCE Haddo Eric Von	26-07-42	35 Sqn
R/70448	F/S	BRYANT Harry Douglas	6-01-42	12 Sqn
R/89943	F/S	BRYDEN Herbert	29-07-42	419 Sqn
R/58102	F/S	BUCHANAN Alexander Gibson	6-01-42	102 Sqn
R/92487	F/S	BUCHANAN Stanley Lloyd George	12-08-42	57 Sqn
R/109346	F/S	BUCHNER Charles Wesley	27-08-42	15 OTU
J/12988	P/O	BUCK Frederick Walter	15-10-42	420 Sqn
R/56144	F/S	BUCKLEY John Peter Burton Richard	31-03-42	35 Sqn
J/6158	P/O	BUDD Phil Clive	27-04-42	149 Sqn
R/111658	F/S	BUECHLER Maurice Emanuel [USA]	16-09-42	9 Sqn
R/17591	P/O	BULANDA Joseph Peter	10-11-42	7 Sqn
J/16565	P/O	BUNT James Edward	18-12-42	97 Sqn
R/95743	F/S	BURCHELL Donald Fred	9-11-42	425 Sqn
J/16054	F/S	BURKE John Richard Powell	1-10-42	405 Sqn
R/102904	F/S	BURKE Roy Norman Victor	9-11-42	425 Sqn
R/102612	LAC	BURNS John Francis	27-09-42	12 OTU
R/97521	F/S	BURRILL Frank	10-06-42	75 Sqn
J/8102	P/O	BURTON Howard Houston [USA]	20-09-42	9 Sqn
R/54303	F/S	BUSSELL Arthur Allen	2-04-42	57 Sqn
R/6968	F/S	BUSTIN John William Arthur	30-06-42	57 Sqn
R/91290	Sgt	BYE John Henry	25-01-42	23 OTU
R/129019	F/S	BYRD Clifford Howard John	25-08-42	83 Sqn
R/83541	WO2	CACHIA John	7-12-42	425 Sqn
R/64713	F/S	CADGER William John	31-03-42	76 Sqn
R/68128	F/S	CALDERWOOD Donald John	11-09-42	83 Sqn
R/127719	Sgt	CALDWELL Gordon Miles	16-09-42	12 OTU
R/90563	F/S	CALLAN Morris Kolesky	10-11-42	102 Sqn
R/103468	F/S	CAMERON Douglas Charles	5-12-42	1658 HCU
C/1403	F/L	CAMERON Wilfred Lawrie	31-05-42	14 OTU
R/71752	F/S	CAMP Sydney Clarence	15-01-42	51 Sqn
J/10769	F/O	CAMPBELL Alexander Bruce	17-12-42	115 Sqn
R/61803	F/S	CAMPBELL Douglas Reid	28-01-42	78 Sqn
R/88552	Sgt	CAMPBELL James Bertram	1-08-42	25 OTU
J/15888	P/O	CAMPBELL John Thompson	1-10-42	405 Sqn
R/127800	F/S	CAPTON Leslie James	29-08-42	49 Sqn
C/1613	F/L	CARDELL John Sommerville	16-08-42	408 Sqn
J/7197	P/O	CARDINAL Barrie Phillip	7-06-42	214 Sqn
R/53908	F/S	CAREY John Joseph	29-08-42	103 Sqn
J/9143	F/O	CARLYLE Walter Beattie	21-07-42	106 Sqn
R/116332	Sgt	CARON Aime Leon	17-09-42	49 Sqn
R/82511	F/S	CARPENTER Charles Arthur	1-10-42	405 Sqn
J/10186	F/O	CARRICK John Hammond	1-10-42	78 Sqn
R/77956	F/S	CARROLL Bernard	30-07-42	102 Sqn
R/65245	F/S	CARROLL Charles Edward	7-02-42	50 Sqn
R/54101	F/S	CARRUTHERS Carl Stuart	9-03-42	15 Sqn
R/96134	F/S	CARRUTHERS Ford Ross	6-09-42	12 Sqn
R/130033	F/S	CARSWELL James Cannon	17-09-42	23 OTU
R/91412	F/S	CARTER Albert Martin	1-10-42	405 Sqn
J/15883	P/O	CARTMELL Robert Joseph	14-09-42	214 Sqn
J/11102	F/O	CARTWRIGHT George Stevenson	9-11-42	425 Sqn
R/74777	F/S	CARYLL Ian Brian [Jamaica]	29-07-42	156 Sqn
R/54313	WO2	CASEY Raymond Francis	14-07-42	35 Sqn
J/15844	P/O	CASIMIRI Harry	16-09-42	22 OTU
R/74701	F/S	CASSIDY Frederick William	3-09-42	419 Sqn
J/15105	P/O	CASTON Thomas Walker	28-02-42	110 Sqn
R/78926	F/S	CATON Archie Ernest	28-08-42	419 Sqn
R/53364	F/S	CATTLE Thomas Robert Manard	9-06-42	405 Sqn
R/55408	F/S	CAUCHY Louis Augustin Marie	28-06-42	150 Sqn
R/120674	Sgt	CAUSIER Russell George	14-12-42	22 OTU
J/6167	P/O	CAVAGHAN Eric Graham	30-05-42	419 Sqn
R/135149	Sgt	CAVANAUGH Robert Joseph [USA]	17-11-42	405 Sqn
J/7473	P/O	CHAFFEY George Henry	31-05-42	142 Sqn
R/78950	F/S	CHALKEN Christopher Norman	29-08-42	408 Sqn
R/82327	F/S	CHALLIS Albert Clifford	5-10-42	425 Sqn
R/113527	Sgt	CHAPMAN Donald Harold	10-09-42	14 OTU
R/69135	F/S	CHARBONNEAU Ivan Lee	9-05-42	15 Sqn
R/82859	Sgt	CHARBONNEAU Joseph Milton Lorraine	7-05-42	23 OTU
R/59571	F/S	CHARLES John Hamilton	31-05-42	61 Sqn
R/90686	F/S	CHARRON Joseph Hilarion	11-09-42	25 OTU
R/96359	F/S	CHARTON Moses	6-10-42	19 OTU
J/9349	P/O	CHASE Robert Fleming	17-09-42	106 Sqn
R/77559	WO2	CHASTON Lionel Greer	28-08-42	408 Sqn
J/10179	F/O	CHERNIUK George	7-11-42	7 Sqn
R/93562	F/S	CHESSOR Edward William	21-10-42	21 OTU
J/6653	P/O	CHEVALIER Joseph Frederic	29-03-42	61 Sqn
R/65313	F/S	CHIASSON John Charles	24-07-42	207 Sqn
R/56204	F/S	CHICOINE MiD Joseph Vincent	3-07-42	103 Sqn
R/58481	F/S	CHISHOLM Roderick James	6-06-42	35 Sqn
R/101535	F/S	CHISLETT Herbert Alfred	16-08-42	50 Sqn
J/16502	P/O	CHOLETTE Joseph Henri Jacques	20-12-42	425 Sqn
J/16081	P/O	CHOUINIERE Eugene Edward [USA]	25-11-42	207 Sqn
R/91312	F/S	CHRISTIE Allen Frederick	28-08-42	44 Sqn
R/86747	F/S	CLARE Norman Austin	28-08-42	14 OTU
R/122070	F/S	CLARK Darwin Jackson [USA]	12-12-42	26 OTU
R/67811	F/S	CLARK Gerald Madison [USA]	29-07-42	156 Sqn
R/81023	WO1	CLARK James Anderson	15-09-42	419 Sqn
J/19450	P/O	CLARK Samuel Stuart	29-11-42	405 Sqn
J/5703	P/O	CLARKE Harold William	21-01-42	408 Sqn

145

ID	Rank	Name	Date	Unit	ID	Rank	Name	Date	Unit
R/92256	Sgt	CLARKE Ralph	14-09-42	19 OTU	R/79077	F/S	CROKE Francis Bernard	22-08-42	10 OTU
J/11210	P/O	CLARKE Robert Edward	17-09-42	7 Sqn	J/17056	P/O	CRONK George Edward [USA]	7-12-42	425 Sqn
R/54784	F/S	CLARKE Thomas Henry	11-06-42	83 Sqn	R/74718	F/S	CROSS William Andrew	9-03-42	15 Sqn
J/15667	P/O	CLARKE Wilfrid Victor	1-08-42	9 Sqn	R/95095	F/S	CROSSING John Keith	26-06-42	23 OTU
R/16871	P/O	CLARKSON Robert Guy	21-12-42	9 Sqn	R/85907	F/S	CROSSLAND Harry [United Kingdom]	1-06-42	12 OTU
R/91302	F/S	CLEMENT Roger Albert	28-08-42	207 Sqn	R/127686	F/S	CROSSTHWAITE Daniel	31-12-42	83 Sqn
J/9366	F/O	CLEMENTS Desmond Bracken	9-11-42	22 OTU	R/55836	F/S	CROTEAU Joseph Fernand Raymond	16-11-42	425 Sqn
R/93336	F/S	CLEMENTS John Gordon	6-12-42	102 Sqn	R/69734	F/S	CROTHERS Thomas Edward	3-07-42	420 Sqn
R/97434	F/S	CLOUTIER Joseph Edmond	22-12-42	105 Sqn	R/102208	Sgt	CROZIER Lloyd Donald James	23-03-42	1518 Flt
R/54295	F/S	COBBETT Charles Howard	18-08-42	101 Sqn	R/75722	F/S	CULP Reginald Harley	5-09-42	142 Sqn
R/96163	F/S	COLBRAN Lester Owen	7-09-42	115 Sqn	R/87313	F/S	CUMMING Alister Godfrey	6-11-42	218 Sqn
R/106892	Sgt	COLDRON George Edward Cragg	14-09-42	14 OTU	J/15985	P/O	CUNNINGHAM Francis Leo	1-10-42	405 Sqn
J/6799	P/O	COLDWELL Gordon Willard	17-05-42	149 Sqn	R/15531	F/L	CYBULSKI DFC Stanley Julian	21-12-42	156 Sqn
R/106062	F/S	COLE Frederick Marsden	26-06-42	24 OTU	J/15608	P/O	DABBS DFC Howard Earl	7-12-42	101 Sqn
R/64719	F/S	COLE James Edward	28-06-42	405 Sqn	R/76568	F/S	DADSON Victor Charles	25-01-42	408 Sqn
R/106214	F/S	COLE Robert John Levi	16-10-42	142 Sqn	J/15417	P/O	DAFOE Jack Stanley	9-05-42	408 Sqn
R/77433	WO2	COLLARD Cornelious	9-11-42	420 Sqn	R/94887	Sgt	DAKIN Thomas Dunbar	23-03-42	1518 Flt
R/77329	WO2	COLLETT Russell Thomas Joshua	20-09-42	218 Sqn	R/58211	F/S	DANIELS Arthur	29-07-42	57 Sqn
R/91184	F/S	COLLINS John Robert	28-07-42	107 Sqn	R/130187	F/S	DAOUST Richard Cecil	10-09-42	16 OTU
R/64727	F/S	COLPITTS John William	3-01-42	99 Sqn	R/56446	F/S	DARLEY Henry Francis Stain	14-04-42	419 Sqn
R/83851	Sgt	COLQUHOUN Ray Ormond	11-02-42	10 OTU	R/77327	F/S	DAUGHNEY John Haliburton	22-04-42	408 Sqn
R/110138	F/S	COLVIN Richard John Todd	10-10-42	419 Sqn	R/62265	F/S	DAVENPORT John Joseph	13-04-42	408 Sqn
R/90227	Sgt	COLWILL William Clifford	24-10-42	207 Sqn	J/16866	P/O	DAVIDSON Edward Ian Ross	30-11-42	22 OTU
R/88022	F/S	CONGDON Donald Willard	13-10-42	156 Sqn	R/62936	F/S	DAVIDSON Frank Edwards	18-09-42	15 Sqn
R/64825	F/S	CONNELL Joseph Walter	26-02-42	16 OTU	R/91650	F/S	DAVIDSON Roy	21-06-42	420 Sqn
R/60557	F/S	CONNELL William Paterson	16-02-42	77 Sqn	R/97987	F/S	DAVIES Roy Percival	11-08-42	14 OTU
R/72553	Sgt	CONSTABLE Melvyn Ralph	8-09-42	115 Sqn	R/78493	WO1	DAVIES William Robert	17-06-42	102 Sqn
R/76122	WO2	CONTER David	17-06-42	102 Sqn	R/85807	F/S	DAVIS Henry Lawrence	28-05-42	1443 Flt
J/6161	P/O	CONVEY Leo Joseph	28-03-42	109 Sqn	R/81403	F/S	DAVIS Hershel Homer [USA]	20-04-42	420 Sqn
J/6152	P/O	COOK Albert	28-08-42	35 Sqn	R/97448	F/S	DAVIS Norman	9-11-42	425 Sqn
J/15258	P/O	COOK Harold Leslie	10-04-42	12 Sqn	R/54528	F/S	DAVIS Philip Weir	30-09-42	51 Sqn
R/62860	F/S	COOK Robert Douglas	25-05-42	22 OTU	R/90329	F/S	DAWDY Louis Donald	2-09-42	405 Sqn
R/70432	F/S	COOKE Leonard Frank	31-05-42	156 Sqn	R/67521	F/S	DAWES Spencer Sidney [United Kingdom]	1-04-42	214 Sqn
R/61123	P/O	COONE Ernest Herbert	2-06-42	97 Sqn					
R/54828	F/S	COONEY James Daniel O'Leary	16-08-42	106 Sqn	J/8099	P/O	DAY John Francis	26-07-42	35 Sqn
R/106593	F/S	COOPER Arthur Douglas	15-09-42	14 OTU	R/93140	Sgt	DEARLOVE Lewis Nelson	30-06-42	405 Sqn
J/7986	P/O	COOPER George Albert	29-07-42	9 Sqn	R/139948	Sgt	DEATHERAGE Walter David	10-09-42	14 OTU
R/80234	F/S	COOPER Hector Thomas Moore	3-04-42	101 Sqn	J/15701	P/O	DELL Harley James	29-07-42	419 Sqn
R/55387	F/S	COOPER James Francis	5-09-42	61 Sqn	R/69265	F/S	DEMPSAY Ronald	13-10-42	214 Sqn
R/97274	Sgt	COOPER John Donald	21-10-42	7 Sqn	R/71782	F/S	DEMPSEY Philip Damon	29-07-42	57 Sqn
R/72104	F/S	COOPER John Robert	5-06-42	150 Sqn	R/102185	F/S	DERBYSHIRE George Edward	4-09-42	25 OTU
R/79564	Sgt	COPELAND Ben Bales	1-10-42	405 Sqn	R/107000	Sgt	DERRICK Melvin Ralph	19-08-42	21 OTU
A/65	F/S	COPELAND Herbert Redvers	8-06-42	420 Sqn	R/56151	F/S	DERRY Richard Ironmonger	2-06-42	26 OTU
R/59294	F/S	CORMACK John	15-04-42	405 Sqn	R/85302	Sgt	DESJARDINS Joseph Ernest	17-10-42	23 OTU
R/81453	F/S	CORMACK William Thomas	31-05-42	156 Sqn	J/85163	P/O	de NEVERS Frank Holmes	14-09-42	22 OTU
J/15537	P/O	CORRIGAN Robert James	19-08-42	226 Sqn	J/15717	P/O	DE BARTOK DFC Ernest Akos Frederic		
R/61096	F/S	COSTIGAN Edward Norman	17-06-42	419 Sqn				20-09-42	101 Sqn
R/82472	F/S	COTE Joseph John Edward	7-10-42	115 Sqn	R/84563	F/S	DICKINSON Winston James [USA]	30-06-42	405 Sqn
J/4885	P/O	COTTIER Thomas George	16-01-42	419 Sqn	R/67803	F/S	DILLON Raymond James [USA]	15-05-42	408 Sqn
R/94968	F/S	COUBROUGH George Thomas	30-11-42	98 Sqn	R/119135	F/S	DION Raymond Bernard	10-12-42	57 Sqn
J/5791	F/L	COULTER James Stewart	12-08-42	408 Sqn	R/82839	F/S	DIXON Calvin Daniel	21-08-42	218 Sqn
R/86910	F/S	COWAN Leo Martin	29-08-42	61 Sqn	R/102275	Sgt	DIXON Garth Lavain	13-09-42	22 OTU
J/15418	P/O	COWELL Richard Bryan	6-07-42	419 Sqn	R/92079	F/S	DOBIE Robert Charles	26-03-42	16 OTU
R/109687	F/S	COWLEY Stuart Harold	17-09-42	1654 CU	R/62688	F/S	DOE Bruce Elbert	26-03-42	12 Sqn
R/65319	F/S	COX David Reid	14-04-42	1652 CU	R/93162	F/S	DOHERTY Robert	5-10-42	419 Sqn
R/72605	F/S	COX Robert Leith	2-06-42	142 Sqn	R/81079	F/S	DOHERTY Robert Spencer	22-07-42	408 Sqn
R/53847	F/S	CRAIG Robert Kenneth	26-01-42	102 Sqn	R/101954	F/S	DOLDING Arthur John	17-11-42	405 Sqn
R/63057	WO2	CRAIG William Warren	21-07-42	35 Sqn	R/84823	F/S	DONAHUE Walter Vernard	1-08-42	24 OTU
R/100225	F/S	CRANE Beverley Dwight	29-09-42	20 OTU	R/77810	WO2	DONALD Robert Stewart	18-12-42	97 Sqn
R/93683	Sgt	CRANNA William Thomas	10-09-42	22 OTU	R/97047	F/S	DONALDSON John	16-09-42	23 OTU
R/74850	F/S	CRANSWICK Douglas	28-06-42	150 Sqn	R/78064	F/S	DONALDSON William Robert	8-02-42	12 OTU
R/68063	F/S	CRAWFORD Orville Everett	30-05-42	419 Sqn	J/15419	PO	DONNISON Frederick Ritchie	17-06-42	419 Sqn
R/87315	F/S	CRAWFORD Thomas Alvin	6-05-42	13 Sqn	R/54393	F/S	DONOGHUE John Granville [USA]	17-04-42	97 Sqn
J/15665	F/L	CRAWFORD William Samuel	21-12-42	156 Sqn	J/9570	P/O	DONOVAN William Harry	20-09-42	61 Sqn
R/83409	Sgt	CREEDE Joseph Daniel	27-07-42	405 Sqn	J/11594	P/O	DORAY Joseph Leonard	9-11-42	22 OTU
R/59557	F/S	CRESWELL Ralph Nelson Adams	31-05-42	22 OTU	R/77809	F/S	DOTEN Glen Oscar	8-06-42	10 OTU
R/110435	F/S	CROCKER Murray Rowe	17-09-42	1654 CU	R/73262	F/S	DOW James Robert	26-03-42	61 Sqn
R/83002	WO2	CROFT Wesley Bethel	14-10-42	420 Sqn	R/106416	Sgt	DOWLAND Frederick Henry	7-09-42	22 OTU

Service #	Rank	Name	Date	Unit
R/90540	F/S	DOYLE John Peter	26-07-42	97 Sqn
R/88694	Sgt	DRAKE Donald Frank	24-03-42	19 OTU
R/93310	F/S	DRENNAN Alfred Thomas	11-09-42	405 Sqn
R/99619	Sgt	DREW Thomas Alexander	17-09-42	15 OTU
R/70723	F/S	DREYER Raymond Wesley	15-05-42	408 Sqn
R/99962	F/S	DRINKWATER John Willard	19-09-42	44 Sqn
J/5792	P/O	DRYSDALE Robert Elmer	12-02-42	114 Sqn
R/78389	F/S	DUFF Frederick Francis	26-06-42	102 Sqn
R/68670	F/S	DUFFIELD John Alvin	25-09-42	61 Sqn
R/94590	F/S	DUNAJSKI Francis Xavier Joseph	13-10-42	10 Sqn
R/61792	F/S	DUNCAN Mervyn	26-03-42	12 Sqn
J/15986	P/O	DUNCAN William Howard	1-10-42	405 Sqn
R/102045	F/S	DUNLOP James Mather	7-09-42	12 Sqn
R/82518	F/S	DUNLOP John Leonard	11-12-42	10 Sqn
J/16668	P/O	DUNLOP Thomas Edwin	9-11-42	102 Sqn
R/65409	F/S	DUNN Charles Douglas	27-03-42	408 Sqn
R/78393	Sgt	DUNN Sidney Gordon Ellis	4-10-42	102 Sqn
R/60552	F/S	DUTTON Joseph Mervyn	6-06-42	419 Sqn
R/82074	F/S	DU BROY Joseph William	15-10-42	10 Sqn
R/83536	F/S	EAGLES Clarence Gordon	2-09-42	405 Sqn
R/83563	F/S	EASTWOOD Clarence Alfred	28-07-42	51 Sqn
J/9417	F/O	EDGETT George Hammond	6-10-42	142 Sqn
R/91707	F/S	EDWARDS John Frederick	22-12-42	9 Sqn
R/97583	F/S	EDWARDS Theodore Ian Mardon	3-12-42	102 Sqn
R/92046	F/S	EGAN Edward Byron	1-08-42	44 Sqn
R/83220	F/S	EGGLETON Cleveland John	11-09-42	25 OTU
R/87296	F/S	EINARSON Harold Bjorn	10-09-42	207 Sqn
R/77565	WO2	EKELUND John Herbert	16-10-42	149 Sqn
R/65845	F/S	ELDER William John	16-01-42	214 Sqn
J/5332	F/L	ELIOTT John Livingstone Hopkins [United Kingdom]	9-05-42	9 Sqn
R/75861	F/S	ELKINGTON Clarence Scott	25-08-42	101 Sqn
J/5318	F/O	ELLIOTT John William	16-03-42	57 Sqn
R/92690	F/S	ELLIS Arden Ivan	11-08-42	75 Sqn
R/92181	F/S	ELLIS George Henry	21-06-42	420 Sqn
R/66341	F/S	ELLSWORTH Gordon Leroy	10-09-42	158 Sqn
R/67644	F/S	ELMSLIE James Arthur [USA]	29-07-42	9 Sqn
R/92023	Sgt	EMERSLUND William Young	25-09-42	61 Sqn
J/15265	P/O	EMOND Joseph Edouard Hector	10-07-42	142 Sqn
R/82867	F/S	EMPEY Herbert Carl	28-08-42	142 Sqn
J/10174	P/O	ENGLAND Peter Ayrton Visart	10-09-42	102 Sqn
R/86298	Sgt	ENGLISH Marshall Frederick	31-05-42	10 Sqn
J/10008	F/S	ENNS Benjamin Hugo	29-11-42	405 Sqn
J/9259	F/O	ERICKSON Roy Stanley	6-10-42	405 Sqn
R/85838	F/S	ERNST Lloyd Sylvester	27-09-42	78 Sqn
R/84123	F/S	EUBANK Frederick Henry	24-06-42	9 Sqn
R/91535	F/S	EVANS Clarence Ernest	26-07-42	35 Sqn
R/71697	F/S	EVANS Geoffrey Charles	24-06-42	103 Sqn
J/15580	P/O	EVANS Ivan Thomas Hugel	7-07-42	419 Sqn
R/83398	F/S	EVANS James Spencer	28-07-42	22 OTU
R/77426	F/S	EVANS William Walter	18-09-42	10 OTU
R/64755	F/S	EWING Arthur Colin	3-09-42	405 Sqn
R/85957	F/S	FAHEY Robert Edward	29-07-42	16 OTU
R/62715	F/S	FAIRBROTHER Wendell Wilburn	16-02-42	61 Sqn
R/84029	F/S	FARGHER George Frederick	10-09-42	102 Sqn
R/60963	F/S	FARLEY Leo Louis Joseph	4-06-42	218 Sqn
J/15541	P/O	FAWCETT Albert H. John	16-09-42	22 OTU
R/68576	F/S	FAWCETT Milton Argue	28-06-42	150 Sqn
R/67976	F/S	FEDIGAN James Gerald Joseph [USA]	29-06-42	22 OTU
R/86326	F/S	FEDIRCHYK Michael William	29-06-42	22 OTU
R/93377	F/S	FEE Gordon Isaac	13-09-42	22 OTU
R/104215	F/S	FEINSTEIN Sam	30-09-42	12 Sqn
R/78046	F/S	FELLOWS John	17-12-42	75 Sqn
J/7072	P/O	FELT Donald Orlo	26-07-42	115 Sqn
R/85955	F/S	FENTON David	29-07-42	156 Sqn
R/110171	F/S	FERGUSON Duncan Comrie	9-11-42	20 OTU
R/80008	F/S	FERGUSON James McMillan	7-07-42	419 Sqn
R/87884	Sgt	FERNIE Peter John	26-06-42	102 Sqn
R/92966	F/S	FETHERSTON Thomas Richard Norman	9-11-42	102 Sqn
J/4530	F/L	FETHERSTON William Hugh	4-04-42	405 Sqn
R/83103	F/S	FIDDLER George Layton	14-09-42	44 Sqn
R/56351	F/S	FIELD William Ewart Nixon	27-06-42	405 Sqn
J/15423	P/O	FINDLAY William Scott	27-07-42	142 Sqn
R/80168	F/S	FINKBEINER Clarence Henry	9-05-42	408 Sqn
R/110336	F/S	FINLEY Clarence Bruce	8-11-42	76 Sqn
R/69808	F/S	FIRMAN George Albert [USA]	5-08-42	44 Sqn
J/15136	P/O	FISHER John Cobeau	28-02-42	110 Sqn
R/66159	F/S	FISK George Charles	9-04-42	83 Sqn
R/88211	F/S	FITZGERALD John Chisholm	26-07-42	15 Sqn
R/69615	WO2	FITZGERALD Rowan Charles	27-06-42	405 Sqn
R/62401	F/S	FLAVELLE Robert Ernest	21-10-42	7 Sqn
R/77881	F/S	FLEMING Andrew	18-08-42	214 Sqn
R/133282	Sgt	FLEMING John Brown	24-07-42	214 Sqn
R.75715	F/S	FLESCH Arnold Leo	29-03-42	419 Sqn
R/64470	F/S	FLETCHER Dickenson	28-08-42	142 Sqn
J/15691	P/O	FLETCHER James Lester	6-12-42	226 Sqn
R/57839	F/S	FLETCHER Leonard Watson	31-03-42	76 Sqn
J/7541	P/O	FLYNN Francis Larry	26-06-42	1651 CU
R/56267	F/S	FOGG Kenneth Andrew	6-05-42	460 Sqn
R/79246	F/S	FOLTZ Raymond Rogers [USA]	9-11-42	425 Sqn
R/117007	Sgt	FORAN Martin Raymond	24-09-42	22 OTU
R/62650	F/S	FORBES John Gordon	30-05-42	419 Sqn
R/79656	WO2	FORD George Edward [United Kingdom]	1-08-42	9 Sqn
R/58540	F/S	FORD Harry Kennedy	9-06-42	83 Sqn
R/80334	F/S	FORMAN John	6-10-42	75 Sqn
R/87980	F/S	FORMAN Robert William	20-12-42	76 Sqn
R/92075	WO2	FORSTER John Joseph William	3-11-42	1484 Flt
R/86422	F/S	FORSYTH John Hamilton	6-06-42	21 OTU
R/54940	F/S	FORTIN Edmour	22-07-42	101 Sqn
2510	F/S	FORTIN Joseph Maxwell Wenceslas	2-06-42	405 Sqn
R/111815	Sgt	FOSTER Alfred Merrill	15-10-42	21 OTU
J/16685	P/O	FOSTER Leslie	30-07-42	50 Sqn
J/9420	P/O	FOUNTAIN Irwin Dale	11-09-42	7 Sqn
R/86362	F/S	FOURNIER Rene Joseph Ludger	30-10-42	10 OTU
J/85331	P/O	FOX Albert Lloyd	20-12-42	78 Sqn
J/10404	P/O	FOY Dennis Fitzmaurice	1-09-42	14 OTU
R/101501	F/S	FRAME George Murray	12-09-42	408 Sqn
R/86255	F/S	FRANCHUK Stefan	7-12-42	101 Sqn
R/77217	F/S	FRANCOEUR William Cecil	25-06-42	76 Sqn
R/68080	F/S	FRANKLIN Harold Ralph	30-03-42	10 Sqn
J/3271	F/O	FRASER Alexander James	3-01-42	106 Sqn
R/76371	F/S	FRASER Chipman Cameron Dawson	2-09-42	142 Sqn
J/15238	P/O	FRASER William Macmillan	27-03-42	408 Sqn
R/64633	F/S	FRASER William Mann	2-04-42	57 Sqn
J/15424	P/O	FREESTONE John Handel	3-09-42	419 Sqn
R/70881	F/S	FREYSTEINSSON Harry Theodore Franklin	28-07-42	57 Sqn
J/15686	P/O	FROST William David	1-08-42	420 Sqn
R/65663	Sgt	FUGERE Michael William	20-12-42	405 Sqn
R/87427	F/S	FUNK Mervin	11-11-42	425 Sqn
R/78336	LAC	GALBRAITH Archibald Murray	26-03-42	Tempsford
R/110413	F/S	GALIPEAU Robert Henry [USA]	14-09-42	22 OTU
R/102761	F/S	GALLAGHER Frank John	11-09-42	25 OTU
J/16499	P/O	GALLAWAY Lloyd George	1-10-42	61 Sqn
R/90157	F/S	GAMMON Rex Thomas	28-07-42	22 OTU
R/98016	F/S	GANES Joseph Wayne [USA]	28-07-42	88 Sqn
R/56406	WO2	GANNON Stephen Frederic	29-11-42	405 Sqn
R/101865	F/S	GARDNER John	20-12-42	106 Sqn
R/76113	WO2	GARDNER Norman Alexander	6-11-42	21 Sqn
R/67982	F/S	GARDNER William Hawksworth	25-06-42	22 OTU
J/15721	P/O	GARNER Leslie Lewis	29-08-42	408 Sqn
R/78621	F/S	GARNETT Francis Campbell [USA]	10-03-42	405 Sqn
R/90072	F/S	GARTSIDE Wallace Mallory	12-08-42	408 Sqn

ID	Rank	Name	Date	Sqn
R/74829	F/S	GATES Billy Orin [USA]	15-04-42	214 Sqn
18039A	Sgt	GAYFER John Burton	5-01-42	405 Sqn
R/69897	F/S	GELLATLY Charles Dewitt [USA]	9-04-42	83 Sqn
R/98366	F/S	GENNETTE Francis Wayne [USA]	11-09-42	20 OTU
R/100105	F/S	GEORGE Richard Melvin	11-09-42	25 OTU
R/117661	Sgt	GEORGES Gregory Manuel [USA]	17-12-42	101 Sqn
R/61672	F/S	GEREIN Adam Jacob	11-07-42	101 Sqn
R/78315	F/S	GERMAIN George Harvey	23-06-42	420 Sqn
J/15170	F/O	GERTY Frederick Arthur George Wilmott	2-06-42	405 Sqn
J/15815	P/O	GERVAIS Edward Emile	24-09-42	405 Sqn
R/61613	F/S	GIBBONS Francis Earl	10-08-42	405 Sqn
R/91886	F/S	GIBBONS James Reginald	19-09-42	50 Sqn
R/91205	F/S	GIBBS Jack Edward	3-07-42	420 Sqn
R/70724	F/S	GIBSON Albert Graham	21-07-42	106 Sqn
R/102011	F/S	GIBSON Alexander Cameron	17-07-42	158 Sqn
R/76541	F/S	GIBSON Robert Dudley	20-09-42	150 Sqn
R/68672	F/S	GIBSON Rodney David	1-08-42	16 OTU
R/86412	F/S	GIBSON William Graham	20-07-42	10 Sqn
R/66046	F/S	GIDDENS Harold Richard	21-07-42	35 Sqn
R/76036	F/S	GIFFIN John Winslow Alexander	16-02-42	77 Sqn
R/109675	Sgt	GILBERT John Richard [USA]	6-08-42	78 Sqn
R/60244	F/S	GILFOY James Eugene	12-03-42	77 Sqn
R/62821	F/S	GILL John Davidson	5-09-42	101 Sqn
R/95484	F/S	GILLESPIE Hugh Gordon	14-11-42	405 Sqn
J/10175	F/O	GILLIES Gordon Menhennick	1-10-42	78 Sqn
R/79099	F/S	GILMOUR Donald McMurtie	6-09-42	21 OTU
J/10886	P/O	GILMOUR William	21-08-42	19 OTU
R/76533	WO2	GILSON Edmond William John	28-08-42	15 Sqn
R/101641	F/S	GIROUARD Donald Alfred	22-09-42	425 Sqn
R/62704	F/S	GIROUX Gerald Grant	2-04-42	57 Sqn
R/54903	F/S	GIROUX Joseph Antonio Lucien	13-03-42	12 Sqn
R/103565	F/S	GISLASON Norman	6-10-42	405 Sqn
R/70094	F/S	GITTINGS William George	12-08-42	408 Sqn
R/71415	F/S	GLINZ Donald Frederick	7-05-42	22 OTU
R/68696	F/S	GLOVER Robert Bell	18-01-42	142 Sqn
R/77436	F/S	GODBEHERE James Herbert	31-05-42	1502 Flt
R/75207	WO2	GOODFELLOW Lloyd Truman	25-08-42	83 Sqn
J/15745	P/O	GOOLD George Clarence	16-09-42	22 OTU
R/83552	F/S	GORDON Richard Lawrence	29-04-42	408 Sqn
R/66094	WO2	GORDON William Frederick	9-11-42	7 Sqn
R/109531	Sgt	GORDON-KAY Douglas	6-11-42	10 OTU
R/62217	F/S	GORIEU Raymond Albert Aime	30-06-42	405 Sqn
R/93025	F/S	GORMAN Ralph Ernest [USA]	10-09-42	75 Sqn
R/55226	WO2	GOSSELIN Joseph Simeon David Benoit	22-06-42	218 Sqn
R/84216	F/S	GOULD Jay Randall	16-11-42	101 Sqn
R/105633	F/S	GOURLAY Robert Francis	1-10-42	10 Sqn
R/105796	F/S	GRABEK Roman	14-09-42	14 OTU
J/5058	F/L	GRAHAM Arthur James	24-10-42	102 Sqn
J/8607	P/O	GRAHAM Richard Robert	30-07-42	149 Sqn
J/6306	P/O	GRAHAM Robert Macfarlane	9-05-42	158 Sqn
R/79042	F/S	GRANT William John Peter	28-05-42	1443 Flt
R/84623	F/S	GRANT William Seaman	17-09-42	405 Sqn
R/92093	F/S	GRATTAN Noel	31-05-42	22 OTU
R/65174	F/S	GRAVES Grant Russell	12-04-42	405 Sqn
R/67287	F/S	GRAY George Armstrong	28-08-42	14 OTU
R/62780	Sgt	GRAY Harry Joseph Thomas	14-10-42	420 Sqn
R/58225	F/S	GRAY John Balfour	27-02-42	144 Sqn
R/93121	F/S	GRAY Robert Reid	27-08-42	214 Sqn
R/79093	F/S	GRAY Stanley Goddard [USA]	27-09-42	78 Sqn
J/16009	P/O	GREEN Arthur Monson [USA]	1-10-42	405 Sqn
R/64484	F/S	GREEN Everett Stevenson	13-10-42	419 Sqn
R/120946	Sgt	GREGORY Bruce Durward	4-12-42	19 OTU
R/74809	F/S	GREGORY Richard St. Julien	3-04-42	16 OTU
4199	F/S	GREY-NOBLE Henry	26-01-42	51 Sqn
R/85633	F/S	GRIFFIN John Richard	13-07-42	7 Sqn
J/15231	P/O	GRIFFITH Allan George	16-04-42	156 Sqn
R/84183	F/S	GRIFFITH Robert Kitchen	16-09-42	101 Sqn
R/77592	F/S	GRIMES Donald Leonard	8-11-42	9 Sqn
R/76024	F/S	GROFF Wilfred Rodgers	26-03-42	420 Sqn
R/84043	F/S	GROVER Henry Arthur	15-10-42	419 Sqn
J/15126	P/O	GRUNDY Franklin Burton	28-04-42	150 Sqn
R/55316	F/S	GUDGEON Alan Harold	22-06-42	218 Sqn
R/83204	WO2	GUICHARD James Louis [USA]	25-11-42	207 Sqn
R/120164	Sgt	GUNN Harold William	15-12-42	405 Sqn
R/104946	F/S	GUNNING Kenneth Stewart	16-11-42	149 Sqn
R/77348	F/S	GURR Edward James Henry	29-07-42	9 Sqn
R/89449	Sgt	HACKETT David George	2-10-42	405 Sqn
R/72081	F/S	HACKNEY Charles	26-02-42	158 Sqn
R/97845	F/S	HADLEY James Caldwell [USA]	25-06-42	22 OTU
R/71111	F/S	HAGEL Francis Eldon	15-04-42	408 Sqn
R/93443	F/S	HAIG Gordon Carruthers	9-12-42	102 Sqn
R/58480	F/S	HALE Edward Everett [USA]	15-01-42	214 Sqn
R/60003	F/S	HALEY James Franklin	16-06-42	150 Sqn
R/74348	WO1	HALL Clement William	16-09-42	12 OTU
R/78889	F/S	HALL George	4-08-42	142 Sqn
J/6652	P/O	HALLIDAY Robert Balfour	15-04-42	214 Sqn
R/58198	F/S	HALSTEAD David Harry	16-09-42	22 OTU
R/80540	F/S	HALWARD James Frederick	5-05-42	420 Sqn
R/117309	Sgt	HAMEL Orlando Delmar Conrad	29-11-42	405 Sqn
R/92180	F/S	HAMILTON Edward Robert	18-05-42	20 OTU
R/64416	F/S	HAMILTON Harry Robert	22-07-42	12 Sqn
J/10176	F/O	HAMILTON William Caldwell [USA]	24-10-42	57 Sqn
R/68734	F/S	HAMMOND Arthur Edward	17-06-42	35 Sqn
R/76975	F/S	HANCOCK John Patrick	6-05-42	16 OTU
J/8615	P/O	HANNA George Robert	21-07-42	106 Sqn
R/85918	F/S	HANNABY John	1-08-42	9 Sqn
R/83873	F/S	HANNAH Thomas John	13-07-42	420 Sqn
R/85155	F/S	HANSFORD Albert Henry	1-10-42	15 Sqn
R/71321	F/S	HARDESTY Benedict Joseph	6-10-42	103 Sqn
R/59562	F/S	HARDESTY Gilbert Peter Mallon	15-01-42	103 Sqn
R/69887	WO2	HARE Thomas William	7-04-42	15 Sqn
R/99637	F/S	HARGREAVES Mason Hand	16-10-42	19 OTU
R/73175	WO2	HARGROVE Basil Eldon	31-12-42	83 Sqn
J/9411	P/O	HARLEY John William Morrison	19-07-42	22 OTU
R/74244	F/S	HARNEY Edmund Murray	15-09-42	419 Sqn
R/58690	F/S	HARP Thomas Allen	29-07-42	218 Sqn
R/70534	F/S	HARPER Alan Buchan	23-06-42	57 Sqn
J/18525	P/O	HARPER Milton Alexander	20-12-42	97 Sqn
R/85966	Sgt	HARPER Robert Henry	25-08-42	22 OTU
R/83419	F/S	HARRELL William Jessup [USA]	30-06-42	405 Sqn
J/15584	P/O	HARRIS Arnold Harvey	17-06-42	419 Sqn
R/62960	F/S	HARRIS Carl Clark	26-06-42	102 Sqn
R/80735	F/S	HARRIS Herbert Allenby	3-12-42	214 Sqn
J/5082	P/O	HARRIS William Arthur	9-03-42	83 Sqn
R/100702	F/S	HARRISON Gordon Llewelyn	23-11-42	161 Sqn
R/61664	F/S	HARRISON Harold Hugh	14-07-42	12 Sqn
R/73765	F/S	HARRISON Ronald Richard	31-05-42	22 OTU
C/15720	P/O	HART Gerald Charles	3-09-42	419 Sqn
R/64799	F/S	HARTNETT Francis Leon Joseph	28-07-42	103 Sqn
R/75667	F/S	HARTNETT Thomas Joseph	31-05-42	9 Sqn
R/88469	F/S	HARVEY Beverley Morton [USA]	6-12-42	464 Sqn
R/83885	F/S	HARVIE Lloyd Gordon	1-08-42	16 OTU
R/79281	F/S	HASEKIAN Charles Robert [USA]	7-11-42	83 Sqn
R/98055	Sgt	HAWK Denzil Clair [USA]	31-10-42	30 OTU
R/129349	F/S	HAWKE William Edward	7-12-42	102 Sqn
J/15286	P/O	HAY John Arthur	15-09-42	419 Sqn
R/82352	Sgt	HAYES James Patrick	6-07-42	22 OTU
J/18550	P/O	HAYES Ronald [USA]	7-12-42	425 Sqn
R/104769	F/S	HEATH Harold Edgar	2-09-42	142 Sqn
J/7776	P/O	HEDLEY William James	13-10-42	83 Sqn
J/6137	P/O	HEGGIE Robert	25-03-42	61 Sqn
R/77394	Sgt	HELGESEN Thorstein Enevold	13-07-42	7 Sqn
R/59371	F/S	HENDERSON Donald Louden	10-01-42	408 Sqn

R/69157	F/S	HENMAN Arthur Reginald	30-03-42	10 Sqn	R/106511	Sgt	HUNT Ernest Page	13-10-42	22 OTU
R/106552	F/S	HENRY John Magwood	16-08-42	14 OTU	R/92325	WO2	HUNTER James Albert	20-12-42	78 Sqn
R/92225	WO2	HENRY Victor Roy	7-11-42	21 Sqn	R/69856	F/S	HUNTER John Thompson	17-06-42	419 Sqn
R/107685	F/S	HENSCHEL Walter Adolf	20-12-42	76 Sqn	R/98980	F/S	HUNTER Thomas McLennan Miller	1-10-42	10 Sqn
R/88475	Sgt	HENSHAW Douglas Bernard	29-07-42	218 Sqn	R/75946	F/S	HUTCHISON Jack Leon	3-06-42	115 Sqn
J/5676	P/O	HEPBURN Donald Stuart Reddy	17-04-42	97 Sqn	R/104434	Sgt	HYSON Arnold Wentworth	12-08-42	405 Sqn
J/11955	P/O	HERBERT Anthony Albert	9-11-42	22 OTU	R/111773	Sgt	IRISH Jack William	1-08-42	405 Sqn
R/93513	F/S	HERON Frank Brown Graham	7-07-42	21 Sqn	R/103273	F/S	IRVINE James Frederick	10-09-42	16 OTU
J/7039	P/O	HESLOP James Robert	21-06-42	7 Sqn	R/75436	F/S	IRVINE Walter Harrison	29-08-42	75 Sqn
R/86357	F/S	HESP William John	29-08-42	115 Sqn	R/123215	Sgt	IVERS Ronald Arthur [USA]	1-10-42	10 Sqn
R/68055	F/S	HEXTER Robert William	24-07-42	405 Sqn	J/7462	F/O	IZZARD Laurence Theodore	8-12-42	149 Sqn
R/56250	F/S	HIBBARD Howard Robert	9-05-42	419 Sqn	J/16883	P/O	JACKES James Connacher	20-12-42	156 Sqn
R/75890	F/S	HICKEY Norman George	2-04-42	214 Sqn	R/62219	F/S	JACKSON Kenneth Robert	19-08-42	61 Sqn
R/113252	F/S	HICKS Herbert Ernest	10-10-42	419 Sqn	R/73034	F/S	JACKSON Leonard Douglas	2-06-42	405 Sqn
R/68516	Sgt	HICKS Joseph Melvin	24-04-42	420 Sqn	J/15950	P/O	JACKSON DFC Leonard Thomas	31-12-42	83 Sqn
J/13418	P/O	HIGGINS Anthony	16-12-42	23 OTU	R/83904	Sgt	JACKSON Robert James	19-01-42	20 OTU
R/141503	F/S	HIGGINSON John Blake	11-09-42	26 OTU	R/101378	Sgt	JACKSON Ronald Adey	7-09-42	22 OTU
J/15279	P/O	HIGGINSON Lloyd George	9-06-42	405 Sqn	R/6172	P/O	JACKSON Rutherford James	29-06-42	57 Sqn
J/16537	P/O	HILL Hugh Ernest	16-12-42	15 Sqn	R/102789	F/S	JACKSON William	6-12-42	102 Sqn
R/62261	F/S	HILL James Benson Harvey	18-01-42	142 Sqn	R/56201	F/S	JACOBSON Joseph Alfred	28-01-42	106 Sqn
J/85167	P/O	HILL Robert George	14-09-42	22 OTU	R/76606	F/S	JACQUES Douglas Harold Morton	15-04-42	214 Sqn
J/16087	P/O	HILL Swante Oliver	29-07-42	18 Sqn	R/85212	LAC	JAHNKE Walter Robert	15-09-42	419 Sqn
R/7775	Sgt	HILL Walter Alexander	10-08-42	405 Sqn	J/7214	P/O	JAMES Alan Frederick	24-04-42	150 Sqn
J/6380	F/L	HILLIER Lawrence David	3-09-42	405 Sqn	R/114619	F/S	JAMES Robert Frederick	14-12-42	22 OTU
R/88319	F/S	HILTZ Lawrence Donald	28-08-42	75 Sqn	R/95238	Sgt	JAMES William Patrick	12-08-42	24 OTU
R/81085	F/S	HINCKS Claude Harvey	28-08-42	97 Sqn	R/125364	F/S	JAMIESON John Bourne	28-11-42	28 OTU
R/59536	WO2	HINKS Cecil Charles David	29-07-42	16 OTU	R/77307	F/S	JANISZEWSKI Franciszek	29-08-42	61 Sqn
R/70156	F/S	HIRST James Frederick	13-07-42	7 Sqn	R/54831	F/S	JEFFRIES Ernest Norman	9-06-42	405 Sqn
J/4903	P/O	HOBSON Kenneth Edward	29-03-42	419 Sqn	R/87576	F/S	JEMMETT Joseph	29-08-42	115 Sqn
R/75663	F/S	HODGE William John	14-02-42	16 OTU	R/56125	WO2	JENKINS Alger [USA]	27-03-42	408 Sqn
R/92164	F/S	HODGES Ronald George Renouf	12-08-42	75 Sqn	R/78631	F/S	JENNER Edward George	8-02-42	22 OTU
R/95943	F/S	HODGINS Adam Kidd	9-11-42	405 Sqn	R/95369	Sgt	JENSEN Oscar Knud Lerche	9-08-42	20 OTU
R/82340	F/S	HODGINS Leslie Nellis	27-04-42	7 Sqn	R/78061	WO2	JENSON Stanley	22-11-42	10 Sqn
R/111255	F/S	HOGAN Francis Joseph	13-10-42	10 Sqn	R/84820	F/S	JOHNSON Albert Morse Borden	3-12-42	115 Sqn
R/91395	F/S	HOGBEN Donald Lorne	22-12-42	466 Sqn	R/84187	F/S	JOHNSON Douglas Graeme Harrison		
J/5694	P/O	HOIDAS Irvine Frank	20-05-42	7 Sqn				16-11-42	115 Sqn
R/60261	F/S	HOLLAND Lloyd Ellison	16-09-42	142 Sqn	R/95038	F/S	JOHNSON Frank Edward	28-07-42	22 OTU
R/77422	WO2	HOLLINSWORTH Jack Atheslton	17-12-42	103 Sqn	R/70600	F/S	JOHNSON Harry Laverne	16-06-42	1651 CU
R/76189	F/S	HOLMES Andrew	28-08-42	419 Sqn	R/137467	F/S	JOHNSON Howard Edward [USA]	16-09-42	26 OTU
R/61031	WO2	HOLMES Frank Alex	3-06-42	102 Sqn	J/7901	P/O	JOHNSON Melvin Florin	28-08-42	142 Sqn
R/68171	F/S	HOLMES John Gordon	7-07-42	419 Sqn	R/82881	F/S	JOHNSON Wallace Hayden	11-09-42	22 OTU
J/16538	P/O	HOLMES Russell Neal	16-12-42	15 Sqn	R/84435	F/S	JOHNSON William Ernest	16-09-42	15 Sqn
R/97505	F/S	HOLMES William Edward Wall	1-08-42	14 OTU	R/86418	F/S	JOHNSON William Ross Campbell	31-05-42	23 OTU
R/10250	P/O	HOLUB Michael	14-09-42	21 OTU	R/59551	F/S	JOHNSTON Arthur George	7-08-42	78 Sqn
J/16717	P/O	HOOPER George Camps	30-07-42	142 Sqn	R/105687	F/S	JOHNSTON Edward Irvine	20-12-42	49 Sqn
R/60349	F/S	HOPPER Earl Edwin	4-08-42	142 Sqn	R/92229	F/S	JOHNSTON Hubert Clodomir	17-09-42	106 Sqn
R/82817	F/S	HORNIDGE Joseph Noel Charles	17-12-42	218 Sqn	R/79842	F/S	JOHNSTON James Kenneth	2-09-42	14 OTU
R/71714	F/S	HORNING Robert Lewis	14-01-42	22 OTU	R/72399	F/S	JOHNSTONE Andrew Taylor	27-07-42	420 Sqn
R/101342	F/S	HORNSETH Alvin Marvin	12-08-42	23 OTU	J/8101	P/O	JOHNSTONE Earl Ernest Edward	20-07-42	10 Sqn
J/15033	P/O	HOSEA DFC Russel Lloyd George	8-03-42	115 Sqn	R/94638	F/S	JOLLEY John Percy	15-10-42	419 Sqn
J/15150	P/O	HOWARD Ernest Richard	9-04-42	419 Sqn	R/90284	WO2	JONES Edmund George	20-12-42	428 Sqn
R/67896	F/S	HOWARD Kenneth Laverne	9-11-42	7 Sqn	R/95326	Sgt	JONES Edward James	1-08-42	24 OTU
R/70896	F/S	HOWARD William Ross	7-05-42	22 OTU	R/62366	F/S	JONES Joseph	29-11-42	405 Sqn
J/9437	P/O	HOWARTH Edward Paul	30-09-42	14 OTU	R/105354	F/S	JONES Leslie Leather	28-08-42	29 Sqn
R/79659	F/S	HOWE Martin Charles	1-04-42	405 Sqn	J/15726	P/O	JONES William James	14-10-42	420 Sqn
R/85922	F/S	HOWE Percival Eric John	12-07-42	101 Sqn	R/85622	WO2	JORDAN Lawrence Henry	10-12-42	9 Sqn
R/93192	F/S	HOWELLS John Gordon	5-10-42	425 Sqn	R/64869	F/S	JOWETT Harold Ernest	10-02-42	11 OTU
R/86111	WO2	HREHORAK Nickolas	22-09-42	103 Sqn	J/4822	F/O	JOYCE David Dudley Plaister	2-06-42	10 Sqn
R/66086	F/S	HUBBERT John Monteith	23-04-42	9 Sqn			[Argentina]		
R/87541	F/S	HUDEMA Michael	6-10-42	405 Sqn	R/82442	F/S	JOYNT John Millar	15-10-42	420 Sqn
J/15491	F/L	HUDOCK John George [USA]	29-07-42	156 Sqn	7671	WO2	JUNEAU Alfred Roger	11-12-42	10 Sqn
R/68744	F/S	HUESTON Elden Francis	1-08-42	16 OTU	R/75691	WO2	KAUFMAN William John	1-08-42	420 Sqn
J/4819	F/L	HUGHES MiD George Pryce [Argentina]	11-07-42	105 Sqn	R/65242	F/S	KEARNS MiD Gerald John Patrick	20-05-42	7 Sqn
					J/16681	P/O	KEDDY Charles William	28-08-42	142 Sqn
R/99971	F/S	HUGHES Raymond Woods	10-09-42	22 OTU	R/85916	F/S	KEDWELL Horace Russell	29-07-42	1651 CU
J/4825	F/O	HUGHES Richard Pryce [Argentina]	15-04-42	10 Sqn	R/6393	P/O	KEELE Gordon Frederick	13-03-42	16 OTU
J/9527	F/O	HUMPHRIES Harry Lancaster	6-11-42	78 Sqn	R/90459	F/S	KEENE Arthur George Wilson	9-08-42	20 OTU
R/78903	F/S	HUNKING Elwin Thomas	1-08-42	14 OTU	R/106392	F/S	KEHL Edward Carl	6-11-42	218 Sqn

ID	Rank	Name	Date	Unit
R/125770	F/S	KELLEY Alfred Theodore [USA]	8-12-42	15 Sqn
R/76125	F/S	KELLEY Harry Joseph	19-01-42	20 OTU
R/73181	WO2	KELLY Lloyd Franklin	27-07-42	408 Sqn
R/88687	F/S	KEMP John Beverley	6-07-42	22 OTU
J/3762	F/O	KENNEDY Frederick James	30-05-42	15 Sqn
R/69561	F/S	KENNEDY Gordon	19-05-42	35 Sqn
R/68661	F/S	KENNEDY Jack Matthew	8-04-42	23 OTU
J/15431	P/O	KENNEDY John Robert	4-05-42	78 Sqn
R/93149	F/S	KEOGH William George	12-09-42	408 Sqn
J/6175	P/O	KEOUGH William Joseph [USA]	2-06-42	97 Sqn
R/99687	F/S	KERR James Carl	10-09-42	14 OTU
R/84533	F/S	KERTSON Richard Arthur	5-09-42	419 Sqn
R/92307	F/S	KIDSON Frank Wilfred	10-09-42	61 Sqn
J/16319	P/O	KIESWETTER Emerson Harvey [USA]	16-12-42	15 Sqn
R/95729	F/S	KINCAID John Joseph	28-08-42	101 Sqn
R/69338	F/S	KINCH James Henry	28-06-42	61 Sqn
R/71446	F/S	KING Arnold William Charles Ernest	22-04-42	22 OTU
J/10413	P/O	KING Donald Chesley	14-09-42	22 OTU
R/106627	F/S	KING Francis Edward	6-12-42	487 Sqn
R/83545	F/S	KING John Clifton	9-05-42	419 Sqn
R/75603	F/S	KING John Nelson Secord	17-09-42	1654 CU
R/74447	F/S	KINGSLAND Edwin Herbert	10-11-42	102 Sqn
R/73760	F/S	KINGSLEY Joseph Leopold Rene	20-12-42	78 Sqn
R/91915	F/S	KINNEE Ronald Alfred	15-09-42	419 Sqn
R/95300	Sgt	KIRBY Alfred	9-08-42	20 OTU
R/76971	F/S	KIRBY Erlyn Everard	6-05-42	150 Sqn
R/74930	F/S	KIRBY Walter Grenfell	30-11-42	7 Sqn
R/77036	F/S	KIRKPATRICK Herbert Joseph	6-06-42	419 Sqn
J/15997	P/O	KITCHEN John Colwell	1-10-42	405 Sqn
R/101804	F/S	KITSON Charles Albert	17-09-42	405 Sqn
J/10411	F/O	KOEHN Arthur Ferdinand	28-10-42	1651 HCU
R/121565	Sgt	KOSTENUK William Michael	29-11-42	405 Sqn
R/75325	F/S	KOSTYSHYN William Martin	27-07-42	115 Sqn
R/60959	F/S	KOWALSKI Louis	11-03-42	149 Sqn
R/59132	WO2	KRAUSE Joseph Anthony	25-08-42	7 Sqn
J/7530	P/O	KREFTING Raymond Marenus	6-08-42	419 Sqn
R/71532	F/S	KRIGER Louis	2-09-42	156 Sqn
R/85956	F/S	KUCHERYK Peter	1-10-42	405 Sqn
R/75874	F/S	KURTZ Dennis Haig	1-08-42	16 OTU
R/76994	WO2	KUZYK MiD Eugene	22-09-42	425 Sqn
R/71497	F/S	KYLE William Thomas	20-02-42	17 OTU
J/15165	P/O	LACELLE Joseph Harvey Milton	28-06-42	405 Sqn
R/96120	F/S	LAFLAMME Joseph Yves Camille Charles Auguste	16-11-42	425 Sqn
J/15432	P/O	LAING Norman Leslie	27-07-42	405 Sqn
J/5334	P/O	LAING Richard Arthur	12-02-42	419 Sqn
J/7422	P/O	LAMB Thomas Fraser	26-06-42	27 OTU
R/84347	F/S	LAMONT Ian Craigie	5-09-42	142 Sqn
R/86614	F/S	LANCELEY Charles Henry	8-09-42	115 Sqn
J/85241	P/O	LAND James Edward [USA]	19-09-42	15 Sqn
J/16053	P/O	LANG Andrew Alexander	1-10-42	405 Sqn
R/64323	F/S	LANG Sydney Stephen [USA]	14-01-42	17 OTU
R/55403	F/S	LANGLOIS Louis Marie	14-04-42	419 Sqn
R/65194	F/S	LANTZ George Malcolm	13-04-42	408 Sqn
R/120083	F/S	LAPORTE Joseph Eugene Raymond	12-11-42	425 Sqn
R/95499	F/S	LARCHE Joseph Armand	11-11-42	425 Sqn
J/13075	P/O	LASBY Lawrence Edly	14-12-42	22 OTU
J/11807	F/O	LAUT William George	16-11-42	426 Sqn
R/83468	F/S	LAVERS William Wilfred Henry	10-09-42	75 Sqn
R/79640	WO2	LAW Harold Naismith	27-07-42	420 Sqn
R/62488	LAC	LAWLEY Edward Douglas	15-09-42	419 Sqn
R/55798	F/S	LAWRENCE John Buchanan	7-04-42	101 Sqn
R/60620	F/S	LAWRENCE Reginald Marcus	15-04-42	214 Sqn
R/70294	Sgt	LAWRENCE William Joseph	18-04-42	75 Sqn
J/15200	P/O	LAWSON MiD John Stephen	2-06-42	78 Sqn
R/86144	F/S	LAWTON Harry [USA]	9-06-42	97 Sqn
R/72939	F/S	LAWTON Richard Woffendale	16-12-42	23 OTU
R/85382	F/S	LAXDAL Hugh Lawrence	1-08-42	12 Sqn
R/119546	F/S	LA BOSSIERE Jules Joseph	16-09-42	12 OTU
R/69114	F/S	LA RONDE Gerald Grenville Joseph	19-04-42	420 Sqn
R/77173	F/S	LA SALLE Joseph Daniel Leo	24-07-42	207 Sqn
R/85565	F/S	LEA Stephen Alfred William	30-09-42	51 Sqn
J/7227	P/O	LEACH Leonard Charles Robert	14-10-42	61 Sqn
R/85630	Sgt	LEAN Richard Harvey	11-02-42	10 OTU
R/81225	F/S	LEATHERMAN Russel Quince [USA]	21-09-42	115 Sqn
R/95574	Sgt	LEBANO Vincent Joseph Louis	30-09-42	9 Sqn
R/76272	F/S	LEBLANC Charles Emile	17-06-42	419 Sqn
R/92116	F/S	LEE Arthur Geoffrey	15-10-42	405 Sqn
R/79839	F/S	LEE Charles Campbell	18-08-42	76 Sqn
J/5490	P/O	LEECH Lawrence Malcolm	16-04-42	214 Sqn
R/85786	F/S	LEETHER Albert	25-08-42	22 OTU
R/62661	F/S	LEFEBVRE Gordon Randolph	30-04-42	158 Sqn
R/54052	F/S	LEFTLY Nelson	8-04-42	405 Sqn
R/7735	WO1	LEMOINE Lorne James	16-09-42	22 OTU
R/70507	F/S	LENICHEK Victor Raymond	27-07-42	57 Sqn
R/77507	F/S	LENNOX Andrew	26-03-42	103 Sqn
J/15980	P/O	LENOVER Charles Stephen	12-08-42	156 Sqn
R/77298	F/S	LESLIE Percy Cartshore	26-07-42	114 Sqn
R/77456	F/S	LEVESQUE Fernand Joseph	22-08-42	15 Sqn
R/85962	F/S	LEWIS Gerald Edwin	15-10-42	405 Sqn
R/56879	F/S	LEWIS Richard James Hammelsten	14-03-42	77 Sqn
R/77455	F/S	LE BLANC Ernest Joseph	30-07-42	149 Sqn
R/50333	F/S	LE FURGEY Osborne Bayfield	5-01-42	405 Sqn
J/15698	P/O	LE PAGE Joseph Louis Phillippe	1-10-42	405 Sqn
R/62370	F/S	LINDSAY Frank Donald	6-06-42	149 Sqn
J/9555	F/O	LINDSAY John David	13-10-42	10 Sqn
R/69761	F/S	LINDSEY Donald Cole [USA]	26-03-42	16 OTU
R/72363	F/S	LINES Walter John Edward	21-04-42	138 Sqn
R/62095	F/S	LINWOOD William	30-06-42	115 Sqn
R/84681	WO2	LISSON Harris Mansel	20-11-42	150 Sqn
R/68140	F/S	LITTLE Kingsley Clarence	23-06-42	420 Sqn
R/81065	Sgt	LLEWELLYN Frank [USA]	8-02-42	12 OTU
R/62683	F/S	LLOYD Clarence Franklin	1-08-42	408 Sqn
J/5799	P/O	LOCKE Richard Philip	8-04-42	405 Sqn
R/71545	Sgt	LOCKHART Robert Alexander	14-09-42	19 OTU
C/15019	P/O	LOMAS Clifford Herbert	16-01-42	419 Sqn
R/50377	WO1	LONG Vaughan Ross	7-11-42	83 Sqn
R/97582	F/S	LONGLEY John Arthur	15-10-42	405 Sqn
R/92183	F/S	LORD David Frank	26-06-42	23 OTU
J/11109	P/O	LOREE James William	17-12-42	44 Sqn
R/99690	F/S	LOTT William Wesley	13-10-42	156 Sqn
J/16312	P/O	LOUGHEAD Eric Crowe	12-12-42	28 OTU
R/80935	WO2	LOUNT Robert Marr	21-10-42	1657 HCU
R/83249	F/S	LOVE Jnr Claude Lorraine [USA]	4-08-42	142 Sqn
R/95024	WO2	LOVE James Hawthorne	20-12-42	103 Sqn
R/91655	WO2	LOW Douglas Dunbar	8-11-42	9 Sqn
R/50712	F/S	LOWE Francis John	26-03-42	12 Sqn
R/86751	F/S	LOWE John Manley	12-08-42	50 Sqn
R/65904	F/S	LOWE Levi	15-10-42	405 Sqn
R/77585	F/S	LUCAS John James	2-09-42	156 Sqn
J/8342	P/O	LUCKI Albin	31-05-42	12 OTU
R/71746	WO1	LUNAN William Everett	12-08-42	78 Sqn
R/66181	F/S	LUNDY Harvey William	2-04-42	57 Sqn
R/63733	F/S	LUPTON Stanley Raymond	6-08-42	102 Sqn
R/94598	LAC	LUTEN Leo Owen	15-09-42	419 Sqn
R/91236	F/S	LYONS Frederick Erwin Edgar	7-09-42	101 Sqn
R/61124	F/S	L'HIRONDELLE Patrick Bernard	2-06-42	114 Sqn
C/169	W/C	MacALLISTER Gordon Dale	26-02-42	405 Sqn
R/85762	Sgt	MacARTHUR Harry Francis [USA]	14-09-42	22 OTU
R/76219	F/S	MacDONALD Harry Alexander	17-06-42	419 Sqn
J/7523	P/O	MacDONALD Mado Henry Donald [USA]	8-05-42	44 Sqn
R/82429	F/S	MacDONELL Archibald Bernard	24-06-42	9 Sqn
R/76083	F/S	MacDOUGALL Neil	20-06-42	101 Sqn

Service No.	Rank	Name	Date	Unit
J/10168	F/O	MacGILLIVRAY Aubrey Lawrence	1-10-42	102 Sqn
J/15383	P/O	MacKENZIE Maurice Doherty	9-06-42	109 Sqn
R/86313	WO2	MacKENZIE Norman Angus	2-09-42	405 Sqn
R/68538	F/S	MacKINNON Fernand Fagan	9-03-42	408 Sqn
R/72893	Sgt	MacKINNON John Reginald	16-10-42	19 OTU
J/4767	F/O	MacLEAN Donald Stewart	31-05-42	22 OTU
R/65201	F/S	MacLEAN Stephen Joseph	1-02-42	61 Sqn
R/65421	F/S	MacLENNAN Charles Grant	16-10-42	142 Sqn
J/10161	P/O	MacLEOD John Donald	16-09-42	106 Sqn
R/92778	F/S	MacLEOD Thomas Norman	12-12-42	57 Sqn
R/91524	Sgt	MacPHAIL John Franklin	8-03-42	14 OTU
R/113324	F/S	MacPHERSON Cyril Haig	1-10-42	10 Sqn
J/10329	F/O	MacPHERSON Duncan James	9-11-42	150 Sqn
J/8439	P/O	MacQUEEN Ian Andrew James [Argentina]	5-08-42	44 Sqn
R/72714	Sgt	MacRAE George Kenneth	24-03-42	19 OTU
R/71574	F/S	MACAULAY Donald Archie	30-07-42	419 Sqn
R/86116	F/S	MACAULAY William James	6-08-42	419 Sqn
R/65534	F/S	MACAULEY Frank Alfred Conway [Bahamas]	16-09-42	22 OTU
R/73010	Sgt	MACAULEY John Walker	27-07-42	405 Sqn
R/72529	WO2	MACDONALD Angus Daniel	17-12-42	103 Sqn
R/104467	Sgt	MACDONALD Eric William	7-11-42	83 Sqn
R/86838	F/S	MACDONALD Frank McLeod	20-09-42	161 Sqn
R/76227	WO2	MACDONALD Joseph Camillus	20-09-42	9 Sqn
R94992	LAC	MACDONALD Ronald Douglas Jeffrey	5-06-42	1443 Flt
J/10698	P/O	MACGREGOR Alexander Edward	18-08-42	20 OTU
J/5050	F/O	MACKENZIE DFC Kenneth Alex	8-11-42	9 Sqn
R/64474	F/S	MACLEOD Norman Kenneth	24-04-42	150 Sqn
R/83189	F/S	MACNAB David Charles	16-05-42	16 OTU
J/8950	P/O	MADSON John Emmett	20-08-42	61 Sqn
R/74322	F/S	MAGLADRY Harold Ernest	2-07-42	218 Sqn
R/74704	WO2	MAIN Faris Clyde [USA]	26-06-42	11 OTU
R/86164	WO2	MAKAY Albert George	31-10-42	150 Sqn
J/11451	F/O	MALLETT Ronald Frederick	30-11-42	22 OTU
J/8596	P/O	MALOFIE Daniel	3-07-42	214 Sqn
R/86225	WO2	MALONE Edward Cecil	20-12-42	78 Sqn
R/68700	F/S	MALUISH George Douglas	7-07-42	21 Sqn
R/80326	F/S	MANCHUR Carl Albert	29-07-42	12 Sqn
R/56422	F/S	MANDER William Eric	27-07-42	102 Sqn
J/5084	P/O	MANDERS Robert Emmett [China]	17-03-42	49 Sqn
R/75471	F/S	MANDIN Emile Francois Bruno	9-06-42	150 Sqn
J/15638	F/O	MANN DFC Lloyd Robertson	21-12-42	156 Sqn
R/92040	F/S	MARCHANT Robert Cresswell	25-06-42	20 OTU
R/83550	F/S	MARGRETT Alan Arthur [USA]	10-06-42	107 Sqn
R/71494	F/S	MARKLE Jack Wellington	9-05-42	408 Sqn
J/15139	F/O	MARKS Edward Michael	7-06-42	214 Sqn
R/56238	WO2	MARKS George Henry Herbert	3-06-42	102 Sqn
R/105553	F/S	MARLER Donald Thomas	10-11-42	102 Sqn
J/6801	P/O	MAROK Joseph Mitchell [USA]	26-01-42	14 OTU
R/131262	Sgt	MARONEY Paul Jones	9-11-42	405 Sqn
R/75097	Sgt	MARSHALL William John	13-04-42	49 Sqn
J/16503	P/O	MARTEL Pierre Augustin Guy	20-12-42	425 Sqn
R/72512	F/S	MARTIN Allistair Bruce	1-08-42	9 Sqn
R/76682	Sgt	MARTIN Chester Thomas	5-01-42	22 OTU
R/62763	F/S	MARTIN Emerson Hubert	22-04-42	22 OTU
R/11121	F/O	MARTIN Eric	29-11-42	1446 Flt
J/15225	P/O	MARTIN DFC Stanley Sinclair	1-06-42	20 OTU
R/92660	F/S	MARTIN William Bradley	21-09-42	115 Sqn
R/85779	F/S	MARTIN William McKenzie	7-11-42	7 Sqn
R/67931	F/S	MASKILL Donald Joseph [USA]	15-01-42	115 Sqn
R/56128	F/S	MASSE George Joseph [USA]	17-01-42	405 Sqn
R/82826	F/S	MASSEY Clarence Ames	8-12-42	102 Sqn
J/15164	P/O	MASUR Dennis Stanley [South Africa]	27-08-42	15 Sqn
R/85609	F/S	MATHIESON Donald	20-05-42	156 Sqn
R/103575	F/S	MATSON Mervin Keith	11-09-42	25 OTU
J/11847	P/O	MATTHEWS Philip Malcolm	9-11-42	408 Sqn
R/113277	F/S	MATTOON Stanley Finace	17-12-42	97 Sqn
R/66051	F/S	MAXIM William Leonard	14-07-42	419 Sqn
R/95390	F/S	MAXWELL Arnold Grant	6-05-42	16 OTU
R/93957	F/S	MAXWELL James David	29-10-42	10 OTU
R/60219	Sgt	MAY Thomas Irving	22-01-42	408 Sqn
R/119960	Sgt	MAZIER Michael William	22-09-42	19 OTU
J/15435	P/O	McALEAVEY Joseph Morgan	31-05-42	142 Sqn
R/68396	Sgt	McALPINE Douglas Haig	17-04-42	44 Sqn
R/66054	F/S	McAROY Michael	9-05-42	419 Sqn
R/87459	F/S	McARTER Glenville	3-09-42	75 Sqn
R/100790	F/S	McBEAN William Charles	17-09-42	23 OTU
J/85161	P/O	McBRATNEY William Thomas Beilby	10-09-42	22 OTU
R/58174	WO2	McBRIDE Thomas	18-08-42	101 Sqn
J/8785	F/O	McBURNEY Samuel Lorne	17-12-42	97 Sqn
R/75315	F/S	McCALLUM John Francis	24-10-42	207 Sqn
J/9780	F/O	McCANN Charles Curtis Merrel	17-12-42	218 Sqn
R/10138	F/S	McCANN John Warren	1-10-42	405 Sqn
R/86355	F/S	McCANN William Alexander	28-06-42	115 Sqn
J/7796	P/O	McCARTHY Murray Lorne	10-08-42	102 Sqn
J/6361	P/O	McCARTHY William Francis	14-04-42	420 Sqn
R/105512	F/S	McCARTNEY John	6-12-42	102 Sqn
R/110750	Sgt	McCASKY Eddie Stanley Joseph	11-09-42	22 OTU
R/86622	F/S	McCAUSLAND William Alfred Delorme	12-08-42	15 Sqn
R/56256	F/S	McCAW Cameron Francis	6-06-42	419 Sqn
J/11118	F/O	McCLEERY Raymond Norman	17-12-42	44 Sqn
R/85669	F/S	McCLENNAN Bruce Wallace	28-05-42	20 OTU
R/80175	F/S	McCLINTOCK Archibald	15-04-42	408 Sqn
R/81878	LAC	McCONNELL Andrew Lloyd	2-09-42	408 Sqn
J/4881	S/L	McCORMACK John	4-04-42	405 Sqn
R/82657	F/S	McCORMICK Hugh Roderick Neil	21-06-42	24 OTU
R/62439	F/S	McCOY Alfred Ernest	9-05-42	419 Sqn
R/93497	WO2	McCRAE Athol Malver William	3-12-42	115 Sqn
R/93516	WO2	McCREADY George Donald	20-12-42	44 Sqn
R/91332	F/S	McCRON William Grainger	1-10-42	405 Sqn
R/107653	F/S	McCULLOCH Robert Lyle	22-09-42	103 Sqn
J/3766	F/O	McCULLOCH William Donald	23-06-42	61 Sqn
J/16133	P/O	McDONALD Arthur Joseph	8-11-42	9 Sqn
R/76973	F/S	McDONALD Charles George	24-06-42	23 OTU
J/6711	P/O	McDONALD Donald Patrick [USA]	2-06-42	142 Sqn
J/9524	P/O	McDONALD Gordon Cameron	24-08-42	44 Sqn
R/90083	F/S	McDONALD Jack Thompson	28-12-42	23 OTU
R/92286	F/S	McDONALD James Edward	2-06-42	10 OTU
R/107349	F/S	McDONALD John Duncan	9-11-42	420 Sqn
J/5059	F/O	McDONALD DFC John Gordon	11-09-42	83 Sqn
R/71718	F/S	McDONALD John Melville	23-07-42	51 Sqn
R/86634	F/O	McDONOGH Athol Ian	20-08-42	75 Sqn
R/73006	F/S	McDOUGALL Vernon Estey	6-05-42	419 Sqn
R/61678	WO2	McDOWELL Kenneth Lendon	17-05-42	419 Sqn
R/82438	F/S	McELROY Guy James Herman	5-10-42	419 Sqn
J/5087	F/O	McEWEN Alan James	9-06-42	405 Sqn
R/69829	F/S	McEWEN William Tripp	10-04-42	12 Sqn
R/91235	Sgt	McFEE Allan Garfield	30-06-42	405 Sqn
R/69352	F/S	McGEE Thomas Bartley	26-07-42	19 OTU
R/58817	F/S	McGILL Edmund Thomas	9-06-42	405 Sqn
R/61819	Sgt	McGILLIVRAY Earl Lewis	29-11-42	405 Sqn
R/89516	F/S	McGRATH Bernard Arthur	3-09-42	405 Sqn
R/59351	WO1	McGRATH Dennis Brien	29-04-42	115 Sqn
R/59361	F/S	McGRATH Robert Kenneth	22-07-42	142 Sqn
R/54884	F/S	McHUGH Gerald Finnbarr	30-09-42	149 Sqn
R/85920	F/S	McILVEEN Archibald Edwin	1-08-42	9 Sqn
J/11945	F/O	McINTOSH Douglas Young	29-11-42	1446 Flt
R/101201	F/S	McINTYRE Robert Francis	2-10-42	149 Sqn
R/73282	F/S	McKAY Daniel Archibald	28-08-42	75 Sqn
R/68423	F/S	McKEE Kenneth Gilbert	16-05-42	16 OTU
R/81410	F/S	McKEITH Allan Barnby	6-04-42	16 OTU
R/76201	WO2	McKENNA Gerald Lewis	28-08-42	97 Sqn

R/62807	F/S	McKENZIE John Draper	31-05-42	12 OTU		R/100177	F/S	MITCHELL Wallace [USA]	20-05-42	103 Sqn
R/80200	Sgt	McKENZIE Orville Wilbert	2-06-42	408 Sqn		R/71725	F/S	MITTELL Ernest Edward	6-07-42	22 OTU
R/61025	WO2	McKINNON Donald Ross	29-07-42	18 Sqn		R/85993	F/S	MOLESWORTH James	24-10-42	103 Sqn
R/81478	F/S	McKINNON William Gordon	6-08-42	102 Sqn		R/106468	F/S	MOLLARD William John	16-10-42	115 Sqn
R/53905	F/S	McLACHLAN William Macintyre	20-07-42	158 Sqn		R/77464	F/S	MONROE Edward Francis [USA]	29-07-42	419 Sqn
J/11630	P/O	McLAREN Jack	14-10-42	22 OTU		R/69146	F/S	MONTGOMERY George Raymond	9-06-42	405 Sqn
J/15748	P/O	McLAREN Robert Perrin	18-08-42	57 Sqn		R/54098	F/S	MOODIE Donald Malcolm	30-05-42	12 Sqn
J/16387	P/O	McLAUGHLIN Andrew Joseph	10-12-42	57 Sqn		J/1211	P/O	MOODIE Kenneth William Byron	5-05-42	149 Sqn
J/9506	P/O	McLEAN David Gerald	1-08-42	14 OTU		J/10139	P/O	MOOR Maurice Gordon	6-12-42	464 Sqn
R/93450	F/S	McLEAN Ernest Caldwell	8-12-42	101 Sqn		R/85295	F/S	MOORE James Roland	17-10-42	61 Sqn
R/69782	F/S	McLEAN George Arthur	5-05-42	103 Sqn		J/7065	P/O	MOORE James Russel	6-04-42	20 OTU
R/69027	WO2	McLEAN George Percy	27-03-42	408 Sqn		R/78024	F/S	MOORE John Lyndon [USA]	13-03-42	77 Sqn
R/66065	F/S	McLEAN John Andrew	17-08-42	207 Sqn		R/74456	WO2	MOORE Noel McHenry [USA]	30-07-42	419 Sqn
R/64893	F/S	McLELLAN Albert Benjamin	10-09-42	61 Sqn		R/80811	WO2	MORELLY Max Louis	16-09-42	15 Sqn
R.62633	F/S	McLENNAN Hilbert Alexander	3-01-42	22 OTU		R/82076	Sgt	MORGAN Bruce	4-07-42	61 Sqn
R/68643	LAC	McLEOD Norman Richard [United Kingdom]	29-03-42	405 Sqn		C/1608	F/L	MORGAN John Elcock	20-04-42	16 OTU
						R/113280	LAC	MORGAN Joseph Evan	29-06-42	Swinderby
R/79941	LAC	McMAHON John Franklin	24-04-42	408 Sqn		R/66350	WO2	MORGAN Rhys Hallam	2-09-42	97 Sqn
R/56323	F/S	McMANAMAN Edward Carroll	17-01-42	27 OTU		R/87814	WO2	MORIARTY Louis Edmund	20-12-42	103 Sqn
R/78058	F/S	McMENOMY Sydney	7-09-42	101 Sqn		R/92143	Sgt	MORIN Ralph William	9-05-42	10 OTU
R/76601	F/S	McMILLAN Alexander	14-04-42	419 Sqn		R/82328	F/S	MORLEY George Allen	24-06-42	9 Sqn
R/82882	F/S	McMULLIN Cecil Robert	16-11-42	149 Sqn		J/9762	F/O	MORLIDGE Arthur Bryan	2-10-42	419 Sqn
J/5484	F/O	McMURCHY William Archibald	26-07-42	97 Sqn		J/8794	P/O	MORRIS Claude Reginald Frederick	5-09-42	419 Sqn
R/56297	Sgt	McNALLY William Carlisle	4-01-42	82 Sqn		J/15342	P/O	MORRIS David Gordon	9-06-42	405 Sqn
C/1482	S/L	McNAUGHTON Ian George Armour	23-06-42	61 Sqn		R/79504	F/S	MORRIS George Thomas	11-07-42	101 Sqn
						R/73169	F/S	MORRIS Vernon Lewis	8-04-42	22 OTU
R/75116	WO2	McPHEE Allan Jeremiah	14-07-42	97 Sqn		J/9634	P/O	MORRISON Lloyd George	24-06-42	23 OTU
R/90725	F/S	McPHEE Ewan Cameron	17-12-42	57 Sqn		R/77068	F/S	MORRISON Stewart Alexander	22-01-42	106 Sqn
R/92407	F/S	McPHEE John Allen	12-12-42	102 Sqn		J/8627	P/O	MORRISON Vincent Merrill Macdonald		
R/104097	Sgt	McPHEE Stephen David	10-10-42	1654 HCU					29-08-42	103 Sqn
r/67249	f/s	McQUAID William Vincent	30-07-42	61 Sqn		R/100533	F/S	MORRISSY DFM Harry [USA]	3-12-42	102 Sqn
J/7088	F/O	McRAE Lynds Farquhar	5-10-42	102 Sqn		R/81473	F/S	MORROW Donald Lloyd	15-10-42	150 Sqn
R/107564	Sgt	McRITCHIE Ronald Edwin	14-09-42	19 OTU		R/91335	F/S	MORROW John Robert	28-08-42	419 Sqn
J/9915	F/O	McROBERTS Clarence Arthur	11-12-42	10 Sqn		R/106236	F/S	MORTIMER Arthur	20-12-42	97 Sqn
R/93977	F/S	McWILLIAM Robert James	28-11-42	75 Sqn		R/54309	F/S	MOULE Wallace Alfred Richard	13-04-42	76 Sqn
R/107667	F/S	MEANWELL Victor	30-11-42	22 OTU		R/78998	F/S	MOWBRAY Alexander Mackenzie	1-10-42	10 Sqn
R/62957	F/S	MEECH William Ian	13-04-42	408 Sqn		R/89025	Sgt	MUIR Alexander Douglas	3-09-42	405 Sqn
R/82503	F/S	MEERS Frank Edward	4-09-42	25 OTU		J/15671	P/O	MULHAUSER Robert Samuel [USA]	4-06-42	76 Sqn
R/81078	F/S	MELLISH Richard Lewis	24-05-42	207 Sqn		J/7067	P/O	MULLINS James Doran	29-07-42	9 Sqn
R/54985	F/S	MENARD Joseph Donat Romeo	1-10-42	218 Sqn		J/5687	P/O	MURDOCK John Maclean	28-03-42	7 Sqn
R/68709	F/S	MENSHEK Francis Joseph [USA]	9-03-42	12 Sqn		R/67977	WO2	MURPHY Edward Warren [USA]	2-10-42	405 Sqn
R/6143A	F/S	MERCER Keith Paterson	13-11-42	97 Sqn		R/67905	F/S	MURPHY Patrick Louis	7-07-42	419 Sqn
R/73304	F/S	MESHEAU George Lawson Macintosh				R/77771	F/S	MURPHY Thomas Francis	1-08-42	57 Sqn
			7-05-42	23 OTU		R/75144	F/S	MURPHY William Arthur	12-03-42	77 Sqn
R/78978	F/S	MEYER John Emerson	25-06-42	76 Sqn		R/79506	F/S	MURPHY William Morgan	29-10-42	115 Sqn
R/95104	F/S	MEYERS Norman Clifford	10-10-42	150 Sqn		R/95318	F/S	MURRAY Donald	14-09-42	22 OTU
R/91294	F/S	MIDDLETON Robert John	7-12-42	101 Sqn		R/93062	F/S	MURRAY George Douglas	13-10-42	214 Sqn
R/62407	F/S	MILLAR George Ronald	16-02-42	77 Sqn		J/8623	P/O	MURRAY George Weyman	2-06-42	23 OTU
R/90451	F/S	MILLARD Donald Albert	25-06-42	22 OTU		8163A		MURRAY Joseph George	6-05-42	419 Sqn
J/16197	P/O	MILLEN Frank Severne [USA]	16-12-42	15 Sqn		R/92114	F/S	MURRAY William Frederick	17-09-42	405 Sqn
J/15579	P/O	MILLER Bruce Armstrong	29-06-42	57 Sqn		J/5991	P/O	MURRAY William James	14-04-42	420 Sqn
R/94347	LAC	MILLER Gordon Stewart	9-07-42	15 OTU		J/9587	P/O	MYRICK John Frederick	11-08-42	78 Sqn
J/4697	F/O	MILLER Hubert Harvey	12-02-42	420 Sqn		J/16486	P/O	NADEAU Laurent Joseph Onesime	3-08-42	405 Sqn
J/15213	P/O	MILLER Ivan Anderson	21-04-42	138 Sqn		R/90775	Sgt	NASH Albert Edward	10-12-42	22 OTU
R.72545	F/S	MILLER Terris Haggie	28-08-42	78 Sqn		R/69378	WO2	NAULT Joseph Borden	17-10-42	218 Sqn
J/10692	P/O	MILLER William Adam	18-08-42	20 OTU		R/92365	Sgt	NAVEY Gordon	4-08-42	20 OTU
R/58166	F/S	MILLERD William Francis	16-05-42	408 Sqn		R/78543	F/S	NAVIN Donald Joseph	10-08-42	78 Sqn
J/15307	P/O	MILLICHAMP Harold Reuben	26-04-42	218 Sqn		R/67970	F/S	NEAL Harry Alyn [USA]	11-04-42	214 Sqn
R/76763	WO2	MILLIGAN Geoffrey Eaton	10-09-42	218 Sqn		R/100587	F/S	NEEDLER John	16-09-42	23 OTU
R/128672	F/S	MILLIKEN Ralph Elliott	29-11-42	405 Sqn		J/15441	F/O	NEILL Robert Walter	6-11-42	21 Sqn
R/86929	F/S	MILLS Russel Wilbert Lewis	5-09-42	12 Sqn		R/85152	F/S	NELMS Edward James	15-06-42	19 OTU
R/107580	F/S	MILNE William Stanley	29-11-42	405 Sqn		R/132976	F/S	NEUBERT Charles Joseph [USA]	2-10-42	405 Sqn
R/81762	Sgt	MILOT Albert Victor Bolduc	15-10-42	405 Sqn		R/102474	F/S	NEULS Philip Carl	15-09-42	14 OTU
R/113992	Sgt	MILTON Carl William	8-11-42	22 OTU		R/54986	F/S	NEVEU Charles Stacey	9-05-42	158 Sqn
R/87341	Sgt	MIREAU Albert Onide	22-06-42	10 Sqn		R/82708	F/S	NEVILLE Gerald Anthony	9-11-42	102 Sqn
J/15022	P/O	MITCHELL DFM George Eric [USA]	6-04-42	75 Sqn		R/80124	F/S	NEVILLE John Oliver Hugh	2-04-42	57 Sqn
R/93972	Sgt	MITCHELL John Arnold	11-08-42	78 Sqn		R/88706	F/S	NEWMAN James William	20-08-42	115 Sqn
R/77146	F/S	MITCHELL Norman Rae	28-08-42	49 Sqn		R/95759	F/S	NIBBLET Joseph Linwood [USA]	16-09-42	23 OTU

Service #	Rank	Name	Date	Sqn
R/64786	F/S	NICKERSON Alden Ernest	11-07-42	97 Sqn
J/7784	P/O	NICOLLE John Frederick	11-09-42	106 Sqn
R/78054	F/S	NIDELMAN Bernard Davis	21-06-42	420 Sqn
R/57743	F/S	NIXON Frederick William	12-08-42	15 Sqn
R/83366	F/S	NOEL Patrick Cluney [USA]	28-07-42	22 OTU
R/72641	F/S	NORRIE Thomas Lloyd Joseph [USA]	2-06-42	23 OTU
R/69125	F/S	NORRIS James Royden	14-04-42	419 Sqn
R/92493	F/S	NORRIS Peter Vincent	2-09-42	14 OTU
R/123004	Sgt	NORTH William James	5-09-42	142 Sqn
R/70090	F/S	NORTON James Shield	9-05-42	408 Sqn
R/59356	F/S	NOTON Reginald Frederick	2-07-42	218 Sqn
R/64912	F/S	NUGENT Charles Gerard	1-10-42	44 Sqn
J/16099	P/O	OLIVER Thomas Edward	22-10-42	158 Sqn
J/8777	F/O	OLSEN Edward Carl [USA]	1-10-42	405 Sqn
R/51998	F/S	OMILIANOUSKI Peter Christopher	26-06-42	24 OTU
R/56246	F/S	ONESON Paul Patrick Augustus	30-06-42	405 Sqn
J/15865	P/O	ORR Harry Edward	14-09-42	214 Sqn
R/98836	F/S	ORR James Samuel	1-09-42	115 Sqn
J/6359	P/O	OSTEN Max Martin	5-05-42	22 OTU
4418	F/S	OTT John	24-09-42	405 Sqn
R/56284	Sgt	OULSTER Norman Maxwell	26-06-42	10 OTU
R/79143	F/S	OWENS Thomas Reid	24-07-42	405 Sqn
R/76409	F/S	O'BRIEN Donald Kempton	6-05-42	16 OTU
R/70461	WO1	O'BRIEN John William	16-09-42	22 OTU
J/15750	P/O	O'BRIEN Ralph Connors	31-05-42	158 Sqn
R/79053	F/S	O'CONNOR John Henry	11-08-42	14 OTU
R/101932	F/S	O'DELL Austin Roy	20-12-42	428 Sqn
R/90547	F/S	O'DRISOLL Michael Francis	5-10-42	425 Sqn
J/9136	F/O	O'GRADY John Earl	6-12-42	139 Sqn
R/95736	F/S	O'GRADY Joseph Leonard	5-10-42	419 Sqn
R/92556	WO2	O'LEARY Jack Robert	1-11-42	138 Sqn
R/54187	F/S	O'LEARY Robert Joseph	26-03-42	16 OTU
R/122572	F/S	O'NEIL Edward Thomas	6-09-42	20 OTU
J/15443	P/O	O'SULLIVAN Michael Joseph	16-09-42	106 Sqn
R/109023	F/S	PABLO Daniel Lawrence [USA]	11-09-42	22 OTU
R/8215	P/O	PAFFORD Clifford Wilbert	29-08-42	115 Sqn
R/55438	F/S	PAGE Raoul Omer Joseph	1-04-42	405 Sqn
R/69723	F/S	PAGE Walter David	1-04-42	214 Sqn
J/7338	P/O	PALIN Peter James Arnold Huke	7-05-42	23 OTU
R/95316	F/S	PALMASON Stefan Douglas	6-07-42	419 Sqn
C/15803	P/O	PALMER Edward McGee	3-09-42	15 Sqn
R/75611	F/S	PALMER Herbert James	6-06-42	20 OTU
R/91651	F/S	PALMER Sidney Alexander	5-10-42	419 Sqn
R/78112	Sgt	PARHAM Robert Nelson	20-06-42	7 Sqn
R/50775	Sgt	PARK John Edward	6-10-42	405 Sqn
R/64434	F/S	PARKE Charles Arthur	25-04-42	11 OTU
R/83152	Sgt	PARKER John Austin	28-09-42	115 Sqn
J/16080	P/O	PARKYN Alfred Joseph [USA]	25-11-42	207 Sqn
R/58117	F/S	PARRY Thomas Campbell	28-06-42	218 Sqn
R/56118	F/S	PARSONS Ernest Albert	10-01-42	12 Sqn
R/135770	Sgt	PATENAUDE Raymond Armond [USA]	16-10-42	142 Sqn
R/102339	F/S	PATERSON Alexander Gordon	6-12-42	487 Sqn
R/80866	F/S	PATERSON James	28-08-42	142 Sqn
R/58431	F/S	PATERSON Stewart Thomas	9-05-42	10 OTU
J/15251	P/O	PATEY Jack Douglas	31-05-42	61 Sqn
R/77966	LAC	PATMORE Allen William	6-07-42	419 Sqn
R/93472	F/S	PATON Charles Anderson	17-09-42	405 Sqn
R/60348	F/S	PATRICK Alexander Granton	28-01-42	106 Sqn
R/79238	Sgt	PATRY Joseph Adelard Frederic Evariste	16-11-42	425 Sqn
R/55148	F/S	PATRY Joseph Jean Edmond Gustave Renee	28-08-42	14 OTU
J/7464	P/O	PATTERSON Eric Courtney	28-08-42	15 Sqn
J/8343	P/O	PATTINSON William Shearer	29-08-42	61 Sqn
R/110977	F/S	PATTON Charles Reginald	31-10-42	150 Sqn
R/85752	F/S	PAUDASH Robert Elmer	21-09-42	115 Sqn
R/108688	F/S	PAYIE Everett Garfield	22-11-42	115 Sqn
R/83558	F/S	PEARCE Bsil Vincent	14-07-42	419 Sqn
R/80774	F/S	PEARCE Robert Charles	4-08-42	142 Sqn
R/54196	F/S	PEARSON Alexander Francis Jack	28-07-42	103 Sqn
R/78288	F/S	PEARSON Robert Wakefield	6-07-42	419 Sqn
R/100368	F/S	PECK DFM Charles Woodrow Wilson	7-11-42	207 Sqn
R/77370	Sgt	PECK George James [USA]	15-01-42	214 Sqn
R/98793	F/S	PEDERSEN Walter Carl	14-09-42	21 OTU
R/59671	F/S	PEEBLES Francis Garfield	17-06-42	102 Sqn
R/82350	F/S	PEIRCEY Arthur Charles Campbell	6-06-42	20 OTU
J/9759	P/O	PELLETT Keith Thomas	29-08-42	408 Sqn
R/131821	F/S	PENN William Harvey [USA]	17-12-42	9 Sqn
R/65152	F/S	PENNEY William Alfred	26-07-42	142 Sqn
R/107561	F/S	PENNEY William Francis	1-08-42	25 OTU
R/75636	Sgt	PEREIRA Jnr William	5-06-42	156 Sqn
J/11440	F/O	PERROT Herbert Frederick	6-12-42	7 Sqn
J/15202	P/O	PETERS Donald Howard	6-06-42	419 Sqn
R/107123	F/S	PETERS Kevin Arthur	5-10-42	76 Sqn
R/143149	Sgt	PETERS Roy Donald	24-07-42	57 Sqn
R/82876	Sgt	PETERS Roy James	1-10-42	102 Sqn
R/78123	F/S	PETERSEN Reginald Bruce	9-05-42	420 Sqn
R/86320	Sgt	PETHYBRIDGE William John	9-06-42	405 Sqn
R/86743	F/S	PHALEMPIN Gerald Francis Joseph	13-10-42	214 Sqn
R/60733	F/S	PHALEMPIN Henri	26-03-42	408 Sqn
R/60734	F/S	PHILLIPS Edmund Cecil	26-02-42	405 Sqn
R/62639	WO2	PHILLIPS Gordon McLean	28-06-42	405 Sqn
R/60210	F/S	PHILLIPS John Leonard Hartley	9-03-42	15 Sqn
R/79163	WO2	PHILLIPS Neil Seymour Hunter [United Kingdom]	7-11-42	107 Sqn
R/103788	Sgt	PHILLIPS Thomas Bowman	16-08-42	14 OTU
R/78379	F/S	PHILLIPS William Herbert Edward	17-04-42	16 OTU
R/90469	F/S	PHILP Donald Robert [USA]	16-09-42	23 OTU
R/108369	Sgt	PHIPPS George Robert	5-08-42	26 OTU
R/77269	F/S	PICHER Wilfred Clarence	29-03-42	142 Sqn
R/95667	F/S	PICKARD Clarence Eugene	1-10-42	10 Sqn
R/87334	F/S	PICKEL Gordon Edgar	12-07-42	14 OTU
R/97561	F/S	PICKERING Walter Henry	15-09-42	419 Sqn
R/66308	F/S	PICKERING William Vincent	30-07-42	149 Sqn
R/98484	Sgt	PICKETT Warren Fyan [USA]	31-05-42	405 Sqn
R/56087	F/S	PIERS William Stapleton	26-02-42	405 Sqn
J/8168	P/O	PIGGOTT Jack Edward	3-04-42	16 OTU
R/67563	F/S	PIKULA Frank	17-05-42	419 Sqn
R/56441	F/S	PILBOROUGH William Edgar	8-06-42	35 Sqn
R/78467	F/S	PIPHER William Melville	26-03-42	142 Sqn
R/69669	WO2	PLATT William Lloyd	9-06-42	405 Sqn
R/74360	F/S	PLAYER James Kelleher	9-11-42	102 Sqn
R/67907	F/S	PLEASANCE John Beverly	22-07-42	408 Sqn
J/8611	P/O	POCH Louis	10-09-42	61 Sqn
R/90109	Sgt	POCOCK James Jerome	1-10-42	405 Sqn
R/55385	F/S	POIRIER Joseph William	12-02-42	419 Sqn
R/123260	Sgt	POLLARD Charles Edward	11-09-42	22 OTU
R/107334	F/S	POLLOCK Robert Joseph	3-09-42	19 OTU
R/100460	F/S	POPE William James	9-11-42	20 OTU
R/80033	F/S	POPPLESTONE William Maurice	26-03-42	114 Sqn
R/72543	F/S	PORTER Aulden Claire	10-08-42	78 Sqn
J/6667	P/O	PORTER Cornelius James	8-05-42	419 Sqn
R/86124	F/S	POST Ralph Ainsworth	19-05-42	106 Sqn
R/70841	F/S	POTTER John Victor	27-07-42	405 Sqn
R/59709	F/S	POWELL Lloyd Charles	16-01-42	419 Sqn
J/5226	P/O	POWELL Norman Nelson	11-02-42	12 Sqn
R/78675	WO2	POWELL Thomas Edward	5-10-42	419 Sqn
J/7334	P/O	POWER John Gerald	18-06-42	12 Sqn
R/82744	F/S	PRENDERGAST Albert Edward	20-10-42	115 Sqn
R/105300	Sgt	PRENTICE Robert Bruce	27-07-42	405 Sqn
J/9150	P/O	PRESTON John Allan	25-06-42	24 OTU
R/98205	Sgt	PRICE George Edward [USA]	16-07-42	13 OTU
R/79132	F/S	PRICE Hubert Douglas	2-10-42	419 Sqn
R/67111	F/S	PRICE John James	27-07-42	420 Sqn
C/920	S/L	PRICE DFC Lyall Basil Burman	29-07-42	408 Sqn

ID	Rank	Name	Date	Unit	ID	Rank	Name	Date	Unit
R/79255	Sgt	PRIME Peter [USA]	1-08-42	25 OTU	R/70737	F/S	ROBERTSON George Murray	2-04-42	144 Sqn
R/76625	F/S	PRITCHARD Joseph Corbin	20-04-42	420 Sqn	R/63605	Sgt	ROBERTSON Harry Malcolm	30-04-42	99 Sqn
R/74972	F/S	PROBERT William Douglas	19-09-42	15 Sqn	R/59266	F/S	ROBERTSON William Alan	5-01-42	405 Sqn
R/104801	F/S	PROSSER Douglas Vary	9-11-42	150 Sqn	R/85447	F/S	ROBINSON Cecil Raymond	25-06-42	24 OTU
J/8440	P/O	PYE Franklyn Richard Samuel	27-08-42	142 Sqn	R/93774	F/S	ROBITAILLE Arthur Hector	20-08-42	75 Sqn
J/6130	F/O	QUINLAN Dennis John	17-08-42	207 Sqn	R/90158	F/S	ROBSON George Erwin	5-10-42	419 Sqn
R/82607	WO2	QUINN Francis Paul Desmond	8-12-42	101 Sqn	R/65815	F/S	ROBSON Melvin Peter Frederick	26-02-42	405 Sqn
J/15447	P/O	QUINN Walter Lewis	28-08-42	142 Sqn	R/78960	F/S	ROBSON Sidney Bentley	17-09-42	15 OTU
R/86314	F/S	RAE James Douglas	6-12-42	115 Sqn	R/70049	F/S	ROCHE John Joseph	12-02-42	419 Sqn
R/93321	F/S	RAITBLAT Norman	9-11-42	425 Sqn	R/78242	F/S	RODDY Frederick Duggan	9-05-42	12 Sqn
R/95017	Sgt	RALPH Cuthbert Percy	19-07-42	22 OTU	R/95149	F/S	RODDY William George	7-07-42	156 Sqn
R/84321	WO2	RAMEY Gordon Howard	10-12-42	57 Sqn	J/16394	P/O	RODGER John David James	7-12-42	425 Sqn
R/67847	F/S	RAMEY Warren Thomas [USA]	23-04-42	9 Sqn	R/92207	F/S	RODGERS Joseph Eli	21-09-42	101 Sqn
R/62139	Sgt	RANKIN John Maxwell	24-09-42	405 Sqn	R/99252	Sgt	ROGERS Barney Andrew	11-09-42	16 OTU
R/78363	F/S	RATCLIFF Alfred Frank Chilvers	6-08-42	9 Sqn	R/57608	Sgt	ROLLINS Richard Alan	15-12-42	405 Sqn
J/5301	F/O	RATCLIFFE Carson Stewart	29-07-42	1651 CU	R/76127	F/S	ROMAS James Arthur Easterbrooks	29-04-42	408 Sqn
R/66130	WO2	RATCLIFFE DFM John Thomas	15-10-42	97 Sqn	R/67269	F/S	RONEY George William	22-07-42	115 Sqn
R/104129	F/S	RATHE Donald Stuart [USA]	29-10-42	115 Sqn	R/64340	F/S	ROSS Alfred Edgar	17-04-42	44 Sqn
R/66437	F/S	RATTRAY Norman McInnes	27-07-42	35 Sqn	J/9288	P/O	ROSS Donald Wingrove	10-09-42	207 Sqn
R/139127	F/S	RAUSCH William Stanley	24-10-42	78 Sqn	R/76228	F/S	ROSS Douglas McRae	26-07-42	35 Sqn
R/77340	WO2	RAYMOND Jean Paul Alban	20-12-42	425 Sqn	R/76634	F/S	ROSS Godfrey Hyde Stewart	12-02-42	419 Sqn
R/107555	F/S	READ Frederick Wilson	10-11-42	102 Sqn	R/85385	F/S	ROSS John	27-07-42	57 Sqn
R/107162	F/S	READ Kenneth Neville	22-12-42	44 Sqn	R/95429	F/S	ROSS Leslie Jack Willis	1-09-42	115 Sqn
R/69516	F/S	READ Robert George Dunlop	3-06-42	460 Sqn	R/99245	F/S	ROSS Norman Wilbur	29-11-42	405 Sqn
J/7203	P/O	REASON Wilson Albert	31-05-42	158 Sqn	R/71069	F/S	ROSS Samuel	28-08-42	78 Sqn
J/9777	P/O	REAUME Clarence William	7-09-42	101 Sqn	R/54032	F/S	ROWE Gordon Harry	20-09-42	102 Sqn
R/79231	F/S	RECCHIA Edward Albert	29-10-42	15 Sqn	R/80558	WO2	ROWNEY John Hoskin	29-08-42	57 Sqn
R/86394	F/S	REEVES William Neil	21-05-42	25 OTU	R/84376	F/S	ROY Alexander	5-09-42	142 Sqn
R/101761	F/S	REGIMBAL Leo Joseph	13-07-42	7 Sqn	R/55159	WO2	ROY Charles William Hurley	20-12-42	425 Sqn
R/86620	F/S	REID Ian Maclaren	8-06-42	420 Sqn	R/82377	F/S	ROYLE James Arthur	5-09-42	419 Sqn
R/95363	F/S	REID James Thomas	13-09-42	22 OTU	J/15648	P/O	RUDDY William James	28-06-42	61 Sqn
R/64381	F/S	REID Max Alfred	12-02-42	419 Sqn	J/15172	P/O	RUNNER DFM Joseph Moore	8-03-42	115 Sqn
R/53909	F/S	REID Stanleigh Lowry	2-06-42	405 Sqn	R/85469	F/S	RUSSELL Henry Millen	27-08-42	218 Sqn
R/67824	F/S	REID Wilbert George [USA]	1-04-42	20 OTU	R/91885	F/S	RUSSELL John De Forest	15-10-42	57 Sqn
R/74884	Sgt	REILLY Kenneth William	1-01-42	22 OTU	R/100818	F/S	RUSSELL Richard Anderson [USA]	28-07-42	107 Sqn
R/61467	F/S	REIMER Alvin Wilbert	12-01-42	138 Sqn	J/4758	F/O	RYAN John Patrick [New Zealand]	18-05-42	15 Sqn
R/126898	F/S	REYBURN Gerald Thomas [USA]	25-10-42	142 Sqn	R/125902	Sgt	SABOURIN Franklin Thomas	7-11-42	83 Sqn
R/62684	F/S	REYNOLDS William Douglas	24-09-42	102 Sqn	R/62910	F/S	SADLER John Murray	7-05-42	23 OTU
R/65338	F/S	RICE Walter Ruben	6-06-42	419 Sqn	R/105629	F/S	SAGE William Bruce	4-09-42	25 OTU
R/77962	WO2	RICHARDS Gordon Hubert	17-11-42	405 Sqn	R/103664	Sgt	SALCHENBERGER Robert Andrew	14-09-42	16 OTU
J/15450	P/O	RICHARDS William Mortimer	2-06-42	21 OTU	J/16066	P/O	SALMON Victor Nelson	27-07-42	226 Sqn
J/6134	P/O	RICHARDSON Denis John	8-02-42	22 OTU	J/5790	P/O	SANDERSON George Frederick	3-06-42	7 Sqn
R/78229	F/S	RICHARDSON Douglas Roy	6-01-42	57 Sqn	R/58359	F/S	SANDERSON John Wright	8-04-42	405 Sqn
R/82608	F/S	RICHARDSON Edmund St. Aubin [United Kingdom]	15-10-42	12 Sqn	R/102803	Sgt	SANDHAM Richard	30-09-42	23 OTU
					R/83908	F/S	SANDIFORD James Bertram	5-10-42	425 Sqn
R/58721	F/S	RICHARDSON James Patrick	14-07-42	142 Sqn	J/4814	F/O	SANDYS John Frederick Kelly [United Kingdom]	12-03-42	75 Sqn
R/54463	F/S	RIDDER Warren Henry [USA]	5-09-42	419 Sqn					
R/66334	F/S	RIEDY Robert Harvey [USA]	18-03-42	15 OTU	R/72286	WO1	SARGANT Warren Langton	14-07-42	419 Sqn
J/15938	P/O	RIOUX Raoul Joseph	22-09-42	425 Sqn	R/55599	F/S	SAVAGE Donald	15-01-42	10 Sqn
R/107812	F/S	ROBB George Barclay	7-09-42	22 OTU	R/106599	F/S	SAWATZKY George Gerhard	8-11-42	76 Sqn
R/56387	WO2	ROBB George Spence	14-07-42	158 Sqn	R/74880	F/S	SCARFF John William	8-04-42	22 OTU
R/72335	F/S	ROBB Reginald Francis	26-02-42	158 Sqn	R/79036	Sgt	SCHMELTZ Francis Donald [USA]	1-07-42	21 OTU
R/65294	F/S	ROBBINS Max Feindel	28-08-42	35 Sqn	R/85216	F/S	SCHWEITZER Jacob Adam	28-04-42	22 OTU
R/77310	F/S	ROBERT Allan Dease	5-06-42	150 Sqn	R/87422	Sgt	SCOBIE Lewis William	10-10-42	419 Sqn
R/74926	F/S	ROBERTS Angus Frederick	21-05-42	25 OTU	J/8838	F/O	SCOTT Donald Phillips	13-10-42	83 Sqn
R/82059	F/S	ROBERTS David Phillips	22-07-42	101 Sqn	R/80514	F/S	SCOTT Frank Raymond	5-10-42	102 Sqn
R/98501	F/S	ROBERTS George William	3-09-42	405 Sqn	J/4112	P/O	SCOTT John Grant	20-01-42	142 Sqn
R/77364	F/S	ROBERTS Harry Edwards	28-08-42	101 Sqn	R/85161	F/S	SCOTT Robert Thomas	11-03-42	19 OTU
R/74225	F/S	ROBERTS Lloyd John Osborne	6-05-42	419 Sqn	R/137578	F/S	SCOTT Roy Harold	11-10-42	75 Sqn
R/87325	WO2	ROBERTS Maurice Luther	7-11-42	83 Sqn	R/77223	F/S	SCOTT Stanley Walter	7-09-42	115 Sqn
R/58215	WO2	ROBERTS Melvin Harry	24-06-42	76 Sqn	R/82221	F/S	SCOTT Walter Edward	30-09-42	23 OTU
R/90445	Sgt	ROBERTSHAW William John	9-01-42	19 OTU	R/61631	WO2	SCOTT William Lawrence	28-06-42	405 Sqn
R/93119	F/S	ROBERTSON Andrew Crawford Stark	5-09-42	419 Sqn	R/101980	Sgt	SCOTTEN Jack Clarence	11-09-42	405 Sqn
					J/9782	F/O	SCOURFIELD Leslie Rowland	15-10-42	419 Sqn
R/98882	F/S	ROBERTSON Donald Roy	10-10-42	16 OTU	R/85408	F/S	SCRIMES Frank John Barnes	2-06-42	23 OTU
R/83401	F/S	ROBERTSON Eugene Garland [USA]	1-08-42	16 OTU	R/69704	F/S	SEBERRAS Joseph	23-04-42	9 Sqn
R/79164	F/S	ROBERTSON George Macklin Lascelles	17-04-42	22 OTU	R/82658	F/S	SEGUIN Joseph Joffre Marc	24-10-42	425 Sqn
					J/5794	P/O	SEIBOLD Elwood Raymond	3-06-42	61 Sqn

ID	Rank	Name	Date	Unit
R/80202	F/S	SEIFERT Arnold Adolf	31-05-42	12 Sqn
R/79111	F/S	SENEZ Joseph Wilfred Alderic	9-11-42	57 Sqn
J/11358	P/O	SHADLE Charles Corbett [USA]	15-10-42	21 OTU
R/80520	F/S	SHANNON Charles Melville	9-05-42	419 Sqn
R/78148	WO2	SHAPTER William James Aubrey	6-08-42	207 Sqn
J/9636	P/O	SHAW George Leigh	25-08-42	22 OTU
R/51824	WO1	SHAW Joseph Harold Gourley	5-10-42	419 Sqn
R/115190	F/S	SHAW Robert James Abadore	15-12-42	405 Sqn
J/10132	F/S	SHAW Robert Simpson	4-11-42	1518 Flt
R/83056	F/S	SHEFFLER Lew Wallace [USA]	14-04-42	21 OTU
R/91663	F/S	SHELSON Archie Edward	13-11-42	97 Sqn
R/78934	F/S	SHEPHERD Austin	19-08-42	61 Sqn
R/65215	F/S	SHEPPARD Edward Edmond	19-08-42	61 Sqn
R/105877	Sgt	SHERMAN Charles Arthur	11-09-42	20 OTU
J/7532	P/O	SHIRES Reginald Albert	1-09-42	115 Sqn
J/7035	P/O	SHOEMAKER DFC Wilbert Andrew	26-07-42	15 Sqn
R/92301	F/S	SHORT Thomas Henry	16-11-42	149 Sqn
R/52504	WO2	SHRINER Charles Percival	19-08-42	61 Sqn
R/68751	WO2	SHUMSKY William Nelson	25-08-42	7 Sqn
R/58531	WO2	SIDNEY Lawrence	30-06-42	405 Sqn
R/79014	F/S	SIDORCHUCK Nicholas	9-11-42	102 Sqn
R/76610	F/S	SIMBALIST Eugene	3-12-42	115 Sqn
J/15474	P/O	SIMMONS Cecil William [USA]	30-06-42	149 Sqn
R/77458	F/S	SIMONEAU Joseph Ludovic Rodolphe	24-10-42	425 Sqn
R/85420	F/S	SIMONSON Veron Leray	1-08-42	25 OTU
R/59701	F/S	SINCLAIR Marcel Stanley	8-05-42	408 Sqn
R/78077	F/S	SINCLAIR Wilbert Lome	14-02-42	12 OTU
R/118216	F/S	SINCLAIR William Robert Campbell	13-10-42	22 OTU
R/86398	F/S	SIWAK Adolph Antonio	24-10-42	149 Sqn
R/80198	F/S	SLEZAK Henry Maximilian	27-07-42	405 Sqn
R/77069	WO1	SMARDON Donald Martin	10-12-42	22 OTU
R/92605	F/S	SMART William James	14-07-42	158 Sqn
R/73007	F/S	SMITH Albert Alexander	16-05-42	408 Sqn
R/79500	F/S	SMITH Armand Joseph Marcel	9-11-42	420 Sqn
J/9675	P/O	SMITH Carl Edward	13-08-42	77 Sqn
R/74365	F/S	SMITH Cecil Baker	7-07-42	419 Sqn
R/76192	Sgt	SMITH David Macneil	17-06-42	102 Sqn
R/73247	F/S	SMITH Douglas Richard	11-09-42	16 OTU
J/6235	F/O	SMITH Edward Arthur	6-06-42	156 Sqn
R/78895	F/S	SMITH Frederick John	31-10-42	150 Sqn
R/82895	F/S	SMITH Garnet Floyd	11-08-42	149 Sqn
R/53943	WO2	SMITH George Hilliard	19-08-42	61 Sqn
R/84385	Sgt	SMITH Jack Arthur Charles	16-09-42	23 OTU
R/74480	F/S	SMITH James Edgar	29-07-42	57 Sqn
R/77150	F/S	SMITH James Henry	25-04-42	420 Sqn
J/10310	F/O	SMITH Leonard Ian	6-10-42	115 Sqn
J/15451	P/O	SMITH Ray Branton	26-07-42	106 Sqn
4349	F/S	SMITH Raymond Frank	9-09-42	77 Sqn
R/73287	F/S	SMITH Robert Ainslie	26-07-42	114 Sqn
R/93318	F/S	SMITH Robert Gordon	7-12-42	101 Sqn
R/86146	Sgt	SMITH Walter Graham	8-02-42	12 OTU
R/61660	F/S	SMYTH David Beverley	15-10-42	420 Sqn
R/80105	F/S	SMYTH James William	31-05-42	142 Sqn
R/73321	WO2	SNARR Lloyd Ellsworth	20-12-42	405 Sqn
R/83354	F/S	SNIDER Charles Solomon [USA]	9-11-42	420 Sqn
R/91316	F/S	SNOW William Oliver	16-09-42	9 Sqn
R/106059	F/S	SOKOL William	11-11-42	425 Sqn
R/102246	F/S	SOTKOWY Stanley Walter	17-12-42	115 Sqn
J/85160	P/O	SOUTAR James Ronald Fairbank	18-08-42	218 Sqn
R/59327	F/S	SPAFFORD Alvin Leslie	3-07-42	103 Sqn
R/86211	Sgt	SPARROW Bruce Harry	10-10-42	16 OTU
R/84639	Sgt	SPEARS Edmund Thomas	25-08-42	22 OTU
J/5136	F/O	SPEIR John Garfield	11-08-42	207 Sqn
R/88087	Sgt	SPINNEY James William	16-11-42	101 Sqn
R/71030	F/S	SPOULER Joseph George	14-09-42	214 Sqn
R/59112	F/S	SPRATT Cecil Robert	30-07-42	149 Sqn
R/97062	F/S	SPRINGHAM Ernest Richard	7-11-42	7 Sqn
R/98121	F/S	STAGEMAN Richard Elmer [USA]	29-07-42	16 OTU
R/78073	F/S	STALKER Leonard Ogilvy	26-03-42	420 Sqn
R/59841	F/S	STAMMERS Ernest Frank	6-12-42	115 Sqn
R/87945	F/S	STANDFAST John Percy	12-10-42	12 Sqn
R/67711	WO2	STANLEY Melville James	29-11-42	405 Sqn
R/92640	F/S	STARK William McBain James	17-12-42	44 Sqn
R/76063	F/S	STARRETT Clarence William	28-03-42	7 Sqn
R/70825	F/S	STEINHAUER George Henry	31-03-42	35 Sqn
R/75683	F/S	STELMAN Alexander	22-06-42	218 Sqn
R/84432	F/S	STEPHENSON Thomas Aitken	2-10-42	78 Sqn
R/79018	F/S	STEWART Donald Ross	25-06-42	10 Sqn
R/77459	F/S	STEWART Frederick William	20-07-42	10 Sqn
J/9881	P/O	STEWART James Gethings	12-08-42	23 OTU
R/111808	Sgt	STEWART Moodie Morris	9-11-42	20 OTU
R/73095	WO2	STEWART Robert Reginald	1-08-42	420 Sqn
R/85506	WO2	STEWART Robert William	15-12-42	405 Sqn
R/102451	F/S	STILBORN Kenneth Elwood	13-11-42	107 Sqn
R/128083	F/S	STOCKTON Robert White	8-11-42	158 Sqn
J/10078	P/O	STOLL Ernest Frederick Johann	25-08-42	22 OTU
J/10706	F/O	STOLLERY Ernest	20-12-42	405 Sqn
J/15485	P/O	STOREY Robert Lorne	4-07-42	61 Sqn
R/87673	WO1	STOWE Sidney Vernon	2-10-42	419 Sqn
R/92290	F/S	STRAIN Robert Peter	7-11-42	207 Sqn
J/9585	P/O	STREET Douglas Alfred	27-07-42	405 Sqn
14033A	F/S	STREETING Joseph Fletcher	13-10-42	419 Sqn
J/7540	P/O	STRONG George Frederick	24-07-42	405 Sqn
J/9289	F/O	STUART Harding James	2-10-42	419 Sqn
R/81084	F/S	STUART Richard Charles	20-08-42	75 Sqn
J/7219	P/O	STURGESS John Lee	13-08-42	15 Sqn
R/55593	Sgt	ST. CYR Edouard Wilfred	22-09-42	425 Sqn
R/54325	F/S	ST. LOUIS Joseph Gordon	17-09-42	405 Sqn
R/69204	F/S	ST. LOUIS Michael Bertram	10-09-42	75 Sqn
R/77228	F/S	ST. PIERRE Josph Alphonse Maurice	15-09-42	14 OTU
J/6030	P/O	SUGRUE William Donald	22-02-42	19 OTU
J/85162	P/O	SULLIVAN Clifford Roy	11-09-42	22 OTU
J/6841	F/O	SULLIVAN Joseph Patrick	21-12-42	156 Sqn
J/15454	P/O	SUMPTON John Emmanuel	17-06-42	102 Sqn
R/70757	F/S	SUTHERBY Charles Andrew Levern	29-08-42	408 Sqn
R/81424	F/S	SUTHERLAND George Keith	30-07-42	149 Sqn
R/95344	F/S	SUTHERLAND Peter	14-09-42	22 OTU
R/102438	F/S	SUTTILL William	10-12-42	22 OTU
R/107046	F/S	SVEINSON Helgi Sveinn	2-10-42	419 Sqn
R/97371	F/S	SWAIN Aubrey Russell	25-10-42	12 Sqn
R/76207	F/S	SWANSBURG Arthur Douglas	27-07-42	405 Sqn
R/77417	WO2	SWARBRICK Joseph Cecil	3-12-42	115 Sqn
J/8938	F/O	SWEET Julian Frederic	21-11-42	150 Sqn
R/60293	F/S	SWIDERSKI Alexander	12-06-42	9 Sqn
J/7916	P/O	SZUMLINSKI Charles Leonard	1-08-42	24 OTU
R/70913	F/S	TAIT Francis Alexander	28-01-42	214 Sqn
R/83538	F/S	TAIT John	1-08-42	25 OTU
R/69866	WO2	TAIT William	25-06-42	16 OTU
R/98436	F/S	TANNER Kenneth Boyd [USA]	16-09-42	23 OTU
R/55549	F/S	TAPP Joseph Norbert	5-09-42	101 Sqn
R/74067	WO2	TASSE Joseph Hector Georges	9-11-42	425 Sqn
R/70586	Sgt	TATHAM Gordon Bertram	28-06-42	405 Sqn
R/65251	F/S	TAYLOR Donald Theodore	24-10-42	150 Sqn
J/15649	P/O	TAYLOR Frederick John	28-08-42	35 Sqn
R/108843	F/S	TAYLOR George Robert Ian [Cuba]	29-11-42	405 Sqn
R/95405	F/S	TAYLOR Hermann John	19-08-42	61 Sqn
J/7076	P/O	TAYLOR Kenneth Henry	3-06-42	408 Sqn
R/75732	F/S	TAYLOR Leonard Clayton	20-05-42	103 Sqn
J/7221	P/O	TAYLOR Talbot Jones [USA]	6-06-42	35 Sqn
R/91300	F/S	TAYLOR Thomas Ross	17-10-42	15 Sqn
R/80890	Sgt	TAYLOR William Edward George	6-02-42	21 OTU
R/83544	F/S	TAYNEN Donald Jack	20-04-42	16 OTU
J/10284	F/O	TEAGUE Denis Frank	24-10-42	78 Sqn
R/62467	WO2	TELFER Robert Lloyd	28-08-42	103 Sqn
R/100369	Sgt	TEMPLE Albert John	7-09-42	22 OTU

Service No.	Rank	Name	Date	Unit
R/97834	F/S	TEMPLETON Pat Neff [USA]	7-09-42	22 OTU
R/77521	F/S	TERRIS Thomas Meldram	7-06-42	156 Sqn
R/83416	F/S	TERWILLIGER William Henry [USA]	31-08-42	24 OTU
R/77091	F/S	THEBERGE Jean Marie Marcel Raymond	29-07-42	156 Sqn
R/67674	F/S	THOMAS Thomas Joseph	12-02-42	419 Sqn
J/9551	F/O	THOMAS Wilbert Harry	23-10-42	158 Sqn
J/9588	P/O	THOMPSON Duncan Gordon	15-10-42	57 Sqn
R/93193	F/S	THOMPSON Harry Victor	9-11-42	150 Sqn
J/7225	F/O	THOMPSON Harry William	3-09-42	419 Sqn
R/57930	F/S	THOMPSON John Albert	2-06-42	405 Sqn
R/51638	F/S	THOMPSON Joseph Michael	13-03-42	83 Sqn
J/10239	F/O	THOMPSON Walter McNaught	24-10-42	218 Sqn
R/71841	F/S	THOMSON James Anderson	13-07-42	420 Sqn
J/9862	P/O	THOMSON James Handiside	27-04-42	149 Sqn
R/84167	F/S	THOMSON William	17-05-42	419 Sqn
R/78983	WO2	THORNEYCROFT Leonard Everett	17-12-42	97 Sqn
R/70102	WO2	THURLOW William Charles	24-07-42	405 Sqn
R/74264	WO2	THURSTON Harold Jason	20-09-42	9 Sqn
R/61115	WO2	TIGHE Lawrence Joseph	30-09-42	149 Sqn
R/86352	F/S	TITUS Gerald Robert	27-07-42	405 Sqn
J/10185	F/O	TODD Francis Lionel	5-10-42	419 Sqn
J/9575	F/O	TOMLINSON Mansell Matthew	15-10-42	405 Sqn
R/80180	WO2	TORKELSON Donald Leroy	25-06-42	22 OTU
R/94722	F/S	TORONCZUK Constantin	10-08-42	22 OTU
R/83273	WO2	TOUGH John George Ross	23-11-42	44 Sqn
J/7202	P/O	TRAPP Byron Adair	21-06-42	7 Sqn
R/93386	F/S	TREADWELL William Henry	1-08-42	25 OTU
R/66697	F/S	TRITT Jack	16-11-42	425 Sqn
J/15829	P/O	TROWBRIDGE Vincent Charles William	27-08-42	218 Sqn
R/83089	WO2	TRUDELL Chester Charles	17-12-42	97 Sqn
R/87850	F/S	TUCK John Frederick	29-08-42	115 Sqn
R/77248	F/S	TULLER John Olmstead	20-09-42	61 Sqn
R/85200	WO2	TURCOTTE Garnet Hartford [USA]	10-12-42	21 Sqn
R/82814	F/S	TURNER Jean Albert Marc	9-06-42	103 Sqn
R/60962	F/S	TURNER John Blackwell	16-01-42	104 Sqn
R/55384	F/S	TURPIN Thomas Edward	1-10-42	78 Sqn
C/167	W/C	TWIGG John Despard	28-08-42	408 Sqn
J/15855	P/O	TYLER William Stone [USA]	15-04-42	405 Sqn
R/68167	WO2	UDELL Donald	16-09-42	142 Sqn
R/119542	F/S	URQUHART David Smith	7-12-42	425 Sqn
R/82332	F/S	URQUHART Ronald Neil [USA]	26-06-42	11 OTU
J/15861	P/O	USHER Moses Lewis	31-03-42	35 Sqn
R/82046	F/S	UTMAN Keith Barkley	2-06-42	26 OTU
R/99576	Cpl	VAIL Donald	9-07-42	15 OTU
R/78640	F/S	VALKENIER William Joseph [USA]	6-05-42	419 Sqn
R/74630	WO2	VANDERVOORT William John	25-11-42	207 Sqn
R/64920	WO2	VAUTOUR Albeni Camille	1-08-42	101 Sqn
R/110223	F/S	VAN BRUNT Norman Albert	20-12-42	405 Sqn
R/54999	F/S	VAN GEUN Furneaux Montague	14-07-42	419 Sqn
R/103930	F/S	VAN NORMAN Hugh Duncan	17-09-42	15 OTU
R/78273	F/S	VEARNCOMBE Reginald Howard	28-01-42	22 OTU
R/62799	F/S	VEZINA Joseph Fernand Paul	12-02-42	419 Sqn
R/86125	Sgt	VIAU Joseph Rene	14-02-42	16 OTU
J/6995	P/O	VIPOND Dalton Eastman	26-03-42	408 Sqn
R/67738	F/S	WADDELL Woodrow Wilcox [USA]	9-11-42	405 Sqn
R/90299	F/S	WADDLE Ward Ralph	9-11-42	405 Sqn
R/76357	F/S	WADMAN Leonard Alfred	31-05-42	405 Sqn
R/101328	F/S	WAGNER Elmer Leroy [USA]	28-07-42	22 OTU
R/124697	F/S	WAGNER Gerald Edward	20-12-42	405 Sqn
R/91255	F/S	WAKELIN Raymond Lloyd	30-09-42	12 Sqn
R/95061	F/S	WAKEMAN William Arthur	13-10-42	419 Sqn
J/10056	F/O	WALKER Arthur Douglas	15-10-42	97 Sqn
R/77410	F/S	WALKER John Edward Stuart	21-07-42	106 Sqn
R/10183	F/O	WALLACE George Ernest	22-11-42	115 Sqn
R/107254	Sgt	WALLAND Allan Clarance	9-11-42	405 Sqn
R/87781	F/S	WALLS Raymond Ben	2-09-42	97 Sqn
R/54847	Sgt	WALSH Cecil Stephen	30-06-42	405 Sqn
R/75183	F/S	WALSH Patrick Charles	29-03-42	83 Sqn
R/95093	Sgt	WALTERS Ronald George	8-08-42	29 OTU
J/12796	P/O	WARDROP Alexander McBirnie	14-10-42	420 Sqn
R/97662	F/S	WARDROP John Jamieson Patrick	2-09-42	14 OTU
R/84138	F/S	WARNICK Eugene Edward	26-07-42	114 Sqn
R/4285	WO2	WARREN Robert Orville Orson [USA]	21-09-42	10 OTU
R/91963	F/S	WATERS Jnr George Henry [USA]	14-09-42	12 Sqn
R/69360	F/O	WATKINSON James Lester	16-11-42	115 Sqn
R/98140	WO2	WATSON Harry Raeburn	11-09-42	83 Sqn
R/70107	F/S	WATSON Howard Cameron	19-05-42	103 Sqn
R/77490	F/S	WATSON Ian Reay	26-06-42	1652 CU
J/16430	F/O	WATSON Rayden Frederic	11-12-42	158 Sqn
R/68126	Sgt	WATTERWORTH Mack William	5-10-42	218 Sqn
R/92534	F/S	WEBB Wilbert George	10-08-42	150 Sqn
J/15991	P/O	WEBB William Miskiman	24-09-42	405 Sqn
J/5471	P/O	WEBSTER George Hamilton	28-01-42	214 Sqn
R/88208	F/S	WEBSTER Walter Hopkins [USA]	17-05-42	419 Sqn
C/15021	P/O	WEIR James Chapman	28-06-42	97 Sqn
R/62398	F/S	WELSH Gerald Arthur	31-05-42	405 Sqn
R/72357	F/S	WENT Henry Edward	9-05-42	419 Sqn
J/16716	P/O	WEST Donald Coburn	27-07-42	142 Sqn
R/76959	F/S	WEST William Robert	2-04-42	214 Sqn
J/15812	P/O	WESTGATE Robert John	11-07-42	97 Sqn
R/68698	F/S	WHEAR John Willard	16-09-42	142 Sqn
R/83079	F/S	WHITE Douglas Arthur	16-09-42	26 OTU
R/85938	F/S	WHITE Ernest Griffith	28-07-42	22 OTU
J/5085	F/O	WHITE Kenneth	30-06-42	149 Sqn
R/87390	F/S	WHITE Lloyd Ernest	15-10-42	420 Sqn
R/67591	F/S	WHITLEY Robert Widdop	30-05-42	419 Sqn
R/56325	F/S	WHYTOCK Robert William Rowland	2-07-42	420 Sqn
R/77557	F/S	WIBERG Raymond Daniel	20-12-42	106 Sqn
R/85433	F/S	WILDE Charles Garnett	3-07-42	420 Sqn
R/78721	F/S	WILEY Charles Gordon	18-03-42	15 OTU
R/122393	F/S	WILKEN Garnet Willard	9-11-42	22 OTU
R/65170	F/S	WILKIE Gordon John	13-04-42	408 Sqn
R/78711	WO2	WILKINSON Gordon Lea	26-06-42	10 OTU
R/67530	F/S	WILLIAMS Arthur Frederick	26-03-42	420 Sqn
R/75063	F/S	WILLIAMS Charles Franklin	6-07-42	419 Sqn
R/77986	F/S	WILLIAMS David Garth	6-12-42	115 Sqn
R/56348	F/S	WILLIAMS Harry Robinson	8-05-42	22 OTU
R/79368	F/S	WILLIAMS John Daniel	10-09-42	22 OTU
R/77403	F/S	WILLIAMS John Patrick	28-04-42	22 OTU
R/122012	F/S	WILLIAMS Lionel Harry	2-10-42	405 Sqn
J/7204	P/O	WILLIAMS Maldwyn Wyn	20-05-42	103 Sqn
R/93550	F/S	WILLIAMSON Harry Robert	1-10-42	61 Sqn
R/71602	WO2	WILLIAMSON Harry Ward	16-07-42	158 Sqn
R/68142	F/S	WILLIAMSON Neil	12-02-42	419 Sqn
R/73086	F/S	WILLIGAR Lloyd Edgar	18-04-42	101 Sqn
J/85159	P/O	WILLOUGHBY Edwin Bertram	1-08-42	25 OTU
R/92803	F/S	WILSON Alan John	6-12-42	7 Sqn
R/76046	F/S	WILSON Ernest George	3-07-42	214 Sqn
R/51067	Sgt	WILSON George Watson	15-09-42	419 Sqn
R/71741	WO1	WILSON Harold Eric	6-12-42	107 Sqn
R/106968	F/S	WILSON Harold Gilchrist	25-10-42	12 Sqn
R/59976	Sgt	WILSON James Murray	9-01-42	19 OTU
R/67917	F/S	WILSON Robert Edwin	22-04-42	408 Sqn
R/82838	F/S	WILSON Stanley Allen	27-08-42	12 Sqn
J/8129	P/O	WILSON Thompson Lawrie	20-08-42	61 Sqn
R/67312	F/S	WILSON William Bruce Milne	6-04-42	16 OTU
J/9925	F/O	WINDER Robert Gledhill	21-10-42	7 Sqn
R/84099	F/S	WISHART Robert	22-07-42	408 Sqn
J/10182	F/S	WITHERS Joseph Alan William	6-12-42	487 Sqn
R/79045	F/S	WITHERS Jnr Thomas Austin [USA]	27-07-42	405 Sqn
J/16089	P/O	WITHINGTON DFM David Thomas	8-11-42	22 OTU
R/80002	F/S	WITYCK Peter	5-01-42	405 Sqn

J/8619	P/O	WOOD Frederick Francis Andrew	29-06-42	14 OTU	
R/75098	F/S	WOODLEY Donald Schlueter	8-04-42	22 OTU	
J/11232	F/O	WOODMAN James Donald	17-12-42	115 Sqn	
R/106876	F/S	WOODRUFF Richard John	30-09-42	23 OTU	
J/15546	P/O	WOOF Reginald	1-08-42	156 Sqn	
R/59555	F/S	WOOLGAR James Harold Boston	10-09-42	61 Sqn	
R/110246	Sgt	WOOLLIAMS Russell Hale	31-10-42	30 OTU	
R/80999	F/S	WOOLNER Robert Ward	8-07-42	106 Sqn	
R/79316	F/S	WRIGHT Frederick Herbert Richard	6-09-42	20 OTU	
J/9698	P/O	WRIGHT James Allister	29-08-42	61 Sqn	
R/73309	F/S	WRIGHT William Mitchell	30-11-42	149 Sqn	
J/7472	F/S	WYNN Eric Pierce	24-08-42	149 Sqn	
R/80041	F/S	YANKOSKI Anthony	25-06-42	22 OTU	
R/101059	F/S	YAPP Thomas Walter [USA]	12-10-42	12 Sqn	
R/70975	F/S	YATES Albert Cranston	10-09-42	61 Sqn	
R/118035	F/S	YEATES George Reginald	8-09-42	78 Sqn	
R/66080	F/S	YORKE Wilbert George	6-01-42	12 Sqn	
R/102932	F/S	YOUMANS Frederick Aleck	24-09-42	102 Sqn	
R/87403	F/S	YOUNG James Roslyn	2-05-42	13 OTU	
R/106035	Sgt	YUILL Kenneth Ferguson	6-07-42	22 OTU	
R/86810	F/S	ZAPARYNUK Peter Karil	28-08-42	419 Sqn	
J/8781	P/O	ZAVADOWSKY Harry George	13-05-42	17 OTU	
J/16639	P/O	ZEALAND John Herbert	10-11-42	102 Sqn	

Note

The entry for R/102011 F/S Alexander Cameron Gibson may be erroneous as his name does not appear in the records pertaining to 158 Squadron, neither is he identified as such in the Commonwealth War Graves Commission register for burials in Jurby (St. Patrick) Churchyard on the Isle of Man. However, in Les Allison and Harry Hayward's *magnum opus* commemorating the airmen and airwomen of Canada who lost their lives, and published under the title *They Shall Grow Not Old* shows this airman as belonging to 158 Squadron and that he was killed on 17th July, 1942, when his Anson I R9640 of the Staff Pilots Training Unit flew into a hill, in cloud, near Park Lewellwen Farm on North Barrule, Isle of Man. It is possible that F/S Gibson had been posted to 158 Squadron, though his movement had yet to take place, but it is more likely that his details have been confused with the next entry in the book which is in respect of J/87558 P/O Arnold Roy Alexander Gibson who was killed while flying with 158 Squadron on 11th April, 1944. This is certainly accurate and P/O Gibson's name is commemorated in Part 8 of this Roll of Honour.

Some documentation has been brought to my attention that show F/S King and F/S Martin who disappeared without trace on the 22nd April, 1942, as belonging to 106 Squadron, though this is not borne out by their entries in the Runnymede Memorial registers. It is thought that their aircraft, reported as a Wellington (a type not issued to 106 Squadron) came down in the Bay of Biscay whilst flying out to Malta.

I have, in previous observations, remarked upon parents losing both a son and a daughter and in respect of the airmen perpetuated in this section such a tragedy befell the Shermans of Fort Saskatchewan in Alberta. Their son Charles lost his life in the final stages of his bomber pilot training while his sister, Sgt Edna Alice Sherman, a clerk in service at No.5 CMB Dartmouth, died from natural causes on the 2nd November, 1944. Charles now rests in Holland at Groesbeek Canadian War Cemetery, while Edna was brought back to Alberta to lie in a churchyard close to her home.

Other Canadians perpetuated in this section and whose parents would mourn the death of another son (serving in Bomber Command) later in the war are P/O Birchall, brother Roland being killed in April 1943; the air gunner trained Deatherage brothers from Smiley, Saskatchewan, George being killed late in 1944, while flying with 101 Squadron. The Einarson twins, meanwhile, graduated as pilots but neither lived to hear the cheers of victory; Harold, here commemorated, has no known grave, while Johann, dying over France in 1944, gained a Distinguished Flying Cross and a Distinguished Flying Medal in his all too brief life of 23 years.

For the family and friends of the Stuarts, Richard and Reginald, sad tidings arrived in less than a year; Richard serving with 75 (New Zealand) Squadron was lost in the August of 1942, while Reginald died the following April when his 405 (City of Vancouver) Squadron Halifax failed to make it home from a mine laying sortie over the Bay of Biscay.

Life, sadly, was all too short for the Kowalski boys, Louis and John with neither surviving to celebrate a 22nd birthday and for their parents, just a year between the loss of their two dear sons. Such remarks are almost mirrored in the deaths of the Woolgar boys, James and William, 21 and 20 years of age respectively, though it was two years almost to the day that separate their passing.

An expensive visit to the battleship *Tirpitz* resulted in the death of Harold Franklin, while a little over two years later his younger brother, Lloyd, was posted missing from a trip to the railway yards at Somain; neither has a known grave over which to reflect upon their memory but their names are remembered in perpetuity on the panels of the Runnymede Memorial.

And finally an observation of some interest, it was not until 1942, that the first Royal Canadian Air Force airman, serving in any Command, whose surname commenced with the letter 'U' (37 are reported) died while on active service. Perhaps not surprisingly, this sad distinction settles on P/O Moses Lewis Usher of 35 Squadron, a wireless operator, serving with 35 Squadron (see Volume 3 page 57 for the circumstances of his death).

ROYAL NEW ZEALAND AIR FORCE personnel

NZ404522	P/O	ABBOTT Alexander Richard	12-02-42	455 Sqn
NZ405215	Sgt	AINGER Thomas Brian	19-04-42	156 Sqn
NZ402974	F/S	AITCHISON Campbell Ewen Justin	12-03-42	75 Sqn
NZ412309	P/O	ALDERTON Kivell Harold William	18-08-42	57 Sqn
NZ411734	Sgt	ALPE James Frederick	19-12-42	149 Sqn
NZ41617	Sgt	ANDERSON William James	17-09-42	7 Sqn
NZ405217	Sgt	ARMORY Sydney	29-06-42	11 OTU
NZ404586	Sgt	ARNOLD Albert Edgar	11-09-42	78 Sqn
NZ41563	Sgt	ASHWIN Eric Lumley Durham	17-12-42	75 Sqn
NZ39857	F/L	BABER MiD Czechoslovak War Medal Thomas James Desmond	12-03-42	75 Sqn
NZ412467	Sgt	BADCOCK Alan Frederick	9-11-42	57 Sqn
NZ403565	Sgt	BADLEY John Warren	12-08-42	106 Sqn
NZ40640	W/O	BAGNALL Trevor Horace	17-12-42	75 Sqn
NZ404014	F/S	BAIRD William Alan	20-05-42	12 Sqn
NZ414380	F/O	BANNERMAN Douglas Robert	21-12-42	467 Sqn
NZ41564	Sgt	BARBER Frederick George	26-06-42	11 OTU
NZ411358	F/S	BARCLAY Thomas Smith [United Kingdom]	12-08-42	75 Sqn
NZ41975	F/S	BARNES William James	5-06-42	57 Sqn
NZ405130	Sgt	BARRY James Harold	11-11-42	57 Sqn
NZ41300	Sgt	BAXTER Lawrence Heaton	17-04-42	44 Sqn
NZ404477	P/O	BEATSON Rex Vivian	9-05-42	44 Sqn
NZ403566	Sgt	BEAVEN James Wilfred	22-05-42	75 Sqn
NZ402237	P/O	BEAVER Gordon Findlay	27-03-42	408 Sqn
NZ402158	P/O	BECK DFM Richard Colvin Seddon	24-07-42	25 OTU
NZ405364	F/O	BELL Leslie Edwin	17-09-42	1654 CU
NZ404882	P/O	BELL Maurice Perrott	29-03-42	75 Sqn
NZ41302	F/O	BENEFIELD Victor Dominic	16-09-42	11 OTU
NZ404526	P/O	BILLING Kelvin Cholwill	2-06-42	83 Sqn
NZ403773	P/O	BIRNIE Robert	9-01-42	458 Sqn
NZ404051	Sgt	BISSELL Albert Frank	24-06-42	103 Sqn
NZ404994	Sgt	BLAIR Noel Hensley	13-04-42	115 Sqn
NZ401164	F/O	BLAKE DFC Harold Roger	31-05-42	20 OTU
NZ405221	F/O	BLEASE John Thomas	14-07-42	97 Sqn
NZ403419	F/O	BLUNDEN Neil Ralph	30-03-42	10 Sqn
NZ411852	P/O	BOADEN Frank Bruce	14-09-42	115 Sqn
NZ41566	Sgt	BOLAND Thomas Lindsay	20-08-42	61 Sqn
NZ413808	F/O	BOMFORD John Hamilton	28-10-42	1651 HCU

ID	Rank	Name	Date	Unit	ID	Rank	Name	Date	Unit
NZ402450	F/S	BOWIE Valance Trent	30-11-42	149 Sqn	NZ41638	Sgt	CROUCH Herbert Charles	28-04-42	22 OTU
NZ405366	F/S	BOWKER Thomas Layton	23-10-42	218 Sqn	NZ411742	Sgt	CROZIER Noel Henry	24-09-42	9 Sqn
NZ401954	P/O	BRADEY George Edward Francis	11-08-42	75 Sqn	NZ41574	F/S	CUMMOCK Vincent Patrick	3-06-42	57 Sqn
NZ401302	Sgt	BRADLEY Douglas Reginald	16-01-42	104 Sqn	NZ412469	P/O	CUNNINGHAM Alan Henry	15-10-42	156 Sqn
NZ404587	Sgt	BRAILEY Clifton Robert	21-06-42	75 Sqn	NZ41314	F/S	DALE Geoffrey Ernest	1-10-42	61 Sqn
NZ411204	Sgt	BRISCO Robert Hylton	29-07-42	75 Sqn	NZ402438	F/S	DALEY Bernard Joseph	1-06-42	20 OTU
NZ39691	Sgt	BROADY Raymond Herbert John	28-11-42	75 Sqn	NZ411377	P/O	DALLENGER Ben	17-09-42	7 Sqn
NZ405224	F/S	BROCKET John Crawford	15-10-42	149 Sqn	NZ405746	Sgt	DALLY Aubrey Raymond	1-08-42	101 Sqn
NZ39082	P/O	BROUGH Valentine George	14-09-42	156 Sqn	NZ411378	P/O	DALZELL Errol Thomas Paterson	28-08-42	75 Sqn
NZ405367	P/O	BROUN Alan Stewart	9-07-42	75 Sqn	NZ403954	F/S	DARLING Richard Maxwell	28-08-42	156 Sqn
NZ411364	F/S	BROWN George Thirlwell	27-08-42	101 Sqn	NZ404852	F/S	DAVIES Ian Wynn	9-05-42	158 Sqn
NZ404527	Sgt	BROWN Hugh Stainger	26-01-42	51 Sqn	NZ403569	F/S	DAVIS Ronald Fraser	29-07-42	75 Sqn
NZ402534	F/S	BROWN John Lukies	12-03-42	75 Sqn	NZ403760	F/S	DEAN Frederick Spendlove	28-10-42	1651 HCU
NZ404995	F/S	BROWN Kenneth Charles	29-08-42	57 Sqn	NZ415064	Sgt	DENHAM Maurice Thorpe	17-12-42	10 OTU
NZ40859	F/S	BRYSON Norman Albert	26-07-42	75 Sqn	NZ413334	P/O	DEVLIN Kevin John	11-09-42	75 Sqn
NZ391379	P/O	BUCKLEY Wallace Edward	21-06-42	75 Sqn	NZ412317	Sgt	DIMOCK Vallance Albert Oliver	25-10-42	75 Sqn
NZ41977	P/O	BUDGE William Finlay	6-04-42	75 Sqn	NZ414265	F/O	DIXON Maxwell Wintringham	6-12-42	115 Sqn
NZ41868	F/O	BULLOCK Derek Vaughan	21-08-42	218 Sqn	NZ401375	F/L	DOBBIN Laurence St. George	12-08-42	75 Sqn
NZ41140	Sgt	BURGESS James Michael	6-11-42	15 Sqn	NZ41980	F/O	DOBSON Charles Dudley	29-08-42	149 Sqn
NZ404478	P/O	BURNHAM Wilfred Henry	11-01-42	12 Sqn	NZ39965	Sgt	DOWNS Harry Chapman	10-01-42	82 Sqn
NZ414239	Sgt	BURROWES Thomas Bernard	4-09-42	15 OTU	NZ402172	F/S	DROMGOOLE Sydney Houston	22-04-42	75 Sqn
NZ405228	F/S	BUSSELL Henry Chaytor	29-03-42	106 Sqn	NZ402859	P/O	DUFF DFC Peter Stanley	14-09-42	16 OTU
NZ402848	Sgt	BUTLER-WILLIAMS Geoffrey Hugh			NZ404344	P/O	DUNCKLEY Raymond Harold	27-08-42	214 Sqn
			3-07-42	12 Sqn	NZ401756	P/O	EARLE John	12-03-42	75 Sqn
NZ401751	F/L	BUTT Charles Henry	4-11-42	1518 Flt	NZ405515	Sgt	EDWARDS Denis Henry	31-05-42	22 OTU
NZ412201	P/O	BYERS Robert William	27-08-42	156 Sqn	NZ411720	Sgt	ELLIOTT Max Hilton	30-09-42	149 Sqn
NZ404529	F/S	BYRNE Martin John	29-07-42	75 Sqn	NZ41887	P/O	ELLIS Alexander Leslie	16-04-42	149 Sqn
NZ402437	F/S	CAIRNS Louvain Trevor	26-07-42	75 Sqn	NZ403955	Sgt	ELLIS John	21-12-42	7 Sqn
NZ404016	Sgt	CAITCHEON Gordon Edwin	29-07-42	75 Sqn	NZ405264	Sgt	ENRIGHT Leo Daniel	21-12-42	7 Sqn
NZ412313	Sgt	CALLAGHAN Douglas	25-05-42	22 OTU	NZ413831	Sgt	ENSOR Weiland Fairfax	15-10-42	158 Sqn
NZ403940	F/S	CAMERON Gordon Russell	6-02-42	21 Sqn	NZ402989	F/O	EVANS Arthur William Smith	29-04-42	35 Sqn
NZ391857	F/S	CAMPBELL Alan	29-07-42	75 Sqn	NZ411870	Sgt	EVERETT George Walter James	9-11-42	57 Sqn
NZ411718	P/O	CARNCROSS Murray Ellis	29-07-42	75 Sqn	NZ401492	F/O	FAIRBAIRN Leonard John	17-11-42	158 Sqn
NZ403941	F/S	CARREL Noel Ernest Robertson	27-07-42	142 Sqn	NZ403571	Sgt	FALK Victor Arthur Bullecourt	26-06-42	11 OTU
NZ403425	F/O	CASEY DFC John Edwin	28-06-42	11 OTU	NZ403119	P/O	FARROW James Ralph	26-06-42	83 Sqn
NZ402981	F/S	CASKEY Robin William	12-08-42	106 Sqn	NZ404023	Sgt	FENTON James Watt	10-11-42	107 Sqn
NZ41875	P/O	CASTLING John Graham	6-01-42	19 OTU	NZ412218	Sgt	FIRTH Ellison George	13-10-42	75 Sqn
NZ392015	Sgt	CATO Malcolm Vernon	16-07-42	149 Sqn	NZ39097	P/O	FITZSIMONS Harold Douglas John		
NZ40914	F/S	CHAMBERLAIN Lloyd Montgomery						29-07-42	115 Sqn
			12-03-42	75 Sqn	NZ402454	F/S	FLEMING James Alexander	26-01-42	12 Sqn
NZ413024	F/O	CHAMBERS Frank [United Kingdom]	9-12-42	11 OTU	NZ412472	Sgt	FLOWER William Harvey	26-06-42	11 OTU
NZ41978	F/S	CHAPMAN John Wynne	4-06-42	115 Sqn	NZ41319	F/S	FOLLETT James Douglas	28-08-42	101 Sqn
NZ411369	F/S	CHAPMAN Kenneth Dudley	6-11-42	15 Sqn	NZ404631	F/S	FOSTER Claude Allan	7-11-42	83 Sqn
NZ414246	F/O	CHARTERIS Walter Ian	29-10-42	19 OTU	NZ41981	F/S	FOUNTAIN Cedric Niel	23-04-42	75 Sqn
NZ402982	F/S	CHRISTIE Arthur Stafford	21-06-42	75 Sqn	NZ41320	P/O	FOX John Joseph	1-06-42	114 Sqn
NZ414249	F/S	CLARE Cedric William	20-11-42	11 OTU	NZ411753	Sgt	FRAMPTON Laurie Albert	29-07-42	75 Sqn
NZ404894	F/S	CLARK Lloyd Denzil	23-10-42	158 Sqn	NZ414277	Sgt	FRANKLIN Benjamin Allan	16-12-42	75 Sqn
NZ404895	P/O	CLARK Mervyn Oliver	17-12-42	75 Sqn	NZ405030	F/O	FRASER Allen Armistice	21-06-42	75 Sqn
NZ402983	F/S	CLARK Terence George	16-09-42	106 Sqn	NZ403437	F/S	FRASER Myles Frederick Gordon	16-05-42	75 Sqn
NZ401753	P/O	CLIFFORD Daniel Joseph	18-01-42	142 Sqn	NZ404350	Sgt	FRIEND Ian Ignatius [Australia]	9-11-42	218 Sqn
NZ404442	P/O	CLOTHIER Henry Garfield	2-06-42	10 Sqn	NZ412322	Sgt	FULLER John Alexander	31-10-42	150 Sqn
NZ402852	P/O	COAKLEY Kenneth James	14-01-42	21 Sqn	NZ411969	Sgt	FULLER Richard John	15-10-42	11 OTU
NZ40161	Sgt	COLES Thomas Edward	7-09-42	75 Sqn	NZ402177	P/O	FULTON William John	20-05-42	12 Sqn
NZ412468	Sgt	COLLETT Henry William Amner	16-11-42	101 Sqn	NZ403599	F/S	GANDERTON John Raymond Francis		
NZ416097	Sgt	COLLINS Wilford John	6-12-42	14 OTU				2-06-42	10 Sqn
NZ412887	Sgt	CONNELLY Harry Ian Forsyth	10-10-42	149 Sqn	NZ412877	Sgt	GARDINER Kenneth Frederick	9-11-42	57 Sqn
NZ40736	P/O	COOK Bryan Manssen	24-07-42	18 Sqn	NZ403440	F/S	GARLAND John Francis	3-12-42	115 Sqn
NZ403951	F/S	COONEY Patrick John Denis	13-03-42	460 Sqn	NZ402128	P/O	GAVEGAN Jack Ralph	9-07-42	75 Sqn
NZ391697	Sgt	COPPERSMITH Raymond Patrick	26-07-42	75 Sqn	NZ401265	Sgt	GEORGE Hylton Carlyle	17-02-42	11 OTU
NZ412207	F/S	CORLETT Edmund Murray	21-11-42	214 Sqn	NZ404353	F/O	GILBERD Morris Searle	16-10-42	149 Sqn
NZ39902	W/O	COWLRICK Andrew Jack	3-06-42	7 Sqn	NZ41894	F/S	GILBERTSON John Edward	29-07-42	75 Sqn
NZ411741	Sgt	CRABTREE Ronald Hugh	17-09-42	7 Sqn	NZ404024	Sgt	GILL Adrian Harold Cooper	17-08-42	214 Sqn
NZ411064	Sgt	CRAILL David George	29-08-42	57 Sqn	NZ403362	Sgt	GILL John Trevor Vivian	4-09-42	75 Sqn
NZ405237	Sgt	CRAN Franklyn Bertram	29-03-42	75 Sqn	NZ404547	Sgt	GODDARD Harry Oldfield	17-09-42	7 Sqn
NZ405475	Sgt	CRARER Thomas Eric	29-07-42	75 Sqn	NZ405482	Sgt	GODFREY Herbert Edward	20-07-42	158 Sqn
NZ404339	Sgt	CRAWFORD Henry Varley Gibb	7-09-42	75 Sqn	NZ412225	P/O	GOODWIN Grahame Cyril Ralph	16-09-42	11 OTU
NZ411066	Sgt	CRAY Trevor Haughton	29-07-42	16 OTU	NZ39099	F/S	GOORD Stephen Bryan	10-08-42	460 Sqn
NZ40618	F/L	CRESWELL MiD Philip Henry	19-01-42	9 Sqn			[United Kingdom]		

Service No	Rank	Name	Date	Sqn
NZ413408	Sgt	GORDON Douglas Huntly	16-10-42	115 Sqn
NZ411233	Sgt	GOULD James Douglas	10-07-42	75 Sqn
NZ405483	Sgt	GOULD Robert John	24-09-42	102 Sqn
NZ411897	F/O	GOULD William Herbert	29-08-42	408 Sqn
NZ404483	Sgt	GRAHAM Raymond Edgar	10-09-42	218 Sqn
NZ405254	Sgt	GRANT Horace Llewellyn	4-09-42	75 Sqn
NZ414283	P/O	GRANT Ian Alexander	17-09-42	11 OTU
NZ405255	Sgt	GRAY James Cornwall	24-09-42	9 Sqn
NZ405484	Sgt	GRAY Wilfred John	7-08-42	158 Sqn
NZ402997	F/S	GREEN Cyril Vincent	11-08-42	75 Sqn
NZ404026	Sgt	GRENFELL Richard John	29-06-42	75 Sqn
NZ403574	F/S	GROVES Alpheus Leslie	7-09-42	75 Sqn
NZ404866	Sgt	GRUT Harvey Jennings	26-01-42	51 Sqn
NZ404867	F/O	HADEN Francis Seymour	17-11-42	11 OTU
NZ404073	Sgt	HALL James Milton	31-05-42	26 OTU
NZ403547	F/S	HAMILTON Donald Albert Stanley	2-04-42	214 Sqn
NZ41328	Sgt	HAMILTON Robert Alfred	26-01-42	51 Sqn
NZ437013	Sgt	HAMLIN Percy John Havelock	17-02-42	11 OTU
NZ412683	F/S	HANNAH Wilfred James	6-11-42	15 Sqn
NZ403788	Sgt	HARKINS Roy Gordon	25-02-42	27 OTU
NZ404028	Sgt	HARRIS Claude Joseph	29-03-42	75 Sqn
NZ413065	P/O	HARRIS Herbert Adams	10-11-42	7 Sqn
NZ402999	Sgt	HARRIS Richard James	23-04-42	75 Sqn
NZ41902	Sgt	HARVEY Edgar William	16-12-42	75 Sqn
NZ411891	Sgt	HAWKEN Everard Howard	24-03-42	1515 Flt
NZ404484	P/O	HAYES Peter [Australia]	27-08-42	156 Sqn
NZ405742	F/S	HAYNES Owen	19-08-42	61 Sqn
NZ404359	F/O	HEALD Kenneth Fenton	29-04-42	57 Sqn
NZ411075	Sgt	HEGAN John Gordon George	29-06-42	75 Sqn
NZ404361	Sgt	HENDRY Keith Alexander	29-06-42	11 OTU
NZ405266	Sgt	HENRY John Wallace	24-09-42	9 Sqn
NZ411721	Sgt	HERBERT Ronald Ernest	25-05-42	22 OTU
NZ403576	F/S	HEURTLEY John Theodore	20-06-42	15 Sqn
NZ404029	F/S	HIBELL Bert Gordon	27-02-42	77 Sqn
NZ404030	F/S	HIGGINS Robert Henry	13-04-42	15 Sqn
NZ41329	F/S	HIGGOTT Frederick Rex	24-10-42	218 Sqn
NZ404067	Sgt	HIRST Raymond John Finlay	10-07-42	75 Sqn
NZ404068	F/S	HODSELL John Herbert	15-08-42	150 Sqn
NZ403603	F/O	HODSON Nathaniel Edmund	27-07-42	57 Sqn
NZ412331	Sgt	HOGAN Denis Patrick	28-08-42	75 Sqn
NZ405274	Sgt	HOLMES Stanley	17-12-42	218 Sqn
NZ413417	Sgt	HOOD Walter Huson	29-10-42	15 Sqn
NZ404366	Sgt	HOOPER Percival James	24-07-42	207 Sqn
NZ414627	P/O	HOSKINS William Arthur	16-09-42	11 OTU
NZ402823	F/S	HOWELL Ernest Hallright	16-10-42	149 Sqn
NZ403605	P/O	HUGGETT Arthur Gordon	6-02-42	142 Sqn
NZ414293	Sgt	HUGILL Howard James	25-10-42	75 Sqn
NZ405489	Sgt	HUNT Albert John Victor	24-10-42	207 Sqn
NZ405278	Sgt	HUNT Laurence Warren	16-01-42	150 Sqn
NZ402060	F/O	HUNTER Harold Eric	16-03-42	57 Sqn
NZ411076	Sgt	HURLEY Thomas Pearse	10-09-42	11 OTU
NZ402188	F/S	HUTCHINSON Geoffrey Douglas	9-04-42	83 Sqn
NZ41914	F/S	HUTT George Alister	29-07-42	75 Sqn
NZ402189	F/S	IBBOTSON Jack Kendrick [United Kingdom]	4-02-42	21 Sqn
NZ403008	F/S	INDER Eric Charles	27-04-42	27 OTU
NZ411758	Sgt	INGLIS William Gordon Lloyd	12-08-42	75 Sqn
NZ41332	Sgt	INSKIP Jack	10-09-42	11 OTU
NZ41987	P/O	IRVINE John George	6-01-42	19 OTU
NZ405378	Sgt	IRVING Thomas Walter	15-01-42	150 Sqn
NZ412529	Sgt	IVES Sidney Horace	14-09-42	218 Sqn
NZ41333	F/O	JACOBSON Gerald Howard	17-12-42	75 Sqn
NZ401387	W/O	JANNINGS Derek Frederick Paterson	15-09-42	1484 Flt
NZ411761	Sgt	JARVIS Alfred William	6-11-42	15 Sqn
NZ411722	Sgt	JARVIS Claude Joseph Frederick	7-09-42	75 Sqn
NZ401765	F/S	JASPER John Whiteside	23-04-42	9 Sqn
NZ413077	F/O	JAY Charles Henry Ernest [United Kingdom]	9-12-42	11 OTU
NZ412885	Sgt	JENKIN Bryant Leonard McKenzie	25-11-42	207 Sqn
NZ411763	Sgt	JENNINGS George Smith	5-09-42	101 Sqn
NZ41907	F/S	JOHNS Arthur Grahame	29-07-42	75 Sqn
NZ404445	W/O	JOHNSON Edward Owen	8-07-42	19 OTU
NZ41481	Sgt	JOHNSON Henry Peter	16-07-42	149 Sqn
NZ415700	Sgt	JONES Rothesay Linton	18-11-42	21 OTU
NZ41591	Sgt	JONES Louis Arthur	27-08-42	218 Sqn
NZ411217	Sgt	JONES Rex Nigel Hugh [United Kingdom]	2-10-42	115 Sqn
NZ404540	Sgt	JONES Russell Royl Alwyn	4-06-42	207 Sqn
NZ413336	Sgt	JUDD Douglas Howard	10-09-42	75 Sqn
NZ411764	Sgt	JURY Jack Leslie	12-08-42	75 Sqn
NZ39557	F/S	KAY Thomas	5-06-42	150 Sqn
NZ405739	Sgt	KEANE James William	1-08-42	103 Sqn
NZ411765	Sgt	KEARNS Frank Ernest	28-08-42	101 Sqn
NZ411908	Sgt	KELCHER Walter Foch	11-09-42	75 Sqn
NZ403580	Sgt	KELLY Reginald Joseph Stephen	22-04-42	75 Sqn
NZ404494	Sgt	KEMP Reginald Andrew	16-02-42	77 Sqn
NZ412342	Sgt	KENDAL Christopher James	17-12-42	75 Sqn
NZ403012	F/S	KENNEDY Isaac [United Kingdom]	9-11-42	142 Sqn
NZ402874	F/S	KENNEDY John Bernard	13-02-42	455 Sqn
NZ404070	F/S	KENNEDY Maurice Young	10-04-42	144 Sqn
NZ401499	F/S	KERRISK Albert Williams	20-01-42	142 Sqn
NZ405492	Sgt	KILPATRICK Norman Robert	29-07-42	1651 CU
NZ404378	P/O	KING Douglas George	1-06-42	115 Sqn
NZ414640	F/S	KIRBY Vincent Xavier	15-10-42	11 OTU
NZ411219	Sgt	KIRKLAND Douglas James	15-10-42	21 Sqn
NZ413091	F/S	KIRKPATRICK Ernest Samuel	10-12-42	11 OTU
NZ405494	Sgt	KNIGHT Leon Gaston	9-06-42	75 Sqn
NZ403457	F/S	KNOBLOCH Reginald Eric	2-04-42	57 Sqn
NZ403458	Sgt	KRALJEVICH Mark	29-07-42	75 Sqn
NZ41540	F/S	LAMB Donald Trevor	17-09-42	7 Sqn
NZ413710	Sgt	LAMONT Charles Derrick	17-12-42	115 Sqn
NZ416122	Sgt	LAPSLEY Robert Balfour	12-12-42	12 OTU
NZ41338	Sgt	LARKINS James Beattie	23-06-42	57 Sqn
NZ404907	Sgt	LEES Reginald Sidney	27-07-42	75 Sqn
NZ403965	P/O	LELAND Patrick Henry Francis William	6-05-42	115 Sqn
NZ404384	F/S	LEWIS Jeffrey	6-05-42	7 Sqn
NZ402877	F/S	LIDDELL David Lloyd Carney	12-04-42	144 Sqn
NZ41341	Sgt	LINCOLN Lloyd John Holmes	7-04-42	61 Sqn
NZ41342	Sgt	LINCOLN Stanley Holmes	3-06-42	61 Sqn
NZ401396	P/O	LINDSAY Royal George	15-01-42	104 Sqn
NZ413438	Sgt	LLOYD John Llewellyn	15-10-42	11 OTU
NZ404908	F/O	LOGAN James Allan	10-11-42	107 Sqn
NZ404909	F/O	LONGUET Russell Stronach	15-10-42	156 Sqn
NZ412242	P/O	LONSDALE Ralph [Canada]	6-10-42	149 Sqn
NZ405290	F/O	LOWRIE John [United Kingdom]	28-08-42	49 Sqn
NZ403583	P/O	LOWTHER Peter Desmond	10-07-42	75 Sqn
NZ405497	Sgt	LUMSDEN James Flers	10-09-42	149 Sqn
NZ411912	Sgt	LUND Clarence Patrick	29-07-42	7 Sqn
NZ41920	Sgt	MACGREGOR Allan James	22-04-42	408 Sqn
NZ411919	Sgt	MACKAY Andrew Donald	22-05-42	75 Sqn
NZ404491	P/O	MACKENZIE Angus Carr	9-06-42	35 Sqn
NZ41597	Sgt	MACPHERSON MiD John Anderson	18-08-42	218 Sqn
NZ404916	F/S	MAHOOD Thomas Stanley	22-04-42	75 Sqn
NZ413102	Sgt	MANSON Thomas Irvine	17-12-42	57 Sqn
NZ404488	P/O	MARSHALL Raymond Keith	15-10-42	106 Sqn
NZ405737	Sgt	MARTIN Angus	16-10-42	149 Sqn
NZ411236	Sgt	MARTIN George Edward	10-09-42	149 Sqn
NZ405302	Sgt	MARTIN George Wilfred	2-10-42	115 Sqn
NZ412346	Sgt	MARTIN Leslie Hunter	29-10-42	115 Sqn
NZ411429	P/O	MASON Leonard Martin	29-07-42	115 Sqn
NZ403551	P/O	McALPINE Walter Duncan	17-12-42	75 Sqn

Service No	Rank	Name	Date	Unit
NZ411222	P/O	McCARTHY Arthur [United Kingdom]	5-09-42	214 Sqn
NZ401470	P/O	McCARTHY John Justin Neville	24-07-42	207 Sqn
NZ403976	P/O	McCARTHY Morris Donald Darwin	27-02-42	77 Sqn
NZ415072	Sgt	McCARTHY Robert George	16-09-42	12 OTU
NZ414646	Sgt	McCONNELL James Allison	25-10-42	75 Sqn
NZ413264	Sgt	McCORD Edward Alexander [Eire]	15-10-42	11 OTU
NZ411422	Sgt	McFARLAND Robert Louis Andrew	25-10-42	115 Sqn
NZ403465	P/O	McGREGOR John Dunlop	29-07-42	1651 CU
NZ411079	Sgt	McGREGOR Murdoch Gordon	30-06-42	75 Sqn
NZ405298	Sgt	McINTYRE Monte Alan Gray	17-12-42	101 Sqn
NZ412891	Sgt	McISAAC Alexander	28-11-42	75 Sqn
NZ40922	P/O	McKAY Ronald Victor Neal	13-04-42	15 Sqn
NZ41918	P/O	McKEEN Cyril James	24-09-42	9 Sqn
NZ404078	F/S	McKENNA Edwin Francis	18-12-42	1474 Flt
NZ404388	Sgt	McKENZIE Donald John	6-05-42	13 OTU
NZ391085	Sgt	McKENZIE Frank Edwin	9-07-42	75 Sqn
NZ404571	Sgt	McKENZIE Kenneth George	10-10-42	149 Sqn
NZ401440	P/O	McKEOWN James Day	23-06-42	61 Sqn
NZ404389	Sgt	McKILLOP Robert Hugh	16-12-42	15 Sqn
NZ411724	F/O	McLEAN Albert William	28-10-42	1651 HCU
NZ404616	Sgt	McLEAN Andrew Fraser	31-05-42	1652 CU
NZ404392	Sgt	McLEAN Sydney Stewart	17-12-42	101 Sqn
NZ403019	F/S	McMAHON Henry Thomas Owen	22-04-42	75 Sqn
NZ405539	Sgt	McMURCHY James Gordon	29-07-42	75 Sqn
NZ411083	Sgt	McNAUGHTAN Irvine Norman John	19-12-42	149 Sqn
NZ40239	F/O	McNEIL Mervyn George	1-08-42	27 OTU
NZ404912	F/S	McPHERSON Colin Valentine	26-07-42	75 Sqn
NZ402559	F/O	MEE Leo George	24-09-42	102 Sqn
NZ412252	F/O	MEREDITH James Lloyd	1-10-42	15 Sqn
NZ411768	F/S	MEREDITH Richmond Lovett	29-10-42	115 Sqn
NZ414386	Sgt	METCALFE Thomas Otto	11-09-42	75 Sqn
NZ405303	F/S	MEYER Noel Roy	25-08-42	61 Sqn
NZ404617	F/S	MILLER Donald	17-09-42	15 OTU
NZ411769	F/O	MILLS George William Alfred	7-09-42	75 Sqn
NZ41601	Sgt	MITCHELL Leonard Allen	26-06-42	11 OTU
NZ404084	Sgt	MITCHELL Norman	29-06-42	75 Sqn
NZ411924	F/S	MOLLER John Hope	1-10-42	10 Sqn
NZ411087	Sgt	MONCRIEF Ernest Francis Sydney	30-06-42	75 Sqn
NZ411432	F/S	MONK Walter Jack	30-06-42	75 Sqn
NZ403970	F/O	MONRO James Brian	26-06-42	24 OTU
NZ404085	Sgt	MOORE Francis Perrie George	1-08-42	16 OTU
NZ41928	F/S	MORGAN James Auld	24-08-42	218 Sqn
NZ411088	Sgt	MORGAN William Wynne	9-11-42	218 Sqn
NZ404987	Sgt	MORRISON Hugh	2-05-42	13 OTU
NZ404397	P/O	MORSE Noel Percy	8-04-42	57 Sqn
NZ411725	P/O	MORTON Robin William	3-07-42	18 Sqn
NZ403556	Sgt	MOSS Leonard Edward	28-08-42	15 Sqn
NZ415005	Sgt	MUNRO Thomas Fraser	10-09-42	11 OTU
NZ411927	P/O	MURDOCK Graham Edward	9-06-42	75 Sqn
NZ403585	F/S	MURPHY John William	17-09-42	158 Sqn
NZ403766	Sgt	MUTTON Wilfred George	27-04-42	27 OTU
NZ404088	F/S	NEILL Berry Arthur	2-04-42	20 OTU
NZ412476	Sgt	NELSON George	2-10-42	115 Sqn
NZ41994	F/S	NEWLOVE Cyril Charles	16-08-42	156 Sqn
NZ405309	Sgt	NEWMAN Richard Alfred William	4-09-42	75 Sqn
NZ403625	F/S	NICOL Jack Napier	16-07-42	149 Sqn
NZ411929	Sgt	NICOL Trafford McRae	23-04-42	75 Sqn
NZ413988	Sgt	OLDRIDGE Donald Stuart	25-10-42	115 Sqn
NZ404934	F/S	OLLIVER Edward Alan	18-04-42	158 Sqn
NZ403610	F/O	OPENSHAW Edward Basil Hamilton	6-06-42	10 Sqn
NZ41524	F/S	ORGAN George Geoffrey	10-02-42	138 Sqn
NZ403558	Sgt	ORME Selwyn Charles	7-11-42	83 Sqn
NZ404935	W/O	OSMAN Aubrey William	17-09-42	61 Sqn
NZ413277	Sgt	OUTEN Ernest Joseph	16-09-42	11 OTU
NZ402210	F/S	O'CONNELL Carroll Frederick	10-01-42	12 Sqn
NZ41544	Sgt	O'DOWD Albert William	9-06-42	75 Sqn
NZ414666	Sgt	O'HALLORAN Charles Ambrose	6-09-42	21 OTU
NZ41352	Sgt	O'HALLORAN William Peter	14-09-42	1651 CU
NZ413278	Sgt	O'MALLEY Michael James	17-12-42	101 Sqn
NZ413308	Sgt	O'MALLEY Walter Archibald	10-09-42	11 OTU
NZ411226	F/S	O'NEIL Ronald	9-11-42	57 Sqn
NZ411096	Sgt	O'SHEA William Clerken	29-07-42	75 Sqn
NZ411773	Sgt	O'SULLIVAN Francis William	15-10-42	149 Sqn
NZ411932	F/O	PAAPE John Mitchell	9-06-42	214 Sqn
NZ41546	Sgt	PARISH Richard John	25-06-42	11 OTU
NZ411440	P/O	PARKER Reginald Alfred Stewart	13-03-42	16 OTU
NZ403822	F/S	PARKES William Ronald	7-09-42	75 Sqn
NZ411774	Sgt	PARKINSON Alan Irwin	1-10-42	218 Sqn
NZ412518	Sgt	PARKINSON Lewis Harry	13-10-42	75 Sqn
NZ411932	P/O	PARTON William James	12-03-42	75 Sqn
NZ41490	Sgt	PARTRIDGE Frederick Stanley	16-02-42	61 Sqn
NZ404936	Sgt	PATERSON William John	2-04-42	57 Sqn
NZ403628	Sgt	PEACOCK Thomas William	1-10-42	76 Sqn
NZ411776	Sgt	PELLOW Ernest Trevor	14-09-42	218 Sqn
NZ411934	F/S	PERKS Eric	29-08-42	75 Sqn
NZ412350	Sgt	PETERSON Bernard Leslie	21-12-42	7 Sqn
NZ403985	Sgt	PIERARD Arthur Walter	27-07-42	57 Sqn
NZ402525	Sgt	PIKE Henry William	29-08-42	57 Sqn
NZ412351	Sgt	PIKE Trevor Charles Beckett	15-10-42	149 Sqn
NZ39882	Sgt	POLE Leslie Ernest	16-07-42	149 Sqn
NZ412267	P/O	POTTS Donald Norman	9-07-42	75 Sqn
NZ404095	F/S	PRICE Henry John	12-03-42	75 Sqn
NZ411777	Sgt	PULLAR Henry Welsh	17-12-42	75 Sqn
NZ402541	F/S	PULLEN Clifford George	7-08-42	7 Sqn
NZ405507	Sgt	PULLINGER David	16-08-42	44 Sqn
NZ401031	F/O	PURCIVALL DFC John William	22-09-42	460 Sqn
NZ405508	Sgt	RAMSAY William Robertson	9-06-42	75 Sqn
NZ405454	Sgt	RANDLE Douglas Haig	30-06-42	75 Sqn
NZ403987	F/S	REED Dudley Herman	20-05-42	35 Sqn
NZ404944	P/O	REENBERG John Reginald	14-02-42	12 OTU
NZ411100	Sgt	REEVES Ivan Harry	26-06-42	11 OTU
NZ411778	Sgt	REID George Ernest	2-09-42	218 Sqn
NZ412352	Sgt	RENTON Rupert Ernest	4-09-42	75 Sqn
NZ41997	P/O	RICHARDSON Frederick Burns	14-02-42	12 OTU
NZ411449	F/S	RIDDELL Robert	12-08-42	57 Sqn
NZ414680	Sgt	RIDGWAY George Francis	3-09-42	11 OTU
NZ411101	P/O	ROBERTSON Norman Bruce	27-07-42	75 Sqn
NZ413545	Sgt	ROBINSON Stephen Harry	24-03-42	1515 Flt
NZ411939	Sgt	ROGERS Kenneth Stanley	17-01-42	12 OTU
NZ391713	Sgt	ROSE George Herbert	7-09-42	75 Sqn
NZ41359	F/S	ROSS Stanley David	26-07-42	75 Sqn
NZ403768	F/S	ROWE Nelson Raymond	12-08-42	150 Sqn
NZ414344	Sgt	ROWE Norman John	10-09-42	11 OTU
NZ41361	Sgt	ROY John Charles	26-06-42	50 Sqn
NZ40209	F/S	RUSSELL Leslie Plimmer	20-05-42	35 Sqn
NZ41999	F/S	RYAN Keith Forbes	2-09-42	218 Sqn
NZ401411	F/O	RYAN Patrick Hugh	6-10-42	44 Sqn
NZ414682	Sgt	SALE Edward Desmond	6-09-42	21 OTU
NZ412593	Sgt	SAMPSON Henry Woolls	30-07-42	149 Sqn
NZ411730	Sgt	SAUL Norman Priestley [South Africa]	7-09-42	75 Sqn
NZ404620	Sgt	SAVAGE John Henry	29-07-42	75 Sqn
NZ411491	P/O	SCANSIE Milan Roy	16-06-42	1651 CU
NZ404412	W/O	SCHAW Frederick Arthur	5-10-42	102 Sqn
NZ404950	Sgt	SCHOFIELD Siddle Henry	28-07-42	107 Sqn
NZ413484	Sgt	SCOTT Alexander	3-12-42	75 Sqn
NZ401291	F/S	SCOTT Leslie McKenzie	13-03-42	12 Sqn
NZ401413	F/S	SCRAGG Reuben Acton	9-03-42	12 Sqn
NZ413897	Sgt	SHALFOON Charles John	11-10-42	75 Sqn
NZ412746	Sgt	SHARMAN George William	7-09-42	75 Sqn
NZ405513	Sgt	SHARP Richard Edwin	10-07-42	75 Sqn
NZ404414	P/O	SHEPHERD Ian James	27-07-42	75 Sqn

NZ403994	F/S	SHEPHERD Leonard Clarence	17-12-42	218 Sqn
NZ41946	P/O	SLIGO John Adam	8-05-42	57 Sqn
NZ411006	P/O	SMART Randolp Cruickshank	10-09-42	75 Sqn
NZ405331	P/O	SMEATON Wilfred Hubert	22-05-42	75 Sqn
NZ402221	F/S	SMITH Albert Ivan	16-05-42	75 Sqn
NZ403032	F/S	SMITH Glen Allen	28-08-42	15 Sqn
NZ41641	F/O	SMITH Harry Francis Burton	24-09-42	9 Sqn
NZ403040	F/L	SMITH DFM Jack Menzies	7-09-42	7 Sqn
NZ41950	P/O	SMITH Rupert John	9-06-42	75 Sqn
NZ41952	Sgt	SMITH Selwyn Clarence	25-10-42	75 Sqn
NZ41953	P/O	SMITH Trevor Harry	9-07-42	75 Sqn
NZ404960	F/S	SNOOK Ronald Vernon	26-03-42	57 Sqn
NZ411950	P/O	SPEEDY James Lyders	17-09-42	11 OTU
NZ41371	Sgt	SPENCE Charles Ronald	12-03-42	58 Sqn
NZ41552	Sgt	SPENCER Kenneth Stuart	29-07-42	1651 CU
NZ404420	P/O	SPITTAL Philip Charles	26-07-42	75 Sqn
NZ41553	Sgt	STANLEY Jack Foden	10-09-42	11 OTU
NZ404623	Sgt	STEWART Ian Gordon	29-07-42	75 Sqn
NZ405337	P/O	STEWART Jack Graham	30-07-42	61 Sqn
NZ411785	Sgt	STEWART Leslie Ian	29-07-42	75 Sqn
NZ39946	S/L	STEWART Russell Redway	6-02-42	21 Sqn
NZ403997	W/O	STIRLING DFM Colin John	26-06-42	26 OTU
NZ412362	Sgt	STOKES Wallace Frederick	17-12-42	75 Sqn
NZ413309	Sgt	STONE Noel Edward	17-10-42	15 Sqn
NZ405338	F/S	STONE Ronald Francis	30-07-42	102 Sqn
NZ413505	Sgt	STREETER Lawrence William	16-09-42	26 OTU
NZ414356	Sgt	STUART Charles Alexander	26-09-42	24 OTU
NZ412363	F/S	STUART Joseph William	27-08-42	156 Sqn
NZ412364	P/O	STUBBINGS Robert James	28-07-42	101 Sqn
NZ413282	Sgt	STYLES Ivan Raymond	15-10-42	11 OTU
NZ404567	P/O	SUCKLING Oswald William	9-03-42	150 Sqn
NZ411469	F/O	SUCKLING Russell Henry	28-08-42	44 Sqn
NZ405340	F/S	SUTHERLAND Alexander George	29-07-42	75 Sqn
NZ41631	F/S	SUTHERLAND Norman James	16-08-42	207 Sqn
NZ402223	F/L	SUTHERLAND Vernon Elton	31-12-42	16 OTU
NZ411103	Sgt	SWANN Murray	28-08-42	101 Sqn
NZ41610	Sgt	SWINDLEHURST Reginald Frederick	10-09-42	149 Sqn
NZ411104	Sgt	TABOR Adrian Oscar	29-07-42	75 Sqn
NZ411229	F/S	TAIT George Edward [Australia]	19-12-42	149 Sqn
NZ413148	Sgt	TANNER Arthur James	17-10-42	15 Sqn
NZ41611	Sgt	TATE Maurice Varey	10-09-42	218 Sqn
NZ402912	F/S	THOMPSON Harry Malfroy	25-08-42	150 Sqn
NZ41612	Sgt	THOMSON DFM Adam Haddon	9-11-42	218 Sqn
NZ40667	F/O	THOMSON DFC James Williamson	19-01-42	20 OTU
NZ413285	Sgt	TONKIN Douglas Noel	25-10-42	75 Sqn
NZ404970	Sgt	TORRANCE Maurice Allan	16-10-42	149 Sqn
NZ411473	P/O	TOTTMAN David James	7-11-42	7 Sqn
NZ411474	F/S	TOVEY John Alexander	10-12-42	138 Sqn
NZ40927	P/O	TRENGROVE Raymond Wickliffe John	21-06-42	75 Sqn
NZ411788	Sgt	TUNBRIDGE Victor Arthur	28-08-42	75 Sqn
NZ411475	Sgt	TURNER Ernest Henry	28-10-42	1651 HCU
NZ405346	F/S	URWIN Reginald William	29-10-42	115 Sqn
NZ41637	Sgt	USHER Benson	31-05-42	61 Sqn
NZ403615	P/O	VAN DADELSZEN Michael	15-01-42	10 Sqn
NZ391872	P/O	VIVIAN Patrick Aylmer	14-09-42	1654 CU
NZ404577	F/S	VOGAN George Hillary	8-04-42	57 Sqn
NZ41382	P/O	WAGSTAFF Eric Gordon	22-12-42	26 OTU
NZ411108	Sgt	WAKEMAN Hector John	18-08-42	57 Sqn
NZ412912	Sgt	WALSHE Desmond James	11-09-42	75 Sqn
NZ402000	F/S	WAPLE Eric	20-07-42	12 Sqn
NZ413162	Sgt	WARNER Kenneth John	14-09-42	115 Sqn
NZ402231	P/O	WARNOCK John Mervyn	8-04-42	22 OTU
NZ41632	Sgt	WARREN Lewis John	10-10-42	149 Sqn
NZ411110	Sgt	WARRING Robert John	12-08-42	75 Sqn
NZ405531	Sgt	WATERS Edward Ashton	23-11-42	44 Sqn
NZ411111	P/O	WATERS Laurence John Braithwaite	19-08-42	226 Sqn
NZ404847	P/O	WATKINS MiD Frank Vernon	20-12-42	156 Sqn
NZ404543	F/S	WATSON Hugh Arthur Thomas	30-06-42	7 Sqn
NZ413522	Sgt	WATTERS Ventry	13-10-42	75 Sqn
NZ403780	P/O	WEBSTER John Colin	17-10-42	61 Sqn
NZ41709	Sgt	WELCH Harold Rangi	16-12-42	75 Sqn
NZ411112	Sgt	WELLS Charles Easton	29-07-42	1651 CU
NZ41969	F/S	WELLS Stuart Daniel	30-09-42	149 Sqn
NZ411797	Sgt	WEST Frederick Robert	26-06-42	12 OTU
NZ41970	F/S	WESTERMAN Victor Kenneth	29-07-42	75 Sqn
NZ403630	Sgt	WESTGATE Arthur William	25-03-42	14 OTU
NZ411561	Sgt	WHITCOMBE William Henry	16-12-42	75 Sqn
NZ411003	F/S	WHITE Owen Beamish	24-09-42	9 Sqn
NZ41717	Sgt	WHITE William George Henry	17-12-42	75 Sqn
NZ404107	Sgt	WHITING Norman Edward	16-05-42	75 Sqn
NZ412372	Sgt	WHITWELL Hugh Clarence	10-10-42	149 Sqn
NZ40613	F/O	WHITWELL DFM Peter Coulson [United Kingdom]	7-11-42	7 Sqn
NZ405532	Sgt	WILKINSON Mervyn	25-05-42	22 OTU
NZ411230	Sgt	WILLIAMS John Charles	18-08-42	57 Sqn
NZ404977	Sgt	WILLIAMS John Syddall	25-05-42	22 OTU
NZ411487	F/S	WILLIAMSON Alan Campbell	29-07-42	115 Sqn
NZ411962	Sgt	WILMSHURST John Charles	10-07-42	75 Sqn
NZ411963	Sgt	WILSON Arthur Roy	17-01-42	12 OTU
NZ403035	F/S	WILSON Eric Glover	7-09-42	75 Sqn
NZ402475	F/L	WILSON Peter John	29-07-42	75 Sqn
NZ404438	F/S	WILSON Warwick St. George Ruxton	18-04-42	57 Sqn
NZ403631	Sgt	WILTON Stanley Lyell	26-06-42	11 OTU
NZ412373	Sgt	WINSTANLEY James Francis	27-07-42	75 Sqn
NZ412779	F/S	WISELY Bruce Alexander	20-11-42	76 Sqn
NZ404985	Sgt	WOODCOCK Roy Joffre Desmond	12-03-42	75 Sqn
NZ402449	Sgt	WOODHAM Henry William	28-02-42	75 Sqn
NZ403487	P/O	WOODROW Henry Joseph	16-01-42	214 Sqn
NZ401800	P/O	WRIGHT Lewis Alfred	10-03-42	455 Sqn
NZ411998	Sgt	WRIGHTSON Cyril Charles	22-04-42	75 Sqn
NZ403787	F/O	YATES Eric John Robert	27-07-42	142 Sqn
NZ41626	Sgt	YDE Trevor Victor	14-04-42	21 OTU
NZ41389	Sgt	YEOMAN Kenneth Harry	25-10-42	115 Sqn
NZ404629	Sgt	YOUNG Allen Norman	31-05-42	26 OTU
NZ405771	Sgt	YOUNG George Anthony	9-07-42	75 Sqn

Note

In the first volume of his outstanding research into the deaths of New Zealand airmen, Errol Martyn indicates that Sgt Hawken and Sgt Robinson, at the time of their deaths, had been attached from 15 (Pilots) Advanced Flying Unit to 1515 Beam Approach Training Flight but as both aviators are commemorated on the Roll of Honour for No.2 Group, dedicated at Ely Cathedral on Sunday the 6th of November, 1955, I have decided to include their names in the main Roll and not in the attached personnel.

Errol also makes an important observation regarding the death of F/O Blake in that although he was the captain of a 22 Operational Training Unit Wellington participating in the first of the '1,000 plan' raids, his parent unit was 20 Operational Training Unit based at Lossiemouth, where he had been serving as an instructor since completing a tour of duty shared between 103 and 150 Squadrons.

Another example of a cross-unit transfer for the Cologne raid concerns Sgts James Hall and Allen Young, both perishing in a 27 Operational Training Unit aircraft, though they were on the strength of 26 Operational Training Unit.

It is also important to note that 1942 was the worst year for Royal New Zealand Air Force casualties in respect of Bomber Command, a total of 531 deaths being recorded. Although serving with all the bomber groups, most lost their lives while posted to squadrons operating under the aegis of No.3 Group of which 75 Squadron was a prominent formation. Originally a Royal Flying Corps squadron of the Great War, 75 Squadron had reformed during the expansionist years of the late 1930s, but early in April 1940 the squadron merged with 148 Squadron and Station Headquarters Harwell to become No.15 Operational Training Unit. On the same day, the 4th, the Royal New Zealand Heavy Bomber flight based at Feltwell was elevated to squadron status as 75 (New Zealand) Squadron. In his analysis of the performance of bomber squadrons, Martin Middlebrook reports that 75 (New Zealand) Squadron flew the most sorties, not only in its parent group, but in the whole of Bomber Command, sustaining casualties second only to 115 Squadron, also of No.3 Group.*

Finally, Errol Martyn also comments on the deaths of the Lincoln brothers, Lloyd and Stanley, both of whom died while posted to 61 Squadron and both being recorded in this section, while in similar vein he reports the double tragedy that befell the parents of Denis and Norman Edwards (his details are recorded in the Royal Air Force section), a mere four days being the span of their loss on Bomber Command duties. For the O'Halloran family of Waikouaiti eight days passed between the deaths of Charles and William, both losing their lives at training formations that had been pressed into support of Main Force operations.

There are, of course, many such references to these sad occasions where more than one member of a family died while serving their country and I beg forgiveness for not mentioning every such example in this particular section.

* These statistics have been taken from the Operational Statistics section of *The Bomber Command War Diaries* by Martin Middlebrook and Chris Everitt (Viking, 1985).

The worst 24-hours in the history of the Royal New Zealand Air Force came on the night of the 28th-29th July, when the port city of Hamburg was the focus of the Command's attention; twixt dusk and dawn a total of 32 airmen perished, all bar two coming from No.3 Group squadrons and where 75 (New Zealand) Squadron bore the brunt of the deaths with 21 of its personnel lost. One more airman from this gallant air force died during this period, namely F/S Peter Masters Gawith DFM who failed to return in his Hurricane from an intruder sortie over Holland. Including the last named, who had 37 operational sorties to his credit, the 33 airmen concerned were, in the main, highly experienced with over 400 operations under their belts, F/S Alan Campbell being the veteran whose score ended on his 52nd.

POLISH AIR FORCE
personnel

P.794237	Sgt	ABRAHAM Julian	11-09-42	18 OTU
P.793752	Sgt	ARDELLI Kazimierz Jan	20-06-42	305 Sqn
P.1538	P/O	ASSMAN Ludwik Karol	6-04-42	304 Sqn
P.780935	Sgt	BABRAJ Zdzislaw	6-04-42	304 Sqn
P.1700	P/O	BACZKIEWICZ Egon	17-05-42	18 OTU
P.76826	F/L	BAK Jan	15-01-42	300 Sqn
P.780721	Sgt	BALA Eugeniusz	14-03-42	305 Sqn
P.1591	P/O	BALICKI Roman	26-06-42	18 OTU
P.783597	Sgt	BALUCKI Jozef	13-04-42	300 Sqn
P.780722	Sgt	BARTECZKO Michal	22-07-42	301 Sqn
P.0079	F/O	BARZDO Stanislaw	4-05-42	305 Sqn
P.792075	Sgt	BAY Franciszek	18-04-42	300 Sqn
P.1541	P/O	BERDYS Stefan	15-01-42	300 Sqn
P.792267	F/S	BIALY Czeslaw	6-02-42	300 Sqn
P.794993	Sgt	BIALY Lech Jozef	16-10-42	300 Sqn
P.1368	P/O	BIEGANSKI Tadeusz Jan	30-01-42	18 OTU
P.782806	Sgt	BIELEC Stanislaw	9-10-42	301 Sqn
P.783721	Sgt	BLACHOWSKI Marian	13-10-42	301 Sqn
P.781526	Sgt	BLACHOWSKI Zygfryd	5-09-42	300 Sqn
P.783942	Sgt	BLASZCZAK Kazimierz	20-06-42	300 Sqn
P.782688	Sgt	BOBER Mieczyslaw Eugeniusz	7-06-42	301 Sqn
P.1592	P/O	BOCK Harry Ludomir	27-07-42	301 Sqn
P.780855	Sgt	BOCHACZEK Antoni	27-03-42	301 Sqn
P.782812	Sgt	BOGUSIAK Jozef	17-05-42	18 OTU
P.1853	P/O	BOGUSZEWSKI Boleslaw	27-07-42	300 Sqn
P.792083	Sgt	BORECKI Boleslaw Andrzej	23-01-42	301 Sqn
P.0586	F/O	BOROWICZ Ludomir Kazimierz	9-11-42	300 Sqn
P.782481	Sgt	BOSEK Henryk Gerwazy Jozef	22-01-42	305 Sqn
P.792176	Sgt	BRILL Eugeniusz	8-11-42	18 OTU
P.783077	Sgt	BRYCH Ryszard	14-10-42	300 Sqn
P.782608	Sgt	BUJAK Wincenty	26-02-42	301 Sqn
P.792203	Sgt	CACKO Kazimierz	26-06-42	18 OTU
P.784624	Sgt	CEGLOWSKI Edward	27-02-42	305 Sqn
P.781046	Sgt	CHRZANOWSKI Gustaw	15-06-42	300 Sqn
P.792071	Sgt	CHYLEWSKI Franciszek	15-01-42	300 Sqn
P.1301	F/O	CICHOWICZ Stanislaw	7-12-42	300 Sqn
P.794200	Sgt	CIESZYNSKI-NALECZ Jan Leszek	9-11-42	300 Sqn
P.0120	F/O	CIOLEK Jakub	6-08-42	301 Sqn
P.782344	Sgt	CZAPSKI Zdzislaw	3-07-42	301 Sqn
P.780641	F/S	CZERWONKA Jozef	6-06-42	301 Sqn
P.794333	Sgt	CZOPIK Roman Stefan	19-08-42	18 OTU
P.794118	Sgt	DANIK Jan	6-06-42	301 Sqn
P.793486	Sgt	DERULSKI Zdzislaw	7-12-42	300 Sqn
P.0100	F/O	DOBROMIRSKI Krzysztof Leon	17-12-42	138 Sqn
P.792927	Sgt	DOLATA Edmund	26-02-42	301 Sqn
P.1658	P/O	DOMANSKI Ludwik	6-08-42	301 Sqn
P.1796	P/O	DRANICKI Mieczyslaw Kazimierz	14-03-42	305 Sqn
P.792600	Sgt	DROZDZIK Karol Jozef	26-02-42	301 Sqn
P.0932	F/O	DUBAS Zbigniew Jan Kazimierz	23-06-42	301 Sqn
P.782231	F/S	DUSZA Stanislaw	19-08-42	18 OTU
P.780454	Cpl	DYMEK Stanislaw	21-12-42	300 Sqn
P.780037	Sgt	DZIEKONSKI Czeslaw	20-06-42	300 Sqn
P.1717	P/O	DZIERZBICKI Lech Stanislaw	24-04-42	304 Sqn
P.780726	Sgt	ERDT Jozef	4-05-42	300 Sqn
P.1701	P/O	EUSTACHIEWICZ Kazimierz Marian	2-06-42	18 OTU
P.793780	Sgt	FATYGA Stanislaw	19-08-42	18 OTU
P.781954	Sgt	FENGER Augustyn	7-12-42	301 Sqn
P.792687	Sgt	FERENC Stefan	28-04-42	304 Sqn
P.783238	Sgt	FRANKOWSKI Antoni	6-08-42	301 Sqn
P.1034	F/O	FUGIEL Franciszek	26-02-42	301 Sqn
P.780860	Sgt	FURMANIAK Jozef	7-12-42	300 Sqn
P.782519	Cpl	GAJOSINSKI Jerzy	29-04-42	301 Sqn
P.781505	Sgt	GARBACZ Wincenty	28-04-42	304 Sqn
P.783661	Sgt	GARSTKA Stanislaw	11-01-42	304 Sqn
P.781591	Sgt	GAWLAK Feliks	28-08-42	305 Sqn
P.784359	Sgt	GEBACZKA Czeslaw	25-11-42	300 Sqn
P.1798	P/O	GIDASZEWSKI Walerian Feliks	27-02-42	305 Sqn
P.1659	P/O	GLOWACKI Adam Kazimierz	22-07-42	301 Sqn
P.1553	P/O	GLOWACKI Wincenty	3-06-42	301 Sqn
P.784073	Sgt	GOHRES Walenty	6-08-42	301 Sqn
P.792069	Sgt	GOLASZEWSKI Mieczyslaw	27-03-42	301 Sqn
P.0758	F/O	GOLCZEWSKI Aleksander Roman	27-02-42	305 Sqn
P.0739	F/O	GORECKI Jerzy	1-11-42	305 Sqn
P.780991	Sgt	GORNY Kazimierz Maciej	29-08-42	305 Sqn
P.0070	F/O	GORZENSKI Mieczyslaw	26-02-42	305 Sqn
P.783452	Sgt	GRAJNERT Dominik Marian	6-04-42	304 Sqn
P.0755	F/O	GRODZKI Alfred	7-12-42	301 Sqn
P.703902	Sgt	GROSS Jozef	20-11-42	305 Sqn
P.793004	Sgt	GROSS Stanislaw	4-05-42	305 Sqn
P.1556	P/O	GRYCZ Czeslaw	27-03-42	301 Sqn
P.782821	Sgt	GUSOWSKI Alojzy Pawel	20-06-42	305 Sqn
P.1661	P/O	HALASTRA Jan	3-06-42	301 Sqn
P.783205	Sgt	HESSE Henryk	2-10-42	18 OTU
P.792653	Sgt	HIPP Tadeusz Adolf	14-03-42	18 OTU
P.1399	W/C	HIRSZBANDT OBE DFC Robert Juliusz	2-06-42	305 Sqn
P.783646	Sgt	HORBAJCZUK Emil	27-03-42	301 Sqn

P.794285	Sgt	HOROCH Jan Wojciech	11-09-42	300 Sqn	P.783106	Sgt	LAGONSKI Jerzy	14-10-42	300 Sqn
P.782753	Sgt	HUPALO Aleksander	18-04-42	300 Sqn	P.1433	F/O	LECH Eugeniusz Marian	20-06-42	300 Sqn
P.0742	F/O	IDZIKOWSKI Zbigniew August	17-12-42	138 Sqn	P.784000	Sgt	LECH-PIEROZYNSKI Juliusz Brunon Herbert		
P.0046	F/O	JABLONSKI Jan	26-02-42	301 Sqn				26-06-42	18 OTU
P.794222	Sgt	JAKUBIEC Jozef	5-09-42	300 Sqn	P.76827	F/O	LEWALD-JEZIERSKI Norbert Andrzej Waldemar		
P.1001	F/O	JAKUBOWSKI Franciszek	27-03-42	300 Sqn				4-05-42	300 Sqn
P.1847	P/O	JANAS Stanislaw	14-10-42	300 Sqn	P.0968	F/O	LEWICKI Cezary	22-07-42	301 Sqn
P.794580	Sgt	JANEK Stanislaw	26-07-42	300 Sqn	P.783107	Sgt	LEWKOWICZ Sykstus Marian	6-06-42	301 Sqn
P.781970	F/S	JANIK Jozef	28-08-42	305 Sqn	P.1192	F/O	LIPOWCZAN Wiktor	22-07-42	301 Sqn
P.784142	Sgt	JANIK Jozef	11-04-42	304 Sqn	P.792920	Sgt	LIS Stanislaw	19-08-42	18 OTU
P.0444	F/O	JANKIEWICZ Henryk Aleksander	20-06-42	305 Sqn	P.794284	Sgt	LOZINSKI Marian Jozef	3-07-42	301 Sqn
P.0117	F/O	JANKOWIAK Wiktor	27-03-42	301 Sqn	P.781601	Sgt	LUBOJANSKI Konrad	13-04-42	300 Sqn
P.0484	F/O	JANKOWSKI Antoni	4-05-42	305 Sqn	P.1845	F/O	LUBOJEMSKI Stanislaw	20-11-42	305 Sqn
P.782335	Sgt	JANKOWSKI Wladyslaw	24-04-42	304 Sqn	P.783877	Sgt	LUGOWSKI Stanislaw	3-07-42	301 Sqn
P.1560	P/O	JAROSZYK Witold Stanislaw	27-03-42	301 Sqn	P.1054	F/O	LUKASIK Fidelis Jozef	6-06-42	301 Sqn
P.782281	Sgt	JASKIEWICZ Jozef Emil Franciszek	26-06-42	18 OTU	P.1443	P/O	MACZYNSKI Jozef	11-01-42	304 Sqn
P.76726	F/O	JEZEWSKI Konrad	20-06-42	300 Sqn	P.780189	F/S	MADEJSKI Tadeusz	30-10-42	138 Sqn
P.0933	F/O	JOSZT Kazimierz	1-11-42	305 Sqn	P.780118	Sgt	MADRACKI Czeslaw	21-04-42	138 Sqn
P.794213	Sgt	KACZMARCZYK Stanislaw	20-06-42	300 Sqn	P.0308	F/O	MALEC Franciszek Tadeusz	9-06-42	300 Sqn
P.784277	Sgt	KALICIECKI Eugeniusz Ludwik	17-05-42	18 OTU	P.780393	Sgt	MALISZEWSKI Robert Bronislaw	22-07-42	301 Sqn
P.781276	Sgt	KAPA Kazimierz Jerzy	23-06-42	301 Sqn	P.1706	P/O	MAZURKIEWICZ Michal	11-07-42	18 OTU
P.793737	Sgt	KARBOWSKI Bronislaw	21-04-42	138 Sqn	P.794275	Sgt	MELLER Jozef Alojzy	23-06-42	301 Sqn
P.794923	Sgt	KARNY Jan	15-10-42	18 OTU	P.1371	F/O	MICHALIK Waclaw Stanislaw	23-06-42	301 Sqn
P.780181	Sgt	KEDZIERSKI Stanislaw	3-07-42	301 Sqn	P.0313	F/L	MICHALOWSKI Marian Stanislaw Kostka		
P.794280	Sgt	KEMPSKI Wojciech Jerzy	18-05-42	18 OTU				9-06-42	300 Sqn
P.1967	P/O	KEPINSKI Stefan Kryspin	19-08-42	18 OTU	P.783148	Sgt	MICHALSKI Ludwik	20-06-42	300 Sqn
P.793014	Sgt	KERYLUK Julian	9-06-42	300 Sqn	P.780902	Sgt	MIELCAREK Stanislaw	20-06-42	300 Sqn
P.1447	F/O	KIWACZ Rajmund	3-06-42	301 Sqn	P.793975	F/S	MIELNIK Michal	16-10-42	300 Sqn
P.780711	F/S	KLENIEWSKI Alfred Edmund	17-12-42	138 Sqn	P.794437	Sgt	MIKOS Wlodzimierz Jerzy	26-06-42	18 OTU
P.1226	F/O	KLEWICZ Tadeusz Jozef	11-01-42	304 Sqn	P.794315	Sgt	MISTECKI Edmund Stanislaw	2-10-42	18 OTU
P.1601	F/O	KLIMCZYK Jan	18-05-42	18 OTU	P.0999	F/L	MLYNARSKI Edward Jerzy	13-04-42	304 Sqn
P.0720	F/O	KLOCEK Jan Tadeusz	29-08-42	305 Sqn	P.1156	F/O	MOSIEWICZ Waclaw	15-01-42	300 Sqn
P.782574	Sgt	KONDERAK Izydor	22-08-42	300 Sqn	P.783756	Sgt	NAJDA Roman	7-12-42	305 Sqn
P.783164	Sgt	KOREPTA Jan Stanislaw	29-08-42	305 Sqn	P.76775	F/L	NATKANSKI Zygmunt	6-04-42	304 Sqn
P.794342	Sgt	KORNAFEL Florian	15-10-42	18 OTU	P.1664	P/O	NEULINGER Stefan Jan	20-06-42	300 Sqn
P.780475	Sgt	KORZON Zbigniew	13-03-42	301 Sqn	P.784833	Sgt	NICZEWSKI Stefan	6-02-42	300 Sqn
P.781829	Sgt	KOSIOR Edmund Stanislaw	13-03-42	301 Sqn	P.1611	P/O	NIEMCZYK Maksymilian	26-06-42	18 OTU
P.781721	Sgt	KOSMALSKI Czeslaw	22-01-42	301 Sqn	P.792834	Sgt	NIEMECZEK Teofil	27-03-42	300 Sqn
P.793332	F/S	KOSTURKIEWICZ DFM Antoni	11-04-42	18 OTU	P.781661	Sgt	NIEWIADOMSKI Stanislaw	15-04-42	301 Sqn
P.0766	F/O	KOWAL Cezary	27-03-42	301 Sqn	P.792042	Sgt	NOCON Piotr	22-01-42	301 Sqn
P.792828	Sgt	KOWALAK Tadeusz	5-09-42	300 Sqn	P.794000	Sgt	NOGAJ Zygmunt	6-06-42	301 Sqn
P.0131	F/O	KOWALSKI Edward	28-04-42	304 Sqn	P.781492	Sgt	NOWAK BEM Jan Michal	22-07-42	301 Sqn
P.76772	F/O	KOZAK Jan	6-06-42	301 Sqn	P.783663	Sgt	NOWAKOWSKI Henryk	15-10-42	18 OTU
P.703029	Sgt	KOZAKIEWICZ Adam	7-12-42	300 Sqn	P.781399	Sgt	NOWICKI Boguslaw	4-05-42	300 Sqn
P.1562	P/O	KOZIEL Andrzej	26-02-42	301 Sqn	P.782245	Sgt	NOWOTARSKI Mieczyslaw	4-05-42	305 Sqn
P.784220	Sgt	KOZLOWSKI Czeslaw	30-10-42	138 Sqn	P.793334	Sgt	OBIOREK Stanislaw	11-01-42	304 Sqn
P.0625	F/O	KOZLOWSKI Wladyslaw Aleksander			P.794818	Sgt	OLES Kazimierz	11-09-42	18 OTU
			14-03-42	18 OTU	P.793829	Sgt	ORLEWSKI Jan	18-04-42	300 Sqn
P.794276	Sgt	KOZLOWSKI Zdzislaw	18-05-42	18 OTU	P.1441	F/O	ORSZA-MATYSEK Jan	18-04-42	301 Sqn
P.792679	Sgt	KOZLOWSKI Zenobiusz	4-11-42	300 Sqn	P.76681	F/O	ORZECHOWSKI Jan	27-02-42	305 Sqn
P.1206	F/O	KRASNODEBSKI Henryk	3-07-42	301 Sqn	P.1570	P/O	OSADZINSKI Alfred	6-04-42	304 Sqn
P.780831	F/S	KRENZEL Pawel Konrad	15-01-42	300 Sqn	P.784659	Sgt	OSCIAK Mieczyslaw	4-11-42	300 Sqn
P.783089	F/S	KROPACZ Jan	20-06-42	300 Sqn	P.784083	Sgt	OSOWSKI Bronislaw	1-11-42	305 Sqn
P.794444	Sgt	KRUKOWSKI Leonard	30-11-42	18 OTU	P.1230	F/O	OSTASZEWSKI Leon	24-09-42	305 Sqn
P.781174	Sgt	KUBERA Wladyslaw	17-05-42	18 OTU	P.0093	F/O	OSTASZEWSKI Stanislaw Marian	14-03-42	305 Sqn
P.792432	F/S	KUBIAK Teofil Jerzy	3-07-42	301 Sqn	P.794728	Sgt	OSTROWSKI Antoni	24-09-42	305 Sqn
P.1476	F/O	KUCZA Kazimierz	22-07-42	301 Sqn	P.1336	F/O	PAJER Piotr	13-04-42	300 Sqn
P.1724	P/O	KUDERSKI Piotr	22-07-42	301 Sqn	P.0858	F/O	PANKIEWICZ Stanislaw	17-12-42	138 Sqn
P.0115	F/L	KUJAWA Czeslaw	30-01-42	18 OTU	P.1571	P/O	PANTKOWSKI DFC Franciszek	30-10-42	138 Sqn
P.1662	P/O	KULAKOWSKI Andrzej	6-06-42	301 Sqn	P.784835	Sgt	PASICH Kazimierz	15-04-42	305 Sqn
P.0035	F/O	KUREK Janusz Augustyn Henryk	11-01-42	304 Sqn	P.793868	Sgt	PASZKOT Kazimierz	11-09-42	18 OTU
P.794272	Sgt	KUROWSKI Ludwik Tadeusz Jozef	6-08-42	301 Sqn	P.1436	F/O	PASZKOWSKI Aleksander Jan	9-06-42	300 Sqn
P.0675	F/O	KUSEK Franciszek	26-06-42	18 OTU	P.792360	Sgt	PATEK Boleslaw Kazimierz	11-01-42	304 Sqn
P.0751	F/O	KUSMIERZ Jozef Jan	18-04-42	300 Sqn	P.794053	Sgt	PAWLAK Jan	22-07-42	301 Sqn
P.0608	F/O	KWAK Jan Tadeusz	24-04-42	304 Sqn	P.793713	Sgt	PECZKOWSKI Wojciech	14-10-42	300 Sqn
P.782129	F/S	KWIECIEN Andrzej	11-04-42	304 Sqn	P.0113	F/O	PERKOWSKI Prot Jacek	13-03-42	301 Sqn
P.780881	Sgt	KWIECINSKI Jerzy	27-03-42	300 Sqn	P.1097	F/O	PESZKOWSKI Boleslaw Eugeniusz	22-07-42	301 Sqn
P.784658	Sgt	LAGODZINSKI Marian Wojciech	15-01-42	300 Sqn	P.784660	Sgt	PIATEK Stanislaw	16-10-42	300 Sqn

Ref	Rank	Name	Date	Unit
P.780342	Sgt	PIECZYNSKI Zdzislaw Stanislaw	28-04-42	304 Sqn
P.784062	Sgt	PIETROW Jerzy	27-03-42	301 Sqn
P.794347	Sgt	PILARSKI Waclaw Jozef	1-11-42	305 Sqn
P.0218	F/O	PLAWSKI Daniel	6-06-42	301 Sqn
P.784965	Sgt	PODGORSKI Kazimierz Andrzej	6-06-42	301 Sqn
P.780012	W/O	PODGORZAK Jozef	7-06-42	301 Sqn
P.793111	Sgt	POKRANT Longin	3-07-42	301 Sqn
P.782119	Sgt	POKRZYWA Rajmund Antoni	11-01-42	304 Sqn
P.794249	Sgt	POLAK Edmund	9-06-42	300 Sqn
P.1615	P/O	POLCZYK Jerzy	30-01-42	18 OTU
P.781551	Sgt	PONIATOWSKI Czeslaw	29-08-42	305 Sqn
P.780197	Sgt	PONULAK Wladyslaw	7-12-42	301 Sqn
P.782940	F/S	PORADA Franciszek Stanislaw	27-03-42	301 Sqn
P.0349	F/O	POWIERZA Stanislaw	7-06-42	301 Sqn
P.0788	F/O	PRASCHILL Stefan Leopold Alojzy	3-06-42	301 Sqn
P.783112	Sgt	PRUCHNIEWICZ Aleksander	24-09-42	305 Sqn
P.782620	Sgt	PSUJA Alfred	20-11-42	305 Sqn
P.780702	Sgt	PYTLAK Jan	28-08-42	305 Sqn
P.793030	Sgt	RADECKI Roman	6-06-42	301 Sqn
P.794046	Sgt	RAUSINSKI Zygmunt Ludwik	9-11-42	300 Sqn
P.792938	Sgt	RAWSKI Jan	9-07-42	300 Sqn
P.0088	P/O	REDA Waclaw	22-01-42	301 Sqn
P.1617	P/O	RETUR Zdzislaw	27-03-42	301 Sqn
P.0310	F/O	RODZYNKIEWICZ Ryszard Waclaw	24-09-42	305 Sqn
P.780748	Sgt	ROGOWSKI Adam	11-01-42	304 Sqn
P.0843	F/O	ROGOWSKI Andrzej	1-11-42	305 Sqn
P.782240	Sgt	ROKUS Albert August	23-01-42	301 Sqn
P.792755	Sgt	ROZDZYNSKI Aleksander	26-06-42	18 OTU
P.792577	F/S	RUDEL Andrzej	22-07-42	301 Sqn
P.794248	Sgt	RUEGER Stefan Piotr	29-08-42	305 Sqn
P.0518	F/O	RYMKIEWICZ Czeslaw	14-03-42	305 Sqn
P.1970	P/O	RYSZTOK Jan	15-10-42	18 OTU
P.1575	P/O	RZEMYK Mieczyslaw	15-04-42	301 Sqn
P.792642	Sgt	SADOWSKI Jan	30-01-42	18 OTU
P.784033	Sgt	SADURSKI Zygmunt	7-11-42	300 Sqn
P.782441	Sgt	SAMULSKI Zygmunt	4-05-42	300 Sqn
P.781127	Sgt	SANKOWSKI Alojzy	11-01-42	304 Sqn
P.793963	Sgt	SAPETA Stanislaw Ryszard	9-10-42	301 Sqn
P.792836	Sgt	SAPIEHA Florian	7-06-42	301 Sqn
P.781680	Sgt	SAPKO Boleslaw	7-12-42	300 Sqn
P.781342	Sgt	SASIN Waclaw	14-03-42	305 Sqn
P.781411	Sgt	SAWCZUK Borys Karol	11-09-42	300 Sqn
P.1620	P/O	SAWICKI Ireneusz	4-11-42	300 Sqn
P.780511	Sgt	SEDZIMIR Bronislaw Wladyslaw	2-06-42	305 Sqn
P.780916	Sgt	SEKOWSKI Tadeusz	24-09-42	305 Sqn
P.782659	Sgt	SIUDA Eugeniusz	13-03-42	301 Sqn
P.794876	Sgt	SIUDAK Wladyslaw	7-12-42	305 Sqn
P.1252	G/C	SKARZYNSKI Stanislaw Jakub	26-06-42	Lindholme
P.1671	P/O	SKORA Aleksander Kazimierz	18-05-42	18 OTU
P.781592	Sgt	SLABIKOWSKI Mieczyslaw	27-03-42	300 Sqn
P.780420	F/S	SOBKOWIAK Franciszek	30-10-42	138 Sqn
P.1256	P/O	SOBOLEWSKI Piotr	16-10-42	300 Sqn
P.780515	Sgt	SOROKO Konstanty	23-01-42	301 Sqn
P.784804	Sgt	SPORNY Antoni	29-01-42	106 Sqn
P.793105	Sgt	STACHURSKI Wladyslaw	27-03-42	300 Sqn
P.0365	F/O	STAPOR Jan	9-10-42	301 Sqn
P.780066	Sgt	STENGIERSKI Jan	14-03-42	18 OTU
P.784805	Sgt	STRAIGIS Stanley Walter	2-06-42	18 OTU
P.784864	Sgt	STRZELCZYK Wladyslaw	13-04-42	300 Sqn
P.784302	Sgt	STRZYZEWSKI Jacek	11-01-42	304 Sqn
P.793778	Sgt	SWIATKOWSKI Czeslaw	11-09-42	18 OTU
P.794273	Sgt	SWIDERSKI Marian J	20-06-42	305 Sqn
P.0869	F/O	SWITALSKI Aleksander Brunon	17-05-42	18 OTU
P.792429	Sgt	SZCZEPANSKI Stanislaw	9-10-42	301 Sqn
P.76788	F/O	SZCZUROWSKI Ryszard Zygmunt	28-04-42	304 Sqn
P.0007	F/O	SZELA Zbigniew	2-06-42	305 Sqn
P.793957	Sgt	SZLENK Eugeniusz	20-11-42	305 Sqn
P.0612	F/O	SZNIDEL Stefan	15-04-42	305 Sqn
P.0135	F/O	SZPAK Adam Szymon Stanislaw	5-09-42	300 Sqn
P.792539	LAC	SZTUBA Stanislaw Mieczyslaw	14-01-42	301 Sqn
P.0465	F/O	SZUMBARSKI Wiktor	11-09-42	18 OTU
P.793835	Sgt	SZYCHOWIAK Leon	5-09-42	300 Sqn
P.793978	Sgt	SZYKOWNY Tadeusz	7-06-42	301 Sqn
P.0300	F/O	SZYMANOWSKI Wladyslaw	22-07-42	301 Sqn
P.784051	Sgt	SZYMEN Czeslaw	16-10-42	300 Sqn
P.0439	F/O	SZYSZKOWSKI Antoni Kazimierz	20-06-42	300 Sqn
P.781546	AC1	TKACZUK Mateusz	2-08-42	18 OTU
P.784068	Sgt	TOBOLA Jan Marian	27-03-42	301 Sqn
P.782024	Sgt	TOKARZEWSKI Jan Andrzej	30-01-42	18 OTU
P.0340	F/O	TOMASZEWSKI Jozef	20-06-42	300 Sqn
P.793742	Sgt	TREUTLER Janusz	4-11-42	300 Sqn
P.781549	Sgt	TRUSZKOWSKI Janusz Piotr	15-04-42	301 Sqn
P.793782	Sgt	TULISZKA Edmund	19-08-42	18 OTU
P.1580	P/O	TURSKI Stanislaw Konrad	29-08-42	305 Sqn
P.792054	Sgt	TWARKOWSKI Zdzislaw Zygmunt	23-06-42	301 Sqn
P.794201	Sgt	ULICKI Jozef	2-06-42	305 Sqn
P.0523	F/O	URBANIAK Jan	18-04-42	300 Sqn
P.1629	P/O	USZPOLEWICZ Boleslaw	27-03-42	300 Sqn
P.1630	P/O	VEIT Wojciech	6-02-42	300 Sqn
P.76802	F/L	VOELLNAGEL Antoni Henryk	21-04-42	138 Sqn
P.792219	Sgt	WARDYNSKI Stanislaw	20-06-42	300 Sqn
P.76615	F/L	WASZKIEWICZ Stanislaw	11-09-42	300 Sqn
P.783227	Sgt	WERSCHNER Ludwik	20-11-42	305 Sqn
P.792279	Sgt	WESOLOWSKI Zygmunt	2-07-42	301 Sqn
P.1431	F/O	WIECZOREK Zygmunt	26-06-42	18 OTU
P.0341	F/O	WIELICZKO GM Kazimierz Zygmunt	2-06-42	305 Sqn
P.783363	Sgt	WIERASZKA Wladyslaw	4-05-42	305 Sqn
P.1047	F/O	WIERZBICKI Jerzy Aleksander	11-09-42	300 Sqn
P.781183	Sgt	WILCZYNSKI Zenon	14-10-42	300 Sqn
P.781191	Sgt	WILMANSKI Leon	21-04-42	138 Sqn
P.1222	F/O	WISNIEWSKI Andrzej	18-05-42	18 OTU
P.1273	F/O	WITAKOWSKI Franciszek Andrzej	6-06-42	301 Sqn
P.76627	F/O	WODZICKI DFC Mariusz	30-10-42	138 Sqn
P.76656	F/O	WOJCICKI Kazimierz Jan	25-10-42	305 Sqn
P.780095	Sgt	WOJCIECHOWSKI Mieczyslaw	21-04-42	138 Sqn
P.76650	F/L	WOJCIK DFC Jozef	14-10-42	300 Sqn
P.0043	F/L	WOJCIK Stanislaw Marian	24-04-42	304 Sqn
P.784126	Sgt	WOJTECZKO Stefan	7-07-42	301 Sqn
P.782395	Sgt	WOLSKI Stanislaw	26-06-42	18 OTU
P.0144	F/L	WOLSKI Waclaw	4-05-42	300 Sqn
P.780835	Sgt	WOZNIAK Lucjan Jan Stanislaw	24-04-42	304 Sqn
P.0355	F/O	WYBRANIEC Pawel Jan	6-06-42	301 Sqn
P.780214	Sgt	WYSOCKI Roman	17-12-42	138 Sqn
P.794336	Sgt	ZACHEL Henryk	15-10-42	18 OTU
P.792058	Sgt	ZAGORSKI Tadeusz	4-05-42	305 Sqn
P.1585	P/O	ZAJAC Jan	11-01-42	304 Sqn
P.784108	Sgt	ZAKIELARZ Edward Kazimierz	11-09-42	300 Sqn
P.0852	F/O	ZAKRZEWSKI Stefan	13-03-42	301 Sqn
P.780146	Sgt	ZALEJKO Wladyslaw	13-04-42	300 Sqn
P.784574	Sgt	ZALEWSKI Jaroslaw	3-06-42	301 Sqn
P.793239	Sgt	ZALEWSKI Leon Ignacy	9-06-42	300 Sqn
P.76830	F/O	ZAMOYSKI Zdzislaw Franciszek	15-04-42	301 Sqn
P.780216	W/O	ZAREMBA Franciszek	30-10-42	138 Sqn
P.793168	Sgt	ZAWISTOWSKI Jozef	2-06-42	305 Sqn
P.76733	F/O	ZELAZINSKI Bogumil	27-03-42	300 Sqn
P.781872	Sgt	ZELIGOWSKI Waclaw	3-06-42	301 Sqn
P.1636	P/O	ZEROMSKI Stanislaw Jozef	27-02-42	305 Sqn
P.784774	Sgt	ZIAJSKI Mieczyslaw	13-03-42	301 Sqn
P.0830	F/O	ZIELENIEWSKI Stanislaw	24-04-42	304 Sqn
P.781151	F/S	ZIELINSKI Oskar Franciszek	17-12-42	138 Sqn
P.1586	P/O	ZIEMIANSKI Kazimierz	6-04-42	304 Sqn
P.0230	F/O	ZUBRYCKI Walenty	4-11-42	300 Sqn
P.793039	F/S	ZUK Waclaw	30-10-42	138 Sqn
P.0291	F/O	ZYGMUNTOWICZ Ryszard	21-04-42	138 Sqn

Note

Further to the remarks in my summary for the loss of G/C Skarzynski's aircraft (see Volume 3, page 137), it has been brought to my attention that the dinghy was successfully launched and boarded by the four surviving members of the crew though the sea state is described as being extremely rough. It was some while before G/C Skarzynski was spotted leaving the stricken bomber and for reasons that cannot be firmly established, he emerged not from the starboard side of the cockpit but on the opposite side whereupon he took the full force of a wave and was quickly swept some distance from the Wellington. Despite the heroic efforts by those in the dinghy to steer in the direction of his cries for help, they were unable to reach him and thus perished an extremely brave and very well respected officer of the Polish Air Force.

F/O Wojcicki lost his life during the course of an enemy air raid on Torquay when bombs struck the requisitioned hotel that was being used as a hospital and in which he was a patient. He is buried in the large Polish plot at Newark. Similar to my footnote remarks at the end of the Royal New Zealand Air Force section, 1942 was the worst year for Polish Air Force casualties, a total of 354 being recorded. The majority died in the service of their national squadrons but as will be seen from the tables, more than a few perished while flying the arduous special duty missions that were part of the remit given to No.138 Squadron.

WOMEN'S AUXILIARY AIR FORCE
personnel

1696	S/O	BLAKISTON-HOUSTON Barbara Kathleen		
			16-03-42	Feltwell
450565	ACW2	CADDICK Grace	19-10-42	Stradishall
2062466	ACW2	GLOVER Ethel	1-08-42	Tempsford
2052156	ACW2	GOLDSBROUGH Nora	27-04-42	Honington
2097411	ACW2	GORMAN Margaret Taylor	25-03-42	2 Group
2058675	ACW1	ORTON Betty	11-06-42	11 OTU
2020315	ACW1	PERHAM Ivy Emily	25-08-42	Stradishall
426755	Cpl	SKINNER Marjorie Joyce	23-01-42	Watton
447215	ACW1	WHITLOCK Joan Eileen	21-01-42	8 Group
2002675	ACW2	WRIGHT Jean Dibby	8-02-42	5 Group

Note

ACW2 Gorman's entry in the Commonwealth War Graves Commission register for Godmanchester (St. Mary) Churchyard, Huntingdonshire, indicates that she was only sixteen years of age when she died. Assuming her entry is correct, then Margaret Taylor Gorman must rank as one of the youngest to die on active service in the Second World War.

Attached personnel

ROYAL AIR FORCE

61948	F/L	BATTEN Hector Austin Charles	31-05-42	CGS
621339	F/S	CONNOR Josiah Robert	31-05-42	CGS
1381469	Sgt	COX Gordon William	26-06-42	13 Sqn
923289	F/S	ENNA Peter Fini Pentland	2-06-42	13 Sqn
111953	P/O	FRITH Peter George	26-06-42	13 Sqn
787441	W/O	JAMBOR Oldrich [Czechoslovakia]	31-05-42	CGS
103511	P/O	JOHNSON David Malcolm	31-05-42	CGS
45539	F/O	LOOKER Peter Huxley	26-06-42	13 Sqn
968453	F/S	McLEAN John McKenzie [Canada]	31-05-42	CGS
1291941	Sgt	PLANT Robert Tenant	26-06-42	13 Sqn
42980	F/L	REDMAN Douglas Grant	2-06-42	13 Sqn
550766	F/S	TRIMMER Thomas Frederick	2-06-42	13 Sqn
1250069	Sgt	VINTER Henry Herbert William	26-06-42	13 Sqn

ROYAL NEW ZEALAND AIR FORCE

NZ404884	P/O	BOX Denis Grant	30-05-42	9 AOS
NZ404496	F/S	O'NEILL William George	26-06-42	13 Sqn

Note

13 Squadron Army Co-operation Command and the Central Gunnery School of Flying Training Command participated in the three '1,000 plan' raids of May and June 1942, the former being tasked for intruder missions while the latter was included in the Main Force bombing of Cologne. P/O Box had been attached to 1502 Beam Approach Training Flight, Driffield and died on his first operational sortie.

UNITED STATES ARMY AIR FORCE

–	2Lt	GRANT Boyd S.	4-07-42	226 Sqn
11019157	Cpl	KRAMAREWICZ Charles P.	4-07-42	226 Sqn
O-432079	1Lt	LOEHRL Frederick A.	4-07-42	226 Sqn
O-432081	1Lt	LYNN William O.	4-07-42	226 Sqn
O-434829	1Lt	MENTE C. R.	1-07-42	226 Sqn
–	Sgt	MURPHY William E.	1-07-42	226 Sqn
–	Capt	STRACHEN S. F.	1-07-42	226 Sqn
–	Sgt	WHITHAM Robert L.	4-07-42	226 Sqn
–	Sgt	WILLIAMS Murphy K.	4-07-42	226 Sqn
19000376	Sgt	WRIGHT James W.	4-07-42	226 Sqn

Note

All had been attached to 226 Squadron based at Swanton Morley from the recently arrived 15th Bomb Squadron. For further information concerning those who died on the 4th of July, America's Independence Day, please consult pages 243 and 244 of Michael J. F. Bowyer's indispensable history of No.2 Group. Capt Strachen, 1Lt Mente and Sgt Murphy perished in a training accident.

ARMY

179138	Capt	BUTTERWORTH Harold Macrae	11-04-42	214 Sqn
64403	Capt	MAIR Alfred Peter	26-03-42	214 Sqn
194495	2Lt	MURRAY Louis Bingham	26-02-42	7 Sqn
97866	Capt	NOEL John Cecil	13-04-42	15 Sqn
77532	Capt	ROGERS Frank Leslie	14-03-42	51 Sqn
88507	Capt	TINGLE MC Howard Grantley	2-04-42	214 Sqn
89769	Capt	WHITE Donald Roderick	24-05-42	109 Sqn
170143	Capt	WYN GRIFFITH John Frimston	28-03-42	7 Sqn

Note

In all cases the Commonwealth War Graves Commission registers show that the above were attached to the Royal Air Force. It is likely they were serving in the dual capacity of anti-aircraft and searchlight liaison officers; Capt Tingle's entry being annotated 327 Bty (6th Bn City of London Regt) Searchlight Regt. It is further observed that 2Lt Murray had been attached to 7 Squadron with effect from the 15th of December, 1941, from 12 Operational Training Unit.

CIVILIAN

–	Mr HALFORD Glynn		17-01-42
–	Mr TAGG K.		18-07-42

Note

The deaths of these two civilians are described respectively in Volume 7, page 94 and Volume 3, page 152. Both men were meteorologists, the former serving at Lichfield and the latter at Wattisham.

Postscript

Bomber Command's casualties for the year total, at least, 9,397 officers, airmen and airwomen, plus a minimum of 34 attached personnel. In the previous part I concluded the Royal Canadian Air Force section by drawing attention to the many American citizens crossing the border to enlist in the RCAF; their sacrifice in 1942 was considerable.

A high proportion of the year's casualties who perished during the course of bombing operations fell victim to the Luftwaffe's increasingly efficient night fighter arm and though force of circumstance would eventually curtail the effectiveness of the night fighter units, this would not be until almost the end of the war. Training accidents continued to take their toll of victims, while others killed on operations but in circumstances that did not witness the destruction of their aircraft (hence their exclusion from previous volumes) are here commemorated.

As has been my wont, I will close this account for 1942, with a selection of citation reports gleaned from various editions of *The London Gazette*. In the previous section, I reported the award made to a New Zealand pilot, Sgt James Allen Ward VC, remarking that such a prestigious award should receive pride of place; now I record the tributes paid to F/O Leslie Thomas Manser and F/S Rawdon Hume Middleton RAAF, both being pilots and serving with 50 Squadron and 149 Squadron respectively. F/O Manser gained his VC for his outstanding valour during the night of 30th/31st May, 1942, when Cologne was the target for the first '1,000 plan' raid of the war.'*Flying Officer Manser was captain and first pilot of a Manchester aircraft which took part in the mass raid on Cologne on the night of May 30th, 1942.*

'*As the aircraft was approaching its objective it was caught by searchlights and subjected to intense and accurate anti-aircraft fire. Flying Officer Manser held on his dangerous course and bombed the target successfully from a height of 7,000 feet.*

'*Then he set course for base. The Manchester had been damaged and was still under heavy fire. Flying Officer Manser took violent evasive action, turning and descending to under 1,000 feet. It was of no avail. The searchlights and flak followed him until the outskirts of the city were past. The aircraft was hit repeatedly and the rear gunner was wounded. The front cabin filled with smoke; the port engine was over-heating badly.*

'*Pilot and crew could all have escaped safely by parachute. Nevertheless, Flying Officer Manser, disregarding the obvious hazards, persisted in his attempt to save aircraft and crew from falling into enemy hands. He took the aircraft up to 2,000 feet. Then the port engine burst into flames. It was ten minutes before the fire was mastered, but then the engine went out of action for good, part of one wing was burnt, and the air-speed of the aircraft became dangerously low.*

'*Despite all the efforts of pilot and crew, the Manchester began to lose height. At this critical moment, Flying Officer Manser once more disdained the alternative of parachuting to safety with his crew. Instead, with grim determination, he set a new course for the nearest base, accepting for himself the prospect of almost certain death in a firm resolve to carry on to the end.*

'*Soon, the aircraft became extremely difficult to handle and, when a crash was inevitable, Flying Officer Manser ordered the crew to bale out. A sergeant handed him a parachute but he waved it away, telling the non-commissioned officer to jump at once as he could only hold the aircraft steady for a few seconds more. While the crew were descending to safety they saw the aircraft, still carrying their gallant captain, plunge to earth and burst into flames.*

'*In pressing home his attack in the face of strong opposition, in striving, against heavy odds, to bring back his aircraft and crew and, finally, when in extreme peril, thinking only of the safety of his comrades, Flying Officer Manser displayed determination and valour of the highest order.*'

How, you may wonder, was it possible for such detail to be known of this heroic flight with the crew parachuting over enemy occupied territory and Flying Officer Manser dead at the controls of his shattered bomber? Fortunately, apart from the navigator who was soon captured having landed awkwardly and, thereby, injuring himself, the others were quickly rounded up by local Belgians and, with the assistance of many brave patriots, were ushered south to cross the Pyrenees into Spain and on, eventually, to the safe haven of Gibraltar from whence they were flown back to England. Here, under close interrogation, they related the completely unselfish actions of their skipper's final operation, thus enabling the authorities to recommend he receive the nation's highest honour.

And it was a similar tale of devotion to duty, despite being grievously wounded, and a steely determination to overcome quite overwhelming odds that led to the award of the VC, again posthumously, to a young Australian, F/S Rawdon Hume Middleton. The occasion was the long haul across France and over the Alps to attack an industrial target in northern Italy, late in November, 1942.

'*Flight Sergeant Middleton was captain and first pilot of a Stirling aircraft detailed to attack the Fiat Works at Turin one night in November, 1942. Great difficulty was experienced in climbing to 12,000 feet to cross the Alps, which led to excessive consumption of fuel. So dark was the night that the mountain peaks were almost invisible.*

'*During the crossing Flight Sergeant Middleton had to decide whether to proceed or turn back, there being barely sufficient fuel for the return journey. Flares were sighted ahead and he continued his mission and even dived to 2,000 feet to identify the target, despite the difficulty of regaining height. Three flights were made over Turin at this low altitude before the target was identified. The aircraft was then subjected to fire from light anti-aircraft guns.*

'*A large hole appeared in the port main plane which made it difficult to maintain lateral control. A shell then burst in the cockpit, shattering the windscreen and wounding both pilots. A piece of shell splinter tore into the side of Flight Sergeant Middleton's face, destroying his right eye and exposing the bone over the eye. He was probably wounded also in the body or legs. The second pilot received wounds in the head and both legs which bled profusely. The wireless operator was also wounded in the leg.*

'*Flight Sergeant Middleton became unconscious and the aircraft dived to 800 feet before control was regained by the second pilot, who took the aircraft up to 1,500 feet and released the bombs. There was still light flak, some very intense, and the aircraft was hit many times. The three gunners replied continuously until the rear turret was put out of action.*

'*Flight Sergeant Middleton had now recovered consciousness and, when clear of the target, ordered the second pilot back to receive first aid. Before this was completed the latter insisted on returning to the cockpit, as the captain could see very little and could only speak with loss of blood and great pain.*

'*Course was set for base and the crew now faced an Alpine crossing and a homeward flight in a damaged aircraft, with insufficient fuel. The possibilities of abandoning the aircraft or landing in Northern France were discussed but Flight Sergeant Middleton expressed his intention of trying to make the English coast, so that his crew could leave the aircraft by parachute. Owing to his wounds and diminishing strength, he knew that, by then, he would have little or no chance of saving himself. After four hours, the French coast was reached and here the aircraft, flying at 6,000 feet, was once more engaged and hit by intense light anti-aircraft fire. Flight Sergeant Middleton was still at the controls and mustered sufficient strength to take evasive action.*

'*After crossing the Channel there was only sufficient fuel for 5 minutes flying. Flight Sergeant Middleton ordered the crew to abandon the aircraft while he flew parallel with the coast for a few* miles, after which he intended to head out to sea. Five of the crew left the aircraft safely, while two remained to assist Flight Sergeant Middleton. The aircraft crashed in the sea and the bodies of the front gunner and flight engineer were recovered the following day. Their gallant captain was apparently unable to leave the aircraft and his body has not been traced.

'Flight Sergeant Middleton was determined to attack the target regardless of the consequences and not to allow his crew to fall into enemy hands. While all the crew displayed heroism of a high order, the urge to do so came from Flight Sergeant Middleton, whose fortitude and strength of will made possible the completion of the mission. His devotion to duty in the face of overwhelming odds is unsurpassed in the annals of the Royal Air Force.'

This last citation appeared on Friday, the 15th of January, 1943, just two weeks before the sea gave up the body of this spirited Australian. Following a period of lying on a catafalque at Mildenhall, from whence he had taken off for his final sortie, F/S Middleton RAAF was buried, with full military honours, on the 5th of February, 1943, in Beck Row (St. John) Churchyard. Those from his crew who survived were also honoured, receiving DFCs or DFMs as appropriate.

The edition that bore the news of Middleton's award also recorded details of a DSO awarded to F/L William Templeton Christie DFM of 7 Squadron, a PFF pilot who gave his life in circumstances not too dissimilar to that of Middleton and, by coincidence, while attacking Turin a fortnight after the action recorded above. Hit by flak, while flying at 7,000 feet over the target area, Christie managed to steer his crippled Stirling away from Turin but was unable to gain sufficient height to make the crossing of the Alps viable. Heading south, he ordered his crew to bale out but was unable to do so himself before the Stirling crashed at Fossano. 'Since being awarded the Distinguished Flying Medal this officer has taken part in 27 operational flights. Flight Lieutenant Christie has always displayed courage and determination of a very high order, pressing home his attacks on the most heavily defended targets. On one occasion he was detailed to attack Mannheim. In the face of heavy opposition he first dropped flares and then made his attack from a very low level. He is an outstanding captain of aircraft who has consistently displayed skill and judgement of a high order, while his devotion to duty has inspired his fellow pilots.'

The DFM gained by F/L Christie had been Gazetted on Christmas Eve 1940, following a successful tour of operations with 58 Squadron. Initially, he would have flown as a second pilot to a seasoned captain before making his operational debut in charge of his own crew on the 8th/9th of September, 1940, attacking invasion barges waiting in the port of Ostend. It was not an auspicious start for the weather proved to be dreadful and of the 13 crews, drawn from three squadrons, only two were able to locate and identify the docks area. Christie was not amongst them and, furthermore, it is noted that he was obliged to forced land his Whitley on return.

My next citation offering, published on the 8th of May, 1942, is also in respect to a DSO, this time concerning F/L Peter Nixby of 214 Squadron.'One night in April, 1942, this officer was the captain of an aircraft detailed to attack a target in the Ruhr. During the operation his aircraft was subjected to heavy anti-aircraft fire whilst held in the glare of numerous searchlights. The starboard engine, the mainplane and aileron, the bomb doors and the tail plane were damaged. The navigator was dangerously wounded in the abdomen and thigh, the front gunner was injured about the eye and Flight Lieutenant Nixey himself was hit in the right arm by a shell-splinter. In the face of harassing circumstances, although deprived of the assistance of his navigator, Flight Lieutenant Nixey coolly and skilfully flew the damaged aircraft back to this country where he made a safe landing with the undercarriage retracted. This officer has completed numerous sorties and he has always displayed outstanding courage, leadership and skill.'

April, 1942, had been a torrid month for 214 Squadron, seven of their Wellingtons being lost on the 1st/2nd of the month when Hanau was their objective. Of the 42 aircrew reported missing, only one survived to sit the rest of the war out as a reluctant guest of the German prison guards. F/L Nixey, however, made a good recovery from his injuries, only to be killed in action on the 20th of June, 1942, when his Stirling (conversion to the type having taken place during April and May) was shot down by a night-fighter over Holland.

Finally, a triple citation for the award of the British Empire Medal (Military Division), published on the 29th of December, 1942, recognising the valour of F/S John Philp, Sgt George Kenneth Reardon RCAF and Sgt Louis Victor Fossleitner, all of 149 Squadron and who found themselves in very serious trouble while returning in their Stirling from operations on the 19th/20th of September, 1942. 'Flight Sergeant Philp and Sergeants Reardon and Fossleitner were captain, front gunner and navigator respectively of an aircraft which attacked Munich one night in September, 1942. On the return flight the engineer reported that there would only be sufficient spare fuel to operate for 15 minutes on arrival at base. Flight Sergeant Philp therefore obtained permission to land at a nearer airfield. When nearing the airfield, however, one of the engines failed and it was necessary to descend on to the sea off the coast. Although the aircraft was kept level, it broke in four parts on impact with the water and these three airmen, together with the wireless operator and the mid-upper gunner, were thrown into the sea. Flight Sergeant Philp, who is a strong swimmer, volunteered to swim to shore alone to get help. He abandoned this intention, however, as it was necessary to help the mid-upper gunner, and in company with Sergeant Reardon, started to swim to shore, taking the mid-upper gunner with them.

'They were picked up by a fishing boat after swimming for 3½ hours, but unfortunately the gunner was found to be dead. In the meantime, Sgt Fossleitner, although badly shaken, had volunteered to remain behind on one of the wings and support the wireless operator, whose spine was fractured. He supported him for 2½ hours, until eventually both were picked up by an Air/Sea Rescue Launch. The courage and fortitude displayed by Flight Sergeant Philp and Sergeants Reardon and Fossleitner were of the highest order.'

Tragically, as so often was the case in the grim middle years of the war, F/S Philp (now commissioned) was killed, along with his entire crew, on the 8th of December, 1942, when his Stirling crashed in Suffolk, having turned back from a minelaying sortie with technical problems. Fossleitner was, by this time, already dead, being one of seven killed when their Stirling crashed near Mildenhall while being air tested on the 10th of November. Sgt Reardon RCAF, to the best of my knowledge, survived and returned home to his native Canada.

* Please refer to my comments at the end of the Royal Canadian Air Force section and if my suspicions that an error has been made prove to be correct, then the casualty total for 1942 should read 9,284.

Part 7

Bomber Command
Roll of Honour – 1943

Any student of Bomber Command's history cannot help but observe the number of occasions when its Air Officer Commanding-in-Chief was diverted from the primary aim of bombing the industrial heartland of Nazi Germany. From the very outset of hostilities in 1939, these interruptions seemed designed to thwart the ambitions of the most industrious of commanders and for Harris, in January 1943, coming towards the end of his first full year in office, little would change. It will be recalled that Harris's priority on succeeding Sir Richard Peirse was to convince his military and political masters that he could deliver on the perceived effectiveness of his Command. This initial objective was achieved most demonstrably within six months of taking up his appointment by the heavy assaults on Cologne, Essen and Bremen, though only the first these raids is now acknowledged as being a success.

However, Harris had stamped his mark and for the better part of the last six months of 1942, he was able to concentrate on the task in hand, which was getting to grips with destroying Germany's industrial base. However, commencing in late October, he was obliged to divert his attention towards targets in northern Italy in support of *Operation Torch* and within weeks of the dawning of the New Year, he found himself drawn into committing his forces to raids on the submarine base at Lorient, and at other Brittany ports, from where Grossadmiral Karl Doenitz was despatching his U-boat packs to join battle with the Atlantic convoys. Compared to previous raids this new offensive brought about considerable destruction of the infrastructure that supported these targets and by late March, when a halt was called, Lorient and much of St. Nazaire lay in ruins, though no great material damage had been caused to the submarine pens which lay beneath many metres of protective reinforced concrete and steel.

As this ordered phase in the bombing campaign ended, another had begun and it was this offensive, pressed home with much vigour between early March and late July 1943, that Bomber Command left an indelible mark on Germany's industrial base, the Ruhr. The opening raid was launched against Essen during the night of 5th/6th March 1943, with the despatch of over 400 aircraft, including eight *Oboe*-equipped Mosquitoes, and in the wake of perfect marking the Main Force made their contribution by inflicting damage upon the Krupp factories on a scale never previously achieved. Destruction was assessed in terms of acres and reconnaissance photographs showed vast swathes of the town centre had been destroyed by the twin combination of high-explosive and incendiaries, the latter making up two-thirds of the bomb tonnage carried by the Main Force. Psychologically, this stunning assault on Essen came at a time when the German population at large was still coming to terms with the traumatic defeat inflicted by the Soviets at Stalingrad upon General Friedrich Paulus's Sixth Army, added to which was the knowledge that Rommel's once indefatigable Afrika Korps was in full retreat across the sands of North Africa. Now with the coming of spring a chill foreboding of what lay ahead settled upon those living in the major towns and cities of homeland Germany. With the strength of Bomber Command growing by the day Harris, now secure in his position at High Wycombe, was able to pursue his goal of trying to bomb Germany out of the war and with his American counterparts joining the offensive by day, he had every reason to feel confident of the final outcome.

Much has been written about the Battle of the Ruhr and it is not within the remit of this volume to comment greatly on the myriad of attacks that took place in the spring and summer of 1943. However, it is appropriate to remark on the outcome of a few of the raids that mark this period in the Command's history. All took place in the May and though it was the headline grabbing 'Dams' operation by nineteen Lancasters from the specially formed 617 Squadron, it was the visit to Dortmund on the 23rd/24th of the month that signalled to the German authorities what they might expect from future Bomber Command incursions. A total of 826 aircraft were made ready, four-fifths of this number being the four-engined 'heavies'. Mostly, the raid went smoothly; the weather over Dortmund was favourable thus enabling the Pathfinders to mark accurately and the Main Force pressed home the bombing, and with scant evidence of any serious creepback developing, vast areas of the centre, north and east of this major industrial centre were destroyed. Such success was not gained without pain with close on forty bombers failing to return and of those lost investigations by historians delving into surviving Luftwaffe records suggest that over fifty percent fell to the defending night fighters. Then, as a precursor as to what would be inflicted upon Hamburg before the summer was over, the Barmen district of Wuppertal buckled beneath a welter of heavy and accurate bombing on the night of 29th/30th May which left over 3,000 dead and near on eighty percent of the town little more than heaps of fire-blackened rubble. It was, as already hinted at in the last paragraph, a battle of great intensity which drew in equal parts upon the stamina and resolve of the bomber crews charged with having to go forth time and time again against the best defended targets in Europe and the determination of the Luftwaffe's night fighter units to inflict as crippling a loss as possible on their adversaries. Both would achieve a measure of success; the bomber squadrons pounded their objectives in even greater weight of numbers, though being subjected to very serious losses inflicted upon them by the fighters and the flak, while the defenders, bereft of a system that rarely allowed them to be stood down from operations, had to contend with a steady attrition of experienced crews. In this respect, the Luftwaffe did not have the benefit of the still-expanding Empire Air Training Scheme that enabled the Royal Air Force to replenish its losses in aircrews, no matter how severe a drubbing was being handed out.

And so the year continued. With the closing down of the Battle of the Ruhr, Harris, with support on two days from the Americans, turned his attention towards the port of Hamburg and in a series of four night raids tore the heart from this ancient city in the process of which one attack created a firestorm of hitherto unknown intensity, claiming the lives of approximately 40,000 of Hamburg's population. The ferocity of this single operation, carried out by less than 800 bombers, eclipsed all that had gone before and in the annals of bombing history would not be surpassed until the Dresden raid in 1945.

With high summer giving way to autumn and in turn the long nights of winter, Bomber Command girded its loins in readiness for the offensive that its commander-in-chief hoped would convince the German High Command that a continuation of the war from their prospective was untenable. The Battle of Berlin upon which such high aspirations hinged began on the night of the 18th/19th of November and it would continue, practically unabated, until the early spring of 1944. In total, thirty-two major night bombing operations would be mounted in this period, sixteen of these being directed at Germany's capital city. For the aircrews concerned the winter of 1943-1944 was to prove the most difficult period of the bombing campaign to date. Practically every operation flown in the four-and-a-half months of the Battle was a long-distance slog through skies thick with cloud and heavy with ice and as if the inclement weather was not enough to contend with, crews were only too aware that the Luftwaffe was dogging their progress every mile of the way. Without any shadow of a doubt, Berlin and its associated attacks; Leipzig, Magdeburg and Frankfurt, to name but a trio, came close to sapping the strength of Bomber Command and it speaks volumes for the toughness and the courage of all involved that despite the heavy losses in both men and material the aircrews stuck manfully to their task. It is also fair to recognise that like our own people in the grim days of 1940 and 1941 when London and numerous other towns across the United Kingdom were being blitzed, the German civilians were now showing that they, too, could shoulder the immense pain and heartache in witness to the death and destruction taking place around them. Many years ago, certainly before embarking on this series of books detailing the losses incurred by Bomber Command, I exchanged correspondence with Guss Lerch who, as a child, witnessed at first hand the severe attacks on the city of Frankfurt which, as he would recall, on one occasion created fires of such intentsity that those living near the river Main and who were sheltering in basements were forced to break through the dividing walls between their apartment blocks until they reached the river banks where they found partial comfort from the insufferable heat in the water. Mothers, he remembered, would constantly duck their children beneath the surface in order to give them some relief from the suffocating heat. In another attack on the city he learned of a British airman coming down by parachute to finish up on, or close to a building complex into which he entered to escape the numerous explosions that were occurring in his immediate vicinity. Soon, he found himself in a cellar with the inhabitants of the apartments and sharing in their misery until the all-clear was sounded and his subsequent arrest.

The end result of such unrelenting activity was resulting in aircrew casualties frequently running to three-figure totals after each major operation. For example, in the wake of the opening raid of the *Battle of Berlin* on the 18th/19th November 1943, and during which a sizeable force of bombers attacked the city of Mannheim, over 230 telegrams had to be sent to next of kin informing them that a husband or son was missing from air operations. In the months to follow, for delay was inevitable, similar messages brought the dread tidings that over 160 had been killed. Throughout the United Kingdom and across the span of our great Commonwealth countless families were having to contend with the mounting toll of service casualties. Unlike today there was no great sharing of collective grief; each family, large or small suffered within themselves and amongst their circle of close-knit friends. Some parents, particularly where it was the elder son, never fully came to terms with such news and thus lived out their remaining years in silent suffering.

ROYAL AIR FORCE, AUXILIARY AIR FORCE and ROYAL AIR FORCE (VOLUNTEER RESERVE) personnel

1458181	F/S	AARON VC DFM Arthur Louis	14-08-43	218 Sqn
1332230	Sgt	AARON Cyril Edgar	11-01-43	81 OTU
82184	F/L	ABBISS Leslie William	30-05-43	218 Sqn
1098896	Sgt	ABBOTT Clifford	29-04-43	75 Sqn
129038	F/L	ABBOTT Cyril Howard	22-10-43	78 Sqn
1335643	Sgt	ABEL Sydney	1-05-43	106 Sqn
1498310	Sgt	ABELL Frank	24-08-43	115 Sqn
1461188	Sgt	ABLETT John Stephen Robinson	25-06-43	102 Sqn
1433368	Sgt	ABLEWHITE Edward John	17-04-43	460 Sqn
1336188	Sgt	ABRAHAM Brian Alfred	22-06-43	90 Sqn
1035724	Sgt	ABRAHAM Charles Frederick	7-02-43	61 Sqn
1385479	Sgt	ABREY Gerald John	20-01-43	487 Sqn
1065899	Sgt	ACHESON John McFarland	25-07-43	460 Sqn
148756	P/O	ACKERLEY Douglas Baldwin	26-06-43	10 Sqn
1801770	Sgt	ACKLAND Albert	22-11-43	428 Sqn
114192	F/L	ACKLAND DFC Leslie James	26-03-43	109 Sqn
1109915	Sgt	ACKROYD Harold	27-09-43	166 Sqn
1206608	Sgt	ACLAND Woodward Russell	24-08-43	100 Sqn
638104	Sgt	ACTON-HILL Ian Rex Locke	15-07-43	158 Sqn
1483499	Sgt	ADAIR Robert	30-05-43	115 Sqn
1365001	Sgt	ADAM George Chirrey	4-02-43	90 Sqn
655432	Sgt	ADAM James Dick	29-01-43	408 Sqn
1029111	Sgt	ADAM James Green	15-04-43	431 Sqn
1340346	Sgt	ADAM John Caldwell	3-02-43	214 Sqn
124637	F/O	ADAM Kenneth Alexander	10-03-43	77 Sqn
1575169	F/S	ADAMS Dene	22-10-43	103 Sqn
146446	P/O	ADAMS Derrick Henry George	24-05-43	10 Sqn
1393765	Sgt	ADAMS Derrick John Edwin	8-10-43	9 Sqn
1339868	Sgt	ADAMS Donald Albert	9-10-43	431 Sqn
1395215	Sgt	ADAMS Frank Henry	19-12-43	138 Sqn
1336525	Sgt	ADAMS Frederick Thomas	12-06-43	158 Sqn
1078804	Sgt	ADAMS George	14-05-43	419 Sqn
54003	P/O	ADAMS DFC Gilbert Ernest	16-12-43	625 Sqn
1100855	F/S	ADAMS Howard Victor	12-03-43	1661 HCU
1814270	Sgt	ADAMS John Andrew	26-11-43	102 Sqn
1077026	Sgt	ADAMS John Gerald Patrick	25-04-43	29 OTU
1576379	Sgt	ADAMS Kenneth Arthur	6-09-43	77 Sqn
1222832	Sgt	ADAMS Kenneth Cyril Christopher	25-06-43	156 Sqn
1233375	Sgt	ADAMS Norman Ellis	16-12-43	9 Sqn
1383398	Sgt	ADAMS Percy William	9-01-43	103 Sqn
1332481	Sgt	ADAMS Peter Maurice	9-10-43	12 Sqn
1332933	F/S	ADAMS Sidney George	4-04-43	51 Sqn
656049	F/S	ADAMS Stanley Bean	22-10-43	10 Sqn
150243	P/O	ADAMS Walter Waldron	9-08-43	82 OTU
1238639	Sgt	ADAMS Wilfred	29-01-43	23 OTU
39263	S/L	ADAMSON Donald Edward William	5-01-43	20 OTU
1012730	Sgt	ADAMSON William Thompson	9-10-43	12 Sqn
131831	P/O	ADCOCK Lawrence Rockliffe	17-01-43	35 Sqn
1389800	F/S	ADDIS Harold William	3-12-43	1409 Flt
1821990	Sgt	ADDISON Hugh Alexander Stewart	26-11-43	102 Sqn
1358415	Sgt	ADDISON John Edward	3-05-43	487 Sqn
1313919	Sgt	ADDISON William Walter George	28-08-43	207 Sqn
1369466	Sgt	ADGER Andrew Syme	2-03-43	97 Sqn
655624	Sgt	ADLAM Oscar Philip Edwin Ronald John	12-02-43	427 Sqn

134701	F/O	ADLARD Ernest Edward	2-06-43	20 OTU
531481	Sgt	ADSETTS Jack	29-06-43	619 Sqn
1391419	Sgt	AGATE George Edward	6-09-43	405 Sqn
646478	Sgt	AGER Ernest Douglas	24-05-43	214 Sqn
576419	Sgt	AGER Vernon Roderick	13-04-43	101 Sqn
1285977	Sgt	AGGETT Alfred Henry Reginald	27-02-43	166 Sqn
1551188	Sgt	AGNEW Thomas Watson	10-03-43	14 OTU
975465	Sgt	AINSCOW William	2-12-43	103 Sqn
1079641	Sgt	AINSWORTH Brian Cyrus	26-05-43	101 Sqn
145718	F/O	AINSWORTH George	23-11-43	83 Sqn
49737	F/O	AINSWORTH Norman	5-05-43	101 Sqn
1338524	F/S	AINSWORTH Stanley	4-12-43	51 Sqn
1502749	Sgt	AIRD James Storey	18-02-43	9 Sqn
1301560	Sgt	AITCHISON Alexander Smith	18-02-43	158 Sqn
1367354	Sgt	AITKEN Andrew	28-05-43	51 Sqn
1322354	Sgt	AITKEN Donald Paget	23-11-43	1658 HCU
1110660	Sgt	AITKEN John [Canada]	13-06-43	50 Sqn
1051227	Sgt	AITKENHEAD William	6-11-43	138 Sqn
1007571	Sgt	AKEISTER Clifford Walter	15-06-43	44 Sqn
1536320	Sgt	AKERS Roland Graham	24-06-43	214 Sqn
1436220	Sgt	AKRILL William Eric	13-03-43	115 Sqn
136454	F/O	ALBISTON Kenneth	23-09-43	75 Sqn
532245	Sgt	ALCOCK MiD Frank Kitchener [Australia]	24-08-43	75 Sqn
120401	F/O	ALDERDICE George Frederick	26-07-43	61 Sqn
123518	F/O	ALDERSON-HILLER Jonah	26-11-43	83 Sqn
1331632	F/S	ALDERTON Peter Henry	13-05-43	61 Sqn
545761	Sgt	ALDERTON Philip William	17-12-43	103 Sqn
1334286	Sgt	ALDISS Harry Derek Gordon	17-12-43	12 Sqn
1527318	Sgt	ALDOUS George Edward	7-10-43	426 Sqn
1202459	Sgt	ALDRIDGE Eric William	3-04-43	166 Sqn
1238970	Sgt	ALEXANDER Denis William	5-03-43	12 OTU
146301	P/O	ALEXANDER DFM Felix Norman	4-10-43	97 Sqn
1361331	Sgt	ALEXANDER Henry	22-06-43	57 Sqn
1311746	Sgt	ALEXANDER Leopold Gordon	2-02-43	49 Sqn
1340990	Sgt	ALEXANDER Thomas	17-06-43	12 Sqn
1393222	Sgt	ALFORD Donald Eric	24-05-43	214 Sqn
1377990	Sgt	ALISON Walter Herbert David	13-05-43	419 Sqn
1389808	Sgt	ALLAIS Louis Paul Edwin	20-12-43	576 Sqn
1459143	Sgt	ALLAN Albert James	19-08-43	1658 HCU
523635	F/S	ALLAN Andrew	12-03-43	50 Sqn
1368090	Cpl	ALLAN Harry	29-05-43	23 OTU
124401	F/O	ALLAN Leslie Alexander	3-03-43	76 Sqn
1098639	Sgt	ALLAN Robert	19-02-43	166 Sqn
1555479	Sgt	ALLAN Robert	19-05-43	310 FTU
553739	Sgt	ALLATSON Daniel	16-09-43	617 Sqn
127293	F/O	ALLBERRY Charles Robert Cecil Austin	3-04-43	78 Sqn
159057	P/O	ALLDEN Basil Eric Edward	22-10-43	78 Sqn
1376825	Sgt	ALLEN Albert George	27-01-43	429 Sqn
936019	Sgt	ALLEN Francis Frederick	3-02-43	75 Sqn
1332207	Sgt	ALLEN Francis Henry	14-02-43	49 Sqn
1315775	Sgt	ALLEN Francis John	7-02-43	424 Sqn
144928	F/O	ALLEN Francis McIvor	29-12-43	467 Sqn
1338136	Sgt	ALLEN Frederick Thomas	12-05-43	29 OTU
1030279	Sgt	ALLEN George	10-03-43	44 Sqn
1054029	W/O	ALLEN Harold Edward	24-08-43	83 Sqn
1330670	Sgt	ALLEN Henry William	10-04-43	11 OTU
971456	W/O	ALLEN John	23-06-43	429 Sqn
1431960	Sgt	ALLEN Leonard	6-09-43	424 Sqn
1543290	Sgt	ALLEN Norman	5-07-43	10 OTU
129579	F/O	ALLEN Reginald Edward Charles	30-05-43	102 Sqn
146982	P/O	ALLEN Reginald Ellithorne	12-06-43	15 Sqn
610851	Sgt	ALLEN Robert Edward	12-05-43	20 OTU
1448941	Sgt	ALLEN Ronald Burnip	20-08-43	10 Sqn
901540	Sgt	ALLEN Ronald Sidney	3-03-43	214 Sqn
1023445	Sgt	ALLEN Stanley	18-01-43	44 Sqn
1815960	Sgt	ALLEN Vaughan Stacey	3-03-43	12 OTU
1214350	Sgt	ALLEN Vernon	28-07-43	101 Sqn
1719924	Sgt	ALLEN William	22-11-43	77 Sqn
113902	F/O	ALLIN Ronald	14-02-43	49 Sqn
1336064	Sgt	ALLISON Geoffrey Frank	22-10-43	12 Sqn
953183	Sgt	ALLISON Richard	5-05-43	101 Sqn
135683	F/O	ALLISON Robert Frederick William	28-07-43	102 Sqn
115784	S/L	ALLISON DFC William Ezekiel	28-11-43	16 OTU
144047	F/O	ALLISTON Eric Austin	4-12-43	35 Sqn
1338809	Sgt	ALLOM Sidney	29-12-43	467 Sqn
1238809	Sgt	ALLOWAY Frederick Victor George	24-05-43	166 Sqn
62267	F/L	ALLSEBROOK DSO DFC Ralf Athelsie Pole	16-09-43	617 Sqn
1151764	F/S	ALLSO Gerald Walter	2-12-43	35 Sqn
115341	F/L	ALLUM DFM Leslie James	24-11-43	7 Sqn
157072	P/O	ALLWRIGHT Ernest Frank	30-07-43	57 Sqn
132389	F/O	ALP Frederick Arthur	13-05-43	207 Sqn
1020978	Sgt	ALSOP Eric Brandreth	5-03-43	156 Sqn
1104327	Sgt	AMBLER Kenneth	1-05-43	77 Sqn
646000	Sgt	AMBRIDGE Ernest Edward Alexander	26-07-43	156 Sqn
40040	S/L	AMBROSE Benjamin Southam [Eire]	12-06-43	467 Sqn
937514	Sgt	AMBROSE Eric	23-11-43	44 Sqn
145522	P/O	AMESBURY Roy Locke	23-06-43	466 Sqn
1392604	Sgt	AMOND Kenneth Alfred	3-03-43	139 Sqn
752196	Sgt	AMOR Edward William John 'Eddy'	9-07-43	106 Sqn
138881	F/O	AMOS Cyril Rowland	31-12-43	21 OTU
1314428	Sgt	AMOS George	27-01-43	429 Sqn
1320473	Sgt	AMOS Henry Edwin	11-02-43	102 Sqn
1483128	Sgt	AMOS John	26-01-43	29 OTU
1330644	Sgt	AMOS Reginald John	8-04-43	419 Sqn
1550957	Sgt	AMOS Robert Glass	14-07-43	102 Sqn
1455709	Sgt	AMSTELL Raymond Henry	7-08-43	75 Sqn
129920	P/O	ANASTASSIADES Michael Cyriates [Cyprus]	16-04-43	156 Sqn
1399793	Sgt	ANCELL Robert Hasting [Argentina]	24-05-43	49 Sqn
143758	P/O	ANDERSEN DFC Harold Roy	17-04-43	156 Sqn
1347713	Sgt	ANDERSON Adam	21-04-43	49 Sqn
1557295	Sgt	ANDERSON Alexander McNeil	20-12-43	158 Sqn
955870	Sgt	ANDERSON Charles Basil	28-05-43	77 Sqn
52024	P/O	ANDERSON Cyril Thorpe	23-09-43	49 Sqn
129172	F/O	ANDERSON David James	30-07-43	35 Sqn
132958	F/O	ANDERSON Francis Victor	2-10-43	5 Group
626653	Sgt	ANDERSON Frederick	12-06-43	12 Sqn
573205	Sgt	ANDERSON George Henry	21-01-43	103 Sqn
1435918	Sgt	ANDERSON Harry	28-05-43	76 Sqn
157131	P/O	ANDERSON James	4-12-43	405 Sqn
656484	Sgt	ANDERSON James John	12-06-43	51 Sqn
1559088	Sgt	ANDERSON John	23-06-43	30 OTU
1553367	Sgt	ANDERSON John McIntosh	4-11-43	12 Sqn
127890	F/L	ANDERSON John Thomas	20-10-43	115 Sqn
1585397	Sgt	ANDERSON John Winton	5-12-43	101 Sqn
942664	Sgt	ANDERSON Robert	27-03-43	214 Sqn
1561599	Sgt	ANDERSON Ronald Morrison	30-05-43	460 Sqn
572444	Sgt	ANDERSON Stewart McKenzie	15-01-43	161 Sqn
1348529	Sgt	ANDERSON Thomas Johnstone	17-02-43	14 OTU
1219022	Sgt	ANDERSON Walter	23-06-43	78 Sqn
156592	P/O	ANDERSON DFC William	23-11-43	156 Sqn
966497	Sgt	ANDERSON William	22-06-43	83 Sqn
1431266	Sgt	ANDERTON James Henry	23-09-43	15 Sqn
1203309	Sgt	ANDERTON James Joseph	12-06-43	83 Sqn
62315	F/L	ANDERTON John Theodore	23-08-43	100 Sqn
1451460	Sgt	ANDERTON John Thomas	11-06-43	22 OTU
115930	S/L	ANDREW DFC Charles Frederick	30-07-43	35 Sqn
645577	Sgt	ANDREW Denys	30-03-43	196 Sqn
1335131	Sgt	ANDREW Douglas Seymour	11-04-43	115 Sqn
1307153	Sgt	ANDREW Edward Slaven	9-10-43	51 Sqn
1365392	Sgt	ANDREW Eric James	5-04-43	21 Sqn
1042366	Sgt	ANDREW Jack	15-02-43	28 OTU
1332841	Sgt	ANDREWS Albert Stanley	22-06-43	90 Sqn
1562044	Sgt	ANDREWS Albert Victor	26-09-43	24 OTU
1319131	Sgt	ANDREWS Edgar James	3-10-43	103 Sqn

1376955	Sgt	ANDREWS Francis Bernard		17-01-43	61 Sqn	1316463	Sgt	ASHDOWN Herbert Ivor	15-06-43	9 Sqn
134073	F/O	ANDREWS Frank George		20-10-43	115 Sqn	657089	Sgt	ASHDOWN Leslie Edward	11-03-43	158 Sqn
634968	Sgt	ANDREWS James Samuel		13-05-43	75 Sqn	1320551	Sgt	ASHDOWN Michael Henry Charles	26-07-43	75 Sqn
155491	P/O	ANDREWS Peter Ronald		22-10-43	100 Sqn	656235	F/S	ASHDOWN Richard	26-02-43	1651 HCU
1263093	Sgt	ANDREWS Reginald Frederick		16-08-43	75 Sqn	1337699	Sgt	ASHLEY Terrance Claude	19-08-43	1658 HCU
651327	Sgt	ANDREWS William		12-03-43	103 Sqn	1337269	Sgt	ASHMAN Frederick Edward	26-11-43	49 Sqn
87066	S/L	ANEKSTEIN DFC Cyril		31-08-43	7 Sqn	138796	F/O	ASHMAN Graham Leslie	2-12-43	106 Sqn
1439554	Sgt	ANGELL Dennis Walter		29-10-43	97 Sqn	1578202	Sgt	ASHMORE Kenneth	14-08-43	19 OTU
148401	P/O	ANGELL Leonard Arthur Charles		22-06-43	83 Sqn	148442	P/O	ASHPLANT CGM George	25-07-43	166 Sqn
1385016	Sgt	ANGUS Charles William		16-12-43	466 Sqn	1399659	Sgt	ASHTON Cyril James	22-11-43	10 Sqn
1387376	Sgt	ANGUS Jack Norman		12-06-43	78 Sqn	1609829	Sgt	ASHTON Derek Ellis	7-10-43	149 Sqn
1386110	Sgt	ANGWIN Gordon Arthur		15-08-43	61 Sqn	1394127	Sgt	ASHTON Herbert George	24-05-43	10 Sqn
1390280	Sgt	ANSELL Albert Victor		1-05-43	57 Sqn	41814	F/L	ASHTON Ronald Hugh [Eire]	29-04-43	12 Sqn
1472439	Sgt	ANSELL Horace George		17-08-43	138 Sqn	1870675	Sgt	ASHWIN Harold James Bowen	14-09-43	115 Sqn
126831	S/L	ANSET DFC Douglas Campbell		22-11-43	156 Sqn	1529817	Sgt	ASHWORTH Alan	3-08-43	75 Sqn
1183277	Sgt	ANSLEY Dennis		28-03-43	419 Sqn	124708	F/O	ASHWORTH Charles Henry	29-06-43	431 Sqn
1187326	Sgt	ANTCLIFFE William		24-05-43	27 OTU	1697462	Sgt	ASHWORTH Denys	26-11-43	7 Sqn
1315996	Sgt	ANTHONY Daniel Thomas		11-04-43	75 Sqn	533104	Sgt	ASHWORTH Leslie	23-06-43	83 Sqn
124745	F/O	ANTHONY Thomas Henry		27-01-43	57 Sqn	156554	P/O	ASHWORTH William Storey	9-07-43	49 Sqn
1314645	Sgt	APLIN William Gilbert John		30-03-43	429 Sqn	1477972	Sgt	ASKEW Raymond	16-12-43	75 Sqn
1337474	Sgt	APPERLEY Norman Hubert		4-07-43	431 Sqn	1535621	Sgt	ASKEW Robert	10-06-43	428 Sqn
1334568	Sgt	APPLEGARTH Henry		31-03-43	13 OTU	936478	Sgt	ASKHAM Clarence	13-05-43	156 Sqn
1101248	F/S	APPLETON John		9-04-43	76 Sqn	989186	Sgt	ASKWITH Robert	24-08-43	78 Sqn
1005599	Sgt	APPLETON Robert Mitchell		2-10-43	207 Sqn	1236891	Sgt	ASPDEN Ernest Joseph	30-03-43	431 Sqn
1604813	Sgt	APPLEYARD Donald Robert Cox		29-12-43	10 Sqn	531185	Sgt	ASPDEN James Henry	18-04-43	138 Sqn
1332097	Sgt	ARCH Percy		31-08-43	100 Sqn	1336697	W/O	ASPDEN Leonard Wilson	28-08-43	12 Sqn
1287148	F/S	ARCHER Arthur Dorrien		2-10-43	207 Sqn	60283	F/L	ASTELL DFC William	17-05-43	617 Sqn
658103	Sgt	ARCHER Donald William McGlashan		3-08-43	35 Sqn	1675694	Sgt	ASTIN Alan	6-09-43	10 Sqn
591125	F/S	ARCHER Kenneth		26-07-43	103 Sqn	130527	P/O	ASTIN Herbert Whitaker	2-03-43	115 Sqn
1382654	Sgt	ARCHER Ralph Edgar		29-06-43	76 Sqn	1430634	Sgt	ASTLE Charles Wilson	24-05-43	20 OTU
641651	Sgt	ARCHER Victor Harry		23-05-43	214 Sqn	1209308	Sgt	ASTON James Carleton	3-04-43	83 Sqn
1551096	Sgt	ARCHIBALD John		13-07-43	156 Sqn	1127674	F/S	ASTON DFM John Edward Griffiths	27-09-43	103 Sqn
1344176	Sgt	ARCHIBALD William		27-11-43	619 Sqn	1394397	Sgt	ASTON Maurice Robert	25-06-43	12 Sqn
125650	F/O	ARCHIBALD William Alexander McLean		14-02-43	15 Sqn	118570	F/O	ASTROSKY Peter Clyde	3-02-43	218 Sqn
						1436421	Sgt	ATHA John Leonard	28-05-43	158 Sqn
1379537	Sgt	ARDRON Walter Frederick		3-08-43	61 Sqn	1147597	F/S	ATHEY Stanley Tallintire	20-10-43	166 Sqn
1389316	F/S	ARGENT Ronald Jack		4-12-43	102 Sqn	1215470	Sgt	ATKIN James Sidney	17-01-43	83 Sqn
1293850	Sgt	ARGENT Sidney John		10-04-43	9 Sqn	1318855	Sgt	ATKINS Eric	4-02-43	57 Sqn
1288844	Sgt	ARLETT George William		3-12-43	619 Sqn	749747	Sgt	ATKINS John Frederick	29-04-43	196 Sqn
151047	F/O	ARLISS Frank George		8-10-43	9 Sqn	1317866	Sgt	ATKINS Oswald Morgan	18-08-43	100 Sqn
624543	Sgt	ARLOW James Henry [USA]		22-06-43	44 Sqn	1815273	Sgt	ATKINS Raymond	16-12-43	426 Sqn
1220830	Sgt	ARMER George William		2-03-43	9 Sqn	1672429	Sgt	ATKINSON Donald John	28-08-43	156 Sqn
1561872	Sgt	ARMET Ian George		28-07-43	106 Sqn	149561	P/O	ATKINSON Edward Smith	24-11-43	1656 HCU
1434609	Sgt	ARMITAGE Douglas		25-06-43	75 Sqn	1454621	Sgt	ATKINSON Edwin	29-09-43	17 OTU
1014935	Sgt	ARMITAGE John Douglas		9-04-43	76 Sqn	1485104	F/S	ATKINSON George Addison	23-11-43	214 Sqn
138796	P/P	ARMSTRONG Chester		14-07-43	115 Sqn	47360	F/L	ATKINSON Herbert Philipson	1-05-43	405 Sqn
1380542	Sgt	ARMSTRONG John Hubert		15-06-43	44 Sqn	1391253	Sgt	ATKINSON Jack Holder	2-01-43	1658 HCU
74586	F/O	ARMSTRONG John Robert		30-03-43	77 Sqn	1017417	Sgt	ATKINSON John	22-06-43	149 Sqn
134072	P/O	ARMSTRONG Thomas		5-05-43	57 Sqn	1052661	Sgt	ATKINSON John Bruce	23-09-43	50 Sqn
1390997	Sgt	ARMSWORTH Ronald George		4-07-43	214 Sqn	52640	P/O	ATKINSON Joseph Henry	25-05-43	180 Sqn
1393146	Sgt	ARNOLD Ernest Arthur		20-02-43	90 Sqn	1500580	Sgt	ATKINSON Maurice	31-08-43	207 Sqn
909128	Sgt	ARNOLD James Peter		7-09-43	76 Sqn	1266030	Sgt	ATKINSON Thomas Martin	26-06-43	466 Sqn
155801	P/O	ARNOTT Alfred Percy		1-09-43	158 Sqn	1337107	Sgt	AUDLEY Denis James	30-07-43	51 Sqn
1333984	Sgt	ARNOTT Patrick		25-05-43	15 Sqn	1576642	Sgt	AUDLEY Dennis Sydney	3-09-43	1661 HCU
1514783	Sgt	ARROWSMITH John Critchley		12-11-43	102 Sqn	134681	P/O	AULD John	27-03-43	10 OTU
1256391	F/S	ARTER Albert Ernest		24-08-43	35 Sqn	134675	F/O	AULT Roy Elkington	22-10-43	166 Sqn
50778	P/O	ARTHUR Douglas Invicta		12-03-43	100 Sqn	1333889	F/S	AUSTEN Frank John	23-09-43	57 Sqn
1394300	Sgt	ARTHUR Jackson Dunbar [Grenada]		17-09-43	10 OTU	710101	Sgt	AUSTIN Frederick Hugh [Rhodesia]	4-04-43	51 Sqn
1551651	Sgt	ARTHUR Stanley		16-07-43	10 Sqn	948573	Sgt	AUSTIN George Frederick	2-10-43	51 Sqn
1371842	Sgt	ARTHUR William George		25-05-43	427 Sqn	1390546	Sgt	AUSTIN George Henry	18-11-43	622 Sqn
613886	Sgt	ARTHURS Michael Raymond Jack		17-06-43	1656 HCU	1580167	Sgt	AUSTIN Harry	18-10-43	44 Sqn
1241805	Sgt	ASBURY Reginald Arthur		8-04-43	44 Sqn	1331903	Sgt	AUSTIN Horace William	24-05-43	199 Sqn
530930	Sgt	ASH Arthur Frederick		3-03-43	12 OTU	109358	F/O	AUSTIN John	24-08-43	78 Sqn
128583	F/O	ASHBURNER Norman		24-08-43	12 Sqn	1319425	Sgt	AUSTIN Kenneth Henry	7-02-43	30 OTU
1313797	Sgt	ASHBY Frederick Charles		25-06-43	427 Sqn	1516660	Sgt	AUSTIN Leslie	12-11-43	78 Sqn
1699995	Sgt	ASHCROFT Bernard Patrick		27-04-43	156 Sqn	1087065	Sgt	AUSTIN Leslie Ernest	18-01-43	12 Sqn
126517	F/O	ASHCROFT Eric Richard Victor		1-04-43	103 Sqn	591214	F/S	AUSTIN DFM William Frank	1-03-43	103 Sqn
1512556	Sgt	ASHCROFT John Herbert		25-11-43	26 OTU	778987	Sgt	AUSTIN William Henry [Rhodesia]	23-08-43	103 Sqn
999214	Sgt	ASHCROFT Thomas Alfred		9-10-43	431 Sqn	1457372	Sgt	AUSTIN William Stanley	16-12-43	1661 HCU

Service #	Rank	Name	Date	Sqn/Unit
1337605	Sgt	AUSTIN William Thomas	9-10-43	51 Sqn
1336690	Sgt	AVENT John William	14-05-43	10 Sqn
1030271	Sgt	AVERY Cyril	1-03-43	51 Sqn
1063033	Sgt	AVERY John	5-05-43	7 Sqn
1336681	Sgt	AVERY Reginald Arthur Charles	12-06-43	12 Sqn
1323894	F/S	AVIS Roy Frederick	24-08-43	78 Sqn
1335145	Sgt	AXBY Leslie Frederick	30-01-43	466 Sqn
626794	Sgt	AXTELL DFM Dennis	17-04-43	51 Sqn
1620118	Sgt	AXUP George Arthur	18-01-43	97 Sqn
1377776	Sgt	AYERST Francis Donovan	29-06-43	12 Sqn
657684	Sgt	AYLARD Arthur Charles	17-06-43	12 Sqn
129173	F/O	AYLING Kenneth Arthur Charles	6-09-43	196 Sqn
1334489	Sgt	AYRES George Alfred	13-06-43	57 Sqn
1314327	Sgt	AYRES George William	29-01-43	21 OTU
656967	Sgt	AYRES Leonard Edward	3-04-43	15 OTU
1333632	F/S	AYRES Richard Joseph	28-05-43	35 Sqn
84333	F/L	AYSCOUGH Peter Edwin	13-02-43	158 Sqn
1338704	Sgt	BABER Stanley Ernest	31-08-43	166 Sqn
658123	Sgt	BABINGTON Raymond Vivian	14-01-43	466 Sqn
50038	P/O	BABINGTON-BROWNE Kenneth Douglas	8-08-43	61 Sqn
1393720	Sgt	BACKHOUSE Francis Langhorne [Chile]	28-07-43	106 Sqn
1029538	Sgt	BACKLER Alec Frederick	4-07-43	9 Sqn
141331	P/O	BACKLOG Cyril Peter	23-08-43	207 Sqn
1320220	Sgt	BACON Basil Albert	13-05-43	90 Sqn
1383765	Sgt	BACON James Edward	20-10-43	97 Sqn
1386461	Sgt	BACON John Andrew	13-08-43	77 Sqn
1393865	Sgt	BACON Leonard William	7-07-43	21 OTU
1392379	Sgt	BACON Peter Frederick	3-03-43	460 Sqn
1612703	Sgt	BACON Richard Ernest Charles	24-11-43	1658 HCU
1239676	Sgt	BADCOCK Richard	28-01-43	14 OTU
155766	P/O	BADGE Horace	12-07-43	207 Sqn
1436522	Sgt	BAGGALEY Robert Frederick Fletcher	24-05-43	10 Sqn
44775	S/L	BAGGULEY DFC Robert Beck	9-03-43	139 Sqn
1236213	Sgt	BAGLEY Arthur Eddie	2-04-43	57 Sqn
996788	Sgt	BAGLEY John Watts	21-04-43	57 Sqn
1237237	F/S	BAGLEY Ronald William	7-08-43	28 OTU
636153	Sgt	BAILES Robert James	15-06-43	103 Sqn
1081675	Sgt	BAILEY Alfred	29-06-43	10 Sqn
1039496	Sgt	BAILEY Arthur	8-10-43	9 Sqn
143799	P/O	BAILEY Arthur Wilfred	7-09-43	1658 HCU
1231732	Sgt	BAILEY Clifford John	9-10-43	51 Sqn
1385068	Sgt	BAILEY Christopher Albert	28-07-43	102 Sqn
1395673	Sgt	BAILEY Denis Reginald	19-11-43	90 Sqn
937025	Sgt	BAILEY Douglas	28-08-43	83 Sqn
1235308	Sgt	BAILEY Eric	24-11-43	460 Sqn
1448910	LAC	BAILEY Frederick John	26-11-43	83 Sqn
1236325	Sgt	BAILEY George Irvine	25-07-43	103 Sqn
1431774	Sgt	BAILEY James	26-06-43	166 Sqn
48551	F/O	BAILEY DFC John Brian Godfrey	22-06-43	431 Sqn
1575646	Sgt	BAILEY John Francis Albury	3-10-43	77 Sqn
1312380	Sgt	BAILEY Peter	3-03-43	103 Sqn
1104712	Sgt	BAILEY Ronald	20-02-43	467 Sqn
1332267	Sgt	BAILEY Sydney Arthur James	26-05-43	12 Sqn
1412311	Sgt	BAILEY Thomas	8-04-43	1654 Sqn
1440585	Sgt	BAILEY Wilfred	9-07-43	106 Sqn
136031	F/O	BAILEY Wilfred Edward	11-08-43	158 Sqn
155786	P/O	BAILIE Cyril Philip	3-08-43	75 Sqn
547782	Sgt	BAILY John Herbert	3-08-43	115 Sqn
658930	Sgt	BAIN Andrew	24-08-43	75 Sqn
1347034	Sgt	BAIN Frederick James Ross	23-06-43	78 Sqn
1148681	Sgt	BAINBRIDGE Roland Barnsley	22-11-43	102 Sqn
651014	F/S	BAINBRIDGE Thomas James	12-06-43	7 Sqn
1600016	Sgt	BAIRD Donald Robert	4-07-43	12 Sqn
1562177	Sgt	BAIRD Robert 'Ronnie'	7-08-43	620 Sqn
70789	S/L	BAIRD The Hon. Robert Alexander Graville	14-07-43	115 Sqn
1585825	Sgt	BAKER Albert Ronald	4-04-43	156 Sqn
952283	Sgt	BAKER Arthur Vernon	26-11-43	115 Sqn
576634	Sgt	BAKER Charles Patrick	30-05-43	419 Sqn
169107	P/O	BAKER Donald	16-12-43	625 Sqn
1177976	Sgt	BAKER Edward Gordon	26-06-43	115 Sqn
578114	Sgt	BAKER Eric Gordon Fay Beaumont	28-05-43	115 Sqn
100585	F/L	BAKER Ernest Thomas	18-11-43	35 Sqn
156607	P/O	BAKER Frederick John	4-12-43	51 Sqn
1380947	F/S	BAKER Frederick William	11-01-43	12 Sqn
570635	Sgt	BAKER George William Frederick	30-03-43	106 Sqn
657594	Sgt	BAKER Gilbert Campbell	30-01-43	466 Sqn
1699340	Sgt	BAKER Herbert	13-06-43	76 Sqn
1652940	Sgt	BAKER Herbert Charles	18-08-43	419 Sqn
1395957	Sgt	BAKER John Alexander	4-10-43	100 Sqn
144360	P/O	BAKER DFC Robert Arthur	20-09-43	50 Sqn
128588	F/O	BAKER Robert Edward	9-10-43	431 Sqn
1318696	Sgt	BAKER Ronald Dennis	5-03-43	466 Sqn
1286156	Sgt	BAKER Ronald Valentine	7-02-43	199 Sqn
1211171	Sgt	BAKER Thomas	20-09-43	1485 Flt
149084	P/O	BAKER Valentine	11-08-43	97 Sqn
156698	P/O	BAKER Vernon Reginald	6-09-43	78 Sqn
658156	F/S	BAKER Victor James	28-10-43	1656 HCU
932842	Sgt	BAKER Wilfred Eric	4-02-43	106 Sqn
642079	W/O	BAKER DFM William Charles	24-08-43	83 Sqn
1334345	Sgt	BAKER William James	3-10-43	467 Sqn
1195460	Sgt	BAKEWELL James Henry	17-01-43	101 Sqn
119887	F/L	BAKEWELL Tom	25-07-43	102 Sqn
1216503	Sgt	BALA Edward Stanley	28-01-43	20 OTU
657240	Sgt	BALDOCK Harry William	5-03-43	214 Sqn
1315271	Sgt	BALDWIN Arthur	10-07-43	50 Sqn
1293595	Sgt	BALDWIN Harold Victor	16-07-43	432 Sqn
1861770	Sgt	BALDWIN Peter	9-08-43	82 OTU
124761	F/O	BALDWIN Stanley Alfred	18-08-43	35 Sqn
1296659	Sgt	BALDWIN William Albert John	22-11-43	218 Sqn
1338274	Sgt	BALE Aubrey Herbert	4-12-43	7 Sqn
141333	F/O	BALE Charles Francis 'Paddy'	2-10-43	619 Sqn
1396828	Sgt	BALFOUR Raymonde Derek	28-04-43	101 Sqn
1531807	Sgt	BALICH Leonard	20-12-43	576 Sqn
1268240	Sgt	BALL Christopher Francis 'Doogie'	4-04-43	16 OTU
575670	Sgt	BALL Derrick John	17-01-43	101 Sqn
1385837	Sgt	BALL Douglas Albert	14-05-43	138 Sqn
1334656	Sgt	BALL Edward Frank	29-03-43	97 Sqn
1427907	F/S	BALL Frank	20-12-43	576 Sqn
1198317	Sgt	BALL Fred	24-08-43	97 Sqn
1549453	Sgt	BALL Frederick	30-07-43	102 Sqn
916429	F/S	BALL Leonard William [Australia]	20-12-43	51 Sqn
130156	F/O	BALL Robert Lionel Harman	22-10-43	10 Sqn
1580260	Sgt	BALL Robert William	13-07-43	106 Sqn
1620011	Sgt	BALL Thomas	26-06-43	166 Sqn
971137	Sgt	BALL William	12-02-43	427 Sqn
148012	P/O	BALLAMY Norman Lewis	15-06-43	44 Sqn
639777	Sgt	BALLANTYNE Angus Granger	15-06-43	106 Sqn
1697871	Sgt	BALLARD George Edward John [Canada]	26-11-43	166 Sqn
1390845	Sgt	BALLAUFF Roland Walter	9-08-43	82 OTU
122321	F/L	BALLEY Julien William Noel	9-04-43	77 Sqn
1232989	Sgt	BALSDON Roland Charles	17-06-43	156 Sqn
575897	Sgt	BAMFORD Charles Glendinning	17-04-43	49 Sqn
1428219	Sgt	BAMFORD John	16-12-43	100 Sqn
1417073	AC2	BAND George Rupert	29-05-43	23 OTU
1374522	Sgt	BANDEEN Frank Alexander	30-03-43	57 Sqn
1318948	F/S	BANDY Frederick Alexander	30-05-43	75 Sqn
567344	Sgt	BANFIELD Alfred John	17-06-43	100 Sqn
1891699	Sgt	BANGS Archibald Robert	27-09-43	75 Sqn
1802052	Sgt	BANGS George Charles	23-10-43	15 OTU
1391087	Sgt	BANKS Alan Raymond	7-09-43	1663 HCU
1338445	Sgt	BANKS David Frank Rawlinson	21-04-43	158 Sqn
1153128	Sgt	BANKS Desmond John	13-07-43	467 Sqn
777836	F/S	BANKS DFM Edward William [Rhodesia]	13-05-43	156 Sqn

142349	F/O	BANKS George Graham	18-10-43	103 Sqn		132190	P/O	BARNETT Herbert William	17-04-43	10 OTU
1113233	Sgt	BANKS George Leslie	27-01-43	218 Sqn		1319840	Sgt	BARNETT Laurence Philip	14-05-43	149 Sqn
1073681	F/S	BANKS James	25-02-43	424 Sqn		1575833	Sgt	BARNETT Thomas	31-08-43	207 Sqn
1531755	Sgt	BANKS Leslie	16-12-43	619 Sqn		1332114	Sgt	BARNEVELD Robert	14-07-43	408 Sqn
1529841	F/S	BANKS Richard Hooton	2-12-43	630 Sqn		1432057	Sgt	BARNFATHER Douglas Allen [Argentina]	28-07-43	106 Sqn
1374377	LAC	BANNATYNE Hugh	19-06-43	Snaith						
1564310	Sgt	BANNATYNE William Watson	17-04-43	467 Sqn		927683	Sgt	BARNS Frederick William	25-05-43	1652 HCU
170654	P/O	BANNING Albert Edward Frederick	29-12-43	431 Sqn		1370380	Sgt	BARNSLEY Percy	4-09-43	7 Sqn
578325	Sgt	BANNISTER Hugh George	18-11-43	115 Sqn		149985	P/O	BARR Keith Alec	16-07-43	50 Sqn
107990	F/L	BANNON James	24-11-43	7 Sqn		1081897	Sgt	BARRASS Richard	24-08-43	12 Sqn
1321638	Sgt	BANTING Stanley James	23-08-43	61 Sqn		1863079	AC2	BARRELL Francis George	4-09-43	5 Group
1039743	F/S	BANYER James	5-05-43	15 Sqn		78524	W/C	BARRELL DSO DFC* Robert George 'Bob'		
1621592	Sgt	BARAS Mark Sidney	24-08-43	199 Sqn					25-06-43	7 Sqn
1200694	Sgt	BARBER Alfred Lionel	1-05-43	106 Sqn		83979	F/L	BARRETT Cuthbert Roderick	16-04-43	1657 HCU
1354869	Sgt	BARBER Dennis Robert	1-05-43	9 Sqn		143425	P/O	BARRETT Harold Brisco	25-06-43	218 Sqn
133831	F/O	BARBER Frederick Albert	8-06-43	16 OTU		115775	F/O	BARRETT DFC Jack Kenneth	17-05-43	617 Sqn
1386599	Sgt	BARBER George William	4-07-43	15 Sqn		577074	Sgt	BARRETT Jack Leslie	16-12-43	576 Sqn
1330147	Sgt	BARBER Herbert Francis	22-01-43	98 Sqn		932772	Sgt	BARRETT John Gerald [Australia]	9-07-43	101 Sqn
131081	F/O	BARBER John Stuart	22-10-43	77 Sqn		1429689	Sgt	BARRETT John Raymond	1-03-43	76 Sqn
134720	F/O	BARBER Kenneth Arthur	27-09-43	76 Sqn		1267993	Sgt	BARRETT John William	3-08-43	103 Sqn
113908	F/O	BARBEZAT Charles Lawrence	18-08-43	10 Sqn		123848	F/O	BARRETT Kenneth Alan	16-04-43	158 Sqn
157645	P/O	BARDEN Alfred Vernon Cecil	22-10-43	76 Sqn		1425570	Sgt	BARRETT Peter William	31-01-43	19 OTU
754583	Sgt	BARDEN John Leslie Emery	31-01-43	101 Sqn		1164249	Sgt	BARRETT Ronald Charles	9-07-43	106 Sqn
1587540	Sgt	BARDILL Cecil	1-09-43	101 Sqn		541539	Sgt	BARRETT William	9-01-43	44 Sqn
1575269	Sgt	BARFOOT Thomas Bertram	25-02-43	102 Sqn		1313503	Sgt	BARRIE BEM Alexander	20-04-43	51 Sqn
1319073	Sgt	BARHAM Edward Frederick Maurice	20-10-43	166 Sqn		132743	F/O	BARRIE Alexander Chalmers	17-05-43	19 OTU
1270788	Sgt	BARHAM Harry Frederick	22-06-43	158 Sqn		1392878	Sgt	BARRIE Frederick William	1-12-43	199 Sqn
1127161	Sgt	BARHAM Sam	4-07-43	12 Sqn		1010564	Sgt	BARRIE John Irvine	22-06-43	35 Sqn
50226	F/O	BARKER Atholl	22-11-43	7 Sqn		1366519	Sgt	BARRIE Tom Brown	18-08-43	619 Sqn
1514792	Sgt	BARKER Charles Dennis	7-07-43	30 OTU		1393993	Sgt	BARRINGTON John Edward	20-12-43	76 Sqn
1233899	Sgt	BARKER Dennis	30-07-43	51 Sqn		1813827	Sgt	BARRON Alfred Victor Martin	17-09-43	158 Sqn
40070	S/L	BARKER Derrick Maxwell	10-03-43	100 Sqn		1027587	Sgt	BARROTT Clarence Bertram	21-04-43	90 Sqn
931976	Sgt	BARKER Eric Harry Frederic	26-05-43	207 Sqn		1321447	Sgt	BARROW Leonard Richard	12-06-43	199 Sqn
1586363	F/S	BARKER Jeffrey William	26-11-43	463 Sqn		1386172	Sgt	BARROW Stanley Francis	26-05-43	166 Sqn
968735	Sgt	BARKER Leslie	12-03-43	10 Sqn		138469	F/O	BARROW Sydney	24-08-43	100 Sqn
156042	P/O	BARKER Ralph Francis George	27-09-43	10 Sqn		1047258	Sgt	BARROW William Henry	1-03-43	466 Sqn
989712	Sgt	BARKER Robert Walton	4-04-43	408 Sqn		1390368	Sgt	BARRY Ernest Thomas	30-07-43	77 Sqn
1338327	Sgt	BARKER Stanley Frank	25-06-43	101 Sqn		950236	Sgt	BARRY William 'Bill'	25-06-43	78 Sqn
1377348	Sgt	BARKER William Arthur	10-04-43	9 Sqn		159713	P/O	BARTHELEMY Jasques	4-11-43	138 Sqn
1390740	Sgt	BARLEGS Stanley George	18-10-43	9 Sqn		1188499	Sgt	BARTHOLOMEW Douglas Wallace	13-06-43	100 Sqn
1337932	Sgt	BARLEY David Llewellyn	1-03-43	15 OTU		1322036	Sgt	BARTHOLOMEW Kenneth Frederick	2-03-43	115 Sqn
1389145	F/S	BARLEY Frederick Norman	11-04-43	7 Sqn		949381	Sgt	BARTLE Harold Garside	28-07-43	102 Sqn
1125516	Sgt	BARLEY Walter Ernest	17-06-43	100 Sqn		126837	F/O	BARTLEET Francis Walter	3-03-43	429 Sqn
1314768	Sgt	BARLOW Arnold Thomas	25-06-43	156 Sqn		578277	Sgt	BARTLETT Edward	31-08-43	427 Sqn
1321808	F/S	BARLOW Raymond William	1-09-43	77 Sqn		1383206	Sgt	BARTLETT Edward Albert	31-07-43	218 Sqn
1318256	F/S	BARLOW Ronald Alfred	26-06-43	196 Sqn		1586437	Sgt	BARTLETT Ernest George William	6-09-43	61 Sqn
1392675	Sgt	BARNARD Frederick Vernon	22-06-43	35 Sqn		1339319	Sgt	BARTLETT Frank Arthur	31-08-43	434 Sqn
1293974	Sgt	BARNARD James Arthur	3-03-43	51 Sqn		605496	Sgt	BARTLETT Vivian Herbert	29-09-43	158 Sqn
1389302	Sgt	BARNARD Michael Stanley	15-08-43	192 Sqn		1525488	F/S	BARTLETT William Henry	22-06-43	466 Sqn
109004	F/O	BARNES Anthony Drew Ashby	13-03-43	102 Sqn		1321459	Sgt	BARTLEY Donald	20-10-43	166 Sqn
1678058	Sgt	BARNES Arthur Mallinson	27-09-43	460 Sqn		1382842	Sgt	BARTON Benjamin Joseph	28-08-43	199 Sqn
1333926	Sgt	BARNES Derryck	1-09-43	622 Sqn		1582468	Sgt	BARTON Percy	9-10-43	218 Sqn
1586006	Sgt	BARNES Edwin Charles Albert	31-07-43	218 Sqn		1271695	Sgt	BARTON Ronald James	29-04-43	218 Sqn
1429176	Sgt	BARNES Eric Raymond	16-11-43	28 OTU		1585435	Sgt	BARTON Thomas George	26-06-43	51 Sqn
1052254	Sgt	BARNES Frederick	13-07-43	100 Sqn		1177728	Sgt	BARTON William Kenneth	29-01-43	408 Sqn
546801	Sgt	BARNES George Kenneth	3-10-43	467 Sqn		161601	P/O	BARTON-SMITH Reginald Lionel	11-11-43	1654 HCU
1382125	Sgt	BARNES Henry Lewis	27-04-43	158 Sqn		61988	F/L	BARTRUM Jack Edward	16-05-43	161 Sqn
1412081	Sgt	BARNES Herbert Rhys	17-04-43	50 Sqn		654128	Sgt	BASELEY Arthur Leonard	4-07-43	12 Sqn
1179334	Sgt	BARNES Louis Harold	26-11-43	76 Sqn		1319553	F/S	BASEY Roger William	24-12-43	514 Sqn
1803122	Sgt	BARNES Peter Adin	26-11-43	103 Sqn		1054927	Sgt	BASNETT Harold	7-09-43	77 Sqn
1312128	F/S	BARNES Reginald Henry	27-04-43	158 Sqn		1388099	Sgt	BASS Eric George	13-05-43	149 Sqn
1311751	Sgt	BARNES Robin Harold	25-06-43	102 Sqn		1395324	Sgt	BASS John William	14-11-43	10 OTU
656215	F/S	BARNES Sidney James	25-06-43	7 Sqn		89591	F/L	BASSAGE Charles Thomas	2-12-43	12 Sqn
1545325	Sgt	BARNES Sydney	18-08-43	426 Sqn		1317135	Sgt	BASSETT Joseph Henry	18-08-43	44 Sqn
1317678	Sgt	BARNES Sydney Roy	19-05-43	310 FTU		1238546	Sgt	BASSETT Ronald Herbert	1-10-43	1660 HCU
1811513	Sgt	BARNES Victor Joseph	22-10-43	77 Sqn		134569	F/O	BASTEN John	24-08-43	623 Sqn
1266491	Sgt	BARNES William	25-07-43	214 Sqn		126739	P/O	BASTIAN Peter Spencer	26-03-43	429 Sqn
1379802	Sgt	BARNES William Geoffrey	2-04-43	57 Sqn		1385600	Sgt	BASTICK Howard Anthony	19-02-43	166 Sqn
1319045	Sgt	BARNETT Conrad Alfred Stanley	15-06-43	49 Sqn		169468	P/O	BATCHELOR George William	16-12-43	625 Sqn

Number	Rank	Name	Date	Unit	Number	Rank	Name	Date	Unit
138400	F/O	BATCHELOR Harold Ockenden	18-08-43	49 Sqn	1385801	Sgt	BEATON Robert Allen	15-06-43	106 Sqn
1461147	Sgt	BATE Frederick Walter	3-10-43	623 Sqn	1456992	Sgt	BEATSON Jack	14-04-43	101 Sqn
1066641	W/O	BATES Albert Peter	16-08-43	166 Sqn	1335569	Sgt	BEATTIE Frederick Donald	2-12-43	12 Sqn
1586116	Sgt	BATES Cyril Walter	26-05-43	101 Sqn	1347709	Sgt	BEATTIE Stanley Grieve	28-05-43	10 Sqn
1623026	Sgt	BATES Eric William Hardy	3-11-43	429 Sqn	1390141	Sgt	BEAUCHAMP Alfred	1-03-43	51 Sqn
1398599	Sgt	BATES Frederick William Alfred	7-09-43	158 Sqn	138150	F/O	BEAUMONT Gerard Anthony	26-11-43	7 Sqn
1301762	Sgt	BATES James Dennis	17-08-43	218 Sqn	1601542	Sgt	BEAUMONT Ronald Francis	16-04-43	460 Sqn
1078000	Sgt	BATES John Alec	17-04-43	50 Sqn	1358410	Sgt	BEAVEN Albert Edward	12-03-43	102 Sqn
1294682	Sgt	BATES John Frederick	26-06-43	106 Sqn	626944	F/S	BEAVEN DFM Roy	17-04-43	83 Sqn
1800729	Sgt	BATES John Sydney	5-12-43	623 Sqn	144644	P/O	BEAZLEIGH Arthur James	7-09-43	78 Sqn
570468	Sgt	BATES Michael	13-05-43	50 Sqn	37538	S/L	BECK Anthony	25-06-43	218 Sqn
1338950	Sgt	BATES Raymond George	7-07-43	15 OTU	1380833	Sgt	BECK George Henry	31-07-43	15 Sqn
650588	Sgt	BATEY George	13-07-43	50 Sqn	1237059	Sgt	BECK Howard	27-04-43	102 Sqn
656918	F/S	BATKIN William Charles	14-07-43	419 Sqn	131167	F/L	BECK Hubert John	30-03-43	76 Sqn
621459	Sgt	BATTEN Gilbert Herbert McDonald	20-10-43	115 Sqn	641951	Sgt	BECK James Andrew	28-08-43	467 Sqn
1318361	Sgt	BATTEN Gordon George	9-11-43	90 Sqn	155341	P/O	BECK Leslie Thomas	26-07-43	50 Sqn
1333486	Sgt	BATTEN Harold Royston	11-11-43	161 Sqn	1580106	Sgt	BECK Ronald Cecil Victor	3-08-43	12 Sqn
1432288	Sgt	BATTERBEE Roy	26-05-43	166 Sqn	1128694	Sgt	BECK William Christie	30-05-43	90 Sqn
1349459	Sgt	BATTRAM Arthur	2-03-43	115 Sqn	970018	W/O	BECKETT Samuel Nicoll	11-04-43	429 Sqn
1111947	F/S	BATTY Edgar	23-06-43	431 Sqn	1390334	Sgt	BEDBROOK Anthony Richard Duncan		
1415510	Sgt	BATTY George	14-05-43	44 Sqn				4-09-43	50 Sqn
1289921	Sgt	BATTY William James	6-09-43	49 Sqn	904734	Sgt	BEDDOE Anthony Claude	11-04-43	35 Sqn
1398938	Sgt	BAUGHEN Clifford Walter Henry	10-11-43	1660 HCU	1338439	F/S	BEDWARD Alfred Arthur Charles	3-08-43	35 Sqn
1320428	Sgt	BAUMAN Donald Compton	12-06-43	156 Sqn	1059604	Sgt	BEE Robinson	3-04-43	83 Sqn
1293621	Sgt	BAUMANN Albert Elvin	16-12-43	9 Sqn	658479	F/S	BEEBE John	23-11-43	44 Sqn
146417	P/O	BAWDEN Edward Semmens	24-05-43	76 Sqn	1144928	Sgt	BEECH Frederick Ronald	5-05-43	35 Sqn
1320943	Sgt	BAXTER Alan Russell	24-08-43	77 Sqn	1545047	Sgt	BEECH Jack Stear	3-10-43	17 OTU
1011881	Sgt	BAXTER David	13-05-43	78 Sqn	1318329	Sgt	BEECH Kenneth Albert	24-12-43	44 Sqn
1390065	Sgt	BAXTER Jack Alexander	1-09-43	77 Sqn	1330837	Sgt	BEECH Leslie Joseph	14-05-43	57 Sqn
1537044	Sgt	BAXTER James	8-09-43	29 OTU	948008	Sgt	BEECHER John Edward Arthur	3-10-43	76 Sqn
1020127	Sgt	BAXTER James William	29-06-43	77 Sqn	1133751	Sgt	BEEDIM James Arthur	5-05-43	166 Sqn
127296	F/O	BAXTER John	5-05-43	102 Sqn	1060143	Sgt	BEEDLE Stanley	3-11-43	101 Sqn
1266661	F/S	BAXTER Malcolm	12-06-43	78 Sqn	1864120	Sgt	BEEKEN Graham	9-10-43	431 Sqn
50894	F/O	BAXTER Malcolm Wilfred	23-01-43	12 Sqn	151229	F/O	BEELEY David	18-09-43	1658 HCU
124108	F/O	BAXTER Montague Frank	22-11-43	10 Sqn	1600187	Sgt	BEER Ernest Jack	2-05-43	24 OTU
1050918	F/S	BAXTER Stanley	6-02-43	90 Sqn	1052604	Sgt	BEER Norman	18-10-43	9 Sqn
1381903	Sgt	BAXTER William Parker	24-05-43	166 Sqn	1304013	Cpl	BEER Philip Jack Frank	24-09-43	166 Sqn
1072872	Sgt	BAYBUT Richard William	4-07-43	103 Sqn	47763	F/O	BEESLEY Peter Leslie	7-02-43	158 Sqn
900952	Sgt	BAYFIELD Sidney Albert	30-03-43	76 Sqn	1425681	Sgt	BEESTON Frank Lynford	26-06-43	115 Sqn
156689	P/O	BAYLDON Richard Anthony	16-12-43	9 Sqn	126624	F/O	BEETON Edwin Harold	12-03-43	102 Sqn
1002401	Sgt	BAYLES Thomas Richard	23-05-43	57 Sqn	1215939	Sgt	BEEVER Joe	17-12-43	156 Sqn
613449	Sgt	BAYLIS Gerald Percy	3-11-43	467 Sqn	552516	Sgt	BEGGS William John	1-09-43	44 Sqn
136528	F/O	BAYLIS Harry William	24-08-43	78 Sqn	89843	F/L	BELCHER George	4-12-43	405 Sqn
1041555	Sgt	BAYLISS Edward Percy George	19-02-43	156 Sqn	1387091	Sgt	BELDON Eric Nigel Nicholson	31-08-43	7 Sqn
1300620	Sgt	BAYLISS Jack	1-05-43	9 Sqn	2216229	Sgt	BELFIELD James Philip	3-10-43	77 Sqn
1393907	Sgt	BAYLY Reginald Sydney	22-09-43	214 Sqn	1027864	Sgt	BELL Charles Armstrong	29-03-43	218 Sqn
161307	P/O	BAYRAM Clarence Herbert	4-12-43	576 Sqn	1270241	Sgt	BELL Claude Stephen	14-06-43	199 Sqn
127292	F/O	BAYS Leslie	10-08-43	102 Sqn	1334843	Sgt	BELL Derek Reginald	25-07-43	76 Sqn
1282642	Sgt	BEACH George Henry	4-10-43	419 Sqn	1432116	Sgt	BELL Douglas	3-01-43	24 OTU
1338277	Sgt	BEACHAM Ernest George Ronald	13-05-43	106 Sqn	122394	F/O	BELL Douglas Mackenzie [USA]	24-11-43	408 Sqn
1863537	Sgt	BEACOCK Eric Charles	19-11-43	149 Sqn	1558567	Sgt	BELL Eric James	3-08-43	115 Sqn
647383	Sgt	BEADON Stanley David	2-02-43	50 Sqn	548637	Sgt	BELL Ernest	30-05-43	35 Sqn
1380112	Sgt	BEADSMOORE Wilfred Reginald	28-05-43	77 Sqn	1130938	Sgt	BELL Ernest	30-07-43	57 Sqn
1384926	F/S	BEAKE Harry James	10-08-43	103 Sqn	1371967	Sgt	BELL Francis Douglas	14-03-43	161 Sqn
562976	W/O	BEALE MBE James William	18-12-43	Croft	1288776	F/S	BELL Geoffrey	26-05-43	192 Sqn
53081	P/O	BEALE Norman Nice 'Bubs'	14-11-43	1652 HCU	966932	Sgt	BELL George	9-03-43	7 Sqn
1322230	Sgt	BEALES William Arthur	23-09-43	149 Sqn	1318653	Sgt	BELL George Hutchinson Rennie	6-09-43	106 Sqn
1465966	Sgt	BEALEY Donald Jack	4-12-43	576 Sqn	126807	F/O	BELL DFM James	26-06-43	106 Sqn
137540	F/O	BEAMES Kenneth Herbert	29-09-43	9 Sqn	1127149	Sgt	BELL James Richard	12-06-43	431 Sqn
1357541	Sgt	BEAN Harold Dennis	22-09-43	115 Sqn	131959	F/O	BELL James Rutherford Hutton	17-06-43	61 Sqn
170433	P/O	BEANE Harold	26-11-43	57 Sqn	1097964	Sgt	BELL John	18-01-43	97 Sqn
1535181	Sgt	BEARD Alvery	1-05-43	9 Sqn	1330611	Sgt	BELL John Anthony Martin	9-01-43	44 Sqn
1438808	Sgt	BEARD Leslie Thomas	13-06-43	97 Sqn	121435	F/O	BELL John Morling	13-02-43	199 Sqn
1379617	Sgt	BEARD Oliver	4-07-43	90 Sqn	1165211	Sgt	BELL Kenneth Foster	13-05-43	196 Sqn
1334654	Sgt	BEARDWELL Frederick George	18-10-43	467 Sqn	1627841	Sgt	BELL Robert Ernest	15-06-43	106 Sqn
72334	F/O	BEARE Adrian	7-07-43	30 OTU	1021071	Sgt	BELL Ronald	13-05-43	12 Sqn
846474	Sgt	BEASLEY Herbert William	26-06-43	61 Sqn	1077692	Sgt	BELL Ronald	24-05-43	75 Sqn
1433340	Sgt	BEASLEY John Henry	31-01-43	16 OTU	157196	P/O	BELL Stanley John	21-10-43	83 Sqn
655653	Sgt	BEATH James Hay Armstrong	30-01-43	466 Sqn	1163588	Sgt	BELL Thomas Hylton [Rhodesia]	23-06-43	78 Sqn

Service No	Rank	Name	Date	Sqn
1075168	Sgt	BELL Tom	18-10-43	103 Sqn
1038441	Sgt	BELL William	3-10-43	90 Sqn
1134764	Sgt	BELL William	27-03-43	101 Sqn
1585877	Sgt	BELL William	26-11-43	115 Sqn
1126437	Sgt	BELLAMY Charles Edward	2-03-43	97 Sqn
903979	Sgt	BELLAMY Dudley William	3-08-43	115 Sqn
1181118	W/O	BELLAMY John Edward	2-12-43	103 Sqn
1439058	Sgt	BELLHOUSE William Henry	12-06-43	199 Sqn
1585669	Sgt	BELLINGER William James	17-12-43	57 Sqn
1451971	Sgt	BELLIS Sydney	9-02-43	19 OTU
125665	F/O	BELLMAN George Charles	3-02-43	218 Sqn
1387037	Sgt	BELSHAM David William	28-02-43	49 Sqn
1795491	Sgt	BELSHAW Arthur Ernest	6-09-43	12 Sqn
147743	P/O	BELSHAW DFM Richard Watt	25-07-43	214 Sqn
145774	P/O	BELSHER Harold Donovan	24-06-43	10 OTU
1851875	Sgt	BELTON Robert Edward	4-09-43	15 Sqn
1459357	Sgt	BELTON William	26-11-43	460 Sqn
1332098	F/S	BEMBRIDGE John William	23-06-43	156 Sqn
1809240	Sgt	BENDER Laurie George	23-09-43	419 Sqn
1197228	Sgt	BENDING Dennis Ronald	1-03-43	15 OTU
1277051	Sgt	BENEY Eric Thomas	8-03-43	7 Sqn
550323	F/S	BENFIELD MiD Victor Harold	19-06-43	Snaith
1331554	Sgt	BENJAMIN Kenneth	30-03-43	428 Sqn
1076715	LAC	BENN James	4-11-43	3 Group
1079703	Sgt	BENNETT Cecil Gordon	13-02-43	30 OTU
1384833	Sgt	BENNETT Eric Walter John	27-04-43	158 Sqn
1388734	Sgt	BENNETT George Alfred	25-11-43	1678 HCU
1474654	Sgt	BENNETT George Herbert	22-10-43	51 Sqn
1339124	F/S	BENNETT Herbert Sidney	2-12-43	550 Sqn
1372493	Sgt	BENNETT James Lindsay	22-11-43	77 Sqn
1319079	Sgt	BENNETT John Henry	6-09-43	51 Sqn
650929	Sgt	BENNETT Leonard	26-06-43	100 Sqn
957663	F/S	BENNETT Michael John	9-04-43	101 Sqn
1608215	Sgt	BENNETT Michael Oliver Douglas	1-10-43	44 Sqn
1254325	Sgt	BENNETT Norman Reginald	21-01-43	158 Sqn
1338150	Sgt	BENNETT Robert William	3-08-43	115 Sqn
1322262	F/S	BENNETT DFM Ronald Sidney	22-11-43	97 Sqn
975636	Sgt	BENNETT Rowland	3-10-43	158 Sqn
1410655	Sgt	BENNETT Stanley George	31-08-43	218 Sqn
1386459	Sgt	BENNETT Terence	23-06-43	51 Sqn
927900	Sgt	BENNETT Walter James	23-05-43	57 Sqn
1028937	Sgt	BENNETT William	1-09-43	101 Sqn
1102644	Sgt	BENNETT William Alan	28-01-43	102 Sqn
1281626	Sgt	BENNETTON Frederick Horace	5-05-43	75 Sqn
1531878	Sgt	BENNING Ronald Douglas	9-04-43	9 Sqn
1338480	Sgt	BENNY John Henry	27-09-43	15 Sqn
1450256	Sgt	BENSON Arthur	24-05-43	166 Sqn
1143366	Sgt	BENSON George Edward	12-03-43	78 Sqn
1333625	Sgt	BENTLEY George William	18-08-43	426 Sqn
658077	Sgt	BENTLEY Harry	12-03-43	78 Sqn
952706	Sgt	BENTLEY Leslie George	28-07-43	100 Sqn
1583723	Sgt	BERESFORD John Bosworth	28-09-43	75 Sqn
130590	P/O	BERNSTEIN Ralph Isaac	5-01-43	20 OTU
1211846	Sgt	BERRESFORD Derrick Lewis	26-05-43	101 Sqn
47736	F/L	BERRIDGE Gordon Frederick	28-08-43	218 Sqn
658784	W/O	BERRY Alan	12-11-43	78 Sqn
1162200	Sgt	BERRY Albert Warren	17-04-43	50 Sqn
1380078	Sgt	BERRY Eric	23-01-43	75 Sqn
1604340	Sgt	BERRY Frank	31-07-43	408 Sqn
1578408	Sgt	BERRY Harold Arthu James	14-05-43	149 Sqn
975799	Sgt	BERRY Kenneth George	30-05-43	115 Sqn
1339099	Sgt	BERRY Sidney Albert	20-12-43	10 Sqn
1081914	Sgt	BERRY Walter	10-04-43	81 OTU
1368760	Sgt	BERRY William Glover	13-05-43	467 Sqn
1068137	F/S	BERRY Winston Seymour	13-03-43	7 Sqn
1813511	Sgt	BERTRAM Arthur Edward	18-10-43	115 Sqn
43195	S/L	BERTRAM Frederick Clifford	1-05-43	77 Sqn
1050195	Sgt	BERTRAM Lorenzo	8-04-43	428 Sqn
144198	P/O	BERTRAM Norman	5-04-43	10 Sqn
51682	P/O	BERWICK DFM George Alfred	20-09-43	138 Sqn
1353851	Sgt	BERWICK Thomas Alfred	18-02-43	9 Sqn
580838	W/O	BESANT DFM Ronald Cuthbert	11-08-43	192 Sqn
908515	Sgt	BEST Arthur Edwin	24-08-43	83 Sqn
148464	P/O	BEST Charles Henry	3-08-43	100 Sqn
1245321	Sgt	BESTWICK Frank	9-03-43	61 Sqn
1473247	Sgt	BESTWICK William Henry	23-05-43	57 Sqn
156574	P/O	BESZANT Peter Theobald	24-08-43	83 Sqn
1169920	Sgt	BETTANEY Leslie	22-11-43	156 Sqn
1387742	Sgt	BETTERTON Victor Edward	5-05-43	1663 HCU
1235499	Sgt	BETTINSON Donald William	13-07-43	49 Sqn
1811721	Sgt	BETTS Albert Edward	7-09-43	158 Sqn
642091	Sgt	BETTS Elmer	4-07-43	103 Sqn
1219830	Sgt	BETTS Eric William	13-05-43	426 Sqn
115097	F/L	BETTS Leslie Robert	12-06-43	467 Sqn
2203093	Sgt	BETTS Ronald	17-12-43	101 Sqn
1234732	LAC	BETTS Stanley	18-11-43	622 Sqn
1812409	Sgt	BETTS Sydney James	7-07-43	12 Sqn
1231505	Sgt	BETTS Thomas Ivan	31-08-43	166 Sqn
50678	F/O	BEVAN Clifford John William	28-09-43	149 Sqn
1380060	Sgt	BEVAN William Hughes	26-02-43	90 Sqn
146337	P/O	BEVERIDGE Graham Thomas	29-06-43	35 Sqn
1171184	Sgt	BEVIS Kenneth Jack	28-08-43	12 Sqn
146345	P/O	BEVIS Peter Edward	26-06-43	106 Sqn
643736	Sgt	BICK Douglas Louvain	27-09-43	166 Sqn
64287	S/L	BICKERDIKE DFC Herbert Frank	20-12-43	77 Sqn
49977	F/O	BICKHAM Charles John	28-04-43	75 Sqn
1380667	F/S	BICKLE William Douglas	23-09-43	49 Sqn
1212556	Sgt	BICKLEY John Frederick	12-10-43	90 Sqn
1292839	Sgt	BICKNELL George Alfred	23-09-43	49 Sqn
1266090	Sgt	BIDDLE Frederick John	12-06-43	51 Sqn
1482431	Sgt	BIDDULPH Sidney	18-05-43	149 Sqn
1313932	Sgt	BIFFIN Albert Samuel	3-08-43	214 Sqn
577845	Sgt	BIGG Peter	21-04-43	57 Sqn
1430145	Sgt	BIGGIN Harry	15-06-43	49 Sqn
1210605	Sgt	BIGGS Edwin Arthur	30-03-43	408 Sqn
1264148	Sgt	BIGGS Jack	30-12-43	50 Sqn
155227	P/O	BIGGS DFM William	7-09-43	427 Sqn
569401	Sgt	BIGGS William Frank	12-06-43	12 Sqn
656218	F/S	BIGHAM Douglas John	24-08-43	100 Sqn
1293131	Sgt	BILHAM Reginald Percival	4-04-43	149 Sqn
151454	F/O	BILKE George Edward	8-09-43	29 OTU
1320794	Sgt	BILLETT Cyril William	27-11-43	50 Sqn
1391974	Sgt	BILLINGHAM John Anthony Geoffrey	30-09-43	619 Sqn
1502415	Sgt	BILLINGTON Cedric Leslie	3-04-43	83 Sqn
131956	F/O	BILLINGTON Edward Norman	22-06-43	15 Sqn
1097982	Sgt	BILLINGTON John	3-09-43	101 Sqn
751750	F/S	BILLINGTON DFM Walter	3-03-43	429 Sqn
1080356	Sgt	BILLINGTON William	3-04-43	83 Sqn
129024	F/O	BILNEY Raymond Thomas James	4-09-43	467 Sqn
126821	F/O	BILSON Frederick William	9-10-43	405 Sqn
1211327	Sgt	BINGLEY Dennis Gordon	15-07-43	158 Sqn
134044	F/O	BINHAM Ronald James	11-01-43	81 OTU
137664	P/O	BINNING Lionel Hubert Rogers	12-03-43	149 Sqn
149339	P/O	BINNS Harry	11-08-43	78 Sqn
129640	F/O	BINNS John Bentley	12-06-43	78 Sqn
124612	F/O	BINT DFM Dennis Edward John	11-04-43	26 OTU
116801	F/L	BIRBECK DFC John Lancelot	25-07-43	218 Sqn
1284722	F/S	BIRCH Harry Vincent	27-11-43	619 Sqn
129764	P/O	BIRCH John Dudley [Eire]	28-01-43	20 OTU
1076673	Sgt	BIRCHALL Eric	24-12-43	44 Sqn
1407182	Sgt	BIRD Arthur Reginald	20-12-43	514 Sqn
1386978	F/S	BIRD Eric Norman	26-07-43	214 Sqn
142562	F/O	BIRD Frank	14-07-43	81 OTU
1677697	Sgt	BIRD Henry James	21-10-43	83 Sqn
1339867	Sgt	BIRD John Edward Henry	18-10-43	101 Sqn
125987	F/O	BIRD Kenneth Sidney	17-04-43	218 Sqn
80369	F/O	BIRD Newton [Rhodesia]	10-04-43	9 Sqn

133726	F/O	BIRD Peter Charles Stuart	12-05-43	20 OTU	1334224	Sgt	BLANC Thomas Walter	23-11-43	630 Sqn
139610	P/O	BIRD Raymond Harry	3-01-43	61 Sqn	1234784	Sgt	BLANCH Keith Charles	17-09-43	10 OTU
547208	Sgt	BIRD Stanley George	22-11-43	78 Sqn	903776	Sgt	BLANCHARD Norman	23-06-43	161 Sqn
1578167	Sgt	BIRD Thomas Aldroyd	18-11-43	10 Sqn	1339896	Sgt	BLANCHARD Rex	3-10-43	15 Sqn
1337140	Sgt	BIRD Thomas Arthur	8-04-43	101 Sqn	778988	Sgt	BLAND Joseph Arthur [Rhodesia]	23-04-43	9 Sqn
124844	F/O	BIRDSALL William	23-09-43	90 Sqn	1393703	Sgt	BLANDFORD Stanley Kendal [Chile]	22-10-43	10 Sqn
50786	F/O	BIRKBECK Eric Gordon	30-07-43	166 Sqn	658328	F/S	BLANKS Edwin Henry	24-11-43	7 Sqn
1336750	Sgt	BIRKBY Tom	1-09-43	149 Sqn	1890052	Sgt	BLATCH Norman William Edward	20-12-43	76 Sqn
1115374	F/S	BIRKETT Sydney Edmund	1-09-43	620 Sqn	124718	F/O	BLAZER Alec Hayward	11-08-43	619 Sqn
1218839	Sgt	BIRKHEAD Denis	24-05-43	10 Sqn	1232224	Sgt	BLISS John Miller	18-11-43	15 Sqn
621280	F/S	BIRKIN Frank	29-06-43	12 Sqn	1535273	Sgt	BLOOD Ronald Geoffrey	31-08-43	166 Sqn
1430538	Sgt	BIRKS Frederick Richard	26-11-43	83 Sqn	1269421	Sgt	BLOOM Roy Benjamin Charles	7-02-43	425 Sqn
1127582	Sgt	BIRRELL James Briggs Elder	3-10-43	77 Sqn	1331745	Sgt	BLOOMFIELD Frank Harry	23-10-43	467 Sqn
1550840	Sgt	BIRRELL James Wingate Sellars	30-05-43	10 Sqn	1447364	Sgt	BLOOMFIELD George William	1-09-43	78 Sqn
1567298	Sgt	BIRT Phillip McLaughlin	23-09-43	100 Sqn	1337223	Sgt	BLOOMFIELD Michael	2-07-43	30 OTU
955619	Sgt	BIRTLES Cyril	11-04-43	50 Sqn	928126	Sgt	BLOXHAM John Lewis	1-09-43	90 Sqn
751476	F/S	BIRTWISTLE Frederick Richard	30-03-43	97 Sqn	552574	Sgt	BLOXHAM Malcolm Victor	23-09-43	75 Sqn
1891314	Sgt	BISCOE James Walter	12-11-43	90 Sqn	1432654	Sgt	BLOXWICH James Henry	30-05-43	431 Sqn
1199609	Sgt	BISH Arthur Reginald	31-08-43	12 Sqn	963808	Sgt	BLUE Dugald	26-11-43	103 Sqn
1147352	Sgt	BISHELL Henry Stuart Fell	12-03-43	106 Sqn	148798	P/O	BLUM Denis [France]	22-06-43	408 Sqn
1386398	Sgt	BISHOP Alfred Thomas	4-07-43	51 Sqn			(served as BROOKE)		
1271480	Sgt	BISHOP Arthur John	1-09-43	75 Sqn	967176	F/S	BLUNDELL Derek Webb	27-11-43	619 Sqn
1602232	Sgt	BISHOP Charles Clifford	22-10-43	15 OTU	1385376	Sgt	BLUNDELL Harold Edwin	5-04-43	21 Sqn
574641	Sgt	BISHOP Donald Robert	13-02-43	50 Sqn	1027741	Sgt	BLUNDELL Phillip	26-06-43	51 Sqn
124671	F/O	BISHOP Douglas Vernon	22-05-43	1656 HCU	1380227	Sgt	BLUNDELL William James	30-05-43	466 Sqn
1200299	Sgt	BISHOP Edwin Charles	26-06-43	9 Sqn	1547352	Sgt	BLUNT Leonard	27-11-43	16 OTU
130572	F/O	BISHOP Reginald Charles	22-06-43	77 Sqn	69448	F/L	BLURTON DFC Philip Jones	22-10-43	103 Sqn
1425199	Sgt	BISHOP Robert	2-10-43	57 Sqn	630246	Sgt	BLYTH George	18-08-43	419 Sqn
1312303	Sgt	BISHOP Roy	9-04-43	207 Sqn	1483382	Sgt	BLYTH Jack Samuel	24-08-43	218 Sqn
1252904	F/S	BISHOP Thomas David	24-08-43	35 Sqn	133459	F/O	BLYTHE Ronald Charles	17-06-43	49 Sqn
127013	F/O	BISSET George Alexander	2-03-43	207 Sqn	936333	Sgt	BOAK Roderick Cawthorn	25-11-43	Graveley
1165342	Sgt	BLABER Arthur Clarence	25-02-43	9 Sqn	1390587	Sgt	BOAR Arthur John	22-06-43	83 Sqn
526799	Sgt	BLACK Alastair Milner Hood	24-05-43	51 Sqn	1319146	Sgt	BOARD Ronald William Henry	9-10-43	429 Sqn
1344487	Sgt	BLACK David	5-03-43	11 OTU	1523267	Sgt	BOARDMAN Edward James	21-10-43	83 Sqn
155222	F/O	BLACK Ian Campbell Bennett	16-12-43	9 Sqn	1495951	Sgt	BOARDMAN Gerald Mortimer	9-04-43	7 Sqn
1331729	Sgt	BLACK John	9-10-43	432 Sqn	1028039	Sgt	BOARDMAN Robert Cecil	14-05-43	44 Sqn
1317476	Sgt	BLACKBAROW Ernest Bernard	28-05-43	10 Sqn	1438273	Sgt	BOARDMAN Ronald	15-06-43	44 Sqn
655425	W/O	BLACKBURN Ian Harold	22-10-43	76 Sqn	1336666	F/S	BODDINGTON Jack Thomas Stillman	20-12-43	76 Sqn
623092	LAC	BLACKBURN Jack	26-02-43	Langar	1029429	Sgt	BODEN Stanley	26-02-43	158 Sqn
1387462	Sgt	BLACKBURN John Sydney	17-04-43	15 Sqn	658465	Sgt	BODY James Howard	13-05-43	78 Sqn
1555057	Sgt	BLACKBURN Robert Allan McCulloch			1293282	Sgt	BOESE Frank Arthur	3-02-43	75 Sqn
			3-10-43	76 Sqn	1127216	Sgt	BOGLE Ernest Anthony	15-06-43	460 Sqn
1092940	Sgt	BLACKETT Jack	1-09-43	61 Sqn	1415741	Sgt	BOHN Arthur Reginald	23-09-43	428 Sqn
134081	F/O	BLACKHURST Sydney	23-06-43	97 Sqn	1450623	Sgt	BOLAM Warwick Hall	25-07-43	158 Sqn
802586	Sgt	BLACKIE William [Canada]	25-06-43	51 Sqn	1219810	Sgt	BOLAND Donald Edward Joseph	1-03-43	103 Sqn
170425	P/O	BLACKLEY Edward John	24-12-43	44 Sqn	1558122	Sgt	BOLAND Thomas	20-04-43	460 Sqn
1801521	Sgt	BLACKMAN Donald William	4-12-43	576 Sqn	1349988	Sgt	BOLES Francis	17-08-43	138 Sqn
1921967	F/S	BLACKMAN Eric Charles	4-07-43	429 Sqn	1211045	Sgt	BOLITHO Richard	17-05-43	617 Sqn
1398967	Sgt	BLACKMAN George Joseph	22-11-43	75 Sqn	169030	P/O	BOLSWORTH DFM Bernard	20-12-43	78 Sqn
149556	P/O	BLACKMORE DFC Alfred Henry	20-10-43	49 Sqn	1836087	Sgt	BOLT Nelson	26-11-43	625 Sqn
578348	Sgt	BLACKMORE John Charles	16-03-43	44 Sqn	1333378	Sgt	BOLTON John Albert	28-04-43	218 Sqn
1377328	F/S	BLACKWELL Arthur Edward	5-03-43	78 Sqn	989205	F/S	BOLTON Kenneth	6-03-43	49 Sqn
1227154	Sgt	BLACKWELL Hubert Leslie	17-12-43	100 Sqn	1391746	Sgt	BOLTON Lawrence William	14-05-43	77 Sqn
134678	F/O	BLACKWELL Ronald Arthur	22-11-43	78 Sqn	1392125	Sgt	BONAR Colin Niven	27-04-43	156 Sqn
1278728	LAC	BLACKWELL Stephan	19-06-43	Snaith	39487	F/L	BONARD Ian Numa	29-04-43	196 Sqn
1272014	Sgt	BLACKWELL William Alfred	28-05-43	460 Sqn	1164636	Sgt	BOND Alfred Leslie	8-02-43	44 Sqn
1055854	Sgt	BLACKWOOD James Lawson	2-12-43	90 Sqn	1301892	Sgt	BOND Arthur William	28-04-43	61 Sqn
656138	F/S	BLACKWOOD John Gladstone	3-11-43	625 Sqn	1338770	Sgt	BOND Bernard John	31-07-43	78 Sqn
944213	Sgt	BLAGDEN Arthur Sanderson	23-01-43	12 Sqn	149049	P/O	BOND Edward Hunter	13-06-43	460 Sqn
55025	F/O	BLAIN David Edward	18-11-43	90 Sqn	1198997	Sgt	BOND Leslie James	17-01-43	50 Sqn
132955	F/O	BLAIR David Carmichael	12-11-43	1659 HCU	1393302	Sgt	BOND Stanley George	28-08-43	620 Sqn
151237	F/O	BLAIR John	20-12-43	76 Sqn	1024724	Cpl	BOND Thomas John	18-06-43	83 Sqn
548871	Sgt	BLAKE Ernest Cecil Allan	16-09-43	617 Sqn	48898	F/O	BONE Alexander Victor	17-04-43	49 Sqn
151622	F/O	BLAKE Frederick John	20-12-43	44 Sqn	1029629	Sgt	BONE Arthur	21-04-43	12 Sqn
1338590	Sgt	BLAKE Peter Reginald James	13-05-43	51 Sqn	1381738	Sgt	BONE Henry George	15-02-43	207 Sqn
1220818	Sgt	BLAKE Ronald Sydney	26-05-43	214 Sqn	126961	P/O	BONEST Harry Edwin	26-01-43	466 Sqn
1219955	F/S	BLAKE Walter Steward	20-12-43	103 Sqn	904699	Sgt	BONHAM Frank Oliver	18-04-43	1659 HCU
40202	S/L	BLAKE Wilfred Albert [Canada]	21-04-43	7 Sqn	124717	F/O	BONNER Albert Carey	26-05-43	431 Sqn
1267121	Sgt	BLAKE-HALES George [Belgium]	23-10-43	467 Sqn	132804	F/O	BONNER Harry Frederick Charles	2-12-43	207 Sqn

Service No	Rank	Name	Date	Sqn
1622347	Sgt	BONNER Sidney	29-06-43	51 Sqn
657619	Sgt	BONSON James Edward	5-03-43	106 Sqn
128460	P/O	BOODRIE James Clinton	15-01-43	16 OTU
1413457	Sgt	BOOKER David Robert	29-09-43	156 Sqn
610543	Sgt	BOOKER Dennis	14-02-43	158 Sqn
126945	F/O	BOOKER William Richard	29-06-43	149 Sqn
1585666	Sgt	BOOLS Martin	22-11-43	115 Sqn
1162710	W/O	BOONE Cecil Jack Walton	27-09-43	166 Sqn
1331310	Sgt	BOONE Ronald Henry	12-06-43	35 Sqn
1424526	Sgt	BOOTH Albert William	29-06-43	10 Sqn
906085	F/S	BOOTH Alfred Ernest	6-02-43	424 Sqn
124861	F/L	BOOTH DFC Arnold	31-08-43	12 Sqn
1378781	Sgt	BOOTH Derek Arnold	19-02-43	467 Sqn
139949	P/O	BOOTH Ernest	20-04-43	149 Sqn
143910	F/O	BOOTH Geoffrey	26-11-43	103 Sqn
1078315	Sgt	BOOTH Harry	24-08-43	158 Sqn
1281328	Sgt	BOOTH Peter Waring	20-12-43	49 Sqn
1096896	Sgt	BOOTH Ronald	7-08-43	75 Sqn
649831	Sgt	BOOTH Stanley Thomas	23-06-43	427 Sqn
132706	F/O	BOOTH Thomas	12-05-43	20 OTU
1048079	Sgt	BOOTHMAN Robert Arthur	4-12-43	625 Sqn
636558	Sgt	BOOTHROYD Stanley	22-05-43	138 Sqn
141711	P/O	BOOY Frank Edward	10-04-43	466 Sqn
139927	P/O	BORDYCOTT DFC DFM Kenneth Winchcombe	17-04-43	156 Sqn
1366071	Sgt	BOREHAM Alfred Norman	10-03-43	10 Sqn
1723161	Sgt	BOREHAM Edward Roy	9-10-43	156 Sqn
1057662	Sgt	BORLAND John Hinds	2-08-43	28 OTU
1437293	Sgt	BORTHWICK Robert	15-06-43	9 Sqn
1559228	Sgt	BORTHWICK William [Brazil]	20-12-43	10 Sqn
1541998	Sgt	BOSTOCK Albert	29-12-43	434 Sqn
1579672	Sgt	BOSTOCK James Trueman	3-02-43	218 Sqn
1445497	Sgt	BOSTOCK Leslie Frederick	24-12-43	514 Sqn
1376911	Sgt	BOSTOCK William Charles	1-05-43	77 Sqn
132413	F/O	BOSTON Douglas James	20-10-43	115 Sqn
1432357	Sgt	BOSWELL George Thomas	22-10-43	158 Sqn
1673550	Sgt	BOSWELL Herbert Geoffrey	27-11-43	49 Sqn
1378416	Sgt	BOSWELL Robert McBain [Argentina]	27-02-43	180 Sqn
944091	Sgt	BOSWORTH Norman	30-06-43	1513 Flt
51975	P/O	BOTTING DFC Norman Arthur	16-09-43	617 Sqn
1604911	Sgt	BOTTLE Robert Edward Charles	16-12-43	1662 HCU
1437922	Sgt	BOTTOMLEY George Langdon	26-05-43	207 Sqn
1256133	Sgt	BOTTOMLEY Handel	24-08-43	15 Sqn
1215757	LAC	BOTTOMLEY Ronald	7-08-43	199 Sqn
1315053	Sgt	BOUCHER George Edwin	3-11-43	101 Sqn
1579567	Sgt	BOUCHER William Royce	22-11-43	428 Sqn
1339109	Sgt	BOUGHTON Clifford	17-06-43	100 Sqn
1318605	Sgt	BOUGOURD William George	20-10-43	1664 HCU
1457473	Sgt	BOUNDY John Gordon	17-09-43	10 OTU
134161	F/O	BOUNDY William Henry	23-06-43	620 Sqn
933423	F/S	BOURNE Cyril	16-04-43	35 Sqn
967727	Sgt	BOURNE David Barclay	13-05-43	83 Sqn
79226	F/L	BOUSFIELD DFC Jack Matthew	2-02-43	50 Sqn
1339908	Sgt	BOUSFIELD John Henry	14-02-43	158 Sqn
1615075	Sgt	BOUSHER Frederick Leonard	18-10-43	101 Sqn
1318648	Sgt	BOUTLE Cecil Norman	9-10-43	78 Sqn
647190	Sgt	BOUTTELL Roy Hedley David	14-09-43	138 Sqn
145177	P/O	BOVIS Denis Clarke	12-06-43	467 Sqn
89593	S/L	BOWDEN DFC* Frederick Harold	10-07-43	428 Sqn
1528496	Sgt	BOWDEN Geoffrey	14-08-43	78 Sqn
621553	F/S	BOWDEN Irvine Charles Randolph	27-09-43	432 Sqn
55064	F/O	BOWDEN Peter Lewis	18-11-43	15 Sqn
142347	F/O	BOWDEN Ronald Sydney	4-12-43	576 Sqn
1418000	Sgt	BOWEN David Benjamin	27-09-43	15 Sqn
1336468	Sgt	BOWEN Edwin Stanley	30-03-43	77 Sqn
109017	F/L	BOWEN Raymond Thomas	13-09-43	12 OTU
1378175	Sgt	BOWEN William Donald	2-03-43	15 Sqn
1318945	Sgt	BOWER Ernest William	31-08-43	149 Sqn
1575473	Sgt	BOWER Frank Geoffrey	4-04-43	16 OTU
1551769	Sgt	BOWER William Houston	21-01-43	158 Sqn
1602905	Sgt	BOWERMAN Kenneth Ivor	15-06-43	50 Sqn
1452264	F/S	BOWERS Arthur	11-04-43	214 Sqn
1402265	Sgt	BOWERS Reginald Hubert	11-08-43	102 Sqn
1450547	Sgt	BOWERS Robert Sidney	18-11-43	15 Sqn
1098656	Sgt	BOWES Kenneth	12-06-43	12 Sqn
1194726	Sgt	BOWKER Arthur Patrick	10-08-43	35 Sqn
1163245	Sgt	BOWLES Frederick James	21-04-43	21 Sqn
1219595	Sgt	BOWLES Gordon Stanley	5-05-43	102 Sqn
1676288	Sgt	BOWLES Harry	24-12-43	44 Sqn
943966	Sgt	BOWLES Thomas Patrick	9-01-43	97 Sqn
968910	Sgt	BOWLEY Kenneth	7-02-43	158 Sqn
155846	P/O	BOWLING Thomas John	18-08-43	405 Sqn
1395762	Sgt	BOWMAN Edward Albert	22-06-43	156 Sqn
1042659	Sgt	BOWN George	23-09-43	77 Sqn
1481016	AC1	BOWN George Archie	7-09-43	49 Sqn
339844	Sgt	BOWN Gerald Macness [Newfoundland]	5-02-43	50 Sqn
116522	F/O	BOWRING Norman Harvey	4-12-43	405 Sqn
1333462	Sgt	BOWRING Robert Abner Hugh	4-07-43	35 Sqn
1053096	Sgt	BOWS Thomas	26-02-43	207 Sqn
118812	S/L	BOWYER Clifford Charles John [Eire]	14-05-43	15 Sqn
1800778	Sgt	BOWYER Raymond Marshall	30-07-43	7 Sqn
123153	F/O	BOWYER The Hon. Richard Laurence Grenville	29-01-43	226 Sqn
1393248	Sgt	BOXALL Charles Henry George	28-04-43	75 Sqn
1387360	Sgt	BOXALL James Roy	29-06-43	12 Sqn
1110637	Sgt	BOXALL John	22-11-43	102 Sqn
1501911	Sgt	BOXER George Ernest	3-11-43	49 Sqn
1601807	Sgt	BOXSHALL Stuart Osmond Joseph	2-12-43	12 Sqn
1387514	Sgt	BOYCE John Scott	27-04-43	51 Sqn
1316442	Sgt	BOYCE William James	4-10-43	419 Sqn
1376657	Sgt	BOYD Albert Bartram	30-03-43	76 Sqn
1203145	F/S	BOYD Cecil Ritchie	4-12-43	77 Sqn
652467	Sgt	BOYD Daniel David	15-08-43	420 Sqn
1891353	Sgt	BOYD Gordon John Percy	4-10-43	115 Sqn
577658	Sgt	BOYD James	16-04-43	156 Sqn
125482	F/O	BOYD Peter Delamere	3-04-43	419 Sqn
1308219	Sgt	BOYD Raymond Vernon	29-06-43	51 Sqn
1379357	Sgt	BOYD William James Stonard	28-03-43	419 Sqn
1486601	Sgt	BOYDELL Alfred	15-06-43	100 Sqn
989148	Sgt	BOYDELL Ronald	4-05-43	78 Sqn
1393311	Sgt	BOYDEN William Henry	27-09-43	199 Sqn
1101061	Sgt	BOYES James Riby	27-04-43	90 Sqn
1482187	Sgt	BOYES Joseph Edward	18-05-43	149 Sqn
949475	Sgt	BOYES William Henry	9-10-43	51 Sqn
1568673	Sgt	BOYLAN Martin	4-12-43	625 Sqn
1482429	Sgt	BOYLE Michael John	15-01-43	10 Sqn
1080704	F/S	BOYNTON Thomas William	23-11-43	12 Sqn
144715	P/O	BOZIER George Alfred	11-04-43	76 Sqn
1322480	Sgt	BOZIER Reginald Thomas	12-02-43	101 Sqn
128869	F/O	BRACE Adrian Colebrook	23-09-43	218 Sqn
964963	Sgt	BRACE Aubrey Ronald	22-10-43	35 Sqn
1542786	Sgt	BRACEY Arthur	20-09-43	1485 Flt
1527091	Sgt	BRACKEN Edward	30-07-43	57 Sqn
1457457	Sgt	BRACKEN William David	22-11-43	428 Sqn
1610166	Sgt	BRADBURY Robert Douglas	18-01-43	44 Sqn
1621894	Sgt	BRADBURY Robert Stanley	5-12-43	101 Sqn
147221	P/O	BRADFORD Jack	31-08-43	15 Sqn
156591	P/O	BRADFORD DFC John Dennis	23-09-43	97 Sqn
1252341	Sgt	BRADFORD Thomas William	6-09-43	9 Sqn
52928	P/O	BRADLEY Eric George	26-11-43	158 Sqn
653563	Sgt	BRADLEY George Beedham	20-12-43	50 Sqn
620508	Sgt	BRADLEY Herbert	28-07-43	467 Sqn
569239	Sgt	BRADLEY Ivor Hall	24-06-43	156 Sqn
1291023	F/S	BRADLEY Robert Cecil	1-09-43	428 Sqn
1212989	Sgt	BRADLEY Snowdon Cawood	27-01-43	57 Sqn
1259352	Sgt	BRADLEY Victor Thomas	31-08-43	76 Sqn
658341	Sgt	BRADLEY William Frederick	12-06-43	100 Sqn

1450741	Sgt	BRADSHAW Bernard	8-08-43	22 OTU
115108	F/O	BRADSHAW Dennis Charles	4-07-43	103 Sqn
1083274	Sgt	BRADSHAW Eric	22-06-43	90 Sqn
1313652	Sgt	BRADSHAW Gordon Charles Arthur	23-09-43	90 Sqn
1078965	Sgt	BRADSHAW Henry Easton	26-02-43	102 Sqn
1474536	Sgt	BRADSHAW John Olav	14-07-43	90 Sqn
148755	P/O	BRADSHAW Reginald Eric	29-06-43	10 Sqn
1480790	Sgt	BRADSHAW Ronald	23-06-43	207 Sqn
1673635	Sgt	BRADSHAW William	1-09-43	1662 HCU
657501	Sgt	BRADY George	21-04-43	12 Sqn
1319845	Sgt	BRADY Thomas George	26-11-43	626 Sqn
145473	P/O	BRAGG Richard Edward	13-05-43	78 Sqn
1735039	Sgt	BRAGG Ronald Vincent	2-08-43	57 Sqn
621785	Sgt	BRAGG Wilfred Spencer	8-04-43	15 Sqn
970033	Sgt	BRAID Alexander	30-12-43	106 Sqn
940787	W/O	BRAINES Murray Ronald	3-10-43	61 Sqn
1684804	Sgt	BRAMALL Frank	18-11-43	192 Sqn
653941	Sgt	BRAMBLE James Alfred	30-05-43	218 Sqn
130450	P/O	BRAMHAM Charles Orfeur	26-03-43	460 Sqn
1239593	Sgt	BRAMLEY Terence Charles	2-12-43	101 Sqn
1051374	Sgt	BRAMWELL Walter	30-05-43	75 Sqn
962835	F/S	BRANCH DFM Albert Charles	20-10-43	83 Sqn
1353125	Sgt	BRAND Adam Cubie	18-08-43	467 Sqn
1355955	Sgt	BRAND Ronald Charles Henry	15-06-43	44 Sqn
1586424	Sgt	BRANDON Alan Alfred	23-11-43	51 Sqn
42792	S/L	BRANDON-TRYE Philip	18-07-43	1485 Flt
52826	P/O	BRANNAN John Robert	2-10-43	15 OTU
156946	P/O	BRANNIGAN Augustine	28-08-43	77 Sqn
574488	Sgt	BRANSCOMBE John Viner	3-04-43	51 Sqn
120951	F/O	BRANSGROVE Alfred Ernest	30-07-43	166 Sqn
1607031	Sgt	BRANSON Geoffrey Victor	26-06-43	101 Sqn
939924	Sgt	BRASON James	23-05-43	90 Sqn
127175	F/L	BRASSINGTON John Gordon	22-11-43	82 OTU
1546821	Sgt	BRATT Douglas Stuart	6-03-43	49 Sqn
1320783	Sgt	BRAUND Charles Gage	29-09-43	17 OTU
1380936	Sgt	BRAWN Leonard Thomas	22-10-43	76 Sqn
516576	F/S	BRAY Charles Henry	25-02-43	102 Sqn
1339912	Sgt	BRAY Edward Raymond	26-07-43	158 Sqn
1315878	Sgt	BRAY Frederick John	18-02-43	158 Sqn
1315003	Sgt	BRAY Leonard Redvers	10-04-43	30 OTU
1159492	Sgt	BRAY Leslie Robert	17-04-43	51 Sqn
1850199	Sgt	BRAY William Richard	27-09-43	218 Sqn
137669	P/O	BRAYBROOK DFM Frederick Arthur	17-01-43	35 Sqn
653562	Sgt	BRAYBROOK Stanley	17-04-43	76 Sqn
118056	F/O	BRAYSHAW Graham	27-02-43	16 OTU
1319137	Sgt	BREAM Eric James	27-09-43	78 Sqn
658952	Sgt	BREAR Basil	24-08-43	156 Sqn
148473	P/O	BRECHIN James Maxwell	11-08-43	158 Sqn
1093893	W/O	BRECKON DFM Kenneth	23-08-43	103 Sqn
52753	F/O	BREMNER Archibald Ferguson	2-10-43	207 Sqn
942037	Sgt	BRENNAN Charles [Canada]	17-05-43	617 Sqn
118387	F/L	BRENNAN Patrick	19-02-43	15 Sqn
1600210	Sgt	BRENNEN Dennis	3-04-43	83 Sqn
1612568	Sgt	BRENT James Lawrence	18-11-43	514 Sqn
1477508	Sgt	BRENTNALL Kenneth Thomas	15-08-43	61 Sqn
1561437	F/S	BRESLIN DFM Daniel	18-07-43	1485 Flt
1312833	Sgt	BRETT Bruce Thomas	20-04-43	51 Sqn
130599	F/O	BRETT James Albert	4-10-43	50 Sqn
577164	Sgt	BRETT John	23-09-43	97 Sqn
118090	P/O	BRETT Michael Kerslake	29-01-43	158 Sqn
135502	F/O	BREVITT Robert William	27-11-43	103 Sqn
1604493	Sgt	BREWER John Harrison	27-09-43	166 Sqn
1600029	Sgt	BREWER Stanley Charles	21-01-43	103 Sqn
1035972	Sgt	BREWSTER James Edward	23-01-43	75 Sqn
1567853	Sgt	BREWSTER John Walker	24-12-43	103 Sqn
1380917	Sgt	BRIANT Victor George Edward	17-09-43	158 Sqn
922835	Sgt	BRICE Kenneth Oliver	4-04-43	408 Sqn
1580102	Sgt	BRICK George	5-05-43	101 Sqn
1377689	Sgt	BRIDGE Basil Dewdrey	22-01-43	487 Sqn
570570	Sgt	BRIDGE Bernard Stanley	17-06-43	61 Sqn
1384583	Sgt	BRIDGE William Mortimer	28-12-43	20 OTU
136048	P/O	BRIDGER Lawrence Mattinson	10-03-43	77 Sqn
537128	Sgt	BRIERLEY Fred	27-09-43	76 Sqn
1499412	Sgt	BRIERLEY John Robert	26-01-43	460 Sqn
1402515	Sgt	BRIFFETT Sydney John	17-04-43	51 Sqn
1546261	Sgt	BRIGGS Arthur	9-03-43	61 Sqn
1577617	Sgt	BRIGGS Horace Alfred	1-05-43	51 Sqn
1227721	Sgt	BRIGGS Thomas	31-12-43	21 OTU
1609673	Sgt	BRIGHT Henry George	27-09-43	11 OTU
67597	F/L	BRIGHT Twice MiD John Alexander	19-02-43	83 Sqn
946701	Sgt	BRIGHT Joseph Allen	10-08-43	103 Sqn
648514	Sgt	BRIGHT Kenneth Ernest	4-09-43	106 Sqn
147921	P/O	BRIGHTON William Job	25-07-43	218 Sqn
106881	F/L	BRILL David James	16-12-43	97 Sqn
136327	F/L	BRIND James Robert	30-07-43	166 Sqn
657693	Sgt	BRINDLE Eric	7-02-43	158 Sqn
1238304	Sgt	BRINDLEY Kenneth Lindon	18-10-43	103 Sqn
1604770	Sgt	BRINE Frederick Reginald	9-10-43	7 Sqn
132736	P/O	BRINKWORTH Rowland George	29-01-43	408 Sqn
1850112	Sgt	BRINTON Eric Alfred	9-10-43	7 Sqn
85935	F/L	BRINTON Reginald Herbert	4-07-43	429 Sqn
125668	F/O	BRISBANE William Christie	17-04-43	51 Sqn
1333752	F/S	BRISTOW Arthur George	9-07-43	106 Sqn
1393357	Sgt	BRISTOW Lester Jack Duncan [USA]	31-08-43	149 Sqn
1268417	Sgt	BRISTOW William Frederick	4-10-43	100 Sqn
1020217	Sgt	BRITTAIN John Charles	18-01-43	97 Sqn
1191968	Sgt	BRITTLE George Henry	2-12-43	626 Sqn
1333706	Sgt	BRITTON Arthur James	20-04-43	57 Sqn
1431391	Sgt	BRITTON Charles Alfred	26-06-43	103 Sqn
1336022	F/S	BRITTON Frederick James	15-04-43	7 Sqn
1182532	F/S	BRITTON Joseph John	6-04-43	16 OTU
1338484	Sgt	BRITTON Maurice Henry	20-12-43	10 Sqn
1321592	Sgt	BROAD Ernest Roy	11-06-43	1654 HCU
156321	P/O	BROADBENT Alec Bridgewater	22-10-43	50 Sqn
1491322	Sgt	BROADBENT Gerald Francis	13-05-43	24 OTU
143698	P/O	BROADBENT Harold	13-05-43	214 Sqn
52829	P/O	BROADBENT John Frank	11-08-43	57 Sqn
1137645	Sgt	BROADHEAD Eric	26-05-43	7 Sqn
1581597	Sgt	BROADHURST James	2-12-43	12 Sqn
1132427	Sgt	BROADHURST Kenneth	29-06-43	149 Sqn
1067031	Sgt	BROADLEY John William Robinson	18-01-43	9 Sqn
937347	Sgt	BROADLEY Ronald	26-07-43	75 Sqn
1212129	Sgt	BROADMORE Alfred George	25-07-43	103 Sqn
1615700	Sgt	BROCK Derek Guy	31-08-43	15 Sqn
1207000	Sgt	BROCK Herbert	10-03-43	100 Sqn
517587	Sgt	BROCKLEHURST Thomas	18-08-43	49 Sqn
1310694	Sgt	BROCKWAY Alfred James	24-05-43	419 Sqn
1254086	Sgt	BRODERICK John	4-04-43	214 Sqn
658031	Sgt	BRODIE Albert Edwin	12-06-43	51 Sqn
149883	P/O	BRODIE Ian James Duncan	8-03-43	75 Sqn
121730	F/O	BRODIE John Duncan	5-01-43	101 Sqn
1393089	Sgt	BROGAN Patrick George	8-01-43	9 Sqn
1451959	Sgt	BROMBY Arthur	16-08-43	166 Sqn
629129	Sgt	BROMLEY Reginald	13-06-43	97 Sqn
625668	Sgt	BROMLEY Thomas Leslie	27-04-43	15 Sqn
1392030	Sgt	BROMWICH Alfred Theodore Cuthbert	14-05-43	44 Sqn
1392087	Sgt	BRONSKY Harold	26-11-43	49 Sqn
1549548	Sgt	BROOK Charles Edward	16-08-43	115 Sqn
148571	P/O	BROOK Dennis Herbert	22-06-43	101 Sqn
658265	Sgt	BROOK Eric	15-02-43	28 OTU
924868	Sgt	BROOK Patrick 'Pat'	2-03-43	1654 HCU
1340648	Sgt	BROOKE Edward George	30-05-43	90 Sqn
573732	F/S	BROOKER DFM Robin Neville Benedict	2-02-43	7 Sqn
155004	P/O	BROOKES Dennis William	22-10-43	102 Sqn
574090	Sgt	BROOKES Melvin John Halls	14-05-43	77 Sqn
1415865	Sgt	BROOKES Reginald	28-02-43	49 Sqn

1337041	Sgt	BROOKMAN Herbert John Redrup	4-12-43	431 Sqn		778810	Sgt	BROWN Malcolm Penvil [Rhodesia]	27-04-43	429 Sqn
908789	Sgt	BROOKS Arthur James	11-04-43	1660 HCU		1347708	Sgt	BROWN Mathew Parkinson	17-06-43	1656 HCU
657597	Sgt	BROOKS John Henry	27-01-43	51 Sqn		72105	F/L	BROWN Nigel Stuart Hally	7-04-43	166 Sqn
1193006	Sgt	BROOKS Wilfred Stanley	25-06-43	156 Sqn		144183	P/O	BROWN Ralph	23-04-43	9 Sqn
1438247	Sgt	BROOKSBANK Alfred Clifton	1-09-43	623 Sqn		581266	W/O	BROWN Ralph Chaytor	22-01-43	180 Sqn
545146	Sgt	BROOME Alfred Thomas	17-12-43	12 Sqn		746335	Sgt	BROWN Reginald Thomas	6-11-43	138 Sqn
578880	Sgt	BROOMFIELD Leonard Stuart	5-05-43	90 Sqn		658431	Sgt	BROWN Reginald William	30-03-43	49 Sqn
658866	F/S	BROTHERS George	16-12-43	9 Sqn		944643	Sgt	BROWN Richard	2-03-43	207 Sqn
1528408	Sgt	BROTHERTON Alwyn	26-05-43	7 Sqn		1059977	Sgt	BROWN Roland	16-04-43	1409 Flt
135042	F/O	BROTHWELL Jack	22-11-43	75 Sqn		1285031	Sgt	BROWN Ronald	14-08-43	19 OTU
1239045	Sgt	BROTHWELL George William	15-01-43	29 OTU		131965	P/O	BROWN Roy	11-04-43	166 Sqn
1339242	Sgt	BROUGH Derek Walter	15-06-43	9 Sqn		1213064	Sgt	BROWN Roy	25-06-43	156 Sqn
1561520	Sgt	BROUGH Iam Clark	10-11-43	1660 HCU		1322948	Sgt	BROWN Sidney	14-05-43	102 Sqn
1390807	Sgt	BROUGH Robert	14-04-43	101 Sqn		1199948	Sgt	BROWN Stanley Kenneth	22-06-43	460 Sqn
1179979	Sgt	BROUGH Ronald	30-03-43	77 Sqn		1336567	Sgt	BROWN Stephen Hugh Colin	17-04-43	76 Sqn
577758	Sgt	BROUGHAM-FADDY Patrick Langston				1034865	Sgt	BROWN Sydney Crowther	27-04-43	156 Sqn
			17-04-43	156 Sqn		127127	F/O	BROWN Thomas	13-05-43	419 Sqn
1216884	Sgt	BROUGHTON Geoffrey James	12-08-43	28 OTU		124924	F/O	BROWN Thomas David	28-05-43	166 Sqn
1310565	Sgt	BROWN Abraham Lawson	2-03-43	61 Sqn		131998	P/O	BROWN Thomas Henry	27-03-43	7 Sqn
61007	F/L	BROWN Alan McKeand	15-06-43	103 Sqn		1588721	Sgt	BROWN Vincent De Paul	24-12-43	100 Sqn
1860203	Sgt	BROWN Alfred	26-05-43	51 Sqn		990520	Sgt	BROWN Walter	14-07-43	102 Sqn
1349635	F/S	BROWN Andrew Angus	6-09-43	149 Sqn		151776	P/O	BROWN Walter Gowans	7-09-43	102 Sqn
147318	P/O	BROWN Andrew James Ewen	24-08-43	83 Sqn		1340249	Sgt	BROWN William	30-07-43	77 Sqn
170737	P/O	BROWN Arthur Edward	17-12-43	166 Sqn		1496924	Sgt	BROWN William Alfred	27-09-43	10 Sqn
1245320	Sgt	BROWN Bromley John William	18-08-43	61 Sqn		1052824	F/S	BROWN William Austin	11-02-43	107 Sqn
411576	Sgt	BROWN Charles Bernard	30-07-43	214 Sqn		155006	P/O	BROWN William Gordon Leslie	22-06-43	35 Sqn
131769	P/O	BROWN Charles Douglas	30-01-43	28 OTU		616402	F/S	BROWN William John	13-08-43	78 Sqn
1208683	Sgt	BROWN Charles Frederick	3-08-43	115 Sqn		1320679	F/'S	BROWN William Richard	22-10-43	103 Sqn
1192773	Sgt	BROWN Charles Victor	11-03-43	44 Sqn		1384984	Sgt	BROWN William George	20-06-43	10 Sqn
1272049	F/S	BROWN Cyril Douglas	30-07-43	61 Sqn		1418678	Sgt	BROWNE David Ronald	3-09-43	101 Sqn
149639	P/O	BROWN Cyril Macdonald	10-08-43	103 Sqn		1323595	Sgt	BROWNE Edward Whitby Henry	26-06-43	106 Sqn
1386316	Sgt	BROWN David	29-06-43	10 Sqn		1336517	Sgt	BROWNE John Bonser	1-05-43	44 Sqn
51130	P/O	BROWN Denis James	29-04-43	218 Sqn		1337351	Sgt	BROWNE John Geoffrey Stewart	24-10-43	14 OTU
1337080	Sgt	BROWN Denis Norman	4-05-43	78 Sqn		55102	F/O	BROWNE Richard William	7-09-43	81 OTU
1125561	Sgt	BROWN Dennis	31-07-43	15 Sqn		1219663	F/S	BROWNING Anthony Charles	2-08-43	57 Sqn
1549636	Sgt	BROWN Dennis	30-03-43	106 Sqn		657584	Sgt	BROWNING William	10-03-43	10 Sqn
124415	F/O	BROWN Derek Frank Paston	20-06-43	115 Sqn		1289968	Sgt	BROWNLEE John Peter Hughes	1-05-43	77 Sqn
133716	F/O	BROWN Donald Arthur	18-11-43	90 Sqn		1554013	Sgt	BROWNLIE Archibald Halliday	7-10-43	49 Sqn
1576940	Sgt	BROWN Donald Arthur	29-01-43	9 Sqn		1074262	Sgt	BROWNLESS Thomas	3-08-43	405 Sqn
1004817	Sgt	BROWN Douglas	1-05-43	106 Sqn		1611324	Sgt	BROWNLOW Frederick Charles	27-04-43	158 Sqn
1317926	Sgt	BROWN Douglas	8-08-43	61 Sqn		1818551	Sgt	BRUCE Donald	23-09-43	77 Sqn
52566	P/O	BROWN Edward James	31-08-43	35 Sqn		1347044	Sgt	BRUCE George	27-11-43	103 Sqn
1148680	Sgt	BROWN Eric Gregson	13-05-43	51 Sqn		124216	F/O	BRUCE DFM James George	28-03-43	105 Sqn
1579075	Sgt	BROWN Eric Wilfred	11-12-43	26 OTU		1068572	Sgt	BRUCE Norman	17-04-43	196 Sqn
1081280	Sgt	BROWN Francis Joseph	6-09-43	196 Sqn		1512554	Sgt	BRUCE Wallace	31-08-43	106 Sqn
1313225	Sgt	BROWN Frank Charles	26-07-43	102 Sqn		967187	F/S	BRUCE William	13-07-43	467 Sqn
751279	F/S	BROWN Geoffrey	17-04-43	76 Sqn		1566041	Sgt	BRUCE William Stewart	27-11-43	428 Sqn
1318730	F/S	BROWN George Frederick	4-12-43	431 Sqn		1382778	Sgt	BRUM Frederick Miller	8-03-43	21 OTU
1451031	Sgt	BROWN George Henson	9-10-43	51 Sqn		1205942	LAC	BRUNDELL MiD John Henry	26-11-43	83 Sqn
1578580	Sgt	BROWN George Wilfred	22-06-43	156 Sqn		1063579	Sgt	BRUNNING Walter Henry	31-01-43	97 Sqn
1437124	Sgt	BROWN Gordon Harry	28-07-43	102 Sqn		1288015	W/O	BRUNT Ronald	26-11-43	49 Sqn
1689518	Sgt	BROWN Harry	2-12-43	103 Sqn		1302138	Sgt	BRUNTON Alexander Brodie	18-10-43	460 Sqn
1481118	Sgt	BROWN Hedley	23-09-43	419 Sqn		658381	Sgt	BRUNTON Alexander Cunningham	6-09-43	405 Sqn
1382768	Sgt	BROWN Henry David	26-03-43	460 Sqn		1444326	Sgt	BRUNTON Ronald Lewis	4-11-43	12 Sqn
545569	Sgt	BROWN Herbert George	4-05-43	15 Sqn		1389594	Sgt	BRYAN Albert George	23-06-43	9 Sqn
1187561	Sgt	BROWN James	26-06-43	103 Sqn		841200	Sgt	BRYAN Arthur	11-08-43	77 Sqn
136035	F/O	BROWN DFM James Wilfred Henry	20-09-43	138 Sqn		131166	F/O	BRYAN Charles Edward Thomas	3-08-43	103 Sqn
144933	P/O	BROWN James Wood	22-11-43	158 Sqn		1375818	F/S	BRYAN Walter Joseph	1-02-43	226 Sqn
1645687	AC2	BROWN John	19-06-43	Snaith		1063523	Sgt	BRYANS William Robert	10-07-43	408 Sqn
1303478	Sgt	BROWN John Arthur	13-05-43	214 Sqn		1451681	Sgt	BRYANT Charles Edward	23-05-43	218 Sqn
1432404	Sgt	BROWN John George	13-06-43	76 Sqn		1622899	Sgt	BRYANT Edward Oscar	24-09-43	57 Sqn
109028	F/O	BROWN John Hilton	9-03-43	35 Sqn		1384167	Sgt	BRYANT Eric William Capel	11-08-43	30 OTU
1482424	Sgt	BROWN John James	3-05-43	81 OTU		530868	Sgt	BRYANT James	20-04-43	57 Sqn
156611	F/O	BROWN John Thomas	17-12-43	97 Sqn		1312458	Sgt	BRYANT Llyn David	26-05-43	35 Sqn
1138903	Sgt	BROWN Joseph Henry	8-10-43	97 Sqn		1334545	Sgt	BRYANT Robert George Frederick	28-02-43	90 Sqn
146430	F/L	BROWN DFM Kenneth	4-10-43	97 Sqn		1294010	Sgt	BRYANT William Harry	26-05-43	90 Sqn
138498	P/O	BROWN Kenneth Joseph	1-03-43	420 Sqn		1567478	Sgt	BRYSON William Armit	3-10-43	77 Sqn
1615648	Sgt	BROWN Leonard Charles	2-12-43	57 Sqn		1561508	Sgt	BUCHAN Alexander	22-11-43	10 Sqn
1496117	Sgt	BROWN Louis	30-07-43	102 Sqn		1345035	Sgt	BUCHAN David McDougall	13-06-43	50 Sqn

986703	Sgt	BUCHAN George Banks	4-09-43	50 Sqn	158342	P/O	BURGESS John	5-12-43	1409 Flt
1565131	Sgt	BUCHAN John Sydney	27-10-43	11 OTU	1274974	Sgt	BURGESS Neville Edward	4-09-43	467 Sqn
655439	Sgt	BUCHAN Torrance	10-08-43	76 Sqn	124881	F/O	BURGESS Philip Sidney	16-05-43	617 Sqn
108149	F/O	BUCHANAN Frederick	3-02-43	78 Sqn	1391096	Sgt	BURGESS Roy Eric	9-10-43	106 Sqn
1567888	Sgt	BUCHANAN John George	13-11-43	51 Sqn	1389310	Sgt	BURGESS Thomas Mountford Adie	13-06-43	57 Sqn
1123751	Sgt	BUCHANAN Thomas Alexander Stuart			1331062	Sgt	BURGESS William Charles	10-03-43	44 Sqn
			5-05-43	166 Sqn	139206	P/O	BURGHER Reginald Silvester	26-02-43	102 Sqn
1372826	Sgt	BUCHANAN William Stewart	13-07-43	467 Sqn	1613718	Sgt	BURGOINE Michael Charles	21-04-43	61 Sqn
1305690	Sgt	BUCK Arthur William	23-09-43	49 Sqn	1379057	Sgt	BURINI Kenneth Alan	30-03-43	429 Sqn
1313328	Sgt	BUCK Edward Samuel	28-05-43	10 Sqn	1331917	Sgt	BURKE Arnold Bradley	24-12-43	100 Sqn
1399457	Sgt	BUCK John Anthony	22-10-43	78 Sqn	632396	F/S	BURKE Dennis	24-08-43	35 Sqn
137256	F/O	BUCK Leslie Albert	17-09-43	10 OTU	129140	F/O	BURKE DFM Hugh	20-09-43	138 Sqn
1391079	Sgt	BUCK Peter Leighton	24-08-43	158 Sqn	1109609	F/S	BURKILL Clifford	8-03-43	15 Sqn
1385277	Sgt	BUCK Robert Alfred	22-05-43	431 Sqn	1377962	F/S	BURLEY William Charles	4-12-43	431 Sqn
1378810	F/S	BUCK Robert Moscrop	27-11-43	428 Sqn	1077981	Sgt	BURMAN Richard Thomas	22-10-43	10 Sqn
156099	P/O	BUCKEL William	23-11-43	44 Sqn	1281850	Sgt	BURN Arthur Henry	13-05-43	24 OTU
133113	F/O	BUCKLAND Ronald William	26-07-43	158 Sqn	1388532	Sgt	BURN Robert Horace	3-08-43	61 Sqn
1120118	Sgt	BUCKLE Charles Joseph	15-06-43	50 Sqn	139960	F/O	BURNAM-RICHARDS Sydney George		
1686318	Sgt	BUCKLE Kenneth Ronald	11-08-43	214 Sqn				9-10-43	7 Sqn
1218154	Sgt	BUCKLE Michael John	11-01-43	81 OTU	131029	F/O	BURNE Colin	28-07-43	207 Sqn
1335598	F/S	BUCKLE Ronald Oswald	22-11-43	156 Sqn	540272	Sgt	BURNELL William	4-09-43	7 Sqn
1865368	Sgt	BUCKLE Roy William John	26-11-43	102 Sqn	1218402	Sgt	BURNETT Eric George	18-10-43	100 Sqn
1229779	Sgt	BUCKMAN Henry Ernest	1-09-43	622 Sqn	145469	P/O	BURNETT Ernest John	13-07-43	50 Sqn
657468	F/S	BUCKNER Ronald George Edwin	20-12-43	10 Sqn	574662	Sgt	BURNETT Laurence	3-03-43	12 Sqn
1199615	Sgt	BUCKSEY Valentine Richard	9-10-43	429 Sqn	1550978	Sgt	BURNETT Reginald	13-07-43	49 Sqn
1314591	Sgt	BUDD Colin Anthony	17-09-43	158 Sqn	155579	P/O	BURNS Aaron	11-08-43	57 Sqn
655615	F/S	BUDDEN Frederick Alfred	18-02-43	139 Sqn	655643	F/S	BURNS Andrew	5-05-43	78 Sqn
1194248	Sgt	BUFFERY William Henry	10-08-43	102 Sqn	115731	F/O	BURNS DFM Ian Crawford	1-04-43	103 Sqn
1581096	Sgt	BUFFHAM Roy	28-11-43	16 OTU	119906	F/O	BURNS John Joseph Wilfred	29-04-43	196 Sqn
1396272	Sgt	BUGG Bernard Stanley George	11-04-43	7 Sqn	1217692	F/S	BURNS Stephen	20-12-43	617 Sqn
1247330	Sgt	BUGG Leslie William	14-07-43	81 OTU	1033054	Sgt	BURNS Walter Eric	11-02-43	107 Sqn
1391064	Sgt	BULL Edward George	6-09-43	623 Sqn	1148682	Sgt	BURNSIDE John	17-06-43	49 Sqn
1585407	Sgt	BULL Ronald Bernard	15-08-43	192 Sqn	1039031	Sgt	BURNSIDE John Lawrence	29-06-43	76 Sqn
1375194	Sgt	BULL Walter Charles	23-07-43	24 OTU	637240	F/S	BURR William Cecil	12-03-43	97 Sqn
983356	Sgt	BULLEN William	10-03-43	166 Sqn	135685	F/O	BURRAS Charles Eric	30-07-43	78 Sqn
1215473	Sgt	BULLOCK Jack	27-09-43	166 Sqn	1392530	Sgt	BURRELL Reginald Arthur	16-07-43	10 Sqn
129475	F/O	BULLOCK James Rodolph	24-05-43	102 Sqn	137469	F/O	BURRELL Robert	20-12-43	44 Sqn
1334618	Sgt	BULMER Albert Derek	12-06-43	115 Sqn	1336905	Sgt	BURRETT Hugh Faringdon	1-09-43	90 Sqn
116940	F/O	BULPITT Arthur Norman	3-03-43	139 Sqn	149497	P/O	BURRIDGE Harold James [Canada]	14-07-43	78 Sqn
573198	Sgt	BUNCE Jack	27-02-43	12 Sqn	1385003	F/S	BURRIDGE Robert	13-05-43	196 Sqn
117580	S/L	BUNCLARK DFC DFM Peter	24-08-43	78 Sqn	1047345	Sgt	BURROUGHS Jeffrey	26-07-43	156 Sqn
1319521	F/S	BUNDLE DFM James Thomas	18-10-43	97 Sqn	147470	P/O	BURROW Joseph Howard	12-06-43	431 Sqn
1390343	Sgt	BUNDY Francis William	20-10-43	405 Sqn	1536322	Sgt	BURROWS Kenneth Reginald	2-07-43	30 OTU
1501434	Sgt	BUNKER John Dennis Gordon	16-07-43	10 Sqn	1503094	Sgt	BURROWS Norman Rupert	17-05-43	617 Sqn
366029	W/O	BUNT Edward Trezise	18-02-43	57 Sqn	929453	Sgt	BURROWS Stanley Herbert	22-06-43	218 Sqn
1822100	Sgt	BUNTAIN William Robert	16-12-43	7 Sqn	1271016	Sgt	BURSON Aaron	3-04-43	106 Sqn
1550979	Sgt	BUNTIN James	13-05-43	9 Sqn	1284770	Sgt	BURSTON Maynard Hargrave	22-06-43	57 Sqn
1384948	Sgt	BUNTING Barnard Angus	13-05-43	51 Sqn	1336282	Sgt	BURT Raymond Charles	17-04-43	51 Sqn
		[New Zealand]			524215	Sgt	BURT Vernon Clifford	6-04-43	1663 HCU
51326	F/O	BURBECK Kenneth Rees	23-09-43	100 Sqn	1047849	Sgt	BURTON Arthur Blackburn	22-10-43	10 Sqn
126016	F/O	BURBRIDGE DFC Frank Peter	22-11-43	97 Sqn	1332563	Sgt	BURTON Barry Charles	27-02-43	16 OTU
1315519	Sgt	BURCH Bertram Sidney	20-09-43	138 Sqn	1199686	Sgt	BURTON Charles	24-08-43	149 Sqn
50040	F/L	BURCHETT AFC Arthur Robert	20-12-43	51 Sqn	612357	Sgt	BURTON Cyril	23-11-43	207 Sqn
1575805	Sgt	BURDETT Donald Wiliam	6-09-43	49 Sqn	1314108	Sgt	BURTON Cyril Kitchener	12-06-43	76 Sqn
51730	P/O	BURDON John	10-08-43	102 Sqn	1515874	Sgt	BURTON Derrick Percy	20-10-43	10 OTU
1890406	Sgt	BURFIELD John Ray Richard	3-08-43	428 Sqn	1576202	Sgt	BURTON Edward	14-06-43	199 Sqn
1320913	Sgt	BURGE Dennis John	22-09-43	434 Sqn	1300347	Sgt	BURTON Frederick	22-06-43	619 Sqn
1315388	Sgt	BURGESS Alan Stewart	23-09-43	106 Sqn	1389244	Sgt	BURTON Frederick Ronald	11-04-43	15 Sqn
1370149	Sgt	BURGESS Alexander Rennie	3-03-43	12 OTU	1612869	Sgt	BURTON George Charles	28-08-43	620 Sqn
1230174	Sgt	BURGESS Alfred Brian	7-02-43	166 Sqn	1186818	Sgt	BURTON Harold William	5-05-43	90 Sqn
1385792	Sgt	BURGESS Alfred Charles	9-01-43	103 Sqn	913376	Sgt	BURTON Herbert Frank	13-01-43	61 Sqn
1315656	Sgt	BURGESS Anthony Richard	12-03-43	1661 HCU	1395372	Sgt	BURTON John Francis	27-11-43	16 OTU
1270390	Sgt	BURGESS Arthur	1-09-43	77 Sqn	1385331	Sgt	BURTON DFM Kenneth Reginald	4-04-43	214 Sqn
1382415	Sgt	BURGESS Arthur	22-06-43	166 Sqn	139618	F/O	BURTON Robert Edward Halliburton	2-10-43	57 Sqn
156616	P/O	BURGESS Charles Sidney	31-08-43	434 Sqn	1331548	W/O	BURTON Royce Reginald	3-08-43	166 Sqn
995291	Sgt	BURGESS Cornelius	24-12-43	44 Sqn	1335190	Sgt	BURTON Stanley George	5-12-43	101 Sqn
51898	P/O	BURGESS Edgar Heaton	21-01-43	103 Sqn	907876	F/S	BURTON-BURGESS Frederick Edward		
1311769	Sgt	BURGESS George Richard	29-04-43	196 Sqn				23-11-43	83 Sqn
128714	F/O	BURGESS John	4-04-43	158 Sqn	138333	F/O	BUSBY Arthur Edward	4-12-43	115 Sqn

Service #	Rank	Name	Date	Sqn
1391156	Sgt	BUSBY Denis George	4-02-43	57 Sqn
147211	P/O	BUSBY CGM Desmond Clive Camden [Ceylon]	17-06-43	156 Sqn
1138659	Sgt	BUSBY Stanley	26-05-43	51 Sqn
1317349	Sgt	BUSCOMBE Edwin George	29-04-43	12 Sqn
136704	F/O	BUSH Kenneth Stanley	27-05-43	105 Sqn
521148	Sgt	BUSH William Alfred [Canada]	26-06-43	101 Sqn
1385767	Sgt	BUSH William Charles	27-01-43	466 Sqn
1079812	Sgt	BUSHELL Henry Bernard	16-12-43	7 Sqn
1393670	Sgt	BUSHILL Arthur Sidney	24-05-43	44 Sqn
1602942	Sgt	BUSSELL Raymond Harold	26-11-43	103 Sqn
88143	F/O	BUSSEY Richard Selwyn	3-10-43	78 Sqn
1578256	Sgt	BUTCHER Arthur William	31-01-43	9 Sqn
1604241	Sgt	BUTCHER Kenneth Richard	4-12-43	115 Sqn
649905	Sgt	BUTLER Charles	2-12-43	156 Sqn
1804215	Sgt	BUTLER Donald Frederick	17-12-43	57 Sqn
1484118	Sgt	BUTLER Harold	31-08-43	218 Sqn
1268653	Sgt	BUTLER John Joseph	24-08-43	35 Sqn
130518	P/O	BUTLER John Perceval	9-01-43	14 OTU
139948	P/O	BUTLER Kenneth Frank	18-01-43	12 Sqn
1573300	Sgt	BUTLER Lionel Wembley Henry	27-09-43	166 Sqn
985083	Sgt	BUTLER Maurice	1-09-43	214 Sqn
1577781	Sgt	BUTLER Ralph Blackton	13-06-43	100 Sqn
1388968	Sgt	BUTLER Reginald Eric	28-09-43	1667 HCU
1112316	Sgt	BUTLER Richard	3-05-43	107 Sqn
139687	F/O	BUTLER Robert	16-12-43	97 Sqn
941135	F/S	BUTLER Robert	26-11-43	103 Sqn
1554168	Sgt	BUTLER William Cairns	29-06-43	51 Sqn
547514	Sgt	BUTLIN Dennis Charles	1-05-43	1663 HCU
961492	Sgt	BUTT Jack Eric	14-05-43	149 Sqn
801506	Sgt	BUTT Thomas Alfred George	15-02-43	90 Sqn
162505	P/O	BUTTERFIELD Derek William Hanson	3-10-43	12 Sqn
2206621	Sgt	BUTTERFIELD Frank	14-05-43	57 Sqn
1233713	F/S	BUTTERFIELD Thomas	3-12-43	9 Sqn
1336746	Sgt	BUTTERLEY Thomas	30-01-43	28 OTU
1623599	Sgt	BUTTERLY John Desmond [Eire]	7-07-43	12 Sqn
1425005	F/S	BUTTERWORTH Cyril	17-08-43	57 Sqn
656801	Sgt	BUTTERWORTH Peter	29-06-43	149 Sqn
1339068	Sgt	BUTTON Cyril	3-08-43	115 Sqn
1516920	Sgt	BUTTON Denis George	12-11-43	35 Sqn
917093	Sgt	BUTTON Edward Lionel	16-12-43	9 Sqn
133704	F/O	BUTTON Gordon William Frederick	18-07-43	10 OTU
991263	Sgt	BUTTREY Harold	17-06-43	49 Sqn
785082	Sgt	BUXTON Arthur John [Far East]	13-05-43	90 Sqn
1034932	F/S	BUXTON Bernard John	31-08-43	427 Sqn
1177603	Sgt	BUXTON Harold	15-04-43	106 Sqn
1850646	Sgt	BUXTON Harry Gilbert	19-12-43	433 Sqn
529409	W/O	BUXTON John Edward	13-06-43	76 Sqn
1199580	Sgt	BUXTON Martin Levi	30-05-43	431 Sqn
149464	P/O	BUXTON DFM Reginald Kenneth	18-08-43	61 Sqn
1801432	Sgt	BUZAN Wilfred Claud	26-11-43	103 Sqn
134381	F/O	BYE Verner Charles	24-08-43	12 Sqn
933155	Sgt	BYGRAVE Leonard	7-02-43	158 Sqn
1388520	Sgt	BYRNE Edward Leslie	24-07-43	1652 HCU
156954	P/O	BYRNE James Ian Francis	28-08-43	77 Sqn
1385599	Sgt	BYSOUTH Dennis Norman	10-04-43	9 Sqn
49875	F/O	BYWATER DFC Arthur Harold	12-03-43	7 Sqn
139683	P/O	CABLE John Duncan Skelton	18-08-43	115 Sqn
169109	P/O	CABLE William Douglas Vernon	20-12-43	76 Sqn
1187011	Sgt	CADD John Jesse	16-01-43	61 Sqn
1111482	Sgt	CADDEN Edward	18-01-43	12 Sqn
1389837	Sgt	CADE William Harry	24-08-43	619 Sqn
1411702	Sgt	CADEL William Arthur	3-05-43	81 OTU
1331075	Sgt	CADMORE Edgar	12-06-43	76 Sqn
1600368	Sgt	CAHILL Edward James	28-07-43	156 Sqn
1495745	Sgt	CAHILL John	22-10-43	158 Sqn
856537	Sgt	CAIN Thomas Edward	17-12-43	100 Sqn
1575959	Sgt	CAINE Bernard James	8-03-43	21 OTU
1051616	F/S	CAIRNS Thomas Robert	13-05-43	83 Sqn
1801478	Sgt	CALCRAFT Norman James	24-08-43	199 Sqn
50437	F/O	CALCUTT Fred Irving	13-07-43	44 Sqn
778483	Sgt	CALCUTT Richard [Rhodesia]	18-01-43	44 Sqn
131954	F/O	CALDECOURT Ronald Dennis	23-06-43	78 Sqn
1370276	Sgt	CALDWELL John Hamilton	16-12-43	576 Sqn
655402	F/S	CALDWELL William Reginald	13-07-43	100 Sqn
549996	Sgt	CALE Adrian Laurence William	27-01-43	50 Sqn
1377873	Sgt	CALEY Arthur Ashton	25-06-43	7 Sqn
1459176	Sgt	CALLAGHAN James Edward	1-04-43	103 Sqn
542701	Sgt	CALLAN James Richard [Eire]	14-04-43	138 Sqn
1120882	Sgt	CALLANAN James	13-02-43	12 Sqn
1480159	Sgt	CALLAWAY Joseph Aloysius	26-11-43	626 Sqn
155479	P/O	CALLAWAY Martin Philp	1-09-43	90 Sqn
517656	Sgt	CALLCUT Jack Sidney	22-06-43	460 Sqn
130287	F/O	CALMAN Denis Henry	26-11-43	61 Sqn
137298	P/O	CALVERT DFM Cyril Desmond	3-04-43	83 Sqn
1393627	Sgt	CALVERT John Reginald Gallimore	15-04-43	196 Sqn
857444	Sgt	CALVERT Joseph	24-12-43	115 Sqn
1349352	Sgt	CALVERT William	11-06-43	467 Sqn
1337068	Sgt	CALWAY Frederick George	9-10-43	218 Sqn
1092905	Sgt	CAMBURN Alec Reginald	1-05-43	77 Sqn
127843	P/O	CAMERON DFM Alexander	1-02-43	11 OTU
126508	F/O	CAMERON Andrew Greenhill	9-01-43	44 Sqn
1320110	Sgt	CAMERON David Ian	25-07-43	103 Sqn
591992	Sgt	CAMERON Douglas	9-07-43	97 Sqn
1304742	Sgt	CAMERON Gibson	23-06-43	75 Sqn
1342504	Sgt	CAMERON Ian Nicol Ferguson	27-09-43	50 Sqn
1555813	Sgt	CAMERON James Barkess	22-10-43	158 Sqn
971743	Sgt	CAMERON Leslie Charles	17-04-43	75 Sqn
155800	P/O	CAMERON Robert	3-11-43	10 Sqn
165635	F/O	CAMERON William Johnstone [Canada]	7-09-43	78 Sqn
155127	P/O	CAMILLE Philippe Emmanuel [Mauritius]	22-10-43	57 Sqn
1098538	Sgt	CAMM Gilbert Simpson	23-11-43	460 Sqn
1339016	Sgt	CAMMIES Donald Thomas William	27-09-43	19 OTU
1605423	Sgt	CAMP Edgar William	7-11-43	1663 HCU
1235252	Sgt	CAMPAIN Gordon	13-01-43	12 OTU
1071521	Sgt	CAMPBELL Alexander	4-03-43	51 Sqn
1498151	Sgt	CAMPBELL Allan	21-01-43	51 Sqn
994017	Sgt	CAMPBELL Archibald Thomas Wilson	18-08-43	90 Sqn
1239952	Sgt	CAMPBELL Arnold	24-05-43	102 Sqn
1333017	Sgt	CAMPBELL Colin Desmond Harry	26-06-43	90 Sqn
1370062	Sgt	CAMPBELL Daniel	24-12-43	550 Sqn
658529	F/S	CAMPBELL Douglas	13-07-43	424 Sqn
1345600	Sgt	CAMPBELL Douglas Noel	12-06-43	12 Sqn
126966	F/O	CAMPBELL Edmund Fraser	28-05-43	76 Sqn
1287460	Sgt	CAMPBELL Eric Archibald Owen	17-01-43	101 Sqn
1147377	Sgt	CAMPBELL Eric William	27-01-43	57 Sqn
1366510	Sgt	CAMPBELL George Law	27-09-43	156 Sqn
87059	S/L	CAMPBELL DFC Halan Donald Richard Leroy [Canada]	14-05-43	408 Sqn
1007245	Sgt	CAMPBELL Hugh	17-12-43	218 Sqn
1065510	Sgt	CAMPBELL James Kenneth	21-04-43	102 Sqn
1690312	Sgt	CAMPBELL John Archibald	22-07-43	1657 HCU
122910	F/O	CAMPBELL John Michael	29-03-43	218 Sqn
614965	Sgt	CAMPBELL Kenneth Munro	30-05-43	218 Sqn
978248	Sgt	CAMPBELL Robert Allison	23-11-43	97 Sqn
149528	P/O	CAMPBELL Robert McMillan	18-08-43	44 Sqn
548217	Sgt	CAMPBELL Thomas	30-07-43	78 Sqn
1281944	Sgt	CAMPBELL Thomas Joseph	15-05-43	30 OTU
1133327	Sgt	CAMPS Albert	21-05-43	149 Sqn
149523	P/O	CANDY Ernest	14-07-43	90 Sqn
1802920	Sgt	CANE William George	21-10-43	103 Sqn
1190095	Sgt	CANN Stanley Richard	15-02-43	90 Sqn
1392582	Sgt	CANNELL Stanley William Charles	17-02-43	14 OTU
1271645	Sgt	CANNING Jack	29-06-43	424 Sqn
1397680	Sgt	CANT Leslie Ronald	24-06-43	75 Sqn

1397376	Sgt	CANTIN Richard Claud Harold	26-11-43	61 Sqn	1312636	Sgt	CASSELL John Edwin O'Neil	22-06-43	460 Sqn
142555	F/O	CAPLAN DFM Maynard Meyer	7-09-43	1658 HCU	1481549	Sgt	CASSELL Stephen Joseph	18-08-43	100 Sqn
1333385	Sgt	CAPLIN Vivian Max	26-02-43	427 Sqn	1312310	Sgt	CASSELL William Arthur	22-10-43	434 Sqn
1333550	Sgt	CAPON Maurice George Wilfred	16-04-43	460 Sqn	1067061	F/S	CASSIDY James	24-08-43	218 Sqn
751463	F/S	CAPON Philip John	18-08-43	103 Sqn	1802082	Sgt	CASSIDY Patrick	8-10-43	97 Sqn
126833	F/O	CAPON Reginald Brian	22-06-43	35 Sqn	1558450	Sgt	CASSIDY Thomas Cornelius	31-08-43	149 Sqn
1350937	Sgt	CAPP Leslie Stanley	4-07-43	12 Sqn	1335447	F/S	CASSINGHAM Ernest	12-06-43	35 Sqn
131489	P/O	CAPPLEMAN DFM Walter Henry	22-01-43	180 Sqn	1039199	Sgt	CASSTLES John Hamilton	17-05-43	10 OTU
127066	F/O	CAPRON Roderick Halliley	1-05-43	467 Sqn	1152895	LAC	CASTELL Ronald William	25-07-43	Graveley
1331878	Sgt	CARD Benjamin William	15-06-43	44 Sqn	631242	F/S	CASTELLARI Reginald Lionel	11-04-43	166 Sqn
1522196	Sgt	CARDOO Alexander Rodger	30-05-43	75 Sqn	1339076	F/S	CASTELLS Nigel Paul Ivan	28-07-43	50 Sqn
567350	Sgt	CARDWELL Douglas Eric	16-02-43	103 Sqn	526097	Sgt	CASTLE Alfred	24-08-43	619 Sqn
1580617	Sgt	CARDY Dennis Alfred	12-08-43	28 OTU	142892	P/O	CATCH Henry	13-05-43	214 Sqn
1214849	Sgt	CARE Donald Burton	2-03-43	15 Sqn	1384413	Sgt	CATER Frederick William	18-01-43	9 Sqn
125672	F/O	CAREY Basil	23-04-43	9 Sqn	1384736	Sgt	CATER Ronald Charles George	1-02-43	425 Sqn
129334	P/O	CAREY Peter Denzil O'Donoghue	28-01-43	20 OTU	155019	P/O	CATES Lawrence Reginald	1-09-43	51 Sqn
1321055	Sgt	CAREY Peter Leslie	2-04-43	16 OTU	1808380	Sgt	CATON George Anthony Carlisle 'Tony'		
64295	F/L	CARFOOT Norman Henry	3-11-43	49 Sqn				17-12-43	17 OTU
137554	F/O	CARLING Peter	28-08-43	76 Sqn	1313217	Sgt	CAUDELL William Ernest	4-09-43	44 Sqn
1515883	Sgt	CARLON Ronald	16-08-43	166 Sqn	112387	F/L	CAUDREY Dennis Edward	23-11-43	630 Sqn
42672	S/L	CARLYON DFC Paul Winstanley Manners			1454107	Sgt	CAULTON Ivan	7-04-43	166 Sqn
		[Canada]	15-03-43	214 Sqn	2209008	Sgt	CAUSER Edward	16-08-43	21 OTU
798585	Sgt	CARNELL Basil [Newfoundland]	12-03-43	214 Sqn	1267471	Sgt	CAUSER George Thomas	13-07-43	100 Sqn
115116	F/O	CARPENTER David James	3-09-43	101 Sqn	573801	Sgt	CAVADINO Francis Anthony	29-01-43	408 Sqn
142131	F/O	CARPENTER George Ralph	18-08-43	12 Sqn	646879	Sgt	CAVANAGH Edward	3-08-43	115 Sqn
1503460	Sgt	CARPENTER James Clement	30-07-43	57 Sqn	1029887	Sgt	CAVE Ronald	22-09-43	12 OTU
1323063	Sgt	CARPENTER John Alexander	13-07-43	57 Sqn	1130074	Sgt	CAVENEY Thomas James	3-03-43	15 Sqn
139490	P/O	CARR Albert	6-02-43	1657 HCU	1330185	Sgt	CAVIE Jack George	27-09-43	10 Sqn
998856	Sgt	CARR Edward	8-03-43	61 Sqn	654206	Sgt	CAVILL Edward	28-05-43	35 Sqn
612438	Sgt	CARR Frank Emmerson	30-10-43	5 Group	1400551	Sgt	CAWTHORNE Donald	6-10-43	19 OTU
933802	Sgt	CARR Frederick George	7-02-43	158 Sqn	649855	Sgt	CAWTHORNE John Thomas	6-09-43	51 Sqn
1491624	Sgt	CARR Harry	27-11-43	49 Sqn	1096561	Sgt	CAWTHRA Norman Algar Musgrove	25-06-43	166 Sqn
1121598	Sgt	CARR Lawrence	15-01-43	214 Sqn	1456974	Sgt	CAYLESS George Reuben Stacey	29-06-43	467 Sqn
127260	F/O	CARR Robert Henry	11-03-43	44 Sqn	132388	F/O	CAZALY Cuthbert Keith	28-05-43	467 Sqn
1378749	F/S	CARR DFM Robert Stonehouse	12-03-43	207 Sqn	1623574	Sgt	CERVI Louis	13-07-43	103 Sqn
658715	Sgt	CARR Walter	30-03-43	49 Sqn	1483582	Sgt	CHADFIELD George Edward	30-05-43	44 Sqn
514361	F/S	CARRINGTON Charles Gordon	28-08-43	51 Sqn	1214519	Sgt	CHADWICK Alfred	21-04-43	90 Sqn
1333287	Sgt	CARRINGTON Dennis John	18-08-43	620 Sqn	1622527	Sgt	CHADWICK Cyril	24-08-43	156 Sqn
119522	F/O	CARRINGTON Lawrence Vernon	22-01-43	98 Sqn	1020104	Sgt	CHADWICK Harold	23-08-43	100 Sqn
1484120	Sgt	CARROLL Bernard	2-12-43	156 Sqn	1453551	Sgt	CHADWICK Stanley	23-11-43	1658 HCU
936076	Sgt	CARROLL James Maurice	17-06-43	103 Sqn	1537059	Sgt	CHADWICK Thomas Noel	28-03-43	105 Sqn
50691	F/O	CARROTT Hubert Edward	9-10-43	61 Sqn	1237680	Sgt	CHAFFEY Frederic Munroe	24-05-43	78 Sqn
1345462	F/O	CARRUTHERS James Thomson	4-09-43	57 Sqn	1322049	Sgt	CHALK Albert Edward	31-07-43	408 Sqn
1344908	Sgt	CARSCADDEN Andrew Steel	4-09-43	106 Sqn	574277	Sgt	CHALKER Charles Leslie	4-07-43	15 Sqn
1108682	F/S	CARSON David Ellis Murray	3-08-43	166 Sqn	1330438	Sgt	CHALKLEY John	24-08-43	102 Sqn
1271552	Sgt	CARTER Edwin	21-10-43	7 Sqn	140914	P/O	CHALLIS Edward	27-03-43	214 Sqn
1515873	Sgt	CARTER Ernest	21-04-43	77 Sqn	1614936	Sgt	CHALLIS John Frederick	22-10-43	431 Sqn
146404	P/O	CARTER Mathew Cecil	13-06-43	50 Sqn	131995	P/O	CHALLONER Charles Stuart	4-03-43	100 Sqn
126747	F/O	CARTER Norman Henry	7-09-43	156 Sqn	50465	P/O	CHALLONER DFC Thomas William	19-03-43	161 Sqn
1331481	Sgt	CARTER Stanley Charles	25-06-43	7 Sqn	1321621	Sgt	CHALMERS John Geoffrey	8-04-43	466 Sqn
1545420	Sgt	CARTER Stephen Hodge	23-07-43	24 OTU	1401894	Sgt	CHALMERS Thomas	26-05-43	467 Sqn
652517	Sgt	CARTER Thomas	21-04-43	100 Sqn	1476619	Sgt	CHAMBERLAIN William Eric	12-03-43	100 Sqn
1300587	Sgt	CARTER Thomas	15-06-43	12 Sqn	1392393	Sgt	CHAMBERLAIN Willie Austin 'Bill'	8-08-43	26 OTU
1071349	Sgt	CARTER Wallace	3-04-43	166 Sqn	1578098	Sgt	CHAMBERS Arthur Alfred	19-04-43	22 OTU
1454154	Sgt	CARTER William Harry	24-12-43	463 Sqn	656382	Sgt	CHAMBERS Colin Frederick	15-03-43	138 Sqn
577959	Sgt	CARTER William Jesse	18-01-43	467 Sqn	1330903	Sgt	CHAMBERS Douglas Edward Cyril	12-06-43	419 Sqn
1129644	Sgt	CARTMELL Joseph Leadbetter	15-04-43	101 Sqn	150000	F/O	CHAMBERS Geoffrey	8-07-43	17 OTU
1672469	Sgt	CARTMELL Mark Watson	27-11-43	103 Sqn	1434966	Sgt	CHAMBERS Jack Harvey	2-12-43	57 Sqn
747242	LAC	CARTWRIGHT Charles Henry	18-01-43	218 Sqn	942459	Sgt	CHAMBERS Richard	22-10-43	57 Sqn
124313	F/O	CARTWRIGHT David I'Anson	10-03-43	429 Sqn	1620466	Sgt	CHAMBERS William Henry	16-12-43	103 Sqn
659124	Sgt	CARTWRIGHT Harold	1-09-43	90 Sqn	1508677	Sgt	CHAMBERS William John	26-05-43	51 Sqn
1318994	Sgt	CARTWRIGHT Leslie Henry	27-11-43	49 Sqn	1294119	Sgt	CHAMP Wilfred Stanley	12-06-43	15 Sqn
1334945	Sgt	CARTY Harry Dennis Gordon	30-03-43	429 Sqn	1315034	Sgt	CHAMPION Wilfred Albert	1-03-43	29 OTU
1466576	Sgt	CARVER John	11-03-43	15 OTU	53774	P/O	CHAMPION William James	4-11-43	75 Sqn
1393968	F/S	CARVER Reginald Walter	29-12-43	61 Sqn	1800725	Sgt	CHANDLER Albert William	29-09-43	419 Sqn
159068	P/O	CASELEY Reginald Job	4-12-43	77 Sqn	639605	Sgt	CHANDLER Alfred George	23-11-43	100 Sqn
1801923	Sgt	CASELTON Victor John	4-09-43	15 Sqn	1032376	Sgt	CHANDLER Frederick John	1-05-43	76 Sqn
998689	F/S	CASEY William Anthony	24-12-43	514 Sqn	1699810	Sgt	CHANLDER James John	30-05-43	75 Sqn
1334740	Sgt	CASH George Henry Joseph	4-04-43	214 Sqn	1313346	Sgt	CHANDLER John Noel Thomas	30-07-43	214 Sqn

Number	Rank	Name	Date	Unit
1219494	Sgt	CHANDLER Rowland John Paul	23-06-43	30 OTU
1197641	Sgt	CHANNING Denys William Birkett	29-06-43	149 Sqn
1007496	Sgt	CHAPLIN Jack	14-07-43	78 Sqn
1035098	Sgt	CHAPLIN Kenneth Walter	6-09-43	44 Sqn
1579639	Sgt	CHAPMAN Alfred Charles Richard	18-08-43	619 Sqn
1160856	Sgt	CHAPMAN Anthony William	30-05-43	106 Sqn
128617	F/O	CHAPMAN Chelmsford Edward	6-03-43	426 Sqn
1425936	F/S	CHAPMAN Cyril	16-12-43	576 Sqn
1585448	Sgt	CHAPMAN Ernest Harrington	9-10-43	429 Sqn
1322050	Sgt	CHAPMAN Ernest John	21-01-43	101 Sqn
1023437	F/S	CHAPMAN Frank Lewis	22-11-43	7 Sqn
1388554	Sgt	CHAPMAN Frederick George	24-08-43	158 Sqn
132777	F/O	CHAPMAN Frederick John	17-10-43	196 Sqn
127265	F/O	CHAPMAN Frederick Russell Forbes [Australia]	13-02-43	420 Sqn
2208993	Sgt	CHAPMAN George	20-12-43	103 Sqn
1395829	Sgt	CHAPMAN George Charles	23-06-43	83 Sqn
1397248	Sgt	CHAPMAN George Ernest	4-10-43	419 Sqn
125992	F/O	CHAPMAN John Henry	13-02-43	158 Sqn
617652	Sgt	CHAPMAN Kenneth Herbert	1-03-43	103 Sqn
134746	F/O	CHAPMAN Twice MiD Maurice Allen	26-06-43	15 Sqn
1861645	Sgt	CHAPMAN Philip Albert	10-07-43	50 Sqn
1380243	Sgt	CHAPMAN Philip Arthur	12-06-43	115 Sqn
1397807	Sgt	CHAPMAN Richard James	29-07-43	218 Sqn
1238906	Sgt	CHAPMAN Ronald Ellis	10-08-43	102 Sqn
1522573	Sgt	CHAPMAN Russell Jesse	20-04-43	460 Sqn
658677	Sgt	CHAPMAN Sidney William	1-09-43	78 Sqn
646335	F/S	CHAPMAN Stanley	27-11-43	50 Sqn
930738	Sgt	CHAPMAN Stanley	18-08-43	12 Sqn
571423	Sgt	CHAPMAN Thomas Arnold	20-05-43	207 Sqn
1316314	Sgt	CHAPMAN William Patrick Delaney	30-03-43	460 Sqn
976906	Sgt	CHAPPELL Douglas Stanley Knox	9-10-43	106 Sqn
1094495	Sgt	CHAPPELL Harry	16-12-43	97 Sqn
625153	Sgt	CHAPPELL Stanley Frederick Walter	8-04-43	100 Sqn
1257583	F/S	CHAPPLE Walter James	15-06-43	9 Sqn
1386718	Sgt	CHARLEBOIS Edward William Leon	12-03-43	102 Sqn
1095725	Sgt	CHARLES Eric Arthur	30-07-43	7 Sqn
969366	W/O	CHARLESWORTH Alan	18-11-43	77 Sqn
1684079	Sgt	CHARLESWORTH Derek	3-08-43	428 Sqn
128692	P/O	CHARLESWORTH Edgar Richard	15-01-43	427 Sqn
1394791	Sgt	CHARLIER Peter Joseph	4-08-43	16 OTU
1318463	Sgt	CHARLTON Herbert Percy Durtnall	9-10-43	1664 HCU
621023	Sgt	CHARLTON John Thomas	5-03-43	218 Sqn
1333575	Sgt	CHARLTON Leslie Albert	2-08-43	18 OTU
644136	F/S	CHARLTON Ronald	4-11-43	75 Sqn
1601866	Sgt	CHARROTT Charles William	6-11-43	138 Sqn
1039009	F/S	CHARTERS John Bennett	28-07-43	106 Sqn
1380306	Sgt	CHASMAR Maurice Dudley	27-09-43	434 Sqn
1576209	Sgt	CHATTERTON Haigh	8-04-43	49 Sqn
82955	F/L	CHAVE Owen Cecil	14-02-43	15 Sqn
1128782	Sgt	CHEADLE George	4-09-43	101 Sqn
1336014	Sgt	CHEADLE Richard John	22-09-43	77 Sqn
1262889	Sgt	CHEAL William Edward	2-12-43	103 Sqn
1425127	Sgt	CHEASMAN Harold Alma	14-02-43	102 Sqn
948084	Sgt	CHECKETTS Frank Reginald William	2-02-43	44 Sqn
134030	F/O	CHEETHAM Alfred	11-04-43	50 Sqn
949236	Sgt	CHEETHAM James Arthur	2-05-43	11 OTU
1332233	Sgt	CHERRY Frederick John	30-03-43	408 Sqn
1336708	Sgt	CHESHIRE Harry William	18-06-43	83 Sqn
138785	F/O	CHESSER Ronald Etheridge	11-08-43	115 Sqn
1336122	Sgt	CHESSON Frederick John Charles	28-09-43	75 Sqn
1153105	Sgt	CHESSON Lawrence George	24-08-43	158 Sqn
1254680	Sgt	CHESTER Arthur John	14-01-43	466 Sqn
50232	F/O	CHESTER Herbert William	29-06-43	76 Sqn
1214512	F/S	CHESTER Ralph Owen	1-09-43	77 Sqn
26198	S/L	CHESTERMAN AFC Humphrey William Albert	11-04-43	7 Sqn
1383472	W/O	CHESTERTON DFC Paul Fulton	27-09-43	166 Sqn
1678429	Sgt	CHEW Bernard	16-12-43	44 Sqn
1810131	Sgt	CHEW Norman Alfred Pinxton	28-08-43	12 Sqn
1303121	Sgt	CHILCOTT Fernley Graham	27-09-43	10 Sqn
968999	Sgt	CHILD Roy Craven	24-05-43	214 Sqn
1294046	F/S	CHILDS Jack Whitney	18-11-43	15 Sqn
128604	F/L	CHILDS John Rowlison	28-07-43	15 Sqn
1076367	Sgt	CHILVER Kenneth Graham	28-05-43	428 Sqn
1235580	Sgt	CHILVERS George Alfred	2-12-43	1664 HCU
1335221	Sgt	CHILVERS John George Bruce	18-01-43	9 Sqn
1586498	Sgt	CHINN Richard Thomas	20-09-43	138 Sqn
1105193	Sgt	CHIPCHASE Kenneth William	11-03-43	83 Sqn
658368	Sgt	CHIPMAN Charles Anthony	11-03-43	15 OTU
127842	F/O	CHIPPENDALE Geoffrey Brian	21-04-43	21 Sqn
43929	S/L	CHISHOLM DFC Alexander Frederick	23-11-43	83 Sqn
1052247	Sgt	CHISHOLM Donald Alexander	13-07-43	467 Sqn
159042	P/O	CHISLETT Kenneth Edwin	9-10-43	51 Sqn
1384670	F/S	CHISLETT Raymond Colin	1-09-43	214 Sqn
1530103	Sgt	CHISNALL James	5-05-43	1663 HCU
1324736	Sgt	CHISNALL Leslie Malcolm	26-05-43	166 Sqn
128516	F/O	CHITTY Donald James Dupree	21-04-43	77 SQN
1181053	Sgt	CHITTY Richard Lawrence	14-01-43	9 Sqn
1389214	AC1	CHITTY Ronald James	30-03-43	1483 Flt
134570	P/O	CHIVERTON Harold George Raymond	5-05-43	102 Sqn
932412	Sgt	CHORLEY Robert Alexander	31-08-43	9 Sqn
146033	P/O	CHORLEY Verdun James	22-10-43	61 Sqn
129489	F/O	CHRISTIE William Douglas	3-08-43	100 Sqn
1335516	Sgt	CHRISTMAS James William	17-12-43	100 Sqn
638164	Sgt	CHRISTON James Frederick	6-02-43	90 Sqn
143398	P/O	CHRISTY Robert	24-05-43	49 Sqn
155352	P/O	CHUBB Alfred William	27-09-43	432 Sqn
1395990	Sgt	CHUMBLEY Robert Alfred	20-10-43	57 Sqn
148123	P/O	CHURCH Bernard Henry	26-06-43	214 Sqn
1196564	Sgt	CHURCH David	28-04-43	75 Sqn
1270457	Sgt	CHURCH Eric Cyril	24-05-43	10 Sqn
1586295	Sgt	CHURN Thomas Bernard	2-10-43	15 OTU
1399230	Sgt	CIPRIANI Mervyn Eugene [Trinidad]	22-10-43	158 Sqn
910303	Sgt	CLACK Matthew Henry	25-06-43	102 Sqn
1293199	Sgt	CLACK Norman William Stanley	12-06-43	76 Sqn
1070408	Sgt	CLAGUE William Francis Collister	30-05-43	460 Sqn
156067	F/O	CLAGUE William Henry	31-08-43	218 Sqn
1130711	Sgt	CLAPHAM Thomas Herbert	1-02-43	1659 HCU
1587325	Sgt	CLAPP Thomas Hill	3-10-43	103 Sqn
162785	P/O	CLAPPERTON John	23-11-43	630 Sqn
1330221	Sgt	CLARE Richard	27-01-43	139 Sqn
1351276	F/S	CLARK Alan John	27-09-43	156 Sqn
1389325	Sgt	CLARK Albert Brinley	28-08-43	77 Sqn
1600432	Sgt	CLARK Albert Edward	12-03-43	1661 HCU
1387144	Sgt	CLARK Alfred William	17-04-43	460 Sqn
1203348	Sgt	CLARK Arthur Harold	5-05-43	101 Sqn
1331499	Sgt	CLARK Charles Henry Arthur	28-09-43	90 Sqn
657815	F/S	CLARK Douglas	23-11-43	103 Sqn
1578459	Sgt	CLARK Ernest Leslie	15-05-43	27 OTU
128520	F/O	CLARK Frederick Allan	13-05-43	77 Sqn
1850565	Sgt	CLARK Frederick George	17-12-43	12 Sqn
1442665	F/S	CLARK Geoffrey Francis	24-12-43	625 Sqn
628471	Sgt	CLARK George Ellis	26-07-43	61 Sqn
116208	F/O	CLARK Harold Arthur	28-08-43	83 Sqn
151632	F/O	CLARK Harry	17-12-43	57 Sqn
1093765	Sgt	CLARK Henry Alan	4-07-43	214 Sqn
1348909	Sgt	CLARK James	29-07-43	218 Sqn
1343392	F/S	CLARK DFM James Crichton	4-07-43	166 Sqn
954596	Cpl	CLARK John George	23-09-43	7 Sqn
81051	F/L	CLARK John Hope	26-01-43	29 OTU
658415	Sgt	CLARK John William Cockbain	5-01-43	101 Sqn
1341114	Sgt	CLARK Norman Will Hilton	18-08-43	61 Sqn
1369751	Sgt	CLARK Robert	3-03-43	427 Sqn
1051117	Sgt	CLARK Robert Mair	7-11-43	1663 HCU
1337671	F/S	CLARK DFM Stanley Percy	4-12-43	115 Sqn

Service No	Rank	Name	Date	Sqn
1581159	Sgt	CLARK Thomas Jackson	18-10-43	467 Sqn
116802	F/L	CLARK Walter Alexander Graham	22-11-43	156 Sqn
636060	Sgt	CLARK Walter Henry	5-03-43	156 Sqn
1385841	Sgt	CLARK Wilfred Ernest Fuller [Spain]	14-04-43	12 Sqn
156304	P/O	CLARK William Alfred	2-12-43	630 Sqn
1437777	Sgt	CLARK William Arthur	3-04-43	15 OTU
1356741	Sgt	CLARK William Henry Robert	16-07-43	10 Sqn
940903	Sgt	CLARKE Albert	28-08-43	75 Sqn
1497822	Sgt	CLARKE Cecil	28-05-43	77 Sqn
144446	P/O	CLARKE Charles William	13-05-43	50 Sqn
1216733	Sgt	CLARKE Clifford	27-01-43	21 OTU
1397327	Sgt	CLARKE Douglas	22-10-43	14 OTU
129352	F/O	CLARKE Francis Desmond	11-04-43	166 Sqn
1334192	Sgt	CLARKE Frederick Francis	16-12-43	166 Sqn
128546	F/O	CLARKE George McFerran	28-07-43	102 Sqn
139592	F/O	CLARKE Gordon Harvey	12-08-43	620 Sqn
1206892	Sgt	CLARKE Harold Thomas	28-06-43	101 Sqn
151170	F/O	CLARKE Henry Thomas	24-11-43	405 Sqn
50666	P/O	CLARKE John Clifford Alfred	31-01-43	57 Sqn
1803722	Sgt	CLARKE John Edward	16-12-43	101 Sqn
1483604	Sgt	CLARKE John Raymond Joseph	2-06-43	20 OTU
126043	P/O	CLARKE John Tully	13-03-43	431 Sqn
1230788	Sgt	CLARKE Joseph Gordon	6-09-43	106 Sqn
127957	F/O	CLARKE Michael Wilfred Peter	22-06-43	35 Sqn
102139	F/O	CLARKE Raymond	15-07-43	139 Sqn
1586132	Sgt	CLARKE Stephen Frank	23-09-43	77 Sqn
70132	S/L	CLARKE William	3-02-43	214 Sqn
1439792	Sgt	CLARKE William Leslie	24-08-43	78 Sqn
1554278	Sgt	CLARKSON George Henry	2-08-43	28 OTU
1217763	Sgt	CLAXTON Ebenezer Roy	3-12-43	166 Sqn
1379629	Sgt	CLAY Charles Norris	14-04-43	12 Sqn
135718	F/O	CLAY Leonard Douglas	27-09-43	199 Sqn
1583071	Sgt	CLAYDON Gordon William	24-12-43	100 Sqn
1315110	Sgt	CLAYDON Richard George	13-06-43	101 Sqn
1685180	Sgt	CLAYTON Edward	22-09-43	460 Sqn
1006016	Sgt	CLAYTON Eric Wilfred	28-08-43	12 Sqn
157684	P/O	CLAYTON DFM Frank	14-11-43	1409 Flt
1265211	F/S	CLAYTON Harold Leonard	2-12-43	44 Sqn
1126817	F/S	CLAYTON Thomas James	22-07-43	27 OTU
1377386	Sgt	CLAYTON William Hugh	12-03-43	149 Sqn
116769	F/O	CLEAR DFC Gordon Sampson	20-03-43	139 Sqn
516664	Sgt	CLEASBY Frederick James	5-05-43	83 Sqn
1338423	Sgt	CLEAVER Frank Charles	28-05-43	35 Sqn
574703	Sgt	CLEAVER Norman Claude	24-07-43	18 OTU
1315213	Sgt	CLEEVE Ronald George	17-12-43	97 Sqn
947632	Sgt	CLEGG Herbert	28-04-43	101 Sqn
656810	Sgt	CLEGG Jack	27-04-43	76 Sqn
1493160	Sgt	CLEGHORN Alan Hall	23-09-43	75 Sqn
146022	P/O	CLELLAND Harry James	12-06-43	158 Sqn
1569956	Sgt	CLELLAND Thomas	19-09-43	1658 HCU
149152	F/L	CLEMENT DFC Edward John	18-11-43	7 Sqn
127970	F/O	CLEMENT Henry Eifion	15-04-43	101 Sqn
1602118	Sgt	CLEMENTS Gerard William	17-09-43	10 OTU
124440	F/O	CLEMENTS John Sinclair	26-07-43	214 Sqn
1242362	Sgt	CLEMENTS Maurice Freeman	7-02-43	166 Sqn
124706	Sgt	CLEMENTS Raymond Frederick	17-04-43	51 Sqn
134106	F/O	CLEMENTS Ronald Cyril Saville	20-10-43	115 Sqn
1817088	Sgt	CLENTON James Sidney	31-08-43	158 Sqn
112739	F/L	CLEVELAND Cyril Herbert	2-10-43	61 Sqn
1128375	Sgt	CLEVERLY George Edward	9-10-43	460 Sqn
1379816	Sgt	CLIFFE Jack	15-06-43	103 Sqn
1338085	Sgt	CLIFFORD Arnold Charles	12-02-43	427 Sqn
1332298	Sgt	CLIFFORD Dennis John	13-03-43	199 Sqn
1851281	Sgt	CLIFFORD Ralph Colin	16-12-43	166 Sqn
1272678	Sgt	CLIFFORD Richard	16-08-43	115 Sqn
1206512	F/S	CLIFT DFM Alexander	12-03-43	7 Sqn
1387289	Sgt	CLIFTON Charles Thomas	28-02-43	83 Sqn
1048381	Sgt	CLIFTON DFM Leonard	31-07-43	90 Sqn
1352806	Sgt	CLINCH Desmond Henry	19-06-43	77 Sqn
655142	W/O	CLINCH Ernest James	13-08-43	77 Sqn
1384438	Sgt	CLINGING Brodie John	17-04-43	76 Sqn
116125	F/O	CLITHEROE DFC Brendan	12-03-43	207 Sqn
1459710	Sgt	CLOSE James Joseph	4-07-43	15 Sqn
1386024	Sgt	CLOTHIER Robert Alfred	23-09-43	101 Sqn
1473128	Sgt	CLOUD Allan	28-07-43	156 Sqn
130286	F/O	CLOUGH Fred	16-08-43	61 Sqn
1393499	Sgt	CLOUT Charles Frederick	11-02-43	57 Sqn
1324101	Sgt	CLOVER Arthur James	2-02-43	49 Sqn
1292995	Sgt	CLUTTERBUCK Robert Frank	17-04-43	100 Sqn
161037	P/O	CLUTTERBUCK William George	3-11-43	49 Sqn
924233	F/S	CLYDE Eric Alston	18-04-43	1659 HCU
1377364	W/O	CLYNES CGM Michel George	26-11-43	431 Sqn
1212410	Sgt	COADE Charles Frederick	29-07-43	218 Sqn
1276786	Sgt	COAKER John	18-02-43	61 Sqn
127277	F/O	COALES Daniel	14-08-43	431 Sqn
146344	P/O	COATES Arthur Henry	17-07-43	207 Sqn
130651	F/O	COATES Harold Kenneth	4-09-43	49 Sqn
1125972	Sgt	COATES Sidney	14-01-43	9 Sqn
1251081	F/S	COATES William Edward	23-11-43	50 Sqn
145671	P/O	COBB Joseph Albert George	5-05-43	35 Sqn
651458	Sgt	COBBY Arthur Victor Edward	31-07-43	15 Sqn
1080615	Sgt	COBLEY Clifford	23-09-43	77 Sqn
1198596	Sgt	COBLEY Frank	18-10-43	7 Sqn
1370576	Sgt	COCHRANE Alexander Wilson	29-04-43	207 Sqn
43847	S/L	COCHRANE DFC Archibald George Alexander	20-10-43	83 Sqn
997456	Sgt	COCHRANE George Noel [Eire]	23-06-43	161 Sqn
1586300	Sgt	COCHRANE John Henry Forrester	4-12-43	7 Sqn
1575884	Sgt	COCHRANE Spencer George	11-08-43	30 OTU
1001188	Sgt	COCKBURN William Atkinson	20-12-43	77 Sqn
1605760	Sgt	COCKCROFT Bernard Harold	7-09-43	102 Sqn
149904	P/O	COCKING Arthur Bernard	27-09-43	78 Sqn
1338031	Sgt	COCKING Leslie	30-07-43	102 Sqn
1312110	Sgt	COCKING Ronald Francis	27-04-43	90 Sqn
1314800	Sgt	COCKRAM Ronald Alfred William	28-02-43	20 OTU
1532960	Sgt	COCKROFT John	2-12-43	101 Sqn
137221	P/O	COCKS Charles Wilfred Hurman	29-01-43	9 Sqn
1216483	Sgt	COCKS Frank Robert	17-04-43	408 Sqn
1163110	Sgt	COCKSHOTT Robert John [Canada]	29-06-43	149 Sqn
1316152	Sgt	CODD William Reginald Leslie	26-05-43	77 Sqn
1649543	Sgt	COE David Richard	16-09-43	427 Sqn
1578186	Sgt	COFFIN Albert Glyn	26-05-43	9 Sqn
159885	P/O	COGDELL Charles James Bertram	26-11-43	61 Sqn
1352803	Sgt	COGDELL Cyril Norman Victor	13-05-43	51 Sqn
975634	Sgt	COGGANS George Muirhead	20-12-43	78 Sqn
1321293	Sgt	COGGINS Roland John	29-06-43	76 Sqn
1321547	Sgt	COHEN Herbert Cyril	20-12-43	76 Sqn
1331552	Sgt	COHEN Leonard	20-10-43	100 Sqn
1235344	Sgt	COHEN Murray	3-10-43	18 OTU
1134101	Sgt	COLBERT Edward	31-08-43	9 Sqn
1165025	Sgt	COLBERT Stanley Riswin	9-01-43	97 Sqn
1474360	Sgt	COLBOURNE Andrew	29-12-43	10 Sqn
1239511	W/O	COLBURN Claude Maurice	14-07-43	78 Sqn
45813	F/L	COLDICOTT DFM Albert Douglas	13-05-43	207 Sqn
127276	F/O	COLDWELL William Francis	30-03-43	83 Sqn
1311910	Sgt	COLE Arthur George	2-12-43	460 Sqn
957041	Sgt	COLE Edward	28-11-43	16 OTU
616283	F/S	COLE DFM Frank William Richard	8-03-43	7 Sqn
1388306	Sgt	COLE George Stanley	15-06-43	49 Sqn
1382074	Sgt	COLE George William	20-04-43	158 Sqn
1215655	Sgt	COLE James Frederick	3-12-43	12 Sqn
1282599	LAC	COLE James William	30-08-43	15 Sqn
1575873	Sgt	COLE John	8-08-43	106 Sqn
118067	F/L	COLE John Denis [Egypt]	3-04-43	158 Sqn
116103	F/O	COLE John Stuart	26-07-43	51 Sqn
1317878	Sgt	COLE Robert Arnold	31-07-43	76 Sqn
1201005	Sgt	COLE Robert Henry	24-08-43	620 Sqn
1126336	Sgt	COLE Robert Longster	27-03-43	44 Sqn

Service #	Rank	Name	Date	Squadron
553895	Sgt	COLE Walter Douglas	16-11-43	21 OTU
1874034	Sgt	COLEBROOKE John Roy	22-11-43	10 Sqn
1389344	Sgt	COLEGATE Donald Alfred Ross	20-10-43	12 OTU
137555	F/O	COLEMAN John Wallace	24-05-43	76 Sqn
906887	Sgt	COLEMAN Leaonard Walter	17-11-43	10 OTU
1229472	Sgt	COLES Dennis	29-06-43	76 Sqn
1332380	Sgt	COLES Raymond Martin	27-09-43	15 Sqn
124952	F/O	COLES Samuel Albert	5-05-43	35 Sqn
569527	Sgt	COLES Trevor Charles	11-02-43	102 Sqn
67023	F/L	COLLEDGE Maule William	14-09-43	139 Sqn
1354131	Sgt	COLLEN Desmond Owen	22-11-43	426 Sqn
1286366	F/S	COLLENET Francois Benigne	18-11-43	115 Sqn
742200	W/O	COLLENETTE DFM Michael de Beauchamp	28-04-43	61 Sqn
1379918	Sgt	COLLIER Thomas	1-09-43	149 Sqn
1500013	Sgt	COLLIER William	29-04-43	428 Sqn
1026403	Sgt	COLLINGE John Desmond	5-05-43	35 Sqn
1575031	Sgt	COLLINGRIDGE John	28-01-43	20 OTU
655677	Sgt	COLLINGS Leonard George	13-03-43	115 Sqn
1433512	Sgt	COLLINGWOOD Peter Edward	24-06-43	218 Sqn
625920	Sgt	COLLINS DFM Arthur Victor	27-11-43	166 Sqn
1200432	Sgt	COLLINS Cecil Howard	1-05-43	9 Sqn
1376372	Sgt	COLLINS Dennis	12-03-43	218 Sqn
1649688	Sgt	COLLINS Dennis James	10-08-43	103 Sqn
158425	P/O	COLLINS Derek	31-08-43	432 Sqn
107924	F/L	COLLINS Francis George Tims	27-11-43	101 Sqn
1285155	Sgt	COLLINS Glencoe Henry George	3-02-43	21 Sqn
1391602	F/S	COLLINS Howard Frank	20-10-43	1664 HCU
519890	Sgt	COLLINS James Joseph Frederick	18-10-43	115 Sqn
1518242	Sgt	COLLINS John	31-08-43	149 Sqn
129356	F/O	COLLINS Leonard John	12-06-43	100 Sqn
1351313	Sgt	COLLINS Leslie Felix	8-10-43	9 Sqn
1333918	Sgt	COLLINS Norman Pine	24-08-43	15 Sqn
1316430	Sgt	COLLINS Norman Sidney	26-05-43	218 Sqn
1395711	Sgt	COLLINS Peter Ambrose	25-10-43	20 OTU
1810921	Sgt	COLLINS Peter Robert	31-08-43	106 Sqn
1312950	Sgt	COLLINS Richard Arthur	12-02-43	101 Sqn
1337346	F/S	COLLINS Ronald Alfred	9-10-43	12 Sqn
1392410	Sgt	COLLINS MiD Ronald George	31-08-43	78 Sqn
149592	P/O	COLLINS Thomas	24-08-43	100 Sqn
1600763	Sgt	COLLINS William	26-07-43	10 Sqn
1216717	Sgt	COLLIS Raoul Derek	6-09-43	77 Sqn
1807326	Sgt	COLLISHAW Charles William	17-12-43	97 Sqn
138457	Sgt	COLLMAN Edward George	30-05-43	429 Sqn
1208872	Sgt	COLONNA Adrian Robert Alfred	9-01-43	44 Sqn
141201	F/L	COLSON DFM William Alfred	17-12-43	97 Sqn
1317783	Sgt	COLSTON Thomas James	22-10-43	57 Sqn
617284	Sgt	COLVERSON Raymond Leonard	3-03-43	76 Sqn
577324	Sgt	COLWELL Thomas Bell	19-03-43	161 Sqn
1600059	Sgt	COLWILL Wallace James	21-04-43	12 Sqn
1809432	Sgt	COLYER Gordon William	25-06-43	75 Sqn
1601106	Sgt	COMBER Douglas Ralph	18-11-43	622 Sqn
1388894	Sgt	COMBES John Cresswell	4-09-43	460 Sqn
1395190	Sgt	COMER Lionel Frederick	29-09-43	166 Sqn
1089983	Sgt	COMMON Eric Norman	7-02-43	11 OTU
1322681	Sgt	COMPTON DFM Francis Cyril	29-06-43	35 Sqn
1023509	Sgt	CONDRON John	26-06-43	15 Sqn
139888	P/O	CONE George Herbert	15-05-43	27 OTU
113752	F/O	CONGDON DFM Sydney John	15-08-43	138 Sqn
1091325	F/S	CONLON John Ralph	27-11-43	50 Sqn
1005899	Sgt	CONNAH Cyril	26-06-43	100 Sqn
1085201	Sgt	CONNEFF Sidney Robert [Eire]	9-07-43	101 Sqn
1370941	Sgt	CONNEL James Hamilton	3-08-43	166 Sqn
133730	F/O	CONNOLLY Francis Martin	24-12-43	100 Sqn
1119137	Sgt	CONNOR David Gordon	6-09-43	9 Sqn
1553860	Sgt	CONNOR John Norman	21-10-43	44 Sqn
911845	Sgt	CONNOR Leslie Norman	13-06-43	460 Sqn
1451682	Sgt	CONNOR Robert Henry	28-07-43	207 Sqn
658849	Sgt	CONNOR Terence William	25-06-43	101 Sqn
1079115	W/O	CONNOR Walter Campbell	18-11-43	7 Sqn
1078040	Sgt	CONROY John	22-03-43	101 Sqn
141019	F/O	CONROY Patrick Hector	26-07-43	90 Sqn
636547	Sgt	CONSTABLE John Edgar	12-06-43	12 Sqn
1332902	Sgt	CONSTABLE Thomas Alfred	20-02-43	90 Sqn
571115	Sgt	CONUEL Reginald William	5-05-43	7 Sqn
1218971	Sgt	CONWAY Frank Ronald	20-03-43	27 OTU
1127145	Sgt	CONWAY John	23-06-43	10 Sqn
1235964	Sgt	CONWELL Philip Joseph	15-04-43	196 Sqn
550013	F/S	COOK Alan Ronald	19-06-43	101 Sqn
130588	F/O	COOK Alec Victor Ibbetson	26-06-43	90 Sqn
1378841	Sgt	COOK Arthur James	4-01-43	21 OTU
940791	F/S	COOK Brian Alistarre	5-07-43	1660 HCU
1387411	Sgt	COOK Charles Henry David	11-03-43	44 Sqn
1351535	F/S	COOK Charles Smith	27-11-43	619 Sqn
1338457	Sgt	COOK Edward	19-09-43	1658 HCU
1025304	Sgt	COOK Edward John	1-03-43	103 Sqn
141794	P/O	COOK Eric Charles	24-09-43	12 Sqn
130615	F/O	COOK Eric John	31-08-43	166 Sqn
906747	Sgt	COOK Eric William	3-04-43	9 Sqn
1609864	Sgt	COOK Ernest Desmond	15-04-43	75 Sqn
1382496	Sgt	COOK Francis Stewart Crichton	26-02-43	103 Sqn
131765	P/O	COOK George	12-03-43	139 Sqn
1094187	Sgt	COOK George Thomas	21-05-43	149 Sqn
1319564	Sgt	COOK George Victor	28-08-43	149 Sqn
524567	Sgt	COOK James Falshaw	14-02-43	15 Sqn
1332552	Sgt	COOK Leslie Frank	10-06-43	24 OTU
1409174	Sgt	COOK Patrick Joseph	9-06-43	619 Sqn
1322755	Sgt	COOK Percy Victor	4-07-43	466 Sqn
538725	Sgt	COOK Reginald John	13-06-43	158 Sqn
127864	F/O	COOK Ronald Hermond Downes	13-05-43	199 Sqn
1257739	Sgt	COOK Stanley Arthur James	25-05-43	207 Sqn
129353	F/O	COOK Victor	14-04-43	101 Sqn
1116625	Sgt	COOK Walter Randall	24-05-43	101 Sqn
1005936	Sgt	COOK William Alexander	21-04-43	49 Sqn
1174531	Sgt	COOK William Walter Rufus	29-06-43	207 Sqn
132914	F/O	COOKE Aubrey Stanley [USA]	18-08-43	139 Sqn
1312387	Sgt	COOKE Edgar Jack	18-09-43	15 OTU
572721	Sgt	COOKE Eric Thomas	16-07-43	10 Sqn
1334284	Sgt	COOKE Harry William Frederick	27-09-43	50 Sqn
576371	Sgt	COOKE Hubert William	18-08-43	405 Sqn
914766	Sgt	COOKE Kenneth Bryan	27-04-43	420 Sqn
1323297	Sgt	COOKE Robert	29-12-43	12 Sqn
1382059	Sgt	COOKE Roy Edward	3-02-43	106 Sqn
1339096	Sgt	COOKE William	19-06-43	77 Sqn
1335476	Sgt	COOKSEY Robert Frederick	4-04-43	460 Sqn
40894	S/L	COOKSON Arthur Alan	4-07-43	166 Sqn
129479	F/O	COOKSON John	24-05-43	51 Sqn
658137	Sgt	COOKSON Reginald Harry	25-06-43	50 Sqn
1542878	Sgt	COOKSON Stanley	15-01-43	29 OTU
1623145	Sgt	COOMBE Antony Paul	24-12-43	44 Sqn
1319785	Sgt	COOMBES Donald George John	2-03-43	44 Sqn
911475	Sgt	COOMBES Harold James	11-04-43	57 Sqn
144181	F/L	COOMBS Cyril Ernest	14-07-43	90 Sqn
1334427	Sgt	COOMBS George Edward William	24-08-43	97 Sqn
1338475	Sgt	COOMBS Robert Victor	13-02-43	12 Sqn
134716	F/O	COOMES Roy John	22-05-43	1656 HCU
1455215	Sgt	COOPER Alan Norman	25-06-43	90 Sqn
49280	F/O	COOPER Alexander Nicholson	17-04-43	76 Sqn
1377124	Sgt	COOPER Bernard William David	20-04-43	100 Sqn
1129034	Sgt	COOPER Bertram George Arthur	16-07-43	10 Sqn
1373880	Sgt	COOPER Charles Joseph	1-09-43	103 Sqn
145306	P/O	COOPER Dennis Ray	13-05-43	28 OTU
1384132	Sgt	COOPER Douglas John	26-03-43	460 Sqn
1219550	Sgt	COOPER Edwin George	24-08-43	35 Sqn
1055977	Sgt	COOPER Ernest	9-01-43	103 Sqn
1321258	Sgt	COOPER Ernest George	13-05-43	24 OTU
1546822	Sgt	COOPER Frank	11-02-43	102 Sqn
1492388	Sgt	COOPER George	20-04-43	57 Sqn

Service No.	Rank	Name	Date	Sqn
1604429	Sgt	COOPER George Hartley [Australia]	2-12-43	460 Sqn
124578	F/O	COOPER George William	28-05-43	115 Sqn
112376	F/L	COOPER Gerald Charles	20-10-43	106 Sqn
1313990	Sgt	COOPER Godfrey Storian	18-04-43	156 Sqn
1335995	Sgt	COOPER Jack	18-08-43	10 Sqn
542661	Sgt	COOPER James	21-04-43	103 Sqn
1323023	Sgt	COOPER Kenneth Thomas	24-12-43	44 Sqn
1398968	Sgt	COOPER Leon Harvey	23-11-43	630 Sqn
170735	P/O	COOPER Norman Maylin	17-12-43	101 Sqn
658348	Sgt	COOPER Raymond Lester	30-09-43	619 Sqn
1394523	Sgt	COOPER Reginald Gordon	4-09-43	50 Sqn
1699772	Sgt	COOPER Robert Alfred	29-06-43	149 Sqn
1335912	Sgt	COOPER Ronald Bertram	23-06-43	101 Sqn
1863524	AC2	COOPER Roy William	9-08-43	149 Sqn
1602272	Sgt	COOPER William Allen	6-09-43	10 Sqn
115186	F/O	COOPER William George	30-03-43	214 Sqn
1338065	F/S	COOPER William Richard	24-12-43	100 Sqn
1317251	Sgt	COOPEY Wilfred Martin	2-07-43	620 Sqn
1579993	Sgt	COOPMAN Peter	16-12-43	103 Sqn
1334120	F/S	COPAS Kenneth Richard	6-11-43	138 Sqn
1715960	Sgt	COPE Francis Sidney	16-12-43	9 Sqn
1321550	Sgt	COPE Horace Clarence	6-03-43	76 Sqn
1086776	Sgt	COPE Ronald	17-04-43	49 Sqn
1166829	Sgt	COPELAND Arthur Alfred	4-11-43	75 Sqn
638850	F/S	COPLEY Leonard	11-04-43	214 Sqn
1377041	Sgt	COPP Phillip Bernard	2-02-43	44 Sqn
1804993	Sgt	COPPING Frederick Stanley	16-12-43	103 Sqn
628893	Sgt	COPPINS Leonard John	20-03-43	27 OTU
1691471	Sgt	COPSEY Leonard George	1-12-43	75 Sqn
1553400	Sgt	CORBETT James Brownlie	26-05-43	9 Sqn
1321331	Sgt	CORBETT John Joseph	18-08-43	115 Sqn
1591475	Sgt	CORBITT Daniel	16-12-43	619 Sqn
751063	W/O	CORBY Geoffrey Raymond	4-07-43	97 Sqn
1586198	Sgt	CORDELL Ronald Arthur	27-09-43	15 Sqn
570212	Sgt	CORDERY Sidney	9-04-43	106 Sqn
1008290	Sgt	CORDINGLEY Ronald	30-04-43	460 Sqn
1510733	Sgt	CORFIELD Norman	1-09-43	101 Sqn
1331079	Sgt	CORK Kenneth James	13-08-43	214 Sqn
1378184	Sgt	CORKE Jim	18-01-43	12 Sqn
1021230	F/S	CORLESS Thomas	2-07-43	620 Sqn
1019076	Sgt	CORLETT Arthur Stanley	23-09-43	77 Sqn
1259575	Sgt	CORLEY Percival Maurice	14-02-43	426 Sqn
1123977	Sgt	CORMACK Archibald McKay	13-03-43	199 Sqn
149530	P/O	CORNELL Eric Raymond Ivan	24-08-43	15 Sqn
1064514	Sgt	CORNES Howard Melville	31-07-43	218 Sqn
1131924	Sgt	CORNS Alexander	26-06-43	115 Sqn
1338129	Sgt	CORNWELL Frederick William	23-09-43	57 Sqn
1723530	Sgt	CORNWELL Herbert Leonard	17-12-43	405 Sqn
1169754	Sgt	CORNWELL Robert	3-10-43	623 Sqn
1017680	Sgt	CORPS Alfred George Shelton	3-05-43	51 Sqn
1386280	Sgt	CORRIE Cyril Charles	2-12-43	44 Sqn
1133737	Sgt	CORRIE William Pulteney	28-02-43	20 OTU
947720	Sgt	CORRIGAN William	17-04-43	405 Sqn
155894	P/O	CORSBY Arthur Gilbert	29-09-43	78 Sqn
1163277	Sgt	COSFORD Frederick	19-08-43	1658 HCU
1244294	Sgt	COSFORD Thomas	4-02-43	57 Sqn
1585898	Sgt	COSGROVE Peter Michael	28-05-43	100 Sqn
46911	F/O	COSHALL Stanley	3-05-43	487 Sqn
1575352	Sgt	COSNETT Eric William	30-05-43	106 Sqn
1086971	Sgt	COSSEY Sidney	23-10-43	15 OTU
1310087	Sgt	COSSINS Albert John	24-12-43	97 Sqn
1671282	Sgt	COSTELLO Joseph John	4-07-43	51 Sqn
46332	S/L	COSTELLO-BOWEN AFC Edgar Alfred	9-08-43	1655 MTU
659040	Sgt	COSTER Edgar Stanley	30-05-43	158 Sqn
1807761	Sgt	COSTER William Robert	6-10-43	19 OTU
130513	P/O	COTTER Patrick Claud	17-04-43	50 Sqn
1411408	F/S	COTTERELL Cyril Harold William	20-12-43	156 Sqn
936161	Sgt	COTTERILL Arthur	1-09-43	77 Sqn
945026	Sgt	COTTERILL Ronald	11-11-43	161 Sqn
160845	P/O	COTTLE William Waterson	22-11-43	102 Sqn
1376525	Sgt	COTTON Kenneth Albert Charles	22-06-43	460 Sqn
1516171	Sgt	COTTON Leonard	23-09-43	428 Sqn
155939	P/O	COTTON Leslie John Victor	31-08-43	78 Sqn
1078832	Sgt	COTTON Willie	31-01-43	106 Sqn
135402	F/L	COTTRELL Bernard	6-09-43	149 Sqn
144293	F/O	COUGHLAN DFM John [Eire]	12-10-43	82 OTU
1098267	Sgt	COULDWELL Edward	15-02-43	90 Sqn
1559064	Sgt	COULL Alexander	22-06-43	149 Sqn
1050302	Sgt	COULSEY John Robert	15-06-43	49 Sqn
1496446	Sgt	COULSON Kenneth	19-04-43	156 Sqn
155507	P/O	COULSON Raymond [Australia]	9-10-43	61 Sqn
1212998	Sgt	COULSON Ronald	11-04-43	50 Sqn
1076266	Sgt	COULTER Kenneth Boyd	28-06-43	101 Sqn
1147868	Sgt	COULTHARD Alan Maxwell	9-04-43	9 Sqn
525073	F/S	COULTON James	16-12-43	106 Sqn
1077010	F/S	COUPE Harold	28-05-43	199 Sqn
1530957	Sgt	COUPE Harry	28-08-43	10 OTU
1458000	F/S	COUPE Leonard Peter	20-12-43	428 Sqn
1126438	F/S	COUPER James Robert	5-03-43	419 Sqn
1393683	Sgt	COURT Kenneth Owen	25-02-43	106 Sqn
1046519	Sgt	COURT Patrick James	25-06-43	620 Sqn
1086282	Sgt	COURTNEY John Joseph	15-04-43	408 Sqn
1352306	Sgt	COUSIN Harry	25-07-43	51 Sqn
1479455	AC2	COUSIN Joseph Ridley	19-06-43	Snaith
1495456	Sgt	COUSIN James Muir	17-02-43	14 OTU
1324365	Sgt	COUSINS Alfred	24-08-43	83 Sqn
1050802	Sgt	COUSINS Andrew Smeaton	10-07-43	50 Sqn
1430231	Sgt	COUSINS Arthur James	20-04-43	460 Sqn
1242954	LAC	COUSINS John Desmond	7-09-43	49 Sqn
1336969	Sgt	COVELL Donald Walpole	14-07-43	466 Sqn
33133	W/C	COVENTRY DFC Henry Reginald [Canada]	14-07-43	102 Sqn
27048	W/C	COVERDALE MiD John	22-06-43	431 Sqn
1324110	Sgt	COVERDALE Reginald Francis	30-05-43	106 Sqn
1077677	Sgt	COWAN Andrew	1-09-43	214 Sqn
545154	Sgt	COWAN Hamilton	17-01-43	49 Sqn
1361185	Sgt	COWAN John	3-08-43	166 Sqn
1319861	Sgt	COWAN Robert William McGavin	19-11-43	431 Sqn
514413	Sgt	COWAP John	6-09-43	149 Sqn
1332058	Sgt	COWARD Ernest Charles	22-09-43	434 Sqn
1863808	Sgt	COWCHER Sidney Frederick	22-10-43	1657 HCU
643825	Sgt	COWDREY Alfred George Robert	16-12-43	115 Sqn
938828	Sgt	COWELL Roy	25-07-43	76 Sqn
1036940	Sgt	COWEN John Robert	23-11-43	97 Sqn
1555819	Sgt	COWEN John Robert	12-11-43	78 Sqn
1134233	Sgt	COWGILL Stanley	26-06-43	106 Sqn
1578147	Sgt	COWHAM Stanley William	29-04-43	207 Sqn
1553773	Sgt	COWIE Alexander Bruce	8-03-43	21 OTU
45949	F/L	COWIE DFM Arthur	13-02-43	199 Sqn
967384	Sgt	COWIE Douglas	14-03-43	9 Sqn
1252153	F/S	COWIE Frank Norman Simpson	20-10-43	115 Sqn
1822254	Sgt	COWIE John Campbell	22-10-43	51 Sqn
1083783	Sgt	COWIE Robert Norman	3-07-43	19 OTU
1087690	Sgt	COWLER Frederick George	15-09-43	10 Sqn
120216	F/O	COWLEY DFM John Albert	12-06-43	156 Sqn
645715	Sgt	COWLING Donald Leonard	22-09-43	115 Sqn
1391652	Sgt	COWLING Peter Radford	20-10-43	100 Sqn
1378312	Sgt	COWLISHAW Harold	14-01-43	9 Sqn
549530	F/S	COWMAN William Harris	7-02-43	408 Sqn
1271839	Sgt	COWPER Edwin Francis	7-02-43	158 Sqn
1384312	Sgt	COX Anthony Graham	4-07-43	35 Sqn
952028	F/S	COX DFM Peter	8-04-43	405 Sqn
1175980	Sgt	COX Arthur	24-08-43	158 Sqn
778591	W/O	COX Clive Arthur [Rhodesia]	3-12-43	166 Sqn
1575287	Sgt	COX Douglas Graham	18-08-43	619 Sqn
1334812	Sgt	COX Ernest Walter	17-04-43	51 Sqn
149332	P/O	COX Frank Geoffrey	2-12-43	44 Sqn

657865	Sgt	COX Frederick William	14-02-43	102 Sqn	1210978	Sgt	CRESSWELL Andrew	13-05-43	431 Sqn
156106	P/O	COX DFM Geoffrey Lewis	22-09-43	207 Sqn	1575726	Sgt	CRESSWELL Arthur Bryce	31-07-43	78 Sqn
1230240	Sgt	COX Gerald Norman	12-11-43	78 Sqn	1678544	AC2	CRESSWELL Donald William	6-04-43	1663 HCU
578383	Sgt	COX Godfrey Denis	31-08-43	218 Sqn	572760	Sgt	CRESSWELL John Douglas	25-06-43	620 Sqn
569405	F/S	COX Godfrey Hippesley	25-06-43	7 Sqn	141549	P/O	CRESSWELL Vernon	11-08-43	106 Sqn
1578285	Sgt	COX Harold	8-10-43	21 OTU	143426	F/O	CRIBBIN George	28-05-43	467 Sqn
1586740	Sgt	COX Henry William	13-05-43	467 Sqn	1424703	Sgt	CRICK George Walter William	17-11-43	10 OTU
1333683	Sgt	COX Horace James	2-05-43	11 OTU	1399693	Sgt	CRIMMINS Martin Alexander	6-11-43	26 OTU
156916	P/O	COX John Edward	23-10-43	467 Sqn	1383133	Sgt	CRIPPS Basil Robert	13-06-43	49 Sqn
1685621	Sgt	COX Leslie Robert	16-12-43	1667 HCU	1215484	Sgt	CRISP Basil George	16-08-43	75 Sqn
1030470	Sgt	COX Lisle	2-02-43	44 Sqn	1473085	Sgt	CRISP Claud Eric	22-09-43	77 Sqn
1384385	Sgt	COX Ralph James Mitchell	23-04-43	9 Sqn	1377224	Sgt	CRISWICK Maurice Leonard Charles	4-07-43	15 Sqn
1542162	LAC	COX Ronald	19-08-43	18 OTU	1515736	Sgt	CRITCHLEY George Gordon	16-12-43	576 Sqn
1254141	Sgt	COX Ronald Harry	27-01-43	105 Sqn	1456862	Sgt	CRITCHLOW Richard Noel Pickwell	24-11-43	405 Sqn
1383830	F/S	COX Samuel Thomas	22-06-43	7 Sqn	1324627	Sgt	CROAD Leslie Herbert	29-07-43	78 Sqn
1575418	Sgt	COX Thomas	5-05-43	10 Sqn	114241	F/O	CROCKFORD Anthony	4-09-43	7 Sqn
1193709	Sgt	COX Trevor John	26-02-43	102 Sqn	991772	Sgt	CROFT Albert Francis William Noble	23-10-43	100 Sqn
1370416	Sgt	COX William	25-06-43	78 Sqn	1316145	Sgt	CROFT Donald Edward	30-07-43	97 Sqn
1395774	Sgt	COX William Augustus	2-12-43	156 Sqn	974572	Sgt	CROFT John Ernest Norman	15-02-43	100 Sqn
1492748	Sgt	COX William Frederick	18-10-43	103 Sqn	1801134	Sgt	CROFT Leonard George 'Len'	3-08-43	44 Sqn
1811872	Sgt	COX William Henry	10-06-43	24 OTU	1193969	Sgt	CROFTS Donald Albert	2-03-43	149 Sqn
1621891	Sgt	COX William Roland	4-12-43	102 Sqn	1231276	Sgt	CROFTS Reginald	9-10-43	51 Sqn
156106	P/O	COXON DFM Geoffrey Lew	22-09-43	207 Sqn	1891269	Sgt	CRONCHEY Henry Richard	2-10-43	61 Sqn
945356	Sgt	COY Donald	31-01-43	106 Sqn	1377657	F/S	CRONK Leslie William	13-01-43	106 Sqn
49719	P/O	COYLE DFM Michael George	22-01-43	180 Sqn	1331344	Sgt	CROOK Basil John France	23-03-43	196 Sqn
159015	P/O	COYLE DFC Michael John	4-10-43	156 Sqn	1447786	Sgt	CROOK Eric Charles	26-06-43	106 Sqn
1494494	Sgt	COYNE Stephen George	28-08-43	620 Sqn	1320902	Sgt	CROOK Roger Ernest	15-06-43	460 Sqn
1385661	Sgt	COZENS Geoffrey Eric	29-09-43	17 OTU	1455496	Sgt	CROOKES Raymond	29-06-43	1659 HCU
148793	P/O	COZENS DFM George Arthur	4-07-43	149 Sqn	1677821	Sgt	CROOKES Vincent	18-10-43	619 Sqn
1309272	Sgt	CRABBE Ernest Stanley	28-07-43	156 Sqn	1802161	Sgt	CROOKS Leonard Arthur	26-11-43	101 Sqn
1338850	Sgt	CRACKNELL Harold Edward	3-10-43	77 Sqn	44054	W/C	CROOKS DSO DFC Leslie	18-08-43	426 Sqn
1585934	Sgt	CRAIG David George	2-12-43	156 Sqn	1333929	Sgt	CROOKS Reginald Herbert	1-09-43	619 Sqn
621658	W/O	CRAIG DFM James Ferrie	22-10-43	103 Sqn	1321533	Sgt	CROOKS Stanley Edward	3-04-43	156 Sqn
159088	P/O	CRAIG William Howie	20-12-43	51 Sqn	1305841	Sgt	CROSLAND Douglas	29-09-43	17 OTU
1123747	Sgt	CRAIGIE Douglas Hugh	26-11-43	83 Sqn	143801	P/O	CROSS Herbert Ernest	29-06-43	10 Sqn
1354608	Sgt	CRAM Duncan	14-05-43	44 Sqn	1092054	Sgt	CROSS James Arthur	30-03-43	49 Sqn
1533234	Sgt	CRAM William	15-06-43	100 Sqn	929899	Sgt	CROSS John	22-09-43	434 Sqn
1124348	Sgt	CRAMB Peter William	1-09-43	158 Sqn	1029597	Sgt	CROSS Leslie	21-10-43	103 Sqn
798741	Sgt	CRAMM Reginald Harrison [Newfoundland]	23-06-43	218 Sqn	148485	P/O	CROSS Walter Herbert	31-08-43	7 Sqn
					1580165	Sgt	CROSSLAND Tom	9-04-43	77 Sqn
1675338	Sgt	CRAMMOND John	31-07-43	408 Sqn	996783	F/S	CROSSLEY Richard	18-08-43	619 Sqn
113332	F/L	CRAMP Dennis	13-07-43	44 Sqn	1386952	Sgt	CROSSON Arthur James	30-03-43	149 Sqn
1196620	Sgt	CRAMPTON Charles Ernest	24-08-43	428 Sqn	135886	F/O	CROUCH Eric	10-07-43	408 Sqn
124479	F/O	CRAMPTON Leonard Robert	27-07-43	156 Sqn	1874592	Sgt	CROUCH Ernest Walter	17-12-43	156 Sqn
1104323	Sgt	CRANE Barrie Lincoln	15-03-43	161 Sqn	1320612	Sgt	CROUCH Leonard Robert	2-05-43	11 OTU
1265082	LAC	CRANE Charles	25-11-43	Graveley	130507	F/O	CROUCH Robert Geoffrey	2-05-43	424 Sqn
48908	F/O	CRANE Laurence George 'Larry'	4-11-43	12 Sqn	1433486	Sgt	CROUCH Walter	21-10-43	161 Sqn
537108	Sgt	CRANHAM Jasper Robert	30-05-43	10 Sqn	1555573	Sgt	CROW Martin Harvey Christie	12-03-43	102 Sqn
1210039	Sgt	CRANK Arthur Allan	22-06-43	83 Sqn	641113	Sgt	CROW Percy	4-09-43	44 Sqn
1187563	Sgt	CRAPPER-BOVEY Derrick Roy Lionel	3-10-43	12 Sqn	1206970	Sgt	CROWE Edward James	25-07-43	214 Sqn
1565815	Sgt	CRAVEN Thomas Lockerbie	1-09-43	158 Sqn	576432	Sgt	CROWE George Alfred	2-12-43	630 Sqn
127903	F/O	CRAWFORD Albert Victor	15-06-43	50 Sqn	1386792	Sgt	CROWHURST Eric Frank	19-02-43	466 Sqn
121135	F/O	CRAWFORD Douglas	11-03-43	166 Sqn	1036177	Sgt	CROWLEY Michael John	9-01-43	44 Sqn
631115	Sgt	CRAWFORD Frank Patrick	12-03-43	10 Sqn	1319268	Sgt	CROWSLEY Dennis Arthur	4-07-43	115 Sqn
1543229	Sgt	CRAWFORD Frederick Arthur	3-08-43	103 Sqn	1335788	Sgt	CROWTHER Alan Ross	6-09-43	149 Sqn
841109	Sgt	CRAWFORD George Ernest	24-12-43	103 Sqn	1339159	Sgt	CROWTHER Frederick Edward William		
1560532	F/S	CRAWFORD George Morris	29-07-43	218 Sqn				3-10-43	75 Sqn
973264	Sgt	CRAWFORD Harry James	21-10-43	161 Sqn	1514591	Sgt	CROWTHER Joshua	26-07-43	51 Sqn
634710	Sgt	CRAWFORD Ian Douglas	1-05-43	77 Sqn	1414489	Sgt	CROWTHER Thomas Raymond	28-07-43	57 Sqn
1082106	Sgt	CRAWFORD Ian Kieran	9-01-43	158 Sqn	655726	F/S	CROXFORD Donald Stanyon	18-08-43	10 Sqn
1795797	Sgt	CRAWFORD William Arthur [Eire]	1-09-43	199 Sqn	1318163	Sgt	CRUDGINGTON John Arthur	18-09-43	1658 HCU
542456	F/S	CRAWLEY John Sidney Francis Victor	23-06-43	156 Sqn	136732	P/O	CRUICKSHANK George	16-04-43	35 Sqn
1542378	Sgt	CREAMER Keith Thornton	2-10-43	15 OTU	1129716	Sgt	CRUMMEY Patrick Joseph	28-08-43	620 Sqn
48603	F/L	CREBBIN DFC John Percival	23-11-43	83 Sqn	977000	Sgt	CRUTTENDEN Cyril Leslie	21-04-43	90 Sqn
1090311	Sgt	CREBBIN Ronald	1-03-43	12 OTU	1547554	Sgt	CRUXTON George Henry	21-04-43	77 Sqn
1114834	Sgt	CREDLAND Ralph Hilton	28-01-43	20 OTU	143859	P/O	CRYER Robert Pickering	21-04-43	12 Sqn
1330741	Sgt	CREEVY Douglas William	26-05-43	12 Sqn	931386	Sgt	CUBEY John Kenneth	27-11-43	103 Sqn
1331396	F/S	CREIGHTON-KELLY Geoffrey Keith Henry			1453409	Sgt	CUBITT Thomas	22-11-43	83 Sqn
			3-08-43	428 Sqn	1388584	F/S	CUDD Alan Francis	22-09-43	434 Sqn

187

Service No	Rank	Name	Date	Sqn
1312113	Sgt	CUFF Edward Harold	24-08-43	199 Sqn
1386752	F/S	CUFFEY Frederick	13-06-43	115 Sqn
1230164	Sgt	CUGLEY Sidney	24-08-43	405 Sqn
125676	F/O	CULFF Edward Richard	30-03-43	196 Sqn
1814522	Sgt	CULL Stanley Victor	16-12-43	576 Sqn
1813997	Sgt	CULLEN James Alderson	4-11-43	12 Sqn
798691	Sgt	CULLETON John David [Canada]	15-04-43	10 Sqn
1320560	Sgt	CULLEY Arthur Leslie	2-09-43	81 OTU
1031824	Sgt	CULLEY Edward James	28-04-43	158 Sqn
1330446	Sgt	CULLUM James Frederick William	13-07-43	156 Sqn
1437100	Sgt	CULSHAW John Richard	28-08-43	75 Sqn
1383404	Sgt	CUMBERBATCH Grey Doyle [Barbados]	5-03-43	100 Sqn
998050	Sgt	CUMMING John	30-07-43	97 Sqn
971807	Sgt	CUMMINGS Edward Nicholas	12-06-43	100 Sqn
1334212	Sgt	CUMMINGS Jack William	29-09-43	166 Sqn
1431931	F/S	CUMMINGS James Maurice	3-11-43	101 Sqn
1653296	Sgt	CUMMINS Richard Charles Luke	23-09-43	90 Sqn
1192627	Sgt	CUMMINS Thomas Francis	14-07-43	466 Sqn
965489	Sgt	CUNLIFFE James	6-09-43	106 Sqn
1453475	Sgt	CUNLIFFE William Edward	12-06-43	12 Sqn
1369229	F/S	CUNNINGHAM Gordon Strachan	1-12-43	199 Sqn
1212445	Sgt	CUNNINGHAM John Charles	16-08-43	207 Sqn
643601	Sgt	CUNNINGHAM Leonard Roy	11-04-43	75 Sqn
119842	F/O	CUNNINGHAM Pennell Stilis	28-09-43	90 Sqn
1494009	Sgt	CUNNINGHAM Richard Frederick	14-03-43	9 Sqn
1577976	Sgt	CURE George Arthur	15-05-43	30 OTU
121280	F/L	CURLE Richard Alexander	4-03-43	100 Sqn
1568236	Sgt	CURLE Robert	2-12-43	514 Sqn
1610909	Sgt	CURLING Edwin Donald	29-04-43	196 Sqn
1316951	Sgt	CURNOW Richard	17-11-43	10 OTU
1016904	Sgt	CURRAH George	29-01-43	226 Sqn
130412	P/O	CURRALL Howard Brian	31-03-43	10 OTU
995156	F/S	CURRAN John	24-08-43	623 Sqn
1821749	Sgt	CURRAN John Graham	5-09-43	1661 HCU
1045746	Sgt	CURRAN Joseph	24-09-43	428 Sqn
1237454	Sgt	CURREY John Armstrong	24-08-43	101 Sqn
1367283	Sgt	CURRIE James	30-05-43	115 Sqn
1697046	Sgt	CURRIE William Bryce	2-12-43	44 Sqn
1316120	Sgt	CURRIER Wilfred Herbert	18-10-43	115 Sqn
1521801	Sgt	CURRY David	18-11-43	15 Sqn
1021538	F/S	CURRY DFM James	4-10-43	97 Sqn
1567974	Sgt	CURRY John Veitch	25-11-43	28 OTU
151411	P/O	CURRY Thomas Bertram	11-05-43	24 OTU
51291	P/O	CURSLEY Leslie Jack	30-03-43	76 Sqn
1580055	Sgt	CURSON John	28-08-43	218 Sqn
128012	F/O	CURTIE Edward Robert	28-05-43	10 Sqn
51673	P/O	CURTIS DFM Basil Arthur	29-04-43	196 Sqn
549252	Sgt	CURTIS Charles Dennis	3-08-43	214 Sqn
814139	Sgt	CURTIS Duncan	16-04-43	460 Sqn
142853	P/O	CURTIS Eric Frederick	22-06-43	15 Sqn
1483600	Sgt	CURTIS John Richard	12-06-43	156 Sqn
1313229	Sgt	CURTIS Leslie Harold	8-02-43	44 Sqn
149063	P/O	CURTIS Lewis William	4-07-43	149 Sqn
1386838	Sgt	CURTIS Stanley Arthur	9-04-43	75 Sqn
1615703	Sgt	CUSHING Charles	16-12-43	166 Sqn
1388747	Sgt	CUST Philip Gordon	8-02-43	10 OTU
1396887	Sgt	CUSTANCE Robert Corrie	17-12-43	101 Sqn
1573822	Sgt	CUTHBERT David Duncan	22-06-43	158 Sqn
1384688	Sgt	CUTHBERTSON Alfred	4-07-43	77 Sqn
133560	F/O	CUTLER Stanley Albert Charles	23-06-43	78 Sqn
652428	Sgt	CUTTER George Robert	12-08-43	620 Sqn
1099128	Sgt	DABBS John	9-08-43	149 Sqn
162864	P/O	DABNOR Roy Alfred	22-11-43	102 Sqn
1330174	Sgt	DABSON Cyril Claude	17-06-43	100 Sqn
569552	Sgt	DADD Roy Ernest	21-04-43	12 Sqn
1168383	Sgt	DADGE William George Henry	15-08-43	420 Sqn
1315406	Sgt	DAFT Christopher Harry George	26-07-43	78 Sqn
1035453	Sgt	DAGG Theodore Ivan Lishman	29-06-43	78 Sqn
1600759	Sgt	DAGNALL Thomas Stanley Roy	20-12-43	428 Sqn
741554	W/O	DAINTY DFM Eric	13-06-43	100 Sqn
1579189	Sgt	DAKER Leslie John	26-05-43	9 Sqn
128962	F/O	DALE George Raynor	4-04-43	9 Sqn
1670732	Sgt	DALE John	5-09-43	30 OTU
155092	P/O	DALE John Albert Harold	28-07-43	100 Sqn
141548	F/O	DALE Kenneth Thornton	20-12-43	50 Sqn
47871	F/O	DALEY DFM Arthur	21-04-43	103 Sqn
1129286	Sgt	DALEY Thomas James	29-04-43	103 Sqn
125494	F/O	DALLIMORE Clifford Stephen	6-10-43	19 OTU
1318874	Sgt	DALLIMORE Leonard William	13-07-43	156 Sqn
636611	F/S	DALTON Albert Colin	7-09-43	156 Sqn
1396464	Sgt	DALTON Dennis Edward	3-08-43	61 Sqn
1295229	Sgt	DALTON Frank Albert	4-07-43	15 Sqn
161782	P/O	DALTON Jack Proctor	2-12-43	57 Sqn
1800945	Sgt	DALTON Joseph Michael	22-06-43	77 Sqn
551847	Sgt	DALY Peter	23-05-43	57 Sqn
574870	Sgt	DALZELL William Madine	28-08-43	199 Sqn
1432841	Sgt	DALZIEL Thomas William Hodgson	3-10-43	18 OTU
942345	Sgt	DAMMS Robert Arthur	5-04-43	405 Sqn
1156717	Sgt	DAMPIER Ronald Eric Arthur	9-04-43	207 Sqn
1310902	Sgt	DANBY Francis	19-06-43	77 Sqn
1322837	F/S	DANDO Ronald William	27-09-43	78 Sqn
146425	P/O	DANE MiD Gerald Herbert	13-05-43	78 Sqn
1027306	Sgt	DANGERFIELD Edwin	15-06-43	49 Sqn
1473420	Sgt	DANIEL Jack Bays	2-12-43	103 Sqn
1318026	F/S	DANIEL Robert Norman Victor	24-12-43	156 Sqn
1129987	Sgt	DANIEL Thomas Steadman	20-12-43	49 Sqn
1315951	Sgt	DANIEL Thomas William Reynold	12-06-43	78 Sqn
564614	Sgt	DANIELS David Richard	28-07-43	101 Sqn
132723	F/O	DANIELS Sam Tunnicliffe 'Peter'	8-06-43	16 OTU
1321773	Sgt	DARAGON John Alexander	27-01-43	51 Sqn
1324474	Sgt	DARBY Robert John	8-10-43	9 Sqn
1385490	Sgt	DARBYSHIRE Eric	3-08-43	405 Sqn
126819	F/O	DARBYSHIRE Frank	6-07-43	196 Sqn
60303	F/L	DARE Henry William Julius	3-08-43	405 Sqn
1389500	F/S	DARKIN Victor Alfred	23-09-43	50 Sqn
40368	S/L	DARLING DFC Donald Frederick William	30-01-43	105 Sqn
1452908	Sgt	DARLINGTON Ralph William	18-02-43	9 Sqn
1396028	Sgt	DARRAH Kenneth William	24-08-43	77 Sqn
121551	F/L	DARROCH John Baillie	5-04-43	408 Sqn
1392050	Sgt	DARROCH John William	25-06-43	97 Sqn
1811761	Sgt	DARTNALL John Victor	30-05-43	75 Sqn
1320478	Sgt	DARVALL Joseph Henry James	20-12-43	51 Sqn
986740	Sgt	DARWISH Derwish Haj	28-07-43	12 Sqn
657600	W/O	DASH Ronald	3-08-43	103 Sqn
1316701	Sgt	DASH Rowland Josiah	26-06-43	44 Sqn
130517	F/O	DATTA Ramesh Chandra [India]	9-07-43	97 Sqn
1034778	Sgt	DAVANY Edward Francis	9-11-43	90 Sqn
1386048	Sgt	DAVENPORT Roy Victor Malcolm	3-03-43	12 Sqn
1389014	Sgt	DAVEY Arthur Ernest	15-06-43	50 Sqn
127314	F/O	DAVEY Edwin Francis	16-06-43	460 Sqn
1394020	Sgt	DAVEY Eric James	26-02-43	103 Sqn
1396457	Sgt	DAVEY Herbert Charles	30-11-43	30 OTU
1375549	Sgt	DAVEY Percival James	31-01-43	97 Sqn
120435	F/O	DAVEY Walter Edwin	5-05-43	149 Sqn
1296897	Sgt	DAVID Evan George	24-05-43	10 Sqn
1803836	Sgt	DAVIDGE John James	7-08-43	28 OTU
1355496	Sgt	DAVIDSON Alan	27-09-43	103 Sqn
1550371	Sgt	DAVIDSON Alan Fleming	4-04-43	20 OTU
1566671	Sgt	DAVIDSON Alexander McNaught	21-10-43	20 OTU
1321868	W/O	DAVIDSON Brian Bruce	29-09-43	166 Sqn
1338539	Sgt	DAVIDSON Edward Reginald	16-04-43	61 Sqn
1590344	Sgt	DAVIDSON Francis Joseph	18-11-43	419 Sqn
142844	F/O	DAVIDSON DFM George Russell	29-12-43	35 Sqn
1369345	Sgt	DAVIDSON John	3-01-43	24 OTU
984107	Sgt	DAVIDSON John Charles	26-06-43	90 Sqn
628831	F/S	DAVIDSON DFM Henry Eugene	14-04-43	138 Sqn

Service No	Rank	Name	Date	Unit
1385043	Sgt	DAVIDSON Thomas Raymond	8-04-43	218 Sqn
1349734	F/S	DAVIE Andrew	11-08-43	97 Sqn
1561886	Sgt	DAVIE Donald Cameron Stewart	18-11-43	76 Sqn
1005717	W/O	DAVIE George Alexander	11-04-43	214 Sqn
981492	Sgt	DAVIES Arthur Haydn	18-10-43	207 Sqn
1337881	Sgt	DAVIES Arthur Illingworth	10-01-43	10 OTU
155854	P/O	DAVIES Arthur William	1-09-43	158 Sqn
125498	F/O	DAVIES Brian Tristram	18-04-43	1659 HCU
1313708	Sgt	DAVIES Brinley Oliver	15-06-43	12 Sqn
142446	P/O	DAVIES Cecil Harold	4-04-43	156 Sqn
1235336	Sgt	DAVIES Charles	27-01-43	429 Sqn
1412831	Sgt	DAVIES Cyril	3-03-43	51 Sqn
978626	Sgt	DAVIES David Edward	6-09-43	44 Sqn
1135384	Sgt	DAVIES David Gwyn	24-12-43	550 Sqn
1330671	Sgt	DAVIES David John	22-06-43	90 Sqn
1392889	Sgt	DAVIES David Oswald	24-12-43	207 Sqn
139303	P/O	DAVIES David Tudor	26-07-43	77 Sqn
1334007	Sgt	DAVIES Digby Gwilym St. John	9-10-43	90 Sqn
1420122	Sgt	DAVIES Edgar William	26-11-43	106 Sqn
134694	F/O	DAVIES Edward Raymond	23-09-43	9 Sqn
1578847	Sgt	DAVIES Ellis	13-09-43	12 OTU
1490509	Sgt	DAVIES Eric	22-03-43	101 Sqn
101537	F/L	DAVIES Evan Arthur	13-02-43	50 Sqn
116794	F/O	DAVIES Francis Arnold	3-02-43	78 Sqn
1503365	Sgt	DAVIES Frank	9-10-43	51 Sqn
815114	Sgt	DAVIES Frank Wells	27-04-43	207 Sqn
1259385	Sgt	DAVIES Frederick Herbert	8-05-43	460 Sqn
641112	Sgt	DAVIES Frederick Ronald	15-08-43	138 Sqn
137587	P/O	DAVIES Garfield	13-05-43	102 Sqn
1027862	Sgt	DAVIES George Chamberlain	31-07-43	75 Sqn
158798	P/O	DAVIES Glyndwr	7-10-43	426 Sqn
1578179	Sgt	DAVIES Gordon Ernest	11-04-43	81 OTU
1314365	Sgt	DAVIES Gwynn Towyn	26-05-43	214 Sqn
1317697	F/S	DAVIES Hiram Edwin	25-06-43	106 Sqn
1078918	Sgt	DAVIES Hughie Francis	4-02-43	427 Sqn
1338693	F/S	DAVIES Ivor Glyn	4-12-43	51 Sqn
998630	Sgt	DAVIES James Owen	6-09-43	49 Sqn
1318543	Sgt	DAVIES John	13-05-43	218 Sqn
1682448	Sgt	DAVIES John Francis Matthew	24-11-43	166 Sqn
1315508	Sgt	DAVIES John Herbert	29-06-43	100 Sqn
1283912	F/S	DAVIES John Malcolm	12-06-43	7 Sqn
1332402	Sgt	DAVIES Lancelot Walter	28-08-43	199 Sqn
1112193	Sgt	DAVIES Leslie	5-01-43	101 Sqn
138148	F/O	DAVIES Max Howard	31-08-43	78 Sqn
932083	F/S	DAVIES Peter Howard Rowe Barrington	3-05-43	487 Sqn
1152952	Sgt	DAVIES Philip Thomas	31-08-43	166 Sqn
67648	F/L	DAVIES Richard Edward	1-09-43	61 Sqn
1206039	Sgt	DAVIES Robert	11-04-43	1660 HCU
1648079	Sgt	DAVIES Robert Thomas Edward	30-09-43	619 Sqn
1338839	Sgt	DAVIES Roderick	30-03-43	431 Sqn
1032360	Sgt	DAVIES Ronald	9-10-43	166 Sqn
1178654	LAC	DAVIES Ronald Allison	26-02-43	9 Sqn
1600566	Sgt	DAVIES Ronald Cecil	3-08-43	35 Sqn
546698	Sgt	DAVIES Thomas Albert	12-06-43	78 Sqn
991591	Sgt	DAVIES Thomas Henry	18-10-43	103 Sqn
159934	P/O	DAVIES Thomas Herbert	9-10-43	106 Sqn
1064824	Sgt	DAVIES Thomas Lynn	13-01-43	12 Sqn
1232668	Sgt	DAVIES Thomas Stanley	7-09-43	10 Sqn
1339176	Sgt	DAVIES Trevor	29-09-43	434 Sqn
1316984	Sgt	DAVIES Wilfred	7-08-43	26 OTU
937521	F/S	DAVIES MiD William Arthur	18-08-43	49 Sqn
1160814	Sgt	DAVIES William Arthur	22-06-43	619 Sqn
967345	Sgt	DAVIES William Daniel Roydon	20-12-43	44 Sqn
2209522	Sgt	DAVIES William John	24-11-43	7 Sqn
657964	Sgt	DAVIES William Price	26-05-43	51 Sqn
941487	Sgt	DAVIES William Stuart	19-08-43	138 Sqn
1425083	Sgt	DAVIES Wyndham Henry	23-06-43	218 Sqn
1152398	Sgt	DAVIS Arthur	22-09-43	101 Sqn
120803	F/O	DAVIS Arthur Joseph [Fiji Islands]	25-06-43	7 Sqn
127541	F/O	DAVIS Derek Henry Victor	26-06-43	51 Sqn
575812	Sgt	DAVIS Edward Strangways	28-05-43	467 Sqn
1254697	Sgt	DAVIS Ernest John Walter	18-02-43	9 Sqn
1832294	Sgt	DAVIS Frederick Peter	18-08-43	419 Sqn
953242	Sgt	DAVIS Frederick William	29-06-43	15 Sqn
1027022	F/S	DAVIS DFM George Albert	4-12-43	405 Sqn
1335915	Sgt	DAVIS Gordon Alfred	22-10-43	12 Sqn
626837	W/O	DAVIS Herbert Percy	17-12-43	101 Sqn
1352674	Sgt	DAVIS Jack	1-09-43	158 Sqn
629241	Sgt	DAVIS Jim Jack	16-04-43	75 Sqn
643447	Sgt	DAVIS John	3-01-43	61 Sqn
1333716	Sgt	DAVIS John Bernard	7-08-43	9 Sqn
126678	F/O	DAVIS John Campbell	3-04-43	50 Sqn
125310	F/O	DAVIS Lewis George	17-08-43	619 Sqn
1809975	Sgt	DAVIS Louis Leslie	25-06-43	97 Sqn
1385696	Sgt	DAVIS Ronald	27-09-43	166 Sqn
132626	F/O	DAVIS Ronald Jack	5-05-43	90 Sqn
574589	Sgt	DAVIS Roy Thomas	22-06-43	15 Sqn
1577165	F/S	DAVIS Stanley James	23-11-43	83 Sqn
658478	Sgt	DAVIS Thomas	26-07-43	61 Sqn
1456334	F/S	DAVIS Thomas Rhodes	23-11-43	9 Sqn
1254297	Sgt	DAVIS Thomas Robert	14-03-43	1651 HCU
1384245	Sgt	DAVIS Thomas William	3-11-43	76 Sqn
1551245	Sgt	DAVIS William	17-04-43	10 OTU
1522697	Sgt	DAVIS William Alderson	23-09-43	460 Sqn
1384993	Sgt	DAVIS William Thomas	26-06-43	214 Sqn
1066331	Sgt	DAVISON Charles Clement	3-10-43	78 Sqn
1606469	Sgt	DAVISON George William John	13-04-43	101 Sqn
1143278	Sgt	DAVISON John Ronald	24-12-43	115 Sqn
1123089	Sgt	DAVISON Robert Fairbairn	8-04-43	1654 HCU
991400	Sgt	DAVISON Rogert William	3-12-43	9 Sqn
1450992	Sgt	DAVISON Thomas	23-08-43	103 Sqn
1444291	Sgt	DAWE Harry Victor	1-12-43	199 Sqn
1335335	Sgt	DAWE John Alexander Goad	17-06-43	156 Sqn
1389130	Sgt	DAWE Wallace Arthur	1-03-43	50 Sqn
659048	Sgt	DAWES Henry Dennis	23-01-43	12 Sqn
132775	F/O	DAWKINS James Jeremiah	3-10-43	51 Sqn
1811130	Sgt	DAWKINS Leslie John	27-09-43	158 Sqn
1365781	Sgt	DAWSON Alexander Robertson	12-06-43	420 Sqn
1813538	Sgt	DAWSON Archibald Douglas	14-07-43	428 Sqn
141810	P/O	DAWSON Clifford George	3-04-43	158 Sqn
1077766	F/S	DAWSON Frank	11-08-43	619 Sqn
1315442	Sgt	DAWSON James George	27-01-43	105 Sqn
1386587	Sgt	DAWSON John	3-10-43	623 Sqn
1125488	Sgt	DAWSON Sydney	16-04-43	1657 HCU
1006135	Sgt	DAWSON Thomas	30-03-43	158 Sqn
1116784	Sgt	DAWSON Thomas Brown	28-07-43	15 Sqn
1501161	Sgt	DAWSON William Gorden	14-07-43	90 Sqn
1123166	F/S	DAWSON William Waller	17-04-43	61 Sqn
1330448	Sgt	DAY Alfred Frederick Sidney	23-06-43	9 Sqn
1528083	Sgt	DAY Douglas Edward	20-10-43	106 Sqn
1280658	Sgt	DAY Edward George Havelock	9-10-43	106 Sqn
1447790	Sgt	DAY Frank William	21-04-43	102 Sqn
1333356	Sgt	DAY Frederick William Robert	24-08-43	149 Sqn
124456	F/O	DAY Herbert Harry	17-04-43	50 Sqn
1872295	Sgt	DAY Joseph Robert George	6-11-43	138 Sqn
1433929	Sgt	DAY Leonard Frederick Charles	13-06-43	460 Sqn
1891503	Sgt	DAY Michael Irvine Ryder	19-11-43	75 Sqn
1319108	Sgt	DAY Michael John	2-12-43	35 Sqn
1379869	Sgt	DAY Richard Harvey	31-08-43	102 Sqn
1452920	Sgt	DAY Wilfred Robert	16-12-43	49 Sqn
1385312	Sgt	DAY William George Thomas	25-06-43	57 Sqn
1720260	AC2	DAY William John	1-03-43	1657 HCU
1387351	Sgt	DAYE Ronald Ernest	18-10-43	101 Sqn
916891	Sgt	DEACOCK Victor Alfred	28-08-43	149 Sqn
1316200	Sgt	DEACON Edwin Albert	3-07-43	19 OTU
25042	W/C	DEACON John William	27-02-43	105 Sqn
1535807	Sgt	DEACON John William	15-06-43	49 Sqn

1049243	Sgt	DEACON Robert	5-05-43	1663 HCU	864810	Sgt	DEUGARD Robert Douglas	18-08-43	619 Sqn
975224	Sgt	DEACON Thomas [Eire]	20-10-43	97 Sqn	990042	Sgt	DEVENEY Patrick Joseph	19-11-43	15 OTU
139373	F/O	DEACON Victor George	22-10-43	166 Sqn	1224414	Sgt	DEVEREUX Sidney John	29-06-43	15 Sqn
1380721	Sgt	DEACON William Rees	29-01-43	17 OTU	1005338	Sgt	DEVEREUX-MACK Norman Sydney	27-01-43	21 OTU
1314016	Sgt	DEAN Alec Charles	9-07-43	166 Sqn	45546	S/L	DEVERILL DFC AFC* DFM Ernest Alfred		
576664	Sgt	DEAN Dennis Lawrence	22-09-43	214 Sqn				17-12-43	97 Sqn
1209112	Sgt	DEAN Edward Victor	6-09-43	76 Sqn	114251	F/O	DEVILLE Edward Patrick	12-06-43	7 Sqn
2211152	Sgt	DEAN Eric Alfred	29-12-43	30 OTU	1386648	Sgt	DEVINE Bernard Peter	6-09-43	9 Sqn
120672	F/O	DEAN George Ernest	27-05-43	139 Sqn	1369741	Sgt	DEVITT Robert Francis	23-09-43	15 Sqn
1314707	Sgt	DEAN Gordon William Davidson	16-08-43	166 Sqn	658578	Sgt	DEW Thomas Albert	30-03-43	196 Sqn
1579863	Sgt	DEAN Harold	1-09-43	18 OTU	1604149	Sgt	DEWDNEY Peter Frank	3-08-43	12 Sqn
2216248	Sgt	DEAN John Ellis	25-06-43	428 Sqn	1391811	Sgt	DEWEY Ronald	14-05-43	44 Sqn
1452042	Sgt	DEAN John Gordon Kennedy	16-04-43	156 Sqn	127249	F/O	DEXTER Keith Inger	17-06-43	103 Sqn
1383733	Sgt	DEAN Richard Edward	26-02-43	426 Sqn	701975	F/S	de BOTTE Leo	24-06-43	218 Sqn
1811198	Sgt	DEAN Richard Philip	22-09-43	158 Sqn	138197	P/O	de GARIS Derek Gordon	3-02-43	214 Sqn
1605270	Sgt	DEAN Roderick John Charles	26-07-43	158 Sqn			[Channel Islands]		
1385334	Sgt	DEAN Sidney John	5-02-43	26 OTU	139692	F/O	de JONGH Oscar Geoffrey	22-11-43	82 OTU
1445870	Sgt	DEAN Stanley Frederick	13-05-43	214 Sqn	139579	P/O	DE MEILLAC Guy Maurice Marie Lagarrigue		
127164	F/L	DEAN Wilfred Thomas	12-06-43	158 Sqn				9-04-43	7 Sqn
1197803	Sgt	DEANE Alick George	30-03-43	57 Sqn	1397457	Sgt	DE MEILLAC Yves	3-10-43	90 Sqn
133334	F/O	DEANE John William Frederick	2-12-43	101 Sqn	1571654	Sgt	DE SACHY Maurice Paul	5-09-43	20 OTU
1039634	Sgt	DEANS Donald	17-08-43	218 Sqn	1385877	Sgt	DE SILVA Joe Herbert Wejies	17-01-43	9 Sqn
127926	F/O	DEANS DFC James Lyall	17-10-43	196 Sqn	89122	P/O	DE VILLIERS Paul	30-07-43	97 Sqn
1343832	F/S	DEANS Robert	15-07-43	158 Sqn	134208	F/O	DE VRIES Henry Andrew	16-12-43	619 Sqn
1590663	Sgt	DEARDEN Robert Francis	16-12-43	619 Sqn	1601679	Sgt	DHERING Robert Joseph William	28-11-43	16 OTU
1321244	Sgt	DEASLEY George Leonard Albert	13-07-43	12 Sqn	1820673	Sgt	DICK Alexander McDonald	18-10-43	7 Sqn
1434590	Sgt	DEAVES Edmund James	23-09-43	100 Sqn	1383312	Sgt	DICK Hugh Robert	13-05-43	207 Sqn
946818	Sgt	DEAVIN Frank Ernest	23-11-43	7 Sqn	1613337	Sgt	DICKENS Frederick Donald	29-09-43	156 Sqn
1609880	Sgt	DEBBEN Roy Ernest	4-07-43	51 Sqn	134077	P/O	DICKER Albert Raymond	24-03-43	16 OTU
943098	Sgt	DEBENHAM Alfred Gordon	28-04-43	19 OTU	1544971	Sgt	DICKIE Thomas Lynas	4-10-43	196 Sqn
778128	Sgt	DEBEURIER Wilfred Eric	31-01-43	101 Sqn	1821247	Sgt	DICKIE William	20-12-43	576 Sqn
		[South Africa]			626974	Sgt	DICKINS Thomas Edward	13-07-43	156 Sqn
1394588	Sgt	DECK Paul Dalralph	13-06-43	115 Sqn	1576380	Sgt	DICKINSON Arthur Cyril	5-09-43	1663 HCU
157194	P/O	DEE Eric Hubert	6-09-43	10 Sqn	629265	Sgt	DICKINSON Cecil	23-09-43	77 Sqn
1459666	Sgt	DEE Timothy I'anson	16-12-43	408 Sqn	142572	P/O	DICKINSON John	12-03-43	10 Sqn
1383346	Sgt	DEIGHTON Andrew Peter	21-04-43	77 Sqn	1331953	Sgt	DICKINSON William Henry	4-07-43	15 Sqn
1649902	Sgt	DEKKERS Zeger William Casper	20-10-43	12 OTU	1313177	Sgt	DICKMAN Ewart Wentworth	20-12-43	77 Sqn
		[Holland]			1550321	Sgt	DICKSON Desmond	22-10-43	1657 HCU
1313004	Sgt	DELAHAY Hedley Robert	6-09-43	623 Sqn	1824449	Sgt	DICKSON Harry	27-09-43	19 OTU
1397003	Sgt	DELANEY William Edward	14-04-43	426 Sqn	1368890	Sgt	DICKSON John Edwin	29-06-43	419 Sqn
		[New Zealand]			49686	F/O	DIGBY MiD Percy William	3-04-43	76 Sqn
134692	F/O	DELL Frederick Arthur	2-12-43	44 Sqn	1315999	Sgt	DIGBY Wilfred Charles	14-05-43	44 Sqn
1575924	Sgt	DEMAINE Douglas	20-10-43	619 Sqn	1577037	Sgt	DIGGLE Frank Charles	26-11-43	100 Sqn
1392262	Sgt	DEMPSEY William Charles Thomas	22-06-43	158 Sqn	1607238	Sgt	DIGGLE John Wilson	20-10-43	625 Sqn
1559214	Sgt	DEMPSTER David Dand	20-12-43	51 Sqn	1129136	Sgt	DIGGLE Raymond	23-09-43	57 Sqn
1256582	Sgt	DENBY John William	19-02-43	156 Sqn	975031	Sgt	DIGNUM Robert Edward	11-02-43	57 Sqn
1438344	Sgt	DENBY Lawrence	15-04-43	431 Sqn	155545	P/O	DILLINGHAM Horace Charles	4-07-43	15 Sqn
1129595	Sgt	DENHAM Walter	26-05-43	7 Sqn	1078529	Sgt	DILLNUTT George Walter	20-10-43	619 Sqn
157440	P/O	DENHOLM James	20-06-43	408 Sqn	1397293	Sgt	DILLON George William	12-03-43	97 Sqn
1319761	Sgt	DENMAN Gilbert Charles	17-12-43	100 Sqn	1126212	Sgt	DILLON John	26-06-43	100 Sqn
655634	Sgt	DENMAN Percival Lawrence	24-06-43	10 OTU	2209717	Sgt	DILLON Philip	16-12-43	1661 HCU
1336450	Sgt	DENNEHY Patrick Daniel	1-03-43	10 OTU	1850638	Sgt	DIMOND Francis John	4-12-43	35 Sqn
147533	P/O	DENNESS Kenneth	23-06-43	9 Sqn	148893	P/O	DINES Frederick Albert	24-11-43	1656 HCU
756167	Sgt	DENNEY George Albert	29-06-43	44 Sqn	1344874	Sgt	DINGWALL Thomas Melville Law	26-02-43	1658 HCU
151309	F/O	DENNEY Ronald Frederick	3-12-43	166 Sqn	137565	P/O	DINNAGE Frederick Henry	1-02-43	226 Sqn
906461	F/S	DENNIS Frank Harry	8-10-43	9 Sqn	1337405	Sgt	DINNIS Arthur Desmond	5-03-43	83 Sqn
659116	Sgt	DENNIS Harry	5-02-43	75 Sqn	1384309	Sgt	DIPPLE Richard Walter Albert	6-07-43	1660 HCU
126041	F/O	DENSLOW Donald George	10-03-43	166 Sqn	134568	F/O	DISBROWE Henry Alington	26-07-43	90 Sqn
146316	P/O	DENT Jack Banfield	24-05-43	10 Sqn	149510	P/O	DISBURY Geoffrey Francis	9-07-43	106 Sqn
1384029	Sgt	DENT Harold Charles [Guatemala]	15-04-43	214 Sqn	143890	F/O	DIVALL William George	16-09-43	617 Sqn
1399712	Sgt	DENTON Albert Henry	22-10-43	429 Sqn	143800	F/L	DIVE-ROBINSON Leonard Charles	31-07-43	75 Sqn
1262911	Sgt	DENYER Ernest Claude	26-07-43	75 Sqn	1254892	F/S	DIXON Alan Norris	17-04-43	49 Sqn
1208830	Sgt	DENYER John	14-03-43	27 OTU	1695195	Sgt	DIXON Arnold	18-08-43	419 Sqn
1324875	Sgt	DENYER William George	21-09-43	12 OTU	1800277	Sgt	DIXON Cyril William	25-06-43	90 Sqn
1333519	Sgt	DENZEY Albert Ronald	14-05-43	218 Sqn	1340494	Sgt	DIXON David Albert Henry	18-08-43	139 Sqn
1086924	Sgt	DERBYSHIRE Arthur	29-06-43	149 Sqn	2216204	Sgt	DIXON George Alexander	20-10-43	1664 HCU
1451160	Sgt	DERBYSHIRE Harold	17-04-43	81 OTU	125643	F/O	DIXON Herbert Donald	16-04-43	78 Sqn
1352654	Sgt	DERRINGTON Trevor Radley	20-12-43	78 Sqn	1810602	Sgt	DIXON Herbert Edwin	20-04-43	460 Sqn
085002	Sgt	DETLEY Frederick Charles	29-05-43	149 Sqn	1338080	Sgt	DIXON John	3-10-43	51 Sqn

Service No.	Rank	Name	Date	Unit
1124086	Sgt	DIXON John Alfred	10-03-43	23 OTU
155913	P/O	DIXON Kenneth Thomas	24-08-43	78 Sqn
1085416	Sgt	DIXON Morris	4-07-43	196 Sqn
1046330	Sgt	DIXON Richard Norman	28-04-43	101 Sqn
1120687	Sgt	DIXON Stanley	9-04-43	44 Sqn
1527169	Sgt	DIXON Thomas Wilkinson	30-05-43	218 Sqn
1178204	Sgt	DOBBINS Ronald William	28-08-43	12 Sqn
979710	Sgt	DOBIE John Scott	10-03-43	103 Sqn
68816	F/O	DOBLE DFC Michael Eugene	12-03-43	207 Sqn
1090929	Sgt	DOBSON George Granville	8-04-43	460 Sqn
1437825	Sgt	DOBSON Herbert	7-10-43	15 Sqn
1320688	Sgt	DOBSON James	1-10-43	44 Sqn
1331638	F/S	DOBSON Ronald Frank Alfred	17-06-43	156 Sqn
106875	F/L	DOBSON Thomas Reginald	28-08-43	51 Sqn
1336361	Sgt	DOCK Frank William	9-10-43	50 Sqn
155782	P/O	DOCKER Richard John Robert	18-08-43	61 Sqn
1107057	Sgt	DODD John	24-05-43	214 Sqn
1295445	Sgt	DODD Leslie Joseph	3-02-43	218 Sqn
1030115	Sgt	DODDS George Noon [Australia]	1-09-43	12 Sqn
1126307	Sgt	DODDS James Keith	6-04-43	427 Sqn
576830	F/S	DODDS John David	30-07-43	9 Sqn
1432169	Sgt	DODSON George David	2-10-43	424 Sqn
1129601	Sgt	DODSON John	10-08-43	76 Sqn
135751	F/O	DOHERTY John Christopher	4-12-43	630 Sqn
1336841	Sgt	DOIDGE George Lewis	21-04-43	102 Sqn
542725	Sgt	DOLAN John	28-07-43	101 Sqn
1052038	Sgt	DOLLARD Edward John	5-01-43	101 Sqn
1337861	Sgt	DOLLING Raymond Edgar	18-09-43	17 OTU
638615	Sgt	DOLBEAR Ronald	30-03-43	429 Sqn
1210049	Sgt	DOMLEO Stanley Victor	20-12-43	49 Sqn
657952	Sgt	DOMNITZ Jacob	12-06-43	76 Sqn
996625	Sgt	DONALD James Middleton	30-03-43	77 Sqn
710150	Sgt	DONALD Kenneth Neville [Rhodesia]	12-08-43	620 Sqn
43934	F/L	DONALDSON David James	20-04-43	158 Sqn
1127694	Sgt	DONALDSON David Stuart	22-06-43	7 Sqn
1397543	Sgt	DONALDSON James	28-07-43	50 Sqn
574813	Sgt	DONALDSON Vincent John Mervyn	9-01-43	57 Sqn
1535683	Sgt	DONBAVAND Brian Gray	26-08-43	20 OTU
1582238	Sgt	DONCASTER Ivan Keith	22-10-43	166 Sqn
1338185	Sgt	DONE George Francis	31-01-43	9 Sqn
138397	P/O	DONKIN Dixon David	7-08-43	620 Sqn
1369188	Sgt	DONLEVY Patrick	13-07-43	467 Sqn
1554638	Sgt	DONNACHIE John	18-09-43	17 OTU
132810	P/O	DONNELLY Joseph	1-03-43	15 OTU
129159	F/O	DONNELLY William Archibald	28-06-43	428 Sqn
132034	F/O	DONOVAN Robert Leonard	4-07-43	115 Sqn
1505512	Sgt	DOOLITTLE Edward Francis	1-05-43	9 Sqn
523425	Sgt	DORAN John	29-01-43	9 Sqn
1345599	F/S	DORAN William Henry Charles [Australia]	13-07-43	57 Sqn
1171809	Sgt	DOREY William Donald	9-01-43	12 Sqn
1391523	AC1	DORMON Oliver Richard Edward	19-06-43	Snaith
551841	F/S	DORMON Robert Edwin	7-03-43	51 Sqn
1036353	Sgt	DORN Thomas Andrew Cuthbertson	27-09-43	78 Sqn
169445	P/O	DORRELL Stanley George	23-11-43	7 Sqn
1330802	Sgt	DORRINGTON Frank William	29-03-43	102 Sqn
529468	F/S	DORSETT John William Albert	8-03-43	156 Sqn
131827	F/O	DOUGLAS Angus Ward	27-11-43	408 Sqn
130983	F/L	DOUGLAS Archibald Gordon	7-09-43	10 Sqn
531628	Sgt	DOUGLAS Donald Harold [Canada]	3-10-43	77 Sqn
1098313	Sgt	DOUGLAS George	2-10-43	460 Sqn
980831	Sgt	DOUGLAS John	31-01-43	19 OTU
1076330	Sgt	DOUGLAS Joseph	29-06-43	149 Sqn
1411154	Sgt	DOUGLAS Norman	13-05-43	214 Sqn
611793	Sgt	DOUGLAS Robert Cooper Mills	21-04-43	77 Sqn
134674	F/O	DOUGLAS Ronald Thomas	26-05-43	199 Sqn
845654	Sgt	DOUGLAS Stanley Ernest Ross	28-07-43	15 Sqn
1343507	Sgt	DOUGLAS William John	9-06-43	619 Sqn
1270967	Sgt	DOVE Arthur Reginald	30-03-43	427 Sqn
1219582	Sgt	DOVE William	2-05-43	424 Sqn
126836	F/O	DOWDALL Leonard James	26-02-43	102 Sqn
132025	F/O	DOWDELL William James	29-04-43	12 Sqn
145672	P/O	DOWDING Kenneth Butler	13-06-43	57 Sqn
127304	F/O	DOWLING Victor John	30-03-43	51 Sqn
1464831	Sgt	DOWNES Arnold Richard	24-08-43	77 Sqn
989136	Sgt	DOWNES Cecil William Sinclair	29-04-43	12 Sqn
907282	Sgt	DOWNES David William	28-07-43	106 Sqn
125931	F/O	DOWNEY George	26-07-43	10 Sqn
574259	Sgt	DOWNING Dennis	28-02-43	49 Sqn
1027411	Sgt	DOWNING George Neville [Australia]	4-07-43	196 Sqn
131604	F/O	DOWNING Tom	15-08-43	61 Sqn
1388558	Sgt	DOWNS Albert Edward	3-05-43	487 Sqn
1101786	Sgt	DOWNS Charles Harold	18-11-43	101 Sqn
162544	P/O	DOWNS Ernest John Hamlin	16-12-43	115 Sqn
1053593	Sgt	DOWNS James Leslie	29-01-43	1652 HCU
1456871	Sgt	DOWNS Robert	1-09-43	12 Sqn
1119224	Sgt	DOWNS Robert Vernon	19-11-43	10 Sqn
655505	Sgt	DOWNTON George Edgar	16-08-43	29 OTU
88035	F/L	DOWSE DFC Arthur Patrick	16-04-43	78 Sqn
1078821	Sgt	DOWSE Bewick Johnston	22-06-43	35 Sqn
1201264	Sgt	DOWSETT DFM Alfred William	4-12-43	115 Sqn
975343	Sgt	DOWSON Derek Oswald	11-04-43	214 Sqn
1590162	Sgt	DOWSON William	2-12-43	550 Sqn
1397808	Sgt	DOWTHWAITE Basil Philip	14-07-43	102 Sqn
1222300	Sgt	DOY Jack	14-04-43	138 Sqn
987167	Sgt	DOYLE Dennis Thomas Frank	6-09-43	78 Sqn
120248	F/O	DOYLE Edward	27-01-43	139 Sqn
1323519	Sgt	DOYLE John Patrick	30-07-43	460 Sqn
1588990	Sgt	DOYLE Joseph William	28-07-43	106 Sqn
1088094	Sgt	DOYLE William Edward	13-06-43	97 Sqn
975397	Sgt	DRABBLE Maurice Louis Seth	23-05-43	218 Sqn
1391710	Sgt	DRAGO Richard Edward	28-01-43	1659 HCU
136363	F/O	DRAKE George	16-12-43	166 Sqn
1380012	Sgt	DRAKE William John	12-06-43	156 Sqn
1025320	Sgt	DRANSFIELD Maurice	18-02-43	106 Sqn
1303626	Sgt	DRAPER Edwin	2-12-43	90 Sqn
1312186	F/S	DRAY Dennis Bernard	30-03-43	115 Sqn
1436076	Sgt	DRAYCOTT George Arthur	16-12-43	625 Sqn
105169	F/O	DRAYTON Philip Charles Bradley	26-05-43	207 Sqn
1390450	Sgt	DRAYTON Victor Alfred	28-08-43	199 Sqn
1157212	Sgt	DREDGE Eric William	1-09-43	77 Sqn
1316195	Sgt	DREW William Albert	12-06-43	28 OTU
155245	P/O	DREW William John	18-08-43	44 Sqn
129462	F/O	DRING DFC Thomas	3-04-43	467 Sqn
1497401	Sgt	DRINKWATER Robert James	27-09-43	78 Sqn
1542966	Sgt	DRIVER James	7-07-43	15 OTU
130571	F/O	DRUCE Geoffrey Henry David	15-04-43	21 OTU
138230	Sgt	DRUETT Dennis James	12-03-43	102 Sqn
45806	F/L	DRUMMOND DFM James Anthony Patrick	3-08-43	100 Sqn
1577281	F/S	DRUMMOND Leonard Arthur	18-10-43	97 Sqn
1576835	Sgt	DRURY Allen	24-05-43	27 OTU
1663138	Sgt	DRURY Dennis	3-11-43	466 Sqn
1033594	Sgt	DRYDEN Frank Charles	31-08-43	619 Sqn
572670	Sgt	DUCHENE Edmund Alexis	23-06-43	156 Sqn
1457983	Sgt	DUCKERS Peter Ernest	18-10-43	100 Sqn
1817920	Sgt	DUCKETT George William Francis	17-08-43	138 Sqn
569983	Sgt	DUDLEY Cecil Thomas Oswald	17-06-43	61 Sqn
1236721	Sgt	DUDLEY Charles William	13-06-43	49 Sqn
1333020	Sgt	DUDLEY John	25-02-43	102 Sqn
1037801	Sgt	DUFFY Thomas	23-09-43	106 Sqn
1802454	Sgt	DUFTY Arthur David	9-10-43	12 Sqn
125680	F/O	DUGARD Harry Welland	12-03-43	103 Sqn
920070	Sgt	DUGARD Leonard James	30-07-43	78 Sqn
39071	S/L	DUGDALE DFC Joseph	26-07-43	90 Sqn
1090679	Sgt	DUKES Frederick James Benjamin	22-06-43	7 Sqn
658873	F/S	DULIEU Henry George Middleton [St. Lucia]	22-11-43	83 Sqn

Service No	Rank	Name	Date	Sqn
1386442	F/S	DUMBRILL Herbert Charles	20-12-43	428 Sqn
1002583	Sgt	DUNBAR Alexander	13-01-43	106 Sqn
1348084	F/S	DUNBAR John Alexander	30-07-43	97 Sqn
155918	P/O	DUNCAN Allan Uriah [Jamaica]	2-12-43	9 Sqn
102115	F/O	DUNCAN John Bryce	1-03-43	51 Sqn
1346422	Sgt	DUNCAN John Gilchrist	17-04-43	50 Sqn
1459879	Sgt	DUNCAN John Hubert	3-12-43	619 Sqn
1554603	Sgt	DUNCANSON William	28-08-43	15 Sqn
1391637	Sgt	DUNGER Kenneth James	20-12-43	102 Sqn
130271	F/O	DUNGER Peter John	13-05-43	429 Sqn
1750728	Sgt	DUNKERLEY Kenneth	28-12-43	20 OTU
1450680	Sgt	DUNKERLEY William	24-05-43	426 Sqn
149984	P/O	DUNLOP Charles John Lindsay	15-09-43	10 Sqn
159470	P/O	DUNLOP James Miller	15-09-43	10 Sqn
1320264	Sgt	DUNMORE Leslie Allan	13-05-43	106 Sqn
126469	F/O	DUNN Bryan	12-02-43	427 Sqn
1319229	Sgt	DUNN Frederick Thomas	22-11-43	102 Sqn
1527436	Sgt	DUNN George	25-04-43	29 OTU
1148911	Sgt	DUNN Joseph Richard	4-09-43	100 Sqn
944720	Sgt	DUNN Robert	17-04-43	467 Sqn
701861	Sgt	DUNNE James [Eire]	22-01-43	464 Sqn
85661	F/L	DUNNET Charles William	17-06-43	49 Sqn
1435865	Sgt	DUNNING Walter Thomas	22-06-43	158 Sqn
1602348	Sgt	DUNSTAN Reginald Herbert	21-04-43	90 Sqn
937812	W/O	DURHAM DFM Robert	12-06-43	12 Sqn
1253915	F/S	DURLING Maurice Leonard	10-03-43	77 Sqn
144930	P/O	DURNE Ronald Richard Frank	30-08-43	26 OTU
658365	Sgt	DUROE William Henry	28-08-43	620 Sqn
577654	Sgt	DURRANT Harold Vivian	21-04-43	12 Sqn
1389406	Sgt	DURRANT Norman Wilfred	26-11-43	102 Sqn
1349970	Sgt	DUTHIE William	13-05-43	214 Sqn
1393374	Sgt	DUTTON Edward John	22-10-43	427 Sqn
1209360	Sgt	DUTTON John George Stanley	5-05-43	102 Sqn
1316241	Sgt	DUTTON Kenneth Trevor	11-02-43	57 Sqn
1338700	Sgt	DUTTON Robert Ernest	15-04-43	214 Sqn
1239969	Sgt	DUTTON William Arthur	17-06-43	49 Sqn
143759	F/O	DUVAL Bernard Paul	2-12-43	57 Sqn
157252	P/O	DUXBURY Norman Thomas	5-09-43	1661 HCU
127141	F/L	DUXBURY DFC Vincent	1-10-43	1660 HCU
656639	Sgt	DU-PLAT-TAYLOR Philip Corbet	29-09-43	158 Sqn
1383116	Sgt	DWELLY Esmond Dassett	14-05-43	426 Sqn
1450690	Sgt	DWYER Walter	26-11-43	57 Sqn
139848	P/O	DYBALL Douglas Arthur	26-07-43	158 Sqn
518808	F/S	DYDE Frederick William	2-10-43	207 Sqn
533448	Sgt	DYER Charley Gordon [Canada]	12-03-43	78 Sqn
1606353	Sgt	DYER Edward Harold George	22-11-43	51 Sqn
1339128	Sgt	DYER John Henry	26-02-43	90 Sqn
987897	Sgt	DYKES Fred	29-05-43	158 Sqn
1453171	Sgt	DYKES Ralph Eric	9-10-43	156 Sqn
137546	P/O	DYKES Stanley Clarence	18-07-43	1661 HCU
1290666	Sgt	DYMICK Alfred George	22-01-43	429 Sqn
1501437	Sgt	DYNES George Charles	27-03-43	35 Sqn
1338865	F/S	DYSON Arthur George	11-11-43	102 Sqn
147481	P/O	DYSON Robert Samuel	10-07-43	61 Sqn
1218403	Sgt	DYSON Ronald	30-03-43	420 Sqn
134070	F/O	DE'ATH Leslie James	24-08-43	218 Sqn
144788	P/O	D'EATH Denis Murray	6-09-43	156 Sqn
1621889	Sgt	EADE Lionel Walter	3-08-43	115 Sqn
136523	P/O	EADES Alan Howard	13-05-43	139 Sqn
64264	F/L	EADES George Hadley Templeton	27-03-43	431 Sqn
1123826	Sgt	EADES William Frederick	23-06-43	77 Sqn
1531353	Sgt	EAGLAND Kenneth Cook	21-04-43	12 Sqn
629071	Sgt	EAGLEN Edgar Louis	12-03-43	214 Sqn
148443	P/O	EAGLESHAM William Dunsmore	12-06-43	431 Sqn
1397129	Sgt	EALDEN Frederick William	26-06-43	90 Sqn
1319738	Sgt	EAMES Percy George	24-05-43	101 Sqn
1804045	Sgt	EARL Henry James	30-07-43	156 Sqn
1332585	Sgt	EARLE Frederick Joseph	21-04-43	75 Sqn
162608	P/O	EARLE Jack	4-12-43	625 Sqn
1339874	Sgt	EARNSHAW Frank	20-10-43	83 Sqn
1331999	Sgt	EASEY George	13-02-43	199 Sqn
1332145	Sgt	EASTBURY Alfred Raymond	19-01-43	20 OTU
143096	P/O	EASTHAM Edward Victor	24-06-43	192 Sqn
1381717	Sgt	EASTLAKE Maurice Gillman	12-07-43	1656 HCU
1575713	Sgt	EASTMAN John Bernard	1-10-43	1660 HCU
1334954	Sgt	EASTOE Leslie Frank	18-02-43	158 Sqn
1330123	Sgt	EASTON Cecil	25-06-43	156 Sqn
1127456	Sgt	EASTON David	18-08-43	61 Sqn
120442	F/O	EASTWOOD Eric Douglas	4-07-43	196 Sqn
1078947	Sgt	EASTWOOD Geoffrey	5-05-43	101 Sqn
1114338	Sgt	EASTWOOD Jack	17-01-43	50 Sqn
1301034	Sgt	EASTWOOD Stanley	16-08-43	115 Sqn
1583178	Sgt	EATON Henry Allen	4-09-43	7 Sqn
1802250	Sgt	EATON Walter	22-11-43	77 Sqn
149506	P/O	EAUDE Leo	18-10-43	619 Sqn
156938	P/O	EAVES Arthur James Douglas	26-11-43	61 Sqn
1042163	Sgt	ECCLES Joseph	4-07-43	15 Sqn
1476724	Sgt	ECCLESTON John Travers	31-08-43	466 Sqn
1376454	Sgt	ECKETT Bernard James	12-03-43	106 Sqn
127283	P/O	ECKTON Alfred Raymond	15-01-43	427 Sqn
553011	Sgt	EDDINGTON William	13-05-43	196 Sqn
1334389	Sgt	EDE Albert James	26-07-43	156 Sqn
1147643	Sgt	EDEN Charles	29-07-43	218 Sqn
1478935	Sgt	EDEN John Francis	31-01-43	16 OTU
1304070	Sgt	EDGAR Alec	15-05-43	30 OTU
1380422	Sgt	EDGAR Allan Knowles	17-04-43	77 Sqn
1822324	Sgt	EDGAR Charles Roder Melville	3-11-43	434 Sqn
1452815	Sgt	EDGOOSE Raymond Lynn	24-06-43	218 Sqn
1217917	Sgt	EDMEADES Jack Edward	18-02-43	158 Sqn
145800	P/O	EDMOND William	14-07-43	158 Sqn
142522	P/O	EDMONDS DFC James William	4-07-43	466 Sqn
656269	Sgt	EDMONDS Ronald Albert	30-03-43	44 Sqn
1625218	Sgt	EDMONDSON Sydney	6-11-43	26 OTU
1026801	Sgt	EDMONDSON Thomas Eric	4-07-43	12 Sqn
1392733	Sgt	EDMUNDS John	3-11-43	57 Sqn
1335488	Sgt	EDSER Frederick John	6-09-43	78 Sqn
1432354	Sgt	EDWARDS Albert Victor	13-05-43	90 Sqn
989879	Sgt	EDWARDS Albert William Frederick	3-09-43	44 Sqn
1313119	Sgt	EDWARDS Cadfan	26-01-43	15 OTU
138891	P/O	EDWARDS Charles Arthur	17-06-43	49 Sqn
1456665	Sgt	EDWARDS Clifford Beecroft	6-09-43	44 Sqn
1305137	Sgt	EDWARDS Cyril Bert	28-08-43	103 Sqn
1198784	Sgt	EDWARDS David Roy	18-04-43	156 Sqn
1315509	Sgt	EDWARDS Desmond	24-12-43	514 Sqn
948474	Sgt	EDWARDS Edward William	16-07-43	9 Sqn
1236492	Sgt	EDWARDS Ellis Drury	30-03-43	149 Sqn
159033	P/O	EDWARDS Francis Bernard	3-10-43	428 Sqn
1219680	Sgt	EDWARDS Frank George Gibling	10-03-43	100 Sqn
1331491	Sgt	EDWARDS Frank John	13-01-43	106 Sqn
1066933	F/S	EDWARDS Frederick	2-12-43	97 Sqn
1321557	Sgt	EDWARDS Frederick Arthur James	26-07-43	51 Sqn
509879	Sgt	EDWARDS Frederick John	25-07-43	102 Sqn
1386296	Sgt	EDWARDS George Alfred Philip	22-06-43	156 Sqn
1078045	Sgt	EDWARDS George Harold	1-05-43	467 Sqn
1522340	Sgt	EDWARDS Gordon Cull	1-10-43	1660 HCU
1286321	Sgt	EDWARDS Haydn Winston	6-03-43	76 Sqn
143652	P/O	EDWARDS DFM John Frederick	17-04-43	61 Sqn
1256599	Sgt	EDWARDS John Leonard	24-05-43	51 Sqn
130636	F/O	EDWARDS John Lloyd	15-06-43	75 Sqn
1167329	W/O	EDWARDS Joseph Gilbert	17-04-43	51 Sqn
1577779	Sgt	EDWARDS Kenneth	24-07-43	18 OTU
1118711	Sgt	EDWARDS Kenneth Williams	7-02-43	166 Sqn
1873490	Sgt	EDWARDS Leslie Edward	6-07-43	27 OTU
1384142	Sgt	EDWARDS Montague	14-07-43	428 Sqn
1289974	Sgt	EDWARDS Patrick John	27-03-43	101 Sqn
1379731	Sgt	EDWARDS Reginald George	11-04-43	166 Sqn
1657665	Sgt	EDWARDS Reginald John	4-12-43	51 Sqn
1387240	Sgt	EDWARDS Ronald Patrick	27-01-43	50 Sqn

Service No	Rank	Name	Date	Unit
1322675	Sgt	EDWARDS Terry	20-10-43	90 Sqn
142008	P/O	EDWARDS Thomas	30-03-43	76 Sqn
1229956	Sgt	EDWARDS Thomas Eric	10-03-43	77 Sqn
1332515	F/S	EDWARDS Thomas Chapman	24-08-43	158 Sqn
966317	Sgt	EDWARDS Tudor Lewis	11-04-43	166 Sqn
1808351	Sgt	EDYVEAN-WALKER Peter Geoffrey	17-11-43	166 Sqn
1531789	Sgt	EELES Frank	28-08-43	620 Sqn
1320283	Sgt	EFEMEY Frederick Albert Charles	3-12-43	166 Sqn
1433364	Sgt	EGAN Edward	16-12-43	9 Sqn
658234	Sgt	EGAN John Francis	24-08-43	78 Sqn
1338021	Sgt	EGAN Patrick Joseph	4-02-43	90 Sqn
576406	Sgt	EGGLETON Dennis Louis Noke [Canada]	8-04-43	218 Sqn
964374	Sgt	EHRHART Loring Charles	27-01-43	218 Sqn
1332191	Sgt	EKE Edward William	13-05-43	90 Sqn
1817130	Sgt	EKINS George Edward	2-06-43	24 OTU
949211	Sgt	ELCOX Anthony Graham	30-07-43	57 Sqn
129355	F/O	ELDER Douglas Cunningham	3-08-43	103 Sqn
1430252	Sgt	ELDER Edward Vladimir Austin	27-09-43	434 Sqn
1672923	Sgt	ELDER Richard Walker	3-11-43	76 Sqn
1091022	Sgt	ELDER Sidney	22-11-43	77 Sqn
88431	F/L	ELDER AFC William Alexander Stevenson	25-02-43	207 Sqn
125506	F/O	ELDERFIELD Henry	17-04-43	50 Sqn
133201	P/O	ELDERTON Clarence William	4-08-43	138 Sqn
67652	F/L	ELDRIDGE DFC* John Gordon	24-05-43	166 Sqn
1293257	Sgt	ELDRIDGE Philip Henry	3-04-43	158 Sqn
1579640	Sgt	ELEY Alban Kenneth	18-04-43	156 Sqn
1334842	Sgt	ELEY Anthony Edward	24-12-43	57 Sqn
976368	Sgt	ELKINS Raymond George	21-04-43	103 Sqn
1330229	Sgt	ELKINS Victor Norman	12-03-43	102 Sqn
1218856	Sgt	ELKS George Reginald	28-08-43	76 Sqn
1539475	Sgt	ELLACOTT Norman Ernest	4-06-43	26 OTU
117133	F/O	ELLDRED Peter John	18-11-43	192 Sqn
1283829	Sgt	ELLEN Charles Victor	3-03-43	103 Sqn
1579899	Sgt	ELLICK Frank	2-10-43	61 Sqn
1383884	Sgt	ELLINGHAM Thomas Edward	29-04-43	207 Sqn
1509658	Sgt	ELLINS Charles Percival	23-09-43	75 Sqn
1360106	F/S	ELLINS John Francis	9-10-43	106 Sqn
656764	Sgt	ELLIOT Peter Arthur Frank	31-08-43	466 Sqn
1218608	Sgt	ELLIOT Robert Hugh	23-06-43	51 Sqn
135633	F/O	ELLIOTT Daniel Valentine	23-06-43	158 Sqn
1435429	Sgt	ELLIOTT Harry	11-04-43	166 Sqn
657205	F/S	ELLIOTT John Herbert	11-06-43	207 Sqn
1659630	AC1	ELLIOTT John James Farley	27-07-43	Horsham St. Faith
117489	F/O	ELLIOTT Maurice Alec Stanley	8-04-43	76 Sqn
42401	S/L	ELLIOTT DFC Peter Campbell	1-03-43	35 Sqn
1002912	Sgt	ELLIOTT Thomas	23-11-43	460 Sqn
1527934	Sgt	ELLIS Alfred James	19-02-43	15 Sqn
1031023	Sgt	ELLIS David Morgan	24-08-43	101 Sqn
1233887	Sgt	ELLIS David Walter	9-07-43	166 Sqn
1320286	Sgt	ELLIS Gordon George	27-01-43	21 OTU
1270431	Sgt	ELLIS Herbert Charles	1-05-43	44 Sqn
1224945	Sgt	ELLIS John Charles	3-11-43	426 Sqn
121140	F/O	ELLIS Kenneth Hector	3-03-43	106 Sqn
1318147	Sgt	ELLIS Leonard James	24-09-43	12 Sqn
1313959	Sgt	ELLIS Leslie	11-04-43	7 Sqn
145792	P/O	ELLIS Leslie James	1-05-43	44 Sqn
147094	P/O	ELLIS Leslie Jewitt	2-12-43	460 Sqn
1454670	Sgt	ELLIS Norman	22-06-43	101 Sqn
1388790	F/S	ELLIS Peter Martin Crowle	16-12-43	576 Sqn
159481	P/O	ELLIS Ronald	9-10-43	102 Sqn
918424	Sgt	ELLIS Royston Hazeldine George	31-08-43	199 Sqn
132386	P/O	ELLIS DFC William Claude	10-08-43	76 Sqn
1021328	F/S	ELLIS William Henry	21-04-43	75 Sqn
147969	P/O	ELLISON Richard Campbell	12-06-43	429 Sqn
1294158	Sgt	ELLMER Harold Roy	22-09-43	57 Sqn
1075913	Sgt	ELLWOOD William Ernest	1-10-43	1660 HCU
1206613	Sgt	ELPHICK Harry Eli	31-08-43	199 Sqn
1317012	Sgt	ELSON Peter Jeffrey	27-09-43	78 Sqn
1315743	Sgt	ELSWORTHY George	29-04-43	12 Sqn
961061	Sgt	ELTON Percy John	3-03-43	15 Sqn
1125626	Sgt	ELVIDGE Clifford	7-07-43	15 OTU
1332186	Sgt	ELVIN Ronald Edward	27-01-43	21 OTU
519416	Sgt	ELWELL Bertram	15-04-43	75 Sqn
1203925	Sgt	ELWELL John Edwin	31-03-43	10 OTU
141791	P/O	EMANS Albert Edward	28-08-43	156 Sqn
1254332	Sgt	EMBERSON Frank James	28-01-43	14 OTU
143225	P/O	EMBERSON Thomas Edward	4-05-43	15 Sqn
1300003	Sgt	EMERSON John	26-06-43	51 Sqn
1678504	Sgt	EMERSON John Maple	27-09-43	76 Sqn
574341	Sgt	EMERSON Richard Vincent	20-04-43	57 Sqn
37762	S/L	EMERTON Peter James	14-11-43	1652 HCU
45801	F/L	EMERY DFM Alan Arnold	4-04-43	51 Sqn
1316711	Sgt	EMERY Alfred Keith	18-10-43	207 Sqn
1144841	Sgt	EMMERSON Maurice	7-09-43	78 Sqn
157736	P/O	EMMERSON Peter	28-11-43	28 OTU
1259229	Sgt	EMMETT John Henry	16-06-43	460 Sqn
1576201	Sgt	EMMS Arthur Edward	1-05-43	7 Sqn
1813155	Sgt	EMMS Philip Leslie	22-10-43	428 Sqn
1434258	Sgt	EMSON Joseph William	18-10-43	44 Sqn
1381754	Sgt	ENGEL Paul	2-10-43	619 Sqn
1511673	Sgt	ENGLAND George Alfred	2-12-43	103 Sqn
1130657	Sgt	ENGLAND Norman Nicholas	22-06-43	44 Sqn
1001372	Sgt	ENGLISH Leslie	29-09-43	166 Sqn
635420	Sgt	ENOCH Dillwyn	16-07-43	10 Sqn
1385891	Sgt	ENRIGHT Brian Patrick [Eire]	26-01-43	23 OTU
147316	P/O	ENRIGHT Gerard William Board	26-06-43	106 Sqn
988200	Sgt	ENRIGHT Jethro Nathaniel	11-04-43	78 Sqn
129576	F/O	ENTWHISTLE Harry	28-05-43	102 Sqn
634999	Sgt	ENTWISLE Dangan Mervyn Robert Bertin	27-09-43	76 Sqn
1113359	Sgt	ENTWISTLE Clifford	29-06-43	10 Sqn
1538482	Sgt	ENTWISTLE Harold	23-09-43	78 Sqn
1288043	Sgt	EPATHITE John William	26-02-43	158 Sqn
1037117	Sgt	ERDBEER William John	28-05-43	158 Sqn
160059	P/O	ERICKSON David William [Rhodesia]	30-05-43	44 Sqn
1204724	Sgt	ERNE Arthur William	24-06-43	218 Sqn
574108	Sgt	ERNE Kenneth Frank	28-04-43	218 Sqn
1531620	Sgt	ERRINGTON George	16-04-43	466 Sqn
1080349	Sgt	ERRINGTON John Blackburn	17-11-43	405 Sqn
1507631	Sgt	ERRINGTON Sydney Arthur	25-06-43	7 Sqn
125507	F/O	ERWIN John Francis Henry	11-08-43	115 Sqn
1814421	Sgt	ERWOOD Frank Alfred	4-11-43	12 Sqn
118575	F/O	ESPY Harl J. [USA]	27-03-43	35 Sqn
1258658	Sgt	ESSEN Stanley Frederick	26-02-43	9 Sqn
142009	P/O	ETHELSTON John George	19-02-43	15 Sqn
136881	F/O	ETHERINGTON Harry Mark	11-08-43	77 Sqn
129058	F/O	ETIENNE Hugh Terence [St. Lucia]	5-03-43	214 Sqn
923169	Sgt	ETTLE Walter Idris	20-06-43	10 OTU
1018567	F/S	EVANS Albert Edward	20-10-43	83 Sqn
1492250	Sgt	EVANS Albert Rowland	5-04-43	57 Sqn
1580410	Sgt	EVANS Albert William	26-07-43	102 Sqn
1318804	F/S	EVANS Anthony Henry	3-11-43	101 Sqn
1311553	F/S	EVANS Arthur	4-11-43	12 Sqn
160674	P/O	EVANS Arthur Frederick	12-11-43	158 Sqn
1031846	Sgt	EVANS Benjamin Kenneth Hall	12-07-43	467 Sqn
50665	F/O	EVANS DFM Brynmor Granville	25-05-43	180 Sqn
1338188	Sgt	EVANS David Ivor James	26-11-43	103 Sqn
130699	F/O	EVANS Douglas Arthur Norman	24-05-43	35 Sqn
128977	F/O	EVANS Douglas William Henry [Channel Islands]	13-05-43	207 Sqn
1162655	Sgt	EVANS Eric Stanley	15-03-43	11 OTU
1480303	Sgt	EVANS Ernest	4-12-43	78 Sqn
1473151	Sgt	EVANS George Edward	12-06-43	51 Sqn
960709	Sgt	EVANS George William	24-08-43	156 Sqn
1393533	Sgt	EVANS Gerald Douglas	17-05-43	10 OTU

1317037	Sgt	EVANS Gerwyn Howell	3-04-43	9 Sqn	656329	Sgt	FARE Edward Frederick	10-07-43	77 Sqn
1218571	Sgt	EVANS Gordon Joseph	21-04-43	49 Sqn	132184	P/O	FARLA France Louis	30-01-43	16 OTU
1196508	Sgt	EVANS Gwilyn Richard	24-05-43	49 Sqn	1575746	Sgt	FARLEY Dennis Charles	21-04-43	7 Sqn
658854	F/S	EVANS Harold Thomas	20-12-43	49 Sqn	159066	P/O	FARLEY Horace Frank	22-11-43	51 Sqn
1551799	Sgt	EVANS Harry John	6-08-43	51 Sqn	143877	P/O	FARLEY Stanley Robert	29-03-43	166 Sqn
1387863	Sgt	EVANS Henry	17-04-43	101 Sqn	1338093	Sgt	FARMER John Ernest	28-09-43	428 Sqn
1653812	Sgt	EVANS Herbert Denis	22-09-43	77 Sqn	1118254	Sgt	FARMER Leslie	2-03-43	44 Sqn
1677156	Sgt	EVANS Jack	22-09-43	101 Sqn	158305	P/O	FARMER Victor Douglas	5-05-43	57 Sqn
145515	P/O	EVANS John	15-06-43	9 Sqn	1482428	Sgt	FARMERY Raymond Brown	3-08-43	158 Sqn
1315359	Sgt	EVANS John	6-02-43	14 OTU	1399312	Sgt	FARNDELL Brian Harold	23-11-43	12 Sqn
149139	P/O	EVANS DFM John Colin	26-06-43	57 Sqn	1038623	Sgt	FARNELL Frank William	24-05-43	10 Sqn
619407	Sgt	EVANS John James	3-08-43	214 Sqn	1212594	Sgt	FARNELL Paul Richardson	11-06-43	1654 HCU
1334798	Sgt	EVANS John Warwick Craven	24-05-43	101 Sqn	985405	Sgt	FARNEN Edward	15-04-43	149 Sqn
1652992	Sgt	EVANS Leonard Thomas	3-08-43	115 Sqn	121554	F/O	FARQUHARSON LEY Henry	11-02-43	102 Sqn
1577745	Sgt	EVANS Leslie Robert	12-06-43	12 Sqn	149148	P/O	FARR Edward George	24-08-43	426 Sqn
1412730	Sgt	EVANS Lionel Frderick	5-05-43	21 OTU	1318284	Sgt	FARR Francis Roy	17-12-43	97 Sqn
1312502	F/S	EVANS Myrddin	3-08-43	428 Sqn	1237623	Sgt	FARR Norman Sidney	30-03-43	428 Sqn
1197361	Sgt	EVANS Peter Charles	30-07-43	97 Sqn	1390989	Sgt	FARRELL Charles Alfred	25-09-43	29 OTU
1317417	Sgt	EVANS Reginald Charles	24-01-43	20 OTU	653824	Sgt	FARRELLY James Francis	8-03-43	15 Sqn
547680	Sgt	EVANS Robert Ormond	27-09-43	434 Sqn	1316196	Sgt	FARREN Percy Eric	29-01-43	21 OTU
1390444	Sgt	EVANS Ronald Charles George	31-07-43	75 Sqn	1562923	Sgt	FARRER Edgar	3-10-43	18 OTU
530757	Sgt	EVANS Ronald David	13-05-43	149 Sqn	133785	P/O	FARROW Ernest George	15-05-43	30 OTU
635327	Sgt	EVANS Ronald Frank	3-02-43	214 Sqn	1803112	Sgt	FATHERS Richard Thomas	23-11-43	97 Sqn
119223	F/O	EVANS Ronald Herbert Aitchison	25-01-43	226 Sqn	1391293	Sgt	FAULCONBRIDGE Kenneth Richard	20-04-43	218 Sqn
946822	Sgt	EVANS Stanley William	1-09-43	158 Sqn	1030315	Sgt	FAULKNER Arthur	16-06-43	405 Sqn
1134492	Sgt	EVANS Sydney Frederick	11-08-43	15 Sqn	1336161	Sgt	FAULKNER Dennis Edwin	2-06-43	20 OTU
1321223	F/S	EVANS Thomas Lynn	20-12-43	158 Sqn	578345	Sgt	FAULKNER Donald Frederick	17-12-43	57 Sqn
1005138	Sgt	EVANS William David	31-08-43	9 Sqn	136885	F/O	FAULKNER Ronald Norman	27-09-43	103 Sqn
1313826	Sgt	EVANS William Harold Vaughan	1-03-43	466 Sqn	931566	Sgt	FAUVEL Norman Louis	21-04-43	90 Sqn
1421169	Sgt	EVANS William Herbert	31-08-43	78 Sqn			[Channel Islands]		
1187983	Sgt	EVERDEN Leslie Leonard	17-04-43	75 Sqn	139690	F/O	FAVIER Ralph Enrique	7-09-43	106 Sqn
119783	F/O	EVERILL Jerrold Mountford	11-04-43	166 Sqn	1081397	Sgt	FAY Francis Joseph	22-11-43	83 Sqn
963888	Sgt	EVERITT David Bertram	15-04-43	10 Sqn	655452	F/S	FAZACKERLEY Frederick	25-06-43	7 Sqn
1119284	Sgt	EVERTON Leslie Harold	4-07-43	12 Sqn	1083876	Sgt	FAZACKERLEY Horace Cyril	20-04-43	57 Sqn
657231	Sgt	EVISON Peter	3-03-43	207 Sqn	614144	Sgt	FAZAKERLEY Thomas	30-03-43	49 Sqn
1576002	Sgt	EWAN Eric	23-09-43	49 Sqn	1316492	Sgt	FEAR Brian Albert	7-09-43	10 Sqn
1030547	F/S	EWEN Thomas Robertson	7-10-43	15 Sqn	1317167	W/O	FEAR Trevor	24-08-43	75 Sqn
574356	Sgt	EWING Warren Morgan	14-05-43	57 Sqn	1292205	Sgt	FEARN Bert Henry	29-12-43	408 Sqn
		[New Zealand]			1570056	Sgt	FEARN John Murdoch	14-09-43	115 Sqn
1506936	Sgt	EXLEY Harry	27-09-43	218 Sqn	933831	Sgt	FEATHERSTONE Henry	3-10-43	103 Sqn
146972	P/O	EYLES Stanley Clarence	9-07-43	49 Sqn	1150572	Sgt	FEATHERSTONE William	11-06-43	1654 HCU
1071970	Sgt	EYRE Kenneth Cedric	3-03-43	75 Sqn	1527088	Sgt	FEE Thomas	13-04-43	101 Sqn
928328	Sgt	EYRE Leslie Frank	26-11-43	514 Sqn	1162929	Sgt	FEELEY Roy Reginald	3-04-43	9 Sqn
1022285	Sgt	EYRE Samuel	3-11-43	10 Sqn	1571107	Sgt	FEELY Desmond Robert	21-10-43	161 Sqn
1067501	Sgt	EZARD George	3-09-43	199 Sqn	632983	Sgt	FEENAN Andrew James	8-03-43	75 Sqn
115153	F/L	FAGAN DFC Leslie William Dudley	22-10-43	10 Sqn	1318266	Sgt	FEENEY Herbert	27-11-43	101 Sqn
129115	F/L	FAIRCHILD John Edwin	13-09-43	12 OTU	1161980	Sgt	FELCE Hugh Morris	3-03-43	214 Sqn
1021583	F/S	FAIRFIELD Edward	22-10-43	427 Sqn	1379924	Sgt	FELL Hayden	5-03-43	83 Sqn
51686	P/O	FAIRGRIEVE DFM Thomas Darling	25-07-43	218 Sqn	1193202	Sgt	FELLOWS Graham	21-04-43	61 Sqn
1493165	Sgt	FAIRHURST James Albert	29-08-43	29 OTU	1390228	Sgt	FELLS Donald	23-08-43	207 Sqn
1498587	Sgt	FAIRHURST Norman Louis	20-04-43	218 Sqn	1396129	Sgt	FELSENSTEIN Gerald Cecil	12-03-43	102 Sqn
1145813	Sgt	FAIRHURST Stanley	20-10-43	29 OTU	1846665	AC1	FENNELL Samuel	5-10-43	5 Group
632330	Sgt	FAIRLIE David Gow	6-03-43	49 Sqn	658569	Sgt	FENNING Ernest Hatfield	5-10-43	51 Sqn
1602476	Sgt	FAIRMANER Alfred William	26-06-43	51 Sqn	569932	Sgt	FENTIMAN Douglas Charles	30-07-43	97 Sqn
931694	Sgt	FALCK George Frederick Alfred Edward			1304421	Sgt	FENTON Charles Henry	4-07-43	90 Sqn
			22-11-43	49 Sqn	522339	Sgt	FENWICK Clifford Richard	23-06-43	90 Sqn
1681266	Sgt	FALCKH Charles William	22-06-43	77 Sqn	139598	F/L	FERGUSON Alan Egerton	6-09-43	78 Sqn
139689	P/O	FALEIJEVAS Jurgis	11-08-43	77 Sqn	1565261	Sgt	FERGUSON Duncan Alexander	15-06-43	103 Sqn
		(served as COCKAYNE George)			1322786	Sgt	FERGUSON Ian Woodman	26-09-43	14 OTU
570198	Sgt	FALKINGHAM Peter	25-05-43	207 Sqn	137127	F/O	FERGUSON James Robb	20-12-43	50 Sqn
1395644	Sgt	FALL Geoffrey	8-06-43	26 OTU	1554441	Sgt	FERGUSON John	31-07-43	218 Sqn
656451	F/S	FALL Roy	7-09-43	158 Sqn	1344019	Sgt	FERGUSON Philip	22-01-43	76 Sqn
139843	P/O	FALLON Joseph	2-06-43	20 OTU	1222496	Sgt	FERMANIAN Edwin Carlo	12-03-43	103 Sqn
552269	Sgt	FALLON Leo Patrick	13-03-43	115 Sqn	1399826	Sgt	FERNANDO Vincent Francis [Ceylon]	3-08-43	166 Sqn
1239601	Sgt	FALLOWS Stanley	25-06-43	57 Sqn	1383533	Sgt	FERNEE George Richard	17-04-43	77 Sqn
1796300	Sgt	FALLS Henri Hugh	26-11-43	115 Sqn	1337210	Sgt	FERRIER John Philip	26-11-43	463 Sqn
1673319	Sgt	FANNAN Lawrence Peter	11-08-43	115 Sqn	1495558	Sgt	FERRIS Douglas Claude	13-05-43	9 Sqn
1576328	Sgt	FARAHAR Roy Albert James	7-07-43	15 OTU	1376974	F/S	FERRIS William	20-12-43	466 Sqn
159580	F/O	FARE Arthur Russell	4-10-43	419 Sqn	130288	F/O	FEWTRELL Ronald Norman	28-05-43	102 Sqn

143396	P/O	FIDDES Henry Crelling	17-04-43	15 Sqn		922593	Sgt	FITZGERALD Michael Joseph	20-04-43	158 Sqn
1415512	Sgt	FIDDES Louis Stanley	11-04-43	9 Sqn		1499616	Sgt	FITZPATRICK Arthur Allan	28-04-43	218 Sqn
1554261	F/S	FIDDES Robert	20-12-43	102 Sqn		1699809	Sgt	FITZSIMMONS John	23-06-43	77 Sqn
633093	Sgt	FIDDLER Jack	11-08-43	35 Sqn		1318429	Sgt	FLACK John Herbert	2-12-43	90 Sqn
1196513	Sgt	FIDGEON Francis Christopher	17-04-43	76 Sqn		1318786	Sgt	FLAHERTY Michael John	24-05-43	15 Sqn
628161	Sgt	FIELD Ernest James	15-04-43	466 Sqn		1336859	Sgt	FLATMAN Stephen Thomas	17-09-43	196 Sqn
1320541	Sgt	FIELD Francis	4-07-43	214 Sqn		631814	Sgt	FLATTERS Albert Reginald	6-11-43	138 Sqn
611676	Sgt	FIELD Leon John George	31-08-43	9 Sqn		142563	F/O	FLEET Alfred Gerald	23-11-43	105 Sqn
41164	F/L	FIELD Robert Howard Byers	24-01-43	20 OTU		591603	Sgt	FLEMING Albert Ronald	24-12-43	103 Sqn
149478	P/O	FIELDEN Derrick	18-08-43	467 Sqn		1576515	Sgt	FLEMING Alfred Reginald	6-09-43	78 Sqn
755751	F/S	FIELDER Gordon Brown	26-07-43	214 Sqn		132773	F/O	FLEMING Charles Bernard	12-06-43	100 Sqn
141159	F/L	FIELDER Roland John	3-11-43	10 Sqn		1349738	Sgt	FLEMING Charles Roughead	30-05-43	115 Sqn
1111801	F/S	FIELDHOUSE Leslie	3-04-43	83 Sqn		1129762	Sgt	FLEMING John	6-08-43	192 Sqn
2216185	Sgt	FIELDING Anthony Hudson Ramsden				1891783	Sgt	FLEMING Joseph Charles Frederick	12-11-43	158 Sqn
			29-12-43	431 Sqn		992509	F/S	FLEMING Laurence Michael	13-02-43	22 OTU
132145	F/O	FIELDING Francis Edwin	29-06-43	207 Sqn		129158	F/O	FLEMING Noel Douglas	27-04-43	76 Sqn
162606	P/O	FIELDING Geoffrey	27-11-43	408 Sqn		978488	Sgt	FLEMING Norman	23-09-43	49 Sqn
1022019	Sgt	FIELDING James	4-02-43	102 Sqn		1335053	Sgt	FLEMING Ronald Arthur	25-07-43	51 Sqn
1332345	Sgt	FIELDING Kenneth John	3-01-43	24 OTU		1343175	Sgt	FLEMING William	4-04-43	51 Sqn
1079323	Cpl	TOMLINSON Leslie Tomlinson	2-07-43	158 Sqn		1527064	F/S	FLETCHER Arthur	30-07-43	51 Sqn
1383094	Sgt	FIELDING Ronald Vincent	13-06-43	101 Sqn		1389587	F/S	FLETCHER Dennis Walter Cleveland	22-06-43	83 Sqn
574056	Sgt	FIELDS Harold Walter	24-05-43	166 Sqn		1383620	Sgt	FLETCHER George Frederick	27-04-43	196 Sqn
1196129	Sgt	FILLEUL George Arthur	3-08-43	9 Sqn		1334452	Sgt	FLETCHER Gordon William George	15-06-43	460 Sqn
132872	F/O	FILMER Eric	8-08-43	61 Sqn		156598	P/O	FLETCHER DFM Jack	7-09-43	156 Sqn
1355652	Sgt	FINCH Henry Thomas	9-10-43	97 Sqn		1579349	Sgt	FLETCHER James Frederick	17-04-43	49 Sqn
1413665	Sgt	FINCH Stanley Eric	4-07-43	115 Sqn		1092331	Sgt	FLETCHER John	23-09-43	77 Sqn
577642	Sgt	FINCHAM Arthur William	26-05-43	218 Sqn		44065	S/L	FLETCHER DFM MiD John Lawrence	2-03-43	76 Sqn
921069	Sgt	FINCHAM Roy Eppy	3-08-43	44 Sqn		150150	F/O	FLETCHER Leslie	16-12-43	1663 HCU
998702	Sgt	FINDLAY John	1-09-43	101 Sqn		1333953	F/S	FLETCHER Neville Egerton	6-09-43	427 Sqn
1342595	Sgt	FINDLAY Peter Wright	30-05-43	460 Sqn		1269967	Sgt	FLETCHER Phillip Owen	31-08-43	149 Sqn
1365331	F/S	FINDLAY William	4-09-43	44 Sqn		1088071	Sgt	FLETCHER Reginald	15-06-43	12 Sqn
1451563	Sgt	FINDLEY Roy Charles Samuel	17-04-43	81 OTU		1322503	Sgt	FLETCHER Robert	26-11-43	1658 HCU
944476	Sgt	FINDLEY William	9-10-43	51 Sqn		1811231	Sgt	FLETCHER Robert Bernard	24-08-43	78 Sqn
1331566	Sgt	FINK Harry Richard	22-06-43	35 Sqn		1255237	Sgt	FLETCHER Stanley George	25-07-43	103 Sqn
1045568	Sgt	FINLAY George Prosser	22-10-43	158 Sqn		44063	S/L	FLETCHER DFC DFM William	14-02-43	158 Sqn
1686496	Sgt	FINLAY William Armstrong	23-08-43	460 Sqn		1222635	Sgt	FLETTON William Stephen	23-08-43	100 Sqn
1374446	LAC	FINLAYSON Hugh	19-06-43	Snaith		1321784	Sgt	FLOOD Percy Eric Charles	5-05-43	7 Sqn
1218851	F/S	FINN Michael Joseph Thomas	6-09-43	620 Sqn		124712	P/O	FLOOD Reginald	14-02-43	158 Sqn
146984	P/O	FIRTH Christopher	20-10-43	619 Sqn		577867	Sgt	FLOREY Edwin John Charles	8-01-43	467 Sqn
1330260	Sgt	FIRTH Dennis William	28-08-43	102 Sqn		79541	S/L	FLOWER Frank Thiompson	3-04-43	83 Sqn
1383746	Sgt	FISH Eddie	10-01-43	10 Sqn		1295414	Sgt	FLOWER Peter John	24-09-43	428 Sqn
1288872	Sgt	FISH Reginald Stanley	30-07-43	156 Sqn		37542	S/L	FLOWERDEW John Bernard	5-05-43	102 Sqn
925124	Sgt	FISHER Albert Leslie	26-05-43	7 Sqn		1384586	Sgt	FLOYD Alan St. John	11-08-43	57 Sqn
143669	P/O	FISHER Alfred Ernest	30-03-43	57 Sqn		1333213	Sgt	FLOYD Denys	22-06-43	158 Sqn
1576883	Sgt	FISHER Arthur George	22-10-43	49 Sqn		1338298	Sgt	FLOYD Robert William	12-03-43	102 Sqn
1055777	Sgt	FISHER Charles Harold	5-05-43	35 Sqn		970979	W/O	FLYNN James	3-08-43	103 Sqn
1603546	Sgt	FISHER Denis Alexander John	24-12-43	57 Sqn		158411	F/O	FLYNN John William	20-12-43	426 Sqn
1496421	Sgt	FISHER Donald Coulthard	5-03-43	29 OTU		128613	F/O	FLYNN Leslie George	25-06-43	218 Sqn
1332036	Sgt	FISHER Ernest Herbert	22-06-43	158 Sqn		1174414	F/S	FLYNN Patrick	9-03-43	35 Sqn
87183	F/S	FISHER Frederick Warren	13-05-43	28 OTU		145699	P/O	FOALE William Charles Robert	12-06-43	78 Sqn
1238789	Sgt	FISHER Guy	27-04-43	51 Sqn		1454500	Sgt	FODEN Frederick Francis	23-06-43	83 Sqn
1139038	Sgt	FISHER Harry	4-09-43	106 Sqn		1240718	Sgt	FOGG Arthur	3-11-43	101 Sqn
132807	F/O	FISHER John Robinson	18-10-43	467 Sqn		577754	Sgt	FOGGON John	14-07-43	408 Sqn
1335417	Sgt	FISHER Leonard Robert	1-09-43	149 Sqn		1016942	F/S	FOLEY John	22-10-43	49 Sqn
1321583	Sgt	FISHER Leonard William	2-07-43	30 OTU		918300	Sgt	FOLEY Reginald Douglas	1-03-43	103 Sqn
1339294	Sgt	FISHER Lewis William	2-12-43	156 Sqn		1348986	Sgt	FOLEY William	27-04-43	102 Sqn
644404	Sgt	FISHER Phillip Stanley	8-01-43	50 Sqn		1176166	Sgt	FOLKER Percy John	2-03-43	61 Sqn
124316	F/O	FISHER Ronald Victor	9-10-43	431 Sqn		1334913	Sgt	FONTAINE Ronald William	18-11-43	514 Sqn
701854	Sgt	FISHER Stanley George	20-02-43	90 Sqn		1212342	Sgt	FOOT Raymond George	15-06-43	44 Sqn
517185	Sgt	FISHER William Robert	21-01-43	196 Sqn		1437370	LAC	FOOTE Robert	12-05-43	1658 HCU
1098374	F/S	FISHER William Starkey	16-12-43	156 Sqn		973384	Sgt	FORBES Douglas	8-03-43	61 Sqn
1375457	Sgt	FISK Leslie Claude Alec	29-03-43	97 Sqn		1256940	Sgt	FORBES Robert George Cameron	24-08-43	199 Sqn
1632361	F/S	FITCH Edward William	28-08-43	10 OTU		148437	P/O	FORBES Thomas Benzie	13-07-43	12 Sqn
138391	P/O	FITCHETT Arthur James	25-06-43	51 Sqn		1421773	Sgt	FORD Albert Edward	25-11-43	26 OTU
1150600	Sgt	FITCHETT James Parker	28-05-43	100 Sqn		142518	P/O	FORD Albert Leonard	23-06-43	466 Sqn
1332433	Sgt	FITT Leonard Charles	11-04-43	115 Sqn		921623	Sgt	FORD Arthur George Henry	22-06-43	158 Sqn
1075399	Sgt	FITTON Jeffrey	13-05-43	218 Sqn		1603153	Sgt	FORD David	18-10-43	101 Sqn
148128	P/O	FITZGERALD Arthur Marcus	28-08-43	207 Sqn		1218711	Sgt	FORD Douglas Courtney	25-07-43	51 Sqn
1337889	Sgt	FITZGERALD Michael John	22-06-43	77 Sqn		1334076	F/S	FORD Ernest Charles Allenby	23-08-43	434 Sqn

Service #	Rank	Name	Date	Sqn
1031742	Sgt	FORD Harold Joseph	6-11-43	1659 HCU
1206989	Sgt	FORD Herbert Charles	16-02-43	103 Sqn
1108540	Sgt	FORD John	2-12-43	630 Sqn
916310	Sgt	FORD John Edward	1-03-43	29 OTU
51286	P/O	FORD John Ireland Pearson	29-04-43	196 Sqn
1462092	Sgt	FORD Roy Arthur	22-10-43	49 Sqn
1330672	Sgt	FORD Sidney Lazarus	12-06-43	12 Sqn
1293009	Sgt	FORD William Henry	30-07-43	77 Sqn
657853	Sgt	FORD William John	31-07-43	620 Sqn
1136637	Sgt	FORDE Patrick John	3-08-43	428 Sqn
61478	S/L	FOREMAN DFC Douglas Montague	13-01-43	12 OTU
656378	Sgt	FORGAN William John	3-08-43	103 Sqn
1333660	Sgt	FORMAN Bernard Frank	2-03-43	44 Sqn
656323	Sgt	FORREST James	8-04-43	218 Sqn
1390229	Sgt	FORREST James	23-11-43	7 Sqn
658923	Sgt	FORREST John Reid 'Jack'	1-09-43	61 Sqn
77913	S/L	FORREST DSO DFC Joseph Neville	24-08-43	97 Sqn
1386815	Sgt	FORSDICK Ronald Victor Stuart	6-09-43	619 Sqn
127976	F/O	FORSHAW Harry	15-06-43	619 Sqn
1036858	LAC	FORSTER Charles Storey	2-07-43	620 Sqn
1581900	Sgt	FORSTER Kenneth	21-12-43	1679 HCFlt
644295	Sgt	FORSTER Robert	22-06-43	77 Sqn
1411102	Sgt	FORSTER Thomas Ridley	23-06-43	158 Sqn
1533997	Sgt	FORSTER William	12-06-43	156 Sqn
1382045	F/S	FORSYTH DFM Albert Victor	28-09-43	35 Sqn
49575	F/O	FORT DFC John	15-09-43	617 Sqn
1329885	Sgt	FORTH William Norman	4-05-43	218 Sqn
1179661	Sgt	FORTUNE Herbert	17-04-43	15 Sqn
1811229	Sgt	FORWARD Alexander Harold	2-12-43	12 Sqn
568299	Sgt	FORWARD Edward John	27-01-43	218 Sqn
1337461	Sgt	FOSKETT John Bartholomew	26-06-43	102 Sqn
126581	F/L	FOSTER DFC Alfred Francis	12-06-43	161 Sqn
1550850	F/S	FOSTER Clarence William	20-10-43	83 Sqn
1583333	Sgt	FOSTER Eric William	19-03-43	161 Sqn
1318113	Sgt	FOSTER Henry Orlando	27-04-43	26 OTU
1061305	Sgt	FOSTER Kenneth	14-05-43	12 Sqn
1455838	Sgt	FOSTER Kenneth	10-07-43	77 Sqn
77915	S/L	FOSTER DFC* Kenneth Jack	23-09-43	97 Sqn
545719	Sgt	FOSTER Raymond Norman Percy	17-04-43	49 Sqn
1390814	Sgt	FOSTER Roy	30-07-43	61 Sqn
1144201	Sgt	FOSTER Stanley	4-07-43	103 Sqn
1331516	Sgt	FOSTER Thomas Charles	6-09-43	196 Sqn
1560291	Sgt	FOTHERINGHAM Norman	25-06-43	101 Sqn
1600996	Sgt	FOUET Edward Thomas	27-02-43	166 Sqn
136345	F/O	FOULDS Leonard	29-04-43	207 Sqn
1034817	Sgt	FOULKES Eric Lewis	26-11-43	625 Sqn
1215328	Sgt	FOWELL Edwin	31-01-43	16 OTU
1324047	Sgt	FOWLER Frederick Robert	15-06-43	49 Sqn
1394170	F/S	FOWLER Joseph Arthur	27-11-43	619 Sqn
1320278	Sgt	FOWLER Peter Douglas	23-01-43	75 Sqn
1063009	F/S	FOWLER Raymond Jack	25-05-43	180 Sqn
1347405	F/S	FOWLER Richard	22-10-43	102 Sqn
1893913	Sgt	FOWLER Ronald Charles	27-09-43	19 OTU
1377062	Sgt	FOWLER Ronald Frank	19-02-43	15 Sqn
1558029	Sgt	FOWLER Thomas Kirk	12-06-43	15 Sqn
1576327	Sgt	FOWLES John Sidney Wilson	14-05-43	102 Sqn
110139	F/O	FOWLIE William Alexander	5-03-43	90 Sqn
1191332	Sgt	FOWLSTON Reginald	18-08-43	49 Sqn
141853	P/O	FOX Albert Reginald	5-05-43	21 OTU
1322943	Sgt	FOX Allan Maynard	24-08-43	100 Sqn
1815826	Sgt	FOX Arthur William George	30-07-43	77 Sqn
132146	F/O	FOX Basil John	3-08-43	61 Sqn
102099	F/L	FOX Charles William	30-07-43	9 Sqn
1111948	Sgt	FOX Cyril John	11-04-43	26 OTU
61479	S/L	FOX Douglas Park	12-06-43	115 Sqn
1455705	Sgt	FOX Eric Charles	30-07-43	35 Sqn
123109	F/O	FOX George	26-03-43	429 Sqn
1392764	Sgt	FOX George Francis	22-09-43	428 Sqn
1034049	Sgt	FOX Herbert	2-12-43	103 Sqn
1348527	Sgt	FOX Patrick	9-06-43	619 Sqn
575854	Sgt	FOX Philip Robert	27-09-43	78 Sqn
1230170	Sgt	FOX Ronald Richard	15-04-43	7 Sqn
143802	P/O	FOX Sydney Frederick Norman	30-07-43	460 Sqn
864838	Sgt	FOX Terence Rochfort	6-09-43	427 Sqn
1230508	Sgt	FOY John Edwin	4-07-43	12 Sqn
127111	F/O	HOY Stanley	12-02-43	5 Group
1540341	Sgt	FRADLEY John Richard	14-07-43	102 Sqn
1392756	Sgt	FRAME William Steel	24-08-43	15 Sqn
658374	Sgt	FRAMPTON Charles Edward James	8-04-43	460 Sqn
1382502	Sgt	FRANCE Lyle Albert [Cuba]	6-02-43	90 Sqn
1815847	Sgt	FRANCIS Alan John	17-05-43	75 Sqn
1335172	Sgt	FRANCIS Clarence Bedbrook	18-08-43	619 Sqn
1399078	Sgt	FRANCIS Edward John	7-10-43	15 Sqn
511509	Sgt	FRANCIS Ernest David	19-06-43	Snaith
143571	P/O	FRANCIS Ernest George	27-04-43	196 Sqn
656057	Sgt	FRANCIS Ernest George	18-08-43	61 Sqn
126038	F/O	FRANCIS Gordon Charles Wardlaw	30-03-43	97 Sqn
575484	Sgt	FRANCIS Harold	28-12-43	22 OTU
1025976	Sgt	FRANCIS Ivor	4-04-43	9 Sqn
1269078	Sgt	FRANCIS Jack Thomas	26-05-43	166 Sqn
1032171	Sgt	FRANCIS John	18-08-43	100 Sqn
1212997	Sgt	FRANCIS John Albert	26-06-43	106 Sqn
1269942	Sgt	FRANCIS Ronald Douglas	3-04-43	9 Sqn
1339184	Sgt	FRANCIS Thomas Harry Grinstead	25-07-43	158 Sqn
1424559	Sgt	FRANCIS Thomas Terrance Blewett	23-09-43	467 Sqn
1387239	Sgt	FRANK Norman Harry	14-05-43	149 Sqn
1071461	Sgt	FRANKISH Charles	16-12-43	106 Sqn
144261	P/O	FRANKLAND Eric Vernon	4-04-43	10 Sqn
1482156	Sgt	FRANKLAND Richard Henry	26-02-43	158 Sqn
1384378	Sgt	FRANKLIN Arthur William	22-10-43	100 Sqn
1377502	F/S	FRANKLIN Kleon Donald	11-04-43	429 Sqn
524705	Sgt	FRANKLIN Robert	29-06-43	149 Sqn
125434	F/O	FRANKLIN DFC William Harry	19-03-43	161 Sqn
998499	Sgt	FRANKS John Robert	4-04-43	158 Sqn
62319	F/O	FRANKS Tom	6-01-43	10 OTU
1316158	Sgt	FRAPWELL Arthur Wesley	13-04-43	81 OTU
1554308	Sgt	FRASER Alexander Ramsay	4-09-43	7 Sqn
710169	Sgt	FRASER Edward [Rhodesia]	27-09-43	61 Sqn
139620	P/O	FRASER George Eitaro	23-08-43	106 Sqn
1486625	Sgt	FRASER George Robert	18-11-43	10 Sqn
1292708	Sgt	FRASER Henry Alexander Shaw	24-01-43	20 OTU
126958	F/O	FRASER Kennedy Emslie	5-04-43	9 Sqn
1345138	Sgt	FRASER William John	11-06-43	467 Sqn
1551131	Sgt	FRASER William Kemp	23-10-43	15 OTU
972338	Sgt	FRAZER Robert	1-03-43	103 Sqn
127338	F/L	FRAZER-HOLLINS DFC George Albert James	2-12-43	101 Sqn
1126762	Sgt	FREEL James	12-03-43	10 Sqn
1553565	Sgt	FREELAND Robert	4-07-43	90 Sqn
141990	P/O	FREEMAN Albert Eric Barley	31-08-43	166 Sqn
1575231	Sgt	FREEMAN Frank Morris	24-08-43	75 Sqn
932778	Sgt	FREEMAN Henry Alfred	22-09-43	207 Sqn
902545	Sgt	FREEMAN Leslie Frank	18-08-43	49 Sqn
1322558	Sgt	FREEMAN Lionel Gerald	24-05-43	214 Sqn
39626	S/L	FREEMAN Max Ingram [Canada]	28-09-43	90 Sqn
1332204	Sgt	FREEMAN Reginald Clifford Herbert	27-09-43	76 Sqn
1389597	Sgt	FREEMAN Richard Albert	28-08-43	149 Sqn
1315706	Sgt	FREEMAN Robert Leslie	3-09-43	460 Sqn
134156	F/O	FREEMAN Roger Nelson	22-06-43	158 Sqn
1210564	Sgt	FREEMAN Ronald William	4-07-43	103 Sqn
1394987	Sgt	FREEMAN Trevor James	31-12-43	21 OTU
1311073	F/S	FREEMAN William Edwin	29-04-43	12 Sqn
1393824	F/S	FREEZE William Fillmor [Canada]	28-08-43	83 Sqn
1332367	Sgt	FRENCH DFM Edward George Owen	6-09-43	77 Sqn
1890470	Sgt	FRENCH Ernest Lawrence	2-12-43	12 Sqn
1337669	F/S	FRENCH Herbert John	24-08-43	149 Sqn
1376200	Sgt	FRESHWATER John Matthew	5-03-43	83 Sqn
1020907	Sgt	FRETWELL Reginald Austin	3-02-43	226 Sqn

Service No	Rank	Name	Date	Unit
1370267	Sgt	FREW Harry McCaulay	2-03-43	97 Sqn
1193096	F/S	FREWER John Henry	27-09-43	7 Sqn
129176	F/O	FREWIN Lawrence William Arthur	16-06-43	405 Sqn
581211	W/O	FRIENDLY DFM Jocelyn	21-05-43	139 Sqn
657022	Sgt	FRITH Edwin John	26-02-43	102 Sqn
651754	Sgt	FROST Keith John	26-05-43	207 Sqn
49214	P/O	FROST Reginald Jeffrey	10-01-43	20 OTU
1387211	Sgt	FROST Robert Cooper	20-02-43	90 Sqn
1332384	Sgt	FROSTWICK Ernest Samuel	27-04-43	26 OTU
974822	Sgt	FROUD Kenneth Percy	26-07-43	77 Sqn
658467	Sgt	FRY Antony Hare	1-04-43	103 Sqn
1338820	F/S	FRY Arthur Frank	23-10-43	434 Sqn
156081	P/O	FRY Francis John	9-10-43	156 Sqn
613175	F/S	FRY Peter Austin	17-12-43	161 Sqn
1575584	Sgt	FRY Ronald Sidney	3-08-43	76 Sqn
1442302	Sgt	FRYER Peter Henry	23-11-43	50 Sqn
754360	W/O	FRYER Ronald Joseph	25-11-43	28 OTU
128008	F/O	FUCHS DFC Cecil Carl Albert	12-03-43	226 Sqn
1312340	Sgt	FUDGE Donald Charles Holmes	22-06-43	149 Sqn
155994	P/O	FULLAGER Dennis Raymond	9-07-43	49 Sqn
1287154	Sgt	FULLER Arthur Ronald	3-10-43	90 Sqn
149517	P/O	FULLER DFC Cyril	18-10-43	619 Sqn
1321598	Sgt	FULLER Frank Anthony	23-11-43	100 Sqn
1321959	Sgt	FULLER Geoffrey William	28-06-43	101 Sqn
1318951	Sgt	FULLER Godfrey Purdon	12-11-43	1659 HCU
1333900	Sgt	FULLER Leslie Ernest	3-08-43	115 Sqn
143760	P/O	FULLER Michael John David	17-05-43	617 Sqn
745940	F/S	FULLER Michael O'Donovan	26-05-43	35 Sqn
1319889	Sgt	FULLER Russell Edwards	24-08-43	77 Sqn
1338084	Sgt	FULTHORPE Richard	4-06-43	28 OTU
1559794	Sgt	FULTON Hugh	22-09-43	207 Sqn
138658	P/O	FULTON Ian Thomson Stirrat [USA]	30-03-43	149 Sqn
1387101	Sgt	FULTON James Kenneth	26-05-43	180 Sqn
1292366	Sgt	FUNNELL Donald Ernest	15-04-43	10 Sqn
1330590	Sgt	FUNNELL Ronald Eric	27-04-43	156 Sqn
142880	F/O	FURLONG DFC Norman John	9-10-43	20 OTU'
2206880	Sgt	FURNISS Harry Taylor	30-07-43	166 Sqn
980286	Sgt	FURRIE Francis Andrew	16-12-43	103 Sqn
1551806	Sgt	FYFE Norman Watt	15-06-43	49 Sqn
1322336	Sgt	FYFIELD Basil Raymond	14-05-43	51 Sqn
136884	F/O	GADD DFC Albert William	26-11-43	101 Sqn
1216729	Sgt	GADD George Edward	3-04-43	101 Sqn
1576049	Sgt	GADSBY Albert Edwin	8-10-43	97 Sqn
1144460	Sgt	GADSDEN David	23-11-43	7 Sqn
1803066	Sgt	GADSDON Kenneth William	28-06-43	101 Sqn
907386	Sgt	GAFFEE Leonard	5-09-43	149 Sqn
1542807	Sgt	GAFFNEY Robert Myles Joseph	17-12-43	100 Sqn
1321285	W/O	GAFFORD Roy	28-07-43	100 Sqn
1385897	Sgt	GAGE Donald Francis	10-04-43	466 Sqn
1318498	Sgt	GAGE Frank Harry	20-12-43	576 Sqn
1337997	Sgt	GAIGER Alfred Richard John	16-09-43	427 Sqn
1315144	Sgt	GAIT Leslie John	12-03-43	10 Sqn
1499876	Sgt	GAIT Ronald Clifford	3-01-43	61 Sqn
1574286	Sgt	GALBRAITH George Murray	26-07-43	35 Sqn
141551	P/O	GALE Alex Edward	26-07-43	78 Sqn
1490465	F/S	GALE John Kennah	3-10-43	467 Sqn
1271102	Sgt	GALE John William	31-07-43	75 Sqn
1384752	Sgt	GALE Leslie Charles	1-09-43	214 Sqn
151013	F/O	GALE Norman Hathway	8-09-43	75 Sqn
134066	F/O	GALL Robert Strachan	24-12-43	463 Sqn
1135122	Sgt	GALLAGHER John	3-02-43	218 Sqn
1561595	Sgt	GALLAGHER Patrick	26-11-43	103 Sqn
1289114	Sgt	GALLANTREE Frederick John	13-08-43	77 Sqn
967826	Sgt	GALLOWAY David Albert	18-08-43	10 Sqn
651974	Sgt	GALLOWAY James	22-06-43	428 Sqn
1368326	Sgt	GALLOWAY James	30-07-43	428 Sqn
1393558	Sgt	GAMAGE Walter George	22-10-43	166 Sqn
1391617	Sgt	GAMBLE Alfred John	7-09-43	1658 HCU
1235889	Sgt	GANLY Harry	24-11-43	1656 HCU
1338420	Sgt	GANNON John	11-03-43	15 OTU
132096	F/O	GARAI Earle Stanley	30-05-43	218 Sqn
1081660	Sgt	GARBUTT John	25-06-43	620 Sqn
1377510	Sgt	GARD Gilbert Lesley	18-11-43	15 Sqn
527199	Sgt	GARDEN Alexander	12-03-43	207 Sqn
1118792	Sgt	GARDINER Alexander McDonald	5-05-43	226 Sqn
1289316	Sgt	GARDNER Albert John	30-07-43	158 Sqn
130580	F/O	GARDNER DFC Alfred Edward Walter	18-11-43	57 Sqn
1313789	Sgt	GARDNER Ernest Edward	3-08-43	100 Sqn
1029631	Sgt	GARDNER Henry	7-07-43	103 Sqn
1349554	Sgt	GARDNER Henry	3-08-43	405 Sqn
1108687	Sgt	GARDNER John Campbell	25-06-43	90 Sqn
657746	Sgt	GARDNER Leslie	24-08-43	619 Sqn
1388174	Sgt	GARDNER Michael	17-06-43	1656 HCU
120704	F/L	GARDNER Norman Joseph	27-03-43	431 Sqn
132378	F/O	GARDNER Norman Philip	11-08-43	115 Sqn
993649	Sgt	GARFIT Joseph Leslie	29-06-43	15 Sqn
1272498	Sgt	GARGRAVE Donald Frederick	17-04-43	408 Sqn
1074974	Sgt	GARLAND John Patrick McMillan	13-07-43	424 Sqn
1818877	Sgt	GARLAND John William	2-12-43	101 Sqn
1387309	Sgt	GARLICK Albert Edward	4-07-43	102 Sqn
45425	S/L	GARLICK DFC* John Munro	2-12-43	97 Sqn
145021	F/O	GARMENT Hedley Howard	16-12-43	460 Sqn
1320205	Sgt	GARMENT Raymond Kenneth	11-08-43	57 Sqn
530348	F/S	GARNER Colin Henry	30-05-43	35 Sqn
937568	Sgt	GARNER Edward	26-05-43	35 Sqn
1191173	Sgt	GARNER George Charles	5-04-43	21 Sqn
1284050	Sgt	GARNER George Harry Marriner	1-11-43	19 OTU
1393192	Sgt	GARNER Wilfred Frank	3-09-43	100 Sqn
1095175	F/S	GARNETT Kenneth	2-12-43	9 Sqn
1382466	Sgt	GARNETT Kenneth Peter	29-04-43	428 Sqn
1036702	Sgt	GARNHAM John Stephen	4-07-43	51 Sqn
1295534	Sgt	GARNHAM Leslie Henry	12-04-43	81 OTU
1338242	Sgt	GARNHAM Phillip William	2-03-43	61 Sqn
1330009	Sgt	GARRARD Geoffrey Herbert	28-05-43	77 Sqn
1144424	Sgt	GARRATT William Goodman	11-07-43	77 Sqn
1154625	F/S	GARRETT Francis Beesley	18-08-43	467 Sqn
140881	P/O	GARRINGTON Alan Mello	23-09-43	12 Sqn
1331174	Sgt	GARROD Ralph Frederick	24-06-43	218 Sqn
1684808	Sgt	GARSIDE Raymond	29-12-43	460 Sqn
1125865	Sgt	GARSIDE Ronald Francis	7-07-43	103 Sqn
128972	F/O	GARTERY Douglas	24-05-43	419 Sqn
1568245	Sgt	GARTLAND John Aloysius	22-11-43	218 Sqn
1077126	Sgt	GARVIN William Henry	25-07-43	75 Sqn
1507792	Sgt	GASKIN Stanley	26-06-43	166 Sqn
1392668	Sgt	GASKINS Leonard Charles	4-11-43	75 Sqn
1338711	Sgt	GASTON John Sydney	30-07-43	102 Sqn
1446136	Sgt	GATES Eric	13-09-43	12 OTU
126623	F/O	GATES DSO Frederick William	5-05-43	101 Sqn
1333380	Sgt	GATES Geoffrey John	5-03-43	12 OTU
1483399	Sgt	GATES Thomas	26-07-43	158 Sqn
118636	F/O	GAUNTLETT Herbert Horatio	3-05-43	107 Sqn
1316475	Sgt	GAUNTLETT Norman Richard	28-08-43	102 Sqn
1265877	F/S	GAVAGAN James Morris	12-06-43	78 Sqn
156937	P/O	GAWLER Harold Evans Vivian	1-09-43	77 Sqn
1295418	F/S	GAWLER DFM Stanley Alfred	3-09-43	1661 HCU
536350	Sgt	GAWTHORP Walter Gordon	18-02-43	207 Sqn
1209435	Sgt	GAY Leonard Charles	15-09-43	138 Sqn
1270591	Sgt	GAYTON James Donald	10-03-43	44 Sqn
1393160	Sgt	GAYWOOD Samuel James	24-05-43	10 Sqn
1315082	Sgt	GAZZARD Cedric Brian	23-09-43	90 Sqn
129152	P/O	GEACH Leslie Hoyle	2-03-43	9 Sqn
131641	F/O	GEALE Basil Alfred Alexander	13-05-43	429 Sqn
1384115	Sgt	GEARING Alfred James	13-05-43	419 Sqn
1295163	Sgt	GEARING Lawrence Charles	13-06-43	76 Sqn
44485	F/L	GEARY Cornelius Vincent Joseph	12-06-43	83 Sqn
1212477	Sgt	GEE Laurence Geoffrey Earl	29-09-43	166 Sqn
1332441	F/S	GEE Paul	4-07-43	196 Sqn

Service No	Rank	Name	Date	Sqn
1549838	Sgt	GELL Henry Joseph Fitzgerald	3-03-43	115 Sqn
51687	P/O	GENESIS DFM Robert Harry	11-04-43	7 Sqn
1320927	Sgt	GENEVER Douglas Alan	26-05-43	207 Sqn
1334520	Sgt	GENT Donald Samuel	17-06-43	460 Sqn
1396922	Sgt	GENTLE Horace Henry	29-06-43	100 Sqn
1345755	Sgt	GEORGE Arthur	30-01-43	466 Sqn
658532	Sgt	GEORGE Gordon	23-06-43	161 Sqn
1577632	Sgt	GEORGE James Barrie Diggle	1-02-43	1659 HCU
1349772	Sgt	GEORGE William	30-05-43	158 Sqn
1256384	Sgt	GERAGHTY Eric William	23-06-43	9 Sqn
1392628	Sgt	GERRARD Ronald Alfred	12-03-43	103 Sqn
146302	P/O	GERRARD Victor Charles	22-10-43	1657 HCU
1394459	Sgt	GERRARD William Valentine [Canada]	14-07-43	78 Sqn
1456340	Sgt	GESS John Edgar Melrose	6-10-43	19 OTU
1082024	Sgt	GETTINGS Frank	25-06-43	102 Sqn
991605	Sgt	GIBB Clarence William	20-10-43	100 Sqn
1559476	Sgt	GIBB George Leash	25-07-43	214 Sqn
1111494	Sgt	GIBB George Muir	30-07-43	78 Sqn
80374	P/O	GIBBINGS Graham John [Rhodesia]	10-04-43	9 Sqn
1527965	Sgt	GIBBNEY Raymond Mordue	14-05-43	214 Sqn
617297	Sgt	GIBBONS Alfred Norman	30-07-43	97 Sqn
1393405	F/S	GIBBONS Cyril	18-10-43	101 Sqn
1500187	Sgt	GIBBONS Michael Gerrard	26-02-43	102 Sqn
636305	W/O	GIBBONS William John Patrick	29-08-43	29 OTU
1200710	Sgt	GIBBS Alec Ernest John	13-06-43	102 Sqn
1293272	Sgt	GIBBS Dennis Francis	13-02-43	12 Sqn
1577754	Sgt	GIBBS Ernest Alfred	20-10-43	115 Sqn
1268389	Sgt	GIBBS Frederick George Roscoe	29-04-43	12 Sqn
1290012	Sgt	GIBBS Henry John	24-05-43	51 Sqn
40468	F/L	GIBBS Robert Winton Arnold	13-07-43	467 Sqn
1602054	Sgt	GIBBS Sidney George	27-09-43	15 Sqn
1079181	Sgt	GIBBY William David	25-09-43	29 OTU
61043	S/L	GIBSON DFC Arthur	16-12-43	7 Sqn
39981	S/L	GIBSON DFC Croix de Guerre avec Palme Christopher Francis	14-03-43	138 Sqn
135412	P/O	GIBSON George Brian	24-03-43	16 OTU
1349486	F/S	GIBSON Gordon	7-09-43	1658 HCU
1138669	Sgt	GIBSON Hugh	3-05-43	487 Sqn
151310	F/O	GIBSON James	17-09-43	10 OTU
1397245	Sgt	GIBSON John Charles	31-07-43	78 Sqn
137520	F/O	GIBSON Kenneth	15-08-43	467 Sqn
1585098	Sgt	GIBSON Maurice Albert	28-04-43	158 Sqn
1036711	Sgt	GIBSON Robert Trevor	12-11-43	1659 HCU
1526809	Sgt	GIBSON William Stanley	1-03-43	15 OTU
996048	Sgt	GIELTY Anthony Patrick	17-04-43	408 Sqn
1323461	Sgt	GIGGS Ernest Gordon Leonard	13-05-43	466 Sqn
1393472	Sgt	GILBERT Albert Owen	14-02-43	102 Sqn
1047153	Sgt	GILBERT George Robert	3-04-43	9 Sqn
117396	F/O	GILBERT John Trevor	31-07-43	23 OTU
1264739	Sgt	GILBERT Ronald	25-06-43	156 Sqn
156089	P/O	GILBERT Ronald Reid	24-08-43	78 Sqn
1221820	Sgt	GILBERT Wilfred Arthur	17-09-43	196 Sqn
1375675	Sgt	GILBEY Kenneth	3-09-43	44 Sqn
145172	F/O	GILDING Leonard Cecil	22-10-43	10 Sqn
1309196	Sgt	GILES Bernard Robert	6-09-43	620 Sqn
1384234	Sgt	GILES Evan David	3-08-43	103 Sqn
144766	P/O	GILES DFM Frank	13-05-43	156 Sqn
138329	P/O	GILES John Cecil	31-08-43	75 Sqn
1322691	Sgt	GILES Montague Ewart	24-12-43	550 Sqn
1194020	Sgt	GILES Walter Edward James	4-10-43	100 Sqn
1569298	Sgt	GILFILLAN William	18-11-43	75 Sqn
1810627	Sgt	GILKES Leslie Francis [Trinidad]	3-08-43	9 Sqn
1452106	Sgt	GILL Alan Arthur	12-06-43	12 Sqn
125984	F/O	GILL Christopher James John	31-01-43	106 Sqn
940017	F/S	GILL George	17-04-43	429 Sqn
613186	Sgt	GILL Hector McNeill	28-08-43	78 Sqn
1351297	Sgt	GILL Leonard	1-05-43	12 Sqn
1336802	Sgt	GILL Robert Edward	6-06-43	30 OTU
1459774	Sgt	GILL Ronald Luscombe	18-11-43	623 Sqn
149605	P/O	GILL Thomas Henry	6-09-43	9 Sqn
1211980	Sgt	GILLAM Reginald Alan Frederick	27-11-43	83 Sqn
1511671	Sgt	GILLANDERS William Andrew	12-06-43	12 Sqn
938834	Sgt	GILLARD John William	24-06-43	75 Sqn
751698	Sgt	GILLARD Kenneth Sydney	23-06-43	214 Sqn
144205	P/O	GILLESPIE DFM Alan	16-05-43	617 Sqn
1554372	Sgt	GILLESPIE Albert Webb	1-03-43	29 OTU
117679	F/L	GILLETT David Stapylton	13-01-43	61 Sqn
74331	F/L	GILLIAT Christopher David	9-03-43	156 Sqn
547631	Sgt	GILLICKER Thomas	11-08-43	78 Sqn
121503	F/L	GILLIES Alexander McMillan	27-05-43	14 OTU
1387485	F/S	GILLIES Neil	23-05-43	158 Sqn
1585244	Sgt	GILLIES Raymond	24-12-43	550 Sqn
1336396	F/S	GILLINGHAM Leslie Frederick	20-12-43	76 Sqn
1025077	Sgt	GILLIS David [Canada]	22-06-43	90 Sqn
1601131	Sgt	GILLIVER Frederick Leonard Reginald	13-05-43	57 Sqn
34042	W/C	GILLMAN James Robert	5-05-43	83 Sqn
52912	P/O	GILLMORE James Horatio	22-09-43	7 Sqn
148843	P/O	GILMOUR Andrew Patrick	4-07-43	90 Sqn
968152	F/S	GILPIN DFM William Cleghorn [Canada]	1-02-43	11 OTU
1512418	Sgt	GILVARY John Kevin [Eire]	18-08-43	419 Sqn
1291765	Sgt	GINN Edwin Robert	20-04-43	149 Sqn
1391642	Sgt	GINSBERG Reuben	26-11-43	1658 HCU
1148144	Sgt	GIRDLER Alfred	22-09-43	158 Sqn
127972	F/O	GIRDWOOD William McCall	22-06-43	619 Sqn
1210420	F/S	GITTINS DFM George Herbert	18-11-43	101 Sqn
1337875	Sgt	GITTINS Lumley Hugh Ellis	7-09-43	76 Sqn
1067871	F/S	GITTINS Thomas Henry	7-08-43	75 Sqn
1330780	Sgt	GLADWISH Reginald Edwin	9-01-43	44 Sqn
657118	Sgt	GLARE Geoffrey John	27-04-43	207 Sqn
1802673	Sgt	GLASS George Eric	27-10-43	1656 HCU
1382321	Sgt	GLASSMAN David	12-06-43	51 Sqn
133082	F/L	GLASSPOOL Sidney Arthur Henry	27-11-43	408 Sqn
1179830	Sgt	GLAZZARD John James Horatio	30-05-43	115 Sqn
655120	Sgt	GLEESON Thomas James	24-08-43	12 Sqn
1370858	Sgt	GLEN Andrew	12-06-43	158 Sqn
1367274	Sgt	GLENDINNING John Renwick	13-06-43	115 Sqn
1070166	Sgt	GLENDINNING John Thomas	29-04-43	75 Sqn
1379631	Sgt	GLENTWORTH Lewis	27-09-43	76 Sqn
957981	Sgt	GLOTHAM William John	1-05-43	57 Sqn
1528101	Sgt	GLOVER Charles Henry	13-07-43	100 Sqn
1061009	Sgt	GLOVER Davis William	28-05-43	199 Sqn
1385248	Sgt	GLOVER Gordon	12-06-43	100 Sqn
1335742	Sgt	GLOVER Henry Raymond	25-06-43	7 Sqn
1321791	Sgt	GLOVER Patrick Edward 'Paddy'	26-06-43	115 Sqn
49935	P/O	GLOVER Ronald Haigh	20-04-43	51 Sqn
1464583	Sgt	GLOVER Thomas Francis John	5-03-43	29 OTU
1652528	Sgt	GLOVER-PRICE Leonard John	29-06-43	76 Sqn
129643	F/O	GLUCK Mark	24-05-43	405 Sqn
655464	Sgt	GODBOLD Kenneth Herbert	8-04-43	419 Sqn
1316480	F/S	GODDARD Charles Albert	6-09-43	619 Sqn
1622398	Sgt	GODDARD Harry	13-05-43	51 Sqn
1030197	Sgt	GODDARD Jack	9-03-43	7 Sqn
1319988	Sgt	GODDARD Joseph Eric	28-07-43	101 Sqn
1088307	Sgt	GODDEN Frank Leslie	30-03-43	115 Sqn
658613	Sgt	GODDEN Richard Lewis	17-06-43	467 Sqn
46212	F/O	GODFREY Henry Jack	6-01-43	10 OTU
1272401	Sgt	GODFREY Samuel Henry	22-11-43	51 Sqn
1146107	Sgt	GODFREY Stanley	22-05-43	1656 HCU
130595	F/L	GODFREY DFC Stephen Clifford Paul	4-10-43	156 Sqn
134571	F/O	GODLEY Aaron George William	11-08-43	106 Sqn
1074276	Sgt	GODLEY John	12-07-43	1663 HCU
1476178	Sgt	GODSEFF Gerald James	20-10-43	100 Sqn
1576836	Sgt	GODSON DFM Samuel	29-08-43	29 OTU
158709	P/O	GOFF Cyril Charles	18-10-43	100 Sqn
1454431	Sgt	GOFF Reginald George William	16-07-43	50 Sqn

1264837	Sgt	GOFFIN Richard William	2-02-43	102 Sqn	1586313	Sgt	GOSNELL Walter Henry	12-03-43	78 Sqn
1095873	F/S	GOFTON Cyril Campbell	31-08-43	427 Sqn	147359	P/O	GOSPEL Leslie Warren	16-08-43	49 Sqn
141470	P/O	GOLD David Alan	17-01-43	76 Sqn	1607025	Sgt	GOSS John Edward	24-11-43	405 Sqn
1312265	F/S	GOLD Edmund Harry	7-10-43	15 Sqn	42562	F/L	GOUDGE Ivor Philip Chester	30-05-43	12 Sqn
146830	P/O	GOLD Edward Maurice	12-06-43	466 Sqn	133219	P/O	GOUGH Arthur Edward	27-01-43	218 Sqn
131960	F/O	GOLDBERG Woolf William	6-09-43	76 Sqn	1575135	Sgt	GOUGH David Albert Harris	26-06-43	102 Sqn
1604513	Sgt	GOLDEN John Gordon	31-08-43	149 Sqn	1050457	Sgt	GOUGH Edward	28-07-43	102 Sqn
1330847	Sgt	GOLDFINGER Zanwel [Israel]	24-05-43	214 Sqn	123684	F/O	GOUGH Kenneth Adrian	15-08-43	7 Sqn
1272586	Sgt	GOLDFLUST Julius	24-05-43	78 Sqn	1318923	F/S	GOUGH Raymond Victor	6-09-43	9 Sqn
1216316	Sgt	GOLDIE Neil	25-06-43	432 Sqn	1184858	Sgt	GOUGH Roy	6-09-43	77 Sqn
517511	Sgt	GOLDING Richard Charles Sydney	4-07-43	97 Sqn	1085952	Sgt	GOUGH William Ellis	2-12-43	9 Sqn
110589	F/O	GOLDING William Ronald	3-03-43	76 Sqn	1255195	Sgt	GOULD D'Arcy [New Zealand]	9-04-43	101 Sqn
1575355	Sgt	GOLDRICK Martin	20-02-43	90 Sqn	645547	Sgt	GOULD Frank Hustler	28-08-43	102 Sqn
133411	F/O	GOLDRING James David Spencer	18-07-43	10 OTU	1182265	Sgt	GOULD John	16-04-43	15 Sqn
1040030	F/S	GOLDSBROUGH William	6-09-43	77 Sqn	1262308	Sgt	GOULD Joseph William	5-03-43	466 Sqn
46702	F/L	GOLDSMITH Geoffrey	2-12-43	12 Sqn	1384731	Sgt	GOULD Stanley Francis	15-04-43	90 Sqn
1254181	W/O	GOLDSPINK Walter Eric	28-09-43	405 Sqn	591244	Sgt	GOULDEN Donald	18-08-43	10 Sqn
1394118	Sgt	GOLDSTEIN Dennis Harold	9-10-43	51 Sqn	658400	Sgt	GOULDING James	21-04-43	12 Sqn
1021749	Sgt	GOLDSTRAW Ernest Edward	12-07-43	57 Sqn	576269	Sgt	GOULDING Norman James Yates [USA]	23-11-43	630 Sqn
921667	F/S	GOLDSTRAW Reginald	13-06-43	50 Sqn					
1349422	F/S	GOLLOGLY Robert Wallace	31-08-43	619 Sqn	813163	Sgt	GOURD Albert Ernest Edwin	28-08-43	428 Sqn
1768162	Sgt	GOMERSALL Ernest Edward Roberts	28-07-43	15 Sqn	1258721	Sgt	GOWARD Raymond Percy	22-06-43	218 Sqn
34123	W/C	GOMM DSO DFC Cosme Lockwood [Brazil]	15-08-43	467 Sqn	1323289	Sgt	GOWER Frank Patrick Charles	13-05-43	98 Sqn
					941531	Sgt	GOWING Ronald	3-04-43	158 Sqn
146157	P/O	GONCE Hugh Bernard [USA]	16-04-43	156 Sqn	1335182	Sgt	GRACE Michael James	1-05-43	57 Sqn
1336491	Sgt	GOOCH Daniel Last	4-03-43	100 Sqn	614065	Sgt	GRACE Raymond Archibald	29-06-43	619 Sqn
1476182	Sgt	GOOD Charles Alfred	15-04-43	21 OTU	1444939	Sgt	GRAHAM Albert Edward	30-05-43	12 Sqn
900793	Sgt	GOOD George James	17-04-43	100 Sqn	1369996	Sgt	GRAHAM Andrew	28-04-43	75 Sqn
1207073	Sgt	GOODACRE William Ernest	30-07-43	78 Sqn	1211042	Sgt	GRAHAM Edwin	18-10-43	460 Sqn
1085013	Sgt	GOODALL Frederick George	29-12-43	431 Sqn	1344743	Sgt	GRAHAM Harry George	5-05-43	196 Sqn
1236214	Sgt	GOODCHILD Cyril Noel	19-02-43	15 Sqn	655372	Sgt	GRAHAM James	23-11-43	97 Sqn
1382764	Sgt	GOODE Harold Frederick	23-04-43	467 Sqn	1390603	Sgt	GRAHAM James	21-12-43	427 Sqn
591500	Sgt	GOODE Kenneth Frank	18-08-43	100 Sqn	1555242	Sgt	GRAHAM James Edward	30-11-43	14 OTU
1210554	Sgt	GOODE Wilfred George	29-01-43	420 Sqn	1063129	Sgt	GRAHAM John	18-08-43	44 Sqn
125513	F/O	GOODERHAM Douglas Samuel	14-05-43	431 Sqn	1540496	F/S	GRAHAM John	3-12-43	9 Sqn
649870	Sgt	GOODFELLOW Ernest Gilbert	27-04-43	158 Sqn	134669	F/O	GRAHAM John Crichton	26-11-43	106 Sqn
1101483	Sgt	GOODHAND Arthur	29-04-43	12 Sqn	1603188	Sgt	GRAHAM Leslie Thompson	3-10-43	15 Sqn
1331855	Sgt	GOODING Bernard Hamilton	17-04-43	156 Sqn	1289237	Sgt	GRAHAM Newell	23-06-43	90 Sqn
1851689	Sgt	GOODING Brian Liell	26-11-43	625 Sqn	1132761	Sgt	GRAHAM Robert	28-08-43	90 Sqn
126584	F/L	GOODLEY DFC Leslie Grahame	9-03-43	156 Sqn	1393572	Sgt	GRAHAM Robert Coats	3-11-43	158 Sqn
1337423	F/S	GOODSELL Kenneth Edward	13-08-43	207 Sqn	1370182	Sgt	GRAHAM Thomas	18-08-43	61 Sqn
1535711	Sgt	GOODWILL Herbert Ivor	9-01-43	158 Sqn	1601124	Sgt	GRAHAM Thomas Elliot Brydon	23-09-43	9 Sqn
131493	F/O	GOODWIN Denis Charles	13-06-43	101 Sqn	1025312	Sgt	GRAHAM Vickers	29-08-43	29 OTU
1813726	Sgt	GOODWIN Ernest Charles	18-11-43	76 Sqn	151100	F/O	GRAHAM William Henry	27-08-43	1663 HCU
1603332	Sgt	GOODWIN John	28-08-43	207 Sqn	1345277	Sgt	GRAHAM William Shearer Lindsay	10-04-43	1661 HCU
49147	F/O	GOODWIN DFC Ronald Edward	30-07-43	156 Sqn	135747	F/O	GRAHAM BELL Frank	9-08-43	82 OTU
628839	Sgt	GOODWIN Stanley Leonard	12-05-43	207 Sqn	1807481	Sgt	GRAIN John William	18-10-43	9 Sqn
1281353	Sgt	GOODWIN Thomas George	7-09-43	106 Sqn	625045	Sgt	GRAINGER Eric	23-06-43	75 Sqn
1586434	Sgt	GOODWIN Thomas Ivor	31-08-43	78 Sqn	1541260	Sgt	GRAINGER James	22-10-43	10 Sqn
957450	Sgt	GOODYEAR Paul Arnold Urquhart	13-07-43	49 Sqn	1615904	Sgt	GRANGE Leslie John	22-09-43	78 Sqn
929591	Sgt	GOODYEAR Ronald Edward	24-05-43	78 Sqn	1323448	Sgt	GRANGE Terence	1-09-43	75 Sqn
1337540	Sgt	GOOM Harry Ernest St. Hill	29-09-43	78 Sqn	133564	P/O	GRANT Donald Edward	5-05-43	102 Sqn
552903	W/O	GOOZEE John Thomas	4-10-43	100 Sqn	127969	F/O	GRANT Douglas Munroe [Newfoundland]	23-06-43	103 Sqn
1028523	F/S	GORBETT Edward	24-08-43	15 Sqn					
1376471	Sgt	GORDON Albert John	4-04-43	214 Sqn	1474209	Sgt	GRANT Frank	29-04-43	12 Sqn
1349618	Sgt	GORDON Douglas Baxter	30-05-43	460 Sqn	1365657	Sgt	GRANT Frederick Douglas	10-11-43	1660 HCU
658700	Sgt	GORDON Douglas Travell	16-12-43	9 Sqn	572554	Sgt	GRANT George Alan Ashley	30-05-43	218 Sqn
1684376	Sgt	GORDON Hugh Alexander	28-08-43	428 Sqn	127489	F/O	GRANT DFC Jacob Maurice	16-09-43	617 Sqn
1564384	Sgt	GORDON James Frederick	3-10-43	51 Sqn	1118853	Sgt	GRANT John William	18-02-43	419 Sqn
86721	F/L	GORDON DFC John	5-11-43	105 Sqn	1473338	Sgt	GRANT Leslie Collier	8-11-43	623 Sqn
971675	Sgt	GORDON Wilson Hebenton	23-06-43	156 Sqn	930059	Sgt	GRANT Richard Columba	29-04-43	12 Sqn
656682	Sgt	GORE Kenneth	21-10-43	7 Sqn	1388923	Sgt	GRANT William Joseph	23-09-43	77 Sqn
1431059	Sgt	GORE Kenneth	26-06-43	102 Sqn	1026588	Sgt	GRANT William McKinlay	3-08-43	61 Sqn
1607030	Sgt	GORE Peter Aubrey Joseph	26-07-43	61 Sqn	1351568	Sgt	GRATTON John James	24-08-43	75 Sqn
124505	F/O	GORICK Norman	31-01-43	428 Sqn	1324750	Sgt	GRATWICK Ronald Ernest	9-10-43	166 Sqn
1311363	Sgt	GORMAN Bernard	28-07-43	101 Sqn	1411885	AC2	GRAVELL William Alyn	29-05-43	23 OTU
1134562	Sgt	GORTON Clifford	25-06-43	428 Sqn	1306906	Sgt	GRAVES Edward William	2-12-43	57 Sqn
114785	F/L	GORTON Walter Albert	1-09-43	158 Sqn	124868	F/O	GRAY Charles William Gilbert	14-04-43	429 Sqn
906488	F/S	GOSDEN Eric Bertram	22-11-43	77 Sqn	1215330	Sgt	GRAY Cecil William	22-10-43	103 Sqn

Service No.	Rank	Name	Date	Unit
1330750	Sgt	GRAY Derek Milner	8-03-43	460 Sqn
1375699	Sgt	GRAY Douglas Murray	9-06-43	619 Sqn
1391377	Sgt	GRAY Edward James	2-03-43	50 Sqn
1454671	Sgt	GRAY Edward Stephen Andre	14-08-43	19 OTU
124318	F/O	GRAY Harry	17-04-43	425 Sqn
1270428	Sgt	GRAY James Nicol	1-03-43	419 Sqn
620057	F/S	GRAY John	16-12-43	619 Sqn
629214	Sgt	GRAY John Edwin	6-09-43	90 Sqn
1314934	Sgt	GRAY John Phillip	24-12-43	576 Sqn
1499067	Sgt	GRAY Myrddin	13-08-43	77 Sqn
142040	P/O	GRAY Robert Malcolm	29-01-43	166 Sqn
137441	P/O	GRAY Ronald	15-01-43	161 Sqn
125739	F/L	GRAY Stanley Nicholson	17-12-43	161 Sqn
1263851	Sgt	GRAY Sydney John	13-02-43	115 Sqn
1416025	Sgt	GRAY Thomas Leslie	29-01-43	158 Sqn
1098526	F/S	GRAY William Dixon	30-05-43	35 Sqn
149986	P/O	GRAY William Leslie	31-07-43	90 Sqn
1344792	Sgt	GRAY William Mitchell	20-12-43	78 Sqn
1194273	Sgt	GREASLEY William Edmund	12-03-43	101 Sqn
1099278	F/S	GREAVES Thomas Henry	30-07-43	77 Sqn
1624484	Sgt	GREAVES William Henry	18-08-43	103 Sqn
1379098	Sgt	GREAVISON Harry Elliott	6-09-43	83 Sqn
944129	F/S	GREEN Bernard	13-09-43	12 OTU
614909	Sgt	GREEN Charles	13-05-43	90 Sqn
1622553	Sgt	GREEN Charles Alexander	4-10-43	100 Sqn
911355	Sgt	GREEN Cyril John	22-09-43	101 Sqn
1581444	Sgt	GREEN Ernest	26-06-43	115 Sqn
1467551	Sgt	GREEN George Albert Frank	18-06-43	158 Sqn
1255176	Sgt	GREEN George Charles	26-06-43	466 Sqn
1215632	Sgt	GREEN George Edward	3-03-43	106 Sqn
132744	F/O	GREEN George Francis Rowland	26-11-43	625 Sqn
1322942	F/S	GREEN Gilbert John	23-09-43	49 Sqn
1390947	Sgt	GREEN Henry Thomas	22-10-43	1654 HCU
157406	P/O	GREEN Herbert	22-09-43	434 Sqn
1310815	Sgt	GREEN James William	9-04-43	199 Sqn
1036569	Sgt	GREEN John	23-08-43	106 Sqn
574948	Sgt	GREEN Kenneth Frederick	29-03-43	97 Sqn
2216002	Sgt	GREEN Lawrence	23-08-43	106 Sqn
1317497	W/O	GREEN Leonard Edward Frank	1-09-43	12 Sqn
1615038	Sgt	GREEN Leonard Herbert William	21-08-43	1658 HCU
1865995	Sgt	GREEN Leslie Lloyd	22-11-43	77 Sqn
627752	Sgt	GREEN Malcolm Lionel	4-07-43	12 Sqn
1556996	Sgt	GREEN Paul Brian	29-12-43	10 Sqn
1379175	Sgt	GREEN Peter Harry Barrowclough Parkinson	18-01-43	76 Sqn
1211032	Sgt	GREEN Reginald Thomas Charles	15-04-43	75 Sqn
112481	F/O	GREEN Thomas Herbert	24-05-43	51 Sqn
551444	Sgt	GREEN Vernon Guy	24-08-43	77 Sqn
1217286	Sgt	GREEN Walter Richard	23-06-43	158 Sqn
1383040	F/S	GREEN Wilfred Malvern	17-12-43	101 Sqn
155206	P/O	GREEN William	11-08-43	158 Sqn
1021000	Sgt	GREEN William	16-09-43	15 Sqn
1081353	Sgt	GREEN William	28-07-43	467 Sqn
1591531	Sgt	GREEN William Arthur	26-11-43	166 Sqn
1157570	Sgt	GREENAWAY Claude Charles	6-02-43	90 Sqn
1109116	F/S	GREENE Peter Alexander	9-04-43	77 Sqn
1444784	Sgt	GREENFIELD Ernest Edwin	3-10-43	44 Sqn
1315254	F/S	GREENFIELD Jack	13-05-43	196 Sqn
1001217	Sgt	GREENHALGH Cyril	24-05-43	76 Sqn
1379905	Sgt	GREENHALGH Eric	27-03-43	214 Sqn
1345865	Sgt	GREENHORN William	3-05-43	51 Sqn
1317229	Sgt	GREENING Frederick Charles	13-05-43	50 Sqn
1313492	Sgt	GREENING Gilbert John	10-07-43	77 Sqn
149108	P/O	GREENLEES Samuel	22-10-43	78 Sqn
1003229	Sgt	GREENMON Philip John	29-12-43	10 Sqn
46221	F/L	GREENUP Douglas Ronald	30-03-43	1483 Flt
1550613	Sgt	GREENWAY John	15-06-43	103 Sqn
933268	Sgt	GREENWELL John	16-12-43	426 Sqn
1494130	Sgt	GREENWELL John	30-12-43	50 Sqn
1059993	F/S	GREENWOOD Francis Joseph	12-06-43	35 Sqn
980381	Sgt	GREENWOOD Jack	13-07-43	467 Sqn
1360248	Sgt	GREENWOOD John William	17-04-43	15 Sqn
544783	Sgt	GREENWOOD Norman	12-06-43	83 Sqn
1319236	Sgt	GREEP DFM Robert Sidney	18-02-43	106 Sqn
611098	Sgt	GREER Samuel John	26-07-43	214 Sqn
1388948	Sgt	GREEST Thomas Henry	27-09-43	10 Sqn
1314252	Sgt	GREGORY Albert Frank	3-08-43	405 Sqn
576245	F/S	GREGORY Cyril Elvett	28-08-43	199 Sqn
141285	F/O	GREGORY DFM George Henry Ford Goodwin	17-05-43	617 Sqn
658271	Sgt	GREGORY Leslie	27-02-43	166 Sqn
996725	Sgt	GREGORY Thomas Joseph	13-05-43	57 Sqn
977863	Sgt	GREGSON Leslie Harold	2-03-43	76 Sqn
131902	F/O	GREGSON William Victor	28-08-43	78 Sqn
656907	Sgt	GREIG Alexander	3-03-43	103 Sqn
1230512	Sgt	GREW Gordon Charles	13-07-43	57 Sqn
1244614	Sgt	GREY Duncan	13-05-43	106 Sqn
1317456	Sgt	GREY Frank	18-08-43	467 Sqn
50952	F/L	GREY Robert	13-05-43	78 Sqn
819180	Sgt	GRIEVSON Frank Charles	7-07-43	21 OTU
116771	F/O	GRIFFIN Arthur Cecil Montagu	28-05-43	21 Sqn
132959	P/O	GRIFFIN David Neil Allen	3-04-43	15 OTU
953947	Sgt	GRIFFIN Harold Claude	18-01-43	9 Sqn
1153700	Sgt	GRIFFIN James John	15-08-43	61 Sqn
848335	F/S	GRIFFIN James Russell	31-08-43	35 Sqn
1396113	Sgt	GRIFFIN Norman Nowell	17-12-43	166 Sqn
111157	F/L	GRIFFITH John Gordon	17-10-43	196 Sqn
1023959	Sgt	GRIFFITH Thomas	5-05-43	83 Sqn
1237253	Sgt	GRIFFITH William Donald	27-04-43	51 Sqn
1454411	Sgt	GRIFFITHS Alan	9-07-43	101 Sqn
1620469	Sgt	GRIFFITHS David	3-08-43	51 Sqn
1296693	Sgt	GRIFFITHS David Emmanuel	14-08-43	1662 HCU
156084	P/O	GRIFFITHS David George	27-09-43	76 Sqn
117360	F/O	GRIFFITHS Edward Ivor	18-02-43	158 Sqn
138591	P/O	GRIFFITHS Eric	23-06-43	103 Sqn
1399828	Sgt	GRIFFITHS Ernest Reginald Hylton	26-06-43	44 Sqn
140916	P/O	GRIFFITHS George	16-04-43	1409 Flt
572592	Sgt	GRIFFITHS John Edwards Lewis	9-01-43	51 Sqn
1337841	Sgt	GRIFFITHS John Howard	24-05-43	166 Sqn
160874	P/O	GRIFFITHS Leslie Mayberry	9-11-43	90 Sqn
1263470	Sgt	GRIFFITHS Malcom	13-08-43	77 Sqn
116501	F/O	GRIFFITHS Robert Williams	17-08-43	35 Sqn
1316333	Sgt	GRIFFITHS Wilfred Ambrose	21-04-43	102 Sqn
900986	Sgt	GRIFFITHS-BUCHANAN Alexander Neill	9-10-43	78 Sqn
1141059	Sgt	GRIGGS Charles	23-12-43	15 OTU
1375614	Sgt	GRIGGS Fred William	15-04-43	10 Sqn
138314	F/O	GRIMES DFM Walter Crawford	18-11-43	617 Sqn
1601228	Sgt	GRIMMOND Joseph Ronald	17-09-43	10 OTU
1127071	Sgt	GRIMSHAW Charles Edward	15-06-43	460 Sqn
649407	Sgt	GRIMSHAW Cyril James	8-04-43	100 Sqn
84667	S/L	GRIMSTON DFC The Hon. Brian	4-04-43	156 Sqn
1438024	Sgt	GRIMWOOD Leslie	4-11-43	75 Sqn
1331835	Sgt	GRIMWOOD Peter	24-05-43	10 Sqn
1159783	Sgt	GRIMWOOD Philip Jack William	4-04-43	156 Sqn
1375739	F/S	GRIST Thomas Charles James	21-04-43	61 Sqn
644474	Sgt	GRIVELL Mervyn Stanley	24-08-43	156 Sqn
1383142	Sgt	GROCOCK Denis Charles	15-04-43	196 Sqn
1443282	Sgt	GROCOCK Joseph Stanley	28-04-43	19 OTU
1382101	Sgt	GROOM Frank	23-06-43	161 Sqn
1222829	Sgt	GROOM Philip	6-09-43	78 Sqn
568210	Sgt	GROOM Stanley	24-05-43	35 Sqn
1350336	Sgt	GROUT Dennis	6-09-43	156 Sqn
1379957	Sgt	GROVE Albert Stanley	15-01-43	29 OTU
127318	F/O	GROVE Eric George	23-06-43	156 Sqn
1579893	Sgt	GROVE Norman Frederick	14-11-43	20 OTU
1581242	Sgt	GROVE Richard Frederick	31-08-43	75 Sqn
1576028	Sgt	GROVES Ivor Francis	2-12-43	57 Sqn

Service No.	Rank	Name	Date	Sqn
1509486	Sgt	GROZIER James Edwin	20-12-43	51 Sqn
1526055	F/S	GRUNDY Eric Granville	16-12-43	106 Sqn
155369	P/O	GRUNDY Fred	3-10-43	158 Sqn
1487533	Sgt	GRUNDY George	17-12-43	97 Sqn
106872	F/L	GRUNDY James Alfred	3-10-43	51 Sqn
1435512	F/S	GRUNDY Robert	18-08-43	15 Sqn
626664	F/S	GRUNDY DFM Stanley [South Africa]	9-04-43	101 Sqn
1174669	Sgt	GRUNTMAN Herbert John	2-03-43	76 Sqn
568519	Sgt	GUERRIER Glyndwr	2-02-43	102 Sqn
1122799	Sgt	GUEST Donald Charles Lionel	8-04-43	218 Sqn
1603378	Sgt	GUEST Douglas Anthony Percy	6-09-43	149 Sqn
1167534	Sgt	GUEST Percy	28-05-43	166 Sqn
1458306	Sgt	GULEY Harry Raymond Robertson	3-08-43	51 Sqn
1378136	Sgt	GULLERY Hugh Francis	4-02-43	9 Sqn
1602960	Sgt	GULLIVER John Derek	28-09-43	101 Sqn
1379214	Sgt	GUMMER Leo	13-05-43	431 Sqn
1389502	Sgt	GUNN John Fraser McKenzie	22-09-43	90 Sqn
927129	Sgt	GUNN John Leonard	18-04-43	1659 HCU
578387	Sgt	GUNN Kelsall George	28-08-43	15 Sqn
122307	F/O	GUNNILL Bernard	24-12-43	141 Sqn
139201	P/O	GUNNING Leslie George	3-01-43	61 Sqn
1314180	F/S	GUNNINGHAM George Rex Lilburn	4-12-43	78 Sqn
131992	P/O	GUNTER Bernard John	8-03-43	61 Sqn
130730	P/O	GUNTER Geoffrey Ian	31-03-43	13 OTU
919478	Sgt	GURDON John Robert	11-04-43	166 Sqn
1581644	Sgt	GURNEY Arthur Edwin	22-06-43	218 Sqn
932499	Sgt	GURNEY Francis William	15-02-43	28 OTU
143231	P/O	GURR Anthony John	8-04-43	15 Sqn
1284804	Sgt	GURRY Albert Henry	19-06-43	77 Sqn
1677210	Sgt	GUSTARD Henry Noble	9-10-43	106 Sqn
1172550	Sgt	GUTERMAN DFM Jack	17-05-43	617 Sqn
1086663	Sgt	GUTH Eric John	31-01-43	16 OTU
122495	F/O	GUTHRIE Alan	24-09-43	12 Sqn
1335916	Sgt	GUY Frank	29-04-43	196 Sqn
1365885	Sgt	GUY Robert Kerr	3-04-43	51 Sqn
1211944	Sgt	GUY Ronald Stevens	6-02-43	199 Sqn
1217158	Sgt	GWILLAM Douglas Victor	2-02-43	102 Sqn
1413343	F/S	GWYNNE Elfod	22-10-43	429 Sqn
1319315	Sgt	HACKER Gordon Mayo	29-06-43	431 Sqn
1132947	Sgt	HACKETT Frank Joseph	3-04-43	101 Sqn
1600315	F/S	HACKETT Roy Edward	16-12-43	106 Sqn
949263	Sgt	HADDEN Leslie George	26-05-43	149 Sqn
1365803	Sgt	HADDOW Alan	5-04-43	57 Sqn
143857	P/O	HADDOW James Love	29-04-43	12 Sqn
147654	F/O	HADDOW John	26-11-43	102 Sqn
1185774	Sgt	HADEN Albert Frederick	13-01-43	61 Sqn
1450378	Sgt	HADFIELD Howard	26-07-43	620 Sqn
1132867	Sgt	HADFIELD John Milner	5-05-43	101 Sqn
572631	Sgt	HADLAND Maurice Richard	17-04-43	431 Sqn
658149	Sgt	HADLEY Raymond	13-08-43	166 Sqn
102608	S/L	HADLEY DFC Ronald	16-12-43	156 Sqn
1601759	Sgt	HADLOW Douglas William	9-10-43	51 Sqn
1606982	Sgt	HADLOW Hubert Alfred	17-12-43	156 Sqn
1436394	Sgt	HADWIN Derrick	31-07-43	78 Sqn
911279	Sgt	HAFFENDEN Maurice Ernest	23-09-43	77 Sqn
135666	F/O	HAGAN John Frederick Lawrence	4-11-43	12 Sqn
569504	Sgt	HAGEMAN Ronald	28-05-43	35 Sqn
42500	S/L	HAGGARTY DFC Patrick Archibald	17-08-43	35 Sqn
1626815	Sgt	HAGGER Peter Charles	26-11-43	158 Sqn
1498307	Sgt	HAGUE Jack Phillip	28-08-43	102 Sqn
1768277	AC1	HAIGH Arthur	2-07-43	620 Sqn
1590382	Sgt	HAIGH Geoffrey	1-09-43	101 Sqn
1295400	Sgt	HAIGH John Davidson	12-03-43	102 Sqn
1587219	Sgt	HAIGH Ronald Charles	1-09-43	15 Sqn
143386	P/O	HAILEY Kenneth Sidney	29-04-43	218 Sqn
133331	F/O	HAINES Frank Rees	29-06-43	51 Sqn
149607	P/O	HAINES Frederick John	25-06-43	7 Sqn
1257965	F/S	HAINES Ivan Charles	8-04-43	44 Sqn
1267828	Sgt	HAININ Leslie	29-04-43	90 Sqn
1198942	Sgt	HAIR Gavin McMurray [Canada]	17-01-43	61 Sqn
1291772	Sgt	HALDEMAN William Cyril	4-04-43	156 Sqn
52116	F/O	HALE Charles Noel	30-12-43	50 Sqn
145835	P/O	HALE Ronald Reginald	13-06-43	102 Sqn
937612	Sgt	HALES Alfred	13-07-43	12 Sqn
1464887	Sgt	HALESTRAP Ronald Alfred	14-05-43	77 Sqn
1313051	Sgt	HALEY Michael Frederick	17-06-43	49 Sqn
152239	P/O	HALFPENNY William John	8-11-43	20 OTU
149519	P/O	HALKIER Henry	8-08-43	61 Sqn
957304	Sgt	HALL Alfred Douglas	29-06-43	149 Sqn
577780	Sgt	HALL Aubrey	24-05-43	10 Sqn
1046228	Sgt	HALL Daniel William	22-10-43	434 Sqn
1564377	Sgt	HALL David Hastings	17-11-43	57 Sqn
1483259	Sgt	HALL Douglas Sinclair	20-12-43	50 Sqn
950798	Sgt	HALL Edwin John	29-09-43	158 Sqn
1216854	Sgt	HALL Eric	26-03-43	426 Sqn
1576096	Sgt	HALL Eric	12-03-43	1661 HCU
1527080	Sgt	HALL Ernest [Eire]	30-05-43	419 Sqn
908561	Sgt	HALL Ernest Alfred	16-08-43	61 Sqn
1215546	Sgt	HALL Ernest William	21-05-43	149 Sqn
1585186	Sgt	HALL George Alfred	6-11-43	26 OTU
1396863	Sgt	HALL George John Charles	5-05-43	149 Sqn
1527061	W/O	HALL Gilbert Eric	31-08-43	9 Sqn
1369293	Cpl	HALL Grenville Charles	12-05-43	1658 HCU
118413	F/O	HALL Harold Patterson	12-03-43	226 Sqn
1436050	F/S	HALL BEM Harry Ernest	22-09-43	214 Sqn
1314646	Sgt	HALL Ivor Edwin George	26-05-43	207 Sqn
1527292	Sgt	HALL James	8-04-43	15 Sqn
1432645	Sgt	HALL John	4-07-43	15 Sqn
1590860	Sgt	HALL John Donald	24-11-43	14 OTU
635059	F/S	HALL DFM Kenneth	1-05-43	12 Sqn
1538483	Sgt	HALL Kenneth	8-01-43	50 Sqn
1810528	Sgt	HALL Leslie Ronald	20-10-43	166 Sqn
1446090	F/S	HALL Malcolm Thomas Tudor	29-07-43	156 Sqn
539562	Sgt	HALL Patrick	17-06-43	9 Sqn
1312003	Sgt	HALL Philip Raymond	11-04-43	166 Sqn
1049999	Sgt	HALL Robert Clifford	23-05-43	158 Sqn
575290	Sgt	HALL Robert Kirby	2-03-43	61 Sqn
1810453	Sgt	HALL Ronald Alfred	16-04-43	460 Sqn
1230947	W/O	HALL Stanley Gordon William	21-10-43	83 Sqn
51335	F/O	HALL Thomas	22-11-43	10 Sqn
1359883	Sgt	HALL Thomas Edwin	21-04-43	90 Sqn
1585136	Sgt	HALL Thomas Joseph	23-09-43	57 Sqn
1254960	Sgt	HALL Walter Douglas	29-12-43	10 Sqn
1054394	Sgt	HALL Wilfred	2-09-43	81 OTU
1819415	Sgt	HALLAM James William	18-09-43	17 OTU
1416860	Sgt	HALLAM Myrddin Walter	25-10-43	20 OTU
1176108	Sgt	HALLETT Benjamin Thomas	5-03-43	100 Sqn
658907	Sgt	HALLETT John Frederick	2-08-43	57 Sqn
1410281	Sgt	HALLETT Norman Frank	11-04-43	100 Sqn
146010	P/O	HALLIDAY Chalmers	4-07-43	466 Sqn
1335256	Sgt	HALLIDAY Kenneth Ronald	18-12-43	311 FTU
966650	Sgt	HALLIDAY William	11-02-43	57 Sqn
1498721	Sgt	HALLIWELL Eric	17-12-43	405 Sqn
1147706	Sgt	HALLIWELL Joe Hilton	19-02-43	166 Sqn
2209228	Sgt	HALLIWELL William	10-11-43	1660 HCU
858236	Sgt	HALLOWS Walter	13-06-43	102 Sqn
1331376	Sgt	HALLWORTH Alan Walter	6-09-43	419 Sqn
991197	Sgt	HALSALL William	14-02-43	49 Sqn
1313054	Sgt	HALSTED Arthur Fitzgerald	13-05-43	429 Sqn
1392507	Sgt	HALSTON Edward George	28-05-43	10 Sqn
127243	F/O	HAM MiD Harry Douglas	1-09-43	106 Sqn
1575323	F/S	HAMBLIN Reginald	11-08-43	35 Sqn
1389996	Sgt	HAMBLING Harold Charles	13-07-43	106 Sqn
141713	P/O	HAMER Douglas Vincent	28-04-43	75 Sqn
1685662	Sgt	HAMER Jack	22-10-43	103 Sqn
523827	Sgt	HAMILL Edward	28-07-43	12 Sqn
1085741	Sgt	HAMILTON Charles Lambert	4-09-43	100 Sqn
115244	F/O	HAMILTON George Cecil	18-07-43	10 OTU

Number	Rank	Name	Date	Unit
146105	F/L	HAMILTON DFC Gordon	2-10-43	61 Sqn
1379006	Sgt	HAMILTON James	30-07-43	158 Sqn
1368785	Sgt	HAMILTON James Crane	25-07-43	103 Sqn
1259434	Sgt	HAMILTON John Leopold [Jamaica]	17-05-43	10 OTU
1043580	Sgt	HAMILTON Robert Gordon	15-04-43	101 Sqn
129614	F/O	HAMILTON William	16-12-43	426 Sqn
1552712	Sgt	HAMILTON William Warnock Black	4-12-43	51 Sqn
1270391	Sgt	HAMILTON-FOX Robert Sydney	9-04-43	7 Sqn
1282690	Sgt	HAMLYN Denis Edward	21-04-43	15 OTU
1290150	Sgt	HAMMETT Edwin George	14-04-43	138 Sqn
131082	F/L	HAMMOND DFC Charles Neville	22-10-43	166 Sqn
125985	F/O	HAMMOND George Noel	30-07-43	97 Sqn
138827	P/O	HAMMOND Kenneth Charles	29-01-43	158 Sqn
1335044	Sgt	HAMMOND Reginald	23-06-43	90 Sqn
1031693	Sgt	HAMMOND Samuel	15-04-43	90 Sqn
1809320	Sgt	HAMMOND Stanley Frederick	12-06-43	77 Sqn
170426	P/O	HAMPSON Kenneth Clifford	16-12-43	1661 HCU
1231035	F/S	HAMPSON Maurice	4-12-43	51 Sqn
1131389	Sgt	HAMPTON George	20-12-43	78 Sqn
136895	F/O	HAMPTON John	19-11-43	90 Sqn
1312179	Sgt	HAMPTON Reginald Thomas	22-09-43	460 Sqn
60812	S/L	HANAFY John Theodore	25-05-43	180 Sqn
155500	P/O	HANAVAN Philip	20-10-43	106 Sqn
1585534	Sgt	HANBERGER Peter Frederick	4-05-43	15 Sqn
1414141	Sgt	HANCE Lawrence Ernest	3-11-43	22 OTU
348493	W/O	HANCOCK Ernest Augustus	18-11-43	Bourn
576889	Sgt	HANCOCK Gordon William	15-04-43	106 Sqn
1032799	F/S	HANCOCK James	25-06-43	106 Sqn
1375756	Sgt	HANCOCK James Eric George	15-04-43	10 Sqn
1395875	Sgt	HANCOCK Peter George	20-12-43	103 Sqn
942217	Cpl	HAND Charles Fenton	6-07-43	16 OTU
1456811	Sgt	HAND Desmond Terence	27-09-43	10 Sqn
1446459	Sgt	HAND Roy Owen	22-10-43	77 Sqn
144203	P/O	HANDLEY DFM Christopher Dinsdale	21-04-43	139 Sqn
137652	F/L	HANDLEY DFM Rowland Ernest	16-12-43	97 Sqn
1065511	Sgt	HANDS Kenneth	14-02-43	49 Sqn
1609447	Sgt	HANDS Philip Leslie	28-09-43	101 Sqn
1332473	Sgt	HANDS Roy Ladbrooke	24-12-43	44 Sqn
40822	F/L	HANKEY Stephen Alers	17-12-43	161 Sqn
1553397	Sgt	HANNAH James Johnstone	17-12-43	138 Sqn
1383305	Sgt	HANNAM Leon	1-05-43	77 Sqn
1511886	Sgt	HANNAWAY Bernard	17-01-43	1654 HCU
1388875	Sgt	HANNELL Edward	9-07-43	106 Sqn
1106835	Sgt	HANRAHAN George Joseph [New Zealand]	22-06-43	158 Sqn
49951	F/O	HANRAHAN John Filmer	25-06-43	7 Sqn
135507	F/O	HANSCOMB Charles Keyte	24-11-43	44 Sqn
162538	P/O	HANSELL Horace James	22-11-43	218 Sqn
1377043	Sgt	HANSFORD Roland Philip	22-06-43	158 Sqn
1114059	Sgt	HANSON Frank	18-01-43	467 Sqn
1458347	F/S	HANSON Harry	24-12-43	141 Sqn
992659	Cpl	HANSON Herbert	7-02-43	51 Sqn
2207081	Sgt	HANSON Robert Hugh	21-06-43	81 OTU
1177722	F/S	HANSTOCK Colin	10-03-43	77 Sqn
1092623	Sgt	HAPPOLD William Bernard Johnson	5-05-43	102 Sqn
538409	Sgt	HARBOTTLE George Raymond	5-04-43	57 Sqn
52803	P/O	HARBOUR Eric Hugh Milbourn	30-07-43	61 Sqn
1312847	Sgt	HARBOUR Henry Peter Gordon	14-11-43	10 OTU
657882	Sgt	HARBOUR Reginald	3-08-43	100 Sqn
577177	Sgt	HARCOMBE Cledwyn Mathew	22-06-43	35 Sqn
41790	S/L	HARCOURT DFC Vernon Ralph Garcia	21-05-43	139 Sqn
1125265	F/S	HARDAKER William	24-12-43	115 Sqn
155893	P/O	HARDCASTLE John Walter	22-10-43	78 Sqn
1382065	Sgt	HARDEE Eric Thomas Dunn	27-04-43	196 Sqn
128911	F/L	HARDEN Lawrence Arthur	3-11-43	10 Sqn
577986	Sgt	HARDING Arthur Regent	7-03-43	51 Sqn
1531330	Sgt	HARDING Edwin Thomas	26-06-43	106 Sqn
1589233	Sgt	HARDING John	6-09-43	12 Sqn
1286788	Sgt	HARDING William	18-02-43	207 Sqn
133330	F/O	HARDING-HAYDON William John	12-06-43	103 Sqn
927795	Sgt	HARDINGHAM Robert Edward	27-04-43	90 Sqn
1394564	W/O	HARDMAN Gordon Edmund Bernard	25-07-43	103 Sqn
1508882	Sgt	HARDMAN Joseph	30-05-43	12 Sqn
1332273	Sgt	HARDS William Frederick Walter	13-05-43	214 Sqn
1212995	Sgt	HARDY Douglas Ernest James	29-01-43	166 Sqn
943042	Sgt	HARDY Gordon	4-04-43	16 OTU
1032217	Sgt	HARDY Joseph	20-10-43	7 Sqn
1272168	Sgt	HARDY Leslie George	30-05-43	432 Sqn
1738601	Sgt	HARDY William	14-07-43	102 Sqn
1441087	Sgt	HARGEST James Philip Vaughan	14-05-43	218 Sqn
149621	P/O	HARGRAVE George Melton 'Tim'	28-09-43	57 Sqn
155583	P/O	HARGREAVES Edward Thompson	3-12-43	619 Sqn
1126171	Sgt	HARGREAVES James	20-10-43	620 Sqn
1310051	Sgt	HARGREAVES James McGhee	13-05-43	83 Sqn
1210201	Sgt	HARGREAVES Ronald	3-02-43	218 Sqn
1124468	Sgt	HARGREAVES William Henry	11-04-43	100 Sqn
1477379	Sgt	HARKER Maurice	3-05-43	24 OTU
1563753	Sgt	HARKER Thomas Nathaniel	2-05-43	11 OTU
1550367	Sgt	HARKNESS John Furniss	17-08-43	57 Sqn
1127681	Sgt	HARKNESS William	5-05-43	75 Sqn
50605	F/O	HARLEY Edward Vincent	2-12-43	207 Sqn
1578786	Sgt	HARLEY Robert William	17-04-43	103 Sqn
1324251	Sgt	HARMAN James	22-09-43	77 Sqn
975077	Sgt	HARMAN Ronald Thomas	17-06-43	460 Sqn
1547702	Sgt	HARMES George Edwin	17-05-43	466 Sqn
1323843	Sgt	HARMES John Frederick	3-12-43	106 Sqn
1308078	Sgt	HARMES Sydney Edward	3-03-43	15 OTU
536477	Sgt	HARNER George Henry	9-10-43	12 Sqn
1435658	Sgt	HARNETT Ronald Edward	22-10-43	49 Sqn
1239175	Sgt	HARPER Alan Bert	31-07-43	76 Sqn
145811	P/O	HARPER Anthony Vyvian	30-05-43	466 Sqn
1196615	Sgt	HARPER Douglas Hayden	30-03-43	83 Sqn
127313	F/O	HARPER Douglas William Francis	29-03-43	102 Sqn
134213	F/O	HARPER Eric	29-06-43	619 Sqn
1816632	Sgt	HARPER Eric	25-06-43	76 Sqn
1191736	F/S	HARPER Geoffrey Cyril	18-11-43	427 Sqn
1231237	Sgt	HARPER James Henry	3-11-43	101 Sqn
1393719	Sgt	HARPER James Henry Roy	24-05-43	1654 HCU
1083168	Sgt	HARPER John Francis	31-07-43	78 Sqn
572648	Sgt	HARPER John Perryer	15-06-43	49 Sqn
60540	F/L	HARPER Leonard Hugh Acland	23-09-43	12 Sqn
538154	Sgt	HARRETT Leonard	9-10-43	78 Sqn
84889	F/L	HARRIES John Roderick	21-04-43	77 Sqn
1303978	Sgt	HARRIES Reginald Eric Rees	9-01-43	103 Sqn
951610	Sgt	HARRIES Wyndham Hadrian	14-07-43	78 Sqn
157285	P/O	HARRILL Edward Charles	4-09-43	100 Sqn
1263308	F/S	HARRINGTON William Walter	2-12-43	460 Sqn
1210390	Sgt	HARRIS Alan Raymond	9-07-43	97 Sqn
1389947	Sgt	HARRIS Albert Charles	1-09-43	419 Sqn
1207018	Sgt	HARRIS Arthur	31-08-43	7 Sqn
1319009	Sgt	HARRIS Aubrey Charles	25-06-43	90 Sqn
1233698	Sgt	HARRIS Bertram Stanley	3-08-43	166 Sqn
1818535	Sgt	HARRIS Dion Clive	23-09-43	460 Sqn
1833605	Sgt	HARRIS Edward Charles	1-09-43	103 Sqn
1582089	Sgt	HARRIS Edwin Fuller	1-09-43	12 Sqn
1802331	Sgt	HARRIS Eric	11-12-43	16 OTU
1024179	Sgt	HARRIS Frank William	23-11-43	7 Sqn
1291074	Sgt	HARRIS Frederick George	27-04-43	102 Sqn
136362	F/O	HARRIS George Henry Richard Forrest	26-11-43	100 Sqn
1506081	Sgt	HARRIS Henry Philip George	18-09-43	15 OTU
1312247	Sgt	HARRIS Jack Sidney	1-05-43	12 Sqn
1035756	Sgt	HARRIS Jessel Hyam	12-03-43	10 Sqn
1339498	Sgt	HARRIS John	11-03-43	158 Sqn
1452502	Sgt	HARRIS John	22-11-43	115 Sqn

118128	F/O	HARRIS John Frederick	29-03-43	218 Sqn	1459940	Sgt	HARTLEY Ronald	17-05-43	19 OTU
1431077	Sgt	HARRIS John Sidney	12-05-43	29 OTU	1567021	Sgt	HARTLEY William	22-10-43	158 Sqn
1099749	LAC	HARRIS Kenneth William	19-06-43	Snaith	1358147	F/S	HARTSHORN Alfred Henry	16-12-43	7 Sqn
1377951	Sgt	HARRIS Leonard Francis James	15-04-43	7 Sqn	655162	F/S	HARTSHORN James Leslie	14-02-43	102 Sqn
1600130	Sgt	HARRIS Leonard Stanley [Eire]	19-11-43	15 OTU	158031	P/O	HARTSTEIN Phillip	9-10-43	7 Sqn
1335461	F/S	HARRIS Leslie	29-06-43	76 Sqn	1213407	Sgt	HARTWELL Ronald Alfred	19-05-43	19 OTU
1819039	Sgt	HARRIS Leslie Norman	18-11-43	9 Sqn	105183	F/L	HARVEY DFC MiD Charles Vincent	23-11-43	156 Sqn
1193140	Sgt	HARRIS Martin	14-01-43	466 Sqn	133456	F/O	HARVEY Dennis	26-05-43	100 Sqn
953174	Sgt	HARRIS Myer	12-06-43	12 Sqn	1394496	Sgt	HARVEY Donald Bruce	16-12-43	101 Sqn
1653119	Sgt	HARRIS Norman Thomas	29-09-43	434 Sqn	161482	P/O	HARVEY Eric Bertram	4-09-43	100 Sqn
130388	P/O	HARRIS Peter Graham	12-03-43	103 Sqn	1083371	Sgt	HARVEY Jack	1-03-43	466 Sqn
2203780	Sgt	HARRIS Raymond Albert	22-10-43	1664 HCU	1874061	Sgt	HARVEY John William	23-11-43	7 Sqn
124802	F/O	HARRIS Raymond George	30-03-43	51 Sqn	998848	Sgt	HARVEY Walter	3-04-43	15 OTU
1384334	Sgt	HARRIS Robert Ernest	25-11-43	1678 HCU	1314276	Sgt	HARVEY Wilfred Gerald	9-04-43	106 Sqn
1270693	Sgt	HARRIS Robert Henry	30-05-43	10 Sqn	142910	P/O	HARWOOD DFM Henry	8-03-43	7 Sqn
1451522	Sgt	HARRIS Sidney	28-09-43	101 Sqn	1231532	Sgt	HARWOOD John	23-08-43	103 Sqn
1315161	Sgt	HARRIS Stanley De Gruchy	1-09-43	426 Sqn	1390412	Sgt	HARWOOD John Leonard	31-08-43	466 Sqn
1244545	Sgt	HARRIS Stanley James	27-09-43	218 Sqn	656219	Sgt	HARWOOD William Edward	26-02-43	427 Sqn
1258716	Sgt	HARRIS Thomas Arthur	18-08-43	61 Sqn	1388573	Sgt	HASEMAN Patrick James	26-03-43	460 Sqn
1432430	Sgt	HARRIS Thomas William	30-03-43	408 Sqn	44563	W/C	HASKELL DFC Walter Ralph	17-08-43	57 Sqn
1316851	Sgt	HARRIS Walter John	3-01-43	207 Sqn	1436349	Sgt	HASKINGS Gordon Edward	3-11-43	10 Sqn
1558802	AC2	HALL William Gordon	12-05-43	1658 HCU	1437309	Sgt	HASLAM Herbert Charles	2-12-43	103 Sqn
993514	Sgt	HARRIS William Gothwaite	6-02-43	90 Sqn	1494074	Sgt	HASLAM Ronald	19-02-43	467 Sqn
560630	W/O	HARRIS MiD William Henry	17-12-43	100 Sqn	657450	F/S	HASLAM Wilfred Eric	18-10-43	100 Sqn
131027	F/O	HARRISON Charles	28-05-43	460 Sqn	1142302	Sgt	HASLAM William Leslie	18-07-43	1661 HCU
1281951	F/S	HARRISON Charles Ronald	24-12-43	625 Sqn	1582945	F/S	HASLEGRAVE Merrik	4-10-43	156 Sqn
1601591	Sgt	HARRISON Clifford Maundrell	6-09-43	101 Sqn	1138074	Sgt	HASTINGS Thomas Edward	13-03-43	7 Sqn
1430273	Sgt	HARRISON Cyril	12-08-43	620 Sqn	161747	P/O	HASTINGS Thomas Herbert	20-12-43	426 Sqn
641277	Sgt	HARRISON Daniel	28-07-43	102 Sqn	1398671	Sgt	HATCH Norman Morgan	30-05-43	12 Sqn
1455360	Sgt	HARRISON Edgar David	13-05-43	12 Sqn	1392608	Sgt	HATCHARD Vincent Herbert [New Zealand]	14-05-43	102 Sqn
126177	Sgt	HARRISON Frank Everett	8-07-43	17 OTU	1145025	Sgt	HATELEY Aubrey Peter	24-11-43	405 Sqn
1158748	Sgt	HARRISON Frederick Vaughan	26-03-43	460 Sqn	1322131	Sgt	HATHAWAY Herbert Thomas	28-08-43	199 Sqn
1611886	AC1	HARRISON George Henry	14-11-43	1652 HCU	1334032	Sgt	HATHAWAY Robert Froude	4-07-43	149 Sqn
1333052	Sgt	HARRISON Henry Basil	13-04-43	81 OTU	1330482	Sgt	HATHAWAY Stanley Alfred	13-05-43	83 Sqn
1271406	Sgt	HARRISON Jack	11-04-43	15 Sqn	132167	P/O	HATT Ronald Henry William	13-01-43	61 Sqn
994787	Sgt	HARRISON John	18-02-43	158 Sqn	1436033	Sgt	HATTON John	3-04-43	15 OTU
1485062	Sgt	HARRISON John Bennett	23-09-43	467 Sqn	1304766	F/S	HATTON Sydney	24-08-43	83 Sqn
1081356	Sgt	HARRISON John Reginald	15-08-43	61 Sqn	1013557	Sgt	HATTON William	15-09-43	617 Sqn
1439229	Sgt	HARRISON Kenneth Cecil	13-05-43	156 Sqn	156043	P/O	HATWELL Stanley Wilfrid	27-09-43	156 Sqn
1386784	Sgt	HARRISON Leonard Arthur	22-06-43	44 Sqn	1218136	Sgt	HAVELOCK Robert Chapman	9-01-43	14 OTU
643364	Sgt	HARRISON Maurice	24-05-43	10 Sqn	1459226	Sgt	HAVENHAND Leonard	30-03-43	76 Sqn
1194276	Sgt	HARRISON Michael Arthur	24-05-43	419 Sqn	1243203	Sgt	HAVERCROFT Walter Crampton	28-08-43	149 Sqn
36029	W/C	HARRISON Ralph Armine Ignatius	12-06-43	100 Sqn	1578211	Sgt	HAWES Albert Henry	26-06-43	51 Sqn
1210696	Sgt	HARRISON Ronald	19-04-43	156 Sqn	1386521	Sgt	HAWES Frank	23-06-43	51 Sqn
1514814	Sgt	HARRISON William	2-09-43	81 OTU	909086	Sgt	HAWGOOD Gerald	23-11-43	7 Sqn
943302	Sgt	HARRISON William Edmund	12-07-43	1656 HCU	1433516	Sgt	HAWKES Sydney Percival	18-08-43	11 OTU
1225093	Sgt	HARROLD Edward George	2-02-43	44 Sqn	1872798	Sgt	HAWKES Tom Bailey	17-12-43	138 Sqn
1199490	Sgt	HARROLD Frederick	11-05-43	24 OTU	145836	P/O	HAWKES William Dick	13-05-43	207 Sqn
1335706	Sgt	HARROLD Ronald Kenneth	26-07-43	75 Sqn	919527	Sgt	HAWKINS Albert James	4-04-43	408 Sqn
655301	F/S	HARROP Frank Sleigh	3-05-43	107 Sqn	949897	F/S	HAWKINS Arthur Thomas	17-05-43	19 OTU
1377395	Sgt	HARROWER Charles Malcolm	1-05-43	106 Sqn	135658	F/O	HAWKINS Eric Henry	13-07-43	103 Sqn
617248	Sgt	HARROWER Thomas 'Tommy'	9-01-43	50 Sqn	1299618	Sgt	HAWKINS Frederick John	12-06-43	75 Sqn
1272474	Sgt	HARRUP Arthur Roy	28-08-43	166 Sqn	658138	Sgt	HAWKINS Henry Victor	28-07-43	467 Sqn
1380381	F/S	HARSLEY James Henry Smith	26-11-43	83 Sqn	976658	Sgt	HAWKINS James Alfred	27-04-43	196 Sqn
1439959	Sgt	HARSTON Cyril Thomas	20-10-43	57 Sqn	1369127	Sgt	HAWKINS John Henry	20-10-43	625 Sqn
1335639	Sgt	HART Basil Graham	10-03-43	10 Sqn	1585262	Sgt	HAWKINS Ronald	16-12-43	115 Sqn
567377	Sgt	HART David Adrian	4-03-43	100 Sqn	1314531	Sgt	HAWKINS Ronald Eric	1-05-43	77 Sqn
1314586	Sgt	HART Edgar Desmond	22-06-43	218 Sqn	633506	Sgt	HAWKINS Samuel	27-04-43	51 Sqn
130641	F/O	HART Edward Chichester	15-09-43	138 Sqn	1272083	Sgt	HAWKINS Victor Barnett	18-10-43	103 Sqn
1115910	F/S	HART Eric Kelvin	30-03-43	429 Sqn	1316309	Sgt	HAWKINS William David	3-04-43	158 Sqn
1290777	Sgt	HART Ernest John Ronald	18-02-43	158 Sqn	1432434	Sgt	HAWKRIDGE Harold Joseph	4-07-43	9 Sqn
143867	P/O	HART DFM Frederick William	5-03-43	156 Sqn	961437	Sgt	HAWKSWORTH William Ernest	20-10-43	29 OTU
1194214	Sgt	HART Norman John	19-08-43	1663 HCU	814218	Sgt	HAWLEY Albert	1-05-43	76 Sqn
1480803	Sgt	HART Robert	27-11-43	16 OTU	1269142	Sgt	HAWLEY Sydney Buchanan	14-05-43	405 Sqn
1337459	Sgt	HART William Arthur	22-09-43	218 Sqn	1483107	Sgt	HAWORTH Jack Rodney	23-09-43	101 Sqn
1265973	Sgt	HART William John	21-02-43	405 Sqn	1081225	Sgt	HAWORTH John	20-07-43	1662 HCU
1432989	Sgt	HARTIN Charles William	23-06-43	161 Sqn	577705	Sgt	HAXTON Andrew Scott	27-09-43	218 Sqn
1199430	Sgt	HARTLEY Edward	27-01-43	106 Sqn	1023216	F/S	HAY DFM Francis	30-05-43	466 Sqn
1450365	F/S	HARTLEY Matthew	16-12-43	103 Sqn					

1002505	F/S	HAY Frederick	15-04-43	35 Sqn	1169045	W/O	HEARD John William	18-07-43	1485 Flt
778764	F/S	HAY George [Rhodesia]	26-06-43	101 Sqn	1339187	Sgt	HEARN John William	26-02-43	218 Sqn
817198	W/O	HAY Peter John	9-10-43	431 Sqn	1457812	Sgt	HEARN Stanley Cyril Henry	22-09-43	434 Sqn
1874077	Sgt	HAYCOCK Christopher Jack	6-10-43	19 OTU	1240536	Sgt	HEATH Denis Graham	3-02-43	218 Sqn
117422	F/L	HAYCOCK DFC Dennis Henry	17-04-43	15 Sqn	1214771	F/S	HEATH Geoffrey	22-09-43	214 Sqn
44407	F/L	HAYDEN DFC Charles Kenneth	9-03-43	139 Sqn	921793	Sgt	HEATH Reginald Baron Percy Henry	12-03-43	218 Sqn
1294654	Sgt	HAYDEN John Gregory	17-12-43	101 Sqn	134917	P/O	HEATHCOTE-PEIRSON Gerald Frederick		
1244010	Sgt	HAYDEN Thomas Frederick	17-04-43	51 Sqn				29-04-43	90 Sqn
746694	Sgt	HAYES Albert	6-10-43	76 Sqn	1456983	Sgt	HEATON Bernard	16-12-43	100 Sqn
1277063	Sgt	HAYES Alfred Edward	12-06-43	78 Sqn	1699714	Sgt	HEATON Francis Patrick	3-11-43	57 Sqn
518809	Sgt	HAYES Bernard Alfred	26-02-43	83 Sqn	1494685	Sgt	HEATON Roy William	20-12-43	408 Sqn
105177	F/O	HAYES DFC Ernest Spencer	17-06-43	156 Sqn	632591	F/S	HEBDEN William Andrew	31-07-43	90 Sqn
1322284	Sgt	HAYES George Alfred	9-10-43	90 Sqn	1212184	Sgt	HEDGE Herbert	16-08-43	49 Sqn
1507661	Sgt	HAYES John Desmond	2-08-43	28 OTU	1552095	Sgt	HEDGE John Clem	15-05-43	30 OTU
1507633	F/S	HAYES Peter Mill	20-12-43	10 Sqn	1800194	Sgt	HEDGES Raymond Edgar	16-12-43	7 Sqn
120087	F/O	HAYES DFC Ralph Gamble	5-11-43	105 Sqn	1318167	Sgt	HEDICKER Ronald Walter	9-04-43	77 Sqn
1531493	Sgt	HAYES Ronald William	2-12-43	101 Sqn	1126573	F/S	HEDLEY William Henry	20-10-43	405 Sqn
1269598	Sgt	HAYES Stanley George Benjamin	22-06-43	158 Sqn	110617	F/L	HEELEY Frank Richard	4-10-43	83 Sqn
1674540	Sgt	HAYHURST Clifford	30-08-43	26 OTU	778991	F/S	HEFFERON Alfred Victor [Rhodesia]	6-09-43	83 Sqn
1153818	Sgt	HAYLE John Reginald	26-06-43	106 Sqn	1030026	Sgt	HEGARTY Terence James	23-09-43	75 Sqn
130637	F/O	HAYLEY Colin	13-07-43	106 Sqn	118668	F/L	HEIN Werner John	23-06-43	214 Sqn
1332269	Sgt	HAYLLAR William Frederick	25-05-43	207 Sqn	1098278	Sgt	HELLIWELL Anthony Ribour	12-06-43	51 Sqn
1339597	Sgt	HAYMAN Francis Ernest	22-09-43	90 Sqn	128521	F/O	HELVARD Arne Rhoar [Denmark]	22-06-43	1651 HCU
1431797	Sgt	HAYNES Colin	23-09-43	90 Sqn	1593684	Sgt	HEMBROUGH Harry Longdon	22-10-43	14 OTU
1087533	Sgt	HAYNES Kenneth William	5-04-43	408 Sqn	1773024	Sgt	HEMINGWAY Fred	18-11-43	76 Sqn
1205271	Sgt	HAYNES Reginald Frank	15-06-43	57 Sqn	1392967	Sgt	HEMINGWAY Peter	23-05-43	57 Sqn
125824	F/O	HAYNES Rodney	10-04-43	30 OTU	1235070	Sgt	HEMMINGS Cyril Benjamin	23-06-43	75 Sqn
33405	S/L	HAYTER DFC John Edward Ross [South Africa]	4-10-43	83 Sqn	610854	Sgt	HEMMINGS Edward	13-02-43	12 Sqn
					1334168	Sgt	HEMMINGS Frank	12-06-43	78 Sqn
1333343	Sgt	HAYTON John William	4-09-43	100 Sqn	1578243	Sgt	HEMPSTOCK Donald Roy	23-08-43	158 Sqn
1119824	Sgt	HAYTON Joseph Banks	16-11-43	28 OTU	1232887	Sgt	HEMUS Leslie James	9-04-43	106 Sqn
1413029	Sgt	HAYWARD Clifford Henry	5-10-43	434 Sqn	632926	Sgt	HENCE John	9-04-43	101 Sqn
651764	Sgt	HAYWARD Desmond David	3-02-43	75 Sqn	634581	Sgt	HENDEN Henry Edward	12-03-43	10 Sqn
86633	S/L	HAYWARD DFC Eric Lewis	30-03-43	106 Sqn	1125769	Sgt	HENDERSON Alexander Keir	23-05-43	57 Sqn
1322145	Sgt	HAYWARD Ian	22-10-43	14 OTU	1294468	Sgt	HENDERSON George	28-05-43	158 Sqn
1464967	Sgt	HAYWARD Lawrence Charles 'Laurie'			1346643	Sgt	HENDERSON Hector	10-03-43	14 OTU
			18-08-43	467 Sqn	133003	P/O	HENDERSON James	12-03-43	405 Sqn
1270441	F/S	HAYWARD Leonard William	30-03-43	428 Sqn	1042115	Sgt	HENDERSON James Robert	26-11-43	419 Sqn
41408	S/L	HAYWOOD Geoffrey Brandrick	15-06-43	44 Sqn	1019301	Sgt	HENDERSON John	20-12-43	50 Sqn
1209070	Sgt	HAYWOOD George	13-07-43	57 Sqn	143404	P/O	HENDERSON John Harold	26-02-43	83 Sqn
905022	Sgt	HAYWOOD Ronald Edward	29-04-43	12 Sqn	156121	P/O	HENDERSON DFM Ralph	22-11-43	83 Sqn
1313768	Sgt	HAZARD CGM Ivan Henry	20-01-43	101 Sqn	2201250	Sgt	HENDERSON Thomas Cook	29-12-43	103 Sqn
1525171	Sgt	HAZEL Stanley Thomas	22-11-43	158 Sqn	1072483	Sgt	HENDERSON William Frederick	29-05-43	218 Sqn
1268287	Sgt	HAZELDEN-FRENCH Edmund	14-05-43	149 Sqn	146015	P/O	HENDON William Roy	30-05-43	466 Sqn
974288	Sgt	HAZELDINE Walter	23-11-43	12 Sqn	146447	P/O	HENDRY Alfred Jones	13-05-43	51 Sqn
130282	F/O	HAZELL Albert William	2-12-43	44 Sqn	534084	Sgt	HENDRY Douglas Hunter	27-09-43	15 Sqn
1586956	Sgt	HAZELL Gordon Robert	23-06-43	77 Sqn	1010647	Sgt	HENDRY James	20-12-43	51 Sqn
937603	F/S	HAZELWOOD Kevin Robert	4-04-43	156 Sqn	1478299	Sgt	HENDRY John Kevin	1-05-43	77 Sqn
1337670	Sgt	HEAD Dennis Harold	20-07-43	1662 HCU	145508	P/O	HENDRY Robert Lawrence	10-07-43	50 Sqn
1302953	Sgt	HEAD James Alfred	29-04-43	218 Sqn	338378	Sgt	HENLEY Leslie James	18-08-43	49 Sqn
143900	P/O	HEAD DFM Laurence Walter George	29-04-43	12 Sqn	128547	F/O	HENLEY MiD Philip Ernest	4-09-43	467 Sqn
1603770	Sgt	HEAD Leslie Ronald	9-10-43	429 Sqn	102972	F/L	HENRY Cyril Reginald	19-03-43	109 Sqn
53736	P/O	HEAD Peter Ewan	17-12-43	101 Sqn	1021115	Sgt	HENRY Thomas Joseph	29-01-43	9 Sqn
1321178	Sgt	HEADFORD Reginald Thomas Henry	20-12-43	466 Sqn	126503	F/O	HENRY William	11-02-43	106 Sqn
1600351	Sgt	HEAL John James Victor	18-08-43	10 Sqn	1318060	Sgt	HENSHALL Hubert James	5-10-43	434 Sqn
1603283	Sgt	HEAL Reginald Jack	24-12-43	115 Sqn	1311513	Sgt	HENSHAW Ronald	13-08-43	166 Sqn
909074	Sgt	HEAL William Albert	23-09-43	50 Sqn	1578815	Sgt	HENSON Kenneth	22-06-43	101 Sqn
160862	P/O	HEALD Sydney	26-11-43	61 Sqn	1563332	Sgt	HENSON Leslie Allan	20-12-43	166 Sqn
1130063	Sgt	HEALEY Alfred	11-03-43	44 Sqn	778954	Sgt	HENWOOD Thomas Henry Edward [Rhodesia]	4-02-43	26 OTU
1314164	Sgt	HEALEY Clifford	12-11-43	102 Sqn					
116140	F/L	HEALEY DFC DFM Everard Frank Gray			149945	P/O	HEPPELL John William	22-10-43	10 Sqn
			13-01-43	106 Sqn	528021	Sgt	HEPTONSTALL Albert	30-03-43	51 Sqn
1582388	Sgt	HEALEY Joseph Michael	22-10-43	103 Sqn	1212641	Sgt	HERBERT Arthur	24-05-43	199 Sqn
145302	F/O	HEALEY Lawrence	22-10-43	61 Sqn	1438154	Sgt	HERBERT Carl Donald	29-06-43	149 Sqn
1335475	F/S	HEALY Bernard James	18-11-43	35 Sqn	1397124	Sgt	HERBERT Charles	11-01-43	12 Sqn
144329	P/O	HEANEY Leslie George	9-10-43	78 Sqn	1425487	Sgt	BERBERT Dennis	26-02-43	196 Sqn
947067	Sgt	HEAP DFM Donald	5-03-43	156 Sqn	133392	F/O	HERBERT Derrick Wilson	24-12-43	50 Sqn
1816110	Sgt	HEAP DFM Eric	2-12-43	101 Sqn	142149	P/O	HERBERT DFM George Racine	12-06-43	35 Sqn
128665	F/O	HEARD Edwin Francis Hamilton	13-05-43	467 Sqn	116456	F/O	HERBERT Gerald Bevill	14-02-43	158 Sqn

Service No	Rank	Name	Date	Sqn
1377606	Sgt	HERBERT Leonard Victor William	25-02-43	102 Sqn
1380131	Sgt	HERBERT Sidney Eric	14-05-43	426 Sqn
1575212	Sgt	HERBERT Trevor Charles	12-06-43	466 Sqn
1190213	Sgt	HERMON Samuel Robert Outra	23-03-43	196 Sqn
158583	P/O	HERON Henry Wilson	31-08-43	166 Sqn
1047013	Sgt	HERON James	4-12-43	630 Sqn
125471	F/O	HERRIN Philip Gerard	23-06-43	207 Sqn
1575657	Sgt	HERRING Kenneth	3-10-43	76 Sqn
160733	P/O	HERRINGTON William James	24-06-43	192 Sqn
130130	F/O	HERRIOTT DFM Arthur James	1-03-43	419 Sqn
124703	F/O	HESKETH Eric	9-04-43	9 Sqn
1063367	Sgt	HESKETH Thomas Griffith	9-01-43	97 Sqn
1144359	Sgt	HESLOP Robert Arthur	17-06-43	103 Sqn
1501112	Sgt	HESLOP Ronald	12-03-43	50 Sqn
1143480	Sgt	HESLOP Thomas	28-05-43	102 Sqn
1231807	Sgt	HESTER George Denby	9-01-43	12 Sqn
1683293	Sgt	HETHERINGTON John	22-06-43	460 Sqn
127354	F/O	HETHERINGTON Stanley	22-04-43	10 OTU
131990	F/O	HETTERLEY Harry Oswald	22-11-43	51 Sqn
610183	F/S	HEWESTON Eugene	3-10-43	158 Sqn
1266114	F/S	HEWITSON Kenneth	22-09-43	218 Sqn
146012	P/O	HEWITT Cecil William	23-06-43	466 Sqn
1197665	Sgt	HEWITT Dennis Arthur	24-08-43	622 Sqn
133098	F/O	HEWITT Frank	22-10-43	10 Sqn
955034	Sgt	HEWITT George Walter	4-12-43	7 Sqn
1601582	Sgt	HEWITT Richard William	2-07-43	620 Sqn
1417486	Sgt	HEWITT Walter Frank	2-01-43	1658 HCU
156343	P/O	HEWSON George Peter	22-10-43	1657 HCU
1292990	Sgt	HEYDON John Ernest Walter	10-03-43	429 Sqn
577141	F/S	HEYES Adrian Bernard	16-08-43	115 Sqn
655460	W/O	HEYES DFM Thomas Sidney	7-08-43	22 OTU
157454	P/O	HEYWORTH Charles	25-11-43	428 Sqn
1583173	Sgt	HIBBERT Eric	2-12-43	57 Sqn
1199434	F/S	HIBBURT Edward Charles	27-03-43	158 Sqn
162589	P/O	HICKLIN DFM Kenneth Norman	26-11-43	101 Sqn
1185786	Sgt	HICKLING Bernard George	13-05-43	467 Sqn
155088	P/O	HICKLING George Edward	27-09-43	78 Sqn
155795	P/O	HICKLING John	31-08-43	207 Sqn
911628	Sgt	HICKLING John Desmond	5-12-43	623 Sqn
1272101	Sgt	HICKLING Norman Victor	22-06-43	77 Sqn
146867	P/O	HICKMAN Stewart William	27-09-43	76 Sqn
1809662	Sgt	HICKMOTT Edward	9-10-43	51 Sqn
1393333	Sgt	HICKS Arthur Brian	20-12-43	158 Sqn
104530	F/O	HICKS Gerald Lambert	21-04-43	21 Sqn
1316957	Sgt	HICKS Harold James	22-09-43	218 Sqn
1451908	Sgt	HICKS Thomas Arthur	25-06-43	102 Sqn
656250	F/S	HIDDLESTON George Adam	25-06-43	12 Sqn
950684	Sgt	HIGGINS Edward	12-07-43	207 Sqn
143695	P/O	HIGGINS Robert Geoffrey	23-06-43	161 Sqn
1501767	Sgt	HIGGINS Thomas Gibson	22-12-43	207 Sqn
1430315	Sgt	HIGGINS Thomas Patrick	28-10-43	1656 HCU
47665	F/L	HIGGINSON DFM Ronald Yarwood	23-04-43	9 Sqn
1291126	Sgt	HIGGS Donald Richard	5-05-43	149 Sqn
1380052	Sgt	HIGGS Kenneth George	26-05-43	428 Sqn
641244	Sgt	HIGGS Percy William Charles	24-08-43	620 Sqn
1394458	Sgt	HIGGS Ronald Fassnidge	28-08-43	10 OTU
1335138	F/S	HIGGS William Charles	24-11-43	405 Sqn
1318117	Sgt	HIGGS William James	3-02-43	78 Sqn
744714	Sgt	HIGH Dennis	5-05-43	166 Sqn
1523110	Sgt	HIGHAM Stanley	19-12-43	138 Sqn
1048176	Sgt	HIGHET Robert	12-06-43	12 Sqn
611325	Sgt	HILDITCH William Webster	25-06-43	75 Sqn
121330	S/L	HILES DSO DFC Waldo Harry Bentley	24-08-43	623 Sqn
1269266	Sgt	HILL Archibald Eric Thomas	24-08-43	101 Sqn
132380	F/O	HILL Cecil George	2-08-43	57 Sqn
127356	F/O	HILL Charles Ellison	23-11-43	44 Sqn
130564	F/O	HILL David	25-07-43	102 Sqn
1812104	Sgt	HILL Donald Colin	6-09-43	90 Sqn
1810331	Sgt	HILL Eric	18-10-43	103 Sqn
1334006	Sgt	HILL Eric Bertram	5-05-43	10 Sqn
1699994	Sgt	HILL Frank	29-06-43	78 Sqn
1435573	Sgt	HILL Geoffrey Maxted	17-04-43	408 Sqn
1526249	Sgt	HILL George Alexander	22-06-43	158 Sqn
1575532	Sgt	HILL George Roland	23-06-43	77 Sqn
1350603	F/S	HILL Gordon Leslie	26-07-43	50 Sqn
1819780	Sgt	HILL Ivan Henry	17-11-43	10 OTU
1396171	Sgt	HILL John	24-12-43	156 Sqn
1317863	Sgt	HILL John Edwin	19-06-43	50 Sqn
1062419	F/S	HILL John Stewart	21-01-43	103 Sqn
148446	P/O	HILL Norman Ernest	4-07-43	12 Sqn
1202448	Sgt	HILL Roland	24-08-43	158 Sqn
1218294	Sgt	HILL Ronald	27-09-43	78 Sqn
959541	F/S	HILL Roy	17-04-43	196 Sqn
1331545	Sgt	HILL Samuel Henry	7-09-43	10 Sqn
1388792	F/S	HILL Thomas William	11-06-43	467 Sqn
1315729	F/S	HILL Victor	15-09-43	617 Sqn
1412570	Sgt	HILL William Walter	29-06-43	100 Sqn
976567	Sgt	HILLHOUSE John Brown	7-02-43	61 Sqn
972195	Sgt	HILLIER Trevor [Canada]	26-11-43	83 Sqn
142020	F/O	HILLS DFM Gordon Leonard	20-12-43	77 Sqn
997003	Sgt	HILLS Leslie Frederick	20-03-43	27 OTU
50475	F/O	HILLS William John	4-07-43	97 Sqn
957788	Sgt	HILT Frederick Stanley	27-03-43	10 OTU
1208584	Sgt	HILTON Charles Henry	24-08-43	78 Sqn
158247	P/O	HILTON George Robert	12-10-43	90 Sqn
60073	W/C	HILTON DSO DFC* Raymond	23-11-43	83 Sqn
1147367	Sgt	HINCHCLIFFE Harold	17-04-43	50 Sqn
170430	P/O	HINDE John Walter	17-12-43	57 Sqn
1685429	Sgt	HINDLEY Frank	18-10-43	100 Sqn
1277651	Sgt	HINDLEY James	15-06-43	106 Sqn
1058762	Sgt	HINDLEY James Theodore	23-06-43	429 Sqn
1080447	Sgt	HINDMARCH John Ernest	7-07-43	12 Sqn
1032071	Sgt	HINDMARCH Robert	28-08-43	90 Sqn
1029913	Sgt	HINDS John Frederick	23-05-43	158 Sqn
159051	P/O	HINE Alan	18-11-43	218 Sqn
1335229	Sgt	HINE Charles Joseph James	24-05-43	10 Sqn
118483	F/L	HINE Douglas Alfred	23-06-43	431 Sqn
1394419	Sgt	HINE Henry George Alfred	16-12-43	166 Sqn
804158	Sgt	HINES Arthur Vivian Derrick	26-02-43	90 Sqn
1163590	F/S	HINGLEY Lancelot George Howard	27-02-43	180 Sqn
1496520	Sgt	HINKS Jeffrey Charles	18-11-43	434 Sqn
550977	F/S	HINSHELWOOD George Allan	4-05-43	218 Sqn
1249131	Sgt	HINSON Peter	6-09-43	78 Sqn
155038	F/O	HINTON Charles Godfrey	23-11-43	9 Sqn
1319154	Sgt	HIRD Ernest Graham	22-06-43	149 Sqn
1042116	Sgt	HIRSCH Simon	22-06-43	77 Sqn
1320056	Sgt	HIRST Cyril Gordon	18-07-43	1661 HCU
1217352	Sgt	HIRST Donald Samuel	23-09-43	460 Sqn
1451452	Sgt	HIRST-GEE Vincent	22-09-43	9 Sqn
778876	F/S	HISCOCK Reuben Oliver [Rhodesia]	24-11-43	408 Sqn
1567321	Sgt	HISLOP John Carmichael	18-08-43	426 Sqn
1270145	Sgt	HITCHCOCK Reginald Charles	14-03-43	9 Sqn
1335371	Sgt	HITCHCOCK Thomas Leonard Victor	24-05-43	76 Sqn
131601	F/O	HITCHCOCK William Joseph John	28-07-43	102 Sqn
843241	Sgt	HITCHCOX Edward James	5-09-43	1663 HCU
1505123	Sgt	HITCHEN Kenneth	3-03-43	76 Sqn
647480	F/S	HITCHEN Samuel	16-09-43	617 Sqn
1890009	Sgt	HITCHIN Maurice Walter	9-10-43	429 Sqn
1323326	Sgt	HITCHINS John Alfred	24-06-43	214 Sqn
1056981	Sgt	HITCHMOUGH Robert James Henry	1-09-43	149 Sqn
576765	Sgt	HITCHON George Arthur	18-02-43	61 Sqn
49032	F/O	HITT Charles George	6-03-43	76 Sqn
1035815	Sgt	HOARE William Patrick	21-04-43	15 OTU
1452681	Sgt	HOBAN John Francis	18-10-43	101 Sqn
1204788	Sgt	HOBBIS William Alfred	13-06-43	102 Sqn
1383998	Sgt	HOBBS Arthur Roy	10-04-43	9 Sqn

648328	Sgt	HOBBS David George	1-03-43	50 Sqn	1015613	F/S	HOLDSWORTH Benjamin	19-11-43	10 Sqn
1321379	Sgt	HOBBS Dennis John	2-12-43	460 Sqn	1545876	Sgt	HOLDSWORTH Clifford William	5-10-43	429 Sqn
574609	Sgt	HOBBS Desmond Frank Augustus	26-07-43	90 Sqn	144654	P/O	HOLDSWORTH Donald Alfred	17-04-43	61 Sqn
1338119	Sgt	HOBBS Douglas Edward John	23-09-43	90 Sqn	1576102	Sgt	HOLDSWORTH Eric	3-03-43	115 Sqn
1329575	Cpl	HOBBS Edward William	4-02-43	7 Sqn	1338760	Sgt	HOLE Arthur Charles	26-02-43	158 Sqn
1609558	Sgt	HOBBS Frederick Johns	23-06-43	75 Sqn	922300	Sgt	HOLE Harry Ernest	27-01-43	21 OTU
1600365	Sgt	HOBBS Jack Allen	24-08-43	149 Sqn	1337529	Sgt	HOLE Jack Gordon	29-06-43	467 Sqn
148175	P/O	HOBBS Peter	11-08-43	77 Sqn	1623418	Sgt	HOLEY Osborne	7-07-43	15 OTU
126646	P/O	HOBDAY Wallace Thomas	29-03-43	101 Sqn	41704	W/C	HOLFORD DSO DFC David William	17-12-43	100 Sqn
1091719	Sgt	HOBKIRK Kenneth Stewart	13-05-43	51 Sqn	1624700	Sgt	HOLLAMBY Douglas Leon	19-11-43	90 Sqn
576564	Sgt	HOBSON Lionel	4-09-43	101 Sqn	1440278	Sgt	HOLLAMBY Eric	6-09-43	77 Sqn
49285	F/O	HOBSON Stuart Melbourne	5-04-43	9 Sqn	1210474	Sgt	HOLLAND Albert Edward	27-01-43	106 Sqn
1509809	Sgt	HOCKEY Leslie	2-10-43	23 OTU	132994	P/O	HOLLAND Francis	12-03-43	405 Sqn
655423	F/S	HOCKLEY Terence Frederick	13-03-43	199 Sqn	132094	F/O	HOLLAND Frank Wilfred	13-08-43	214 Sqn
34124	W/C	HODDER AFC Cyril Charles	22-01-43	180 Sqn	53318	P/O	HOLLAND George Charles	4-12-43	405 Sqn
19243	G/C	HODDER Francis Samuel	6-09-43	Syerston	1493771	Sgt	HOLLAS Raymond	7-07-43	103 Sqn
1585048	Sgt	HODDINOTT John Robert	17-12-43	138 Sqn	1331061	F/S	HOLLEDGE Norman Reginald	19-06-43	77 Sqn
1538261	Sgt	HODDLE Robert Leslie 'Bob'	30-05-43	102 Sqn	1577048	Sgt	HOLLERON Laurence John	2-03-43	44 Sqn
1588682	Sgt	HODGE John	8-11-43	20 OTU	1382650	Sgt	HOLLETT William Alfred	27-04-43	207 Sqn
1097285	Sgt	HODGE Ronald William	30-05-43	35 Sqn	911325	Sgt	HOLLEY Henry Thomas	20-03-43	27 OTU
1339519	Sgt	HODGES Alfred Malcolm	20-04-43	100 Sqn	626498	Sgt	HOLLEY Raymond Walter Ernest	3-03-43	207 Sqn
923732	Sgt	HODGES Charles Walter	27-09-43	156 Sqn	577168	Sgt	HOLLIDAY Malcolm Keith	16-06-43	405 Sqn
1581728	Sgt	HODGES George Austin	3-08-43	61 Sqn	1154990	Sgt	HOLLIDGE Harry Keith	28-08-43	156 Sqn
630317	Sgt	HODGES George Samwell	26-06-43	57 Sqn	128621	F/O	HOLLIMAN Sidney Michael	29-04-43	218 Sqn
158788	P/O	HODGES Henry Fitzgerald	4-11-43	138 Sqn	1579315	Sgt	HOLLINGSWORTH Cyril Henry	23-11-43	7 Sqn
1301508	Sgt	HODGES Oliver Hughes	4-09-43	467 Sqn	574960	Sgt	HOLLINGWORTH Cyril Ernest	9-01-43	103 Sqn
1332624	Sgt	HODGES Oswald William Douglas	18-10-43	9 Sqn	591645	Sgt	HOLLOWAY Alfred	23-10-43	15 OTU
754928	Sgt	HODGES Ronald Horace	23-11-43	156 Sqn	146695	P/O	HOLLOWAY Arthur John	13-07-43	50 Sqn
1388688	Sgt	HODGES William Henry	3-08-43	115 Sqn	1580024	Sgt	HOLLOWAY Edward	16-12-43	49 Sqn
1316915	Sgt	HODGKINS Albert John	3-10-43	428 Sqn	147192	P/O	HOLLOWAY Ian Allison Mervyn	20-04-43	149 Sqn
1046400	Sgt	HODGKINSON Alan	22-10-43	49 Sqn	1714832	Sgt	HOLLOWAY Peter	1-09-43	12 Sqn
577048	Sgt	HODGKINSON Patrick	4-07-43	149 Sqn	129609	F/O	HOLLOWAY Ronald Thomas	7-09-43	1663 HCU
1506082	Sgt	HODGSON Ernest	12-03-43	100 Sqn	135418	P/O	HOLLOWELL Ernest Maurice	1-03-43	420 Sqn
142857	P/O	HODGSON James Robert Arthur	29-03-43	166 Sqn	1383322	Sgt	HOLLYWOOD Ronald Leslie	26-06-43	103 Sqn
1130071	Sgt	HODGSON Joseph	1-05-43	57 Sqn	160839	P/O	HOLMAN Horace	28-07-43	156 Sqn
656856	Sgt	HODGSON Roger Leslie	4-04-43	101 Sqn	143938	P/O	HOLMAN Sidney George	1-09-43	103 Sqn
1523752	Sgt	HODGSON Ronald William	27-11-43	101 Sqn	149902	P/O	HOLMAN Tony Angelo	3-08-43	61 Sqn
1030199	Sgt	HODGSON Thomas	26-02-43	158 Sqn	1190817	Sgt	HOLMAN William James	13-05-43	102 Sqn
987572	Sgt	HODSON Frederick	1-09-43	619 Sqn	1301281	Sgt	HOLME Harry Pears	28-04-43	75 Sqn
170129	P/O	HODSON Maurice Albert Nicholas	27-09-43	199 Sqn	139880	F/O	HOLME Kenneth	31-08-43	76 Sqn
52119	P/O	HODSON William Henry	30-07-43	9 Sqn	126601	F/O	HOLMES Alan Lionel	7-03-43	51 Sqn
656134	Sgt	HOEY Joseph Edwards	23-09-43	75 Sqn	1600328	Sgt	HOLMES Anthoney Ernest Harry	27-09-43	76 Sqn
158337	P/O	HOGAN DFM Leslie	29-09-43	105 Sqn	998612	Sgt	HOLMES Deryck	22-01-43	76 Sqn
1390972	Sgt	HOGAN Patrick Raymond	30-08-43	26 OTU	1394757	Sgt	HOLMES Eric Howeth	26-02-43	90 Sqn
710078	F/S	HOGAN William Edmund [Rhodesia]	30-07-43	77 Sqn	1029217	Sgt	HOLMES Francis Bernard	13-05-43	218 Sqn
1055990	Sgt	HOGARTH Kenneth Herbert	25-02-43	207 Sqn	1139371	Sgt	HOLMES Frank	23-06-43	10 Sqn
76910	F/L	HOGG George Frank	14-07-43	102 Sqn	37013	S/L	HOLMES DFC Frederick Arthur	17-04-43	429 Sqn
1390159	Sgt	HOGG Jack	26-05-43	35 Sqn	157280	P/O	HOLMES Frederick William	13-07-43	100 Sqn
651799	Sgt	HOGG Peter John Howlett	11-12-43	12 Sqn	1433551	Sgt	HOLMES Howard Miles	21-04-43	15 OTU
158281	P/O	HOGG DFM Richard Munro	4-10-43	97 Sqn	656099	F/S	HOLMES Hugh Victor	22-06-43	429 Sqn
1345063	Sgt	HOGG William Stanley	5-01-43	20 OTU	1091687	Sgt	HOLMES Jack	4-07-43	432 Sqn
1387125	Sgt	HOLBECH Kenneth Alfred	10-03-43	429 Sqn	977737	Sgt	HOLMES James	28-05-43	405 Sqn
937362	Sgt	HOLBROOK Ivor George	22-11-43	75 Sqn	1559295	Sgt	HOLMES James Maxwell	30-12-43	18 OTU
926963	W/O	HOLCOMBE Harry	30-03-43	158 Sqn	102602	P/O	HOLMES DFC Joseph Sydney	19-02-43	83 Sqn
132347	F/S	HOLDAWAY Ronald David	1-09-43	101 Sqn	135023	F/O	HOLMES Laurence Henry	17-04-43	408 Sqn
1259359	F/S	HOLDAWAY Roy Frederick	24-08-43	467 Sqn	1335294	Sgt	HOLMES Nevil Temple	10-08-43	61 Sqn
591390	Sgt	HOLDEN Abraham	11-04-43	431 Sqn	1477342	Sgt	HOLMES Robert	26-11-43	431 Sqn
1334010	Sgt	HOLDEN Alfred Eric Ancel	28-07-43	15 Sqn	1530766	Sgt	HOLMES Ronald William	28-08-43	166 Sqn
624070	Sgt	HOLDEN Cecil Charles	31-08-43	218 Sqn	619492	Sgt	HOLT Alec	20-02-43	90 Sqn
103484	S/L	HOLDEN DSO DFC* MiD George Walton	16-09-43	617 Sqn	1217084	F/S	HOLT Derek Arthur	1-12-43	75 Sqn
					1279234	Sgt	HOLT Kenneth	4-12-43	35 Sqn
1388081	Sgt	HOLDEN Henry Walter	2-04-43	16 OTU	578060	Sgt	HOLTHAM Raymond Henry	30-03-43	408 Sqn
651668	Sgt	HOLDEN Matthew Bean	3-02-43	218 Sqn	137054	F/O	HOMERSHAM Geoffrey John	30-07-43	97 Sqn
1204312	F/S	HOLDER Clement Maurice	4-12-43	405 Sqn	1387002	F/S	HOMERSHAM William Percy	1-09-43	77 Sqn
1250340	F/S	HOLDERNESS Jack Arthur	4-04-43	156 Sqn	1282166	Sgt	HONE Sydney Francis	20-10-43	97 Sqn
1810435	Sgt	HOLDING Dennis Charles Herbert	9-07-43	97 Sqn	1483215	Sgt	HONEYBILL Ernest	18-08-43	15 Sqn
1386349	Sgt	HOLDING John Lockwood	22-09-43	207 Sqn	658674	Sgt	HOOD Frank Anderson Wallace	4-04-43	20 OTU
1672121	Sgt	HOLDING Leslie	5-09-43	1661 HCU	1431222	Sgt	HOOD Geoffrey	22-10-43	12 Sqn
1078836	Sgt	HOLDING William	27-04-43	51 Sqn	1142161	Sgt	HOOD James Breeds	13-01-43	106 Sqn

1383547	Sgt	HOOD William James	16-07-43	50 Sqn
982209	Sgt	HOOFE Mark	9-04-43	460 Sqn
1602507	Sgt	HOOK Jack Beverley Jonathan	5-05-43	7 Sqn
84339	W/C	HOOKWAY DFC Stanley Gordon	5-03-43	156 Sqn
1392028	Sgt	HOOPER Arthur Edward	24-12-43	576 Sqn
129598	F/O	HOOPER Cecil Bertie 'Bob'	26-05-43	12 Sqn
1234152	Sgt	HOOPER Frederick George	30-05-43	75 Sqn
1318454	Sgt	HOOPER Harold Francis	24-08-43	218 Sqn
574248	Sgt	HOOPER Herbert Cecil	5-05-43	101 Sqn
151897	F/O	HOOPER Ralph	25-10-43	14 OTU
49586	F/O	HOOS Ronald	30-05-43	35 Sqn
158427	P/O	HOOSON DFM Joseph	29-12-43	35 Sqn
122129	F/L	HOPE DFC Robert Bernard [Australia]	3-04-43	83 Sqn
1584837	Sgt	HOPE Walter	30-12-43	50 Sqn
61281	F/L	HOPGOOD DFC* John Vere	17-05-43	617 Sqn
1392079	Sgt	HOPKIN Gwyn	22-06-43	101 Sqn
158677	P/O	HOPKIN Samuel David	1-09-43	44 Sqn
1317702	Sgt	HOPKINS Daniel	4-09-43	101 Sqn
1415465	Sgt	HOPKINS George	30-07-43	467 Sqn
1604617	Sgt	HOPKINS Stanley Harold	1-09-43	214 Sqn
1550305	Sgt	HOPKINS William Ernest	1-02-43	11 OTU
1451050	Sgt	HOPKINSON Clifford	2-10-43	44 Sqn
127817	F/O	HOPKINSON Donald	17-05-43	617 Sqn
1544310	Sgt	HOPKINSON Leslie	7-07-43	12 Sqn
133250	F/L	HOPPS DFC Francis Thomas	2-12-43	103 Sqn
117427	F/O	HOPSON David Joseph	19-02-43	15 Sqn
138816	P/O	HOPSON George Edward	24-05-43	207 Sqn
1386575	Sgt	HOPSON Sydney Howell	22-10-43	427 Sqn
1379644	Sgt	HORDON Ronald	2-02-43	44 Sqn
132659	F/O	HORKHEIMER Milton	27-09-43	158 Sqn
1231981	Sgt	HORLEY Alfred Charles	7-07-43	26 OTU
1387726	F/S	HORN Derrick Leslie Walter	20-10-43	115 Sqn
1304938	F/S	HORNBY Eric	16-09-43	617 Sqn
1586200	Sgt	HORNE Albert James	4-04-43	196 Sqn
641601	Sgt	HORNE George Hubert Charles	12-11-43	78 Sqn
155799	P/O	HORNE James	18-10-43	619 Sqn
1320949	Sgt	HORNE Kenneth George	29-04-43	90 Sqn
1323974	Sgt	HORNE Leslie Albert	2-03-43	97 Sqn
133536	F/O	HORNE DFC Wallace James	1-05-43	105 Sqn
988537	F/S	HORNER Malcolm David	29-06-43	97 Sqn
127862	F/O	HOROBIN Arthur James	9-10-43	106 Sqn
1352833	Sgt	HORRELL Harold Alfred	26-06-43	103 Sqn
1176649	Sgt	HORRIGAN William Hadley	31-08-43	75 Sqn
1233316	W/O	HORROCKS Peter	14-07-43	78 Sqn
568924	Sgt	HORSFALL David Taylor	17-05-43	617 Sqn
574342	Sgt	HORSHAM Peter John	18-08-43	619 Sqn
951152	Sgt	HORSLEY John Herbert Victor	2-10-43	207 Sqn
658990	Sgt	HORSLEY Victor	15-06-43	49 Sqn
1198644	Sgt	HORSLEY William Arthur	14-03-43	1651 HCU
1623297	Sgt	HORSWILL Robert Edward	3-08-43	419 Sqn
1380418	Sgt	HORTON Charles	18-11-43	10 Sqn
1575213	Sgt	HORTON Ernest	13-07-43	106 Sqn
1318975	F/S	HORTON George John Thomas	4-10-43	83 Sqn
1438845	Sgt	HORTON John Stanley	8-03-43	21 OTU
1294067	Sgt	HORTON Roy Cyril	3-04-43	101 Sqn
1289611	F/S	HORWOOD Albert Joseph	27-03-43	44 Sqn
1337229	F/S	HORWOOD Ronald William	23-08-43	61 Sqn
1283824	F/S	HOSFORD GM George Lynas	30-01-43	16 OTU
865141	Sgt	HOSKING Arthur Leslie Thomas	22-06-43	460 Sqn
136064	F/L	HOSKING Leslie Dennis	12-11-43	35 Sqn
133518	F/O	HOTSON John Dunsmore	13-08-43	420 Sqn
145180	P/O	HOUGH Edward	13-05-43	50 Sqn
1058798	W/O	HOUGH Gerald	5-05-43	101 Sqn
118105	F/L	HOUGH DFC James	18-11-43	7 Sqn
1271588	Sgt	HOUGHAM Jack	9-07-43	106 Sqn
1543667	Sgt	HOUGHTON Harold Maitland	19-12-43	138 Sqn
1336140	F/S	HOUGHTON John Thomas	6-04-43	16 OTU
1037662	Sgt	HOULGRAVE John William	30-03-43	149 Sqn
974219	Sgt	HOULISTON George Watson	14-04-43	103 Sqn
52068	P/O	HOULSTON DFM John Lofthouse Robinson	29-06-43	51 Sqn
121569	F/O	HOUSTON Alexander Millar	8-04-43	76 Sqn
1531156	Sgt	HOUSTON Samuel James	20-04-43	100 Sqn
1391094	Sgt	HOVELL George Albert	3-03-43	15 OTU
1392470	Sgt	HOVER Alfred Walter	31-01-43	9 Sqn
658131	Sgt	HOWARD Basil Leonard	29-06-43	76 Sqn
129579	Sgt	HOWARD Douglas William	6-02-43	90 Sqn
1260589	Sgt	HOWARD Eric John Charles	14-05-43	10 Sqn
1167366	Sgt	HOWARD Ernest Thomas Raymond	29-03-43	218 Sqn
1208813	Sgt	HOWARD Frederick George	7-07-43	21 OTU
1622642	Sgt	HOWARD George	1-09-43	1662 HCU
1132050	Sgt	HOWARD John Salisbury	14-05-43	218 Sqn
1686652	Sgt	HOWARD Leslie	20-12-43	77 Sqn
1029361	Sgt	HOWARD Leslie Pinnington	18-08-43	115 Sqn
652711	Sgt	HOWARTH Arnold	3-04-43	51 Sqn
1479264	Sgt	HOWARTH John	28-05-43	10 Sqn
655475	Sgt	HOWARTH John Kershaw	3-04-43	76 Sqn
1048811	Sgt	HOWARTH Joseph	23-09-43	90 Sqn
1146906	Sgt	HOWARTH Leslie	29-06-43	78 Sqn
1080129	Sgt	HOWARTH Ronald	23-09-43	57 Sqn
1132279	Sgt	HOWARTH Ronald Lewis	13-06-43	100 Sqn
979354	F/S	HOWAT Adam Black Seaton	25-07-43	218 Sqn
1430996	Sgt	HOWE Amos	1-03-43	51 Sqn
1313057	Sgt	HOWE Bernard	22-06-43	619 Sqn
1416423	Sgt	HOWE Frank Cecil	14-02-43	158 Sqn
137472	F/O	HOWE Jack	26-11-43	166 Sqn
149545	P/O	HOWE John	23-11-43	630 Sqn
1149218	Sgt	HOWE John Thompson	21-01-43	207 Sqn
1175171	Sgt	HOWE Maurice Richard	3-08-43	100 Sqn
132816	F/L	HOWE DFC Stanley George	12-06-43	35 Sqn
156349	F/O	HOWE-BROWNE Francis David Kilmaine [Tanganyika Territory]	2-12-43	460 Sqn
1395412	Sgt	HOWELL Arthur	28-09-43	1667 HCU
1386465	Sgt	HOWELL Donald James	26-11-43	166 Sqn
1386452	Sgt	HOWELL Edward William	23-09-43	49 Sqn
1384397	Sgt	HOWELL Francis James	13-05-43	106 Sqn
1389535	Sgt	HOWELL Richard Herbert	10-04-43	103 Sqn
1380180	F/S	HOWELL Robert Geoffrey	10-12-43	617 Sqn
1419577	Sgt	HOWELLS Arthur	8-02-43	44 Sqn
1254491	Sgt	HOWES Alfred John	18-08-43	426 Sqn
1295447	Sgt	HOWES Eric Yeomans	11-08-43	77 Sqn
1214675	Sgt	HOWES William 'Billy'	27-09-43	620 Sqn
1284892	Sgt	HOWES William Robert	30-05-43	218 Sqn
124407	F/L	HOWGILL DFC Richard Raymond	3-08-43	100 Sqn
1284957	Sgt	HOWIE James Cyril	14-05-43	10 Sqn
1105929	Sgt	HOWITT Eric John	25-07-43	158 Sqn
659180	F/S	HOWLAND Harold Stanley	2-03-43	15 Sqn
528778	Sgt	HOWLETT Arthur Edgar	8-03-43	75 Sqn
138684	P/O	HOWLETT David Frederick	17-04-43	218 Sqn
1575692	Sgt	HOWORTH John Hitchin	14-03-43	9 Sqn
40115	S/L	HOWROYD David William Southam	9-10-43	106 Sqn
146295	P/O	HOWSAM Harold Elvin	13-06-43	83 Sqn
133877	F/O	HOWSE Derek George	26-06-43	51 Sqn
125164	F/O	HOWSON Paul Terence	19-02-43	15 Sqn
1316783	Sgt	HOY Cyril	10-01-43	11 OTU
162611	P/O	HOYLE Frank Henry	29-12-43	408 Sqn
647729	Sgt	HOYLE Tom	3-09-43	156 Sqn
159717	P/O	HOYNE Henry Charles	13-08-43	77 Sqn
1342928	F/S	HOYNES Robert Brackenridge	20-12-43	102 Sqn
1477239	F/S	HUBBARD Edward George	17-12-43	97 Sqn
1331086	Sgt	HUBBARD Henry Thomas George	27-05-43	218 Sqn
1377312	Sgt	HUBBARD John Gordon	30-03-43	166 Sqn
1488523	Sgt	HUBBARD John Thomas	18-08-43	619 Sqn
927540	Sgt	HUBBARD Kenneth	14-05-43	138 Sqn
1682045	Sgt	HUBBERT Eric	4-12-43	630 Sqn
1585982	Sgt	HUCKER Frederick Walter	27-09-43	78 Sqn
1319885	Sgt	HUDDY Walter Agar Leopold	26-07-43	51 Sqn
1434083	Sgt	HUDSON Colin Frederick	18-08-43	15 Sqn

Service No	Rank	Name	Date	Sqn
1213915	Sgt	HUDSON Dennis	4-12-43	10 Sqn
1393093	Sgt	HUDSON Edward Victor	11-04-43	115 Sqn
1581611	Sgt	HUDSON Eric Francis	4-10-43	75 Sqn
129518	F/O	HUDSON Francis James	17-04-43	103 Sqn
998980	F/S	HUDSON Harry	21-04-43	21 Sqn
1131558	Sgt	HUDSON Herbert John	6-09-43	419 Sqn
1145881	F/S	HUDSON John	23-09-43	90 Sqn
1457263	Sgt	HUDSON John	26-05-43	100 Sqn
128045	F/O	HUDSON John Melvill	26-07-43	156 Sqn
1268207	F/S	HUDSON Laurence Gilbert	5-03-43	106 Sqn
576853	Sgt	HUDSON Malcolm John	11-04-43	138 Sqn
1473515	Sgt	HUDSON Richard Taylor Anthony	28-05-43	199 Sqn
1378108	F/S	HUDSON DFM William Peel	8-03-43	7 Sqn
1126718	Sgt	HUDSPITH Norman	14-05-43	426 Sqn
573249	Sgt	HUGGAN Brinley	26-06-43	51 Sqn
131487	F/O	HUGGARD John Basil O'Connell	10-03-43	7 Sqn
970899	F/S	HUGHES MC [Czechoslovakia] Albert	20-09-43	138 Sqn
1581631	Sgt	HUGHES Albert Frederick	17-12-43	218 Sqn
1221156	Sgt	HUGHES Cecil William	30-05-43	90 Sqn
1382173	Sgt	HUGHES Clewin Arthur	27-09-43	19 OTU
152393	F/O	HUGHES Clifford	24-12-43	50 Sqn
1036179	F/S	HUGHES Cyril Duggan	30-07-43	35 Sqn
1831558	Sgt	HUGHES Desmond Howard	22-11-43	115 Sqn
1467789	Sgt	HUGHES Ernest Arthur	12-03-43	102 Sqn
146707	P/O	HUGHES Eric Charles	26-06-43	218 Sqn
1333200	Sgt	HUGHES Francis Albert	22-01-43	76 Sqn
1579190	F/S	HUGHES Frederick Arthur	18-10-43	97 Sqn
1381323	F/S	HUGHES James Hywel	10-03-43	77 Sqn
1175887	Sgt	HUGHES John	2-03-43	50 Sqn
1025996	Sgt	HUGHES John McGary	28-09-43	77 Sqn
1318634	Sgt	HUGHES Leslie Edgar	27-09-43	78 Sqn
1808927	Sgt	HUGHES Raymond	16-12-43	432 Sqn
144946	F/O	HUGHES Richard Lloyd	24-12-43	576 Sqn
2215990	Sgt	HUGHES Robert	2-12-43	630 Sqn
1450608	Sgt	HUGHES Ronald	13-05-43	199 Sqn
1333407	Sgt	HUGHES Ronald William	21-08-43	82 OTU
155802	P/O	HUGHES Squire Ronald	22-10-43	61 Sqn
1021591	Sgt	HUGHES Stuart Fred	14-07-43	35 Sqn
1368747	Sgt	HUGHES Thomas	9-04-43	9 Sqn
1684906	Sgt	HUGHES Thomas Idwell	30-07-43	428 Sqn
1215478	Sgt	HUGHES Thomas Vesteinn	13-02-43	420 Sqn
1796312	Sgt	HUGHES Victor Stanley	22-11-43	75 Sqn
159070	P/O	HUGHES Walter	22-11-43	102 Sqn
136545	F/O	HUGHES William	18-08-43	61 Sqn
1494700	Sgt	HUGHES William	29-06-43	35 Sqn
1091670	Sgt	HUGHES William Charles	18-11-43	76 Sqn
916677	Sgt	HUGHES William Edward	23-06-43	77 Sqn
1378874	Sgt	HUGILL Noble	1-09-43	622 Sqn
1431980	Sgt	HUISH Ronald John	11-11-43	1654 HCU
1384738	Sgt	HUKE Richard	23-06-43	76 Sqn
1334066	Sgt	HULBERT Charles Vernon Leslie Ravenhill	29-06-43	44 Sqn
83244	F/L	HULL Arthur Horace	11-04-43	76 Sqn
1541699	Sgt	HULL George	22-06-43	57 Sqn
977041	Sgt	HULMES Arthur	16-08-43	61 Sqn
1538484	Sgt	HUMBLE Albert Lawson	22-09-43	158 Sqn
1820248	Sgt	HUMBLE George	18-08-43	49 Sqn
1811429	Sgt	HUMBLES Roy James	5-09-43	149 Sqn
1818989	Sgt	HUMPAGE Ronald George	4-11-43	26 OTU
1395877	Sgt	HUMPHREY Leonard Joseph	28-02-43	90 Sqn
1416813	F/S	HUMPHREY Walter Henry	18-08-43	619 Sqn
147911	P/O	HUMPHREYS Albert Edward	23-06-43	427 Sqn
1164578	Sgt	HUMPHREYS Gwyn Fryn	30-05-43	419 Sqn
533882	F/S	HUMPHREYS DFM Hugh	12-06-43	7 Sqn
1575436	Sgt	HUMPHREYS Sydney James	1-09-43	12 Sqn
1035927	Sgt	HUMPHREYS William Stanley	16-04-43	1657 HCU
1389976	Sgt	HUMPHRIES Douglas Oswald	4-07-43	15 Sqn
133641	F/O	HUMPHRIES Francis Peter	18-10-43	101 Sqn
1318034	Sgt	HUMPHRIES James William	8-01-43	467 Sqn
1236942	F/S	HUMPHRIES Kenneth Albert	20-12-43	50 Sqn
1318660	Sgt	HUMPHRIES Peter Rowland	28-08-43	77 Sqn
1629519	AC2	HUMPHRIES Stephen Alfred	30-09-43	Bourn
1375694	Sgt	HUNT Anthony Robert John	25-06-43	7 Sqn
1385303	Sgt	HUNT Bernard Alan Cavendish	14-09-43	138 Sqn
1809449	Sgt	HUNT Charles Roy East	3-11-43	429 Sqn
49307	F/L	HUNT Colin Herbert James	16-07-43	50 Sqn
911975	Sgt	HUNT Cyril	23-06-43	9 Sqn
1378420	Sgt	HUNT Dennis Cecil Harry	22-01-43	76 Sqn
1336268	Sgt	HUNT Dennis Cyril	3-07-43	19 OTU
1268390	Sgt	HUNT Eric George	30-03-43	149 Sqn
1216145	Sgt	HUNT Frederick William	6-11-43	1679 Flt
1338292	Sgt	HUNT Graham James	31-01-43	97 Sqn
615956	Sgt	HUNT John William	26-02-43	102 Sqn
1515438	Sgt	HUNT Oswald	23-09-43	15 OTU
913763	Sgt	HUNT Peter Henry Russell	15-04-43	100 Sqn
1271097	Sgt	HUNT Raymond Edward Joseph	17-04-43	100 Sqn
1214081	Sgt	HUNT Ronald Leslie	1-03-43	103 Sqn
1384991	Sgt	HUNT Stanley Gordon	2-03-43	115 Sqn
1585820	Sgt	HUNT Terence William	5-05-43	7 Sqn
571223	Sgt	HUNTER Aubrey	13-06-43	50 Sqn
1345736	Sgt	HUNTER Fergus John	26-06-43	427 Sqn
1332920	Sgt	HUNTER Henry Philip	2-04-43	57 Sqn
1568637	Sgt	HUNTER James	14-09-43	158 Sqn
1018437	Sgt	HUNTER James Stewart	18-01-43	100 Sqn
617249	Sgt	HUNTER John	8-02-43	44 Sqn
652116	Sgt	HUNTER John	1-05-43	1663 HCU
1090357	Sgt	HUNTER Maurice	23-08-43	106 Sqn
79562	F/L	HUNTER Richard Theobald	6-09-43	78 Sqn
651596	Sgt	HUNTER Robert	31-08-43	77 Sqn
1344511	Sgt	HUNTER Robert	26-11-43	158 Sqn
1396315	Sgt	HUNTER William Alexander Wilson	15-04-43	431 Sqn
1358198	Sgt	HUNTING Ernest Francis	3-08-43	75 Sqn
1396068	Sgt	HUNTINGFORD Archie Edwin	16-08-43	49 Sqn
1335432	Sgt	HUNTLEY Eric Douglas	18-09-43	15 OTU
143453	P/O	HUNTLEY DFM Francis Hindmarch	13-05-43	50 Sqn
1300534	Sgt	HUNTLEY Walter Roy	6-09-43	78 Sqn
62322	S/L	HUNTLEY-WOOD DFC Ian McArtair [New Zealand]	3-09-43	207 Sqn
657140	Sgt	HURL William Thomas	5-03-43	218 Sqn
1193559	Sgt	HURLE Cecil Herbert	13-05-43	102 Sqn
1501801	Sgt	HURN Henry Andrew Ronald	22-11-43	115 Sqn
1219204	F/S	HURRELL Raymond	2-10-43	460 Sqn
1384018	Sgt	HURSON James Munro	23-06-43	83 Sqn
1315897	F/S	HURST David Picton Phillips	28-07-43	101 Sqn
130533	F/O	HURST DFC George Gerard	27-09-43	218 Sqn
1817269	Sgt	HURST James	16-12-43	7 Sqn
156781	P/O	HURST John Russell	7-09-43	156 Sqn
1387540	Sgt	HUTCHINSON John Albert	17-08-43	138 Sqn
853608	Sgt	HUTCHINSON John Henry	1-07-43	1654 HCU
568986	Sgt	HUTCHINSON Jonathan	9-01-43	44 Sqn
1108506	Sgt	HUTCHINSON Walter Gilbey	7-05-43	29 OTU
1606864	Sgt	HUTCHINSON William	3-08-43	405 Sqn
52151	P/O	HUTCHISON John	13-06-43	49 Sqn
120854	F/L	HUTCHISON DFC* Robert Edward George 'Hutch'	16-09-43	617 Sqn
1028048	Sgt	HUTTON George Cairns	23-06-43	15 Sqn
1312748	Sgt	HUTTON John	3-11-43	10 Sqn
632578	Sgt	HUTTON Robert	22-09-43	7 Sqn
1585578	Sgt	HUXHAM Herbert John	9-01-43	50 Sqn
820050	Sgt	HUXLEY Norman Jones	31-08-43	427 Sqn
135873	F/O	HUXTER Ellis Edward	1-09-43	623 Sqn
1271580	Sgt	HYAM Jack Louis	13-06-43	57 Sqn
1318574	Sgt	HYATT George Albert	12-03-43	10 Sqn
132394	F/O	HYATT Vincent Longmead	3-10-43	102 Sqn
1249758	Sgt	HYDE Donald James Arthur	16-04-43	15 Sqn
1129625	Sgt	HYDES Douglas	9-10-43	61 Sqn
135115	F/O	HYETT Edward	28-08-43	76 Sqn
655968	F/S	HYETT Horace William Enoch	24-05-43	44 Sqn

124201	F/O	HYLAND Basil Paul Malcolm	27-04-43	207 Sqn
778292	F/S	HYMAN Basil [Rhodesia]	30-07-43	214 Sqn
969248	Sgt	HYND William	12-03-43	101 Sqn
1391347	Sgt	HYNDS Herbert John William	2-10-43	57 Sqn
160841	P/O	HYNE David Alan	20-12-43	78 Sqn
1187888	Sgt	HYRONS Albert Leslie	2-03-43	15 Sqn
655431	Sgt	IBBOTSON Wilfred	17-05-43	617 Sqn
1576588	Sgt	ILIFF John Maxwell	27-01-43	51 Sqn
1079192	Sgt	ILLINGWORTH Irvine	28-08-43	78 Sqn
1387760	Sgt	ILLINGWORTH William	16-04-43	78 Sqn
134082	F/O	ILLIUS Andrew Bruce Warwick	24-08-43	156 Sqn
1480164	Sgt	IMESON Robert Stanton	2-12-43	103 Sqn
640842	Sgt	IMMS James	13-06-43	427 Sqn
110952	F/L	INCE DFC* Clarence Desmond	22-06-43	7 Sqn
1271750	Sgt	INCH Douglas Frederick	17-04-43	51 Sqn
133088	F/O	INGHAM Frederick Gordon	21-08-43	82 OTU
132331	F/O	INGHAM John Paul	23-09-43	75 Sqn
1435162	Sgt	INGLE James Peter Hardy	25-07-43	1659 HCU
1459839	Sgt	INGLE Stanley Lionel	27-11-43	103 Sqn
1569642	Sgt	INGLIS David Wilson	17-12-43	166 Sqn
1052249	Sgt	INGLIS George John	3-01-43	61 Sqn
1343173	Sgt	INGLIS Ian Bethune	24-05-43	10 Sqn
979322	Sgt	INGLIS James Robertson	11-04-43	75 Sqn
1348907	Sgt	INGLIS Robert	23-11-43	630 Sqn
1127598	Sgt	INGRAM Arthur England	7-04-43	9 Sqn
527257	F/S	INGRAM John Ogilvie	10-07-43	61 Sqn
1388776	Sgt	INGRAM John Paton	10-03-43	10 OTU
1607348	Sgt	INGRAM Roy Henry	4-07-43	103 Sqn
656917	Sgt	INNES Andrew	2-03-43	97 Sqn
128662	F/L	INNES DFC Hugh Gault	27-09-43	156 Sqn
978314	LAC	INNES Norman	18-03-43	90 Sqn
1551722	Sgt	INNES Ronald McKenzie	18-11-43	9 Sqn
1503644	Sgt	INNESS George Matthew	13-06-43	10 Sqn
1255764	Sgt	INNOCENT Oliver Henry Thomas	4-09-43	100 Sqn
1074776	Sgt	INNS George	6-09-43	623 Sqn
1265045	Sgt	INSOLE James Cornelius	19-03-43	161 Sqn
1207661	Sgt	INWOOD Eric William	11-02-43	57 Sqn
139625	F/O	IRELAND Dennis Barton [Australia]	14-09-43	138 Sqn
1435308	Sgt	IRELAND John	16-12-43	101 Sqn
1468380	Sgt	IRONS George Harold	31-07-43	78 Sqn
1134386	Sgt	IRONS Sidney Walter	24-12-43	576 Sqn
1546937	Sgt	IRVIN Kenneth	22-10-43	1664 HCU
1374412	LAC	IRVINE Alfred	19-06-43	Snaith
144005	P/O	IRVINE John Lawrence	9-04-43	106 Sqn
1342403	Sgt	IRVING James Bolton McMillan	21-04-43	102 Sqn
936723	Sgt	IRVING John Addley	10-08-43	102 Sqn
1194272	Sgt	IRVING Sydney	18-11-43	76 Sqn
1411984	Sgt	IRWIN Jack Edward	14-09-43	138 Sqn
1221258	Sgt	IRWIN John	10-07-43	12 Sqn
1186092	Sgt	IRWIN Patrick [Eire]	31-08-43	1651 HCU
127920	F/L	IRWIN William Thomas	3-10-43	51 Sqn
656562	Sgt	ISAACS Ralph	2-03-43	207 Sqn
1502733	Sgt	ISHERWOOD Joseph	3-08-43	75 Sqn
134108	F/O	ISRAEL Leslie	18-11-43	192 Sqn
1876512	Sgt	IVERSON James Edward William	24-11-43	166 Sqn
1198853	Sgt	IVORY Lawrence	22-10-43	207 Sqn
1550129	Sgt	JACK Henry	4-09-43	49 Sqn
1187970	Sgt	JACK Vincent Edward	25-02-43	106 Sqn
1075889	F/S	JACKETT DFM William George	11-08-43	35 Sqn
1322187	Sgt	JACKSON Albert James	8-04-43	156 Sqn
946403	Sgt	JACKSON Claude Roy	27-09-43	166 Sqn
658448	Sgt	JACKSON Donald	27-03-43	10 OTU
158648	P/O	JACKSON Edward Laming	22-10-43	207 Sqn
1029143	Sgt	JACKSON Frank	3-08-43	51 Sqn
1580041	Sgt	JACKSON Frank	28-08-43	166 Sqn
1577059	Sgt	JACKSON Frank Bertram	4-07-43	432 Sqn
1337232	Sgt	JACKSON Frank Charles	27-09-43	428 Sqn
130647	F/O	JACKSON Frank Whitford	12-06-43	196 Sqn
1291366	Sgt	JACKSON Frederick John	25-07-43	76 Sqn
1263933	Sgt	JACKSON George William	29-01-43	166 Sqn
1342206	Sgt	JACKSON Gordon Hunter	4-10-43	619 Sqn
139721	P/O	JACKSON James Archibald	8-07-43	17 OTU
1564702	Sgt	JACKSON John	3-10-43	12 Sqn
1312983	Sgt	JACKSON Lionel Francis	12-08-43	76 Sqn
85250	F/L	JACKSON Robert Arthur	2-02-43	49 Sqn
1807141	Sgt	JACKSON Robert Sidney	16-11-43	28 OTU
1098586	Sgt	JACKSON Roy [Eire]	23-06-43	620 Sqn
1112663	Sgt	JACKSON Thomas Henry	12-02-43	1660 HCU
1093291	Sgt	JACKSON Thomas James	20-12-43	51 Sqn
1385644	Sgt	JACKSON Thomas Richard	2-12-43	626 Sqn
127008	F/O	JACKSON Trevor Hugh	4-12-43	102 Sqn
1379812	F/S	JACKSON Wilfred	30-01-43	466 Sqn
1219223	Sgt	JACKSON William Edward	12-06-43	199 Sqn
651866	Sgt	JACKSON William John	24-11-43	61 Sqn
133512	F/O	JACKSON-BAKER Terence Walter	16-12-43	7 Sqn
1384790	Sgt	JACOB Vernon Russell	28-07-43	106 Sqn
649808	F/S	JACOBS John Arthur Charles	14-05-43	51 Sqn
1318066	Sgt	JACOBSEN Alexander	9-01-43	57 Sqn
1575014	Sgt	JACQUES George Ronald	26-06-43	218 Sqn
1380526	Sgt	JACQUES John Charles	31-01-43	101 Sqn
51701	P/O	JAGGER David Colin Tansley	4-04-43	10 Sqn
930627	Sgt	JAKES Leslie	13-05-43	78 Sqn
1320164	Sgt	JAKEWAY William Roy	10-04-43	9 Sqn
1555849	AC1	JAMES Albert John	7-02-43	51 Sqn
1178891	Sgt	JAMES Albert Maldwyn	5-05-43	57 Sqn
1577790	Sgt	JAMES Allan	21-05-43	149 Sqn
158917	P/O	JAMES Arthur William	9-10-43	51 Sqn
1579656	Sgt	JAMES Aubrey Rex	26-02-43	102 Sqn
1335785	Sgt	JAMES Brian Hugh	27-04-43	51 Sqn
138920	F/O	JAMES Brynley	18-08-43	49 Sqn
1181424	Sgt	JAMES Charles Geoffrey	4-09-43	44 Sqn
1452712	Sgt	JAMES Charles Lawrence	17-04-43	49 Sqn
645849	Sgt	JAMES Clifford William	19-02-43	15 Sqn
1419008	Sgt	JAMES Daniel Gwyn	27-11-43	16 OTU
1132025	Sgt	JAMES Douglas Anthony	23-09-43	90 Sqn
148180	P/O	JAMES Ernest	1-09-43	158 Sqn
1174187	Sgt	JAMES George William	5-05-43	196 Sqn
1268838	Sgt	JAMES Leonard Charles	20-10-43	139 Sqn
1128455	Sgt	JAMES Leslie	26-11-43	102 Sqn
1332170	Sgt	JAMES Leslie Arthur	16-04-43	15 Sqn
1652915	Sgt	JAMES Raymond Godfrey	22-09-43	214 Sqn
614587	Sgt	JAMES Ronald	16-08-43	49 Sqn
992896	Sgt	JAMES Stanley	13-05-43	90 Sqn
1334586	Sgt	JAMES Stanley William	18-08-43	61 Sqn
615300	Sgt	JAMES Thomas Ithel	27-02-43	12 Sqn
1385904	Sgt	JAMES Thomas Sidney	30-07-43	156 Sqn
710231	Sgt	JAMES Timothy Henry Russell [Rhodesia]	18-08-43	44 Sqn
156324	P/O	JAMES William Henry	14-09-43	138 Sqn
860478	F/S	JAMESON Derek Bellingham	24-12-43	100 Sqn
1374372	LAC	JAMIESON John	19-06-43	Snaith
1333534	Sgt	JAMIESON Thomas Arthur	14-05-43	218 Sqn
1370277	Sgt	JAMIESON William Burt	23-08-43	100 Sqn
129179	P/O	JAPP Anthony Albert	13-02-43	10 OTU
136865	F/O	JAQUES Charles Reginald	16-12-43	576 Sqn
1691928	Sgt	JARDINE Thomas Traverse	1-05-43	77 Sqn
1017022	Sgt	JARMAN Arthur	22-06-43	100 Sqn
1419269	Sgt	JARMAN Ernest James Emrys	27-09-43	10 Sqn
1721809	Sgt	JARMAN John Albert James	18-07-43	10 OTU
27088	S/L	JARRETT Geoffrey William Jones	3-04-43	9 Sqn
1058757	Sgt	JARVIE Charles McAllister	16-05-43	617 Sqn
1344192	Sgt	JARVIE William Baird	3-10-43	18 OTU
128010	F/O	JARVIS George	31-08-43	432 Sqn
567590	Sgt	JARVIS Frederick James	30-05-43	35 Sqn
1316326	Sgt	JASPER Ralph Owen	23-06-43	214 Sqn
1319877	Sgt	JAY Francis Norman	13-06-43	103 Sqn
1299446	Sgt	JAYE Thomas	17-05-43	617 Sqn
658612	F/S	JEAL Jasper Lionel	12-06-43	78 Sqn

650191	Sgt	JEE Douglas Thomas	31-07-43	50 Sqn	933612	F/S	JOHNSEN John Martin Claridge	3-03-43	51 Sqn
1036500	Sgt	JEFFCOCK Cyril	27-09-43	460 Sqn	1380770	Sgt	JOHNSON Alan Morton	12-06-43	115 Sqn
1410474	Sgt	JEFFERIES Basil	3-08-43	12 Sqn	655716	W/O	JOHNSON Alfred Henry	23-09-43	15 OTU
1280562	Sgt	JEFFERIES Michael Charles	26-05-43	431 Sqn	1872886	Sgt	JOHNSON Alfred Henry	17-12-43	100 Sqn
908611	W/O	JEFFERIS Douglas William	11-04-43	429 Sqn	138812	P/O	JOHNSON Arthur Denis	28-05-43	166 Sqn
1319892	F/S	JEFFERY Albert Edgar	25-07-43	166 Sqn	127493	F/O	JOHNSON Bernard	3-03-43	207 Sqn
1338726	Sgt	JEFFERY Alfred Henry	11-04-43	50 Sqn	1116830	Sgt	JOHNSON Cecil	26-11-43	626 Sqn
1862968	Sgt	JEFFERY Donald Ernest	23-09-43	428 Sqn	135112	F/O	JOHNSON Charles Alfred	25-06-43	51 Sqn
128889	F/O	JEFFERY John Denzil	28-05-43	102 Sqn	1577601	Sgt	JOHNSON Ernest Walter Haynes	13-06-43	49 Sqn
1314398	Sgt	JEFFERY John Richard	22-03-43	101 Sqn	1219540	Sgt	JOHNSON Frank	5-09-43	1663 HCU
1300036	Sgt	JEFFERY Leon McNeill	23-09-43	50 Sqn	146606	P/O	JOHNSON Frank Robert	12-06-43	158 Sqn
1101027	Sgt	JEFFREY Douglas Robert	23-03-43	196 Sqn	1066778	Sgt	JOHNSON Fred	5-05-43	83 Sqn
1537056	Sgt	JEFFREY Francis Walter	3-08-43	115 Sqn	1511990	Sgt	JOHNSON George	23-11-43	156 Sqn
142511	P/O	JEFFREY DFM Ralph Ernest	6-04-43	1663 HCU	1124496	Sgt	JOHNSON George Eric	3-02-43	214 Sqn
1440434	Sgt	JEFFREYS Gordon Clarence	24-08-43	90 Sqn	1435337	Sgt	JOHNSON George Ronald	26-06-43	466 Sqn
101546	F/O	JEFFREYS DFC Gordon Sidney	17-01-43	49 Sqn	1818684	Sgt	JOHNSON Graham	29-12-43	115 Sqn
1383288	Sgt	JEFFREYS Ronald Eric	29-03-43	218 Sqn	1623412	Sgt	JOHNSON Harold	24-12-43	576 Sqn
1386466	Sgt	JEFFRIES Leonard Frank	10-07-43	12 Sqn	1235558	Sgt	JOHNSON Harry	2-12-43	12 Sqn
1303397	Sgt	JEFFS Eric	22-06-43	166 Sqn	1270417	Sgt	JOHNSON Howard Edward	31-01-43	106 Sqn
1575981	Sgt	JELFS Arthur Stanley	14-07-43	78 Sqn	1087702	Sgt	JOHNSON Jack Raymond	24-05-43	35 Sqn
1287313	Sgt	JELLEY William Charles Ivor	12-02-43	427 Sqn	1463377	Sgt	JOHNSON James Arthur	8-10-43	21 OTU
147752	P/O	JENKINS DFC Griffith Llewellyn	28-08-43	623 Sqn	570989	Sgt	JOHNSON Kenneth Roy	25-02-43	207 Sqn
1379148	Sgt	JENKINS Harold	23-04-43	9 Sqn	1685159	Sgt	JOHNSON Lionel Trevor	7-09-43	77 Sqn
1186208	Sgt	JENKINS Harry Goodwin	18-01-43	9 Sqn	80238	F/O	JOHNSON Noel Charles [Rhodesia]	30-03-43	83 Sqn
1129497	Sgt	JENKINS Islyn	3-10-43	623 Sqn	1583490	Sgt	JOHNSON Philip Henry	28-08-43	149 Sqn
134207	F/O	JENKINS James Peter Julian	26-11-43	106 Sqn	125426	F/O	JOHNSON Philip Robert	31-07-43	218 Sqn
1336930	Sgt	JENKINS John Henry	24-08-43	158 Sqn	941850	F/S	JOHNSON Raymond	6-01-43	10 OTU
1380739	Sgt	JENKINS Kenneth Avon	13-06-43	10 Sqn	127914	F/O	JOHNSON Raymond James	25-06-43	218 Sqn
577165	Sgt	JENKINS Leslie Howard	4-02-43	90 Sqn	1212114	Sgt	JOHNSON Raymond Sydney	6-09-43	427 Sqn
1600405	Sgt	JENKINS Leslie Seaborn	26-11-43	1658 HCU	1130408	Sgt	JOHNSON Robert Eric Lowden	17-05-43	10 OTU
1314184	Sgt	JENKINS Richard John	12-03-43	50 Sqn	1453416	Sgt	JOHNSON Ronald Joseph	17-04-43	467 Sqn
1321940	Sgt	JENKINS Ronald Lascelles	22-10-43	10 Sqn	124414	F/O	JOHNSON Ronald Norton	3-04-43	101 Sqn
1187305	F/S	JENKINS Rufus George	4-07-43	102 Sqn	1318338	Sgt	JOHNSON Ronald Theodore	9-10-43	78 Sqn
1382585	Sgt	JENKINS Samuel	9-07-43	101 Sqn	900321	Sgt	JOHNSON Stanley Charles	12-03-43	1661 HCU
1314715	Sgt	JENKINS Terence	20-03-43	101 Sqn	145822	P/O	JOHNSON DFM Thomas Frederick Edward		
129161	F/O	JENKINS William Hugh	29-03-43	102 Sqn				5-09-43	1661 HCU
1380237	Sgt	JENKINSON Arnold	21-04-43	102 Sqn	52112	P/O	JOHNSON Thomas William	16-09-43	617 Sqn
1025847	Sgt	JENKINSON Harry	8-04-43	100 Sqn	1220311	Sgt	JOHNSON William	3-04-43	467 Sqn
139033	P/O	JENKINSON Leslie	17-01-43	1654 HCU	1316302	Sgt	JOHNSON William Gordon	29-06-43	15 Sqn
88871	F/L	JENKS Ian Shirley	20-04-43	57 Sqn	710117	Sgt	JOHNSON William Paul [Rhodesia]	2-12-43	44 Sqn
1332167	Sgt	JENNINGS Bernard Arthur William	26-06-43	218 Sqn	1485790	Sgt	JOHNSTON George Arthur Francis [Eire]	30-05-43	90 Sqn
1215579	Sgt	JENNINGS Brian Roland	12-03-43	214 Sqn					
1148932	Sgt	JENNINGS Gordon	30-03-43	408 Sqn	976714	Sgt	JOHNSTON Henry	16-09-43	138 Sqn
1818122	Sgt	JENNINGS Harold	28-08-43	75 Sqn	138152	F/O	JOHNSTON John David	23-11-43	103 Sqn
1134672	Sgt	JENNINGS Jack	31-08-43	100 Sqn	68139	S/L	JOHNSTON DFC Peter	30-05-43	35 Sqn
1325772	W/O	JENNINGS Percy Joseph	9-10-43	156 Sqn	141803	P/O	JOHNSTON Reginald Renouf	9-04-43	76 Sqn
1337496	Sgt	JENNINGS Ralph Vincent	15-04-43	7 Sqn	1393440	Sgt	JOHNSTON Robert Alexander	20-02-43	90 Sqn
1322986	Sgt	JENNINGS William	5-05-43	15 Sqn	1060657	F/S	JOHNSTON Thomas Barr	17-05-43	617 Sqn
1318565	F/S	JENNINGS William George	24-08-43	102 Sqn	533353	Sgt	JOHNSTON Tom	12-09-43	12 OTU
127311	P/O	JEPP Dudley William Charles	13-01-43	12 OTU	1320754	Sgt	JOHNSTONE Alan David	31-08-43	78 Sqn
45724	F/L	JEPPS Arthur Charles	12-07-43	207 Sqn	1566488	Sgt	JOHNSTONE James Aikman	8-11-43	623 Sqn
1575100	Sgt	JEPSON Reginald Andrew Bown	19-07-43	28 OTU	948736	Sgt	JOHNSTONE Norman Burt	4-02-43	106 Sqn
1211239	Sgt	JEPSON Sydney	24-05-43	426 Sqn	530175	F/S	JOHNSTONE Thomas	26-06-43	44 Sqn
1237319	Sgt	JERVIS Ivor Armstrong	23-05-43	57 Sqn	567921	Sgt	JOISCE Leslie	13-03-43	199 Sqn
1288682	Sgt	JERVIS Terence Ernest	10-04-43	30 OTU	50612	P/O	JOLLEY Herbert Francis	13-05-43	156 Sqn
1334688	Sgt	JEWELL John Gillian	30-03-43	49 Sqn	1320077	Sgt	JOLLIFFE DFM Charles Benjamin	20-10-43	7 Sqn
1852027	Sgt	JEWELL Norman William	1-09-43	426 Sqn	1129588	Sgt	JOLLY John	4-07-43	35 Sqn
129153	F/O	JIMINEZ Derick	11-08-43	158 Sqn	1302163	Sgt	JOLLY Thomas	24-09-43	12 Sqn
146941	P/O	JOBES Stanley Buchan	24-05-43	166 Sqn	1211847	Sgt	JONES Aeron	14-05-43	10 Sqn
1379410	Sgt	JOBLING Philip Percy	12-03-43	218 Sqn	1234135	Sgt	JONES Albert	15-04-43	425 Sqn
120547	F/O	JOBLING DFC Walter Stephen	1-09-43	1654 HCU	1456857	Sgt	JONES Alfred William	8-10-43	21 OTU
1545475	Sgt	JOBSON Ronald	3-11-43	12 Sqn	1297209	Sgt	JONES Arthur	4-07-43	97 Sqn
1338580	Sgt	JOEL Dennis Cecil 'Bill'	7-07-43	15 OTU	1388330	Sgt	JONES Arthur Sidney	12-06-43	466 Sqn
1378473	Sgt	JOHN Alan Jordan Clement	21-12-43	14 OTU	1183725	Sgt	JONES Benjamin Bryn	27-04-43	207 Sqn
1498305	Sgt	JOHN Glanville Owen	1-03-43	12 OTU	126511	F/O	JONES Cecil Gordon	3-02-43	106 Sqn
1153102	Sgt	JOHN John Elwyn	17-08-43	57 Sqn	130652	F/O	JONES Charles Edwin	23-11-43	12 Sqn
135284	F/O	JOHN DFC William Frederick	14-11-43	1409 Flt	1727096	Sgt	JONES Charles Robert William	4-12-43	97 Sqn
1332379	Sgt	JOHNS Charles Phillip	23-06-43	78 Sqn	1375410	Sgt	JONES Claude William	23-08-43	103 Sqn
1338520	Sgt	JOHNS James Stuart	9-07-43	106 Sqn	1337506	Sgt	JONES Daniel Vernon	11-04-43	75 Sqn

Service No	Rank	Name	Date	Unit
1335684	F/S	JONES David George Charles	10-08-43	49 Sqn
1338696	Sgt	JONES David John	22-06-43	35 Sqn
1816948	Sgt	JONES David Owen	18-11-43	460 Sqn
1430702	Sgt	JONES David Vincent	13-08-43	619 Sqn
134069	F/O	JONES Denzil Gordon	28-07-43	100 Sqn
158408	P/O	JONES Edward Ellis	22-10-43	166 Sqn
1087736	Sgt	JONES Edward Neilan	1-09-43	1654 HCU
1062590	F/S	JONES Elwyn Knowles	13-02-43	199 Sqn
1248002	F/S	JONES Eric James	26-07-43	51 Sqn
646251	Sgt	JONES Ernest Llewellyn	15-08-43	192 Sqn
842484	Sgt	JONES Frederick	14-09-43	115 Sqn
1135264	Sgt	JONES Frederick Arthur	6-09-43	620 Sqn
1465761	Sgt	JONES Glyndwr	9-08-43	149 Sqn
128518	F/O	JONES Gordon Francis	21-04-43	12 Sqn
942633	Cpl	JONES Gordon Victor	3-05-43	51 Sqn
1125794	Sgt	JONES Goronwy Wyn	3-04-43	101 Sqn
1651232	Sgt	JONES Griffiths Gwyn	31-07-43	44 Sqn
646237	Sgt	JONES Gwynfryn	26-07-43	620 Sqn
629048	Sgt	JONES Harold	25-06-43	156 Sqn
1375844	Sgt	JONES Harold Ernest	16-04-43	466 Sqn
656183	F/S	JONES Henry Newman	29-09-43	166 Sqn
1419935	Sgt	JONES Henry Raymond	24-08-43	78 Sqn
1192740	Sgt	JONES Henry Summers	31-01-43	9 Sqn
570542	Sgt	JONES Herbert Llewelyn	5-04-43	9 Sqn
1126466	Sgt	JONES Howell Rees	26-02-43	15 Sqn
1436993	Sgt	JONES Hugh Ivor	4-09-43	57 Sqn
1337890	Sgt	JONES Iorwerth Beynon	27-04-43	207 Sqn
1054939	Sgt	JONES Ivor Glyn	16-09-43	617 Sqn
1314731	Sgt	JONES Ivor Gordon	8-07-43	17 OTU
133565	F/O	JONES James	17-08-43	57 Sqn
1451275	Sgt	JONES John	24-05-43	51 Sqn
1386043	Sgt	JONES John Ceredig	3-04-43	158 Sqn
1500880	Sgt	JONES John Glynn	1-09-43	12 Sqn
1164197	Sgt	JONES John Haydn	1-03-43	15 Sqn
929585	Sgt	JONES John Ivor	27-09-43	428 Sqn
1319384	F/S	JONES John James	31-08-43	102 Sqn
650138	Sgt	JONES John Morris	24-08-43	467 Sqn
1062633	Sgt	JONES John Whyford Marsh	23-06-43	103 Sqn
1294775	Sgt	JONES Joseph Edwin	24-03-43	16 OTU
1684563	Sgt	JONES Kenneth	18-11-43	101 Sqn
1390633	Sgt	JONES Kenneth Victor	3-03-43	106 Sqn
120550	F/O	JONES Kenneth William	22-09-43	428 Sqn
1576162	Sgt	JONES Laurence Havard	29-12-43	115 Sqn
1113094	Sgt	JONES Lawrence	15-04-43	149 Sqn
1420919	Sgt	JONES Leonard	13-02-43	12 Sqn
1206582	Sgt	JONES Leonard Gordon	29-03-43	420 Sqn
1809928	Sgt	JONES Leslie James	30-04-43	156 Sqn
1337745	Sgt	JONES Leslie Morgan	12-03-43	199 Sqn
1653104	Sgt	JONES Mervyn	14-07-43	115 Sqn
1425102	Sgt	JONES Michael John	4-10-43	115 Sqn
1602070	Sgt	JONES Myrddin	20-10-43	619 Sqn
656955	F/S	JONES Norman Elsdon	13-05-43	51 Sqn
1391954	Sgt	JONES Philip Cyril	7-09-43	427 Sqn
1337681	Sgt	JONES Philip Frederick	17-09-43	102 Sqn
155094	P/O	JONES Ralph Neville	10-12-43	617 Sqn
1424723	Sgt	JONES Rhys	1-09-43	619 Sqn
626828	Sgt	JONES Richard Emrys	3-12-43	9 Sqn
1652042	Sgt	JONES Richard Glyn	26-11-43	460 Sqn
620761	Sgt	JONES Robert Hugh	3-08-43	9 Sqn
159052	P/O	JONES Robert John	3-11-43	77 Sqn
1218431	Sgt	JONES Robert Warren	2-12-43	44 Sqn
1334155	Sgt	JONES Ronald Albert	10-04-43	30 OTU
971236	Sgt	JONES Ronald Lloyd	24-08-43	90 Sqn
1057537	Sgt	JONES Samuel	24-05-43	44 Sqn
1038767	Sgt	JONES Stanley	4-12-43	76 Sqn
65537	F/O	JONES Sydney Rhys	12-02-43	1660 HCU
1515860	F/S	JONES Thomas	26-11-43	102 Sqn
1622196	Sgt	JONES Thomas	24-06-43	214 Sqn
1483420	Sgt	JONES Thomas Eric	26-11-43	1658 HCU
610787	Sgt	JONES Thomas Evan	17-04-43	100 Sqn
1379595	Sgt	JONES Thomas Rees [Argentina]	29-06-43	44 Sqn
657750	Sgt	JONES Thomas William	18-01-43	9 Sqn
1314494	F/S	JONES Wallace Edgar	20-10-43	90 Sqn
1459867	Sgt	JONES Walter	5-11-43	199 Sqn
1192438	Sgt	JONES Walter Edward	30-03-43	429 Sqn
979839	Sgt	JONES Walter Espley	23-11-43	9 Sqn
1814011	Sgt	JONES Wilbert Blake	22-11-43	419 Sqn
124510	F/L	JONES William Arthur	20-04-43	100 Sqn
650318	F/S	JONES William Frederick	9-04-43	460 Sqn
1300297	Sgt	JONES William Owen	7-09-43	1663 HCU
1026151	Sgt	JONES William Richard	12-03-43	103 Sqn
1316509	Sgt	JONES William Trevor	29-04-43	218 Sqn
148459	P/O	JONES Wilton	26-07-43	10 Sqn
1289195	F/S	JOPLING John Thomas	18-08-43	44 Sqn
657303	Sgt	JOPLING Thomas	20-04-43	218 Sqn
901880	Sgt	JORDAN Donald Valentine	22-06-43	619 Sqn
1397047	Sgt	JORDAN Eric Bernard	28-06-43	106 Sqn
1275767	Sgt	JORDAN Eric Ronald Edward	16-12-43	101 Sqn
1377409	Sgt	JORDAN Leonard Cecil	27-09-43	50 Sqn
1292151	Sgt	JORDAN Reginald Matthew	31-07-43	44 Sqn
1393659	Sgt	JORDAN Sidney John	27-09-43	15 Sqn
1398262	Sgt	JORDAN Wilbur Haldane [Bahamas]	12-06-43	78 Sqn
128952	F/O	JOSS Derek McLean	2-10-43	619 Sqn
1685619	Sgt	JOWETT Herbert Freeman	4-09-43	460 Sqn
1481271	Sgt	JOWETT John Hall	23-11-43	50 Sqn
945664	Sgt	JOWITT Harold	12-03-43	100 Sqn
658682	W/O	JOY Francis Richard	9-10-43	12 Sqn
1238563	Sgt	JOYCE George Robert	1-09-43	1654 HCU
1334423	Sgt	JOYCE James Vivian	25-07-43	460 Sqn
1323846	Sgt	JOYCE Thomas Baden	29-12-43	30 OTU
107718	F/O	JOYCE Trevor Francis	1-09-43	61 Sqn
1315154	Sgt	JUBB Brian McMahon	26-05-43	214 Sqn
1385055	Sgt	JUDD Cecil Norman	16-01-43	61 Sqn
119300	F/O	JUDD George Gordon	31-07-43	15 Sqn
1233573	Sgt	JUDD Thomas Eric	26-06-43	102 Sqn
1379544	F/S	JUGGINS Francis Ernest	26-07-43	103 Sqn
1079475	F/S	JULIAN William Bailes	31-08-43	199 Sqn
1178447	Sgt	JULYANS Percy	3-02-43	226 Sqn
119301	F/O	JUNIPER Kenneth Stanley	13-07-43	44 Sqn
1476365	Sgt	JURGENSEN Casper Harold	13-01-43	106 Sqn
1260533	Sgt	JURY Kenneth William	29-04-43	12 Sqn
132953	F/O	JUSTICE Derrick Lionel Paul	31-08-43	196 Sqn
1307170	Sgt	KANE Gordon Esmond	17-09-43	196 Sqn
1376851	Sgt	KAU Joseph Reginald John	21-01-43	158 Sqn
623848	Sgt	KAY Harold	14-02-43	10 Sqn
1375551	Sgt	KAY DFM Harry	14-02-43	158 Sqn
1073023	Sgt	KAY Herbert	28-02-43	49 Sqn
1079407	Sgt	KAY Jack	17-04-43	76 Sqn
129348	F/O	KAY John	13-06-43	76 Sqn
1451293	Sgt	KAY John	5-05-43	90 Sqn
1590013	Sgt	KAYE George Henry	3-12-43	576 Sqn
1295228	Sgt	KEABLE Bertie Frederick	27-04-43	76 Sqn
1682195	Sgt	KEALEY Derek Henry	31-07-43	90 Sqn
162520	P/O	KEAN James Thomas McCormick	28-11-43	192 Sqn
913467	Sgt	KEARNES Robert Thomas Harden	6-09-43	10 Sqn
1116344	W/O	KEARNLEY DFM Vincent	28-11-43	16 OTU
1589516	Sgt	KEARSLEY Harold	22-10-43	10 Sqn
1418911	AC2	KEAT Leonard Charles	3-01-43	428 Sqn
623478	F/S	KEAY James Spy	3-04-43	83 Sqn
1114757	Sgt	KEEBLE Kenneth Stuart 'Ken'	19-02-43	15 Sqn
1455487	LAC	KEECH James Cecil	17-11-43	5 Group
925015	Sgt	KEEDWELL John	4-04-43	158 Sqn
1334003	Sgt	KEELE John Kenneth	31-08-43	102 Sqn
149998	P/O	KEEN Jack Bradshaw	29-06-43	15 Sqn
1384067	Sgt	KEEN Kenneth William	19-02-43	12 OTU
1376154	Sgt	KEENAN David	29-03-43	166 Sqn
127317	F/O	KEENE George William Lansdowne	27-09-43	76 Sqn
1334731	Sgt	KEENE Ronald Ernest	15-01-43	16 OTU

1239640	Sgt	KEETON Anthony Edward	7-02-43	199 Sqn	1349717	Sgt	KERR Douglas Paterson	21-01-43	103 Sqn
1084438	Sgt	KEIGHLEY James Arthur	17-06-43	103 Sqn	1558163	W/O	KERR George John Stewart	1-12-43	75 Sqn
1078101	Sgt	KEIGHTLEY Angus Clifford	22-06-43	101 Sqn	1332511	Sgt	KERR John	11-01-43	27 OTU
1803747	Sgt	KEIR Kenneth George Vincent	2-12-43	460 Sqn	1378669	Sgt	KERR Joseph William	30-03-43	429 Sqn
113026	F/O	KEIRL Charles James	24-08-43	78 Sqn	979213	Sgt	KERR Roderick Watson	3-03-43	460 Sqn
129552	F/O	KELLETT John	27-11-43	619 Sqn	1324340	Sgt	KERR Thomas Carmichael	28-09-43	101 Sqn
138337	F/O	KELLOW Arthur Leonard	24-08-43	100 Sqn	1369391	Sgt	KERRIGAN Aloysius Barclay	17-06-43	156 Sqn
1384311	Sgt	KELLY Denis	1-03-43	35 Sqn	1685384	Sgt	KERSHAW Charles	22-10-43	103 Sqn
1312800	Sgt	KELLY Dennis Patrick	29-06-43	431 Sqn	1622112	Sgt	KERSHAW John Bailey	24-08-43	623 Sqn
701906	F/S	KELLY Desmond Henry Russell	23-06-43	77 Sqn	1077003	Sgt	KERSHAW Joseph	26-05-43	77 Sqn
655704	Sgt	KELLY Ernest Alexander	15-01-43	29 OTU	1359595	Sgt	KERSHAW William	6-09-43	619 Sqn
569345	Sgt	KELLY Francis Clifford	11-02-43	106 Sqn	1580784	Sgt	KERSHAW William Dyson	7-09-43	81 OTU
573042	Sgt	KELLY Fred Leslie Cecil	20-04-43	149 Sqn	1338260	Sgt	KERSLAKE Herbert William Ralph	27-09-43	620 Sqn
1502127	Sgt	KELLY James Andrew [Eire]	28-02-43	49 Sqn	777739	Sgt	KERWIN Reginald Sydney [Rhodesia]	12-06-43	460 Sqn
1230179	Sgt	KELLY John	23-09-43	419 Sqn	1331427	Sgt	KETLEY Leonard Arthur	2-03-43	50 Sqn
1534905	Sgt	KELLY John Gerard	6-10-43	19 OTU	1653208	Sgt	KETTLETY Stanley Thomas	9-10-43	90 Sqn
1559792	F/S	KELLY Ronald Glendinning	9-10-43	106 Sqn	1432344	Sgt	KEVIS Allen James	17-12-43	100 Sqn
1544208	Sgt	KELSALL James Neil	21-04-43	21 Sqn	1494966	Sgt	KEWLEY Charles Henry	24-12-43	50 Sqn
1315685	Sgt	KEMM Jack	28-08-43	115 Sqn	133406	F/O	KEY Evelin Leon Joseph	4-12-43	102 Sqn
1314838	F/S	KEMMETT John Arthur Colin	3-12-43	1691 Flt	1124499	Sgt	KEYMER Harry George	2-12-43	460 Sqn
1123389	Sgt	KEMP Alexander	29-03-43	97 Sqn	1154466	Sgt	KIBBY Robert Henry	2-12-43	101 Sqn
1162793	Sgt	KEMP Donald William	28-08-43	51 Sqn	2210121	Sgt	KIDD Cyril Addison	19-12-43	138 Sqn
994709	Sgt	KEMP George	22-11-43	428 Sqn	1096827	Sgt	KIDD William	1-09-43	158 Sqn
547753	Sgt	KEMP George Samuel	2-10-43	44 Sqn	1293092	F/S	KIERNAN Joseph	8-01-43	50 Sqn
655779	F/S	KEMP Graham Alexander	24-09-43	166 Sqn	1322297	Sgt	KILBURN Herbert Edward	31-08-43	619 Sqn
1235720	Sgt	KEMP John Laurence	15-01-43	214 Sqn	1351860	Sgt	KILLAN John Leslie	18-10-43	467 Sqn
1451590	Sgt	KEMP John Leigh	28-08-43	199 Sqn	1851581	Sgt	KILLE Peter Frederick	9-10-43	460 Sqn
1457206	Sgt	KEMPSON Eric	9-10-43	7 Sqn	1055997	F/S	KILLEN John	17-12-43	97 Sqn
1233859	Sgt	KEMPTON John Henry	14-03-43	161 Sqn	1331007	Sgt	KILLICK Charles Kingston	25-06-43	432 Sqn
1603664	Sgt	KEMP-WECH Ralph	18-10-43	103 Sqn	928731	Sgt	KILLICK Donald Eddie	26-07-43	35 Sqn
2207084	Sgt	KENDALL Kenneth	14-08-43	1662 HCU	1461557	Sgt	KILNER Charles Frederick	25-08-43	103 Sqn
656267	F/S	KENDALL Norman	24-08-43	199 Sqn	1300139	Sgt	KILPATRICK Joseph Henry Clark	6-09-43	419 Sqn
1072258	Sgt	KENDLAN Michael	24-06-43	75 Sqn	1270585	Sgt	KILSBY Gordon Frederick	23-06-43	9 Sqn
1076759	Sgt	KENDREW Clarence	4-09-43	49 Sqn	1007374	F/S	KILVERT Norman Ernest	17-02-43	1482 Flt
936286	Sgt	KENDRICK John [Canada]	2-04-43	16 OTU	1380825	Sgt	KILVINGTON Howard	9-03-43	7 Sqn
1204535	Sgt	KENNARD Harold Moore	20-02-43	90 Sqn	617334	Sgt	KILYON Joseph William	14-02-43	102 Sqn
40715	S/L	KENNARD DFC John Herbert	27-09-43	103 Sqn	1290705	Sgt	KIMBER John Evan Samuel	8-04-43	15 Sqn
1387785	Sgt	KENNEDY Daniel	18-08-43	428 Sqn	1319181	Sgt	KIMBER John Henry	30-03-43	431 Sqn
965752	Sgt	KENNEDY Frederick Smith	29-06-43	15 Sqn	1336307	Sgt	KIMBER Peter Roy	5-03-43	214 Sqn
1551514	Sgt	KENNEDY James	15-02-43	90 Sqn	1385099	Sgt	KIMBERLEY Edward Joseph	14-04-43	138 Sqn
948904	Sgt	KENNEDY James Stuart	29-12-43	61 Sqn	1793063	Sgt	KINCAID Robert Frew	1-11-43	19 OTU
1083975	Sgt	KENNEDY John Gerard	30-05-43	35 Sqn	1576573	Sgt	KIND Alan William	11-08-43	158 Sqn
1389031	Sgt	KENNEDY Patrick Arthur	25-06-43	78 Sqn	1670066	Sgt	KINDER Henry Richard	24-03-43	16 OTU
1003148	Sgt	KENNEDY Raymond Anthony	23-06-43	75 Sqn	1213091	Sgt	KINERMAN Edward Frederick	13-05-43	51 Sqn
1487492	Sgt	KENNEDY Ronald	29-03-43	218 Sqn	1316916	F/S	KING Albert Aubrey	23-10-43	467 Sqn
1260526	Sgt	KENNEDY Stephen William	23-06-43	51 Sqn	1332284	Sgt	KING Alec Percy	26-08-43	20 OTU
1449867	Sgt	KENNELL Brian James	1-09-43	199 Sqn	1579313	Sgt	KING Alfred Leslie	6-09-43	83 Sqn
122989	F/O	KENNETT Leslie George	18-08-43	620 Sqn	755203	F/S	KING Archie Ernest	14-04-43	138 Sqn
1158838	Sgt	KENNINGTON George Thomas	3-02-43	218 Sqn	1376608	Sgt	KING Benjamin	30-05-43	431 Sqn
1375175	Sgt	KENNY John Joseph [Eire]	7-02-43	30 OTU	1382661	Sgt	KING Charles Lionel	13-05-43	51 Sqn
1052337	Sgt	KENSALL George	20-12-43	428 Sqn	1383417	Sgt	KING Charles Parnell	26-06-43	9 Sqn
1448022	Sgt	KENT Arthur Leonard	3-09-43	100 Sqn	1544099	Sgt	KING Charles Victor	9-07-43	97 Sqn
1333800	Sgt	KENT Edward	29-06-43	51 Sqn	634371	Sgt	KING Edward George	4-04-43	149 Sqn
1176581	Sgt	KENT Edward Cecil	2-10-43	51 Sqn	1314015	Sgt	KING Edward Woodrow	13-02-43	158 Sqn
1092493	Sgt	KENT Edwin	20-12-43	408 Sqn	1246101	F/S	KING Francis Peter	23-11-43	156 Sqn
1863958	Sgt	KENT Owen Vernon	4-12-43	625 Sqn	123223	F/O	KING Frank	26-07-43	78 Sqn
700760	Sgt	KENT Robert Benjamin Lyon [Middle East]	28-07-43	50 Sqn	119303	F/L	KING DFC Frederick Edward	14-07-43	102 Sqn
					1293398	Sgt	KING George Charles	22-10-43	429 Sqn
1093341	Sgt	KENT Stanley Wilfred	24-08-43	78 Sqn	134722	F/O	KING Graham	28-08-43	12 Sqn
2204598	Sgt	KENYON Norman Ainscough	25-11-43	28 OTU	1025718	Sgt	KING Henry	10-08-43	405 Sqn
1586059	Sgt	KEOGH Michael	26-05-43	100 Sqn	1586586	Sgt	KING Herbert Donald	17-12-43	138 Sqn
122064	F/O	KEOGH Patrick Gregory	22-10-43	10 Sqn	134158	P/O	KING James Frederick	6-04-43	16 OTU
1079113	Sgt	KEOWN Frederick James	3-02-43	27 OTU	1128416	Sgt	KING John	4-09-43	103 Sqn
572001	F/S	KERCKHOVE Robert Alfred	25-06-43	97 Sqn	1609738	Sgt	KING John	29-03-43	102 Sqn
644129	Sgt	KEREVAN John James	15-06-43	103 Sqn	121250	F/O	KING Joseph William Trainor	24-05-43	10 Sqn
1333840	Sgt	KERLEY Robert Charles	13-06-43	50 Sqn	578808	Sgt	KING Kerry George	26-11-43	514 Sqn
657663	Sgt	KERMODE Brian	22-06-43	218 Sqn	1332051	Sgt	KING Leslie John	21-02-43	424 Sqn
1814365	Sgt	KERNER John Richard William	4-12-43	76 Sqn	52286	P/O	KING DFM Leslie Ronald	24-08-43	405 Sqn
1338395	Sgt	KERNICK Reginald John	3-04-43	78 Sqn	1335800	F/S	KING Maurice Henry	26-11-43	83 Sqn

Number	Rank	Name	Date	Unit
127784	F/O	KING Michael Henham	26-11-43	103 Sqn
1315580	F/S	KING Michael Rodney Warr	28-07-43	467 Sqn
103831	P/O	KING Oswald Theodore Percy	8-01-43	50 Sqn
1604310	Sgt	KING Peter James	4-10-43	427 Sqn
1601208	Sgt	KING Reginald Alfred John	18-02-43	467 Sqn
1270913	Sgt	KING Stanley Alfred	3-08-43	44 Sqn
1384545	Sgt	KING William Albert 'Bill'	1-09-43	214 Sqn
41712	F/L	KING William John	13-03-43	199 Sqn
1321389	F/S	KING William Joseph	6-09-43	51 Sqn
129146	F/O	KINGHAM Alfred John	14-03-43	161 Sqn
127104	F/O	KINGHAM Ronald Frederick	13-05-43	149 Sqn
1185185	Sgt	KINGS Richard George	22-07-43	1657 HCU
658993	Sgt	KINGSLAND Raymond Geoffrey	22-06-43	77 Sqn
1393685	Sgt	KINGSNORTH Cyril Leslie	24-09-43	57 Sqn
1333157	Sgt	KINGSNORTH David John	11-06-43	207 Sqn
946017	Sgt	KINNEAR James Addie	13-06-43	100 Sqn
635123	Sgt	KINNEAR John	17-05-43	617 Sqn
656290	Sgt	KINNIBURGH William	11-04-43	166 Sqn
658321	F/S	KINSEY William Noel	24-11-43	7 Sqn
657159	Sgt	KIPLING Guy	23-06-43	90 Sqn
1392399	Sgt	KIRBY Arthur James	4-12-43	100 Sqn
127173	F/O	KIRBY DFC Herbert Harry	14-08-43	19 OTU
1237264	Sgt	KIRBY James	27-09-43	428 Sqn
1237646	Sgt	KIRBY James	27-01-43	106 Sqn
1453264	Sgt	KIRBY Jeffrey George	3-11-43	76 Sqn
1234614	Sgt	KIRBY John	16-07-43	10 OTU
1383370	Sgt	KIRBY John Henry George	2-07-43	29 OTU
1441108	Sgt	KIRBY Phillip George	28-09-43	77 Sqn
121510	F/O	KIRBY Ronald	15-06-43	44 Sqn
1385246	Sgt	KIRBY William George	23-05-43	218 Sqn
1582272	Sgt	KIRK Edwin	11-06-43	1654 HCU
149830	P/O	KIRK Eric	24-08-43	102 Sqn
42007	F/L	KIRK William John Rennie	14-02-43	466 Sqn
1010024	Sgt	KIRKHAM Bertie	29-09-43	78 Sqn
1035586	Sgt	KIRKMAN Jack	16-08-43	207 Sqn
132995	P/O	KIRKPATRICK William Watson	12-03-43	405 Sqn
157115	P/O	KIRKUP John Elliott	22-10-43	207 Sqn
990083	Sgt	KIRKUP Ralph Donkin	10-03-43	44 Sqn
146119	F/O	KIRKWOOD DFC James	17-12-43	97 Sqn
611336	Sgt	KIRSCH Charles Frederick	27-11-43	408 Sqn
145786	P/O	KITCHEN Antony Derek	17-04-43	51 Sqn
1387038	Sgt	KITCHEN Peter William	1-09-43	77 Sqn
1398614	Sgt	KITCHENER Henry Richard	20-12-43	102 Sqn
1384066	Sgt	KITCHING Alfred Lawrance	27-01-43	50 Sqn
1215487	Sgt	KITCHING Stephen Tom	7-08-43	75 Sqn
1150992	Sgt	KITE Edwin Dennis	22-09-43	207 Sqn
983012	LAC	KITE Evan John	28-04-43	76 Sqn
1393059	Sgt	KITE Frederick William	16-12-43	106 Sqn
129117	F/L	KITNEY DFM Raymond Kirby	7-07-43	15 OTU
946806	Sgt	KITSON George Graham	22-06-43	57 Sqn
130501	F/O	KLEINBERG Georges [Belgium]	23-06-43	207 Sqn
1455874	Sgt	KLEINER Harry	23-05-43	57 Sqn
965184	Sgt	KLEINHORN Maurice	17-04-43	83 Sqn
778837	F/S	KLEYNHANS Cornelius William [Rhodesia]	9-04-43	207 Sqn
1149159	F/O	KNAGGS Kenneth	30-08-43	26 OTU
1312487	Sgt	KNAPMAN Reginald Arthur	1-05-43	9 Sqn
144325	P/O	KNAPP Charles Francis	24-10-43	19 OTU
1450874	Sgt	KNEALE Derek	3-11-43	76 Sqn
142881	P/O	KNEESHAW Arthur Clifford	8-04-43	466 Sqn
1393510	Sgt	KNIGHT Frank Charles Richard	25-07-43	158 Sqn
1380457	Sgt	KNIGHT Frank Henry	4-04-43	51 Sqn
40304	S/L	KNIGHT Frederick John	29-06-43	12 Sqn
1236043	Sgt	KNIGHT Frederick Joseph	17-04-43	218 Sqn
1817301	Sgt	KNIGHT George Ernest	24-08-43	622 Sqn
963535	Sgt	KNIGHT John Geoffrey	13-08-43	214 Sqn
136036	F/O	KNIGHT DFC Kenneth Joseph	3-09-43	207 Sqn
128902	F/L	KNIGHT Leslie Herbert	23-06-43	78 Sqn
658117	F/S	KNIGHT Reginald Arthur	6-09-43	9 Sqn
1332400	Sgt	KNIGHT Reginald Frederick	10-04-43	30 OTU
938121	Sgt	KNIGHT Ronald Frank	4-07-43	51 Sqn
1311941	Sgt	KNIGHT Samuel James	11-04-43	35 Sqn
1575506	Sgt	KNIGHT Sidney	23-11-43	12 Sqn
149349	P/O	KNIGHT Thomas Henry	24-12-43	44 Sqn
155475	P/O	KNIGHT DFC William Francis Cyril	27-09-43	218 Sqn
926621	F/S	KNILL Leslie	19-02-43	83 Sqn
1383477	Sgt	KNOCK Thomas James	29-03-43	101 Sqn
148868	P/O	KNOESEN Benjamin Gabriel	30-07-43	97 Sqn
1294782	Sgt	KNOPE Thomas George	1-02-43	11 OTU
127847	F/O	KNOTT Leslie Sidney	11-04-43	429 Sqn
656356	F/S	KNOWLES MiD John Alfred	1-12-43	199 Sqn
1575223	Sgt	KNOWLES Maurice Henry	8-04-43	100 Sqn
46131	F/L	KNOWLES Robert Langley	20-02-43	90 Sqn
1029237	Sgt	KNOX Clifford Morrell	16-09-43	617 Sqn
1068554	Sgt	KNOX John Clarence	2-12-43	100 Sqn
127962	F/O	KRISH Felix Maurice	12-02-43	1660 HCU
125533	F/O	KUJUNDZIC Nebojsa [Yugoslavia]	4-03-43	103 Sqn
1128371	Sgt	KURRING Edwin	14-05-43	419 Sqn
1575932	Sgt	KYNNERSLEY Graeme James	28-07-43	50 Sqn
941667	Sgt	LACKENBY Andrew	6-07-43	75 Sqn
1590747	Sgt	LACKENBY Thomas	4-10-43	75 Sqn
1272458	Sgt	LACKEY Henry Joseph Patrick	17-06-43	12 Sqn
547135	Sgt	LACY John Percy	16-04-43	15 Sqn
1550660	Sgt	LAFFERTY Thomas	3-12-43	166 Sqn
945774	Sgt	LAFFORD Cecil	10-08-43	102 Sqn
910591	Sgt	LAGNA Noel	26-05-43	7 Sqn
1344401	Sgt	LAIDLAW David Douglas	3-03-43	115 Sqn
127911	F/L	LAING Brian McMenamen	3-08-43	61 Sqn
1366694	Sgt	LAING James Readdie	24-08-43	90 Sqn
1396120	Sgt	LAKE Aston Crawford	12-06-43	15 Sqn
135654	F/O	LAKE William John	9-10-43	12 Sqn
655914	F/S	LAMACRAFT Harry Charles	3-05-43	487 Sqn
1295572	Sgt	LAMB Charles James Joseph Whitton	13-05-43	115 Sqn
936947	Sgt	LAMB Frank Morrison	4-07-43	97 Sqn
655748	F/S	LAMB George	3-10-43	17 OTU
655956	Sgt	LAMB James Gordon	2-03-43	15 Sqn
1094107	Sgt	LAMB Leslie	18-01-43	76 Sqn
130389	F/O	LAMB Robert Kenneth	4-07-43	103 Sqn
146864	P/O	LAMBERT DFM Cecil Agar	6-08-43	51 Sqn
927685	Sgt	LAMBERT Dudley Noel	22-10-43	10 Sqn
127064	F/O	LAMBERT Edward	10-04-43	1661 HCU
1339473	Sgt	LAMBERT Frederick George	8-04-43	15 Sqn
1586401	F/S	LAMBERT Leslie Ernest	29-12-43	467 Sqn
1066420	W/O	LAMBERT DFM Oliver	1-09-43	97 Sqn
1525044	Sgt	LAMBERT Raymond	13-03-43	199 Sqn
1323203	Sgt	LAMBERT Reginald Walter	21-04-43	77 Sqn
127063	F/O	LAMBIE William Crichton	4-05-43	15 Sqn
657444	Sgt	LAMONT Joseph Ballard	26-07-43	620 Sqn
1311504	Sgt	LAMPEN Leslie Charles	11-04-43	105 Sqn
1507263	Sgt	LANCASTER Harold	14-05-43	218 Sqn
1136610	Sgt	LANCASTER Thomas	30-07-43	57 Sqn
1131694	Sgt	LANCASTER William Newton	19-06-43	50 Sqn
1320387	Sgt	LANCE Kenneth	22-11-43	10 Sqn
1305535	Sgt	LANCELOTT Robert George 'Bob'	2-07-43	620 Sqn
1332099	Sgt	LAND Charles Richard	4-02-43	9 Sqn
1392263	Sgt	LAND Cyril Arthur	25-07-43	166 Sqn
1699658	Sgt	LAND James	28-07-43	101 Sqn
1425942	Sgt	LANDER Robert Otley	4-09-43	15 Sqn
611578	Sgt	LANDER Victor James	22-09-43	15 Sqn
1607349	Sgt	LANDERS Roger Desmond	19-06-43	50 Sqn
1098418	Sgt	LANDING Harold	29-12-43	408 Sqn
128589	P/O	LANE Albert William	2-02-43	49 Sqn
88241	F/L	LANE Anthony Winter	30-01-43	28 OTU
1386890	Sgt	LANE Arthur Frederick	21-05-43	466 Sqn
1394728	Sgt	LANE Arthur John	22-09-43	90 Sqn
1583419	Sgt	LANE Eric George	5-10-43	51 Sqn
1451579	Sgt	LANE Frederick John	18-08-43	77 Sqn
1851312	Sgt	LANE James Lionel	17-10-43	196 Sqn

Service #	Rank	Name	Date	Unit
1875446	Sgt	LANE John Edward	30-12-43	26 OTU
1390339	Sgt	LANE John Edward William	25-06-43	101 Sqn
575359	Sgt	LANE Peter	18-01-43	97 Sqn
1260753	Sgt	LANGELAND Arthur Bruce	14-02-43	158 Sqn
1323838	Sgt	LANGFORD Roland Eric	4-09-43	100 Sqn
1337179	Sgt	LANGHAM Louis John	26-02-43	102 Sqn
134377	P/O	LANGHORNE Kenneth Robert	26-05-43	467 Sqn
1043901	Sgt	LANGLANDS Howard	4-07-43	196 Sqn
1603246	Sgt	LANGLEY Cecil Raymond	30-07-43	78 Sqn
1804334	Sgt	LANGLEY Cyril Caister	24-11-43	44 Sqn
1253310	F/S	LANGLEY Denis Paul	18-02-43	57 Sqn
1511061	Sgt	LANGLEY John Birkett	3-04-43	419 Sqn
1080691	Sgt	LANGLEY John Frederick	30-05-43	428 Sqn
1122669	F/S	LANGLEY Lawrence	12-10-43	90 Sqn
1261372	Sgt	LANGLEY William Corner	8-04-43	460 Sqn
1314232	Sgt	LANGLEY-ELLIS Struan Anthony	9-01-43	50 Sqn
1314455	Sgt	LANGRELL James	31-01-43	106 Sqn
1455580	Sgt	LANGSTAFF Kenneth William	26-06-43	44 Sqn
1333518	F/S	LANGSTON Stanley Charles	1-09-43	77 Sqn
1239621	Sgt	LANKESTER Ronald	7-04-43	166 Sqn
47652	F/O	LAPPING James Balam	8-04-43	49 Sqn
2208869	Sgt	LARGE Ronald	2-10-43	57 Sqn
149555	P/O	LARGE Ronald Dive	7-09-43	106 Sqn
904570	Sgt	LARKIN Cyril Walter	30-05-43	75 Sqn
1575497	Sgt	LARKIN Kenneth Richard	26-07-43	158 Sqn
117353	F/O	LARKINS Raymond Henry	27-04-43	429 Sqn
1759180	AC2	LARMAN Herbert	7-02-43	51 Sqn
149693	P/O	LARNACH Conrad	15-08-43	61 Sqn
131957	F/O	LASKIE William	3-11-43	76 Sqn
51721	F/O	LATHAM DFM Thomas Coulton	27-09-43	103 Sqn
39286	S/L	LATIMER DFC Jerrard	15-04-43	106 Sqn
1396732	Sgt	LATTER Tom Emund Wynn	22-06-43	101 Sqn
40625	S/L	LAUD Ronald Hugh [New Zealand]	12-06-43	75 Sqn
1331489	Sgt	LAUDER Frederick James	3-05-43	51 Sqn
980462	Sgt	LAUGHLIN Samuel	13-05-43	57 Sqn
1165343	Sgt	LAUGHTON Richard	18-08-43	61 Sqn
1395121	Sgt	LAURENCE Alan Robert	24-12-43	550 Sqn
1578703	Sgt	LAVENDER William Edwin Frederick	5-09-43	20 OTU
142579	F/L	LAVER Edward Alfred James	12-06-43	158 Sqn
132846	F/O	LAVERICK Harold	24-08-43	12 Sqn
545207	Sgt	LAVERICK DFM William	29-12-43	35 Sqn
626292	Sgt	LAW Alexander McIntyre	13-06-43	101 Sqn
1504180	Sgt	LAW John Douglas	11-04-43	100 Sqn
1581950	Sgt	LAW John Downing	22-09-43	90 Sqn
1077194	Sgt	LAW DFM Norman	27-04-43	115 Sqn
1350613	Sgt	LAWN George Stanley	20-12-43	49 Sqn
1582751	Sgt	LAWRANCE Laurence Bert	16-12-43	1661 HCU
1317859	Sgt	LAWRENCE Cyril John	20-10-43	166 Sqn
1396413	Sgt	LAWRENCE Dion Patrick [Grand Duchy of Luxembourg]	4-12-43	100 Sqn
1237208	Sgt	LAWRENCE Ernest Frederick	29-06-43	12 Sqn
1376010	W/O	LAWRENCE Leonard	2-12-43	12 Sqn
1853883	Sgt	LAWRENCE Robert Anthony	17-08-43	97 Sqn
591258	Sgt	LAWRENCE Thomas Raymond	6-04-43	1663 HCU
1266105	Sgt	LAWRENCE Vincent	18-01-43	44 Sqn
1388668	Sgt	LAWRENCE Walter Henry	8-09-43	12 OTU
1439516	Sgt	LAWRENSON Frederick	6-11-43	138 Sqn
157192	P/O	LAWRENSON George Ashley	27-09-43	218 Sqn
1431816	Sgt	LAWS Reginald Walter	27-11-43	50 Sqn
655647	Sgt	LAWS Thomas Charles	11-03-43	158 Sqn
46731	F/L	LAWSON MiD Christopher Daniel	16-06-43	405 Sqn
1389676	Sgt	LAWSON Donald Allen	14-09-43	158 Sqn
658406	Sgt	LAWSON George Henry	24-05-43	10 Sqn
1011861	Sgt	LAWSON George Witham	23-06-43	90 Sqn
1029770	Sgt	LAWSON Kenneth	30-01-43	16 OTU
1145407	Sgt	LAWSON Ralph	4-09-43	15 Sqn
1048604	F/S	LAWSON Robert	4-09-43	7 Sqn
133097	F/O	LAWTON Ernest Edward	29-06-43	97 Sqn
1216916	Sgt	LAX Eric	18-06-43	12 Sqn
573105	Sgt	LAX Frederick Thomas	3-02-43	15 Sqn
134183	F/O	LAXTON Charles Sidney	24-11-43	44 Sqn
987264	Sgt	LAY Henry Frederick Daniel	20-04-43	158 Sqn
1447813	Sgt	LAY Philip Maurice	2-10-43	15 OTU
1585575	Sgt	LAYBOURN George Wilfred	18-04-43	207 Sqn
1549850	Sgt	LAYCOCK Arthur L.	30-03-43	1651 HCU
1696963	AC1	LAYCOCK Jack Ezra	2-07-43	158 Sqn
1392825	Sgt	LAYCOCK Raymond Leon	14-03-43	9 Sqn
137342	P/O	LAYLEY Geoffrey Charles	27-01-43	218 Sqn
613142	Sgt	LAY-FLURRIE Frank George	12-06-43	158 Sqn
1611281	Sgt	LAZARUS Louis	3-10-43	18 OTU
1624263	Sgt	LEA James Frank	28-10-43	1656 HCU
577749	Sgt	LEA Roland William	2-10-43	57 Sqn
129599	F/O	LEA Ronald Percy	12-06-43	196 Sqn
109093	F/L	LEA DFC Thomas Sidney	21-04-43	77 Sqn
345474	Sgt	LEACH Charles Willis Eric	5-05-43	149 Sqn
1237320	Sgt	LEADBETTER Joseph	30-05-43	106 Sqn
625778	Sgt	LEADBITTER Leonard Arthur	5-03-43	106 Sqn
919585	Sgt	LEADER James Lionel	27-07-43	156 Sqn
21350	F/L	LEADER WILLIAMS Derek George	6-09-43	12 Sqn
149229	P/O	LEADLEY Thomas Jeffrey	31-08-43	15 Sqn
1194348	Sgt	LEAK Victor George	27-04-43	90 Sqn
1699563	Sgt	LEAKE Lawrence	14-05-43	214 Sqn
131903	P/O	LEAN Geoffrey William	23-01-43	15 OTU
1600961	Sgt	LEANEY Leonard Henry	5-05-43	57 Sqn
139408	P/O	LEAR Antony Frederick	25-02-43	106 Sqn
126018	F/O	LEAR Edward 'Teddy'	28-02-43	90 Sqn
135628	F/O	LEAR Kenneth Seymour	20-12-43	10 Sqn
1456975	Sgt	LEATHER Harold	3-05-43	81 OTU
1034351	Sgt	LEATHLEY William Trevor	21-04-43	90 Sqn
1393387	Sgt	LECOMBER Joseph Edward	14-05-43	83 Sqn
1478810	Sgt	LEDBURY William James	26-05-43	218 Sqn
128586	F/O	LEDDIMAN William Ernest	13-07-43	100 Sqn
1330439	Sgt	LEDGER Roy Victor	1-03-43	35 Sqn
1535227	Sgt	LEDSHAM Ronald	23-11-43	44 Sqn
961573	Sgt	LEE Alan William	12-06-43	12 Sqn
1134570	Sgt	LEE Arthur	24-08-43	78 Sqn
1535178	Sgt	LEE Clarence Norman	18-08-43	103 Sqn
1132944	Sgt	LEE Eric Markham	17-04-43	214 Sqn
1132146	Sgt	LEE Frank	12-06-43	158 Sqn
578282	Sgt	LEE Frederick Ernest	14-05-43	57 Sqn
921759	Sgt	LEE Geoffrey	31-08-43	102 Sqn
1316014	Sgt	LEE Gordon Stone	15-05-43	27 OTU
1638331	LAC	LEE Herbert	27-08-43	80 Wing
1217066	Sgt	LEE Jack	11-02-43	106 Sqn
1382920	Sgt	LEE John Patrick	28-07-43	12 Sqn
158711	P/O	LEE DFC Kenneth Reuben	22-10-43	103 Sqn
1623490	Sgt	LEE Leslie	26-11-43	1658 HCU
162786	P/O	LEE Peter Alan	2-12-43	550 Sqn
1289185	F/S	LEE Peter Edward	18-10-43	101 Sqn
804397	Sgt	LEE Reuben Frederick	5-10-43	434 Sqn
127921	F/O	LEE William George	5-03-43	420 Sqn
577037	Sgt	LEE William Tressillian	14-05-43	102 Sqn
1809766	Sgt	LEECH Charles Henry	18-10-43	103 Sqn
1453597	Sgt	LEEDHAM Geoffrey	7-09-43	77 Sqn
1169134	Sgt	LEEDHAM Geoffrey Ernest	24-05-43	101 Sqn
1291992	Sgt	LEEDHAM John	14-05-43	102 Sqn
157410	P/O	LEEDHAM William John	23-09-43	149 Sqn
1684485	Sgt	LEEMING John	8-09-43	103 Sqn
155018	P/O	LEEPER Robert Ernest	11-08-43	51 Sqn
1573459	Sgt	LEES Archibald Thomson	3-08-43	76 Sqn
1004486	Sgt	LEES Jack	21-04-43	7 Sqn
1058896	Sgt	LEES Kenneth Richard	11-2-43	106 Sqn
1578183	Sgt	LEES Peter	29-04-43	12 Sqn
572694	Sgt	LEES Peter Middleton	23-11-43	44 Sqn
1214347	Sgt	LEES Reginald George	29-09-43	16 OTU
131951	F/O	LEES Sydney	18-07-43	10 OTU
1870018	Sgt	LEEVES Eric Kenneth	3-10-43	90 Sqn
125695	F/L	LEE-BROWN Edward Claude	14-04-43	103 Sqn

1384549	Sgt	LEFORT Albert Edward	23-08-43	103 Sqn	1425912	Sgt	LEWIS Richard	26-05-43	77 Sqn
1287735	Sgt	LEGG Brian	4-05-43	78 Sqn	1719956	Sgt	LEWIS Robert Alfred	18-08-43	428 Sqn
539691	Sgt	LEGG Kenneth George	24-05-43	12 Sqn	1333112	Sgt	LEWIS Ronald Ernest	7-09-43	76 Sqn
571682	Sgt	LEGGOTT George	4-12-43	49 Sqn	161699	P/O	LEWIS Roy Arthur	2-12-43	57 Sqn
135451	P/O	LEIGH John Lewis	22-01-43	180 Sqn	1653157	Sgt	LEWIS Thomas George	30-07-43	214 Sqn
1077886	Sgt	LEIGH John Robert	5-05-43	83 Sqn	131994	P/O	LEWIS Thomas Glendenning Harries	24-05-43	49 Sqn
616090	Sgt	LEIGH Samuel	9-07-43	106 Sqn	1337949	Sgt	LEWIS Thomas Vardare	22-10-43	51 Sqn
1232161	Sgt	LEIGHTON George Kenneth	28-03-43	105 Sqn	1481299	F/S	LEWIS Trevor Washington	21-10-43	161 Sqn
1113522	Sgt	LEITCH Andrew Christie [Canada]	2-12-43	619 Sqn	570550	F/S	LEWIS DFM Vernon Charles	24-08-43	83 Sqn
1487121	Sgt	LEITH-ROSS Thomas	13-06-43	408 Sqn	1551000	Sgt	LEWIS William	17-01-43	101 Sqn
132410	P/O	LELEU James Frederick	7-04-43	9 Sqn	1490344	Sgt	LEWIS William Cecil	26-06-43	77 Sqn
1312026	Sgt	LENAHAN Dennis	15-04-43	149 Sqn	63071	S/L	LEWIS DFC William James	3-11-43	467 Sqn
143988	P/O	LENG Illtyd French	30-03-43	44 Sqn	909501		LEWIS-STANTIFORD Ronald Stanley Victor		
1323750	Sgt	LENNARD Frank	1-09-43	12 Sqn			(served as LEWIS)	30-03-43	408 Sqn
950013	Sgt	LENNOX George Len	28-04-43	75 Sqn	1435154	Sgt	LEYLAND Ronald	28-05-43	10 Sqn
149672	P/O	LENS Aubrey	24-08-43	75 Sqn	1147126	Sgt	LE HURAY Eric	17-09-43	158 Sqn
147224	P/O	LEONARD Antony Maynard	26-11-43	7 Sqn	577884	Sgt	LE PAGE Rex Lake [Channel Islands]	1-05-43	44 Sqn
1811706	Sgt	LEONARD Arthur Frederick Robert	4-07-43	90 Sqn	611624	Sgt	LIDDELL Harold	22-01-43	180 Sqn
122723	F/O	LEONARD Frank Redman	18-01-43	1654 HCU	1338282	Sgt	LIDDELL Jack Robert George	16-05-43	617 Sqn
1314807	Sgt	LEONARD Mervyn	21-04-43	90 Sqn	1390957	Sgt	LIDDLE George	25-06-43	432 Sqn
1678529	Sgt	LEONARD Thomas Marshall	18-08-43	115 Sqn	129581	F/O	LIDDLE Peter Harold [South Africa]	24-05-43	214 Sqn
1397923	Sgt	LEPETIT Ronald George	13-06-43	10 Sqn	1025185	Sgt	LIDSTER Eric	22-06-43	83 Sqn
657098	Sgt	LEPPARD Alan Charles	4-05-43	78 Sqn	653613	Sgt	LIGHTFOOT John Henry	9-01-43	44 Sqn
1551139	Sgt	LESLIE Alan Ramsay	23-05-43	57 Sqn	1477306	Sgt	LILLEY George Alfred	4-07-43	431 Sqn
1351975	Sgt	LESLIE Angus Earle	3-10-43	9 Sqn	1580187	Sgt	LILLEY Herbert Walter	13-08-43	420 Sqn
155934	P/O	LESLIE David Bruce	1-09-43	51 Sqn	1391041	Sgt	LILLEY James Charles	29-04-43	103 Sqn
1214074	Sgt	LESTER Albert Eric	24-08-43	78 Sqn	1387539	Sgt	LILLYMAN Bernard	23-07-43	24 OTU
338714	Sgt	LESTER John Finsterbush	24-05-43	44 Sqn	1354876	Sgt	LILLYWHITE DFM Ronald Frank	2-02-43	102 Sqn
1098112	Sgt	LESTER Ralph Thomas Gurden	9-10-43	106 Sqn	1187598	Sgt	LIMBRICK Arthur Moseley	20-02-43	90 Sqn
1389462	Sgt	LETBE Thomas James	11-04-43	15 Sqn	946593	Sgt	LINACRE Jack	5-03-43	466 Sqn
1315524	Sgt	LETHERBARROW Edward John	11-04-43	75 Sqn	1386011	Sgt	LIND Norman Ernest	29-04-43	12 Sqn
128953	F/O	LETTERS Robert William John	30-05-43	90 Sqn	123960	F/L	LIND Robert Frood	29-01-43	9 Sqn
946122	Sgt	LETTS Leslie	31-08-43	77 Sqn	1063005	Sgt	LINGARD Derek	24-06-43	10 OTU
1077731	Sgt	LEVEN William	13-05-43	428 Sqn	1261280	Sgt	LINDLEY John	25-06-43	620 Sqn
1601778	Sgt	LEVER Neville Alfred	26-03-43	460 Sqn	1585760	Sgt	LINDREA John Desmond	21-04-43	90 Sqn
118166	F/O	LEVERONI John Emile [Eire]	23-09-43	15 OTU	106366	F/L	LINDSAY Bruce Keith	28-01-43	102 Sqn
1577248	Sgt	LEVERTON Dennis George	18-07-43	1661 HCU	532556	Sgt	LINDSAY Harold	27-09-43	434 Sqn
142513	P/O	LEVI Frederick Howard	4-07-43	466 Sqn	131905	F/O	LINDSEY Leopold Ernest	27-04-43	156 Sqn
658831	Sgt	LEVINE Hyman	25-06-43	90 Sqn	1817558	Sgt	LINE Austin Raymond	24-08-43	115 Sqn
1077553	Sgt	LEVINS George	10-04-43	426 Sqn	1815307	Sgt	LINEHAM William Alf	29-09-43	156 Sqn
658924	Sgt	LEVITUS Sydney	13-04-43	81 OTU	1383508	F/S	LINEHAN Cornelius Charles	22-11-43	77 Sqn
127244	F/O	LEVY Paul Albert	28-08-43	57 Sqn	1239286	Sgt	LINEKER Ivan Wildman	3-01-43	207 Sqn
1402321	Sgt	LEWINGDON Christopher John	11-08-43	158 Sqn	133727	F/O	LINFORD Jack Victor	2-10-43	44 Sqn
1153956	Sgt	LEWINGTON Leslie Owen	6-07-43	75 Sqn	1171532	Sgt	LING Donald Robert	20-04-43	100 Sqn
946288	F/S	LEWIS Alun Gwyn	11-04-43	429 Sqn	573996	Sgt	LINGWOOD Leslie David	15-03-43	78 Sqn
1387933	Sgt	LEWIS Alun Oliver	17-04-43	51 Sqn	51295	P/O	LINKLATER DFM Ian Alistair Hardy	12-03-43	207 Sqn
1193204	F/S	LEWIS Arthur Rupert	9-04-43	207 Sqn	1569397	Sgt	LINTERN Henry Rose	17-12-43	101 Sqn
969331	Sgt	LEWIS Brynley Edmond	29-06-43	97 Sqn	1383809	F/S	LIPSHITZ DFM Arthur	23-12-43	15 OTU
575832	Sgt	LEWIS Clifford Howard	2-03-43	50 Sqn	1397331	Sgt	LIPTROTT Edward Jack	1-09-43	51 Sqn
1581747	Sgt	LEWIS Dennis Mansell	29-06-43	44 Sqn	1385054	Sgt	LISSNER Peter Richard	4-07-43	35 Sqn
1414771	Sgt	LEWIS Desmond	27-01-43	429 Sqn	1504644	Sgt	LISTER David Blackburn	11-01-43	81 OTU
1097776	Sgt	LEWIS Eric	21-04-43	149 Sqn	136878	F/O	LISTER Dennis	2-07-43	29 OTU
573570	Sgt	LEWIS George Edward	30-03-43	460 Sqn	131168	F/L	LISTER Eric Leslie	4-12-43	431 Sqn
1230404	Sgt	LEWIS George Raymond	22-03-43	101 Sqn	1064071	Sgt	LISTER George Pearson	27-05-43	105 Sqn
1080678	Sgt	LEWIS Harry	26-07-43	156 Sqn	776126	Sgt	LITCHFIELD Edwin Giles	27-04-43	429 Sqn
130701	F/O	LEWIS Herbert Frank	15-06-43	103 Sqn			[Middle East]		
1312584	Sgt	LEWIS Herbert James	8-10-43	97 Sqn	979995	Sgt	LITOLFF Bernard Leo	12-03-43	207 Sqn
1314450	F/S	LEWIS Islwyn	16-12-43	115 Sqn	127796	F/O	LITTELL Lemuel George	1-02-43	226 Sqn
139836	P/O	LEWIS Ivor Rees	13-08-43	166 Sqn	1365959	Sgt	LITTLE Alexander	3-01-43	24 OTU
41035	F/L	LEWIS Jack Maurice	18-08-43	102 Sqn	1398493	Sgt	LITTLE David Henry William	26-11-43	97 Sqn
129357	F/O	LEWIS James Edgar	25-06-43	102 Sqn	37573	W/C	LITTLE DFC Three times MiD Edwin John		
1283419	Sgt	LEWIS Jenkin Gildas	18-06-43	12 Sqn				1-09-43	623 Sqn
1526100	Sgt	LEWIS John	31-07-43	76 Sqn	984813	Sgt	LITTLE John	2-03-43	44 Sqn
109536	F/O	LEWIS John Clifford North	2-05-43	24 OTU	1126807	Sgt	LITTLE John	2-03-43	97 Sqn
1260659	Sgt	LEWIS Leonard James	23-11-43	207 Sqn	932521	W/O	LITTLE John Frederick	30-08-43	139 Sqn
1394840	Sgt	LEWIS Louis Montague	30-08-43	26 OTU	1294785	Sgt	LITTLEFAIR Robert William	13-05-43	106 Sqn
1315566	Sgt	LEWIS Malcolm Harold Victor	7-04-43	166 Sqn	1268196	Sgt	LITTLEHALES Reginald	3-11-43	625 Sqn
540757	Sgt	LEWIS DFM Ralph [Australia]	7-02-43	158 Sqn	1670565	Sgt	LITTLEWOOD Denys	26-05-43	214 Sqn
1380317	Sgt	LEWIS Reginald Lawrence	12-06-43	460 Sqn	1028329	Sgt	LIVERMORE Reginald Ernest	25-07-43	51 Sqn

Service No	Rank	Name	Date	Unit
1352400	F/S	LIVESEY Joseph	24-06-43	192 Sqn
1330159	Sgt	LIVETT George Alfred	22-06-43	83 Sqn
1346263	Sgt	LIVINGSTON David	5-02-43	50 Sqn
1125844	Sgt	LLEWELLYN Idris	31-08-43	196 Sqn
1338144	Sgt	LLEWELLYN Idrys Wyn Lloyd	3-04-43	101 Sqn
540353	Sgt	LLEWELLYN Sidney	15-01-43	158 Sqn
131972	P/O	LLEWELYN Dilwyn	27-01-43	21 OTU
1304616	Sgt	LLOYD Albert Eric	24-08-43	90 Sqn
1112720	Sgt	LLOYD David Allen	18-08-43	419 Sqn
1716135	Sgt	LLOYD Glyn Weatherley	9-07-43	101 Sqn
1332039	Sgt	LLOYD Griffith Arthur	18-02-43	419 Sqn
1058003	Sgt	LLOYD Harry	4-04-43	460 Sqn
1716240	Sgt	LLOYD Henry Alexander	12-07-43	1656 HCU
147904	P/O	LLOYD Henry Simon Raoul	30-05-43	466 Sqn
621384	Sgt	LLOYD Herbert	30-05-43	149 Sqn
1586374	Sgt	LLOYD James Thomas	29-06-43	207 Sqn
1816030	Sgt	LLOYD Kenneth	26-06-43	61 Sqn
122507	F/O	LLOYD Michael	22-10-43	12 Sqn
130016	F/O	LLOYD Neville Mellor	14-09-43	61 Sqn
1863637	Sgt	LLOYD Ronald	27-11-43	626 Sqn
654033	Sgt	LLOYD Stanley	7-09-43	427 Sqn
979965	Sgt	LLOYD Thomas Evan	24-06-43	218 Sqn
1813938	Sgt	LLOYD William Eric	23-11-43	100 Sqn
983952	Sgt	LOACH Kenneth [USA]	3-02-43	106 Sqn
1038226	Sgt	LOAR Victor	31-01-43	97 Sqn
1399459	Sgt	LOBB Robert	27-07-43	156 Sqn
1361506	F/S	LOCHHEAD John Campbell	4-12-43	429 Sqn
1271461	Sgt	LOCK Benjamin Charles	3-03-43	15 OTU
1801878	Sgt	LOCK David	4-07-43	158 Sqn
1317140	F/S	LOCK Leslie George Kitchener	4-12-43	97 Sqn
1142645	Sgt	LOCKEY George	23-06-43	75 Sqn
130280	F/O	LOCKIE George	13-07-43	49 Sqn
143389	P/O	LOCKSMITH George William	13-05-43	51 Sqn
1040500	Sgt	LOCKWOOD Charles Thomas	3-10-43	102 Sqn
143430	P/O	LOCKWOOD John Norman	28-05-43	467 Sqn
940414	Sgt	LODGE Maurice Albert	25-07-43	103 Sqn
983568	Sgt	LOFTHOUSE John Donald	7-08-43	9 Sqn
655598	F/S	LOFTHOUSE Maurice William	3-02-43	102 Sqn
1600812	Sgt	LOFTUS Thomas Henry	18-07-43	1661 HCU
778801	Sgt	LOGIE Frank [Rhodesia]	18-01-43	467 Sqn
1575942	Sgt	LOKE Thomas Harold	1-09-43	620 Sqn
1077211	F/S	LOMAS Kenneth	22-11-43	10 Sqn
149948	P/O	LONG Arthur John Echlin	18-08-43	10 Sqn
1332091	Sgt	LONG Charles Alexander	14-07-43	90 Sqn
40722	S/L	LONG DFC AFC Donald George	31-01-43	57 Sqn
1335994	Sgt	LONG Francis Albert	4-12-43	431 Sqn
1081853	Sgt	LONG Joseph Sidney	7-10-43	15 Sqn
1324064	Sgt	LONG Kenneth Hughes	5-03-43	29 OTU
126471	F/O	LONG Lewis Charles	12-06-43	431 Sqn
988528	Sgt	LONG Norman	5-05-43	57 Sqn
916450	Sgt	LONG Sydney Robert	31-07-43	15 Sqn
1600540	Sgt	LONG William Charles Arthur	17-05-43	617 Sqn
27229	W/C	LONGFIELD Geoffrey Phelps	26-02-43	105 Sqn
49736	F/O	LONGHORN DFM Robert Henry	22-01-43	180 Sqn
1283056	Sgt	LONGLEY Charles Henry	1-05-43	51 Sqn
1602674	Sgt	LONGMAN Leslie Wilfred	3-10-43	90 Sqn
546539	Sgt	LONGSTER Robert Elston	12-06-43	100 Sqn
1538877	Sgt	LONGWORTH Alfred	3-10-43	17 OTU
61283	F/L	LONSDALE DFC Douglas Herbert Scott	3-01-43	9 Sqn
658361	W/O	LOOP DFC David Halstead	18-10-43	103 Sqn
1395954	Sgt	LOOSE Reginald Victor	4-04-43	158 Sqn
152720	P/O	LORRIMORE James Wallace	29-12-43	30 OTU
1004605	Sgt	LOUDON Arthur	11-04-43	15 Sqn
1198324	Sgt	LOUTH William Robert	1-05-43	77 Sqn
1123009	Sgt	LOVATT Leslie Sutcliffe	3-02-43	21 Sqn
1290988	Sgt	LOVE Geoffrey Spencer	11-03-43	44 Sqn
1552158	F/S	LOVE Hugh	17-06-43	156 Sqn
1811507	Sgt	LOVEGROVE Frank Edward	28-10-43	1656 HCU
577026	Sgt	LOVELADY Douglas William	12-03-43	1661 HCU
1318280	Sgt	LOVELAND Donald Stephen	15-07-43	158 Sqn
1324523	Sgt	LOVELL Bernard Desmond	22-10-43	7 Sqn
50667	P/O	LOVELL Derek Graham	12-03-43	83 Sqn
1320899	F/S	LOVELL Eric James	23-11-43	218 Sqn
1582638	Sgt	LOVELOCK James Henry	20-10-43	405 Sqn
1388965	Sgt	LOVERIDGE Gilbert Dalton	3-08-43	214 Sqn
950159	Sgt	LOVEROCK Edward John	18-02-43	61 Sqn
1198322	Sgt	LOVERSEED Richard Bruce	13-05-43	57 Sqn
1458314	Sgt	LOVESAY Allan George	26-11-43	101 Sqn
1333957	Sgt	LOVEWELL Jack Edmond	16-08-43	75 Sqn
1379210	W/O	LOVIS DFC John Alfred Cronin	22-11-43	156 Sqn
1290929	Sgt	LOWDELL James Stephen	12-03-43	102 Sqn
28252	G/C	LOWE Brian Everard	18-07-43	1485 Flt
657721	Sgt	LOWE Evan Robert	24-08-43	218 Sqn
115129	F/O	LOWE DFC Harold	3-02-43	75 Sqn
657928	Sgt	LOWE James William	3-05-43	487 Sqn
1497432	Sgt	LOWE John William	24-08-43	101 Sqn
916013	Sgt	LOWE Joseph	2-10-43	619 Sqn
1218582	Sgt	LOWE Peter	18-08-43	467 Sqn
658480	Sgt	LOWE Robert	26-05-43	166 Sqn
1683548	Sgt	LOWE William	1-09-43	623 Sqn
1479071	Sgt	LOWE William Ewart	26-11-43	429 Sqn
1288402	Sgt	LOWER Alfred William Nelson	20-10-43	100 Sqn
155010	P/O	LOWERY James Harold	24-08-43	78 Sqn
1515134	Sgt	LOWEY Walter Harvey	30-05-43	1651 HCU
1322699	Sgt	LOWINGS Jack Louis Stanley	28-05-43	102 Sqn
1485071	Sgt	LOWIS Charles	4-05-43	78 Sqn
148179	P/O	LOWRIE James	22-06-43	149 Sqn
1321590	Sgt	LOWRY Peter Sydney	19-11-43	431 Sqn
1502000	LAC	LOWRY Robert	12-05-43	1658 HCU
1380534	Sgt	LOWTHER Richard William	11-04-43	75 Sqn
1673273	Sgt	LUCAS Alan	24-08-43	426 Sqn
1135766	Sgt	LUCAS Arthur	30-03-43	196 Sqn
1388785	Sgt	LUCAS Arthur James Wadd	28-09-43	428 Sqn
1431954	Sgt	LUCAS Charles Philip	6-07-43	1660 HCU
1081361	Sgt	LUCAS David	29-09-43	419 Sqn
1814763	Sgt	LUCAS Frederick John	31-08-43	218 Sqn
975066	Sgt	LUCAS DFM George Emile Garton	26-11-43	106 Sqn
1250557	Sgt	LUCAS George William Thomas	1-12-43	75 Sqn
1536584	Sgt	LUCAS Leonard	18-08-43	61 Sqn
1800889	Sgt	LUCKETT Frederick John	28-09-43	1664 HCU
1812408	Sgt	LUCY Thomas James	24-08-43	149 Sqn
1323682	Sgt	LUDBROOK William George	3-03-43	106 Sqn
1333442	F/S	LUDGATE Arthur Charles	13-08-43	420 Sqn
128653	F/O	LUDLOW Arthur Ronald	13-07-43	44 Sqn
47914	F/O	LUFF Edmund	5-03-43	156 Sqn
632405	Sgt	LUFF George	12-06-43	51 Sqn
1350846	Sgt	LUKE Albert George	2-12-43	626 Sqn
1339381	Sgt	LUKE Anthony	21-04-43	77 Sqn
1380482	Sgt	LUKE Sydney Charles	30-05-43	466 Sqn
1271876	F/S	LULHAM Reginald Bertram Sidney	16-09-43	617 Sqn
646710	Sgt	LUMLEY John Godfrey	17-06-43	156 Sqn
128373	F/O	LUMLEY Michael Hope	13-01-43	106 Sqn
534284	Sgt	LUNN John Wilson [Canada]	3-08-43	428 Sqn
1603982	Sgt	LUNN Sidney James	20-12-43	149 Sqn
1167033	Sgt	LUNN Thomas Reginald	22-06-43	218 Sqn
52039	F/O	LUNNISS Robert Henry Herbert	20-12-43	466 Sqn
125539	F/O	LUPTON Selwyn Jaques	16-04-43	166 Sqn
633691	Sgt	LUPTON Sydney	13-05-43	61 Sqn
1330619	Sgt	LUSCOMBE Percival Harold	3-03-43	115 Sqn
1170005	Sgt	LUSCOMBE Thomas Henry	3-04-43	166 Sqn
1376013	F/S	LUSH Albert Leonard	4-04-43	464 Sqn
1338934	Sgt	LUTHER Terence Wilfred Charles	23-06-43	77 Sqn
125696	F/O	LUTHER Wallace Clifford [Newfoundland]	29-05-43	158 Sqn
132180	P/O	LUTON DFC Ronald Stockwell	12-03-43	7 Sqn
1235760	Sgt	LUTWYCHE Percy	8-04-43	15 Sqn
1622053	Sgt	LUXFORD Alan George	16-08-43	57 Sqn

Service No	Rank	Name	Date	Sqn
1086977	Sgt	LUXTON John Russell	12-08-43	76 Sqn
1285678	Sgt	LYALL Richard	13-01-43	12 Sqn
649159	Sgt	LYE Mervyn Courtney	22-10-43	100 Sqn
1384157	Sgt	LYGO Henry John	11-06-43	207 Sqn
1231203	Sgt	LYLE Leslie Holden	8-06-43	16 OTU
937541	Sgt	LYNAM Percy	11-08-43	9 Sqn
1001787	F/S	LYNCH DFM Alexander	11-03-43	83 Sqn
999000	F/S	LYNCH James	28-07-43	100 Sqn
1561219	Sgt	LYNCH John	17-12-43	138 Sqn
904871	Sgt	LYNCH Martin John	27-11-43	619 Sqn
131908	F/O	LYNCH Paul	28-07-43	12 Sqn
125540	F/O	LYNE Donald Harrison	22-06-43	149 Sqn
1336379	Sgt	LYNN Ronald William	5-05-43	196 Sqn
1615745	Sgt	LYNN Walter Stanley	28-08-43	57 Sqn
1336486	Sgt	LYON Anthony Jules Lawson	5-05-43	101 Sqn
143403	P/O	LYON Philip Grenville	11-03-43	158 Sqn
130633	F/O	LYON Richard	3-08-43	61 Sqn
1265233	Sgt	LYONS Geoffrey	14-01-43	9 Sqn
924920	Sgt	LYONS Peter John	9-10-43	12 Sqn
1802900	Sgt	LYSAGHT Joseph George	20-07-43	1662 HCU
1090703	Sgt	LYSTER Roland Felix [Eire]	20-04-43	51 Sqn
1129954	Sgt	LYTHGOE Leslie George	3-08-43	432 Sqn
1562678	Sgt	L'ARGENT John George	4-12-43	431 Sqn
1096832	Sgt	MABEN William Snowball	28-07-43	106 Sqn
581232	Sgt	MacANINCH Hugh Caven	18-08-43	44 Sqn
127172	F/O	MacDONALD Ian Roy	16-12-43	7 Sqn
1365713	Sgt	MacDONALD James Jenkins	25-06-43	102 Sqn
1199028	Sgt	MacDONALD Joseph Mannix	10-07-43	408 Sqn
1295086	Sgt	MacDONALD William Henry	23-09-43	103 Sqn
126044	F/O	MacFARLANE Richard	20-12-43	617 Sqn
1558318	Sgt	MacINTYRE Andrew	25-11-43	28 OTU
43706	S/L	MacKENZIE DFC Donald Carr [New Zealand]	12-06-43	467 Sqn
82671	S/L	MacKENZIE DFC Donald Forbes	17-12-43	97 Sqn
1367215	Sgt	MacKENZIE Gordon William	3-08-43	61 Sqn
1557233	F/S	MacKINLEY William Buthart	4-10-43	156 Sqn
121205	F/L	MacLACHLAN DFC Alastair Robert Anderson	7-09-43	156 Sqn
1330142	Sgt	MacLEAN Clement	3-10-43	467 Sqn
1545886	Sgt	MacLEAN David	2-10-43	51 Sqn
541514	Sgt	MacLEOD Neil	4-04-43	149 Sqn
1558645	Sgt	MacLEAY Farquhar	26-06-43	101 Sqn
1587745	Sgt	MacNISH PORTER John Anthony	22-10-43	207 Sqn
1116913	F/S	MacPHEDRAN James Cumming	26-05-43	51 Sqn
1573466	Sgt	MacRAE Duncan Hugh Cameron	31-07-43	44 Sqn
1560316	Sgt	MacRITCHIE Malcolm John	22-09-43	9 Sqn
1582436	Sgt	MacWILLIAM Robert Blair [Brazil]	27-01-43	106 Sqn
1347046	Sgt	MACADAM John Swanson	14-05-43	10 Sqn
656568	Sgt	MACAULAY Cecil Hill	1-09-43	158 Sqn
1324876	Sgt	MACAULEY Frederick Norman	22-10-43	103 Sqn
1340793	Sgt	MACAULAY Wilfred Chalmers	23-06-43	15 Sqn
980916	Sgt	MACDONALD Arthur	11-06-43	467 Sqn
1578548	Sgt	MACDONALD Derrick William	24-08-43	115 Sqn
139297	F/O	MACDONALD Duncan	18-11-43	9 Sqn
610265	Sgt	MACDONALD Frederick	2-03-43	408 Sqn
132735	P/O	MACDONALD Hamish Turner	3-04-43	419 Sqn
948318	LAC	MACDONALD James Alexander	2-07-43	620 Sqn
1369115	Sgt	MACDONALD James Smith	23-09-43	78 Sqn
156663	P/O	MACDONALD Joseph Widger Murphy	1-09-43	1654 HCU
1349985	Sgt	MACDONALD Samuel	28-08-43	103 Sqn
1225368	Sgt	MACE John Rust	14-02-43	158 Sqn
1803191	Sgt	MACE Leslie Reginald	9-12-43	77 Sqn
566978	Sgt	MACFARLANE James	12-03-43	83 Sqn
142540	P/O	MACFARLANE William	17-04-43	61 Sqn
1604641	Sgt	MACHAN Raymond John Kellett [South Africa]	22-10-43	76 Sqn
1166970	Sgt	MACHIN Harry	1-09-43	12 Sqn
134567	F/O	MACHIN Leonard William	25-07-43	103 Sqn
873863	Sgt	MACINTYRE Alexander John	19-12-43	138 Sqn
148279	P/O	MACINTYRE John Francis Bell	18-08-43	12 Sqn
1183352	F/S	MACK Arthur Cyril	22-07-43	27 OTU
91224	S/L	MACK DFC Michael Charles Xavier	24-08-43	35 Sqn
131976	F/O	MACKAY Alexander	29-06-43	619 Sqn
1559316	Sgt	MACKAY Archibald Ian	21-04-43	103 Sqn
126037	P/O	MACKAY George	3-04-43	83 Sqn
1567819	Sgt	MACKAY James	26-11-43	57 Sqn
659021	Sgt	MACKAY Neil	18-11-43	115 Sqn
125698	F/O	MACKELDEN Frank	12-06-43	466 Sqn
971820	Sgt	MACKENZIE Alexander	27-03-43	156 Sqn
149962	P/O	MACKENZIE David	3-08-43	9 Sqn
1347924	Sgt	MACKENZIE Donald	22-11-43	10 Sqn
123952	F/O	MACKENZIE Ian Fraser	27-04-43	90 Sqn
119333	F/O	MACKENZIE James Noble	25-06-43	51 Sqn
1821945	Sgt	MACKENZIE Kenneth	22-09-43	12 OTU
1355437	Sgt	MACKENZIE Matthew Walker	12-03-43	405 Sqn
135885	F/O	MACKENZIE Roderick Alexander	15-08-43	138 Sqn
1391917	Sgt	MACKINTOSH Edward Donald Charles	4-07-43	158 Sqn
1430161	Sgt	MACKINTOSH John	29-04-43	12 Sqn
40727	S/L	MACKINTOSH John Cameron	17-06-43	156 Sqn
1515864	Sgt	MACKINTOSH Kenneth	26-05-43	166 Sqn
959456	Sgt	MACKLIN William Henry	19-02-43	15 Sqn
1620313	Sgt	MACKRELL Sidney	1-09-43	622 Sqn
1261086	Sgt	MACLAREN William Finlay	29-09-43	158 Sqn
125300	F/O	MACLEAN DFC Ian	14-09-43	138 Sqn
950711	Sgt	MACLEOD Alister Campbell	22-06-43	35 Sqn
81062	F/L	MACLEOD DFC Arthur George	20-10-43	7 Sqn
1366232	F/S	MACMILLAN John	25-06-43	106 Sqn
1508454	Sgt	MACNEALL Joseph	30-03-43	1483 Flt
1331712	F/S	MACQUARIE Thomas Albert	30-07-43	102 Sqn
111483	F/L	MACQUEEN DFC Alexander Fraser	12-03-43	83 Sqn
124539	F/L	MACPHERSON DFM Alexander Niven	24-08-43	83 Sqn
140922	F/O	MACPHERSON Bruce Edwin Cornwall [Canada]	9-10-43	7 Sqn
115553	F/O	MACPHERSON Colin Jesse	26-11-43	102 Sqn
1115141	Sgt	MACPHERSON Finlay	26-11-43	76 Sqn
1553551	Sgt	MACRAE Ian	25-06-43	78 Sqn
1394138	Sgt	MACSWAYNE Leslie Thomas	20-10-43	90 Sqn
1552454	Sgt	MACTAVISH Claud Gordon Humphrey	4-02-43	90 Sqn
1365036	Sgt	MACTIER David Henry	9-04-43	9 Sqn
112021	F/L	MACWATT Ian Fraser [Canada]	11-08-43	158 Sqn
1355158	Sgt	MADDAFORD Leslie Thomas Christian	13-08-43	619 Sqn
1216741	Sgt	MADDEN Frederick	9-10-43	78 Sqn
137176	F/O	MADDEX John Douglas	17-11-43	166 Sqn
1135821	Sgt	MADDISON Amos Ryder	14-01-43	426 Sqn
635352	Sgt	MADDOCK James Edward	2-08-43	57 Sqn
1600507	Sgt	MADDOCKS George Samuel	30-07-43	57 Sqn
1696999	Sgt	MADELEY Leonard	17-12-43	97 Sqn
1237419	Sgt	MADEN John	15-08-43	138 Sqn
147519	P/O	MADGETT DFM Hedley Robert	18-08-43	61 Sqn
1384719	Sgt	MAGILL Alfred Benjamin	12-06-43	100 Sqn
1581919	Sgt	MAGSON Edmund	23-09-43	149 Sqn
614099	F/S	MAGUIRE Austin Gabriel [Eire]	3-04-43	50 Sqn
549483	Sgt	MAHER Michael	16-12-43	408 Sqn
1511663	Sgt	MAHER William Patrick [Eire]	23-09-43	419 Sqn
129466	F/L	MAHONEY John Philip	24-08-43	101 Sqn
577547	Sgt	MAHONY John Desmond [Eire]	13-05-43	77 Sqn
1381950	Sgt	MAHONY John Frederick Hamilton	9-01-43	14 OTU
1483123	Sgt	MAIDMENT Leslie Edward	28-07-43	78 Sqn
1045726	Sgt	MAILEY Richard	4-07-43	214 Sqn
149352	P/O	MAIR Arthur	8-10-43	9 Sqn
1366952	Sgt	MAIR George Derrick	1-09-43	90 Sqn
134184	F/O	MAIR Robert Edward	23-11-43	207 Sqn
625386	Sgt	MAIRS Thomas	14-03-43	138 Sqn

Service No	Rank	Name	Date	Sqn
999158	Sgt	MAISNER Stanley	22-06-43	100 Sqn
1335760	Sgt	MAITLAND Hugh	12-08-43	620 Sqn
1336854	Sgt	MAJOR Gordon Cecil	11-08-43	57 Sqn
141709	P/O	MAJOR Wilfred Roy	26-02-43	1657 HCU
128577	F/O	MAKIN Dennis	26-05-43	199 Sqn
625581	Sgt	MALCOLM James Berkley	22-09-43	218 Sqn
1315318	Sgt	MALE Gerald Arthur Harold	23-06-43	207 Sqn
1577515	Sgt	MALE Hugh Millett	28-08-43	10 OTU
1577578	Sgt	MALLABER John	23-09-43	97 Sqn
652146	F/S	MALLETT DFM Charles Lucas	26-06-43	106 Sqn
1456067	Sgt	MALLEY Donald George	28-08-43	15 Sqn
941933	Sgt	MALLIN Ernest	9-10-43	12 Sqn
1245952	F/S	MALLIN DFM James Henry	3-11-43	467 Sqn
1207245	Sgt	MALPASS John	25-06-43	156 Sqn
1055780	Sgt	MALTBY Charles	14-05-43	10 Sqn
60335	S/L	MALTBY DSO DFC David John Hatfield	15-09-43	617 Sqn
41443	S/L	MANAHAN DFC James Ross [Canada]	12-06-43	100 Sqn
990668	Sgt	MANDERSON James	21-10-43	83 Sqn
1238240	Sgt	MANDY Vincent	20-12-43	149 Sqn
50977	F/O	MANIFOLD Norman	30-07-43	156 Sqn
1410557	Sgt	MANLEY Frederick John	24-12-43	156 Sqn
1490978	Sgt	MANLEY George Heathcote	24-11-43	1658 HCU
1210634	Sgt	MANLEY Leonard Francis	23-09-43	77 Sqn
158249	P/O	MANN Arthur	2-12-43	207 Sqn
1437312	Sgt	MANN Durston	23-06-43	427 Sqn
1199260	F/S	MANN John James	5-11-43	61 Sqn
1509131	Sgt	MANN John William	1-11-43	19 OTU
657260	Sgt	MANN Peter	23-09-43	57 Sqn
126960	F/O	MANNING Albert John	23-06-43	427 Sqn
148492	P/O	MANNING Cecil Walter Alvin	18-08-43	12 Sqn
149484	P/O	MANNING James Edward Albert Power	13-07-43	50 Sqn
1320934	Sgt	MANNING Leslie Percy	15-01-43	161 Sqn
139637	F/O	MANNING DFC Peter William	17-08-43	405 Sqn
1300611	Sgt	MANNING William Alfred	28-05-43	77 Sqn
1190925	Sgt	MANSELL John George Herbert	10-07-43	102 Sqn
1385811	Sgt	MANSFIELD John James	23-06-43	97 Sqn
925934	F/S	MANSFIELD Peter Lawford	11-04-43	50 Sqn
1068163	Sgt	MANSLEY John Kenneth	1-05-43	57 Sqn
1291991	Sgt	MANTELL Eric Charles	8-01-43	50 Sqn
141279	P/O	MANTLE DFM* Eric Harry	30-03-43	106 Sqn
39599	S/L	MANTON Richard John	20-10-43	83 Sqn
1691966	Sgt	MANUEL Charles Lewis	22-06-43	57 Sqn
124457	F/O	MAPPIN Howard	22-06-43	83 Sqn
655660	Sgt	MARCHANT William Bunney	23-09-43	100 Sqn
1152393	Sgt	MARFLEET Stanley Mordaunt	7-05-43	29 OTU
1335003	Sgt	MARGERUM Charles Alfred	28-04-43	101 Sqn
1336916	Sgt	MARGETSON George Sydney	9-03-43	207 Sqn
161356	P/O	MARKHAM Frank	18-11-43	623 Sqn
55012	F/O	MARKS Bertie James	24-12-43	576 Sqn
148897	P/O	MARKS DFM Douglas James	30-07-43	97 Sqn
161746	P/O	MARKS Robert Philip	16-12-43	426 Sqn
1370445	Sgt	MARKS Sydney John	1-09-43	622 Sqn
1395042	Sgt	MARLIN Cecil George Lewin	30-03-43	44 Sqn
1199710	Sgt	MARLOW Arthur	27-02-43	427 Sqn
1353768	Sgt	MARLOW John Leslie	16-04-43	75 Sqn
1177760	Sgt	MARLOW Wilfred	2-08-43	57 Sqn
129522	F/O	MARNOCH James Murray	26-05-43	100 Sqn
1095055	Sgt	MARR Cyril	14-04-43	429 Sqn
1223111	Sgt	MARRIOTT Donald Alfred	2-06-43	24 OTU
1003474	Sgt	MARRIOTT DFM John	17-05-43	617 Sqn
119348	F/L	MARRIOTT DFM Philoip Samuel	11-03-43	15 OTU
129617	F/O	MARRIOTT Robert	10-03-43	10 OTU
1458137	Sgt	MARSDEN Denis	15-02-43	28 OTU
156915	F/O	MARSDEN James	23-11-43	44 Sqn
1218635	F/S	MARSDEN James Arthur	25-06-43	102 Sqn
568415	Sgt	MARSDEN Ronald	17-05-43	617 Sqn
127010	F/O	MARSDEN William Allan	24-05-43	44 Sqn
1322114	Sgt	MARSH Alan Claude	10-08-43	102 Sqn
542744	Sgt	MARSH Albert William	22-09-43	207 Sqn
107993	F/O	MARSH DFC Alfred Beazley	4-04-43	156 Sqn
1324504	Sgt	MARSH Charles Kenneth	23-08-43	106 Sqn
162788	P/O	MARSH Eric George James	27-09-43	10 Sqn
1303848	F/S	MARSH Frederick Cecil	18-01-43	100 Sqn
1080667	Sgt	MARSH Joseph	14-07-43	35 Sqn
1312151	Sgt	MARSH Wilfrid Charles	21-04-43	102 Sqn
1339165	W/O	MARSHALL Alan Matthew	18-10-43	7 Sqn
1339496	Sgt	MARSHALL Alexander John	22-05-43	431 Sqn
1366808	Sgt	MARSHALL Andrew Heriot	30-07-43	100 Sqn
1575371	F/S	MARSHALL Angus Herbert	31-07-43	78 Sqn
159048	P/O	MARSHALL Barrington Horsfield	22-10-43	158 Sqn
1074162	Sgt	MARSHALL Bernard	30-07-43	156 Sqn
111112	F/L	MARSHALL Colin Carswell	23-06-43	77 Sqn
134371	F/O	MARSHALL Geoffrey Lawrence	14-09-43	139 Sqn
1096252	Sgt	MARSHALL George	1-03-43	15 OTU
983679	Sgt	MARSHALL Leonard	28-05-43	35 Sqn
549755	Sgt	MARSHALL Norman	31-01-43	106 Sqn
817293	Sgt	MARSHALL Norman	29-04-43	90 Sqn
147956	P/O	MARSHALL Oswald Peter	16-07-43	78 Sqn
1550307	Sgt	MARSHALL Robert	17-12-43	138 Sqn
1380401	Sgt	MARSHALL Stanley Wallis	8-02-43	10 OTU
39618	S/L	MARSHALL Thomas Bingham	14-05-43	431 Sqn
1214303	Sgt	MARSLAND Albert Edgar 'Arthur'	16-12-43	49 Sqn
127310	F/O	MARSLAND Kenneth	29-06-43	424 Sqn
1289368	Sgt	MARSON Wilfred Henry	3-11-43	49 Sqn
1210368	Sgt	MARTIN Alan Edward	13-04-43	81 OTU
656129	Sgt	MARTIN Bernard	29-01-43	166 Sqn
1576759	Sgt	MARTIN Charles Frederick	27-11-43	626 Sqn
1382408	Sgt	MARTIN Denys Philip	24-08-43	78 Sqn
1393417	Sgt	MARTIN Deryk Bramley	20-04-43	51 Sqn
1810891	Sgt	MARTIN Douglas George Gordon	8-04-43	1654 HCU
1577953	Sgt	MARTIN Frederick Harry	12-06-43	100 Sqn
1551120	Sgt	MARTIN George Ladly	20-12-43	156 Sqn
1320191	Sgt	MARTIN Harold James	7-02-43	425 Sqn
1127476	F/S	MARTIN Harry	20-06-43	10 OTU
143898	P/O	MARTIN James	13-02-43	12 Sqn
1479054	Sgt	MARTIN James Patrick	22-06-43	15 Sqn
1100006	Sgt	MARTIN Joseph	17-01-43	83 Sqn
129198	F/O	MARTIN Leslie Charles	11-05-43	15 OTU
124513	F/O	MARTIN Leslie Cyril	14-05-43	149 Sqn
1294190	Sgt	MARTIN Lionel	24-05-43	214 Sqn
1576432	Sgt	MARTIN Maurice Jack	16-12-43	106 Sqn
1600285	Sgt	MARTIN Norman	23-11-43	1658 HCU
1334936	Sgt	MARTIN Reginald Arthur	15-06-43	106 Sqn
1171555	Sgt	MARTIN Reginald George	27-03-43	214 Sqn
1361267	Sgt	MARTIN Reginald Gray	3-10-43	44 Sqn
136815	F/O	MARTIN Robert John	13-07-43	16 OTU
1010657	Sgt	MARTIN Ronald	1-05-43	12 Sqn
156635	F/L	MARTIN Roy Frank	23-11-43	78 Sqn
1104290	Sgt	MARTIN Sydney	2-12-43	207 Sqn
636646	Sgt	MARTIN Thomas	17-04-43	467 Sqn
1126214	F/S	MARTIN Thomas A.	21-10-43	83 Sqn
956091	Sgt	MARTIN William Alfred	2-03-43	15 Sqn
1377906	Sgt	MARTIN William George	8-10-43	158 Sqn
1382848	F/S	MARTINS Hedley Geoffrey	15-01-43	161 Sqn
1028891	Sgt	MARTLAND John	30-05-43	102 Sqn
1365973	Sgt	MARWICK George Edward	31-01-43	57 Sqn
1202453	Sgt	MARWOOD William Arthur 'Billy'	15-02-43	22 OTU
141862	P/O	MARX Paul Manfred Daniel [USA]	27-02-43	180 Sqn
1601545	Sgt	MASKELL Cecil Arthur	20-10-43	166 Sqn
624676	Sgt	MASON Anthony Lawrence	12-08-43	149 Sqn
1376810	Sgt	MASON Arthur James Cedric	16-02-43	103 Sqn
1230433	Sgt	MASON Frederick David	16-08-43	75 Sqn
1385000	Sgt	MASON Geoffrey Adams	15-06-43	100 Sqn
1007560	F/S	MASON DFM George Edward	20-12-43	156 Sqn
1319670	F/S	MASON Harold Vrede	18-11-43	10 Sqn
1380052	Sgt	MASON Herbert	1-05-43	78 Sqn

Service #	Rank	Name	Date	Sqn
123834	F/O	MASON John Edward	14-02-43	466 Sqn
1802311	Sgt	MASON Richard Coombe	28-08-43	156 Sqn
129350	P/O	MASON Richard Patrick	3-01-43	24 OTU
1333188	Sgt	MASON Richard William	17-04-43	408 Sqn
162612	P/O	MASON Robert Edward	16-12-43	100 Sqn
1336934	Sgt	MASON William	7-05-43	29 OTU
1818080	Sgt	MASON William	4-12-43	100 Sqn
156947	P/O	MASSIE Alexander	24-08-43	77 Sqn
1322528	Sgt	MASSIE Charles John	4-10-43	75 Sqn
134543	F/O	MASSIE Robert John	24-08-43	199 Sqn
48894	P/O	MASSIE Ronald	27-05-43	105 Sqn
121055	F/O	MASSIP de TURVILLE Gerald Oliver Marcel	13-05-43	51 Sqn
1852880	Sgt	MASTERS Albert Henry	26-11-43	103 Sqn
135294	P/O	MASTERS Peter William	24-03-43	16 OTU
1395905	Sgt	MASTIN John Henry	28-05-43	51 Sqn
1266729	Sgt	MATCHES Rodger David	13-05-43	78 Sqn
1575596	Sgt	MATHER Reginald	9-10-43	431 Sqn
29258	W/C	MATHESON Alister William Stewart	18-07-43	1485 Flt
1558725	F/S	MATHESON Hugh Martin	3-08-43	100 Sqn
136890	F/O	MATHESON Walter Roderick	16-11-43	21 OTU
131964	F/O	MATHEWS Gerard	30-07-43	57 Sqn
1566697	Sgt	MATHIESON Alexander James	22-11-43	49 Sqn
157573	P/O	MATHISON William Thomas	6-09-43	49 Sqn
112440	F/L	MATKIN DFC Sidney George	15-08-43	7 Sqn
129519	F/O	MATON Edward Thomas	13-05-43	90 Sqn
155803	P/O	MATTHEWS Arthur James	23-11-43	630 Sqn
1320673	F/S	MATTHEWS Charles William	21-12-43	76 Sqn
1809779	Sgt	MATTHEWS Cyril James	23-06-43	51 Sqn
1385943	Sgt	MATTHEWS Cyril Percy	4-12-43	97 Sqn
1457373	Sgt	MATTHEWS Edgar Leslie	26-05-43	9 Sqn
1377383	Sgt	MATTHEWS Eric William	25-05-43	180 Sqn
149907	F/O	MATTHEWS Ernest Frederick Charles	24-08-43	78 Sqn
1851986	Sgt	MATTHEWS Frank	26-11-43	626 Sqn
1333334	Sgt	MATTHEWS Glyndwr Edward	29-06-43	15 Sqn
1318179	Sgt	MATTHEWS Harold	14-07-43	115 Sqn
1287638	F/S	MATTHEWS James Richard George	20-12-43	466 Sqn
575309	Sgt	MATTHEWS Kenneth Edwin William	2-03-43	9 Sqn
53821	P/O	MATTHEWS Leonard Henry	27-11-43	408 Sqn
1290987	F/S	MATTHEWS Leslie Ronald Bruce	4-12-43	576 Sqn
1322010	Sgt	MATTHEWS Philip Edwin	11-04-43	76 Sqn
1187176	Sgt	MATTHEWS Reginald John	8-04-43	76 Sqn
993623	Sgt	MATTHEWS Richard Ayerst	26-02-43	9 Sqn
798639	Sgt	MATTHEWS Robert Francis [Newfoundland]	18-01-43	9 Sqn
1419572	Sgt	MATTHEWS Thomas Granville	13-05-43	90 Sqn
122230	F/O	MATTHEWS Vernon James	11-04-43	35 Sqn
575342	Sgt	MAUDLING Peter Howard	22-10-43	427 Sqn
62275	S/L	MAUDSLAY DFC Henry Eric	17-05-43	617 Sqn
1580261	Sgt	MAUND Roland	22-09-43	102 Sqn
151179	P/O	MAUND Ronald Albert Charles	23-06-43	158 Sqn
646817	Sgt	MAUNDER William Richard	18-01-43	12 Sqn
1310472	F/S	MAUNDERS Geoffrey Frank Stuart	3-11-43	101 Sqn
1334206	Sgt	MAVROMATIS Alexander	26-11-43	103 Sqn
124200	F/O	MAWSON Eric	17-07-43	207 Sqn
1344526	Sgt	MAXWELL Frederick Charles	5-05-43	90 Sqn
1432779	Sgt	MAXWELL James Francis	1-09-43	158 Sqn
1600416	Sgt	MAY Albert James Francis	23-10-43	15 OTU
656422	F/S	MAY Arthur Ernest	24-08-43	149 Sqn
1335225	Sgt	MAY Bernard Louis	21-06-43	619 Sqn
129022	F/O	MAY George	13-06-43	100 Sqn
1500660	Sgt	MAY Leslie	29-03-43	101 Sqn
40409	S/L	MAY Robert Seayers [Canada]	29-04-43	90 Sqn
1439176	Sgt	MAY Ronald George	27-11-43	626 Sqn
162590	P/O	MAYER CGM Stanley	26-11-43	101 Sqn
1383527	Sgt	MAYNARD Derek Charles	26-05-43	218 Sqn
1719973	Sgt	MAYNARD Peter	7-07-43	103 Sqn
1386420	F/S	MAYNARD Thomas William	20-12-43	617 Sqn
1049725	Sgt	MAYNE Thomas Dunwoody	22-10-43	408 Sqn
1211529	F/S	MAYO George William	6-09-43	77 Sqn
1128672	Sgt	MAYOH William Dennis	21-04-43	460 Sqn
1600686	Sgt	MAZIN Francis Montague	22-06-43	35 Sqn
547995	Sgt	McADAM Henry James	1-09-43	77 Sqn
1065235	Sgt	McADAM James	13-08-43	420 Sqn
1567091	Sgt	McADAM James Paterson	22-11-43	83 Sqn
635873	Sgt	McADIE William	20-12-43	149 Sqn
1294414	Sgt	McALEESE Patrick	7-03-43	51 Sqn
525353	F/S	McALLAN Alexander	25-07-43	Wyton
1079144	F/S	McALLISTER John	19-02-43	83 Sqn
118079	F/L	McALPINE Donald Gordon	30-12-43	50 Sqn
134095	F/O	McARA Ronald Stenhouse	16-12-43	576 Sqn
1241848	Sgt	McARDLE Patrick Desmond	22-06-43	218 Sqn
638671	Sgt	McARTHUR George Arthur	24-08-43	218 Sqn
1551189	F/S	McARTHUR Robert Campbell	16-09-43	617 Sqn
1349571	Sgt	McAULAY Robert James	29-06-43	76 Sqn
147496	P/O	McAUSLAND Henry Tudor	12-06-43	431 Sqn
1108568	Sgt	McBAY Arthur Cave [Argentina]	26-02-43	50 Sqn
51909	P/O	McBRIAR William Robert	17-04-43	51 Sqn
152200	P/O	McBRIDE Andrew Mather	22-09-43	83 OTU
113888	F/L	McBRIDE James McAllister [Trinidad]	17-12-43	161 Sqn
1552437	Sgt	McCABE Andrew	18-01-43	9 Sqn
129597	F/O	McCALL Thomas McKean	3-08-43	9 Sqn
338707	Sgt	McCALL Tom	26-02-43	103 Sqn
651839	Sgt	McCALL William	14-05-43	149 Sqn
1497332	Sgt	McCALLUM Douglas Izett	18-11-43	218 Sqn
574552	Sgt	McCALLUM George Loudon Ker	29-04-43	103 Sqn
1821899	Sgt	McCALLUM Robert Grigor	18-08-43	428 Sqn
147957	P/O	McCANN Bryan Stanley	12-08-43	76 Sqn
657131	Sgt	McCARRON William	18-02-43	57 Sqn
553871	Sgt	McCARTHY Denis Joseph [Eire]	22-10-43	431 Sqn
1896850	Sgt	McCARTHY Edward	27-11-43	16 OTU
151083	F/O	McCARTHY Henry	24-11-43	1658 HCU
40239	S/L	McCARTHY Raymond William [New Zealand]	15-04-43	7 Sqn
1146785	Sgt	McCARTIE Edward Leo	7-09-43	1658 HCU
1190922	Sgt	McCARTNEY Daniel Blake	13-04-43	81 OTU
134650	P/O	McCARTNEY John	28-02-43	83 Sqn
1473499	Sgt	McCARTNEY Peter William Streeter	7-09-43	434 Sqn
1370097	Sgt	McCARTNEY William Crawford	4-09-43	467 Sqn
126826	F/O	McCAUGHEY Peter Skinner	11-04-43	15 Sqn
134062	F/O	McCLEAVE George Richard	6-09-43	106 Sqn
1384317	Sgt	McCLELLAN Stanley Stuart	1-05-43	44 Sqn
41596	S/L	McCLURE DFC David Alston Johnstone [Belgium]	12-03-43	83 Sqn
1552700	Sgt	McCOLL Donald	30-05-43	44 Sqn
1118712	F/S	McCOLL Frederick Donald	17-01-43	35 Sqn
161589	P/O	McCOMB John Graham	18-11-43	9 Sqn
1822623	Sgt	McCONNELL John	24-12-43	550 Sqn
1563789	Sgt	McCONNELL William	4-07-43	102 Sqn
1335542	Sgt	McCONNELL William Alexander Dalziel	26-05-43	24 OTU
1365426	Sgt	McCOO Oliver	1-09-43	75 Sqn
1550786	Sgt	McCORMACK John Millar	9-10-43	12 Sqn
639959	Sgt	McCORMICK John	3-04-43	78 Sqn
570381	Sgt	McCOY Alan James	7-04-43	9 Sqn
126510	F/O	McCRACKEN Ronald George	28-02-43	49 Sqn
1388067	Sgt	McCREADIE Daniel	24-12-43	463 Sqn
68770	F/L	McCRORIE Thomas Fraser	23-06-43	75 Sqn
146317	P/O	McCROSSAN DFM John Michael	13-06-43	50 Sqn
1061413	Sgt	McCULLAGH James Irvine	22-10-43	427 Sqn
1344081	Sgt	McCULLOCH Duncan McMillan	28-07-43	207 Sqn
1567335	Sgt	McCULLOCH George Duffett	20-07-43	1662 HCU
645957	Sgt	McCULLOCH Henry	9-03-43	61 Sqn
145513	P/O	McCULLOCH Kenneth	15-06-43	619 Sqn
984102	F/S	McCULLOCH Thomas Oswald Steele	3-09-43	460 Sqn
1802253	Sgt	McDERMOTT Leonard Frank	18-08-43	44 Sqn
647941	Sgt	McDERMOTT Thomas George	4-12-43	166 Sqn
1518118	Sgt	McDONAGH Kevin [Eire]	6-09-43	9 Sqn

Service #	Rank	Name	Date	Unit
1338233	Sgt	McDONALD Albert Frederick	17-04-43	467 Sqn
1545464	Sgt	McDONALD Arnold Brough	2-12-43	426 Sqn
1366019	Sgt	McDONALD Daniel	30-07-43	97 Sqn
657379	Sgt	McDONALD David Alex John [USA]	1-02-43	26 OTU
143390	P/O	McDONALD George William	24-08-43	620 Sqn
1346452	Sgt	McDONALD William Davies	19-08-43	12 OTU
1502383	Sgt	McDONALD-HUNTER Donald Sydney	23-09-43	15 OTU
132142	F/O	McDONNELL Ian Lochiel	11-06-43	207 Sqn
1287949	Sgt	McDONNELL Terence	17-10-43	196 Sqn
1083266	Sgt	McDONOUGH William	29-04-43	196 Sqn
143982	F/L	McDOUGAL George Horne	28-07-43	408 Sqn
1349603	Sgt	McDOUGALL Alexander	8-03-43	21 OTU
1560454	Sgt	McDOUGALL Alexander	2-12-43	460 Sqn
1348093	Sgt	McDOWALL Andrew	10-07-43	50 Sqn
40142	S/L	McDOWELL Alexander Lyons [Canada]	22-10-43	207 Sqn
122720	F/O	McDOWELL Walter Harry	22-10-43	61 Sqn
1350620	F/S	McELLENBOROUGH Samuel John	24-08-43	100 Sqn
535709	Sgt	McELROY William	10-07-43	77 Sqn
655814	Sgt	McEWEN Douglas	3-04-43	83 Sqn
1242821	Sgt	McFARLANE Alexander Duncan	26-06-43	51 Sqn
1348644	Sgt	McFARLANE Gordon Barrie	29-03-43	83 Sqn
1347222	Sgt	McFARLANE John Fleming	22-01-43	76 Sqn
1378907	Sgt	McGEOWN George Ernest	1-02-43	26 OTU
129456	F/L	McGHIE Henry	27-09-43	166 Sqn
32201	W/C	McGHIE Irwin John	18-08-43	619 Sqn
1049404	Sgt	McGILL Donald Estcourt	17-06-43	103 Sqn
1325037	Sgt	McGILL William	1-09-43	619 Sqn
1337039	Sgt	McGINLEY Alexander Patrick	4-07-43	90 Sqn
128888	F/O	McGINN William Bryden	13-08-43	166 Sqn
1024009	Sgt	McGINNES John	7-02-43	30 OTU
1560563	Sgt	McGLOIN Edward	4-04-43	214 Sqn
1796255	Sgt	McGLOIN Thomas [Eire]	22-11-43	75 Sqn
574982	Sgt	McGLORY Stanley	24-05-43	405 Sqn
1554452	Sgt	McGONIGAL Francis Victor	4-02-43	9 Sqn
972243	Sgt	McGOVERN John	27-09-43	218 Sqn
1551754	Sgt	McGOWAN William McIlwee	26-06-43	115 Sqn
1021081	Sgt	McGRANE James	3-03-43	15 Sqn
120663	F/O	McGRATH Bernard Christopher	28-05-43	77 Sqn
641119	F/S	McGRATH Denis [Eire]	16-12-43	103 Sqn
1130425	Sgt	McGRATH Louis Renton	22-06-43	44 Sqn
1365664	Sgt	McGRATH William Joseph	29-03-43	102 Sqn
538142	Sgt	McGRAY Victor Wallace	26-11-43	429 Sqn
52922	P/O	McGREGOR Alexander Aloyisius	28-08-43	51 Sqn
1602585	Sgt	McGREGOR Duncan Roy	5-05-43	102 Sqn
1077860	Sgt	McGREGOR George	28-08-43	620 Sqn
1125722	Sgt	McGUIRE William	4-07-43	90 Sqn
1816967	Sgt	McGUIRK John	2-10-43	57 Sqn
1133853	Sgt	McHENDRY Joseph Brown	15-06-43	50 Sqn
1105617	F/S	McHUGH Edward Thomas	4-04-43	156 Sqn
657874	Sgt	McHUGH Francis Bernard	11-04-43	26 OTU
133706	F/O	McINNES Robert Gemmell	1-09-43	158 Sqn
539090	F/S	McINTOSH James Ritchie	27-09-43	10 Sqn
137543	P/O	McINTYRE Andrew	26-07-43	61 Sqn
1437780	Sgt	McINTYRE Donald Carstairs	26-02-43	9 Sqn
1796352	Sgt	McIVOR Joseph Henry	26-11-43	460 Sqn
1391576	Sgt	McKAY William John	20-06-43	10 Sqn
1522883	Sgt	McKEAG Robert	4-09-43	50 Sqn
577186	Sgt	McKEAG Thomas Henry Richard	22-11-43	10 Sqn
1352452	Sgt	McKECHAN Alexander	4-07-43	103 Sqn
1089032	Sgt	McKEE John	19-02-43	467 Sqn
997977	Sgt	McKEE Robert	6-09-43	9 Sqn
1552385	Sgt	McKEITH Thomas Elder Charles Kinnoch	23-08-43	207 Sqn
1075572	Sgt	McKELVIE Charles Dale [Canada]	21-04-43	90 Sqn
29110	G/C	McKENNA Austin Flower	3-09-43	Langar
137470	F/O	McKENNA John	4-08-43	16 OTU
1316585	Sgt	McKENNA John Henry	28-02-43	83 Sqn
1166981	Sgt	McKENNY John	30-03-43	115 Sqn
1367442	Sgt	McKENZIE Alexander John	17-06-43	1656 HCU
573805	Sgt	McKENZIE John	16-12-43	460 Sqn
950891	Cpl	McKENZIE John Williamson	25-07-43	Graveley
1475337	Sgt	McKENZIE Kenneth	8-08-43	26 OTU
526812	Sgt	McKENZIE Leslie John Andrew	3-09-43	106 Sqn
1334022	Sgt	McKENZIE Munro	8-01-43	9 Sqn
1382646	Sgt	McKEON John Patrick Valentine	7-08-43	26 OTU
1620745	Sgt	McKEOWN Ronald Daniel	16-07-43	10 Sqn
1079134	Sgt	McKERNIN Harry Francis	3-11-43	57 Sqn
1303883	Sgt	McKERRELL Robert	27-03-43	7 Sqn
1295318	Sgt	McKIERNAN Stanislaus Cyril 'Stan'	3-08-43	35 Sqn
1007370	Sgt	McKILLOP Alexander Walker	14-05-43	77 Sqn
1349733	Sgt	McKINLAY Alexander McAuslan	3-10-43	76 Sqn
69440	S/L	McKINNA DFC* Robert Alexander	23-09-43	97 Sqn
986700	Sgt	McKINNIE James McDonald	1-03-43	29 OTU
1008695	LAC	McKUNE James Glen	19-04-43	21 Sqn
656999	Sgt	McLACHLAN Alexander Lachan	25-01-43	192 Sqn
1340993	Sgt	McLACHLAN Dugald	28-04-43	19 OTU
970305	Sgt	McLAREN Alexander Stewart	30-03-43	49 Sqn
988491	F/S	McLAREN Ian Nichol	31-08-43	199 Sqn
1343837	Sgt	McLAREN Robert Allan	17-04-43	51 Sqn
1065812	Sgt	McLAUCHLAN John	26-07-43	620 Sqn
1550125	Sgt	McLAUGHLIN Andrew	3-10-43	90 Sqn
657589	Sgt	McLAUGHLIN Thomas	25-07-43	51 Sqn
656143	Sgt	McLEAN John	10-03-43	14 OTU
1568363	Sgt	McLEAN John Cook	21-10-43	103 Sqn
1456213	Sgt	McLEAN Raymond Tasker	25-11-43	28 OTU
929866	Sgt	McLEAN Stanley Frederick	31-01-43	9 Sqn
1365143	Sgt	McLEAN William James	27-11-43	426 Sqn
1551176	Sgt	McLEAN William Thomas	15-04-43	106 Sqn
1558044	Sgt	McLELLAN William Whitelaw	25-07-43	103 Sqn
626056	Sgt	McLELLAND Alexander Boyd	3-10-43	467 Sqn
644941	Sgt	McLELLAND William John	12-03-43	78 Sqn
1443130	Sgt	McLENNAN Kenneth Hector Crichton	30-07-43	158 Sqn
1551036	Sgt	McLENNAN William Thomas	8-01-43	9 Sqn
1382656	Sgt	McLEOD James Reginald	26-05-43	77 Sqn
1803388	F/S	McLEOD Kenneth Gordon	28-09-43	622 Sqn
1076873	Sgt	McLOUGHLIN George	19-02-43	467 Sqn
1262086	Sgt	McLOUGHLIN John Bernard	6-07-43	75 Sqn
131658	F/O	McLOUGHLIN Thomas	3-04-43	102 Sqn
1697680	AC2	McLOUGHLIN Thomas Alexander [Eire]	2-07-43	620 Sqn
990173	Sgt	McLUSKEY James Fraser	12-06-43	467 Sqn
1344489	Sgt	McMACKIN Francis Edward	25-07-43	76 Sqn
1334932	Sgt	McMANUS Alfred George	22-05-43	431 Sqn
133410	F/O	McMANUS Charles Patrick [Eire]	18-11-43	101 Sqn
50436	F/O	McMASTER John	17-04-43	429 Sqn
115658	F/O	McMASTER DFM Wilson Frederick	17-12-43	161 Sqn
1568151	Sgt	McMEEKAN Thomas Robert	19-08-43	1658 HCU
1338724	Sgt	McMILLAN Eric John	22-10-43	1657 HCU
1345984	Sgt	McMILLAN Ewen Cameron	15-06-43	106 Sqn
118616	F/O	McMILLAN Gordon Hunt	18-01-43	9 Sqn
1551039	Sgt	McMILLAN John	22-11-43	10 Sqn
1187788	Sgt	McMILLAN Malcolm	28-01-43	14 OTU
139489	P/O	McMULLAN William Austin	17-01-43	35 Sqn
1088074	Sgt	McMULLAN William Neill	24-05-43	1654 HCU
1323735	Sgt	McMULLIN Hugh	2-10-43	44 Sqn
156914	P/O	McNAIR Alexander	6-09-43	44 Sqn
80418	F/O	McNAIR DFC Brian Robert [South Africa]	17-04-43	467 Sqn
1021169	Sgt	McNAIR Charles Aitchison	18-02-43	107 Sqn
147680	P/O	McNAIR Patrick Colin	23-06-43	90 Sqn
1028538	Sgt	McNALLY Robert William Stephen	23-09-43	419 Sqn
1366992	Sgt	McNAUGHT William James Bryden	22-10-43	57 Sqn
614340	Sgt	McNEIL Francis	3-10-43	106 Sqn
1038619	Sgt	McNEIL Ronald	21-01-43	158 Sqn
1025811	Sgt	McNEILL Douglas	4-02-43	57 Sqn

1550627	Sgt	McNEILL Joseph Francis	21-04-43	61 Sqn	1398030	Sgt	MERRIGAN William John	13-05-43	51 Sqn
155095	P/O	McNESS John Henry	26-06-43	408 Sqn	1005888	Sgt	MERRILL George	2-12-43	35 Sqn
1452090	Sgt	McNULTY Peter	4-05-43	15 Sqn	1336498	Sgt	MERRITT Frederick Henry	11-08-43	115 Sqn
1346461	Sgt	McPHERSON James Johnston	22-06-43	77 Sqn	1252255	Sgt	MERRITT John James	4-04-43	51 Sqn
1349156	Sgt	McPHERSON Matthew	6-09-43	9 Sqn	1338421	Sgt	MERRY Patrick Edward Kevin Daly	12-06-43	199 Sqn
1574058	Sgt	McPHILLIPS Francis	21-04-43	12 Sqn	962998	Sgt	MESSENGER Frank Vero	24-08-43	434 Sqn
1783085	Sgt	McQUADE Hugh	3-09-43	101 Sqn	130665	F/O	MESSENT John Staughton	14-04-43	15 OTU
1349542	Sgt	McQUADE Hugh Steel	12-06-43	75 Sqn	125424	F/O	METCALF Anthony	30-03-43	77 Sqn
1501290	Sgt	McQUADE John Eric	7-10-43	149 Sqn	1529124	Sgt	METCALF Keith Addingley	6-09-43	619 Sqn
1369879	Sgt	McQUATER Alick	26-05-43	75 Sqn	1416068	Sgt	METCALFE Dennis William	25-07-43	460 Sqn
591584	F/S	McQUILLAN Francis Dennis	22-06-43	15 Sqn	156065	P/O	METCALFE DFM Frederick Gerard	31-08-43	619 Sqn
1345092	Sgt	McSHANE John Joseph	3-10-43	102 Sqn	127290	F/O	METCALFE John Leslie	22-03-43	101 Sqn
1375108	Sgt	McSTAY Thomas Smith	9-04-43	77 Sqn	68145	F/L	METCALFE DFC Leonard Walter	11-08-43	30 OTU
144212	F/L	McSWEENEY DFC Conal Brenden Thomas	4-10-43	156 Sqn	1477557	Sgt	METCALFE Norman	22-06-43	44 Sqn
					1698546	Sgt	METCALFE Ralph	22-06-43	83 Sqn
149702	P/O	McTERNAGHAN Kenneth Wilson	28-08-43	78 Sqn	1459019	Sgt	METCALFE Ronald Arthur	22-09-43	214 Sqn
1367705	Sgt	McVEY Francis Gerrard	9-10-43	78 Sqn	656658	F/S	METCALFE Rowland Stafford	30-05-43	419 Sqn
1371651	Sgt	McVICAR Angus	15-04-43	75 Sqn	923584	Sgt	MEYER Claude Jean Philippe [France]	10-07-43	12 Sqn
131165	P/O	McVITTY George	12-06-43	100 Sqn	1330620	Sgt	MEYER Reginald Charles	13-05-43	207 Sqn
630736	Sgt	McWILLIAM Albert Ernest [Eire]	22-06-43	83 Sqn	1534900	Sgt	MEYNELL Aubrey Denys	21-12-43	78 Sqn
142494	P/O	McWILLIAM George	14-03-43	161 Sqn	1353345	Sgt	MEYRICK Granville	25-09-43	29 OTU
1550725	Sgt	McWILLIAMS Robert	28-07-43	207 Sqn	1551320	Sgt	MICHAELS Albert Edward	13-05-43	467 Sqn
655561	F/S	MEAD James	3-03-43	103 Sqn	1386272	Sgt	MICHELL Frederick Charles Walter	13-06-43	10 Sqn
1726789	Sgt	MEAD William Robert	26-11-43	158 Sqn	1388185	Sgt	MICHELL William Eric Thomas	26-11-43	514 Sqn
1024031	Sgt	MEADOW Leonard	28-09-43	622 Sqn	78731	F/L	MICHIE James Barnett	19-02-43	467 Sqn
1212282	Sgt	MEADS Alfred Victor	26-07-43	61 Sqn	1079596	Sgt	MIDDLEBROOK Reginald Frank	17-06-43	49 Sqn
1389013	Sgt	MEAKER Frederick	18-08-43	11 OTU	1670757	Sgt	MIDDLETON Ernest	14-08-43	1662 HCU
1211173	Sgt	MEAKIN George Stephen	1-10-43	44 Sqn	1476465	Sgt	MIDDLETON Harvey Johnson	4-10-43	75 Sqn
128666	F/O	MEAKIN Leonard	29-04-43	103 Sqn	1576529	Sgt	MIDDLETON John Irwin	7-07-43	30 OTU
1583462	Sgt	MEAKIN Maurice	28-08-43	620 Sqn	1601445	Sgt	MIDDLETON Kenneth Percy	31-07-43	15 Sqn
126748	F/O	MEAKINS Geoffrey	29-04-43	428 Sqn	1822930	Sgt	MIDDLETON William John George	22-11-43	158 Sqn
149942	P/O	MEARIS Eric	30-09-43	619 Sqn	127005	F/O	MIDGLEY Ellis Ronald	13-06-43	51 Sqn
156086	P/O	MEARS Kenneth James	27-11-43	619 Sqn	1803243	Sgt	MIDWINTER George William	7-09-43	1663 HCU
659110	F/S	MEARS Ronald Albert	29-03-43	218 Sqn	1139905	Sgt	MILBURN Charles	3-02-43	78 Sqn
1321140	Sgt	MEASOR Ronald Lawrence	31-10-43	619 Sqn	1590726	Sgt	MILBURN Charles	24-12-43	576 Sqn
139376	P/O	MEATYARD Michael James	7-05-43	29 OTU	1339546	Sgt	MILES Arthur Charles Reece	23-12-43	15 OTU
613005	Sgt	MEDLYN Jack Haig	8-01-43	5 Group	1335238	Sgt	MILES Donald William	23-01-43	15 OTU
1244865	Sgt	MEECH Albert William George	30-05-43	460 Sqn	1312077	F/S	MILES Francis John	26-02-43	90 Sqn
1191334	Sgt	MEECH James Matthew	25-06-43	429 Sqn	156040	P/O	MILES Gerald Stanley	16-09-43	617 Sqn
551830	Sgt	MEEHAN Noel Stephen Joseph	29-12-43	61 Sqn	1237269	Sgt	MILES Henry Edwin	16-12-43	166 Sqn
1370430	Sgt	MEEK William Alexander	26-11-43	7 Sqn	777922	Sgt	MILES Jack [South Africa]	4-04-43	9 Sqn
1819478	Sgt	MEGRAHANAN John Francis (served as MEGRAN)	26-11-43	1658 HCU	1129300	Sgt	MILES Leslie James	28-05-43	35 Sqn
					908026	Sgt	MILES Leslie Roy	4-12-43	10 Sqn
126127	P/O	MEIJER Dutch Cross of Merit Adolf Philip [Holland]	3-03-43	15 Sqn	1377449	Sgt	MILES Ronald George	13-05-43	77 Sqn
					1553503	Sgt	MILLAR Harry Walker	13-07-43	106 Sqn
1457139	F/S	MEIKLE David William	12-10-43	90 Sqn	1341185	Sgt	MILLAR James Arthur	25-02-43	19 OTU
52913	P/O	MEIKLE DFM Thomas Alfred	16-09-43	617 Sqn	126710	F/O	MILLAR John Guy	13-07-43	49 Sqn
1102605	Sgt	MEIKLEJOHN William Miller	13-03-43	7 Sqn	927578	Sgt	MILLAR Robert Harvey	3-03-43	15 OTU
658495	Sgt	MEIN John Gustard	6-09-43	78 Sqn	1560123	Sgt	MILLAR Thomas Frame	10-03-43	100 Sqn
1495870	Sgt	MELBOURNE Leslie Edmund	18-10-43	97 Sqn	657781	F/S	MILLARD Harry 'Hal'	20-10-43	166 Sqn
161688	P/O	MELIA Thomas Bernard	16-12-43	44 Sqn	1321984	Sgt	MILLEDY Thomas Patrick Gore	3-03-43	460 Sqn
124949	F/O	MELLER Harry Lewis	2-03-43	15 Sqn	1345237	Sgt	MILLER Archibald [USA]	3-10-43	77 Sqn
1382734	Sgt	MELLISH Percy Edward	4-05-43	78 Sqn	158294	P/O	MILLER DFC Bruce Fitzgerald Henry	22-10-43	103 Sqn
943914	Sgt	MELLOR Albert Leslie	8-09-43	75 Sqn	1497411	Sgt	MILLER Charles Kenneth	24-06-43	214 Sqn
658718	Sgt	MELLOR Harry Briggs	16-07-43	10 Sqn	156958	P/O	MILLER David	22-10-43	57 Sqn
1230793	Sgt	MELLOR Kenneth	18-11-43	9 Sqn	925232	Sgt	MILLER Donald William	18-10-43	103 Sqn
139845	F/O	MELLOR Walter Fanning	22-10-43	77 Sqn	1066777	Sgt	MILLER Frank	28-05-43	21 Sqn
1322282	Sgt	MELVILLE David Henry	5-03-43	218 Sqn	1394400	Sgt	MILLER Frank Cyril Edward	2-03-43	57 Sqn
1127575	Sgt	MENSFORTH Maurice	4-04-43	50 Sqn	50188	P/O	MILLER DFM George Henry	14-02-43	158 Sqn
1387214	Sgt	MEPSTED Ronald William	26-06-43	100 Sqn	1205929	F/S	MILLER Gifford Benjamin Coles	14-02-43	49 Sqn
148054	P/O	MERCER Robert Edward	23-06-43	431 Sqn	1049098	LAC	MILLER Harold James	10-02-43	Watton
1684899	Sgt	MEREDITH Kenneth	22-09-43	76 Sqn	1470915	Sgt	MILLER Horace William	29-12-43	30 OTU
1122826	Sgt	MEREDITH Philip	28-09-43	101 Sqn	158404	P/O	MILLER James	4-12-43	77 Sqn
1587160	Sgt	MEREFIELD Victor John	17-04-43	103 Sqn	155221	P/O	MILLER James Henry	15-08-43	61 Sqn
1210234	W/O	MERRALLS DFM Ernest	17-11-43	166 Sqn	147190	P/O	MILLER Robert Ballantine	17-06-43	156 Sqn
1387096	F/S	MERRETT Raymond Leslie	19-02-43	83 Sqn	1313750	Sgt	MILLER Robert Sydney George	24-05-43	12 Sqn
156005	P/O	MERRICKS Leslie Frank	28-08-43	51 Sqn	1503799	Sgt	MILLER Stanley Frederick	16-12-43	166 Sqn
1148277	F/S	MERRIDEW Arthur	11-12-43	26 OTU	1086156	Sgt	MILLER Thomas Richard	7-10-43	90 Sqn
1366380	Sgt	MERRIE John Weir	28-07-43	15 Sqn	777923	Sgt	MILLER Tom [South Africa]	16-01-43	61 Sqn

Service No.	Rank	Name	Date	Unit
156006	P/O	MILLIGAN Henry William	6-09-43	78 Sqn
1097417	Sgt	MILLIN Alfred John Henry	1-09-43	623 Sqn
656624	Sgt	MILLING DFM Edward	27-09-43	166 Sqn
115317	F/L	MILLNS Ralph Frederick	26-02-43	105 Sqn
1038740	Sgt	MILLNS Thomas Desmond	26-06-43	101 Sqn
553832	F/S	MILLS Alan John	13-06-43	50 Sqn
1048627	Sgt	MILLS Frederick	26-06-43	214 Sqn
1386526	Sgt	MILLS Frederick	18-07-43	10 OTU
1440297	Sgt	MILLS Kenneth Alfred	12-03-43	10 Sqn
156338	P/O	MILLS Kenneth Perram	22-10-43	429 Sqn
572504	Sgt	MILLS Peter	23-06-43	207 Sqn
1385980	Sgt	MILLS Peter Banister	20-04-43	149 Sqn
1030747	AC2	MILLS Robert George	2-07-43	158 Sqn
159426	P/O	MILLS Sidney George	29-09-43	78 Sqn
1500154	Sgt	MILLS Stanley Thomas	23-09-43	419 Sqn
1487391	Sgt	MILLS William	10-03-43	10 OTU
655255	F/S	MILLS William David	27-05-43	218 Sqn
1385557	Sgt	MILLWARD Eddie	3-08-43	75 Sqn
1088096	Sgt	MILLWARD Harry	13-05-43	20 OTU
139491	P/O	MILLWARD Joseph	12-03-43	218 Sqn
1372639	Sgt	MILNE Alexander Meek	11-06-43	1654 HCU
138662	F/L	MILNE DFC Angus Joyhn Mathewson	14-09-43	138 Sqn
995124	Sgt	MILNE Ernest	30-03-43	158 Sqn
950601	Sgt	MILNE George Dakers	20-12-43	51 Sqn
41606	F/L	MILNE Roderick Fairweather [New Zealand]	14-02-43	196 Sqn
149050	P/O	MILNER George Sabathu	26-11-43	431 Sqn
51800	P/O	MILTON DFM Frank Cyril	17-04-43	83 Sqn
577846	Sgt	MILTON George Edwin	28-07-43	156 Sqn
1583502	Sgt	MILTON Leslie John	3-09-43	1661 HCU
1181097	Sgt	MINCHIN John William	17-05-43	617 Sqn
914451	Sgt	MINDEL Samuel David	22-06-43	44 Sqn
1270648	Sgt	MINNS Cederic Roland	23-06-43	218 Sqn
1393358	Sgt	MINNS Gilbert Robert	3-04-43	156 Sqn
528466	Sgt	MINNS Herbert	3-11-43	49 Sqn
658922	Sgt	MINTON John Dyfrig	24-05-43	51 Sqn
1391833	F/S	MIRAMS Stanley Percy	20-12-43	78 Sqn
573564	Sgt	MISSELDINE Jack	12-03-43	149 Sqn
1349419	Sgt	MITCHELL Alexander Lillie	28-08-43	428 Sqn
1003659	Sgt	MITCHELL Andrew	18-01-43	12 Sqn
138789	F/O	MITCHELL Clifford	9-11-43	90 Sqn
778210	Sgt	MITCHELL Colin Patrick [Rhodesia]	18-01-43	44 Sqn
134375	F/O	MITCHELL Desmond George	24-08-43	15 Sqn
1234582	Sgt	MITCHELL Eric	28-04-43	19 OTU
142506	F/O	MITCHELL DFM Ernest Raymond	23-11-43	156 Sqn
127494	F/L	MITCHELL DFC Ernest William	3-10-43	61 Sqn
1079029	Sgt	MITCHELL Frederick Henry	26-06-43	102 Sqn
616838	F/S	MITCHELL George	8-03-43	61 Sqn
1062559	Sgt	MITCHELL George	8-01-43	9 Sqn
1479975	Sgt	MITCHELL Gilbert Frank	23-01-43	75 Sqn
150116	F/O	MITCHELL Harold	17-11-43	166 Sqn
1210726	F/S	MITCHELL Harold George	23-09-43	97 Sqn
1637351	Sgt	MITCHELL Hubert Stanley	24-12-43	576 Sqn
1080459	Sgt	MITCHELL Jack	10-03-43	10 OTU
1210334	Sgt	MITCHELL James Henry	12-06-43	100 Sqn
1397975	Sgt	MITCHELL John Charles	28-09-43	1664 HCU
1801303	Sgt	MITCHELL John Ian	14-03-43	9 Sqn
124006	F/O	MITCHELL AFM Joseph Arthur	26-02-43	9 Sqn
131953	F/O	MITCHELL Neville Sladen	28-08-43	620 Sqn
1567835	Sgt	MITCHELL Norman Rhine	18-08-43	428 Sqn
1809346	Sgt	MITCHELL Peter William 'Pepe'	18-08-43	61 Sqn
1233734	Sgt	MITCHELL Raymond Arthur	26-07-43	77 Sqn
1565530	Sgt	MITCHELL Robert	6-07-43	26 OTU
1060145	Sgt	MITCHELL Robert Caven	17-07-43	207 Sqn
1568420	Sgt	MITCHELL Robert Charles	6-11-43	1679 HCFlt
1503006	Sgt	MITCHELL Sydney James	28-08-43	207 Sqn
952826	Cpl	MITCHELL William	25-07-43	Graveley
1426572	Sgt	MITCHELL William Arthur	18-08-43	619 Sqn
1054919	Sgt	MITCHELL William Connell	3-09-43	199 Sqn
1389928	Sgt	MITCHENER George James	26-05-43	166 Sqn
1085812	AC1	MITHAN William	2-07-43	158 Sqn
549090	Sgt	MITTON Clifford Harry	30-03-43	76 Sqn
2220959	Sgt	MITTONETTE Frederick William	23-12-43	15 OTU
1575533	Sgt	MOBLEY Innis Edward	13-05-43	431 Sqn
145353	P/O	MOCKFORD Patrick Alfred Kingsley	29-04-43	207 Sqn
117429	F/O	MOFFAT William Ian	3-03-43	15 Sqn
1219556	Sgt	MOFFATT Alan Raymond	3-08-43	44 Sqn
520643	Sgt	MOGER William Henry	3-01-43	207 Sqn
1394856	Sgt	MOGG Dennis Bryant	9-01-43	44 Sqn
137208	F/O	MOIR DFC Alastair Ian Taylor	25-05-43	1652 HCU
1661438	Sgt	MOLESWORTH John William	22-11-43	434 Sqn
1107377	Sgt	MOLLISON Angus McKay	5-03-43	90 Sqn
1621707	Sgt	MOLLOY Joseph Anthony	4-03-43	28 OTU
1043869	Sgt	MONAGHAN Albert	29-06-43	97 Sqn
542252	Sgt	MONAGHAN Michael	22-10-43	166 Sqn
530301	Sgt	MONAGHAN Terence	2-10-43	619 Sqn
641993	Sgt	MONCRIEFF Robert Sinclair	21-08-43	1658 HCU
52539	P/O	MONEY John Edward	13-07-43	44 Sqn
656686	Sgt	MONEY Kenneth Gerald	13-05-43	218 Sqn
1890036	Sgt	MONK Thomas Albert	26-11-43	115 Sqn
1451283	Sgt	MONKS Jack	17-04-43	101 Sqn
1395645	Sgt	MONTEITH John	10-06-43	24 OTU
1119211	Sgt	MONTGOMERY David	12-06-43	78 Sqn
1331520	Sgt	MONTIGUE Richard James Bruce	8-04-43	100 Sqn
1317395	Sgt	MOODEY Ronald Alec	26-11-43	166 Sqn
1380727	Sgt	MOODEY Ronald Percy	3-02-43	21 Sqn
160129	P/O	MOODIE Arthur Thane	16-12-43	44 Sqn
1087282	Sgt	MOODY Bernard	5-05-43	405 Sqn
1801481	Sgt	MOODY Edward Thomas Guy	27-09-43	434 Sqn
920127	Sg	MOODY Malcolm Charles	18-01-43	76 Sqn
1398344	Sgt	MOODY Peter Michael Bernard	25-07-43	158 Sqn
1609499	Sgt	MOODY Ronald Frank	2-12-43	50 Sqn
1321404	Sgt	MOODY Victor Charles George	4-05-43	78 Sqn
1305672	Sgt	MOON Arthur	12-06-43	161 Sqn
658627	Sgt	MOON Donald Francis	13-05-43	102 Sqn
145662	P/O	MOON DFM Donald Reading	5-09-43	20 OTU
46396	F/L	MOON DFC Douglas Charles	26-07-43	102 Sqn
951417	Sgt	MOON John William	3-04-43	50 Sqn
50039	F/O	MOON Kenneth Edward	29-06-43	76 Sqn
655855	Sgt	MOONEY Hugh Harvey	29-06-43	467 Sqn
1032093	Sgt	MOONEY John Edward	19-12-43	138 Sqn
151848	P/O	MOORBY Frank Preston	26-09-43	14 OTU
127974	F/O	MOORCROFT William James	14-07-43	115 Sqn
1205347	Sgt	MOORE Albert	4-09-43	57 Sqn
657599	Sgt	MOORE Arthur Duncan	12-06-43	467 Sqn
1106308	Sgt	MOORE Bernard Arthur Riley	13-05-43	75 Sqn
937174	Sgt	MOORE Charles William	24-08-43	78 Sqn
1801946	Sgt	MOORE Dennis Maurice	4-12-43	97 Sqn
1379514	Sgt	MOORE Eric Louis Bowen	31-01-43	57 Sqn
1379660	Sgt	MOORE Ernest Raymond	14-07-43	35 Sqn
1510059	Sgt	MOORE Frank	4-05-43	78 Sqn
529282	Sgt	MOORE George Edward	27-03-43	101 Sqn
1322934	Sgt	MOORE Harold William	26-05-43	77 Sqn
155481	P/O	MOORE Herbert Allen	1-09-43	149 Sqn
156433	P/O	MOORE James Stirling	24-08-43	78 Sqn
137996	F/O	MOORE John William	1-10-43	1660 HCU
42071	F/L	MOORE DFC Joseph Laurence	25-06-43	97 Sqn
115080	F/O	MOORE Joseph Stanley	11-05-43	15 OTU
1215410	Sgt	MOORE Kenneth	24-06-43	192 Sqn
1668709	AC1	MOORE Lewis David	2-07-43	158 Sqn
122964	F/O	MOORE Maurice William	17-09-43	10 OTU
1042799	Sgt	MOORE Maurice William	30-05-43	106 Sqn
1450860	Sgt	MOORE Peter John	22-10-43	427 Sqn
570619	F/S	MOORE Phillip	16-09-43	617 Sqn
52074	P/O	MOORE DFM Raymond Edward	13-06-43	83 Sqn
130634	F/L	MOORE Richard William George	20-10-43	106 Sqn
1040804	Sgt	MOORE Robert	11-03-43	405 Sqn
1383811	F/S	MOORE Robert Arthur	25-07-43	103 Sqn

Service No.	Rank	Name	Date	Squadron
1199640	Sgt	MOORE Ronald Thomas	15-06-43	49 Sqn
130330	F/O	MOORE Ronald Victor	22-04-43	10 OTU
1225511	Sgt	MOORE Stanley	27-05-43	218 Sqn
1811627	Sgt	MOORE Thomas George	31-08-43	207 Sqn
1081184	Sgt	MOORE Thomas Watson	16-12-43	103 Sqn
1054827	Sgt	MOORE Vernon	22-09-43	428 Sqn
524207	Sgt	MOORE Victor Clague	1-09-43	12 Sqn
1235122	Sgt	MOORE Walter	11-04-43	7 Sqn
1339757	Sgt	MOORSHEAD Henry Berryman	29-01-43	158 Sqn
1095964	Sgt	MORAN Harry	31-08-43	100 Sqn
1025415	Sgt	MORDECAL David Gwynne	8-04-43	460 Sqn
1411197	Sgt	MORDECAL Kenneth David Selwyn	28-06-43	101 Sqn
139725	F/O	MORDUE Henry	30-09-43	50 Sqn
1809983	Sgt	MORE Robert McLeod [Brazil]	22-11-43	75 Sqn
1610496	Sgt	MOREL Ronald Henry	18-10-43	207 Sqn
129636	P/O	MORGAN Brinley Ewart	18-01-43	1654 HCU
124467	F/O	MORGAN Douglas Henry Wain	9-04-43	166 Sqn
1434778	Sgt	MORGAN Eric	2-06-43	20 OTU
633789	Sgt	MORGAN Frank Arthur	29-01-43	21 OTU
929015	F/S	MORGAN Frederick Henry	24-12-43	156 Sqn
1322390	Sgt	MORGAN Iorwerth Beynon	27-11-43	103 Sqn
143666	P/O	MORGAN Ivor Malcolm Payne	17-04-43	196 Sqn
1403486	Sgt	MORGAN Joffre Leige	22-09-43	214 Sqn
969408	F/S	MORGAN John Charles	13-01-43	61 Sqn
1338378	Sgt	MORGAN John Iorwerth Palmer	14-05-43	77 Sqn
1333266	Sgt	MORGAN Joseph Keenan	13-06-43	50 Sqn
658473	Sgt	MORGAN Joshua	10-03-43	100 Sqn
126512	F/O	MORGAN Kenneth Llewellyn	7-02-43	61 Sqn
1154112	Sgt	MORGAN Raymond Hardie	30-07-43	102 Sqn
2220391	Sgt	MORGAN Ronald Berkley	26-09-43	24 OTU
134667	F/O	MORGAN Walter Henry	12-07-43	467 Sqn
1651941	Sgt	MORGAN William Alfred	22-09-43	90 Sqn
1539846	Sgt	MORGAN William George	29-09-43	419 Sqn
1663229	Sgt	MORGAN William John	2-12-43	1664 HCU
1313895	Sgt	MORGANS Evan Maunder	24-08-43	115 Sqn
711065	Sgt	MORLEY Christopher Searle Hamilton	18-01-43	467 Sqn
1186852	Sgt	MORLEY Edgar Harry	15-06-43	103 Sqn
1322146	Sgt	MORLEY Robert Edward	23-09-43	50 Sqn
1238594	Sgt	MORPETH William Lewis	22-10-43	434 Sqn
1023575	Sgt	MORRALL George	20-02-43	90 Sqn
1750577	Sgt	MORRELL Francis William	4-07-43	214 Sqn
1556121	Sgt	MORRICE George John	11-06-43	207 Sqn
1383392	F/S	MORRIS Alexander Frederick Henry	24-09-43	428 Sqn
1337838	Sgt	MORRIS Cecil Andrew [Eire]	29-06-43	78 Sqn
1140092	Sgt	MORRIS Charles Bertram	19-01-43	20 OTU
658459	F/S	MORRIS Davis Gwynne	20-12-43	10 Sqn
656599	Sgt	MORRIS Edward Silas	24-05-43	166 Sqn
1245949	Sgt	MORRIS Frank	18-02-43	139 Sqn
1120735	Sgt	MORRIS Frederick Allan	28-05-43	21 Sqn
578187	Sgt	MORRIS Frederick Thomas	24-08-43	15 Sqn
1230528	Sgt	MORRIS Geoffrey Eli	12-03-43	20 OTU
1393640	Sgt	MORRIS Harold Alexandra	25-07-43	76 Sqn
1334931	Sgt	MORRIS Hugh	20-12-43	514 Sqn
1370964	Sgt	MORRIS Hugh John	25-05-43	15 Sqn
1152974	Sgt	MORRIS James Ivor	3-01-43	9 Sqn
1558377	Sgt	MORRIS John	23-09-43	419 Sqn
134363	P/O	MORRIS John Ernest	27-05-43	139 Sqn
1271185	Sgt	MORRIS Norman Henry	26-06-43	44 Sqn
798534	F/S	MORRIS Ralph Calasanctis [Newfoundland]	18-01-43	9 Sqn
119221	F/O	MORRIS DFC Reginald Charles	16-03-43	139 Sqn
1216163	Sgt	MORRIS Reginald Henry	9-01-43	103 Sqn
571812	Sgt	MORRIS Roger Marshall	13-05-43	9 Sqn
1344250	Sgt	MORRIS Thomas	26-07-43	78 Sqn
1325871	Sgt	MORRIS Thomas Benjamin	30-05-43	149 Sqn
133734	P/O	MORRISH Ronald	6-11-43	138 Sqn
1560135	Sgt	MORRISON George	3-11-43	76 Sqn
1333473	F/S	MORRISON Malcolm Lionel Brian	4-07-43	90 Sqn
1085990	AC2	MORROW John	3-01-43	428 Sqn
521097	Sgt	MORROW Patrick William John	29-04-43	196 Sqn
1196256	Sgt	MORROW Stanley Samuel	31-03-43	10 OTU
1413656	Sgt	MORSE Arthur Lawrence	3-08-43	51 Sqn
1297114	Sgt	MORSE Ronald Alfred William	16-07-43	10 Sqn
127978	F/O	MORSE Walter Edwin Lawrence	26-05-43	149 Sqn
622725	Sgt	MORSE Willie	10-07-43	102 Sqn
117484	F/L	MORTENSON Edward George	16-04-43	78 Sqn
1332299	F/S	MORTHAM Richard Sidney	23-11-43	97 Sqn
1499905	Sgt	MORTIMER Alfred	26-06-43	166 Sqn
169038	P/O	MORTIMER Cecil Henry	2-12-43	101 Sqn
1576506	Sgt	MORTIMER Geoffrey Charles	26-06-43	51 Sqn
1506921	Sgt	MORTIMER Leonard	20-10-43	29 OTU
515976	Sgt	MORTIMER Sidney Harold	3-08-43	61 Sqn
1392722	Sgt	MORTIMORE George	9-03-43	207 Sqn
1324729	F/S	MORTLOCK Kenneth George	2-10-43	619 Sqn
1214528	Sgt	MORTON Frank	30-03-43	12 Sqn
139401	P/O	MORTON Hubert William Howe	29-01-43	44 Sqn
159046	P/O	MORTON John	26-11-43	431 Sqn
1436644	Sgt	MORTON John	29-12-43	101 Sqn
947789	Sgt	MORTON John Edward Hipwell	28-08-43	76 Sqn
129550	P/O	MORTON John Robert	23-05-43	57 Sqn
1068361	Sgt	MORTON Robert	29-01-43	226 Sqn
658719	Sgt	MORTON Stanley James	8-08-43	26 OTU
1384487	Sgt	MORTON William Alexander	6-09-43	9 Sqn
944593	Sgt	MOSELEY Leonard Granville 'Len'	8-02-43	51 Sqn
1351789	Sgt	MOSELEY Stanley	14-04-43	103 Sqn
1207069	Sgt	MOSES George	6-02-43	199 Sqn
531870	Sgt	MOSEY Ernest	6-09-43	44 Sqn
632033	Sgt	MOSEY Stanley Ryder	5-05-43	21 OTU
142054	F/O	MOSLEY Harold Edwin	23-09-43	218 Sqn
807289	Sgt	MOSS Albert Edward	3-11-43	428 Sqn
130874	P/O	MOSS Dennis Oswald	27-02-43	16 OTU
142335	F/O	MOSS Edwin John Barnes	24-11-43	405 Sqn
1384606	Sgt	MOSS George Arthur	2-03-43	15 Sqn
1406740	Sgt	MOSS Glynville William	6-09-43	196 Sqn
1213548	Sgt	MOSS Reginald Vincent Newton	5-03-43	12 OTU
1576133	F/S	MOSS Stephen Vincent	2-12-43	9 Sqn
632357	F/S	MOSSOP William	31-01-43	428 Sqn
88428	F/L	MOTT Guy Leslie	28-08-43	115 Sqn
148375	P/O	MOTT Kenneth George	26-06-43	9 Sqn
1322107	Sgt	MOTT Leslie Oswald	22-09-43	460 Sqn
657070	Sgt	MOTTERSHEAD Harold	6-04-43	16 OTU
1314162	Sgt	MOULD Charles Cyril	25-06-43	75 Sqn
1297129	Sgt	MOULD Norman Stanley	26-06-43	101 Sqn
1272021	Sgt	MOULDING Kenneth Ernest	12-08-43	620 Sqn
1292879	Sgt	MOULTON Frederick Arthur	28-04-43	75 Sqn
1593475	Sgt	MOUNCEY Matthew	16-11-43	28 OTU
148050	P/O	MOUNSEY Harold George Pete	1-09-43	214 Sqn
124550	F/O	MOUNSEY William Norman	24-05-43	12 Sqn
648133	Sgt	MOWLES Felix James	14-03-43	161 Sqn
138471	F/O	MOXHAM Peter Clement	11-08-43	619 Sqn
159683	P/O	MOYLER DFM Leslie Ernest	7-09-43	427 Sqn
139959	F/O	MOYNIHAN Francis Henry	22-11-43	51 Sqn
912056	Sgt	MUDGE William Henry	15-09-43	138 Sqn
1802465	Sgt	MUFFETT Guy Anthony	6-09-43	77 Sqn
1600330	Sgt	MUGRIDGE Herbert Gladstone	4-05-43	15 Sqn
1479869	Sgt	MUIR Alexander Edward	13-06-43	102 Sqn
982053	Sgt	MUIR James	12-06-43	78 Sqn
1565941	Sgt	MUIR James Hogg	27-11-43	428 Sqn
1331575	Sgt	MUIR John Henry	30-06-43	425 Sqn
124744	F/O	MUIR John Neville Macmillan	14-02-43	15 Sqn
1388470	Sgt	MUIR Reginald William Lingfield	9-07-43	106 Sqn
1127204	Sgt	MUIR Robert Kennedy Buchanan	15-06-43	49 Sqn
979323	Sgt	MUIRHEAD Muro McKenzie	16-04-43	156 Sqn
1468681	AC1	MULCAHY Edward Stephen	25-07-43	Wyton
1382671	Sgt	MULDOON Reginald Arthur	22-06-43	83 Sqn
37202	S/L	MULFORD William Edwin	12-06-43	431 Sqn
1332768	Sgt	MULHOLLAND Henry Stephen	12-06-43	75 Sqn

1253419	Sgt	MULLANE Harold Victor	3-08-43	76 Sqn	1334122	Sgt	NASH Leslie John	9-04-43	44 Sqn
536072	Sgt	MULLANY John Thomas	1-09-43	419 Sqn	1109844	Sgt	NASH Ronald Harry	31-08-43	7 Sqn
938998	Sgt	MULLARKEY Richard Patrick Michael			1397903	Sgt	NASON Reginald Albert	11-04-43	35 Sqn
			28-08-43	620 Sqn	1504432	F/S	NAYLOR Arthur Edward	24-12-43	625 Sqn
1068145	Sgt	MULLETT Brendan Francis [Eire]	5-03-43	29 OTU	1484092	Sgt	NAYLOR Bernard	18-01-43	9 Sqn
1455851	Sgt	MULLIGAN James Lawrence Anthony			1310478	Sgt	NAYLOR Harry John	2-02-43	102 Sqn
			14-04-43	12 Sqn	1074000	Sgt	NAYLOR Jack Hempshall	7-09-43	76 Sqn
132954	F/O	MULLIGAN Michael	18-10-43	103 Sqn	1132574	Sgt	NAYLOR John Herbert	31-08-43	77 Sqn
1393122	Sgt	MULLIN Joseph	10-08-43	103 Sqn	1380344	Sgt	NAYLOR Ronald Sydney	20-08-43	10 Sqn
1129398	Sgt	MULLIS George William	4-06-43	26 OTU	1539922	Sgt	NEAL Basil Leonard	21-04-43	90 Sqn
700735	F/S	MUMME Robin Morris [Middle East]	17-04-43	51 Sqn	920484	Sgt	NEAL Dennis William	9-07-43	49 Sqn
1321629	Sgt	MUNDAY Douglas Robert	30-05-43	460 Sqn	985412	Sgt	NEAL Frederick Stephen	14-05-43	419 Sqn
657170	Sgt	MUNN Andrew McKenzie	14-04-43	103 Sqn	1601305	Sgt	NEAL James William	13-08-43	432 Sqn
1575881	Sgt	MUNN Derrick Ivor Thomas	3-12-43	9 Sqn	1218784	Sgt	NEAL Ronald	3-08-43	51 Sqn
1349759	Sgt	MUNN Hugh	28-09-43	75 Sqn	1621821	Sgt	NEALE Jack	8-03-43	156 Sqn
610306	Sgt	MUNN Stanley Walter	4-07-43	15 Sqn	1711578	Sgt	NEALE William George	2-12-43	103 Sqn
1217276	Sgt	MUNNERY Harold	21-04-43	90 Sqn	134162	F/O	NEATHWAY William Sidney	7-09-43	106 Sqn
148178	P/O	MUNNS Reginald William Frederick	7-09-43	77 Sqn	128584	F/L	NEIL Gilbert John Bingham	22-11-43	7 Sqn
125353	F/O	MUNRO Alexander Lyon	8-04-43	49 Sqn	158248	P/O	NEIL Ronald Frederick	2-12-43	106 Sqn
1566746	Sgt	MUNRO Charles	24-08-43	75 Sqn	531666	Sgt	NEILL William Frederick	3-11-43	57 Sqn
1381934	Sgt	MUNRO Henry Duncan	15-01-43	427 Sqn	1627274	Sgt	NELSON Charles Storer	2-10-43	51 Sqn
1803564	Sgt	MUNT Donovan	14-07-43	81 OTU	1553494	Sgt	NELSON Donald Cecil	15-01-43	29 OTU
157628	P/O	MURFITT Cyril Marshall	22-10-43	76 Sqn			[Channel Islands]		
1044231	Sgt	MURPHY Derick	14-07-43	115 Sqn	1341933	Sgt	NELSON Gordon Abraham	22-10-43	78 Sqn
157194	P/O	MURPHY Patrick Terence	7-09-43	10 Sqn	1210274	Sgt	NELSON Harry	25-07-43	76 Sqn
976496	Sgt	MURPHY Peter Thomas	29-04-43	12 Sqn	1002811	Sgt	NELSON James	28-09-43	1664 HCU
1331482	Sgt	MURPHY Phillip James Peter	24-08-43	427 Sqn	1319095	Sgt	NELSON Reginald	6-09-43	51 Sqn
1246721	F/S	MURPHY Terence Peter	29-06-43	619 Sqn	1371110	Sgt	NELSON Robert Gilchrist	6-09-43	9 Sqn
121571	F/O	MURRAY Angus Mackay	17-01-43	83 Sqn	1108813	Sgt	NESBIT James Robert	24-04-43	16 OTU
135153	F/O	MURRAY Daniel James	22-01-43	180 Sqn	43535	S/L	NESBITT Eric Hugh Montgomery	22-11-43	7 Sqn
1388680	Sgt	MURRAY Edward Alan 'John'	3-11-43	12 Sqn	133519	F/L	NESBITT John Douglas	14-07-43	78 Sqn
1320579	Sgt	MURRAY Eric Anthony	17-07-43	467 Sqn	136688	F/O	NESDEN John	28-08-43	156 Sqn
990575	Sgt	MURRAY George Ernest	16-11-43	28 OTU	1320693	Sgt	NETTLE Desmond John	15-08-43	420 Sqn
1340096	Sgt	MURRAY George Maxwell	17-06-43	156 Sqn	41452	W/C	NETTLETON VC John Dering	13-07-43	44 Sqn
632757	Sgt	MURRAY Hugh	4-07-43	90 Sqn	1335481	Sgt	NEVE Henry John James	5-07-43	10 OTU
1000346	W/O	MURRAY Hugh	6-02-43	14 OTU	1812845	Sgt	NEVILLE James Paterson	21-10-43	103 Sqn
979186	Sgt	MURRAY James Redi	27-09-43	158 Sqn	142564	P/O	NEVILLE Wilfred Ronald	16-02-43	103 Sqn
1467008	Sgt	MURRAY John Thomson	13-05-43	77 Sqn	1083960	Sgt	NEWALL John Geoffrey	13-05-43	149 Sqn
658018	Sgt	MURRAY William	13-05-43	90 Sqn	1312030	Sgt	NEWBERY Hugh Donald	24-05-43	102 Sqn
657378	Sgt	MURRAY William John	25-07-43	51 Sqn	1549717	Sgt	NEWBOLT George Henry	26-07-43	103 Sqn
1338275	F/S	MURRELL Laurence Victor	2-12-43	101 Sqn	1084684	Sgt	NEWBON John James	18-08-43	419 Sqn
908204	Sgt	MURTAGH Anthony Jack	3-10-43	76 Sqn	161280	P/O	NEWCOMB Richard William [Chile]	18-11-43	57 Sqn
1120343	Sgt	MURTAGH John	31-01-43	9 Sqn	925177	Sgt	NEWCOMBE Roy	28-07-43	100 Sqn
778810	Sgt	MURTON Walter George	31-01-43	9 Sqn	1391936	F/S	NEWELL Albert Victor	25-06-43	156 Sqn
		[South Africa]			108067	F/L	NEWELL Walter Francis	2-12-43	44 Sqn
1381332	F/S	MUSGROVE Thomas	24-05-43	76 Sqn	1578528	Sgt	NEWEY Henry Derrick	19-11-43	434 Sqn
1254843	F/S	MUSK DFM Percy John	12-03-43	83 Sqn	1199800	Sgt	NEWEY Leonard	4-12-43	76 Sqn
1037820	Sgt	MUSKETT Ralph	27-01-43	97 Sqn	1294257	Sgt	NEWLAND Harold Cedric Alan	12-03-43	102 Sqn
618204	Sgt	MUSSEN William Edward	28-09-43	428 Sqn	959476	Sgt	NEWLAND John Alfred Ernest	15-08-43	467 Sqn
658293	Sgt	MUSSON Charles Ronald	10-08-43	49 Sqn	53012	P/O	NEWLAND Peter Edward	7-10-43	426 Sqn
578264	Sgt	MUSTCHIN John Frederick	13-06-43	115 Sqn	1600295	Sgt	NEWMAN Albert Edwin	30-07-43	214 Sqn
1390823	Sgt	MUSTON Leonard Charles	26-01-43	15 OTU	1201836	F/S	NEWMAN Charles Hugh	30-03-43	77 Sqn
142328	P/O	MUSTO Clifford Erich	31-08-43	166 Sqn	1530092	Sgt	NEWMAN Clifford	24-05-43	51 Sqn
575761	Sgt	MUTCH George Connelly	17-08-43	35 Sqn	1266270	Sgt	NEWMAN Frederick Rosslyn	10-08-43	102 Sqn
650875	Sgt	MUTTON Rodney Roy	24-12-43	57 Sqn	1067709	Sgt	NEWMAN George Albert	17-01-43	83 Sqn
1078078	Sgt	MYCOCK George Beardmore	22-06-43	158 Sqn	131000	F/O	NEWMAN James Frederick	5-07-43	10 OTU
632110	Sgt	MYCOCK William George	31-08-43	619 Sqn	156120	P/O	NEWMAN John Arthur Cyril	28-08-43	166 Sqn
1023525	Sgt	MYERS George	10-04-43	466 Sqn	1109887	Sgt	NEWMAN John Lawrence	22-09-43	7 Sqn
1533554	Sgt	MYERS Leonard	18-08-43	12 Sqn	1382409	Sgt	NEWMAN Peter Frank Edward	9-01-43	158 Sqn
119287	F/O	MYERS Peter Rodney Vincent	18-02-43	106 Sqn	1146100	Sgt	NEWMAN Phillip Joseph	17-01-43	1654 HCU
1230232	F/S	MYERSCOUGH Thomas	23-11-43	44 Sqn	136531	P/O	NEWMAN Raymond Edgar	26-05-43	15 Sqn
1148269	Sgt	MYERSCOUGH William	9-04-43	166 Sqn	985618	F/S	NEWNES Leslie	18-10-43	115 Sqn
1392196	Sgt	MYHILL William Raymond	24-10-43	75 Sqn	1383342	Sgt	NEWPORT Jack William	23-06-43	15 Sqn
1316536	Sgt	NAILE Ronald Sydney	4-07-43	196 Sqn	79755	F/L	NEWSHAM DFC George	31-08-43	35 Sqn
1385433	Sgt	NAIMAN Harry	25-06-43	57 Sqn	1381184	Sgt	NEWTON Arthur Thomas	3-09-43	199 Sqn
1551450	Sgt	NAPIER Henry	1-09-43	622 Sqn	1802894	Sgt	NEWTON Charles Stephen	8-08-43	26 OTU
1319053	Sgt	NASH Harold	3-08-43	166 Sqn	1801399	Sgt	NEWTON Frederick George	18-10-43	467 Sqn
1377535	Sgt	NASH Henry Charles William	20-06-43	10 Sqn	1601296	Sgt	NEWTON John Albert Thomas	14-07-43	115 Sqn
979904	Sgt	NASH Leonard	27-03-43	7 Sqn	1398368	Sgt	NEWTON Joseph William	1-03-43	466 Sqn

Graves in the Reichswald Forest War Cemetery where over 7,500 Allied servicemen are buried, nearly 4,000 of this total being airmen. Chris Lofty / CWGC

Rheinberg War Cemetery where close to 3,000 airmen lie, many of whom died during raids on the Ruhr targets. Chris Lofty / CWGC

Hanover War Cemetery where over 1,800 Allied airmen are buried, most falling in the last 24 months of the bombing campaign. CWGC

Sage War Cemetery, the foreground dominated by the shadow from the Cross of Sacrifice. CWGC

Luxembourg (Hollerich) Communal Cemetery. CWGC

Charleroi Communal Cemetery where almost every grave is the final resting place for a Bomber Command airman. CWGC

Bergen-op-Zoom War Cemetery where a high percentage of the air force graves concern Bomber Command victims. CWGC

Eindhoven (Woensel) General Cemetery, the graves shaded by a tree that lends an air that could be quintessentially English. CWGC

Trondheim (Stavne) Cemetery guarding 34 Bomber Command airmen, many of whom died trying to sink the *Tirpitz*. CWGC

Choloy War Cemetery with the Cross of Sacrifice in the background. CWGC

Poznan Old Garrison Cemetery. CWGC

Neaufles-Ste-Martin Memorial. 207 Squadron Archive via Raymond Glynne-Owen

Newark-upon-Trent Cemetery, final resting place for many of the Polish Air Force airmen who gave their lives for freedom. Brian Walker

Harrogate (Stonefall) Cemetery where the majority of the 3,300 air force graves mark the sacrifice of the Commonwealth Air Forces and in particular the Royal Canadian Air Force. CWGC

Oxford (Botley) Cemetery where most of the 457 air force graves contain the remains of those who died while training for Bomber Command. CWGC

Scampton (St. John the Baptist) Church stands silent sentinel to close on 100 air force graves. Brian Walker

Boldre (St. John) Church where a lovingly tended plot holds the remains of 15 Canadian airmen from 405 Squadron. Andrew Chorley

1319126	Sgt	NEWTON Stanley John	22-01-43	464 Sqn	147954	P/O	NORRIS Frederick	6-09-43	196 Sqn
1119116	Sgt	NEWTON Thomas Raine	18-02-43	61 Sqn	142348	P/O	NORRIS John Edward	12-06-43	28 OTU
1554049	Sgt	NEWTON Walter	5-09-43	30 OTU	1149026	Sgt	NORRIS Keith	20-04-43	57 Sqn
1388302	Sgt	NEWTON William Richard	23-06-43	51 Sqn	1083372	Sgt	NORRIS Robert	22-09-43	7 Sqn
1433565	Sgt	NICHOL Leslie	2-10-43	15 OTU	149219	P/O	NORRIS Samuel	28-08-43	78 Sqn
1316582	Sgt	NICHOLAS Albert Thomas	14-09-43	158 Sqn	132148	F/O	NORRIS Sidney Gordon	13-07-43	467 Sqn
1299451	LAC	NICHOLAS John Thomas	26-11-43	83 Sqn	129109	F/O	NORRIS Stanley	3-08-43	12 Sqn
136821	P/O	NICHOLLS Cecil Aspland	3-06-43	10 OTU	744724	Cpl	NORRIS Thomas John	27-05-43	14 OTU
1319393	Sgt	NICHOLLS Douglas Hartley	19-06-43	50 Sqn	1115797	Sgt	NORTH Edward	2-12-43	101 Sqn
1214010	Sgt	NICHOLLS Eric Ernest	6-09-43	619 Sqn	1231672	Sgt	NORTH Frederick James	23-05-43	214 Sqn
927758	Sgt	NICHOLLS James Ernest [Canada]	14-02-43	15 Sqn	1627763	Sgt	NORTH Geoffrey	27-11-43	101 Sqn
1413556	Sgt	NICHOLLS James Robert	30-07-43	78 Sqn	116791	F/O	NORTH Harold	3-04-43	467 Sqn
107893	F/L	NICHOLLS William Arthur	14-03-43	Harwell	1318678	Sgt	NORTH Stuart Albert James	26-07-43	77 Sqn
657751	Sgt	NICHOLS Alan George Holroyd	23-01-43	15 OTU	998917	Sgt	NORTH Thomas Leslie	24-12-43	50 Sqn
101051	F/L	NICHOLS Alan Hone	3-04-43	50 Sqn	114391	F/O	NORTH DFC Wilfred Ronald Eli	27-11-43	408 Sqn
133460	P/O	NICHOLS Charles Henry	27-02-43	16 OTU	119289	F/O	NORTHEND John Edward	13-01-43	61 Sqn
1565538	Sgt	NICHOLS Frederick	11-12-43	16 OTU	1601428	Sgt	NORTHOVER George William Henry		
1318759	Sgt	NICHOLS John Francis	28-08-43	620 Sqn				15-04-43	101 Sqn
1377941	Sgt	NICHOLS Lawrence William	16-05-43	617 Sqn	1258052	Sgt	NORTON Alan George	5-12-43	623 Sqn
1336897	Sgt	NICHOLS Leonard William	29-09-43	78 Sqn	129558	P/O	NORTON Edward Albert	30-05-43	90 Sqn
1318088	Sgt	NICHOLS Roy Arthur	17-11-43	149 Sqn	127794	F/O	NORTON DFC Francis Dunsford	18-08-43	61 Sqn
1098136	Sgt	NICHOLSON Arthur Dennis	29-04-43	103 Sqn	1441506	Sgt	NORTON George Charles William	22-06-43	100 Sqn
120421	F/O	NICHOLSON Charles Edward	14-02-43	103 Sqn	645642	F/S	NORTON Leonard Walter James	17-07-43	424 Sqn
1800467	Sgt	NICHOLSON Jack Ernest	24-08-43	75 Sqn	116782	F/O	NORTON Peter Hilary	30-03-43	97 Sqn
658284	Sgt	NICHOLSON Thomas	23-06-43	620 Sqn	1580969	Sgt	NORTON Reginald Raymond	20-12-43	10 Sqn
1144183	F/S	NICHOLSON DFM Vivian	15-09-43	617 Sqn	1391075	Sgt	NOSWORTHY Leonard Christopher	29-12-43	431 Sqn
86533	F/L	NICHOLSON Walter Hills	15-02-43	Harwell	1321158	Sgt	NOTMAN Ashley William Frederick	3-10-43	623 Sqn
919205	Sgt	NICHOLSON William	5-05-43	101 Sqn	1458872	Sgt	NOTON Leslie Williamson	22-10-43	10 Sqn
1811748	Sgt	NICKELS Edward George	30-07-43	78 Sqn	1223860	Sgt	NOWELL Colin William	24-07-43	1652 HCU
657425	W/O	NICOL Henry	25-07-43	75 Sqn	1265662	F/S	NUGENT John Percival	23-09-43	49 Sqn
1374808	Sgt	NICOL Ian Brodie	13-06-43	76 Sqn	1523977	Sgt	NUGENT William	1-05-43	57 Sqn
1555319	Sgt	NICOL William Logan	4-08-43	16 OTU	146436	P/O	NUNEZ George Albert [Trinidad]	1-05-43	9 Sqn
1002233	W/O	NICOLL Ivan Kenealy	20-10-43	10 OTU	132381	F/O	NUNN Charles William	23-11-43	44 Sqn
161716	P/O	NICOLL Thomas	19-11-43	192 Sqn	1160293	Sgt	NUNN Douglas Arthur	13-03-43	199 Sqn
702262	Sgt	NIELSEN Gordon Cornelius	28-01-43	14 OTU	1202182	Sgt	NUNN John Henry	15-04-43	100 Sqn
1376119	Sgt	NIPPER George Robert	13-05-43	207 Sqn	1378662	Sgt	NUNN Robert Arthur	2-03-43	149 Sqn
1348699	Sgt	NISBET William Noble	25-06-43	90 Sqn	141403	F/O	NUNN Victor William Joseph	27-11-43	83 Sqn
1429329	W/O	NIXON Denis John	2-12-43	90 Sqn	751569	W/O	NUTT Joseph Frederick	9-07-43	57 Sqn
1134784	Sgt	NIXON Francis William	2-09-43	11 OTU	655641	Sgt	NUTTALL Fred	17-01-43	1654 HCU
1232054	W/O	NIXON Norman	15-06-43	49 Sqn	1600601	Sgt	NUTTALL Frederick Thomas	23-06-43	10 Sqn
957106	Sgt	NIXON Peter Francis	12-06-43	115 Sqn	1672295	Sgt	NUTTALL Harry	6-09-43	419 Sqn
651655	Sgt	NOAKES Stanley Lawrence 'Larry'	9-08-43	149 Sqn	1132714	Sgt	NUTTALL John	17-06-43	61 Sqn
977618	Sgt	NOAR Harry	15-04-43	90 Sqn	1801284	Sgt	NUTTMAN Douglas John	2-12-43	9 Sqn
1239310	Sgt	NOAR Joseph	31-08-43	466 Sqn	1384582	Sgt	NYE Donald Edwin	17-08-43	57 Sqn
1805674	F/S	NOBLE Francis Edward	20-10-43	7 Sqn	2202158	Sgt	NYLAND James Patrick [Eire]	27-09-43	166 Sqn
648188	Sgt	NOBLE George Bernard	7-02-43	51 Sqn	1040150	F/S	OAKES Albert Joseph	30-08-43	29 OTU
146104	P/O	NOBLE John Isaac	13-05-43	51 Sqn	1230795	Sgt	OAKES Arthur Stanley	25-01-43	226 Sqn
1579991	Sgt	NOBLE John William	6-09-43	9 Sqn	1201575	Sgt	OAKES Percy Pugh	12-03-43	214 Sqn
1111561	Sgt	NOBLE Lister	17-01-43	61 Sqn	757915	Sgt	OAKLEY Alfred Warner	5-05-43	1663 HCU
777884	F/S	NOBLE Mervyn Parnaby [Rhodesia]	29-06-43	12 Sqn	143878	F/O	OAKLEY Charles Edward	22-10-43	427 Sqn
113393	F/O	NOBLE Thomas	14-05-43	138 Sqn	1130826	Sgt	OAKLEY Frederick	14-07-43	78 Sqn
1059835	Sgt	NOBLE William	14-02-43	49 Sqn	127353	F/O	OATES Harold Denis	15-06-43	106 Sqn
1271711	Sgt	NODES Peter Arnold	22-01-43	464 Sqn	1410437	Sgt	OATRIDGE Kenneth	27-04-43	102 Sqn
1255244	Sgt	NOLAN Joseph George	14-02-43	103 Sqn	1430645	Sgt	OATS Rundle Houston	26-05-43	35 Sqn
159690	P/O	NOLL Ludwig Otto	27-09-43	7 Sqn	17030	G/C	ODBERT Reginald Vere Massey	18-07-43	1485 Flt
127018	P/O	NONO Vincent Anthony	1-05-43	106 Sqn	111481	F/O	ODDIE Major Hugh	26-06-43	78 Sqn
130503	P/O	NOON Frank	29-01-43	420 Sqn	1220163	Sgt	ODGERS George Louvain	6-09-43	90 Sqn
1087857	Sgt	NORDHOFF Christopher Frank	3-09-43	97 Sqn	1252002	Sgt	OFFEN Edwin Marley	21-04-43	90 Sqn
1380915	Sgt	NORGATE Morris John	7-02-43	199 Sqn	1434396	Sgt	OFFER Kenneth James	18-10-43	103 Sqn
1312417	Sgt	NORGROVE Eric Stanley Raymond	15-08-43	420 Sqn	1457209	Sgt	OFIELD Douglas Gordon Miles	15-06-43	100 Sqn
619724	Sgt	NORIE Kenneth Ross	15-09-43	138 Sqn	1573298	Sgt	OGDEN George	24-08-43	75 Sqn
1386374	F/S	NORLEY DFM Ronald William	26-11-43	49 Sqn	1473356	Sgt	OGDEN Sydney	13-05-43	207 Sqn
999350	F/S	NORMAN Frank	13-06-43	50 Sqn	139614	P/O	OGLE Terik Godfrey	15-04-43	149 Sqn
541519	Sgt	NORMAN Jack	28-04-43	61 Sqn	1140418	Sgt	OGLE Thomas	23-06-43	77 Sqn
1129071	Sgt	NORMAN James	27-09-43	78 Sqn	1392579	Sgt	OKILL Percy Cyril	7-09-43	10 Sqn
1214816	Sgt	NORMAN William Edwin	4-04-43	149 Sqn	130266	P/O	OLD Melvyn Frederick	25-02-43	19 OTU
1603160	Sgt	NORREYS Paul John	14-08-43	427 Sqn	134657	P/O	OLDE William James	19-03-43	109 Sqn
48516	F/O	NORRINGTON DFM Derrick	26-02-43	83 Sqn	953465	Sgt	OLDERSHAW John Leivers [Newfoundland]	28-08-43	103 Sqn
646162	Sgt	NORRINGTON Harold Sidney	25-07-43	75 Sqn					

1322967	Sgt	OLDFIELD Harold Sewell	26-11-43	61 Sqn	1174901	F/S	OWEN Roger	9-01-43	158 Sqn
1438969	Sgt	OLDFIELD Ronald	3-03-43	460 Sqn	160664	P/O	OWEN Stanley	18-11-43	622 Sqn
135035	F/O	OLDHAM Eric Bertram	10-07-43	12 Sqn	1194377	Sgt	OWEN Stanley	13-05-43	90 Sqn
126832	F/O	OLDHAM Lawrence Philip	4-07-43	103 Sqn	1410618	Sgt	OWENS Richard Arthur	7-08-43	28 OTU
574359	Sgt	OLDHAM Paul Thomas Cyril	14-02-43	149 Sqn	1250494	F/S	OWENS William Alfred	30-05-43	75 Sqn
913181	Sgt	OLDING Jack Douglas	1-05-43	77 Sqn	1334159	Sgt	OXENBRIDGE Edward William	19-02-43	15 Sqn
1084594	Sgt	OLDROYD Benjamin	21-04-43	214 Sqn	1412229	Sgt	OXLEY Thomas Raymond	3-11-43	77 Sqn
1124471	Sgt	OLDROYD William	1-05-43	78 Sqn	1087359	Sgt	OXSPRING Henry Utley	10-04-43	1661 HCU
159704	P/O	OLIVE Roy Eric [Channel Islands]	28-08-43	77 Sqn	1254722	F/S	OYLER Potter George	5-04-43	408 Sqn
161605	P/O	OLIVER Albert Alwyn	18-10-43	101 Sqn	134679	F/O	O'BOYLE Terence Donovan 'Terry'	31-08-43	78 Sqn
658522	Sgt	OLIVER Donald Charles	24-05-43	78 Sqn	55024	F/O	O'BRIEN Desmond Henry Patrick [Eire]	26-11-43	166 Sqn
1386980	Sgt	OLIVER Ernest Fred Jesse	28-05-43	307 FTU	1028910	Sgt	O'BRIEN Gilbert John	23-11-43	44 Sqn
124860	F/O	OLIVER Francis Edward	5-12-43	101 Sqn	551549	F/S	O'BRIEN DFM James Joseph	14-04-43	103 Sqn
135415	F/O	OLIVER Frank	13-06-43	158 Sqn	145848	P/O	O'BRIEN DFM James Thomas	12-06-43	161 Sqn
1130155	Sgt	OLIVER Gilbert Edward	11-08-43	115 Sqn	159672	P/O	O'BRIEN John Bernard	20-12-43	156 Sqn
1312946	Sgt	OLIVER Jack Russell	27-03-43	7 Sqn	1030890	Sgt	O'BRIEN Joseph John [Eire]	19-08-43	1658 HCU
1238185	Sgt	OLIVER William Edgar	24-05-43	10 Sqn	142835	P/O	O'BRIEN Patrick Peter Gordon	4-07-43	466 Sqn
147766	P/O	OLSON Charles Stanley	13-06-43	49 Sqn	1065692	Sgt	O'BRIEN Raymond	3-04-43	83 Sqn
576163	Sgt	ONION Walter George	31-08-43	78 Sqn	1436222	Sgt	O'BRIEN William	17-07-43	207 Sqn
120489	F/O	OPENSHAW Frederick	27-05-43	139 Sqn	1323095	Sgt	O'BRIEN William David George	9-04-43	101 Sqn
1215561	Sgt	OPENSHAW Oliver Ormrod	8-02-43	10 OTU	52767	P/O	O'CARROLL Francis [Eire]	13-07-43	50 Sqn
1380977	Sgt	ORAM William John	22-01-43	427 Sqn	1430146	Sgt	O'CONNELL Bernard	3-11-43	12 Sqn
580706	W/O	ORCHARD Derek Henry	17-06-43	156 Sqn	126607	F/O	O'CONNELL Cornelius Frederick	26-05-43	90 Sqn
148698	P/O	ORCHARD Edward Albert	6-07-43	1660 HCU	1030449	Sgt	O'CONNOR Cornelius	23-11-43	207 Sqn
1335620	Sgt	ORCHARD Edward Peter	10-08-43	16 OTU	925406	Sgt	O'CONNOR George Ernest Patrick	13-01-43	106 Sqn
1391877	Sgt	ORCHARD Eric Leslie	14-05-43	44 Sqn	1670354	Sgt	O'CONNOR Harold Widdrington	6-04-43	1663 HCU
1609625	Sgt	ORCHARD Thomas Charles Lewis	26-05-43	15 Sqn	1600881	AC2	O'DONNELL Anthony Charles	19-06-43	Snaith
1548857	Sgt	ORD Alan	3-08-43	166 Sqn	156627	P/O	O'DONNELL Peter Joseph	18-08-43	103 Sqn
156711	P/O	ORD Robert Charles	23-09-43	9 Sqn	39828	S/L	O'DONOGHUE Charles	1-04-43	103 Sqn
134688	F/O	ORGAN Arthur Joseph	16-08-43	57 Sqn	933194	Sgt	O'DONOGHUE Donald	9-10-43	460 Sqn
541922	Sgt	ORGAN John Lewis	5-03-43	83 Sqn	1796256	Sgt	O'DONOVAN Michael John [Eire]	9-10-43	427 Sqn
129182	F/O	ORME Alan Bert	24-05-43	78 Sqn	1796043	Sgt	O'FARRELL John Hubert	31-07-43	75 Sqn
542399	Sgt	ORME Alexander Colin	17-12-43	218 Sqn	1305606	Sgt	O'HAGAN James Joseph	15-04-43	431 Sqn
147981	F/O	ORME Geoffrey Charles	24-12-43	550 Sqn	657662	W/O	O'HANLON Felix Francis	25-07-43	103 Sqn
1530815	Sgt	ORMEROD Tom Lawrence	30-07-43	57 Sqn	51838	P/O	O'HARE Francis Edward	27-04-43	405 Sqn
1132242	Sgt	ORR John	26-06-43	166 Sqn	1479311	Sgt	O'KANE Edward	25-02-43	467 Sqn
991727	F/S	ORR John Ronald	30-03-43	76 Sqn	1330779	Sgt	O'LEARY John	20-10-43	57 Sqn
159514	P/O	OSBORN Arthur William	16-12-43	7 Sqn	1515353	Sgt	O'LEARY Timothy Thomas [Eire]	7-10-43	49 Sqn
657839	Sgt	OSBORN James Albert	12-06-43	12 Sqn	1352708	Sgt	O'LOUCHLIN Dennis	20-04-43	57 Sqn
1613719	Sgt	OSBORNE Alfred George	20-10-43	619 Sqn	1430879	Sgt	O'MALLEY Wilfred	27-11-43	166 Sqn
1295241	Sgt	OSBORNE Cyril James	9-01-43	51 Sqn	659011	P/O	O'NEILL Bernard Desmond	22-06-43	460 Sqn
1533381	Sgt	OSBORNE George	17-12-43	138 Sqn	1821708	Sgt	O'NEILL Charles	16-12-43	103 Sqn
1539830	Sgt	OSBORNE Jack	23-06-43	101 Sqn	1822516	Sgt	O'NEILL George Clark	22-12-43	207 Sqn
1172557	Sgt	OSBORNE James Leslie	12-06-43	12 Sqn	1033308	Sgt	O'NEILL James Joseph	5-05-43	149 Sqn
149557	P/O	OSMER George William	23-08-43	207 Sqn	1367121	Sgt	O'NEILL William	13-05-43	196 Sqn
1390052	Sgt	OSMOND Anthony	26-06-43	51 Sqn	46527	F/O	O'REGAN Denis Patrick [Eire]	4-04-43	20 OTU
1391764	Sgt	OSMOND Sydney Frederick	17-04-43	408 Sqn	1549441	Sgt	O'REILLY James	9-10-43	166 Sqn
1333605	Sgt	OTT Henry George	13-08-43	214 Sqn	549434	Sgt	O'RIORDAN Dennis Patrick	26-05-43	15 Sqn
132742	F/O	OTTER Bernard	16-12-43	9 Sqn	624585	Sgt	O'SULLIVAN Denis	26-06-43	218 Sqn
1036446	Sgt	OTTER Eric	27-09-43	218 Sqn	36192	S/L	PAAPE DFC* Arthur Mitchell [New Zealand]	3-04-43	467 Sqn
156599	P/O	OTTER DFC John Clifford	18-11-43	156 Sqn					
1118735	Sgt	OTTEY Joseph Arthur	22-06-43	156 Sqn	1333597	Sgt	PACE Ronald McMurray	12-03-43	139 Sqn
141460	P/O	OTTLEY DFC Warner	17-05-43	617 Sqn	1339883	Sgt	PACK Ernest Albert	27-09-43	166 Sqn
1387817	Sgt	OTTLEY Geoffrey George	26-01-43	15 OTU	901009	Sgt	PACKER Ronald Jack	4-02-43	9 Sqn
1391065	Sgt	OTTOLANGUI Aaron	15-04-43	101 Sqn	2207373	Sgt	PACKHAM Stanley	27-07-43	16 OTU
1310459	Sgt	OTTY Spencer	3-10-43	103 Sqn	1800480	Sgt	PADDON Frederick David	4-09-43	101 Sqn
1397140	Sgt	OUDINOT Albert James	19-11-43	10 Sqn	650462	W/O	PADDON George Frederick	28-05-43	467 Sqn
1812760	Sgt	OUGH Alan Andrew	18-11-43	622 Sqn	1394579	Sgt	PADLEY John Paty	3-08-43	61 Sqn
1358312	Sgt	OUSLEY Joseph William	16-06-43	460 Sqn	1515141	Sgt	PAE Philip Rex	24-12-43	50 Sqn
1189925	Sgt	OVERINGTON Oliver John	31-08-43	9 Sqn	1395720	Sgt	PAGE Albert George	21-04-43	15 OTU
534934	Sgt	OWEN David Elwyn	28-08-43	90 Sqn	1135765	Sgt	PAGE Alfred Henry	7-04-43	9 Sqn
538488	Sgt	OWEN Hugh	26-07-43	214 Sqn	1377777	W/O	PAGE Arthur William Horace	3-08-43	103 Sqn
1387138	Sgt	OWEN Hugh George	15-04-43	10 Sqn	1318669	Sgt	PAGE Charles Michael	27-01-43	51 Sqn
954124	Sgt	OWEN John Charles	13-05-43	9 Sqn	1336423	Sgt	PAGE Donald Alfred	28-07-43	50 Sqn
1068297	Sgt	OWEN John Elwyn	4-07-43	9 Sqn	1332712	F/S	PAGE Frank Ronald	24-11-43	7 Sqn
26062	W/C	OWEN MiD John Jervis	6-07-43	466 Sqn	1316109	F/S	PAGE Henry Reuben	23-09-43	97 Sqn
1223682	Sgt	OWEN Joseph Edward	3-11-43	434 Sqn	1280548	F/S	PAGE John Henry	25-07-43	102 Sqn
1269604	Sgt	OWEN Norman Frederick	3-05-43	51 Sqn	749356	F/S	PAGE Kenneth John	25-11-43	26 OTU
1437145	Sgt	OWEN Robin Cecil Carrow	12-03-43	106 Sqn	47738	F/O	PAGE Lawrence Higgin	13-04-43	81 OTU

Service No	Rank	Name	Date	Unit
143377	P/O	PAGE Peter John	26-06-43	106 Sqn
1390505	Sgt	PAGE Ronald Arthur	7-05-43	29 OTU
1675979	Sgt	PAGE Sidney Percival	20-12-43	428 Sqn
656429	Sgt	PAGE Victor	12-03-43	149 Sqn
1809479	Sgt	PAGETT Henry Samuel	26-06-43	218 Sqn
1140287	Sgt	PAGETT Thomas Robert	12-06-43	12 Sqn
151630	F/O	PAGETT William George Simpson	22-11-43	75 Sqn
1318427	Sgt	PAICE Norman Frederick	29-09-43	16 OTU
152004	F/O	PAICE Peter Reginald	26-11-43	625 Sqn
1394734	Sgt	PAIN Arthur Douglas	22-06-43	57 Sqn
1314628	Sgt	PAINTER Charles Frederick	28-08-43	102 Sqn
146391	F/O	PAINTER Kenneth	20-10-43	97 Sqn
143985	P/O	PAINTER Walter John	11-04-43	76 Sqn
127105	F/O	PAISLEY Ronald	26-05-43	214 Sqn
1167098	Sgt	PALGRAVE Thomas George	9-10-43	102 Sqn
1578718	Sgt	PALING Thomas	20-12-43	10 Sqn
155927	P/O	PALK Stanley George	18-08-43	61 Sqn
1872542	Sgt	PALLANCA Joseph	26-11-43	115 Sqn
640100	Sgt	PALLENDER Ralph Henry	17-04-43	467 Sqn
627672	F/S	PALLISTER William Richard	10-08-43	35 Sqn
128509	F/O	PALMER Alan Cairns	3-04-43	106 Sqn
1323654	Sgt	PALMER Cyril William Edwy	22-09-43	428 Sqn
1386162	Sgt	PALMER Francis Charles William	29-01-43	21 OTU
1583498	Sgt	PALMER George	23-09-43	9 Sqn
1319822	Sgt	PALMER George Edward	24-07-43	18 OTU
1804862	Sgt	PALMER George James	18-11-43	10 Sqn
1040061	Sgt	PALMER James	4-04-43	149 Sqn
155842	P/O	PALMER James Walter	26-06-43	57 Sqn
1289435	Sgt	PALMER Phillip John	26-11-43	7 Sqn
131597	F/O	PALMER Robert Bertram Douglas	9-07-43	97 Sqn
1230761	Sgt	PALMER Robert John	15-04-43	90 Sqn
1457804	Sgt	PALMERLEY John	25-05-43	180 Sqn
547328	Sgt	PAPE Horace	29-06-43	10 Sqn
151465	P/O	PAPINEAU Roderic Winston	4-08-43	16 OTU
127031	F/O	PARAMORE Arthur Frederick	9-04-43	9 Sqn
1321973	Sgt	PARGETER Thomas Alan	18-08-43	405 Sqn
1332576	Sgt	PARISH Cecil Reginald	24-08-43	75 Sqn
81927	F/L	PARISH Charles Woodbine	21-04-43	7 Sqn
1067882	Sgt	PARK Alexander Muir	17-06-43	103 Sqn
1294117	Sgt	PARK Donald Jasper [South Africa]	28-04-43	101 Sqn
162548	P/O	PARK Douglas	2-12-43	57 Sqn
1361100	Sgt	PARK James	24-05-43	101 Sqn
1259549	Sgt	PARKER Alfred Michael	3-04/43	78 Sqn
908599	Sgt	PARKER Alfred Raymond	7-02-43	61 Sqn
144042	P/O	PARKER Arthur Thomas	3-10-43	77 Sqn
1300008	Sgt	PARKER Brace Henry	26-01-43	15 OTU
1318622	Sgt	PARKER Edward	22-10-43	51 Sqn
76465	S/L	PARKER GC DFC Edward Donald	16-01-43	61 Sqn
1129440	F/S	PARKER Edward Norman	29-12-43	429 Sqn
655812	Sgt	PARKER Eric	12-03-43	214 Sqn
53732	P/O	PARKER Frank Alfred George	18-11-43	7 Sqn
52880	P/P	PARKER Frank Ernest Saville	20-10-43	57 Sqn
157408	P/O	PARKER Geoffrey Albert Norris	30-07-43	57 Sqn
140882	Sgt	PARKER Geoffrey Cuming	9-07-43	101 Sqn
1293717	Sgt	PARKER George Albert	28-05-43	115 Sqn
139526	F/O	PARKER Gordon Ernest Malbon	27-09-43	10 Sqn
1335926	Sgt	PARKER Harry	4-06-43	26 OTU
1386266	Sgt	PARKER James William George	24-05-43	51 Sqn
1042441	F/S	PARKER John	29-06-43	431 Sqn
132041	F/O	PARKER Lancelot Herbert	24-05-43	1654 HCU
161042	P/O	PARKES Geoffrey Edward	22-10-43	12 Sqn
1600874	Sgt	PARKES William James	22-06-43	619 Sqn
137406	Sgt	PARKIN Charles Edwin	26-07-43	51 Sqn
1506302	Sgt	PARKIN Dennis	18-08-43	49 Sqn
1434589	Sgt	PARKIN Philip	23-05-43	57 Sqn
1078306	Sgt	PARKINSON James	17-04-43	426 Sqn
1098353	Sgt	PARKINSON Jeffery Cyril Bert	24-08-43	199 Sqn
1682651	Sgt	PARKINSON Ralph	24-12-43	625 Sqn
144180	P/O	PARKINSON Ronald Albert	29-04-43	428 Sqn
149958	P/O	PARKINSON Ronald Chesterton	18-07-43	1661 HCU
121057	F/L	PARNHAM DFC Percy	14-05-43	51 Sqn
1302064	Sgt	PARR Cyril George	20-02-43	90 Sqn
1431080	Sgt	PARR John Martland	15-08-43	420 Sqn
133463	F/O	PARR Robert Henry	15-06-43	106 Sqn
1395274	Sgt	PARR Sydney Westall	24-10-43	19 OTU
1313333	Sgt	PARRITT Geoffrey Charles	29-06-43	76 Sqn
119175	S/L	PARROTT Eric Horace	24-08-43	97 Sqn
1174427	Sgt	PARROTT Peter Cross	19-08-43	1663 HCU
1333567	Sgt	PARROTT Sidney George	17-12-43	97 Sqn
643093	Sgt	PARRY DFM Edward	19-02-43	106 Sqn
1183623	Sgt	PARRY Edward William David	22-09-43	218 Sqn
137569	F/O	PARRY Emlyn	28-05-43	10 Sqn
131560	F/O	PARRY Frederick	26-06-43	115 Sqn
133704	F/O	PARRY Henry Weston	4-07-43	97 Sqn
2208915	Sgt	PARRY James Leo	27-09-43	620 Sqn
126019	F/L	PARRY Martyn Hope	18-08-43	467 Sqn
1383146	Sgt	PARRY Norman Ronald	26-06-43	166 Sqn
1501195	Sgt	PARRY Robert Richard	10-03-43	429 Sqn
120735	F/O	PARSLOE Cyril Vincent	28-08-43	218 Sqn
146687	P/O	PARSLOW DFM George Charles William	22-06-43	431 Sqn
1807286	Sgt	PARSONS Arthur Richard John	27-09-43	10 Sqn
124214	F/O	PARSONS Cuthbert Michael	4-02-43	427 Sqn
1673114	Sgt	PARSONS Eric	31-08-43	1651 HCU
1334357	Sgt	PARSONS Gilbert Kenneth	10-04-43	30 OTU
1332551	Sgt	PARSONS Harry Michael	4-04-43	214 Sqn
1319479	Sgt	PARSONS Henry Edward	3-10-43	78 Sqn
1813276	Sgt	PARSONS Jack	3-11-43	101 Sqn
1576472	Sgt	PARSONS James Barry	6-09-43	51 Sqn
124756	F/O	PARSONS John	3-04-43	50 Sqn
120073	F/L	PARSONS Wilfred John	20-04-43	158 Sqn
102536	F/O	PARTON Frederick Arthur	4-02-43	90 Sqn
1257165	Sgt	PARTOS John Emil	27-02-43	427 Sqn
1317682	Sgt	PARTRIDGE Charles Arthur	27-03-43	51 Sqn
1802712	Sgt	PARTRIDGE Richard John	7-09-43	77 Sqn
1585869	Sgt	PASCOE George Edgar	15-04-43	100 Sqn
1312779	Sgt	PASKINS Howard George	4-10-43	50 Sqn
1547158	Sgt	PASQUAL William Anthony	13-05-43	77 Sqn
1396394	Sgt	PASQUINS Richard Leonard	3-08-43	115 Sqn
1036236	Sgt	PASS Ernest Vincent	26-05-43	77 Sqn
990571	F/S	PASS DFM Joseph	25-06-43	106 Sqn
656720	Sgt	PASSEY Sydney John	3-08-43	405 Sqn
1367322	Sgt	PATE Alexander Waddell	27-04-43	424 Sqn
639330	Sgt	PATERSON Alan	1-09-43	61 Sqn
155393	P/O	PATERSON James Burges	15-08-43	7 Sqn
127471	F/O	PATERSON James Kinnell	4-07-43	214 Sqn
151636	F/O	PATERSON John Kidston Law	10-11-43	1660 HCU
656974	F/S	PATERSON Leslie Francis	25-05-43	180 Sqn
628327	Sgt	PATERSON Robert Campbell	23-09-43	49 Sqn
1152080	Sgt	PATES Walter Henry	15-01-43	427 Sqn
1804153	Sgt	PATON James Eric Frederick	24-12-43	576 Sqn
1071891	F/S	PATON John Campbell	3-03-43	103 Sqn
162550	P/O	PATRICK Ernest Harold	2-12-43	57 Sqn
124740	F/O	PATRICK Ernest Henry	26-06-43	57 Sqn
1216471	Sgt	PATRICK George Edward	4-07-43	214 Sqn
155834	P/O	PATTERSON George Barnes Penny [Eire]	11-08-43	619 Sqn
644823	Sgt	PATTERSON William Joseph	27-09-43	158 Sqn
632331	Sgt	PATTISON Charles	27-03-43	35 Sqn
146098	P/O	PATTISSON Leslie Herbert	5-05-43	15 Sqn
1384483	Sgt	PATTON Sydney William	16-04-43	78 Sqn
1218542	Sgt	PAUL Brian Charles	18-11-43	431 Sqn
129501	F/O	PAUL Douglas Ewen	12-06-43	28 OTU
139298	F/L	PAUL George Graham [Argentina]	27-09-43	78 Sqn
138879	F/O	PAUL Robert Victor	7-07-43	15 OTU
125563	F/O	PAUL Ronald James	12-03-43	10 Sqn
1801011	Sgt	PAULING Douglas Albert [New Zealand]	26-01-43	29 OTU

Service No	Rank	Name	Date	Sqn	Service No	Rank	Name	Date	Sqn
1387643	Sgt	PAULL Robert William	1-03-43	466 Sqn	658210	F/S	PEEK DFM Samuel Joseph	17-12-43	97 Sqn
1320174	Sgt	PAVELEY Derek Arthur Frank	23-05-43	218 Sqn	1392710	Sgt	PEEL George Henry	26-06-43	106 Sqn
50509	P/O	PAVELY DFM Robert Frank	26-06-43	15 Sqn	1042200	Sgt	PEEL James Alexander	30-03-43	97 Sqn
124814	F/O	PAVEY Donald Louis	5-04-43	139 Sqn	1067704	Sgt	PEERS William Alan	24-08-43	77 Sqn
1231279	Sgt	PAVITTE Derek Raymond	1-10-43	1660 HCU	1393511	Sgt	PEGG Eric Henry	11-08-43	77 Sqn
928713	Sgt	PAWSEY James John	12-06-43	76 Sqn	1238512	Sgt	PEGG Ronald George	3-04-43	83 Sqn
1455178	Sgt	PAWSON George Stanley	4-09-43	49 Sqn	1322280	Sgt	PEGG Stanley Eldridge	2-07-43	30 OTU
137522	F/O	PAXTON Archibald Hugh George	30-03-43	76 Sqn	1615594	Sgt	PEGGS Geoffrey Charles	28-07-43	467 Sqn
126015	F/O	PAYLING Edwin	29-01-43	408 Sqn	573474	Sgt	PEGLER Guy	17-05-43	617 Sqn
1577810	Sgt	PAYNE Albert Lewis	13-06-43	100 Sqn	1536156	Sgt	PELL Charles Harry	23-11-43	630 Sqn
1426357	Sgt	PAYNE Cecil William	12-06-43	78 Sqn	1800826	Sgt	PELLATT Frederick James	14-08-43	19 OTU
1475694	Sgt	PAYNE Cyril	17-04-43	50 Sqn	1504281	Sgt	PELMEAR Laurence	22-09-43	428 Sqn
1317460	Sgt	PAYNE Donald William	29-04-43	12 Sqn	158990	P/O	PENDERGREST Robert William	20-12-43	77 Sqn
1579828	Sgt	PAYNE Geoffrey George	31-08-43	466 Sqn	1507479	Sgt	PENDLEBURY Norman	24-08-43	100 Sqn
1583937	Sgt	PAYNE Geoffrey Oswald	8-11-43	623 Sqn	1217783	F/S	PENDLETON James Edward	31-08-43	432 Sqn
138436	F/O	PAYNE John William	22-10-43	7 Sqn	1806842	Sgt	PENFOLD Alfred	18-11-43	35 Sqn
1339292	Sgt	PAYNE Kenneth Sidney Albert	15-04-43	149 Sqn	1194474	W/O	PENFOLD DFM Donald Jamieson	17-12-43	97 Sqn
1231503	Sgt	PAYNE Peter Henry	27-09-43	158 Sqn	136396	F/O	PENMAN Archibald McLeod	4-07-43	431 Sqn
155906	P/O	PAYNE Raymond Stanley	28-08-43	78 Sqn	37362	W/C	PENMAN DFC AFC MiD William Mitchell	3-10-43	61 Sqn
1376668	Sgt	PAYNE Sidney Alfred	5-05-43	21 OTU	1010416	Sgt	PENNELL Harold	17-09-43	158 Sqn
1304123	Sgt	PAYNE Thomas Samuel	25-06-43	78 Sqn	1391441	F/S	PENNELLS DFM Robert Henry	26-11-43	83 Sqn
1257191	F/S	PAYNE Trevor Herrington	16-09-43	617 Sqn	923761	Sgt	PENNEY Dennis William	19-02-43	106 Sqn
1150780	F/S	PAYNE William Francis	22-06-43	166 Sqn	1497495	Sgt	PENNINGTON Eric	7-09-43	1663 HCU
1649641	Sgt	PAYTON Ronald	22-09-43	90 Sqn	1040748	Sgt	PENNINGTON Jack	16-12-43	1667 HCU
1272044	Sgt	PAYTON Stanley	23-06-43	207 Sqn	118726	F/O	PENNINGTON DFC John Ray	13-01-43	106 Sqn
1458970	LAC	PEACE Fred	25-11-43	106 Sqn	1463189	F/S	PENNY George Edward	28-09-43	57 Sqn
1580573	Sgt	PEACE Walter Thomas	24-08-43	12 Sqn	1552510	Sgt	PENNYCOOK David Coventry	7-02-43	199 Sqn
1379768	Sgt	PEACH George Herbert William	26-06-43	196 Sqn	1187020	Sgt	PENNYCORD Albert Douglas	8-04-43	466 Sqn
1221520	Sgt	PEACHEY Norman Arthur	1-05-43	7 Sqn	1385187	Sgt	PENRY David Trevor	17-04-43	49 Sqn
1315380	Sgt	PEACHEY Stanley Frank	6-02-43	14 OTU	1549732	Sgt	PEPLOE Frank George	27-09-43	158 Sqn
1339367	Sgt	PEACOCK Arthur David	5-12-43	623 Sqn	138308	P/O	PEPPER Charles William Valentine	3-03-43	214 Sqn
1295569	Sgt	PEACOCK Eric James	11-04-43	166 Sqn	1375738	Sgt	PEPPER James Harry [Canada]	23-11-43	7 Sqn
1305916	Sgt	PEACOCK Ronald William Ernston	11-06-43	1654 HCU	567959	Sgt	PERCH Douglas William	3-03-43	103 Sqn
119014	F/O	PEACOCK William Oliver	3-04-43	139 Sqn	1600739	Sgt	PERCIVAL Charles John	25-05-43	149 Sqn
1330631	Sgt	PEAD Ivor Francis William	2-09-43	81 OTU	1016163	Sgt	PERCIVAL Roy	23-01-43	12 Sqn
1578531	Sgt	PEADON Alec Henry	31-08-43	78 Sqn	144692	P/O	PERCY Gerard	9-03-43	156 Sqn
642436	Sgt	PEAK James	26-02-43	102 Sqn	127264	F/L	PERFECT DFC Jack	22-11-43	7 Sqn
1029848	Sgt	PEAKE Fergus Thomas	21-04-43	12 Sqn	1315838	Sgt	PERIDES Charles George	3-10-43	158 Sqn
1382481	Sgt	PEARCE Alan Raymond	31-08-43	102 Sqn	128669	F/O	PERKINS Albert Joseph	18-08-43	35 Sqn
161402	P/O	PEARCE Alfred John	18-08-43	619 Sqn	1601353	Sgt	PERKINS Eric Norman	4-02-43	57 Sqn
130290	F/O	PEARCE James Edmund	13-07-43	467 Sqn	130511	F/O	PERKINS Jack Austin	25-06-43	102 Sqn
162553	P/O	PEARCE Kenneth David	24-12-43	115 Sqn	1384395	Sgt	PERKINS Kenneth	20-12-43	78 Sqn
1237466	Sgt	PEARCE Norman Alfred John	26-07-43	35 Sqn	953431	Sgt	PERKINS Richard Dowding	18-01-43	44 Sqn
1585059	Sgt	PEARCE Peter Henry	18-01-43	1654 HCU	1075785	Sgt	PERKINS William	4-01-43	21 OTU
1817261	Sgt	PEARCE William Edward	20-07-43	1662 HCU	553248	Sgt	PERRETT Jack Dale	23-01-43	12 Sqn
155212	P/O	PEARCEY Robert George	16-08-43	207 Sqn	1049981	LAC	PERRIN Arthur Nasmith	14-09-43	158 Sqn
625593	Sgt	PEARMAN Thomas Frederick	6-09-43	83 Sqn	1295070	Sgt	PERRIN Ronald James	3-08-43	166 Sqn
940650	Sgt	PEARS Victor Herbert	21-08-43	100 Sqn	143422	P/O	PERRING Clive Bolas	16-04-43	15 Sqn
574692	F/S	PEARSE Leslie	27-11-43	619 Sqn	144215	P/O	PERROTT Arthur Frederick James	4-07-43	103 Sqn
1577869	Sgt	PEARSON Derek Edward Percy	2-12-43	426 Sqn	1313763	Sgt	PERRY Bernard William Alfred	12-04-43	425 Sqn
1394169	Sgt	PEARSON Douglas Milward	26-11-43	102 Sqn	1439469	Sgt	PERRY John William 'Bill'	2-08-43	18 OTU
1628361	Sgt	PEARSON Edward Henry	13-06-43	49 Sqn	1324106	Sgt	PERRY Leslie Dennis	17-12-43	166 Sqn
1125798	F/S	PEARSON Fred Alwyn	12-03-43	149 Sqn	980250	Sgt	PERRY Percy	30-03-43	460 Sqn
1219649	Sgt	PEARSON Geoffrey	29-09-43	16 OTU	1315441	Sgt	PERRY Robert Leonard	25-07-43	103 Sqn
1387656	F/S	PEARSON Gerald	28-08-43	76 Sqn	1386608	Sgt	PERRY Ronald Bertram	6-08-43	425 Sqn
134671	F/O	PEARSON Horace Horatio	29-06-43	10 Sqn	1321960	Sgt	PERRY Sidney Edward	21-01-43	103 Sqn
1110204	Sgt	PEARSON DFM Kenneth	7-09-43	156 Sqn	1578961	Sgt	PERRY Wilfred Harry	18-11-43	218 Sqn
1288177	Sgt	PEARSON Leslie Charles	3-03-43	51 Sqn	121049	F/O	PERY KNOX GORE Edmond Arthur	7-09-43	427 Sqn
1377412	Sgt	PEARSON Peter Braithwaite	16-04-43	75 Sqn	657052	Sgt	PETERS George Clare	27-04-43	51 Sqn
1123153	Sgt	PEARSON Thomas	21-04-43	77 Sqn	1297050	F/S	PETERS Kenneth George	2-03-43	207 Sqn
1892378	Sgt	PEART Andrew Frederick	8-11-43	20 OTU	1323630	Sgt	PETERS Maurice Dawbry	29-04-43	103 Sqn
1032659	Sgt	PEARY Charles Dennis	20-10-43	29 OTU	149158	P/O	PETERS DFM Robert William	15-08-43	138 Sqn
1559144	Sgt	PEAT Thomas Dunlop	1-05-43	467 Sqn	1563653	Sgt	PETERS Thomas Kennedy Prentice	16-09-43	15 Sqn
1739039	Sgt	PEATE Norman Walter	7-09-43	81 OTU	133705	F/O	PETERS Victor Charles	28-08-43	97 Sqn
117424	F/O	PEATE Stanley	29-06-43	10 Sqn	1453792	Sgt	PETHER Donald Hector	23-09-43	419 Sqn
1332790	Sgt	PECK Geoffrey Francis	10-03-43	10 Sqn	1112332	Sgt	PETHERBRIDGE Cyril	27-02-43	12 Sqn
1807584	Sgt	PECK Gordon Harry	12-07-43	1656 HCU	1385866	Sgt	PETRE Alfred Charles	27-09-43	218 Sqn
1212563	Sgt	PECK Joseph	4-07-43	102 Sqn	1499191	Sgt	PETTEFAR George	11-08-43	57 Sqn
1212081	Sgt	PEDDER Robert Edward	22-10-43	427 Sqn					

1083351	Sgt	PETTET Walter Bell	16-08-43	115 Sqn	1284001	Sgt	PINK Frederick Norman	12-06-43	12 Sqn
145158	P/O	PETTIGREW George May	21-04-43	103 Sqn	1345595	Sgt	PINKERTON Robert Mitchell	23-06-43	10 Sqn
1043274	Sgt	PETTINGER George	26-02-43	90 Sqn	155762	P/O	PIPER Henry Charles George	18-10-43	44 Sqn
1321179	Sgt	PETTS Laurence Alfred Herbert	3-08-43	115 Sqn	1219322	Sgt	PIPER John	30-07-43	9 Sqn
156355	P/O	PETTY Alfred Herbert	3-11-43	10 Sqn	53097	P/O	PIRIE David Leslie	24-12-43	115 Sqn
1542943	Sgt	PETTY Norman Farrar	2-12-43	207 Sqn	1336315	Sgt	PITHARA Stelois Petron [Cyprus]	2-08-43	28 OTU
137375	F/O	PETYT Barry Kingsley	18-11-43	101 Sqn	1337565	F/S	PITMAN Bertram John	23-11-43	9 Sqn
1334693	Sgt	PEVERLEY Kenneth William	24-03-43	1652 HCU	1578344	Sgt	PITMAN Donald Alfred	16-04-43	78 Sqn
81650	F/L	PEXTON DFC Harold Cass	30-07-43	35 Sqn	984566	Sgt	PITMAN DFM Donald Thane	18-01-43	61 Sqn
1583515	Sgt	PEZARO Louis	18-11-43	622 Sqn	1176419	Sgt	PITT Charles Arthur	7-02-43	166 Sqn
1698514	Sgt	PHELAN Francis	22-11-43	156 Sqn	1578317	Sgt	PITT James Andrew	24-08-43	218 Sqn
128913	F/O	PHILIP David Walter Alexander	1-09-43	103 Sqn	1198978	Sgt	PITT Stanley Thomas	3-08-43	405 Sqn
1139924	LAC	PHILIP Stanley	27-05-43	14 OTU	1192387	Sgt	PITT William Charles	3-04-43	76 Sqn
1616244	Sgt	PHILIP William	18-08-43	44 Sqn	572542	Sgt	PITTARD Frederick Stanley Tristram Seymour		
1313665	Sgt	PHILLIPS Arthur James	5-05-43	7 Sqn				31-01-43	49 Sqn
1317759	W/O	PHILLIPS Charles	28-08-43	90 Sqn	1387554	Sgt	PITTARD Ronald William	26-05-43	15 Sqn
1201720	Sgt	PHILLIPS Cyril George	5-02-43	75 Sqn	1602397	Sgt	PLAMPTON Cyril Walter	16-12-43	576 Sqn
1319969	Sgt	PHILLIPS Cyril William	4-12-43	102 Sqn	135887	F/O	PLANT Fred	18-08-43	49 Sqn
1652804	Sgt	PHILLIPS David Elwyn	24-11-43	1658 HCU	1209375	Sgt	PLANT Horace	13-05-43	83 Sqn
1313912	Sgt	PHILLIPS Dennis Stuart	12-06-43	76 Sqn	145328	P/O	PLASKETT Stanley	1-05-43	106 Sqn
1801951	Sgt	PHILLIPS Edwin Roylance	18-12-43	311 FTU	1455822	Sgt	PLATONI Rino Guiseppe Arturo	24-03-43	1652 HCU
136525	F/O	PHILLIPS Frederick Edward	24-08-43	101 Sqn	137558	P/O	PLATT Edward	24-08-43	78 Sqn
577156	Sgt	PHILLIPS Geoffrey Michael	23-06-43	214 Sqn	969970	Sgt	PLATT Frederick James	30-03-43	76 Sqn
930235	Sgt	PHILLIPS George	29-04-43	75 Sqn	139424	F/L	PLATT Robert Charles	4-07-43	90 Sqn
1530967	Sgt	PHILLIPS George Edwin	24-12-43	44 Sqn	1384338	Sgt	PLATT Victor Stanley	30-05-43	35 Sqn
1458031	Sgt	PHILLIPS James Michael	22-11-43	158 Sqn	51285	P/O	PLEASANCE Roy Victor Charles	11-04-43	9 Sqn
124870	F/O	PHILLIPS John	24-05-43	218 Sqn	1504640	Sgt	PLENDERLEITH Norman Peter	24-05-43	10 Sqn
643976	Sgt	PHILLIPS John	22-06-43	77 Sqn	1850602	Sgt	PLOWMAN Eric William	10-11-43	1660 HCU
1631900	Sgt	PHILLIPS John	5-12-43	623 Sqn	110161	Sgt	PLOWRIGHT Peter	11-04-43	100 Sqn
138829	F/O	PHILLIPS John Douglas	12-12-43	105 Sqn	1585718	Sgt	PLUMMER John Edward	6-06-43	30 OTU
1451351	Sgt	PHILLIPS John Henry	24-08-43	101 Sqn	1338940	Sgt	PLUMMER Kenneth George	23-11-43	434 Sqn
145145	P/O	PHILLIPS John Montague	30-07-43	61 Sqn	142890	P/O	PLUMRIDGE Eric James	12-07-43	158 Sqn
1836048	Sgt	PHILLIPS Mansel Vernal	4-12-43	431 Sqn	1214884	Sgt	PLUMRIDGE Eric John	20-10-43	106 Sqn
591875	Sgt	PHILLIPS Richard Stanley 'Ted'	2-06-43	24 OTU	1320385	Sgt	POCKNELL Ernest Charles	21-10-43	7 Sqn
1442651	Sgt	PHILLIPS Sidney	26-02-43	15 Sqn	647914	W/O	POINTER DFM Edward George 'Jimmie'		
126448	F/O	PHILLIPS Thomas John	15-08-43	467 Sqn				25-06-43	7 Sqn
1581447	Sgt	PHILLIPS Walter	24-12-43	100 Sqn	1485923	Sgt	POLLAND Joseph Norman	19-12-43	138 Sqn
1811870	Sgt	PHILLIPS William John	28-09-43	101 Sqn	1546295	Sgt	POLLARD Francis	15-08-43	138 Sqn
658017	Sgt	PHILLIS Bruce Arthur	7-09-43	76 Sqn	143577	P/O	POLLARD George William	26-06-43	196 Sqn
120580	F/L	PHILPS John Albert	30-07-43	156 Sqn	1434975	Sgt	POLLARD Maurice Arthur	4-02-43	115 Sqn
1349598	Sgt	PHIN Crawford Kier	27-03-43	214 Sqn	926860	Sgt	POLLARD William John	12-10-43	90 Sqn
622605	Sgt	PHIPPS William	12-11-43	35 Sqn	133390	F/O	POLLETT Peter Walter Robert	16-12-43	166 Sqn
1214025	Sgt	PICKARD Raymond Stuart	30-07-43	218 Sqn	1624430	Sgt	POLLITT Alan James	20-12-43	576 Sqn
127967	F/O	PICKARD Wilfrid Harold James	29-06-43	424 Sqn	1229401	Sgt	POLLITT Derek Bryan	18-01-43	12 Sqn
80222	F/L	PICKEN DFC William James [Rhodesia]	5-03-43	106 Sqn	134209	F/O	POLMAN Douglas John	30-09-43	78 Sqn
1438919	Sgt	PICKERSGILL Donald	3-10-43	76 Sqn	1390134	Sgt	POLSON David Bannerman	3-10-43	78 Sqn
998431	Sgt	PICKFORD Leslie	17-07-43	196 Sqn	966164	Sgt	POMFRET John	20-04-43	460 Sqn
1457107	Sgt	PICKLES John Hayden	30-05-43	10 Sqn	1600465	Sgt	POND Albert Leonard William	27-04-43	51 Sqn
527356	Sgt	PICKUP Herbert	3-08-43	35 Sqn	1586779	Sgt	PONSFORD Albert Ernest	23-06-43	103 Sqn
144185	P/O	PICKUP Robert Leslie	2-04-43	57 Sqn	60087	F/L	PONT Donald Samuel	22-11-43	10 Sqn
658095	Sgt	PICTON Jack	23-06-43	90 Sqn	149168	P/O	POOL Douglas Leonard Arthur	30-07-43	7 Sqn
39562	W/C	PIDDINGTON DFC James Arthur	28-07-43	429 Sqn	1075546	Sgt	POOLE David John	24-12-43	50 Sqn
		[Canada]			1392927	Sgt	POOLE Frank Percival George	11-08-43	15 Sqn
1333026	Sgt	PIERCE Ernest William Victor	29-04-43	51 Sqn	1105804	Sgt	POOLE Harry	16-12-43	1667 HCU
982034	Sgt	PIERCE George Trevor	10-02-43	1657 HCU	1190686	Sgt	POOLE Jack	24-08-43	75 Sqn
1181213	Sgt	PIERPOINT Harry	24-05-43	12 Sqn	1239482	Sgt	POOLE Raymond William	9-08-43	149 Sqn
1376120	Sgt	PIERSON Rodney Leslie	17-04-43	75 Sqn	1036160	Sgt	POOLE Roy Francis	18-01-43	12 Sqn
1282904	Sgt	PIGGOTT Joseph	13-05-43	429 Sqn	1698523	Sgt	POOLE Stanley	27-03-43	156 Sqn
132042	P/O	PIGGS Albert Harry	17-01-43	76 Sqn	1456718	Sgt	POOLEY Frank Henry Edward	26-05-43	214 Sqn
1345233	Sgt	PIKE Douglas William	16-11-43	21 OTU	1331271	Sgt	POOLEY James Thomas	5-05-43	90 Sqn
657492	Sgt	PIKE Ronald James	1-05-43	78 Sqn	1313650	Sgt	POPE Ronald George	12-06-43	158 Sqn
1673064	Sgt	PILBEAM Alexander Bernard	17-11-43	149 Sqn	1431087	Sgt	POPE Stanley James	3-12-43	166 Sqn
1607271	Sgt	PILBEAM Edwin George	18-10-43	103 Sqn	130268	F/O	POPPERWELL Lionel George	18-08-43	44 Sqn
1388935	Sgt	PILGRIM Brian Gordon	8-04-43	1654 HCU	51888	P/O	PORTCH Albert Leonard Stanley	4-04-43	156 Sqn
1474216	Sgt	PILKINGTON Frank Elliot	4-07-43	214 Sqn	132018	F/O	PORTEOUS Peter Simpson	20-10-43	57 Sqn
553810	Sgt	PIMM John Ernest William	28-08-43	83 Sqn	124823	F/O	PORTER Arthur Robert	29-06-43	149 Sqn
656841	Sgt	PIMM Ronald William Belmont	7-08-43	28 OTU	134075	F/O	PORTER Edwin David	9-10-43	51 Sqn
1313873	Sgt	PINCHIN Kenneth Albert	9-04-43	199 Sqn	1415866	Sgt	PORTER Frederick Allan	20-10-43	625 Sqn
568487	Sgt	PINE-COFFIN Geoffrey Tristram	14-07-43	102 Sqn	1349394	Sgt	PORTER John Smith	23-06-43	90 Sqn

1078562	Sgt	PORTER Thomas Geoffrey	4-07-43	9 Sqn	1317199	Sgt	PRICE John Caradoc Lewis	23-09-43	12 Sqn
1030622	Sgt	PORTREY Thomas Lloyd	30-05-43	218 Sqn	1580639	Sgt	PRICE Leonard Austin	4-09-43	467 Sqn
1267082	Sgt	PORTSMOUTH Robert James	11-08-43	15 Sqn	1454385	Sgt	PRICE Leslie Frederick	26-06-43	115 Sqn
1220372	Sgt	POSTLETHWAITE Donald	2-10-43	15 OTU	1206397	Sgt	PRICE Leslie Rezin	2-12-43	460 Sqn
1029774	Sgt	POTHECARY James William	31-07-43	76 Sqn	1579634	Sgt	PRICE Norman Albert	3-05-43	487 Sqn
143772	P/O	POTTER Albert Robert	29-04-43	196 Sqn	1210898	Sgt	PRICE Thomas	26-07-43	35 Sqn
1585887	Sgt	POTTER Eric Bradley	14-07-43	90 Sqn	1314497	Sgt	PRICE William Edward	3-10-43	76 Sqn
130724	P/O	POTTER Frank Slaney	4-02-43	115 Sqn	1702083	Sgt	PRICE William John	4-09-43	15 Sqn
1386331	Sgt	POTTER George Henry	22-05-43	1656 HCU	1312544	Sgt	PRIEST Allan	30-01-43	28 OTU
1322696	Sgt	POTTER Peter Henry	3-11-43	77 Sqn	161360	P/O	PRIEST Cyril	20-12-43	10 Sqn
1586102	Sgt	POTTER Thomas Frank	12-06-43	158 Sqn	1579077	Sgt	PRIEST Geoffrey Frederick	31-01-43	16 OTU
1149021	Sgt	POTTS Douglas Errington	6-09-43	83 Sqn	111118	F/O	PRIESTLEY Geoffrey Douglas	13-05-43	50 Sqn
1302756	Sgt	POTTS Eric Thomas	16-09-43	427 Sqn	1214073	Sgt	PRIESTLEY Harold	22-10-43	431 Sqn
123653	F/L	POTTS James Wallace [New Zealand]	1-05-43	12 Sqn	1517817	Sgt	PRIESTLEY John Peter	26-06-43	166 Sqn
151236	F/O	POTTS John William	18-11-43	431 Sqn	929736	Sgt	PRIESTLEY John Shields	27-03-43	101 Sqn
909213	Sgt	POTTS Norman	22-05-43	1656 HCU	1112179	Sgt	PRIGENT Gustave	1-03-43	76 Sqn
1534581	Sgt	POULTER James Leeman	26-05-43	90 Sqn	1217983	Sgt	PRINCE George Dennis	16-06-43	460 Sqn
1424279	Sgt	POULTER Reginald James	29-12-43	460 Sqn	1218594	Sgt	PRINCE Ralph Gregory	8-04-43	44 Sqn
1397028	Sgt	POULTON Alfred Arthur	1-09-43	214 Sqn	657628	F/S	PRING Alfred Stanley	27-09-43	76 Sqn
1813936	SGt	POULTON Christopher Joseph	3-11-43	101 Sqn	656957	Sgt	PRING George Stanley	8-04-43	49 Sqn
119902	F/O	POUNDER George	11-04-43	139 Sqn	118900	F/O	PRINGLE DFC Henry James	16-09-43	617 Sqn
1231293	Sgt	POUNDER Thomas John	8-10-43	9 Sqn	1211131	Sgt	PRINGLE Nicholas	29-01-43	158 Sqn
633299	Sgt	POUNDS Ernest Henry John	13-02-43	158 Sqn	41061	F/L	PRIOLEAU Antony Seton Wombwell	21-04-43	90 Sqn
130974	F/O	POVEY Eric Albert	3-08-43	61 Sqn	115734	F/L	PRIOR DFM Alfred Ellis	14-03-43	161 Sqn
1024139	Sgt	POW Leslie	4-10-43	75 Sqn	1375981	F/S	PRIOR John Henry	6-03-43	49 Sqn
37984	S/L	POWDRELL Walter Harry [New Zealand]	14-02-43	103 Sqn	1431810	Sgt	PRITCHARD Edwin	13-05-43	78 Sqn
					1261039	Sgt	PRITCHARD Edwin Walter	2-12-43	12 Sqn
1076894	Sgt	POWELL Dennis Howitt	20-02-43	90 Sqn	52099	P/O	PRITCHARD Henry Nigel	15-08-43	467 Sqn
644741	Sgt	POWELL Dennis John Dean	16-09-43	617 Sqn	1511162	Sgt	PRITCHARD Robert George	24-05-43	35 Sqn
905173	Sgt	POWELL Douglas Gordon Jackson	31-08-43	76 Sqn	1230791	Sgt	PRITCHARD Thomas Henry	14-07-43	428 Sqn
1082026	Sgt	POWELL Edward Temple	26-05-43	12 Sqn	1205018	F/S	PRITCHARD DFM Thomas James	13-05-43	156 Sqn
1391524	Sgt	POWELL Frederick William Albert	9-07-43	101 Sqn	1259008	Sgt	PRITCHARD William Henry 'Harry'	2-03-43	15 Sqn
122735	F/O	POWELL George Roland	4-02-43	106 Sqn	759255	W/O	PROCKTER John Reginald	1-09-43	428 Sqn
1338127	Sgt	POWELL Graham James	5-03-43	106 Sqn	1123963	Sgt	PROCTER John Henry	22-10-43	427 Sqn
1585571	Sgt	POWELL Jack	17-12-43	97 Sqn	1320356	Sgt	PROCTER Norman William	13-06-43	115 Sqn
1419217	AC2	POWELL Joseph Edward	19-06-43	Snaith	1520443	Sgt	PROCTOR John Alston	1-05-43	467 Sqn
123965	F/L	POWELL Kenneth	7-02-43	199 Sqn	1333029	Sgt	PROTHERO Raymond Price	2-12-43	106 Sqn
159444	P/O	POWELL Leonard James	3-10-43	158 Sqn	133419	F/O	PROUDFOOT Robert Laval	16-12-43	100 Sqn
144037	P/O	POWELL Leslie	15-04-43	214 Sqn	1322305	Sgt	PROUTEN Kenneth	29-12-43	61 Sqn
1199942	Sgt	POWELL Norman Ernest	22-01-43	464 Sqn	1836365	Sgt	PROVIS Gilbert George	22-10-43	9 Sqn
104352	F/O	POWELL Roger Hubert	29-04-43	98 Sqn	1258424	F/S	PRUDHOE John Kenneth	4-10-43	83 Sqn
130526	P/O	POWELL Sidney James	26-01-43	29 OTU	151019	F/O	PRYCE-WILLIAMS Wilfrid Selwyn	23-09-43	218 Sqn
1396149	Sgt	POWER Arthur Patrick	15-08-43	467 Sqn	1212929	Sgt	PRYDE Francis George	31-08-43	218 Sqn
1547055	Sgt	POWIS Frank	11-08-43	30 OTU	1572859	Sgt	PRYDE-WATSON Robin Douglas	23-06-43	161 Sqn
650303	Sgt	POWIS Glenville George	30-05-43	460 Sqn	648137	Sgt	PRYKE George Arthur	29-06-43	15 Sqn
1809127	Sgt	POYNTER Herbert Francis	17-06-43	9 Sqn	142021	P/O	PRYOR DFM Geoffrey Victor	30-03-43	106 Sqn
1219197	F/S	PRAGNELL Thomas Walter	16-12-43	432 Sqn	136541	F/O	PUDDEPHATT Dennis Percival	14-05-43	77 Sqn
111779	F/L	PRANGLEY Peter John Matcham	26-11-43	100 Sqn	1813231	Sgt	PUDDLE Raymond	22-10-43	12 Sqn
1262759	Sgt	PRATT Benjamin	3-08-43	467 Sqn	618980	F/S	PUGH Edward Lockington	15-06-43	44 Sqn
1314020	Sgt	PRATT Cyril Herbert	28-08-43	207 Sqn	1583491	Sgt	PUGH Ifor Wyn	18-08-43	427 Sqn
1189940	Sgt	PRATT Frank Theodore	27-04-43	196 Sqn	1310320	Sgt	PUGH Kenneth Henry	3-01-43	207 Sqn
1271556	Sgt	PRATT Frank William	5-09-43	1661 HCU	1323043	Sgt	PUGH Leonard Stephen	31-07-43	44 Sqn
1390630	F/S	PRATT Henry John	6-09-43	78 Sqn	123636	F/O	PUGH DFM Richard Elwyn Vaughan	26-11-43	103 Sqn
53269	P/O	PRATT DFM John Towler	17-12-43	97 Sqn	1317561	Sgt	PUGH Ronald	26-06-43	101 Sqn
523915	W/O	PRATT Richard William [Eire]	31-08-43	1651 HCU	1317570	Sgt	PUGH Thomas George Griffiths	23-09-43	97 Sqn
531170	Sgt	PRECIOUS Harold	4-04-43	9 Sqn	145859	P/O	PULLAN Alan William	17-06-43	61 Sqn
1174086	Sgt	PREECE Robert John	18-02-43	61 Sqn	646201	Sgt	PULLEN Dick Irvin	17-04-43	77 Sqn
1234556	F/S	PREECE Wallace John	9-10-43	51 Sqn	44315	W/C	PULLEN Edward	20-12-43	50 Sqn
1304420	F/S	PRENDERGAST John	22-11-43	83 Sqn	1258731	Sgt	PULLEN Lionel Groves	25-11-43	26 OTU
155580	P/O	PRENDERGAST Leslie	18-08-43	44 Sqn	133087	F/O	PULLING Ronald Kedward	4-11-43	138 Sqn
1391016	Sgt	PRESCOTT George William	26-11-43	103 Sqn	1398388	Sgt	PUNTER Jack	23-08-43	61 Sqn
1263575	Sgt	PRESTON Eric Alfred Richard	31-08-43	207 Sqn	591849	Sgt	PURCELL Cecil Joseph	24-08-43	90 Sqn
1541030	Sgt	PRESTON Stephen	28-08-43	207 Sqn	1179990	Sgt	PURCELL Douglas John	28-08-43	78 Sqn
1567257	Sgt	PRETSELL John	22-10-43	77 Sqn	1475172	Sgt	PURCELL George Albert	1-09-43	12 Sqn
572090	F/S	PRICE Arthur Philip	9-06-43	619 Sqn	1341671	AC1	PURDEN Peter	27-09-43	10 OTU
1338508	Sgt	PRICE Avon Emrys Gomer	6-09-43	196 Sqn	1554949	Sgt	PURDIE Thomas	3-05-43	75 Sqn
134664	F/O	PRICE Eric Raymond	22-10-43	77 Sqn	1613094	Sgt	PURDY Hugh Patrick	6-09-43	106 Sqn
1310592	Sgt	PRICE Henry	18-08-43	419 Sqn	1324355	Sgt	PURRINGTON Arthur	18-08-43	49 Sqn
520838	W/O	PRICE Howell Ward	28-05-43	10 Sqn	612040	Sgt	PURSELL Ernest	30-08-43	26 OTU

Number	Rank	Name	Date	Sqn
1394531	F/S	PURVIS Bertram Lambert	20-12-43	78 Sqn
120587	F/O	PUSEY Frederick Ronald Charles	18-08-43	115 Sqn
108949	F/L	PUTTOCK John Albert	8-10-43	20 OTU
621910	Sgt	PYE Edward Alexander	29-04-43	12 Sqn
1213196	Sgt	PYLE Rodney Henry	22-06-43	100 Sqn
1024949	Sgt	PYLE Tom	1-09-43	12 Sqn
1312130	F/S	PYLE William Frank	16-07-43	10 Sqn
657375	Sgt	PYM Frederick Reginald	28-05-43	199 Sqn
1890859	Sgt	PYNE William Edward	23-11-43	51 Sqn
1819377	Sgt	PYOTT Graham Francis	17-09-43	196 Sqn
564567	Sgt	PYPER John Robert	18-02-43	57 Sqn
130235	F/O	PYRAH Arthur	30-07-43	7 Sqn
910228	Sgt	QUAIFE Alfred Edward	14-05-43	431 Sqn
1213933	Sgt	QUANCE William Henry	18-08-43	44 Sqn
1392702	Sgt	QUAR Alfred John	27-09-43	199 Sqn
1501100	Sgt	QUAYLE James	14-07-43	158 Sqn
156633	P/O	QUAYLE Peter Geoffrey	6-09-43	620 Sqn
1317194	Sgt	QUICK Edward George	29-04-43	196 Sqn
1322348	Sgt	QUICK Leonard Arthur	10-03-43	44 Sqn
624571	Sgt	QUICKFALL John Francis	24-08-43	90 Sqn
1061861	F/S	QUIGLEY Francis	2-02-43	7 Sqn
48947	F/O	QUILTER Harold Denis	23-06-43	431 Sqn
1113656	Sgt	QUINE Frank Septimus	26-11-43	1658 HCU
1267977	Sgt	QUINLIVAN William Patrick	12-03-43	102 Sqn
1675148	Sgt	QUINN Joseph	23-12-43	1664 HCU
1523625	Sgt	QUINN Walter	9-10-43	78 Sqn
121240	F/O	QUINNEY Robert Alfred	24-11-43	408 Sqn
1333360	Sgt	RABBITT Kenneth Eric	27-04-43	429 Sqn
1317904	W/O	RABETT DFC Reginald Paul	9-10-43	166 Sqn
1313369	Sgt	RADBOURN Bertram George	25-07-43	103 Sqn
1385949	Sgt	RADBOURNE Arthur Henry	3-04-43	166 Sqn
1484662	Sgt	RADCLIFFE Alfred Bryden	31-07-43	78 Sqn
646713	Sgt	RADDALL Philip Smythe	22-09-43	218 Sqn
1437419	Sgt	RADFORD Charles Edward	25-07-43	75 Sqn
1206438	Sgt	RADFORD Horace Stanley Pullen	17-04-43	420 Sqn
1389706	Sgt	RADFORD Reginald William	28-02-43	427 Sqn
1396256	Sgt	RAE John	8-11-43	20 OTU
1318335	Sgt	RAE Thorold Esmond	7-09-43	1663 HCU
1120014	Sgt	RAESIDE William Turnbull	12-02-43	1660 HCU
1028751	Sgt	RAFFERTY George Newton	13-02-43	30 OTU
1391333	Sgt	RAGGETT Albert William	30-08-43	29 OTU
149324	P/O	RAGGETT Peter Roland	18-08-43	35 Sqn
80131	F/O	RAIL William Douglas [Rhodesia]	14-05-43	44 Sqn
1476472	Sgt	RAILTON Alfred Joseph	26-05-43	166 Sqn
134553	F/O	RAINFORD Robert Gorman	31-08-43	75 Sqn
1558903	Sgt	RAISBECK Robert	20-07-43	1662 HCU
1341342	Sgt	RAIT Thomas Gilmour	13-02-43	115 Sqn
149829	P/O	RALPH Frederick Sydney	30-07-43	460 Sqn
1346417	Sgt	RALSTON David Ballantyne	3-04-43	51 Sqn
1539979	Sgt	RAMM Ernest Charles	18-08-43	419 Sqn
777891	F/S	RAMSAY Sydney Vincent [South Africa]	9-01-43	12 Sqn
1238287	Sgt	RAMSAY Walter Dennis	21-04-43	103 Sqn
1059364	Sgt	RAMSDEN John	21-10-43	161 Sqn
1456815	Sgt	RAMSEY Herbert Arthur	3-04-43	101 Sqn
1149217	Sgt	RAMSHAW John George	7-03-43	51 Sqn
905742	W/O	RANDALL Douglas William Graham	3-10-43	102 Sqn
119813	F/O	RANDALL Harry John	18-08-43	49 Sqn
1202224	Sgt	RANDALL William James	22-06-43	428 Sqn
148392	F/O	RANDS Douglas Findlay	26-11-43	431 Sqn
1052516	Sgt	RANKEN George Alexander Aitken	26-02-43	196 Sqn
146332	P/O	RANKIN Andrew	24-08-43	75 Sqn
1322952	Sgt	RANSOM Bernard Stanley	29-03-43	101 Sqn
994313	Sgt	RANSOM Charles Edgar Clarke	15-01-43	214 Sqn
1079156	Sgt	RANSOME Laurence Henry	3-04-43	419 Sqn
1850117	Sgt	RANSON Barrie Stanley	29-12-43	429 Sqn
68155	S/L	RAPHAEL DFC Alfred Sydney	18-08-43	467 Sqn
656896	Sgt	RAPHAEL Victor Edward Richard	25-07-43	103 Sqn
1336152	Sgt	RASHLEY Colin Edward	7-08-43	620 Sqn
1336977	Sgt	RASHLEY Ronald Frederick	26-06-43	115 Sqn
121160	F/O	RASMUSSEN Edward Christian Carl	11-01-43	12 Sqn
743397	Sgt	RATCLIFF Reginald Edward	12-06-43	156 Sqn
118621	F/O	RATCLIFFE Edward Lloyd George	19-02-43	15 Sqn
138648	P/O	RATCLIFFE George Arthur	5-03-43	218 Sqn
158689	P/O	RATCLIFFE Gordon Lennox	16-12-43	49 Sqn
141332	P/O	RATCLIFFE John Robert Francis	3-08-43	405 Sqn
1077190	Sgt	RATCLIFFE Joesph Edward	7-07-43	30 OTU
1577332	Sgt	RATE Bernard Stanley	28-07-43	15 Sqn
1314304	Sgt	RATHBONE John Desmond	26-07-43	620 Sqn
1235704	Sgt	RATHBONE Kenneth Graham	13-07-43	106 Sqn
701032	Sgt	RAVEN Ronald	30-05-43	90 Sqn
144762	P/O	RAVEN Ronald Edward	5-04-43	9 Sqn
1271610	Sgt	RAVEN Roy Desmond	26-07-43	158 Sqn
569748	Sgt	RAVINE Donald Charles	19-08-43	1663 HCU
1491394	Sgt	RAW John	14-07-43	102 Sqn
1238965	Sgt	RAWCLIFFE John	3-04-43	51 Sqn
136317	P/O	RAWLING DFC Stockton Gowland	6-04-43	1663 HCU
1312985	Sgt	RAWLINGS Donald Peter Jack	17-08-43	218 Sqn
158413	P/O	RAWLINGS Frederick Donald	27-11-43	426 Sqn
1122816	Sgt	RAWLINGS Thomas	22-10-43	419 Sqn
1219018	Sgt	RAWLINS Alexander George	12-06-43	466 Sqn
134366	F/O	RAWLINS Kenrick Wyville [Trinidad]	13-08-43	139 Sqn
128872	F/O	RAWLINSON George	28-05-43	10 Sqn
1601751	Sgt	RAWNSLEY William Barrymore	23-05-43	57 Sqn
1591338	Sgt	RAWSON Jack	24-12-43	100 Sqn
1391599	Sgt	RAY Frederick Harry	29-09-43	156 Sqn
1323244	Sgt	RAY Geoffrey Arthur William	16-12-43	115 Sqn
658424	Sgt	RAY Harry	17-04-43	51 Sqn
145801	P/O	RAY John Frederick 'Johnny'	6-07-43	466 Sqn
1128117	Sgt	RAY Kenneth	17-04-43	10 OTU
1212711	Sgt	RAY Louis John	22-06-43	57 Sqn
50657	F/L	RAYMENT Ronald David	27-11-43	619 Sqn
1385954	Sgt	RAYNER Norman Percival	28-05-43	166 Sqn
1202331	Sgt	RAYNER Sturgess Herbert	13-07-43	50 Sqn
132174	F/O	REA DFM Alan James	27-05-43	105 Sqn
50611	F/O	READ Aubrey William	26-11-43	106 Sqn
127125	F/O	READ Crosby Frank	14-07-43	102 Sqn
1389067	Sgt	READ Dudley Herbert	3-08-43	115 Sqn
128958	P/O	READ DFC Frederick Arthur	18-01-43	1654 HCU
1323640	Sgt	READ Frederick David	19-08-43	1663 HCU
1304578	Sgt	READ George Green	6-09-43	623 Sqn
133200	P/O	READ George Patrick	31-08-43	15 Sqn
1671157	Sgt	READ Graham	20-10-43	166 Sqn
1335292	Sgt	READ Harry George John Heaps	13-07-43	49 Sqn
1179121	Sgt	READ Howard Jack	6-02-43	199 Sqn
156615	P/O	READ Joseph	7-09-43	427 Sqn
1394386	Sgt	READ Kenneth William	23-06-43	620 Sqn
1390976	Sgt	READ Raymond Gordon	17-12-43	100 Sqn
542180	Sgt	READ Ronald William	17-01-43	83 Sqn
51669	F/O	READ William Ralph	29-12-43	460 Sqn
657755	Sgt	READE John Joseph [Eire]	26-03-43	426 Sqn
1331432	Sgt	READER Edgar Henry	23-06-43	75 Sqn
131647	P/O	READHEAD Harry Sanford	15-01-43	161 Sqn
1127540	Sgt	READMAN James Leo	27-04-43	51 Sqn
1316515	Sgt	READY Arthur William	18-08-43	77 Sqn
124183	F/L	READY Charles Peter	2-12-43	103 Sqn
135136	F/L	REAY Derek Edward	23-11-43	207 Sqn
1025301	Sgt	REAY John Bowman	13-02-43	12 Sqn
1109402	Sgt	REAY Reginald Herbert	18-08-43	158 Sqn
1543666	Sgt	REAY Robert Gordon	23-08-43	100 Sqn
1335751	Sgt	REDBOURN Peter Reginald	4-12-43	10 Sqn
1425265	Sgt	REDDELL Cyril	4-07-43	90 Sqn
1030797	Sgt	REDDICLIFFE Francis Henry	9-04-43	75 Sqn
1211258	Sgt	REDDISH John	13-05-43	9 Sqn
1128544	Sgt	REDDY Harold	14-03-43	420 Sqn
938010	LAC	REDFERN Elijah Reginald	12-02-43	1660 HCU
1035035	F/S	REDFERN James Gordon	2-12-43	156 Sqn
1819376	Sgt	REDFERN Ronald	26-11-43	550 Sqn
125567	F/O	REDMAN DFC Ernest George	4-07-43	149 Sqn

231

1248099	Sgt	REDMAN Ivan Arthur	17-12-43	100 Sqn	1533893	Sgt	RENTON Reginald James	6-09-43	90 Sqn
1251710	Sgt	REDMAN John	24-05-43	78 Sqn	1533201	Sgt	RENWICK James	15-06-43	103 Sqn
917340	Sgt	REDMAN Walter George	13-06-43	57 Sqn	1339894	Sgt	RETTER Denis Cyril	10-03-43	10 Sqn
1572718	Sgt	REDPATH Stephen	26-05-43	75 Sqn	637292	Sgt	REVELEY George Henry	2-12-43	12 Sqn
1451970	Sgt	REDSHAW Anthony Cantell	29-06-43	51 Sqn	1187995	Sgt	REW Arthur Ernest	30-01-43	466 Sqn
710081	Sgt	REED Clarence Darlington [Rhodesia]	26-03-43	426 Sqn	1094046	Sgt	REX Francis Douglas	1-09-43	77 Sqn
1293332	Sgt	REED David Marlow	30-03-43	51 Sqn	118712	F/O	REYNOLDS Benjamin Frank	12-12-43	105 Sqn
49649	F/O	REED DFC Frederick Charles	31-01-43	57 Sqn	132095	F/O	REYNOLDS Charles Pharaoh	26-06-43	100 Sqn
1189480	W/O	REED Frederick William	19-06-43	11 OTU	1074002	F/S	REYNOLDS David Raymond Nicholas		
1098655	Sgt	REED Philip Noel	3-02-43	106 Sqn				25-05-43	180 Sqn
1388490	Sgt	REED William George	15-06-43	50 Sqn	1497496	Sgt	REYNOLDS Frank	7-09-43	1658 HCU
1330193	Sgt	REED William Lewis	31-07-43	408 Sqn	1333394	Sgt	REYNOLDS Jack Albert George	3-09-43	44 Sqn
1335612	Sgt	REEDER Kenneth Jack	13-02-43	158 Sqn	1172613	Sgt	REYNOLDS John Henry	17-04-43	10 OTU
1432571	AC1	REEKS William Thomas	23-03-43	88 Sqn	1438887	Sgt	REYNOLDS Leslie Thomas	28-08-43	207 Sqn
1316996	Sgt	REES Alun	14-01-43	9 Sqn	777783	Sgt	REYNOLDS Lorimer Seymour	4-09-43	100 Sqn
1653285	Sgt	REES David Gareth	22-10-43	166 Sqn			[Rhodesia]		
1314623	Sgt	REES David John	6-04-43	1663 HCU	1132708	F/S	REYNOLDS Richard Patrick	25-06-43	620 Sqn
1321234	Sgt	REES Jack Valentine	17-04-43	61 Sqn	1380860	Sgt	RHODES Harold Frank	12-04-43	428 Sqn
1317618	Sgt	REES John	24-05-43	10 Sqn	1038105	Sgt	RHODES Harry Robert	15-06-43	49 Sqn
1317602	F/S	REES John Charles Eynon	23-11-43	50 Sqn	1380554	W/O	RHODES John Thomas Campbell	22-10-43	103 Sqn
961005	Sgt	REES John Vernon	8-10-43	21 OTU	1126993	Sgt	RHYND Douglas Dick	10-07-43	50 Sqn
930246	W/O	REES Kenneth Royston	29-04-43	207 Sqn	141465	P/O	RIACH George	3-04-43	78 Sqn
1316649	Sgt	REES Leonard	28-08-43	102 Sqn	1337819	Sgt	RICE Vincent Arthur	25-04-43	29 OTU
657547	Sgt	REES Lewis William	26-05-43	77 Sqn	1283558	Sgt	RICH Peter Colin William	13-05-43	51 Sqn
1386919	F/S	REES Roland Ernest James	28-08-43	199 Sqn	139952	P/O	RICH Ronald Stanley	4-07-43	166 Sqn
1277699	Sgt	REES Thomas Emrys	24-12-43	156 Sqn	658035	Sgt	RICH Thomas	29-04-43	218 Sqn
1317610	Sgt	REES William John	3-07-43	460 Sqn	1585241	Sgt	RICHARDS Alan John George	22-10-43	158 Sqn
1313451	Sgt	REES William Thomas	16-12-43	49 Sqn	1418379	Sgt	RICHARDS David John	13-05-43	35 Sqn
1130993	LAC	REES Willie	6-08-43	51 Sqn	106862	F/O	RICHARDS Francis	8-03-43	61 Sqn
1058557	F/S	REESON Frederick George	23-09-43	432 Sqn	124113	F/O	RICHARDS Frank Mansell	15-06-43	44 Sqn
1388458	Sgt	REEVE Basil Horace	29-04-43	90 Sqn	1602799	Sgt	RICHARDS Fred James	3-08-43	115 Sqn
1396187	Sgt	REEVE Charles Henry	17-12-43	156 Sqn	159008	P/O	RICHARDS Ivor Lloyd	21-10-43	83 Sqn
1264864	Sgt	REEVE George Edward	22-09-43	101 Sqn	996588	F/S	RICHARDS John	3-04-43	51 Sqn
1335974	Sgt	REEVE Ronald Walter John	8-08-43	26 OTU	37480	S/L	RICHARDS John Colverd	21-04-43	12 Sqn
1581814	Sgt	REEVE William	28-09-43	57 Sqn	1211347	Sgt	RICHARDS John Hamlyn	11-08-43	97 Sqn
1501872	Sgt	REEVES Arthur	24-11-43	44 Sqn	129228	F/O	RICHARDS John Henry	24-12-43	576 Sqn
1860969	Sgt	REEVES Arthur Alfred	31-08-43	78 Sqn	1271196	F/S	RICHARDS John Thomas	27-11-43	619 Sqn
1118706	Sgt	REFFIN Joseph	29-06-43	100 Sqn	1356283	Sgt	RICHARDS Kenneth	25-06-43	156 Sqn
1350043	Sgt	REFFLES Albert William	22-06-43	158 Sqn	1395771	Sgt	RICHARDS Norman Conrad	15-06-43	619 Sqn
1890102	Sgt	REGAN Patrick James	4-12-43	78 Sqn	1336553	Sgt	RICHARDS Roderick Henry	2-07-43	620 Sqn
656535	Sgt	REID Arthur William	3-02-43	27 OTU	128667	F/O	RICHARDS William Harold	15-08-43	61 Sqn
1459932	Sgt	REID Charles Clifford	17-12-43	83 Sqn	615979	Sgt	RICHARDSON Alex Henry	23-06-43	466 Sqn
1316069	Sgt	REID Donald Harold	17-04-43	51 Sqn	1020385	Sgt	RICHARDSON Arnold	16-12-43	9 Sqn
118486	F/L	REID DFC Dougal Hamish	26-06-43	57 Sqn	1294108	Sgt	RICHARDSON Arthur William	10-12-43	617 Sqn
1438909	Sgt	REID Douglas Harbinson	1-09-43	77 Sqn	1315873	Sgt	RICHARDSON Arthur William	29-06-43	207 Sqn
149302	P/O	REID Henry James Arthur	25-07-43	166 Sqn	1585002	Sgt	RICHARDSON Christopher Arthur	26-05-43	51 Sqn
125568	F/L	REID James	11-08-43	158 Sqn	1385126	Sgt	RICHARDSON Colin Arthur	3-06-43	10 OTU
1568125	Sgt	REID James Douglas McGill	18-08-43	44 Sqn	1123968	Sgt	RICHARDSON David Bracken	4-09-43	467 Sqn
144464	P/O	REID John Alexander	24-08-43	83 Sqn	169470	P/O	RICHARDSON Desmond Albert	2-12-43	35 Sqn
1592054	Sgt	REID Kenneth	18-10-43	24 OTU	1213853	Sgt	RICHARDSON Douglas David	9-01-43	97 Sqn
125422	F/O	REID Norman Stewart Matthew	16-07-43	78 Sqn	1387194	Sgt	RICHARDSON Eric Ryder	26-06-43	115 Sqn
543427	W/O	REID Richard [Eire]	4-12-43	625 Sqn	1366787	Sgt	RICHARDSON Frank Joseph	16-07-43	10 Sqn
657577	Sgt	REID Robert	3-08-43	9 Sqn	1147351	Sgt	RICHARDSON Harry	30-03-43	57 Sqn
130931	F/O	REID Robert Ryland	28-05-43	115 Sqn	1376652	Sgt	RICHARDSON Harry Reginald Jack	28-08-43	149 Sqn
1560929	Sgt	REID Thomas	12-07-43	1663 HCU	932166	Sgt	RICHARDSON Jack Lewis	19-02-43	15 Sqn
1367429	Sgt	REID William	26-07-43	51 Sqn	1090533	Sgt	RICHARDSON John	23-11-43	207 Sqn
1367967	Sgt	REID William Martin Ewing	23-08-43	207 Sqn	1062514	Sgt	RICHARDSON John Walton	26-05-43	77 Sqn
1005145	Sgt	REILLY Anthony	5-05-43	97 Sqn	1300201	Sgt	RICHARDSON John Wilson	19-11-43	90 Sqn
1566048	Sgt	REILLY James Black	23-11-43	103 Sqn	1043804	Sgt	RICHARDSON Leslie	24-08-43	620 Sqn
1559119	Sgt	REILLY Michael Norman	11-02-43	102 Sqn	1216870	Sgt	RICHARDSON Leslie Henry	18-01-43	12 Sqn
119261	F/O	REILY Richard Louis	28-03-43	105 Sqn	2207432	Sgt	RICHARDSON Ronald William	12-08-43	466 Sqn
861885	Sgt	RELPH Henry Charles	12-06-43	15 Sqn	1481205	Sgt	RICHARDSON Sidney James	5-09-43	20 OTU
47411	F/O	REMBRIDGE Lewis Garnier	4-07-43	97 Sqn	949104	Sgt	RICHARDSON Stanley	8-04-43	44 Sqn
1387475	F/S	RENELT Kenneth Bert	20-12-43	166 Sqn	1231188	Sgt	RICHARDSON Stanley Arthur	22-10-43	77 Sqn
984007	Sgt	RENFREW Robert	28-08-43	75 Sqn	951197	Sgt	RICHARDSON Thomas Frank	11-04-43	214 Sqn
1564365	Sgt	RENNIE James Hynd	14-11-43	20 OTU	88671	F/L	RICHARDSON Thomas Herbert Ottewill		
535117	Sgt	RENSHAW Anthony Steven	14-05-43	83 Sqn				3-04-43	78 Sqn
1396721	Sgt	RENSHAW John Herbert	26-01-43	29 OTU	1188860	Sgt	RICHARDSON William George [USA]	3-04-43	51 Sqn
136395	F/O	RENTON Paul	28-07-43	429 Sqn	1443062	Sgt	RICHARDSON William George	24-07-43	1652 HCU

Service No	Rank	Name	Date	Sqn
119220	F/O	RICHBELL Leonard Edmund	3-05-43	487 Sqn
1183680	Sgt	RICHINGS Dennis Stanley	26-02-43	102 Sqn
115542	F/L	RICHMAN DFM Rowland Edward	2-03-43	149 Sqn
1315723	Sgt	RICHMOND Arthur	5-11-43	199 Sqn
145332	P/O	RICHMOND Arthur William 'Bill'	21-04-43	21 Sqn
1059399	F/S	RICHMOND James	2-12-43	156 Sqn
658703	Sgt	RICHMOND John Roderick	2-05-43	11 OTU
1391946	Sgt	RICHMOND Norman Percy	16-04-43	460 Sqn
1348445	Sgt	RICHMOND Ronald Stuart	30-05-43	12 Sqn
1271609	F/S	RICHTER Valentine 'Val'	16-12-43	576 Sqn
900643	Sgt	RICKETTS Harold William	2-03-43	57 Sqn
638601	Sgt	RICKETTS Richard Frank	22-10-43	49 Sqn
45901	F/L	RICKINSON DFC Leslie Arthur	13-05-43	83 Sqn
137523	P/O	RIDD John Horace	3-04-43	83 Sqn
1314248	Sgt	RIDD Thomas John	3-04-43	106 Sqn
1345041	Sgt	RIDDELL James Crawford Duncan	18-08-43	158 Sqn
991490	Sgt	RIDDELL John Smith	12-06-43	161 Sqn
992727	Sgt	RIDDELL Walter	18-11-43	427 Sqn
798620	Sgt	RIDEOUT Harry Alfred [Newfoundland]	20-03-43	101 Sqn
1219496	Sgt	RIDER John William	3-03-43	214 Sqn
1056063	Sgt	RIDGE Arthur	8-04-43	218 Sqn
1323884	Sgt	RIDGE William Ernest	26-11-43	158 Sqn
1320885	Sgt	RIDGLEY Ronald William	25-06-43	101 Sqn
540625	Sgt	RIDGWAY Roy Cyril	17-06-43	103 Sqn
1058367	Sgt	RIDLEY Andrew	7-09-43	102 Sqn
111535	F/O	RIDLEY Frank	31-01-43	49 Sqn
1018378	Sgt	RIDLEY Norman	21-01-43	158 Sqn
1457270	Sgt	RIDSDALE Brnard	29-09-43	50 Sqn
1244450	Sgt	RIGBY Henry	25-02-43	106 Sqn
127881	F/O	RIGBY John Edward	24-05-43	51 Sqn
137374	P/O	RIGBY Kenneth Craiglaw	3-08-43	405 Sqn
745328	F/S	RIGDEN John Stanley	14-03-43	138 Sqn
1148459	Sgt	RIGG Roy Commer	4-12-43	115 Sqn
943320	Sgt	RILES Henry	30-01-43	426 Sqn
1253689	Sgt	RILEY Albert Thomas	3-01-43	9 Sqn
1090148	Sgt	RILEY George Hector	9-08-43	149 Sqn
1389192	F/S	RILEY John Coates	18-11-43	35 Sqn
1352461	Sgt	RILEY Joseph	25-04-43	29 OTU
1538446	Sgt	RILEY Milton	29-06-43	100 Sqn
1185099	Sgt	RILEY Richard George	9-03-43	156 Sqn
1032154	Sgt	RILEY Thomas	4-07-43	408 Sqn
1283533	F/S	RINGE Wallace Anthony	26-02-43	83 Sqn
1320553	Sgt	RINGER Cyril James	18-09-43	1658 HCU
1379717	Sgt	RIPPINGALE George	28-08-43	158 Sqn
1066150	Sgt	RISHTON William	22-03-43	101 Sqn
1095177	Sgt	RISINGHAM Charles	22-01-43	429 Sqn
1341377	Sgt	RITCHIE John	26-07-43	51 Sqn
1177423	Sgt	RIVERS Cecil Frederick Archie	2-07-43	29 OTU
1330344	Sgt	RIVERS Norman Evans	29-06-43	619 Sqn
1295092	Sgt	RIVERS Royce William	15-06-43	44 Sqn
1804254	Sgt	RIVETT Francis Edgar Arthur	24-12-43	576 Sqn
630984	F/S	RIXON Alfred	4-04-43	156 Sqn
1232122	Sgt	ROADLEY George Stephen	24-08-43	102 Sqn
656009	Sgt	ROBB David Arthur	23-05-43	57 Sqn
116074	F/O	ROBB John William	15-05-43	27 OTU
906980	Sgt	ROBBINS George Alfred	8-06-43	16 OTU
1338962	Sgt	ROBBINS Sidney Aaron	3-11-43	625 Sqn
1670155	Sgt	ROBBINS Thomas Manuel	2-12-43	103 Sqn
1374376	LAC	ROBERTON James	19-06-43	Snaith
1330745	Sgt	ROBERTS Albert Ernest	3-05-43	50 Sqn
1818062	Sgt	ROBERTS Albert William	26-11-43	429 Sqn
2213691	Sgt	ROBERTS Arnold	13-06-43	51 Sqn
1269945	F/S	ROBERTS Charles Walpole	17-05-43	617 Sqn
1064318	Sgt	ROBERTS Edward	13-01-43	61 Sqn
1452782	Sgt	ROBERTS Eric James	20-12-43	514 Sqn
649066	Sgt	ROBERTS Frederick	24-08-43	78 Sqn
651771	Sgt	ROBERTS Geoffrey Evan	17-04-43	51 Sqn
1168071	Sgt	ROBERTS George Frederick	5-01-43	101 Sqn
1056193	F/S	ROBERTS Hugh Alan	13-05-43	51 Sqn
1008845	Sgt	ROBERTS Jack	26-06-43	51 Sqn
1585875	Sgt	ROBERTS Kenneth Bysshe	29-09-43	17 OTU
52038	P/O	ROBERTS DFM Llewellyn	12-06-43	161 Sqn
1511208	Sgt	ROBERTS Phillip	6-09-43	106 Sqn
2209068	Sgt	ROBERTS Phillip Grenville	8-11-43	623 Sqn
128510	F/L	ROBERTS DFC Reginald	18-11-43	156 Sqn
143094	P/O	ROBERTS DFM Richard David	28-04-43	158 Sqn
1124720	Sgt	ROBERTS Richard Hywel	11-04-43	57 Sqn
1389926	Sgt	ROBERTS Robert Elwyn	9-01-43	57 Sqn
2207091	Sgt	ROBERTS Robert William	20-12-43	103 Sqn
1301559	F/S	ROBERTS Ronald Frank	24-08-43	102 Sqn
1331594	Sgt	ROBERTS Ronald Harold Percival	2-03-43	57 Sqn
1333459	Sgt	ROBERTS Ronald James	27-03-43	10 OTU
1005778	Sgt	ROBERTS Thomas Ainslie	17-09-43	158 Sqn
1653106	Sgt	ROBERTS Thomas George	18-11-43	431 Sqn
1677382	Sgt	ROBERTS Thomas Glyn	19-09-43	1658 HCU
1413356	Sgt	ROBERTS Trevor	9-10-43	166 Sqn
1323253	Sgt	ROBERTS William Augustus	13-05-43	50 Sqn
1380839	Sgt	ROBERTS William Stanley	30-07-43	15 OTU
1824708	Sgt	ROBERTSON Alexander	24-10-43	19 OTU
145512	P/O	ROBERTSON Angus Alan	6-09-43	106 Sqn
1395178	Sgt	ROBERTSON Charles William	28-07-43	78 Sqn
1270871	Sgt	ROBERTSON Desmond Charles	16-05-43	466 Sqn
653317	Sgt	ROBERTSON Frank	28-07-43	106 Sqn
657521	F/S	ROBERTSON Harry	29-09-43	158 Sqn
116210	F/O	ROBERTSON Hector	10-04-43	9 Sqn
1374201	Sgt	ROBERTSON James	30-03-43	49 Sqn
1607210	Sgt	ROBERTSON James	26-11-43	61 Sqn
1565878	Sgt	ROBERTSON John	22-11-43	77 Sqn
53343	P/O	ROBERTSON John Alexander	1-09-43	44 Sqn
1367800	Sgt	ROBERTSON John James	16-12-43	408 Sqn
1559474	Sgt	ROBERTSON John Kennedy	26-11-43	101 Sqn
1620748	Sgt	ROBERTSON Stanley	7-08-43	9 Sqn
1379852	Sgt	ROBERTSON Thomas Charles	17-04-43	49 Sqn
1365292	F/S	ROBERTSON Thomas Jack	2-12-43	106 Sqn
778953	Sgt	ROBERTSON Tudor Robert Musgrave [Rhodesia]	20-10-43	29 OTU
1365148	Sgt	ROBERTSON William Alexander	8-10-43	9 Sqn
1306838	Sgt	ROBERTSON William Downie	22-06-43	35 Sqn
530734	Sgt	ROBERTSON William Mitchell	29-03-43	218 Sqn
1096843	Sgt	ROBINSON Alfred	7-10-43	149 Sqn
34089	G/C	ROBINSON DSO DFC* AFC Basil Vernon	24-08-43	35 Sqn
1324276	Sgt	ROBINSON Benjamin	3-08-43	61 Sqn
987906	Sgt	ROBINSON Brook	10-12-43	617 Sqn
578359	Sgt	ROBINSON Charles William	25-06-43	12 Sqn
1677459	Sgt	ROBINSON Clifford	16-12-43	625 Sqn
778674	Sgt	ROBINSON Derrick Joseph Rishworth [Rhodesia]	3-04-43	467 Sqn
1239036	Sgt	ROBINSON Donald Hubert	13-05-43	90 Sqn
1267632	Sgt	ROBINSON Douglas Cory	3-05-43	487 Sqn
1530031	Sgt	ROBINSON Edward	4-09-43	7 Sqn
1330303	Sgt	ROBINSON Eric Arthur	31-03-43	14 OTU
538137	Sgt	ROBINSON Frank James	23-11-43	1658 HCU
1094894	Sgt	ROBINSON Frank Norman	4-05-43	218 Sqn
989538	Sgt	ROBINSON George	5-02-43	50 Sqn
1699156	Sgt	ROBINSON George Albert	22-06-43	57 Sqn
52820	P/O	ROBINSON Harry	18-08-43	61 Sqn
1576239	Sgt	ROBINSON Harry	30-05-43	44 Sqn
1380701	F/S	ROBINSON Humphrey Peter	22-10-43	103 Sqn
1024294	Sgt	ROBINSON John	5-03-43	100 Sqn
155261	P/O	ROBINSON Norman John [Eire]	24-11-43	9 Sqn
1394512	Sgt	ROBINSON Peter Brindley	23-06-43	427 Sqn
1384272	Sgt	ROBINSON Reginald Warren	8-01-43	9 Sqn
1332631	Sgt	ROBINSON Robert Walter	17-04-43	77 Sqn
45617	S/L	ROBINSON DFM MiD Samuel	26-02-43	83 Sqn
124758	F/O	ROBINSON Stuart Quentin	14-06-43	199 Sqn
1080327	Sgt	ROBINSON Thomas	12-03-43	20 OTU

120669	F/O	ROBINSON Thomas Collis	17-04-43	51 Sqn		1623561	Sgt	ROOKS Albert	22-10-43	1654 HCU
1199109	Sgt	ROBINSON Thomas Norman	30-07-43	9 Sqn		549120	LAC	ROONEY Hugh	2-07-43	620 Sqn
1073018	LAC	ROBINSON Walter	26-02-43	196 Sqn		1238955	Sgt	ROONEY Raymond Joseph	17-04-43	49 Sqn
162592	P/O	ROBINSON Walter Ernest	2-12-43	156 Sqn		1392398	Sgt	ROOTS Harry	26-05-43	77 Sqn
1602056	Sgt	ROBINSON William	14-07-43	78 Sqn		1322042	Sgt	ROOTS Kenneth George	13-05-43	149 Sqn
142019	P/O	ROBINSON William Albert	3-04-43	158 Sqn		145911	P/O	ROOT-REED Maurice	3-10-43	61 Sqn
1504635	Sgt	ROBINSON William Arthur	9-06-43	619 Sqn		1623211	Sgt	ROPER Ernest Anthony	13-07-43	467 Sqn
1577597	Sgt	ROBINSON William Stephen	27-09-43	19 OTU		1185420	F/S	ROPER John Victor	10-03-43	103 Sqn
1496426	Sgt	ROBOTHAM Kenneth James	1-12-43	199 Sqn		1358058	Sgt	RORISON James	26-06-43	51 Sqn
1553859	Sgt	ROBSON Eric	4-09-43	467 Sqn		113328	F/O	ROSAM DFC DFM Edward William George		
1451671	Sgt	ROBSON Frank Weldon	23-11-43	1658 HCU					31-01-43	57 Sqn
1314570	Sgt	ROBSON Jack Henry	15-01-43	23 OTU		575202	Sgt	ROSE Derrick John	16-08-43	57 Sqn
1044114	F/S	ROBSON James Allan	23-06-43	90 Sqn		124400	F/O	ROSE Desmond James	13-02-43	115 Sqn
1079549	Sgt	ROBSON Joseph	18-11-43	218 Sqn		1387015	Sgt	ROSE Frederick Charles	24-05-43	10 Sqn
1109207	Sgt	ROBSON Joseph Jeffrie	15-02-43	466 Sqn		1356376	Sgt	ROSE George	5-05-43	102 Sqn
631432	Sgt	ROBSON Keith	24-04-43	218 Sqn		1318644	Sgt	ROSE Gilbert Ernest	23-06-43	218 Sqn
1160792	LAC	ROBSON Kenneth Thomas	12-03-43	1661 HCU		1541546	Sgt	ROSE Peter John	1-03-43	50 Sqn
1049564	Sgt	ROBSON DFM Stanley	26-07-43	103 Sqn		1150866	Sgt	ROSE Stanley John	10-03-43	103 Sqn
1518240	Sgt	ROBSON Thomas William Eric	22-01-43	76 Sqn		1071860	Sgt	ROSE Thomas Leslie	3-08-43	428 Sqn
1294066	Sgt	ROCHE Stephen Joseph	3-02-43	226 Sqn		1554345	Sgt	ROSE William	28-11-43	16 OTU
1685967	Sgt	ROCHECOUSTE Jean Maxime Herve	20-12-43	10 Sqn		1144632	Sgt	ROSEN Anthony Ezra	18-11-43	101 Sqn
		[Mauritius]				655247	F/S	ROSENBLATT Nathan	6-08-43	192 Sqn
1206439	Sgt	ROCHESTER Aubrey Edgar Perrin	24-05-43	51 Sqn		1387181	Sgt	ROSENTHAL Saul Austin Roy	11-08-43	106 Sqn
1236544	Sgt	ROCK Douglas Harry	5-05-43	83 Sqn		1393143	Sgt	ROSS Anthony Edward Deighton	7-07-43	21 OTU
1620922	Sgt	ROCKETT Tom	11-08-43	158 Sqn		132098	F/O	ROSS Colin Patrick [Grenada]	3-11-43	49 Sqn
520821	Sgt	ROCKNEAN Horace	17-06-43	103 Sqn		1371363	Sgt	ROSS James Hamilton	12-03-43	218 Sqn
339812	Sgt	ROCKWOOD Gerald Wilfred	20-06-43	10 Sqn		1804080	Sgt	ROSS Joesph William	16-12-43	576 Sqn
		[Newfoundland]				127015	F/O	ROSS Robert Craig	25-07-43	76 Sqn
1386124	F/S	RODD Jack Arnold	30-08-43	139 Sqn		1313694	Sgt	ROSSER Russell Verran	15-04-43	196 Sqn
1226671	Sgt	RODEN Ernest Howard	10-08-43	49 Sqn		139685	F/O	ROSSER Trevor	2-12-43	44 Sqn
37893	S/L	RODEN DFC George Alan	2-12-43	626 Sqn		128011	F/O	ROSSIE Anthony Alexander	30-07-43	9 Sqn
		[New Zealand]				130612	F/O	ROSSIGNOL Allen Theodore Lewis	2-06-43	20 OTU
121558	F/O	RODGER James Alexander	16-09-43	617 Sqn				[USA]		
131066	F/L	RODGER Robert Young	9-11-43	90 Sqn		1330740	F/S	ROSS THOMSON Hugh Alexander	2-02-43	102 Sqn
1381145	Sgt	RODGERS Jack	17-04-43	83 Sqn		1499353	Sgt	ROSTRON Alfred	27-09-43	10 Sqn
960866	Sgt	RODGERS John Harris	23-09-43	100 Sqn		1029458	Sgt	ROSTRON Joseph	29-01-43	408 Sqn
657967	F/S	RODGERS Ronald	28-08-43	77 Sqn		1399303	Sgt	ROTHER Louis Anthony [Trinidad]	25-10-43	20 OTU
1292168	Sgt	RODWAY George Albert	4-05-43	15 Sqn		1387403	F/S	ROTHERA Peter Geoffrey	4-07-43	429 Sqn
1576603	Sgt	ROE George	9-01-43	57 Sqn		1107777	Sgt	ROTHERAY Lewis	29-01-43	1652 HCU
1384342	Sgt	ROGERS Brian Arthur	27-04-43	75 Sqn		1334592	Sgt	ROUGHAN John Patrick	26-05-43	218 Sqn
146027	F/L	ROGERS Derek Ralph	22-10-43	78 Sqn		1431821	Sgt	ROUGHLEY John	18-06-43	83 Sqn
1338400	Sgt	ROGERS Edgar Ronald	27-09-43	19 OTU		1671697	Sgt	ROULSON Arthur Dewhirst	4-12-43	576 Sqn
138792	P/O	ROGERS Frank	1-06-43	26 OTU		1318732	Sgt	ROUSE John Ernest	20-03-43	27 OTU
1382746	Sgt	ROGERS Gilbert Humphreys	5-05-43	75 Sqn		1380943	Sgt	ROUSE Raymond Gerrard	30-01-43	28 OTU
113484	F/O	ROGERS DFM Harold Humphrey	8-04-43	76 Sqn		1810021	Sgt	ROUSE Richard William	14-07-43	78 Sqn
1890385	Sgt	ROGERS Harry George	3-11-43	12 Sqn		148785	F/L	ROUTEN DFM Dennis Arthur	27-09-43	7 Sqn
120595	F/O	ROGERS John Arthur	7-08-43	620 Sqn		964395	F/S	ROUTLEDGE DFM Frank William Thomas		
1545048	Sgt	ROGERS John Hill	4-10-43	100 Sqn					3-04-43	83 Sqn
1462732	AC1	ROGERS Leonard James	12-03-43	5 Group		1178835	F/S	ROUTLEDGE Thomas Anthony	26-05-43	12 Sqn
1380939	Sgt	ROGERS Peter	26-02-43	15 Sqn		80412	P/O	ROUX Theunis Christoffel [Rhodesia]	29-01-43	408 Sqn
1724911	AC1	ROGERS Reginald Arthur Charles	8-08-43	214 Sqn		1508403	Sgt	ROWAND William	27-11-43	101 Sqn
1183329	Sgt	ROGERS Robert James	27-01-43	460 Sqn		658656	Sgt	ROWBOTHAM Douglas	3-08-43	405 Sqn
818036	F/S	ROGERS Samuel Phillip	22-11-43	10 Sqn		1294895	F/S	ROWBOTTOM Edward Thomas Samuel		
141459	P/O	ROGERS Sidney Clifford	10-02-43	1657 HCU					31-08-43	102 Sqn
1377421	Sgt	ROGERS William Augustus	17-04-43	51 Sqn		1094047	Sgt	ROWBOTTOM Harold	5-05-43	1663 HCU
156417	P/O	ROGERSON John Turner	3-10-43	427 Sqn		1078082	Sgt	ROWE Harry Dawson	16-04-43	156 Sqn
108001	S/L	ROHDE DFC Douglas Oscar	17-01-43	3 GComFlt		1149033	Sgt	ROWELL Arnold William	25-02-43	19 OTU
1681963	Sgt	ROLFE Arthur	4-09-43	460 Sqn		659085	Sgt	ROWEN Frederick Robert	24-08-43	78 Sqn
1601535	Sgt	ROLFE Henry Edmund	5-09-43	20 OTU		1323502	Sgt	ROWLAND Derek Lawson	3-05-43	487 Sqn
136361	F/O	ROLFE Phillip Neville	23-09-43	57 Sqn		1040539	Sgt	ROWLANDS Eric	24-05-43	460 Sqn
1180657	F/S	ROLFE Raymond Robert Seppings	19-03-43	161 Sqn		1330566	Sgt	ROWLANDS Thomas Philip	3-10-43	623 Sqn
155787	F/S	ROLLIN DFC Donald Albert	16-12-43	44 Sqn		1575968	Sgt	ROWLANDS Walter Clive	26-06-43	9 Sqn
124946	F/O	ROLLINGS Charles Richard George	24-08-43	77 Sqn		1434822	Sgt	ROWLEY Dennis William	5-05-43	101 Sqn
149921	P/O	ROLLINS Philip Eaton	14-09-43	138 Sqn		1237461	Sgt	ROWSON Geoffrey Harold	18-01-43	97 Sqn
1575725	Sgt	ROLLINSON Samuel Dudley	29-06-43	424 Sqn		125572	F/O	ROXBURGH Stephen	12-06-43	466 Sqn
1335420	Sgt	ROLPH Cecil George	23-09-43	419 Sqn		1247245	Sgt	ROYANS Bernard	23-09-43	106 Sqn
1377787	Sgt	ROME Edwin	13-05-43	12 Sqn		118604	F/O	ROYDE DFC George Reicher	14-05-43	149 Sqn
1077030	Sgt	ROOKE James Wesley	28-07-43	102 Sqn		1314292	Sgt	ROYNON Edward John	16-12-43	466 Sqn
1376950	Sgt	ROOKE Ronald Vivian Steven	28-02-43	90 Sqn		1397659	Sgt	ROYSE Alfred Peter	3-10-43	158 Sqn

1451982	Sgt	ROZA Henry Francis	18-08-43	77 Sqn		1555790	LAC	SALKELD Robert	7-08-43	199 Sqn
546586	Sgt	RUANE Patrick Joseph	15-06-43	619 Sqn		159430	P/O	SALMON Frank Edward Gordon	23-11-43	78 Sqn
1676327	Sgt	RUDDEN Terence	16-12-43	166 Sqn		1416753	Sgt	SALMON Laurence Cyril	29-08-43	29 OTU
1419688	Sgt	RUDDY Brian Hartley	24-08-43	75 Sqn		1550383	Sgt	SALMOND Peter Miller Hamilton	16-08-43	61 Sqn
1319221	Sgt	RUDGE Desmond	22-06-43	408 Sqn		1316986	Sgt	SALT Albert Walter	5-09-43	1663 HCU
1011171	LAC	RUDGE Herbert	19-06-43	Snaith		149344	P/O	SALT Gordon Geoffrey	27-11-43	619 Sqn
926842	F/S	RUDKIN Peter Alfred James	9-01-43	51 Sqn		125986	F/O	SALT JuIın Hamilton	9-04-43	44 Sqn
155921	P/O	RUDKIN Samuel Ivan	17-08-43	44 Sqn		657679	Sgt	SALT Reginald James Peter	7-02-43	408 Sqn
129613	F/O	RUDMAN Albert John	20-12-43	426 Sqn		1263273	Sgt	SALTER Francis George	13-05-43	149 Sqn
520333	F/S	RUDMAN Charles Thomas	12-07-43	10 OTU		1434098	W/O	SALTHOUSE Wilfrid	28-07-43	12 Sqn
1387054	Sgt	RUGERONI-HOPE Joseph Raymond Charles				156123	P/O	SALVAGE Arthur Jack	4-12-43	51 Sqn
			2-02-43	19 OTU		1125185	Sgt	SALVAGE Fred 'Freddie'	10-03-43	100 Sqn
1564807	F/S	RUMBLE Cyril	22-08-43	1658 HCU		1459749	Sgt	SAMPSON Cyril	23-06-43	427 Sqn
1321620	Sgt	RUMMERY Laurence Arthur	21-04-43	12 Sqn		1337716	Sgt	SAMPSON Kennth John	17-05-43	19 OTU
1810353	Sgt	RUNCIMAN Kenneth	24-09-43	12 Sqn		106546	F/O	SAMS John Hamilton	26-06-43	9 Sqn
1383593	Sgt	RUOCCO Domenico	30-05-43	75 Sqn		1600605	Sgt	SAMUEL Alec Cecil	12-08-43	76 Sqn
1697335	Sgt	RUSH Arthur Anthony	13-06-43	115 Sqn		591204	Sgt	SAMUEL Gwilym John	29-06-43	78 Sqn
1337178	Sgt	RUSHBY Alfred Sugden	2-12-43	207 Sqn		656180	Sgt	SANDARS Alan McGeoch	26-06-43	57 Sqn
1250272	Sgt	RUSHTON Ian Peter Douglas	29-04-43	428 Sqn		1196410	Sgt	SANDERS Daniel	23-06-43	90 Sqn
1621269	Sgt	RUSHTON Rodney	11-08-43	77 Sqn		1434069	Sgt	SANDERS Harold George	30-06-43	1513 Flt
131938	F/O	RUSSEL Gordon	26-05-43	100 Sqn		146937	P/O	SANDERS John Fryon	24-05-43	166 Sqn
653110	F/S	RUSSELL Alexander	17-12-43	97 Sqn		1319816	Sgt	SANDERS Lawrence Anthony Wykeham		
1317088	Sgt	RUSSELL Emrys	12-06-43	103 Sqn					5-05-43	57 Sqn
1432656	Sgt	RUSSELL Ernest Edward	13-05-43	24 OTU		1302205	Cpl	SANDERSON Christopher Shields	28-05-43	Feltwell
1331291	Sgt	RUSSELL Harold William Frederick	1-10-43	1660 HCU		102108	F/L	SANDERSON Eric	29-06-43	97 Sqn
1320125	Sgt	RUSSELL Harry	13-05-43	466 Sqn		573844	Sgt	SANDERSON Fred William	26-06-43	9 Sqn
1522694	Sgt	RUSSELL John	24-12-43	50 Sqn		149461	P/O	SANDERSON Frederick Richard	28-08-43	78 Sqn
1338131	Sgt	RUSSELL John Herbert	12-06-43	75 Sqn		1339053	Sgt	SANDERSON John Edward	19-05-43	14 OTU
1391528	Sgt	RUSSELL Robin Francis	31-07-43	76 Sqn		1062023	Sgt	SANDFIELD Gordon	5-05-43	419 Sqn
924224	Sgt	RUSSELL Stanley Ernest	30-07-43	9 Sqn		138793	P/O	SANDHAM Thomas	30-07-43	214 Sqn
1183357	Sgt	RUSSELL Stanton Eric Arthur	5-05-43	35 Sqn		1315036	Sgt	SANDOVER Peter	4-02-43	427 Sqn
1266850	Sgt	RUSSELL Thomas Edward	26-02-43	102 Sqn		1455048	Sgt	SANDOW Alfred	1-03-43	50 Sqn
1347861	Sgt	RUSSELL Thomas Pollock	30-05-43	460 Sqn		612042	F/S	SANKEY DFM Thomas Neville	1-03-43	35 Sqn
1214848	Sgt	RUSSOM Eric	16-12-43	576 Sqn		129535	F/O	SANSOM Geoffrey	24-06-43	192 Sqn
146988	P/O	RUST Maurice Edgar	23-06-43	83 Sqn		992386	F/S	SARGENT Charles Frederick	30-07-43	9 Sqn
1022420	Sgt	RUSTON Donald	13-08-43	432 Sqn		1321977	Sgt	SARGENT Walter Leonard	2-12-43	103 Sqn
1074263	Sgt	RUTH William	14-02-43	158 Sqn		142055	P/O	SARGINSON John	26-07-43	51 Sqn
1585062	Sgt	RUTHERFORD George	4-05-43	15 Sqn		1801758	Sgt	SATCHELL John Walter	28-09-43	428 Sqn
133718	F/O	RUTHERFORD Robert Henry	22-07-43	1657 HCU		1307696	Sgt	SAUNDERS Alan Richard	18-01-43	76 Sqn
927349	F/S	RUTHERFORD MiD Stuart John Gascoyne				1394719	Sgt	SAUNDERS Anthony Francis	31-08-43	75 Sqn
			31-03-43	10 OTU		149206	P/O	SAUNDERS Arthur Foreman	29-06-43	15 Sqn
1535677	Sgt	RUTTER John	17-04-43	100 Sqn		1605321	Sgt	SAUNDERS Eric	31-08-43	75 Sqn
1379190	Sgt	RYAN Daniel	1-02-43	11 OTU		1380702	Sgt	SAUNDERS Frank	19-02-43	166 Sqn
614624	Sgt	RYAN James Joseph	14-05-43	149 Sqn		151429	F/O	SAUNDERS Frederick	18-08-43	11 OTU
1386032	Sgt	RYAN Mervyn John Rees	12-07-43	10 OTU		1286414	Sgt	SAUNDERS Frederick Henry	23-01-43	105 Sqn
135110	F/O	RYAN Patrick Joseph	24-08-43	101 Sqn		785073	Sgt	SAUNDERS Harold Edward Richard	11-02-43	102 Sqn
1803233	Sgt	RYAN Simon John [Eire]	22-11-43	156 Sqn				[Australia]		
617495	Sgt	RYDER Frederick Ernest	4-12-43	77 Sqn		649405	Sgt	SAUNDERS Henry Arthur	6-09-43	149 Sqn
1458224	Sgt	RYDER Haydn Deryk	11-11-43	1654 HCU		1293909	F/S	SAUNDERS John Arthur	30-05-43	10 Sqn
1075560	Sgt	RYDER Jack	2-03-43	76 Sqn		1577848	Sgt	SAUNDERS Kenneth	9-10-43	106 Sqn
143402	P/O	RYDER Thomas Joseph	11-04-43	7 Sqn		1627455	AC2	SAUNDERS Leslie Albert	25-07-43	Graveley
1809922	Sgt	RYE Robert Kenneth	17-04-43	101 Sqn		1809920	Sgt	SAUNDERS Philip James	24-08-43	620 Sqn
646001	Sgt	SABELL Ronald Sidney	3-04-43	106 Sqn		996259	Sgt	SAUNDERS Raymond Charles	3-04-43	139 Sqn
1338727	Sgt	SACH Dennis Bertram	13-05-43	149 Sqn		1601119	Sgt	SAUNDERS Raymond Percy Thomas	30-03-43	149 Sqn
967831	F/S	SACKVILLE-GOLDEN Ronald Edmund				139677	Sgt	SAUNDERS William Henry	6-09-43	76 Sqn
			9-01-43	419 Sqn		1585455	W/O	SAUNDERS William Thomas	4-10-43	97 Sqn
1515172	Sgt	SACRE John George	4-09-43	49 Sqn		1080386	Sgt	SAVAGE Maurice	29-04-43	12 Sqn
1346909	F/S	SADDLER William George Fyfe	26-11-43	514 Sqn		1503913	Sgt	SAVAGE Willis Arthur	16-12-43	75 Sqn
1288558	Sgt	SADLEIR Robert Edgar	6-07-43	1660 HCU		170452	P/O	SAVILLE Bernard John	20-12-43	49 Sqn
545242	Sgt	SADLER Alfred Arthur	30-12-43	26 OTU		74738	W/C	SAVILLE DSO DFC Donald Teale	25-07-43	218 Sqn
1186870	Sgt	SADLER Frank	4-07-43	10 Sqn		1253947	Sgt	SAVILLE James Harold	15-06-43	103 Sqn
1893262	Sgt	SADLER William James	8-10-43	20 OTU		1235571	Sgt	SAVILLE Kenneth	22-09-43	207 Sqn
1601078	Sgt	SAFFREY John	22-10-43	166 Sqn		988963	F/S	SAVORY Augustus William	27-11-43	83 Sqn
1292880	Sgt	SAGE Gordon Charles	20-12-43	156 Sqn		1268571	Sgt	SAVOY Derrick William	7-09-43	106 Sqn
572568	Sgt	SAGE Robert James	23-06-43	158 Sqn		1558937	Sgt	SAVUKEVITCH John	31-08-43	102 Sqn
1130523	Sgt	SALAD Joseph	3-05-43	51 Sqn				(served as HARRIS)		
1491828	Sgt	SALE Leslie	16-12-43	426 Sqn		123355	F/O	SAWDY William Ernest	14-06-43	199 Sqn
1803655	Sgt	SALES George Alastair	22-09-43	9 Sqn		1322090	Sgt	SAWKINGS Herbert Ward	4-05-43	218 Sqn
1178553	Cpl	SALISBURY Albert	21-11-43	61 Sqn		125574	F/L	SAWYER Rupert Claude	13-05-43	35 Sqn

Service #	Rank	Name	Date	Sqn
137545	F/O	SAXBY Thomas William Allan	4-09-43	106 Sqn
1127441	Sgt	SAXON Edward	18-07-43	1661 HCU
137557	P/O	SAXON Joseph	24-08-43	77 Sqn
1499180	Sgt	SAXTON George Henry	13-05-43	9 Sqn
1233720	W/O	SAXTON John Harold	23-11-43	50 Sqn
130260	P/O	SAY Ronald Victor	19-01-43	20 OTU
1337045	Sgt	SAYER Derrick Balcombe	20-02-43	90 Sqn
1293575	Sgt	SAYER George Charles Daniel	3-03-43	76 Sqn
1322634	Sgt	SAYERS Arthur William	15-05-43	27 OTU
814160	Sgt	SAYERS Frank Gordon	14-04-43	12 Sqn
120525	F/O	SCALES John	20-12-43	466 Sqn
798725	Sgt	SCAMMELL Bernard Thomas [Newfoundland]	24-06-43	10 OTU
49314	F/O	SCAMMELL DFC Geoffrey Wynne	18-08-43	426 Sqn
1089365	Sgt	SCANLON William Ernest [Eire]	5-04-43	10 Sqn
1399058	Sgt	SCARBOROUGH Herbert Edgar	17-09-43	10 OTU
1383823	Sgt	SCARBROUGH William Edward	15-02-43	100 Sqn
144714	P/O	SCARCLIFFE George Albert	7-09-43	78 Sqn
1261331	Sgt	SCARFE Leslie Thomas	28-04-43	75 Sqn
1109741	Sgt	SCARGALL Fred Raithby	17-01-43	1654 HCU
1219656	Sgt	SCARISBRICK Leonard Everard	16-09-43	15 Sqn
149982	P/O	SCARLES Jack Robert	14-09-43	138 Sqn
1027850	Sgt	SCARLETT DFM William	4-07-43	166 Sqn
1624092	Sgt	SCARR Frederick George	28-08-43	90 Sqn
1268317	Sgt	SCHEDDLE Max	4-07-43	90 Sqn
928921	F/S	SCHILDKNECHT Albert Edmond [Belgium]	19-02-43	83 Sqn
141827	P/O	SCHOFIELD Arthur Reginald	28-04-43	158 Sqn
1088089	Sgt	SCHOFIELD James William	23-01-43	75 Sqn
1124862	Sgt	SCHOFIELD Samuel	4-08-43	16 OTU
50978	P/O	SCHOLEY Albert Bloomer	20-02-43	90 Sqn
644477	Sgt	SCHOLEY Leslie Harry	18-08-43	61 Sqn
1339266	F/S	SCHROEDER Leslie Charles	26-05-43	12 Sqn
1334705	Sgt	SCHUBERT Guy Edgar	24-05-43	78 Sqn
572620	Sgt	SCHULTZ Louis William John	27-03-43	44 Sqn
1054722	Sgt	SCOBIE William	9-01-43	103 Sqn
1628705	Sgt	SCOREY Ernest Bertram Frank	24-08-43	78 Sqn
531018	Sgt	SCOTNEY Cecil Claude Daniels	18-05-43	149 Sqn
159896	P/O	SCOTT Alan John	3-11-43	467 Sqn
948645	Sgt	SCOTT Alexander Suttie	27-07-43	156 SQN
1107845	Sgt	SCOTT Arthur Daniel	15-02-43	28 OTU
1386189	Sgt	SCOTT Bertram Leslie	26-06-43	101 Sqn
127166	F/O	SCOTT Edward Henry	15-04-43	214 Sqn
1272216	Sgt	SCOTT Eric Desmond	2-05-43	11 OTU
1392922	Sgt	SCOTT Frank Frederick	4-12-43	115 Sqn
1345479	Sgt	SCOTT George	27-09-43	76 Sqn
1346873	Sgt	SCOTT Harry	26-07-43	158 Sqn
901570	Sgt	SCOTT Horace Stephen	26-05-43	149 Sqn
1335856	Sgt	SCOTT James Albert	12-05-43	20 OTU
578312	Sgt	SCOTT James Clark	24-12-43	550 Sqn
1347014	Sgt	SCOTT James Davidson	19-11-43	149 Sqn
1370641	Sgt	SCOTT James Waugh	3-12-43	619 Sqn
1369058	Sgt	SCOTT James William	3-05-43	81 OTU
1550748	Sgt	SCOTT John	30-08-43	29 OTU
118600	F/O	SCOTT John Wardle	29-04-43	218 Sqn
1094144	Sgt	SCOTT Joseph	17-06-43	12 Sqn
1289554	Sgt	SCOTT Kenneth William	13-02-43	158 Sqn
158004	P/O	SCOTT Peter John Macintyre	23-11-43	405 Sqn
1126204	Sgt	SCOTT Robert Eccles	30-03-43	429 Sqn
1467914	Sgt	SCOTT Robert Edward	20-10-43	166 Sqn
575419	Sgt	SCOTT Robert Matthew	22-06-43	35 Sqn
1439048	Sgt	SCOTT Roland Kenneth	29-06-43	149 Sqn
1545020	Sgt	SCOTT Sydney	3-02-43	21 Sqn
1785281	Sgt	SCOTT Thomas Mackie	26-03-43	199 Sqn
1035757	Sgt	SCOTT William	25-02-43	19 OTU
157423	F/O	SCOTT William Henry	9-10-43	78 Sqn
1346099	Sgt	SCOTT William Leslie	10-08-43	419 Sqn
1385756	F/S	SCOTT William Robert	30-05-43	10 Sqn
1081067	Sgt	SCRAGG Denis	29-06-43	207 Sqn
1331581	F/S	SCRATCHLEY Ronald Maversley	21-01-43	158 Sqn
1235968	Sgt	SCRATON Ernest Harry	9-10-43	427 Sqn
52599	P/O	SCRUTON Derrick George	30-07-43	460 Sqn
1582262	Sgt	SCUDDER Bertram Thomas	29-09-43	434 Sqn
1291875	Sgt	SCUDDER John William	9-04-43	75 Sqn
1219445	Sgt	SCULLY Gerard	13-05-43	77 Sqn
159569	P/O	SCUTT Sidney George	10-11-43	1660 HCU
1254727	F/S	SEAGER Dennis Ernest Arthur	13-07-43	44 Sqn
1337616	Sgt	SEAGER Peter	8-11-43	20 OTU
658294	Sgt	SEAL Leonard Lawrence	25-06-43	50 Sqn
131979	F/O	SEALL Ernest George	15-06-43	106 Sqn
1516234	Sgt	SEAMAN Austin Alec Middleton	24-11-43	44 Sqn
842721	Sgt	SEARLE John Ernest	26-11-43	158 Sqn
930345	Sgt	SEARLE Leonard Walter	21-10-43	7 Sqn
1201914	Sgt	SEARS Edward Kenneth	28-08-43	77 Sqn
1818726	Sgt	SEARSTON Raymond	6-08-43	23 OTU
1461723	Sgt	SEATTER Harcus	16-12-43	115 Sqn
1534670	Sgt	SEDDON Cyril	29-12-43	460 Sqn
2203354	Sgt	SEDDON James	28-08-43	207 Sqn
1445550	Sgt	SEDDON Reginald Derek	20-12-43	514 Sqn
1673504	F/S	SEDGWICK John Frederick	22-09-43	460 Sqn
1002165	Sgt	SEDMAN Kenneth William	4-09-43	101 Sqn
1112458	F/S	SEERY Clifford James	16-12-43	7 Sqn
577651	Sgt	SEES Richard George Henry	27-04-43	51 Sqn
1315145	Sgt	SEFTON Laurence Henry	18-08-43	10 Sqn
1810747	Sgt	SEGAL Abraham	29-04-43	103 Sqn
1399211	Sgt	SEIGAL David	17-05-43	10 OTU
1860983	Sgt	SELBY Frederick George	4-12-43	10 Sqn
1691986	Sgt	SELBY Maurice John	4-09-43	7 Sqn
1377760	F/S	SELBY Richard Charles	3-02-43	218 Sqn
1585667	Sgt	SELBY-LOWNDES Richard Montacute William	17-06-43	49 Sqn
1449163	Sgt	SELF Alfred Arthur	14-02-43	15 Sqn
1513331	Sgt	SELKIRK James Lynch	2-12-43	12 Sqn
1893889	Sgt	SELLARS Robert Bryson	22-11-43	1664 HCU
1529258	Sgt	SELLERS John	4-07-43	214 Sqn
129106	S/L	SELLS DFC Gordon Arthur	22-10-43	78 Sqn
109922	F/L	SELMAN DFC Crofton Lustleigh	8-03-43	7 Sqn
1394045	Sgt	SELTH Ronald Cecil	7-07-43	26 OTU
1392938	Sgt	SENGER James Ernest	13-06-43	10 Sqn
1021679	Sgt	SEPHTON Arthur	25-01-43	192 Sqn
86637	F/L	SEWARD Frederick Phillip	29-06-43	97 Sqn
1356712	Sgt	SEWARD Solomon	24-06-43	214 Sqn
1810154	Sgt	SEWELL Kenneth George	22-10-43	102 Sqn
1672888	Sgt	SEWELL William Arthur 'Bill'	3-08-43	44 Sqn
46223	F/L	SEYMOUR MiD Affyn	22-11-43	7 Sqn
124711	F/O	SEYMOUR Andrew Grenville	4-04-43	9 Sqn
143393	F/O	SEYMOUR Colin	9-10-43	20 OTU
1267833	Sgt	SHACKLADY Albert	22-06-43	156 Sqn
1507344	Sgt	SHACKLETON Ernest	16-05-43	101 Sqn
110567	F/O	SHADBOLT DFC Ronald Reginald	6-09-43	106 Sqn
1375964	Sgt	SHADGETT Terence William	24-05-43	166 Sqn
49298	F/O	SHADWELL Lancelot Rodney Cayley	3-04-43	78 Sqn
1386247	Sgt	SHAKESPEARE Michael David	22-06-43	408 Sqn
1216168	Sgt	SHAKESPEARE Norman John	3-11-43	101 Sqn
33285	W/C	SHAND DFC William Peter	20-04-43	139 Sqn
1380892	F/S	SHANDLEY Eric L'Estrange Lightfoot	3-04-43	83 Sqn
136889	F/O	SHANNON Wilfred Tasman	4-07-43	103 Sqn
1586732	Sgt	SHAPLEY Niel	22-09-43	460 Sqn
1329764	Sgt	SHARMAN Arthur Albert	9-07-43	101 Sqn
577192	Sgt	SHARMAN Peter Robinson	5-05-43	15 Sqn
1246257	Sgt	SHAROOD Harold John	14-03-43	138 Sqn
1566236	Sgt	SHARP David	12-11-43	1659 HCU
145476	P/O	SHARP Derek Minden	26-06-43	44 Sqn
629132	Sgt	SHARP Gerald David	23-06-43	427 Sqn
1498349	Sgt	SHARP Harry	6-02-43	14 OTU
1530450	Sgt	SHARP Robert Thomas Cartmel	29-01-43	166 Sqn
1435229	Sgt	SHARP Wilfred	13-06-43	10 Sqn
919134	Sgt	SHARPE Antony Cecil	12-03-43	76 Sqn

144690	P/O	SHARPE Donald Ernest	14-05-43	149 Sqn	577950	Sgt	SHEPPARD Harold Francis	17-06-43	156 Sqn
168970	P/O	SHARPE Geoffrey Owen	9-12-43	77 Sqn	1391502	Sgt	SHEPPARD Henry Alan	12-12-43	61 Sqn
1293926	Sgt	SHARPE John Henry	3-12-43	1409 Flt	1332395	F/S	SHEPPARD Kenneth Robert William	25-06-43	102 Sqn
1451615	Sgt	SHARPE Thomas Henry	30-09-43	78 Sqn	159072	P/O	SHERER DFM Harry Hamblin	20-12-43	51 Sqn
964253	Sgt	SHARPLEY Matthew Irons	21-01-43	101 Sqn	1322599	Sgt	SHERGOLD Frederick Cecil	22-09-43	207 Sqn
1234786	Sgt	SHARRATT George Vivian	18-11-43	115 Sqn	1149715	Sgt	SHERGOLD Tom Graham	17-04-43	75 Sqn
80461	P/O	SHATTOCK Nicholas Coryndon [Rhodesia]	9-01-43	44 Sqn	1556644	Sgt	SHERIDAN George McCurrach	27-03-43	44 Sqn
					1338999	Sgt	SHERRATT Francis Charles	30-05-43	460 Sqn
1127874	Sgt	SHAW Alexander	12-06-43	78 Sqn	1454837	Sgt	SHERRATT Harold	3-03-43	15 Sqn
1064277	Sgt	SHAW Arthur Edwin	22-10-43	10 Sqn	126554	F/O	SHERRING Victor Charles	26-02-43	9 Sqn
132268	Sgt	SHAW Edwin Arthur	15-04-43	90 Sqn	524675	F/S	SHERRINGTON Frederick Arthur	10-08-43	102 Sqn
1074934	Sgt	SHAW Eric	12-03-43	101 Sqn	908776	Sgt	SHERRINGTON Stanley Victor	30-07-43	51 Sqn
624836	F/S	SHAW DFM Ernest	15-06-43	103 Sqn	1063769	Sgt	SHERWOOD Charles Henry	26-05-43	77 Sqn
1436866	Sgt	SHAW Francis Graham	17-09-43	158 Sqn	1330133	F/S	SHERWOOD Norman Louis	20-09-43	138 Sqn
1438055	Sgt	SHAW Frank	23-09-43	12 Sqn	622411	Sgt	SHERYN MiD Malcolm James	2-12-43	106 Sqn
1321440	F/S	SHAW Frank William	3-10-43	467 Sqn	146274	P/O	SHEWARD Kenneth George	1-09-43	77 Sqn
1338184	Sgt	SHAW Frederick Harold	9-07-43	166 Sqn	1338228	Sgt	SHIBKO Maurice	4-04-43	16 OTU
1130438	Sgt	SHAW John Hatfield	18-08-43	619 Sqn	1148284	Sgt	SHIELD Norman	21-04-43	90 Sqn
1132866	Sgt	SHAW Kenneth Fazackerley	23-06-43	35 Sqn	570643	Sgt	SHIELDS Charles Robert	24-05-43	35 Sqn
1628459	AC2	SHAW Michael	25-11-43	Graveley	143451	P/O	SHIELLS DFM James Lauder	16-04-43	15 Sqn
160842	P/O	SHAW Noel Reginald	18-11-43	115 Sqn	1320623	Sgt	SHIMEILD Eric Henry	18-11-43	207 Sqn
1585786	Sgt	SHAW Percy	8-10-43	9 Sqn	2204168	Sgt	SHIMWELL Harry Bernard	3-11-43	428 Sqn
1576981	F/S	SHAW Raymond George	10-08-43	102 Sqn	141989	P/O	SHINN Herbert William	1-09-43	103 Sqn
1379174	Sgt	SHAW Ronald	27-01-43	106 Sqn	1865142	Sgt	SHIPP James Keith	19-11-43	431 Sqn
575244	Sgt	SHAW Royce Selwyn	13-05-43	90 Sqn	1197149	Sgt	SHIPP William Henry	30-03-43	44 Sqn
1576142	F/S	SHAW Stanley	18-08-43	44 Sqn	1388684	Sgt	SHIRLEY Francis William [Eire]	9-06-43	619 Sqn
1331022	Sgt	SHAW Stuart Patrick	30-03-43	115 Sqn	1385355	Sgt	SHIRLEY Leonard Frank	3-11-43	434 Sqn
1190732	Sgt	SHAW Wilfred	26-02-43	15 Sqn	1058899	Sgt	SHIRLEY Thomas Robert Doake	17-01-43	101 Sqn
1451308	Sgt	SHAW William	3-11-43	77 Sqn	1602329	Sgt	SHIRLEY Wilfred James	5-05-43	21 OTU
1603334	Sgt	SHEA Ronald George Barclay	24-11-43	408 Sqn	1851652	Sgt	SHIRVELL Leonard John Wesley	27-11-43	428 Sqn
41480	F/L	SHEAD Derrick Alan [Canada]	22-01-43	427 Sqn	136394	F/O	SHONE John Oswald	10-08-43	103 Sqn
1320427	Sgt	SHEAD Harry Leonard	2-04-43	19 OTU	128654	F/O	SHOOTER DFM Francis Arthur Mallett	28-02-43	83 Sqn
1174332	Sgt	SHEARER Hugh	15-03-43	161 Sqn					
1361268	Sgt	SHEARER William	2-07-43	620 Sqn	1586857	Sgt	SHORE-MARSTON Walter Roy	26-11-43	102 Sqn
146112	P/O	SHEARMAN Peter James	15-06-43	44 Sqn	131009	F/L	SHORT Albert Robert	31-08-43	78 Sqn
653935	Sgt	SHEARON Robert William	27-01-43	106 Sqn	1540792	Sgt	SHORT Arthur	3-02-43	102 Sqn
542963	F/S	SHEARS Ronald	4-02-43	57 Sqn	1398053	Sgt	SHORT Boris Karl	5-10-43	51 Sqn
1387684	Sgt	SHEEDY Michael	22-10-43	103 Sqn	1319336	Sgt	SHORT Eric	28-05-43	100 Sqn
1395112	Sgt	SHEEHAN Leonard Lawrence	11-08-43	158 Sqn	1043825	Sgt	SHORT Joseph	29-04-43	12 Sqn
151328	F/O	SHEERMAN Maurice Gordon	3-10-43	76 Sqn	1290625	F/S	SHORT Leslie Edwin	1-09-43	199 Sqn
1334923	Sgt	SHEERMAN Philip Hudd	30-05-43	102 Sqn	1295112	Sgt	SHORT Leslie Frederick John	21-04-43	15 OTU
1147315	Sgt	SHEFFIELD William	6-09-43	78 Sqn	639991	Sgt	SHORT Robert	3-10-43	467 Sqn
1214227	Sgt	SHEFFORD Frank Edward	18-08-43	77 Sqn	1333478	Sgt	SHORT Samuel George	9-10-43	12 Sqn
52713	P/O	SHEIL Eric Gordon	13-08-43	7 Sqn	1178784	F/S	SHORTLAND Bertram Arthur	27-09-43	76 Sqn
745491	F/S	SHELDON Derek	1-05-43	12 Sqn	1123560	Sgt	SHORTLAND Peter	20-04-43	51 Sqn
1378962	Sgt	SHELLEY William Oliver	2-03-43	207 Sqn	1321156	Sgt	SHOWLER Roy Arthur Collins	12-06-43	158 Sqn
1451976	Sgt	SHELMERDINE Thomas Pender	28-08-43	83 Sqn	125421	F/O	SHREEVES Edward George	10-03-43	77 Sqn
1484074	Sgt	SHELTON Ronald	31-07-43	78 Sqn	1322043	Sgt	SHRIMPTON Eric Sheldon	22-09-43	158 Sqn
1575168	Sgt	SHELVINGTON Walter Henry Arthur	21-05-43	149 Sqn	1251519	Sgt	SHRUBSALL Leonard Richard James	29-05-43	218 Sqn
1578088	Sgt	SHEPHARD Cyril William	7-09-43	29 OTU	66495	F/L	SHUFFLEBOTHAM Reginald James	15-04-43	100 Sqn
1072962	F/S	SHEPHARD Herbert	11-10-43	1684 Flt	539314	F/S	SHUTTLEWORTH Frank	14-09-43	138 Sqn
130261	P/O	SHEPHERD Alfred Raymond	19-02-43	12 OTU	1049563	Sgt	SIBBALD Clyde Maxwell	26-06-43	115 Sqn
1800264	Sgt	SHEPHERD Eric George	28-08-43	199 Sqn	1383168	Sgt	SIBLEY John Henry	22-03-43	101 Sqn
1330349	Sgt	SHEPHERD Gordon George	9-07-43	49 Sqn	152298	P/O	SIBLEY Leslie Reginald Vincent	20-10-43	10 OTU
1114117	F/S	SHEPHERD Horace	12-06-43	12 Sqn	1579481	Sgt	SIBLEY Walter Thomas	24-12-43	550 Sqn
146166	F/O	SHEPHERD James	30-05-43	149 Sqn	1586893	Sgt	SICKELMORE Henry Herbert George	13-07-43	156 Sqn
1321126	Sgt	SHEPHERD John Edward	23-09-43	50 Sqn	1499834	Sgt	SIDAWAY Norman	3-10-43	467 Sqn
132393	F/O	SHEPHERD John Frederick	26-07-43	620 Sqn	1450558	Sgt	SIDDALL Eric Smith	26-11-43	103 Sqn
1071280	F/S	SHEPHERD John Goodwillie	27-03-43	156 Sqn	1330259	Sgt	SIDDELL John Edward	11-03-43	15 OTU
929961	Sgt	SHEPHERD Raymond	1-05-43	77 Sqn	1558641	Sgt	SIDDOWAY William	28-11-43	16 OTU
130259	P/O	SHEPHERD Stanley Walker	3-03-43	12 OTU	129162	P/O	SIDEY Arthur	1-03-43	10 OTU
573650	Sgt	SHEPHERD Thomas	15-04-43	214 Sqn	946455	Sgt	SIDHU Devinder Singh	28-04-43	75 Sqn
1546655	Sgt	SHEPHERD Thomas George William	1-09-43	5 Group	1197663	Sgt	SIDWELL Roland Stanley	21-04-43	100 Sqn
1551889	Sgt	SHEPHERD William	8-09-43	12 OTU	1332421	F/S	SIGOURNAY Dennis William	29-06-43	51 Sqn
1390821	Sgt	SHEPHERD William Thomas	17-06-43	103 Sqn	1582936	Sgt	SILCOCK Trevor	31-08-43	75 Sqn
537395	Sgt	SHEPLEY Robert Malcolm	28-07-43	50 Sqn	145423	F/L	SILK DFM Arthur James Wyndham	22-11-43	97 Sqn
1267634	Sgt	SHEPPARD Charles Phillip	6-04-43	1663 HCU	156594	P/O	SILVERMAN DFM David Mark Claude		
1412878	Sgt	SHEPPARD Edward Stanley	29-09-43	158 Sqn				18-11-43	156 Sqn
1322316	Sgt	SHEPPARD Frederick	20-04-43	149 Sqn	148478	P/O	SILVESTER Cyril Albert Henry	10-08-43	51 Sqn

237

1579710	F/S	SILVESTER Cyril Harold	28-08-43	83 Sqn	613594	Sgt	SLADE Edwin Douglas	30-07-43	57 Sqn
977392	F/S	SILVESTER DFM George Bernard	18-08-43	49 Sqn	43416	S/L	SLADE DSO Fraser Burstock	18-08-43	12 Sqn
937931	Sgt	SIM Leslie Alexander	2-10-43	460 Sqn	121451	F/L	SLADE DFC Ivor Charles Brian	24-08-43	83 Sqn
945654	Sgt	SIMM Clifford	9-07-43	106 Sqn	1260188	Sgt	SLADE Kenneth Edward	17-01-43	61 Sqn
115545	F/L	SIMMONDS Cyril John	30-01-43	466 Sqn	143997	P/O	SLADE Stanley John	28-09-43	405 Sqn
1378201	Sgt	SIMMONDS Frederick Henry 'Pete'	20-10-43	7 Sqn	1235596	Sgt	SLANEY Arthur Ronald	6-09-43	419 Sqn
1248156	Sgt	SIMMONDS Harold Thomas	15-09-43	617 Sqn	1516173	Sgt	SLATER John Patrick	20-12-43	428 Sqn
1702067	Sgt	SIMMONDS Kenneth Charles	16-11-43	432 Sqn	1626592	Sgt	SLATER Leslie	25-11-43	1678 HCU
551578	Sgt	SIMMONDS Kenneth Rupert William	3-03-43	12 Sqn	1579284	F/S	SLATER Victor Matthew	28-11-43	16 OTU
1389545	Sgt	SIMMONS Alec	15-02-43	90 Sqn	1575183	Sgt	SLATER William	26-06-43	9 Sqn
1006398	Sgt	SIMMONS Bernard	14-01-43	9 Sqn	1589390	Sgt	SLATER Roger Vincent	26-07-43	77 Sqn
1335631	Sgt	SIMMONS Donald John	30-03-43	57 Sqn	1565787	Sgt	SLATTER George	7-09-43	1663 HCU
1334759	Sgt	SIMMONS John	28-05-43	158 Sqn	1292478	Sgt	SLATTERY Terence Michael	19-01-43	20 OTU
980521	Sgt	SIMMONS Thomas Charles Eugene	26-05-43	35 Sqn	1392646	F/S	SLAUGHTER Laurence George	4-12-43	10 Sqn
957593	Sgt	SIMMS Herbert William Charles	3-08-43	100 Sqn	910908	Sgt	SLAUGHTER Robert William	18-08-43	49 Sqn
1436631	Sgt	SIMMS William Walter	3-02-43	226 Sqn	996958	Sgt	SLINGER Douglas Hope Newton	17-06-43	100 Sqn
1536980	Sgt	SIMONS Albert	26-07-43	620 Sqn	658262	Sgt	SLINGSBY Fred Noel	27-04-43	76 Sqn
1380680	Sgt	SIMONS Frank Charles	28-06-43	78 Sqn	1089371	Sgt	SLOAN Robert Edward	13-05-43	61 Sqn
848625	Sgt	SIMPKIN Albert Henry	27-09-43	50 Sqn	1544915	Cpl	SLOSS Francis Neville	18-06-43	83 Sqn
1321760	Sgt	SIMPKIN Gordon Ivor	25-06-43	76 Sqn	1632077	Sgt	SLY Arthur Ernest	18-11-43	622 Sqn
2216150	Sgt	SIMPSON Albert Frederick	2-10-43	51 Sqn	1377300	Sgt	SMALE Gordon Joseph	21-01-43	101 Sqn
159073	P/O	SIMPSON Arnold Galloway	17-11-43	57 Sqn	1812351	Sgt	SMALE Thomas	23-08-43	460 Sqn
106561	S/L	SIMPSON DFM Ernest Robert	26-02-43	83 Sqn	1317420	Sgt	SMALE Thomas Gerald	13-06-43	12 Sqn
1238939	Sgt	SIMPSON Frederick	27-03-43	426 Sqn	149316	P/O	SMALL Albert Richard George	31-07-43	90 Sqn
156270	P/O	SIMPSON George	22-10-43	78 Sqn	1313073	Sgt	SMALL Ronald John [Canada]	10-08-43	49 Sqn
1183567	Sgt	SIMPSON Harry	29-05-43	158 Sqn	51893	F/L	SMALLEY DFC Robert Matthew	27-11-43	83 Sqn
630257	F/S	SIMPSON James Stevenson	16-09-43	617 Sqn	1177130	F/S	SMALLEY William Bertram Hammond		
1507630	Sgt	SIMPSON John Hilton	11-08-43	158 Sqn				13-02-43	166 Sqn
1045724	Sgt	SIMPSON John Johnston	15-06-43	12 Sqn	1314228	Sgt	SMALLRIDGE Maxwell George	9-10-43	7 Sqn
1185795	F/S	SIMPSON John Thompson	27-09-43	7 Sqn	51914	P/O	SMART DFM Arthur Bertram	13-06-43	83 Sqn
127980	F/O	SIMPSON Joseph William	3-04-43	106 Sqn	1322742	Sgt	SMART Eric Shirley	25-09-43	29 OTU
659008	Sgt	SIMPSON Malcolm	22-10-43	100 Sqn	144753	P/O	SMART James	14-04-43	103 Sqn
1601327	Sgt	SIMPSON Michael John Christopher	3-09-43	460 Sqn	1318312	Sgt	SMART Kenneth Charles	22-06-43	158 Sqn
1101417	Sgt	SIMPSON Raymond Brinley	25-06-43	57 Sqn	112534	F/O	SMART Kenneth Flaxman	30-03-43	196 Sqn
157319	P/O	SIMPSON Theodore Leonard	20-10-43	100 Sqn	1324892	Sgt	SMART Leonard George	31-08-43	102 Sqn
1272597	Sgt	SIMPSON Waldo	2-05-43	424 Sqn	124547	F/O	SMART Neville	26-02-43	196 Sqn
1017292	Sgt	SIMPSON William	7-09-43	156 Sqn	945683	Sgt	SMART Philip	1-03-43	103 Sqn
130239	F/O	SIMPSON William Rhymer	6-09-43	77 Sqn	1333204	Sgt	SMART Philip John	2-12-43	156 Sqn
1316116	Sgt	SIMS Robert Alfred	1-09-43	77 Sqn	1815430	Sgt	SMART Richard James	23-09-43	12 Sqn
1292124	Sgt	SINCLAIR Anthony James	1-03-43	15 Sqn	125579	F/O	SMEATON Alexander Bruce	27-11-43	83 Sqn
657717	Sgt	SINCLAIR Stanley	3-08-43	12 Sqn	1310982	Sgt	SMEATON Robert	11-01-43	81 OTU
644138	Sgt	SINCLAIR William Alexander Roy	28-07-43	102 Sqn	1345207	Sgt	SMELLIE David Mackenzie	17-04-43	50 Sqn
577701	Sgt	SINDEN Robert	19-02-43	467 Sqn	1062645	Sgt	SMETHURST James	20-12-43	514 Sqn
1315664	Sgt	SINDREY Arthur George Percival	29-04-43	218 Sqn	983888	Sgt	SMIRK William Cecil	7-09-43	77 Sqn
131254	P/O	SINGER William	5-01-43	20 OTU	979749	Sgt	SMITH Alan	10-01-43	10 Sqn
975582	Sgt	SINGLETON Bernard Mario	12-03-43	78 Sqn	1378794	F/S	SMITH Alan Keilier	17-04-43	460 Sqn
1391610	Sgt	SINGLETON Ronald Alfred	21-01-43	101 Sqn	139847	P/O	SMITH Albert	12-05-43	20 OTU
1444720	Sgt	SITCH Ronald Stephen	22-10-43	51 Sqn	1690693	AC2	SMITH Albert	25-04-43	Wyton
572445	Sgt	SIXSMITH Arthur Cyril	15-03-43	138 Sqn	1852352	Sgt	SMITH Alfred Jack	22-10-43	1657 HCU
1432835	Sgt	SKEELES Frederick John	21-02-43	424 Sqn	1265587	Sgt	SMITH Alfred Percy	18-01-43	467 Sqn
1235073	Sgt	SKELLY Albert Arthur	27-03-43	429 Sqn	657644	F/S	SMITH Albert Ralph	1-09-43	44 Sqn
1503603	Sgt	SKELTON Cecil Mark	3-04-43	50 Sqn	954610	Sgt	SMITH Allen Kenneth	26-06-43	15 Sqn
1545950	Sgt	SKELTON George Leslie	22-11-43	10 Sqn	982880	F/S	SMITH Archibald Flemington	30-03-43	77 Sqn
1584644	Sgt	SKELTON Raymond	3-11-43	625 Sqn	120028	F/O	SMITH Arthur	17-06-43	467 Sqn
1331635	Sgt	SKELTON Thomas Henry	13-05-43	207 Sqn	653815	Sgt	SMITH Arthur	29-06-43	51 Sqn
1500666	Sgt	SKELTON William	14-04-43	138 Sqn	1694468	Sgt	SMITH Arthur	28-07-43	76 Sqn
1348258	Sgt	SKILLIN Robert	16-09-43	15 Sqn	1589096	Sgt	SMITH Arthur Edward	2-10-43	207 Sqn
1112266	F/S	SKINNER Bernard Kenneth	18-01-43	9 Sqn	1430417	Sgt	SMITH Arthur Layton	18-11-43	35 Sqn
1566923	Sgt	SKINNER David	28-08-43	199 Sqn	126548	F/L	SMITH DFC Basil Francis	30-07-43	156 Sqn
1269101	F/S	SKINNER Desmond	7-02-43	44 Sqn	1475502	Sgt	SMITH Ben	20-04-43	460 Sqn
1431924	Sgt	SKINNER Frank Edward	22-10-43	431 Sqn	1684936	Sgt	SMITH Bernard	20-12-43	408 Sqn
110849	F/O	SKINNER Leonard John	23-01-43	105 Sqn	122746	F/O	SMITH Bernard James	11-04-43	9 Sqn
900261	Sgt	SKIPP Thomas Frank	28-10-43	1656 HCU	156956	P/O	SMITH Bertram Charles	2-10-43	44 Sqn
155489	P/O	SKIPPER Desmond Wallace	28-09-43	101 Sqn	1331504	Sgt	SMITH Brian Thomas Campbell	11-03-43	44 Sqn
135632	F/O	SKITT Eric Duckinson	24-08-43	100 Sqn	530021	Sgt	SMITH Charles Derrick	26-02-43	103 Sqn
1400880	Sgt	SKYRME Thomas John	2-12-43	1664 HCU	1338514	Sgt	SMITH Charles Edward	19-11-43	10 Sqn
1029611	Sgt	SLACK Arthur	14-07-43	78 Sqn	1335889	Sgt	SMITH Charles John Herbert	5-03-43	466 Sqn
1496119	Sgt	SLACK George Rowland	28-07-43	106 Sqn	151244	F/O	SMITH Clifford	23-09-43	12 Sqn
1316054	Sgt	SLADE Arthur Dennis	12-03-43	101 Sqn	148587	P/O	SMITH Cyril Frankham	22-10-43	61 Sqn

751618	F/S	SMITH	Cyril James Drane	25-02-43	102 Sqn	1386548	Sgt	SMITH Kenneth Gordon	26-11-43	460 Sqn
1062133	Sgt	SMITH	David	7-09-43	106 Sqn	932945	F/S	SMITH Kenneth Ivor	29-06-43	97 Sqn
1559352	Sgt	SMITH	David Crawford	30-05-43	428 Sqn	1509397	Sgt	SMITH Kenneth Joseph	28-05-43	102 Sqn
1239555	F/S	SMITH	David Crofton	13-05-43	51 Sqn	1322298	Sgt	SMITH Kenneth William	31-08-43	78 Sqn
134995	P/O	SMITH	Denis Hedley	3-02-43	214 Sqn	1450592	F/S	SMITH Lees	9-11-43	90 Sqn
1435614	Sgt	SMITH	Dennis	14-08-43	1662 HCU	1385192	Sgt	SMITH Leonard George	17-04-43	10 OTU
574049	Sgt	SMITH	Derek Clowes	14-03-43	1651 HCU	1446946	Sgt	SMITH Leonard Ray	25-05-43	15 Sqn
1272560	Sgt	SMITH	Donald Fred	21 05-43	1654 HCU	1672344	Sgt	SMITH Leonard Thomas	19-11-43	15 OTU
1235284	Sgt	SMITH	Donald Jack	7-02-43	166 Sqn	1351056	Sgt	SMITH Leonard William	24-06-43	192 Sqn
658902	F/S	SMITH	Donald Sinclair	18-11-43	622 Sqn	144922	P/O	SMITH Leopold Alfred	22-11-43	158 Sqn
1211893	Sgt	SMITH	Douglas John	28-05-43	51 Sqn	1312940	Sgt	SMITH Leslie Alfred	13-01-43	50 Sqn
1809782	Sgt	SMITH	Edward	2-12-43	49 Sqn	1271374	Sgt	SMITH Leslie Charles	17-04-43	460 Sqn
540655	F/S	SMITH	Edward Clarence	20-12-43	617 Sqn	136933	F/O	SMITH DFC Leslie Frederick	8-09-43	1657 HCU
1811495	Sgt	SMITH	Edward Victor	16-12-43	166 Sqn	1110714	F/S	SMITH Leslie Rowland	15-03-43	138 Sqn
1312690	Sgt	SMITH	Edwin	23-06-43	101 Sqn	658928	Sgt	SMITH Maurice James	17-12-43	218 Sqn
1330882	Sgt	SMITH	Edwin	14-07-43	115 Sqn	1349535	Sgt	SMITH Norman Campbell	13-07-43	467 Sqn
1139609	Sgt	SMITH	Eric	26-11-43	61 Sqn	1219354	Sgt	SMITH Paul Anthony	8-04-43	425 Sqn
1314202	Sgt	SMITH	Eric John	3-09-43	44 Sqn	1460283	Sgt	SMITH Peter	30-05-43	102 Sqn
1331063	Sgt	SMITH	Eric Ronald	11-08-43	214 Sqn	1290933	Sgt	SMITH Peter Tristan	21-04-43	61 Sqn
646905	F/S	SMITH	Eric Sidney	6-06-43	30 OTU	126613	F/O	SMITH Philip Ritchie	5-05-43	83 Sqn
1133208	Sgt	SMITH	Ernest	13-06-43	10 Sqn	1377817	Sgt	SMITH Reginald Charles	27-03-43	35 Sqn
632681	Sgt	SMITH	Ernest Frederick	11-03-43	158 Sqn	1293036	Sgt	SMITH Reginald Ernest	20-04-43	460 Sqn
1380953	Sgt	SMITH	Francis Andrew	9-04-43	106 Sqn	1270242	W/O	SMITH DFC Richard Bradley	20-12-43	7 Sqn
136954	F/O	SMITH	Francis Melville	7-07-43	12 Sqn	1503916	Sgt	SMITH Robert	24-12-43	100 Sqn
1025977	F/S	SMITH	Frank	2-12-43	9 Sqn	1339131	Sgt	SMITH Robert Gordon	17-06-43	49 Sqn
1454835	Sgt	SMITH	Frank	16-06-43	460 Sqn	1435478	Sgt	SMITH Robert Vivian Duncan	4-12-43	7 Sqn
138424	P/O	SMITH DFM	Frederick	17-04-43	156 Sqn	1380261	Sgt	SMITH Robert William	10-02-43	1657 HCU
62395	F/L	SMITH	Frederick Charles	17-12-43	8 Group	1239376	Sgt	SMITH Ronald	1-12-43	75 Sqn
1578941	Sgt	SMITH	Frederick Charles	18-02-43	57 Sqn	1333412	Sgt	SMITH Ronald Albert Hurworth	24-06-43	214 Sqn
1802554	Sgt	SMITH	Frederick George	20-10-43	106 Sqn	1810805	Sgt	SMITH Ronald Alfred	27-09-43	78 Sqn
155192	P/O	SMITH	Geoffrey Charles	4-07-43	90 Sqn	1575673	Sgt	SMITH Ronald Henry	2-08-43	18 OTU
129363	F/O	SMITH	Geoffrey Salter	26-07-43	102 Sqn	1483072	Sgt	SMITH Ronald Stanley	30-07-43	51 Sqn
53583	P/O	SMITH	George	26-11-43	97 Sqn	1425790	Sgt	SMITH Samuel	30-07-43	26 OTU
142872	P/O	SMITH	George	4-04-43	9 Sqn	1152993	Sgt	SMITH Sidney John	15-09-43	138 Sqn
151332	F/O	SMITH	George Henry Ivor	23-07-43	24 OTU	1390791	W/O	SMITH Sidney Walter	6-09-43	90 Sqn
1813182	Sgt	SMITH	George William	23-11-43	7 Sqn	126462	F/O	SMITH Stanley	20-10-43	106 Sqn
124700	F/O	SMITH	Harold	31-08-43	7 Sqn	1455802	Sgt	SMITH Stanley	27-05-43	218 Sqn
1379615	F/S	SMITH	Harold	24-11-43	408 Sqn	138070	F/O	SMITH Stanley David	18-10-43	9 Sqn
522461	F/S	SMITH	Harry	4-11-43	138 Sqn	1331034	Sgt	SMITH Stanley Gordon	12-03-43	101 Sqn
1466653	Sgt	SMITH	Harry Arthur	9-01-43	51 Sqn	1128846	F/S	SMITH DFM Sydney	9-10-43	78 Sqn
628540	F/S	SMITH DFM	Harold	3-10-43	17 OTU	1021395	Sgt	SMITH Thomas	18-05-43	149 Sqn
126887	F/O	SMITH	Harold Eric	17-04-43	76 Sqn	993817	Sgt	SMITH Thomas Haig	13-05-43	431 Sqn
1318937	Sgt	SMITH	Harry Richard	24-08-43	427 Sqn	1045872	Sgt	SMITH Thomas Reginald Maxwell	4-07-43	35 Sqn
149906	P/O	SMITH	Hedley Millard	16-07-43	10 Sqn	1178195	Sgt	SMITH Vincent George Louvaine	15-06-43	9 Sqn
1374424	LAC	SMITH	Hugh	19-06-43	Snaith	980905	Sgt	SMITH Vivian	18-08-43	467 Sqn
1550719	Sgt	SMITH	Hugh	22-11-43	115 Sqn	1129590	Sgt	SMITH Walter Leonard	6-09-43	149 Sqn
1317049	Sgt	SMITH	Ivor Melvyn	22-10-43	77 Sqn	144291	P/O	SMITH William	9-04-43	44 Sqn
1534965	Sgt	SMITH	Jack	10-03-43	103 Sqn	1034418	Sgt	SMITH William	26-05-43	9 Sqn
1096819	Sgt	SMITH	James	31-08-43	166 Sqn	63414	S/L	SMITH DFC William Arthur	2-02-43	7 Sqn
1094915	Sgt	SMITH	James Colin	24-05-43	102 Sqn	1289965	F/S	SMITH William Edward	14-02-43	466 Sqn
658984	Sgt	SMITH	James Griffiths	18-10-43	100 Sqn	1586966	Sgt	SMITH William Frank	28-09-43	428 Sqn
1053959	Sgt	SMITH	James Thomas	21-04-43	102 Sqn	1319671	Sgt	SMITH William Henry James	14-07-43	102 Sqn
1475434	F/S	SMITH DFM	James William Taylor Mason			542580	F/S	SMITH William James	2-12-43	44 Sqn
				5-04-43	408 Sqn	131886	F/L	SMITH DFC William John	30-07-43	156 Sqn
1313558	Sgt	SMITH	Joe	13-05-43	207 Sqn	943798	Sgt	SMITH William John	18-01-43	12 Sqn
928040	Sgt	SMITH	John	10-08-43	76 Sqn	936175	Sgt	SMITH William Patrick	23-06-43	156 Sqn
1028126	Sgt	SMITH	John	14-04-43	101 Sqn	143806	P/O	SMITH William Settle 'Bill'	12-06-43	158 Sqn
1699158	Sgt	SMITH	John	18-11-43	35 Sqn	576784	Sgt	SMITH William Stanley	9-10-43	61 Sqn
1308482	Sgt	SMITH	John Beaty Lamson	18-08-43	77 Sqn	1049079	Sgt	SMITH William Thomas	27-09-43	50 Sqn
63467	F/L	SMITH	John Cecil	20-08-43	20 OTU	159705	P/O	SMITH William Walter	7-09-43	77 Sqn
1263058	Sgt	SMITH	John Ernest	12-03-43	10 Sqn	1293011	Sgt	SMITHDALE Alan	20-04-43	57 Sqn
1810132	Sgt	SMITH	John George	23-11-43	630 Sqn	1334611	Sgt	SMITHERMAN Arthur Douglas	3-01-43	9 Sqn
649887	Sgt	SMITH	John Richard Godfrey	14-07-43	102 Sqn	1395928	Sgt	SMITHERS Ronald	3-12-43	619 Sqn
1603576	Sgt	SMITH	John Thomas	31-08-43	199 Sqn	930340	Sgt	SMITHSON Edward Stephen	2-03-43	9 Sqn
958374	Sgt	SMITH	Joseph	2-08-43	57 Sqn	1520153	AC1	SMOLLAN Dennis	7-02-43	51 Sqn
121951	F/L	SMITH DFC	Joseph Taber	22-11-43	156 Sqn	1216233	Sgt	SMURTHWAITE Joseph	18-02-43	207 Sqn
940574	Sgt	SMITH MiD	Keith Wilson	20-12-43	78 Sqn	644566	Sgt	SMYTH Edward Joseph	14-09-43	138 Sqn
36042	W/C	SMITH DSO Twice MiD Kenneth Brooke Farley				139301	P/O	SMYTH John Stanley	26-07-43	51 Sqn
				11-04-43	9 Sqn	149676	P/O	SMYTH Wallace Robert	30-07-43	57 Sqn

Service No	Rank	Name	Date	Sqn
143667	P/O	SMYTHE Noel Bentley	26-06-43	196 Sqn
1434323	Sgt	SNAPE Peter Francis	30-07-43	78 Sqn
1553974	Sgt	SNEDDON James	28-09-43	77 Sqn
1342219	Sgt	SNEDDON James Wilson	3-08-43	75 Sqn
1381732	Sgt	SNEESBY Reginald	25-06-43	12 Sqn
130194	F/O	SNELL Albert Dennis Serpell	16-07-43	50 Sqn
1388725	Sgt	SNELL Henry Roy	24-08-43	619 Sqn
161695	P/O	SNOOK Jack William	19-11-43	90 Sqn
655955	Sgt	SNOOK William Charles	27-04-43	115 Sqn
1091872	Sgt	SNOW Albert George	3-03-43	51 Sqn
1037458	Sgt	SNOWDON John Henry William	26-06-43	101 Sqn
647800	Sgt	SOANG Charles Catto	30-07-43	158 Sqn
657878	Sgt	SOBER Benny	13-01-43	12 OTU
1384232	Sgt	SOLLY Frederick Albert	20-04-43	460 Sqn
155021	P/O	SOLOMON Edmund	3-08-43	35 Sqn
748642	Sgt	SOLOMONS Louis John (served as SOMERS)	17-11-43	149 Sqn
116679	F/O	SOLON Paul Gerard	22-01-43	98 Sqn
658354	Sgt	SOMERFORD Bernard Welby	13-02-43	420 Sqn
155189	P/O	SOMERS Frederick Ernest	6-09-43	623 Sqn
1376410	Sgt	SOMERVILLE Thomas Clarkson [New Zealand]	30-03-43	44 Sqn
124190	F/L	SOULSBY Guy	23-11-43	12 Sqn
1522992	Sgt	SOULSBY William John Riddle	1-09-43	428 Sqn
156955	P/O	SOUTER Arthur William Avis	18-08-43	61 Sqn
1612608	Sgt	SOUTH Douglas Reynold	26-02-43	103 Sqn
1284694	Sgt	SOUTHAM George Henry	3-05-43	487 Sqn
1212023	Sgt	SOUTHAM Leslie Arthur	4-06-43	26 OTU
921349	Sgt	SOUTHCOTT Charles Philip	8-08-43	61 Sqn
107910	F/O	SOUTHERN DFM Derek John Nigel	8-04-43	49 Sqn
1127777	Sgt	SOUTHERN Frederick	22-10-43	76 Sqn
1450396	Sgt	SOUTHERN William James	29-09-43	11 OTU
1217694	Sgt	SOUTHGATE Victor Jack	5-11-43	199 Sqn
67049	F/O	SOUTHON Frederick Albert	3-04-43	83 Sqn
1334699	Sgt	SOUTHWELL John	24-12-43	115 Sqn
1813414	Sgt	SOUTHWELL William Arthur	4-09-43	101 Sqn
637314	Sgt	SOWERBY Leslie Thomas	25-07-43	214 Sqn
1253037	Sgt	SOWTER John York	7-08-43	26 OTU
145022	P/O	SPAIN Harold Scott [Brazil]	18-11-43	460 Sqn
1323191	Sgt	SPANTON Derek Richard	25-06-43	7 Sqn
1392394	Sgt	SPARKES George Henry	3-05-43	487 Sqn
133774	F/O	SPARKES Peter John	18-08-43	419 Sqn
1318964	Sgt	SPARROW Herbert Alfred	3-08-43	115 Sqn
1516058	Sgt	SPEAKE John Buckland	3-10-43	17 OTU
542000	Sgt	SPEAR Albert Clavey	18-01-43	9 Sqn
1555010	F/S	SPEEDIE DFM William Fisher	6-09-43	77 SQN
1104674	Sgt	SPEIGHT Norman Gwynne	23-11-43	434 Sqn
1500014	Sgt	SPEIRS Eric	16-12-43	166 Sqn
947859	Sgt	SPEIRS James	17-04-43	50 Sqn
1196260	Sgt	SPELLER Wilfred Albert	12-07-43	10 OTU
1456979	Sgt	SPELMAN Reginald William Melville	17-12-43	101 Sqn
1076957	F/S	SPENCE Alan	30-05-43	431 Sqn
1535230	Sgt	SPENCE Alan Havelock	5-03-43	100 Sqn
1559800	Sgt	SPENCE David Lambert	22-09-43	83 OTU
1230748	Sgt	SPENCE James Arthur	12-07-43	207 Sqn
1574008	Sgt	SPENCE Robert Barclay	24-08-43	77 Sqn
1123753	Sgt	SPENCE William John	30-07-43	35 Sqn
1079010	Sgt	SPENCER Arthur Raymond	9-03-43	61 Sqn
574332	Sgt	SPENCER Bernard	26-05-43	467 Sqn
151074	F/O	SPENCER Frank	29-12-43	431 Sqn
759324	W/O	SPENCER Frederick James	31-10-43	139 Sqn
552410	Sgt	SPENCER John Scott	10-04-43	30 OTU
124650	F/O	SPENCER John Frederick	29-03-43	428 Sqn
149541	Sgt	SPENCER Joseph Aloysius	23-08-43	61 Sqn
1320167	Sgt	SPENCER Maurice Frank	3-08-43	428 Sqn
954342	Sgt	SPENCER Milton	26-07-43	102 Sqn
1775014	Sgt	SPENCER Robert William	18-10-43	460 Sqn
1438166	Sgt	SPENCER Thomas Roy	9-10-43	7 Sqn
1265249	F/S	SPENCER William Ernest Arthur	22-10-43	102 Sqn
1393578	Sgt	SPICER Benjamin Ernest	5-04-43	57 Sqn
1424787	Sgt	SPIERLING Raymond	5-12-43	101 Sqn
710256	Sgt	SPIERS Allan Douglas 'Bob' [South Africa]	27-11-43	50 Sqn
1319678	Sgt	SPIERS Harry James	3-05-43	81 OTU
1578587	Sgt	SPIERS Joseph	23-09-43	49 Sqn
1487715	Sgt	SPIERS Wilfred Roland	22-09-43	78 Sqn
1474213	Sgt	SPINK Charles Leonard	22-10-43	103 Sqn
975262	F/S	SPIRES DFM Alan Seblery	12-06-43	115 Sqn
1378279	Sgt	SPIVEY Fred Travis	12-02-43	101 Sqn
137217	P/O	SPOONER Daniel	5-05-43	15 Sqn
1231251	Sgt	SPOONER Kenneth	4-02-43	115 Sqn
156601	P/O	SPOONER Robert	30-07-43	35 Sqn
51543	P/O	SPRACK DFM Charles Frederick John	13-06-43	83 Sqn
116671	F/O	SPRACKLING Leonard William	5-03-43	83 Sqn
1315858	Sgt	SPRACKMAN Richard Stephen	18-10-43	619 Sqn
84278	F/L	SPRATT Edward Devereux	3-03-43	12 OTU
1271792	Sgt	SPRECKLY Phillip George	12-06-43	51 Sqn
1193053	Sgt	SPRIGGS George William Sidney	10-08-43	61 Sqn
1078608	Sgt	SPRINGETT Alfred Bakes	22-11-43	51 Sqn
1336371	Sgt	SPRINGETT Eric Turner	28-09-43	428 Sqn
1219801	Sgt	SPROAT Gordon	28-08-43	102 Sqn
121548	F/L	SPROSEN Arthur Thomas	30-01-43	426 Sqn
1446838	Sgt	SPURGEON Leslie Graham	3-08-43	103 Sqn
1581551	Sgt	SPURR Alan	22-11-43	51 Sqn
655184	Sgt	SPURR Frank	31-01-43	97 Sqn
985455	Sgt	SPURR Lloyd	15-08-43	467 Sqn
140877	F/O	SPYERS Guy Dermot	18-11-43	101 Sqn
1574376	Sgt	SQUAIR Fred Robert Maxwell	16-12-43	166 Sqn
1411892	Sgt	SQUIBBS Frank Owen	5-10-43	51 Sqn
1478651	Sgt	SQUIERS Myles Christian Campbell [South Africa]	29-03-43	102 Sqn
1302829	Sgt	SQUIRE Harry	26-06-43	75 Sqn
1803573	Sgt	SQUIRE William Albert Henry	29-12-43	460 Sqn
654516	Sgt	SQUIRES Bernard William	5-05-43	101 Sqn
1388828	Sgt	SQUIRES Maurice Brian	13-05-43	467 SQN
1784108	Sgt	STABLER Ernest	23-11-43	1658 HCU
902017	W/O	STABLES William Roy	22-09-43	101 Sqn
623214	Sgt	STACEY Mervyn	31-08-43	12 Sqn
1169401	W/O	STACEY DFC Stanley Thomas	26-11-43	83 Sqn
1269939	Sgt	STACEY William Henry	27-04-43	51 Sqn
644879	Sgt	STAFFORD Alfred Douglas	20-08-43	10 Sqn
138810	F/O	STAFFORD DFM Arthur Oswald	23-09-43	101 Sqn
1182873	W/O	STAFFORD DFM Graham Campbell	4-04-43	156 Sqn
1033931	Sgt	STAFFORD Septon	1-04-43	103 Sqn
1332705	Sgt	STAGG Harry Herbert	18-11-43	514 Sqn
1528611	Sgt	STAINSBY Raymond Frederick	27-08-43	1663 HCU
1576580	Sgt	STAIT Stuart Donald	3-10-43	44 Sqn
133773	F/O	STALKER John Lawrence	22-10-43	1657 HCU
1383228	W/O	STALLY Ernest Charles	23-06-43	83 Sqn
1031832	F/S	STAMP Thomas Edward	18-10-43	97 Sqn
1130080	Sgt	STANCLIFFE Cecil	18-08-43	49 Sqn
1397365	Sgt	STANDING Reginald	16-12-43	44 Sqn
1458478	Sgt	STANDISH John Ward	23-08-43	207 Sqn
1035770	Sgt	STANDRING William	30-03-43	97 Sqn
80378	F/O	STANFORD Nicholas James [Rhodesia]	5-05-43	101 Sqn
70877	F/L	STANHOPE Gilbert William	1-03-43	103 Sqn
1525019	Sgt	STANIFORTH John	5-05-43	196 Sqn
123637	F/L	STANILAND Brian James	2-12-43	156 Sqn
1387764	Sgt	STANLEY Ernest	22-06-43	619 Sqn
1286323	F/S	STANLEY Phillip Francis	24-04-43	199 Sqn
1095183	Sgt	STANLEY Thomas	3-08-43	103 Sqn
113849	F/L	STANLEY DFC Thomas Albert	25-07-43	218 Sqn
903139	Sgt	STANNARD Francis Donald	14-05-43	214 Sqn
1038690	Sgt	STANNERS Frederick Wade	12-03-43	10 Sqn
1127348	Sgt	STANSFIELD Arthur	23-08-43	100 Sqn
1604584	Sgt	STANTON Arthur John	24-11-43	7 Sqn

1375253	F/S	STANTON David	23-09-43	49 Sqn
48863	F/O	STANTON Eugene Joseph	29-01-43	420 Sqn
1542987	Sgt	STANWORTH Henry Arthur	27-09-43	10 Sqn
1291030	Sgt	STAPLES Horace	17-06-43	103 Sqn
1807327	Sgt	STAPLEY Robert McKie	2-08-43	28 OTU
1030871	Sgt	STARK Arthur Irving	5-05-43	166 Sqn
1536256	Sgt	STATHAM Walter George	18-11-43	9 Sqn
1080326	Sgt	STEARMAN Thomas	1-09-43	1662 HCU
1322158	Sgt	STEED Ernest Alfred	12-03-43	101 Sqn
1307887	Sgt	STEED Peter Donovan	15-04-43	101 Sqn
1338571	Sgt	STEEDMAN Charles William	13-02-43	158 Sqn
1409336	Sgt	STEEL Alexander	13-05-43	57 Sqn
1162703	Sgt	STEEL Harold Jack	26-02-43	427 Sqn
1374039	F/S	STEEL John Minorgan	25-06-43	90 Sqn
578363	Sgt	STEEL Raymond James Harry	19-11-43	10 Sqn
1443406	Sgt	STEELE Harry Ernest	2-12-43	90 Sqn
127895	F/L	STEELE James	3-11-43	76 Sqn
1419176	Sgt	STEELE Leslie Arthur	20-10-43	166 Sqn
655242	F/S	STEELE Robert James	26-05-43	12 Sqn
1316139	F/S	STEER Geoffrey Sturtridge	28-08-43	149 Sqn
922222	Sgt	STEER George	14-05-43	51 Sqn
624670	Sgt	STEER Francis John Maddock	25-06-43	57 Sqn
147998	P/O	STEER Ronald	16-08-43	61 Sqn
141802	P/O	STEMP Ronald Claude	3-04-43	158 Sqn
1268035	F/S	STENHOUSE John David William	1-03-43	51 Sqn
52311	P/O	STENHOUSE Thomas	13-07-43	50 Sqn
145346	P/O	STENHOUSE William Elliott	22-09-43	7 Sqn
1455230	Sgt	STENNING Charles Clifford	1-09-43	78 Sqn
129370	P/O	STENNING Sidney John	31-01-43	19 OTU
89622	F/L	STENT Norman Sydney Lionel	15-02-43	100 Sqn
1059267	F/S	STEPHEN William	15-04-43	149 Sqn
51895	P/O	STEPHEN DFM William James	25-06-43	97 Sqn
1576447	Sgt	STEPHENS Arthur Francis	22-06-43	15 Sqn
1318904	Sgt	STEPHENS Frederick	12-03-43	50 Sqn
138689	P/O	STEPHENS Gerald	4-02-43	90 Sqn
1179576	Sgt	STEPHENS John Ackroyd	13-05-43	12 Sqn
39135	W/C	STEPHENS DFC John Douglas	30-08-43	15 Sqn
1585561	Sgt	STEPHENS John Thomas	17-04-43	156 Sqn
1316715	Sgt	STEPHENS Paul	14-05-43	44 Sqn
900043	Sgt	STEPHENS Ronald Edwin	7-05-43	29 OTU
1601045	Sgt	STEPHENS Stanley Vine	14-07-43	81 OTU
162534	P/O	STEPHENS DFM Trevor George	22-11-43	156 Sqn
1437794	Sgt	STEPHENS William	9-07-43	97 Sqn
1190561	Sgt	STEPHENSON Bernard Hamilton	12-06-43	431 Sqn
148892	P/O	STEPHENSON George Noel	1-09-43	44 Sqn
149569	P/O	STEPHENSON Kenneth John	3-10-43	61 Sqn
620520	Sgt	STEPHENSON Leslie	12-06-43	12 Sqn
1088249	Sgt	STEPHENSON Maxwell Wilson	8-01-43	9 Sqn
1684544	Sgt	STEPHENSON Peter	25-06-43	428 Sqn
1231524	Sgt	STEPHENSON William George	10-04-43	1661 HCU
127278	F/O	STEPNEY Cyril George	18-11-43	35 Sqn
1380632	F/S	STETTINER Henry Frederick Roger	30-03-43	158 Sqn
979723	Sgt	STEVEN Andrew John Kerr	24-08-43	78 Sqn
1092305	F/S	STEVEN Robert Redpath	4-12-43	431 Sqn
1024938	Sgt	STEVENS Alan	3-05-43	487 Sqn
1294635	Sgt	STEVENS Arthur William	13-05-43	51 Sqn
1289680	Sgt	STEVENS Edward Arthur	31-07-43	218 Sqn
1383561	Sgt	STEVENS James Henry	7-08-43	9 Sqn
1397811	Sgt	STEVENS John Charles William	14-06-43	199 Sqn
1401047	Sgt	STEVENS John Henry	3-10-43	44 Sqn
149698	P/O	STEVENS Reginald	18-10-43	619 Sqn
1337465	W/O	STEVENS Robert	18-10-43	103 Sqn
1331708	Sgt	STEVENS Ronald	11-03-43	1660 HCU
548169	W/O	STEVENS William John	24-06-43	10 OTU
1210218	Sgt	STEVENSON Alexander Bertram	22-05-43	1656 HCU
929350	Sgt	STEVENSON Donald Arthur	9-07-43	101 Sqn
131126	F/O	STEVENSON Donald Leslie	15-06-43	207 Sqn
1380989	Sgt	STEVENSON George William	25-07-43	1659 HCU
158717	P/O	STEVENSON Louis	23-09-43	97 Sqn
1076636	Sgt	STEVENSON Mathew Waddell	24-08-43	434 Sqn
1024896	Sgt	STEVENSON Richard William	25-06-43	51 Sqn
1369435	Sgt	STEVENSON William	27-03-43	426 Sqn
1808246	Sgt	STEVENTON Ronald	3-10-43	158 Sqn
116785	P/O	STEWARD Albert Edward	24-05-43	166 Sqn
120646	F/O	STEWARD Maurice James	13-02-43	50 Sqn
517058	F/S	STEWART DFM Charles	12-03-43	7 Sqn
1722688	Sgt	STEWART Eric Peter	17-06-43	1656 HCU
566943	F/S	STEWART MiD Frank	12-06-43	35 Sqn
547841	Sgt	STEWART Francis Barkhouse	3-03-43	75 Sqn
575014	Sgt	STEWART James	26-07-43	419 Sqn
1522531	Sgt	STEWART James	26-07-43	158 Sqn
636350	Sgt	STEWART James Alexander	4-09-43	467 Sqn
1537758	Sgt	STEWART James Dixon	29-09-43	158 Sqn
131071	F/O	STEWART James Henry [USA]	4-07-43	196 Sqn
1391507	Sgt	STEWART John Alistair	30-05-43	102 Sqn
1346451	Sgt	STEWART John Cameron	13-05-43	156 Sqn
131808	F/O	STEWART AFM John Maxwell	3-04-43	467 Sqn
1368456	Sgt	STEWART John McLean	11-12-43	617 Sqn
1361082	Sgt	STEWART Robert Charles	17-12-43	97 Sqn
1117389	Sgt	STEWART Thomas	23-09-43	75 Sqn
1343848	Sgt	STEWART William	26-02-43	102 Sqn
1391941	Sgt	STILES Edwin James Christopher	18-08-43	1656 HCU
1430814	Sgt	STILES William John	18-08-43	49 Sqn
1234599	Sgt	STILL Cecil Edgar Pollard	13-07-43	57 Sqn
1016380	Sgt	STILL George Thomas	30-03-43	83 Sqn
1312924	Sgt	STIMPSON Leonard Allen	13-05-43	77 Sqn
1307399	Sgt	STINTON Alan Victory David	18-01-43	76 Sqn
1551278	Sgt	STIRLING Alexander McLennan	9-08-43	149 Sqn
120887	F/O	STIRTON Ian Nicoll	22-01-43	429 Sqn
658070	Sgt	STOBBS William Edward	6-07-43	75 Sqn
1812792	Sgt	STOCK Edward Percy	22-10-43	1654 HCU
1021498	Sgt	STOCK Jack	3-04-43	166 Sqn
138479	P/O	STOCK Ronald William Harry	22-04-43	10 OTU
1140185	Sgt	STOCKBURN Robert Emmerson	2-03-43	50 Sqn
1386848	Sgt	STOCKLEY Harold Handley	16-07-43	10 Sqn
1568288	Sgt	STOCKS Robert Blythe	24-12-43	103 Sqn
1028166	Sgt	STOCKS DFM Thomas	22-11-43	156 Sqn
1544089	Sgt	STOCKS Thomas Frederick	14-02-43	15 Sqn
1150881	Sgt	STOCKTON Raymond William	27-04-43	428 Sqn
1323851	Sgt	STOCKWELL Charles Stanley	1-12-43	199 Sqn
109381	F/O	STOCKWELL Laurence Edwin	18-01-43	1654 HCU
1351487	Sgt	STODDART Raymond Tarlton	30-05-43	44 Sqn
936820	Sgt	STODDART Thomas William Tremble	26-05-43	207 Sqn
1209732	Sgt	STOKER Frederick James	15-06-43	106 Sqn
551369	F/S	STOKES DFM Arthur	14-03-43	138 Sqn
1394064	Sgt	STOKES Edgar Arthur	29-12-43	102 Sqn
158139	P/O	STOKES Geoffrey John Hamley	22-11-43	156 Sqn
1164343	Sgt	STOKES George William	1-09-43	158 Sqn
1809371	Sgt	STOKES Ronald Walter	25-02-43	19 OTU
1239665	Sgt	STOKES-ROBERTS Bennett	4-07-43	115 Sqn
1160153	Sgt	STOLBERG Geoffrey Charles	22-09-43	77 Sqn
1270148	Sgt	STONE Alfred Reginald	4-07-43	196 Sqn
1387857	Sgt	STONE Allan Gaskell	11-04-43	9 Sqn
1311959	F/S	STONE Antony Joseph	15-09-43	617 Sqn
1451978	Sgt	STONE David Campbell	25-05-43	100 Sqn
146277	F/O	STONE DFC Eric John	29-12-43	35 Sqn
933382	Sgt	STONE Harold Raymond	13-06-43	50 Sqn
1333951	Sgt	STONE Jack Richard	14-05-43	83 Sqn
993803	Sgt	STONE James	12-06-43	78 Sqn
572912	Sgt	STONE John	16-12-43	97 Sqn
1270251	Sgt	STONE John Dennis	28-01-43	1659 HCU
1313099	Sgt	STONE Leighton Mansel	8-03-43	75 Sqn
1804541	Sgt	STONE Leslie Leonard	7-09-43	434 Sqn
1308435	Sgt	STONE Marcus Walter	12-06-43	12 Sqn
66031	F/L	STONE DFC Philip John	13-06-43	50 Sqn
1585207	Sgt	STONE Reginald 'Reg'	31-01-43	106 Sqn

Service No	Rank	Name	Date	Squadron
1076018	Sgt	STONEHOUSE James	8-10-43	9 Sqn
158258	P/O	STONELEY DFM Michael John Ernest	18-11-43	156 Sqn
1336851	W/O	STONEMAN John Stafford	3-08-43	103 Sqn
912203	Sgt	STONEMAN Reginald Tarbat	16-12-43	1667 HCU
1325380	Sgt	STONESTREET Alfred Newman	27-05-43	139 Sqn
1559479	Sgt	STONEY Francis Oliver	22-11-43	218 Sqn
656400	Sgt	STOPFORD Newman Gee	8-04-43	156 Sqn
149617	P/O	STORER Colin Harrison	16-12-43	106 Sqn
1145662	F/S	STOREY Alan Everard	10-08-43	102 Sqn
1809725	Sgt	STOREY Derrick George Amos	24-05-43	75 Sqn
37615	S/L	STOREY George Gerard	17-06-43	49 Sqn
650050	Sgt	STOREY Robert Albert	23-04-43	9 Sqn
1238263	Sgt	STOTHARD Frederick	22-09-43	76 Sqn
985652	Sgt	STOTT DFM Alan	13-05-43	50 Sqn
130569	F/O	STOTT Joseph	4-12-43	76 Sqn
162588	P/O	STOTT DFM Robert	26-11-43	101 Sqn
1379702	Sgt	STOTT Thomas Frederick	18-10-43	103 Sqn
1302662	Sgt	STOTTER Joseph William	28-04-43	101 Sqn
1072451	LAC	STOUT Kenneth Hindley	22-12-43	9 Sqn
1312210	Sgt	STOWE Dennis	21-04-43	90 Sqn
1341911	Sgt	STRACHAN Alexander Taylor	11-01-43	81 OTU
1013892	Sgt	STRACHAN John	17-04-43	76 Sqn
1320655	F/S	STRACHAN John Philip	27-09-43	78 Sqn
1312207	Sgt	STRAKER Paul Gilbert	23-09-43	90 Sqn
145733	P/O	STRAND Cyril	30-05-43	158 Sqn
1343141	Sgt	STRANG John Calderhead Bruce	31-08-43	139 Sqn
155793	P/O	STRANGE Andrew Paul Edmund	26-11-43	61 Sqn
157142	P/O	STRANGE Harold Arthur	14-11-43	10 OTU
1395453	Sgt	STRANGE Harry John	17-05-43	617 Sqn
1551143	Sgt	STRATH David John Duthie	17-06-43	460 Sqn
996460	Sgt	STRATHEARN James Hill	4-04-43	214 Sqn
1396511	Sgt	STRATON Peter David	25-06-43	214 Sqn
1166593	Sgt	STRATTON Raymond Walter John	4-11-43	75 Sqn
1113682	F/S	STREET Donald Edward	13-03-43	7 Sqn
1458835	Sgt	STREET Erick Thomas Charles	29-07-43	218 Sqn
139622	P/O	STREET Frank	31-08-43	78 Sqn
1319512	Sgt	STREET Harry	17-12-43	101 Sqn
1456889	Sgt	STREET Leslie Charles John	2-12-43	626 Sqn
141090	F/O	STREET DFM Peter Robert	30-12-43	18 OTU
1313967	Sgt	STREET Reginald Victor	18-10-43	207 Sqn
1575811	Sgt	STREET Ronald Victor	24-05-43	115 Sqn
949546	Sgt	STRETTON James Hornby	5-05-43	101 Sqn
1389698	Sgt	STREVENS Frederick Charles	24-08-43	622 Sqn
1605487	Sgt	STRIBLEY Derick Waters	22-10-43	77 Sqn
137364	F/O	STRINGER Albert William	18-10-43	207 Sqn
1581536	Sgt	STRINGER Clement	14-05-43	51 Sqn
1047255	F/S	STRINGER George Clifford	23-09-43	15 Sqn
1467653	Sgt	STRINGER Ronald Amos Charles Martin	18-08-43	57 Sqn
1817407	Sgt	STRINGER Roy Alan	11-06-43	207 Sqn
1045932	Sgt	STRINGFELLOW John Michael	1-09-43	15 Sqn
2209335	Sgt	STROLIN Alfred Charles	2-09-43	81 OTU
1214453	Sgt	STRONG Donald Hugh	3-10-43	12 Sqn
1126658	Sgt	STRONG Elliott Eggleston	7-09-43	427 Sqn
1114468	Sgt	STRONG Thomas William Kitchener	15-02-43	207 Sqn
1311955	Sgt	STROUD Douglas Edward Henry	24-07-43	18 OTU
149534	P/O	STRUTHERS Donald MacLean	26-06-43	44 Sqn
1121371	Sgt	STUART Alfred	28-09-43	428 Sqn
72476	S/L	STUART Antony Charles Letteblere Akroyd	31-08-43	76 Sqn
158306	F/O	STUART CGM Frederick John	20-12-43	426 Sqn
1350310	Sgt	STUART John	22-01-43	429 Sqn
655800	F/S	STUART Joseph Gordon	23-09-43	77 Sqn
1385971	Sgt	STUART Lloyd Lincoln	26-02-43	218 Sqn
1681268	Sgt	STUART Richard	29-12-43	61 Sqn
1337433	Sgt	STUBBINGS Frederick William	9-10-43	431 Sqn
1590086	Sgt	STUBBS George Henry	2-12-43	106 Sqn
145679	P/O	STUBBS Leonard Emmerson	17-07-43	207 Sqn
61461	F/L	STUBBS DFC Richard Noel	27-02-43	103 Sqn
1312076	AC1	STUBBS Sidney Miller	19-06-43	Snaith
51042	P/O	STUCKEY MiD William	23-06-43	75 Sqn
49983	F/O	STUFFIN Harry George	26-11-43	106 Sqn
1316753	Sgt	STURGESS James William	10-07-43	408 Sqn
1542840	Sgt	STYLER Gordon Herbert	9-10-43	78 Sqn
1716536	AC2	STYLES John Albert	1-03-43	West Raynham
1322545	Sgt	STYLES Robert Griffiths Alan	5-01-43	20 OTU
126886	F/O	ST. JOHN John Henry Roy Sarano	22-06-43	35 Sqn
131774	P/O	ST. LEDGER Charles Patrick	17-06-43	103 Sqn
127923	F/O	SUCH George	25-07-43	76 Sqn
137526	F/O	SUFFIELD James	23-09-43	15 OTU
1623604	Sgt	SUFFIELD James Arthur	31-07-43	78 Sqn
127055	F/O	SUGAR Gordon Robert	13-06-43	83 Sqn
1385108	Sgt	SUGDEN Frank Arthur	24-12-43	625 Sqn
1119079	Sgt	SUGDEN Thomas Mitchell	26-06-43	102 Sqn
1481508	Sgt	SUGDEN Vincent	23-06-43	101 Sqn
631997	Sgt	SULLIVAN Douglas Charles	3-10-43	90 Sqn
1890218	Sgt	SULLIVAN Eric	2-12-43	460 Sqn
1215235	Sgt	SULLIVAN James	28-07-43	100 Sqn
1395407	F/S	SULLIVAN DFM John Timothy	4-10-43	97 Sqn
1275819	Sgt	SUMMERS Robert	28-12-43	20 OTU
1057133	Sgt	SUMMERSON William Anderson	14-02-43	149 Sqn
126845	F/L	SUMNER DFC Alan Henry John	17-08-43	35 Sqn
125711	F/O	SUMNER Anthony John [Argentina]	26-11-43	103 Sqn
1128947	Sgt	SUMNER Francis	6-09-43	619 Sqn
1302029	Sgt	SUNLEY Allen	10-08-43	35 Sqn
759008	W/O	SUNLEY Guy	9-01-43	50 Sqn
1388224	Sgt	SURGEY Charles Kenneth [Uruguay]	30-05-43	158 Sqn
944647	Sgt	SURTEES Andrew George	29-04-43	218 Sqn
649134	Sgt	SUTCLIFFE Arthur	4-09-43	57 Sqn
1324374	Sgt	SUTCLIFFE Jack	20-06-43	10 Sqn
1678635	Sgt	SUTHERLAND John William Elwison	18-10-43	100 Sqn
117689	F/L	SUTHERLAND Willdon Simpson Drysdale	27-05-43	139 Sqn
156620	P/O	SUTHERST Jack	31-08-43	7 Sqn
1324003	Sgt	SUTTON Alexander Robert	21-01-43	207 Sqn
1434193	Sgt	SUTTON Arnold John	22-06-43	7 Sqn
1209339	Sgt	SUTTON George	29-04-43	218 Sqn
1384354	F/S	SUTTON George Henry	30-07-43	77 Sqn
1033490	Sgt	SUTTON Thomas Henry	31-08-43	35 Sqn
647531	F/S	SWAIN Donald Arthur Alfred	26-11-43	35 Sqn
119477	F/O	SWAIN Egbert Horace	6-07-43	466 Sqn
1336737	Sgt	SWAIN Frederick Charles [Canada]	29-04-43	196 Sqn
39136	W/C	SWAIN MiD James George Wilson	20-04-43	100 Sqn
1389005	Sgt	SWAIN Rex	17-06-43	12 Sqn
1699589	Sgt	SWAINSTON Bernard Shade	29-06-43	149 Sqn
1219652	Sgt	SWALLOW Bryan Milton	31-01-43	9 Sqn
127306	F/O	SWALLOW Paul Douglas	14-07-43	90 Sqn
1184889	Sgt	SWAN George	12-06-43	28 OTU
1587352	Sgt	SWEET Dennis William	1-09-43	419 Sqn
1230519	Sgt	SWEET Harold	26-05-43	431 Sqn
1321457	F/S	SWEET Harold Lewis	26-11-43	61 Sqn
1587150	Sgt	SWEET Sandom	5-05-43	90 Sqn
990927	Sgt	SWEETING Charles William	1-09-43	623 Sqn
1029829	Sgt	SWEETLOVE Ronald Spencer	8-04-43	100 Sqn
1240819	Sgt	SWIFT Clement Roland	8-03-43	156 Sqn
1283491	Sgt	SWIFT Frederick John	3-08-43	103 Sqn
104764	S/L	SWIFT DFC James Eric	12-06-43	83 Sqn
1699713	Sgt	SWINCHATT Kenneth	4-12-43	630 Sqn
1210606	Sgt	SWINDALE Raymond Leslie	9-10-43	434 Sqn
1675628	Sgt	SWINDLE Maurice Noel Graham	22-11-43	1664 HCU
1087538	F/S	SWINNEY Arthur	27-09-43	156 Sqn
967340	Sgt	SWINTON John	25-07-43	102 Sqn
144641	P/O	SWIRE William Hallewell	3-04-43	9 Sqn
1239644	F/S	SYKES Eric Whitton	18-11-43	90 Sqn
1081986	Sgt	SYKES Harry	21-10-43	103 Sqn

1575179 Sgt	SYKES James Thomas	22-11-43	158 Sqn	
957643 Sgt	SYKES John	6-02-43	14 OTU	
1078563 Sgt	SYKES John Walter	25-06-43	57 Sqn	
657255 Sgt	SYKES Joshua Alan	29-06-43	44 Sqn	
1085070 Sgt	SYKES Ralph	22-10-43	102 Sqn	
1387788 Sgt	SYMONDS Douglas James	24-12-43	44 Sqn	
1397027 Sgt	SYMONS John Westlake	26-11-43	102 Sqn	
126677 F/O	TABBERER Thomas Henry	28-08-43	78 Sqn	
1274037 Sgt	TABENOR Geoffrey	22-11-43	49 Sqn	
1293166 Sgt	TABNER Lawrence Harry	14-01-43	466 Sqn	
1332966 Sgt	TAGG Kenneth John	12-06-43	12 Sqn	
1425260 Sgt	TAGG Lancelot	21-04-43	90 Sqn	
1533637 Sgt	TAIT Alan John	3-10-43	103 Sqn	
1063628 Sgt	TAIT John McCalla	26-03-43	78 Sqn	
1151777 Sgt	TAIT John Robert	8-04-43	218 Sqn	
1408456 Sgt	TAKLE Ernest John	16-12-43	207 Sqn	
1030278 Sgt	TALGAM Edward	3-08-43	51 Sqn	
1337370 Sgt	TANN Roy Arthur	3-11-43	10 Sqn	
551240 F/S	TANNER Anthony George	26-07-43	50 Sqn	
1312384 Sgt	TANNER Leonard Victor	22-06-43	83 Sqn	
1361367 Sgt	TANNOCK Alexander	30-05-43	35 Sqn	
149542 P/O	TANSLEY Ernest Henry	2-12-43	57 Sqn	
1333864 Sgt	TARBIN Clifford Edward	3-10-43	77 Sqn	
1810812 Sgt	TARLING Robert	2-12-43	460 Sqn	
1383325 Sgt	TARR Vincent John	15-06-43	9 Sqn	
1094117 Sgt	TARRAN George Bussey	27-01-43	21 OTU	
1450019 Sgt	TARRANT Alfred Bertram	8-03-43	75 Sqn	
1850925 Sgt	TARRANT Stanley George	4-12-43	51 Sqn	
1238778 Sgt	TARREN Robert James	6-04-43	1663 HCU	
1575752 Sgt	TARVER John	3-08-43	100 Sqn	
1232838 Sgt	TASKER Albert	28-08-43	620 Sqn	
130434 F/O	TATE Francis Richard Harry	20-04-43	57 Sqn	
650164 Sgt	TATE Kenneth Charles	26-07-43	103 Sqn	
1575776 Sgt	TATE Lawrence James	9-04-43	106 Sqn	
1146823 Sgt	TATE Ronald Edward	7-09-43	10 Sqn	
138889 P/O	TATE Stanley O'Connor [Eire]	13-07-43	467 Sqn	
1467770 Sgt	TATTAM George Thomas	3-05-43	487 Sqn	
1129472 Sgt	TATTERSALL Rowland	11-08-43	27 OTU	
1433374 Sgt	TATTERSALL Sydney Richard	1-09-43	77 Sqn	
155792 P/O	TAVERNER Philip Ackroyd	22-10-43	49 Sqn	
145472 P/O	TAY John Perton	29-06-43	51 Sqn	
1321755 Sgt	TAYLER Douglas Arthur Allen	6-07-43	75 Sqn	
1318170 Sgt	TAYLER Reginald Harry	29-04-43	196 Sqn	
575430 Sgt	TAYLOR Alastair James	16-05-43	617 Sqn	
1374466 Sgt	TAYLOR Albert	30-03-43	51 Sqn	
1603089 Sgt	TAYLOR Albert Edward	1-09-43	620 Sqn	
1385739 Sgt	TAYLOR Albert James	18-09-43	1658 HCU	
1561460 Sgt	TAYLOR Alexander Munro	30-05-43	35 Sqn	
1399348 Sgt	TAYLOR Alexander Sargant	17-09-43	196 Sqn	
1431243 Sgt	TAYLOR Allan Henry	4-07-43	196 Sqn	
966000 Sgt	TAYLOR Arthur	19-11-43	622 Sqn	
156273 P/O	TAYLOR Arthur Edwin [USA]	6-09-43	106 Sqn	
1333164 Sgt	TAYLOR Arthur John	10-03-43	44 Sqn	
1578977 Sgt	TAYLOR Arthur Norman	9-07-43	166 Sqn	
1601091 Sgt	TAYLOR Arthur William Ernest	12-03-43	97 Sqn	
1391298 Sgt	TAYLOR Aubrey Bramley	2-10-43	44 Sqn	
1296656 Sgt	TAYLOR Basil Frank	24-11-43	1658 HCU	
710151 Sgt	TAYLOR Bertie Edward [Rhodesia]	5-05-43	196 Sqn	
1390419 Sgt	TAYLOR Charles Edward	17-08-43	218 Sqn	
1219035 Sgt	TAYLOR Cyril	13-05-43	429 Sqn	
910576 F/S	TAYLOR Edgar Francis	22-10-43	57 Sqn	
1070060 Sgt	TAYLOR Eric	7-08-43	9 Sqn	
110642 F/O	TAYLOR Eric Alfred	1-03-43	76 Sqn	
80477 F/O	TAYLOR Ewart Arthur [Rhodesia]	2-12-43	12 Sqn	
1017135 F/S	TAYLOR Frank	21-04-43	21 Sqn	
1735147 Sgt	TAYLOR Frank Richard	20-12-43	426 Sqn	
1430565 Sgt	TAYLOR George	17-06-43	100 Sqn	
1236706 Sgt	TAYLOR George Rolling	27-02-43	427 Sqn	
143385 F/O	TAYLOR CGM DFC Harry Forbes McPherson	5-12-43	1409 Flt	
533766 Sgt	TAYLOR Herbert	24-08-43	218 Sqn	
1334645 Sgt	TAYLOR Hubert Stanley	5-05-43	10 Sqn	
1239660 Sgt	TAYLOR Jack	9-10-43	432 Sqn	
1624512 Sgt	TAYLOR Jack	27-09-43	199 Sqn	
655553 Sgt	TAYLOR James	27-08-43	1663 HCU	
1676093 Cpl	TAYLOR James Henry	1-07-43	5 Group	
156318 P/O	TAYLOR Jeffrey Charles May	4-07-43	408 Sqn	
1851668 Sgt	TAYLOR John	23-11-43	44 Sqn	
1606590 Sgt	TAYLOR John Edward	12-11-43	78 Sqn	
1028370 Sgt	TAYLOR John George	14-09-43	158 Sqn	
1434892 Sgt	TAYLOR John Peter	3-08-43	214 Sqn	
751507 F/S	TAYLOR John Thomas	5-05-43	57 Sqn	
124553 P/O	TAYLOR Kenneth Alsey	27-01-43	218 Sqn	
1131423 AC1	TAYLOR Kenneth Darwin	2-07-43	158 Sqn	
1238522 Sgt	TAYLOR Kenneth Gordon	3-10-43	90 Sqn	
1237051 Sgt	TAYLOR Kenneth Mirfin	17-06-43	467 Sqn	
938779 Sgt	TAYLOR Kenneth Norman	30-09-43	9 Sqn	
647282 Sgt	TAYLOR Kenneth William	4-04-43	156 Sqn	
617940 Sgt	TAYLOR Leslie Alfred	26-07-43	51 Sqn	
1475722 Sgt	TAYLOR Nicholas Daunt	26-11-43	103 Sqn	
1330788 Sgt	TAYLOR Norman Edwin	14-05-43	44 Sqn	
1336198 Sgt	TAYLOR Norman Phillip	3-03-43	51 Sqn	
1346152 Sgt	TAYLOR Patrick James	25-06-43	90 Sqn	
1525616 F/S	TAYLOR Robert Edward	31-07-43	218 Sqn	
1462395 Sgt	TAYLOR Robert George	23-11-43	9 Sqn	
1374432 LAC	TAYLOR Robert Menzies	19-06-43	Snaith	
648472 Sgt	TAYLOR Ronald	21-01-43	103 Sqn	
914436 Sgt	TAYLOR Ronald Frederick [Canada]	21-12-43	76 Sqn	
1187123 Sgt	TAYLOR Roy Herbert George	30-03-43	57 Sqn	
1318833 F/S	TAYLOR Roy Leonard	20-10-43	83 Sqn	
1583320 Sgt	TAYLOR Sidney Alan	16-12-43	625 Sqn	
1458100 Sgt	TAYLOR William	5-03-43	214 Sqn	
1532521 Sgt	TAYLOR William Arthur	25-06-43	90 Sqn	
1292832 Sgt	TAYLORSON Harry	25-06-43	90 Sqn	
1579780 Sgt	TEAGUE Kenneth Joseph	22-01-43	487 Sqn	
1536280 Sgt	TEASDALE Norman	22-09-43	158 Sqn	
121255 P/O	TEASDEL Arthur John	27-02-43	166 Sqn	
131492 F/O	TEBBLE George Graham	17-06-43	103 Sqn	
1577297 Sgt	TEBBUTT William	28-09-43	622 Sqn	
1371009 Sgt	TELFER Adam	21-04-43	49 Sqn	
1390942 F/S	TELFER Clive	19-11-43	10 Sqn	
1586042 Sgt	TELFER Douglas	26-06-43	57 Sqn	
1046346 Sgt	TELFER Robert Martin	27-09-43	78 Sqn	
1099681 F/S	TELFORD Harry	23-10-43	467 Sqn	
127971 F/O	TEMPLE Harold Luttrell	10-08-43	35 Sqn	
1395482 Sgt	TEMPLEMAN Norman Ralph	16-11-43	16 OTU	
1559351 Sgt	TEMPLETON Alexander George	28-08-43	77 Sqn	
1071533 Sgt	TEMPLETON Arthur Moore	4-02-43	427 Sqn	
656607 Sgt	TEMPLETON William George Mitchell	21-11-43	192 Sqn	
1336557 Sgt	TEMPLE-MURRAY Alan Michael Terence David	17-06-43	1656 HCU	
139509 P/O	TERRY Frank Arthur	11-04-43	7 Sqn	
1800644 Sgt	TERRY George Louis	28-08-43	218 Sqn	
1091871 Sgt	TERRY Harry	5-03-43	11 OTU	
1387301 Sgt	TERRY James Richard	10-01-43	10 OTU	
1019953 Sgt	TESSICK Francis	20-12-43	76 Sqn	
1397311 Sgt	TESTER Kenneth Arthur	2-04-43	57 Sqn	
1081182 Sgt	TETLEY John Charlton	18-10-43	103 Sqn	
81378 F/L	TETLEY DFC William Abbotson	30-05-43	35 Sqn	
1367316 Sgt	TEVIOTDALE Thomas	12-02-43	101 Sqn	
1801167 Sgt	TEW George Charles	6-09-43	427 Sqn	
1334754 Sgt	TEWFIK Raymond Khalil	17-05-43	10 OTU	
155199 P/O	THACKER Frederick Harold	1-09-43	158 Sqn	
138109 F/O	THACKWAY Edward	17-12-43	97 Sqn	
1385945 Sgt	THALLON Robert Erle	4-07-43	214 Sqn	

Service #	Rank	Name	Date	Squadron
1386971	Sgt	THEOBALD Robert Walter	24-12-43	100 Sqn
116418	F/L	THEOBALD DFC Wilfred Murray	12-06-43	7 Sqn
142371	P/O	THEW Harry Scott	7-09-43	427 Sqn
1576424	Sgt	THEWLIS Alec Carson	24-08-43	78 Sqn
1217817	Sgt	THIRKETTLE Ernest Albert Cecil	4-09-43	460 Sqn
1512169	Sgt	THIRSK David Wilkie	8-08-43	61 Sqn
1368871	Sgt	THOM DFM James Myles	6-03-43	49 Sqn
1236390	Sgt	THOMAS Alan Jeffery	29-06-43	100 Sqn
1410272	Sgt	THOMAS Albert Edward Glyn	26-11-43	463 Sqn
1276953	Sgt	THOMAS Alfred	23-09-43	218 Sqn
149999	P/O	THOMAS Alfred John	31-07-43	75 Sqn
1312656	Sgt	THOMAS Arthur Brinley	11-04-43	115 Sqn
648382	F/S	THOMAS Arthur Gwilyn	17-01-43	50 Sqn
1382457	Sgt	THOMAS Arthur Leslie	24-08-43	77 Sqn
1437035	Sgt	THOMAS Arthur William	3-02-43	106 Sqn
623547	Sgt	THOMAS Benjamin James	23-09-43	90 Sqn
127240	F/L	THOMAS Cecil George	3-11-43	49 Sqn
117691	F/O	THOMAS Clifford Stanley	29-01-43	226 Sqn
124699	F/O	THOMAS Daniel Owen	12-06-43	83 Sqn
655982	Sgt	THOMAS David	2-03-43	50 Sqn
1379101	Sgt	THOMAS David John Dudley	25-01-43	226 Sqn
1336716	Sgt	THOMAS Dennis Arthur	13-06-43	460 Sqn
544114	Sgt	THOMAS Donald George	17-01-43	101 Sqn
1217614	Sgt	THOMAS Douglas	29-06-43	15 Sqn
1446824	Sgt	THOMAS Douglas Arthur	3-08-43	405 Sqn
1331633	Sgt	THOMAS Edward	26-05-43	426 Sqn
1270671	Sgt	THOMAS Edwin Gordon	16-04-43	78 Sqn
137365	F/O	THOMAS Ernest Arthur	9-10-43	61 Sqn
1048366	Sgt	THOMAS Frank	18-11-43	514 Sqn
1238300	Sgt	THOMAS Frank Heydon	24-03-43	1652 HCU
977593	Sgt	THOMAS Hamilton John	23-09-43	15 Sqn
1335963	Sgt	THOMAS Harold Gwyn	17-06-43	103 Sqn
1170573	Sgt	THOMAS Harold Henry	18-10-43	44 Sqn
2216159	Sgt	THOMAS Harold Parry	20-12-43	44 Sqn
612466	Sgt	THOMAS Hopkin George	30-05-43	115 Sqn
126001	F/O	THOMAS Jeffrey Stuart	5-09-43	1663 HCU
980825	Sgt	THOMAS John	31-08-43	106 Sqn
1313122	Sgt	THOMAS John	28-08-43	158 Sqn
1386883	Sgt	THOMAS John	13-05-43	61 Sqn
620927	Sgt	THOMAS John Charles	29-05-43	218 Sqn
1384314	Sgt	THOMAS John James	7-09-43	427 Sqn
975702	Sgt	THOMAS Joseph Edmund	26-11-43	463 Sqn
1291773	Sgt	THOMAS Leonard Evan	12-03-43	10 Sqn
132176	F/O	THOMAS Leslie Howard	17-12-43	161 Sqn
658115	Sgt	THOMAS Leslie Raymond	6-05-43	19 OTU
1414728	LAC	THOMAS Morgan David	17-02-43	1482 Flt
1422017	Sgt	THOMAS Phillip John Cecil	31-01-43	97 Sqn
1316730	Sgt	THOMAS Reginald James	4-11-43	75 Sqn
647506	Sgt	THOMAS Richard Henry	10-04-43	9 Sqn
575820	Sgt	THOMAS Ronald Albert Henry	27-03-43	35 Sqn
1334293	Sgt	THOMAS Roy	2-12-43	103 Sqn
108829	F/O	THOMAS Roy Dudley Clifton	3-05-43	487 Sqn
915352	Sgt	THOMAS Stanley Alan	18-11-43	622 Sqn
156310	P/O	THOMAS Stanley Philip Iltid	18-11-43	514 Sqn
1813914	Sgt	THOMAS Thomas Stanley	24-08-43	158 Sqn
1286345	Sgt	THOMAS Urien	27-03-43	156 Sqn
1331876	Sgt	THOMAS William Charles	22-09-43	214 Sqn
1203830	Sgt	THOMAS William Charles Marcus	28-08-43	57 Sqn
1217408	Sgt	THOMAS William Frank	13-07-43	12 Sqn
149471	P/O	THOMPSON Alan Henry	18-08-43	44 Sqn
1515448	Sgt	THOMPSON Alexander	14-09-43	158 Sqn
1097549	Sgt	THOMPSON Alfred	23-06-43	90 Sqn
1495077	Sgt	THOMPSON Arthur Robert Hollinshead [Eire]	11-04-43	9 Sqn
148761	P/O	THOMPSON Charles Edward	22-06-43	100 Sqn
1637596	Sgt	THOMPSON Charles George	17-12-43	166 Sqn
1214018	Sgt	THOMPSON Edward Alec	30-05-43	44 Sqn
132382	F/L	THOMPSON DFC Edward Mackson	18-11-43	156 Sqn
144266	P/O	THOMPSON Frank Malcolm	17-04-43	51 Sqn
1242384	Sgt	THOMPSON Frederick	24-05-43	408 Sqn
120392	F/L	THOMPSON DFC* Frederick Denzil James	12-03-43	7 Sqn
658258	Sgt	THOMPSON Frederick William	27-11-43	626 Sqn
1063365	Sgt	THOMPSON Geoffrey	25-06-43	7 Sqn
1800334	Sgt	THOMPSON George Clark	26-07-43	51 Sqn
1038224	Sgt	THOMPSON George Kenneth	27-04-43	429 Sqn
1587646	Sgt	THOMPSON Gerald	24-08-43	623 Sqn
1385555	Sgt	THOMPSON Glyn John Davies	22-06-43	428 Sqn
1483381	Sgt	THOMPSON Harold Blamire	24-05-43	166 Sqn
138393	P/O	THOMPSON Harold Geoffrey Allen	19-05-43	310 FTU
1578271	Sgt	THOMPSON Harry Edward	21-10-43	103 Sqn
52755	P/O	THOMPSON Hugh Conn	22-06-43	44 Sqn
143217	P/O	THOMPSON James Burdett	9-03-43	156 Sqn
1365303	F/S	THOMPSON James William	20-12-43	466 Sqn
1311822	Sgt	THOMPSON John Jocelyn [Eire]	3-03-43	76 Sqn
141457	P/O	THOMPSON John Rawson	5-03-43	78 Sqn
657132	Sgt	THOMPSON John Robert	13-05-43	218 Sqn
160916	P/O	THOMPSON DFM Joseph Watson	27-11-43	50 Sqn
1129556	Sgt	THOMPSON Leonard William	24-08-43	156 Sqn
1004634	Sgt	THOMPSON Leslie	17-04-43	426 Sqn
116203	F/L	THOMPSON Leslie Edward	5-10-43	429 Sqn
1253760	Sgt	THOMPSON Lewis Reginald	3-03-43	207 Sqn
1334603	Sgt	THOMPSON Norman	27-04-43	51 Sqn
136456	F/O	THOMPSON Peter	22-09-43	78 Sqn
130160	P/O	THOMPSON Ralph William	11-04-43	424 Sqn
1385570	Sgt	THOMPSON Reginald Herbert William	26-06-43	44 Sqn
1590783	Sgt	THOMPSON Roland	9-10-43	427 Sqn
621155	Sgt	THOMPSON Ronald Ernest	18-08-43	620 Sqn
1351019	Sgt	THOMPSON Tom	24-12-43	103 Sqn
1219352	Sgt	THOMPSON Vincent Percival	1-03-43	29 OTU
1476771	Sgt	THOMPSON William Harris	26-06-43	214 Sqn
1041279	F/S	THOMPSON William Harrison	28-08-43	620 Sqn
1484375	Sgt	THOMPSON William Howard	3-08-43	75 Sqn
1077841	F/S	THOMSON Albert John	12-11-43	35 Sqn
1551466	Sgt	THOMSON Andrew	10-07-43	77 Sqn
160040	F/L	THOMSON Douglas Lindsay [Rhodesia]	3-10-43	61 Sqn
910599	Sgt	THOMSON Douglas Menzies	2-07-43	620 Sqn
1313414	Sgt	THOMSON Eric Wilson [Canada]	13-05-43	51 Sqn
1562966	Sgt	THOMSON George	4-07-43	115 Sqn
1052427	Sgt	THOMSON James	24-06-43	218 Sqn
1710027	Sgt	THOMSON John Charles	24-08-43	15 Sqn
1374282	Sgt	THOMSON John Smith	23-09-43	75 Sqn
1556094	Sgt	THOMSON Thomas	17-11-43	405 Sqn
1111480	Sgt	THOMSON William	11-04-43	9 Sqn
1680443	Sgt	THOMSON William Guthrie	22-11-43	77 Sqn
1377796	Sgt	THOMSON William Henry	26-05-43	199 Sqn
649194	Sgt	THORN Ronald	23-11-43	51 Sqn
159225	P/O	THORNE Arthur George [Jamaica]	20-12-43	78 Sqn
850080	F/S	THORNE Eric John	15-07-43	139 Sqn
1266197	F/S	THORNE Robert George	9-03-43	7 Sqn
1315558	Sgt	THORNE William James	24-07-43	18 OTU
1433249	Sgt	THORNHILL William	27-09-43	460 Sqn
1464625	Sgt	THORNHILL William Henry	23-10-43	467 Sqn
1690020	Sgt	THORNLEY Douglas Leslie	23-10-43	434 Sqn
1577977	Sgt	THORNTON James Henry	26-07-43	103 Sqn
155349	P/O	THORNTON Richard Andrew	22-10-43	408 Sqn
577022	Sgt	THORNTON Richard Leonard	1-05-43	1663 HCU
1213543	Sgt	THORNTON Ronald	12-08-43	620 Sqn
1488238	Sgt	THORNYCROFT Peter Mytton	23-06-43	77 Sqn
131898	P/O	THOROGOOD Frederick Keith	13-02-43	30 OTU
1812195	Sgt	THOROGOOD Ronald	18-10-43	101 Sqn
1270263	Sgt	THOROGOOD Stanley	31-08-43	7 Sqn
156078	P/O	THORP Arthur	3-10-43	76 Sqn
1317387	Sgt	THORPE Bernard	9-10-43	90 Sqn

1800350	Sgt	THORPE Charles Edward	27-04-43	115 Sqn		1314002	Sgt	TOMS Charles Cecil	17-12-43	218 Sqn
1514349	Sgt	THORPE Ernest	4-10-43	75 Sqn		1396656	Sgt	TOMS Ernest Charles	20-12-43	166 Sqn
1389321	Sgt	THORPE Leslie John	3-09-43	30 OTU		1317569	Sgt	TOMS Peter Alfred	15-06-43	49 Sqn
1515965	Sgt	THRALL Frederick	12-11-43	102 Sqn		130269	F/O	TONER Kenneth	10-07-43	50 Sqn
1457394	Sgt	THREADGOLD Ronald Walter	26-07-43	75 Sqn		156045	P/O	TONKIN DFM Thomas	18-08-43	49 Sqn
52222	P/O	THURLBY MiD Lucius Thorpe	18-10-43	101 Sqn		51064	F/L	TONKINSON Donald Thomas	28-05-43	166 Sqn
1286488	Sgt	THURLOW Arthur Leonard	12-03-43	102 Sqn		1383991	Sgt	TOOMEY Henry Albert	28-08-43	207 Sqn
1320616	Sgt	THURLOW Edward	13-06-43	158 Sqn		1438888	Sgt	TOOTH Arthur	29-06-43	44 Sqn
1510800	Sgt	THWAITE John Fisher	22-10-43	1654 HCU		1818440	Sgt	TOPHAM Edward Arthur	2-12-43	550 Sqn
125888	F/O	THWAITES Colin	17-04-43	10 OTU		1802973	Sgt	TORBETT Clifford William	18-08-43	100 Sqn
79550	S/L	THWAITES DFC Michael Edward	12-03-43	7 Sqn		1319178	Sgt	TORRANCE Bernard	23-01-43	75 Sqn
1600509	Sgt	TIBBLE Derek Bewlay	12-06-43	76 Sqn		1044676	Sgt	TOUGH George Herbert [Eire]	1-09-43	1654 HCU
1873950	Sgt	TIBBLES Thomas Henry	8-10-43	9 Sqn		1337153	Sgt	TOULSON Reginald	26-07-43	50 Sqn
1138805	Sgt	TICE Alan	18-08-43	158 Sqn		146093	P/O	TOUZEL Norman Bernard	25-06-43	166 Sqn
119747	F/O	TICKLE Harold John Robert	3-01-43	61 Sqn		657647	Sgt	TOVEY Albert George	25-06-43	102 Sqn
1601720	Sgt	TICKNER Arthur Raymond	30-05-43	115 Sqn		553608	Sgt	TOWE Eric	26-06-43	218 Sqn
132746	F/O	TIDBALL Walter Roy	26-07-43	158 Sqn		130237	F/O	TOWERS Albert Frank	15-04-43	100 Sqn
1579975	Sgt	TIDMARSH Arthur Donald	17-01-43	76 Sqn		37334	W/C	TOWLE John Gordon	31-08-43	12 Sqn
127147	F/L	TILBURY Eric Arthur	13-06-43	83 Sqn		975798	Sgt	TOWLER Edwin	13-02-43	30 OTU
1337416	Sgt	TILBURY Reginald Arthur	28-05-43	158 Sqn		1217965	Sgt	TOWN Gerland Albert Raymond	21-04-43	75 Sqn
578008	Sgt	TILEY Charles John	8-04-43	49 Sqn		702576	Sgt	TOWN John Newton	26-02-43	103 Sqn
1803748	Sgt	TILEY Frederick Aubrey	9-10-43	434 Sqn		1307856	Sgt	TOWN Joseph Alfred	23-09-43	15 Sqn
1175445	Sgt	TILLEN Frank Ivan	15-02-43	207 Sqn		1484117	Sgt	TOWNSEND Ernest	20-08-43	10 Sqn
158600	P/O	TILLER Henry	2-12-43	101 Sqn		121412	F/O	TOWNSEND Francis Eric	1-03-43	50 Sqn
576698	Sgt	TILLER Peter Edward	5-05-43	102 Sqn		1385329	Sgt	TOWNSEND Frank Cecil	15-04-43	21 OTU
1167927	F/S	TILLEY Arthur Francis Edward	1-03-43	15 Sqn		1568521	Sgt	TOWNSEND John Howison	19-08-43	1663 HCU
127792	F/O	TILSON MiD Cyril Garnett	18-01-43	9 Sqn		1577926	Sgt	TOWNSEND Ronald Reginald	25-09-43	29 OTU
924220	W/O	TIMLIN Glyn Anthony	12-11-43	90 Sqn		1804594	Sgt	TOWNSON Thomas Glyn	20-12-43	466 Sqn
1777401	F/S	TIMMINS John James 'Jim'	28-09-43	1664 HCU		149211	P/O	TOWSE DFM Wilfred	26-07-43	15 Sqn
147272	P/O	TIMMINS Raymond Alfred	31-07-43	44 Sqn		128915	F/O	TOY MiD Gordon Frederick	1-09-43	622 Sqn
1576649	Sgt	TIMMS Dennis William	26-11-43	101 Sqn		1218772	Sgt	TOZE Harold James	26-06-43	101 Sqn
1312358	Sgt	TIMMS Lionel	15-06-43	619 Sqn		1237749	Sgt	TOZER Ronald Henry	24-08-43	622 Sqn
1220111	Sgt	TIMMS DFM Wilfred Arthur	27-04-43	115 Sqn		144884	P/O	TRAFFORD Hugh Jenkin	22-06-43	460 Sqn
125606	F/O	TIMNEY Thomas Cuthbert	5-05-43	149 Sqn		1586008	Sgt	TRAHAIR Roy	18-10-43	619 Sqn
616470	Sgt	TINCH Peter Arnaud	6-04-43	1663 HCU		37580	W/C	TRAILL DFC Anthony William Tarleton		
1480799	Sgt	TINDALE Vernon John Sheldrake	26-05-43	101 Sqn					14-08-43	1662 HCU
1654833	Sgt	TINGLE Cyril Brynmore	24-07-43	1652 HCU		657397	Sgt	TRAILL Daniel Anthony	13-05-43	466 Sqn
1320307	Sgt	TINKLER Sidney Richard	14-05-43	214 Sqn		986255	Sgt	TRAILL MiD Ian Craig	2-02-43	44 Sqn
656206	F/S	TIPLER Ernest Arthur	23-06-43	78 Sqn		1094818	Sgt	TRAINOR Owen Joseph	6-03-43	76 Sqn
1803626	Sgt	TIPPIN Norman Guy	13-07-43	103 Sqn		130859	P/O	TRAMSON Lex Arthur	5-01-43	20 OTU
1796161	F/S	TITTERINGTON James	24-11-43	1658 HCU		658957	Sgt	TRAVIS Donald Armitage	27-02-43	12 Sqn
525494	Sgt	TOAL Leslie	15-06-43	50 Sqn		1077299	Sgt	TRAVIS Jack	31-03-43	10 OTU
1312182	Sgt	TOBIN Martin Patrick	25-06-43	432 Sqn		1055872	Sgt	TRAYNOR Frank Morley	30-05-43	35 Sqn
1372393	F/S	TOCHER Eric James	16-12-43	44 Sqn		139400	P/O	TRAYNOR James Mellon	28-04-43	218 Sqn
1579135	Sgt	TODD Cyril Douglas	1-05-43	57 Sqn		1267812	Sgt	TREHEARN John Frederick Alfred	30-07-43	102 Sqn
1254715	Sgt	TODD John Alexander	10-03-43	103 Sqn				[South Africa]		
1390129	Sgt	TODD John Peter	9-10-43	78 Sqn		1261299	Sgt	TREMAIN James Thomas 'Jim'	7-02-43	51 Sqn
1385587	Sgt	TODD John Simpson	26-01-43	15 Sqn		1600600	Sgt	TREMBLE Francis John Martin	8-06-43	16 OTU
37368	S/L	TODD-WHITE Richard Nevil	18-08-43	1660 HCU		121339	F/O	TREMEAR James Hedley	12-07-43	1656 HCU
1525042	Sgt	TODKILL George	27-09-43	434 Sqn		68742	F/L	TRENCH DSO John Patrick	8-03-43	7 Sqn
1268610	Sgt	TOFT William Eric	2-03-43	44 Sqn		1324586	Sgt	TRENERY George Walter	3-05-43	487 Sqn
1122560	Sgt	TOFTS Robert Edward	15-06-43	619 Sqn		127120	F/O	TREVARTHEN Albert William Arnold	17-04-43	196 Sqn
1378392	Sgt	TOLSON Ernest	11-04-43	7 Sqn		1291380	Sgt	TREVAYNE Paul Rodney	3-02-43	75 Sqn
1389282	Sgt	TOMACHEPOLSKY Favel	3-11-43	101 Sqn		44674	F/L	TREVES Stanley Leonard	3-02-43	218 Sqn
1037931	Sgt	TOMBE George	7-03-43	51 Sqn		1808747	Sgt	TREW Bernard Frederick	1-09-43	103 Sqn
143676	P/O	TOMKINS Douglas Arthur Sydney	8-04-43	218 Sqn		1394248	Sgt	TREW Percival Edwin	12-03-43	103 Sqn
131897	F/O	TOMKINS Thomas Beavan	23-06-43	101 Sqn		1381877	Sgt	TREW Victor George	4-07-43	431 Sqn
1435137	Sgt	TOMLIN Cyril Edward	21-05-43	149 Sqn		1316038	Sgt	TREZISE Eric John	11-04-43	15 Sqn
1196426	Sgt	TOMLIN Richard Henry	2-12-43	103 Sqn		1194209	Sgt	TRIGG David Richard	15-03-43	11 OTU
145156	P/O	TOMLIN DFC Thomas Edwin	18-08-43	49 Sqn		1578630	Sgt	TRIGG Norman Frederick	3-03-43	103 Sqn
151313	F/O	TOMLINS Frederick William Ernest	20-06-43	10 OTU		149616	P/O	TRILL Stanley Richard	23-09-43	106 Sqn
630845	F/S	TOMLINSON Alan	25-06-43	97 Sqn		1239637	Sgt	TRIMBY Frederick	7-09-43	434 Sqn
1233323	Sgt	TOMLINSON Clifford Wyatt	7-09-43	77 Sqn		1320028	Sgt	TRINDER Louis Arthur	2-03-43	76 Sqn
591747	Sgt	TOMLINSON Leonard Ralph	3-04-43	83 Sqn		133803	F/O	TRITTON John Frederick	26-04-43	214 Sqn
1430802	Sgt	TOMLINSON Leslie	23-09-43	149 Sqn		1708058	Sgt	TROAKE Kenneth Edward	16-06-43	12 OTU
1232284	Sgt	TOMPKINS Edward Stanley	13-05-43	207 Sqn		156077	P/O	TROAKE Stephen John	26-11-43	76 Sqn
137665	F/L	TOMPKINS DFC Frederick Arthur George				1352234	Sgt	TROLLOPE Thomas Victor	3-04-43	158 Sqn
			22-06-43	7 Sqn		129360	P/O	TROTT Arthur	13-06-43	51 Sqn

Service №	Rank	Name	Date	Unit
1546300	Sgt	TROTTER Alexander Denholm	30-08-43	29 OTU
1056289	F/S	TROTTER DFM John Frederick	18-08-43	61 Sqn
1128155	Sgt	TROTTER William Hedley	5-03-43	214 Sqn
658650	Sgt	TROWBRIDGE Frank William Noel	25-06-43	432 Sqn
1192341	Sgt	TROWBRIDGE William George	16-07-43	50 Sqn
990159	Sgt	TROWER-FOYAN Ivor Raymond	14-09-43	158 Sqn
1132042	Sgt	TROWSDALE George Edward	13-07-43	103 Sqn
50285	P/O	TRUE James Bernard	27-05-43	218 Sqn
977703	Sgt	TRUMAN Edward George	23-09-43	90 Sqn
1394829	Sgt	TRUSCOTT Henry	22-11-43	156 Sqn
125301	F/O	TRUSCOTT Thomas Olver	18-01-43	467 Sqn
657050	Sgt	TUCK Stanley Ernest	13-06-43	57 Sqn
1385164	Sgt	TUCKER Alfred Arthur	16-12-43	7 Sqn
1155015	F/S	TUCKER DFM Bertram George	23-11-43	83 Sqn
1332550	Sgt	TUCKER Dennis Arthur	4-09-43	101 Sqn
1457344	Sgt	TUCKER Eric Hector	26-01-43	21 OTU
577958	Sgt	TUCKER Ivor	30-05-43	44 Sqn
155165	P/O	TUCKER Richard Charles	24-08-43	35 Sqn
1398791	Sgt	TUDDENHAM Douglas Eric	23-06-43	78 Sqn
1524686	Sgt	TULLY James Robert	26-07-43	77 Sqn
633057	Sgt	TUNLEY James	23-09-43	49 Sqn
1813154	Sgt	TUNNICLIFF Frederick James	24-12-43	463 Sqn
146287	P/O	TUNSTALL Reginald	13-05-43	51 Sqn
1804525	Sgt	TUPPEN Peter Joseph Alexander	20-12-43	44 Sqn
42542	S/L	TURGEL DFC Philip Raymond	26-05-43	100 Sqn
118613	F/O	TURK Ronald Douglas	5-03-43	156 Sqn
1392051	Sgt	TURKENTINE Herbert Henry	2-03-43	57 Sqn
1387018	Sgt	TURLEY Lawrence Richard William	28-09-43	1667 HCU
1131177	Sgt	TURNBULL George Ian	13-08-43	166 Sqn
1017385	Sgt	TURNBULL James Edward	29-03-43	218 Sqn
649185	Sgt	TURNBULL Neil Mackintosh	17-06-43	467 Sqn
1391320	Sgt	TURNER Albert	9-10-43	218 Sqn
1316391	Sgt	TURNER Albert Edward	7-08-43	75 Sqn
125631	F/O	TURNER Arnold James	11-04-43	9 Sqn
1220247	Sgt	TURNER Blackmore	22-09-43	101 Sqn
1316452	Sgt	TURNER Derek Wilfrid	6-02-43	199 Sqn
1606517	Sgt	TURNER Desmond Frank Oswald	7-07-43	103 Sqn
131600	F/O	TURNER Donald Stuart	23-09-43	101 Sqn
1335872	Sgt	TURNER Francis William	22-06-43	83 Sqn
37775	S/L	TURNER DFC MiD Francis William Scott [Canada]	22-09-43	76 Sqn
1685409	Sgt	TURNER Frank	2-12-43	550 Sqn
149678	P/O	TURNER Frederick Thomas	31-07-43	44 Sqn
130700	F/O	TURNER Fulliott Victor Polhill	24-05-43	1654 HCU
113498	F/O	TURNER Geoffrey Austin	10-08-43	76 Sqn
950345	F/S	TURNER Harry	26-07-43	102 Sqn
1267135	Sgt	TURNER Jack Sydney	19-02-43	467 Sqn
614960	Sgt	TURNER James	5-03-43	218 Sqn
1577497	Sgt	TURNER Leslie	3-10-43	76 Sqn
149548	P/O	TURNER Ronald Vincent	4-04-43	467 Sqn
1576975	Sgt	TURNER Ronald Vincent	12-07-43	10 OTU
120671	F/O	TURNER Ronald William	3-03-43	15 Sqn
156119	P/O	TURNER Stanley Charles	1-09-43	51 Sqn
1369730	Sgt	TURNER William	1-09-43	12 Sqn
1476394	Sgt	TURPIN William James	5-05-43	460 Sqn
149611	P/O	TURP Kenneth Charles	28-08-43	83 Sqn
656192	Sgt	TURVEY Leonard	20-04-43	57 Sqn
1385286	Sgt	TURVILLE Leslie Gordon	2-07-43	620 Sqn
1384140	Sgt	TUTT Bernard Frederick	26-11-43	97 Sqn
1176067	Sgt	TUTT George Bertie	24-12-43	44 Sqn
812184	Sgt	TUTT Norman Percy	10-04-43	9 Sqn
1546219	Sgt	TWEDDLE Sidney	22-11-43	77 Sqn
1063624	Sgt	TWEEDALE Fred	4-10-43	50 Sqn
1067394	Sgt	TWEEDIE James	17-06-43	156 Sqn
1333546	Sgt	TWIDDY Robert	30-03-43	44 Sqn
1810044	Sgt	TWITCHEN Ronald Bertram	29-06-43	76 Sqn
1235304	Sgt	TWITTY Geoffrey William	12-06-43	12 Sqn
702593	Sgt	TWOHY Albert	25-06-43	101 Sqn
1027584	F/S	TYAS Harold Empsall	28-05-43	307 FTU
1033927	Sgt	TYLDESLEY Jack	28-02-43	20 OTU
576427	Sgt	TYLER Edward Ernest	25-06-43	106 Sqn
70691	S/L	TYLER Edward Frederick	29-04-43	12 Sqn
642761	Sgt	TYLER John Alfred	28-07-43	102 Sqn
51097	F/O	TYLER John Vincent	22-11-43	97 Sqn
1318148	Sgt	TYREMAN Norman Allen	3-09-43	44 Sqn
546505	Sgt	TYRER Geoffrey Prescott	15-04-43	100 Sqn
952938	Sgt	TYSALL Frederick William	6-09-43	106 Sqn
1623946	Sgt	TYTHERLEIGH Alan Edwin	3-07-43	460 Sqn
120851	F/O	TYTHERLEIGH DFC William John	17-05-43	617 Sqn
1334077	Sgt	UDEN Jack Henry	26-05-43	149 Sqn
957871	Sgt	UFTON DFM Edward George	6-04-43	16 OTU
131775	P/O	ULRICH Jack Eric	7-03-43	51 Sqn
1528690	Sgt	UNDERDOWN Thomas	18-08-43	619 Sqn
1581877	Sgt	UNDERHILL Clifford Reginald	16-12-43	7 Sqn
1271149	Sgt	UNDERLIN George Samuel	17-06-43	49 Sqn
1062161	LAC	UNDERWOOD Fred	12-05-43	1658 HCU
1267926	F/S	UNDERWOOD James Noel	22-11-43	97 Sqn
1000940	Sgt	UNDERWOOD Norman Kenneth	14-05-43	44 Sqn
1073810	Sgt	UNSWORTH John Neville	3-03-43	214 Sqn
1318328	Sgt	UNWIN Peter Henry	30-07-43	97 Sqn
642206	Sgt	UNWIN Ronald	2-03-43	97 Sqn
1318579	Sgt	UPPERTON Leslie Raymond	8-04-43	1654 HCU
1258142	Sgt	UPSON Victor James	15-04-43	149 Sqn
651156	Sgt	UPTON Harold Albert	17-04-43	101 Sqn
142129	F/O	URE John Neville	24-08-43	623 Sqn
141415	P/O	URQUHART Alexander	30-03-43	106 Sqn
142864	P/O	URQUHART Alexander	11-04-43	166 Sqn
1348237	Sgt	URQUHART John Watson	9-01-43	105 Sqn
1380640	Sgt	URRY Leopold	13-05-43	90 Sqn
1014657	F/S	URWIN Robert Matthew	12-03-43	7 Sqn
2206972	Sgt	UTTLEY Graham Howard	14-09-43	1656 HCU
1350774	Sgt	VAISEY Ronald Noel	27-02-43	12 Sqn
656860	F/S	VALENTINE Herbert Malcolm	13-08-43	139 Sqn
1395959	Sgt	VALENTINE Kenneth William	15-2-43	90 Sqn
517088	Sgt	VALLANCE Charles George Leonard	29-06-43	76 Sqn
1316342	Sgt	VANDY Clifford	20-04-43	51 Sqn
1334882	Sgt	VANDY Raymond Victor	22-09-43	158 Sqn
1443790	Sgt	VANLINT James Arthur	17-08-43	23 OTU
1128891	Sgt	VANSTON Norman	17-04-43	100 Sqn
1438521	Sgt	VARDY Gordon	4-09-43	7 Sqn
1381736	Sgt	VAUGHAN Leonard George	13-03-43	199 Sqn
1388329	Sgt	VAUGHAN Ronald Oliver	13-06-43	460 Sqn
562927	Sgt	VAUGHAN William Johnson	11-04-43	97 Sqn
1485877	Sgt	VAULKHARD James Jardine	19-04-43	156 Sqn
131136	F/O	van HOBOKEN DFC Jacques Robert Christian [Belgium]	26-11-43	106 Sqn
148830	F/O	van WALWYK DFM Reginald Alfred	17-12-43	100 Sqn
1624363	Sgt	VAN HAL Henri Antonius	2-12-43	626 Sqn
1348043	Sgt	VEAL James Kevin Barry	4-04-43	51 Sqn
574382	Sgt	VEALE William Henry	20-12-43	78 Sqn
1079916	Sgt	VEALL Bernard	25-06-43	50 Sqn
1378911	Sgt	VEECK Albert Charles August	30-03-43	196 Sqn
1516659	Sgt	VEITCH Alfred Robert	15-06-43	100 Sqn
710084	Sgt	VELDSMAN Johannes Jacobus	28-04-43	101 Sqn
1314161	Sgt	VENN Frederick Martin	5-05-43	156 Sqn
1390418	Sgt	VENTHAM Jack Allen	3-05-43	51 Sqn
1576901	Sgt	VENTON Peter Frederick Penn	29-06-43	15 Sqn
119179	S/L	VERDON-ROE DFC Lighton	13-05-43	156 Sqn
131988	F/O	VERNEY Stanley John Huxtable	27-09-43	218 Sqn
649196	Sgt	VICCARS Eric Clifford	14-07-43	75 Sqn
575997	Sgt	VICKERS Harold William George	29-06-43	100 Sqn
1653453	Sgt	VIGGERS Sidney David	16-12-43	100 Sqn
1180892	Sgt	VINCENT George Taylor	8-02-43	44 Sqn
1819902	Sgt	VINCENT Kenneth	23-11-43	1658 HCU
1313855	Sgt	VINCENT Leslie Reginald	10-07-43	12 Sqn
70827	S/L	VINCENT DFC Peter Ree	27-09-43	156 Sqn

Service #	Rank	Name	Date	Unit
1021215	F/S	VINCENT Raymond George	26-11-43	158 Sqn
1624673	Sgt	VINE Eric	26-11-43	61 Sqn
1032516	Sgt	VINE Henry Bookless	19-02-43	467 Sqn
1865092	Sgt	VINER Frederick Alfred	20-12-43	156 Sqn
1316193	Sgt	VINES Frank Harry Liddon	6-03-43	49 Sqn
1055354	Sgt	VINT John Reuben	18-08-43	77 Sqn
139657	F/O	VIVIAN Sidney Richard	10-08-43	102 Sqn
1339114	Sgt	VODDEN John Thomas	4-07-43	103 Sqn
143771	P/O	VOLANTE DFM Stewart James	4-04-43	156 Sqn
656175	Sgt	VOLLANS Derek	15-04-43	425 Sqn
1813390	Sgt	VOSS William	9-10-43	78 Sqn
1393810	Sgt	WADDING Patrick [Eire]	15-08-43	7 Sqn
1380140	Sgt	WADDINGTON William Edwin	5-03-43	218 Sqn
943745	Sgt	WADE Alan Cartwright	11-04-43	214 Sqn
145656	F/O	WADE BEM Eric	23-11-43	105 Sqn
1393987	Sgt	WADE George Herbert Casebourne	3-11-43	77 Sqn
568514	Sgt	WADE Gordon	15-04-43	7 Sqn
1236350	AC1	WADE Neville	10-11-43	1660 HCU
1318520	F/S	WADE-SEYMOUR John Charles	18-11-43	76 Sqn
1489406	Sgt	WADESON Thomas Edward	3-08-43	75 Sqn
1387152	Sgt	WADSWORTH Eric Charles	3-10-43	78 Sqn
996981	Sgt	WADSWORTH Jack	2-12-43	432 Sqn
1376718	Sgt	WADSWORTH Richard	26-05-43	90 Sqn
1581818	Sgt	WAGGETT William Emerson	28-05-43	10 Sqn
519643	Sgt	WAGHORN Ernest Solomon	10-03-43	103 Sqn
655937	F/S	WAGSTAFF Thomas Kenneth	8-04-43	76 Sqn
126745	F/O	WAINER Harold Keith	5-05-43	101 Sqn
1695286	Sgt	WAINWRIGHT Timothy	26-11-43	429 Sqn
1481843	Sgt	WAITE Alan Wilson	15-06-43	9 Sqn
575638	Sgt	WAITE Aubrey Reginald	12-06-43	75 Sqn
1531151	Sgt	WAITE David	14-07-43	81 OTU
1163802	Sgt	WAITE Derrick Norman Duckers	1-03-43	103 Sqn
1279016	Sgt	WAITE Ernest Claude	22-06-43	149 Sqn
577724	Sgt	WAITE Henry George Charles	24-05-43	15 Sqn
125423	F/O	WAITE Laurence	29-03-43	101 Sqn
158032	P/O	WAITT William Thomas	3-10-43	76 Sqn
141792	F/O	WAKEFIELD Arthur James	2-12-43	103 Sqn
1411732	Sgt	WAKEFIELD Harry	11-04-43	15 Sqn
155359	P/O	WAKEFIELD John James	18-08-43	61 Sqn
101565	F/L	WAKEFORD DFC John Alfred	4-07-43	9 Sqn
1295216	Sgt	WAKEMAN William Edward	26-04-43	156 Sqn
1319771	Sgt	WAKERELL Leslie James	31-08-43	166 Sqn
1410336	Sgt	WAKLEY Harry Reginald	17-01-43	1654 HCU
1324776	Sgt	WALDER Dennis Marshall	24-08-43	101 Sqn
1386586	Sgt	WALDER Frederick James	27-03-43	156 Sqn
1383863	Sgt	WALDORF Leonard	13-05-43	199 Sqn
1496737	Sgt	WALES Jack Rowland	4-09-43	100 Sqn
1530950	Sgt	WALKDEN Terence Anthony	5-09-43	20 OTU
1338105	F/S	WALKE William Arthur	2-12-43	49 Sqn
1389686	Sgt	WALKER Anthony Patrick Leslie	8-08-43	26 OTU
89607	S/L	WALKER DFC Antony De Quincey	12-06-43	161 Sqn
1112914	Sgt	WALKER Archibald	15-04-43	7 Sqn
85276	F/L	WALKER Arthur	17-12-43	12 Sqn
1077177	Sgt	WALKER Charles Raymond	27-09-43	76 Sqn
1320280	Agt	WALKER Clifford	20-04-43	100 Sqn
1323891	Sgt	WALKER Donald William	24-12-43	625 Sqn
149970	P/O	WALKER Frederick John Thomas 'Freddy'	4-12-43	10 Sqn
1332840	Sgt	WALKER George Albert	3-08-43	75 Sqn
566666	Sgt	WALKER George Frederick Maurice	8-04-43	1654 HCU
1551590	Sgt	WALKER Gordon Boyd	7-04-43	9 Sqn
533846	Sgt	WALKER James	17-06-43	100 Sqn
117425	F/O	WALKER John	8-04-43	109 Sqn
162591	P/O	WALKER John	22-11-43	156 Sqn
748494	Sgt	WALKER John Alan	13-07-43	156 Sqn
145851	P/O	WALKER DFM John Albert	24-05-43	1654 HCU
1550332	AC2	WALKER Joseph Spence	1-01-43	12 Sqn
1487606	Sgt	WALKER Kenneth Wylam	18-10-43	101 Sqn
129766	F/O	WALKER Leslie Alexander	14-04-43	429 Sqn
1610270	Sgt	WALKER Peter	29-12-43	431 Sqn
127545	F/O	WALKER Philip Alsop	27-04-43	90 Sqn
658252	Sgt	WALKER Reginald William	10-03-43	100 Sqn
1085432	Sgt	WALKER Richard Samuel Augustus	14-05-43	44 Sqn
1235107	Sgt	WALKER Robert Alfred	14-07-43	115 Sqn
129607	F/O	WALKER Robert Frank	19-08-43	1658 HCU
151250	F/O	WALKER Stanley Herbert	9-10-43	431 Sqn
755649	Sgt	WALKER Thomas	17-02-43	14 OTU
969796	F/S	WALKER Thomas Jack	12-03-43	207 Sqn
1380192	Sgt	WALKER Victor Norman	23-05-43	214 Sqn
1371707	Sgt	WALKER William	16-09-43	617 Sqn
1252022	Sgt	WALL Eric George	3-11-43	101 Sqn
927481	Sgt	WALL John Sidney	15-02-43	100 Sqn
1457095	Sgt	WALL Samuel David	31-01-43	101 Sqn
1301837	Sgt	WALLACE George	31-08-43	7 Sqn
1030121	Sgt	WALLACE John	8-04-43	1654 HCU
130163	F/O	WALLACE John Douglas	13-05-43	57 Sqn
1138965	Sgt	WALLACE John Horix	26-07-43	620 Sqn
1609264	Sgt	WALLACE Kenneth Leonard	17-10-43	196 Sqn
1078029	Sgt	WALLACE Kenneth Richard	24-08-43	619 Sqn
1333384	Sgt	WALLACE Lionel Robert	7-04-43	405 Sqn
657762	Sgt	WALLACE William Charles	26-07-43	51 Sqn
33350	S/L	WALLAGE Stanley Norman Tuttell	5-04-43	57 Sqn
1385455	Sgt	WALLEN Emanuel	31-08-43	15 Sqn
1097035	Sgt	WALLER Henry Stewart	26-11-43	101 Sqn
1333615	Sgt	WALLER John Roland Smith	28-05-43	199 Sqn
1266776	Sgt	WALLER Peter Anthony	18-02-43	57 Sqn
168663	P/O	WALLER Peter Raymond	20-12-43	78 Sqn
1434167	F/S	WALLER William George	22-11-43	97 Sqn
1578208	Sgt	WALLIS Albert Edwin	24-05-43	10 Sqn
143228	P/O	WALLIS Reginald John	27-03-43	156 Sqn
1340054	Sgt	WALLS John Anderson	10-08-43	102 Sqn
1287750	Sgt	WALNE Robert Neville	26-11-43	514 Sqn
1383413	Sgt	WALROND Arthur Adolphus	29-06-43	15 Sqn
1691368	Sgt	WALSH Bernard Thomas	25-07-43	51 Sqn
1084155	Sgt	WALSH Herbert	13-05-43	419 Sqn
778564	F/S	WALSH John Harvey Courtney [Rhodesia]	5-04-43	9 Sqn
138590	F/O	WALSH Michael William Boyes	6/-09-43	78 Sqn
161010	P/O	WALSH DFC Terence John Patrick	18-11-43	7 Sqn
1213720	Sgt	WALSHAW David Humphrey	23-08-43	434 Sqn
1527573	Sgt	WALSHAW Kenneth	18-11-43	218 Sqn
1294708	Sgt	WALTER Ronald Frederick	20-12-43	77 Sqn
1802702	Sgt	WALTER Stanley Alan	28-09-43	434 Sqn
1385752	Sgt	WALTER William Edward	26-06-43	90 Sqn
1330701	Sgt	WALTERS Arthur George	19-01-43	20 OTU
1415639	Sgt	WALTERS Clifford Stanley	13-09-43	12 OTU
1253897	Sgt	WALTERS Frances Llewellyn D'Oyly	9-03-43	61 Sqn
858772	Sgt	WALTERS Frederick Philip Cavendish	6-09-43	427 Sqn
1271369	Sgt	WALTERS Gerard Stanley	3-04-43	158 Sqn
1313880	Sgt	WALTERS Harold	15-04-43	149 Sqn
1579168	Sgt	WALTERS Kenneth Eric	22-06-43	100 Sqn
1261427	Sgt	WALTERS Leonard Charles Arthur	27-09-43	76 Sqn
49233	F/O	WALTERS Lionel	17-04-43	51 Sqn
1231534	Sgt	WALTERS Louis Edward	30-07-43	57 Sqn
1377506	Sgt	WALTERS Vivian	9-04-43	7 Sqn
1261582	Sgt	WALTERS William David Ronald	30-07-43	35 Sqn
1240033	F/S	WALTON Charles Frederick	23-09-43	49 Sqn
1047593	Sgt	WALTON Clifford	6-09-43	12 Sqn
1436208	Sgt	WALTON Frederick	10-08-43	76 Sqn
651948	Sgt	WALTON Frederick Henry	4-07-43	158 Sqn
1380500	Sgt	WALTON George Samuel	14-05-43	77 Sqn
1316540	Sgt	WALTON James Daniel	22-10-43	12 Sqn
1320461	Sgt	WALTON John Christopher	31-03-43	10 OTU
952997	F/S	WALTON Raymond	8-02-43	44 Sqn
1523018	Sgt	WALTON Richard Charles	18-08-43	61 Sqn
1336410	F/S	WALTON Ronald	3-11-43	77 Sqn

ID	Rank	Name	Date	Sqn
129362	F/O	WALTON Sidney Arthur	30-07-43	158 Sqn
144757	P/O	WALTON William Highmoor	17-04-43	100 Sqn
654069	Sgt	WALTON William Scrimgrough	27-11-43	83 Sqn
1321739	Sgt	WANNELL Robert James	22-11-43	82 OTU
656462	Sgt	WANSTALL Richard Fleury	17-04-43	75 Sqn
1212244	Sgt	WARBEY Terence Eugene	26-06-43	15 Sqn
1493593	Sgt	WARBURTON Frank	23-05-43	158 Sqn
1565412	Sgt	WARBURTON John Stanley	21-05-43	149 Sqn
1074938	Sgt	WARD Albert	3-04-43	158 Sqn
1607007	Sgt	WARD Alan Kenneth	26-11-43	100 Sqn
920078	Sgt	WARD David Scott	19-11-43	51 Sqn
1321748	Sgt	WARD Frank Frederick	14-07-43	35 Sqn
1020872	Sgt	WARD Frank Glenister	8-04-43	44 Sqn
1641825	Sgt	WARD George Frederick	5-05-43	10 Sqn
1060035	F/S	WARD Harold	24-05-43	214 Sqn
991198	Sgt	WARD Herbert	22-10-43	166 Sqn
155509	P/O	WARD James Francis	3-12-43	619 Sqn
743589	Sgt	WARD John	17-01-43	76 Sqn
156122	P/O	WARD Kenneth	1-09-43	158 Sqn
1482480	Sgt	WARD Leo Peter	14-03-43	138 Sqn
1508955	AC2	WARD Norman	7-02-43	51 Sqn
1622666	Sgt	WARD Robert Sugden	2-12-43	12 Sqn
51648	P/O	WARD DFC Robert Weavers	14-04-43	138 Sqn
1388250	Sgt	WARD Ronald Aslin	30-05-43	102 Sqn
1335502	F/S	WARD Walter Philling	28-08-43	76 Sqn
1585762	Sgt	WARD William James	27-11-43	50 Sqn
1553630	Sgt	WARD William Middleton	12-06-43	12 Sqn
1312826	Sgt	WARDLE John	11-08-43	619 Sqn
1108658	Sgt	WARDLEY Tom Kenneth	20-10-43	166 Sqn
157829	P/O	WARDMAN Norman Percy	27-09-43	10 Sqn
1366325	Sgt	WARDROP Robert	8-01-43	9 Sqn
148476	P/O	WARDROP William	24-08-43	83 Sqn
538177	Sgt	WARDROPE Sydney McWilliams	25-01-43	Snaith
143227	F/O	WARFIELD DFM Norman John	24-12-43	156 Sqn
1451359	Sgt	WARHURST Robert Wallace	20-06-43	10 OTU
1439524	Sgt	WARHURST Thomas	27-09-43	166 Sqn
155948	P/O	WARINER Stanley Truman	29-09-43	78 Sqn
635944	Sgt	WARING John Cyril	20-04-43	51 Sqn
1348637	Sgt	WARING William Henry	17-06-43	49 Sqn
1090550	Sgt	WARNE Cecil Wallace	1-05-43	77 Sqn
1318828	Sgt	WARNER Alexander Felix	21-04-43	102 Sqn
1801861	Sgt	WARNER Charles Herbert Albert	3-09-43	101 Sqn
128619	F/O	WARNER James Herbert	16-05-43	617 Sqn
2209337	Sgt	WARNER John Albert	16-12-43	75 Sqn
960814	Sgt	WARNES Charles Arthur	24-05-43	27 OTU
1288529	F/S	WARNES Jack	20-04-43	218 Sqn
1391138	Sgt	WARR Bertram James [Canada]	3-04-43	158 Sqn
161366	P/O	WARRELL Alan Henry William	27-09-43	10 Sqn
1291689	Sgt	WARRELL Ronald Henry	4-07-43	15 Sqn
1385391	Sgt	WARREN Alan Leonard	4-04-43	214 Sqn
1315426	Sgt	WARREN Frederick Hensher	6-04-43	1663 HCU
1580874	Sgt	WARREN George Charles William	30-03-43	12 Sqn
1465627	Sgt	WARREN Gerald Alfred	6-08-43	51 Sqn
1388638	Sgt	WARREN Harold John	26-05-43	9 Sqn
1028640	Sgt	WARREN Harry Edwin	28-08-43	156 Sqn
129595	F/O	WARREN John Michael	18-08-43	619 Sqn
136720	P/O	WARREN Llewellyn Edgar	12-03-43	83 Sqn
842606	Sgt	WARREN Richard Hall	9-03-43	207 Sqn
1586065	Sgt	WARREN Ronald Leslie	27-10-43	11 OTU
581545	F/S	WARTNABY George	30-01-43	16 OTU
155215	P/O	WARWICK Kenneth Edgar	3-12-43	9 Sqn
1293070	Sgt	WARWICK Phillip Albert George	25-06-43	102 Sqn
1079709	Sgt	WATERHOUSE Ronald	29-03-43	101 Sqn
1338722	Sgt	WATERHOUSE Roy Arthur	23-06-43	101 Sqn
141788	P/O	WATERMAN James Frederick	3-09-43	101 Sqn
1312274	Sgt	WATERMAN Jeffery James	6-09-43	75 Sqn
1601324	Sgt	WATERS Reginald Arthur	3-10-43	12 Sqn
1334179	Sgt	WATERSTON John Hunter	26-06-43	77 Sqn
1530030	Sgt	WATKIN Cuthbert	30-07-43	51 Sqn
116992	F/L	WATKIN Ralph	22-01-43	180 Sqn
1601336	Sgt	WATKINS Arthur Emlyn	4-12-43	115 Sqn
1652776	Sgt	WATKINS David Aubrey	16-04-43	78 Sqn
938881	F/S	WATKINS DFM Dennis Arthur	21-04-43	419 Sqn
1505043	Sgt	WATKINS Frederick Arthur	3-11-43	625 Sqn
1390906	Sgt	WATKINS John George	26-05-43	166 Sqn
1582961	Sgt	WATKINS John Gwilyn	18-08-43	44 Sqn
106145	F/L	WATKINS Kenneth Bernard	3-09-43	156 Sqn
544249	Sgt	WATKINS Stanley	19-11-43	75 Sqn
1261508	Sgt	WATKINS Thomas Frank	23-08-43	61 Sqn
536785	Sgt	WATKINS Victor Henry John	29-06-43	207 Sqn
548859	F/S	WATKINS William Humphrey	17-12-43	156 Sqn
1333776	Sgt	WATKINSON Reginald	12-06-43	103 Sqn
131969	F/O	WATKINSON Reginald Thomas	3-10-43	51 Sqn
840146	Sgt	WATLING Frederick	6-09-43	76 Sqn
1213427	Sgt	WATMOUGH Kenneth	16-12-43	625 Sqn
155594	P/O	WATSON DFC Alexander McCracken	2-12-43	50 Sqn
1157517	Sgt	WATSON Arthur William	17-12-43	57 Sqn
1112190	Sgt	WATSON Christopher	23-11-43	50 Sqn
1800433	Sgt	WATSON Derick Shand	17-12-43	100 Sqn
1316881	F/S	WATSON Donald Moulton	21-10-43	7 Sqn
1127753	Sgt	WATSON Edward	6-08-43	51 Sqn
1490237	AC1	WATSON Edward	18-07-43	Downham Market
1383608	Sgt	WATSON Gordon	1-05-43	77 Sqn
570569	Sgt	WATSON Jack	1-09-43	51 Sqn
1239046	Sgt	WATSON Jack	20-06-43	10 Sqn
546010	Sgt	WATSON Jack Hill	4-01-43	460 Sqn
1578677	Sgt	WATSON John Alan	17-12-43	156 Sqn
1043277	F/S	WATSON John George Addison	17-12-43	138 Sqn
1369957	Sgt	WATSON John Knox	1-09-43	61 Sqn
29029	S/L	WATSON John Russell	16-08-43	115 Sqn
124488	F/O	WATSON Joseph Henry Gray	15-05-43	30 OTU
1433407	Sgt	WATSON Kenneth Ernest	18-08-43	49 Sqn
152507	P/O	WATSON Michael Hilary	17-11-43	10 OTU
1336115	Sgt	WATSON Reginald Ernest	15-06-43	460 Sqn
1290604	Sgt	WATSON Richard George	3-03-43	106 Sqn
1561631	Sgt	WATSON Robert	21-04-43	77 Sqn
33074	S/L	WATSON Robert Grant [Rhodesia]	3-09-43	44 Sqn
652631	F/S	WATSON Ronald	21-04-43	21 Sqn
1346290	Sgt	WATSON Samuel Black	9-10-43	12 Sqn
119462	F/O	WATSON Terrance George	30-01-43	466 Sqn
161042	P/O	WATSON Thomas	26-11-43	97 Sqn
1340991	Sgt	WATSON Thomas David	2-01-43	1658 HCU
149098	P/O	WATSON William Joshua	3-10-43	51 Sqn
110643	F/L	WATT DSO DFC James Stanley [Argentina]	22-06-43	7 Sqn
1349949	Sgt	WATT John Burt	21-04-43	77 Sqn
710235	Sgt	WATT Kenneth [Rhodesia]	2-10-43	44 Sqn
925584	Sgt	WATT Samuel Frederick	18-02-43	57 Sqn
1349236	Sgt	WATTERS William	23-09-43	103 Sqn
49120	F/O	WATTS Christopher Anthony	17-01-43	49 Sqn
1312572	Sgt	WATTS David Michael Turner [Canada]	16-04-43	75 Sqn
1250352	Sgt	WATTS Donald Ernest	2-05-43	24 Sqn
1388097	F/S	WATTS Ernest Reginald	11-11-43	161 Sqn
1238503	Sgt	WATTS Francis William	3-09-43	199 Sqn
1381437	F/S	WATTS George Edward	30-01-43	466 Sqn
967613	F/S	WATTS Herbert	6-01-43	10 OTU
122766	F/O	WATTS Peter Arthur	20-12-43	156 Sqn
52700	P/O	WATTS Sidney Henry Charles	14-07-43	158 Sqn
216038	F/S	WATTS Stanley Langford Conway	1-03-43	35 Sqn
1011474	Sgt	WATTS Walter	3-04-43	9 Sqn
1260942	Sgt	WATTS Wilfred Gordon	12-06-43	100 Sqn
1282147	Sgt	WAUDBY Ronald	17-01-43	61 Sqn
130999	F/O	WAUGH Harley George	8-11-43	20 OTU
1295368	Sgt	WAY Herbert Henry	5-05-43	10 Sqn

Service #	Rank	Name	Date	Squadron
1389078	Sgt	WAY Kenneth Andrew [British Guiana]	4-04-43	149 Sqn
89359	F/L	WAYMAN DFC Michael Myers	20-03-43	139 Sqn
1391814	Sgt	WAYMAN Stanley John	24-05-43	75 Sqn
1032406	Sgt	WEAKNER Simon Hughes	22-09-43	214 Sqn
1391460	Sgt	WEARN William John	23-08-43	103 Sqn
1409013	Sgt	WEAVER Emrys Herbert	3-03-43	75 Sqn
141796	P/O	WEAVER John	18-08-43	100 Sqn
931679	Sgt	WEAVER Ronald George	19-02-43	15 Sqn
960685	F/S	WEAVER Victor Alfred	24-08-43	90 Sqn
943636	Sgt	WEAVING Lionel George Henry	28-09-43	622 Sqn
1804007	Sgt	WEBB Charles Francis	28-08-43	156 Sqn
1585688	Sgt	WEBB Douglas Vernon	7-09-43	77 Sqn
1375146	Sgt	WEBB Ernest Charles	18-01-43	1654 HCU
116652	F/L	WEBB DFM Frank Charles	4-10-43	83 Sqn
1448647	Sgt	WEBB Frederick Herbert	30-07-43	7 Sqn
1398010	Sgt	WEBB Henry George Ogilvy	30-07-43	15 OTU
49997	F/O	WEBB James Frederick	17-04-43	76 Sqn
657412	Sgt	WEBB John	11-04-43	75 Sqn
1521786	Sgt	WEBB John Scott	18-08-43	11 OTU
133086	F/O	WEBB Joseph Arthur 'Joe'	24-08-43	100 Sqn
1315766	Sgt	WEBB Kenneth Ernest	17-04-43	76 Sqn
1381435	Sgt	WEBB Lawrence Edward Victor	20-03-43	101 Sqn
124760	F/L	WEBB DFC Leonard Sidney	4-10-43	97 Sqn
1153676	Sgt	WEBB Norman George	23-08-43	102 Sqn
1395154	Sgt	WEBB Richard William	2-12-43	101 Sqn
932584	Sgt	WEBB Robert Charles Henry	3-04-43	106 Sqn
1149761	Sgt	WEBB Ronald	24-01-43	20 OTU
1430274	Sgt	WEBB Roy	30-07-43	35 Sqn
955673	Sgt	WEBB Sidney George	30-03-43	460 Sqn
169387	P/O	WEBB Stanley	29-12-43	10 Sqn
1266998	Sgt	WEBB Stanley Lawrence	23-06-43	75 Sqn
1382258	Sgt	WEBB Thomas Henry	3-04-43	78 Sqn
1576212	F/S	WEBB William John Henry	4-12-43	77 Sqn
1377524	Sgt	WEBBER Jack	9-01-43	57 Sqn
1605166	Sgt	WEBBER Peter Rodney	2-12-43	460 Sqn
1167097	Sgt	WEBBER Royston Robert Isaac	3-03-43	76 Sqn
1169330	Sgt	WEBER Arthur John	13-06-43	50 Sqn
1320777	Sgt	WEBSTER Denis	17-06-43	9 Sqn
137191	F/L	WEBSTER DFC Harry	24-08-43	35 Sqn
1292688	Sgt	WEBSTER Henry Francis	16-08-43	61 Sqn
1320839	Sgt	WEBSTER John Walter	2-03-43	207 Sqn
110633	F/L	WEBSTER Keith	23-06-43	427 Sqn
523101	Sgt	WEBSTER Leigh Gordon	27-04-43	115 Sqn
1699504	Sgt	WEBSTER Morven	23-06-43	15 Sqn
814232	Sgt	WEBSTER Vincent	18-08-43	35 Sqn
1603571	Sgt	WEDDELL Cornelius	23-09-43	467 Sqn
137107	F/O	WEDDELL Denis Max	26-07-43	214 Sqn
1385532	Sgt	WEDDELL Robert Edmund Stanley	15-06-43	100 Sqn
1335713	Sgt	WEDDERBURN Brian Walter Edward	17-04-43	76 Sqn
657657	Sgt	WEDDERSPOON Alan Bayne	1-02-43	1659 HCU
1174998	Sgt	WEEKS Philip Ian	26-11-43	76 Sqn
1481511	Sgt	WEIGH Allan Desmond	3-11-43	428 Sqn
567856	Sgt	WEIGHELL George Myron	20-10-43	619 Sqn
1094049	Sgt	WEIGHELL Norman Edwin	27-09-43	78 Sqn
940463	Sgt	WEIGHT James Walter	2-09-43	106 Sqn
119155	F/O	WEIGHT Robert Ernest	29-03-43	97 Sqn
982527	Sgt	WEIR John Alexander Maclean	24-07-43	1652 HCU
1217620	Sgt	WEIR Michael Frederick	15-04-43	76 Sqn
136714	P/O	WEIR William Kenneth McFarlane	27-03-43	10 OTU
1645012	Sgt	WELBY Wilfred	17-12-43	101 Sqn
132711	F/O	WELCH Douglas Clement	5-11-43	199 Sqn
1318580	W/O	WELCH Douglas Harold	22-10-43	427 Sqn
1251211	F/S	WELCH John Charles	25-06-43	106 Sqn
744932	W/O	WELCH DFM John Lawrence	15-09-43	617 Sqn
1291444	Sgt	WELCH Stanley Henry	26-07-43	103 Sqn
51330	F/O	WELDON DFM Arnold	2-12-43	101 Sqn
130519	P/O	WELDON Faber Ernest Frederick [Eire]	5-04-43	57 Sqn
131125	P/O	WELLARD Cyril Ernest	21-04-43	100 Sqn
40965	S/L	WELLBURN DFC Dennis Crosby	1-09-43	61 Sqn
1487005	Sgt	WELLER Douglas Arthur Wallace	10-04-43	426 Sqn
142507	P/O	WELLER Leonard George	17-05-43	617 Sqn
1604505	Sgt	WELLS Albert Douglas	5-12-43	101 Sqn
1286485	Sgt	WELLS Alexander George	25-07-43	166 Sqn
1578532	Sgt	WELLS Charles Frederick Simpson	24-05-43	27 OTU
953542	Sgt	WELLS Francis George	8-09-43	12 OTU
1332103	Sgt	WELLS Frank Alan	30-05-43	90 Sqn
1304641	Sgt	WELLS Harold James	23-06-43	620 Sqn
1413221	Sgt	WELLS Henry	7-04-43	9 Sqn
631311	W/O	WELLS Jack	18-10-43	101 Sqn
1231537	Sgt	WELLS James Franklin	26-07-43	620 Sqn
1600931	Sgt	WELLS John Raymond	27-04-43	77 Sqn
1604457	Sgt	WELLS Laurence Ernest Percival	9-10-43	460 Sqn
1432681	Sgt	WELLS Phillip Eric	2-12-43	156 Sqn
122249	F/L	WELLS Robert Frederick	2-12-43	9 Sqn
1331819	Sgt	WELLS Ronald Herbert	21-04-43	21 Sqn
1318974	Sgt	WELLS Roy Horace	2-12-43	35 Sqn
1448179	Sgt	WELLS Thomas Alfred	27-04-43	102 Sqn
1113723	Sgt	WELLS Victor	30-05-43	12 Sqn
123044	F/L	WELLS Walter Basil	17-04-43	83 Sqn
624682	Sgt	WELLS William Alfred	31-07-43	15 Sqn
1123739	Sgt	WELSBY Frank Johnes	16-06-43	12 OTU
1001961	Sgt	WELSH Joseph	27-11-43	626 Sqn
149518	P/O	WELSH Lawrence Sinclair	22-06-43	44 Sqn
1369334	Sgt	WELSH William Miller	3-08-43	9 Sqn
1344329	Sgt	WEMYSS John James	9-06-43	619 Sqn
997249	Sgt	WENMOTH Percival Jack	28-08-43	78 Sqn
548014	Sgt	WENSLEY Harry Hargreaves	29-04-43	12 Sqn
1188359	Sgt	WERNER Harry Victor	25-02-43	218 Sqn
527172	Sgt	WESCOMBE Stanley	18-01-43	9 Sqn
1803260	Sgt	WEST Arthur Dennis	22-11-43	77 Sqn
939187	Sgt	WEST Arthur Douglas	23-11-43	7 Sqn
1680420	Sgt	WEST Brian	22-09-43	78 Sqn
1316504	Sgt	WEST Clifford George	16-04-43	78 Sqn
1311887	Sgt	WEST Dudley Frank	14-05-43	138 Sqn
1331511	Sgt	WEST Frank Edward	8-08-43	61 Sqn
139516	F/O	WEST DFM Gerald Arthur	2-12-43	44 Sqn
1283890	Sgt	WEST Harold John	18-02-43	207 Sqn
1254233	Sgt	WEST John Edgar	18-01-43	97 Sqn
1337149	Sgt	WEST Robert Eric Percival	6-06-43	30 OTU
129921	F/O	WEST Sidney Herbert	15-04-43	100 Sqn
1314467	Sgt	WESTALL Edward George	12-06-43	78 Sqn
1394339	Sgt	WESTALL Frederick Ronald	16-12-43	101 Sqn
1455546	Sgt	WESTBARN John	23-06-43	77 Sqn
1112260	Sgt	WESTERDALE Jack	30-03-43	57 Sqn
1206109	Sgt	WESTLAKE John Wilfred Noel	17-06-43	12 Sqn
1293482	Sgt	WESTON James Alexander	26-11-43	61 Sqn
1131503	Sgt	WESTON Roger Pickering	28-09-43	1667 HCU
1379790	Sgt	WESTON Thomas Neville	18-08-43	44 Sqn
1046328	Sgt	WESTTHORP Kenneth	19-02-43	467 Sqn
1333598	Sgt	WESTWOOD Charles William Henry	24-05-43	166 Sqn
1210748	Sgt	WESTWOOD John	12-02-43	1660 HCU
953203	Sgt	WETHERELL Dennis	29-12-43	467 Sqn
575378	Sgt	WETHERELL Ronald Bainbridge	27-01-43	57 Sqn
82716	F/L	WETHERLY DFC MiD Jack Harold	30-03-43	76 Sqn
1226975	Sgt	WHALEN Leonard	25-07-43	103 Sqn
1314155	Sgt	WHALLEY Thomas James	26-01-43	23 OTU
1817321	Sgt	WHALLEY William Arthur	3-10-43	44 Sqn
1473130	Sgt	WHALLEY William Stephen	8-09-43	103 Sqn
1236751	Sgt	WHARMBY Tom	13-05-43	199 Sqn
1031763	Sgt	WHARTON Charles	20-10-43	57 Sqn
623524	Sgt	WHATLEY Ronald James	29-03-43	97 Sqn
1314153	Sgt	WHATLEY Timothy	6-09-43	75 Sqn
936166	Sgt	WHATMORE Alexander	15-08-43	7 Sqn
1059932	F/S	WHATMOUGH Thomas	12-06-43	75 Sqn
117361	F/O	WHEAL Herbert Clifford	4-07-43	196 Sqn

1254714	Sgt	WHEATLEY Albert	29-04-43	196 Sqn	964185	Sgt	WHITEHART John Herbert	28-04-43	75 Sqn
42290	F/L	WHEATLEY Arthur Thomas	2-03-43	76 Sqn	1385142	F/S	WHITEHEAD Arthur John Charles	3-09-43	207 Sqn
1677247	Sgt	WHEATLEY George Rogerson	27-08-43	1663 HCU	1317727	Sgt	WHITEHEAD Frederick Alan	26-06-43	115 Sqn
1623279	Sgt	WHEATLEY James Frederick	2-10-43	57 Sqn	1530099	Sgt	WHITEHEAD George	15-06-43	103 Sqn
1213729	Sgt	WHEATLEY William Horace	10-08-43	103 Sqn	975551	Sgt	WHITEHEAD James Milton	18-02-43	61 Sqn
120231	F/O	WHEEKER Lionel Cottrell	9-04-43	199 Sqn	1318491	Sgt	WHITEHEAD John Alfred	18-10-43	115 Sqn
1489514	Sgt	WHEELDON Frank	29-06-43	100 Sqn	1333569	Sgt	WHITEHEAD John Eric	22-11-43	51 Sqn
1379371	Sgt	WHEELER Harry Sidney	23-08-43	103 Sqn	1313044	Sgt	WHITEHEAD John Smith	17-06-43	1656 HCU
1335675	Sgt	WHEELER Nathaniel John Edward	2-10-43	61 Sqn	1456667	Sgt	WHITEHEAD Joseph	29-12-43	30 OTU
132788	F/O	WHEELER Walter John	26-06-43	57 Sqn	1213624	Sgt	WHITEHEAD Norman	27-01-43	218 Sqn
119901	F/O	WHEELHOUSE Thomas Charles	28-04-43	218 Sqn	155020	P/O	WHITEHOUSE James Newell	26-07-43	102 Sqn
144260	F/O	WHEEN Henry	5-04-43	10 Sqn	138340	F/O	WHITEHOUSE James William	22-10-43	1657 HCU
1818212	Sgt	WHELDON Cyril Terence	3-11-43	101 Sqn	636622	Sgt	WHITEHOUSE William Leslie	9-04-43	207 Sqn
1333520	Sgt	WHELLAMS Reginald Alfred	20-04-43	100 Sqn	1336444	Sgt	WHITELAND William Frederick	30-03-43	429 Sqn
1255976	Sgt	WHETTON Arthur Herbert	28-08-43	207 Sqn	1451555	Sgt	WHITELEY Cyril George	30-07-43	102 Sqn
1096809	Sgt	WHETTON Jack Adam	31-08-43	218 Sqn	1382323	Sgt	WHITELOCK Stewart	4-07-43	12 Sqn
1249500	Sgt	WHILES George William	7-02-43	158 Sqn	657522	Sgt	WHITELOCK Tom	3-01-43	149 Sqn
144619	P/O	WHILLIS Samuel Leslie	16-05-43	617 Sqn	1332011	Sgt	WHITEMAN Alfred Charles	29-06-43	424 Sqn
144777	P/O	WHITAKER Arthur Neville	16-05-43	617 Sqn	1234862	Sgt	WHITEMAN John Charles Lawrence	26-05-43	75 Sqn
570495	Sgt	WHITAKER Denis Edward	9-04-43	207 Sqn	1335378	Sgt	WHITEMAN Robert Ernest	13-01-43	12 Sqn
130019	Sgt	WHITAKER Joseph	25-09-43	29 OTU	1149749	Sgt	WHITEOAK Arthur Wilson	13-05-43	207 Sqn
1384532	F/S	WHITAKER Richard Frederick	5-05-43	149 Sqn	1511156	Sgt	WHITESIDE Frank	27-09-43	460 Sqn
130596	F/O	WHITAKER William Butler	24-05-43	12 Sqn	1018060	Sgt	WHITESIDE Leslie	18-01-43	9 Sqn
1433955	Sgt	WHITBY Maxwell	17-04-43	100 Sqn	1268702	Sgt	WHITFIELD Ernest	24-08-43	158 Sqn
1393852	Sgt	WHITBY Sydney Arthur	24-09-43	428 Sqn	1496432	Sgt	WHITFIELD Robert	25-06-43	428 Sqn
1601565	Sgt	WHITCOMBE Keith Robert Arthur	20-04-43	57 Sqn	1299235	Sgt	WHITFIELD William Dennis	1-09-43	620 Sqn
1386561	Sgt	WHITE Albert Edward George	30-07-43	61 Sqn	1063748	Sgt	WHITFIELD William Forster	17-04-43	166 Sqn
1445443	Sgt	WHITE Albert John	15-04-43	149 Sqn	1653049	Sgt	WHITFORD Reginald	12-10-43	90 Sqn
1333972	Sgt	WHITE Alfred William	25-05-43	207 Sqn	1199977	Sgt	WHITING Norman Geoffrey	23-06-43	427 Sqn
1386049	Sgt	WHITE Arthur Nathaniel Edward	12-02-43	23 OTU	1601035	Sgt	WHITING William Henry	30-03-43	97 Sqn
1335970	Sgt	WHITE Basil Talbot	21-02-43	424 Sqn	1547703	Sgt	WHITLEY George Valentine	28-09-43	428 Sqn
1339032	Sgt	WHITE Bernard Charles John	21-04-43	102 Sqn	1604580	Sgt	WHITLEY Ronald Alfred	17-12-43	12 Sqn
1312741	Sgt	WHITE Cyril Frank	13-03-43	199 Sqn	157834	F/L	WHITMARSH DFM Alan Walter	20-12-43	10 Sqn
133725	F/O	WHITE David Conway [Kenya]	26-11-43	61 Sqn	1609269	Sgt	WHITMARSH Ronald Gordon	2-12-43	90 Sqn
1610619	Sgt	WHITE Eric William	5-07-43	10 OTU	1334488	Sgt	WHITMARSH William Edmund	24-12-43	625 Sqn
1396247	Sgt	WHITE Ernest Alfred	31-08-43	78 Sqn	651215	Sgt	WHITMORE Harold William	2-12-43	626 Sqn
570403	Sgt	WHITE Frank Edward	21-10-43	7 Sqn	1350487	Sgt	WHITNEY Stanley William	24-12-43	44 Sqn
1852320	Sgt	WHITE Frederick Charles	18-11-43	218 Sqn	127067	F/O	WHITTAKER Alan Ewart	15-06-43	49 Sqn
1308157	Sgt	WHITE Geoffrey	29-06-43	115 Sqn	1231515	F/S	WHITTAKER Frank William	14-07-43	35 Sqn
1084519	Sgt	WHITE Gordon Roy	4-07-43	103 Sqn	1315940	Sgt	WHITTAKER Gordon Charles	27-04-43	15 Sqn
1773015	Sgt	WHITE Graham	23-11-43	460 Sqn	1080547	Sgt	WHITTAKER James Robert	29-06-43	166 Sqn
941955	Sgt	WHITE Jack	22-06-43	35 Sqn	1219858	Sgt	WHITTAKER Willie Jackson	14-04-43	429 Sqn
1397951	Sgt	WHITE James Stanley	16-08-43	207 Sqn	1864357	Sgt	WHITTER Phillip Arthur	23-08-43	100 Sqn
991230	Sgt	WHITE John Edward	27-01-43	50 Sqn	144575	P/O	WHITTICKS Henry John	24-11-43	44 Sqn
161723	P/O	WHITE John Freebairn	23-11-43	630 Sqn	2202386	Sgt	WHITTINGHAM Jack Dandridge	26-11-43	419 Sqn
37620	W/C	WHITE DFC John Henry	18-11-43	156 Sqn	159886	P/O	WHITTINGHAM DFM Sam James	18-11-43	617 Sqn
1375718	Sgt	WHITE Joseph Alexander	27-02-43	180 Sqn	1315989	Sgt	WHITTLE Arthur Henry James	30-03-43	76 Sqn
1535795	Sgt	WHITE Kenneth	15-02-43	207 Sqn	1392934	Sgt	WHITTLESEA Herbert Thomas	11-08-43	76 Sqn
961265	Sgt	WHITE Kenneth Ernest Gordon	22-06-43	158 Sqn	44540	F/L	WHITWELL AFM Jack Martindale	11-04-43	1660 HCU
1390403	Sgt	WHITE Kenneth Thomas	11-06-43	467 Sqn	1314530	Sgt	WHYATT Hugh Richard Belcher	30-05-43	106 Sqn
120889	F/L	WHITE Morris John Alfred	17-08-43	35 Sqn	541136	Sgt	WHYATT Leonard	20-04-43	158 Sqn
1405182	Sgt	WHITE Paget Derick	4-07-43	214 Sqn	910596	W/O	WHYBROW Horace	16-12-43	100 Sqn
1030030	Sgt	WHITE Peter Adolphus	4-04-43	27 OTU	995669	Sgt	WHYTE George Hugh	21-01-43	51 Sqn
1314559	Sgt	WHITE Raymond Charles	17-04-43	49 Sqn	1345473	Sgt	WHYTE James Logan	18-02-43	207 Sqn
160524	P/O	WHITE Raymond Christmas	31-08-43	432 Sqn	1332147	F/S	WICKERSHAM Albert James	26-11-43	35 Sqn
1331366	Sgt	WHITE Raymond William	26-02-43	218 Sqn	124521	F/O	WIDDECOMBE Ronald James	24-08-43	199 Sqn
1181067	F/S	WHITE Reginald John	21-04-43	77 Sqn	656756	Sgt	WIDDOP John Kendall	16-12-43	9 Sqn
1193463	Sgt	WHITE Richard Kitchener	16-04-43	466 Sqn	125598	F/O	WIDDOWSON Thomas Ingram	20-12-43	51 Sqn
1388298	Sgt	WHITE Robert Stirratt	29-06-43	10 Sqn	1379326	Sgt	WIDGERY Edward Leslie	25-02-43	102 Sqn
655917	Sgt	WHITE Ronald Edward John	2-03-43	78 Sqn	536586	Sgt	WIGGETT Clarence Edgar	22-06-43	83 Sqn
1318824	Sgt	WHITE Stephen George	26-06-43	106 Sqn	1321793	Sgt	WIGGINS Richard	25-02-43	467 Sqn
138691	P/O	WHITE Sydney Henry John	29-01-43	158 Sqn	642881	Sgt	WIGHTMAN Kenneth	16-12-43	7 Sqn
1112318	F/S	WHITE Thomas	23-09-43	106 Sqn	132874	F/O	WIGLEY George Alexander	17-12-43	97 Sqn
1128697	Sgt	WHITE Walter Leslie	22-04-43	10 OTU	1819124	Sgt	WIGLEY John Thomas	18-10-43	101 Sqn
152154	P/O	WHITE William Alfred	25-10-43	20 OTU	1393205	Sgt	WIGMORE Victor Henry	1-09-43	18 OTU
1382599	F/S	WHITECROSS James Standley [Bermuda]	22-10-43	61 Sqn	1075891	Sgt	WIGNALL Clifford	19-02-43	467 Sqn
					1503859	Sgt	WILBRAHAM Norman	10-08-43	102 Sqn
1415511	Sgt	WHITEHALL Charles Douglas	13-05-43	61 Sqn	1452153	Sgt	WILBY Frank Paul	6-09-43	49 Sqn

Service No	Rank	Name	Date	Unit
1214692	Sgt	WILBY Jack	26-02-43	102 Sqn
1312013	Sgt	WILCHER Aubrey Ralph	27-11-43	619 Sqn
128624	F/O	WILCOCK Ernest Douglas	13-06-43	102 Sqn
1007194	Sgt	WILCOCK Herbert	15-04-43	196 Sqn
985040	Sgt	WILCOCK Kenneth	15-06-43	106 Sqn
1586239	Sgt	WILCOCKSON Robert William	16-08-43	207 Sqn
567872	Sgt	WILCOX David Oliver	4-07-43	115 Sqn
537936	Sgt	WILCOX Francis William	18-06-43	83 Sqn
122767	F/O	WILD Dennis Paul Reginald	10-02-43	81 OTU
1601483	Sgt	WILD Leonard	20-10-43	625 Sqn
1458993	Sgt	WILD Reginald	27-09-43	166 Sqn
1218849	Sgt	WILD Robert	26-07-43	620 Sqn
1504089	Sgt	WILD William Henry	22-05-43	138 Sqn
1321712	Sgt	WILDBORE Ralph	31-08-43	12 Sqn
1004224	Sgt	WILDE Colin	15-06-43	49 Sqn
1812044	Sgt	WILDE Cyril James	20-11-43	57 Sqn
1578782	Sgt	WILDE James Alec	24-12-43	44 Sqn
149950	P/O	WILDEN DFC Allan Ralph	3-08-43	100 Sqn
1158064	Sgt	WILDMAN Leslie Harold	7-11-43	1663 HCU
1001023	Sgt	WILES Alan	2-12-43	12 Sqn
1209651	Sgt	WILES Alfred Albert	25-02-43	424 Sqn
1334775	Sgt	WILES Laurence Henry Victor	22-09-43	214 Sqn
935454	Sgt	WILFORD Henry	29-04-43	12 Sqn
1575740	Sgt	WILKES Arthur Edwin	23-06-43	431 Sqn
141103	P/O	WILKES DFM Ronald Edward	15-04-43	35 Sqn
1322035	Sgt	WILKES Thomas William Albert	28-08-43	199 Sqn
941414	F/S	WILKES Walter Ian Leslie	28-08-43	97 Sqn
147357	F/O	WILKIE CGM Cecil James Morley	4-10-43	50 Sqn
539504	Sgt	WILKIE DFM David Lessels	4-10-43	156 Sqn
1399267	Sgt	WILKIN George William	23-09-43	218 Sqn
1250736	Sgt	WILKINS Edward	26-02-43	9 Sqn
146788	P/O	WILKINS Edward Jack Austin	6-08-43	51 Sqn
1231499	Sgt	WILKINS Percy Eric	4-07-43	103 Sqn
1495945	Sgt	WILKINSON Digby Moor	19-07-43	22 OTU
145900	F/L	WILKINSON BEM Douglas Arthur Clarence	3-10-43	61 Sqn
1581403	Sgt	WILKINSON Frank	22-10-43	158 Sqn
2208870	Sgt	WILKINSON Fred	27-11-43	426 Sqn
1212271	Sgt	WILKINSON George Cornelius	16-07-43	10 OTU
642538	F/S	WILKINSON George Stanley	6-09-43	75 Sqn
110542	F/L	WILKINSON Herbert Henry Vincent	22-10-43	10 Sqn
1025280	Sgt	WILKINSON John	16-05-43	617 Sqn
935356	Sgt	WILKINSON DFM John Thomas	13-06-43	50 Sqn
1522786	Sgt	WILKINSON John William	23-09-43	12 Sqn
536891	Sgt	WILKINSON Roy Albert Wilfred	16-07-43	50 Sqn
109372	F/O	WILKINSON Stanley	13-05-43	139 Sqn
993249	Sgt	WILKINSON DFM Stanley	4-10-43	50 Sqn
1123748	Sgt	WILKINSON Thomas Gerard	25-06-43	50 Sqn
156357	P/O	WILKINSON DFC Wilfred	18-11-43	156 Sqn
1417280	Sgt	WILKS Ronald	23-09-43	75 Sqn
1333621	Sgt	WILLARS Peter Clifford	30-05-43	460 Sqn
1236693	Sgt	WILLATT John	29-04-43	12 Sqn
1262570	Sgt	WILLBOURN Bertram Wallace	19-02-43	15 Sqn
1387115	F/S	WILLCOCKS Edgar Harold	21-10-43	103 Sqn
1322553	Sgt	WILLETT Frederick John	22-06-43	156 Sqn
848286	Sgt	WILLETTS Francis	18-08-43	10 Sqn
134699	P/O	WILLETTS Stanley	18-11-43	622 Sqn
1677696	Sgt	WILLIAMS Alan	9-10-43	106 Sqn
1653142	Sgt	WILLIAMS Alan Basil Granville	7-09-43	1658 HCU
1714933	Sgt	WILLIAMS Alfred James	24-09-43	12 Sqn
1392748	F/S	WILLIAMS Alfred John Charles	23-11-43	207 Sqn
1391272	Sgt	WILLIAMS Allan Arthur Frederick	31-01-43	9 Sqn
1112414	Sgt	WILLIAMS Arthur James Heppel	15-03-43	11 OTU
1539602	Sgt	WILLIAMS Austin Ainsworth	16-09-43	617 Sqn
573577	Sgt	WILLIAMS Carey	23-08-43	102 Sqn
123048	F/O	WILLIAMS Cyril Frederick	16-04-43	61 Sqn
1193026	Sgt	WILLIAMS Cyril Percy	18-08-43	103 Sqn
149466	P/O	WILLIAMS David	31-07-43	78 Sqn
931403	F/S	WILLIAMS David	20-12-43	102 Sqn
576733	Sgt	WILLIAMS David Dennis	25-07-43	103 Sqn
1380623	Sgt	WILLIAMS David Ellis	23-06-43	97 Sqn
618117	F/S	WILLIAMS David Hugh	13-05-43	12 Sqn
1083911	Sgt	WILLIAMS David Reginald	3-04-43	15 OTU
130932	F/O	WILLIAMS David Stuart	28-05-43	115 Sqn
553822	Sgt	WILLIAMS David Winston	10-04-43	466 Sqn
1585028	Sgt	WILLIAMS Denis Leslie	10-06-43	24 OTU
657696	F/S	WILLIAMS Dennis	17-12-43	218 Sqn
149140	P/O	WILLIAMS DFM Derek	26-07-43	103 Sqn
1316166	Sgt	WILLIAMS Douglas	20-03-43	27 OTU
1337753	Sgt	WILLIAMS Edward Charles Bert	5-03-43	78 Sqn
122828	F/O	WILLIAMS Edward Trevor	3-05-43	487 Sqn
1130519	Sgt	WILLIAMS Enoch Jones	28-08-43	78 Sqn
134704	F/O	WILLIAMS Eric	22-10-43	1654 HCU
1337304	Sgt	WILLIAMS Ernest	3-04-43	106 Sqn
952308	Sgt	WILLIAMS Francis Henry	23-06-43	15 Sqn
1295227	Sgt	WILLIAMS Frederick Arthur	26-05-43	149 Sqn
1130624	Sgt	WILLIAMS Frederick Ernest	22-01-43	76 Sqn
613496	Sgt	WILLIAMS Frederick George	28-05-43	10 Sqn
1304115	Sgt	WILLIAMS Frederick George	3-04-43	76 Sqn
146607	P/O	WILLIAMS Frederick Lionel	12-06-43	161 Sqn
1684611	Sgt	WILLIAMS Frederick Stanley	18-08-43	428 Sqn
1379610	Sgt	WILLIAMS George Henry	25-06-43	166 Sqn
136044	F/O	WILLIAMS GM Graham George	17-04-43	102 Sqn
1237135	Sgt	WILLIAMS Harold Edward	11-04-43	166 Sqn
531347	Sgt	WILLIAMS Harry	10-07-43	77 Sqn
1801135	Sgt	WILLIAMS Henry Albert	17-12-43	166 Sqn
1222755	Sgt	WILLIAMS Henry Gordon	31-08-43	9 Sqn
1499052	Sgt	WILLIAMS Howard Llewellyn	7-02-43	61 Sqn
1394323	Sgt	WILLIAMS Hubert Gwyn	19-12-43	138 Sqn
1389188	Sgt	WILLIAMS Hugh Charles	22-05-43	431 Sqn
1414532	Sgt	WILLIAMS Ivor George	24-08-43	199 Sqn
1504193	Sgt	WILLIAMS Ivor Wyn	8-04-43	15 Sqn
1606375	Sgt	WILLIAMS James Richard	31-07-43	76 Sqn
115798	F/O	WILLIAMS DFC John	19-02-43	15 Sqn
136407	F/O	WILLIAMS John Alfred	2-12-43	57 Sqn
1029551	AC1	WILLIAMS John Clyde	12-02-43	9 Sqn
1316732	Sgt	WILLIAMS John Gareth Vaughan	26-06-43	106 Sqn
1601743	Sgt	WILLIAMS John Loxton	26-11-43	463 Sqn
1387840	Sgt	WILLIAMS John Peter	27-08-43	1663 HCU
1029717	Sgt	WILLIAMS John Richard	4-12-43	429 Sqn
1094029	Sgt	WILLIAMS John William	15-04-43	214 Sqn
1394555	F/S	WILLIAMS Kenneth	9-10-43	429 Sqn
1315633	Sgt	WILLIAMS Kenneth Rees George	17-04-43	76 Sqn
126857	F/L	WILLIAMS Leslie Kenneth	12-08-43	620 Sqn
40584	S/L	WILLIAMS Mark Arthur Lotherington	15-01-43	427 Sqn
1321906	Sgt	WILLIAMS Maurice Norman	22-11-43	156 Sqn
1388418	Sgt	WILLIAMS Maurice Roy	17-06-43	12 Sqn
1654794	Sgt	WILLIAMS Melville Sidney	2-10-43	51 Sqn
931715	F/S	WILLIAMS Montagu Normington	29-05-43	307 FTU
1077619	Sgt	WILLIAMS Peter	14-07-43	115 Sqn
1239188	Sgt	WILLIAMS Rees Arthur	22-05-43	431 Sqn
43262	F/L	WILLIAMS Reginald Frank [Canada]	9-10-43	78 Sqn
657974	Sgt	WILLIAMS Richard Stanley	6-01-43	10 OTU
1149195	Sgt	WILLIAMS Richard Thompson	4-02-43	90 Sqn
974495	Sgt	WILLIAMS Robert	1-05-43	44 Sqn
1385800	Sgt	WILLIAMS Robert	26-02-43	426 Sqn
1653153	Sgt	WILLIAMS Robert	1-09-43	428 Sqn
1136286	Sgt	WILLIAMS Robert Salisbury	30-07-43	102 Sqn
1437991	Sgt	WILLIAMS Ronald	19-02-43	166 Sqn
146333	F/O	WILLIAMS DFC Ronald Charles	29-12-43	35 Sqn
1350714	F/S	WILLIAMS Ronald Franklin	13-05-43	57 Sqn
1434986	F/S	WILLIAMS Ronald George	24-11-43	408 Sqn
541394	Sgt	WILLIAMS Ronald Mayhew	5-07-43	Wyton
45374	S/L	WILLIAMS DFC Ronald Sidney	14-07-43	158 Sqn
1604637	Sgt	WILLIAMS Rowland Arthur	23-09-43	9 Sqn
140912	P/O	WILLIAMS Roy Arthur	13-02-43	75 Sqn

Number	Rank	Surname	Given names	Date	Unit
1410459	Sgt	WILLIAMS	Stanley	2-12-43	103 Sqn
1386325	Sgt	WILLIAMS	Stanley Ernest	25-06-43	101 Sqn
1484363	Sgt	WILLIAMS	Stanley John	3-08-43	428 Sqn
1381181	Sgt	WILLIAMS	Sydney	23-06-43	83 Sqn
1452582	Sgt	WILLIAMS	Sydney	9-10-43	102 Sqn
965881	Sgt	WILLIAMS	Trevor Lloyd	12-03-43	97 Sqn
155480	P/O	WILLIAMS	Walter Stanley	24-08-43	218 Sqn
1410983	Sgt	WILLIAMS	William Cyril	6-07-43	1660 HCU
1452447	Sgt	WILLIAMS	William Philip	31-08-43	78 Sqn
637252	Sgt	WILLIAMS	William John	4-07-43	149 Sqn
1563261	Sgt	WILLIAMSON	Adam Ness	3-11-43	10 Sqn
1036493	Sgt	WILLIAMSON	Arthur Fenwick	18-11-43	9 Sqn
39092	W/C	WILLIAMSON	Edgar Arthur	31-07-43	44 Sqn
1365974	Sgt	WILLIAMSON	Henry Rochead	14-05-43	83 Sqn
1343703	Sgt	WILLIAMSON	James [Canada]	18-10-43	103 Sqn
148444	F/O	WILLIAMSON	James Vaughan	22-11-43	1664 HCU
591366	Sgt	WILLIAMSON	John Paul	22-10-43	103 Sqn
1571134	Sgt	WILLIAMSON	Lawrence Arthur	26-11-43	57 Sqn
1808063	Sgt	WILLIAMSON	Richard Oliver	22-10-43	12 Sqn
1074636	Sgt	WILLIAMSON	Ronald Frederick	24-05-43	166 Sqn
1814576	Sgt	WILLIG	Aubrey Ernest Charles	23-09-43	419 Sqn
925963	Sgt	WILLIS	Anthony Marshall	21-01-43	103 Sqn
1394695	Sgt	WILLIS	Charles Albert	20-04-43	460 Sqn
573470	Sgt	WILLIS	Ernest Frederick John	30-07-43	35 Sqn
1382215	F/S	WILLIS	Frederick Arthur William	3-03-43	75 Sqn
124109	P/O	WILLIS	George Harold	20-04-43	158 Sqn
1434099	F/S	WILLIS DFM	Herbert John	9-10-43	115 Sqn
1194896	Sgt	WILLIS	James Albert	3-03-43	12 OTU
80259	F/O	WILLIS	Ivan Reginald [Rhodesia]	21-01-43	158 Sqn
1331200	Sgt	WILLIS	William Alfred	27-04-43	102 Sqn
142482	P/O	WILLMOTT	Ronald Arthur Bertram	1-03-43	51 Sqn
49765	F/O	WILLOUGHBY	Stephen Alan	13-05-43	429 Sqn
640916	Sgt	WILLS	Frederick Roy	23-08-43	106 Sqn
1170594	Sgt	WILLSHER	Frederick Phillip	26-05-43	75 Sqn
1268645	Sgt	WILLSHIRE	Raymond Hedley	29-06-43	431 Sqn
134747	P/O	WILSON	Alan Bert	25-01-43	192 Sqn
1434808	Sgt	WILSON	Alexander	22-10-43	115 Sqn
129361	F/O	WILSON	Alexander Bell Pate	28-05-43	51 Sqn
532057	F/O	WILSON	Andrew	26-03-43	78 Sqn
1501266	Sgt	WILSON	Andrew James Normandale	12-06-43	76 Sqn
1196327	Sgt	WILSON	Arthur William Ernest	30-03-43	196 Sqn
1264302	Sgt	WILSON	Charles Henry Morgan	22-10-43	158 Sqn
1335658	F/S	WILSON	David	26-11-43	7 Sqn
631262	Sgt	WILSON	David Strachan	21-10-43	7 Sqn
1316141	Sgt	WILSON	Dennis Raymond	1-05-43	51 Sqn
656188	Sgt	WILSON	Donald Charles	13-03-43	7 Sqn
1452163	Sgt	WILSON	Edward David	26-11-43	49 Sqn
1320727	Sgt	WILSON	Edward George	18-09-43	1658 HCU
1029925	Sgt	WILSON	Edward Joseph	4-09-43	77 Sqn
995196	Sgt	WILSON	Ernest	26-06-43	90 Sqn
546293	Sgt	WILSON	Ernest John	1-05-43	78 Sqn
522964	F/S	WILSON	George	3-09-43	156 Sqn
1345905	Sgt	WILSON	George	4-08-43	16 OTU
1349775	Sgt	WILSON	George	27-03-43	101 Sqn
1161605	Sgt	WILSON	George Arthur	18-10-43	619 Sqn
1383005	Sgt	WILSON	George Joseph	16-04-43	460 Sqn
156129	P/O	WILSON	George William	29-09-43	78 Sqn
1804275	Sgt	WILSON	George William	11-08-43	106 Sqn
118566	F/L	WILSON	Harold Sydney	16-09-43	617 Sqn
909231	Sgt	WILSON	Harry Leonard	4-07-43	9 Sqn
1813184	Sgt	WILSON	Henry Robert	22-10-43	103 Sqn
576865	Sgt	WILSON	Jack William George	26-07-43	103 Sqn
612661	Sgt	WILSON	James Ferguson Lindsay	5-03-43	106 Sqn
1336604	Sgt	WILSON	Jesse Thomas	13-07-43	50 Sqn
1080434	Sgt	WILSON	John	23-09-43	9 Sqn
1386132	Sgt	WILSON	John Guyie	13-05-43	199 Sqn
658464	Sgt	WILSON	John Leslie	26-02-43	102 Sqn
1128900	F/S	WILSON	John Lindsay	12-06-43	7 Sqn
1053443	Sgt	WILSON	John Rodger	23-11-43	434 Sqn
1372169	Sgt	WILSON	Joseph	27-04-43	90 Sqn
131566	F/O	WILSON	Kenneth	30-07-43	78 Sqn
120422	F/O	WILSON	Kenneth James Barclay	24-08-43	100 Sqn
1621809	Sgt	WILSON	Leonard Dinsdale	16-12-43	101 Sqn
1302847	Sgt	WILSON	Ralph	9-04-43	7 Sqn
1125318	Sgt	WILSON	Richard Reginald	7-09-43	77 Sqn
1104498	Sgt	WILSON	Robert	12-03-43	50 Sqn
1349747	Sgt	WILSON	Robert	3-10-43	77 Sqn
1578403	Sgt	WILSON	Robert	9-11-43	90 Sqn
1480719	F/S	WILSON	Robert Alexander Cooper	17-12-43	101 Sqn
620764	Sgt	WILSON	Robert Francis	11-04-43	50 Sqn
120627	F/L	WILSON	Robert Hay	11-08-43	57 Sqn
1070425	Sgt	WILSON	Robert McGregor	30-03-43	158 Sqn
1492741	Sgt	WILSON	Roy	5-09-43	1661 HCU
1521081	Sgt	WILSON	Samuel James	28-08-43	77 Sqn
1388746	Sgt	WILSON	Stuart	11-12-43	26 OTU
1498723	Sgt	WILSON	Thomas John 'Jack'	28-09-43	428 Sqn
144265	P/O	WILSON	Thomas Richardson	14-09-43	138 Sqn
1389001	Sgt	WILSON	Valentine Robertson	11-04-43	115 Sqn
126985	F/O	WILSON	Victor Albert	13-05-43	57 Sqn
990531	F/S	WILSON	William	15-01-43	161 Sqn
1098032	F/S	WILSON	William Mark	22-11-43	7 Sqn
1452338	Sgt	WILSON	William Primrose	16-12-43	7 Sqn
128514	F/O	WINCHESTER	Howard Stephen	26-05-43	149 Sqn
1333599	Sgt	WINCHESTER	Ronald Gordon	17-06-43	103 Sqn
156358	P/O	WINCHURCH	John Ivor	31-08-43	15 Sqn
116092	F/O	WINDSOR	Reginald John Frederick	25-02-43	106 Sqn
132698	F/O	WINFIELD	Ronald Walter	23-06-43	9 Sqn
159043	P/O	WINN DFM	Albert Edward	3-10-43	158 Sqn
1212281	Sgt	WINN	John Edwin	1-04-43	103 Sqn
1080262	Sgt	WINN	Robert	29-06-43	100 Sqn
139527	P/O	WINN	Ronald Arthur	24-08-43	78 Sqn
1697127	Sgt	WINSTANLEY	Jack	5-11-43	10 Sqn
134723	P/O	WINSTANLEY	Thomas	1-03-43	15 OTU
1491459	AC1	WINTER	David Milne	27-02-43	49 Sqn
1314142	Sgt	WINTER	Ronald Harry	17-04-43	408 Sqn
2201670	Sgt	WINTERBOTTOM	Cyril Raymond	4-10-43	419 Sqn
1439760	Sgt	WINTERBURN	Norman Percy	29-09-43	156 Sqn
1796389	Sgt	WINTERS	John Owens	2-12-43	1664 HCU
1570461	Sgt	WINTON	Alexander John	24-11-43	1658 HCU
925214	Sgt	WISDOM	William Frederick Charles	29-09-43	16 OTU
1392746	Sgt	WISE	Frederick Reuben	18-11-43	77 Sqn
1551786	Sgt	WISHART	George Sinclair	23-05-43	218 Sqn
969171	Sgt	WISHART	Thomas	29-01-43	9 Sqn
141334	F/O	WISSLER	Richard Peter	22-10-43	431 Sqn
1269601	Sgt	WITCHLOW	George Charles	25-07-43	103 Sqn
1332048	Sgt	WITHAM	Harold Edmund	11-03-43	158 Sqn
1332130	Sgt	WITHAM	Herbert William	2-12-43	101 Sqn
656822	Sgt	WITHAM	William Kenneth	14-08-43	1662 HCU
1431233	Sgt	WITTON	Anthony	5-03-43	12 OTU
1575633	Sgt	WITTS	Thomas Edward	25-07-43	103 Sqn
1804500	Sgt	WIX	George Frank Albert	22-07-43	1657 HCU
129565	F/O	WODEHOUSE	Frank George	8-08-43	106 Sqn
39805	S/L	WOLFE DFC	Denzil Lloyd [Canada]	14-07-43	405 Sqn
1531814	Sgt	WOLFF	Harold Joseph	25-09-43	29 OTU
1117841	Sgt	WOLSTENCROFT	Kenneth	4-07-43	35 Sqn
155159	P/O	WOLSTENHOLME DFM	Cyril Hayworth	27-09-43	7 Sqn
143996	P/O	WOLTON DFM	James Herbert	8-04-43	1654 HCU
1230388	Sgt	WOOD	Alan Richard	5-04-43	57 Sqn
641465	Sgt	WOOD	Albert Joseph	25-07-43	405 Sqn
1149750	Sgt	WOOD	Arthur Charles	12-07-43	207 Sqn
656588	F/S	WOOD	Benjamin Brinley	23-06-43	75 Sqn
135657	P/O	WOOD	Christopher Barton	29-04-43	100 Sqn
37920	S/L	WOOD MiD	Clifford Sinclair Farquhar	22-10-43	103 Sqn
151327	F/O	WOOD	Donald	12-11-43	35 Sqn

1351620	F/S	WOOD Douglas Stewart		18-08-43	35 Sqn	120667	P/O	WOODS Ronald George	29-01-43	158 Sqn
1367826	Sgt	WOOD Dugald Gillies		27-09-43	199 Sqn	1337097	Sgt	WOODS Ronald Victor	3-11-43	77 Sqn
1331631	Sgt	WOOD Edward John		26-02-43	1658 HCU	1337005	Sgt	WOODS Ronald William	5-09-43	1663 HCU
1311885	Sgt	WOOD Edwin Hall		1-05-43	76 Sqn	112437	F/O	WOODS Roy Desmond	22-01-43	98 Sqn
953122	Sgt	WOOD Eric Sharpe		5-04-43	9 Sqn	1150953	Sgt	WOODS William Harold	27-04-43	18 OTU
1149392	Sgt	WOOD Frank		15-04-43	101 Sqn	129042	F/O	WOODSEND Hugh William	27-07-43	156 Sqn
1047841	Sgt	WOOD Galen		4-12-43	431 Sqn	131966	F/O	WOODWARD Arthur	26-06-43	15 Sqn
1099748	Sgt	WOOD George		22-06-43	77 Sqn	1333246	Sgt	WOODWARD James Ernest	23-06-43	78 Sqn
1514614	Sgt	WOOD George		18-08-43	77 Sqn	1316223	Sgt	WOODWARD John Charles	16-02-43	103 Sqn
658403	Sgt	WOOD George Robert Yorston		13-05-43	431 Sqn	139846	P/O	WOODWARD Noel George	21-04-43	15 OTU
1583465	Sgt	WOOD George Stanley		6-09-43	427 Sqn	1218440	Sgt	WOODWARD Thomas John	4-04-43	156 Sqn
1338068	Sgt	WOOD Harold		1-03-43	50 Sqn	1316601	Sgt	WOOLCOCK Roy Henry	16-12-43	1661 HCU
1578075	Sgt	WOOD Henry Leonard		3-11-43	49 Sqn	1290189	Sgt	WOOLCOTT Douglas George	24-08-43	75 Sqn
742752	W/O	WOOD Herbert Edward		12-06-43	9 Sqn	1336795	Sgt	WOOLDRIDGE Frederick John	19-11-43	15 OTU
1255050	F/S	WOOD Ivor		9-03-43	207 Sqn	146938	P/O	WOOLDRDIGE Hugh Telfer	13-06-43	158 Sqn
755138	F/S	WOOD James Currie		25-05-43	100 Sqn	1323920	Sgt	WOOLFORD Reginald John	28-07-43	12 Sqn
1047244	Sgt	WOOD John		27-04-43	76 Sqn	50230	F/O	WOOLHOUSE Edward Barrie	26-11-43	115 Sqn
1375501	F/S	WOOD John		6-02-43	90 Sqn	950313	W/O	WOOLHOUSE Stanley	3-10-43	51 Sqn
2216037	Sgt	WOOD Kenneth		2-12-43	156 Sqn	1438573	Sgt	WOOLLAM James Edward Lucas	10-03-43	10 OTU
1606542	Sgt	WOOD Kenneth Roy		16-12-43	408 Sqn	1389559	Sgt	WOOLLARD Thomas Henry	12-07-43	1663 HCU
1086890	Sgt	WOOD Maurice		29-06-43	51 Sqn	155858	P/O	WOOLLDRIDGE Cyril Arthur	19-12-43	138 Sqn
1435587	Sgt	WOOD Neville Henry [New Zealand]		5-05-43	156 Sqn	1488741	Sgt	WOOLLEY George William	18-10-43	101 Sqn
1295568	Sgt	WOOD Owen William		24-08-43	77 Sqn	1213595	Sgt	WOOLNOUGH Ronald Clifford	4-09-43	106 Sqn
553971	Sgt	WOOD Peter John		24-05-43	78 Sqn	519840	F/S	WOOLNOUGH William Oldfield	17-04-43	156 Sqn
130506	F/O	WOOD Raymond George		17-04-43	426 Sqn	1316368	Sgt	WOOSNAM Richard Gordon	12-08-43	466 Sqn
991246	Sgt	WOOD Robert		12-07-43	207 Sqn	1203965	Sgt	WOOSNAM William	4-04-43	51 Sqn
655224	Sgt	WOOD Ronald Douglas		9-04-43	9 Sqn	1603969	Sgt	WOOSTER Douglas Leonard Herbert	19-08-43	1658 HCU
578238	Sgt	WOOD Samuel		13-06-43	51 Sqn	1138238	Sgt	WORRALL Frank	7-04-43	9 Sqn
143087	P/O	WOOD Sidney Midgley		8-04-43	466 Sqn	1214527	Sgt	WORRALL Raymond	30-07-43	51 Sqn
1335616	Sgt	WOOD Stanley Walter		19-08-43	12 OTU	1377805	Sgt	WORROW John Henry	17-01-43	61 Sqn
1236752	F/S	WOOD Terence Albert		10-04-43	49 Sqn	1577574	Sgt	WORSDALE Albert	26-06-43	115 Sqn
1280220	Sgt	WOOD Victor Jack		21-01-43	207 Sqn	1392269	Sgt	WORSEY Ralph Frederick	4-10-43	100 Sqn
1002202	F/S	WOOD Victor Ronald		3-02-43	78 Sqn	130162	P/O	WORSLEY Arthur Lesley	7-02-43	425 Sqn
1324081	Sgt	WOOD William Charles		31-01-43	49 Sqn	1384017	Sgt	WORSLEY Frank Ernest	1-09-43	90 Sqn
1271145	Sgt	WOOD William Charles Luke		4-09-43	7 Sqn	142320	F/O	WORSNOP Fred	11-08-43	158 Sqn
128447	F/L	WOOD William George		22-10-43	105 Sqn	1083323	Sgt	WORSNOP Frederick Arthur	14-05-43	83 Sqn
1136273	Sgt	WOOD William Haseltine		27-01-43	57 Sqn	1585034	Sgt	WORT Donald Frank	1-12-43	75 Sqn
135659	F/O	WOOD William Henry		23-06-43	103 Sqn	574819	Sgt	WORTHINGTON Jack Herbert	9-04-43	75 Sqn
1030901	Sgt	WOODACRE Albert Edwin		24-09-43	12 Sqn	1126476	Sgt	WORTHINGTON Wilfred	9-07-43	106 Sqn
1384980	Sgt	WOODARD Amos Alfred Thomas		23-06-43	620 Sqn	139947	P/O	WRAGGE Geoffrey	1-05-43	7 Sqn
1138811	F/S	WOODCOCK DFM Geoffrey		27-09-43	7 Sqn	1264399	Sgt	WRATTEN Jack	26-02-43	15 Sqn
1588938	Sgt	WOODCOCK Norman		18-06-43	83 Sqn	1452340	Sgt	WRAY Ranson	22-09-43	76 Sqn
997011	F/S	WOODCOCK Peter		17-06-43	156 Sqn	1061805	Sgt	WREAKES Jack	1-03-43	420 Sqn
1288645	Sgt	WOODFIELD Hugh		26-02-43	103 Sqn	655863	Sgt	WRIGHT Alexander Thomas Mitchel	26-05-43	101 Sqn
1439456	Sgt	WOODFIELD Ronald George		4-04-43	149 Sqn	159087	P/O	WRIGHT Allan French	20-12-43	408 Sqn
1232134	Sgt	WOODFORD Reginald Edgar		2-10-43	460 Sqn	1149750	Sgt	WRIGHT Arthur Charles	12-07-43	207 Sqn
155878	P/O	WOODGATE Joseph Eric		24-08-43	101 Sqn	1293733	W/O	WRIGHT Bernard Christian Naylor	31-10-43	139 Sqn
995589	Sgt	WOODHALL Ronald		16-04-43	78 Sqn	33129	W/C	WRIGHT Christopher Louis Yser	23-11-43	51 Sqn
1032548	Sgt	WOODHOUSE Arthur		2-04-43	16 OTU	1622986	Sgt	WRIGHT David Hartnoll	18-12-43	311 FTU
110587	F/O	WOODHOUSE Harold Walter		26-05-43	9 Sqn	1576730	Sgt	WRIGHT Douglas	9-01-43	97 Sqn
142611	P/O	WOODHOUSE Robert Beck		23-09-43	218 Sqn	156351	P/O	WRIGHT Edric George	23-11-43	44 Sqn
1452094	F/S	WOODHOUSE Roland Reuben		2-10-43	207 Sqn	1044677	Sgt	WRIGHT Edward John	1-09-43	15 Sqn
1337539	Sgt	WOODING William Russell 'Bobs'		7-07-43	15 OTU	1473923	Sgt	WRIGHT Eric	12-06-43	78 Sqn
1318406	Sgt	WOODLAND William		1-05-43	12 Sqn	992607	Sgt	WRIGHT Eric Charles	22-05-43	1656 HCU
1434664	Sgt	WOODLEY Albert		2-12-43	44 Sqn	526692	Sgt	WRIGHT Ernest Albert	5-03-43	214 Sqn
1335010	Sgt	WOODLEY Arthur Charles		13-06-43	102 Sqn	1292308	Sgt	WRIGHT Ernest Edward	30-07-43	102 Sqn
1211129	Sgt	WOODLEY James William Robert Henry				1043180	Sgt	WRIGHT George Arthur	22-11-43	218 Sqn
				9-04-43	77 Sqn	1213927	F/S	WRIGHT George Clifford	17-04-43	76 Sqn
127130	F/O	WOODROFFE Derrick Roy		29-05-43	158 Sqn	148758	P/O	WRIGHT George Roland	22-06-43	166 Sqn
931971	Sgt	WOODROFFE George Percy		30-07-43	102 Sqn	953453	Sgt	WRIGHT Gordon	11-08-43	106 Sqn
1448727	Sgt	WOODROW Edward Bert		24-08-43	102 Sqn	1590868	Sgt	WRIGHT James	23-09-43	428 Sqn
591524	Sgt	WOODROW Harold		18-01-43	1656 HCU	1388972	Sgt	WRIGHT John Harold	26-06-43	102 Sqn
933968	Sgt	WOODROW Stanley Alfred		27-03-43	214 Sqn	610312	Sgt	WRIGHT John Henry Bernard	3-03-43	106 Sqn
1190385	F/S	WOODRUFF Harold Eunson		13-02-43	199 Sqn	1199164	Sgt	WRIGHT Leonard Frederick	24-12-43	550 Sqn
1184099	Sgt	WOODS Donald Walter		30-07-43	460 Sqn	1319421	F/S	WRIGHT Leslie Alfred	24-05-43	51 Sqn
1339079	Sgt	WOODS Hubert Frederick John		24-12-43	550 Sqn	1294453	Sgt	WRIGHT Leslie Charles	17-05-43	75 Sqn
542030	Sgt	WOODS James		14-05-43	138 Sqn	132198	F/O	WRIGHT Maurice Winter	22-11-43	49 Sqn
1330321	Sgt	WOODS Joseph Byrne		11-04-43	214 Sqn	37589	S/L	WRIGHT Noel William	24-08-43	77 Sqn

1274019	Sgt	WRIGHT Ralph Henry	18-11-43	35 Sqn		1236143	Sgt	YOUNG Robert Anthony	8-08-43	26 OTU
33366	S/L	WRIGHT Robert Brian	24-08-43	156 Sqn		1852472	Sgt	YOUNG Russell Clare Stedman	20-10-43	12 OTU
142491	P/O	WRIGHT Robert Graham	30-03-43	76 Sqn		572343	Sgt	YOUNG Stanley	14-02-43	49 Sqn
1534380	Sgt	WRIGHT Sidney	12-06-43	15 Sqn		1581582	Sgt	YOUNG Thomas Bertram	21-10-43	161 Sqn
1499893	Sgt	WRIGHT Sydney	9-01-43	44 Sqn		1383984	Sgt	YOUNG Walter	30-05-43	44 Sqn
116695	F/O	WRIGHT William	30-01-43	105 Sqn		1795688	Sgt	YOUNG William	11-12-43	82 OTU
591755	Sgt	WRIGHTSON Robert	2-03-43	61 Sqn		1480146	F/S	YOUNG William Arthur	2-12-43	460 Sqn
1684109	Sgt	WUNDERLEY Joseph	17-12-43	100 Sqn		658237	Sgt	YOUNG William Stanley	10-03-43	10 OTU
547504	Sgt	WURR Donald	14-05-43	218 Sqn		113351	F/L	YOUSEMAN DFC Edward Ernest George		
1464425	Sgt	WYATT Eric George	2-12-43	103 Sqn					18-11-43	617 Sqn
1332914	Sgt	WYATT Peter Clifford Wilfred	7-08-43	9 Sqn		1191524	Sgt	YOXALL Charles Henry	3-02-43	218 Sqn
1166714	Sgt	WYATT-MATTHEWS Ronald Joseph 26-07-43		158 Sqn		757254	Sgt	YUILL Archibald	24-09-43	428 Sqn
1127228	Sgt	WYKES Joseph	13-05-43	75 Sqn		1343026	Sgt	YULE James	22-09-43	218 Sqn
982917	Sgt	WYLIE Robert McKenzie	25-02-43	467 Sqn		908648	F/S	ZAHL Ronald Aaron	29-09-43	434 Sqn
1625511	Sgt	WYNN Hamer Rex	22-09-43	214 Sqn		1321233	F/S	ZANCHI Paul Rudolph	26-11-43	101 Sqn
146838	P/O	WYNN Ian Archer	26-05-43	100 Sqn		1603263	Sgt	ZASTROW William Robert	22-11-43	10 Sqn
129105	F/O	WYNNE DFM Herbert Lloyd	19-03-43	161 Sqn		908724	Sgt	ZEDY Gordon Clifford Andrew	15-06-43	44 Sqn
1319559	Sgt	WYNNIATT Raymond Lewis	7-07-43	26 OTU		1428439	Sgt	ZOELLER Peter Ernest	29-05-43	23 OTU
1583664	Sgt	YALE Robert Alec	29-12-43	467 Sqn		1699349	Sgt	ZUIDMULDER John Thomas	3-10-43	76 Sqn
1578659	Sgt	YARDLEY Dennis George	31-08-43	218 Sqn						
1049789	Sgt	YARE George William	26-07-43	158 Sqn						
1063311	Sgt	YARKER Percy	29-01-43	21 OTU						
979987	Sgt	YARWOOD Thomas Samuel	30-07-43	102 Sqn						
1439441	Sgt	YATES Colin	11-08-43	30 OTU						
1510347	Sgt	YATES David Bennett	26-02-43	158 Sqn						
1132141	Sgt	YATES Eric Ashley	26-02-43	50 Sqn						
820019	Sgt	YATES Frank	10-04-43	30 OTU						
131977	F/O	YATES Frederick Leonard	14-07-43	115 Sqn						
1499051	Sgt	YATES George Arthur	20-10-43	90 Sqn						
133420	F/L	YATES Keith Riley	9-10-43	90 Sqn						
1545898	Sgt	YATES Richard Donald	3-11-43	625 Sqn						
130879	F/O	YATES Sidney Herbert	15-06-43	103 Sqn						
1390540	Sgt	YEATES George Harold	27-03-43	35 Sqn						
1398916	Sgt	YEATMAN Albert Reginald Charles	24-12-43	44 Sqn						
1578189	Sgt	YELLAND Cyril William	17-04-43	49 Sqn						
1317656	Sgt	YEO Gordon Arthur	16-05-43	617 Sqn						
1314128	Sgt	YEO Louis John	8-04-43	44 Sqn						
137226	F/O	YEO William Hector John	24-08-43	90 Sqn						
1322153	Sgt	YETTON William Charles	1-03-43	50 Sqn						
1126332	F/S	YIELDER Alfred Campbell	5-03-43	466 Sqn						
1318051	Sgt	YORK Alfred Raymond	19-02-43	12 OTU						
1467118	Sgt	YORKE Donald Henry	15-03-43	21 Sqn						
1582011	Sgt	YORKE Leslie George	12-11-43	102 Sqn						
156416	P/O	YOUNG Alan Edward	31-08-43	427 Sqn						
1443591	Sgt	YOUNG Alexander McDonald	12-06-43	78 Sqn						
36135	S/L	YOUNG Alfred Markham [Australia]	26-06-43	106 Sqn						
130565	F/O	YOUNG Arnold William Stephen	19-06-43	77 Sqn						
2206984	Sgt	YOUNG Arthur	3-09-43	1661 HCU						
1074494	Sgt	YOUNG Charles	3-07-43	460 Sqn						
1537408	Sgt	YOUNG Charles Edward	21-10-43	161 Sqn						
132851	F/O	YOUNG Charles William Ross	13-06-43	460 Sqn						
122905	F/O	YOUNG Denis	14-02-43	103 Sqn						
1600095	Sgt	YOUNG Dennis Alfred	18-08-43	434 Sqn						
1515649	Sgt	YOUNG Eric	7-09-43	81 OTU						
1380959	Sgt	YOUNG George Edward	7-02-43	61 Sqn						
72478	S/L	YOUNG DFC* Henry Melvin [USA]	17-05-43	617 Sqn						
1376146	Sgt	YOUNG Horace Derrick	29-05-43	158 Sqn						
1561575	Sgt	YOUNG James Arthur	3-10-43	12 Sqn						
138835	F/O	YOUNG DFM James Lawson	3-09-43	207 Sqn						
156657	P/O	YOUNG John Murray	1-09-43	622 Sqn						
61960	F/L	YOUNG DFC John Oswald	30-03-43	106 Sqn						
1216336	Sgt	YOUNG Joseph William	16-04-43	35 Sqn						
572584	Sgt	YOUNG Kenneth Roland Joseph	13-03-43	106 Sqn						
125603	F/O	YOUNG Leslie	30-03-43	166 Sqn						
1265860	Sgt	YOUNG Norman	27-03-43	7 Sqn						
1238951	Sgt	YOUNG Norman Albert	26-07-43	90 Sqn						
1265193	Sgt	YOUNG Ralph Charles	2-07-43	620 Sqn						
142551	F/O	YOUNG Raymond Albert Lewis	9-10-43	20 OTU						

Note

Interestingly, the three airmen with the surname 'Bowen', commemorated in this section, had in common 'George' as their first Christian name, the last, George Macness, being a Newfoundland army transfer in July 1940.

The 18 airmen with Snaith entered as their unit title, and who died on the 19th of June, 1943, all lost their lives in a terrible ammunition dump explosion, the aftermath of which led to the immediate despatch on Air Ministry orders of John Rowlands GC to assess the situation and take the requisite action to return Snaith to its operational role. This process took Rowlands and his team ten days to complete. Subsequently, he was knighted and rose in rank to that of Air Marshal before retiring from the Royal Air Force in July 1973. He died, aged 90, on the 4th of June, 2006, his obituary being reported in the leading newspapers. A further point of interest, nine of those who perished in the explosion are buried in Selby Cemetery and nine are commemorated on the Runnymede Memorial while it is further observed that seven, all Leading Aircraftman in rank, came from Scotland, their service numbers ranging between 1374372 (LAC Jamieson) and 1374446 (LAC Finlayson) thus identifying them all as enlisting in August 1940 at an Edinburgh recruitment office.

Remaining with the recruitment theme, F/S Hefferon's service number indicates that he enlisted in Rhodesia during the month of June 1940; interestingly, however, Les Allison and Harry Hayward show him as coming from Toronto, Ontario. His entry in the Rheinberg War Cemetery register gives no hint as to his place of birth, merely noting that his parents were Charles and Susan Hefferon.

Another Canadian serving with the Royal Air Force and who died during 1943, concerns W/C Coventry whose elder brother, Robert, had died almost three years previous. Their service numbers were 33133 and 33023 respectively, thus suggesting they arrived in the United Kingdom at the same time and may well have completed their pilot training together. Henry Coventry is buried in France, while Robert, who lost his life while flying with 17 Operational Training Unit (see Volume 7 page page 29 for further details), rests in Down Hatherley (St. Mary and Corpus Christi) Churchyard, Gloucestershire. In addition, both are commemorated on the Oak Bay Memorial, Victoria, British Columbia.

Amongst the more than a handful of New Zealanders reported above is the name of Douglas Pauling who, from the copious notes provided by Errol Martyn, enlisted in New Zealand with the aim of becoming a Fleet Air Arm pilot but following his arrival in the United Kingdom he failed to qualify in the profession of his choice and in January 1942 he transferred to the Royal Air Force, eventually remustering as an air gunner. At the time of his death he had flown a total of 103 hours, some of which (I suspect) had been logged during his attempts to become a pilot. Another unusual observation concerns F/L Harper who died with 12 Squadron during an attack on Mannheim in late September; Leonard Harper had commenced his operational career with 56 Squadron (Fighter Command) before crossing the Atlantic to Canada on a staff pilot posting from which he returned in the early months of 1943, joining Bomber Command. At the time of his death at the age of 30 he had added 19 operational bomber sorties to the 17 operations flown with '56'.

The entry in respect of AC1 Herbert Lee is most interesting in that at the time of his death 80 Wing was still being controlled by No.60(Signals) Group which, in turn, came under the authority of Headquarters Fighter Command. However, on the 8th of November, 1943, 80 Wing was transferred to No.100(Special Duties) Group, at Radlett, and coming under the control of Bomber Command. Lee's entry on the casualty return slip indicates his parent Command as 'Bomber', hence his inclusion in this Roll.

It is further observed that Herman Edwin and Ethel Rosamund Surgey of Montevideo, Uruguay, the parents of Sgt Charles Kenneth Surgey, lost a second son, Cpl John Eady Surgey in 1944. Like his younger brother, Cpl Surgey lost his life while serving in Bomber Command. Although many parents lost more than one son or daughter, I have drawn attention to this particular tragedy as their entries in the cemetery registers do not indicate a family relationship.

Of the handful of airmen that died during the year as prisoners of war, F/L Jack Maurice Lewis had been shot down in July 1940 (see Volume 1, page 85) and his death was the consequence of being struck by a train. He is buried in Poland in Poznan Old Garrison Cemetery.

I consider it appropriate to make a few general observations concerning 617 Squadron, forever remembered in Royal Air Force history as the squadron specially formed for the purpose of breaching the Ruhr dams, an operation mounted in May 1943, and which cost the squadron dearly in losses to both aircraft and crews (see Volume 4 pages 151 and 152 for details). Although coming under the umbrella of No.5 Group, the role for '617' was mainly in the sphere of special operations and in the aftermath of the dams raid was regarded by some members of the command as a *'one op. unit'*. This was rather an unfair judgement for in carrying out their special assignments '617' sustained quite serious casualties, six experienced crews (most were survivors from the dams operation) being lost over a period of 48 hours in mid-September after being tasked to breach the Dortmund-Ems canal near Ladbergen. The subject of many books (the first from the pen of Guy Gibson VC, who led the raid, appearing within months of the attack taking place) including a two-volume history by Alan W. Cooper, films and television documentaries, the achievements of 617 Squadron are destined to interest aviation writers for generations yet to come.

ROYAL AUSTRALIAN AIR FORCE
personnel

427631	F/S	ABERLE Douglas Buchanan	23-11-43	460 Sqn
11615	F/S	ADAIR Charles Edward	23-09-43	467 Sqn
410586	F/S	ADDINSALL Geoffrey William	10-07-43	12 Sqn
406634	W/O	AIRY Andrew Basil Reginald	26-06-43	466 Sqn
416918	P/O	ALEXANDER Wilfred Wilson	14-03-43	27 OTU
420333	F/L	ALFORD Thomas Derek Hudson	2-12-43	460 Sqn
409786	P/O	ALLAN Francis Barker	6-09-43	419 Sqn
416404	F/S	ALLAN Stanley Gordon	29-05-43	218 Sqn
408558	F/S	ALLSOPP William Frederick	9-04-43	460 Sqn
416819	F/S	ALTUS Hector Ferdinand	18-11-43	9 Sqn
427788	Sgt	ANDERSON Alexander Henry	6-11-43	27 OTU
416735	F/O	ANDERSON DFC Charles Beatty	30-07-43	460 Sqn
412606	F/O	ARCHIBALD DFC Thomas	13-05-43	77 Sqn
414333	P/O	ARMOUR William John	20-12-43	428 Sqn
413522	F/S	ASHLEY Aubrey George	25-07-43	460 Sqn
426486	F/S	ATHERTON John Carman	24-12-43	550 Sqn
12316	F/S	ATKIN Charles Carr	5-03-43	28 OTU
403490	F/L	AUBERT DFM Charles Oscar	16-11-43	156 Sqn
405618	F/S	AUSTIN Walter Edmund Joseph	27-01-43	460 Sqn
409881	F/S	AYERS Ralph James	20-12-43	149 Sqn
401730	F/S	BAKER Robert Henry	17-04-43	460 Sqn
408948	F/L	BALDING DFC Keith Todd	27-09-43	218 Sqn
22230	F/S	BALDWIN Edward Alexander	13-06-43	460 Sqn
408949	Sgt	BALL John Howard	8-04-43	460 Sqn

414289	F/O	BALLARD Victor Norman	24-03-43	16 OTU
405803	F/S	BANKS Ivan William	26-06-43	101 Sqn
16249	P/O	BANKS Malcolm James	27-09-43	50 Sqn
401899	F/L	BARLOW DFC Robert Norman George		
			16-05-43	617 Sqn
409649	F/S	BARR Donald Leighton Spence	7-07-43	103 Sqn
406912	F/S	BARRETT-LENNARD Michael Godfrey		
			22-09-43	460 Sqn
20047	F/S	BARRY John Lawrence	5-05-43	460 Sqn
422103	F/S	BARTLE Peter Chadwick	27-08-43	1663 HCU
414382	Sgt	BATTERHAM Jack Alexander	25-11-43	1678 HCU
413943	F/S	BATTLE Ernest John	16-12-43	97 Sqn
415212	F/S	BAVIN Douglas Frederick	3-06-43	10 OTU
412098	F/S	BAYLISS Jack Bernard	30-03-43	166 Sqn
425263	F/O	BEATTIE Glen Patrick	29-12-43	460 Sqn
401884	Sgt	BELL Frederick George	3-02-43	27 OTU
205848	Sgt	BELL John Courtney	17-04-43	460 Sqn
414457	F/S	BELL Keith Selwyn	29-12-43	115 Sqn
40597	F/S	BELLMAN Norman Edwin	4-09-43	44 Sqn
408382	F/S	BELOT Theodore Albert	14-06-43	27 OTU
420637	F/O	BENNETT Bruce William	12-06-43	460 Sqn
415066	F/S	BENT Thomas Edward	30-07-43	460 Sqn
410436	F/S	BERRY Edwin Henry	31-08-43	466 Sqn
33396	F/S	BERRY Weston Robert	12-06-43	12 Sqn
409887	F/S	BETSON John Louis Ward	23-09-43	100 Sqn
426012	F/O	BEYER Harry Malcolm	14-08-43	21 OTU
410589	F/S	BEYER Maxwell Sydney	25-11-43	1678 HCU
413710	F/S	BICKNELL Aubrey Griffith	15-10-43	27 OTU
411839	F/S	BIFFEN Jack Stanley	24-05-43	460 Sqn
1316618	Sgt	BIGGS Albert Henry	27-11-43	428 Sqn
413476	F/S	BIGGS Ernest Roy	18-08-43	103 Sqn
14228	F/S	BIRK Doric Phillip	15-06-43	460 Sqn
412334	F/O	BIRTLES Alfred John	28-08-43	78 Sqn
406557	Sgt	BISHOP Benjamin Harvey	11-03-43	158 Sqn
405437	P/O	BLACK Charles Noola	4-04-43	408 Sqn
409519	F/O	BLACK Gregory James	3-04-43	156 Sqn
422388	F/O	BLACKMORE Geoffrey Livingstone	16-12-43	576 Sqn
416114	P/O	BLIGHT Ambrose Edward	29-12-43	460 Sqn
405819	F/S	BOASE Peter Leonard	17-04-43	467 Sqn
408418	Sgt	BOCK Allan James Henry	22-07-43	27 OTU
409888	F/S	BOLGER Christopher Kevin	27-09-43	460 Sqn
414193	F/S	BOLGER Hugh Burke	12-07-43	467 Sqn
412099	F/S	BOND John Keith	18-01-43	12 Sqn
420334	F/S	BOOTH John Milton	3-12-43	576 Sqn
413518	F/S	BORTHWICK John Mayo	1-09-43	1662 HCU
406769	Sgt	BORRETT Arnold Harvey	19-02-43	15 Sqn
412101	F/S	BOYD Frank Lawrence	21-01-43	103 Sqn
426823	P/O	BOYD Harold William	28-12-43	20 OTU
410830	F/O	BOYD James Owen	2-12-43	460 Sqn
408244	F/S	BOYES Gordon Ediss	21-04-43	15 OTU
409500	F/S	BOYLE Daniel Patrick	15-05-43	30 OTU
411478	F/S	BRADFORD Michael Albert Edward	15-04-43	35 Sqn
412892	F/S	BRASSEL Terence Joseph	21-05-43	466 Sqn
420611	P/O	BRAWN Roy Arthur	3-11-43	76 Sqn
410646	F/S	BRETT Ronald Oswald Charles	12-07-43	207 Sqn
411281	F/S	BRIEN Henry Herbert	3-03-43	12 Sqn
411439	F/S	BRIGDEN Clifton Macleay	27-04-43	51 Sqn
403160	P/O	BRITTINGHAM Raymond Arthur	27-01-43	460 Sqn
409287	F/S	BROCK John Alexander	25-06-43	50 Sqn
401739	F/S	BRODIE Ian George	27-01-43	460 Sqn
421563	F/S	BROOK Philip Munro	1-09-43	15 Sqn
414460	F/S	BROOK Roy Edward	4-10-43	467 Sqn
407040	F/O	BROOKER Gordon Roy	24-11-43	139 Sqn
400450	W/O	BROOKS Charles Willie	7-07-43	15 OTU
405156	F/S	BROOKS Hiram George	4-01-43	460 Sqn
412054	F/S	BROWN Allan John James	2-12-43	460 Sqn
416018	P/O	BROWN Leo Frederick Joseph	24-06-43	156 Sqn
427113	F/S	BROWN Ronald	23-09-43	90 Sqn

412003	F/S	BROWN Roy	23-11-43	460 Sqn		418632	F/S	CONROY Desmond James	26-11-43	26 OTU
405997	P/O	BROWN Seymour Villiers	31-08-43	12 Sqn		426317	F/S	CONROY Reginald Matthew	18-11-43	622 Sqn
404849	Sgt	BROWNE James Arthur Gerald	31-01-43	49 Sqn		413829	F/S	CONWAY Norman James	4-09-43	460 Sqn
414914	F/S	BROWNE William Joseph	31-08-43	158 Sqn		406614	S/L	COOK DFC DFM Arthur Sydney	4-10-43	156 Sqn
405823	F/S	BROWNJOHN Hilton George	22-10-43	100 Sqn		403502	F/S	COOPER Eric Neil	30-03-43	460 Sqn
411748	F/O	BRYANT Robert Maxwell	11-06-43	156 Sqn		408628	P/O	COOPER John Albert Basil	26-07-43	103 Sqn
414195	P/O	BRYDE Geoffrey Nigel James	24-05-43	1654 HCU		411680	F/S	COPE George Robert	15-06-43	460 Sqn
422121	F/S	BRYDEN William Edward	31-08-43	158 Sqn		411124	Sgt	CORFE Dudley Anstruther	18-01-43	460 Sqn
405998	P/O	BUCHANAN James Thomas	28-07-43	467 Sqn		422138	F/S	CORKILL Charles William Maxwell	20-12-43	149 Sqn
425115	F/S	BUCHANAN Norman William	18-08-43	49 Sqn		405122	S/L	CORSER DFC MiD Edward Geoffrey Manson		
426524	F/S	BUCKBY Ernest Middleton	5-09-43	1661 HCU					2-12-43	460 Sqn
414196	F/S	BUCKERIDGE Clement Ralph	15-06-43	460 Sqn		410459	F/S	COWAN Charles Robert	26-07-43	466 Sqn
413924	F/S	BULL Henry Ellis	30-05-43	460 Sqn		416935	F/S	COX Dudley Vincent	22-09-43	460 Sqn
409503	F/S	BULLEN Noel Joseph	24-08-43	101 Sqn		409385	P/O	CRABTREE Edward Jeptha	22-09-43	9 Sqn
411440	W/O	BURCHER Reginald Maxwell	30-07-43	460 Sqn		405676	F/S	CRAMER Patrick Joseph	21-04-43	103 Sqn
413820	F/S	BURGE Walter Francis	18-11-43	431 Sqn		422536	F/S	CRAMP Roy	9-10-43	61 Sqn
414463	F/S	BURGUM William Arnold	24-08-43	158 Sqn		420155	F/S	CRANFIELD Astley Arthur	22-09-43	460 Sqn
417333	F/S	BURTON John Raymond	20-10-43	10 OTU		411113	F/O	CRAPP Errol Clifton	4-03-43	100 Sqn
411739	P/O	BURROWS William Gordon	18-01-43	12 Sqn		423657	Sgt	CRIBB Stanley Bridson	22-10-43	1657 HCU
408306	F/S	BUTTERWORTH John	16-12-43	7 Sqn		400969	F/S	CRIPPS Raymond Frank	9-01-43	12 Sqn
406992	F/S	BUXTON Alfred William	8-09-43	103 Sqn		412114	Sgt	CROSS William Norman	11-06-43	467 Sqn
416410	F/S	BYASS Reginald Anderson	3-04-43	156 Sqn		415021	F/S	CROUCH Douglas Henry	15-06-43	460 Sqn
409506	F/O	CAFFYN Murray Cameron	8-10-43	460 Sqn		414338	F/S	CUMMING Allen Royce	23-09-43	460 Sqn
416649	F/S	CALVESBERT John Frederick	8-06-43	26 OTU		408904	P/O	CUMMINGS Max Keiran	18-06-43	83 Sqn
415115	W/O	CAMPBELL Hugh	16-12-43	103 Sqn		402789	F/S	CURTIS DFC Desmond De Burgh	7-09-43	156 Sqn
420454	F/O	CAMPBELL Macquarie James	1-09-43	620 Sqn		412231	P/O	CURTIS John Franklin	3-09-43	1661 HCU
420335	F/S	CAMPBELL Robert Hugh	11-11-43	102 Sqn		401744	F/S	CURTIS Stanley Noel	30-03-43	166 Sqn
412479	F/S	CANDISH Eugene John	5-05-43	460 Sqn		415310	Sgt	CUTHBERTSON William Tait	31-03-43	14 OTU
412391	F/L	CARMICHAEL Reginald	4-09-43	467 Sqn		409668	F/S	DALDY Gordon Alfred Joffre	8-09-43	103 Sqn
414642	F/S	CARNE Roy Dempsey	16-05-43	466 Sqn		409669	F/S	DALLWITZ Raymond Ernest	4-10-43	467 Sqn
10169	Sgt	CARR John	21-01-43	101 Sqn		414339	P/O	DALZIEL James Samuel Kevin	4-09-43	101 Sqn
413167	P/O	CARRINGTON James Llewellyn	28-07-43	467 Sqn		403012	F/L	DAMPIER-CROSSLEY DFC Edward	11-08-43	619 Sqn
410304	F/O	CARTER Leonard Thomas	18-10-43	460 Sqn				[New Zealand]		
407963	W/O	CARTHEW Ewin Garth	4-09-43	460 Sqn		407965	Sgt	DANGERFIELD John Charles	21-01-43	207 Sqn
420141	Sgt	CASHION Patrick Leslie	14-06-43	27 OTU		413967	P/O	DARGIE Leo Malcolm	27-09-43	460 Sqn
409080	Sgt	CATRON William Alan	30-01-43	27 OTU		411096	F/S	DARKEN Raymond de Champfleur	21-01-43	207 Sqn
415377	F/S	CAVANAGH Leonard Ernest	23-06-43	158 Sqn		18071	F/O	DAVENPORT Frank Sydney	18-10-43	467 Sqn
426046	F/S	CHADWICK Thomas Patrick	24-09-43	57 Sqn		413357	F/S	DAVEY Allan John	1-09-43	199 Sqn
413712	F/S	CHALMERS Ivor Ramsay	9-10-43	431 Sqn		405678	F/O	DAVIE John Henry Clarence	26-07-43	214 Sqn
414764	F/S	CHAPMAN Arthur Edward	28-05-43	100 Sqn		417460	F/S	DAVIES George Bruce	22-10-43	1654 HCU
415117	P/O	CHAPMAN Cedric Arthur	13-07-43	467 Sqn		405966	F/S	DAVIS Beresford Milton Troy	24-05-43	460 Sqn
414992	F/S	CHAPMAN Jack Routledge	30-07-43	467 Sqn		412921	F/S	DAVIS Noel Michael	28-08-43	218 Sqn
415118	F/S	CHAPPELL John Arnold	31-08-43	102 Sqn		408278	F/S	DAVIS William Athur Mathias	30-05-43	218 Sqn
416322	F/S	CHARLICK David Harold Victor	30-03-43	460 Sqn		403913	F/S	DAY Edwin Atholwood	27-01-43	460 Sqn
411121	P/O	CHARLTON William Roy Kenneth	17-04-43	460 Sqn		408307	F/S	DEAN David Erskine Ellis	28-07-43	467 Sqn
408564	F/S	CHITTOCK Wesley Victor	27-04-43	51 Sqn		413550	Sgt	DEARING Lysle Herbert Hungerford	7-07-43	15 OTU
275328	F/S	CHIVERS Ernest Keele	23-05-43	57 Sqn		424741	Sgt	DEATH Ernest Norman	10-09-43	27 OTU
416324	F/S	CHRISTIE Robert Stanley	12-06-43	460 Sqn		415467	F/O	DEDMAN Harold George Day	16-12-43	460 Sqn
415119	P/O	CLARKE John Yorke	28-08-43	158 Sqn		402590	F/S	DELATORRE Melville George	3-03-43	207 Sqn
413362	F/S	CLARKE Kenneth Roy	5-07-43	10 OTU		409522	F/S	DELLAR Thomas George	12-06-43	30 OTU
408968	F/O	CLARKE Roy Leslie	1-09-43	61 Sqn		413178	F/O	DENNETT William James	15-06-43	460 Sqn
420337	F/S	CLEGG Roy Richard	15-09-43	1659 HCU		405175	P/O	DENNIS Ernest Arthur	26-07-43	50 Sqn
403687	F/O	CLEMENT George Bruce	7-09-43	156 Sqn		413552	P/O	DENYER Neil Howard	3-09-43	156 Sqn
424119	Sgt	CLIFFORD Ronald John	2-09-43	11 OTU		406641	F/L	DESMOND John Matthew	28-05-43	467 Sqn
416932	P/O	CLUCAS Frank Cottier	20-12-43	428 Sqn		410221	F/S	DEVERELL Eric Ernest	31-08-43	78 Sqn
414001	P/O	COCKREM Harry William George	27-09-43	10 Sqn		405300	F/S	DIMMOCK Thomas Frank	23-01-43	12 Sqn
401302	F/S	COLE Elliot Livesey	31-01-43	49 Sqn		411243	P/O	DODDS David Laing	3-09-43	156 Sqn
408329	F/S	COLE Ray Osmond	2-12-43	460 Sqn		417348	F/O	DODSON Alfred Shurrock	28-08-43	467 Sqn
409462	F/O	COLE Stuart Vivian	27-09-43	460 Sqn		400698	F/S	DOGSHUN John Henry	9-04-43	460 Sqn
409665	P/O	COLEMAN Alan Joseph	4-12-43	97 Sqn		419461	F/S	DOHERTY Nicholas	11-12-43	26 OTU
401184	W/O	COLLENS William Wallace	4-04-43	464 Sqn		416552	F/O	DOLLAR Ralph Edmund	20-04-43	460 Sqn
413826	F/S	COLLESS Gordon Sydney	30-06-43	466 Sqn		420614	F/S	DONOHOE James Blackman	12-06-43	467 Sqn
414446	P/O	COLLIER Albert Thomas Stanley	2-12-43	550 Sqn		425493	F/S	DOONAN Francis William	21-12-43	78 Sqn
404749	F/S	COLLINS James Geoffrey	23-08-43	460 Sqn		405842	F/S	DOUDS Douglas	15-06-43	460 Sqn
406772	F/S	COLLINS John Cyril	3-09-43	156 Sqn		420924	Sgt	DOUGLAS John Angus	12-05-43	29 OTU
413532	F/S	COLLIS Robert Humphrey	7-07-43	21 OTU		418088	F/S	DOW John Charles De Burgh	23-10-43	207 Sqn
411084	Sgt	CONLON John Vincent	23-01-43	460 Sqn		426066	Sgt	DOWIE Nevill William	3-11-43	466 Sqn
420152	F/S	CONROY Bernard Keith	30-06-43	466 Sqn		409392	P/O	DRIPPS Donald Campbell	24-12-43	550 Sqn

425622	F/S	DUANE Gregory Terence	23-10-43	1657 HCU	425009	F/S	FOWLER Gordon Charles	23-09-43	9 Sqn
413078	P/O	DUFF Gordon Alexander	21-09-43	57 Sqn	416646	P/O	FOWLER James Walter	26-11-43	463 Sqn
413838	P/O	DUFFY Rodney Ernest	23-09-43	218 Sqn	427313	F/S	FOXCROFT Kenneth Edgar	17-12-43	97 Sqn
411217	W/O	DUGAN John Henry	15-08-43	7 Sqn	409579	F/S	FRANCIS John Edmund	4-10-43	467 Sqn
14855	Sgt	DUNKIN Frank	9-04-43	1661 HCU	415130	F/S	FRANKISH Robert Walter Wetherall	18-09-43	1658 HCU
420164	F/S	DUNLOP Edward Anzac	3-11-43	434 Sqn	416561	F/S	FRASER Albert Thomas	10-07-43	102 Sqn
413555	F/S	DUNN Douglas Ashton	30-06-43	466 Sqn	419177	Sgt	FRASER James Munro Mearns	26-09-43	14 OTU
415315	F/S	DUNN Norman Neville	18-09-43	17 OTU	413756	F/S	FRASER Peter Aird	30-07-43	78 Sqn
411010	F/S	DUNN Phillip Wesley	30-03-43	460 Sqn	423710	Sgt	FRAZER Jack Edward	28-09-43	16 OTU
416149	F/S	DURDIN Garnet Walter	4-03-43	100 Sqn	420653	F/S	FRAZER Lancelott James	3-07-43	460 Sqn
412411	Sgt	DYCE Kenneth Douglas	24-05-43	460 Sqn	408585	P/O	FRAZER Norman Roscoe	31-08-43	12 Sqn
414129	P/O	EBELING Frederick Clive	6-09-43	78 Sqn	413561	P/O	FREEMAN Maurice Joseph	23-11-43	460 Sqn
409034	F/S	EBBOTT Edwin Cyril	17-04-43	460 Sqn	425147	F/S	FRENCH Gordon Albert	11-08-43	106 Sqn
414664	Sgt	ECCLES John Stoppard [United Kingdom]	11-01-43	27 OTU	415518	F/S	FRENCH Keeble Charles	28-08-43	207 Sqn
					426572	F/S	FRIZZELL Cecil Roland	5-12-43	467 Sqn
413180	P/O	EDIS Herbert George	1-09-43	101 Sqn	415079	P/O	FUHRMANN DFM Herbert Leonard	30-07-43	460 Sqn
411685	F/S	EDMONDS Neville John	2-12-43	156 Sqn	406975	F/S	FULFORD Dudley Francis	4-04-43	464 Sqn
408644	W/O	EDMONDS Roy Marmaduke	18-10-43	7 Sqn	417632	F/S	FULLER Kenneth Rosslyn	26-11-43	61 Sqn
414919	Sgt	EDMONDS William Edward	2-10-43	460 Sqn	411890	Sgt	FULTON Edgar Claude	3-03-43	460 Sqn
411885	P/O	EDWARDS Clifford	3-07-43	460 Sqn	407349	F/S	FUSS Newton Hasalby	31-08-43	466 Sqn
24574		EDWARDS Colin Howard	2-12-43	460 Sqn	410595	F/S	GALLAGHER Anthony Joseph	7-11-43	1663 HCU
413748	F/S	EDWARDS Patrick John	20-12-43	466 Sqn	403464	Sgt	GALLAGHER Francis Alexander Kevin		
415126	F/S	EGAN John Joseph	24-05-43	214 Sqn				21-01-43	207 Sqn
415024	F/S	ELIOT Ivan Aubrey	31-08-43	1651 HCU	425149	F/S	GALLIGAN Edwin Richard	1-09-43	623 Sqn
412501	P/O	ELLIOTT Stanley Brown	26-06-43	103 Sqn	425298	F/S	GALLIGAN Patrick James	29-06-43	44 Sqn
415076	F/S	ELLIS Thomas Douglas	23-09-43	218 Sqn	409683	F/S	GALT Kenneth Rae	22-09-43	460 Sqn
411686	F/S	ELSLEY Henry Cecil	24-08-43	199 Sqn	413976	F/O	GARBUTT Milton Edwin	3-10-43	467 Sqn
420551	F/S	ELSTUB Thomas Clifford	22-10-43	1657 HCU	403806	F/S	GARVEN Arthur Anderson	8-04-43	460 Sqn
410593	F/O	EMERY William Edward	15-06-43	460 Sqn	415132	F/S	GATES Robert Ingersole	29-06-43	467 Sqn
410330	F/S	EMMERSON Ronald Harry	16-12-43	75 Sqn	401939	P/O	GEDDES Roy Hamilton	29-06-43	10 Sqn
413843	P/O	ENGLISH DFC James Herbert John	2-12-43	460 Sqn	412129	F/S	GEE Frank Ernest	31-08-43	199 Sqn
409398	F/S	EVANS David Geoffrey	26-07-43	90 Sqn	421899	F/S	GEHRIG Roy Lawrence	23-09-43	218 Sqn
420651	F/S	FAIRBAIRN George Stuart	4-09-43	101 Sqn	426871	Sgt	GEHRMANN Kenneth Joseph	20-10-43	12 OTU
414011	P/O	FAIRLIE Kenneth	24-08-43	97 Sqn	415245	F/S	GIBBONS Arthur Leonard	28-07-43	467 Sqn
402233	W/O	FARLAM Alan Kenneth	14-08-43	19 OTU	402922	P/O	GIBBS William Lionel	13-05-43	83 Sqn
416843	P/O	FARMER Walter Theodore	23-09-43	467 Sqn	426082	F/S	GIBNEY James Crompton	6-09-43	78 Sqn
422157	F/S	FEAKES Rex	14-07-43	466 Sqn	420465	F/S	GIBSON James Geoffrey	18-11-43	460 Sqn
404716	P/O	FERGUSON Noel	8-04-43	156 Sqn	402858	P/O	GIBSON Trevor Leslie	18-01-43	9 Sqn
416844	P/O	FERME Harold	27-09-43	78 Sqn	407712	F/O	GIRRBACH Karl	4-04-43	156 Sqn
420652	F/S	FERNANCE Darcy James	10-09-43	27 OTU	402334	F/L	GILES DFC Clifford Argo	8-03-43	61 Sqn
12174	F/S	FETTELL Mervyn Byron	16-06-43	27 OTU	414483	F/S	GILKESON Fenwick Moseley	16-08-43	21 OTU
424169	Sgt	FIETZ Clive Henry Charles	7-08-43	26 OTU	409042	F/S	GILLAN Frank Bruce	1-05-43	12 Sqn
403864	P/O	FINCH Colin Geoffrey	6-11-43	27 OTU	415135	F/S	GLIDDON Arthur William Howard	30-07-43	460 Sqn
406674	F/S	FINCH Edward Henry	5-05-43	149 Sqn	420875	F/S	GLOVER Kenneth Robert Ralph	24-12-43	463 Sqn
412941	F/S	FINDLEY John Ellis	16-12-43	1662 HCU	418387	F/S	GODFREY Lloyd William Lewis	3-12-43	576 Sqn
408569	W/O	FINLAYSON DFM Alexander Douglas	31-08-43	199 Sqn	413370	F/O	GODLEY Colin Cortland	3-08-43	61 Sqn
408907	F/S	FINLAYSON Donald Scott	15-06-43	460 Sqn	401845	F/O	GODWIN DFC Gerald Patrick	23-10-43	467 Sqn
413482	F/S	FINNANE Brian	21-04-43	460 Sqn	5015	P/O	GOLDSMITH Peter Mylrea	18-08-43	619 Sqn
401933	F/O	FISHER Russel Gardiner	24-08-43	199 Sqn	285324	F/O	GOOD Melville Ross	28-08-43	467 Sqn
422640	F/S	FITZGERALDN Kenneth George	2-09-43	11 OTU	417068	F/S	GOOD Peter Raymond	1-09-43	1662 HCU
414548	Sgt	FITZGERALD Patrick John	12-03-43	20 OTU	401209	W/O	GOODING Ronald	4-04-43	460 Sqn
414014	F/S	FITZGERALD William Hugh	1-09-43	460 Sqn	409404	F/S	GORDON Andrew	13-06-43	460 Sqn
414667	F/S	FITZNER Leonard Charles	24-08-43	467 Sqn	417069	F/S	GORDON Colin Ross	31-08-43	100 Sqn
413079	F/O	FLASHMAN Alfred Charles Ronald	15-06-43	460 Sqn	409472	F/O	GORDON Hugh Lyons	15-06-43	460 Sqn
425293	F/S	FLEISCHFRESSER Colin Albert	4-09-43	7 Sqn	402985	P/O	GOSPER DFC Lee Gordon	8-03-43	7 Sqn
413113	F/L	FLEMING Raymond Charles	9-07-43	101 Sqn	404582	F/S	GRACE James Pearce Massey	8-04-43	156 Sqn
405547	F/S	FLETCHER Eric John Benjamin	4-01-43	460 Sqn	411312	Sgt	GRAHAM Ross Clive	3-03-43	460 Sqn
414782	F/S	FLETCHER Kenneth Edwin	12-06-43	466 Sqn	403169	F/S	GRAINGER Athol Richard	15-02-43	207 Sqn
403691	F/S	FLETT Roderick Henry	8-04-43	156 Sqn	426437	F/S	GRANT David Charles	20-12-43	10 Sqn
414549	F/S	FLITCROFT Noel Oliver Boyd	17-06-43	460 Sqn	413307	F/S	GRANT Donald Ross	15-06-43	460 Sqn
403045	W/O	FOGDEN Edmund Daniel	12-08-43	466 Sqn	420661	F/S	GRANT John Alexander	28-05-43	460 Sqn
419171	F/S	FORBES John Ronald	19-11-43	15 OTU	410483	F/O	GRANT Joseph Peter	29-12-43	460 Sqn
401498	F/S	FORBES William Dennis Keith	20-03-43	27 OTU	414931	F/S	GRANT Sinclair August	1-09-43	1662 HCU
414132	F/L	FORD Patrick Raymond	12-06-43	12 Sqn	413373	F/S	GRAY George Henderson	14-06-43	27 OTU
401688	F/S	FORREST James Lowrie	9-04-43	460 Sqn	405443	F/S	GRAY Herbert Peace	4-01-43	90 Sqn
416558	F/O	FORRESTER Sidney Milton	4-09-43	460 Sqn	406804	F/S	GREEN Bryant Francis Kingdom	27-04-43	51 Sqn
414293	F/S	FORSYTH Francis Smith	25-07-43	460 Sqn	408829	F/S	GREEN Fletcher William Randall	12-06-43	466 Sqn
409587	F/S	FORSYTH Thomas Kevin	20-10-43	139 Sqn	415732	F/S	GREENWELL Francis William	25-11-43	28 OTU

Number	Rank	Name	Date	Unit
401503	Sgt	GREGORY Eric Otho	30-06-43	466 Sqn
408348	F/S	GREGORY Raymond Trevor	4-09-43	44 Sqn
403735	F/L	GRENFELL Kenneth Hugh	30-03-43	460 Sqn
403187	F/S	GREY Llewellyn	31-01-43	49 Sqn
413577	P/O	GRIBBLE Edward Henry	16-12-43	466 Sqn
410327	F/S	GRIEVE Ronald McLennan	14-06-43	27 OTU
416761	F/S	GRIFFITH Hugh Phillip	16-06-43	12 OTU
30185	Sgt	GRIFFITHS Daniel Brooke	28-04-43	19 OTU
425154	F/S	GROB Nicholas Charles	9-12-43	77 Sqn
425301	F/S	GUNDERS Ernest Harold	15-08-43	61 Sqn
413856	F/S	GUNNING William Alfred	14-07-43	466 Sqn
417364	F/S	GUY William Trevor	3-10-43	90 Sqn
401236	P/O	GYLES Nathaniel Robert	28-04-43	61 Sqn
413989	F/O	HADLEY George Arthur	23-09-43	460 Sqn
404704	P/O	HADLEY DFC Lloyd Henry Moorehead	13-06-43	460 Sqn
414348	F/S	HALLAM Raymond Henry	28-08-43	467 Sqn
414558	F/S	HALLAS John William	28-09-43	434 Sqn
400276	F/O	HALLETT DFC Peter Thomas Leeds	5-11-43	1655 MTU
414349	F/S	HALSTEAD William Kevin	16-12-43	460 Sqn
400255	F/S	HAMMOND Louis James	27-01-43	51 Sqn
409046	F/S	HAMOOD Frank Norman	12-08-43	466 Sqn
408578	F/S	HAMPTON Gordon Vivian	30-03-43	460 Sqn
414560	F/S	HANSEN James Foster	7-07-43	15 OTU
22001		HANSEN Ronald Hans	22-09-43	460 Sqn
421595	F/S	HARBER Harley Cecil	24-08-43	158 Sqn
420941	Sgt	HARDAKER Francis Ira	14-08-43	21 OTU
417072	F/S	HARDY Maxwell Henry	23-11-43	44 Sqn
408833	F/S	HARLEM Athol Asher	31-08-43	199 Sqn
421975	F/S	HARPER John	19-11-43	10 Sqn
415379	F/S	HARPER Wilfred	26-07-43	466 Sqn
413862	P/O	HARRIS Alan Grant	3-11-43	466 Sqn
417837	F/S	HARRIS Albert Alfred	16-12-43	576 Sqn
410861	F/O	HARRIS Edwin Arthur	22-10-43	158 Sqn
404606	W/O	HARRIS George Albert	22-10-43	1657 HCU
414024	P/O	HARRIS Hector William	26-11-43	61 Sqn
408163	Sgt	HARRIS Kennington John Hythe	4-01-43	460 Sqn
412954	P/O	HARRIS Lloyd George	11-08-43	106 Sqn
413993	F/S	HARRISON Ernest	11-11-43	161 Sqn
416669	F/O	HARRISON Leonard Eric	22-06-43	460 Sqn
400392	W/O	HARRISON-OWEN Jack	26-07-43	466 Sqn
409698	F/S	HART Kevin Leslie	22-09-43	12 OTU
416571	F/O	HARVEY Alain Morison	24-05-43	35 Sqn
412957	F/S	HARVEY Bruce Harold	21-04-43	460 Sqn
414025	F/L	HARVEY George Henry	29-12-43	61 Sqn
415789	F/S	HASKINS Ronald Henry	16-08-43	57 Sqn
417482	F/S	HASTINGS Ian Angus	23-11-43	7 Sqn
409542	F/S	HATFIELD Ronald Arthur	14-06-43	27 OTU
407287	F/O	HAWKINS Frank Bryce	2-03-43	207 Sqn
412958	P/O	HAY John Edwin	9-10-43	106 Sqn
411906	F/S	HAYES John Henry Terence	24-05-43	101 Sqn
415082	P/O	HAYMES Leslie Jack	1-09-43	460 Sqn
412439	F/S	HAYTER Norman Wood	17-08-43	138 Sqn
19907	F/S	HAZELDENE Jack Archer	7-10-43	21 OTU
417483	F/O	HEADING Bronson Donald	21-12-43	78 Sqn
414027	F/S	HEAP Arthur William	24-12-43	463 Sqn
415531	F/S	HEASON Leonard William	18-11-43	90 Sqn
408309	F/S	HEATH Jack	12-06-43	460 Sqn
405310	F/S	HEATLEY Ian Victor	3-03-43	12 Sqn
421272	F/S	HEBBLEWHITE Geoffrey Alfred	23-12-43	15 OTU
412442	P/O	HECKENDORF John Llewelyn	20-12-43	50 Sqn
409544	F/O	HEFFERNAN Robert Jarvis	22-06-43	460 Sqn
403586	P/O	HEINRICH Esmond Peter	17-01-43	50 Sqn
413765	F/O	HEINS Alfred Ronald	16-03-43	27 OTU
412443	F/S	HELLYER Colin Cecil Oliver	20-08-43	139 Sqn
400612	F/S	HEMING Keith Ronald	5-03-43	218 Sqn
420013	F/S	HENDERSON Robert Malcolm	23-11-43	460 Sqn
404904	F/S	HENDERSON William Douglas	17-01-43	1654 HCU
415144	F/S	HENNESSY James [Eire]	23-06-43	30 OTU
425158	Sgt	HENRY Hugh Patrick	27-08-43	1663 HCU
428007	F/S	HERBERT James Joseph	6-11-43	27 OTU
411783	F/O	HERRING Guy Bamford	20-04-43	100 Sqn
414137	P/O	HEWERDINE James Joseph	12-07-43	156 Sqn
414237	F/S	HEWITT Kenneth Hemsley	15-04-43	27 OTU
400433	W/O	HICKLING DFC William Liness Charles	20-12-43	156 Sqn
32782	F/S	HIGHLAND William Thomas Emmerick	3-10-43	15 Sqn
405586	F/S	HILEY Alan Ernest	11-02-43	101 Sqn
414238	F/S	HILL Eric Allan	4-09-43	15 Sqn
416674	F/S	HILL Frederick Lewis Ian	26-06-43	101 Sqn
420566	F/S	HILLIER Henry Outred	30-07-43	467 Sqn
412139	F/S	HILTON Alan	5-05-43	460 Sqn
415982	F/S	HINES Albert Henry	22-10-43	1657 HCU
414239	P/O	HINTON Leonard John	18-10-43	103 Sqn
411910	P/O	HOCKING James Douglas	1-09-43	460 Sqn
413999	Sgt	HODSON Raymond Knight	3-02-43	27 OTU
414798	P/O	HOFFMAN Kevin Herbert	28-07-43	467 Sqn
422559	F/S	HOGAN Austin John	19-08-43	12 OTU
413866	F/S	HOGAN Peter John	12-06-43	460 Sqn
416574	F/S	HOGBEN Reginald Stanley	20-04-43	460 Sqn
406977	P/O	HOLDEN Edmund Geoffrey	14-06-43	27 OTU
414564	F/S	HOLLINGWORTH Robert Mead	4-12-43	77 Sqn
414866	P/O	HOLMES Ian Mervyn Patterson	7-09-43	10 Sqn
414351	F/S	HOLMES Ross Primrose	28-07-43	467 Sqn
403268	F/O	HOOD DFM Robert Thomas	3-09-43	156 Sqn
420753	F/S	HOOKER Allan	1-09-43	15 Sqn
402461	P/O	HORNE DFM Albert Elliott	14-05-43	408 Sqn
400470	F/O	HORNE DFC Urquhart Douglas Haig	13-06-43	460 Sqn
409306	F/S	HORNER Edward Thomas	21-05-43	466 Sqn
414034	F/L	HORNIBROOK Harold Kevin	24-08-43	158 Sqn
414352	F/S	HORWOOD John Harold	12-06-43	460 Sqn
425940	Sgt	HOSKIN Richard Chessel Lister	20-12-43	158 Sqn
425014	F/S	HOSKINGS Edward	16-12-43	1662 HCU
413386	F/S	HOTCHKIS George Stewart	27-09-43	149 Sqn
420469	F/S	HOUGHTON Douglas Conway	1-09-43	214 Sqn
405737	Sgt	HOWES Kevin Vincent	3-02-43	27 OTU
414938	F/S	HOWIE Charles Gordon	16-12-43	460 Sqn
403742	P/O	HUDSON Richard Julian	24-06-43	156 Sqn
35488	F/S	HUGGARD John Stephen	29-04-43	12 Sqn
417487	F/S	HUGHES Gordon Henry	23-09-43	90 Sqn
409971	P/O	HUGHES Peter Francis	19-11-43	622 Sqn
413601	P/O	HUNT Walter James	28-09-43	622 Sqn
409411	P/O	HURLE William Grover	24-08-43	467 Sqn
411327	P/O	HUTCHINSON Francis Ebsworth	4-01-43	460 Sqn
21442	P/O	INGLIS Robert Ernest	2-12-43	156 Sqn
410236	F/S	INGRAM Lester Neil	22-04-43	10 OTU
410338	F/S	INNES Frank Faulks	3-08-43	115 Sqn
412010	P/O	IRELAND Stanley James	29-12-43	460 Sqn
422031	F/S	IRVIN George Henry	29-12-43	460 Sqn
409550	F/S	ISAACS Gerald Henry	7-07-43	103 Sqn
400989	F/O	JACKSON DFM Frederick Roy	22-10-43	109 Sqn
416679	F/S	JACKSON Sydney Edward	4-10-43	467 Sqn
416680	F/S	JAEKEL Desmond Nelson	5-05-43	460 Sqn
408656	F/S	JAMES Kenneth	21-04-43	460 Sqn
414691	F/S	JARVIS William Louis	23-09-43	75 Sqn
403745	F/O	JAY Brinley Pearce	17-04-43	158 Sqn
415149	P/O	JEFFREYS John Alan	3-11-43	61 Sqn
420836	F/S	JENNINGS Murray Noel	3-12-43	576 Sqn
402507	F/O	JOHNSON Alan James	30-07-43	460 Sqn
15467	P/O	JOHNSON Leslie Joseph	2-12-43	156 Sqn
412967	F/S	JOHNSON Leslie Ronald	9-07-43	106 Sqn
404684	F/S	JOHNSTON Alexander Clive	13-05-43	156 Sqn
409125	F/O	JOHNSTON Allan Stewart	7-11-43	1663 HCU
425166	P/O	JOHNSTON Stanley Maxwell	2-09-43	11 OTU
425322	F/S	JOHNSTON William Whitelaw	3-11-43	466 Sqn

413775	F/S	JONES Howell Idris	9-11-43	90 Sqn		412552	P/O	LLOYD DFM Frank Leathley Robinson	2-10-43	460 Sqn
417959	F/S	JONES Maurice William	3-12-43	576 Sqn		401508	Sgt	LLOYD Hugh Herbert	1-02-43	1661 HCU
402508	W/O	JONES Pax Lloyd Evan	30-07-43	460 Sqn		412553	F/S	LOCKREY Ronald John	22-06-43	460 Sqn
411699	F/S	JONES Trevor John	1-09-43	460 Sqn		412160	F/L	LODER DFC George Bruce	20-12-43	156 Sqn
406621	P/O	JONES Trevor Tudor	6-11-43	27 OTU		405918	F/O	LOGAN Clifford Charles Pownall	23-09-43	75 Sqn
400415	F/O	JOSEPH Graham Harris	17-06-43	467 Sqn		22643	F/S	LOGUE Stanley Ernest	18-01-43	1656 HCU
420816	F/S	JOYCE Leslie	19-11-43	622 Sqn		413396	P/O	LONG Arthur	23-09-43	467 Sqn
409716	F/S	KAN Alexander Elias	2-12-43	460 Sqn		413622	F/S	LONGMORE Kenneth William	24-08-43	90 Sqn
413390	F/S	KAY Thomas Leslie Hobson	16-12-43	103 Sqn		403273	F/S	LONSDALE Ronald Thomas	4-01-43	460 Sqn
415995	F/S	KEALY John William	3-10-43	90 Sqn		38780	F/S	LOUTHEAN Donald	23-11-43	460 Sqn
410498	F/S	KEARNEY Augustine Michael	18-11-43	622 Sqn		413624	F/S	LOVELLE-DRAPER Adrian Mervyn	19-08-43	12 OTU
400804	F/L	KEARNS John Howard	26-01-43	460 Sqn		400559	F/O	LOWRY Samuel Keith	3-09-43	1661 HCU
15302	Sgt	KEAY Peter John	16-04-43	61 Sqn		414710	F/S	LOXTON Alan Frederick	28-08-43	467 Sqn
413208	F/S	KEEFFE Norbert Clement	21-04-43	12 Sqn		410504	P/O	LUCAS Stephen John	3-11-43	466 Sqn
267504	S/L	KELAHER Carl Richard	4-09-43	460 Sqn		409560	F/S	LUCY Harry Kenloch	22-09-43	460 Sqn
425314	F/S	KELLY Brian Arthur	1-09-43	158 Sqn		6756	Sgt	LUKER Henry Whitfield	18-06-43	83 Sqn
404789	F/O	KENNEDY DFC Frederick Robert Anthony				413779	F/S	LUMSDEN Oswald John	23-09-43	467 Sqn
			16-09-43	156 Sqn		412986	F/S	LUNDIE David Crawford Paterson	13-06-43	460 Sqn
404296	W/O	KENT DFC Leslie Arnold	2-12-43	460 Sqn		424546	F/O	LUTHER Clive Prosdocimi	16-12-43	7 Sqn
413610	F/S	KERLIN Bernard	28-08-43	467 Sqn		406532	F/L	LUTZ DFC Alan Montgomery	7-09-43	156 Sqn
401646	F/S	KERR Donald	3-03-43	12 Sqn		408909	F/S	LYNCH Geoffrey Augustine	28-08-43	207 Sqn
414697	F/S	KERR Ernest James	28-05-43	460 Sqn		426230	F/S	LYNCH John	31-08-43	218 Sqn
409144	F/S	KERR Robert Albert	26-05-43	214 Sqn		406458	F/O	MacDONALD Robert Haynes 'Ronnie'		
410674	F/S	KIFT Robert Stanley	22-10-43	35 Sqn					23-11-43	156 Sqn
413210	Sgt	KILLEEN Kenneth Barton	30-01-43	27 OTU		405593	P/O	MACDONALD Donald Ian	9-04-43	460 Sqn
411335	F/S	KING Edwin Robert	17-04-43	460 Sqn		409162	F/S	MACDONALD Leonard Howell	14-06-43	27 OTU
423760	F/S	KING Bede James Veitch	16-12-43	49 Sqn		410357	F/S	MACFARLANE Murray Armstrong	27-11-43	626 Sqn
409146	F/S	KING Robert Samuel	20-04-43	460 Sqn		403146	P/O	MACKENZIE Evan Seaforth	13-05-43	156 Sqn
410675	F/S	KING Sidney James	10-07-43	50 Sqn		405005	P/O	MACKENZIE Ian Cumming	15-04-43	408 Sqn
410347	F/S	KITCHEN Stanley Charles	22-10-43	57 Sqn		411469	F/S	MACKENZIE Peter Murchison	20-04-43	460 Sqn
403519	Sgt	KNIGHT Alan	8-02-43	44 Sqn		414810	F/S	MACKIE Clarence Desmond	30-07-43	100 Sqn
401449	F/L	KNIGHT DSO MiD Leslie Gordon	16-09-43	617 Sqn		416875	F/S	MACPHERSON Donald Malcolm	18-08-43	419 Sqn
30159	F/S	KNIGHTS Walter William Nelson	27-11-43	619 Sqn		409844	F/S	MAHER John Martin	12-07-43	467 Sqn
403348	F/O	KNIGHT-BROWN Noel Henry	26-10-43	1481 Flt		405921	F/O	MAHONEY Edward Alan	21-04-43	460 Sqn
9431	Sgt	KNILANDS Bruce	17-04-43	460 Sqn		416223	F/S	MAHONEY Kevin Eugene	13-05-43	467 Sqn
22170	W/O	KNOX DFC Cyril William	20-12-43	156 Sqn		409723	F/S	MALCOLM John Douglas	18-11-43	460 Sqn
401699	F/S	KRAEMER John Robert	24-08-43	97 Sqn		410606	F/S	MANNING Walter Frederick James	18-11-43	460 Sqn
34017	F/S	KROHN Henry John	22-06-43	35 Sqn		405131	P/O	MANT Graeme Smyth	11-03-43	467 Sqn
406693	F/S	LAING Edward Vivian	21-01-43	103 Sqn		400677	F/S	MARFELL Archibald John	3-03-43	12 Sqn
421737	F/S	LAKE Donald Carmichael	18-10-43	460 Sqn		413315	F/S	MARONEY Robert William	12-06-43	466 Sqn
412527	F/S	LAMOND Alexander Campbell	16-04-43	1657 HCU		420697	F/S	MARRIAGE Stanley Joseph	16-06-43	460 Sqn
413617	F/S	LANCASTER Eric Edward	7-04-43	166 Sqn		414359	F/S	MARSH John	23-08-43	460 Sqn
408770	F/S	LANCASTER Ernest Lee	17-04-43	51 Sqn		405260	Sgt	MARTIN Alfred Henry	19-02-43	12 OTU
417496	F/S	LANGLEY Keith Albert	4-10-43	620 Sqn		416876	F/S	MARTIN Lewis William	1-09-43	1662 HCU
412543	Sgt	LATHAM Francis Graham	5-05-43	466 Sqn		417096	P/O	MARTIN Virgil Austin	26-11-43	61 Sqn
8686	F/S	LAWSON John William	16-05-43	466 Sqn		404987	F/S	MASON Neville Ray	13-05-43	156 Sqn
408724	F/S	LAY Kenneth Laurence William	11-06-43	156 Sqn		404975	F/S	MASON Norman Talbot	26-01-43	460 Sqn
426353	F/S	LA FRENTZ Sylvester Stuart Lyndhurst				403396	P/O	MATCHETT William Mervyn James	27-01-43	460 Sqn
			6-11-43	27 OTU		413221	P/O	MATHERS CGM Francis Edwin	6-09-43	77 Sqn
411919	F/S	LEAN Leonard Wentworth	9-04-43	1661 HCU		413628	F/S	MATHESON Ross Henley	19-11-43	15 OTU
421602	Sgt	LEE Jack Stuart	14-06-43	27 OTU		412465	P/O	MATTHEWS Frederick George	13-08-43	214 Sqn
403363	P/O	LEE John Gordon	4-04-43	460 Sqn		408859	F/S	MATTHEWS Frederick James	4-08-43	27 OTU
400592	F/L	LEEK Willoiam Douglas	11-01-43	12 Sqn		14444	Sgt	MATTHEWS Stanley James	27-01-43	460 Sqn
409060	F/O	LEITCH DFC James Westwood	20-10-43	7 Sqn		412166	Sgt	MATTHEWS William Roy	27-02-43	15 Sqn
425172	F/S	LESEBERG Ernest	11-12-43	16 OTU		402531	W/O	MATTRESS Charles Alfred	26-06-43	166 Sqn
412458	F/S	LEWIS Alfred Edward	28-04-43	75 Sqn		408917	P/O	McALPINE John Gilbert	26-11-43	61 Sqn
416587	F/S	LEWIS Robert Driscoll	7-02-43	30 OTU		409478	F/S	McBEAN Ronald Charles	30-07-43	467 Sqn
400811	F/O	LEY Trevor Arthur	15-05-43	27 OTU		401388	F/S	McCARTHY John Herbert	14-02-43	50 Sqn
419319	F/S	LE GRAND Anthony Murray	20-12-43	466 Sqn		410712	P/O	McCOLL Kenneth Septimus	4-04-43	408 Sqn
9027	P/O	LIERSCH Rex Vinitius	28-09-43	101 Sqn		410251	P/O	McCORMACK William Thomas	5-05-43	21 OTU
408725	F/S	LIMBRICK Frederick William George	9-04-43	106 Sqn		408661	P/O	McCORMICK George William	27-02-43	105 Sqn
411109	Sgt	LINDSAY David John	18-01-43	1656 HCU		403144	P/O	McCRAE Frederick Charles	12-12-43	27 OTU
409874	P/O	LINDSEY Angus Macdonald	18-11-43	10 Sqn		422033	F/S	McCUDDEN Reginald Thomas	23-09-43	57 Sqn
413621	P/O	LINE Murray Alfred	11-11-43	161 Sqn		403754	F/O	McCULLAGH Stephen Falcon Scott	30-03-43	460 Sqn
410615	F/S	LINTON Norman Royce	22-07-43	27 OTU		410698	F/O	McCULLOCH Hugh John	28-08-43	207 Sqn
425175	F/S	LIST Stephen McCarthy	3-11-43	49 Sqn		420978	Sgt	McDONAGH John Henry William	12-03-43	20 OTU
420762	F/S	LITTLE Leslie Thomas	16-06-43	460 Sqn		418456	F/S	McDONALD Alan Harvey	22-09-43	158 Sqn
421540	F/S	LIVINGSTONE David	4-09-43	57 Sqn		403069	P/O	McDONALD Arthur Lennox	12-03-43	106 Sqn

408737	Sgt	McDONALD Ian Ross	11-01-43	27 OTU		421436	F/S	MORRISON D'Arcy Edward	23-09-43	460 Sqn
418760	Sgt	McDONALD William Harold	30-08-43	30 OTU		22395	F/S	MORRISON Kenneth William	10-07-43	77 Sqn
414255	F/S	McDONNELL Leslie Maxwell	17-06-43	460 Sqn		423162	F/S	MORRISON William Hugh [New Zealand]	24-09-43	199 Sqn
421664	F/S	McDOWELL Harold Russell	17-12-43	12 Sqn						
403200	F/O	McEGAN Eugene Francis	22-11-43	97 Sqn		409727	F/S	MORTON Oswald Percy	21-05-43	466 Sqn
412633	F/S	McGLINCHY Francis	20-04-43	460 Sqn		407847	F/O	MOYLE Ronald Albert	31-01-43	97 Sqn
415268	F/S	McGRATH Thomas William Newport	28-08-43	97 Sqn		407391	F/S	MOYNAGH Reginald Albert	16-12-43	460 Sqn
420703	P/O	McINTYRE Frederick Goodwin	24-08-43	467 Sqn		409175	F/S	MUIR Bruce Montague	21-04-43	460 Sqn
414154	F/O	McINTYRE Norman Gregor	16-12-43	97 Sqn		26117	Sgt	MULLER Harold Frederick	18-01-43	1656 HCU
414721	F/O	McINTYRE Ronald Keith	29-12-43	460 Sqn		411595	P/O	MULLINGER Robert Bruce	18-01-43	12 Sqn
412636	P/O	McIVER DFC Kenneth Archibald	3-10-43	467 Sqn		410846	F/S	MUNTZ Joseph William	23-11-43	460 Sqn
400328	F/O	McKECHNIE Douglas Alexander	6-11-43	27 OTU		401457	F/S	MURPHY Edward Francis	3-03-43	460 Sqn
413645	F/S	McKEE John Irvine	2-12-43	460 Sqn		425337	F/S	MURPHY John Henry	16-12-43	166 Sqn
416270	W/O	McKENNY Lancelot Loxton	15-08-43	467 Sqn		411226	W/O	MURRAY Hugh George	22-10-43	199 Sqn
415087	F/L	McKENZIE Frederick Charles	26-06-43	90 Sqn		423208	F/S	MURRAY John Ambrose McCormack	19-11-43	15 OTU
407530	P/O	McKIGGAN Malcolm Eric	6-11-43	27 OTU		411043	F/L	MYERS Bernard Francis	21-04-43	100 Sqn
420353	F/S	McLACHLAN James Barber	31-08-43	466 Sqn		416601	F/S	NAFFIN Robert Clarence	24-08-43	101 Sqn
417092	F/S	McLAREN Clarence Ray	2-12-43	630 Sqn		415174	F/S	NAILE Leslie Jack	26-06-43	100 Sqn
404519	F/O	McLEAN DFC John MacArthur	11-08-43	619 Sqn		411936	F/S	NAIRN Clifford Morton	24-08-43	199 Sqn
401243	P/O	McLENNAN DFM Hugh Alexander	19-02-43	156 Sqn		401528	F/S	NEALE Alan Frank	18-01-43	12 Sqn
12840	F/S	McLEOD Graham Albert George	24-08-43	158 Sqn		1580879	Sgt	NEEDHAM Frederick	25-06-43	166 Sqn
414070	P/O	McMAHON Michael	24-12-43	103 Sqn		413015	P/O	NEEDS Lancelot Kenneth	3-08-43	100 Sqn
422243	F/S	McMAHON Michael Joseph	30-07-43	467 Sqn		414072	P/O	NEGUS Bruce Lindsay	18-10-43	207 Sqn
425409	F/S	McMILLAN Ronald Robert	16-12-43	7 Sqn		5553	Sgt	NELSON Colin Alexander	24-05-43	1654 HCU
405381	F/O	McNEILL Thomas Hector	30-03-43	460 Sqn		421667	F/S	NELSON Raymond Stuart	27-11-43	83 Sqn
413788	F/S	McPHAN Robert Barr	3-09-43	460 Sqn		415088	P/O	NELSON Wallace Cyril	23-09-43	50 Sqn
412024	F/S	McQUADE Victor Carl	14-06-43	27 OTU		425541	F/S	NETHERSOLE William Frederick	9-10-43	115 Sqn
414816	F/S	McWHA Reginald Douglas	16-12-43	7 Sqn		420842	F/S	NEVILLE Frederick Gordon	6-11-43	27 OTU
8939	Sgt	MEADOWS Allan Keith	9-04-43	460 Sqn		424305	Sgt	NEWNHAM Henry Arthur	18-09-43	17 OTU
414248	F/S	MEDHURST Malcolm Graeme	18-08-43	103 Sqn		416780	F/S	NEWSTEAD Trevor	24-11-43	460 Sqn
413222	F/S	MEIKLEJOHN Robert Bruce	22-06-43	7 Sqn		419205	F/S	NEWTON Lyndsay Thomas	24-10-43	14 OTU
413631	F/S	MELL John Francis	12-06-43	466 Sqn		409581	F/S	NIELD Robert Alexander	22-10-43	158 Sqn
413876	F/S	MENERE Douglas	5-11-43	199 Sqn		409578	Sgt	NIXON James Edwin	2-10-43	51 Sqn
416594	F/S	MENZIES Colin Kerr	17-04-43	101 Sqn		410009	P/O	NOLAN William George	7-09-43	10 Sqn
421921	F/S	MERES Frank	7-08-43	9 Sqn		412176	F/S	NORMAN Ernest Edward	20-07-43	1662 HCU
400391	P/O	METHVEN Stuartson Charles	23-01-43	460 Sqn		405645	P/O	NORTH Charles Peter	3-11-43	466 Sqn
425183	F/S	MIENERT Victor	17-12-43	405 Sqn		416512	P/O	NORTON Hartley Graham	3-10-43	44 Sqn
426961	F/S	MIGNER Alexander	30-12-43	26 OTU		406029	P/O	NOSEDA DFC Arthur Raymond	9-01-43	105 Sqn
401848	F/S	MILLER Colin McDowell	18-01-43	12 Sqn		425736	F/S	NOTT Reginald Lance	4-11-43	138 Sqn
411165	F/S	MILLER Ian Gordon	16-04-43	460 Sqn		1313076	Sgt	NOTT William Hugh John	13-01-43	12 OTU
412438	F/S	MILLER Reginald James	5-05-43	21 OTU		425347	F/S	NOWLAND Francis Edward	26-11-43	166 Sqn
415261	F/S	MILLER William Anderson	3-10-43	102 Sqn		401659	P/O	ODGERS Thomas Rex	28-08-43	199 Sqn
404884	F/S	MILLETT Graham Henry	11-03-43	467 Sqn		403368	Sgt	OLIVER Harold Bruce	27-01-43	460 Sqn
420233	F/S	MILLIKEN Edward David	12-06-43	466 Sqn		427017	F/S	O'DEA Ronald Patrick	26-11-43	49 Sqn
415040	F/S	MILLS John Franklin	14-05-43	10 Sqn		418558	F/S	O'DEA Walter David Barry	20-12-43	514 Sqn
416596	F/S	MILNE Donald Harold	4-07-43	35 Sqn		416697	F/S	O'DONNELL John Patrick	28-12-43	20 OTU
421039	F/S	MINTER William Raymond	22-10-43	57 Sqn		410716	P/O	O'DWYER Frank	6-09-43	78 Sqn
409933	F/O	MITCHELL Alan Roy	2-12-43	460 Sqn		409216	F/S	O'FARRELL Patrick Thomas	22-09-43	115 Sqn
409567	P/O	MITCHELL Alan Seabrook	2-10-43	460 Sqn		411811	F/S	O'GRADY Francis John	28-05-43	77 Sqn
404654	F/O	MITCHELL Frank Howard	27-01-43	21 OTU		421850	F/S	O'HARE Terence Patrick	29-12-43	102 Sqn
416693	F/O	MITCHELL Graham Douglas	12-07-43	467 Sqn		425205	F/S	O'NEILL Howard Charles	14-09-43	158 Sqn
415167	W/O	MOLLOY Andrew	21-12-43	78 Sqn		403397	F/O	O'RIORDAN Clifford Timothy	30-07-43	460 Sqn
416383	P/O	MONK Peter Vivian	17-04-43	100 Sqn		415736	P/O	O'SULLIVAN Thomas Charles	9-10-43	7 Sqn
410908	P/O	MOON James Joseph	20-12-43	428 Sqn		26228	Sgt	PAGE Thomas William	25-06-43	50 Sqn
421995	F/S	MOORE Arthur Nelson	6-09-43	78 Sqn		425208	F/S	PANOS Peter	27-09-43	10 Sqn
410555	F/S	MOORE Cyril James	5-07-43	75 Sqn		414118	F/S	PARK Robert William	30-07-43	467 Sqn
412627	P/O	MOORE Donald Francis	5-11-43	199 Sqn		412265	P/O	PARKER Alfred Kenneth	17-04-43	460 Sqn
410689	F/S	MOORE John Francis	20-12-43	166 Sqn		426381	F/S	PARKER Edwin Earle	22-10-43	49 Sqn
400595	F/O	MOORE DFC Kay	4-04-43	460 Sqn		416886	P/O	PARKER Jeffrey Felgate	6-11-43	27 OTU
420900	F/O	MOORE William Gordon	18-11-43	623 Sqn		9359	Sgt	PARKER Laurence Maurice	4-12-43	467 Sqn
415264	F/O	MORCOMBE William James	18-11-43	622 Sqn		415090	Sgt	PARKES Jack Elliott	19-02-43	12 OTU
401074	F/O	MOREY DFC Stanley Allan	27-09-43	103 Sqn		409274	F/S	PARSONS John Maxwell	26-05-43	467 Sqn
412618	F/S	MORGAN Frederick William	14-05-43	12 Sqn		411372	Sgt	PATERSON Frederick Harley	11-02-43	101 Sqn
408610	F/S	MORGAN Laurence Alfred	31-01-43	9 Sqn		412028	P/O	PATRICK DFC Maxwell Morley	23-11-43	156 Sqn
411593	F/S	MORLEY Arthur	4-07-43	10 Sqn		415912	F/S	PAULL Ronald Joseph	22-10-43	10 Sqn
425719	F/S	MORLEY Daniel Charles	22-11-43	115 Sqn		408871	Sgt	PEAKE Ronald Moseley	12-03-43	100 Sqn
406573	F/S	MORPHETT Douglas Clarke	18-01-43	12 Sqn		414425	P/O	PEATE Raymond Ernest Lee	18-11-43	115 Sqn
404873	F/S	MORRIS Victor James	8-06-43	1659 HCU		408873	F/S	PEKIN Stanley Thomas	18-08-43	419 Sqn

Number	Rank	Name	Date	Unit
23113	F/S	PEPPERRELL Archibald James	4-09-43	101 Sqn
404983	W/O	PERRETT Rex Gordon	30-07-43	35 Sqn
410721	F/S	PERRY John Charles	28-08-43	57 Sqn
414077	P/O	PETERS Herbert Norman	22-06-43	90 Sqn
413890	F/S	PETERSEN Harry Harcourt	16-12-43	460 Sqn
408459	F/S	PETERSON Kermit Joseph	26-11-43	102 Sqn
410255	F/S	PHELAN Ian Rupert	2-12-43	460 Sqn
415273	F/S	PHILLIPS Everard John	24-08-43	101 Sqn
412338	F/S	PHILLIPS Frank Gale	16-06-43	460 Sqn
409600	F/S	PHILLIPS Keith Balfour	28-08-43	166 Sqn
409451	F/O	PHILLIPS Phillip Henry	18-08-43	12 Sqn
18297	F/S	PHILLIPS Thomas David	3-09-43	1661 HCU
408779	F/O	PIETSCH Leonard	12-06-43	467 Sqn
23729	F/S	PLANT Bruce Albert	23-09-43	460 Sqn
413249	P/O	PLANT Henry Edward Morgan	22-10-43	10 Sqn
420050	F/S	PLUMMER John Clement	17-06-43	460 Sqn
421852	F/O	POOLE James	29-12-43	460 Sqn
410088	F/S	POTTER Graham Ernest	3-10-43	467 Sqn
406680	F/S	POTTER Robert Lincoln	30-03-43	460 Sqn
409940	F/O	POULTER Henry Alfred	15-09-43	1664 HCU
400820	F/L	POULTON DFM Norman Thomas Riggall	16-12-43	156 Sqn
406873	F/L	POWELL DFC Leslie John	16-12-43	156 Sqn
407972	P/O	PRESTON Francis Albert	23-08-43	100 Sqn
414426	F/S	PRICE Julius	3-10-43	158 Sqn
409221	F/S	PRIDGEON Walter Frank	20-04-43	460 Sqn
409592	P/O	PRINGLE Lawrence James	22-10-43	76 Sqn
21144	Sgt	PROWSE Alexander Alwyn	26-05-43	12 Sqn
417232	F/S	PRYDE William	23-09-43	57 Sqn
414161	F/S	PULLOM Frank	3-10-43	467 Sqn
404262	F/O	PYE John Downing	27-04-43	77 Sqn
425053	P/O	QUAITE DFM Lorraine John	6-11-43	27 OTU
411378	F/O	QUANCE Peter Reginald	20-06-43	408 Sqn
401567	F/O	QUICK Arthur William Frederick	5-11-43	1655 MTU
411259	Sgt	QUINLAN Sydney George	11-02-43	101 Sqn
409443	F/O	QUINTON Lloyd Frederick	6-09-43	44 Sqn
406681	Sgt	RAE Donald James	27-03-43	214 Sqn
405502	W/O	RANCLAUD Walter Boscawen	4-04-43	460 Sqn
413896	F/O	RANDALL DFC Francis Archibald	16-12-43	460 Sqn
415917	F/S	RASHBROOK Robert William	1-09-43	1654 HCU
423325	F/S	RATCLIFFE Peter John	19-11-43	622 Sqn
413032	P/O	RATCLIFFE Robert James	11-08-43	57 Sqn
420270	F/S	RAYS Ronald James	23-09-43	101 Sqn
417118	F/S	READ Graham Sydney	28-09-43	405 Sqn
426155	F/S	READ John Knox	20-10-43	57 Sqn
421463	F/S	READING Edgar George	24-10-43	14 OTU
411520	F/O	REARDON Alfred Henry	15-08-43	467 Sqn
420596	F/S	REDDY Douglas Edward Lanyon	27-09-43	1657 HCU
413426	F/S	REDWAY Thomas Edward Nagle	16-07-43	10 OTU
414080	F/S	REID Douglas Angus	30-07-43	467 Sqn
420055	F/S	RENDLE Patrick William James	29-06-43	78 Sqn
411381	P/O	RENNO DFM James Darcy William	3-08-43	100 Sqn
417416	F/S	REU Robert Garth	28-07-43	467 Sqn
414083	P/O	RICH Donald Robert	22-06-43	218 Sqn
30005	F/O	RICHARDS Austin Oliver George	20-04-43	10 OTU
413754	F/S	RICHARDS Robert Edward Duncan	3-12-43	576 Sqn
410382	Sgt	RICHARDSON Harold James	22-07-43	27 OTU
421081	P/O	RICHARDSON Roy Joseph	27-11-43	49 Sqn
420272	F/S	RICKERSEY Sydney George	2-09-43	11 OTU
411383	P/O	RICKETTS DFC Stanley John	14-08-43	1662 HCU
403699	F/O	RIDING Harry	4-03-43	100 Sqn
402754	F/O	RIDLEY DFM John Kenneth	19-02-43	83 Sqn
415182	F/S	RILEY John Richmond	9-04-43	101 Sqn
414960	F/S	RILEY William Eric	26-06-43	466 Sqn
412189	F/O	RITCHIE DFC Eric Whitby	20-12-43	156 Sqn
412843	F/O	RITCHIE Norman James	9-04-43	101 Sqn
407909	Sgt	ROBERTS Arthur Reece	12-03-43	100 Sqn
404657	P/O	ROBERTSON Ian Ronald	28-04-43	61 Sqn
413256	F/S	ROBERTSON Russell Leslie	16-05-43	466 Sqn
425220	F/S	ROBINSON Allan Blakiston	17-08-43	138 Sqn
412270	F/S	ROBINSON Charles Lloyd	16-12-43	7 Sqn
406795	F/S	ROBINSON Nicholas Auber Benjamin	14-07-43	115 Sqn
405771	Sgt	RODGERS Leslie Lindsay	27-01-43	429 Sqn
407036	P/O	ROLLINS James Leslie	8-04-43	49 Sqn
414089	P/O	ROOKE William James	18-08-43	49 Sqn
409597	F/O	ROPER Leslie Walter	4-09-43	106 Sqn
405605	P/O	ROSE DFC Walter Henry	23-11-43	156 Sqn
24818	F/S	ROSS Angus Donald Mackay	21-05-43	466 Sqn
412844	F/S	ROSS David	28-05-43	156 Sqn
409278	F/S	ROSS Frederick James	20-08-43	139 Sqn
405233	F/S	ROSS Herbert John	30-05-43	35 Sqn
408339	F/S	ROSS Hugh Robert Hector	17-12-43	12 Sqn
418052	F/S	ROSS Neil Colin	18-12-43	311 FTU
410729	F/S	ROSSITER James Louis	4-12-43	630 Sqn
415683	F/S	ROURKE Gerald Alan	31-07-43	78 Sqn
421128	F/S	ROWAN Douglas John	3-10-43	158 Sqn
401196	F/L	ROWCROFT Oscar Gladwin	25-02-43	467 Sqn
416288	F/S	RUDD DFM James Chadd	1-05-43	78 Sqn
416791	F/O	RUNDLE Samuel Thomas John	4-09-43	44 Sqn
30245	F/O	RUSH Francis William	16-12-43	7 Sqn
421512	F/S	RUSHTON Arthur Noel Forrester	22-09-43	460 Sqn
414506	F/O	RUSS Sidney Michael	5-05-43	460 Sqn
415684	F/S	RUSSELL David	19-08-43	12 OTU
411192	F/O	RUST Bruce Kinley	4-04-43	460 Sqn
420500	F/S	RUTTER Donald Malcolm	22-11-43	83 Sqn
421399	F/S	RYALL Cecil Ernest	22-12-43	207 Sqn
405217	P/O	RYALLS John Richard	28-05-43	467 Sqn
409452	F/O	RYAN Leo Michael	24-12-43	463 Sqn
425224	F/S	SAKER Ernest Henry Benjamin	22-07-43	1657 HCU
415186	Sgt	SAMSON Louis Frederick	9-04-43	77 Sqn
400999	F/S	SAMUEL DFC John Frederick	16-12-43	156 Sqn
423386	F/S	SANSOME George Hilton	7-11-43	1663 HCU
14472	Sgt	SAUNDERS Lewis Albert	4-09-43	467 Sqn
406814	W/O	SAUNDERS Raymond Kenneth	16-12-43	432 Sqn
402882	S/L	SAVAGE John Ronald	25-06-43	7 Sqn
414602	F/S	SCHUBERT Derek Percival Robert	24-08-43	467 Sqn
417123	F/S	SCOTT Ian Macdonald	17-12-43	97 Sqn
413903	F/S	SCOTT Frederick Roy	16-12-43	576 Sqn
405884	P/O	SCOTT Stuart Nicholson	30-07-43	460 Sqn
413277	F/O	SCOTT William Verdun	16-12-43	7 Sqn
403701	Sgt	SEDGER Gordon Robert	27-01-43	460 Sqn
416619	P/O	SEDUNARY DFC Alan Joseph Lyall	24-08-43	75 Sqn
409454	P/O	SELLARS Leonard Gerrard	22-07-43	1657 HCU
420066	F/S	SELLEN Leonard George	14-08-43	21 OTU
419344	F/S	SEMMENS Ernest Jack William	18-12-43	21 OTU
409951	F/O	SHALLESS Alan Merris	23-07-43	24 OTU
412714	F/O	SHANAHAN Michael O'Meara	3-09-43	156 Sqn
415055	F/L	SHANNON DFC Colin McTaggart	10-08-43	76 Sqn
410014	F/S	SHEEAN Lorin James	21-12-43	76 Sqn
425810	Sgt	SHERIDAN James Patrick	6-09-43	106 Sqn
410739	F/S	SHERMAN Eric Hempel	2-08-43	18 OTU
425766	F/S	SHERWIN William Thornton	26-11-43	463 Sqn
412846	P/O	SHILLINGLAW William Golder	22-06-43	218 Sqn
413674	F/S	SHORT Joseph Henry	31-08-43	12 Sqn
5148	F/S	SIBBIT Edward Moore	22-09-43	460 Sqn
412850	Sgt	SIDES Roger Fisher Rowe	12-03-43	100 Sqn
414604	F/S	SIMPSON Harry James	6-09-43	156 Sqn
411375	P/O	SIMPSON Kenneth John	1-09-43	214 Sqn
405504	F/S	SIMPSON Noel Ryder	13-06-43	460 Sqn
401053	F/S	SIMPSON Norman Henry	27-01-43	460 Sqn
415279	P/O	SIMPSON Ross McCulloch	18-11-43	90 Sqn
413676	F/S	SIMS Edwin Alfred	23-06-43	77 Sqn
421133	P/O	SINDEN Robert William	26-11-43	97 Sqn
413144	F/S	SINGLE Alan Roy	18-12-43	75 Sqn
409240	F/S	SKERRETT Charles Raymond	27-09-43	78 Sqn

261

Service #	Rank	Name	Date	Squadron
425369	F/O	SLENNETT Christopher Gordon	18-11-43	460 Sqn
403036	F/S	SLOMAN George Sarsfield	1-03-43	35 Sqn
417006	F/S	SMART Edmond Rhys	8-08-43	61 Sqn
416798	F/S	SMART Mervin John	31-08-43	466 Sqn
415056	P/O	SMILY Frank Walton	3-11-43	466 Sqn
415879	F/S	SMITH Albert John	11-12-43	21 OTU
413665	P/O	SMITH Charles Keightley	22-09-43	460 Sqn
409241	F/S	SMITH Henry Keith	26-06-43	101 Sqn
416630	F/S	SMITH James Brooks Hamilton	23-06-43	218 Sqn
418489	F/S	SMITH Laurence Stanley	22-10-43	10 Sqn
416521	F/L	SMITH Leonard Anthony	19-11-43	90 Sqn
414377	Sgt	SMITH Norman George	27-01-43	21 OTU
420780	F/S	SMITH Raymond Purser	21-09-43	57 Sqn
403766	F/O	SMITH DFC Robert Sidney	16-12-43	156 Sqn
412853	P/O	SMITHERS Jack	16-08-43	57 Sqn
6878	Sgt	SMITHSON John Clayton	31-01-43	57 Sqn
415743	F/S	SNOOK Graham Ernest	17-09-43	138 Sqn
411398	P/O	SOMERS James Karl	22-06-43	166 Sqn
407380	F/O	SPAFFORD DFC DFM Frederick Michael 'Spam'	16-09-43	617 Sqn
410177	F/S	SPEECHLEY David Poole	26-07-43	466 Sqn
421135	F/S	SPENCE John Andrew	3-09-43	460 Sqn
421093	F/O	SPIER Walter Frank	3-07-43	460 Sqn
421518	F/S	SQUIRES Maxwell Hope	29-12-43	460 Sqn
413037	P/O	STABELL Victor George	18-08-43	619 Sqn
402412	F/S	STACK Edward Francis	9-01-43	44 Sqn
409485	F/L	STAFFORD Hume Meliville	3-09-43	156 Sqn
402619	F/O	STAIN DFM Roy Roberts	24-12-43	156 Sqn
412739	F/S	STANLEY John Vernon	13-06-43	460 Sqn
409331	F/S	STEWART James Scott	17-04-43	460 Sqn
405189	W/O	STEWART Maxwell Phillip	25-02-43	467 Sqn
400497	F/O	STEWART DFM Neil Gordon	10-09-43	27 OTU
412744	Sgt	STOCKBRIDGE Howard Sydney	12-03-43	20 OTU
417529	F/O	STOECKEL Oswald Ian Hamilton	6-11-43	27 OTU
421097	F/S	STONES Edward John	26-11-43	460 Sqn
426927	Sgt	STRAWBRIDGE Eric John	16-12-43	1662 HCU
410745	F/S	STRINGER Frank Craven	10-09-43	27 OTU
413274	F/S	STUART James	25-11-43	460 Sqn
406702	F/S	STUART Raymond Clarence	17-04-43	467 Sqn
420715	F/S	STUBBINGS John Lloyd Russell	4-09-43	101 Sqn
401568	P/O	STUBBS Alexander William	16-02-43	103 Sqn
414737	F/O	ST. GEORGE Harold Raymond	12-07-43	467 Sqn
425375	F/O	ST. LEDGER Peter Sylvester Anthony	30-07-43	75 Sqn
408713	F/S	SULLIVAN Charles Barry	7-02-43	199 Sqn
404909	F/L	SULLIVAN John McDowall	15-08-43	467 Sqn
407994	F/S	SWAIN John Kenneth	27-01-43	460 Sqn
414169	F/S	SWANSON Arnold Hildrew	27-04-43	13 OTU
404555	F/L	SWEENEY DFC Gordon	22-10-43	105 Sqn
421642	P/O	SWINNEY Tasman Foskett	10-09-43	27 OTU
416725	P/O	SYME John	4-12-43	630 Sqn
415364	F/O	SYMONS Harold Frederick	1-09-43	460 Sqn
409252	F/O	TAIT Bruce Alexander	29-12-43	467 Sqn
410269	F/S	TANKARD Vincent Gregory	17-12-43	83 Sqn
11689	Sgt	TANNER Clarence Edgar	28-02-43	83 Sqn
414170	F/S	TANNER Oliver James	1-09-43	623 Sqn
418584	F/S	TASKIS Douglas Richard Gordon	3-12-43	576 Sqn
420406	F/S	TAYLOR Colin William	16-08-43	49 Sqn
16482	P/O	TAYLOR Ewan Moore	22-10-43	1654 HCU
412860	F/S	TAYLOR Frederick Cecil	25-07-43	460 Sqn
412735	P/O	TAYLOR John	5-09-43	106 Sqn
414967	F/S	TAYLOR Laurence Alexander	3-09-43	1661 HCU
408888	F/O	TAYLOR Thomas Maxwell	17-04-43	101 Sqn
413803	F/S	TAYLOR Tom	30-05-43	460 Sqn
16774	F/S	TEEDE Walter Henry	25-06-43	90 Sqn
414436	F/S	TEERMAN Alfred Walter	22-06-43	460 Sqn
19117	F/S	TERRY Anthony David	12-07-43	467 Sqn
410271	F/O	THOM Donald Seymour	26-11-43	103 Sqn
416466	F/S	THOMAS Bruce Wainwright	1-05-43	76 Sqn
413688	F/S	THOMAS David Sterrit	9-10-43	460 Sqn
411563	F/S	THOMAS Jack Findlay	31-01-43	9 Sqn
417903	F/S	THOMAS John Edwin	28-12-43	20 OTU
416296	W/O	THOMAS Robert Kyffin	2-12-43	156 Sqn
415909	F/S	THOMPSON Edward Claude	3-08-43	27 OTU
409256	F/S	THOMSON Daniel McNicol	12-06-43	12 Sqn
409862	F/S	THOMSON Russell James	18-11-43	622 Sqn
416794	F/S	THORPE Raoul Ellery	26-07-43	466 Sqn
3183	F/S	THROWER Samuel Harrington Considine	16-11-43	16 OTU
414102	Sgt	THURECHT Norman Ray	3-04-43	156 Sqn
417249	F/S	TIMPERON Joseph Banks	16-11-43	28 OTU
422012	F/S	TINMAN Walter Robert	2-12-43	156 Sqn
416631	F/S	TONKIN John Ramsay	7-07-43	15 OTU
406964	Sgt	TOWNSEND Charles Richard	13-03-43	199 Sqn
414851	F/S	TOY Noel Richard Brittan	16-12-43	1662 HCU
406585	P/O	TOZER Colin Foley	16-04-43	466 Sqn
423939	F/S	TREADGOLD John	16-11-43	15 OTU
415104	F/S	TRESIDDER Douglas John	24-08-43	101 Sqn
415000	Sgt	TRIGWELL Russell Seymour	3-04-43	156 Sqn
411970	F/S	TRINDER Charlie Wilson	13-05-43	466 Sqn
22378	F/S	TRUSCOTT Cyril Francis Joseph	3-07-43	460 Sqn
411060	F/O	TUCK DFC Albert Thomas	28-09-43	35 Sqn
417433	F/S	TUCKER Jack Charleton	27-08-43	10 OTU
416633	F/S	TUCKER William John	15-06-43	12 Sqn
416809	P/O	TURNBULL Jack	18-10-43	460 Sqn
408379	F/S	TURNER Robert Campbell	20-12-43	50 Sqn
415286	P/O	TYLER Geoffrey	16-12-43	7 Sqn
410273	F/S	VAUTIER Gernault Mervyn	16-12-43	1662 HCU
412765	P/O	VEECH Neville John	5-12-43	623 Sqn
411620	F/S	VENESS Daniel Edward	25-05-43	1652 HCU
418597	F/S	VICKERMAN Alan John	10-09-43	27 OTU
413049	P/O	VIDLER Alfred Newton	18-08-43	61 Sqn
416635	F/O	VINCENT Howard Russell	24-08-43	467 Sqn
405986	P/O	VIVERS Reobert James Francis	23-09-43	103 Sqn
425911	Sgt	WACHTER Norman Leslie	8-09-43	12 OTU
412217	Sgt	WADDELL Harold Theodore	8-02-43	44 Sqn
28053	Sgt	WADE James Christopher	25-02-43	218 Sqn
1695286	Sgt	WAINWRIGHT Timothy	26-11-43	429 Sqn
425386	F/S	WALDEN John Edward	15-08-43	61 Sqn
415060	F/S	WALLACE David Lawson	28-05-43	156 Sqn
413464	F/L	WALLACE John Phillip Henry	18-11-43	623 Sqn
401605	W/O	WALSH Cyril Augustine	4-09-43	460 Sqn
416110	F/S	WALTER Keith Benjamin	18-01-43	1656 HCU
412043	F/S	WALTON David Claude Melville	24-08-43	78 Sqn
418487	F/S	WALTON Trevor Paul	7-10-43	149 Sqn
416812	F/S	WARD Cornelius David	22-09-43	115 Sqn
411207	F/S	WARD DFM Francis Henry	17-04-43	460 Sqn
406890	W/O	WARD Guydon Whitfield	10-08-43	102 Sqn
415061	W/O	WATERMAN William Maitland	16-12-43	7 Sqn
420327	F/S	WATKINS Marcel Alfred Barnard	20-04-43	100 Sqn
402813	F/S	WATSON Leonard David	20-03-43	27 OTU
425560	F/S	WATSON Leroy Anwyll	4-09-43	7 Sqn
420328	F/O	WATSON Maxwell Thomas Lockwood	22-09-43	460 Sqn
412327	W/O	WATSON Wallace Arthur	16-12-43	7 Sqn
415456	F/S	WATT Maxwell Birdwood	26-06-43	106 Sqn
413495	F/S	WATTERS Leslie Harold	27-04-43	156 Sqn
416469	P/O	WATTS Robert Hamilton	21-10-43	44 Sqn
412778	F/S	WEARNE John Frederick Bice	31-08-43	1651 HCU
409191	Sgt	WEARNE William Raymond	11-01-43	27 OTU
422330	F/S	WEAVER Frank	7-09-43	106 Sqn
401259	F/O	WEAVING Kenneth Arnold Charles	18-01-43	1656 HCU
411562	F/S	WEBBER Keith Robert	21-01-43	103 Sqn
408200	F/L	WEDD DFC Rex Henry	20-12-43	156 Sqn
15851	F/S	WEIR William David	14-06-43	27 OTU
413918	F/O	WELCH John Richard	28-08-43	207 Sqn
405370	F/S	WELLESLEY Charles John Jay	19-02-43	15 Sqn

403389	P/O	WENDON William Murray	13-05-43	156 Sqn
420319	F/S	WESTERBERG Bruce Wilfred	31-07-43	427 Sqn
417917	F/S	WESTERN Malcolm George	16-12-43	576 Sqn
416471	P/O	WESTWOOD Reginald Francis	5-05-43	75 Sqn
412053	F/O	WHEATLEY Ronald	15-04-43	35 Sqn
415291	P/O	WHITAKER Richard Robert	6-09-43	196 Sqn
420091	F/O	WHITE Aubrey James	14-08-43	21 OTU
410402	F/O	WHITE Cedric Gordon	18-10-43	460 Sqn
408896	P/O	WHITE DFM David Edward	17-04-43	460 Sqn
15319	Sgt	WHITE Stanley Musgrave	8-04-43	156 Sqn
413058	P/O	WHITTING Kenneth George	24-12-43	514 Sqn
416815	F/S	WICKS Brian Price	16-12-43	576 Sqn
409356	W/O	WICKS Reginald Russell	2-12-43	156 Sqn
420369	F/S	WICKS DFM William Ross	27-09-43	12 Sqn
417610	F/S	WIGHTMAN Kevin Frederick	16-12-43	1667 HCU
420322	P/O	WILDMAN Ronald William	31-08-43	158 Sqn
425253	F/S	WILKES Kevin John	1-09-43	199 Sqn
413810	F/S	WILKINS John Selwyn	27-09-43	78 Sqn
408557	F/O	WILLIAMS Alexander Frederick	30-07-43	102 Sqn
405224	F/O	WILLIAMS DFC Charles Rowland	16-05-43	617 Sqn
411566	F/S	WILLIAMS Douglas George	21-01-43	103 Sqn
21213	F/S	WILLIAMS Francis Alfred	22-11-43	97 Sqn
401341	F/S	WILLIAMS John Muir	29-04-43	75 Sqn
416135	F/S	WILLIAMS John Norman	17-04-43	460 Sqn
412785	F/S	WILLIAMS Thomas	15-06-43	460 Sqn
6946	Sgt	WILLIAMS Thomas Henry	27-01-43	460 Sqn
405597	F/S	WILLIAMS William	5-05-43	460 Sqn
1231055	Sgt	WILMORE Hubert Roy	30-03-43	196 Sqn
401083	F/S	WILMOT Basil Frederick	11-06-43	467 Sqn
416310	Sgt	WILSON Adrian Grey	25-01-43	226 Sqn
413329	F/S	WILSON Jack Oliphant	26-05-43	15 Sqn
412788	F/L	WILSON John Leslie	1-09-43	77 Sqn
413468	F/S	WILSON Robinson Edward	26-03-43	460 Sqn
420094	F/O	WILSON William Stuart	17-11-43	76 Sqn
409265	F/S	WINCHESTER William Victor Bryan	12-08-43	466 Sqn
420419	F/S	WINDUS Keith Neville	27-11-43	626 Sqn
413469	F/S	WINTERBON John Trevor	23-06-43	156 Sqn
403704	F/L	WOOD Ian Milne	13-07-43	44 Sqn
411977	F/O	WOOD Kemble Russell	20-10-43	405 Sqn
403616	W/O	WOOD Kenneth Alan	2-12-43	156 Sqn
400337	P/O	WOOD Stuart	15-02-43	100 Sqn
402941	F/O	WOODS DFM Clarence William	31-08-43	1651 HCU
410584	F/S	WOODS Jack William	26-09-43	14 OTU
417551	Sgt	WORDEN Frank Elliott	19-08-43	12 OTU
418609	F/S	WRIGHT Allan Walter	3-10-43	467 Sqn
421066	F/S	WRIGHT Charles Sinclair	24-05-43	460 Sqn
414371	Sgt	WRIGHT Stuart Ronald	12-03-43	20 OTU
405001	Sgt	WYLLIE MiD Maxwell Joseph Andrew	22-04-43	460 Sqn
408605	F/S	WYNN Ronald Gordon	13-05-43	156 Sqn
425401	F/S	WYNNE Richard Ivor	20-12-43	156 Sqn
421954	F/S	YENSEN George Louis	31-08-43	1651 HCU
409268	F/S	YEO Howard Garfield	25-06-43	12 Sqn
420098	F/S	YORK Leslie Bennett	26-07-43	51 Sqn
403065	P/O	YOUNG John Charles Harley	16-02-43	103 Sqn
401344	F/S	YOUNGER Robert Graham [Canada]	8-04-43	156 Sqn

Note

On page 122 of Volume 4, the book that is relevant to this section, I observed that of the nine Lancasters lost in the month of April from 460 Squadron, not a single airman survived. Of the 64 aircrew killed, 35 were Australian born and serving with their country's air force.

Amongst the deaths reported above is that of John Yorke Clarke from Roelands in Western Australia; in the early 1970s I was contacted by a survivor from his crew who wrote that his skipper sacrificed his life by remaining at the controls of their stricken bomber in order to give those who had survived the night fighter attack the best possible chance to escape. His last words were *'I can't hold her much longer'*. Tragically, in 1945, his parents, Raymond and Marjorie Clarke, received a second awful telegram, this time informing them that John's brother, Robert, was missing from air operations (his details are reported in Part 9).

ROYAL CANADIAN AIR FORCE
personnel

R/100271	F/S	ABBOTT William Geoffrey	23-05-43	408 Sqn
R/180521	F/S	ABRAMS Stanley William	24-08-43	77 Sqn
R/91189	WO1	ACKER James Gordon	28-04-43	419 Sqn
R/160310	F/S	ACKLAND William Eric [USA]	22-11-43	77 Sqn
R/112252	WO2	ACORN George Warburton	4-12-43	405 Sqn
J/18289	P/O	ACTON George Nelson	26-06-43	408 Sqn
R/161411	F/S	ADAM Russell Edwin	1-09-43	199 Sqn
J/21975	P/O	ADAM Thomas Wilkie	16-06-43	12 OTU
R/136460	F/S	ADAMS Frank Edward	26-08-43	20 OTU
R/186477	Sgt	ADAMSON John McLean	24-12-43	57 Sqn
R/225303	Sgt	ADDISON Douglas Gordon	18-11-43	431 Sqn
C/16683	P/O	ADDISON Joseph Horace	26-06-43	103 Sqn
J/18155	P/O	AFFLECK Walter Raymond	8-03-43	156 Sqn
R/105759	F/S	AGAR Beverley William	3-04-43	419 Sqn
J/14194	F/O	AGASSIZ Roland Ernest Garnault	16-06-43	405 Sqn
R/121039	F/S	AGATE James Victor	29-04-43	428 Sqn
J/21038	F/O	AGNEW David Renwick	29-06-43	419 Sqn
R/100760	F/S	AGNEW Ross Maddaugh	11-02-43	106 Sqn
J/18207	P/O	AIKEN David	26-06-43	408 Sqn
R/86972	F/S	AITKEN Alexander Patterson Morris	10-03-43	1659 HCU
R/127496	F/S	AITKEN Gordon Edward	23-10-43	427 Sqn
R/134836	F/S	ALBERT John Amos	31-08-43	427 Sqn
R/4607	F/S	ALDER Clarence David	27-04-43	420 Sqn
R/123174	F/S	ALDERSON Ernest Henry	24-05-43	408 Sqn
R/89283	Sgt	ALDERSON John Gordon	1-05-43	106 Sqn
R/115197	Sgt	ALDERSON Robert Carson 'Bob'	29-01-43	23 OTU
R/177535	Sgt	ALDRIDGE Thomas	25-07-43	158 Sqn
R/66126	WO1	ALEO Joseph	13-01-43	106 Sqn
J/21716	P/O	ALEXANDER Ralph Leonard	3-02-43	102 Sqn
J/21609	F/O	ALEY Harry Charles	26-11-43	97 Sqn
R/80235	Sgt	ALLAN James Arthur Laurence	28-04-43	419 Sqn
J/20440	F/O	ALLAN John	5-10-43	434 Sqn
R/64851	Sgt	ALLAN McKeen	31-01-43	9 Sqn
J/16754	P/O	ALLAN Ralph Grant [United Kingdom]	28-05-43	432 Sqn
R/114255	WO2	ALLAN Walter Howden	3-09-43	22 OTU
J/6935	F/L	ALLAN William Cosmo	28-12-43	405 Sqn
J/92604	P/O	ALLEN Eric Alexander	11-04-43	7 Sqn
R/147588	LAC	ALLEN Herb John	7-07-43	424 Sqn
R/78939	WO2	ALLEN Hugh Garfield	30-03-43	196 Sqn
R/127565	F/S	ALLEN Sidney	18-10-43	115 Sqn
R/179370	Sgt	ALLEN Ward William James	16-12-43	166 Sqn
R/88416	F/S	AMIRAULT Alphe Baptiste	5-03-43	214 Sqn
J/22362	P/O	AMYS Spencer Hewitt	13-02-43	22 OTU
R/112706	F/S	ANDERSON Billie Albert	28-08-43	90 Sqn
J/18417	P/O	ANDERSON Clarence Howard	31-08-43	9 Sqn
R/159275	F/S	ANDERSON Evan Macdonald	8-10-43	20 OTU
R/98929	F/S	ANDERSON Floyd Roger Willis	7-04-43	405 Sqn
R/193090	Sgt	ANDERSON Howard Leroy	22-11-43	10 Sqn
R/99890	F/S	ANDERSON John Albert	4-07-43	419 Sqn
R/111471	Sgt	ANDERSON Norman Thomas	4-12-43	431 Sqn
R/70849	WO2	ANDERSON Sydney Andrew	18-11-43	115 Sqn
R/178345	F/S	ANDERSON Wallace Dorrance	7-09-43	78 Sqn
J/19070	F/O	ANDREW George Varnum	20-12-43	426 Sqn
R/108563	F/S	ANDREWS Clifford Raymond	12-06-43	199 Sqn
J/14390	F/O	ANDREWS Edward Joseph	3-08-43	428 Sqn
J/18204	P/O	ANDREWS James Wesley	22-06-43	35 Sqn
R/104597	F/S	ANDREWS Wilfred	25-06-43	51 Sqn
R/95701	WO2	ANGLIN William Sherron	30-05-43	429 Sqn
R/136581	F/S	ANGUS David Colin Brodie	18-08-43	405 Sqn
R/157737	F/S	ANTIFAEV Michael	21-10-43	20 OTU
R/103626	F/S	APPLEGATE Ernest Arthur	14-04-43	12 Sqn

ID	Rank	Name	Date	Sqn
R/108014	F/S	ARCHAMBAULT Joseph Rene	22-06-43	408 Sqn
R/141130	F/S	ARCHER Jack Colin	5-05-43	408 Sqn
J/2207	P/O	ARCHER Ross James	29-01-43	23 OTU
J/18858	P/O	ARCHIBALD Lewis Percival	16-12-43	426 Sqn
R/139949	Sgt	ARCHIE Steve	17-04-43	408 Sqn
R/106448	Sgt	ARGO William	29-01-43	23 OTU
R/84152	WO2	ARLEN Anthony	8-03-43	75 Sqn
R/156931	F/S	ARLIDGE Wallace Gale	30-07-43	428 Sqn
J/22059	F/O	ARMITAGE Irving	23-11-43	434 Sqn
R/54363	F/S	ARMSTRONG Edward Lawrence	30-05-43	419 Sqn
R/125223	F/S	ARMSTRONG George Ernest	5-05-43	166 Sqn
J/17547	P/O	ARMSTRONG George Wesley	23-06-43	97 Sqn
J/27607	P/O	ARMSTRONG Gerald Henry	4-12-43	431 Sqn
R/161129	Sgt	ARMSTRONG Thomas Reginald	26-08-43	81 OTU
R/131602	F/S	ARMSTRONG William Ernest	4-07-43	432 Sqn
R/112872	F/S	ARMSTRONG Willis Henry	11-07-43	1489 Flt
J/23347	F/O	ARNEIL Douglas James	28-11-43	16 OTU
R/133584	WO2	ARNOLD William Henry	24-09-43	57 Sqn
R/179877	Sgt	ARNOTT George Donald [USA]	26-11-43	460 Sqn
R/117504	F/S	ARPIN Joseph Jean Charles	20-02-43	424 Sqn
R/145976	F/S	ARRIL William McKenzie	6-08-43	23 OTU
R/83431	WO2	ARSENAULT Joseph Gaspard	1-02-43	1659 HCU
R/119416	WO2	ARTHUR James Lamb	17-05-43	617 Sqn
R/118066	Sgt	ASH Albert Charles	6-04-43	427 Sqn
J/17262	P/O	ASHDOWN Frederick James Mackenzie	21-04-43	21 Sqn
R/134348	F/S	ASKEW George William	26-07-43	419 Sqn
R/134417	F/S	ASKEW John Ruskin	28-01-43	1659 HCU
R/120876	F/S	ASSAF George	23-05-43	408 Sqn
R/134035	Sgt	ATKINSON Albert Earl	14-05-43	429 Sqn
R/124949	F/S	ATKINSON Robert Elmer	2-07-43	620 Sqn
J/18229	P/O	ATKINSON Stanley Kyle	27-09-43	432 Sqn
R/107425	F/S	ATTREE Vincent Eardley	24-08-43	156 Sqn
R/172425	Sgt	ATWELL Kenneth Dudley	16-11-43	15 OTU
R/101920	P/O	ATWOOD Bertram Edwin	13-01-43	12 Sqn
R/152693	F/S	AUBIN John George Marcel	22-09-43	158 Sqn
R/117869	Sgt	AUCLAIR Joseph Arsene Roch Tancrede	29-01-43	23 OTU
R/120256	Sgt	AUDY Joseph Engelbert	3-03-43	425 Sqn
R/99993	F/S	AVEY Gerald Russell	5-03-43	100 Sqn
J/15639	F/L	AWAD Charles Mohamed Slyman	27-04-43	429 Sqn
R/106054	F/S	BAGG Arthur James	8-03-43	15 Sqn
J/22534	F/O	BAHT Ralph Edmund	9-10-43	97 Sqn
R/101346	WO2	BAILEY Albert George	28-05-43	432 Sqn
J/20211	F/L	BAILEY George Cooley [USA]	22-11-43	49 Sqn
R/82988	F/S	BAILEY Harry Russell	19-02-43	426 Sqn
R/141776	Sgt	BAILEY John Arthur	29-03-43	426 Sqn
R/119568	F/S	BAILEY Martin	28-08-43	75 Sqn
R/113936	F/S	BAILEY Robert Gordon [USA]	30-05-43	429 Sqn
R/86191	F/S	BAILEY Wesley Glenn	29-09-43	434 Sqn
J/17942	F/O	BAILLIE Ralph Cameron	30-07-43	78 Sqn
R/106671	WO2	BAIN David Lachlan	30-03-43	429 Sqn
R/141597	F/S	BAKEMAN Edward Henry [USA]	14-04-43	12 Sqn
R/66134	WO1	BAKER Carl George	31-08-43	7 Sqn
R/107959	WO2	BAKER Douglas Charles	9-10-43	432 Sqn
J/17661	P/O	BAKER Frank Greenaway	26-05-43	428 Sqn
R/16767	F/S	BAKER George Raymond	9-03-43	426 Sqn
J/17766	P/O	BAKER Jonial William	4-07-43	432 Sqn
J/23600	F/L	BAKER Shirley Waldemar Frank	2-12-43	432 Sqn
J/17747	P/O	BALCER Cyril Rene	29-04-43	428 Sqn
J/18378	F/O	BALCOMBE Alfred Alexander	15-08-43	7 Sqn
R/133749	F/S	BALDERSTON John Percival Ernest	30-06-43	425 Sqn
R/163624	F/S	BALDWIN Robert William	16-12-43	1661 HCU
J/15169	S/L	BALDWIN DFC William Henry	24-08-43	405 Sqn
J/22479	F/O	BALKAM Marshall Edwin [USA]	3-08-43	432 Sqn
R/98593	F/S	BALLANTYNE Wallace Bruce	9-10-43	434 Sqn
J/23131	F/O	BALLOCH James Hamilton	22-10-43	427 Sqn
R/147187	F/S	BAMBRIDGE James Henry	9-06-43	619 Sqn
R/107703	WO2	BANCESCU George	24-05-43	405 Sqn
R/122571	F/S	BANKS Lloyd Marshall	18-08-43	428 Sqn
R/110597	Sgt	BARBE Maurice Jean	27-01-43	50 Sqn
R/172004	Sgt	BARCLAY William Richmond	28-06-43	22 OTU
R/160730	LAC	BARDGETT Nelson Lemar	6-07-43	424 Sqn
R/149418	Sgt	BARIBEAU Leo Joseph	9-03-43	426 Sqn
R/103678	WO2	BARKER Frank Harvey	9-01-43	419 Sqn
J/17650	P/O	BARKER Myron Edward	14-05-43	57 Sqn
R/163850	F/S	BARKWELL John Herbert	11-11-43	78 Sqn
R/100983	F/S	BARLOW Reginald Newman	24-07-43	420 Sqn
R/138574	WO2	BARLOW Ronald Malcolm	23-09-43	432 Sqn
R/150671	F/S	BARNES John Francis	30-03-43	408 Sqn
R/87330	WO2	BARNES Raymond James	16-04-43	75 Sqn
R/91572	LAC	BARNSON Arthur Theodore	3-12-43	1691 Flt
R/196074	Sgt	BARONI Raymond John [USA]	16-12-43	9 Sqn
R/180672	Sgt	BARR Robert Allan	8-10-43	149 Sqn
R/148801	Sgt	BARR Willis Eric	15-01-43	23 OTU
R/107341	F/S	BARRETT Frederick Howard	27-01-43	51 Sqn
R/135579	F/S	BARRETT Martin	9-07-43	49 Sqn
R/107770	F/S	BARRON Percival Edward	29-03-43	420 Sqn
R/157138	F/S	BARSKE Paul Jack	26-11-43	428 Sqn
R/103506	WO2	BARTMAN Gordon Harold	21-04-43	102 Sqn
R/92543	WO2	BARTMAN Lloyd Wallace	15-04-43	7 Sqn
J/25015	F/O	BARTON Hugh Hartil	9-11-43	23 OTU
R/114520	Sgt	BATEMAN Albert Leroy	1-03-43	419 Sqn
R/137694	WO2	BATEMAN James Richard	17-12-43	100 Sqn
R/131551	F/S	BATES David Henderson [USA]	30-07-43	428 Sqn
R/129242	F/S	BATTERTON John Martin	18-08-43	419 Sqn
J/14701	F/O	BAUM William George Rex	24-08-43	427 Sqn
J/14523	F/O	BAUMGARTEN Raymond Lamport	13-05-43	428 Sqn
R/86923	WO2	BEAIRSTO Carl Phillips	23-06-43	427 Sqn
J/13842	F/O	BEATON Alexander Farquhar	28-05-43	428 Sqn
R/67642	F/S	BEATON Charles Norman	5-04-43	426 Sqn
R/161665	F/S	BEATTIE Harold James	27-11-43	166 Sqn
J/10119	P/O	BEATTIE Hugh Donald	14-05-43	405 Sqn
R/124012	WO2	BEATTY Donald Lyall	26-05-43	426 Sqn
R/152879	F/S	BEATTY James Murray	2-12-43	1664 HCU
R/119427	WO1	BEATTY Walter Stanley	4-04-43	405 Sqn
J/18308	P/O	BEAVO William Edward	17-08-43	405 Sqn
R/68061	Sgt	BEBENSEE DFM Douglas Glenn	14-07-43	405 Sqn
R/120117	F/S	BECKETT Robert Francis	28-03-43	419 Sqn
R/77965	WO2	BECKTHOLD William	9-10-43	50 Sqn
R/96932	F/S	BEEBE Henry Craig	18-01-43	97 Sqn
J/22698	F/O	BEGBIE Kendall Bell	16-09-43	427 Sqn
R/91319	WO2	BELANGER Frank James	31-01-43	101 Sqn
R/96685	Sgt	BELANGER Joseph Leonin Lionel	11-04-43	26 OTU
R/143569	Sgt	BELEC Gordon	13-05-43	81 OTU
R/77189	F/S	BELIVEAU Joseph Henri Alphonse	28-01-43	1659 HCU
J/23490	F/O	BELL Angus Fyfe	2-10-43	23 OTU
J/17340	P/O	BELL Angus Hugh	4-07-43	419 Sqn
R/70130	F/S	BELL Bruce Edwin	21-08-43	1658 HCU
J/79393	F/S	BELL Ernest Maxwell	5-03-43	429 Sqn
R/62147	WO2	BELL Frank George	12-11-43	35 Sqn
R/153884	F/S	BELL Malcolm Owen Morley	3-11-43	429 Sqn
R/202312	Sgt	BELLEW Henry Benedict	2-12-43	1664 HCU
J/13120	F/O	BELLINGER William George	29-09-43	434 Sqn
J/8657	F/O	BELLINGHAM Adam Sidney	24-07-43	420 Sqn
R/74917	WO2	BEMI Frederick	8-04-43	420 Sqn
J/9406	P/O	BENNETT Cecil Joseph	30-01-43	427 Sqn
J/12978	F/O	BENNETT Donald Edward	5-03-43	420 Sqn
R/143404	F/S	BENNETT James Gordon	27-11-43	101 Sqn
J/17158	F/O	BENNETT John	30-07-43	432 Sqn
J/11949	F/O	BENSON Robert Lowell	26-02-43	196 Sqn
R/70608	WO2	BENTLEY Thomas Lloyd	27-04-43	405 Sqn
R/77334	WO2	BERESFORD George James	19-02-43	420 Sqn
R/16782	F/L	BERG George Theodore	3-10-43	434 Sqn
R/151425	F/S	BERNARD David	20-12-43	166 Sqn
R/182015	F/S	BERNDT Evan James	26-11-43	76 Sqn

ID	Rank	Name	Date	Sqn
R/62500	WO2	BERNICK Lloyd Adolf	26-02-43	9 Sqn
J/17079	P/O	BERTHIAUME Joseph Francois Exavier Gilles	26-05-43	7 Sqn
R/167515	F/S	BESSE Claude Andrew	16-12-43	408 Sqn
R/198740	Sgt	BESSENT Henry Roberts	17-12-43	405 Sqn
R/94993	F/S	BESSETTE Bertie Joseph August	16-04-43	15 Sqn
J/12047	F/O	BESWICK Herbert Russell	24-11-43	23 OTU
R/161867	F/S	BETTRIDGE Oliver Augustus	11-08-43	115 Sqn
R/90407	WO2	BETTS Donald	1-09-43	44 Sqn
R/134551	F/S	BETTS Norman Garnet	23-08-43	434 Sqn
J/14791	F/O	BEYAK Alexander Edward	22-10-43	429 Sqn
R/110092	F/S	BILLING James William	2-03-43	487 Sqn
J/22033		BINGHAM Clifford Marvin	20-06-43	10 OTU
J/17924	P/O	BINNIE Colin Muir	29-07-43	424 Sqn
R/90351	WO2	BIRCHALL Roland	17-04-43	408 Sqn
R/115881	F/S	BIRD Colin Ray	3-03-43	115 Sqn
R/145007	F/S	BIRD Derry Gates [USA]	12-06-43	28 OTU
R/60554	WO2	BIRD Robert Francis	16-01-43	61 Sqn
R/115874	F/S	BIRD Sydney Dennis	15-06-43	49 Sqn
R/102142	F/S	BIRKBECK Alburn Frederick	26-05-43	467 Sqn
R/125848	F/S	BIRTCH George Ernest Percy	1-09-43	419 Sqn
J/18162	P/O	BISHEFF George Edward	22-06-43	408 Sqn
J/22393	F/O	BISHOP Gordon Eugene	29-12-43	431 Sqn
R/133344	F/S	BISHOP John Philpott	4-07-43	429 Sqn
J/13118	F/O	BISHOP Stanley Adolfson	28-05-43	100 Sqn
R/136065	F/S	BISSET William McManus	30-03-43	427 Sqn
R/97262	F/S	BITTEN Frederick Charles	7-02-43	425 Sqn
R/137089	F/S	BITTNER John Drake [USA]	29-01-43	420 Sqn
J/14746	F/O	BITTNER Joseph Francois Xavier Jean	10-07-43	424 Sqn
R/100110	WO2	BJARNASON Albert Lloyd	29-07-43	424 Sqn
R/84830	Sgt	BLACK Douglas Allan	10-08-43	405 Sqn
R/75540	Sgt	BLACK Gordon Ronald	11-03-43	44 Sqn
R/62820	WO2	BLACK Harry Gordon	8-02-43	44 Sqn
R/118059	Sgt	BLACK John Hannah	3-03-43	429 Sqn
R/123878	WO2	BLACK Roland Edward	2-12-43	103 Sqn
J/7980	F/L	BLACK William Andrew	3-02-43	408 Sqn
J/17313	P/O	BLACKHALL Robert Orin [USA]	5-05-43	408 Sqn
R/131688	F/S	BLACKMORE Winston Woolley	18-08-43	428 Sqn
J/12854	F/O	BLAGBORNE Charles Ward	4-11-43	429 Sqn
R/150542	F/S	BLAKE Eric Stuart	28-04-43	19 OTU
R/78495	WO1	BLAKE Frederick Henry [USA]	3-04-43	158 Sqn
R/190770	Sgt	BLAKE John Michael	21-12-43	78 Sqn
R/9529	WO2	BLAKE Richard Barnett	15-04-43	90 Sqn
R/180851	Sgt	BLAKELEY Wallace John Robert	5-09-43	1663 HCU
R/130420	Sgt	BLAKELY Wallace Bennett	29-12-43	29 OTU
C/157	W/C	BLANCHARD Sedley Stewart	14-02-43	426 Sqn
R/123873	Sgt	BLENKHORN Charles Robert Sayre	4-05-43	22 OTU
J/3989	F/L	BLIGHT Leslie Edwin	30-05-43	432 Sqn
R/115483	WO2	BLIGHT William Gerald	14-04-43	420 Sqn
R/88244	WO1	BLISS DFC Osborne Lloyd	24-08-43	35 Sqn
J/23312	F/O	BLOCH Willys Roland	26-11-43	429 Sqn
R/92475	F/S	BODLEY William	11-04-43	100 Sqn
R/96901	F/S	BOILY Joseph Omer Emile Jules	16-12-43	408 Sqn
R/123477	F/S	BOIVIN John Louis	1-02-43	1659 HCU
J/18781	P/O	BOLES William Harold	27-11-43	426 Sqn
R/129641	WO2	BOLES William Robert King	4-12-43	76 Sqn
J/21430	F/O	BOLSTAD Kenneth Wallace	24-11-43	23 OTU
J/17396	P/O	BONENFANT Joseph Oscar Rosario	23-06-43	429 Sqn
J/19370	P/O	BONESS Herman Peter	19-10-43	7 Sqn
J/21902	F/O	BONNER Murray Wallace	19-08-43	1663 HCU
R/172874	F/S	BOOTH Donald George	28-08-43	149 Sqn
R/135580	F/S	BOOTH George Arnold	11-04-43	431 Sqn
J/21469	F/O	BOOTH Gordon B. [USA]	16-06-43	12 OTU
R/172283	F/S	BORTOLUSSI Aldo	4-10-43	419 Sqn
J/16957	F/L	BOTKIN Richard Trent [USA]	9-10-43	405 Sqn
R/130745	Sgt	BOULTON Russell Charles Heath	13-02-43	22 OTU
R/136109	F/S	BOUNDY William Allan	29-01-43	22 OTU
J/18164	P/O	BOURDON Gregory Ross	23-09-43	57 Sqn
C/5577	F/L	BOURGEOIS Laurie Alban	12-06-43	432 Sqn
R/143278	F/S	BOURNE Kenneth Charles George	4-05-43	22 OTU
J/18957	P/O	BOURNE Kenneth Reid	13-08-43	432 Sqn
J/22810	F/O	BOUSFIELD George Raymond	4-07-43	432 Sqn
J/18377	P/O	BOUVIER DFM Joseph Maurice Leopold	18-08-43	426 Sqn
R/148574	F/S	BOVACONTI Michael Joseph	31-08-43	78 Sqn
R/113737	F/S	BOVAIRD Walter Le Roy	14-05-43	419 Sqn
R/141583	F/S	BOWCOCK Frederick Hamilton	29-07-43	218 Sqn
R/135010	F/S	BOWDEN William Heyer	14-05-43	419 Sqn
R/104755	WO1	BOWER Graham Westwood	1-09-43	619 Sqn
J/20584	F/O	BOWER MiD John Frank	2-12-43	619 Sqn
R/89348	WO2	BOX John Alexander	31-08-43	434 Sqn
J/12480	F/O	BOYCE William John	12-06-43	419 Sqn
R/126478	Sgt	BOYD Charles Arthur	30-03-43	427 Sqn
R/90535	Sgt	BOYER Gilbert Davies	4-04-43	408 Sqn
R/79608	Sgt	BRACKENRIDGE Douglas Matthew	7-02-43	408 Sqn
J/18170	P/O	BRADEY John Charles	18-08-43	61 Sqn
R/125961	WO2	BRADFORD John McKinnon	30-03-43	115 Sqn
R/80033	WO1	BRADLEY Gordon Clark	3-08-43	103 Sqn
J/10044	F/O	BRADLEY James Reid	16-09-43	138 Sqn
R/87029	WO2	BRADLEY John Edward	9-01-43	12 Sqn
J/17675	P/O	BRADLEY Robert	18-08-43	61 Sqn
R/128173	F/S	BRADSHAW Sidney Victor	29-03-43	420 Sqn
J/18523	P/O	BRADY Francis Joseph Desmond	18-08-43	427 Sqn
R/93554	WO2	BRADY Joseph Gordon 'Joe'	17-05-43	617 Sqn
J/18863	P/O	BRAGER Kenneth Lloyd	20-12-43	408 Sqn
R/135031	F/S	BRAND Peter Healey	22-05-43	428 Sqn
R/134525	Sgt	BRANDOW Roy Leonard	29-03-43	420 Sqn
R/89558	F/S	BRAY Earl Clarence	30-07-43	218 Sqn
J/21541	F/O	BRAY Ward	24-08-43	427 Sqn
R/78842	WO1	BRAYFORD Lloyd Willis	11-02-43	57 Sqn
R/108675	WO2	BREEN James Gerald	12-06-43	431 Sqn
R/58998	Sgt	BREEN William John	31-08-43	427 Sqn
J/28551	P/O	BREHN Thomas John	24-11-43	23 OTU
R/117600	F/S	BRENNAN Cornelius Alfred	13-08-43	218 Sqn
R/87243	WO2	BRIDGEMAN Robert Vale	8-01-43	1443 Flt
R/113427	WO1	BRIEGEL James Stuart	16-12-43	432 Sqn
R/108275	Sgt	BRIFFETT George William	21-12-43	427 Sqn
R/184725	Sgt	BRISCO Frederick Lionel	2-12-43	207 Sqn
R/156384	F/S	BRISLAN John Glen	26-08-43	424 Sqn
R/89802	Sgt	BRIGGS-JUDE Robert William	1-09-43	428 Sqn
R/176158	Sgt	BROADBENT Robert Charles	31-07-43	620 Sqn
R/109822	WO2	BRODERICK Leo Joseph Martin	6-09-43	405 Sqn
R/132570	Sgt	BRODIE William	17-06-43	460 Sqn
R/121901	F/S	BROEMELING Alvin John	16-01-43	467 Sqn
R/130553	WO2	BRONDGEEST Lloyd John	1-09-43	51 Sqn
R/108021	LAC	BROOKES Thomas Robert	1-06-43	420 Sqn
R/110293	F/S	BROUGHTON Douglas Oliver	13-05-43	429 Sqn
J/9906	F/O	BROWN Arthur	15-08-43	420 Sqn
R/133263	F/S	BROWN Benjamin Francis [USA]	1-03-43	44 Sqn
J/24007	F/O	BROWN Brian Edward [USA]	17-09-43	10 OTU
J/20377	F/L	BROWN Carlos Manuel [USA] Croix de Guerre [France]	26-11-43	97 Sqn
R/106507	F/S	BROWN Cecil Allan	18-08-43	434 Sqn
R/83255	F/S	BROWN Clayton Perry	23-10-43	434 Sqn
R/109630	WO2	BROWN David Lloyd George	14-07-43	408 Sqn
R/194139	Sgt	BROWN Douglas Roy	28-09-43	1667 HCU
J/17621	F/O	BROWN Douglas Stewart	15-06-43	106 Sqn
R/125229	F/S	BROWN Harry Lyle	20-02-43	467 Sqn
R/124176	F/S	BROWN Ian Stewart	17-04-43	100 Sqn
R/179452	F/S	BROWN James Herbert	24-08-43	100 Sqn
J/22403	P/O	BROWN James Moyes	20-06-43	24 OTU
J/8793	F/O	BROWN John Henry	11-04-43	139 Sqn
R/146053	Sgt	BROWN Norman Conway	26-08-43	22 OTU
J/22358	F/O	BROWN Robert Burns	30-06-43	425 Sqn
J/15744	F/O	BROWN Sydney	15-04-43	424 Sqn

ID	Rank	Name	Date	Sqn
R/111993	F/S	BROWN William	24-05-43	51 Sqn
R/128905	F/S	BROWN William McIntosh	7-09-43	428 Sqn
R/108322	WO2	BRUNET Ernest Charles	20-10-43	405 Sqn
J/22495	F/O	BRUTON Cecil Gilbert	18-08-43	115 Sqn
J/17097	P/O	BRYANS Robert John	13-05-43	218 Sqn
J/10154	F/O	BRYDON James Stenhouse	16-02-43	90 Sqn
R/20911	F/O	BUCHANAN George Harry	27-11-43	426 Sqn
J/20349	F/O	BUCK Frederick Sinclair	28-06-43	101 Sqn
R/83572	F/S	BUCK Kenneth Howard	5-05-43	102 Sqn
R/81059	Sgt	BUCKINGHAM Arthur Victor McDonald	27-01-43	21 OTU
R/120100	F/S	BUCKWELL Walter Herbert Secretan	13-04-43	419 Sqn
R/85483	WO2	BUDD Henry Ellwood	15-04-43	7 Sqn
J/24730	F/O	BUDD Robert William Harry	24-11-43	23 OTU
J/17497	P/O	BUDREAU Jack Gale	10-04-43	426 Sqn
R/87708	WO2	BUICK John Albert	9-01-43	12 Sqn
R/103913	WO2	BUIE Robert Montgomery	11-04-43	424 Sqn
R/102867	F/S	BUNN Myrl Ellwood	17-06-43	49 Sqn
R/154061	Sgt	BURGESS Joseph Emil Leo	5-05-43	22 OTU
J/19346	P/O	BURGESS Raymond Charles	16-11-43	432 Sqn
R/175118	Sgt	BURKE Bernard William	21-10-43	24 OTU
R/95765	WO2	BURKE Cuthbert Worcester Graham [USA]	8-04-434	25 Sqn
R/104185	F/S	BURKE Franklyn Roy	4-04-43	408 Sqn
J/14554	F/O	BURKE Reginald Joseph	25-06-43	620 Sqn
J/20261	F/O	BURKE Robert Weaver [USA]	6-09-43	419 Sqn
R/18329	P/O	BURNETT Leslie Gordon Emanuel	24-08-43	426 Sqn
R/144158	WO2	BURNS James [USA]	12-06-43	429 Sqn
R/140724	F/S	BURNS William	22-10-43	431 Sqn
R/166252	Sgt	BURNSIDE David George Davidson	3-09-43	30 OTU
J/17115	P/O	BURPEE DFM Lewis Johnstone	17-05-43	617 Sqn
J/24484	F/O	BURTON Earl Allen	26-11-43	429 Sqn
R/162245	F/S	BURTON William Harvey	22-10-43	434 Sqn
J/22487	F/O	BUTCHER Charles Merton	27-09-43	428 Sqn
R/15234	F/S	BUTLER Gerald James	19-05-43	19 OTU
R/111601	F/S	BUTLER Ronald Harris	22-10-43	166 Sqn
R/88361	WO2	BUTTS DFM Nolan	17-10-43	196 Sqn
R/133135	F/S	BYERS Colin Edward	22-11-43	49 Sqn
R/57631	F/S	BYERS George James	3-11-43	429 Sqn
J/17474	P/O	BYERS Vernon William	17-05-43	617 Sqn
J/19381	F/O	CABANA Joseph Louis Etienne	4-12-43	429 Sqn
R/131235	F/S	CADEAU Albert Joseph	3-10-43	428 Sqn
J/16783	P/O	CADMUS George Austen [Argentina]	23-06-43	427 Sqn
R/102903	WO2	CAHILL Clement Bernard	31-08-43	427 Sqn
R/85910	WO2	CAIN William Edward	3-03-43	207 Sqn
J/122397	Sgt	CAIRNS Richard Foote	15-02-43	22 OTU
J/17246	P/O	CALDER Gordon Alexander	13-05-43	98 Sqn
99456	F/S	CALDER James Reginald	9-07-43	106 Sqn
R/116334	WO2	CALDER William Henry	22-06-43	429 Sqn
J/16785	P/O	CALDWELL Robert George	12-03-43	424 Sqn
J/25525	F/O	CAMERON Allan Reid [Argentina]	16-12-43	1667 HCU
R/65249	WO1	CAMERON Donald Alexander Joseph	12-08-43	138 Sqn
J/18517	P/O	CAMERON Donald John	28-08-43	51 Sqn
R/149565	F/S	CAMERON John Edward	28-08-43	76 Sqn
R/116979	WO2	CAMERON William Donald Leslie	1-09-43	419 Sqn
R/140390	Sgt	CAMERON William Douglas	9-01-43	419 Sqn
J/21453	F/O	CAMERON William Parmenas	20-10-43	625 Sqn
R/105794	F/S	CAMERON William Wilson	26-02-43	426 Sqn
J/15235	F/L	CAMPBELL DFC Colin Summers	3-03-43	429 Sqn
J/22215	F/O	CAMPBELL Donald Allister	28-07-43	106 Sqn
R/142311	F/S	CAMPBELL Donald Edward	26-06-43	15 Sqn
R/128774	F/S	CAMPBELL Duncan Eric	12-06-43	429 Sqn
R/123725	F/S	CAMPBELL Frederick Archibald	31-08-43	100 Sqn
R/85722	F/S	CAMPBELL Gordon Ernest	23-01-43	12 Sqn
R/95404	Sgt	CAMPBELL John Gilbert	13-02-43	22 OTU
R/162832	Sgt	CAMPBELL John Louis	22-10-43	1664 HCU
R/142015	F/S	CAMPBELL Joseph William	16-07-43	432 Sqn
R/127938	F/S	CAMPBELL Keith Lauchlan	27-02-43	427 Sqn
R/76460	WO2	CAMPBELL Ralph Patrick	31-01-43	101 Sqn
J/18331	P/O	CAMPBELL William Clayton	14-07-43	432 Sqn
R/134429	F/S	CAMSELL Philip Stuart	2-10-43	61 Sqn
J/4894	F/L	CANDLISH John Muir	12-11-43	35 Sqn
R/182457	Sgt	CANNON Ernest Albert	4-09-43	106 Sqn
J/20214	F/O	CANTIN Maurice Raoul	26-11-43	514 Sqn
R/73825	F/S	CANTLEY Alexander Crawford	17-04-43	408 Sqn
R/133638	F/S	CAPIN Edward Butler	1-09-43	103 Sqn
R/121511	F/S	CARDER David Clayton	1-02-43	1659 HCU
J/10796	F/O	CAREFOOT Garnet Oliver	19-11-43	431 Sqn
R/125005	Sgt	CAREY Leslie Ernest	29-06-43	35 Sqn
R/98829	F/S	CARLEY John William	28-04-43	419 Sqn
J/17331	P/O	CARNEY Richard Alexander	17-08-43	405 Sqn
R/73173	WO2	CARPENTER Leonard Stanley	13-02-43	22 OTU
R/58600	F/S	CARR Clarence Milton	3-10-43	623 Sqn
R/84695	WO2	CARRIGAN Joseph Thomas	3-10-43	158 Sqn
J/16064	P/O	CARRUTHERS Alexander [USA]	12-03-43	214 Sqn
J/8442	F/O	CARSON Lawrence Bartlett	19-02-43	15 Sqn
J/22472	F/O	CARTER Fred Moncrieff	1-09-43	622 Sqn
R/106765	WO2	CARTER John Thomas	7-10-43	15 Sqn
J/15862	F/S	CARTER DFC Ronald George	18-08-43	467 Sqn
J/17165	P/O	CARTIER Joseph Louis Raymond Ferrier	29-03-43	428 Sqn
R/124106	F/S	CARVAJAL Earl Randolph [USA]	12-04-43	425 Sqn
R/183870	Sgt	CASE Emerson Earl	19-11-43	431 Sqn
J/17539	P/O	CASE Thomas Edward	19-02-43	156 Sqn
R/91856	F/S	CASEY Theadore Edgar James	11-02-43	57 Sqn
J/17643	P/O	CASTLE John Gordon	24-08-43	78 Sqn
R/97729	Sgt	CATTO John Harrison	2-12-43	1664 HCU
R/118082	F/S	CAULDERWOOD John Samuel Davidson	30-06-43	425 Sqn
J/24505	F/O	CAULFIELD William James	18-10-43	24 OTU
J/13482	F/O	CAVANAUGH Frank Napolean Smith	30-03-43	408 Sqn
R/191994	Sgt	CHALK Everett William	26-11-43	419 Sqn
J/18123	P/O	CHALLENGER Clifford James	13-06-43	57 Sqn
R/96292	WO2	CHAMBERS Patrick Kelly [USA]	4-07-43	432 Sqn
R/9845	F/S	CHAMBERS Walter Owen Earl	7-09-43	156 Sqn
R/87480	F/S	CHAMNEY Burnet Montieth	26-02-43	420 Sqn
R/164692	Sgt	CHAMPION Dudley Sydney	2-10-43	30 OTU
R/72856	WO1	CHAMPION Ellwin Clair	4-10-43	427 Sqn
J/17069	P/O	CHAMPION Harry Mathew	2-03-43	61 Sqn
J/22485	F/O	CHANDLER John Joseph	28-09-43	622 Sqn
R/88749	F/S	CHAPMAN Robert Alfred	27-01-43	57 Sqn
R/99842	F/S	CHATFIELD Walter Lawrence	15-06-43	49 Sqn
J/3491	F/L	CHEETHAM Gerald Harry	25-06-43	76 Sqn
R/117497	WO2	CHEPIL DFM Mack	3-08-43	428 Sqn
R/67557	Sgt	CHERKINSKY Arthur David	2-03-43	419 Sqn
J/14677	F/O	CHERKINSKY Joseph	5-05-43	22 OTU
R/94989	WO1	CHESTER John William	3-09-43	30 OTU
R/141536	F/S	CHEVALIER Joseph Bruno Vianney	26-11-43	23 OTU
J/147645	F/S	CHIBANOFF Alexander	16-09-43	427 Sqn
R/186823	Sgt	CHISNELL Robert Hilliard	18-08-43	23 OTU
R/185428	Sgt	CHOMA Constantin Robert	23-12-43	1664 HCU
J/21984	F/O	CHORNEYKO Athanazie	22-10-43	429 Sqn
R/150742	WO2	CHRISTENSON Floyd Raymond	22-10-43	429 Sqn
R/159411	F/S	CHRISTIANSON Chris Zane Robert	9-10-43	7 Sqn
J/28782	P/O	CHRISTIE John	12-10-43	82 OTU
J/18884	F/O	CHRISTIE DFM Robert Gunn	23-09-43	97 Sqn
R/151669	Sgt	CHRISTIE William James	21-10-43	24 OTU
R/210612	Sgt	CHRISTIEN William Roderic	21-12-43	16 OTU
J/18248	P/O	CHUDZIK Stanley Frank	16-08-43	218 Sqn
R/114617	F/S	CHURCH James Mayson	30-07-43	156 Sqn
R/114615	WO2	CHURCH Maurice Gordon	3-04-43	408 Sqn
R/114787	F/S	CLAMPITT Edward Blake	12-03-43	106 Sqn
R/158763	F/S	CLARK Basil Elliott	26-08-43	20 OTU
J/20627	F/O	CLARK Clarence Taylor	24-11-43	405 Sqn

ID	Rank	Name	Date	Squadron
R/92687	WO2	CLARK Glenn Greaves	14-02-43	196 Sqn
R/175980	F/S	CLARK James	4-09-43	101 Sqn
R/50428	F/S	CLARK Judson Robert Ernest	14-04-43	429 Sqn
J/20082	F/O	CLARK Lawrence Maurice [USA]	29-04-43	166 Sqn
J/14771	F/O	CLARK Ross Edgerton	6-08-43	425 Sqn
J/20183	F/O	CLARK Russell Stanley	21-12-43	408 Sqn
10118	Sgt	CLARKE George Edward	10-03-43	1659 HCU
R/128436	F/S	CLARKE Samuel Edward	26-11-43	419 Sqn
R/147572	WO2	CLARKE William Robertson	2-12-43	156 Sqn
R/169994	Sgt	CLEMENHAGEN Thomas Frederick	22-10-43	428 Sqn
R/172270	Sgt	CLEMENT Harry	16-08-43	207 Sqn
R/104277	F/S	CLEMENTS Horace Herbert	27-03-43	44 Sqn
J/18408	F/O	CLEMENTS Robert Kelly	2-10-43	57 Sqn
R/167518	WO2	CLEVELAND Archie	26-07-43	75 Sqn
R/174455	Sgt	CLEVELAND Scott Grover [USA]	14-05-43	218 Sqn
R/156760	F/S	CLEVELAND Vincent Alton Francis	31-08-43	419 Sqn
J/21295	F/O	CLIFFORD Lewis Banks	7-09-43	77 Sqn
R/141625	WO2	CLIMIE William Benzie Forbes [USA]	23-08-43	434 Sqn
R/108256	F/S	CLITHEROE Roger Victor	5-05-43	408 Sqn
R/22692	F/O	CLOUTIER Joseph Darie Louis	15-09-43	138 Sqn
R/107456	Cpl	COATES Allan Cyrenius James	1-06-43	420 Sqn
R/73428	WO2	COATES Eddie Donald	7-02-43	424 Sqn
J/11566	F/O	COATES Percy Hornby	4-09-43	50 Sqn
J/16276	F/L	COBB DFC Nelson Alexander	29-06-43	35 Sqn
R/102186	WO2	COCHRANE Arnold Wallace	2-03-43	408 Sqn
J/19167	P/O	COCHRANE Thomas Donald	20-12-43	408 Sqn
R/99552	Sgt	COCKADAY Cecil William	29-03-43	420 Sqn
R/127940	F/S	COCKIN Edwin Mills	29-09-43	419 Sqn
R/109811	WO2	COE George Demetrius	22-06-43	429 Sqn
R/100606	WO2	COGGER Walter Leonard	18-08-43	428 Sqn
R/142054	WO2	COGHILL Clarence Malcolm McGregor	3-04-43	83 Sqn
J/17259	P/O	COKER Charles Kenneth	30-05-43	115 Sqn
R/100737	F/S	COLANGELO William	1-03-43	51 Sqn
J/20039	F/O	COLE Edward Mortimer	23-09-43	15 Sqn
R/87628	WO2	COLE Eric Walter	4-04-43	464 Sqn
R/118109	WO2	COLE Frank Murray	3-08-43	100 Sqn
J/16476	F/O	COLES George Henry	16-09-43	617 Sqn
R/76749	Sgt	COLLETT Joseph Harrington	12-05-43	22 OTU
J/23592	F/O	COLLIER Clarence Melville	16-12-43	405 Sqn
J/16769	F/S	COLLINS Albert Charles	27-06-43	420 Sqn
R/190935	Sgt	COLLINS Neil James	22-11-43	1664 Sqn
R/156379	F/S	COLLINS Rae Warren Buddy	4-09-43	50 Sqn
J/21614	F/O	COLLINS Roy Frederick	20-04-43	57 Sqn
J/17934	F/O	COLQUHOUN Carman MacKenzie	22-09-43	218 Sqn
J/6032	F/L	COLQUHOUN Ian Lorne	18-08-43	434 Sqn
J/7430	F/O	COLVIN James Mackenzie	24-05-43	408 Sqn
R/147647	F/S	COMBRES Maurice Emile	4-07-43	12 Sqn
R/117670	WO2	COMEAU Joseph Napoleon Pascal Eugene	28-05-43	408 Sqn
R/95452	WO2	COMRIE Wilfrid Phelps 'Bill' [USA]	29-03-43	102 Sqn
R/88546	WO2	CONNER Alfred Norman	14-02-43	102 Sqn
R/114897	F/S	CONNOR George Ronald	18-08-43	434 Sqn
J/22199	F/O	CONNOR James Gibson [USA]	2-10-43	51 Sqn
R/157058	F/S	COOK Alexander	12-06-43	103 Sqn
R/144405	F/S	COOK Leo Frederick	27-09-43	432 Sqn
J/24619	P/O	COOK Lorne Frankland	24-11-43	23 OTU
J/6276	S/L	COOK DFC Robert Geoffrey	4-12-43	431 Sqn
J/10020	F/O	COOK Russel Gordon	8-04-43	425 Sqn
R/92573	F/S	COONS Dexter Brand	9-03-43	426 Sqn
R/87128	F/S	COOPER Eugene Joseph	23-09-43	101 Sqn
R/145758	F/S	COOPER Frederick Terrance	26-08-43	22 OTU
R/86182	WO2	COOPER Jack	29-05-43	158 Sqn
R/184379	Sgt	COPEGOG Allan Joseph	2-10-43	23 OTU
R/129552	WO2	COPELAND Thomas William John	29-06-43	467 Sqn
R/54352	WO2	COPPING Harold James Langford	26-11-43	429 Sqn
R/88388	F/S	CORBETT John Alexander	14-03-43	420 Sqn
R/126738	F/S	CORLEY Louie Elmo [USA]	16-04-43	156 Sqn
J/19245	P/O	CORNELIUS Ernest Dean	24-08-43	427 Sqn
R/122947	Sgt	CORNFIELD Joseph Samuel	27-01-43	23 OTU
J/10884	F/O	CORNISH Oliver Mansell	5-05-43	83 Sqn
R/115498	F/S	CORRELL John Dunham	27-02-43	12 Sqn
R/78953	WO2	CORRIE Glen Howard	28-02-43	83 Sqn
J/11240	F/O	CORY Gordon Johnson	12-03-43	424 Sqn
R/155334	Sgt	COSTELLO John Terrance	22-10-43	166 Sqn
R/123094	F/S	COSTELLO Michael	15-08-43	75 Sqn
R/99818	WO2	COSTELLO Ralph Matthew [USA]	24-05-43	199 Sqn
R/142131	F/S	COTE Joseph Richard	2-10-43	424 Sqn
R/93558	WO2	COTTAM Alden Preston	17-05-43	617 Sqn
J/21625	F/O	COTTINGHAM Cyril Morgan	22-11-43	49 Sqn
R/88868	F/S	COTTON Ernest James	28-05-43	51 Sqn
R/105693	F/S	COUCH John Edmund	25-07-43	103 Sqn
R/96684	F/S	COULOMBE Joseph Rosario Arthur Rolland	3-02-43	106 Sqn
J/9324	F/O	COULSON Robert Frederick	24-05-43	420 Sqn
J/16713	P/O	COURTNEY James Boyd [USA]	5-03-43	90 Sqn
R/123973	F/S	COUTTS Lorne Ronald	27-04-43	428 Sqn
R/95345	F/S	COWAN Robert John Alexander	9-01-43	51 Sqn
J/16786	F/O	COX Edmund Thomas	7-02-43	424 Sqn
R/105169	WO2	COZENS Paul Joseph	14-04-43	420 Sqn
J/18448	P/O	CRAIG DFM Walter David	24-08-43	35 Sqn
J/22535	F/O	CRAIGIE James Edgar Donald	26-06-43	106 Sqn
R/110957	WO2	CRAIK Murray Clayton	23-09-43	467 Sqn
R/143665	F/S	CRAIN William Gilbert	22-10-43	427 Sqn
R/186496	Sgt	CRAWFORD John Joseph	18-11-43	429 Sqn
R/128786	WO2	CREBBIN Gordon James	3-10-43	431 Sqn
R/131089	WO2	CRIMMINS Raymond Thomas [USA]	13-05-43	429 Sqn
J/16533	F/L	CRIMMINS DFC William Dennis	16-12-43	625 Sqn
J/17418	P/O	CROCKATT David Edward	27-04-43	405 Sqn
J/11952	F/L	CROCKETT Earle Grant	28-08-43	97 Sqn
R/152605	F/S	CROSSLAND Dan	30-09-43	1667 HCU
R/97071	F/S	CROUSE Henry Arthur	24-05-43	76 Sqn
R/85550	F/S	CROWE James Franklin Karl	23-06-43	10 Sqn
R/107739	WO2	CROWE Leo Ralph	8-04-43	466 Sqn
J/11953	F/O	CROWLEY John William	27-07-43	156 Sqn
J/16383	P/O	CROZIER DFM David Macleod	13-01-43	106 Sqn
R/147569	F/S	CROZIER William James	3-08-43	405 Sqn
J/22866	F/O	CUDNEY Herbert Wilfred	22-10-43	434 Sqn
J/13839	F/O	CULBERT Frederick Campbell	26-06-43	408 Sqn
R/84400	WO2	CULVER Donald George	5-03-43	420 Sqn
R/158185	F/S	CUMMINE Gordon	29-12-43	431 Sqn
R/128687	F/S	CUMMING John William	9-08-43	149 Sqn
R/106631	WO2	CUMMING Leonard Allan	5-02-43	50 Sqn
J/26608	F/O	CUMMING-BART Jerome Thomas Ellis [Trinidad]	2-12-43	426 Sqn
R/141707	WO2	CUMMINGS Robert [USA]	11-12-43	617 Sqn
R/162693	Sgt	CUMMINS Victor Charles	7-07-43	30 OTU
R/113684	F/S	CURRIE Alfred Ross	22-06-43	77 Sqn
R/130188	F/S	CURRIE John	27-01-43	50 Sqn
J/17355	P/O	CURRIE Robert Eldyrn	25-06-43	166 Sqn
J/22532	F/O	CURRIE William Matthew	13-02-43	115 Sqn
J/9340	F/L	CURTIN DFC* Donald Joseph [USA]	25-02-43	106 Sqn
R/90186	F/S	CURTIS Kenneth George	21-01-43	103 Sqn
R/150545	F/S	CZAJKOWSKI Mieczstaw	18-08-43	158 Sqn
R/102105	F/S	DAHL Calvin Warren	2-04-43	57 Sqn
J/22865	F/O	DALE Jack Ralph	4-10-43	419 Sqn
R/126429	WO2	DALEY Charles Francis	9-03-43	61 Sqn
R/111753	WO2	DALLY James William	18-08-43	419 Sqn
J/17164	P/O	DALTON George William Rupert	13-06-43	427 Sqn
R/120612	F/S	DALTON Gordon Edwin	3-10-43	90 Sqn
J/20887	F/S	DALTON John Anthony	29-04-43	166 Sqn
J/20481	F/O	DANCE John James	23-10-43	434 Sqn
J/16385	P/O	DANAHY DFC Sylvester	28-02-43	83 Sqn
J/22617	F/O	DANNIGER Harry Allen [USA]	6-09-43	419 Sqn
R/142365	F/S	DARBY Alan	7-05-43	29 OTU

ID	Rank	Name	Date	Sqn
R/108258	F/S	DARLINGTON Frank Lawrence	4-02-43	106 Sqn
R/132181	F/S	DAUK Heronimus Dominick Alouise	2-10-43	424 Sqn
R/62274	Sgt	DAVENPORT Harold	30-03-43	408 Sqn
R/129865	F/S	DAVEY William Harold	10-08-43	102 Sqn
J/13085	F/O	DAVID John Martin	18-10-43	7 Sqn
R/79102	WO2	DAVID Joseph Jean Baptiste Sylviel Paul Henri	23-06-43	97 Sqn
R/181120	F/S	DAVIDSON Alexander	24-08-43	75 Sqn
A/14035	F/S	DAVIDSON Edward Vicary	3-10-43	434 Sqn
J/20818	F/O	DAVIDSON Gideon	26-06-43	115 Sqn
R/115668	F/S	DAVIDSON Keith Benedict	12-06-43	12 Sqn
R/104824	WO2	DAVIDSON Lyall James	27-06-43	432 Sqn
J/10328	F/O	DAVIDSON William Cameron	13-07-43	424 Sqn
R/180070	F/S	DAVIE James Anderson	4-07-43	15 Sqn
R/113216	LAC	DAVIES Dennis William	29-08-43	427 Sqn
J/21939	F/O	DAVIES Ralph Perry	12-06-43	429 Sqn
R/14421	F/O	DAVIES Walter Cecil	16-06-43	405 Sqn
R/104057	F/S	DAVIES William John Ross	5-03-43	426 Sqn
R/143433	Sgt	DAVIS Chester Andith	6-09-43	9 Sqn
R/125221	F/S	DAVIS Delmar Murray	12-06-43	30 OTU
R/126892	WO2	DAVIS Fred Hugh [USA]	4-09-43	100 Sqn
R/92672	WO2	DAVIS Harry Llewellyn	1-06-43	420 Sqn
R/117353	WO1	DAVIS DFM Kenneth George	26-11-43	83 Sqn
R/140082	F/S	DAVIS Martin David [USA]	5-05-43	101 Sqn
J/19412	P/O	DAVIS Robert Henry	26-11-43	429 Sqn
R/17308	F/O	DAVIS Russell Alfred	6-11-43	1679 HCFlt
R/16186	F/O	DAWE Robert William	11-08-43	158 Sqn
R/178318	Sgt	DAWSON Harold Clyde	26-07-43	75 Sqn
R/147410	Sgt	DAWSON Leon Wilfred Joseph	12-06-43	15 Sqn
R/171307	Sgt	DAY Douglas George Black	17-11-43	166 Sqn
R/178676	F/S	DAY Raymond Samuel Louis	28-07-43	207 Sqn
J/14885	F/O	DAY Richard Chester	24-08-43	427 Sqn
J/24498	F/O	DAYMAN Harold Gordon	12-10-43	82 OTU
R/143327	F/S	DAYTON James Edward	23-09-43	419 Sqn
R/108725	WO2	DEAN MiD Cyril Armstrong	14-11-43	82 OTU
R/186039	Sgt	DEAN George Albert Earl	28-08-43	77 Sqn
R/98396	WO2	DEANE Anthony David	23-06-43	427 Sqn
R/78952	WO1	DEANE Kenneth Ignatius Joseph	2-09-43	419 Sqn
J/17245	F/O	DEERING DFC George Andrew 'Tony'	16-09-43	617 Sqn
R/79066	WO2	DELLAR Joseph Charles Edward	5-03-43	106 Sqn
R/70694	Sgt	DELORME Louis Thomas	30-05-43	106 Sqn
R/225014	Sgt	DEMPSTER Richard	23-09-43	419 Sqn
R/83543	WO2	DEMPSTER DFM William Joseph	2-02-43	7 Sqn
R/151903	F/S	DENNIS Pierce James Axel	23-06-43	427 Sqn
J/17486	P/O	DENSMORE George Robert	12-06-43	429 Sqn
R/89376	Sgt	DENT Walter Gilbert	28-04-43	158 Sqn
J/15820	F/O	DESROCHES DFC Joseph Omer Leopold	15-04-43	425 Sqn
R/79377	F/S	DESROSIERS Joseph Claude Marcel	29-01-43	420 Sqn
R/158749	F/S	DEVERELL Mansell Ramsay	25-06-43	432 Sqn
R/115406	Sgt	DEWAR Douglas Robertson	17-01-43	76 Sqn
J/16386	P/O	DEWAR Duncan Hugh Alexander	13-01-43	106 Sqn
J/12158	F/O	de MACEDO John Bernard Joseph	3-10-43	23 OTU
R/88357	F/S	de MOLITOR William Daniel	10-08-43	419 Sqn
R/154021	F/S	DE BELLEFEUILLE Joseph Paul Guy Marcel	6-08-43	23 OTU
J/17554	P/O	DE BUSSAC George Henri	22-06-43	429 Sqn
R/59717	F/S	DE SIEYES Jean Galt	28-09-43	434 Sqn
R/95750	WO2	DE SILVA DFM Desmond Michael [British Guiana]	24-08-43	218 Sqn
R/65419	WO2	DICKIE Alexander McKeen	28-02-43	49 Sqn
R/97638	F/S	DICKIE Robert Lloyd	3-01-43	9 Sqn
R/11845	F/O	DICKINSON Earl Willard	15-08-43	420 Sqn
R/141249	F/S	DICKISON Albert William	26-06-43	106 Sqn
R/156913	F/S	DICKSON Walter Edward	23-09-43	428 Sqn
R/82496	F/S	DILLON John Henry	30-03-43	158 Sqn
R/109988	F/S	DILLON John Vinton	26-11-43	419 Sqn
R/108786	WO2	DILLOW Wallace Edward Charles	29-12-43	35 Sqn
J/22480	F/O	DINGLEY Leonard Douglas	12-11-43	102 Sqn
J/20822	F/O	DINGLEY Linwood Alton [USA]	13-05-43	428 Sqn
J/17798	P/O	DINGWALL Fred Thompson	30-05-43	432 Sqn
J/21426	F/O	DITZLER Donald Willoughby	3-11-43	426 Sqn
R/176201	Sgt	DIXON Albert	13-06-43	427 Sqn
R/181570	F/S	DIXON Alfred Ross	3-07-43	214 Sqn
J/17446	P/O	DIXON Chester Brockie	27-04-43	405 Sqn
R/99543	F/S	DIXON Michael Ralph	11-04-43	166 Sqn
R/113007	F/S	DIXON Robert	19-11-43	427 Sqn
R/114740	F/S	DMYTRUK Croix de Guerre [France] Peter	9-12-43	405 Sqn
R/99045	WO2	DOBSON Warren Lee	17-12-43	405 Sqn
J/18226	P/O	DOCKERILL John Peter	22-06-43	408 Sqn
R/84638	WO2	DOHANEY George Francis	4-07-43	9 Sqn
J/17239	P/O	DOHERTY Francis Aloysius	24-05-43	44 Sqn
J/17608	P/O	DOLBY DFC Earle George	1-09-43	97 Sqn
R/122130	F/S	DONALD Charles Douglas	1-02-43	26 OTU
J/22209	F/O	DONALDSON Gordon Edward	29-09-43	419 Sqn
R/194186	Sgt	DONALDSON Malcolm Forrest	22-11-43	428 Sqn
R/59859	WO2	DONEY Sydney Robert	22-11-43	1664 HCU
R/115752	WO2	DONNELLY Earl Brown	22-09-43	77 Sqn
J/14637	F/O	DORWARD David Taylor	3-06-43	10 OTU
R/135853	F/S	DORZEK Anthony Alloysius	12-04-43	23 OTU
J/26605	P/O	DOS SANTOS Theophilus [Trinidad]	18-08-43	426 Sqn
J/15960	F/O	DOUCETTE DFC Joseph Alexander Theodore	15-04-43	425 Sqn
J/20854	F/O	DOUGLAS Arlie Berton	22-05-43	428 Sqn
J/22691	F/O	DOUGLAS Eric Hayden	17-08-43	420 Sqn
R/173933	Sgt	DOUGLAS Harry Lawrence	7-09-43	434 Sqn
R/102484	WO2	DOUGLAS William Ernest	26-05-43	428 Sqn
R/78364	F/S	DOUGLASS William Ewart	29-01-43	22 OTU
J/20831	P/O	DOWDS Herbert Joseph	17-08-43	420 Sqn
R/109725	F/S	DOWN Alfred James	2-03-43	115 Sqn
R/97522	F/S	DOWNTON Charles Murray	29-01-43	420 Sqn
J/12307	F/O	DRAKE Frederick Douglas	20-01-43	487 Sqn
J/14815	F/O	DRAKE Howard Ralph	13-05-43	426 Sqn
R/52121	Sgt	DRAKE James Isaac	26-02-43	1658 HCU
R/143069	F/S	DRAKE William Bruce	3-03-43	427 Sqn
R/182652	Sgt	DRAPER Thomas William	18-09-43	6(RCAF)Gp
R/58262	F/S	DRESSER Robert Edward	7-09-43	427 Sqn
R/152345	F/S	DRIES Paul William [USA]	23-11-43	97 Sqn
R/169017	Sgt	DRISCOLL Edgar Smith	27-09-43	428 Sqn
J/27314	P/O	DRISCOLL Stanley Albert	9-10-43	218 Sqn
R/149761	F/S	DRISCOLL Thomas John	6-08-43	425 Sqn
R/57794	Sgt	DRURY Robert William	8-02-43	44 Sqn
J/17333	P/O	DRYSDALE James Leonard	24-05-43	44 Sqn
R/55961	F/S	DUBE Joseph Paul Henri	17-11-43	405 Sqn
R/76935	F/S	DUBETZ Lawrence	1-05-43	77 Sqn
R/159966	Sgt	DUBORD Joseph Emilien Jean Cyriaque	26-11-43	23 OTU
R/75458	WO2	DUCKER Benjamin Victor Lloyd	27-03-43	431 Sqn
8009A	WO2	DUCLOS Joseph Jean	24-07-43	1652 HCU
R/51858	F/S	DUDLEY Gordon Howard	21-12-43	427 Sqn
R/115915	F/S	DUFFY Francis John	27-04-43	420 Sqn
R/119305	WO2	DUFTON MiD Donald William	13-08-43	77 Sqn
R/79463	WO2	DUGAL Joseph Jean Baptist Albert	3-03-43	425 Sqn
R/195135	Sgt	DUHAMEL Joseph Andrew Jean	17-10-43	23 OTU
J/21361	F/O	DUKE Allan Thomas [USA]	17-08-43	23 OTU
R/106616	F/S	DUKE Harvey McKerr	7-02-43	424 Sqn
J/10667	F/O	DUNAND Emile Joseph Francis	2-02-43	49 Sqn
R/108858	Sgt	DUNBAR George Irving Herbert	27-02-43	419 Sqn
R/95497	WO2	DUNCAN Frederick Colin	28-02-43	49 Sqn
J/26696	P/O	DUNLOP Dawson Aubrey	24-11-43	23 OTU
J/20568	F/O	DUNLOP Lawrence Gray	7-09-43	1658 HCU
R/70006	Sgt	DUNLOP Robert Osbourne Mitchell	4-04-43	78 Sqn
R/99798	F/S	DUNN Harvey Adam	9-01-43	419 Sqn
R/141380	F/S	DUNN Ralph Gordon	22-10-43	207 Sqn

ID	Rank	Name	Date	Sqn
R/101556	Sgt	DUNPHY Clifford Alexander	21-01-43	420 Sqn
J/13814	F/O	DUNPHY Robert Ronald	26-06-43	425 Sqn
J/13843	F/L	DUNPHY DFC Roderick James	20-12-43	426 Sqn
R/122199	F/S	DUPLIN Wilfred Joseph Alexander	15-01-43	23 OTU
R/177109	Sgt	DUPONT Joseph Arthur Charles	22-10-43	434 Sqn
J/16408	P/O	DUPRE Frederick Louis Edward	29-03-43	166 Sqn
J/14745	F/O	DURNELL Archibald Bertram Charles	20-06-43	10 OTU
R/110088	Sgt	DURRELL Donald	22-10-43	49 Sqn
R/58766	Sgt	DUTHIE William Peter	3-02-43	419 Sqn
R/136360	F/S	DUTTON Leonard	14-04-43	420 Sqn
R/61271	WO2	DUTTON Thomas Alexander	3-03-43	427 Sqn
J/26607	P/O	du BOULAY Denis Claude Desmond [St. Lucia]	24-08-43	426 Sqn
R/129312	WO2	DU BOSE Thomas Coke [USA]	5-04-43	21 Sqn
R/102350	F/S	DYER Harold George	8-01-43	50 Sqn
J/21817	P/O	DYNARSKI Edward Frank [USA]	14-04-43	12 Sqn
R/122956	F/S	DYSON Carson Lyle	14-07-43	432 Sqn
R/73846	WO2	d'APERNG Hans	1-09-43	419 Sqn
J/17626	F/O	EAGER DFC William Hedley	16-12-43	1661 HCU
J/10891	F/O	EARNSHAW Kenneth	17-05-43	617 Sqn
R/118286	WO2	EAST Michael George King	26-05-43	90 Sqn
J/8202	F/O	EAST Ronald Clark	22-07-43	420 Sqn
C/20879	F/O	EATON Robert George	3-11-43	428 Sqn
R/157924	F/S	EATON William Bligh	9-10-43	7 Sqn
R/121772	F/S	EBBERS Henry Bernard	23-08-43	434 Sqn
J/27315	P/O	EBERLE Raymond Frederick	22-09-43	218 Sqn
R/86661	P/O	ECCLESTONE Edwin Clifford [United Kingdom]	28-09-43	77 Sqn
J/24430	F/O	EDGAR Alexander William	4-12-43	431 Sqn
R/105371	F/S	EDWARDS Emery Kenneth	22-05-43	428 Sqn
J/21216	F/O	EDWARDS John Harvey	7-04-43	405 Sqn
R/184880	F/S	EDWARDS Mason Argue	22-10-43	158 Sqn
R/125516	Sgt	EDWARDS Robert George	31-07-43	408 Sqn
R/153973	F/S	EDWARDS Russell Irwin	13-03-43	199 Sqn
R/191580	Sgt	EDWARDS William Earl	21-12-43	78 Sqn
R/51529	Sgt	ELLARD Cameron William	5-05-43	408 Sqn
R/79270	WO2	ELLIOT Donald Emil	12-05-43	22 OTU
R/139294	Sgt	ELLIOTT Donald Christopher	7-09-43	77 Sqn
J/13369	F/O	ELLIOTT Gordon William	12-04-43	425 Sqn
J/14678	F/O	ELLIOTT Harry Bertram	19-04-43	22 OTU
J/23147	F/O	ELLIOTT Thomas John	4-10-43	428 Sqn
J/14866	F/O	ELLIOTT William Gerald	5-05-43	419 Sqn
J/15925	F/O	ELLIS Albert James	4-10-43	83 Sqn
R/190987	Sgt	ELLIS Arthur William	11-12-43	26 OTU
R/84903	Sgt	ELLIS John Valentine	10-03-43	23 OTU
R/95905	F/S	ELLIS William Mason	29-05-43	158 Sqn
J/20855	F/O	ELMORE Bruce Alan	3-11-43	428 Sqn
J/18062	P/O	EMERSON DFM Thomas Henry Navin	14-07-43	405 Sqn
R/52795	Sgt	EMMONS Kenneth Edward	5-05-43	408 Sqn
J/20582	F/O	ERICKSON Earl Henry	22-09-43	77 Sqn
R/116318	F/S	ERICKSON Harry	29-06-43	10 Sqn
J/9574	F/O	ERLY William Jerome	27-09-43	158 Sqn
J/7023	F/O	ERZINGER John Dartry	13-05-43	102 Sqn
R/130078	P/O	ESTE John Douglas Alexander	1-09-43	428 Sqn
R/55816	F/S	ETHIER Joseph Paul Oliver	14-05-43	426 Sqn
R/95730	WO2	EVANS David Finlay	8-04-43	420 Sqn
R/225302	Sgt	EVANS Harold Evan	9-10-43	431 Sqn
R/138303	F/S	EVANS James Henry	10-08-43	405 Sqn
J/18037	F/O	EVANS John Wesley	24-05-43	214 Sqn
R/192899	Sgt	EVANS William Harry	29-09-43	11 OTU
R/130109	F/S	EVELINE Joseph Henry	14-02-43	426 Sqn
R/173859	Sgt	EVEREST Dennis	22-09-43	9 Sqn
R/54015	F/S	EVERSFIELD Sydeny Eric	4-07-43	12 Sqn
J/16328	F/L	EWER DFC Harold Frederick	26-07-43	103 Sqn
J/21535	P/O	FAIRWEATHER Edgar Lloyd	15-08-43	420 Sqn
J/16905	P/O	FALLIS John	18-01-43	12 Sqn
R/144200	F/S	FALLOWDOWN Kenneth Ross	22-11-43	82 OTU
J/16216	P/O	FANSHER Harry Frederick	18-01-43	12 Sqn
J/21265	F/L	FANSON Gordon William Neil	18-04-43	428 Sqn
R/85961	WO2	FARAH George	14-02-43	102 Sqn
R/188765	Sgt	FARMER Kenneth Albert	18-11-43	419 Sqn
J/12974	F/O	FARNHAM John Arlo	28-05-43	432 Sqn
J/14805	F/O	FARQUHAR Allan Ronald Armitage	28-07-43	429 Sqn
J/14209	F/O	FARR Harry Prior	23-10-43	434 Sqn
R/152210	F/S	FARREL John Alexander	5-05-43	419 Sqn
R/127628	Sgt	FARRELL Douglas Joseph	28-01-43	14 OTU
R/103820	WO2	FARRELL John Miller	14-05-43	78 Sqn
R/112769	WO2	FARRELL William Robert	4-12-43	77 Sqn
J/24533	P/O	FARRER Hiram	18-09-43	17 OTU
J/11241	F/O	FARRINGTON Harry Gregory	29-03-43	218 Sqn
J/3737	F/L	FARROW Leslie Richard	22-09-43	7 Sqn
R/93489	WO2	FAWNS Herman Stanley	22-06-43	431 Sqn
R/93202	Sgt	FAYLE John Stanley	25-02-43	207 Sqn
R/90344	F/S	FEAGAN Jack Walter	19-06-43	50 Sqn
R/118550	F/S	FEAKES George Stanley	1-09-43	428 Sqn
R/154156	F/S	FEARNELEY Francis Newton Salisbury	12-11-43	1659 HCU
R/172702	F/S	FEDI Eric	7-09-43	77 Sqn
R/67976	F/S	FEDIGAN James Gerald Joseph [USA]	29-06-43	22 OTU
J/17260	P/O	FELSEN Marcus Richards	13-06-43	50 Sqn
R/75877	WO2	FENTON Roy Cook	18-01-43	44 Sqn
R/101891	F/S	FERGUSON Donald Alexander	28-2-43	427 Sqn
R/102082	F/S	FERGUSON Lawrence Arkwright	29-06-43	424 Sqn
R/115045	WO2	FERGUSON Robert Chrysler	14-05-43	149 Sqn
R/105725	WO2	FERRIER Roy Wilson	19-02-43	426 Sqn
J/19463	P/O	FERRIER Walter Robert	20-12-43	434 Sqn
J/128607	F/O	FERRIS Ernest Robert	26-06-43	425 Sqn
R/129539	WO2	FERRIS John Sherman	22-10-43	78 Sqn
R/106063	F/S	FETHERSTONHAUGH Charles Brian	10-01-43	10 Sqn
R/106603	WO2	FIGHTER Kenneth Franklin	13-05-43	426 Sqn
R/81030	Sgt	FILL Harold Walter	17-04-43	408 Sqn
J/9635	F/O	FILLINGHAM Thomas Ashton	12-06-43	405 Sqn
J/6386	F/L	FILLMORE Stuart Reginald	11-08-43	218 Sqn
J/24182	F/O	FINDLAY Jack Chisholm	30-10-43	427 Sqn
R/97647	WO2	FIRTH Joseph Arthur	13-07-43	100 Sqn
J/20482	F/O	FISCHER Alfred Austin	20-12-43	434 Sqn
J/22786	P/O	FISHER Ernest Edward	14-01-43	22 OTU
R/157039	F/S	FITCH James Henry	17-04-43	101 Sqn
R/83848	F/S	FITCH James Richard	26-07-43	103 Sqn
J/14775	F/O	FITZGERALD Gerald William	3-08-43	166 Sqn
R/80915	WO1	FITZPATRICK Charles Phillip	18-08-43	434 Sqn
J/15533	F/O	FITZ-GIBBON George Desmond	30-01-43	426 Sqn
J/13419	F/O	FLATT William Henry	23-06-43	207 Sqn
J/17802	F/O	FLETCHER Arthur Gordon	13-06-43	83 Sqn
J/17222	P/O	FLETCHER Grant Alexander	4-04-43	408 Sqn
J/170220	Sgt	FLETCHER James Leonard	18-08-43	427 Sqn
J/22074	F/O	FLETT Stewart Mackenzie	6-11-43	1659 HCU
R/138384	WO2	FLEWIN Charles Edward	3-11-43	426 Sqn
J/15718	F/O	FODERINGHAM DFC Clifford	3-09-43	156 Sqn
J/23051	F/O	FOGG Edgar Delyra	18-11-43	419 Sqn
J/14741	F/O	FOLEY Bruce Gregory [USA]	3-10-43	77 Sqn
R/90930	F/S	FOLEY William Joseph	5-04-43	405 Sqn
J/22796	F/O	FOLKERSEN Victor Roy	5-09-43	1661 HCU
R/176962	Sgt	FOLLETT Albert	7-11-43	15 OTU
J/12302	F/O	FOLLOWS William Arthur	22-06-43	429 Sqn
R/102678	WO2	FOOTE Alan Dick	8-01-43	9 Sqn
R/187590	Sgt	FOOTE John	11-12-43	16 OTU
R/121566	F/S	FORAN Theodore Willson	15-04-43	149 Sqn
J/17200	F/O	FORBES Allan Leighton	30-07-43	7 Sqn
R/83127	WO2	FORBES William Clyde	3-03-43	425 Sqn
R/116865	WO2	FORDYCE Gordon William	23-11-43	156 Sqn
J/19350	P/O	FOREST John Kenneth	9-12-43	77 Sqn
J/17672	P/O	FORSYTH Harold Earl	14-05-43	149 Sqn

ID	Rank	Name	Date	Sqn
R/117476	WO2	FORTIN Jean Gilbert Felix	4-10-43	51 Sqn
J/17453	P/O	FOSTER Alfred Louis	15-04-43	7 Sqn
R/85356	WO1	FOSTER Allan Gerald	12-08-43	138 Sqn
J/22793	F/O	FOSTER Arthur Baker	4-07-43	408 Sqn
R/70200	F/S	FOSTER Charles St. Clair	28-03-43	419 Sqn
J/17091	P/O	FOSTER DFC Edward Austin Nixon	27-04-43	115 Sqn
J/11615	P/O	FOSTER Leslie Charles	27-06-43	420 Sqn
J/25075	F/O	FOULSTON James Arthur	2-12-43	1664 HCU
R/151463	Sgt	FOURNIER Roger Moise	22-10-43	429 Sqn
R/91889	WO2	FOWELL Albert Edward	12-06-43	408 Sqn
C/14078	F/O	FOWLER AFM Harry Wilfred	29-06-43	419 Sqn
J/22529	F/O	FOWLER Reginald John Leake	25-06-43	428 Sqn
J/11234	F/O	FOX Morgan David	14-02-43	196 Sqn
R/112757	F/S	FRANCIS Wilfred George	2-03-43	419 Sqn
R/84415	F/S	FRANK Ralph	30-03-43	97 Sqn
J/8216		FRASER Douglas Gordon	13-05-43	426 Sqn
R/65162	F/S	FRASER George William	24-08-43	12 Sqn
R/64674	WO1	FRASER Hugh Scott	18-11-43	49 Sqn
R/4236A	F/S	FRASER Iain	17-01-43	50 Sqn
R/121015	F/S	FRASER James Kenneth	20-10-43	1664 HCU
R/129563	F/S	FRASER John Hugh Murdock	29-03-43	218 Sqn
R/119693	F/S	FRASER Richard Douglas	13-05-43	12 Sqn
R/176127	Sgt	FRASER Robert Anton	31-08-43	427 Sqn
J/6659	F/O	FREBERG DFC Philip Gustave	11-04-43	7 Sqn
R/61217	WO2	FREELAND Warren Walter	9-03-43	7 Sqn
J/16400	F/O	FREEMAN Averell Whitman	17-08-43	420 Sqn
R/133119	F/S	FREEMAN Henry Graham	24-05-43	51 Sqn
R/137079	F/S	FREEMAN James William	4-05-43	22 OTU
J/10162	F/O	FREEMAN William Joseph	13-02-43	35 Sqn
R/120897	F/S	FREWEN Stanley Douglas	22-05-43	428 Sqn
R/123239	Sgt	FREZELL Edward Gerrard	13-02-43	30 OTU
J/11609	F/O	FRIZZELL James Clifford	28-08-43	97 Sqn
R/188092	Sgt	FROST Harold William	16-09-43	427 Sqn
R/115677	F/S	FROST John Bert	18-02-43	106 Sqn
J/18454	P/O	FROUD Harold Garfield	26-06-43	427 Sqn
J/16944	P/O	FRY Ernest John	6-03-43	76 Sqn
J/17663	F/O	FUDGE Bruce Samuel	22-06-43	431 Sqn
R/76310	F/S	FUDGE Howard Philip	14-05-43	149 Sqn
R/61529	Sgt	FULCHER Louis Thomas	3-04-43	467 Sqn
C/17965	P/O	FULLER William Homer	2-10-43	23 OTU
R/163567	Sgt	FULTON Douglas Bloom	9-10-43	218 Sqn
R/87122	Sgt	FULTON Roy Oswald	5-03-43	83 Sqn
J/7036	F/O	FUNKHOUSE Harvey George	3-08-43	428 Sqn
J/17917	P/O	FURMAN Russel Max [USA]	17-07-43	207 Sqn
J/17025	P/O	GAGNON Gerald Alban	27-06-43	427 Sqn
J/21254	P/O	GAIN Andrew Macfarlane Harrison	15-01-43	23 OTU
J/18832	P/O	GALAVAN Cyril Vincent	29-09-43	166 Sqn
R/92353	F/S	GALBRAITH John Eldon	18-01-43	9 Sqn
R/107927	F/S	GALE George Claremont	9-04-43	7 Sqn
J/27392	P/O	GALLAGHER Gordon John	9-11-43	23 OTU
R/138591	LAC	GALLANT Joseph Fernand Roger	12-09-43	425 Sqn
R/141634	F/S	GALLOWAY James	3-11-43	426 Sqn
J/9337	F/L	GAMBLE Robert Hodgson Perry	4-04-43	408 Sqn
R/169746	Sgt	GANDER Arthur Frederick	19-11-43	427 Sqn
J/18065	P/O	GARALICK Alexander	3-08-43	428 Sqn
R/103201	F/S	GARBAS Francis Anthony	17-05-43	617 Sqn
R/108830	F/S	GARBUTT William Harrison	15-08-43	420 Sqn
R/123021	WO2	GARDINER Allan Thomas	26-11-43	429 Sqn
J/15548	F/L	GARDINER DFC Raymond Arthur	23-11-43	405 Sqn
J/22218	F/O	GARDNER William Austin	4-09-43	100 Sqn
R/65741	WO1	GARDNER Norman William	7-11-43	1663 HCU
R/111417	F/S	GARLAND Douglas Haig Armour	1-09-43	419 Sqn
R/134226	F/S	GARMAN Keith Lavon [USA]	13-05-43	218 Sqn
R/122401	WO2	GAROUTTE Bryon Norman [USA]	4-07-43	432 Sqn
R/190537	Sgt	GARRICK Charles Ross	3-10-43	102 Sqn
R/84377	WO2	GARSHOWITZ Abram	17-05-43	617 Sqn
R/148364	F/S	GAUDRY Harold Prentiss	3-08-43	432 Sqn
R/107473	F/S	GAUTHIER Joseph Omer Romain	19-02-43	426 Sqn
J/17108	P/O	GAUTHIER Joseph Victor Leo	3-03-43	425 Sqn
J/18380	P/O	GAWTHROP Kenneth Gordon	18-08-43	426 Sqn
J/16487	F/O	GEBHARD Claude William	27-04-43	158 Sqn
J/17721	P/O	GEDAK Joseph Isador	13-05-43	90 Sqn
R/184067	Sgt	GEE Melvin Ellis	3-11-43	426 Sqn
R/180825	Sgt	GEMMEL Keith Pratt	3-07-43	19 OTU
J/22054	F/O	GENNIS Max	16-12-43	619 Sqn
R/95479	F/S	GEORGE William Harris	17-04-43	100 Sqn
R/115979	F/S	GERDING Cecil Louis	13-05-43	57 Sqn
R/114715	F/S	GERGLEY Steve John	21-01-43	420 Sqn
J/10730	F/O	GERMAN AFM Harold Wallace	3-10-43	434 Sqn
R/78050	Sgt	GEROW Wilbur John	18-11-43	419 Sqn
C/6318	P/O	GIBAULT Joseph Leon	24-11-43	23 OTU
J/124889	F/S	GIBBONS Anthony James	31-07-43	15 Sqn
J/21735	F/O	GIBSON Abraham Joseph	24-08-43	426 Sqn
R/158800	F/S	GIBSON Donald James	17-12-43	101 Sqn
R/75614	WO2	GIBSON John William	17-04-43	408 Sqn
J/20374	F/O	GIBSON Leo Garth	13-02-43	420 Sqn
J/22069	F/O	GIERULSKI Ted Charles	17-12-43	408 Sqn
R/134457	F/S	GIFFIN Stephen Graham	14-04-43	420 Sqn
R/53388	Sgt	GIGUERE George Joseph	1-02-43	425 Sqn
R/117691	F/S	GIGUERE Joseph Emery Romeo	7-02-43	408 Sqn
J/21298	F/O	GILBERT Reginald Campbell	3-09-43	199 Sqn
R/152522	F/S	GILCHRIST David Ronald	26-05-43	77 Sqn
J/139912	Sgt	GILCHRIST William Carter	18-11-43	431 Sqn
R/123266	F/S	GILES David Edward	29-04-43	166 Sqn
R/135059	F/S	GILLEN William Albert [USA]	9-01-43	57 Sqn
R/56637	Sgt	GILLESPIE John	27-04-43	207 Sqn
R/155552	F/S	GILLIES Donald James	3-07-43	19 OTU
R/115910	F/S	GILLIES Kenneth Malcolmson	1-06-43	420 Sqn
R/89875	WO2	GILLIN James William	13-07-43	49 Sqn
R/97720	Sgt	GILLIS Norman Montague	17-12-43	138 Sqn
C/1036	S/L	GILMORE DFC Edward Gerard	5-04-43	408 Sqn
R/184720	Sgt	GILVERSON Albert Edward	19-08-43	1663 HCU
R/90668	F/S	GIMBY William Edwin	18-08-43	405 Sqn
J/22212	F/O	GINGRAS Joseph Rene Guy	26-06-43	432 Sqn
J/13143	F/O	GIPSON Aaron Henry	17-04-43	103 Sqn
J/22568	P/O	GIRTY Lloyd George	5-04-43	21 Sqn
R/143186	F/S	GLADWIN Francis Edmund	28-06-43	22 OTU
R/103897	F/S	GLADWIN Lewis Lee	14-02-43	1651 HCU
R/120563	Sgt	GLASCOCK Orval Kenneth	27-04-43	420 Sqn
R/180232	F/S	GLASS Ronald Frank	10-07-43	102 Sqn
J/18551	P/O	GLASSBERG Jack	3-03-43	425 Sqn
J/10212	F/O	GLINZ Harvey Sterling	16-05-43	617 Sqn
R/110773	WO2	GLOVER Charles Gordon	6-09-43	83 Sqn
R/118056	F/S	GOLDNEY Robert Edward	5-04-43	405 Sqn
R/148539	Sgt	GOLDSPINK Joseph John	28-03-43	419 Sqn
J/12863	F/O	GOLDSTEIN Robert Philip	3-10-43	428 Sqn
R/77325	WO2	GONNETT Lennox Alwin	3-02-43	419 Sqn
R/90240	WO2	GOODFELLOW James Richard	14-07-43	428 Sqn
R/149073	F/S	GOODWIN James Robertson	2-12-43	432 Sqn
J/15706	P/O	GOODWIN Robert Oscar Evans	25-06-43	419 Sqn
R/61133	Sgt	GORDON Archibald Don	7-04-43	405 Sqn
R/135048	F/S	GORDON John Peter Campbell	23-09-43	57 Sqn
J/21894	F/O	GORDON Macdonald Stuart	3-09-43	199 Sqn
R/16260	P/O	GORDON DFC William Campbell	3-09-43	156 Sqn
R/90290	WO1	GORING Curtis Albert	1-09-43	405 Sqn
R/150741	Sgt	GORRIE Harvey Frank	1-02-43	1659 HCU
R/138599	WO2	GOTT Alfred Norman	20-12-43	51 Sqn
R/139157	F/S	GOUDY DFM Cameron McKenzie	17-07-43	77 Sqn
J/21429	F/O	GOULD Howard James	18-10-43	9 Sqn
R/156749	F/S	GOULD William Norman	22-09-43	12 OTU
R/134921	F/S	GOURDE Robert Russell [USA]	28-04-43	419 Sqn
R/71815	Sgt	GOWEN Charles Gerard	13-05-43	102 Sqn
R/139047	F/S	GOWLING George Robert	24-05-43	419 Sqn
R/93601	WO2	GOWRIE Chester Bruce	20-12-43	617 Sqn
J/21043	F/O	GRACIE Byron McGie	23-06-43	427 Sqn
J/18225	P/O	GRAHAM Gordon Allan	18-11-43	9 Sqn

Service No.	Rank	Name	Date	Unit
R/91900	WO1	GRAHAM Harold Richmond	13-07-43	103 Sqn
J/16414	P/O	GRAHAM Robert	5-03-43	420 Sqn
R/78456	WO2	GRAINGER James George	27-04-43	102 Sqn
J/18431	P/O	GRANGE Edward Alexander McDougall [United Kingdom]	15-08-43	467 Sqn
J/27696	P/O	GRANT Alexander	22-11-43	82 OTU
J/17223	P/O	GRANT Arthur Gordon	12-06-43	408 Sqn
J/21941	P/O	GRANT Bruce Angus	29-03-43	420 Sqn
J/24632	F/O	GRANT Leslie Kenneth Alexander	17-12-43	97 Sqn
J/22204	F/O	GRANT William Angus	5-05-43	408 Sqn
C/10383	F/L	GRAY Kenneth MacGregor	10-08-43	405 Sqn
R/140935	F/S	GRAY Peter Ritchie	2-12-43	1664 HCU
R/91855	WO2	GRAY William Reid	18-02-43	419 Sqn
J/22586	F/O	GREAVES Roy	9-10-43	90 Sqn
R/107004	WO2	GREEN Arthur Stanley	24-05-43	419 Sqn
R/160583	F/S	GREEN Charles	12-08-43	28 OTU
J/18353	P/O	GREEN Frank Stanford	6-09-43	106 Sqn
R/147218	F/S	GREEN Hans Asmussen	23-09-43	467 Sqn
R/168797	F/S	GREEN Roy Leslie	6-11-43	1679 HCFlt
R/86903	F/S	GREEN Thomas Kendall	1-09-43	428 Sqn
R/225224	Sgt	GREEN William Henry	2-12-43	432 Sqn
J/20077	F/O	GREEN William John Russel	25-07-43	1659 HCU
R/7534	F/O	GREENAN John Fergus	2-03-43	57 Sqn
R/106204	F/S	GREENGRASS Roy Stanley	10-03-43	1659 HCU
R/125227	F/S	GREER James Miller	29-03-43	420 Sqn
J/20881	F/O	GREIG Patrick Joseph McCrohan	1-06-43	420 Sqn
R/119705	F/S	GRENON Alfred Joseph	22-05-43	428 Sqn
R/98989	WO2	GRICE Ivor Charles	2-03-43	408 Sqn
R/163282	Sgt	GRIESE Leonard David	19-12-43	433 Sqn
J/22270	F/O	GRIEVE John Melrose	21-12-43	427 Sqn
R/161439	F/S	GRIFFIN Edward Herbert William	4-10-43	419 Sqn
R/80654	WO2	GRIFFIN Robert George	11-04-43	57 Sqn
R/98563	F/S	GRIFFITHS Robert Thomas	23-09-43	419 Sqn
R/58484	Sgt	GRIMSON Albert Marino	26-11-43	103 Sqn
J/18200	P/O	GRINDLEY William Edward	4-09-43	57 Sqn
R/97707	F/S	GROGAN Barrington Philip	27-02-43	419 Sqn
J/23517	F/O	GROSE Carl	19-07-43	22 OTU
R/107592	F/S	GRUCHY Charles Albert	17-01-43	76 Sqn
R/125963	F/S	GUAY Francis John	23-10-43	434 Sqn
R/55551	WO2	GUAY Joseph Jacques Alfred	17-04-43	408 Sqn
R/145232	Sgt	GUBB John Franklin	29-03-43	426 Sqn
R/108356	WO2	GUEPIN Yvon Jean Baptiste	14-05-43	149 Sqn
J/16807	F/O	GUEST Charles Hugh	15-11-43	139 Sqn
R/162319	F/S	GUEST George William	24-12-43	100 Sqn
R/79076	WO2	GUILD Fred Winslow	27-03-43	44 Sqn
R/79306	F/S	GUILLEMETTE Alfred Frederic	7-02-43	425 Sqn
R/104187	F/S	GULLISON Frederick Eugene	8-02-43	10 OTU
J/23112	F/O	GUPPY Frederick John Sydney	2-10-43	23 OTU
R/149918	F/S	GUSTAFSON Roy Gosta Helmer	7-10-43	15 Sqn
R/113728	F/S	GUSTAVSEN Preben Brandt	29-03-43	428 Sqn
R/156742	Sgt	HACKETT William James	15-02-43	22 OTU
R/127714	WO2	HADDEN Eldred Blakely	18-03-43	156 Sqn
J/16232	F/O	HADDEN William Anderson	24-09-43	428 Sqn
R/178279	F/S	HADIKEN Alexander Alan	24-08-43	218 Sqn
R/120914	F/S	HAGAN Robert Edward	22-05-43	428 Sqn
R/99069	F/S	HAGEN Harris Gordon	2-06-43	24 OTU
R/152439	F/S	HAHN Henry Joseph	23-08-43	100 Sqn
R/117684	F/S	HAINES Lloyd George	17-04-43	408 Sqn
C/1322	F/L	HAINES Victor Yelverton	26-11-43	429 Sqn
R/131435	F/S	HALEY Byron Leo	13-05-43	467 Sqn
R/95419	WO2	HALIKOWSKI Joseph Walter	3-04-43	405 Sqn
R/126388	F/S	HALL Allan Avand Fisher	5-05-43	22 OTU
R/73485	F/S	HALL Clowes Edwin	22-10-43	51 Sqn
R/108359	F/S	HALL George Langley	29-01-43	22 OTU
R/108825	F/O	HALL George Robert Douglas	14-03-43	420 Sqn
J/19432	P/O	HALL Joseph William Kenneth	28-09-43	622 Sqn
J/16063	P/O	HALL Maxwell Palmer	5-04-43	408 Sqn
R/65638	Sgt	HALL Serbert Norman	3-04-43	419 Sqn
J/20375	F/O	HALL Thomas Frederick	26-06-43	425 Sqn
J/17288	P/O	HALLDING Ernest Claude	1-05-43	7 Sqn
J/14216	F/O	HALPIN Maurice Patrick	27-09-43	434 Sqn
R/129750	Sgt	HALVORSEN John Detrick [USA]	12-06-43	28 OTU
R/92131	WO2	HAMBROOK Mark David Willis	26-02-43	83 Sqn
R/118223	F/S	HAMER Jack Thomas	28-08-43	428 Sqn
R/164468	Sgt	HAMIL Walter Henry	9-10-43	431 Sqn
R/137725	WO2	HAMILTON Donald Grant	4-12-43	429 Sqn
R/102390	F/S	HAMILTON James Douglas	23-06-43	427 Sqn
J/21291	F/O	HAMILTON William Harry	4-10-43	419 Sqn
J/15425	F/O	HAMILTON William Norman	27-09-43	218 Sqn
J/23298	F/O	HAMPTON William Edward	4-12-43	429 Sqn
R/101482	WO2	HANAN Samuel [USA]	27-04-43	429 Sqn
J/16661	P/O	HANBIDGE Ralph Trever	8-01-43	467 Sqn
J/8376	F/O	HANDFORTH Stanley Willard	26-07-43	419 Sqn
R/158965	F/S	HANEY Bruce Wismer	16-12-43	166 Sqn
R/110175	F/S	HANNA James	10-08-43	405 Sqn
R/142418	WO2	HANNAH Robert Stanley	25-02-43	207 Sqn
R/115553	F/S	HANNAY Albert Edward	12-03-43	1661 HCU
R/160789	F/S	HANSELL Harry Ernest	27-09-43	434 Sqn
R/103842	WO2	HANSEN Harry Alwin	26-02-43	420 Sqn
R/196069	Sgt	HANTON Lloyd George	24-11-43	408 Sqn
R/131571	Sgt	HARALSON Oliver John	14-05-43	419 Sqn
J/16700	F/L	HARDING DFC Andrew Crawford	18-11-43	7 Sqn
J/17338	P/O	HARDING Reginald Clifford	18-08-43	44 Sqn
J/22551	F/O	HARDY John Edward	9-04-43	166 Sqn
J/10054	F/O	HARDY William Albert George	1-05-43	405 Sqn
J/15655	F/O	HARMAN Frank Albert	24-08-43	405 Sqn
R/128052	WO2	HARRINGTON John	12-06-43	7 Sqn
R/199529	Sgt	HARRINGTON Myron Clarence	9-10-43	427 Sqn
J/9742	F/L	HARRIS Victor Henry	26-02-43	15 Sqn
R/132541	WO2	HARRIS Victor Keith	20-10-43	620 Sqn
R/114556	WO2	HARRIS William Scott	15-04-43	428 Sqn
J/18007	P/O	HARRISON DFM Arthur	27-09-43	103 Sqn
R/130740	F/S	HARRISON Bruce Robert	1-09-43	428 Sqn
J/13416	F/O	HARRISON Frank Percival	24-05-43	405 Sqn
R/76374	F/S	HARRISON Gordon Rudolph	24-08-43	158 Sqn
J/26639	P/O	HARRISON Jack Eckersley	25-11-43	20 OTU
J/21400	F/O	HARRISON James Robert [USA]	22-10-43	427 Sqn
R/70275	Sgt	HARRISON John McLaren	14-05-43	408 Sqn
J/18220	P/O	HARRISON John Wilfred	12-11-43	35 Sqn
J/25841	P/O	HARRISON Orton Douglas	22-09-43	158 Sqn
J/18463	F/O	HARRISON Richard Samuel	23-08-43	434 Sqn
R/4196	F/S	HARRISON Stewart	24-07-43	420 Sqn
R/115276	F/S	HARRON William Rehfeld	29-01-43	23 OTU
R/111333	F/S	HART Gordon Gerald	28-05-43	428 Sqn
R/95244	F/S	HART Ralph Eric	14-05-43	405 Sqn
R/140156	F/S	HARTMAN Clifford Lawrence	23-11-43	7 Sqn
J/10412	F/O	HARTNEY Norman John Patrick	16-02-43	90 Sqn
R/103722	WO2	HARTNEY William Douglas	28-02-43	427 Sqn
J/132700	F/S	HARVEY Benjamin Campbell [USA]	30-03-43	1651 HCU
J/8127	P/O	HARVIE Robert	17-01-43	50 Sqn
J/10657	F/O	HASLAM Charles Broadbent	18-01-43	9 Sqn
R/120614	F/S	HATCH Alan Edgar	13-05-43	428 Sqn
J/21631	F/O	HATCHWELL James Gaston	21-12-43	427 Sqn
J/9407	F/L	HATLE Clifford Oscar	17-04-43	408 Sqn
R/114914	F/S	HAUGEN Willard Melvin	18-08-43	405 Sqn
R/139686	F/S	HAVARD Donald Ivor	14-05-43	429 Sqn
J/16775	F/O	HAWKINS John David	17-08-43	405 Sqn
J/17659	P/O	HAYES Norman Dennis	12-06-43	426 Sqn
R/116546	F/S	HAYES Russell Daniel	6-09-43	419 Sqn
R/101345	WO2	HAYWARD Victor Charles	11-02-43	106 Sqn
R/96161	WO2	HEALEY Harold Arthur	9-04-43	207 Sqn
R/82526	WO1	HEALEY Allan	22-09-43	434 Sqn
R/74590	WO1	HEARD John William Harold	10-03-43	23 OTU
R/5535	F/L	HEARD Stanley Mervyn	18-08-43	419 Sqn
J/16756	P/O	HEATHER Roderick John	12-03-43	427 Sqn

Service No.	Rank	Name	Date	Sqn
R/88174	WO2	HEBB Warren St. Clair	28-08-43	97 Sqn
J/17480	P/O	HEDEN Philip Gustave	29-07-43	424 Sqn
J/19730	P/O	HEHIR John [USA]	10-04-43	426 Sqn
R/54915	Sgt	HEIDER Georges	4-12-43	431 Sqn
R/178656	Sgt	HEINIG John Peter	6-09-43	10 Sqn
R/115171	F/S	HELE Carroll Telfer	26-06-43	425 Sqn
R/65921	Sgt	HELM Edward James	3-11-43	429 Sqn
R/70986	P/S	HEMING Cecil Davis	17-04-43	408 Sqn
R/120606	P/S	HEMING George Chetwynd	17-04-43	408 Sqn
R/94132	F/S	HEMMING Edward Frank John 'Eddie'	9-12-43	77 Sqn
R/98354	WO2	HENCKE Jnr Werner Charles [USA]	27-04-43	428 Sqn
R/75353	Sgt	HENDERSON Charles Orrin	12-03-43	405 Sqn
R/139159	WO2	HENRY Ernest Frank	30-07-43	75 Sqn
J/18530	P/O	HENRY Robert Lloyd	29-08-43	427 Sqn
J/21468	P/O	HEPBURN Elmer James	7-10-43	49 Sqn
R/92042	F/S	HERBERT Garnet McMillan	3-10-43	428 Sqn
R/128322	WO2	HERMAN George Philip	18-11-43	101 Sqn
R/137373	F/S	HERRINGTON Granite William [USA]	30-03-43	408 Sqn
J/8380	F/S	HERRON Arnold Raymond	4-07-43	12 Sqn
J/17171	P/O	HESLIP William Daylor	5-04-43	428 Sqn
J/22526	F/O	HETHERINGTON Patrick Michael	7-08-43	22 OTU
R/132100	F/S	HETHERINGTON William Moffatt Tattersall	30-07-43	78 Sqn
R/175904	Sgt	HEWER Lorne Barrie	6-06-43	30 OTU
R/78896	WO2	HEWITT William Robert Harold	1-05-43	51 Sqn
R/131460	F/S	HEXIMER Harry Pliley	23-06-43	427 Sqn
J/22556	F/O	HICKEY Arthur Reginald	8-04-43	419 Sqn
J/22450	F/L	HICKS Donald Elliott	3-11-43	76 Sqn
R/155731	F/S	HICKS Harold Stanley	25-06-43	429 Sqn
J/10024	F/O	HICKS Murray Drysdale Stephen	13-06-43	50 Sqn
R/82956	F/S	HICKS Reginald McLeod	4-07-43	408 Sqn
R/98109	WO2	HIGGINS DFM Francis Joseph	26-06-43	427 Sqn
R/89625	WO2	HIGGINS James Herbert	2-03-43	408 Sqn
J/26984	F/O	HIGHSTED Raymond Harold	28-09-43	1664 HCU
C/18022	P/O	HIGHTOWER DFC Cecil Earl	26-07-43	10 Sqn
R/93410	WO2	HIGNELL Wilbert Scott	9-01-43	97 Sqn
R/145781	F/S	HILDRETH Charles Clifford	13-05-43	428 Sqn
J/8621	F/L	HILL Allan Myrick	27-03-43	431 Sqn
J/15522	S/L	HILL DFC Howard Stephenson	18-04-43	1659 HCU
R/157756	F/S	HILL Lawrence Merwin	26-04-43	419 Sqn
R/79024	WO2	HILL Raymond Hepton	3-02-43	419 Sqn
R/87742	WO1	HILL DFM Wellington	23-11-43	97 Sqn
R/100778	F/S	HILL William Frederick Irvine	17-08-43	420 Sqn
R/139366	F/S	HILL William Grant	7-08-43	22 OTU
R/115769	F/S	HILL William Hiram 'Bill'	13-05-43	106 Sqn
C/8680	P/O	HILLHOUSE James Robert	3-10-43	76 Sqn
J/19173	P/O	HILLIARD Tom William	4-11-43	408 Sqn
R/88514	WO2	HILLMAN Gordon Thomas	27-03-43	156 Sqn
R/176395	F/S	HILLS James Oliver	23-06-43	429 Sqn
R/107211	WO2	HILLS William James	26-05-43	7 Sqn
J/9188	F/O	HINCHCLIFFE William Edward	24-08-43	426 Sqn
J/18885	P/O	HINGSTON Fayette Williams Brown George	4-12-43	429 Sqn
J/17189	F/O	HOAR William George	29-03-43	218 Sqn
R/115666	WO2	HOAR William Joseph	28-09-43	90 Sqn
J/16996	F/O	HODGE Frederick William	22-06-43	405 Sqn
J/22156	F/O	HODGKINSON Allen Keith	3-11-43	428 Sqn
R/108386	F/S	HODGSON Keith Jonathan	13-02-43	50 Sqn
R/107715	Sgt	HODGSON Kenneth	4-05-43	22 OTU
J/14676	F/O	HODGSON Russell	4-07-43	102 Sqn
R/107769	WO2	HOEY James William Douglas	24-06-43	218 Sqn
J/9740	F/O	HOFFMAN Theodore Robert	30-07-43	77 Sqn
J/21411	F/O	HOGAN Joe Douglas	24-09-43	57 Sqn
R/79184	WO2	HOGAN Richard Wilfred Charles	27-03-43	101 Sqn
R/149420	Sgt	HOGARTH William Elder	28-08-43	467 Sqn
J/21352	F/O	HOGG Donald Allan	26-11-43	429 Sqn
R/141441	F/S	HOGG Douglas Allen	4-07-43	432 Sqn
R/97033	F/S	HOGG William James	13-02-43	50 Sqn
R/197059	Sgt	HOLBECK John Edmund	6-11-43	26 OTU
J/17213	P/O	HOLDEN William	5-05-43	7 Sqn
R/140533	F/S	HOLDITCH Gordon William	17-08-43	23 OTU
R/53029	Sgt	HOLLAND Joseph John Francis	22-06-43	428 Sqn
R/86757	WO2	HOLLINGSHEAD Charles William	21-01-43	420 Sqn
J/17511	P/O	HOLLOWELL Robert Spencer	1-06-43	420 Sqn
R/156906	Sgt	HOLLYER Percy	12-06-43	78 Sqn
R/86847	WO1	HOLM George Russel	11-04-43	57 Sqn
R/143622	Sgt	HOLMES Joseph Andrew Cletus	24-08-43	75 Sqn
R/104814	F/S	HOLNESS Nelson Earl	5-02-43	50 Sqn
J/12470	F/O	HOLT Peter Grattan	30-05-43	44 Sqn
R/76130	Cpl	HOLT William Phillip	29-08-43	427 Sqn
J/21529	F/O	HOLTBY Robert Armstrong	29-12-43	431 Sqn
R/90950	WO2	HOME Allan Lockwood	13-05-43	57 Sqn
R/104231	F/S	HOOD William Andrew	29-06-43	419 Sqn
J/25592	F/O	HOOK Alan Thomas	2-12-43	57 Sqn
J/22746	F/O	HOOPCHUK George	18-10-43	24 OTU
R/197102	F/S	HOOPER George Robert	4-12-43	429 Sqn
R/177542	F/S	HOOPER George Thomas	3-11-43	10 Sqn
R/70806	Sgt	HOOPER John	24-05-43	408 Sqn
R/173734	Sgt	HOPE Clifford Lionel	17-12-43	97 Sqn
R/180665	Sgt	HOPKINS George William James	7-09-43	29 OTU
R/136282	F/S	HOPLEY Albert Frederick	14-05-43	426 Sqn
R/115081	F/S	HOPPING Arthur Stanley	24-07-43	420 Sqn
R/127784	F/S	HORAHAN Lawrence Melville	17-04-43	420 Sqn
R/95448	WO1	HORN Walter Wilfred	27-06-43	432 Sqn
R/76770	WO2	HORNE DFM Alexander Manson	6-03-43	49 Sqn
J/17468	P/O	HORNER Douglas Carter	20-06-43	408 Sqn
R/135101	F/S	HORTON Harold Albert [USA]	8-01-43	467 Sqn
R/127814	F/S	HORWOOD Douglas Ray	13-05-43	428 Sqn
J/21895	F/O	HOSKEN Charles Douglas Alexander	14-07-43	78 Sqn
R/90327	F/S	HOUSTON James Young	28-05-43	405 Sqn
J/14171	F/O	HOVINEN Melvin Olaf [USA]	13-07-43	106 Sqn
R/132630	F/S	HOW Thomas Ferguson	14-05-43	426 Sqn
R/130873	F/S	HOWARD Graham Wilson	22-10-43	429 Sqn
J/16792	F/O	HOWARD Maurice William	31-08-43	434 Sqn
J/22496	F/O	HOWARD Robert John	12-04-43	425 Sqn
R/81305	F/S	HOWDEN Charles Victor	29-06-43	149 Sqn
R/225109	Sgt	HOWITSON George Alexander	22-11-43	419 Sqn
J/26309	P/O	HOWL Alfred William	8-10-43	20 OTU
R/97208	WO2	HOWSON William Harold	21-10-43	24 OTU
J/51021	P/O	HOYT Gordon Ray	22-01-43	427 Sqn
J/13422	F/O	HUBBELL George Henry	1-06-43	420 Sqn
R/63841	WO2	HUCKER John Alfred Nelson	9-10-43	405 Sqn
R/131974	WO2	HUETHER Harold Logan	10-04-43	9 Sqn
J/21575	F/O	HUFFMAN George Lawrence	24-11-43	426 Sqn
J/3990	S/L	HUGHES Alfred Johnstone	27-11-43	426 Sqn
J/26610	P/O	HUGHES Griffith Lewis	9-10-43	78 Sqn
R/90778	F/S	HUGLI Vincent Armand	9-01-43	419 Sqn
R/116029	F/S	HUME Raymond Graham	21-04-43	77 Sqn
R/225311	Sgt	HUMPHRIES Alick Victor Douglas	7-09-43	427 Sqn
R/140397	F/S	HUMPHRYS Peter Robert	19-12-43	433 Sqn
J/16904	F/O	HUNT James Turner	11-02-43	106 Sqn
J/17251	F/L	HUNT Leslie William	4-07-43	15 Sqn
R/61035	WO1	HUNTER Donald Campbell	26-02-43	9 Sqn
R/55617	F/S	HUNTER Dwain Nowell	30-07-43	61 Sqn
J/18041	P/O	HUNTER John Douglas	26-06-43	408 Sqn
J/16516	P/O	HUNTER Russell John	22-06-43	15 Sqn
J/86851	P/O	HUNTER William Langenbeck	22-11-43	419 Sqn
R/102768	WO1	HURL Carl Norman	9-10-43	432 Sqn
J/19164	P/O	HURLEY Harold James	16-12-43	426 Sqn
R/149121	F/S	HURTEAU Alfred Eujene	14-05-43	419 Sqn
R/144839	Sgt	HUTCHINS Martin Lawrence [USA]	13-06-43	51 Sqn
R/91860	WO2	HUTCHINSON Gordon James	31-01-43	101 Sqn
J/15652	F/O	HYNAM DFC Graham Stanley [USA]	29-05-43	23 OTU

Service No	Rank	Name	Date	Unit
J/24024	P/O	IBBOTT Herbert	9-08-43	82 OTU
J/22494	F/O	INGRAHAM Walter Crowe	22-09-43	428 Sqn
R/119142	F/S	INGRAM Eric Harold	15-04-43	214 Sqn
R/138030	Sgt	INGRAM William John Bowser	6-09-43	424 Sqn
R/155366	F/S	INNES Arthur Gordon	29-12-43	429 Sqn
R/79766	F/S	INNES Gordon Arthur	3-09-43	30 OTU
R/107044	Sgt	IRELAND Percy John	8-04-43	419 Sqn
R/165031	F/S	IRVINE Douglas Raymond	17-12-43	97 Sqn
J/11956	F/O	IRWIN Howard Clinton	5-04-43	428 Sqn
R/124524	F/S	ISAACS James Earl	17-04-43	420 Sqn
J/16895	F/O	ISFELD Ivan Andrew	31-08-43	139 Sqn
J/17654	F/O	IVATT Harold Moseley	13-05-43	50 Sqn
J/11217	F/O	JACKSON Alan Hamilton	9-04-43	7 Sqn
R/116342	F/S	JACKSON Allan Benjamin	7-09-43	434 Sqn
J/20125	F/O	JACKSON Charles Warner	11-04-43	420 Sqn
J/18801	P/O	JACKSON Henry Alfred	7-09-43	427 Sqn
J/19031	F/O	JACKSON Ross Banting	22-10-43	408 Sqn
R/144258	F/S	JACOB Jack Morton	22-11-43	428 Sqn
J/16184	P/O	JACOBS Michael Stein	13-02-43	22 OTU
R/106534	WO2	JACOBSEN Harold Thomas	18-02-43	419 Sqn
R/56096	Sgt	JAMES James Clair Rouse	29-06-43	76 Sqn
R/188839	Sgt	JAMES Russell George	6-09-43	419 Sqn
R/90781	WO2	JARRETT Donald Leslie	4-04-43	408 Sqn
J/10565	F/O	JARVIS Ambury Newton	26-02-43	50 Sqn
J/11443	F/O	JEANNERET Paul Winstanley	14-02-43	426 Sqn
R/130022	F/S	JENNINGS Ivor Derrick	4-09-43	467 Sqn
R/124657	F/S	JENNINGS Roland Warren	24-05-43	405 Sqn
R/141694	F/S	JENSKY Jacob [USA]	31-08-43	432 Sqn
R/156981	F/S	JEROME John Orville	18-08-43	419 Sqn
R/68645	Sgt	JESSIMAN George Herkis	20-12-43	428 Sqn
R/135170	F/S	JETTE Joseph Charles Etienne	11-06-43	428 Sqn
J/21026	F/O	JEWELL Victor John	30-07-43	432 Sqn
R/123858	F/S	JOHANNESSON Gudmundur Arnpot	5-05-43	408 Sqn
R/149284	F/S	JOHN Merlin Lindsay	23-12-43	1664 HCU
J/11119	F/O	JOHNS Kenneth William	22-01-43	487 Sqn
R/83461	Sgt	JOHNSON Charles Martin	6-08-43	51 Sqn
R/120884	F/S	JOHNSON Dennis Wilbert	5-05-43	428 Sqn
R/178385	F/S	JOHNSON Einar	23-08-43	61 Sqn
R/103555	F/S	JOHNSON Frederick David	17-08-43	23 OTU
R/126451	WO2	JOHNSON Harold Winthrop	22-11-43	82 OTU
R/116340	WO2	JOHNSON Jack Lawrence	4-06-43	10 Sqn
R/117549	WO2	JOHNSON John William [USA]	9-07-43	101 Sqn
R/71026	Sgt	JOHNSON Julius Bjorn	25-06-43	419 Sqn
R/128381	F/S	JOHNSON Leonard John	30-07-43	156 Sqn
R/102710	WO2	JOHNSON Phillip Shuttleworth	30-05-43	419 Sqn
J/17660	P/O	JOHNSON William Quinton	24-05-43	15 Sqn
J/19288	P/O	JOHNSTON Angus Augustus	16-12-43	426 Sqn
R/149773	WO2	JOHNSTON Ernest Gerald	25-11-43	1678 HCU
J/18087	P/O	JOHNSTON Gregg McIntyre	18-08-43	434 Sqn
J/16067	F/O	JOHNSTON Keith McLean	26-07-43	429 Sqn
J/23738	P/O	JOHNSTONE Thomas	4-08-43	16 OTU
R/129230	WO2	JOLLIFFE Percy George	18-11-43	427 Sqn
R/180403	Sgt	JONASSON Leonard Norman [USA]	17-04-43	76 Sqn
J/14774	F/O	JONES Benjamin Stanley	27-09-43	434 Sqn
J/18865	P/O	JONES George MacDonald	16-12-43	426 Sqn
R/137406	F/S	JONES James Rundle	24-12-43	100 Sqn
R/106431	F/S	JONES Robert John	7-04-43	405 Sqn
R/151472	Sgt	JORDAN Gordon Richard	22-09-43	101 Sqn
R/135639	F/S	JORDAN Herbert Charles	14-07-43	466 Sqn
R/187567	Sgt	JORDAN Joseph Anthony	24-12-43	100 Sqn
R/137382	F/S	JORDAN Robert Carson [USA]	18-08-43	434 Sqn
R/69379	WO2	JORDAN William Francis	5-04-43	405 Sqn
R/149986	Sgt	JORGENSEN Stanley Johannes	17-04-43	408 Sqn
J/7433	S/L	JOST DFC Burton Norris	25-06-43	419 Sqn
R/104836	F/S	JUPE Royden Martin	26-02-43	420 Sqn
R/133968	F/S	KAHN Melvin Samuel [USA]	19-02-43	1661 HCU
J/22773	F/O	KAIN George Donald	23-08-43	106 Sqn
R/101947	F/S	KAISER Walter Bruce	25-07-43	1659 HCU
R/80897	Sgt	KAPUSCINSKI William George	17-04-43	408 Sqn
R/176146	F/S	KARCZA George	28-08-43	620 Sqn
R/119924	WO2	KASHMAR William	26-06-43	427 Sqn
J/17135	P/O	KAVANAGH John Patrick	10-03-43	166 Sqn
R/67163	WO2	KAVANAUGH Joseph Garnet Stewart	23-11-43	405 Sqn
J/25845	F/O	KAY Gordon Harry	2-12-43	44 Sqn
R/111354	LAC	KEARNS Thomas Melville	16-07-43	432 Sqn
R/186394	Sgt	KEAST Harry Arnold	2-12-43	426 Sqn
R/139292	F/S	KEATING John Patrick	14-05-43	138 Sqn
R/150902	F/S	KEAY Charles William	25-06-43	429 Sqn
J/15518	P/O	KEE John Richard	12-03-43	101 Sqn
R/86226	WO2	KEE Robert James	3-01-43	61 Sqn
R/116462	F/S	KEELER Russell Ross	12-08-43	28 OTU
R/151311	Sgt	KEHOE Gerald Desmond	29-12-43	431 Sqn
R/84478	Cpl	KEIGHAN James Edmond	29-08-43	427 Sqn
R/119175	F/S	KELLAWAY Lorne Edward	26-02-43	420 Sqn
J/18252	P/O	KELLNER Norman	22-06-43	408 Sqn
R/115923	F/S	KELLOWAY Edward	28-08-43	12 Sqn
J/22193	P/O	KELLY Alan Douglas	14-07-43	81 OTU
J/18189	P/O	KELLY Albert Edward	4-07-43	408 Sqn
R/113903	F/S	KELLY Donald Herbert	2-06-43	24 OTU
R/55516	F/S	KELLY Donald Robert	12-06-43	432 Sqn
R/141262	F/S	KELLY Francis Joseph	9-10-43	427 Sqn
R/117367	Sgt	KELLY Michael John	29-01-43	23 OTU
J/19451	P/O	KELLY Paul Grant	13-05-43	428 Sqn
J/18860	P/O	KELSO Stuart Ross	4-12-43	429 Sqn
R/178673	F/S	KENDALL John Topham	10-08-43	61 Sqn
J/10426	F/O	KENDEL Ewald George	21-01-43	420 Sqn
J/20024	F/O	KENNEDY Donald Lloyd	5-04-43	426 Sqn
J/14521	F/O	KENNEDY Elmer Earl	5-05-43	419 Sqn
R/116232	F/S	KENNEDY Gerald William 'Bunny'	12-02-43	1660 HCU
J/22693	P/O	KENNEDY James Carlyle	10-07-43	424 Sqn
R/109126	WO2	KENNEDY John Clayton	17-04-43	426 Sqn
R/117380	F/S	KENNEDY Michael Joseph	27-11-43	101 Sqn
J/20079	F/O	KENNEDY Patrick	18-11-43	427 Sqn
R/143849	Sgt	KENNEDY Roy	13-02-43	22 OTU
R/117107	F/S	KENNY Arthur Joseph	14-01-43	9 Sqn
R/85474	WO2	KENNY William Booker	27-02-43	12 Sqn
J/11963	F/O	KENT Hugh Benjamin	30-01-43	427 Sqn
R/96909	Sgt	KENT Joseph Charles	4-06-43	26 OTU
C/472	W/C	KERBY Harold Wilmer	30-07-43	432 Sqn
R/82326	WO1	KERBY Michael Joseph Stuart	12-05-43	22 OTU
R/128981	F/S	KERNAGHAN Clarence Gerald	26-05-43	180 Sqn
J/18390	P/O	KERR Lloyd Wilson	31-08-43	434 Sqn
R/135114	WO2	KERR Louis Noel Lyndon [Trinidad]	23-09-43	76 Sqn
J/19112	P/O	KERSLAKE Walter	22-10-43	408 Sqn
R/128147	Sgt	KESTER John Douglas	15-02-43	22 OTU
R/97604	WO2	KETTLEY Clifford John Vosper	25-07-43	405 Sqn
R/135246	F/S	KEW Allan Alfred	13-05-43	78 Sqn
J/9738	F/O	KEYES Robert Joseph	13-02-43	199 Sqn
R/136318	Sgt	KILLHAM Richard Archibald	12-04-43	23 OTU
R/118065	F/S	KILPATRICK James Augustus	28-02-43	427 Sqn
R/98960	F/S	KIMBER Michael Patrick	25-06-43	428 Sqn
R/9561	F/S	KIMMEL Spencer Griffith [USA]	26-02-43	105 Sqn
R/82402	F/S	KIMMERLY Amos Walter	11-04-43	424 Sqn
R/109235	WO2	KINDT Cecil John Edgar	26-11-43	626 Sqn
R/126316	F/S	KING Clement Lawrence Clifford	10-01-43	10 Sqn
R/142247	F/S	KING George McGowan	22-09-43	218 Sqn
R/109695	WO2	KING Rolph Henry	22-06-43	77 Sqn
J/17510	P/O	KING William Robert	1-06-43	420 Sqn
R/155969	F/S	KIRK Raymond Arthur	24-08-43	427 Sqn
J/22566	F/O	KIRKHAM Ernest Bruce	3-08-43	44 Sqn
R/157559	F/S	KIRKHAM Thomas Yarwood	3-08-43	432 Sqn
J/10427	F/O	KIRKLAND Harry Nettleton	26-02-43	105 Sqn
R/106357	F/S	KISSICK Victor Robert David Joseph	12-03-43	50 Sqn
J/14801	F/O	KITCHEN Harold Allen Nelson	17-09-43	196 Sqn

ID	Rank	Name	Date	Sqn
J/13838	F/O	KITT Elliott	12-04-43	425 Sqn
R/149019	F/S	KLAUER Aloysius William	4-05-43	22 OTU
J/14999	S/L	KNEALE Thomas Matthew	16-12-43	426 Sqn
R/179319	F/S	KNOX Roy Vincent Bernard	3-10-43	623 Sqn
R/166769	F/S	KNOX Vincent Cooke Lindsay	20-12-43	9 Sqn
R/134193	F/S	KNUUTTILA Arne Gabriel	1-09-43	426 Sqn
J/11218	F/O	KOMAIKO William Kadison [USA]	20-02-43	467 Sqn
R/137398	F/S	KOPACZ Walter Anthony [USA]	30-03-43	408 Sqn
R/132169	F/S	KOPCHUK John	22-06-43	429 Sqn
R/76759	Sgt	KOWALSKI John	1-03-43	419 Sqn
R/166030	F/S	KOZOCKI William Walter	9-10-43	429 Sqn
R/112534	Sgt	KROTZ Percy Earl	6-11-43	1659 HCU
R/89611	WO2	KRULICKI Louis John	21-04-43	7 Sqn
R/141400	F/S	KUCINSKY Joseph Wendelin [USA]	25-06-43	405 Sqn
R/149879	Sgt	KULYK Nick	10-03-43	23 OTU
R/134910	F/S	KWASNEY William	17-04-43	408 Sqn
J/16635	P/O	LABARGE Bernard Henry	12-03-43	405 Sqn
R/131388	F/S	LABBE Joseph Paul Roland	6-08-43	23 OTU
R/150233	F/S	LABELLE Joseph Napoleon Emile Roger	3-10-43	12 Sqn
R/79494	WO1	LABERGE Joseph Claude Albert	23-06-43	429 Sqn
R/182511	F/S	LABIUK George	23-06-43	218 Sqn
R/178430	F/S	LABRIE Reginald Edmund	9-07-43	49 Sqn
R/111482	F/S	LACASSE Florian Mercier	18-01-43	9 Sqn
J/18922	P/O	LACHANCE Joseph Leonidas Roger Rolland	16-12-43	426 Sqn
R/107026	Sgt	LACINA Emanuel George	12-03-43	405 Sqn
10542	F/S	LAFONTAINE Theodore	5-05-43	166 Sqn
R/55654	F/S	LAGACE Joseph Maurice Conrad	25-06-43	432 Sqn
R/73968	F/S	LAIDLAW Joseph Stanley	5-04-43	21 Sqn
J/23273	F/O	LAING Keith Nesbitt	26-08-43	81 OTU
R/134599	F/S	LAKE John William	12-06-43	100 Sqn
R/190919	Sgt	LAKE Kenneth Neville	19-12-43	433 Sqn
R/82280	WO2	LALONDE Lawrence Joseph	11-04-43	57 Sqn
R/164563	F/S	LAMB James Lawrence	18-08-43	57 Sqn
R/70699	Sgt	LAMBERT Milford Alexander	11-04-43	115 Sqn
R/146714	LAC	LAMMERSE Joseph Jack	3-01-43	23 OTU
R/142748	F/S	LAMOND James Crawford	26-05-43	218 Sqn
R/158735	Sgt	LAMOURE Lawrence Ronald	30-05-43	419 Sqn
J/15308	F/O	LANCASTER Hector Beattie	10-07-43	408 Sqn
R/117657	WO2	LANCTIN Joseph Wilfred Maurice Emond	3-03-43	425 Sqn
R/100254	F/S	LANDRY Rene Rodger	5-03-43	100 Sqn
R/81411	F/S	LANE Frank Sydney	27-04-43	429 Sqn
R/119753	F/S	LANG James Murray Reginald	12-06-43	408 Sqn
R/157801	LAC	LANGDALE Frank	27-04-43	426 Sqn
R/108482	WO1	LANGLOIS Joseph Albert Roger	6-09-43	424 Sqn
R/108441	F/S	LAPOINTE Jean Paul Claude	18-08-43	434 Sqn
R/136601	F/S	LAPOINTE Joseph Omer Andre	22-10-43	427 Sqn
R/73774	WO2	LARIN Joseph Louis Bernard	25-02-43	467 Sqn
R/70848	Sgt	LARSEN Peder	1-02-43	1659 HCU
R/102165	WO2	LARSON Alfred Perry	12-03-43	424 Sqn
J/19262	P/O	LARSON Richard Henry	17-11-43	405 Sqn
J/22357	F/O	LAUDER Jack Morgan	4-09-43	50 Sqn
R/97538	F/S	LAUGHLAN Harmon Wendelyn	3-02-43	78 Sqn
J/19334	F/O	LAUGHLAND DFM Alan Macneiley	18-11-43	617 Sqn
R/104713	F/S	LAURENCE Joseph Fernand Rolland	26-05-43	77 Sqn
J/22363	F/O	LAURIN Jean Paul	17-06-43	61 Sqn
J/18759	P/O	LAVALLEE Louis Max	23-07-43	161 Sqn
R/87497	Sgt	LAVIGNE Joseph Edward Robert	9-01-43	158 Sqn
R/54941	Sgt	LAVOIE Marcel	1-09-43	426 Sqn
J/20168	F/O	LAW Albert Clayton	10-07-43	405 Sqn
R/109583	Sgt	LAW Robert Ronald	22-06-43	90 Sqn
R/93290	WO2	LAWRENCE Edward Charles	2-02-43	44 Sqn
J/14351	F/O	LAWRENCE Glyn James	30-07-43	166 Sqn
J/20164	F/O	LAWRENCE William John	23-11-43	405 Sqn
J/12970	F/O	LAWRY Gordon Williams	3-04-43	419 Sqn
R/101307	F/S	LAWSON Harry Taylor Anderson	5-03-43	420 Sqn
R/147471	F/S	LAWSON Kenneth William	12-06-43	76 Sqn
R/124427	WO2	LAZENBY Thomas Henry	17-08-43	420 Sqn
R/54685	Sgt	LA FLAMME Joseph George Euclid	26-11-43	431 Sqn
R/79419	F/S	LEACH Charles Francis [USA]	26-02-43	427 Sqn
R/144066	F/S	LEACH John Anthony	27-09-43	434 Sqn
R/155623	Sgt	LEADBEATER Gordon Bruce	24-05-43	218 Sqn
J/18900	P/O	LEAVER Francis Henry	31-08-43	434 Sqn
R/113437	F/S	LEBIHAN Gabriell Emile Joseph	28-05-43	405 Sqn
R/95511	F/S	LEBLANC John Maurice	17-04-43	425 Sqn
R/139393	F/S	LECKIE Albert Wordie [USA]	10-03-43	1659 HCU
R/98963	WO1	LEDFORD DFM William Holt	23-08-43	434 Sqn
R/105328	F/S	LEDGETT Milton Ray	28-08-43	434 Sqn
J/16270	F/O	LEDOUX Georges Paul Henri	15-04-43	425 Sqn
J/22569	F/O	LEE Everett Victor	27-04-43	156 Sqn
R/142160	F/S	LEE Howard Osborne	14-07-43	432 Sqn
R/68499	WO1	LEE James Livingston	30-05-43	35 Sqn
J/17759	P/O	LEE Richard John	5-05-43	156 Sqn
J/7598	F/L	LEFROY DFC Henry Keith	23-11-43	405 Sqn
R/136403	Sgt	LEGAULT Jean Breboeuf Laurent	4-12-43	426 Sqn
R/99179	F/S	LEGERE Joseph Reginald Evariste	24-12-43	550 Sqn
R/64510	Sgt	LEGGE Robert Colin	5-02-43	75 Sqn
R/184282	Sgt	LEHMAN Leonard Wilfred	6-11-43	1679 HCFlt
R/146475	F/S	LEIGHTON James Alan	18-08-43	428 Sqn
R/63913	WO1	LEITCH Glenn Arthur	12-06-43	429 Sqn
R/115117	LAC	LEITCH John Bruce	1-06-43	420 Sqn
J/16796	P/O	LEMIEUX Joseph Henri Thomas Jacques	22-06-43	405 Sqn
R/106948	F/S	LEMKE John Julius	30-01-43	426 Sqn
R/123711	Sgt	LEMMERICK John Albert	8-04-43	14 OTU
R/85651	WO1	LEMON John Harold	11-04-43	57 Sqn
J/16481	P/O	LENNOX John Watt	5-05-43	405 Sqn
J/17329	P/O	LEROUX Romeo Lionel	27-06-43	420 Sqn
R/65939	WO2	LESAGE Joseph Alexander	22-11-43	419 Sqn
R/117456	F/S	LESSER Raymond	4-09-43	467 Sqn
R/84617	WO2	LEVASSEUR Benoit Albert	18-02-43	419 Sqn
R/225002	F/S	LEVENE Alfred Barish	26-10-43	30 OTU
R/55503	F/S	LEVESQUE Joseph Thomas	4-02-43	9 Sqn
R/116417	F/S	LEVINS Milford Glen Thomas	13-05-43	57 Sqn
R/135017	F/S	LEVITT Isadore Samuel	30-05-43	429 Sqn
R/106451	WO2	LEWIS Albert Bennett	22-06-43	408 Sqn
J/10317	F/O	LEWIS DFC Frank Edward	4-09-43	7 Sqn
R/133341	F/S	LEWIS Glen Edwin [USA]	4-07-43	432 Sqn
R/102653	F/S	LEWIS Herbert Dalton	7-02-43	61 Sqn
R/83454	WO2	LEWIS Howard Clark [USA]	14-03-43	9 Sqn
R/139045	F/S	LEWIS Jack Edwin	20-06-43	10 Sqn
J/18274	P/O	LEWIS James Melford	18-08-43	61 Sqn
R/115799	F/S	LEWIS Raymond David	10-04-43	1661 HCU
R/140521	F/S	LEWIS Richard Hubert	27-02-43	427 Sqn
J/16982	F/O	LEWIS DFM William Thomas	5-05-43	101 Sqn
R/115974	F/S	LE BLANC Joseph Renee Alexis	28-07-43	408 Sqn
J/18873	P/O	LE BROCK Joseph Willy Odessa Roger Garry	19-10-43	103 Sqn
J/8782	F/O	LE CLAIRE Eugene Joffre Kenneth	11-06-43	22 OTU
R/196094	Sgt	LE PAGE Adrian Roland Joseph	3-09-43	30 OTU
J/13829	F/O	LIDSTER Perry Desmond	28-06-43	22 OTU
R/147416	F/S	LIFMAN Thornhall Baldur	18-08-43	428 Sqn
R/180436	WO2	LIGHTHEART Alvin Ernest	19-04-43	22 OTU
R/84482	WO1	LINDSAY Basil Edward	4-09-43	7 Sqn
R/108705	F/S	LINDSAY Magnus James	27-11-43	428 Sqn
R/73337	WO1	LISSON Douglas Clark	14-03-43	138 Sqn
J/25849	F/O	LITTLE Gordon James [USA]	16-12-43	97 Sqn
R/157090	F/S	LITYNESKY Stephen Williams	22-11-43	1664 HCU
J/17974	F/O	LIVERMORE Texas Roy	24-05-43	408 Sqn
J/17110	P/O	LIVINGSTON DFC Robert Athway	22-06-43	405 Sqn
R/70722	WO1	LOCKER Robert Lorne	18-04-43	1659 HCU
J/17599	P/O	LOGAN Ray Hutchings	28-05-43	109 Sqn
J/5710	F/L	LOGGIE James Roy [USA]	24-11-43	429 Sqn
J/18815	P/O	LONEY Glen Benson	16-12-43	619 Sqn

ID	Rank	Name	Date	Unit
J/17237	P/O	LONG Albert Morgan	6-07-43	466 Sqn
J/14874	F/O	LONG Arthur Bebbington	15-08-43	420 Sqn
R/157864	Sgt	LONG Charles Robert Gaudet [USA]	9-11-43	23 OTU
J/11238	F/O	LONG Clarence Roy	19-02-43	15 Sqn
R/156117	Sgt	LONG George Albert	7-08-43	28 OTU
J/17407	P/O	LONG Stuart Hermon	28-09-43	405 Sqn
R/135092	F/S	LONGSTAFF Emmett Jay [USA]	17-04-43	218 Sqn
R/93461	F/S	LONGWELL Arthur Grant	14-02-43	426 Sqn
J/6829	F/L	LORD Frederick Charles	27-09-43	434 Sqn
R/154427	F/S	LOSA Ricardo	16-12-43	49 Sqn
R/82621	WO2	LOUGH William Herbert	7-02-43	408 Sqn
J/14178	P/O	LOVE Robert Portor	26-01-43	23 OTU
J/22488	F/O	LOW George Stewart	24-08-43	427 Sqn
J/17294	F/O	LOW James	7-09-43	1658 HCU
J/23465	P/O	LOWE Harry [USA]	27-11-43	49 Sqn
R/134497	WO2	LOWE Irvin Melville	4-12-43	76 Sqn
J/15046	F/S	LOWE Robert Henry	30-01-43	426 Sqn
R/131761	WO2	LOWLE Gordon Pomeroy	2-12-43	432 Sqn
J/13992	F/O	LOWN John Lionel Frederick	22-06-43	429 Sqn
R/94724	WO2	LOWTHER David Wesley	3-03-43	103 Sqn
J/10021	F/O	LOWTHER John Clair	28-09-43	405 Sqn
R/184001	F/S	LOYST Morley Percival	9-11-43	90 Sqn
R/115798	WO2	LUCYK Steven William	3-11-43	76 Sqn
J/22787	F/O	LUDLOW Michael Thomas Robert	10-08-43	419 Sqn
J/10683	F/L	LUNDBERG Torkel Torkelsson	21-01-43	103 Sqn
R/91200	Sgt	LUNDY Ernest Edward	13-05-43	428 Sqn
R/187630	Sgt	LUNDY James	3-10-43	428 Sqn
J/10875	F/L	LUNN Gerald Alfred	17-04-43	429 Sqn
R/99088	WO2	LUTES Allison Roy	14-07-43	78 Sqn
J/15434	F/L	LUXFORD Floyd Edward	3-04-43	405 Sqn
R/122558	F/S	LYMBURNER Leo McClellan	3-03-43	427 Sqn
R/103922	F/S	LYNASS James Cunningham	3-05-43	487 Sqn
J/22422	F/O	LYNCH John Donald	26-11-43	625 Sqn
J/24525	F/O	LYNCH Raymond Victor	1-11-43	19 OTU
R/102004	WO2	LYNN Robert John Thomas [USA]	3-02-43	218 Sqn
J/13423	P/O	LYONS Henry Neelin	23-05-43	15 Sqn
J/18694	P/O	LYTLE Orville	27-09-43	434 Sqn
J/19020	P/O	LYTTLE William Alex	21-04-43	21 Sqn
R/148356	F/S	L'HOMMEDIEU George Martin [USA]	26-09-43	24 OTU
J/12562	F/O	MABEE George Floyd	30-03-43	49 Sqn
R/104425	F/S	MacASKILL Timothy Leo	23-06-43	10 Sqn
J/121633	WO2	MacAULAY Neil Thomas	22-06-43	35 Sqn
J/15309	F/O	MacCAUSLAND Vincent Sanford	17-05-43	617 Sqn
R/124964	WO2	MacDONALD Alexander Hugh	6-11-43	1679 HCFlt
R/153012	F/S	MacDONALD Archibald Stewart	26-11-43	626 Sqn
J/6029	F/L	MacDONALD Bertram Alexander	11-08-43	109 Sqn
R/116520	F/S	MacDONALD Colin Murray	4-11-43	408 Sqn
R/110187	F/S	MacDONALD Donald Andrew	13-02-43	420 Sqn
R/225104	Sgt	MacDONALD Donald John	18-11-43	419 Sqn
J/22619	F/O	MacDONALD Duncan Hildrain	9-10-43	434 Sqn
R/88100	F/S	MacDONALD Irving	17-04-43	408 Sqn
R/138932	F/S	MacDONALD James Clarence	22-06-43	408 Sqn
J/13076	F/O	MacDONALD James Kenneth	5-03-43	420 Sqn
R/115757	F/S	MacDONALD Joseph Roderick Gerald	26-07-43	620 Sqn
J/16935	P/O	MacDONALD Kenneth Watson Baker	8-04-43	420 Sqn
R/131442	Sgt	MacDONALD Ronald Edwin	19-06-43	77 Sqn
R/124685	F/S	MacDONALD Wallace Reginald	14-05-43	9 Sqn
J/22497	F/O	MacDOUGALL Dalton Ross Alexander	26-01-43	23 OTU
R/104348	F/S	MacEACHEN Hugh Archibald	29-04-43	166 Sqn
R/88370	F/S	MacFARLANE David William	26-05-43	77 Sqn
J/13815	F/O	MacFARLANE John Donald	14-03-43	420 Sqn
J/16696	F/L	MacFARLANE DFM Ronald Ernest	16-12-43	101 Sqn
R/143002	F/S	MacGILLIVRAY John James	24-11-43	1658 HCU
J/17089	F/O	MacGREGOR Rob Roy	22-11-43	434 Sqn
J/20832	F/O	MacKAY James	16-12-43	426 Sqn
R/153207	Sgt	MacKENNA William Frank	15-09-43	10 Sqn
J/18334	P/O	MacKENZIE Alan Edward	3-11-43	428 Sqn
R/143462	F/S	MacKENZIE Donald Andrew	12-06-43	426 Sqn
R/61187	Cpl	MacKENZIE James Foster	1-06-43	420 Sqn
R/124707	F/S	MacKILLOP William	28-08-43	57 Sqn
R/135643	F/S	MacLELLAN Alexander Neil [USA]	12-04-43	23 OTU
R/172701	F/S	MacLENNAN Stuart Cameron	31-08-43	76 Sqn
J/12160	F/O	MacMILLAN David John	14-05-43	431 Sqn
R/121431	F/S	MacMILLAN Harry	30-05-43	428 Sqn
R/146794	F/S	MacMILLAN Hugh Coles	6-09-43	90 Sqn
J/20833	P/O	MacMURCHY Edward Douglas	27-09-43	428 Sqn
R/195938	Sgt	MacNEIL Donald Glendon Ellsworth	28-11-43	16 OTU
R/103992	F/S	MacNEILL Rodney Warren	30-03-43	76 Sqn
J/19144	P/O	MacQUEEN Fred Calder	18-12-43	23 OTU
R/103766	F/S	MACDONALD Aeneas Francis	3-02-43	78 Sqn
R/124691	F/S	MACDONALD Robert Gray	12-03-43	405 Sqn
R/16619	P/O	MACDOUGALL George Douglas	4-02-43	90 Sqn
R/81119	Sgt	MACHELL Harry George	17-04-43	408 Sqn
J/10050	F/O	MACINTYRE John Scott	23-06-43	429 Sqn
R/188443	Sgt	MACKAY George Laing	22-11-43	434 Sqn
J/10211	P/O	MACKAY Jack Galloway	17-06-43	83 Sqn
J/16924	P/O	MACKENZIE Jack Douglas	3-02-43	419 Sqn
J/9770	F/O	MACKENZIE John Irven	3-02-43	214 Sqn
R/110747	F/S	MACKSIMCHUK John Theo	5-05-43	166 Sqn
R/128077	F/S	MACLACHLAN Albert James	12-06-43	429 Sqn
R/127864	F/S	MACLAREN Alexander Stewart	10-08-43	419 Sqn
J/17016	F/O	MACNEIL Hugh Columba	13-05-43	57 Sqn
R/124501	F/S	MACPHERSON Harold Stanton	3-03-43	427 Sqn
J/13710	F/O	MADGE Roy Gibson	26-05-43	428 Sqn
R/69500	F/S	MAGDER Hiam Murray	2-02-43	49 Sqn
J/26206	P/O	MAGNES Julius Harold	9-11-43	23 OTU
R/124246	F/S	MAGNUSSON Clarence Narris	22-05-43	428 Sqn
J/20912	F/O	MAGSON Philip John Ashworth	24-08-43	405 Sqn
R/55910	WO2	MAHEU Francois Gabriel	30-06-43	425 Sqn
J/18896	P/O	MAIN Lennox Cameron	3-10-43	431 Sqn
C/1635	W/C	MAIR DFC Alexander Campbell	27-11-43	408 Sqn
R/137144	F/S	MAISENBACHER William Malcolm [USA]	4-04-43	10 Sqn
J/15405	F/L	MAITLAND DFM William John	16-12-43	408 Sqn
J/21628	F/O	MAJOR Thomas Ernest	21-12-43	1679 HCFlt
R/131168	F/S	MALE John Frederick	26-06-43	408 Sqn
R/70158	Sgt	MALLETT John Burns	2-03-43	57 Sqn
R/94772	WO2	MALLORY Leslie Allan	24-08-43	78 Sqn
R/124412	F/S	MANDERS Clarence Delrose	24-11-43	426 Sqn
J/17769	P/O	MANG Ronald Franz	13-07-43	424 Sqn
J/16626	P/O	MANK Matthew [USA]	15-04-43	7 Sqn
R/79067	Sgt	MANN Douglas	9-01-43	158 Sqn
R/107981	F/S	MANN Walter Edward	13-05-43	428 Sqn
J/14239	F/O	MANNERS Frank Thorburn	27-09-43	428 Sqn
R/115267	F/S	MANSER Raymond Earl	26-05-43	180 Sqn
R/112619	F/S	MANSON William Mackenzie	29-04-43	428 Sqn
R/151473	Sgt	MANTHA Rene Real	28-05-43	158 Sqn
R/96762	F/S	MARCHAND Joseph Eric Ritchie	11-06-43	428 Sqn
R/61972	F/S	MARCHANT James Earl	4-12-43	97 Sqn
R/164704	Sgt	MARCHESSAULT Joseph Jean Marie Paul	17-04-43	23 OTU
R/107744	F/S	MAREAN Fred Aten	12-03-43	78 Sqn
R/134206	WO2	MARKS Edward Reginald	18-08-43	428 Sqn
J/12984	F/O	MARKS Walter Douglas	29-01-43	420 Sqn
J/17600	P/O	MARRIOTT John Robert	27-04-43	405 Sqn
J/15643	F/L	MARSH DFC Francis Peter	18-08-43	426 Sqn
R/92466	WO2	MARSHALL Donald Courtenay	9-01-43	12 Sqn
R/86762	WO2	MARSHALL James Stanley	21-04-43	7 Sqn
R/129522	F/S	MARSHALL John Glenford Alexander	30-05-43	428 Sqn
R/138078	WO2	MARSHALL Walter Farquhar	20-12-43	434 Sqn
R/199556	Sgt	MARTIN Daniel Montgomery	7-08-43	22 OTU

Service No.	Rank	Name	Date	Sqn
R/173738	F/S	MARTIN Harold Stuart	12-08-43	76 Sqn
R/128247	F/S	MARTIN Irwin Andrew	2-10-43	424 Sqn
R/122787	WO1	MARTIN James	24-05-43	405 Sqn
R/165286	F/S	MARTIN John Roddick	20-12-43	149 Sqn
J/21567	F/O	MARTIN Stephen Henry	26-10-43	1664 HCU
R/118020	WO2	MARTIN Thomas Edwin	1-09-43	426 Sqn
R/184683	F/S	MARTIN Thomas McPhaile	3-10-43	623 Sqn
J/18332	P/O	MARTIN William	24-08-43	218 Sqn
R/200832	Sgt	MARTIN William Edward	11-12-43	26 OTU
R/133280	F/S	MARTYN John Reid	16-04-43	35 Sqn
R/93458	WO2	MARUGG Stephen James	30-05-43	158 Sqn
J/22410	F/O	MARYNOWSKI Michael Edmund	16-12-43	408 Sqn
R/130273	F/S	MASSON Eugene Shadrack	14-03-43	138 Sqn
R/110339	F/S	MASTERMAN Wallace Alfred Lawrence	26-01-43	424 Sqn
R/90238	WO2	MASTERSON Kenneth Howard	24-05-43	426 Sqn
R/112402	Sgt	MATHESON Alexander Colin	23-05-43	12 OTU
R/79239	WO2	MATHEWS George	26-02-43	218 Sqn
R/103796	F/S	MATLOCK Elmer Keith	8-03-43	15 Sqn
R/193148	Sgt	MATTHEWS Donald Willis	27-09-43	428 Sqn
J/13072	F/O	MATYNIA George Theodore	26-06-43	427 Sqn
J/18315	P/O	MAUGHAN Herbert Francis	28-08-43	51 Sqn
J/18269	P/O	MAUNDER Clifford Leigh	21-04-43	90 Sqn
R/136041	F/S	MAW Clifford Charles	3-09-43	199 Sqn
R/116235	F/S	MAWSON James Alexander	21-08-43	1658 HCU
R/125618	F/S	MAXWELL David Chester	13-05-43	426 Sqn
R/123227	F/S	MAY Bruce Herbert	5-04-43	21 Sqn
R/197082	Sgt	MAY George Alexander	22-11-43	419 Sqn
R/112710	F/S	MAY Russell Edward	25-07-43	103 Sqn
R/92088	WO2	MAYER Harry Edward	29-06-43	424 Sqn
J/14770	F/O	MAYES Warren Bretall [USA]	29-06-43	419 Sqn
R/57637	WO2	MAYNARD Howard Charles Alan	9-10-43	12 Sqn
J/26623	F/O	MAYO John Raymond	23-11-43	434 SQN
R/145926	F/S	MAYO William James	16-11-43	432 Sqn
R/11183	F/O	McALLISTER Leslie Duncan	30-03-43	196 Sqn
R/93277	WO2	McALPINE William James	3-04-43	405 Sqn
R/77162	WO1	McARTHUR DFM Edwin Matthew	1-09-43	405 Sqn
R/115019	WO2	McARTHUR Kenneth Alexander Bernard	4-10-43	428 Sqn
R/104008	WO2	McARTHUR Leo Neil	3-04-43	83 Sqn
J/9850	F/O	McBRIDE John Dugald	4-04-43	408 Sqn
R/142177	F/S	McBRIDE Leslie Brooks	1-09-43	426 Sqn
J/19414	P/O	McCABE Dennis Albert	29-12-43	408 Sqn
J/22070	F/O	McCABE Robert Morrison	20-12-43	158 Sqn
R/172877	F/S	McCALLUM Peter Thomson	26-11-43	429 Sqn
R/154939	Sgt	McCANN Thomas Daniel [USA]	31-08-43	466 Sqn
R/115429	WO2	McCARLDE Frederick Grant	17-04-43	51 Sqn
R/225377	Sgt	McCART Robert Opal Patrick Joseph	23-10-43	429 Sqn
R/181387	Sgt	McCARTNEY Harold Samuel	22-10-43	427 Sqn
R/105454	F/S	McCARTY Daniel John	3-08-43	419 Sqn
R/126326	F/S	McCAUSLAND James Waldo	29-01-43	21 OTU
R/105188	F/S	McCAW John Francis James	29-03-43	218 Sqn
R/147010	F/S	McCLAY Murton Lawrence	31-08-43	102 Sqn
J/20104	F/O	McCLEARY George Frederick	26-07-43	214 Sqn
R/166291	F/S	McCLELLAND David Stuart	21-12-43	76 Sqn
J/21036	F/O	McCLINTOCK George Austin	12-06-43	432 Sqn
R/69464	F/S	McCLUNG John Henry Colin	10-07-43	408 Sqn
J/18814	P/O	McCOMB Roy Ernest	22-10-43	408 Sqn
R/121293	F/S	McCONNELL James Lawrence	29-01-43	22 OTU
R/120653	F/S	McCORMICK Joseph Roy	2-03-43	487 Sqn
R/98027	WO2	McCORMICK Lee Henry Alexander	4-07-43	432 Sqn
R/123498	WO2	McCOY Allan Frank [USA]	14-05-43	10 Sqn
J/14192	F/O	McCRACKEN Alexander Purves	25-07-43	405 Sqn
R/100701	WO2	McCREERY Harry Kenneth	2-03-43	408 Sqn
R/100257	WO2	McCUBBIN Francis Cole	2-12-43	35 Sqn
R/110280	F/S	McCULLAGH Robert Desmond	30-03-43	83 Sqn
R/130254	F/S	McCULLOCH Everett Elmer Stuart	24-08-43	427 Sqn
J/20352	F/O	McCULLOCH Gordon Saunders	1-06-43	420 Sqn
R/134714	WO2	McCULLOCH Robert Lloyd	20-12-43	158 Sqn
R/113382	WO2	McCURDY Max Albert	20-12-43	408 Sqn
J/21030	F/O	McCUTCHEON Ernest Borden	22-07-43	420 Sqn
R/139233	F/S	McCUTCHEON Franklin Tees	19-11-43	51 Sqn
R/96960	F/S	McDERMOTT Edward	3-02-43	75 Sqn
J/19392	P/O	McDERMOTT Edwin Terrance	23-10-43	427 Sqn
J/16764	P/O	McDONALD Devereaux Richard Cecil	3-08-43	432 Sqn
R/93881	F/S	McDONALD Donald Francis	14-05-43	149 Sqn
R/73542	Sgt	McDONALD Gerald Edwin	4-04-43	51 Sqn
J/12329	F/O	McDONALD Howard William	28-07-43	408 Sqn
R/175198	F/S	McDONALD James	7-09-43	434 Sqn
J/17042	P/O	McDONALD Melvyn Alexander	5-04-43	21 Sqn
R/180883	Sgt	McDONALD Wesley Earl	26-08-43	1659 HCU
J/22548	F/O	McDOUGALL Colin Angus	12-06-43	431 Sqn
R/146698	F/S	McDOUGALL Gerard Daniel	1-06-43	420 Sqn
R/101749	F/S	McDOWELL James	16-05-43	617 Sqn
R/116194	F/S	McDOWELL Thomas Alexander	20-04-43	57 Sqn
R/155911	F/S	McEACHERN Reginald Milton	21-10-43	20 OTU
R/193028	Sgt	McEWEN John Alexander	19-11-43	428 Sqn
R/120920	F/S	McEWEN Lawrence David	14-05-43	419 Sqn
R/99534	F/S	McFADDEN Donald Franklin	30-03-43	427 Sqn
J/27316	P/O	McFARLANE Clifford Wallace	20-10-43	625 Sqn
J/17116	F/O	McGAVOCK DFC John Joseph	21-12-43	1679 HCFlt
J/85248	P/O	McGILLIVRAY Craig Edward 'Sonny'	19-11-43	431 Sqn
R/154434	Sgt	McGINN John Henry	10-03-43	1659 HCU
J/6843	F/O	McGLADREY DFC George Glover	14-07-43	405 Sqn
R/108260	WO2	McGRATH Francis Gerard	11-04-43	50 Sqn
R/99387	F/S	McGRATH Gerald	28-03-43	419 Sqn
R/129069	F/S	McGROGAN John Edward	10-07-43	424 Sqn
R/189734	Sgt	McGURTY Albert	20-10-43	1664 HCU
R/118176	Sgt	McHARG Vernon Frederick	26-01-43	424 Sqn
R/112735	F/S	McILRATH Stanley James	30-06-43	425 Sqn
R/128075	F/S	McINNES John George	8-10-43	149 Sqn
R/127620	F/S	McINTOSH John William	5-05-43	419 Sqn
J/18231	P/O	McINTOSH DFM William Philip Macdonald	24-08-43	35 Sqn
J/27451	P/O	McINTYRE Alexander Russell	13-12-43	23 OTU
J/7418	F/O	McINTYRE Harry Starkey	18-08-43	405 Sqn
R/131704	F/S	McINTYRE John Duncan	15-02-43	196 Sqn
R/168726	Sgt	McINTYRE Orville Malcolm	18-08-43	427 Sqn
J/21537	F/O	McKAY Allan Charles	30-09-43	619 Sqn
J/22806	F/O	McKAY Donald Hugh	1-09-43	426 Sqn
R/124347	F/S	McKAY Douglas George	14-07-43	408 Sqn
R/129636	WO2	McKAY Gordon Campbell	17-08-43	405 Sqn
R/115725	F/S	McKAY Harry Robertson	4-02-43	115 Sqn
R/94589	Sgt	McKEE William Ellis	27-09-43	428 Sqn
R/157077	F/S	McKELLAR Malcolm Archie	22-11-43	419 Sqn
R/131929	F/S	McKENDRY John Wilbur	14-07-43	432 Sqn
J/6665	F/O	McKENNA Charles Daniel	8-04-43	109 Sqn
R/110872	F/S	McKENNIE Gerald Baird	5-04-43	21 Sqn
R/116753	WO2	McKENZIE John Andrew Whitmore	4-12-43	35 Sqn
R/92054	Sgt	McKENZIE Lloyd George	27-06-43	432 Sqn
R/79107	F/S	McKEOWN Francis James	13-01-43	12 Sqn
J/24801	P/O	McKERCHER William Dunne Coldicott	25-07-43	1659 HCU
R/156796	F/S	McKERNAN Frank Thomas Andrew	2-12-43	426 Sqn
R/111483	F/S	McKERNS Charles	21-04-43	90 Sqn
R/129152	Sgt	McKIBBON Mervin George	18-08-43	115 Sqn
J/10893	F/O	McKINNON Campbell Archibald	19-02-43	426 Sqn
R/62913	WO1	McKINNON Gerald Frederick	3-11-43	77 Sqn
J/4965	S/L	McKINNON John Arnott	8-04-43	100 Sqn
R/156063	F/S	McKITTERICK Donald Harvey	3-10-43	90 Sqn
R/94736	WO2	McLACHLAN Donald Parker	9-03-43	426 Sqn
R/197506	Sgt	McLACHLAN Russell William	28-11-43	16 OTU
R/21335	F/O	McLAUGHLIN George Lloyd	18-11-43	419 Sqn
J/13807	F/O	McLAUGHLIN William George	10-03-43	1659 HCU

J/20010	F/O	McLEAN Donald Rae	25-04-43	29 OTU
R/54088	Sgt	McLEAN Gordon Mitchell	22-06-43	408 Sqn
R/124704	WO2	McLEAN John James	31-08-43	427 Sqn
R/109281	F/S	McLEAN Kenneth Hector 'Wally'	9-07-43	106 Sqn
R/79756	Sgt	McLEAN Roy Victor	21-02-43	405 Sqn
J/9562	F/O	McLEISH John Alexander MacTavish	28-08-43	428 Sqn
11549	WO2	McLELLAN Cyril Cobb	2-08-43	405 Sqn
J/8807	F/O	McLELLAN Norman Milton	17-04-43	83 Sqn
R/126941	Sgt	McLELLAN Ross Campbell	22-07-43	420 Sqn
R/99282	F/S	McLENAHAN Arthur Cedric	26-08-43	424 Sqn
J/20576	F/O	McLENNAN Burus Alexander	17-12-43	405 Sqn
R/128853	F/S	McLEOD Donald Hugh	9-07-43	106 Sqn
R/119526	F/S	McLEOD Ellis George	28-07-43	106 Sqn
R/105778	F/S	McLEOD Ivan Gordon	30-01-43	426 Sqn
R/134200	WO2	McLEOD Norman Stanley	3-11-43	426 Sqn
R/119623	F/S	McLEOD Roderic Murray	28-03-43	419 Sqn
J/17314	P/O	McMAHON Daryl Owen	11-04-43	57 Sqn
J/26840	F/O	McMANAMAN MiD Reginald Willis	2-12-43	619 Sqn
J/18285	P/O	McMANUS Patrick Joseph Howard	29-06-43	424 Sqn
J/21788	F/O	McMANUS Samuel	9-10-43	78 Sqn
R/163746	Sgt	McMASTER James Herbert	21-10-43	24 OTU
R/86951	Cpl	McMASTER Robert Andrew	5-08-43	1664 HCU
J/14772	F/O	McMILLAN George	13-05-43	426 Sqn
R/79669	WO1	McMILLAN Glen Allen	13-05-43	419 Sqn
J/8437	S/L	McMILLIN James Parker	25-06-43	97 Sqn
R/116366	F/S	McMURACHY William Douglas	13-06-43	101 Sqn
J/4534	W/C	McMURDY Gordon Archibald	22-10-43	419 Sqn
R/166512	F/S	McNAIR Nathaniel Wesley	26-11-43	460 Sqn
R/84846	WO2	McNAIR William Archibald	13-05-43	207 Sqn
R/88342	WO2	McNEIL Roderick	23-06-43	214 Sqn
J/18982	P/O	McNEILL Donald John	18-08-43	428 Sqn
J/17109	F/O	McNICHOL Glen Alexander	17-04-43	83 Sqn
R/84998	WO2	McNUTT Frank Arthur	30-03-43	49 Sqn
J/16505	P/O	McPHEE John Aird	16-01-43	61 Sqn
J/14996	F/O	McPHERSON Coran Cyman	6-09-43	10 Sqn
10748	Sgt	McQUEEN Howard John	3-04-43	405 Sqn
J/180964	F/S	McQUESTION Leslie Arthur	20-12-43	408 Sqn
J/10550	F/O	McQUILLIN George Andrew	14-01-43	426 Sqn
R/147326	F/S	McRAE Christopher Frederick 'Bud'	23-09-43	75 Sqn
R/153528	F/S	McRAE Daniel Sinclair	12-06-43	432 Sqn
J/20195	F/O	McRAE Hector Earl	23-09-43	428 Sqn
R/112668	F/S	McRAE Ronald Cameron	24-05-43	405 Sqn
J/21393	F/O	McSORLEY Rob	26-11-43	625 Sqn
J/85654	P/O	McSWEEN Peter Oswald	18-08-43	419 Sqn
J/14784	F/O	McTAGGART George Ernest	16-12-43	9 Sqn
R/188529	Sgt	McVEAN Alexander Basil	6-11-43	1659 HCU
R/161462	F/S	MECHIN Ralph Franklin	6-11-43	1659 HCU
R/184871	Sgt	MEGIT Reginald Keith	18-11-43	460 Sqn
R/135024	F/S	MEILLEUR Joseph Gonzague Andre Gilles		
			17-10-43	23 OTU
J/14320	F/O	MELLISH Thomas Roland	10-07-43	408 Sqn
J/26209	P/O	MELLOR Richard Hopwood Ogden	26-09-43	24 OTU
J/10046	F/O	MELROSE James Adam Witherbee	22-07-43	420 Sqn
R/112570	F/S	MENZIES Allan	24-08-43	405 Sqn
R/89099	Sgt	MENZIES George Douglas	5-05-43	419 Sqn
R/181017	Sgt	MERCER John Duncan	28-09-43	428 Sqn
R/135156	F/S	MERCIER Joseph Jacques Charles	25-05-43	432 Sqn
J/16457	P/O	MERRITT Edward Miles	15-04-43	149 Sqn
R/129438	Sgt	MERTON John Paul [USA]	16-04-43	166 Sqn
R/108499	F/S	MESSIER Horace Daniel Eugene	18-04-43	1659 HCU
J/21737	P/O	METCALFE Hugh Morland	5-05-43	419 Sqn
R/104383	F/S	METCALFE Malcolm Roy Edgar	5-05-43	408 Sqn
R/191533	Sgt	METZ Donald James	26-11-43	429 Sqn
C/17344	P/O	MEYER Melvin Maier	23-06-43	427 Sqn
J/14502	F/O	MIDDLETON Allan John	10-08-43	405 Sqn
R/117228	WO2	MIDDLETON Franklin	31-08-43	218 Sqn
R/107619	WO1	MIEYETTE Lloyd	16-09-43	617 Sqn
R/92878	WO2	MILAN Clifford Arthur	6-03-43	76 Sqn
J/20816	F/O	MILBURN Francis Lloyd	13-06-43	408 Sqn
J/9415	F/O	MILLAR John Whitela	8-02-43	44 Sqn
J/18310	P/O	MILLAR Kenneth Robert Grant	26-11-43	83 Sqn
J/22360	F/O	MILLAR Raymond Norman	24-09-43	57 Sqn
R/106358	WO2	MILLAR Robert Victor	26-06-43	425 Sqn
R/156897	F/S	MILLER Charles Percy	4-11-43	408 Sqn
J/10662	F/O	MILLER Christian Godfrey	12-06-43	83 Sqn
R/69640	WO2	MILLER David Henry	10-03-43	44 Sqn
R/183626	Sgt	MILLER Edward George Ferdinand	23-09-43	428 Sqn
R/119377	WO2	MILLER George William	12-03-43	149 Sqn
R/165173	F/S	MILLER Harry Lewis	19-12-43	433 Sqn
R/151487	F/S	MILLER James Arthur	24-08-43	405 Sqn
R/73707	Sgt	MILLER Malcolm Stephen	16-08-43	405 Sqn
R/153026	F/S	MILLER Ronald William	22-10-43	434 Sqn
R/113977	F/S	MILLER William Douglas	29-09-43	419 Sqn
R/91771	Sgt	MILLER William John	26-08-43	1659 HCU
R/131449	WO1	MILLIDGE Edwin Gilpin	18-11-43	7 Sqn
J/18184	P/O	MILLIGAN Bruce Ryerson	26-06-43	408 Sqn
R/139843	WO2	MILLIKEN Douglas Wilson	4-12-43	51 Sqn
R/111746	F/S	MILLIKEN Robert Clifton	5-04-43	21 Sqn
R/98892	F/S	MILLSON Harold Roy	3-03-43	427 Sqn
J/13068	F/O	MILNE Douglas Stewart	22-06-43	429 Sqn
J/9355	F/O	MILNE George	14-01-43	426 Sqn
J/10210	F/L	MILNER Guy Benedict	13-06-43	103 Sqn
R/79162	WO1	MILNER Joseph Emmett	1-09-43	15 Sqn
J/16658	P/O	MINNIS DFC Harvey B.	27-04-43	115 Sqn
R/178390	F/S	MINOR Orton	28-07-43	50 Sqn
R/110879	F/S	MINTER Sydney Aubrey	22-10-43	427 Sqn
R/105365	F/S	MITCHELL Albert Ardagh	29-01-43	17 OTU
R/91993	Sgt	MITCHELL Alexander	22-10-43	427 Sqn
R/88029	WO2	MITCHELL Douglas Seldon	13-05-43	106 Sqn
R/171550	Sgt	MITCHELL Henry Osmond	11-12-43	16 OTU
R/86750	WO2	MITCHELL Philip Hubert	26-02-43	420 Sqn
J/23126	F/O	MITCHELL William Alexander	26-11-43	115 Sqn
R/157293	F/S	MITCHELL William George	28-06-43	22 OTU
J/17075	P/O	MIX Reginald Donovan	28-04-43	61 Sqn
R/134973	F/S	MOAD Harold Alexander	2-12-43	57 Sqn
R/80237	WO2	MOFFATT Bertram Augustus	9-04-43	75 Sqn
R/105883	F/S	MOFFATT Curtis MacKinnon	13-03-43	115 Sqn
R/17464	F/O	MOFFATT Murray Quinn	13-05-43	102 Sqn
R/150855	F/S	MOFFATT William Henry	11-08-43	158 Sqn
R/173948	F/S	MOLNAR Gregory	18-10-43	115 Sqn
R/83527	WO2	MOLOZZI George Andrew	13-02-43	22 OTU
J/16554	P/O	MONAHAN Joseph Earl	22-06-43	408 Sqn
J/10892	F/O	MONCKTON John Philip	26-02-43	426 Sqn
R/87074	WO2	MONCRIEFF Stanley Richard	26-11-43	429 Sqn
J/18012	P/O	MONK Eric Joseph [Brazil]	17-06-43	156 Sqn
J/17258	P/O	MONK William Greenhalgh	29-04-43	90 Sqn
R/133810	F/S	MONOGHAN Allan Davis	14-05-43	57 Sqn
J/16396	P/O	MONTEITH John Charles	19-02-43	15 Sqn
R/133519	F/S	MONTEITH John Herbert Tweedale	27-09-43	434 Sqn
J/12811	F/L	MOODIE DFC Duncan McNaught	18-10-43	97 Sqn
		[United Kingdom]		
J/14674	P/O	MOORBY Robert Graham	10-03-43	23 OTU
R/138918	F/S	MOORE Ernest Nixon	5-05-43	166 Sqn
R/119531	WO2	MOORE Franklin Guy	28-04-43	61 Sqn
R/134338	WO2	MOORE George Wallace	22-09-43	90 Sqn
J/17007	F/O	MOORE Harold Barbour [USA]	2-03-43	76 Sqn
R/74326	WO2	MOORE John Alwin	17-01-43	50 Sqn
R/141174	F/S	MOORE Maynard Hazlett	23-06-43	161 Sqn
R/87868	WO2	MOORE Robert Richmond	3-01-43	9 Sqn
R/139779	F/S	MOORE Roger	7-09-43	434 Sqn
J/17804	P/O	MOORE Roy Frederick	4-07-43	432 Sqn
R/119562	Sgt	MOORS Arthur Anthony	8-04-43	14 OTU
R/105579	WO2	MORAN Thomas Matheson	13-05-43	77 Sqn
R/98422	F/S	MORAN William Linkous Cameron	23-06-43	103 Sqn
		[USA]		
R/136820	F/S	MORAND Raymond Florent	26-11-43	23 OTU

ID	Rank	Name	Date	Sqn
J/17617	P/O	MORE Eric Gordon	1-09-43	44 Sqn
R/120226	F/S	MOREY Wesley	13-05-43	90 Sqn
R/133751	WO2	MORGAN Albert Raymond 'Bert'	2-12-43	432 Sqn
R/140186	WO2	MORGAN Charles Earle	27-09-43	156 Sqn
J/90155	P/O	MORGANS Edward Allen	23-08-43	434 Sqn
J/22745	F/O	MORISSETTE Joseph Arthur Lucien	17-10-43	23 OTU
R/136408	F/S	MORLEY Robert Stinson	17-06-43	61 Sqn
R/117063	Sgt	MORRIS Francis Kempton	20-11-43	429 Sqn
R/152214	F/S	MORRIS Harold Urbin	18-08-43	419 Sqn
J/14392	F/O	MORRIS Howard Paul	16-12-43	426 Sqn
J/14326	F/O	MORRIS James Elmer	16-07-43	432 Sqn
R/125703	Sgt	MORRIS John Hubert	8-04-43	419 Sqn
R/184515	Sgt	MORRISON John Murray	27-09-43	428 Sqn
J/18881	P/O	MORRISON Norman Byng	16-12-43	426 Sqn
R/140004	F/S	MORRISON Norman Robert	25-06-43	7 Sqn
J/9764	F/L	MORRISON DFC Roy Gordon	14-07-43	405 Sqn
R/149327	F/S	MORRO Frank Peter	4-12-43	429 Sqn
R/129107	WO2	MORROW Claire Keith	30-07-43	61 Sqn
R/163708	Sgt	MORROW George Donald Hector	8-09-43	12 OTU
R/75596	F/S	MORTON William Cuthbert	16-02-43	90 Sqn
J/21553	F/O	MOSHER Keith Maxwell	20-12-43	428 Sqn
R/193899	Sgt	MOULD George Baker	25-11-43	26 OTU
R/74234	WO1	MOULTON Robert Benjamin	5-05-43	428 Sqn
R/135983	F/S	MOULTON Robert Douglas Webster	29-06-43	100 Sqn
R/108483	F/S	MOUNT Kenneth Herbert	29-01-43	23 OTU
R/150882	Sgt	MUCKLOW Roy	27-04-43	420 Sqn
J/21330	F/O	MUIR Thomas James	3-10-43	623 Sqn
R/89110	Sgt	MUIRHEAD Archie Allen	10-03-43	10 Sqn
R/154030	F/S	MULLEN Adam William [USA]	28-09-43	1667 HCU
R/151170	Sgt	MULLEN Daniel Joseph	28-08-43	218 Sqn
R/131647	F/S	MUNRO George Alexander	6-09-43	9 Sqn
J/17499	F/L	MUNRO DFC James Francis	23-11-43	97 Sqn
R/125923	F/S	MUNRO John Oswald	19-04-43	22 OTU
R/76838	Sgt	MUNSTERMAN Ernest	26-08-43	424 Sqn
R/79291	WO2	MURDOCH William McKenzie	3-02-43	214 Sqn
R/128432	F/S	MURDOCK Raymond Henry	22-07-43	1657 HCU
R/100833	F/S	MURDOCK Reginald English	25-06-43	51 Sqn
R/147182	F/S	MURPHY Kenneth William	9-07-43	106 Sqn
R/76910	WO2	MURPHY Lawrence	9-03-43	426 Sqn
R/146613	F/S	MURPHY Lloyd Joseph Charles	28-04-43	419 Sqn
R/128648	F/S	MURPHY Merton Barnabas	18-08-43	428 Sqn
J/16152	F/O	MURPHY MiD Patrick Scott James	30-07-43	432 Sqn
R/92790	F/S	MURPHY William Gorman	9-01-43	419 Sqn
J/17498	P/O	MURRAY Charles	17-06-43	83 Sqn
R/157619	F/S	MURRAY Kenneth Duncan	1-09-43	51 Sqn
J/17209	P/O	MURRAY Ross Marshall	28-05-43	432 Sqn
J/16203	F/L	MURRELL DFC Sidney Leon [USA]	22-06-43	405 Sqn
12122A	F/S	MUSIC Frederick Warren	2-03-43	57 Sqn
R/140846	F/S	MUSSO Paul Antoine	1-09-43	619 Sqn
J/19183	P/O	MUTCH Robert Douglas	17-11-43	405 Sqn
R/97058	WO1	MUTTON Gerald Thompson	3-11-43	426 Sqn
R/77338	WO2	MYERS Maurice Tallier Peter	14-03-43	138 Sqn
J/18997	P/O	NADEAU Joseph Antoine Maurice	22-10-43	434 Sqn
R/81864	F/S	NADEAU Joseph Roger Emil	4-12-43	76 Sqn
J/20717	F/O	NAISMITH Douglas Arthur	3-11-43	429 Sqn
R/114490	F/S	NAPIER Mathew Simpson	5-02-43	50 Sqn
R/90884	WO2	NASH Charles Arthur	12-06-43	83 Sqn
R/106380	WO2	NAULT Donat Cyprien Romain	5-05-43	408 Sqn
R/161983	Sgt	NAULT George Conrad	30-07-43	428 Sqn
R/123716	F/S	NEAL Francis John	7-10-43	426 Sqn
R/115981	F/S	NEALE Douglas	13-03-43	7 Sqn
J/27938	F/O	NEALE William Percival [USA]	4-12-43	426 Sqn
10786	F/S	NEILSON Eric Haakon	3-06-43	10 OTU
R/79092	WO2	NELSON Frank Goheen [USA]	31-01-43	9 Sqn
R/105521	WO2	NELSON Gordon Arthur	12-06-43	429 Sqn
J/5444	F/L	NELSON Jack Norrin	29-12-43	431 Sqn
R/172037	F/S	NELSON Per Arne Theodore	24-12-43	514 Sqn
R/123738	F/S	NESBITT Gordon Brydon	16-07-43	432 Sqn
R/90501	WO2	NESBITT Harold Earle	11-04-43	7 Sqn
R/70337	Sgt	NESBITT Murray Hudley	13-05-43	51 Sqn
R/104261	WO2	NESS William	23-09-43	149 Sqn
R/138123	F/S	NESS William Bonar	18-08-43	61 Sqn
R/159321	F/S	NESVOLD Millard Leon	18-11-43	622 Sqn
R/120905	F/S	NEWBURG Earl Lloyd	27-04-43	420 Sqn
R/58803	WO2	NEWCOMBE Jack Dunbar	16-12-43	426 Sqn
J/25070	F/O	NEWEL Walter David	20-10-43	12 OTU
R/69385	Sgt	NEWLOVE Henry	22-10-43	434 Sqn
J/21637	F/O	NEWMAN Richard John	22-11-43	419 Sqn
R/78908	WO2	NEWTON Jack McArthur	27-03-43	44 Sqn
R/114904	WO2	NICHOL William Bruce	13-05-43	50 Sqn
J/17634	P/O	NICHOLS BEM Arthur Willard	22-06-43	405 Sqn
R/130836	WO2	NICKERSON William James Murdoch	18-11-43	431 Sqn
R/115841	F/S	NICOL James Charles	1-06-43	420 Sqn
R/124574	F/S	NICOLL Douglas Grant	4-04-43	16 OTU
R/155845	Sgt	NISBET George David	24-05-43	10 Sqn
R/147502	F/S	NIVEN Charles Morrison	4-09-43	467 Sqn
J/17729	P/O	NIXON DFC Robert William	24-08-43	35 Sqn
R/119448	WO2	NOBLE Nelson Albert	22-09-43	9 Sqn
J/17345	P/O	NOBLE Steven [USA]	13-08-43	432 Sqn
R/78909	Sgt	NORMAN Ernest Albert	5-04-43	21 Sqn
R/152593	F/S	NORQUAY Charles John Cameron	3-10-43	77 Sqn
J/92475	P/O	NORTHWAY Henry George	7-09-43	77 Sqn
R/103340	F/S	NOTLEY Norman Frederick	23-06-43	427 Sqn
J/7891	F/L	NOVICK Alexander	22-10-43	57 Sqn
J/7800	F/O	NUSSBAUM Lambert Richard	29-06-43	424 Sqn
R/94118	WO2	NUTIK Louis	1-05-43	7 Sqn
J/17555	P/O	NUTTER Richard Eric 'Dick'	29-06-43	1659 HCU
R/153350	F/S	OAKLEY William Herbert	17-11-43	10 OTU
J/19278	P/O	ODELL James Gilmour	23-11-43	405 Sqn
R/97923	F/S	OGILVY James Sutherland	16-07-43	10 OTU
R/179719	F/S	OGSTON Robert Wilson	7-09-43	408 Sqn
R/66305	WO2	OKE Harold Donald	15-04-43	7 Sqn
R/134468	F/S	OLMSTEAD Leonard Thomas	7-09-43	434 Sqn
R/95308	Sgt	OLSEN Alvin Gustaf	21-01-43	420 Sqn
R/136224	LAC	OLSON Herbert Oswald	26-10-43	427 Sqn
R/131859	Sgt	OPIE Edward Alan	13-09-43	12 OTU
R/134317	F/S	ORLINSKI Casimir Frank	22-06-43	429 Sqn
J/14181	F/O	ORR Donald Hugh	18-08-43	428 Sqn
J/20704	F/O	ORR Richard Herbert	28-08-43	78 Sqn
J/13989l	WO2	ORR Ruben Seymour	26-11-43	76 Sqn
R/97152	F/S	OWALD Ronald Earl [USA]	29-01-43	23 OTU
R/113091	F/S	OTTERHOLM William George	29-06-43	419 Sqn
R/90400	WO2	OWEN Brock Laverne	4-07-43	432 Sqn
J/14520	F/O	O'BRIEN Wallace Wesley	13-05-43	428 Sqn
R/97362	F/S	O'CONNELL Eusebins William	15-06-43	103 Sqn
C/20465	F/O	O'CONNELL Thomas Harold	17-04-43	408 Sqn
R/68264	WO2	O'CONNOR James Michael Barry	28-04-43	419 Sqn
R/114634	F/S	O'CONNOR Stafford Thomas	4-04-43	487 Sqn
R/89111	Cpl	O'CONNOR Wilfrid Martin Joseph	19-12-43	433 Sqn
J/109157	Sgt	O'DONNELL Bernard James	2-03-43	487 Sqn
J/25518	F/O	O'DONOGHUE Maurice Edmund	21-10-43	20 OTU
R/93372	F/S	O'DONOHOE Frank James	21-02-43	405 Sqn
R/77353	WO1	O'GRADY John Brian De Courcy [USA]	17-11-43	617 Sqn
R/188976	Sgt	O'GRADY John Edward	6-11-43	1659 HCU
R/125941	F/S	O'HAIR Orville Stotts [USA]	13-01-43	12 Sqn
R/124579	F/S	O'HALLORAN William Edward	14-05-43	44 Sqn
J/10184	F/L	O'HANLEY Gerald James	28-01-43	102 Sqn
R/128741	F/S	O'HARA Basil Morgan	28-09-43	434 Sqn
R/110283	F/S	O'HARA Gerald Churchill Patrick	28-05-43	428 Sqn
J/17065	F/O	O'HARA James Warren	15-08-43	7 Sqn
R/90360	WO1	O'LEARY Leo Frederick	25-06-43	429 Sqn
J/17836	P/O	O'LEARY Owen Arthur	18-08-43	619 Sqn
R/161662	Sgt	O'NEIL Alton James	9-11-43	23 OTU
J/93063	P/O	O'NEILL Daniel	3-02-43	214 Sqn

R/154098	F/S	O'REILLY James Patrick Gallery	22-06-43	429 Sqn
R/148749	F/S	O'ROURKE Arthur Francis	28-05-43	428 Sqn
R/148808	F/S	PADDISON Robert Edward	4-10-43	419 Sqn
R/148071	LAC	PADVEEN Issie	23-10-43	434 Sqn
R/90773	F/S	PAIGE Milton James	9-01-43	44 Sqn
R/188003	F/S	PAINTER Frederick George	24-08-43	427 Sqn
R/173953	Sgt	PALAVA Edward Henry	8-06-43	26 OTU
R/116471	WO2	PALMATIER David Edwin	22-06-43	429 Sqn
R/98515	WO2	PALMER John	13-05-43	419 Sqn
J/9256	F/O	PALMER Wendell McLean	12-03-43	405 Sqn
R/105866	WO2	PAPLOWSKI John	14-04-43	420 Sqn
R/112301	F/S	PAQUET John Elmer	4-10-43	427 Sqn
R/90548	WO2	PAQUIN Joseph Hector	9-04-43	199 Sqn
J/14193	F/O	PARISEAU Armand Alphonse	23-06-43	427 Sqn
R/141705	Sgt	PARK Ellis Hamilton [USA]	4-05-43	22 OTU
R/101927	F/S	PARKER Benjamin Frederick John	21-02-43	405 Sqn
J/18313	P/O	PARKER Elbert Frank	28-07-43	408 Sqn
R/144024	F/S	PARKER Gordon Francis	18-08-43	419 Sqn
J/11842	F/O	PARKER James Courtland [USA]	14-02-43	408 Sqn
R/92418	F/S	PARKER Leslie Alfred	13-03-43	424 Sqn
R/132048	F/S	PARKER Samuel Rutherford	7-09-43	1658 HCU
R/155748	F/S	PARKER William Glen	3-10-43	103 Sqn
R/105126	F/S	PARKINSON William George	22-06-43	429 Sqn
J/11636	F/O	PARSONS Arthur Edward	1-05-43	77 Sqn
R/157795	Sgt	PARTRIDGE Frederick Herbert	2-10-43	23 OTU
R/134563	F/S	PARTRIDGE Gordon John	17-11-43	405 Sqn
J/16966	P/O	PARTRIDGE Henry Albert	5-03-43	83 Sqn
R/114771	F/S	PARTRIDGE William Norman	14-05-43	166 Sqn
J/14569	F/O	PASCOE Philip Jocelyn	29-06-43	100 Sqn
R/111185	F/S	PATERSON Norman Fraser	5-03-43	426 Sqn
R/163264	Sgt	PATERSON William	21-10-43	24 OTU
J/18941	P/O	PATMAN George Keith	12-11-43	1659 HCU
R/98423	F/S	PATRICK Leslie Cayliss	31-08-43	434 Sqn
J/18374	P/O	PATRICK Michael	22-01-43	427 Sqn
J/17175	P/O	PATRY Joseph Gaudias Albert	22-06-43	408 Sqn
R/55289	F/S	PATTERSON George William Alex	10-07-43	424 Sqn
J/11799	F/O	PATTERSON Joseph Moses	7-02-43	424 Sqn
J/18092	P/O	PATTESON John Grant	26-07-43	620 Sqn
R/151615	F/S	PEARSON Arthur Keith	29-11-43	1657 HCU
R/123129	WO2	PEARSON William	25-06-43	50 Sqn
R/133222	F/S	PEART Edward Burgess	25-06-43	429 Sqn
J/23633	F/O	PEASLAND Charles Willcox [United Kingdom]	29-12-43	429 Sqn
J/16748	P/O	PECK John Nelson	15-01-43	214 Sqn
R/130658	WO2	PEDLAR Robert Clinton	27-09-43	434 Sqn
R/144487	F/S	PEETS Thomas William	30-05-43	419 Sqn
J/135100	F/S	PELLAND Louis Joseph Roger Andre	30-07-43	428 Sqn
R/84289	Sgt	PENFOLD Harold Thomas	4-11-43	138 Sqn
R/87263	F/S	PENNER Alvin Harold	30-03-43	83 Sqn
R/61926	Sgt	PENNER Isaac Abraham	27-04-43	405 Sqn
J/18125	P/O	PENNINGTON DFM Stuart	26-05-43	426 Sqn
R/137421	F/S	PENNYCOOK Charles	4-10-43	75 Sqn
R/57798	Sgt	PENROSE William Henry	27-03-43	158 Sqn
J/22032	P/O	PEPPER Harold Douglas	3-06-43	10 OTU
R/105665	WO1	PEPPER William George	26-05-43	428 Sqn
R/115239	WO2	PERDUE Vincent Thomas	31-08-43	7 Sqn
R/105148	WO2	PERKINS Kenneth Mitchell	8-02-43	44 Sqn
R/148537	WO2	PERRIN John Lyle	4-10-43	427 Sqn
R/86190	F/S	PERRON Antoine Joseph Elphege	25-07-43	460 Sqn
R/79470	F/S	PERRON Joseph Marcel Gaston	3-02-43	425 Sqn
R/58888	F/S	PERRY Harry	4-09-43	15 Sqn
R/131937	F/S	PERRY Joseph J. [USA]	5-01-43	101 Sqn
R/87712	WO1	PERRY Keith Oliver	23-08-43	405 Sqn
J/14027	F/O	PETCH Douglas Hartley	18-11-43	623 Sqn
J/139493	F/S	PETERKIN Francis Weatherford [USA]	22-10-43	419 Sqn
R/185706	F/S	PETERSEN Homer Ejner	23-11-43	12 Sqn
R/114943	F/S	PETERSON Lloyd Harvey	13-02-43	50 Sqn
J/17383	P/O	PETTIGREW James Bruce	14-05-43	426 Sqn
R/142882	F/S	PETTITT Roland	17-12-43	408 Sqn
J/22555	F/S	PETTS Henry Neville	26-05-43	100 Sqn
R/101179	WO2	PHAIR Maurice Andrew [USA]	13-01-43	106 Sqn
R/132641	F/S	PHILLIPS Chester Frank	7-09-43	434 Sqn
R/161985	Sgt	PHILLIPS Derrick Stephen	24-08-43	427 Sqn
R/110054	F/S	PHILLIPS Lloyd Watson	30-01-43	427 Sqn
R/88414	F/S	PHILPOTT James Albert Mason	12-06-43	432 Sqn
R/132192	F/S	PHOENIX Owen Harvey	26-07-43	419 Sqn
J/17357	P/O	PICHE Kenneth Mark [USA]	16-04-43	15 Sqn
R/128307	F/S	PICK Clarence Frank	26-08-43	22 OTU
J/15641	F/S	PICKARD DFC David Leslie	26-11-43	57 Sqn
R/105745	F/S	PICKERING Charles William	10-08-43	405 Sqn
R/102844	WO2	PIERCE Bland Joseph [Eire]	31-08-43	432 Sqn
R/126066	F/S	PIERCE Charles Phillips	1-09-43	196 Sqn
R/130299	F/S	PIGEAU Joseph David	16-08-43	61 Sqn
R/120847	Sgt	PIKET Jacob	12-05-43	22 OTU
J/17738	F/O	PILDREM Robert Alexander	29-12-43	408 Sqn
R/146665	F/S	PILKEY John David	21-12-43	434 Sqn
R/90867	F/S	PILON Francois Rolland Joseph	17-04-43	408 Sqn
R/88005	Sgt	PINCHESS Leslie Austin	2-10-43	23 OTU
J/16143	P/O	PINDER Peter Francis	15-01-43	214 Sqn
R/94997	LAC	PIOTROFSKY Paul	2-05-43	424 Sqn
J/18462	P/O	PIPER MiD Frederick James	18-08-43	434 Sqn
R/108000	F/S	PIRIE James Allan	30-05-43	75 Sqn
R/101308	WO2	PITHIE Harold Chase	31-08-43	427 Sqn
J/14205	F/O	PITKETHLY Alexander	6-09-43	424 Sqn
J/14636	F/O	PITMAN Leslie Charles [United Kingdom]	23-09-43	106 Sqn
R/116161	F/S	PITT Ernest William	18-04-43	1659 HCU
R/113191	F/S	PLANK Lester Kenneth	17-04-43	420 Sqn
R/103187	WO2	PLAUNT Donald Cameron	12-03-43	97 Sqn
J/13121	F/O	PLEASANCE Walter Norman	21-02-43	424 Sqn
J/17388	P/O	PLISHKA Leonard	17-11-43	617 Sqn
R/182077	F/S	PLOUFFE Ernest John Cecil	22-10-43	434 Sqn
R/186875	Sgt	PODBOROCHINSKI Edmund	29-12-43	12 Sqn
R/86547	WO2	PODOLSKY Alex	17-04-43	83 Sqn
J/18748	P/O	POIRIER John Augustin Albert	7-02-43	425 Sqn
R/173896	Sgt	POLLITT Kenneth William	20-10-43	90 Sqn
R/108564	Sgt	POLLOCK James Andrew	14-01-43	426 Sqn
R/124287	WO2	POLLON Ernest Sinclair	26-05-43	90 Sqn
J/16305	F/O	POPPLEWELL Chetwin Hamre	29-09-43	434 Sqn
R/121256	F/S	PORTEOUS Henry Mitchell	4-09-43	57 Sqn
R/152563	F/S	PORTER Allan Lloyd	26-07-43	419 Sqn
J/20814	F/O	PORTER Allister Wilson	20-10-43	106 Sqn
J/9668	F/O	PORTER MiD Charles Edward	27-03-43	419 Sqn
J/23942	F/O	POTTS David [USA]	6-11-43	26 Sqn
R/104609	LAC	POUDRETTE Joseph Gillies Alfred	23-10-43	432 Sqn
R/128171	F/S	POULIN William John	1-09-43	158 Sqn
R/82995	F/S	POWELL David Haynes Barcham	8-01-43	467 Sqn
R/71536	WO2	POWELL William Obediah	3-02-43	214 Sqn
J/9418	F/O	POWER David Allan	2-02-43	50 Sqn
R/76139	F/S	POWER Lawrence Fabien	18-08-43	419 Sqn
R/176903	Sgt	POWER Warren Michael	20-12-43	149 Sqn
J/9245	F/O	PRATT David	28-05-43	21 Sqn
R/91398	F/S	PRENTICE William Ronald	10-07-43	408 Sqn
J/15788	F/O	PREST Elmont Gasper	18-08-43	619 Sqn
R/119661	F/S	PRESTON Charles William	4-07-43	158 Sqn
R/60745	Sgt	PRICE Charles William Patterson	25-06-43	405 Sqn
J/17470	P/O	PRICE John Hugh [USA]	6-09-43	83 Sqn
R/82703	F/S	PRICE Kenneth Ether	5-04-43	21 Sqn
R/74230	WO2	PRIDDIN William Edward Ernest Bethell [USA]	28-04-43	158 Sqn
R/193077	Sgt	PRIDHAM Edward Stanley	21-12-43	434 Sqn
R/132590	F/S	PRIEUR Joseph Fernard Jacques Paul	24-05-43	419 Sqn
J/18880	P/O	PRILL Maurice Milton	16-12-43	426 Sqn

ID	Rank	Name	Date	Sqn
J/11133	F/O	PRINGLE Bertram Hamilton	5-11-43	405 Sqn
R/110932	F/S	PROSNYCK John	5-05-43	428 Sqn
J/16407	P/O	PROSPERINE Frank	27-03-43	101 Sqn
R/139022	F/S	PUDNEY GM Clinton Landis [USA]	16-06-43	405 Sqn
J/13142	F/O	PULLEY Harry Clinton	1-03-43	103 Sqn
R/105100	WO2	PURCHASE Frederick Hugh	27-04-43	429 Sqn
J/12967	F/O	PUSHOR Dale Ernest	30-07-43	7 Sqn
R/107016	F/S	PUTNAM Max Ernest	26-01-43	424 Sqn
R/99568	WO2	PYM William Harold	4-07-43	166 Sqn
J/19930	F/O	PYNISKY Peter	18-08-43	44 Sqn
R/98092	Sgt	QUEEN Harold Allen	31-08-43	207 Sqn
R/54698	Sgt	QUENET Pierre Louis Joseph Marie	4-10-43	427 Sqn
J/17768	P/O	QUEVILLON Raoul	13-06-43	102 Sqn
R/128475	F/S	QUICKFALL Clarke Edward	2-12-43	90 Sqn
R/90077	WO2	QUINN James Edward	13-01-43	106 Sqn
R/100441	WO2	RABAN William Edward	29-12-43	408 Sqn
R/156140	F/S	RADBOURNE Allen Bruce	22-11-43	428 Sqn
R/118160	WO2	RADCLIFF Kenneth Edward	29-04-43	428 Sqn
J/5901	F/L	RAINE Almer Clement	29-06-43	419 Sqn
R/79295	Sgt	RAINVILLE Joseph Lucien Roger	23-09-43	419 Sqn
R/137366	F/S	RAKOCZY Paul Leopold [USA]	29-06-43	10 Sqn
R/152317	F/S	RALPH Frederick Wilson [USA]	24-05-43	460 Sqn
R/196627	WO2	RAMAGE Lawrence Hunter	20-10-43	29 OTU
R/93418	WO2	RAMSAY James Alexander	29-04-43	75 Sqn
R/130158	F/S	RAMSAY Ralph Carlton	19-02-43	426 Sqn
R/105715	F/S	RANDS Harold	26-02-43	426 Sqn
R/115530	F/S	RANGER Raymond	4-10-43	427 Sqn
J/17005	P/O	RANKIN Jnr John [USA]	4-07-43	405 Sqn
R/101981	F/S	RANKMORE Gordon John	28-05-43	307 FTU
R/120191	F/S	RATELLE Roger Emile Lucien	13-05-43	419 Sqn
R/180461	Sgt	RATTIGAN Wilfred James	4-12-43	431 Sqn
R/108752	F/S	RAVEN Harold Roy	3-08-43	100 Sqn
J/20373	F/O	RAWSON James Leslie	12-06-43	426 Sqn
J/11851	F/O	RAY Edmund Rothell [USA]	4-04-43	408 Sqn
J/24590	F/O	RAYMOND Donald Eugene	23-12-43	15 OTU
R/121029	F/S	RAYMOND Lloyd Kenneth	23-09-43	15 Sqn
R/108696	F/S	REA Robert William	27-01-43	97 Sqn
J/22628	F/O	READY Robert Franklin	29-06-43	22 OTU
R/90121	WO2	REANSBURY John Joseph	23-06-43	427 Sqn
R/113223	F/S	RECTOR Vernon Francis	16-07-43	432 Sqn
R/144142	F/S	REDFERN Donald Leroy	4-08-43	16 OTU
R/185698	Sgt	REDMOND Bernard Nicholas	11-12-43	16 OTU
R/77912	Sgt	REDMOND Jack Edward	20-12-43	576 Sqn
J/21915	F/O	REDPATH John Norman Ralston	20-10-43	405 Sqn
R/85313	WO2	REED Clifford Harold	16-01-43	61 Sqn
R/130233	WO2	REED Norman Lloyd	23-09-43	428 Sqn
J/13362	F/O	REEVES Jonah Bruce [USA]	4-07-43	9 Sqn
J/18083	P/O	REICHERT Clifford Clarence	22-06-43	408 Sqn
R/92645	F/S	REID George Vivian Vincent	10-07-43	1659 HCU
J/18163	P/O	REID Kenneth Maxime [USA]	31-07-43	106 Sqn
J/10353	F/O	REID AFC Norman Duncan	23-06-43	427 Sqn
J/16195	P/O	REID Robert James Maxwell Frederick	25-02-43	21 OTU
R/152399	F/S	REID William Cecil	26-09-43	24 OTU
R/92794	WO2	REID William John	10-04-43	9 Sqn
R/142433	F/S	REID William John	14-05-43	429 Sqn
R/93374	WO2	REID William Joseph	13-05-43	61 Sqn
J/16970	P/O	REIF Alfred Frederick	1-03-43	103 Sqn
R/163707	Sgt	REIST Charles Andrew	7-08-43	425 Sqn
R/169475	F/S	RENAUD Joseph Harvey	26-07-43	61 Sqn
R/82532	F/S	RENAUD Joseph Isidore Ronald Roland	18-08-43	434 Sqn
R/99592	F/S	RENNICK John Stanley	25-06-43	12 Sqn
R/128406	F/S	RENWICK Clifford William	24-09-43	428 Sqn
R/127905	WO2	RENWICK John William McLeod	28-08-43	103 Sqn
R/104432	F/S	REYNOLDS Clarence Cecil	22-10-43	434 Sqn
J/9637	F/L	REYNOLDS Fred Albert	4-07-43	429 Sqn
R/131490	F/S	REYNOLDS George William Francis	5-05-43	101 Sqn
R/135119	F/S	REYNOLDS Robert Peter	22-09-43	434 Sqn
J/20351	F/O	REYNOLDS William Cassin	26-05-43	207 Sqn
R/111159	F/S	RHEAUME Earl Stewart	12-06-43	431 Sqn
R/131818	F/S	RHODES Alfred Spencer	22-06-43	429 Sqn
R/168536	Sgt	RICE James Orville	3-08-43	405 Sqn
J/26847	P/O	RICH George Henry [USA]	26-11-43	431 Sqn
J/14785	F/O	RICHARD Russell Bernard	22-11-43	49 Sqn
J/11860	F/O	RICHARDS Robert Cranston	14-01-43	426 Sqn
R/146946	F/S	RICHARDSON Desmond Gerald	26-04-43	426 Sqn
R/86416	WO2	RICHARDSON Jack Graydon	12-03-43	199 Sqn
C/20348	F/O	RICHARDSON John William	10-07-43	1659 HCU
J/19279	P/O	RICHARDSON Murray Lincoln	18-11-43	115 Sqn
R/122409	F/S	RICHARDSON Thornton Edward	11-04-43	166 Sqn
R/81607	F/S	RICHER Joseph George Paul Emille	22-06-43	35 Sqn
J/21221	F/O	RICHMOND Bruce Andrew	30-05-43	429 Sqn
R/97633	WO2	RICHMOND Henry	17-04-43	408 Sqn
R/114345	F/S	RICHMOND John Reginald	14-05-43	12 Sqn
R/163554	Sgt	RICHMOND Kenneth Lyle	19-07-43	22 OTU
R/153603	F/S	RICKETTS Roy Munro	30-05-43	419 Sqn
R/180597	Sgt	RIDDELL Raymond Reid	12-07-43	10 OTU
R/140266	F/S	RIEP Karl	22-10-43	1657 HCU
R/60321	F/S	RIMMER Clarence Flint	11-04-43	100 Sqn
J/21024	F/O	RINN Leonard Rodmond	2-12-43	630 Sqn
J/16519	P/O	RIPLEY Jack Graham	8-03-43	15 Sqn
R/86912	WO2	RISPIN Ronald George	8-04-43	420 Sqn
J/10305	F/O	RITCH Alister Frank Gray	4-02-43	57 Sqn
R/104442	F/S	RITCHIE Douglas Samuel	17-04-43	429 Sqn
R/119578	WO2	RITCHIE Robert William	4-12-43	431 Sqn
R/108468	WO2	RIVEST Levie Afrien	24-05-43	426 Sqn
R/137561	WO2	ROACH James Theodore	11-08-43	158 Sqn
R/122884	F/S	ROBB Fraser Allan	17-04-43	76 Sqn
R/125806	F/S	ROBERTS David Eric	17-04-43	218 Sqn
R/80174	WO1	ROBERTS David Rozell	11-01-43	81 OTU
R/102988	F/O	ROBERTS Ernest Wilson David	9-01-43	51 Sqn
R/119606	F/S	ROBERTS Frank Duncan	7-04-43	405 Sqn
J/18831	P/O	ROBERTS DFM Frederick John	2-12-43	103 Sqn
J/21027	F/O	ROBERTS Leone Joseph	22-10-43	207 Sqn
R/110955	F/S	ROBERTS Norman William	30-03-43	408 Sqn
R/126403	F/S	ROBERTS Walter Raymond	29-06-43	424 Sqn
R/102097	F/S	ROBERTSON Donald Lawrence	3-04-43	156 Sqn
J/10178	F/O	ROBERTSON Ernest Drever	14-07-43	428 Sqn
R/103625	WO2	ROBERTSON John	31-08-43	427 Sqn
J/10302	F/L	ROBERTSON DFC Oliver Brock	28-08-43	97 Sqn
J/50179	F/O	ROBINSON Clifford	24-08-43	83 Sqn
J/10704	F/O	ROBINSON George Creighton	18-08-43	426 Sqn
R/50471	F/S	ROBINSON Neil Owen	19-04-43	156 Sqn
8142A	F/S	ROBINSON Ralph Lavis	22-06-43	405 Sqn
R/50788	Sgt	ROBINSON William Albert	18-02-43	419 Sqn
R/115295	WO2	ROCHE Thomas Joseph	28-07-43	106 Sqn
R/186781	Sgt	RODEN Albert Edward	19-11-43	431 Sqn
R/92002	WO2	RODIN Ivan	2-12-43	460 Sqn
R/141566	F/S	ROE Frank Haviland	1-10-43	1660 HCU
R/85301	WO2	ROGAL Joseph Michael	27-03-43	431 Sqn
R/121900	F/S	ROGERS Eric	9-10-43	218 Sqn
R/131020	F/S	ROGERS Frank Edward	12-04-43	23 OTU
J/7469	F/O	ROGERS Frederick Lennox	3-08-43	428 Sqn
J/21818	F/O	ROLLINGS William Arnold	1-05-43	44 Sqn
R/189695	Sgt	ROOBROECK Maurice Francis Victor	17-12-43	405 Sqn
R/56172	WO1	ROONEY James Joseph	2-03-43	61 Sqn
R/145968	WO2	ROOS Robert Edward	29-12-43	10 Sqn
R/91883	WO2	ROSENBERRY Willard Kennedy	16-02-43	90 Sqn
R/103151	F/S	ROSEVEAR Kenneth Willard	5-04-43	428 Sqn
R/115601	F/S	ROSS Allen Roderick	17-04-43	76 Sqn
R/79133	Sgt	ROSS Donald Robin	14-03-43	138 Sqn
R/176649	Sgt	ROSS Douglas Alexander	28-08-43	218 Sqn
R/99150	F/S	ROSS Francis Owen	17-04-43	76 Sqn
J/16873	P/O	ROSS Herbert John	30-03-43	115 Sqn

R/102337	WO2	ROSS Horace Robert	3-09-43	156 Sqn
R/129274	F/S	ROSS Keith Douglas	12-11-43	1659 HCU
R/127990	F/S	ROSS Walter Eugene	26-07-43	419 Sqn
J/16747	P/O	ROSSIGNOL James Louis [USA]	21-04-43	61 Sqn
R/123638	F/S	ROTHSTEIN Irvine Sydney	6-08-43	75 Sqn
R/185468	Sgt	ROUSSEAU Joseph Henri Fernand	27-09-43	434 Sqn
J/18505	P/O	ROWE Earl Dwyre	22-06-43	405 Sqn
R/154101	F/S	ROWE Ernest Frederick Alan	18-10-43	101 Sqn
R/58798	F/S	ROY Charles Napoleon	10-07-43	12 Sqn
R/56194	WO2	ROY Joseph Tancrede Robert Jean	15-04-43	7 Sqn
J/16141	P/O	ROY William Wallace	15-01-43	161 Sqn
R/187471	Sgt	RUDD Francis	9-10-43	431 Sqn
R/140995	F/S	RUDICK Peter	17-04-43	100 Sqn
R/193610	Sgt	RUSSELL Harry	22-10-43	427 Sqn
R/147158	F/S	RUSSELL Leonard Bruce	23-10-43	431 Sqn
J/12826	F/O	RUSSELL Philip Campion Digby	29-06-43	207 Sqn
R/169893	Sgt	RUTHVEN James Roy Addison	29-12-43	431 Sqn
J/14738	F/O	RUTO Edward Basil [USA]	14-05-43	419 Sqn
R/21709	F/O	RUXTON William Smart	5-10-43	434 Sqn
R/93563	F/S	RUZYCKI Frank	19-02-43	426 Sqn
R/67919	WO1	RYAN John Edward	9-10-43	431 Sqn
R/98510	F/S	RYAN Lawrence Dennis	5-04-43	428 Sqn
R/137429	F/S	RYAN Thomas Joseph [USA]	1-09-43	15 Sqn
R/140616	Sgt	SADESKI John	3-08-43	419 Sqn
R/97340	F/S	SALISBURY Harold Jackson	5-05-43	166 Sqn
R/137609	F/S	SALMERS Eugene	18-06-43	12 Sqn
J/16941	P/O	SAMMET John Henry	10-04-43	426 Sqn
R/17087	F/L	SAMUELS Max	20-06-43	408 Sqn
R/103915	WO2	SANDERSON Delmer Ray	29-01-43	420 Sqn
R/154764	F/S	SANDERSON Kimble Calvin	3-09-43	28 OTU
J/22255	F/O	SANDES Charles Richard	20-12-43	428 Sqn
R/126444	F/O	SANITSKY Irving Louis [USA]	25-02-43	102 Sqn
R/70901	WO1	SANTO Frank Robert	5-05-43	22 OTU
R/109394	Sgt	SARGENT Harry Bertram John	5-04-43	405 Sqn
R/130592	F/S	SAUNDERS Harold Max	17-12-43	405 Sqn
R/126367	WO2	SAUNDERS Joseph Evans	16-12-43	408 Sqn
J/17053	F/O	SAUVE James Earl	3-11-43	408 Sqn
C/1664	W/C	SAVARD DFC Joseph Logan	23-06-43	429 Sqn
R/164404	F/S	SAWYER Kenneth William	27-11-43	426 Sqn
R/53361	F/S	SAYERS Joseph Fisher	7-02-43	408 Sqn
R/186452	Sgt	SAYERS William Horton	28-11-43	16 OTU
C/18817	P/O	SCANES Andrew Franklin	22-10-43	408 Sqn
R/95040	F/S	SCARFF Thomas Deuel	1-05-43	77 Sqn
J/19379	F/O	SCHADE Harvey Maurice	4-12-43	429 Sqn
R/119136	F/S	SCHAMEHORN Clifford Earl	12-06-43	426 Sqn
J/14203	F/O	SCHILANSKY Ivor [South Africa]	22-10-43	427 Sqn
R/129316	WO2	SCHILLER Kenneth Robert	9-12-43	1660 HCU
R/152251	F/S	SCHLEGEL Kenneth Eckert	3-08-43	115 Sqn
R/121591	F/S	SCHMIDT Lester Charles	3-10-43	90 Sqn
R/121528	WO2	SCHNEIDER Gordon Raymond	17-12-43	405 Sqn
J/16432	S/L	SCHNEIDER Murray Stanley Fuller	9-10-43	405 Sqn
R/120845	F/S	SCHULL Frederick Harold	27-06-43	432 Sqn
J/19312	P/O	SCHULZ Olivier Edouard Emile [Switzerland]	8-04-43	425 Sqn
R/165175	F/S	SCOTT David	1-09-43	199 Sqn
J/27608	P/O	SCOTT David Gilbert	26-11-43	429 Sqn
R/140573	F/S	SCOTT Gordon Douglas	7-09-43	29 OTU
R/95664	F/S	SCOTT Robert Alexander Leslie	16-08-43	61 Sqn
R/144237	Sgt	SCOTT William Charles	19-04-43	22 OTU
R/53011	F/S	SCRIMGEOUR William Wilson	8-02-43	44 Sqn
R/66593	Sgt	SCULLION Maurice Patrick	11-06-43	428 Sqn
R/93087	F/S	SEALY Harold Hogarth	29-01-43	420 Sqn
R/140842	Sgt	SEAMAN William Tom	10-06-43	24 OTU
J/18245	P/O	SEARLE William	22-06-43	408 Sqn
R/94570	F/S	SEBELIUS Cecil Lester	22-06-43	408 Sqn
R/141113	F/S	SEDGWICK Arthur Louis	18-11-43	419 Sqn
R/139715	F/S	SEE Douglas Raymond	10-08-43	419 Sqn
R/82362	WO2	SEELEY Duncan Elwin	19-02-43	15 Sqn
R/101853	F/S	SELLAR Ernest Harold	21-02-43	405 Sqn
J/13767	F/O	SELLERS Jnr Greaton Wesley [USA]	12-03-43	149 Sqn
J/20028	F/O	SERGENT Joseph Raymond Louis	17-04-43	408 Sqn
J/20411	F/S	SEWALL William Stuart	22-10-43	434 Sqn
J/8974	F/O	SEXTON Murray Kerr	25-02-43	207 Sqn
J/11948	F/O	SHAGENA Jnr Carl John [USA]	21-02-43	405 Sqn
R/194853	Sgt	SHANKS Arnold Blane	29-09-43	17 OTU
J/21901	F/O	SHANN Harry Pritchard [USA]	30-07-43	214 Sqn
J/21917	F/O	SHANNON George Arnold	6-09-43	419 Sqn
R/115004	WO2	SHARPE Frank Prescott	23-09-43	428 Sqn
R/108329	F/S	SHARPE Richard Allan Whitaker	13-03-43	7 Sqn
R/142181	F/S	SHAW Denis Tolman	31-07-43	76 Sqn
J/17677	F/O	SHAW Malcolm Crimmins	2-12-43	426 Sqn
J/13021	F/L	SHAW Wilfred Lawrence	24-08-43	426 Sqn
R/99460	F/S	SHEA Victor Harrison	4-07-43	15 Sqn
R/57576	F/S	SHEEHAN Francis	2-10-43	460 Sqn
R/81445	WO2	SHEEHAN Henry Augustine	13-05-43	57 Sqn
R/171843	WO2	SHELDON Paul Howard	5-10-43	434 Sqn
R/102895	WO2	SHELNUTT Frank Lee [USA]	30-05-43	428 Sqn
C/6040	F/L	SHELTON Paul Arthur [USA]	28-09-43	77 Sqn
J/14170	F/O	SHEPPARD Walter Fitzgerald	17-12-43	405 Sqn
J/6181	F/L	SHERBACK Ronald Hubert	27-09-43	428 Sqn
R/63606	F/S	SHERIDAN John Francis	18-08-43	428 Sqn
R/155373	WO2	SHERK James Gordon	18-10-43	24 OTU
R/85566	WO2	SHIELDS Thomas Joseph	19-06-43	50 Sqn
J/13020	F/S	SHIVES Arnold Belden	10-03-43	1659 HCU
J/17452	F/O	SHNIER Clifford Charles	30-07-43	97 Sqn
J/7979	F/L	SHOCKLEY Harold Gordon	12-03-43	405 Sqn
4417	F/S	SHORE Wilfred Raymond Russ [United Kingdom]	11-11-43	161 Sqn
J/12691	F/O	SHORT Desmond Robert Parke	26-11-43	431 Sqn
R/102169	WO2	SHORTEN Albert George	13-03-43	199 Sqn
R/115984	F/S	SHORTRIDGE Raymond Francis	24-08-43	427 Sqn
R/147012	F/S	SHTITZ David Jacob	30-05-43	419 Sqn
R/136292	Sgt	SHULMAN Philip Murray	7-09-43	434 Sqn
J/13018	F/L	SHUTTLEWORTH DFC Douglas Dalton	18-08-43	426 Sqn
J/22206	F/O	SHVEMAR Max	25-06-43	427 Sqn
J/20883	F/O	SIBBALD Lloyd Elmer	24-08-43	90 Sqn
J/15700	F/L	SIBBALD DFC William John	22-06-43	101 Sqn
R/175992	Sgt	SIBSON Owen Hugh [USA]	24-05-43	101 Sqn
R/119786	F/S	SIEFFERT Arthur James	22-06-43	429 Sqn
R/159480	F/S	SILLITO Leroy	22-09-43	12 OTU
R/138354	F/S	SILLS John Loring	6-09-43	424 Sqn
R/11617	F/S	SILVER James Seaforth	28-08-43	77 Sqn
R/134345	F/S	SIMMONS Hugh Robertson	22-10-43	1664 HCU
R/70265	Sgt	SIMONETT William Allan	13-05-43	419 Sqn
R/114570	F/S	SIMPSON Alexander James	22-05-43	428 Sqn
J/17113	P/O	SIMPSON John Alexander	15-04-43	420 Sqn
R/153561	F/S	SINCLAIR Cecil Horace	26-06-43	106 Sqn
J/21037	F/O	SINCLAIR David James	28-09-43	434 Sqn
J/16946	F/O	SIRETT Ebenezer Alfred	4-04-43	408 Sqn
J/18375	P/O	SKELTON Oliver Henry	26-02-43	427 Sqn
1050	F/S	SKERRY Leo Clayton	9-10-43	427 Sqn
R/92454	Sgt	SKINNER David Beatty Evans	30-01-43	16 OTU
R/115543	WO2	SKLARCHUK Edward Robert	3-08-43	51 Sqn
R/129209	F/S	SLEEP Howard Cephus	29-03-43	420 Sqn
R/84338	WO2	SLEETH MiD Stewart [USA]	27-04-43	405 Sqn
R/135879	F/S	SLEGG Albert Edward	2-12-43	432 Sqn
R/94489	F/S	SLOBOTSKY David	24-05-43	408 Sqn
J/20847	F/S	SMALL Frederick George	9-10-43	434 Sqn
R/148889	WO2	SMALL James Roy Robert	26-11-43	626 Sqn
R/139880	F/S	SMALLEY Kenneth George	9-10-43	218 Sqn
R/105312	WO2	SMALLWOOD George Kenneth Alfred	28-04-43	419 Sqn
R/143723	WO2	SMART James Augustus	22-11-43	77 Sqn
R/129757	F/S	SMILLIE William Ellwood	20-10-43	1664 HCU
C/15771	F/O	SMITH DFC Albert	13-06-43	50 Sqn

J/16380	P/O	SMITH Alexander John	12-03-43		97 Sqn
R/84121	WO2	SMITH Campbell Murray	11-04-43		115 Sqn
R/91151	Sgt	SMITH Charles Chester	22-10-43		429 Sqn
R/120710	F/S	SMITH Charles Joseph	30-01-43		427 Sqn
R/84977	WO2	SMITH Charles Thomas	26-05-43		15 Sqn
R/94982	WO2	SMITH Dean William	7-02-43		408 Sqn
R/127875	Sgt	SMITH Donald Henry	12-04-43		23 OTU
R/79401	WO2	SMITH Earl George [USA]	3-08-43		428 Sqn
R/51480	Sgt	SMITH Edwin	20-12-43		10 Sqn
R/166678	Sgt	SMITH Frederick Percy	3-10-43		17 OTU
R/139774	F/S	SMITH Frederick William	3-10-43		90 Sqn
R/128614	WO2	SMITH George	17-10-43		23 OTU
R/58116	F/S	SMITH George Russell	27-09-43		166 Sqn
R/109986	F/S	SMITH Glen Frank [USA]	8-10-43		20 OTU
J/18388	P/O	SMITH Henry Maxwell	18-08-43		426 Sqn
R/123492	F/S	SMITH James Allan [Dominican Republic]	27-04-43		428 Sqn
R/94963	WO2	SMITH James Francis	8-04-43		425 Sqn
R/186445	Sgt	SMITH James McGregor	3-11-43		625 Sqn
J/23641	F/O	SMITH James Scott	18-11-43		419 Sqn
R/69401	F/S	SMITH John Wilmer	10-01-43		10 Sqn
R/97918	WO2	SMITH Kenneth Cunliffe	19-11-43		434 Sqn
J/8603	F/O	SMITH Kenneth Read	3-01-43		9 Sqn
R/155648	F/S	SMITH Leslie Gordon	24-05-43		101 Sqn
J/18222	P/O	SMITH Mitchell	13-08-43		432 Sqn
R/120129	F/S	SMITH Neville George	19-06-43		50 Sqn
R/75465	Sgt	SMITH Robert Clifford	4-11-43		408 Sqn
R/131214	F/S	SMITH Russell Harry	27-09-43		434 Sqn
R/151503	F/S	SMITH Stanley	18-11-43		429 Sqn
J/23734	F/O	SMITH Stanley Maurice	22-11-43		115 Sqn
R/161620	F/S	SMITH Stuart Elmer	26-11-43		514 Sqn
J/14174	F/O	SMITH Sydney Kent	29-09-43		156 Sqn
R/108246	Sgt	SMITH Sydney Stuart	21-12-43		434 Sqn
R/113431	F/S	SMITH Theo Curtis	26-02-43		427 Sqn
R/139347	Sgt	SMITH William Alexander	15-11-43		12 OTU
R/107964	F/S	SMITH-JONES Henry Vaynor	29-04-43		428 Sqn
J/15677	F/O	SMUCK Alan Osborn	14-07-43		408 Sqn
R/116935	F/S	SMYTH Clarence Reginald	10-08-43		419 Sqn
J/18088	P/O	SMYTH Michael Sydney	25-07-43		405 Sqn
J/26839	P/O	SNEAD Samuel Thomas	25-07-43	1659 HCU	
J/17777	P/O	SNEATH William Alfred	23-06-43		429 Sqn
J/22065	F/O	SNOOK Albert Veron	20-10-43		625 Sqn
J/16804	F/O	SNOW Morley Vivian	4-12-43		431 Sqn
R/146094	F/S	SNYDER Charles William	24-08-43		434 Sqn
R/122037	Sgt	SNYDER James Joseph [USA]	26-01-43		23 OTU
R/133756	F/S	SOBEL Harold	1-05-43		7 Sqn
R/123719	F/S	SOBIN Joseph Stanley	3-08-43		419 Sqn
R/124548	F/S	SODERO Alexander Theodore	1-06-43		420 Sqn
J/20892	F/O	SOLOMKA Nicholas	6-08-43		23 OTU
R/130819	F/S	SOLUK Paul	25-06-43		12 Sqn
J/8219	F/O	SOMERS Lou Warren	25-06-43		427 Sqn
R/109492	F/S	SONDERGAARD Svend	21-12-43		427 Sqn
R/156843	F/S	SOOS Julien Louis	23-05-43		408 Sqn
J/16825	F/O	SOUCH DFC George Allan	29-07-43		424 Sqn
R/90794	Sgt	SOUTAR Kenneth Gordon	26-08-43		20 OTU
R/149408	F/S	SPANKE Edwin Herman	3-08-43		12 Sqn
J/15722	F/O	SPANNER DFC Frederick Gordon Charles	3-09-43		207 Sqn
R/129739	Sgt	SPARLING John Lewis	22-01-43		427 Sqn
R/128162	WO2	SPARLING Lawson Frederick	26-06-43		106 Sqn
R/80605	F/S	SPARROW William Albert	25-06-43		432 Sqn
J/12979	F/O	SPECTOR Samuel	1-03-43		420 Sqn
R/144263	F/S	SPEICHER George Wilson	23-09-43		57 Sqn
R/154088	F/S	SPENCE Harold Omond [British Guiana]	20-10-43		90 Sqn
J/17487	P/O	SPENCE Malcolm Burgess	22-06-43		429 Sqn
J/173981	F/S	SPENCER Ervine Eugene	20-10-43		90 Sqn
R/139365	F/S	SPENCER Francis Arthur	29-12-43		467 Sqn
R/100196	F/S	SPENCER Hugh Phair	1-05-43		51 Sqn
J/25528	F/O	SPENCER Jack Samuel	18-10-43		24 OTU
R/122306	F/S	SPENCER Norman Vincent	22-09-43		218 Sqn
R/122267	WO2	SPONSLER Harry [USA]	30-05-43		149 Sqn
R/102127	WO2	SPRING Kenneth Loren	12-06-43		115 Sqn
R/92104	WO2	SPROULE Edward Alan	26-05-43		166 Sqn
C/1201	F/L	SPURR Alfred Eugene	23-06-43		103 Sqn
J/21532	F/O	STAMERS Douglas Hazen	16-12-43		405 Sqn
R/134212	F/S	STANLEY Frederick Thomas	5-05-43		419 Sqn
J/17008	P/O	STANLEY Grenville Gordon	2-03-43		76 Sqn
R/95347	WO2	STANLEY Richard Walter	30-05-43		149 Sqn
J/17698	P/O	STAPLES Murray Clement	29-07-43		156 Sqn
R/131714	F/S	STAR Ernest Alexander	22-06-43		429 Sqn
R/114527	WO2	STEADMAN Aubrey David	7-09-43		434 Sqn
R/122165	F/S	STEEDMAN Robert	4-04-43		487 Sqn
R/94702	WO2	STEELE John David	9-04-43		101 Sqn
R/156911	F/S	STEELS Arthur Douglas	8-10-43		149 Sqn
R/58757	F/S	STEFANCHUK John James	10-07-43		408 Sqn
R/191510	Sgt	STEINACKER Alvin Joseph	9-10-43		434 Sqn
R/193107	Sgt	STEMMLER Lorne Alfred	6-09-43		427 Sqn
J/20202	F/O	STEPHENS James Anthony	26-11-43		61 Sqn
R/140746	F/S	STERRETT Joseph Roger Lawrence	21-01-43		207 Sqn
J/17321	F/O	STEVENS DFC George Alfred Harding	28-11-43		16 OTU
J/16687	P/O	STEVENSON Alfred William	17-01-43		76 Sqn
R/129380	F/S	STEVENSON Edward Barnes	15-06-43		100 Sqn
J/16926	F/O	STEWART DFM Angus William	3-09-43		156 Sqn
R/72715	F/S	STEWART Frank Campbell	3-02-43		218 Sqn
R/105711	F/S	STEWART Herbert William	14-01-43		466 Sqn
J/15536	F/L	STEWART DFC Herbert William Joseph	23-11-43		156 Sqn
J/14573	F/O	STEWART John Edgar	24-12-43		550 Sqn
R/138281	F/S	STEWART Joseph Robert	24-05-43		166 Sqn
J/9196	P/O	STEWART Leonard James	9-04-43		7 Sqn
R/163697	Sgt	STEWART Lorne Glen	5-07-43		10 OTU
R/130152	WO2	STEWART Reginald Donald	16-12-43		426 Sqn
J/18281	F/O	STEWART Robert	31-08-43		419 Sqn
R/133336	F/S	STEWART Robert	14-07-43		432 Sqn
J/17100	P/O	STEWART Ronald Henry	17-04-43		51 Sqn
J/27921	P/O	STEWART Verne Allison	23-09-43		428 Sqn
J/16779	F/O	STEWART Walter Ferguson	14-07-43		428 Sqn
R/113188	F/S	STEWART William Henry	11-01-43		81 OTU
R/103778	WO2	STICKNEY Robert Randolph	26-06-43		427 Sqn
J/19157	P/O	STINSON Harley Vernon	2-12-43		35 Sqn
J/17695	P/O	STINSON Lloyd Albert	14-05-43		408 Sqn
R/188037	Sgt	STINSON Wilmer Edmond	2-12-43		432 Sqn
J/18138	P/O	STIVER Donald Ewart	6-09-43		44 Sqn
R/59411	Sgt	STONE Douglas Bryant	27-09-43		428 Sqn
R/109714	F/S	STONE Oscar Wilson [USA]	24-01-43		20 OTU
R/161496	F/S	STONE Robert James	16-12-43		207 Sqn
R/104320	F/S	STORDY John Lawrence	27-04-43		405 Sqn
J/16703	P/O	STOREY Anderson [USA]	18-01-43		9 Sqn
R/68628	WO2	STOREY Douglas Simpson	20-10-43		100 Sqn
R/112684	WO2	STORMER Lloyd Martin	24-08-43		90 Sqn
J/16835	F/L	STOVEL DFC Clifford Campbell	28-07-43		408 Sqn
R/91336	WO2	STOVER Russell Roberts	15-04-43		149 Sqn
R/124535	F/S	STRACHAN James Anthony Osborne	9-10-43		12 Sqn
R/127567	Sgt	STRAIN Clifford Clarence	27-04-43		76 Sqn
R/134019	WO2	STRANDBERG Edwin [USA]	8-04-43		44 Sqn
R/171882	Sgt	STRANG Gerald Lee	16-12-43		405 Sqn
R/169836	F/S	STRICKLAND Roy Cecil	24-11-43		44 Sqn
R/102783	WO2	STRONG Robert Douglas	8-03-43		156 Sqn
J/17228	P/O	STROUTS DFC Frederick Stanley	26-03-43		109 Sqn
R/93568	F/S	STUART Phillip Gordon	9-04-43		75 Sqn
R/133386	F/S	STUART Reginald Victor	7-04-43		405 Sqn
J/14875	P/O	STUDER James Arthur [USA]	6-09-43		419 Sqn
R/151922	F/S	STURLEY Ross Griffin	4-12-43		426 Sqn
7817	F/S	ST. GERMAIN Ernest Joseph	13-06-43		101 Sqn

J/23301	P/O	ST. JOHNS William Ivan [USA]	3-09-43	22 OTU
J/14059	F/O	ST. LOUIS Bruce Anderson	28-09-43	405 Sqn
R/106277	F/S	SULLIVAN William Joseph	14-01-43	426 Sqn
J/18532	P/O	SUMMERS Malcolm Barnes	7-10-43	426 Sqn
R/190551	Sgt	SUTHERLAND George Wills	7-09-43	434 Sqn
R/99732	WO2	SUTHERLAND Leslie Gordon	25-05-43	426 Sqn
R/143237	F/S	SUTHERLAND Wilfred Kastner	5-12-43	623 Sqn
J/17692	P/O	SUTTON Albert James	5-05-43	408 Sqn
J/3722	F/L	SUTTON DFC Harold Ransom	27-05-43	139 Sqn
R/144189	F/S	SUTTON Walter Charles	22-05-43	428 Sqn
R/131686	WO2	SVEINSON Glen Geoffrey	22-10-43	103 Sqn
J/14504	F/O	SWALLOW Robert Philpot	16-08-43	166 Sqn
J/18243	P/O	SWAN Norman Cecil	26-05-43	426 Sqn
R/90888	F/S	SWEENEY James Vincent	15-06-43	106 Sqn
R/90889	F/S	SWEENEY Joseph Gerald	29-06-43	10 Sqn
R/79844	F/S	SWEENEY Wilfred	23-11-43	214 Sqn
J/14813	F/S	SWEET Lawrence Thomas Edwin	30-03-43	427 Sqn
R/76563	WO2	SWEITZER Leonard James	6-02-43	199 Sqn
R/89162	F/S	SWINDELLS Eric Russell	6-06-43	30 OTU
J/17282	P/O	SYLVESTER Victor Thomas	3-08-43	428 Sqn
J/17043	F/O	SYMONS John Ritchie	29-04-43	419 Sqn
J/16688	F/L	TAERUM DFC Torger Harlo 'Terry'	16-09-43	617 Sqn
R/108469	WO2	TAILLEFER Louis Phillipe Roma	12-06-43	429 Sqn
R/156125	F/S	TAIT Hugh Matheson	16-12-43	1667 HCU
R/123539	Sgt	TALMAN Richard Ellwood	26-05-43	426 Sqn
J/13421	F/O	TANNER Harold Edward	30-03-43	408 Sqn
R/146158	F/S	TATE George Douglas Watson	27-06-43	432 Sqn
J/16978	P/O	TAYLOR Arthur Edward	27-04-43	158 Sqn
J/10890	F/O	TAYLOR Finlay Russell	29-07-43	424 Sqn
J/20217	F/O	TAYLOR Frederick Stuart	27-06-43	12 OTU
R/73856	F/S	TAYLOR Garth Shearly	4-10-43	83 Sqn
J/143910	Sgt	TAYLOR Glenwood Alexander	16-02-43	16 OTU
R/98145	WO2	TAYLOR James	29-03-43	76 Sqn
R/130695	F/S	TAYLOR James Alexander Campbell	5-04-43	405 Sqn
J/18624	P/O	TAYLOR John Alexander	17-12-43	218 Sqn
R/159957	F/S	TAYLOR Joseph [USA]	17-08-43	23 OTU
R/77972	F/S	TAYLOR Lawrence	10-03-43	1659 HCU
J/19427	P/O	TAYLOR Leonard Keith	11-04-43	424 Sqn
J/12075	F/O	TAYLOR Malcolm Stout	21-12-43	434 Sqn
R/84381	WO1	TAYLOR Norman Henry Arthur	12-06-43	405 Sqn
J/18109	P/O	TAYLOR DFM Ralph Edgar [USA]	28-05-43	432 Sqn
J/15535	F/O	TAYLOR DFC* Richard Winter	14-03-43	161 Sqn
R/113958	F/S	TAYLOR Robert Allan	18-06-43	83 Sqn
C/18110	F/O	TAYLOR William Bryce	4-07-43	419 Sqn
J/17662	F/O	TAYLOR William Howard	4-07-43	432 Sqn
J/24309	F/O	TAYLOR William John	2-12-43	1664 HCU
J/17609	P/O	TEDFORD Bernard Laird	13-06-43	427 Sqn
R/84505	F/S	TEDFORD Blair Vincent	23-11-43	434 Sqn
R/106683	WO2	TELFER Thomas Wilfred	5-04-43	9 Sqn
J/16322	P/O	TENNIS Howard Allen	13-05-43	429 Sqn
J/13810	P/O	TEW Edmond McLeod	29-01-43	22 OTU
J/124683	F/S	THAYER Robert Francis	17-07-43	424 Sqn
R/104805	WO2	THERIEN Francois Cecilius Jean-Louis	6-08-43	23 OTU
R/94389	F/S	THIBAUDEAU Joseph Evaniste Adrian	5-05-43	428 Sqn
J/122988	F/S	THIESSEN Arley Henry	3-02-43	214 Sqn
R/162252	F/S	THOMASBERG Balder	2-12-43	57 Sqn
R/72344	WO1	THOMPSON Denison Hilton	28-05-43	428 Sqn
R/82736	WO1	THOMPSON Ford Arnold	18-08-43	619 Sqn
R/146160	WO2	THOMPSON George Welland	9-10-43	432 Sqn
R/115765	F/S	THOMPSON Gordon William	30-05-43	432 Sqn
J/166511	Sgt	THOMPSON Harold Robert	22-10-43	14 OTU
J/17581	F/O	THOMPSON Lorne Edgar	16-12-43	101 Sqn
R/111346	F/S	THOMPSON Lyle Harold	18-08-43	61 Sqn
J/25843	P/O	THOMPSON Maxwell Hartley	9-10-43	61 Sqn
J/149306	F/S	THOMPSON Osborne David	23-06-43	77 Sqn
R/164440	Sgt	THOMPSON Thomas Walter	21-12-43	427 Sqn
R/89257	Sgt	THOMPSON William Lloyd George	12-03-43	10 Sqn
R/112455	Sgt	THOMSON Arthur Sylvanus	26-05-43	101 Sqn
J/15487	F/O	THOMSON Ivan Samuel	26-05-43	15 Sqn
R/121044	F/S	THOMSON James Austin	14-05-43	426 Sqn
J/3524	S/L	THOMSON William Nairne	22-10-43	434 Sqn
J/20231	F/O	THORN Stanley Edgar Crosby	9-10-43	427 Sqn
J/13792	F/O	THORNBER Ernest Garfield	3-05-43	487 Sqn
10395	F/O	THORNTON David	18-08-43	419 Sqn
R/117355	WO2	THORPE Donald Menzies	11-12-43	617 Sqn
R/116497	WO2	THOULD Thomas Frank	28-08-43	434 Sqn
J/19337	P/O	THRASHER John William	20-12-43	617 Sqn
J/17471	P/O	THURLOW John Robert	22-06-43	100 Sqn
R/104208	WO2	THURSTON Howard Frederick	18-08-43	12 Sqn
R/108882	F/S	TIDY Charles Harrison	14-03-43	420 Sqn
J/9416	F/L	TIGHE Robert George	5-04-43	428 Sqn
J/21573	F/O	TINDAL Charles Arthur	13-08-43	420 Sqn
J/26842	P/O	TITOF Leon Abraham	18-10-43	9 Sqn
R/91741	WO2	TOD Richard Douglas	23-06-43	75 Sqn
R/91742	WO2	TOD DFM Robert Ernest	23-06-43	75 Sqn
R/155739	F/S	TODD Arthur Francis	6-09-43	76 Sqn
R/114310	F/S	TODD Oliver William	23-06-43	158 Sqn
R/126792	F/S	TODD Richard Earl [USA]	29-03-43	426 Sqn
R/145403	F/S	TODD Robert Mercer	5-09-43	1663 HCU
R/144252	F/S	TODHUNTER Thomas Ralph Henry [United Kingdom]	3-11-43	12 Sqn
R/110876	F/S	TOMCHYSHYN Peter	14-08-43	1662 HCU
J/21899	F/O	TOMCZAK Marcel Emmett	25-07-43	405 Sqn
J/16659	P/O	TOMLINSON Frank Morton	10-03-43	7 Sqn
R/157029	F/S	TOMLINSON James Gordon	23-11-43	434 Sqn
R/130533	F/S	TOMYN Steve	17-04-43	427 Sqn
R/103890	F/S	TONGUE Jack	29-03-43	97 Sqn
R/103535	WO2	TOOMBS Harry Wallace	3-05-43	487 Sqn
R/130140	WO2	TOOMBS John Blackstock	26-11-43	61 Sqn
R/74721	WO1	TOON James Willis	14-04-43	103 Sqn
R/103759	F/S	TOPPING William Frederick	12-03-43	424 Sqn
R/117511	F/S	TOUPIN Joseph Onesime Thomas Ange Albert Gerard	12-04-43	23 OTU
J/17295	P/O	TOUPIN Lionel Louis Victor	9-03-43	7 Sqn
R/92996	F/S	TOVEY James Harold	7-09-43	434 Sqn
R/185559	Sgt	TOWLE Sidney Elmer	1-09-43	428 Sqn
J/16397	P/O	TOWNSEND Leslie Robert	9-04-43	199 Sqn
J/16876	P/O	TOWNSEND Philip Edward Thompson	1-03-43	420 Sqn
R/92330	F/S	TOWNSEND William Russell	29-06-43	78 Sqn
R/157548	F/S	TRACE Jack Richdale	6-09-43	78 Sqn
R/84804	F/S	TRACEY Harold Vernon	30-03-43	158 Sqn
J/16651	P/O	TRASK Cyril Randolph	5-03-43	426 Sqn
R/133834	F/S	TRAVER Howard William [USA]	3-02-43	218 Sqn
R/16069	F/O	TREHERNE Howard Cedric	29-06-43	12 Sqn
R/123752	F/S	TREMBLAY David Gerald	17-06-43	9 Sqn
R/117594	F/S	TREMBLAY Joseph Neree Andre Maurice	10-03-43	429 Sqn
J/17540	P/O	TREMBLAY Pierre Yves Camille	19-02-43	156 Sqn
J/10163	F/L	TRILSBECK DFC Theodore	16-12-43	156 Sqn
R/68175	WO1	TRIPP Herbert Andrew	12-06-43	419 Sqn
J/16827	P/O	TRIPPE Temple Dawson [USA]	28-09-43	405 Sqn
R/121469	F/S	TROFANENKO William	10-07-43	424 Sqn
R/109393	WO2	TROMAN John Lewis	18-08-43	427 Sqn
R/126445	Sgt	TROWBRIDGE Stuart Urquhart	31-01-43	16 OTU
R/169016	Sgt	TRUAX James Lyall	26-11-43	419 Sqn
R/79441	WO2	TRUDEAU Pierre Paul	15-04-43	425 Sqn
R/144193	F/S	TSCHANTRE Albert Andrew [USA]	17-04-43	408 Sqn
R/122089	F/S	TUCKER Gordon Leslie	23-06-43	427 Sqn
J/16947	P/O	TUCKER Thomas Ernest Jeffrey	27-06-43	420 Sqn
J/16242	P/O	TUMA Charles	4-02-43	115 Sqn
R/109798	Sgt	TURNER Jnr Benjamin Warren [USA]	21-02-43	405 Sqn
R/134252	F/S	TURNER Clarence Alvin	6-11-43	1659 HCU
R/111837	F/S	TURNER Dalton Arnold	9-07-43	106 Sqn

ID	Rank	Name	Date	Unit	ID	Rank	Name	Date	Unit
R/106197	WO2	TURNER Frederick Oswald	22-06-43	77 Sqn	J/22200	F/O	WARD Arthur William	23-09-43	218 Sqn
J/7326	F/L	TURNER DFC Geoffrey	23-09-43	75 Sqn	R/105321	F/S	WARD Frederick	12-03-43	50 Sqn
18079A	WO2	TURNER Herbert Albert	16-12-43	432 Sqn	J/11359	F/O	WARD Harold Bramley	14-07-43	428 Sqn
J/8378	F/L	TURNER Wilbur Lewis	4-05-43	218 Sqn	R/115679	F/S	WARD John Langmeael	28-02-43	427 Sqn
R/91408	WO2	TUTTON Kenneth William	14-02-43	426 Sqn	R/86739	WO2	WARD Robert Harvey	8-03-43	156 Sqn
R/128073	WO2	TYCOLES Elmer Lawrance	24-12-43	428 Sqn	R/191206	Sgt	WARDROPE Caluin Hudson	3-10-43	431 Sqn
14063A	Sgt	TYLER George	29-04-43	207 Sqn	J/22431	F/O	WARE Everlyn Leonard	7-09-43	81 OTU
J/86662	P/O	TYMCHUK Metro Daniel	28-09-43	77 Sqn	J/19309	P/O	WAREHAM Harold Baxter	16-12-43	100 Sqn
R/147160	F/S	TYRONE Gordon Louis [USA]	23-06-43	427 Sqn	J/16662	P/O	WARK Albert Mercier [USA]	8-01-43	467 Sqn
R/135043	F/S	UDITSKY Andrew Peter [USA]	5-05-43	166 Sqn	R/102085	WO2	WARNE Thomas Herbert	18-02-43	61 Sqn
R/180464	Sgt	UREN Edwin Florence	17-11-43	405 Sqn	J/18605	P/O	WARNER Harry Dale	12-06-43	432 Sqn
J/14818	F/O	URETZKY Harry	24-05-43	408 Sqn	R/89237	Sgt	WARNICK Arthur Raymond	4-07-43	408 Sqn
R/90824	F/S	URQUHART Robert	18-08-43	61 Sqn	R/156101	F/S	WARR Edward Francis	2-10-43	424 Sqn
J/9163	F/O	URQUHART DFC Robert Alexander	17-05-43	617 Sqn	R/152436	F/S	WARREN George Richard Marr	28-08-43	10 Sqn
R/137759	F/S	USHER Gregory Alphonse	6-09-43	419 Sqn	J/11112	F/O	WARWICK Douglas William	16-09-43	617 Sqn
J/10684	F/O	VALLANCE Lloyd George	15-04-43	149 Sqn	J/7520	F/L	WATERBURY DFC Orville Ray	12-03-43	83 Sqn
R/143973	WO2	VALLEY William Allan	19-11-43	78 Sqn	J/5689	F/L	WATERMAN DFC Thomas John Davies		
J/16604	P/O	VANCE Elmer Robert	21-04-43	7 Sqn				3-09-43	207 Sqn
J/17326	F/O	VANDEKERCKHOVE DFC George Pierre Cornelius			R/107768	WO2	WATERS Norman James	26-05-43	428 Sqn
			31-08-43	427 Sqn	R/74057	WO2	WATSON Donald Alexander	9-01-43	419 Sqn
R/120070	WO2	VANDERBECK Roger Edwin [USA]	13-07-43	424 Sqn	R/97267	WO2	WATSON Floyd Bertram	23-10-43	434 Sqn
R/109924	WO2	VAN BUREN Russell Benson [USA]	6-03-43	76 Sqn	R/140083	WO2	WATSON Herbert George	12-06-43	9 Sqn
R/134679	F/S	VAN CAMP Ralph Hughes	15-06-43	619 Sqn	J/22809	F/O	WATSON John Kaye	26-05-43	426 Sqn
J/17409	P/O	VAN CLEAF Raymond Kenneth	19-05-43	310 FTU	R/54861	F/S	WATSON Peter	5-11-43	199 Sqn
R/182204	F/S	VAREY Bryan Henry	26-11-43	61 Sqn	R/164504	Sgt	WATSON Robert Martin	3-10-43	76 Sqn
J/10677	F/O	VEIRA DFC Basil Vernon Lancelot	29-04-43	12 Sqn	R/90946	P/O	WATT Bruce Emmott	17-04-43	49 Sqn
		[St. Kitts]			R/67910	WO2	WATT Douglas Hubert	2-02-43	102 Sqn
R/136704	F/S	VENNES Joseph Jules Jean Jacques	26-11-43	23 OTU	R/122699	F/S	WATTS Rae McGee	13-07-43	103 Sqn
R/176396	F/S	VERAAS Audfinn	30-07-43	102 Sqn	R/108809	F/S	WAUGH Donald Herbert	27-04-43	156 Sqn
R/104910	F/S	VEYS Joseph Vincent John Raymond	28-05-43	408 Sqn	R/92992	F/S	WAY Delmar Cyril	8-04-43	419 Sqn
R/95518	F/S	VIAU Joseph Alfred Jean Louis	12-03-43	97 Sqn	R/102353	WO2	WAY James Oscar	17-04-43	75 Sqn
J/15727	F/O	VICARY George Thomas	23-06-43	427 Sqn	R/67735	WO1	WEAKLEY Lawrence O'Neill [USA]	27-01-43	51 Sqn
R/92411	WO2	VIDAL Aymeric Essex	29-06-43	51 Sqn	R/77581	F/S	WEAVER Sylvan Ellwood	4-04-43	487 Sqn
J/14229	P/O	VIETTO Romeo Dominick Louis	28-08-43	620 Sqn	J/17776	P/O	WEBB Cyrus Wilfred	11-08-43	97 Sqn
J/11355	F/O	VINEY Frederick Harold	16-08-43	405 Sqn	R/93492	WO2	WEBB Francis Arthur	18-01-43	9 Sqn
R/161045	F/S	VITCH Michael Nancy	27-09-43	434 Sqn	J/14505	F/O	WEBB Frederick Vere	16-09-43	427 Sqn
R/93441	WO2	VOSE James Samuel	13-05-43	429 Sqn	R/106709	WO2	WEBBER Rodney [USA]	3-04-43	158 Sqn
R/123285	Sgt	VYSE Cecil Edward	27-02-43	16 OTU	R/116719	WO2	WEBER Harry Arthur	22-10-43	77 SQN
J/14393	F/O	WADDINGTON Robert Frederick	2-12-43	426 Sqn	R/147246	WO1	WEBSTER Lloyd Pierson	26-11-43	419 Sqn
R/161159	F/S	WADE William Harold	27-11-43	428 Sqn	J/17287	F/O	WEEDEN Gordon Herbert	10-12-43	617 Sqn
J/11120	F/O	WADMAN Lester McBride	8-03-43	15 Sqn	R/87956	WO2	WEEDY Raymond Cuthbert	13-05-43	419 Sqn
J/16323	P/O	WAGNER Robert Eugene [USA]	14-05-43	426 Sqn	R/166149	F/S	WEEKS Edward Howard	26-08-43	20 OTU
J/20354	F/O	WAHL William	14-05-43	166 Sqn	J/15549	F/L	WEEKS William George	14-07-43	428 Sqn
R/107124	F/S	WALEN George	5-03-43	426 Sqn	J/17467	P/O	WEESE Robert Allen	29-03-43	166 Sqn
R/146393	F/S	WALKEM George Rodney Alexander	20-10-43	166 Sqn	R/123705	F/S	WEIR Alexander Cuthbert	21-04-43	102 Sqn
J/25527	F/O	WALKER Donald Cameron	2-12-43	1664 HCU	R/102418	F/S	WEISS Ross	2-03-43	408 Sqn
R/64856	F/S	WALKER John Harvey William	29-06-43	619 Sqn	J/16600	P/O	WELCH Harry William	19-02-43	156 Sqn
R/63806	Sgt	WALKERDINE Frederick William	14-05-43	419 Sqn	J/19121	P/O	WELCH Henry Maxwell	3-11-43	76 Sqn
J/16151	P/O	WALKINSHAW William Alexander	8-04-43	420 Sqn	R/101969	F/S	WELCH Robert Thomas James	23-12-43	1679 HCFlt
R/91311	F/S	WALLACE Dalton James Kenneth	21-04-43	21 Sqn	J/17138	P/O	WELLER Allen Lewis	10-03-43	166 Sqn
J/22912	F/O	WALLACE George Albert	28-09-43	81 OTU	R/125266	F/S	WELLS Roy Arthur	22-10-43	427 Sqn
R/176389	F/S	WALLACE John	2-12-43	1664 HCU	R/122275	WO2	WELLWOOD Kenneth Douglas	4-09-43	106 Sqn
J/24145	F/O	WALLACE John William	27-09-43	19 OTU	R/79382	F/S	WELSH Ronald Hanson	21-01-43	420 Sqn
R/78305	F/S	WALLACE Robert Noble	27-09-43	434 Sqn	J/10523	F/O	WESLEY Ralph Eric	3-03-43	106 Sqn
R/107040	F/S	WALLACE Willard Warren	30-01-43	427 Sqn	J/14997	P/O	WESTON George	29-01-43	23 OTU
R/127739	Sgt	WALLACE William Bruce	10-03-43	23 OTU	C/22671	F/O	WESTON William James	22-10-43	427 Sqn
R/92287	WO2	WALLACE William Victor	3-03-43	207 Sqn	R/53979	WO2	WHALEN Edward Ambrose	17-04-43	426 Sqn
J/13830	F/O	WALLEY Keith Minshull	5-04-43	426 Sqn	J/10045	F/O	WHEELER George Howard	25-02-43	207 Sqn
R/143738	F/S	WALLNER John Isidore	18-08-43	49 Sqn	R/128074	F/S	WHEELER William Bernard	25-07-43	1659 HCU
R/138602	F/S	WALLS Bruce Woodrow	13-07-43	103 Sqn	R/194061	Sgt	WHELAN John Joseph	29-12-43	431 Sqn
R/225386	Sgt	WALSH Richard James Hartland	29-12-43	429 Sqn	J/8406	F/L	WHISTON Arthur James	22-10-43	408 Sqn
		[United Kingdom]			R/158113	Sgt	WHITE Ashley Bertram	22-10-43	1664 HCU
R/76467	F/S	WALSH William Duncan	22-06-43	408 Sqn	J/16896	P/O	WHITE Dominic Bernard	15-04-43	149 Sqn
R/146066	F/S	WALTER Gordon Stanley	18-08-43	419 Sqn	R/150887	F/S	WHITE Edward Kenneth 'Eddie'	25-07-43	405 Sqn
R/131192	WO2	WALTERS Edward Joseph [USA]	10-12-43	617 Sqn	R/91819	WO2	WHITE John Day	3-04-43	405 Sqn
R/137620	F/S	WALTON Jonathan Harvey	25-06-43	424 Sqn	R/114141	F/O	WHITE Joseph	5-05-43	428 Sqn
J/21545	F/O	WALTON Lloyd Henry	22-07-43	420 Sqn	J/17541	P/O	WHITE DFM Murray Edward	8-03-43	156 Sqn
J/9543	F/O	WANN John Allistair	4-04-43	10 Sqn	R/109372	F/S	WHITEHEAD Samuel Leenoy	13-05-43	207 Sqn

J/22492	F/O	WHITHAM Lester Lyle	3-11-43	428 Sqn
R/164046	F/S	WHITNEY William John	22-10-43	207 Sqn
R/120681	LAC	WHYTE David Allen	7-07-43	424 Sqn
R/97867	F/S	WICKSON Gordon Conrad	22-06-43	83 Sqn
J/18537	P/O	WILDE James	7-10-43	426 Sqn
R/16872	P/O	WILE Floyd Alvin	17-05-43	617 Sqn
J/6026	S/L	WILKIN DFC MiD MC [Czechoslovakia] Richard Pennington	20-09-43	138 Sqn
R/128622	Sgt	WILKINS Russell Frederick	19-01-43	20 OTU
R/182329	F/S	WILKINSON Arthur Morley	29-12-43	115 Sqn
R/139975	Sgt	WILKINSON Bernard Elliott	15-02-43	22 OTU
J/17145	F/O	WILLAN John Davis	10-09-43	14 OTU
R/133812	Sgt	WILLARD William Ross	2-07-43	23 OTU
R/130791	Sgt	WILLIAMS James Dennis	1-03-43	103 Sqn
J/18379	P/O	WILLIAMS John	24-08-43	426 Sqn
R/116322	WO2	WILLIAMS Percy Gordon	25-02-43	207 Sqn
R/137111	Sgt	WILLIAMS Robert Earl [USA]	5-03-43	426 Sqn
J/18908	P/O	WILLIAMS Tracy Arthur Thomas	24-08-43	78 Sqn
R/186329	Sgt	WILLIAMSON Jack	4-12-43	431 Sqn
R/95454	F/S	WILLIAMSON John Andrew	4-04-43	487 Sqn
R/138346	F/S	WILLINGTON David	22-11-43	102 Sqn
R/128764	WO2	WILLSON Arthur Bruce	22-10-43	419 Sqn
R/117584	F/S	WILSON Arthur William	10-01-43	10 Sqn
R/186094	Sgt	WILSON Donald Wesley	22-10-43	434 Sqn
J/21729	F/O	WILSON Frank Porter	26-08-43	424 Sqn
J/14175	F/O	WILSON George Stephen	28-05-43	405 Sqn
J/16117	P/O	WILSON Ian Marr	25-01-43	192 Sqn
R/106028	F/S	WILSON James Averd	29-01-43	23 OTU
R/186325	Sgt	WILSON James Ivan	20-10-43	166 Sqn
R/102722	F/S	WILSON John Wallace	27-01-43	50 Sqn
J/10887	F/O	WILSON Kevin Davies	27-06-43	420 Sqn
J/18828	P/O	WILSON Robert James	29-07-43	424 Sqn
R/120027	F/S	WILSON Robert Potter [USA]	18-02-43	419 Sqn
R/113265	F/S	WILSON Wesley William	5-02-43	75 Sqn
R/165360	Sgt	WILTON Leo	2-12-43	514 Sqn
J/20218	F/L	WILTON Walter Torrance	29-12-43	408 Sqn
R/99861	F/S	WINDERS Bruce Dean	27-09-43	218 Sqn
R/103246	F/S	WINDIBANK Frank Richard	14-05-43	429 Sqn
6141A		WINDSOR Kenneth Charles	15-09-43	138 Sqn
R/109935	F/S	WINEGARDEN Frank Ellsworth	30-05-43	419 Sqn
J/22453	F/O	WINNING Walter Fry	4-12-43	434 Sqn
J/14238	F/O	WINTER Francis William	19-11-43	427 Sqn
R/136425	F/S	WINTZER Victor Joseph August	1-09-43	419 Sqn
J/17710	P/O	WITT Ernest Maurice	14-07-43	405 Sqn
R/122133	F/S	WITTS David Douglas	7-09-43	434 Sqn
J/25589	F/O	WOLFE Richard Warren [USA]	3-09-43	22 OTU
R/193118	Sgt	WOLKOWSKI Anthony	4-12-43	426 Sqn
R/105398	F/S	WOOD Albert Leonard	25-07-43	102 Sqn
J/18772	P/O	WOOD Duncan Andrew	6-08-43	425 Sqn
J/19027	F/O	WOOD Ernest Morgan	27-09-43	10 Sqn
J/10688	F/O	WOOD George	31-01-43	428 Sqn
R/82786	WO2	WOOD John Kenneth	22-06-43	429 Sqn
J/22547	F/O	WOOD Julian Vernon Orison	13-05-43	61 Sqn
R/91595	F/S	WOOD Keith Robertson	26-06-43	51 Sqn
J/11864	F/S	WOOD Thomas Clinton Stuart	15-02-43	196 Sqn
R/140867	F/S	WOODCOCK Gerald Harvey	30-07-43	78 Sqn
R/115213	F/S	WOODHOUSE Alexander Trevor	1-03-43	419 Sqn
J/16388	P/O	WOOLFORD James [USA]	17-01-43	61 Sqn
R/77317	WO2	WOOLLEY Robert Stanley	25-02-43	467 Sqn
R/113195	F/S	WORDEN Arthur Cephas	26-05-43	51 Sqn
R/85180	P/O	WORLEY Robert Stephen Borden	25-02-43	424 Sqn
R/193651	Sgt	WORRAD Alfred William Leonard	22-10-43	434 Sqn
J/17985	P/O	WORTHINGTON Robert Franklin	25-06-43	156 Sqn
R/93302	F/S	WOYCE Stanley Verdun	8-01-43	467 Sqn
J/21828	F/S	WRIGHT Charles Austin	10-08-43	419 Sqn
R/131827	WO2	WRIGHT Charles Notley Dawson	20-10-43	619 Sqn
R/153606	WO2	WRIGHT Harold Redfern	4-12-43	78 Sqn
J/17943	P/O	WRIGHT James Russell	17-06-43	156 Sqn
J/22531	F/O	WRIGHT Ralph James	5-04-43	405 Sqn
R/99557	F/S	WYATT William Hubert	28-05-43	158 Sqn
J/21717	F/O	WYGLE Hugh Manson	26-05-43	180 Sqn
R/129010	WO2	WYLIE Douglas McKay	22-09-43	218 Sqn
J/21470	F/O	WYTON Arnold Edwin	9-10-43	90 Sqn
R/117043	WO2	YACKISON Frank	22-10-43	419 Sqn
R/77427	WO2	YELLIN Philip Frank	30-03-43	431 Sqn
R/91899	WO1	YONKER Zenon	14-07-43	78 Sqn
R/102677	WO2	YOUNG Archibald Kay	26-06-43	427 Sqn
J/19577	P/O	YOUNG Gerald Arthur	9-03-43	61 Sqn
R/90189	WO2	YOUNG Gordon Kenneth	16-04-43	466 Sqn
J/16906	P/O	YOUNG DFC Gordon William	26-05-43	90 Sqn
R/74870	F/S	YOUNG Jack Paton	30-03-43	51 Sqn
R/75118	WO2	YOUNG Kenneth Ian	26-02-43	218 Sqn
R/114096	WO2	YOUNG Robert Allen	4-11-43	408 Sqn
J/18352	P/O	YOUNG Stanford Grant	31-08-43	434 Sqn
R/115908	F/S	ZALESCHUK Demetre	17-04-43	408 Sqn
R/115850	F/S	ZANDER Donald	31-08-43	102 Sqn
R/139842	F/S	ZAPFE Merton Earl	24-05-43	51 Sqn
J/17716	P/O	ZAREIKIN Samuel [USA]	28-05-43	102 Sqn
R/90314	WO2	ZAVITZ Russell	13-01-43	106 Sqn
R/56703	Sgt	ZAYETS Stephen	14-07-43	428 Sqn
J/24802	F/O	ZDAN Russell Terres	23-09-43	428 Sqn
R/111112	F/S	ZEAVIN Max	9-03-43	426 Sqn
R/148402	F/S	ZEIDEL Rudolph	12-06-43	429 Sqn
R/107172	WO2	ZUNTI James Joseph	23-11-43	50 Sqn

Note

Concerning WO2 George Mathews, the Durnbach War Cemetery register, as prepared by the Commonwealth War Graves Commission, reports his surname in the manner noted here and in the above Canadian air force Roll. However, other documents against which this Roll is being cross-referred spell his surname as 'Matthews'. It will also be observed that the Tod brothers from St. Vital, Manitoba, twins Richard and Robert, died on the same day and with same squadron. Most unusually, the authorities appear to have sanctioned that both would be allowed to fly together, and in doing so they perished when their Stirling was shot down by a night fighter (see Volume 4, page 199 for further information). For Percy and Jean Kirkham of Vancouver, it is possible that they received twin telegrams on the same day informing them that their sons, Ernest and Thomas were missing from air operations. Ernest had trained as a navigator and was serving with 44 Squadron, while Thomas had become an air gunner and was stationed at Skipton-on-Swale where 432 Squadron was still equipped with Wellingtons. Both squadrons were participants in the fourth and final raid in what historians refer to as *The Battle of Hamburg* and from this operation in early August 1943 both failed to return, their names now being recorded on the panels of the Runnymede Memorial. Although not dying on the same day, the MacGregor boys, Rob from Burnaby and Gordon of Vancouver, both died on the same date in the month, namely the 22nd with Rob's death reported in November 1943 and Gordon's in June of the following year. Also from Vancouver were the O'Hara brothers, Basil and Gerald, and who like the MacGregors lost their lives on the same date, though not in the same month. Gerald was first to go down, missing on the 28th of May while attacking Essen with Basil following four months later during what was to be a costly visit to Hannover. No identifiable remains have ever been found; thus both are now commemorated on panel 185 of the Runnymede Memorial.

Two brothers who served and died on the same unit, 426 (Thunderbird) Squadron, were Norman (commemorated in this section) and Allister McLeod. Both were age 22 at the time of their passing, Allister being killed in action almost a year to the day after Norman. Meanwhile, the McPhee boys from Kirkland Lake, Ontario perished during their tours of duty with No.5 Group squadrons, John being reported missing in mid-January, a month following the death of Ewan whose name is perpetuated in the previous section.

The 23-year-old Bird twins from Lashburn, Saskatchewan, died during the year under review, both being buried in Germany with Colin lying in Becklingen War Cemetery and Sydney resting in the Reichswald Forest War Cemetery.

Staying with the vexed subject of brothers who died in Bomber Command service, George and John Askew were both killed within six months of each other, George while flying with 419 Squadron and John during the training phase of his service, while in the case of the Bartman boys, Gordon and Lloyd, their deaths were reported in the space of less than a week. Both are believed to have trained together as wireless operators before going their separate ways; Lloyd to pathfinders and Gordon to No.4 Group. In the alphabetical order of surnames, the Bartmans are followed by the Bartons and in just a little over six months following the loss of Hugh his younger brother, Thomas, disappeared without trace while flying with 425 Squadron. Death separates the Hill brothers, Howard and Raymond (both remembered in this section) by approximately 10 weeks, Howard having been decorated and screened from operations while Raymond, the first of the two boys to die, was still engaged on his tour with 419 Squadron. In the sad cases of the Marchants, James and John from Clair, Saskatchewan, well over a year passed following the loss of James before their parents received news that John had failed to return in late March 1945, victory in Europe being less than two months away.

And, concerning this section, these awful tragedies continued with telegrams being despatched to the Church family of Dilke, Saskatchewan, informing them that their sons James and Maurice were missing from air operations. As will be seen from their service numbers they had joined the air force on the same day but following basic training their paths went in differing directions, James to become an air gunner and Maurice a navigator. The Chudzik boys, Stanley and William lost their lives on missions that took them over France; Stanley's 218 Squadron Stirling falling victim in August 1943, to a night fighter when outbound to Turin and William being posted missing in June of the following year following a sortie to Versailles. Trained as pilots, Frank and Frederick Rogers from Colborne, Ontario, perished four months apart and at 17 years of age Frank was amongst the youngest from his country to lose his life on active service in the Second World War, while Frederick was only 21 when his aircraft was lost without trace four months after the death of Frank. Two more brothers who followed the same aircrew trade, in their case air gunners, were Frank and Charles Roberts from Homewood, Manitoba. Frank is remembered in this section, while Charles who died in August 1944, will be commemorated in the next part.

David Lowther and his younger sibling John died in this year; David in the March over Germany and John being lost without trace whilst on Path Finder duties over Hannover in late September. And it was operations over the Third Reich that brought the ultimate in dread news to Julius and Vida Prill of Minburn, Alberta for within a month of being informed that their son Maurice was missing came news that their younger boy, Berle, had been killed. Both brothers had died within a month either side of Christmas 1943, when the Battle of Berlin was at its height. By a terrible coincidence, it was operations over France that cut short the young lives of James and Albert Pollock, James dying in January 1943, while raiding the submarine pens at Lorient, while in the summer of 1944, Albert was lost during a strike on rail communications at Saintes.

In most cases here recorded, the loss of loved ones occurred over Germany or the Occupied Countries, but the Mitchell brothers, Henry and James, were destined to be killed in the United Kingdom though their graves are in cemeteries some distance apart with Henry resting in Botley Cemetery after losing his life at 16 Operational Training Unit and James, killed in a midair collision in August 1944, lying with so many of his fellow countrymen in Harrogate (Stonefall) Cemetery. And it was a fighter affiliation training exercise on the 24th April, 1944, that led to the death of David Pickering, his elder brother, Charles having been posted missing from operations to Mannheim in August 1943.

The pain that some parents felt after receiving news that their children were either missing or killed while serving overseas was, in countless cases, too much to bear and this, at times, led to a reluctance to include their parental details in the cemetery registers. Thus, in the case of Lorne and Walter Stewart from Oxbow, Saskatchewan, it is only their entries in *They Shall Grow Not Old* that enables me to establish that they were related, both boys dying within the space of a fortnight in July 1943. Also killed within 14 days of each other were James and Joseph Sweeney from Cobalt, Ontario. From their entries in Commonwealth War Graves Commission registers and Canadian documents they appear to be unrelated, though astute readers will realise that they must have stood next to each other for attestation as their service numbers are consecutive; furthermore, it is almost certain that they trained together as air gunners.

The year here documented witnessed the death in September of F/L Torger Taerum of 617 Squadron who in the May had been the navigator for Guy Gibson on the epic operation to breach the Mohne Dam; a little short of 18 months later his 18-year-old brother, Lorne, failed to return while flying as an air gunner with 550 Squadron.

I have remarked on several occasion the preference shown by the many Americans to remain with the air force of their choice, after their own country entered the war in December 1941. And thus it was with the Zareikin brothers, Samuel and Joseph of Los Angeles, California. Neither would return to their homeland; Samuel being remembered in this section, while his elder brother (Joseph was 36 when he was killed by a night fighter attack on his 433 Squadron Halifax) is commemorated in Part 8.

In respect of F/S Whitehead, some documents spell his second Christian name as Lee-noy, while in the case of F/S Czajkowski (almost certain to be of Polish extraction) his Christian name is interpreted either as Mieczstaw (as shown in this section) or Mieczystaw. Concerning F/S Macdonald's (R/103766) first Christian name, here shown as 'Aeneas,' other records give his name as 'James'.

To conclude the notes for 1943, although it is impossible to comment upon every death, while compiling this section my attention was brought to the comments reported in *They Shall Grow Not Old* in respect of F/S Hadden of 156 Squadron. It seems he was walking across the airfield at Warboys when he was struck from behind by the propeller of a taxying Spitfire.

ROYAL NEW ZEALAND AIR FORCE
personnel

NZ42284	Sgt	ABERCROMBIE Laurence Norman	3-03-43	15 OTU
NZ415052	F/O	ADAMSON David Maurice	28-09-43	75 Sqn
NZ414372	Sgt	AICKEN Kenneth Roy	18-01-43	467 Sqn
NZ39668	P/O	ALEXANDER Ian Hamilton	13-05-43	12 Sqn
NZ411717	F/S	AMOS Orison Edwin	3-03-43	15 Sqn
NZ415980	Sgt	ANDERSON Ronald Claude	17-04-43	467 Sqn
NZ41174	Sgt	ANDREWS Clifford Bruce	28-09-43	149 Sqn
NZ404092	F/S	ASHBY-PECKHAM Douglas Joseph		
			22-06-43	218 Sqn
NZ416075	Sgt	ATKINSON Donald Keith	17-04-43	100 Sqn
NZ416996	F/S	AUBREY MiD David George	15-08-43	192 Sqn
NZ414575	Sgt	AUSTIN John Albert	14-01-43	466 Sqn
NZ421312	F/S	BADCOCK David Herbert William	6-09-43	149 Sqn
NZ41142	F/S	BAKER James Guthrie	1-09-43	75 Sqn
39786	S/L	BALL DFC MiD William Arthur Coleman		
			9-03-43	156 Sqn
NZ414226	Sgt	BANKS-MARTIN Robert Alexander	9-01-43	51 Sqn
NZ413700	F/S	BARTON Arthur James Douglas	5-02-43	75 Sqn
NZ403932	F/O	BATHGATE DFC James Robertson Grant		
			11-12-43	161 Sqn
NZ416077	Sgt	BAULF Ivan Harry William	21-02-43	424 Sqn
NZ417263	F/S	BAXTER Alexander Kirk	3-08-43	76 Sqn
NZ39078	P/O	BAYNTON Thomas James	3-05-43	487 Sqn
NZ417003	F/S	BEAVIS Hugh Walter	25-07-43	218 Sqn
NZ413373	Sgt	BEER Norman Clive	18-02-43	207 Sqn
NZ42361	F/S	BELL George Goodall	24-08-43	78 Sqn
NZ415282	P/O	BENNETT Raymond Frederick	30-05-43	75 Sqn
NZ415055	F/S	BENNETT Thomas Samuel Eric	21-04-43	102 Sqn
NZ414580	P/O	BENTLEY Robert Henry Waldron	5-05-43	75 Sqn
NZ424964	F/S	BERNARD Arthur George	22-11-43	75 Sqn
NZ415737	F/S	BISHOP Leon Eric Gordon	11-06-43	207 Sqn
NZ415738	F/S	BISSET Stuart Richard	23-06-43	75 Sqn
NZ415056	F/O	BLACK Norman Scott	2-03-43	76 Sqn
NZ416445	F/O	BLANCHARD Cyril Francis	26-05-43	218 Sqn
NZ422175	F/S	BLANK John Frederick	23-06-43	75 Sqn
NZ412194	P/O	BLINCOE DFC Kenneth Edward	3-02-43	75 Sqn

Service No	Rank	Name	Date	Squadron
NZ40364	P/O	BLUCK Norman Bradford	24-06-43	75 Sqn
NZ414491	Sgt	BOSWELL John McLaren	5-05-43	75 Sqn
NZ413248	F/S	BOWMAN James Ferguson	26-07-43	90 Sqn
NZ413221	F/S	BOYD Ronald Gordon	24-08-43	622 Sqn
NZ415742	F/S	BRADFORD Edward Albert John	14-09-43	115 Sqn
NZ411737	F/S	BRIAN William Leslie Fred	28-04-43	75 Sqn
NZ417192	F/S	BRIDGER Cyril Jack	28-08-43	75 Sqn
NZ41866	P/O	BRIDGMAN Arthur Mervyn	3-03-43	75 Sqn
NZ416629	Sgt	BRIMS John	15-03-43	11 OTU
NZ416083	Sgt	BROOKES George Henry	1-02-43	11 OTU
NZ421669	F/O	BROSNAHAN Frederick Timothy	4-09-43	7 Sqn
NZ416084	Sgt	BROUGH MiD Richmond	6-04-43	1663 HCU
NZ39740	Sgt	BROWN Francis Henry	5-05-43	1663 HCU
NZ413376	F/S	BROWNING James Ronald	5-05-43	101 Sqn
NZ411059	Sgt	BROWNLEE Colin Crawford	26-01-43	466 Sqn
NZ411206	F/S	BUCKLEY Ross Cameron	28-04-43	75 Sqn
NZ412200	F/S	BURBIDGE Kenneth Alfred	23-06-43	75 Sqn
NZ411789	Sgt	BURT Harry Leister	29-03-43	214 Sqn
NZ414493	Sgt	BURTON Clarence Sydney	3-03-43	75 Sqn
NZ422256	F/S	BURTON Owen Albert	25-11-43	1678 HCU
NZ405472	F/S	CAINS Sidney William	14-02-43	158 Sqn
NZ416453	P/O	CALDER James Stanley	18-11-43	15 Sqn
NZ416087	P/O	CALDWELL William Donaldson	18-08-43	158 Sqn
NZ421676	P/O	CALVERT Frank Ian	3-10-43	623 Sqn
NZ403757	F/S	CAMPBELL Colin James	12-03-43	218 Sqn
NZ414242	F/S	CAREY John Henry Roy	30-05-43	75 Sqn
NZ421961	F/S	CLARK Andrew William	4-10-43	115 Sqn
NZ414252	Sgt	CLARK Richard	4-01-43	21 OTU
NZ417265	F/S	CLARK William Douglas	1-09-43	149 Sqn
NZ402539	Sgt	CLARKE John Ernest	30-05-43	10 Sqn
NZ412314	Sgt	CLEARWATER Desmond	3-02-43	75 Sqn
NZ414593	F/O	CLUBB Selwyn James	13-05-43	75 Sqn
NZ421318	Sgt	COATES Dudley Dobson	26-05-43	75 Sqn
NZ412315	F/S	COBB Cyril Thomas	21-04-43	75 Sqn
NZ413738	F/S	COLLINGWOOD Ernest William Joseph	25-06-43	78 Sqn
NZ414961	Sgt	COLLINS Owen Eastwood	30-03-43	166 Sqn
NZ412514	Sgt	COOK George Wood	3-02-43	75 Sqn
NZ414595	P/O	COOK William Arthur	14-04-43	138 Sqn
NZ416460	F/S	COOKSEY James Brett	24-06-43	75 Sqn
NZ424429	F/S	CORBY Sidney Charles	27-10-43	11 OTU
NZ417269	Sgt	CORIN Henry George	28-04-43	75 Sqn
NZ42289	F/S	CORLETT Geoffrey Scott [United Kingdom]	3-08-43	75 Sqn
NZ413818	F/S	COTTON Robert George	31-08-43	1651 HCU
NZ417027	F/S	COUPER James Arthur	3-08-43	75 Sqn
NZ412209	P/O	COUTTS Andrew Edward	3-05-43	487 Sqn
NZ411861	F/L	COWAN DFC James	12-03-43	1661 HCU
NZ42322	F/S	COWIE James Lindis	22-11-43	75 Sqn
NZ41218	F/S	COWIN Thomas Lewis	25-07-43	102 Sqn
NZ414256	F/O	CRAWFORD Bernard Verdun	19-02-43	15 Sqn
NZ42734	F/S	CRAWFORD-WATSON Lewis Stanley	4-11-43	75 Sqn
NZ417270	F/S	CRAWSHAW Robert Ashworth	16-08-43	115 Sqn
NZ412867	Sgt	CRIDGE Alfred Victor Gordon	3-03-43	214 Sqn
NZ413031	F/S	CROKER Leonard Francis	7-02-43	11 OTU
NZ402516	P/O	CROMIE Noel George	19-06-43	11 OTU
NZ414258	P/O	CROSS Sydney Nelson	21-04-43	90 Sqn
NZ411068	P/O	CROSSGROVE DFM Ralph	17-12-43	97 Sqn
NZ415519	F/S	CROZIER Alexander Walter	23-06-43	15 Sqn
NZ413386	P/O	CUMPSTY Frederic William Raukawa	31-07-43	75 Sqn
NZ404338	W/O	CUNNOLD-COOK Arthur Ronald	19-05-43	19 OTU
NZ421575	F/O	CUTHBERT Elias	19-02-43	156 Sqn
NZ42495	F/O	DANCE Alfred Thomas	4-11-43	75 Sqn
NZ42376	F/S	DARNEY Jack Neville	31-08-43	75 Sqn
NZ416465	F/S	DARTON Thomas William	26-05-43	75 Sqn
NZ413937	Sgt	DAVEY Charles Raglan	8-03-43	75 Sqn
NZ411865	Sgt	DAVIDSON Douglas Arthur Mark	13-05-43	466 Sqn
NZ412211	P/O	DEBENHAM Kevin Frederick	16-04-43	75 Sqn
NZ416468	F/L	DILLICAR John Collins	31-07-43	15 Sqn
NZ414600	F/O	DILLON Spencer Inglis	3-08-43	76 Sqn
NZ439022	F/S	DOBSON MiD Peter Gerald	8-09-43	75 Sqn
NZ39907	F/L	DOEL Alfred William	12-06-43	12 Sqn
NZ411746	Sgt	DONALDSON John Clifford	30-03-43	428 Sqn
NZ405262	F/S	DONNELLY James Patrick	28-08-43	620 Sqn
NZ403620	F/S	DOUGHERTY George Switzer	4-09-43	7 Sqn
NZ403617	W/O	DOUGLAS Adrian Vincent	6-09-43	149 Sqn
NZ40916	P/O	DREAVER DFC Bruce Colin	13-08-43	49 Sqn
NZ414603	F/S	DUCKMANTON Henry Cavell	23-03-43	196 Sqn
NZ414604	F/O	DUFFILL James Gilbert	17-01-43	101 Sqn
NZ413702	Sgt	DURHAM Donald	30-01-43	466 Sqn
NZ412872	F/S	DURWARD James Sydney	21-01-43	101 Sqn
NZ415298	F/S	DUTHIE George Robert James	14-07-43	158 Sqn
NZ426083	F/S	EAST Patton Mason	24-10-43	75 Sqn
NZ416009	F/S	EDGAR Frank Shepley	24-08-43	622 Sqn
NZ417275	F/O	EDGE Bernard Frederick	4-09-43	7 Sqn
NZ416196	P/O	ELLIOTT Reginald Frederick	21-04-43	90 Sqn
NZ414269	F/L	ELLIS George Ivan	20-04-43	149 Sqn
NZ413397	F/S	ELLIS Stanley James	4-10-43	115 Sqn
NZ413703	Sgt	ELLIS William Tidswell	22-06-43	428 Sqn
NZ415524	F/S	ENGLISH Lloyd Francis	18-08-43	619 Sqn
NZ416103	P/O	ERICKSEN Mervin Arthur	24-08-43	75 Sqn
NZ417042	F/S	ESTCOURT Kenneth Trevor	30-05-43	90 Sqn
NZ40380	F/S	FARRELLY Raymond James	22-10-43	158 Sqn
NZ422698	F/S	FAWCETT Arnold Goodrick	4-11-43	75 Sqn
NZ401823	F/O	FERGUSON Victor William	13-06-43	50 Sqn
NZ412874	F/S	FISK Joseph George Arkless	1-09-43	75 Sqn
NZ42294	F/O	FITZGERALD William Vincent	27-05-43	218 Sqn
NZ413833	P/O	FLACK Alfred William	30-05-43	149 Sqn
NZ411796	F/S	FLANSBURGH-WASHBOURNE Alvah Wilkie	11-02-43	102 Sqn
NZ421038	F/S	FLEMING John Stuart Selby	19-11-43	90 Sqn
NZ41577	P/O	FLORENCE DFM Ronald	18-11-43	617 Sqn
NZ421321	P/O	FRANCE Ralph Stanley	31-08-43	15 Sqn
NZ413305	Sgt	FREEMAN Patrick Paul Deane	5-02-43	75 Sqn
NZ415756	F/L	FRENCH DFC Richard Otway	4-09-43	7 Sqn
NZ403619	P/O	FUGGLE DFM Reginald	22-09-43	115 Sqn
NZ417279	F/O	GLENDAY Lindsay David	16-09-43	15 Sqn
NZ414278	Sgt	GOING Raymond Cyril	3-03-43	75 Sqn
NZ40919	W/O	GOLDSMITH Lionel Manuel	22-09-43	115 Sqn
NZ41696	F/S	GOODFELLOW William Desmond Laurence	3-05-43	487 Sqn
NZ417047	P/O	GOULDING John	31-08-43	77 Sqn
NZ411396	F/S	GOW John Graham	14-02-43	149 Sqn
NZ42295	P/O	GRAINGER James Kennedy	15-04-43	75 Sqn
NZ404998	F/L	GRAY DFC Edward McLeod	5-05-43	156 Sqn
NZ402589	F/S	GRAY Roderick Walter	31-08-43	15 Sqn
NZ415077	F/S	GRIFFITHS Rex Vernon	14-09-43	115 Sqn
NZ415819	P/O	GROVES Kelvin Havelock Green	17-04-43	75 Sqn
NZ422656	F/O	GUSTOFSON John Vernon	30-05-43	90 Sqn
NZ421149	F/O	GWYNNE Lloyd John	23-06-43	15 Sqn
NZ415411	Sgt	HALLIBURTON Keith	28-04-43	75 Sqn
NZ414977	F/S	HAMBLYN Douglas Charles William	6-09-43	77 Sqn
NZ422705	F/S	HAMBLYN Eric Charles	4-10-43	115 Sqn
NZ417053	F/S	HANNAH Charles William	19-11-43	622 Sqn
NZ415692	P/O	HARDER Robert	3-10-43	467 Sqn
NZ405265	P/O	HARDING-SMITH Dudley	13-02-43	75 Sqn
NZ414286	Sgt	HARRAP Horace Robert	14-03-43	138 Sqn
NZ415069	F/S	HARRIES Harold	18-08-43	11 OTU
NZ415529	F/S	HARRIS Albert Douglas	13-08-43	214 Sqn
NZ416635	F/S	HARRIS Leo Frederick	6-09-43	90 Sqn
NZ416483	Sgt	HARVEY Robert Frederick	13-05-43	75 Sqn
NZ403525	W/O	HATCHARD Thomas Harold	4-09-43	7 Sqn
NZ42326	F/S	HAUB Darcy Leslie Conrad	31-08-43	75 Sqn

Serial	Rank	Name	Date	Unit
NZ416111	F/O	HAWKINS John Vincent	23-06-43	15 Sqn
NZ41903	F/O	HEATH John Hawarth	29-08-43	29 OTU
NZ416113	P/O	HELM George Vincent	1-09-43	75 Sqn
NZ42327	F/S	HENDERSON Gordon	25-06-43	90 Sqn
NZ416114	F/S	HENDRY John Lawrence	31-08-43	106 Sqn
NZ414622	P/O	HENLEY MiD Douglas Charles	1-09-43	75 Sqn
NZ415760	F/S	HIGGINSON Brian Purdy	27-09-43	199 Sqn
NZ416116	F/S	HIGHAM Frank Douglas	28-08-43	75 Sqn
NZ41330	F/L	HILTON DFC Frederick	25-06-43	7 Sqn
NZ40230	S/L	HOBBS DFC Alan Murray	26-06-43	9 Sqn
NZ421717	Sgt	HOLMES Keith Vivian Arkle	23-09-43	11 OTU
NZ421933	F/S	HOLMS Alexander Hunter	6-09-43	149 Sqn
NZ40975	F/L	HOOD MiD Sefton Douglas Lisle	18-01-43	1656 HCU
NZ416425	F/S	HORROBIN Boothroyd Pascoe 'Royd'	24-06-43	10 OTU
NZ421934	F/S	HOTHERSALL Francis Edward	21-12-43	78 Sqn
NZ405276	F/O	HOTSON Bryan Frank Robert	1-03-43	214 Sqn
NZ392104	Sgt	HOWELL Alexander Clunie	28-04-43	75 Sqn
NZ413418	Sgt	HOWES Victor Charles	28-04-43	75 Sqn
NZ413335	F/O	HOWLETT Arthur Douglas	23-09-43	75 Sqn
NZ414630	F/O	HUMPHREYS MiD Noel Robert Shakespeare	6-09-43	623 Sqn
NZ42297	Sgt	HUNTER Patrick Torre	28-04-43	75 Sqn
NZ421279	F/S	HURDLE Walter	4-11-43	75 Sqn
NZ422676	F/S	IMRIE George Burns	4-11-43	75 Sqn
NZ421935	Sgt	INNES Owen Alfred	30-05-43	75 Sqn
NZ416498	F/O	JACKSON Bernard Lionel	31-07-43	15 Sqn
NZ42330	F/S	JACKSON Kensington Campbell	31-08-43	75 Sqn
NZ413422	F/O	JACOMBS Eric William Mitchell	18-01-43	9 Sqn
NZ426333	F/S	JAMES Charles	4-11-43	75 Sqn
NZ416119	F/O	JENKIN Ralph Francis	16-12-43	75 Sqn
NZ405780	W/O	JENKINS Ernest Roy	29-04-43	75 Sqn
NZ417063	Sgt	JOBLIN Frederick John Leigh	24-05-43	75 Sqn
NZ414634	F/O	JOHANSON Keith Campbell	5-02-43	50 Sqn
NZ42298	Sgt	JOHNS Lionel Fairfax Furner	30-04-43	90 Sqn
NZ414635	P/O	JOHNSON DFM Albert Andrew	18-11-43	97 Sqn
NZ415300	F/O	JOHNSON Ian Sinclair	22-01-43	429 Sqn
NZ414986	Sgt	JOHNSON Kenneth James	30-03-43	44 Sqn
NZ416198	F/O	JOHNSTON John	13-05-43	75 Sqn
NZ40921	F/O	JONES Owen Kenyon	12-06-43	12 Sqn
NZ403579	W/O	KAVANAGH Stanley Leo	30-05-43	75 Sqn
NZ412341	F/S	KEELEY James Hamilton	26-07-43	90 Sqn
NZ411766	P/O	KELL William Robert	19-11-43	78 Sqn
NZ41336	F/O	KIBBLE Kenneth Stanton	21-01-43	101 Sqn
NZ415261	F/S	KILBY William Adam	1-09-43	75 Sqn
NZ417069	F/O	KINROSS Colin John	16-12-43	75 Sqn
NZ414990	F/S	KIRKPATRICK Laurence John	23-09-43	75 Sqn
NZ414992	F/S	LAING Maurice Basil	8-11-43	623 Sqn
NZ413709	Sgt	LAMB Erwin Henry Reubin	5-05-43	75 Sqn
NZ422662	F/S	LAMB John Alexander	21-12-43	76 Sqn
NZ41136	Sgt	LANGDALE-HUNT Maurice Richard	30-03-43	1651 HCU
NZ403582	W/O	LAVIN Norman Henry	13-06-43	101 Sqn
NZ415434	Sgt	LAWSON John Henry	15-03-43	11 OTU
NZ42420	F/S	LEWIS Aubrey Lewin	11-08-43	15 Sqn
NZ414642	F/S	LINDLEY Tom	7-02-43	11 OTU
NZ413436	F/S	LINDUP John Broomfield	18-06-43	12 Sqn
NZ415538	F/S	LISTER Hilton Arthur	28-05-43	156 Sqn
NZ417671	P/O	LITTLE Eoin Graham	7-09-43	76 Sqn
NZ417284	F/O	LODGE Tom	4-11-43	75 Sqn
NZ413096	P/O	LORD Martin	27-03-43	7 Sqn
NZ392049	F/S	LOVE Reginald Vivian	8-11-43	623 Sqn
NZ416324	F/O	LOVELOCK James Benjamin	1-09-43	75 Sqn
NZ416508	F/O	LOWE Gordon Thomas	17-11-43	149 Sqn
NZ415541	F/S	LOWER Roy Wolseley	1-09-43	149 Sqn
NZ404718	F/S	LUNDON Francis Patrick	24-08-43	75 Sqn
NZ404079	F/S	MacLEOD Norman Alexander	30-04-43	75 Sqn
NZ41194	Sgt	MacPHAIL Allan Corson Anderson	30-05-43	75 Sqn
NZ421737	F/O	MACDONALD Allan Gordon	24-12-43	103 Sqn
NZ422418	F/O	MACKENZIE Stanley Henry	22-11-43	75 Sqn
NZ402557	F/S	MACKIE John Duncan Duthie	28-04-43	158 Sqn
NZ413713	F/L	MACKIE DFC Sydney Colin Rive	20-12-43	35 Sqn
NZ422665	F/S	MARGETTS John Edward Stanley	22-11-43	75 Sqn
NZ414656	P/O	MARKLAND Edward Roy	18-02-43	106 Sqn
NZ414657	Sgt	MARSH Giles Bacchus	27-01-43	106 Sqn
NZ413769	Sgt	MARSHALL Frank Wilfred	30-03-43	115 Sqn
NZ416136	P/O	MARSON John Adam	22-06-43	156 Sqn
NZ403790	F/L	MARTIN DFC Barry	2-02-43	7 Sqn
NZ413872	F/S	MARTIN Donald Ernest	23-06-43	75 Sqn
NZ415001	Sgt	MARTYN John Basil	30-03-43	428 Sqn
NZ421077	P/O	MASTERS William Stuart	4-11-43	75 Sqn
NZ392057	F/O	MATHESON Farquhar Duncan	26-07-43	77 Sqn
NZ415073	F/S	MATHIAS Geoffrey Alan	27-05-43	218 Sqn
NZ414318	F/S	MAUNSELL Leslie Cormac	26-05-43	100 Sqn
NZ417085	F/S	MAYO John Russell	7-08-43	75 Sqn
NZ422663	F/S	McCALLUM Lawrence Bruce	29-06-43	149 Sqn
NZ413573	P/O	McCASKILL Donald Gordon	15-04-43	75 Sqn
NZ40410	F/O	McCULLOUGH DFC John	3-02-43	75 Sqn
NZ415336	F/O	McDONALD Ninian Robson	30-07-43	158 Sqn
NZ417077	F/S	McEWIN Andrew James	23-06-43	75 Sqn
NZ411989	P/O	McGEEHAN DFM Peter John Dickson	16-03-43	139 Sqn
NZ414996	F/O	McGOWAN Stuart	3-05-43	487 Sqn
NZ415770	F/S	McGREGOR Keith Alexander	1-09-43	75 Sqn
NZ39570	F/S	McKAY Frank Gordon	15-06-43	12 Sqn
NZ414726	Sgt	McKENZIE Donald Maxwell Lang	26-01-43	466 Sqn
NZ41344	F/O	McKENZIE Francis Max	23-06-43	75 Sqn
NZ402544	F/O	McKINLEY DFC Terence	14-11-43	1652 HCU
NZ415416	Sgt	McNAB Donald Gordon	27-04-43	76 Sqn
NZ405299	F/L	McNAREY David Ian	20-04-43	149 Sqn
NZ416586	Sgt	McWILLIAM Allan	30-05-43	75 Sqn
NZ416520	F/O	MELDRUM Hector William	14-11-43	10 OTU
NZ415002	F/O	MENZIES Ian Robert	8-09-43	75 Sqn
NZ413451	F/L	MILLIKEN Robert Eric	17-04-43	100 Sqn
NZ416141	P/O	MOONEY James Owen Beggs [Eire]	17-04-43	103 Sqn
NZ413106	F/S	MOORE Acel Theodore Walter	26-05-43	100 Sqn
NZ416013	F/S	MORGAN Arthur Henry John	23-09-43	218 Sqn
NZ41993	Sgt	MORGAN John Gilbert	10-04-43	466 Sqn
NZ414887	F/S	MORRIS Leslie Francis [United Kingdom]	25-07-43	214 Sqn
NZ417092	F/S	MORRISON Kenneth Forbes	25-06-43	78 Sqn
NZ422306	F/O	MORSE Colin Rutherford	14-09-43	115 Sqn
NZ41350	P/O	MOSEN Robert John	3-08-43	115 Sqn
NZ404653	F/O	MOSS Douglas Hamilton	24-08-43	75 Sqn
NZ37213	W/O	MURPHY Maurice Joseph	26-11-43	83 Sqn
NZ413307	Sgt	MURPHY Terence Austin	3-02-43	75 Sqn
NZ413111	F/O	NAYLOR James Hubert	27-03-43	35 Sqn
NZ411771	F/O	NEAL Bruce	30-03-43	1483 Flt
NZ413339	F/O	NELSON Ronald Herbert	22-09-43	214 Sqn
NZ413462	F/O	NEWCOMB Robert Clayton	4-10-43	115 Sqn
NZ403021	F/S	NEWLAND Kenneth Mitchell	30-03-43	1483 Flt
NZ416526	P/O	NEWTON DFC Norman Thomas	16-12-43	115 Sqn
NZ404928	W/O	NIALL Alexander William	16-09-43	15 Sqn
NZ415006	F/O	NIMMO Robert Anderson	4-10-43	115 Sqn
NZ416145	F/S	NORMAN Raymond Fraser	30-05-43	75 Sqn
NZ413773	F/S	NORTHCOAT Douglas Haig	23-06-43	427 Sqn
NZ426337	F/S	NORTON Philip	22-10-43	14 OTU
NZ404932	Sgt	O'CARROLL Patrick Samuel	10-02-43	1657 HCU
NZ402063	F/O	O'DONNELL David Keith	15-01-43	214 Sqn
NZ414889	F/S	O'SHAUGHNESSY Eric	3-08-43	76 Sqn
NZ416540	W/O	PARGETER Aubrey Huia	21-10-43	103 Sqn
NZ412420	F/S	PARKER Barton Thomas Eric	28-08-43	199 Sqn
NZ421090	F/S	PARKIN Victor Trevor	31-08-43	75 Sqn
NZ41931	P/O	PARKINSON Gerald Andrew	12-03-43	218 Sqn
NZ416150	F/S	PARTON Austen Bristow	29-06-43	149 Sqn
NZ416151	Sgt	PARTRIDGE Frederick Andrew	11-04-43	100 Sqn

NZ417290	F/O	PATTISON John	3-08-43	76 Sqn	NZ415204	F/S	SMITH Arthur Holdsworth	30-05-43	431 Sqn
NZ421987	F/S	PAYNE Frederick	31-08-43	1651 HCU	NZ415563	Sgt	SMITH Cyril Richard	3-05-43	487 Sqn
NZ414671	P/O	PEARCE DFM Colin Rees	22-06-43	428 Sqn	NZ421614	F/S	SMITH Ian Hector Ross	1-09-43	75 Sqn
NZ421940	F/O	PEATTIE Robert James	29-06-43	149 Sqn	NZ415378	F/S	SMITH Ronald Alexander	15-04-43	75 Sqn
NZ414672	F/L	PERRERS Frederick Leonard	23-11-43	630 Sqn	NZ416177	F/L	SMITH William Brian	27-09-43	78 Sqn
NZ416155	F/O	PERROTT William Rosser	25-06-43	75 Sqn	NZ417243	F/S	SOWERBY Geoffrey Phillips	23-09-43	75 Sqn
NZ416534	F/O	PERRY Edward Alexander	31-03-43	13 OTU	NZ413499	P/O	SPAIN Vernon Enright	28-02-43	90 Sqn
NZ413469	F/O	PERYMAN Stanley Bailey	3-05-43	487 Sqn	NZ415426	F/O	SPIERS Howard Ivan	18-08-43	100 Sqn
NZ403611	F/S	PETERSEN Leo	25-06-43	90 Sqn	NZ417244	F/S	SQUIRE Lewis Alfred	4-09-43	7 Sqn
NZ414337	F/L	PETRIE DFC John Russell	16-12-43	7 Sqn	NZ42194	F/O	STEVENSON Ian Sydney Alexander	16-09-43	15 Sqn
NZ415200	Sgt	PHELOUNG Charles Edward	4-04-43	51 Sqn	NZ421336	F/S	STEWART Donald MacKay	1-09-43	75 Sqn
NZ411899	P/O	PHELPS HOPKINS Ronald Vivian	25-06-43	218 Sqn	NZ415383	F/S	STONE Robert James	31-07-43	75 Sqn
NZ414673	F/S	PICKETT John	13-07-43	57 Sqn	NZ413281	Sgt	STONE Ronald Charles	17-04-43	75 Sqn
NZ415714	F/O	POLGLASE David	11-04-43	105 Sqn	NZ415384	P/O	STOWELL James Hampton	5-05-43	15 Sqn
NZ416537	P/O	POOLE Francis McDonald	23-09-43	78 Sqn	NZ413718	P/O	STRANG Evan Rankin	23-06-43	427 Sqn
NZ416016	F/S	PORRITT Lawrence George	26-06-43	100 Sqn	NZ411614	Sgt	STRONG Donald Percy	30-05-43	218 Sqn
NZ42106	F/S	POTTER Edward Vivian	1-09-43	12 Sqn	NZ413905	F/S	STRONG Geoffrey Walter	24-06-43	75 Sqn
NZ415782	P/O	PRINS Harvey George	23-09-43	100 Sqn	NZ414697	F/L	SULLIVAN DFC Michael Acton	20-12-43	156 Sqn
NZ416163	P/O	PULLAN Arthur Alfred Henri	13-06-43	76 Sqn	NZ422670	F/S	SUTHERLAND James	18-10-43	103 Sqn
NZ422207	F/S	PURVES James John	25-10-43	75 Sqn	NZ414357	F/O	SUTHERLAND Owen Kenneth	1-09-43	77 Sqn
NZ412736	F/O	PYE Halford Douglas	28-05-43	115 Sqn	NZ413907	P/O	TABOR Lionel William	15-02-43	90 Sqn
NZ416017	F/S	RAMSAY Ian Grant	31-07-43	15 Sqn	NZ42192	F/S	TALBOT Harold George [Eire]	22-09-43	158 Sqn
NZ416539	F/S	RANDLE James Robert	24-10-43	75 Sqn	NZ42113	F/S	TALBOT James Leonard Keith	3-08-43	115 Sqn
NZ416164	F/L	RAWLINGS DFC Raymond Charles	9-10-43	20 OTU	NZ425446	Sgt	TANNER Thomas Bayly	27-10-43	11 OTU
NZ414678	Sgt	REDDING Randolph Ernest	5-02-43	75 Sqn	NZ413283	Sgt	TAYLOR Gordon Arthur	11-04-43	9 Sqn
NZ414679	F/S	REDWOOD Charles Henry Gerard	22-06-43	7 Sqn	NZ413149	F/O	TAYLOR Joseph Greig	9-10-43	405 Sqn
NZ42339	F/S	REEVES Sydney Cecil Oliver	3-08-43	75 Sqn	NZ404426	F/L	TAYLOR Royston Charles Clifford	15-08-43	7 Sqn
NZ416578	F/S	REID Alexander Millson	31-07-43	90 Sqn	NZ422671	P/O	THIRD James	24-08-43	75 Sqn
NZ42457	F/S	RICHARDS Harold Leslie Raymond	18-11-43	622 Sqn	NZ422001	F/S	THOMAS Charles Frank	19-11-43	622 Sqn
NZ404946	F/S	RICHARDS James Leonard	23-06-43	75 Sqn	NZ40586	F/S	THOMAS Raymond	6-07-43	75 Sqn
NZ41190	F/O	RIDDLE Charles Hudson	30-05-43	75 Sqn	NZ413152	P/O	THOMPSON Desmond Lewis	29-04-43	75 Sqn
NZ424999	Sgt	RIDDLER Stanley Winston	3-10-43	75 Sqn	NZ401791	F/O	THOMPSON DFM Onslow Waldo	1-05-43	105 Sqn
NZ412354	F/S	RIDINGS Desmond George	5-05-43	156 Sqn	NZ411107	Sgt	THOMPSON Wilfred Strachan	3-02-43	102 Sqn
NZ422668	Sgt	RIORDAN John Milton Patrick	26-05-43	75 Sqn	NZ42317	F/S	THOMSON Gordon Douglas	25-06-43	75 Sqn
NZ417107	F/S	ROBERTS Eric John	31-08-43	75 Sqn	NZ421145	F/S	THOMSON Jack	3-08-43	75 Sqn
NZ41549	F/S	ROBERTS Peter George	1-03-43	103 Sqn	NZ40109	F/S	THORNLEY Sydney Russell	30-05-43	75 Sqn
NZ405321	F/S	ROBINSON Allan Launcelot	2-04-43	16 OTU	NZ414529	F/S	THORSTENSEN Frederick William	24-08-43	75 Sqn
NZ415786	P/O	ROBINSON DFC Colin Harben	22-06-43	158 Sqn	NZ416183	F/S	TICKLE Dalton Joseph	23-06-43	15 Sqn
NZ412903	P/O	ROBSON Edgar Lester	22-06-43	428 Sqn	NZ415640	Sgt	TIETJENS Stephen Muir	24-05-43	75 Sqn
NZ414893	P/O	ROBSON DFC Thomas Andrew	20-12-43	35 Sqn	NZ417128	F/S	TINDLE George William	23-11-43	7 Sqn
NZ415788	F/S	ROLLETT Noel Charles	24-08-43	622 Sqn	NZ411954	P/O	TOLLEY Alan Gray	21-04-43	75 Sqn
NZ416542	F/S	ROSE Alistair Frederick	13-08-43	214 Sqn	NZ41615	F/S	TOMOANA Tamaturanga Te Rakai-a-Hawea	29-06-43	149 Sqn
NZ411451	Sgt	ROSS Desmond Ray	28-04-43	75 Sqn	NZ416648	F/O	TONG Harold	30-05-43	75 Sqn
NZ413778	Sgt	ROWSE Deryck Charles	7-02-43	30 OTU	NZ415206	W/O	TOON Kenneth Alan	14-07-43	78 Sqn
NZ411046	F/S	RUFF Ian Richard Victor	13-06-43	115 Sqn	NZ405001	W/O	TUCKER Kenneth Guilfoyle	30-12-43	26 OTU
NZ414346	P/O	RUNDLE John Reginald	18-02-43	214 Sqn	NZ421342	Sgt	TURNBULL George Watson	24-05-43	75 Sqn
NZ404046	F/S	SALT Ian Charles	21-04-43	75 Sqn	NZ42490	F/O	TURNBULL John George [United Kingdom]	16-08-43	75 Sqn
NZ402029	F/O	SALTER Edward William Huia	11-08-43	192 Sqn	NZ421115	F/S	TURNER John Cecil	22-11-43	75 Sqn
NZ411032	P/O	SAMPSON Thomas	14-05-43	466 Sqn	NZ422215	F/S	TURNER Vincent Nicholas Walter	4-12-43	97 Sqn
NZ402563	F/S	SAMSON George King	23-06-43	75 Sqn	NZ416579	F/S	TURNER William	3-08-43	75 Sqn
NZ403287	F/O	SANDS Hugh Powell	23-09-43	75 Sqn	NZ41378	F/S	TWIGG Edward James	27-02-43	166 Sqn
NZ404949	F/S	SAUNDERCOCK Charles Little	26-05-43	90 Sqn	NZ404002	F/O	TYE Ralph Holland	11-01-43	27 OTU
NZ415372	F/S	SAYWELL Edward Wright	14-04-43	35 Sqn	NZ427237	Sgt	UNDERWOOD John Michael	29-09-43	11 OTU
NZ42461	P/O	SCHMIDT Stanley Thomas	6-09-43	76 Sqn	NZ404430	F/S	UPTON Frank Wakefield	21-04-43	75 Sqn
NZ421992	F/S	SCHOLLUM Bernard Joseph	27-09-43	149 Sqn	NZ39590	F/S	USSHER Owen Neville	18-11-43	90 Sqn
NZ417238	F/O	SCHULTZ Kenneth Owen	8-11-43	623 Sqn	NZ415566	F/S	VERCOE Terrance James	31-07-43	75 Sqn
NZ414685	P/O	SCOTT Andrew James Newell	3-02-43	75 Sqn	NZ416185	F/S	VERNAZONI Richard Barry	30-05-43	75 Sqn
NZ416173	F/S	SCOTT Desmond Francis	9-07-43	166 Sqn	NZ404583	Sgt	VEYSEY William John	31-01-43	9 Sqn
NZ42310	F/S	SHARP Victor James	28-09-43	90 Sqn	NZ413286	F/S	VINICOMBE Stanley Seymour	9-03-43	35 Sqn
NZ415815	P/O	SHAW Keith Fred	3-10-43	623 Sqn	NZ42313	Sgt	WADE Horton Neilson	30-05-43	218 Sqn
NZ416210	F/S	SHEDDAN Alexander Bernard	20-12-43	166 Sqn	NZ421300	P/O	WAEREA Tame Hawaikirangi	28-09-43	75 Sqn
NZ415375	Sgt	SHOGREN Malcolm Edward John	28-04-43	75 Sqn	NZ417132	F/S	WAKELY Noel Nathaniel	17-09-43	196 Sqn
NZ421995	F/S	SIMPSON Stuart Edward	19-11-43	90 Sqn	NZ416028	F/S	WALLIS Albert Baulcombe	31-07-43	90 Sqn
NZ425022	F/S	SINCLAIR Rodney Herbert	4-12-43	576 Sqn	NZ401294	W/O	WALSH John Arthur Ernest	9-04-43	75 Sqn
NZ404574	Sgt	SISSON Ernest Arthur	8-01-43	50 Sqn	NZ414705	Sgt	WARLOW David Stanley	9-01-43	57 Sqn
NZ41498	F/S	SKINNER Phillip Holmes	12-03-43	149 Sqn	NZ414363	Sgt	WARNER Timothy William James	3-05-43	487 Sqn
NZ404116	F/O	SMALLFIELD Ernest Ian	31-08-43	102 Sqn					
NZ39267	F/S	SMIT Russell Theodore	30-06-43	466 Sqn					

NZ411960	P/O	WATERHOUSE Leslie James	5-01-43	101 Sqn
NZ421946	F/O	WATSON Clifford Arnold	1-09-43	75 Sqn
NZ415569	F/S	WATSON Percy Fisher	26-07-43	158 Sqn
NZ417299	F/S	WATTERS Terrence	31-08-43	75 Sqn
NZ405459	F/S	WELLINGTON Daniel	27-03-43	7 Sqn
NZ404108	Sgt	WHITCOMBE Rupert Sutton	2-03-43	50 Sqn
NZ402918	W/O	WHITE Arthur Miles	10-04-43	9 Sqn
NZ416188	F/S	WHITELAW Clifford James	25-06-43	75 Sqn
NZ421123	P/O	WHITMORE Richard Charles	28-09-43	75 Sqn
NZ416566	F/S	WHITTA Neville Bruce	16-08-43	75 Sqn
NZ416030	F/S	WHITTINGTON Eric Richmond	22-11-43	75 Sqn
NZ413294	F/S	WHYMAN Owen Kenneth	12-06-43	12 Sqn
NZ42314	F/S	WILCOCKSON Walter Frederick	23-06-43	75 Sqn
NZ416581	Sgt	WILKINS Jack Kenneth	24-05-43	214 Sqn
NZ417138	P/O	WILKINSON Ernest Stanley	6-09-43	75 Sqn
NZ413923	Sgt	WILSON James Archibald	26-03-43	78 Sqn
NZ417300	F/S	WILSON John Gordon	25-07-43	158 Sqn
NZ417139	F/O	WILSON Norman Clarence Bruce	4-11-43	75 Sqn
NZ413165	Sgt	WILTSHIRE Peter Thomas Windsor	21-01-43	101 Sqn
NZ414713	P/O	WITHELL Eric Bayly	18-01-43	12 Sqn
NZ414535	F/S	WOOD Alan William	31-05-43	180 Sqn
NZ411964	Sgt	WOODS Robert Albert Francis	30-05-43	44 Sqn
NZ414536	F/S	WORKMAN Leslie Edmund	13-06-43	49 Sqn
NZ414717	F/L	WRIGHT DFC James Henry	20-12-43	35 Sqn
NZ415049	F/S	WRIGHT DFM Raymond Johnston	26-10-43	1481 Flt

Note

The name of P/O Dreaver is included in this section (and in the statistics for 1943), though it is possible that he was no longer serving with 49 Squadron as he met his death in an air accident involving a Wellington belonging to the Central Gunnery School.

When 75 Squadron lost Stirling III EF340 AA-Q on a minelaying sortie in early May 1943, for the parents of the navigator, Robert Bentley, the telegram informing them that he was missing from air operations was the second that they had received in less than five months, for on the 12th January Robert's younger brother, Sgt Murray Waldron Bentley, had vanished without trace after taking off from Deversor in Egypt with the intention of delivering Spitfire VB ER544 to Agedabia, Libya. Thus, both of their sons are commemorated on memorials to the missing with no known grave, namely Alamein and Runnymede. And by an awful quirk of fate, family and friends of the Stirling's air bomber, Erwin Lamb, would twelve months on be informed that his brother, Ronald, serving on pathfinder duties with 582 Squadron had failed to return from operations over France.

In June 1942, with The Battle of the Atlantic raging in intensity, enemy U-boats were the prime cause in the sinking of 650,000 tons of Allied shipping, one of the U-boats many victims being the S. S. *Waiwera* which was torpedoed while crossing the Atlantic east to west on the 29th June and carrying a large contingent of Royal New Zealand Air Force personnel. Such are the fickle fortunes of fate, that more than a handful of the survivors from the sinking were destined to lose their lives as the war progressed including Norman Bluck, Noel Rollett (Rollett had received a head wound when the *Waiwera* was struck), Noel Humphreys and Keith Shaw, all commemorated in this section.

And 1943 was also a year in which many operationally experienced New Zealanders lost their lives, some after being screened and posted to training formations, while others perished after returning for a second spell of bombing duty. For two sparsely-populated islands, New Zealand was continuing to bear a heavy burden of pain.

POLISH AIR FORCE
personnel

P.0031	F/L	ALBERTI Stefan Karol	21-10-43	18 OTU
P.781725	Sgt	BARTOSIAK Eugeniusz	25-06-43	300 Sqn
P.782464	Sgt	BARZDO Wladyslaw	17-09-43	138 Sqn
P.0538	F/O	BASTER Bronislaw	25-05-43	305 Sqn
P.792895	Sgt	BEDNARSKI Piotr	12-05-43	138 Sqn
P.793097	Sgt	BEEGER Pawel	3-08-43	305 Sqn
P.784001	Sgt	BELINA-PRAZMOWSKI Janusz Jozef	23-04-43	300 Sqn
P.781055	Cpl	BERDECHA Jan	25-05-43	305 Sqn
P.782554	F/S	BIALOBROWKA Mikolaj	22-06-43	300 Sqn
P.703895	Sgt	BIALOBRZESKI Kazimierz	25-05-43	305 Sqn
P.784148	Sgt	BIELAWSKI Jozef	22-05-43	18 OTU
P.794235	Sgt	BIELSKI Antoni	25-06-43	300 Sqn
P.781203	Sgt	BIJOWSKI Jan	25-06-43	300 Sqn
P.2014	P/O	BLAJDA Jozef	22-06-43	300 Sqn
P.704195	Sgt	BLAZEJEWSKI Henryk Lech	15-08-43	300 Sqn
P.794721	Sgt	BLUJ Feliks Antoni	19-12-43	300 Sqn
P.1976	F/O	BOGUSLAWSKI Stefan	29-06-43	300 Sqn
P.792591	F/S	BONK Leon Stanislaw	13-07-43	138 Sqn
P.703153	Sgt	BORKOWSKI Stanislaw	22-05-43	18 OTU
P.780940	Sgt	BRONICKI Mieczyslaw	22-06-43	300 Sqn
P.780664	Sgt	BUDA Franciszek Jan	31-08-43	300 Sqn
P.793667	Sgt	BURDA Jerzy	15-01-43	300 Sqn
P.781969	F/S	CIESLIK Maksymilian	29-06-43	300 Sqn
P.781076	Sgt	CIUCHCINSKI Jan Stefan	22-05-43	300 Sqn
P.794403	Sgt	CZARKOWSKI Henryk Kazimierz	21-06-43	300 Sqn
P.781264	Sgt	DEBOWSKI Ireneusz	23-04-43	300 Sqn
P.781693	Sgt	DOROSZ Stanislaw	13-01-43	305 Sqn
P.783307	Sgt	DRAPALA Roman	12-05-43	18 OTU
P.794313	Sgt	DUTKIEWICZ Karol Zygmunt	13-01-43	305 Sqn
P.780559	W/O	FELUS Kazimierz	6-08-43	1485 Flt
P.704431	Sgt	FOJER Henryk	15-09-43	138 Sqn
P.783556	F/S	FORMANIEWICZ Edmund	27-09-43	18 OTU
P.783091	Sgt	FRANKIEWICZ Mieczyslaw Jozef	12-05-43	18 OTU
P.781695	Sgt	GADOMSKI Stefan	18-04-43	138 Sqn
P.784113	F/S	GALAS Mieczyslaw	13-05-43	300 Sqn
P.783260	Sgt	GALICZYN Stanislaw	26-07-43	300 Sqn
P.782805	Sgt	GARCZYNSKI Edmund	26-07-43	300 Sqn
P.793471	F/S	GASTOL Edward	8-10-43	300 Sqn
P.703431	Sgt	GAWLIK Jan	13-11-43	18 OTU
P.0116	F/L	GEBIK DFC Karol Piotr	15-09-43	138 Sqn
P.793221	Sgt	GERMASINSKI Karol	12-05-43	138 Sqn
P.1552	F/O	GINTER Tadeusz	18-04-43	138 Sqn
P.794632	Sgt	GLASS Mieczyslaw	22-06-43	300 Sqn
P.794329	Sgt	GLOWCZYNSKI Tadeusz	30-01-43	305 Sqn
P.783087	F/S	GOLASZEWKI Jerzy Marian	9-08-43	305 Sqn
P.792204	Sgt	GOSIEWSKI Stanislaw	15-01-43	300 Sqn
P.1599	F/O	GOZDZ Czeslaw	27-09-43	18 OTU
P.794422	Sgt	GRABARCZYK Stanislaw	29-03-43	18 OTU
P.793837	F/S	GRZESKOWIAK Marian Stefan	3-08-43	305 Sqn
P.781188	Sgt	GZELL Henryk Leon	4-02-43	305 Sqn
P.781370	Sgt	IMIOLEK Henryk	15-01-43	300 Sqn
P.792964	F/S	JABLONSKI Wiktor	15-09-43	138 Sqn
P.703492	Sgt	JACENIK Roman	22-06-43	300 Sqn
P.784500	Sgt	JACEWICZ Sergiusz	25-06-43	300 Sqn
P.76696	F/L	JAKUSZ-GOSTOMSKI Franciszek Jozef	15-09-43	138 Sqn
P.794546	Sgt	JAMA Stefan	22-06-43	300 Sqn
P.0053	S/L	JANKOWSKI Jan	5-03-43	300 Sqn
P.2017	F/O	JANKOWSKI Witold	24-05-43	300 Sqn
P.784058	Sgt	JAWOSZEK Stanislaw	25-06-43	300 Sqn
P.793701	Sgt	JEDNAKI Jozef	15-01-43	300 Sqn
P.782677	F/S	JONSKI Edward	13-07-43	138 Sqn
P.0765	F/O	KALINA Stefan	4-02-43	300 Sqn
P.1905	F/O	KALKUS Waclaw Stanislaw	24-06-43	138 Sqn
P.783767	Sgt	KAMINSKI Stanislaw	20-02-43	300 Sqn
P.783202	Sgt	KASPRZAK Eugeniusz Piotr	16-09-43	138 Sqn
P.780650	F/S	KIDZIAK Kazimierz	24-06-43	138 Sqn
P.782266	F/S	KLEINSCHMIDT Marian	29-06-43	300 Sqn
P.0193	F/L	KLOSINSKI Antoni	22-05-43	18 OTU
P.793149	F/S	KNEBLOCH Tadeusz	29-06-43	300 Sqn
P.780782	Sgt	KNIAZYCKI Tadeusz Wladyslaw Zbigniew	8-04-43	300 Sqn

P.1830	P/O	KOCZAPSKI Wladyslaw Karol	25-05-43	305 Sqn
P.792991	LAC	KOPKA Jozef	11-07-43	138 Sqn
P.782530	F/S	KORDYS Wladyslaw	8-10-43	300 Sqn
P.0216	F/L	KORECKI Edward Roman	11-11-43	300 Sqn
P.782472	Sgt	KORZENIOWSKI Antoni Eugeniusz	2-01-43	18 OTU
P.704008	Sgt	KOT Bernard	21-06-43	300 Sqn
P.794211	Sgt	KOT Boleslaw	8-03-43	300 Sqn
P.780470	Sgt	KOT Roman	21-10-43	18 OTU
P.780430	F/S	KOWALSKI Alfons	4-02-43	305 Sqn
P.794283	Sgt	KOZLOWSKI Bernard	4-02-43	305 Sqn
P.1966	P/O	KOZLOWSKI Tolimir	30-01-43	305 Sqn
P.780226	F/S	KRAMARCZYK Kazimierz Jerzy	14-03-43	300 Sqn
P.780580	Sgt	KRAMARZ Julian	20-02-43	300 Sqn
P.1722	F/O	KRAWCZYK Franciszek Kazimierz	13-01-43	305 Sqn
P.794182	Sgt	KRELOWSKI Czeslaw Krzysztof	23-04-43	300 Sqn
P.1834	F/O	KRETKOWSKI Zbigniew Leon Andrzej	21-06-43	300 Sqn
P.781774	Sgt	KUCZKOWSKI Zdzislaw	15-09-43	138 Sqn
P.703387	Sgt	KULIKOWSKI Eugeniusz	24-05-43	300 Sqn
P.794647	Sgt	KUNKA Feliks	22-05-43	18 OTU
P.793785	Sgt	KURZAK Jerzy	12-05-43	138 Sqn
P.783169	Sgt	KUZMINSKI Tadeusz	14-03-43	300 Sqn
P.794039	F/S	LASKOWSKI Jan	13-01-43	305 Sqn
P.780753	F/S	LASKOWSKI DFM Franciszek	13-01-43	305 Sqn
P.0073	F/L	LAWRENCZUK Bogdan Seweryn	18-04-43	138 Sqn
P.780109	Sgt	LAZOWSKI Feliks	4-02-43	300 Sqn
P.794322	Sgt	LERCEL Henryk Wladyslaw	13-05-43	300 Sqn
P.0479	F/O	LESISZ Edward	4-02-43	305 Sqn
P.792916	Sgt	LESNIEWICZ Jan	12-04-43	138 Sqn
P.780882	LAC	LEWCZUK Michal	5-03-43	18 OTU
P.0967	P/O	LEWICKI Henryk	24-05-43	300 Sqn
P.0395	F/L	LEWICKI Napoleon Stanislaw	13-07-43	138 Sqn
P.784315	Sgt	LEZUCH Jan Tadeusz Feliks	22-06-43	300 Sqn
P.783846	Sgt	MAJEWSKI Stefan Jerzy	27-09-43	18 OTU
P.780898	Sgt	MAKARSKI Leopold	22-06-43	305 Sqn
P.1848	P/O	MALICKI Tadeusz Juliusz	4-02-43	300 Sqn
P.793407	Sgt	MALINOWSKI Edmund Jerzy	30-01-43	305 Sqn
P.782886	Sgt	MARCINISZYN Pawel Boleslaw	4-02-43	300 Sqn
P.794308	Sgt	MARCZUK Wladyslaw	8-04-43	300 Sqn
P.794865	Sgt	MARTYNIEC Jozef Kazimierz	15-08-43	300 Sqn
P.783855	Sgt	MATELOWSKI Jozef Karol	4-02-43	300 Sqn
P.794544	Sgt	MAZGAJ Piotr	29-06-43	300 Sqn
P.793235	F/S	MICHALSKI Julian	17-09-43	138 Sqn
P.794086	Sgt	MIERZWA Jakub	4-02-43	300 Sqn
P.794664	F/S	MIKSZA Edward	25-05-43	305 Sqn
P.780600	F/S	MIRONOW Jan Kazimierz	18-04-43	138 Sqn
P.793614	F/S	MISIAK Ludwik Henryk	15-09-43	138 Sqn
P.792226	Sgt	MOLENDA Jozef	15-01-43	305 Sqn
P.1096	F/L	MORAWSKI Julian	13-07-43	138 Sqn
P.1326	S/L	MORAWSKI Stanislaw	8-10-43	300 Sqn
P.1767	F/O	MOSKWA Antoni Julian	8-10-43	300 Sqn
P.784479	Cpl	MUCHA Henryk	18-07-43	18 OTU
P.782764	Sgt	NAPORA Stanislaw	14-03-43	300 Sqn
P.781688	F/S	NAWROT Jan	13-07-43	138 Sqn
P.780193	Sgt	NENKO Jozef	22-05-43	18 OTU
P.783625	Sgt	NIZNIK Adam	25-05-43	305 Sqn
P.784506	Sgt	NOGACKI Stanislaw	22-06-43	300 Sqn
P.0916	F/L	OBRYCKI Karol Jan	25-06-43	300 Sqn
P.1729	F/O	OCHEDZAN Jan Andrzej	19-12-43	300 Sqn
P.794660	Sgt	OGRODNIK Teodor	4-02-43	300 Sqn
P.1091	F/O	OPULSKI Tadeusz Michal	12-05-43	18 OTU
P.0111	F/L	OSMIALOWSKI Leon Ryszard	31-08-43	300 Sqn
P.781757	W/O	PACUT Kazimierz	15-09-43	138 Sqn
P.794373	F/L	PALUSZKIEWICZ Wladyslaw	3-08-43	305 Sqn
P.1731	F/L	PANKIEWICZ Adam	30-01-43	305 Sqn
P.703539	Sgt	PAPKOW Atanazy	14-03-43	300 Sqn
P.794026	Sgt	PASIERSKI Jozef	9-01-43	301 Sqn
P.704094	Sgt	PASTERNAK Tadeusz	12-05-43	18 OTU
P.780909	Sgt	PATLEWICZ Wladyslaw Stanislaw	17-09-43	138 Sqn
P.1733	F/O	PIATKOWSKI Henryk	25-05-43	300 Sqn
P.782899	Sgt	PIATKOWSKI Edward	12-05-43	138 Sqn
P.703858	Sgt	PIOREK Stanislaw Lukasz	27-09-43	18 OTU
P.1969	P/O	PLUSA Andrzej Jozef	13-01-43	305 Sqn
P.0086	F/O	POKORNIEWSKI Fabian Jozef	21-06-43	300 Sqn
P.0438	F/O	POLKOWSKI Jerzy Henryk	12-05-43	138 Sqn
P.76792	P/O	POLNIK Jan	12-05-43	138 Sqn
P.794726	Sgt	POLOM Franciszek	14-03-43	300 Sqn
P.76635	F/L	PRZYSIECKI Eugeniusz	23-04-43	300 Sqn
P.781417	Sgt	RAJPOLD Czeslaw	26-08-43	18 OTU
P.783028	Sgt	RATAJCZYK Czeslaw	24-05-43	300 Sqn
P.1838	F/O	ROUBO Jozef	15-08-43	300 Sqn
P.2021	P/O	RUDEK Jan	8-04-43	300 Sqn
P.1138	F/O	RUNIEWICZ Marian Emanuel	3-08-43	305 Sqn
P.783974	F/S	RUSINSKI Edmund	13-07-43	138 Sqn
P.704144	Sgt	RUTKOWSKI Stanislaw	3-08-43	305 Sqn
P.793799	Sgt	SAWICKI Jerzy	21-10-43	18 OTU
P.780137	F/S	SICINSKI Walenty	24-06-43	138 Sqn
P.793324	Sgt	SIENKIEWICZ Zenon	4-02-43	300 Sqn
P.2113	P/O	SKALISZ Tadeusz Stanislaw	3-08-43	300 Sqn
P.792624	Sgt	SKONIECZNY Jozef	6-02-43	300 Sqn
P.781577	Sgt	SKOSKIEWICZ Franciszek	25-06-43	300 Sqn
P.793899	Sgt	SKWAREK Stanislaw Jozef	26-07-43	300 Sqn
P.792051	Sgt	SLUSARSKI Stanislaw	8-04-43	300 Sqn
P.0846	F/O	SMYK Witold	3-08-43	300 Sqn
P.0204	F/O	SOKOLINSKI Tadeusz Wlodzimierz Bronislaw	9-01-43	301 Sqn
P.793230	Sgt	SOLECKI Mieczyslaw	21-10-43	18 OTU
P.784778	Sgt	SOWA Wladyslaw	4-02-43	300 Sqn
P.782528	Sgt	SROKA Wiktor	30-01-43	305 Sqn
P.781875	Cpl	STANCZUK Edmund	10-09-43	18 OTU
P.1026	F/L	STEININGER Aleksander	31-08-43	300 Sqn
P.792832	Sgt	STEPIEN Stanislaw	8-04-43	300 Sqn
P.2051	P/O	SWIECH Stanislaw	31-08-43	300 Sqn
P.783434	W/O	SZAFRAN Edward Jerzy	20-02-43	300 Sqn
P.784796	Sgt	SZCZURZYNSKI Tadeusz Jozef	21-06-43	300 Sqn
P.703599	Sgt	SZERMETA Tadeusz	23-04-43	300 Sqn
P.782788	Sgt	SZPALINSKI Stanislaw Krzysztof	22-06-43	305 Sqn
P.794517	Sgt	SZYMANOWICZ Henryk	13-05-43	300 Sqn
P.0368	F/O	TABACZYNSKI Rudolf	13-05-43	300 Sqn
P.793717	Sgt	TABACZYNSKI Ernest Ryszard	9-01-43	301 Sqn
P.784540	Sgt	TOMASZEWSKI Konrad Jozef	13-07-43	138 Sqn
P.1916	P/O	TOMICKI Stefan	8-04-43	300 Sqn
P.794311	Sgt	TRZEBUCHOWSKI Jerzy Tadeusz	22-06-43	300 Sqn
P.1128	F/O	TYRALA Tadeusz Jan	9-01-43	301 Sqn
P.793098	Sgt	ULASIUK Franciszek	18-04-43	138 Sqn
P.0839	F/O	WASILEWSKI Wincenty	17-09-43	138 Sqn
P.782668	Sgt	WERNER Stanislaw	13-05-43	300 Sqn
P.794338	F/S	WINIARCZYK Henryk	11-11-43	300 Sqn
P.787743	F/S	WOJNO Bronislaw	12-05-43	138 Sqn
P.792781	Sgt	WYDRZERZECKI Waclaw	4-02-43	300 Sqn
P.794044	Sgt	ZABAL Jozef Mieczyslaw	31-08-43	300 Sqn
P.781302	F/S	ZABICKI Tadeusz Piotr	24-06-43	138 Sqn
P.0062	S/L	ZAKRZEWSKI Edward Pawel	12-05-43	18 OTU
P.784772	Sgt	ZAREBOWICZ Michal	29-03-43	18 OTU
P.794425	Sgt	ZARNIEWSKI Kazimierz	25-06-43	300 Sqn
P.782744	Sgt	ZIELINSKI Walerian Jozef	4-02-43	300 Sqn
P.1982	P/O	ZUKOTYNSKI Stefan	15-01-43	300 Sqn
P.792392	Sgt	ZUKOWSKI Roman	8-10-43	300 Sqn

Note

Betty Clements reports that F/L Przysiecki was a Doctor of Medicine. LAC Kopka while riding a bicycle on Narden Hill, Everton, was hit by a private car. Critically injured, he was taken to RAF Hospital Henlow where he died the same day from his injuries. Unusually, he was not taken for burial in the Polish plot at Newark but interred in Newmarket Road cemetery, Cambridge.

FREE FRENCH AIR FORCE
personnel

30705	S/C	COHEN Lionce	22-05-43	342 Sqn
30019	Cpl	DESERTEAUX Charles Andre	22-05-43	342 Sqn
30386	Lt	de GRAMONT Count Gabriel Antoine Armand	10-04-43	342 Sqn
30528	P/O	JACQUINOT Roland Robert Simon	22-05-43	342 Sqn

Note
For a description of how the Free French Air Force names have been collated, please refer to the footnote appended at the end of the Free French Air Force section reported in Part 8 (1944).

ROYAL NORWEGIAN AIR FORCE
personnel

1581	Sgt	BJERCKE Arne Reidar	29-07-43	76 Sqn
253	2Lt	ECKOFF Nils Darre Stockfleth	3-10-43	76 Sqn
5369	Sgt	FJAERVOLL Birger	22-09-43	76 Sqn
5154	Lt	HOVERSTAD Gunnar	2-12-43	35 Sqn
349	2Lt	HULTHIN Leif Erik Woodrow	22-10-43	76 Sqn
1126	Lt	INDSETH Bjarne	17-01-43	76 Sqn
5133	2Lt	LINDAAS Knut	25-11-43	76 Sqn
1147	Lt	LOCHEN Kjel	18-07-43	1655 MTU
-	Lt	MOE T. D. C.	26-02-43	139 Sqn
1120	Capt	NAESS Bjorn	17-01-43	76 Sqn
5170	Sgt	OSNES Arthur Gustav	22-09-43	76 Sqn
2053	Sgt	PLAHTE Viktor Moinichen	11-12-43	16 OTU
5132	2Lt	SMEDSAAS Ottar	22-09-43	76 Sqn
-	2Lt	SMEDSAAS O.	26-02-43	139 Sqn
1014	Capt	STENE Olav Baake	18-07-43	1655 MTU

Note
I am indebted to Lt Col Eiliv Thorheim RNAF (Retd) for helping to identify those members of the Royal Norwegian Air Force who lost their lives while serving with Bomber Command formations. As will be noted, the majority of RNAF personnel that lost their lives in 1943 served with 76 Squadron. However, as will be seen from the next section (1944), their numbers were more evenly spread amongst Bomber Command units. In due course, following the cessation of hostilities, the bodies of those named above were exhumed from where they had been buried and returned to Norway. For example, Sgt Plahte now rests in Haslum Churchyard, Baerum, just to the west of Oslo.

SOUTH AFRICAN AIR FORCE
personnel

47222	Lt	INGLE DFC Arthur Ray	31-07-43	15 Sqn

WOMEN's AUXILIARY AIR FORCE
personnel

2135303	ACW2	AUSTIN Phyllis	8-04-43	467 Sqn
2102569	LACW	ALMOND Florence	1-11-43	10 Sqn
2062173	ACW1	CLOWES Vera Armistice	1-06-43	Langar
2986	S/O	EASTON Joan Marjorie	8-09-43	Waterbeach
476799	ACW2	FFOULKES Kathleen Megan	7-09-43	Sleap
2144297	ACW2	HARDCASTLE Rosina Doreen	22-05-43	35 Sqn
6552	S/O	HUGHES Karin Lia	6-11-43	27 OTU
470079	ACW2	HUGHES Vera	7-09-43	Sleap
2041172	ACW1	LAWRENCE Jean	6-11-43	12 OTU
2061857	ACW2	LORD Joan Mary	1-10-43	83 OTU
2040839	Cpl	McDOWELL Marion White	26-11-43	Wyton
2040538	Sgt	MORSE Olive Mary	14-09-43	Lissett
2110495	ACW2	SCARGILL Jean	8-07-43	1652 HCU
469853	ACW2	WARREN Edna Eileen	7-08-43	103 Sqn
468262	ACW2	WOODWARD Edna	14-11-43	Tempsford

Note
Although I have reported S/O Easton's parent unit as Waterbeach (as indicated in the 3 Group Roll of Honour), other reports indicate she died at Mepal when a 75 Squadron crashed taking off for operations to Boulogne (see Volume 4, page 319). Cpl McDowell's husband, Gdsm James Alexander McDowell was killed in Italy on the 6th of July, 1944, while serving with the 1st Battalion, Scots Guards. He is buried in Arezzo War Cemetery.

Attached personnel

ROYAL AIR FORCE

746977	W/O	BAILEY John Howard	13-02-43	10(O)AFU
2207345	AC2	HILL Norman Clifford	8-12-43	
		(serving with 5013 Airfield Construction Sqn)		
1568667	AC1	ROBERTSON Frank Hughes	27-07-43	
		(serving with 2746 Sqn RAF Regt)		
988785	Sgt	SUTHERLAND Andrew	19-10-43	
		(serving with 2754 Sqn RAF Regt)		

FLEET AIR ARM

–	S/Lt	COOPER Dudley Stuart	5-05-43
		(detached from HMS *Midge*)	
–	S/Lt	McGRATH Patrick Myles	25-02-43
		(detached from HMS *Daedalus*)	
–	Lt	MUTTRIE Gerard	15-04-43
		(detached from HMS *Daedalus*)	

Note
The two officers from HMS *Daedalus* lost their lives while attached to 106 Squadron. The former is buried in Germany at Durnback War Cemetery, while his colleague lies in France on the Somme at Souvillers-Mongival Communal Cemetery. Lt Muttrie died in a flying accident involving a 226 Squadron Boston (see Volume 4, page 138 for details).

UNITED STATES ARMY AIR FORCE

10201028	Sgt	BRANT J. W.	4-10-43	50 Sqn
O-885970	2Lt	CARLSON AM PH Carl	1-12-43	199 Sqn
O-886052	1Lt	DEVINEY PH Harold A.	31-08-43	149 Sqn
O-430995	Capt	ESTES DFC SM AM James A.	3-11-43	138 Sqn
10601018	T/S	FISHER PH Eastman G.	17-06-43	156 Sqn
T-190910	F/O	FISHER PH William C.	16-12-43	432 Sqn
–	1Lt	GROSS B. W.	11-11-43	161 Sqn
10601041	Sgt	JOHNSON AM*** PH Edward F.	26-11-43	61 Sqn
–	Sgt	KELLY J. J.	3-12-43	101 Sqn
–	1Lt	KELLY L. M.	20-12-43	78 Sqn
T-190798	F/O	MORGAN Thomas H.	4-10-43	100 Sqn
T-190844	F/O	OIEN AM PH Henry S.	4-11-43	408 Sqn
–	Lt	PEDERSON J. M. K.	18-11-43	405 Sqn
O-886059	Lt	ROBERTS E. G.	7-10-43	9 Sqn
O-885994	1Lt	ROSNER PH Eugene L.	9-07-43	106 Sqn
–	Lt	STILLER N.	20-12-43	408 Sqn
T-190803	F/O	THOMAS PH Tod J.	4-10-43	427 Sqn
10601391	M/S	WALTON PH John M.	22-10-43	166 Sqn
O-886088	Lt	WEST D.	4-11-43	57 Sqn
O-885993	1Lt	WILLIAMS John D.	12-07-43	10 OTU

Note

In the majority of cases where American airmen served with formations outside of their own command structure and who are buried in war cemeteries outside America, their entries are frequently annotated *12th Replacement Depot*. For ease of understanding, however, I have reported the squadron or training establishment in which they were serving at the time of their deaths. Capt Estes and 1Lt Gross had been attached from the 22nd Anti-Submarine Squadron.

F/O Fisher is commemorated in *They Shall Grow Not Old* without any reference to the serial number that he was issued with whilst a member of the Royal Canadian Air Force. His birth place is reported as 'Missouri'.

The abbreviations AM and PH are for Air Medal and Purple Heart respectively; asterisks indicate that the award was made on other occasions, three times in the case of Sgt Johnson. The DFC awarded to Capt Estes is, I assume, an American Distinguished Flying Cross.

ARMY

261757	2Lt	FENWICK Thomas Edward		7-07-43	30 OTU
158707	Lt	ROBERTS Philip Andrew		15-05-43	30 OTU

Note

It is believed that both were liaison officers attached for guidance on anti-aircraft and searchlight procedures. Further information concerning their deaths are recorded in Volume 7, pages 233 and 220 respectively.

CIVILIAN (BRITISH)

–	Miss ROBSON BSc Dorothy		3-11-43	RAE

Note

Miss Robson was an acknowledged expert in her specialist field of bomb sight development and had been attached from her Farnborough base to Holme-on-Spalding Moor where she had joined F/L Steele on a pre-operations test flight of a 76 Squadron Halifax. During the flight disaster overtook the crew and all perished when their aircraft crashed 300 yards north-east of Allotment Farm between Goodmanham and Middleton-on-the-Wolds. Miss Robson is buried in Yorkshire at Pocklington Rural Cemetery.

CIVILIAN (AUSTRALIAN)

–	Mr STOCKTON Norman		2-12-43	460 Sqn

Note

A war correspondent for the *Sydney Sun* newspaper, Norman Stockton lost his life while flying in a Lancaster belonging to 460 Squadron and tasked for operations over Berlin. Three members of the crew, who were captained by P/O English RAAF, managed to parachute to safety but the remainder were killed and their remains now lie in Berlin 1939-1945 War Cemetery.

Postscript

In this year of terrible attrition with the Command's losses in material and manpower rising at an alarming rate, two deaths deserve special mention. Both were holders of the Victoria Cross and both perished within a month of each other, the first being W/C John Dering Nettleton and the second F/S Arthur Louis Aaron. In April 1942, Nettleton, then a squadron leader, had led a force of twelve Lancasters (drawn equally from 44 and 97 Squadrons) on a daring deep penetration raid by day to attack the M.A.N. works at Augsburg. Over half the force failed to return, four crews, all from 44 Squadron, fell victim to enemy fighters over France while over the target area three more bombers were shot from the sky by the intense light flak. For his outstanding leadership S/L Nettleton was awarded the Victoria Cross, details being promulgated in the *Third Supplement to The London Gazette* and dated the 28th of April, 1942. *'Squadron Leader Nettleton was the leader of one of two formations of six Lancaster heavy bombers detailed to deliver a low-level attack in daylight on the diesel engine factory at Augsburg in Southern Germany on April 17th, 1942. The enterprise was daring, the target of high military importance. To reach it and get back, some 1,000 miles had to be flown over hostile territory.*

'Soon after crossing into enemy territory his formation was engaged by 25 to 30 fighters. A running fight ensued. His rear guns went out of action. One by one the aircraft of his formation were shot down until in the end only his own and one other remained. The fighters were shaken off but the target was still far distant. There was formidable resistance to be faced.

'With great spirit and almost defenceless, he held his two remaining aircraft on their perilous course and after a long and arduous flight, mostly at only 50 feet above the ground, he brought them to Augsburg. Here anti-aircraft fire of great intensity and accuracy was encountered. The two aircraft came low over the roof tops. Though fired at from point blank range, they stayed their course to drop their bombs true on the target. The second aircraft, hit by flak, burst into flames and crash-landed. The leading aircraft, though riddled with holes, flew safely back to base, the only one of the six to return.

'Squadron Leader Nettleton, who has successfully undertaken many other hazardous operations, displayed unflinching determination as well as leadership and valour of the highest order.'

F/S Aaron's award was posthumous and in terms of outstanding courage and devotion to duty stands amongst the highest in the annals of self sacrifice. Showing total disregard for his own well being Aaron strove against near insurmountable odds to bring his crew to safety and in doing pushed his wounded and broken frame beyond all hope of recovery. Well into his tour of operations with 218 Squadron, F/S Aaron had been briefed to participate in an attack by 152 aircraft (principally Stirlings) on Turin, while a much heavier force comprising of Lancasters and Halifaxes bombed industrial targets in Milan. It is likely that Aaron and his crew viewed the forthcoming sortie as one which gave them a reasonable chance of survival, particularly when matched against their recent run of operations and, initially, little occurred to alter this view. Then, having crossed the spectacular barrier of the Alps and with the crew making ready for the task in hand the situation changed in a matter of seconds from one of comparative ease to one of extreme concern and which, ultimately, would result in the death of Arthur Louis Aaron. Thus, the *Fourth Supplement to The London Gazette* duly reported on the 5th of November, 1943: *'On the night of 12th August, 1943, Flight Sergeant Aaron was the captain and pilot of a Stirling aircraft detailed to attack Turin. When approaching to attack, the bomber received devastating bursts of fire from an enemy fighter. Three engines were hit, the windscreen shattered, the front and rear turrets put out of action and the elevator control damaged, causing the aircraft to become unstable and difficult to control. The navigator (F/S Cornelius Alfred Brennan RCAF) was killed and other members of the crew were wounded.*

'A bullet struck Flight Sergeant Aaron in the face, breaking his jaw and tearing away part of his face. He was also wounded in the lung and his right arm was rendered useless. As he fell forward over the control column, the aircraft dived several thousand feet. Control was regained by the flight engineer at 3,000 feet. Unable to speak, Flight Sergeant Aaron urged the bomb aimer by signs to take over the controls. Course was then set southwards in an

endeavour to fly the crippled bomber, with one engine out of action, to Sicily or North Africa.

'Flight Sergeant Aaron was assisted to the rear of the aircraft and treated with morphia. After resting for some time he rallied and, mindful of his responsibility as captain of aircraft, insisted on returning to the pilot's cockpit, where he was lifted into his seat and had his feet placed on the rudder bar. Twice he made determined attempts to take control and hold the aircraft to its course but his weakness was evident and with difficulty he was persuaded to desist. Though in great pain and suffering from exhaustion, he continued to help by writing directions with his left hand.

'Five hours after leaving the target the petrol began to run low, but soon afterwards the flare path at Bone airfield was sighted. Flight Sergeant Aaron summoned his failing strength to direct the bomb aimer in the hazardous task of landing the damaged aircraft in the darkness with undercarriage retracted. Four attempts were made under his direction; at the fifth Flight Sergeant Aaron was so near to collapsing that he had to be restrained by the crew and the landing was completed by the bomb aimer.

'Nine hours after landing, Flight Sergeant Aaron died from exhaustion. Had he been content, when grievously wounded, to lie still and conserve his failing strength, he would probably have recovered, but he saw it as his duty to exert himself to the utmost, if necessary with his last breath, to ensure that his aircraft and crew did not fall into enemy hands. In appalling conditions he showed the greatest qualities of leadership and, though wounded and dying, he set an example of devotion to duty which has seldom been equalled and never surpassed.'

Although the citation cites an enemy fighter as being responsible it was, in fact, fire from another Stirling that caused this terrible tragedy. Subsequently, a Conspicuous Gallantry Medal was awarded to F/S Allan Larden RCAF for his part in flying the crippled Stirling to Bone, while Sgts Malcolm Mitchem, the flight engineer, and 'Jimmy' Guy, wireless operator, received Distinguished Flying Medals.

There are many instances when my eye has settled on coincidences during the preparation of this section of the Roll but none more so than when examining the first of the seven registers published in respect of service burials in Yorkshire. On the 7th of September, 1943, two airmen lost their lives in training accidents that involved Halifaxes from the heavy conversion units; in an horrific crash at Newsholme Plantation near Howden ten were killed when a 1658 HCU aircraft came down at midday while roughly 40 miles away to the north-east seven perished when their 1663 HCU Halifax smashed into the ground north of Bridlington (see page 64 of Volume 8 for further details pertaining to these losses). The navigator in the 1658 HCU bomber was Sgt Frank Reynolds from Eccleshill, Bradford, while the wireless operator in the second aircraft was Sgt Eric Pennington of Airedale, Castleford and though neither were related, except that both were Yorkshiremen living some 15 miles apart, they had joined the air force on the same day and they must have stood next to each other at the same recruiting office for Pennington had been issued with the service number 1497485 while Reynolds was given 1497486. For certain both would have gone through the initial stages of their training together before going their separate ways to complete the specialist sections of their aircrew profession only to die on the same day during the final stages of their pursuit to become operational aircrew in Bomber Command.

Finishing now with an example of the many gallantry awards that were given in 1943, I present a joint citation published in the Second Supplement to the London Gazette issued on the 23rd of March, 1943. Five were awarded Conspicuous Gallantry Medals while P/O Frederick William Gates, the aircraft's wireless operator, received a Distinguished Service Order. 'On the night of 14th February, 1943, Pilot Officer Gates, Flight Sergeant Dove and Sergeants Williams, Bain and Airey were members of the crew of an aircraft captained by Sergeant Hazard, which was detailed to attack Milan. Whilst over the target area, the aircraft was attacked by an enemy fighter from close range. Its gunfire exploded some incendiary bombs which had failed to release and a fire quickly developed in the bomber. The fuselage became a mass of flames reaching through the mid-upper turret manned by Flight Sergeant Dove. Ammunition in the turret boxes and ducts commenced to explode in all directions. In the face of an appalling situation, Flight Sergeant Dove coolly remained at his post. Although he was burned about the hands and face, he manned his guns with grim resolution, skill and accuracy. He delivered a devastating burst at the attacker, which had already been engaged and hit by the rear gunner and succeeded in destroying it. Disregarding the roaring flames, he then descended from his turret and went to the assistance of Sergeant Airey, the rear gunner, who had been wounded, and extricated him from the rear turret. The situation had become extremely critical and Sergeant Hazard ordered the crew to prepare to abandon aircraft. When informed that one of his comrades was helpless he decided, in spite of the grave risk entailed, to attempt a forced landing. Meanwhile, Pilot Officer Gates, assisted by Sergeants Williams and Bain bravely tackled the fire with extinguishers and succeeded in getting it under control. The aircraft was now down to 800 feet but, as the fire had subsided, Sergeant Hazard quickly decided to attempt to fly the badly damaged bomber home. He regained height and displaying fine airmanship crossed the Alps in safety, although 1 engine failed whilst so doing.

'On the remainder of the journey Pilot Officer Gates, rendered valuable assistance to his captain and frequently ministered to his wounded comrade, although this necessistated clambering over a hole in the floor of the aircraft in darkness. Aided by the skilful navigation of Sergeant Williams and good work by Sergeant Bain, the flight engineer, Sergeant Hazard succeeded in flying the seriously damaged aircraft back to this country. In circumstances of the greatest danger, this aircraft crew displayed courage, fortitude and devotion to duty with the highest traditions of the Royal Air Force.'

Of this sextet of gallant airmen, only F/S Dove and Sgt Airey survived the war. Three died in a flying accident just three days prior to their awards being promulgated, while P/O Gates lost his life in the early hours of the 5th of May, 1943, when his Lancaster, which had been hit by flak during an attack on Dortmund, crashed between Hotham and North Cave.

In closing this section, it is observed that F/L Curtin RCAF was the first American national, flying in Bomber Command, to gain a first bar to his DFC, while in the case of F/S Kozocki, named in the same section, is reported in the publication They Shall Grow Not Old as having the surname Kozicki.

Note: Between May and October, 1943, 420, 424 and 425 Squadrons of No.6(RCAF) Group and their Wellingtons were despatched to the Middle East theatre where they carried out bombing operations in support of No.205 Group. Although, technically, outside of the sphere of Bomber Command's control, I have decided to include their casualties in this Roll of Honour.

Part 8

Bomber Command
Roll of Honour – 1944

The New Year began in much the same vein as the last two months of the old. More oft than not the target map screens in briefing rooms at bomber bases across the country were pulled aside revealing to the assembled airmen strands of ribbons snaking eastwards in the direction of Berlin. Six major assaults on Germany's capital city were launched in the January and apart from the fifth attack when some ground detail was visible, the bomber crews saw little of the earth beneath as they battled their way through skies leaden with cloud to release their bombs into the hazy smudge left by the sky-markers. Not surprisingly, the effectiveness of these raids were, in general, minimal and the disappointment of such poor results could not be offset by a reduction in casualty figures which averaged out at around 6 per cent for each operation. Neither, in respect of the mounting casualty toll, could any comfort be gained from the occasions when attention was turned to other centres of importance and, in the main, it was the Lancaster equipped squadrons that were bearing the brunt of this considerable pain. Such was the case when Brunswick was raided in strength during the night of 14th/15th January, resulting in 38 Lancasters failing to return, 7.6 per cent of the force of 498 bombers despatched. Depressingly, from the Command's view point, little damage was inflicted on this relatively small target and it was a similar story on the 21st/22nd January, when a mixed bag of Lancasters and Halifaxes attempted to get to grips with Magdeburg. Losses rose to over 8 per cent and it is a near certainty that skilful handling of the Luftwaffe's night fighter force accounted for most of the 57 aircraft missing, 35 of these being Halifaxes. And as if these sobering statistics were not enough for the planning staff to contend with, February and March would bring little respite.

The first half of February was relatively quiet but in the middle of the month Harris sanctioned the heaviest raid yet sent to the German capital when a force comprised of 561 Lancasters, 314 Halifaxes and 16 twin-engined Mosquitoes bore down from the north and in the face of an extremely hostile flak barrage released their bomb loads though banks of cloud to cause extensive damage in the central and south-western districts of the city. Numerous night fighter combats were witnessed and over 40 crews failed to make it home. Then, less than a week later over 70 bombers were shot down during a raid on the industrial centre of Leipzig. An almost unimaginable strain was being felt by all concerned and but for the output of fresh and willing faces from the training formations, such crippling losses would have been near unsustainable. As it was, considerable numbers of experienced bomber crews were being lost, particularly from Path Finder Force squadrons. But a form of salvation was at hand for the current round of operations, referred to by military historians as the *Battle of Berlin*, drew to a close the entire direction of Bomber Command was set to change and for the foreseeable future the man to whom Harris would now be answerable was the recently appointed Allied Supreme Commander, General Dwight D. Eisenhower. But before making some observations on what would become one of the most productive periods in Bomber Command's history the outcome of the raid to Nuremberg on the night of the 30th/31st March cannot be allowed to pass without comment. A week previous the Command's Main Force squadrons, mustering for the occasion 811 aircraft, had flown to Berlin, by way of a northern approach, for the last time. Throughout the seven to eight hours that it took to fly this torturous operation crews faced winds far in excess of what had been forecast and as a result the bomber stream became scattered, particularly after leaving Berlin and commencing the long leg towards the North Sea and relative safety. Usually it was the scourge of the German night fighters that sealed the fate of so many bomber crews during this grim phase of operations but on this particular night it was the minimally less feared flak batteries that inflicted the most damage. The respected historian, Martin Middlebrook, believes that approximately 50 of the 72 aircraft lost that night fell victim to flak, an inordinately high total. A series of operations, begun in earnest the previous November with the desired aim of destroying the will of the enemy to continue the war had ended in failure.

And so we come by way of an extremely effective visit to Essen on the night of the 26th/27th March, to Nuremberg. Normally, as it was the full moon cycle all Main Force squadrons would have been stood-down but the weather experts forecast conditions of high cloud for the outward route but with clearing conditions to allow for ground marking of the target area. However, this prediction was called into question following the presentation of evidence gathered by the daily Meteorological Flight Mosquito. Nonetheless, despite the ominous portents of danger in the offing, the raid went ahead and close on 800 bombers were sent out in conditions of bright moonlight. Consequently, having picked up and identified the main thrust of intent, the German controllers were able to marshal their forces to great effect and for the bomber crews there was scant respite from attack all the way to the target. In the space of roughly an hour, 82 bombers were shot down and it was only through being forced to break off their engagements and land for refuelling that the night fighters were unable to repeat their success as the survivors braced themselves for the long flight home. Again, I turn to the historian Martin Middlebrook for a resume of the night's terrible losses; 97 aircraft classified as missing, 10 destroyed in crashes on return (or written off with battle damage) and one lost in a take-off accident. In terms of aircrew casualties, I draw attention to my fifth volume of Bomber Command losses which show 540 killed in action or dying as a result of injuries received, 157 were prisoners of war (one, F/S D. Bauldie, was killed on the 19th of April, 1945, when a flight of Typhoon fighter-bombers, in a tragic case of mistaken identity, strafed a large column of prisoners of war near the village of Gresse) and 10 in the early stages of evading capture.

Since the previous autumn it had not been all gloom and despondency, though the straws of comfort were few and far between. Kassel, Frankfurt, Leipzig (the December raid being particularly concentrated), Stettin, Stuttgart and the split raids in late February on Schweinfurt and Augsburg had all produced results that ranged between reasonably effective and very damaging. It was, however, an inescapable fact that since the introduction of *Window* as a protective measure, followed by the undeniable success of the Hamburg operations in the summer of 1943, the Luftwaffe had recovered strongly and any lingering hopes that the war could be brought to a conclusion by bombing alone had by the early spring of 1944 completely evaporated. Nonetheless, despite the crippling losses over the past six months, Bomber Command was gaining in both material strength and in the capacity to defend the bomber streams by means of radio countermeasures. Thus, with operational direction now being dictated by the needs of the Allied Supreme Commander as he prepared his forces for the invasion of Europe, Harris's squadrons were about to enter into a campaign of tactical bombing that would help immeasurably in denying the enemy an effective response to any seaborne landings. Working in partnership with the might of the American Eighth Air Force and the tactical day-bomber forces, Bomber Command set about helping to destroy the key railway centres in France and Belgium that were vital to the free movement of supplies and reinforcements to the occupying military but in order that the enemy should not gain any firm hint as to where the Allies intended their armies to come ashore, much subterfuge had to be employed and a most intricate plan of operations was set in train. Throughout the ten weeks twixt Nuremberg and the Normandy landings, the Main Force squadrons were obliged to operate in their night bombing capacity and many in authority were, rightfully, fearful that by doing so numerous casualties would be inflicted on the long-suffering citizens of those towns that were about to be targeted. Although it would be wrong to say that every operation was a success, in the main Bomber Command rose magnificiently to the challenge and deaths to civilians in these areas, although at times substantial, were nowhere near as high as had once been feared. As well as attacking the myriad of rail centres spread across France and Belgium, attention was also paid to military camps, the long chain of coastal defences, supply dumps (many of these being hidden deep inside forested areas), armament factories and, when conditions were deemed favourable and there was a stand-down from the pre-invasions plans, familiar targets in Germany were visited. Thus, during April, Aachen, Cologne, Dusseldorf, Karlsruhe and Essen, to name a random five, were raided in some strength and to good effect with losses being regarded as minimal when compared to those of the first three months of the year.

It would, however, be erroneous to believe that Bomber Command's terrible losses were behind them. True, with the diversity of targets now being prosecuted, crews found themselves operating at a much higher frequency and, as a consequence, some found themselves completing a tour of duty within three months of starting. However, many were flying well in excess of the recognised '30' sorties, principally because many of the targets now on offer were of relatively short duration. For example, raids on the V-1 flying bomb sites in the area of the Pas-de-Calais might be completed within a span of four hours from take off to landing. Furthermore, the plethora of targets under attack on any one night reduced the capabilities of the Luftwaffe to concentrate its forces in any particular area but, it has to be said, when their fighters did penetrate one of the many bomber streams the results could be quite harrowing. An example of such success, from the enemy's point of view, occurred on the night of the 3rd/4th of May, when 346 Lancasters, aided by 16 Mosquitoes acting as markers, bombed a Panzer training camp near the village of Mailly. Due to problems in radio communications the orbiting Main Force was seriously delayed and though the ensuing bombing was extremely accurate the night fighters enjoyed a field day, accounting for the majority of the 42 Lancasters destroyed (460 Squadron lost six aircraft [one being crewed by airmen from 101 Squadron] and of the 42 airmen involved just three, all evaders, survived while 12 Squadron, 50 Squaron and 101 Squadron each sustained a quartet of losses). Similarly, the raid on the Trappes marshalling yards near Paris in early June resulted in 15 of the 105 participating Halifaxes being shot down as the fighters harried their prey all the way to the coast. And it was on such occasions that individual squadrons could suffer the most appalling losses. Staying with the visit to Trappes, an operation that principally involved No.4 Group, 158 Squadron, operating from Lissett, despatched a total of 23 aircraft, of which five were shot down and a sixth, captained by P/O B. D. Bancroft, an Australian, was so badly damaged that it was written off as beyond economical repair. In his post raid report, Bancroft stated that after bombing the yards and while heading towards their exit point near Le Havre, flying at 7,500 feet, a Ju 88 pounced, its cannon fire blasting a hole in the floor of the fuselage and causing extensive damage to the aircraft's hydraulic system and rendering most of his flying instruments unserviceable. In the immediate confusion three members of his crew either fell through the hole ripped in the fuselage floor, or baled out, these including his badly wounded wireless operator, Sgt L. S. Dwan, who did not survive, his mid-upper air gunner, Sgt K. L. G. Le Heup, subsequently reported as a prisoner of war and the flight engineer, Sgt L. Cottrell who, eventually, made his way home to England. The remaining members of Bancroft's crew fought the flames that had engulfed most of the centre section, bringing them under control before making an emergency landing at Hurn airfield near Bournemouth. 76 Squadron, based at Holme-on-Spalding Moor lost three Halifaxes and Leconfield's two resident units, 466 Squadron and 640 Squadron reported two and three crews missing respectively.

Following the invasion, Bomber Command would endure many more difficult nights as the squadrons continued to lend tactical support to the armies on the ground but with Allied air supremacy of the skies over the battle front it became possible to introduce all of the bomber groups to daylight operations and thus realise, at last, the terrible potential of round the clock attack. Although the ground fighting remained tense and for several months territorial advantage was restricted to inch-by-inch gains rather than spectacular advance, the inevitable breakout from the Normandy battle area was never in serious doubt and when, at last, the armoured columns broke through the German lines the rout of the once all-conquering Wehrmacht was spectacular. Bomber Command's part in all this cannot be over emphasised and, as many historians have remarked, during an average week the Command would despatch as many sorties (5,000 on average) as had been possible in the first nine months of the war. Not only were the aircrews working at full stretch but their ground staff counterparts were performing their duties to the highest order of the service.

Before leaving the summer of 1944 to history, a few examples illustrating the pain still being inflicted by the Luftwaffe on the Command's night operations. During the night of the 12th/13th of June, Harris authorised over 1,000 sorties, mainly to disrupt rail communications leading to the battle area, but a sizeable force numbering 303 aircraft went to Germany, carrying out an extremely accurate attack on the Nordstern synthetic-oil producing plant at Gelsenkirchen and it was here that the night fighters got to work on the bomber stream, accounting for the majority of the 17 Lancasters shot down. Before the month was out a similar operation was mounted, this time by 321 bombers raiding the Holten synthetic-oil complex at Sterkrade. Of the 32 bombers reported missing from all operations flown this night, no less than 31 were victims of the Sterkrade attack, 77 Squadron being particular hard hit with the loss of seven of its 23 participating Halifaxes. Then, in July, the railway yards at Revigny were visited on three occasions and it was during the course of the third attack that the night fighters infiltrated the relatively small bomber stream of Lancasters and shot down 24 of their number. In percentage terms this was an horrific 22 per cent of the crews involved, 619 Squadron, based at Dunholme Lodge, losing five from the 13 sent. Little wonder that the historian Oliver Clutton-Brock titled his 1994 account of the three raids as *Massacre over the Marne*.

Thus, it came about that Harris was released from Eisenhower's dictate in mid-September and the scene was set for the most intensive series of bombing operations yet witnessed in the war to date. This would result in the near total destruction of Germany's major towns and cities, though throughout the remaining months of conflict tactical operations would be flown as and when required by the ground commanders. With little to fear from the Luftwaffe's day fighter units and with the prospect of being able to call upon our own fighter squadrons to provide escort protection, Bomber Command commenced to flex its strength, by day, over the Ruhr. Somewhat surprisingly, it was not the much-vaunted Lancaster squadrons that led the way but 216 Halifaxes drawn from No.4 Group that left their Yorkshire bases shortly before midday on Sunday the 27th of August to attack the Rheinpreussen synthetic-oil refining plant in the Meerbeck district of Homberg. Marking, by *Oboe*, was provided by Path Finder Force Mosquitoes and Lancasters and despite rather copious amounts of cloud over the target area, most crews report seeing enough ground detail to enable them to carry out a good bombing run. Throughout the operation, crews witnessed the unfamiliar sight of large numbers of Spitfires milling around, as many as nine squadrons being employed for the outward leg and seven for the withdrawal phase. Flak over the target is described as intense but despite several bombers being hit, none were brought down. In recognition of this historic occasion, I report the impressions of two of the Australian pilots involved. First, F/S J. Espie's reminiscences of the outbound leg to Homberg in his 76 Squadron Halifax; *'We approached with the aircraft in a race course pattern all jockeying for position. Some of the leading crews seemingly impatient and firing many Verey cartridges as if to order lesser aircraft to heel. Then all the smaller gaggles started to interweave into compact groups. Slowly at first the groups built up, until we neared the Ruhr and everyone was in tight formation. To me it looked like mile upon mile of aircraft, those in the distance like motionless insects. The gentle relative movement of the nearer aircraft sometimes changing abruptly into swift crossovers which were quite stunning to see.'* Then, on reaching the target area F/S Espie was aware that his wireless operator, Sgt 'Wally' Waddington who had been busy dispersing *Window*, had broken off from his task and had come up into the cockpit. *'A Halifax, slightly higher and in front of us filled the windscreen. Black balls of expended explosives from anti-aircraft shells sped past and fresh black puffs kept appearing from all directions. That was enough for 'Wally' and he disappeared back to the Window chute and the timely despatch of those thousands of silvered-paper strips. To my knowledge, 'Wally' never put his head up in my office again while we were over enemy territory.'* Next, a much terser report from F/S T. S. Powe whose 158 Squadron Halifax was hit by flak before he could withdraw from the target area. *'Sparks and smoke were seen coming from the starboard engines and there was smoke and a pungent odour inside the aircraft. We were unable to return to base and I crash landed at Bodney in Norfolk.'*

The die was now cast; Bomber Command was no longer restricted to a night bombing campaign over the German mainland. For the next few weeks, however, a round of tactical operations precluded any great attention to targets in Germany. Final attention was paid to the remaining flying-bomb sites in the Pas-de-Calais, followed by a lengthy series of raids on the German garrison at Le Havre, bypassed by the Allies in their haste to exploit the break out from Normandy. Then, on the night of 11th/12th September, a relatively small force of Lancasters and Mosquitoes, all from No.5 Group, dealt a crushing blow on the city of Darmstadt. Such was the accuracy of marking and concentration of bombing that followed, the central parts of the city and the districts immediately south and east of the centre were reduced to near total destruction as the fire storm took hold. Then, over the next 48-hours synthetic-oil centres in the Ruhr were bombed by day before, once again, tactical operations in support of Operation Market Garden were flown, as well as a series of raids against the beleaguered German garrison at Calais.

On the ground the impetus that had expelled the occupation forces from the capitals of Paris and Brussels, and the capture on the 4th of September of the key Belgian port of Antwerp, had slowed as the Allied armies' lines of communication became critically extended. Though the French port of Brest was functioning, the distance over which supplies had to be moved was, in some cases, over 500 miles and, therefore, it was absolutely vital that the entrances to the Scheldt were secured in order to bring Antwerp into use. Unfortunately, the reversal of fortune experienced at Arnhem and the consequences that followed resulted in nearly three months of delay before the port could be opened up to shipping. As had been the pattern of late, Bomber Command played its part with a series of precision raids against the island of Walcheren which guarded the entrance to the Scheldt, these operations being interwoven with a series of stunning attacks on the Ruhr cities of Duisburg and Essen. The strikes on Duisburg, in particular, well illustrates the overwhelming strength of Bomber Command and the inability of the Luftwaffe to make any serious intervention, at least by day. The first raid by over a thousand bombers, heavily protected by fighter escort, struck at just after 9 a.m. on the 14th of October and such was the concentration of bombing that the flak defences buckled under the sheer weight of attack. Nonetheless, 14 bombers were brought down and a further seven aircraft failed to return when Duisburg was hit for the second time in the early hours of the 15th, again with over a thousand bombers participating. These quite spectacular attacks were followed by twin operations against Essen, the first of these by night on the 23rd/24th of October and the second by day on the 25th. In total, losses from Essen amounted to a dozen aircraft while the city itself was very severely damaged with acres of near total destruction and substantial losses in war production being reported (steel output from Krupps plummeted as a direct result of these raids).

For the remainder of the year the pattern of attacks established in the autumn months continued and rarely a day or night went by without Bomber Command's presence being felt in some part of the German mainland, either in the shape of a substantial Main Force attack or the equally effective strikes by the Mosquitoes of the Light Night Striking Force (a total of nine Mosquito equipped squadrons were operating under the authority of No.8 (PFF) Group). The familiar names of Cologne, Dusseldorf (raided in strength for the final time during the night of the 2nd/3rd of November), Gelsenkirchen, Dortmund and their like continued to appear on the briefing room boards, but less well known targets also began to appear; Kaiserslautern, Bonn, Aschaffenburg and Neuss to name but a quartet and from time to time Harris was called upon to lend support to land operations, particularly in the wake of the surprise German counter-attack in mid-December which for a few days rang very serious alarm bells at all Allied headquarters. It proved, however, to be merely a false dawn of hope though it would be the New Year before the Allied ground forces could say that they had successfully repelled the Wehrmacht's last serious throw of the dice. As December 1944 gave way to the New Year, Bomber Command was at the peak of its operational strength and the terrible memories of the Battle of Berlin period and the first three months of the year had been, in the most part, firmly assuaged.

ROYAL AIR FORCE, AUXILIARY AIR FORCE and ROYAL AIR FORCE (VOLUNTEER RESERVE) personnel

Service No	Rank	Name	Date	Squadron
130719	F/O	ABBOTT Arthur Frank	22-01-44	83 Sqn
1804051	Sgt	ABBOTT Douglas Alan	14-01-44	166 Sqn
1580720	Sgt	ABBOTT Harry	10-04-44	12 Sqn
1626469	Sgt	ABBOTT Norman William Stanley	22-06-44	214 Sqn
127346	F/O	ABBOTT Peter John	13-07-44	103 Sqn
1880551	Sgt	ABBOTT Stanley James	25-06-44	9 Sqn
175843	P/O	ABBOTT Wilfred	18-07-44	431 Sqn
1615651	Sgt	ABEL Leslie Francis	21-01-44	207 Sqn
44911	W/C	ABERCROMBY DFC* William	2-01-44	83 Sqn
1862629	Sgt	ABERY Frederick James	24-02-44	405 Sqn
1356442	Sgt	ABLETT Charles	3-01-44	61 Sqn
1850013	Sgt	ABRAHAM Kenneth James	26-07-44	1657 HCU
1186223	W/O	ABRAHAM Robert George	23-10-44	44 Sqn
928572	Sgt	ABRAHAMS Aleck	22-01-44	76 Sqn
1605926	Sgt	ABRAMS Ronald Walter	6-06-44	149 Sqn
2203439	Sgt	ACE John Henry	10-11-44	97 Sqn
185019	P/O	ACHESON George Victor	16-09-44	239 Sqn
1595296	Sgt	ACKCRAL Alfred Edwin	15-11-44	1666 HCU
1537792	Sgt	ACKROYD Ben	27-01-44	1660 HCU
1586706	Sgt	ACOMBE-HILL Cyril Arthur	28-01-44	61 Sqn
649091	Sgt	ACOURT Burleigh Charles	29-06-44	76 Sqn
141163	F/O	ACWORTH DFC Dennis Herbert	28-05-44	627 Sqn
1671613	Sgt	ADAIR Stanley	13-08-44	61 Sqn
1450691	Sgt	ADAMS Clifford	15-06-44	425 Sqn
1391578	F/S	ADAMS Daniel Gilbert	25-04-44	49 Sqn
1345972	F/S	ADAMS David	31-10-44	90 Sqn
173518	F/O	ADAMS Douglas Alan Moore	7-08-44	149 Sqn
1851113	Sgt	ADAMS Ernest James	8-05-44	15 Sqn
629232	Sgt	ADAMS Frederick Thomas Henry	30-01-44	463 Sqn
187726	P/O	ADAMS George	14-10-44	419 Sqn
1201006	F/S	ADAMS George Roughton Carver Gilroy	31-01-44	103 Sqn
174599	P/O	ADAMS Henry Harris	19-04-44	57 Sqn
1890680	Sgt	ADAMS Jack	15-02-44	115 Sqn
178513	F/O	ADAMS Joseph Edward	6-11-44	207 Sqn
1553944	Sgt	ADAMS Kenneth	19-07-44	630 Sqn
1852722	Sgt	ADAMS Kenneth Ernest Charles	19-08-44	51 Sqn
1322911	Sgt	ADAMS Louis Robert	31-03-44	51 Sqn
1608426	Sgt	ADAMS Percy Alfred Oliver	29-07-44	550 Sqn
1185991	W/O	ADAMS Reginald Hartley	31-03-44	51 Sqn
120247	F/L	ADAMS DFC Robert	22-06-44	630 Sqn
1324495	F/S	ADAMS DFM Roland Arthur	20-01-44	83 Sqn
1391532	Sgt	ADAMS William Alfred	23-09-44	166 Sqn
168511	P/O	ADAMSON John	27-01-44	408 Sqn
148447	F/O	ADAMSON DFC William Ian	31-03-44	101 Sqn
156744	F/O	ADAMS-LANGLEY Juan Alberto [Chile]	8-07-44	106 Sqn
575659	Sgt	ADDEMS Clifford Charles	27-08-44	576 Sqn
175073	P/O	ADDER Mervyn	15-03-44	44 Sqn
1835722	AC1	ADDICOTT Alfred Tudor	17-03-44	31 Base
1684394	Sgt	ADDY Donald	31-03-44	101 Sqn
184147	P/O	ADDYMAN Dennis Edwalds	26-12-44	10 Sqn
1600694	Sgt	ADKIN Lawrence Sidney John	30-01-44	514 Sqn
160648	F/O	AFFLECK Douglas	30-01-44	640 Sqn
1503655	F/S	AGAR DFM Gilbert Harry	12-05-44	103 Sqn
1874688	Sgt	AGER Peter Dennis Victor	17-06-44	434 Sqn
1260468	W/O	AGG DFM Richard William	25-06-44	9 Sqn
155576	F/O	AGNEW DFC James Thompson	20-04-44	1655 MTU
136364	F/O	AGNEW Kenneth Len	14-01-44	550 Sqn
1434385	Sgt	AIANO Robert Harold	28-04-44	431 Sqn
1061336	LAC	AIKEN John	13-09-44	617 Sqn
1349585	F/S	AIKMAN William McAlister	31-03-44	12 Sqn
3011067	Sgt	AINSWORTH Richard Eric	2-12-44	433 Sqn
1338301	F/S	AINSWORTH Sydney Wilson	4-05-44	101 Sqn
1816445	F/S	AIREY Robert William	24-02-44	78 Sqn
141023	F/O	AIRS Wilfred	29-06-44	7 Sqn
176489	P/O	AISTON Aidan	5-07-44	192 Sqn
1532964	Sgt	AISTON Alfred William	16-03-44	625 Sqn
1824340	Sgt	AITCHISON Robert	17-09-44	102 Sqn
1001191	W/O	AITKEN Robertson Brown	8-06-44	15 Sqn
1805343	Sgt	AKEHURST Bernard Spencer John	15-02-44	115 Sqn
1397504	Sgt	AKERS John Archer	30-08-44	630 Sqn
658229	Sgt	AKHURST Sidney John	15-10-44	626 Sqn
533661	Sgt	ALBERY Albert Richard	1-07-44	12 Sqn
152969	F/O	ALBON Eric	13-06-44	78 Sqn
1576661	Sgt	ALBONE Arthur Ronald	20-02-44	51 Sqn
151080	F/O	ALBUTT Oliver Leslie	10-05-44	550 Sqn
2209054	Sgt	ALCOCK Eric Henry	27-01-44	101 Sqn
127192	F/O	ALCOCK John Perry	5-08-44	161 Sqn
88402	F/L	ALCOCK DFC Selwyn Henry	27-01-44	83 Sqn
955354	Sgt	ALCOCK Sidney Radford	5-08-44	166 Sqn
176042	P/O	ALCOTT Arthur John	22-05-44	100 Sqn
122956	F/L	ALCUIN JONES Ivor	30-08-44	1655 MTU
1850102	Sgt	ALDEN Arthur John	25-08-44	640 Sqn
109107	F/L	ALDERSON Edward	21-04-44	30 OTU
1853664	Sgt	ALDERSON William Cecil	31-08-44	166 Sqn
1873795	Sgt	ALDRED Frank George	27-01-44	622 Sqn
183600	F/O	ALDRED Norman Frederick	23-09-44	61 Sqn
175106	F/O	ALDRIDGE Arthur James	12-09-44	576 Sqn
1853526	Sgt	ALDRIDGE Frank Henry	22-06-44	106 Sqn
45274	F/L	ALDUS Reginald Major	14-10-44	626 Sqn
651372	Sgt	ALEXANDER Christopher	30-08-44	83 Sqn
170100	P/O	ALEXANDER CGM James Michie	15-02-44	7 Sqn
1672382	Sgt	ALEXANDER John Campbell	1-09-44	138 Sqn
1607283	Sgt	ALEXANDER Raymond George	31-08-44	1654 HCU
172294	P/O	ALEXANDER Richard Colton	8-05-44	44 Sqn
989463	F/S	ALEXANDER Robert Lawson	30-08-44	635 Sqn
1896003	Sgt	ALEXANDER Thomas Edward	9-06-44	50 Sqn
1479414	Sgt	ALEXANDER William Edward	25-04-44	97 Sqn
168697	F/O	ALFORD MiD Reginald William	8-11-44	1655 MTU
1471670	Sgt	ALLAKER Kenneth Herbert	25-05-44	76 Sqn
1562335	Sgt	ALLAN Alexander	15-07-44	460 Sqn
1821830	Sgt	ALLAN Harry Bain	23-04-44	78 Sqn
151061	F/O	ALLAN Ian Godfrey	3-01-44	83 Sqn
1487859	Sgt	ALLAN James Morton	11-04-44	622 Sqn
1524157	Sgt	ALLAN John Stanley	30-10-44	21 OTU
966502	F/S	ALLAN Norman Sinclair	15-03-44	625 Sqn
1075879	Sgt	ALLAN Sidney	27-01-44	149 Sqn
1590136	Sgt	ALLANSON Thomas	14-10-44	153 Sqn
1132284	Sgt	ALLDIS Stanley	13-06-44	166 Sqn
1591743	Sgt	ALLDRITT Terence	25-05-44	640 Sqn

1850401	Sgt	ALLEN Anthony Peter	28-05-44	460 Sqn
1399042	Sgt	ALLEN Arthur Joseph	13-07-44	1662 HCU
1601202	Sgt	ALLEN Basil John	15-02-44	622 Sqn
1385431	Sgt	ALLEN Charles Martin	30-06-44	51 Sqn
128426	F/O	ALLEN Charles Reginald	19-03-44	578 Sqn
148787	F/L	ALLEN Clifford Arthur Lawrence	27-04-44	10 Sqn
1604285	Sgt	ALLEN Clifford Frank	29-07-44	625 Sqn
170941	F/O	ALLEN Clifford Leslie Eldridge	25-03-44	630 Sqn
1321334	Sgt	ALLEN Dennis Geoffrey	8-05-44	106 Sqn
1586581	Sgt	ALLEN Dennis Roy	29-07-44	50 Sqn
1025717	F/S	ALLEN Francis	19-08-44	576 Sqn
643123	Sgt	ALLEN Frank Norman	1-07-44	625 Sqn
1853859	Sgt	ALLEN Frederick	19-07-44	115 Sqn
183343	P/O	ALLEN John Guy	31-10-44	90 Sqn
1672972	Sgt	ALLEN Kenneth	25-02-44	12 Sqn
1310572	Sgt	ALLEN Lawrence	22-04-44	1654 HCU
1428471	Sgt	ALLEN Norman John	24-01-44	14 OTU
658419	F/S	ALLEN Norman William	30-01-44	467 Sqn
1529131	Sgt	ALLEN Richard William	2-01-44	83 Sqn
1594928	Sgt	ALLEN Sidney Walpole	30-08-44	103 Sqn
170268	P/O	ALLEN Thomas Arthur	28-05-44	101 Sqn
1836509	Sgt	ALLEN William Ebenezer	25-02-44	12 Sqn
540956	F/S	ALLEN William Morton	14-01-44	75 Sqn
1590978	Sgt	ALLENBY George	19-07-44	78 Sqn
178946	P/O	ALLFORD Frederick Charles	19-08-44	7 Sqn
51349	F/O	ALLINSON DFM John	4-08-44	635 Sqn
1672238	F/S	ALLISON DFM Arthur Hayes	30-07-44	57 Sqn
2220851	Sgt	ALLISON Edward Charles	23-12-44	90 Sqn
141772	F/O	ALLISON DFM Frank	29-01-44	97 Sqn
110791	F/L	ALLISON George Edmund	22-07-44	23 Sqn
1593445	Sgt	ALLISON John	19-07-44	138 Sqn
1800530	Sgt	ALLISON John	4-12-44	189 Sqn
570541	Sgt	ALLISON Robert Alexander	14-01-44	101 Sqn
1388172	Sgt	ALLISON Robert Francis Neil	15-02-44	100 Sqn
153326	F/O	ALLMAN Henry Edward	30-08-44	90 Sqn
1803538	Sgt	ALLPORT Howard	12-10-44	21 OTU
146712	F/L	ALLSON Alan Ernest	10-02-44	199 Sqn
1583449	Sgt	ALLSOP Alfred	15-02-44	622 Sqn
1343996	F/S	ALLWELL Peter	3-01-44	426 Sqn
54973	P/O	ALP Percy Leonard	18-07-44	431 Sqn
977330	W/O	ALSBURY William Thomas	13-08-44	156 Sqn
1488179	Sgt	ALSOP Ernest Clifford	2-09-44	1656 HCU
1668424	Sgt	ALSOPP Kenneth George	8-07-44	50 Sqn
48871	F/O	ALSTON Eric Robert	25-04-44	61 Sqn
1509278	LAC	ALSTON William Arthur George	23-09-44	582 Sqn
1548356	F/S	ALTON James Poe	29-04-44	12 Sqn
170028	P/O	ALVES Joseph Emmanuel	29-01-44	625 Sqn
1321473	F/S	AMES Richard Harry	16-06-44	582 Sqn
146973	F/O	AMEY DFC Ronald Ernest	31-12-44	50 Sqn
1424918	F/S	AMEYE Emile Rene Lucien Maria [Belgium]	6-11-44	463 Sqn
169719	F/L	AMIES Alan	12-05-44	15 Sqn
1445907	Sgt	AMIES Philip	13-08-44	630 Sqn
1397358	F/S	AMORY Richard Gore [British Guiana]	21-07-44	100 Sqn
1322346	F/S	AMOS Leslie Edward	23-04-44	90 Sqn
2210672	Sgt	AMOS Norman	4-11-44	640 Sqn
161781	F/O	AMPHLETT William Victor	22-05-44	50 Sqn
1590890	Sgt	ANDERSON Alan Herbert	8-06-44	115 Sqn
1547680	Sgt	ANDERSON Alfred	30-08-44	550 Sqn
172970	P/O	ANDERSON Arthur Leslie	8-05-44	49 Sqn
1317943	Sgt	ANDERSON David Angus	31-03-44	207 Sqn
1591979	Sgt	ANDERSON Edmund Dawson	31-07-44	57 Sqn
156267	F/O	ANDERSON Edward	20-01-44	83 Sqn
1875010	Sgt	ANDERSON Frank Iron	27-04-44	57 Sqn
1217743	F/S	ANDERSON Jack	3-01-44	405 Sqn
1823158	Sgt	ANDERSON John Stodart	31-10-44	9 Sqn
1396592	Sgt	ANDERSON John William Thompson	14-01-44	576 Sqn
1531860	F/S	ANDERSON Kenneth	22-03-44	49 Sqn
1388016	F/S	ANDERSON Lionel David	27-04-44	515 Sqn
1566518	Sgt	ANDERSON Peter Alexander	9-09-44	17 OTU
991776	Sgt	ANDERSON Richard	27-01-44	57 Sqn
170283	F/O	ANDERSON Stanley Milton	21-07-44	514 Sqn
1821629	Sgt	ANDERSON William Andrew Melrose	31-01-44	626 Sqn
1501026	Sgt	ANDERSON William Gowland	28-04-44	101 Sqn
1685678	Sgt	ANDERTON John Brian	6-10-44	78 Sqn
188601	P/O	ANDRE Edmond Gabriel Fernand Ghislan [Belgium]	7-12-44	227 Sqn
148330	F/O	ANDREWES Peter Lancelot	13-06-44	166 Sqn
154833	F/O	ANDREWS James Horace	6-12-44	460 Sqn
1199065	Sgt	ANDREWS MiD John Francis	9-09-44	426 Sqn
1461939	Sgt	ANDREWS John Neville	15-03-44	550 Sqn
533383	Sgt	ANDREWS Leslie Arthur	15-10-44	90 Sqn
1853736	Sgt	ANDREWS Richard Walter	4-05-44	625 Sqn
1336644	Sgt	ANDREWS Ronald Albert	13-01-44	15 Sqn
1314936	W/O	ANDREWS Ronald James	1-06-44	156 Sqn
105186	F/L	ANDREWS Ronald John	20-01-44	7 Sqn
1893084	Sgt	ANGLES William George	14-10-44	166 Sqn
3066380	Sgt	ANGUS Frederick John	15-12-44	12 Sqn
1581067	F/S	ANGUS Kenneth	28-12-44	576 Sqn
1507990	Sgt	ANKERS Edward	14-06-44	11 OTU
1507625	Sgt	ANNAN Harry Barton	10-01-44	1652 HCU
162871	F/O	ANNETT MiD Hugh Crawford	11-11-44	97 Sqn
1458450	F/S	ANSDELL Geoffrey Ronald	22-06-44	57 Sqn
1893412	Sgt	ANSELL Allan Alfred	19-07-44	49 Sqn
1397244	Sgt	ANSELL Benjamin Edward	18-03-44	115 Sqn
1416947	Sgt	ANSELL Dennis John	23-09-44	101 Sqn
1895351	Sgt	ANSELL Frederick Neale	16-06-44	514 Sqn
572304	Sgt	ANSELL Kenneth Raymond	7-06-44	550 Sqn
903498	W/O	ANSELL Washington Henry Samuel	30-08-44	550 Sqn
124803	F/O	ANSTEE Jack	6-01-44	97 Sqn
1652768	Sgt	ANSTEY William James	11-04-44	158 Sqn
1809483	F/S	ANTHONY Colin Richard	2-11-44	576 Sqn
1580805	Sgt	ANTHONY Ernest	10-05-44	106 Sqn
1196006	Sgt	ANTHONY Ernest Alfred	24-03-44	12 Sqn
176446	P/O	ANTHONY Henry Roy	15-07-44	103 Sqn
1566046	Sgt	ANTHONY William Young	21-07-44	514 Sqn
1270708	Sgt	APLIN John Howard	14-01-44	432 Sqn
186317	P/O	APPERLEY Peter Samuel Glover	12-09-44	467 Sqn
2221619	Sgt	APPLEBY Charles William	13-08-44	76 Sqn
1583410	Sgt	APPLEBY Eric Ernest	29-01-44	15 Sqn
145692	F/L	APPLEBY DFC Robert Reginald George	6-01-44	35 Sqn
1600645	Sgt	APPLEGARTH Kenneth	4-05-44	460 Sqn
1724254	Sgt	APPLETON Roy Henry	31-01-44	1660 HCU
1869934	Sgt	ARBON Frederick James	2-05-44	51 Sqn
1852354	Sgt	ARBON Harold Edward	13-08-44	166 Sqn
153879	F/O	ARBON Henry George	4-11-44	51 Sqn
1894301	Sgt	ARCHARD Leonard Thomas	25-06-44	102 Sqn
135740	F/O	ARCHARD Theodore Edward	4-05-44	50 Sqn
1211168	Sgt	ARCHER Albert John Owen	30-01-44	207 Sqn
1089147	Sgt	ARCHER Alfred	12-09-44	619 Sqn
1029029	F/S	ARCHER Austin William	27-01-44	9 Sqn
1578115	Sgt	ARCHER John Derick	25-06-44	50 Sqn
1095103	AC1	ARCHER John Richard	10-04-44	Spilsby
1572931	F/S	ARCHIBALD Kenneth	13-08-44	582 Sqn
1672758	Sgt	ARCHER John Thomas	3-06-44	10 Sqn
1808696	Sgt	ARCHER Kenneth Arthur	20-02-44	49 Sqn
1822059	Sgt	ARCUS Leslie Drummond	21-07-44	467 Sqn
156647	F/O	ARGENT Edward James	14-01-44	9 Sqn
1593410	Sgt	ARGENT James William	17-06-44	3 LFS
152343	F/O	ARKLESS Leonard Nixon	20-09-44	514 Sqn
1077100	Sgt	ARLOW Thomas Alone	4-11-44	640 Sqn
568867	Sgt	ARMIN Arthur Meakin	23-05-44	57 Sqn
1685660	Sgt	ARMITAGE Brian Holt	21-07-44	12 Sqn
1548659	Sgt	ARMITAGE John Edward	11-02-44	21 OTU
172478	P/O	ARMON Arthur John Thomas	25-04-44	100 Sqn

Number	Rank	Name	Date	Sqn
142201	F/L	ARMOUR Clifford Harold	20-02-44	630 Sqn
129136	F/O	ARMOUR DFC DFM James Alexander	8-05-44	138 Sqn
1591807	Sgt	ARMSTRONG Arthur	22-06-44	49 Sqn
1317510	Sgt	ARMSTRONG Ashley John	22-03-44	100 Sqn
1795827	Sgt	ARMSTRONG David	15-06-44	115 Sqn
1673357	Sgt	ARMSTRONG Derek Souter	14-08-44	103 Sqn
2204557	Sgt	ARMSTRONG Francis Thomas	15-07-44	103 Sqn
1570702	Sgt	ARMSTRONG George	29-01-44	10 Sqn
991466	Sgt	ARMSTRONG George Robert	7-06-44	578 Sqn
953912	Sgt	ARMSTRONG John	23-04-44	77 Sqn
54454	P/O	ARMSTRONG Joseph	10-03-44	90 Sqn
1684332	Sgt	ARMSTRONG Joseph	21-07-44	75 Sqn
188127	P/O	ARMSTRONG Kenneth Robert	18-11-44	578 Sqn
1382421	F/S	ARMSTRONG Phillip Heriot	15-03-44	77 Sqn
172414	F/O	ARMSTRONG Robert	29-07-44	103 Sqn
1135120	F/S	ARMSTRONG Robert	6-08-44	50 Sqn
1567337	Sgt	ARMSTRONG Robert	31-03-44	101 Sqn
111560	F/L	ARMSTRONG DFC Robert Gow	27-04-44	49 Sqn
1674487	Sgt	ARMSTRONG Robert Lionel	6-11-44	106 Sqn
177963	P/O	ARMSTRONG DFM Thomas Alan	13-09-44	1655 MTU
173604	P/O	ARNEIL Adam Scott	31-03-44	76 Sqn
154683	F/O	ARNETT Dennis Sullivan	11-11-44	44 Sqn
1861330	Sgt	ARNOLD Frederick Robert	27-07-44	630 Sqn
1330980	F/S	ARNOLD Leonard William John	9-05-44	83 Sqn
125382	F/O	ARNOLD Philip Sydney	7-06-44	106 Sqn
1890774	Sgt	ARNOLD Ronald Frank	4-05-44	166 Sqn
1000377	Sgt	ARNOLD Sydney John	16-03-44	12 Sqn
1515414	Sgt	ARNOLD Thomas	27-03-44	10 Sqn
1425524	F/S	ARTHUR Douglas Alexander	20-01-44	10 Sqn
1584922	Sgt	ARTHUR Lewis John	3-08-44	166 Sqn
1393681	Sgt	ARTHUR Robert Geoffrey	24-03-44	578 Sqn
1821788	Sgt	ARTHUR Robert Peter	21-01-44	578 Sqn
46630	F/L	ASH Cedric John Keenth	12-06-44	635 Sqn
129520	F/L	ASH DFC George Henry [USA]	27-11-44	161 Sqn
1399276	Sgt	ASH John Thomas	1-07-44	625 Sqn
574407	Sgt	ASHBY Arthur	26-07-44	49 Sqn
1817180	Sgt	ASHCROFT Albert John	27-10-44	49 Sqn
112736	F/L	ASHCROFT DFC Alfred Edward 'David'	6-10-44	157 Sqn
151325	F/O	ASHCROFT Charles	16-05-44	576 Sqn
1578476	F/S	ASHCROFT Francis Robert	16-07-44	15 Sqn
1581428	Sgt	ASHCROFT Philip Kennedy	24-12-44	103 Sqn
151215	F/O	ASHFORD Albert Henry [USA]	30-01-44	405 Sqn
574775	Sgt	ASHFORD Christopher Maurice	21-07-44	158 Sqn
1048795	Sgt	ASHLEY Cecil	29-11-44	12 Sqn
1581756	Sgt	ASHLEY William George	25-07-44	1655 MTU
106567	F/L	ASHMAN Herbert Leonard	25-05-44	7 Sqn
1866432	Sgt	ASHPOLE Gerald John James	6-06-44	97 Sqn
1396278	Sgt	ASHTON Derek Kilgour [Peru]	27-01-44	166 Sqn
1892578	Sgt	ASHTON Edwin	13-07-44	166 Sqn
172209	P/O	ASHTON DFM John Norman Stephen	12-02-44	419 Sqn
1459213	Sgt	ASHTON Leo	21-01-44	77 Sqn
1437584	F/S	ASHTON Tom	31-03-44	44 Sqn
1439160	Sgt	ASHURST William	15-02-44	625 Sqn
1594580	Sgt	ASHWELL Harry	14-07-44	77 Sqn
519749	Sgt	ASHWORTH Earnshaw	6-12-44	61 Sqn
169692	P/O	ASHWORTH DFM Harry	17-02-44	1409 Flt
1389734	F/S	ASKER William Francis	8-07-44	83 Sqn
1399198	F/S	ASKIE Richard Edward Leslie	12-09-44	625 Sqn
1682446	Sgt	ASKWITH Dennis	13-06-44	578 Sqn
54222	P/O	ASLETT Percy Ronald	23-04-44	7 Sqn
1579265	F/S	ASPELL Kenneth James	22-11-44	630 Sqn
1437583	W/O	ASPEY DFM William	8-08-44	7 Sqn
171216	P/O	ASPIN DFM James Desmond	20-02-44	625 Sqn
1457155	F/S	ASPIN Vincent Earle	31-03-44	635 Sqn
1800248	Sgt	ASPINALL Glyn Robert 'Bob'	14-04-44	5 LFS
1101769	F/S	ASPINALL DFM Harry	23-04-44	61 Sqn
1453321	Sgt	ASPINALL Kenneth	3-01-44	156 Sqn
1606369	Sgt	ASPINELL Derek Charles Ernest	30-08-44	115 Sqn
1331865	Sgt	ASPLEN Raymond John	31-03-44	622 Sqn
1143274	Sgt	ASQUITH David Beaumont	20-02-44	166 Sqn
1684723	Sgt	ASQUITH Denis	23-05-44	166 Sqn
2211524	Sgt	ASTALL Clifford	12-08-44	76 Sqn
172418	P/O	ASTBURY Thomas Edwin	23-04-44	103 Sqn
177562	P/O	ASTLE DFC Alfred	24-09-44	156 Sqn
2211645	Sgt	ASTLEY William Edward	8-06-44	115 Sqn
1866959	Sgt	ASTON Ronald Leonard 'Ron'	23-05-44	90 Sqn
161591	P/O	ATCHESON DFC Samuel Cunningham	16-03-44	57 Sqn
1542940	Sgt	ATHA Phil	22-03-44	100 Sqn
1358514	Sgt	ATHERTON Cyril	28-01-44	199 Sqn
162805	P/O	ATHERTON James Lever	28-04-44	166 Sqn
1575432	Sgt	ATHEY Rex Ward	11-06-44	7 Sqn
1451056	Sgt	ATKIN Ronald James	5-07-44	9 Sqn
172115	P/O	ATKIN Samuel Stephen	20-05-44	115 Sqn
1603538	Sgt	ATKINS Frederick Thomas George	18-04-44	1657 HCU
144756	F/O	ATKINS Kenneth Leslie	15-02-44	103 Sqn
1895451	Sgt	ATKINS Norman Arthur	16-10-44	115 Sqn
148720	F/O	ATKINS Reginald Clifford Cooke	26-08-44	97 Sqn
1582830	Sgt	ATKINS William Goodson	21-01-44	432 Sqn
169678	P/O	ATKINSON Cyril (served as REED)	4-05-44	101 Sqn
1396885	F/S	ATKINSON Dennis	31-03-44	115 Sqn
1603962	F/S	ATKINSON Edgar David	4-11-44	640 Sqn
2216077	Sgt	ATKINSON Eric	2-01-44	626 Sqn
1622202	Sgt	ATKINSON Eric Raymond	30-08-44	90 Sqn
150377	F/O	ATKINSON Herbert Thomas George	27-08-44	12 Sqn
1022291	Sgt	ATKINSON John	21-04-44	619 Sqn
970210	Sgt	ATKINSON John Anthony	22-01-44	467 Sqn
173151	P/O	ATKINSON John Latimer [Portugal]	13-02-44	169 Sqn
173072	P/O	ATKINSON John Leslie	31-03-44	635 Sqn
613970	Sgt	ATKINSON Joseph	28-12-44	419 Sqn
1893014	Sgt	ATKINSON Ralph Ian	17-08-44	433 Sqn
1525378	Sgt	ATKINSON Richard Graham	24-03-44	207 Sqn
132865	F/O	ATKINSON Thomas Ralston	21-02-44	640 Sqn
187342	P/O	ATKINSON Wilfred George	19-10-44	161 Sqn
1580420	Sgt	ATTENBORROW Eric	16-07-44	15 Sqn
1817884	Sgt	ATTER Cyril Ernest	11-12-44	514 Sqn
182784	P/O	ATTERTON Alfred William	9-08-44	138 Sqn
1292143	Sgt	AULT William George	23-04-44	101 Sqn
143845	F/L	AUNGIERS Graham Bice	20-07-44	109 Sqn
1267017	Sgt	AUSTIN Derrick	8-07-44	50 Sqn
1005440	F/S	AUSTIN Herbert Ingle	23-04-44	429 Sqn
176233	F/O	AUSTIN John Prescott	18-08-44	103 Sqn
1320627	F/S	AUSTIN John William	29-06-44	582 Sqn
1872833	F/S	AUSTIN Kenneth Herbert	31-12-44	626 Sqn
1603415	Sgt	AUSTIN Maxwell	20-10-44	550 Sqn
175050	P/O	AUSTIN William Herbert	12-06-44	101 Sqn
1675798	Sgt	AUTY Eric	15-02-44	12 Sqn
628423	Sgt	AVER Francis Alfred	29-01-44	467 Sqn
1041908	F/S	AVERY James Victor	2-03-44	15 OTU
1808102	Sgt	AVIET Philip Bodein	30-08-44	460 Sqn
54664	P/O	AXTON Robert Henry	11-04-44	640 Sqn
658985	Sgt	AYRE Algernon Early William	12-05-44	61 Sqn
922274	F/S	AYRES Alfred	25-03-44	640 Sqn
1865089	Sgt	AYRES Alfred William Walter	11-04-44	625 Sqn
1817751	Sgt	AYRES Cyril George	5-10-44	1666 HCU
1505092	Sgt	AYRES Leonard	6-12-44	61 Sqn
1623324	F/S	AYRES Leonard Reuben	24-12-44	166 Sqn
170269	P/O	AYRES Robert Frederick	28-05-44	626 Sqn
1575190	Sgt	BACHE Dennis Frederick	20-01-44	622 Sqn
1800174	Sgt	BACHELOR Albert Ernest	25-05-44	576 Sqn
2210786	Sgt	BACKHOUSE Leslie	14-06-44	11 OTU
115404	F/L	BACON Arthur Albert	17-09-44	1652 HCU
132592	F/L	BACON DFC Donovan John	11-04-44	49 Sqn
151232	F/O	BACON Douglas Alfred	22-05-44	50 Sqn
1581501	Sgt	BADGER Victor John	26-07-44	166 Sqn
152517	F/O	BAGG Robert Percy McMillan	14-01-44	101 Sqn

Service No	Rank	Name	Date	Sqn
1492185	Sgt	BAGGALEY Joseph	6-11-44	463 Sqn
1577534	Sgt	BAGNALL George	16-03-44	35 Sqn
820005	F/S	BAGSHAW Charles	20-02-44	103 Sqn
1165133	Sgt	BAGULEY Peter	13-09-44	218 Sqn
1852464	Sgt	BAIGENT Peter Henry	8-07-44	61 Sqn
152530	F/O	BAILES Richard	30-04-44	460 Sqn
1603676	Sgt	BAILEY Albert Ronald	20-02-44	166 Sqn
1048169	Sgt	BAILEY Anthony John Martin Francis	2-07-44	1667 HCU
1319907	Sgt	BAILEY Charles Ronald	30-01-44	207 Sqn
1235079	Sgt	BAILEY Clifford	26-03-44	49 Sqn
1060826	F/S	BAILEY Eric	4-05-44	101 Sqn
1818101	Sgt	BAILEY Eric Hargreaves	28-10-44	1661 HCU
1537395	F/S	BAILEY George	20-02-44	158 Sqn
1868473	Sgt	BAILEY George Edward	19-04-44	115 Sqn
1601442	Sgt	BAILEY Harry James	6-12-44	550 Sqn
1591915	Sgt	BAILEY James	4-05-44	101 Sqn
153630	F/O	BAILEY Paul Bernard	11-09-44	514 Sqn
1338873	F/S	BAILEY Peter Alan Gainsford	23-05-44	100 Sqn
1297999	F/S	BAILEY DFM Reginald Charles	22-06-44	83 Sqn
1398336	F/S	BAILEY Reginald Charles	22-01-44	35 Sqn
3006845	Sgt	BAILEY Robert Arthur George	14-08-44	20 OTU
1807199	Sgt	BAILEY Roger Francis Geoffrey	1-09-44	138 Sqn
170965	P/O	BAILEY Ronald Walter	22-05-44	630 Sqn
153012	F/O	BAILEY Sydney James	25-06-44	102 Sqn
2220975	Sgt	BAILEY Thomas William	26-03-44	460 Sqn
1585910	Sgt	BAILEY Victor George	9-01-44	16 OTU
1821620	Sgt	BAIN James Stuart	22-12-44	630 Sqn
1334065	W/O	BAINES Alfred Peter	29-07-44	582 Sqn
1051646	F/S	BAINES William	15-02-44	77 Sqn
168515	P/O	BAIRD John Humphreys	21-02-44	640 Sqn
1567843	Sgt	BAIRD Ronald Jackson	14-04-44	9 Sqn
1676545	Sgt	BAKE Edmund	31-03-44	640 Sqn
1087406	F/S	BAKER Alfred	25-04-44	619 Sqn
1724295	Sgt	BAKER Alfred Douglas	13-07-44	550 Sqn
1895850	Sgt	BAKER Arthur Charles Henry	8-07-44	57 Sqn
2235491	Sgt	BAKER Arthur Fred	28-10-44	12 OTU
1397018	Sgt	BAKER Arthur Stanley	6-01-44	576 Sqn
1600504	Sgt	BAKER Charles Henry	16-03-44	115 Sqn
55889	P/O	BAKER Charles Richard Henry	12-09-44	158 Sqn
1583703	Sgt	BAKER Christopher Thomas	20-02-44	463 Sqn
175921	F/O	BAKER Cyril	8-07-44	49 Sqn
152761	F/O	BAKER David	25-09-44	576 Sqn
54076	P/O	BAKER Francis William	4-05-44	460 Sqn
656153	F/S	BAKER Frederick Basil	25-04-44	626 Sqn
146594	F/O	BAKER Frederick John	25-04-44	619 Sqn
1710506	Sgt	BAKER Frederick Robert William	23-09-44	207 Sqn
162508	F/O	BAKER Geoffrey Anthony	22-06-44	619 Sqn
157833	F/O	BAKER George	4-05-44	101 Sqn
1358880	F/S	BAKER George Arthur	29-01-44	30 OTU
1814627	Sgt	BAKER Henry George	26-08-44	75 Sqn
1602984	Sgt	BAKER Herbert Samuel	12-05-44	15 Sqn
151315	F/L	BAKER Howard Warburton	8-09-44	582 Sqn
116391	F/O	BAKER Hugh Anthony Ballantine [Jamaica]	30-07-44	97 Sqn
120393	S/L	BAKER DSO DFC John	20-05-44	7 Sqn
1852412	Sgt	BAKER Keith Russell	13-06-44	514 Sqn
174632	P/O	BAKER Leslie Jack	23-05-44	9 Sqn
1265506	Sgt	BAKER Reginald Wilfred	24-12-44	103 Sqn
1624103	Sgt	BAKER Robert Charles	25-07-44	75 Sqn
1354336	W/O	BAKER Ronald Charles William Gibson	23-05-44	97 Sqn
151360	F/O	BAKER Roy Barry	2-01-44	44 Sqn
1399043	Sgt	BAKER Terence Charles	31-03-44	49 Sqn
1719963	Sgt	BAKER Victor George	21-01-44	434 Sqn
1809164	Sgt	BAKER William George	25-03-44	78 Sqn
1240198	Sgt	BALAAM Ernest	22-01-44	44 Sqn
1583083	Sgt	BALDRY Cecil Malcolm	22-01-44	578 Sqn
1579824	Sgt	BALDWIN Albert Hankinson	13-08-44	467 Sqn
130728	F/L	BALDWIN DFM Alexander James	17-05-44	571 Sqn
1411466	Sgt	BALDWIN Bernard Henry John	20-02-44	207 Sqn
176493	P/O	BALDWIN Bernard Oliver	25-05-44	158 Sqn
1492362	Sgt	BALDWIN George Jesse	23-08-44	1657 HCU
1818187	Sgt	BALDWIN John	31-03-44	156 Sqn
1396686	F/S	BALDWIN Leonard Stanley	26-08-44	97 Sqn
1825182	Sgt	BALDWIN Leslie Harold	18-03-44	51 Sqn
1894597	Sgt	BALE Alan Dennis	17-04-44	5 LFS
976784	Sgt	BALE Frank Edwin Fricker	6-09-44	57 Sqn
150127	F/O	BALES Peter Richard	21-01-44	35 Sqn
1438060	Sgt	BALL Alex William Charles	3-01-44	57 Sqn
1322511	F/S	BALL Donald Faulkner	11-05-44	50 Sqn
1161312	Sgt	BALL Frederick Charles	12-02-44	50 Sqn
170964	F/L	BALL DFC George Edward	8-07-44	49 Sqn
46312	F/L	BALL John Potter	8-08-44	15 Sqn
658450	F/S	BALL Kenneth Richard	30-01-44	156 Sqn
169125	F/O	BALL Peter William	22-06-44	207 Sqn
1587414	Sgt	BALL Robert Walter	22-05-44	576 Sqn
1082323	Sgt	BALLANTYNE John Robinson	3-02-44	84 OTU
47517	F/L	BALLANTYNE DFM Raymond Robert Stanley	15-02-44	7 Sqn
1823293	Sgt	BALLANTYNE Thomas	12-09-44	467 Sqn
978237	F/S	BALLARD William Arthur	16-03-44	578 Sqn
1836236	Sgt	BALLINGER William Stanley	13-08-44	101 Sqn
1853283	Sgt	BALLS Donald Albert Oliver	31-12-44	150 Sqn
1852397	Sgt	BALMAN John Henry	11-12-44	514 Sqn
1589924	F/S	BALMER James	8-07-44	106 Sqn
1591013	Sgt	BALMFORTH Dennis	8-06-44	78 Sqn
160069	F/O	BALSDON Desmond Ernest [Rhodesia]	9-06-44	44 Sqn
933476	Sgt	BALSER Charles Arthur	8-07-44	61 Sqn
177515	F/O	BAMBEROUGH Robert	23-09-44	12 Sqn
153126	F/O	BAMBURY Joseph John	26-07-44	141 Sqn
1043241	W/O	BAMFORD Philip Edward	9-07-44	622 Sqn
626388	F/S	BAMFORD Tom	8-06-44	115 Sqn
1439184	F/S	BANCROFT William Stuart	13-07-44	103 Sqn
1832773	Sgt	BANFIELD Clive Walter	11-04-44	514 Sqn
1357410	F/S	BANHAM Alan	8-06-44	166 Sqn
1580816	Sgt	BANKS Charles	26-03-44	626 Sqn
149056	F/L	BANKS Cyril Alfred	18-12-44	227 Sqn
1428222	Sgt	BANKS Eric George	8-07-44	106 Sqn
1091782	Sgt	BANKS Joseph	3-01-44	83 Sqn
2205640	Sgt	BANKS Peter	15-12-44	625 Sqn
147209	F/L	BANKS Robert	13-09-44	625 Sqn
173519	F/L	BANKS Robert James Lloyd	12-09-44	7 Sqn
1755008	Sgt	BANKS Ronald Frederick	20-02-44	466 Sqn
1007262	F/S	BANNAN Joseph Bernard	10-04-44	635 Sqn
3040779	Sgt	BAPTIST Robert	6-08-44	51 Sqn
1458414	F/S	BARBER Albert Roy	11-05-44	467 Sqn
1425737	Sgt	BARBER Arthur	25-06-44	149 Sqn
1819384	Sgt	BARBER Brian Samuel	13-08-44	101 Sqn
1339953	Sgt	BARBER Dennis Albert	25-04-44	12 OTU
1455924	Sgt	BARBER George Peter	27-09-44	1654 HCU
1589519	Sgt	BARBER John Douglas	22-06-44	44 Sqn
1593780	Sgt	BARBER Joseph	22-05-44	100 Sqn
1807492	Sgt	BARBER Josiah Trevor	8-08-44	90 Sqn
1620366	Sgt	BARBER Lewis Randall	21-07-44	578 Sqn
1577217	Sgt	BARBER Raymond Charles	13-06-44	12 Sqn
1216017	Sgt	BARBER Sidney Basil	9-04-44	460 Sqn
1349602	Sgt	BARBOUR Robert Ross	2-01-44	61 Sqn
1569993	Sgt	BARCLAY Arthur	14-01-44	576 Sqn
173589	P/O	BARCLAY James	22-03-44	44 Sqn
1451841	F/S	BARDEN Henry Keith	24-03-44	78 Sqn
3000648	Sgt	BAREHAM Maurice Archibald Victor	1-11-44	429 Sqn
147510	F/O	BARHAM Douglas Reginald	22-03-44	207 Sqn
137581	F/O	BARHAM Leonard Alfred	25-09-44	199 Sqn
1307841	Sgt	BARHAM Stanley George Rayner	13-06-44	78 Sqn
1437565	F/S	BARK Eric Walter	25-05-44	7 Sqn
1896771	Sgt	BARKER Anthony	27-07-44	44 Sqn
1621971	Sgt	BARKER Arthur	9-12-44	21 OTU
1392337	Sgt	BARKER Bernard Andrew	11-07-44	1666 HCU

156282	F/O	BARKER Ernest William Henry	13-09-44	158 Sqn		1538450	F/S	BARRINGTON George Henry	29-01-44	630 Sqn
1623707	Sgt	BARKER Frederick Cecil	26-02-44	427 Sqn		527275	Sgt	BARRON Cedric Jack	29-01-44	466 Sqn
1894666	Sgt	BARKER Gerald Gordon	13-06-44	460 Sqn		1556406	Sgt	BARRON Harry	30-06-44	51 Sqn
1624738	Sgt	BARKER John Douglas	21-01-44	514 Sqn		1345933	Sgt	BARRON John Faulds	18-04-44	433 Sqn
1893502	Sgt	BARKER John Skinner	26-02-44	207 Sqn		1822881	Sgt	BARRON Robert James	21-11-44	78 Sqn
146946	F/O	BARKER DFM Kenneth Stowell Harrison				1669770	AC1	BARROW Royston Clifford	28-12-44	347 Sqn
			21-07-44	97 Sqn		1010397	F/S	BARRY George	2-01-44	156 Sqn
916712	Sgt	BARKER Leonard William	8-07-44	17 OTU		1490130	Sgt	BARRY Kenneth Walter	30-01-44	106 Sqn
1896457	Sgt	BARKER Norman	19-07-44	630 Sqn		1391654	W/O	BARRY Terence Patrick	29-07-44	576 Sqn
1238928	Sgt	BARKER Raymond	4-05-44	207 Sqn		1880819	Sgt	BARSBY George Edward	22-12-44	189 Sqn
2220930	Sgt	BARKER Robert Grainger	12-09-44	625 Sqn		1324529	Sgt	BARSON Jack Frank Macdonald	21-07-44	75 Sqn
131052	F/O	BARKLEY Hugh Alastair	16-02-44	640 Sqn		1864380	Sgt	BARSS Monty	13-08-44	101 Sqn
1893996	Sgt	BARKSHIRE Albert Leslie	8-08-44	15 Sqn		152006	F/O	BARTER Stuart Percival	28-05-44	626 Sqn
176232	P/O	BARLEY Edward	5-07-44	1667 HCU		1391800	F/S	BARTHOLOMEW Ernest Frederick	27-01-44	7 Sqn
1579353	Sgt	BARLOW Albert Kenneth	20-02-44	166 Sqn		53826	P/O	BARTHOLOMEW DFC John Arthur	21-02-44	97 Sqn
2206468	Sgt	BARLOW Donald Vincent	9-07-44	622 Sqn				[South Africa]		
1450108	Sgt	BARLOW Edward Stanley	5-01-44	431 Sqn		1605920	Sgt	BARTHOLOMEW Kenneth	27-01-44	101 Sqn
1603320	F/S	BARLOW Leonard	6-08-44	97 Sqn		1386260	Sgt	BARTINGTON John Percival	21-01-44	1653 HCU
1318860	Sgt	BARLOW Peter Sidney	8-01-44	138 Sqn		2220686	Sgt	BARTLE Charles Mayo	6-12-44	227 Sqn
1807428	Sgt	BARLOW Reginald Dennis	15-03-44	11 OTU		145148	F/L	BARTLEET John Peter Dennis	14-08-44	103 Sqn
1578220	F/S	BARLOW Ronald Kenneth 'Ron'	11-04-44	12 Sqn		39928	W/C	BARTLETT DFC* Christopher Smales	13-06-44	434 Sqn
178232	P/O	BARNARD Leslie James	23-06-44	76 Sqn				[USA]		
1313002	F/S	BARNARD Michael Charles	14-01-44	1653 HCU		170963	P/O	BARTLETT Cyril Alfred	8-05-44	106 Sqn
1800728	Sgt	BARNDEN John Walton	7-10-44	166 Sqn		1608803	Sgt	BARTLETT Kenneth Charles	6-01-44	103 Sqn
1323215	F/S	BARNES Alan Douglas	3-01-44	156 Sqn		1850398	F/S	BARTLETT Rodney Claude	6-11-44	214 Sqn
54095	P/O	BARNES Albert Edward	14-01-44	166 Sqn		1311036	F/S	BARTLEY Frederick William	15-02-44	424 Sqn
1803398	Sgt	BARNES Charles Clarence	12-06-44	101 Sqn		168669	F/O	BARTON VC Cyril Joe	31-03-44	578 Sqn
1819399	Sgt	BARNES Clarence	14-08-44	103 Sqn		1814488	Sgt	BARTON Donald Edward	2-03-44	156 Sqn
958297	F/S	BARNES Donald Arthur	27-08-44	576 Sqn		1622233	Sgt	BARTON John	31-12-44	218 Sqn
1867595	Sgt	BARNES Kenneth Victor	22-06-44	207 Sqn		1385704	F/S	BARTON Kenneth Frederick Fisher	6-01-44	576 Sqn
542608	Sgt	BARNES Raymond	30-07-44	106 Sqn		1894713	Sgt	BARTON Ronald Pascoe	6-10-44	106 Sqn
1385975	F/S	BARNES Robert Edward	23-04-44	15 Sqn		1621407	Sgt	BARTON Thomas	30-08-44	103 Sqn
1337287	F/S	BARNES Roy Haywood	21-07-44	9 Sqn		1523188	Sgt	BARTRAM Ronald	17-06-44	102 Sqn
127345	F/L	BARNES DFC Roy Laurence	15-02-44	7 Sqn		187752	P/O	BARTY William Edward Heaton	6-12-44	429 Sqn
135727	F/L	BARNES DFC William George	11-04-44	10 Sqn		156340	F/O	BASEDEN Geoffrey Thomas	8-07-44	9 Sqn
1577045	F/S	BARNETT Alfred John	25-02-44	467 Sqn		1223167	Sgt	BASFORD Leslie Eric	17-06-44	640 Sqn
1431543	F/S	BARNETT Frederick William	23-04-44	12 Sqn		1580529	Sgt	BASFORD Ronald Barnard	2-03-44	76 Sqn
1624095	Sgt	BARNETT Kenneth Gordon	1-07-44	625 Sqn		151158	F/O	BASHI Edward [Iraq]	28-04-44	100 Sqn
1584724	Sgt	BARNETT Stanley Sutton	30-08-44	300 Sqn		1044212	Sgt	BASKOTT Anthony William	29-04-44	12 Sqn
1174351	Sgt	BARNETT Thomas James	24-03-44	158 Sqn		2203637	Sgt	BASSETT Derek Alfred	21-07-44	90 Sqn
1571360	Sgt	BARNETT Thomas Scott	21-07-44	578 Sqn		1423298	Sgt	BASSMAN Leon Asher	4-10-44	550 Sqn
2235180	Sgt	BARNETT William John	5-09-44	84 OTU		1399763	Sgt	BASTEN Henry George	25-02-44	408 Sqn
1665785	Sgt	BARNICOAT Ronald Ernest	29-07-44	425 Sqn		1581875	Sgt	BATCHELOR Christopher Richard	21-02-44	115 Sqn
155493	F/L	BARNSDALE Frank Sharpe	11-04-44	576 Sqn		1324664	Sgt	BATCHOUSKI William Joseph	31-03-44	78 Sqn
1389866	Sgt	BARON Donald John Kelsall	30-08-44	300 Sqn		1584852	Sgt	BATE Howard Joseph	16-11-44	15 Sqn
149632	F/O	BARON Edgar Harold	18-12-44	51 Sqn		1865972	Sgt	BATEMAN Charles Geoffrey Gordon	24-03-44	626 Sqn
658353	F/S	BARON Ernest Emmanuel	27-01-44	101 Sqn		1482192	Sgt	BATEMAN John William	3-01-44	103 Sqn
177680	P/O	BARR Adam John McDowall	17-06-44	102 Sqn		146944	F/O	BATEMAN Kenneth	8-06-44	138 Sqn
1522161	F/S	BARR David Murray	13-09-44	166 Sqn		1447334	Sgt	BATEMAN Lawrence David	25-07-44	207 Sqn
179995	F/O	BARR Dennis	13-08-44	640 Sqn		632703	Sgt	BATEMAN Robert	14-01-44	101 Sqn
905950	Sgt	BARR Larry Howard Jesse	19-03-44	578 Sqn		175422	P/O	BATES Albert	25-05-44	429 Sqn
1027529	Sgt	BARR Peter	26-08-44	622 Sqn		1082214	F/S	BATES Edwin	31-03-44	138 Sqn
1475695	Sgt	BARR Stanley James	4-05-44	576 Sqn		1622071	Sgt	BATES Fred	31-05-44	1654 HCU
134083	F/L	BARRASS John Morgan	24-12-44	166 Sqn		1479898	Sgt	BATES John Esprey [Eire]	31-03-44	156 Sqn
55950	F/O	BARRATT Edgar	16-12-44	106 Sqn		1391048	Sgt	BATES Philip Charles	1-03-44	76 Sqn
1890310	Sgt	BARRATT Roy Stanley	15-03-44	149 Sqn		1600459	Sgt	BATES Raymond Leonard	26-02-44	431 Sqn
1684379	Sgt	BARRATT Thomas	16-06-44	7 Sqn		1816580	Sgt	BATES Sidney	14-01-44	12 Sqn
2209552	Sgt	BARRATT Wilfrid	31-03-44	550 Sqn		1044422	W/O	BATES Wilfrid Armstrong	18-12-44	51 Sqn
992916	F/S	BARRELL Ernest Rowe Newton	20-04-44	635 Sqn		1585341	Sgt	BATES William Alexander	20-02-44	514 Sqn
1277169	F/S	BARRET Hugh	23-04-44	640 Sqn		1851600	Sgt	BATHAM Raymond John	29-04-44	15 Sqn
1018655	LAC	BARRETT Alfred Gallagher	10-04-44	Spilsby		1395700	F/S	BATHE John Raymond	25-04-44	76 Sqn
1896411	Sgt	BARRETT Arthur Courtney	8-07-44	207 Sqn		1892488	Sgt	BATHMAKER Francis Henry	28-04-44	101 Sqn
61470	S/L	BARRETT DFC Charles Rene	13-09-44	608 Sqn		146951	F/O	BATT Harold Weston	3-05-44	550 Sqn
150205	F/O	BARRETT Ernest Malcolm	21-04-44	30 OTU		171042	P/O	BATTEN-SMITH DFC John [India]	31-03-44	101 Sqn
1516278	Sgt	BARRETT Fred	30-01-44	467 Sqn		1873692	F/S	BATTERBEE Ernest Arthur	19-08-44	7 Sqn
1623973	F/S	BARRETT George Arthur	28-11-44	166 Sqn		998897	F/S	BATTERSBY Geoffrey Wilkinson	30-08-44	550 Sqn
1467119	Sgt	BARRETT Leonard Charles	26-02-44	12 Sqn		549512	Sgt	BATTY Ronald John Morton	21-07-44	75 Sqn
1315330	Sgt	BARRETT Robert Dennis Parker	28-04-44	1658 HCU		1593608	Sgt	BATTYE Edmund	21-11-44	49 Sqn
1338081	F/S	BARRINGER Ronald Alfred	13-08-44	83 Sqn		151367	F/O	BATTYE Harold Knowles	20-02-44	630 Sqn

131985	F/O	BAUGHAN Robert Leonard	28-03-44	161 Sqn
1893164	Sgt	BAWTREE Joseph Eric	13-06-44	166 Sqn
1079189	F/S	BAXENDALE Robert	30-08-44	635 Sqn
1750006	P/O	BAXTER George	22-06-44	44 Sqn
1392861	Sgt	BAXTER Henry Alfred	16-03-44	463 Sqn
1251291	W/O	BAXTER DFM John Charles	31-03-44	156 Sqn
1388976	Sgt	BAXTER Kenneth William John	21-01-44	115 Sqn
1821358	Sgt	BAXTER William Allan	1-09-44	138 Sqn
185783	P/O	BAYES Joseph Thomas	4-11-44	75 Sqn
531871	Sgt	BAYFORD Cyril	11-11-44	57 Sqn
55015	F/L	BAYLEY Alan Frederick	22-06-44	57 Sqn
658573	F/S	BAYLEY Richard Frederick	31-03-44	12 Sqn
1580230	F/S	BAYLISS Cyril Ernest	1-11-44	106 Sqn
1106297	Sgt	BAYLISS Dennis Alfred	27-11-44	189 Sqn
1622664	Sgt	BAYLISS Donald George	16-03-44	625 Sqn
1054757	Sgt	BAYNES Charles James	25-07-44	103 Sqn
3031437	Sgt	BAYTON Jack Colbrook	12-12-44	195 Sqn
118131	S/L	BAZALGETTE VC DFC Ian Willoughby [Canada]	4-08-44	635 Sqn
907053	Sgt	BEACH Alfred Kenneth	6-11-44	57 Sqn
1567112	Sgt	BEACH William	28-01-44	61 Sqn
1587896	Sgt	BEACHAM Ernest Cecil	22-05-44	550 Sqn
172304	P/O	BEADLE Robert Eugene	16-05-44	625 Sqn
1891000	Sgt	BEAGLEY John Oliver	23-05-44	100 Sqn
1803550	Sgt	BEAL George	20-02-44	78 Sqn
1891083	Sgt	BEAN David Arthur	16-03-44	76 Sqn
48487	F/L	BEAN Harry	17-08-44	97 Sqn
138406	F/O	BEARCROFT Albert Bramwell	3-01-44	619 Sqn
1591348	Sgt	BEARD Eric	15-07-44	103 Sqn
1601748	Sgt	BEARD Peter Franklyn	22-03-44	78 Sqn
1818755	Sgt	BEARDMORE John Thomas	4-11-44	75 Sqn
1578410	F/S	BEARDSHAW John George	17-12-44	57 Sqn
1580939	F/S	BEARDSMORE William James Henry	29-07-44	103 Sqn
1609756	Sgt	BEARE Eric Sydney	21-07-44	51 Sqn
152243	F/O	BEARNE Hugh William Vaughan	4-05-44	12 Sqn
144343	F/O	BEATON John Mackenzie	29-07-44	467 Sqn
152544	F/O	BEATSON Cyril	6-10-44	49 Sqn
1824754	Sgt	BEATTIE Alan	27-04-44	156 Sqn
1822489	Sgt	BEATTIE James Elliot	30-01-44	156 Sqn
1852569	F/S	BEATTIE Leonard Frank	12-09-44	626 Sqn
1544120	F/L	BEATTIE William Henry Taylor	10-05-44	90 Sqn
1532959	Sgt	BEATTIE William Walker	15-07-44	576 Sqn
1107864	F/S	BEAUMONT Arthur	22-03-44	432 Sqn
140860	F/O	BEAUMONT John Edward	31-03-44	460 Sqn
162506	F/L	BEAUMONT DFC Ronald Alfred William	22-06-44	57 Sqn
1626908	Sgt	BEBINGTON Ernest Egerton	16-03-44	12 Sqn
1681254	Sgt	BECHEREL Roland Jean [Mauritius]	10-05-44	50 Sqn
1381726	W/O	BECK DFC Dennis Maurice	13-08-44	83 Sqn
710131	Sgt	BECKLEY Maurice George [Rhodesia]	4-11-44	44 Sqn
134748	F/L	BECKLEY Robert James	11-10-44	1655 MTU
1399602	Sgt	BECKWITH Frederick William Walter	28-06-44	460 Sqn
913881	F/S	BEDDISON Brian Derek	25-06-44	50 Sqn
129540	F/L	BEDELL DFC* Cecil Ford	14-08-44	83 Sqn
169914	P/O	BEDFORD Frank Reginald	7-03-44	18 OTU
1543670	Sgt	BEDFORD Horace	9-08-44	138 Sqn
1853408	F/S	BEDGGOOD Arthur Henry	27-11-44	138 Sqn
1250631	Sgt	BEDWELL George Frederick Kenneth	2-01-44	9 Sqn
1125712	Sgt	BEEBY Frank	27-08-44	1661 HCU
1584473	Sgt	BEECH Cyril	5-03-44	75 Sqn
658022	Sgt	BEECH James	25-07-44	207 Sqn
1606782	Sgt	BEECHEY David Henry	19-04-44	625 Sqn
176445	F/O	BEECHEY Walter Ronald	4-11-44	640 Sqn
1438194	F/S	BEECROFT Jack	8-09-44	582 Sqn
2201738	Sgt	BEECROFT Robert Gordon	13-08-44	115 Sqn
1594241	Sgt	BEEDLE George	5-07-44	1667 HCU
126822	F/O	BEER DFC Bernard Arthur William	30-01-44	115 Sqn
178145	P/O	BEER Gordon William	4-05-44	420 Sqn
172469	P/O	BEER Howard Ernest	31-03-44	101 Sqn
179985	F/O	BEER Leslie William	18-12-44	50 Sqn
151422	F/O	BEER Raymond Henry	28-05-44	103 Sqn
1170688	Sgt	BEER Reginald Henry	5-12-44	84 OTU
619840	F/S	BEERE Walter Harold	15-02-44	77 Sqn
1391522	F/S	BEESLEY Douglas Richard	11-04-44	61 Sqn
1874381	Sgt	BEESON Jack Edward	29-06-44	76 Sqn
1594564	Sgt	BEESON Joseph	2-11-44	576 Sqn
1389096	Sgt	BEESON William Joseph	16-06-44	635 Sqn
145379	F/O	BEETCH Alan Victor	27-01-44	61 Sqn
1595071	Sgt	BEEVERS George Henry	29-06-44	12 Sqn
149515	F/O	BEGERNIE Albert Henry James	19-07-44	619 Sqn
1436510	F/S	BEGG James	29-01-44	429 Sqn
179702	F/O	BEGG William	23-09-44	9 Sqn
1318936	Sgt	BEILBY Peter Raymond	31-03-44	625 Sqn
1175252	Sgt	BELL Alistair Walker	3-01-44	83 Sqn
147665	F/O	BELL Andrew Allan	27-04-44	78 Sqn
1050826	Sgt	BELL Arthur	15-01-44	626 Sqn
1677308	Sgt	BELL Brian Atkinson	1-04-44	1656 HCU
151471	F/O	BELL Bryan Esmond	10-06-44	49 Sqn
173058	P/O	BELL Cyril	4-05-44	207 Sqn
1566466	F/S	BELL David McFarlane Forsyth	22-06-44	49 Sqn
1558691	Sgt	BELL David Robertson	28-05-44	78 Sqn
592073	F/S	BELL Duncan Neilson	27-04-44	103 Sqn
972074	W/O	BELL Frederick James	22-12-44	83 Sqn
1115113	F/S	BELL Frederick Joseph	4-05-44	101 Sqn
1396956	F/S	BELL George William	11-11-44	227 Sqn
47578	F/L	BELL DFC Gilbert	10-05-44	9 Sqn
1473823	Sgt	BELL Harold Barnard	27-01-44	166 Sqn
1567138	Sgt	BELL Ian	26-02-44	78 Sqn
1796420	Sgt	BELL James	27-08-44	97 Sqn
1537760	Sgt	BELL James Hogg	9-12-44	21 OTU
51820	F/O	BELL DFC John	27-08-44	12 Sqn
1133841	F/S	BELL John	2-01-44	156 Sqn
1564498	Sgt	BELL John Beaumont	12-09-44	622 Sqn
1811656	Sgt	BELL John Peter Ogilvie	11-06-44	15 Sqn
173943	F/O	BELL John Robson	20-11-44	75 Sqn
1621754	Sgt	BELL Maurice	27-08-44	115 Sqn
129748	F/O	BELL Peter Anthony Charles	24-03-44	103 Sqn
1606089	Sgt	BELL Peter Edwin	6-11-44	622 Sqn
63454	F/L	BELL Raisbeck Dennis	6-10-44	51 Sqn
1526928	Sgt	BELL Richard	3-03-44	1666 HCU
1509479	Sgt	BELL Thomas	6-01-44	619 Sqn
174025	F/L	BELL DFC Walter John	21-07-44	15 Sqn
1385160	Sgt	BELL William Henry	24-02-44	578 Sqn
172301	P/O	BELL William John	28-04-44	100 Sqn
1625609	Sgt	BELLAMY Frank William	6-06-44	149 Sqn
2211409	Sgt	BELLAMY William Henry 'Bill'	21-07-44	115 Sqn
1080344	F/S	BELLHOUSE Edward Whitley	21-07-44	158 Sqn
126639	F/O	BELLINGHAM Kenneth George	22-06-44	106 Sqn
1038227	Sgt	BELTON Alfred Johnson	27-01-44	426 Sqn
1582863	Sgt	BELTON John	22-04-44	635 Sqn
1046454	Sgt	BENBOW Hubert Francis	28-04-44	138 Sqn
1867969	Sgt	BENDER Joseph [Canada]	17-06-44	102 Sqn
173405	F/O	BENDER DFC Milton Harold	10-04-44	460 Sqn
1511190	F/S	BENGSTON John	4-05-44	619 Sqn
1580616	Sgt	BENHAM Albert Clifford	13-06-44	514 Sqn
1671182	Sgt	BENJAMIN Maurice	12-09-44	44 Sqn
1255181	Sgt	BENJAMIN Thomas Evan Edward	8-05-44	15 Sqn
1149235	Sgt	BENNETT Alfred	19-04-44	625 Sqn
1603741	Sgt	BENNETT Alfred Edwin	20-02-44	514 Sqn
151351	F/O	BENNETT Arthur	10-05-44	9 Sqn
1602216	F/S	BENNETT Edmund	16-10-44	115 Sqn
127220	F/L	BENNETT Edward	25-09-44	576 Sqn
2220133	Sgt	BENNETT George	10-05-44	467 Sqn
2222266	Sgt	BENNETT George Frederick	12-09-44	1653 HCU
153741	F/O	BENNETT Harry James	24-07-44	1660 HCU
145380	F/O	BENNETT Henry Edward	2-01-44	460 Sqn
778022	F/S	BENNETT John Galway [Rhodesia]	19-06-44	44 Sqn
190398	P/O	BENNETT Leonard William	11-11-44	619 Sqn

Service No	Rank	Name	Date	Sqn
1334810	F/S	BENNETT Paul Kenneth Ernest	23-01-44	1667 HCU
1579389	Sgt	BENNETT Percy James	14-01-44	97 Sqn
1601570	F/S	BENNETT Peter Anthony	25-04-44	115 Sqn
1613599	Sgt	BENNETT Peter Edward	9-10-44	76 Sqn
1579492	Sgt	BENNETT Philip Charles Knill	24-03-44	514 Sqn
651521	F/S	BENNETT Reginald Joseph	8-12-44	630 Sqn
1498749	W/O	BENNETT Ronald	3-08-44	619 Sqn
1579544	Sgt	BENNETT Ronald William	17-12-44	61 Sqn
1620198	F/S	BENNETT Stanley Claude	2-11-44	49 Sqn
1601205	Sgt	BENNETT Vickers Lavender	3-06-44	640 Sqn
1581863	Sgt	BENNETT Victor	25-02-44	44 Sqn
989053	Sgt	BENSON George Henry	12-09-44	214 Sqn
171065	P/O	BENSON Herbert John 'Jack'	25-02-44	100 Sqn
627862	Sgt	BENSON John Edward	28-05-44	101 Sqn
177792	P/O	BENSON DFM Leslie Bernard	22-06-44	49 Sqn
182038	P/O	BENTING Alan William	25-09-44	617 Sqn
1698420	Sgt	BENTLEY Ronald	5-07-44	106 Sqn
1388598	Sgt	BENTLEY Stanley George	24-03-44	12 Sqn
1098060	Sgt	BERESFORD Douglas Harold	6-07-44	635 Sqn
171591	F/O	BERESFORD Graham	5-08-44	425 Sqn
639890	Sgt	BERESFORD Ronald William	26-03-44	49 Sqn
129551	F/O	BERG DFC John Joseph	17-06-44	550 Sqn
182161	F/O	BERKELEY Nicholas George [Canada]	30-08-44	115 Sqn
990488	F/S	BERNARD William	6-12-44	77 Sqn
1890825	Sgt	BERRETT Reginald Hughes	27-11-44	138 Sqn
160000	F/O	BERRINGTON John Raynor [Rhodesia]	15-03-44	44 Sqn
1861471	Sgt	BERRY Alexander Mitchell	13-05-44	466 Sqn
919485	F/S	BERRY Arnold	16-12-44	106 Sqn
2212872	Sgt	BERRY Eric	18-12-44	51 Sqn
1133453	Sgt	BERRY Ernest	2-01-44	626 Sqn
993248	Sgt	BERRY John	4-05-44	12 Sqn
1318968	Sgt	BERRY John Charles	13-09-44	20 OTU
140907	F/L	BERRY DFM Kenneth Herbert	15-02-44	103 Sqn
186901	P/O	BERRY Leonard	4-11-44	51 Sqn
1865875	Sgt	BERRY Robert William	22-05-44	49 Sqn
173187	F/O	BERRY Royston Willett	4-11-44	49 Sqn
1391597	F/O	BERRY Thomas Cromwell	13-08-44	467 Sqn
913231	Sgt	BERRY Thomas George	21-01-44	77 Sqn
1868459	Sgt	BERRY William Arthur	14-10-44	12 Sqn
1600195	F/S	BERRY William Charles	14-01-44	115 Sqn
158336	F/O	BERTENSHAW Clifford	19-10-44	105 Sqn
41366	S/L	BEST DFC Charles Brian	16-09-44	515 Sqn
175398	F/O	BEST Derek Wilfred	10-08-44	50 Sqn
185713	P/O	BEST Frederick Gordon Stuart	18-12-44	227 Sqn
151751	F/O	BESTWICK Richard Bernard	26-03-44	460 Sqn
1336195	Sgt	BETHELL Peter Edwin	16-03-44	420 Sqn
162867	P/O	BETT Raymond Cecil	15-02-44	7 Sqn
926074	Sgt	BETTERTON David	22-06-44	44 Sqn
1851822	Sgt	BETTRIDGE Ronald Stacey	20-02-44	61 Sqn
1581858	Sgt	BETTRIDGE Thomas William	17-06-44	3 LFS
1618081	Sgt	BETTS Reginald Claude	22-01-44	102 Sqn
51501	F/O	BETTY Rowland David	29-01-44	50 Sqn
170892	F/L	BEVERIDGE DFC Robert Walter	4-08-44	635 Sqn
1880277	F/S	BEVERTON Harry Albert	12-09-44	15 Sqn
1685716	F/S	BEVIN Arthur	28-10-44	35 Sqn
154627	F/O	BIBB Neville Urbane	5-11-44	1660 HCU
1870102	LAC	BICHARD Derrick Gordon	29-12-44	514 Sqn
122345	S/L	BICKERS DFC Kenneth George	24-03-44	103 Sqn
1893452	Sgt	BICKNELL Edward Stanley	6-11-44	619 Sqn
144998	F/O	BIDDISCOMBE Laurence George	20-01-44	427 Sqn
1666864	Sgt	BIDWELL Jack	18-11-44	51 Sqn
622666	Sgt	BIEHL William McKay [Canada]	13-06-44	78 Sqn
153189	F/O	BIGGS David Louis	10-04-44	515 Sqn
1308284	W/O	BIGGS Kenneth Stanley	13-06-44	100 Sqn
1044838	Sgt	BILLINGTON Thomas Hornby	12-09-44	214 Sqn
1818136	Sgt	BILLSON Dennis Roland	31-03-44	101 Sqn
1291037	Sgt	BILNEY Frank George Stanley	22-03-44	158 Sqn
1337685	Sgt	BINDER Jack Percival George	31-03-44	51 Sqn
941122	W/O	BINGHAM John Michael	12-09-44	207 Sqn
1684683	Sgt	BINGHAM Norman	17-05-44	1661 HCU
52508	F/O	BINGHAM Robert Byron	21-08-44	1655 MTU
1519992	Sgt	BINGHAM William	25-04-44	9 Sqn
53926	F/L	BINGHAM William Nicholas	30-12-44	156 Sqn
1824919	Sgt	BINNIE James	23-09-44	630 Sqn
49732	F/L	BINNS Herbert Denis	19-07-44	138 Sqn
1430234	F/S	BINNS Stanley	1-06-44	622 Sqn
1853424	Sgt	BINT Thomas William	25-03-44	626 Sqn
1685263	Sgt	BIRBECK Douglas Brigg	16-03-44	49 Sqn
1509133	Sgt	BIRCH Eric	25-03-44	12 Sqn
1600760	Sgt	BIRCH Jack	22-05-44	514 Sqn
187731	P/O	BIRCH Sidney Harold	6-11-44	207 Sqn
1409579	Sgt	BIRCHLEY Henry William	21-01-44	78 Sqn
1590882	Sgt	BIRD Charles	22-05-44	100 Sqn
1585460	Sgt	BIRD Edgar George	21-01-44	76 Sqn
1494307	Sgt	BIRD Sydney	4-05-44	1662 HCU
40361	S/L	BIRD Walter Douglas Wilberforce	26-08-44	692 Sqn
1395146	F/S	BIRDSEYE Alexander Frederick	9-11-44	138 Sqn
1320903	Sgt	BIRKBECK Howard Derek	15-07-44	103 Sqn
1549729	Sgt	BIRKBY Ronnie	12-09-44	214 Sqn
151757	F/O	BIRKETT John	1-04-44	1656 HCU
169533	F/O	BIRKIN William	5-07-44	192 Sqn
173326	P/O	BIRNIE John	19-04-44	115 Sqn
1392403	F/S	BIRT Peter John	25-07-44	466 Sqn
993153	Sgt	BIRTWHISTLE James	3-01-44	166 Sqn
177254	F/O	BISCHOFF John Nicolas	24-09-44	51 Sqn
1333658	Sgt	BISH Claude Frederick	16-05-44	103 Sqn
178508	P/O	BISHOP Alfred William	21-11-44	Fiskerton
1608815	Sgt	BISHOP Cecil Thomas	20-04-44	218 Sqn
172471	P/O	BISHOP Cyril Arthur	27-04-44	106 Sqn
947234	F/S	BISHOP Denzil Yorke	21-04-44	625 Sqn
1394165	F/S	BISHOP George Thomas	18-07-44	158 Sqn
1580733	Sgt	BISHOP Norman Derek	1-07-44	626 Sqn
1578199	Sgt	BISHOP Norman Reginald	4-05-44	101 Sqn
1860463	Sgt	BISHOP Peter William	25-05-44	51 Sqn
1334892	F/S	BISHOP Ronald William	18-08-44	630 Sqn
1322249	Sgt	BISHOP Sidney Thomas	14-03-44	75 Sqn
1337955	F/S	BISHOP William John Barrie	5-02-44	115 Sqn
1686150	Sgt	BISHOP Willie Beaumont	8-06-44	138 Sqn
650022	Sgt	BISSET David	4-05-44	50 Sqn
121430	F/L	BISSET Thomas Neish Watters	8-06-44	78 Sqn
1696431	LAC	BITHELL Frederick	29-11-44	5 Group
152948	F/O	BLABER Herbert Sidney William	26-07-44	166 Sqn
107476	S/L	BLACK Allan	1-02-44	239 Sqn
1592077	Sgt	BLACK Harold John	17-12-44	101 Sqn
1823613	Sgt	BLACK Harry Penrice	4-05-44	460 Sqn
153665	F/O	BLACK Henry	14-10-44	550 Sqn
1002830	Sgt	BLACK James	29-07-44	434 Sqn
1531244	Sgt	BLACK Joseph	16-06-44	514 Sqn
1606715	Sgt	BLACK Percy Alfred William	23-10-44	625 Sqn
168636	F/L	BLACK DFC Thomas Wilson	23-09-44	97 Sqn
170204	F/O	BLACKBAND AFC Norman Charles	18-11-44	35 Sqn
1622469	Sgt	BLACKBURN Edward	22-05-44	100 Sqn
1438682	F/S	BLACKBURN Edward Arnold	9-06-44	51 Sqn
186889	P/O	BLACKBURN Joseph	18-12-44	425 Sqn
165034	P/O	BLACKBURN Robert Guy	19-08-44	635 Sqn
543703	Sgt	BLACKFORD Leonard Douglas	23-03-44	514 Sqn
142196	F/O	BLACKHAM Peter Douglas	8-07-44	9 Sqn
2205827	Sgt	BLACKIE David	22-06-44	44 Sqn
183893	P/O	BLACKLOCK Henry Wales	12-09-44	218 Sqn
1103498	Sgt	BLACKLOCK Thomas	3-06-44	10 Sqn
134380	F/O	BLACKMAN Henry Francis	20-02-44	429 Sqn
136588	F/O	BLADEN William Egbert Trevor	2-03-44	630 Sqn
143580	F/O	BLAHA DFM Oldrich Dennis	2-01-44	44 Sqn
1605312	Sgt	BLAIKE Donald Victor	9-06-44	49 Sqn
1796405	Sgt	BLAIR Ernest Bramwell	15-02-44	578 Sqn
153893	F/O	BLAIR George Alexander	4-05-44	101 Sqn
136172	S/L	BLAIR DFC DFM John Edward	22-05-44	156 Sqn

Service No	Rank	Name	Date	Sqn
1263138	Sgt	BLAKE Arthur William	5-10-44	115 Sqn
1892602	Sgt	BLAKE Edward George	26-11-44	49 Sqn
151084	F/O	BLAKE Robert Johnstone	28-04-44	102 Sqn
162660	F/O	BLAKE Ronald Ernest	14-10-44	626 Sqn
1389836	F/S	BLAKE William Enos	31-03-44	61 Sqn
972379	Sgt	BLAKE William Percy	12-09-44	514 Sqn
130328	F/O	BLAKEMAN DFC Alec William	3-01-44	83 Sqn
1837046	Sgt	BLAKEMAN Ernest Walter	31-05-44	12 OTU
1685551	Sgt	BLANCHARD Arthur	11-12-44	49 Sqn
1677489	Sgt	BLANCHARD James William	22-06-44	106 Sqn
1583395	Sgt	BLANCHARD Raymond Arthur Oswald	26-07-44	103 Sqn
158670	P/O	BLANCHETTE Charles Edward	2-01-44	156 Sqn
1865666	Sgt	BLANCKLEY George William	17-08-44	158 Sqn
1673627	Sgt	BLAND Eric Boys	25-06-44	102 Sqn
1896258	Sgt	BLAND Ernest Arthur	26-03-44	15 Sqn
153468	F/O	BLANDFORD Gerald Edward	13-08-44	115 Sqn
1347849	F/S	BLANE James Higgins	19-07-44	61 Sqn
1436860	Sgt	BLANKSBY Allan	21-01-44	1667 HCU
178645	P/O	BLATCHFORD Basil Farrel	19-08-44	7 Sqn
1881482	Sgt	BLATCHFORD Leonard Glendenning	22-12-44	189 Sqn
169133	F/O	BLAYDON DFM Reginald William	8-08-44	582 Sqn
135741	F/O	BLENCOWE John Dawson	24-02-44	149 Sqn
1474283	Sgt	BLENKARN Alexander Neil	22-05-44	50 Sqn
1595390	F/S	BLENKINSOP Mathew	26-11-44	115 Sqn
1869923	Sgt	BLERKOM Francis Alfred William	13-09-44	101 Sqn
3025172	Sgt	BLEWETT Alwyn	26-08-44	12 OTU
1339575	F/S	BLEWETT Hubert	15-02-44	77 Sqn
1876647	Sgt	BLIGH Norman Nicholas	30-01-44	463 Sqn
1716531	LAC	BLINMAN Hugh Cecil	27-04-44	Bungay
81376	F/L	BLOCKEY Robert Charles	3-01-44	156 Sqn
175588	P/O	BLOCKLEY DFM David Ellis	19-07-44	76 Sqn
1582340	F/S	BLOCKLEY Maurice William	5-10-44	115 Sqn
1414792	Sgt	BLOOM Benjamin	16-06-44	514 Sqn
574661	F/S	BLOOMER John Edwin	25-04-44	635 Sqn
1604008	F/S	BLOOMFIELD Alec Peter	21-11-44	192 Sqn
914304	Sgt	BLOOMFIELD Dennis Bertram	31-03-44	156 Sqn
1334268	Sgt	BLOOMFIELD Harry William	21-01-44	76 Sqn
2221318	Sgt	BLORE William Edward	21-07-44	514 Sqn
1684056	Sgt	BLOY Ronald Frederick	30-12-44	76 Sqn
1393228	F/S	BLUMFIELD Dennis William	19-07-44	49 Sqn
1717468	Sgt	BLUMIRE William	14-03-44	11 OTU
1602657	F/S	BLUNDELL Cecil Leonard	24-12-44	35 Sqn
2205143	Sgt	BLUNDELL John James	21-07-44	75 Sqn
1811667	Sgt	BLUNDEN Arthur Thomas	20-05-44	514 Sqn
151908	F/O	BLUNT Donald Edward	27-01-44	84 OTU
133000	F/O	BLUTE DFM Frederick John	21-04-44	100 Sqn
1521247	Sgt	BLYTH Jack	9-07-44	622 Sqn
1895914	Sgt	BLYTH Kenneth Digby	17-06-44	640 Sqn
50036	F/O	BOAD Albert Alan	10-03-44	207 Sqn
1554282	F/S	BOAG DFM George	26-08-44	214 Sqn
1233242	F/S	BOAM Alfred George	9-05-44	35 Sqn
1873573	F/S	BOANSON John George Shepherd	8-06-44	514 Sqn
1549458	Sgt	BOARDLEY Harold	27-01-44	467 Sqn
1813576	Sgt	BOARDMAN Frederick	30-04-44	460 Sqn
549441	Sgt	BOARDMAN Harry	11-11-44	467 Sqn
1399616	Sgt	BOCKING Ronald John	19-07-44	100 Sqn
119232	F/O	BODDEN Geoffrey	15-02-44	77 Sqn
1521634	Sgt	BODGER Harry	13-08-44	166 Sqn
1050107	F/S	BODIN Hugh Alexander Andrew	2-09-44	1656 HCU
1722687	Sgt	BODKIN Frank Sidney	24-03-44	57 Sqn
1575448	Sgt	BODSWORTH George Henry	4-03-44	20 OTU
1853136	Sgt	BODSWORTH Jack Arthur William	4-05-44	101 Sqn
100086	F/L	BODY Geoffrey Deller	18-12-44	10 Sqn
1467695	Sgt	BODY James Joseph	4-01-44	11 OTU
1624767	Sgt	BODYCOT Gordon Harry	20-02-44	626 Sqn
1582576	Sgt	BOFFEY George Henry	16-02-44	106 Sqn
1582849	Sgt	BOFFEY Ronald	8-05-44	138 Sqn
625459	Sgt	BOGAN Amos Frederick [Eire]	4-03-44	11 OTU
134125	F/O	BOIVIN Leslie Claude William	30-08-44	106 Sqn
1672925	Sgt	BOLAND John	21-01-44	102 Sqn
3000725	Sgt	BOLDERSTONE DFM Peter Frederick	30-11-44	429 Sqn
132852	F/O	BOLSOLVER Alan Richard	2-01-44	156 Sqn
1609017	Sgt	BOLT Bobbie	24-02-44	100 Sqn
642443	Sgt	BOLT Ellis William	20-02-44	408 Sqn
1318081	F/S	BOLT Leslie Arthur	10-03-44	90 Sqn
1594020	F/S	BOLT Ronald	24-12-44	166 Sqn
1587851	Sgt	BOLT William Frederick Donald	20-02-44	101 Sqn
155377	F/O	BOLT William Thomas	26-08-44	7 Sqn
124812	F/O	BOLTER Sidney Ronald	9-06-44	1652 HCU
1835068	F/S	BOLTON Derek	21-11-44	514 Sqn
1867066	Sgt	BOLTON Douglas Charles	20-01-44	10 Sqn
157916	F/O	BOLTON Eric	5-11-44	102 Sqn
2208887	Sgt	BOLTON Frank	22-03-44	9 Sqn
178848	P/O	BOLTON John Henry	17-06-44	434 Sqn
1581788	Sgt	BOLTON John Stanley	31-03-44	424 Sqn
1459379	Sgt	BOLTON Kenneth Stanley	12-08-44	76 Sqn
1639785	LAC	BOLTON Samuel	29-12-44	514 Sqn
1890153	Sgt	BOLTON Sidney David	21-11-44	49 Sqn
149966	P/O	BOND DFC Gerald Peter Robert	2-01-44	156 Sqn
40666	S/L	BOND Kenneth Frank Pennington	22-04-44	77 Sqn
1411265	Sgt	BOND Raymond James	12-05-44	166 Sqn
1722655	Sgt	BOND Ronald Sidney	23-06-44	100 Sqn
1473244	Sgt	BONE Edmund Douglas	12-09-44	619 Sqn
1541373	Sgt	BONE Eric	24-12-44	103 Sqn
1131466	Sgt	BONE George	29-01-44	625 Sqn
1449499	Sgt	BONE John Henry	15-03-44	90 Sqn
1445581	Sgt	BONES Frank Leonard	20-02-44	77 Sqn
53840	P/O	BONNAR George Alexander	19-03-44	20 OTU
1523916	Sgt	BONNER Charles Aidan	28-05-44	550 Sqn
171344	F/O	BONNER Kenneth Harding	6-11-44	515 Sqn
169906	P/O	BONNETT Henry John	11-06-44	7 Sqn
1580635	Sgt	BONSER Maurice Reginald	5-06-44	1658 HCU
1686264	Sgt	BOOCOCK John Hargrave	13-09-44	158 Sqn
145424	F/L	BOOKER DFC Alan John	22-12-44	83 Sqn
1627930	F/S	BOOKER Frank Louis	30-07-44	102 Sqn
1388994	Sgt	BOOKER John Owen	17-06-44	102 Sqn
1866190	Sgt	BOOKER Sidney James	7-02-44	1663 HCU
1603498	Sgt	BOON Roy James Alfred	31-03-44	576 Sqn
1869230	Sgt	BOORMAN Robert James	26-08-44	419 Sqn
1866449	Sgt	BOOT Wilfred Charles	27-01-44	576 Sqn
3030323	Sgt	BOOTH Alfred Bertram Ernest	25-07-44	514 Sqn
1801590	F/S	BOOTH Alfred Stanley	16-11-44	15 Sqn
1034046	Sgt	BOOTH Clifford	25-07-44	75 Sqn
1583384	Sgt	BOOTH Denis	27-04-44	44 Sqn
1056832	Sgt	BOOTH Eric	29-10-44	463 Sqn
1083386	Sgt	BOOTH Ernest	11-12-44	1662 HCU
182236	F/O	BOOTH Frank Josiah	25-12-44	166 Sqn
1473057	Sgt	BOOTH Fred	8-07-44	207 Sqn
56364	P/O	BOOTH Frederick Oliver [Australia]	22-12-44	578 Sqn
1588960	Sgt	BOOTH Frederick William	28-01-44	115 Sqn
2206432	Sgt	BOOTH Jack	8-05-44	619 Sqn
1625225	Sgt	BOOTH John Calvert	13-06-44	100 Sqn
174620	P/O	BOOTH John Herbert	20-05-44	166 Sqn
1549743	Sgt	BOOTH Norman Robert	5-11-44	166 Sqn
1549733	Sgt	BOOTH Ronald	20-02-44	35 Sqn
1621356	Sgt	BOOTH Sydney	13-02-44	15 OTU
154279	F/O	BOOTH Thomas Burton	13-08-44	12 Sqn
1359010	F/S	BOOTHROYD James Kenneth	25-02-44	550 Sqn
133371	F/O	BOOTH-SMITH Peter William	11-04-44	161 Sqn
56231	P/O	BORDER William	4-11-44	432 Sqn
136427	F/O	BORDISS Ronald John	10-04-44	35 Sqn
1390586	Sgt	BORE Herbert Frederick	25-02-44	61 Sqn
1289573	F/S	BORE Stanley Robert	22-06-44	207 Sqn
1390575	Sgt	BOREHAM Clifford John	4-05-44	44 Sqn
157303	P/O	BORLAND DFC James	3-01-44	156 Sqn
1057662	Sgt	BORLAND John Hinds	2-08-44	28 OTU
1864945	Sgt	BORLEY Leonard Henry James	13-08-44	578 Sqn

Service No.	Rank	Name	Date	Sqn
1332645	Sgt	BORRADAILE Gavin Carfrae	30-01-44	463 Sqn
169546	P/O	BORROW DFM Herbert Edward	20-01-44	83 Sqn
132740	F/L	BORTHWICK DFC George Wilson Syme	29-01-44	97 Sqn
1868872	Sgt	BORTON Eric Edward	4-05-44	101 Sqn
1352419	Sgt	BOSS Ronald William	7-07-44	166 Sqn
151905	F/O	BOSTON Brian James	26-08-44	635 Sqn
1385337	Sgt	BOSTON Jack Northwood	24-03-44	640 Sqn
125638	F/L	BOSWELL Alan	27-04-44	83 Sqn
1673546	Sgt	BOSWELL George William	10-06-44	207 Sqn
1807185	Sgt	BOSWORTH Ronald Albert John	25-08-44	640 Sqn
1393762	Sgt	BOSWORTH Sidney	23-04-44	405 Sqn
1566670	Sgt	BOTHWELL James Roger	29-01-44	431 Sqn
1765035	F/S	BOTT James Wilfred	23-04-44	7 Sqn
1852754	Sgt	BOTT Raymond John	11-06-44	100 Sqn
1580780	Sgt	BOTT William James	10-06-44	630 Sqn
2201400	Sgt	BOTTERILL William Henry	25-02-44	420 Sqn
156341	F/O	BOTTING Hubert Edwin	10-05-44	9 Sqn
158790	F/O	BOTTRELL William John	2-01-44	207 Sqn
1336604	F/S	BOUCH DFM Albert	15-06-44	582 Sqn
1682242	Sgt	BOULGER Kevin	24-06-44	7 Sqn
52159	F/O	BOULTER Philip Pullyn [Canada]	14-01-44	514 Sqn
925505	W/O	BOULTON Alfred	23-05-44	207 Sqn
115339	F/L	BOULTON Frank Nelson	19-04-44	640 Sqn
1609134	Sgt	BOULTON Raymond Herbert	10-05-44	463 Sqn
1582055	Sgt	BOURNE Leonard Bertie	17-12-44	49 Sqn
1315094	Sgt	BOURNE Percy Roy	25-02-44	100 Sqn
1627444	Sgt	BOURNE Roy Stuart	25-03-44	630 Sqn
1869652	Sgt	BOURNER Derrick Lawrence	5-12-44	426 Sqn
153873	F/O	BOURTON Eric	6-10-44	49 Sqn
1237935	F/S	BOUSFIELD Derick	4-11-44	625 Sqn
1300901	Sgt	BOUTLE Jack	5-10-44	101 Sqn
1892607	Sgt	BOUTTELL Robert Lawrence	24-06-44	7 Sqn
157902	F/O	BOVETT George William	8-08-44	15 Sqn
3005645	Sgt	BOWD Lawrence William	12-09-44	1653 HCU
1682849	Sgt	BOWDEN George Vernon	7-06-44	1654 HCU
182602	F/O	BOWDEN Samuel	11-11-44	57 Sqn
1591660	Sgt	BOWDEN Terence	28-01-44	61 Sqn
1170874	Sgt	BOWDEN Woodrow Wilson	6-10-44	105 Sqn
1322645	Sgt	BOWDITCH Bryan Robert	25-02-44	626 Sqn
1877102	Sgt	BOWEN Alan George	11-12-44	514 Sqn
1330289	F/S	BOWEN Bryan Victor	12-09-44	207 Sqn
161261	F/O	BOWEN Geoffrey Hugh	13-05-44	1655 MTU
1581233	Sgt	BOWEN Harry Elizah	11-06-44	625 Sqn
1653166	Sgt	BOWEN Henry John	22-03-44	44 Sqn
122988	F/L	BOWEN Jack	20-02-44	429 Sqn
2220386	Sgt	BOWEN James Arthur	27-08-44	35 Sqn
1522821	Sgt	BOWEN John Beedie	21-04-44	15 Sqn
42481	F/L	BOWEN Peter Duncan	13-02-44	169 Sqn
1322148	F/S	BOWEN Philip Hubert	8-07-44	50 Sqn
54028	P/O	BOWEN Roland John	2-01-44	156 Sqn
1455428	Sgt	BOWEN-CHENNELL Philip	22-06-44	9 Sqn
1866493	Sgt	BOWER Frederick Norman	25-02-44	1662 HCU
1338406	F/S	BOWER Thomas Charles	20-07-44	109 Sqn
1605444	Sgt	BOWERMAN Richard Venville Thomas	30-01-44	97 Sqn
178512	F/L	BOWERS Evelyn George William	27-08-44	630 Sqn
1581065	Sgt	BOWERS Frank	26-07-44	1657 HCU
1815873	Sgt	BOWERS William	22-03-44	158 Sqn
1394105	Sgt	BOWES Laurence	30-01-44	463 Sqn
1095610	Sgt	BOWEY William	24-03-44	115 Sqn
1577716	F/S	BOWKER Norman Charles	20-02-44	12 Sqn
1182712	Sgt	BOWLER Fred Ernest	27-04-44	100 Sqn
1448125	F/S	BOWLER John Alfred	22-03-44	158 Sqn
1626590	Sgt	BOWLER Reginald Patrick	11-04-44	103 Sqn
1223079	F/S	BOWLER Ronald Edgar	26-02-44	408 Sqn
1590669	Sgt	BOWLES Arthur James	4-05-44	101 Sqn
1600205	Sgt	BOWLES Herbert Reginald	30-01-44	576 Sqn
1800366	Sgt	BOWLES Mervyn Alan	25-02-44	1662 HCU
1592827	Sgt	BOWLEY Irvin	29-07-44	106 Sqn
151227	F/O	BOWLING Harold	31-03-44	51 Sqn
1594409	Sgt	BOWMAN Fred	17-06-44	102 Sqn
1126757	Sgt	BOWMAN Ninian	3-01-44	100 Sqn
1815156	F/S	BOWN Thomas	12-12-44	635 Sqn
1622424	F/S	BOWRING Eric	5-11-44	166 Sqn
40363	S/L	BOWS Ronald	20-02-44	166 Sqn
1488974	Sgt	BOWTELL James Henry Raymond [Eire]	1-09-44	90 Sqn
1470144	Sgt	BOWTHORPE Dennis Frederick	24-03-44	51 Sqn
1463805	Sgt	BOWYER DFM Norman Hugh	31-03-44	101 Sqn
1578935	F/S	BOX DFM George Walter	30-01-44	100 Sqn
69472	F/L	BOXALL Charles Frank	22-03-44	105 Sqn
1432345	Sgt	BOYCE Donald George Neville	23-04-44	578 Sqn
179322	P/O	BOYCE Kenneth Arthur	8-07-44	207 Sqn
1865370	Sgt	BOYCE Robert James	27-04-44	49 Sqn
1591070	Sgt	BOYD Frederick	31-03-44	158 Sqn
125427	F/L	BOYD DFC George Kilpatrick	30-01-44	514 Sqn
1290787	Sgt	BOYD George Patrick	15-10-44	61 Sqn
1474359	Sgt	BOYD James Thomas	5-08-44	166 Sqn
1479287	Sgt	BOYDE Russell	24-03-44	166 Sqn
1435862	Sgt	BOYDON Ronald Arthur Blake	21-03-44	207 Sqn
1078689	F/S	BOYES Henry	21-01-44	76 Sqn
187754	P/O	BOYLAN Michael Joseph	18-12-44	432 Sqn
1750635	Sgt	BOYLE Francis Patrick	23-09-44	207 Sqn
89389	S/L	BOYLE DFC Michael Innes	27-04-44	57 Sqn
170182	F/O	BOYLE DFM Samuel	22-06-44	83 Sqn
1874522	Sgt	BOYTER Peter Vincent	16-07-44	76 Sqn
1463968	Sgt	BOZIER Laurence Herbert	22-06-44	44 Sqn
2209182	Sgt	BRACEGIRDLE Julian Charles	26-08-44	101 Sqn
122351	F/L	BRACEWELL DFC John Hopkinson	25-03-44	12 Sqn
109905	F/L	BRACHI Basil John	29-01-44	239 Sqn
175008	F/O	BRADBURN George	11-09-44	35 Sqn
2220590	Sgt	BRADBURN James Leslie	4-05-44	12 Sqn
1343450	W/O	BRADBURN John Henry	6-10-44	78 Sqn
157696	F/O	BRADBURN DFC Joseph	10-05-44	44 Sqn
143735	F/O	BRADBURY Frederick Shaw [Argentina]	21-06-44	1661 HCU
1425774	Sgt	BRADBURY Hugh	10-06-44	10 Sqn
1601578	Sgt	BRADBURY Roy Charles	14-01-44	1656 HCU
177394	P/O	BRADD Dennis George	22-06-44	630 Sqn
177675	P/O	BRADDOCK Eric Frederick	17-06-44	102 Sqn
49100	F/L	BRADFORD Cyril Samuel	27-05-44	692 Sqn
1897114	Sgt	BRADFORD James Gibson	27-08-44	115 Sqn
1814075	Sgt	BRADFORD Robert Fred	8-07-44	17 OTU
1594893	Sgt	BRADLEY Alfred	5-07-44	106 Sqn
118225	F/O	BRADLEY Anthony Alfred Arthur	13-08-44	51 Sqn
53275	F/O	BRADLEY DFM George Richard	29-08-44	582 Sqn
1622746	Sgt	BRADLEY Harold	5-07-44	630 Sqn
1314683	F/S	BRADLEY James Sydney	28-04-44	405 Sqn
1129431	Sgt	BRADLEY William Leslie	20-02-44	103 Sqn
182554	P/O	BRADSHAW George William	29-07-44	432 Sqn
1338925	Sgt	BRADSHAW Gordon Hamer	11-04-44	83 Sqn
1192320	F/S	BRADSHAW John Richard	23-01-44	161 Sqn
1216161	Sgt	BRADSHAW Neville	29-07-44	103 Sqn
1209681	Sgt	BRADY DFM Henry George	4-05-44	619 Sqn
135684	F/L	BRADY Thomas Scullion	30-08-44	635 Sqn
1896765	Sgt	BRAGG Clifford George	9-08-44	161 Sqn
178527	F/O	BRAIN Dennis Ingham	2-09-44	57 Sqn
1875233	Sgt	BRAINE Alfred Richard	29-07-44	514 Sqn
1605017	Sgt	BRAMBLE Anthony John	26-07-44	100 Sqn
1493019	Sgt	BRAMHALL John Vincent	28-04-44	101 Sqn
1579009	Sgt	BRAMLEY Francis Peter	15-02-44	622 Sqn
1367871	F/S	BRAMLEY George William	14-01-44	156 Sqn
2220988	Sgt	BRAMLEY Reginald	13-06-44	622 Sqn
151568	F/O	BRAMMER Dennis Archibald	18-10-44	630 Sqn
1431825	F/S	BRAMWELL Cecil Arthur	9-06-44	51 Sqn
1322104	Sgt	BRANCHFLOWER Ronald William 'Ron'	20-01-44	10 Sqn

Number	Rank	Name	Date	Sqn
154594	F/O	BRANDON Alan George	7-10-44	51 Sqn
1585663	F/S	BRANDON Francis Donald	21-07-44	622 Sqn
1644180	AC2	BRANDON Sydney John	23-03-44	22 OTU
1578489	Sgt	BRANDRICK Derek Malcolm	9-05-44	90 Sqn
133217	F/O	BRANDWOOD Frank Bertram	16-06-44	571 Sqn
173633	P/O	BRANT Roy Robert	22-05-44	626 Sqn
1868334	Sgt	BRAWN Bernard John	24-05-44	1656 HCU
1601100	F/S	BRAWN Henry	11-08-44	51 Sqn
173004	P/O	BRAY Douglas	11-04-44	149 Sqn
1582655	Sgt	BRAY Edward Raymond	9-05-44	90 Sqn
88650	F/L	BRAY Geoffrey Edward	7-10-44	627 Sqn
174002	P/O	BRAY Jack	13-06-44	408 Sqn
1079279	Sgt	BRAY Kenneth	29-01-44	7 Sqn
1323878	F/S	BRAY Kenneth Arthur	31-03-44	158 Sqn
1234370	Sgt	BRAZIER Alfred John	13-06-44	166 Sqn
1588551	Sgt	BRAZIER George	18-06-44	1663 HCU
1815577	Sgt	BREAKER John	31-03-44	578 Sqn
1521636	Sgt	BREAR James	31-03-44	51 Sqn
948979	F/S	BREEDON Samuel Henry Dennis	22-06-44	467 Sqn
1797554	Sgt	BREEN Michael Joseph [Eire]	11-02-44	21 OTU
151344	F/S	BREMNER Ian Mackenzie	4-05-44	101 Sqn
1567605	Sgt	BREMNER John	20-01-44	102 Sqn
977174	F/S	BREMNER William Sinclair	22-03-44	7 Sqn
1058585	Sgt	BRENNAN James Bernard	21-07-44	15 Sqn
552912	Sgt	BRERETON Charles James	7-09-44	103 Sqn
1212930	Sgt	BRETSCHER Eric Maxwell	23-03-44	115 Sqn
1625074	Sgt	BRETT Allan Francis	27-01-44	149 Sqn
183918	P/O	BRETT Anthony Leonard	15-08-44	207 Sqn
1867875	Sgt	BRETT Arthur Charles	11-11-44	57 Sqn
1807476	Sgt	BRETT Raymond William	22-06-44	44 Sqn
1493262	Sgt	BRETTELL Arthur	22-01-44	514 Sqn
1418695	Sgt	BREWER Cyril	30-11-44	75 Sqn
1874022	Sgt	BREWER David John	20-02-44	61 Sqn
1893614	AC2	BREWER Donald Victor	29-12-44	514 Sqn
130220	F/O	BREWER Leslie Francis	21-01-44	1667 HCU
1301456	F/S	BREWER Lewis	11-10-44	19 OTU
1774080	Sgt	BREWSTER Clifford Moore	30-01-44	576 Sqn
811164	F/S	BRICE Albert	31-03-44	158 Sqn
1260504	F/S	BRICK Eric David	12-12-44	218 Sqn
179791	F/O	BRICKWOOD William Douglas	12-09-44	514 Sqn
1394634	F/S	BRIDEWELL Maurice Edward	20-02-44	429 Sqn
1393427	Sgt	BRIDGEMAN Edward Garrod Joshua	27-05-44	1656 HCU
2219145	Sgt	BRIERLEY John Harrison	8-09-44	14 OTU
1815067	Sgt	BRIERS John William	26-08-44	101 Sqn
1590037	Sgt	BRIGGS David Abel	6-01-44	467 Sqn
1609862	Sgt	BRIGGS Godfrey Henry James	21-11-44	460 Sqn
1132443	Sgt	BRIGGS James	24-03-44	15 Sqn
1133469	F/S	BRIGGS John	20-02-44	640 Sqn
53303	F/O	BRIGGS Harry Rowan	10-06-44	207 Sqn
55018	F/O	BRIGGS Thomas Watt	15-02-44	57 Sqn
1875531	Sgt	BRIGHT Frederick Charles	19-07-44	619 Sqn
1392836	Sgt	BRIGHT Leslie Raymond	29-01-44	77 Sqn
1800892	F/S	BRIGHT Reginald Francis Jack	20-10-44	35 Sqn
1042582	Sgt	BRIGHT Stanley	7-02-44	1663 HCU
1393046	F/S	BRIGNELL Cyril	6-11-44	61 Sqn
1800930	Sgt	BRIGNELL Dennis Horace Albert	24-03-44	78 Sqn
1521828	Sgt	BRIMELOW Ronald	11-04-44	625 Sqn
1324836	F/S	BRIMICOMBE Ronald Alfred James	12-09-44	635 Sqn
150360	F/O	BRINDLEY Anthony Harley	19-09-44	106 Sqn
1583646	Sgt	BRINING John	12-09-44	77 Sqn
3050808	Sgt	BRISBOURNE Edward	5-09-44	84 OTU
1811837	Sgt	BRISTOW Alfred John	20-02-44	103 Sqn
639378	Sgt	BRISTOW Anthony Edwin	11-04-44	149 Sqn
135973	Sgt	BRISTOW Donald Alexander	13-06-44	427 Sqn
1098212	F/S	BRITCHFORD Arthur Thomas	11-09-44	35 Sqn
188990	P/O	BRITTAIN Eric James	23-05-44	9 Sqn
1272180	W/O	BRITTAIN Francis Charles	17-06-44	199 Sqn
1587323	Sgt	BRITTAN Donald William	7-11-44	128 Sqn
144279	F/O	BRITTON Eric Ivor	4-12-44	227 Sqn
169733	P/O	BROAD Harold Douglas	30-01-44	207 Sqn
1205696	F/S	BROAD John Thomas	13-08-44	582 Sqn
1876207	Sgt	BROAD Leslie Henry	31-03-44	49 Sqn
1593830	Sgt	BROADBENT Alan Stewart	28-05-44	166 Sqn
130884	F/O	BROADBENT Allan Robinson	14-01-44	7 Sqn
136513	F/L	BROADBENT Eric	29-07-44	103 Sqn
1437834	Sgt	BROADMORE Wilfred Henry	25-03-44	625 Sqn
1825415	Sgt	BROCKETT William Dunbar	27-08-44	15 Sqn
141687	F/O	BROCKLEHURST Norman	28-03-44	161 Sqn
1399152	F/S	BRODEN Malcolm Henry	23-09-44	101 Sqn
2208864	Sgt	BRODERICK William	25-03-44	61 Sqn
1862111	Sgt	BRODIE Basil Hubert	6-11-44	619 Sqn
174302	P/O	BRODIE James	22-06-44	106 Sqn
1795365	Sgt	BRODIE William James Totten	30-01-44	622 Sqn
1450090	Sgt	BROE Bernard	26-05-44	5 LFS
1690453	F/S	BROLL James	24-07-44	619 Sqn
1413551	F/S	BROMHAM Clifford George	6-01-44	35 Sqn
1247614	F/S	BROMLEY Alan Stevens	23-05-44	75 Sqn
1601558	F/S	BROMLEY Harold Herbert Joseph	23-09-44	9 Sqn
33158	W/C	BROMLEY OBE DFC Neil Ballingal Reid	6-09-44	169 Sqn
1193941	LAC	BROOK Cyril William Hugh	26-03-44	22 OTU
115765	F/L	BROOK John Edward	6-10-44	105 Sqn
1379465	W/O	BROOK Norman	13-08-44	77 Sqn
174668	F/L	BROOK DFC Robert	16-09-44	405 Sqn
1674979	Sgt	BROOK Stanley	25-07-44	35 Sqn
1486403	F/S	BROOKE Kenneth Arba	15-07-44	103 Sqn
150235	F/O	BROOKE Peter Upton	24-03-44	576 Sqn
1395647	Sgt	BROOKER Dennis Frank	24-03-44	626 Sqn
122416	F/L	BROOKER Gregory Bernard	19-10-44	85 Sqn
1600214	F/S	BROOKER Philip Leonard	14-10-44	550 Sqn
955093	Sgt	BROOKES Charles Albert	22-03-44	100 Sqn
2206928	Sgt	BROOKES Eric	29-01-44	50 Sqn
1275686	F/S	BROOKES Eric William	21-01-44	158 Sqn
160528	F/O	BROOKES John Robert	13-05-44	466 Sqn
1684909	Sgt	BROOKFIELD Thomas Sandford	21-07-44	15 Sqn
175043	F/O	BROOKS Alexander Campbell	8-08-44	90 Sqn
1836404	Sgt	BROOKS Arthur George	4-05-44	626 Sqn
1654521	Sgt	BROOKS Brynley Howell	13-07-44	1662 HCU
2209373	Sgt	BROOKS Dennis	25-06-44	77 Sqn
1320768	Sgt	BROOKS Douglas Arthur	7-02-44	19 OTU
777769	Sgt	BROOKS Francis Gilbert [Rhodesia]	20-02-44	166 Sqn
159065	F/O	BROOKS James	31-03-44	51 Sqn
182033	P/O	BROOKS John Alfred	11-09-44	156 Sqn
151987	F/O	BROOKS John McCallum	31-05-44	1654 HCU
1570097	Sgt	BROOKS Maxwell Anderson	14-01-44	626 Sqn
164831	F/O	BROOKSBANK John Parrington	6-12-44	103 Sqn
1395746	Sgt	BROOME Derek Christopher	25-07-44	622 Sqn
1078667	W/O	BROOMFIELD Albert Edward	29-01-44	630 Sqn
1451239	F/S	BROOMFIELD Ernest John Adams	15-07-44	515 Sqn
54634	P/O	BROOMFIELD John	24-04-44	619 Sqn
1398296	Sgt	BROOMFIELD Leslie Alfred	12-09-44	630 Sqn
1892203	Sgt	BROTHERHOOD Harry William	26-08-44	626 Sqn
1835172	Sgt	BROTHERHOOD Leonard	14-10-44	428 Sqn
1622969	Sgt	BROTHERTON Denis James	18-03-44	463 Sqn
1576786	Sgt	BROTHERTON Leslie Arthur	10-06-44	10 Sqn
952410	F/S	BROTHERTON Robert	21-01-44	115 Sqn
1544100	Sgt	BROUGH Robert Horace	7-06-44	578 Sqn
1815266	Sgt	BROUGHTON James William	22-05-44	7 Sqn
1525205	Sgt	BROUGHTON Walter	21-07-44	578 Sqn
1318489	Sgt	BROWETT Donald Henry Gilbert	9-06-44	50 Sqn
2205529	Sgt	BROWN Alan John	22-11-44	1660 HCU
1292798	Sgt	BROWN Albert Henry	6-06-44	149 Sqn
2209356	Sgt	BROWN Albert Henry	28-05-44	550 Sqn
1578712	Sgt	BROWN Alfred Charles	25-02-44	1661 HCU
1399195	Sgt	BROWN Arthur Charles	5-07-44	463 Sqn
182555	P/O	BROWN Arthur Reginald	14-10-44	550 Sqn
1581033	Sgt	BROWN Charles Derek	3-01-44	101 Sqn
1867213	Sgt	BROWN Charles Thomas	4-05-44	50 Sqn

Service No	Rank	Name	Date	Sqn
1620541	Sgt	BROWN Clifford Althea	16-02-44	622 Sqn
1875016	Sgt	BROWN Cyril	25-07-44	514 Sqn
1831716	Sgt	BROWN Daniel Frank	2-09-44	57 Sqn
2209219	Sgt	BROWN David	24-03-44	12 Sqn
993434	Sgt	BROWN David Robert	19-07-44	78 Sqn
1867211	Sgt	BROWN Derek Murray Arthur	15-02-44	640 Sqn
130272	F/O	BROWN DFC Donald	8-05-44	138 Sqn
136897	F/O	BROWN Edward George	4-03-44	199 Sqn
1322611	F/S	BROWN Edward Sharrott	14-01-44	166 Sqn
1318339	Sgt	BROWN Eric Ronald	28-07-44	101 Sqn
2206599	Sgt	BROWN Eric William	24-03-44	77 Sqn
1561578	F/S	BROWN Francis George Chaplin	4-08-44	635 Sqn
1583464	Sgt	BROWN Francis Patrick	25-04-44	50 Sqn
1537052	Sgt	BROWN Frank Colin	28-04-44	51 Sqn
1338347	F/S	BROWN George Henry	28-04-44	460 Sqn
1419009	F/S	BROWN George James	23-10-44	76 Sqn
1520541	Sgt	BROWN George Kennedy	13-06-44	514 Sqn
1568787	Sgt	BROWN George Spalding	4-11-44	195 Sqn
1851490	Sgt	BROWN Gerald Edwin	20-02-44	466 Sqn
850186	Sgt	BROWN Herbert	11-08-44	102 Sqn
1735535	Sgt	BROWN Hubert Henry	27-08-44	622 Sqn
1415876	F/S	BROWN Hugh McBeath	21-07-44	90 Sqn
3020057	Sgt	BROWN James	5-11-44	10 Sqn
153303	F/O	BROWN James Edward	16-09-44	90 Sqn
173626	P/O	BROWN James Nelson	1-07-44	101 Sqn
1351491	Sgt	BROWN James William	26-02-44	102 Sqn
1575151	F/S	BROWN John	17-06-44	576 Sqn
1487397	Sgt	BROWN John Alderton	7-02-44	19 OTU
1163091	F/S	BROWN John Francis	24-02-44	51 Sqn
2209145	Sgt	BROWN John Henry	17-06-44	77 Sqn
1710052	Sgt	BROWN John William	24-02-44	61 Sqn
1614345	AC1	BROWN Lawrence Rex Frank	21-06-44	626 Sqn
1800176	F/S	BROWN Maurice George	21-04-44	15 Sqn
115788	F/L	BROWN Norman [USA]	23-12-44	35 Sqn
1323802	F/S	BROWN Norman Wells	25-06-44	9 Sqn
1822936	Sgt	BROWN Owen McDavid	18-04-44	158 Sqn
1217562	Sgt	BROWN Percy James	23-09-44	101 Sqn
145370	F/O	BROWN Peter Charles Russell	15-03-44	463 Sqn
1305927	Sgt	BROWN Peter Henry	31-03-44	166 Sqn
1316156	Sgt	BROWN Reginald George	29-01-44	7 Sqn
1650995	Sgt	BROWN Reginald John	17-04-44	5 LFS
104694	S/L	BROWN DFC MiD Reginald Wiseman [Canada]	24-06-44	7 Sqn
1145879	Sgt	BROWN Richard	22-06-44	619 Sqn
756017	W/O	BROWN Richard William	15-02-44	101 Sqn
1076492	F/S	BROWN Robert	30-11-44	578 Sqn
1802002	Sgt	BROWN Robert Thomas	3-06-44	640 Sqn
154592	F/O	BROWN Ronald	14-10-44	115 Sqn
159659	F/L	BROWN Ronald Joshua	30-01-44	622 Sqn
1399174	F/S	BROWN Stanley Albert	9-12-44	171 Sqn
1171420	Sgt	BROWN Thomas	23-09-44	61 Sqn
1367292	Sgt	BROWN Thomas Anderson	20-02-44	429 Sqn
1549104	F/S	BROWN Thomas Anthony Victor	9-12-44	171 Sqn
1389618	Sgt	BROWN Walter Edward	16-02-44	97 Sqn
945000	W/O	BROWN William Donald	20-01-44	7 Sqn
141689	F/O	BROWNE Alaric	3-06-44	158 Sqn
1396177	Sgt	BROWNE Herbert John	23-06-44	626 Sqn
124523	F/L	BROWNE DFC William Desmond	13-07-44	14 OTU
1560442	F/S	BROWNLEE William	22-06-44	106 Sqn
1337430	F/S	BRUCE Derek James	14-01-44	101 Sqn
1605997	Sgt	BRUCE John	5-12-44	84 OTU
1566967	Sgt	BRUCE John Henry	17-09-44	75 Sqn
86600	F/L	BRUCE John Samuel [USA]	17-08-44	405 Sqn
551988	Sgt	BRUCE William	15-03-44	90 Sqn
1815134	Sgt	BRUCK Raymond Athol	22-12-44	630 Sqn
1580408	Sgt	BRUMWELL Richard Arthur	16-10-44	207 Sqn
185379	P/O	BRUNNING Joseph Charles	14-10-44	115 Sqn
1587881	Sgt	BRUNSDON Edward Ronald	6-09-44	7 Sqn
1514782	Sgt	BRUNSKILL Edward	19-10-44	186 Sqn
1575724	F/S	BRUNT Edward	25-04-44	619 Sqn
133372	F/L	BRUNT Sidney Percival	17-12-44	692 Sqn
1570543	Sgt	BRUNTON John Fraser	19-04-44	149 Sqn
1153961	Sgt	BRUTY Donald Sidney	22-05-44	550 Sqn
655790	F/S	BRYAN Eric	3-06-44	76 Sqn
143853	F/O	BRYAN John William	25-02-44	550 Sqn
1089339	F/S	BRYAN Lawrence Stanley	3-06-44	76 Sqn
1897813	Sgt	BRYAN Robert Harry	19-03-44	101 Sqn
77103	S/L	BRYAN-SMITH DFC* MiD Martin	6-06-44	97 Sqn
152776	F/O	BRYANT Donald June	8-06-44	78 Sqn
143598	F/O	BRYANT DFC Harold Cherberd	2-05-44	514 Sqn
1160208	W/O	BRYANT Richard William George	25-06-44	149 Sqn
1851276	Sgt	BRYANT Sydney Herbert	22-06-44	214 Sqn
1850867	F/S	BRYANT William Henry	20-01-44	429 Sqn
1497914	Sgt	BRYCE Alec	27-01-44	467 Sqn
149705	F/O	BRYCE Alexander Frederick	8-05-44	138 Sqn
646633	Sgt	BRYCE William	11-08-44	640 Sqn
1874880	Sgt	BRYER Dennis George Albert	20-11-44	75 Sqn
134999	F/O	BRYSON James Gilmour	2-01-44	550 Sqn
1568011	Sgt	BRYSON William Sutherland	30-08-44	106 Sqn
1572193	Sgt	BUCHAN Frank	24-09-44	57 Sqn
1801638	Sgt	BUCHAN Frederick	21-01-44	35 Sqn
954002	Sgt	BUCHAN William Alexander	24-03-44	158 Sqn
640503	F/S	BUCHANAN DFM Alexander Keir	15-02-44	7 Sqn
1577875	F/S	BUCHANAN Ian Archibald	5-07-44	9 Sqn
176094	F/O	BUCHANAN Walter John Fergus	26-07-44	49 Sqn
1398205	F/S	BUCKBY John Alan	22-06-44	44 Sqn
1580378	Sgt	BUCKBY Noel	15-10-44	90 Sqn
1382937	F/S	BUCKINGHAM Eric Montague	31-03-44	51 Sqn
1314518	Sgt	BUCKLAND Ernest	14-03-44	78 Sqn
1626710	Sgt	BUCKLE Terence Arthur	13-06-44	158 Sqn
1600800	Sgt	BUCKLER Henry Charles Joseph	3-08-44	166 Sqn
1396829	Sgt	BUCKLEY Edgar William	11-04-44	1661 HCU
1685014	Sgt	BUCKLEY Herbert Samuel	24-07-44	1660 HCU
2202638	F/S	BUCKLEY James Mathew	9-05-44	405 Sqn
1451456	F/S	BUCKLEY John Arthur	22-06-44	619 Sqn
1813417	Sgt	BUCKLEY Percy William	29-07-44	622 Sqn
1332032	F/S	BUCKMAN Ronald Frank William	13-06-44	434 Sqn
1232279	Sgt	BUCKNALL Geoffrey James	22-01-44	51 Sqn
1895576	Sgt	BUDD Peter Antony	25-06-44	149 Sqn
1869819	Sgt	BUDDEN Aubrey Ernest Walter	3-02-44	84 OTU
188996	P/O	BUGDEN Arthur Wilbert Chesley [Newfoundland]	22-05-44	57 Sqn
138465	F/O	BUJAC Bernard Gordon David	10-06-44	207 Sqn
46089	F/L	BULCRAIG DFM John Alec	19-07-44	57 Sqn
142336	F/O	BULL Arthur David	31-03-44	61 Sqn
1593511	Sgt	BULL Ernest	26-08-44	103 Sqn
68766	F/L	BULL Ernest James	15-04-44	30 OTU
578353	Sgt	BULL Francis Charles William	29-01-44	463 Sqn
1600151	F/S	BULL Francis William	13-07-44	103 Sqn
1806789	Sgt	BULL Joseph Bagnall	15-03-44	101 Sqn
1398431	F/S	BULL Kenneth Frederick	5-11-44	166 Sqn
1606722	F/S	BULL Leonard James	28-12-44	576 Sqn
43932	F/L	BULL Leslie George	29-03-44	109 Sqn
637026	Sgt	BULL Ronald	13-05-44	419 Sqn
641665	W/O	BULL William Charles	10-05-44	50 Sqn
1591602	Sgt	BULLAMORE Stanley	27-01-44	83 Sqn
1623269	Sgt	BULLEN Royston William	1-09-44	138 Sqn
1805873	Sgt	BULLIVANT Albert Edward	22-03-44	7 Sqn
1815790	Sgt	BULLOCK Donald	30-08-44	115 Sqn
1093742	LAC	BULMAN Harry	4-08-44	Woodbridge
67193	F/L	BULMER Edward Charles	1-06-44	Westcott
1852441	Sgt	BUMSTEAD George William	21-07-44	514 Sqn
1610917	Sgt	BUNCHER James Arthur	28-04-44	166 Sqn
1336293	F/S	BUNKER Ronald Ralph	22-05-44	460 Sqn
159427	P/O	BUNN Ivor George	20-02-44	78 Sqn
145317	F/O	BUNN Kenneth James	29-06-44	76 Sqn
171856	P/O	BUNNAGAR Maurice	12-05-44	9 Sqn
136328	F/O	BUNNEY Kenneth Ralph	6-07-44	161 Sqn

Service No	Rank	Name	Date	Unit
1320651	F/S	BUNTING Dennis Ernest Victor	14-01-44	7 Sqn
173443	P/O	BUNTING DFM William Frederick	29-07-44	582 Sqn
159512	F/O	BURCH George John	23-09-44	582 Sqn
162551	P/O	BURCHAM Alfred John	29-01-44	15 Sqn
1803818	Sgt	BURCHELL Peter	1-04-44	1656 HCU
1439217	Sgt	BURDEN Daniel	3-01-44	619 Sqn
753568	Sgt	BURDEN Joseph William Samuel	16-03-44	35 Sqn
1737563	Sgt	BURDETT Frank William	20-02-44	12 Sqn
1334420	Sgt	BURDETT John Charles	24-03-44	640 Sqn
133462	F/L	BURGER DFC Thomas	29-01-44	7 Sqn
1819813	Sgt	BURGESS Alan	2-11-44	622 Sqn
1566930	Sgt	BURGESS Alexander Addison	29-01-44	102 Sqn
152917	F/O	BURGESS Arnold George	25-07-44	514 Sqn
1436225	F/S	BURGESS Fred	4-05-44	576 Sqn
1624834	Sgt	BURGESS George Frederick	6-10-44	115 Sqn
1589723	Sgt	BURGESS John Raymond	4-05-44	619 Sqn
1591083	Sgt	BURGESS Noel Vincent	24-03-44	576 Sqn
2216202	Sgt	BURGESS Robin Harold Croucher	30-08-44	97 Sqn
649037	Sgt	BURGESS Ronald Frank	18-07-44	158 Sqn
1874815	Sgt	BURGESS Roy	14-01-44	1656 HCU
1853294	Sgt	BURGON Peter Gordon	26-02-44	420 Sqn
54592	P/O	BURGLASS Gilbert Clark	17-06-44	102 Sqn
1394350	Sgt	BURGUM Robert Edward	28-04-44	51 Sqn
1523987	Sgt	BURKE James	3-08-44	460 Sqn
1652303	Sgt	BURKE John William	24-03-44	115 Sqn
1281933	W/O	BURKE Joseph Yancey	18-03-44	692 Sqn
1313837	Sgt	BURKE Ronald Ernest 'Ron'	27-01-44	9 Sqn
1057178	Sgt	BURKE Thomas Herbert	21-04-44	625 Sqn
1147248	Sgt	BURKE William	10-06-44	44 Sqn
1238968	Sgt	BURKITT Harry	24-03-44	578 Sqn
1320846	Sgt	BURKITT William Frederick	23-03-44	9 Sqn
179369	P/O	BURKWOOD Robert William	25-06-44	61 Sqn
1874533	Sgt	BURLEIGH Terence John	23-04-44	101 Sqn
1814741	Sgt	BURLEY Albert Royston	23-09-44	101 Sqn
149874	F/L	BURLEY DFC Philip Kenneth	8-07-44	692 Sqn
1215321	Sgt	BURMAN Leslie	22-04-44	1660 HCU
173083	P/O	BURNABY Michael Adrian	4-05-44	405 Sqn
177502	P/O	BURNELL Aubrey William Alexander	21-07-44	97 Sqn
1230225	Sgt	BURNELL Sidney	6-01-44	12 Sqn
171640	P/O	BURNETT Walter Henry	31-03-44	166 Sqn
1550824	F/S	BURNETT Walter McGregor Halliday	27-08-44	44 Sqn
1062754	Sgt	BURNETT William Alexander	28-06-44	90 Sqn
1796555	Sgt	BURNS Gerald Joseph	9-06-44	44 Sqn
1606652	Sgt	BURNS Raymond Edmund Thomas	7-10-44	166 Sqn
1107230	W/O	BURNS Robert	14-07-44	24 OTU
1617065	Sgt	BURNSIDE Henry Charles	8-11-44	218 Sqn
521847	F/S	BURNSIDE DFM John Kean	13-08-44	61 Sqn
1822420	Sgt	BURNSIDE Samuel	16-10-44	14 OTU
1582165	Sgt	BURR Percy William	11-11-44	227 Sqn
1393262	F/S	BURR Terence Michael Vaughan	20-08-44	169 Sqn
1583288	Sgt	BURRELL Roy	30-01-44	207 Sqn
1853296	Sgt	BURROUGHS Keith Douglas	18-03-44	44 Sqn
1282840	LAC	BURROWES Bertram Errol	9-09-44	139 Sqn
118027	F/L	BURT DFC Eric Cyril	21-07-44	97 Sqn
1551748	F/S	BURT Peter	26-08-44	635 Sqn
120036	F/L	BURT DFC Philip Richmond	5-07-44	35 Sqn
1321486	F/S	BURTENSHAW Dennis Frederick	3-01-44	156 Sqn
1283980	Sgt	BURTON Albert William	4-05-44	192 Sqn
1593192	Sgt	BURTON Dennis Henry Francis	19-09-44	467 Sqn
1431822	F/S	BURTON Douglas	13-06-44	76 Sqn
1494673	Sgt	BURTON Edward Nichols	2-01-44	106 Sqn
1483336	Sgt	BURTON Francis John	25-04-44	12 OTU
1803031	Sgt	BURTON Frederick William	4-05-44	626 Sqn
151079	F/O	BURTON John Raymond	28-04-44	101 Sqn
1591487	Sgt	BURTON Ronald	12-09-44	622 Sqn
1801606	F/S	BURTON Ronald George	1-06-44	156 Sqn
158541	F/O	BURTON DFC Stanley	9-03-44	1667 HCU
21249	F/L	BURTT Robert Petchell	29-01-44	50 Sqn
172072	P/O	BURWOOD Geoffrey Hubert Stephen	3-06-44	640 Sqn
1382569	Sgt	BURY Stanley William	14-01-44	7 Sqn
139961	F/L	BUSH DFC Cyril	20-02-44	7 Sqn
1324130	Sgt	BUSH William Andrew	11-04-44	84 OTU
168795	F/O	BUSH William Henry	18-11-44	578 Sqn
3030346	Sgt	BUTCHER Kenneth Charles	30-08-44	463 Sqn
1320767	F/S	BUTCHER Norman	11-04-44	622 Sqn
1394318	F/S	BUTCHER Peter John	13-06-44	158 Sqn
1877190	Sgt	BUTCHER Spencer Christopher John	21-07-44	90 Sqn
1808830	Sgt	BUTCHER Stanley Clifford	28-06-44	640 Sqn
901752	F/S	BUTCHER William Albert	29-07-44	630 Sqn
1836613	Sgt	BUTLER Arthur Cecil	3-12-44	138 Sqn
1892533	Sgt	BUTLER Arthur Leslie Truelove	27-01-44	84 OTU
2204679	Sgt	BUTLER Dennis Raymond	29-07-44	619 Sqn
1359064	Sgt	BUTLER Francis Charles	24-03-44	57 Sqn
1585469	Sgt	BUTLER George Herbert	25-05-44	78 Sqn
87395	F/L	BUTLER Harry Clegg	23-03-44	239 Sqn
1593289	Sgt	BUTLER James Henry	10-05-44	9 Sqn
1282513	W/O	BUTLER James William	12-08-44	30 OTU
1451567	Sgt	BUTLER Kenneth	21-01-44	1667 HCU
1811369	F/S	BUTLER Maurice Percival	27-04-44	57 Sqn
1453947	Sgt	BUTLER Noel	20-01-44	622 Sqn
1384944	Sgt	BUTLER Patrick Frederick	23-04-44	75 Sqn
139994	F/O	BUTLER Peter Ross	12-04-44	619 Sqn
170230	P/O	BUTLER Robert John	21-01-44	15 Sqn
1318348	W/O	BUTLER William Valentine	14-01-44	166 Sqn
1310755	Sgt	BUTSON Charles	24-03-44	7 Sqn
178809	P/O	BUTSON James Frederick	27-08-44	7 Sqn
131169	F/L	BUTT Leslie George	1-09-44	157 Sqn
1589861	Sgt	BUTTERFIELD John	26-08-44	83 OTU
67056	S/L	BUTTERFIELD DFC MiD William Ronald	6-06-44	515 Sqn
1622660	F/S	BUTTERS Uriah Bernard	17-09-44	115 Sqn
1509113	F/S	BUTTERWORTH Henry Roy	31-03-44	101 Sqn
1379184	W/O	BUTTERWORTH James William	21-07-44	90 Sqn
1673376	Sgt	BUTTERWORTH John	8-07-44	207 Sqn
1891917	Sgt	BUTTLING Anthony George	23-04-44	514 Sqn
148028	F/O	BUXTON Gordon	27-04-44	207 Sqn
1614503	Sgt	BUXTON Lawrence	22-05-44	514 Sqn
2203174	Sgt	BUZZA Reginald Ernest	21-07-44	75 Sqn
1822196	Sgt	BYARS John Adams	20-02-44	630 Sqn
1578875	Sgt	BYATT Colin Victor	31-03-44	78 Sqn
1866301	Sgt	BYFORD Edward Thomas William	24-03-44	78 Sqn
973375	Sgt	BYNG Clarence Aden	25-08-44	10 Sqn
1553021	Sgt	BYRNE Felix	31-01-44	1664 HCU
1547072	Sgt	BYRNE Grayham Bancroft	19-07-44	138 Sqn
1521794	F/S	BYRNE Patrick Joseph John	4-11-44	101 Sqn
1262672	Sgt	BYRNE Roy Michael	24-03-44	429 Sqn
1338284	Sgt	BYRNE Terence Patrick	30-08-44	463 Sqn
1867078	Sgt	BYSOUTH Raymond Walter	30-08-44	50 Sqn
1105202	Sgt	BYTH Robert	31-03-44	514 Sqn
175482	P/O	CABLE DFM George	8-05-44	138 Sqn
122999	F/L	CADDIE John Worthington	26-07-44	157 Sqn
1874339	Sgt	CADGE Thomas	15-03-44	578 Sqn
45207	F/L	CADMAN DFM Arthur Robert	31-03-44	97 Sqn
145333	F/L	CADMAN DFC Peter Eric	10-04-44	105 Sqn
1739534	F/S	CADMAN MiD Robert	26-08-44	635 Sqn
169502	P/O	CAFFERY Norman	20-02-44	158 Sqn
1892512	Sgt	CAFFREY Francis	5-11-44	466 Sqn
174879	P/O	CAGIENARD Robert Roland	25-04-44	115 Sqn
1353265	Sgt	CAHILL Dennis	4-10-44	44 Sqn
1018880	F/S	CAILE Albert	22-01-44	166 Sqn
1525642	Sgt	CAINE Gerrard	16-02-44	199 Sqn
1605460	Sgt	CAILES Norman George	21-04-44	17 OTU
135871	F/O	CAIRNS DFM Charles Gordon	3-01-44	156 Sqn
135753	F/O	CAIRNS Herbert Laurence Wray	29-01-44	630 Sqn
1891428	Sgt	CAIRNS John	20-02-44	61 Sqn
53886	P/O	CAIRNS John Caldwell	10-04-44	12 Sqn
1894992	Sgt	CAIRNS John Desmond	12-05-44	15 Sqn
1824099	Sgt	CAIRNS Thomas David Stoddart	8-08-44	90 Sqn

Number	Rank	Name	Date	Sqn
629445	Sgt	CAIRNS William Denmark	11-06-44	90 Sqn
142923	F/O	CALDER Thomas Sawers	22-06-44	44 Sqn
157632	F/O	CALDERHEAD Raymond Francis	29-07-44	550 Sqn
1777282	Sgt	CALLAN John Patrick	30-08-44	75 Sqn
1061420	W/O	CALLENDER DFM Edward	7-03-44	115 Sqn
1452884	F/S	CALLON Gordon Frederick	17-12-44	49 Sqn
3032826	Sgt	CALLOW Gerald Ivor	26-08-44	83 OTU
160630	F/O	CALVERT DFC Arthur	27-03-44	21 OTU
1491264	F/S	CALVERT Edward Hilary	25-05-44	103 Sqn
151583	F/O	CALVERT Ernest Norman	13-08-44	77 Sqn
1623515	Sgt	CALVERT DFM Thomas	2-01-44	101 Sqn
1896872	Sgt	CAMBRIDGE William James Cecil	19-07-44	460 Sqn
153722	F/O	CAMERON Forbes	24-09-44	166 Sqn
1553854	F/S	CAMERON Gregor	11-04-44	149 Sqn
1323158	Sgt	CAMERON John Charles	10-07-44	630 Sqn
1823538	Sgt	CAMERON John Wesley	25-04-44	16 OTU
1077716	F/S	CAMERON Norman Davidson	2-01-44	97 Sqn
1573066	Sgt	CAMERON Scott	29-01-44	51 Sqn
544768	Sgt	CAMM Philip Otley	3-01-44	49 Sqn
2210277	Sgt	CAMP John Henry	6-05-44	11 OTU
2208436	Sgt	CAMPBELL Alistair	23-09-44	78 Sqn
1346811	Sgt	CAMPBELL Archibald Sinclair	23-05-44	408 Sqn
1565575	F/S	CAMPBELL Charles Gerrard	28-12-44	576 Sqn
1574529	Sgt	CAMPBELL Clelland Mackenzie	19-03-44	625 Sqn
1560116	Sgt	CAMPBELL Colin Ian Duncan	7-06-44	115 Sqn
174998	P/O	CAMPBELL DFC Colin Macaulay	8-09-44	14 OTU
179543	F/O	CAMPBELL Donald	12-09-44	35 Sqn
1314892	F/S	CAMPBELL Donald Stirling	13-05-44	640 Sqn
1142447	F/S	CAMPBELL Edward	15-02-44	7 Sqn
536164	Sgt	CAMPBELL Ernest	23-10-44	44 Sqn
658147	Sgt	CAMPBELL Everard	29-01-44	102 Sqn
1342122	Sgt	CAMPBELL George McNeill	20-02-44	166 Sqn
1822580	Sgt	CAMPBELL Ian	8-06-44	156 Sqn
1821979	Sgt	CAMPBELL James	22-03-44	432 Sqn
145182	F/O	CAMPBELL DFC James Easdale	2-11-44	15 Sqn
1489683	F/S	CAMPBELL John Gordon	24-03-44	619 Sqn
1349336	Sgt	CAMPBELL John McDougal	22-05-44	207 Sqn
1568628	Sgt	CAMPBELL John McLeod	2-03-44	44 Sqn
1386525	Sgt	CAMPBELL Kenneth Alfred John	6-01-44	35 Sqn
1366029	Sgt	CAMPBELL Robert Alexander	15-02-44	625 Sqn
1301496	F/S	CAMPBELL Robert George	8-08-44	582 Sqn
917815	W/O	CAMPBELL MiD Robert Jackson	13-06-44	78 Sqn
179864	P/O	CAMPBELL Sydney	31-10-44	90 Sqn
1475547	Sgt	CAMPBELL Thomas	30-01-44	100 Sqn
1355935	Sgt	CAMPBELL William	2-09-44	1656 HCU
1853822	Sgt	CAMPBELL William Robert	30-08-44	50 Sqn
1568600	Sgt	CAMPBELL William Smith	28-05-44	12 Sqn
578247	F/S	CAMPBELL William Wright	13-04-44	90 Sqn
42049	W/C	CAMPLING DSO DFC Frank Knowles	8-04-44	1 LFS
47364	S/L	CAMPLING DSO DFC Richard David	15-02-44	7 Sqn
2210997	Sgt	CANDAY Charles Richard	6-07-44	15 Sqn
146286	F/O	CANDLIN DFC DFM Geoffrey William Clifton	25-01-44	83 Sqn
137471	F/O	CANDY Arthur Albert	11-04-44	635 Sqn
1321351	Sgt	CANHAM George James	12-09-44	1653 HCU
136936	F/L	CANN DFC Lindsay Northcote Beavis	17-12-44	156 Sqn
158021	P/O	CANNING Donald	21-01-44	115 Sqn
1819894	F/S	CANNING Geoffrey Maurice	31-08-44	166 Sqn
1833215	Sgt	CANNOCK George	26-02-44	207 Sqn
1394438	F/S	CANNON DFM Charles Henry	27-04-44	101 Sqn
1880283	Sgt	CANNON Cornelius Charles	21-07-44	90 Sqn
1320615	F/S	CANNON Dennis	24-03-44	103 Sqn
161795	P/O	CANNON Leslie	18-03-44	61 Sqn
1623025	Sgt	CANNON William	29-01-44	77 Sqn
173273	F/O	CANSELL George Edward	7-10-44	617 Sqn
128923	F/O	CANT James Sutherland	20-02-44	640 Sqn
1716088	Sgt	CANT William Joseph	2-01-44	207 Sqn
1314134	F/S	CANTLE Arthur Basil	4-11-44	51 Sqn
1387255	Sgt	CANTLE-JONES Allan	14-03-44	78 Sqn
1600636	Sgt	CANTLIN Charles Patrick	10-04-44	10 OTU
1247573	Sgt	CANTOR Jack Marshall	31-01-44	550 Sqn
1493381	Sgt	CANTWELL Christopher Felix	15-06-44	15 Sqn
1894616	Sgt	CANTWELL Reginald Horace	12-03-44	199 Sqn
1531915	Sgt	CANTY Arthur William	29-01-44	51 Sqn
1653342	Sgt	CAPEL Brinley George	14-01-44	408 Sqn
1387274	Sgt	CAPEL Michael George	2-01-44	550 Sqn
1483697	F/S	CAPEWELL Denis Claude	10-04-44	10 OTU
1684410	Sgt	CAPON John	18-12-44	50 Sqn
1624412	Sgt	CAPSTICK Nicholas Jackson	16-03-44	115 Sqn
54303	P/O	CARBUTT Denis	24-03-44	61 Sqn
1330794	F/S	CARE Ernest Charles	28-10-44	76 Sqn
1348658	F/S	CAREY Gordon Hunter McKenzie	28-06-44	640 Sqn
1069049	Sgt	CAREY John James	30-08-44	166 Sqn
1501828	Sgt	CARLESS John	5-02-44	115 Sqn
1586665	Sgt	CARLICK David Brynmor	20-02-44	9 Sqn
171073	P/O	CARLILE Derek Reginald	15-02-44	630 Sqn
934352	Sgt	CARLING Ronald David John Campbell	28-06-44	44 Sqn
130876	F/L	CARLTON DFC Arthur Ernest	4-05-44	97 Sqn
808181	Sgt	CARLYLE James Clifford	25-11-44	12 OTU
170257	P/O	CARLYLE DFM Stanley	4-05-44	97 Sqn
1892690	Sgt	CARMAN Dennis Mark	2-09-44	57 Sqn
1832828	Sgt	CARMICHAEL Ernest Donald	16-07-44	15 Sqn
1684223	Sgt	CARMICHAEL Harry	1-06-44	515 Sqn
1624833	Sgt	CARNCROSS Norman	5-08-44	166 Sqn
70117	F/L	CARNEGIE Ronald Forbes	8-07-44	44 Sqn
1294200	Sgt	CARPENTER Cecil Thomas William	18-07-44	158 Sqn
1395962	F/S	CARPENTER Charles Louis	8-07-44	57 Sqn
147119	F/O	CARPENTER Eric James Lovelace	30-01-44	97 Sqn
1385287	Sgt	CARPENTER George Henry	16-02-44	619 Sqn
1382644	Sgt	CARPENTER Reginald William	6-01-44	619 Sqn
659081	Sgt	CARR Charles	12-02-44	1658 HCU
177718	P/O	CARR DFM David Hounsell	22-06-44	49 Sqn
2202047	Sgt	CARR George Robert	31-07-44	103 Sqn
1393365	Sgt	CARR James Baxter	8-06-44	101 Sqn
2209563	Sgt	CARR James Henry	31-03-44	44 Sqn
145812	F/O	CARR Kenneth Stanway	19-08-44	7 Sqn
1316832	Sgt	CARR Lewis Francis	15-02-44	102 Sqn
1319244	F/S	CARRELL DFM Gerald [Channel Islands]	20-02-44	35 Sqn
1862974	Sgt	CARRINGTON George Edward	11-11-44	467 Sqn
137405	F/O	CARROLL Gerald Dennis	8-02-44	138 Sqn
21326	F/L	CARROLL Richard Valentine	11-06-44	100 Sqn
1894153	Sgt	CARROTT Derek Charles	29-07-44	405 Sqn
1500995	F/S	CARROTT James Edward	26-02-44	15 Sqn
1590317	Sgt	CARRUTHERS John Robert	13-05-44	419 Sqn
133396	F/L	CARRUTHERS William Maurice	26-02-44	78 Sqn
44553	S/L	CARTER DFC Albert Leslie	23-12-44	582 Sqn
1398317	Sgt	CARTER Donald John	20-09-44	619 Sqn
1819918	Sgt	CARTER Douglas	8-07-44	57 Sqn
70770	W/C	CARTER DFC Edward James	6-06-44	97 Sqn
1499168	Sgt	CARTER George Frederick	29-01-44	431 Sqn
546667	Sgt	CARTER Harold Gordon	29-07-44	514 Sqn
1458092	Sgt	CARTER Joe	29-05-44	1657 HCU
1591447	Sgt	CARTER John Arthur	15-12-44	12 Sqn
172825	P/O	CARTER John Denis	4-05-44	12 Sqn
576282	F/S	CARTER John Noel	22-03-44	9 Sqn
1819883	Sgt	CARTER Joseph Burnett	13-06-44	166 Sqn
1321264	Sgt	CARTER Leonard Charles	25-06-44	77 Sqn
1866694	Sgt	CARTER Leslie Thomas	21-11-44	51 Sqn
116945	F/O	CARTER Richard Douglas	25-04-44	97 Sqn
55210	F/O	CARTER Victor Charles	17-05-44	138 Sqn
1543208	Sgt	CARTER Walter Frederick	21-07-44	75 Sqn
1478946	Sgt	CARTLIDGE Richard Matthew	12-05-44	630 Sqn
640625	LAC	CARTWRIGHT Cecil William	26-05-44	18 OTU
2220594	Sgt	CARTWRIGHT Frank	1-06-44	149 Sqn
1474347	Sgt	CARTWRIGHT George Alfred	20-02-44	625 Sqn
3050652	Sgt	CARTWRIGHT John Edward	19-08-44	51 Sqn
2221707	Sgt	CARTY Martin	7-12-44	1651 HCU

Service No	Rank	Name	Date	Sqn/Unit
1880342	Sgt	CARVELL Reginald Cecil	25-05-44	158 Sqn
176877	F/O	CARVER Anthony Hugh	30-08-44	50 Sqn
1595839	Sgt	CARVER Joseph	31-12-44	218 Sqn
161393	F/O	CARYER Paul Arthur Charles	11-11-44	44 Sqn
1577079	F/S	CASAJUANA Ramon Dennis	22-04-44	635 Sqn
1541433	Sgt	CASE James Godfrey	22-04-44	1654 HCU
1316080	F/S	CASEBROOK Joseph	25-07-44	83 Sqn
1797954	Sgt	CASEY James [Eire]	21-04-44	115 Sqn
39024	F/L	CASEY Michael James	31-03-44	57 Sqn
1522440	Sgt	CASH Desmond Terence	24-03-44	78 Sqn
1392257	Sgt	CASPER Leonard Charles	24-02-44	115 Sqn
161396	F/O	CASS Douglas Arthur	17-05-44	10 OTU
573138	F/S	CASS Ernest George	27-04-44	619 Sqn
1586515	F/S	CASS Jeremy	12-12-44	149 Sqn
158903	P/O	CASS Raymond	30-01-44	83 Sqn
182155	P/O	CASS Robert Marwood	9-08-44	640 Sqn
109074	F/L	CASS Ronald Foster	2-11-44	622 Sqn
1337722	F/S	CASS Sydney Evan Wallace [Canada]	13-06-44	578 Sqn
172119	P/O	CASSAN John Douglas	22-06-44	214 Sqn
1821042	Sgt	CASSELS James Jackson	6-02-44	149 Sqn
1523882	Sgt	CASSIN James Patrick	30-08-44	50 Sqn
154240	F/O	CASSINI Carl Winston [India]	18-12-44	51 Sqn
1322250	Sgt	CASSY Colin Campbell	21-01-44	434 Sqn
1191263	Sgt	CASTLE Frederick John	25-04-44	49 Sqn
122360	S/L	CASTLE Hugh Wilfred	15-11-44	115 Sqn
1893225	Sgt	CASTLE-HALL Reginald Alfred	17-06-44	77 Sqn
1627211	Sgt	CASTON Cyril Leon	24-09-44	166 Sqn
134311	F/O	CATERER James	16-06-44	635 Sqn
1802374	F/S	CATCHPOLE Walter John	15-02-44	156 Sqn
1351915	Sgt	CATLEY Basil MacCormack	13-09-44	218 Sqn
1685413	Sgt	CATLOW Ronald	24-03-44	102 Sqn
2203362	Sgt	CATO Donald Antony	10-05-44	9 Sqn
1808380	Sgt	CATON George Anthony Carlisle 'Tony'	17-12-44	17 OTU
176420	F/O	CATT Henry Nathaniel	13-08-44	158 Sqn
1876698	Sgt	CATTERWELL John Thomas George	9-06-44	102 Sqn
117960	F/L	CATTLE Aubrey Edward Henderson	13-05-44	1655 MTU
2216054	Sgt	CATTRALL Philip Rodney	15-03-44	51 Sqn
1895558	Sgt	CAULFIELD Gordon John Joseph	26-08-44	214 Sqn
1199994	Sgt	CAUSLEY Herbert William	30-08-44	75 Sqn
1671657	Sgt	CAVE Edward James	23-03-44	50 Sqn
174881	F/O	CAVE Raymond	12-09-44	77 Sqn
1315026	F/S	CAWDERY Victor Norman	14-01-44	156 Sqn
637564	F/S	CAWSON Hugh Desmond	25-06-44	90 Sqn
238520	Cpl	CAWTHORN Lewis Charles Liversedge	5-11-44	Spilsby
1557429	F/S	CHADWICK John Grant	8-06-44	138 Sqn
1891349	Sgt	CHADWICK Ronald William	22-01-44	102 Sqn
1322729	F/S	CHAFER Stanley Robert	23-04-44	640 Sqn
1652522	Sgt	CHAFFE Arthur Ernest	22-01-44	1662 HCU
1602209	F/S	CHAFFE George	1-07-44	12 Sqn
1600514	F/S	CHALK Kenneth William	29-01-44	77 Sqn
1332610	Sgt	CHALKLIN Stanley Kenneth	30-01-44	207 Sqn
1623295	Sgt	CHALLINOR Arthur Frederick	24-02-44	115 Sqn
2220400	Sgt	CHALLINOR George	5-11-44	166 Sqn
929397	Sgt	CHALLIS Norman David	26-08-44	622 Sqn
984297	F/S	CHALMERS DFM David	23-09-44	97 Sqn
1685320	Sgt	CHALONER George	29-10-44	50 Sqn
966881	Sgt	CHALTON Harold	13-02-44	15 OTU
113350	F/L	CHAMBERS DFC* Albert	6-06-44	97 Sqn
1451459	Sgt	CHAMBERS John Albert	12-05-44	9 Sqn
1125452	Sgt	CHAMBERS John McDonald	17-06-44	3 LFS
1482755	Sgt	CHAMBERS Ralph	2-01-44	467 Sqn
157673	P/O	CHAMBERS William John	21-02-44	9 Sqn
138801	F/L	CHAMPION DFM Frederick John Joseph	27-11-44	161 Sqn
1874746	Sgt	CHAMPKIN Douglas George	28-04-44	460 Sqn
47598	F/L	CHANDLER George Neville	31-12-44	218 Sqn
1896632	Sgt	CHANDLER Joseph	4-05-44	460 Sqn
1162631	Sgt	CHANDLER Kenneth Ernest	29-06-44	10 Sqn
1279002	Sgt	CHANDLER Ronald William	24-03-44	626 Sqn
1588080	Sgt	CHANNON Gordon	29-01-44	76 Sqn
1315456	F/O	CHANT Leslie	2-12-44	35 Sqn
146748	F/O	CHANT William Morton	3-06-44	158 Sqn
172981	P/O	CHANTLER Robert Edward	23-04-44	115 Sqn
1812960	Sgt	CHAPLIN Ronald James	20-02-44	78 Sqn
152933	F/O	CHAPLIN Sidney John	4-05-44	1662 HCU
1434611	Sgt	CHAPMAN Arthur Stanley	10-08-44	50 Sqn
1805624	Sgt	CHAPMAN David	5-11-44	166 Sqn
1346174	Sgt	CHAPMAN Edward Ferguson	8-06-44	77 Sqn
1606661	Sgt	CHAPMAN Frank Edward Walter	15-02-44	622 Sqn
110639	F/L	CHAPMAN Gordon Lawrence	21-11-44	51 Sqn
1876520	Sgt	CHAPMAN Harold Edward	15-03-44	625 Sqn
86517	F/L	CHAPMAN Henry Charles Alfred	29-07-44	514 Sqn
157869	F/O	CHAPMAN Henry Godfrey	19-07-44	463 Sqn
635546	F/S	CHAPMAN John William	23-04-44	76 Sqn
1393162	Sgt	CHAPMAN Joseph Ernest	25-02-44	61 Sqn
1421743	F/S	CHAPMAN Kenneth Sidney James	3-01-44	156 Sqn
1577320	F/S	CHAPMAN Leonard Arthur	27-03-44	10 Sqn
1149773	F/S	CHAPMAN William	25-03-44	97 Sqn
175750	P/O	CHAPMAN William Risden	17-06-44	431 Sqn
1820359	Sgt	CHAPMAN William Stevenson	12-06-44	635 Sqn
1097462	F/S	CHAPPEL Albert James Aidan	29-01-44	115 Sqn
1591968	F/S	CHAPPELL Albert	21-02-44	9 Sqn
133724	F/O	CHAPPELL Charles Lancelot	20-02-44	463 Sqn
1431223	F/S	CHAPPELL Howard Douglas	26-08-44	97 Sqn
1603984	Sgt	CHAPPELL Leonard Arthur	31-03-44	635 Sqn
1510807	Sgt	CHAPPELL Leslie Frank	22-05-44	9 Sqn
1890699	Sgt	CHAPPELL Sidney	4-04-44	5 LFS
1602941	Sgt	CHAPPELL William Harold	16-10-44	12 OTU
2221730	Sgt	CHARLES Edward Christopher	11-12-44	49 Sqn
1131655	Sgt	CHARLES Gwilym	28-10-44	19 OTU
1874041	Sgt	CHARLES Ralph Terence	16-02-44	97 Sqn
2225458	Sgt	CHARLESWORTH Harold Walley	6-12-44	460 Sqn
1459565	F/S	CHARLESWORTH Tom	5-07-44	192 Sqn
170224	P/O	CHARLESWORTH Trevor George William	31-03-44	44 Sqn
1457348	Sgt	CHARLIER John Marcel	24-02-44	9 Sqn
1590660	Sgt	CHARLTON Douglas	14-01-44	101 Sqn
1188067	Sgt	CHARLTON Eric Howard	4-05-44	44 Sqn
1581860	Sgt	CHARLTON Raymond	21-01-44	77 Sqn
1594899	Sgt	CHARLTON Ronald	1-11-44	426 Sqn
183027	P/O	CHARLTON Thomas Trevor	30-08-44	514 Sqn
1348547	Sgt	CHARTERS Robert John	30-01-44	106 Sqn
1323849	Sgt	CHASE Albert John	13-08-44	115 Sqn
175174	P/O	CHASE Derek John	23-04-44	156 Sqn
1138357	F/S	CHASE Wilmot George	24-03-44	578 Sqn
1578591	Sgt	CHASTON Dennis Alfred	31-03-44	50 Sqn
179033	F/O	CHATWIN Francis Reginald	25-09-44	199 Sqn
3050018	Sgt	CHATWIN Rex Joseph	19-09-44	106 Sqn
162870	P/O	CHAULK Artillus [Newfoundland]	29-01-44	115 Sqn
1820306	Sgt	CHAUNDY Maurice Leonard	25-04-44	16 OTU
1894195	Sgt	CHECKLEY Ivor Arthur	7-07-44	26 OTU
1812377	F/S	CHEESEMAN Kenneth Leslie 'Kell'	13-08-44	78 Sqn
1804108	Sgt	CHEESEMAN Raymond Edward William	14-01-44	166 Sqn
1473152	W/O	CHEETHAM Ronald William	28-08-44	239 Sqn
1807401	Sgt	CHELU Robert William	29-06-44	582 Sqn
1486586	Sgt	CHENEY Frederick	4-03-44	20 OTU
1852728	Sgt	CHERRY Arthur John	26-08-44	7 Sqn
2209539	Sgt	CHERRY James Stuart	26-06-44	1667 HCU
639762	F/S	CHESHIRE Kenneth William	3-01-44	619 Sqn
652219	Sgt	CHESHIRE William John	8-06-44	138 Sqn
1607353	Sgt	CHESTER Augustus Bryan	15-02-44	426 Sqn
187842	P/O	CHESTER Joseph Harold	18-11-44	51 Sqn
647351	Sgt	CHESTERS Ralph Sherwin	27-01-44	426 Sqn
1575850	F/S	CHEW Alan David	13-08-44	218 Sqn
1339297	Sgt	CHICK Donald Walter	27-04-44	619 Sqn

139891	F/O	CHILCOTT DFC Roy Anthony	16-02-44	50 Sqn	1603824	Sgt	CLARK Ross Lewis	28-04-44	166 Sqn
1800835	Sgt	CHILD James Sydney	21-01-44	427 Sqn	124482	F/L	CLARK Sydney Ewan Carswell	29-06-44	7 Sqn
149060	P/O	CHILD DFC Royston James	6-01-44	35 Sqn	934072	Sgt	CLARK Thomas Henry	6-06-44	426 Sqn
168690	P/O	CHILDS Edward Horace	30-01-44	576 Sqn	1233900	Sgt	CLARK Wilfred	8-07-44	57 Sqn
1890418	Sgt	CHILDS Victor George	1-05-44	514 Sqn	1371877	Sgt	CLARK William	25-03-44	625 Sqn
1834661	Sgt	CHILES Kenneth	14-08-44	103 Sqn	150037	F/O	CLARK William George	15-02-44	10 Sqn
155993	F/O	CHILMAN Peter Ernest	28-04-44	75 Sqn	1321803	Sgt	CLARK William George	28-04-44	51 Sqn
568065	F/S	CHINERY Roy William	2-01-44	100 Sqn	156593	F/O	CLARKE DFM Alfred George	10-05-44	44 Sqn
138076	F/O	CHIRIGHIN Cecil David	8-06-44	622 Sqn	175596	P/O	CLARKE Alfred Thomas	23-06-44	76 Sqn
39652	S/L	CHISHOLM John Harry MacKellar	16-09-44	157 Sqn	1896551	Sgt	CLARKE Arthur Tracey	25-06-44	106 Sqn
1896735	Sgt	CHISMAN Arthur Langley	19-10-44	460 Sqn	1867619	Sgt	CLARKE Brian Edward	14-01-44	576 Sqn
1865965	Sgt	CHITTENDEN Peter	2-01-44	463 Sqn	2220842	Sgt	CLARKE Cecil Amos	26-08-44	514 Sqn
1896571	Sgt	CHITTOCK Isaiah Lewis	25-05-44	51 Sqn	1585274	Sgt	CLARKE Claude Venables	20-02-44	57 Sqn
70126	S/L	CHOPPING DFC Ralph Campbell	26-08-44	7 Sqn	1600718	Sgt	CLARKE Derek John Stanley	21-07-44	626 Sqn
151348	F/O	CHRIMES Oswald Kenneth	16-03-44	466 Sqn	160076	F/O	CLARKE Desmond De Villiers [South Africa]	8-09-44	29 OTU
1049057	Sgt	CHRISTIE Charles	18-04-44	158 Sqn					
1128392	F/S	CHRISTIE Charles Cecil	25-03-44	626 Sqn	129448	F/L	CLARKE Douglas Augustine William	30-08-44	1655 MTU
53421	F/O	CHRISTIE John	27-07-44	627 Sqn	107142	F/L	CLARKE MiD Ernest Summer	30-01-44	97 Sqn
1115377	W/O	CHRISTIE Leslie	29-01-44	630 Sqn	1581727	Sgt	CLARKE Eric Stanley	21-07-44	578 Sqn
170702	P/O	CHURCH Eric Arthur	20-01-44	102 Sqn	1463568	Sgt	CLARKE Frederick Charles	4-05-44	625 Sqn
163986	F/O	CHURCHER Gerald Leonard	29-10-44	515 Sqn	161322	P/O	CLARKE George	27-01-44	15 Sqn
965799	Sgt	CHURCHER William John	2-01-44	61 Sqn	940365	Sgt	CLARKE Harold William	16-10-44	115 Sqn
1332240	F/S	CHURCHILL Dennis Arthur	31-03-44	51 Sqn	184538	P/O	CLARKE Henry	12-09-44	218 Sqn
124782	F/L	CHURCHILL DFC* Henry Dixie	7-05-44	156 Sqn	621717	Sgt	CLARKE Henry James	15-02-44	10 Sqn
575146	Sgt	CHURCHOUSE David John Kenneth	23-05-44	207 Sqn	1600754	F/S	CLARKE MiD Herbert George	7-10-44	617 Sqn
1067662	F/S	CHURCHMAN Maurice	20-02-44	576 Sqn	2204244	Sgt	CLARKE James Ernest	26-08-44	83 OTU
152041	F/O	CLACK Basil Alfred	16-06-44	61 Sqn	1300857	Sgt	CLARKE John	28-05-44	432 Sqn
124623	S/L	CLACK DFM Kenneth Arthur	31-03-44	76 Sqn	177263	P/O	CLARKE DFC John Anthony Creemer	20-10-44	35 Sqn
1603396	Sgt	CLACK Leslie Reginald	24-03-44	578 Sqn	983710	Cpl	CLARKE John Ashley	28-12-44	347 Sqn
151413	F/O	CLACK Sidney Arthur	27-08-44	12 Sqn	177011	P/O	CLARKE John Seymour Macleod	25-05-44	158 Sqn
1396004	LAC	CLAESSEN Rupert Settatree	3-12-44	44 Sqn	1162204	F/S	CLARKE Joseph Desmond	3-01-44	405 Sqn
1509139	Sgt	CLAMP Clifford	11-04-44	576 Sqn	1602946	Sgt	CLARKE Kenneth William	23-09-44	207 Sqn
104541	F/L	CLANCEY Richard William	8-11-44	1655 MTU	134715	F/O	CLARKE Leslie Francis	15-03-44	51 Sqn
1795884	Sgt	CLANCY Robert Peter	21-11-44	192 Sqn	1380159	F/S	CLARKE Ralph William	12-05-44	115 Sqn
143739	F/O	CLAPHAM Philip Charles	11-11-44	619 Sqn	56445	P/O	CLARKE Richard Joseph [Fire]	23-12-44	35 Sqn
1022894	F/S	CLAPHAM William Paterson	31-03-44	427 Sqn	51703	F/L	CLARKE Richard Towers	31-07-44	57 Sqn
2205668	Sgt	CLAPTON Ian Rosse	15-12-44	625 Sqn	184151	P/O	CLARKE Robert Barclay	30-08-44	106 Sqn
1588531	F/S	CLAQUE John Edward	18-07-44	578 Sqn	1823047	Sgt	CLARKE Robert Joseph	24-04-44	102 Sqn
144607	F/O	CLARE Frederick William	28-05-44	75 Sqn	50765	F/O	CLARKE Sydney Mervyn	23-04-44	550 Sqn
1568239	Sgt	CLARENCE Arthur	4-05-44	101 Sqn	1807084	Sgt	CLARKE Victor William	12-09-44	1658 HCU
2210061	Sgt	CLARK Albert Arthur	23-01-44	1667 HCU	747313	Sgt	CLARKE William	21-04-44	57 Sqn
1473146	Sgt	CLARK Albert Dennis	26-05-44	5 LFS	1685389	Sgt	CLARKE William Harold	29-01-44	166 Sqn
1826183	Sgt	CLARK Andrew	2-11-44	153 Sqn	1796193	Sgt	CLARKIN Philip Peter [Eire]	21-01-44	550 Sqn
1578273	Sgt	CLARK Bernard	27-01-44	61 Sqn	151846	F/O	CLARKSON Andrew	29-07-44	106 Sqn
1004554	W/O	CLARK Brian	5-08-44	425 Sqn	1007251	Sgt	CLARKSON Francis	20-02-44	460 Sqn
106151	F/L	CLARK MiD Charles Peter	29-09-44	161 Sqn	169318	F/O	CLARSON Ian David Henry	19-07-44	78 Sqn
1717165	Sgt	CLARK Donald Carpenter	18-07-44	115 Sqn	1628570	Sgt	CLASSEN William George	28-12-44	101 Sqn
1324105	F/S	CLARK Ernest William	26-08-44	100 Sqn	1338676	Sgt	CLATWORTHY Douglas Roy	27-08-44	115 Sqn
168675	P/O	CLARK Frank	25-04-44	49 Sqn	1815821	Sgt	CLAXTON Ronald	2-05-44	51 Sqn
172551	P/O	CLARK Geoffrey John Reader	12-05-44	166 Sqn	1594522	Sgt	CLAY Cain	13-08-44	101 Sqn
1330373	F/S	CLARK George Charles	20-02-44	102 Sqn	1852931	Sgt	CLAY Ronald Edgar	22-06-44	44 Sqn
1335626	Sgt	CLARK George Frederick	15-02-44	166 Sqn	1591635	Sgt	CLAY Thomas Spender	26-08-44	83 Sqn
1575494	Sgt	CLARK Gerard	15-03-44	44 Sqn	1039740	Sgt	CLAYDEN Ernest	2-07-44	1667 HCU
2212860	F/S	CLARK Gilbert Milroy	18-12-44	227 Sqn	179031	F/O	CLAYDEN Frank Arthur	15-10-44	90 Sqn
1851602	Sgt	CLARK Grahame Gordon	5-10-44	101 Sqn	130537	P/O	CLAYDON Frank Edward	14-01-44	166 Sqn
1122986	Sgt	CLARK Henry David	27-04-44	106 Sqn	47351	F/L	CLAYES DFC Norman	13-05-44	105 Sqn
2218400	Sgt	CLARK Herbert Edgar	21-11-44	408 Sqn	1811224	Sgt	CLAYTON Alfred James Herbert	31-03-44	101 Sqn
159223	F/O	CLARK Hilary Daniel	10-06-44	49 Sqn	16-2352	Sgt	CLAYTON Ernest	4-01-44	11 OTU
1346415	Sgt	CLARK James	12-03-44	199 Sqn	1133484	Sgt	CLAYTON Henry	16-11-44	15 Sqn
1545681	Sgt	CLARK James	22-03-44	50 Sqn	1624688	Sgt	CLAYTON Jack	6-12-44	77 Sqn
144761	F/O	CLARK John	27-01-44	101 Sqn	1739516	Sgt	CLAYTON James B.	22-12-44	189 Sqn
1853346	Sgt	CLARK John David	21-11-44	51 Sqn	1563552	AC2	CLAYTON Joseph Thomas	22-03-44	102 Sqn
169584	P/O	CLARK Joseph James Richard	20-02-44	207 Sqn	1896425	Sgt	CLAYTON Kenneth	27-09-44	1654 HCU
1605215	Sgt	CLARK Kenneth Edward	16-02-44	78 Sqn	139962	F/L	CLAYTON DFC Ralf John Henry	15-02-44	7 Sqn
573413	F/S	CLARK Maurice Arthur	22-06-44	57 Sqn	1545659	Sgt	CLAYTON Samuel Joseph	2-05-44	218 Sqn
1356191	Sgt	CLARK Raymond Ernest William	26-08-44	622 Sqn	626938	F/S	CLAYTON Thomas Roy [Canada]	4-05-44	57 Sqn
1564949	F/S	CLARK Robert	14-10-44	12 Sqn	1603691	Sgt	CLAYTON Victor Neville	13-07-44	103 Sqn
651129	F/S	CLARK Robert Charles	3-05-44	35 Sqn	171432	P/O	CLAYTON William Robert	21-06-44	1661 HCU
2208987	Sgt	CLARK Ronald	2-01-44	207 Sqn	1621688	Sgt	CLAYWORTH Albert	26-08-44	300 Sqn

171637	P/O	CLEGG GM James	15-03-44	101 Sqn		1850361	Sgt	COHEN Lionel	23-04-44	424 Sqn
1578868	Sgt	CLEGG Richard	16-03-44	625 Sqn				(served as WALTERS)		
169494	P/O	CLEGG William Arthur	14-01-44	7 Sqn		1668508	F/S	COHEN Louis	5-10-44	626 Sqn
1532013	F/S	CLEMENT Charles Roy	6-10-44	78 Sqn		1811276	Sgt	COHEN Samuel George	29-01-44	7 Sqn
1800987	Sgt	CLEMENT Charles Thomas Leslie	26-02-44	207 Sqn		1468060	Sgt	COKER Frederick Charles	25-04-44	12 OTU
150238	F/L	CLEMENT DFC Frederick Cecil Walter	8-07-44	106 Sqn		149304	F/O	COKER Hugh	15-07-44	156 Sqn
1393760	Sgt	CLEMENT Ronald Denis	8-02-44	138 Sqn		143257	F/O	COLAN Anthony Owen	26-02-44	166 Sqn
1573051	Sgt	CLEMENTS Howard Glen	14-01-44	101 Sqn		148102	F/S	COLBERT DFC Sydney	14-01-44	156 Sqn
1875077	Sgt	CLEMENTS Reginald George	9-12-44	21 OTU		174672	P/O	COLBORN Edward Albert	26-03-44	10 Sqn
2210186	Sgt	CLEMINSON-PASSEY John Harold	10-04-44	PFNTU		956180	Sgt	COLBOURNE John Leslie	6-01-44	576 Sqn
175564	P/O	CLENAHAN DFC Robert Lonsdale	15-06-44	582 Sqn		1437045	F/S	COLBURN Francis Leman Jesse	6-11-44	550 Sqn
611721	Sgt	CLETHEROE Charles	16-08-44	625 Sqn		1583876	Sgt	COLDICOTT Dennis John	4-05-44	103 Sqn
1266119	F/S	CLEVEY William Alfred	28-05-44	103 Sqn		977625	F/S	COLDICUTT Edward Cecil	25-05-44	640 Sqn
1584554	AC1	CLEWS Walter	10-04-44	Spilsby		137578	S/L	COLDWELL DSO DFM Philip Robert	20-05-44	7 Sqn
169587	P/O	CLIBURN Eric Percy	25-03-44	57 Sqn		1543965	Sgt	COLDWELL Walter	27-05-44	5 LFS
2220679	Sgt	CLIFFORD Ronald Henry	30-08-44	50 Sqn		127557	F/O	COLDWELL-HORSFALL George David		
1825003	Sgt	CLIFF-McCULLOCH Alexander Peter							16-05-44	12 OTU
			1-06-44	138 Sqn		151428	F/O	COLE Albert Stanley	29-07-44	49 Sqn
123289	F/O	CLIFTON Albert Edwin	11-04-44	169 Sqn		1800713	F/S	COLE Douglas Arthur	15-03-44	77 Sqn
171392	P/O	CLIFTON Charles	28-01-44	199 Sqn		1600897	F/S	COLE Douglas Neville	5-11-44	76 Sqn
142062	F/O	CLIFTON Frederic Allan Newell	23-05-44	49 Sqn		1716749	Sgt	COLE John Percival Victor	16-02-44	619 Sqn
1146496	Sgt	CLIFTON Leslie	31-01-44	97 Sqn		1486632	Sgt	COLE Richard Derrick	23-09-44	61 Sqn
1031305	Sgt	CLIMO Rendle George William	20-01-44	97 Sqn		1387235	F/S	COLE Robert Samuel	2-05-44	514 Sqn
2210367	Sgt	CLINCH Frederick William	23-12-44	90 Sqn		1578101	Sgt	COLEBATCH Norman Henry	3-01-44	156 Sqn
1288144	Sgt	CLINCH Kenneth	28-05-44	75 Sqn		178780	F/O	COLEMAN Gerald	9-10-44	462 Sqn
1336818	F/S	CLISBY Derek	6-08-44	83 Sqn		144359	F/O	COLEMAN Phillip James	16-04-44	619 Sqn
1614648	Sgt	CLITHEROE Thomas Craske	29-07-44	12 Sqn		1582838	Sgt	COLEMAN Ronald F.	22-05-44	49 Sqn
1193544	Sgt	CLOUGH David [USA]	12-05-44	75 Sqn		1894491	Sgt	COLEMAN Ronald Frank	25-06-44	61 Sqn
162049	F/O	CLOUGH Denis Graham	17-09-44	1652 HCU		147097	F/O	COLEMAN Sidney Harry	6-08-44	51 Sqn
1671810	Sgt	CLOUGH Henry Denton	5-02-44	115 Sqn		1339954	Sgt	COLEMAN Sydney Francis	24-09-44	85 OTU
1483603	Sgt	CLOUGH Kenneth	10-04-44	166 Sqn		1397422	F/S	COLEMAN Thomas Arthur	25-05-44	158 Sqn
1523112	Sgt	CLOUGH Kenneth	17-06-44	102 Sqn		150042	F/L	COLENUTT Hubert James	6-02-44	149 Sqn
1591628	Sgt	CLOUGH Winston Pescod	18-03-44	630 Sqn		1624295	F/S	COLES Eric Charles	30-06-44	514 Sqn
1652839	Sgt	CLOUTER Geoffrey Thomas	26-02-44	12 Sqn		1894366	Sgt	COLES Leslie Peter	21-11-44	514 Sqn
1595006	Sgt	CLOWES Wallace Arthur	4-11-44	425 Sqn		1895090	Sgt	COLEY Raymond Charles	31-10-44	460 Sqn
1520775	Sgt	CLUCAS Philip Harold	13-08-44	50 Sqn		1605311	Sgt	COLGATE Harold George	30-05-44	11 OTU
1391077	F/S	CLULOW George Frederick	31-03-44	207 Sqn		139595	F/O	COLHOUN William Andrew Lawrence	31-03-44	49 Sqn
1319227	F/S	CLUTTERBUCK Leonard Charles	22-05-44	166 Sqn		1811940	F/S	COLLENS Reginald Joseph	3-01-44	156 Sqn
1798065	Sgt	CLYDE William	6-11-44	106 Sqn		45448	S/L	COLLETT AFC Albert Leslie	27-04-44	83 Sqn
1890818	Sgt	COAKER Ronald Lee	15-08-44	207 Sqn		1103799	Sgt	COLLEY Edward Leslie	10-08-44	619 Sqn
1670149	Sgt	COATES James Arthur	16-03-44	463 Sqn		1802370	Sgt	COLLEY Ronald Jack 'Ron'	24-02-44	51 Sqn
1483125	F/S	COATES Raymond	22-05-44	630 Sqn		1894963	Sgt	COLLIER Richard Alfred James	31-03-44	101 Sqn
1593142	Sgt	COATES Walter	23-06-44	77 Sqn		1384914	Sgt	COLLIER Ronald Frank	28-04-44	102 Sqn
161794	P/O	COATES DFM William Darby	25-03-44	97 Sqn		1567439	Sgt	COLLIER William Roy	3-01-44	432 Sqn
1801058	F/S	COBB Dennis	26-08-44	83 Sqn		1822863	Sgt	COLLIN Thomas	9-06-44	467 Sqn
1315286	F/S	COBB William	3-08-44	619 Sqn		1800837	Sgt	COLLINGS Ronald Charles	8-07-44	207 Sqn
150100	F/O	COBBIN David Webb	14-01-44	550 Sqn		1595173	Sgt	COLLINGWOOD Charles Norman	5-12-44	428 Sqn
1797997	Sgt	COBURN Albert Joseph	16-09-44	78 Sqn		1823042	Sgt	COLLINGWOOD Lewis	22-01-44	158 Sqn
122441	F/O	COCHRAN Dennis Herbert	31-03-44	10 OTU		1603327	Sgt	COLLINS Anthony Thomas	27-09-44	1654 HCU
1550734	Sgt	COCHRANE John	25-04-44	622 Sqn		144941	F/L	COLLINS Arthur Vincent	24-02-44	149 Sqn
1600118	F/S	COCKBAINE Michael William	21-11-44	51 Sqn		1603108	Sgt	COLLINS David Norman	27-04-44	207 Sqn
1569223	Sgt	COCKBURN John Thomas	4-05-44	166 Sqn		967795	F/S	COLLINS Ernest Lewis	30-08-44	106 Sqn
1880173	Sgt	COCKER Eric Royston	13-06-44	90 Sqn		1389556	Sgt	COLLINS Frederick Charles	14-01-44	166 Sqn
1620633	Sgt	COCKSHOTT Wright	12-06-44	101 Sqn		1896249	Sgt	COLLINS Frederick James	13-07-44	166 Sqn
1892631	Sgt	CODD John Herbert	29-07-44	576 Sqn		1186834	Sgt	COLLINS George Edward	15-03-44	90 Sqn
1818737	Sgt	CODLING Ronald	21-01-44	207 Sqn		177516	P/O	COLLINS Gilson Edmund	30-07-44	1656 HCU
1593244	Sgt	CODY Martin	3-08-44	619 Sqn		1869001	Sgt	COLLINS Gordon Robert	31-03-44	622 Sqn
1507583	Sgt	COE Cecil Robert	5-10-44	115 Sqn		1808961	Sgt	COLLINS Henry William	23-04-44	582 Sqn
1409939	Sgt	COE Cyril Rupert	17-05-44	1661 HCU		1593956	Sgt	COLLINS Leslie	22-01-44	166 Sqn
1600455	F/S	COE Eric John	24-09-44	61 Sqn		2220310	Sgt	COLLINS Reginald Noah	27-08-44	35 Sqn
1126098	F/S	COE George Ernest	12-05-44	432 Sqn		1461479	Sgt	COLLINS Robert William	25-06-44	102 Sqn
621726	Sgt	COFFEY Frederick	15-02-44	10 Sqn		3010060	Sgt	COLLINS Timothy [Eire]	29-07-44	103 Sqn
158848	P/O	COGBILL Arthur Jems	22-03-44	Riccall		2220002	Sgt	COLLINS William Bernard	12-08-44	76 Sqn
151239	F/O	COGGINS Ronald William Welch	24-02-44	578 Sqn		1549496	F/S	COLLINSON Bernard	15-11-44	115 Sqn
183800	P/O	COGHLAN Lawrence William	17-08-44	102 Sqn		1211264	W/O	COLLINSON George Thomas	23-08-44	692 Sqn
655617	Sgt	COHEN Abraham	3-01-44	57 Sqn		1233362	Sgt	COLLISON George Alec	28-06-44	106 Sqn
1523141	Sgt	COHEN Benjamin	25-04-44	166 Sqn		1284701	F/S	COLLIS Leslie John	25-03-44	576 Sqn
1391163	F/S	COHEN David Isadore	21-02-44	9 Sqn		152401	F/O	COLLYER Cyril Thomas	7-10-44	51 Sqn
1893247	Sgt	COHEN Isaac Ivan	4-11-44	195 Sqn		1398722	Sgt	COLMAN Percival Leonard	25-02-44	550 Sqn

143466	F/O	COLOMBO DFC Donald Arthur	25-03-44	12 Sqn	1586233	Sgt	COOPER Alfred Frank	21-01-44	1661 HCU
143762	F/O	COLTHURST John Buller	24-02-44	115 Sqn	1586469	F/S	COOPER Arthur John Macfarlane	30-12-44	156 Sqn
158802	F/O	COLVILLE Fred	31-03-44	97 Sqn	1383683	F/S	COOPER Arthur Wilfred	22-05-44	576 Sqn
54235	P/O	COLVIN DFC Alfred	25-02-44	156 Sqn	575301	Sgt	COOPER Basil John	18-09-44	57 Sqn
171275	P/O	COLVIN John	25-05-44	7 Sqn	1819329	Sgt	COOPER Dennis John	27-04-44	49 Sqn
1600445	Sgt	COLWELL Harry George	13-06-44	78 Sqn	2221308	Sgt	COOPER Edward Roy	28-12-44	75 Sqn
1129817	F/S	COMBE George Ernest	15-02-44	7 Sqn	1876629	Sgt	COOPER George James	25-05-44	576 Sqn
1823102	Sgt	COMBE Thomas Smith	22-05-44	514 Sqn	1852306	Sgt	COOPER Gerald Douglas	8-07-44	207 Sqn
1220626	F/S	COMER Leonard John	24-03-44	103 Sqn	174945	F/O	COOPER Herbert Wright	19-07-44	61 Sqn
108944	S/L	COMPTON Anthony Wilfred Alwyne [Canada]	29-09-44	161 Sqn	172104	P/O	COOPER Hugh Boys	23-04-44	7 Sqn
					1308375	Sgt	COOPER James Henry	23-05-44	75 Sqn
1600146	F/S	COMPTON Stanley James	25-07-44	83 Sqn	1384316	Sgt	COOPER John	20-04-44	1657 HCU
1398070	Sgt	COMPTON William Walter Stanley	20-02-44	49 Sqn	152008	F/O	COOPER Norman Ernest	15-06-44	78 Sqn
140891	F/O	COMYN Reginald Daniel [Eire]	3-08-44	239 Sqn	1600217	Sgt	COOPER Norman Leslie	24-03-44	640 Sqn
2235489	Sgt	CONCHIE James Edward	28-09-44	29 OTU	1474128	F/S	COOPER Roger Hughes	7-06-44	103 Sqn
156769	F/O	COND Rex Hinton	31-03-44	101 Sqn	68807	F/L	COOPER Thomas Noel	6-11-44	515 Sqn
133539	F/L	CONLON DFC William Michael	8-06-44	156 Sqn	1489922	Sgt	COOPER William	21-11-44	49 Sqn
1128106	F/S	CONNATTY Terence Robert	25-04-44	49 Sqn	1893358	Sgt	COOPER William James	21-07-44	101 Sqn
2211503	Sgt	CONNELL Peter	9-11-44	625 Sqn	1295109	F/S	COOTE Arthur William	20-01-44	83 Sqn
1567790	Sgt	CONNELL Thomas Samuel	31-03-44	51 Sqn	1425976	Sgt	COOTE Frederick Samuel	21-02-44	9 Sqn
1370843	F/S	CONNELLY Joseph	11-05-44	467 Sqn	1610044	Sgt	COOTE George Alfred	4-05-44	626 Sqn
1236363	Sgt	CONNETT Ernest Lewis	25-06-44	75 Sqn	3000114	Sgt	COOTE Kenneth Percy	27-08-44	115 Sqn
1587763	Sgt	CONNOLLY Cyril William	27-08-44	625 Sqn	1588638	Sgt	COPE John Francis	9-06-44	51 Sqn
1569111	Sgt	CONNOLLY Hugh Henry Mills	31-03-44	550 Sqn	622353	Sgt	COPELAND George Lewis	31-07-44	100 Sqn
37385	W/C	CONNOLLY Patrick Edward Geoffrey Gunnell	14-07-44	550 Sqn	1215324	Sgt	COPLEY Dennis	22-02-44	218 Sqn
					1600555	F/S	COPP Peter Frederick John	30-10-44	85 Sqn
1566901	Sgt	CONNON George Christie	2-01-44	101 Sqn	1335846	Sgt	COPPING Peter George	29-01-44	115 Sqn
1819154	Sgt	CONNOR Anthony Charles	1-06-44	622 Sqn	1582857	F/S	CORBETT Kenneth Raymond	29-01-44	10 Sqn
1268145	F/S	CONNOR Robert Owen	8-06-44	78 Sqn	923564	Sgt	CORDERY John Charles	18-11-44	51 Sqn
1549439	Sgt	CONNOR Thomas William	23-05-44	630 Sqn	2211649	Sgt	CORDON Leslie Theodore	7-06-44	1654 HCU
1295094	Sgt	CONRAD Henry	3-01-44	49 Sqn	2216220	Sgt	CORKILL Ronald Blair	23-04-44	431 Sqn
1890908	Sgt	CONSTABLE John Charles	18-10-44	115 Sqn	613736	Sgt	CORLESS John	8-08-44	103 Sqn
1563542	F/S	CONSTABLE Patrick Millar	23-04-44	514 Sqn	1383128	F/S	CORLETT Arthur Ian	20-02-44	12 Sqn
1824996	Sgt	CONVY Michael	6-10-44	115 Sqn	1354726	Sgt	CORLETT Arthur Leonard	27-08-44	1657 HCU
1585116	Sgt	COOCH Charles William	5-05-44	7 Sqn	2209824	Sgt	CORLETT John Norman	24-10-44	18 OTU
1044705	Sgt	COOGAN James Patrick [Eire]	13-06-44	166 Sqn	1317111	F/S	CORNELIUS Raymond Summers	22-05-44	9 Sqn
R/110020	LAC	COOK Albert Royal Felken	16-07-44	61 Base	168812	F/L	CORNELL DFC Norman James	22-06-44	83 Sqn
87071	F/L	COOK Alastair John	31-03-44	12 Sqn	152793	F/O	CORNELL Reginald Henry	19-10-44	627 Sqn
1503607	F/S	COOK Anthony Martindale	26-02-44	12 Sqn	2220039	Sgt	CORNER Frank Leonard	7-06-44	106 Sqn
143852	F/O	COOK Aubrey Edgar	27-01-44	166 Sqn	1593000	Sgt	CORNER William	24-02-44	30 OTU
1336408	F/S	COOK Charles	21-01-44	427 Sqn	1522542	Sgt	CORNES Denis Claridge	30-01-44	100 Sqn
1624847	Sgt	COOK Cyril	8-12-44	90 Sqn	1866629	F/S	CORNISH Dennis James	9-11-44	138 Sqn
1158471	Sgt	COOK Donald Herbert William	14-01-44	97 Sqn	575796	F/S	CORNISH Eric	24-06-44	7 Sqn
1579359	Sgt	COOK Harry	20-02-44	626 Sqn	1609419	Sgt	CORNISH Vernon Charles	21-07-44	75 Sqn
1551870	F/S	COOK Harry William	21-07-44	578 Sqn	168642	P/O	CORNWELL DFC Kenneth Frank	29-01-44	166 Sqn
1334466	Sgt	COOK Joseph Thomas	4-05-44	19 OTU	1330214	Sgt	CORNWELL Reginald Sydney	14-01-44	101 Sqn
1813397	Sgt	COOK Leonard George	18-10-44	630 Sqn	183071	P/O	CORRAN Stanley	13-08-44	427 Sqn
1853768	Sgt	COOK Michael John	17-12-44	50 Sqn	1087422	Sgt	CORRIGAN Peter	26-08-44	626 Sqn
139650	F/L	COOK Ralph Edward	17-06-44	102 Sqn	1501099	Sgt	CORRIS Douglas	21-07-44	75 Sqn
1696030	Sgt	COOK Robert	14-07-44	158 Sqn	148858	P/O	CORRY John Simpson Blair	28-10-44	76 Sqn
168676	F/O	COOK DFM Roy James [Canada]	28-01-44	625 Sqn	149591	F/O	COSENS DFC Frank William	15-02-44	207 Sqn
1836629	Sgt	COOK Royston Garfield	2-08-44	51 Sqn	1447261	Sgt	COSGROVE David James Clark	13-08-44	622 Sqn
1183804	Sgt	COOK Wilfred Julian	24-07-44	102 Sqn	1025606	Sgt	COSGROVE Gilbert	16-03-44	514 Sqn
2209173	Sgt	COOKE Alfred	31-03-44	514 Sqn	1875013	Sgt	COSSEY Hedley John	22-06-44	619 Sqn
162972	F/O	COOKE David Clifford	12-09-44	207 Sqn	1880733	Sgt	COSSINS Geoffrey Douglas	20-05-44	83 OTU
1383704	F/S	COOKE Frank Stewart	26-02-44	207 Sqn	153208	F/O	COSSINS John Gordon	28-10-44	76 Sqn
46790	F/L	COOKE John Grant	5-07-44	35 Sqn	902774	W/O	COSSINS Reginald Frederick Henry	23-05-44	207 Sqn
1816385	F/S	COOKE John Peter	5-10-44	75 Sqn	1804430	Sgt	COSTIN Philip Eric	7-12-44	1651 HCU
1336866	F/S	COOKE John Robert Alfred	30-06-44	51 Sqn	2206578	Sgt	COTTAM Sylvester	3-08-44	625 Sqn
178710	P/O	COOKE Raymond Joseph	13-08-44	158 Sqn	1348052	Sgt	COTTAR Robert	17-06-44	77 Sqn
1451038	Sgt	COOKMAN Harry	27-01-44	149 Sqn	1527411	Sgt	COTTER Fred	22-01-44	166 Sqn
1591119	Sgt	COOKSEY Joseph	3-01-44	619 Sqn	1821266	Sgt	COTTER Douglas Andrew	12-09-44	44 Sqn
2210045	Sgt	COOKSON Thomas Phillip	2-09-44	57 Sqn	1430072	F/S	COTTERELL Eric	31-05-44	12 OTU
1587024	F/S	COOLE Douglas Albert Frederick	29-06-44	582 Sqn	1378318	Sgt	COTTERILL William Hobson	20-02-44	429 Sqn
177978	P/O	COOLES Douglas Reginald	16-06-44	7 Sqn	1898325	Sgt	COTTON Jesse Ernest	22-11-44	640 Sqn
1549199	F/S	COOLING John	15-10-44	90 Sqn	1575755	Sgt	COTTON Leslie	28-04-44	166 Sqn
1582983	Sgt	COOMBE Douglas James	28-01-44	467 Sqn	1392583	Sgt	COTTON Walter	18-03-44	434 Sqn
179081	F/O	COOMBS Grahame Frederick	6-08-44	50 Sqn	172470	P/O	COTTON MINCHIN Christopher Humphrey [USA]	31-03-44	12 Sqn
172298	P/O	COOPER Alfred Ernest Stanley	28-04-44	166 Sqn					

1607868	Sgt	COTTRELL Dennis Owen	27-03-44	78 Sqn
1897803	Sgt	COTTRELL Edward Cyril	4-05-44	192 Sqn
1350378	F/S	COTTRELL Gilbert Valentine	15-06-44	582 Sqn
1425970	F/S	COTTRELL Norman	20-01-44	57 Sqn
755107	Sgt	COTTRELL Norman Richard	31-03-44	207 Sqn
1850861	Sgt	COTTRELL Royston William	24-02-44	1664 HCU
2209452	Sgt	COUGHLAN Leo	28-04-44	51 Sqn
1523070	Sgt	COUGHLIN Bernard	16-02-44	77 Sqn
1871450	Sgt	COUGHTREY James Algernon	6-09-44	1667 HCU
1582477	Sgt	COULING Herbert John	7-02-44	1656 HCU
1890267	Sgt	COULSON Joseph Frederick	11-04-44	635 Sqn
1560932	Sgt	COULTER James	21-04-44	57 Sqn
1234081	Sgt	COULTER Frederick Thomas	22-03-44	97 Sqn
1600454	Sgt	COUP John	31-03-44	622 Sqn
1388349	F/S	COURT Frederick John	25-07-44	102 Sqn
132022	F/O	COURT DFC Thomas Roger	9-09-44	138 Sqn
2220217	Sgt	COURTENAY Ernest John	27-07-44	44 Sqn
1578974	Sgt	COURTENAY Stanley William	23-04-44	550 Sqn
1424977	Sgt	COURTOIS Jean Eugeine Joseph Alphonso [Belgium]	23-05-44	166 Sqn
44076	W/C	COUSENS DSO DFC MC [Czechoslovakia] Alan George Seymour	22-04-44	635 Sqn
164909	P/O	COUSIN Cyril	30-08-44	101 Sqn
1866747	Sgt	COUSIN Robert Frederick	29-07-44	630 Sqn
1321669	F/S	COUSINS Alec Henry	24-12-44	35 Sqn
1237485	Sgt	COUSINS Frank William	11-06-44	75 Sqn
1295276	LAC	COVE Donald Charles	2-01-44	76 Sqn
2208026	Sgt	COVELL George	25-08-44	218 Sqn
1600580	F/S	COVENEY Albert James	19-10-44	161 Sqn
1322554	Sgt	COVERLEY John Charles	30-08-44	619 Sqn
67107	F/L	COWAN Hugh Wilson	28-09-44	627 Sqn
1803789	F/S	COWAN DFM John Edward	23-09-44	97 Sqn
1348489	Sgt	COWAN William Robertson	1-07-44	101 Sqn
1622516	F/S	COWARD Bernard	28-10-44	90 Sqn
171192	P/O	COWARD Clifford William	11-04-44	49 Sqn
1317812	Sgt	COWDREY Reginald Sidney William	20-01-44	57 Sqn
1860362	Sgt	COWELL Albert Edward	3-01-44	463 Sqn
1823215	Sgt	COWELL John Roger	1-07-44	12 Sqn
144617	F/O	COWEN Wilfred James	11-11-44	97 Sqn
169485	F/O	COWGILL DFC Peter James	18-12-44	85 Sqn
1308596	Sgt	COWIE John Boyle	25-06-44	576 Sqn
177640	P/O	COWIE Peter	11-06-44	625 Sqn
1074033	Cpl	COWIN Albert	28-12-44	347 Sqn
156559	F/O	COWLES DFC Reginald Clifford Andrew	11-12-44	514 Sqn
955374	Sgt	COWLEY Thomas Baxter	25-02-44	44 Sqn
176488	P/O	COWLING Aubrey Francis	6-08-44	51 Sqn
1534158	Sgt	COWLING Herbert Edwin	25-07-44	103 Sqn
1314241	F/S	COX Albert William	23-05-44	35 Sqn
175483	P/O	COX Alwyn Trevor	27-04-44	57 Sqn
182638	P/O	COX Arthur Cromwell Llewellyn	12-09-44	626 Sqn
1891838	Sgt	COX Dennis Bertram	25-04-44	100 Sqn
1602435	Sgt	COX James Lawford	5-07-44	49 Sqn
1869548	Sgt	COX James William	23-09-44	12 Sqn
118138	F/L	COX John Kevin	3-01-44	619 Sqn
113418	S/L	COX Leonard Edgar	22-06-44	49 Sqn
44189	F/L	COX AFC Maurice Ivan	28-04-44	103 Sqn
1821808	Sgt	COX Richard Belton	19-07-44	619 Sqn
1624744	Sgt	COX Thomas Hugh	26-03-44	192 Sqn
1607195	F/S	COX William Edwin John	31-08-44	1654 HCU
1583248	Sgt	COXHEAD Frank Ernest	23-06-44	97 Sqn
1900036	Sgt	COYLE John James	12-09-44	622 Sqn
1601560	F/S	COZENS Alan Duncan	24-12-44	100 Sqn
1590633	Sgt	COZENS Reginald Herbert	23-05-44	106 Sqn
133615	F/O	COZENS William Arthur	21-01-44	427 Sqn
155075	F/O	COZENS-HARDY Graham Sydney	9-11-44	625 Sqn
1607297	Sgt	CRABB Ronald George 'Ron'	21-07-44	100 Sqn
1510828	Sgt	CRABTREE Harry	25-02-44	419 Sqn
1324859	Sgt	CRABTREE James Douglas	6-10-44	635 Sqn
171003	P/O	CRABTREE John Athelstan	30-01-44	100 Sqn
1493180	F/S	CRABTREE John Calverley	21-11-44	75 Sqn
1676417	Sgt	CRABTREE Thomas James	12-09-44	635 Sqn
1544879	Sgt	CRACKNELL Albert Wilfred	29-07-44	420 Sqn
1575892	F/S	CRADDOCK Ronald Gerrard	25-04-44	626 Sqn
1867543	Sgt	CRADDOCK Thomas Finbar [Eire]	5-11-44	76 Sqn
159902	P/O	CRADDOCK William John	6-01-44	97 Sqn
1338713	Sgt	CRAGG Kenneth Leonard	20-02-44	514 Sqn
142375	F/O	CRAGG William Philip	22-02-44	218 Sqn
651886	F/S	CRAGGS David	29-07-44	582 Sqn
1825324	Sgt	CRAIG Angus	25-08-44	218 Sqn
659080	F/S	CRAIG Hugh Howie	27-01-44	622 Sqn
622827	Sgt	CRAIG John MacDonald	13-08-44	102 Sqn
1868383	Sgt	CRAIG John Nicol	12-05-44	427 Sqn
1390151	Sgt	CRAIG John Richard	22-01-44	640 Sqn
150617	F/O	CRAIG Lawrence William Harward	22-11-44	1660 HCU
1357411	Sgt	CRAIG Peter	6-06-44	76 Sqn
1823190	Sgt	CRAIG Robert	25-07-44	50 Sqn
171334	P/O	CRAIG Ronald Henry	25-06-44	9 Sqn
1341584	Sgt	CRAIG William	25-02-44	61 Sqn
1395725	Sgt	CRAIGIE Colin	22-03-44	626 Sqn
338549	Sgt	CRAIL William David	12-10-44	692 Sqn
134759	F/L	CRAMER Oscar Rene	12-08-44	76 Sqn
139688	F/O	CRAMP DFC Douglas Louis 'Duggie'	22-06-44	83 Sqn
1587965	Sgt	CRANE Clifford John	26-07-44	49 Sqn
1425973	F/S	CRANE Jack Henry	25-05-44	640 Sqn
1532034	Sgt	CRANE Thomas	28-07-44	101 Sqn
996215	F/S	CRANE William Edward	18-12-44	207 Sqn
201196	P/O	CRANEFIELD Robert Arthur Godwin	12-09-44	630 Sqn
1452911	Sgt	CRANSTON Gordon	28-04-44	460 Sqn
42696	S/L	CRANSWICK DSO DFC Alec Panton	5-07-44	35 Sqn
1608732	Sgt	CRATE Stanley Ralph	25-04-44	463 Sqn
1138526	F/S	CRAVEN Alfred	25-03-44	460 Sqn
1896929	Sgt	CRAVEN Alfred	27-07-44	44 Sqn
1454842	Sgt	CRAVEN Leonard	11-05-44	50 Sqn
1455595	Sgt	CRAVEN Louis James	31-03-44	158 Sqn
183801	F/O	CRAWFORD Charles Wallace	6-10-44	78 Sqn
175311	F/O	CRAWFORD Christopher Nigel Charles	15-10-44	7 Sqn
2211693	Sgt	CRAWFORD Foreer Douglas	26-07-44	432 Sqn
42197	F/L	CRAWFORD Jack Simon Gustave	15-03-44	550 Sqn
1566714	Sgt	CRAWFORD John	28-08-44	19 OTU
1392529	W/O	CRAWFORD John Mitchell	11-11-44	97 Sqn
1545675	Sgt	CRAWFORD Nathaniel Hugh	31-05-44	1654 HCU
1626265	Sgt	CRAWFORD Peter John Sprague	25-03-44	78 Sqn
1515079	Sgt	CRAWFORD Robert John	4-05-44	101 Sqn
929824	Sgt	CRAWFORD Ronald Aubrey	17-06-44	10 Sqn
2206157	Sgt	CRAWFORD Walter Edmond	27-04-44	35 Sqn
1134045	F/S	CRAWFORD William Andrew	8-06-44	115 Sqn
1615729	Sgt	CRAWLEY Clifford Charles	28-03-44	20 OTU
1294373	Sgt	CRAWLEY Samuel Edward	17-08-44	431 Sqn
1077115	Sgt	CRAWSHAW Maurice Smith	29-01-44	166 Sqn
1593188	Sgt	CRAWSHAW Stanley Raynor	4-11-44	49 Sqn
578032	Sgt	CRAZE Henry Edward Lawrence	21-07-44	158 Sqn
139886	F/L	CREASE DFC Ronald	14-01-44	7 Sqn
1594993	Sgt	CREASER George	12-12-44	195 Sqn
1354856	Sgt	CREBER Ronald Gordon	3-01-44	103 Sqn
188647	P/O	CREBBIN William Donald	26-11-44	115 Sqn
951791	F/S	CREER George Edward	25-04-44	78 Sqn
1429155	F/S	CREIGHTON DFM Noel Vaughan	27-04-44	101 Sqn
1586074	F/S	CREMINS Thomas David	21-12-44	97 Sqn
1561150	F/S	CRERAR Daniel	6-10-44	78 Sqn
1609239	Sgt	CRESSWELL Kenneth John	21-04-44	57 Sqn
28066	F/L	CREW DFC George Cecil	25-05-44	7 Sqn
1474210	Sgt	CRIBBIN George Norman	8-06-44	78 Sqn
656214	W/O	CRIBBS Henry Lanwarne	23-06-44	76 Sqn
1851867	Sgt	CRICK Lawrence Eric	4-03-44	199 Sqn
1507997	F/S	CRIMES Brian Francis Frederick	9-11-44	138 Sqn
1864307	Sgt	CRINGLE Robert Morrison	25-03-44	12 Sqn

1592241	Sgt	CRISFIELD Kenneth Solman	21-01-44	102 Sqn	1322496	F/S	CRYSTAL Rowland Henry	25-04-44	626 Sqn
1814423	Sgt	CRISP John Anthony	1-11-44	106 Sqn	171463	P/O	CUBBAGE DFM Brion Stanley	15-02-44	7 Sqn
1822207	Sgt	CRITCHLEY Lawrence Archibald	7-07-44	44 Sqn	170096	P/O	CUDE Basil Vincent	20-02-44	625 Sqn
1627552	Sgt	CRO David Harry	4-05-44	101 Sqn	1606835	Sgt	CUDLIPP Leonard William	28-05-44	582 Sqn
1890979	Sgt	CROAD George Partridge	28-04-44	138 Sqn	1896078	Sgt	CUFFEY Jonathan	29-06-44	10 Sqn
124256	W/C	CROCKER DFC* Malcolm [USA]	22-06-44	49 Sqn	1109838	F/S	CULLEN Peter Guthrie	24-12-44	166 Sqn
1801911	Sgt	CROCKETT Ronald Charles	30-01-44	156 Sqn	51053	F/O	CULLING Maurice Ferguson	15-03-44	149 Sqn
1388525	Sgt	CROCKFORD William Stanley	20-02-44	83 Sqn	51876	F/O	CULLINGTON Augustine Frederick	11-11-44	207 Sqn
915189	F/S	CROFT Arthur Cornelius	28-06-44	106 Sqn	1880199	Sgt	CULLUM Douglas Cyril	12-12-44	195 Sqn
925330	W/O	CROFT Claude William	4-05-44	12 Sqn	1348049	F/S	CULLY Wilbert	28-04-44	15 Sqn
154538	F/O	CROFT Peter Frederick	18-12-44	106 Sqn	962422	Sgt	CULVERWELL DFM Oswald Drury	29-01-44	434 Sqn
172205	P/O	CROFTS Fred	26-02-44	408 Sqn	1867838	Sgt	CUMBERLAND Walter James Eric	26-03-44	192 Sqn
1077090	F/S	CROKER Desmond Rimmer	15-07-44	207 Sqn	120434	F/L	CUMBERWORTH Leslie	2-09-44	1662 HCU
1825824	Sgt	CROLL James MacGregor	6-11-44	106 Sqn	1591862	Sgt	CUMBOR Thomas Shaftsbury	11-08-44	51 Sqn
613136	F/S	CROMAR DFM Donald	3-01-44	83 Sqn	1343298	Sgt	CUMMING James Craig	23-04-44	433 Sqn
162647	P/O	CROMARTY John Donald Range	3-01-44	156 Sqn	1569151	Sgt	CUMMING James Duncan	15-10-44	207 Sqn
1567127	Sgt	CROMARTY Joseph Fraser	4-12-44	1652 HCU	130528	F/O	CUMMINS Alfred Peter	31-03-44	51 Sqn
1593722	F/S	CROMPTON Frank	24-12-44	100 Sqn	1812153	Sgt	CUNDICK George William	12-10-44	166 Sqn
1095831	Sgt	CROMPTON William Roland	28-05-44	166 Sqn	1436622	Sgt	CUNDIFF Victor Ronald	11-02-44	158 Sqn
1390847	Sgt	CROMWELL Leonard Neil	21-02-44	640 Sqn	168967	P/O	CUNLIFFE Henry Norman	25-02-44	408 Sqn
1624601	F/S	CRONAN Thomas	18-12-44	207 Sqn	1566379	Sgt	CUNNINGHAM Charles Allan	11-06-44	460 Sqn
1762053	Sgt	CROOK Ronald Derek	4-05-44	44 Sqn	1812949	Sgt	CUNNINGHAM Donald Henry James	20-02-44	103 Sqn
157897	F/O	CROOK Walter Marshall	22-06-44	44 Sqn	1339759	Sgt	CUNNINGHAM Edward Andrew	15-03-44	101 Sqn
1493915	Sgt	CROOKE Arthur Woodrow	29-07-44	103 Sqn	1365361	Sgt	CUNNINGHAM George	25-07-44	75 Sqn
1591244	Sgt	CROOKS John Measor	4-05-44	626 Sqn	1803037	Sgt	CUNNINGHAM James Alfred	11-06-44	166 Sqn
1687739	Sgt	CROOKS John Hodgson	5-11-44	166 Sqn	1353624	Sgt	CUNNINGHAM John	8-06-44	622 Sqn
1587077	Sgt	CROOM Lionel Pearcey	7-06-44	460 Sqn	1568454	Sgt	CUNNINGHAM John	20-01-44	622 Sqn
1795076	Sgt	CRORY Weir	31-03-44	640 Sqn	182544	P/O	CUNNINGHAM John Meynell	18-07-44	429 Sqn
1671851	Sgt	CROSBY Bertram	19-03-44	101 Sqn	2209399	Sgt	CUNNINGHAM Robert Nixon	24-03-44	61 Sqn
1593845	Sgt	CROSBY Charles Gordon	3-01-44	61 Sqn	110558	F/L	CUNNINGHAM Ronald Percy	2-01-44	61 Sqn
179049	P/O	CROSBY DFM Vincent Brian [Eire]	15-06-44	582 Sqn	177256	P/O	CURLESS George	27-08-44	625 Sqn
151798	F/O	CROSIER Frank	5-07-44	106 Sqn	1512109	Sgt	CURPHEY Albert Leonard	13-08-44	102 Sqn
1196326	Sgt	CROSLAND Elwyn	23-03-44	26 OTU	2204864	Sgt	CURRAN Andrew Peter	25-04-44	12 OTU
1593233	Sgt	CROSS Arthur	16-03-44	12 Sqn	1566601	Sgt	CURRIE Andrew	14-03-44	78 Sqn
1596177	Sgt	CROSS Charles	1-11-44	57 Sqn	145701	F/O	CURRIE Edgar James	31-03-44	97 Sqn
1815434	F/S	CROSS Charles William	12-12-44	150 Sqn	1569077	Sgt	CURRIE James	21-01-44	77 Sqn
1313572	W/O	CROSS Dennis Harold James	9-05-44	83 Sqn	169469	P/O	CURRIE DFC William	3-01-44	7 Sqn
1314436	F/S	CROSS Frederick Thomas	25-04-44	16 OTU	1553148	Sgt	CURRIE William	8-05-44	106 Sqn
39305	S/L	CROSS DFC Ian Kingston Pembroke	31-03-44	103 Sqn	1685011	Sgt	CURRUMS William Norman	13-06-44	578 Sqn
151248	F/O	CROSS John Stanley	20-02-44	630 Sqn	1570690	Sgt	CURSITER John Robert	23-05-44	35 Sqn
1314932	W/O	CROSS Michael Govier	16-07-44	83 Sqn	1398725	Sgt	CURTIS Arthur Ernest	19-07-44	619 Sqn
1451670	F/S	CROSS Raymond Jack	4-05-44	207 Sqn	1295055	Sgt	CURTIS Donald Wilfred	31-05-44	1654 HCU
174670	P/O	CROSSLEY Edmund Forbes	19-04-44	57 Sqn	955429	F/S	CURTIS Douglas	18-03-44	44 Sqn
185784	F/S	CROSSLEY Ernest	2-11-44	428 Sqn	638981	Sgt	CURTIS Frazer	24-03-44	78 Sqn
1039308	Sgt	CROSSTHWAITE Ernest	19-03-44	1667 HCU	178241	P/O	CURTIS Gilbert Alfred John	8-06-44	431 Sqn
169572	P/O	CROTHERS Frederick	20-01-44	10 Sqn	55805	P/O	CURTIS Kenneth Lawrence	22-03-44	408 Sqn
1436260	Sgt	CROTHERS Kenneth Denzel	23-05-44	103 Sqn	1396192	Sgt	CURTIS Maurice Henry James	16-10-44	207 Sqn
149983	F/O	CROUCH DFM Alan John	13-05-44	76 Sqn	120090	F/L	CURTIS DFM Robert Julian	2-05-44	514 Sqn
1437428	Sgt	CROUCH John Lowes	9-04-44	460 Sqn	46406	F/L	CURTIS Roy	24-3-44	51 Sqn
655586	W/O	CROWE Matthew	21-08-44	1655 MTU	1629379	Sgt	CURTIS Stanley Raymond	9-08-44	138 Sqn
1824369	Sgt	CROWE Robert Frederick	25-07-44	15 Sqn	1691959	Sgt	CURZON Ernest William	20-02-44	83 Sqn
1510703	F/S	CROWTHER Ernest	21-07-44	622 Sqn	55957	P/O	CUSACK Charles	30-07-44	420 Sqn
1819387	Sgt	CROWTHER Frederick Stephen	5-10-44	101 Sqn	1505655	Sgt	CUSHING Keith	23-01-44	161 Sqn
150099	F/O	CROXFORD Reginald John Claude	14-01-44	7 Sqn	162810	P/O	CUSSON Thomas Frederick	17-06-44	77 Sqn
1893473	Sgt	CROXON Kenneth Eric	25-08-44	75 Sqn	1869160	Sgt	CUSTANCE Charles	21-07-44	101 Sqn
2213869	Sgt	CROZIER Gilbert	30-09-44	1651 HCU	1315283	Sgt	CUTHBERT John Edward Ashfield	7-08-44	149 Sqn
1596731	Sgt	CROZIER Peter	13-09-44	20 OTU	1470775	Sgt	CUTHBERT John Rowland	29-07-44	576 Sqn
620947	Sgt	CRUICKSHANK Douglas	15-03-44	408 Sqn	1043255	Sgt	CUTHBERTSON James Gordon	18-03-44	463 Sqn
1564167	Sgt	CRUICKSHANK James Alexander	26-08-44	103 Sqn	144345	F/O	CUTHBERTSON William Roberts	1-07-44	101 Sqn
1568887	F/S	CRUICKSHANK John Mitchell	29-11-44	35 Sqn	1391319	Sgt	CUTLER Dennis George	31-03-44	640 Sqn
129767	F/O	CRUMBLEY William Michael	16-06-44	405 Sqn	149504	F/O	CUTLER James Ferdinand	30-01-44	640 Sqn
701241	Sgt	CRUMP Gilbert Frederick	12-05-44	61 Sqn	1459698	Sgt	CUTLER Nelson Harcourt	17-04-44	5 LFS
1464302	Sgt	CRUMPLER George Edward	1-06-44	115 Sqn	1880022	Sgt	CUTTING John	22-06-44	619 Sqn
152750	F/O	CRUTCHER Ronald William	18-06-44	1663 HCU	154246	F/O	DACK Kenneth Peter	12-09-44	214 Sqn
1324786	Sgt	CRUTCHFIELD Peter Neller	12-05-44	103 Sqn	1592260	Sgt	DACRE James Harold	4-04-44	1657 HCU
135442	F/O	CRUWYS Croix de Guerre avec Palme Gerald Herbert	20-04-44	635 Sqn	553003	F/S	DADDS Kenneth	31-03-44	51 Sqn
					1678501	Sgt	DADSWELL John Douglas	16-03-44	625 Sqn
1323152	F/S	CRUX Cecil Charles	18-12-44	207 Sqn	1616793	Sgt	DAGGER Douglas Walter	21-07-44	9 Sqn
1606768	Sgt	CRYER Eric Alfred	28-04-44	166 Sqn	1750491	Sgt	DAGGETT Harry	15-02-44	166 Sqn

Service No	Rank	Name	Date	Sqn
169391	P/O	DAGGETT Sydney	29-01-44	10 Sqn
948192	Sgt	DAGLESS Leonard Eagles	13-07-44	550 Sqn
1804130	Sgt	DAINES Albert Henry	20-02-44	103 Sqn
1591465	Sgt	DAINES Arthur Henry	24-03-44	576 Sqn
182712	F/O	DAINTY Frederick William	11-11-44	626 Sqn
1577127	F/S	DAITZ Leslie Bernard	6-08-44	97 Sqn
1771175	Sgt	DALBY Jack	11-12-44	57 Sqn
2210202	Sgt	DALE Henry	9-05-44	35 Sqn
1623580	Sgt	DALES Douglas Frank	29-06-44	102 Sqn
1890562	Sgt	DALEY Daniel	1-07-44	10 Sqn
1622390	Sgt	DALEY Ernest	28-10-44	35 Sqn
161283	F/O	DALGARNO William	23-12-44	582 Sqn
177620	F/O	DALGLEISH Edward	16-07-44	207 Sqn
1390391	Sgt	DALLAWAY Douglas Demas Russell	3-01-44	49 Sqn
174550	F/O	DALLEN Jesse Gray	19-07-44	207 Sqn
1454372	Sgt	DALMAN Alan Charles	22-06-44	619 Sqn
112765	F/L	DALRYMPLE Angus	25-04-44	78 Sqn
1114763	Sgt	DALTON George Arthur	6-11-44	101 Sqn
1338225	Sgt	DALTON George William	25-07-44	622 Sqn
1681855	Sgt	DALY Henry	16-05-44	12 OTU
1457698	F/S	DALZELL Johnstone Christian	20-02-44	77 Sqn
1499774	Sgt	DALZIEL John Routedge	15-02-44	7 Sqn
1605219	Sgt	DANBURY Geoffrey Albert	23-06-44	76 Sqn
1851377	Sgt	DANCE Raymond Ernest	4-05-44	207 Sqn
1685501	Sgt	DAND Robert Matthew	4-05-44	50 Sqn
144340	F/O	DANE Eric John	4-05-44	103 Sqn
151788	F/O	DANIEL Gilbert	10-06-44	10 Sqn
3011016	Sgt	DANIEL Harry	24-11-44	12 OTU
148281	F/L	DANIEL Ronald Basil	1-07-44	101 Sqn
1522943	Sgt	DANIELS Leslie	24-03-44	78 Sqn
1681937	F/S	DANIELS Norman	12-12-44	635 Sqn
962812	Sgt	DANIELS Raymond Valentine Montigue	15-03-44	35 Sqn
2216175	F/S	DANIELS Ronald Denver	9-05-44	405 Sqn
188192	P/O	DANSON Alban Duckett	29-11-44	101 Sqn
1396428	Sgt	DAPLYN Frederick William	20-02-44	433 Sqn
1455379	Sgt	DARBEN Leonard George	31-03-44	61 Sqn
1801128	F/S	DARBON Douglas	2-12-44	23 Sqn
1392961	F/S	DARBY Arthur William Charles	25-04-44	7 Sqn
153895	F/O	DARBY Leslie John	19-09-44	106 Sqn
1737140	Sgt	DARBY William	6-11-44	50 Sqn
1131515	Sgt	DARKIN George William	12-09-44	640 Sqn
1865761	Sgt	DARLINGTON Stanley	23-09-44	1664 HCU
1877735	Sgt	DARLOW Cecil Geoffrey Nigel	31-10-44	90 Sqn
1342842	F/S	DARROCH Sym	23-11-44	195 Sqn
1605327	Sgt	DART Denis	27-01-44	622 Sqn
151317	F/O	DARVALL John Walter Charles	27-04-44	156 Sqn
1164922	Sgt	DARWOOD John Thomas	15-02-44	466 Sqn
1393998	F/S	DATSON John	6-07-44	635 Sqn
1337654	Sgt	DAVENPORT James George	25-04-44	76 Sqn
515421	Sgt	DAVENPORT John Bruce Thornley	30-07-44	106 Sqn
967316	F/S	DAVENPORT John Johnson	3-01-44	7 Sqn
1354430	Sgt	DAVENPORT Thomas	21-07-44	405 Sqn
3025201	Sgt	DAVEY Albert Arthur	10-08-44	50 Sqn
3010409	Sgt	DAVEY Douglas William Henry	30-08-44	90 Sqn
1873833	F/S	DAVEY Frederick James	13-08-44	83 Sqn
170183	F/O	DAVEY George Albert	19-07-44	61 Sqn
1560241	Sgt	DAVIDSON Daniel	17-07-44	149 Sqn
1895851	Sgt	DAVIDSON Francis Henry	12-09-44	35 Sqn
1003978	Sgt	DAVIDSON John	30-06-44	12 Sqn
1372843	Sgt	DAVIDSON Robert Cunningham Foss	24-03-44	578 Sqn
1573660	Sgt	DAVIDSON Ronald 'Ronnie'	31-08-44	21 OTU
1227419	LAC	DAVIDSON Trevor Ewart	10-04-44	207 Sqn
179853	P/O	DAVIDSON Walter Cecil	5-11-44	424 Sqn
179653	P/O	DAVIDSON William	21-07-44	578 Sqn
170752	F/O	DAVIE Peter	15-07-44	1651 HCU
1435786	Sgt	DAVIES Arthur Henry	12-09-44	207 Sqn
1100499	Sgt	DAVIES Arthur James	7-06-44	1654 HCU
1891883	Sgt	DAVIES Charles Christopher	21-04-44	100 Sqn
1313600	F/S	DAVIES DFM David Fisher	8-01-44	138 Sqn
1836072	Sgt	DAVIES David Gwynne	6-02-44	149 Sqn
1705248	Sgt	DAVIES Dennis	25-05-44	158 Sqn
569444	F/S	DAVIES Dennis Albert	8-07-44	50 Sqn
1652786	Sgt	DAVIES Dennis Vivian	16-03-44	408 Sqn
170453	P/O	DAVIES Denzil Meecham	14-01-44	156 Sqn
1575462	Sgt	DAVIES Desmond Roy Morgan	22-05-44	550 Sqn
157062	F/O	DAVIES DFC Donald Leslie	30-07-44	57 Sqn
1437282	Sgt	DAVIES Douglas Graham	5-03-44	218 Sqn
1880665	Sgt	DAVIES Edward Whelan	17-12-44	153 Sqn
188992	P/O	DAVIES Edwin Charles Thomas	3-08-44	619 Sqn
935690	F/S	DAVIES Eric McHugh	5-07-44	35 Sqn
1322400	F/S	DAVIES Ernest Arthur	23-05-44	83 Sqn
50773	F/O	DAVIES Ernest Edgar Cyril	24-02-44	149 Sqn
1652436	Sgt	DAVIES Evan Hugh	20-02-44	434 Sqn
1315680	F/S	DAVIES Geoffrey Stuart	22-03-44	97 Sqn
1537068	F/S	DAVIES George Henry	25-04-44	626 Sqn
1833018	Sgt	DAVIES Griffith John	21-01-44	61 Sqn
171929	P/O	DAVIES DFC Harry Nevill	22-03-44	44 Sqn
1388039	F/S	DAVIES Hiram Tom	2-03-44	76 Sqn
1456033	Sgt	DAVIES Idris	21-01-44	102 Sqn
2207029	Sgt	DAVIES James	29-01-44	166 Sqn
175652	F/O	DAVIES James Glyn	24-09-44	166 Sqn
1802683	Sgt	DAVIES James McDowell	4-05-44	101 Sqn
2204830	Sgt	DAVIES John Albert	17-04-44	5 LFS
141523	F/O	DAVIES John Charles Henry	22-01-44	83 Sqn
176652	F/O	DAVIES John Edwin Henry	13-07-44	550 Sqn
1317991	F/S	DAVIES John Montague	20-09-44	619 Sqn
1580941	Sgt	DAVIES John Richard	3-08-44	166 Sqn
1833380	Sgt	DAVIES Lewis Ivor	23-10-44	625 Sqn
53642	F/O	DAVIES Norman Arthur	13-07-44	550 Sqn
143143	F/O	DAVIES Peter Groucutt	29-01-44	83 Sqn
1819560	Sgt	DAVIES Peter Morley	12-04-44	50 Sqn
1317623	Sgt	DAVIES Raymond David	14-03-44	75 Sqn
156998	F/O	DAVIES Reginald Ivor Havard	23-05-44	115 Sqn
182167	F/O	DAVIES Richard	19-10-44	9 Sqn
2206026	Sgt	DAVIES Robert Meirion	6-10-44	640 Sqn
1515730	Sgt	DAVIES Robert Thomas	30-01-44	100 Sqn
1684489	Sgt	DAVIES Robert Wray	17-08-44	78 Sqn
1128796	LAC	DAVIES MiD Ronald	29-12-44	617 Sqn
575723	Sgt	DAVIES Roy Joseph	24-07-44	625 Sqn
1603898	Sgt	DAVIES Roy Joseph	23-05-44	75 Sqn
1315090	F/S	DAVIES Royston George	23-06-44	97 Sqn
1605840	Sgt	DAVIES Sidney Frank	30-09-44	1651 HCU
1874074	Sgt	DAVIES Thomas John Glanville	20-02-44	83 Sqn
1314093	W/O	DAVIES Trefor	31-07-44	12 OTU
146291	F/O	DAVIES Trevor Rhys	17-06-44	77 Sqn
1656202	Sgt	DAVIES Tudor	29-06-44	424 Sqn
2210654	Sgt	DAVIES Vaughan	23-05-44	103 Sqn
170955	P/O	DAVIES Warwick George	20-02-44	57 Sqn
179238	P/O	DAVIES William Alfred Cyril	22-06-44	630 Sqn
127814	F/L	DAVIES William George	18-07-44	158 Sqn
1018309	F/S	DAVIES William Gordon	19-03-44	97 Sqn
144996	F/O	DAVIES William Haydn	20-01-44	622 Sqn
616191	W/O	DAVIES William John	21-07-44	75 Sqn
1388248	Sgt	DAVIS Arthur Sydney	6-01-44	576 Sqn
1896494	Sgt	DAVIS Bertram George	19-10-44	1651 HCU
1603333	Sgt	DAVIS Clifford Francis Charles	31-03-44	207 Sqn
1257683	Sgt	DAVIS Eric Alfred	23-05-44	12 Sqn
1567913	Sgt	DAVIS Frederick Victor	17-07-44	28 OTU
515502	W/O	DAVIS Gerald Joseph	18-10-44	630 Sqn
154512	F/O	DAVIS Harry Samuel	24-12-44	635 Sqn
1606693	Sgt	DAVIS John Harry	17-03-44	578 Sqn
1431230	F/S	DAVIS Joseph Anthony	26-02-44	15 Sqn
40569	S/L	DAVIS Kenneth Graham	20-02-44	7 Sqn
156354	F/O	DAVIS DFM Leonard George	22-06-44	630 Sqn
120736	F/L	DAVIS Leslie George	27-01-44	83 Sqn
174023	P/O	DAVIS Mark Anthony Hamilton	22-06-44	619 Sqn
1322108	Sgt	DAVIS Norman	11-06-44	15 Sqn

134179	F/O	DAVIS Percy George	27-04-44	100 Sqn		155114	F/O	DEIGHTON Frederick Ernest	13-05-44	105 Sqn
1833877	Sgt	DAVIS Percy Reginald	23-06-44	1666 HCU		1375320	F/S	DEIGHTON Garry	14-01-44	408 Sqn
1581083	Sgt	DAVIS Raymond Walter	3-06-44	76 Sqn		1875601	Sgt	DELANEY Lincoln William	11-08-44	12 Sqn
171203	P/O	DAVIS Sidney Hubert	29-01-44	57 Sqn		1330376	W/O	DELL John Franklin	30-08-44	21 OTU
617912	Sgt	DAVIS Trevor Hugh	30-08-44	166 Sqn		170294	P/O	DEMPSEY James Henry	15-03-44	405 Sqn
1172743	W/O	DAVIS DFM Victor Allenby	11-09-44	582 Sqn		958053	Sgt	DENBY Alfred William	28-10-44	90 Sqn
1750343	Sgt	DAVIS William	25-05-44	101 Sqn		1890830	Sgt	DENCH Frederick Kenneth	25-02-44	622 Sqn
2214945	Sgt	DAVISON Alan	27-04-44	100 Sqn		50231	F/L	DENMAN Brian	20-02-44	78 Sqn
1497368	F/S	DAVISON Colin	19-07-44	49 Sqn		1605654	Sgt	DENNEHY Desmond John	20-02-44	166 Sqn
1891953	Sgt	DAVISON David Arthur Keith	25-06-44	9 Sqn		135674	F/O	DENNESS Bernard	5-03-44	218 Sqn
1677871	Sgt	DAVISON George	26-02-44	1661 HCU		1589160	Sgt	DENNETT Ronald George	7-06-44	550 Sqn
1480506	Sgt	DAVISON James	12-09-44	619 Sqn		1549174	Sgt	DENNETT Thomas Arthur	23-10-44	44 Sqn
1310158	F/S	DAVISON John Leslie	27-04-44	630 Sqn		1592515	Sgt	DENNING Leslie Watson	22-03-44	432 Sqn
178725	P/O	DAVISON Richard	1-07-44	625 Sqn		41783	S/L	DENNIS DSO DFC John Mervyn	20-05-44	7 Sqn
146432	F/O	DAVISON Robert	20-04-44	1655 MTU		2204350	Sgt	DENNIS George Charles	6-12-44	550 Sqn
1367521	Sgt	DAVISON Thomas Riddle	7-02-44	1662 HCU		1279754	Sgt	DENNIS Robert George	25-02-44	115 Sqn
1447529	Sgt	DAW Percy John	27-04-44	106 Sqn		162836	P/O	DENNIS DFM Roy	17-03-44	17 OTU
1300770	Sgt	DAWKINS Alexander Harold	2-08-44	467 Sqn		1315320	Sgt	DENNIS Terence Raymond	15-03-44	51 Sqn
1624137	Sgt	DAWSON Albert	24-12-44	100 Sqn		1863320	Sgt	DENNY Albert John	7-02-44	1656 HCU
529673	Sgt	DAWSON Arthur	16-03-44	100 Sqn		120438	F/L	DENNY Peter Frederick	11-04-44	83 Sqn
981812	F/S	DAWSON Dennis Arthur	20-02-44	630 Sqn		170954	P/O	DENSON George James	24-02-44	9 Sqn
574270	Sgt	DAWSON Douglas Albert	18-06-44	115 Sqn		1575680	Sgt	DENT Roland	15-02-44	166 Sqn
82210	F/L	DAWSON DFC Eric Sydney	29-10-44	582 Sqn		1877210	Sgt	DEPOTEX Harry James	12-09-44	619 Sqn
1604151	Sgt	DAWSON Frank	25-06-44	77 Sqn		1514432	Sgt	DERBY Frank Kenneth	4-11-44	195 Sqn
1594380	Sgt	DAWSON Frank Lockwood	23-04-44	149 Sqn		170953	P/O	DERBYSHIRE James Edward	26-02-44	207 Sqn
1875339	F/S	DAWSON George William	15-10-44	466 Sqn		1896733	Sgt	DERHAM Norman	21-07-44	514 Sqn
183922	P/O	DAWSON Leonard Bert	6-07-44	424 Sqn		1862158	Sgt	DESBOROUGH William Edward	29-07-44	431 Sqn
159010	P/O	DAWSON Raymond	22-01-44	427 Sqn		1390210	Sgt	DEVENISH James William	25-02-44	61 Sqn
1684836	F/S	DAWSON Reginald	23-10-44	76 Sqn		129331	F/L	DEVEREAU George Stephen	12-12-44	150 Sqn
1578763	Sgt	DAWSON Roy	11-01-44	17 OTU		1891641	Sgt	DEVINE Edward James	21-01-44	97 Sqn
160725	P/O	DAWSON Stanley [Canada]	14-01-44	408 Sqn		627399	W/O	DEVLIN John	16-06-44	7 Sqn
179283	F/O	DAWSON Thomas Clough	24-10-44	576 Sqn		1673439	Sgt	DEVLIN Peter	30-08-44	514 Sqn
1372580	F/S	DAWSON Tom	31-03-44	460 Sqn		136397	F/O	DEVON Harold Alan	31-03-44	44 Sqn
1616285	Sgt	DAWSON Walter	25-03-44	166 Sqn		1540030	Sgt	DEW James Victor	13-06-44	100 Sqn
150228	F/O	DAY Alfred George	6-01-44	619 Sqn		749538	Sgt	DEW Norman Hylton	11-06-44	75 Sqn
1896250	Sgt	DAY Douglas Frederick Gordon	4-11-44	101 Sqn		1094980	Sgt	DEWHURST Harold	12-05-44	75 Sqn
1800687	Sgt	DAY Eric Charles	5-07-44	630 Sqn		1880897	Sgt	de ANGELIS John Alexander	20-09-44	622 Sqn
1420668	Sgt	DAY Harold Henry	21-11-44	460 Sqn		1398843	Sgt	de CASAGRANDE Raphael Edward	22-06-44	207 Sqn
1896335	Sgt	DAY Joseph William	23-03-44	26 OTU		517767	Sgt	de LENGERKIE Kenneth Harold Fontain		
172955	F/L	DAY Maurice Charles	21-07-44	578 Sqn					28-05-44	550 Sqn
1324940	F/S	DAY Norman Leslie Terrett	4-12-44	207 Sqn		148018	F/O	de MARIGNY Galtan Joseph George	24-03-44	12 Sqn
1898443	Sgt	DAY Raymond Edward Buckenham	16-12-44	106 Sqn				[Amirante Islands]		
1238125	Sgt	DAY Richard Jock	22-03-44	514 Sqn		FX117431		F/Ode MENTEN de HORNE Georges Marie Ghislain		
1892715	Sgt	DAY Stanley Valentine	29-07-44	12 Sqn				[Belgium]	2-01-44	550 Sqn
3005518	Sgt	DAY Walter Frederick	5-11-44	76 Sqn		1578959	F/S	de la HAYE Nelson John	25-06-44	90 Sqn
155911	F/O	DAY William Edward	22-06-44	49 Sqn				[Channel Islands]		
151214	F/O	DAYNES Harold Eric	29-01-44	50 Sqn		171730	P/O	DIBBINS Douglas Robert	25-04-44	76 Sqn
1798041	Sgt	DEA Martin [Eire]	13-06-44	622 Sqn		1825388	Sgt	DICERBO Philip	25-07-44	582 Sqn
710323	F/S	DEACON Norman Tudor [Rhodesia]	4-12-44	57 Sqn		1798176	Sgt	DICK Thomas	30-08-44	12 Sqn
170739	P/O	DEACON Ronald Albert	20-01-44	622 Sqn		1470499	F/S	DICKEL Alfred Henry	2-06-44	138 Sqn
1590148	Sgt	DEAKIN Harry	30-01-44	463 Sqn		1819788	Sgt	DICKEN Albert Edward	22-06-44	49 Sqn
152754	F/O	DEAN Arnold Keith Michael	28-08-44	161 Sqn		158584	P/O	DICKERSON Reginald William	16-02-44	106 Sqn
1456092	Sgt	DEAN Arthur	15-02-44	102 Sqn		1224113	Sgt	DICKHART Edgar Alfred [South Africa]	6-01-44	57 Sqn
1892263	Sgt	DEAN Bryan Charles Frederick	9-08-44	161 Sqn		1739072	Sgt	DICKIN Roy Caswell	12-09-44	97 Sqn
1852388	Sgt	DEAN Frederick Bert	12-08-44	625 Sqn		134058	F/O	DICKINS Kenneth Shirley	14-01-44	115 Sqn
1651555	LAC	DEAN George Walker	5-06-44	460 Sqn		143854	F/L	DICKINSON Albert	31-03-44	7 Sqn
2202752	Sgt	DEAN Kenneth Henry	18-03-44	61 Sqn		1511926	Sgt	DICKINSON Clifford	28-06-44	44 Sqn
1459135	Sgt	DEAN Robert Geoffrey	27-07-44	44 Sqn		1034670	Sgt	DICKINSON Frank	1-07-44	625 Sqn
1271352	Sgt	DEAN Stanley Thomas	27-01-44	84 OTU		1491703	F/S	DICKINSON Harry	16-09-44	515 Sqn
1582658	Sgt	DEAN William Henry	26-03-44	15 Sqn		1624199	Sgt	DICKINSON John Edward William	21-07-44	90 Sqn
1393542	F/S	DEAR Jack	25-03-44	78 Sqn		170191	P/O	DICKINSON John Russell	27-04-44	49 Sqn
161700	P/O	DEARMAN DFC Derrick Roy	21-04-44	207 Sqn		1609924	Sgt	DICKINSON Kenneth	22-05-44	630 Sqn
87060	W/C	DEAS DSO DFC* William Inglis	8-07-44	630 Sqn		1549113	Sgt	DICKINSON Raymond Stuart	25-05-44	576 Sqn
		[South Africa]				1487374	Sgt	DICKINSON Ronald	2-01-44	44 Sqn
1250525	Sgt	DEATH Leslie Frederick	9-06-44	44 Sqn		987302	Sgt	DICKINSON Sydney	1-06-44	149 Sqn
168843	F/O	DEBROCK DFC Fernand Camille Guillaume				170952	P/O	DICKINSON Vernon Francis	29-01-44	1660 HCU
		[Belgium]	15-07-44	156 Sqn		1821789	Sgt	DICKSON Alexander David	31-03-44	101 Sqn
48419	F/L	DEE Frederick James	27-08-44	166 Sqn		1564075	Sgt	DICKSON Allan	24-07-44	619 Sqn
1579913	Sgt	DEELEY Geoffrey Raymond	13-06-44	578 Sqn		1823811	Sgt	DICKSON David	22-05-44	166 Sqn

Number	Rank	Name	Date	Unit
1897116	Sgt	DICKSON Harry Thomson	6-10-44	115 Sqn
910935	Sgt	DIGBY Ronald Ernest	21-07-44	514 Sqn
2205876	Sgt	DIGGIN Thomas Stephen [Eire]	30-08-44	14 OTU
1536835	Sgt	DIGGLE Arthur	25-03-44	115 Sqn
1454679	F/S	DIGGLE Lawrence	10-05-44	97 Sqn
1584011	Sgt	DILKES Maurice Francis	13-06-44	78 Sqn
1583059	Sgt	DILLEY Dennis Arthur	20-11-44	1656 HCU
80106	F/O	DILL-RUSSELL John David [Rhodesia]	15-02-44	115 Sqn
40044	W/C	DILWORTH DFC John Frederick	25-02-44	100 Sqn
1437880	F/S	DINEEN Bertrand Patrick	27-01-44	622 Sqn
53475	F/O	DINEEN Cecil John	24-03-44	35 Sqn
2202492	Sgt	DINEEN Jerimiah Francis	21-07-44	90 Sqn
153261	F/O	DINNAGE Harold Ernest	20-05-44	83 OTU
1380408	W/O	DING Leslie Arthur	30-07-44	514 Sqn
1445548	F/S	DISS Robert William	11-04-44	158 Sqn
1822288	Sgt	DIVENS John	6-10-44	78 Sqn
1892030	Sgt	DIX Albert Llewellyn	16-05-44	625 Sqn
1861605	Sgt	DIXEY Henry Charles [Canada]	10-05-44	9 Sqn
1603118	Sgt	DIXON Derek Arthur	3-01-44	57 Sqn
172882	P/O	DIXON Harold	27-04-44	57 Sqn
1079152	W/O	DIXON Harry	29-08-44	50 Sqn
2211099	Sgt	DIXON Herbert Horace	13-05-44	576 Sqn
1602182	F/S	DIXON John Arthur Glanville	28-06-44	106 Sqn
1321050	Sgt	DIXON Leonard Henry Joseph	31-03-44	467 Sqn
1125643	F/S	DIXON DFM Norman	8-09-44	14 OTU
1438149	F/S	DIXON Norman Frederick	2-01-44	9 Sqn
155761	F/L	DIXON DFC Reginald Robinson	21-01-44	10 Sqn
173521	P/O	DIXON John Roy	19-03-44	101 Sqn
1678171	Sgt	DIXON William Beattie	22-03-44	626 Sqn
1835971	Sgt	DIXON William Dennis	4-05-44	50 Sqn
1874696	Sgt	DOBBIE Fred	13-09-44	20 OTU
1529674	F/S	DOBSON Alexander	27-08-44	90 Sqn
1442409	F/S	DOBSON Edwin	12-09-44	214 Sqn
1504526	F/S	DOBSON Frederick Arthur	20-01-44	102 Sqn
1331818	Sgt	DOBSON Norman James John	23-04-44	90 Sqn
1777217	Sgt	DOCHERTY Norman	20-02-44	207 Sqn
125501	F/O	DOCHERTY Thomas	2-01-44	156 Sqn
1562816	Sgt	DOCHERTY William	25-04-44	424 Sqn
173926	P/O	DOD Harold Frederick	5-07-44	49 Sqn
1591349	Sgt	DODD Allen	23-09-44	12 Sqn
152259	F/O	DODDS Harry	14-10-44	550 Sqn
146377	F/O	DODDS Martin	8-06-44	115 Sqn
172519	P/O	DODDS Robert Leslie	12-09-44	214 Sqn
1479658	Sgt	DODGSON David James	5-11-44	76 Sqn
130916	F/O	DODSON DFM Herbert Leslie George	20-01-44	83 Sqn
1332730	Sgt	DODSON Ronald Eric	7-06-44	115 Sqn
115307	S/L	DODWELL DFC* Terence Edgar	19-07-44	571 Sqn
1316836	Sgt	DOE Leslie Hubert	20-01-44	434 Sqn
178475	P/O	DOHERTY Hilary Louis [Eire]	30-06-44	514 Sqn
527589	F/S	DOLAMORE DFM Frank Leonard [New Zealand]	22-05-44	514 Sqn
1228751	Cpl	DOLAN Edward Robert	18-08-44	Tempsford
1090708	F/S	DOLBY Harold	21-04-44	15 Sqn
945635	Sgt	DOLBY Lawrence Albert	25-06-44	9 Sqn
652653	Sgt	DOLDEN Robert Herbert	14-01-44	1656 HCU
1602251	Sgt	DOLLERY Arthur George	6-10-44	433 Sqn
1553633	Sgt	DONALD George	22-03-44	44 Sqn
1568395	Sgt	DONALDSON George Barr	27-08-44	15 Sqn
972603	F/S	DONALDSON Leslie John	15-02-44	166 Sqn
1013809	Sgt	DONCASTER Francis Herbert	28-01-44	467 Sqn
182009	F/O	DONKIN Alfred Victor	17-12-44	57 Sqn
542206	F/S	DONKIN Ernest William	6-08-44	51 Sqn
1057454	Sgt	DONNACHIE Joseph James	12-10-44	1657 HCU
2208992	Sgt	DONNELLY Hugh McLauglin	31-03-44	156 Sqn
1520549	Sgt	DONNELLY Patrick	12-09-44	50 Sqn
1530698	Sgt	DONOGHUE Daniel Anthony	13-07-44	550 Sqn
1556976	Sgt	DONOGHUE Patrick	25-06-44	61 Sqn
172554	P/O	DONOVAN Charles Albert	31-03-44	578 Sqn
1836270	Sgt	DONOVAN John Henry	22-06-44	57 Sqn
126763	F/O	DONOVAN DFM Walter Spruce	27-06-44	1655 MTU
189628	P/O	DOOLEY Peter Lawrence	17-09-44	115 Sqn
977328	Sgt	DOOLEY Vincent	29-01-44	90 Sqn
1032035	F/S	DOOTSON Herbert	28-04-44	138 Sqn
1315291	F/S	DORAM Eric Colston	27-04-44	630 Sqn
183947	F/O	DOREY Edmund Henry Stephen	12-12-44	149 Sqn
991687	Sgt	DORRITY John	28-04-44	103 Sqn
1682296	Sgt	DOTT Hugh Fraser	13-08-44	115 Sqn
1388107	Sgt	DOUGAN Stephen Nelson	27-04-44	630 Sqn
1386802	Sgt	DOUGHTY James Charles	13-08-44	102 Sqn
1802798	Sgt	DOUGHTY Reginald James	11-10-44	101 Sqn
933062	Sgt	DOUGHTY Sidney William	1-06-44	1667 HCU
1670363	Sgt	DOUGHTY Walter James Bernard	25-07-44	50 Sqn
1685113	Sgt	DOUGLAS Herbert Walter	26-08-44	626 Sqn
158022	P/O	DOUGLAS Kenneth Alfred Reid	6-01-44	57 Sqn
138075	F/O	DOUGLAS-PULLEYNE Ian Richard Montagu [Canada]	20-02-44	78 Sqn
1449870	Sgt	DOULL Ronald Henry	2-01-44	626 Sqn
820031	F/S	DOVE George	29-01-44	630 Sqn
1075279	Sgt	DOVE James	20-01-44	434 Sqn
577055	Sgt	DOVE Roy Kenneth	26-07-44	100 Sqn
2235927	Sgt	DOVETON Jack Lambe	12-10-44	83 OTU
1335580	F/S	DOVEY Cyril William	29-06-44	7 Sqn
159677	P/O	DOWDING Alexander Francis	15-02-44	424 Sqn
1382810	Sgt	DOWDING John	30-01-44	514 Sqn
165070	F/O	DOWDING Michael McLoughlin	27-12-44	75 Sqn
1725436	Sgt	DOWE David Jesse	25-06-44	463 Sqn
542574	Sgt	DOWLING Joseph Ronald	5-04-44	11 OTU
1805739	Sgt	DOWLING Reginald Albert	12-10-44	21 OTU
130207	F/O	DOWNER DFC George Lionel	14-01-44	115 Sqn
1671293	Sgt	DOWNES Patrick	20-01-44	18 OTU
921113	F/S	DOWNES Stanley William	15-02-44	625 Sqn
1800550	Sgt	DOWNEY James Michael	14-08-44	20 OTU
116504	F/L	DOWNEY DFM Joseph	11-06-44	571 Sqn
136351	F/O	DOWNING John Wallace	23-05-44	75 Sqn
170437	P/O	DOWNS James Arthur	16-02-44	102 Sqn
153656	F/O	DOWSE Charles Douglas	15-11-44	115 Sqn
630916	Sgt	DOWSE Condor Charles	9-08-44	138 Sqn
1162453	W/O	DOWSE Henry James	9-08-44	115 Sqn
1484106	Sgt	DOWSE Leonard	4-01-44	1658 HCU
1607202	Sgt	DOYE Peter James	15-02-44	57 Sqn
128562	F/O	DOYLE Desmond Patrick	26-02-44	239 Sqn
154086	P/O	DOYLE Douglas Robert [Eire]	19-04-44	28 OTU
1065830	Sgt	DOYLE John	18-04-44	428 Sqn
137611	F/O	DOYLE John Christopher Patrick	31-03-44	103 Sqn
174773	F/L	DOYLE DFM Kenneth Patrick Cochrane	24-09-44	156 Sqn
517789	F/S	DRAKE Alan George	31-03-44	630 Sqn
1049379	Sgt	DRAKE Albert	2-03-44	76 Sqn
184671	P/O	DRAPER Cornelius George	14-10-44	153 Sqn
120439	S/L	DREDGE Walter Frank	11-04-44	158 Sqn
1557840	Sgt	DREVER Frederick Irving	20-05-44	50 Sqn
912475	F/S	DREW Corbett Norman George	7-05-44	576 Sqn
1396993	Sgt	DREW Cornelius Stanley	6-06-44	515 Sqn
145376	F/O	DREW Douglas McMillan	23-04-44	115 Sqn
174635	P/O	DREW Thomas John	4-05-44	101 Sqn
1852711	Sgt	DREWETT Ronald Edwin	29-01-44	429 Sqn
1620920	Sgt	DREWETT Walter Andrew	12-09-44	622 Sqn
1817454	Sgt	DRING Frederick Frank	10-05-44	619 Sqn
161594	F/L	DRINKALL Austin	6-08-44	83 Sqn
1815438	Sgt	DRISCOLL Robert Douglas	11-11-44	44 Sqn
160678	F/O	DRIVER DFM Donald Arthur	31-05-44	12 OTU
1318434	Sgt	DRIVER Leonard George	22-01-44	76 Sqn
1821635	Sgt	DRUMMOND David Watt	8-06-44	138 Sqn
1429179	Sgt	DRURY Ronald Archibald	28-05-44	550 Sqn
1568203	Sgt	DRYBURGH William Reid	6-10-44	640 Sqn
1503335	Sgt	DRYER Leslie	20-01-44	10 Sqn
1895943	Sgt	DRYLAND Edward James	20-09-44	622 Sqn
1578790	Sgt	DUCK Robert Edward	22-06-44	630 Sqn

Number	Rank	Name	Date	Squadron
1890080	Sgt	DUCKWORTH Ernest Richard	24-06-44	149 Sqn
532588	F/S	DUCKWORTH Herbert	21-02-44	640 Sqn
1589150	Sgt	DUCKWORTH Maurice	15-03-44	51 Sqn
1439747	Sgt	DUDLEY Cyril George	4-05-44	101 Sqn
138406	F/O	DUDLEY Leonard Charles	22-05-44	7 Sqn
1388344	F/S	DUDLEY DFM Ronald	21-01-44	97 Sqn
1001732	F/S	DUDLEY Thomas Kem	29-01-44	10 Sqn
174032	P/O	DUDMAN James	11-06-44	625 Sqn
2204002	Sgt	DUERDEN Charles	27-04-44	10 Sqn
153572	F/O	DUERR Ernest Augustus	18-08-44	576 Sqn
1059197	W/O	DUFF Peter	18-06-44	115 Sqn
1372916	Sgt	DUFF Robert	31-10-44	460 Sqn
1509136	F/S	DUFF Thomas	31-03-44	61 Sqn
1562929	F/S	DUFF Thomas Handley	22-06-44	101 Sqn
1805514	Sgt	DUFFETT James	22-12-44	630 Sqn
1891039	Sgt	DUFFIELD Richard Arthur	25-07-44	622 Sqn
1568139	Sgt	DUFFIN James	18-12-44	3 LFS
1583091	Sgt	DUFFY Edward Colin	23-04-44	640 Sqn
2211362	Sgt	DUFFY Michael Hugh	4-05-44	97 Sqn
1343829	Sgt	DUFFY Robert	10-04-44	207 Sqn
1852960	Sgt	DUFTY Thomas Brian	30-08-44	12 Sqn
1487796	Sgt	DUGGAN Daniel Patrick [Eire]	23-05-44	50 Sqn
1397590	Sgt	DUGGAN Denis Cecil	22-01-44	44 Sqn
1004177	Sgt	DUGGAN Thomas Dennis	1-07-44	101 Sqn
1439832	F/S	DUGGAN Thomas Douglas	13-04-44	90 Sqn
1822307	Sgt	DUGUID John	15-02-44	100 Sqn
1383442	Sgt	DUKE Ronald Edward	31-01-44	1660 HCU
170280	P/O	DUKELOW Peter James	22-05-44	550 Sqn
145279	F/O	DULAIT Andre Joseph Julien Christain [Belgium]	13-06-44	408 Sqn
1456993	F/S	DULLAGHAN Stephen Patrick	23-04-44	149 Sqn
1827113	Sgt	DUMARESQUE John Anley [Canada]	20-09-44	622 Sqn
1866298	Sgt	DUMMER Cyril Albert Reginald	17-06-44	10 Sqn
1585541	Sgt	DUNBAR James Laird	22-05-44	514 Sqn
614225	F/S	DUNBAR DFM William Alexander [Canada]	21-01-44	10 Sqn
1346999	Sgt	DUNCAN John Williamson	12-08-44	76 Sqn
1676156	Sgt	DUNCAN Leslie	12-09-44	102 Sqn
1826247	Sgt	DUNCAN Malcolm	21-07-44	514 Sqn
2205769	Sgt	DUNCAN William	13-06-44	78 Sqn
1105973	F/S	DUNCAN William Garfield	21-02-44	97 Sqn
152406	F/O	DUNCAN-SMITH Anthony	4-05-44	19 OTU
52798	F/O	DUNCANSON Robert Hay	19-07-44	78 Sqn
1608657	F/S	DUNFORD Edward Roy	11-10-44	101 Sqn
1853351	Sgt	DUNFORD Edward William Albert	24-08-44	1666 HCU
1575081	Sgt	DUNFORD John William	23-04-44	433 Sqn
154276	F/O	DUNHAM Leslie Ronald	22-05-44	550 Sqn
160014	F/O	DUNK Thomas William [Rhodesia]	8-06-44	15 Sqn
1608128	Sgt	DUNKLEY Robert Henry	17-09-44	51 Sqn
1891534	Sgt	DUNLOP Cyril Ernest	17-12-44	50 Sqn
989158	W/O	DUNLOP James	20-02-44	77 Sqn
1822043	Sgt	DUNLOP John McClymont	24-02-44	460 Sqn
1559306	Sgt	DUNLOP John McIntyre	3-01-44	83 Sqn
1033386	F/S	DUNLOP Leslie Horton	15-02-44	207 Sqn
151051	F/O	DUNLOP Robert	11-04-44	640 Sqn
1559799	F/S	DUNLOP Thomas Russell	10-04-44	166 Sqn
40897	W/C	DUNN DFC Albert Robinson [Canada]	22-06-44	83 Sqn
155196	F/O	DUNN DFC Cyril John	12-09-44	83 Sqn
1542934	Sgt	DUNN Henry	20-02-44	626 Sqn
171076	F/O	DUNN DFC DFM James	27-07-44	139 Sqn
1337677	Sgt	DUNN John Henry	24-04-44	21 OTU
1650666	Sgt	DUNN Leslie Turner	11-06-44	625 Sqn
1824300	Sgt	DUNN Thomas	11-04-44	1661 HCU
1520456	Sgt	DUNN William Joseph	21-07-44	75 Sqn
1511063	Sgt	DUNNE John Kevin	3-06-44	158 Sqn
1395778	F/S	DUNNETT Stanley Edward	12-09-44	626 Sqn
174043	P/O	DUNNING DFM Guy Ernest	6-06-44	97 Sqn
174022	P/O	DUNSTAN Percy James	10-04-44	166 Sqn
145908	F/O	DUNSTAN Ronald James	4-12-44	227 Sqn
1798286	Sgt	DUNSTER Reuben Joseph [Eire]	11-12-44	57 Sqn
126830	F/L	DUNTON Frederick Ross	30-08-44	166 Sqn
128701	F/O	DURANT Edward Robinson	3-08-44	61 Sqn
1592562	Sgt	DURHAM John George	23-10-44	625 Sqn
156302	F/O	DURHAM DFC Lennox [Australia]	25-04-44	50 Sqn
1822445	Sgt	DURIE Thomas Wilkie	21-01-44	101 Sqn
130448	F/O	DURINGER DFC DFM Alfred Herbert	2-01-44	101 Sqn
2209756	Sgt	DURKIN James Alexander	25-04-44	619 Sqn
1389300	Sgt	DURMAN Peter Edward	16-11-44	214 Sqn
1622745	F/S	DURN Maurice	23-06-44	97 Sqn
1335535	F/S	DURRANT Edmund Anthony	5-06-44	1658 HCU
1801052	Sgt	DURRANT Kenneth Michael Garton	16-09-44	582 Sqn
151418	F/O	DURRANT Stanley Frederick	23-09-44	576 Sqn
657694	Sgt	DUSHMAN David	22-03-44	97 Sqn
133386	F/O	DUSSON Neville John	29-10-44	515 Sqn
1431527	Sgt	DUTHOIT Cyril	10-05-44	467 Sqn
136823	F/O	DUTTON John Arthur	6-01-44	7 Sqn
151020	F/O	DUTTON Kenneth	22-06-44	49 Sqn
1032629	F/S	DUTTON Thomas Royle	15-02-44	156 Sqn
1582673	Sgt	DUTTON Wilfred	15-07-44	166 Sqn
1335418	Sgt	DWAN Leonard Stanley	3-06-44	158 Sqn
1324551	F/S	DWELLY John Aldridge	2-01-44	100 Sqn
1172812	Sgt	DYCKHOFF George Edward	10-04-44	166 Sqn
1892315	Sgt	DYE Kenneth Reginald	3-05-44	550 Sqn
153308	F/O	DYER Francis James	18-07-44	158 Sqn
1217992	Sgt	DYER John Harold	2-01-44	106 Sqn
1399766	Sgt	DYER William Augustus	25-08-44	218 Sqn
1504327	Sgt	DYERSON Harold Edward	27-04-44	12 Sqn
1095605	F/S	DYKE George Clifford	6-08-44	97 Sqn
132869	F/O	DYKE William Horace	3-01-44	83 Sqn
1575431	Sgt	DYKES William Arthur	20-02-44	166 Sqn
1111961	Sgt	DYSON John Duncan	31-03-44	207 Sqn
1356909	Sgt	D'ARCY Jack Basil	31-03-44	50 Sqn
1605781	Sgt	EADES Aubrey Edward	26-10-44	166 Sqn
150244	F/L	EAMES Edwin Laurence [USA]	22-05-44	100 Sqn
950584	W/O	EAMES Leslie James	19-08-44	635 Sqn
1438577	F/S	EARL Harold	13-06-44	76 Sqn
1415516	F/S	EARL DFM James Charles	4-05-44	101 Sqn
524033	Sgt	EARLE Thomas	26-03-44	426 Sqn
134761	F/L	EARLEY DFM MiD Bernard	2-11-44	15 Sqn
172946	P/O	EARNSHAW Reginald	28-04-44	640 Sqn
1398359	Sgt	EARWALKER Percival Henry	11-02-44	21 OTU
174553	P/O	EASBY Norman Wilson	28-06-44	106 Sqn
2206647	Sgt	EASDON Leonard	14-01-44	101 Sqn
1636431	Sgt	EASTER Richard John Harry	16-03-44	630 Sqn
1215300	Sgt	EASTERLOW Bernard Gordon	12-05-44	9 Sqn
2209361	Sgt	EASTHAM James Stanley	13-07-44	103 Sqn
1235342	W/O	EASTMENT Frederick Arthur	8-06-44	15 Sqn
183867	P/O	EASTHOPE Hiram	12-09-44	7 Sqn
1586348	Sgt	EASTMAN John Gordon	28-04-44	15 Sqn
1535785	F/S	EASTMAN John Watson	3-06-44	640 Sqn
1251915	Sgt	EASTMAN Reginald Arthur	31-03-44	640 Sqn
161266	F/O	EASTMENT Arthur Herbert	4-05-44	19 OTU
1340743	F/S	EASTON Alexander	23-10-44	463 Sqn
1456823	Sgt	EASTON Ronald Herbert	21-01-44	83 Sqn
1522162	F/S	EASTON Samuel	18-12-44	463 Sqn
1535672	Sgt	EASTWOOD George Harry	20-02-44	625 Sqn
171333	P/O	EASTWOOD Jack Hilton	12-05-44	61 Sqn
136429	F/O	EASTWOOD Kenneth	18-09-44	23 Sqn
2226284	Sgt	EASTWOOD Thomas Philip	19-10-44	29 OTU
1326107	Sgt	EATON Edward Denis	24-06-44	149 Sqn
37224	G/C	EATON DFC Eric Cecil	28-04-44	156 Sqn
1822142	Sgt	EATON George Howard	13-08-44	101 Sqn
1274722	Sgt	EATON Harold	24-02-44	156 Sqn
155592	F/L	EATON Harry Charles	20-01-44	10 Sqn
1283604	F/S	EATON John David	26-02-44	90 Sqn
1608502	Sgt	EATON John James	28-04-44	166 Sqn
1670569	Sgt	EATON Joseph Roy	7-07-44	166 Sqn
52485	F/O	EATON Walter	21-04-44	97 Sqn

Service No.	Rank	Name	Date	Sqn
1590859	Sgt	EAYRES Raymond	14-10-44	115 Sqn
49993	F/L	EBERT DFC George Henry	6-01-44	207 Sqn
1337413	F/S	EBSWORTH Edwin William	27-01-44	576 Sqn
1378087	Sgt	EBSWORTH William Nowell	12-03-44	199 Sqn
1890696	Sgt	EBURNE Terence Alexander	28-05-44	102 Sqn
2209021	F/S	ECCLESTON Arthur	18-12-44	432 Sqn
1684843	F/S	ECCLESTON Stanley	16-11-44	207 Sqn
1268286	Sgt	ECCLESTONE Stanley	2-01-44	207 Sqn
176416	P/O	ECCLESTONE Thomas Stanley	11-05-44	515 Sqn
3021658	Sgt	EDDIE Keith Summers	29-07-44	626 Sqn
1594592	Sgt	EDDISON Raymond	16-03-44	625 Sqn
628555	W/O	EDE John Ernest Richard	21-07-44	467 Sqn
1740049	Sgt	EDEN Stanley James	26-02-44	420 Sqn
1026434	W/O	EDGAR Frank	29-11-44	128 Sqn
1074118	Sgt	EDGE Eric	2-01-44	106 Sqn
1324941	Sgt	EDGE Leslie James	24-03-44	78 Sqn
1112606	W/O	EDGE Stanley Patrick	13-07-44	14 OTU
1313034	F/S	EDGECOMBE George Edward	30-01-44	463 Sqn
1585145	F/S	EDGELL Thomas Robert	1-11-44	426 Sqn
1508681	Sgt	EDGEWORTH Robert	25-02-44	626 Sqn
1379496	W/O	EDINBURGH William Henry	24-09-44	156 Sqn
1677608	Sgt	EDMANDS Derek Roy	29-01-44	115 Sqn
1290934	W/O	EDMONDS Arthur Frederick	16-02-44	77 Sqn
1816413	Sgt	EDMONDS John Alun	25-07-44	1661 HCU
133096	F/O	EDMONDS Patrick John	7-06-44	115 Sqn
1336890	Sgt	EDSALL Douglas William Henry	6-06-44	76 Sqn
51120	F/L	EDWARD DFC John Andrew	24-06-44	617 Sqn
2220578	Sgt	EDWARDS David Alderson	19-03-44	1667 HCU
1586160	Sgt	EDWARDS David James	20-01-44	166 Sqn
169193	P/O	EDWARDS Douglas Hinton	31-03-44	76 Sqn
929365	W/O	EDWARDS Edward Thomas	15-02-44	625 Sqn
169113	P/O	EDWARDS Elwyn Hinton	5-03-44	218 Sqn
1321526	F/S	EDWARDS Ernest Charles	11-04-44	576 Sqn
1316995	Sgt	EDWARDS Francis Joseph	18-04-44	427 Sqn
578280	Sgt	EDWARDS Frederick Charles	25-06-44	50 Sqn
1869475	Sgt	EDWARDS Frederick William	14-04-44	5 LFS
177700	P/O	EDWARDS DFC Gordon James	16-09-44	405 Sqn
591941	Sgt	EDWARDS Gordon Mackenzie	8-06-44	115 Sqn
157108	F/O	EDWARDS Hubert William Joseph	21-07-44	97 Sqn
174351	P/O	EDWARDS Iorwerth Pierce	11-06-44	7 Sqn
1113619	W/O	EDWARDS James Patterson	26-08-44	514 Sqn
172240	F/O	EDWARDS Jeffrey Neil	22-12-44	157 Sqn
1897034	Sgt	EDWARDS John Francis Patrick	5-07-44	207 Sqn
1900724	F/S	EDWARDS John Ogilvy [Eire]	11-12-44	1651 HCU
119780	F/L	EDWARDS Philip John	26-08-44	622 Sqn
1853863	Sgt	EDWARDS Richard	28-05-44	427 Sqn
1257237	Sgt	EDWARDS Sidney	10-04-44	460 Sqn
170938	P/O	EDWARDS Sidney Albert	10-05-44	97 Sqn
1430281	Sgt	EDWARDS Thomas	22-05-44	57 Sqn
1861350	Sgt	EDWARDS Thomas Ernest	29-01-44	77 Sqn
179057	F/O	EDWARDS Thomas John	4-11-44	101 Sqn
1082724	F/S	EDWARDS Thomas William	22-01-44	83 Sqn
924350	Sgt	EDWARDS Walter Victor Lawrence	21-02-44	115 Sqn
1579083	F/S	EDWARDS Wilfred Ernest	21-07-44	12 Sqn
1652947	Sgt	EDWARDS William Austin	28-05-44	103 Sqn
1804079	Sgt	EDWARDS William Frank	22-03-44	49 Sqn
1607130	Sgt	EDWARDS William Randolph	8-12-44	1652 HCU
40811	S/L	EGAN-WYER Bernard Owen	6-12-44	77 Sqn
1802344	Sgt	EGGBEER Harry George	23-05-44	90 Sqn
120444	S/L	EGGINS DFC Robert Kingdon	27-07-44	83 Sqn
1333561	Sgt	EGGLESON Frederick Charles	2-01-44	463 Sqn
752767	Sgt	EGGLESTON Douglas	6-07-44	582 Sqn
126033	F/L	EHRMAN DFC Leopold 'Leo'	29-01-44	630 Sqn
1594944	Sgt	EKE Raymond	22-11-44	61 Sqn
1585302	Sgt	EKERS Leonard Charles B.	1-07-44	625 Sqn
1293121	Sgt	EKINS Edward Henry	5-07-44	106 Sqn
1594431	Sgt	ELAND Alfred	13-05-44	576 Sqn
1141778	Sgt	ELAND Fred	24-03-44	578 Sqn
1811531	Sgt	ELCOMBE Robert	7-06-44	460 Sqn
1525615	F/S	ELDER Thomas Wilfred	29-01-44	97 Sqn
748485	F/S	ELDERS George Stanley	26-10-44	166 Sqn
1895127	Sgt	ELDRIDGE Peter Charles	3-06-44	640 Sqn
145829	F/O	ELEY Frederick Eric	30-08-44	619 Sqn
771810	Sgt	ELIOT Eric Marshall [India]	6-07-44	161 Sqn
1166810	Sgt	ELKINGTON Alfred	16-02-44	640 Sqn
1437743	F/S	ELKINGTON Kenneth Neal	14-01-44	626 Sqn
3030988	Sgt	ELL Derek Eugene	17-09-44	1652 HCU
1622371	Sgt	ELLA James Maurice	25-03-44	44 Sqn
1233499	Sgt	ELLAM Kenneth	31-03-44	49 Sqn
858945	Sgt	ELLAMS Thomas	23-04-44	1659 HCU
1798090	Sgt	ELLARD George Cornelius [Eire]	13-08-44	90 Sqn
186688	P/O	ELLEMAN Charles	27-11-44	138 Sqn
1816199	Sgt	ELLENOR John	27-04-44	49 Sqn
1396585	Sgt	ELLENOR William	25-01-44	PFNTU
152950	F/O	ELLERKER Lancelot Herbert	13-07-44	166 Sqn
1818990	Sgt	ELLERSLIE Roy	13-05-44	426 Sqn
1431392	Sgt	ELLICK Maitland	31-03-44	106 Sqn
1806072	Sgt	ELLICOTT Denis Alfred Gilbert	6-07-44	635 Sqn
1211502	Sgt	ELLIOTT Albert Edward	21-01-44	408 Sqn
141982	F/O	ELLIOTT Alfred Charles	21-04-44	57 Sqn
1179569	F/S	ELLIOTT Arthur John	23-03-44	514 Sqn
1594207	Sgt	ELLIOTT Bernard Stanley Winskill	25-07-44	166 Sqn
1860419	Sgt	ELLIOTT George Algernon	2-05-44	429 Sqn
1217619	F/S	ELLIOTT James Reginald	11-05-44	50 Sqn
1650667	Sgt	ELLIOTT John Norman	19-04-44	149 Sqn
162597	P/O	ELLIOTT Raymond William	20-01-44	426 Sqn
1523249	Sgt	ELLIOTT Robert	15-03-44	578 Sqn
2210866	Sgt	ELLIOTT Thomas Woodman	21-07-44	9 Sqn
1604178	Sgt	ELLIS George Stanley	30-01-44	100 Sqn
171502	P/O	ELLIS Harold Thomas	21-01-44	102 Sqn
39510	F/L	ELLIS Jack Llewellyn	7-11-44	128 Sqn
1052736	Sgt	ELLIS James	3-05-44	550 Sqn
1528092	AC1	ELLIS James	9-09-44	156 Sqn
1410921	Sgt	ELLIS James Edwin	20-02-44	49 Sqn
1471352	Sgt	ELLIS John Robert	19-03-44	50 Sqn
157529	P/O	ELLIS Robert Thomas Harold	21-01-44	18 OTU
537642	Sgt	ELLIS Ronald	4-05-44	207 Sqn
1897461	Sgt	ELLIS Ronald Arthur	12-10-44	14 OTU
1456863	Sgt	ELLISON Harold	16-03-44	100 Sqn
56151	P/O	ELLISON Thomas Arthur	23-10-44	1656 HCU
939956	Sgt	ELLWOOD Gerald	4-05-44	420 Sqn
1331956	F/S	ELLWOOD Reginald	3-01-44	83 Sqn
51911	F/O	ELLYATT John	10-06-44	10 Sqn
1806889	Sgt	ELMES Dennis Walter	6-08-44	207 Sqn
1521641	Sgt	ELMS Arthur Ernest	30-01-44	115 Sqn
159691	F/O	ELMY Gordon	31-03-44	156 Sqn
1852639	Sgt	ELSBURY Harold Ralph	22-05-44	460 Sqn
165181	F/O	ELSON Frank Raymond	12-12-44	635 Sqn
171397	P/O	ELTON Colin	4-05-44	35 Sqn
543937	Sgt	ELVISH Norman	16-10-44	115 Sqn
1438270	Sgt	EMENY Kenneth	21-01-44	77 Sqn
1795670	Sgt	EMERSON John Frederick Wallace [Eire]	16-12-44	106 Sqn
66558	F/L	EMERSON Roderick Stanley 'Derick'	21-02-44	97 Sqn
1393444	F/S	EMERY Gordon Frederick	18-07-44	158 Sqn
3040593	Sgt	EMERY Horace Samuel	20-11-44	1656 HCU
1041920	Sgt	EMMETT Joseph Edward	22-06-44	467 Sqn
1869004	F/S	EMMOTT Douglas	27-08-44	12 Sqn
538244	Sgt	EMMS Peter Cawthorn	24-03-44	12 Sqn
1894515	Sgt	EMSLEY Ernest George	24-04-44	619 Sqn
1500221	Sgt	EMSON Ronald	19-03-44	166 Sqn
1415222	Sgt	ENDEAN Douglas Edgar	27-04-44	49 Sqn
1895899	Sgt	ENGLEHARDT Wolf Herman	28-07-44	101 Sqn
1602359	Sgt	ENGLAND Richard William	23-05-44	9 Sqn
1591922	Sgt	ENGLAND Ronald	25-07-44	466 Sqn
1394919	Sgt	ENGLEFIELD Donald	13-08-44	78 Sqn
117836	F/L	ENGLISH William	15-02-44	630 Sqn
1614413	Sgt	ENNALS George Frederick	29-07-44	207 Sqn

Number	Rank	Name	Date	Sqn
155207	F/O	ENNIS DFC Clifford John	8-06-44	138 Sqn
1582755	Sgt	ENNIS John Frederick	15-03-44	101 Sqn
1339743	Sgt	ENNOR John Reginald	23-12-44	90 Sqn
40096	S/L	ENO DSO DFC MiD Lloyd Higgs [Canada]	15-03-44	51 Sqn
1512552	Sgt	ENSOR James	23-04-44	100 Sqn
759042	W/O	ENTWISLE Herbert	15-02-44	15 Sqn
1394106	F/S	ENTWISTLE Donnel	22-01-44	51 Sqn
1622341	Sgt	ERATT Robert Edward	29-12-44	419 Sqn
992684	Sgt	ERICKSON Charles	5-07-44	35 Sqn
655068	W/O	ERICKSON William	6-10-44	115 Sqn
179210	F/O	ERRITT DFC Cyril	13-08-44	83 Sqn
1071465	Sgt	ESCRITT Benjamin	4-05-44	625 Sqn
154961	F/O	ESCRITT William Henry	11-10-44	101 Sqn
160680	F/O	ESDALE Jack	2-09-44	1662 HCU
1593823	Sgt	ESPIN-HEMPSALL Brian	9-11-44	625 Sqn
49845	F/O	ESPLEY Eric Charles	31-03-44	576 Sqn
151969	F/O	ESSENHIGH Edward Gordon	17-12-44	49 Sqn
1578474	Sgt	ESSEX Kenneth Albert	22-05-44	550 Sqn
1578038	F/S	ESSON Patrick Alexander	31-03-44	578 Sqn
1176109	Sgt	ESTCOURTE Arthur Henry	15-03-44	90 Sqn
1801712	Sgt	ETHERIDGE James Frederick	24-03-44	625 Sqn
1457188	F/S	ETHERIDGE Joseph Arthur	23-11-44	195 Sqn
157299	F/O	EVANS Albert	25-03-44	44 Sqn
42745	F/L	EVANS MiD Brian Herbert [Australia]	31-03-44	49 Sqn
1492815	F/S	EVANS Christmas Deiniol	4-11-44	78 Sqn
1339689	Sgt	EVANS Clifford James	25-03-44	44 Sqn
1312674	Sgt	EVANS Clifford John	18-10-44	630 Sqn
1473693	Sgt	EVANS Cyril Edwards	22-01-44	158 Sqn
2210016	Sgt	EVANS David	30-11-44	578 Sqn
3025155	Sgt	EVANS David Douglas	26-08-44	12 OTU
149057	F/L	EVANS David George	21-07-44	15 Sqn
1337333	Sgt	EVANS David Jones	1-07-44	12 Sqn
1502460	Sgt	EVANS Denis	15-03-44	427 Sqn
1873611	Sgt	EVANS Dennis Thomas	30-08-44	21 OTU
1836534	Sgt	EVANS Desmond Charles	23-09-44	582 Sqn
2204517	Sgt	EVANS Eric	12-10-44	83 OTU
1603609	F/S	EVANS Eric Franklyn	27-08-44	12 Sqn
710241	F/S	EVANS Eric Vincent [Rhodesia]	22-06-44	207 Sqn
1800212	F/S	EVANS Ernest Edward	12-12-44	582 Sqn
1853237	Sgt	EVANS Ernest Edward	12-09-44	158 Sqn
127520	F/O	EVANS DFM Francis Kent	8-01-44	627 Sqn
1146235	Sgt	EVANS Frank	19-10-44	186 Sqn
1297469	LAC	EVANS Fred Arnold	19-12-44	85 Sqn
1578573	Sgt	EVANS Frederick Edward Raymond	18-03-44	1657 HCU
656618	F/S	EVANS George Rhys	3-01-44	405 Sqn
1602267	F/S	EVANS George William	4-05-44	50 Sqn
1025594	Sgt	EVANS Graham Herbert	26-03-44	425 Sqn
1274257	Sgt	EVANS Hubert John	28-05-44	166 Sqn
1835451	AC2	EVANS Jack	4-09-44	Tempsford
145371	F/O	EVANS Ivor Glyndwr	22-05-44	50 Sqn
1395420	Sgt	EVANS John Edmond	20-08-44	169 Sqn
132710	F/O	EVANS John Emlyn	15-02-44	630 Sqn
1678129	Sgt	EVANS John George Furness [South Africa]	26-07-44	100 Sqn
175064	P/O	EVANS John Kevin [Newfoundland]	16-09-44	1655 MTU
183073	P/O	EVANS John Thomas	29-07-44	431 Sqn
1605227	Sgt	EVANS Kenneth Edgar	14-01-44	432 Sqn
1836030	Sgt	EVANS Lionel John	31-03-44	44 Sqn
177452	P/O	EVANS Mathias	6-07-44	635 Sqn
1836528	Sgt	EVANS Meurig	9-08-44	640 Sqn
1393145	Sgt	EVANS Noel Reginald James	14-01-44	156 Sqn
176567	F/O	EVANS Norman Joseph	4-10-44	44 Sqn
1037397	Sgt	EVANS Norman Shallcross	18-11-44	460 Sqn
1385774	F/S	EVANS Percival Edric	27-08-44	635 Sqn
1386058	Sgt	EVANS Raymond John	28-05-44	101 Sqn
1426660	Sgt	EVANS Robert William John	6-01-44	467 Sqn
1581757	Sgt	EVANS Ronald George	12-09-44	625 Sqn
142213	F/L	EVANS Stanley	31-03-44	7 Sqn
159086	F/O	EVANS Thomas Arthur	31-03-44	578 Sqn
137624	F/O	EVANS Thomas Ieuan Milner	18-11-44	578 Sqn
1655924	Sgt	EVANS Thomas John	25-03-44	57 Sqn
1299215	Sgt	EVANS Thomas Randall	20-02-44	625 Sqn
573381	F/S	EVANS Thomas Tomley	22-03-44	166 Sqn
902284	F/S	EVANS William Frederick	27-04-44	106 Sqn
151142	F/O	EVANS William James	14-01-44	7 Sqn
1026577	Sgt	EVANS William Leonard	28-04-44	100 Sqn
1580430	F/S	EVANSON William George	1-08-44	101 Sqn
1609448	Sgt	EVELEIGH Harold Peter Frank	5-07-44	9 Sqn
1809566	Sgt	EVERED Frederick William	26-08-44	100 Sqn
174693	F/O	EVERETT DFM Arthur Charles	24-12-44	635 Sqn
1594197	Sgt	EVERETT Donald Charles	20-02-44	207 Sqn
1209151	Sgt	EVERETT Edwin William	8-07-44	49 Sqn
751065	W/O	EVERETT DFM Jack	13-07-44	14 OTU
1501830	Sgt	EVERITT John Oliver	15-03-44	51 Sqn
179609	P/O	EWART Samuel	22-06-44	57 Sqn
1896427	Sgt	EWING James Peter	4-07-44	12 Sqn
1613477	F/S	EWING Leslie Ernest	6-11-44	207 Sqn
1394192	F/S	EYRES Eric Gordon Morrice	25-04-44	626 Sqn
1802351	Sgt	FABB Douglas Ernest	17-06-44	576 Sqn
1813220	Sgt	FAGG John Richard	8-06-44	15 Sqn
172210	P/O	FAHY Edward	17-06-44	419 Sqn
1175373	Sgt	FAINT Reginald David	27-08-44	15 Sqn
173760	P/O	FAIRBAIRN Douglas Thomas George	11-06-44	100 Sqn
1456224	F/S	FAIRBAIRN John	23-06-44	97 Sqn
1393603	F/S	FAIRBAIRN Kenneth McLean	25-02-44	550 Sqn
50478	F/O	FAIRBAIRN Neil Joseph	25-04-44	622 Sqn
747317	Sgt	FAIRBROTHER Arthur Lawrence	15-02-44	77 Sqn
1615345	Sgt	FAIRCLOTH Alfred Williams	1-07-44	1 GpSDFlt
1450687	F/S	FAIRCLOUGH Leonard Thomas	20-02-44	9 Sqn
140862	F/S	FAIRES Douglas John	22-06-44	207 Sqn
2210638	Sgt	FAIRHURST Thomas Arthur	11-06-44	100 Sqn
591778	Sgt	FAIRLEY Ronald Victor	29-01-44	576 Sqn
1394032	F/S	FAIRPLAY Roy	22-03-44	158 Sqn
1691254	Sgt	FAIRSERVICE James Brown	15-07-44	1651 HCU
128618	F/O	FAIRWEATHER DFC Gilbert Walter [British Honduras]	22-06-44	83 Sqn
77912	F/L	FALCONER Daniel John	16-10-44	12 OTU
87052	W/C	FALCONER DFC AFC Donald Buchan [Rhodesia]	30-12-44	156 Sqn
1822105	Sgt	FALCONER James	27-01-44	463 Sqn
1750250	Sgt	FALLON Dennis	30-08-44	460 Sqn
1608414	Sgt	FANCY Ernest John	25-04-44	626 Sqn
143472	F/O	FARARA DFC DFM George Grafron Haig	8-07-44	630 Sqn
641603	F/S	FARBRACE William John James	12-09-44	640 Sqn
2209556	Sgt	FARDOE Thomas Eric	29-07-44	44 Sqn
188313	P/O	FARISH Fraser	10-11-44	97 Sqn
909914	Sgt	FARLEY Albert Walter Verdun	31-03-44	101 Sqn
1382100	F/S	FARLEY Anthony Frederick William	13-06-44	115 Sqn
629251	Sgt	FARLEY Charles Frederick	5-10-44	626 Sqn
1594250	Sgt	FARLEY Cyril Frank	18-12-44	3 LFS
1728946	Sgt	FARLEY Ernest Richard	4-11-44	44 Sqn
1897257	Sgt	FARLEY Thomas Reuben	29-05-44	1657 HCU
749863	F/S	FARMELO Kenneth Edmund Leonard	20-01-44	83 Sqn
2204356	Sgt	FARMER Alan	21-04-44	44 Sqn
636504	Sgt	FARMER Kenneth	23-04-44	115 Sqn
2220935	Sgt	FARMER Leslie Desmond	6-08-44	97 Sqn
1624880	Sgt	FARMER Thomas William	6-11-44	550 Sqn
1603478	Sgt	FARMER William Walter	10-04-44	PFNTU
128687	S/L	FARMERY DFM Clifford John	21-01-44	77 Sqn
1824896	Sgt	FARNDALE Bernard	30-08-44	115 Sqn
1605101	Sgt	FARNDEN Kenneth	29-11-44	12 Sqn
1390007	F/S	FARNELL Ernest Arthur	31-03-44	630 Sqn
172990	P/O	FARNHAM DFM Frank	15-07-44	103 Sqn
169016	F/O	FARNHILL Jack	17-08-44	57 Sqn
1147012	F/S	FARNWORTH John	26-08-44	75 Sqn

Service No	Rank	Name	Date	Unit
1532220	Sgt	FARTHING Cyril	1-04-44	1656 HCU
1654183	Sgt	FARR Forrest Alan Luigi Angove	24-03-44	100 Sqn
146341	F/O	FARR Michael Anthony	11-07-44	138 Sqn
2209858	Sgt	FARRALL Dennis	16-06-44	635 Sqn
1049271	Sgt	FARRALL Frederick Arthur	25-05-44	640 Sqn
1395425	Sgt	FARRANT Colin William	6-01-44	12 Sqn
1388878	F/S	FARRANT Douglas James	10-04-44	635 Sqn
1238840	F/S	FARRELL Arthur Harkness	17-04-44	5 LFS
1349742	F/S	FARRELL John McFarlane	11-11-44	97 Sqn
1386762	Sgt	FARRELL Richard Joseph	20-02-44	463 Sqn
1138457	Sgt	FARRELL William Noel	7-03-44	1667 HCU
40046	S/L	FARRINGTON Allan Leonard [Australia]	29-08-44	582 Sqn
1389162	Sgt	FARRINGTON George	30-08-44	101 Sqn
178519	F/O	FAULKNER Charles Robson	12-09-44	630 Sqn
849211	Sgt	FAULKNER George	29-12-44	170 Sqn
84712	F/L	FAULKNER John Geoffrey	23-12-44	35 Sqn
1660558	Sgt	FAULKNER Reginald James	24-03-44	156 Sqn
1897104	Sgt	FAULKNER Robert Edward	24-09-44	50 Sqn
1126175	Sgt	FAULKNER William John	30-08-44	50 Sqn
1473895	Sgt	FAVAGER Victor	16-03-44	100 Sqn
1485213	Sgt	FAWCETT Dudley Sydney	2-01-44	100 Sqn
1685718	Sgt	FAWCETT James Charles	30-08-44	101 Sqn
1439198	Sgt	FAWCETT John Randall	12-09-44	218 Sqn
43032	S/L	FAWCETT DFC Rowland Eden [Canada]	2-01-44	156 Sqn
1238637	F/S	FAWCETT Selwyn	27-04-44	207 Sqn
1594824	Sgt	FAWKES John	29-08-44	50 Sqn
1230376	F/S	FAZACKERLEY Raymond	22-06-44	44 Sqn
1473318	Sgt	FEAKINS Frederick John	11-09-44	35 Sqn
2216622	Sgt	FEAR Joseph	8-07-44	207 Sqn
1768132	Sgt	FEARNLEY Jack	29-10-44	50 Sqn
2201584	Sgt	FEARNS Francis	29-07-44	408 Sqn
1459770	Sgt	FEATHER Edgar	2-05-44	7 Sqn
1098626	F/S	FEAVER Thomas Edward	15-10-44	7 Sqn
951326	F/S	FEE Joseph Edward David	18-07-44	158 Sqn
142914	F/L	FEELEY DFC Arthur	6-06-44	582 Sqn
1214953	Sgt	FELDMAN Israel	8-07-44	9 Sqn
1684693	Sgt	FELL Jack Clarke	27-04-44	78 Sqn
1472950	F/S	FELL James Anthony	6-10-44	106 Sqn
1581317	Sgt	FELLOWS Joseph Harold	16-07-44	207 Sqn
1540769	Sgt	FELTHAM Harry Kitchener	25-06-44	467 Sqn
1853244	Sgt	FELTHAM Peter Bernard	19-09-44	106 Sqn
138139	F/O	FENLEY John	20-02-44	15 Sqn
160932	F/O	FENNELL Ronald William Jack	29-11-44	12 Sqn
1318683	F/S	FENNELL Roy Barton	31-03-44	166 Sqn
1058300	Sgt	FENNER Peter Owen	24-03-44	166 Sqn
1488561	Sgt	FENSON Richard Henry	12-09-44	635 Sqn
1861579	Sgt	FENTON John Alan	5-11-44	166 Sqn
1283600	Sgt	FENTON John Thomas	4-05-44	35 Sqn
1620104	Sgt	FENTON Maurice Frederick	23-04-44	166 Sqn
996901	Sgt	FENWICK Albert	2-03-44	76 Sqn
1395122	F/S	FENWICK John Handley David	25-02-44	514 Sqn
1520986	Sgt	FENWICK Thomas	7-10-44	514 Sqn
1431356	F/S	FENWICK Thomas Philip	20-05-44	44 Sqn
1234319	Sgt	FEREDAY Sidney Lascelles	22-03-44	9 Sqn
1826549	Sgt	FERGUS George Alexander	24-10-44	576 Sqn
1522934	Sgt	FERGUS Thomas	19-07-44	138 Sqn
1818698	Sgt	FERGUSON Alexander Young	3-06-44	76 Sqn
1678323	Sgt	FERGUSON David Anderson	22-01-44	44 Sqn
975699	Sgt	FERGUSON David Joseph	20-01-44	419 Sqn
131132	F/O	FERGUSON George [Canada]	22-05-44	57 Sqn
1782105	Sgt	FERGUSON Harold Ian	29-07-44	626 Sqn
1591340	Sgt	FERGUSON Jack	19-04-44	115 Sqn
1349124	F/S	FERGUSON Peter James Hughes	15-02-44	10 Sqn
1330850	Sgt	FERGUSON Robert	6-01-44	97 Sqn
1578284	F/S	FERGUSON Thomas William	30-08-44	103 Sqn
1826294	Sgt	FERGUSON William Brisbane	22-10-44	1659 HCU
3020425	Sgt	FERNIE Crawford	14-10-44	12 Sqn
1568204	Sgt	FERNIE Ronald Patience Heriot	17-12-44	17 OTU
2202536	LAC	FERNSBY Guy	14-06-44	61 Sqn
1566749	Sgt	FERRANS Robert Jeffrey	28-06-44	90 Sqn
102590	F/L	FERRY Twice MiD Leslie Howard	30-03-44	20 OTU
1126142	Sgt	FETTIS Richard James	16-03-44	625 Sqn
157430	P/O	FEW George Frederick William	6-01-44	7 Sqn
1133610	F/S	FEWSTER Herbert	14-01-44	166 Sqn
1396105	Sgt	FIDLER Edwin Gordon	22-03-44	35 Sqn
135040	F/O	FIDLER Frederick George	30-01-44	463 Sqn
1543138	Sgt	FIDLER Gordon Alwyn	20-02-44	460 Sqn
155125	F/O	FIELD Dennis Arthur	11-12-44	105 Sqn
1606624	Sgt	FIELD Leonard Alfred	15-02-44	207 Sqn
149554	F/O	FIELD Thomas Bertram	20-02-44	83 Sqn
1852280	Sgt	FIELDER Ronald Ernest	8-06-44	115 Sqn
1642303	Sgt	FIELDHOUSE Cyril William	15-06-44	115 Sqn
1035033	F/S	FIELDING Leslie	29-07-44	576 Sqn
1620500	Sgt	FIELDING Salvin	2-11-44	576 Sqn
159006	P/O	FILBEY Ronald Harry	3-01-44	426 Sqn
1600078	Sgt	FILBY James Alfred	20-02-44	158 Sqn
55086	F/O	FILBY Walter George Frederick	17-08-44	630 Sqn
1337166	Sgt	FILER Frederick Albert Walter	3-12-44	138 Sqn
1387614	F/S	FILER William Gordon	28-01-44	426 Sqn
33383	F/L	FILLEUL Philip Richard Steuart	12-09-44	214 Sqn
1258276	F/S	FILMER Frank William	13-07-44	1662 HCU
1577956	F/S	FINCH Arthur	23-03-44	9 Sqn
1894312	Sgt	FINCH Ernest Arthur	17-06-44	102 Sqn
1132101	Sgt	FINCH Harold Charles	13-07-44	1652 HCU
1582444	Sgt	FINCH John Aidan Butler	28-08-44	19 OTU
1331869	Sgt	FINCH Thomas Arthur	14-01-44	12 Sqn
1814408	Sgt	FINCH William James Thomas	22-01-44	166 Sqn
1821527	Sgt	FINDLATER Stuart Alexander	29-07-44	1654 HCU
1556361	F/S	FINDLAY Alexander McGeoch	2-11-44	49 Sqn
1807884	Sgt	FINDLAY Dennis John	22-03-44	103 Sqn
571711	F/S	FINDLAY James	15-10-44	207 Sqn
1566283	Sgt	FINDLAY James Addie 'Jimmy'	19-07-44	207 Sqn
1568579	Sgt	FINDLAYSON Robert Hamilton	26-08-44	90 Sqn
176090	P/O	FINDLEY Stanley	8-07-44	57 Sqn
1802888	F/S	FINDLOW Colin Peter	12-11-44	23 Sqn
1672926	Sgt	FINGLETON James	29-06-44	102 Sqn
1339325	Sgt	FINIGHAN Clifford Leslie	12-05-44	103 Sqn
176585	P/O	FINK Jan Frederick	18-07-44	578 Sqn
164363	F/O	FINLAYSON William Peter Cobbaw	30-10-44	21 OTU
54207	P/O	FINN DFM Thomas Victor	27-01-44	463 Sqn
1533514	Sgt	FINNERTY Thomas	20-02-44	576 Sqn
1522018	Sgt	FINNEY Jack Vernon	13-08-44	102 Sqn
1803168	Sgt	FINNIGAN Brian Bernard Melrose	16-05-44	16 OTU
1823313	Sgt	FINNIGAN Patrick	4-11-44	640 Sqn
1390489	F/S	FIRTH Charles Morton	5-07-44	207 Sqn
1439601	F/S	FIRTH Eric	21-01-44	76 Sqn
999710	Sgt	FIRTH Geoffrey	3-01-44	166 Sqn
1322490	Sgt	FISHER Alick Charles	4-02-44	82 OTU
1564156	Sgt	FISHER Anthony	11-06-44	460 Sqn
125430	S/L	FISHER DFC DFM David Roy	17-06-44	102 Sqn
182582	P/O	FISHER Donald Iain Begbie	9-11-44	138 Sqn
172728	P/O	FISHER Eric Thomas	30-07-44	115 Sqn
1602365	Sgt	FISHER Frederick Graham	6-12-44	103 Sqn
1896156	Sgt	FISHER Frederick William	26-07-44	166 Sqn
1434607	F/S	FISHER Leonard	21-07-44	100 Sqn
1451885	Sgt	FISHER Norman	23-01-44	1667 HCU
170281	P/O	FISHER Norman James	4-05-44	626 Sqn
187033	P/O	FISHER DFM Raymond Victor	17-12-44	156 Sqn
645165	Sgt	FISHER Ronald Albert	12-09-44	44 Sqn
1592874	Sgt	FISHPOOL Robert Vincent	16-09-44	582 Sqn
157741	F/O	FISHWICK Kenneth William	13-05-44	635 Sqn
1583115	Sgt	FITCHETT Roland	17-06-44	103 Sqn
1897158	F/O	FITTALL Ronald Ernest	22-06-44	463 Sqn
2209093	Sgt	FITTON Alfred Frederick	21-02-44	427 Sqn
3040322	Sgt	FITTON Edmond	5-11-44	76 Sqn
176576	P/O	FITZGERALD Maurice Isidore Joseph	28-05-44	75 Sqn

1671698	Sgt	FITZPATRICK James	26-07-44	166 Sqn	3010665	Sgt	FORRESTER James Leonard	20-11-44	75 Sqn
1575467	Sgt	FITZPATRICK John Christopher	18-10-44	630 Sqn	1038479	Sgt	FORSHAW Basil	28-04-44	460 Sqn
632592	Sgt	FITZSIMMONS Felix	21-02-44	9 Sqn	111102	S/L	FORSHAW John Charles Noel	27-04-44	141 Sqn
149951	F/O	FLACK Victor Samuel	6-01-44	97 Sqn	134683	F/O	FORSHEW Frederick Edward	14-01-44	9 Sqn
155505	F/O	FLAHERTY Dennis Kieran	27-07-44	627 Sqn	645750	F/S	FORSTER Douglas	30-08-44	106 Sqn
1219836	Sgt	FLAHERTY Edward John	21-07-44	90 Sqn	1480362	Sgt	FORSTER Douglas George	22-01-44	102 Sqn
179006	P/O	FLANAGAN Maurice	21-07-44	10 Sqn	1897586	Sgt	FORSTER Fred	6-12-44	635 Sqn
1346200	Sgt	FLAVELL Joseph	24-03-44	166 Sqn	1876702	Sgt	FORSTER Frederick Douglas	4-07-44	12 Sqn
1559757	Sgt	FLAVELL Samuel	23-05-44	166 Sqn	123200	F/L	FORSTER John	20-09-44	622 Sqn
1073035	Cpl	FLELLO Arthur Edward	21-08-44	52 Base	1592020	Sgt	FORSTER Thomas Harrison Armstrong		
2220983	Sgt	FLELLO James Charles	6-12-44	57 Sqn				26-02-44	12 Sqn
1595708	Sgt	FLEMING Alexander Stewart	23-12-44	35 Sqn	1593433	Sgt	FORSTER William	6-11-44	463 Sqn
1568942	Sgt	FLEMING John Mc. M.	20-01-44	466 Sqn	1894970	Sgt	FORSYTH Alexander	9-03-44	1667 HCU
1795114	AC1	FLEMING Thomas	10-04-44	Spilsby	1597691	Sgt	FORSYTH William Bratton	20-11-44	14 OTU
1294322	Sgt	FLEMING William	2-01-44	460 Sqn	1565064	Sgt	FORTE Rudolph Angel Antonio	21-01-44	76 Sqn
149055	F/O	FLETCHER Alfred	21-01-44	51 Sqn	1510806	Sgt	FORTH Norman Louis	25-04-44	115 Sqn
179580	F/O	FLETCHER Derrick	28-12-44	576 Sqn	1898863	Sgt	FORTUNE Daniel Joseph	7-09-44	17 OTU
52570	F/O	FLETCHER Edward Eric	30-08-44	106 Sqn	113416	S/L	FOSTER DFC Arthur Edgar	22-06-44	630 Sqn
1890601	Sgt	FLETCHER Edward John	27-04-44	83 Sqn	1800552	F/S	FOSTER Austin Joseph	27-08-44	192 Sqn
151988	F/O	FLETCHER Edwin McGilvary	12-04-44	50 Sqn	624078	F/S	FOSTER Charles Leslie	23-05-44	100 Sqn
1515478	Sgt	FLETCHER Eric	27-04-44	156 Sqn	1397833	Sgt	FOSTER Charles Sidney	20-02-44	77 Sqn
172309	P/O	FLETCHER Harold	17-06-44	419 Sqn	133357	P/O	FOSTER David Kay	28-05-44	515 Sqn
1420555	Sgt	FLETCHER Ian Douglas Wolfe	12-01-44	14 OTU	1851274	Sgt	FOSTER Dennis Reginald	29-10-44	50 Sqn
186736	F/O	FLETCHER James	15-12-44	625 Sqn	119550	F/L	FOSTER Donovon John	3-11-44	550 Sqn
1593916	Sgt	FLETCHER John	12-10-44	166 Sqn	159149	P/O	FOSTER Douglas Arthur	12-09-44	35 Sqn
115198	F/L	FLETCHER John David	23-06-44	97 Sqn	1414503	Sgt	FOSTER Francis Charles	12-09-44	626 Sqn
151475	F/O	FLETCHER Joseph Ambrose	9-07-44	622 Sqn	1321968	Sgt	FOSTER Frederick Albert	25-04-44	115 Sqn
1880697	Sgt	FLETCHER Kenneth Joseph	6-11-44	214 Sqn	177401	P/O	FOSTER Harold Arthur	8-06-44	115 Sqn
1320358	F/S	FLETCHER Thomas Santola	31-03-44	9 Sqn	1558684	Sgt	FOSTER James	18-12-44	3 LFS
2209502	Sgt	FLETCHER William	25-05-44	640 Sqn	1581957	F/S	FOSTER James Joseph William	13-08-44	622 Sqn
910709	W/O	FLETT DFM Adam Herd	14-01-44	109 Sqn	1004570	Sgt	FOSTER Jeffrey Bernard	29-01-44	10 Sqn
1544755	F/S	FLETT Donald Angus	8-06-44	431 Sqn	985156	Sgt	FOSTER John	25-03-44	460 Sqn
129347	F/O	FLINT Clifford Sheldon	13-05-44	635 Sqn	143467	F/O	FOSTER DFC John Douglas	7-05-44	156 Sqn
1852349	Sgt	FLINT Harry Thomas George	21-04-44	100 Sqn	1593330	Sgt	FOSTER Kenneth	17-05-44	1661 HCU
171865	P/O	FLITCROFT Frank Chester	1-03-44	76 Sqn	1579040	Sgt	FOSTER Sidney Frederick	27-04-44	49 Sqn
1467806	F/S	FLITTON Derek Noel	8-06-44	408 Sqn	571591	F/S	FOTHERGILL Wilfred Brydon	21-04-44	15 Sqn
130660	F/L	FLOOD Michael Thomas [Argentina]	4-12-44	189 Sqn	1591122	Sgt	FOULDS Reuben Edward	8-06-44	101 Sqn
1449273	Sgt	FLORENT Vivian Bertram	9-06-44	102 Sqn	1852446	Sgt	FOULKES Eric Dudley	3-06-44	640 Sqn
1010304	Sgt	FLOWER Frank William	27-01-44	622 Sqn	3010396	Sgt	FOULKES Lawrence	22-05-44	49 Sqn
1389901	F/S	FLOWERS Kenneth William	20-02-44	103 Sqn	37345	S/L	FOULSHAM DFC AFC James	20-07-44	109 Sqn
161272	F/O	FLOYD Herbert George	23-12-44	90 Sqn	132829	F/O	FOUNTAIN William Arthur Horace	8-06-44	115 Sqn
902602	Sgt	FLUDE Frank William	30-08-44	50 Sqn	1231027	Sgt	FOUNTAINE Frank Edward	24-03-44	166 Sqn
177272	P/O	FLYNN DFC Denis	15-06-44	582 Sqn	1620148	Sgt	FOWEATHER Edmund	13-09-44	101 Sqn
1322156	Sgt	FODDERING Eric John	23-06-44	460 Sqn	1036349	Sgt	FOWLER Dennis Philip	20-01-44	158 Sqn
168808	F/O	FOGDEN Edward Sydney	13-09-44	608 Sqn	1850070	Sgt	FOWLER Francis Henry	24-03-44	7 Sqn
152573	F/O	FOLEY Kenneth Albert	6-12-44	57 Sqn	1826506	Sgt	FOWLER Henry	18-12-44	463 Sqn
170237	F/O	FOLLEY Frank Smith	27-04-44	141 Sqn	1623556	Sgt	FOWLER Maurice	23-04-44	156 Sqn
1575665	Sgt	FONTAINE David Jack Ervin	27-07-44	630 Sqn	1873581	Sgt	FOWLER Peter	22-01-44	78 Sqn
1391733	F/S	FOOTMAN Walter Alec Clarence	4-05-44	625 Sqn	1083705	Sgt	FOWLS Robert Leslie	8-05-44	49 Sqn
133401	F/O	FOOTTIT Keith Alan Murray	21-01-44	77 Sqn	184123	P/O	FOX Albert Edward	30-08-44	463 Sqn
1690225	Sgt	FORBES Hugh	13-05-44	466 Sqn	1542113	F/S	FOX Alfred	7-03-44	1667 HCU
1348902	W/O	FORBES James Francis	8-08-44	7 Sqn	146839	F/L	FOX DFM Cedric Charles	25-05-44	158 Sqn
1826864	Sgt	FORBES John Duff	17-09-44	1652 HCU	138131	F/O	FOX Charles Lawrence	17-09-44	617 Sqn
1801152	Sgt	FORD Alfred James	13-09-44	218 Sqn	1202748	F/S	FOX Charles Victor	7-05-44	576 Sqn
139587	F/O	FORD Arthur Hanley	17-06-44	77 Sqn	1332445	Sgt	FOX Clifford Edward Robert	31-03-44	635 Sqn
1578261	Sgt	FORD Douglas Maxwell	19-03-44	192 Sqn	537696	F/S	FOX Ernest Clive	28-06-44	106 Sqn
147218	F/L	FORD Frederick John	9-11-44	138 Sqn	173268	P/O	FOX Francis Edward	26-03-44	426 Sqn
154079	F/O	FORD Harry Thomas	14-10-44	115 Sqn	1322257	Sgt	FOX Frederick George Michael	13-08-44	158 Sqn
53153	F/O	FORD James Camp	6-05-44	11 OTU	1449165	F/S	FOX Harold William	18-04-44	433 Sqn
1827160	Sgt	FORD John Wood	28-10-44	1661 HCU	1517617	Sgt	FOX Harry	8-06-44	77 Sqn
1211751	Sgt	FORD William Vernon	31-03-44	103 Sqn	149196	F/O	FOX James Lewis	17-09-44	1652 HCU
170975	F/O	FORDE Edmond Gerard	16-02-44	434 Sqn	177086	P/O	FOX DFC John Elston	10-07-44	105 Sqn
1527398	Sgt	FORDE Frank Michael	30-01-44	622 Sqn	2201592	Sgt	FOX Kenneth Edward Arthur	30-06-44	514 Sqn
1198516	Sgt	FORDER John Royston	16-02-44	78 Sqn	1593043	Sgt	FOX Norman	24-07-44	1660 HCU
1866501	Sgt	FORDHAM Arthur Stanley	1-07-44	10 Sqn	959865	Sgt	FOX Sydney William	3-06-44	158 Sqn
1873791	Sgt	FOREMAN George Henry	22-02-44	218 Sqn	1433606	Sgt	FOX Thomas Austin	16-03-44	630 Sqn
1365898	F/S	FORMAN George	20-02-44	35 Sqn	955609	Sgt	FOX Willoughby	6-01-44	103 Sqn
1826053	Sgt	FORREST Douglas Thomas	12-09-44	622 Sqn	128047	F/O	FOXCROFT DFC Phillip Spencer	28-05-44	627 Sqn
2205836	Sgt	FORREST Ronald Arthur	3-08-44	619 Sqn	1313948	F/S	FOY Thomas Joseph	6-08-44	83 Sqn

Service No.	Rank	Name	Date	Squadron
653929	Sgt	FOY Victor Basil	28-05-44	626 Sqn
1853072	Sgt	FOYLE Gordon Victor	16-06-44	61 Sqn
1686490	Sgt	FOYLE Kenneth	21-01-44	514 Sqn
1457002	Sgt	FRADLEY George	14-01-44	9 Sqn
1560058	F/S	FRAME Robert Day	27-04-44	44 Sqn
1591940	Sgt	FRANCE Walter	27-08-44	166 Sqn
1439592	Sgt	FRANCE William Edward	31-03-44	630 Sqn
1422866	F/S	FRANCIS Dilwyn	22-03-44	100 Sqn
118646	F/L	FRANCIS DFC Eric	31-03-44	138 Sqn
1652846	Sgt	FRANCIS John David	12-06-44	102 Sqn
1580571	Sgt	FRANCIS John Stevens	22-06-44	101 Sqn
1387022	Sgt	FRANCIS Kenneth Geoffrey	31-03-44	7 Sqn
186468	P/O	FRANCIS Leonard Thomas	12-11-44	49 Sqn
54718	P/O	FRANCIS Sydney Frederick	8-06-44	115 Sqn
1894710	Sgt	FRANCIS William Henry	16-09-44	466 Sqn
1590367	Sgt	FRANK Kenneth	27-04-44	619 Sqn
1591171	Sgt	FRANKISH Ronald	20-01-44	102 Sqn
1895945	Sgt	FRANKLIN Frederick John	7-06-44	115 Sqn
142089	F/O	FRANKLIN Geoffrey Edward	29-07-44	49 Sqn
1313274	Sgt	FRANKLIN James Joseph	16-11-44	15 Sqn
41009	S/L	FRANKLIN Robert Harcourt	16-10-44	115 Sqn
1615606	Sgt	FRANKLIN Ronald Frederick John	19-08-44	51 Sqn
552916	F/S	FRANKLIN Trevor Gordon	22-05-44	166 Sqn
1443752	F/S	FRASER Bertram	11-05-44	463 Sqn
970100	F/S	FRASER David Alexander	21-04-44	97 Sqn
171020	P/O	FRASER David Carruthers	4-05-44	101 Sqn
152915	F/O	FRASER Gordon	25-06-44	102 Sqn
935921	Sgt	FRASER James	22-05-44	514 Sqn
1821059	Sgt	FRASER James Sidney	21-01-44	102 Sqn
1569101	Sgt	FRASER Stephen	14-08-44	20 OTU
983910	Sgt	FRASER Thomas Douglas Safely	22-06-44	630 Sqn
1559186	Sgt	FRASER William	29-01-44	7 Sqn
53739	F/O	FRAZER DFC Robert	27-04-44	83 Sqn
156827	F/O	FREARSON Frederick John	2-11-44	15 Sqn
149671	F/O	FRECKLETON DFM James McGregor	22-06-44	49 Sqn
51678	F/O	FREDERICK Arthur Alfred	13-09-44	640 Sqn
115624	F/L	FREDMAN DFC Norman Henry	6-05-44	109 Sqn
1891501	Sgt	FREEBORN John William	2-11-44	153 Sqn
1868786	Sgt	FREEBORN William Charles	14-01-44	1653 HCU
1670597	Sgt	FREEBURN Alexander Henry	22-05-44	514 Sqn
1896087	Sgt	FREEMAN Carl Robert	20-11-44	75 Sqn
172828	F/O	FREEMAN DFC Desmond Clayton	24-09-44	61 Sqn
1331538	F/S	FREEMAN Gordon Ernest	25-06-44	9 Sqn
1483956	Sgt	FREEMAN John Anthony	22-05-44	207 Sqn
1396618	Sgt	FREEMAN John Archibald	5-04-44	11 OTU
150240	F/L	FREEMAN Reginald John	23-04-44	149 Sqn
917954	Sgt	FREEMAN William Thomas	21-04-44	44 Sqn
1603837	Sgt	FREEMANTLE Alfred Basil	17-06-44	77 Sqn
153721	F/O	FREER Kenneth Burdett	12-09-44	35 Sqn
1488529	LAC	FREER Ronald Percy	8-04-44	5 LFS
1580825	Sgt	FREER William Harold	15-06-44	78 Sqn
151308	F/L	FRENCH Cyril Vincent	5-03-44	90 Sqn
1148278	F/S	FRENCH George Robert	2-05-44	51 Sqn
798778	Sgt	FRENCH Gerard Francis [Newfoundland]	25-04-44	83 Sqn
144954	F/L	FRENCH Leonard Arthur	8-08-44	90 Sqn
173135	P/O	FRENCH Peter Henry	21-04-44	619 Sqn
1892504	Sgt	FRENCH Ronald Wilfred	23-04-44	166 Sqn
632441	Sgt	FRENCH William Dennis	16-02-44	97 Sqn
1624312	Sgt	FRETTER George John	15-10-44	101 Sqn
1577087	F/S	FRETWELL Alan	6-07-44	582 Sqn
2207037	Sgt	FETWELL Desmond	19-04-44	28 OTU
1132241	F/S	FREW Andrew McWilliams	8-07-44	61 Sqn
50286	F/L	FREW DFC William Elmslie	27-08-44	83 Sqn
1895662	Sgt	FRICKER Herbert Wilfred	5-06-44	1658 HCU
1570522	Sgt	FRIEL Patrick	8-05-44	106 Sqn
1323802	F/S	FRIEND John Douglas	11-11-44	626 Sqn
2215315	Sgt	FRIESNER Alec	3-06-44	640 Sqn
1527303	Sgt	FRISBY Albert John	18-12-44	50 Sqn
1817031	Sgt	FRISBY Leonard	11-04-44	1661 HCU
1579241	F/S	FRITH Arthur	23-03-44	426 Sqn
1583023	F/S	FRITH Peter	6-07-44	12 Sqn
1589935	Sgt	FRITH Sanford Peter	31-03-44	514 Sqn
1787720	Sgt	FRIZZELL Gordon Abercromby Center	18-12-44	463 Sqn
153321	F/O	FROBISHER Martin Peter	5-11-44	102 Sqn
1320636	F/S	FROGGATT Douglas William	30-01-44	101 Sqn
1609273	Sgt	FROGLEY DFM Terence Frederick	19-07-44	619 Sqn
1801136	Sgt	FROST Arthur Henry	15-10-44	7 Sqn
169741	P/O	FROST Charles Albert	31-03-44	44 Sqn
613715	Sgt	FROST George Edward	29-06-44	102 Sqn
138508	F/O	FROST Herbert Charles	31-03-44	156 Sqn
1580431	Sgt	FROST Reginald Roy	23-05-44	57 Sqn
1390463	F/S	FROUD Denis Percy John 'Denny'	20-02-44	9 Sqn
1800278	Sgt	FROUD Percy	12-09-44	35 Sqn
1603443	F/S	FRY Edward Charles	8-05-44	106 Sqn
130598	F/L	FRY Harold Leonard	29-01-44	467 Sqn
1895898	Sgt	FRY Leslie Joseph	30-11-44	429 Sqn
1801193	Sgt	FRY Peter Denis	4-05-44	460 Sqn
50229	F/O	FRY Peter William	29-09-44	157 Sqn
1623205	Sgt	FRYER Hubert	5-07-44	1667 HCU
1383302	F/S	FRYER Robert	23-05-44	100 Sqn
115221	F/L	FULFORD Geoffrey Underhill	7-10-44	166 Sqn
1601768	Sgt	FULFORD Roy Warren Melvin	26-08-44	90 Sqn
1873877	Sgt	FULLER Denis James	22-05-44	100 Sqn
1804809	Sgt	FULLER Frank Tilden	31-03-44	7 Sqn
61991	S/L	FULLER Frederick Edgar	8-05-44	619 Sqn
148490	F/L	FULLER DFC Kenneth William Lipscombe	15-07-44	550 Sqn
137606	F/O	FULLER Ronald Harry	20-02-44	103 Sqn
2204572	Sgt	FULLERTON Elliott	10-05-44	9 Sqn
1481142	Sgt	FULTON James Gerald	28-03-44	20 OTU
1500300	Sgt	FULTON John	4-11-44	626 Sqn
1079160	Sgt	FULTON Joseph	8-06-44	166 Sqn
3025228	Sgt	FURBER Alan George	6-12-44	550 Sqn
2214118	Sgt	FURLONG Peter [Eire]	31-03-44	425 Sqn
178724	P/O	FURNISS Brian Bruce	14-08-44	83 Sqn
1818904	Sgt	FURNIVAL Albert	12-09-44	619 Sqn
1673341	Sgt	FURNIVAL James	28-09-44	115 Sqn
171169	P/O	FUSSELL Llewellyn Vivian	15-02-44	630 Sqn
177861	P/O	FUTCHER Stanley Montague	5-07-44	106 Sqn
1340922	Sgt	FYFE Jack Leslie	8-06-44	115 Sqn
650314	Sgt	FYFE William	21-04-44	57 Sqn
152574	F/O	GADD Harry Albert George	3-11-44	550 Sqn
1445080	F/S	GADSBY William Charles	14-01-44	97 Sqn
151085	F/O	GAGE John Watson	3-01-44	463 Sqn
1549492	Sgt	GAINES Philip	10-06-44	10 Sqn
138128	F/O	GAINS Francis George	2-03-44	156 Sqn
1394287	F/S	GAINSBOROUGH-ALLEN John Herbert	20-01-44	83 Sqn
185948	P/O	GALBRAITH William	3-11-44	424 Sqn
174617	P/O	GALE Charles Henry George	11-03-44	30 OTU
1297387	F/S	GALE DFM Norman Leslie Ernest	19-07-44	57 Sqn
154202	F/O	GALE Stanley	28-11-44	166 Sqn
1607032	Sgt	GALLACHER Peter James	16-03-44	625 Sqn
1555986	Sgt	GALLAGHER Denis Charles	23-05-44	57 Sqn
157083	F/L	GALLAGHER DSO Frederick Whitton	22-06-44	207 Sqn
1823530	Sgt	GALLAGHER John	22-05-44	514 Sqn
1568955	Sgt	GALLAGHER Michael	15-02-44	77 Sqn
1621052	F/S	GALLAGHER Vincent	19-07-44	49 Sqn
1600952	F/S	GALLIARD John Douglas	4-12-44	619 Sqn
171215	P/O	GALLOP Roy	30-01-44	625 Sqn
2209841	Sgt	GALLOWAY John	21-01-44	434 Sqn
1681085	Sgt	GAMBLE William A.	22-12-44	189 Sqn
1549193	Sgt	GAMMAGE Leslie	25-03-44	166 Sqn
1836364	Sgt	GANDERTON Raymond Llewelyn	17-06-44	3 LFS
172928	P/O	GARBUTT Richard Henry	18-03-44	466 Sqn
1280538	W/O	GARCIA-WEBB Joseph	16-11-44	109 Sqn

Service No	Rank	Name	Date	Sqn
1801142	Sgt	GARDE Joseph Michael	15-02-44	100 Sqn
54461	P/O	GARDINER Frederick George	13-04-44	90 Sqn
1199405	Sgt	GARDINER Kenneth	31-03-44	156 Sqn
1626043	Sgt	GARDINER Leslie Theodore	21-01-44	514 Sqn
1446552	Sgt	GARDINER Stanley Robert George	20-02-44	166 Sqn
1320619	Sgt	GARDNER Carol Ernest Woodridge	25-02-44	115 Sqn
1336804	Sgt	GARDNER Charles Clifford Allen	28-05-44	626 Sqn
1801671	Sgt	GARDNER Herbert Charles	13-08-44	622 Sqn
1399997	F/S	GARDNER John	12-09-44	207 Sqn
171094	P/O	GARDNER Raymond Henry	24-03-44	1656 HCU
68776	F/L	GARDNER Reginald George	9-10-44	608 Sqn
1389521	Sgt	GARDNER Robert Cecil	05-05-44	61 Sqn
1324764	Sgt	GARDNER Spencer Arthur Grafton	11-04-44	61 Sqn
627184	W/O	GARDNER DFM Victor	31-03-44	156 Sqn
1851578	Sgt	GARFIELD Benjamin Robert	20-02-44	77 Sqn
2206796	Sgt	GARFORTH Eric	25-08-44	75 Sqn
132868	F/O	GARLAND George Frederick	25-03-44	44 Sqn
1873620	Sgt	GARLAND James Douglas	20-10-44	550 Sqn
133619	F/O	GARLETTE Peter James	21-01-44	77 Sqn
176966	F/L	GARLICK Graham Robert	21-07-44	9 Sqn
154595	F/O	GARLING John Roger	17-12-44	57 Sqn
1295076	Sgt	GARNER Charles William	30-08-44	630 Sqn
1627183	Sgt	GARNER Kenneth	4-05-44	625 Sqn
169000	F/O	GARNETT Bateman Redge	18-07-44	158 Sqn
1564458	F/S	GARNETT Frank Hailstones [USA]	27-09-44	115 Sqn
158579	P/O	GARNETT Frederick Horace	2-01-44	106 Sqn
1876662	Sgt	GARNHAM Alan Hugh	21-07-44	578 Sqn
1139617	Sgt	GARNSEY John Edwin	20-05-44	44 Sqn
2218803	Sgt	GARRAD Ralph	20-10-44	550 Sqn
1577074	F/S	GARRATT John Charles	31-03-44	550 Sqn
1686892	Sgt	GARRATT Leslie	12-12-44	15 Sqn
175558	P/O	GARRAWAY Derek Peter	27-04-44	78 Sqn
1543513	F/S	GARRETT Arthur Thomas	25-02-44	61 Sqn
1896238	Sgt	GARRETT Charles William	31-08-44	433 Sqn
1031817	W/O	GARRETT Robert Anthony	11-08-44	51 Sqn
1206061	F/S	GARRICK Francis Julian Herbert	10-04-44	57 Sqn
1565479	Sgt	GARROD Lawrence Emmerson	19-04-44	28 OTU
1324243	F/S	GARROD Robert Stanley	4-05-44	50 Sqn
1177605	Sgt	GARSIDE Douglas Whitehead	4-11-44	626 Sqn
173609	P/O	GARSIDE James	24-03-44	102 Sqn
182267	P/O	GARSIDE Robert Barry	29-07-44	103 Sqn
532483	Sgt	GARTLAND James	7-10-44	51 Sqn
117420	F/L	GARVEY DSO DFC Frederick James [Canada]	15-02-44	83 Sqn
1506937	Sgt	GASKELL Tom	23-05-44	100 Sqn
1405852	Sgt	GATE Joseph	28-03-44	20 OTU
1581986	Sgt	GATENSBURY Richard Peter	1-07-44	625 Sqn
1836678	Sgt	GATES Derek Picken	31-08-44	550 Sqn
640843	W/O	GAUGHRAN Wilfred	8-08-44	582 Sqn
1365820	Sgt	GAULD Edgar Alexander	31-03-44	9 Sqn
2220609	Sgt	GAUT Richard Arthur	16-07-44	207 Sqn
1193341	Sgt	GAWLER Ellis Robert	23-01-44	1667 HCU
152823	F/O	GAY Dennis Frederick	30-08-44	619 Sqn
1436052	F/S	GAY John Charles	19-08-44	7 Sqn
154954	F/O	GAYFORD Alfred William	31-10-44	1661 HCU
1494816	Sgt	GAYTHORPE Kenneth	13-07-44	103 Sqn
1894914	Sgt	GAZLEY Edward Frank	10-10-44	1667 HCU
1174459	Sgt	GEAKE Sidney Harry	24-02-44	578 Sqn
1893333	Sgt	GEARING Leonard Thomas	1-06-44	15 Sqn
1567832	Sgt	GEDDES Alexander McPherson	19-04-44	149 Sqn
1827129	Sgt	GEDDES Peter Innes	20-09-44	622 Sqn
1228595	Sgt	GEDGE Edward	20-02-44	12 Sqn
1544388	Sgt	GEDLING Ernest	24-10-44	576 Sqn
2210666	Sgt	GEE Henry	12-09-44	44 Sqn
1517079	Sgt	GEE Herbert William	11-06-44	100 Sqn
1592752	Sgt	GEE Leslie Robert	13-05-44	640 Sqn
1895133	Sgt	GEEN Kenneth Roy	19-10-44	29 OTU
1717745	Sgt	GEEVES John	6-07-44	582 Sqn
2222028	Sgt	GENNO Eric Neil	16-11-44	1663 HCU
1383081	Sgt	GENT Alfred Charles Dempsey	12-09-44	90 Sqn
1615002	Sgt	GENT Patrick Noel	12-10-44	83 OTU
1647557	Sgt	GEORGE Gordon Victor	12-09-44	100 Sqn
1801357	Sgt	GEORGE Herbert Royston	10-02-44	199 Sqn
1869090	Sgt	GEORGE John Joseph	3-06-44	466 Sqn
1029427	W/O	GEORGE Matthew Glyn	20-11-44	514 Sqn
1333458	F/S	GEORGE Ronald V.	23-04-44	61 Sqn
67077	W/C	GEORGESON DSO DFC Gordon Forbes	27-07-44	83 Sqn
1434588	Sgt	GERAGHTY William Albert	26-02-44	15 Sqn
1803074	Sgt	GERMING John William	28-04-44	75 Sqn
1561517	Sgt	GETTINGS Thomas	20-02-44	419 Sqn
1612557	Sgt	GHISLETTA Albert Dennis	23-09-44	207 Sqn
632040	W/O	GIBB DFC John Webster	20-02-44	156 Sqn
1821194	Sgt	GIBB John William	23-01-44	1667 HCU
851417	F/S	GIBBERSON Frank Hubert	7-07-44	44 Sqn
1817726	Sgt	GIBBON Homfray Reece	29-01-44	166 Sqn
1591851	Sgt	GIBBON BROWN John Alan	30-01-44	101 Sqn
1819251	Sgt	GIBBS Henry	25-04-44	78 Sqn
1585370	F/S	GIBBS John William	5-07-44	207 Sqn
175484	F/O	GIBBS DFC Kenneth	28-12-44	101 Sqn
1801366	F/S	GIBBS Leslie Edward	8-06-44	156 Sqn
1654812	Sgt	GIBBS Robert Charles	3-03-44	1666 HCU
169764	F/O	GIBBS Walter Ernest	30-08-44	514 Sqn
134061	F/O	GIBSON Christopher	25-02-44	156 Sqn
1393163	Sgt	GIBSON David	16-03-44	100 Sqn
1894952	Sgt	GIBSON Eric John	6-12-44	207 Sqn
1896098	Sgt	GIBSON George Frederick	30-08-44	101 Sqn
1699599	Sgt	GIBSON Granville Butterworth	17-09-44	102 Sqn
39438	W/C	GIBSON VC DSO* DFC* Legion of Merit (Commander) Guy Penrose	19-09-44	54 Base
162808	P/O	GIBSON Jack Saddington	6-07-44	12 Sqn
1564373	F/S	GIBSON James	20-04-44	622 Sqn
1564654	Sgt	GIBSON John Cowan	17-06-44	102 Sqn
1565824	Sgt	GIBSON Marshall Gow	1-11-44	619 Sqn
138048	F/O	GIBSON Raymond Leslie	28-04-44	15 Sqn
1601726	Sgt	GIBSON Robert Charles	30-01-44	405 Sqn
984464	F/S	GIBSON Thomas Lipsey	22-05-44	514 Sqn
2209930	Sgt	GIBSON William Maurice	31-03-44	158 Sqn
187030	P/O	GIBSON Thomas Herbert	23-09-44	97 Sqn
966851	Sgt	GIDDINGS Robert Gifford	12-04-44	619 Sqn
1464954	F/S	GIDMAN DFM Cyril	29-07-44	57 Sqn
1528612	Sgt	GIFFARD Clive Allen	30-01-44	576 Sqn
173328	P/O	GIGGER Derrick John	16-03-44	635 Sqn
525662	Sgt	GILBERT Cyril Stanley	13-08-44	90 Sqn
1588803	Sgt	GILBERT James Harry	27-04-44	408 Sqn
1178418	Sgt	GILBERT James Walter	25-02-44	156 Sqn
1582850	Sgt	GILBERT Patrick Neil	21-07-44	405 Sqn
1698349	F/S	GILBERTSON John Booth	30-01-44	83 Sqn
1213210	F/S	GILCHRIST John Thomas	20-01-44	466 Sqn
186330	P/O	GILCHRIST Thomas	7-10-44	514 Sqn
1824389	Sgt	GILCHRIST William James	18-04-44	158 Sqn
1867645	Sgt	GILDARE Anthony John Byron	20-01-44	10 Sqn
1070752	Sgt	GILDER Stanley	8-06-44	624 Sqn
1605178	Sgt	GILES Douglas William May	2-05-44	1659 HCU
1317796	F/S	GILES Reginald Frederick Arthur	20-05-44	115 Sqn
1337733	Sgt	GILES Ronald	20-02-44	630 Sqn
1600994	F/S	GILES William Henry	22-05-44	7 Sqn
1371853	F/S	GILFEATHER Patrick Anthony	20-02-44	429 Sqn
1462241	Sgt	GILL Albert James 'Bert'	8-05-44	15 Sqn
55220	F/O	GILL Alexander Thomas	20-09-44	622 Sqn
1895985	Sgt	GILL Charles Frederick	16-09-44	432 Sqn
133484	F/L	GILL George Robert	12-12-44	1662 HCU
151989	F/O	GILL Jack Norman	18-03-44	630 Sqn
1129870	Sgt	GILL James	16-09-44	466 Sqn
1675512	Sgt	GILL John	20-02-44	625 Sqn
1575600	F/S	GILL John Thomas	9-05-44	405 Sqn
2209425	Sgt	GILL Joseph	1-07-44	12 Sqn
53946	P/O	GILL Leslie Frank	2-01-44	156 Sqn

Number	Rank	Name	Date	Squadron
1681271	Sgt	GILL Leslie Mathers	16-09-44	90 Sqn
2210653	Sgt	GILL Richard	28-05-44	514 Sqn
1020043	Cpl	GILL William Edward	9-09-44	156 Sqn
1607197	Sgt	GILLAM David James	21-01-44	434 Sqn
172290	P/O	GILLARD Gordon Peter	10-05-44	44 Sqn
1796391	Sgt	GILLESPIE Edward Albert	26-08-44	83 Sqn
182168	P/O	GILLESPIE John Ronald	7-10-44	78 Sqn
1800716	Sgt	GILLHAM Roy William Patrick	6-07-44	635 Sqn
54452	P/O	GILLIARD Joseph [Eire]	16-02-44	432 Sqn
648452	Sgt	GILLIATT Edward George	16-06-44	75 Sqn
1457266	Sgt	GILLIATT Percy Arthur	27-07-44	630 Sqn
572714	Sgt	GILLIBRAND Arthur Douglas Ward	15-11-44	115 Sqn
184908	P/O	GILLINGHAM Eric Thornton	15-12-44	12 Sqn
1393396	Sgt	GILLINGS George Frank	20-02-44	158 Sqn
170350	F/L	GILLIS DFC Hartley David	8-06-44	156 Sqn
1577951	Sgt	GILLIVER Joseph Harry	27-07-44	619 Sqn
520265	Sgt	GILMARTIN Thomas	13-06-44	78 Sqn
1677587	Sgt	GILMORE David	23-03-44	426 Sqn
45842	F/L	GILMOUR DFC John	27-07-44	83 Sqn
174554	P/O	GILMOUR John	9-06-44	50 Sqn
610020	Sgt	GILPIN George Edward	4-05-44	50 Sqn
1896753	Sgt	GILPIN Sidney Roy	23-10-44	625 Sqn
1590120	Sgt	GILROY Clive	21-01-44	431 Sqn
902433	Sgt	GILSON Kenneth Edric	26-02-44	50 Sqn
1586191	Sgt	GILSON Kenneth Eric	25-07-44	57 Sqn
1582933	Sgt	GINGOLD Sidney David	31-08-44	21 OTU
1895342	Sgt	GINN Raymond Henry	13-08-44	115 Sqn
1594791	Sgt	GIRDWOOD John Edward	8-06-44	101 Sqn
173147	P/O	GIRLING Cyril Ernest	26-03-44	10 Sqn
153015	F/O	GISBY Michael	12-12-44	582 Sqn
1064890	Sgt	GITTOES Jenkin Morgan	29-07-44	57 Sqn
1368438	F/S	GIVENS Robert Logie	29-06-44	76 Sqn
1434388	Sgt	GIZZI Peter Carmino	22-01-44	76 Sqn
1835119	Sgt	GLADSTONE William Bert	8-07-44	106 Sqn
141116	F/O	GLADWELL Michael George	30-01-44	115 Sqn
1542381	Sgt	GLANSFORD Harry Matthews	21-07-44	514 Sqn
1316279	Sgt	GLANVILL James Ernest	25-02-44	97 Sqn
1581293	Sgt	GLASGOW John James	28-10-44	1661 HCU
1699735	Sgt	GLASPER Hubert	12-10-44	30 OTU
1605575	Sgt	GLASS Roy	16-06-44	635 Sqn
1372859	F/S	GLASS Stewart	31-03-44	51 Sqn
110789	S/L	GLASSPOOL DFC Leslie Henry	28-04-44	156 Sqn
536667	F/S	GLAUS Louis Godfrey	15-02-44	7 Sqn
175730	P/O	GLAYSHER Victor Robert	24-03-44	578 Sqn
1526801	Sgt	GLEADLE Arthur Frederick	2-01-44	61 Sqn
1516394	Sgt	GLEDHILL Ernest	23-04-44	514 Sqn
1386450	F/S	GLEDHILL James Leslie	22-05-44	9 Sqn
1623866	Sgt	GLEDHILL Peter Aspinall	18-12-44	3 LFS
1592716	Sgt	GLEDHILL Victor	17-06-44	77 Sqn
1378355	F/S	GLEDSTONE Robert	1-07-44	625 Sqn
176522	P/O	GLEESON Alfred George	13-07-44	103 Sqn
179415	P/O	GLEESON DFC Peter Augustine	13-08-44	83 Sqn
1821597	Sgt	GLEN Cecil	15-02-44	166 Sqn
639111	Sgt	GLEN Thomas	23-06-44	76 Sqn
1525469	Sgt	GLENN William Denis	19-07-44	460 Sqn
1615064	Sgt	GLIBBERY Edward Henry	20-02-44	78 Sqn
1819740	Sgt	GLITHERO George Norton	3-06-44	76 Sqn
144606	F/O	GLOSSOP Charles Horace	21-01-44	7 Sqn
177572	P/O	GLOSSOP Victor Thomas	21-07-44	578 Sqn
1588485	Sgt	GLOVER Brian	15-03-44	9 Sqn
1199702	F/S	GLOVER Fred	4-05-44	50 Sqn
151103	F/O	GLOVER Harry Drinen	31-03-44	61 Sqn
2210429	Sgt	GLOVER Raymond	9-11-44	625 Sqn
1319846	Sgt	GODDARD Alan Arthur Frank	31-03-44	57 Sqn
1602239	Sgt	GODDARD Anthony Henry John	5-11-44	51 Sqn
1323147	Sgt	GODDARD Arthur Ernest John	21-07-44	75 Sqn
1339439	Sgt	GODDARD Arthur Parvin	1-11-44	619 Sqn
1582369	Sgt	GODDARD Frank	23-06-44	626 Sqn
1049548	Sgt	GODDARD Geoffrey	23-04-44	514 Sqn
152303	F/O	GODDARD Horace Raymond	23-04-44	78 Sqn
139402	F/O	GODDARD Kenneth Douglas	25-05-44	15 Sqn
145387	F/L	GODDARD Wilfred	26-09-44	405 Sqn
577818	Sgt	GODDEN Dennis Albert	26-08-44	622 Sqn
1210979	F/S	GODDEN Frank Stephen	24-02-44	578 Sqn
1807618	F/S	GODFRAY DFM Marcus George	27-08-44	7 Sqn
1454589	Sgt	GODREY Maurice Frederick	20-02-44	640 Sqn
1893355	Sgt	GODFREY Robert Frederick	4-05-44	626 Sqn
175487	P/O	GODFREY Stewart James	24-06-44	50 Sqn
183562	F/O	GOEMANS Cornelis Jacobus Maria [Holland]	4-11-44	640 Sqn
1865819	Sgt	GOGGIN David Anthony	22-05-44	100 Sqn
2206617	Sgt	GOLDBERG Hyman [Canada]	27-04-44	619 Sqn
1086976	Sgt	GOLDBERG Norman Myer	23-05-44	49 Sqn
1644548	Sgt	GOLDER James William	3-06-44	76 Sqn
1601186	Sgt	GOLDING Derrick Walter	25-04-44	619 Sqn
945043	F/S	GOLDING Joseph Albert	3-12-44	138 Sqn
1481558	F/S	GOLDING Roland	16-03-44	76 Sqn
130244	F/L	GOLDINGAY DFC Leslie Dennis	28-04-44	7 Sqn
1393901	Sgt	GOLDMAN Maurice [Belgium]	25-02-44	460 Sqn
170420	P/O	GOLIGHTLY John William	20-02-44	61 Sqn
1566258	Sgt	GOLLOP Cecil Ralph	28-09-44	29 OTU
1438518	F/S	GOMERSALL Jack	19-03-44	97 Sqn
1585090	Sgt	GOMMO John	28-04-44	115 Sqn
653945	Sgt	GOOCH Frederick John	23-09-44	12 Sqn
552951	Sgt	GOOCH Robert William	14-01-44	97 Sqn
1439501	Sgt	GOOD Wilfred	21-01-44	405 Sqn
1458094	Sgt	GOODACRE Arthur	22-06-44	106 Sqn
2209795	Sgt	GOODACRE Ralph	29-07-44	103 Sqn
1234133	F/S	GOODALE Frederick James	23-05-44	103 Sqn
91090	P/O	GOODALL Alan Fletcher	28-05-44	420 Sqn
1552815	Sgt	GOODALL DFM James Alexander	31-03-44	101 Sqn
1700117	Sgt	GOODBRAND William	17-09-44	1652 HCU
1245670	F/S	GOODE Cyril Arthur	6-06-44	578 Sqn
1705245	Sgt	GOODE Edmund Charles William	16-07-44	467 Sqn
1317752	Sgt	GOODFELLOW Wallace Albert	20-01-44	10 Sqn
1673585	Sgt	GOODIER Sidney	15-12-44	625 Sqn
1337662	F/S	GOODING Norman Frederick Walter	15-02-44	77 Sqn
1416452	F/S	GOODING Thomas Robert Terence	12-10-44	83 OTU
176436	P/O	GOODMAN Edwin Arthur [South Africa]	22-06-44	207 Sqn
33252	W/C	GOODMAN Royal Hellenic Air Force Cross Hubert Reginald [South Africa]	12-05-44	103 Sqn
1398590	Sgt	GOODMAN Kenneth Martin	30-08-44	514 Sqn
1319008	W/O	GOODMAN Robert Frederick	22-12-44	83 Sqn
1153626	Sgt	GOODRIDGE Eric Sidney	20-02-44	12 Sqn
658283	F/S	GOODWIN Alistair Chisholm	21-01-44	77 Sqn
2216790	Sgt	GOODWIN Colin William	22-06-44	619 Sqn
1336800	Sgt	GOODWIN Frederick Albert	25-02-44	156 Sqn
54670	P/O	GOODWIN Kenneth	10-05-44	619 Sqn
912395	F/S	GOODWIN William Roland	2-03-44	15 OTU
1836414	Sgt	GOODYEAR William John	5-07-44	630 Sqn
1894979	Sgt	GOORAVITCH Jack Bernard	2-01-44	100 Sqn
1321812	F/S	GORDGE Henry	31-07-44	57 Sqn
1591936	Sgt	GORDON Harold	30-08-44	428 Sqn
1486294	Sgt	GORDON Harry	6-01-44	57 Sqn
1057611	W/O	GORDON DFM James Roberts	19-08-44	635 Sqn
1431591	F/S	GORDON James Sidney	29-07-44	207 Sqn
914858	F/S	GORDON Norman	5-07-44	49 Sqn
185116	F/O	GORDON Ronald	20-11-44	75 Sqn
963494	Sgt	GORDON Terence Michael	19-07-44	9 Sqn
168781	P/O	GORMAN John Joseph	4-05-44	101 Sqn
1490579	Sgt	GORMAN Leonard	6-01-44	57 Sqn
2207003	Sgt	GORNALL Edward Cuthbert	16-02-44	50 Sqn
1342577	Sgt	GORRIE James	22-01-44	76 Sqn
120984	S/L	GORTON Harold	12-11-44	49 Sqn
1822442	Sgt	GOSKIRK John Doherty	31-03-44	51 Sqn
552339	Sgt	GOSLING Graham Noel	6-02-44	149 Sqn
176529	P/O	GOSLING Keith	21-07-44	101 Sqn

Service No.	Rank	Name	Date	Sqn
1783240	Sgt	GOSNAY Wilfred Arnold	25-05-44	51 Sqn
1891510	Sgt	GOSNOLD Peter Andrew	21-11-44	514 Sqn
1605337	Sgt	GOSS Eric Arthur	23-04-44	429 Sqn
1318695	Sgt	GOSS Norman Joseph	23-03-44	106 Sqn
1275643	Sgt	GOTHAM Arthur William	20-02-44	428 Sqn
1620754	Sgt	GOTT Frank Vennard	28-05-44	460 Sqn
1563229	Sgt	GOUDIE Ernest Albert	5-11-44	76 Sqn
129664	F/O	GOUGH DFC Cedric Dennis	20-02-44	156 Sqn
1652948	Sgt	GOUGH Patrick Francis	20-04-44	420 Sqn
1819441	Sgt	GOUGH Ronald	23-08-44	20 OTU
1034195	F/S	GOULBOURN Jack William	24-02-44	156 Sqn
1819416	Sgt	GOULD Raymond Dennis	25-05-44	158 Sqn
141399	F/O	GOULD DFM Thomas	13-09-44	640 Sqn
1806619	F/S	GOULDING Albert Leonard	11-06-44	7 Sqn
1190810	Sgt	GOULDING William	13-08-44	61 Sqn
1892933	Sgt	GOULDSTONE Victor Charles William Arras	14-04-44	5 LFS
46342	S/L	GOULE DFC Haydn William	27-01-44	12 Sqn
1603639	Sgt	GOVER George Henry Francis	20-01-44	102 Sqn
1320000	F/S	GOW Charles Henry	30-01-44	44 Sqn
1567621	Sgt	GOWANS Joseph George	24-02-44	149 Sqn
1813553	F/S	GOWDEY Alan William	16-09-44	405 Sqn
1512471	Sgt	GOWDY William John	21-01-44	35 Sqn
186476	P/O	GOWER Jack Gerald	26-12-44	10 Sqn
1894705	Sgt	GOWER Leslie Percy	26-08-44	207 Sqn
176556	P/O	GOWING Kenneth Joseph	8-07-44	44 Sqn
1818907	Sgt	GOWLAND Alfred William	27-03-44	166 Sqn
160154	P/O	GRAAFF Dewhurst [Rhodesia]	7-07-44	44 Sqn
155208	P/O	GRACEY Herbert	21-01-44	10 Sqn
1345468	Sgt	GRACEY Robert Johnstone	4-05-44	463 Sqn
29090	W/C	GRACIE DFC Edward John	15-02-44	169 Sqn
1076548	Sgt	GRADY John	23-03-44	115 Sqn
1391860	W/O	GRAHAM Ambrose Alexander [Trinidad]	12-09-44	1690 Flt
1077700	Sgt	GRAHAM Benjamin Alexander Blackie	21-01-44	77 Sqn
950628	Sgt	GRAHAM Cecil George	4-05-44	460 Sqn
171278	P/O	GRAHAM Charles William George	20-02-44	77 Sqn
159937	F/O	GRAHAM MiD Clive Evans Miles	23-09-44	617 Sqn
1595293	Sgt	GRAHAM Edward	27-07-44	619 Sqn
1585636	Sgt	GRAHAM Francis James	3-08-44	166 Sqn
573068	F/S	GRAHAM Harold	20-01-44	622 Sqn
1825076	Sgt	GRAHAM James	1-06-44	115 Sqn
1875912	Sgt	GRAHAM James	28-04-44	431 Sqn
1345209	Sgt	GRAHAM James Banks 'Jimmy'	11-04-44	158 Sqn
136874	F/O	GRAHAM James Percy	25-07-44	35 Sqn
1568451	Sgt	GRAHAM Neil	22-03-44	103 Sqn
1868113	Sgt	GRAHAM Neil	28-09-44	29 OTU
1570906	Sgt	GRAHAM Robert	11-04-44	78 Sqn
915348	LAC	GRAHAM Thomas Edward Henry	9-09-44	156 Sqn
622825	Sgt	GRAHAM William Brodie 'Bill'	23-04-44	103 Sqn
155255	F/L	GRAIN DFM Arthur James	3-05-44	550 Sqn
1048620	F/S	GRAINGER Harry	23-04-44	106 Sqn
2213920	Sgt	GRAINGER John Walker	29-05-44	1657 HCU
1127595	W/O	GRANGE DFM Albert	21-02-44	7 Sqn
116087	F/L	GRANGER Peter Coram	12-09-44	35 Sqn
1464570	Sgt	GRANSDEN Laurence Wilfred	23-01-44	20 OTU
1721656	AC1	GRANT Alan	3-11-44	80 Wing
1323260	Sgt	GRANT Albert Edward	21-01-44	77 Sqn
527237	Sgt	GRANT Donald Cameron Kitchener	23-05-44	75 Sqn
1512532	F/S	GRANT Harold	10-05-44	97 Sqn
1567523	Sgt	GRANT Hugh Kerr [USA]	23-05-44	103 Sqn
40220	S/L	GRANT MiD John Ritchie [Canada]	12-05-44	115 Sqn
1573980	Sgt	GRANT Joseph	31-03-44	50 Sqn
1824018	Sgt	GRANT Robert Band	21-06-44	15 Sqn
152306	F/O	GRANT BEM William George	13-06-44	166 Sqn
138764	F/O	GRANTHAM Jack Howard	15-03-44	169 Sqn
1814726	Sgt	GRANTHAM John Raymond	2-05-44	218 Sqn
172419	F/L	GRANTHAM William Edwin	8-07-44	61 Sqn
1288313	Sgt	GRATWICKE Bernard Francis	24-03-44	619 Sqn
1817484	Sgt	GRAVES Charles Septimus Aliband	24-06-44	101 Sqn
186550	P/O	GRAVES Edward George	23-05-44	57 Sqn
1336898	Sgt	GRAVES Reginald Gordon	8-02-44	18 OTU
172589	P/O	GRAVES-HOOK Philip Rodney	23-05-44	49 Sqn
155069	F/O	GRAY Jack Gillard	13-06-44	408 Sqn
1542873	Sgt	GRAY James Kilvington	17-06-44	576 Sqn
905574	Sgt	GRAY John Shirra	26-12-44	76 Sqn
1332583	F/S	GRAY Richard Ernest	29-05-44	141 Sqn
1874063	Sgt	GRAY Richard William	21-02-44	78 Sqn
1090796	F/S	GRAY Robert Irwin	20-11-44	514 Sqn
1586855	Sgt	GRAY Ronald Frank	14-06-44	11 OTU
1288766	F/S	GRAY William Ernest	9-11-44	625 Sqn
1394653	F/S	GRAYSON Victor Henry	5-07-44	9 Sqn
1895732	Sgt	GREB Henry Charles	1-07-44	626 Sqn
592078	Sgt	GREEN Alan Roy	3-06-44	640 Sqn
1576157	F/S	GREEN Alan William	23-04-44	514 Sqn
1851219	Sgt	GREEN Arthur	13-08-44	156 Sqn
649190	Sgt	GREEN Arthur Leslie	22-05-44	576 Sqn
1450549	F/S	GREEN Bryan George	2-05-44	514 Sqn
657872	F/S	GREEN Douglas Keller	24-09-44	156 Sqn
1178717	W/O	GREEN Edmund William	27-04-44	83 Sqn
66532	F/L	GREEN Gerald Wilson	11-12-44	49 Sqn
1576896	Sgt	GREEN Herbert Wilfred	7-03-44	1667 HCU
1499229	Sgt	GREEN James Alfred	24-03-44	156 Sqn
33253	W/C	GREEN John Dale	10-04-44	PFNTU
1605300	Sgt	GREEN Joseph Leonard	15-02-44	77 Sqn
1604776	Sgt	GREEN Kenneth Edwin	31-03-44	460 Sqn
1582001	Sgt	GREEN Louis Henry	25-03-44	57 Sqn
1581709	Sgt	GREEN Michael Elliott	16-02-44	50 Sqn
985847	Sgt	GREEN Noel William	25-05-44	576 Sqn
1898548	Sgt	GREEN Percy Edward	16-12-44	106 Sqn
160589	P/O	GREEN Percy Wilfred	2-03-44	630 Sqn
1650030	Sgt	GREEN Raymond Albert	8-09-44	14 OTU
1587182	Sgt	GREEN Robert Alfred	4-05-44	166 Sqn
1581870	Sgt	GREEN Ronald Ernest	5-02-44	115 Sqn
1585525	F/S	GREEN Sidney Charles	11-11-44	57 Sqn
3030259	Sgt	GREEN Thomas Frederick	5-12-44	84 OTU
1393051	Sgt	GREEN William James	15-03-44	550 Sqn
156083	F/O	GREENACRE Gordon Charles George	31-03-44	76 Sqn
1580227	Sgt	GREENAN John	17-06-44	3 LFS
1549632	F/S	GREENAWAY Charles William	25-06-44	61 Sqn
1449845	Sgt	GREENAWAY William Reginald	27-01-44	432 Sqn
1673038	Sgt	GREENER Thomas	18-10-44	115 Sqn
151197	F/O	GREENFIELD Alfred Charles Allwood	7-06-44	44 Sqn
710171	Sgt	GREENFIELD Harry Moxon [Rhodesia]	22-06-44	44 Sqn
2215845	Sgt	GREENFIELD Henry	27-04-44	103 Sqn
1321982	F/S	GREENFIELD Rex Edward	31-03-44	7 Sqn
158535	F/O	GREENGRASS Stanley Walter	27-08-44	12 Sqn
1503641	F/S	GREENHALGH Jack	16-03-44	57 Sqn
577287	Sgt	GREENHILL Bernard Owen	6-01-44	207 Sqn
1567926	Sgt	GREENHILL George Dalgetty	2-03-44	76 Sqn
1836309	Sgt	GREENING Gordon Valentine	17-09-44	102 Sqn
1591783	Sgt	GREENLEY David	12-09-44	619 Sqn
1866929	Sgt	GREENSMITH John David	24-08-44	1666 HCU
2206988	Sgt	GREENWELL Clement Ralph	3-01-44	103 Sqn
131550	F/O	GREENWOOD Alfred	8-05-44	44 Sqn
642804	Sgt	GREENWOOD Ernest	26-07-44	49 Sqn
1461091	F/S	GREENWOOD Ernest Walter	25-04-44	83 Sqn
1169099	Sgt	GREENWOOD George Edward	28-01-44	49 Sqn
1550138	AC1	GREENWOOD John Johnson	26-03-44	239 Sqn
1818238	Sgt	GREENWOOD Kenneth Hartley	5-01-44	431 Sqn
650233	Sgt	GREENWOOD Stanley Stuart	23-05-44	576 Sqn
1436515	F/S	GREGG Henry	20-02-44	166 Sqn
1603720	Sgt	GREGO Cyril Charles	30-08-44	21 OTU
1283636	F/S	GREGORY Frederick	31-03-44	514 Sqn
1065035	Sgt	GREGORY Henry Thomas	3-06-44	166 Sqn
1005552	Sgt	GREGORY Jack	13-08-44	51 Sqn
1324747	Sgt	GREGORY Jack Phillip	29-06-44	76 Sqn
151983	F/O	GREIG John Frederick James	13-08-44	83 Sqn

Service No	Rank	Name	Date	Unit
133050	F/L	GREIG DFC John Mortimer	29-01-44	1660 HCU
1144831	F/S	GREIG Ronald	22-03-44	49 Sqn
1553997	Sgt	GREIG Stanley	18-03-44	1657 HCU
1000908	Sgt	GREIG Walter Henry Mills	13-07-44	576 Sqn
1587665	Sgt	GREMS Arthur Charles	20-02-44	49 Sqn
1626370	Sgt	GRESSWELL Ronald	21-07-44	578 Sqn
1685127	Sgt	GRESTY James	20-07-44	582 Sqn
159102	F/O	GREW William Thomas	23-09-44	78 Sqn
1119682	Sgt	GREY Felix Bernard	2-01-44	97 Sqn
1333297	Sgt	GRIBBEN Thomas	13-06-44	12 Sqn
1397763	F/S	GRIBBLE Arthur Horace	15-11-44	115 Sqn
2209891	Sgt	GRICE Harold	12-09-44	622 Sqn
1485173	Sgt	GRIER James	11-04-44	83 Sqn
1822215	Sgt	GRIEVE Allan Fleming	13-07-44	9 Sqn
577530	Sgt	GRIEVE Francis George	11-07-44	408 Sqn
1521456	Sgt	GRIFFIN Arthur Desmond	22-06-44	49 Sqn
1321616	F/S	GRIFFITH John Arthur Thomas	15-02-44	158 Sqn
1652544	Sgt	GRIFFITHS Alan Curnow	7-06-44	550 Sqn
1474286	F/S	GRIFFITHS Arthur	3-08-44	619 Sqn
1578754	Sgt	GRIFFITHS Basil	16-06-44	75 Sqn
1389070	F/S	GRIFFITHS David	16-06-44	635 Sqn
168661	F/O	GRIFFITHS DFC Frank	8-07-44	83 Sqn
1835969	Sgt	GRIFFITHS George Henry	20-02-44	630 Sqn
1313245	F/S	GRIFFITHS Gilbert Frank	13-06-44	76 Sqn
612907	Sgt	GRIFFITHS Glyn	3-01-44	156 Sqn
2211356	Sgt	GRIFFITHS Harold De Gray	22-05-44	57 Sqn
655697	W/O	GRIFFITHS Harry Ernest Lloyd	1-07-44	139 Sqn
1140787	Sgt	GRIFFITHS John William	15-02-44	622 Sqn
1813603	Sgt	GRIFFITHS Michael Edmund	17-12-44	17 OTU
175662	F/O	GRIFFITHS Oscar	24-12-44	100 Sqn
171170	P/O	GRIFFITHS Sidney John	29-01-44	467 Sqn
1589581	Sgt	GRIFFITHS Sydney George	16-10-44	10 Sqn
1339216	Sgt	GRIFFITHS Thomas Rhys Llewellyn	30-08-44	166 Sqn
1399035	F/S	GRIFFITHS William Edward	19-07-44	630 Sqn
176583	P/O	GRIGG George Alan	24-07-44	619 Sqn
1419839	Sgt	GRIGG George Ernest	21-01-44	35 Sqn
177073	P/O	GRIGGS Raymond William	8-06-44	408 Sqn
86729	F/L	GRILLAGE Frederick George	3-12-44	582 Sqn
1119613	F/S	GRIMES George Lionel	25-03-44	7 Sqn
631689	W/O	GRIMSON MiD George John William	14-04-44	37 Sqn
130333	F/L	GRIMWOOD Francis Leonard	22-07-44	23 Sqn
172155	P/O	GRINDROD John Carter	24-02-44	100 Sqn
946690	Sgt	GRINT Joseph Robert	25-07-44	207 Sqn
2206408	Sgt	GRISDALE Harold	21-07-44	101 Sqn
45148	F/L	GRISMAN William Jack	6-04-44	109 Sqn
918972	Sgt	GRIST Ronald James	29-01-44	463 Sqn
1375424	W/O	GRITTY George Kenneth	4-05-44	460 Sqn
1320894	F/S	GROGAN Gordon Stuart	6-10-44	106 Sqn
1890169	Sgt	GRONOW Kenneth Edward	25-07-44	622 Sqn
1814429	Sgt	GROOM Peter William	17-09-44	617 Sqn
1603566	Sgt	GROSS Arthur William Ronald	16-06-44	50 Sqn
1581803	Sgt	GROUCOTT Stanley Joseph	29-01-44	434 Sqn
1818243	Sgt	GROVE Stephen	23-04-44	9 Sqn
146424	F/L	GROVE William George	24-03-44	15 Sqn
1444895	Sgt	GROVER Sydney Herbert	13-08-44	158 Sqn
1586410	Sgt	GROVES John Denis	21-01-44	115 Sqn
1387958	F/S	GROVES John Victor	31-03-44	61 Sqn
182368	P/O	GROVES Philip Henry	12-09-44	102 Sqn
151259	F/L	GRUBB Anthony Edward	5-07-44	57 Sqn
2206212	Sgt	GRUNDY Elson Holland	2-11-44	426 Sqn
1393695	F/S	GRUNDY Ernest George	25-03-44	61 Sqn
657840	F/S	GUBBINS Cyril John	6-06-44	1651 HCU
1684645	F/S	GUEST Frank	11-12-44	514 Sqn
1801227	Sgt	GUEST Thomas Henry	11-04-44	550 Sqn
151891	F/O	GUILE James	8-05-44	106 Sqn
1675093	Sgt	GUILE Ronald	25-04-44	463 Sqn
2202756	F/S	GUINAN Edmund	17-06-44	431 Sqn
174686	P/O	GUIVER Sydney Jack	13-08-44	14 OTU
1627470	Sgt	GULLY Ernest Gordon	23-09-44	50 Sqn
1342935	Sgt	GUNN Edward Sandilands	20-02-44	103 Sqn
1433278	Sgt	GUNN Thomas Reginald	21-07-44	578 Sqn
1602200	F/S	GUNNING Edwin Charles	4-11-44	51 Sqn
169429	F/L	GUNZI Guy Godfrey Charles 'Nip'	27-04-44	619 Sqn
152296	F/O	GURDEN Frederick Ernest Rex	22-12-44	626 Sqn
1291835	Sgt	GURDEN Leslie Norman	26-05-44	19 OTU
1878210	AC2	GURNEY Aubrey Nigel	15-07-44	57 Sqn
1335009	F/S	GURTON DFM John Leonard	15-02-44	156 Sqn
1036918	Sgt	GUTHRIE John Charles	31-03-44	635 Sqn
3020081	Sgt	GUTHRIE Thomas Crerar	21-08-44	415 Sqn
1600730	Sgt	GUTTERIDGE Don	13-08-44	115 Sqn
1867802	Sgt	GUTTRIDGE Derek Vernon	9-05-44	431 Sqn
1820355	Sgt	GUY Charles Mathieson	30-07-44	514 Sqn
172461	P/O	GUY Guilyn Penry	22-06-44	57 Sqn
1617737	Sgt	GUY John Patrick	25-07-44	15 Sqn
1565396	F/S	GUY Robert Calder	8-06-44	514 Sqn
1029598	F/S	GUY Walter Austin	31-03-44	51 Sqn
163713	F/O	GWYER Herbert Harry Stephen	11-12-44	49 Sqn
1447821	Sgt	GWYN Herbert John Compton	29-01-44	51 Sqn
1764165	Sgt	GWYNNE John Vernon	20-02-44	426 Sqn
1872636	Sgt	GWYNNE Phillip John Bentley	7-12-44	463 Sqn
1566687	Sgt	GWYNNE William James	31-03-44	103 Sqn
1416572	Sgt	HABERFIELD Ivor Ronald Frank	11-04-44	619 Sqn
1028882	Sgt	HABBERSHAW Frederick	30-01-44	156 Sqn
1129143	F/S	HABERGHAM Arnold William	19-07-44	619 Sqn
1602535	Sgt	HABGOOD Frederic Harold	31-07-44	550 Sqn
1399598	Sgt	HABGOOD Guy Wilfred	6-10-44	78 Sqn
564683	F/S	HACK Ernest James	21-07-44	514 Sqn
1303836	Sgt	HACKETT Arthur John	3-01-44	156 Sqn
1430823	Sgt	HADDEN Dennis Allen	4-05-44	103 Sqn
135016	F/O	HADDOCK Robert Edward	4-05-44	625 Sqn
184184	P/O	HADDRELL Herbert George	15-10-44	1667 HCU
1431390	F/S	HADEN William	31-03-44	640 Sqn
1047949	Sgt	HADFIELD Gerald	17-06-44	102 Sqn
1851439	Sgt	HADLAND James Thomas	20-01-44	76 Sqn
177379	F/O	HADLEY Neville	21-07-44	10 Sqn
1303266	F/S	HADLINGTON John Douglas	25-06-44	97 Sqn
974950	Sgt	HADLOW Bernard	8-07-44	17 OTU
1394214	F/S	HAGERTY Cyril William	27-04-44	10 Sqn
1284877	Sgt	HAGGER Cyril Leslie	23-06-44	77 Sqn
128907	F/L	HAGGIS Douglas Charles	25-08-44	218 Sqn
156385	P/O	HAGON DFC William Henry Frederick George	21-01-44	77 Sqn
1452134	F/S	HAGUE John	19-07-44	207 Sqn
1819687	Sgt	HAGUES George Thomas	13-09-44	625 Sqn
1822622	Sgt	HAIG David Beattie	23-05-44	630 Sqn
811039	Sgt	HAIGH Ernest Walter	22-05-44	514 Sqn
101522	F/L	HAIGH DFM Fred	22-03-44	35 Sqn
925316	F/S	HAINE Richard	6-06-44	50 Sqn
1350032	Sgt	HAINES Anthony Oliver	20-02-44	103 Sqn
1852300	Sgt	HAINES Stanley Sidney John	23-04-44	149 Sqn
1594915	Sgt	HAINSWORTH Norman	24-09-44	467 Sqn
1677148	Sgt	HAINSWORTH Richard Beetham	27-04-44	49 Sqn
160855	F/O	HALBERT DFC Thomas David	27-04-44	83 Sqn
1457196	Sgt	HALE Charles Thiepval	22-06-44	77 Sqn
1606173	Sgt	HALE Dennis William	2-11-44	622 Sqn
146250	F/O	HALE Frederick Leslie	20-02-44	625 Sqn
1541335	Sgt	HALES Harold Frederick	3-01-44	166 Sqn
1533561	Sgt	HALES Joseph Harold England	22-05-44	49 Sqn
1810455	Sgt	HALES Richard Benjamin	21-11-44	192 Sqn
1895806	Sgt	HALES Ronald Douglas	8-06-44	15 Sqn
1583147	Sgt	HALES Walter Richard	21-02-44	78 Sqn
127308	F/O	HALESTRAP DFC Geoffrey George	13-05-44	1655 MTU
1127618	Sgt	HALEY John	31-10-44	460 Sqn
1802238	Sgt	HALKE Donald John	25-02-44	460 Sqn
1812871	Sgt	HALL Albert Ernest	30-08-44	90 Sqn
2218394	Sgt	HALL Albert Frederick	15-10-44	207 Sqn
1544769	Sgt	HALL Albert Howard	21-07-44	622 Sqn
151580	F/O	HALL Alexander Henry	24-04-44	102 Sqn

Service No	Rank	Name	Date	Sqn
1535797	Sgt	HALL Arthur Graham	28-05-44	550 Sqn
1869433	Sgt	HALL Donald William Herbert	20-11-44	14 OTU
1895735	Sgt	HALL Douglas Robert William	9-03-44	1667 HCU
1869287	Sgt	HALL Eric George	18-12-44	207 Sqn
1391531	Sgt	HALL Ernest Ronald	7-06-44	550 Sqn
1582161	F/S	HALL Frank Horace	29-07-44	619 Sqn
1342144	Sgt	HALL James	30-01-44	626 Sqn
1553897	F/S	HALL James	7-12-44	1651 HCU
129005	F/O	HALL DFC James Arthur	6-06-44	578 Sqn
174020	P/O	HALL John Ernest	8-06-44	622 Sqn
1163754	W/O	HALL John William	11-09-44	514 Sqn
179851	P/O	HALL John William Frank	4-10-44	419 Sqn
161613	F/O	HALL Lawrence Ambrose	10-08-44	619 Sqn
1495938	F/S	HALL Leslie	16-03-44	630 Sqn
978968	F/S	HALL Norman	20-02-44	514 Sqn
976475	W/O	HALL Raymond Frank Joseph Cyril	2-05-44	514 Sqn
149572	F/O	HALL Robert Buchan	5-08-44	161 Sqn
1392121	Sgt	HALL Robert Ewen	24-02-44	75 Sqn
1581458	Sgt	HALL Robert Henry	23-04-44	101 Sqn
1457899	F/S	HALL Roberts	18-12-44	51 Sqn
1431397	Sgt	HALL Ronald Charles	15-02-44	77 Sqn
1331030	F/S	HALL DFM Stanley John	23-05-44	83 Sqn
944380	Sgt	HALL Thomas Albert	22-06-44	49 Sqn
1895157	Sgt	HALL Thomas John	8-08-44	75 Sqn
1333525	F/S	HALL DFM Thomas William John	31-03-44	106 Sqn
621942	Sgt	HALL William	10-05-44	106 Sqn
106323	F/O	HALLAM DFC Herbert Leslie	21-11-44	514 Sqn
545834	Sgt	HALLAM Reginald	20-01-44	1653 HCU
1393049	Sgt	HALLETT Clement Arthur	5-07-44	207 Sqn
1602270	Sgt	HALLETT Ronald Tom	23-09-44	166 Sqn
1485099	F/S	HALLIDAY George Robert Shield	25-02-44	44 Sqn
175048	F/O	HALLIWELL Albert Edward	12-12-44	195 Sqn
1523572	Sgt	HALLIWELL Harvey	12-04-44	432 Sqn
2206039	Sgt	HALLIWELL James Furness Clayton	12-09-44	44 Sqn
151077	F/O	HALLOWS DFC George	23-05-44	576 Sqn
1286551	Sgt	HALLS Alexander James Frank	23-10-44	467 Sqn
162792	P/O	HALPERIN DFC Ronald	21-02-44	156 Sqn
177923	P/O	HALPIN John Lawrence	22-06-44	619 Sqn
1450069	F/S	HALSHAW John Edward	25-06-44	9 Sqn
999346	W/O	HALSTEAD William Derek Taylor	27-08-44	90 Sqn
1890071	Sgt	HALY Reginald Frank Edwin	7-06-44	44 Sqn
928499	F/S	HAMBLING DFM Ernest	20-04-44	635 Sqn
144652	F/O	HAMBLY Alfred	22-06-44	49 Sqn
3010857	Sgt	HAMBLY Leslie Joseph	24-09-44	9 Sqn
170729	P/O	HAMBY Peter Hanson	15-03-44	7 Sqn
1683268	Sgt	HAMER Derek	27-08-44	1657 HCU
1392998	F/S	HAMILTON Archibald	25-03-44	57 Sqn
184878	P/O	HAMILTON Derek Alexander Clemence	12-09-44	44 Sqn
1238004	Sgt	HAMILTON Ernest William	20-02-44	103 Sqn
1119701	Sgt	HAMILTON Henry	29-06-44	467 Sqn
1568684	Sgt	HAMILTON Hugh Graham	26-08-44	207 Sqn
1126670	Sgt	HAMILTON James Robertson	20-02-44	429 Sqn
1822772	Sgt	HAMILTON John	3-01-44	166 Sqn
1825268	Sgt	HAMILTON John Bryce	30-08-44	300 Sqn
1806460	Sgt	HAMILTON Kenneth James	12-09-44	100 Sqn
1335338	F/S	HAMILTON Paul Jameson	1-06-44	115 Sqn
1566443	Sgt	HAMILTON Robert	14-10-44	115 Sqn
1739618	Sgt	HAMILTON Stanley	18-08-44	103 Sqn
1826261	Sgt	HAMILTON Thomas	31-08-44	550 Sqn
128054	F/O	HAMLIN Arthur Ronald	5-05-44	139 Sqn
1600719	Sgt	HAMLIN John	31-03-44	44 Sqn
1622724	F/S	HAMMOND Ernest Vernon	27-08-44	166 Sqn
1576457	Sgt	HAMMOND John Edwin	25-03-44	115 Sqn
1890035	Sgt	HAMMOND Leonard Douglas	29-01-44	102 Sqn
153748	F/L	HAMMOND Richard Alfred Charles	10-05-44	106 Sqn
927501	Sgt	HAMMOND William Alfred	16-03-44	426 Sqn
1809627	Sgt	HAMONIAUX Gordon Ernest	19-03-44	463 Sqn
114329	F/L	HAMPSHIRE Herbert Robin	28-06-44	141 Sqn
1853986	Sgt	HAMPSON John William	8-06-44	420 Sqn
179285	P/O	HAMPSON Royston Percy	21-07-44	51 Sqn
1537060	Sgt	HAMPSON Seddon	22-03-44	78 Sqn
145468	F/O	HANCHAR Charles Armand Georges [Belgium]	13-06-44	408 Sqn
1337513	Sgt	HANCOCK Douglas	21-07-44	115 Sqn
2206033	Sgt	HANCOCK Jesse	11-06-44	100 Sqn
1396104	F/S	HANCOCK Stanley Albert	22-05-44	75 Sqn
172481	F/O	HANCOX Reginald Sidney	13-08-44	12 Sqn
116100	F/L	HAND Vernon Terence Joseph	12-08-44	1665 HCU
1091175	F/S	HANDCOCK William George	14-01-44	101 Sqn
2204315	Sgt	HANDFORD Alan John	22-06-44	619 Sqn
173341	P/O	HANDLEY Albert	4-05-44	50 Sqn
156428	P/O	HANDLEY DFC Christopher Mark	2-01-44	156 Sqn
1895656	Sgt	HANDS Gordon Ernest Deryvk	19-07-44	49 Sqn
1390983	F/S	HANDS John	13-07-44	415 Sqn
1576688	F/S	HANDS John Edward	22-01-44	166 Sqn
1819763	Sgt	HANET Jean Pierre	12-09-44	214 Sqn
1314595	F/S	HANFORD Leonard	27-08-44	1661 HCU
1819276	Sgt	HANKIN William Ernest	26-08-44	12 OTU
2209952	Sgt	HANKINSON Eric	13-08-44	101 Sqn
1609340	Sgt	HANKS Charles Raymond	10-04-44	207 Sqn
159005	F/O	HANKS James Edward	23-04-44	640 Sqn
171364	P/O	HANKS Reginald Alfred	24-03-44	425 Sqn
1802118	Sgt	HANLEY James Johnston	24-02-44	61 Sqn
573620	F/S	HANLEY Matthew William	22-11-44	1660 HCU
1803007	Sgt	HANMER Vernon Albert	23-09-44	207 Sqn
605539	Sgt	HANNA Charles Murray [USA]	12-12-44	149 Sqn
1796357	Sgt	HANNA James	7-06-44	630 Sqn
640248	W/O	HANNAFORD William Albert	6-06-44	149 Sqn
1570758	Sgt	HANNAH Andrew James	15-10-44	101 Sqn
1824317	Sgt	HANNAH Neil	19-07-44	9 Sqn
1347355	Sgt	HANNAH Norman Marshall	7-06-44	9 Sqn
155897	F/O	HANNAH DFC William	21-07-44	97 Sqn
2210062	Sgt	HANNELL Kenneth	1-07-44	101 Sqn
965557	F/S	HANNON William Gerrard	12-11-44	49 Sqn
1163911	Cpl	HANRAHAN Thomas Frederick	8-11-44	3 Group
173340	F/O	HANSELL DFC Richard Neville	26-08-44	300 Sqn
179265	P/O	HANSFORD Arthur	25-04-44	420 Sqn
1851362	Sgt	HANSFORD Cyril Edward	25-06-44	9 Sqn
172950	P/O	HANSON Cyril Richard	8-06-44	166 Sqn
1601317	Sgt	HANSON George Charles	1-09-44	138 Sqn
1284645	W/O	HANSON John Richard	20-04-44	635 Sqn
1131665	F/S	HANSON Leslie	23-04-44	424 Sqn
1899499	Sgt	HANSON Robert Laurence	4-12-44	189 Sqn
171336	P/O	HANSON Ronald Stanley	4-05-44	50 Sqn
1818459	Sgt	HARBIDGE William Ernest	26-02-44	15 Sqn
1607419	Sgt	HARBOUR William	23-04-44	12 Sqn
1591194	Sgt	HARBRON Harry	25-04-44	166 Sqn
1811226	Sgt	HARD Frederick Hubert	5-07-44	630 Sqn
151165	F/O	HARDCASTLE William Gordon	8-07-44	106 Sqn
61077	F/O	HARDEN DFC George James	25-04-44	617 Sqn
1336781	F/S	HARDEN James Lane	23-04-44	463 Sqn
1324291	Sgt	HARDER Frank Norman	7-06-44	9 Sqn
1402410	Sgt	HARDEY Ronald Redfern	29-07-44	103 Sqn
184768	P/O	HARDIE David	6-11-44	214 Sqn
1603957	Sgt	HARDING Arthur Charles	16-06-44	635 Sqn
89991	F/O	HARDING Frank William	14-01-44	7 Sqn
1691596	Sgt	HARDING George Frederick	4-11-44	78 Sqn
1602968	F/S	HARDING Henry George	6-12-44	61 Sqn
1865691	Sgt	HARDING Kenneth Lovell	29-01-44	90 Sqn
143293	F/O	HARDING DFC Leslie William	23-09-44	166 Sqn
574158	F/S	HARDING Louis Arthur	24-09-44	9 Sqn
89808	F/L	HARDING Maurice Frederick Cleave	26-08-44	207 Sqn
39519	F/L	HARDING Nelson Maxwell	16-09-44	78 Sqn
1705084	Sgt	HARDING Ronald William	21-11-44	514 Sqn
3005903	Sgt	HARDING Stanley	25-11-44	463 Sqn
152513	F/O	HARDING Walter Thomas	19-07-44	78 Sqn
184635	P/O	HARDING William Ralph	6-11-44	214 Sqn

Service #	Rank	Name	Date	Unit
1233577	Sgt	HARDMAN Fred	19-03-44	20 OTU
151349	F/O	HARDMAN John	28-05-44	460 Sqn
635378	Sgt	HARDMAN Thomas	10-04-44	149 Sqn
1325790	F/S	HARDWICK Robert Edward	25-05-44	158 Sqn
183072	P/O	HARDWICK William John	13-08-44	428 Sqn
650489	Sgt	HARDY Douglas William Edward	22-06-44	49 Sqn
647883	Sgt	HARDY Frederick Ralph	17-06-44	103 Sqn
1684385	F/S	HARDY Harry	12-09-44	218 Sqn
170251	F/O	HARDY John Edward Cecil	6-12-44	608 Sqn
2209289	Sgt	HARDY Terence Edward	19-07-44	61 Sqn
1323620	F/S	HARDY Walter	6-11-44	106 Sqn
1321865	Sgt	HARDY William Edgar	16-03-44	49 Sqn
1439383	Sgt	HARE John	25-06-44	44 Sqn
647127	Sgt	HARE John Alfred	6-01-44	97 Sqn
132390	F/L	HARE DFC Walter Roy	11-05-44	467 Sqn
161805	F/O	HARFORD Peter Edward George	2-11-44	49 Sqn
1427039	Sgt	HARGILL Allen	30-08-44	106 Sqn
1155026	Sgt	HARGOOD Charles Arthur	25-04-44	12 OTU
178830	P/O	HARGRAVE Alan Bright	19-08-44	7 Sqn
142090	F/O	HARGREAVES Dennis	2-06-44	138 Sqn
575689	Sgt	HARGREAVES John Alfred	28-04-44	166 Sqn
169452	P/O	HARLAND Ian William	25-06-44	149 Sqn
171813	F/O	HARLAND John Herbert Gerard	20-11-44	514 Sqn
571071	F/S	HARLEY William Thomas	12-09-44	635 Sqn
1399617	Sgt	HARLING John Edward	27-08-44	515 Sqn
1623143	Sgt	HARLING John Edwin	7-02-44	19 OTU
1804459	Sgt	HARMAN Arthur Samuel	11-04-44	466 Sqn
1391110	Sgt	HARMAN Fred	20-02-44	9 Sqn
1853662	Sgt	HARMAN James	20-09-44	514 Sqn
1406404	F/S	HARMAN DFM Leslie Thomas	6-07-44	635 Sqn
1232350	Sgt	HARMER Kenneth Wilfred	22-05-44	619 Sqn
1608330	F/S	HARMSWORTH Desmond Aubrey	28-04-44	432 Sqn
620288	F/S	HARMSWORTH-SMITH Frederick Ronald	12-09-44	35 Sqn
1595185	Sgt	HARNELL Albert	10-04-44	10 OTU
1874594	Sgt	HARPER Benjamin George	22-03-44	166 Sqn
1829682	Sgt	HARPER Charles	24-09-44	85 OTU
631720	Sgt	HARPER Edward	20-02-44	466 Sqn
172183	P/O	HARPER Edward Charles Bisset	27-04-44	106 Sqn
1339897	F/S	HARPER Geoffrey Kelvin	29-01-44	97 Sqn
1817318	F/S	HARPER Jeffrey Francis Pryce	28-10-44	35 Sqn
2205720	Sgt	HARPER John	26-07-44	619 Sqn
186700	P/O	HARPER John Derrick	4-10-44	44 Sqn
1601730	Sgt	HARPER Kenneth Archibald	23-04-44	149 Sqn
1678239	Sgt	HARPER Kenneth Horridge	3-01-44	57 Sqn
2205712	Sgt	HARPER Robert Noel	8-07-44	50 Sqn
1672145	Sgt	HARPER Ronald Thomas	31-03-44	156 Sqn
1594534	Sgt	HARPER Sidney Sutherland	14-10-44	166 Sqn
900315	Sgt	HARRIS Alfred	1-11-44	106 Sqn
176237	P/O	HARRIS Arnold Reginald	13-07-44	1662 HCU
1615832	Sgt	HARRIS Clifford Alfred	17-08-44	57 Sqn
1603373	Sgt	HARRIS David George	24-03-44	100 Sqn
1580053	Sgt	HARRIS Dennis William	18-12-44	3 LFS
1423759	Sgt	HARRIS Emmanuel Henry	26-08-44	78 Sqn
1583153	Sgt	HARRIS Ernest Charles Elam	23-03-44	106 Sqn
1582210	Sgt	HARRIS Ernest Edward James	22-06-44	57 Sqn
545284	Sgt	HARRIS Frank Albert Charles	21-02-44	427 Sqn
1806356	Sgt	HARRIS Frank George	30-08-44	50 Sqn
1485057	W/O	HARRIS George	31-12-44	138 Sqn
144712	F/O	HARRIS George Richard	3-01-44	83 Sqn
188312	P/O	HARRIS George Walter	21-11-44	429 Sqn
1458651	F/S	HARRIS Harold	16-06-44	582 Sqn
1581276	F/S	HARRIS Harvey Roy	15-10-44	466 Sqn
1615781	Sgt	HARRIS Jack Frank	31-03-44	106 Sqn
1399950	F/S	HARRIS John George	3-12-44	138 Sqn
937401	Sgt	HARRIS John James	6-10-44	51 Sqn
133607	F/L	HARRIS Keith	29-01-44	115 Sqn
1584722	Sgt	HARRIS Kenneth Ephraim	22-03-44	35 Sqn
184362	P/O	HARRIS Leonard George	9-11-44	625 Sqn
2221167	Sgt	HARRIS Manning Robert Frederick	20-10-44	550 Sqn
1311906	Sgt	HARRIS Peter	16-02-44	50 Sqn
176168	P/O	HARRIS Reginald Bernard Victor	25-07-44	622 Sqn
1629001	Sgt	HARRIS Reginald Jack	14-01-44	115 Sqn
1333587	Sgt	HARRIS Robert Percy	15-02-44	10 Sqn
650776	F/S	HARRIS Thomas	10-05-44	50 Sqn
1397160	Sgt	HARRIS Warrington	27-03-44	166 Sqn
1029330	F/S	HARRIS William Alfred	4-05-44	12 Sqn
657748	W/O	HARRISON Bernard Harley	21-11-44	192 Sqn
171684	P/O	HARRISON Bernard Silverius	22-03-44	158 Sqn
118127	F/L	HARRISON Charles Melville	10-12-44	139 Sqn
1384966	F/S	HARRISON DFM David Ernest	15-02-44	7 Sqn
1590368	Sgt	HARRISON Denis	6-10-44	49 Sqn
1129675	F/S	HARRISON Edward Arthur	13-04-44	90 Sqn
141544	F/O	HARRISON Ernest Henry	25-07-44	15 Sqn
1516172	Sgt	HARRISON Farewell	7-06-44	460 Sqn
2205992	Sgt	HARRISON Geoffrey	31-12-44	138 Sqn
2203348	Sgt	HARRISON Graham	25-06-44	149 Sqn
1581921	Sgt	HARRISON Henry Selwyn	21-01-44	1667 HCU
110412	F/L	HARRISON DFC Hugh Raymond	24-07-44	625 Sqn
1173702	Sgt	HARRISON James	12-09-44	218 Sqn
1582271	F/S	HARRISON James Arthur	6-11-44	619 Sqn
173612	P/O	HARRISON John Albert	13-07-44	103 Sqn
54541	P/O	HARRISON John Douglas	23-04-44	514 Sqn
1620624	Sgt	HARRISON John Lomax	8-02-44	18 OTU
1267694	Sgt	HARRISON Laurence Edwin	28-10-44	12 OTU
1819564	Sgt	HARRISON Norris Mervyn	25-04-44	76 Sqn
1128211	Sgt	HARRISON Robert	25-02-44	514 Sqn
1652715	Sgt	HARRISON Stanley John	30-01-44	625 Sqn
177077	F/O	HARRISON Trevor Gordon	21-07-44	578 Sqn
1396448	Sgt	HARRISON William Frederick	23-04-44	75 Sqn
1196227	W/O	HARRISON William George	23-05-44	207 Sqn
178049	F/O	HARROP Kenneth	6-10-44	49 Sqn
1601839	Sgt	HARRY James William	24-02-44	75 Sqn
174555	P/O	HART Claude	13-07-44	576 Sqn
1382283	F/S	HART Eric George	29-01-44	576 Sqn
1192149	LAC	HART George William Frederick	19-05-44	50 Sqn
1053592	F/S	HART Kenneth Frederick Hill	4-03-44	138 Sqn
1804387	Sgt	HART Leonard James	15-12-44	625 Sqn
1671946	F/S	HART Robert Henry Standing	6-06-44	149 Sqn
1391453	Sgt	HART Ronald Arthur	21-01-44	101 Sqn
48420	S/L	HART Stanley William	15-10-44	10 Sqn
951579	F/S	HARTHILL John Cameron	24-02-44	51 Sqn
1851465	Sgt	HARTLAND William Thomas	12-12-44	195 Sqn
2216066	Sgt	HARTLEY Arthur	25-02-44	149 Sqn
178002	P/O	HARTLEY Eric Albert	7-10-44	617 Sqn
1425781	F/S	HARTLEY Frank	5-07-44	630 Sqn
1582326	F/S	HARTLEY Henry Herbert	27-08-44	115 Sqn
1620932	Sgt	HARTLEY Jack	17-12-44	17 OTU
954358	Sgt	HARTLEY John Leonard	17-09-44	128 Sqn
1579399	Sgt	HARTLEY Martin	16-02-44	50 Sqn
1685744	Sgt	HARTLEY Sylvester	28-05-44	626 Sqn
1585484	Sgt	HARTLEY Thomas John Charles	2-05-44	10 Sqn
3025176	Sgt	HARTMAN Ernest John	17-12-44	101 Sqn
657578	F/S	HARTMAN Lawrence Charles	14-01-44	7 Sqn
184006	P/O	HARTSTEIN Emmanuel	23-08-44	83 OTU
1580365	F/S	HARVEY Charles Elmer	15-03-44	51 Sqn
174533	P/O	HARVEY DFM Donald Edmund Dunning	10-05-44	97 Sqn
1330253	F/S	HARVEY Frederick Walter	23-04-44	77 Sqn
1800650	Sgt	HARVEY George Richard	29-07-44	408 Sqn
1431604	F/S	HARVEY James	23-04-44	12 Sqn
1825211	Sgt	HARVEY Lyal	23-01-44	161 Sqn
1393041	F/S	HARVEY Owen Stuart	23-04-44	51 Sqn
1607906	Sgt	HARVEY Roy Charles Walter Henry	30-11-44	578 Sqn
1078296	W/O	HARVEY William	11-06-44	78 Sqn
1582500	Sgt	HARVEY William Mawrey	4-05-44	1662 HCU
1189052	F/S	HARWOOD Raymond Guy	22-06-44	630 Sqn
178759	P/O	HARWOOD Rupert Thomas William	19-07-44	619 Sqn

2211443	Sgt	HASKINS Eric	23-09-44	9 Sqn		1181648	W/O	HAZLEHURST Alan	30-01-44	405 Sqn
1079636	Sgt	HASLAM Edwin	22-03-44	7 Sqn		1322062	Sgt	HEAD Albert Edward	14-01-44	156 Sqn
2219498	Sgt	HASLAM George Frederick	27-12-44	75 Sqn		1801075	Sgt	HEAD Gerard John	25-04-44	76 Sqn
2201240	Sgt	HASLETT Stewart	25-05-44	101 Sqn		1819907	F/S	HEADLAND Donald George	28-10-44	90 Sqn
160744	F/O	HASTE Douglas Frederick	29-11-44	12 Sqn		2206703	F/S	HEADLEY George Mathew	2-01-44	156 Sqn
1593365	Sgt	HASTIE Edward Hope	28-04-44	51 Sqn		1514328	Sgt	HEAHER William	23-04-44	90 Sqn
1337802	F/S	HASSETT Graham Arthur	2-05-44	218 Sqn		1337707	F/S	HEAL Frank Sidney George	17-08-44	102 Sqn
575792	Sgt	HASWELL George William	8-06-44	15 Sqn		130972	F/O	HEAL Ronald William	27-01-44	149 Sqn
185204	P/O	HATCH DFM Cyril Frederick [Australia]	13-09-44	640 Sqn		153200	F/O	HEALAS Harold Edward Hewitt	12-09-44	35 Sqn
						172917	F/O	HEALD Robert	18-07-44	431 Sqn
933266	Sgt	HATCH Ernest Ambrose	27-04-44	106 Sqn		170211	F/L	HEALEY DFC Francis William	30-08-44	635 Sqn
129148	S/L	HATCHER DFC AFM Leslie	22-12-44	83 Sqn		533694	Sgt	HEALEY Harry Reginald	27-04-44	106 Sqn
1580729	Sgt	HATFIELD Arthur	25-02-44	550 Sqn		1876797	Sgt	HEALEY William Leonard	6-08-44	51 Sqn
1399719	Sgt	HATFIELD Peter Albert	26-03-44	115 Sqn		1892821	Sgt	HEALY Jeremiah	8-07-44	57 Sqn
1396651	Sgt	HATTON Noel	4-05-44	626 Sqn		1463267	F/S	HEALY Joseph	4-05-44	463 Sqn
1266780	F/S	HATTON Peter James	25-03-44	44 Sqn		3012270	Sgt	HEAP Jeffery	25-11-44	12 OTU
188725	P/O	HATZFELD Emile	30-08-44	467 Sqn		1477459	F/S	HEAP Robert	10-05-44	97 Sqn
2209203	Sgt	HAUGH George	23-03-44	115 Sqn		54037	P/O	HEARD Eric Thome	25-05-44	158 Sqn
67123	F/O	HAWDON John Oldham	29-12-44	170 Sqn		1393141	F/S	HEARD Philip Thomas	11-04-44	158 Sqn
1504897	F/S	HAWES Stanley	22-06-44	49 Sqn		1471160	F/S	HEARN Douglas Charles Norman	16-11-44	15 Sqn
156366	F/O	HAWKEN Donald William Carylon	19-03-44	166 Sqn		127875	F/O	HEARN James White	23-03-44	9 Sqn
1354388	W/O	HAWKER Edwin James	8-08-44	582 Sqn		1867389	Sgt	HEARN Eric Richard	19-07-44	138 Sqn
1804587	Sgt	HAWKER Ronald Francis	20-02-44	429 Sqn		151490	F/O	HEARN William Edgar	6-12-44	635 Sqn
1602334	F/S	HAWKES Eric Peter	7-06-44	44 Sqn		1571747	Sgt	HEARTON David Houston	24-02-44	30 OTU
1324754	F/S	HAWKES Richard James Travers	28-06-44	90 Sqn		1607798	Sgt	HEASMAN Gordon Edward	3-01-44	61 Sqn
1876684	Sgt	HAWKES Ronald George	6-11-44	622 Sqn		1390980	F/S	HEASMAN James Henry Charles	24-09-44	61 Sqn
1035546	Sgt	HAWKINGS William Ewart	28-10-44	419 Sqn		1575948	F/S	HEASON Herbert Leonard	13-08-44	83 Sqn
1894528	Sgt	HAWKINS Alfred David	23-06-44	626 Sqn		994607	F/S	HEATH Alan Douglas	20-05-44	7 Sqn
168619	F/O	HAWKINS Edward George	2-05-44	218 Sqn		170948	P/O	HEATH Allan Frank	23-05-44	207 Sqn
184075	P/O	HAWKINS Frederick Charles	7-10-44	617 Sqn		1590875	Sgt	HEATH Ernest	12-08-44	1667 HCU
1604329	Sgt	HAWKINS Geoffrey Hamilton	1-03-44	76 Sqn		1337216	F/S	HEATH Frank	18-04-44	9 Sqn
120119	F/L	HAWKINS James Addison	14-04-44	1521 Flt		1443366	Sgt	HEATH Gilbert Thomas James	30-01-44	101 Sqn
1576122	F/S	HAWKINS Vernon Henry	11-04-44	78 Sqn		1891988	Sgt	HEATH Ronald William Charles	11-11-44	467 Sqn
1556207	Sgt	HAWKSWORTH Frank	31-03-44	115 Sqn		1582590	Sgt	HEATH William George Noel	30-08-44	101 Sqn
1592514	Sgt	HAWKSWORTH Ralph James	22-05-44	9 Sqn		153571	F/O	HEATHER Derek Cecil	23-09-44	61 Sqn
1699416	AC1	HAWORTH Frank	10-04-44	Spilsby		169319	F/O	HEATLEY William George	18-11-44	35 Sqn
160208	F/O	HAWORTH John Hereward Titley [Rhodesia]	1-11-44	44 Sqn		1549534	Sgt	HEATON Edward	23-01-44	161 Sqn
						1494490	Sgt	HEATON Eric William	4-12-44	1661 HCU
1863381	LAC	HAYDEN Geoffrey Graham	29-12-44	514 Sqn		1601049	F/S	HEAVENER Harvey Joseph [Eire]	29-06-44	12 Sqn
913140	F/S	HAYDEN Randolph James	26-08-44	300 Sqn		1449642	F/S	HEBBES Arthur Percy	17-05-44	1661 HCU
980744	Sgt	HAYDOCK Douglas	26-02-44	15 Sqn		168829	F/O	HEBDITCH Frank Fearnley	26-08-44	514 Sqn
169583	P/O	HAYES Bernard Michael	25-03-44	44 Sqn		145109	F/O	HEDGES Peter Oscar	5-02-44	105 Sqn
1580268	Sgt	HAYES Eric William	19-07-44	100 Sqn		1604542	Sgt	HEDGES William Norman	16-03-44	76 Sqn
1431388	F/S	HAYES Robert Jeffrey	26-01-44	115 Sqn		1394245	Sgt	HEDLEY Daniel Henry	11-06-44	7 Sqn
175961	F/O	HAYES Ronald Thomas	24-07-44	630 Sqn		1349989	F/S	HEGGISON Andrew Dempster	16-09-44	199 Sqn
2208054	Sgt	HAYES Stanley	24-02-44	578 Sqn		177029	P/O	HELLEGERS Paul Constant Marie [Belgium]	11-08-44	640 Sqn
1623029	Sgt	HAYES Thomas Eric	25-06-44	576 Sqn						
1078009	F/S	HAYHURST Joseph	25-05-44	7 Sqn		2211367	Sgt	HELLIWELL Frank	18-07-44	630 Sqn
1495341	F/S	HAYHURST Thomas Stanley	4-05-44	12 Sqn		1549598	Sgt	HELLIWELL John Alfred	24-07-44	630 Sqn
1892380	Sgt	HAYLER Edwin John	8-08-44	75 Sqn		1437898	F/S	HELM Francis	30-01-44	100 Sqn
1316474	F/S	HAYLES DFM Raymond Percival	21-02-44	15 Sqn		2209214	Sgt	HELSBY Derek Leonard	29-01-44	1660 HCU
1385509	Sgt	HAYLOCK John Andrew [Canada]	22-01-44	640 Sqn		174783	P/O	HEMBRY Jack	29-06-44	432 Sqn
153006	F/O	HAYMAN Kenneth Charles Morris	13-06-44	78 Sqn		1492963	Sgt	HEMINGWAY Harry	19-09-44	467 Sqn
1352506	Sgt	HAYMAN William John	23-05-44	101 Sqn		152478	F/O	HEMINGWAY William Eric	20-05-44	83 OTU
1454945	F/S	HAYNES Arthur	31-03-44	101 Sqn		152583	F/O	HEMMENS Philip Derek	18-10-44	49 Sqn
1320572	F/S	HAYNES Geoffrey Thomas	25-02-44	44 Sqn		84918	S/L	HEMMINGS Garrard Clutton	13-08-44	156 Sqn
1591247	Sgt	HAYS George Arthur	8-07-44	207 Sqn		980268	Sgt	HEMMINGS Harold	20-02-44	78 Sqn
1384255	F/S	HAYWARD Frederick Arthur	8-06-44	15 Sqn		1592635	Sgt	HEMPSEED Maurice	2-12-44	428 Sqn
1151568	Sgt	HAYWARD Herbert Stanley	23-03-44	514 Sqn		168620	P/O	HEMSLEY Derek Joseph	24-03-44	158 Sqn
152963	F/O	HAYWARD Hugh Walter	21-11-44	Fiskerton		152065	F/O	HEMSLEY Gordon William	1-06-44	138 Sqn
139986	F/O	HAYWARD John Victor	20-05-44	115 Sqn		1825899	Sgt	HENDERSON Alastair Millar	7-06-44	630 Sqn
1602875	Sgt	HAYWARD Maurice Edward	24-09-44	9 Sqn		1623053	Sgt	HENDERSON Arthur Ian	12-05-44	9 Sqn
1810699	Sgt	HAYWOOD Albert George	25-04-44	78 Sqn		1823120	Sgt	HENDERSON David	19-07-44	100 Sqn
2220923	Sgt	HAYWOOD James Douglas	12-09-44	77 Sqn		141569	F/O	HENDERSON Frank	27-03-44	78 Sqn
649966	W/O	HAYWOOD CGM Ronald	14-01-44	7 Sqn		127350	F/O	HENDERSON George Simpson	13-08-44	635 Sqn
1802564	Sgt	HAYWOOD William Edward	21-09-44	9 Sqn		1565053	F/S	HENDERSON James Mitchell	22-05-44	630 Sqn
147122	F/O	HAZELL Arthur	6-01-44	97 Sqn		1825541	Sgt	HENDERSON James Williamson	7-03-44	1667 HCU
1896138	Sgt	HAZELL Herbert William	13-09-44	90 Sqn		1075987	F/S	HENDERSON John	14-08-44	83 Sqn
918657	F/S	HAZELL Leslie Albert	15-02-44	35 Sqn		1071348	F/S	HENDERSON Joseph	25-05-44	78 Sqn

Service No	Rank	Name	Date	Sqn
1092311	F/S	HENDERSON Kenneth Michael	5-10-44	115 Sqn
1592119	Sgt	HENDERSON Leslie	31-07-44	103 Sqn
172206	P/O	HENDERSON Maxwell	23-05-44	408 Sqn
144341	F/O	HENDERSON Norman Randall	10-06-44	10 Sqn
1084292	Sgt	HENDERSON Stanley	2-01-44	626 Sqn
1126958	F/S	HENDERSON Thomas Donald	20-02-44	35 Sqn
1592198	Sgt	HENDERSON William	5-11-44	15 Sqn
1711746	Sgt	HENDON Peter George William	24-03-44	12 Sqn
141570	F/O	HENDRY Andrew Gillespie	27-04-44	10 Sqn
1348243	Sgt	HENDRY Gordon Hewett	3-01-44	100 Sqn
1572688	Sgt	HENDRY James	27-03-44	10 Sqn
2215589	Sgt	HENDRY Thomas	4-07-44	463 Sqn
172463	P/O	HENLEY Francis Norman	23-05-44	57 Sqn
1211299	Sgt	HENLEY Maurice Benjamin	22-11-44	630 Sqn
1028076	Sgt	HENNAN Sydney	22-01-44	466 Sqn
1802604	Sgt	HENNESSEY John Patrick	11-04-44	49 Sqn
1497963	F/S	HENNESSY Francis Edward	29-07-44	44 Sqn
165194	F/O	HENNESSY Joseph William	17-12-44	156 Sqn
172573	P/O	HENNESSY Maurice Clement	13-06-44	100 Sqn
1308671	Sgt	HENNIS John William	14-01-44	514 Sqn
171932	F/L	HENRIQUEZ Alfred George [Jamaica]	17-08-44	630 Sqn
2204861	Sgt	HENRY Alan Paul Telford	11-12-44	1651 HCU
131970	F/O	HENRY Andrew Alexander	10-05-44	50 Sqn
136057	F/O	HENRY John Waite	31-03-44	156 Sqn
46126	F/L	HENRY MiD Percy Reginald	14-01-44	7 Sqn
171394	P/O	HENRY Walter	20-02-44	514 Sqn
1605140	Sgt	HENSEY Charles Arthur	28-04-44	640 Sqn
1583433	Sgt	HENSHALL Peter	31-08-44	21 OTU
151014	F/O	HENSHAW Donald Frank	22-01-44	514 Sqn
1350968	Sgt	HENSON George William	24-03-44	12 Sqn
1899116	Sgt	HENSON Rex William	11-12-44	49 Sqn
148014	F/O	HENTSCH Frederick Charles	25-03-44	12 Sqn
1268878	LAC	HENWOOD Hugh	20-04-44	Gransden Lodge
182151	P/O	HEPBURN William Hendry	2-11-44	576 Sqn
1216360	Sgt	HEPWORTH Harold Leslie	31-03-44	156 Sqn
1624606	Sgt	HEPWORTH Ronald	24-03-44	51 Sqn
1029248	W/O	HEPWORTH William Mackie	20-02-44	10 Sqn
1806771	Sgt	HERBERT Frederick William	8-06-44	138 Sqn
2211697	Sgt	HERBERT George Alan	30-07-44	102 Sqn
1822275	Sgt	HERBERT Henry Ernest	14-04-44	5 LFS
142135	F/L	HERBERT DFC Peter Norman	7-10-44	627 Sqn
1178839	W/O	HERBERT DFM Wallace	25-07-44	83 Sqn
1561487	Sgt	HERKES James	22-05-44	460 Sqn
133094	F/O	HERON Allan Gleave	2-05-44	75 Sqn
1143288	Sgt	HERON Kenneth Royston	30-06-44	514 Sqn
1306239	Sgt	HESKETH John	10-03-44	207 Sqn
147672	F/O	HESKETH Louis Milsom	6-12-44	77 Sqn
179215	P/O	HESKETH Noel	23-08-44	1657 HCU
1897455	Sgt	HESKETH Robert Roderick [Mexico]	7-09-44	17 OTU
129549	F/O	HESLOP DFC Desmond Baker Feapon	25-05-44	7 Sqn
1677689	F/S	HESLOP Norman	15-10-44	7 Sqn
1569035	Sgt	HESLOP Thomas	10-04-44	207 Sqn
1880052	Sgt	HETHERINGTON David	28-06-44	106 Sqn
1534026	F/S	HETHERINGTON George Dennis	23-05-44	207 Sqn
172423	P/O	HETHERINGTON Joseph	27-05-44	1656 HCU
179430	P/O	HETHERINGTON Lewis Wilfred	15-08-44	428 Sqn
123955	F/L	HETHERWICK Peter	6-10-44	640 Sqn
1568930	Sgt	HEUGH Robert	6-10-44	78 Sqn
1600431	Sgt	HEWARD William John	28-04-44	15 Sqn
1819684	Sgt	HEWES Maurice Hardy	12-06-44	101 Sqn
139712	F/O	HEWETSON Alan Joseph	29-07-44	625 Sqn
109307	F/L	HEWETT DFM Ronald James	20-05-44	7 Sqn
129480	F/O	HEWISH Frank Leonard	22-06-44	630 Sqn
1565879	Sgt	HEWITSON John	25-02-44	100 Sqn
1490563	F/S	HEWITT Dennis	16-03-44	625 Sqn
1286775	Sgt	HEWITT Herbert	27-01-44	1660 HCU
1450742	F/S	HEWITT Herbert Henry	8-07-44	49 Sqn
161083	F/L	HEWITT DFC John Henry	15-06-44	582 Sqn
183777	P/O	HEWITT DFM Kenneth William	23-12-44	582 Sqn
1320539	Sgt	HEWITT Leslie Bertram	8-08-44	630 Sqn
148737	P/O	HEWITT Mark	6-01-44	12 Sqn
1812711	Sgt	HEWITT Peter Neville	16-10-44	12 OTU
173119	P/O	HEWITT Stanley	4-05-44	582 Sqn
1549452	Sgt	HEWITT Thomas Raymond	15-03-44	90 Sqn
1027513	F/S	HEWITT William	22-04-44	635 Sqn
1609263	Sgt	HEWLETT Roy Douglas	25-04-44	635 Sqn
747760	W/O	HEWSON John Frederick	8-05-44	627 Sqn
54937	F/S	HEYES James	18-04-44	158 Sqn
173145	P/O	HEYS Daniel Sutcliffe	31-03-44	7 Sqn
2221199	Sgt	HEYWOOD Eric William	24-09-44	50 Sqn
170404	F/O	HEYWOOD John Edmund	18-03-44	1657 HCU
149827	F/L	HIBBERT DFC Ivan Alderwin	4-08-44	635 Sqn
1238246	F/S	HIBBERT Keith	24-07-44	582 Sqn
176419	P/O	HICKEN Philip	25-05-44	192 Sqn
153282	F/O	HICKLING Alan William	13-08-44	115 Sqn
1576582	F/S	HICKLING Francis Charles	14-01-44	576 Sqn
1187085	Sgt	HICKLING Roy Ernest	10-05-44	619 Sqn
1331452	F/S	HICKMAN Frederick William	20-01-44	76 Sqn
1321823	Sgt	HICKS Cecil William	25-03-44	12 Sqn
1397995	Sgt	HICKS Douglas Frederick	31-01-44	97 Sqn
1323145	Sgt	HICKS Kenneth Arthur	21-01-44	76 Sqn
2220764	Sgt	HICKS Mervyn Jack	25-04-44	427 Sqn
130619	F/O	HICKS Richard Edward	27-01-44	166 Sqn
1390386	F/S	HICKSON Frederick James Noel	19-04-44	419 Sqn
1442924	Sgt	HICKSON William Henry	29-03-44	1652 HCU
1103376	F/S	HIE Eric	21-01-44	35 Sqn
1522515	Sgt	HIGDON Joseph William	27-04-44	57 Sqn
2205657	Sgt	HIGGINBOTHAM Walter Christopher	6-12-44	434 Sqn
1805365	Sgt	HIGGINBOTTOM John Critchley	17-06-44	199 Sqn
1808537	Sgt	HIGGINS Alfred Arthur John	24-04-44	425 Sqn
984434	Sgt	HIGGINS Charles	19-07-44	207 Sqn
1876641	Sgt	HIGGINS George Albert	8-07-44	50 Sqn
1514419	Sgt	HIGGINS John James Villiers	9-12-44	171 Sqn
169454	P/O	HIGGINS Leslie William	9-05-44	90 Sqn
1109234	Sgt	HIGGINS Patrick	4-05-44	44 Sqn
150335	F/O	HIGGINS Robert Josephus Constable	28-10-44	90 Sqn
1319732	Sgt	HIGGINS Sidney William	13-08-44	578 Sqn
657489	Sgt	HIGGINS Wilfred	8-07-44	49 Sqn
1595916	Sgt	HIGGISON James Lugton	6-10-44	466 Sqn
133333	F/O	HIGGS DFC Douglas George Joseph	14-01-44	101 Sqn
53148	S/L	HIGGS DFC Richard Marcellus	23-09-44	97 Sqn
1615906	Sgt	HIGH Robert Maurice	25-11-44	12 OTU
1390721	F/S	HIGHTON Christopher	11-04-44	635 Sqn
171454	P/O	HIGNETT Kenneth Kinsey	26-02-44	427 Sqn
1383970	W/O	HILDEBRAND Harold William John	18-12-44	51 Sqn
1397651	Sgt	HILDER Charles Alfred	24-03-44	115 Sqn
1520932	F/S	HILDER Sydney Napier	6-11-44	106 Sqn
1250293	F/S	HILDERSLEY Ronald	12-12-44	195 Sqn
1565222	F/S	HILDRETH John Angus	31-03-44	576 Sqn
137168	F/O	HILDREW Francis Daglish Richardson	10-06-44	44 Sqn
1372387	Sgt	HILL Charles Burton	30-08-44	75 Sqn
1574600	Sgt	HILL Charles Martin	20-02-44	10 Sqn
986204	Sgt	HILL Clifford Austin	20-02-44	640 Sqn
185478	F/O	HILL Ellis	11-12-44	514 Sqn
1109630	F/S	HILL Eric	31-03-44	97 Sqn
1352851	Sgt	HILL Eric Reginald	10-05-44	467 Sqn
1436352	F/S	HILL Ernest	23-09-44	61 Sqn
134661	F/L	HILL OBE DFC Farnham	23-05-44	576 Sqn
154358	F/O	HILL Frank	7-10-44	78 Sqn
132036	F/O	HILL Frank David	23-09-44	582 Sqn
158285	F/O	HILL Frederick Brearley	28-05-44	514 Sqn
60532	S/L	HILL DFC Frederick Peter	31-03-44	51 Sqn
1817129	F/S	HILL George John	10-05-44	97 Sqn
1579675	Sgt	HILL Harold Roy	31-03-44	514 Sqn
1810334	Sgt	HILL Harry	27-01-44	626 Sqn
1318035	F/S	HILL Harry Walter	16-03-44	578 Sqn
171887	P/O	HILL Henry Bolton [Eire]	20-01-44	434 Sqn

Service #	Rank	Name	Date	Sqn
1324959	F/S	HILL Henry Oliver	15-03-44	77 Sqn
656631	F/S	HILL John	8-05-44	619 Sqn
1590143	Sgt	HILL John	14-11-44	51 Sqn
126789	F/L	HILL John Rowland	22-06-44	49 Sqn
1023531	Sgt	HILL Joseph	21-01-44	115 Sqn
1601477	Sgt	HILL Ronald Charles	22-05-44	49 Sqn
1323823	F/S	HILL Ronald Patrick Grenville	31-03-44	44 Sqn
2220769	Sgt	HILL Rowland Theodore	25-08-44	101 Sqn
172421	F/O	HILL Stanley Albert	25-09-44	1661 HCU
1535267	Sgt	HILL Thomas Arthur	6-07-44	578 Sqn
1397469	Sgt	HILL Thomas Ernest	17-06-44	102 Sqn
146617	F/O	HILL DFM Thomas Herbert Archibald	13-08-44	156 Sqn
169912	P/O	HILL Thomas William	22-01-44	35 Sqn
1040830	F/S	HILL DFM Thomas William	8-06-44	166 Sqn
1605753	Sgt	HILL Walter Maxwell	30-08-44	463 Sqn
1084513	Sgt	HILL William James	2-03-44	156 Sqn
1600602	F/S	HILLIER Henry Roy	18-12-44	207 Sqn
1851609	Sgt	HILLIER Raymond	11-04-44	619 Sqn
1567503	Sgt	HILLIS John	31-03-44	78 Sqn
1245750	Sgt	HILLMAN Leonard Wesley	7-06-44	460 Sqn
1601538	Sgt	HILLMAN Ronald Victor	3-01-44	156 Sqn
151071	F/O	HILLS Henry Thomas	13-06-44	78 Sqn
147663	F/O	HILLS Michael	11-06-44	15 Sqn
1391337	Sgt	HILLS Walter Charles	16-02-44	106 Sqn
1803216	Sgt	HILLYARD Edward Peter	29-01-44	166 Sqn
1321806	F/S	HILL-COTTINGHAM Edward Francis	21-04-44	57 Sqn
150105	F/L	HILTON Arthur	15-02-44	102 Sqn
1390746	Sgt	HILTON Francis	21-01-44	7 Sqn
1496574	Sgt	HILTON John	9-06-44	51 Sqn
3034356	Sgt	HILTON Kenneth Lawrence	12-10-44	14 OTU
1337618	F/S	HINCH Laurence Alexander	9-06-44	49 Sqn
175573	P/O	HINDE Geoffrey William	22-05-44	550 Sqn
1391619	F/S	HINDE Ronald	22-03-44	97 Sqn
1386334	Sgt	HINDER John Grimes	1-04-44	1656 HCU
2206229	Sgt	HINDLE Henry	14-08-44	550 Sqn
154673	F/O	HINDLE Jack	6-12-44	10 Sqn
144450	F/O	HINDLEY DFC Norman	24-03-44	158 Sqn
747867	W/O	HINES Charles Robert	31-12-44	150 Sqn
1397984	Sgt	HINES John Charles	13-08-44	90 Sqn
1235097	Sgt	HINETT William Frederick	19-07-44	619 Sqn
1074123	F/S	HINKS Brinley Charles	2-01-44	156 Sqn
1651235	Sgt	HINTON Frederick William	25-04-44	16 OTU
1893290	Sgt	HINTON John Herbert	9-12-44	171 Sqn
148029	F/O	HINTON John Norman	19-03-44	578 Sqn
1602893	Sgt	HINVES Geoffrey Charles	23-08-44	1657 HCU
1101877	F/S	HIRST Thomas Johnson	31-03-44	7 Sqn
928092	Sgt	HISCOX Henry John	21-07-44	75 Sqn
187942	P/O	HISLOP Edward	24-12-44	102 Sqn
1594952	Sgt	HISLOP Gilbert Leslie	16-11-44	214 Sqn
1581832	Sgt	HITCHCOCK Norman Peter	5-12-44	84 OTU
157742	P/O	HITCHEN John Thomas	3-01-44	83 Sqn
2203456	Sgt	HITCHEN Roy Challinor	18-12-44	51 Sqn
1175274	Sgt	HOAD John Norman	23-09-44	61 Sqn
108544	F/L	HOAD DFC Kenneth Charles	25-04-44	9 Sqn
576677	Sgt	HOARE Herbert Dennis	16-07-44	44 Sqn
1099356	Sgt	HOARTY John	25-05-44	419 Sqn
1587621	F/S	HOBBS Edward George	23-09-44	50 Sqn
1430022	Sgt	HOBBS Edward Joseph	22-12-44	97 Sqn
1314314	F/S	HOBBS Frank	31-03-44	51 Sqn
1262633	F/S	HOBBS Frank James	16-03-44	630 Sqn
1816098	Sgt	HOBBS Vivian George	23-12-44	582 Sqn
1394703	F/S	HOBBS William John	8-07-44	61 Sqn
975241	F/S	HOBBY Geoffrey	20-02-44	49 Sqn
151739	F/O	HOCKEN Frederick Robert	24-03-44	77 Sqn
1377231	F/S	HOCKING James Charles	13-06-44	578 Sqn
1623536	Sgt	HOCKLEY Peter Desmond	18-11-44	515 Sqn
1628242	Sgt	HODDER-WILLIAMS Geoffrey	11-06-44	166 Sqn
1826605	Sgt	HODGE James	23-10-44	467 Sqn
1561655	Sgt	HODGE James Gerrard	25-04-44	626 Sqn
157045	F/O	HODGE John Sydney	7-07-44	44 Sqn
1321993	F/S	HODGES Edwin Jack	2-05-44	61 Sqn
1675389	Sgt	HODGES James	18-12-44	227 Sqn
574399	F/S	HODGKINS Frank Grafton	15-03-44	625 Sqn
1079224	F/S	HODGKINS John	1-06-44	149 Sqn
1393662	F/S	HODGKINSON John Gordon	29-01-44	10 Sqn
1549777	Sgt	HODGKINSON Kenneth Harold	25-05-44	576 Sqn
1403973	LAC	HODGKINSON Roy	19-05-44	61 Sqn
1104619	Sgt	HODGKINSON Sidney	6-10-44	49 Sqn
1686419	Sgt	HODGSON Arthur	25-02-44	626 Sqn
81736	F/L	HODGSON Francis Everard	29-12-44	170 Sqn
1686216	Sgt	HODGSON Geoffrey	1-04-44	20 OTU
172181	P/O	HODGSON Harold Seth	26-03-44	49 Sqn
984920	Sgt	HODGSON John	28-07-44	101 Sqn
1625672	Sgt	HODGSON John	11-06-44	467 Sqn
154238	F/O	HODGSON Kenneth	29-10-44	582 Sqn
134076	F/O	HODGSON Peter Noel	6-01-44	207 Sqn
135647	F/O	HODGSON Richard	25-03-44	640 Sqn
169014	P/O	HODGSON Walter	14-01-44	97 Sqn
129945	F/L	HODGSON DFC AFM William McKellar [Uruguay]	27-12-44	109 Sqn
1819663	Sgt	HODSON Alfred Arthur Henry	4-05-44	576 Sqn
130663	F/L	HODSON DFC Alfred John Shirley	7-02-44	1663 HCU
1582498	Sgt	HODSON Arthur Reginald	20-02-44	514 Sqn
1822830	Sgt	HOFFIE William	17-05-44	1661 HCU
1520414	Sgt	HOGAN John	11-04-44	9 Sqn
1424592	Sgt	HOGAN Russell Eugene	4-05-44	626 Sqn
1394176	F/S	HOGBEN Robert	27-11-44	115 Sqn
1561925	F/S	HOGG George	4-05-44	12 Sqn
147626	F/O	HOGG Murray Leonard [New Zealand]	20-09-44	622 Sqn
2211120	Sgt	HOGG Robert John	6-11-44	619 Sqn
42310	F/L	HOGG DFC Thomas Leslie	7-05-44	627 Sqn
1191808	F/S	HOLBOROW Richard Frank Bernard	21-01-44	15 Sqn
156071	P/O	HOLBOURN Edwin Cecil	2-01-44	106 Sqn
158423	F/O	HOLBROOK DFC Frederick	15-07-44	156 Sqn
1300859	Sgt	HOLBROOK James Charles	26-02-44	166 Sqn
1622836	F/S	HOLBROOK William Henry	28-11-44	166 Sqn
39823	F/L	HOLBROW Stanley Charles	21-05-44	1655 MTU
1819155	Sgt	HOLDCROFT John Stanley	26-08-44	90 Sqn
1392190	Sgt	HOLDEN Clifton Charles	22-06-44	49 Sqn
1521290	Sgt	HOLDEN John	10-06-44	49 Sqn
173327	P/O	HOLDEN John Edgar	4-05-44	103 Sqn
1394468	Sgt	HOLDEN Joseph Gerald	3-01-44	61 Sqn
2209331	Sgt	HOLDEN Kenneth David	15-04-44	1664 HCU
173631	P/O	HOLDEN Leslie	27-04-44	100 Sqn
1853476	Sgt	HOLDER John Arthur	20-02-44	434 Sqn
1332814	F/S	HOLDER Norman Lionel	15-02-44	77 Sqn
1671139	Sgt	HOLDEN Richard	18-12-44	51 Sqn
133575	F/O	HOLDING Arthur David	20-01-44	617 Sqn
1325933	Sgt	HOLDOM Anthony Joe	27-01-44	166 Sqn
1089015	LAC	HOLDRIDGE Eric	10-08-44	80 Wing
152225	F/O	HOLDSWORTH Dennis Harrington	26-08-44	622 Sqn
1896665	Sgt	HOLE Mervyn	11-02-44	21 OTU
140864	F/O	HOLES Peter William Raymond	14-04-44	5 LFS
1585928	Sgt	HOLFORD George William	24-07-44	1660 HCU
942236	Sgt	HOLFORD William Leslie	27-04-44	83 Sqn
1028124	W/O	HOLLAND Arthur	7-07-44	44 Sqn
702440	Sgt	HOLLAND Arthur Noel Ellis	22-12-44	189 Sqn
1874064	Sgt	HOLLAND Basil Featherstone	5-08-44	161 Sqn
115325	F/L	HOLLAND Christopher	13-08-44	100 Sqn
1580714	Sgt	HOLLAND Frank	2-01-44	207 Sqn
1320772	F/S	HOLLAND Frank George	24-03-44	15 Sqn
1458358	Sgt	HOLLAND Gordon Reginald	29-01-44	90 Sqn
2210768	Sgt	HOLLAND Reginald Frederick	4-11-44	195 Sqn
1396475	F/S	HOLLAND Richard John	6-10-44	78 Sqn
171204	P/O	HOLLANDER Robert Henry Phillip	23-04-44	61 Sqn
1801850	Sgt	HOLLANDS DFM Alan Stanley	27-04-44	101 Sqn
1318586	F/S	HOLLEDGE Francis Reginald	13-08-44	635 Sqn

Service No	Rank	Name	Date	Sqn
3000576	Sgt	HOLLIDAY Robert Henry	24-12-44	103 Sqn
1604186	Sgt	HOLLIDAY William Dennis	6-01-44	619 Sqn
177033	P/O	HOLLINGSWORTH Derrick Reginald	7-06-44	103 Sqn
1800740	Sgt	HOLLINGUM Ronald Stanley	12-05-44	626 Sqn
1623303	Sgt	HOLLINRAKE Keith	21-06-44	15 Sqn
1866571	Sgt	HOLLIS John Henry	22-06-44	463 Sqn
1324480	F/S	HOLLIS William John	25-02-44	156 Sqn
1606440	Sgt	HOLLOW John Theodore	25-02-44	463 Sqn
132882	F/L	HOLLOWAY DFM Frederick George	30-11-44	115 Sqn
1816266	Sgt	HOLLOWAY Joseph Horace	4-05-44	460 Sqn
1891437	Sgt	HOLLOWAY Vincent Sydney	31-03-44	427 Sqn
119215	F/L	HOLMAN Walter Frank Marschlier	5-08-44	166 Sqn
1802916	Sgt	HOLMES Alan John	8-07-44	207 Sqn
1581012	Sgt	HOLMES Albert Ernest	22-06-44	101 Sqn
1056540	Sgt	HOLMES Alexander	1-08-44	101 Sqn
519212	Sgt	HOLMES Arthur Albert	16-06-44	514 Sqn
165695	P/O	HOLMES Cecil Frank	28-10-44	12 OTU
1590154	Sgt	HOLMES Charles Herbert	27-04-44	626 Sqn
1576329	Sgt	HOLMES Dennis Aubrey	6-11-44	463 Sqn
1585099	Sgt	HOLMES Dudley White	30-12-44	76 Sqn
1577142	F/S	HOLMES Frank Norman	4-05-44	582 Sqn
1281476	W/O	HOLMES Geoffrey Charles Christie	6-06-44	149 Sqn
129368	F/O	HOLMES Geoffrey Vernon	14-01-44	432 Sqn
164590	P/O	HOLMES Harold James	8-09-44	29 OTU
162039	F/O	HOLMES John Richard	31-12-44	150 Sqn
132792	F/L	HOLMES Kenneth Thomas Shaw	22-03-44	158 Sqn
1322068	F/S	HOLMES Robert	22-04-44	635 Sqn
1567476	Sgt	HOLMES Robert	25-05-44	103 Sqn
49192	F/L	HOLMES Stanley William [Eire]	20-02-44	158 Sqn
1891514	Sgt	HOLMES Terence	26-07-44	429 Sqn
1810022	Sgt	HOLMES Sydney Charles	10-06-44	49 Sqn
1629647	Sgt	HOLMES William Henry	14-01-44	7 Sqn
1825958	Sgt	HOLMES Wilson	22-03-44	44 Sqn
656947	W/O	HOLMWOOD Jack Norman	25-03-44	635 Sqn
1803277	Sgt	HOLMWOOD Ronald Charles	21-04-44	30 OTU
1131680	Sgt	HOLROYD Frederick William	8-06-44	78 Sqn
2209128	Sgt	HOLT Alan	25-04-44	115 Sqn
1159886	F/S	HOLT Albert Arthur	31-07-44	617 Sqn
1795306	F/S	HOLT Alwyn Evelyn Stuart	19-07-44	207 Sqn
1306958	Sgt	HOLT Blake	31-10-44	15 Sqn
1127147	Sgt	HOLT George Henry	21-07-44	514 Sqn
1681673	Sgt	HOLT Stanley	8-07-44	44 Sqn
1590007	Sgt	HOLT William Alexander	27-08-44	166 Sqn
183746	P/O	HOLTON Jack	9-11-44	625 Sqn
1218832	F/S	HOLYOAK Dennis Gordon	18-10-44	630 Sqn
1585756	Sgt	HOMER Terence William George	30-12-44	156 Sqn
1392321	F/S	HOMEWOOD John Walter	22-01-44	630 Sqn
1321438	F/S	HOMEWOOD Ronald William	3-01-44	57 Sqn
1214443	Sgt	HOND Reginald Samuel	5-10-44	75 Sqn
51154	F/O	HONE DFC Edward	14-01-44	156 Sqn
2221190	Sgt	HONE Sidney George	20-11-44	75 Sqn
1608258	Sgt	HONEY John Richard	24-03-44	625 Sqn
151110	F/O	HONIG Herbert Walter	7-10-44	617 Sqn
172595	P/O	HONOR Leonard	1-07-44	12 Sqn
1319886	F/S	HONOUR Stanley James	29-07-44	103 Sqn
1339243	F/S	HOOD Charles Cliffe Owen	23-04-44	78 Sqn
153235	F/O	HOOD Ivor Harold Robin	30-08-44	550 Sqn
1157678	F/S	HOOD Louis Henry	8-06-44	15 Sqn
1318967	Sgt	HOOD Robin	29-07-44	576 Sqn
1667076	Sgt	HOOD Rubin Iain	7-06-44	9 Sqn
2216027	Sgt	HOOKER Alfred Donald	9-04-44	578 Sqn
137938	F/O	HOOKER DFM Ernest Leslie	20-09-44	622 Sqn
1684873	Sgt	HOOLE Ronald	16-03-44	49 Sqn
1836153	Sgt	HOOPER David Henry	17-06-44	640 Sqn
1394825	Sgt	HOOPER John William	4-05-44	626 Sqn
172176	P/O	HOOPER DFC Robert Cecil	22-06-44	630 Sqn
182014	F/O	HOOPER Terence Dudley	11-11-44	227 Sqn
2217010	Sgt	HOOPER Thomas Joseph	6-12-44	550 Sqn
1577726	Sgt	HOPCRAFT Ernest	20-02-44	156 Sqn
1052269	F/S	HOPE Allan Roland	21-07-44	514 Sqn
54711	P/O	HOPE Thomas William	12-06-44	635 Sqn
127900	F/L	HOPE-ROBERTSON Alastair Tennant	21-07-44	578 Sqn
1546820	F/S	HOPKINS Donald	23-04-44	103 Sqn
1399683	F/S	HOPKINS Eric George	25-07-44	57 Sqn
65997	F/L	HOPKINS Harry	14-07-44	158 Sqn
1337740	Sgt	HOPKINS Herbert Peter	21-01-44	77 Sqn
171701	P/O	HOPKINS Mervyn	4-05-44	169 Sqn
1590534	Sgt	HOPKINSON Eric	23-05-44	50 Sqn
1500726	Sgt	HOPKINSON Samuel	24-02-44	156 Sqn
1890043	Sgt	HOPPER Dennis Albert	15-02-44	419 Sqn
1399532	Sgt	HOPPER William Walter	10-05-44	550 Sqn
175577	F/O	HORDLEY Trevor John	8-07-44	207 Sqn
710203	Sgt	HORE Clive [Rhodesia]	10-06-44	44 Sqn
1266367	F/S	HORLER William	12-12-44	150 Sqn
574273	Sgt	HORN Joseph Kenneth	28-06-44	90 Sqn
152049	F/O	HORNBY James Brooks	6-06-44	149 Sqn
150016	F/L	HORNBY John Clement	24-02-44	115 Sqn
1591255	Sgt	HORNBY Norman	28-05-44	429 Sqn
150111	F/O	HORNBY Norman Henry	12-10-44	692 Sqn
1641609	Sgt	HORNER Arthur William	14-03-44	75 Sqn
123859	F/L	HORNER DFC Cyril Frank	2-01-44	156 Sqn
1321534	Sgt	HORNER Leon	5-07-44	49 Sqn
2211444	Sgt	HORRIDGE Albert	5-10-44	115 Sqn
2209732	Sgt	HORROCKS James	25-05-44	76 Sqn
2208986	Sgt	HORROCKS Leslie	21-04-44	61 Sqn
650027	F/S	HORROCKS Thomas	7-10-44	617 Sqn
1459233	F/S	HORROCKS Thomas	13-08-44	101 Sqn
1588162	Sgt	HORROCKS Thomas Bruce Rushworth	13-08-44	218 Sqn
155866	F/O	HORSBURGH DFM George	8-08-44	7 Sqn
1451575	Sgt	HORSFIELD Arthur	31-03-44	50 Sqn
1387835	F/S	HORSFORD Ray Steele	25-07-44	75 Sqn
161592	F/O	HORSLEY DFC Joseph	29-01-44	166 Sqn
177911	F/O	HORSPOOL Jack Higginson	29-08-44	50 Sqn
1701036	Sgt	HORSWELL Kenneth Alfred	25-06-44	149 Sqn
1851892	Sgt	HORTON Edward Derek	23-05-44	432 Sqn
142461	F/O	HORTON George Aubrey James	8-05-44	15 Sqn
1471891	Sgt	HORTON James	8-07-44	57 Sqn
1219651	F/O	HORTON Leslie Alfred	20-02-44	158 Sqn
175003	P/O	HORTON Peter Kenneth	11-06-44	467 Sqn
957175	Sgt	HORTON Ronald Arthur	31-03-44	78 Sqn
1545049	F/S	HORTON Thomas	23-04-44	7 Sqn
2210688	Sgt	HORTON William Henry	18-12-44	50 Sqn
1873278	AC2	HORWOOD Frederick Alfred	7-05-44	Little Snoring
1852744	Sgt	HOSGOOD Frederick Ernest	21-02-44	115 Sqn
152765	F/O	HOSIER Francis	29-07-44	576 Sqn
1570479	Sgt	HOSSACK Crawford McKerrow	25-02-44	156 Sqn
1321888	F/S	HOUBEN Denis Arthur	22-06-44	207 Sqn
1546277	F/S	HOUGH John	14-08-44	550 Sqn
1819715	Sgt	HOUGH Maurice	7-06-44	1654 HCU
135510	F/O	HOUGH William John	16-07-44	44 Sqn
176435	P/O	HOUGHTON AFM Claud Morley	10-06-44	630 Sqn
1620799	F/S	HOUGHTON Clifford Henry	6-10-44	207 Sqn
2205576	Sgt	HOUGHTON John	21-11-44	49 Sqn
67682	F/L	HOULDEN Sidney Jack	23-05-44	106 Sqn
1580028	F/S	HOULDSWORTH DFM Harold Edward	22-06-44	83 Sqn
1582003	Sgt	HOULTON Louis Verdon	30-01-44	101 Sqn
1443135	W/O	HOUNSOME Harry	5-11-44	15 Sqn
1323885	Sgt	HOUSDEN Ernest George	4-05-44	103 Sqn
1591726	Sgt	HOUSEMAN Ronald	5-07-44	44 Sqn
751251	W/O	HOUSTON John Kesson	1-02-44	239 Sqn
1111046	Sgt	HOUSTON Stephen	15-07-44	1651 HCU
1322132	Sgt	HOWARD Bernard Victor	14-01-44	101 Sqn
104406	F/L	HOWARD Christopher John Geoffrey	7-10-44	617 Sqn
1896784	Sgt	HOWARD Cyril	8-07-44	61 Sqn

1577657	Sgt	HOWARD Eric MacPherson	20-02-44	576 Sqn		1312982	W/O	HUGHES Dennis James	22-01-44	514 Sqn
1313807	Sgt	HOWARD Francis Henry George	9-06-44	426 Sqn		1709121	Sgt	HUGHES Elwyn Rees	21-02-44	630 Sqn
1119630	Sgt	HOWARD Frederick	13-08-44	625 Sqn		2215955	Sgt	HUGHES Eryl Rowlands	3-01-44	57 Sqn
1453876	Sgt	HOWARD Stanley Clifford	27-09-44	1654 HCU		1431375	Sgt	HUGHES Frederick	23-11-44	630 Sqn
997285	F/S	HOWARTH Alwyn Victor	27-08-44	83 Sqn		1672885	Sgt	HUGHES Frederick	22-01-44	76 Sqn
50972	F/O	HOWARTH DFM John	31-03-44	460 Sqn		173818	P/O	HUGHES Gordon John Henry	15-05-44	1653 HCU
2204859	Sgt	HOWARTH Norman	17-06-44	102 Sqn		1893436	Sgt	HUGHES Harold	25-01-44	466 Sqn
1863748	Sgt	HOWARTH William Ley	4-12-44	1661 HCU		1066930	Sgt	HUGHES Humphrey Watkin	20-02-44	156 Sqn
1592318	Sgt	HOWCROFT Albert	23-04-44	431 Sqn		1566653	Sgt	HUGHES James Patrick	9-06-44	426 Sqn
591724	F/S	HOWE Edward Albert	20-02-44	7 Sqn		1120984	Sgt	HUGHES John	16-06-44	61 Sqn
1380267	F/S	HOWE Edward Frederick	14-01-44	432 Sqn		145336	F/O	HUGHES John Douglas	1-02-44	627 Sqn
1461728	Sgt	HOWE Harry William Frederick	12-09-44	35 Sqn		1077667	F/S	HUGHES Laurie Frederick	4-05-44	97 Sqn
1368876	Sgt	HOWE John Tennant	19-03-44	50 Sqn		1442941	F/S	HUGHES Leonard William	29-06-44	10 Sqn
993314	Sgt	HOWE Ronald	16-06-44	75 Sqn		133874	F/O	HUGHES Michael Henry	1-06-44	161 Sqn
1317047	F/S	HOWELL Edward Leonard Colston	16-06-44	635 Sqn		1575442	Sgt	HUGHES Patrick	11-04-44	514 Sqn
144914	F/L	HOWELL DFC Ernesto	9-11-44	138 Sqn		175594	F/O	HUGHES DFM Patrick Anthony	12-12-44	582 Sqn
1851966	Sgt	HOWELL Gordon Charles	11-04-44	10 Sqn		1894389	Sgt	HUGHES Peter Herbert Frederick	14-10-44	115 Sqn
187222	P/O	HOWELL Gordon Robert	8-07-44	106 Sqn		158625	F/O	HUGHES Peter Malcolm	23-05-44	408 Sqn
1316825	Sgt	HOWELL John Glyn	15-02-44	158 Sqn		1317701	F/S	HUGHES Peter Rees	14-01-44	44 Sqn
1581325	Sgt	HOWELL Kenneth Brian	15-10-44	186 Sqn		1591723	Sgt	HUGHES Raymond	11-09-44	51 Sqn
1875086	Sgt	HOWELL Ronald Frederick	25-07-44	640 Sqn		1572188	Sgt	HUGHES Richard	6-09-44	1667 HCU
1102739	Sgt	HOWELLS David	16-05-44	103 Sqn		1451198	Sgt	HUGHES Robert	29-01-44	207 Sqn
160514	F/O	HOWELLS Gerwyn Evan William	30-07-44	97 Sqn		2209477	Sgt	HUGHES Robert John	25-05-44	15 Sqn
1266769	W/O	HOWELLS Ronald	24-03-44	115 Sqn		1797514	Sgt	HUGHES Thomas	31-03-44	630 Sqn
1814315	Sgt	HOWES Charles David	27-05-44	1654 HCU		1818114	Sgt	HUGHES William	27-08-44	1657 HCU
1399427	Sgt	HOWES Cyril	20-02-44	83 Sqn		1893220	Sgt	HUGHES William Austin	25-05-44	158 Sqn
1393541	F/S	HOWES Henry George	31-03-44	635 Sqn		107974	F/L	HUGHES William Edward	3-04-44	80 Wing
1624757	Sgt	HOWIE Harold Salisbury	27-01-44	12 Sqn		175288	P/O	HUGILL Herbert	8-06-44	408 Sqn
945986	Sgt	HOWIE James Napier	19-07-44	630 Sqn		1890106	Sgt	HULL Alexander John	25-03-44	115 Sqn
1626531	Sgt	HOWITT Ian	13-09-44	15 Sqn		657390	F/S	HULL George James	18-03-44	61 Sqn
1584671	Sgt	HOWLES Henry Howard	13-07-44	103 Sqn		1623956	Sgt	HULL Henry	24-03-44	429 Sqn
1614728	Sgt	HOWLETT Thomas Samuel	8-01-44	138 Sqn		125522	F/L	HULL DFC William Edgar	4-05-44	101 Sqn
1867384	Sgt	HOWSER Laurence Arthur	15-10-44	1664 HCU		171901	P/O	HULLAH Alfred Henry	24-02-44	166 Sqn
1592372	Sgt	HOWSON Charles Ashton	28-04-44	1658 HCU		967597	Sgt	HULLEY George	21-02-44	115 Sqn
1570900	Sgt	HOWSON Herbert	29-01-44	429 Sqn		145292	F/O	HULME John	9-09-44	138 Sqn
1437112	F/S	HOWSON Ronald Edward	28-05-44	75 Sqn		1896080	Sgt	HULME Raymond Cecil	23-05-44	106 Sqn
1670542	Sgt	HOY Arthur	6-11-44	622 Sqn		1323051	Sgt	HULSE Arthur Leslie	10-02-44	158 Sqn
174139	F/O	HOYLAND John	2-11-44	61 Sqn		1339681	Sgt	HUMBER Ernest John	21-07-44	12 Sqn
150061	F/O	HOYLE Harold	21-10-44	84 OTU		170143	P/O	HUMBLE John Wensley	13-08-44	578 Sqn
188894	P/O	HOYLE John Isaac	18-12-44	426 Sqn		173448	P/O	HUME George William	13-05-44	692 Sqn
1503849	Sgt	HOYLE John William	25-04-44	635 Sqn		1207777	F/S	HUMPHREY Alec Frank	25-05-44	7 Sqn
161253	F/O	HUBAND Richard Francis 'Dick'	9-06-44	26 OTU		144604	F/O	HUMPHREYS Douglas George William		
1225889	F/S	HUBBARD Frank William	25-04-44	49 Sqn					24-03-44	7 Sqn
1333708	Sgt	HUBBARD Stanley George	25-02-44	550 Sqn		44177	F/L	HUMPHREYS Edgar Spottiswoode	31-03-44	107 Sqn
1323518	Sgt	HUBBARD George Alfred	11-09-44	514 Sqn		1592990	Sgt	HUMPHREYS Gordon	7-06-44	576 Sqn
186586	P/O	HUBBLE James Claude	12-10-44	83 OTU		1449377	Sgt	HUMPHREYS Hugh William	14-06-44	466 Sqn
2205182	Sgt	HUDDLESTON Tom	2-10-44	19 OTU		1395757	F/S	HUMPHRIES Peter Leslie	10-06-44	169 Sqn
1126973	F/S	HUDSON Benjamin Johnson	16-05-44	576 Sqn		1897209	Sgt	HUNNISETT Harry Richard Stuart	21-07-44	90 Sqn
1376055	Sgt	HUDSON Edward Bancroft	10-05-44	9 Sqn		176483	P/O	HUNT Basil Oliver	30-07-44	57 Sqn
1801746	Sgt	HUDSON Francis William	26-08-44	692 Sqn		1586187	F/S	HUNT Clifford Oliver Victor	11-08-44	51 Sqn
1080378	F/S	HUDSON George	15-03-44	11 OTU		1609266	Sgt	HUNT Desmond Edward	25-03-44	166 Sqn
1813316	Sgt	HUDSON Harold Desmond	16-10-44	12 OTU		1582257	Sgt	HUNT Kenneth	3-01-44	156 Sqn
156996	F/O	HUDSON James Victor	24-08-44	1666 HCU		164211	F/O	HUNT Kenneth Alfred Isaac	24-12-44	103 Sqn
1500264	F/S	HUDSON Raymond John	2-01-44	156 Sqn		1396680	Sgt	HUNT Kenneth William Percival	24-04-44	619 Sqn
156283	F/O	HUDSON Robert Frederick	5-11-44	102 Sqn		172474	P/O	HUNT DFC Leonard	28-06-44	166 Sqn
1305510	Sgt	HUDSON DFM Robert Hall	27-04-44	49 Sqn		1577634	Sgt	HUNT Leslie	12-12-44	12 Sqn
3050160	Sgt	HUDSON Robert Henry	15-03-44	408 Sqn		1898110	Sgt	HUNT Leslie Albert Victor	12-12-44	149 Sqn
1594181	Sgt	HUDSPETH Basil	30-11-44	578 Sqn		1218968	Sgt	HUNT Reginald	14-01-44	1653 HCU
1261850	Sgt	HUGGETT Douglas John David	9-11-44	625 Sqn		1319408	W/O	HUNT Reginald Thomas	20-05-44	7 Sqn
1684923	Sgt	HUGGINS Kenneth	2-02-44	432 Sqn		1867689	Sgt	HUNT Stanley Price	4-11-44	195 Sqn
1622403	Sgt	HUGHES Aereon	31-08-44	1654 HCU		1891862	Sgt	HUNT Terence Edward	8-07-44	61 Sqn
921975	Sgt	HUGHES Allen Wakley	31-03-44	166 Sqn		152730	F/L	HUNT William James	23-06-44	97 Sqn
107912	F/L	HUGHES Bernard John	27-08-44	12 Sqn		151249	F/O	HUNTER Andrew Burnet	25-03-44	12 Sqn
1685192	Sgt	HUGHES Cyril Armstrong	20-02-44	408 Sqn		1358626	F/S	HUNTER Anthony Ivor Gwynne	10-04-44	635 Sqn
175342	P/O	HUGHES David	23-04-44	149 Sqn		85249	S/L	HUNTER Colin Harvard	8-05-44	44 Sqn
1133959	F/S	HUGHES David	22-05-44	550 Sqn		1566763	Sgt	HUNTER Edward Hope	29-07-44	619 Sqn
570033	Sgt	HUGHES David Maurice	7-10-44	166 Sqn		1825464	Sgt	HUNTER Ernest William	13-08-44	156 Sqn
526346	W/O	HUGHES David Thomson	16-09-44	199 Sqn		1567746	Sgt	HUNTER George Thomson	19-03-44	20 OTU
982845	Sgt	HUGHES David William	13-08-44	77 Sqn		151099	F/O	HUNTER James	22-01-44	77 Sqn

Service No	Rank	Name	Date	Sqn
1577090	F/S	HUNTER Kenneth	4-10-44	44 Sqn
1531347	Sgt	HUNTER Leonard	11-09-44	51 Sqn
1826736	Sgt	HUNTER Robert	6-11-44	622 Sqn
1084601	F/S	HUNTER Robert John	3-01-44	83 Sqn
1895550	Sgt	HUNTER Thomas Kelloch	13-09-44	15 Sqn
1823886	Sgt	HUNTER Thomas Wyper	12-09-44	1653 HCU
1567320	Sgt	HUNTER William	12-09-44	50 Sqn
1573177	Sgt	HUNTER William	2-11-44	15 Sqn
633310	Sgt	HUNTER William Thomas Robert	1-07-44	101 Sqn
1388025	Sgt	HUNTLEY John Leonard George	12-09-44	640 Sqn
1890773	Sgt	HUNTLEY William James	21-01-44	77 Sqn
1239780	F/S	HURDISS Thomas James	7-10-44	617 Sqn
156012	F/O	HURLEY Alec Richard	26-02-44	239 Sqn
1294364	W/O	HURLEY Charles Henry Thomas	22-06-44	57 Sqn
1457547	Sgt	HURLEY Dennis James	23-01-44	20 OTU
1323550	F/S	HURLEY Ivor Edward	25-07-44	35 Sqn
128524	F/O	HURLEY John Daniel	25-05-44	192 Sqn
1435265	Sgt	HURR Ernest John	28-04-44	1658 HCU
54585	P/O	HURSEY Frederick George	25-03-44	640 Sqn
132848	F/O	HUSSEY John Eric	29-01-44	15 Sqn
1374948	Sgt	HUTCHENS James McArthur	23-08-44	1657 HCU
652906	Sgt	HUTCHEON Robert	26-03-44	10 Sqn
37177	S/L	HUTCHINS MiD Charles John Kenneth	6-06-44	149 Sqn
1825513	Sgt	HUTCHINSON Daniel John	27-11-44	115 Sqn
1439958	Sgt	HUTCHINSON Eric Stanley	4-05-44	12 Sqn
2206021	Sgt	HUTCHINSON Harold James	23-08-44	1657 HCU
1594050	Sgt	HUTCHINSON John	4-11-44	51 Sqn
1874082	Sgt	HUTCHINSON Leslie John Harry	25-06-44	44 Sqn
1533378	Sgt	HUTCHINSON Robert Anthony	14-01-44	432 Sqn
110553	F/L	HUTCHISON Alexander	16-09-44	466 Sqn
1560875	Sgt	HUTCHISON David John [Australia]	8-06-44	77 Sqn
1802804	Sgt	HUTCHISON Tom Atwell [USA]	30-04-44	460 Sqn
1579061	Sgt	HUTSON Kenneth Frank	20-01-44	76 Sqn
176159	P/O	HUTT Geoffrey	18-03-44	434 Sqn
1575248	F/S	HUTT Raymond Harold	16-06-44	514 Sqn
1822192	Sgt	HUTTON John Watson	18-12-44	3 LFS
1378696	W/O	HUTTON DFC John William	31-07-44	617 Sqn
178775	P/O	HUTTON Kenneth Thomas	21-07-44	578 Sqn
1337245	Sgt	HUXEN Frederick Joseph	10-03-44	90 Sqn
148788	F/L	HYDE Charles [Canada]	31-12-44	150 Sqn
118161	F/L	HYDE Horace Robert	29-01-44	83 Sqn
149552	F/L	HYDE DFC Leonard Victor	31-03-44	97 Sqn
1591817	Sgt	HYDES Ronald	23-04-44	9 Sqn
177687	P/O	HYLAND Peter Joseph	28-07-44	101 Sqn
1624645	Sgt	HYMAS Colin	19-07-44	463 Sqn
1494571	F/S	HYNDMAN George Blackwood	25-05-44	51 Sqn
1246104	Sgt	HYNES Thomas Joseph	20-02-44	61 Sqn
1018307	F/S	IBALL William Harold	16-06-44	635 Sqn
1684589	Sgt	IBBOTSON Geoffrey	21-01-44	77 Sqn
176482	P/O	IBBOTSON Harry	9-05-44	432 Sqn
2216149	Sgt	IDDON William	16-02-44	78 Sqn
1324570	Sgt	IDLE Harry	4-07-44	12 Sqn
1375322	F/S	IFE Alan	23-05-44	57 Sqn
1852528	Sgt	ILES John Bickerstaff	24-08-44	1666 HCU
1293340	F/S	ILES Ronald Charles James	28-01-44	115 Sqn
183122	F/O	ILLINGWORTH George Ernest	12-11-44	49 Sqn
1091212	Sgt	ILLINGWORTH John	13-04-44	158 Sqn
1387549	Sgt	ILLINGWORTH Peter Bartley	22-04-44	1660 HCU
1609563	Sgt	IMBER Basil George	2-01-44	61 Sqn
1853808	Sgt	IMPEY William	28-05-44	466 Sqn
1853097	Sgt	IND Roy Victor	19-07-44	463 Sqn
144953	F/O	INESON James Frank	4-05-44	9 Sqn
150115	F/O	INGHAM Eric	27-11-44	115 Sqn
2216043	Sgt	INGHAM Francis William	23-04-44	7 Sqn
1479625	F/S	INGHAM James Roy	4-05-44	582 Sqn
2211981	Sgt	INGLE Geoffrey	11-04-44	158 Sqn
1683129	F/S	INGLE Thomas Dennis	28-11-44	166 Sqn
137140	F/O	INGLEBY Philip	7-08-44	617 Sqn
1711742	Sgt	INGRAM Dennis James	29-07-44	90 Sqn
1851864	Sgt	INGRAM Douglas St. Clair	11-05-44	50 Sqn
116714	S/L	INGRAM DFC George Francis Henry	24-06-44	35 Sqn
160955	F/O	INGRAM John Herbert	22-06-44	49 Sqn
1400819	F/S	INGRAM Kenneth Herschel Callender	1-10-44	50 Sqn
160179	P/O	INGRAM Stuart Biddulph [Rhodesia]	20-05-44	44 Sqn
55287	F/O	INGREY MiD Philip Alan	8-08-44	7 Sqn
174019	F/O	INGS Robert Verdun	13-08-44	76 Sqn
175657	P/O	INNES Arthur Joseph	3-06-44	76 Sqn
117458	F/L	INNS John Howard	21-04-44	100 Sqn
151635	F/O	INSTON John	30-01-44	106 Sqn
1592559	Sgt	IRELAND John Ronald	8-06-44	138 Sqn
174243	P/O	IRELAND Nicolas Arthur	6-07-44	635 Sqn
1361132	Sgt	IRONS John	27-04-44	1667 HCU
1493121	Sgt	IRVINE Charles Alexander	8-02-44	19 OTU
1063368	Sgt	IRVINE John Purcell	21-07-44	101 Sqn
1349829	F/S	IRVING George Roan	30-09-44	23 Sqn
174403	P/O	IRVING John Robert	20-05-44	50 Sqn
153129	F/O	IRWIN James Thomas	9-06-44	1652 HCU
131135	F/L	IRWIN DFC John Gordon	4-08-44	635 Sqn
183398	F/O	ISAAC James	23-09-44	106 Sqn
151994	F/O	ISHAM Stanley Alfred	26-02-44	463 Sqn
634050	F/S	ISHERWOOD Samuel	24-06-44	617 Sqn
1667376	Sgt	ISON Horace	10-06-44	630 Sqn
1631368	Sgt	ISTERLING Eric Frederick	25-11-44	12 OTU
1388628	W/O	IVES James Kenneth	30-01-44	100 Sqn
1873929	Sgt	IZOD Leonard George Alfred	27-04-44	106 Sqn
1822606	Sgt	JACK George McPherson	1-09-44	138 Sqn
1369112	Sgt	JACK Peter	31-03-44	115 Sqn
1553039	Sgt	JACK Robert Davidson	27-04-44	1667 HCU
1365209	Sgt	JACK William Cameron	15-03-44	44 Sqn
1389970	Sgt	JACKS Alfred Ernest	29-02-44	10 OTU
174250	P/O	JACKSON Albert Edward	9-05-44	426 Sqn
1494300	Sgt	JACKSON Alfred Clifford	14-01-44	576 Sqn
1451476	Sgt	JACKSON Alfred Leslie	11-04-44	640 Sqn
172175	P/O	JACKSON Alfred Thomas	12-05-44	630 Sqn
1324269	F/S	JACKSON Arthur Leslie	21-11-44	49 Sqn
1324500	Sgt	JACKSON Arthur Ronald	23-04-44	15 Sqn
33261	W/C	JACKSON Twice MiD Ashley Duke	6-01-44	207 Sqn
1506834	F/S	JACKSON Clifford	8-07-44	50 Sqn
1039306	F/S	JACKSON Crossley	23-05-44	103 Sqn
1892759	Sgt	JACKSON Cyril Alfred Leonard	19-10-44	29 OTU
171902	P/O	JACKSON DFC David Stuart	4-05-44	626 Sqn
159059	P/O	JACKSON Douglas	24-02-44	51 Sqn
1625077	Sgt	JACKSON Eric Hartley Gordon	30-08-44	103 Sqn
186695	P/O	JACKSON Gordon Arthur	6-12-44	77 Sqn
1593864	Sgt	JACKSON Harold	28-11-44	166 Sqn
1684020	Sgt	JACKSON Harold	16-03-44	12 Sqn
655767	F/S	JACKSON Henry	25-03-44	78 Sqn
127619	P/O	JACKSON James Alexander	16-02-44	199 Sqn
928428	Sgt	JACKSON John Douglas Rugg	18-06-44	1663 HCU
917861	F/S	JACKSON John Henry 'Jack'	26-12-44	101 Sqn
171668	F/O	JACKSON John Malcolm Shand	6-11-44	214 Sqn
1459023	Sgt	JACKSON John Robert	23-03-44	50 Sqn
177048	P/O	JACKSON Kenneth Hawley	25-05-44	429 Sqn
1589176	F/S	JACKSON DFM Leslie	28-10-44	35 Sqn
1339328	F/S	JACKSON Leslie Frederick	22-06-44	207 Sqn
1434566	F/S	JACKSON Norman	25-04-44	50 Sqn
1593230	Sgt	JACKSON Robert	6-12-44	227 Sqn
1035003	Sgt	JACKSON Sidney [Channel Islands]	25-05-44	158 Sqn
1072879	W/O	JACKSON Thomas	17-12-44	57 Sqn
1681086	Sgt	JACKSON Thomas Leslie	5-07-44	44 Sqn
134514	F/O	JACKSON Walter Walton	14-10-44	139 Sqn
1577169	F/S	JACKSON William Neville	16-02-44	640 Sqn
1390466	F/S	JACOBS Edgar Royston	20-01-44	83 Sqn
1338808	F/S	JACOBS Peter Alan	29-07-44	1654 HCU
1321651	Sgt	JACQUES Beresford Matthew	8-07-44	207 Sqn
134697	F/O	JACQUES Ronald	11-05-44	463 Sqn
1331468	Sgt	JAEGER John Henry	4-01-44	11 OTU
39634	S/L	JAGGARD Harold Royston	2-01-44	7 Sqn

171172	F/O	JAGGER DFM Brian	30-04-44	BDU	1835953	Sgt	JEFFERY Arthur John	9-11-44	138 Sqn
2205762	Sgt	JAGGER Donald	22-06-44	101 Sqn	1320877	Sgt	JEFFERY George William	31-03-44	630 Sqn
1074626	F/S	JAGGER George Edward	22-05-44	50 Sqn	159898	F/O	JEFFERY DFM Henry William Edward	6-06-44	97 Sqn
123520	S/L	JAGGER DFC John Johnstone	21-01-44	35 Sqn	1870799	Sgt	JEFFERY Kenneth Arthur	31-03-44	44 Sqn
1505659	Sgt	JAKEMAN Laurence	28-04-44	100 Sqn	1800571	Sgt	JEFFERY William George	11-98-44	640 Sqn
136730	F/O	JAMES Brian Andrew	29-01-44	83 Sqn	1896555	Sgt	JEFFREE William John Roy	12-12-44	218 Sqn
1869076	Sgt	JAMES Charles Albert	28-04-44	1658 HCU	1582911	Sgt	JEFFREY Charles Colin	30-08-44	106 Sqn
54855	F/O	JAMES Claud Roy	20-09-44	622 Sqn	1323904	F/S	JEFFRIES Frederick	15-07-44	460 Sqn
64299	F/L	JAMES Clement Hugh Lawton [South Africa]	11-03-44	97 Sqn	1436258	F/S	JEFFRIES Leonard Arthur	6-01-44	467 Sqn
					1863403	Sgt	JEFFS Philip John	25-05-44	192 Sqn
1399446	F/S	JAMES Cyril Henry Robert	31-12-44	218 Sqn	1455075	Sgt	JEFFS Raymond William	6-01-44	103 Sqn
1419573	Sgt	JAMES Cyril Thomas	25-02-44	1662 HCU	972553	Sgt	JELLEY Christopher	21-04-44	625 Sqn
1603174	F/S	JAMES Donald Seymour	6-01-44	35 Sqn	161735	P/O	JENKINS Alfryn James	24-03-44	100 Sqn
1267376	Sgt	JAMES Douglas Edward	29-01-44	630 Sqn	1419911	Sgt	JENKINS David Winston	29-01-44	77 Sqn
182100	P/O	JAMES Frank Edward	27-08-44	625 Sqn	1852243	F/S	JENKINS Ernest Herbert	6-08-44	83 Sqn
1293097	Sgt	JAMES Frank Lancelot	14-08-44	103 Sqn	144925	F/O	JENKINS Martin	22-03-44	97 Sqn
1896671	Sgt	JAMES Frederick Henry William	15-10-44	186 Sqn	1338028	F/S	JENKINS Richard Howell	13-08-44	101 Sqn
1867002	Sgt	JAMES Frederick Thomas	12-09-44	106 Sqn	1451229	F/S	JENKINS Stanley	25-08-44	640 Sqn
55017	F/O	JAMES Geoffrey Watkin	14-01-44	207 Sqn	1262364	Sgt	JENKINS Stanley Hugh	16-03-44	578 Sqn
658864	F/S	JAMES George Lloyd	2-01-44	9 Sqn	1807425	Sgt	JENKINS Sydney Herbert	15-02-44	10 Sqn
1577614	Sgt	JAMES George Widderington	20-01-44	101 Sqn	1585758	Sgt	JENKINS Tom Edward	27-08-44	44 Sqn
659059	F/S	JAMES Joseph Davis Stephen	11-06-44	90 Sqn	2216450	Sgt	JENKINS Wallace Henry 'Wally'	27-04-44	630 Sqn
1818259	Sgt	JAMES Kenneth Thomas	16-05-44	12 OTU	978344	F/S	JENKINS William	2-01-44	630 Sqn
146930	F/O	JAMES DFC Mervyn	22-06-44	49 Sqn	1865677	Sgt	JENKINS Wycliffe	31-03-44	7 Sqn
1604711	Sgt	JAMES Raymond Edwin	22-03-44	158 Sqn	1811733	F/S	JENNER Edward William	30-07-44	514 Sqn
1601379	Sgt	JAMES Raymond George	23-05-44	77 Sqn	1540656	Sgt	JENNINGS Albert Edward	12-02-44	1659 HCU
1896179	Sgt	JAMES Ronald	17-06-44	101 Sqn	2221231	Sgt	JENNINGS David Wilfred	17-06-44	102 Sqn
128908	F/L	JAMES Stanley	27-01-44	9 Sqn	1579944	Sgt	JENNINGS Herbert Maxwell	12-05-44	115 Sqn
145058	F/O	JAMES Thomas Cecil	22-11-44	61 Sqn	411560	Sgt	JENNINGS Herbert William	23-09-44	61 Sqn
135088	F/O	JAMES Walter John	2-01-44	83 Sqn	1590072	Sgt	JENNINGS John Edward	7-06-44	103 Sqn
989723	W/O	JAMES DFM MiD William Birdsall	10-11-44	51 Sqn	1576042	F/S	JENNINGS Norman	23-03-44	50 Sqn
1293578	F/S	JAMES William Douglas	21-01-44	61 Sqn	157100	P/O	JENNINGS Peter Milton	20-02-44	158 Sqn
152150	F/O	JAMES William Kelso	31-03-44	51 Sqn	118399	F/O	JENNINGS Richard Harvey Brooke	20-01-44	18 OTU
163644	F/S	JAMES William McPherson	22-12-44	630 Sqn	174541	P/O	JENNISON George Clifton	13-05-44	466 Sqn
1338403	Sgt	JAMES William Norton	31-03-44	61 Sqn	1585814	Sgt	JERVIS Anthony	23-04-44	103 Sqn
169723	F/L	JAMESON Andrew	25-04-44	622 Sqn	979438	F/S	JERVIS DFM Frederick Joseph Patrick	25-01-44	PFNTU
1280638	F/S	JAMESON George Walter	19-07-44	49 Sqn	1397145	F/S	JERWOOD Cedric Raymond	19-07-44	630 Sqn
1048295	Sgt	JAMESON James Gilroy Baty	16-03-44	463 Sqn	1389427	Sgt	JESSAMY Stephen Richard	22-01-44	76 Sqn
973079	Sgt	JAMESON Norman	26-08-44	90 Sqn	1390320	Sgt	JESSOP David Richard	2-01-44	100 Sqn
1823518	Sgt	JAMIESON Allan James Nolf	31-03-44	640 Sqn	1330507	Sgt	JEWELL Edwin Jack	22-06-44	207 Sqn
1635559	Sgt	JAMIESON Anthony Leslie	22-06-44	619 Sqn	1506251	F/S	JEWELL Francis Douglas	20-05-44	50 Sqn
1007433	Sgt	JAMIESON John	31-03-44	106 Sqn	1401468	F/S	JEWELL Kenneth James	30-08-44	300 Sqn
1551751	F/S	JAMIESON Ronald David Whamond	24-03-44	625 Sqn	1294813	Sgt	JILLINGS John Albert	23-06-44	460 Sqn
168517	P/O	JANES Frederick William	15-02-44	424 Sqn	1601203	Sgt	JOB Donald James	12-12-44	195 Sqn
151458	F/O	JANNINGS John Gordon	29-06-44	76 Sqn	186381	P/O	JOHN Frederick Edwin	12-11-44	49 Sqn
178781	F/O	JARDINE Basil Robinson	29-06-44	102 Sqn	1316412	Sgt	JOHN Glyn	2-01-44	100 Sqn
185218	P/O	JARDINE William	15-10-44	10 Sqn	1656081	Sgt	JOHN Howell	22-03-44	514 Sqn
1432745	Sgt	JARMAN William John	19-07-44	630 Sqn	143416	F/O	JOHNS DFC Frederick Charles	24-07-44	23 Sqn
116797	F/L	JARVIE Rodger Bingham	14-01-44	405 Sqn	909215	Sgt	JOHNS Ronald George	31-03-44	550 Sqn
173911	F/L	JARVIS Arthur	21-06-44	15 Sqn	1897760	Sgt	JOHNSON Adolphus Sylvanus Akinpelu [Nigeria]	24-07-44	1660 HCU
804377	Sgt	JARVIS Barry Wentworth	8-06-44	622 Sqn					
1436651	Sgt	JARVIS Frank	29-01-44	77 Sqn	1580932	Sgt	JOHNSON Albert	25-05-44	51 Sqn
144201	F/O	JARVIS George Frederick	27-05-44	139 Sqn	1812937	Sgt	JOHNSON Albert Alexander	14-01-44	626 Sqn
1319044	F/S	JARVIS Peter Woolvin	17-08-44	630 Sqn	1607088	Sgt	JOHNSON Albert William	22-03-44	514 Sqn
1808378	F/S	JARVIS Sidney Alfred	22-05-44	550 Sqn	161590	F/O	JOHNSON Allan George Garth	31-05-44	630 Sqn
151148	F/O	JARVIS William Leonard	21-04-44	625 Sqn	171726	P/O	JOHNSON Arthur Douglas	20-02-44	7 Sqn
937799	Sgt	JAUNCEY Cyril James	2-11-44	102 Sqn	1578421	Sgt	JOHNSON Arthur James	31-03-44	44 Sqn
1875005	Sgt	JAY Bernard Leslie	9-11-44	625 Sqn	1819247	Sgt	JOHNSON Colin	20-10-44	35 Sqn
106165	F/L	JAYES John Arthur	8-09-44	14 OTU	1013070	W/O	JOHNSON DFC David Walter Thomas	30-01-44	625 Sqn
1324638	F/S	JEAL Ernest	19-04-44	149 Sqn					
174615	P/O	JEANS George Rex	22-04-44	1654 HCU	48317	F/L	JOHNSON DFC Dennis	6-06-44	582 Sqn
170687	P/O	JEAPES Sidney Arthur	25-04-44	9 Sqn	1592490	Sgt	JOHNSON Duncan Alfred	11-04-44	161 Sqn
1390404	Sgt	JEEVES Geoffrey Eugene	19-04-44	625 Sqn	1395353	F/S	JOHNSON Edward	13-05-44	576 Sqn
1811014	Sgt	JEFFCOATE Frederick Robert	25-02-44	149 Sqn	1507974	F/S	JOHNSON Edward Arnold	25-06-44	50 Sqn
1313283	F/S	JEFFERIES CGM Arthur Harrington	31-03-44	550 Sqn	1036704	Sgt	JOHNSON Erod Gordon	31-03-44	101 Sqn
1408444	Sgt	JEFFERIES Henry	14-10-44	626 Sqn	1390712	Sgt	JOHNSON Frederick Walter	13-08-44	9 Sqn
1580896	F/S	JEFFERIES Jack	12-09-44	100 Sqn	1590858	Sgt	JOHNSON George	21-07-44	578 Sqn
1590889	Sgt	JEFFERSON John	13-04-44	90 Sqn	170252	P/O	JOHNSON DFM George Albert	2-01-44	97 Sqn
1482478	F/S	JEFFERSON Thomas	17-06-44	576 Sqn	1611879	F/S	JOHNSON DFM Granville Cyril	14-01-44	156 Sqn

Service No	Rank	Surname	Name	Date	Sqn
146308	F/O	JOHNSON	Harry	16-09-44	90 Sqn
172880	P/O	JOHNSON	Harry	24-03-44	578 Sqn
112784	F/S	JOHNSON DFC	Herbert Oxley	11-05-44	83 Sqn
176437	F/O	JOHNSON	James	21-10-44	75 Sqn
1556755	F/S	JOHNSON	James	23-06-44	76 Sqn
901978	Sgt	JOHNSON	John Alfred	24-03-44	15 Sqn
1591067	Sgt	JOHNSON	John Elliot	28-04-44	7 Sqn
1339937	Sgt	JOHNSON	Joseph William	23-05-44	101 Sqn
957399	Sgt	JOHNSON	Kenneth Lewis	14-01-44	156 Sqn
1530508	Sgt	JOHNSON	Leslie	4-05-44	12 Sqn
2204527	Sgt	JOHNSON	Leslie	23-10-44	625 Sqn
1802410	Sgt	JOHNSON	Michael Arthur	4-05-44	97 Sqn
1398602	F/S	JOHNSON	Norman Hugh	27-04-44	106 Sqn
173903	P/O	JOHNSON	Peter	22-06-44	619 Sqn
169067	P/O	JOHNSON	Peter Lister	4-05-44	169 Sqn
641334	Sgt	JOHNSON	Richard Anthony	4-05-44	460 Sqn
1555812	F/S	JOHNSON	Robert	31-03-44	550 Sqn
1488745	Sgt	JOHNSON	Robert Newton	8-05-44	106 Sqn
650531	Sgt	JOHNSON	Ronald	11-04-44	12 Sqn
1090092	Sgt	JOHNSON	Ronald	15-03-44	44 Sqn
1600380	Sgt	JOHNSON	Ronald Mortimer William	29-07-44	576 Sqn
1314210	Sgt	JOHNSON	Stanley Gordon	8-02-44	18 OTU
1518362	LAC	JOHNSON	Wallace	6-01-44	30 OTU
1835421	Sgt	JOHNSON	William	20-09-44	619 Sqn
1392448	F/S	JOHNSON	William Frederick	16-02-44	102 Sqn
1595015	Sgt	JOHNSON	William Frederick	11-08-44	12 Sqn
1590138	Sgt	JOHNSON	William Harold	25-02-44	156 Sqn
1851675	Sgt	JOHNSTON	Alexander Oliver	31-03-44	101 Sqn
1568398	Sgt	JOHNSTON	Andrew	28-01-44	199 Sqn
1554598	F/S	JOHNSTON	Arthur Gordon	28-08-44	239 Sqn
53267	P/O	JOHNSTON	Donald Charles	20-01-44	7 Sqn
1672996	Sgt	JOHNSTON	Edward William Hargreaves	14-01-44	207 Sqn
1565817	Sgt	JOHNSTON	James	25-09-44	463 Sqn
135076	F/O	JOHNSTON	James Guy	31-03-44	103 Sqn
1821340	Sgt	JOHNSTON	John	13-01-44	15 Sqn
1048606	Sgt	JOHNSTON	John Oswald	22-06-44	619 Sqn
1807870	Sgt	JOHNSTON	Kenneth Harold	18-07-44	158 Sqn
1387379	F/S	JOHNSTON	Thomas Frederick	20-02-44	103 Sqn
1523033	Sgt	JOHNSTON	Thomas Nicholson Cowan	28-10-44	1661 HCU
659129	F/S	JOHNSTONE	Andrew	23-09-44	50 Sqn
1119201	Sgt	JOHNSTONE	Henry	10-04-44	PFNTU
153834	F/O	JOHNSTONE	James	23-09-44	576 Sqn
2203179	F/S	JOHNSTONE	John Martin	30-12-44	76 Sqn
1822545	Sgt	JOHNSTONE	John Peacock Craig	23-05-44	630 Sqn
1115129	Sgt	JOHNSTONE	John Thomas Hughes	5-06-44	1658 HCU
1323968	Sgt	JOHNSTONE	Reginald James	25-05-44	207 Sqn
952397	Sgt	JOHNSTONE	Ronald Sidney	20-02-44	103 Sqn
1523241	Sgt	JOHNSTONE	William	25-02-44	550 Sqn
1522494	Sgt	JOINT	Harry Arthur	3-01-44	103 Sqn
1026509	LAC	JOLLANDS	James John	12-12-44	5 Group
2206449	Sgt	JOLLEY	Joseph Isaac	25-05-44	429 Sqn
1851711	Sgt	JOLLY	Alexander Arthur	12-08-44	12 OTU
1871640	Sgt	JOLLY	Eric Noel	17-08-44	405 Sqn
629823	W/O	JOLLY DFM	Herbert Alfred William	25-01-44	35 Sqn
88240	F/L	JOLLY	Kenneth Frank	7-01-44	1655 MTU
1815824	Sgt	JONES	Albert Christopher	13-05-44	426 Sqn
929021	F/S	JONES	Albert Patrick	31-03-44	166 Sqn
149560	F/O	JONES	Albert Victor Morgan	28-03-44	103 Sqn
1450382	Sgt	JONES	Alfred Cecil	8-02-44	18 OTU
53785	P/O	JONES	Alfred Ernest	27-01-44	408 Sqn
2220848	Sgt	JONES	Archibald Donald	23-09-44	9 Sqn
1739017	Sgt	JONES	Arthur Henry	10-05-44	44 Sqn
571686	Sgt	JONES	Aubrey Thomas Grenville	28-04-44	460 Sqn
1175759	Sgt	JONES	Basil	8-08-44	419 Sqn
142452	F/O	JONES	Benjamin Cynddylan	24-03-44	166 Sqn
701653	W/O	JONES DFM	Charles Augustus	17-08-44	97 Sqn
1338323	F/S	JONES	Charles John	26-09-44	85 Sqn
1391880	F/S	JONES	Charles John	21-01-44	434 Sqn
1494661	Sgt	JONES	Clifford Leighton	13-07-44	576 Sqn
546999	Sgt	JONES	Colin Edward	20-02-44	77 Sqn
1384743	Sgt	JONES	Cyril	1-06-44	138 Sqn
182806	P/O	JONES	Daniel George	19-08-44	635 Sqn
954868	Sgt	JONES	David	25-04-44	100 Sqn
178696	P/O	JONES	David Faulkner	21-07-44	578 Sqn
144926	F/O	JONES	David Gwynfor	4-05-44	50 Sqn
1316138	Sgt	JONES	David John	25-05-44	103 Sqn
975131	F/S	JONES	David Lloyd	19-04-44	115 Sqn
1652460	Sgt	JONES	David Lynn	15-02-44	550 Sqn
1601614	F/S	JONES	David Martyn	19-07-44	100 Sqn
1602369	Sgt	JONES	David Rhys	15-12-44	625 Sqn
186680	P/O	JONES	David Thomas William	1-11-44	434 Sqn
1583686	Sgt	JONES	Dennis	6-09-44	7 Sqn
155338	F/O	JONES	Dennis Stanley	25-07-44	35 Sqn
1412783	F/S	JONES	Denzil	3-03-44	578 Sqn
1867932	Sgt	JONES	Derek Ernest William	17-07-44	149 Sqn
148382	F/O	JONES	Elwyn	30-11-44	115 Sqn
1321095	F/S	JONES	Eric Stanley	25-04-44	50 Sqn
152737	F/O	JONES	Ernest	16-06-44	61 Sqn
1651532	Sgt	JONES	Ernest George	23-05-44	49 Sqn
570004	F/S	JONES	Ernest Thomas	12-05-44	15 Sqn
1012895	Sgt	JONES	Francis Reginald	3-09-44	1656 HCU
630810	W/O	JONES	Frank Price	14-01-44	7 Sqn
1334090	F/S	JONES	Frank Stanley	29-07-44	514 Sqn
2209024	Sgt	JONES	Frank Thomas Edward	13-08-44	101 Sqn
1472177	Sgt	JONES	Frederick Edward	12-11-44	49 Sqn
152726	F/O	JONES	Frederick Walter	27-01-44	84 OTU
54294	P/O	JONES	Geoffrey David	3-06-44	166 Sqn
1420376	Sgt	JONES	George Henry	21-02-44	427 Sqn
127237	F/L	JONES	George Leeson	16-07-44	207 Sqn
2209509	Sgt	JONES	Glyn	24-04-44	77 Sqn
1684714	Sgt	JONES	Glynn	31-03-44	460 Sqn
1892748	Sgt	JONES	Gordon Baden	26-08-44	75 Sqn
1677036	F/S	JONES	Goronwy	13-08-44	83 Sqn
1108838	W/O	JONES	Graham Marsden	19-08-44	83 Sqn
1811331	Sgt	JONES	Graham Randall	23-04-44	514 Sqn
1709001	Sgt	JONES	Gwilyn Teifi	16-05-44	419 Sqn
1125703	F/S	JONES	Gwyn Hughes	21-07-44	578 Sqn
176137	P/O	JONES	Gwynfor	25-05-44	582 Sqn
1397321	F/S	JONES	Halwood Thomas	22-05-44	115 Sqn
1397694	Sgt	JONES	Harold	30-07-44	1656 HCU
1537023	F/S	JONES	Harold Elfed	20-02-44	158 Sqn
54704	F/O	JONES	Harold Frederick	6-11-44	622 Sqn
171287	F/O	JONES DFM	Harry	24-08-44	1652 HCU
176650	F/O	JONES	Harry	29-07-44	550 Sqn
1229734	LAC	JONES	Herbert Bromley	9-09-44	156 Sqn
1652873	Sgt	JONES	Howard Cullimore	4-05-44	207 Sqn
1413674	F/S	JONES	Howard Dennis	21-01-44	408 Sqn
619144	Sgt	JONES	Howard William	25-02-44	156 Sqn
1866363	F/S	JONES	Hugh Brenton	18-12-44	51 Sqn
1661195	AC1	JONES	Idris Eurfyl	10-04-44	207 Sqn
120982	F/L	JONES	Ieuan Iorwerth	2-05-44	218 Sqn
1317668	Sgt	JONES	Inigo Malcolm	15-02-44	115 Sqn
1647936	Sgt	JONES	Jack	4-11-44	625 Sqn
1869815	F/S	JONES	Jack	29-07-44	1654 HCU
610918	F/S	JONES DFM	James Ellis	2-04-44	35 Sqn
1836046	Sgt	JONES	James Ivor	22-01-44	427 Sqn
1384281	Sgt	JONES	James Michael	27-01-44	460 Sqn
1398082	Sgt	JONES	John	26-02-44	12 Sqn
1022998	F/S	JONES	John Albert	18-12-44	51 Sqn
1337834	F/S	JONES	John Anthony	23-05-44	83 Sqn
1530697	Sgt	JONES	John Elias	25-06-44	9 Sqn
1332717	Sgt	JONES	Joseph	30-04-44	460 Sqn
2203542	Sgt	JONES	Kenneth	12-12-44	218 Sqn
170923	P/O	JONES	Lawrence George	29-01-44	97 Sqn
138589	F/L	JONES DFC	Leonard Cyril	10-05-44	97 Sqn
1669239	Sgt	JONES	Luther John	24-09-44	51 Sqn

Service No	Rank	Name	Date	Squadron
1800137	Sgt	JONES Martin Luther	6-07-44	15 Sqn
1212311	Sgt	JONES Michael Nichols	12-09-44	1658 HCU
1605143	Sgt	JONES Norman Owen	15-02-44	166 Sqn
1507140	F/S	JONES Ogwen	23-05-44	419 Sqn
1390870	F/S	JONES DFM Percival Henry Minton	22-06-44	463 Sqn
1622133	Sgt	JONES Percy William	13-08-44	90 Sqn
151767	F/O	JONES Philip Chambers	8-05-44	15 Sqn
1515485	F/S	JONES Philip Griffith	15-07-44	166 Sqn
865682	F/S	JONES Phillip Llewellyn	25-02-44	61 Sqn
139585	F/L	JONES Randall Vincent 'Joey'	20-02-44	35 Sqn
990103	W/O	JONES Raymond	29-11-44	153 Sqn
2208899	Sgt	JONES Reginald Victor	26-03-44	426 Sqn
1547292	Sgt	JONES Richard [Eire]	25-06-44	61 Sqn
127236	F/L	JONES Robert	29-07-44	514 Sqn
1464205	F/S	JONES Robert Hugh	3-08-44	460 Sqn
1694037	Sgt	JONES Robert William	4-11-44	463 Sqn
646212	Sgt	JONES Ronald Claude Hamilton	25-04-44	61 Sqn
151373	F/O	JONES Rowland Woolley	17-06-44	431 Sqn
179429	P/O	JONES Roy Cyril Morgan	27-08-44	44 Sqn
1589217	Sgt	JONES Roy Rees	27-01-44	463 Sqn
45065	S/L	JONES DFC Samuel Davis	31-03-44	158 Sqn
1235025	F/S	JONES Stanley	22-01-44	640 Sqn
2211337	Sgt	JONES Stanley	31-03-44	207 Sqn
148022	F/O	JONES Stanley Edward	26-08-44	514 Sqn
1652966	Sgt	JONES Stanley Lewis	20-02-44	9 Sqn
1431519	Sgt	JONES Sydney James Louis	21-01-44	550 Sqn
3010723	Sgt	JONES Thomas	5-11-44	102 Sqn
970374	F/S	JONES Thomas Derek	25-07-44	514 Sqn
1271373	Sgt	JONES Thomas Edward	20-09-44	514 Sqn
1379411	Sgt	JONES Thomas Evans	28-04-44	460 Sqn
174018	P/O	JONES Thomas George	8-05-44	15 Sqn
1461755	Sgt	JONES Thomas Henry	16-03-44	463 Sqn
1521627	Sgt	JONES Thomas Henry	27-01-44	1660 HCU
171649	P/O	JONES Thomas Ivor	22-05-44	103 Sqn
1578097	F/S	JONES Thomas John	26-08-44	207 Sqn
3031716	Sgt	JONES Thomas William	24-09-44	85 OTU
1414894	Sgt	JONES Tom Milford	30-01-44	44 Sqn
926315	Sgt	JONES Trevor Morgan	28-06-44	166 Sqn
133632	F/O	JONES Vernon Llewelyn Bowen	24-02-44	100 Sqn
1523059	Sgt	JONES Willian Donnan	31-03-44	630 Sqn
1061382	Sgt	JONES William Ernest	22-05-44	103 Sqn
1602237	Sgt	JONES William Frederick Whitehouse	7-10-44	166 Sqn
1131932	Sgt	JONES William Joseph	31-01-44	97 Sqn
135670	F/O	JONES William Llewellyn Wynn	2-05-44	514 Sqn
1317736	F/S	JONES William Patrick	4-05-44	166 Sqn
1312306	F/S	JORDAN Albert Henry James	21-04-44	15 Sqn
3005766	Sgt	JORDAN Harold William Fleetwood	4-12-44	189 Sqn
187254	P/O	JORDAN John Warder	6-12-44	635 Sqn
1586087	F/S	JORDAN John William Frank	18-12-44	227 Sqn
1853154	Sgt	JORDAN Ronald Merrick	22-06-44	630 Sqn
1317098	F/S	JORY Anthony	16-03-44	115 Sqn
126938	F/L	JOSEPH Lawrence	10-05-44	90 Sqn
1419221	Sgt	JOSHUA William Desmond	7-02-44	1656 HCU
149633	F/O	JOSLING DFC John Basil	24-07-44	1660 HCU
1600557	Sgt	JOSLYN Kenneth Sidney	14-01-44	405 Sqn
1603167	Sgt	JOWETT George	3-01-44	426 Sqn
1508672	LAC	JOWETT Leonard	30-03-44	207 Sqn
155924	F/O	JOWETT Rayner Francis	2-03-44	630 Sqn
1339790	Sgt	JOY David Victor	5-07-44	460 Sqn
1397521	Sgt	JOY DFM Frederick Henry	4-05-44	619 Sqn
3012024	Sgt	JOYCE Neville	24-09-44	51 Sqn
162865	F/L	JOYNSON John Lewis	28-10-44	23 Sqn
1393694	Sgt	JUDD James	11-04-44	640 Sqn
53448	F/O	JUDD James Frederick	25-06-44	49 Sqn
1594312	Sgt	JUDSON Donald	29-07-44	100 Sqn
1583474	Sgt	JUKES Alfred Edgar	30-06-44	51 Sqn
1581666	Sgt	JULIAN Richard Henry	23-09-44	106 Sqn
1398872	F/S	JULIER Ernest William	13-07-44	166 Sqn
171626	P/O	JUPP Harold Edward	26-02-44	166 Sqn
3032199	Sgt	JURY Jack Kenneth	6-12-44	460 Sqn
136955	F/O	KADWILL Henry John	25-04-44	78 Sqn
1803280	Sgt	KAHLER Hyman Chaim Mordecai	19-04-44	75 Sqn
1600536	Sgt	KALMS Michael Yorke Zisslin	16-03-44	408 Sqn
1601185	Sgt	KANO Peter Hogan	22-06-44	630 Sqn
1592239	Sgt	KASHER Frank	31-03-44	51 Sqn
1795814	AC2	KAVANAGH Annesley Richard [Eire]	25-01-44	Upwood
1437600	F/S	KAY Alfred	25-02-44	514 Sqn
42006	S/L	KAY DFC* Desmond Hayward Sidley	19-10-44	109 Sqn
1530097	Sgt	KAY Levi Livesey	1-07-44	101 Sqn
121553	F/L	KAYLL Anthony George Randall	27-04-44	156 Sqn
132840	F/O	KAYSER Ronald Peter Nicolas	12-05-44	61 Sqn
1896606	Sgt	KEAN Augustus Martin	28-06-44	166 Sqn
82700	F/L	KEARD John Alexander	4-05-44	101 Sqn
159653	P/O	KEARLEY Bernard John	29-01-44	77 Sqn
1396608	Sgt	KEARLEY John William 'Jack'	24-03-44	115 Sqn
1233707	Sgt	KEARNEY James Joseph	5-07-44	106 Sqn
1584132	Sgt	KEARNEY John Edward	29-07-44	576 Sqn
141566	F/O	KEARNEY Raymond	24-03-44	156 Sqn
1894016	Sgt	KEARNEY Robert [Eire]	24-12-44	640 Sqn
1853799	Sgt	KEATES Henry Mostyn	10-04-44	12 Sqn
1338063	Sgt	KEATING Raymond	22-05-44	156 Sqn
1880365	Sgt	KEATLEY Henry Cyril	30-08-44	619 Sqn
1429335	Sgt	KEATLEY Robert Samuel	20-09-44	622 Sqn
1896361	Sgt	KEAY Edward Thomas Joseph	23-11-44	195 Sqn
137607	F/O	KEAY John Morrice	23-01-44	161 Sqn
1535168	Sgt	KEDWARD Douglas	12-09-44	218 Sqn
850281	Sgt	KEEL Arnold Thomas	28-01-44	115 Sqn
101474	F/L	KEEL Paul Ulrik	4-06-44	16 OTU
110837	F/L	KEELE DFC Brian Rushworth	12-11-44	85 Sqn
1381057	Sgt	KEELEY Donald	24-03-44	115 Sqn
1685186	Sgt	KEELING Harry Vernon	2-11-44	622 Sqn
139378	F/O	KEELING Leslie Charles	3-01-44	619 Sqn
2206220	Sgt	KEEN Derrick	11-11-44	44 Sqn
1578976	F/S	KEEN Richard Thomas	13-09-44	15 Sqn
909313	Sgt	KEEN Victor Albert	5-07-44	49 Sqn
1388826	Sgt	KEENAN Patrick [Eire]	28-04-44	51 Sqn
1114253	F/S	KEENAY Thomas	24-11-44	12 OTU
1577631	Sgt	KEENE Eric Douglas	2-01-44	9 Sqn
1570038	Sgt	KEENEN James Richard	22-01-44	514 Sqn
1126908	Sgt	KEENEN Samuel David	23-06-44	460 Sqn
1890710	F/S	KEENOR Alfred George Alexander	25-06-44	90 Sqn
1892749	Sgt	KEENS George Archer	23-09-44	50 Sqn
1456997	Sgt	KEEP Eric Macdonald	1-04-44	138 Sqn
659155	F/S	KEEPING Kenneth Stanley	28-04-44	100 Sqn
1216415	Sgt	KEETCH Roy Albert Webster	14-01-44	156 Sqn
994243	Sgt	KEIGHTLEY Frederick	31-03-44	207 Sqn
162868	P/O	KELLEHER Francis Mostyn	27-01-44	12 Sqn
54310	P/O	KELLOW Leslie George [Canada]	31-03-44	49 Sqn
1594719	Sgt	KELLY Benjamin	20-11-44	14 OTU
2204866	Sgt	KELLY Charles Philip	25-04-44	115 Sqn
1521682	Sgt	KELLY Daniel	10-06-44	30 OTU
1586432	W/O	KELLY DFM David Richard	22-06-44	83 Sqn
1875358	Sgt	KELLY Ernest George	6-11-44	214 Sqn
1575589	Sgt	KELLY Michael Thomas	10-06-44	207 Sqn
1892357	Sgt	KELLY Patrick	19-10-44	161 Sqn
130515	S/L	KELLY DFC* Philip	21-11-44	Fiskerton
1321703	Sgt	KELLY Robert Frederick [India]	31-03-44	51 Sqn
1605468	Sgt	KELLY Sidney Lionel William	1-06-44	622 Sqn
1553988	F/S	KELLY William	16-05-44	103 Sqn
1568466	Sgt	KELMAN William Ronald	30-01-44	207 Sqn
1795060	F/S	KELSO James Guthrie Wallace	17-06-44	102 Sqn
1081023	Sgt	KELSO Thomas	29-07-44	12 Sqn
1814573	Sgt	KEMBER Henry George	22-06-44	630 Sqn
1214631	F/S	KEMISH DFM Edward James	25-06-44	61 Sqn
1417183	Sgt	KEMP Cyril Raymond	10-04-44	149 Sqn
1861978	Sgt	KEMP Douglas James Ashley	8-06-44	138 Sqn
149253	F/O	KEMP DFC Edward Alexander Louis	14-08-44	83 Sqn
1866112	Sgt	KEMP George Edward	6-10-44	78 Sqn

1592001	Sgt	KEMP George Henry	22-05-44	514 Sqn	174614	P/O	KETTLES-ROY Peter [Kenya]	18-04-44	158 Sqn
1652040	Sgt	KEMP Jack	30-09-44	1651 HCU	1532576	Sgt	KEWIN Alfred	14-01-44	115 Sqn
805412	W/O	KEMP Joseph Charles	9-05-44	35 Sqn	141882	F/O	KEWLEY George Douglas	22-03-44	626 Sqn
1335126	Sgt	KEMP Phillip Alaric	11-06-44	100 Sqn	1587235	Sgt	KEWN Peter Robert	13-07-44	103 Sqn
1397621	Sgt	KEMP Robert Reginald	15-03-44	11 OTU	3010600	Sgt	KEY John	14-06-44	11 OTU
1801055	Sgt	KEMP Robert William	22-05-44	626 Sqn	151424	F/O	KEYTE Donald Frederick Westfield	13-06-44	12 Sqn
1873545	Sgt	KEMPEN Percy George	29-01-44	630 Sqn	1587588	Sgt	KIBBEY Keith Dawson	29-07-44	103 Sqn
1603550	Sgt	KEMPSON John	25-04-44	28 OTU	1894490	Sgt	KIBBLE Denzil Charles	13-06-44	90 Sqn
1585078	Sgt	KEMPTHORNE Ronald Dunstan	30-08-44	21 OTU	1391158	W/O	KIDBY Dennis Alfred	30-07-44	75 Sqn
1276250	Sgt	KENDALL Horace Henry	25-02-44	97 Sqn	151849	F/O	KIDD Alfred	22-06-44	9 Sqn
1593933	Sgt	KENDREW Leslie	6-11-44	550 Sqn	42952	F/L	KIDD Colin Alfred	28-04-44	156 Sqn
1585679	F/S	KENDRICK Arthur Charles	31-03-44	156 Sqn	145374	F/O	KIDD Harold	20-02-44	630 Sqn
2220126	Sgt	KENDRICK Harry	31-03-44	115 Sqn	1621496	Sgt	KIDD Harry Hewitt	13-07-44	166 Sqn
3031120	Sgt	KENDRICK William Patrick	14-11-44	51 Sqn	152342	F/O	KIDD John Allan	19-07-44	138 Sqn
971349	Sgt	KENNEDY Andrew	26-03-44	10 Sqn	2206292	Sgt	KIDD Philip Sidney	8-06-44	115 Sqn
1801582	F/S	KENNEDY David Robert	17-12-44	50 Sqn	1149461	Sgt	KIDLEY Robert Arthur	2-01-44	44 Sqn
1620864	Sgt	KENNEDY Desmond William	18-04-44	51 Sqn	1396509	Sgt	KIDMAN James Herbert	20-01-44	622 Sqn
1822421	Sgt	KENNEDY Donald Thomson	13-08-44	115 Sqn	1475966	F/S	KIEFF Maurice	26-08-44	90 Sqn
54250	F/O	KENNEDY DFM Falconer Milne	6-11-44	550 Sqn	2211230	Sgt	KIELY Edmond Joseph [Eire]	20-10-44	35 Sqn
169432	P/O	KENNEDY Harry Murray	8-01-44	138 Sqn	1650202	Sgt	KILBY Leslie Howard	18-09-44	12 OTU
148471	F/O	KENNEDY DFC James Alphonsus	13-09-44	239 Sqn	1592352	Sgt	KILCOYNE Terry	7-08-44	149 Sqn
2211438	F/S	KENNEDY John	30-08-44	101 Sqn	1568496	Sgt	KILGOUR James	13-07-44	103 Sqn
1323689	F/S	KENNEDY John James O'Neil	16-02-44	77 Sqn	170959	P/O	KILGOUR Joseph Seddon	27-04-44	630 Sqn
1875897	Sgt	KENNEDY Joseph Donald	27-01-44	84 OTU	147636	F/O	KILLE Reginald Herbert	5-07-44	35 Sqn
1784070	Sgt	KENNEDY Leslie	6-11-44	619 Sqn	2235144	AC2	KILLICK George Valentine Frank	8-04-44	1 LFS
162542	P/O	KENNEDY Ronald William	26-03-44	192 Sqn	1615908	Sgt	KILLINGBACK John Harold Bruce	15-06-44	78 Sqn
132867	F/O	KENNEDY DFC Sidney Ivor	2-01-44	101 Sqn	1547059	F/S	KILNER Donald Joseph	16-03-44	514 Sqn
2212847	Sgt	KENNEDY William	17-12-44	17 OTU	979520	Sgt	KILNER Ronald Henry	9-06-44	1652 HCU
1892843	Sgt	KENNEDY William Richard	8-05-44	106 Sqn	2206500	Sgt	KILPATRICK Leslie Charles	30-03-44	20 OTU
1439053	Sgt	KENNETT Stanley Burton	30-01-44	640 Sqn	1437393	F/S	KILSBY Albert Gothian	8-09-44	115 Sqn
1805144	F/S	KENNINGHAM Derek Allen	31-12-44	138 Sqn	1575038	Sgt	KILSBY Horace Sidney	15-07-44	460 Sqn
523674	Sgt	KENNISON James Edward	6-01-44	576 Sqn	1215916	F/S	KILSBY Peter Henry	5-03-44	218 Sqn
542541	Sgt	KENNY Douglas	20-02-44	514 Sqn	1822765	Sgt	KILTIE Alexander Murphie	18-03-44	630 Sqn
1835809	Sgt	KENNY Gerald Patrick [Trinidad]	2-11-44	195 Sqn	986311	Sgt	KILTIE James	22-05-44	166 Sqn
67700	F/L	KENNY DFC* John Henry	7-08-44	139 Sqn	1595368	Sgt	KILVINGTON Lewis	6-10-44	640 Sqn
651216	Sgt	KENNY Joseph Patrick	4-05-44	166 Sqn	1592750	Sgt	KIMBER Bernard Michael	25-04-44	626 Sqn
1388233	Sgt	KENRICK DFM Bernard	23-04-44	61 Sqn	1835657	Sgt	KIMBER Frederick Charles	25-04-44	626 Sqn
1033566	Sgt	KENRICK John Milton	28-06-44	640 Sqn	1581438	Sgt	KIMBERLEY John Kenneth	22-06-44	630 Sqn
1319497	Sgt	KENSETT James Henry	31-03-44	115 Sqn	60132	S/L	KINCHIN Ernest William	21-04-44	239 Sqn
1527435	F/S	KENT Bryan Stanley	12-09-44	100 Sqn	1596079	Sgt	KINCHIN Harry	8-07-44	17 OTU
144046	F/O	KENT Dennis Harold	21-01-44	35 Sqn	1338708	Sgt	KINCHINGTON Keith James	10-06-44	625 Sqn
1575940	F/S	KENT Howard Matthew	10-05-44	97 Sqn	1540685	Sgt	KINDER William Royle	28-04-44	51 Sqn
870252	Sgt	KENT Sidney	31-12-44	150 Sqn	1365195	Sgt	KINDLEN Philip	27-05-44	1656 HCU
172207	P/O	KENT Walter Harris	19-04-44	432 Sqn	1582218	Sgt	KINDRED Eric Warnford	11-04-44	9 Sqn
185554	F/O	KENYON Arthur Thomas	24-12-44	35 Sqn	1801474	Sgt	KING Arthur James George 'Jimmy'	22-04-44	1654 HCU
642691	Sgt	KENYON Ernest	2-03-44	156 Sqn	176014	P/O	KING Clifford Roy	7-06-44	9 Sqn
1527502	Sgt	KENYON John	23-04-44	51 Sqn	1398998	Sgt	KING Colin Rupert	3-01-44	156 Sqn
1865927	Sgt	KENYON Redvers	29-10-44	50 Sqn	978905	Sgt	KING Constant	12-02-44	50 Sqn
1589152	Sgt	KENYON Wilfred Owen	27-08-44	576 Sqn	1590536	Sgt	KING Desmond	28-04-44	15 Sqn
653560	Sgt	KEOGH John Edward	22-06-44	101 Sqn	145501	F/O	KING Donald Hugh	19-04-44	28 OTU
1473056	F/S	KERFOOT Albert Henry	14-10-44	153 Sqn	1802260	Sgt	KING Frank Benjamin Gregory	20-10-44	460 Sqn
1490317	Sgt	KERFOOT John	31-07-44	9 Sqn	1892896	Sgt	KING Frank Desmond	25-04-44	115 Sqn
1341586	Sgt	KERMACK James Thomson	15-07-44	550 Sqn	1602002	Sgt	KING George Edward	8-06-44	166 Sqn
177752	P/O	KERNAHAN John	8-07-44	49 Sqn	152912	F/O	KING James Charles	6-10-44	49 Sqn
172462	P/O	KERNAHAN Kenneth Ian [Trinidad]	28-05-44	12 Sqn	1395486	Sgt	KING John James	11-04-44	622 Sqn
1826297	Sgt	KERR Alexander George	26-08-44	626 Sqn	149202	F/O	KING DFC Kenneth Henry	31-10-44	128 Sqn
1503951	AC1	KERR Malcolm Gilbert	13-10-44	149 Sqn	149660	F/O	KING DFC Leslie William John	24-06-44	617 Sqn
1392387	F/S	KERR Peter Graham Lamont	6-01-44	97 Sqn	1331323	F/S	KING Peter Charles	14-01-44	156 Sqn
1495199	Sgt	KERR Samuel Taylor	13-09-44	625 Sqn	1394149	Sgt	KING Peter Charles Morrell	28-05-44	550 Sqn
171678	F/O	KERR William Thomson	21-12-44	109 Sqn	1321023	Sgt	KING Robert Joseph	27-01-44	18 OTU
178829	P/O	KERRUISH George Archibald	28-06-44	640 Sqn	1892478	Sgt	KING Ronald	28-12-44	101 Sqn
2221041	Sgt	KERRY John	27-01-44	1660 HCU	37857	S/L	KING MiD Terence Sydney Raymond	10-03-44	90 Sqn
1324503	F/S	KERSEY Douglas William Anthony	24-04-44	619 Sqn	924601	AC1	KING Thomas	8-04-44	1 LFS
1509854	LAC	KERSLAKE John	26-12-44	73 Base	1148328	Sgt	KING DFM Thomas	21-01-44	77 Sqn
183589	F/O	KERSLAKE Thomas Edward	27-09-44	619 Sqn	1802538	Sgt	KING Trevor Reginald	27-01-44	426 Sqn
1540856	Sgt	KERWIN Ernest	19-04-44	115 Sqn	1269972	Sgt	KING Walter Charles William	24-03-44	432 Sqn
1897268	F/S	KESTEN George	4-11-44	101 Sqn	93613	Cpl	KING William	22-05-44	33 Base
168963	P/O	KETCHER DFM Gerald Ralph	20-01-44	426 Sqn	1316912	F/S	KING William Joseph	10-08-44	50 Sqn
591864	F/S	KETLEY-ROLPH Reginald John	12-12-44	218 Sqn	1035031	Sgt	KING William Patrick Joseph	25-02-44	419 Sqn

Service No.	Rank	Name	Date	Unit
174119	P/O	KINGHAM Ernest Arthur	16-06-44	514 Sqn
1351436	Sgt	KINGHAM William	21-01-44	431 Sqn
1334271	Sgt	KINGMAN Eric Ronald	12-05-44	61 Sqn
1871565	Sgt	KINGMAN Phillip Reginald	3-11-44	550 Sqn
1394618	Sgt	KINGSMILL Stanley George	28-04-44	11 OTU
133610	F/L	KINGWELL Leonard John	20-02-44	514 Sqn
150440	F/O	KINMAN Jack	12-12-44	582 Sqn
1569829	Sgt	KINNEAR Robert Peebles	19-07-44	425 Sqn
1522824	Sgt	KINNES William Duncan	19-04-44	57 Sqn
151245	F/O	KINSELLA Patrick	21-02-44	78 Sqn
1582720	Sgt	KINSEY John Spencer	25-08-44	101 Sqn
635898	W/O	KINSEY William Edmund	26-08-44	635 Sqn
1692998	Sgt	KINVIG Clifford Clarke	2-07-44	103 Sqn
172900	P/O	KIPPEN DFC Ernest McClure	31-03-44	101 Sqn
185652	P/O	KIRBY Charles Frederick	23-10-44	463 Sqn
1860956	Sgt	KIRBY Eric Raymond Sidney	23-06-44	626 Sqn
1333680	F/S	KIRBY George Bowering	6-10-44	106 Sqn
1811158	Sgt	KIRBY Terence	23-04-44	166 Sqn
39103	S/L	KIRBY-GREEN Thomas Gresham	29-03-44	40 Sqn
1459772	F/S	KIRK Andrew Joseph	20-02-44	576 Sqn
1602413	Sgt	KIRK Charles William	8-06-44	15 Sqn
1827419	Sgt	KIRK John	22-07-44	20 OTU
1334735	F/S	KIRK Ronald George Henry	28-06-44	166 Sqn
1117305	Sgt	KIRKHAM Leonard	25-04-44	166 Sqn
182189	P/O	KIRKLAND David Sinclair	13-08-44	640 Sqn
1581273	F/S	KIRKLAND Samuel Edward	21-07-44	115 Sqn
1184749	Sgt	KIRKPATRICK George Edward	29-07-44	49 Sqn
143805	F/L	KIRKPATRICK DFC John	9-12-44	171 Sqn
144459	F/O	KIRKPATRICK William Leopold Carver	2-03-44	630 Sqn
41771	S/L	KIRTON James Hughes	27-01-44	84 OTU
174112	P/O	KIRTON John Stanley	13-06-44	166 Sqn
1591092	Sgt	KIRTON William David	25-05-44	103 Sqn
1067998	Sgt	KIRWAN DFM John Anthony [Eire]	8-07-44	49 Sqn
173155	P/O	KITCHEN DFC Alfred Edward	28-11-44	109 Sqn
1199896	F/S	KITSON William	20-02-44	576 Sqn
619400	W/O	KITTO DFM Henry	6-06-44	582 Sqn
1332685	F/S	KITTO Philip Malcolm	26-07-44	49 Sqn
523468	Sgt	KNAPMAN Charles Robert	29-07-44	467 Sqn
1604544	Sgt	KNAPP Alan Wilfred	16-05-44	576 Sqn
1607110	Sgt	KNAPP Francis Norman	29-07-44	576 Sqn
1681317	F/S	KNAPTON Ronald	21-07-44	75 Sqn
1608360	Sgt	KNELLER Alan Francis	18-04-44	158 Sqn
126681	F/O	KNIGHT Bernard Ellis	17-05-44	571 Sqn
52153	F/O	KNIGHT Earl Allan	26-02-44	239 Sqn
1895706	Sgt	KNIGHT Ernest Percival	7-10-44	78 Sqn
1396522	Sgt	KNIGHT George Edward	20-02-44	514 Sqn
1867701	Sgt	KNIGHT Henry Robert	7-10-44	514 Sqn
1549787	Sgt	KNIGHT John	27-08-44	625 Sqn
1090507	F/S	KNIGHT John Bernard	22-06-44	97 Sqn
1602007	F/S	KNIGHT Kenneth	20-02-44	35 Sqn
1395508	F/S	KNIGHT Roy Harry	26-03-44	460 Sqn
938113	F/S	KNIGHT Walter David	8-06-44	101 Sqn
1674986	Sgt	KNIGHTON Leslie	5-12-44	84 OTU
1044234	F/S	KNIGHTS Jack	24-03-44	514 Sqn
858763	Sgt	KNOTT John Edward	20-10-44	550 Sqn
1468044	Sgt	KNOTT John Marsland	21-04-44	625 Sqn
1052000	W/O	KNOWLES Donald Russell	16-03-44	12 Sqn
1324832	Sgt	KNOWLES Douglas John	2-05-44	10 Sqn
55042	F/O	KNOWLES John Joseph	16-03-44	49 Sqn
1684763	Sgt	KNOWLES Robert Henry	23-06-44	100 Sqn
172412	P/O	KNOWLES Wilfred Martin	1-07-44	1 GpSDFlt
2209802	Sgt	KNOX Kenneth Frederick	5-11-44	15 Sqn
1640191	Sgt	KOFOED Peter Joseph John	20-05-44	7 Sqn
158038	P/O	KULARATNE Ananda	16-02-44	102 Sqn
1179762	Sgt	KUMAR Vijendra	3-06-44	10 Sqn
1332603	Sgt	LABERN Stephen Francis	13-07-44	103 Sqn
1820269	Sgt	LACKIE George	22-06-44	207 Sqn
1576434	F/S	LACEY-JOHNSON Nigel Arthur	4-05-44	101 Sqn
173283	F/O	LACY DFC Clifford	19-07-44	49 Sqn
931729	W/O	LAGDON Stanley Alfred	12-02-44	419 Sqn
3021455	Sgt	LAIDLAW Albert	14-10-44	550 Sqn
1055861	F/S	LAIDLAW Douglas Batholomew	26-03-44	626 Sqn
152788	F/O	LAING Geoffrey	23-10-44	625 Sqn
147526	F/O	LAING John Rollo	24-03-44	514 Sqn
135875	F/O	LAING Thomas Charles	27-01-44	576 Sqn
177512	P/O	LAIRD Sinclair Mackay	25-07-44	1667 HCU
158131	F/O	LAISHLEY Charles Edwin	26-09-44	405 Sqn
1583806	Sgt	LAISHLEY Ronald Frederick	14-01-44	514 Sqn
1573789	Sgt	LAMB George Brown	1-02-44	1660 HCU
3040171	Sgt	LAMB Gerald	15-10-44	90 Sqn
1324182	F/S	LAMB John George	20-11-44	14 OTU
1320433	Sgt	LAMB Leonard Ernest	23-04-44	7 Sqn
1852855	Sgt	LAMB Michael George	16-09-44	582 Sqn
1019200	F/S	LAMB Thomas Leslie	23-05-44	207 Sqn
1594880	Sgt	LAMBELL James	31-08-44	1654 HCU
1387055	F/S	LAMBERT Frederick Walter	23-04-44	218 Sqn
63419	S/L	LAMBERT DFC George Frank [Australia]	5-07-44	35 Sqn
152790	F/O	LAMBERT George Stanley	11-10-44	101 Sqn
1549739	Sgt	LAMBERT Herbert	29-07-44	50 Sqn
1339964	Sgt	LAMBERT John James	19-03-44	192 Sqn
148827	F/O	LAMBERT DFC Kenneth James	28-05-44	640 Sqn
1637396	Sgt	LAMBERT Percival Harold	31-03-44	12 Sqn
145181	F/O	LAMBERT DFM William Tharves	23-12-44	109 Sqn
150466	F/L	LAMBERTON James Alan	29-09-44	161 Sqn
145594	F/O	LAMBTON Donald Bell	29-07-44	630 Sqn
1581207	F/S	LAMMAS Robert Charles Ernest	14-10-44	153 Sqn
947546	W/O	LAMONBY Joseph	20-05-44	7 Sqn
973493	Sgt	LAMOND William Hopkirk	1-05-44	514 Sqn
1432986	F/S	LAMPKIN William Alfred	25-02-44	12 Sqn
1384535	F/S	LAMPREY Peter Henry	14-01-44	101 Sqn
155909	P/O	LANAGHAN John	22-01-44	51 Sqn
1522817	Sgt	LANAGHAN Leo	31-03-44	78 Sqn
1150826	Sgt	LANCASTER Eric	26-08-44	635 Sqn
1455345	Sgt	LANCASTER John Asplin	10-03-44	11 OTU
149692	F/O	LANCE DFC Adrian Charles Edward	17-05-44	29 OTU
1869132	Sgt	LANCELEY Stanley Eric	9-07-44	622 Sqn
657030	Sgt	LANDAU Henry	22-01-44	166 Sqn
1536715	Sgt	LANDEN Arthur	20-01-44	102 Sqn
1082729	Sgt	LANDLES John	15-02-44	115 Sqn
1266011	Sgt	LANDON John Conybeare	20-02-44	625 Sqn
651329	Sgt	LANE Eric Arthur	14-01-44	405 Sqn
932746	F/S	LANE Ernest Allan [Canada]	22-01-44	514 Sqn
1682895	F/S	LANE DFM George William	17-12-44	50 Sqn
1853600	Sgt	LANE Henry Joseph Lawrence Michael	8-06-44	115 Sqn
1376435	W/O	LANE John Frederick	22-06-44	50 Sqn
1609246	Sgt	LANE John William	8-06-44	640 Sqn
174127	P/O	LANE Leslie George	15-02-44	630 Sqn
1895981	Sgt	LANE Robert	29-07-44	514 Sqn
1890849	Sgt	LANE Robert Myall	31-03-44	97 Sqn
613629	F/S	LANE William	21-07-44	90 Sqn
1894750	Sgt	LANE William	24-04-44	21 OTU
1892373	Sgt	LANG Henry G.	12-04-44	619 Sqn
1823515	Sgt	LANG John Archibald	16-03-44	1664 HCU
1896528	Sgt	LANG Raymond Stanley	21-07-44	75 Sqn
1303972	Sgt	LANGAN Thomas	7-06-44	115 Sqn
171907	P/O	LANGFORD DFC Denis	24-06-44	156 Sqn
173918	P/O	LANGFORD George Albert	25-05-44	576 Sqn
1575129	F/S	LANGFORD Robert Donald	22-05-44	514 Sqn
158023	P/O	LANGFORD Victor Arthur Reginald	20-07-44	83 Sqn
132813	F/L	LANGHAM DFC Douglas Frank	15-02-44	7 Sqn
156735	P/O	LANGLEY Frank	27-01-44	61 Sqn
1605104	Sgt	LANGLEY Norman Isaac	26-11-44	49 Sqn
1897749	Sgt	LANGRIDGE Alan Ambrose Michael	27-08-44	630 Sqn
1812710	Sgt	LANGRIDGE Alfred Frank	19-04-44	115 Sqn
141691	F/O	LANGSTON Francis Samuel	11-04-44	158 Sqn
45973	S/L	LANGTON AFC DFM Robert Thomas	28-10-44	76 Sqn

1822461	Sgt	LANGTON James	1-11-44	426 Sqn
1852359	Sgt	LANGSTONE Albert Frederick	4-12-44	207 Sqn
53279	P/O	LANGWORTHY DFM Alfred Leslie	10-01-44	1652 HCU
1821076	Sgt	LANNIGAN Willliam	20-02-44	514 Sqn
1459947	Sgt	LAPES Joseph Jackson	22-03-44	100 Sqn
2210592	F/S	LAPPIN Robert George	19-07-44	207 Sqn
1295704	F/S	LAPTHORNE Leonard Norman	3-01-44	156 Sqn
1586818	Sgt	LARBY Alfred Jack	3-01-44	103 Sqn
138133	F/O	LARBY Harold Joseph	22-05-44	207 Sqn
151726	F/O	LARCEY George Frederick	26-07-44	157 Sqn
1332939	Sgt	LARCOME Raymond	23-09-44	50 Sqn
151473	F/O	LARGE Cyril	29-01-44	10 Sqn
1189479	W/O	LARKINS Alfred Robert Patrick	8-06-44	156 Sqn
151847	F/O	LARMAN Kenneth Thomas	4-05-44	626 Sqn
1206400	F/S	LARNER Ronald James	29-02-44	10 OTU
1895307	Sgt	LAROCHE Robert Bernard	28-04-44	51 Sqn
151852	F/O	LARSEN John Larsenius	31-03-44	207 Sqn
1594764	Sgt	LARVIN William Patrick	26-03-44	49 Sqn
1332109	W/O	LASSAM John Ludlow	21-07-44	514 Sqn
173614	P/O	LASSEY George	2-05-44	10 Sqn
1038622	Sgt	LATCHFORD Philip	18-04-44	51 Sqn
1576723	Sgt	LATHAM Alan	31-03-44	207 Sqn
1535809	Sgt	LATHAM Malcolm	20-02-44	626 Sqn
54355	P/O	LATHAM MiD Robert	29-01-44	625 Sqn
1850362	Sgt	LATHAM Warren Herbert	19-07-44	50 Sqn
1570743	Sgt	LATIMER William McCreadie	17-06-44	199 Sqn
1570546	Sgt	LAUDER John Adam	17-06-44	77 Sqn
1334234	Sgt	LAUGHLIN Ivor Eugene	27-03-44	10 Sqn
171908	P/O	LAURENS DFM John	20-02-44	101 Sqn
1398485	Sgt	LAVENDER John Charles Anthony	25-03-44	625 Sqn
1808343	Sgt	LAVER Leslie Norman John	14-01-44	97 Sqn
1528071	Sgt	LAVERICK Raymond	14-01-44	550 Sqn
143286	F/O	LAW Derek Cunningham	12-09-44	90 Sqn
171852	P/O	LAW Frank	20-02-44	103 Sqn
1537400	F/S	LAW James	25-05-44	640 Sqn
1246248	F/S	LAW Robert George	8-08-44	7 Sqn
623480	Sgt	LAWLER Douglas John	17-06-44	103 Sqn
1579443	F/S	LAWLEY Raymond	31-03-44	635 Sqn
1234719	Sgt	LAWN Percy Reginald	19-03-44	101 Sqn
1268110	W/O	LAWRANCE DFM Charles Henry	14-01-44	156 Sqn
1319292	F/S	LAWRENCE Alfred George	20-05-44	7 Sqn
175640	P/O	LAWRENCE George Cathness	13-06-44	578 Sqn
153629	F/O	LAWRENCE Gordon	30-08-44	50 Sqn
1661026	Sgt	LAWRENCE Harold Raymond	31-03-44	576 Sqn
575685	F/S	LAWRENCE Keith Gilbert	23-05-44	50 Sqn
1147982	F/S	LAWRENCE DFM Leonard	22-06-44	630 Sqn
1818865	Sgt	LAWRENCE Neville	14-10-44	153 Sqn
1850459	Sgt	LAWRENCE Percival Alfred Dowding	23-06-44	626 Sqn
1581062	Sgt	LAWRENCE Ronald Victor	22-05-44	630 Sqn
1030402	Sgt	LAWRIE Alexander William	2-01-44	207 Sqn
1568089	Sgt	LAWRIE George Law	12-09-44	630 Sqn
1822199	Sgt	LAWRIE James Bell	13-07-44	166 Sqn
1450070	Sgt	LAWRY Kenneth	11-04-44	158 Sqn
149628	F/O	LAWSON George Simpson	23-12-44	35 Sqn
1668021	Sgt	LAWSON Gerald Bennett	24-01-44	14 OTU
1595595	Sgt	LAWSON John	8-11-44	218 Sqn
1590008	Sgt	LAWSON Thomas	23-10-44	76 Sqn
533023	Sgt	LAWSON Wilfred	27-01-44	626 Sqn
101561	F/L	LAWSON-TANCRED Anthony Thomas	14-01-44	49 Sqn
2209661	Sgt	LAWTON Walter Joseph	31-05-44	1654 HCU
1852128	Sgt	LAX Douglas Graham	31-03-44	460 Sqn
1816757	Sgt	LAXTON Kenneth Edgar	18-06-44	115 Sqn
1695288	Sgt	LAYBOURNE Roy William	27-04-44	12 Sqn
152935	F/O	LAYCOCK Derrick	26-08-44	626 Sqn
129404	F/L	LAYLEY Ronald George	14-01-44	7 Sqn
183715	P/O	LAYTON-SMITH Michael Stuart	19-08-44	7 Sqn
121466	F/L	LAZENBY DFC Alan Lansdale	3-01-44	101 Sqn
1472369	Sgt	LEA Jack Vernon	11-06-44	75 Sqn
159456	F/O	LEACH Gordon Noble	27-05-44	1654 HCU
1429200	AC1	LEACH Harry George	29-12-44	514 Sqn
154354	F/O	LEADBEATER Jack	30-08-44	90 Sqn
1483819	LAC	LEADBITTER George	26-10-44	5 Group
153567	F/O	LEAH Edmund	8-08-44	15 Sqn
1801148	F/S	LEAHY Anthony Fenton Gillman	22-03-44	7 Sqn
173969	P/O	LEAHY Frank George	31-03-44	408 Sqn
1295928	Sgt	LEAME Albert Henry	11-08-44	51 Sqn
623992	Sgt	LEANEY Francis Michael [Australia]	13-06-44	622 Sqn
2220239	Sgt	LEATHAM Leonard Granville	6-07-44	578 Sqn
2209059	F/S	LEATHAM Robert Edward	16-05-44	576 Sqn
2209647	Sgt	LEATHER Peter John	27-08-44	90 Sqn
1802905	Sgt	LEATHERBARROW Dyson	6-01-44	12 Sqn
85674	S/L	LEATHERLAND AFC Douglas	21-04-44	97 Sqn
1575439	F/S	LEAVESLEY William Desmond	16-09-44	405 Sqn
934222	Sgt	LEBATT William Henry Garrett	19-07-44	619 Sqn
1593894	Sgt	LEDGER Anthony	23-09-44	463 Sqn
1821552	Sgt	LEDINGHAM William Ferguson	29-01-44	576 Sqn
1874595	Sgt	LEE Augustus Ernest	23-05-44	103 Sqn
1895651	Sgt	LEE Bernard Jack	7-06-44	115 Sqn
1144562	Sgt	LEE Charles Geoffrey	13-05-44	640 Sqn
1677312	Sgt	LEE Eric	22-03-44	49 Sqn
1835870	Sgt	LEE Ernest Roy	16-03-44	420 Sqn
1128432	F/S	LEE Jack	6-10-44	115 Sqn
128936	F/L	LEE DFC James Henry Stallwood	23-04-44	106 Sqn
1528812	Sgt	LEE John Cottis	27-01-44	626 Sqn
1614168	Sgt	LEE Raymond Leslie	19-07-44	138 Sqn
1398774	Sgt	LEE Roy	27-08-44	576 Sqn
154088	F/O	LEE Samuel Tudor	12-12-44	15 Sqn
1497200	Sgt	LEE Stanley	28-04-44	15 Sqn
1676235	Sgt	LEE Thomas Robson	21-01-44	434 Sqn
1521133	Sgt	LEE William	22-04-44	635 Sqn
1592493	Sgt	LEEMING Cyril	23-10-44	44 Sqn
2219210	Sgt	LEEMING Thomas	12-12-44	195 Sqn
138084	F/O	LEES Alexander	24-03-44	78 Sqn
174542	P/O	LEES Archibald Macpherson	22-04-44	1660 HCU
1566424	Sgt	LEES Charles Grey	4-12-44	57 Sqn
1521116	Sgt	LEES David Morrison	11-04-44	83 Sqn
2216226	Sgt	LEES Harry	5-07-44	57 Sqn
2211846	Sgt	LEES Harvey Edward	11-04-44	158 Sqn
1821316	Sgt	LEES John Richard	28-04-44	115 Sqn
118164	S/L	LEE-WARNER DFC AFC Henry Philip	26-08-44	90 Sqn
1819854	Sgt	LEFT Edward	27-12-44	75 Sqn
911476	Sgt	LEFTLY Donald Arthur William	23-04-44	103 Sqn
150349	F/O	LEGARD Peter Eric	31-03-44	166 Sqn
909926	Sgt	LEGG Joseph Edward	17-06-44	550 Sqn
1603547	Sgt	LEGG Noel	20-01-44	78 Sqn
1894509	Sgt	LEGGETT Alfred Edward	31-03-44	460 Sqn
124775	F/O	LEGGETT Edward Richard Freeman	20-02-44	106 Sqn
182015	P/O	LEGGETT Thomas Edward	9-08-44	115 Sqn
117474	F/L	LEGGETT Thomas Gordon	28-05-44	103 Sqn
1582866	Sgt	LEGGITT Russell Frederick	12-05-44	9 Sqn
185670	P/O	LEIGH Eric	23-10-44	463 Sqn
2210791	Sgt	LEIGH Robert	24-09-44	166 Sqn
46462	F/L	LEIGH Thomas Barker [Australia]	30-03-44	76 Sqn
2209941	Sgt	LEIGHTON Bernard	25-07-44	75 Sqn
1819797	Sgt	LEIGHTON Peter James	27-08-44	115 Sqn
1800193	Sgt	LEISHMAN John James	12-06-44	635 Sqn
1801415	Sgt	LEITCH John Traill	16-09-44	466 Sqn
1090739	Sgt	LEITCH Thomas Graham	16-02-44	640 Sqn
128409	F/L	LEITHEAD DFM Thomas	26-02-44	102 Sqn
1819426	Sgt	LEIVERS Ernest William	17-10-44	19 OTU
151978	F/O	LELLIOTT Jack Cyril	1-07-44	10 Sqn
123242	F/L	LEMMON Reginald Arthur Montague	23-04-44	76 Sqn
1895244	Sgt	LEMON Jack Benjamin	8-08-44	17 OTU
1468946	F/S	LENOX DFM Leonard Alfred	30-07-44	97 Sqn
1398773	Sgt	LENTON Kenneth Frank	8-12-44	630 Sqn
778694	W/O	LEO Arthur John Owen [Rhodesia]	20-08-44	35 Sqn
152791	F/O	LEONARD Andrew Burgess	13-06-44	166 Sqn

160715	F/O	LEONARD Arthur		6-12-44	550 Sqn	1006198	F/S	LIGERTWOOD James Alexander	29-06-44	102 Sqn
1057682	Sgt	LEONARD James		4-11-44	195 Sqn	157334	F/O	LIGHT Leslie Edward	27-11-44	115 Sqn
2218704	Sgt	LEONARD James		3-11-44	550 Sqn	116893	F/L	LIGHTBODY Hugh Arthur	15-07-44	515 Sqn
138895	F/O	LEONARD Kenneth Alexander		22-03-44	158 Sqn	1485692	F/S	LIGHTFOOT Thomas James	24-02-44	57 Sqn
176559	F/O	LEONARD Leslie William		20-09-44	619 Sqn	1076061	Sgt	LIGHTLEY Thomas William	27-09-44	1654 HCU
2217448	Sgt	LERIGO Norman Henry		25-02-44	460 Sqn	2202534	Sgt	LIGHTOWLER Frederick William	2-11-44	102 Sqn
1893217	Sgt	LESTER Albert Thomas		22-01-44	578 Sqn	1892003	Sgt	LILLEY Alfred Frederick James	8-06-44	15 Sqn
1257765	Sgt	LETHBRIDGE Richard		28-05-44	102 Sqn	186658	P/O	LILLEY Geoffrey William	2-11-44	15 Sqn
1593256	Sgt	LETTEN Lennard		31-08-44	166 Sqn	1571830	Sgt	LILLEY George Henry	17-08-44	433 Sqn
1592026	Sgt	LETTS John		26-08-44	300 Sqn	1591109	Sgt	LILLEY Lawrence Edward	29-07-44	619 Sqn
173763	P/O	LETTS Sydney Albert		18-07-44	115 Sqn	801556	W/O	LILLEY DFC Robert	28-04-44	141 Sqn
174647	F/O	LEUTY Brian Stewart		27-08-44	12 Sqn	152713	F/O	LILLEY William Raymond	13-05-44	640 Sqn
184303	P/O	LEVENE David		23-09-44	106 Sqn	1590345	F/S	LILLICO Charles William	8-06-44	78 Sqn
150453	F/O	LEVENS Edward David		23-11-44	195 Sqn	1894974	F/S	LILLICRAP Herbert Edgar	17-06-44	576 Sqn
1324366	F/S	LEVERINGTON Dennis Walter		13-06-44	158 Sqn	151193	F/O	LILLINGTON David	9-06-44	102 Sqn
2211822	Sgt	LEVERITT Terence		27-11-44	115 Sqn	1126218	W/O	LILLY William James	24-09-44	50 Sqn
147010	F/O	LEVIN DFC Martin Henry Ove		7-08-44	139 Sqn	1150477	F/S	LILLYWHITE William Henry	11-10-44	19 OTU
1606948	Sgt	LEVINGS Grahame Arthur		16-11-44	625 Sqn	143269	F/O	LIMBERT DFC Ronald F.	21-11-44	514 Sqn
160142	F/O	LEVY Frank		17-09-44	617 Sqn	1399207	F/S	LINCOLN David John	4-11-44	625 Sqn
1893404	Sgt	LEVY George Arthur		21-07-44	75 Sqn	1814569	Sgt	LINCOLN James Alfred	24-03-44	78 Sqn
1396396	F/S	LEVY Sidney		10-05-44	619 Sqn	1293195	F/S	LINDENBOON Kevin Patrick	24-12-44	102 Sqn
1279022	Sgt	LEWARNE Horace Arnold		25-06-44	44 Sqn	1577356	F/S	LINDHARD Sten [Denmark]	10-04-44	149 Sqn
1608368	Sgt	LEWENDON Alan Richard		12-09-44	576 Sqn	1378157	F/S	LINDLEY LLOYD William Desmond	20-02-44	83 Sqn
1898698	Sgt	LEWIN William Ashlin		17-07-44	28 OTU	1562812	Sgt	LINDSAY Douglas Sinclair	2-05-44	515 Sqn
1587162	Sgt	LEWINGTON Clarence Ralph Benjamin				1624589	Sgt	LINDSAY George	21-11-44	75 Sqn
				17-06-44	10 OTU	1869698	Sgt	LINDSAY Horace	4-11-44	158 Sqn
1464956	F/S	LEWIS Arthur Jack		25-06-44	9 Sqn	1556238	Sgt	LINDSAY James	22-05-44	630 Sqn
1243743	Sgt	LEWIS Arthur Sydney		13-08-44	101 Sqn	1562901	Sgt	LINDSAY William	31-03-44	635 Sqn
1656317	Sgt	LEWIS Cecil Frederick		15-02-44	625 Sqn	1583771	Sgt	LINE Arthur Richard	25-04-44	78 Sqn
177392	P/O	LEWIS Ernest Frederick		13-06-44	76 Sqn	1579769	Sgt	LINE Edward John	21-07-44	115 Sqn
1585091	Sgt	LEWIS Ernest George		23-06-44	626 Sqn	175601	P/O	LINES Charles Henry	1-05-44	420 Sqn
970467	W/O	LEWIS Ernest Philip		1-08-44	10 Sqn	112751	F/L	LINES Peter	30-07-44	106 Sqn
1419042	Sgt	LEWIS Frank Reginald		20-02-44	514 Sqn	1582834	Sgt	LINFOOT John William	26-02-44	207 Sqn
147958	F/O	LEWIS Geoffrey William		11-05-44	139 Sqn	1477129	Sgt	LINFORD Kenneth	26-02-44	463 Sqn
658833	F/S	LEWIS Gordon Florence		13-06-44	514 Sqn	1393994	F/S	LING Derrick Francis	29-01-44	10 Sqn
1317924	Sgt	LEWIS Gwilym John		12-04-44	1654 HCU	158028	F/O	LING James Gordon Richmond	31-03-44	9 Sqn
3005380	Sgt	LEWIS Harold		14-10-44	550 Sqn	153190	F/O	LING Robert Stanley	28-05-44	515 Sqn
1391807	Sgt	LEWIS Harry		15-02-44	57 Sqn	1427911	Sgt	LING Samuel Wardley	19-07-44	619 Sqn
2213864	Sgt	LEWIS Harry		12-10-44	166 Sqn	1323146	Sgt	LINGLEY Norman Frank	20-02-44	102 Sqn
964128	Sgt	LEWIS Idris Wynne		29-07-44	50 Sqn	2212899	Sgt	LISHMAN Norman	12-06-44	102 Sqn
147660	F/O	LEWIS John Iorwerth Gedrych		28-04-44	115 Sqn	1520883	Sgt	LINT Gordon Seymour	1-07-44	10 Sqn
163556	F/O	LEWIS John Thomas		16-11-44	1663 HCU	158128	F/O	LINTON DFC Adam	20-10-44	35 Sqn
1445360	Sgt	LEWIS Johnny		25-06-44	44 Sqn	648465	Sgt	LISTER Christopher	22-05-44	576 Sqn
1869643	Sgt	LEWIS Kenneth Buckler		3-02-44	84 OTU	1801710	Sgt	LISTER Derek Edward	25-04-44	16 OTU
1479413	F/S	LEWIS Leonard Raymond		29-01-44	77 Sqn	2208842	Sgt	LISTER Stanley	23-05-44	207 Sqn
1324641	Sgt	LEWIS Leslie Albert		9-05-44	35 Sqn	1579416	Sgt	LITCHFIELD George Andrew	2-01-44	467 Sqn
1850225	Sgt	LEWIS Leslie George		30-08-44	166 Sqn	174760	P/O	LITCHFIELD Maurice Jacques	15-02-44	207 Sqn
153471	F/O	LEWIS Norman John		26-08-44	103 Sqn	149608	F/O	LITHERLAND DFC* Henry Allen	16-02-44	50 Sqn
1441139	F/S	LEWIS Reginald Charles Lindfield		29-07-44	582 Sqn	1589059	Sgt	LITTERICK Robert	19-09-44	106 Sqn
1893209	Sgt	LEWIS Reginald Ivon		21-07-44	622 Sqn	972007	W/O	LITTLE Allan	20-05-44	7 Sqn
129118	F/L	LEWIS Rendel Forrest		8-12-44	630 Sqn	1519810	Sgt	LITTLE Arthur James	10-03-44	207 Sqn
135660	F/O	LEWIS Ronald Hugh		16-02-44	106 Sqn	151620	F/O	LITTLE Bryan Spofforth	19-07-44	61 Sqn
1583580	Sgt	LEWIS Samuel		3-01-44	57 Sqn	1451930	F/S	LITTLE George Henry	23-05-44	49 Sqn
934272	F/S	LEWIS Samuel James Ross		11-04-44	635 Sqn	154679	F/O	LITTLE Henry Alvis	4-12-44	189 Sqn
1604730	Sgt	LEWIS Stanley Alfred		22-03-44	103 Sqn	1568726	Sgt	LITTLE Lockhart Beatson	28-04-44	166 Sqn
1454475	LAC	LEWIS Victor Ernest		12-09-44	1690 Flt	1233167	Sgt	LITTLE Norman Douglas	7-07-44	166 Sqn
151896	F/O	LEYLAND Joseph Vincent		24-03-44	619 Sqn	1389680	F/S	LITTLE Robert Harrison	16-02-44	619 Sqn
1494059	Sgt	LEYLAND Robert		25-07-44	102 Sqn	1450191	F/S	LITTLE Stanley William George	25-07-44	207 Sqn
1002296	Sgt	LE BRUN Chris Harry		6-05-44	11 OTU	1063432	Sgt	LITTLEWOOD Walter Acklam	31-03-44	78 Sqn
1819125	Sgt	LE MEE-POWER Colin Adrian Cowper 'Bob'				144612	F/L	LIVELY Frank	24-06-44	7 Sqn
				3-06-44	76 Sqn	175822	P/O	LIVESEY Martin	29-06-44	10 Sqn
1509891	Sgt	LE NEVE FOSTER Bernard Peter		22-03-44	514 Sqn	802523	F/S	LIVINGSTON DFM Mathew	23-01-44	161 Sqn
151640	F/O	LIDBETTER Cecil John		15-02-44	115 Sqn	1349096	F/S	LIVINGSTONE George Frederick	6-06-44	50 Sqn
1572466	Sgt	LIDDLE Alastair Fraser		22-12-44	626 Sqn	1895678	Sgt	LIVINGSTONE Ian Brown	24-07-44	1666 HCU
153931	F/O	LIDDLE Norman		17-05-44	29 OTU	103849	F/O	LLEWELLYN DFC William Glyn	15-07-44	166 Sqn
1357726	Sgt	LIDDLE Thomas Burgess		31-03-44	7 Sqn	1603206	Sgt	LLOYD Cyril William	19-03-44	166 Sqn
2209744	Sgt	LIDDY Thomas Anthony		22-03-44	78 Sqn	1661180	Sgt	LLOYD David Glanville	26-02-44	102 Sqn
2208850	Sgt	LIDERTH Robert		15-03-44	101 Sqn	2209263	Sgt	LLOYD Dewi	13-06-44	12 Sqn
1701209	Sgt	LIFE Stephen Richard		11-07-44	115 Sqn	1293920	Sgt	LLOYD Edgar Charles Prytherch	8-07-44	50 Sqn

Service #	Rank	Name	Date	Squadron
1430128	F/S	LLOYD Frank	25-02-44	460 Sqn
1352500	Sgt	LLOYD Howard Norman	25-07-44	466 Sqn
153933	F/O	LLOYD Joseph William	19-09-44	106 Sqn
1324223	F/S	LLOYD Leslie Harold	1-07-44	625 Sqn
1399625	Sgt	LLOYD Raymond William	22-06-44	207 Sqn
84133	S/L	LLOYD DSO Thomas Williams	13-02-44	617 Sqn
1876588	Sgt	LOADES Stanley Robert	29-01-44	630 Sqn
104336	S/L	LOBB DFC Herbert Cecil	26-08-44	635 Sqn
937648	Sgt	LOCK Thomas	29-07-44	426 Sqn
1600299	F/S	LOCK William Edward	25-04-44	622 Sqn
1375830	W/O	LOCKE Horace Leonard [Canada]	17-09-44	102 Sqn
1874060	Sgt	LOCKE Robert Ernest	31-03-44	57 Sqn
182693	P/O	LOCKE Roland James	8-07-44	630 Sqn
1818729	Sgt	LOCKETT Douglas Sydney	26-03-44	626 Sqn
1593872	Sgt	LOCKETT Harold	6-10-44	76 Sqn
1594980	Sgt	LOCKEY Thomas Arthur Stanley	21-11-44	433 Sqn
141787	F/O	LOCKHART John	21-01-44	77 Sqn
112728	W/C	LOCKHART DSO DFC* William Guy	28-04-44	7 Sqn
151370	F/O	LOCKTON Patrick Arthur	15-03-44	550 Sqn
131879	F/O	LOCKWOOD DFC Frederick James	15-07-44	156 Sqn
1451159	F/S	LOCKWOOD Leonard	31-03-44	101 Sqn
67610	F/L	LOCKYER Clement Charles	29-01-44	83 Sqn
124321	F/L	LODER Kenneth Hedley	29-07-44	514 Sqn
136816	F/O	LODGE Abraham Gordon	23-05-44	57 Sqn
1891173	Sgt	LODGE Ernest Arthur	24-03-44	576 Sqn
1615775	Sgt	LODGE Roy Edward	2-05-44	218 Sqn
1592543	Sgt	LODGE Vincent	28-04-44	115 Sqn
778107	Sgt	LOEWENSON Louis Jack [Rhodesia]	3-01-44	100 Sqn
1064629	W/O	LOFTHOUSE Frank	17-06-44	199 Sqn
135108	F/O	LOGAN DFC John James	11-04-44	550 Sqn
1399075	Sgt	LOGAN Kenneth Victor	27-08-44	15 Sqn
128702	F/O	LOGAN Robert	19-07-44	619 Sqn
1342051	Sgt	LOGUE Daniel	20-01-44	10 Sqn
1819350	F/S	LOKE Robert Dennis	24-04-44	102 Sqn
152644	F/O	LOMAS Edward Henry	29-09-44	157 Sqn
1581882	Sgt	LOMAS Philip Edwin	21-04-44	30 OTU
171913	P/O	LOMBARD Michael Ferdinand	2-05-44	75 Sqn
150433	F/L	LONDON Ronald	6-12-44	227 Sqn
160682	P/O	LONG DFM Duncan Albert	24-03-44	578 Sqn
1620472	Sgt	LONG Ernest	8-05-44	106 Sqn
1537907	Sgt	LONG Geoffrey	4-05-44	12 Sqn
983714	Sgt	LONGSTAFF Thomas	27-03-44	14 OTU
3030276	Sgt	LONG Harold Edwin	21-07-44	514 Sqn
89375	F/L	LONG James Leslie Robert	13-04-44	9 Sqn
930245	W/O	LONG Robert William	8-05-44	49 Sqn
1595256	Sgt	LONG Samuel	13-02-44	15 OTU
1595130	Sgt	LONGBOTTOM Frank	6-10-44	51 Sqn
591397	Sgt	LONGDEN Wilfred	24-03-44	77 Sqn
1651990	F/S	LONGHURST Bernard Ewart	22-11-44	61 Sqn
1891298	Sgt	LONGHURST Bertram Stephen	10-05-44	467 Sqn
1396844	F/S	LONGLAND Charles Alfred	25-07-44	103 Sqn
1893672	F/S	LONGLAND Geoffrey Alan	12-12-44	635 Sqn
1897867	Sgt	LONGMAN Francis David Pemberton	19-07-44	207 Sqn
1815829	Sgt	LONGMATE George Stanley	27-04-44	207 Sqn
1819806	Sgt	LONGMORE William	8-08-44	419 Sqn
138083	F/O	LONGSON Francis	30-06-44	514 Sqn
997223	Sgt	LONGTON Henry	31-03-44	166 Sqn
974506	Sgt	LONGWORTH Herbert	24-03-44	15 Sqn
1388549	F/S	LONG-HARTLEY Paul	16-06-44	582 Sqn
149847	F/L	LOOS DFC Edward Albert	5-08-44	161 Sqn
1591901	Sgt	LOOSE William Arthur	22-06-44	619 Sqn
1594457	Sgt	LOOSLI Max	19-07-44	619 Sqn
748357	W/O	LORD Roland Thornton	10-04-44	635 Sqn
137385	F/O	LORD William Charles John	3-01-44	619 Sqn
1295153	F/S	LORETAN Robert Antoine Frederick	8-05-44	106 Sqn
1607068	Sgt	LORRAIN Alfred Dennis	4-12-44	44 Sqn
178572	P/O	LOTT John Ernest	7-06-44	619 Sqn
39743	S/L	LOUGHBOROUGH Arthur James	22-06-44	106 Sqn
1685541	Sgt	LOUGHLIN Thomas	19-07-44	57 Sqn
1796421	Sgt	LOUGHRIN Robert Thomas Garth	29-02-44	1666 HCU
1892195	Sgt	LOUIS Ernest Albert	12-05-44	630 Sqn
169200	F/O	LOUSADA Gerald Gilbert Ormonde	30-11-44	115 Sqn
1504268	F/S	LOVATT Frank	27-03-44	78 Sqn
549261	F/S	LOVE James William	31-03-44	78 Sqn
1850343	Sgt	LOVEDAY David Arthur	27-04-44	207 Sqn
1607117	F/S	LOVEGROVE Geoffrey Lionel	30-11-44	578 Sqn
967425	Sgt	LOVEGROVE Reginald George	4-05-44	582 Sqn
1896159	Sgt	LOVELAND Ambrose William	25-09-44	199 Sqn
1387188	Sgt	LOVELAND John Thomas	20-02-44	49 Sqn
1386515	F/S	LOVELL George Thomas Alfred	24-03-44	78 Sqn
85649	S/L	LOVELL DFC Victor Charles	28-04-44	141 Sqn
1897777	Sgt	LOVERIDGE Frederick Robert	21-07-44	101 Sqn
1819711	Sgt	LOVEROCK William Henry	24-04-44	77 Sqn
624950	F/S	LOVETT Joseph James	23-04-44	640 Sqn
184363	F/O	LOVETT Michael Joseph	4-12-44	207 Sqn
1604339	Sgt	LOVETT Stuart John	6-11-44	550 Sqn
1561331	Sgt	LOW George Jack	31-03-44	578 Sqn
965562	Sgt	LOW William	23-05-44	57 Sqn
1860066	Sgt	LOWBRIDGE DFM Harold Oxspring	26-08-44	300 Sqn
1583613	F/S	LOWE Derek Stanley	17-12-44	156 Sqn
652649	Sgt	LOWE Edward Sidney	21-01-44	514 Sqn
1646186	Sgt	LOWE George Frederick	25-03-44	61 Sqn
1575855	Sgt	LOWE John Ernest	12-04-44	1654 HCU
2220521	Sgt	LOWE Peter Charles	27-09-44	619 Sqn
657895	W/O	LOWE DFC Robert William	6-07-44	635 Sqn
173593	P/O	LOWE Wilfred Jim	23-06-44	76 Sqn
151082	F/O	LOWE William	25-07-44	75 Sqn
1590245	Sgt	LOWERY John	23-05-44	207 Sqn
1622243	Sgt	LOWERY Kenneth Arthur	22-01-44	514 Sqn
1862913	Sgt	LOWIN William John Clifford	11-04-44	1661 HCU
1602820	Sgt	LOWLETT Norman Bernard	24-03-44	578 Sqn
54943	P/O	LOWREY Ralph William	8-06-44	408 Sqn
1056079	Sgt	LOWRIE Campbell	3-06-44	76 Sqn
1594991	Sgt	LOWSON George Stanley	26-06-44	626 Sqn
177738	P/O	LUCAN DFM Richard Dennis	7-10-44	617 Sqn
900811	Sgt	LUCAS Donald George Jack	21-01-44	7 Sqn
149943	F/O	LUCAS DFC Geffrey William	11-10-44	19 OTU
1713648	Sgt	LUCAS George Henry	25-07-44	619 Sqn
1576075	F/S	LUCAS George Morley	19-03-44	192 Sqn
172355	P/O	LUCAS DFC Norman Harold Brian	29-07-44	1654 HCU
1895744	Sgt	LUCAS Ronald Paul	29-06-44	76 Sqn
1601882	Sgt	LUCAS Ronald William	29-06-44	102 Sqn
2216237	Sgt	LUCAS Stanley	15-02-44	424 Sqn
952787	Sgt	LUCAS Stanley Douglas	20-11-44	514 Sqn
1822712	Sgt	LUCAS Thomas Kelly Douglas	2-05-44	10 Sqn
1395654	F/S	LUCHA Peter August	25-02-44	1661HCU
171068	P/O	LUCKETT Bernard Montague	25-03-44	97 Sqn
1465160	Sgt	LUCY Alfred Henry	27-09-44	115 Sqn
186182	F/O	LUDLOW Cyril John	29-07-44	57 Sqn
2221055	Sgt	LUKEMAN Alex Ernest	20-10-44	550 Sqn
1812113	Sgt	LUKER Nevil Ralph	16-09-44	21 OTU
148749	F/O	LUMBY Clifford Craven	3-02-44	84 OTU
1061816	F/S	LUMSDEN DFM William	2-01-44	156 Sqn
146459	F/L	LUNAN William Robb	10-09-44	239 Sqn
158000	F/O	LUND Edmund Thornley	20-05-44	7 Sqn
152743	F/O	LUNDIE Alan Robert Lionel	21-11-44	514 Sqn
1520042	Sgt	LUNDY Richard	21-04-44	467 Sqn
1874918	Sgt	LUNNISS Edward	2-01-44	61 Sqn
1684477	F/S	LUNT Phillip	18-09-44	57 Sqn
179649	P/O	LUPTON Harry	30-08-44	300 Sqn
1338521	Sgt	LUSCOMBE-ARMSTRONG Peter	24-02-44	100 Sqn
542814	Sgt	LUTON Herbert Charles	21-07-44	115 Sqn
1578970	F/S	LUTWYCHE Leslie Richard	19-07-44	9 Sqn
1893984	Sgt	LUXFORD Frederick Jesse	17-05-44	29 OTU
1569054	Sgt	LYALL George	23-04-44	582 Sqn
1467578	F/S	LYFORD Francis Philip	3-08-44	619 Sqn
1409875	LAC	LYFORD Leonard George	28-04-44	Old Buckenham

159425	P/O	LYFORD DFC Percy Robert	2-01-44	156 Sqn	56034	P/O	MACKAY Huntley David Shaw Mann Jack		
152007	F/O	LYNAM Francis John	1-07-44	101 Sqn				15-08-44	207 Sqn
152457	F/O	LYNAM William	7-06-44	460 Sqn	1522815	Sgt	MACKAY Peter George	9-08-44	466 Sqn
1262223	W/O	LYNES DFM Peter John	7-06-44	83 Sqn	1827719	Sgt	MACKENZIE David Geddes	7-12-44	1651 HCU
910937	Sgt	LYNCH James	22-01-44	166 Sqn	2202271	Sgt	MACKENZIE Clarence Dunkin Fraser	31-03-44	514 Sqn
1832292	Sgt	LYNCH John Patrick	16-10-44	115 Sqn	655473	F/S	MACKEW Gerald Victor	23-04-44	49 Sqn
162991	P/O	LYNCH Michael Shaun	15-02-44	158 Sqn	1881129	Sgt	MACKEY Stanley Herbert	12-09-44	207 Sqn
646452	Sgt	LYNCH Patrick Joseph	31-03-44	103 Sqn	147522	F/O	MACKIE John Dennis	23-09-44	101 Sqn
1373580	Sgt	LYNCH Phillip	21-01-44	115 Sqn	171615	P/O	MACKIE Peter Hendry Jones	20-02-44	77 Sqn
1389429	Sgt	LYNCH William Edward	13-08-44	625 Sqn	1804016	Sgt	MACKILLIGIN Julian Pelham	31-03-44	106 Sqn
1386808	Sgt	LYNE Donald Edward	24-06-44	12 Sqn	1569752	Sgt	MACKINNON Kenneth Ewan	6-11-44	207 Sqn
1360209	W/O	LYON Abraham Thomson	13-08-44	218 Sqn	969833	Sgt	MACKINTOSH David Thomson	12-04-44	50 Sqn
1320186	F/L	LYON Aubrey Kenneth Lawson	21-01-44	77 Sqn	1819311	Sgt	MACKINTOSH Jeremy Ernest	19-07-44	619 Sqn
127908	F/L	LYON Charles Anthony	31-03-44	635 Sqn	115298	F/L	MACLEAN Alistair	10-06-44	30 OTU
1335701	F/S	LYON John Douglas	15-03-44	578 Sqn	1823590	Sgt	MACLEAN Archibald	25-04-44	622 Sqn
2206480	Sgt	LYON Maurice Mitchell	21-07-44	24 OTU	183628	P/O	MACLEOD William Ross Douglas	26-12-44	10 Sqn
1582633	Sgt	LYONS Henry Anthony Montagu	24-02-44	100 Sqn	1675090	Sgt	MACNAMARA John Robert	12-12-44	150 Sqn
1822738	Sgt	LYONS John Edward	20-01-44	102 Sqn	1604049	Sgt	MACNAUGHTON-SMITH Michael John		
177259	F/O	LYONS John Mortimer	29-11-44	101 Sqn				22-06-44	630 Sqn
1089359	W/O	LYONS Joseph	17-12-44	156 Sqn	1566921	Sgt	MACPHERSON Angus Alexander	8-05-44	138 Sqn
1804046	Sgt	LYSSINGTON DFM William Henry	29-01-44	625 Sqn	1346622	Sgt	MACPHERSON George John	24-02-44	149 Sqn
1491299	Sgt	LYTH Thomas	1-07-44	101 Sqn	135103	F/O	MACPHERSON John	10-04-44	207 Sqn
964480	W/O	LYTHGOE George Edward	8-09-44	582 Sqn	1822917	Sgt	MACRAE Finlay	30-01-44	44 Sqn
133267	F/L	L'AMIE DFC Frederick Theulis	21-11-44	515 Sqn	1528613	Sgt	MADDEN Joseph	3-08-44	625 Sqn
1676974	Sgt	MABBOTT Gerland Walter Charles	25-03-44	425 Sqn	1874494	Sgt	MADDEN Michael	18-04-44	158 Sqn
1610176	F/S	MABBUTT John William Charles	20-09-44	619 Sqn	2226577	Sgt	MADDOCKS John Eaton	12-10-44	83 OTU
1507161	Sgt	MABEY Walter John	5-03-44	426 Sqn	1334594	F/S	MADDOX Peter John Edward	19-04-44	115 Sqn
176721	P/O	MABON Adam [Canada]	13-06-44	408 Sqn	1896030	Sgt	MADGE Eric Arthur	9-09-44	626 Sqn
1496442	F/S	MABON William	28-04-44	640 Sqn	1398434	W/O	MADGE John George	11-11-44	97 Sqn
1135105	Sgt	MacDONALD John Wilson	30-01-44	44 Sqn	1606117	Sgt	MADGWICK Norman Victor	6-11-44	214 Sqn
1605055	Sgt	MacDONALD Ronald James	31-03-44	103 Sqn	148510	F/O	MAGAN Daniel William	23-04-44	550 Sqn
1802341	Sgt	MacDONALD William John Charles	14-01-44	12 Sqn	1579523	Sgt	MAGNESS Charles Graham	5-02-44	115 Sqn
1319513	F/S	MacDOUGALL Charles James Ross	25-08-44	10 Sqn	1671268	F/S	MAGUIRE Denis Joseph	14-08-44	44 Sqn
1550855	Sgt	MacFADYEN Colin	22-05-44	44 Sqn	1538238	Sgt	MAGUIRE Joseph	3-06-44	166 Sqn
1550897	F/S	MacFARLANE James	6-06-44	149 Sqn	148856	F/O	MAGUIRE Martin Malcolm	16-09-44	78 Sqn
710158	Sgt	MacFARLANE Kenneth Lowe [Rhodesia]	12-04-44	1654 HCU	152802	F/O	MAHER James	29-07-44	103 Sqn
					1336772	F/S	MAHONEY Rex Cecil	29-10-44	582 Sqn
1451336	F/S	MacGIBBON Peter Alexander	21-07-44	622 Sqn	643941	F/S	MAIDEN Leonard	18-08-44	576 Sqn
1566360	Sgt	MacGILLIVRAY Alexander Donald	26-02-44	431 Sqn	132722	F/O	MAIDSTONE Raymond Joseph Alfred	2-01-44	467 Sqn
1624784	Sgt	MacINNES Peter James	25-03-44	57 Sqn	183046	P/O	MAIR William Gordon	30-08-44	90 Sqn
1372381	Sgt	MacIVER Angus McLeod	29-07-44	415 Sqn	1801805	Sgt	MAITLAND Andrew Priest	13-09-44	166 Sqn
159055	P/O	MacKENZIE DFC Alasdair Leslie	21-01-44	51 Sqn	184621	P/O	MAJAKI DFC Bert Alex	9-10-44	578 Sqn
179236	P/O	MacKENZIE Alastair Lewis	19-07-44	78 Sqn	151851	F/O	MAJOR Denis William	23-05-44	207 Sqn
1566634	Sgt	MacKENZIE Andrew Wilson	27-01-44	460 Sqn	154763	F/O	MAKEWELL Charles Leslie	11-12-44	1651 HCU
163827	F/O	MacKENZIE Donald Graham	24-11-44	1655 MTU	1575592	F/S	MAKING Lewis John	22-05-44	635 Sqn
1424160	Sgt	MacKENZIE Douglas Bowman	20-07-44	550 Sqn	1819794	Sgt	MALABAND Sidney Joseph	22-06-44	106 Sqn
991795	Sgt	MacKENZIE Duncan Benjamin Grant			2205033	Sgt	MALCOLM John Alexander	13-07-44	1662 HCU
			3-01-44	156 Sqn	151550	F/O	MALIN Alfred Ernest George	11-06-44	625 Sqn
153582	F/O	MacLEAN Andrew Glassford	30-08-44	50 Sqn	1817408	Sgt	MALLABONE John	23-10-44	419 Sqn
710159	F/S	MacLEOD Alexander	9-06-44	50 Sqn	2211358	Sgt	MALLEN Herbert Joseph	6-08-44	50 Sqn
63376	F/O	MacLEOD Angus Peter	29-01-44	239 Sqn	158594	F/O	MALLETT DFC Ronald Spencer	28-06-44	141 Sqn
149317	F/L	MacLEOD Ian	28-10-44	19 OTU	1484062	Sgt	MALLETT Thomas Henry	2-01-44	106 Sqn
970783	Sgt	MacLEOD Roderick	13-08-44	158 Sqn	1566862	Sgt	MALLON Peter	24-02-44	460 Sqn
1823751	Sgt	MacLEOD Ronald	31-08-44	550 Sqn	136723	F/L	MALONEY DFM Patrick	18-08-44	83 Sqn
1797001	Sgt	MacMAHON James Kevin [Eire]	30-08-44	434 Sqn	1592172	Sgt	MALTBY DFM Jack Harrison	4-05-44	619 Sqn
150306	F/O	MacMASTER Ian Edgar [USA]	19-03-44	625 Sqn	1386763	Sgt	MALTHOUSE Reuben Horace Frederick		
1430818	Sgt	MacMILLAN-CLARK John	9-03-44	1667 HCU				10-04-44	635 Sqn
1018514	F/S	MacPHERSON DFM Ewen Dugald	20-01-44	83 Sqn	1852383	Sgt	MALTMAN William Hunter	27-07-44	83 Sqn
1823549	Sgt	MacPHERSON John Duncan	13-05-44	431 Sqn	147939	F/O	MAMOUTOFF George [Russia]	20-06-44	141 Sqn
154743	F/O	MacPHERSON Robert	4-11-44	158 Sqn	1867033	Sgt	MANSELL Philip John	26-12-44	10 Sqn
1579079	W/O	MacPHERSON William Reddington	29-07-44	61 Sqn	960800	W/O	MANDALL James Branthwaite	21-02-44	9 Sqn
173265	P/O	MACDONALD DFC Murdo	6-08-44	83 Sqn	1385495	W/O	MANDER Frederick Arthur	28-05-44	166 Sqn
1410722	F/S	MACE Arthur George	22-12-44	626 Sqn	148461	F/O	MANDER DFC Geoffrey Wilson	26-02-44	1655 MTU
1320991	F/S	MACEY Kenneth Joseph	25-02-44	626 Sqn	1814477	Sgt	MANGAN Denis Patrick	6-06-44	50 Sqn
1343646	Sgt	MACFIE John	25-06-44	61 Sqn	1455687	Sgt	MANLEY John Dennington	27-04-44	156 Sqn
1685261	Sgt	MACDONALD Edward Dixon	26-04-44	30 OTU	512750	F/S	MANLEY Walter John	26-08-44	97 Sqn
160214	F/O	MACGREGOR John Richard [Rhodesia]	12-09-44	44 Sqn	934780	W/O	MANLOW Gerald James	7-10-44	514 Sqn
1825581	Sgt	MACKAY Alexander	9-08-44	427 Sqn	147960	F/O	MANN Albert Oswald	22-05-44	115 Sqn
1823109	Sgt	MACKAY David	23-04-44	578 Sqn	1339382	Sgt	MANN Donald George	14-01-44	576 Sqn

Number	Rank	Name	Date	Unit
1672599	Sgt	MANN Ernest Edward	16-10-44	14 OTU
1601233	F/S	MANN Peter Douglas	6-12-44	57 Sqn
1584717	Sgt	MANN William George	30-01-44	106 Sqn
127251	F/O	MANNING Albert Edward	23-03-44	9 Sqn
1520513	Sgt	MANNING Gordon Edward [Eire]	8-09-44	29 OTU
2203524	Sgt	MANNING John [Eire]	23-12-44	90 Sqn
2209405	Sgt	MANNION John	25-06-44	576 Sqn
1562926	F/S	MANNION Kevin	22-12-44	97 Sqn
45151	S/L	MANSBRIDGE AFC Donald William	20-04-44	635 Sqn
1876639	Sgt	MANSBRIDGE Ronald	4-05-44	582 Sqn
118342	F/O	MANSER Jack Purcell	25-09-44	576 Sqn
1876425	Sgt	MANSFIELD Alexander Andrew 'Alex'	20-01-44	166 Sqn
1398799	Sgt	MANSFIELD Dennis Leslie	21-01-44	1667 HCU
1804226	Sgt	MANSFIELD James Arthur Augustus	4-05-44	582 Sqn
43707	W/C	MANSFIELD DFC Nelson Reuben [New Zealand]	14-01-44	156 Sqn
1322731	F/S	MANSFIELD Sydney	23-06-44	100 Sqn
1097851	Sgt	MANSON John	23-05-44	57 Sqn
1601439	Sgt	MANT Kenneth Victor	13-05-44	576 Sqn
1615950	Sgt	MANTHORPE Anthony John	27-01-44	149 Sqn
51737	F/L	MANVELL DFC DFM Robert Edward	24-06-44	156 Sqn
178892	P/O	MAPLESON Dennis	12-09-44	7 Sqn
1579978	F/S	MARAVAN-WILLIAMS Thomas Ronald	6-10-44	207 Sqn
158046	F/O	MARCHAND Chester Joseph Francis [British Honduras]	26-08-44	7 Sqn
1603363	Sgt	MARCHANT Edward George	25-02-44	514 Sqn
1393299	F/S	MARCHANT Walter Sidney	16-06-44	405 Sqn
159899	F/L	MARDEN DFC Frederick Alexander	27-07-44	83 Sqn
1874914	Sgt	MARDLING Dennis Charles	13-08-44	115 Sqn
1323693	F/S	MARDON-MOWBRAY Kenneth David	24-03-44	158 Sqn
1893899	Sgt	MARFIL Lorenzo	21-10-44	75 Sqn
115985	F/L	MARGACH DFC Donald Sinclair	29-07-44	582 Sqn
1576746	F/S	MARGETTS Keith Harry	24-03-44	626 Sqn
188929	P/O	MARGETTS Leonard Charles	4-05-44	9 Sqn
1146271	Sgt	MARKLAND James Robert	7-07-44	166 Sqn
187079	P/O	MARKOVITCH Alfred Abraham	2-11-44	15 Sqn
1591085	Sgt	MARKS Dennis	31-07-44	12 OTU
1581483	F/S	MARKS Joseph	14-10-44	626 Sqn
1676946	Sgt	MARKS William James	1-07-44	100 Sqn
2211419	Sgt	MARKSON Ellis	9-08-44	161 Sqn
170960	F/O	MARLAND John Colin	23-05-44	57 Sqn
2220018	Sgt	MARLER James Henry	5-07-44	433 Sqn
1677033	Sgt	MARLEY George Percival	16-03-44	460 Sqn
1592882	Sgt	MARLEY Norman	4-08-44	434 Sqn
1579439	Sgt	MARLOW Alfred	12-09-44	106 Sqn
1085425	F/S	MARLOW DFM George Edward	21-01-44	51 Sqn
1581034	Sgt	MARPER Arnold	19-07-44	619 Sqn
163554	F/O	MARR Donald James Taylor	4-11-44	158 Sqn
1553611	F/S	MARR Robert	23-10-44	9 Sqn
155122	F/O	MARRIAN Norman	31-03-44	101 Sqn
1432314	F/S	MARRIOTT Dennis	25-05-44	640 Sqn
1398464	F/S	MARRIOTT Frederick James	22-03-44	35 Sqn
2220086	Sgt	MARRIOTT George Clifford	14-07-44	158 Sqn
1581586	Sgt	MARRIOTT James Roy	15-10-44	207 Sqn
130224	F/O	MARRIOTT DFM Kenneth	20-02-44	7 Sqn
1850509	Sgt	MARRIOTT Kenneth Robert	31-03-44	57 Sqn
171697	P/O	MARRIS Kenneth George	9-05-44	426 Sqn
184624	P/O	MARRON Edward	23-12-44	83 Sqn
1425192	Sgt	MARROW Alfred Allan	11-06-44	467 Sqn
1430280	F/S	MARROWS Dennis	8-07-44	50 Sqn
47708	F/L	MARROWS George Arthur	8-06-44	78 Sqn
1059533	Sgt	MARSDEN Denys George	8-07-44	50 Sqn
2221244	Sgt	MARSDEN John	23-03-44	26 OTU
1892516	Sgt	MARSH Beresford	13-05-44	640 Sqn
957721	F/S	MARSH Charles Harry	21-02-44	15 Sqn
145303	F/O	MARSH Henry Herbert	11-06-44	75 Sqn
152610	F/L	MARSH Roy Frederick	12-12-44	15 Sqn
170636	P/O	MARSH Thomas Gordon	26-03-44	15 Sqn
1699568	Sgt	MARSHALL Arthur Forster	21-07-44	90 Sqn
646886	Sgt	MARSHALL David Waldie	24-02-44	9 Sqn
1430700	F/S	MARSHALL Ernest	15-02-44	7 Sqn
936381	Sgt	MARSHALL George Robert	9-03-44	1667 HCU
576242	Sgt	MARSHALL Harold William Hughes	30-01-44	463 Sqn
632513	Sgt	MARSHALL Harry William	21-02-44	640 Sqn
151613	F/O	MARSHALL James Brown	31-03-44	51 Sqn
1565267	Sgt	MARSHALL John	4-11-44	640 Sqn
1565759	Sgt	MARSHALL John	20-02-44	10 Sqn
170386	F/O	MARSHALL John Frank Vale	19-09-44	106 Sqn
1593190	Sgt	MARSHALL Joseph	22-05-44	9 Sqn
126683	F/L	MARSHALL Kenneth	29-07-44	207 Sqn
1893252	Sgt	MARSHALL Noris Sydney	19-03-44	101 Sqn
1544531	Sgt	MARSHALL Reginald	20-05-44	514 Sqn
151917	F/O	MARSHALL Robert Keith	10-06-44	10 Sqn
1295549	Sgt	MARSHALL Ronald	29-07-44	44 Sqn
1812780	F/S	MARSHALL Stanley Edward William	5-07-44	9 Sqn
539072	Sgt	MARSHALL Sydney	24-12-44	166 Sqn
39671	S/L	MARSHALL DFC MiD Trevor Owen [New Zealand]	8-07-44	106 Sqn
137835	F/O	MARSHALL William Edge	11-05-44	424 Sqn
179203	P/O	MARSLAND Jack	27-08-44	1657 HCU
157900	F/O	MARSTON Leonard Frederick Arthur	27-08-44	44 Sqn
136912	F/O	MARSTON DFC Norman Allan	25-05-44	78 Sqn
121946	F/L	MARTENS Arthur Tempest [Canada]	27-01-44	426 Sqn
153897	F/O	MARTIN Alan	26-08-44	90 Sqn
185419	P/O	MARTIN Alexander	31-12-44	166 Sqn
1604936	Sgt	MARTIN Basil George	14-01-44	626 Sqn
574263	F/S	MARTIN Beric John Chivalle	14-03-44	77 Sqn
52313	F/O	MARTIN MiD David Charles	4-05-44	625 Sqn
1667417	Sgt	MARTIN Eric	31-03-44	640 Sqn
1342599	F/S	MARTIN Francis	21-01-44	97 Sqn
919965	Sgt	MARTIN Francis Arnold	17-06-44	1660 HCU
1398507	Sgt	MARTIN Frank Samuel	26-08-44	12 OTU
1415676	F/S	MARTIN Glynn James Owen	8-07-44	83 Sqn
1649052	Sgt	MARTIN Harold Sidney	6-12-44	227 Sqn
1183447	F/S	MARTIN DFM Harry	23-10-44	625 Sqn
1685635	Sgt	MARTIN Henry	3-01-44	156 Sqn
1871426	F/S	MARTIN Hubert Edward	25-04-44	7 Sqn
1880935	Sgt	MARTIN Hugh Patrick	26-08-44	100 Sqn
654574	Sgt	MARTIN DFM James George Louis	18-09-44	57 Sqn
1040315	F/S	MARTIN John James	29-01-44	83 Sqn
106968	S/L	MARTIN DFC* John Lionel	28-04-44	7 Sqn
1514078	F/S	MARTIN Kenneth	16-11-44	625 Sqn
1873541	Sgt	MARTIN Kenneth Mark	12-05-44	103 Sqn
153528	F/O	MARTIN Leonard Arthur	20-11-44	75 Sqn
1821748	Sgt	MARTIN Mark Addy	29-01-44	51 Sqn
1377847	W/O	MARTIN Owen Harwood	5-11-44	10 Sqn
1270135	Sgt	MARTIN Raymond Henri	4-05-44	625 Sqn
1579977	F/S	MARTIN Reuben	29-01-44	10 Sqn
176912	P/O	MARTIN Sidney	15-07-44	166 Sqn
1390977	F/S	MARTIN Stanley Edward	1-02-44	1660 HCU
1032632	Sgt	MARTIN Stanley Frank	2-05-44	514 Sqn
1437908	Sgt	MARTIN Tom	21-01-44	61 Sqn
1079614	F/S	MARTIN William Frederick	22-03-44	35 Sqn
1602856	Sgt	MARTIN William Percy	24-02-44	166 Sqn
1454683	Sgt	MARTINDALE Peter Drake	30-01-44	514 Sqn
1392648	Sgt	MARTINEZ Mariano	6-12-44	227 Sqn
176037	P/O	MARVIN DFC Douglas William James	28-05-44	75 Sqn
1125814	Sgt	MARWOOD Arthur Rex	25-06-44	9 Sqn
1819771	Sgt	MARWOOD John	8-07-44	207 Sqn
114383	F/L	MARWOOD TUCKER Neville	13-08-44	101 Sqn
1891721	Sgt	MARY Marcel Paul	13-09-44	625 Sqn
127532	F/O	MASKELL DFC Arthur George	1-06-44	161 Sqn
139295	F/O	MASKELL Harold Thomas	23-05-44	35 Sqn
2211801	Sgt	MASON Albert	10-06-44	10 Sqn
177529	P/O	MASON Archibald	5-10-44	101 Sqn

1538414 F/S	MASON Charles	20-01-44	10 Sqn
1324605 F/S	MASON Douglas Walter	6-12-44	77 Sqn
923438 W/O	MASON Eric Arthur	25-05-44	576 Sqn
1814786 Sgt	MASON Eric Thomas	18-10-44	115 Sqn
130794 F/O	MASON DFM Hugh	27-04-44	83 Sqn
1881521 Sgt	MASON John Frederick	25-10-44	115 Sqn
175361 P/O	MASON DFC John Herbert	10-05-44	50 Sqn
1304507 Sgt	MASON Kenneth George	23-06-44	460 Sqn
1816001 F/S	MASON Ronald Lloyd	23-03-44	50 Sqn
1894780 Sgt	MASON Stanley	27-04-44	57 Sqn
185875 P/O	MASON Thomas Donald Lawson	15-10-44	7 Sqn
1260719 Sgt	MASON William Charles	24-03-44	166 Sqn
1575137 Sgt	MASSEY Charles William	11-04-44	84 OTU
1585804 Sgt	MASSEY Joseph Edward	1-07-44	12 Sqn
1483341 F/S	MASSEY Wilfred Joseph	13-06-44	100 Sqn
141336 F/L	MASSY Michael Ingoldsby [Eire]	4-08-44	635 Sqn
1291811 Sgt	MASTERS Herbert Alfred	24-02-44	9 Sqn
1590753 Sgt	MATE Victor Hugo	15-02-44	550 Sqn
1892084 Sgt	MATHER Henry James	6-06-44	149 Sqn
1042788 F/S	MATHER James John	4-08-44	635 Sqn
173890 P/O	MATHER Kenneth Richard	20-05-44	115 Sqn
157746 F/O	MATHER DFM William	22-06-44	49 Sqn
158113 F/O	MATHESON Andrew	27-09-44	627 Sqn
183423 P/O	MATHEWS DFC Albert Cyril	11-11-44	83 Sqn
1387793 F/S	MATHEWS Arthur	28-04-44	15 Sqn
116727 F/L	MATHEWS DFC Robert Noel	12-02-44	24 OTU
54378 F/O	MATHIAS Glyn Davies	25-08-44	218 Sqn
1344764 F/S	MATHISON James Alexander	29-11-44	35 Sqn
1819744 Sgt	MATON James Alfred Thomas	22-06-44	49 Sqn
1239496 Sgt	MATON Ronald John	31-03-44	578 Sqn
1397613 Sgt	MATTHES Alfred George	6-01-44	7 Sqn
1621498 Sgt	MATTHEWMAN Leslie	21-07-44	578 Sqn
156039 F/L	MATTHEWS DFC Albert Edward Anderson		
		22-06-44	49 Sqn
1333744 Sgt	MATTHEWS Albert Stanley	6-01-44	103 Sqn
1602064 Sgt	MATTHEWS Cecil Arthur William	31-03-44	106 Sqn
1035560 Sgt	MATTHEWS Charles Hadland	30-07-44	102 Sqn
1580013 F/S	MATTHEWS Douglas Garnet 'Doug'	5-05-44	7 Sqn
2221540 Sgt	MATTHEWS Ernest William	4-12-44	227 Sqn
47719 S/L	MATTHEWS George Dixon	11-10-44	101 Sqn
1322267 Sgt	MATTHEWS Harold William	10-05-44	9 Sqn
2220485 Sgt	MATTHEWS Jeffrey	5-07-44	207 Sqn
1065498 Sgt	MATTHEWS Kenneth Forshaw	18-12-44	10 Sqn
1204048 F/S	MATTHEWS Phillip Marcus	23-09-44	61 Sqn
108052 F/L	MATTHEWS Thomas William	26-03-44	1655 MTU
1030709 Sgt	MATTHEWS Walter Howard Hill	6-10-44	51 Sqn
109492 F/L	MATTHEWS William John	16-11-44	1663 HCU
1446208 Sgt	MATTHEWS William Victor	6-07-44	15 Sqn
1315894 F/S	MATTICK DFM Stanley Richard	2-01-44	106 Sqn
1390388 F/S	MATTOCKS Bernard Charles	22-05-44	207 Sqn
174531 P/O	MAUDE Ronald Peter	8-06-44	115 Sqn
1592224 Sgt	MAUGHAN Douglas	31-03-44	50 Sqn
1320941 Sgt	MAUGHAN Norman Hepple	15-07-44	103 Sqn
179277 F/O	MAUL Edwin Charles	21-11-44	49 Sqn
153013 F/O	MAULE John	27-08-44	35 Sqn
70457 W/C	MAW DFC Michael Trentham	13-08-44	640 Sqn
1494278 Sgt	MAWHINNEY James	3-02-44	16 OTU
150102 F/O	MAWLE Roger Hanson	2-01-44	550 Sqn
1892092 Sgt	MAWSON George William	29-07-44	103 Sqn
1591864 Sgt	MAWSON Harry	12-12-44	582 Sqn
2210542 Sgt	MAWSON William Ernest	18-12-44	10 Sqn
1286456 F/S	MAXTED Charles Henry	20-02-44	207 Sqn
171441 P/O	MAXWELL David Clerk Hill	23-05-44	12 Sqn
1593960 Sgt	MAXWELL James Frederick	4-11-44	51 Sqn
1345994 Sgt	MAXWELL William Cochrane	4-05-44	460 Sqn
1431403 F/S	MAY Frederick James	24-06-44	7 Sqn
1468242 F/S	MAY Ivor David James	20-02-44	640 Sqn
575531 F/S	MAY John Albert	31-03-44	432 Sqn
1620247 Sgt	MAY Leonard Douglas	4-01-44	11 OTU
145698 F/L	MAY DFM Percival Thomas Frederick	30-12-44	76 Sqn
1803334 Sgt	MAY Sidney Frank	14-01-44	156 Sqn
1684015 Sgt	MAY William Bronwhill	13-05-44	635 Sqn
1899304 Sgt	MAYCOCK Dennis Walter	31-12-44	218 Sqn
1391763 F/S	MAYCOCK John Robert	30-01-44	83 Sqn
1078833 F/S	MAYES Albert	29-01-44	83 Sqn
1821101 Sgt	MAYGER James Douglas	25-04-44	626 Sqn
1414791 F/S	MAYHEW Denis John	5-05-44	7 Sqn
171740 P/O	MAYHEW Frederick Ethelbert William	17-05-44	29 OTU
975391 F/S	MAYHEW MiD Leonard Charles George		
		25-06-44	97 Sqn
1604575 Sgt	MAYNARD Kenneth Edmund	13-06-44	158 Sqn
1339967 Sgt	MAYNARD Leslie Douglas	24-03-44	102 Sqn
1583327 Sgt	MAYNARD William Herbert	18-09-44	8 Group
1601056 Sgt	MAYNE Cyril Edward	3-06-44	166 Sqn
1576545 Sgt	MAYO David Alfred William	22-05-44	550 Sqn
175703 P/O	MAYO Wilfred Haydn	6-06-44	149 Sqn
1262062 W/O	MAYOW Theodore David	10-04-44	10 OTU
1867597 Sgt	MAYS John Charles	23-12-44	35 Sqn
2210689 Sgt	McADAM Robert Douglas	21-07-44	75 Sqn
1334138 Sgt	McAINSH John	29-10-44	463 Sqn
1311744 Sgt	McALLISTER Alan Joseph	10-05-44	106 Sqn
1078235 Sgt	McALLISTER John	21-04-44	97 Sqn
1684019 F/S	McARDLE John	26-08-44	78 Sqn
1823181 Sgt	McARTHUR Ronald Charles	22-06-44	207 Sqn
1348047 Sgt	McCABE John	23-09-44	61 Sqn
1374780 Sgt	McCAFFERY John Thomas Eardley	22-05-44	156 Sqn
174060 P/O	McCALL Antony Patrick	16-03-44	57 Sqn
1574131 Sgt	McCALL Thomas	24-02-44	578 Sqn
173828 F/O	McCALLUM DFC Joseph Archibald Wilson		
		12-09-44	44 Sqn
553785 F/S	McCALLUM Murray William	12-12-44	635 Sqn
1397486 Sgt	McCALLUM Simon	28-04-44	166 Sqn
184087 P/O	McCANNON James [Eire]	21-11-44	78 Sqn
1483480 F/S	McCARROLL William John	17-06-44	10 Sqn
169703 F/O	McCARTHY Anthony Gerard	21-07-44	405 Sqn
1893589 Sgt	McCARTHY George Francis Peter	30-07-44	1656 HCU
3031377 Sgt	McCARTHY James Robert	17-09-44	1652 HCU
1836186 Sgt	McCARTHY John Emmanuel	21-02-44	460 Sqn
1797927 Sgt	McCARTHY John Michael	19-07-44	100 Sqn
177120 F/O	McCARTHY Leonard John Thomas	6-11-44	550 Sqn
1802226 Sgt	McCARTHY Mark Charles	18-04-44	51 Sqn
173522 F/L	McCARTHY DFC Patrick George	19-08-44	7 Sqn
31398 F/O	McCARTNEY James	25-04-44	78 Sqn
1568681 Sgt	McCASH Thomas Kinnoch	29-01-44	83 Sqn
1804429 Sgt	McCAULEY William Arthur	21-01-44	460 Sqn
1795998 Sgt	McCLAY Thomas Findlay	28-05-44	432 Sqn
653636 Sgt	McCLEAN Cecil	13-06-44	166 Sqn
1322963 F/S	McCLEAN John Allen	31-03-44	622 Sqn
160597 F/O	McCLELLAND DFM Gerald	23-04-44	77 Sqn
1822320 Sgt	McCLENAGHAN Hugh Fleming	31-03-44	101 Sqn
1566407 Sgt	McCLENAHAN James Stark	6-10-44	49 Sqn
1088075 F/S	McCLUNE William Joseph	27-11-44	189 Sqn
1573323 Sgt	McCLURE Robert Milligan	23-05-44	101 Sqn
1832010 Sgt	McCLUSKEY Thomas	1-06-44	138 Sqn
1823784 Sgt	McCLUSKIE Alexander	19-04-44	432 Sqn
1899023 Sgt	McCONKEY John Crawford	23-10-44	625 Sqn
1137800 Sgt	McCONNELL Andrew Leslie	30-01-44	463 Sqn
158915 S/L	McCONNELL DFC David Whiteside	15-02-44	101 Sqn
1685386 Sgt	McCONNELL Stanley	31-03-44	156 Sqn
159570 F/O	McCONNELL Victor	11-04-44	83 Sqn
149143 F/O	McCONNELL-JONES Adam Carter Hay		
		22-07-44	1655 MTU
658240 Sgt	McCOOL Jeremiah	4-05-44	576 Sqn
1455591 F/S	McCORMACK Dennis Patrick	31-03-44	51 Sqn
1334685 F/S	McCORMICK Alexander Ernest	25-03-44	630 Sqn
1493956 Sgt	McCORMICK John Payne	25-02-44	514 Sqn
710079 F/S	McCORMICK William Hugo	20-02-44	35 Sqn
	[South Africa]		

Service #	Rank	Name	Date	Sqn
1590743	Sgt	McCOURT John Robert	29-01-44	166 Sqn
55793	P/O	McCOY William Christopher	6-06-44	149 Sqn
61308	S/L	McCREANOR Maurice	31-03-44	578 Sqn
1497501	Sgt	McCREVEY Joseph	24-03-44	61 Sqn
54776	P/O	McCRUDDEN Denis Joseph	22-06-44	57 Sqn
1822819	Sgt	McCUDDEN Robert	13-08-44	14 OTU
1367884	F/S	McCULLOCH William	7-03-44	35 Sqn
1821083	Sgt	McCULLOCH William	25-05-44	103 Sqn
1540678	Sgt	McCULLY Edwin	31-03-44	103 Sqn
1301467	Sgt	McCURRY James	21-01-44	76 Sqn
1111437	Sgt	McDERMOTT Derrick	10-05-44	1658 HCU
1332060	F/S	McDONAGH GM Bernard [Eire]	8-07-44	619 Sqn
1339376	F/S	McDONALD Alphonsus Mary Bonaventure	27-09-44	619 Sqn
154199	F/O	McDONALD Peter Frank	23-11-44	195 Sqn
1822095	Sgt	McDONALD Peter Gordon	7-02-44	1663 HCU
1606602	Sgt	McDONALD Reginald James	8-07-44	44 Sqn
1813167	Sgt	McDONNELL Dennis	30-01-44	156 Sqn
1895574	Sgt	McDONOUGH John Joseph	24-03-44	115 Sqn
1821121	Sgt	McDOUGALL William Armour	25-06-44	149 Sqn
54387	P/O	McDOWELL Ian Hugh	23-04-44	101 Sqn
1511670	F/S	McENEANEY Terence Conlon	16-03-44	49 Sqn
1337238	Sgt	McEVOY James Patrick	28-05-44	12 Sqn
1552110	F/S	McEWAN George	18-04-44	158 Sqn
1492885	Sgt	McEWAN George Alan	22-05-44	626 Sqn
115593	F/L	McFADDEN Albert Stanley	31-03-44	97 Sqn
627945	Sgt	McFADDEN Charles Henry	25-02-44	622 Sqn
1523124	Sgt	McFADDEN Terence Christopher	31-03-44	640 Sqn
182296	P/O	McFADDEN Thomas Joseph Aloysius	18-07-44	427 Sqn
1820043	Sgt	McFARLANE James	30-08-44	428 Sqn
171854	P/O	McFARLIN Frank Stuart	11-05-44	50 Sqn
1421544	Sgt	McGAHEY James	31-03-44	514 Sqn
191924	P/O	McGARRITY Bernard	5-11-44	424 Sqn
1382146	F/S	McGARVA James George	27-04-44	83 Sqn
173338	P/O	McGAW Neil McArthur	4-05-44	625 Sqn
152740	F/O	McGEORGE John Ronald	21-07-44	75 Sqn
1332995	Sgt	McGHEE Douglas William	14-01-44	115 Sqn
1521465	Sgt	McGHIE John	31-03-44	550 Sqn
1820458	Sgt	McGHIE John Alexander Johnstone Mills	29-07-44	106 Sqn
542658	Sgt	McGIFFEN Herbert	11-04-44	622 Sqn
1317896	F/S	McGILL Arthur Henry	31-03-44	630 Sqn
1824436	Sgt	McGILL Tom David	21-11-44	192 Sqn
150505	F/O	McGILLIVRAY William	2-11-44	61 Sqn
134533	S/L	McGILVRAY DFC John William Eunson Duncan	11-04-44	619 Sqn
998505	W/O	McGINLAY John	6-01-44	7 Sqn
1590360	Sgt	McGINN Joseph Peter	23-04-44	582 Sqn
2203660	Sgt	McGLADE John Herbert	8-06-44	420 Sqn
110887	F/L	McGLASHAN Alexander Neill	3-01-44	156 Sqn
176028	F/O	McGLONE Frank	21-07-44	90 Sqn
1100822	Sgt	McGLYNN Alphonsus Bede	31-10-44	692 Sqn
1590573	Sgt	McGLYNN John	28-04-44	51 Sqn
638160	Sgt	McGOLDRICK Joseph	7-06-44	1652 HCU
132396	F/O	McGONAGLE DFC Bernard Pierce	8-05-44	138 Sqn
1861916	Sgt	McGOWAN John	21-01-44	427 Sqn
992535	LAC	McGOWAN Owen Joseph	23-03-44	22 OTU
83277	F/L	McGOWAN Robert Henry	22-12-44	189 Sqn
1825130	Sgt	McGRAIN Robert Wood	28-10-44	76 Sqn
1795204	Sgt	McGRATH Edward Walter [Eire]	29-11-44	103 Sqn
169673	P/O	McGREGOR Donald	10-04-44	149 Sqn
978853	F/S	McGREGOR James Harvey	31-05-44	12 OTU
569429	W/O	McGREVY DFM Dennis	8-08-44	7 Sqn
1097178	Sgt	McGUIGAN Hugh	21-07-44	101 Sqn
1777473	F/S	McGUIRE Ernest	24-12-44	100 Sqn
1345937	F/S	McGUIRE George Muir	17-09-44	617 Sqn
657932	W/O	McHAFFIE David	22-03-44	7 Sqn
1800890	Sgt	McHUGH John Francis	13-07-44	576 Sqn
1684767	Sgt	McILROY Alfred	15-06-44	78 Sqn
1821827	Sgt	McILVENEY James Gerald	16-11-44	207 Sqn
1796516	Sgt	McILWAINE William Ernest	23-05-44	50 Sqn
1568493	Sgt	McINNES Daniel	27-03-44	14 OTU
1820970	Sgt	McINROY John Joseph	27-03-44	166 Sqn
174949	F/O	McINTOSH Donald Cameron	30-11-44	115 Sqn
147774	F/O	McINTOSH Douglas Berry	31-03-44	166 Sqn
171930	F/O	McINTOSH Peter Cameron	25-07-44	207 Sqn
951312	F/S	McINTOSH Robert	24-03-44	15 Sqn
550259	F/S	McINTOSH William James	13-08-44	514 Sqn
3030075	Sgt	McINTYRE Andrew	18-07-44	158 Sqn
1562888	Sgt	McINTYRE Francis Cassidy	25-06-44	75 Sqn
1576770	W/O	McINTYRE John	29-10-44	463 Sqn
1568125	Sgt	McINTYRE John McDougal	15-03-44	625 Sqn
939112	F/S	McINTYRE Reginald Colin	21-04-44	57 Sqn
1785330	Sgt	McINTYRE William Meikle	6-11-44	106 Sqn
1562336	Sgt	McIVER James	29-01-44	431 Sqn
2210005	Sgt	McIVER Patrick Louis	22-05-44	550 Sqn
1580154	Sgt	McJANNETT Alexander Strathearn	27-04-44	12 Sqn
138480	F/O	McKAY Alfred Thompson	27-04-44	12 Sqn
1591313	Sgt	McKAY Donald	16-10-44	10 Sqn
591199	Sgt	McKAY James Morris	17-06-44	550 Sqn
1351466	Sgt	McKAY Ronald Alexander	22-05-44	619 Sqn
1823066	Sgt	McKEAND Robert Allison	9-08-44	115 Sqn
160193	F/O	McKECHNIE Donald Neil [Rhodesia]	27-07-44	44 Sqn
1820939	Sgt	McKECHNIE Douglas	27-01-44	467 Sqn
26144	G/C	McKECHNIE GC William Neil	30-08-44	Metheringham
2200086	Sgt	McKEE Jeffrey Hodgson	5-11-44	76 Sqn
151850	F/O	McKEE Joseph	23-05-44	9 Sqn
1567526	Sgt	McKELVIE William	25-04-44	115 Sqn
155542	P/O	McKENDRY Denis Charles James	3-01-44	83 Sqn
1795560	Sgt	McKENNA Charles Cecil	12-04-44	50 Sqn
1672365	F/S	McKENNA Joseph Niall [Eire]	23-05-44	103 Sqn
1594165	Sgt	McKENZIE Alan	17-08-44	630 Sqn
914855	Sgt	McKENZIE John	31-01-44	550 Sqn
1562476	Sgt	McKENZIE John Gilmour	6-10-44	49 Sqn
1812777	Sgt	McKENZIE Vincent	22-06-44	44 Sqn
1337038	F/S	McKEOWN John Joseph	25-02-44	514 Sqn
1820965	Sgt	McKERLAY Robert	29-01-44	83 Sqn
1381921	F/S	McKERROW John Andrew	27-04-44	44 Sqn
2219045	Sgt	McKIE Kenneth Moffatt	13-09-44	15 Sqn
1361194	F/S	McKILLOP John Allan	6-10-44	78 Sqn
1826753	Sgt	McKILLOP Robert Shaw	6-12-44	57 Sqn
151995	F/O	McKINNON Leslie John	22-06-44	619 Sqn
1566471	Sgt	McKINSTRY Thomas	10-04-44	460 Sqn
755362	W/O	McKNIGHT James Bernard	31-01-44	1660 HCU
1827919	Sgt	McLACHLAN David Christie	30-08-44	21 OTU
159447	P/O	McLACHLAN DFC James Thornton Douglas	15-02-44	7 Sqn
1821453	Sgt	McLACHLAN John Matthew	8-07-44	106 Sqn
1891777	Sgt	McLAREN Alistair Stuart	23-05-44	35 Sqn
1824962	Sgt	McLAREN Edward Laurie	19-08-44	51 Sqn
171644	P/O	McLAREN John	13-07-44	166 Sqn
1515312	Sgt	McLAREN Robert Charles	14-01-44	626 Sqn
1893585	Sgt	McLAREN Robert McGuire	13-08-44	76 Sqn
1672260	F/S	McLAREN William Alistair	16-11-44	214 Sqn
161690	P/O	McLAREN DFC William Graham Kerr	15-02-44	7 Sqn
1349943	Sgt	McLATCHIE George Thomas	14-01-44	101 Sqn
127223	F/L	McLAUGHLIN DFC Benjamin Edward	5-07-44	1667 HCU
2204122	Sgt	McLAUGHLIN Edward Colhoun	3-01-44	100 Sqn
1562810	Sgt	McLAUGHLIN James Aloysius	11-11-44	57 Sqn
171284	F/O	McLEAN Alexander George [Malaya]	31-10-44	90 Sqn
949983	Sgt	McLEAN David	2-01-44	106 Sqn
185130	P/O	McLEAN James	6-11-44	608 Sqn
1566319	F/S	McLEAN John	29-10-44	207 Sqn
1580558	Sgt	McLEAN Thomas Fisk	29-01-44	115 Sqn
170615	P/O	McLEISH DFC James Campbell	15-03-44	97 Sqn
1339244	Sgt	McLENNAN Alexander William	31-03-44	578 Sqn
1616782	Sgt	McLEOD Benjamin	8-05-44	49 Sqn

Service No	Rank	Name	Date	Sqn
1101950	Sgt	McLEOD John Gerard	25-07-44	1667 HCU
160641	P/O	McLEOD Williams Colins	24-03-44	640 Sqn
1399054	Sgt	McLOUGHLIN Charles James	21-01-44	514 Sqn
173060	P/O	McMANUS Philip Joseph	17-06-44	419 Sqn
1672812	Sgt	McMILLAN DFM Douglas William	14-03-44	78 Sqn
1383001	Sgt	McMILLAN William Henry	20-02-44	625 Sqn
1144727	Sgt	McMINN John	17-06-44	103 Sqn
164928	F/O	McNABNEY Samuel	8-08-44	7 Sqn
152971	F/O	McNALLY Francis Herbert Thomas	27-08-44	35 Sqn
1582886	Sgt	McNAMARA Anthony John	26-08-44	214 Sqn
1342754	Sgt	McNAUGHTON John	11-04-44	640 Sqn
176729	F/O	McNAUGHTON William Ross	19-07-44	207 Sqn
1825327	Sgt	McNEE John	13-09-44	15 Sqn
1458251	Sgt	McNEIGHT Hubert Graham	31-03-44	158 Sqn
1559057	Sgt	McNEILL Robert Findlay	16-03-44	625 Sqn
1825964	Sgt	McPAKE Henry	27-11-44	115 Sqn
154653	F/O	McQUADE William	6-12-44	207 Sqn
1550193	Sgt	McQUATER John	28-04-44	51 Sqn
1802314	Sgt	McQUEENEY Peter	21-01-44	514 Sqn
645384	Sgt	McRANN Peter Brendon	25-06-44	50 Sqn
1570384	Sgt	McROBBIE Thomas Andrew	6-06-44	76 Sqn
151768	F/O	McRUER David Winchester	14-04-44	5 LFS
527682	Sgt	McSPADYEN James	15-02-44	622 Sqn
1595923	Sgt	McSPORRAN Niel Graham	30-08-44	103 Sqn
157510	P/O	McTEER Donald	5-04-44	11 OTU
1825292	Sgt	McVEY James	4-10-44	550 Sqn
1556369	Sgt	McVEY John Harold	25-04-44	626 Sqn
1670355	Sgt	McWATT Francis	2-11-44	576 Sqn
1821553	Sgt	McWHIRTER Andrew Whitelaw	22-05-44	550 Sqn
1124861	Sgt	MEACHEN Robert Stanley	23-09-44	61 Sqn
1862131	Sgt	MEAD Norman Eric	27-09-44	1654 HCU
1337023	Sgt	MEAD Stuart John	16-03-44	460 Sqn
1398775	F/S	MEAD Walter Percy	23-04-44	166 Sqn
1582835	Sgt	MEADE Frank	1-07-44	625 Sqn
69435	F/L	MEADOWS Albert Edwards	20-05-44	139 Sqn
517497	Sgt	MEADOWS Stanley Allen	6-11-44	101 Sqn
1456465	Sgt	MEAGER William Harry	12-09-44	463 Sqn
153017	F/O	MEAKER Edward Thomas	29-07-44	550 Sqn
1573695	Sgt	MEANEY John McBean	21-07-44	626 Sqn
1607727	Sgt	MEARS Lawrence Ernest	20-02-44	78 Sqn
1805442	Sgt	MEDCALF Arthur David	2-09-44	57 Sqn
1812678	Sgt	MEDLOCK Horace Ernest	6-12-44	635 Sqn
153446	F/O	MEDRINGTON Henry Noel Trevor	17-12-44	57 Sqn
143849	F/O	MEDWAY Leslie Frank	4-05-44	625 Sqn
900604	F/S	MEEGHAN Frederick Arthur	17-06-44	77 Sqn
1600595	F/S	MEEHAN Kenneth Gladwin	18-07-44	158 Sqn
1335005	Sgt	MEEHAN Terence John	22-05-44	166 Sqn
1896332	Sgt	MEERING Eric	6-10-44	51 Sqn
135667	F/O	MEESON William George	18-04-44	51 Sqn
155071	P/O	MEGAINEY Rowland Henry	22-01-44	433 Sqn
161804	F/L	MEGGESON DFC Oliver John	26-08-44	83 Sqn
1572413	Sgt	MEIKLE William	23-01-44	161 Sqn
1195317	F/S	MEIR Thomas Matthew	12-09-44	100 Sqn
1493493	Sgt	MELBOURNE Lawrence Rex	15-03-44	101 Sqn
1594035	Sgt	MELL Ernest	15-02-44	57 Sqn
1592717	Sgt	MELLARD Raymond Henry	8-07-44	83 Sqn
1017778	Sgt	MELLING Joseph James	28-01-44	467 Sqn
1602828	Sgt	MELLISH Arthur Donald	8-08-44	50 Sqn
1046421	Sgt	MELLISH John Thomas	14-03-44	11 OTU
142199	F/O	MELLOR Abel Jocelyn	11-11-44	582 Sqn
1671436	Sgt	MELLOR Alec Lee	13-06-44	432 Sqn
1580333	Sgt	MELLOR John	10-05-44	467 Sqn
2211651	Sgt	MELLOR Philip George	9-05-44	432 Sqn
1199382	F/S	MELLORS Stanley	25-06-44	90 Sqn
1344712	W/O	MELROSE Alan Andrew Watt	28-06-44	141 Sqn
1577288	Sgt	MELTON Ronald	21-02-44	115 Sqn
1594563	Sgt	MELVILLE James	26-07-44	100 Sqn
1237634	Sgt	MENARY Basil Hughes	31-03-44	51 Sqn
1804251	Sgt	MENELL David Victor	31-03-44	630 Sqn
1565321	Sgt	MENZIES Colin Sutherland	16-07-44	76 Sqn
3020036	Sgt	MENZIES David	6-10-44	78 Sqn
108868	F/L	MENZIES DFC John Watherston	6-07-44	161 Sqn
1853114	Sgt	MEPHAM Denis Norman	27-12-44	75 Sqn
1287371	W/O	MERCER Ernest	11-04-44	161 Sqn
1897326	Sgt	MERCER Leslie Harry	7-08-44	149 Sqn
1320448	F/S	MERCER Richard Arthur	19-04-44	625 Sqn
1823010	Sgt	MERCER Robert Denhohm	5-07-44	57 Sqn
1801225	Sgt	MERCER Roy Victor	20-02-44	166 Sqn
1602737	Sgt	MERCES Ainsley Charles George	20-02-44	156 Sqn
1313396	Sgt	MERCY William Trevor	12-09-44	207 Sqn
1836004	Sgt	MEREDITH Edward Lewis	26-08-44	83 Sqn
116897	F/L	MEREDITH DFC John Andrew Trevor	10-05-44	83 Sqn
151469	F/L	MERRICK Francis Xavier	28-06-44	44 Sqn
1323482	Sgt	MERRICKS Arthur John Howard	25-02-44	100 Sqn
1468776	Sgt	MERRIFIELD Kenneth Francis	19-07-44	61 Sqn
3025139	Sgt	MERRITT Kenneth	31-12-44	150 Sqn
1588224	Sgt	MESSENGER Donald Kenneth	11-04-44	466 Sqn
1890126	Sgt	MESSENGER Hubert Alexander	28-05-44	640 Sqn
1351107	Sgt	MESSENGER Maurice Herbert	24-02-44	100 Sqn
1803300	Sgt	MESSENGER Reginald Alan	19-03-44	578 Sqn
162854	P/O	MESSER Robert Grainger	20-02-44	78 Sqn
177070	P/O	MESSER Robert John	29-06-44	102 Sqn
1683577	Sgt	METCALF Edward Roseby	26-02-44	431 Sqn
1515747	F/S	METCALFE Edward Arthur	4-05-44	103 Sqn
1595069	Sgt	METCALFE Hugh Swales	21-11-44	460 Sqn
1001891	Sgt	MEWBURN Hugh Harrison	27-01-44	626 Sqn
1896033	Sgt	MEYER Robert Charles Mawby	12-09-44	622 Sqn
124514	F/L	MEYER DFC William Alexander	15-03-44	97 Sqn
151321	F/O	MEYLER John Kingsley	7-02-44	1663 HCU
1892881	Sgt	MICALLEF Joseph Albert	21-06-44	1661 HCU
1612517	Sgt	MICHELL Leslie Ronald Herbert	27-01-44	576 Sqn
129283	F/O	MICHIELSEN Erik Fritz Karel [Holland]	26-08-44	83 OTU
618349	Sgt	MICKLEBOROUGH-SAUNDERS Eric Walter	16-07-44	76 Sqn
1216702	Sgt	MICKLEFIELD George Cyril Rowland	5-07-44	460 Sqn
521064	Sgt	MICKUS Anthony	21-01-44	115 Sqn
1319096	F/S	MIDDLEDITCH Harold Joseph	25-06-44	77 Sqn
1822037	Sgt	MIDDLEMAS James Graham	26-05-44	5 LFS
171185	P/O	MIDDLETON Albert Charles [Eire]	26-02-44	427 Sqn
1569017	Sgt	MIDDLETON Arthur Walter	21-07-44	115 Sqn
1031088	W/O	MIDDLETON Edward	12-05-44	61 Sqn
619089	W/O	MIDDLETON George Henry	31-08-44	83 Sqn
1570263	Sgt	MIDDLETON Robert	27-04-44	630 Sqn
1881082	Sgt	MIDDLETON Ronald	12-12-44	149 Sqn
1438733	W/O	MIDDLETON DFM Rowland	12-09-44	83 Sqn
50885	F/O	MIDDLETON Thomas James	25-07-44	514 Sqn
155486	F/O	MIFFLIN DFC Frederick Manuel [Newfoundland]	27-04-44	106 Sqn
1390244	Sgt	MILBURN Douglas John	11-09-44	408 Sqn
168625	P/O	MILES Bertram William	10-02-44	199 Sqn
56010	P/O	MILES Cyril Frederick Thomas	19-07-44	138 Sqn
172293	P/O	MILES George Robert	8-05-44	44 Sqn
187426	P/O	MILES John	20-11-44	75 Sqn
1396768	Sgt	MILES Leonard	21-07-44	578 Sqn
1192828	Sgt	MILES Ronald Edward	13-06-44	78 Sqn
114578	F/L	MILLAR Alexander	11-09-44	156 Sqn
53841	F/O	MILLAR Douglas	21-07-44	514 Sqn
177977	P/O	MILLAR George	8-07-44	49 Sqn
1897364	Sgt	MILLAR John Cleland	2-11-44	15 Sqn
1568573	Sgt	MILLAR Neil Grant	12-12-44	1662 HCU
1825218	Sgt	MILLAR Robert	5-08-44	166 Sqn
1343965	Sgt	MILLAR Russell Scott	11-06-44	100 Sqn
1487423	F/S	MILLAR Wilfred Sydney	23-04-44	463 Sqn
1314400	F/S	MILLARD DFM Alfred Edwin	20-01-44	83 Sqn
1466020	F/S	MILLARD Charles William Roy	14-11-44	51 Sqn
1165720	Sgt	MILLARD Harold George	9-05-44	83 Sqn
1289479	F/S	MILLEN Beresford Bruce	25-02-44	156 Sqn

1349064	F/S	MILLER Alexander Montgomery	28-01-44	115 Sqn	1622128	Sgt	MITCHELL Edward	13-07-44	576 Sqn
1621743	Sgt	MILLER Aubrey Harris	6-01-44	207 Sqn	129679	F/O	MITCHELL Frank Ernest	18-07-44	431 Sqn
1573710	Sgt	MILLER Charles Edward	7-10-44	78 Sqn	1684063	Sgt	MITCHELL Fred	12-09-44	50 Sqn
1559389	F/S	MILLER George Robert Shaw	29-07-44	467 Sqn	189118	P/O	MITCHELL George Clarke	15-07-44	103 Sqn
900230	Sgt	MILLER Gordon [Canada]	13-07-44	103 Sqn	1395992	Sgt	MITCHELL Harry Douglas	11-06-44	75 Sqn
141748	F/L	MILLER Hugh John [Canada]	29-01-44	7 Sqn	134693	F/O	MITCHELL Ivor	29-01-44	207 Sqn
1552376	F/S	MILLER Ian Graham Campbell	27-08-44	115 Sqn	1514804	Sgt	MITCHELL Jack	4-12-44	44 Sqn
133956	F/O	MILLER John	16-06-44	571 Sqn	1825675	Sgt	MITCHELL James Baird	2-11-44	49 Sqn
968796	F/S	MILLER John	8-07-44	207 Sqn	1388627	Sgt	MITCHELL James Lewis	13-09-44	158 Sqn
1013132	Sgt	MILLER John Ashworth	30-08-44	90 Sqn	1390301	Sgt	MITCHELL James Thomas Arthur	21-01-44	102 Sqn
172075	P/O	MILLER John Irving	20-02-44	550 Sqn	544389	F/S	MITCHELL DFM John Sandiford	30-07-44	97 Sqn
186702	F/O	MILLER Kenneth Archibald Willison	12-12-44	149 Sqn	751705	F/S	MITCHELL Kenneth Gordon	24-03-44	166 Sqn
710272	Sgt	MILLER Kenneth Silver Mylne [Rhodesia]	22-12-44	189 Sqn	172974	P/O	MITCHELL Kenneth Walter	16-05-44	103 Sqn
					1580437	F/S	MITCHELL Norman	12-09-44	44 Sqn
932588	Sgt	MILLER Kenneth Victor	25-03-44	44 Sqn	1088025	Sgt	MITCHELL Norman Harold	15-02-44	630 Sqn
1622551	Sgt	MILLER Lawrence Ayrton	31-07-44	100 Sqn	1077420	Sgt	MITCHELL Peter	14-01-44	101 Sqn
1603616	Sgt	MILLER Leslie George Robert	3-01-44	405 Sqn	135429	F/O	MITCHELL DFC Peter Edward	5-04-44	109 Sqn
1587685	Sgt	MILLER Nelson William Conway	2-05-44	10 Sqn	1690176	Sgt	MITCHELL Thomas	22-04-44	1660 HCU
1604765	Sgt	MILLER Robert Gordon	17-12-44	17 OTU	1101923	Sgt	MITCHELL Thomas Durward	24-12-44	622 Sqn
1802543	F/S	MILLER Stanley Isidore	24-02-44	156 Sqn	1337491	LAC	MITCHELL William Irvine George	9-08-44	Snaith
1880698	Sgt	MILLER William Henry	21-01-44	1661 HCU	1290938	Sgt	MITCHELL William Niven	8-07-44	17 OTU
1551842	Sgt	MILLIGAN Andrew Aitken	29-04-44	90 Sqn	1517301	Sgt	MITCHINSON Joseph Martin	13-07-44	103 Sqn
1600847	Sgt	MILLIGAN Lionel Herbert	23-05-44	101 Sqn	657027	F/S	MITCHINSON William	24-03-44	166 Sqn
1272279	Sgt	MILLIGAN Robert Arbuthnot	8-06-44	115 Sqn	1595302	Sgt	MITCHISON John	24-07-44	1660 HCU
1197021	Sgt	MILLINER Eric Albert	26-03-44	460 Sqn	1560689	Sgt	MITRA Bejoy Krishna [India]	25-01-44	PFNTU
1874036	Sgt	MILLINGTON Peter Edward	8-06-44	115 Sqn	657731	Sgt	MITTON Arthur Westwood	20-02-44	626 Sqn
1334196	F/S	MILLIS Leslie Noel	22-01-44	514 Sqn	1319639	F/S	MITTON Harold Bertram	11-02-44	425 Sqn
1819685	Sgt	MILLNS Reginald	26-03-44	49 Sqn	1053665	W/O	MITTON William Edward	15-02-44	103 Sqn
2220740	Sgt	MILLS Arnold William	4-03-44	20 OTU	1874047	Sgt	MOBBS Richard Sidney	13-06-44	15 Sqn
1601802	Sgt	MILLS Cecil Albert	22-03-44	97 Sqn	127786	F/O	MOFFAT DFC James	21-02-44	156 Sqn
1350976	F/S	MILLS Charles Bernard	22-03-44	626 Sqn	1564978	Sgt	MOFFAT Thomas	26-08-44	61 Sqn
54364	F/O	MILLS David Guy	21-07-44	100 Sqn	1366117	Sgt	MOFFATT David Drylie	19-07-44	630 Sqn
1509562	F/S	MILLS DFM Dennis Arthur	2-01-44	156 Sqn	1567557	Sgt	MOFFATT John	22-05-44	166 Sqn
1625986	Sgt	MILLS Dennis Raymond	20-01-44	57 Sqn	1896779	Sgt	MOGGRIDGE George Harry	22-06-44	619 Sqn
1812769	Sgt	MILLS Derek Arthur	6-08-44	207 Sqn	153714	F/O	MOHR Martin Jack Stanley	6-10-44	51 Sqn
145367	F/O	MILLS Douglas Henry	6-02-44	149 Sqn	1894400	Sgt	MOIR Alexander	27-09-44	619 Sqn
1465875	Sgt	MILLS Frank William	21-07-44	9 Sqn	168506	F/O	MOLE Douglas John	18-12-44	10 Sqn
1716353	Sgt	MILLS Geoffrey Edgar	12-12-44	150 Sqn	1182706	Cpl	MOLE James Albert	9-09-44	156 Sqn
1891587	Sgt	MILLS Geoffrey Laurence	11-06-44	625 Sqn	1797494	Sgt	MOLLOY Joseph Francis	19-07-44	100 Sqn
1593533	Sgt	MILLS Leonard	11-04-44	158 Sqn	1802369	Sgt	MOLYNEUX Harry Law	11-05-44	463 Sqn
2221099	Sgt	MILLS Mark	13-08-44	158 Sqn	1436972	Sgt	MOLYNEUX Keith	27-01-44	467 Sqn
1320716	Sgt	MILLS Roy Colin	31-03-44	61 Sqn	1579556	Sgt	MOLYNEUX Kenneth William	13-08-44	626 Sqn
1852086	Sgt	MILLS Stanley Harry	10-04-44	207 Sqn	1528746	Sgt	MONAGHAN Eric Samuel	29-01-44	97 Sqn
1681717	Sgt	MILLWARD Clement Richard	30-08-44	50 Sqn	1318155	Sgt	MONCK Peter	11-04-44	49 Sqn
178237	P/O	MILLWARD Maxwell Benjamin	22-06-44	207 Sqn	1574423	Sgt	MONCUR Alfred Keith	20-07-44	1661 HCU
2209050	Sgt	MILLWARD Norman Robert	23-05-44	207 Sqn	1867911	Sgt	MONEY Edward Thomas	30-07-44	115 Sqn
1697372	Sgt	MILNE Alexander	29-07-44	576 Sqn	1390097	Sgt	MONK Edmund Joseph Paul	31-03-44	51 Sqn
1892981	Sgt	MILNE James David	28-10-44	12 OTU	749827	Sgt	MONK Guy	2-01-44	100 Sqn
576911	W/O	MILNE John George	30-11-44	115 Sqn	52571	F/O	MONK Royston Edwards	26-07-44	100 Sqn
132625	F/L	MILNE DFC Owen Strachan	23-12-44	109 Sqn	1500257	Sgt	MONKS Harold	31-03-44	78 Sqn
129931	F/O	MILNE Robert Alexander	22-03-44	207 Sqn	1505068	Sgt	MONKS Harry	6-12-44	227 Sqn
1825462	Sgt	MILNE William Andrew Gardner	12-09-44	90 Sqn	152996	F/O	MONKS Maurice Arnold	13-06-44	166 Sqn
1346699	Sgt	MILNE Williamson Gray	30-01-44	640 Sqn	1667930	Sgt	MONNINGTON Alfred Gordon	12-08-44	1667 HCU
160860	F/O	MILNER Leon	12-12-44	460 Sqn	1394482	F/S	MONSEN-ELVIK Harold Annalls	8-06-44	138 Sqn
173331	F/O	MILNER Michael Nicholson	8-07-44	207 Sqn	1367497	Sgt	MONTEITH Thomas	23-04-44	106 Sqn
617405	Sgt	MILNER William	28-04-44	460 Sqn	1820975	Sgt	MONTGOMERY Campbel McKay William		
158791	F/L	MILTON James Roy George	26-02-44	427 Sqn				18-07-44	158 Sqn
1394305	F/S	MILTON Kenneth Brice	4-05-44	44 Sqn	149797	F/L	MONTGOMERY George Henry	15-10-44	207 Sqn
136386	F/O	MILWARD Arthur Hewitt	25-04-44	9 Sqn	170961	P/O	MONTGOMERY Robert	27-04-44	49 Sqn
1796309	Sgt	MINNS Stanley	12-09-44	622 Sqn	1366420	Sgt	MONTGOMERY Robert	30-01-44	514 Sqn
138467	F/O	MINNS Douglas Frank	21-04-44	15 Sqn	1481555	Sgt	MOODY Edward	14-08-44	550 Sqn
1404706	Sgt	MINNS Terry James	23-09-44	101 Sqn	177085	P/O	MOODY Francis Harold Rowlands	22-05-44	625 Sqn
1852200	Sgt	MINOR Donald	28-01-44	103 Sqn	173596	P/O	MOODY Frank Alfred	26-04-44	10 Sqn
2205779	Sgt	MINSHULL Leonard	24-03-44	619 Sqn	1114037	W/O	MOODY George David	31-03-44	460 Sqn
1385854	F/S	MINTJENS William Jack	12-09-44	35 Sqn	657036	F/S	MOODY George Thomas	29-01-44	431 Sqn
1338928	Sgt	MIRAMS Douglas Charles	22-03-44	44 Sqn	1576882	Sgt	MOODY James Revill	19-07-44	138 Sqn
1338959	Sgt	MIRAMS Reginald Arthur Duncan	30-01-44	514 Sqn	1626105	Sgt	MOON Derrick Leonard Desmond	30-08-44	75 Sqn
48966	F/L	MIRFIN Ernest	27-04-44	83 Sqn	120499	F/O	MOONEY DFM Robert Leo	2-01-44	97 Sqn
658855	F/S	MIRIAMS Jack Leonard	20-01-44	76 Sqn	1869940	Sgt	MOORE Alan John	25-07-44	57 Sqn

351

Service No	Rank	Name	Date	Sqn
155794	F/O	MOORE Arthur	30-01-44	207 Sqn
1330136	W/O	MOORE Donald Charles	13-09-44	15 Sqn
1800381	Sgt	MOORE Ernest Donald	12-02-44	50 Sqn
1586101	Sgt	MOORE Ernest Percy	23-03-44	17 OTU
1608629	Sgt	MOORE Graham Bernard Charles	8-06-44	138 Sqn
1187056	W/O	MOORE Harold John	11-11-44	97 Sqn
1399452	Sgt	MOORE Herbert Louis	17-06-44	77 Sqn
1615731	Sgt	MOORE Jack Morris	25-07-44	166 Sqn
1117487	Sgt	MOORE James Alexander	23-05-44	57 Sqn
1605107	Sgt	MOORE James Ernest	4-05-44	103 Sqn
131881	F/L	MOORE DFM James Gilhulme	10-03-44	207 Sqn
1898038	Sgt	MOORE James Worrall	17-12-44	49 Sqn
526578	Sgt	MOORE John Charles	4-11-44	195 Sqn
1582062	Sgt	MOORE John Thomas Victor	28-07-44	101 Sqn
1894318	Sgt	MOORE Kenneth William Charles	8-06-44	115 Sqn
1235401	Sgt	MOORE Peter William Lewis	27-08-44	57 Sqn
1319944	F/S	MOORE Roy Skilton	25-04-44	622 Sqn
1868952	Sgt	MOORE Thomas	29-07-44	49 Sqn
182035	P/O	MOORE William English [Newfoundland]	13-08-44	12 Sqn
1406490	Sgt	MOORE William John	24-03-44	100 Sqn
2216165	Sgt	MOORES Walter	20-02-44	576 Sqn
109518	F/L	MOORHEAD DFC Brian	29-07-44	463 Sqn
160760	F/O	MORAN Hubert	17-05-44	29 OTU
1344096	Sgt	MORAN James Francis	4-05-44	625 Sqn
1239323	F/S	MORAN Leslie Victor	22-03-44	158 Sqn
161088	P/O	MORASSI Allan	2-01-44	156 Sqn
175625	F/O	MORCOM Stephen Bickford	19-07-44	619 Sqn
1389740	Sgt	MORELAND Thomas	8-06-44	115 Sqn
1591886	Sgt	MOREMAN George	12-10-44	14 OTU
1684628	Sgt	MORETON James	23-09-44	9 Sqn
169313	F/O	MORETON Michael Patrick	19-07-44	78 Sqn
1578513	Sgt	MOREY Jeffrey Thomas	20-02-44	207 Sqn
541709	Sgt	MORFEY Ainslie Henry	10-08-44	50 Sqn
1486732	Sgt	MORGAN Arthur Ronald	31-03-44	50 Sqn
1867863	Sgt	MORGAN Bernard Reginald	25-05-44	419 Sqn
1868859	Sgt	MORGAN Edward Henry John	17-06-44	576 Sqn
1306780	Sgt	MORGAN Frank	2-01-44	207 Sqn
1853794	Sgt	MORGAN Frederick	8-06-44	115 Sqn
3050011	Sgt	MORGAN Gordon	27-08-44	1657 HCU
646041	Sgt	MORGAN Harry James	30-06-44	514 Sqn
1424536	Sgt	MORGAN Ieuan Glynne	13-02-44	15 OTU
1337960	F/S	MORGAN Ivor	18-07-44	578 Sqn
1433267	Sgt	MORGAN James	28-04-44	1568 HCU
182018	F/O	MORGAN James Edward	27-08-44	115 Sqn
1836700	Sgt	MORGAN James Islwyn	24-12-44	100 Sqn
1417169	Sgt	MORGAN John Fisher	22-01-44	466 Sqn
1852381	F/S	MORGAN John Hubert	13-08-44	635 Sqn
1396983	F/S	MORGAN Leonard	19-07-44	619 Sqn
1801125	Sgt	MORGAN Leonard	18-04-44	433 Sqn
1414772	Sgt	MORGAN Leonard Robert	24-03-44	578 Sqn
1394772	Sgt	MORGAN Maurice Frederick	25-06-44	75 Sqn
1893132	Sgt	MORGAN Ronald David	18-07-44	158 Sqn
1416979	Sgt	MORGAN Stanley Baldwin	22-12-44	97 Sqn
1578981	F/S	MORGAN Saunders Eiragwyn	12-06-44	101 Sqn
1415228	F/S	MORGAN Victor Charles	3-11-44	550 Sqn
1577083	Sgt	MORGAN Walter John	15-07-44	1651 HCU
1316806	F/S	MORGAN William Graham	29-01-44	166 Sqn
1651121	Sgt	MORGAN William Norman	21-07-44	90 Sqn
1413306	Sgt	MORGAN William Thomas	22-01-44	427 Sqn
1895616	Sgt	MORGANSTEIN Isadore Maurice	13-09-44	166 Sqn
151873	F/O	MORGAN-OWEN Maurice Linden	23-04-44	514 Sqn
1851259	Sgt	MORGON Rupert Frank Reginald	30-01-44	199 Sqn
1593856	Sgt	MORLEY James	23-10-44	44 Sqn
1531492	Sgt	MORLEY Kenneth	24-02-44	115 Sqn
1866330	Sgt	MORLEY Roy	31-12-44	218 Sqn
173188	F/O	MORONEY William John	4-11-44	49 Sqn
158922	P/O	MORONEY William Patrick	22-03-44	97 Sqn
1389016	Sgt	MORONI Hubert Frank	20-02-44	15 Sqn
151734	F/O	MORRAD Neville	25-05-44	640 Sqn
1450679	F/S	MORRAL Harold	15-02-44	622 Sqn
1686362	Sgt	MORRELL Alan Thompson Tait	25-06-44	576 Sqn
1397720	Sgt	MORRELL Kenneth	15-10-44	186 Sqn
1126931	F/S	MORRICE Colin	20-02-44	640 Sqn
164083	F/O	MORRICE Walter	9-11-44	20 OTU
539116	Cpl	MORRIS Allen	6-08-44	80 Wing
1168349	F/S	MORRIS Arthur Charles Norman	28-01-44	115 Sqn
1321632	Sgt	MORRIS Charles Thomas Richard	3-01-44	156 Sqn
81055	F/L	MORRIS Cyril Lascelles	13-08-44	12 Sqn
1591938	Sgt	MORRIS Derek	31-12-44	218 Sqn
185979	P/O	MORRIS Eric Meudway	4-11-44	195 Sqn
1199619	F/S	MORRIS Ernest	22-11-44	61 Sqn
1384599	W/O	MORRIS George William	2-11-44	15 Sqn
1583482	Sgt	MORRIS Grenville Malcombe	11-04-44	576 Sqn
129619	F/O	MORRIS Harry Donald Geoffrey	21-01-44	76 Sqn
1544587	Sgt	MORRIS Isaac	18-07-44	115 Sqn
1430151	F/S	MORRIS Ivor James	29-07-44	207 Sqn
1851391	Sgt	MORRIS James Arthur	24-03-44	115 Sqn
156959	F/L	MORRIS James Trevor Willis	7-12-44	640 Sqn
1389993	Sgt	MORRIS James William	24-09-44	61 Sqn
1652943	Sgt	MORRIS John Desmond	22-01-44	630 Sqn
171018	F/O	MORRIS John Edward	26-09-44	463 Sqn
1607592	Sgt	MORRIS John George	22-04-44	635 Sqn
1589893	Sgt	MORRIS John William	31-03-44	78 Sqn
130129	F/O	MORRIS Joseph Phillip	6-12-44	550 Sqn
1867900	Sgt	MORRIS Peter	4-12-44	166 Sqn
1399831	Sgt	MORRIS Reginald Arthur	30-01-44	166 Sqn
188459	P/O	MORRIS Richard Hartlebury	23-11-44	195 Sqn
1892968	Sgt	MORRIS Robert	3-06-44	640 Sqn
1494879	F/S	MORRIS Ronald Robert Curphey	31-08-44	460 Sqn
1503563	F/S	MORRIS Samuel Price	20-02-44	158 Sqn
567720	Sgt	MORRIS Sydney	23-05-44	57 Sqn
153583	F/O	MORRIS William	24-09-44	50 Sqn
136872	F/L	MORRISH DFC Harold Frederick	24-09-44	156 Sqn
1603335	Sgt	MORRISH Jack Stanley Francis	21-07-44	578 Sqn
1587515	Sgt	MORRISH John Anthony	14-01-44	207 Sqn
2210235	Sgt	MORRISON George	8-08-44	15 Sqn
150107	F/L	MORRISON DSO Godfrey Arnold	23-05-44	103 Sqn
127904	F/O	MORRISON Hew	27-07-44	83 OTU
159666	F/O	MORRISON DFC John	20-04-44	427 Sqn
1543162	Sgt	MORRISON Joshua Hebden	29-07-44	106 Sqn
1384400	LAC	MORRISON William Henry	10-08-44	49 Sqn
1251048	W/O	MORROW James Patrick [Canada]	20-01-44	466 Sqn
150313	F/O	MORSHEAD Owen Henry	23-10-44	625 Sqn
1800371	Sgt	MORTER Ernest Leonard	25-07-44	300 Sqn
1436379	Sgt	MORTIMER Arthur Woodburn	14-01-44	156 Sqn
1685107	Sgt	MORTIMER Ernest	20-01-44	460 Sqn
124264	F/L	MORTIMER DFM Godfrey Ernest	10-05-44	44 Sqn
1322900	F/S	MORTLOCK Vivien Vincent	25-03-44	7 Sqn
2220632	Sgt	MORTON Albert Edward	19-07-44	115 Sqn
52754	F/L	MORTON AFC Arthur Samuel	25-07-44	35 Sqn
1398980	Sgt	MORTON Charles Alfred	21-07-44	578 Sqn
1458241	F/S	MORTON Charles Gregory	22-06-44	49 Sqn
1575470	F/S	MORTON Clifford Keith	6-11-44	619 Sqn
1337604	Sgt	MORTON Ernest Leonard	20-02-44	166 Sqn
1803719	Sgt	MORTON Frank Ronald	24-02-44	156 Sqn
1108570	F/S	MORTON John Kenneth	6-01-44	7 Sqn
2204952	Sgt	MOSELEY William Edward	31-07-44	9 Sqn
1396082	F/S	MOSEN Frederick Hugh	30-01-44	166 Sqn
1581577	Sgt	MOSLEY Frank	20-01-44	622 Sqn
1032889	Sgt	MOSLEY Rupert	14-01-44	576 Sqn
1803621	F/S	MOSLEY-LEIGH Peter James	21-07-44	10 Sqn
1569206	Sgt	MOSMAN James Kelly	14-01-44	576 Sqn
1115114	Sgt	MOSS Alan	6-10-44	78 Sqn
2205500	Sgt	MOSS Colin	15-10-44	432 Sqn
1578638	F/S	MOSS Dennis Elvet	18-04-44	9 Sqn
106228	S/L	MOSS DFC Edward Henry	31-03-44	61 Sqn
1537417	Sgt	MOSS Fred	20-01-44	102 Sqn

Service #	Rank	Name	Date	Sqn
1606781	Sgt	MOSS John Morris	8-07-44	49 Sqn
159579	F/O	MOSS Joseph Barker	29-07-44	103 Sqn
2202493	Sgt	MOSS Leonard	31-03-44	9 Sqn
1686131	Sgt	MOSS Maurice Henry	24-11-44	128 Sqn
1449858	Sgt	MOSS Stanley Eric	7-06-44	578 Sqn
1891643	Sgt	MOTLEY Kevin Patrick Royston	23-08-44	1657 HCU
1593482	Sgt	MOTTISHAW Herbert Edward	14-01-44	97 Sqn
1101314	Sgt	MOTTRAM Philip Gascoyne	20-02-44	630 Sqn
1869623	Sgt	MOTTRAM Reginald James 'Reg'	18-03-44	463 Sqn
1623131	Sgt	MOTTS George Edwin	31-03-44	76 Sqn
1378208	Sgt	MOUAT Archibald James	9-10-44	462 Sqn
1382104	W/O	MOULD Geoffrey Arthur Douglas	22-05-44	635 Sqn
173597	P/O	MOULDEN Erice Henry	10-03-44	207 Sqn
1618889	Sgt	MOULDING Edward Robert Reginald	31-03-44	635 Sqn
1652638	Sgt	MOULE David Howell	6-12-44	460 Sqn
1853428	Sgt	MOULE John Herbert	26-08-44	300 Sqn
1305263	Sgt	MOULT Albert	13-06-44	76 Sqn
1891923	Sgt	MOUNT Albert George Edward	8-06-44	115 Sqn
1391128	F/S	MOUNT DFM Jesse Presley Robert	3-01-44	156 Sqn
149351	F/O	MOUSDELL Norman Albert Roberts	26-04-44	30 OTU
1046348	Sgt	MOWBRAY Frederick	20-01-44	102 Sqn
1194956	Sgt	MOWBRAY Joseph	24-03-44	166 Sqn
1042640	Sgt	MOXEN Eric	22-01-44	78 Sqn
160518	F/L	MOYES DFC Peter James	8-06-44	156 Sqn
2219023	Sgt	MOYLE Richard Henry	16-05-44	12 OTU
66643	F/L	MOY-THOMAS James Alan	29-02-44	1692 Flt
2210468	Sgt	MUAT Albert Ernest	30-08-44	101 Sqn
549273	W/O	MUCKART DFC Grant	21-04-44	97 Sqn
1576768	F/S	MUDDIMAN Denis Walter	12-05-44	630 Sqn
1875817	Sgt	MUFFETT Raymond Ernest	22-05-44	550 Sqn
1821736	Sgt	MUIR Alexander Rattray	27-04-44	57 Sqn
115170	S/L	MUIR DFC Andrew	21-02-44	156 Sqn
1563302	Sgt	MUIR David Thomson	17-12-44	61 Sqn
1670588	Sgt	MUIR David Vallance	10-08-44	50 Sqn
162811	F/O	MUIR David Walker	27-04-44	166 Sqn
135095	F/L	MUIR James Findlay 'Jim' [India]	27-04-44	207 Sqn
146137	F/O	MUIR Kenneth William Angus	4-05-44	101 Sqn
802563	Sgt	MUIR Malcolm	13-07-44	550 Sqn
1312876	Sgt	MULCUCK Illtyd Melville	21-02-44	9 Sqn
1568209	Sgt	MULLEN Thomas	19-07-44	619 Sqn
153056	F/O	MULLETT Peter Derek	15-11-44	115 Sqn
1600129	Sgt	MULLINS Michael	27-01-44	18 OTU
1601793	Sgt	MULLINS Norman Edward	25-05-44	51 Sqn
1586139	Sgt	MUMFORD David George	19-07-44	9 Sqn
50097	F/O	MUNBY DFC Joseph Leonard	20-02-44	692 Sqn
1390520	Sgt	MUNDAY Arnold	15-02-44	57 Sqn
1380855	Sgt	MUNDAY William Alfred	22-03-44	103 Sqn
1894649	Sgt	MUNDY Dennis Andrew Frederick	11-06-44	90 Sqn
947565	Sgt	MUNDY Hector MacDonald	25-05-44	576 Sqn
1804821	Sgt	MUNNS Harold Charles	21-04-44	625 Sqn
1075155	W/O	MUNRO DFM Alexander Armstrong	11-04-44	619 Sqn
1567515	Sgt	MUNRO David McArthur	16-03-44	463 Sqn
132760	F/O	MUNRO Neil	26-02-44	239 Sqn
153903	F/O	MUNSEY Roy Hensman	26-08-44	7 Sqn
911937	W/O	MUNSLOW Eric	11-04-44	101 Sqn
1395912	Sgt	MUNSON Donald William	29-01-44	76 Sqn
1866562	Sgt	MUNTON Gordon Charles	25-04-44	97 Sqn
632298	LAC	MURDIE Thomas Sydney Walker	3-02-44	5 Group
40414	S/L	MURDOCH Anthony O'Shea [New Zealand]	27-04-44	106 Sqn
1896046	Sgt	MURDOCH Isaac Lynas	23-10-44	625 Sqn
1345478	W/O	MURDOCH Thomas Talbot	21-10-44	75 Sqn
1685275	Sgt	MURGATROYD Jack	12-09-44	35 Sqn
33346	W/C	MURPHY DSO* DFC Croix de Guerre avec Palme Alan Michael	2-12-44	23 Sqn
1894787	Sgt	MURPHY Alfred George	16-03-44	10 Sqn
1622959	Sgt	MURPHY Desmond Norman	10-03-44	90 Sqn
1263101	F/S	MURPHY Francis Art	12-09-44	44 Sqn
1182077	Sgt	MURPHY James Christopher [Eire]	12-09-44	44 Sqn
1890850	Sgt	MURPHY John Joseph	20-02-44	433 Sqn
1532407	Sgt	MURPHY Leo	23-04-44	51 Sqn
1823639	Sgt	MURPHY Peter	12-12-44	1662 HCU
172485	P/O	MURPHY Robert	6-07-44	141 Sqn
153830	F/O	MURPHY Roger William	12-09-44	1653 HCU
1390564	Sgt	MURPHY Stanley Thomas	6-05-44	11 OTU
2210907	Sgt	MURPHY Thomas	26-12-44	10 Sqn
133523	F/O	MURPHY DFC William	23-05-44	576 Sqn
2206546	Sgt	MURPHY William Leslie	19-04-44	115 Sqn
1213498	F/S	MURRAY Albert	9-06-44	51 Sqn
630659	W/O	MURRAY Alexander	20-11-44	97 Sqn
145681	F/O	MURRAY Alexander Archibald	3-06-44	10 Sqn
1826555	Sgt	MURRAY Alexander George	24-10-44	576 Sqn
535937	Sgt	MURRAY Charles Malachi	30-08-44	166 Sqn
170229	P/O	MURRAY Edgar John	20-02-44	630 Sqn
639500	F/S	MURRAY Ernest George	25-08-44	218 Sqn
182133	P/O	MURRAY Harold Duncan	27-08-44	576 Sqn
1433884	W/O	MURRAY Henry Francis Graham	1-06-44	138 Sqn
132847	F/O	MURRAY Henry Ross	25-06-44	149 Sqn
152733	F/O	MURRAY Hugh McWilliam	10-06-44	207 Sqn
1502110	F/S	MURRAY Jack	2-01-44	156 Sqn
1560136	F/S	MURRAY James Francis Joseph	24-07-44	630 Sqn
1581654	Sgt	MURRAY John Patrick	11-06-44	460 Sqn
1559341	Sgt	MURRAY Kenneth	7-02-44	1656 HCU
658837	Sgt	MURRAY Peter	3-01-44	166 Sqn
1348949	Sgt	MURRAY Thomas McKay Arnand	2-11-44	576 Sqn
125146	F/L	MURRAY William John	15-06-44	78 Sqn
1607910	Sgt	MURRAY William Valentine	27-01-44	460 Sqn
1322747	Sgt	MURTON Harold Sidney	6-01-44	103 Sqn
1892309	Sgt	MURTON Martin Ernest	22-05-44	630 Sqn
1580876	Sgt	MUSSETT Dennis Roland	13-05-44	635 Sqn
1339911	F/S	MUSTOE Frederick Charles	28-05-44	103 Sqn
1850302	Sgt	MUTCH Ernest	30-08-44	50 Sqn
1499642	Sgt	MUTTOCK Alan	15-12-44	12 Sqn
1590607	Sgt	MUXLOW Denis Roy	9-10-44	462 Sqn
1382834	F/S	MYER Edward Michael	22-01-44	432 Sqn
157518	F/O	MYERS David	15-10-44	101 Sqn
2209603	Sgt	MYERS Francis	13-08-44	90 Sqn
201467	P/O	MYERS James Henry	23-05-44	207 Sqn
2205934	Sgt	MYERS Robert William	30-08-44	50 Sqn
1486415	Sgt	MYERS Stanley George	18-04-44	51 Sqn
172358	P/O	MYERS William Mornington Edmund	4-05-44	166 Sqn
1027466	F/S	MYLES Alan Peter	25-03-44	44 Sqn
183075	P/O	MYLES George	31-03-44	424 Sqn
1232857	F/S	MYLES James	13-08-44	101 Sqn
1378626	F/S	NAGALINGAM Kadir Kamn [Ceylon]	15-10-44	166 Sqn
134212	F/O	NAIFF Ronald Arthur	15-10-44	692 Sqn
1591232	Sgt	NAINBY Thomas	6-05-44	35 Sqn
1122824	F/S	NAIRN Andrew Swanston	6-10-44	640 Sqn
1685736	Sgt	NAIRN George Henry	29-07-44	103 Sqn
1549173	Sgt	NAISMITH Francis Findley	4-05-44	460 Sqn
1865537	F/S	NALDRETT Henry John	22-12-44	83 Sqn
748818	Cpl	NALL Reuben	14-05-44	Tuddenham
1609250	Sgt	NANSON Reginald William	26-07-44	103 Sqn
170713	P/O	NAPIER John McDonald	25-04-44	7 Sqn
1076653	F/S	NAPIER DFM Walter Alexander	27-04-44	83 Sqn
2221020	Sgt	NASH Charles Arthur	10-05-44	467 Sqn
1654190	Sgt	NASH Clifford George	26-08-44	75 Sqn
1575026	Sgt	NASH Donald Percy	23-04-44	115 Sqn
1610167	Sgt	NASH Frederick Desmond	23-04-44	514 Sqn
1438715	Sgt	NASH Harry Dennis	18-04-44	51 Sqn
1409323	LAC	NASH Jack Charlton	4-12-44	Little Snoring
172182	P/O	NASH Peter Albert	15-05-44	630 Sqn
1584193	Sgt	NASH Robert Brotherstone	10-05-44	90 Sqn
928627	F/S	NATHANSON Cecil	25-03-44	626 Sqn
1808639	Sgt	NAUNTON John Douglas	15-07-44	550 Sqn
1499247	Sgt	NAYLOR Arthur	4-05-44	619 Sqn

Number	Rank	Name	Date	Sqn
1433131	Sgt	NAYLOR Donald	30-01-44	106 Sqn
54372	F/O	NAYLOR James Fraser	17-09-44	617 Sqn
2216119	Sgt	NAYLOR James Willie	16-03-44	57 Sqn
1898463	Sgt	NAYLOR John William	25-09-44	199 Sqn
1622999	F/S	NAYLOR Kenneth	27-11-44	138 Sqn
2212864	Sgt	NAYLOR Reginald Percy	21-07-44	90 Sqn
1215795	F/S	NEAL David Robert	22-03-44	50 Sqn
1850090	Sgt	NEAL Donald Albert	14-01-44	156 Sqn
1523593	Sgt	NEAL Harold James	24-03-44	78 Sqn
1801910	F/S	NEAL Herbert Reginald	19-07-44	49 Sqn
1159697	Sgt	NEAL Norman John	6-06-44	76 Sqn
182745	F/O	NEALE Conrad Denis	6-11-44	106 Sqn
1874706	Sgt	NEALE Donald John	27-08-44	12 Sqn
54940	P/O	NEARY Charles Henry	11-06-44	434 Sqn
139724	F/O	NEARY Edward Patrick	29-01-44	1660 HCU
2209019	Sgt	NEARY Leonard Gerard	20-01-44	158 Sqn
1306694	Sgt	NEEDHAM Arthur	16-09-44	15 Sqn
1325312	Sgt	NEESON Robert John	30-07-44	1656 HCU
1673669	Sgt	NEEVE James William	6-01-44	467 Sqn
172039	F/O	NEGUS John	10-11-44	97 Sqn
170744	P/O	NEIGHBOUR Stanley William George	24-02-44	156 Sqn
1534938	Sgt	NEIL Percy	28-01-44	115 Sqn
1571102	Sgt	NEIL William	20-02-44	77 Sqn
118473	S/L	NEIL William Alexander Stevenson [New Zealand]	6-12-44	57 Sqn
138890	F/L	NEISON DFC Thomas	22-06-44	630 Sqn
1823742	Sgt	NELSON Donald Alexander	13-08-44	12 Sqn
183617	P/O	NELSON Eric	3-06-44	138 Sqn
1896358	F/O	NELSON Harold	31-01-44	1660 HCU
641893	Sgt	NELSON Horatio Robert	24-03-44	78 Sqn
134166	F/O	NELSON James	20-01-44	102 Sqn
1796160	Sgt	NELSON John Frederick	7-02-44	1663 HCU
971413	Sgt	NELSON John Weir	11-04-44	9 Sqn
1451354	F/S	NELSON Kenneth	19-07-44	630 Sqn
1801584	Sgt	NELSON Roger	29-01-44	466 Sqn
1515342	F/S	NELSON Ronald	28-06-44	106 Sqn
623923	Sgt	NELSON Thomas	20-02-44	158 Sqn
153298	F/O	NETHERCOTT Kenneth John	16-09-44	78 Sqn
1876635	Sgt	NETTLETON Kenneth William	14-10-44	550 Sqn
1802280	Sgt	NEVILL Ronald	19-07-44	76 Sqn
1880703	Sgt	NEVILLE Edward	12-09-44	50 Sqn
1796917	Sgt	NEVILLE Gerald Purcelle [Eire]	15-10-44	101 Sqn
131567	F/L	NEVILLE John	30-08-44	635 Sqn
1296378	Sgt	NEW Norman Charles	10-03-44	207 Sqn
188154	P/O	NEWBERRY Frederick	9-11-44	426 Sqn
1586987	F/S	NEWBERY Harry George	4-11-44	195 Sqn
1387525	Sgt	NEWBERY Patrick	20-02-44	419 Sqn
1590064	Sgt	NEWBOULT Ronald	23-09-44	207 Sqn
1812145	F/S	NEWBURY Dennis William	20-02-44	514 Sqn
200723	P/O	NEWCOMBE Frederick Parkinson	3-11-44	550 Sqn
1171725	Sgt	NEWCOMBE Henry John	13-06-44	100 Sqn
135399	F/O	NEWCOMBE MiD Jack	13-05-44	76 Sqn
647142	F/S	NEWELL Albert Joseph	21-02-44	97 Sqn
1565600	Sgt	NEWELL Alfred James	24-07-44	625 Sqn
1576971	F/S	NEWELL Alfred Rowe	26-03-44	15 Sqn
168745	P/O	NEWELL Francis George	11-04-44	30 OTU
577927	F/S	NEWELL Harold	19-07-44	463 Sqn
1237683	Sgt	NEWELL Leonard Alfred	25-07-44	166 Sqn
1377357	F/S	NEWELL Victor Louis John	28-05-44	166 Sqn
152717	F/O	NEWENS Reginald John	28-05-44	101 Sqn
610521	Sgt	NEWEY Harold James	20-02-44	61 Sqn
187760	P/O	NEWLAND Derek Gordon	24-11-44	419 Sqn
1520585	Sgt	NEWLANDS John	29-07-44	106 Sqn
1823350	Sgt	NEWLANDS John	28-05-44	1659 HCU
161648	P/O	NEWLYN Raymond Victor	29-01-44	15 Sqn
172752	P/O	NEWMAN Charles William Joseph	25-04-44	61 Sqn
1339270	F/S	NEWMAN Douglas Cecil	25-06-44	61 Sqn
1109109	F/S	NEWMAN Ernest	19-10-44	9 Sqn
925797	Sgt	NEWMAN Hubert Ernest	26-08-44	90 Sqn
1575537	Sgt	NEWMAN James Arthur	24-03-44	115 Sqn
1850048	Sgt	NEWMAN Percy	31-03-44	622 Sqn
1399876	Sgt	NEWMAN Peter Dennis	24-03-44	1656 HCU
2202209	Sgt	NEWMAN Terence	8-06-44	78 Sqn
923554	Sgt	NEWMAN Thomas Charles	24-12-44	460 Sqn
1576554	Sgt	NEWMAN Walter	28-01-44	199 Sqn
1318514	F/S	NEWNAM Leonard Edward	27-08-44	115 Sqn
1172993	Sgt	NEWNHAM Alfred	14-03-44	75 Sqn
132864	F/O	NEWSON Frank William	21-01-44	1667 HCU
171269	P/O	NEWSTEAD Frank Leonard	31-03-44	51 Sqn
53834	F/O	NEWTON DFM Albert John	4-05-44	97 Sqn
173546	P/O	NEWTON Clifford	13-06-44	578 Sqn
1805911	Sgt	NEWTON Edward William	13-08-44	429 Sqn
129719	F/O	NEWTON Frederick William	10-04-44	10 OTU
1480974	Sgt	NEWTON Harry	26-03-44	425 Sqn
1896256	Sgt	NEWTON Harry	8-06-44	115 Sqn
155991	F/O	NEWTON Robert Alexander	8-09-44	582 Sqn
1678297	Sgt	NEWTON Thomas	30-01-44	405 Sqn
1292158	Sgt	NEWTON William Albert Edward 'Bill'	16-06-44	7 Sqn
134882	F/O	NIBLETT Charles Joseph	3-06-44	158 Sqn
1897417	Sgt	NIBLETT Frank William	23-10-44	12 Sqn
162951	P/O	NICE Patrick Eric Norman	21-02-44	9 Sqn
138588	F/O	NICE Ronald Frank	25-02-44	115 Sqn
1298586	Sgt	NICHOLAS Bertram Horace	25-03-44	97 Sqn
1301629	Sgt	NICHOLL Jack	31-03-44	51 Sqn
1821022	Sgt	NICHOLL Robert	11-04-44	1661 HCU
1852333	Sgt	NICHOLLS Dereck	26-05-44	5 LFS
1314684	F/S	NICHOLLS Edwin Clifford	6-01-44	103 Sqn
1602187	Sgt	NICHOLLS Frederick Roy	25-04-44	78 Sqn
172425	P/O	NICHOLLS George Edwin	27-04-44	12 Sqn
1863129	Sgt	NICHOLLS James	23-04-44	149 Sqn
3006475	Sgt	NICHOLLS John	15-12-44	12 Sqn
1576493	F/S	NICHOLLS Joseph William	9-08-44	161 Sqn
111973	S/L	NICHOLLS Thomas Musgrove	31-03-44	625 Sqn
1225686	F/S	NICHOLS Arthur Leslie	27-04-44	103 Sqn
175089	F/O	NICHOLS George Frederick	3-12-44	138 Sqn
1581185	Sgt	NICHOLS Howard William	16-07-44	44 Sqn
1801158	F/S	NICHOLS DFM William David	15-02-44	7 Sqn
981579	Sgt	NICHOLSON Alexander	30-01-44	514 Sqn
1057527	Sgt	NICHOLSON Esmond	18-12-44	10 Sqn
1523535	Sgt	NICHOLSON Gerald Thomas	18-07-44	578 Sqn
1597145	Sgt	NICHOLSON John Stanley Alexander	8-09-44	29 OTU
1338154	F/S	NICHOLSON Joseph John Gordon	12-04-44	1654 HCU
1594726	Sgt	NICHOLSON Kenneth	21-07-44	578 Sqn
1624728	Sgt	NICHOLSON Norman	29-05-44	1657 HCU
1333659	F/S	NICOL James Cochran	14-01-44	97 Sqn
1134746	F/S	NICOLSON Cecil	16-06-44	7 Sqn
1555268	Sgt	NICOLSON George Pierrie	25-02-44	44 Sqn
1583156	Sgt	NIELSEN John	15-10-44	1667 HCU
1714926	Sgt	NIGHTINGALE Henry Arthur	23-05-44	408 Sqn
1386933	Sgt	NIGHTINGALE Linton Henry	22-03-44	49 Sqn
1875420	Sgt	NINEHAM Ronald Eric	8-07-44	49 Sqn
1800386	Sgt	NISBETT William George	25-08-44	101 Sqn
1796275	Sgt	NIXON Charles Alexander	24-12-44	166 Sqn
170344	P/O	NIXON DFM Ernest Charles	6-01-44	35 Sqn
156085	F/O	NIXON Francis John	25-02-44	61 Sqn
612488	Sgt	NIXON George	6-12-44	57 Sqn
1595438	Sgt	NIXON George	11-11-44	619 Sqn
115143	F/L	NIXON Graham William	16-09-44	582 Sqn
171083	P/O	NIXON John	30-01-44	467 Sqn
1898832	Sgt	NIXON Joseph Henry	31-05-44	12 OTU
1682465	Sgt	NIXON Joseph Terence	5-07-44	7 Sqn
1571977	F/S	NIXON Ralph	24-06-44	7 Sqn
1671453	Sgt	NIXON Richard Kenneth	8-07-44	57 Sqn
1796296	F/S	NIXON Thomas Lowry	15-06-44	15 Sqn
2214130	LAC	NIXON Thomas Simpson	30-10-44	1667 HCU
46028	S/L	NIXON DFC DFM Thomas Reginald	20-02-44	7 Sqn
152339	F/O	NIXON William	30-08-44	103 Sqn

Service No	Rank	Name	Date	Sqn
1559169	F/S	NIXON William	31-08-44	103 Sqn
1392350	F/S	NOAD Charles Arthur Shears	31-01-44	626 Sqn
171457	P/O	NOAKES DFC Leon Francis George	23-04-44	7 Sqn
562236	W/O	NOBLE Twice MiD Bertram Bernard	28-04-44	101 Sqn
1801049	F/S	NOBLE Collinson Alfred Peter	12-12-44	150 Sqn
1684346	Sgt	NOBLE Dennis	15-10-44	101 Sqn
747740	Sgt	NOBLE William Fred	30-08-44	166 Sqn
1397479	F/S	NOLAN Francis Thomas	11-04-44	625 Sqn
87027	F/L	NORBURY Peter Wingate	8-06-44	115 Sqn
1620610	Sgt	NORGATE John Kenneth	28-08-44	550 Sqn
2220879	Sgt	NORGROVE John	31-03-44	103 Sqn
2211863	Sgt	NORMAN Cecil Barber	2-07-44	1667 HCU
1614469	Sgt	NORMAN Dennis Stanley	7-09-44	17 OTU
173875	P/O	NORMAN Gerald Harry	10-05-44	44 Sqn
1586301	Sgt	NORMAN Howard James	4-05-44	35 Sqn
1868905	Sgt	NORMAN DFM James	25-07-44	419 Sqn
1394301	F/S	NORMAN Robert Henry	5-07-44	463 Sqn
1136617	Sgt	NORMAN Robert John	5-07-44	207 Sqn
1582499	F/S	NORMAN Vincent Edward	21-11-44	460 Sqn
153934	F/O	NORMAN William	20-05-44	83 OTU
1592453	Sgt	NORMAN William Christopher	5-10-44	626 Sqn
1543005	Sgt	NORMANTON Peter Hugh	25-01-44	16 OTU
1541523	Sgt	NORMINGTON John Edward	11-05-44	515 Sqn
1589308	Sgt	NORRIS Alick Clem	6-11-44	619 Sqn
1588202	Sgt	NORRIS Allan Bretherton	31-03-44	578 Sqn
1459937	Sgt	NORRIS Eric	22-06-44	44 Sqn
1836940	Sgt	NORRIS Eustace Vincent	19-11-44	1666 HCU
2221452	Sgt	NORRIS Frank William Bates	5-06-44	1658 HCU
1900179	Sgt	NORRIS James	28-12-44	576 Sqn
175851	P/O	NORRIS DFM John Thomas Webster Green	16-09-44	582 Sqn
1602554	Sgt	NORRIS Raymond Geoffrey	1-06-44	15 Sqn
1801492	Sgt	NORRIS Ronald William	23-04-44	514 Sqn
1384133	W/O	NORRIS Samuel	1-06-44	622 Sqn
135750	F/L	NORRIS DFC Stanley George	25-07-44	83 Sqn
1316674	F/S	NORRIS William Thomas Nichol	23-05-44	57 Sqn
1497697	Sgt	NORTH Leslie	15-02-44	57 Sqn
1807029	Sgt	NORTHCOTE Douglas Roland	29-07-44	576 Sqn
798768	Sgt	NORTHCOTT David George [Newfoundland]	27-08-44	12 Sqn
162782	P/O	NORTHOVER DFC Dudley Leonard	11-04-44	149 Sqn
1254684	F/S	NORTON Arthur	13-05-44	640 Sqn
1801045	Sgt	NORTON George Henry	4-05-44	57 Sqn
1575441	Sgt	NORTON Harry Arthur	2-01-44	44 Sqn
942326	Sgt	NORTON Henry Norman	25-03-44	12 Sqn
1872390	Sgt	NORTON Leslie Valentine	31-03-44	635 Sqn
1322116	F/S	NOTLEY Alan	22-05-44	622 Sqn
1867212	Sgt	NOTLEY John	23-03-44	166 Sqn
1450078	Sgt	NOTT Eric Charles	21-02-44	78 Sqn
1801172	Sgt	NOTTAGE Kenneth Ernest	29-07-44	100 Sqn
1576650	F/S	NOTTINGHAM Thomas George	17-08-44	630 Sqn
1614464	Sgt	NOVELL John Edward	27-01-44	576 Sqn
53223	F/O	NOWELL DFM David Clifford	31-03-44	76 Sqn
1585902	Sgt	NOWLAN Joseph Edwin George	7-02-44	1662 HCU
1662098	Sgt	NOYES Frederick John	12-09-44	90 Sqn
173773	P/O	NOYES Peter Raymond	18-03-44	76 Sqn
1895775	Sgt	NUGENT James	11-11-44	207 Sqn
1671822	F/S	NUNDY Bert	23-12-44	109 Sqn
152240	F/O	NUNNS Norman	15-07-44	550 Sqn
1496525	F/S	NURSE Reginald Sydney	25-02-44	408 Sqn
1594041	Sgt	NUTBROWN Robert Lawrence	23-09-44	78 Sqn
1234174	Sgt	NUTLEY Basil	31-03-44	61 Sqn
954362	Sgt	NUTMAN John Runniff	24-03-44	425 Sqn
1210237	F/S	NUTT Joseph Henry	14-01-44	12 Sqn
1515745	F/S	NUTTALL Fred	4-11-44	640 Sqn
1592205	Sgt	NUTTALL Reginald George	18-12-44	463 Sqn
1504558	F/S	NUTTALL Stanley	25-03-44	97 Sqn
1218760	Sgt	NUTTER David Edward	15-03-44	550 Sqn
1894334	F/S	OAKES Thomas Leslie	13-08-44	640 Sqn
152203	F/O	OAKLEY John Williamson	25-05-44	158 Sqn
158226	F/O	OAKLEY Maurice Alvey	26-09-44	463 Sqn
1439442	Sgt	OATES Stanley	13-04-44	158 Sqn
1721802	Sgt	OCLEE Kenneth Ealy	22-03-44	158 Sqn
179200	P/O	ODDEN Ronald George	22-06-44	57 Sqn
1314770	Sgt	ODGERS Ross [Canada]	23-05-44	57 Sqn
1877334	Sgt	OFFORD Charles Stanley	12-10-44	166 Sqn
1808316	F/S	OFFORD Peter Anthony Joseph	24-12-44	166 Sqn
1892332	Sgt	OFFORD William	1-07-44	101 Sqn
1587940	Sgt	OGBORNE Reginald Henry Frederick	31-03-44	50 Sqn
54597	P/O	OGDEN DFC Cecil Harold	15-07-44	103 Sqn
621667	Sgt	OGILVIE Charles Gordon Mackay [Newfoundland]	16-11-44	214 Sqn
1565909	Sgt	OGILVIE George Charles	21-01-44	84 OTU
1896061	Sgt	OGLEY Herbert	13-08-44	78 Sqn
1506017	Sgt	OLDFIELD James	4-05-44	12 Sqn
1853239	Sgt	OLDFIELD Leonard Arthur	11-11-44	97 Sqn
1582625	Sgt	OLDHAM Edward Ashley	3-01-44	166 Sqn
160013	F/O	OLDHAM DFC Gordon William [Rhodesia]	27-04-44	44 Sqn
155566	F/O	OLDHAM DFM James Wolstenholme	30-07-44	97 Sqn
1516167	Sgt	OLDROYD Edward	25-05-44	158 Sqn
1892056	Sgt	OLDROYD Trafford Henry	16-10-44	431 Sqn
1630903	Sgt	OLIVE Ernest Edward	25-02-44	467 Sqn
1802544	Sgt	OLIVE Jack Percival	23-05-44	97 Sqn
1800202	Sgt	OLIVER David Reuben	22-05-44	50 Sqn
1006958	Sgt	OLIVER Frederick	24-06-44	622 Sqn
1422977	F/S	OLIVER Gordon Anthony O'Neil	22-12-44	97 Sqn
1822471	Sgt	OLIVER John Alexander	31-05-44	12 OTU
151326	F/O	OLIVER Mostyn William	9-11-44	138 Sqn
1562387	Sgt	OLIVER William	20-02-44	434 Sqn
50687	S/L	OLLIER DFC AFM Leonard	28-05-44	103 Sqn
1320477	Sgt	OLLIFFE Jack Charles William	29-01-44	434 Sqn
151238	F/O	OLYOTT Walter Thomas	4-06-44	635 Sqn
172991	P/O	OMAN Samuel Walker	13-08-44	640 Sqn
1344854	Sgt	OMNETT William Houston Pollock	28-01-44	115 Sqn
102560	F/L	ONLEY Ronald Charles	11-12-44	128 Sqn
1590386	Sgt	OPENSHAW Roy	25-02-44	44 Sqn
1312291	Sgt	OPIE John James	28-04-44	166 Sqn
1346171	F/S	ORAM Alfred Wishart	25-05-44	582 Sqn
144455	F/O	ORAM Louis Lawrence	25-01-44	PFNTU
50234	F/O	ORBELL Ronald William	25-07-44	619 Sqn
926349	Sgt	ORCHARD Eustace Henry	15-03-44	77 Sqn
1387790	F/S	ORCHARD Gordon Arthur	30-01-44	100 Sqn
1675402	Sgt	ORD Edward	25-07-44	102 Sqn
1530987	Sgt	ORD Jack	31-03-44	78 Sqn
171616	P/O	ORD Thomas Edward	28-01-44	199 Sqn
1755424	Sgt	ORFORD John	4-11-44	195 Sqn
1836099	Sgt	ORME David Cooke	16-11-44	166 Sqn
1603414	Sgt	ORME Dennis David	15-03-44	44 Sqn
1520717	F/S	ORMONDROYD Stanley	12-09-44	576 Sqn
148800	F/O	ORMROD James Henry	4-05-44	12 Sqn
54772	P/O	ORR Archibald	1-07-44	626 Sqn
1551656	F/S	ORR George	22-06-44	214 Sqn
1346229	Sgt	ORR John	27-01-44	84 OTU
155396	F/O	ORR DFC John Allan	15-10-44	626 Sqn
1073290	Sgt	ORR William	24-03-44	207 Sqn
1819567	Sgt	ORRELL Stuart Charles	25-06-44	50 Sqn
1592436	Sgt	ORRICK Alan	2-07-44	1667 HCU
1592923	Sgt	ORRICK Basil	13-08-44	640 Sqn
139639	F/L	ORTON Edwin	23-11-44	622 Sqn
1895092	Sgt	OSBORN Albert James	22-06-44	57 Sqn
1880797	Sgt	OSBORN Arthur	31-07-44	100 Sqn
1715000	Sgt	OSBORN Henry Albert	16-06-44	514 Sqn
1875824	Sgt	OSBORNE Clement Basil	29-07-44	103 Sqn
160669	F/O	OSBORNE Edward Walter	16-09-44	239 Sqn
1210239	Sgt	OSBORNE George Thomas	5-07-44	57 Sqn
2204231	Sgt	OSBORNE Ernest	24-03-44	433 Sqn
1395421	Sgt	OSBORNE Frederick George Francis	20-02-44	103 Sqn

Service #	Rank	Name	Date	Sqn
49749	F/O	OSBORNE Joseph Campbell	2-01-44	7 Sqn
1208875	F/S	OSBORNE Raymond George	27-04-44	49 Sqn
1577092	F/S	OSBORNE DFM Roderick	8-06-44	166 Sqn
182213	P/O	OSBORNE Roy Robert	13-08-44	102 Sqn
1602493	Sgt	OSMAN Eric Ahmed	11-08-44	51 Sqn
1209008	Sgt	OSMAN Ronald Charles	4-12-44	57 Sqn
548094	W/O	OSTERLOH Victor George	27-01-44	83 Sqn
1332102	F/S	OSWALD Kenneth Anthony	4-05-44	35 Sqn
1493028	Sgt	OSWALD Kenneth Craven	25-04-44	76 Sqn
1438718	F/S	OSWALD Roy	24-06-44	44 Sqn
1337810	Sgt	OTTEWELL Richard Thomas	27-01-44	101 Sqn
1397336	Sgt	OUGHTON Leonard Percival	28-04-44	166 Sqn
1693952	Sgt	OULTON Thomas	4-05-44	460 Sqn
1339346	F/S	OUTRAM Ernest Joseph	25-04-44	61 Sqn
1320609	Sgt	OVEREE John Walter William	27-08-44	12 Sqn
1891732	Sgt	OVEREND Laurence William Frederick	15-03-44	550 Sqn
102525	F/L	OVERGAAUW Geert Adrianus Cornelis [Holland]	15-08-44	207 Sqn
1882274	Sgt	OVIS Ronald Dennis	6-12-44	419 Sqn
1315346	Sgt	OWEN Anthony Guy	15-02-44	207 Sqn
76117	S/L	OWEN Arthur Stanhope	12-12-44	Chedburgh
1316375	F/S	OWEN Cyril Malcolm	16-10-44	10 Sqn
1338653	F/S	OWEN Frederick Charles	27-08-44	635 Sqn
1102986	Sgt	OWEN Frederick Gordon	26-08-44	90 Sqn
1622728	F/S	OWEN George	23-12-44	582 Sqn
1880694	Sgt	OWEN George Frederick	28-12-44	428 Sqn
157392	F/O	OWEN George William	12-09-44	622 Sqn
1664252	Sgt	OWEN Harold Edgar Frank	12-05-44	630 Sqn
1397974	Sgt	OWEN Kenneth William	4-05-44	463 Sqn
162950	F/O	OWEN DFC Norman	13-08-44	14 OTU
1395854	F/S	OWEN Reginald John	8-08-44	50 Sqn
1301771	Sgt	OWEN Thomas Robert	23-06-44	78 Sqn
1316364	Sgt	OWEN Thomas Yeandle	16-03-44	514 Sqn
652199	F/S	OWEN Trevor Roebeck Glandon	27-08-44	97 Sqn
1602371	Sgt	OWEN Walter Ronald	29-01-44	576 Sqn
654599	W/O	OWEN William	30-08-44	101 Sqn
1395893	Sgt	OWEN William George	29-08-44	50 Sqn
151397	F/O	OWENS Gordon Count	11-08-44	12 Sqn
1573888	Sgt	OWENS William Struthers	12-08-44	30 OTU
176017	F/L	OXBORROW DFC John Edgar Percival	12-09-44	44 Sqn
1853210	Sgt	OXBORROW Roy	25-09-44	467 Sqn
1383796	F/S	OXENBURGH DFM James David	2-05-44	51 Sqn
176286	P/O	OXENHAM Albert Ronald	22-05-44	100 Sqn
3031334	Sgt	OXLADE Frank Albert	18-12-44	3 LFS
1437185	Sgt	OXLEY Peter Reginald	25-03-44	57 Sqn
1594315	Sgt	OYSTON Leslie	8-12-44	630 Sqn
1319093	F/S	O'BREE Harry George John	28-05-44	460 Sqn
1801508	Sgt	O'BRIEN Jeremiah	20-03-44	10 OTU
41053	F/O	O'BRIEN MiD John Thompson	18-11-44	7 Sqn
1399507	Sgt	O'BRIEN Peter Loda	19-03-44	192 Sqn
1135938	F/S	O'CALLAGHAN Joseph	7-12-44	640 Sqn
1167201	Sgt	O'CALLAGHAN Patrick Joseph Anthony	22-05-44	467 Sqn
1217981	F/S	O'CONNELL Richard James	22-01-44	44 Sqn
1896465	Sgt	O'CONNOR Armel Gordon	11-04-44	30 OTU
1629068	Sgt	O'CONNOR Arthur Bryant	12-09-44	625 Sqn
984462	Sgt	O'CONNOR Arthur Sidney	29-01-44	10 Sqn
1474265	Sgt	O'CONNOR Edward Albert	21-07-44	622 Sqn
1852461	Sgt	O'CONNOR Michael [Eire]	21-04-44	207 Sqn
2220291	Sgt	O'CONNOR William Lawrence	17-07-44	28 OTU
1652692	Sgt	O'DONNELL Terence Brendon	6-11-44	622 Sqn
143498	F/O	O'KEEFE Michael Patrick	22-04-44	1660 HCU
1896029	Sgt	O'LEARY Gerald	3-06-44	10 Sqn
536970	W/O	O'LOUGHLIN Vincent John	21-10-44	75 Sqn
1795144	Sgt	O'MAHONY Joseph Clement	2-01-44	207 Sqn
916300	Sgt	O'MEARA Patrick Peter [Eire]	2-01-44	550 Sqn
1713620	Sgt	O'NEILL George Edward	4-05-44	460 Sqn
1312312	F/S	O'NEILL BEM Joseph Herbert Patrick	28-04-44	51 Sqn
153719	F/O	O'NEILL Ronald	15-04-44	30 OTU
1853904	Sgt	O'NEILL William Francis	22-05-44	460 Sqn
1385976	F/S	O'NEILL William Patrick Heremon	31-03-44	156 Sqn
130132	F/L	O'SHAUGHNESSY Thomas Vincent	20-01-44	617 Sqn
151430	F/O	O'SULLIVAN Desmond Francis [Eire]	27-08-44	115 Sqn
984533	Sgt	O'SULLIVAN John	22-01-44	51 Sqn
1481831	Sgt	O'TOOLE Lawrence	17-08-44	102 Sqn
1717146	Sgt	PACK Alan William	31-08-44	1664 HCU
1631760	Sgt	PACK Frederick John	31-05-44	12 OTU
1894637	Sgt	PACKHAM Robert Eward Swain	30-08-44	463 Sqn
1604035	Sgt	PADLEY Eric Arthur	5-07-44	192 Sqn
1376742	W/O	PAGE Albert Leonard	21-07-44	578 Sqn
172299	F/L	PAGE Aubrey James	25-07-44	102 Sqn
1579628	Sgt	PAGE Cecil Arthur	11-06-44	90 Sqn
1869699	Sgt	PAGE Charles John	19-04-44	625 Sqn
1649720	Sgt	PAGE Dennis Arthur	2-06-44	138 Sqn
1713536	Sgt	PAGE Henry Fredrick	31-03-44	622 Sqn
1432806	Sgt	PAGE Herbert Peter	7-06-44	44 Sqn
1814068	Sgt	PAGE Leonard Augustus Alfred	8-07-44	630 Sqn
1380018	F/S	PAGE Leonard Gordon	24-09-44	51 Sqn
1581304	Sgt	PAGE Leslie Trevor John	25-07-44	300 Sqn
1395217	Sgt	PAGET Arthur Thopmas	17-06-44	550 Sqn
1335547	F/S	PAIGE Richard James	15-02-44	102 Sqn
1390491	Sgt	PAIN Henry William John	25-02-44	61 Sqn
1466662	Sgt	PAIN Ronald George	27-08-44	35 Sqn
1633408	Sgt	PAINE Kenneth	19-07-44	207 Sqn
151098	F/O	PAINTER Arthur Joseph	24-04-44	102 Sqn
135140	F/O	PAINTER William Henry	17-06-44	19 OTU
55026	F/L	PALANDRI Richard Silvio	8-08-44	50 Sqn
1542325	Sgt	PALFREY Joseph	23-04-44	550 Sqn
1651048	Sgt	PALLETT Frederick Cecil	1-06-44	149 Sqn
643812	W/O	PALMER DFM Albert Stanley	20-04-44	635 Sqn
1721835	Sgt	PALMER Allan George	28-01-44	103 Sqn
124807	F/L	PALMER Cecil John Edward	3-01-44	49 Sqn
1852440	Sgt	PALMER Dennis Burton	27-01-44	84 OTU
961254	Sgt	PALMER Dennis William	22-06-44	49 Sqn
1474541	Sgt	PALMER Edward William	8-07-44	207 Sqn
138398	F/L	PALMER DFC Eric Hewett	31-03-44	97 Sqn
155490	F/O	PALMER George	14-01-44	156 Sqn
1896993	Sgt	PALMER George Edmund	30-03-44	20 OTU
153386	F/O	PALMER George Stanley	27-08-44	166 Sqn
1515657	Sgt	PALMER Jack	18-03-44	630 Sqn
1891238	Sgt	PALMER James	8-07-44	106 Sqn
1797778	Sgt	PALMER Patrick Joseph [Eire]	4-08-44	77 Sqn
543152	Sgt	PALMER Philip Fred	5-02-44	115 Sqn
951869	Sgt	PALMER Robert	25-07-44	466 Sqn
115772	S/L	PALMER VC DFC* Robert Anthony Maurice	23-12-44	109 Sqn
1322330	Sgt	PALMER William Arthur	12-05-44	626 Sqn
169421	F/L	PALMER William Edward	8-06-44	15 Sqn
1583509	Sgt	PALMER William Reginald	30-01-44	405 Sqn
918780	Sgt	PANES Clifford David	14-01-44	101 Sqn
1314367	F/S	PANNIERS Edward Douglas	14-01-44	156 Sqn
1880849	Sgt	PANTHER Arnold John Porter	14-10-44	153 Sqn
175557	P/O	PANTON Christopher Witton	31-03-44	433 Sqn
1154981	F/S	PANTRY Thomas [Switzerland]	16-05-44	141 Sqn
169510	P/O	PAPWORTH DFC John Norris	6-06-44	582 Sqn
1896648	Sgt	PARADISE Edward George	2-11-44	195 Sqn
1316665	F/S	PARDOE Albert Alfred	20-02-44	61 Sqn
177439	P/O	PARFITT Reginald	6-07-44	578 Sqn
922824	F/S	PARFITT Walter Robert Charles	13-08-44	582 Sqn
1853953	Sgt	PARHAM Derick Arthur Roland	21-07-44	578 Sqn
1593220	Sgt	PARISH Frank	22-05-44	100 Sqn
1567907	Sgt	PARK David	13-07-44	1652 HCU
912468	Sgt	PARKER Alan Charles	20-01-44	1657 HCU
1381898	Sgt	PARKER Brian	28-09-44	463 Sqn
1623312	Sgt	PARKER Donald	12-10-44	7 Sqn
54422	F/O	PARKER DFM Edward	2-11-44	576 Sqn

Service #	Rank	Name	Date	Unit
173067	P/O	PARKER Edward Albert	26-07-44	431 Sqn
1471658	Sgt	PARKER Edward George Lancelot	30-08-44	106 Sqn
1677776	Sgt	PARKER Ernest	29-01-44	434 Sqn
1869920	Sgt	PARKER Ernest William	30-08-44	550 Sqn
2207123	F/S	PARKER Geoffrey	21-06-44	15 Sqn
1817628	Sgt	PARKER George Oliver	11-04-44	161 Sqn
1803778	Sgt	PARKER George Robert	30-01-44	44 Sqn
1875343	Sgt	PARKER Harold Colin	20-02-44	207 Sqn
1174732	Sgt	PARKER Jack William Logg	10-05-44	9 Sqn
658844	F/S	PARKER Jeremiah	10-05-44	467 Sqn
173134	F/O	PARKER John	24-07-44	619 Sqn
1146642	Sgt	PARKER John Lewis	11-04-44	61 Sqn
1819805	Sgt	PARKER Leonard Edward	24-02-44	9 Sqn
2208900	Sgt	PARKER Peter James Northen	17-06-44	102 Sqn
1585229	Sgt	PARKER Peter Thomas	13-02-44	15 OTU
1466283	F/S	PARKER Raymond	6-06-44	149 Sqn
1851671	Sgt	PARKER Raymond William	24-07-44	1660 HCU
150097	F/O	PARKER Richard Morgan	30-01-44	100 Sqn
1892552	Sgt	PARKER Robert Ronald Smithie	12-08-44	75 Sqn
116394	F/L	PARKER MiD Thomas George John	30-08-44	463 Sqn
1817340	F/S	PARKES Gerald	22-12-44	578 Sqn
114010	S/L	PARKES DSO Stuart Martin Parkeshouse	26-08-44	97 Sqn
1670523	Sgt	PARKHILL Alfred Corrothers	21-07-44	101 Sqn
1592560	Sgt	PARKIN Donald	25-04-44	192 Sqn
1678439	Sgt	PARKIN John Edmund	26-11-44	115 Sqn
1567334	Sgt	PARKIN Richard	11-06-44	75 Sqn
1410923	Sgt	PARKIN Terence	27-04-44	49 Sqn
1873911	F/S	PARKINSON DFM Gordon James William	8-07-44	49 Sqn
172426	P/O	PARKINSON Jack	13-05-44	576 Sqn
2204260	Sgt	PARKINSON William Ronald	22-06-44	57 Sqn
948804	Sgt	PARKMAN John Alfred	29-01-44	50 Sqn
1393242	F/S	PARKYN Ronald	13-06-44	115 Sqn
1804750	Sgt	PARMENTER Richard Sydney	31-03-44	460 Sqn
622838	F/S	PARR Sidney	16-06-44	582 Sqn
2212825	Sgt	PARR Thomas	31-05-44	1654 HCU
1851463	Sgt	PARRISH Edward Lionel	26-02-44	90 Sqn
182674	P/O	PARROTT Herbert	26-07-44	619 Sqn
1649552	Sgt	PARROTT James Harrison	29-01-44	419 Sqn
1052458	F/S	PARRY Edward	11-04-44	61 Sqn
1862502	Sgt	PARRY Eric	3-06-44	138 Sqn
1378220	Sgt	PARRY Eric Frank	27-04-44	100 Sqn
55216	F/O	PARRY James Francis	12-09-44	619 Sqn
2203123	Sgt	PARRY Oswald Albert	30-11-44	578 Sqn
1086157	Sgt	PARRY William Grainger	12-05-44	115 Sqn
154808	F/O	PARSONS Douglas Edwin	18-12-44	3 LFS
1275550	Sgt	PARSONS Harold Walter	26-03-44	626 Sqn
1099391	Sgt	PARSONS Peter Anstiss	19-03-44	578 Sqn
1387279	Sgt	PARSONS Ronald	15-02-44	100 Sqn
1836455	Sgt	PARSONS Thomas Victor	13-08-44	77 Sqn
156772	F/O	PARTINGTON Ian	20-09-44	514 Sqn
1524275	Sgt	PARTINGTON Ralph	23-04-44	49 Sqn
1394153	W/O	PARTRIDGE Denis Gilbert	23-06-44	97 Sqn
1623818	Sgt	PARTRIDGE Clarence Arthur	3-06-44	640 Sqn
1395024	Sgt	PARTRIDGE Ronald Anthony	27-01-44	1660 HCU
1852206	Sgt	PARTRIDGE William Norman	29-06-44	102 Sqn
1410630	Sgt	PASCOE Archie	4-12-44	619 Sqn
1579595	Sgt	PASCOE Cyril Joseph	29-01-44	12 OTU
1213898	Sgt	PASFIELD Leonard John 'Len'	14-01-44	626 Sqn
1803633	Sgt	PASKELL Frederick Alfred	15-02-44	102 Sqn
1196414	F/S	PASSAGE Thomas Eugene	5-08-44	166 Sqn
148090	F/O	PASSINGHAM DFM Clifford	13-05-44	635 Sqn
1316032	Sgt	PATCHETT Herbert Desmond 'Sonnie'	25-03-44	78 Sqn
151062	F/O	PATEMAN William Henry Charles	16-02-44	619 Sqn
126709	F/L	PATERSON David Clark	18-09-44	515 Sqn
1552814	Sgt	PATERSON George Inglis	20-02-44	83 Sqn
1550628	Sgt	PATERSON John	29-07-44	619 Sqn
1823399	Sgt	PATERSON John	23-12-44	582 Sqn
1824999	Sgt	PATERSON John Sinclair	24-09-44	15 Sqn
175168	P/O	PATERSON Philip Lionel Bennett	14-08-44	20 OTU
1823505	Sgt	PATERSON Robert McKinstray	20-11-44	514 Sqn
1601152	Sgt	PATES Edward Frank	24-03-44	166 Sqn
1896477	Sgt	PATEY Frank Benjamin	31-03-44	50 Sqn
1893740	Sgt	PATIENCE William Ronald	6-08-44	97 Sqn
1585454	Sgt	PATMORE Arthur Frederick	22-05-44	166 Sqn
1214901	F/S	PATMORE Ernest Edward James	25-04-44	9 Sqn
1389061	F/S	PATMORE DFM Ronald Marshall	27-04-44	101 Sqn
1566514	Sgt	PATON David Ferguson	13-07-44	166 Sqn
1394069	F/S	PATON Euan Harvey	27-01-44	149 Sqn
1545237	Sgt	PATRICK Henry	2-01-44	61 Sqn
1583253	F/S	PATRICK Reginald James	26-09-44	463 Sqn
2211183	Sgt	PATTEN Frederick Hubert	25-07-44	75 Sqn
1876219	Sgt	PATTEN James Cyril	22-03-44	425 Sqn
1323721	Sgt	PATTENDEN Bernard Hugh	2-03-44	15 OTU
1491419	F/S	PATTERSON David Gordon	5-08-44	161 Sqn
630907	Sgt	PATTERSON Gerald Joseph	18-04-44	427 Sqn
161641	F/O	PATTERSON DFC John William	27-07-44	83 Sqn
1438245	F/S	PATTERSON Maxwell Chambers	14-01-44	101 Sqn
1594123	Sgt	PATTERSON Reginald	11-11-44	619 Sqn
1553418	Sgt	PATTERSON Stanley	25-05-44	76 Sqn
1576385	F/S	PATTI Samuel Roger	8-05-44	106 Sqn
1427569	Sgt	PATTISON Eric Stephen	6-12-44	103 Sqn
1812157	Sgt	PATTISON Ernest	25-07-44	83 Sqn
1499309	Sgt	PAUL Frank Henry James	8-06-44	15 Sqn
1320130	Sgt	PAUL Henry Alfred	21-01-44	10 Sqn
1608094	Sgt	PAUL Jack Hastings	21-01-44	405 Sqn
1593431	Sgt	PAUL Ronald James	6-10-44	106 Sqn
1392466	F/S	PAULEY Felix Owen Warboys	16-02-44	106 Sqn
1377692	W/O	PAWSEY Owen John	11-12-44	57 Sqn
1329560	Sgt	PAXTON Robert Henry	31-03-44	550 Sqn
1134608	F/S	PAYNE Claude Charles	31-03-44	514 Sqn
1337267	Sgt	PAYNE Cyril George	3-01-44	619 Sqn
1569124	Sgt	PAYNE Edward James	2-11-44	77 Sqn
187217	P/O	PAYNE Gordon Arthur	6-10-44	207 Sqn
1271687	Sgt	PAYNE Herbert Frederick	20-02-44	77 Sqn
710275	Sgt	PAYNE John Graham Phillipson [Rhodesia]	10-06-44	44 Sqn
1491571	F/S	PAYNE Leslie Frank	16-10-44	207 Sqn
1528967	Sgt	PAYNE Richard John	7-02-44	1662 HCU
1083964	W/O	PAYNE Sydney William	4-05-44	12 Sqn
963274	Sgt	PAYNE Victor Douglas	13-05-44	515 Sqn
1627385	Sgt	PAYNE Victor Edmond	4-01-44	11 OTU
1869457	Sgt	PAYTON Alfred William	14-11-44	51 Sqn
1547679	Sgt	PAYTON Arthur	29-07-44	622 Sqn
1434302	F/S	PEACE Eric Henry	23-06-44	97 Sqn
1592073	Sgt	PEACE George	8-07-44	50 Sqn
524666	Sgt	PEACE Leslie [Canada]	29-07-44	106 Sqn
1872747	Sgt	PEACH Dermott Frederick Arthur	25-05-44	15 Sqn
989685	F/S	PEACOCK Clarence	22-03-44	49 Sqn
1484053	Sgt	PEACOCK Edward	25-03-44	61 Sqn
160601	P/O	PEACOCK Francis James	29-01-44	630 Sqn
152783	F/O	PEACOCK Henry Frank	8-06-44	101 Sqn
1318159	F/S	PEACOCK James John	15-02-44	103 Sqn
162822	P/O	PEACOCK Kenneth	25-03-44	630 Sqn
1818530	Sgt	PEAD Ronald	15-03-44	463 Sqn
35917	F/O	PEAKE Charles Edward	31-03-44	635 Sqn
1533257	Sgt	PEAKE James Henry	30-08-44	166 Sqn
1891075	Sgt	PEAKE Kenneth Edwin	16-03-44	514 Sqn
1606629	Sgt	PEAKE Stanley William	10-06-44	10 Sqn
1335550	Sgt	PEALL Leslie Wilfred Arthur	31-03-44	76 Sqn
1816429	Sgt	PEARCE Arthur Joseph	4-10-44	550 Sqn
1893142	Sgt	PEARCE Bernard	23-05-44	90 Sqn
1603564	F/S	PEARCE Donald Maurice	17-12-44	57 Sqn
125871	F/L	PEARCE John Mansfield	19-08-44	1655 MTU
1316948	F/S	PEARCE Maurice Edward	12-09-44	83 Sqn
161468	F/O	PEARCE Merlin	13-09-44	640 Sqn

Service No	Rank	Name	Date	Sqn
1737174	Sgt	PEARCE Norman	24-04-44	102 Sqn
1880404	Sgt	PEARCE Ronald Ernest	23-09-44	576 Sqn
1339551	Sgt	PEARCE Ronald Francis	17-06-44	10 Sqn
52032	F/O	PEARCE Wilfred	22-03-44	49 Sqn
1653773	Sgt	PEARCE William Charles	25-04-44	622 Sqn
177550	P/O	PEARCEY William Gordon	17-06-44	434 Sqn
1313836	W/O	PEARN Peter Francis Cory	27-08-44	192 Sqn
1892105	Sgt	PEARSALL Peter Francis Gordon	13-06-44	15 Sqn
646992	F/S	PEARSE Derek Charles	18-03-44	630 Sqn
175491	P/O	PEARSE Geoffrey Frank	22-05-44	100 Sqn
1436390	F/S	PEARSON Charles Ernest	20-02-44	625 Sqn
1385830	Sgt	PEARSON Clifford	30-08-44	467 Sqn
1135624	Sgt	PEARSON Francis Joseph	25-02-44	463 Sqn
1337855	Sgt	PEARSON Gilbert	24-03-44	100 Sqn
126002	F/L	PEARSON DFC Ian Maclaren	3-01-44	7 Sqn
1296342	Sgt	PEARSON Lawrence	22-03-44	426 Sqn
1836265	Sgt	PEARSON Maxwell John	27-08-44	115 Sqn
1066692	F/S	PEARSON Monteith Samuel	15-02-44	622 Sqn
1579725	Sgt	PEARSON DFM Robert Arthur	27-04-44	101 Sqn
1141403	F/S	PEARSON Robert Edward	2-03-44	630 Sqn
1132796	Sgt	PEARTON Kingsley	21-04-44	100 Sqn
1436156	Sgt	PEASE Ernest Montague John	2-01-44	106 Sqn
1390188	W/O	PEASGOOD George Knight	21-01-44	550 Sqn
1620868	Sgt	PEAT Austin	27-01-44	84 OTU
1338511	F/S	PECK Eric Edward Stephen	17-09-44	617 Sqn
170605	P/O	PECK Frederick Leslie	22-05-44	626 Sqn
1812386	Sgt	PECK Gordon Joseph William	11-04-44	51 Sqn
'187059'	Sgt	PECK Joseph Edward	12-10-44	21 OTU
1487387	F/S	PECKETT Henry Mitchell	4-05-44	57 Sqn
1389552	F/S	PECKHAM William Thomas George	24-03-44	429 Sqn
1520817	Sgt	PEDLEY John Desmond	24-03-44	619 Sqn
156773	F/O	PEDLOW William	17-08-44	102 Sqn
1375587	W/O	PEDRAZZINI Richard	13-08-44	635 Sqn
1585830	F/S	PEEL Edwin	29-07-44	207 Sqn
1496607	F/S	PEEL Ronald William	17-06-44	102 Sqn
1750374	Sgt	PEERS John	25-02-44	97 Sqn
1338509	Sgt	PEGG Leonard Frederick	16-09-44	608 Sqn
1525908	LAC	PEGG Robert	2-02-44	35 Sqn
1603302	Sgt	PEGLER Maurice Stanley	23-06-44	100 Sqn
1800767	Sgt	PEGRUM Douglas Frank	16-05-44	103 Sqn
1890440	Sgt	PELHAM Maurice Bernard	13-06-44	15 Sqn
1262146	Sgt	PEMBERTON William Leslie	12-02-44	12 OTU
1059734	Sgt	PENDER James	5-07-44	576 Sqn
645711	Sgt	PENHALIGON William John 'Bill'	10-05-44	90 Sqn
150252	F/O	PENMAN Ernest Richard 'Dickie'	8-05-44	106 Sqn
1251477	Sgt	PENN Charles Frederick	25-06-44	463 Sqn
138453	F/L	PENNINGTON Allen	27-04-44	83 Sqn
1822618	Sgt	PENNYKID Robert	24-03-44	77 Sqn
80123	F/O	PENROSE DFC George William [Rhodesia]	14-01-44	156 Sqn
1880020	Sgt	PENTON Douglas	12-0-44	44 Sqn
702672	Sgt	PENTON Jack Ronald	15-07-44	550 Sqn
1607978	Sgt	PENTON Kenneth	8-06-44	115 Sqn
1608061	Sgt	PEPPER Ernest George Richard	10-05-44	550 Sqn
1453939	Sgt	PEPPER Jack Desmond	28-06-44	106 Sqn
1682572	F/S	PEPPER James	23-05-44	75 Sqn
1147343	Sgt	PERCIVAL Samuel	31-03-44	44 Sqn
553063	Sgt	PERCIVAL Walter Reginald	28-04-44	75 Sqn
621831	F/S	PERCIVAL William	21-01-44	35 Sqn
128053	S/L	PERKINS DFC Albert Sydney	27-08-44	83 Sqn
1461925	Sgt	PERKINS Alfred Charles	10-06-44	10 Sqn
1896164	Sgt	PERKINS David James	31-12-44	138 Sqn
53366	F/L	PERKINS Edward Leslie John	23-06-44	97 Sqn
1181759	Sgt	PERKINS Harry	30-06-44	51 Sqn
1393016	F/S	PERKINS Harry	18-03-44	463 Sqn
137552	F/O	PERKINS Ronald Percy David	20-02-44	83 Sqn
55959	P/O	PERRETT Anthony Lambert	12-09-44	90 Sqn
1586043	Sgt	PERRETT Frederick Charles	21-01-44	10 Sqn
1552400	Sgt	PERRIE William Griffin	25-03-44	44 Sqn
1809153	Sgt	PERRING Arthur	23-09-44	463 Sqn
1312857	F/S	PERRY Geoffrey John	19-07-44	49 Sqn
1823401	Sgt	PERRY George	21-07-44	12 Sqn
183588	F/O	PERRY James Percival	16-10-44	115 Sqn
160761	F/O	PERRY Leslie Walter	1-11-44	106 Sqn
1392734	F/S	PERRY Victor Leonard	27-03-44	166 Sqn
1238492	Sgt	PERSSE Donald Robert	27-05-44	1656 HCU
1578440	Sgt	PESTELL Arthur	16-02-44	97 Sqn
1339137	F/S	PESTER Leo Ernest George	28-06-44	460 Sqn
1654156	Sgt	PESTICCIO Guglielmo	16-09-44	78 Sqn
1592800	Sgt	PETCH Basil Harry	4-11-44	625 Sqn
179597	F/O	PETERS Cyril Edwin Thomas	10-11-44	97 Sqn
115353	F/L	PETRIDES DFM Basil Oliver	21-02-44	156 Sqn
1247027	Sgt	PETTIFER John Gilbert	2-05-44	75 Sqn
1022473	Sgt	PETTIGREW Bruce	22-12-44	463 Sqn
1851255	Sgt	PETTIS William George Sydney	31-03-44	166 Sqn
1895178	Sgt	PETTIT Douglas Darrah	23-10-44	462 Sqn
1627623	Sgt	PETTIT Norman George Valentine	22-06-44	49 Sqn
1803782	Sgt	PETTITT Geoffrey Leslie	10-04-44	10 OTU
1803071	F/S	PETTMAN William Henry Thomas	12-09-44	218 Sqn
157326	F/L	PETTS DFC Hubert Thomas	23-04-44	463 Sqn
151756	F/O	PETTS Leslie William	27-04-44	44 Sqn
1148877	Sgt	PEVERELLE Bernard John	30-08-44	50 Sqn
158697	F/O	PEZARO James Bernard George 'Jim'	25-04-44	83 Sqn
1272508	F/S	PHELAN Daniel John	20-01-44	83 Sqn
1568737	Sgt	PHILIP Sydney	11-04-44	30 OTU
1583796	Sgt	PHILLIPS Alfred Arthur	15-05-44	626 Sqn
151843	F/O	PHILLIPS Charles Ronald	13-07-44	103 Sqn
154247	P/O	PHILLIPS Cyril James Benjamin	4-05-44	19 OTU
186745	P/O	PHILLIPS Denis Nigel	24-08-44	18 OTU
1280695	Sgt	PHILLIPS Dennis Herbert	24-07-44	582 Sqn
1866742	Sgt	PHILLIPS Desmond Kenneth James	29-07-44	467 Sqn
1581809	Sgt	PHILLIPS Frank	31-03-44	101 Sqn
1128364	F/S	PHILLIPS Frank David Thomas	20-10-44	35 Sqn
2208843	Sgt	PHILLIPS Fred	19-07-44	76 Sqn
2200275	F/S	PHILLIPS Herbert Weston	22-03-44	158 Sqn
1353834	Sgt	PHILLIPS James John	23-05-44	97 Sqn
2203535	Sgt	PHILLIPS John	8-09-44	14 OTU
1324960	Sgt	PHILLIPS Joseph Frederick	4-01-44	1657 HCU
1836349	Sgt	PHILLIPS Leonard	19-10-44	9 Sqn
1315084	F/S	PHILLIPS Leslie John	22-03-44	49 Sqn
1593422	F/S	PHILLIPS Ralph	15-10-44	7 Sqn
932117	F/S	PHILLIPS Ralph Clifford George	12-09-44	90 Sqn
2211498	Sgt	PHILLIPS Victor Thomas	31-12-44	218 Sqn
1420250	F/O	PHILLIPS William David	31-07-44	9 Sqn
2209715	Sgt	PHILLIPS William Myles	11-04-44	640 Sqn
1822774	F/S	PHILP Charles	17-06-44	576 Sqn
155969	F/O	PHILPOT William George	23-05-44	408 Sqn
1380036	Sgt	PHIPPS Roger	14-01-44	49 Sqn
2215390		PHOENIX George Denis	11-04-44	158 Sqn
1621258	Sgt	PICK Sydney	3-11-44	550 Sqn
1075888	Sgt	PICKEN James	16-10-44	10 Sqn
1580355	Sgt	PICKER George William	26-07-44	49 Sqn
1623919	Sgt	PICKERING Alan Leslie	23-05-44	630 Sqn
1198988	Sgt	PICKERING Douglas Arthur	28-05-44	1659 HCU
1434290	Sgt	PICKERING Walter	23-05-44	75 Sqn
2209296	Sgt	PICKFORD Henry	4-05-44	166 Sqn
1339536	F/S	PICKFORD Victor Jack	15-03-44	101 Sqn
174147	P/O	PICKIN Eric	31-03-44	622 Sqn
1590407	Sgt	PICKLES Maurice	22-05-44	103 Sqn
185504	P/O	PICKLES Robert	30-08-44	635 Sqn
1436408	F/S	PICKSTONE Alan	27-04-44	619 Sqn
182123	F/O	PICOT Philip Mourant	12-12-44	103 Sqn
1801735	Sgt	PICTON Horace Sydney	28-08-44	550 Sqn
129769	F/L	PICTON DFC Richard William	11-04-44	550 Sqn
151087	F/O	PICTON Roy Geoffrey	13-06-44	514 Sqn
1586848	Sgt	PICTON Sydney Arthur	29-07-44	514 Sqn
3000833	F/S	PICTON Walter Charles	8-11-44	1662 HCU
1559966	F/S	PIEDOT Victor Wilfred	21-01-44	76 Sqn

Number	Rank	Name	Date	Sqn
1496522	Sgt	PIERCE John Dawson Holland	22-06-44	207 Sqn
177335	P/O	PIERCE Leonard William Aldridge	15-06-44	78 Sqn
976406	Sgt	PIGGIN Arthur Ernest	20-11-44	186 Sqn
147781	F/O	PIGGIN Peter John	2-03-44	630 Sqn
1320920	Sgt	PIGGOTT William David	27-09-44	115 Sqn
68183	S/L	PIKE MiD Dudley George Hart	10-03-44	207 Sqn
1606158	Sgt	PIKE Norman Reginald	23-05-44	9 Sqn
161470	P/O	PIKE DFM Reginald Charles	15-03-44	97 Sqn
1853897	Sgt	PILBEAM Anthony Stopher	3-01-44	57 Sqn
1800970	Sgt	PILGRIM Augustus Walter Edward	29-01-44	166 Sqn
1605288	Sgt	PILL Maxwell John	19-10-44	29 OTU
1322324	F/S	PILLINGER Leonard Charles	24-02-44	156 Sqn
1397188	Sgt	PINCH Francis James	8-05-44	49 Sqn
1623092	Sgt	PINDER Charles Alan	21-01-44	77 Sqn
1590862	Sgt	PINDER Willie 'Bill'	4-01-44	1658 HCU
1303878	Sgt	PINFOLD Frederick Charles	13-04-44	1663 HCU
1322624	F/S	PINK Philip Claude	21-07-44	578 Sqn
1307767	Sgt	PINKARD Donald Ernest	21-01-44	76 Sqn
1394869	F/S	PINKETT Roy	27-04-44	100 Sqn
1463004	F/S	PINKS Albert Edward	31-03-44	578 Sqn
2220566	Sgt	PINNOCK James Edward	29-07-44	103 Sqn
1880334	Sgt	PIPER John Simpson	15-08-44	1663 HCU
1604993	Sgt	PIPER Mervyn Kenneth	15-02-44	578 Sqn
1077652	Sgt	PIPER Patrick Michael	10-11-44	97 Sqn
62260	S/L	PIPKIN DFC* Leonard Charles	30-08-44	Lindholme
1583163	Sgt	PITCHER Peter James Vincent	21-02-44	9 Sqn
1653141	F/S	PITCON Robert Charles	26-08-44	635 Sqn
1318780	Sgt	PITFIELD Albert Stanley	31-03-44	460 Sqn
1578738	F/S	PITHOUSE Kenneth Henry	31-08-44	103 Sqn
1313419	Sgt	PITMAN Edward James	21-01-44	514 Sqn
171789	P/O	PITMAN Reginald Henry	31-03-44	625 Sqn
1621271	Sgt	PITTS Thomas Frederick	6-07-44	578 Sqn
1520039	Sgt	PITTY Edwin Hesketh	13-09-44	20 OTU
174690	P/O	PIZZEY Herbert Rex	19-04-44	57 Sqn
1867724	Sgt	PLACE Ian Alistair	22-06-44	630 Sqn
999504	Sgt	PLANT Clarence Victor	13-08-44	83 Sqn
1819448	Sgt	PLANT Cyril Leslie	27-08-44	625 Sqn
1636803	Sgt	PLANT Henry John	13-06-44	12 Sqn
1896100	Sgt	PLANT Joseph Raymond	26-08-44	514 Sqn
1576639	Sgt	PLANT Ronald	24-03-44	12 Sqn
1474275	F/S	PLASTOW Alfred Henry John	12-09-44	100 Sqn
185771	P/O	PLATT Frederick Patrick	1-11-44	429 Sqn
141887	F/L	PLATTEN John Anthony	21-07-44	158 Sqn
908932	W/O	PLAYER Samuel Thomas	2-01-44	101 Sqn
135090	F/O	PLEASANCE Nigel Leslie St. George	19-07-44	138 Sqn
22172	G/C	PLEASANCE Norman Charles	23-03-44	Bardney
1198121	F/S	PLESTED Jack Gardener	24-09-44	51 Sqn
1811104	F/S	PLEYDELL Horace John	29-01-44	97 Sqn
1620607	F/S	PLIMMER DFM Albert Leslie	12-12-44	582 Sqn
1522065	Sgt	PLOWMAN Frederick George	30-08-44	50 Sqn
1575092	F/S	PLUMB Cyril Fred	20-01-44	83 Sqn
1804691	Sgt	PLUMB Ivor Collins	20-05-44	115 Sqn
1332775	F/S	PLUMLEY Douglas William	5-11-44	76 Sqn
125161	F/O	PLUMMER DFC Cyril John	24-03-44	103 Sqn
1606785	Sgt	PLUMMER John Frederick	25-04-44	115 Sqn
151195	F/O	PLUNKETT Cyril Keith	8-05-44	619 Sqn
1594267	Sgt	PLUNKETT William Henry	30-10-44	21 OTU
177157	P/O	POCOCK Francis Anthony	30-08-44	101 Sqn
1805762	Sgt	POCOCK Michael Casey	15-04-44	30 OTU
185749	P/O	POCOCK Robert Leslie	29-10-44	582 Sqn
1606873	Sgt	POINTER Leslie Allan	29-07-44	626 Sqn
151152	F/O	POINTON Charles Ellis	30-01-44	207 Sqn
658309	F/S	POLAND Robert George	19-01-44	76 Sqn
902730	Sgt	POLDEN George Edward	10-04-44	12 Sqn
1648307	Sgt	POLE Henry	26-03-44	460 Sqn
151608	F/O	POLKINGHORNE Howard Clifford	9-07-44	622 Sqn
1135505	F/S	POLLARD Charles Leslie	15-10-44	90 Sqn
1109146	F/S	POLLARD Herbert Clare	6-11-44	214 Sqn
1890626	Sgt	POLLARD Herbert Eugene	27-04-44	57 Sqn
172428	P/O	POLLARD Ormond Harold	1-07-44	12 Sqn
170947	P/O	POLLEY Gordon Frederick	24-03-44	207 Sqn
1458528	Sgt	POLLITT William	7-10-44	51 Sqn
1894985	Sgt	POMEROY James Sydney	31-01-44	626 Sqn
1392396	Sgt	POMFRET Walter Charles	29-07-44	90 Sqn
1893522	Sgt	POMROY Reginald William	30-08-44	514 Sqn
1320161	Sgt	POND Eric Raymond William	31-03-44	514 Sqn
1389967	Sgt	PONDER Cyril Arthur	21-01-44	61 Sqn
1588511	Sgt	POOK Ernest	23-08-44	1657 HCU
1382229	F/S	POOL Reginald Howard	5-08-44	617 Sqn
1576962	Sgt	POOLE Colin Francis	29-06-44	76 Sqn
2220167	Sgt	POOLE Gilbert Anthony	31-03-44	106 Sqn
1576815	F/S	POOLE Harry Raymond	23-04-44	76 Sqn
1334787	F/S	POOLE Jack Sealy	22-01-44	432 Sqn
1399489	F/S	POPE Albert William	10-08-44	619 Sqn
1803039	Sgt	POPE Arthur Charles	21-01-44	76 Sqn
170284	P/O	POPE George Alfred	24-03-44	578 Sqn
1433634	F/S	POPE Ronald Edward	25-12-44	640 Sqn
1317822	F/S	POPE Walter Charles	23-03-44	115 Sqn
1898903	Sgt	POPLE Leonard Ambrose	7-10-44	51 Sqn
1594519	Sgt	PORRELL John	16-06-44	514 Sqn
551572	Sgt	PORRITT Arnold	25-02-44	97 Sqn
1386730	Sgt	PORTEOUS Francis William	2-01-44	207 Sqn
1369004	Sgt	PORTEOUS James Hardman	23-10-44	625 Sqn
1506078	F/S	PORTEOUS Kenneth Alexander	21-01-44	15 Sqn
171282	F/L	PORTEOUS DSO DFM* William Ford Watson	20-05-44	7 Sqn
1603789	Sgt	PORTER Albert Glanville	25-05-44	51 Sqn
1098275	Sgt	PORTER Alexander	22-05-44	9 Sqn
1608252	Sgt	PORTER Edward Joseph Charles	20-01-44	434 Sqn
113389	W/C	PORTER DFC* Edward Leach	17-08-44	97 Sqn
26243	W/C	PORTER Eric Frederick	25-02-44	156 Sqn
1390856	Sgt	PORTER George Alfred	27-01-44	576 Sqn
1307116	Sgt	PORTER Harold Robert	7-10-44	78 Sqn
1322181	Sgt	PORTER Kenneth George	18-07-44	158 Sqn
158699	P/O	PORTER Kenneth Leslie	28-03-44	9 Sqn
630524	F/S	PORTER Reginald Edward	22-05-44	550 Sqn
185050	P/O	PORTER Reginald Herbert	15-10-44	10 Sqn
2211553	Sgt	PORTER William Charles	29-07-44	12 Sqn
1217077	Sgt	POSTINS Gerald Harry	29-07-44	61 Sqn
2209316	Sgt	POSTON John Joseph	26-08-44	83 OTU
1269614	W/O	POTTER Albert Loos	29-05-44	141 Sqn
1676178	Sgt	POTTER James	16-05-44	625 Sqn
3006136	Sgt	POTTER Leslie Arthur Raymond	18-12-44	3 LFS
1538445	Sgt	POTTER Ralph Desmond	8-07-44	106 Sqn
1392545	Sgt	POTTER Ronald George	15-02-44	166 Sqn
1861337	Sgt	POTTS Alec Raymond	22-05-44	467 Sqn
1867154	Sgt	POTTS John Frederick	13-06-44	28 OTU
658783	F/S	POTTS Joseph	30-10-44	85 Sqn
39755	S/L	POULTER MiD Cecil Wardman	23-04-44	218 Sqn
142340	F/O	POULTER John	28-06-44	44 Sqn
1575525	F/S	POULTON Alan James	20-01-44	158 Sqn
1510041	Sgt	POUND George Albert Alexander	25-04-44	424 Sqn
1624676	Sgt	POUND Henry Watkin	10-04-44	166 Sqn
1818557	F/S	POUNTNEY Roy Stanley	28-04-44	460 Sqn
1850139	Sgt	POUT Peter Ernest	3-01-44	156 Sqn
164204	F/O	POVEY Derek John	20-11-44	1656 HCU
164543	F/O	POVEY John Herbert	24-11-44	12 OTU
122734	F/L	POW William Renton	29-11-44	153 Sqn
1818899	Sgt	POWELL Edwin Sampson	8-11-44	158 Sqn
53935	P/O	POWELL Eric Nash	25-04-44	619 Sqn
1603981	Sgt	POWELL Frank Alfred	24-07-44	625 Sqn
1107452	Sgt	POWELL George Edmund	15-01-44	626 Sqn
1894686	Sgt	POWELL Henry George Coles	15-04-44	1664 HCU
1818344	Sgt	POWELL James Henry	11-04-44	90 Sqn
1604522	Sgt	POWELL James Vincent	20-01-44	1657 HCU
998039	F/S	POWELL John Lynden	25-02-44	550 Sqn
967233	Sgt	POWELL John Reginald	15-03-44	550 Sqn
1608500	F/S	POWELL Richard John	29-06-44	7 Sqn

1654832	Sgt	POWELL Terence	11-04-44	83 Sqn	1582517	Sgt	PRITCHARD William Leslie	27-01-44	426 Sqn
1322456	Sgt	POWELL Thomas Trevor	2-01-44	106 Sqn	1621153	F/S	PROBERT Alan Charles	27-11-44	189 Sqn
121347	F/L	POWELL William Leonard	29-07-44	49 Sqn	1517303	Sgt	PROBERT Geoffrey Thomas	24-03-44	626 Sqn
141455	F/O	POWELL-WIFFEN Twice MiD Arthur William [New Zealand]	17-02-44	1409 Flt	114400	F/L	PROCTER Gordon Arbuthnot	31-03-44	166 Sqn
					1313237	F/S	PROCTOR Edgar William	22-01-44	44 Sqn
1579586	Sgt	POWER Kenneth John	28-05-44	101 Sqn	1029514	Sgt	PROFFITT William John	19-03-44	166 Sqn
182853	P/O	POWIS Leslie William	12-08-44	76 Sqn	135744	F/O	PRONGER Norman Ronald George	24-03-44	576 Sqn
153204	F/O	POWNER James Henry	15-11-44	115 Sqn	1365162	Sgt	PROPHET Clifford Beaty	8-07-44	83 Sqn
1671803	F/S	POYNTON Alfred Fred	20-02-44	35 Sqn	931998	Sgt	PROSSER James Edward	29-07-44	431 Sqn
1390154	Sgt	PRADA Italo	31-03-44	9 Sqn	902514	Sgt	PROUTEN Herbert John	29-02-44	10 OTU
1131229	Sgt	PRANKETT Royce	20-02-44	156 Sqn	177531	P/O	PROWLES Charles Frank 'Ted'	16-06-44	514 Sqn
914246	Sgt	PRATT Arthur	22-01-44	514 Sqn	1867428	Sgt	PRUSHER Derek Francis	3-01-44	49 Sqn
1598625	Sgt	PRATT Dennis	30-10-44	21 OTU	1582778	Sgt	PRYCE Raymond William	22-05-44	100 Sqn
1325000	F/S	PRATT Edgar Walter Roslyn	20-07-44	582 Sqn	1801978	Sgt	PRYOR James Robert	13-08-44	158 Sqn
1202339	F/S	PRATT Herbert Gordon	8-05-44	106 Sqn	1853943	Sgt	PUCKETT Ralph Lionel	7-06-44	106 Sqn
1576863	Sgt	PRATT Norman Ernest	14-01-44	1653 HCU	1806702	Sgt	PUDDUCK Harry George	12-02-44	50 Sqn
1480812	F/S	PRATT-ROBINSON Ronald	2-02-44	432 Sqn	1396289	F/S	PUGH Ambrose Christopher	21-07-44	578 Sqn
1319896	Sgt	PREATOR Lewis Sylvester	19-03-44	166 Sqn	1581750	Sgt	PUGH Derrick Rowley Owen	23-10-44	625 Sqn
151813	F/O	PREECE Reginald Roderic	22-12-44	626 Sqn	658462	F/S	PUGH Harold Edward George	19-04-44	115 Sqn
1594326	Sgt	PRENTICE George	27-01-44	18 OTU	136696	F/O	PUGH Sidney James	15-04-44	30 OTU
1350917	Sgt	PRESCOTT Albert Ivor	21-11-44	514 Sqn	1604653	Sgt	PUIU Arnold Gordon	28-05-44	460 Sqn
158971	F/L	PRESLAND DFC Ernest James	16-05-44	576 Sqn	652403	F/S	PULFORD DFM John	13-02-44	617 Sqn
1581026	Sgt	PRESLAND John Raymond	10-05-44	619 Sqn	148869	F/O	PULFREY Leslie	17-06-44	550 Sqn
1055466	Sgt	PREST William	31-03-44	467 Sqn	1311450	F/S	PULLEE Leonard William	11-06-44	7 Sqn
1356244	LAC	PRESTON Arthur Charles	26-01-44	PFNTU	924992	Sgt	PULLEN William Alfred	28-04-44	640 Sqn
133520	F/O	PRESTON DFC Wilfred	23-01-44	161 Sqn	1861808	Sgt	PULLEN William Edward	27-08-44	12 Sqn
1199316	W/O	PRETLOVE Norman Leslie	12-10-44	1687 Flt	175556	P/O	PULLIN DFC Bernard Arthur	13-08-44	582 Sqn
1344599	Sgt	PRETSWELL Ian Arras	23-05-44	626 Sqn	144691	F/O	PULLMAN John Howard	23-04-44	61 Sqn
1681110	Sgt	PREWER David	21-04-44	44 Sqn	948791	Sgt	PULLMAN Thomas Joseph	20-02-44	626 Sqn
54651	P/O	PRICE Albert	20-05-44	7 Sqn	2208923	Sgt	PULMAN Arthur	30-01-44	207 Sqn
1273886	F/S	PRICE Allan Selwyn	14-10-44	12 Sqn	1836889	Sgt	PURBRICK Harold Desmond	26-04-44	30 OTU
184715	P/O	PRICE Arthur Daniel	12-09-44	7 Sqn	1713564	Sgt	PURDIE William Smith	20-02-44	49 Sqn
1335208	Sgt	PRICE Arthur William	10-04-44	100 Sqn	129554	F/O	PURKIS Basil Laird	25-08-44	101 Sqn
137473	F/O	PRICE Basil Newton John	14-01-44	576 Sqn	152439	F/O	PURKIS Charles Sidney	12-06-44	635 Sqn
130644	F/O	PRICE Charles Cleveland	25-05-44	158 Sqn	1663282	Sgt	PURKISS Royston Frederick	29-01-44	102 Sqn
1317522	F/S	PRICE David Maldwyn	30-01-44	640 Sqn	605673	Sgt	PURNELL-EDWARDS William Paston Liddon [Eire]	15-10-44	186 Sqn
1458348	Sgt	PRICE Denis Walter	27-01-44	12 Sqn					
1866332	Sgt	PRICE Ernest Frederick	16-06-44	61 Sqn	1850315	Sgt	PURSE Donald William George 'Don'	25-09-44	576 Sqn
1507522	Sgt	PRICE Gerald	29-07-44	12 Sqn	1238611	Sgt	PURSGLOVE Henry Robert	22-06-44	44 Sqn
1496337	Sgt	PRICE Harold Gordon	18-03-44	466 Sqn	1595081	Sgt	PURVES James	29-07-44	626 Sqn
125472	F/O	PRICE James Alfred	22-01-44	51 Sqn	1612021	Sgt	PURVIS Leonard	11-02-44	21 OTU
1578804	Sgt	PRICE James Thomas	8-07-44	9 Sqn	158090	F/O	PURVIS DFC Victor Davenant	7-07-44	44 Sqn
1807491	Sgt	PRICE Reginald Joseph	26-07-44	103 Sqn	173542	P/O	PUTT Maurice Emerson	31-03-44	97 Sqn
1836656	Sgt	PRICE Vivian Graham	25-09-44	576 Sqn	1585983	Sgt	PUTT Ronald Leslie	17-06-44	102 Sqn
151337	F/O	PRICKETT Terrence Helyer	22-03-44	626 Sqn	1807665	Sgt	PUTTICK Derek Ronald	24-11-44	12 OTU
1610620	F/S	PRIDDLE Terence Jack	5-11-44	15 Sqn	175906	P/O	PUTTOCK Alec Lenard	17-06-44	576 Sqn
187227	P/O	PRIDGETT Henry John Francis	29-06-44	467 Sqn	130823	F/O	PUVER James	31-03-44	635 Sqn
1591317	Sgt	PRIEST Michael Joseph Louis	25-06-44	77 Sqn	985279	Sgt	PYBUS Alfred	29-01-44	15 Sqn
1399105	F/S	PRIEST Raymond Eric	24-03-44	578 Sqn	122983	F/L	PYE Thomas James	13-08-44	156 Sqn
182783	P/O	PRIESTLEY Leonard	16-07-44	44 Sqn	1801298	Sgt	PYKE Cyril Martin	13-07-44	550 Sqn
1435334	Sgt	PRIESTLEY Reginald Bateman	15-03-44	149 Sqn	1602985	Sgt	PYKE Norman	21-01-44	405 Sqn
1338043	F/S	PRIGG George Arthur John	30-01-44	625 Sqn	175907	F/O	PYLE John Edgar Alexander	21-07-44	622 Sqn
31459	P/O	PRINCE Allan Leslie	29-01-44	115 Sqn	1852477	Sgt	PYNE John Septimus	9-04-44	460 Sqn
1609895	Sgt	PRINCE Eric Richard	29-01-44	77 Sqn	1582386	F/S	QUANBOROUGH Cyril	17-06-44	3 LFS
1425704	Sgt	PRINCE Thomas John	6-08-44	83 Sqn	134898	F/O	QUAYLE Thomas	7-06-44	57 Sqn
913891	Sgt	PRING Albert George	22-07-44	20 OTU	1600345	F/S	QUELCH Charles Sidney	16-09-44	78 Sqn
134724	F/O	PRINGLE Henry Brian Deopard	28-01-44	115 Sqn	1389820	F/S	QUELCH Leonard Sidney	13-04-44	90 Sqn
2211889	Sgt	PRINGLE John Wellington Gordon	15-07-44	576 Sqn	1594157	Sgt	QUICK Eldred William	4-11-44	101 Sqn
1459044	Sgt	PRINGLE Leonard Edgar	10-05-44	463 Sqn	1320468	Sgt	QUICKE John Raymond	16-03-44	76 Sqn
1819099	Sgt	PRIOR Dennis Charles	11-09-44	35 Sqn	1524562	Sgt	QUINE Thomas Frederick	25-02-44	550 Sqn
37611	S/L	PRIO DFC Garfield Wallace [Canada]	22-01-44	218 Sqn	1874439	Sgt	QUINLIVAN John Henry	22-12-44	630 Sqn
173394	F/O	PRIOR Jack Edgar	31-03-44	12 Sqn	649485	W/O	QUINN DFC DFM Charles Edward	15-02-44	7 Sqn
1575451	Sgt	PRIOR John Adolphe	7-08-44	149 Sqn	1622355	Sgt	QUINN Ronald Charles	12-09-44	630 Sqn
1334363	F/S	PRIOR Leonard	30-08-44	630 Sqn	175619	P/O	QUINTON Charles Henry	8-06-44	115 Sqn
992691	Sgt	PRITCHARD Douglas	18-06-44	1663 HCU	1570380	AC1	QUINTON Harold	8-04-44	1 LFS
1322271	F/S	PRITCHARD George Sydney	3-06-44	640 Sqn	998929	Sgt	RACE George Albert	30-01-44	156 Sqn
1578502	F/S	PRITCHARD Howard	4-06-44	635 Sqn	178006	P/O	RACKLEY Geoffrey Norman	22-06-44	619 Sqn
54285	P/O	PRITCHARD John Leonard	11-04-44	619 Sqn	634738	W/O	RADCLIFFE George	11-06-44	15 Sqn
114399	F/L	PRITCHARD Marcus Sydney Francis	18-12-44	106 Sqn	1576117	Sgt	RADFORD Kenneth William	25-02-44	1661 HCU

Service#	Rank	Name	Date	Sqn
1890982	Sgt	RADFORD Kenneth William	8-02-44	138 Sqn
1564682	Sgt	RADLEY Arthur	20-01-44	158 Sqn
1876928	Sgt	RADLEY Peter	22-12-44	626 Sqn
1016155	Sgt	RAE George Patrick	24-03-44	156 Sqn
1894736	Sgt	RAE John	19-07-44	630 Sqn
955666	Sgt	RAFFERTY Joseph	20-05-44	115 Sqn
138068	F/O	RAGLESS John Scott	15-02-44	15 Sqn
1386397	Sgt	RAINBOW Leslie John Clifford	9-06-44	49 Sqn
998435	W/O	RAINE Arthur Thomas	19-08-44	635 Sqn
1565370	Sgt	RAINE William	19-10-44	186 Sqn
1861857	F/S	RALPH Basil William	15-02-44	15 Sqn
910510	Sgt	RALPH Frederick George	8-08-44	106 Sqn
171396	P/O	RALPH James William	15-02-44	115 Sqn
1863365	Sgt	RAMAGE Keith Lund	12-05-44	103 Sqn
34248	G/C	RAMPLING DSO DFC Kenneth Johnson	22-03-44	7 Sqn
1684235	Sgt	RAMSAY David	23-01-44	1667 HCU
52871	F/O	RAMSAY Gerald Longfield	6-06-44	582 Sqn
571776	F/S	RAMSAY Howard William	11-09-44	1690 Flt
1822163	Sgt	RAMSAY James	11-04-44	625 Sqn
1570005	Sgt	RAMSAY William Halkett	15-03-44	90 Sqn
52128	F/O	RAMSAY William Hannah Clingen	5-07-44	106 Sqn
2210406	Sgt	RAMSBOTTOM Eric	15-10-44	90 Sqn
55792	P/O	RAMSDEN Benjamin	13-08-44	100 Sqn
1801882	Sgt	RAMSEY Ronald Henry	8-02-44	18 OTU
54081	P/O	RAMWELL William Gayter	19-03-44	192 Sqn
133214	F/O	RAND Kenneth Peter	6-01-44	97 Sqn
1880956	Sgt	RAND Michael Arthur	5-11-44	1660 HCU
2204816	Sgt	RANDALL Arthur Bernard	28-04-44	434 Sqn
135720	F/L	RANDALL Francis Reginald	1-06-44	622 Sqn
1880924	Sgt	RANDALL Henry	27-08-44	90 Sqn
1438572	Sgt	RANDALL James William	21-04-44	619 Sqn
1216626	Sgt	RANDALL Robert William	12-09-44	44 Sqn
1575025	Sgt	RANDLE Dennis	25-04-44	626 Sqn
1832973	Sgt	RANGER James William	4-05-44	460 Sqn
171474	P/O	RANKIN Charles	21-01-44	408 Sqn
175934	P/O	RANKIN Denis Henderson	14-08-44	20 OTU
153309	F/O	RANKIN George Wallace	21-06-44	1661 HCU
173840	P/O	RANKIN DFM Herbert [Eire]	25-02-44	61 Sqn
1795202	Sgt	RANKIN William Black	22-05-44	166 Sqn
1583033	Sgt	RANN George Gordon Graham	14-01-44	1653 HCU
633193	F/S	RAPERE Nelson John	21-01-44	35 Sqn
1801807	Sgt	RASEY William George	30-08-44	101 Sqn
1801563	Sgt	RATCLIFF Leslie	8-06-44	166 Sqn
2213842	Sgt	RATCLIFFE Jack	15-02-44	115 Sqn
2209639	Sgt	RATCLIFFE Jacky	22-06-44	57 Sqn
1494609	F/S	RATCLIFFE Terence	24-03-44	78 Sqn
178322	P/O	RATHBONE John	15-06-44	433 Sqn
1521088	F/S	RATTRAY Peter Wyper	18-11-44	51 Sqn
1585338	Sgt	RATTRAY Stanley Herbert	14-01-44	207 Sqn
1873868	Sgt	RAVEN Arthur John Edward	20-01-44	76 Sqn
1387476	Sgt	RAVENSCROFT James Thomas	27-01-44	166 Sqn
67624	S/L	RAW DFC AFC Anthony William	11-09-44	156 Sqn
1235510	F/S	RAWLEY Edward George	16-12-44	57 Sqn
1805814	Sgt	RAWLINGS Francis John William	12-10-44	21 OTU
1583233	Sgt	RAWLINGS George William	28-01-44	115 Sqn
1323852	F/S	RAWLINGS Peter	30-01-44	625 Sqn
1710329	Sgt	RAWLINSON David Joseph	20-02-44	431 Sqn
2216259	F/S	RAWLINSON Neville Ayrton	25-05-44	582 Sqn
168670	F/L	RAWLINSON DFC Thomas	25-05-44	429 Sqn
1592699	Sgt	RAWSON Donald William	5-07-44	207 Sqn
1324690	F/S	RAWSON Frank Sidney	25-06-44	44 Sqn
1683124	Sgt	RAWSON Peter Dearnley	21-02-44	460 Sqn
1465842	Sgt	RAY Dennis Kenneth	23-04-44	90 Sqn
1483955	Sgt	RAY John	28-05-44	103 Sqn
1138809	Sgt	RAY Wilfred	19-07-44	76 Sqn
122402	S/L	RAYBOULD DSO DFM Arthur William	6-06-44	582 Sqn
2221557	Sgt	RAYBOULD Charles Francis	28-10-44	115 Sqn
1266460	Sgt	RAYMEN Frederick James	4-11-44	195 Sqn
151138	F/O	RAYMENT Donald Frederick	19-07-44	78 Sqn
2214194	Sgt	RAYMER Eric Andrew James	16-11-44	1663 HCU
1237388	Sgt	RAYMOND Anthony Frank	13-05-44	576 Sqn
134804	F/O	RAYMOND Geoffrey Thomas	24-02-44	149 Sqn
1578650	F/S	RAYMOND Verant Garth	24-03-44	77 Sqn
1338914	F/S	RAYNER Eric James	22-01-44	1662 HCU
756083	F/S	RAYNER Sidney Walter	3-01-44	7 Sqn
1394183	Sgt	RAYNER Stanley Ernest	25-03-44	640 Sqn
151064	F/O	RAYNHAM Harry Frederick [Bechuanaland]	22-06-44	463 Sqn
159692	F/O	REA George Malcolm	21-05-44	1655 MTU
1233459	LAC	READ Albert Le Gordon	8-01-44	1678 HCU
1853103	Sgt	READ Eric Richard	22-05-44	626 Sqn
2215997	Sgt	READ George Irving	15-10-44	186 Sqn
161606	P/O	READ Jack Montague	21-01-44	207 Sqn
154193	F/O	READ John James	7-06-44	460 Sqn
1813759	Sgt	READ John James	4-05-44	12 Sqn
1601667	F/S	READ John Thornton	6-04-44	207 Sqn
1410481	Sgt	READ Kenneth Norman	4-05-44	12 Sqn
1218563	F/S	READ Leo Erle	31-03-44	622 Sqn
1442773	F/S	READ Robert Arthur	19-03-44	97 Sqn
1684805	Sgt	READDY Arthur Philip	28-01-44	426 Sqn
2221251	Sgt	READMAN Norman Arthur	11-12-44	514 Sqn
178065	F/O	READY Denis William	16-10-44	207 Sqn
1421525	Sgt	REARDON Harold Roger	15-02-44	625 Sqn
2220712	Sgt	REASON Henry Gordon	2-03-44	15 OTU
1892370	Sgt	REAVELEY William Thomas	11-06-44	75 Sqn
122816	S/L	REAVILL Ralph	25-05-44	158 Sqn
150490	F/O	REAY Geoffrey Norman	4-11-44	51 Sqn
1814703	Sgt	RECABARREN Raul Fernando	26-08-44	428 Sqn
1218557	Sgt	REDALL Roy	23-04-44	77 Sqn
187488	P/O	REDDINGTON James Vincent	21-11-44	78 Sqn
1696297	Sgt	REDFEARN Alan Richardson	23-04-44	149 Sqn
645572	F/S	REDFEARN DFM Ivor Charles	6-01-44	35 Sqn
901789	W/O	REDFERN MiD Alan Timothy	6-07-44	635 Sqn
1639906	F/S	REDFORD DFM George Hossack	18-11-44	35 Sqn
656698	F/S	REDFORD Keith George	16-03-44	578 Sqn
1048952	Sgt	REDHEAD James	2-01-44	405 Sqn
531268	Sgt	REDHEAD Nathaniel Ernest	22-05-44	115 Sqn
159718	F/O	REDMAN Alan Harry	19-04-44	432 Sqn
1321969	Sgt	REDMAN Anthony George	16-03-44	100 Sqn
1866972	F/S	REDMAYNE Albert	11-10-44	101 Sqn
172972	F/O	REDMOND John	2-11-44	102 Sqn
123236	F/O	REDSHAW Robert Hall	22-05-44	619 Sqn
1575074	F/S	REDSTONE Percy George Frank	24-02-44	405 Sqn
1607108	Sgt	REED Charles John	4-12-44	619 Sqn
1434329	Sgt	REED Douglas	21-07-44	115 Sqn
1165112	F/S	REED Ernest John Watts	11-08-44	12 Sqn
1585306	Sgt	REED Frederick James	13-06-44	31 Base
1181898	Sgt	REED Frederick William	8-06-44	1667 HCU
151078	F/O	REED George Carlisle	24-03-44	166 Sqn
1806981	Sgt	REED John Charles Lewis	21-02-44	156 Sqn
1281835	Sgt	REED Joseph John	10-06-44	49 Sqn
172568	P/O	REED DSO Richard Robert	23-05-44	576 Sqn
1590929	Sgt	REED Robert	28-10-44	1661 HCU
172402	F/O	REEDER Stanley Warren	12-10-44	608 Sqn
1319532	F/S	REEDMAN Alexander William	22-01-44	630 Sqn
1337828	F/S	REES David Robert Harding	22-01-44	78 Sqn
1335744	Sgt	REES Francis George	22-03-44	78 Sqn
1650742	F/S	REES Frederick Bernard	17-12-44	49 Sqn
1580581	Sgt	REES John Howard	27-04-44	106 Sqn
135877	F/O	REES Maurice Owen	30-01-44	100 Sqn
1339107	Sgt	REES Robert Patrick	20-02-44	102 Sqn
1395869	Sgt	REES Sidney George	15-02-44	622 Sqn
1251817	F/S	REES Terence	6-10-44	49 Sqn
1652964	Sgt	REES Thomas Brynnor	11-06-44	15 Sqn
1863157	F/S	REES Walter	20-02-44	57 Sqn
1552703	Sgt	REEVE Albert Edgar	21-02-44	78 Sqn
1583577	Sgt	REEVE Charles George	28-06-44	166 Sqn

Number	Rank	Name	Date	Unit
1465897	Sgt	REEVE Stanley Rickard	27-04-44	106 Sqn
172236	F/L	REEVES Charles William	11-09-44	156 Sqn
1234696	Sgt	REEVES Frederick Sydney Gordon	29-01-44	57 Sqn
1575770	Sgt	REEVES DFM Kenneth Basil	14-01-44	12 Sqn
146103	F/O	REEVES Ralph Leonard	20-02-44	156 Sqn
1653027	Sgt	REGAN Lancelot Thomas Daniel	8-04-44	1 LFS
1800834	Sgt	REGAN Terence Arthur	10-04-44	10 OTU
174080	P/O	REGAN Walter Thomas	31-03-44	10 Sqn
2211424	Sgt	REID Alexander	21-10-44	75 Sqn
1453674	Sgt	REID Alec	29-11-44	12 Sqn
1568216	Sgt	REID Allan McLean	15-03-44	149 Sqn
1800613	F/S	REID Arthur George [Jamaica]	21-11-44	10 Sqn
1368361	Sgt	REID Edward Clark	30-08-44	467 Sqn
1077588	F/S	REID George	23-05-44	50 Sqn
3020819	Sgt	REID George	28-05-44	101 Sqn
127268	F/O	REID Gilmour Murray	21-01-44	408 Sqn
1293545	Sgt	REID Ian Henry Milne	21-07-44	101 Sqn
1570033	F/S	REID James Mercer	13-08-44	626 Sqn
48900	F/L	REID John Alexander [Canada]	22-11-44	627 Sqn
1318282	F/S	REID John Macdonald	26-08-44	101 Sqn
577259	Sgt	REID Reginald Charles	8-05-44	619 Sqn
1800815	Sgt	REID Winston Alverstone Coningsby	17-06-44	102 Sqn
1331709	F/S	REILLY Francis Patrick	29-01-44	419 Sqn
1089622	F/S	REILLY Norman Parry	4-05-44	576 Sqn
55056	F/O	REILLY AFM Terence Desmond	4-05-44	19 OTU
1482369	Sgt	RELTON Albert	13-07-44	166 Sqn
138457	F/L	RELTON Edward Harry Maxwell	13-08-44	9 Sqn
1802332	Sgt	REMSBERY Geoffrey Charles	13-08-44	50 Sqn
55833	P/O	RENDELL Kenneth Louis	6-10-44	571 Sqn
1239172	Sgt	RENEAU Sydney Owen	1-07-44	12 Sqn
1563802	F/S	RENNIE Charles	27-08-44	15 Sqn
1111502	Sgt	RENNIE Sebastian	28-04-44	460 Sqn
1571183	Sgt	RENNIE Stanley Cunningham	16-09-44	199 Sqn
1439513	F/S	RENTON Dennis	21-01-44	77 Sqn
177545	P/O	RENTON William	13-06-44	578 Sqn
1502388	Sgt	RENWICK Richard Alan	22-03-44	78 Sqn
1874029	Sgt	RESTELL Walter Leo Arthur	10-05-44	106 Sqn
2225488	Sgt	RETALLICK Joseph	8-09-44	14 OTU
1335477	F/S	REYNOLDS Benjamin Samuel	25-02-44	156 Sqn
1453495	F/S	REYNOLDS Dennis Leonard	25-04-44	50 Sqn
142887	F/O	REYNOLDS George Edward James	26-08-44	97 Sqn
1415061	Sgt	REYNOLDS George Frederick	20-02-44	78 Sqn
151662	F/O	REYNOLDS George Leonard	24-07-44	77 Sqn
1853432	Sgt	REYNOLDS Gerard Thomas Wilfred	31-03-44	166 Sqn
658826	F/S	REYNOLDS James Cooney	29-01-44	97 Sqn
1508795	Cpl	REYNOLDS Leslie George	27-04-44	Bungay
1850794	Sgt	REYNOLDS Peter Henry	4-12-44	1652 HCU
120589	F/L	REYNOLDS Robert Winter	8-07-44	467 Sqn
1086293	Sgt	REYNOLDS Thomas George	15-10-44	626 Sqn
174153	F/L	REYNOLDS Thomas George Lionel	25-07-44	15 Sqn
2203973	Sgt	RHANEY Francis Victor	31-03-44	158 Sqn
54696	P/O	RHEAD George Edwards	9-08-44	161 Sqn
1585767	F/S	RHODES Alfred Gordon	29-06-44	10 Sqn
1892174	Sgt	RHODES David Charles	9-05-44	35 Sqn
1522850	F/S	RHODES George	31-08-44	166 Sqn
1520430	Sgt	RHODES John	13-07-44	103 Sqn
1623802	Sgt	RHODES Thomas Ernest	31-08-44	21 OTU
1661067	Sgt	RICE Edward Morgan Penry	19-10-44	9 Sqn
1607123	Sgt	RICE Frank Norman	22-05-44	463 Sqn
185745	P/O	RICE James Hedley	21-11-44	78 Sqn
1836758	Sgt	RICE Kenneth Frederick	22-06-44	619 Sqn
1821876	Sgt	RICE Norman Mackenzie	24-07-44	619 Sqn
1393469	F/S	RICE Stanley Douglas Gordon	29-07-44	619 Sqn
136818	F/O	RICH Ivor John Frederick	22-03-44	514 Sqn
147664	F/O	RICH Trevor	21-07-44	10 Sqn
51389	F/L	RICHARDS Arthur Thomas	22-05-44	57 Sqn
1339312	F/S	RICHARDS Clifford Dudley	19-10-44	9 Sqn
1314457	F/S	RICHARDS David Stanley	12-09-44	207 Sqn
1393487	Sgt	RICHARDS Derrick Sydney James	14-01-44	1653 HCU
1338542	Sgt	RICHARDS Ernest Charles	29-01-44	429 Sqn
125875	F/O	RICHARDS Ernest Charles David	7-02-44	1656 HCU
172305	P/O	RICHARDS Frank William	11-04-44	12 Sqn
979317	Sgt	RICHARDS George	5-07-44	192 Sqn
1653605	Sgt	RICHARDS Gomer	14-01-44	101 Sqn
1802168	Sgt	RICHARDS James Arthur	15-07-44	103 Sqn
170946	P/O	RICHARDS John Leslie	15-02-44	630 Sqn
157503	P/O	RICHARDS John Nigel	14-01-44	7 Sqn
1394671	Sgt	RICHARDS Joseph Stewart	19-04-44	57 Sqn
1892836	Sgt	RICHARDS Kenneth Christopher	26-08-44	90 Sqn
1432021	F/S	RICHARDS Leslie Reginald	24-06-44	149 Sqn
1604506	Sgt	RICHARDS Robert	21-01-44	427 Sqn
126893	F/L	RICHARDS Samuel John	13-08-44	156 Sqn
1315209	F/S	RICHARDS Sidney John	21-01-44	550 Sqn
160150	P/O	RICHARDS Thomas Bryan [Rhodesia]	22-06-44	44 Sqn
1896748	Sgt	RICHARDSON Alexander	12-10-44	7 Sqn
910760	W/O	RICHARDSON Arthur John	25-06-44	44 Sqn
1310928	Sgt	RICHARDSON Basil	1-07-44	1 GpSDFlt
1392954	F/S	RICHARDSON Charles Henry	22-05-44	630 Sqn
1600893	F/S	RICHARDSON Dick	25-06-44	77 Sqn
179944	P/O	RICHARDSON Edgar	13-08-44	514 Sqn
138462	F/O	RICHARDSON Edward Albert	20-01-44	102 Sqn
1590570	Sgt	RICHARDSON Edward Robert	23-01-44	161 Sqn
113496	F/L	RICHARDSON DFM Edwin John Clessie	30-08-44	83 Sqn
176866	P/O	RICHARDSON Eric Foster	8-06-44	115 Sqn
1896091	Sgt	RICHARDSON Frederick James	23-06-44	100 Sqn
1376495	Sgt	RICHARDSON Herbert Wilfred	31-03-44	106 Sqn
1385272	F/S	RICHARDSON John Charles	11-11-44	619 Sqn
1485703	F/S	RICHARDSON John Edward	30-07-44	514 Sqn
1609453	Sgt	RICHARDSON Joseph Francis	31-03-44	622 Sqn
1590537	Sgt	RICHARDSON Leslie Joseph	22-05-44	619 Sqn
1580737	Sgt	RICHARDSON Peter Harry	21-07-44	90 Sqn
1483352	Sgt	RICHARDSON Robert	22-01-44	83 Sqn
157522	F/O	RICHARDSON Robert Edwin	31-08-44	103 Sqn
1874495	Sgt	RICHARDSON Robert William	23-05-44	626 Sqn
3005593	Sgt	RICHARDSON Roy Philip	13-10-44	1657 HCU
157884	F/O	RICHARDSON Thomas	18-07-44	115 Sqn
1299973	Sgt	RICHELET Armand [Belgium]	23-05-44	166 Sqn
1390921	F/S	RICHES John Paul	13-02-44	617 Sqn
121448	S/L	RICHES DFC* Wilfrid Cyril	6-07-44	635 Sqn
1895705	Sgt	RICHMAN Herbert Leslie	12-12-44	149 Sqn
1345452	F/S	RICHMOND John	12-11-44	23 Sqn
1283210	Sgt	RICHMOND John Daniel	28-12-44	429 Sqn
1399781	Sgt	RICHMOND Norman Cobban	1-06-44	625 Sqn
143906	F/L	RICHMOND Ronald	24-03-44	156 Sqn
1399324	Sgt	RICHOLD George Henry	11-08-44	640 Sqn
1573141	Sgt	RICHOMME Eric Philip [Channel Islands]	28-06-44	106 Sqn
1863658	Sgt	RICKEARD Arthur John	27-08-44	44 Sqn
1323954	Sgt	RICKETTS Stanley William	20-02-44	514 Sqn
1003849	Sgt	RIDD Herbert George	4-05-44	50 Sqn
185761	F/O	RIDDELL William	6-12-44	57 Sqn
172907	P/O	RIDDLE Horace Albert	4-05-44	626 Sqn
1587493	Sgt	RIDDLE Hoskin Peter	15-03-44	7 Sqn
1873572	Sgt	RIDDLE John Henry	16-03-44	166 Sqn
570829	Sgt	RIDDLE Richard Archibald Kilgour	27-04-44	156 Sqn
1624836	Sgt	RIDGWAY Arthur John	4-05-44	101 Sqn
2216201	F/S	RIDING William Henry	12-05-44	432 Sqn
1334902	Sgt	RIDLEY Albert James	11-09-44	578 Sqn
949503	F/S	RIDLEY George	30-01-44	97 Sqn
1822394	Sgt	RIDLEY John	29-07-44	426 Sqn
79218	F/L	RIDLEY Raymond Nicholas	20-01-44	7 Sqn
1106608	Cpl	RIDPATH Andrew	22-08-44	5 Group
654573	Sgt	RIDYARD Greenwood Gee	23-03-44	50 Sqn
156774	F/O	RIGBY Joseph	25-04-44	635 Sqn
1658848	Sgt	RIGBY Thomas King	25-03-44	427 Sqn
1815835	F/S	RILEY Edward Bonsor	24-06-44	156 Sqn
1584169	Sgt	RILEY Francis Christopher	12-05-44	75 Sqn

Service No	Rank	Name	Date	Unit
153473	F/O	RILEY Frederick Charles	8-08-44	90 Sqn
1685093	Sgt	RILEY Henry	28-05-44	30 OTU
1594504	Sgt	RILEY Thomas Richard	12-09-44	630 Sqn
1515357	Sgt	RILEY William Edward	20-02-44	625 Sqn
1496000	LAC	RILEY William Henry	21-10-44	239 Sqn
3008479	AC2	RIMAN Charles Henry	9-09-44	33 Base
1673522	Sgt	RIMMER Denis Fay	21-04-44	97 Sqn
1495443	Sgt	RIMMER Donald	22-05-44	75 Sqn
2211927	Sgt	RIMMER Herbert	28-04-44	1658 HCU
843261	Sgt	RINGWOOD DFM Jack	28-01-44	625 Sqn
176158	P/O	RIORDAN John	28-04-44	640 Sqn
172870	P/O	RIPPON Dan Carrigan	1-07-44	101 Sqn
577573	Sgt	RITCHIE Frank	12-09-44	100 Sqn
968282	Sgt	RITCHIE George Arklay	18-03-44	427 Sqn
1803787	Sgt	RITCHIE Kenneth Victor	26-08-44	635 Sqn
1389036	Sgt	RIVERS Anthony Albert	9-08-44	161 Sqn
1386079	F/S	RIVERS Ronald Geoffrey	18-03-44	115 Sqn
1293598	Sgt	RIVERS William Marley	25-05-44	158 Sqn
1634350	Sgt	RIX John Albert	2-11-44	49 Sqn
1891954	Sgt	ROACH Basil John	28-05-44	427 Sqn
144544	F/O	ROBBINS DFC Alfred Edward	23-04-44	77 Sqn
1338956	Sgt	ROBBINS Dennis	11-04-44	460 Sqn
623468	Sgt	ROBBINS Dennis George	11-04-44	158 Sqn
1338780	Sgt	ROBBINS Frederick David	14-01-44	576 Sqn
1852263	Sgt	ROBBINS Kenneth Thomas	22-06-44	57 Sqn
634237	F/S	ROBERTS DFM Albert Edward	15-03-44	97 Sqn
1318190	Sgt	ROBERTS Arthur Melvyn	21-01-44	77 Sqn
1819401	F/S	ROBERTS Bleddyn Lloyd	7-10-44	514 Sqn
179401	P/O	ROBERTS Charles William George	20-02-44	408 Sqn
1544887	Sgt	ROBERTS Colin	31-03-44	106 Sqn
1457708	Sgt	ROBERTS Cyril	18-03-44	466 Sqn
1626114	Sgt	ROBERTS Dennis William	16-12-44	115 Sqn
1880379	Sgt	ROBERTS Derek John	31-07-44	12 OTU
1685090	Sgt	ROBERTS Douglas Dean	17-06-44	77 Sqn
970464	W/O	ROBERTS DFM Edward Charles	25-06-44	90 Sqn
1624053	Sgt	ROBERTS Edward Mansell	13-08-44	14 OTU
1320600	Sgt	ROBERTS Eric Wickens	27-03-44	78 Sqn
156707	F/O	ROBERTS Evan	24-12-44	102 Sqn
1422157	F/S	ROBERTS Evan Ephraim Edward	22-05-44	156 Sqn
173964	P/O	ROBERTS DFM Frank Douglas	25-06-44	97 Sqn
149622	F/L	ROBERTS DFC Frank James	21-01-44	97 Sqn
1131282	F/S	ROBERTS DFM Frederick Glyn	7-07-44	103 Sqn
1452334	F/S	ROBERTS George William	27-03-44	1409 Flt
577100	Sgt	ROBERTS Gerald Vincent	2-01-44	7 Sqn
1106717	Sgt	ROBERTS Harry	29-01-44	115 Sqn
1567921	Sgt	ROBERTS James Manderson	10-04-44	103 Sqn
1089013	Sgt	ROBERTS John	6-01-44	97 Sqn
2208978	Sgt	ROBERTS John Andrew	8-05-44	106 Sqn
128948	F/L	ROBERTS John Hubert	27-10-44	239 Sqn
176514	P/O	ROBERTS John Meredith	25-05-44	158 Sqn
2211675	Sgt	ROBERTS Joseph Edward	23-09-44	166 Sqn
1487670	Sgt	ROBERTS Kenneth	29-07-44	207 Sqn
1086767	F/S	ROBERTS Kenneth James	23-01-44	161 Sqn
1431154	Sgt	ROBERTS Kenneth James	12-09-44	158 Sqn
157625	F/L	ROBERTS DFC Leslie	28-10-44	35 Sqn
1622038	F/S	ROBERTS Leslie George	18-12-44	51 Sqn
1603695	Sgt	ROBERTS Leslie William	26-02-44	463 Sqn
1808483	Sgt	ROBERTS Owen Stanley	24-03-44	166 Sqn
2210829	Sgt	ROBERTS Pyrs Owen	25-09-44	199 Sqn
2205622	Sgt	ROBERTS Reginald Alan Wellesley	29-07-44	576 Sqn
1668201	Sgt	ROBERTS Robert Daniel	16-12-44	115 Sqn
1341705	Sgt	ROBERTS Robert Russell	31-03-44	101 Sqn
2205764	Sgt	ROBERTS Tegwyn	23-09-44	61 Sqn
177560	P/O	ROBERTS Thomas Robert Wade	13-06-44	434 Sqn
959101	F/S	ROBERTS Walter James	24-09-44	156 Sqn
2206786	Sgt	ROBERTS William	6-12-44	550 Sqn
1030803	Sgt	ROBERTS William Arthur	5-07-44	57 Sqn
1155381	Sgt	ROBERTS William John Henry	29-10-44	582 Sqn
1592545	Sgt	ROBERTSHAW Arthur Edgar	1-04-44	20 OTU
1379027	F/S	ROBERTSHAW Cecil Burnley	13-08-44	514 Sqn
1392730	F/S	ROBERTSON Alan Weir Struan	23-03-44	239 Sqn
1683527	Sgt	ROBERTSON Alexander	5-12-44	84 OTU
1567775	Sgt	ROBERTSON David Band	28-04-44	102 Sqn
1450693	F/S	ROBERTSON Donald	6-01-44	12 Sqn
1520557	F/S	ROBERTSON Donald	12-09-44	218 Sqn
1821069	Sgt	ROBERTSON George Smith	31-03-44	106 Sqn
112684	S/L	ROBERTSON DFC Ian	2-01-44	101 Sqn
155090	F/O	ROBERTSON DFC James	28-10-44	1661 HCU
1438554	Sgt	ROBERTSON James Donald	7-02-44	427 Sqn
657943	Sgt	ROBERTSON James Miller	11-04-44	1661 HCU
1553559	F/S	ROBERTSON James William	23-01-44	161 Sqn
1109978	Sgt	ROBERTSON John	12-09-44	50 Sqn
1565047	F/S	ROBERTSON John Daly	6-11-44	622 Sqn
1821891	Sgt	ROBERTSON John Murray	25-05-44	51 Sqn
1577452	F/S	ROBERTSON John Neil	4-05-44	1662 HCU
185773	P/O	ROBERTSON John Wadsworth	9-11-44	625 Sqn
1397798	Sgt	ROBERTSON Maurice John	26-08-44	300 Sqn
1565912	Sgt	ROBERTSON William Bertram	15-03-44	550 Sqn
1324986	F/S	ROBEY Leslie James	8-06-44	166 Sqn
176362	P/O	ROBIN Leslie	18-07-44	431 Sqn
1874073	Sgt	ROBINS Peter Cyril	28-06-44	166 Sqn
1545327	F/S	ROBINSON Anthony	28-06-44	106 Sqn
1015525	W/O	ROBINSON Arthur William	3-01-44	405 Sqn
132863	F/L	ROBINSON DFC Benjamin Reginald	17-06-44	640 Sqn
1061193	F/S	ROBINSON DFM Bernard Leo	6-01-44	35 Sqn
2221106	Sgt	ROBINSON Dennis	30-01-44	463 Sqn
1061047	F/S	ROBINSON Donald Stephen	17-03-44	17 OTU
1455045	F/S	ROBINSON Frank	20-09-44	622 Sqn
1623526	AC1	ROBINSON George	1-05-44	514 Sqn
646672	Sgt	ROBINSON George Albert	27-04-44	460 Sqn
1404551	Sgt	ROBINSON Henry Power	10-05-44	550 Sqn
1594686	Sgt	ROBINSON James Edward	24-08-44	1652 HCU
3066983	Sgt	ROBINSON James Goldsmith	15-12-44	12 Sqn
1511210	Sgt	ROBINSON John	23-04-44	166 Sqn
951830	Sgt	ROBINSON John Robert	25-11-44	12 OTU
1318764	F/S	ROBINSON John William	11-06-44	15 Sqn
2205557	Sgt	ROBINSON John William	7-08-44	149 Sqn
649403	F/S	ROBINSON Joseph William	12-09-44	35 Sqn
1082484	F/S	ROBINSON Joseph William Ivan	29-01-44	77 Sqn
178794	P/O	ROBINSON Keith	29-06-44	102 Sqn
1590995	Sgt	ROBINSON Leonard Hugh	20-01-44	1657 HCU
183935	P/O	ROBINSON Norman Kingsley	3-09-44	426 Sqn
184696	P/O	ROBINSON Peter	19-08-44	635 Sqn
135130	F/O	ROBINSON Raymond John	15-02-44	166 Sqn
1037933	Sgt	ROBINSON Robert Calderwood	21-04-44	207 Sqn
2209379	Sgt	ROBINSON Roy	1-06-44	138 Sqn
1725072	Sgt	ROBINSON Roy Edwin Dennis	25-05-44	76 Sqn
1528518	F/S	ROBINSON Stanley	18-12-44	106 Sqn
1503025	Sgt	ROBINSON Thomas James	16-03-44	578 Sqn
3012168	Sgt	ROBINSON William	9-12-44	21 OTU
1022509	Sgt	ROBLIN David Daniel	24-02-44	30 OTU
1671735	Sgt	ROBSON Arthur	16-09-44	582 Sqn
152768	F/O	ROBSON Edward Chatterton	19-07-44	57 Sqn
1576820	Sgt	ROBSON Frederick Ernest	29-01-44	463 Sqn
1683375	Sgt	ROBSON John George	10-04-44	57 Sqn
1624707	Sgt	ROBSON Sidney	25-03-44	97 Sqn
144657	F/O	ROBSON William Bowman	29-01-44	83 Sqn
1293713	Sgt	ROBSON William Charles Walter	16-03-44	76 Sqn
1764138	Sgt	ROBY Thomas Arthur	25-06-44	576 Sqn
1600671	Sgt	ROCHE Gerard Patrick	21-02-44	156 Sqn
1622397	F/S	ROCKINGHAM Peter Hilary	10-05-44	1658 HCU
169004	P/O	RODBOURN Kenneth	16-03-44	630 Sqn
1315683	Sgt	RODDA Douglas Ernest	22-12-44	189 Sqn
568729	Sgt	RODERICK Alan	28-05-44	514 Sqn
171390	P/O	RODGER James Menzies	16-03-44	115 Sqn
1562043	F/S	RODGER Robert	29-07-44	619 Sqn
1387728	Sgt	RODGER Thomas Walter [Argentina]	9-06-44	102 Sqn
153910	F/O	RODGERS Stanley	6-11-44	463 Sqn

Service No	Rank	Name	Date	Sqn
1880035	Sgt	RODGERS Thompson Alfred	24-12-44	166 Sqn
173506	P/O	RODGERSON Jack	12-05-44	115 Sqn
1661997	Sgt	RODHOUSE Raymond Arthur	14-01-44	115 Sqn
1832886	Sgt	RODWAY Stanley John	4-05-44	101 Sqn
176769	P/O	ROE Ernest John	7-06-44	44 Sqn
144200	F/O	ROE Ronald Stuart	20-05-44	7 Sqn
1609482	Sgt	ROE Thomas Edward	20-02-44	12 Sqn
1852080	Sgt	ROFFEY Douglas Archibald Thomas	25-07-44	75 Sqn
1819000	Sgt	ROGERS Albert John	26-03-44	192 Sqn
1616108	Sgt	ROGERS Allan Thomas	18-09-44	57 Sqn
1593178	Sgt	ROGERS Arthur	13-07-44	1662 HCU
937101	Sgt	ROGERS Arthur Mervyn	15-02-44	115 Sqn
1612257	F/S	ROGERS Edward Frank	15-10-44	166 Sqn
184478	P/O	ROGERS Frederick William	13-09-44	218 Sqn
121119	F/L	ROGERS Griffith Gilbert	18-09-44	23 Sqn
173133	P/O	ROGERS Henry	29-06-44	102 Sqn
1130293	Sgt	ROGERS John	30-08-44	21 OTU
171085	F/O	ROGERS DFC Kenneth Roy	27-08-44	100 Sqn
1681948	Sgt	ROGERS Sam Paul [Canada]	20-02-44	207 Sqn
1852120	Sgt	ROGERS Thomas James	31-03-44	424 Sqn
144769	F/O	ROGERS Walter James	25-05-44	158 Sqn
151320	F/O	ROGERS William John Hopkins	4-05-44	50 Sqn
1543271	Sgt	ROGERSON Anthony	20-02-44	158 Sqn
147714	F/L	ROGERSON DFC John Inshaw	17-08-44	97 Sqn
2209393	Sgt	ROGERSON Peter	4-01-44	1658 HCU
159445	P/O	ROHRER Francis Richard	24-02-44	51 Sqn
1601823	Sgt	ROLFE Donald Leslie James	13-08-44	578 Sqn
1469579	Sgt	ROLFE Douglas	25-04-44	49 Sqn
1391433	Sgt	ROLFE Leonard Alfred	4-11-44	626 Sqn
1850207	Sgt	ROLFE Ronald John	15-06-44	15 Sqn
1622914	Sgt	ROLLINSON Arthur	24-09-44	166 Sqn
90391	W/C	ROLLINSON DFC John Dudley	29-01-44	630 Sqn
1176863	W/O	ROLPH Henry Thomas	23-04-44	514 Sqn
1645930	Sgt	ROLPH Raymond Albert	6-07-44	578 Sqn
171066	F/O	ROLTON DFC Leslie George	31-07-44	617 Sqn
152497	F/O	RONAYNE Charles Stanford	11-06-44	141 Sqn
160504	P/O	RONDELET Reve Achille Nicolas [Canada]	22-01-44	427 Sqn
1438865	Sgt	ROOK Ronald	25-05-44	192 Sqn
1324354	Sgt	ROOKER Norman Charles Vezey	7-06-44	106 Sqn
1479035	F/S	ROOKES Allan Lawson	7-08-44	156 Sqn
1809843	Sgt	ROOKWOOD Frank Thomas Harold	4-11-44	195 Sqn
1391821	F/S	ROOTS Leslie Charles	19-07-44	100 Sqn
1590901	Sgt	ROPER Albert Derrick	5-07-44	207 Sqn
1515925	Sgt	ROPER Victor Ronald	4-05-44	626 Sqn
147507	F/O	ROSBOTTOM John Herbert	14-09-44	692 Sqn
153443	F/O	ROSE George Frederick	12-09-44	90 Sqn
1890273	Sgt	ROSE John	22-01-44	76 Sqn
1874808	Sgt	ROSE Reginald Alfred	23-05-44	77 Sqn
1481165	F/S	ROSE Wallace	22-03-44	35 Sqn
710346	Sgt	ROSELT Adrian Ruyseh [South Africa]	4-12-44	57 Sqn
149350	F/O	ROSEN Raymond Arnold	1-07-44	10 Sqn
1586996	Sgt	ROSENBERG Ernest Dennis	11-04-44	635 Sqn
155354	F/O	ROSHER DFM Frank George	14-01-44	514 Sqn
1437982	F/S	ROSHER Horace Sydney	24-09-44	61 Sqn
13698936	Sgt	ROSS Alexander	2-01-44	61 Sqn
174333	P/O	ROSS Alexander Robert	22-06-44	49 Sqn
1344679	F/S	ROSS Allan Henry	31-03-44	101 Sqn
1877036	Sgt	ROSS Charles Herbert	12-09-44	625 Sqn
1491673	Sgt	ROSS Gordon Ernest	29-07-44	626 Sqn
178539	F/O	ROSS Henry	29-12-44	170 Sqn
975825	Sgt	ROSS Ian Hamilton	23-06-44	76 Sqn
1273637	Sgt	ROSS Ian Murray [Canada]	13-06-44	166 Sqn
172466	P/O	ROSS James Albert McLean	10-04-44	12 Sqn
1365859	Sgt	ROSS John Archibald Duncan	9-11-44	625 Sqn
1334400	F/S	ROSS John Henry Charles	13-08-44	635 Sqn
1550710	F/S	ROSS John Hamilton	25-05-44	640 Sqn
1673067	Sgt	ROSS Joesph Beaddie	13-06-44	460 Sqn
32111	W/C	ROSS Quentin Weston Aldridge	25-03-44	626 Sqn
1236337	F/S	ROSS Reginald Norman	15-02-44	419 Sqn
52808	F/O	ROSS MBE MM Ronald Emerson 'Pat'	1-04-44	1656 HCU
1411386	Sgt	ROSS Roy McStuart	24-03-44	100 Sqn
2209009	F/S	ROSS Walter	8-06-44	622 Sqn
1354012	F/S	ROSS William	26-08-44	7 Sqn
139487	F/L	ROSS DFC William George	20-01-44	83 Sqn
151612	F/O	ROSSER John Radford	12-09-44	35 Sqn
1483108	F/S	ROSSER William John	29-01-44	630 Sqn
85791	F/L	ROSSINGTON Philip John	21-07-44	90 Sqn
1578477	Sgt	ROTHERA John Patrick	29-01-44	207 Sqn
2206323	Sgt	ROTHWELL Harold	13-06-44	166 Sqn
171500	F/L	ROTHWELL DFC Lewis	28-04-44	51 Sqn
1253688	LAC	ROULLIER Edward Thomas	10-04-44	Spilsby
48054	F/L	ROUND DFM Frank Desmond	5-07-44	35 Sqn
1239106	Sgt	ROUND John Raymond	2-01-44	550 Sqn
1699385	AC2	ROURKE Edward	10-04-44	207 Sqn
1436301	Sgt	ROUSE Albert Edward John	28-06-44	460 Sqn
174939	P/O	ROUSE John Wallis	23-05-44	100 Sqn
1293573	F/S	ROUSE Reginald James	28-01-44	115 Sqn
137532	F/O	ROUSSEAU Felix Charles	24-03-44	429 Sqn
1591457	Sgt	ROUTLEDGE John	11-11-44	44 Sqn
156075	F/O	ROW James Malcolm	24-03-44	578 Sqn
1579317	Sgt	ROWCLIFFE David	1-04-44	49 Sqn
1271023	Sgt	ROWE Edward John	21-02-44	427 Sqn
1606978	Sgt	ROWE Ernest George	6-05-44	11 OTU
1836885	Sgt	ROWE Norman	29-11-44	12 Sqn
170723	F/O	ROWE DFC Philip Finnis	27-04-44	101 Sqn
56272	P/O	ROWLAND Bernard Lawrence	3-08-44	61 Sqn
127942	F/L	ROWLAND DFC Thomas Wilson	14-01-44	101 Sqn
537312	Sgt	ROWLANDS Albert Raymond	10-05-44	97 Sqn
1624754	Sgt	ROWLANDS Clifford John	5-09-44	85 OTU
122998	F/L	ROWLANDS DFC Desmond Harold	31-03-44	97 Sqn
1515893	Sgt	ROWLANDS Ernest Jones	22-05-44	635 Sqn
1332442	Sgt	ROWLEY Anthony William Herbert	16-03-44	28 OTU
1247821	Sgt	ROWLEY John Edward	22-04-44	1660 HCU
1579631	Sgt	ROWLEY Joseph Peter	26-08-44	101 Sqn
1454675	Sgt	ROWLEY Kenneth	28-04-44	166 Sqn
1890653	Sgt	ROWLEY Leslie George	11-04-44	158 Sqn
1091825	Sgt	ROWNTREE Mathew	25-11-44	427 Sqn
1853111	Sgt	ROWTHORN Peter Robert	12-05-44	630 Sqn
1218669	Sgt	ROXBY Edward	21-07-44	578 Sqn
1676062	Sgt	ROXBY Henry	2-11-44	49 Sqn
1396030	Sgt	ROXBY Thomas Francis Maude	2-01-44	550 Sqn
1456668	Sgt	ROY William	27-01-44	18 OTU
1531800	F/S	ROYAL Ernest William	11-08-44	51 Sqn
3000076	Sgt	ROYAL Robert Eric	23-06-44	76 Sqn
1582033	Sgt	ROYALL Gordon	27-06-44	1655 MTU
1452441	Sgt	ROYSTON Gordon	29-01-44	90 Sqn
55213	P/O	RUDD Donald	29-07-44	550 Sqn
1819118	Sgt	RUDD John Alan	11-12-44	49 Sqn
89839	F/L	RUDDICK James	22-01-44	44 Sqn
1890442	Sgt	RUDELHOFF Henry William	20-01-44	78 Sqn
1834880	Sgt	RUDGE James Henry	28-05-44	427 Sqn
1316548	Sgt	RUDGE Ronald Allen James	20-02-44	83 Sqn
175408	F/O	RUFFLE DFC Frederick Henry	23-11-44	1692 Flt
1397963	Sgt	RUGG George William	24-02-44	156 Sqn
1393799	F/S	RUMBLES Marshall Brian	22-05-44	635 Sqn
2209127	Sgt	RUME Myer	25-5-44	424 Sqn
2209612	F/S	RUMNEY Joseph	21-07-44	97 Sqn
1338135	F/S	RUMNEY Walter Henry	28-04-44	1658 HCU
1565343	Sgt	RUNCIMAN Ian Boyd	4-11-44	51 Sqn
125432	F/L	RUNNACLES John Seymour	11-11-44	97 Sqn
1324628	Sgt	RUNYARD Ronald George	10-05-44	90 Sqn
542730	Sgt	RUSH Leslie Gordon	28-01-44	199 Sqn
1275536	Sgt	RUSHER Norman Ralph	20-11-44	1656 HCU
1880077	Sgt	RUSHTON Edward William	8-05-44	49 Sqn
654193	F/S	RUSHWORTH Frederick	20-01-44	466 Sqn
1399814	Sgt	RUSHWORTH James Donald [Brazil]	16-11-44	207 Sqn
614239	Sgt	RUSSELL Donald Mac	13-06-44	408 Sqn

188136	P/O	RUSSELL Eric Herbert	29-11-44	101 Sqn		1322905	F/S	SANDFORD Arthur James	27-01-44	101 Sqn
1398106	F/S	RUSSELL Frederick William	13-08-44	158 Sqn		1581636	Sgt	SANDILANDS Leslie Gordon	29-01-44	77 Sqn
129583	F/L	RUSSELL DFC George	23-12-44	109 Sqn		1897221	Sgt	SANDILANDS William Law	28-10-44	76 Sqn
1813427	Sgt	RUSSELL Harry	28-05-44	12 Sqn		189653	P/O	SANDOVER Reginald William	13-06-44	158 Sqn
160216	F/O	RUSSELL Henry Alfred Scott [Rhodesia]	23-10-44	44 Sqn		620716	Sgt	SANDS Henry Selwyn	4-12-44	106 Sqn
						1892480	Sgt	SANDY Roy George Emmitt	10-01-44	1652 HCU
842512	Sgt	RUSSELL Philip Charles	16-11-44	207 Sqn		141567	F/O	SANFORD Robert	6-07-44	635 Sqn
1399883	Sgt	RUSSELL Reginald George Samuel	4-05-44	35 Sqn		197338	P/O	SANKEY William George	30-08-44	115 Sqn
1822851	Sgt	RUSSELL Robert Baillie	28-04-44	102 Sqn		1418517	Sgt	SANSOM Kenneth Walter	22-06-44	207 Sqn
1576617	Sgt	RUSSELL Ronald	4-05-44	50 Sqn		1897020	Sgt	SAPSED Henry	16-11-44	625 Sqn
1520931	Sgt	RUSSELL Stanley Roland	4-05-44	460 Sqn		173311	F/O	SARGENT Alexander James	19-07-44	630 Sqn
70594	W/C	RUSSELL DFC* William McFarlane [Canada]	8-05-44	138 Sqn		114047	F/L	SARGENT DFC Eric Wilfred	27-01-44	83 Sqn
						1624840	Sgt	SARGENT Robert Hawley	25-06-44	44 Sqn
1591403	Sgt	RUSSON Harold	7-03-44	1667 HCU		1438714	F/S	SARJANTSON Alan	18-04-44	51 Sqn
68194	F/L	RUTHERFORD AFC Norman Bayne [Australia]	18-09-44	627 Sqn		1896162	Sgt	SAUNDERS Alan Russel	7-02-44	19 OTU
						1117296	F/S	SAUNDERS Alexander Gray Thomas	23-09-44	10 Sqn
1320368	Sgt	RUTHERFORD-BROWNE Anthony	28-01-44	115 Sqn		111991	S/L	SAUNDERS DFC Anthony Douglas	20-02-44	156 Sqn
106375	F/L	RUTLEDGE Arthur William	16-09-44	1655 MTU		943666	Sgt	SAUNDERS Bertram Eric	15-11-44	1666 HCU
1894564	Sgt	RUTSON George Jack	18-10-44	115 Sqn		1130386	Sgt	SAUNDERS Christopher	22-03-44	626 Sqn
1491674	F/S	RUTTER Jack	28-05-44	30 OTU		1803522	Sgt	SAUNDERS Frank Alfred	24-09-44	9 Sqn
1324923	Sgt	RYAN Alfred Allan Joseph	11-06-44	625 Sqn		1896195	Sgt	SAUNDERS Frank Charles	9-08-44	640 Sqn
2220652	Sgt	RYAN Charles Patrick	22-01-44	427 Sqn		1852883	Sgt	SAUNDERS Frederick Charles	24-09-44	85 OTU
174155	P/O	RYAN Dennis William	5-07-44	9 Sqn		1413460	F/S	SAUNDERS George Arthur	24-03-44	100 Sqn
129107	F/O	RYAN Ernest	24-02-44	30 OTU		1607411	Sgt	SAUNDERS George Maurice	10-11-44	97 Sqn
1285937	F/S	RYAN George Thomas	29-07-44	626 Sqn		133458	F/L	SAUNDERS DFC Ian William	29-07-44	12 Sqn
1432798	F/S	RYAN John	10-11-44	61 Sqn		902995	Sgt	SAUNDERS Ronald Arthur Leighton	22-03-44	166 Sqn
1616427	Sgt	RYDER Arthur William	8-06-44	622 Sqn		157140	F/O	SAUNDERSON Christopher William	13-05-44	76 Sqn
643421	Sgt	RYDER Dennis Harvey	10-05-44	97 Sqn		1393629	F/S	SAVAGE Basil Oswald	22-03-44	158 Sqn
1238672	Sgt	RYDER Reginald George	15-03-44	7 Sqn		1386346	Sgt	SAVAGE Donald Percy Judge	30-01-44	100 Sqn
130616	F/L	RYDER William Wallace	28-01-44	115 Sqn		1459486	Sgt	SAVAGE Douglas	24-03-44	77 Sqn
79219	S/L	RYLE DFC George	28-04-44	7 Sqn		1819131	Sgt	SAVAGE Frank William	9-06-44	50 Sqn
1339838	F/S	SABINE David Shirley	27-03-44	1409 Flt		1523833	F/S	SAVAGE George Donald	13-06-44	514 Sqn
1271349	Sgt	SADDLER Robert Campbell	25-09-44	199 Sqn		56045	P/O	SAVAGE Maurice	26-08-44	207 Sqn
535804	Sgt	SADLER Henry	23-07-44	514 Sqn		658651	F/S	SAVAGE Phillip Henry	25-02-44	100 Sqn
1381538	Sgt	SADLER John Russell	6-12-44	460 Sqn		1652979	F/S	SAVERY Clifford	8-11-44	51 Sqn
1526058	F/S	SADLER Robert	4-06-44	635 Sqn		1593727	Sgt	SAVILLE Gerald	6-11-44	57 Sqn
1896102	Sgt	SADLER William Charles	30-08-44	103 Sqn		1318133	Sgt	SAWKINS Kenneth	16-11-44	625 Sqn
2204680	Sgt	SAGAR Joseph	15-03-44	44 Sqn		148865	F/O	SAWYER Ernest William	23-09-44	101 Sqn
1146986	F/S	SAGE Thomas Edwin	13-06-44	460 Sqn		174215	P/O	SAWYER Frederick Charles Archibald	29-07-44	434 Sqn
138072	F/O	SAIDLER James Donald	2-05-44	7 Sqn		1091895	Sgt	SAXBY William John	23-05-44	630 Sqn
1802077	Sgt	SAINES Kenneth Ernest Douglas	14-11-44	51 Sqn		520481	Sgt	SAXTY Albert John William	29-01-44	10 Sqn
1850084	Sgt	SALLIS Jack Henry	4-05-44	103 Sqn		1318013	F/S	SAYCE Stanley Walter	6-04-44	207 Sqn
176036	P/O	SALMON Frederick Arthur	8-05-44	44 Sqn		70604	F/L	SAYER Arthur John	15-02-44	7 Sqn
1602817	Sgt	SALMON John James [Eire]	18-06-44	28 OTU		1870253	Sgt	SAYER Cyril Thomas	28-06-44	90 Sqn
1864687	Sgt	SALMON John William	11-12-44	1651 HCU		1866235	Sgt	SAYERS Albert Laurie	8-07-44	207 Sqn
657616	F/S	SALMOND Frank	18-04-44	158 Sqn		1629785	Sgt	SCALES Frederick Arthur	23-09-44	61 Sqn
1818690	Sgt	SALMONS Robert Henry	23-06-44	77 Sqn		1434761	F/S	SCALES Kenneth James	29-01-44	434 Sqn
54522	P/O	SALT Bernard	31-03-44	12 Sqn		1853075	Sgt	SCAMMELL Arthur	14-10-44	153 Sqn
1451820	Sgt	SALT Charles Arthur	24-03-44	514 Sqn		657203	Sgt	SCAMMELL Kenneth Frederick	20-02-44	7 Sqn
1890999	Sgt	SALTER Anthony Miles	25-07-44	1667 HCU		1032289	F/S	SCARFF Douglas George Bertie	22-06-44	83 Sqn
1826128	Sgt	SALTON Kenneth Ronald	14-10-44	550 Sqn		1322542	F/S	SCHEFFLER St. John Edward Roderick Samuel		
1587294	Sgt	SALWAY Leslie	24-07-44	50 Sqn					18-04-44	51 Sqn
126974	F/L	SAMBIDGE DFC Albert Henry John	30-01-44	83 Sqn		941898	Sgt	SCHNEIDER Arthur William Louis	14-01-44	101 Sqn
1608556	F/S	SAMPSON Graham Mortimer	15-11-44	115 Sqn		1119084	Sgt	SCHOFIELD Basil Henry	31-03-44	101 Sqn
186413	P/O	SAMPSON Louis David	20-11-44	75 Sqn		174944	P/O	SCHOFIELD DFM Derek	25-04-44	619 Sqn
1515480	Sgt	SAMPSON Roger John	28-04-44	640 Sqn		1506088	F/S	SCHOFIELD Eric	26-08-44	101 Sqn
1853730	Sgt	SAMUEL John Charles	29-11-44	153 Sqn		1686166	Sgt	SCHOFIELD Geoffrey	27-03-44	78 Sqn
1321353	Sgt	SAMUELS Reginald Douglas	15-03-44	550 Sqn		1604023	Sgt	SCHOFIELD John Northcott	20-02-44	77 Sqn
2223112	Sgt	SANDALL Bernard	31-03-44	21 OTU		120349	S/L	SCHOFIELD Robert Henry	30-08-44	83 Sqn
1382666	Sgt	SANDER William James	25-03-44	635 Sqn		153717	P/O	SCHOFIELD Stephen Roger	19-03-44	20 OTU
149052	F/O	SANDERS Christopher	12-12-44	460 Sqn		1812070	Sgt	SCHOFIELD William Frank	5-07-44	192 Sqn
1436511	Sgt	SANDERS John George Douglas	11-11-44	619 Sqn		631611	W/O	SCOLES Kenneth	22-06-44	44 Sqn
125979	F/L	SANDERS Richard Vernon	10-04-44	149 Sqn		1112154	Sgt	SCHOLEY John Winston	19-03-44	97 Sqn
1590732	Sgt	SANDERS Thomas Stephen	14-01-44	100 Sqn		160180	P/O	SCHOLTZ Neville John Wingrove [Rhodesia]	22-06-44	44 Sqn
1684681	Sgt	SANDERSON Donald	23-01-44	20 OTU						
1322881	Sgt	SANDERSON Douglas Albert	9-06-44	49 Sqn		1608365	Sgt	SCHORR Max	23-04-44	578 Sqn
1506086	Sgt	SANDERSON Eric	27-08-44	1661 HCU		1876107	F/S	SCHWARZ Hans Heinz (served as Blake H.)	13-08-44	101 Sqn
142852	F/L	SANDERSON DFC John Edward	24-03-44	1656 HCU						
1554662	F/S	SANDERSON Victor Andrew	31-03-44	50 Sqn		147351	F/O	SCOTLAND Ernest Douglas	22-10-44	571 Sqn

Service No.	Rank	Name	Date	Sqn
1341832	Sgt	SCOTLAND Robert Ramsay	20-01-44	10 Sqn
157536	F/O	SCOTT Albert	27-08-44	166 Sqn
54182	P/O	SCOTT Alexander Gregory	13-06-44	625 Sqn
183788	P/O	SCOTT Arthur Charles	12-09-44	7 Sqn
1324631	Sgt	SCOTT Bruce Robert	5-07-44	49 Sqn
176377	F/L	SCOTT Charles Berrie	24-09-44	9 Sqn
1160335	Sgt	SCOTT Donald Charles	17-12-44	57 Sqn
1895973	Sgt	SCOTT Donald Harry	29-11-44	101 Sqn
1816835	Sgt	SCOTT Ernest George	22-06-44	44 Sqn
1307851	Sgt	SCOTT George Walter	31-03-44	44 Sqn
2209627	Sgt	SCOTT George William Dennis	3-06-44	640 Sqn
1023462	F/S	SCOTT Gerald Eagleson	24-03-44	514 Sqn
1323101	Sgt	SCOTT Horace Dawson	13-06-44	15 Sqn
169044	P/O	SCOTT Hugh Mackenzie	2-01-44	207 Sqn
1560052	Sgt	SCOTT James Inglis	24-03-44	625 Sqn
1347303	Sgt	SCOTT James Rattray	25-07-44	619 Sqn
644319	Sgt	SCOTT John	6-12-44	57 Sqn
163951	F/O	SCOTT John Norman Lawrence [Kenya]	6-12-44	10 Sqn
1553200	Sgt	SCOTT John Simpson	3-01-44	156 Sqn
1568179	Sgt	SCOTT John Younger	21-04-44	44 Sqn
1382694	F/S	SCOTT Laurence Alfred	23-04-44	7 Sqn
1899459	Sgt	SCOTT Norman	4-12-44	189 Sqn
1392909	Sgt	SCOTT Reginald Frederick	13-07-44	166 Sqn
1585572	F/S	SCOTT Robert Arthur Simpson	9-11-44	625 Sqn
2205999	Sgt	SCOTT Roger	21-11-44	514 Sqn
1451202	F/S	SCOTT Ronald	8-06-44	78 Sqn
1553209	F/S	SCOTT Ronald Parson	22-06-44	207 Sqn
1823365	Sgt	SCOTT Thomas Ireland	19-07-44	100 Sqn
1474110	F/S	SCOTT Walter	27-11-44	149 Sqn
1486629	F/S	SCOTT William Henry	13-08-44	578 Sqn
1435311	Sgt	SCOTT William Leslie	21-04-44	17 OTU
1861486	Sgt	SCRATCHLEY Peter Arthur	29-07-44	467 Sqn
182431	P/O	SCRIMSHAW Christopher Charles	13-08-44	61 Sqn
160001	F/O	SCRIVENER Rendal Anthony Fenwick [Rhodesia]	4-05-44	57 Sqn
1853985	Sgt	SCRIVENS Victor Frank	8-06-44	115 Sqn
366436	Sgt	SCRUTON John Eric	24-03-44	166 Sqn
177641	P/O	SCUFFINS DFM Gordon John	30-07-44	57 Sqn
69487	F/L	SCUTT Stanley Leslie	17-08-44	57 Sqn
163586	F/O	SEAGER Eric John	12-12-44	195 Sqn
1593067	Sgt	SEAGO Arthur William	12-05-44	630 Sqn
1339301	F/S	SEAGRAVE Kenneth Charles	4-01-44	1657 HCU
1818874	Sgt	SEALTIEL Anthony Ralph	22-05-44	514 Sqn
1484103	F/S	SEAMAN Charles Roland	18-03-44	51 Sqn
152328	F/O	SEARL Jack Laidlaw	11-12-44	57 Sqn
1373660	Sgt	SEARLE Frederick Charles	4-05-44	57 Sqn
1600379	Sgt	SEARLE Peter Frederick	21-01-44	101 Sqn
1853236	Sgt	SEARLE Reginald Victor	22-04-44	1654 HCU
172964	P/O	SEARLES Charles Frederick	8-07-44	17 OTU
1324623	Sgt	SEARLES Ernest Robert	1-06-44	149 Sqn
152995	P/O	SEARS Colin William Owen	20-01-44	18 OTU
1335581	Sgt	SEARS Edward Gordon	23-03-44	106 Sqn
1648584	Sgt	SEARS Peter	18-03-44	1657 HCU
1891837	Sgt	SECRETAN Philip Donald	17-08-44	630 Sqn
1684979	Sgt	SEDDON Clifford	22-03-44	50 Sqn
963130	Sgt	SEDDON John Patrick	29-01-44	90 Sqn
1005463	Sgt	SEDDON Richard Gerard	8-07-44	207 Sqn
983777	F/S	SEDDON Robert	13-08-44	156 Sqn
103558	F/L	SEDGWICK Daniel Leonard	23-04-44	51 Sqn
1800349	Sgt	SEDGWICK Frederick	11-06-44	100 Sqn
1389042	Sgt	SEELEY Frederick John	21-01-44	433 Sqn
983376	Sgt	SEFTON Edward	22-01-44	78 Sqn
1148515	Sgt	SEFTON Frank	28-03-44	20 OTU
1675804	F/S	SEFTON Norman Bennett	15-02-44	7 Sqn
863360	Sgt	SEILER Frederick Maurice	1-11-44	44 Sqn
155821	F/O	SELENYI Robert Vincent	13-08-44	101 Sqn
2206501	Sgt	SELLARS Billie	26-08-44	300 Sqn
169729	F/L	SELLER Howard Thomas	12-09-44	218 Sqn
151884	F/O	SELLERS Harry	21-07-44	578 Sqn
1177392	Sgt	SELLICK Albert John	8-06-44	115 Sqn
47308	F/L	SELLORS Douglas	21-04-44	239 Sqn
1057241	W/O	SENIOR John Raymond	6-04-44	207 Sqn
1044703	Sgt	SERVICE Robert John	15-03-44	77 Sqn
1429948	Sgt	SETCHFIELD Trevor	13-07-44	550 Sqn
1585006	Sgt	SEVIOUR Albert	27-08-44	115 Sqn
47397	S/L	SEWELL Donald Alec	19-03-44	166 Sqn
1336329	Sgt	SEWELL Malcolm Charles	8-05-44	106 Sqn
129615	F/O	SEWELL Peter Redman	25-05-44	51 Sqn
160592	P/O	SEYMOUR Charles Joseph	20-02-44	158 Sqn
1475129	Sgt	SEYMOUR Francis Stanley	19-07-44	49 Sqn
1398483	F/S	SHACKLETON Colin	18-04-44	51 Sqn
1218398	Sgt	SHACKLETON Ernest	26-07-44	49 Sqn
2206050	Sgt	SHACKLETON Roy	17-12-44	50 Sqn
78858	F/L	SHACKMAN AFC Lawrence	31-10-44	692 Sqn
61040	S/L	SHADFORTH DFC Wallace Gordon	13-06-44	115 Sqn
1612001	Sgt	SHAIMAN Leonard	23-04-44	78 Sqn
1545432	Sgt	SHAKESPEARE Howard	18-09-44	57 Sqn
1801992	Sgt	SHANAHAN John James	11-02-44	425 Sqn
179632	P/O	SHAND Norman John	19-07-44	420 Sqn
1814787	F/S	SHANE Frederick John William	29-07-44	7 Sqn
1384669	F/S	SHANKS Ernest Thomas	30-06-44	514 Sqn
1607839	F/S	SHANNON George Ross	25-07-44	207 Sqn
155256	F/L	SHARD DFC DFM Robert Nathan	16-02-44	78 Sqn
1318198	F/S	SHARLAND Clifford Cyril	22-05-44	550 Sqn
138832	F/O	SHARLAND DFC Robert George	28-04-44	156 Sqn
1616582	Sgt	SHARMAN Dennis Raymond	11-10-44	19 OTU
2210322	Sgt	SHARP Edward	4-12-44	207 Sqn
151339	F/O	SHARP Eric Lewis	8-05-44	106 Sqn
1823063	Sgt	SHARP John	11-04-44	158 Sqn
178246	P/O	SHARP Malcolm	13-08-44	78 Sqn
172178	P/O	SHARP Maurice	25-02-44	1661 HCU
1321148	Sgt	SHARP Ralph George	29-01-44	7 Sqn
144580	F/O	SHARP Robert Walter	21-01-44	207 Sqn
1575581	F/S	SHARP William Arthur	24-07-44	619 Sqn
172286	P/O	SHARP William Clark	15-02-44	100 Sqn
1011102	F/S	SHARPE Alex	22-06-44	214 Sqn
1595269	Sgt	SHARPE Francis Philip	30-08-44	21 OTU
1337746	W/O	SHARPE DFM Granville Sidney	24-09-44	97 Sqn
153234	F/O	SHARPE Sidney Harry	9-11-44	138 Sqn
1494813	Sgt	SHARPEN Leslie	23-05-44	90 Sqn
1865144	Sgt	SHARPLES Jack Wilson	11-06-44	405 Sqn
2204552	Sgt	SHARPLEY John Eason	1-07-44	100 Sqn
1125640	Sgt	SHARROCKS Gordon	7-10-44	78 Sqn
1089927	Sgt	SHATWELL Arthur	29-10-44	207 Sqn
1386027	Sgt	SHATZ Edward	16-03-44	100 Sqn
54437	P/O	SHAW MiD Arthur	21-04-44	428 Sqn
1674657	F/S	SHAW DFM Clifford	24-12-44	635 Sqn
1577435	Sgt	SHAW Deryck Harold	14-01-44	49 Sqn
1672605	Sgt	SHAW Frank	25-04-44	49 Sqn
1332113	Sgt	SHAW Frank Everett	13-07-44	9 Sqn
182101	F/O	SHAW George Kenneth	15-10-44	166 Sqn
107593	W/O	SHAW Harold	28-05-44	166 Sqn
1075175	F/S	SHAW Henry Archibald	22-06-44	207 Sqn
70617	F/L	SHAW James	8-07-44	17 OTU
2211323	Sgt	SHAW James	22-03-44	44 Sqn
1577422	F/S	SHAW John	22-06-44	207 Sqn
41479	S/L	SHAW John Leslie	6-06-44	515 Sqn
1050043	Sgt	SHAW John McDonald	29-06-44	405 Sqn
1819375	Sgt	SHAW John William	4-05-44	50 Sqn
1578357	F/S	SHAW Joseph Pickett	22-06-44	207 Sqn
108854	F/L	SHAW Norman Henry	12-12-44	635 Sqn
173547	Sgt	SHAW Peter	11-06-44	166 Sqn
1651549	F/S	SHAW Stanley Bernard	29-12-44	170 Sqn
1322382	Sgt	SHAW Thomas	16-10-44	14 OTU
1039039	F/S	SHAW DFM Thomas Roy	15-03-44	97 Sqn
173548	P/O	SHAW Walter James	23-04-44	100 Sqn
1823003	Sgt	SHAW William	19-07-44	207 Sqn

171598	P/O	SHAW William Muir	12-05-44	432 Sqn	1726836	Sgt	SHORTER Edward Arthur	30-01-44	156 Sqn
1853000	Sgt	SHAYLER Anthony George	2-08-44	467 Sqn	1880037	Sgt	SHORTER Frederick Henry	22-06-44	50 Sqn
146633	F/O	SHEA DFC Denis Charles	17-09-44	617 Sqn	625411	Sgt	SHOTTON Cyril Peter	5-08-44	166 Sqn
1894302	Sgt	SHEAD William Frederick	23-05-44	166 Sqn	67050	S/L	SHOVE DFC Nathaniel Leslie	13-05-44	76 Sqn
1800275	Sgt	SHEAHAN John Leonard	28-05-44	550 Sqn	147118	F/O	SHRIVES Stanley Kenneth	26-07-44	166 Sqn
2202399	Sgt	SHEARD Francis Bernard	15-10-44	10 Sqn	1330851	F/S	SHROPSHALL Keith James	31-03-44	76 Sqn
1823667	Sgt	SHEARER James	28-04-44	432 Sqn	155125	F/O	SHUTE Montague Roger	25-07-44	622 Sqn
1564464	Sgt	SHEARER William Gilchrist Dufferin	24-09-44	15 Sqn	1475487	Sgt	SHUTT Geoffrey	25-05-44	576 Sqn
1388915	F/S	SHEARING Edward Henry John	20-05-44	514 Sqn	174066	P/O	SHUTTLE Frederick William	31-03-44	640 Sqn
1320181	F/S	SHEARING James Sidney	24-10-44	576 Sqn	1522202	Sgt	SHUTTLEWORTH Robert Baxter	29-02-44	10 OTU
1809160	Sgt	SHEARSBY Henry Frederick	12-04-44	619 Sqn	1525067	Sgt	SIDDALL Donald Frank	31-03-44	460 Sqn
134586	F/O	SHEASBY Herbert Keith	15-03-44	9 Sqn	1520715	F/S	SIDEBOTHAM Fred Thomas Murray	6-01-44	207 Sqn
1836565	Sgt	SHEEHAN Donald Brian	23-04-44	90 Sqn	53845	F/O	SIDNELL James Eric	25-05-44	158 Sqn
1863241	Sgt	SHEEHAN John Harold	8-06-44	78 Sqn	1049056	Sgt	SILLENDER John James	12-09-44	50 Sqn
1798718	Sgt	SHEEHY Patrick Joseph	7-10-44	514 Sqn	1216021	Sgt	SILLATOE Kenneth Ernest Dudley	20-01-44	18 OTU
1812007	Sgt	SHEEN Douglas	7-09-44	17 OTU	155368	F/O	SILLITOE Kenneth Edward Ewen	16-07-44	83 Sqn
1578397	Sgt	SHEFFIELD Jack	25-06-44	467 Sqn	54051	P/O	SILLS MiD James Archibald	24-03-44	15 Sqn
1317832	F/S	SHELL John Lander	25-04-44	626 Sqn	1473492	Sgt	SILSON James Alfred	5-11-44	10 Sqn
1895713	Sgt	SHELTON Joseph William 'Joey'	21-01-44	115 Sqn	1890134	Sgt	SILVER Sydney Gordon	31-03-44	49 Sqn
1576638	F/S	SHENTON Arthur Clifford	4-05-44	619 Sqn	128929	F/L	SILVERMAN Alexis Louis	28-04-44	102 Sqn
177165	P/O	SHENTON Donald	17-06-44	431 Sqn	1701327	Sgt	SILVERMAN David Louis	29-01-44	434 Sqn
1853068	Sgt	SHEPHARD Henry Alfred	23-05-44	103 Sqn	1083375	F/S	SILVERMAN Tony	18-07-44	12 Sqn
1576640	F/S	SHEPHERD Eric	10-05-44	106 Sqn	171455	P/O	SILVERWOOD Geoffrey	30-01-44	100 Sqn
172463	P/O	SHEPHERD Frank	27-04-44	103 Sqn	56185	P/O	SILVERWOOD DFM Henry	29-08-44	582 Sqn
2209614	Sgt	SHEPHERD Joseph	31-03-44	514 Sqn	1372600	Sgt	SIM James Kincade	30-08-44	115 Sqn
2211335	Sgt	SHEPPARD Vernon	14-10-44	626 Sqn	169451	P/O	SIMCOX James Albert	13-06-44	15 Sqn
157898	F/O	SHEPSTONE Brinley	23-06-44	78 Sqn	1570435	Sgt	SIME John Lyle	21-07-44	101 Sqn
1606884	Sgt	SHEPSTONE Kenneth Rogers	21-07-44	12 Sqn	146612	F/O	SIMISTER DFM Norman	8-05-44	138 Sqn
3010170	Sgt	SHERBURN John Geoffrey	24-12-44	166 Sqn	1448546	Sgt	SIMKIN Jack Edward	24-09-44	9 Sqn
1864069	Sgt	SHERGOLD Norman Harold	25-06-44	61 Sqn	2211376	Sgt	SIMMONDS Edward George	4-11-44	640 Sqn
1121513	W/O	SHERIDAN Charles Henry	22-06-44	619 Sqn	1605077	Sgt	SIMMONDS Henry John William	19-07-44	115 Sqn
1826246	Sgt	SHERIDAN John Patrick	4-10-44	550 Sqn	1836668	Sgt	SIMMONDS Ivor Herbert	5-07-44	1667 HCU
2209172	Sgt	SHERIDAN Thomas John	3-06-44	158 Sqn	1357238	F/S	SIMMONS Alfred John	6-01-44	207 Sqn
1183717	Sgt	SHERLIKER Herbert	18-03-44	61 Sqn	182455	P/O	SIMMONS Arthur Vernon	26-08-44	90 Sqn
162517	P/O	SHERLOCK DFC Harry	25-02-44	408 Sqn	1395857	F/S	SIMMONS Donald Eric	25-07-44	166 Sqn
172498	P/O	SHERLOCK Kenneth William	16-02-44	102 Sqn	29049	W/C	SIMMONS Henry Augustus	23-03-44	26 OTU
1577535	Sgt	SHERRATT Cecil William	20-02-44	428 Sqn	171331	P/O	SIMMONS Robert Alfred	27-03-44	10 Sqn
1822097	Sgt	SHERRIT James Alexander	9-11-44	625 Sqn	1876124	Sgt	SIMMONS William Albert	31-03-44	49 Sqn
1586167	Sgt	SHERRY Albert William	21-04-44	17 OTU	1392577	Sgt	SIMNETT Brian	14-03-44	75 Sqn
175817	P/O	SHERVINGTON Tyrrell Michael John	7-06-44	550 Sqn	1076298	F/S	SIMONDS Malachy James [Eire]	19-07-44	463 Sqn
1460238	Sgt	SHERWIN Ernest Francis	11-06-44	90 Sqn	1609292	Sgt	SIMONS Frank Edward	24-03-44	433 Sqn
1583794	Sgt	SHERWIN John Edward Loos	15-11-44	1666 HCU	1435840	Sgt	SIMONS Frederick Edward	23-08-44	83 OTU
1088330	Sgt	SHERWOOD Alan Walton	24-03-44	61 Sqn	157097	F/O	SIMPKIN Leslie Norman	22-06-44	49 Sqn
2211742	Sgt	SHEWEN John George	4-12-44	15 Sqn	1388315	Sgt	SIMPKIN Percival Henry	25-03-44	625 Sqn
997852	Sgt	SHIELD George Armstrong	22-01-44	76 Sqn	1031549	Sgt	SIMPSON Abel	24-03-44	35 Sqn
1675802	Sgt	SHIELDS Frank Wells	28-04-44	7 Sqn	1551166	Sgt	SIMPSON Alexander Farquharson	14-11-44	51 Sqn
1086114	Sgt	SHIELDS Fred George	10-04-44	166 Sqn	1593858	Sgt	SIMPSON Alexander Paton	4-05-44	12 Sqn
1795770	Sgt	SHIELDS James	25-05-44	192 Sqn	1096276	F/S	SIMPSON Charles Holsey	26-02-44	12 Sqn
1570549	Sgt	SHIELDS Robert	21-01-44	419 Sqn	2208949	Sgt	SIMPSON Frank Norman	26-03-44	425 Sqn
1825696	Sgt	SHIELDS Robert Duncan Dumbreck	20-09-44	514 Sqn	185530	P/O	SIMPSON Geoffrey	29-11-44	35 Sqn
171796	P/O	SHIELDS William Gibb Johnston	20-01-44	622 Sqn	1824321	Sgt	SIMPSON George Alexander Milne	16-09-44	78 Sqn
1334523	F/S	SHIELDS William Harold	24-03-44	78 Sqn	1549784	Sgt	SIMPSON Harold	31-03-44	550 Sqn
1566808	Sgt	SHIELS Alexander Kelso	27-04-44	12 Sqn	1510042	Sgt	SIMPSON Harold William	1-04-44	1656 HCU
1896561	Sgt	SHILCOCK James Douglas	6-11-44	550 Sqn	1806333	Sgt	SIMPSON DFM Henry Evan Wade	8-06-44	166 Sqn
122927	F/L	SHILLETO Alfred Cecil	13-07-44	14 OTU	1905742	AC2	SIMPSON James	1-10-44	33 Base
1683352	Sgt	SHIMMIN John Harold	11-05-44	515 Sqn	1896343	F/S	SIMPSON John Liberty	24-12-44	102 Sqn
1683367	Sgt	SHINGLES Ivan	19-07-44	49 Sqn	1557627	Sgt	SIMPSON John William	21-07-44	90 Sqn
170943	P/O	SHINN DFC Albert William	22-06-44	49 Sqn	157539	F/O	SIMPSON Leonard Harry	30-08-44	103 Sqn
1684534	Sgt	SHIPLEY Reginald	8-05-44	106 Sqn	155534	F/O	SIMPSON Leslie	31-03-44	101 Sqn
151431	F/O	SHIRLEY Alfred Vernon	2-01-44	61 Sqn	1818121	Sgt	SIMPSON Norman Gordon	22-11-44	61 Sqn
1202160	W/O	SHIRLEY George Frederick Charles Grandfield	27-08-44	635 Sqn	1805752	Sgt	SIMPSON Raymond George Victor	25-05-44	214 Sqn
					182404	P/O	SIMPSON Ronald Marshall	25-07-44	102 Sqn
1436419	Sgt	SHIRLEY Wilfred Henry	20-02-44	9 Sqn	1339616	Sgt	SIMPSON Terence Dennis	27-01-44	101 Sqn
1590650	Sgt	SHORT Alan Douglas	22-04-44	1654 HCU	1836408	Sgt	SIMPSON Theophilus John	25-07-44	622 Sqn
1590755	Sgt	SHORT Anthony Arthur	22-05-44	626 Sqn	1397228	Sgt	SIMS Anthony Bert Hayward	27-04-44	515 Sqn
175220	P/O	SHORT Charles David Angelo	4-05-44	625 Sqn	1810802	F/S	SIMS DFM George Henry	25-07-44	166 Sqn
1806043	F/S	SHORT Harold Edgar	24-03-44	61 Sqn	1577750	F/S	SIMS Kenneth	20-02-44	61 Sqn
1001749	Sgt	SHORT Stanley Harold	7-02-44	427 Sqn	1817708	Sgt	SIMS Raymond John	22-11-44	61 Sqn
1508293	Sgt	SHORTEN William	25-04-44	115 Sqn	1320290	F/S	SIMS Thomas Edward Frederick	11-04-44	158 Sqn

367

176406	F/O	SIMSON Royston Hubert	25-07-44	57 Sqn		914220	Sgt	SLOMAN Robert Gerald	21-07-44	75 Sqn
1071014	Sgt	SINCLAIR Adam Thompson	20-02-44	625 Sqn		147214	F/L	SLOPER DFC* John Lambert	10-04-44	PFNTU
1603358	Sgt	SINCLAIR Alfred Cecil Edgcumbe (served as GALE R. A.)	31-07-44	100 Sqn		1392523	Sgt	SLOW Henry Samuel	24-02-44	61 Sqn
						1382990	F/S	SLOWLY GM Roy Victor Edward	12-09-44	90 Sqn
136838	F/O	SINCLAIR Graham Olaf Barratt	12-09-44	218 Sqn		46091	S/L	SLY DFC AFM Ernest Frank	14-01-44	514 Sqn
1565049	Sgt	SINCLAIR Robert Morton	30-10-44	21 OTU		1621436	LAC	SMAILES Laurence	29-12-44	514 Sqn
1593177	Sgt	SINCLAIR Stephen	25-07-44	619 Sqn		646926	Sgt	SMALE MiD Robert Francis	2-01-44	630 Sqn
151242	F/L	SINCLAIR William	9-05-44	405 Sqn		1131750	Sgt	SMALL Albert	7-06-44	550 Sqn
1822200	Sgt	SINCLAIR William Aeden	29-03-44	419 Sqn		997506	Sgt	SMALL Cyril	10-09-44	103 Sqn
139840	F/O	SINDEN Francis Edward	23-05-44	49 Sqn		1697611	Sgt	SMALL Ernest	17-03-44	28 OTU
1560847	F/S	SINGER John	12-09-44	619 Sqn		1336458	F/S	SMALL Ernest George	1-06-44	622 Sqn
1578129	Sgt	SINGER Leslie Norman	7-02-44	1662 HCU		1670362	Sgt	SMALL George Robert	19-03-44	625 Sqn
1384615	Sgt	SINGER Maurice Raymond 'Bobby'	26-02-44	427 Sqn		1521752	Sgt	SMALL Robert William	13-09-44	625 Sqn
1261285	Sgt	SINGFIELD William George	21-04-44	44 Sqn		906002	Sgt	SMALLBONE Edward	26-06-44	1667 HCU
1324569	Sgt	SINGH Mohna [India]	30-07-44	106 Sqn		1607395	Sgt	SMALLDON Eric John	16-09-44	90 Sqn
171643	F/S	SINGLETON Bernard Townsend	26-07-44	166 Sqn		137311	F/O	SMART Alan Field Grant	20-05-44	7 Sqn
152438	F/O	SINGLETON John Albert	11-04-44	158 Sqn		1494949	Sgt	SMART Gordon [Eire]	12-09-44	101 Sqn
153307	F/O	SINGLETON Malcolm Dick	18-11-44	35 Sqn		984868	F/S	SMART James Howie	16-02-44	640 Sqn
39008	W/C	SISLEY Alan Francis Moir [Australia]	31-08-44	550 Sqn		1581608	Sgt	SMART Owen Edward Gilbert	22-05-44	463 Sqn
1398598	Sgt	SISLEY Owen Frederick	7-06-44	578 Sqn		152645	F/O	SMART Reginald Hannam	31-03-44	57 Sqn
1895505	Sgt	SISLEY Robert Edward James	4-04-44	5 LFS		151288	F/O	SMART DFC Trevor Tressler	22-06-44	207 Sqn
1474748	Sgt	SISSONS Derrick	30-01-44	100 Sqn		1818902	Sgt	SMEDLEY Ivan Edward	30-01-44	405 Sqn
1622340	Sgt	SISSONS John Randolph	29-06-44	10 Sqn		2204600	Sgt	SMEDLEY Robert	10-04-44	57 Sqn
1600791	Sgt	SIZER Claude William Frank	27-04-44	49 Sqn		1670782	F/S	SMELLIE Robert	10-08-44	619 Sqn
1825534	Sgt	SKEA William	7-10-44	166 Sqn		1601321	Sgt	SMEDMORE William Harrold Frederick	31-03-44	12 Sqn
1796390	Sgt	SKEAT John Alfred Edward	25-04-44	78 Sqn						
1322527	Sgt	SKEATES Reginald Victor	24-07-44	102 Sqn		176033	P/O	SMILEY Thomas Stamper	9-06-44	49 Sqn
1284038	W/O	SKEEL John	25-03-44	166 Sqn		150429	F/L	SMITH Alan Leslie	21-07-44	622 Sqn
618386	F/S	SKEET Frederick George	20-02-44	408 Sqn		132712	F/O	SMITH Albert	19-04-44	115 Sqn
1448086	Sgt	SKEITES Donald James	27-04-44	57 Sqn		151615	F/O	SMITH Albert John	11-04-44	158 Sqn
962849	Sgt	SKELCHER Frederick Walter	31-03-44	61 Sqn		1337225	Sgt	SMITH Alec Norman	25-05-44	429 Sqn
2209827	Sgt	SKELLORN Horace	4-05-44	467 Sqn		1823405	Sgt	SMITH Alexander	17-06-44	102 Sqn
1629697	Sgt	SKELLY Frank	25-04-44	626 Sqn		1601144	Sgt	SMITH Alexander Gerald	2-01-44	463 Sqn
1579239	Sgt	SKELTON Arthur Roy	15-03-44	149 Sqn		1527311	Sgt	SMITH Arthur	15-03-44	625 Sqn
1473051	Sgt	SKELTON Edward	2-01-44	550 Sqn		1596824	Sgt	SMITH Arthur Douglas	13-09-44	20 OTU
152714	F/O	SKELTON Ivan George	18-10-44	115 Sqn		1338175	F/S	SMITH Arthur William	25-07-44	207 Sqn
1697217	F/S	SKELTON DFM John	6-12-44	186 Sqn		547611	Sgt	SMITH Augustus Edward	24-03-44	15 Sqn
1684303	Sgt	SKIDMORE Norman Leslie	30-07-44	1656 HCU		1389203	F/S	SMITH Basil Thomas	24-03-44	78 Sqn
134721	F/L	SKINGLEY DFC Jack	21-07-44	97 Sqn		1578569	F/S	SMITH Bert	11-12-44	57 Sqn
912689	W/O	SKINNER Clifford John	14-01-44	97 Sqn		1591474	F/S	SMITH Bert	27-08-44	83 Sqn
108951	F/L	SKINNER John Walrod Seymour	3-06-44	640 Sqn		117761	F/S	SMITH DFM Bertram Leonard	29-07-44	428 Sqn
1880467	Sgt	SKIPPER Edward Wilfred	18-12-44	106 Sqn		917722	Sgt	SMITH Charles Arthur	8-04-44	75 Sqn
2215940	Sgt	SKIRROW Norman	21-04-44	30 OTU		148393	F/O	SMITH DFM Claud Austin	28-05-44	12 Sqn
177552	P/O	SKUCE Peter Grahame	10-06-44	207 Sqn		1542938	F/S	SMITH Clifford Ernest	28-07-44	101 Sqn
1430914	Sgt	SKUTT Harold	16-06-44	635 Sqn		152042	F/O	SMITH Colin Clifton	13-08-44	77 Sqn
1896103	Sgt	SLACK Arthur	24-06-44	1662 HCU		1202361	Sgt	SMITH Cyril Edward	21-01-44	15 Sqn
1593611	Sgt	SLACK Joseph Kitchener	13-08-44	626 Sqn		1602814	Sgt	SMITH Denis Victor George	25-06-44	9 Sqn
173160	P/O	SLADE Albert Edward	16-05-44	576 Sqn		1576461	F/S	SMITH Dennis Frederick	14-01-44	405 Sqn
1896319	Sgt	SLADE James Arthur	17-08-44	625 Sqn		1807478	Sgt	SMITH Dennis George Brailsford	29-06-44	102 Sqn
939810	W/O	SLADE Norman Francis	30-08-44	161 Sqn		1230432	Sgt	SMITH Dennis Leslie	2-01-44	12 Sqn
1815706	Sgt	SLATER Colin Harry	25-06-44	75 Sqn		133507	F/O	SMITH Dennis Ripley	25-02-44	97 Sqn
2210570	Sgt	SLATER Edwin	25-08-44	75 Sqn		1896917	Sgt	SMITH Derek Reginald	14-10-44	12 Sqn
656696	F/S	SLATER Geoffrey	21-02-44	630 Sqn		158984	F/O	SMITH DFC Derrick Albert John	3-06-44	138 Sqn
158716	P/O	SLATER Joseph Walter	14-01-44	101 Sqn		157951	F/O	SMITH Desmond Felix Anthony Faustin	20-09-44	622 Sqn
172026	F/O	SLATER Peter	21-11-44	514 Sqn						
1428062	Sgt	SLATER Walter Herbert	26-08-44	300 Sqn		1348232	Sgt	SMITH Donald	24-03-44	207 Sqn
178950	P/O	SLATTER Albert Lawrence	15-10-44	10 Sqn		1395416	Sgt	SMITH Donald Lawrence	31-03-44	10 Sqn
87660	F/L	SLATTER John Fosbroke	5-02-44	1655 MTU		1837100	Sgt	SMITH Donald William	17-05-44	29 OTU
138082	F/O	SLATTER Leslie John	28-01-44	103 Sqn		1852687	Sgt	SMITH Douglas James	28-06-44	90 Sqn
1806234	Sgt	SLATTER William Frederick	10-08-44	50 Sqn		1323374	Sgt	SMITH Douglas William James	15-03-44	77 Sqn
1580782	Sgt	SLATTERY Edward Kenneth	4-05-44	582 Sqn		1389708	F/S	SMITH Duncan Lewis Thomas	23-09-44	582 Sqn
3041586	Sgt	SLAVEN John Wilson Mitchell	6-12-44	10 Sqn		1684698	F/S	SMITH Edgar	30-08-44	1660 HCU
1189174	Sgt	SLEEP Alfred Burford	30-08-44	90 Sqn		1119114	W/O	SMITH Edmund	13-09-44	218 Sqn
1533681	Sgt	SLEEP Royston	22-06-44	106 Sqn		1818735	Sgt	SMITH Edward	25-03-44	576 Sqn
1684309	Sgt	SLEIGHTHOLM David	23-05-44	75 Sqn		1316567	W/O	SMITH DFM Edward George	6-07-44	582 Sqn
1456690	Sgt	SLEVEN Arthur Edward James	21-02-44	15 Sqn		1600337	Sgt	SMITH Edward George	11-06-44	166 Sqn
1552498	Sgt	SLOAN John Johnstone	30-01-44	156 Sqn		67687	F/L	SMITH Edwin Donald	6-01-44	576 Sqn
3005474	Sgt	SLOANE Frederick Jiohn	6-11-44	57 Sqn		1398972	F/S	SMITH Eric William	16-10-44	10 Sqn
860307	Sgt	SLOCOMBE Leonard	20-11-44	514 Sqn		1219050	W/O	SMITH Ernest	27-08-44	515 Sqn

Service No	Rank	Surname	Name	Date	Squadron
1865935	Sgt	SMITH	Ernest Hamilton Victor	25-02-44	100 Sqn
1625433	Sgt	SMITH	Ernest Leslie	12-09-44	635 Sqn
817196	Sgt	SMITH	Foster Nelson	22-06-44	467 Sqn
1584152	Sgt	SMITH	Francis Bertram	19-07-44	207 Sqn
1564493	Sgt	SMITH	Francis David Matheson	15-12-44	12 Sqn
1801964	Sgt	SMITH	Francis Ernest Albert	16-03-44	408 Sqn
1318281	F/S	SMITH	Francis James William [Canada]	22-05-44	550 Sqn
1631398	Sgt	SMITH	Francis Ronald	3-06-44	640 Sqn
161663	F/O	SMITH	Frank John	13-09-44	218 Sqn
172030	P/O	SMITH	Frank Raymond	31-03-44	625 Sqn
1593160	Sgt	SMITH	Fred Gordon	16-11-44	1663 HCU
1621687	Sgt	SMITH	Frederick Arthur	25-10-44	431 Sqn
1455964	Sgt	SMITH	Frederick James	31-07-44	100 Sqn
1433744	F/S	SMITH	Frederick Kenneth	24-03-44	35 Sqn
1899710	Sgt	SMITH	Frederick Percival John	4-11-44	195 Sqn
1818638	Sgt	SMITH	Frederick Ronald	7-12-44	1651 HCU
108543	S/L	SMITH DFC	Gavin Strang	17-06-44	550 Sqn
165004	F/O	SMITH	George	25-11-44	12 OTU
616653	F/S	SMITH	George Edward	2-01-44	97 Sqn
818186	Sgt	SMITH	George William	29-02-44	10 OTU
150048	F/O	SMITH	Gordon	7-06-44	82 OTU
172926	P/O	SMITH	Gordon John Leslie	27-04-44	57 Sqn
629543	Sgt	SMITH	Harold Ernest	11-08-44	640 Sqn
153441	F/O	SMITH	Harry	29-09-44	157 Sqn
1520956	Sgt	SMITH	Henry Eadsporth	27-09-44	619 Sqn
1872415	Sgt	SMITH	Henry George	29-10-44	207 Sqn
1653074	Sgt	SMITH	Henry Giles	18-06-44	1663 HCU
2211926	Sgt	SMITH	Herbert	1-04-44	1656 HCU
1501417	Sgt	SMITH	Herbert Richard	12-06-44	102 Sqn
941420	Sgt	SMITH	Herbert Walter Lawrence	21-04-44	57 Sqn
172995	P/O	SMITH	Horace James Worthing	22-03-44	158 Sqn
146980	F/L	SMITH	Howard Arthur Frederick	29-07-44	576 Sqn
1535180	F/S	SMITH	Hubert Frederick	22-01-44	83 Sqn
1559802	F/S	SMITH	Hugh McPherson	25-06-44	106 Sqn
157892	F/O	SMITH	Jack	12-06-44	101 Sqn
1383434	Sgt	SMITH	James	25-03-44	78 Sqn
1604615	Sgt	SMITH	James	21-10-44	75 Sqn
1822687	Sgt	SMITH	James	15-02-44	77 Sqn
1333893	Sgt	SMITH	James Alan	18-04-44	51 Sqn
1821681	Sgt	SMITH	James Murdoch	22-03-44	408 Sqn
1351316	Sgt	SMITH	Jesse Charles	29-01-44	10 Sqn
1323064	Sgt	SMITH	John	20-02-44	78 Sqn
1556800	Sgt	SMITH	John	4-12-44	463 Sqn
1866461	Sgt	SMITH	John	21-07-44	578 Sqn
1890212	Sgt	SMITH	John	11-04-44	12 Sqn
153826	F/O	SMITH	John Arthur	1-11-44	106 Sqn
1881209	Sgt	SMITH	John Charles Wilfred	18-11-44	51 Sqn
645575	W/O	SMITH	John Coates	4-05-44	103 Sqn
1813739	Sgt	SMITH	John David	4-08-44	635 Sqn
1211031	Sgt	SMITH	John Edward Noble	21-04-44	207 Sqn
1491254	Sgt	SMITH	John Francis	25-01-44	16 OTU
175502	P/O	SMITH	John Henry George	22-06-44	630 Sqn
1606296	Sgt	SMITH	John Howard	15-12-44	625 Sqn
1398719	Sgt	SMITH	John James Harold	13-07-44	1662 HCU
1455460	Sgt	SMITH	John Joseph	15-01-44	626 Sqn
1425785	Sgt	SMITH	John Stuart	21-01-44	61 Sqn
51068	F/O	SMITH DFC	John William	21-11-44	515 Sqn
1583360	Sgt	SMITH	John William	12-05-44	103 Sqn
1868059	Sgt	SMITH	John William	25-07-44	103 Sqn
1496241	F/S	SMITH	Joseph Morrison	22-01-44	102 Sqn
1603697	Sgt	SMITH	Keith John	18-07-44	115 Sqn
1473345	Sgt	SMITH	Kenneth	26-08-44	57 Sqn
1577088	Sgt	SMITH	Kenneth	7-02-44	1663 HCU
145144	F/O	SMITH	Kenneth Ferris	23-01-44	161 Sqn
1802485	Sgt	SMITH	Kenneth Oliver	6-06-44	50 Sqn
1808582	Sgt	SMITH	Leonard George	12-05-44	166 Sqn
176021	P/O	SMITH	Leonard James Richard [Malaya]	3-06-44	76 Sqn
950136	W/O	SMITH DFC	Leslie Herbert	17-08-44	97 Sqn
1473490	Sgt	SMITH	Leslie Leonard John	8-05-44	138 Sqn
1817166	Sgt	SMITH	Maurice George	28-04-44	101 Sqn
137169	F/O	SMITH	Norman Alfred	4-05-44	57 Sqn
1851601	Sgt	SMITH	Norman Ronald	14-01-44	97 Sqn
102151	F/L	SMITH	Philip Bonnington [Paraguay]	24-09-44	15 Sqn
1575329	F/S	SMITH	Philip Newbould	8-07-44	207 Sqn
1868834	Sgt	SMITH	Philip Raymond	13-08-44	514 Sqn
1151681	F/S	SMITH	Phillip Combles	23-04-44	578 Sqn
1335530	Sgt	SMITH	Raymond Algernon Reeves	15-02-44	166 Sqn
1235250	Sgt	SMITH	Raymond Charles	30-07-44	75 Sqn
1715062	Sgt	SMITH	Reginald John	10-05-44	106 Sqn
1575616	Sgt	SMITH	Robert Charles	11-04-44	30 OTU
1890521	Sgt	SMITH	Robert Edward	23-04-44	7 Sqn
1777269	Sgt	SMITH	Robert Eric	25-05-44	576 Sqn
1569867	Sgt	SMITH	Robert Speedie	23-04-44	12 Sqn
1585911	Sgt	SMITH	Ronald Alfred	1-07-44	101 Sqn
1866711	Sgt	SMITH	Ronald Arthur	29-11-44	460 Sqn
157915	F/O	SMITH	Ronald Leonard	5-07-44	192 Sqn
1615009	Sgt	SMITH	Ronald Victor	11-04-44	30 OTU
1313019	F/S	SMITH	Royston Laurence	20-02-44	576 Sqn
1583052	Sgt	SMITH	Sidney	22-03-44	100 Sqn
1466984	Sgt	SMITH	Sidney George	22-05-44	156 Sqn
1331001	F/S	SMITH	Stanley	27-04-44	49 Sqn
1592691	Sgt	SMITH	Stanley Waring	18-07-44	158 Sqn
1388382	F/S	SMITH	Terence Walter	29-01-44	97 Sqn
1822792	Sgt	SMITH	Thomas Allison	24-03-44	102 Sqn
578014	Sgt	SMITH	Thomas Daniel	30-08-44	467 Sqn
1575907	Sgt	SMITH	Thomas Harry James	25-05-44	419 Sqn
159075	P/O	SMITH	Thomas Henry	20-02-44	78 Sqn
1149674	Sgt	SMITH	Thomas James	14-01-44	49 Sqn
1582261	Sgt	SMITH	Thomas John Roy	18-09-44	515 Sqn
1273841	W/O	SMITH	Thomas Richard William	26-12-44	76 Sqn
1825000	Sgt	SMITH	Thomas Ritchie	27-08-44	625 Sqn
1483335	W/O	SMITH DFC	Walter	15-06-44	582 Sqn
1590321	Sgt	SMITH	Walter Norman	11-04-44	78 Sqn
1504052	F/S	SMITH	William	8-07-44	61 Sqn
1396176	F/S	SMITH	William Charles	25-05-44	640 Sqn
611657	F/L	SMITH	William Henry	15-02-44	156 Sqn
1819575	Sgt	SMITH	William James	29-07-44	61 Sqn
1862828	Sgt	SMITH	William James Reuben	27-03-44	78 Sqn
1368230	Sgt	SMITH	William McKenna	22-03-44	35 Sqn
1504638	F/S	SMYTH	James	31-03-44	166 Sqn
993020	F/S	SMYTH	Robert	12-09-44	207 Sqn
1580584	Sgt	SNEDDON	Robert Alexander	4-05-44	50 Sqn
174376	P/O	SNELL	Alan	28-05-44	166 Sqn
1481857	Sgt	SNELL	Raymond	17-06-44	51 Sqn
1321695	Sgt	SNELL	Richard William	1-07-44	101 Sqn
1389270	F/S	SNELLING	Dennis Cyril George	3-01-44	156 Sqn
1388603	Sgt	SNELLING	Ronald Edward	27-08-44	90 Sqn
1313128	Sgt	SNEYD	Edwin George	28-04-44	460 Sqn
1380349	Sgt	SNOOK	Alfred Arthur	2-05-44	218 Sqn
1100769	Sgt	SNOWBALL	Thomas	4-06-44	635 Sqn
1822845	Sgt	SNOWDEN	William	6-12-44	103 Sqn
1601000	F/S	SNOWDON	Arthur William	24-03-44	578 Sqn
177959	P/O	SNOWDON	John Atherstone	23-05-44	115 Sqn
941781	Sgt	SNOWLING	Harry	22-05-44	50 Sqn
1868375	Sgt	SNOXELL	Douglas Arthur Patrick	4-10-44	44 Sqn
1398223	Sgt	SOAN	Humphrey Rupert Cruse	22-10-44	571 Sqn
173799	P/O	SOLLY	Charles John	22-06-44	207 Sqn
1324217	Sgt	SOLOMAN DFM	Thomas Christopher	21-01-44	51 Sqn
143847	F/O	SOLOMON	Leonard John	1-06-44	138 Sqn
1850393	Sgt	SOMERS	Lawrence Frazer	2-01-44	101 Sqn
136222	S/L	SOMERSCALES DFC	Stanley Alan	23-04-44	76 Sqn
1553634	Sgt	SOMERVILLE	William	11-04-44	158 Sqn
1052600	F/S	SOO	Ronald	14-01-44	166 Sqn
1171961	Sgt	SOPER	Albert Percy	14-10-44	550 Sqn
146152	F/O	SORENSON	Theodore	14-10-44	12 Sqn
1616880	Sgt	SORTON	Morley Frederick Roy	27-01-44	408 Sqn
1675681	Sgt	SOULSBY	Thomas Walter	14-01-44	115 Sqn

Service No	Rank	Name	Date	Sqn/Unit
1672449	Sgt	SOUTAR Robert Alexander	4-11-44	128 Sqn
1613111	F/S	SOUTH Alexander Arthur	7-09-44	17 OTU
1581192	F/S	SOUTHERN Eric Richard	20-11-44	14 OTU
941962	Sgt	SOUTHERN James	22-05-44	44 Sqn
160096	F/O	SOUTHEY Jack Celtic [Rhodesia]	15-02-44	103 Sqn
2209471	Sgt	SOUTHWARD Kenneth Charles	22-01-44	76 Sqn
2209114	F/S	SOUTHWORTH Charles Henry	28-06-44	106 Sqn
2206836	Sgt	SOWDEN James Birch	16-09-44	199 Sqn
1083540	Sgt	SOWERBY Frederick William	3-06-44	466 Sqn
1523529	Sgt	SOWERSBY Ernest Smith	25-04-44	83 Sqn
159951	F/O	SPAKOWSKI Stanley George	29-07-44	550 Sqn
155494	F/L	SPARK DFC George Aytoun	29-01-44	625 Sqn
1320930	Sgt	SPARKES Bernard Kenneth	20-02-44	625 Sqn
1604735	Sgt	SPARKES Eric Cecil	15-02-44	15 Sqn
130251	F/O	SPARKS William Angus 'Peter'	11-11-44	207 Sqn
160507	F/O	SPARROW Michael Robert	20-01-44	466 Sqn
1592133	Sgt	SPAVEN James Leslie	21-07-44	622 Sqn
1080677	Sgt	SPEAKMAN William	28-01-44	103 Sqn
1474290	F/S	SPEAR Leonard Gordon	13-08-44	101 Sqn
1320824	F/S	SPECKMAN John Clement	5-08-44	619 Sqn
2218427	Sgt	SPEDDING John	6-08-44	50 Sqn
1324131	Sgt	SPEECHLY John Charles	5-02-44	115 Sqn
1594467	Sgt	SPEIGHT James	3-03-44	1666 HCU
133029	F/O	SPELLER Thomas Herbert	25-04-44	78 Sqn
1493490	Sgt	SPENCE Alan	20-02-44	630 Sqn
1670414	Sgt	SPENCE Arthur	29-01-44	1660 HCU
1901001	Sgt	SPENCE Samuel Oscar	2-11-44	415 Sqn
1455592	Sgt	SPENCER Alfred Ernest	14-01-44	101 Sqn
1387303	F/S	SPENCER Charles Frederick	5-07-44	57 Sqn
1609905	F/S	SPENCER Cyril Gordon	25-04-44	7 Sqn
1433953	F/S	SPENCER Frank Richard	16-06-44	514 Sqn
1593463	Sgt	SPENCER Frederick Ivan	13-06-44	166 Sqn
1588684	Sgt	SPENCER Harold Arthur	25-03-44	57 Sqn
139384	F/O	SPENCER Howard	22-06-44	83 Sqn
1307935	Sgt	SPENCER Jack	21-07-44	622 Sqn
171853	F/L	SPENCER James Basil Percy	31-07-44	57 Sqn
614042	W/O	SPENCER Kenneth	5-05-44	7 Sqn
1620185	Sgt	SPENCER Paul Ivan	5-12-44	84 OTU
1575186	W/O	SPENCER Ronald Howard	29-07-44	75 Sqn
144457	F/O	SPENCER Ronald Victor	4-05-44	1662 HCU
2209623	Sgt	SPENCER Thomas	8-07-44	57 Sqn
1400658	F/S	SPENCER Victor William	24-03-44	78 Sqn
2209224	Sgt	SPENDELOW Harold Raymond	29-04-44	630 Sqn
153124	F/O	SPETCH John Edward	28-10-44	23 Sqn
1579969	Sgt	SPIBEY William Herbert	21-01-44	1653 HCU
658220	F/S	SPICE Maurice Charles	26-03-44	15 Sqn
130968	F/L	SPICER Ronald George	15-03-44	77 Sqn
950495	Sgt	SPIDEN David Christie	25-10-44	115 Sqn
1818722	Sgt	SPIERS Keith Herbert	23-06-44	460 Sqn
1581963	F/S	SPIERS Kenneth Charles	12-09-44	218 Sqn
1271463	Sgt	SPILLMAN Geoffrey Joseph	15-10-44	166 Sqn
1801595	Sgt	SPINK Edward James Percy	28-06-44	640 Sqn
1817740	Sgt	SPINKS Albert John	27-03-44	14 OTU
1625934	Sgt	SPINKS Frank Edwin	13-06-44	78 Sqn
154056	F/O	SPLANE Edgar Charles	26-06-44	1667 HCU
1868639	Sgt	SPOONER Samuel John	13-08-44	625 Sqn
1851084	Sgt	SPORNE Oscar William	24-03-44	433 Sqn
1522033	F/S	SPOTSWOOD Eric	27-11-44	115 Sqn
1567579	Sgt	SPOWART David	23-09-44	576 Sqn
1485060	F/S	SPOWART John Robinson	4-05-44	101 Sqn
1604485	Sgt	SPRAGG Victor Thomas	14-11-44	51 Sqn
1852228	Sgt	SPREADBURY George	30-12-44	156 Sqn
1320866	Sgt	SPRIGGS Eric William	21-06-44	15 Sqn
1449550	F/S	SPRIGGS John Stanley	23-01-44	1667 HCU
1477332	F/S	SPRING Joseph Vernon	15-03-44	90 Sqn
747845	F/S	SPRINGETT Alan Douglas	25-11-44	12 OTU
185460	P/O	SPRINGGAY James Harry Herbert	11-10-44	101 Sqn
1442428	F/S	SPURDEN George Charles	22-03-44	44 Sqn
151601	F/O	SQUIBB William Albert Frederick	23-04-44	582 Sqn
121396	S/L	SQUIBBS Reginald Arthur	12-09-44	619 Sqn
171911	P/O	SQUIRES Robert Leslie	7-05-44	405 Sqn
1593642	Sgt	STABLER Jim	17-06-44	1660 HCU
1459796	Sgt	STACEY Thomas Herbert	21-04-44	17 OTU
2206324	Sgt	STACK Ronald Desmond	1-07-44	101 Sqn
1592107	Sgt	STAFF Norman Desmond	25-07-44	166 Sqn
1166582	F/S	STAFFORD John Francis	14-01-44	101 Sqn
1399018	Sgt	STAFFORD John Henry	1-04-44	20 OTU
2221029	Sgt	STAFFORD Leonard	13-08-44	578 Sqn
1881894	Sgt	STAFFORD Peter Robert	13-08-44	14 OTU
2203120	Sgt	STAFFORD Richard Winson	25-07-44	514 Sqn
1796370	Sgt	STAFFORD Thomas Joseph Brenden	13-06-44	158 Sqn
152716	F/O	STAINBANK Richard Edmund	12-09-44	90 Sqn
132016	F/O	STAKES Ronald	18-04-44	158 Sqn
1893122	Sgt	STALKER Clifford Neil	5-07-44	57 Sqn
1609434	Sgt	STALLARD Ernest Thomas	18-03-44	466 Sqn
1399911	Sgt	STALLWOOD Ralph	8-06-44	115 Sqn
172642	P/O	STALVIES Bryan Wallis Henshall	25-07-44	1667 HCU
1336172	Sgt	STAMMERS Thomas Geoffrey	21-01-44	77 Sqn
135725	F/L	STAMMERS Wilfrid Jack	22-03-44	166 Sqn
152464	F/O	STAMP Charles Edward	8-07-44	207 Sqn
171503	F/O	STAMP Leslie George	5-08-44	425 Sqn
1492841	Sgt	STAMPER Percy	17-06-44	102 Sqn
1386182	Sgt	STANBRIDGE Alec Arthur	25-03-44	635 Sqn
1445546	Sgt	STANBRIDGE Kenneth Frederick [Australia]	20-01-44	102 Sqn
54874	P/O	STANBURY Frederick Herbert	18-09-44	627 Sqn
1380081	F/S	STANDFIELD Eric Phillip Arthur	7-10-44	51 Sqn
1577005	Sgt	STANDLEY Roy Joseph	20-01-44	158 Sqn
1623168	Sgt	STANDLEY-SMITH Philip	6-06-44	515 Sqn
1602092	Sgt	STANDRING Derrick John	4-12-44	1661 HCU
1022083	W/O	STANDRING Eddie	30-11-44	115 Sqn
1817806	Sgt	STANILAND Philip Arthur	4-05-44	103 Sqn
130880	F/O	STANISLAUS Anthony Frederick	6-01-44	97 Sqn
1582138	Sgt	STANLEY John	3-05-44	550 Sqn
143258	F/O	STANLEY John Bottomley	22-06-44	49 Sqn
1575206	F/S	STANLEY John Frederick	15-01-44	626 Sqn
176376	F/O	STANLEY Raymond Louis	6-10-44	78 Sqn
1581810	Sgt	STANLEY Thomas John	11-04-44	622 Sqn
1338510	Sgt	STANNARD Alfred Richard	30-07-44	75 Sqn
89297	F/L	STANNARD Clifford Robert	14-01-44	156 Sqn
151143	F/O	STANNARD Leslie Frank	8-05-44	138 Sqn
1554370	W/O	STANNERS Ramsay	20-02-44	156 Sqn
1323766	F/S	STANNETT Ernest Frederick	4-05-44	460 Sqn
920528	W/O	STANSFIELD Geoffrey Egerton	11-04-44	101 Sqn
1581889	Sgt	STANTON Fred	31-03-44	44 Sqn
3010595	Sgt	STANTON Henry	9-12-44	171 Sqn
1580213	Sgt	STANTON Samuel	30-08-44	630 Sqn
1437148	Sgt	STAPLETON Clifford	12-09-44	90 Sqn
1874338	Sgt	STAPLETON Cyril	5-07-44	207 Sqn
1653202	Sgt	STAPLETON William Thomas	22-12-44	626 Sqn
1896471	Sgt	STAPLEY Ernest Edwin	18-06-44	115 Sqn
1896761	Sgt	STAPLEY Roy Stuart	4-11-44	101 Sqn
53473	F/O	STAR Joseph	13-06-44	28 OTU
1894243	Sgt	STARBUCK Sydney Dennis	15-10-44	166 Sqn
133485	F/L	STARIE DFC Bernard John	15-03-44	97 Sqn
1863956	Sgt	STARKEY Charles Ronald	21-11-44	75 Sqn
531899	Sgt	STARKEY Raymond Charles	12-12-44	195 Sqn
1777090	Sgt	STARKIE Eric	30-01-44	100 Sqn
548376	F/S	STARKIE Thomas	12-09-44	44 Sqn
623359	Sgt	STARLING Ernest William	29-07-44	463 Sqn
1660591	Sgt	STARR John Reginald	21-01-44	158 Sqn
1898133	Sgt	STARSMORE John James	30-08-44	21 OTU
1600846	Sgt	STARTIN Geoffrey Leonard	25-06-44	75 Sqn
124125	F/L	STEAD MiD Ernest	20-02-44	630 Sqn
183425	P/O	STEAD Walter	24-07-44	630 Sqn
1468683	Sgt	STEAN Jack Leslie	23-04-44	149 Sqn
1195607	F/S	STEANE William	25-05-44	158 Sqn
1813152	Sgt	STEDMAN Edward Henry	10-04-44	460 Sqn

Service #	Rank	Name	Date	Sqn	Service #	Rank	Name	Date	Sqn
1589945	F/S	STEEDMAN William Kenneth	22-05-44	7 Sqn	50448	F/L	STEWART Douglas	6-10-44	106 Sqn
1457502	Sgt	STEEL Harry Stanley Nelson	23-04-44	78 Sqn	1391538	Sgt	STEWART Duncan Ernest	24-02-44	426 Sqn
153263	F/O	STEEL John Harvey	30-07-44	106 Sqn	1233526	F/S	STEWART Edwin	25-07-44	103 Sqn
2206920	Sgt	STEEL William Arthur	5-07-44	427 Sqn	1365996	F/S	STEWART George Ronald	16-03-44	625 Sqn
1486363	Sgt	STEELE Herbert Dennis	23-03-44	106 Sqn	937440	F/S	STEWART Gordon	22-12-44	578 Sqn
1492541	Sgt	STEELE Kenneth	24-09-44	156 Sqn	1448566	Sgt	STEWART Harold	25-04-44	97 Sqn
1612783	F/S	STEELE Michael William Beevor	22-06-44	44 Sqn	1822847	Sgt	STEWART James Angus	20-01-44	78 Sqn
1533388	F	STEELE Norman Thompson	29-01-44	77 Sqn	1802244	Sgt	STEWART John	23-05-44	100 Sqn
1867974	Sgt	STEELE Ronald Arthur William	4-12-44	467 Sqn	129742	F/L	STEWART DFC John Kennedy	23-05-44	35 Sqn
1048665	Sgt	STEELS Harry	23-04-44	463 Sqn	1399585	Sgt	STEWART Kenneth John	11-08-44	640 Sqn
46016	F/L	STEERE DFC DFM Harry	9-06-44	627 Sqn	130452	F/O	STEWART MiD Robert Campbell	31-03-44	77 Sqn
1819122	Sgt	STEERS Albert Henry	6-12-44	61 Sqn	174930	P/O	STEWART Robert Henderson	28-04-44	115 Sqn
3030868	Sgt	STEERS Peter Mervyn	13-06-44	432 Sqn	145856	S/L	STEWART DFC Ronald George Falconar		
2208713	Sgt	STEGER William Edward	13-06-44	514 Sqn				2-01-44	156 Sqn
1347313	F/S	STEIN Angus Wilson	2-05-44	515 Sqn	120044	F/L	STEWART William Alistair McLean Beardmore		
1452226	F/S	STEMBRIDGE Malcolm Mason	31-03-44	51 Sqn				30-08-44	101 Sqn
1323628	F/S	STENNER George Edward	29-07-44	630 Sqn	152408	F/O	STEYLAERTS Louis David	8-05-44	106 Sqn
1572098	Sgt	STEPHEN Andrew	6-10-44	49 Sqn	1444397	Sgt	STICKELLS Anthony Morgan	12-04-44	50 Sqn
123837	F/O	STEPHEN Herbert Ingram	11-04-44	169 Sqn	1601649	F/S	STIEFEL Peter George	24-09-44	51 Sqn
944044	W/O	STEPHEN Raymond Thomas	29-07-44	15 Sqn	142453	F/O	STIGGER James William	19-01-44	161 Sqn
1892588	Sgt	STEPHEN William John	20-01-44	101 Sqn	1864127	Sgt	STILING Frederick Thomas	14-01-44	550 Sqn
3011102	Sgt	STEPHENS Dennis Gwylin	23-03-44	17 OTU	1800197	Sgt	STILL Frederick Albert	17-06-44	3 LFS
1339900	F/S	STEPHENS Donald Carl	29-07-44	49 Sqn	161406	P/O	STILL Wilfred	25-03-44	635 Sqn
1586493	Sgt	STEPHENS Donald Henry	3-01-44	101 Sqn	1588796	Sgt	STILLIARD Michael Martin	31-03-44	640 Sqn
106237	S/L	STEPHENS DFC Harry Bernard	6-05-44	109 Sqn	155249	F/L	STIMPSON DFC Maurice Cecil	15-02-44	156 Sqn
1581851	Sgt	STEPHENS William John	30-08-44	21 OTU	1898037	Sgt	STOBART Hanley	11-12-44	49 Sqn
1592391	Sgt	STEPHENSON Cecil	8-05-44	106 Sqn	178242	P/O	STOBBART William	4-05-44	420 Sqn
1684795	Sgt	STEPHENSON Harry	30-09-44	1651 HCU	1549518	F/S	STOBBS Joseph Kenneth	20-09-44	619 Sqn
2202048	Sgt	STEPHENSON John Leonard	21-07-44	75 Sqn	151063	F/O	STOBO Ronald	3-01-44	49 Sqn
1473150	Sgt	STEPHENSON Kenneth	30-08-44	101 Sqn	1626766	Sgt	STOCK Derek Cecil	3-08-44	460 Sqn
911222	Sgt	STEPNEY Charlie	21-11-44	514 Sqn	1392768	Sgt	STOCK James	3-01-44	61 Sqn
1121985	Sgt	STERRY Sidney	29-05-44	1657 HCU	142550	F/O	STOCKILL Arnold	22-12-44	630 Sqn
1365326	F/S	STEVEN Donald MacConigill	25-06-44	77 Sqn	1880011	Sgt	STOCKWELL William John	24-10-44	576 Sqn
129506	F/L	STEVEN DFC Kenneth Munro	14-01-44	97 Sqn	1898283	Sgt	STODDEN Kenneth	20-11-44	1656 HCU
87717	F/O	STEVENS Arthur	20-02-44	103 Sqn	1577610	F/S	STOKELD Francis Henry	5-07-44	106 Sqn
150017	F/O	STEVENS Donald	10-06-44	21 OTU	1284065	F/S	STOKES Donald Joseph	15-02-44	166 Sqn
1893032	Sgt	STEVENS Donald Nabe	20-02-44	49 Sqn	1029666	W/O	STOKES Fred	21-01-44	101 Sqn
1576847	F/S	STEVENS Douglas Edward John	29-08-44	582 Sqn	1586991	Sgt	STOKES Frederick Charles Albert	29-07-44	427 Sqn
135013	F/O	STEVENS Frederick	7-04-44	139 Sqn	1818871	Sgt	STOKES Victor Clement Arthur	8-07-44	9 Sqn
1388946	F/S	STEVENS Harold John Walter	20-05-44	83 OTU	1677803	AC2	STOKOE Sidney	14-04-44	5 LFS
1263452	Sgt	STEVENS Harold Leslie	21-07-44	626 Sqn	1387998	Sgt	STOLLAR Harry	25-02-44	550 Sqn
125607	F/L	STEVENS Joseph	21-07-44	75 Sqn	152068	F/L	STONE Donald Edward Ross	23-09-44	61 Sqn
1456987	Sgt	STEVENS Joseph	31-03-44	7 Sqn	1335602	F/S	STONE Edwin Andrew	4-05-44	463 Sqn
1321425	F/S	STEVENS Maurice Arthur	30-01-44	463 Sqn	160519	F/O	STONE Frederick Richard	22-06-44	630 Sqn
1523782	Sgt	STEVENS Norman	30-08-44	514 Sqn	174918	P/O	STONE George Bernard	13-08-44	156 Sqn
1813627	Sgt	STEVENS Piers Trevor	2-05-44	75 Sqn	1808611	Sgt	STONE Jack Alfred	29-07-44	626 Sqn
1393048	Sgt	STEVENS Reginald Ralph	21-01-44	405 Sqn	1577215	Sgt	STONE Joseph Ronald	27-08-44	12 Sqn
143597	F/O	STEVENS Richard Hubert	25-03-44	12 Sqn	1259098	Sgt	STONE Leonard	28-01-44	115 Sqn
1472482	Sgt	STEVENS Thomas Albert	11-05-44	467 Sqn	153810	F/O	STONE Leslie Bernard	16-11-44	1663 HCU
1897046	Sgt	STEVENS William Harry Read	6-11-44	207 Sqn	178871	P/O	STONE Richard John	29-07-44	431 Sqn
188909	P/O	STEVENSON Jack	29-12-44	170 Sqn	1816613	Sgt	STONE Sidney	1-07-44	626 Sqn
172088	F/O	STEVENSON John	7-08-44	139 Sqn	1316590	Sgt	STONEMAN Richard Edward Leonard	3-01-44	100 Sqn
1436619	F/S	STEVENSON Ronald	3-01-44	57 Sqn	156739	F/L	STONEMAN Robert Victor	12-09-44	7 Sqn
1480507	F/S	STEVENSON DFM Samuel Brown	14-01-44	97 Sqn	1324455	Sgt	STONEMAN Wilfred George	25-01-44	PFNTU
1621778	AC1	STEVENTON Edward Roland	8-04-44	1 LFS	1084598	Sgt	STONES John Chapman	20-01-44	76 Sqn
1874038	Sgt	STEWARD Arthur Llewellyn	21-02-44	9 Sqn	1174434	Sgt	STONES Thomas Roby	20-01-44	10 Sqn
160646	F/O	STEWARD Harry Michael	16-07-44	76 Sqn	1234185	Sgt	STONES Ramon	18-03-44	61 Sqn
1457149	Sgt	STEWARD John Edwin	4-05-44	101 Sqn	182631	P/O	STONES William	15-10-44	466 Sqn
1344346	Sgt	STEWART Alan Raymond Bryce	25-08-44	75 Sqn	1896104	Sgt	STONHAM Gilbert Arthur	29-07-44	433 Sqn
173882	P/O	STEWART Albert Henry	8-06-44	622 Sqn	1387473	Sgt	STOPP Alexander Charles	22-01-44	630 Sqn
1561509	Sgt	STEWART Alexander	24-10-44	576 Sqn	1892044	Sgt	STOPP Ronald Charles	9-10-44	462 Sqn
1825753	Sgt	STEWART Andrew	30-08-44	101 Sqn	1085739	Sgt	STORER Frank	31-03-44	166 Sqn
659104	F/S	STEWART Angus Roderick Graham	21-02-44	640 Sqn	1348676	F/S	STOREY Gladstone Myers	21-02-44	78 Sqn
1825643	Sgt	STEWART Anthony	13-08-44	578 Sqn	136367	F/O	STOREY John	2-01-44	61 Sqn
169048	F/O	STEWART DFM Charles Fullerton	29-08-44	582 Sqn	1431938	Sgt	STORR John	4-12-44	44 Sqn
138825	F/O	STEWART DFC Charles Hume	13-05-44	76 Sqn	577047	F/S	STOTT Guy Raymond	27-08-44	630 Sqn
152126	F/O	STEWART David Winterburn	17-06-44	576 Sqn	1458650	F/S	STOTT Leonard James	12-10-44	14 OTU
1387541	Sgt	STEWART Donald	31-03-44	424 Sqn	141547	F/O	STOTT Sydney James	8-06-44	101 Sqn
909536	F/S	STEWART Donald George William	31-07-44	617 Sqn	145510	F/L	STOUT DFC Geoffrey Stevenson	23-09-44	617 Sqn

Service #	Rank	Name	Date	Sqn/Unit
2211352	Sgt	STOVOLD Willie	16-06-44	61 Sqn
1263353	Sgt	STOW Harry William	5-06-44	1658 HCU
798810	Sgt	STOWE Bernard [Newfoundland]	4-12-44	1661 HCU
107520	F/L	STOWER John Gifford	31-03-44	142 Sqn
152397	F/L	STRACHAN Richard Lyon	28-11-44	166 Sqn
1825366	Sgt	STRAITON Peter	15-11-44	1666 HCU
1400080	Sgt	STRANGE John Brian	20-01-44	622 Sqn
642061	W/O	STRATFORD George Henry [Canada]	19-07-44	78 Sqn
171030	F/O	STRATFORD DFM Ronald Kenneth	30-08-44	460 Sqn
1051454	Sgt	STRATHEARN James	25-03-44	466 Sqn
171501	F/L	STRATIS DFC William Anthony	7-06-44	44 Sqn
1201942	F/S	STRATTON Bruce Albert	20-02-44	12 Sqn
123026	F/L	STREET Denys Oliver	6-04-44	207 Sqn
1446864	Sgt	STREET Harold John	4-05-44	1662 HCU
1891633	Sgt	STREET James William	27-08-44	35 Sqn
1802950	Sgt	STREET Leonard Arthur	1-08-44	101 Sqn
1320514	Sgt	STREET Peter Alfred	7-03-44	1667 HCU
1638635	Sgt	STREET Richard	27-01-44	1660 HCU
1531787	F/S	STREETING Henry Hutchinson	29-01-44	77 Sqn
1874823	Sgt	STRINGER Victor	23-10-44	625 Sqn
1386539	F/S	STROMBERG Gordon Henry	9-06-44	514 Sqn
141395	F/O	STRONELL Norman John	30-08-44	103 Sqn
1315980	F/S	STROUD Bernard	19-07-44	138 Sqn
1602149	Sgt	STROUD Dennis Frederick	19-11-44	84 OTU
1806766	Sgt	STROWGER James	24-09-44	97 Sqn
1365083	Sgt	STUART Ian Forbes	4-05-44	12 Sqn
1560462	F/S	STUART Kenneth Charles	21-07-44	9 Sqn
1577911	Sgt	STUBBINGS Ronald	16-02-44	199 Sqn
1896200	Sgt	STUBBS Kenneth	18-03-44	1657 HCU
1805250	Sgt	STUBBS Thomas Edward	13-06-44	15 Sqn
1585202	Sgt	STURGEON John Alfred	23-04-44	582 Sqn
1230339	Sgt	STYNES Bernard	8-05-44	138 Sqn
1607227	Sgt	ST. CLAIR Donald	9-03-44	1667 HCU
1802602	Sgt	ST. LEGER Ronald Peter	24-11-44	12 OTU
1495722	F/S	SUDDABY Walter	24-03-44	158 Sqn
1675773	Sgt	SUDDICK Lindsay Snowdon	31-03-44	61 Sqn
136193	F/O	SUDDS Gerald Henry	28-01-44	467 Sqn
1586836	Sgt	SUFFIELD Leonard Thomas Victor	13-06-44	625 Sqn
1576034	Sgt	SUFFOLK John Dennis	18-11-44	51 Sqn
1892572	Sgt	SULLIVAN Edward Thomas Ebenezer	14-01-44	49 Sqn
1314851	Sgt	SULLIVAN George Albert	15-02-44	77 Sqn
1572372	Sgt	SULLIVAN John	30-09-44	426 Sqn
1294908	F/S	SULLIVAN Joseph Henry	24-02-44	100 Sqn
138898	F/O	SULLIVAN Robert Denis [Eire]	20-02-44	77 Sqn
1319318	F/S	SULLOCK Wilfred Albert	25-05-44	101 Sqn
547067	Sgt	SUMMERS Andrew Bernard	21-01-44	15 Sqn
123053	F/L	SUMMERS Geoffrey John	1-06-44	515 Sqn
156999	F/O	SUMMERS John William	17-06-44	640 Sqn
188029	P/O	SUMMERS Kenneth James	6-11-44	207 Sqn
1894502	F/S	SUMMERS Norman	22-12-44	189 Sqn
1373631	Sgt	SUMMERS William	22-01-44	467 Sqn
1395702	Sgt	SUMMERS Woolf Jack	24-02-44	75 Sqn
1862419	Sgt	SUMMERSCALE Kenneth Launcelot	31-03-44	12 Sqn
170015	F/L	SUMMERSCALES DFC Charles	22-12-44	83 Sqn
1335456	Sgt	SUMNER Henry Alan	19-10-44	186 Sqn
1800914	Sgt	SUMNER Kenneth Rowland	15-03-44	550 Sqn
151228	F/O	SUMNER Leslie	4-05-44	460 Sqn
1897833	Sgt	SUMNER Thomas Leslie	18-11-44	51 Sqn
127337	F/L	SUMSION David Hugh	30-08-44	90 Sqn
1624631	Sgt	SUNDERLAND Cecil	6-11-44	463 Sqn
1593402	Sgt	SUNDERLAND Eric Arthur	23-10-44	460 Sqn
1623987	F/S	SUNLEY John Robert	15-10-44	186 Sqn
154310	F/O	SUNTER Arnold	22-07-44	20 OTU
1893432	Sgt	SUPKOVITCH Alfred	19-07-44	207 Sqn
1425387	Cpl	SURGEY John Eady [Urugauy]	6-07-44	20 OTU
1575402	Sgt	SURGEY Walter	11-04-44	83 Sqn
1337739	F/S	SURMAN Roden Wadham	16-02-44	1663 HCU
60792	F/L	SURPLICE DFC Victor Henry	21-01-44	77 Sqn
1390296	Sgt	SURRIDGE John Arthur	10-06-44	207 Sqn
1670154	Sgt	SURTEES Raymond	16-06-44	514 Sqn
1092752	F/S	SUTCLIFFE DFM Albert	23-12-44	35 Sqn
1623937	Sgt	SUTCLIFFE Donald	16-05-44	26 OTU
160749	F/O	SUTHERIN John Garnet	26-08-44	83 OTU
1892870	Sgt	SUTHERLAND Geoffrey Thomas	13-07-44	550 Sqn
173800	P/O	SUTHERLAND Hugh Alastair	10-05-44	106 Sqn
2220532	Sgt	SUTHERLAND John Rennie	20-09-44	619 Sqn
1394668	F/S	SUTHERLAND John Sinclair	21-02-44	78 Sqn
1567609	Sgt	SUTHERLAND Robert Donald John	8-06-44	115 Sqn
1816276	Sgt	SUTTON Arthur Kitchener	5-10-44	75 Sqn
1236027	Sgt	SUTTON Edward John	3-01-44	156 Sqn
1140041	Sgt	SUTTON Jack	2-01-44	9 Sqn
1627424	Sgt	SUTTON James Arthur Ivan	4-05-44	626 Sqn
169579	P/O	SUTTON John	31-03-44	622 Sqn
1181273	W/O	SUTTON John Albert	21-11-44	192 Sqn
1450551	F/S	SUTTON Ronald Walter	20-01-44	166 Sqn
1387861	F/S	SUTTON Stanley	25-02-44	419 Sqn
1601396	F/S	SWADLING Kenneth Matthew Francis	17-06-44	199 Sqn
37658	F/L	SWAIN Cyril Douglas	31-03-44	105 Sqn
1121382	Sgt	SWAINSTON John	12-12-44	15 Sqn
1624377	Sgt	SWANN Joseph William	27-01-44	166 Sqn
2209106	Sgt	SWANN Leslie Ronald	11-06-44	625 Sqn
1576242	Sgt	SWANN Ronald Ezra	14-01-44	207 Sqn
1339960	F/S	SWANNELL John William	27-08-44	115 Sqn
1138377	Sgt	SWANSON John Lonsdale	4-12-44	619 Sqn
161665	F/O	SWANSON John Stewart	23-09-44	78 Sqn
70659	S/L	SWANSTON Harold 'Jock'	4-05-44	103 Sqn
1488758	Sgt	SWANSTON Leslie Seton Dewar	15-02-44	57 Sqn
125743	F/L	SWARBRICK DFC John	20-07-44	109 Sqn
187233	P/O	SWARBRICK Joseph	11-05-44	424 Sqn
1486325	Sgt	SWART Edward Cornelius	5-11-44	102 Sqn
1585694	F/S	SWEATMAN Peter Bramwell	21-07-44	15 Sqn
179538	F/O	SWEETMAN John Edwin [Hong Kong]	23-09-44	50 Sqn
145171	F/O	SWEETMAN DFM Oswald Cuthbert	9-10-44	608 Sqn
1484251	Sgt	SWINBANK Robert Mathias	6-12-44	10 Sqn
1892460	Sgt	SWINGLER Joseph Abraham [Canada]	25-02-44	44 Sqn
52075	F/L	SWINNEY DFC Charles Roy	14-01-44	156 Sqn
40575	S/L	SWYERS James [Newfoundland]	7-06-44	5 Group
2209656	Sgt	SYKES Clifford	16-07-44	15 Sqn
570013	Sgt	SYKES Derek	25-06-44	102 Sqn
1653469	Sgt	SYKES Derek Colin	22-06-44	463 Sqn
1594255	Sgt	SYKES Leonard	11-06-44	625 Sqn
1216818	F/S	SYKES Paul Derrick	24-04-44	77 Sqn
1576517	Sgt	SYKES Terence William	4-05-44	103 Sqn
1582908	Sgt	SYMCOX Reginald	21-01-44	102 Sqn
1491619	Sgt	SYMONDS Arthur	22-05-44	550 Sqn
2235152	Sgt	SYMONDS Cyril	18-12-44	3 LFS
1456322	W/O	SYMONDS Geoffrey	15-10-44	1667 HCU
1832193	AC2	SYMONDS Harold Ernest	7-05-44	90 Sqn
62339	F/L	SYMONS John George	23-03-44	207 Sqn
1796523	Sgt	SYNNOTT Daniel Felix Oliver	22-06-44	630 Sqn
2221473	Sgt	TABUTEAU Oliver [Canada]	30-08-44	550 Sqn
2221328	Sgt	TABERNER Raymond	12-12-44	195 Sqn
1624500	Sgt	TABNER Eric Edward	12-05-44	115 Sqn
1850279	Sgt	TABOR Kenneth Harold	10-05-44	467 Sqn
2221473	Sgt	TABUTEAU Oliver [Canada]	30-08-44	550 Sqn
176763	P/O	TAFT Ralph Norman	5-07-44	630 Sqn
1332880	Sgt	TAILBY Reginald John	4-05-44	625 Sqn
172306	P/O	TAIT David Reid	25-04-44	166 Sqn
1552494	F/S	TAIT Henry Sutherland	19-03-44	97 Sqn
174330	P/O	TAIT Lawrence	11-04-44	78 Sqn
1852475	Sgt	TALBOT Denis George	30-01-44	21 OTU
152410	F/O	TALBOT Derrick	4-11-44	49 Sqn
137222	F/O	TALBOT DFC Edward	5-06-44	692 Sqn
1060663	F/S	TALBOT John Edward	6-11-44	61 Sqn
1232653	Sgt	TALBOT Kenneth	13-01-44	15 Sqn
1392407	F/S	TALBOT Lionel Moore	10-05-44	35 Sqn
1388587	Sgt	TALBY Cyril	25-03-44	635 Sqn

Number	Rank	Name	Date	Sqn
186308	P/O	TALES John Henry	8-11-44	218 Sqn
170352	P/O	TANDY Roy	25-02-44	156 Sqn
171646	P/O	TANNER Charles Evan Raymond	1-06-44	625 Sqn
183732	P/O	TANNER James Roy	9-11-44	138 Sqn
123867	F/L	TANNER Llewellyn Elvet	1-11-44	619 Sqn
578649	Sgt	TANSER Sidney Thomas	8-06-44	78 Sqn
1604944	Sgt	TANSLEY Mervyn Lambert	6-11-44	608 Sqn
1392978	F/S	TAPP Ralph Aubrey	16-05-44	103 Sqn
928795	F/S	TARBARD Victor	26-10-44	166 Sqn
1874644	Sgt	TARBIN Dennis George	16-07-44	15 Sqn
1068226	Sgt	TARR Charles Francis	14-01-44	432 Sqn
39695	F/L	TATAM Noel Curtis	18-12-44	10 Sqn
1378784	W/O	TATE John Frederick Russell	19-07-44	619 Sqn
172570	P/O	TATE Robert Richard Jack	31-03-44	103 Sqn
111526	F/L	TATE Thomas Jobson	7-10-44	617 Sqn
28137	W/C	TATNALL DFC James Benjamin	15-02-44	7 Sqn
659088	F/S	TATTERSALL Clarence	25-02-44	550 Sqn
117655	F/L	TATTERSALL Dennis Boden	30-08-44	467 Sqn
1217551	Sgt	TATTERSFIELD Anthony William	14-01-44	408 Sqn
2210014	Sgt	TATTLER Harry	8-06-44	78 Sqn
1825381	Sgt	TAWSE Alexander Simpson	19-03-44	20 OTU
2216859	Sgt	TAYLOR Alan Armitage	8-05-44	106 Sqn
120348	F/L	TAYLOR DFC Alan George	31-03-44	78 Sqn
159424	F/L	TAYLOR Albert Clement Michael Gibson	5-07-44	35 Sqn
44406	S/L	TAYLOR DFM Albert Edward	2-01-44	7 Sqn
1366936	Sgt	TAYLOR Alexander John	4-12-44	166 Sqn
615242	Sgt	TAYLOR Alfred Leonard	24-03-44	51 Sqn
1868950	Sgt	TAYLOR Archibald William	10-08-44	619 Sqn
1583779	Sgt	TAYLOR DFM Arthur	23-05-44	576 Sqn
1819923	Sgt	TAYLOR Arthur Frederick	23-06-44	77 Sqn
1537765	F/S	TAYLOR Arthur Norman	26-08-44	300 Sqn
152505	F/O	TAYLOR Charles Delaney	3-06-44	10 Sqn
1811247	F/S	TAYLOR DFM Charles Robert	22-06-44	83 Sqn
1880883	Sgt	TAYLOR Charles William	26-08-44	300 Sqn
1581229	Sgt	TAYLOR Charlie	19-07-44	138 Sqn
1671845	Sgt	TAYLOR Clifford	8-09-44	29 OTU
1892039	Sgt	TAYLOR David Richard	7-06-44	578 Sqn
1322386	F/S	TAYLOR David Robert	14-01-44	166 Sqn
1320825	Sgt	TAYLOR Dennis Alfred	27-01-44	467 Sqn
1617065	Sgt	TAYLOR Donald James	7-12-44	1651 HCU
1290706	W/O	TAYLOR Edwin Alexander	13-08-44	83 Sqn
1332670	Sgt	TAYLOR Eric Belmont	11-04-44	12 Sqn
2202861	Sgt	TAYLOR Francis James	20-02-44	103 Sqn
1549593	F/S	TAYLOR Fred	18-04-44	51 Sqn
998259	F/S	TAYLOR Geoffrey David	29-07-44	582 Sqn
1561928	Sgt	TAYLOR George	25-06-44	50 Sqn
1593905	Sgt	TAYLOR George	13-07-44	550 Sqn
1521681	F/S	TAYLOR George Ridley Telford	18-12-44	3 LFS
1581481	Sgt	TAYLOR Harry	20-02-44	514 Sqn
1891931	Sgt	TAYLOR Harry	11-04-44	158 Sqn
1601575	Sgt	TAYLOR Jack Lewis Page	20-02-44	77 Sqn
2211923	Sgt	TAYLOR James	7-06-44	578 Sqn
1377207	F/S	TAYLOR James Jenkins	30-01-44	83 Sqn
1079856	F/S	TAYLOR John	11-06-44	625 Sqn
1551965	F/S	TAYLOR John	15-02-44	207 Sqn
1318181	F/S	TAYLOR John Albert	15-03-44	77 Sqn
135702	F/L	TAYLOR John Gordon	29-01-44	207 Sqn
1419271	F/S	TAYLOR John Meredith	16-11-44	625 Sqn
54339	P/O	TAYLOR John Wilkinson	20-02-44	156 Sqn
143798	F/O	TAYLOR DFC Joseph Thomas	8-07-44	630 Sqn
153350	F/O	TAYLOR Kenneth Edward	5-10-44	626 Sqn
1577966	Sgt	TAYLOR Leslie	30-08-44	115 Sqn
1876619	Sgt	TAYLOR Leslie Arthur	22-03-44	50 Sqn
1616111	Sgt	TAYLOR Maurice John	13-06-44	427 Sqn
113834	F/L	TAYLOR DFM MiD Norman	14-10-44	139 Sqn
1570098	Sgt	TAYLOR Norman	22-01-44	102 Sqn
1825961	F/S	TAYLOR Patrick Joseph	27-08-44	576 Sqn
1084566	Sgt	TAYLOR Percy Weston	28-10-44	115 Sqn
147908	F/O	TAYLOR Peter Alan	13-08-44	156 Sqn
1324017	Sgt	TAYLOR Peter Donald	25-06-44	463 Sqn
1892190	Sgt	TAYLOR Reginald Thomas	25-05-44	101 Sqn
152830	F/O	TAYLOR Rennie	15-03-44	11 OTU
170149	P/O	TAYLOR DFC Richard	31-03-44	97 Sqn
1385234	Sgt	TAYLOR Richard Desmond [British Guiana]	26-03-44	460 Sqn
2207122	Sgt	TAYLOR Richard Edward	16-10-44	14 OTU
1401963	Sgt	TAYLOR Richard Thomas	30-11-44	75 Sqn
1486979	Sgt	TAYLOR Robert Arthur	25-04-44	61 Sqn
1561301	Sgt	TAYLOR Robert Finlay	31-03-44	115 Sqn
1699395	Sgt	TAYLOR Ronald	29-01-44	50 Sqn
1590230	Sgt	TAYLOR Ronald James	8-07-44	467 Sqn
1431888	Sgt	TAYLOR Roy Sidney Custance	25-02-44	622 Sqn
160846	P/O	TAYLOR Stanley Ralph	18-03-44	466 Sqn
3000350	Sgt	TAYLOR Stanley William John	4-12-44	15 Sqn
168850	P/O	TAYLOR Sydney William Herbert	29-01-44	434 Sqn
818137	Sgt	TAYLOR Vincent Nelson	11-12-44	57 Sqn
658221	Sgt	TAYLOR Walter Charles	21-07-44	514 Sqn
102126	F/L	TAYLOR William	22-12-44	157 Sqn
657866	F/S	TAYLOR William	12-09-44	44 Sqn
1321329	Sgt	TAYLOR William Alfred	27-01-44	467 Sqn
1396691	Sgt	TAYLOR William Charles	10-05-44	550 Sqn
1623557	Sgt	TAYLOR William Lee	12-12-44	149 Sqn
1620512	F/S	TAYLOR William Valentine [New Zealand]	2-09-44	57 Sqn
1168418	F/S	TAYTON Victor Henry	20-05-44	514 Sqn
1523709	Sgt	TEAGUE Richard Joseph	20-01-44	1653 HCU
1569460	Sgt	TEAPE William	8-06-44	431 Sqn
1777400	Sgt	TEASDALE Owen Arkle	3-06-44	76 Sqn
158816	F/O	TEBBUT John Alan	24-06-44	12 Sqn
1583675	Sgt	TEBBUTT Allen Parker	26-08-44	103 Sqn
1319032	Sgt	TEBBUTT Geoffrey Norman	25-04-44	83 Sqn
152967	F/O	TEECE Alec Jabez Desmond	20-09-44	514 Sqn
1592342	F/S	TELFORD Phillip	21-11-44	44 Sqn
2212933	Sgt	TELFORD Walter Barton	5-11-44	1660 HCU
1386550	Sgt	TELLING Dennis Edward	28-03-44	20 OTU
1263973	Sgt	TEMPAN Frank	20-01-44	1653 HCU
1623244	F/S	TEMPEST Kenneth	27-08-44	90 Sqn
1811207	Sgt	TEMPLEMAN William Jack Edward	25-10-44	115 Sqn
1822885	Sgt	TEMPLETON John	25-04-44	166 Sqn
158242	F/L	TENNANT Ernest Ingham	13-08-44	50 Sqn
1388158	F/S	TERRELL Alfred George	25-03-44	44 Sqn
188483	P/O	TERRELL Charles Edward	3-12-44	138 Sqn
1515176	Sgt	TERRIERE Claude [Mauritius]	4-11-44	101 Sqn
1398111	Sgt	TERRY Alma Louis	4-12-44	1661 HCU
2220315	Sgt	TERRY John	20-05-44	166 Sqn
1392049	F/S	TERRY Kenneth Valentine Frank	23-04-44	106 Sqn
1290468	Sgt	TERRY Robert James	20-10-44	626 Sqn
614774	Sgt	TETLEY Alfred Douglas	23-04-44	514 Sqn
157563	F/O	TETLOW Royston	26-08-44	622 Sqn
1622143	Sgt	THACKERAY Frank	27-08-44	576 Sqn
1850503	Sgt	THAIR Reginald James	27-07-44	619 Sqn
150329	F/L	THATCHER George Atherton	11-06-44	90 Sqn
1593242	Sgt	THEAKER James Thomas	5-07-44	9 Sqn
1464853	Sgt	THEEDOM Victor Albert Edward	8-01-44	138 Sqn
1591242	Sgt	THEW Robert	5-10-44	427 Sqn
1805377	Sgt	THIELE John Ashford	24-10-44	10 OTU
1652801	Sgt	THOMAS Albert	24-12-44	35 Sqn
1649209	Sgt	THOMAS Brian Henry Maude	16-03-44	57 Sqn
1499060	F/S	THOMAS Daniel Goronwy	17-09-44	617 Sqn
121406	F/L	THOMAS DFC David Latimer Court	14-01-44	7 Sqn
169609	F/O	THOMAS David Selwyn	16-09-44	90 Sqn
1459137	Sgt	THOMAS Douglas Jerome	29-04-44	103 Sqn
1811856	Sgt	THOMAS Edwin Henry	23-04-44	75 Sqn
527414	F/S	THOMAS Edwin Robert	31-03-44	101 Sqn
1255715	F/S	THOMAS Frank Charles	20-02-44	550 Sqn
1226085	F/S	THOMAS Glyn	30-08-44	50 Sqn
174290	P/O	THOMAS Gwilym Rhys	13-09-44	692 Sqn

Service No.	Rank	Name	Date	Unit
1441411	F/S	THOMAS Harold George	31-08-44	550 Sqn
2209027	Sgt	THOMAS Harry	20-02-44	49 Sqn
983327	F/S	THOMAS Henry Samuel	1-06-44	622 Sqn
1339726	F/S	THOMAS Herbert Ronald	4-12-44	227 Sqn
1895708	Sgt	THOMAS Howard Mansel	4-11-44	75 Sqn
1184086	Sgt	THOMAS Ivor Bertram	22-05-44	44 Sqn
178038	P/O	THOMAS Ivor Henry	13-08-44	158 Sqn
1591316	Sgt	THOMAS James Harold	28-04-44	51 Sqn
618895	F/S	THOMAS John Alfred	3-01-44	83 Sqn
1836239	Sgt	THOMAS John Mansel	28-05-44	12 Sqn
1588612	Sgt	THOMAS John William	28-06-44	44 Sqn
919279	F/S	THOMAS Owen	12-08-44	76 Sqn
172593	F/L	THOMAS DFC Peter Alfred	23-12-44	582 Sqn
1671438	Sgt	THOMAS Richard John	15-06-44	115 Sqn
1681745	Sgt	THOMAS Robert	18-12-44	51 Sqn
1536704	F/S	THOMAS Ronald	31-03-44	115 Sqn
1586842	Sgt	THOMAS Ronald	25-03-44	103 Sqn
1621276	Sgt	THOMAS Ronald Edward	19-07-44	50 Sqn
1398046	F/S	THOMAS Stephen Joseph	12-06-44	102 Sqn
1315500	F/S	THOMAS Theophilus John	2-01-44	106 Sqn
168842	F/L	THOMAS Thomas Morgan	3-06-44	138 Sqn
154395	F/O	THOMAS Thomas Yestyn	4-10-44	550 Sqn
119075	F/L	THOMAS DFC Walter	20-02-44	692 Sqn
1356860	F/S	THOMAS Walter Mervyn	5-10-44	101 Sqn
1270084	F/S	THOMAS William John	19-07-44	619 Sqn
1652484	Sgt	THOMAS William Marshall	13-08-44	14 OTU
1117171	W/O	THOMASON Albert	17-12-44	57 Sqn
542295	Sgt	THOMASON Ernest	15-07-44	103 Sqn
1500590	Sgt	THOMPSON Alan	29-01-44	576 Sqn
1111877	F/S	THOMPSON Allan	24-03-44	15 Sqn
109488	F/L	THOMPSON Anthony William	5-07-44	24 OTU
1319740	Sgt	THOMPSON Clifford Henry	23-04-44	12 Sqn
1090928	W/O	THOMPSON DFC Dennis	20-10-44	35 Sqn
338267	Sgt	THOMPSON Douglas Stanley	2-09-44	1656 HCU
630061	Sgt	THOMPSON Edward	31-08-44	103 Sqn
54128	F/L	THOMPSON DFC Edward Noel	23-04-44	77 Sqn
652750	F/S	THOMPSON Frank	26-11-44	115 Sqn
1503915	F/S	THOMPSON Frank	31-03-44	106 Sqn
1590427	Sgt	THOMPSON Frank	25-03-44	97 Sqn
1590591	Sgt	THOMPSON George Adam Nichols	30-01-44	207 Sqn
169311	F/O	THOMPSON George Austin	19-09-44	106 Sqn
1795515	Sgt	THOMPSON Harold Vincent Dick	22-06-44	44 Sqn
169024	F/O	THOMPSON James Edward	17-07-44	28 OTU
1638282	LAC	THOMPSON James Frederick	9-09-44	156 Sqn
1796355	Sgt	THOMPSON James Sturgeon	31-03-44	433 Sqn
1453762	Sgt	THOMPSON John	3-06-44	76 Sqn
127924	F/O	THOMPSON John Bernard	19-07-44	61 Sqn
179541	P/O	THOMPSON John Lionel	5-11-44	76 Sqn
2204008	Sgt	THOMPSON Kenneth	15-03-44	550 Sqn
1125440	Sgt	THOMPSON Leslie	27-08-44	630 Sqn
1818855	Sgt	THOMPSON Leslie	23-01-44	1679 HCFlt
1323406	Sgt	THOMPSON Leslie St. Clair	12-05-44	630 Sqn
1852372	Sgt	THOMPSON Patrick John	12-09-44	90 Sqn
1638225	Sgt	THOMPSON Peter Theodore	8-02-44	138 Sqn
1579307	Sgt	THOMPSON Robert	21-04-44	619 Sqn
1799820	Sgt	THOMPSON Robert	15-10-44	166 Sqn
1593634	Sgt	THOMPSON Robert 'Bobbie'	25-06-44	49 Sqn
656888	F/S	THOMPSON Robert Findye	31-03-44	207 Sqn
2005260	Sgt	THOMPSON Robert John	28-04-44	115 Sqn
156386	P/O	THOMPSON Robert Sidney	21-01-44	427 Sqn
1866655	Sgt	THOMPSON Ronald	20-11-44	1656 HCU
1515655	Sgt	THOMPSON Ronald Granville	1-04-44	138 Sqn
2214099	Sgt	THOMPSON Roy	22-05-44	7 Sqn
1677683	Sgt	THOMPSON Sidney	3-06-44	158 Sqn
658101	Sgt	THOMPSON Thomas Robertson	4-01-44	1657 HCU
1515446	F/S	THOMPSON Thomas Walton	31-03-44	578 Sqn
966222	Sgt	THOMPSON Thomas William	24-07-44	50 Sqn
1553058	Sgt	THOMPSON William	26-02-44	432 Sqn
1670366	Sgt	THOMPSON William Haswell	19-03-44	101 Sqn
1581769	F/S	THOMPSON William Henry	12-09-44	44 Sqn
146601	F/O	THOMPSON William Oliver	24-02-44	30 OTU
1347841	Sgt	THOMSON Alexander	23-10-44	467 Sqn
1682291	Sgt	THOMSON Alexander	5-06-44	1658 HCU
1522204	Sgt	THOMSON Alexander Ritchie	17-06-44	3 LFS
1579103	F/S	THOMSON Alistair Grant	23-06-44	77 Sqn
543645	Sgt	THOMSON Douglas	4-11-44	51 Sqn
1596065	Sgt	THOMSON George Alfred	14-08-44	550 Sqn
1097466	Sgt	THOMSON Gordon	31-03-44	103 Sqn
154228	F/O	THOMSON James Andrew	17-12-44	49 Sqn
1554274	Sgt	THOMSON John	13-05-44	640 Sqn
1572448	Sgt	THOMSON Robert	31-03-44	432 Sqn
1890158	Sgt	THOMSON Stanley Innis	23-04-44	51 Sqn
1565415	Sgt	THOMSON William Baird	11-04-44	1661 HCU
1294394	F/S	THORINGTON Frederick	2-01-44	156 Sqn
1045216	Sgt	THORLEY Joseph	13-08-44	101 Sqn
1586927	Sgt	THORNE Albert Edward John	27-08-44	35 Sqn
186295	P/O	THORNE Christopher James	11-10-44	101 Sqn
2202529	Sgt	THORNE Harold Victor John	22-03-44	432 Sqn
1284560	Sgt	THORNE Jack Wood	4-12-44	207 Sqn
1877598	Sgt	THORNHILL Albert Charles	23-10-44	76 Sqn
1333987	F/S	THORNHILL Martin Arthur	11-06-44	405 Sqn
1618730	Sgt	THORNTON George Henry	31-03-44	514 Sqn
161494	P/O	THORNTON DFC Ronald Charles	22-03-44	50 Sqn
152921	P/O	THORNTON Ronald Edward John	23-03-44	26 OTU
1869857	Sgt	THOROGOOD Walter Cecil	12-09-44	622 Sqn
155998	F/O	THORPE Alfred	31-03-44	76 Sqn
1506851	Sgt	THORPE Bernard	15-02-44	77 Sqn
1323343	F/S	THORPE Derrick Gordon Cobley	25-05-44	576 Sqn
172216	F/O	THORPE DFC John Herbert	29-11-44	35 Sqn
1594817	Sgt	THORPE Ronald	22-03-44	1658 HCU
1336659	Sgt	THORPE Ronald Clive	25-03-44	640 Sqn
1313226	Sgt	THRIPP Edwin	8-01-44	138 Sqn
1818982	Sgt	THROSBY William John	11-04-44	83 Sqn
1818773	Sgt	THURSBY Alfred	27-01-44	1660 HCU
138069	F/O	TIBBITS Walter Gervase	25-02-44	149 Sqn
2235184	Sgt	TIBBLES Richard Edward	28-08-44	19 OTU
149460	F/O	TIBBS Rowland	19-07-44	207 Sqn
1865826	Sgt	TICKNER Gerald	13-09-44	640 Sqn
144615	F/O	TIDBY Charles Henry	23-06-44	100 Sqn
149066	F/O	TIDMARSH DFC Albert Frederick	9-06-44	1652 HCU
1398185	Sgt	TIDMAS Frank Edward	30-01-44	622 Sqn
1591010	Sgt	TILBURN George Henry	6-10-44	78 Sqn
1515872	Sgt	TILL Albert Edward	8-06-44	622 Sqn
1578559	Sgt	TILLAM John Lanes	25-03-44	635 Sqn
1853579	Sgt	TILSED Raymond William Sidney	4-11-44	195 Sqn
1896307	Sgt	TIMMINS Leonard	20-05-44	7 Sqn
1544917	F/S	TIMPERLEY Leonard Joseph	28-10-44	12 OTU
173558	P/O	TIMPERLEY Robert	31-03-44	12 Sqn
1620951	Sgt	TIMSON Arthur Alec	21-01-44	77 Sqn
142454	F/O	TINCLER Geoffrey Claud	21-04-44	100 Sqn
1805768	Sgt	TINDAL Ronald Walter	31-03-44	10 Sqn
1458532	Sgt	TINDALL Kenneth Witty	20-02-44	408 Sqn
1611612	Sgt	TINDELL Derek William	7-03-44	18 OTU
1819840	Sgt	TINGLE Charles Reginald	21-01-44	61 Sqn
188457	P/O	TINGLE Frank	12-11-44	49 Sqn
156693	P/O	TINN Farquhar Gray George	29-01-44	115 Sqn
1822669	Sgt	TIPALDI Rudolph	1-03-44	76 Sqn
1581522	Sgt	TIPPIN Arthur John	6-10-44	115 Sqn
151365	F/O	TIPPING Gerald	25-07-44	15 Sqn
1320873	Sgt	TIPPING Gordon Thomas	8-07-44	467 Sqn
1896743	Sgt	TITCHENER Alec Sidney	30-09-44	1651 HCU
1217960	F/S	TIVEY Gerald	31-03-44	101 Sqn
1814861	Sgt	TIXHON Walther [Belgium]	28-05-44	166 Sqn
112026	F/L	TIZARD St. John	17-06-44	550 Sqn
627852	Sgt	TOBIN John Joseph	25-02-44	115 Sqn
1554137	Sgt	TODD Alexander Crew Lachie	6-10-44	78 Sqn
1331104	Sgt	TODD Cecil Reginald	12-05-44	626 Sqn
1890853	Sgt	TODD Colin Barry	24-02-44	9 Sqn

Service No	Rank	Name	Date	Sqn/Unit
173008	P/O	TODD Cyril James	28-06-44	90 Sqn
1332783	Sgt	TODD Cyril Robert Leslie	29-01-44	115 Sqn
1514704	F/S	TODD Edward Norman	28-06-44	640 Sqn
1115149	Sgt	TODD George Walter	17-08-44	102 Sqn
1343680	Sgt	TODD John	19-07-44	100 Sqn
1523611	Sgt	TODHUNTER Harold	14-08-44	20 OTU
154207	F/O	TOFIELD Philip John	12-09-44	622 Sqn
1677810	Sgt	TOFT Clifford	21-01-44	51 Sqn
177849	P/O	TOINTON David Samuel [Canada]	12-09-44	625 Sqn
544267	Sgt	TOLAND Raymond Foster	10-05-44	106 Sqn
1324335	Sgt	TOLL John George Frederick	13-08-44	78 Sqn
1332795	Sgt	TOLLAST Henry John	14-08-44	9 Sqn
1393284	Sgt	TOLLEY Stanley William	22-03-44	103 Sqn
1143246	Sgt	TOLLIDAY George William	4-11-44	195 Sqn
1673113	Sgt	TOLLIT Alan St. John	25-06-44	90 Sqn
159417	F/O	TOMALIN Herbert Frederick	15-03-44	51 Sqn
145901	F/O	TOMBS Norman	24-03-44	103 Sqn
1686492	Sgt	TOMKINS Herbert Dixon	3-02-44	16 OTU
811121	Sgt	TOMKINSON Claude Vernon	27-01-44	1660 HCU
1750255	Sgt	TOMKINSON Ronald	31-08-44	460 Sqn
2220225	Sgt	TOMLINSON Derrick Reuben	29-07-44	103 Sqn
1301516	Sgt	TOMLINSON Frederick George	13-06-44	78 Sqn
172564	P/O	TOMLINSON George Robert	27-01-44	9 Sqn
1605090	Sgt	TOMLINSON Harry Peer	8-08-44	90 Sqn
1439047	Sgt	TOMLINSON James	21-09-44	9 Sqn
659150	F/S	TOMLINSON Leslie	21-07-44	622 Sqn
644438	Sgt	TOMLINSON William Richard	21-07-44	10 Sqn
1125388	W/O	TOMMIE Laurence	26-07-44	103 Sqn
157922	F/O	TOMPKINS Phillip Edwin	21-07-44	75 Sqn
1697423	Sgt	TONES Eric Boynton	24-03-44	625 Sqn
1411098	Sgt	TONGE Edgar	3-06-44	76 Sqn
979747	F/S	TONGE Herbert	9-08-44	640 Sqn
1870924	Sgt	TONGUE Cyril Wallace Langford	24-02-44	405 Sqn
1569087	F/S	TONKS Kenneth	6-11-44	463 Sqn
173599	P/O	TONKYN John Walter	23-04-44	405 Sqn
1480698	Sgt	TOOLEY James Arthur	11-04-44	101 Sqn
152479	F/O	TOOLEY Paul William	16-09-44	90 Sqn
152236	F/O	TOOMER Ronald	12-09-44	35 Sqn
1583671	Sgt	TOON Stanley Leslie	22-03-44	78 Sqn
1622619	F/S	TOOTH John Ernest	13-09-44	625 Sqn
1419910	Sgt	TOPHAM Lyndon Kenneth	20-02-44	463 Sqn
1211652	F/S	TOPLIS Jack Thomas	6-01-44	207 Sqn
1576629	F/S	TOPPING Walter Eric	13-04-44	90 Sqn
1578567	Sgt	TORBETT Vernon William George	11-04-44	9 Sqn
1253971	Sgt	TORODE James	11-04-44	576 Sqn
1574544	Sgt	TORRANCE John	20-02-44	102 Sqn
169915	P/O	TOSH James Findlay	30-01-44	166 Sqn
1796569	Sgt	TOTTEN John	17-06-44	1660 HCU
128513	F/O	TOTTY Norman George	15-02-44	15 Sqn
1568795	Sgt	TOUGH Francis	21-07-44	10 Sqn
151163	F/O	TOVERY Frank	11-06-44	100 Sqn
55041	F/O	TOVEY Ronald William	8-06-44	115 Sqn
657133	F/S	TOWERS Jack	29-04-44	90 Sqn
1498162	W/O	TOWILL Charles Edgar	23-10-44	44 Sqn
1578957	F/S	TOWLE Edward George	16-12-44	106 Sqn
1431592	F/S	TOWNDROW Ronald	8-07-44	61 Sqn
185161	P/O	TOWNLEY James Raymond	27-09-44	1654 HCU
2220094	Sgt	TOWNS Robert Hunter	11-06-44	467 Sqn
1623085	Sgt	TOWNSEND Cyril Hiram	17-08-44	102 Sqn
1740042	Sgt	TOWNSEND Denys Edward	12-08-44	30 OTU
1321858	F/S	TOWNSEND Donald George	22-06-44	57 Sqn
578126	Sgt	TOWNSEND John	22-01-44	433 Sqn
1078579	F/S	TOWNSEND DFM Ralph	17-06-44	550 Sqn
625503	W/O	TOWNSEND-COLES MiD Roland Brainerd Herbert	15-07-44	18 Sqn
2202697	Sgt	TOWNSLEY Alan	17-04-44	5 LFS
1237476	F/S	TOWSE DFM Christopher Danby	10-05-44	83 Sqn
1890462	Sgt	TOWSE Frederick Albert	10-05-44	619 Sqn
160872	F/O	TRAGHEIM Edward Alfred [Canada]	26-11-44	115 Sqn
1581787	Sgt	TRANTER Albert Royden	4-05-44	35 Sqn
133338	F/L	TRANTER DFC Thomas Eric	13-09-44	640 Sqn
1653603	Sgt	TRAVERS William Samuel	20-01-44	83 Sqn
162794	P/O	TRAVERS-CLARKE Evelyn	20-02-44	12 Sqn
1851762	Sgt	TRAYHORN James Arthur	28-08-44	550 Sqn
634398	Sgt	TRAYLER Victor Nelson	2-01-44	626 Sqn
658044	F/S	TRAYLOR Gerald Walter [Canada]	20-02-44	35 Sqn
614985	F/S	TRAYNOR Patrick	3-01-44	83 Sqn
1323811	Sgt	TREADWELL Arthur Henry	5-07-44	576 Sqn
70880	S/L	TREASURE Guy Benjamin	25-06-44	102 Sqn
1867730	Sgt	TREBY John Arthur	1-06-44	1667 HCU
1587786	Sgt	TREMAYNE Melville John	3-06-44	158 Sqn
1390234	F/S	TRENAMAN Mazzine John	10-01-44	1652 HCU
1801670	Sgt	TRETT Ronald Dennis	2-01-44	460 Sqn
1852878	Sgt	TREVETHAN Roy	22-06-44	467 Sqn
1584991	Sgt	TREVIS Sidney Charles	12-12-44	582 Sqn
47354	F/L	TREVOR-ROPER DFC DFM Richard Dacre	31-03-44	97 Sqn
1391956	Sgt	TRIGWELL George Henry	13-08-44	514 Sqn
1354812	Sgt	TRIMBY Ambrose Frederick Maurice	2-09-44	1656 HCU
1384704	Sgt	TRINDER Thomas Stanley	27-01-44	626 Sqn
1587176	Sgt	TRIVETT Arthur	20-02-44	625 Sqn
1896554	Sgt	TROAKE Randolph Henry Charles	13-08-44	622 Sqn
1414525	F/S	TRODD Geoffrey Wilfred	31-03-44	166 Sqn
1636341	Sgt	TROLLOPE John Edward	3-08-44	460 Sqn
1868451	Sgt	TROTMAN John Leonard Brunner	26-08-44	419 Sqn
169548	P/O	TROTT Bernard Aidan	14-01-44	156 Sqn
1429987	F/S	TROTT Corbyn James	13-06-44	76 Sqn
1595391	Sgt	TRUBY James	6-10-44	115 Sqn
144162	F/O	TRUESDALE Albert Edward 'Bertie'	22-05-44	630 Sqn
1455172	Sgt	TRUFFET Francis Herbert	28-08-44	19 OTU
999898	Sgt	TRUMAN Wilfred Cyril	25-05-44	582 Sqn
1335495	Sgt	TRUMPER Victor Frederick Thomas	29-07-44	576 Sqn
86235	F/L	TRUSCOTT DFC Philip Vincent	6-09-44	169 Sqn
151149	F/O	TUBBS Kenneth John	20-02-44	57 Sqn
916863	F/S	TUCK Frank Cyril Victor	4-08-44	635 Sqn
176410	P/O	TUCK DFC Harry Humphrey	29-07-44	625 Sqn
1895120	Sgt	TUCK Herbert Alfred	17-12-44	61 Sqn
1800484	Sgt	TUCKER Arthur William	14-08-44	550 Sqn
1891569	Sgt	TUCKER Frederick Liege	24-04-44	619 Sqn
1868828	Sgt	TUCKER George Henry	8-07-44	50 Sqn
1321777	F/S	TUCKER John Henry	7-06-44	619 Sqn
173842	P/O	TUCKER John Lovelace	23-04-44	106 Sqn
1587192	Sgt	TUCKER Sidney George	27-01-44	84 OTU
1330876	Sgt	TUCKER William John	27-09-44	115 Sqn
1611657	LAC	TUCKWELL William Henry	25-02-44	105 Sqn
1319075	Sgt	TUDDENHAM Russell James Hammond	29-10-44	207 Sqn
1890869	Sgt	TUFFS Arthur	23-05-44	103 Sqn
1557970	Sgt	TUGMAN Robert	24-03-44	166 Sqn
1711838	Sgt	TULETT Herbert Stanley Douglas	12-05-44	166 Sqn
169425	F/O	TULL DFC Desmond Trevor	18-12-44	85 Sqn
124570	F/O	TULL George Arthur	3-01-44	61 Sqn
1269564	Sgt	TULLETT Henry Thomas	27-03-44	14 OTU
1343077	Sgt	TULLOCH James	26-08-44	635 Sqn
1339538	F/S	TUNBRIDGE Douglas Oliver	19-03-44	97 Sqn
1395660	Sgt	TUNNELL Eric Henry	23-09-44	50 Sqn
1621263	Sgt	TUNNICLIFFE Ralph Wallace	7-03-44	18 OTU
152827	F/O	TUNSTALL Edmund Thomas	13-08-44	51 Sqn
171001	P/O	TUNSTALL Ernest Edwin	15-02-44	100 Sqn
1851985	Sgt	TUPMAN Dennis Henry	11-04-44	635 Sqn
1607041	Sgt	TUPPER Sidney Webb	30-01-44	467 Sqn
1601690	F/S	TURKENTINE Fredrick John	18-12-44	106 Sqn
154091	F/O	TURNBULL Bryan Evason	7-10-44	78 Sqn
139993	F/O	TURNBULL James Alexander Welsh	21-01-44	102 Sqn
1097185	LAC	TURNBULL John	16-04-44	12 Sqn
948285	Sgt	TURNBULL John George	4-05-44	460 Sqn
1044419	F/S	TURNBULL John Mowbray	2-01-44	630 Sqn
1820580	F/S	TURNBULL William	29-11-44	35 Sqn

525573	Sgt	TURNER Bertie Frederick	21-01-44	463 Sqn	1836576	Sgt	VALE Lionel Robert	4-05-44	460 Sqn
1394543	Sgt	TURNER Donald Arthur	29-01-44	207 Sqn	1814417	F/S	VALENCIA Robert Henry	13-08-44	156 Sqn
150167	F/O	TURNER Donald George	22-03-44	49 Sqn	82532	F/L	VALENTA Arnost [Czechoslovakia]	31-03-44	311 Sqn
1263330	F/S	TURNER DFM Frederick	17-01-44	15 OTU	1576668	Sgt	VALLANCE Francis Beardsley	20-02-44	514 Sqn
188991	P/O	TURNER Howard Ernest	19-07-44	49 Sqn	1624485	Sgt	VAMPLOUGH Ernest	5-03-44	218 Sqn
152492	F/O	TURNER Jack	25-05-44	15 Sqn	1799345	Sgt	VANCE Herbert	20-10-44	1666 HCU
1127989	F/S	TURNER Jack	11-04-44	149 Sqn	1823455	Sgt	VANCE Melrose	9-06-44	467 Sqn
749921	Sgt	TURNER James John 'Jimmy'	11-04-44	158 Sqn	1578665	F/S	VANN Donald	21-07-44	51 Sqn
139703	F/O	TURNER John Alfred	13-08-44	101 Sqn	1335144	F/S	van MARLE John Arthur	18-03-44	76 Sqn
1869208	Sgt	TURNER Joseph	31-10-44	90 Sqn	144600	F/O	van STOCKUM William Jacob [Holland]	10-06-44	10 Sqn
1458457	F/S	TURNER Kenneth Henry	20-11-44	186 Sqn					
1389695	Sgt	TURNER Maurice	6-01-44	467 Sqn	1869498	Sgt	VAN DER LINDE John Peter	7-10-44	166 Sqn
1795136	F/S	TURNER Norman	1-05-44	514 Sqn	40273	W/C	VARE AFC Kenneth Frederick [New Zealand]	2-01-44	630 Sqn
176475	P/O	TURNER Oswald John	7-06-44	83 Sqn					
1661472	Sgt	TURNER Patrick Anthony	24-02-44	100 Sqn	1111885	Sgt	VAREY Harry	17-12-44	49 Sqn
1530427	Sgt	TURNER Raymond Valentine	20-01-44	76 Sqn	1116187	Sgt	VAREY Thomas William	11-04-44	9 Sqn
914705	Sgt	TURNER Ronald Archibald George	24-03-44	640 Sqn	178252	F/O	VARLEY Norman	13-06-44	408 Sqn
144357	F/O	TURNER Sidney George	6-06-44	578 Sqn	2210716	Sgt	VARLEY William	8-02-44	18 OTU
1825556	Sgt	TURNER William	19-03-44	20 OTU	959181	F/S	VARRALL Frederick Albert Charles	29-07-44	103 Sqn
1483675	Sgt	TURNER William Francis	4-12-44	207 Sqn	1352859	Sgt	VAUGHAN George Albert	30-08-44	166 Sqn
152501	F/O	TURNIDGE Brian Grahame	6-07-44	578 Sqn	1389416	F/S	VAUGHAN Ivor Charles	30-08-44	300 Sqn
1299326	F/S	TURRELL DFM Ronald Howard	17-06-44	1660 HCU	1505077	F/S	VAUGHTON James	22-06-44	619 Sqn
163561	F/O	TURVEY Edward Robert	11-12-44	1651 HCU	1603709	F/S	VEAL Frederick Ernest William	24-04-44	619 Sqn
1582404	Sgt	TUSTIN Dennis George	17-06-44	77 Sqn	1853807	Sgt	VEALE DFM Alfred Joseph	13-06-44	115 Sqn
2211929	Sgt	TUTHILL Peter Eric	5-10-44	75 Sqn	127901	F/O	VEALE Norman	3-08-44	239 Sqn
808316	F/S	TUTILL John William	30-12-44	156 Sqn	1572134	Sgt	VEDOVATO Marco Joseph Henry	28-05-44	103 Sqn
176275	P/O	TUTT Norman James	16-06-44	582 Sqn	162357	F/O	VEGLIO Julian Arthur Edmund	12-12-44	195 Sqn
1567240	Sgt	TWEEDIE James	24-07-44	582 Sqn	1814362	Sgt	VENABLES William Geoffrey Alexander	21-01-44	1661 HCU
175327	P/O	TWEEDIE John Burns	23-04-44	115 Sqn					
515294	Sgt	TWELL Harry	26-08-44	101 Sqn	1602081	F/S	VENESS Raymond Frank	14-10-44	550 Sqn
1674832	F/S	TWELL Norman	27-08-44	7 Sqn	176925	P/O	VERE-HODGE Hector Matthew Julius	12-09-44	97 Sqn
1473131	Sgt	TWIGG William Edwin	13-08-44	76 Sqn					
151201	F/O	TWILLEY Bernard Mark	18-12-44	51 Sqn	1583710	Sgt	VERNER Norman Arnsby	30-01-44	463 Sqn
158562	F/O	TWINING Robert Ernest Samuel	2-05-44	218 Sqn	1880548	Sgt	VERNON Gordon Ernest	1-11-44	424 Sqn
1874043	Sgt	TWITCHETT Arnold Charles	20-02-44	431 Sqn	1216538	Sgt	VERNON Roger Dunkerley	19-03-44	101 Sqn
1383372	Sgt	TWITCHETT Arthur George	6-01-44	12 Sqn	155333	F/O	VERRIER DFC Alfred Reginald	21-11-44	Fiskerton
618798	Sgt	TWOMEY Dennis Daniel [Eire]	27-03-44	14 OTU	1509446	Sgt	VESSEY William Chapman	12-06-44	635 Sqn
1383995	Sgt	TWOMEY DFM Terence Michael	17-08-44	97 Sqn	1814586	Sgt	VEVERS Eric Frank	11-11-44	467 Sqn
1804729	Sgt	TWYDELL Victor Leonard	22-02-44	218 Sqn	1628411	Sgt	VICARY Cyril Claude	20-01-44	76 Sqn
991577	F/S	TWYNEHAM George	23-09-44	61 Sqn	2209015	Sgt	VICK James Albert	3-06-44	138 Sqn
1594010	Sgt	TYE Jack	20-01-44	97 Sqn	1533843	Sgt	VICKERS Albert	24-03-44	514 Sqn
1076760	Sgt	TYLER Clifford Owen	16-02-44	77 Sqn	158905	P/O	VICKERS DFC Geoffrey	2-01-44	156 Sqn
1812260	Sgt	TYLER Frank Thomas	8-05-44	15 Sqn	1576350	F/S	VICKERS Harry Sidney	11-04-44	83 Sqn
1288811	Cpl	TYLER George David	14-04-44	15 Sqn	710145	Sgt	VICKERS Paul Vernon de Villiers [Rhodesia]	20-01-44	83 Sqn
1397186	Sgt	TYLER George Herbert	5-07-44	630 Sqn					
1323748	Sgt	TYLER Morris Joseph	31-03-44	514 Sqn	168773	P/O	VICKERS Philip Dennis	12-05-44	103 Sqn
1816965	Sgt	TYM Alan	12-03-44	199 Sqn	1646362	LAC	VICKERS Robert Charles	6-05-44	630 Sqn
1385473	Sgt	TYRIE DFM William Richard	2-01-44	630 Sqn	1419019	Sgt	VICKERY Albert Leo Norman	20-02-44	463 Sqn
1461788	Sgt	UDALL Dennis William Albert	28-01-44	103 Sqn	1486527	Sgt	VINCE Bernard Reginald	13-08-44	514 Sqn
1851507	F/S	UDELL William Charles	30-06-44	514 Sqn	1395910	F/S	VINCENT Frank Arthur	25-08-44	75 Sqn
136718	F/L	UNDERHILL Claude Raymond	21-07-44	97 Sqn	1483346	Sgt	VINCENT James Frederick	28-05-44	514 Sqn
152835	F/O	UNDERWOOD Edward Arthur	22-12-44	189 Sqn	1336764	F/S	VINCENT John Keith Robert	3-06-44	138 Sqn
1454510	F/S	UNDERWOOD John Bernard	22-03-44	514 Sqn	1199312	Sgt	VINCENT Norman Douglas John	29-01-44	97 Sqn
176368	P/O	UNDERWOOD Kenneth Alfred	29-06-44	12 Sqn	1603902	Sgt	VINE Gilbert Dennis	2-05-44	7 Sqn
1432425	F/S	UNDERWOOD DFM Ronald	2-01-44	156 Sqn	123505	F/L	VINNELL Henry Victor Alexander	27-11-44	192 Sqn
84710	S/L	UNDRELL DFC Geoffrey Alan Ritchie	11-09-44	156 Sqn	42662	F/L	VINSON Ronald Anthony	14-01-44	115 Sqn
1495465	Sgt	UPFOLD George	15-01-44	626 Sqn	1891957	Sgt	VIOLETT Frederick Frank	22-05-44	9 Sqn
169192	P/O	UPPINGTON DFC Brian Seymour	15-03-44	51 Sqn	1226876	Sgt	VIOLLET Robert Frederick Henry	19-07-44	49 Sqn
1622713	Sgt	UPSALL Walter	27-04-44	207 Sqn	39191	S/L	VIPAN Arthur Lushington	16-10-44	12 OTU
1809229	Sgt	UPTON Eric Basil	15-02-44	76 Sqn	54224	P/O	VIPOND Thomas Elliott	25-03-44	115 Sqn
1336538	F/S	UPTON Peter William	22-01-44	514 Sqn	1524021	Sgt	VIVOUR Bankole Beresford	31-03-44	156 Sqn
1575421	Sgt	UPTON Stanley James	22-03-44	49 Sqn	187497	P/O	VOCE Eric Frederick Leslie	29-11-44	101 Sqn
1382396	F/S	URCH Fred	24-06-44	156 Sqn	906410	F/S	VOELLNER William	26-08-44	103 Sqn
778979	F/S	UREN Peter George [Rhodesia]	8-07-44	61 Sqn	1392293	F/S	VOLCOVITCH Alfred (served as MYERS)	19-07-44	619 Sqn
1815458	Sgt	URQUHART Angus Vass	13-08-44	635 Sqn					
1522473	Sgt	USHER Edgar	21-04-44	100 Sqn	2210136	Sgt	VOSE Peter	23-05-44	429 Sqn
153476	F/S	USHER Reginald William Harold	8-12-44	630 Sqn	1566024	Sgt	WADDELL John Christian	24-06-44	1662 HCU
1676820	F/S	USHER Thomas Norman	22-06-44	83 Sqn	1077103	Sgt	WADDELL John Joseph	14-01-44	405 Sqn
1333681	F/S	UTTING Bernard Thomas	31-03-44	9 Sqn	1622511	Sgt	WADDINGTON Kenneth	22-06-44	207 Sqn

127932	F/L	WADDINGTON Sidney Arthur	29-09-44	157 Sqn	945652	Sgt	WALLBANK Cyril	22-05-44	467 Sqn
1379126	Sgt	WADE Arthur Walter	25-04-44	83 Sqn	1577234	Sgt	WALLBEY Kenneth James	20-02-44	630 Sqn
1694924	Sgt	WADE John Dixon	12-12-44	15 Sqn	1049087	F/S	WALLEN Mathew John	1-07-44	1 GpSDFlt
573758	F/S	WADE Raymond Lister	17-06-44	1660 HCU	1392292	Sgt	WALLER Alan Abraham	3-01-44	156 Sqn
152946	P/O	WADE Robert Frederick	20-01-44	18 OTU	1337807	F/S	WALLER Arthur Alfred	7-06-44	578 Sqn
1318538	F/S	WADGE DFM Francis	24-02-44	100 Sqn	1801943	Sgt	WALLER Charles Peter	11-04-44	90 Sqn
159050	P/O	WADSWORTH DFC Douglas Arnold	4-05-44	619 Sqn	1585328	Sgt	WALLER Cyril	27-04-44	156 Sqn
1040733	LAC	WADSWORTH Eric Alexander	6-06-44	408 Sqn	1320142	Sgt	WALLER Eric Gordon	24-03-44	625 Sqn
1064744	F/S	WADSWORTH Joseph	24-03-44	103 Sqn	1151554	Sgt	WALLER Ernest Victor	5-04-44	11 OTU
53497	F/O	WADSWORTH Philip	28-04-44	156 Sqn	1819414	Sgt	WALLER Harry	11-06-44	420 Sqn
172841	P/O	WAIGHT Cassian Henry	20-02-44	101 Sqn	1291564	Sgt	WALLER Ralph Jesse Sorrey	6-02-44	149 Sqn
178240	P/O	WAIT William Noel	5-08-44	617 Sqn	173892	P/O	WALLER Stanley	12-05-44	115 Sqn
1579832	F/S	WAITE Arthur	29-01-44	83 Sqn	1390000	Sgt	WALLINGER Wallace	13-06-44	12 Sqn
2209456	Sgt	WAITES John	4-05-44	626 Sqn	1802513	Sgt	WALLIS Edwin Valentine	21-11-44	51 Sqn
1295505	Sgt	WAKEFIELD Edmund Donald	9-11-44	625 Sqn	174498	P/O	WALLIS DFC Harry Andre	25-04-44	7 Sqn
47482	F/L	WAKEFIELD Michael Grey	24-06-44	7 Sqn	155510	F/O	WALLIS Hubert	20-02-44	61 Sqn
1582235	Sgt	WAKEFIELD Norman George	14-06-44	11 OTU	1803333	Sgt	WALLIS Jack Ronald	22-06-44	619 Sqn
1897446	Sgt	WAKEFIELD Raymond Victor	6-12-44	103 Sqn	1809799	Sgt	WALLIS Norman Leslie	31-03-44	625 Sqn
2216242	Sgt	WAKEFIELD William	20-02-44	158 Sqn	184879	P/O	WALLNUT Bernard Joseph	30-11-44	141 Sqn
1397471	Sgt	WAKEFORD Hubert Jack	17-06-44	102 Sqn	1090492	Sgt	WALMSLEY Arthur	29-10-44	207 Sqn
160593	F/O	WAKEHAM Norman John	28-05-44	166 Sqn	1673473	Sgt	WALMSLEY Herbert Vincent	2-01-44	106 Sqn
177735	P/O	WAKELEY Reginald Charles Hubert	7-06-44	630 Sqn	1528517	Sgt	WALMSLEY Kenneth	25-02-44	1662 HCU
1579920	Sgt	WAKEMAN Edward Vivian	19-07-44	115 Sqn	1750354	Sgt	WALMSLEY Kenneth Eastwood	1-01-44	28 OTU
161784	P/O	WAKLEY Cyril Arthur	20-01-44	97 Sqn	1588886	Sgt	WALMSLEY Richard	22-03-44	408 Sqn
1684118	Sgt	WALCH William	25-02-44	619 Sqn	1458471	Sgt	WALMSLEY William	25-03-44	433 Sqn
1291223	F/S	WALDEN Peter Horace	31-07-44	12 OTU	651775	Sgt	WALSH Edward	14-08-44	550 Sqn
1877437	Sgt	WALDON Phillip Lawson	22-12-44	626 Sqn	1817555	Sgt	WALSH William Joseph	6-01-44	7 Sqn
156776	F/O	WALDRON John Henry	18-12-44	10 Sqn	55891	P/O	WALSHAM Reginald Thomas	1-08-44	429 Sqn
1065821	W/O	WALDRON William	29-07-44	582 Sqn	153828	F/O	WALTER Francis Peter	25-09-44	576 Sqn
1339815	F/S	WALE Frederick William	27-04-44	49 Sqn	1807788	Sgt	WALTER Frank George	4-05-44	101 Sqn
73022	F/L	WALENN Twice MiD Gilbert William	29-03-44	25 OTU	178076	P/O	WALTERS Ronald Neville Henry	11-07-44	22 OTU
1893593	Sgt	WALES William	3-06-44	158 Sqn	1351227	W/O	WALTERS DFM Henry Leonard	27-05-44	1656 HCU
1249971	Sgt	WALFORD Leonard Ernest	31-03-44	49 Sqn	1652405	Sgt	WALTERS John James Owen	17-03-44	17 OTU
51345	F/L	WALKER Albert Warnforth	24-12-44	635 Sqn	1593388	Sgt	WALTERS Norman	16-05-44	12 OTU
657966	Sgt	WALKER Archibald James	22-06-44	619 Sqn	1587139	Sgt	WALTERS Richard Stuart Lynton	9-06-44	44 Sqn
1515147	Sgt	WALKER Arnold	23-04-44	90 Sqn	974685	Sgt	WALTHAM Cecil	23-10-44	76 Sqn
1550318	F/S	WALKER Arthur Binnie	29-01-44	77 Sqn	1021045	F/S	WALTHAM John Edward	25-04-44	78 Sqn
139686	F/O	WALKER DFC Arthur James	22-12-44	617 Sqn	174051	P/O	WALTON Charles Richard Ernest	4-05-44	50 Sqn
1603285	Sgt	WALKER Bernard Raymond Guy	26-03-44	10 Sqn	1631566	Sgt	WALTON Edward John	30-08-44	630 Sqn
573551	Sgt	WALKER Colin	22-01-44	76 Sqn	174943	F/O	WALTON Eric	25-08-44	10 Sqn
1825930	Sgt	WALKER David Alexander Robertson	28-10-44	90 Sqn	183067	P/O	WALTON Ernest William	25-07-44	420 Sqn
1331539	F/S	WALKER Edward George	21-04-44	625 Sqn	1738008	Sgt	WALTON Geoffrey Alan	14-01-44	207 Sqn
1569932	Sgt	WALKER Ernest Oswald	17-06-44	102 Sqn	1448762	Sgt	WALTON George Fearnley	14-10-44	12 Sqn
937534	Sgt	WALKER Frank Birkett	27-04-44	44 Sqn	571411	Sgt	WALTON Henry Charles	23-01-44	161 Sqn
1533927	F/S	WALKER Garth	21-01-44	550 Sqn	1454058	Sgt	WALTON John Richard Vincent	19-04-44	640 Sqn
1352784	Sgt	WALKER George	24-03-44	102 Sqn	1309536	Sgt	WALTON Norman	16-02-44	78 Sqn
1216533	F/S	WALKER George Arthur	29-07-44	44 Sqn	2208979	Sgt	WALTON Richard	30-01-44	166 Sqn
1594671	Sgt	WALKER George Frederick Wilson	14-07-44	433 Sqn	52211	F/O	WALTON DFC BEM William George Evans		
1212018	Sgt	WALKER George William	31-03-44	106 Sqn				9-09-44	138 Sqn
1873691	Sgt	WALKER Horace John	25-05-44	158 Sqn	1393635	Sgt	WANGLER Arthur Levett	31-03-44	640 Sqn
64897	W/C	WALKER AFC DFM Jesse Holland	12-09-44	83 Sqn	1005427	Sgt	WANNOP John	30-01-44	433 Sqn
179250	P/O	WALKER John William	13-08-44	429 Sqn	131987	F/O	WARBOYS Leslie Victor	3-06-44	138 Sqn
1077032	Sgt	WALKER John William	30-01-44	405 Sqn	1484107	Sgt	WARBURTON Carl Arthur	23-05-44	75 Sqn
174906	F/O	WALKER Kenneth Leslie	13-08-44	102 Sqn	2210063	Sgt	WARBURTON John Arthur	28-04-44	103 Sqn
1852244	Sgt	WALKER Leslie Edward Bowler	8-09-44	29 OTU	173156	P/O	WARBURTON DFC William	6-08-44	83 Sqn
1603383	F/S	WALKER Peter Frank	31-03-44	166 Sqn	1067053	Sgt	WARBURTON William	27-01-44	61 Sqn
149550	F/L	WALKER DFC MiD Ronald Arthur	9-07-44	83 Sqn	1581798	Sgt	WARD Alan James	9-10-44	462 Sqn
658405	Sgt	WALKER Stanley	29-01-44	1660 HCU	1509409	Sgt	WARD Allen Edward Roy	15-03-44	625 Sqn
172592	P/O	WALKER Stanley Arthur Douglas	6-06-44	76 Sqn	1738524	Sgt	WARD Arthur Roy	22-06-44	619 Sqn
960863	Sgt	WALKER Walter	25-02-44	408 Sqn	1460197	Sgt	WARD Dennis Reginald	8-08-44	15 Sqn
1076680	Sgt	WALKER Wilfred Keith	25-03-44	44 Sqn	1893108	Sgt	WARD Donald	12-12-44	149 Sqn
1366864	F/S	WALKER William Robertson	4-05-44	101 Sqn	1815269	Sgt	WARD Frederick	19-07-44	460 Sqn
1812085	Sgt	WALL George William Frederick	16-10-44	14 OTU	1800885	Sgt	WARD Frederick John	30-08-44	1660 HCU
1576531	F/S	WALL William Alfred	2-01-44	83 Sqn	148184	F/O	WARD Geoffrey	2-01-44	9 Sqn
1615678	Sgt	WALLACE Anthony John	22-11-44	1660 HCU	1865789	Sgt	WARD George Ernest	13-08-44	578 Sqn
133403	F/O	WALLACE DFC Edward Peter	4-11-44	128 Sqn	1582145	Sgt	WARD Harold Victor	19-10-44	9 Sqn
1370144	F/S	WALLACE Robert	28-04-44	431 Sqn	1768223	Sgt	WARD Harry	27-05-44	1654 HCU
1388350	F/S	WALLACE Sydney	2-05-44	7 Sqn	2221266	Sgt	WARD Harry	25-08-44	640 Sqn
1824662	Sgt	WALLACE William	24-07-44	630 Sqn	1484108	Sgt	WARD James William	29-01-44	429 Sqn

1483329	F/S	WARD John Bernard	4-05-44	463 Sqn	149100	F/O	WATERHOUSE DFC Victor	2-01-44	156 Sqn
171453	P/O	WARD John Francis	11-05-44	467 Sqn	1315374	Sgt	WATERS George Lawrence	6-01-44	57 Sqn
126716	F/O	WARD John Halliday	23-05-44	115 Sqn	618134	Sgt	WATERS John	2-01-44	626 Sqn
1583182	Sgt	WARD John Richard	20-02-44	49 Sqn	1561612	F/S	WATERS John Joseph	10-05-44	50 Sqn
610229	Sgt	WARD John Ronald	27-07-44	619 Sqn	1801475	Sgt	WATERS Robert Charles	24-03-44	626 Sqn
1001977	F/S	WARD John Thomas	24-06-44	7 Sqn	518019	Sgt	WATKINS Alfred Ernest	22-01-44	83 Sqn
1819348	Sgt	WARD Kenneth Arthur	24-03-44	156 Sqn	174085	F/O	WATKINS Antony Guy Samuel	13-09-44	166 Sqn
1459087	F/S	WARD Kenneth Rookby	11-06-44	166 Sqn	149930	F/O	WATKINS DFC David Trevor	7-10-44	617 Sqn
134564	F/L	WARD DFC Michael	25-07-44	83 Sqn	1399063	F/S	WATKINS Eric Howard Pitt	6-12-44	57 Sqn
977445	F/S	WARD Montagu Arnold	24-03-44	115 Sqn	140880	F/O	WATKINS Gwynfor	19-07-44	76 Sqn
1819837	Sgt	WARD Norman Vincent	23-05-44	425 Sqn	1234938	Sgt	WATKINS Harold James	21-07-44	578 Sqn
1577566	Sgt	WARD Raymond [Canada]	3-06-44	158 Sqn	162607	P/O	WATKINS DFC Herbert John	29-01-44	625 Sqn
139701	F/O	WARD Raymond John	4-05-44	12 Sqn	150388	F/O	WATKINS John Peter	16-05-44	141 Sqn
1898016	Sgt	WARD Richard Edward	31-12-44	138 Sqn	1583322	Sgt	WATKINS Sydney	14-01-44	1653 HCU
957279	Sgt	WARD Robert James	1-11-44	619 Sqn	1594483	Sgt	WATKINS William	13-07-44	166 Sqn
1808911	Sgt	WARD Roger Brockwell	24-09-44	166 Sqn	1651897	Sgt	WATKINS William Kenneth	20-02-44	514 Sqn
1812253	Sgt	WARD Stanley Robert	9-06-44	467 Sqn	1863421	Sgt	WATKINSON Dennis Robert Gordon	14-10-44	153 Sqn
1880385	Sgt	WARD Stephen Henry	12-12-44	150 Sqn	1896150	Sgt	WATKINSON John	25-07-44	102 Sqn
1579650	Sgt	WARD Thomas Dudley	21-04-44	44 Sqn	139524	F/L	WATLING George Alfred	29-01-44	97 Sqn
1824912	Sgt	WARD Thomas Malcolm	23-11-44	195 Sqn	952059	Sgt	WATSON Alan	20-01-44	102 Sqn
915488	Sgt	WARD Victor Jack	13-09-44	101 Sqn	1104163	F/S	WATSON Bertie Alexander	24-09-44	51 Sqn
1049823	Sgt	WARDEN Thomas	10-04-44	149 Sqn	1822918	Sgt	WATSON Cecil John	15-07-44	550 Sqn
175510	F/O	WARDLE DFC Anthony Valentine Hutchinson			1340421	Sgt	WATSON Donald	12-04-44	50 Sqn
			29-07-44	57 Sqn	1567286	Sgt	WATSON Douglas Livingstone	21-07-44	51 Sqn
1819580	Sgt	WARDLE Keith Harry Hackney	2-01-44	207 Sqn	1806714	Sgt	WATSON Edwin Ernest	6-01-44	619 Sqn
1451760	Sgt	WARDMAN Eric	8-07-44	49 Sqn	1271554	Sgt	WATSON Ernest Nelson	8-08-44	630 Sqn
1387736	Sgt	WARE George James	17-06-44	103 Sqn	177547	P/O	WATSON DFM Frank Raymond	6-06-44	97 Sqn
1511389	AC1	WARE James	12-01-44	514 Sqn	1169390	LAC	WATSON Frederick Charles	29-12-44	514 Sqn
1890900	Sgt	WARE Peter Henry Colin	25-08-44	10 Sqn	139715	F/O	WATSON George	19-04-44	149 Sqn
1703303	Sgt	WAREHAM Bertram Edmund	22-05-44	622 Sqn	1493014	Sgt	WATSON Jock Martin	24-06-44	7 Sqn
134370	F/O	WAREHAM Frank Edward	5-07-44	44 Sqn	1477926	Sgt	WATSON John Ernest	27-04-44	619 Sqn
1204189	F/S	WAREHAM Sidney John	30-01-44	44 Sqn	1602170	F/S	WATSON John Maurice Andrews	24-09-44	50 Sqn
1319125	Sgt	WAREHAM William Henry	23-01-44	1667 HCU	173304	P/O	WATSON Leslie Thomas	11-05-44	467 Sqn
1401926	F/S	WARHAM Arthur Simpson	26-09-44	85 Sqn	1343714	Sgt	WATSON Robert	19-07-44	100 Sqn
151745	F/O	WARING John	3-02-44	84 OTU	1822226	Sgt	WATSON Robert	28-04-44	15 Sqn
154092	F/O	WARING Norman Richard	12-12-44	195 Sqn	1892230	Sgt	WATSON Ronald George Thomas	12-05-44	9 Sqn
1621062	Sgt	WARING Tom	29-07-44	12 Sqn	922306	Sgt	WATSON Ronald Somner	20-02-44	625 Sqn
1628087	Sgt	WARLOW Neville Philip	28-05-44	103 Sqn	1594037	Sgt	WATSON Thomas Colbeck	24-03-44	115 Sqn
1653307	Sgt	WARLOW William John	20-11-44	75 Sqn	164281	F/O	WATSON Thomas Mulby	11-12-44	1651 HCU
1391412	Sgt	WARNER Kenneth William	9-06-44	50 Sqn	187732	P/O	WATSON Thomas Nicholson	18-12-44	463 Sqn
169580	F/O	WARNER Sydney George Adolphus	28-08-44	692 Sqn	1851938	Sgt	WATSON Victor John	24-03-44	115 Sqn
176005	P/O	WARREN Alfred	20-04-44	420 Sqn	61983	S/L	WATSON DFC Walter Geoffrey	6-06-44	578 Sqn
1607824	Sgt	WARREN Benjamin David Merrilees	16-09-44	466 Sqn	567222	W/O	WATSON DFM William Alexander 'Sandy'		
150005	F/O	WARREN Collyn Warwick	31-07-44	12 OTU				18-04-44	1657 HCU
151118	F/L	WARREN Derek	12-05-44	75 Sqn	1821732	Sgt	WATSON William Alexander Fernie	13-04-44	90 Sqn
1818249	Sgt	WARREN Edgar William John	24-03-44	115 Sqn	1568847	Sgt	WATSON William Neil	31-12-44	218 Sqn
2201288	Sgt	WARREN Geoffrey Edward	25-08-44	640 Sqn	1824374	Sgt	WATT Alexander Steedman	12-08-44	1667 HCU
1865642	Sgt	WARREN George Henry	27-04-44	460 Sqn	50233	F/O	WATT Charles Burness	22-01-44	78 Sqn
1391942	Sgt	WARREN Henry Robert	4-05-44	9 Sqn	1571083	Sgt	WATT Hance	25-03-44	626 Sqn
126722	F/L	WARREN DFC James Walter	20-02-44	35 Sqn	659103	F/S	WATT John	23-04-44	78 Sqn
1318718	Sgt	WARREN Kenneth Robert James	4-05-44	103 Sqn	1572317	Sgt	WATT John Douglas Duncan	16-07-44	30 OTU
1893040	Sgt	WARREN Lewis Harold David	23-03-44	514 Sqn	625304	F/S	WATTERS James	29-01-44	10 Sqn
174942	P/O	WARREN Merrick George Munday	7-06-44	106 Sqn	2220664	Sgt	WATTON Arthur	27-08-44	57 Sqn
2220811	Sgt	WARRENGER Stanley Joseph	10-04-44	PFNTU	135663	F/O	WATTS Alfred John Spencer	11-04-44	83 Sqn
177190	P/O	WARRINGTON Arthur	17-06-44	434 Sqn	1818467	Sgt	WATTS Bernard Henry	28-04-44	15 Sqn
151648	F/O	WARRINGTON John William	24-09-44	50 Sqn	1653038	Sgt	WATTS Bernard John	5-07-44	463 Sqn
156612	S/L	WARWICK DFC James Brown	19-09-44	627 Sqn	815235	F/S	WATTS Douglas Haig	27-08-44	44 Sqn
1103095	F/S	WARWICK Norman	11-09-44	156 Sqn	1894230	Sgt	WATTS Ernest Leslie	22-05-44	207 Sqn
1434071	F/S	WARWICK Philip Charles	25-05-44	51 Sqn	153578	F/O	WATTS Henry James	14-10-44	12 Sqn
1318846	F/S	WARWICK Robert George	2-01-44	7 Sqn	159708	F/L	WATTS DFC Henry Wager Dixon	6-07-44	635 Sqn
1261897	Sgt	WASH Eric William	31-03-44	550 Sqn	1163515	F/S	WATTS James Edward	16-06-44	7 Sqn
909411	Sgt	WASHER Leonard George	31-03-44	576 Sqn	1874534	Sgt	WATTS John Martin	17-06-44	199 Sqn
183728	P/O	WASHINGTON Clifford George	26-08-44	514 Sqn	1316752	F/S	WATTS Laurence Roy	13-08-44	100 Sqn
1335368	F/S	WASPE Eric John	16-06-44	635 Sqn	158130	F/O	WATTS DFC Leonard Arthur	17-06-44	102 Sqn
1595194	Sgt	WASS William	15-07-44	103 Sqn	1890347	Sgt	WATTS Leonard George William	21-01-44	35 Sqn
1063520	Sgt	WASSON Sydney	16-03-44	625 Sqn	1183531	F/S	WATTS Raymond George	22-05-44	156 Sqn
574815	Sgt	WASTENEY John Walter	24-02-44	100 Sqn	149335	F/O	WATTS Raymond Philip	3-01-44	83 Sqn
169505	P/O	WATCHORN Stanley Ernest	14-01-44	101 Sqn	1851033	Sgt	WATTS Reginald Henry	27-08-44	100 Sqn
1621931	Sgt	WATERHOUSE Alan	30-12-44	76 Sqn	1818766	Sgt	WATTS Ronald Everest	2-01-44	405 Sqn

Service #	Rank	Name	Date	Sqn
1800090	F/S	WATTS Stanley George	18-11-44	35 Sqn
123041	F/L	WAUGH Kenneth Robert [USA]	25-04-44	97 Sqn
175910	F/O	WAUGH Robert John	18-09-44	57 Sqn
172413	P/O	WAUGH Thomas William	16-03-44	49 Sqn
125449	F/O	WAUGH William Robinson	20-02-44	640 Sqn
129744	F/L	WAY DFC William Henry Lewis	6-01-44	35 Sqn
145708	F/L	WAYCOTT DFM William Hugh	11-04-44	550 Sqn
156001	F/O	WEARE DFC Derek Arthur	21-12-44	109 Sqn
1897870	Sgt	WEATHERHEAD Edward Alexander	12-09-44	622 Sqn
605522	Sgt	WEATHERELL John Fenwick [USA]	28-04-44	166 Sqn
148094	F/O	WEATHERILL DFC Douglas Alfred	24-06-44	35 Sqn
1851185	Sgt	WEATHERILL Eric Stanley	21-01-44	7 Sqn
2211887	Sgt	WEATHERLEY Edwin	21-01-44	1667 HCU
175501	P/O	WEAVER Arthur John	6-07-44	635 Sqn
1428641	Sgt	WEAVER Frank Slater	16-03-44	57 Sqn
1836169	Sgt	WEAVER Philip Joseph	4-05-44	467 Sqn
1385225	Sgt	WEBB Angus Phillip	24-03-44	640 Sqn
1876603	Sgt	WEBB Bernard Frank	9-06-44	49 Sqn
1874126	F/S	WEBB Bernard William	25-05-44	582 Sqn
1477068	Sgt	WEBB Charles	23-05-44	166 Sqn
1629973	Sgt	WEBB Cyril Stanley	19-10-44	61 Sqn
1324450	Sgt	WEBB Dennis Anthony	27-08-44	12 Sqn
1894355	Sgt	WEBB Ernest William	17-06-44	550 Sqn
1387510	F/S	WEBB Frank Sidney	28-05-44	582 Sqn
1474327	Sgt	WEBB Frederick James	7-07-44	626 Sqn
1578041	Sgt	WEBB Harry Cyril	25-03-44	427 Sqn
103010	F/L	WEBB Hugh Julian Langdon	31-03-44	635 Sqn
1672977	Sgt	WEBB James Albert	3-02-44	28 OTU
1498781	F/S	WEBB John Cameron Keith	22-03-44	35 Sqn
1434950	Sgt	WEBB Joseph	22-03-44	50 Sqn
924401	Sgt	WEBB Kenneth Graham	18-08-44	103 Sqn
1601171	Sgt	WEBB Leonard Francis	28-04-44	102 Sqn
1866622	Sgt	WEBB Leonard Keith	28-06-44	106 Sqn
1393974	Sgt	WEBB Maurice	27-04-44	57 Sqn
3006137	Sgt	WEBB Peter	4-12-44	227 Sqn
1815316	Sgt	WEBB Peter William	30-01-44	514 Sqn
1473046	F/S	WEBB Richard Arthur	25-03-44	7 Sqn
658394	F/S	WEBB Ronald Bennett	12-05-44	103 Sqn
177636	P/O	WEBB Roy [USA]	6-08-44	83 Sqn
1890518	Sgt	WEBB William Albert	23-04-44	156 Sqn
941457	Sgt	WEBB William James	20-02-44	78 Sqn
146864	F/L	WEBBER DFC Dennis William	13-09-44	625 Sqn
1336908	Sgt	WEBBER Jeffery Francis Mawby	30-08-44	115 Sqn
1814708	Sgt	WEBBER John Charles	21-01-44	433 Sqn
1315671	Sgt	WEBBER Maurice James	27-04-44	44 Sqn
1035856	Sgt	WEBSTER Frank Russell	25-02-44	149 Sqn
1077210	W/O	WEBSTER James	20-09-44	619 Sqn
161587	P/O	WEBSTER James Osmond Rivers	29-01-44	77 Sqn
1559239	Sgt	WEBSTER John	25-03-44	35 Sqn
161469	P/O	WEBSTER John Frederick	14-01-44	156 Sqn
188178	P/O	WEBSTER John Layard Butler	6-11-44	619 Sqn
1285805	Sgt	WEBSTER Joseph Steward	23-06-44	76 Sqn
2219042	Sgt	WEBSTER Leslie Thompson	9-10-44	76 Sqn
1621346	Sgt	WEBSTER Nelson Donald	4-11-44	195 Sqn
617945	F/S	WEBSTER Reginald	4-05-44	101 Sqn
170390	F/O	WEDDELL John	27-11-44	161 Sqn
1502961	Sgt	WEDDLE George Andrew	25-02-44	44 Sqn
139700	F/O	WEEDON Reginald Francis	25-04-44	101 Sqn
1604605	Sgt	WEEDON Sidney Frederick	5-11-44	1660 HCU
1587438	Sgt	WEEDON Stanley William	11-04-44	49 Sqn
173310	F/O	WEEKES Norman Lennox [Kenya]	19-07-44	207 Sqn
168637	P/O	WEEKS Cyril Alfred	27-03-44	78 Sqn
43255	S/L	WEIGHTMAN DFC John Bentley	20-07-44	582 Sqn
1567144	Sgt	WEIR Allan Mackay	28-04-44	166 Sqn
141774	F/O	WEIR Graeme Robert Eric	6-12-44	608 Sqn
133093	F/O	WEIR James Kenneth	15-06-44	15 Sqn
1894060	Sgt	WEIR Leslie George	4-12-44	619 Sqn
1370487	Sgt	WEIR DFM Robert Walker Thomas	13-06-44	115 Sqn
110543	F/L	WEIR Walter	13-08-44	85 Sqn
1391600	Sgt	WELCH Brian Frederick	26-03-44	192 Sqn
170628	F/O	WELCH Eric Albert	6-12-44	10 Sqn
156100	F/L	WELCH Geoffrey Arthur	15-02-44	622 Sqn
2201513	Sgt	WELCH Ian	23-04-44	425 Sqn
175644	P/O	WELCH Robert	5-08-44	617 Sqn
943699	Sgt	WELCH William Harold	7-01-44	44 Sqn
141768	F/O	WELCHMAN Eliot John	13-07-44	166 Sqn
1819970	Sgt	WELDON Sydney Harold	14-01-44	44 Sqn
1396473	F/S	WELHAM Leonard Charles	10-11-44	97 Sqn
1359082	Sgt	WELLER Arthur Henry	16-03-44	35 Sqn
1895614	Sgt	WELLER Leslie Herbert George	20-02-44	460 Sqn
142903	F/O	WELLER DFM Richard James [Canada]	31-03-44	97 Sqn
1397598	Sgt	WELLFARE Richard Henry John	25-03-44	44 Sqn
1600882	Sgt	WELLS Francis Donald	24-03-44	15 Sqn
1334325	F/S	WELLS George Charles	30-07-44	514 Sqn
1836598	F/S	WELLS Jack Douglas	17-08-44	97 Sqn
137551	F/L	WELLS DFC John Hall	22-06-44	83 Sqn
175072	P/O	WELLS John William	11-06-44	625 Sqn
172480	P/O	WELLS Kenneth Arthur	11-06-44	100 Sqn
1802473	Sgt	WELLS Roy Albert	5-10-44	75 Sqn
177936	P/O	WELLS William	12-08-44	1667 HCU
1600789	Sgt	WELLS William Hubert	25-06-44	9 Sqn
1810864	Sgt	WELSH Kenneth Ernest	26-07-44	166 Sqn
1397743	Sgt	WELSTEAD Arthur James	11-02-44	30 OTU
1820590	Sgt	WEMYSS John Michael	23-10-44	429 Sqn
1380740	W/O	WENDES Robert John	16-11-44	109 Sqn
1458038	Sgt	WENHAM Philip Anthony 'Jack'	11-04-44	158 Sqn
1592743	Sgt	WENSLEY Douglas	19-07-44	207 Sqn
1437605	Sgt	WENYON Conrad Gallimore	1-07-44	101 Sqn
1318617	F/S	WERRETT Ronald Arthur	16-03-44	115 Sqn
152067	F/O	WESLEY John Marcus	7-06-44	115 Sqn
42946	F/L	WESSON AFM Richard Edward	6-01-44	619 Sqn
2218652	Sgt	WEST Archibald	4-11-44	625 Sqn
54707	F/O	WEST Arthur	29-07-44	103 Sqn
1316550	Sgt	WEST Arthur Reginald Edgar	29-01-44	97 Sqn
1851950	Sgt	WEST Brian Douglas	8-05-44	106 Sqn
1337836	Sgt	WEST Brian Sidney James	2-01-44	405 Sqn
1502402	Sgt	WEST Cecil Reginald	12-03-44	199 Sqn
1330246	Sgt	WEST Charles Francis	24-04-44	425 Sqn
1605603	Sgt	WEST Charles William	12-10-44	14 OTU
1335412	F/S	WEST Frederick Thomas	20-01-44	83 Sqn
1442340	Sgt	WEST George	27-01-44	576 Sqn
1334079	F/S	WEST George William	31-03-44	51 Sqn
1852405	Sgt	WEST Guidleroy	1-06-44	625 Sqn
1523926	Sgt	WEST Harry	31-03-44	514 Sqn
1517246	Sgt	WEST Harry Bateman	10-04-44	57 Sqn
1852331	Sgt	WEST Harry Charles	15-02-44	15 Sqn
1313737	F/S	WEST Harry George	5-07-44	207 Sqn
1592150	Sgt	WEST John Frederick	29-07-44	49 Sqn
1600034	Sgt	WEST Kenneth Frederick	5-07-44	576 Sqn
170722	P/O	WEST Norman Edward	15-01-44	626 Sqn
1819926	Sgt	WEST Reginald John	24-06-44	12 Sqn
124663	F/O	WEST Robert Alexander	27-01-44	61 Sqn
173984	P/O	WEST Robert John	29-06-44	77 Sqn
1575466	Sgt	WEST Ronald	15-03-44	9 Sqn
1811334	Sgt	WEST Ronald Charles	6-10-44	78 Sqn
1868545	Sgt	WEST William George Edwin	31-07-44	57 Sqn
1465311	Sgt	WESTBROOK Ronald Henry	20-09-44	622 Sqn
175159	F/O	WESTCOTT Lawrence Edward	26-08-44	103 Sqn
1812220	Sgt	WESTCOTT Stanley Anthony	6-12-44	103 Sqn
133578	F/O	WESTERGAARD DFC Niels Erik	2-01-44	630 Sqn
1642409	Sgt	WESTERN Reginald Sydney	21-01-44	76 Sqn
552023	Cpl	WESTGARTH John	29-12-44	514 Sqn
178310	F/O	WESTGATE Ernest [Canada]	12-09-44	44 Sqn
1588698	Sgt	WESTHEAD Francis	20-02-44	630 Sqn
650407	Sgt	WESTHEAD Thomas Henry	31-08-44	1654 HCU
2200207	Sgt	WESTMORELAND Thomas Fowler	29-01-44	207 Sqn
1115103	F/S	WESTON Albert John	20-11-44	75 Sqn
134059	F/L	WESTON Arthur William	10-05-44	97 Sqn

Service No.	Rank	Name	Date	Squadron
1437390	F/S	WESTON Cyril John	16-06-44	7 Sqn
37703	S/L	WESTON Ralph Henry	7-07-44	166 Sqn
1231220	Sgt	WESTON William Roy	29-01-44	57 Sqn
1863967	Sgt	WESTROPE Richard Strickland	29-07-44	408 Sqn
1602927	Sgt	WEVILL Reginald Thomas	31-03-44	61 Sqn
1578857	Sgt	WHALE Leslie Frank	6-12-44	57 Sqn
1894853	Sgt	WHALE Percival Frank	1-05-44	514 Sqn
1212110	Sgt	WHALE Ronald Cecil	6-01-44	97 Sqn
973270	Sgt	WHALLEY Richard	22-03-44	9 Sqn
173131	P/O	WHALLEY DFC Roy	4-05-44	576 Sqn
1034217	Sgt	WHALLEY Wilfred	23-05-44	90 Sqn
2218734	Sgt	WHALLEY Wilfred Fitton	5-11-44	1660 HCU
575752	Sgt	WHAMMOND David Lumgair	17-06-44	103 Sqn
104524	F/L	WHARMBY Roy Bernard	14-01-44	7 Sqn
1610054	Sgt	WHARTON Albert	8-06-44	115 Sqn
1578013	F/S	WHARTON Stanley	4-06-44	635 Sqn
164577	P/O	WHEATLEY Reginald Frank	19-08-44	635 Sqn
1335605	Sgt	WHEATSTONE Cyril Frederick	15-01-44	626 Sqn
1339602	Sgt	WHEELDON Paul Robert	20-02-44	625 Sqn
1393912	Sgt	WHEELER George	20-02-44	83 Sqn
1552002	F/S	WHEELER George William	25-07-44	15 Sqn
1586690	Sgt	WHEELER John Francis Charles	23-10-44	1656 HCU
2208907	F/S	WHEELER Joseph	25-07-44	83 Sqn
1388461	F/S	WHEELER Leslie William Charles	24-03-44	15 Sqn
1561530	Sgt	WHEELER Mark Thomas	4-05-44	12 Sqn
1312367	F/S	WHEELER Raymond Walter	16-02-44	77 Sqn
173594	P/O	WHEELER Reginald Augustus	10-03-44	207 Sqn
656759	Sgt	WHEELER Sidney William	24-03-44	640 Sqn
76594	W/C	WHEELER DFC* MC* Order of St. Stanislaus [Russia] Vashon James	23-03-44	207 Sqn
175807	P/O	WHEELHOUSE Clifford James	20-04-44	420 Sqn
1796208	Sgt	WHELAN John Joseph [Eire]	30-01-44	100 Sqn
1796581	Sgt	WHELAN Leo Patrick [Eire]	13-07-44	103 Sqn
172971	P/O	WHETTON Leonard	26-08-44	626 Sqn
162593	P/O	WHEWAY Ronald James	3-01-44	7 Sqn
1232608	Sgt	WHEWELL Thomas Birtwistle	22-06-44	49 Sqn
1220052	F/S	WHICHELOW Harold Marcus	20-02-44	514 Sqn
81668	F/L	WHIFFEN George Kenneth	5-07-44	105 Sqn
1800084	Sgt	WHIFFIN Douglas James	26-07-44	1657 HCU
2216127	Sgt	WHIMPENNEY Arnold	16-02-44	199 Sqn
980135	F/S	WHINFIELD Robert Ford	27-04-44	619 Sqn
173314	F/O	WHIPP Leonard Priestley	19-10-44	105 Sqn
1549110	Sgt	WHISK Charles Robson 'Peter'	7-03-44	18 OTU
65531	F/L	WHITAKER DFC Leslie Lawrence	4-05-44	161 Sqn
1439598	Sgt	WHITAKER Ralph	16-02-44	102 Sqn
138797	F/O	WHITAKER Richard Arthur	31-03-44	61 Sqn
168796	F/O	WHITAKER Stanley	23-10-44	625 Sqn
1624919	Sgt	WHITBREAD Dennis Lawson	5-08-44	433 Sqn
1437285	F/S	WHITBREAD Leslie James Henry	31-03-44	514 Sqn
1868535	Sgt	WHITE Alan Howard	20-09-44	514 Sqn
1415106	Sgt	WHITE Alan Trevor	29-07-44	12 Sqn
1489085	Sgt	WHITE Alec	28-04-44	51 Sqn
1593166	Sgt	WHITE Alfred Ernest	11-06-44	625 Sqn
1402780	Sgt	WHITE Bernard	12-12-44	195 Sqn
155945	F/O	WHITE Bernard Arthur	28-05-44	166 Sqn
1654063	Sgt	WHITE Bernard Gerrard	20-02-44	12 Sqn
179590	P/O	WHITE Cyril Arthur	25-08-44	640 Sqn
1567188	Sgt	WHITE David	25-05-44	576 Sqn
1534947	F/S	WHITE Douglas	23-03-44	106 Sqn
1579461	Sgt	WHITE Douglas Bertram	22-05-44	622 Sqn
1586005	Sgt	WHITE Douglas John	11-05-44	515 Sqn
169611	F/O	WHITE Douglas John Kenneth	14-10-44	550 Sqn
1203756	Sgt	WHITE Edward	15-02-44	207 Sqn
1452881	Sgt	WHITE Edward	20-02-44	49 Sqn
1593954	Sgt	WHITE Edward Arthur	22-12-44	9 Sqn
653213	Sgt	WHITE Eric	13-06-44	426 Sqn
1892386	Sgt	WHITE Frederick Albert	11-10-44	19 OTU
1806890	Sgt	WHITE Frederick Cyril	25-07-44	1661 HCU
1396093	Sgt	WHITE Frederick Leslie Alan	6-07-44	149 Sqn
161409	F/L	WHITE George Baston	22-12-44	189 Sqn
1801266	Sgt	WHITE George Frederick	25-03-44	460 Sqn
55958	P/O	WHITE Jack	27-08-44	166 Sqn
657977	W/O	WHITE DFM James	25-03-44	630 Sqn
1562042	F/S	WHITE James	11-09-44	35 Sqn
1548168	Sgt	WHITE John Arthur	11-04-44	466 Sqn
153233	F/O	WHITE John Joseph	17-05-44	29 OTU
1595759	Sgt	WHITE Lawrence	23-12-44	35 Sqn
1897615	Sgt	WHITE Leonard Walter John	30-12-44	156 Sqn
1894412	Sgt	WHITE Leslie George	28-06-44	460 Sqn
186863	P/O	WHITE Leslie William	23-10-44	76 Sqn
1836179	Sgt	WHITE Melvyn	27-04-44	630 Sqn
988891	Sgt	WHITE Peter Sigston	2-03-44	630 Sqn
1802994	F/S	WHITE Richard	12-05-44	103 Sqn
1671475	Sgt	WHITE Robert Ian	17-09-44	102 Sqn
1437767	Sgt	WHITE Stanley	28-05-44	51 Sqn
1438267	Sgt	WHITE Terrence	20-02-44	12 Sqn
925205	Sgt	WHITE Thomas	1-07-44	626 Sqn
1765084	Sgt	WHITE Thomas Reginald	11-11-44	227 Sqn
1600618	F/S	WHITE William Albert	18-10-44	630 Sqn
1311804	W/O	WHITE DFM William Courtney	20-04-44	635 Sqn
1099290	Sgt	WHITE William John	25-05-44	78 Sqn
177840	F/O	WHITE William Leslie	29-04-44	12 Sqn
160143	P/O	WHITE William Proffitt	29-01-44	77 Sqn
1393334	F/S	WHITEAR Leslie Henry	14-01-44	7 Sqn
160167	P/O	WHITEBEARD Roy Edward	24-02-44	156 Sqn
1425903	Sgt	WHITEFIELD Cyril Franklyn	25-09-44	463 Sqn
49795	F/L	WHITEFIELD Kenneth William	11-11-44	619 Sqn
1253817	Sgt	WHITEFIELD Leslie Wilfred	25-02-44	156 Sqn
1233064	Sgt	WHITEHALL Raymond Percival	21-07-44	514 Sqn
3000298	F/S	WHITEHAND Thomas William	26-07-44	44 Sqn
2202809	Sgt	WHITEHEAD Alan	15-04-44	30 OTU
2206975	Sgt	WHITEHEAD Alfred	31-03-44	635 Sqn
1542922	Sgt	WHITEHEAD Augustine	1-05-44	514 Sqn
1515878	Sgt	WHITEHEAD Barry	1-07-44	101 Sqn
1621003	F/S	WHITEHEAD Colin	29-10-44	207 Sqn
55845	P/O	WHITEHEAD Colin George William	21-07-44	578 Sqn
126772	F/L	WHITEHEAD Francis Allen	28-01-44	103 Sqn
1333766	F/S	WHITEHEAD Henry Peter	16-06-44	635 Sqn
1214028	W/O	WHITEHOUSE DFC Alfred	27-04-44	83 Sqn
1200847	W/O	WHITEHOUSE DFC Burney Edgar Richard	21-06-44	7 Sqn
1514358	F/S	WHITEHURST Samuel	19-07-44	619 Sqn
1562120	Sgt	WHITELAW Robert	24-03-44	158 Sqn
1591170	Sgt	WHITELEY Jack	23-09-44	101 Sqn
1004530	F/S	WHITELEY Herbert	22-03-44	49 Sqn
1492814	Sgt	WHITELEY Maurice	19-07-44	50 Sqn
2228282	Sgt	WHITELEY Ronald	28-10-44	12 OTU
1474740	Sgt	WHITELEY Stanley	8-01-44	138 Sqn
1380098	Sgt	WHITELEY Thomas	14-01-44	44 Sqn
1146149	Sgt	WHITELOCK Cyril	4-05-44	50 Sqn
1513141	Sgt	WHITESIDE Thomas John	28-05-44	427 Sqn
1851249	Sgt	WHITFIELD Duncan Robert Roland Lewis	22-06-44	44 Sqn
1622364	Sgt	WHITFIELD Eric Norman	31-03-44	166 Sqn
1581969	Sgt	WHITFIELD Harold William	11-04-44	640 Sqn
1595057	Sgt	WHITFIELD James	25-07-44	57 Sqn
2216044	Sgt	WHITFIELD William Ernest	21-01-44	101 Sqn
1568125	Sgt	WHITHAM Jack Howarth	21-07-44	158 Sqn
1893009	Sgt	WHITING Geoffrey Walter	25-07-44	15 Sqn
171177	P/O	WHITING Jack Maxwell	22-05-44	630 Sqn
978030	Sgt	WHITLEY James Woodburn	31-03-44	550 Sqn
1803326	Sgt	WHITLEY Norman George	7-06-44	83 Sqn
173057	P/O	WHITLEY Richard	12-05-44	103 Sqn
154368	F/O	WHITMAN Alfred Albert	8-10-44	11 OTU
149354	F/O	WHITMILL Harry	10-04-44	515 Sqn
152649	F/O	WHITMORE Charles Bernard	30-08-44	103 Sqn
1581406	Sgt	WHITTAKER Dennis Graham	15-02-44	158 Sqn
1877325	Sgt	WHITTAKER Frederick George	28-10-44	76 Sqn

Number	Rank	Name	Date	Unit
1601229	F/S	WHITTAKER James	25-08-44	10 Sqn
1380950	F/S	WHITTALL Eric Charles	27-08-44	90 Sqn
1852098	Sgt	WHITTICK Thomas Leonard John	22-05-44	550 Sqn
1609929	Sgt	WHITTINGTON Frank Henry	25-07-44	622 Sqn
1851166	Sgt	WHITTINGTON Roy	16-09-44	90 Sqn
1106196	Sgt	WHITTLE Cyril	23-04-44	103 Sqn
1851739	Sgt	WHITTLE Geoffrey Rex	3-06-44	76 Sqn
1811022	Sgt	WHITTLE Robert	30-08-44	21 OTU
1836276	Sgt	WHITTLES Gilbert Wheeler	27-04-44	44 Sqn
127109	F/L	WHITTLESTONE DFC Frank Sydney	29-01-44	7 Sqn
1490379	Sgt	WHITTOCK Wallace Frank Alan	21-01-44	51 Sqn
1337437	F/S	WHITTOME John Edward Gifford	22-06-44	619 Sqn
1594668	Sgt	WHITWORTH Arnold	24-09-44	50 Sqn
1170191	Sgt	WHITWORTH John Gibson	25-07-44	103 Sqn
179622	P/O	WHYBRO Russell George	29-07-44	434 Sqn
1217557	Sgt	WHYBROW Leonard Gilbert	24-07-44	582 Sqn
1439043	Sgt	WHYLES Gerard	23-09-44	12 Sqn
171587	P/O	WHYTE Alan Charles	15-02-44	115 Sqn
175620	F/O	WHYTE Gordon Gambley	26-08-44	300 Sqn
1559798	F/S	WHYTE John	23-05-44	90 Sqn
130298	F/S	WHYTE John Anderson	23-01-44	161 Sqn
1569858	Sgt	WHYTE William Shepherd	29-06-44	102 Sqn
179206	F/O	WIBBERLEY Leslie	27-09-44	115 Sqn
116659	F/L	WIBBERLEY Robert David	13-05-44	640 Sqn
1892800	Sgt	WICKENDEN Harold Walter	30-08-44	630 Sqn
151091	F/O	WICKENS Ronald Charles	25-04-44	97 Sqn
186429	P/O	WICKENS Thomas Roy	6-11-44	207 Sqn
52018	F/O	WICKER DFC Edwin Jack	26-08-44	83 Sqn
611981	F/S	WICKHAM Reginald Amesbury	27-04-44	619 Sqn
640170	F/S	WICKLAND Samuel Vernon	23-09-44	61 Sqn
1376921	Sgt	WICKS Edward Charles	10-06-44	10 Sqn
158672	F/O	WIDGER DFM William Henry	4-05-44	101 Sqn
1585086	Sgt	WIDDOWS Maurice Hubert	25-02-44	1661 HCU
157874	F/O	WIENER Derek Abraham	23-05-44	103 Sqn
33203	S/L	WIGG Philip Mervyn	21-04-44	57 Sqn
1582724	F/S	WIGGIN George Harold	28-10-44	115 Sqn
1584679	Sgt	WIGGIN John Charles	8-08-44	90 Sqn
2201712	Sgt	WIGGINS Alan	27-01-44	463 Sqn
1651152	Sgt	WIGGINS Edward Ernest James	7-06-44	106 Sqn
1593975	Sgt	WIGHAM Maurice Hard	7-06-44	106 Sqn
1823065	Sgt	WIGHAM William	19-04-44	149 Sqn
1590994	F/S	WILBY George Arthur	24-06-44	156 Sqn
1595172	Sgt	WILBY Jack Madeley	5-11-44	102 Sqn
1584697	Sgt	WILBY James	15-03-44	463 Sqn
629855	F/S	WILCE Charles John Geoffrey	6-01-44	57 Sqn
1897947	Sgt	WILCOCK Frederick	23-09-44	9 Sqn
52813	F/O	WILCOCK Kenneth	15-02-44	103 Sqn
144458	F/O	WILCOCK Norman Bunker	22-06-44	630 Sqn
3040692	Sgt	WILCOX Ernest	6-12-44	10 Sqn
1583103	F/S	WILCOX William Roland	23-09-44	50 Sqn
2208918	Sgt	WILD Harold	27-04-44	106 Sqn
1451051	F/S	WILDE Edward	23-04-44	514 Sqn
121474	F/L	WILDE Eric Lawless	16-09-44	157 Sqn
143851	F/O	WILDE Kenneth Hubert Dearden	6-01-44	576 Sqn
142148	F/O	WILDEN Robert Fussell	13-06-44	578 Sqn
1334719	Sgt	WILDER Denis Frederick Dean	26-02-44	166 Sqn
1836301	Sgt	WILDING Norman Vaughan	29-07-44	75 Sqn
936016	Sgt	WILDSMITH Percy Arthur	15-08-44	207 Sqn
1575513	Sgt	WILKES Eric Arthur	24-02-44	75 Sqn
156139	F/O	WILKES DFM Harry	9-06-44	26 OTU
947118	F/S	WILKINS Charles Laurence Yorke	14-01-44	7 Sqn
1601570	Sgt	WILKINS Dennis George Edward	25-07-44	1667 HCU
153130	F/O	WILKINS Herbert	16-09-44	582 Sqn
858830	Sgt	WILKINS John	2-08-44	467 Sqn
1396525	Sgt	WILKINS Sidney Charles	4-05-44	50 Sqn
159932	P/O	WILKINS Thomas Ernest	30-01-44	83 Sqn
1622716	Sgt	WILKINSON Albert Henry	16-03-44	630 Sqn
1801871	Sgt	WILKINSON Arthur William	18-04-44	433 Sqn
1684691	Sgt	WILKINSON Cecil	14-10-44	153 Sqn
2220135	Sgt	WILKINSON Dennis	8-08-44	630 Sqn
1029028	Sgt	WILKINSON Edward	16-05-44	625 Sqn
2209695	Sgt	WILKINSON James	4-05-44	9 Sqn
175500	P/O	WILKINSON James Hargreaves	27-04-44	78 Sqn
151058	F/O	WILKINSON John	31-01-44	626 Sqn
1590798	Sgt	WILKINSON Joseph	12-09-44	576 Sqn
175313	P/O	WILKINSON Laurence Edward	22-05-44	115 Sqn
3020214	Sgt	WILKINSON Matthew	15-07-44	1651 HCU
124557	S/L	WILKINSON DFC Flying Cross [Holland] Reginald Eric	27-11-44	161 Sqn
1585068	F/S	WILKINSON Richard John	21-07-44	75 Sqn
1523185	Sgt	WILKINSON Thomas Swinbank	22-01-44	640 Sqn
1338279	F/S	WILKINSON Victor Lawrence	13-09-44	90 Sqn
151361	F/O	WILKINSON DFC William Bertram	8-07-44	106 Sqn
148331	F/O	WILKS Arthur Alexander	28-05-44	103 Sqn
50789	P/O	WILLARD Ernest Arthur Chenery	2-01-44	61 Sqn
1391875	Sgt	WILLCOCKS Herbert Francis	13-04-44	90 Sqn
175985	P/O	WILLES Sidney Hulbert	4-05-44	207 Sqn
1575690	Sgt	WILLETT Kevin Joseph	11-04-44	576 Sqn
1603136	Sgt	WILLETT William Edward Charles	7-09-44	17 OTU
174529	P/O	WILLIAMS DFC Albert	13-06-44	12 Sqn
637452	Sgt	WILLIAMS Alfred Ronald	13-06-44	625 Sqn
1895323	Sgt	WILLIAMS Alfred Thomas	31-03-44	427 Sqn
929571	F/S	WILLIAMS Arthur	15-02-44	10 Sqn
61974	S/L	WILLIAMS DFC Arthur Llewelyn	26-08-44	83 Sqn
1836434	Sgt	WILLIAMS Benjamin Robert	22-05-44	514 Sqn
1853012	Sgt	WILLIAMS Bernard Ivor	8-11-44	27 OTU
1708161	Sgt	WILLIAMS Bertram Trevor	3-06-44	166 Sqn
1316112	F/S	WILLIAMS Celt	31-12-44	218 Sqn
1396380	Sgt	WILLIAMS Cyril	19-04-44	625 Sqn
178568	P/O	WILLIAMS David Gethin	23-06-44	97 Sqn
1386621	F/S	WILLIAMS David Henry	23-04-44	9 Sqn
129004	F/L	WILLIAMS DFC David Laing	27-04-44	83 Sqn
155999	F/O	WILLIAMS DFC Douglas Knight	5-07-44	105 Sqn
171772	P/O	WILLIAMS Edmund Howard	22-03-44	35 Sqn
1836261	Sgt	WILLIAMS Elved Thomas Henry	22-11-44	1660 HCU
157067	F/O	WILLIAMS DFC Eric Albert	11-04-44	61 Sqn
147967	F/O	WILLIAMS DFM Frank	28-05-44	640 Sqn
1896337	Sgt	WILLIAMS Frederick Charles	13-08-44	76 Sqn
1810983	Sgt	WILLIAMS George Henry	14-01-44	44 Sqn
1542376	F/S	WILLIAMS Gordon Deane	21-07-44	90 Sqn
155073	F/O	WILLIAMS Gordon Howard	23-04-44	100 Sqn
173444	P/O	WILLIAMS Graham Harries	31-03-44	101 Sqn
1626195	Sgt	WILLIAMS Gwilym	24-03-44	207 Sqn
651579	F/S	WILLIAMS Gwilym Jones	29-01-44	1660 HCU
1312589	Sgt	WILLIAMS Hadyn George	20-02-44	12 Sqn
1579033	Sgt	WILLIAMS Harold Lees	12-02-44	12 OTU
624020	Sgt	WILLIAMS Harold Lloyd	15-07-44	1651 HCU
1336295	Sgt	WILLIAMS Harold William	21-01-44	77 Sqn
2220951	Sgt	WILLIAMS Harry Roy	12-12-44	218 Sqn
1652120	Sgt	WILLIAMS Idwal	29-07-44	550 Sqn
1415839	F/S	WILLIAMS Ieuan Glyndwyr	24-03-44	115 Sqn
188534	P/O	WILLIAMS Ivor Gordon	21-11-44	49 Sqn
1891702	F/S	WILLIAMS James George	24-12-44	102 Sqn
976202	W/O	WILLIAMS John	3-06-44	10 Sqn
2210669	Sgt	WILLIAMS John	12-12-44	218 Sqn
1866421	Sgt	WILLIAMS John Albert	4-05-44	625 Sqn
1819867	Sgt	WILLIAMS John Clifford	11-04-44	158 Sqn
106173	F/L	WILLIAMS MiD John Francis	6-04-44	107 Sqn
127132	F/O	WILLIAMS DFC John Hubert	10-01-44	1652 HCU
134016	F/L	WILLIAMS John Indoe	29-06-44	432 Sqn
161058	F/O	WILLIAMS John Kenneth	22-01-44	514 Sqn
1404580	F/S	WILLIAMS John Kerwin Stafford	15-02-44	7 Sqn
1585416	Sgt	WILLIAMS John Roland	20-02-44	514 Sqn
1381756	W/O	WILLIAMS John Theodore	2-01-44	7 Sqn
1320247	F/S	WILLIAMS Joseph	25-05-44	103 Sqn
533822	F/S	WILLIAMS Kenneth Hapkin	4-11-44	101 Sqn
908406	Sgt	WILLIAMS DFM Kenneth Percy Charles	11-04-44	550 Sqn

Service No	Rank	Name	Date	Unit
1095530	Sgt	WILLIAMS Leonard	24-12-44	35 Sqn
1627306	F/S	WILLIAMS Leslie Edward	7-06-44	619 Sqn
643674	Sgt	WILLIAMS Mervyn Stephen	2-01-44	61 Sqn
2220606	Sgt	WILLIAMS Norman	4-11-44	51 Sqn
1652811	Sgt	WILLIAMS Raymond George	8-05-44	106 Sqn
649053	Sgt	WILLIAMS Reginald Alfred	16-02-44	199 Sqn
1585239	Sgt	WILLIAMS Reginald George	9-03-44	1667 HCU
1621909	Sgt	WILLIAMS Richard Arthur	27-07-44	44 Sqn
2218917	Sgt	WILLIAMS Robert Gwilym	15-10-44	101 Sqn
1502966	F/S	WILLIAMS Robert Stanley	13-08-44	100 Sqn
859670	Sgt	WILLIAMS Roland	25-07-44	166 Sqn
1853521	Sgt	WILLIAMS Ronald Ernest	17-08-44	630 Sqn
126045	F/L	WILLIAMS DFC Ronald Henry	7-10-44	617 Sqn
1076863	W/O	WILLIAMS Sidney Buxton	2-09-44	57 Sqn
1709098	Sgt	WILLIAMS Thomas Kenneth Morgan	20-02-44	550 Sqn
169155	F/O	WILLIAMS DFC Victor George	23-09-44	97 Sqn
1320281	F/S	WILLIAMS William Frederick	10-03-44	90 Sqn
1750303	Sgt	WILLIAMS William Frederick	27-04-44	44 Sqn
141572	F/O	WILLIAMS William Henry George	22-01-44	578 Sqn
1413546	Sgt	WILLIAMS William Iorwerth	11-06-44	75 Sqn
1338351	Sgt	WILLIAMS William Robert	25-02-44	550 Sqn
53787	F/O	WILLIAMS William Thomas	16-06-44	582 Sqn
1374587	Sgt	WILLIAMSON Alexander Ritchie	12-10-44	166 Sqn
1777442	Sgt	WILLIAMSON Donald	26-08-44	214 Sqn
1084486	Sgt	WILLIAMSON James Ashcroft	4-12-44	189 Sqn
1866698	Sgt	WILLIAMSON Thomas Henry	25-06-44	149 Sqn
646518	F/S	WILLIAMSON-RATTRAY Henry Charles	1-07-44	10 Sqn
1431809	Sgt	WILLIES Joseph William	22-04-44	1654 HCU
1204293	Sgt	WILLIS Frederick Charles	25-02-44	460 Sqn
2208994	Sgt	WILLIS John Frederick	19-04-44	57 Sqn
1321154	Sgt	WILLIS Raymond	14-01-44	550 Sqn
1015771	F/S	WILLIS MiD Robert Arthur	13-08-44	619 Sqn
1318460	F/S	WILLIS Ronald John	13-06-44	100 Sqn
1646386	Sgt	WILLIS Thomas William	1-07-44	12 Sqn
1546247	F/S	WILLIS Victor Sinclair	22-12-44	9 Sqn
1323441	Sgt	WILLIS-CULPITT Peter Frederick	18-03-44	115 Sqn
159468	P/O	WILLMOTT Anthony Patrick	1-02-44	627 Sqn
1585813	Sgt	WILLMOTT Reginald William	29-01-44	7 Sqn
1352077	Sgt	WILLS Frederick David	5-07-44	460 Sqn
1799461	Sgt	WILLS Robert	15-10-44	166 Sqn
1420600	Sgt	WILLSDON Donald	15-02-44	550 Sqn
151016	F/O	WILLSON John Rivers Herbert	11-04-44	161 Sqn
1894529	Sgt	WILLSON John William	23-06-44	100 Sqn
1389663	Sgt	WILLSON William Vernon	24-03-44	51 Sqn
120497	F/L	WILMER John	22-07-44	1655 MTU
1810273	F/S	WILMER Maurice Charles Alfred	25-04-44	192 Sqn
941200	Sgt	WILMSHURST Ernest Arthur	11-05-44	1654 HCU
1332031	Sgt	WILMSHURST Leslie Thomas	3-01-44	7 Sqn
1563280	Sgt	WILSON Alexander	21-07-44	101 Sqn
615819	Sgt	WILSON Arthur	21-07-44	514 Sqn
130614	F/L	WILSON DFC Charles Thomas	29-01-44	97 Sqn
1891616	Sgt	WILSON Colin Francis	5-07-44	424 Sqn
75996	S/L	WILSON DFC Colin Howard	31-03-44	7 Sqn
1894608	Sgt	WILSON Cyril George	15-06-44	78 Sqn
1573648	Sgt	WILSON David Desmond	29-10-44	582 Sqn
1593152	Sgt	WILSON Dennis Alfred	25-06-44	49 Sqn
1768206	Sgt	WILSON Donald Jack [South Africa]	12-05-44	15 Sqn
160162	P/O	WILSON Eric Benjamin	25-05-44	78 Sqn
995612	Sgt	WILSON Francis	20-01-44	57 Sqn
1863415	Sgt	WILSON Francis James	27-08-44	57 Sqn
89417	F/O	WILSON Frank Newton	11-05-44	424 Sqn
1520804	Sgt	WILSON George	26-03-44	192 Sqn
123621	S/L	WILSON DSO DFC George Heath	25-06-44	139 Sqn
1580045	Sgt	WILSON George William	13-05-44	576 Sqn
2213828	Sgt	WILSON George William	13-08-44	622 Sqn
141094	F/L	WILSON DSO DFC DFM Granville	6-09-44	7 Sqn
172790	P/O	WILSON DFM Harry Louis	15-06-44	582 Sqn
1852344	Sgt	WILSON Henry	6-04-44	207 Sqn
1797767	Sgt	WILSON Henry James [Eire]	11-04-44	83 Sqn
1205705	Cpl	WILSON Herbert Charles	9-04-44	3 LFS
178769	P/O	WILSON Hugh	26-08-44	90 Sqn
1691004	Sgt	WILSON Jack	25-04-44	626 Sqn
1079426	F/S	WILSON James	18-12-44	207 Sqn
127202	F/L	WILSON James Maclean [Brazil]	9-11-44	625 Sqn
1521100	Sgt	WILSON John	28-04-44	103 Sqn
1553317	Sgt	WILSON John	30-01-44	207 Sqn
901726	Sgt	WILSON John Joseph	23-05-44	57 Sqn
183037	P/O	WILSON John Leslie [Canada]	7-10-44	426 Sqn
175818	P/O	WILSON John Horsburgh	5-07-44	207 Sqn
150146	F/O	WILSON Joseph Raymond	5-11-44	166 Sqn
1603668	F/S	WILSON Kenneth George	2-03-44	76 Sqn
1394349	Sgt	WILSON Leonard John	21-01-44	102 Sqn
3040116	Sgt	WILSON Patrick Byram	4-12-44	15 Sqn
1806740	Sgt	WILSON Patrick John	12-09-44	214 Sqn
1459231	Sgt	WILSON Peter Collinson	25-04-44	635 Sqn
1602530	Sgt	WILSON Robert Arthur	4-05-44	103 Sqn
1822849	Sgt	WILSON Robert Heddleston Farquhar	29-07-44	50 Sqn
1676659	Sgt	WILSON Ronald	18-04-44	9 Sqn
1804802	Sgt	WILSON Ronald Charles	30-01-44	101 Sqn
149138	F/O	WILSON DFC Ronald Douglas	4-05-44	101 Sqn
134708	F/O	WILSON Ronald John	21-01-44	101 Sqn
1480809	Sgt	WILSON Stanley	4-05-44	166 Sqn
173804	P/O	WILSON Stanley Raymond	31-05-44	1654 HCU
169117	P/O	WILSON Thomas	26-03-44	10 Sqn
1544912	Sgt	WILSON William	23-04-44	514 Sqn
1800221	F/S	WILSON William	2-11-44	102 Sqn
142063	F/O	WILSON William David	21-07-44	626 Sqn
1560313	Sgt	WILSON William Marshall	6-01-44	7 Sqn
1587833	Sgt	WILTON Alan Henry	24-09-44	85 OTU
143921	F/O	WILTON Raymond Howard	13-06-44	15 Sqn
150168	F/O	WIMBERLEY Michael Arabin	24-03-44	78 Sqn
105568	F/O	WIMLETT Denys Ronald	25-03-44	12 Sqn
1377472	W/O	WINCH Charles Alfred	13-09-44	20 OTU
183758	P/O	WINCHESTER Ronald John	13-09-44	90 Sqn
1580762	F/S	WINCOTT Arthur Ronald	6-06-44	149 Sqn
1474215	F/S	WINDER Herbert	23-10-44	76 Sqn
1081479	Sgt	WINDER Roland	29-01-44	166 Sqn
1576263	F/S	WINDLE Albert Edwin	27-08-44	625 Sqn
1590864	Sgt	WINDSOR Walter Richard	10-01-44	1652 HCU
2208906	Sgt	WINFINDALE Robert John	30-01-44	106 Sqn
1547914	Sgt	WINKLEY William	1-05-44	514 Sqn
1503796	F/S	WINLOW David	7-08-44	156 Sqn
2206056	Sgt	WINN Anthony	4-12-44	1661 HCU
938040	Sgt	WINN Thomas	26-02-44	463 Sqn
1608959	Sgt	WINSLADE Henry Charles James	27-08-44	57 Sqn
1614511	Sgt	WINTER Cyril Arthur	24-12-44	35 Sqn
1231043	F/S	WINTER John Seymore	23-12-44	35 Sqn
169680	F/O	WINTER Russell Harry	28-07-44	78 Sqn
153353	F/O	WINTON Edward	20-11-44	186 Sqn
1865130	Sgt	WINZAR Ernest Holmes	11-12-44	1651 HCU
172872	F/L	WISBEY DFC James	28-06-44	640 Sqn
175235	F/O	WISBY Bernard John	17-12-44	156 Sqn
1580499	F/S	WISE Geoffrey Norman	12-09-44	50 Sqn
1835959	Sgt	WISE John Grenfell	16-03-44	49 Sqn
1397932	Sgt	WISE Sidney Frederick	20-01-44	1657 HCU
1603151	Sgt	WISEMAN Basil Guy	11-04-44	460 Sqn
120629	F/L	WISEMAN James Ian	22-02-44	218 Sqn
1323019	Sgt	WITCOMB Leslie John	28-05-44	166 Sqn
1662259	F/O	WITHERDEN Walter Harry	22-12-44	189 Sqn
1340905	Sgt	WITHERS David	19-07-44	630 Sqn
1737508	Sgt	WITHERS Dennis James	6-07-44	161 Sqn
3050215	Sgt	WITHERS Percy Stanley	27-08-44	622 Sqn
1628244	Sgt	WITHINGTON John Alfred	2-01-44	106 Sqn
1578093	F/S	WITHINSHAW Roy	25-04-44	619 Sqn
1434183	Sgt	WITNEY George Henry	22-03-44	207 Sqn
2204999	Sgt	WITTY George Frederick	22-06-44	49 Sqn

1397910	F/S	WITTY Wilfrid Thomas	29-10-44	582 Sqn		1160474	Sgt	WOODMASS Cyril James	22-05-44	57 Sqn
1524174	Sgt	WITZ Stanley Edward	20-11-44	14 OTU		1601319	Sgt	WOODROW Gordon Stanley	8-02-44	138 Sqn
1611961	Sgt	WIVELL Richard Walter John	15-02-44	550 Sqn		649638	Sgt	WOODROW Reginald	25-06-44	50 Sqn
48319	F/L	WODEHOUSE Sydney Edward	17-06-44	77 Sqn		175154	F/O	WOODROW Roy William	31-12-44	218 Sqn
1397330	Sgt	WOLFE Albert John	24-02-44	166 Sqn		156311	F/L	WOODRUFF DFC Dennis Charles	29-01-44	15 Sqn
141988	F/O	WOLFSON Leo	1-07-44	139 Sqn		1234801	F/S	WOODS Albert	16-10-44	14 OTU
1402906	Sgt	WOLSEY Richard	14-10-44	12 Sqn		75403	F/L	WOODS Arthur Bickerstaffe	8-02-44	85 Sqn
1398420	F/S	WOMAR Dennis Henry Peter	30-08-44	635 Sqn		1797545	Sgt	WOODS Charles William	25-07-44	15 Sqn
1502416	Sgt	WOOD Alan	19-03-44	625 Sqn		906385	Sgt	WOODS Edward Harold	31-03-44	106 Sqn
1603433	F/S	WOOD Alfred Harold	5-07-44	35 Sqn		1320640	F/S	WOODS Frank Guy	3-06-44	76 Sqn
1158339	Sgt	WOOD Alfred John	20-01-44	1653 HCU		136862	F/O	WOODS Frederick Walter	31-03-44	640 Sqn
1783228	Sgt	WOOD Bernard Peter	11-08-44	640 Sqn		158426	F/O	WOODS James Wordsworth	2-01-44	44 Sqn
1826216	Sgt	WOOD Blair	4-12-44	227 Sqn		1486640	Sgt	WOODS John Gregory	4-05-44	101 Sqn
1602462	Sgt	WOOD Cyril Charles	20-02-44	460 Sqn		591869	Sgt	WOODS Leonard Frank	7-03-44	1667 HCU
51836	F/L	WOOD DFC David Telfer	8-06-44	156 Sqn		1581815	Sgt	WOODS Peter John	8-07-44	17 OTU
995101	Sgt	WOOD Denis	30-01-44	207 Sqn		1332707	W/O	WOODS Philip Edwin	7-10-44	617 Sqn
963941	F/S	WOOD Derek William	20-05-44	7 Sqn		1386860	F/S	WOODS Ralph Morley	10-03-44	75 Sqn
143222	F/O	WOOD Dudley William Oliver	4-09-44	515 Sqn		778204	Sgt	WOODVINE Arthur Bradley [South Africa]	11-04-44	61 Sqn
168823	P/O	WOOD Edward	27-01-44	149 Sqn						
1816621	Sgt	WOOD Edward Frederick	6-11-44	619 Sqn		1510808	Sgt	WOODWARD Bertie	19-07-44	207 Sqn
1576342	F/S	WOOD MiD Edwin Ernest	16-10-44	115 Sqn		1868328	Sgt	WOODWARD Eric George	10-10-44	1667 HCU
639067	Sgt	WOOD Ernest Albert	5-07-44	57 Sqn		960435	Sgt	WOODWARD Frank	25-02-44	460 Sqn
913872	Sgt	WOOD Frederick George John	12-09-44	90 Sqn		139497	F/L	WOODWARD DFC* Geoffrey Winston	25-10-44	158 Sqn
1810692	F/S	WOOD DFM Geoffrey Walter	21-02-44	97 Sqn						
649881	Sgt	WOOD George	28-04-44	15 Sqn		1549227	Sgt	WOODWARD Gordon Kenneth	22-05-44	514 Sqn
3050138	F/S	WOOD George Frederick	22-06-44	49 Sqn		956437	Sgt	WOODWARD James Edward George	29-06-44	102 Sqn
1549835	Sgt	WOOD Granville	29-05-44	1657 HCU		1811689	Sgt	WOODWARD Leslie Thomas	1-12-44	630 Sqn
176154	P/O	WOOD James Rankin Stratton	25-06-44	61 Sqn		1292153	F/S	WOODWARD Norman	25-02-44	97 Sqn
1528879	Sgt	WOOD John	15-02-44	77 Sqn		147687	F/O	WOODWARD Walter	29-06-44	7 Sqn
1323832	F/S	WOOD John Beresford	3-01-44	83 Sqn		1686529	Sgt	WOODWARD William	29-01-44	97 Sqn
1894948	Sgt	WOOD John Leslie	4-12-44	467 Sqn		1035489	Sgt	WOOLDRIDGE Frederick	30-01-44	463 Sqn
578231	Sgt	WOOD John Stenhouse	30-08-44	101 Sqn		1678701	Sgt	WOOLFREY Allen Henry	17-08-44	158 Sqn
1593500	Sgt	WOOD John William	7-07-44	626 Sqn		1239335	F/S	WOOLHOUSE Alec Thomas Walkington	30-10-44	622 Sqn
174079	P/O	WOOD Kenneth Irvine	25-06-44	50 Sqn						
1338672	F/S	WOOD Leonard George	15-07-44	166 Sqn		1583652	F/S	WOOLISCROFT Albert Kenneth	27-08-44	7 Sqn
175628	F/O	WOOD Leslie John	19-07-44	9 Sqn		1890807	Sgt	WOOLLAM Peter	19-04-44	75 Sqn
1585415	Sgt	WOOD Michael George	13-07-44	166 Sqn		179243	P/O	WOOLLARD Barrington St. John	16-07-44	207 Sqn
1580620	Sgt	WOOD Norman Leslie	5-07-44	207 Sqn		1863504	F/S	WOOLLARD Peter	2-11-44	15 Sqn
135679	F/O	WOOD Peter Michael	12-04-44	619 Sqn		1819373	Sgt	WOOLLEY Arthur Frederick	6-04-44	207 Sqn
182390	P/O	WOOD Philip Ralph	29-07-44	103 Sqn		176049	P/O	WOOLLEY Charles Leonard	10-05-44	44 Sqn
1424336	Sgt	WOOD Reginald Robert	30-08-44	115 Sqn		172310	P/O	WOOLLEY David Edward	28-05-44	420 Sqn
176479	P/O	WOOD Robert Eric Norman	23-05-44	419 Sqn		1805285	F/S	WOOLLEY Robert Arthur	23-06-44	626 Sqn
1607905	Sgt	WOOD Ronald William	26-02-44	12 Sqn		1324142	Sgt	WOOLVEN Frederick Edwin	3-01-44	156 Sqn
1125322	Sgt	WOOD William Arthur	24-02-44	100 Sqn		159688	F/O	WOOLVEN George Leonard	12-06-44	139 Sqn
1450790	Sgt	WOOD William George	10-05-44	50 Sqn		110641	F/L	WOOLVEN Leonard John	17-01-44	15 OTU
1896833	Sgt	WOODBINE William Ernest	3-06-44	76 Sqn		1601449	Sgt	WOOTTEN Walter Francis Stanley	30-01-44	622 Sqn
1318882	F/S	WOODBRIDGE Alan Sidney	18-08-44	1651 HCU		1380933	F/S	WOOTTON-WOOLLEY Brian Thomas	4-05-44	460 Sqn
172563	F/O	WOODBURN James Michael [Eire]	24-02-44	156 Sqn						
1338062	Sgt	WOODCOCK Albert William	20-01-44	622 Sqn		1423134	Sgt	WOPLIN Christopher George	24-04-44	102 Sqn
144040	F/O	WOODCOCK Charles Noel	1-09-44	157 Sqn		1542876	Sgt	WORBOYS Norman	31-03-44	630 Sqn
2208973	Sgt	WOODCOCK John Harold	8-05-44	619 Sqn		1589759	Sgt	WORDEN Eric Stanley	22-06-44	630 Sqn
171650	P/O	WOODCOCK-STEVENS George Arthur	15-10-44	166 Sqn		154603	F/O	WORDEN Harry	2-11-44	102 Sqn
1324073	Sgt	WOODEN Kenneth George	28-04-44	115 Sqn		1595192	Sgt	WORLEY Leonard	10-11-44	97 Sqn
963539	F/S	WOODFIELD Lionel Valentine	27-03-44	166 Sqn		173802	F/O	WORNER Charles Edward Michael	31-07-44	9 Sqn
922095	Sgt	WOODFORD Stanley Alfred George	30-07-44	75 Sqn		2220974	Sgt	WORRALL Lewis Jeremiah	13-07-44	166 Sqn
1806800	Sgt	WOODFORD Thomas Samuel	20-02-44	514 Sqn		1111874	F/S	WORSDALE DFM Jack	2-01-44	97 Sqn
577057	F/S	WOODGER Robert Edward	15-02-44	550 Sqn		1623406	Sgt	WORTH Maurice Leonard	25-02-44	61 Sqn
1685947	Sgt	WOODHEAD Benjamin	23-03-44	17 OTU		156272	F/L	WORTHINGTON DFC James Robert	22-06-44	49 Sqn
1580619	Sgt	WOODHEAD Maxwell	28-09-44	29 OTU		1624968	Sgt	WORTHINGTON Thomas William	18-12-44	51 Sqn
34189	W/C	WOODHOUSE DFC AFC Henry De Clifford Anthony	13-08-44	85 Sqn		1670524	F/S	WORTHINGTON William	23-06-44	460 Sqn
						1684238	Sgt	WORTLEY Allan Edward	27-01-44	460 Sqn
46300	F/L	WOODHOUSE Ronald	7-05-44	627 Sqn		1247336	F/S	WRAGG Alexander	11-04-44	622 Sqn
1436654	Sgt	WOODHOUSE Ronald Letchmere	20-02-44	10 Sqn		1572492	Sgt	WREN Hugh	19-06-44	466 Sqn
1324803	Sgt	WOODHOUSE William Thomas	21-07-44	626 Sqn		652571	Sgt	WRIDE Harold	31-03-44	426 Sqn
160618	F/O	WOODING MiD Frederick Arthur	21-11-44	Fiskerton		161783	P/O	WRIGHT Alfred Edgar	21-02-44	640 Sqn
1626119	Sgt	WOODING Herbert Henry	25-06-44	90 Sqn		158793	F/O	WRIGHT Antony Oliver	27-01-44	57 Sqn
175570	P/O	WOODMAN Frederick Bernard	22-07-44	23 Sqn		1439962	Sgt	WRIGHT DFM Arthur George	16-05-44	576 Sqn
542141	Sgt	WOODMAN Kenneth Benson	8-06-44	466 Sqn		51875	F/O	WRIGHT Basil Owen	15-02-44	166 Sqn
						153605	F/O	WRIGHT Brian Edward	17-12-44	57 Sqn

1616630	Sgt	WRIGHT Charles Henry	19-03-44	625 Sqn
1800924	F/S	WRIGHT DFM Charles Henry Leslie	15-02-44	7 Sqn
174338	P/O	WRIGHT Charles Norman	8-07-44	630 Sqn
161756	P/O	WRIGHT David Leonard	27-01-44	408 Sqn
1467000	Sgt	WRIGHT Dennis William	25-07-44	57 Sqn
159508	F/O	WRIGHT DFC Eric	1-07-44	625 Sqn
1457557	Sgt	WRIGHT Frank	11-04-44	12 Sqn
1339143	Sgt	WRIGHT Frederick John	6-01-44	576 Sqn
1335060	Sgt	WRIGHT George Ernest	26-02-44	207 Sqn
143761	F/O	WRIGHT George Henry	23-05-44	97 Sqn
1578552	F/S	WRIGHT George Leonard	22-06-44	44 Sqn
1681260	F/S	WRIGHT Gilbert Harold	9-06-44	50 Sqn
2203494	Sgt	WRIGHT Harold James	29-01-44	466 Sqn
1595252	Sgt	WRIGHT Herbert	11-09-44	51 Sqn
1390367	Sgt	WRIGHT Herbert Arthur	31-03-44	50 Sqn
1491676	Sgt	WRIGHT John	30-12-44	76 Sqn
50580	F/O	WRIGHT DFC John Hammond	15-02-44	156 Sqn
1466015	F/S	WRIGHT John Llewellyn	8-07-44	9 Sqn
1430225	F/S	WRIGHT DFM Leslie	8-06-44	166 Sqn
171442	P/O	WRIGHT Paul Dempster	20-02-44	12 Sqn
1211932	Sgt	WRIGHT Phillip William	15-02-44	622 Sqn
1579870	Sgt	WRIGHT Raymond Hedley	23-05-44	57 Sqn
130125	F/O	WRIGHT Reginald James	27-05-44	139 Sqn
1309782	Sgt	WRIGHT Robert Henry	4-01-44	1658 HCU
1133855	W/O	WRIGHT Ronald	20-02-44	35 Sqn
1896094	F/S	WRIGHT Stanley John	12-12-44	582 Sqn
1323827	Sgt	WRIGHT Stanley Thomas	25-02-44	12 Sqn
159668	F/O	WRIGHT Stephen Pickering	26-07-44	432 Sqn
161476	P/O	WRIGHT DFC Thomas	2-01-44	101 Sqn
1026044	AC1	WRIGHT Thomas	10-04-44	Spilsby
170619	P/O	WRIGHT Thomas Kitchener	16-05-44	103 Sqn
1678692	F/S	WRIGHT Thomas Leslie	16-11-44	207 Sqn
1892957	Sgt	WRIGHT Victor Stephen	16-10-44	12 OTU
1341391	Sgt	WRIGHT William Edward	6-12-44	57 Sqn
146076	F/O	WYAND Guy Herbert	7-06-44	619 Sqn
1596540	Sgt	WYATT Charles Alfred	8-07-44	17 OTU
152738	F/O	WYATT Henry	22-01-44	76 Sqn
151094	F/O	WYATT John Harker	13-06-44	408 Sqn
1893144	Sgt	WYATT William George	23-01-44	1667 HCU
124519	F/O	WYBORN John Henry	22-03-44	7 Sqn
1386942	Sgt	WYKES Leonard William	22-01-44	466 Sqn
1670532	Sgt	WYLIE William John Crozier	29-07-44	103 Sqn
967562	Sgt	WYNDE Percy Reginald	25-02-44	463 Sqn
103028	S/L	WYNESS DFC Drew Rothwell Cullen	7-10-44	617 Sqn
1814753	Sgt	WYNESS Louis Henry	31-03-44	51 Sqn
1437316	F/S	WYNN Horace George	16-10-44	10 Sqn
185570	P/O	WYNN James Arthur	29-11-44	35 Sqn
108063	F/L	WYNNE-THOMAS Arthur	20-10-44	550 Sqn
171914	P/O	WYN-EVANS John David	25-04-44	7 Sqn
1550746	Sgt	WYPER John	4-12-44	207 Sqn
1432606	Sgt	WYRILL Harold	18-03-44	61 Sqn
1356347	Sgt	YALLOP Roy Frederick Arthur	24-12-44	35 Sqn
1868604	Sgt	YARDLEY Henry William John	22-06-44	57 Sqn
182761	F/O	YATES Bernard	26-12-44	10 Sqn
1895282	Sgt	YATES Bruce Herbert	26-06-44	1667 HCU
152922	F/O	YATES Charles Joseph	24-02-44	30 OTU
1388960	Sgt	YATES George Walter	15-02-44	158 Sqn
1437758	F/S	YATES Robert Francis	28-05-44	166 Sqn
171019	P/O	YATES Robertson Bertrand	22-12-44	617 Sqn
1454669	F/S	YATES Ronald	25-02-44	460 Sqn
1577128	F/S	YATES Ronald Charles	27-01-44	460 Sqn
149373	F/O	YATES William Arthur Churchill	29-05-44	1657 HCU
86941	W/O	YATES William Cave	28-05-44	Langar
161407	P/O	YATES DFC Wilson Birwell	20-02-44	630 Sqn
169449	P/O	YEOMAN John	13-09-44	218 Sqn
1819034	Sgt	YORK Ronald Ivor	16-09-44	405 Sqn
1594296	Sgt	YORK William Lambert	25-03-44	97 Sqn
1439296	F/S	YORKE Eric Oscar Downing	18-04-44	51 Sqn
160033	F/O	YORKE Peter [Rhodesia]	4-12-44	44 Sqn
1802298	Sgt	YORKE William George	22-01-44	630 Sqn
1803648	Sgt	YOUENS Lawrence Walter	23-08-44	692 Sqn
164218	P/O	YOUNG Arthur Alan	19-08-44	1655 MTU
1337510	Sgt	YOUNG Arthur Wilmot	30-07-44	106 Sqn
1825411	Sgt	YOUNG David	27-08-44	57 Sqn
1318927	Sgt	YOUNG David John	15-02-44	115 Sqn
1806956	Sgt	YOUNG Derek Woodcroft	15-02-44	100 Sqn
1083693	W/O	YOUNG DFM Eric	30-11-44	115 Sqn
1487006	F/S	YOUNG Eric	27-08-44	115 Sqn
1479621	F/S	YOUNG DFM George	21-01-44	97 Sqn
134149	F/O	YOUNG George Ambrose	4-06-44	635 Sqn
130882	F/O	YOUNG George Thomas	3-01-44	49 Sqn
1620463	Sgt	YOUNG Jeffrey	5-11-44	76 Sqn
1498989	F/S	YOUNG DFM Leslie	15-02-44	101 Sqn
174106	P/O	YOUNG Leslie Alfred	20-02-44	630 Sqn
135656	F/O	YOUNG Peter Henry Wilson	25-02-44	626 Sqn
753314	Sgt	YOUNG Robert Faulkner	16-08-44	433 Sqn
1376781	Sgt	YOUNG Ronald William	30-01-44	463 Sqn
1876460	Sgt	YOUNG William Arthur John	22-05-44	550 Sqn
1863094	Sgt	YOUNG William Horace	5-05-44	7 Sqn
179795	P/O	YOUNG William James	13-08-44	77 Sqn
1593625	Sgt	YOUNGER Robert Dixon Bruce	19-07-44	463 Sqn
1874065	Sgt	YOUNGS Desmond Claude	24-03-44	57 Sqn
1468058	F/S	YOUNGS Raymond	6-12-44	77 Sqn
184398	P/O	YOXON Albert	7-12-44	1651 HCU
1436512	F/S	YUILL William Houston	14-01-44	101 Sqn
612317	F/S	YUILLE David	23-04-44	76 Sqn
1549198	Sgt	YULE Henry Auld Nisbet	30-08-44	115 Sqn
177540	P/O	ZACCHEO Enrico William	17-06-44	102 Sqn
1811925	Sgt	ZAMMIT John Joseph	23-03-44	9 Sqn
159439	P/O	ZEAL Bernard William	2-01-44	101 Sqn
159153	F/O	ZEFFERTT Leslie Charles	8-07-44	106 Sqn

Note

Although S/L Bazalgette VC (see Postscript for further details pertaining to his death and subsequent award of the Victoria Cross) is shown in this section as hailing from Canada, his parents were of English origin; his education from the age of nine was centred on English schools and private tutelage and I consider it likely that all his formative years up to his joining the army in 1939 were spent in the United Kingdom. Not too dissimilar, though I strongly suspect his parents were Canadian, is the case of W/O George Stratford from Brandon, Manitoba. George arrived in the United Kingdom circa 1938 and joined the regular air force, training as a pilot. His elder brother, meanwhile, received a commission in the Royal Canadian Air Force, losing his life five months after George; both men being commemorated in this Part under their respective air forces.

On the night of the 20th/21st of April, a Wellington belonging to 28 Operational Training Unit left its Castle Donnington base with the intent of dropping leaflets over Northern France. Crewed mainly by Canadians, the last wireless transmission pinpointed the bomber in the vicinity of Brest and flying in a south-westerly direction (see Volume 7, page 287 for details pertaining to its crew). It is believed that within the hour of making this transmission the Wellington was abandoned. Through the good efforts of Oliver Clutton-Brock who in addition to tracing the evasion report (WO208/5583) in respect of the pilot, from which it can be deduced that the rear gunner and wireless operator were injured, has alerted me to details in Roger Huguen's 1993 book *Par Les Nuits Les Plus Longues* which reports that the wireless operator (Sgt John Kempson) parachuted safely but fell over on landing and struck his head on the only rock in the immediate vicinity, fracturing his skull in the process. Despite immediate attention from two local doctors, his injuries proved mortal and he died on the 25th.

F/S Alexander MacLeod's service number (710159) indicates that he enlisted sometime between June and November 1941 in Rhodesia but his entry in the Commonwealth War Graves Commission register shows that his parents were domicile in the United Kingdom. On the 10th of April, 1944, at approximately 1955 hours in the evening a 1,000lb bomb exploded in a fusing shed at Spilsby, killing three armourers and seven assistant armourers. Three are identified within the registers, and repeated in this

Roll, as belonging to 207 Squadron, while the remainder were on the strength of RAF Spilsby though all are commemorated on 207 Squadron's Roll of Honour. This notwithstanding, I am indeed grateful to Raymond Glynne-Owen who, over many years, has painstakingly researched the history of 207 Squadron and delved into records of the various airfields that have hosted '207' over the years. Thus, it was during the course of his investigation of Spilsby's Operations Record Book and a most timely interview with the late Ken Smith who was serving as a station armourer at Spilsby at the time of the tragedy that Raymond was able to ascertain that the most probable cause of the accident was an anti-handling device detonating as an armourer attempted to re-thread a fuse which, inadvertently, had been cross-threaded. The magnitude of the explosion and its aftermath has been reported by Raymond in 207 Squadron Association's newsletter in which he was able to give the names of the six airmen who survived the blast, namely Sgt K. D. Cooper, Cpl A. Vigus, LAC R. Wylie, AC1s W. Brent and W. Caldwell and AC2 F. Walls, all being recovered from the scene in circumstances officially described as extremely hazardous. Such being the urgency of the hour, 207 Squadron was not stood down, though fewer flares than normal were carried that night by the 13 crews briefed to attack the railway yards at Tours (all returned safely) and a continuing degree of momemtum followed with six Lancasters being flown over to East Kirby on the 11th for operations to Aachen.

Two airmen senior in years died during the year; Cpl King, on the strength of 33 Base at Waterbeach, was aged 51 and although he is reported as serving with the volunteer reserve, his service number (93613) indicates he was amongst a large batch of either transfers from other arms or civilian entrants to the RFC between April and October 1917. The second airman, W/O Yates (his age is not shown), is believed to have joined the RFC during this same period.

F/S Ashcroft, who was killed in a flying accident involving a 239 Squadron Mosquito on the 27th of October, is shown in this section as belonging to 49 Squadron, thus adhering to his entry in the Commonwealth War Graves Commission register for Wolverley (St. John The Baptist) Churchyard and my remarks on page 462 of Volume 5.

Finally, in the course of operations against the railway yards at Revigny on 18th/19th July, and which cost the participating 5 Group squadrons 24 Lancasters and 129 aircrew killed, featured two airmen whose surnames suggest Russian/Jewish ancestry. Sgt Supkovitch of 207 Squadron was one and F/S Volcovitch, serving with 619 Squadron, was the other. Both shared a common Christian name, Alfred, and though the former flew under his own name, his compatriot had decided to adopt the surname 'Myers'.

ROYAL AUSTRALIAN AIR FORCE
Personnel

436790	F/S	ABBOTT Stanley Arthur	31-08-44	463 Sqn
417773	P/O	ABELL Douglas Roy	6-10-44	207 Sqn
426482	F/S	ABRAHAM James Hedley	21-07-44	467 Sqn
432081	F/S	ABRAMS Kevin Kenny	12-08-44	1667 HCU
427787	P/O	ACRES Robert Joseph	26-09-44	463 Sqn
410934	F/S	ADAM Walter Joseph	31-03-44	101 Sqn
405513	P/O	ADAMS Eric Kenneth	12-09-44	467 Sqn
434217	F/S	ADAMS Frank Percy	11-06-44	625 Sqn
425819	F/S	ADAMS John Alfred	13-08-44	101 Sqn
434097	F/O	ADCOCK Thomas	30-08-44	103 Sqn
426856	F/S	ADCOCK William Jeffery	1-07-44	625 Sqn
421873	P/O	ALCORN James William	25-06-44	576 Sqn
420109	F/S	ALEXANDER David Sydney	29-01-44	466 Sqn
37691	F/O	ALEXANDER Edward David	12-09-44	622 Sqn
416830	F/S	ALLAN Robert Norman	21-01-44	460 Sqn
409130	Sgt	ALLAN William James	31-03-44	166 Sqn
428898	F/S	ALLBON Douglas George	4-12-44	106 Sqn
434218	F/S	ALLEN Colin Frederick	19-07-44	467 Sqn
410936	F/S	ALLEN Keith Fowler	12-03-44	199 Sqn
5182	F/S	ALLEN Russell	23-04-44	460 Sqn
423033	F/O	ALLSEP Sydney James	23-06-44	460 Sqn
424350	F/S	AMBROSE Patrick Joseph	4-11-44	51 Sqn
414876	F/L	ANDERSEN Robert Charles	22-05-44	115 Sqn
423579	F/S	ANDERSON Eric James	19-08-44	51 Sqn
414121	P/O	ANDERSON Leslie Dean	29-01-44	466 Sqn
28817	P/O	ANDERSON Peter Robert	31-03-44	460 Sqn
24647	F/S	ANDREW William Ronald	13-08-44	9 Sqn
414745	P/O	ANDREWS Reginald Thomas	31-01-44	640 Sqn
429413	F/O	ANGUS Ian Mackenzie	30-07-44	11 OTU
415716	F/O	APPLEYARD William David	19-07-44	49 Sqn
426941	F/O	ARCHAY Kenneth Edgar	22-05-44	463 Sqn
418242	F/S	ARDIS David Corry	24-09-44	467 Sqn
421699	F/S	ARMITT George	14-01-44	44 Sqn
423597	F/O	ARMSTRONG Gordon Arthur	17-06-44	77 Sqn
426447	F/S	ARMSTRONG Herbert Barnard	29-11-44	460 Sqn
423610	F/S	ARMSTRONG James Edward	8-06-44	15 Sqn
410136	F/O	ARNOLD Alan	23-06-44	97 Sqn
429902	F/S	ARTHUR Cecil Glen	15-03-44	101 Sqn
422093	F/S	ARTHUR Paul Druce	31-08-44	1654 HCU
424519	F/S	ASH Richard William	10-05-44	463 Sqn
436598	F/S	ASHTON Robert Alexander	1-09-44	138 Sqn
415958	F/S	AUSTERBERRY Francis Frederick	24-10-44	90 Sqn
429105	F/S	AUSTIN Edward Phillip	23-10-44	462 Sqn
419452	F/O	AUSTIN James	6-11-44	463 Sqn
406988	W/O	AWCOCK Terence Lansdowne	12-09-44	44 Sqn
418496	P/O	A'COURT Gladstone Arthur	22-06-44	467 Sqn
416645	F/O	BAGOT Edward Christopher	14-01-44	156 Sqn
427055	F/O	BAILY George Hadley	4-11-44	49 Sqn
427632	P/O	BAIRSTOW John Leslie	30-08-44	1660 HCU
420808	F/O	BAKER John Albert	11-11-44	207 Sqn
426507	F/S	BAKER DFM Louis Michael Gabriel	8-06-44	166 Sqn
413939	F/S	BAKER Robert Minton	2-03-44	156 Sqn
420825	F/O	BALCOMBE Gordon Robertson	15-02-44	100 Sqn
419948	F/S	BALDWIN Ernest William	17-03-44	17 OTU
412473	F/L	BALDWIN Wilfred Guy	20-01-44	466 Sqn
416402	P/O	BALFOUR Donald Campbell	14-01-44	207 Sqn
68	G/C	BALMER OBE DFC John Raeburn	11-05-44	467 Sqn
426292	F/S	BAMBRICK Virgil Gilbert	4-11-44	195 Sqn
415490	F/L	BANFIELD DFC Raymond Charles	25-07-44	83 Sqn
408433	F/S	BARBER Bramwell Rockliff	25-06-44	463 Sqn
422100	F/S	BARBER George Charles	4-05-44	460 Sqn
427790	F/S	BARLOW Charles Alfred	21-07-44	115 Sqn
417781	F/O	BARLOW David Arnold	21-07-44	467 Sqn
405992	F/L	BARLOW Jack Colclough	6-10-44	106 Sqn
409370	P/O	BARNES DFC Keith Omond	27-01-44	49 Sqn
424554	F/S	BARNES Norman Edward	1-09-44	138 Sqn
30581	F/S	BARNES William Thomas	21-01-44	27 OTU
427611	F/S	BARNETT Kenneth Henry	29-12-44	170 Sqn
418332	F/O	BARNETT Leonard Victor	13-05-44	466 Sqn
418910	F/S	BARR Dennis Ronald	4-05-44	460 Sqn
417275	F/S	BARRETT Douglas George	27-01-44	463 Sqn
409364	W/O	BARRETT Noel Charles	30-08-44	463 Sqn
427405	F/S	BARRETT-LENNARD Francis Graham	12-09-44	90 Sqn
27266	F/S	BARRON Harold Lawrence	22-06-44	57 Sqn
428291	F/O	BARRY David Bernard	22-07-44	20 OTU
417327	F/O	BATEMAN George William	25-06-44	463 Sqn
426426	F/S	BATES Dudley Clive	18-04-44	9 Sqn
426022	F/S	BATH Victor William	25-03-44	466 Sqn
30053	F/S	BATTEN Douglas Walter	22-01-44	640 Sqn
442415	F/S	BATTYE Reginald Harold	4-11-44	463 Sqn
418333	P/O	BAXTER William Samuel	27-08-44	7 Sqn
29888	F/S	BEARD Robert	8-06-44	466 Sqn
435557	Sgt	BEATSON Earl Hume	30-07-44	27 OTU
412360	W/O	BEAVAN William Walter	28-05-44	466 Sqn
432200	F/S	BEAZLEY Alan Osborne	25-07-44	466 Sqn
424354	F/S	BECKHOUSE Gordon Edwin	19-07-44	630 Sqn
422381	F/S	BECKINGHAM Clarence Walter	14-10-44	550 Sqn
418717	F/O	BEDDOE Robert Henry	31-08-44	463 Sqn
410208	W/O	BEECHER Thomas Francis	22-06-44	57 Sqn
424355	F/O	BEESTON James Macfadden	18-11-44	460 Sqn
419081	F/S	BEGG Reginald Kenneth	25-06-44	576 Sqn

418334	F/O	BEHARRIE David	19-07-44	467 Sqn		404623	F/L	BOYLSON DFC* William Wrixon	25-06-44	139 Sqn
414456	Sgt	BEILBY John George	24-04-44	21 OTU		412373	F/S	BRADBURY Keith Robert James	30-01-44	100 Sqn
413945	F/L	BELFORD William Noel	27-01-44	626 Sqn		423050	F/O	BRADLEY Alick Ronald	2-08-44	467 Sqn
413946	W/O	BELL Hilton Craig	8-07-44	106 Sqn		422115	P/O	BRADLEY Thomas Wallace	10-04-44	103 Sqn
434078	F/S	BELL John Hardie	15-03-44	460 Sqn		18098	F/O	BRADY Alan John	30-08-44	467 Sqn
419604	P/O	BENDALL Jabez Kevin	6-12-44	227 Sqn		424361	F/S	BRADY Francis Patrick Joseph	24-06-44	149 Sqn
425264	F/S	BENNETT Brian Percival	20-02-44	463 Sqn		423280	F/O	BRADY John William	23-10-44	625 Sqn
434492	F/S	BENNETT Fred	31-12-44	218 Sqn		408562	W/O	BRAID Alexander Albert	17-06-44	77 Sqn
424117	F/O	BENNETT Kenneth Edwin Harold	18-12-44	463 Sqn		411479	F/O	BRAITHWAITE John Sidney	25-04-44	463 Sqn
424949	F/S	BENSON Philip William	21-07-44	467 Sqn		410443	F/S	BRAND Norman	24-07-44	102 Sqn
413526	F/S	BENZIE James Macadam	15-03-44	463 Sqn		424362	F/S	BRANDER Anthony Phillip	27-01-44	61 Sqn
428900	F/S	BERGELIN Rupert William	23-10-44	460 Sqn		423217	F/S	BRASINGTON George Charles	22-02-44	218 Sqn
410115	F/S	BERNALDO Jack	10-04-44	103 Sqn		426297	P/O	BREMNER Eric	20-02-44	61 Sqn
415495	P/O	BERRYMAN Arthur Albert William	25-06-44	467 Sqn		426030	W/O	BRENNAN Arthur Benjamin	28-10-44	115 Sqn
411987	F/O	BETHEL Stanley James	12-12-44	460 Sqn		405673	W/O	BREWINGTON Robert Alexander	24-03-44	35 Sqn
412306	W/O	BETTINGTON Max Milson	3-06-44	466 Sqn		426496	W/O	BRIGHT Keith Mortimer	6-11-44	214 Sqn
434288	F/S	BEUTEL William	25-06-44	106 Sqn		406636	F/L	BRINE Lindsay Russell	22-06-44	467 Sqn
428902	F/S	BICKFORD Douglas Fitzgerald	31-03-44	158 Sqn		427795	F/S	BROAD Raymond Cecil	6-10-44	463 Sqn
427370	F/S	BIESIOT Leslie Hendrik	30-09-44	1651 HCU		424363	F/S	BROMLEY Reginald Ernest	11-04-44	514 Sqn
414191	F/S	BILLETT Clive	10-04-44	460 Sqn		410144	F/S	BROOKMAN Ronald Charles	26-09-44	463 Sqn
436283	F/S	BILLING Albert Norman James	26-08-44	100 Sqn		426045	F/S	BROOKS James Lennox	10-04-44	460 Sqn
423045	F/O	BILLMAN Douglas Payne	26-07-44	100 Sqn		428396	F/S	BROSNAN John Lane	4-12-44	463 Sqn
414192	W/O	BILTOFT Arthur Henry	7-05-44	576 Sqn		421885	F/S	BROUGHAM Geoffrey Graham	31-03-44	51 Sqn
423602	F/O	BINNIE Keith Cedric	21-07-44	626 Sqn		429645	F/S	BROWN Bruce Harold	6-11-44	57 Sqn
429099	P/O	BINSTEAD Jack	2-11-44	102 Sqn		420436	F/S	BROWN Donald George Wentworth	13-07-44	9 Sqn
429445	F/S	BIRCH Eric Eyles	25-10-44	115 Sqn		414757	F/S	BROWN Edgar Barwood	19-07-44	460 Sqn
38770		BIRCH Ernest Hugh	31-03-44	10 Sqn		426302	P/O	BROWN Edwin Ryland	25-04-44	463 Sqn
418048	F/S	BIRD Campbell David	26-02-44	1661 HCU		415612	P/O	BROWN Ernest	24-03-44	166 Sqn
417330	P/O	BIRD Harold William	17-06-44	77 Sqn		408452	F/O	BROWN Geoffrey Albert	24-09-44	467 Sqn
410619	F/O	BIRD John Powell	25-03-44	460 Sqn		426035	F/O	BROWN Geoffrey William	4-11-44	625 Sqn
416923	F/S	BIRRELL Eric Alfred	15-03-44	9 Sqn		418699	F/S	BROWN Gilbert Francis	8-06-44	1667 HCU
421154	F/S	BIRTLES Ronald Joseph	12-06-44	635 Sqn		434525	F/O	BROWN Harry Arthur Bulger	13-06-44	166 Sqn
415608	P/O	BLACK Clarence Alwin	12-09-44	218 Sqn				[New Zealand]		
426028	P/O	BLACK Douglas John	2-09-44	1656 HCU		423639	F/S	BROWN Herbert Kenith	25-06-44	467 Sqn
410299	F/O	BLACK Dudley Victor	11-06-44	467 Sqn		417809	F/S	BROWN John Eyre	21-04-44	467 Sqn
429371	F/S	BLACK Frank Alexander	6-12-44	57 Sqn		418915	F/S	BROWN John Henry	10-05-44	463 Sqn
418790	F/S	BLACK Stanley Kevin	11-06-44	106 Sqn		414768	F/S	BROWN DFC Robert William	20-10-44	35 Sqn
415497	F/S	BLACKWELL William Donald	2-01-44	467 Sqn		417454	F/O	BROWN Ronald William	29-07-44	576 Sqn
415498	P/O	BLAIR Robert Alexander Walton	17-06-44	77 Sqn		413849	F/L	BROWN Stephen Watson	28-05-44	582 Sqn
428038	F/S	BLAUBAUM Maxwell Bibra	12-09-44	622 Sqn		414903	P/O	BROWN Vivian William	23-05-44	630 Sqn
404648	S/L	BLESSING DSO DFC William Walter	7-07-44	105 Sqn		17786	P/O	BROWN William Norman Waldron	23-04-44	115 Sqn
437364	Sgt	BLOCK Noel Herbert	26-03-44	26 OTU		403643	F/O	BROWNE Adrian Victor	25-10-44	30 OTU
411116	P/O	BLUNDELL Colin Frazer	15-02-44	35 Sqn		418840	F/L	BROWNE David Dorey	12-09-44	467 Sqn
432097	F/S	BOAG Robert James	30-11-44	75 Sqn		415395	W/O	BROWNE Joseph Edward	28-05-44	466 Sqn
409497	F/S	BOAL Harold James	31-01-44	97 Sqn		423780	F/S	BRUCE Frederick Thomas Robert	6-04-44	207 Sqn
424359	F/S	BOATSWAIN James Attewood	26-08-44	100 Sqn		410529	P/O	BRYAN Kenneth Edward	8-06-44	514 Sqn
423214	F/S	BOCK Eric Alan	13-08-44	625 Sqn		414641	F/L	BUCHANAN DFC Malcolm Stjernqvist	21-11-44	78 Sqn
414305	F/S	BOETTCHER Arthur Harold	2-01-44	467 Sqn		419567	F/S	BUCIRDE Reginald John	26-08-44	100 Sqn
427289	F/S	BOGLE Charles Stewart	13-08-44	90 Sqn		430358	F/O	BUCKLAND Edward Cyril	18-09-44	27 OTU
430243	F/S	BOLGER Ray Kethel	30-07-44	27 OTU		429495	F/S	BUCKLAND John William James	31-03-44	207 Sqn
405291	F/O	BOLGER Thomas John	26-09-44	692 Sqn		421311	F/O	BUCKNELL Geoffrey Charles	6-08-44	97 Sqn
442325	F/S	BOLTON Robert John	12-10-44	608 Sqn		430137	F/S	BULL William	21-11-44	460 Sqn
433194	F/O	BOND Alan Campbell	7-12-44	463 Sqn		418917	F/S	BUMPSTEAD Alan	25-03-44	460 Sqn
420433	F/S	BOND John Cecil	11-04-44	466 Sqn		423076	F/S	BURGESS Malcolm Robert	6-06-44	50 Sqn
424080	F/S	BOND John Norman	5-07-44	1667 HCU		432109	F/S	BURGESS Norman George Albert	26-08-44	103 Sqn
426822	F/S	BOURKE Patrick John	11-04-44	466 Sqn		409663	P/O	BURGESS Thomas James	21-04-44	207 Sqn
419550	P/O	BOWE Donald McFarlane	15-08-44	1660 HCU		420438	P/O	BURKE DFC Robert William	10-04-44	460 Sqn
422394	F/O	BOWELL Peter John	6-11-44	463 Sqn		415757	P/O	BURNELL Brian Dudley	26-03-44	460 Sqn
420434	F/S	BOWERN Donald Anderson	13-05-44	466 Sqn		421069	P/O	BURNETT Thomas Alfred	11-06-44	90 Sqn
419253	F/O	BOWES Lyle Edward	22-06-44	207 Sqn		424711	F/S	BURNS Alfred John	17-06-44	77 Sqn
414753	F/O	BOWMAN Nelson Ellis	22-06-44	466 Sqn		417293	W/O	BURNSIDE Harold	11-06-44	7 Sqn
418913	F/O	BOWMAN Norman Jack	26-09-44	463 Sqn		427230	F/S	BURROWS Felix Milton	15-11-44	115 Sqn
406094	F/O	BOWN Leslie Walter	28-04-44	460 Sqn		416824	P/O	BURROWS Frank Reginald	11-04-44	622 Sqn
421239	F/S	BOYCE William George	10-04-44	460 Sqn		421636	P/O	BURROWS Lionel Frederick Walter	9-08-44	466 Sqn
430112	F/S	BOYD Norman Collis	23-12-44	90 Sqn		437212	F/S	BURTON Wallace Bruce	15-05-44	1653 HCU
416041	W/O	BOYD Ronald Howard	4-05-44	103 Sqn		432748	F/S	BURTON Wallace Patrick	20-11-44	186 Sqn
430247	F/S	BOYDELL John Charles Broughton	19-03-44	463 Sqn		415758	W/O	BURY Glyn Norman	12-12-44	149 Sqn
424729	F/S	BOYLE Brian Phillip	31-03-44	103 Sqn		418798	F/O	BUSBY John Harold	13-08-44	622 Sqn
423622	W/O	BOYLE John Joseph	29-10-44	463 Sqn		423625	F/O	BUSH John Francis	19-07-44	630 Sqn

Service #	Rank	Name	Date	Sqn/Unit
432749	F/S	BUTCHER Walter Harvey James	6-11-44	463 Sqn
14734	F/O	BUTLER Neville Edward	29-11-44	460 Sqn
428466	F/S	BUTLER Roy Wallace	13-08-44	101 Sqn
422417	F/S	BUTLER William Charles	2-01-44	61 Sqn
420858	F/O	BUTT Robert Edward	22-03-44	44 Sqn
421158	W/O	BYERS Peter William	26-10-44	166 Sqn
437333	F/S	BYRNE Garry Brendan	18-11-44	460 Sqn
432112	P/O	BYRNE Reginald Elwyn	5-09-44	84 OTU
28766	P/O	BYRNES Robert Wentworth	18-12-44	463 Sqn
432340	F/S	CADDY Peter Giblin	28-08-44	19 OTU
415396	W/O	CAIN Leonard William	28-05-44	466 Sqn
421159	F/S	CALADINE Keith Jervis	29-03-44	1652 HCU
417799	F/S	CALDER Peter John	17-03-44	17 OTU
426531	F/O	CALDERWOOD Leonard John	23-04-44	463 Sqn
432114	F/O	CALLAHAN Peter Ross	27-04-44	460 Sqn
414197	F/S	CALLOW John Karlo	20-01-44	1653 HCU
423445	F/S	CALLOW Peter	12-09-44	467 Sqn
423435	F/S	CALVERT Clive Percival	16-12-44	106 Sqn
415923	F/O	CAMERON Anthony Carlyle	5-11-44	102 Sqn
422423	F/S	CAMERON James William Keith	21-04-44	467 Sqn
408419	F/S	CAMERON Peter Talmage	22-05-44	115 Sqn
419700	F/S	CAMIER Ronald Sutton	13-08-44	90 Sqn
410946	F/O	CAMPBELL Gordon Roch	4-12-44	1661 HCU
414761	P/O	CAMPBELL Hugh Donald	10-05-44	9 Sqn
417335	F/S	CAMPBELL James John	21-02-44	9 Sqn
426774	F/S	CAMPBELL Nigel Douglas	29-06-44	102 Sqn
424286	F/S	CAMPBELL Robert Hepburn	22-05-44	622 Sqn
429922	F/S	CANTWELL Anthony James	28-09-44	29 OTU
414898	P/O	CANTY Edwin Albert	22-06-44	44 Sqn
414622	F/S	CARIUS Leonard Robert	30-01-44	463 Sqn
425120	F/S	CARLILE William David	25-02-44	460 Sqn
429176	F/S	CARLILL Ronald John	22-06-44	467 Sqn
416651	W/O	CARLYLE Hubert George	25-06-44	463 Sqn
420537	F/S	CARMICHAEL John Arthur	24-02-44	51 Sqn
426043	F/S	CARPENTER William James	20-10-44	460 Sqn
400318	F/O	CARR Rex Lionel	19-07-44	460 Sqn
432117	F/O	CARRALL Nigel Bruce	4-11-44	158 Sqn
415508	F/S	CARRAN Frederick Sydney [New Zealand]	27-01-44	12 Sqn
425598	W/O	CARRIER William John	27-08-44	630 Sqn
415761	P/O	CARRINGTON Henry Joseph	22-05-44	49 Sqn
408034	F/O	CARROLL DFC Marmion Wilfred	28-04-44	460 Sqn
421887	F/O	CARTER Alfred Kyrwood	5-07-44	463 Sqn
419556	F/O	CARTER Arnold George	18-11-44	460 Sqn
410145	P/O	CARTER Douglas Alfred	15-03-44	7 Sqn
420638	F/S	CASEY Barry William	19-04-44	466 Sqn
421244	W/O	CASEY James Nelson	2-11-44	576 Sqn
410869	F/S	CASHMAN DFM William Michael	23-04-44	466 Sqn
429774	F/O	CASTLE Percy John	16-10-44	30 OTU
413735	F/S	CASWELL Harry Cosgreave	3-06-44	76 Sqn
424147	F/L	CATO Hugh Orme	5-11-44	15 Sqn
427438	F/S	CAVERIDGE Gergo	28-09-44	463 Sqn
421791	F/S	CHADWICK William Robert	21-01-44	460 Sqn
412480	P/O	CHADWICK-BATES DFC Arthur George Jackson	31-03-44	460 Sqn
434619	F/S	CHALLIS Edgar Glynn	2-08-44	467 Sqn
414465	F/S	CHALMERS Ivor Fredric	29-01-44	207 Sqn
428296	P/O	CHALMERS Robert James	5-11-44	1660 HCU
421858	P/O	CHAMPNESS Edward Frank	23-05-44	630 Sqn
435535	F/S	CHANDLER Roger Staniforth	21-11-44	460 Sqn
408476	F/O	CHANDLER William Charles	25-05-44	15 Sqn
410641	F/S	CHAPMAN Leslie Harold	10-04-44	460 Sqn
417157	F/S	CHAPMAN Wilbur Henry	22-01-44	514 Sqn
422414	F/S	CHAPPLE Ivan	10-05-44	463 Sqn
412902	F/O	CHARLES Thomas Eric	30-01-44	97 Sqn
422133	F/S	CHARLESWORTH Douglas Neal	18-11-44	460 Sqn
424912	F/S	CHARLEY John Ross	6-10-44	78 Sqn
417050	P/O	CHARLICK Dean Gordon	16-08-44	625 Sqn
427184	F/S	CHARMAN Edward George	11-11-44	467 Sqn
409894	F/L	CHASE William McLaurin	9-05-44	405 Sqn
432305	F/S	CHEATLE Allen Leonard	25-07-44	1667 HCU
420146	F/S	CHESTER Lambert Albert	2-01-44	460 Sqn
429846	F/S	CHEYNE George James	22-12-44	463 Sqn
423061	F/O	CHIDGEY Frank Stanley Guest	27-01-44	463 Sqn
28155	F/S	CHIGWIDDEN John Joseph	21-07-44	622 Sqn
429924	F/O	CHINNERY Lavington Edmund John Frederick	13-05-44	466 Sqn
410039	F/L	CHITTY Walter Evan	30-07-44	514 Sqn
432485	F/S	CHRISTIE Alexander Anthony	23-12-44	90 Sqn
423650	F/S	CHRISTIE Sidney Edward	26-02-44	1661 HCU
406292	F/S	CHRISTMASS Lewis Havelock	29-01-44	463 Sqn
417992	F/O	CHURCH David Campbell	29-10-44	207 Sqn
426312	F/O	CLAREY Colin Mervyn	21-07-44	115 Sqn
421347	W/O	CLARK Ivan Henry	5-07-44	460 Sqn
402439	S/L	CLARK DFC AFC MiD James	12-12-44	460 Sqn
408328	P/O	CLARK Ronald Leslie	31-03-44	630 Sqn
423651	P/O	CLARKE Arthur Henry	4-12-44	207 Sqn
421979	F/O	CLARKE Thomas Kenneth	30-08-44	50 Sqn
423063	F/S	CLAYWORTH Eric Raymond	28-04-44	138 Sqn
418069	F/S	CLEARY James Joseph	14-01-44	1656 HCU
410193	F/S	CLEMENT Charles	10-06-44	97 Sqn
408796	F/O	CLEMO William Lindsay	20-01-44	466 Sqn
422261	F/O	CLEVELAND Francis Allan	21-02-44	460 Sqn
418349	F/S	CLIFTON John William	25-03-44	460 Sqn
414337	W/O	CLOSE Douglas Eston	4-05-44	12 Sqn
423641	F/O	CLUBB Frederick John	9-06-44	44 Sqn
415764	F/S	CLUNAS Eric Clark	21-01-44	207 Sqn
410454	F/O	CLYNE Geoffrey Albert	4-05-44	582 Sqn
417699	F/S	COATES Rex	31-08-44	460 Sqn
425605	F/S	COCKROFT Verne Edward	8-07-44	467 Sqn
427870	F/S	CODY Bernard Francis	10-05-44	467 Sqn
417806	F/S	COLE Keenth Ian	12-09-44	100 Sqn
418810	F/S	COLEMAN Kenneth George	3-06-44	466 Sqn
427847	F/S	COLLARD Gartan Gerard	16-08-44	625 Sqn
434777	F/S	COLLAS Cyril	18-11-44	51 Sqn
412112	F/O	COLLINS Allan James	25-02-44	61 Sqn
436900	F/O	COLLINS George Barrowby	11-12-44	128 Sqn
402458	P/O	COLLINS William Frederick	27-04-44	106 Sqn
432125	F/O	COMER George Allen	31-12-44	138 Sqn
412056	F/O	CONDON John James	23-09-44	61 Sqn
425606	F/L	CONLEY DFC Ronald John	6-06-44	97 Sqn
429218	F/O	CONNOLLY Darrell Owen	26-08-44	100 Sqn
409666	F/O	CONNOLLY Frank Andrew	6-01-44	467 Sqn
10981	F/O	CONNOR Arthur Albert	4-07-44	463 Sqn
429450	F/S	CONQUEST Henry John	12-09-44	44 Sqn
409383	F/L	CONSTABLE DFC Donald Frank	24-03-44	78 Sqn
426541	F/S	CONWAY Patrick Joseph	25-07-44	466 Sqn
429526	F/S	COOK Francis John	15-10-44	186 Sqn
423985	F/S	COOK Ronald Anthony	27-01-44	57 Sqn
1510	F/S	COOKE Arthur Wallace	8-11-44	1662 HCU
424152	F/S	COOKE Terence Raymond	1-04-44	20 OTU
433197	F/S	COOMBE Herbert Keith	20-11-44	186 Sqn
26756	F/O	COOPER Joseph Arthur Gordon	6-11-44	57 Sqn
29881	F/L	COOPER Norman Percival	29-01-44	463 Sqn
414769	F/O	CORCORAN Martin Michael	31-03-44	640 Sqn
423648	F/S	CORCORAN Reginald Robert	22-01-44	467 Sqn
412490	F/O	CORLIS John Edwin	12-09-44	218 Sqn
417807	F/O	CORNISH Howard Norman	12-09-44	625 Sqn
429928	F/S	CORNWELL Ross George	16-12-44	115 Sqn
413761	F/O	CORY John Keith	1-07-44	100 Sqn
418737	F/O	COSGRIFF Brian Patrick	21-07-44	51 Sqn
426547	F/S	COTTEW Richard Graham	9-06-44	467 Sqn
432670	F/S	COTTLE John Ronald	8-06-44	466 Sqn
431166	F/S	COVENTRY Roy Cameron	28-09-44	463 Sqn
425278	F/L	COWAN DFC Roland Reginald	25-06-44	467 Sqn
432371	F/S	COWARD Robert	23-10-44	463 Sqn
421250	F/S	COWIN Douglas James	29-01-44	466 Sqn
424379	F/O	COX Maxwell	3-09-44	1656 HCU

411869	P/O	CRADDOCK Thomas Eugene	23-12-44	35 Sqn	410150	P/O	DOMBRAIN Peter Charles Lewis	1-06-44	15 Sqn
415308	P/O	CRAIN Alan Irvine	17-06-44	77 Sqn	420923	F/O	DONALD Harley William Edwards	24-07-44	102 Sqn
421574	F/L	CRANMER Paul Augustus	13-08-44	158 Sqn	426265	F/S	DONALD Keith Courtney	16-09-44	466 Sqn
428098	F/S	CRANSTON Dion Graeme	22-06-44	467 Sqn	403026	F/L	DONNER DFM William John	20-02-44	156 Sqn
23484	P/O	CRAWFORD Kent Elliott	22-06-44	619 Sqn	424827	F/S	DONOWA Rex Valentine	23-04-44	12 Sqn
429179	F/S	CREBER William Henry	20-05-44	83 OTU	421008	F/L	DOOLAN George McGowan	20-04-44	218 Sqn
407199	F/O	CROFT Robert McKerlie	11-05-44	463 Sqn	424566	F/S	DOUGLAS James Watkins	12-09-44	625 Sqn
424855	P/O	CROFT William Denman	25-07-44	466 Sqn	426559	F/S	DOUGLAS Robert James	15-08-44	1660 HCU
414654	P/O	CROMBIE Donald Charles Cameron	31-03-44	514 Sqn	423196	W/O	DOWE Ronald Arthur	24-12-44	166 Sqn
416656	F/L	CROSBY DFC Peter Alan	10-04-44	460 Sqn	419165	F/S	DOWLING Bryan James	3-06-44	466 Sqn
425128	P/O	CROSTHWAITE Douglas Charles	9-05-44	431 Sqn	429881	F/S	DOWLING George Edward	5-07-44	463 Sqn
407821	F/O	CROSTON David Payne	11-05-44	463 Sqn	417058	W/O	DOWLING Terence Eric	18-03-44	44 Sqn
419298	F/O	CROUT Harry Ronald	10-05-44	467 Sqn	414916	F/S	DOWNIE Albert James	21-07-44	467 Sqn
425129	P/O	CULLIFORD Ronald Firth	19-04-44	57 Sqn	427450	F/S	DRAFFIN Ronald John	25-03-44	640 Sqn
417812	F/S	CUMMINGS Ronald Irving	25-03-44	466 Sqn	417817	F/O	DRAYSEY Lloyd	6-11-44	57 Sqn
423661	F/S	CUMMINS Horace Andrew	8-07-44	467 Sqn	417818	F/L	DREWER Clifford Harris	24-06-44	7 Sqn
418038	F/O	CUNNINGHAM Alan Forster	6-10-44	51 Sqn	424862	F/S	DRUMMOND Augustine Francis	26-03-44	626 Sqn
286104	F/L	CURNOW Lancelot Douglas	18-03-44	466 Sqn	425623	P/O	DUEL Allen Robert	5-06-44	27 OTU
419033	F/S	CURREY George Donald	13-08-44	50 Sqn	424863	F/S	DUELL James Baird	29-06-44	102 Sqn
430014	F/S	CURRIE Alan Livingstone	6-09-44	27 OTU	418362	F/O	DUGGAN Gordon William	31-12-44	83 Sqn
437402	F/S	CURRIE Charles Ernest	13-08-44	467 Sqn	418928	F/S	DUGGLEBY Alan Milne	17-06-44	102 Sqn
420157	P/O	CUSICK Milford James	25-03-44	460 Sqn	424162	F/S	DUNBAR Maxwell	25-04-44	630 Sqn
405677	F/S	CUTMORE Maurice Hyde	21-04-44	467 Sqn	418363	F/O	DUNCAN Alan James	29-07-44	44 Sqn
425612	F/S	DALEY John	20-02-44	83 Sqn	38367	P/O	DUNCAN Alexander	4-11-44	466 Sqn
418640	F/S	DALTON John Phillip Sinclair	7-07-44	26 OTU	422459	F/S	DUNCOMBE David Garnet	22-03-44	50 Sqn
415623	F/S	DALY Wilfred Hubert Aloysius	7-02-44	1662 HCU	418258	F/S	DUNFORD Patrick John	4-07-44	463 Sqn
423996	P/O	DANIEL William Neville	8-09-44	582 Sqn	406522	F/O	DUNHAM Donald William	13-08-44	156 Sqn
427445	F/S	DANN George Martin	10-05-44	463 Sqn	423083	P/O	DUNKERLEY Allan Roy Frank	21-11-44	75 Sqn
426059	F/S	DANSIE Jack	19-03-44	466 Sqn	416418	F/O	DUNN Douglas Chapman	30-04-44	463 Sqn
427807	F/O	DATE John Matthew	17-06-44	77 Sqn	414928	P/O	DUNN Leslie William	22-05-44	44 Sqn
416939	F/S	DAVEY Allan Edward Dearlove	26-02-44	90 Sqn	422460	P/O	DUNN Robert Wyndham	11-05-44	1654 HCU
422446	F/S	DAVEY Donald James	13-07-44	166 Sqn	414343	F/L	DURSTON DFC Ivan George	29-01-44	467 Sqn
424158	F/S	DAVIDSON Archibald Cattanach	6-10-44	7 Sqn	433096	F/S	DUTFIELD Ian David	6-11-44	463 Sqn
418355	F/S	DAVIDSON David William	2-11-44	463 Sqn	420648	F/O	DYER Arthur Richard	2-08-44	467 Sqn
422143	F/O	DAVIES Herbert William	13-06-44	166 Sqn	429280	F/S	DYER Bruce Douglas	27-08-44	15 Sqn
411293	F/S	DAVIES Kenneth Nigel Bishop	6-01-44	467 Sqn	422462	F/O	DYER Kenneth Charles	15-03-44	7 Sqn
418816	F/S	DAVIES Sydney Hartley [New Zealand]	25-07-44	466 Sqn	417821	W/O	EARLE Harold Murray	29-10-44	50 Sqn
8905	F/S	DAVIS Lawrence Arthur	23-09-44	463 Sqn	427076	F/S	EASTCOTT Thomas Frederick	15-02-44	466 Sqn
420173	F/O	DAVIS Thomas Edward William	19-07-44	467 Sqn	430019	F/S	EASTGATE Colin Henry	10-05-44	463 Sqn
429452	F/O	DAVIS Vincent	4-12-44	15 Sqn	422467	F/O	EDGINTON William Thomas	25-02-44	467 Sqn
433717	F/S	DAY Graham Fowler	24-12-44	460 Sqn	416941	F/S	EDMONDS Lloyd George	21-01-44	27 OTU
414341	P/O	DEARNALEY DFC Edgar Vincent	22-06-44	467 Sqn	421187	F/O	EDMONDS Stanley Allan	10-04-44	207 Sqn
30953	F/S	DEED Cyril Keith	24-12-44	460 Sqn	19882	P/O	EDMONDS William Alexander	8-11-44	1662 HCU
403983	F/O	DEED DFC Leonard Lawrence	13-08-44	156 Sqn	425626	F/S	EDWARDS Charles Herbert	13-08-44	9 Sqn
425136	F/S	DELACOUR Herbert Samuel	13-06-44	514 Sqn	424830	F/S	EDWARDS George Beith	29-06-44	467 Sqn
419458	F/O	DELAHUNTY James Roderick	2-08-44	467 Sqn	38423	P/O	EDWARDS Peter Colin	26-12-44	10 Sqn
417567	F/S	DENHOLM Robert Russell	18-10-44	115 Sqn	411772	F/O	EDWARDS Philip Edwin	12-12-44	460 Sqn
418927	F/O	DENNETT Peter Buck	19-07-44	630 Sqn	424759	F/S	EDWARDS Stuart Lacey	12-06-44	635 Sqn
403914	F/L	DENNIS DFC Stewart Leigh	13-08-44	156 Sqn	424165	F/S	ELDER Jack Herbert	25-07-44	466 Sqn
425617	F/S	DENT Terence Roy	31-08-44	463 Sqn	426563	F/S	ELGAR William Ralph	4-05-44	460 Sqn
426555	F/S	DESHON Frederick Popham	21-01-44	27 OTU	424397	F/O	ELLENS Herbert Vincent	6-11-44	463 Sqn
415625	P/O	DEVESON Edward Oliver	25-03-44	635 Sqn	419383	F/O	ELLIS Derek Atkinson	11-11-44	49 Sqn
426556	P/O	DEVINE Eena Norman	12-09-44	622 Sqn	412932	F/L	ELLIS DFC Henry Arthur Laurence	20-02-44	77 Sqn
414774	W/O	de FRAINE George Ross	19-03-44	466 Sqn	428569	W/O	ELWOOD John Stephen	31-05-44	1660 HCU
427615	F/S	DIAL Wilfred George Barrett	2-08-44	467 Sqn	409677	P/O	ELY George	3-01-44	57 Sqn
421578	F/S	DICKERSON Kevin Leslie Thomas	15-07-44	460 Sqn	26355	F/S	ELY Ronald Walter	11-05-44	1654 HCU
430773	F/S	DICKIE Robert John	24-12-44	460 Sqn	424263	P/O	EMERY DFC Arthur Francis [New Zealand]	31-10-44	460 Sqn
422038	P/O	DICKSON Colin	4-05-44	467 Sqn					
423079	F/S	DICKSON William Alexander	5-10-44	626 Sqn	418366	F/S	EMERY Simon Grover	21-04-44	467 Sqn
417816	F/S	DIETMAN John Arthur	21-02-44	460 Sqn	427592	F/S	EMROSE Robert Keith	19-09-44	467 Sqn
426253	W/O	DILLON Beresford George Douglas	26-09-44	463 Sqn	409298	W/O	ENGLISH William Newth	23-06-44	460 Sqn
427503	F/S	DILLON James McKenzie	23-09-44	166 Sqn	423087	F/O	ESTELL John Edward	1-07-44	100 Sqn
434607	F/O	DIXON John Russell	10-05-44	1658 HCU	423088	F/S	ETHERTON Ronald Henry	13-08-44	76 Sqn
414211	P/O	DOBBYN Robert Joseph	9-05-44	83 Sqn	428757	F/S	EVANS Harry William	15-07-44	1651 HCU
410467	F/S	DOBINSON Julian	02-01-44	460 Sqn	409678	F/O	EVANS Kenneth Winston	22-03-44	100 Sqn
38380	F/L	DOBSON William	11-06-44	15 Sqn	424563	F/S	EVANS William Stanley	27-11-44	166 Sqn
424861	F/S	DODD Thomas Henry Francis	30-08-44	463 Sqn	427989	F/S	EVEREST Edward James	4-11-44	101 Sqn
403838	F/L	DODDS DFC John Reginald	28-04-44	156 Sqn	422153	F/S	EVERETT John Raymond	20-02-44	51 Sqn
414775	W/O	DOGGETT Gordon Edgar	18-03-44	466 Sqn	423689	F/O	EWEN James Alwyn	16-07-44	467 Sqn

19883	F/S	EWINS Percy Alfred	18-12-44	3 LFS	430750	F/S	FRYER Arthur David	4-11-44	463 Sqn
427077	F/O	EYRE Thomas Frank	11-11-44	467 Sqn	420654	F/O	FRYER Graham	4-05-44	463 Sqn
419464	F/S	FAGG Eric Clifford	20-10-44	460 Sqn	429111	P/O	FURNESS John Howell	4-12-44	15 Sqn
406352	F/O	FAHEY AFM Francis Felix	6-01-44	627 Sqn	423700	F/S	FURNISS Oscar Skelton	4-05-44	467 Sqn
415412	P/O	FAIRCLOUGH Lindsay Samuel	30-01-44	463 Sqn	115476	P/O	FURSE William Walter	6-10-44	207 Sqn
436696	P/O	FAIRHEAD Leslie Herbert Ephraim	4-12-44	227 Sqn	430256	F/S	GADSDEN Noel Wilkinson	13-08-44	625 Sqn
422471	P/O	FAITHORN Lawrence Edward	14-08-44	83 Sqn	425000	P/O	GAGGIN Eric Harry	13-05-44	466 Sqn
414546	F/S	FALLON John James	24-06-44	467 Sqn	404241	F/O	GALE DFC Kenneth William	9-06-44	627 Sqn
410472	P/O	FARDON John Charles	2-06-44	138 Sqn	416947	W/O	GALLAGHER Robert William Francis	13-08-44	83 Sqn
436820	F/S	FARMER Allan	23-10-44	462 Sqn	427459	F/S	GALLAGHER Ronald David	22-01-44	467 Sqn
420928	W/O	FARRAR Allan John	28-04-44	460 Sqn	418382	F/S	GALVIN Kevin Francis	8-06-44	466 Sqn
417824	F/S	FARRER Albert Wilson	16-08-44	625 Sqn	421721	F/S	GAMBLE James Ian	11-06-44	467 Sqn
421860	F/S	FARTHING John Warren Alexander	2-01-44	460 Sqn	426079	F/S	GARDE Douglas Graham	22-05-44	467 Sqn
427861	F/S	FAWCETT Walter Douglas	30-08-44	1660 HCU	413977	P/O	GARDNER James William [New Zealand]	18-03-44	463 Sqn
412936	F/O	FAYLE Ernest Athol	20-02-44	463 Sqn	423095	F/S	GAVIN Howard	22-06-44	106 Sqn
419989	F/O	FEDDERSEN Murray James	11-11-44	467 Sqn	430279	F/S	GAWLER Robert Haynes	23-09-44	12 Sqn
411690	P/O	FEENEY Kenneth George	21-04-44	467 Sqn	418938	F/S	GAY Clifford Samuel	4-05-44	103 Sqn
421192	P/O	FEILBERG Ronald Frederick	22-12-44	466 Sqn	426336	F/S	GEDDES Francis John	16-08-44	625 Sqn
436371	P/O	FELGATE John Mervyn	6-10-44	207 Sqn	404416	Sgt	GEIKIE Walter George McDonald	23-09-44	463 Sqn
413112	F/L	FELL Alwyn Kevin Dudley	15-03-44	51 Sqn	409041	W/O	GELDER Norman Francis	29-07-44	463 Sqn
420870	F/S	FELSTEAD William Eldred	10-05-44	467 Sqn	410885	F/S	GEOGHEGAN John Thomas	4-04-44	630 Sqn
423090	F/S	FERGUSON Eric Kenneth	27-03-44	14 OTU	430654	F/S	GEORGE Charles Leslie	4-12-44	467 Sqn
429544	F/S	FERGUSON George Robert	12-09-44	622 Sqn	434248	F/S	GERAGHTY Gerald Francis	5-10-44	101 Sqn
424914	F/S	FERGUSON Herbert William Reid	10-05-44	467 Sqn	420873	F/S	GERATHY Kevin James	5-11-44	1660 HCU
414996	F/S	FERGUSON Ronald Cedric	24-02-44	460 Sqn	417298	F/S	GERICKE DFM Philip Kenneth Ross	29-01-44	15 Sqn
409037	W/O	FIDGE Harold Stanley	20-02-44	514 Sqn	427460	F/S	GERTZEL William Kevin	13-05-44	466 Sqn
417296	P/O	FIDOCK Robert Clive	3-08-44	460 Sqn	426094	W/O	GIBSON John Richardson	12-10-44	30 OTU
420553	P/O	FINCH Jack	10-04-44	57 Sqn	416949	P/O	GIDDINGS Bryan Wilba	10-06-44	97 Sqn
429079	F/S	FINCH Keith	25-03-44	61 Sqn	419365	F/S	GIDDINGS Lindsay Vernon	24-09-44	467 Sqn
419304	F/S	FINE Bernard David	27-05-44	1654 HCU	415520	F/O	GIFFORD Beverley Hudson	19-07-44	463 Sqn
422942	F/S	FINNEY Keith Macdiarmid	2-08-44	467 Sqn	417464	F/S	GILES Arthur Ronald	12-09-44	576 Sqn
417826	F/S	FISCHER Frank Edgar	29-07-44	463 Sqn	420740	P/O	GILES Edgar Albert James	24-03-44	429 Sqn
419789	F/O	FISHER David Ralston	27-08-44	7 Sqn	417475	F/S	GILES Paul Baily	8-06-44	466 Sqn
415244	P/O	FISHER John William	15-02-44	424 Sqn	27937	P/O	GILES Ronald Leslie	5-06-44	1658 HCU
295249	S/L	FITZGERALD DFC Richard Thomas	24-03-44	35 Sqn	420874	F/S	GILL Henry John	2-01-44	460 Sqn
414015	F/O	FITZPATRICK DFM Allan Thomas	27-09-44	627 Sqn	425001	F/S	GILL Joseph Thomas	31-03-44	106 Sqn
436537	F/S	FLEMING Ian Hunter (served as HUNTER Ian)	23-10-44	12 Sqn	425153	P/O	GILL Phillip Roy	29-01-44	467 Sqn
					408367	F/S	GILL Reginald Thomas	25-02-44	61 Sqn
425644	P/O	FLEMING Jack Byrne	27-05-44	1662 HCU	429849	F/S	GILLARD William Andrew	13-05-44	466 Sqn
421657	F/S	FLEMING Paul Stuart	10-04-44	460 Sqn	417831	F/S	GILLETT Archie Oswald	4-07-44	463 Sqn
431920	F/O	FLETCHER Dennis	18-09-44	27 OTU	404333	F/O	GILLMAN DFC Mervyn Durham	16-01-44	12 Sqn
412942	F/O	FLETCHER Donald	20-02-44	77 Sqn	22776	W/O	GILMOUR Hugh Edward	21-07-44	75 Sqn
414792	F/O	FLETCHER Ernest Gatenby	4-07-44	463 Sqn	419466	P/O	GIRLING Clyde Joseph	24-09-44	97 Sqn
414668	F/S	FLETCHER Joseph John	11-06-44	463 Sqn	430026	F/S	GLANFIELD John Leonard	13-06-44	15 Sqn
402074	F/L	FLETCHER DFC Mervyn Sylvester	2-01-44	156 Sqn	414785	F/S	GLASBY DFC Harvey	30-07-44	97 Sqn
427760	F/S	FLOHM Lionel Wilfred	21-11-44	460 Sqn	417300	P/O	GLASSON Rex Arthur	19-03-44	166 Sqn
422943	F/O	FLORY Maxwell Alfred	31-10-44	460 Sqn	425640	F/S	GLAZEBROOK James George Leslie	25-02-44	619 Sqn
415940	P/O	FONTAINE Peter	19-10-44	460 Sqn	425641	F/S	GLOSTER Edward Fitzgibbon	30-01-44	463 Sqn
424403	F/S	FORDEN Hilton Hardcastle	4-05-44	467 Sqn	436579	F/S	GLOVER Bevil Milton	31-08-44	463 Sqn
415635	F/L	FORREST John Augustus	25-06-44	61 Sqn	426086	F/S	GLOVER Edward Andrew	18-03-44	51 Sqn
413755	F/O	FOSKETT Bruce William	15-02-44	424 Sqn	420658	F/O	GODDARD DFC John Edward	8-09-44	582 Sqn
410649	F/S	FOSTER Max Harvey	20-02-44	166 Sqn	421267	W/O	GODDARD Osmond John	31-03-44	514 Sqn
402737	P/O	FOTHERINGHAM Andrew Henry	4-01-44	1658 HCU	401941	W/O	GODFREY John William	8-06-44	466 Sqn
418378	F/O	FOTHERINGHAM Ian	29-07-44	467 Sqn	415247	F/L	GODFREY Richard Gerard	8-06-44	622 Sqn
420381	P/O	FOULKES Geoffrey Grant	28-04-44	35 Sqn	412945	F/O	GODWIN Kenneth James	20-02-44	460 Sqn
429655	F/O	FRANCIS Alan Henry	18-11-44	460 Sqn	424753	F/S	GOODFELLOW Geoffrey	11-11-44	467 Sqn
422482	F/O	FRANCIS Kenneth William Perry	22-01-44	467 Sqn	410839	P/O	GOODRIDGE Noel	15-06-44	15 Sqn
417356	F/S	FRANCIS Max Gordon	21-04-44	467 Sqn	425094	F/S	GOODERHAM Geoffrey Arthur	29-03-44	1652 HCU
418380	F/O	FRANCIS Raymond Leslie	8-06-44	1667 HCU	32665	W/O	GOODWIN Joseph Ignatious	25-03-44	460 Sqn
427818	F/S	FRANKISH Kenneth Thomas	23-10-44	460 Sqn	423711	P/O	GORDON John Grieve	13-08-44	102 Sqn
434396	F/O	FRASER Bryan Patrick	25-07-44	166 Sqn	412218	F/O	GORDON DFC John Irvine	13-02-44	617 Sqn
422851	F/S	FREAME Edward Jack	21-07-44	467 Sqn	411262	F/O	GOSSIP Arthur Bennett	22-06-44	463 Sqn
417472	F/O	FREEMAN Keith Herbert	21-07-44	10 Sqn	410655	F/S	GOTTO Phillip George	2-03-44	156 Sqn
429404	F/O	FREES John Robert	19-10-44	186 Sqn	423712	F/O	GOUGH Sydney Ernest	13-06-44	15 Sqn
434380	F/S	FRENCH George	11-11-44	467 Sqn	410657	W/O	GOULD Ian Frederick	14-06-44	466 Sqn
427314	F/S	FRIPP Alan Wesley Giles	19-07-44	463 Sqn	427116	F/S	GOULD Robert	27-01-44	626 Sqn
423784	F/O	FROST Kenneth	24-09-44	97 Sqn	413988	P/O	GRAHAM William Alexander	16-03-44	463 Sqn
416945	F/S	FRY Herbert James George	4-05-44	460 Sqn	420185	P/O	GRANT Alan Charles William	16-06-44	7 Sqn
422165	P/O	FRY James Rollo	13-06-44	460 Sqn	432457	Sgt	GRANT Donald Gordon	31-08-44	21 OTU

Number	Rank	Name	Date	Squadron
416953	P/O	GRANT Graham Athol	21-02-44	460 Sqn
417176	F/S	GRASBY Brian Gordon	10-05-44	467 Sqn
420662	P/O	GRAY Harry	22-03-44	35 Sqn
418833	W/O	GRAY Ian Hutchinson	11-11-44	467 Sqn
428772	F/O	GRAY Maurice Claude Norfolk	29-11-44	460 Sqn
419443	F/S	GRAYDON Malcolm Henry	25-05-44	76 Sqn
406618	F/O	GREAM Leonard Arthur	18-03-44	466 Sqn
426337	F/S	GREEN John Michael	18-03-44	61 Sqn
18111	F/S	GREEN Kelvin Carlyle	31-03-44	630 Sqn
430099	Sgt	GREENHILL Thomas John	17-03-44	17 OTU
430375	F/O	GREENWOOD Clement Joseph	22-12-44	463 Sqn
420619	F/O	GREENWOOD John Douglas	29-01-44	90 Sqn
418394	P/O	GREY Linley Joseph	31-08-44	460 Sqn
419307	F/S	GRIEVE Jeffrey James	8-11-44	1662 HCU
429224	F/S	GRIFFIN Felix Ivor	30-08-44	21 OTU
429375	F/S	GRIFFITH John Bryant De Burgh	13-06-44	578 Sqn
413375	F/L	GRIFFITHS Trevor Llewellyn	15-02-44	622 Sqn
427901	F/S	GRIGG Allan Joseph	22-07-44	20 OTU
419308	F/O	GRIMWOOD Frank Lockyer	4-04-44	5 LFS
422269	P/O	GROGAN Kevin Francis	13-08-44	115 Sqn
424901	F/O	GROSE Kenneth	11-09-44	51 Sqn
417954	F/S	GROSVENOR Robert Archer	29-03-44	1652 HCU
428642	F/S	GROVES George Caleb	4-12-44	463 Sqn
43016	F/S	GROVES Reginald Arthur	6-09-44	27 OTU
409992	F/O	GROVES Robert Bruce	7-07-44	44 Sqn
413855	P/O	GRUGEON Stephen Charles	27-01-44	467 Sqn
417833	F/O	GUNDRY Donald Charles	25-07-44	463 Sqn
421861	F/S	GURDON Peter William Bedford	25-02-44	460 Sqn
22067	P/O	GYNTHER Clarence Lloyd	2-01-44	156 Sqn
429948	F/S	HACKETT Michael John	4-05-44	101 Sqn
423789	F/O	HACKNEY Henry Horace	27-05-44	1658 HCU
419467	F/O	HAILEY Keith Ian	22-05-44	467 Sqn
415944	P/O	HALE Harry	1-07-44	625 Sqn
421847	W/O	HALES Hilton Alfred	17-12-44	61 Sqn
410158	P/O	HALL Horace Mervyn	11-04-44	51 Sqn
422504	F/O	HALL Marshall	23-05-44	1658 HCU
432181	F/S	HALL Ronald Norman	4-11-44	463 Sqn
411775	F/O	HALL Stanley George [United Kingdom]	13-02-44	617 Sqn
428694	F/O	HALSTED Roger Hubert	22-12-44	463 Sqn
423722	F/L	HAMILTON Douglas Boyd	20-10-44	460 Sqn
414232	P/O	HAMILTON Mervyn Edgar	15-08-44	463 Sqn
414400	F/O	HAMMOND Peter John	11-05-44	467 Sqn
415527	P/O	HAMPTON George Alfred	24-03-44	57 Sqn
424409	F/S	HANCE John Donald	5-11-44	15 Sqn
422506	F/S	HANCOCK William Stanley	10-05-44	467 Sqn
422174	F/S	HANSCOMBE Donald Edwin	4-12-44	106 Sqn
429431	F/S	HANSEN Vernon Nelson	3-06-44	158 Sqn
415528	P/O	HANSON Peter Edward	30-01-44	463 Sqn
415649	F/O	HARDIE Robert Blackburn	1-09-44	138 Sqn
433103	F/S	HARDING Robert Edward	30-08-44	166 Sqn
419992	F/S	HARE William Henry	3-01-44	16 OTU
421596	F/S	HARGREAVES Charles Haley	31-03-44	460 Sqn
436325	P/O	HARLER Horace William	18-12-44	3 LFS
437415	F/S	HARLEY Harry Kenneth	5-11-44	10 Sqn
418403	F/S	HARRIP Ronald Albert	14-06-44	466 Sqn
11604	P/O	HARRIS James Alfred	22-05-44	622 Sqn
434251	F/S	HARRIS John Osborne	28-05-44	101 Sqn
401690	F/O	HARRIS Robert Maxwell	22-05-44	467 Sqn
404467	F/S	HARRISON Hector Ronald	28-04-44	460 Sqn
420009	W/O	HARRISON Leuncelot	4-07-44	463 Sqn
432668	F/S	HARRISON Mervyn Walter	29-07-44	463 Sqn
413117	W/O	HARRISON Thomas	22-06-44	466 Sqn
415652	F/S	HARRISON Wintfred Patten	3-01-44	166 Sqn
412434	P/O	HART Allan Robert	31-01-44	97 Sqn
426838	F/S	HARTLEY Harry Brian	21-07-44	467 Sqn
423726	F/S	HARVEY Alfred Henry	13-08-44	102 Sqn
420835	F/S	HARVEY Douglas Venning	31-03-44	166 Sqn
418273	F/S	HASELHURST Arthur Wilfred	23-09-44	463 Sqn
417074	P/O	HASTE James Arthur	31-03-44	61 Sqn
432167	F/S	HATHAWAY William Edward	31-08-44	460 Sqn
423287	F/O	HAWKES Frank Sidney	27-08-44	97 Sqn
431448	F/S	HAWTHORN Richard Thurston	7-12-44	463 Sqn
426589	F/S	HAY James	24-03-44	619 Sqn
429152	F/S	HAY John Alexander	10-12-44	21 OTU
407074	F/L	HAY DFC* Robert Claude	13-02-44	617 Sqn
429560	F/S	HAYDEN John Percival	29-01-44	1660 HCU
432172	F/S	HAYES Stuart James	1-09-44	138 Sqn
409996	P/O	HAYMAN Douglas Anthony	2-06-44	138 Sqn
433207	F/S	HAYMAN Geoffrey	4-12-44	467 Sqn
422517	F/O	HAYNES Douglas Leslie	13-08-44	50 Sqn
427830	F/S	HEALY Robert Delmage	28-09-44	463 Sqn
426343	F/S	HEAP Albert Edward	2-08-44	467 Sqn
6025	F/O	HEATH DFM Geoffrey Ernest	29-06-44	627 Sqn
423114	P/O	HEATH Gordon Leonard	25-07-44	166 Sqn
423305	P/O	HEATH Laurence David	30-08-44	166 Sqn
436194	F/O	HEATLEY Wilfred Pearson	16-10-44	30 OTU
24163	W/O	HEDGES DFC Victor Archibald Maudsley	14-01-44	156 SQN
420561	F/O	HEGARTY DFC Dermot John	16-07-44	83 Sqn
423729	F/S	HEIDTMAN Kenneth Frederick	3-08-44	460 Sqn
417839	F/S	HEMINGWAY Colin	3-01-44	463 Sqn
425849	F/O	HENDERSON Bryan John	6-12-44	207 Sqn
433549	F/S	HENDERSON Joslyn Lavarre	7-12-44	463 Sqn
415981	P/O	HENDERSON Thomas Whyndam	10-06-44	10 Sqn
424001	F/S	HENN Clement Herbert	11-04-44	514 Sqn
421332	F/S	HENNESSEY Francis Arthur	20-02-44	460 Sqn
437579	F/S	HENNESSY Kevin William	8-06-44	1667 HCU
412314	F/S	HENNESSY Thomas William	18-03-44	115 Sqn
413194	P/O	HENNINGHAM John Romer	6-01-44	576 Sqn
420385	P/O	HENRY Andrew	10-04-44	460 Sqn
417706	F/L	HERAPATH Ronald Martin	12-12-44	195 Sqn
417639	W/O	HERBERT John Wallace Mills	24-12-44	103 Sqn
424555	F/S	HERBERTSON William	21-11-44	460 Sqn
425439	F/S	HERD Mervyn James	26-03-44	49 Sqn
434645	F/S	HERNE Frank Malcolm	6-10-44	466 Sqn
427118	F/S	HESFORD Brian	6-11-44	57 Sqn
419311	F/S	HEWETT Harold Max	12-05-44	75 Sqn
420565	P/O	HEWITT William Philip Revenall	15-02-44	630 Sqn
411704	F/L	HEWSON William Henry	27-01-44	83 Sqn
426841	F/O	HEYWOOD William Nelson	8-06-44	466 Sqn
400322	F/L	HICKS MiD Stanley Charles	6-01-44	627 Sqn
420192	P/O	HIGGINS Newman Jack	9-05-44	83 Sqn
20076	F/S	HILL Robert Trevor	13-06-44	460 Sqn
409919	F/S	HILL Rowland McPherson	22-06-44	467 Sqn
413195	P/O	HILTON Raymond William	18-02-44	158 Sqn
418275	F/S	HISCOCK William Warren	30-08-44	166 Sqn
414797	P/O	HISLOP Douglas	10-05-44	467 Sqn
424297	F/S	HOBBS Ronald Henry	4-05-44	460 Sqn
429321	P/O	HOCKING James Wallace	28-07-44	1651 HCU
420197	P/O	HOCKLEY Allan James Neville	25-05-44	214 Sqn
413156	F/O	HODDLE Gordon Bruce	25-02-44	550 Sqn
413768	F/O	HODGES Jack Paull	5-07-44	57 Sqn
426598	F/O	HOFFMAN Adolf David Leon	25-04-44	115 Sqn
415658	W/O	HOGAN Edwin Albert	12-09-44	622 Sqn
418949	F/S	HOGAN Michael	27-01-44	84 OTU
414403	F/S	HOGAN Thomas Joseph	20-01-44	1657 HCU
436032	F/S	HOGG Aubrey	23-04-44	103 Sqn
429322	F/S	HOGG William George	11-04-44	460 Sqn
429620	F/S	HOLLANDS James Albert	1-07-44	100 Sqn
423735	F/O	HOGGARD Robert John	2-11-44	15 Sqn
429323	F/S	HOLDEN Richard Paul Percival	13-06-44	622 Sqn
410335	W/O	HOLMES Lester Bertram	19-07-44	49 Sqn
412964	F/O	HOOKWAY Arthur Frederick	22-05-44	7 Sqn
414565	F/S	HOPGOOD Clifford Berger	24-02-44	460 Sqn
430128	F/S	HOPKINS Thomas Alan	13-08-44	101 Sqn
419509	F/S	HORE Ronald Wentworth	13-08-44	467 Sqn
406783	W/O	HORGAN John Byrne	15-02-44	578 Sqn
426346	F/O	HORNIBROOK Albert Keith	23-09-44	61 Sqn

420388 F/S	HOSIER DFM John Stanley	10-04-44	460 Sqn
417377 F/O	HOUGH Leslie Markland	8-11-44	218 Sqn
410668 F/O	HOURIGAN Ivan Patrick	12-09-44	44 Sqn
424634 F/O	HOUSEMAN John William	21-07-44	626 Sqn
423535 F/S	HOUSTON William Leonard	11-11-44	467 Sqn
423536 F/O	HOWARD Bert Charles	4-11-44	463 Sqn
426601 F/S	HOWARD Russell	2-08-44	467 Sqn
430207 F/S	HOWELL Robert Magnay	4-12-44	463 Sqn
418842 F/S	HOWIS William John	25-02-44	460 Sqn
413771 F/S	HUGGETT Norman Grenfell	31-03-44	101 Sqn
413614 P/O	HUGHES DFC Garth Stewart	31-03-44	514 Sqn
26382 W/O	HUGHES Harold Eric	11-05-44	1654 HCU
422204 F/S	HUGHES Mervyn Royce	22-05-44	463 Sqn
427328 F/S	HULLETT William Roy	3-08-44	460 Sqn
417488 P/O	HUMPHREY Vernon Leicester	13-08-44	218 Sqn
428712 F/S	HUMPHREYS Alfred Samuel	16-03-44	463 Sqn
418120 F/S	HUMPHREYS Bruce Lettington	17-04-44	5 LFS
419387 F/S	HUNKIN Gregory Herbert	27-06-44	460 Sqn
422186 P/O	HUNT Colin Charles	15-10-44	101 Sqn
423242 F/S	HUNT Leslie Thomas	13-06-44	166 Sqn
424761 F/S	HUNTER Lionel Gregory Leslie	25-06-44	463 Sqn
421982 P/O	HUNTER Malcolm Ross	22-03-44	35 Sqn
405909 F/S	HURLEY Ernest William Joseph	27-01-44	460 Sqn
420755 P/O	HURLEY Max James	20-02-44	15 Sqn
432190 F/S	HURST Norman George	23-09-44	463 Sqn
432076 F/S	HURSTWAITE Fred Joseph	23-09-44	463 Sqn
422956 F/O	HUTCHINS Kenneth Millett	26-08-44	100 Sqn
416501 F/O	HUTCHINSON DFC Jack Pierce	25-02-44	626 Sqn
408296 F/O	HUTTON Wallace Kenneth	21-01-44	83 Sqn
422187 P/O	HYDE Gordon Leslie	8-06-44	466 Sqn
403514 F/S	HYNES Keith Frederick	19-10-44	109 Sqn
418954 F/S	INCE Roy Alleyne	11-04-44	466 Sqn
420888 F/S	INGLES Arthur Norman	25-02-44	156 Sqn
427833 F/S	ION John Parr	31-08-44	460 Sqn
421221 F/S	IRELAND Lawrence	28-05-44	103 Sqn
431481 F/S	IRVINE John Murray	18-12-44	27 OTU
420950 F/O	IRVING Donald James	31-03-44	101 Sqn
426104 F/S	IRWIN John Percival	20-01-44	57 Sqn
423752 P/O	ISRAEL Jack Lewis	27-06-44	460 Sqn
415331 P/O	IVE George Corbett	20-01-44	76 Sqn
402599 F/O	IVESON Edwin	25-03-44	466 Sqn
434791 F/S	JACKSON Allen Stewart	27-08-44	115 Sqn
429953 F/S	JACKSON Arthur Reginald	7-05-44	576 Sqn
404503 F/O	JACKSON DFC Francis Gordon	28-04-44	460 Sqn
420203 F/S	JACOB Herbert Alfred	11-04-44	466 Sqn
432193 F/S	JACOBS Stanley George	2-09-44	1656 HCU
22102 F/O	JACOBSON George Alexander	23-04-44	514 Sqn
413388 F/O	JACOMBS Richard Mortimer Newark	25-02-44	463 Sqn
409923 F/S	JAGER William Russell	21-01-44	15 Sqn
424763 F/S	JAGO John Leonard	20-10-44	460 Sqn
417490 F/S	JAMES Brian Russell	22-01-44	76 Sqn
409837 P/O	JAMES Stanley Ernest	20-01-44	622 Sqn
424417 F/O	JAMIESON John Robert Umphelby	12-09-44	622 Sqn
429575 F/S	JAMIESON Thomas George	30-08-44	463 Sqn
404507 S/L	JARMAN DFC Eric George Delancey	28-04-44	460 Sqn
27289 F/S	JASPER Alfred George	25-07-44	466 Sqn
426604 F/S	JASPER James Ernest	22-05-44	463 Sqn
412449 F/S	JEFFERY Clarence Bruce	20-01-44	166 Sqn
427420 F/S	JEFFERY Douglas Bruce	21-07-44	467 Sqn
38363 F/S	JEFFERY Keith Edward	8-11-44	1662 HCU
405914 P/O	JEKYLL George Donaldson	9-06-44	102 Sqn
408999 W/O	JENKINS Allan Keith	4-12-44	207 Sqn
424764 F/S	JENKINS Arthur Hedley	16-03-44	467 Sqn
426884 F/S	JENSEN Eric Maxwell	21-04-44	28 OTU
417198 F/S	JOHNS Allan Clyde	22-03-44	9 Sqn
418425 F/O	JOHNSON Clifford James	26-02-44	463 Sqn
425413 F/S	JOHNSTON Alastair Dale	10-05-44	467 Sqn
412066 F/S	JOHNSTON Conrad George	22-01-44	466 Sqn
418535 F/S	JOHNSTON George Alfred	15-03-44	7 Sqn
423762 F/O	JOHNSTONE Geoffrey James Munro	13-08-44	101 Sqn
416967 W/O	JOLLEY DFC Kenroy Alfred	31-03-44	635 Sqn
424299 F/S	JONES Bertram John	23-03-44	17 OTU
417200 W/O	JONES Clarence Archibald	22-06-44	466 Sqn
415032 W/O	JONES Clifford Cecil	8-07-44	467 Sqn
424281 F/S	JONES Clifford Desmond	3-02-44	82 OTU
423786 F/S	JONES Edgar Frederick	6-08-44	51 Sqn
410493 F/O	JONES George Oswald	10-05-44	463 Sqn
436051 F/S	JONES Henry Sylvester	4-12-44	44 Sqn
410365 F/L	JONES Herbert Clifford	8-06-44	138 Sqn
429230 F/S	JONES Ivor Hawkins	30-08-44	1660 HCU
428767 F/O	JONES Jeffrey Ross	19-07-44	100 Sqn
430035 F/S	JONES Maurice Robert	21-07-44	467 Sqn
433334 F/S	JONES Morris Albert	21-11-44	460 Sqn
410064 P/O	JONES Rhys Webb	20-05-44	115 Sqn
419511 F/O	JONES Richard Allan	25-09-44	463 Sqn
430615 F/S	JONES Robert Douglas	18-09-44	12 OTU
426789 F/S	JONES Stanley William	25-03-44	626 Sqn
422206 F/S	JONES Thomas Noel Ian	24-06-44	1662 HCU
429663 F/S	JORDAN Aidan	8-06-44	466 Sqn
418427 F/O	JOWETT Henry Anthony	21-07-44	51 Sqn
421598 F/S	JOYCE Brian Martin	8-07-44	50 Sqn
410496 F/S	JOYCE Eric Albert	6-01-44	467 Sqn
424526 F/S	JOYCE Jack Anthony	4-12-44	166 Sqn
410241 P/O	JUBB Angus James	22-03-44	9 Sqn
429461 F/S	KEATING Robert Henry	6-01-44	467 Sqn
424190 F/S	KEEBLE William Henry	4-04-44	5 LFS
426613 F/S	KELLEY Ronald Rhoades	2-03-44	156 Sqn
415430 W/O	KELLY Bernard Edward	25-06-44	463 Sqn
429341 F/S	KELLY John Edmund Joseph	23-10-44	12 Sqn
414142 P/O	KELLY Lester James	22-05-44	622 Sqn
412970 F/O	KELLY Reginald Stanislaus	24-03-44	78 Sqn
426350 F/S	KELLY Sydney Norris	23-05-44	106 Sqn
419721 F/S	KEMPSON Keith Knowles	19-08-44	51 Sqn
437135 F/O	KENCH Robert Harold	31-12-44	218 Sqn
430890 F/S	KENEALY Edward Joseph	19-10-44	460 Sqn
420237 F/L	KENNEDY Terence William	1-06-44	156 Sqn
422198 F/O	KENNY Colin Joseph	29-10-44	463 Sqn
426439 F/O	KENYON Terence James	6-10-44	466 Sqn
410673 P/O	KERBY James Allan	27-01-44	460 Sqn
409553 P/O	KERR George Jeffreys	29-01-44	463 Sqn
426616 F/O	KERWIN Raymond Thomas	23-09-44	207 Sqn
401459 F/L	KEYS DFC Graeme Connell	5-05-44	139 Sqn
426112 F/S	KEYS John Neville	11-04-44	466 Sqn
426617 F/S	KEYS Noel Richard	27-08-44	97 Sqn
414698 F/O	KIDD Leslie	8-08-44	7 Sqn
417494 F/S	KIDMAN Anthony Sully	24-06-44	1662 HCU
408443 F/S	KILLWORTH William Deldon Douglas	8-07-44	467 Sqn
416862 F/S	KILSBY Neville Western	29-01-44	10 Sqn
15471 F/L	KING Frederick John	25-03-44	12 Sqn
410000 F/S	KING John Granville	19-03-44	166 Sqn
417307 F/S	KING Kenneth Leslie	10-06-44	460 Sqn
413393 W/O	KING Reginald John	15-03-44	460 Sqn
412542 W/O	KING Stanley George Richard	31-03-44	101 Sqn
411336 F/S	KINGHAM John Ernest Thomas Ridgeway	3-06-44	466 Sqn
419758 F/S	KINGSLEY Ronald George	12-10-44	30 OTU
414495 P/O	KINGSTON Patrick Noel	14-01-44	207 Sqn
420817 F/S	KINGSTON Roy Albert	20-02-44	166 Sqn
427123 F/S	KINSMAN William Clifton	5-02-44	26 OTU
434682 F/S	KIRBY Gilbert Thomas	12-09-44	467 Sqn
405246 F/L	KIRBY DFM John Albert	30-03-44	460 Sqn
412972 P/O	KIRKLAND Kenneth Herbert William	30-01-44	106 Sqn
420961 P/O	KIRKLAND Ronald Neville	28-05-44	460 Sqn
425168 F/S	KLEMM Eric James Leopold	12-09-44	467 Sqn
429581 F/S	KLEZEL Ronald Charles	6-10-44	466 Sqn
421601 F/S	KNIGHT Gordon Henry	7-06-44	44 Sqn
422801 P/O	KNIGHT Frederick James	7-06-44	460 Sqn
423420 F/S	KNIGHT Noel Joseph	10-05-44	1658 HCU

391

402869	F/L	KNYVETT DFC Barrington Armitage	2-01-44	460 Sqn
437425	F/S	KRIEG Carl Victor	1-07-44	101 Sqn
413874	W/O	KRONE Henry	15-03-44	460 Sqn
432211	F/S	KRONE John Duncan	8-06-44	466 Sqn
421870	W/O	KRUTLI Reginald Arthur	19-10-44	460 Sqn
426621	F/S	KYDD James	21-01-44	27 OTU
420015	P/O	KYLE Thomas Edmund Bede	24-03-44	7 Sqn
419126	F/S	LACK Maxwell Macdonald	25-06-44	463 Sqn
418130	F/O	LADE Donald Stephen	12-09-44	44 Sqn
435083	F/S	LADLEY John Kevin	11-11-44	101 Sqn
430373	F/S	LAIDLER Gordon James Keith	30-08-44	21 OTU
415800	P/O	LAIDLER Patrick William	14-04-44	5 LFS
429583	F/S	LAING Ainsworth	13-09-44	158 Sqn
424904	F/S	LAKE James Byrne	14-08-44	550 Sqn
400387	F/O	LAMB Colin Neilson	11-04-44	466 Sqn
409318	W/O	LAMBERT Alfred Leonard	23-06-44	97 Sqn
421229	F/S	LAMBERT Jack	22-03-44	7 Sqn
400388	F/O	LAMBLE Francis Stephen	23-06-44	460 Sqn
421428	F/S	LAMBOURNE Henry Edward	16-02-44	199 Sqn
429972	F/O	LANDRIDGE Leslie Keith	2-11-44	467 Sqn
25514	F/S	LANE Jeffrey Gordon	13-06-44	625 Sqn
428720	F/S	LANGDON Francis Charles	29-11-44	463 Sqn
426462	F/O	LANGTON Edwin Kay Lovell	25-10-44	115 Sqn
408157	F/O	LANGWORTHY DFC Walter Dinnathorne	7-01-44	1655 MTU
417855	F/S	LATHLEAN Rex Tidswell	24-07-44	102 Sqn
426355	F/S	LAURIE Lionel George	29-01-44	97 Sqn
425449	F/S	LAVER Leslie Alexander	20-02-44	466 Sqn
426752	F/S	LAVER Thomas Roy	10-05-44	1658 HCU
415432	F/O	LAW Norman Charles	30-01-44	97 Sqn
427652	F/S	LAWN Ronald Herbert	2-01-44	460 Sqn
417085	F/S	LAWRIE Edward Hurtle	21-02-44	460 Sqn
418132	F/S	LAWRY Alan Henry	19-07-44	100 Sqn
410244	P/O	LAWSON Stanley Wallace	2-01-44	463 Sqn
418963	F/S	LEA William Joseph	11-05-44	1654 HCU
429084	F/S	LEAKE Edward John	11-11-44	467 Sqn
424422	F/O	LEAKE Roslyn Downs	6-11-44	622 Sqn
415259	W/O	LEARY Joseph	28-04-44	460 Sqn
412455	W/O	LEAVER James Alfred	18-04-44	158 Sqn
423017	F/O	LEDSAM Douglas George	11-06-44	467 Sqn
426753	F/S	LEE Beverley Gordon	30-06-44	514 Sqn
419688	P/O	LEE David Thomas	5-11-44	15 Sqn
434687	F/S	LEE Desmond Maurice	4-12-44	1652 HCU
419272	F/S	LEEDER Vernon Victor Russell	4-08-44	635 Sqn
434463	F/S	LEES Noel John	19-03-44	466 Sqn
403750	F/S	LEES William Herbert	18-03-44	466 Sqn
419658	F/O	LEIBHARDT Winston Leslie	12-09-44	218 Sqn
434296	F/O	LEIGH James Standish	26-08-44	100 Sqn
427001	P/O	LEITCH Norman Colin Campbell	17-06-44	10 Sqn
427203	F/S	LEMIN William John	2-11-44	467 Sqn
416436	P/O	LEONARD Raymond Haines	11-09-44	156 Sqn
409721	F/S	LESLIE Alan James Durham	27-01-44	463 Sqn
425173	W/O	LESTER Donald Joseph	6-08-44	83 Sqn
412983	W/O	LETT Richard Wilson	29-11-44	460 Sqn
418285	F/S	LEVER Ernest James	7-02-44	19 OTU
429588	F/S	LEVEY Philip Hedley Malcolm	9-10-44	462 Sqn
429464	F/S	LEWIS Neville Ernest	21-11-44	51 Sqn
420759	F/S	LEWIS Victor Kingsbury	27-03-44	15 Sqn
10119	F/O	LEWIS William John	10-05-44	463 Sqn
425475	F/O	LEY Andrew Thomas	29-10-44	463 Sqn
412546	W/O	LE GAY BRERETON Robert	31-08-44	460 Sqn
410070	W/O	LE MAIRE John Sylvester	2-08-44	467 Sqn
421917	F/S	LIERSCH Claude Charles	21-01-44	460 Sqn
426358	P/O	LINCOLN Edward James	24-06-44	149 Sqn
425326	F/S	LINDENBERG Keith Roland	29-01-44	90 Sqn
428723	F/S	LINKLATER Llewellyn William	30-10-44	1667 HCU
423544	F/S	LLEWELLYN Arthur Bevan	23-10-44	12 Sqn
410423	F/O	LLEWELYN Ronald Ernest	31-03-44	467 Sqn
414050	P/O	LLOYD Norman David Livingstone	4-05-44	460 Sqn
419321	F/S	LOCKLIER Norman Edward	13-05-44	466 Sqn
420573	F/L	LOFTUS DFC Watson Temple	9-05-44	83 Sqn
425328	F/S	LONG Arthur Stephen	1-06-44	15 Sqn
423290	F/S	LOONEY Francis Noel	3-01-44	463 Sqn
421603	F/O	LOPEZ Robin Henry	24-09-44	97 Sqn
408486	P/O	LORD Peter Redgrave	6-10-44	466 Sqn
18119	P/O	LOUGHNAN Justin Francis	14-10-44	115 Sqn
429465	F/S	LOUGHNAN Walter Keith	4-11-44	195 Sqn
415339	F/L	LOVE William John Hamilton	24-02-44	578 Sqn
428142	F/S	LOW Peter Morris	20-10-44	460 Sqn
427002	P/O	LOWE James Thomas	4-12-44	15 Sqn
437210	F/O	LOWE Robert Arthur Edward	21-07-44	51 Sqn
414711	P/O	LUDLOW Robert Lanoel	29-01-44	467 Sqn
428278	F/S	LUGTON Reginald Gordon	26-06-44	1667 HCU
428331	P/O	LUPTON James Samuel	12-09-44	514 Sqn
426778	F/S	LUTON Vincent Donovan	22-06-44	467 Sqn
419661	F/S	LYALL William Brian	19-04-44	166 Sqn
420693	P/O	LYFORD Norman Joseph	30-01-44	44 Sqn
410355	F/S	LYNCH Arnold John	20-01-44	460 Sqn
408658	F/O	LYON DFC James Henry Scott	15-03-44	11 OTU
404752	F/L	LYONS DFC Kenneth Marcus Denbigh	30-08-44	463 Sqn
423018	F/S	L'GREEN Neville Alfred	12-12-44	149 Sqn
405955	P/O	MacDOUGALL Allan Douglas	13-09-44	15 Sqn
425178	F/O	MacFADYEN Duncan	10-06-44	49 Sqn
432219	Sgt	MacFARLANE Murdo Donald Davidson	24-04-44	21 OTU
423797	W/O	MacKENZIE Allan Richard	4-11-44	463 Sqn
420354	F/O	MacLEAN Douglas Wallace	23-10-44	12 Sqn
414312	W/O	MacLEOD Eric Ronald Fergus	31-03-44	158 Sqn
419821	F/O	MacMEIKAN Henry Stanley	7-12-44	463 Sqn
423850	F/O	MacPHILLAMY Owen Scott	13-08-44	578 Sqn
426124	P/O	MACDONALD Keith Mitchell	3-01-44	619 Sqn
422633	F/O	MACDONNELL John Hugh Douglas	24-03-44	7 Sqn
434739	F/S	MACGUGAN Ian Fairlie	12-09-44	622 Sqn
412463	F/L	MACK Frank Wharton	29-01-44	466 Sqn
439896	F/S	MACKAY Charles Bede	8-11-44	1662 HCU
414809	F/O	MACKAY Stuart Walter	17-06-44	77 Sqn
417211	F/S	MACKENZIE Douglas John	2-05-44	75 Sqn
414052	P/O	MACKINTOSH Harold Charles Leeton	21-02-44	630 Sqn
410248	F/S	MACKRELL Stanley Vincent	20-02-44	460 Sqn
409166	P/O	MACMILLAN DFC John Ferguson	29-01-44	57 Sqn
426127	F/S	MACOUN George	26-02-44	1661 HCU
439480	F/S	MACPHERSON John Stuart	6-10-44	463 Sqn
428892	F/S	MACRAE Ian Francis	18-12-44	50 Sqn
23723	F/S	MADDALENA Harold James	12-10-44	21 OTU
439657	F/O	MAGGS Arthur Wallace Spencer	8-11-44	1662 HCU
417590	F/S	MAHAR Maurice John	30-08-44	467 Sqn
421812	F/S	MAHER Thomas Francis	5-07-44	463 Sqn
273734	F/L	MAHONEY John Joseph	23-05-44	57 Sqn
423547	F/S	MALONEY John Benedict	4-12-44	207 Sqn
437624	F/S	MANLY Richard Joseph	19-10-44	29 OTU
436085	F/S	MANSELL Jack Peter	24-08-44	1666 HCU
420225	F/S	MANSFIELD Ronald	9-04-44	460 Sqn
401986	F/S	MANUEL William Victor	26-02-44	1661 HCU
423205	W/O	MAPLE James Fraser	23-10-44	463 Sqn
424775	F/S	MARDEN John Barrymore	14-06-44	11 OTU
17520	F/O	MARSH DFC Norman Albert	19-11-44	1656 HCU
424532	F/S	MARSH Norman Edward	25-07-44	622 Sqn
417311	F/S	MARSH Peter Andrew	21-01-44	97 Sqn
422220	F/O	MARSH Walter Ernest	22-05-44	463 Sqn
427527	F/O	MARSHALL Mervyn	31-10-44	460 Sqn
423818	P/O	MARSHALL Roland Maxwell	8-06-44	166 Sqn
413219	F/L	MARTIN Charles James	25-02-44	463 Sqn
417392	F/S	MARTIN Colin Hillier	25-02-44	463 Sqn
417503	F/S	MARTIN Donald Henry	10-04-44	460 Sqn
414812	F/S	MARTIN Douglas Charles	14-04-44	466 Sqn
23503	F/S	MARTIN James Francis	11-02-44	21 OTU
16203	P/O	MARTIN John Francis	25-06-44	463 Sqn

Service No	Rank	Name	Date	Sqn
414313	W/O	MARTIN John Randall	25-03-44	460 Sqn
430626	F/S	MARTIN Kenneth Andrew	12-09-44	90 Sqn
420838	P/O	MARTIN Ronald Cecil	25-02-44	460 Sqn
419806	P/O	MATTINGLEY Albert Frank	22-05-44	463 Sqn
419196	P/O	MAUGHAN Peter Coakes	12-09-44	467 Sqn
412562	W/O	MAUNDER John Henry	11-04-44	466 Sqn
410001	F/S	MAUNSELL Bernard Kingston	27-01-44	12 Sqn
425331	F/O	MAXWELL Gordon Edward	19-04-44	630 Sqn
426130	F/S	MAXWELL Lewis Keith	19-06-44	27 OTU
429831	F/S	MAY Philip Stroud	23-06-44	76 Sqn
428011	P/O	MAYHEAD Jack Maxwell	8-06-44	622 Sqn
408913	W/O	MAYNE Albert Francis	22-05-44	463 Sqn
21660	F/S	McALLISTER Henry Gillon	28-04-44	460 Sqn
411510	F/S	McALLISTER Norman Archibald	15-03-44	149 Sqn
424551	F/S	McALLISTER Ronald	6-08-44	97 Sqn
412623	P/O	McALPINE Keith George	20-02-44	35 Sqn
429122	F/S	McATEER Hilton Henry	12-09-44	90 Sqn
434227	F/O	McCALL Cyril	23-09-44	463 Sqn
410696	P/O	McCARTHY Charles Adrian	24-06-44	7 Sqn
426371	F/S	McCARTHY Leonard James	20-01-44	76 Sqn
419328	F/O	McCARTIN Patrick Leo	20-11-44	75 Sqn
425408	P/O	McCASKER Evered Austin	5-11-44	466 Sqn
428252	F/S	McCAUGHEY Peter Francis	25-02-44	12 Sqn
424110	F/S	McCONVILLE Douglas William	13-08-44	9 Sqn
422631	F/S	McCORMACK Robert Browning	13-08-44	90 Sqn
418722	F/S	McCOY Louis Joseph Patrick	22-06-44	44 Sqn
429607	F/S	McCRAY David William	17-12-44	50 Sqn
433857	F/S	McCULLUM George Roger	4-12-44	106 Sqn
410699	F/O	McCURDY Thomas Neil	27-08-44	97 Sqn
419584	F/O	McDONALD Donald Ian	24-12-44	103 Sqn
426372	F/S	McDONALD Donald James	23-04-44	463 Sqn
433234	F/S	McDONALD Douglas Ross	18-09-44	27 OTU
407529	F/L	McDONALD DFM James Neil	13-08-44	156 Sqn
414419	F/O	McDONALD John Walter	11-02-44	161 Sqn
409729	W/O	McDONALD Norman Neil	22-05-44	463 Sqn
418972	F/S	McDONNELL David Kenneth	22-06-44	207 Sqn
38449	F/S	McDONOUGH Frederick Noel	16-05-44	625 Sqn
421611	F/O	McDOUGALL Raymond Albert James	13-08-44	115 Sqn
410609	F/O	McDOUGALL Robert Bruce	11-04-44	460 Sqn
424303	F/S	McFADDEN Oscar Patrick	28-05-44	166 Sqn
429340	F/O	McGILL John Alexander Douglas	10-06-44	97 Sqn
426895	F/S	McGLADRIGAN Neil Francis Dallaway	10-12-44	57 Sqn
428341	P/O	McGRATH Graham Edward	4-12-44	1652 HCU
418704	F/S	McGRATH James Roch	18-03-44	463 Sqn
432441	F/O	McGRATH Terence James	4-11-44	158 Sqn
424536	F/S	McGREGOR Leslie James	25-06-44	106 Sqn
417714	F/S	McINTYRE Allan David	31-08-44	21 OTU
426653	F/S	McINTYRE James Robert	23-09-44	576 Sqn
425042	F/S	McKAY Malcolm John	24-03-44	158 Sqn
422255	F/O	McKAY William Dennett	25-05-44	15 Sqn
416443	W/O	McKENZIE Lloyd George	10-05-44	463 Sqn
410367	P/O	McKENZIE William Douglas	9-04-44	460 Sqn
407531	F/L	McKINNON DFC Allan Francis	25-03-44	460 Sqn
425881	F/S	McKINNON John Alexander Woodrow	2-08-44	467 Sqn
415347	P/O	McKNIGHT Kevin Harold	26-02-44	463 Sqn
414947	F/S	McLACHLAN William Robertson	27-01-44	460 Sqn
434647	F/S	McLAY John Stirling	5-11-44	466 Sqn
413091	F/L	McLEAN DFC Francis Eric	14-08-44	83 Sqn
424124	F/S	McLEAN Gordon William	28-04-44	100 Sqn
414959	F/S	McLEAN John Gold	30-01-44	463 Sqn
426666	F/S	McLEAN Robert Hudson	30-08-44	106 Sqn
419844	F/S	McLEAN Stanley	7-10-44	514 Sqn
422658	F/S	McLEOD Gordon Wesley	1-09-44	138 Sqn
415672	F/S	McLEOD James	25-02-44	467 Sqn
418296	F/S	McLEOD John Wilbert	7-05-44	576 Sqn
413409	S/L	McLEOD DFC Lewis Arthur John	22-06-44	97 Sqn
12189	F/O	McLEOD Malcolm John	4-07-44	463 Sqn
415269	P/O	McLOUGHLIN James Archibald	30-01-44	115 Sqn
429612	F/S	McMANUS Trevor Alwyn	6-10-44	466 Sqn
423845	F/S	McMASTER Gordon	20-02-44	15 Sqn
434470	P/O	McMASTER Ross Faulkner	21-11-44	460 Sqn
421666	F/O	McMONAGLE Lance Raymond	6-10-44	49 Sqn
425732	F/L	McMULLAN Harcourt Hunter	8-05-44	138 Sqn
406660	S/L	McMULLAN John Francis	22-06-44	466 Sqn
426658	P/O	McNAMARA Michael Frederick John	12-06-44	102 Sqn
413135	W/O	McNAUGHT Donald Hubert	4-05-44	101 Sqn
435175	F/S	McPHAIL Angus Murdock	18-12-44	27 OTU
412261	W/O	McPHEE Athol Neil Douglas	20-02-44	466 Sqn
414267	P/O	McPHIE DFC Keith Cumming	29-01-44	57 Sqn
408338	F/S	McQUITTY Robert John	24-06-44	149 Sqn
425346	F/S	McSWEENEY Gerald Beaumont	5-06-44	27 OTU
422871	F/S	McWHINNEY Joseph	30-08-44	467 Sqn
423152	P/O	MEHDEN Leonard Eugene	20-05-44	115 Sqn
417870	F/O	MELLOWSHIP Rodney James	13-08-44	467 Sqn
418143	P/O	MELVILLE Peter Gordon	26-03-44	192 Sqn
434468	F/S	MENGEL Colin Eric	23-09-44	12 Sqn
424199	W/O	MENZIES Neil Macdonald	4-12-44	106 Sqn
425714	F/O	MERCER Richard Walter	14-08-44	44 Sqn
422609	P/O	MEREDITH Owen Frederick	2-11-44	15 Sqn
426132	F/S	MERRIN Sidney William	9-06-44	467 Sqn
411652	F/O	MESSENGER George Laurie	30-01-44	463 Sqn
437314	F/O	MIDDLETON Charles Gordon	19-10-44	460 Sqn
423153	F/O	MIDDLETON John Hartley	6-10-44	207 Sqn
423833	F/S	MILES Norman Walter	1-07-44	100 Sqn
424432	F/S	MILLER George Thomas	18-12-44	27 OTU
435780	F/S	MILLER Leonard Edric James	22-12-44	463 Sqn
426133	Sgt	MILLER Raymond	3-01-44	11 OTU
13742	F/O	MILLER Russell Johnstone	28-09-44	463 Sqn
417215	W/O	MILLIKAN Kenneth Thomas	23-05-44	106 Sqn
426367	P/O	MILLINER Jack Thomas	25-07-44	75 Sqn
425036	F/S	MILLS Samuel	21-07-44	75 Sqn
410509	F/S	MILLS Thomas George David	12-03-44	199 Sqn
421661	W/O	MINCHIN George Henry	19-07-44	420 Sqn
436054	F/S	MINCHIN Vernon Harold	29-10-44	50 Sqn
412469	W/O	MINEEFF Alexis Charles	25-06-44	463 Sqn
417981	F/S	MITCHELL Colin James	23-09-44	582 Sqn
29132	F/S	MITCHELL David Sneddon	13-06-44	578 Sqn
422619	F/S	MITCHELL Donald Lamont	11-11-44	44 Sqn
60895	P/O	MITCHELL Jack	22-06-44	467 Sqn
408312	P/O	MITCHELL Jack	22-01-44	467 Sqn
422544	F/S	MITCHELL Kenneth Stanley Malcolm	25-06-44	50 Sqn
418452	P/O	MITCHELL Robert Richard	2-11-44	462 Sqn
411099	F/S	MOFFATT Malcolm Douglas	13-08-44	625 Sqn
425454	F/O	MOLINAS DFC Frank Francis	19-07-44	619 Sqn
426369	F/S	MOLLER Augustus Ronald	11-06-44	166 Sqn
417873	F/S	MOLLET Clarence Keith	5-07-44	460 Sqn
421364	P/O	MOLONEY Patrick Murray	25-04-44	424 Sqn
408860	W/O	MOLONY Henry Richardson	24-06-44	1662 HCU
410168	F/S	MONCRIEFF Edwin Douglas	21-01-44	115 Sqn
424271	F/S	MONTGOMERY John William Arthur	3-06-44	640 Sqn
422623	F/O	MOODY William Edgar Laurence	8-06-44	1667 HCU
428256	F/S	MOODY William Joseph	28-05-44	466 Sqn
424435	F/S	MOONEY James Martin	31-03-44	50 Sqn
422625	F/S	MOORE Ernest Roy	31-03-44	158 Sqn
409004	W/O	MOORE Jack Findlay	16-08-44	625 Sqn
423433	F/S	MOORE Richard John William	13-06-44	622 Sqn
432254	F/S	MOORE Stanley James	9-12-44	171 Sqn
415168	W/O	MORAN James Francisco	20-02-44	466 Sqn
437436	F/S	MORAN Laurence Dominic	30-10-44	21 OTU
423822	F/L	MORAN William John	27-08-44	15 Sqn
405465	P/O	MORETON DFC Kenneth	29-01-44	57 Sqn
419096	F/S	MOREY Mervyn Langdon	4-11-44	195 Sqn
429601	F/S	MORGAN Allen	29-01-44	466 Sqn
419274	F/O	MORRIS John Nathan	20-02-44	460 Sqn
422652	W/O	MORRIS Rae Latham	23-10-44	467 Sqn
423824	P/O	MORRISON DFC Alexander Donald	24-12-44	635 Sqn
415435	W/O	MORRISON Roderick de Burgh	29-01-44	77 Sqn

414315	F/O	MORTAL Clive Watson Peter	2-11-44	576 Sqn	420250	P/O	O'BRIEN Cecil	28-01-44	467 Sqn
255684	F/L	MORTIMER DFC Ronald James	25-02-44	463 Sqn	425740	F/S	O'BRIEN John Leo	30-01-44	514 Sqn
423231	F/O	MOSES Keith James	13-06-44	166 Sqn	432451	F/O	O'CONNELL Francis Emanuel	5-07-44	35 Sqn
427533	F/O	MOTTERAM Harry Lawrence	4-11-44	49 Sqn	426377	F/S	O'CONNELL Paul Francis	25-06-44	467 Sqn
423163	P/O	MOULDEN William Robert Harold	22-05-44	115 Sqn	29520	F/S	O'CONNOR Ian	15-11-44	1666 HCU
415482	F/S	MOULSDALE John Russell	11-04-44	514 Sqn	429730	F/S	O'DONNELL Brian John	6-12-44	10 Sqn
421073	P/O	MOXEY Wilfred George	31-03-44	106 Sqn	420906	P/O	O'DONNELL William John	22-01-44	432 Sqn
410845	F/S	MOXHAM Bernard	27-04-44	12 Sqn	429200	F/S	O'DWYER Edmond William	22-07-44	20 OTU
420478	F/S	MOYLAN Patrick	30-01-44	625 Sqn	422978	F/S	O'HALLORAN Desmond Michael Leonid		
423829	F/S	MUDFORD Alan James Wesley	13-07-44	550 Sqn			[Eire]	24-12-44	166 Sqn
29886	F/S	MUDIE James	2-01-44	467 Sqn	434189	F/O	O'LEARY Patrick Joseph	8-07-44	106 Sqn
418864	P/O	MUNDAY Harvey Francis	6-06-44	149 Sqn	410370	W/O	O'MEARA John Patrick	17-06-44	77 Sqn
409210	P/O	MUNRO Duncan John	15-03-44	149 Sqn	415949	F/S	O'NEILL Richard Glasson	20-02-44	78 Sqn
426647	F/O	MUNROE Albert Henry	15-10-44	466 Sqn	415910	P/O	O'SULLIVAN Robert John	15-11-44	115 Sqn
418545	F/S	MURDOCH Robert Daniel	15-02-44	97 Sqn	410171	P/O	PAGE Eric Wilton	25-04-44	463 Sqn
429472	F/O	MURPHY Desmond Eric	4-12-44	44 Sqn	409481	W/O	PAGE Frank Albert	23-05-44	75 Sqn
417399	F/S	MURPHY Eric Reginald Harry	3-02-44	21 OTU	409584	P/O	PAGE Keith Charles	28-05-44	466 Sqn
427394	F/S	MURPHY John Anthony	28-04-44	640 Sqn	425207	F/S	PALFREYMAN Austin Hardcastle	11-04-44	460 Sqn
413020	W/O	MURPHY John Armstrong	31-03-44	156 Sqn	422257	F/O	PALMER John Michael	24-03-44	61 Sqn
419669	F/S	MURPHY William	25-07-44	166 Sqn	420995	F/S	PALMER Kenneth Arthur Malcolm	26-07-44	1657 HCU
413640	F/S	MURRAY John David	4-04-44	5 LFS	415677	F/S	PALMER Stanley John Fielding	15-03-44	463 Sqn
432423	F/O	MURRAY John William	6-10-44	49 Sqn	433753	F/S	PANWICK Keith	3-09-44	1656 HCU
424817	P/O	MURRAY Robert McAuly	12-12-44	15 Sqn	419211	F/S	PARDON Noel Albert	29-06-44	102 Sqn
434406	F/O	MURRAY William Henry	20-02-44	640 Sqn	422680	P/O	PARKER Meredith Burford	22-06-44	466 Sqn
430628	Sgt	MURTON Thomas Dudley	21-01-44	27 OTU	429491	F/S	PARKER Neal Earl	4-05-44	625 Sqn
427535	F/S	MUTTON Leslie	29-07-44	576 Sqn	424451	F/S	PARKER Ralf	30-08-44	463 Sqn
415350	P/O	NAIRN Alex Frederick	2-01-44	83 Sqn	435406	F/O	PARKER Robert Charles	16-10-44	30 OTU
427537	F/S	NALLEN Charles Patrick	4-06-44	635 Sqn	422350	F/S	PARKER Ronald Henry George	31-03-44	106 Sqn
422348	F/S	NAPIER DFM William Conrad	27-04-44	101 Sqn	413416	P/O	PARKINSON George Edward	15-03-44	460 Sqn
419449	F/S	NASH George Edward	8-07-44	61 Sqn	422259	P/O	PARKINSON Herbert Alexander Watson		
425885	F/S	NAYLER Edward Allan	24-04-44	21 OTU				9-06-44	467 Sqn
411227	F/O	NEAL Ronald Leslie	28-04-44	460 Sqn	436658	F/S	PARRY Ernest Arthur	29-11-44	460 Sqn
410557	F/S	NEESON Andrew John	31-01-44	626 Sqn	426757	P/O	PARSONS Albert William Milne	12-09-44	158 Sqn
419561	F/O	NELDER Frank Edward	23-10-44	462 Sqn	434266	F/S	PARSONS Arthur Stuart	31-08-44	550 Sqn
410710	F/S	NELSON Stanley James	26-02-44	463 Sqn	421619	F/O	PASSANT Reginald Herbert	8-07-44	61 Sqn
427015	F/S	NEWBEY Norman Lindsay	30-07-44	11 OTU	423311	F/S	PATE Gilbert Firth	10-05-44	467 Sqn
410253	F/S	NEWELL Edward Sargent	18-03-44	466 Sqn	427726	F/S	PATERSON David Alastair	16-07-44	467 Sqn
428888	F/S	NEWELL Norman Lindsay	16-02-44	77 Sqn	401146	F/L	PATKIN Leo Braham	2-01-44	467 Sqn
423003	F/S	NEWELL Rex John	15-02-44	466 Sqn	13084	W/O	PATON Frederick James Lincoln	2-11-44	576 Sqn
427929	F/S	NEWMAN George Henry	19-10-44	460 Sqn	423326	F/S	PATON John Howie	21-02-44	115 Sqn
426999	F/S	NEWMAN John Bede	31-03-44	101 Sqn	422684	F/S	PATTERSON Arthur Robert	28-04-44	460 Sqn
422083	P/O	NEWMAN Stanley William	28-05-44	514 Sqn	421932	P/O	PATTERSON DFC Donald Richard	24-12-44	635 Sqn
415270	F/L	NEWTON John Verdun	14-01-44	7 Sqn	430939	F/S	PAVEY Kevin Ambrose	26-08-44	100 Sqn
417507	F/S	NICHOLLS Peter William	13-05-44	466 Sqn	423870	F/S	PAUL William	16-07-44	467 Sqn
413886	W/O	NICHOLS Laurence John	13-05-44	466 Sqn	420999	F/S	PAXMAN Leonard Gower	31-03-44	158 Sqn
428765	F/S	NICHOLSON James Arthur	31-03-44	158 Sqn	417512	F/S	PAYNE Malcolm Henry	13-07-44	9 Sqn
417220	F/O	NICHOLSON Ronald Laing	10-06-44	460 Sqn	437695	F/S	PAYNE Richard James	18-11-44	460 Sqn
423855	F/O	NICHOLSON William	4-11-44	466 Sqn	415440	F/O	PEAD Gordon	13-08-44	101 Sqn
26423	F/S	NIELSEN Murray Wilton	30-07-44	102 Sqn	417110	P/O	PEAK Colin Albert	11-04-44	9 Sqn
401638	P/O	NIMMO James Andrew Harold	10-04-44	103 Sqn	427934	F/S	PEARCE Philip John	19-07-44	463 Sqn
424570	F/S	NOAKES Gordon Hughie	25-04-44	463 Sqn	417228	F/S	PEARCE William Robinson	8-06-44	466 Sqn
412660	P/O	NOLAN Allan William	4-06-44	44 Sqn	429017	P/O	PEARMAIN Henry John	2-11-44	102 Sqn
432627	F/S	NORMYLE John Hilary	30-07-44	27 OTU	406550	F/O	PEARSE Lawrence Wilfred	22-01-44	467 Sqn
417875	P/O	NORSWORTHY Robert Keith	23-12-44	35 Sqn	421382	F/S	PEARSON Arthur Barton	2-01-44	83 Sqn
427016	F/S	NOSKE John Alfred	31-03-44	101 Sqn	421453	F/S	PEARSON Laurence Randolph	23-06-44	460 Sqn
421543	F/O	NOTT Jack Stewart	9-07-44	77 Sqn	415913	P/O	PEGGS Robert James	23-05-44	77 Sqn
425199	F/S	NYSTROM Stanley Arthur	1-06-44	15 Sqn	417229	F/O	PELLEW Robert Everard	19-07-44	115 Sqn
422246	F/S	OAKES Ronald Mansfield	14-01-44	115 Sqn	418170	F/S	PEMBERTON Lloyd Lewis	29-07-44	106 Sqn
420493	P/O	OBERG Albert Edward	19-04-44	57 Sqn	423178	F/S	PEPPER Merton George	20-02-44	466 Sqn
426943	F/S	OBERHARDT Edgar	10-04-44	460 Sqn	423313	W/O	PERCY Francis McLeoad	13-08-44	625 Sqn
418559	F/O	OGILVIE James Henderson	18-12-44	463 Sqn	432256	P/O	PERKINS Alan John	27-09-44	467 Sqn
421754	F/S	OHLSON Jack Olof	21-07-44	467 Sqn	434608	F/S	PERRETT Keith Jobson	21-01-44	27 OTU
422671	F/S	OLIVER David James	20-10-44	460 Sqn	417513	F/S	PERRIAM Harold Alan	10-01-44	1652 HCU
436361	F/S	OLSEN George Glenn	6-12-44	460 Sqn	435225	F/S	PERRIE James William	30-08-44	467 Sqn
408733	W/O	OSBORN John Bruce	11-04-44	51 Sqn	423878	P/O	PETERS Walter Thomas	10-05-44	463 Sqn
417877	F/S	OSBORNE John Edward	21-07-44	75 Sqn	418873	W/O	PETERSEN Ernest Arthur [New Zealand]	6-11-44	463 Sqn
418560	F/S	OSBORNE Ronald Henderson	2-05-44	218 Sqn	426675	F/S	PETITT Donald Walker	2-03-44	15 OTU
410560	F/S	OSHLACK Joe	3-06-44	466 Sqn	436274	F/O	PETTIFORD Frederick John	21-11-44	460 Sqn
38181	F/O	OTTAWAY Winton Greer	21-11-44	460 Sqn	434148	F/S	PEUT Robert Henry Christopher	30-08-44	467 Sqn

Service No	Rank	Name	Date	Unit
420045	W/O	PHILIP John	23-10-44	12 Sqn
418299	F/S	PHILIPSON Ernest John	16-03-44	630 Sqn
429855	F/O	PHILLIPS Clement Arthur	29-07-44	467 Sqn
428454	F/S	PHILLIPS Victor Wilfred	3-06-44	466 Sqn
426260	P/O	PHILP Ross Ferrier	7-10-44	161 Sqn
428860	P/O	PICKEN Jacques Andre	2-11-44	102 Sqn
421122	F/O	PICKWORTH Colin Reginald	2-01-44	460 Sqn
424212	F/O	PINN Geoffrey Philip	13-05-44	466 Sqn
424880	P/O	PLOWMAN Arthur Leslie	11-11-44	207 Sqn
427348	W/O	PLUMB William	6-11-44	463 Sqn
428353	P/O	PLUMRIDGE John Bithel	4-12-44	467 Sqn
429482	F/S	PODOSKY Gilbert Graham	8-07-44	467 Sqn
418011	F/S	POGONOWSKI Jeffrey Eugene	15-02-44	35 Sqn
419481	F/S	PORRITT Leonard Haig	8-07-44	467 Sqn
414956	P/O	PORTER John Henry	22-03-44	44 Sqn
427544	W/O	PORTER William Alfred	21-11-44	51 Sqn
40230	F/S	PORTER William Robert Rex	8-06-44	1667 HCU
417313	W/O	POTTER Keith George	7-10-44	460 Sqn
409742	P/O	POTTER Leslie Clifford	29-06-44	102 Sqn
432269	F/S	POTTER Thomas Donovan	8-09-44	29 OTU
424457	P/O	POTTINGER Francis Joseph	29-07-44	467 Sqn
424680	F/S	POULSON Leslie William	3-12-44	138 Sqn
423320	P/O	POWE Trevor Sutherland	9-12-44	171 Sqn
418323	F/S	POWELL Joseph William	14-10-44	166 Sqn
402817	S/L	POWELL DFC Mervyn	11-05-44	463 Sqn
432435	F/S	POWER John Renton	22-12-44	463 Sqn
409590	W/O	POWER Richard John	27-01-44	460 Sqn
430051	F/S	POWERS David Kingsley	30-08-44	166 Sqn
404468	F/S	POYZER DFM Arthur Wallace	7-06-44	83 Sqn
425210	F/S	PRATT Lancelot George	17-06-44	77 Sqn
416994	P/O	PRATTEN Murray Edmund	22-05-44	463 Sqn
421756	F/O	PRESTON James Robert Richard	11-09-44	51 Sqn
413423	F/O	PRITCHARD Jack Stephen	27-04-44	460 Sqn
417913	F/S	PRITCHARD John	1-07-44	101 Sqn
420054	F/O	PROBERT Arthur Harold	11-04-44	460 Sqn
425549	F/S	PRONGER Harold William	31-03-44	61 Sqn
413894	P/O	PROUD Robert John	10-04-44	460 Sqn
412686	W/O	PURCELL Royston William	10-05-44	467 Sqn
425099	F/L	PURRY Ronald Leonard	15-06-44	15 Sqn
421625	F/O	PURSEY DFC Gordon James	27-07-44	83 Sqn
408408	P/O	PURVIS Graham	27-11-44	115 Sqn
429347	F/O	QUAN William Patrick	19-08-44	51 Sqn
418175	F/S	RADLEY Kenneth McDonald	31-03-44	51 Sqn
423323	F/S	RANDELL Norman James	20-02-44	460 Sqn
410725	F/S	RANDS Ian Albert	10-04-44	57 Sqn
9361	F/O	RAPER William	2-01-44	156 Sqn
423256	F/O	RATTLE William Frederick Henry	13-06-44	622 Sqn
424797	F/O	RAWSON George Dudley	4-12-44	467 Sqn
406700	F/S	READ William Neil	11-05-44	463 Sqn
427548	F/S	READER Gordon Sydney	17-09-44	102 Sqn
426157	F/S	REAY Eric Lascelles	29-03-44	1652 HCU
427106	F/S	REECE Bernard	29-07-44	463 Sqn
426685	F/S	REED Charles William	21-01-44	460 Sqn
437544	F/S	REED Keith Arthur George	2-11-44	463 Sqn
409224	F/O	REID DFC Brian Clapham	12-12-44	460 Sqn
434012	F/S	REID Donald Alan	6-12-44	207 Sqn
427044	F/O	REID DFC Edward Forbes	31-10-44	460 Sqn
429738	F/S	REID Frank Bruce	1-06-44	15 Sqn
424799	F/O	REILLY Kevin William	4-11-44	463 Sqn
415276	F/S	REYNOLDS Colin Irwin	6-01-44	467 Sqn
427148	F/S	RICH Warwick William	26-01-44	1652 HCU
415357	F/S	RICHARDS John Edward	19-03-44	466 Sqn
417259	F/O	RICHARDSON Ernest Hartley	23-10-44	462 Sqn
422298	F/O	RICHINS Denis Richard Garth	23-10-44	460 Sqn
426915	F/S	RICHMOND Bruce Stanley	23-05-44	432 Sqn
425752	F/S	RIDGWAY John Thomas	3-06-44	466 Sqn
3717	F/O	RILEY Alexander Douglas	30-01-44	467 Sqn
408595	W/O	RIMINGTON Keith Edward	20-01-44	466 Sqn
418879	F/O	ROBB Laurence William	10-04-44	460 Sqn
416893	F/O	ROBERTS DFC John	15-03-44	463 Sqn
415358	F/L	ROBERTS DFC Kimberley	7-06-44	619 Sqn
417760	P/O	ROBERTS Robert Edward	12-12-44	218 Sqn
423922	F/S	ROBERTS Thomas Leo	21-07-44	467 Sqn
428608	F/S	ROBERTSON Frank Lorne	21-07-44	626 Sqn
420498	F/L	ROBERTSON Ian James	21-01-44	7 Sqn
424821	F/S	ROBERTSON John Maxwell	25-04-44	100 Sqn
416706	F/S	ROBERTSON Ross Lange	25-03-44	466 Sqn
412190	F/O	ROBERTSON William Alfred	2-01-44	156 Sqn
423896	F/S	ROBIN Philip Rollo Aloysius	13-06-44	578 Sqn
420402	F/O	ROBINSON Aubrey	2-01-44	460 Sqn
412304	F/L	ROBINSON DFC Harry George Mason	15-07-44	156 Sqn
416614	P/O	ROBINSON Kevin Alphonsus	16-02-44	199 Sqn
419540	F/S	ROBINSON Nicholas Francis	6-10-44	466 Sqn
434999	F/S	ROBSON Lionel Kenneth	5-10-44	101 Sqn
418571	F/S	ROBSON Phillip Allan	12-06-44	102 Sqn
5136	P/O	ROCHE Austin Frederick	13-06-44	460 Sqn
426161	F/S	ROCHE William Joseph	2-01-44	630 Sqn
437292	F/O	RODERICK Beresford Clayton	25-07-44	1661 HCU
421628	P/O	RODGERS Alexander Gordon	19-07-44	76 Sqn
425809	F/O	ROE Morris James	30-08-44	463 Sqn
419962	F/S	ROGERS David Anderson	24-07-44	102 Sqn
430298	F/S	ROGERS Frank Raymond	19-07-44	467 Sqn
24612	P/O	ROGERS Ormond Roy	22-03-44	49 Sqn
434016	F/O	ROOME Henry Frederick	13-08-44	514 Sqn
424822	F/S	ROPER John	10-05-44	1658 HCU
14464	P/O	ROSE Cyril Ashley	31-03-44	156 Sqn
437319	F/S	ROSE George Henry	13-05-44	640 Sqn
418179	F/O	ROSE Max	8-07-44	57 Sqn
429351	F/O	ROSS Edward Hugh	22-05-44	463 Sqn
407562	P/O	ROSS DFM Edwin John	2-01-44	460 Sqn
410096	P/O	ROSSER Edward Walters	22-03-44	106 Sqn
419608	F/S	ROTHWELL Len	27-07-44	619 Sqn
419140	F/S	ROUTLEY Anthony John	1-07-44	100 Sqn
415830	P/O	ROWE Sydney Lawrence	4-05-44	103 Sqn
422714	F/O	ROWELL Edward Berkley	23-10-44	467 Sqn
424838	F/S	ROWLEY Kenneth Harold	23-10-44	12 Sqn
409747	F/S	ROWLEY Reginald William	2-01-44	460 Sqn
432270	F/S	ROXBY Albert	19-07-44	100 Sqn
437162	F/S	ROY Maxwell Keith Gordon	21-07-44	467 Sqn
434018	F/S	ROYES Robert Henry	31-10-44	460 Sqn
418303	F/S	RUDD Royal Robert	11-04-44	78 Sqn
430056	F/O	RUGLEN John Mortimer	18-09-44	27 OTU
410122	F/O	RUSSELL DFC William Noel Thomsett	23-04-44	466 Sqn
422301	F/S	RUST Kenneth William	12-09-44	622 Sqn
418473	F/S	RYAN David Henry	31-08-44	463 Sqn
426393	F/S	RYAN Douglas James	19-07-44	49 Sqn
416459	F/S	RYAN Edward John	8-08-44	90 Sqn
418695	F/O	RYAN Keith Francis	11-04-44	460 Sqn
422302	F/O	RYAN Leonard Myles	10-04-44	460 Sqn
418012	F/O	RYAN Philip Wyatt	8-07-44	467 Sqn
424923	F/S	RYAN Terrence Russell	30-08-44	463 Sqn
436485	F/S	RYDER Edward Maxwell	5-11-44	466 Sqn
423427	F/S	RYE Clive Arthur	1-03-44	76 Sqn
422008	F/S	SADLER Maurice Edward	2-01-44	463 Sqn
403380	F/O	SAINT-SMITH DFC DFM James Alexander	29-06-44	627 Sqn
434842	F/S	SALIGARI Stanley John	22-06-44	467 Sqn
427153	F/S	SAMPEY William Albert	2-01-44	463 Sqn
417520	F/S	SAMPSON Frederick Richard	27-04-44	78 Sqn
425760	F/S	SAMSON Keith Paul	13-08-44	76 Sqn
423334	F/O	SANDELL David John	30-08-44	467 Sqn
421085	F/O	SANDILANDS Geoffrey Bruce Hope	16-10-44	30 OTU
426690	F/O	SAVAGE John Francis	24-03-44	35 Sqn
425365	F/S	SAVAGE Richard Thomas Percival	25-09-44	199 Sqn
417521	F/S	SAWTELL Arthur Hartley	24-02-44	75 Sqn
433034	F/S	SCHAFER William Mathew	12-10-44	30 OTU
437213	F/S	SCHEADEL Garnet Keith	2-8-44	467 Sqn
426691	F/S	SCHELDT Vernon John	25-07-44	463 Sqn

Number	Rank	Name	Date	Sqn
425061	F/S	SCHMIDT Cleveland Julian	31-03-44	622 Sqn
413798	F/O	SCHOMBERG Charles Copley	23-04-44	463 Sqn
419594	F/S	SCHOTT Keith Jacob	19-07-44	467 Sqn
418685	F/S	SCHULLER Carl Berthold	24-08-44	1666 HCU
432343	F/S	SCHULTZ William Ambrose	23-09-44	463 Sqn
428799	F/S	SCOTT Cyril Thomas	13-08-44	9 Sqn
425226	F/L	SCOTT Eric McLaren	10-05-44	463 Sqn
410611	F/S	SCOTT Henry Douglas	2-01-44	467 Sqn
426166	F/S	SCOTT John Keith	13-08-44	9 Sqn
404043	F/O	SCOTT DFM John Maxwell	12-12-44	460 Sqn
423335	F/S	SCOTT John Symms	24-03-44	51 Sqn
429487	F/S	SCOTT Robert Kenneth	21-07-44	467 Sqn
414603	P/O	SCOTT Thomas William Munro	14-06-44	466 Sqn
423485	F/S	SCOUGALL Frank Stuart Burdett	5-10-44	115 Sqn
422725	F/S	SEALE William John	10-06-44	97 Sqn
425074	W/O	SEDGWICK Herbert William	22-06-44	466 Sqn
420604	F/S	SERGEANT Lindsay Morton	12-02-44	12 OTU
27542	F/O	SHARPE Jack Wellington	27-04-44	460 Sqn
427155	P/O	SHAW Henry Blonin	25-07-44	466 Sqn
424066	F/S	SHAW William Oliver	2-11-44	49 Sqn
409855	F/S	SHEEAN Brian Leo	11-04-44	466 Sqn
423261	F/S	SHEEN Joseph	26-07-44	100 Sqn
426168	F/S	SHELDON Colin	15-02-44	466 Sqn
424224	F/S	SHELTON Douglas Mayall	23-06-44	460 Sqn
432582	F/S	SHEPPARD William Arthur	7-07-44	26 OTU
427559	F/S	SHERWOOD Raymond Collard	15-03-44	460 Sqn
433994	Sgt	SHIELS Allan Warren	19-06-44	27 OTU
413036	W/O	SHIPWAY Raymond George	19-07-44	463 Sqn
427560	F/S	SHOESMITH George Arthur	30-08-44	467 Sqn
430943	F/S	SHORTAL John Lourdes	13-08-44	50 Sqn
412200	F/S	SIMPSON Byron John Joseph	9-04-44	460 Sqn
427954	F/S	SIMPSON Claude Bertram	22-05-44	463 Sqn
414166	P/O	SIMPSON Keith Shambler	24-03-44	158 Sqn
421693	F/S	SIMPSON William John	28-01-44	467 Sqn
415187	W/O	SINCLAIR Kenneth Arthur	23-05-44	630 Sqn
420288	F/L	SINCLAIR DFC Paul Ernest	19-07-44	76 Sqn
410567	F/S	SINCLAIR Peter	29-03-44	1652 HCU
410390	F/O	SINCLAIR William Robert	21-12-44	97 Sqn
432361	F/O	SINDEN George Frederick	4-12-44	467 Sqn
426696	F/S	SINGLETON Russell Percival	12-06-44	102 Sqn
410392	F/S	SISLEY Clive Warren	26-02-44	78 Sqn
420763	F/O	SKARRATT Michael Carleton	24-12-44	460 Sqn
430063	P/O	SKILBECK Robert Wesley	4-12-44	15 Sqn
420289	P/O	SKILLEN Ernest Alfred	12-04-44	50 Sqn
425232	P/O	SKINNER George Alfred	21-04-44	44 Sqn
424888	F/S	SLADE William Allen	10-05-44	463 Sqn
423263	F/O	SLINN Geoffrey Herbert Brandon	27-11-44	138 Sqn
409760	P/O	SMART Joseph William	4-05-44	460 Sqn
422656	F/S	SMITH Alan James	25-09-44	467 Sqn
422309	P/O	SMITH Archibald Lancelot	3-06-44	466 Sqn
425905	F/S	SMITH Arthur Sidney	23-10-44	467 Sqn
424891	F/S	SMITH Benjamin Hartley	24-12-44	166 Sqn
415280	F/L	SMITH Eric Alfred Leith	22-06-44	463 Sqn
410515	F/S	SMITH Harold John	13-05-44	466 Sqn
422321	F/S	SMITH Henry Francis	25-03-44	466 Sqn
423913	F/S	SMITH Ian Harrison	18-06-44	115 Sqn
432577	F/S	SMITH Jeffrey Noel	28-09-44	29 OTU
422722	P/O	SMITH Keith Beresford	25-07-44	466 Sqn
423077	F/O	SMITH Kenneth Victor	18-10-44	115 Sqn
419976	F/S	SMITH Leslie Joseph	26-08-44	100 Sqn
414734	F/O	SMITH DFC Milton Frederick	17-06-44	1660 HCU
415556	F/O	SMITH Neil Joseph	22-06-44	44 Sqn
423344	F/S	SMITH Owen Preston	21-02-44	630 Sqn
427206	F/S	SMITH Phillip Francis	20-11-44	75 Sqn
402757	F/L	SMITH DFC Robert Barnsley	9-04-44	105 Sqn
420793	F/O	SMITH Ronald Richard	5-07-44	57 Sqn
417527	F/S	SMITH Roy Stanley	15-03-44	7 Sqn
410819	P/O	SMITH Sidney Wallace	26-09-44	463 Sqn
35590	F/S	SMITH Stephen Allen	29-07-44	576 Sqn
44993	Sgt	SMYTH Hugh Alexander	30-07-44	27 OTU
420071	P/O	SNAPE Desmon Byrne	24-02-44	141 Sqn
417528	P/O	SOLOMON John Albert	5-07-44	460 Sqn
432281	F/S	SOLOMONS Simon Stanley	30-08-44	166 Sqn
413678	F/S	SORENSEN Neville Lloyd	1-06-44	115 Sqn
429292	F/S	SOUTWOOD Leslie Donald	18-09-44	27 OTU
418689	F/S	SPARGO William Henry	31-03-44	460 Sqn
436108	F/S	SPEAK Leslie George	4-11-44	49 Sqn
434660	F/S	SPEERING Gerard Noel	25-03-44	460 Sqn
427360	F/S	SPENCER Frank George	19-07-44	463 Sqn
425771	F/S	SPENCER Ronald Bernard	16-06-44	514 Sqn
423918	F/O	SPRING Thomas Lavenham	22-05-44	467 Sqn
428566	F/S	STAGG John Leslie	31-12-44	218 Sqn
427160	F/S	STANLEY Morris	1-09-44	138 Sqn
422310	F/O	STAPLES Sydney John	23-09-44	463 Sqn
425238	P/O	STAPLETON Alfred James	15-02-44	102 Sqn
414432	F/O	STARKOFF DFC Victor	18-07-44	578 Sqn
414522	F/L	STARTIN George Charles	28-05-44	50 Sqn
434038	F/S	STEDMAN Mervyn Roger	11-11-44	467 Sqn
429643	F/S	STEFFAN James Pat	8-07-44	467 Sqn
423921	F/O	STEINBECK Arthur Keith	27-04-44	460 Sqn
430067	F/S	STENHOUSE Hugh	26-08-44	7 Sqn
424927	F/S	STEPHENS Frederick Luckman	30-07-44	27 OTU
429247	F/S	STEPHENS William Arthur	5-10-44	626 Sqn
409859	P/O	STEPHENSEN Cyril Edward	4-05-44	50 Sqn
434662	F/S	STERLING Rowan Burgess	19-06-44	27 OTU
422312	F/S	STEVENS Baden Henry	20-01-44	77 Sqn
428371	F/S	STEWART John Galloway	22-06-44	467 Sqn
424101	F/O	STEWART Keith Robert	21-11-44	460 Sqn
434335	F/S	STEWART Russell Ian	24-12-44	460 Sqn
421096	W/O	STIBBARD John Hamilton	8-07-44	49 Sqn
430523	F/S	STICKLAND Ronald Stuart	15-11-44	115 Sqn
423349	W/O	STILES Arthur Edward Jarvis	20-11-44	186 Sqn
420783	W/O	STINSON John Buxton	23-09-44	463 Sqn
421764	W/O	STOBO Wren	23-10-44	460 Sqn
415695	W/O	STOPHER Robert Douglas	5-11-44	466 Sqn
419738	F/O	STOPP John Henry	13-06-44	166 Sqn
426702	F/S	STORER Bernard Kevin	10-05-44	1658 HCU
4048	P/O	STORY Donald William	29-01-44	630 Sqn
425242	F/S	STRANGE Robert Charles	14-01-44	156 Sqn
426790	F/S	STRUTHERS William James	20-04-44	57 Sqn
423925	F/S	STUART Ian Douglas	9-06-44	49 Sqn
419440	F/O	STUART Mark	6-01-44	619 Sqn
418309	F/O	STUART Paul Alfred	25-10-44	115 Sqn
415488	P/O	STUCHBURY Herbert Ronald Houghton	25-02-44	467 Sqn
429001	P/O	STUCKLEY Victor	12-12-44	15 Sqn
429503	F/S	SUMMERS Arthur Albert	25-06-44	467 Sqn
417008	F/S	SUTHERLAND Jack William Alexander	29-01-44	467 Sqn
422750	F/S	SUTTON William Raymond	20-02-44	83 Sqn
419234	F/S	SWAN Jack Edward	19-04-44	466 Sqn
408054	P/O	SYMONDS Peter Louis	3-01-44	463 Sqn
437322	F/S	SYMONDS Richard Gilbert	12-09-44	467 Sqn
421769	F/S	TAGGET Allen Douglas	13-07-44	9 Sqn
418583	F/S	TAINSH Charles Stirling Dundas	13-06-44	625 Sqn
417674	F/S	TALBOT Allan Benjamin	12-08-44	1667 HCU
424230	F/O	TANNER Walter Richard	13-06-44	622 Sqn
428810	F/S	TATE Colin	30-01-44	640 Sqn
429835	F/S	TAVERNER George Alfred Badge	25-07-44	75 Sqn
424894	F/S	TAYLOR Desmond John	23-10-44	467 Sqn
425812	F/L	TAYLOR Lloyd Charles Alexander	28-05-44	514 Sqn
425985	F/S	TAYLOR Neville Alfred	30-08-44	463 Sqn
28072	F/S	TAYLOR Thomas Alfred Peace	28-09-44	463 Sqn
434558	F/S	TAYLOR William Irving	23-05-44	630 Sqn
437684	F/S	TELFORD Angus Reginald	12-10-44	30 OTU
428079	F/S	TEMPLETON Rex Bernard	6-11-44	619 Sqn
431591	F/S	TEMPLETON Robert Park	4-12-44	463 Sqn
426768	P/O	TENNENT Keith George	27-08-44	83 Sqn

409770	W/O	TERRY Arthur Lewis	8-06-44	17 OTU
404725	W/O	TEW Jack Murray	11-03-44	1688 Flt
409973	P/O	THACKRAY Noel William Faulkner	11-04-44	514 Sqn
423929	F/S	THEYER William Justin	27-04-44	460 Sqn
415697	W/O	THOMAS Albert Edward	23-04-44	156 Sqn
426708	P/O	THOMAS Cecil Keith	28-05-44	514 Sqn
403288	P/O	THOMAS Edward George	21-01-44	460 Sqn
434484	F/O	THOMAS Gwynne	7-12-44	463 Sqn
410191	F/S	THOMAS Hubert Cecil Lloyd	15-02-44	466 Sqn
419237	F/O	THOMAS Maxwell Trevethan	25-07-44	622 Sqn
427220	F/S	THOMPSON Eric Moore	28-04-44	166 Sqn
426709	P/O	THOMPSON Ernest	15-10-44	466 Sqn
410398	F/O	THOMPSON Harold John	4-12-44	106 Sqn
32311	F/O	THOMPSON Ian James [New Zealand]	8-07-44	106 Sqn
422757	F/S	THOMPSON John Kevin	22-01-44	466 Sqn
436136	F/S	THOMPSON Wallace	12-08-44	1667 HCU
427768	F/S	THOMSON Clive William	16-09-44	466 Sqn
421118	P/O	THOMSON David McNab	5-07-44	192 Sqn
421771	F/S	THOMSON Ian Alexander	20-02-44	460 Sqn
412774	P/O	THOMSON DFM Jack Hamilton	31-03-44	460 Sqn
436120	F/S	THORNTON Albert Eric	2-11-44	462 Sqn
410792	P/O	THORNTON Arthur Thomas	10-04-44	103 Sqn
426444	P/O	TIBBITS Eric Ronald	19-07-44	115 Sqn
409772	P/O	TICKLE Frank Reginald	16-07-44	207 Sqn
426711	F/S	TIERNAN Patrick Edward Thomas	17-06-44	77 Sqn
417248	P/O	TILBROOK Jeoffrey Maxwell	25-06-44	463 Sqn
410756	W/O	TILL Alwyn Terence	21-08-44	635 Sqn
418889	P/O	TODD John Edward	8-06-44	115 Sqn
418890	F/O	TOINTON Desmonde George	6-10-44	463 Sqn
433279	F/S	TOLHURST Howard Jeffrey	5-11-44	466 Sqn
417286	F/O	TOLLEY Dirk Everard	27-04-44	83 Sqn
419017	F/S	TOMKINS Kenneth James	23-06-44	460 Sqn
426401	F/O	TOOHEY William Donald	3-01-44	463 Sqn
422764	F/S	TOOMEY Leo	22-06-44	106 Sqn
418209	F/L	TOTTENHAM DFC Anthony Bowen Loftus [Eire]	26-09-44	463 Sqn
421105	P/O	TOWERS William Leopold	4-04-44	5 LFS
427041	P/O	TOWLER Lambert Charles	22-05-44	463 Sqn
422765	F/O	TOWNEND Gordon Christopher [United Kingdom]	13-06-44	115 Sqn
417604	F/S	TRAEGER Ernest Hugo	31-03-44	101 Sqn
423186	P/O	TRAILL John Alan	18-06-44	115 Sqn
417678	F/S	TREBILCOCK Colin Eric	29-01-44	10 Sqn
425781	F/S	TREE John Robert	29-01-44	83 Sqn
421524	W/O	TRELOAR John Richings	23-10-44	460 Sqn
424477	F/S	TRESIDDER John Newton	9-10-44	462 Sqn
410182	F/S	TREVENA Alfred Kenneth	14-01-44	9 Sqn
415197	P/O	TREWERN William Charles	18-03-44	466 Sqn
403204	P/O	TRIMBLE Samuel John	6-10-44	207 Sqn
409617	P/O	TROTMAN Clifford John	29-01-44	466 Sqn
416904	F/S	TROUT Malcolm Ralph	21-01-44	460 Sqn
409619	F/O	TRUSCOTT Edward Charles	2-01-44	460 Sqn
428830	F/S	TUBMAN Ronald Vernon	11-04-44	84 OTU
408938	F/O	TUCK George William	24-11-44	128 Sqn
25243	F/O	TUCKER John Francis	10-05-44	467 Sqn
429161	F/S	TUDBERRY William	29-06-44	10 Sqn
416728	F/L	TUGWELL Leonard Ormond	13-08-44	101 Sqn
411968	F/O	TURNER John Curtin	15-10-44	467 Sqn
410017	F/S	TURNER John James Joseph	8-06-44	15 Sqn
408924	F/O	TURNOR Percy Keith	8-05-44	627 Sqn
415595	F/S	TURPIE Eric Dudley	25-02-44	467 Sqn
421645	F/O	TURVEY Ronald George	27-07-44	619 Sqn
422065	F/O	TWYNAM Edward Phipps	4-11-44	625 Sqn
406223	P/O	TYLOR Jack Wilfred	29-01-44	466 Sqn
423359	F/S	TYNE Albert Edward	10-05-44	9 Sqn
424928	F/S	TYTE Owen Leslie	3-06-44	466 Sqn
437236	P/O	UNDERWOOD David	4-11-44	466 Sqn
421420	F/S	UNWIN Alfred Edmund	14-01-44	576 Sqn
410203	W/O	UPTON James Alphonsus	16-07-44	15 Sqn
403438	S/L	UTZ DFC* Eric Arthur Gibson	31-03-44	460 Sqn
401553	P/O	VALE William Searle	6-10-44	157 Sqn
436015	F/S	VALLENDER Phillip Edward Burton	16-10-44	30 OTU
415220	F/L	van RAALTE Henry Stewart	23-06-44	97 Sqn
426716	F/S	VAN COOTEN John William	18-06-44	115 Sqn
421774	P/O	VAUGHAN William Alan Henry	15-07-44	460 Sqn
410494	F/S	VELLENOWETH Henry Morton	6-01-44	467 Sqn
434128	F/S	VIERITZ Clifford Alexander	12-09-44	622 Sqn
416810	F/O	VOWLES John Reuben	22-06-44	44 Sqn
426719	F/S	WADE Peter Stuart	25-05-44	76 Sqn
424239	F/S	WAIGHT Kevin Campbell	10-05-44	467 Sqn
428834	F/S	WALKER Frederic Murray	31-08-44	463 Sqn
410927	F/S	WALKER Kenneth Charles	13-06-44	90 Sqn
423363	P/O	WALKER Lindsay George	3-09-44	1656 HCU
410762	F/S	WALKER Raymond Thomas	23-04-44	149 Sqn
426403	F/S	WALKER Ronald Charles	29-03-44	1652 HCU
408430	F/O	WALKER Ronald Edward	21-01-44	83 Sqn
420087	F/O	WALSH DFC Ronald James	25-07-44	466 Sqn
433631	F/S	WALMSLEY Roy	3-09-44	1656 HCU
420413	F/O	WARD DFC Dudley Francis	10-05-44	463 Sqn
418599	F/O	WARD Henry Thomas	11-05-44	97 Sqn
437237	F/O	WARD John Michael	24-12-44	460 Sqn
409780	F/S	WARD Kenneth William	31-03-44	467 Sqn
422326	P/O	WARD Roland Gilbert	6-06-44	50 Sqn
437033	F/S	WARE Jack Beaumont	30-08-44	467 Sqn
434058	F/O	WARING Jocelyn King	4-12-44	463 Sqn
427047	F/S	WARREN Clifford Young	11-04-44	466 Sqn
410765	P/O	WARREN Kenneth Rowe	8-05-44	106 Sqn
429838	F/S	WARREN Robert James	17-06-44	77 Sqn
437909	F/S	WARRINGTON William Ivon	13-08-44	50 Sqn
427175	F/S	WASHBOURNE Gordon	8-06-44	115 Sqn
425082	F/S	WATSON Cecil John	8-06-44	15 Sqn
430076	Sgt	WATSON David Lancaster	23-03-44	17 OTU
420314	P/O	WATSON Malcolm Douglas	18-03-44	466 Sqn
426245	F/S	WATSON Reginald Kenneth	12-05-44	15 Sqn
424127	F/S	WATTS Raymond Oswell	27-04-44	207 Sqn
425389	P/O	WATTS Richard Herbert	4-05-44	626 Sqn
428873	F/S	WAUGH Maxwell Bruce	17-09-44	1652 HCU
415706	W/O	WAYCOTT William John	6-04-44	207 Sqn
410021	P/O	WEATHERILL Jack	3-01-44	463 Sqn
422774	P/O	WEBB Joseph William	23-12-44	35 Sqn
420726	F/O	WEBB Noel Edwin	4-07-44	463 Sqn
413052	W/O	WEBB William Bryce	10-06-44	97 Sqn
432605	F/S	WEBBER Athol Grant	27-08-44	115 Sqn
417916	F/S	WEEDEN Lionel Warwick	22-05-44	463 Sqn
437606	F/S	WEEKES Richard	29-07-44	576 Sqn
423957	F/S	WEEKES Walter David	9-04-44	460 Sqn
437036	F/S	WEEKS Maxwell Allen	12-08-44	21 OTU
422779	F/S	WEST Andrew Leslie	25-06-44	467 Sqn
425392	F/S	WEST John David	25-03-44	460 Sqn
418779	F/S	WESTERMAN Robert Stephen	11-04-44	466 Sqn
437301	F/S	WESTPHAL Ronald Danford	18-12-44	27 OTU
405511	W/O	WHALE William John Latchford	29-11-44	460 Sqn
426407	F/S	WHAM Dudley	12-12-44	149 Sqn
409807	W/O	WHEELER Lindsay William	19-09-44	106 Sqn
403883	W/O	WHELAN John Patrick	8-06-44	78 Sqn
434299	F/S	WHIMPEY BEM Geoffrey Ray	5-07-44	463 Sqn
410581	F/S	WHITE Alan John	30-01-44	463 Sqn
430524	Sgt	WHITE Athol	8-11-44	1667 HCU
425241	F/S	WHITE Bryan De Bernal [New Guinea]	6-10-44	466 Sqn
430423	F/S	WHITE Desmond Victor	12-10-44	21 OTU
427966	P/O	WHITE Douglas John	12-10-44	30 OTU
410758	W/O	WHITE Frederick William	30-08-44	300 Sqn
421114	W/O	WHITE John Albert	3-09-44	1656 HCU
424497	W/O	WHITE John Paterson	6-12-44	227 Sqn
419495	P/O	WHITE Peter Berchman	9-06-44	44 Sqn
419560	F/S	WHITE Thomas Charles	4-05-44	625 Sqn
425794	F/S	WHITE Walter John	10-05-44	9 Sqn
415563	F/S	WHITELEY Maitland Shackson	25-07-44	466 Sqn

Service#	Rank	Name	Date	Sqn
409632	P/O	WHITESIDE Samuel	27-01-44	460 Sqn
406587	F/L	WHITFORD DFC Allan Pluis	9-05-44	83 Sqn
417920	F/S	WHITTENBURY Mervyn Thomas	13-06-44	460 Sqn
412328	W/O	WHYTE Cecil Harold	23-05-44	106 Sqn
414442	F/S	WILKINS Edward	31-03-44	51 Sqn
30829	P/O	WILKINSON Bruce Gordon	31-08-44	1654 HCU
417547	F/O	WILKINSON John Anthony Howard	29-07-44	463 Sqn
400444	F/L	WILKINSON DFC John Hudson	30-08-44	83 Sqn
419430	F/S	WILKS Geoffrey Talbot	23-04-44	619 Sqn
427164	F/S	WILLIAMS Arthur Henry	31-03-44	51 Sqn
412869	F/S	WILLIAMS Francis Kevin	15-02-44	466 Sqn
416053	F/O	WILLIAMS DFC Gilbert Victor	29-11-44	35 Sqn
421386	F/O	WILLIAMS Henry Edward	4-05-44	463 Sqn
415709	F/S	WILLIAMS James	23-01-44	20 OTU
421398	W/O	WILLIAMS John Robert	6-11-44	463 Sqn
410761	F/S	WILLIAMS Maldwyn David Howell	27-03-44	166 Sqn
417548	F/S	WILLIAMS Raymond George	4-04-44	5 LFS
408462	P/O	WILLIAMS Tasman Leonard	15-10-44	466 Sqn
426933	F/L	WILLIAMSON DFC George Edward	20-11-44	186 Sqn
414741	F/S	WILLIAMSON George Herbert	28-04-44	138 Sqn
408380	W/O	WILLIAMSON James Esca	25-05-44	640 Sqn
424811	F/S	WILLIAMSON Leslie Clarence	18-03-44	466 Sqn
410510	P/O	WILSON Alan William	7-06-44	630 Sqn
421550	F/S	WILSON Allen Howard	31-03-44	101 Sqn
434094	F/S	WILSON Barry	28-05-44	460 Sqn
419370	F/S	WILSON Douglas Harold	15-07-44	1651 HCU
424315	F/S	WILSON James Manning Melville	30-01-44	463 Sqn
432611	P/O	WILSON Michael McIvor	4-11-44	466 Sqn
419354	F/S	WILSON Stanley Alan	13-04-44	90 Sqn
417032	P/O	WINNEKE Leslie Harold	23-05-44	57 Sqn
400907	F/L	WISHART Rodger Peryman	30-01-44	97 Sqn
425800	F/L	WITHAM DFC Reginald Ronald	27-11-44	138 Sqn
406893	P/O	WITHERS Kenneth Fred	14-03-44	78 Sqn
434555	F/S	WIXTED Robert Anthony	5-07-44	1667 HCU
423391	F/O	WONDERS Ronald Reay	29-10-44	50 Sqn
412792	W/O	WOOD George Robert Newton	31-03-44	156 Sqn
410280	F/S	WOOD John Whitham	25-02-44	467 Sqn
435026	F/S	WOOD Malcolm Langley	23-10-44	462 Sqn
28031	F/S	WOOD William Kenneth	21-02-44	115 Sqn
426208	F/S	WOODD George William	8-05-44	106 Sqn
410778	F/S	WOODFORD Alan Mackintosh	20-02-44	15 Sqn
415567	P/O	WOODHAMS Jack Sainsbury	10-05-44	106 Sqn
420731	F/O	WOODS Douglas Austin	30-06-44	514 Sqn
415002	F/O	WOODS William John	19-09-44	467 Sqn
421345	F/S	WOOLF Godfrey	2-01-44	97 Sqn
426412	F/S	WORLEY John Francis	27-01-44	460 Sqn
420326	F/S	WORMALD Jack Dudley	15-02-44	466 Sqn
415713	F/O	WORTH Irwin	21-02-44	97 Sqn
406417	F/O	WORTHINGTON James Robert	19-07-44	463 Sqn
410780	F/S	WRIGHT Robert Wallis	18-04-44	158 Sqn
422329	P/O	WRIGHT Stanley Mountford	25-06-44	106 Sqn
422342	F/O	WRIGHT Wilson Harry Emanuel	16-07-44	467 Sqn
423970	F/S	YABSLEY John Francis	6-01-44	57 Sqn
432329	F/S	YABSLEY Raymond	28-08-44	19 OTU
413471	F/O	YELL DFC Robert Spencer	14-01-44	12 Sqn
428858	P/O	YORK George	13-08-44	102 Sqn
421426	F/S	YOUNG Alan Geoffry	21-02-44	460 Sqn
409963	F/S	YOUNG Ian Cedric	25-02-44	463 Sqn
422825	F/L	YOUNG Philip Edward	13-08-44	102 Sqn
429369	F/O	YOUNG Richard Rodney	7-12-44	463 Sqn
417145	F/O	YOUNG William Archibald	5-07-44	44 Sqn
426944	F/S	ZINGELMANN Leonard William	7-06-44	103 Sqn

Note

Royal Australian Air Force fatalities rose significantly in 1944, falling just short of 1,800 by the year's end. The most senior of their airmen to die was G/C Balmer from Maldon in the State of Victoria whose Lancaster (one of at least ten that fell victim to a fighter) was shot down by a night fighter during an attack on a military camp at Bourg Leopold in Belgium.

ROYAL CANADIAN AIR FORCE personnel

Service#	Rank	Name	Date	Sqn
J/24013	F/L	AALBORG Karl Inge	13-09-44	7 Sqn
J/25067	F/O	AARON Elmer Oscar [USA]	8-05-44	106 Sqn
J/15627	F/O	ABRAMSON Mark Leslie	16-05-44	576 Sqn
J/87053	P/O	ACHTYMICHUK Alexander	23-04-44	429 Sqn
J/29705	F/O	ADAIR David Kenneth	17-06-44	101 Sqn
R/133591	WO1	ADAIR Leslie James	3-01-44	156 Sqn
J/90229	P/O	ADAM Raymond Francis	29-12-44	419 Sqn
R/62722	Cpl	ADAMS MiD Eric Victor	15-09-44	1664 HCU
R/221003	F/S	ADAMS Glenn Prosper	27-09-44	619 Sqn
J/87993	P/O	ADAMS Hugh Alexander	29-07-44	428 Sqn
R/178620	Sgt	ADAMSON Douglas Clayhurst	14-03-44	10 OTU
J/16256	F/O	ADAMSON Robert Hartny	27-01-44	83 Sqn
R/161691	F/S	ADKINSON Thomas James [USA]	24-03-44	57 Sqn
J/88714	P/O	ADLARD William Robert	23-04-44	429 Sqn
J/85822	P/O	AIKEN Douglas Earl	25-06-44	44 Sqn
J/88332	P/O	ALBERT Joseph Henry Yvon	11-02-44	425 Sqn
J/85518	P/O	ALBERTS Edward Lloyd	23-04-44	405 Sqn
J/92032	P/O	ALBRECHT Oscar Jacob	28-04-44	101 Sqn
J/88532	P/O	ALDER William Latham	25-02-44	12 Sqn
J/87553	P/O	ALDRED William Murray	29-07-44	431 Sqn
J/15543	S/L	ALEXANDER DFC DFM Edward Sudbury	14-01-44	156 Sqn
J/27711	F/O	ALEXANDER Ian Sutherland	29-07-44	434 Sqn
J/17186	F/O	ALEXANDER James Richard	13-06-44	434 Sqn
J/24713	F/O	ALLAN Alexander	13-06-44	90 Sqn
J/19942	F/O	ALLAN Francis Frederick George	20-02-44	166 Sqn
J/95201	P/O	ALLAN Robert	21-11-44	433 Sqn
J/86012	P/O	ALLAN Robert Edward	30-01-44	626 Sqn
J/95205	P/O	ALLAN William Bruce	24-12-44	408 Sqn
J/17472	F/O	ALLCROFT DFC Frederick Charles	3-01-44	83 Sqn
J/88053	P/O	ALLEN Jack Beatty	31-03-44	424 Sqn
J/86516	P/O	ALLEN John Francis	20-02-44	61 Sqn
J/14769	F/L	ALLEN DFC Lawrence Arnold	28-04-44	405 Sqn
J/85507	P/O	ALLEYN Foster Richard	20-02-44	426 Sqn
J/6643	F/L	ALLEN John Allardyce	3-01-44	432 Sqn
J/20861	F/L	ALLISON William Joyce 'Joe'	20-11-44	22 OTU
J/93110	P/O	ALMAS Russell Munn	21-11-44	429 Sqn
J/90182	P/O	ALMOND John Neville	25-05-44	424 Sqn
R/143477	Sgt	ALSOP Norman Frederick	15-05-44	419 Sqn
J/89956	P/O	AMSTEIN Norman William	17-06-44	102 Sqn
C/2333	F/L	AMY Harry Thomas	11-05-44	424 Sqn
R/208718	F/S	ANDERSEN Paul	16-07-44	44 Sqn
J/90357	P/O	ANDERSON Alexander John	26-08-44	61 Sqn
R/194889	F/S	ANDERSON Allan Andrew	22-05-44	166 Sqn
J/35534	F/O	ANDERSON Bruce Benjamin	2-11-44	415 Sqn
R/220081	Sgt	ANDERSON Chester Edward	18-12-44	22 OTU
J/98701	Cpl	ANDERSON Clarence Cameron	22-09-44	61 Base
J/86041	P/O	ANDERSON Frederick	30-03-44	138 Sqn
R/168378	Sgt	ANDERSON George McCrommon	16-06-44	22 OTU
J/92358	P/O	ANDERSON Howard Francis	26-08-44	419 Sqn
R/215186	Sgt	ANDERSON John Charles	14-07-44	24 OTU
J/36411	F/O	ANDERSON Leonard Edward	12-09-44	50 Sqn
R/131824	F/S	ANDERSON Lloyd George	31-03-44	625 Sqn
R/193213	Sgt	ANDERSON Neville Joseph	15-11-44	1664 HCU
J/8924	S/L	ANDERSON DFC William Brodie	8-06-44	429 Sqn
J/29202	F/O	ANDERSON William Frank	1-11-44	426 Sqn
J/92722	P/O	ANDERSON William Wallace Eugene	8-11-44	82 OTU
R/185783	F/S	ANDERTON John Alfred	11-06-44	90 Sqn
J/13757	F/L	ANDREW Eric Morrow	24-06-44	7 Sqn
R/201503	Sgt	ANDREW William Arthur Roland	22-03-44	1664 HCU
J/20403	F/O	ANDREWS Edward John	28-05-44	420 Sqn
R/153899	WO2	ANDREWS George Albert	24-02-44	166 Sqn
J/89901	P/O	ANDREWS John French	13-08-44	101 Sqn
J/27301	F/O	ANDREWS Robert John	29-06-44	22 OTU
J/86120	P/O	ANDREWS Walter Harold	29-01-44	57 Sqn
R/100619	WO2	ANNIS Lloyd Dyer	14-01-44	405 Sqn

ID	Rank	Name	Date	Unit
J/92332	P/O	APPLIN Donald John	13-06-44	419 Sqn
J/87413	P/O	ARBOUR Joseph Edward Jean Guy	13-05-44	426 Sqn
J/35033	F/O	ARCHER Robert William	29-07-44	550 Sqn
J/25898	F/O	ARCHIBALD Clyde Glencoe	28-05-44	30 OTU
J/89952	P/O	ARKSEY Walter Lynwood	11-06-44	460 Sqn
C/4685	F/O	ARMOUR Edson Gilroy	18-03-44	434 Sqn
J/92726	P/O	ARMOUR Wilton Garnet	11-11-44	207 Sqn
J/21336	F/O	ARMSTRONG Alexander Thomas	11-06-44	405 Sqn
J/36897	F/O	ARMSTRONG Harold Alexander	25-10-44	428 Sqn
R/202580	Sgt	ARMSTRONG Jack Edward	15-11-44	1664 HCU
J/24240	F/O	ARMSTRONG John Frederick	13-07-44	9 Sqn
J/28574	F/O	ARMSTRONG John Keith	29-07-44	433 Sqn
J/92624	P/O	ARMSTRONG Robert Howard	23-10-44	625 Sqn
J/85254	P/O	ARNELL Algot Leon	8-06-44	101 Sqn
J/13470	S/L	ARNOT DFC Donald Mackenzie	22-01-44	427 Sqn
J/23753	F/O	ARNSTON Frank Arthur	26-02-44	420 Sqn
J/85350	P/O	ARTYNIUK John Peter	8-06-44	431 Sqn
J/95203	P/O	ASH Joseph William	2-12-44	433 Sqn
J/25521	F/O	ASHLEY Borden Bramshott	23-04-44	550 Sqn
J/21524	F/L	ASTBURY John William	14-01-44	405 Sqn
J/86400	P/O	ASTLES John James	20-02-44	408 Sqn
R/169396	Sgt	ASTLES William Wallington	8-06-44	1666 HCU
R/196182	Sgt	ASTRAND Harry	2-05-44	1659 HCU
J/22434	F/O	ATKINS John Ivan	13-05-44	640 Sqn
J/88345	P/O	ATKINS Robert James	31-03-44	424 Sqn
J/94231	P/O	ATKINSON James Neil	21-11-44	426 Sqn
C/87994	P/O	ATTEWELL Arthur Ernest	29-07-44	428 Sqn
J/85928	P/O	AUBIN Joseph Gilbert Dollard	11-02-44	425 Sqn
J/89210	P/O	AUMELL Allan Daniel	24-07-44	619 Sqn
J/90857	P/O	AUSTIN Kenneth Harry	23-12-44	582 Sqn
J/23873	F/O	AVON Joseph Leonidas Gerald	31-07-44	103 Sqn
J/39979	F/O	AWAD Philip Peter [USA]	4-12-44	619 Sqn
J/19610	P/O	AWREY DFC Donald McLean	31-03-44	433 Sqn
J/86457	P/O	AXFORD Cecil	12-08-44	420 Sqn
J/87271	P/O	AXFORD Herbert Frank	21-07-44	578 Sqn
J/12157	F/O	AYRES Audrey Allen [USA]	20-01-44	429 Sqn
R/104790	WO1	BACHAND Joseph Gilles	12-02-44	419 Sqn
C/92467	P/O	BACHANT Joseph Ferdinand Jacques	2-11-44	428 Sqn
R/195442	F/S	BACKLER Herman	18-08-44	576 Sqn
J/87134	F/O	BADGLEY John Clement	1-11-44	434 Sqn
J/24693	P/O	BAILEY Dennis Harold [USA]	22-03-44	432 Sqn
J/90239	P/O	BAILEY Elmer Lincoln	28-05-44	429 Sqn
R/196067	F/S	BAILEY Harold Roy [USA]	23-05-44	57 Sqn
J/28860	P/O	BAILEY Norman	29-07-44	431 Sqn
J/86729	P/O	BAILEY DFC Theodore Reginald	19-11-44	1666 HCU
J/86335	P/O	BAILEY William Alexander	25-05-44	419 Sqn
J/36230	F/L	BAILLARGEON Joseph Louis	17-08-44	433 Sqn
J/18135	F/O	BAILLIE Thomas	30-08-44	428 Sqn
J/27507	F/O	BAIN Ambrose	27-07-44	630 Sqn
J/86239	P/O	BAINBRIDGE George Harvey	25-04-44	626 Sqn
J/25900	F/O	BAIRD William Gordon	5-07-44	433 Sqn
R/182351	Sgt	BAIRD William Oliver Douglas	28-05-44	30 OTU
C/11711	F/O	BAKER Charles Oren	15-04-44	434 Sqn
R/146764	WO2	BAKER Clifford Stanley	30-01-44	467 Sqn
J/25280	F/O	BAKER Herbert Allan	29-01-44	12 OTU
C/7114	F/O	BAKER John Jule	27-01-44	408 Sqn
J/87569	P/O	BAKER Nicholas	31-01-44	101 Sqn
J/89904	P/O	BAKER Thomas Lloyd	17-08-44	433 Sqn
J/92601	P/O	BAKER William Leroy	22-01-44	514 Sqn
J/27511	F/O	BAKER William Long	25-06-44	149 Sqn
R/195726	Sgt	BALDRY Earl Freiman	2-05-44	429 Sqn
J/24527	F/O	BALDWIN John Moody	25-03-44	97 Sqn
R/164036	F/S	BALDWIN John Stanley	3-01-44	61 Sqn
R/132001	WO2	BALDWINSON Walter Baldwin	25-04-44	83 Sqn
J/95200	P/O	BALFOUR Andrew George	1-11-44	426 Sqn
J/86161	P/O	BALL William Sidney	20-02-44	514 Sqn
C/89728	P/O	BALLENTINE Robert Elmer	18-03-44	434 Sqn
J/86128	P/O	BANDLE Leo	24-03-44	432 Sqn
J/88413	P/O	BANDUR Sigmund Bernard	22-05-44	619 Sqn
R/127993	WO1	BANNER William James	8-06-44	1666 HCU
J/23899	F/O	BANNIHR Robert Huston	6-07-44	424 Sqn
R/203391	Sgt	BANNON Carlin Anthony	30-01-44	22 OTU
J/92340	P/O	BARAN Michael	17-06-44	419 Sqn
J/90366	P/O	BARBER James William	25-05-44	101 Sqn
R/180634	Sgt	BARBER Joseph Louis	4-02-44	82 OTU
J/86342	F/O	BARBER Robert John	20-05-44	44 Sqn
J/24738	F/O	BARCLAY Arnold Smedley	20-02-44	640 Sqn
R/222817	Sgt	BARKER Alfred Cyril Seymour	1-07-44	626 Sqn
J/37212	F/O	BARKER Herbert [USA]	1-06-44	138 Sqn
J/29701	F/O	BARKER Kenneth Hubert	21-11-44	514 Sqn
J/88605	P/O	BARKER Lloyd Roger	15-03-44	431 Sqn
J/86069	P/O	BARKWAY Percy James William	4-05-44	626 Sqn
J/39368	F/O	BARLOW Percy	17-12-44	61 Sqn
J/92354	P/O	BARNARD David Russell	26-08-44	419 Sqn
J/92350	P/O	BARNARD Wilfred Stanley	19-07-44	420 Sqn
R/157147	WO2	BARNES Arthur John George	28-04-44	138 Sqn
J/90983	P/O	BARNETT George Howell	30-12-44	432 Sqn
J/92693	P/O	BARNICKE Peter	9-11-44	138 Sqn
J/21045	F/O	BARON Nick John	16-02-44	432 Sqn
R/266446	Sgt	BARR George Henry	30-08-44	19 OTU
R/251406	F/S	BARR Robert James	4-12-44	166 Sqn
R/166590	F/S	BARR Robert Lennox	22-03-44	408 Sqn
J/92196	P/O	BARR William John	10-06-44	630 Sqn
R/271290	LAC	BARRABALL Gordon James	11-09-44	408 Sqn
J/5036	S/L	BARRETT Clayton Keith	12-05-44	432 Sqn
R/174466	F/S	BARRIE Emerson Gordon	24-08-44	1652 HCU
J/86495	P/O	BARRIE John Donald	29-01-44	431 Sqn
J/19345	P/O	BARRONS Harold John	27-01-44	630 Sqn
J/85618	P/O	BARROWMAN DFC Archibald Macarthur	15-03-44	97 Sqn
J/40544	F/O	BARRY George Richard	12-12-44	195 Sqn
J/95199	P/O	BARTLEMAY William Arthur [USA]	25-10-44	428 Sqn
J/35539	F/O	BARTLETT Ralph William	16-05-44	26 OTU
J/24141	F/O	BARTLETT Raymond Neil	28-06-44	44 Sqn
J/88777	P/O	BARTON Thomas Granston	29-07-44	425 Sqn
J/95202	P/O	BASARAB Louis	21-11-44	408 Sqn
J/88192	P/O	BASKERVILLE Norman George	4-05-44	207 Sqn
J/36280	F/O	BATE Arthur John	6-11-44	101 Sqn
J/86432	P/O	BATES John Donald	20-02-44	431 Sqn
J/19670	P/O	BATH Peter Thomas	22-03-44	1658 HCU
J/21182	P/O	BATTY Archie Verdun	14-10-44	428 Sqn
J/86940	P/O	BAUMANN George Robert	29-07-44	431 Sqn
J/94233	P/O	BAXTER Arie Gordon	5-12-44	428 Sqn
J/86085	P/O	BAXTER Douglas Frank Jakes [USA]	5-07-44	576 Sqn
J/87720	P/O	BAXTER William	22-05-44	630 Sqn
J/27270	F/O	BAYER Edward Granville	7-03-44	1667 HCU
R/162352	WO2	BEACH Roy Bernard	31-03-44	427 Sqn
J/89951	P/O	BEALES Ford	10-06-44	10 Sqn
C/1344	S/L	BEALL Gordon Scowcroft	28-05-44	420 Sqn
J/18779	P/O	BEAMES Henry Denys	20-02-44	434 Sqn
J/89967	P/O	BEARD Edwin George	17-08-44	158 Sqn
R/112661	WO2	BEATTIE John Leslie	20-02-44	419 Sqn
R/257898	Sgt	BEATTIE Lyall Kenneth	23-03-44	83 OTU
J/25737	F/O	BEATTY Alvin Marshall	23-05-44	77 Sqn
J/27399	F/O	BEATTY Walter Bennett	1-07-44	101 Sqn
R/155103	F/S	BEAUDOIN Charles Howard Michael	28-06-44	166 Sqn
J/88613	P/O	BEAUREGARD Charles Marie	23-05-44	101 Sqn
J/19855	P/O	BEAZLEY Harry	8-06-44	15 Sqn
R/190101	F/S	BECKER Byron Jeremiah	15-10-44	1664 HCU
R/159331	WO2	BECKETT Arthur Carleton	23-05-44	419 Sqn
R/139887	Sgt	BECKETT Gerald Alfred	3-01-44	101 Sqn
R/96659	Sgt	BEDARD Joseph Jean Paul Marcel	23-04-44	433 Sqn
J/86998	P/O	BEECH Charles Trask	17-06-44	434 Sqn
R/60032	Sgt	BEECH Stanley Percy	25-05-44	51 Sqn
J/85033	P/O	BEER Lloyd Stuart	26-02-44	408 Sqn
J/29575	F/O	BEERS Frederick Kenneth	25-07-44	514 Sqn
J/27853	F/O	BEESLEY Joseph Francis Terence	6-06-44	426 Sqn

ID	Rank	Name	Date	Sqn
J/35867	F/O	BELANGER Jean Joseph Donnelly	30-07-44	22 OTU
J/85548	P/O	BELL Alexander Matthew James	23-03-44	426 Sqn
J/24222	F/O	BELL Alvin Donald Gould	27-01-44	432 Sqn
J/35329	F/O	BELL DFC David	30-11-44	429 Sqn
J/88695	P/O	BELL David Gordon	12-04-44	432 Sqn
J/39888	F/O	BELL Francis Aubrey	22-10-44	1659 HCU
J/86232	P/O	BELL Harold Copeland	16-03-44	578 Sqn
J/19147	P/O	BELL James Bond 'Jimmie'	19-04-44	432 Sqn
J/25954	F/O	BELL James Lloyd	30-03-44	20 OTU
J/88407	WO2	BELL John	22-03-44	97 Sqn
R/157097	WO2	BELL Murray Richard	2-05-44	218 Sqn
R/190751	Sgt	BELL Norman Andrew	29-01-44	431 Sqn
J/21808	F/O	BELL William Alexander	21-07-44	51 Sqn
J/37834	F/O	BELLAMY Glenn Crawford	14-10-44	153 Sqn
J/86414	P/O	BELYEA Allan Conway	31-03-44	103 Sqn
J/37881	F/O	BENNETT Donald Howard	31-12-44	166 Sqn
J/15248	S/L	BENNETT DSO DFC Gordon	25-05-44	405 Sqn
J/91044	P/O	BENNETT Gordon Neil	20-02-44	408 Sqn
R/182006	F/S	BENNETT Jack Norman Ernest	22-03-44	49 Sqn
J/19011	P/O	BENNETT James Gordon	27-01-44	408 Sqn
J/88336	P/O	BENNETT Kenneth Hugh	20-02-44	408 Sqn
R/188356	F/S	BENNETT Lloyd Douglas	14-10-44	625 Sqn
J/87679	P/O	BENNETT Richard Albert John	22-01-44	514 Sqn
J/28685	F/O	BENNETT Richard Jack	29-07-44	514 Sqn
R/178351	F/S	BENNIS Henry	19-04-44	115 Sqn
R/137457	WO2	BENTINCK George Henry [USA]	25-02-44	97 Sqn
J/22576	F/O	BENTLEY Douglas George	12-05-44	432 Sqn
J/87378	P/O	BENTZ Wilbur Boyd	13-05-44	426 Sqn
J/88065	P/O	BERCUSON Bernard	17-08-44	433 Sqn
J/24909	F/O	BERESFORD John Stewart	9-08-44	427 Sqn
J/37812	F/O	BERG Gilbert Louis Oscar	15-11-44	1664 HCU
J/87384	P/O	BERGERON John Albert	13-06-44	408 Sqn
R/118541	LAC	BERGIN James Michael	9-11-44	1659 HCU
J/87767	P/O	BERGLAND Norval	25-02-44	44 Sqn
C/85532	P/O	BERKEY George Robert	23-04-44	405 Sqn
R/219122	Sgt	BERLINGUETTE Joseph Jean Paul Osias	5-12-44	22 OTU
J/29410	F/O	BERMINGHAM Daniel Charles	16-10-44	207 Sqn
J/29331	F/O	BERNASKI Ladimer Jacob	1-07-44	626 Sqn
R/183965	F/S	BERNHARDT Douglas Paul	1-06-44	622 Sqn
J/29412	F/O	BERNIER DFC Joseph Wilfrid Laurier Fernando	18-12-44	425 Sqn
J/38740	F/O	BERNYK Michael	31-12-44	166 Sqn
J/86027	P/O	BERNYK Victor Hector	25-04-44	626 Sqn
J/87476	P/O	BERQUIST Bertil Wilfred	25-02-44	514 Sqn
J/16898	F/L	BERRIGAN DFC Leonard Thomas	25-03-44	7 Sqn
J/90142	P/O	BERRY John La Pointe	31-03-44	424 Sqn
J/27495	F/O	BERRY Keith Gregory	11-01-44	17 OTU
J/9077	F/L	BERTELSEN Frederick Castell	4-05-44	582 Sqn
J/88697	P/O	BERTOIA Ciro	22-03-44	432 Sqn
J/87075	P/O	BERTRAND Joseph Herve Theodore Robert	2-03-44	425 Sqn
R/151914	F/S	BESSETTE Gordon Macmillan	26-02-44	420 Sqn
J/95559	P/O	BEST Alexander Gordon	1-11-44	434 Sqn
J/29515	F/O	BEST Harold Francis Sargent	21-07-44	90 Sqn
J/11043	F/L	BEST John Douglas	11-07-44	1666 HCU
R/221097	F/S	BEST Robert Augusta	9-11-44	138 Sqn
J/89377	P/O	BETTS Bruce George	29-07-44	428 Sqn
J/26756	F/O	BEVERIDGE James Ralph	31-08-44	433 Sqn
J/25920	F/L	BICKELL Peter William [USA]	17-09-44	115 Sqn
J/35094	F/O	BIDWELL Donald David George [USA]	16-05-44	26 OTU
J/89968	P/O	BIELBY Keith Thomas	17-08-44	158 Sqn
J/86395	P/O	BIERS Robert Lloyd	20-02-44	9 Sqn
J/89731	P/O	BIGORAY DFM William Walter	28-04-44	7 Sqn
J/28683	P/O	BILBE John	13-08-44	427 Sqn
J/89270	P/O	BILLINGSLEY Forast Deloise	17-08-44	405 Sqn
R/72273	WO2	BINDER Hector Frederick	25-02-44	626 Sqn
J/26543	F/O	BIOLLO Peter Joseph	29-07-44	576 Sqn
R/193025	F/S	BIRKS William Sidney Atkinson	19-07-44	619 Sqn
J/89900	P/O	BIRMINGHAM Joseph Patrick	13-08-44	578 Sqn
J/19162	F/O	BIRNIE Hugh Waldie	22-08-44	426 Sqn
J/86577	P/O	BISHOP Ernest Howard	29-07-44	432 Sqn
J/88538	P/O	BISHOP James Douglas	8-07-44	50 Sqn
J/16991	S/L	BISSETT DFM Jack Montgomery	31-03-44	427 Sqn
J/27913	F/O	BLACHFORD Glenn Hugh	17-06-44	431 Sqn
J/24704	F/O	BLACK Angus John	22-06-44	57 Sqn
J/24025	F/O	BLACK Bruce Graham [USA]	3-06-44	158 Sqn
J/11844	F/O	BLACK Richard Bursleigh	16-03-44	426 Sqn
J/36399	F/O	BLACKMORE Charles Allen	29-05-44	82 OTU
R/172201	F/S	BLAIR Jack Frederick	21-01-44	102 Sqn
J/28897	F/O	BLAIR Robert Wallace	18-07-44	427 Sqn
R/119545	WO2	BLAIR William	28-05-44	1659 HCU
J/89105	P/O	BLAIS Joseph Laurent Andre	29-07-44	408 Sqn
J/14143	F/O	BLAKE DFC William Vincent	23-04-44	428 Sqn
R/165968	Sgt	BLAKELY William John	3-01-44	405 Sqn
J/14827	F/O	BLAKENEY Lester Ferguson	26-02-44	420 Sqn
R/117405	LAC	BLANCHARD Albert Sheppard	8-03-44	Eastmoor
C/19462	P/O	BLANCHARD Joseph Jerome	15-02-44	434 Sqn
J/89255	P/O	BLANCHARD Westley Lawrence	13-06-44	432 Sqn
J/24016	F/O	BLAND Leonard Alvin	15-03-44	578 Sqn
C/198	W/C	BLANE John Donald	29-07-44	424 Sqn
J/92514	P/O	BLASKO Joseph Arthur	18-07-44	431 Sqn
J/88416	P/O	BLAYDES Herbert	25-06-44	9 Sqn
J/90837	P/O	BLAYNEY Alfred Goodman-Wells	18-12-44	432 Sqn
J/27283	F/O	BLOCK Dalton Irvon	17-08-44	420 Sqn
R/189116	Sgt	BLUNT Walter Leonard	23-07-44	83 OTU
J/89962	F/O	BLYTH Colin John	29-07-44	405 Sqn
R/203369	F/S	BOCK Earl William	22-10-44	626 Sqn
C/87869	P/O	BOEHMER Albert Edward Charles	17-06-44	434 Sqn
J/89406	P/O	BOILEAU Joseph Paul Roger	30-01-44	405 Sqn
J/87272	P/O	BOISSEVAIN Henry Glen	23-04-44	433 Sqn
J/20970	F/O	BOISVERT Wilfred Leger	18-01-44	1659 HCU
J/26382	F/O	BOLDERSTON George Thomas	12-09-44	626 Sqn
J/40378	F/O	BOLTON Vernon Harry	26-08-44	83 OTU
J/86939	F/O	BONAR William Selby Pace	3-11-44	424 Sqn
J/24522	F/O	BONELL William Stewart	30-07-44	514 Sqn
J/86904	P/O	BONNETT Leonard Douglas	15-06-44	433 Sqn
J/25732	F/O	BONNEVILLE John Raymond	20-02-44	408 Sqn
J/90943	P/O	BONOKOSKI Daniel	29-01-44	431 Sqn
R/221856	Sgt	BOOKHOUT Earl Wesley	5-07-44	576 Sqn
J/22097	F/O	BOOTH James Robert	28-01-44	115 Sqn
C/19795	P/O	BOOTH Croix de Guerre avec Palme [Belgium] Robert Alexander	28-04-44	405 Sqn
J/21171	F/O	BORCHARDT Hugo Hysert	21-07-44	90 Sqn
R/204063	Cpl	BORDELEAU Joseph Jacques Bernard	6-10-44	64 Base
R/189482	F/S	BORKOFSKY Edward	6-10-44	78 Sqn
J/19536	P/O	BORROWES DFC Robert Dean	7-05-44	405 Sqn
R/81097	F/S	BORROWMAN William Thomas	11-10-44	1655 MTU
J/23705	F/O	BOSS Norman Holmes	15-11-44	1664 HCU
J/86936	P/O	BOTSFORD Robert Longworth	13-06-44	432 Sqn
R/196196	F/S	BOTTERILL Harold Wallace [USA]	1-11-44	424 Sqn
R/207383	Sgt	BOTTOMLEY Harry Frederick [USA]	11-04-44	625 Sqn
J/88402	P/O	BOTTRELL Gerard Alp	19-02-44	424 Sqn
J/90945	P/O	BOUCHARD Joseph Edmond Yvon	25-03-44	425 Sqn
J/87815	P/O	BOUCHER Gerald Joseph 'Joe'	25-04-44	425 Sqn
J/90953	P/O	BOUCHER Norman Alfred	19-07-44	425 Sqn
J/92616	P/O	BOUCOCK Kenneth George	17-08-44	420 Sqn
J/88809	P/O	BOUDREAU Lawrence Joseph Henry	25-04-44	424 Sqn
J/89284	P/O	BOURGEAULT John Arthur	23-04-44	433 Sqn
J/89946	P/O	BOURQUE Theodore Phillip	25-04-44	78 Sqn
J/88339	P/O	BOUSQUET Elbert Cyril	2-03-44	425 Sqn
J/88414	P/O	BOUTILIER Eric Patrick	23-05-44	432 Sqn
J/9657	F/L	BOW Henry Herbert	23-03-44	426 Sqn
R/159625	F/S	BOWDEN Donald Ivan	20-02-44	408 Sqn
J/88088	P/O	BOWDEN Leonard Douglas	25-04-44	100 Sqn

ID	Rank	Name	Date	Unit
J/92364	P/O	BOWEN Robert Henry	14-10-44	419 Sqn
J/88199	P/O	BOWERING John Ernest Ralph	22-06-44	619 Sqn
J/88409	P/O	BOXALL George Robert	25-04-44	100 Sqn
J/88500	P/O	BOYCE Charles David	22-06-44	207 Sqn
J/90467	P/O	BOYCE Robert Richardson	17-08-44	428 Sqn
J/91105	P/O	BOYD Donald McMillan	12-09-44	630 Sqn
J/88343	P/O	BOYER Maurice William	24-03-44	425 Sqn
J/91059	P/O	BOYLE Ernest Elroy	21-07-44	101 Sqn
J/40079	F/O	BRAATEN Sterling Lorne [USA]	23-08-44	20 OTU
J/27500	F/O	BRAATHEN Harold	5-07-44	44 Sqn
J/88650	P/O	BRAD Harold Arthur	27-04-44	106 Sqn
J/95206	P/O	BRADLEY Charles Raymond	28-12-44	101 Sqn
J/85652	P/O	BRADLEY Jonathan Riley	28-05-44	1659 HCU
J/86966	P/O	BRADLEY Robert Joseph	27-01-44	408 Sqn
J/28537	F/O	BRADLEY Royden Garfield	27-08-44	166 Sqn
R/175313	Sgt	BRADSHAW Allan James	31-03-44	51 Sqn
R/170692	F/S	BRADY Charles John	24-09-44	576 Sqn
J/88405	P/O	BRAMMALL John Alfred	24-03-44	12 Sqn
J/10499	F/L	BRASS James Gladstone	11-12-44	105 Sqn
J/88272	P/O	BRAUN Howard Charles	27-08-44	115 Sqn
J/40677	P/O	BRAUTIGAM Ernest Henry	12-12-44	1664 HCU
J/24720	F/O	BRAYNE Kenneth	13-08-44	429 Sqn
J/24729	F/O	BRAZEAU Joseph Philipe Rene Fernand	24-03-44	425 Sqn
J/87376	P/O	BREEZE Harold Arthur Alexander	28-04-44	434 Sqn
J/41540	P/O	BREHAUT Lowell Milton	5-08-44	86 OTU
J/17271	F/O	BREITHAUPT DFC William Ransom	13-09-44	239 Sqn
R/157928	WO2	BREMNER John Donald	28-04-44	419 Sqn
J/36018	F/O	BRENNAN Herbert John Patrick	1-06-44	138 Sqn
J/86444	P/O	BRENTON Leo Arthur	25-04-44	7 Sqn
J/21331	F/O	BREST Clarence Samuel [Hawaii]	20-01-44	434 Sqn
J/23959	F/O	BRETT Harold Beverly	17-06-44	550 Sqn
J/91055	P/O	BREWER Hedley Royden	5-07-44	433 Sqn
J/93177	P/O	BREWER Thomas James	20-02-44	156 Sqn
R/84002	F/S	BREZINA Frederick George	18-07-44	630 Sqn
J/29586	F/O	BRIAN Edward Joseph	12-09-44	207 Sqn
J/23221	F/L	BRICE Francis Thomas Sargent	13-06-44	408 Sqn
R/175894	F/S	BRIGGS William Edmund	16-03-44	420 Sqn
R/133764	WO1	BRILLINGER Donald Stewart	23-04-44	429 Sqn
J/86180	P/O	BRISSON Joseph Paul Guy	23-04-44	425 Sqn
R/197789	Sgt	BRISTOW Frederick David	31-08-44	22 OTU
2167A	Sgt	BRITLAND George Douglas	11-07-44	408 Sqn
J/88448	P/O	BRITTAIN Paul Herman	21-07-44	10 Sqn
J/27492	F/O	BRITTEN Aubrey Ginders	19-07-44	619 Sqn
J/92636	P/O	BRITTON Clarence William Arthur [USA]	8-11-44	158 Sqn
J/88665	P/O	BRITTS Alfred Joseph	21-07-44	405 Sqn
J/24702	F/O	BROADFOOT Clifford McNeil	20-02-44	434 Sqn
J/18778	F/O	BROADFOOT James Graham	27-01-44	408 Sqn
J/85520	P/O	BROCK DFC Robert George	25-04-44	50 Sqn
J/85535	P/O	BROCKWAY George William	31-03-44	7 Sqn
J/5048	F/L	BRODER John Gordon	24-02-44	1664 HCU
J/35532	F/O	BRODIE Robert Gerald Campbell	21-04-44	30 OTU
J/19860	P/O	BROOKS Alfred	27-01-44	426 Sqn
J/35328	F/O	BROOKS Clare Edward	13-09-44	101 Sqn
J/88793	P/O	BROOKS Glenn Wesley	7-10-44	426 Sqn
J/87931	P/O	BROOKS John Philip	16-03-44	426 Sqn
J/26706	P/O	BROOKS Keith Bishop	4-11-44	78 Sqn
R/191541	Sgt	BROPHEY Burton Orval	26-03-44	15 Sqn
J/28773	P/O	BROSKO Peter Paul	29-07-44	61 Sqn
J/36348	F/O	BROUILLETTE Joseph Ross Eugene	14-10-44	153 Sqn
J/25827	F/O	BROWN Alan Francis	23-05-44	429 Sqn
J/28198	F/O	BROWN Charles Davis [USA]	23-05-44	408 Sqn
J/87009	P/O	BROWN Clement Hector [USA]	12-09-44	100 Sqn
J/89961	P/O	BROWN David Cornfoot	1-07-44	626 Sqn
J/35242	P/O	BROWN David Oscar	21-07-44	514 Sqn
J/95558	P/O	BROWN De Willett Francis	1-11-44	434 Sqn
J/28945	P/O	BROWN Douglas Walter	15-08-44	428 Sqn
J/94612	P/O	BROWN Duncan Stewart	18-12-44	158 Sqn
J/37886	F/O	BROWN Edward John	9-11-44	625 Sqn
R/143614	Sgt	BROWN George	30-08-44	434 Sqn
J/28528	F/O	BROWN George Chahoon	8-08-44	103 Sqn
J/8965	F/L	BROWN Harold Earl [USA]	28-09-44	627 Sqn
J/42283	F/O	BROWN James E. [USA]	1-09-44	1659 HCU
J/28206	F/O	BROWN John Armagh Charles	12-05-44	427 Sqn
C/193	F/O	BROWN John Daniel	23-03-44	426 Sqn
J/86751	P/O	BROWN John Francis	28-05-44	427 Sqn
J/92163	P/O	BROWN John William	14-10-44	550 Sqn
J/35910	F/O	BROWN Leonard George	17-08-44	428 Sqn
J/88160	P/O	BROWN Wesley	29-07-44	432 Sqn
R/194133	F/S	BROWN William Clyde	27-08-44	1661 HCU
R/155985	WO2	BROWN William Earle	22-05-44	514 Sqn
R/180799	F/S	BROWNLEE Irvin Gordon Thomas	13-08-44	76 Sqn
J/27531	F/O	BRUCE Allan	9-11-44	625 Sqn
J/88569	P/O	BRUEGEMAN Raymond Glen	4-08-44	434 Sqn
J/29589	F/O	BRYAN Gerald George	23-09-44	106 Sqn
J/89271	P/O	BRYANS William Stewart	27-08-44	97 Sqn
R/183553	F/S	BRYANT Edward Maines	25-07-44	166 Sqn
J/90923	P/O	BRYDON Francis Samuel	1-06-44	625 Sqn
R/166147	WO2	BRYSON George	27-04-44	106 Sqn
J/39007	F/O	BUCHANAN George David Wills	13-06-44	28 OTU
R/277161	Sgt	BUCHKOWSKI Taras Stefan	2-10-44	19 OTU
J/23022	F/L	BUCK AFC Percy Lloyd	12-09-44	426 Sqn
J/90667	P/O	BUCKBERROUGH Robert Clarke 'Bob'	11-07-44	408 Sqn
J/90464	P/O	BUCKHAM John Alexander	5-07-44	424 Sqn
R/189537	F/S	BUCKINGHAM John Alexander	15-06-44	433 Sqn
J/39274	F/O	BUELL Chester Merrill	28-12-44	101 Sqn
J/85931	P/O	BULGER John Percy	16-03-44	625 Sqn
J/3486	S/L	BULL Charles Gordon	18-07-44	431 Sqn
J/43661	F/O	BULL Frederick Cradock	7-12-44	24 OTU
R/162158	F/S	BULLOCH Earl Kitchener	12-09-44	467 Sqn
J/89261	P/O	BULLOCK Gordon Alan	18-08-44	630 Sqn
R/154844	WO2	BULMAN Frederick Lloyd	23-04-44	166 Sqn
R/261281	Sgt	BUNT Eugene	27-06-44	18 OTU
J/85620	P/O	BURCH Roy Victor	24-03-44	578 Sqn
J/86419	P/O	BURDETT Norman William Ellison	23-04-44	550 Sqn
J/86794	P/O	BURGESS Fred Andrew	29-07-44	432 Sqn
J/90344	P/O	BURGESS Hugh Thomas Blakeley	8-07-44	207 Sqn
J/86415	P/O	BURKE David Warnock	31-03-44	640 Sqn
J/86252	P/O	BURKE John Joseph	6-04-44	408 Sqn
R/153147	F/S	BURKE Joseph Gerard	20-02-44	427 Sqn
R/206904	Sgt	BURKE Joseph Paul Ernest	20-11-44	22 OTU
R/194989	Sgt	BURKE Wesley Ray	3-02-44	16 OTU
J/37803	F/O	BURLEIGH Frank Kenneth [United Kingdom]	4-07-44	24 OTU
R/203545	Sgt	BURNARD Melvin Ellwood	25-03-44	44 Sqn
J/19998	P/O	BURNELL Douglas Arthur	11-09-44	408 Sqn
J/85238	P/O	BURNETT David Mark Tyndall	13-05-44	692 Sqn
J/36277	P/O	BURNIE Glenn David Welsh	24-08-44	1652 HCU
C/86271	P/O	BURNS Edward Robert	26-02-44	102 Sqn
J/16496	F/O	BURNS MiD Gerald Charles	23-04-44	433 Sqn
J/35361	P/O	BURNS Robert James	13-08-44	427 Sqn
J/22423	P/O	BURNS William Stirling	23-09-44	61 Sqn
R/255159	F/S	BURROWS Donald Eugene	4-11-44	51 Sqn
J/22599	P/O	BURROWS John Woollatt	28-04-44	434 Sqn
J/11064	F/L	BURSTON Frank Lorne	5-07-44	82 OTU
J/21807	P/O	BURSTON Glen Richard	5-07-44	82 OTU
J/88261	P/O	BURT Henry Andrew	13-08-44	12 Sqn
R/206418	Sgt	BURT Robert George Alfred	15-03-44	408 Sqn
J/25377	F/O	BURTON James Roberts	26-10-44	166 Sqn
J/87892	F/O	BURTON Robert Elwood	18-07-44	432 Sqn
R/192592	Sgt	BURTON Robert William [USA]	23-01-44	20 OTU
J/39727	F/O	BUSH DFC Douglas Gordon	5-07-44	82 OTU
J/36829	F/O	BUTLER Dell Alfred	14-10-44	425 Sqn
R/167323	WO2	BUTSON Graham Frederick	27-04-44	408 Sqn
J/89955	P/O	BYERS James Edward	13-06-44	78 Sqn
J/13610	F/O	BYRNE Frank Paul [USA]	13-05-44	515 Sqn

Service No.	Rank	Name	Date	Squadron
J/21935	F/O	CALDER Douglas Hector	16-03-44	420 Sqn
R/220155	Sgt	CALDER James Alexander	18-07-44	630 Sqn
J/4695	F/L	CALDER John Philip Sargent	21-07-44	571 Sqn
J/19340	P/O	CALDER Robert George	3-03-44	1666 HCU
J/90282	F/O	CALDWELL Esmond Russell	27-04-44	83 Sqn
J/23966	F/L	CALHOUN DFC Maxwell Boyd	17-08-44	405 Sqn
J/35111	F/O	CALNAN Ronald Frank	20-03-44	82 OTU
R/283317	Sgt	CAMERON Alexander Angus	20-11-44	22 OTU
R/65760	F/S	CAMERON Bruce Clarke	2-01-44	405 Sqn
J/29338	F/O	CAMERON Clare Reid	30-08-44	550 Sqn
J/26595	F/O	CAMERON Douglas Newlands	17-06-44	640 Sqn
J/92129	P/O	CAMERON George	18-08-44	630 Sqn
R/180812	Sgt	CAMERON Gilbert Keith	27-06-44	18 OTU
J/19634	F/O	CAMERON Gordon Everett	29-07-44	408 Sqn
J/19735	P/O	CAMERON Jack Burton	14-01-44	408 Sqn
J/39328	F/O	CAMERON Laurence Emmett	10-10-44	1667 HCU
J/3734	S/L	CAMERON Lloyd Henry	20-02-44	434 Sqn
R/116874	WO1	CAMERON Robert Edgar Hall	25-04-44	626 Sqn
J/89959	P/O	CAMERON Roderick Hugh	23-04-44	149 Sqn
2401A	F/S	CAMERON William Alexander	19-07-44	425 Sqn
J/88363	P/O	CAMMAART Frederick Peter	23-04-44	424 Sqn
J/85824	P/O	CAMPBELL Alexander Grant	11-04-44	576 Sqn
J/21371	F/O	CAMPBELL Allan Paul	2-01-44	405 Sqn
J/90759	P/O	CAMPBELL Charles John	13-05-44	431 Sqn
J/89445	P/O	CAMPBELL Colin Alexander	23-04-44	514 Sqn
J/90306	P/O	CAMPBELL David Sinclair	25-07-44	50 Sqn
J/94493	P/O	CAMPBELL Frederick William	23-12-44	582 Sqn
J/26122	F/O	CAMPBELL James Comodore	15-10-44	626 Sqn
J/95169	P/O	CAMPBELL James Duncan	16-09-44	199 Sqn
J/90947	P/O	CAMPBELL Kenneth Peter	24-04-44	425 Sqn
J/85772	P/O	CAMPBELL Richard Edward John	13-06-44	434 Sqn
J/43615	P/O	CAMPBELL Richard Gladstone	4-10-44	82 OTU
J/22573	F/O	CAMPBELL Robert Roy	13-05-44	419 Sqn
C/95079	P/O	CAMPBELL Russell Archibald	9-10-44	419 Sqn
J/95217	P/O	CAMPBELL Vincent Daniel	9-11-44	625 Sqn
J/35226	F/O	CAMPBELL William	1-06-44	1667 HCU
R/72053	Cpl	CAMPBELL William Howard	24-09-44	408 Sqn
R/54351	WO2	CAMPBELL William Warren	3-03-44	1666 HCU
J/18433	F/O	CAMPSALL Rodney Sigsworth	28-04-44	101 Sqn
J/95160	P/O	CAMPTON Clifden Homer Foch	2-11-44	426 Sqn
R/100359	F/S	CANDLINE Albert Edward	29-07-44	408 Sqn
J/36389	F/O	CANN Robert Leslie	18-12-44	432 Sqn
J/16816	F/O	CANNING Thomas Kenneth	27-10-44	408 Sqn
J/90920	P/O	CANNINGS Kenneth Leverne	9-05-44	432 Sqn
R/81134	Cpl	CANT Norman William	18-09-44	62 Base [United Kingdom]
J/90372	P/O	CANTWELL Michael James Wallace	16-07-44	207 Sqn
C/87643	P/O	CARDINAL Joseph Jacques Bruno	28-05-44	427 Sqn
J/16480	F/L	CAREY DFC Douglas Mintie	31-03-44	12 Sqn
J/90931	P/O	CAREY Robert William Burdell	30-07-44	115 Sqn
J/23360	F/O	CARLETON Reginald Harvey	31-03-44	640 Sqn
J/90059	P/O	CARLSON Alfred	27-01-44	426 Sqn
R/218011	Sgt	CARLSON Elmer Kenneth	12-09-44	619 Sqn
J/90367	P/O	CARLSON Ernest William Bernard	8-06-44	138 Sqn
J/28217	F/O	CARNEGIE Thomas	1-06-44	138 Sqn
J/90183	F/O	CAROL Roy Frank	6-06-44	426 Sqn
J/4918	F/L	CARPENTER Eric Charles	23-12-44	109 Sqn
R/251899	Sgt	CARR Leo Augustave	14-01-44	408 Sqn
R/209938	Sgt	CARR Stuart Allan	23-01-44	1679 HCFlt
R/176860	Sgt	CARRIER Joseph Louis Phillipee Denis [USA]	16-03-44	1664 HCU
R/176957	F/S	CARROLL Ralph William	16-11-44	166 Sqn
J/92333	P/O	CARRUTHERS George William	13-06-44	419 Sqn
J/90068	F/O	CARSON Douglas Alexander	18-07-44	427 Sqn
R/164485	F/S	CARSON Harvey George	13-09-44	166 Sqn
R/109991	WO2	CARSON Lewis Gerard	29-01-44	625 Sqn
J/37796	F/O	CARSON William Donald	17-06-44	426 Sqn
R/190906	F/S	CARTAN Frederick Paul	15-10-44	425 Sqn
J/35424	F/O	CARTER Albert Victor	5-12-44	426 Sqn
J/88161	P/O	CARTER Daniel Newton	17-08-44	630 Sqn
J/89249	P/O	CARTER David Beatty	18-04-44	433 Sqn
J/13993	S/L	CARTER Frank Ernest	15-02-44	434 Sqn
J/94491	P/O	CARTER Henry William Tilson	30-08-44	106 Sqn
J/85969	P/O	CARTER James Alexander	12-05-44	103 Sqn
J/88790	P/O	CARTER Joseph William	17-08-44	405 Sqn
R/164074	F/S	CARTER Laurence Richmond	23-07-44	83 OTU
J/88698	P/O	CARTER Norman Edward [USA]	20-01-44	429 Sqn
J/85344	P/O	CARTER Robert Gordon	26-07-44	431 Sqn
J/28855	F/O	CARTER MiD Roy Edward	9-07-44	431 Sqn
J/93432	P/O	CARTMAN James Edward	30-12-44	161 Sqn
J/28358	F/O	CARTWRIGHT Laird Wallace	13-06-44	427 Sqn
J/89984	P/O	CARY Earl Stanley	7-08-44	149 Sqn
R/180956	WO2	CASAUBON Joseph Noe Gustave Robert	25-04-44	50 Sqn
R/204074	Sgt	CASEY George Francis	4-05-44	103 Sqn
R/275076	Sgt	CASEY Murray Gordon	31-08-44	22 OTU
R/261197	F/S	CASEY Terence Anthony	31-12-44	626 Sqn
R/178671	F/S	CASSADY John Melburne	28-01-44	103 Sqn
R/70340	Sgt	CASSELMAN John Halifax	3-02-44	28 OTU
J/90069	P/O	CASSIDY Lorne Francis	29-07-44	408 Sqn
J/37534	F/O	CATHERALLE Lloyd John Gordon	28-12-44	429 Sqn
J/8759	F/L	CAWKER Douglas Earl	22-03-44	432 Sqn
J/89721	P/O	CAYER Albert Jean William	3-11-44	424 Sqn
R/209550	Sgt	CHALK Jeffrey Thomas Ernest	13-07-44	166 Sqn
R/95021	F/S	CHALMERS Alfred Reid	30-08-44	101 Sqn
J/23463	F/O	CHALMERS Frederick Lorne	20-02-44	15 Sqn
R/89826	WO1	CHALMERS James George William	6-12-44	432 Sqn
J/86747	P/O	CHAMBERS George William	3-06-44	640 Sqn
J/41144	P/O	CHAMBERS Robert Lloyd	30-08-44	14 OTU
J/88244	F/O	CHAMBERS Stanley Victor	4-12-44	619 Sqn
J/95080	P/O	CHAMPAGNE Roland Marcel Joseph	15-10-44	626 Sqn
R/60394	WO2	CHAPLIN Robert	28-04-44	51 Sqn
J/24548	F/O	CHAPMAN Antony Dutton	5-11-44	424 Sqn
J/35119	F/O	CHAPMAN Earl William 'Bill'	29-07-44	434 Sqn
R/85522	WO2	CHAPMAN DFC John Randall	10-05-44	97 Sqn
J/37961	F/O	CHAPMAN Lloyd Edwin	30-08-44	86 OTU
J/88411	P/O	CHAPMAN Robert Scott	25-04-44	424 Sqn
J/87274	P/O	CHAREST Joseph Marie Antoine Laurent	30-01-44	405 Sqn
J/29054	F/O	CHARLAND Robert Albert	15-10-44	626 Sqn
J/19622	P/O	CHARLES William James Donald	23-05-44	103 Sqn
J/25023	F/O	CHARLESWORTH Gilbert Alan	11-04-44	1661 HCU
J/86226	P/O	CHARLTON John Robert	30-01-44	433 Sqn
J/86385	F/O	CHARTRAND John Louis Edmond	2-05-44	419 Sqn
J/24313	F/L	CHATTERTON Edward	30-08-44	115 Sqn
R/196076	F/S	CHAWANSKI Adam Philip	23-05-44	419 Sqn
J/38713	F/O	CHEESMAN Gordon Roy	6-12-44	419 Sqn
J/21428	F/L	CHEQUER George Joseph	30-01-44	514 Sqn
J/86590	P/O	CHESS James Barry	21-01-44	408 Sqn
R/159109	F/S	CHETNEY Rolf Arthur	29-07-44	207 Sqn
R/279581	Sgt	CHEVRIER George Albert	5-12-44	22 OTU
J/91127	P/O	CHINNERY Bruce Charles	30-10-44	158 Sqn
R/191275	F/S	CHORNOUS William	29-11-44	153 Sqn
J/38780	F/O	CHRISTIAN Kenneth Cregeen	6-12-44	434 Sqn
R/168215	F/S	CHRISTIE Charles Wellington	13-01-44	15 Sqn
J/86094	P/O	CHRISTIE Malcolm Keith	13-05-44	640 Sqn
J/88365	P/O	CHRISTIE Robert Foster	25-05-44	429 Sqn
J/27275	F/O	CHRISTIE Trevor Alan Mackenzie	11-06-44	434 Sqn
J/89086	P/O	CHRISTY Elmo Foster	10-08-44	619 Sqn
J/89953	P/O	CHUDZIK William Joseph	11-06-44	420 Sqn
J/24577	F/L	CHURCH Eric Rodger	26-08-44	61 Sqn
J/89451	P/O	CHUTE George Edward	26-03-44	49 Sqn
R/119590	WO1	CLARIDGE William Thomas	28-04-44	419 Sqn
J/91164	P/O	CLARK Ari Bergthor	26-12-44	76 Sqn
J/86332	F/L	CLARK DFC Austin Thomas	27-08-44	57 Sqn
C/89632	P/O	CLARK Edwin Spencer Charles	6-12-44	429 Sqn
J/88161	P/O	CLARK Harold Alexander	31-03-44	426 Sqn

ID	Rank	Name	Date	Unit
J/26760	F/O	CLARK MiD Hollis Andrew Taylor	19-07-44	550 Sqn
R/205305	F/S	CLARK Vernon Edward	7-08-44	1664 HCU
R/193583	Sgt	CLARK William Howard	29-06-44	22 OTU
R/157740	F/S	CLARK William Leonard John	2-01-44	405 Sqn
J/89944	P/O	CLARKE Arthur Kenneth	12-04-44	432 Sqn
J/86873	P/O	CLARKE Donald Wallace	12-09-44	218 Sqn
J/86745	P/O	CLARKE Edward Allan	29-07-44	432 Sqn
J/86980	P/O	CLARKE George Walter	30-11-44	429 Sqn
R/207295	Sgt	CLARKE James Robert	5-08-44	86 OTU
R/192643	F/S	CLARKE John Frederick William	23-09-44	106 Sqn
J/90061	P/O	CLARKSON Robert Leon	31-03-44	432 Sqn
J/88358	P/O	CLAY Harry Charles [USA]	29-01-44	429 Sqn
J/16564	F/L	CLAYDON David Arthur	20-01-44	622 Sqn
R/189379	Sgt	CLEAL Philip Douglas	24-03-44	78 Sqn
J/16865	F/L	CLEARWATER Roy Lloyd	14-10-44	12 Sqn
J/89903	P/O	CLEAVER John Barry	15-08-44	428 Sqn
R/201936	Sgt	CLEGHORNE Howard Herbert	13-10-44	24 OTU
J/24656	F/O	CLEMENT James McVicar	9-08-44	405 Sqn
J/36275	F/O	CLEMENTS John Earl	4-11-44	426 Sqn
J/28197	F/O	CLERC Jacques Robert Oliver [Switzerland]	16-08-44	433 Sqn
J/87453	P/O	CLIFFORD Nicholas Hugh	28-04-44	405 Sqn
J/23522	F/O	CLINKSKILL James Thomas	21-01-44	434 Sqn
J/28346	F/O	CLODE Gordon Elmore	11-01-44	17 OTU
J/20926	F/O	CLOGG Alan Leslie	22-01-44	102 Sqn
J/86891	P/O	CLOUGH George Frederick	22-03-44	408 Sqn
J/35921	F/O	CLOUSTON Ross Cuthbert	15-10-44	626 Sqn
J/10313	F/L	CLOUTIER DFC William Blaise Burke	14-01-44	405 Sqn
J/88734	P/O	CLUFF Robert Fraser	27-04-44	49 Sqn
R/141414	WO2	COATHUP Clifford Harvey	18-04-44	427 Sqn
R/115256	WO1	COATHUP George Richard	16-06-44	22 OTU
J/95409	P/O	COBBETT Bernard Victor	28-12-44	101 Sqn
R/193139	Sgt	COBBETT John Arthur	3-01-44	432 Sqn
J/86710	P/O	COCHRANE James Raymond Henry	25-05-44	429 Sqn
R/68552	LAC	COCKBAIN Henry	11-11-44	Linton on Ouse
J/23605	F/O	COCKWILL Wilfred Glen	3-01-44	57 Sqn
J/89332	P/O	CODE John Edward	2-08-44	425 Sqn
R/201593	Sgt	COFFEY Harry Morley	31-03-44	630 Sqn
J/86225	P/O	COFLIN John George	21-01-44	427 Sqn
J/87301	P/O	COHEN Ashton Irving	9-10-44	419 Sqn
J/4820	S/L	COLDREY George Edwin	3-06-44	405 Sqn
J/25897	F/O	COLE John Arthur	8-06-44	78 Sqn
J/27923	F/O	COLE Kenneth Arthur	15-03-44	405 Sqn
C/87371	P/O	COLE Ralph Stewart	18-07-44	431 Sqn
J/35865	F/O	COLES Edward Thomas	16-06-44	166 Sqn
J/89954	P/O	COLLETT Alfred John	11-06-44	460 Sqn
J/29613	F/O	COLLINGE Frank Donald	7-06-44	1654 HCU
J/38766	F/O	COLLINGWOOD Joseph Vincent	23-10-44	625 Sqn
R/206087	F/S	COLLINS Keith Clayton	4-11-44	78 Sqn
J/22842	P/O	COLLINS Richard Charles	22-03-44	9 Sqn
J/90351	P/O	COLLISTER John William	29-07-44	12 Sqn
J/25297	F/O	COLLVER Joseph Beemer	29-07-44	431 Sqn
J/23976	F/O	COLLYER John William	17-06-44	640 Sqn
J/88213	P/O	COLP Eric Leonard	29-07-44	426 Sqn
J/90922	P/O	COLTMAN Paul Everett	28-05-44	429 Sqn
R/217581	F/S	COLUMBUS Basil Edgar	13-09-44	90 Sqn
J/21864	F/O	COLVILLE Alexander Colborne	16-03-44	408 Sqn
J/95215	P/O	COMMINS Walter Joseph	4-11-44	101 Sqn
J/88175	P/O	COMPTON Orville Francis	13-08-44	429 Sqn
J/93725	P/O	CONLEY Roy Clifford	29-12-44	419 Sqn
J/90932	P/O	CONLY William Morrow	30-07-44	115 Sqn
J/90369	P/O	CONNOLLY Daniel Francis	14-07-44	77 Sqn
R/189736	Sgt	CONNOLLY Thomas Leo	25-02-44	166 Sqn
J/86186	P/O	CONNOR DFC Donald Daubney	1-11-44	431 Sqn
R/198623	F/S	CONOLLY John Louis De Vere	30-08-44	50 Sqn
J/17939	F/O	CONROY Robert Fitzgerald	24-03-44	429 Sqn
R/110020	LAC	COOK Albert Royal Felken	16-07-44	61 Base
R/251484	F/S	COOK Clifford Eugene Leroy	1-11-44	106 Sqn
R/267712	Sgt	COOK Gordon Thomas	15-10-44	432 Sqn
J/92982	P/O	COOK Howard John	25-11-44	427 Sqn
J/88728	P/O	COOK James	29-07-44	432 Sqn
R/263352	F/S	COOK Michael Arthur	6-11-44	50 Sqn
J/19344	P/O	COOK Norman Earl	21-01-44	427 Sqn
J/25395	F/O	COOK Spencer Waddy [USA]	22-06-44	101 Sqn
J/11319	F/L	COOK Walter Herbert	2-12-44	433 Sqn
J/86874	P/O	COOK DFC Walter le Roy	4-11-44	626 Sqn
J/21981	P/O	COOK William Arthur [USA]	29-01-44	429 Sqn
J/37827	F/O	COOK William Wilfred	8-11-44	158 Sqn
R/173576	F/S	COOKE CGM Jackson Chartis	29-11-44	103 Sqn
J/88607	P/O	COOKE John Joseph	28-04-44	431 Sqn
J/35898	F/O	COOKE Matthew John Goldie	5-10-44	1666 HCU
J/87307	P/O	COOMBS Allton John Richard	12-09-44	97 Sqn
R/178848	F/S	COON George Adrian	4-05-44	582 Sqn
J/18201	P/O	COOPER Albert Digby	16-06-44	22 OTU
J/90375	P/O	COOPER Bernard Horace	21-07-44	514 Sqn
J/87015	P/O	COOPER Douglas Alexander	18-07-44	431 Sqn
J/42284	F/O	COOPER Everett Elwyn	5-12-44	428 Sqn
J/23519	F/O	COOPER MiD Thomas William	18-03-44	427 Sqn
J/40083	F/O	COOPER Walter William	5-08-44	86 OTU
J/87454	P/O	COPELAND Donald Johnston	9-05-44	405 Sqn
J/92259	P/O	COPELAND James Coulter	6-12-44	429 Sqn
J/19835	P/O	CORBALLY Joseph Charles	31-03-44	427 Sqn
J/39369	F/O	CORCK Arthur George	8-07-44	17 OTU
J/26477	F/O	CORLESS Alvin Van Dyke	22-06-44	207 Sqn
J/36334	F/O	CORLEY William Arthur	11-07-44	1666 HCU
R/94835	Sgt	CORMAN John Ronald Merwin	1-07-44	14 OTU
R/121343	WO2	CORNFIELD Edward Albert	29-01-44	429 Sqn
J/24503	F/O	CORRIVEAU Arthur Jeffrey	13-05-44	640 Sqn
R/96935	WO2	CORRIVEAU Joseph Thomas Raymond	29-01-44	431 Sqn
J/85244	P/O	COSGROVE Joseph Patrick	19-04-44	625 Sqn
10797	Sgt	COTE Charles Edward	2-03-44	425 Sqn
J/87645	P/O	COTTON David Neville	29-06-44	427 Sqn
R/208208	F/S	COUCH Albert Thomas	1-07-44	101 Sqn
J/95336	P/O	COUGHLIN Gerald Philip	6-12-44	434 Sqn
J/91041	P/O	COULSON Frank	17-12-44	101 Sqn
R/156195	WO2	COULTER Everett Malcolm	20-02-44	78 Sqn
J/157337	Sgt	COULTER Robert Leslie	25-03-44	115 Sqn
J/18508	F/O	COUNTESS Ray Edgerton	28-01-44	426 Sqn
J/90342	P/O	COUPER Mungo William	13-06-44	78 Sqn
R/66744	Sgt	COURNOYER Joseph Jacques Omar	16-03-44	1664 HCU
J/92724	P/O	COURTIS Ernest Edward	1-11-44	426 Sqn
J/197319	Sgt	COUSE George Fitzgerald	23-01-44	20 OTU
J/39588	F/O	COUSINS Norman Edward	26-08-44	83 OTU
J/20061	F/L	COUTURE Joseph Arthur Leo [USA]	21-07-44	578 Sqn
J/85372	P/O	COUTURE Joseph Jean Maurice Marcel	21-01-44	433 Sqn
J/88253	P/O	COWAN Nicholas Edgar John	29-07-44	434 Sqn
J/29529	F/O	COWAN Walter Sidney	2-11-44	186 Sqn
R/151184	Sgt	COWIE Eric Edmond	3-02-44	28 OTU
J/88410	P/O	COWNDEN Vincent Joseph	28-04-44	434 Sqn
J/27318	F/O	COX Henry	29-01-44	433 Sqn
J/11843	F/O	COX Paul Conroy	20-02-44	426 Sqn
J/85152	P/O	CRABTREE Charles Maurice	14-10-44	425 Sqn
R/215305	Sgt	CRACKNELL Richard Stephen	27-06-44	18 OTU
J/8353	F/L	CRACKNELL Walter Charles	31-03-44	426 Sqn
J/21466	F/O	CRAIG DFC James	31-03-44	97 Sqn
J/120025	Sgt	CRAIG Michael Joseph	14-02-44	22 OTU
J/89914	P/O	CRANCH Francis Edward	12-04-44	432 Sqn
J/25081	F/O	CRAWFORD Kenneth	3-01-44	432 Sqn
R/190343	Sgt	CRAWFORD Norman Willard	2-01-44	82 OTU
J/35004	F/O	CRAWFORD Vincent	12-09-44	405 Sqn
J/23127	F/O	CRAWFORD William George	1-06-44	622 Sqn
R/183604	Sgt	CRAWLEY David	25-02-44	420 Sqn
J/90002	F/O	CRAWLEY Edward George	13-07-44	415 Sqn
J/89905	P/O	CRAWLEY Frederick William	17-08-44	158 Sqn

ID	Rank	Name	Date	Sqn
J/95218	P/O	CRAYSTON Kerry Milton	15-11-44	115 Sqn
J/24044	F/O	CREBA John Frederick	15-03-44	427 Sqn
J/19870	P/O	CREIGHTON DFC Allan David	22-06-44	619 Sqn
J/38172	F/O	CROMB Ian Taylor	23-09-44	24 OTU
J/21189	F/O	CROMPTON Richard Clifford	29-01-44	434 Sqn
J/23474	F/O	CRONE Robert Duncan	3-06-44	166 Sqn
J/25978	F/O	CRONIN Patrick Edmund	4-08-44	424 Sqn
R/152808	WO2	CRONK Gavin John	12-05-44	15 Sqn
C/24436	F/L	CRONYN DFC Peter Hume	13-08-44	427 Sqn
J/21660	F/O	CROSBIE Douglas Alexander	25-04-44	424 Sqn
R/161229	WO2	CROSLAND Alfred Hirst	31-03-44	424 Sqn
R/282958	Sgt	CROSS Stanley Esmond	7-12-44	24 OTU
R/76951	WO2	CROSSLEY Frederick Wood	21-01-44	434 Sqn
J/26857	F/L	CROUCHER MiD Gordon	29-07-44	408 Sqn
J/25101	F/O	CROWDY Charles William Cecil	25-04-44	192 Sqn
C/89859	P/O	CROWE Charles David	16-09-44	432 Sqn
R/185340	Sgt	CROWE Eric Arthur	27-06-44	18 OTU
R/195945	F/S	CROWLEY Paul Anthony	13-08-44	428 Sqn
J/90054	P/O	CRUM Wallace Watson	23-05-44	432 Sqn
J/22072	F/O	CRUSE William Lorne	31-03-44	78 Sqn
R/112194	Cpl	CUDMORE Lorne Albert	15-09-44	62 Base
J/27394	F/O	CUFF Roland Walter John	29-07-44	426 Sqn
R/200097	Sgt	CULL Lloyd John	15-04-44	1664 HCU
J/36888	F/O	CULLEN Joseph Patrick Leonard	28-12-44	429 Sqn
J/86606	P/O	CULLEN Sidney Herman	31-03-44	426 Sqn
J/88740	P/O	CULLY Victor Charles [USA]	22-06-44	49 Sqn
J/36932	F/O	CULSHAW Thurston	14-10-44	626 Sqn
R/217185	F/S	CULVERSON Donald Harvey	13-08-44	166 Sqn
J/87849	P/O	CUMING Lloyd Wesley	27-01-44	61 Sqn
U/199090	Sgt	CUMMING Gordon Farrell	2-10-44	1664 HCU
J/19803	P/O	CUMMINGS Kenneth George	20-02-44	102 Sqn
R/190673	Sgt	CUMMINGS Robert Paul	24-05-44	20 OTU
J/88415	P/O	CUNNINGHAM Harry Joseph	23-05-44	408 Sqn
J/92036	P/O	CUNNINGHAM James Adrian	1-07-44	625 Sqn
J/22598	F/O	CUNNINGHAM James Hill	20-02-44	431 Sqn
R/198321	Sgt	CUNNINGHAM Robert Norval [USA]	11-05-44	50 Sqn
R/158319	Sgt	CUNNINGS Ronald Everett	29-02-44	420 Sqn
J/19632	P/O	CURATOLO Louis	14-01-44	44 Sqn
J/88045	P/O	CURLE John Garfield	5-10-44	427 Sqn
J/86491	F/O	CURPHEY Thomas George	29-07-44	50 Sqn
J/40406	F/O	CURRIE Charles	20-11-44	1656 HCU
J/90350	P/O	CURRIE David Fraser	29-07-44	61 Sqn
J/93665	P/O	CURRIE Donald Russell	23-12-44	35 Sqn
J/88815	P/O	CURRIE Gordon	21-01-44	408 Sqn
J/89295	P/O	CUSHMAN Nicholas	25-07-44	420 Sqn
J/88600	P/O	CUTLER Eric Herrington	20-02-44	431 Sqn
J/38340	F/O	CUZNER Ross Llooyd	30-07-44	22 OTU
R/104165	WO1	CYPLES William Harold	17-11-44	24 OTU
J/89882	P/O	DACK Phillip Robert Arthur	20-01-44	434 Sqn
J/87660	P/O	DAGENAIS Joseph Jacques Guy	11-06-44	405 Sqn
J/17647	F/O	DAHLE Truman Helmer	17-08-44	431 Sqn
J/89331	P/O	DALESSANDRO Frank Joseph	29-07-44	425 Sqn
R/223820	Sgt	DALGLISH William Logan	6-08-44	138 Sqn
R/137946	WO2	DALLING James Edwin	2-01-44	82 OTU
J/18270	F/O	DALLYN James Boustead	23-05-44	408 Sqn
J/27493	F/O	DALY James Terence	29-07-44	514 Sqn
R/140423	F/S	DANCEY Glen Allen	24-03-44	433 Sqn
J/192606	Sgt	DANIELS Arnold Douglas	23-08-44	24 OTU
J/38265	F/O	DANIELSON Gordon Daniel	30-08-44	619 Sqn
R/79453	F/S	DAOUST Roger Henry Jules	6-01-44	405 Sqn
J/15601	F/L	DARBY DFM Charles Edmond	28-08-44	608 Sqn
R/261453	F/S	DARLING William Russell	4-12-44	166 Sqn
R/184493	Sgt	DAUPLAISE Joseph Adolphe Maurice	30-07-44	22 OTU
J/88086	P/O	DAVENPORT Frank	20-02-44	10 Sqn
J/87894	P/O	DAVEY Harvey Gordon	13-08-44	427 Sqn
R/118143	WO1	DAVEY Leonard Frank	29-05-44	82 OTU
R/177945	F/S	DAVEY Leslie Gerald	24-03-44	433 Sqn
J/40811	F/O	DAVIDSON George Walker	30-08-44	86 OTU
J/88386	P/O	DAVIDSON John Ewart	20-02-44	433 Sqn
J/26633	F/L	DAVIDSON John William	15-11-44	115 Sqn
J/22514	F/O	DAVIDSON Norman James	13-02-44	617 Sqn
R/156264	WO2	DAVIDSON Norman Sinclair	24-03-44	78 Sqn
J/89890	P/O	DAVIES Douglas Idris	13-06-44	78 Sqn
J/95220	P/O	DAVIES Edmund Alfred John	17-12-44	101 Sqn
J/21363	F/O	DAVIES Gordon Paul	20-02-44	419 Sqn
R/212758	Sgt	DAVIES Herbert Russell	2-05-44	1659 HCU
J/86585	P/O	DAVIES John Cecil	9-06-44	51 Sqn
R/159100	WO2	DAVIES Lawrence Ward	13-08-44	166 Sqn
R/211900	F/S	DAVIES Lorne Graham	29-11-44	153 Sqn
J/87366	P/O	DAVIES Paul Patrick	2-08-44	425 Sqn
J/87194	P/O	DAVIES Robert Henry	17-08-44	420 Sqn
J/86222	P/O	DAVIS Billy	20-01-44	630 Sqn
J/92608	P/O	DAVIS Daniel George	16-06-44	514 Sqn
J/28949	P/O	DAVIS Edward Addy	30-01-44	22 OTU
J/90062	P/O	DAVIS Harry Walter	28-04-44	432 Sqn
J/23609	F/O	DAVIS Kenneth H.	29-06-44	7 Sqn
R/157624	Sgt	DAVIS Robert Siderfin	30-03-44	20 OTU
R/193967	Sgt	DAVIS William Corley	13-06-44	28 OTU
J/35523	F/O	DAVY Harry Denis	22-12-44	405 Sqn
R/107107	WO1	DAVY DFC Henry William [USA]	24-06-44	156 Sqn
J/88704	P/O	DAWSON Donald James Vens	20-02-44	77 Sqn
J/90321	P/O	DAWSON Douglas	17-09-44	115 Sqn
R/202351	Sgt	DAWSON Fabian Richard	23-08-44	1659 HCU
J/89896	P/O	DAWSON Gordon Forbes	15-11-44	115 Sqn
R/82170	F/S	DAZE John Cletus	31-12-44	166 Sqn
R/181350	F/S	DEAN Robert Trevor	1-06-44	1667 HCU
J/40506	F/O	DEANE-FREEMAN Brian	30-08-44	14 OTU
J/19181	P/O	DEATH Arthur Henry	31-03-44	76 Sqn
J/92211	P/O	DEATHERAGE George Edward	17-12-44	101 Sqn
J/22055	F/O	DEEMER Edward John	25-03-44	115 Sqn
J/88384	P/O	DEHOUX Joseph Fernand Gustave Rene		419 Sqn
J/38561	F/O	DELL Ronald Frank	30-08-44	514 Sqn
J/26804	F/O	DELOUGHRY Laurie Daniel	28-04-44	432 Sqn
J/19959	P/O	DEMERS Joseph William Raoul	29-01-44	434 Sqn
J/88686	P/O	DEMPSTER Charles James	13-08-44	429 Sqn
J/17206	F/O	DEMPSTER DFM John McBride	13-02-44	617 Sqn
R/163694	WO2	DENNIS Francis Basil	18-04-44	427 Sqn
J/95222	P/O	DENNIS Frederick Stanley	29-12-44	419 Sqn
J/92123	P/O	DENNIS Russel Edward	10-06-44	630 Sqn
J/95170	P/O	DENNISON Gordon Joshua	16-09-44	199 Sqn
J/24959	F/L	DEPEW Douglas George	13-08-44	429 Sqn
J/86266	P/O	DEPPER Clifford Lloyd	22-01-44	433 Sqn
J/88396	P/O	DERBYSHIRE Donovan Emmerson	23-05-44	419 Sqn
R/264171	Sgt	DERBYSHIRE John	12-10-44	166 Sqn
J/88152	P/O	DESMARAIS Joseph Eugene Gerard	23-05-44	419 Sqn
J/87112	P/O	DESMARAIS DFC Joseph Raymond Jean Marie	18-12-44	425 Sqn
J/88390	P/O	DESROCHES Joseph Paul Lucien Wilfred Leon	23-04-44	433 Sqn
R/225429	Sgt	DESSERTINE Claudien Paul Joseph	23-09-44	1664 HCU
J/19399	P/O	DEVANEY Edward Philip	29-01-44	434 Sqn
J/19592	P/O	DEVEREAUX Frank Gerrard	28-05-44	427 Sqn
C/92768	P/O	DEVITT James Frederick	22-12-44	405 Sqn
J/85650	P/O	DEVOY Alexander Gordon	31-03-44	426 Sqn
J/88395	P/O	DEWAR Peter	13-05-44	419 Sqn
R/171864	WO2	DEWIS Frederick Sayre	22-06-44	630 Sqn
R/210865	F/S	DEWEY Kenneth Welland	24-07-44	625 Sqn
J/90571	P/O	DEY Robert	26-07-44	103 Sqn
J/88388	P/O	de DAUW Andrew Francis	24-03-44	432 Sqn
J/95219	P/O	de MACEDO Joseph Maurice	6-12-44	434 Sqn
J/92028	P/O	DE CELLES Leo Lorne Norman	25-02-44	460 Sqn
J/29580	F/O	DE VRIES Terence [USA]	30-08-44	619 Sqn
J/88389	P/O	DE WITT Arthur Melvin	31-03-44	425 Sqn
J/17187	F/O	DICK La Verne John	30-10-44	627 Sqn
J/9270	F/L	DICKIE Alexander Gordon	10-04-44	100 Sqn

Service No.	Rank	Name	Date	Unit
J/93903	P/O	DICKIE Robert James	21-02-44	97 Sqn
R/281169	Sgt	DICKIE Ross Meredith	30-08-44	19 OTU
R/113573	F/S	DICKIE William James	22-11-44	1660 HCU
J/89013	P/O	DICKINSON Alfred John	13-08-44	427 Sqn
R/185654	LAC	DICKINSON Francis	23-04-44	428 Sqn
J/28488	F/O	DICKINSON Robert Harris	29-06-44	424 Sqn
R/87940	Cpl	DICKSON William Rodger	21-08-44	415 Sqn
J/87465	P/O	DIENO Gustaf Adolph	13-06-44	432 Sqn
J/9497	F/L	DIGNEY Roderick Joseph	31-03-44	424 Sqn
J/18929	P/O	DIMMA DFM Thomas William	24-03-44	22 OTU
R/153186	F/S	DIMOCK Arthur Edward	14-01-44	514 Sqn
R/101473	WO1	DINGWALL John	29-07-44	408 Sqn
R/146964	Sgt	DION Joseph Jacques Louis	15-11-44	1659 HCU
J/89044	P/O	DIONNE Francis Roger	16-03-44	1664 HCU
R/179976	F/S	DITTMER Donald Franklin	24-07-44	1666 HCU
R/209473	F/S	DIVITCOFF Alexander	18-12-44	434 Sqn
J/37706	F/O	DIXON Arthur Allen	28-12-44	428 Sqn
C/35425	F/O	DIXON Frederick Allen	16-06-44	22 OTU
R/142636	F/S	DIXON John	20-02-44	57 Sqn
R/179831	Sgt	DIXON Nelson Alexander	6-01-44	576 Sqn
J/22058	F/O	DIXON William Allison	31-03-44	578 Sqn
J/16455	F/O	DI MARCO Leo John David	19-08-44	429 Sqn
R/188302	Sgt	DI PINTO John Henry	21-01-44	431 Sqn
J/18666	F/O	DOBBYN DFC Joseph Lloyd	23-03-44	50 Sqn
J/36379	F/O	DOBESCH Burghardt Hans	26-05-44	19 OTU
J/35152	F/O	DOCKREY Cyril Bernard	12-09-44	619 Sqn
J/87616	P/O	DODD Thomas Wilfred	22-01-44	514 Sqn
R/133286	WO1	DODDING James David	20-02-44	514 Sqn
J/89743	P/O	DODDS Vernon Fairbank	21-07-44	405 Sqn
J/21046	P/O	DODGE James Harper	28-01-44	426 Sqn
J/29847	F/O	DOE James Harrington	29-07-44	622 Sqn
J/90242	P/O	DOGGETT Harry	17-06-44	426 Sqn
J/16112	F/O	DOIG John	31-03-44	424 Sqn
J/18898	F/L	DOIG Peter Hartley	25-02-44	622 Sqn
J/90917	P/O	DOIRON Harley William [USA]	23-04-44	429 Sqn
J/19999	P/O	DOLTER Francis Wilfred	25-05-44	424 Sqn
J/17152	F/O	DONAHUE DFM Carroll Joseph	2-01-44	7 Sqn
J/87044	P/O	DONALD James Leo	15-02-44	419 Sqn
R/193801	Sgt	DONNELLY Edward John	2-05-44	1659 HCU
J/86162	P/O	DONNELLY James William	20-02-44	434 Sqn
R/200407	Sgt	DONNELLY Thomas Edward Ramsay	25-05-44	19 OTU
J/17137	F/O	DONNELLY DFM Thomas Henry	2-01-44	405 Sqn
J/88382	P/O	DONOGHUE Michael Gerald Edmund	21-01-44	434 Sqn
R/188791	F/S	DONOVAN DFM Irvine Irwin	27-04-44	101 Sqn
J/19725	P/O	DORAN Arthur Joseph	11-06-44	434 Sqn
R/159101	WO2	DORAN Willard Lawrence	2-01-44	9 Sqn
J/86233	P/O	DORAN William Lawrence	15-03-44	408 Sqn
C/90844	P/O	DORRELL Matthew	2-11-44	428 Sqn
J/28201	F/O	DOUGAN Jack Llewelyn	5-10-44	427 Sqn
J/94225	P/O	DOUGLAS Glenn Thomas	21-07-44	101 Sqn
J/42268	F/O	DOUGLAS Norman Evan Paul	31-08-44	22 OTU
J/86117	P/O	DOUGLAS William John [USA]	21-01-44	432 Sqn
J/22588	P/O	DOULL Hedley Forbes	3-01-44	432 Sqn
J/35582	F/O	DOUPE Richard Vernon	5-07-44	82 OTU
J/22851	F/O	DOWD Phillip Paul	22-03-44	626 Sqn
J/85604	P/O	DOWDELL Stanley Geddes	25-03-44	427 Sqn
J/46041	P/O	DOWDING John Frederick	17-10-44	19 OTU
J/35782	F/O	DOWDING Richard Boyd	5-12-44	426 Sqn
J/86196	P/O	DOWE Edward Albert	20-02-44	426 Sqn
R/147950	WO2	DOWLER Norman Garth	20-01-44	101 Sqn
R/270087	F/S	DOWLING Ralph Andrew	6-11-44	50 Sqn
R/183176	Sgt	DOWNEY Bernard	16-02-44	420 Sqn
J/39340	F/O	DOWNING Albert Edward 'Bert'	5-12-44	426 Sqn
J/85797	P/O	DOWNING James	29-07-44	12 Sqn
R/126409	F/S	DOYLE George Temple	11-04-44	161 Sqn
J/88717	P/O	DRAGANIUK William	25-04-44	427 Sqn
J/88338	P/O	DRAMNITZKI Eldore	20-02-44	408 Sqn
J/85398	P/O	DRAPER MiD Clarence Oscar	26-02-44	408 Sqn
J/95179	P/O	DRENNAN Alfred Wallace Jack	17-08-44	433 Sqn
J/19200	F/O	DREW Wendell Pierce	29-07-44	405 Sqn
J/87449	P/O	DREWERY Bertram Ernest	28-12-44	429 Sqn
J/16306	F/O	DRIMMIE DFC Gordon Robert	14-01-44	405 Sqn
J/85612	P/O	DRIVER Paul Edward	28-04-44	434 Sqn
R/272259	Sgt	DROZDIAK William	8-11-44	27 OTU
J/94303	P/O	DRUMM Kenneth Wesley	13-05-44	426 Sqn
J/42654	P/O	DRYER Howard Raymond	29-12-44	405 Sqn
J/86139	P/O	DUBE Henri Edouard	6-11-44	425 Sqn
R/189534	F/S	DUBE Joseph Lucien Marcel	5-12-44	22 OTU
J/90710	P/O	DUBEAU Edward David	13-06-44	427 Sqn
J/88326	P/O	DUBOIS Joseph Edward Lawrence	18-12-44	425 Sqn
J/85409	P/O	DUBROY William Edmond	11-02-44	425 Sqn
J/23906	P/O	DUCHARME Joseph Jean Andre	31-03-44	103 Sqn
J/24048	F/O	DUFFIELD Kenneth Victor	22-03-44	425 Sqn
J/89051	P/O	DUFFIN Edward Roy	13-06-44	427 Sqn
J/92131	P/O	DUFFIN James Douglas	25-08-44	640 Sqn
J/7073	F/L	DUFFY DFC Warren Alvin	7-08-44	617 Sqn
J/88726	P/O	DUFOUR Joseph Theodore Gaston Gerard	19-07-44	425 Sqn
J/29676	F/O	DUGUID James Irving	25-07-44	300 Sqn
R/170623	Sgt	DUGUID James Scott	5-02-44	26 OTU
R/194025	F/S	DUHAMEL Joseph Alphonse Clement	23-09-44	1664 HCU
J/88394	P/O	DUJAY Edmund Ronald	28-04-44	419 Sqn
J/43524	F/O	DUMAS Joseph Laurent Gerrard Gilbert	5-12-44	22 OTU
J/90914	P/O	DUMAS Richard Alexandre	18-03-44	427 Sqn
J/41951	F/O	DUMONT Norman Charles	17-10-44	24 OTU
J/28246	F/O	DUMVILLE Gordon	6-07-44	431 Sqn
R/17186	WO2	DUNAE Alexander	23-05-44	97 Sqn
R/171746	Sgt	DUNBAR William Parker	16-03-44	420 Sqn
R/183624	Sgt	DUNCAN Clarence Delmer	21-04-44	115 Sqn
J/35615	F/O	DUNCAN George Ross	4-10-44	419 Sqn
J/26545	F/O	DUNCAN John	15-03-44	77 Sqn
J/19957	F/O	DUNCAN Robert McIntosh	29-01-44	77 Sqn
J/38266	F/O	DUNFORD Joseph Reginald	15-11-44	115 Sqn
J/95289	P/O	DUNKLEMAN George Amos	6-11-44	50 Sqn
J/22575	F/O	DUNKLEY George Cyril	24-03-44	207 Sqn
J/88861	P/O	DUNLOP Bruce	28-05-44	429 Sqn
J/87195	P/O	DUNLOP George James Talbot	11-06-44	434 Sqn
R/114564	Sgt	DUNN Edric La Dell	24-09-44	24 OTU
J/23117	F/O	DUNN John William Kirkwood	18-07-44	431 Sqn
J/88709	P/O	DUNN Laurie James	15-03-44	427 Sqn
J/19523	P/O	DUNNE James Barry	2-01-44	405 Sqn
R/181089	WO2	DUNNETT Harry Norman	6-01-44	97 Sqn
R/186214	F/S	DUNS Joseph Pearson	7-06-44	103 Sqn
J/21396	F/O	DUNSMUIR John Murray	23-09-44	50 Sqn
R/176437	WO2	DUPUEIS Charles Gordon	20-01-44	102 Sqn
R/184367	Sgt	DUPUIS Irenee Adelard Joseph	3-01-44	432 Sqn
R/198488	Sgt	DURHAM George Henry	27-06-44	18 OTU
J/88078	P/O	DURKIN James Patrick	5-11-44	424 Sqn
J/85681	P/O	DURNIN Alan Howard	29-07-44	408 Sqn
J/89050	P/O	DURNIN Graham William	6-06-44	426 Sqn
J/89213	P/O	DURRANT John Chetwynd	8-08-44	419 Sqn
J/24003	F/O	DURSTON George Henry	19-03-44	578 Sqn
R/190697	F/S	DUTCHAK Peter	18-03-44	630 Sqn
C/86782	F/O	DUTTON James Roy	4-03-44	138 Sqn
R/203037	Sgt	DUTTON Robert Austin	30-08-44	434 Sqn
J/28348	F/O	DUVAL Philip Horace	17-06-44	3 LFS
R/174038	Sgt	DU SABLON Joseph Lionel Underic Gerard	20-11-44	22 OTU
J/19788	F/O	DWYER Earl Stewart	17-06-44	434 Sqn
J/86379	P/O	DWYER Roy Orson	19-04-44	419 Sqn
J/28077	F/O	DYE Jack Ellsworth	3-06-44	77 Sqn
J/90962	P/O	DYELLE Gyles Raymond	12-09-44	405 Sqn
J/85469	F/O	DYER Maurice Ballard	26-07-44	103 Sqn
R/190695	F/S	DYMENT Leslie Roy	27-04-44	78 Sqn

ID	Rank	Name	Date	Sqn
J/87125	P/O	DYMOND Charles Vernon	13-06-44	434 Sqn
J/95221	P/O	D'AMOUR Gerald Roch	24-12-44	408 Sqn
C/95153	P/O	EADE Francis Harvey	14-10-44	425 Sqn
J/92613	P/O	EADINGER John Martin	29-07-44	431 Sqn
J/87921	P/O	EAGLES Philip Brenton	29-07-44	426 Sqn
J/26854	F/O	EAGLESTONE Walter Reginald	21-08-44	415 Sqn
J/19305	P/O	EARLE James Allan [USA]	14-01-44	408 Sqn
J/92606	P/O	EASEN Richard Frederick	1-05-44	514 Sqn
J/36618	F/O	EAST John Douglas Alfred	20-11-44	1656 HCU
C/7735	P/O	EASTHAM Douglas Joseph	24-02-44	405 Sqn
J/25548	F/O	EASTLEY Frederick Charles	9-08-44	640 Sqn
J/37763	F/O	EASTWOOD John Lydbert	30-08-44	434 Sqn
J/28076	F/O	EATON John Burgess	29-02-44	1666 HCU
J/42359	F/O	EBBER Robert Allan	28-12-44	428 Sqn
R/253389	Sgt	EDDIE Lawrence Edgar	3-11-44	1653 HCU
R/158374	F/S	EDGAR Joseph Walter	25-04-44	166 Sqn
J/95046	P/O	EDMISON Kenneth James	9-10-44	76 Sqn
J/5822	F/L	EDMONDS Gerald Boyd	18-04-44	433 Sqn
J/87276	P/O	EDMONDSON Norman Thomson	31-03-44	156 Sqn
J/90345	P/O	EDMUNDS Howard Frederick	19-07-44	207 Sqn
J/24293	F/O	EDWARDS Burdel Frank [USA]	13-05-44	419 Sqn
J/10600	F/L	EDWARDS Peter Charles	15-03-44	77 Sqn
J/21997	F/O	EDWARDS Raymond Fraser	26-05-44	19 OTU
R/180425	Sgt	EDWARDS Robert William	21-01-44	419 Sqn
J/17276	F/L	EINARSON DFC DFM Johann Walter	25-02-44	61 Sqn
J/86556	P/O	EINARSSON Sigurjon	30-01-44	405 Sqn
R/191621	F/S	EITEL Edward Laverne	29-07-44	90 Sqn
J/26295	F/O	ELDRIDGE Arthur Harvey	13-08-44	78 Sqn
J/86764	P/O	ELEY Douglas Raymond	15-03-44	9 Sqn
J/24955	F/O	ELLIOTT Albert Clark	13-06-44	90 Sqn
J/22208	F/O	ELLIOTT Donald James	3-01-44	405 Sqn
J/27133	F/O	ELLIOTT Henry Milton	11-04-44	158 Sqn
J/90281	F/O	ELLIOTT Thomas Harold	25-04-44	192 Sqn
J/86193	P/O	ELLIS Harold	27-01-44	426 Sqn
R/196611	Sgt	ELLIS John William	7-08-44	1664 HCU
J/28202	F/O	ELLIS Ronald Gordon	18-07-44	429 Sqn
J/85047	P/O	ELLIS Ronald Oberlin	16-06-44	405 Sqn
J/89125	P/O	ELLIS Stanley Frederick	12-05-44	427 Sqn
J/24075	F/O	ELLSMERE Ross Orval	4-05-44	97 Sqn
J/25698	F/O	ELLWOOD William Ralph	28-04-44	434 Sqn
C/19960	P/O	ELMS Francis John	29-01-44	434 Sqn
J/28195	F/O	ELPHICK Douglas	8-07-44	9 Sqn
J/19653	P/O	ELSLEY Clarence Irving	16-03-44	420 Sqn
J/35237	F/O	ELWIN Robert Norman [USA]	8-06-44	115 Sqn
R/192677	Sgt	EMERSON Armour John	25-02-44	408 Sqn
J/27577	F/O	EMERSON Ralph Hay	26-12-44	76 Sqn
J/95151	P/O	EMERSON Robert Francis	9-10-44	419 Sqn
R/137530	WO1	EMERY John Francis	19-11-44	1666 HCU
J/22230	F/O	EMERY John Lionel	11-06-44	405 Sqn
J/90085	P/O	EMPEY Earl Blight	13-05-44	431 Sqn
J/22437	F/O	ENGLAND George Albert	21-04-44	428 Sqn
R/177892	F/S	ENGLAND William Henry	17-05-44	1661 HCU
R/251138	Sgt	ENRIGHT Donald Fraser	31-07-44	103 Sqn
J/90181	P/O	EPPLER Edward William	18-04-44	427 Sqn
J/36843	F/O	ERNST William Burton	24-05-44	20 OTU
J/90741	P/O	ESSAR William	11-04-44	550 Sqn
R/203165	Sgt	ETIENNE Francis	25-04-44	192 Sqn
J/89839	P/O	EVANS Conrad Cromer	24-06-44	12 Sqn
J/21016	F/O	EVANS David Carson	18-03-44	434 Sqn
J/35927	F/O	EVANS Douglas John	2-07-44	1667 HCU
J/26336	F/O	EVANS Horace Alexander	11-06-44	625 Sqn
J/35075	F/O	EVANS John Taylor	14-07-44	433 Sqn
R/115196	WO1	EVANS Lloyd George	12-09-44	619 Sqn
J/86832	P/O	EVANS Thomas Govan	29-06-44	10 Sqn
J/35149	F/O	EWART Ross Stuart	13-04-44	1663 HCU
J/88360	P/O	EWEN John Bruce	15-03-44	429 Sqn
J/17210	F/O	EWING Peter Herbert	3-01-44	83 Sqn
J/38699	F/O	EWING William Robert	14-10-44	434 Sqn
J/88618	P/O	FACEY-CROWTHER Lionel Percy	25-06-44	50 Sqn
R/254327	Sgt	FAHSELT Richard Elmer	2-11-44	153 Sqn
J/86024	P/O	FAIR Thomas Worthington	25-04-44	463 Sqn
J/94227	P/O	FAIRALL Maurice Elmer	17-08-44	433 Sqn
J/90956	P/O	FAIREY Earl Roy	29-07-44	425 Sqn
J/25437	F/O	FAIRGRIEVE William Chard	17-08-44	428 Sqn
J/88531	P/O	FAIRHEAD Ernest	12-02-44	1659 HCU
J/87070	P/O	FAIRLESS Alan Gilmore	17-06-44	431 Sqn
R/207621	Sgt	FALAN Ward Thomas	27-04-44	1666 HCU
J/25746	F/O	FALKINS Leonard Marvin	8-05-44	106 Sqn
J/92617	P/O	FARAGHER John	17-08-44	431 Sqn
J/45515	F/O	FARLETTE Joseph Rodolphe Gaston	30-11-44	82 OTU
J/93681	P/O	FARRELL Edward Joseph	18-12-44	432 Sqn
R/144036	F/S	FARRELL James Joseph	23-01-44	1679 HCFlt
J/39321	F/O	FARROW Kenneth Douglas	16-11-44	166 Sqn
J/28229	F/O	FAULKNER Arthur James	13-07-44	103 Sqn
J/86639	P/O	FEINDELL Lewis Leslie	27-04-44	619 Sqn
J/92605	P/O	FELDMAN Arnold Lepine [USA]	19-04-44	115 Sqn
C/95293	P/O	FELDMAN Jacob	29-12-44	419 Sqn
J/22629	F/O	FELDMAN Joseph	12-05-44	630 Sqn
J/28251	F/O	FENNELL Lloyd Richard	19-07-44	207 Sqn
J/25009	F/O	FENNESSEY James Francis	23-04-44	429 Sqn
R/112953	F/S	FERGUSON Gordon Joseph	14-01-44	207 Sqn
J/86519	P/O	FERGUSON John Hugh	4-05-44	35 Sqn
R/153401	F/S	FERGUSON Lloyd Archibald	31-03-44	166 Sqn
J/92615	P/O	FERGUSON Roy Stanley	9-08-44	427 Sqn
J/86015	P/O	FERNANDEZ de LEON Mario Alfred [Guatemala]	25-05-44	429 Sqn
R/218750	Sgt	FERNSTROM Harold Lawson	8-11-44	27 OTU
J/85610	P/O	FERNYHOUGH DFC Walter	29-06-44	432 Sqn
J/23366	F/O	FERRIER James Stewart	31-03-44	7 Sqn
J/92696	P/O	FERRIS Henry William	27-10-44	1666 HCU
J/88486	P/O	FETCHISON Myron	29-07-44	90 Sqn
J/38237	F/O	FICHTNER James Roy	28-10-44	419 Sqn
R/106742	WO2	FIDDES John Duncan	25-04-44	166 Sqn
J/25745	F/O	FIGG Ernest Dyer	29-07-44	12 Sqn
J/14184	F/O	FILMER Jasper Mayton Watson	15-02-44	102 Sqn
J/88383	P/O	FINCH Donald Davies	2-02-44	432 Sqn
R/200704	Sgt	FINCH Gordon Frank	25-07-44	50 Sqn
J/24432	F/O	FINCHAM Leslie Bernard	20-02-44	429 Sqn
R/176113	F/S	FINDLAY Bruce Ebrick	21-01-44	427 Sqn
J/89738	P/O	FINDLAY Lloyd Eby	13-07-44	415 Sqn
J/92132	P/O	FINGLAND Wilfred James	27-08-44	630 Sqn
J/26540	F/O	FINLAYSON Walter Raymond	13-05-44	419 Sqn
J/156084	F/S	FIRTH Ernest James	11-04-44	161 Sqn
J/19844	F/O	FISHER DFC Charles Harold	17-08-44	405 Sqn
J/88232	F/O	FISHER Jack Glen Millan	27-11-44	192 Sqn
J/40190	F/O	FISHER Thomas Francis	15-10-44	432 Sqn
J/19834	P/O	FITTON Norman Frederick	13-06-44	427 Sqn
J/87097	P/O	FitzPATRICK Robert Joseph	13-05-44	426 Sqn
J/215210	F/S	FITZPATRICK DFM John Ernest	27-08-44	166 Sqn
J/25707	P/O	FITZPATRICK Joseph Stanley Paul	21-07-44	578 Sqn
R/210722	Sgt	FITZPATRICK Lambert Joseph	29-11-44	153 Sqn
J/86434	P/O	FITZSIMMONS Gerald Robert	20-02-44	158 Sqn
J/92033	P/O	FLANAGHAN Thomas Edward	28-05-44	550 Sqn
J/87863	P/O	FLATT Alfred Leonard	4-11-44	424 Sqn
J/38270	F/O	FLEGEL Gustaf	27-08-44	166 Sqn
J/20198	F/O	FLEMING Maleon Henry	17-08-44	433 Sqn
R/143004	WO2	FLETCHER William John Kennedy	22-01-44	419 Sqn
R/260951	Sgt	FLETTE Clifford Nicholas	19-11-44	1666 HCU
J/89447	F/O	FLEURY Joseph Oscar Rolland	11-02-44	425 Sqn
J/89772	P/O	FLEWELLING Clarence Clyde [USA]	22-06-44	619 Sqn
J/90719	P/O	FLOOD Donald George	17-09-44	115 Sqn
J/16092	F/L	FLOOD John James	12-09-44	428 Sqn
J/18849	P/O	FLOREN Harold Arthur	14-01-44	405 Sqn
J/25830	F/O	FLOYD Charles Richard 'Dick'	20-03-44	82 OTU
J/24532	F/O	FLOYD George	26-12-44	76 Sqn
J/14167	F/L	FLYNN John Patrick	25-05-44	582 Sqn
J/27421	F/O	FOLLIOTT Eric Walter	29-06-44	424 Sqn

ID	Rank	Name	Date	Unit
J/89123	P/O	FOLLOWS Sidney Wallace	18-04-44	433 Sqn
J/85529	P/O	FONSECA Donald Everton [Jamaica]	21-04-44	207 Sqn
J/24260	F/L	FORBES Allan Patrick	30-08-44	103 Sqn
J/42195	F/O	FORBES Gordon Edmund Bruce	18-12-44	22 OTU
J/27225	F/O	FORD Roy Douglas	28-05-44	427 Sqn
J/11951	F/O	FORREST Frederick	29-01-44	419 Sqn
J/86761	P/O	FORREST William	21-02-44	15 Sqn
J/90086	P/O	FORSBERG Morris Soren	9-06-44	426 Sqn
J/19310	F/O	FORSTER Benjamin Nelson	20-01-44	429 Sqn
J/26693	F/O	FORSTER Richard Hume	19-03-44	625 Sqn
J/19817	P/O	FORSYTH Albert Carmen	20-02-44	429 Sqn
J/24699	F/O	FORSYTH Thomas Rex	28-04-44	431 Sqn
J/24180	F/O	FORTIN Benoit Charles Eugene	23-04-44	425 Sqn
J/87480	P/O	FOSTER Leslie Arthur	28-04-44	405 Sqn
J/25494	F/O	FOSTER Thomas	30-08-44	101 Sqn
J/86593	P/O	FOURNIER Marc Alexander Gerard	15-02-44	419 Sqn
J/24970	F/L	FOWKE Alba Fletcher	29-07-44	514 Sqn
R/264939	F/S	FOWLER Cecil Allen	4-12-44	166 Sqn
R/136319	WO1	FOWLER James Brown [United Kingdom]	16-02-44	78 Sqn
R/155142	WO2	FOX Arthur John Dennis	15-03-44	625 Sqn
J/40225	F/O	FOX Edward George	18-12-44	426 Sqn
J/35831	F/O	FOX Gerald Gordon	29-12-44	405 Sqn
J/90471	P/O	FOX Herbert Ronald Wilkinson	21-08-44	415 Sqn
J/89053	P/O	FOX Howard William George	24-06-44	149 Sqn
R/160403	F/S	FOX John Bruce	12-02-44	1659 HCU
J/90347	P/O	FOY Carson John	25-07-44	61 Sqn
J/35518	F/O	FOY Melville Alfred	23-06-44	1666 HCU
J/24171	F/O	FRAMPTON John Albert	20-02-44	408 Sqn
R/148538	WO1	FRANCIS John Carr	11-06-44	90 Sqn
J/92336	P/O	FRANCIS Richard William	13-06-44	419 Sqn
R/162649	WO2	FRANCIS Robert Lewis	23-04-44	115 Sqn
R/187732	Sgt	FRANK Frank Louis	30-08-44	19 OTU
J/86986	F/O	FRANKFURTH Robert Louis	1-07-44	1GpSDFLt
R/156578	Sgt	FRANKLIN Lloyd Stuart	1-05-44	420 Sqn
J/37166	F/O	FRASER James	1-11-44	424 Sqn
J/88385	F/O	FRASER James Bruce	20-02-44	433 Sqn
R/192437	F/S	FRASER John Michael	1-07-44	625 Sqn
R/219037	Sgt	FRASER John William	2-10-44	19 OTU
R/186053	Sgt	FRASER Lloyd Henderson	11-08-44	24 OTU
J/92015	P/O	FRASER William Frederick	30-08-44	619 Sqn
J/86319	F/O	FRAUTS Clarence William	27-01-44	408 Sqn
J/86863	F/O	FREDERICKSON Turner	30-09-44	426 Sqn
R/160030	WO2	FREEMAN Alexander McCowan	16-03-44	630 Sqn
J/28223	F/O	FREEMAN Elton Eugene	26-08-44	78 Sqn
J/88397	P/O	FREEMAN George Frank	28-05-44	424 Sqn
J/39402	F/O	FREEMAN John Ernest	2-12-44	408 Sqn
R/189238	F/S	FREEMAN William Max	8-11-44	158 Sqn
R/197655	Sgt	FRENCH Kenneth	15-04-44	1664 HCU
J/85493	P/O	FREY Frederick John Alec	26-09-44	405 Sqn
R/158288	WO2	FRIEDT Joseph	28-05-44	101 Sqn
J/13140	F/L	FRIKER Walter Louis	24-12-44	408 Sqn
R/222260	F/S	FRITH Stanley Robert	30-08-44	50 Sqn
J/90080	P/O	FRIZZELL Harvey Albert [USA]	22-03-44	432 Sqn
J/39376	F/O	FRIZZELL Lloyd William	21-11-44	408 Sqn
J/90081	P/O	FUGERE Claude Mercier	25-03-44	427 Sqn
J/26286	F/O	FUHR Harold Arthur	23-06-44	78 Sqn
J/23475	F/O	FULLER Douglas	17-06-44	576 Sqn
J/28902	F/O	FULLERTON Melville Lloyd	20-03-44	82 OTU
R/189530	F/S	FULLUM Walter Joseph	23-05-44	115 Sqn
J/10632	F/L	FULTON Warren Thompson	22-03-44	408 Sqn
J/28887	F/O	FUTIRANSKI Joseph	23-10-44	419 Sqn
J/10954	F/L	FYFE Allan Blake	15-03-44	405 Sqn
J/88608	P/O	GABEL Albert Lloyd	28-04-44	431 Sqn
J/97000	WO2	GABOURY Joseph Alphonse Paul Henri	22-03-44	408 Sqn
R/202350	Sgt	GABRYELSKI Theodore	4-07-44	24 OTU
J/35101	F/O	GADDESS Andrew	4-10-44	419 Sqn
J/19996	P/O	GAGE Donald Irwin	12-05-44	75 Sqn
J/29369	F/O	GAGNEBIN Robert Paul	28-05-44	1659 HCU
C/85188	P/O	GALBRAITH Bernard Edwin	15-03-44	405 Sqn
R/172370	WO2	GALBRAITH Thomas Francis	27-07-44	619 Sqn
J/86981	P/O	GALLAGHER James Cornelius	16-09-44	432 Sqn
J/88398	P/O	GALLAGHER John Douglas	7-06-44	103 Sqn
J/25456	F/O	GALLAGHER Joseph Patrick [USA]	1-06-44	138 Sqn
J/95287	P/O	GALLANT Joseph Lloyd	4-11-44	101 Sqn
J/88710	P/O	GALLAUGHER Ralph Clare	18-03-44	427 Sqn
J/89872	P/O	GALVIN Leo Patrick	13-08-44	115 Sqn
R/276685	Sgt	GALVIN Staniforth Saywell	18-12-44	22 OTU
R/149180	Sgt	GAMBORSKI John	15-11-44	1664 HCU
J/23114	F/O	GAMSBY Austin Gordon	16-06-44	405 Sqn
J/25531	F/O	GANDY Peter Joseph	8-06-44	431 Sqn
R/156933	WO2	GAPP Douglas Edward	12-09-44	50 Sqn
R/163217	F/S	GARBUTT John Albert	19-07-44	619 Sqn
J/18855	F/O	GARDINER DFC Llewellyn Hugh Coverdale	30-08-44	428 Sqn
J/92341	P/O	GARDINER William Henry	17-06-44	419 Sqn
J/87758	P/O	GARDNER John Edward	29-07-44	431 Sqn
J/86329	P/O	GARES Ernest Joseph	19-04-44	419 Sqn
J/27487	F/O	GARLAND William Samuel	27-05-44	1656 HCU
R/194178	Sgt	GARRITY Neville Hugh Banning	22-04-44	1660 HCU
J/39011	F/O	GARTRELL Harold Spencer	14-10-44	12 Sqn
J/8362	F/L	GARVIE Robert Leslie [USA]	15-11-44	1664 HCU
J/29693	F/O	GARWOOD Herbert William	23-06-44	1666 HCU
J/25690	F/O	GATES Arley Sides	27-01-44	432 Sqn
J/92338	P/O	GATES Max Ennis	13-06-44	419 Sqn
R/171191	Sgt	GAUTHIER Joseph Paul Adelard	5-07-44	419 Sqn
J/90899	P/O	GAUTHIER Raymond Charles	18-12-44	425 Sqn
J/25073	F/O	GAUTSCHI DFC Norman Vincent	8-07-44	106 Sqn
J/19119	P/O	GAVIN Thomas Donald	2-01-44	405 Sqn
J/86492	P/O	GAY Wilfred Charles	5-07-44	428 Sqn
K/220611	Sgt	GAZZARD James Frederick	8-11-44	27 OTU
R/209156	Sgt	GEDDES Jack	19-07-44	619 Sqn
J/39029	F/O	GEDDES William Howard	29-05-44	82 OTU
J/36589	F/O	GELINAS Joseph Edward	29-07-44	434 Sqn
J/89894	P/O	GEORGE Andrew Lorne	30-06-44	514 Sqn
J/27881	F/O	GEORGESON Louis Rockford	11-05-44	424 Sqn
J/89877	F/O	GERMIQUET George Edward	17-08-44	431 Sqn
J/86921	P/O	GERRARD Robert Allan	23-04-44	15 Sqn
J/90091	P/O	GERRIE Vernon Chester	4-08-44	424 Sqn
J/85819	P/O	GIBBONS James Walter	20-02-44	429 Sqn
R/136304	F/S	GIBLIN James Raymond	28-12-44	429 Sqn
J/87558	P/O	GIBSON Arnold Roy Alexander	11-04-44	158 Sqn
R/159358	F/S	GIBSON Arthur Leach Patterson	20-01-44	76 Sqn
J/90957	P/O	GIBSON James	29-07-44	425 Sqn
J/85485	P/O	GIBSON John	25-03-44	626 Sqn
R/131971	WO1	GIBSON Robert William	23-12-44	90 Sqn
J/25385	F/O	GIBSON Stanwell John	29-01-44	419 Sqn
J/95158	P/O	GIBSON William James Cameron	1-11-44	424 Sqn
R/111125	WO1	GIFF George Ernest	18-01-44	1659 HCU
J/23078	F/O	GIFFIN Robert Roy	29-07-44	514 Sqn
J/40032	F/O	GILBERT George Lyon	15-10-44	432 Sqn
R/214779	Sgt	GILBERTSON John Harold	24-03-44	1656 HCU
J/17444	F/O	GILBEY James Frank	14-01-44	405 Sqn
R/170620	F/S	GILCHRIST Campbell Colin	6-07-44	15 Sqn
J/24564	F/O	GILCHRIST Donald Ross	17-06-44	3 LFS
J/25813	F/O	GILCHRIST Hugh Gordon	14-08-44	44 Sqn
J/90930	P/O	GILES James Reginald	26-07-44	432 Sqn
J/85996	P/O	GILL Arthur Taylor	8-06-44	1666 HCU
R/134421	WO2	GILLANDER David Stuart	28-03-44	161 Sqn
J/89725	P/O	GILLANDERS Robert Edward	20-02-44	431 Sqn
J/90090	P/O	GILLESPIE William Leaman	18-07-44	429 Sqn
J/24961	F/O	GILLIES John Alexander	24-04-44	425 Sqn
J/87041	P/O	GILLIS Angus Joseph	20-02-44	12 Sqn
J/92584	P/O	GILLIS Robert Rane	25-10-44	431 Sqn
R/191542	Sgt	GILMAR Leslie Kenneth	14-01-44	550 Sqn
J/25797	F/O	GILMORE Francis Ormond	3-08-44	61 Sqn
J/90250	P/O	GILMORE Hugh Boyd	1-08-44	429 Sqn

407

J/88963	P/O	GILSON John	28-04-44	431 Sqn
J/26151	F/O	GILSON Vernon Beverley	2-11-44	408 Sqn
J/12046	F/O	GIROLAMI Adriano Richard	9-05-44	431 Sqn
R/220910	Sgt	GIROUX Joseph Anthony Austin	9-11-44	82 OTU
J/90952	P/O	GIROUX Joseph Zenon	19-07-44	425 Sqn
J/27411	F/O	GLADWELL Willis John	6-07-44	15 Sqn
R/200002	Sgt	GLAISTER Stanley	23-04-44	90 Sqn
2285	WO2	GLASS Ernest Israel	2-01-44	82 OTU
C/87159	P/O	GLASS DFM Harry	8-08-44	429 Sqn
J/89121	P/O	GLASSER Lloyd Charles	25-03-44	427 Sqn
J/27667	F/O	GLEASON Michael Arnold	20-11-44	1656 HCU
J/22136	F/O	GLENDENNING Albert	13-06-44	408 Sqn
J/36021	F/O	GLENN John Alexander	26-08-44	78 Sqn
R/109197	Sgt	GLINZ Kevin Cyril	4-12-44	1661 HCU
J/28762	F/O	GLOECKLER John Ernest 'Jack'	1-08-44	429 Sqn
J/90942	P/O	GLOVER William Albert	21-01-44	434 Sqn
J/95083	P/O	GNIDA Mike	9-10-44	76 Sqn
J/26616	F/O	GNIUS Mike	20-01-44	434 Sqn
J/95159	P/O	GOBLE Cyril Christian	1-11-44	426 Sqn
R/151252	F/S	GODIN John Joseph	6-07-44	578 Sqn
J/18240	P/O	GODIN Joseph Jean Robert Theobald	6-01-44	35 Sqn
R/163651	WO2	GOEHRING Edward Henry	22-06-44	57 Sqn
R/204000	Sgt	GOEHRING Gordon Grant	12-12-44	1664 HCU
R/194962	F/S	GOFF James Alfred	29-11-44	103 Sqn
J/26287	F/O	GOLD Leonard	8-06-44	78 Sqn
J/92362	P/O	GOLDFINCH John Henry Eaton	9-10-44	419 Sqn
R/215319	Sgt	GOLDIE Thomas	1-06-44	1667 HCU
R/196823	Sgt	GOLDING John James	11-01-44	17 OTU
R/82845	LAC	GOLDING Joseph Harold	8-08-44	433 Sqn
R/273033	F/S	GOLDWATER Mark	12-12-44	195 Sqn
J/25981	F/O	GOLUB Matthew Michael	6-07-44	15 Sqn
J/22356	F/O	GOOD Francis Edward	26-08-44	90 Sqn
J/35930	F/O	GOOD Harold Robert	26-08-44	626 Sqn
J/88030	P/O	GOOD Ralph Edward	19-08-44	428 Sqn
J/89736	P/O	GOOD William Adrian	17-06-44	434 Sqn
R/142689	WO2	GOODALL Arthur Manley	14-01-44	626 Sqn
J/19853	P/O	GOODFELLOW Donald Grant	15-02-44	434 Sqn
J/19575	P/O	GOODKEY Leonard Earl	25-02-44	626 Sqn
R/60369	WO1	GOODMAN Arthur Henry	14-02-44	22 OTU
J/25874	F/O	GOODWIN David Webster	23-05-44	24 OTU
R/290583	Sgt	GOODWIN Donald	9-11-44	82 OTU
J/87828	P/O	GOODWIN Ernest Albert	29-07-44	408 Sqn
J/89866	P/O	GOODWIN Vernon Alfred	22-05-44	630 Sqn
J/86923	P/O	GOODWIN William Harvey	13-06-44	408 Sqn
J/10281	F/L	GOODYEAR Hedley Charles Cormick	23-04-44	61 Sqn
J/26415	F/O	GORAK Theodore [USA]	30-08-44	103 Sqn
R/152957	Sgt	GORDON Bruce	29-05-44	82 OTU
J/40766	F/O	GORDON Donald Alexander	30-08-44	14 OTU
J/24299	F/O	GORDON Huntly Parker	29-07-44	427 Sqn
R/259515	Sgt	GORDON James Neil	1-07-44	626 Sqn
R/195719	F/S	GORDON Robert Ernest Douglas	30-08-44	434 Sqn
J/36878	F/O	GORMAN Alexander Thomas	7-08-44	1664 HCU
J/19457	P/O	GOSNEY Leonard David	2-01-44	207 Sqn
J/89449	P/O	GOUDREAU Christian Joseph Jacques Laurier	2-03-44	425 Sqn
J/95288	P/O	GOULD Albert Norman	4-11-44	101 Sqn
J/90089	P/O	GOULD Innis Lindsay Elwin	17-06-44	431 Sqn
J/88393	P/O	GOULDING Stanley Herbert	28-04-44	419 Sqn
J/19617	P/O	GOUNDREY Thomas Alan	12-05-44	432 Sqn
J/24665	F/O	GOURDEAU Arthur Edgar Emile [USA]	31-03-44	427 Sqn
R/210039	Sgt	GOW George	23-05-44	9 Sqn
J/29680	F/O	GOWAN Ronald Burtis	12-09-44	207 Sqn
J/89889	P/O	GOWANS William	8-06-44	158 Sqn
J/35251	F/O	GRACE John Peter	15-10-44	424 Sqn
J/90216	P/O	GRACIE William	5-07-44	433 Sqn
R/114324	F/S	GRACIE William Brown	5-08-44	425 Sqn
J/89985	P/O	GRADY John Bruce	9-08-44	161 Sqn
J/88280	P/O	GRAHAM David Robert	8-06-44	78 Sqn
J/88399	P/O	GRAHAM Frederick George	16-07-44	207 Sqn
J/86290	P/O	GRAHAM James Craig	31-01-44	102 Sqn
J/92095	P/O	GRAHAM Lloyd Thomas	7-12-44	419 Sqn
R/251339	Sgt	GRAHAM Milford Henry	27-01-44	84 OTU
J/87203	P/O	GRAMSON Walter John	29-06-44	76 Sqn
J/89454	P/O	GRANBOIS Wallace Lawrence	23-04-44	514 Sqn
J/27158	F/O	GRANGE Arthur Hugh	6-06-44	582 Sqn
J/89885	P/O	GRANT Alfred Frederick	12-05-44	630 Sqn
J/94549	P/O	GRANT James Vallance	18-12-44	158 Sqn
J/39333	F/O	GRANT John Edward	2-12-44	433 Sqn
J/89906	P/O	GRANT John Joseph	17-08-44	158 Sqn
J/39373	F/O	GRASSIE Chesley Reginald	11-11-44	44 Sqn
J/90084	P/O	GRAVEL Joseph Victor Jacques	9-05-44	431 Sqn
J/88647	P/O	GRAVEL Marcel	5-10-44	427 Sqn
R/58680	WO1	GRAVELET-CHAPMAN John Benjamin	30-08-44	428 Sqn
C/1724	W/C	GRAY Charles	29-07-44	405 Sqn
J/88147	P/O	GRAY Harold Hugh	22-03-44	426 Sqn
R/205856	Sgt	GRAY James Eugene	26-05-44	19 OTU
J/18925	P/O	GRAY Leonard Samuel	22-01-44	427 Sqn
J/37740	F/O	GRAY Robert John	4-07-44	24 OTU
R/146264	Sgt	GRAY Robert Sidney	19-11-44	1666 HCU
J/88692	P/O	GREATREX Douglas Thomas	27-04-44	408 Sqn
J/40431	F/O	GREAVISON Ronald	23-08-44	20 OTU
J/90088	P/O	GREEN Edward Calvin	17-06-44	431 Sqn
J/89296	P/O	GREEN Frank Harold	24-07-44	1666 HCU
J/95292	P/O	GREEN James William	18-12-44	432 Sqn
J/25905	F/O	GREEN Leslie Arthur [USA]	7-08-44	1664 HCU
R/197000	Sgt	GREEN Robert Clarke	23-08-44	24 OTU
J/87726	P/O	GREENE Philip Sanson	16-06-44	405 Sqn
R/224448	F/S	GREENE William	14-10-44	153 Sqn
R/263179	F/S	GREENHALGH Bruce Edward [USA]	28-10-44	419 Sqn
J/86525	P/O	GREENIDGE John Alexander [Trinidad]	30-03-44	419 Sqn
J/22100	F/O	GREENWAY John Kinnaird	3-06-44	158 Sqn
R/209340	Sgt	GREER Clifford Barton	10-10-44	1667 HCU
J/90082	P/O	GREIG Gordon Templeton	28-04-44	431 Sqn
J/24640	F/O	GREVSTAD Melvin Clarence	18-03-44	463 Sqn
R/153562	WO2	GRICE Hubert Gordon	16-05-44	419 Sqn
J/26315	F/O	GRIERSON Quinten Thomas Russell	29-07-44	408 Sqn
J/95286	P/O	GRIFFIN Jack Douglas	2-11-44	415 Sqn
R/128921	WO2	GRIFFiN Terence James	29-01-44	51 Sqn
R/261261	F/S	GRIFFITH Leslie George [USA]	1-11-44	426 Sqn
J/18920	P/O	GRIFFITHS Charles Anthony	3-01-44	426 Sqn
J/36370	F/O	GRIMBLE Henry	17-08-44	433 Sqn
J/85550	P/O	GRODECKI Joseph	23-04-44	405 Sqn
J/90370	P/O	GROH Nelson Hagey	14-07-44	77 Sqn
R/251698	Sgt	GRONBECK Norman	25-07-44	50 Sqn
J/26488	P/O	GROSSER Roy William	23-01-44	1679 HCFlt
R/111476	Sgt	GROULX Joseph Arthur Edmond	20-11-44	22 OTU
J/90092	P/O	GROUT Roy Gordon	9-08-44	427 Sqn
J/85140	P/O	GROVER Don Hernando De Soto	26-03-44	425 Sqn
J/86188	P/O	GUERNSEY Lorne Stanley	31-08-44	433 Sqn
R/191070	Sgt	GUGINS Clarence Walter	24-02-44	1664 HCU
J/18064	F/L	GUILD Robert Douglas	15-10-44	424 Sqn
J/12736	F/O	GUITON Ernest Stuart	30-01-44	405 Sqn
J/88042	P/O	GULEVICH Peter	13-08-44	78 Sqn
R/193562	F/S	GUNN Douglas Alexander	24-11-44	419 Sqn
J/85972	P/O	GUNN Francis Wilburn	25-04-44	626 Sqn
J/85808	P/O	GUSTAFSON John Kenneth	29-07-44	431 Sqn
J/92128	P/O	GUTCHER John Reginald Cecil	27-07-44	630 Sqn
J/24010	F/O	GUTHRIE Archibald Edgar	15-03-44	77 Sqn
J/29230	F/O	GUTHRIE Jerry Taylor	29-07-44	408 Sqn
J/29986	F/O	GUTHRIE Lindsay Leonard	9-11-44	625 Sqn
J/25812	F/O	HAACKE Arthur Paul	23-06-44	1666 HCU

J/87464	P/O	HAALAND Clement Burton	25-07-44	50 Sqn		J/85791	P/O	HARRIS John Alfred	31-03-44	106 Sqn
J/86999	P/O	HABILUK Mike	17-06-44	434 Sqn		J/26803	F/O	HARRIS John Frederick	29-07-44	431 Sqn
R/183946	Sgt	HACKBART Alfred Harvey	20-02-44	419 Sqn		R/115064	Sgt	HARRIS Wilfred Gordon	23-05-44	24 OTU
J/22541	F/O	HACKETT DFC Douglas	30-01-44	405 Sqn		J/89932	P/O	HARRIS William Lane	13-08-44	424 Sqn
J/27167	F/O	HAGELL James Grant	15-10-44	431 Sqn		J/88062	P/O	HARRISON DFC Francis Arthur	14-10-44	428 Sqn
J/86591	P/O	HAGERMAN Gerald Ernest	30-01-44	433 Sqn		J/21448	F/O	HARRISON James Robert	5-08-44	433 Sqn
J/87172	P/O	HAGERTY Norman Earl	21-07-44	12 Sqn		J/37741	F/O	HARRISON Robert William	2-11-44	426 Sqn
J/95154	P/O	HAGGIS Douglas Stewart	14-10-44	115 Sqn		C/86741	P/O	HARROP Frank Grant	11-06-44	420 Sqn
J/88712	P/O	HALBERT Edwin Joseph	25-03-44	427 Sqn		J/86480	P/O	HART Thomas George	22-06-44	630 Sqn
J/11483	F/L	HALCRO James Angus Francis	12-09-44	139 Sqn		J/26313	F/O	HARTLEY Charles Thomas	11-04-44	51 Sqn
J/26179	F/O	HALE Raymond Wallace	24-12-44	419 Sqn		J/14198	F/O	HARTNETT Frederick	15-02-44	419 Sqn
J/6948	F/L	HALE Warren Macaulay	1-06-44	161 Sqn		J/38162	F/O	HARVEY Angus Beverly	23-09-44	50 Sqn
J/90549	P/O	HALEY Alan Wardell	29-12-44	405 Sqn		J/93739	F/O	HARVEY Everard Percival	18-12-44	432 Sqn
J/88320	P/O	HALEY Wilbur St. Clair	18-07-44	427 Sqn		J/85522	P/O	HARVEY Jack Arthur	21-07-44	101 Sqn
J/37151	F/O	HALL Albert Edward	13-06-44	427 Sqn		J/94452	P/O	HARWOOD Edward James Francis	5-12-44	426 Sqn
J/16011	F/O	HALL Alfred Henry Benbow	1-05-44	420 Sqn		R/196364	F/S	HASE Rudolf Carle	4-12-44	227 Sqn
J/22831	F/O	HALL Allan Russell	13-10-44	1657 HCU		J/88705	P/O	HATCH George Charles	20-02-44	434 Sqn
J/21053	F/L	HALL Bertram Edward William	12-12-44	12 Sqn		J/86443	P/O	HATCHMAN Fred [USA]	23-04-44	431 Sqn
J/5492	F/L	HALL James Donald Blanchard	8-08-44	429 Sqn		R/176712	F/S	HAVILL Charles Henry	28-04-44	434 Sqn
J/89283	P/O	HALL Joseph George Brian [USA]	26-03-44	425 Sqn		J/28926	F/O	HAWKE John Elie Fredrick	2-05-44	429 Sqn
J/39298	F/O	HALL Stanley George	25-11-44	427 Sqn		J/86265	P/O	HAWKES DFC Ernest Stewart	20-01-44	426 Sqn
J/89730	F/O	HALL William Churchill	31-03-44	427 Sqn		J/91093	P/O	HAWKES Lloyd Mac	31-03-44	427 Sqn
R/258208	F/S	HALLAM George Theodore	23-10-44	429 Sqn		J/95166	F/O	HAWKINS James Reid	31-08-44	433 Sqn
J/85794	P/O	HALLETT William Alfred Martin	13-07-44	9 Sqn		J/19193	F/O	HAWKINS Stanley Allen	9-05-44	432 Sqn
R/119691	WO2	HALLORAN William Richard	2-01-44	83 Sqn		R/98864	WO1	HAWKINS DFC Walter	15-02-44	7 Sqn
J/35894	F/O	HAMBLIN Maurice Jack	2-10-44	1664 HCU		J/35828	F/O	HAWKINS William Bennett	8-06-44	1666 HCU
J/92169	P/O	HAMEL Charles	20-11-44	22 OTU		J/88340	P/O	HAY Clarence Walter	22-03-44	425 Sqn
J/19965	P/O	HAMILTON Alexander	12-05-44	432 Sqn		J/90944	P/O	HAY Donald Noel	2-03-44	425 Sqn
J/95155	P/O	HAMILTON Dale McGowan	14-10-44	115 Sqn		J/86607	P/O	HAYCOCK Roy Clifford	31-03-44	426 Sqn
J/89908	P/O	HAMILTON Hugh Brannan	26-08-44	78 Sqn		J/23754	F/O	HAYDOCK Philip Frank Charles	5-10-44	427 Sqn
J/95271	P/O	HAMILTON Ian Maccallum	6-11-44	101 Sqn		J/85037	P/O	HAYES John Douglas	16-06-44	405 Sqn
J/19966	P/O	HAMILTON Ian Mackenzie	8-06-44	640 Sqn		J/22592	F/O	HAYTER William Douglas	20-02-44	434 Sqn
R/166270	F/S	HAMILTON John	8-06-44	138 Sqn		J/88609	P/O	HAZEL Royal Edwin	28-04-44	431 Sqn
R/163622	WO2	HAMILTON William Percy	25-02-44	1661 HCU		J/86267	P/O	HEADLY Michael Francis [United Kingdom]	21-01-44	102 Sqn
J/151890	WO2	HAMMETT Lawrence Samuel	29-01-44	51 Sqn						
J/85187	P/O	HAMMOND Albert Ernest	16-03-44	12 Sqn		R/96219	WO1	HEALEY Joseph Michael [USA]	29-02-44	1666 HCU
J/25064	F/O	HAMMOND Douglas William	31-03-44	427 Sqn		J/21121	F/L	HEALEY DFC Wilbert Arley	30-04-44	49 Sqn
J/90362	P/O	HAMPTON William George	24-03-44	429 Sqn		J/20002	F/O	HEATH James	17-06-44	550 Sqn
J/20963	F/O	HANCOCK Harold Alton	20-02-44	426 Sqn		J/19464	P/O	HEATON Albert Kencil	29-01-44	434 Sqn
J/24563	P/O	HANDY William Bertrand	19-03-44	1667 HCU		R/190230	F/S	HEBERT Harold Raymond	25-07-44	420 Sqn
J/88417	P/O	HANDZUK John H.	11-06-44	434 Sqn		J/24011	F/O	HEDRICH John	29-02-44	420 Sqn
J/95269	P/O	HANES William Herbert	2-11-44	77 Sqn		J/20361	F/O	HEFFERNAN John Anthony Foch [USA]	3-01-44	619 Sqn
R/255149	F/S	HANN Douglas Leurensa	11-11-44	227 Sqn						
J/36482	F/O	HANNA Stanley Roy	4-12-44	166 Sqn		J/20660	P/O	HEGY William Norman	21-02-44	427 Sqn
J/87007	P/O	HANNAH Lloyd Albert	14-10-44	625 Sqn		J/90753	P/O	HEIDMAN Wilbert Henry Oliver	16-03-44	420 Sqn
J/87269	P/O	HANNESSON Jack Edward Kristjan	30-06-44	514 Sqn		J/9353	F/L	HEIMBECKER Harry Lyle	15-03-44	429 Sqn
J/89929	P/O	HANON Ingval Millar	21-07-44	101 Sqn		J/91089	P/O	HEIN John	20-02-44	433 Sqn
R/163858	F/S	HANS Stanley William	25-05-44	101 Sqn		J/88189	P/O	HEINEN Frank William	27-01-44	432 Sqn
J/95272	P/O	HANSEN Ezra Mulloy	7-12-44	419 Sqn		R/170494	Sgt	HEMMING Gordon William	25-04-44	16 OTU
R/178083	F/S	HANSEN George Quist	28-04-44	431 Sqn		R/219136	F/S	HENDERSON Arthur James	25-07-44	166 Sqn
J/18692	P/O	HANSEN Lloyd Leonard Hans	14-01-44	408 Sqn		J/19170	P/O	HENDERSON Gerald William	3-01-44	100 Sqn
J/15599	F/L	HANSON DFC James Robert	23-05-44	408 Sqn		J/17722	F/O	HENDERSON Marvin George	25-04-44	1655 MTU
J/29418	P/O	HARACZAY Walter	8-07-44	17 OTU		J/88735	P/O	HENDRY Robert Elliot	27-04-44	408 Sqn
R/182706	F/S	HARBOR Norman Stanley	28-10-44	1661 HCU		R/199823	WO2	HENFREY Jack	2-10-44	82 OTU
J/88359	P/O	HARDING Oscar Leonard Harrington [British Guiana]	25-02-44	433 Sqn		R/64186	Sgt	HENLEY Ernest	21-08-44	415 Sqn
						J/90394	P/O	HENNESSY Thomas Alban	12-09-44	635 Sqn
R/153784	WO2	HARDY Harry Skeet	29-02-44	420 Sqn		R/182289	F/S	HENRY Robert William Garth	2-10-44	19 OTU
J/13731	F/L	HARDY James Thomas	25-11-44	427 Sqn		J/85150	F/O	HERBERT Horace Montague Richard	23-04-44	1659 HCU
J/90529	P/O	HARDY Lloyd Glen	12-09-44	405 Sqn		J/37214	P/O	HERGOTT Gerald Albert	31-03-44	427 Sqn
R/217303	Sgt	HARE Roy Walter	16-05-44	26 OTU		J/92369	P/O	HERMAN William Henry	28-10-44	419 Sqn
R/161116	F/S	HARGREAVES Kenneth [USA]	30-01-44	433 Sqn		J/3747	F/L	HERMITAGE Arthur George	21-01-44	419 Sqn
J/89312	P/O	HARMAN Frederic Cuthbert	31-08-44	433 Sqn		J/25704	P/O	HERON Kenneth	25-07-44	420 Sqn
J/8438	F/L	HARMAN Robert Leonard	13-07-44	415 Sqn		J/22226	F/O	HETHERINGTON Clinton George	23-03-44	426 Sqn
J/87477	P/O	HARNISH Clyde Roderick	31-03-44	101 Sqn		J/38232	F/O	HETHERINGTON George Donald Frederick	17-12-44	153 Sqn
J/95270	P/O	HARPER James Russell	2-11-44	415 Sqn						
J/21023	F/O	HARRIGAN James Francis	29-01-44	115 Sqn		J/28950	F/O	HEUCHERT William Rudolph	4-08-44	424 Sqn
R/113569	Sgt	HARRIGAN Thomas Raymond	29-02-44	405 Sqn		J/36580	F/O	HEUGHAN Allan Watson	22-12-44	189 Sqn
J/90524	P/O	HARRINGTON Timothy Ambrose	23-09-44	9 Sqn		J/19423	P/O	HEWETSON William Russell	29-01-44	429 Sqn

J/20668	F/O	HEWITT Ross Whitten	13-06-44	434 Sqn		R/105586	WO2	HOPPUS Williard Henry	14-01-44	432 Sqn
J/39370	F/O	HEWSON Sydney Dalton	28-12-44	428 Sqn		J/19003	S/L	HOPTON DFC Cecil George	8-06-44	156 Sqn
J/21597	F/O	HEYWORTH Ernest Osborne	3-06-44	10 Sqn		J/21184	F/O	HORN John	29-01-44	115 Sqn
J/88636	P/O	HICKEY James Martin	8-07-44	9 Sqn		J/19466	P/O	HORNBY Albert William	29-01-44	434 Sqn
R/121244	Sgt	HICKOX William	28-05-44	420 Sqn		R/150952	WO2	HORNE James Chandler	27-04-44	619 Sqn
R/145342	F/S	HICKS Lyle Wilmot [USA]	16-02-44	426 Sqn		J/36835	F/O	HORNING Frederick Arthur	6-11-44	50 Sqn
J/88333	P/O	HICKS Orville Wesley	16-02-44	426 Sqn		C/85693	P/O	HORTON Arthur Leslie	9-05-44	426 Sqn
J/22600	F/O	HICKS Winford Gordon [USA]	29-01-44	429 Sqn		J/86837	P/O	HORTON Donald Ellsworth	17-06-44	433 Sqn
R/121488	Sgt	HIGGINS Gerald Frederick	15-11-44	1664 HCU		J/88617	P/O	HORTON Ronald Elmer	22-06-44	106 Sqn
R/130615	F/S	HILKER Donald Ernest	3-01-44	408 Sqn		J/24035	F/O	HOSTETLER Charles Woodrow	29-07-44	426 Sqn
R/185307	WO2	HILL Francis Ignatius Roy Bruce [USA]	29-11-44	103 Sqn		R/205200	Sgt	HOULDEN Eric	4-05-44	50 Sqn
						R/81110	Sgt	HOULDING Elwood Campbell	14-01-44	405 Sqn
J/35779	F/O	HILL James Burleigh	26-10-44	166 Sqn		J/35018	F/O	HOUSTON George Marshall	11-09-44	408 Sqn
R/147614	WO1	HILL John Travers	28-01-44	49 Sqn		J/12683	F/O	HOUSTON John Alan	20-02-44	431 Sqn
J/37792	F/O	HILL Leonard George	17-06-44	426 Sqn		R/138352	F/O	HOUSTON Walter Adams	13-01-44	15 Sqn
J/21914	F/O	HILLMAN James Gordon	25-02-44	408 Sqn		J/17469	F/O	HOW Frederick Winston	28-12-44	419 Sqn
R/252790	Sgt	HILLMAN Ralph Frithjaf [USA]	5-07-44	576 Sqn		R/88689	F/S	HOWARD Burton Dix	21-02-44	630 Sqn
J/22201	F/O	HILLRICH Vincent Phillip	9-06-44	102 Sqn		R/186134	Sgt	HOWARD Donald William	7-02-44	427 Sqn
J/35547	F/O	HILLS Raymond George	28-05-44	30 OTU		J/39324	F/O	HOWARD Douglas Studholme	4-12-44	166 Sqn
R/256204	F/S	HILTS Hugh Donald	29-07-44	90 Sqn		J/28764	F/O	HOWDEN Andrew MacKenzie	7-04-44	139 Sqn
J/89248	P/O	HINDMARSH Felix Campbell	12-04-44	432 Sqn		J/88198	P/O	HOWE Thomas Edward George	22-06-44	619 Sqn
J/38298	F/O	HINE Edward Alexander	19-11-44	1666 HCU		J/91045	P/O	HOWELL Desmond William	25-03-44	433 Sqn
J/91198	P/O	HINE Raymond Ervin	17-12-44	101 Sqn		J/86401	P/O	HOWELL James	20-02-44	431 Sqn
J/22411	F/O	HINSCLIFFE DFC Alfred	7-05-44	405 Sqn		J/90958	P/O	HOWELL John Edward	29-07-44	425 Sqn
J/29374	F/O	HIRST Allan Charles	24-11-44	419 Sqn		J/25977	F/L	HOWES Charles Maurice [United Kingdom]	26-08-44	78 Sqn
R/208993	Sgt	HIRST Harvey Ellis	25-02-44	420 Sqn						
R/209405	F/S	HIRSTWOOD Jesse Ervin	3-08-44	61 Base		J/88603	P/O	HOWEY Edward Clayton	26-02-44	431 Sqn
J/39323	F/O	HITCHCOCK Douglas	18-12-44	432 Sqn		J/92950	P/O	HOWIE Wilfred Herbert	30-08-44	101 Sqn
R/146998	F/S	HITCHCOCK George Edwin	8-06-44	115 Sqn		R/219997	Sgt	HOXFORD Fred Carson	4-05-44	103 Sqn
R/187271	Sgt	HIVON Guy Henry	18-01-44	1659 HCU		R/215102	Sgt	HRYCENKO Arthur Kenneth	17-06-44	3 LFS
J/23121	F/O	HJARTARSON Frederick Jacob	14-01-44	1656 HCU		C/85815	P/O	HUBAND Donald Leslie	27-01-44	426 Sqn
J/28222	F/O	HOAR Archibald MacMaster	23-06-44	77 Sqn		J/29683	F/O	HUBBARD Vincent John	29-07-44	420 Sqn
R/144364	WO2	HOBSON Gordon Herbert	4-05-44	50 Sqn		J/92593	P/O	HUBLEY Cecil David Benjamin	28-12-44	419 Sqn
R/222664	Sgt	HOBSON William Allen	30-01-44	22 OTU		R/106580	WO1	HUDDLESTON John [USA]	15-04-44	1664 HCU
R/266186	Sgt	HODGES Campbell McRae	16-06-44	22 OTU		J/20047	F/L	HUDSON Harry McCormick [USA]	31-03-44	78 Sqn
J/88708	P/O	HODGINS Mervyn Eugene	25-02-44	408 Sqn		J/23947	P/O	HUDSON John Henry	21-08-44	415 Sqn
R/197404	F/S	HODGINS Robert Bruce	11-06-44	625 Sqn		J/89052	P/O	HUFF Walter Donald	16-06-44	405 Sqn
R/134936	F/S	HODGKINS George Arthur	25-07-44	166 Sqn		J/19360	F/O	HUGHES David	11-06-44	434 Sqn
R/191916	F/S	HODGSON George Thomas	21-07-44	578 Sqn		J/93658	P/O	HUGHES Owen Peter	15-06-44	115 Sqn
J/24087	F/O	HODGSON Gordon Ross	5-07-44	419 Sqn		J/14859	F/O	HUGHES William Adrian [USA]	18-04-44	158 Sqn
J/86273	P/O	HODSON Arthur Coles Kitchener	16-03-44	408 Sqn		J/87265	P/O	HUGHES-GAMES Norman Edward	28-09-44	57 Sqn
J/26779	F/O	HOFFMAN William Gladstone	28-07-44	78 Sqn		J/12224	F/O	HUGLI William Paul	25-04-44	424 Sqn
R/149223	Sgt	HOFFORTH Bernard Mathew	29-07-44	408 Sqn		J/87891	P/O	HUISH Gordon Keith	13-07-44	415 Sqn
J/88327	P/O	HOGAN Clyde John	2-10-44	1664 HCU		R/106982	WO1	HUMPHREYS Elmore Oliver Elvidge	30-03-44	419 Sqn
R/160470	F/S	HOGAN Leonard Ignatius	23-01-44	1679 HCFlt						
J/95086	P/O	HOGG John Douglas	15-10-44	432 Sqn		J/21890	F/L	HUNT Robert Bell	20-05-44	7 Sqn
J/95085	P/O	HOGG Leonard Hunter [USA]	14-10-44	425 Sqn		J/88262	P/O	HUNT Thomas John	21-11-44	426 Sqn
J/85619	P/O	HOLENCHUK William	9-06-44	426 Sqn		J/27782	F/O	HUNTER David Renwick	21-01-44	432 Sqn
J/88495	P/O	HOLKE Aldrene Gail	8-05-44	619 Sqn		C/85347	F/O	HUNTER Raymond Orville	9-10-44	424 Sqn
J/90393	P/O	HOLLAND Roy Sidney	12-09-44	635 Sqn		J/25758	F/O	HUNTER William George	23-05-44	429 Sqn
J/92611	P/O	HOLLENBACK Fraser Clarke	19-07-44	115 Sqn		J/25512	F/O	HUNTLEY Sydney Leonard	19-03-44	101 Sqn
J/25803	F/O	HOLLOWAY Donaldson Rendal	15-04-44	1664 HCU		J/88344	P/O	HUOT Joseph Jean Baptiste Benoit	24-03-44	425 Sqn
J/38159	P/O	HOLMES Arthur Sidney Fraser	23-04-44	433 Sqn		R/159901	WO2	HUOT Joseph Wilfred Jean Paul	29-07-44	90 Sqn
J/18161	F/O	HOLMES a'COURT Walter Alexander	2-01-44	44 Sqn		J/19421	F/O	HUPMAN Arnold Freeman	17-06-44	419 Sqn
						R/210041	Sgt	HUPPE Allan Wilfred	17-05-44	1661 HCU
J/86147	P/O	HOLOWAY Lucas	11-06-44	420 Sqn		R/201717	Sgt	HURDER Neil Scott	5-07-44	82 Sqn
J/25929	F/O	HOLSETH Garnet Carlysle	30-08-44	50 Sqn		R/197216	F/S	HURLBUT Nathan Merrill	13-09-44	90 Sqn
J/85593	P/O	HOLTZE Jack	2-11-44	428 Sqn		R/194194	F/S	HURTEAU Joseph Fernand Rolland	23-04-44	425 Sqn
J/37185	F/O	HONG Joseph	23-05-44	24 OTU		J/38161	F/O	HUSKILSON William St. Clair	2-11-44	415 Sqn
J/88657	P/O	HOOD Frederick William	5-07-44	57 Sqn		J/25815	F/O	HUTCHINSON Gordon Frederick	2-07-44	1667 HCU
R/188432	Sgt	HOOD John Spurgeon	8-11-44	22 OTU		J/35209	F/O	HYNDMAN Bruce Douglas	7-12-44	419 Sqn
R/191599	F/S	HOOPER Harry Donald	26-11-44	115 Sqn		R/126404	WO2	HYNES William Joseph	13-01-44	15 Sqn
J/87397	F/O	HOPE DFC William John	26-08-44	90 Sqn		R/223024	Sgt	HYT Nicholas Edward [USA]	25-05-44	101 Sqn
J/88421	P/O	HOPKINS Frederick Randall	8-07-44	50 Sqn		J/91057	P/O	IANUZIELLO Dominic	21-07-44	101 Sqn
J/36267	F/O	HOPPER Garnet Illingsworth	21-11-44	426 Sqn		J/87777	P/O	IMAGE Leslie	29-07-44	425 Sqn
R/80789	Sgt	HOPPER Jack	23-05-44	24 OTU		J/95163	P/O	IMRIE George John	30-07-44	115 Sqn
J/39026	P/O	HOPPER Leo James	4-11-44	426 Sqn		J/88662	P/O	IMRIE John Alexander Kay	28-07-44	408 Sqn
J/86734	P/O	HOPPER Lloyd Hinson	18-07-44	578 Sqn		J/93699	P/O	INESON Allan Clifford	2-11-44	408 Sqn

ID	Rank	Name	Date	Unit
J/90042	P/O	INGELL Leslie Raymond	25-03-44	630 Sqn
R/207365	Sgt	INGLESON Harry William	16-05-44	26 OTU
R/172942	F/S	INMAN Lawrence Melion	11-11-44	227 Sqn
J/92366	F/O	INNES Lloyd John	23-10-44	429 Sqn
J/86381	P/O	INVERARITY John Alexander	8-06-44	408 Sqn
J/88130	F/O	IRELAND Donald George Henry	17-12-44	101 Sqn
R/210291	Sgt	IRELAND Willard Vernon	17-06-44	101 Sqn
J/87468	F/O	IRISH John Roy	1-08-44	429 Sqn
J/21536	F/O	IRVINE Richard Reginald [Eire]	6-06-44	426 Sqn
J/19819	F/O	IRVING Arnold Earle	12-05-44	75 Sqn
J/24814	F/O	IRWIN David Lloyd	23-06-44	78 Sqn
R/206042	F/S	IRWIN Harvey Roland	25-10-44	431 Sqn
R/215775	Sgt	IRWIN James Wesley	24-09-44	24 OTU
J/14212	F/O	IRWIN Robert Aubrey	28-05-44	424 Sqn
J/87543	P/O	IRWIN Robert Murray	11-06-44	420 Sqn
J/16115	F/L	IRWIN Wesley Douglas	22-11-44	627 Sqn
J/90391	F/O	ISAAC George Herbert	29-06-44	424 Sqn
J/24796	F/O	ISFAN John Tudor	12-05-44	9 Sqn
R/176528	F/S	ISLES Harold Elburn	9-05-44	90 Sqn
R/150759	WO2	IVEY Gordon	16-03-44	625 Sqn
J/95268	P/O	JACK Robert Kidd	30-08-44	115 Sqn
R/169959	F/S	JACK Ross Alexander	17-06-44	576 Sqn
J/27118	F/O	JACKMAN Thomas	8-08-44	429 Sqn
J/88322	P/O	JACKSON Alexander James	29-07-44	426 Sqn
J/92355	P/O	JACKSON Alvin Roy	26-08-44	419 Sqn
J/85182	P/O	JACKSON Donald Edward	18-03-44	434 Sqn
J/21979	F/O	JACKSON Duncan John	23-04-44	640 Sqn
J/87979	P/O	JACKSON Gordon	18-07-44	431 Sqn
J/18946	P/O	JACKSON DFC Harold Naylor	15-02-44	156 Sqn
R/128258	WO2	JACKSON Leonard MacCallum	6-01-44	467 Sqn
J/25847	F/O	JACKSON Olavi Leonard	25-03-44	427 Sqn
J/21170	F/O	JACKSON Robert Harold	16-03-44	420 Sqn
J/88163	P/O	JACOBS Avroy	1-11-44	424 Sqn
J/29518	F/O	JACOBS Daniel Louis	20-03-44	82 OTU
C/1629	W/C	JACOBS DFC David Sinclair	23-05-44	408 Sqn
R/108393	WO1	JACQUES Joseph Gaston	23-05-44	24 OTU
J/86240	P/O	JAKEMAN Colin Ian	29-06-44	77 Sqn
J/85073	P/O	JAMES David Eric	18-03-44	433 Sqn
J/220077	F/S	JAMES Norman Thomas	31-08-44	103 Sqn
J/19863	F/O	JAMIESON Donald Sinclair	22-08-44	426 Sqn
J/28677	F/O	JAMIESON Gerald Alexander	6-07-44	15 Sqn
R/104531	Sgt	JANDRON Geoffrey Maynard [Channel Islands]	29-01-44	77 Sqn
J/25852	F/L	JANNEY William Harold	14-10-44	428 Sqn
J/94289	P/O	JANZEN Leslie Homer	18-12-44	434 Sqn
J/21203	P/O	JARDINE Wallace Bell	23-05-44	97 Sqn
R/177084	F/S	JARVIS Everitt Franklyn	31-03-44	622 Sqn
R/153445	Sgt	JEFFERSON John Alan	27-01-44	18 OTU
J/93712	P/O	JEFFERY Kenneth Arthur	21-07-44	514 Sqn
J/27714	F/O	JEFFREY Frank Armstrong	24-06-44	12 Sqn
R/164179	F/S	JEFFREY Wilbur Joseph	1-06-44	138 Sqn
J/38196	P/O	JEFFREYS Herbert Arthur	22-11-44	61 Sqn
J/18996	P/O	JENKINS Spurgeon Delma	15-02-44	434 Sqn
J/90217	P/O	JENKINS Thomas Corson	5-07-44	433 Sqn
J/88334	P/O	JENNINGS Reginald George [USA]	20-02-44	434 Sqn
R/167555	WO2	JEPSON Alan Arthur	22-05-44	635 Sqn
J/88591	P/O	JERMEY Norman Seymore	29-07-44	431 Sqn
R/194134	Sgt	JETTE Joseph Jean Leon	25-03-44	427 Sqn
J/9243	F/L	JIRA Alfred Gisli	21-01-44	433 Sqn
R/189707	F/S	JOBIN Paul Andre Marc	5-12-44	22 OTU
J/27433	P/O	JOBSON Stewart Walter	15-04-44	1664 HCU
R/217129	F/S	JODRELL Norman Francis	4-11-44	78 Sqn
J/8913	F/L	JOHNSON Donald Woodrow [USA]	26-07-44	432 Sqn
J/19424	F/O	JOHNSON Elmer Orville	17-06-44	431 Sqn
R/128478	WO2	JOHNSON Fusi Eirikur 'Sigus'	25-03-44	166 Sqn
J/27956	F/O	JOHNSON Gwynn Wray	29-06-44	424 Sqn
R/186292	Sgt	JOHNSON Harold	30-01-44	100 Sqn
J/35279	F/O	JOHNSON Harry William	6-12-44	103 Sqn
R/178928	F/S	JOHNSON Hubert Clarence	3-06-44	76 Sqn
J/88546	P/O	JOHNSON James Kitchener	19-07-44	619 Sqn
J/85585	P/O	JOHNSON John George	4-05-44	625 Sqn
J/23626	F/O	JOHNSON John Gilbert	25-01-44	16 OTU
J/24921	F/O	JOHNSON Joseph John Raymond	21-07-44	405 Sqn
J/17450	F/O	JOHNSON Kenneth Scott	15-05-44	82 OTU
J/92014	P/O	JOHNSON Leonard Knut	27-08-44	57 Sqn
R/257876	Sgt	JOHNSON Robert Andrew	23-07-44	83 OTU
J/24698	P/O	JOHNSON William George Wesley	23-05-44	49 Sqn
J/86743	P/O	JOHNSON William Kemp	18-04-44	428 Sqn
J/28771	F/O	JOHNSTON Arnold Ney	17-09-44	115 Sqn
J/86171	P/O	JOHNSTON Arthur Leon	13-06-44	76 Sqn
J/85041	P/O	JOHNSTON Clifford Stanley	17-06-44	419 Sqn
R/153793	WO2	JOHNSTON Ernest Carl	31-03-44	625 Sqn
J/28864	F/O	JOHNSTON Jack Harvey	21-11-44	429 Sqn
J/19259	F/O	JOHNSTON DFC James Ian	24-06-44	617 Sqn
C/29783	F/O	JOHNSTON John Armstrong	22-10-44	1659 HCU
J/90924	P/O	JOHNSTON John Markey	17-06-44	434 Sqn
R/222992	F/S	JOHNSTON John William	14-07-44	24 OTU
R/188969	F/S	JOHNSTON Lloyd	18-08-44	576 Sqn
R/110817	Sgt	JOHNSTON Lloyd George	29-02-44	420 Sqn
R/154789	Sgt	JOHNSTON Lorne Herbert	20-03-44	82 OTU
J/85052	P/O	JOHNSTON Norman	3-06-44	405 Sqn
J/95344	P/O	JOHNSTON Thomas Andrew	11-11-44	227 Sqn
J/87253	P/O	JOHNSTONE Ronald Elliott	30-01-44	576 Sqn
C/89437	P/O	JOINER Raymond Conserdine	1-11-44	431 Sqn
J/35757	F/O	JOLLEY Edward Daniel Birch	13-08-44	434 Sqn
J/19581	P/O	JONASSON David Herman	20-02-44	427 Sqn
J/19642	P/O	JONES Allan	16-03-44	76 Sqn
J/25750	F/O	JONES David Richard	25-08-44	101 Sqn
J/25515	F/O	JONES Edward Crowther	3-05-44	550 Sqn
10634	Sgt	JONES George Andrew	4-07-44	24 OTU
J/25913	F/O	JONES Harry Robert	8-06-44	420 Sqn
J/90284	F/O	JONES James Howard	13-05-44	626 Sqn
R/163070	F/S	JONES John Harrison	16-07-44	30 OTU
J/18966	F/O	JONES Lloyd William Wesley	22-01-44	427 Sqn
J/85045	P/O	JONES Norval Hodges	25-03-44	425 Sqn
J/92064	P/O	JONES Paul Reviere	14-10-44	428 Sqn
J/25514	F/O	JONES Robert Roy	16-03-44	625 Sqn
J/17652	F/O	JONES Ronald Marwood	24-11-44	1655 MTU
J/89252	P/O	JONES Walter Stanley	27-04-44	10 Sqn
C/135	G/C	JONES Wilfred Alexander	2-05-44	62 Base
J/24979	F/O	JOPLIN Stanley John	19-07-44	420 Sqn
J/22936	F/O	JORY William Edward	15-10-44	424 Sqn
J/85356	P/O	JOSE Gordon Beverley	8-06-44	431 Sqn
J/90390	F/O	JOYNSON Francis Edward	29-06-44	424 Sqn
J/94152	P/O	JUDGES Gordon	2-11-44	77 Sqn
J/27264	F/O	JULIEN Joseph Albini Gustave	6-10-44	640 Sqn
R/272625	Sgt	JUTZI Curtis	31-08-44	22 OTU
J/89899	P/O	KAESEMODEL Ernest Richard	29-12-44	405 Sqn
J/87268	P/O	KAISER Stanley Keith	17-06-44	434 Sqn
J/27434	F/O	KALHEIM Ben Ingard	30-08-44	103 Sqn
J/90760	P/O	KALYTA Peter	23-05-44	408 Sqn
R/210272	Sgt	KARAIM Tony John	14-02-44	22 OTU
J/88620	P/O	KARREL Curois	29-09-44	431 Sqn
J/92361	P/O	KARSTENS William Russell	4-10-44	419 Sqn
J/89925	P/O	KAWUCHA Joseph Francis	1-07-44	12 Sqn
J/90618	P/O	KAY Lloyd Ronald	9-10-44	76 Sqn
J/95365	P/O	KAY Robert James	1-11-44	424 Sqn
J/87089	P/O	KAY Solomon	24-02-44	405 Sqn
J/18810	F/L	KEARL DFC Eldon Eastman	27-01-44	408 Sqn
J/23901	P/O	KEE Ross James	20-02-44	431 Sqn
J/25842	F/O	KEELER Ervin Leroy	30-01-44	207 Sqn
C/89729	P/O	KEELY Louis John	24-03-44	429 Sqn
R/173638	F/S	KEENAN James Philip	27-04-44	106 Sqn
J/14033	F/O	KEENAN John Ignatius Joseph	16-04-44	405 Sqn
J/90653	P/O	KEEPING Arthur Thomas	8-11-44	424 Sqn
J/38411	F/O	KELLAR David Garfield	24-12-44	408 Sqn

ID	Rank	Name	Date	Sqn
C/88471	P/O	KELLEY David Austin	3-06-44	405 Sqn
J/89258	P/O	KELLEY Stanley Frederick Harding	8-06-44	78 Sqn
J/89392	F/O	KELLIE James William	25-05-44	424 Sqn
J/90307	P/O	KELLUM John Reid [USA]	26-07-44	619 Sqn
J/37186	F/O	KELLY Jack Arthur	4-08-44	434 Sqn
R/200438	F/S	KELLY Karl Emerson	28-12-44	429 Sqn
J/88769	P/O	KELLY Ralph Gordon	20-02-44	408 Sqn
J/19921	F/O	KELLY Thomas Raymond	18-07-44	427 Sqn
J/14241	F/O	KELSO Roger Gordon	13-06-44	434 Sqn
J/86404	P/O	KELTER Herbert Frank	20-02-44	78 Sqn
J/25349	F/O	KEMP Harold Leon	24-02-44	100 Sqn
J/12962	F/L	KEMP Kenneth Donovan	17-08-44	405 Sqn
J/21472	F/O	KEMP Russell William	12-02-44	419 Sqn
J/92949	P/O	KENDALL Francis James	30-08-44	101 Sqn
J/89860	P/O	KENDALL George Herbert	21-12-44	97 Sqn
J/36886	F/O	KENNEDY Carleton Gladstone	30-08-44	434 Sqn
J/91005	P/O	KENNEDY Edward John	24-09-44	24 OTU
J/92027	P/O	KENNEDY Francis Leonard	25-02-44	115 Sqn
J/85673	P/O	KENNEDY Henry John	29-06-44	432 Sqn
J/27157	F/O	KENNEDY Lancelot Stanley	23-05-44	103 Sqn
R/129400	WO2	KENNEDY Leonard Thomas	27-04-44	49 Sqn
J/88743	P/O	KENNEDY William John	18-07-44	115 Sqn
C/85658	P/O	KENT Emil Dan	26-02-44	419 Sqn
C/90305	P/O	KENT Gerald Albion	19-07-44	420 Sqn
J/95371	P/O	KEOWN John Lightfoot	6-12-44	424 Sqn
J/22198	F/O	KERR David Simpson	2-02-44	432 Sqn
J/27159	F/O	KERR Hubert Lloyd	7-02-44	1656 HCU
C/18588	F/O	KERR John William	28-04-44	432 Sqn
J/85910	F/O	KERR Richard Alexander	21-01-44	434 Sqn
J/37220	F/O	KERRY John Nicholas	11-09-44	408 Sqn
J/92274	P/O	KESSELMAN Murray	16-09-44	199 Sqn
R/170747	Sgt	KESTER Noel Thompson	26-05-44	19 OTU
R/209021	F/S	KIDD Earl David	22-06-44	619 Sqn
J/10177	F/L	KIDDER Gordon Arthur	29-03-44	156 Sqn
R/107409	Sgt	KIDNEY Alvin Eric	11-08-44	24 OTU
R/215860	Sgt	KIDNEY Neil John	11-07-44	1666 HCU
R/151549	WO2	KILPATRICK Worthy James	4-01-44	1657 HCU
R/54130	Sgt	KIMBALL Richard George	18-01-44	1659 HCU
J/24229	F/O	KIMMINS Gordon Patrick James	28-05-44	103 Sqn
R/171514	F/S	KING Elmer Charles	16-07-44	44 Sqn
J/26487	F/O	KING Francis Joseph	22-03-44	408 Sqn
J/35114	F/O	KING Harold Herbert	1-07-44	101 Sqn
J/85091	P/O	KING John	29-01-44	115 Sqn
R/93560	WO1	KING William George	31-01-44	1664 HCU
R/126655	WO2	KINGHORN Herbert Helmer	14-01-44	156 Sqn
J/25012	F/O	KINGSLEY William Charles	4-03-44	138 Sqn
J/85533	P/O	KINGSTON Philip Alan	17-06-44	434 Sqn
J/27395	F/O	KINNEAR George Publow	23-04-44	51 Sqn
J/87621	P/O	KIRKPATRICK Roy Nixon	23-04-44	514 Sqn
J/86514	P/O	KIRKWOOD Douglass-Smith	22-05-44	100 Sqn
J/25463	F/L	KIRSCH Abraham Lionel	13-09-44	90 Sqn
J/28245	F/O	KIRSCHNER Irving Jack	26-08-44	419 Sqn
J/88776	P/O	KIRTON Lloyd	28-05-44	429 Sqn
J/91061	P/O	KISILOWSKY Edward	26-08-44	207 Sqn
R/220176	Sgt	KITCHEN Beverley Gordon	6-09-44	1667 HCU
R/222456	F/S	KITCHIN Jack Hurst	30-11-44	429 Sqn
J/87906	P/O	KITE George Robert Graham	23-09-44	10 Sqn
J/86438	F/O	KLEIN Irvine George	15-03-44	431 Sqn
J/37758	F/O	KNAPP Roger Singleton [USA]	20-05-44	83 OTU
J/86435	P/O	KNIGHT Martin Allan	25-02-44	420 Sqn
J/95364	P/O	KNIGHT Ronald Charles	25-10-44	428 Sqn
J/9308	F/L	KNIGHT Ronald Earl	25-07-44	420 Sqn
J/28738	P/O	KNOBOVITCH DFC Harry	2-11-44	415 Sqn
J/95370	P/O	KNOKE Joseph	5-12-44	426 Sqn
R/169674	F/S	KNOWLES Fred	20-11-44	22 OTU
J/92327	P/O	KNOX Victor Alfred	23-04-44	419 Sqn
J/23950	F/L	KNUPP Gordon Winston	9-05-44	405 Sqn
J/89386	P/O	KOHUT Frank	26-08-44	61 Sqn
J/19263	P/O	KOIVU Jack Olavi	26-03-44	426 Sqn
J/37149	F/O	KOLEDA Peter	13-06-44	427 Sqn
J/35077	F/O	KOLOMIC Johnny Peter	11-07-44	1666 HCU
J/35044	F/O	KOMMES Joseph John	25-07-44	619 Sqn
J/43768	F/O	KON William Emil Miroslav	5-10-44	101 Sqn
J/25353	F/O	KORBYL Paul Frank	25-04-44	626 Sqn
J/25524	F/O	KOVACICH Anthony Michael [USA]	30-08-44	115 Sqn
J/27726	F/O	KOWALCHUK Theodore	6-12-44	434 Sqn
R/180195	F/S	KOZLOWSKI Stanley John	15-07-44	576 Sqn
J/43740	P/O	KRAM Meryn	30-08-44	86 OTU
J/85984	P/O	KRAMER Julius [USA]	25-06-44	61 Sqn
J/24321	F/O	KRAMPE William Ernest	25-03-44	424 Sqn
J/90763	P/O	KRAWCHUK Steve Lawrence	29-07-44	100 Sqn
R/178776	WO2	KREWENCHUK Metro Alex	24-12-44	100 Sqn
J/22096	F/O	KRUGER Carl William	31-03-44	12 Sqn
J/90926	P/O	KRYNSKI Tony	28-06-44	460 Sqn
J/87624	P/O	KULESKI Stephen	23-05-44	432 Sqn
R/162250	F/S	KULLBERG Elmer Nels	22-06-44	619 Sqn
J/94600	P/O	KURTZHALS Allan Edward	18-12-44	434 Sqn
J/87091	P/O	KWAS Michael	28-01-44	426 Sqn
C/85505	P/O	KYLE Charles Harrison	13-06-44	434 Sqn
J/86448	P/O	LABACH Peter	16-02-44	426 Sqn
J/90935	P/O	LABELLE Joseph Gaston Gustave Andre	16-09-44	432 Sqn
R/81716	Sgt	LABELLE Joseph Willie Conrad	25-05-44	576 Sqn
R/110907	WO2	LABERGE Daniel Joseph	31-03-44	622 Sqn
J/18279	F/O	LABOW John Irvin	31-03-44	408 Sqn
J/88921	P/O	LABRECQUE Joseph Rosaire Jean Charles	18-12-44	425 Sqn
J/27666	F/O	LACEY William Morris	13-06-44	419 Sqn
J/18906	F/O	LADEROUTE MiD Michael John	11-09-44	434 Sqn
J/86397	P/O	LAFFERTY Albert Ervin	30-01-44	626 Sqn
J/21293	F/L	LAIDLAW David Drysdale	12-02-44	419 Sqn
J/23294	F/O	LAIDLAW James Dutton	31-03-44	640 Sqn
J/18786	F/L	LAINE DFC Sven Roy Walfrid	27-01-44	408 Sqn
J/90517	P/O	LAING John Arthur	23-05-44	425 Sqn
J/90383	P/O	LAIRD David Albert	22-03-44	432 Sqn
J/4896	S/L	LAIRD DFC George Johnstone	31-03-44	427 Sqn
J/87503	P/O	LAIRD John Seddon	23-04-44	424 Sqn
10209	WO2	LALONDE Joseph Alfred Wilfrid Rodrigue	26-01-44	102 Sqn
J/90283	P/O	LAMB Colin Bruce	12-05-44	427 Sqn
R/223672	Sgt	LAMB Leeming Cameron	11-08-44	24 OTU
J/87830	P/O	LAMB Robert Arthur	3-09-44	426 Sqn
J/95165	P/O	LAMB William Alexander	17-08-44	428 Sqn
J/35772	F/O	LAMBERT Edward Roger	14-10-44	166 Sqn
R/194217	Sgt	LAMONTAGNE Joseph Albert Yvon	5-01-44	431 Sqn
J/14517	F/O	LAMPIN Frank Edward	14-01-44	156 Sqn
J/23972	F/O	LANCASTER George Kenneth	13-06-44	78 Sqn
J/21526	F/O	LANCASTER John Douglas	11-06-44	420 Sqn
J/40062	F/O	LANDSKY John Frederick	17-10-44	1664 HCU
J/17144	F/O	LANG Francis Henry	13-06-44	427 Sqn
J/85119	P/O	LANGFORD Frederick George	24-02-44	51 Sqn
C/1631	F/L	LANGFORD MiD Patrick Wilson	31-03-44	16 OTU
J/92155	P/O	LANGLEY Lloyd George	16-09-44	199 Sqn
J/85717	P/O	LANGLOIS John D'Arcy	11-04-44	1661 HCU
J/90385	P/O	LANGRIDGE George James	27-04-44	619 Sqn
J/90933	P/O	LANGRILL William Arthur [USA]	27-08-44	115 Sqn
J/22574	F/O	LANGRISH Harold Keith	23-04-44	106 Sqn
J/94171	P/O	LANKIN William Walford	2-11-44	77 Sqn
R/168038	Sgt	LANOUETTE Joseph Andre	15-05-44	82 OTU
J/91046	P/O	LANSDOWNE Edwin Arthur	18-04-44	433 Sqn
R/135028	F/S	LARIVIERE Joseph Rene	18-12-44	425 Sqn
J/93682	P/O	LARKIN Mark Richard	13-06-44	419 Sqn
J/89982	F/O	LARMOUTH William Oswald Derry	21-07-44	514 Sqn
J/35069	F/O	LARSEN Arnold William	26-08-44	419 Sqn
R/92671	WO1	LARSEN Frederick Albert	6-01-44	576 Sqn

ID	Rank	Name	Date	Sqn
C/88590	P/O	LARSEN George Martin	29-07-44	434 Sqn
R/192316	Sgt	LARSON Ivar	23-04-44	75 Sqn
K/268113	Sgt	LATHAM Horace Roger	10-10-44	1667 HCU
J/88857	P/O	LATHAM Jim	31-03-44	49 Sqn
J/9350	S/L	LATIMER Gerald Bennett	29-07-44	408 Sqn
J/19946	P/O	LATORNELL Maurice Coupland	25-03-44	425 Sqn
J/86453	P/O	LATURNUS Andrew	13-05-44	431 Sqn
J/28208	P/O	LAUDER Gordon Robert	25-05-44	419 Sqn
J/22723	F/O	LAUT Ross K.	21-02-44	427 Sqn
J/10983	F/O	LAVALLEE Joseph Pierre	18-01-44	1659 HCU
J/95177	P/O	LAVALLEY David Henry	6-12-44	434 Sqn
J/89108	P/O	LAVERY Charles Algernon	25-02-44	433 Sqn
J/24534	F/O	LAVERY Thomas Wilbert	31-03-44	50 Sqn
J/19970	P/O	LAVIOLETTE Joseph Alexandre	25-03-44	425 Sqn
J/29840	F/O	LAW Ian	2-11-44	15 Sqn
R/133754	WO2	LAWRENCE Allan Keith	14-01-44	405 Sqn
R/170867	F/S	LAWSON Harry Richard	16-05-44	625 Sqn
J/86493	P/O	LAWSON Victor Mitchell	28-01-44	426 Sqn
J/19672	P/O	LAWSON Wilfred Carroll	25-05-44	51 Sqn
J/38188	F/O	LAYNG William George	4-10-44	419 Sqn
J/90289	P/O	LAYTON Frederick William	8-06-44	433 Sqn
J/95161	P/O	LAZIER Vernon John	2-11-44	77 Sqn
J/85411	P/O	LA POINTE Peter John Orville	4-05-44	420 Sqn
J/25390	F/O	LA PORTE Edmund Elie	23-05-44	425 Sqn
J/88668	P/O	LEACH Roy Arthur	21-07-44	415 Sqn
J/19261	F/O	LEADER Robert Arthur	11-04-44	635 Sqn
J/24215	F/O	LEAMAN James Richard	20-02-44	408 Sqn
R/201700	F/S	LEAMAN Joseph Edmund	16-11-44	166 Sqn
J/26620	F/O	LEARN Robert Bradford	13-06-44	434 Sqn
R/155039	WO2	LEASK Donald Grant	27-04-44	103 Sqn
J/19073	F/O	LEATHERDALE Charles Grant	31-03-44	156 Sqn
J/87266	F/O	LEBANO Frank George	28-05-44	550 Sqn
J/28914	F/O	LEBLANC Joseph Edouard Gerard	16-09-44	432 Sqn
J/61333	Sgt	LEBOLOUS Martin Benedict	20-02-44	419 Sqn
J/38412	F/O	LECKIE John Lyle	17-12-44	153 Sqn
J/28502	F/O	LECKIE Robert Clarke	15-06-44	115 Sqn
J/16096	F/O	LECLAIRE Joseph Jaques Herman Gilde Guy	31-03-44	427 Sqn
J/17478	F/L	LEDDY DFC Gerald Bernard	23-03-44	22 OTU
J/35826	F/O	LEDGER Roy Walton	30-03-44	20 OTU
R/188532	Sgt	LEDUC Joseph Jean Baptiste Laurier	29-01-44	434 Sqn
J/19734	F/O	LEE Carl Thomas Edward	29-01-44	434 Sqn
J/9311	F/L	LEE DFC Jack Griffin	15-10-44	424 Sqn
R/259992	Sgt	LEE John Joseph	5-08-44	86 OTU
J/95372	F/O	LEE John Robert	6-12-44	424 Sqn
J/89415	P/O	LEE Thomas Edwin	5-08-44	425 Sqn
J/38402	F/O	LEE William John	17-10-44	1664 HCU
R/110015	WO1	LEECH Francis James	3-03-44	1666 HCU
J/88346	P/O	LEECH John Peter	24-04-44	425 Sqn
J/36315	F/O	LEEDS Phil [USA]	6-11-44	101 Sqn
R/184325	Sgt	LEES George Douglas	27-04-44	44 Sqn
J/86771	P/O	LEES John Clive	19-09-44	434 Sqn
J/92069	P/O	LEESE William Hewison	18-12-44	10 Sqn
J/88364	F/O	LEFEBVRE John Walter Raymond	9-05-44	425 Sqn
J/22893	F/O	LEGACE Lawrence Firge	21-01-44	432 Sqn
J/92353	F/O	LEGARY Harvey Albert	29-07-44	427 Sqn
J/89453	P/O	LEGAULT Joseph Henri Charles	23-04-44	425 Sqn
J/87061	P/O	LEGGE Preston St. Clair [USA]	13-06-44	434 Sqn
J/89727	P/O	LEHMAN Edgar Clarence	19-03-44	50 Sqn
J/90981	P/O	LEIGH Kenneth	16-10-44	207 Sqn
J/44328	F/O	LEITCH Archibald Havill	16-11-44	214 Sqn
J/89918	F/O	LEITCH John William	23-05-44	429 Sqn
J/27829	F/O	LEITHEAD John Chalmers	18-03-44	692 Sqn
J/92614	P/O	LEMAN Robert Arthur	29-07-44	431 Sqn
R/162667	WO2	LEMKY Ronald George	13-06-44	15 Sqn
J/23462	P/O	LEMMERICK George Earl	29-01-44	419 Sqn
J/88864	P/O	LEMMON Ralph Ernest	7-07-44	460 Sqn
R/153547	WO2	LEONARD Arthur Murray	22-06-44	44 Sqn
J/29987	F/O	LEONARD John	14-08-44	83 Sqn
J/85859	P/O	LEONARD Raymond Gale	20-04-44	420 Sqn
R/53024	WO2	LEONE Nuncie	14-01-44	405 Sqn
J/40879	F/O	LEPPERT Spencer Edwin	7-12-44	24 OTU
J/19296	P/O	LERL Frederick William	16-03-44	578 Sqn
J/92031	P/O	LETCHER Albert Clayton	25-04-44	115 Sqn
J/88830	P/O	LETHBRIDGE John William	27-04-44	100 Sqn
J/89685	P/O	LEVASSEUR Joseph Jean Marie	23-05-44	425 Sqn
J/86441	P/O	LEVESQUE Joseph Pierre Octave Victor	18-03-44	433 Sqn
J/90076	P/O	LEVESQUE Stanley Joseph	9-08-44	427 Sqn
R/85078	F/S	LEVINE David	12-12-44	1664 HCU
R/168700	Sgt	LEWIS Gerwyn Winton	1-04-44	20 OTU
J/85320	P/O	LEWIS Gilbert Allan	13-05-44	640 Sqn
J/87689	P/O	LEWIS Harvey Daniel	29-07-44	432 Sqn
J/28687	F/O	LEWIS William Douglas	27-05-44	5 LFS
J/25353	F/O	LEWIS-WATTS Desmond Loftus	19-04-44	419 Sqn
J/92323	P/O	LEWTHWAITE Donald Clifford	20-02-44	419 Sqn
J/37164	F/O	LEWTHWAITE George Alexander	24-07-44	1666 HCU
R/174719	F/S	LeBLANC Joseph Thomas Lloyd	25-05-44	78 Sqn
J/42865	F/O	LE BLANC Albert Thomas	28-12-44	428 Sqn
J/87669	P/O	LE DREW Donald Alfred Parsons	22-03-44	408 Sqn
J/37183	F/O	LE NOURY Harold Frederick	2-11-44	77 Sqn
J/90129	P/O	LE VASSEUR Lucien Charles	14-10-44	419 Sqn
R/204842	Sgt	LIBBY Otis Wilfrid	17-06-44	3 LFS
J/97888	F/S	LIDDLE Stanley Melville	29-01-44	7 Sqn
J/88775	P/O	LIEBSCHER John Martin Burns	4-05-44	626 Sqn
J/29996	F/O	LILLICO Allan Gainford	14-03-44	10 OTU
J/85364	P/O	LILLICO Gordon William	18-04-44	428 Sqn
J/93687	P/O	LILLICO William Davidson [USA]	26-05-44	419 Sqn
J/22075	F/O	LINDE James Alexander	21-01-44	431 Sqn
J/29690	F/O	LINDENFIELD Alvin Edward	7-06-44	1654 HCU
J/90312	P/O	LINDENSMITH Gordon Leroy	1-08-44	429 Sqn
J/4762	S/L	LINDO DFC Harold Lester [Jamaica]	15-02-44	103 Sqn
J/27248	F/O	LINDSAY Alexander	27-07-44	630 Sqn
J/19994	F/O	LINDSAY James	14-10-44	153 Sqn
J/86650	F/O	LINKLATER Jack Allan	26-08-44	576 Sqn
J/25837	F/O	LINKLATER Raymond Edwin	15-07-44	576 Sqn
J/94444	P/O	LINN Hubert Joseph	30-08-44	101 Sqn
J/2934	S/L	LINNELL Lloyd Martin	29-01-44	434 Sqn
J/86369	P/O	LINTON Francis Malcolm [USA]	23-05-44	50 Sqn
J/89726	P/O	LINTON Leonard Thomas	20-02-44	207 Sqn
J/88772	P/O	LINTON Oswald Adam	15-03-44	427 Sqn
J/90220	P/O	LISTER Gerald Lawrence	12-12-44	1664 HCU
J/25734	F/O	LITCHFIELD Ralph Frank	31-03-44	101 Sqn
J/24320	F/O	LITTLE Martin Stewart	25-05-44	1659 HCU
J/21422	F/L	LITTLE DFC Stuart Walker	25-05-44	582 Sqn
R/169221	F/S	LITTLE Wilfred Robert	27-07-44	44 Sqn
R/180315	Sgt	LIVINGSTONE Robert Douglas	21-01-44	158 Sqn
J/86829	P/O	LIVINGSTONE Samuel George	13-05-44	419 Sqn
R/110978	WO2	LOBB Benjamin Jack	21-01-44	115 Sqn
J/90280	P/O	LOCHHEAD Robert Lachlan [USA]	23-04-44	431 Sqn
J/94346	P/O	LOCKETT James Ernest	18-07-44	431 Sqn
J/27590	F/O	LOEWEN Dale Howard	28-04-44	431 Sqn
J/90278	P/O	LOFTSON Stephan August	24-02-44	9 Sqn
J/88514	P/O	LOGAN DFC Frederick Willis	30-07-44	207 Sqn
R/194248	Sgt	LOGAN James Alexander	11-04-44	83 Sqn
R/149232	Sgt	LOGELIN John Michael	24-05-44	20 OTU
R/115692	WO2	LONG Alfred Joseph	24-02-44	149 Sqn
R/89074	Sgt	LONG Gordon	27-05-44	1656 HCU
J/21366	P/O	LONG Henry Maynard	25-02-44	420 Sqn
J/18760	F/L	LONG DFC Ronald Walter	16-09-44	405 Sqn
J/89159	P/O	LONG Wendell Lyall	31-08-44	433 Sqn
J/25941	F/O	LONG William James [USA]	19-07-44	50 Sqn
J/92038	P/O	LONGLEY Robert Thomas William	5-07-44	433 Sqn
J/95164	P/O	LONIE Jack Maurice	30-07-44	115 Sqn
J/24524	F/O	LORANGER Norman Albert	8-05-44	619 Sqn
R/273608	Sgt	LORD Clifford Allen	2-11-44	153 Sqn

ID	Rank	Name	Date	Unit
R/155256	WO2	LORENZ Dennis Budd Herman	17-08-44	420 Sqn
J/89246	P/O	LOSSING Howard Walter	24-03-44	433 Sqn
J/41054	F/O	LOSZCHUK Peter Paul	30-08-44	86 OTU
J/92127	P/O	LOUGH Ross William	25-07-44	630 Sqn
J/20830	F/O	LOUGH Spencer William	17-06-44	431 Sqn
J/41353	F/O	LOUGHRAN Hugh Joseph	15-10-44	424 Sqn
J/89910	P/O	LOUTH William James	21-01-44	431 Sqn
J/36331	F/O	LOVE Charles Henry	21-11-44	433 Sqn
J/27205	F/O	LOVE Edwin Albert	4-11-44	78 Sqn
J/86496	P/O	LOVE William Kilworthy Murray [USA]	16-02-44	426 Sqn
J/20669	F/O	LOVERING Mervyn Lloyd George	29-07-44	50 Sqn
R/208139	Sgt	LOVETT Charles Edward	15-04-44	1654 HCU
J/16130	F/L	LOVING DFC Leslie Rowland Bond	5-11-44	424 Sqn
J/29520	F/O	LOWE Edward Ronald	13-06-44	419 Sqn
J/93826	P/O	LOWE Herbert	28-10-44	429 Sqn
R/158410	WO2	LOWE Leslie Allen Ralph	13-04-44	90 Sqn
J/87161	P/O	LOWE Thomas Bentley	30-03-44	419 Sqn
J/88783	P/O	LOWICK Morton Albert	29-07-44	426 Sqn
J/92029	P/O	LOWTHER Roy Woodside	19-04-44	149 Sqn
R/105215	F/S	LUCK Jack	20-02-44	103 Sqn
R/209460	Sgt	LUDLOW John Murray	24-07-44	1666 HCU
J/89269	P/O	LUGG Harold William	27-08-44	57 Sqn
J/86440	P/O	LUMGAIR Norman Andrew	15-03-44	408 Sqn
J/28211	F/O	LUMMIS James Cornwallis	17-06-44	434 Sqn
R/144320	Sgt	LUNAN Athol Lorne	23-04-44	1659 HCU
J/92324	P/O	LUNNEY Vernal Norwood	29-03-44	419 Sqn
J/90304	P/O	LUNNIN Thomas Horace	19-07-44	50 Sqn
J/95174	P/O	LUPINSKY Jack	2-11-44	428 Sqn
J/88774	P/O	LYNCH Norman Herbert	23-04-44	431 Sqn
R/212959	Sgt	LYNCH Robert Russell [USA]	27-05-44	5 LFS
J/85084	P/O	LYNE Francis Harold	8-06-44	138 Sqn
J/19590	P/O	LYNG David Thomas	14-01-44	432 Sqn
J/14236	P/O	LYNN Barry Everett	27-01-44	426 Sqn
R/194631	Sgt	LYSAK Leo Mox	11-08-44	24 OTU
J/11486	F/L	MacALLISTER Harvard Darrell Frederick	17-08-44	431 Sqn
J/19100	F/O	MacAULAY Norman Alexander	31-03-44	424 Sqn
J/89699	P/O	MacCARTHY Dermot Reagh	16-09-44	432 Sqn
J/22384	F/L	MacDONALD Alexander	11-06-44	429 Sqn
R/176939	F/S	MacDONALD Donald Alastair	30-08-44	50 Sqn
R/153164	F/S	MacDONALD Fred Whitten	23-04-44	1679 HCFlt
J/87169	P/O	MacDONALD James Ignatius	25-05-44	429 Sqn
R/113794	WO1	MacDONALD James Stewart	1-06-44	1667 HCU
J/85816	P/O	MacDONALD Murdo Norman	27-01-44	426 Sqn
J/89916	P/O	MacDOUGALL Daniel Craig	23-04-44	433 Sqn
R/117210	Sgt	MacDOUGALL John Hillhouse	4-05-44	431 Sqn
J/90647	P/O	MacFARLANE Donald John	29-12-44	405 Sqn
J/28486	P/O	MacFARLANE Matthew Ernest Reid	29-04-44	431 Sqn
J/19277	P/O	MacGILLIVRAY John Campbell	20-01-44	57 Sqn
J/20671	F/O	MacGREGOR David Alton [USA]	22-01-44	35 Sqn
J/26671	F/O	MacGREGOR Donald Stewart	6-10-44	78 Sqn
J/89409	P/O	MacGREGOR Gordon Fraser	22-06-44	49 Sqn
J/92532	P/O	MacGREGOR John Alfred Stuart	28-12-44	419 Sqn
J/22743	P/O	MacGREGOR Peter George Harvey	23-04-44	431 Sqn
J/29691	P/O	MacINTOSH Donald McKenzie	15-07-44	576 Sqn
J/24922	P/O	MacINTOSH Ernest William	7-07-44	166 Sqn
J/86152	P/O	MacKAY Angus Donald	8-06-44	138 Sqn
R/142262	LAC	MacKENZIE David Victor	12-04-44	432 Sqn
J/85814	P/O	MacKENZIE Hugh Fraser	4-05-44	9 Sqn
R/183416	Sgt	MacKINNON Daniel Webster	14-07-44	77 Sqn
J/92039	P/O	MacKINNON John Russell	21-01-44	12 Sqn
J/29267	P/O	MacLAREN Richard Edwardes	13-09-44	90 Sqn
J/86880	P/O	MacLEAN John Angus	28-01-44	408 Sqn
J/88874	P/O	MacLEAN John William	22-03-44	426 Sqn
J/21633	P/O	MacLEAN Roy	29-01-44	431 Sqn
R/141561	WO2	MacLENNAN Hugh [USA]	14-04-44	408 Sqn
R/50312	WO2	MacLENNAN John Alexander	16-07-44	15 Sqn
J/92113	P/O	MacLEOD Alexander Harvey	15-10-44	1664 HCU
J/92030	P/O	MacLEOD Joseph Murdoch	25-04-44	115 Sqn
J/19856	P/O	MacLEOD Malcolm Hinds	25-03-44	425 Sqn
J/95540	P/O	MacLEOD Melvin Joshua	17-12-44	50 Sqn
J/36883	P/O	MacMILLAN John Mervyn	14-10-44	626 Sqn
J/27469	F/O	MacNAIR Elmer Joseph Alexander	12-09-44	619 Sqn
J/28200	P/O	MacNEILL Duncan	29-01-44	12 OTU
J/36326	P/O	MacPHEE John Goodwill	6-10-44	640 Sqn
R/189676	F/S	MacVICAR Donald Irwin	29-07-44	576 Sqn
J/91058	P/O	MACARTHUR George Reginald	20-07-44	582 Sqn
J/14691	F/L	MACDONALD DFC Douglas Allister	2-01-44	630 Sqn
J/28649	F/O	MACDONALD Norman Hector	12-09-44	1653 HCU
J/19534	P/O	MACDUFF Herman Earl	22-05-44	550 Sqn
J/86119	P/O	MACFARLANE Ross Edward	4-05-44	626 Sqn
J/90365	P/O	MACGILLIVRAY Arthur Clarance	25-05-44	192 Sqn
J/19367	P/O	MACGILLIVRAY Ralph Northcliffe	20-03-44	82 OTU
J/89107	P/O	MACHESNEY Gerald Rowland	25-02-44	433 Sqn
R/153082	WO2	MACHUM MiD Donald Blair	29-05-44	82 OTU
J/22602	F/O	MACKAY George Ian	25-03-44	427 Sqn
J/25355	F/L	MACKEIGAN Eion Lloyd	22-01-44	427 Sqn
R/147987	WO2	MACKENZIE Norman Alexander Freeman	27-04-44	49 Sqn
J/35059	F/O	MACKENZIE Samuel Albert	30-08-44	101 Sqn
R/216220	Sgt	MACKEY James Gordon	24-09-44	576 Sqn
J/90349	P/O	MACKIE John Wallace Allan	29-07-44	61 Sqn
R/260780	Sgt	MACKIMMIE Allan Hustead	29-06-44	22 OTU
J/38418	F/O	MACKLAIER Charles Wilbert	4-12-44	166 Sqn
J/26546	F/O	MACLEAN Ian Hector	24-09-44	97 Sqn
J/19971	P/O	MACLEOD Douglas Kenneth	20-02-44	419 Sqn
R/76303	F/S	MACLEOD Gordon Alden	4-10-44	82 OTU
J/22415	F/O	MACLEOD James George	4-01-44	1658 HCU
R/209012	Sgt	MACMILLAN William James	19-04-44	115 Sqn
R/146775	F/S	MADDOCK Frederick Daniel	25-05-44	15 Sqn
J/86422	P/O	MADORE Pierre Joseph Benoit Morel	27-04-44	106 Sqn
J/43513	F/L	MAEDER Paul Allan Cornell	18-12-44	22 OTU
J/10973	F/L	MAFFRE Gerald Frederick	28-04-44	434 Sqn
J/85833	P/O	MAGILL Thomas Eldon	29-07-44	428 Sqn
R/191611	Sgt	MAGOFFIN James Ivan	22-06-44	207 Sqn
R/148733	Sgt	MAGUIRE Edmund Henry Duggan	4-02-44	82 OTU
R/185430	F/S	MAHER Peter James	20-01-44	622 Sqn
J/22594	F/O	MAHONEY John Burke	21-01-44	432 Sqn
J/95352	P/O	MAINPRIZE Harold Kester	6-11-44	101 Sqn
J/58867	P/O	MAJCHROWICZ Frank Robert (served as MACROVIC Frank Robert)	31-03-44	425 Sqn
R/252096	F/S	MALAIDACK Aleck	25-10-44	431 Sqn
J/17107	P/O	MALCOLM Kenneth Bruce	29-01-44	429 Sqn
J/92952	P/O	MALES Charles Harry 'Chuck'	9-10-44	428 Sqn
J/89459	P/O	MALLETTE Joseph Raoul Henri Bernard Clovis	23-05-44	425 Sqn
C/16622	F/O	MALLORY Gordon Ewart	13-06-44	408 Sqn
R/113624	WO2	MALLORY Herbert David	30-04-44	434 Sqn
J/93688	P/O	MALONEY Thomas Joseph	29-12-44	419 Sqn
J/90373	P/O	MALTAIS Francis Giles	19-07-44	50 Sqn
J/89865	P/O	MALYON Douglas Francis	23-04-44	12 Sqn
750	WO2	MALZAN Albert Paul	10-04-44	PFNTU
J/89367	P/O	MANCHIP Francis Walter	30-11-44	429 Sqn
J/94826	P/O	MANCHUL Donald Peter	21-07-44	514 Sqn
J/85595	F/O	MANN DFC Edward James	29-07-44	576 Sqn
J/38736	P/O	MANN Stanley Dickinson	16-07-44	30 OTU
J/92138	P/O	MANN William George	15-10-44	431 Sqn
J/18903	P/O	MANSER William Mason Maxwell	15-02-44	102 Sqn
J/85770	F/O	MANSFIELD DFC Richard Gerard	24-11-44	419 Sqn
J/85487	P/O	MANSON Donald Hendry	6-07-44	582 Sqn
J/89864	P/O	MANSON John George	18-04-44	428 Sqn
J/92365	P/O	MANWELL Robert Gordon	14-10-44	419 Sqn
R/203234	F/S	MARA Joseph Frederick	19-07-44	619 Sqn
R/212967	F/S	MARA Stanley	15-10-44	431 Sqn

ID	Rank	Name	Date	Sqn
J/95393	P/O	MARCELLUS Douglas Loyd	6-12-44	419 Sqn
J/90146	P/O	MARCELLUS Francis Simon	14-07-44	77 Sqn
J/38289	P/O	MARCH Gilbert Horace	18-12-44	432 Sqn
R/193537	Sgt	MARCHINGTON George Frederick	27-06-44	18 OTU
J/27285	F/O	MARDER Moie	30-01-44	101 Sqn
J/25770	F/O	MARK Alfred Rothwell	25-02-44	460 Sqn
R/153059	F/S	MARKS Morris 'Slcok'	22-01-44	630 Sqn
J/95392	F/O	MARLER Norman Gordon	9-11-44	625 Sqn
J/87821	P/O	MARSDEN Arthur Frank	29-07-44	408 Sqn
J/88713	P/O	MARSHALL Lawrence	24-03-44	76 Sqn
R/92517	Sgt	MARSHALL William	4-07-44	24 OTU
R/159991	WO2	MARTEL Joseph Alphonse Leon	29-01-44	576 Sqn
J/90764	P/O	MARTENS Conrad William	29-07-44	100 Sqn
J/27507	F/O	MARTIN Ambrose	26-07-44	432 Sqn
C/782	W/C	MARTIN Arthur Norman	22-01-44	424 Sqn
R/163413	Sgt	MARTIN George	31-01-44	1664 HCU
J/90929	P/O	MARTIN George Bernard	26-07-44	432 Sqn
J/24644	F/O	MARTIN Harry McNaughton	11-04-44	83 Sqn
J/90279	P/O	MARTIN Ivan William	16-03-44	426 Sqn
J/16339	F/O	MARTIN John Livingstone	14-01-44	514 Sqn
R/200158	Sgt	MARTIN Joseph Marcisse Orval	30-07-44	22 OTU
R/182617	Sgt	MARTIN Louis Grover	9-01-44	16 OTU
J/18871	P/O	MARTIN Maurice Allan	16-02-44	432 Sqn
J/89735	P/O	MARTIN Richard Charles	16-06-44	7 Sqn
R/99792	WO1	MARTIN Stanley Douglas	1-11-44	434 Sqn
J/22557	F/L	MARTIN Thomas James	12-09-44	139 Sqn
J/12197	F/O	MARTIN Thomas Russell	9-05-44	432 Sqn
R/176165	F/S	MARTIN Wilfred Bernard	4-05-44	460 Sqn
J/19585	P/O	MARTIN William Henry	29-01-44	431 Sqn
J/88140	P/O	MASON Harry Richard	29-07-44	434 Sqn
J/17624	F/O	MASON DFC James Hubert	1-02-44	1660 HCU
J/23153	F/O	MASON Leonard Eric	23-05-44	57 Sqn
J/89921	P/O	MASSICOTTE George Oswald	17-06-44	431 Sqn
J/92607	P/O	MASSON Joseph Lloyd Clinton	20-05-44	514 Sqn
J/24429	F/O	MATHERLY Jones Monroe [USA]	1-02-44	427 Sqn
J/85929	P/O	MATHESON Alexander McGregor	20-02-44	626 Sqn
R/183751	Sgt	MATHESON Beverley William	14-01-44	1653 HCU
J/88476	P/O	MATHESON Everett Morley	19-07-44	49 Sqn
J/37178	P/O	MATHEWS Arthur George	13-09-44	1658 HCU
R/131915	Sgt	MATKIN Phillip Keith	29-05-44	1666 HCU
J/43053	F/O	MATTHEW Robert Duff	13-10-44	24 OTU
J/17198	F/O	MATTHEWS David Wollaston	30-01-44	22 OTU
J/25198	F/O	MATTHEWS Walter Henry	23-05-44	432 Sqn
R/160410	F/S	MATTIN Leslie Walter	20-01-44	166 Sqn
R/209140	Sgt	MATTLESS William Robert	16-09-44	24 OTU
J/25970	F/L	MAVAUT DFC Paul Raymond Murray	12-09-44	106 Sqn
J/19452	P/O	MAW Arthur Douglas	31-03-44	76 Sqn
J/37480	F/O	MAW Franklin Leonard	23-08-44	20 OTU
J/88628	P/O	MAWHINNEY John Robert	7-06-44	550 Sqn
J/25924	F/O	MAXWELL Austin Vaughan	17-06-44	102 Sqn
J/19401	P/O	MAXWELL Wallace Kingdon	29-01-44	434 Sqn
J/22859	P/O	MAY Alan Edward	6-07-44	424 Sqn
J/86759	P/O	MAY James	20-02-44	12 Sqn
J/88557	P/O	MAYNE Thomas Henry	22-06-44	57 Sqn
J/91171	P/O	MAYOR George William	25-04-44	424 Sqn
R/141896	Sgt	MAYVILLE Joseph Fernard	11-02-44	425 Sqn
J/159249	F/S	McALLISTER Donald James	27-08-44	1661 HCU
J/19854	F/O	McALLISTER Douglas Fraser	17-06-44	434 Sqn
R/128424	WO2	McANEELEY Emmitt Francis	20-02-44	78 Sqn
J/95368	F/O	McARAN Terence Joseph	6-11-44	432 Sqn
J/28898	F/O	McAULAY Martin	14-08-44	44 Sqn
J/23638	F/L	McBAIN DFC Andrew Harold Adelbert	21-08-44	415 Sqn
R/175940	F/S	McBEATH Robert Alexander	25-03-44	427 Sqn
C/87452	P/O	McBRIEN Cecil Howard	29-07-44	431 Sqn
R/194245	Sgt	McCAFFREY Edward William Harold	21-01-44	434 Sqn
J/86046	P/O	McCAFFREY DFC John Harold Alexander	29-07-44	408 Sqn
J/14907	F/L	McCAIG DFC Lelie Neil	20-01-44	426 Sqn
R/214657	Sgt	McCALLUM Arthur Arnold	4-05-44	103 Sqn
R/106339	WO1	McCALLUM John Malcolm	10-04-44	166 Sqn
R/51930	WO1	McCANN Garnet Edward	2-05-44	429 Sqn
R/203261	F/S	McCANN Joseph Maurice Allan	2-11-44	153 Sqn
J/19862	P/O	McCANN Leonard Myles	24-03-44	115 Sqn
J/28883	F/O	McCARTNEY George William	26-08-44	78 Sqn
J/88168	P/O	McCHESNIE Lyle William	12-10-44	166 Sqn
J/21190	F/O	McCLELLAN Robert Bruce	22-01-44	433 Sqn
J/88601	P/O	McCLELLAND James Ronald	28-04-44	102 Sqn
R/107527	WO1	McCLELLAND William Gordon	8-06-44	426 Sqn
J/19845	F/O	McCLINTOCK Patrick Michael	10-12-44	432 Sqn
R/168346	F/S	McCLOSKEY Edward Jerome	5-07-44	576 Sqn
R/87203	WO2	McCLURE James Edward	15-07-44	166 Sqn
R/118907	F/S	McCOLLUM William John	15-07-44	576 Sqn
J/35578	F/O	McCONNELL Norman Edward Henry	11-11-44	619 Sqn
J/88614	P/O	McCORKLE Donald Frederick	3-06-44	158 Sqn
J/88840	F/O	McCORMACK Robert Jamieson	2-11-44	153 Sqn
R/150910	F/S	McCORMICK Kenneth Corbett	4-11-44	626 Sqn
J/95369	P/O	McCOUBREY John Herbert Charles	29-11-44	103 Sqn
J/85104	P/O	McCRAE Donald	28-05-44	550 Sqn
J/91049	P/O	McCREA James Robert	23-04-44	405 Sqn
J/89734	P/O	McCREA Leslie Asa	3-06-44	405 Sqn
J/89471	P/O	McCREARY James Duncan	31-03-44	514 Sqn
R/191097	Sgt	McCRON Samuel Lorne Wilfred	30-11-44	82 OTU
R/202365	Sgt	McCRORY Philip Joseph	23-05-44	90 Sqn
J/35940	F/O	McCULLOUGH David Louis Caskey	6-12-44	424 Sqn
J/37150	F/O	McCUTCHEON William Robert	6-06-44	97 Sqn
J/26645	F/O	McCUTCHION John Alexander	1-07-44	625 Sqn
J/43668	F/O	McDIVITT Keith Oscar	28-12-44	428 Sqn
J/92473	P/O	McDONALD Adam Raeburn	28-12-44	429 Sqn
R/115615	WO2	McDONALD Donald Allan	21-01-44	432 Sqn
R/150801	F/S	McDONALD Harry Thomas	4-01-44	1657 HCU
J/25587	F/O	McDONALD Martin John	13-06-44	408 Sqn
J/23317	F/L	McDONALD Stanley Clayton	4-05-44	405 Sqn
J/22910	F/O	McDONALD William Earl	29-07-44	431 Sqn
J/28550	F/O	McDOUGALL Clarence Francis	29-07-44	408 Sqn
J/87284	F/O	McDOUGALL George	10-05-44	106 Sqn
J/35148	F/O	McDOUGALL Reginald Eugene	22-05-44	460 Sqn
J/85715	P/O	McDOUGALL Ronald Victor	23-04-44	115 Sqn
J/8812	F/L	McDOUGALL DFC* Thom Ross	23-05-44	408 Sqn
J/27407	F/O	McEACHERN Hector Joseph	7-07-44	166 Sqn
C/88589	P/O	McEACHERN Lachlan Neil	29-07-44	434 Sqn
J/90913	P/O	McEACHERN Robert Neil	21-11-44	429 Sqn
J/86482	P/O	McELHERAN John Archibald	13-06-44	432 Sqn
J/90348	P/O	McELROY Lloyd William	29-07-44	415 Sqn
J/88896	P/O	McEVOY DFM Donald Ralph	15-06-44	425 Sqn
J/86800	P/O	McEWAN Ronald Alexander	29-06-44	432 Sqn
J/88350	P/O	McFADDEN Ross John James	29-06-44	77 Sqn
J/88901	P/O	McFEETORS Albert Sydney	14-10-44	428 Sqn
J/95373	P/O	McGEE James	23-12-44	35 Sqn
R/154079	F/S	McGIBBON James Edmund	11-04-44	161 Sqn
J/20908	P/O	McGIBBON Reginald Stewart	29-07-44	576 Sqn
J/5312	F/L	McGILL George Edward	31-03-44	103 Sqn
J/24400	F/O	McGILL Jack Lawrie	24-03-44	166 Sqn
R/210726	Sgt	McGOVERN Joseph Theodore	23-04-44	1659 HCU
R/208585	F/S	McGOWAN John Douglas	29-09-44	576 Sqn
J/15874	F/O	McGOWAN Thomas Campbell	27-05-44	692 Sqn
R/192619	Sgt	McGRATH Anthony William	21-01-44	76 Sqn
C/95172	P/O	McGRAW Anthony Emsley	6-10-44	433 Sqn
J/19304	P/O	McGREGOR Alexander Morvan	19-04-44	432 Sqn
R/258301	F/S	McGREGOR George	30-11-44	429 Sqn
J/95541	P/O	McGREGOR James Bruce	28-12-44	101 Sqn
R/197660	Sgt	McGREGOR Reginald Rothwell	21-03-44	1658 HCU
J/88706	P/O	McGREGOR Robert Edward	20-02-44	434 Sqn

415

ID	Rank	Name	Date	Sqn
J/20233	F/O	McGREGOR Walter Roy	20-01-44	78 Sqn
J/15712	S/L	McGUFFIN DFC William Chester	23-10-44	419 Sqn
J/3716	S/L	McGUGAN Frank Richard	21-04-44	428 Sqn
J/40018	F/O	McGUIGAN Samuel Kellington	12-09-44	1653 HCU
R/213862	Sgt	McGUIGAN William Henry	29-05-44	82 OTU
J/3472	F/L	McGUIRE Michael Kidston	31-08-44	1664 HCU
J/20897	F/O	McGUIRE Patrick Gregory	25-02-44	115 Sqn
J/24741	F/O	McHALE Thomas Patrick	27-11-44	138 Sqn
J/88995	P/O	McHARDY Sidney Alexander Farquharson	15-10-44	10 Sqn
J/25563	F/O	McHENRY James Justin	2-01-44	82 OTU
J/26645	F/O	McHUTCHION John Alexander	1-07-44	625 Sqn
J/88856	P/O	McINNES Jack Ernest	31-03-44	12 Sqn
J/91047	P/O	McINNIS Irvin Neil	18-04-44	433 Sqn
J/86431	F/O	McINTOSH John David	15-02-44	550 Sqn
R/196124	Sgt	McINTYRE Donald Van Norman	31-03-44	101 Sqn
J/88626	P/O	McINTYRE Jack Edwin	13-05-44	426 Sqn
J/22589	F/O	McINTYRE John Alexander	4-05-44	405 Sqn
J/29584	F/O	McINTYRE Lynden Arnold	15-10-44	207 Sqn
J/85615	P/O	McINTYRE Paul Alvin	20-02-44	429 Sqn
J/8169	F/L	McIVER Henry Carbee	13-06-44	408 Sqn
J/11107	F/L	McIVER DFC Malcolm	13-05-44	1655 MTU
J/29531	F/O	McIVOR Clifford Douglas	27-04-44	1667 HCU
J/89043	P/O	McIVOR James	20-02-44	77 Sqn
J/85471	P/O	McIVOR Roderick Austin	28-04-44	419 Sqn
J/92356	P/O	McKAY Harold Lloyd	26-08-44	419 Sqn
R/256266	Sgt	McKAY Harry Whittaker	15-10-44	1664 HCU
R/180114	WO2	McKAY Hugh Robert	20-01-44	7 Sqn
J/86595	P/O	McKAY Robert James	20-01-44	433 Sqn
J/86881	P/O	McKAY Roy Alderson	20-01-44	408 Sqn
R/173301	Sgt	McKENDRY John Allan	23-10-44	625 Sqn
R/188704	Sgt	McKENNA John Andrew	20-01-44	434 Sqn
J/92153	P/O	McKENNA John Leo	22-06-44	630 Sqn
J/89891	P/O	McKENNA Leslie William Joseph	17-06-44	102 Sqn
J/25356	F/O	McKENZIE Alexander Caird	29-01-44	429 Sqn
J/24660	F/O	McKENZIE Daniel Neilson	25-05-44	429 Sqn
J/18887	P/O	McKENZIE James Patrick	20-02-44	427 Sqn
J/86163	P/O	McKENZIE Morris Allan	20-02-44	426 Sqn
J/19969	P/O	McKEOWN Victor Herbert	29-01-44	434 Sqn
J/36019	P/O	McKERRY David Anthony Gregory	20-02-44	431 Sqn
J/26386	P/O	McKIE Donald Galloway Watt	29-05-44	82 OTU
J/24037	F/O	McKILLOP Norman Colin	12-09-44	408 Sqn
J/88558	P/O	McKIM Joseph Arthur	21-07-44	90 Sqn
J/28236	F/O	McKINLEY Curtis David	24-01-44	14 OTU
J/89964	P/O	McKINNEY Robert Francis	31-07-44	9 Sqn
R/2296A	F/S	McKINNON Ian	26-11-44	115 Sqn
J/27633	F/O	McKINNON John Lockwood	2-05-44	1659 HCU
R/62951	Sgt	McKINNON John Ronald	19-05-44	82 OTU
J/92133	P/O	McLAUGHLIN Burton	27-08-44	630 Sqn
J/88621	P/O	McLAUGHLIN George	19-07-44	61 Sqn
J/89163	F/O	McLAUGHLIN Kenneth Alexander	23-09-44	106 Sqn
R/205353	F/S	McLAURIN George Fraser	8-07-44	50 Sqn
J/26324	F/O	McLAY John Milton	28-04-44	432 Sqn
J/95366	P/O	McLEA John Alexander	1-11-44	426 Sqn
J/89689	P/O	McLEAN Archibald Stewart	12-09-44	50 Sqn
R/214452	Sgt	McLEAN Douglas	31-08-44	22 OTU
J/90928	P/O	McLEAN Leslie	5-07-44	460 Sqn
J/86361	P/O	McLEAR Maurice	8-06-44	78 Sqn
R/200655	Sgt	McLELLAN Gordon Keith	15-05-44	82 OTU
J/24650	F/O	McLEOD Alexander Corbett	10-04-44	207 Sqn
J/95367	P/O	McLEOD Allister Currie	1-11-44	426 Sqn
J/87657	P/O	McLEOD Donald George	31-01-44	1664 HCU
J/90934	P/O	McLEOD Hugh Norman	16-09-44	432 Sqn
R/151652	F/S	McLEOD John Malcolm	14-08-44	44 Sqn
R/108649	WO1	McLEOD John Pickles Shaw	21-01-44	431 Sqn
J/7587	F/L	McLEOD Robert Donald	13-09-44	1658 HCU
J/14630	F/O	McLEOD Roy	12-05-44	103 Sqn
J/86882	P/O	McMANUS John Francis	27-01-44	408 Sqn
R/179312	Sgt	McMANUS Rodney Lewis	14-01-44	576 Sqn
J/19923	P/O	McMASTER James Gordon	16-05-44	419 Sqn
J/89943	P/O	McMEEKAN William James	25-03-44	630 Sqn
J/14499	F/O	McMEHEN Robert John	21-01-44	433 Sqn
R/142111	F/S	McMILLAN Clarence Orville	1-07-44	625 Sqn
R/143734	WO2	McMILLAN Roderick	13-06-44	15 Sqn
J/36038	F/O	McMULLEN Douglas James	13-06-44	419 Sqn
J/25893	F/O	McMURCHY Lorne Sinclair	22-06-44	9 Sqn
R/273057	Sgt	McMURTRIE James Crawford	26-08-44	83 OTU
R/250838	Sgt	McMURTRY Allan Fairbairn	12-12-44	1664 HCU
J/89656	P/O	McNABB Robert Hudson	27-08-44	57 Sqn
J/88571	P/O	McNALLY Allan Frank	17-09-44	617 Sqn
J/29858	F/O	McNAMARA Paul Edwin	1-09-44	138 Sqn
J/85395	P/O	McNARY John Crawford	2-05-44	419 Sqn
R/167091	F/S	McNAY Irvin Robert	31-03-44	101 Sqn
R/178854	F/S	McNEIL Robert Willard	25-03-44	78 Sqn
J/25785	F/O	McNEILL Andrew	14-10-44	166 Sqn
J/9201	W/C	McNEILL DFC John Gordon	21-08-44	415 Sqn
J/89407	P/O	McNEILL John Joseph	15-03-44	514 Sqn
J/28557	F/O	McORMOND Charles Robert	13-06-44	419 Sqn
J/93391	F/O	McPHEE Verne Alexander	30-09-44	426 Sqn
J/12340	F/O	McPHEE Walter Norval	31-03-44	427 Sqn
J/90243	P/O	McPHERSON Donald Clifford	17-06-44	431 Sqn
J/90244	P/O	McPHERSON Joseph Maxwell	17-06-44	431 Sqn
J/89285	P/O	McPHERSON Murray Langtry	25-04-44	626 Sqn
J/22449	F/O	McPHERSON William Hugh	15-02-44	434 Sqn
C/91135	P/O	McQUEEN Francis Edmund	17-06-44	426 Sqn
J/19843	F/O	McQUEEN William Melvin	17-06-44	434 Sqn
J/86303	P/O	McRAE Donald Wayne	21-06-44	15 Sqn
J/36381	F/O	McROBB James Keith	29-07-44	427 Sqn
J/14015	S/L	McROBIE Ian Mackenzie	13-06-44	426 Sqn
J/17664	F/L	McSORLEY DFC Bernard Francis [USA]	25-01-44	PFNTU
J/14575	F/O	McTAVISH Archibald Stewart	7-08-44	1664 HCU
J/29220	F/O	McVICAR Reginald Archibald	29-12-44	419 Sqn
J/89887	P/O	McWADE John Robert	1-06-44	149 Sqn
R/262057	Sgt	McWHIRTER Gordon Russell	12-10-44	166 Sqn
J/92159	P/O	McWILLIAM Walter Alexander	6-10-44	7 Sqn
J/7760	F/L	MEAD Robert Frazer [USA]	9-05-44	431 Sqn
R/173960	Sgt	MECHEFSKE Thomas Wilfred	10-04-44	24 OTU
R/206095	F/S	MEDDICK William Ralph	11-06-44	166 Sqn
J/23727	F/O	MEDHURST Reginald Chester Pelham	13-06-44	158 Sqn
R/155027	F/S	MEEK Robert Alexander	28-04-44	434 Sqn
R/159216	Sgt	MEIN Howard Leighton	3-02-44	84 OTU
J/25768	F/O	MELLANDER Ernest William Terence	25-03-44	61 Sqn
J/21183	F/O	MELNICK Nicholas	11-04-44	49 Sqn
J/18235	F/O	MELVILLE Robert Bruce	31-08-44	166 Sqn
R/195958	F/S	MELVILLE Robert Learmonth	17-11-44	24 OTU
J/24256	F/O	MENNIE Oliver Hanton	21-07-44	415 Sqn
J/86541	F/O	MENZIES Howard John	28-05-44	432 Sqn
J/20186	F/O	MERCER Angus Cameron Graeme	19-04-44	432 Sqn
J/38814	F/O	MEREDITH Frederick Leonard	4-12-44	619 Sqn
J/23905	F/O	MERRALL William Robert	16-05-44	625 Sqn
J/29679	F/O	MERRICK Peter William	8-08-44	419 Sqn
J/90073	P/O	MERRITT Cecil Glen	29-07-44	426 Sqn
J/85569	F/O	MERRITT John Percival	31-03-44	622 Sqn
J/87568	P/O	METKA Joseph	26-02-44	102 Sqn
J/5666	S/L	METZLER Harry Warren	31-03-44	424 Sqn
J/88912	P/O	MEYER Lawrence Marius	19-04-44	640 Sqn
J/39015	F/O	MICHALEC John	17-07-44	23 OTU
J/86653	P/O	MICHELL James Lloyd [USA]	25-05-44	429 Sqn
J/86258	P/O	MICHIE Ernest Wilberforce	4-05-44	420 Sqn
R/155997	WO2	MIDDLEMAS Robert James	24-03-44	578 Sqn
J/19034	F/O	MIDDLEMISS DFC Kenneth Robert	14-01-44	12 Sqn
J/23416	F/O	MILBURN Philip Giles	23-04-44	550 Sqn
J/24549	F/O	MILDON Albert Harry	18-03-44	427 Sqn

ID	Rank	Name	Date	Unit
J/28979	F/O	MILES Gordon Ralph	29-07-44	431 Sqn
J/22210	F/O	MILES Vernon Lindsay	29-01-44	10 Sqn
C/6073	P/O	MILLEN Harry Charles	20-03-44	82 OTU
R/143441	F/S	MILLER Alfred Stephen	12-02-44	419 Sqn
J/90050	P/O	MILLER Douglas John	29-07-44	431 Sqn
J/27127	F/O	MILLER Harry James	15-02-44	166 Sqn
R/193144	F/S	MILLER Joseph Mactavish	25-07-44	35 Sqn
J/88256	P/O	MILLER Kenneth Roland	29-07-44	431 Sqn
R/206456	Sgt	MILLER Owen	5-07-44	82 OTU
J/90051	P/O	MILLER Robert Joseph	29-07-44	431 Sqn
J/38112	F/O	MILLER William Cosgrave	31-08-44	22 OTU
J/10425	F/L	MILLIKEN Peter Scott	23-06-44	76 Sqn
J/26745	F/O	MILLMAN Thomas Ralph Bernard	11-05-44	424 Sqn
J/40214	F/O	MILLS Aubrey Melville [USA]	29-07-44	431 Sqn
J/20969	F/O	MILLS Frederick Henry	18-04-44	427 Sqn
R/199345	Sgt	MILNE Frank Alexander	16-05-44	419 Sqn
J/89413	P/O	MILNE John Joseph	12-09-44	207 Sqn
C/88331	P/O	MILNER Evan	29-01-44	419 Sqn
J/86366	F/O	MILNER William Arthur	26-08-44	419 Sqn
J/85866	F/O	MILWARD Leo Victor	31-03-44	433 Sqn
R/189979	Sgt	MINETT Mike	26-02-44	419 Sqn
R/222600	Sgt	MIREAULT Joseph Francis	22-06-44	207 Sqn
J/27721	F/O	MITCHELL Charles Joseph	29-07-44	103 Sqn
R/221524	Sgt	MITCHELL George Donald	25-01-44	16 OTU
R/258551	Sgt	MITCHELL George Willston	28-05-44	30 OTU
R/121261	Sgt	MITCHELL James Walton	21-08-44	415 Sqn
J/18424	F/L	MITCHELL DFC John Maxfield	7-05-44	405 Sqn
R/127883	F/S	MITCHELL Percy Lawrence	31-03-44	425 Sqn
J/92367	P/O	MITCHELL Peter John Felix	23-10-44	429 Sqn
J/86673	P/O	MITCHELL Rex Harris	29-07-44	408 Sqn
C/2106	F/O	MITCHELL William Wilkins	23-05-44	419 Sqn
J/88479	P/O	MOFFAT Archibald Douglas	24-07-44	1666 HCU
R/138175	WO2	MOFFAT Frank Reagh	20-01-44	78 Sqn
J/92010	F/O	MOFFAT James Agnew 'Donald'	27-04-44	106 Sqn
R/206348	F/S	MOFFAT John Winning	16-08-44	433 Sqn
R/208460	Sgt	MOFFAT William Howard	8-06-44	138 Sqn
J/24555	P/O	MOFFIT Francis Wilfred	17-08-44	420 Sqn
R/155573	WO2	MOGALKI Roy Edwards	31-03-44	76 Sqn
R/166138	WO2	MOHLER Otis Judson [USA]	28-05-44	420 Sqn
J/27960	F/O	MOHRING William James	20-03-44	82 OTU
J/92035	P/O	MOLLER Halvar Leo Fred	8-06-44	115 Sqn
J/28476	F/O	MOLLOY Robert	23-10-44	419 Sqn
J/88858	P/O	MOLZAN Otto	4-05-44	626 Sqn
J/86527	P/O	MONAGHAN Richard John Joseph	4-05-44	420 Sqn
J/85942	P/O	MONCRIEFF Harry Reginald	23-05-44	166 Sqn
J/26848	F/O	MONK Ernest Wellington	25-07-44	420 Sqn
J/17208	F/L	MONNIER Henry Charles	18-07-44	158 Sqn
J/28240	F/O	MONTGOMERY Frank Charles	21-07-44	622 Sqn
R/131045	WO1	MONTGOMERY DFC Ralph Joseph	7-05-44	405 Sqn
J/87165	P/O	MOODY Roy William	21-02-44	427 Sqn
J/91139	P/O	MOONEY Richard Edmond	16-11-44	214 Sqn
J/89868	P/O	MOORBY Arthur Robert	17-06-44	434 Sqn
R/201026	Sgt	MOORCROFT Robert Harold	8-09-44	14 OTU
J/88859	P/O	MOORE Arthur Bryson	4-05-44	460 Sqn
R/197236	F/S	MOORE George Edwin	29-06-44	405 Sqn
J/23943	F/O	MOORE James Lambert	13-05-44	419 Sqn
R/254210	F/S	MOORE Lorne Joseph	23-10-44	429 Sqn
J/87131	P/O	MOORE Norman Erick	17-06-44	434 Sqn
R/124087	WO1	MOORE Robert Kirk	11-07-44	1666 HCU
J/26395	F/O	MOORE Walter Norman	6-11-44	101 Sqn
R/195753	F/S	MOORE Walter Raymond	5-07-44	57 Sqn
J/92130	P/O	MORAN Ted James	20-02-44	207 Sqn
J/38717	F/O	MORAN Walter Franklin	4-11-44	101 Sqn
J/90382	P/O	MORE Donald	5-07-44	424 Sqn
R/182168	F/S	MOREAU Bruce Edward	11-12-44	57 Sqn
P/2508	Sgt	MOREAU Joseph Laurent	30-07-44	22 OTU
R/195667	F/S	MOREY James Kenneth	4-05-44	57 Sqn
R/210350	F/S	MORFOOT Lorne Albert	24-07-44	625 Sqn
J/86659	P/O	MORGAN Albert John	13-06-44	434 Sqn
R/76725	Sgt	MORGAN Gwynfryn	7-08-44	1664 HCU
J/19828	F/O	MORGAN James Cuthbert	17-09-44	424 Sqn
J/25000	F/L	MORGAN John Archibald Wynn	16-08-44	433 Sqn
R/57681	Sgt	MORGAN John Robert	20-01-44	434 Sqn
C/10005	F/O	MORGAN Lancelot Eric [Australia]	23-05-44	408 Sqn
R/191341	F/S	MORGAN William George Eaton	29-12-44	419 Sqn
J/26211	F/O	MORIARTY Daniel [USA]	4-05-44	625 Sqn
J/95084	P/O	MORIN Thomas George	9-10-44	76 Sqn
J/38276	F/O	MORLEY Frank Kenneth	27-08-44	166 Sqn
J/12682	F/O	MOROZ Hrykory	22-03-44	408 Sqn
J/89461	P/O	MORRILL Warren Arthur	16-06-44	405 Sqn
J/90364	P/O	MORRIS Frederick William	25-04-44	192 Sqn
R/278665	Sgt	MORRIS Gladstone Clifford	30-11-44	82 OTU
R/106875	Sgt	MORRIS Lawrence Edward	23-05-44	429 Sqn
J/88860	P/O	MORRIS Thomas Harrison	27-04-44	49 Sqn
R/129847	WO2	MORRIS William Penri	21-01-44	550 Sqn
J/28801	F/O	MORRISON Alexander John	13-05-44	103 Sqn
R/133023	F/S	MORRISON Archibald Frew	29-11-44	153 Sqn
R/161244	Sgt	MORRISON Bruce Ralph	21-01-44	405 Sqn
J/19398	F/O	MORRISON Donald	17-06-44	419 Sqn
J/28151	F/O	MORRISON Dugald	29-07-44	415 Sqn
J/21181	F/O	MORRISON Ewart Laverne	19-07-44	619 Sqn
J/14802	F/O	MORRISON Frederick William	1-05-44	420 Sqn
J/28857	P/O	MORRISON Hugh Allan	8-06-44	431 Sqn
R/140271	WO2	MORRISON Hugh Patrick	5-01-44	431 Sqn
R/213960	F/S	MORRISON John Duncan	24-08-44	1652 HCU
J/23207	F/O	MORRISON John Houseal	6-07-44	424 Sqn
J/89924	P/O	MORRISON Martin	22-06-44	619 Sqn
R/85943	P/O	MORRISON Oscar Langdon	20-02-44	429 Sqn
R/121748	Sgt	MORRISON Richard Cecil	21-08-44	415 Sqn
J/27396	F/O	MORRISON William Robinson	18-07-44	158 Sqn
J/90381	P/O	MORRISS John Howard	21-07-44	9 Sqn
J/88110	P/O	MORRITT John Beswick	23-05-44	626 Sqn
J/28294	F/O	MORROW Hugh Francis	17-06-44	434 Sqn
J/26642	F/O	MORROW William Clifford	29-07-44	405 Sqn
J/35773	P/O	MORTIMER George Alexander	4-11-44	195 Sqn
J/24033	F/O	MORTIMER Leslie Lloyd	25-04-44	192 Sqn
J/92620	P/O	MORTON Frank Ernest	27-08-44	115 Sqn
J/88266	P/O	MORTON John Donald	29-07-44	90 Sqn
J/95445	P/O	MORTON Milton Robert	2-11-44	415 Sqn
J/8773	S/L	MOSELEY-WILLIAMS DFC Walter Read	5-10-44	427 Sqn
J/28603	F/O	MOSS Claude Alexander 'Bud'	5-07-44	427 Sqn
J/35065	F/O	MOSS Kenneth Lionel	26-07-44	432 Sqn
J/86439	P/O	MOSS William Victor	15-03-44	550 Sqn
R/157271	WO2	MOTRIUK Stanley Arcadie	8-07-44	50 Sqn
J/85366	P/O	MOUCHET Maurice Rene Nicolas	31-03-44	12 Sqn
R/176899	Sgt	MOULAND Hubert James	3-01-44	408 Sqn
R/143768	F/S	MOULD Gordon Charles	20-01-44	434 Sqn
R/252874	Sgt	MOVOLD Ronald Loughton	14-07-44	433 Sqn
J/90227	P/O	MOXLEY Wilbur Lee	12-09-44	207 Sqn
J/25703	F/O	MOXON Fred Henry	1-07-44	12 Sqn
J/85719	P/O	MUDFORD Vernon	9-05-44	426 Sqn
J/19122	F/O	MUIR Alexander Jamieson	12-05-44	626 Sqn
J/41650	F/O	MUIR John Francis	2-10-44	19 OTU
J/87026	F/O	MUIR Norman Charles	23-10-44	429 Sqn
R/160427	F/S	MUISINER Homer Leroy [USA]	15-04-44	1664 HCU
R/192035	Sgt	MULLEN Albert Lorne	31-01-44	1664 HCU
J/23369	F/O	MULLIGAN George Harold	6-02-44	149 Sqn
R/195834	Sgt	MULLIGAN John	19-04-44	75 Sqn
R/184306	Sgt	MULLIGAN Maurice Gregory	22-01-44	78 Sqn
R/126356	F/S	MULLIN David Sinclair	14-01-44	44 Sqn
J/36947	F/O	MULLIN Gordon Joseph	1-11-44	426 Sqn
J/87245	F/O	MULLIN William Dakin	8-06-44	431 Sqn
R/191400	Sgt	MULLINS Patrick Charles Henry	16-07-44	30 OTU
J/23755	F/O	MUNNERY Norman George Peter	31-03-44	158 Sqn
J/88604	P/O	MUNRO Alexander Milton George	26-02-44	431 Sqn

ID	Rank	Name	Date	Unit
J/24218	F/O	MUNRO George Edmund	31-03-44	425 Sqn
R/150829	WO2	MUNRO Gordon Chapman	21-01-44	1661 HCU
J/36591	F/O	MUNRO James Cameron	17-12-44	101 Sqn
J/94490	P/O	MUNSON David Olaf	25-06-44	149 Sqn
R/116943	WO1	MURDIE Willis Don	5-08-44	86 OTU
J/87750	P/O	MURDOCH Thomas Graham	29-07-44	428 Sqn
J/88711	P/O	MURDOCK Billie Herman	22-03-44	432 Sqn
R/122292	WO1	MURIE James Malcolm	14-07-44	433 Sqn
J/86671	P/O	MURPHY Arthur John	25-05-44	429 Sqn
R/176578	F/S	MURPHY David Matthew	25-07-44	619 Sqn
R/132905	F/S	MURPHY Gerald Francis	2-07-44	1667 HCU
J/36941	F/O	MURPHY Gerald William	9-10-44	419 Sqn
J/36596	F/O	MURPHY Gordon Reginald	29-07-44	514 Sqn
R/151486	WO2	MURPHY Harry Frederick	13-06-44	408 Sqn
J/86753	P/O	MURPHY Henry Arthur	13-08-44	428 Sqn
J/88257	P/O	MURPHY John Francis	29-07-44	434 Sqn
R/201446	F/S	MURPHY John Joseph [USA]	24-11-44	419 Sqn
J/28035	F/O	MURPHY Joseph Arthur	13-06-44	427 Sqn
J/95450	P/O	MURPHY Joseph Harold Michael	29-11-44	128 Sqn
J/26699	F/O	MURPHY Kevin James	8-05-44	138 Sqn
J/92460	P/O	MURPHY Robert Wakely David	1-11-44	434 Sqn
J/22084	F/O	MURPHY William	25-04-44	420 Sqn
J/28935	F/L	MURPHY William Joseph Bernard	16-07-44	467 Sqn
J/15249	F/O	MURRAY Charles Leonard	20-02-44	434 Sqn
J/87658	F/O	MURRAY Clifford Battison	20-02-44	429 Sqn
J/87907	P/O	MURRAY Donald	8-08-44	429 Sqn
J/86896	P/O	MURRAY Frederic Graham	17-05-44	1661 HCU
R/176790	F/S	MURRAY James Lowther	23-08-44	24 OTU
J/12285	F/O	MURRAY John Frank Gordon	13-08-44	427 Sqn
J/86549	P/O	MURRAY John Kay	17-06-44	550 Sqn
J/90052	P/O	MURRAY Kenneth James	29-07-44	431 Sqn
R/175338	F/S	MURRAY Morris Campbell	6-06-44	76 Sqn
J/90358	P/O	MURRAY Jnr William Arnold	29-07-44	425 Sqn
J/93541	P/O	MURRELL William James	5-12-44	426 Sqn
J/88134	P/O	MUSGRAVE Philip Arthur	17-08-44	405 Sqn
J/26289	F/O	MUSKETT George Lindley	29-02-44	1666 HCU
J/19898	P/O	MUSSER John Vernon	29-06-44	432 Sqn
R/114903	WO1	MYDASKI Stanley	15-03-44	427 Sqn
R/157603	WO2	MYERS Theodore Wesley	2-01-44	44 Sqn
J/87544	P/O	MYNARSKI VC Andrew Charles	13-06-44	419 Sqn
J/94453	P/O	MYRON Ian Thomas	5-12-44	426 Sqn
J/37887	P/O	NAFZIGER John Alden	28-10-44	419 Sqn
J/27584	F/O	NAHU Norman Gilbert	28-05-44	427 Sqn
J/89037	P/O	NAIRN Ross Bell	26-08-44	405 Sqn
J/87636	P/O	NARUM Chester Russell	31-03-44	432 Sqn
J/92151	P/O	NAUGLER Gerald Melbourne	23-05-44	630 Sqn
J/27731	F/O	NAZAR Peter	25-05-44	429 Sqn
R/191412	LAC	NAZARKO Walter	28-11-44	61 Base
J/27480	F/O	NEAL John Mason	24-07-44	50 Sqn
J/22062	F/O	NEGRICH Tony	30-06-44	51 Sqn
J/24170	F/O	NEILSON Donald Fullerton [Argentina]	17-06-44	550 Sqn
J/26969	F/L	NELLIGAN Allan Neil	28-10-44	419 Sqn
R/213165	Sgt	NELSON Gordon Howard	28-05-44	1659 HCU
R/170588	F/S	NELSON Joseph Lyle	25-07-44	50 Sqn
J/95449	P/O	NELSON Lloyd William	9-11-44	138 Sqn
R/219944	F/S	NELSON Morley Francis	12-09-44	576 Sqn
J/22624	F/O	NELSON Orvin Kenneth	21-02-44	102 Sqn
J/94226	P/O	NELSON Richard Keary	29-07-44	427 Sqn
J/93997	P/O	NELSON Vincent Emerald	2-11-44	415 Sqn
J/92280	P/O	NEUFELD Edmund	23-10-44	419 Sqn
R/220181	Sgt	NEUMANN Elmer John	17-10-44	1664 HCU
J/26305	F/O	NEVILLE Clifford Gerald	3-06-44	166 Sqn
J/92282	P/O	NEVILLE Robert Thomas	23-10-44	419 Sqn
J/89875	P/O	NEVIN Arthur Francis	13-08-44	61 Sqn
J/24146	F/O	NEVINS John Edmund	11-02-44	158 Sqn
J/35848	P/O	NEWLAND Edward Roy	17-12-44	61 Sqn
R/103037	F/S	NEWTON Oscar Frederick	26-12-44	76 Sqn
R/104146	Sgt	NICHOLS Frederick Arthur	30-01-44	22 OTU
J/18917	P/O	NICKERSON Roland Otis	22-01-44	427 Sqn
J/29618	F/O	NICKLE Russell Karl	28-12-44	419 Sqn
R/139309	WO2	NICOL Albert William	7-02-44	427 Sqn
J/21172	P/O	NICOLSON Ian Hay	15-03-44	7 Sqn
J/89922	P/O	NILES Robert Eugene	17-06-44	426 Sqn
J/94232	P/O	NIMMO Robert Floyd	30-11-44	429 Sqn
J/24535	F/O	NIXON George Franklyn [USA]	3-01-44	57 Sqn
R/175117	F/S	NIXON Harry William	25-03-44	625 Sqn
J/91096	P/O	NIXON Jack Elwin McIntosh	21-07-44	101 Sqn
R/163357	Sgt	NIXON John Leonard	29-02-44	420 Sqn
R/163358	Sgt	NIXON John William	10-04-44	635 Sqn
J/87968	P/O	NOBLE Archibald Thomas	26-05-44	5 LFS
R/193856	F/S	NOBLE George	4-10-44	82 OTU
R/178847	F/S	NOBLE Gordon Harvey	13-09-44	1658 HCU
J/29704	P/O	NOBLE James Albert [USA]	24-09-44	156 Sqn
R/82062	WO2	NOLAN Thomas Harold	3-01-44	405 Sqn
J/90959	P/O	NOONAN Joseph Wilfrid Raymond	29-07-44	425 Sqn
R/149600	F/S	NORDBYE DFM Gordon Leo	8-06-44	166 Sqn
J/26606	F/O	NORDHEIMER Kenneth Albert	17-08-44	405 Sqn
J/89232	P/O	NOREJKO Stephen Lawrence	6-12-44	429 Sqn
R/187486	F/S	NOREN Peter Oliver Kenneth	8-07-44	50 Sqn
J/89120	P/O	NORGAARD John [Denmark]	15-03-44	77 Sqn
R/109152	Sgt	NORMAN Richard Robert	8-06-44	1666 HCU
J/110699	WO1	NORMANDEAU Alphonse Jean-Paul	16-03-44	1664 HCU
R/205216	Sgt	NORMANDEAU Paul Emery	20-08-44	22 OTU
J/27320	F/O	NORMANDIN Alexander James	30-01-44	625 Sqn
J/86645	P/O	NORRIS Donald Mitchell	8-06-44	622 Sqn
J/14566	F/L	NORTHERN DFC Edward	1-05-44	420 Sqn
J/26934	F/O	NORTON Donald Blair	8-06-44	420 Sqn
J/25738	F/O	NOVA Andrew	14-01-44	1653 HCU
J/90310	P/O	NOVACK Nicholas	29-07-44	420 Sqn
J/87120	P/O	NOWLAN Joseph Henry Yvon	11-06-44	434 Sqn
R/159134	WO2	OAKES Fred Glen	21-07-44	15 Sqn
R/190931	Sgt	OAKLEY Ernest James	14-01-44	514 Sqn
J/90421	P/O	OBRIGHT Vernon Patrick	17-06-44	431 Sqn
J/85342	P/O	OCHSNER Robert Duncan	13-06-44	408 Sqn
J/38163	F/O	ODDAN Harold Engman	13-05-44	419 Sqn
J/95168	P/O	ODELL Donald Carr	8-09-44	115 Sqn
R/269308	Sgt	ODOBAS Keith Earl	15-10-44	432 Sqn
R/134373	F/S	OFFER Lloyd	3-01-44	426 Sqn
J/22214	F/O	OGILVIE James McVie	3-01-44	100 Sqn
J/94475	P/O	OGILVIE Scott McCrury	30-11-44	429 Sqn
R/192540	WO2	OLAFSEN Gordon William	18-12-44	434 Sqn
J/36316	F/O	OLIPHANT George Scott	15-05-44	82 OTU
J/89469	P/O	OLIVER John	20-02-44	433 Sqn
J/22436	F/O	OLIVER Melvin Robert	3-05-44	550 Sqn
J/28500	F/O	OLIVER Michael Richard Frewin	29-07-44	103 Sqn
J/88087	P/O	OLIVER William Robert	23-04-44	405 Sqn
J/22702	F/O	OLLETT Ralph William	13-05-44	640 Sqn
R/170661	WO2	OLLINGER John Joseph	21-07-44	51 Sqn
R/213888	Sgt	OLMSTEAD Leslie John	17-10-44	19 OTU
R/186395	F/S	OLMSTED Wilfred Jamieson	18-04-44	428 Sqn
R/175903	F/S	OLSEN George Orlando	13-07-44	103 Sqn
J/19280	P/O	OLSSON Alan Ludvig	26-03-44	426 Sqn
J/18387	F/O	OLSVIK David Osborne	20-02-44	427 Sqn
R/187451	F/S	OMOE Francis Melvin	15-07-44	166 Sqn
R/208669	Sgt	OPIE Glenn Edward	4-10-44	82 OTU
J/37160	P/O	ORCHARD Anthony Brian	2-11-44	415 Sqn
J/89072	P/O	ORR Hubert Francis	31-03-44	426 Sqn
J/95460	P/O	ORR Melvin Osborne	29-11-44	103 Sqn
J/19009	P/O	ORR Robert James	20-01-44	426 Sqn
R/192788	F/S	ORROCK Robert Clifford	17-10-44	24 OTU
R/178725	F/S	OSADCHY William	21-07-44	101 Sqn
J/40491	F/O	OSBORN James Edward	19-11-44	1666 HCU
R/154657	Sgt	OSBORNE Clyde Roswell	24-08-44	1652 HCU
R/181989	Sgt	OSWALD Henry Christian	26-02-44	420 Sqn

Service No.	Rank	Name	Date	Sqn
R/92633	P/O	OUELLETTE Louis Alexander	9-11-44	138 Sqn
J/90386	P/O	OUIMET Joseph Albert Bastien	9-05-44	431 Sqn
R/165026	WO2	OVEREND Gerald Joseph	28-05-44	166 Sqn
R/197141	Sgt	OVERHOLT James Henry	16-03-44	630 Sqn
R/270919	Sgt	OVERLAND John Sven	12-12-44	1664 HCU
R/138002	WO2	OWEN John David	25-03-44	625 Sqn
J/27123	F/O	OWEN Ludey Keshishian	25-06-44	149 Sqn
J/90248	P/O	OWEN Thomas Bruce	29-07-44	432 Sqn
J/86412	P/O	OWENS John Charles	24-03-44	102 Sqn
R/181436	F/S	OZEROFF William Wayne	1-07-44	100 Sqn
J/23895	F/O	O'BRIEN Charles Edward	31-03-44	640 Sqn
J/86201	P/O	O'BRIEN Daniel John	22-03-44	432 Sqn
J/26652	F/O	O'BRIEN Lawrence Francis	5-07-44	424 Sqn
R/203907	F/S	O'CONNELL George Francis Leo	22-06-44	106 Sqn
J/92329	P/O	O'CONNELL Jnr John Carlos	13-05-44	419 Sqn
R/145478	F/S	O'CONNOR Charles Joseph	8-07-44	50 Sqn
J/35008	F/O	O'DONNELL Cecil Frederick [USA]	17-08-44	431 Sqn
J/39724	F/O	O'DONNELL Joseph Norman	19-11-44	1666 HCU
J/19976	P/O	O'DOWDA John Frederick	15-03-44	51 Sqn
R/255038	F/S	O'HARA Leo Francis	9-10-44	419 Sqn
J/26856	F/O	O'HEARE Robert Ernest	18-03-44	427 Sqn
R/160321	F/S	O'LEARY Patrick William	30-08-44	467 Sqn
J/88853	P/O	O'NEIL Grant Murray	30-01-44	405 Sqn
J/22026	F/L	O'NEIL Harold Douglas	6-12-44	429 Sqn
J/87299	P/O	O'NEILL Charles James Erskine	4-05-44	582 Sqn
R/161795	F/S	O'NEILL Edward Lawrence	9-06-44	44 Sqn
J/22703	F/O	O'NEILL Lawrence William	22-01-44	102 Sqn
J/22338	F/O	PADDISON Harold Douglas	20-01-44	429 Sqn
J/14176	F/O	PADGET Richard Elwood	16-02-44	77 Sqn
J/95462	P/O	PAGE Donald Nelson	15-11-44	115 Sqn
J/35427	F/O	PAGE Ernest William	28-12-44	428 Sqn
J/25590	F/O	PAIGE James Willard	23-05-44	97 Sqn
R/161143	WO2	PAIGE John Osborne	3-06-44	76 Sqn
J/14572	F/O	PALIN George Stapleford	3-01-44	103 Sqn
J/15818	W/C	PALMER DFC Charles William	26-09-44	405 Sqn
J/19660	F/O	PALMER Freeman Henry	29-01-44	419 Sqn
J/92063	P/O	PALMER William Frederick	15-10-44	626 Sqn
J/35086	F/O	PALSEN George Joseph Herman	10-04-44	24 OTU
J/90360	P/O	PANTON Charles Lawrence	20-03-44	192 Sqn
J/88855	P/O	PAPINEAU Joseph Paul	25-03-44	427 Sqn
J/87800	P/O	PAPPAJOHN Anthony Peter	4-05-44	166 Sqn
J/22094	F/O	PAQUIN Felix Frederic Florent	31-03-44	424 Sqn
R/62838	F/S	PARADIS Joseph Maurice	18-12-44	425 Sqn
R/108209	LAC	PARANT Joseph Jean Eugene Guy	27-03-44	425 Sqn
J/92716	P/O	PARE Gerrard Leo	30-11-44	429 Sqn
J/86322	P/O	PARE Joseph Alphonse Normand	22-03-44	408 Sqn
J/18806	P/O	PARISE Joseph Paul David	27-01-44	408 Sqn
J/35145	F/O	PARK Arthur Morton	16-10-44	431 Sqn
J/91134	P/O	PARK Edwin Earle Fairgrieve	9-05-44	426 Sqn
J/85817	P/O	PARK William Arnold	27-01-44	426 Sqn
J/12043	F/L	PARKE William Kelvin	28-12-44	101 Sqn
J/19436	P/O	PARKER Andrew Smith	14-01-44	405 Sqn
J/41997	F/O	PARKER Bruce Alexander	12-12-44	635 Sqn
J/17923	F/O	PARKER DFM Donald George Frederick	26-05-44	22 OTU
J/26120	F/O	PARKER Douglas Rendall	9-06-44	426 Sqn
J/85528	P/O	PARKER George	15-03-44	408 Sqn
J/28688	F/O	PARKER Gordon Hewlett	28-04-44	432 Sqn
J/25943	F/O	PARKER Gordon Howard	24-07-44	50 Sqn
J/19583	P/O	PARKER John Allen	15-02-44	419 Sqn
J/88092	P/O	PARKER Robert Carlton	9-06-44	426 Sqn
J/24930	F/O	PARKINSON William Henry	9-05-44	432 Sqn
J/21253	F/L	PARROTT James Murray	18-12-44	434 Sqn
J/19584	P/O	PARROTT Victor	20-01-44	76 Sqn
J/26844	F/O	PARRY Richard Charles	16-02-44	619 Sqn
R/135211	WO2	PARSLEY William Alfred	21-01-44	97 Sqn
J/92330	P/O	PARSONS Ernest Moir	16-05-44	419 Sqn
J/90294	P/O	PARSONS Gordon	13-06-44	427 Sqn
R/110593	Sgt	PARSONS Owen	14-10-44	434 Sqn
J/29191	F/O	PARSONS Reginald	29-07-44	428 Sqn
J/23971	F/O	PARSONS William Earnest	4-05-44	405 Sqn
J/86255	P/O	PASTORIOUS Donald Arthur	28-04-44	434 Sqn
J/16514	F/O	PATERSON Donald John	27-01-44	432 Sqn
R/206161	Sgt	PATERSON Donald Montague	26-08-44	12 OTU
J/28547	F/O	PATERSON Frank Gordon	8-07-44	106 Sqn
J/39880	F/O	PATERSON William	24-12-44	622 Sqn
J/88720	P/O	PATIENCE Kenneth Lorne	28-05-44	427 Sqn
R/182453	Sgt	PATON William Stocks	23-08-44	24 OTU
J/19501	P/O	PATRICK John Walker	10-04-44	149 Sqn
J/85360	P/O	PATTERSON Charles Edmund George	23-05-44	419 Sqn
J/26003	F/O	PATTERSON Edward Douglas	26-02-44	420 Sqn
R/206111	F/S	PATTERSON Gerald William Henry	8-11-44	158 Sqn
J/24226	F/O	PATTERSON Harold McCosh	29-07-44	434 Sqn
J/89893	P/O	PATTERSON John Burton	29-06-44	424 Sqn
J/93274	P/O	PATTERSON John Richard	12-12-44	12 Sqn
J/92920	P/O	PATTERSON John William Lyle	25-11-44	427 Sqn
R/216287	Sgt	PATTERSON Johnston Irwin Stewart 'Jack'	8-07-44	619 Sqn
R/128345	WO2	PATTERSON Leo Harkness	28-01-44	420 Sqn
J/89354	P/O	PATTERSON Ray Edwin	29-07-44	425 Sqn
J/94414	P/O	PATTISON Allen Bruce	31-03-44	514 Sqn
J/86160	P/O	PATTLE Basil William	16-02-44	426 Sqn
J/19028	P/O	PATTON Alvin Alston	31-03-44	408 Sqn
J/28966	F/O	PAWLITZA Elvyn Joseph	13-06-44	427 Sqn
R/178830	F/S	PAWLYK Andrew	30-06-44	15 Sqn
J/22396	F/O	PEABODY Harold Sherman	29-07-44	622 Sqn
J/18009	F/O	PEACOCK DFC Wilfred George	26-09-44	405 Sqn
J/89264	P/O	PEACORE Thomas James	31-07-44	9 Sqn
J/88337	P/O	PEARCE Archibald Gordon	20-02-44	434 Sqn
J/27424	F/O	PEARCE Clarence Walter	30-01-44	22 OTU
R/190936	F/S	PEARCE Jack Gordon	27-07-44	619 Sqn
J/27505	F/O	PEARCE Samuel Henry James	18-12-44	434 Sqn
J/36869	F/O	PEARDON Lloyd George	13-09-44	101 Sqn
J/22368	F/O	PEARL Jack Verner	20-02-44	625 Sqn
J/89814	P/O	PEARSON John Joseph	13-08-44	578 Sqn
J/21980	P/O	PEARSON Robert Allen	8-07-44	405 Sqn
C/24435	P/O	PEARSON Robert Charles	13-06-44	427 Sqn
J/35060	F/O	PECHET Samuel William	5-12-44	428 Sqn
R/183494	Sgt	PECK James Leonard	20-03-44	14 OTU
J/90560	P/O	PEEBLES Henry Thomas	27-04-44	106 Sqn
J/89378	P/O	PEERS Douglas Waldo	13-08-44	101 Sqn
R/279043	Sgt	PEGG Robert Campbell	30-08-44	14 OTU
J/90271	P/O	PELECHATY Ignatius Thomas	30-09-44	426 Sqn
R/136796	F/S	PELLETIER Romeo Arthur	16-03-44	1664 HCU
J/17546	F/O	PELTIER Joseph Ovila	31-07-44	617 Sqn
J/8940	F/L	PENALAGAN Ronald Henry	15-02-44	424 Sqn
J/20187	F/O	PENKURI Kaiho Thomas	16-03-44	514 Sqn
J/85345	P/O	PEPPIATT Franklin Walter	31-03-44	12 Sqn
J/91100	P/O	PERDUE James Alfred	26-08-44	626 Sqn
C/12584	F/L	PERDUE Robert Nelson	24-12-44	622 Sqn
J/28280	F/O	PERKINS George Gordon	4-08-44	434 Sqn
J/6708	F/L	PERRY Davis Hamilton	12-05-44	427 Sqn
K/258127	Sgt	PERRY George Sidney	13-09-44	1658 HCU
J/26300	F/O	PERRY Nap King [USA]	25-01-44	16 OTU
J/95539	P/O	PERRY Nelson Robert	29-11-44	101 Sqn
J/10259	F/L	PERRY Sheldon William Wesley	20-01-44	101 Sqn
J/21539	F/O	PESME Cecil Percy	14-08-44	617 Sqn
R/256474	F/S	PETERS Paul	26-08-44	300 Sqn
J/90075	P/O	PETERS Samuel Leonard	4-08-44	424 Sqn
R/168827	F/S	PETERSON Raymond Floyd	14-01-44	405 Sqn
J/14208	F/O	PETERSON Sidney Glen	25-05-44	78 Sqn
J/90871	F/S	PETERSON William Alexander	21-01-44	432 Sqn
R/51651	F/S	PETRINA Michael Joseph	19-04-44	419 Sqn
R/142756	F/S	PETRY Leslie Lee [USA]	19-01-44	1659 HCU
J/26098	F/O	PETTIGREW Raymond Wilbur	27-09-44	619 Sqn

ID	Rank	Name	Date	Unit	ID	Rank	Name	Date	Unit
J/95167	P/O	PHARIS George William	31-08-44	433 Sqn	R/184114	F/S	PREECE James Harold	12-12-44	1664 HCU
J/89468	P/O	PHILLIPS Cecil	30-01-44	433 Sqn	J/93896	P/O	PREECE Thomas James	20-01-44	426 Sqn
J/28259	P/O	PHILLIPS Clifford Stanley	13-05-44	426 Sqn	J/17637	F/O	PRENTICE James Millar	6-12-44	429 Sqn
J/42729	F/O	PHILLIPS James Murray	29-12-44	405 Sqn	J/22224	F/O	PRESLAND Gordon Richard	29-01-44	50 Sqn
J/87035	P/O	PHILLIPS Ross Joseph	11-06-44	405 Sqn	R/187614	Sgt	PRESTON James Michael	14-01-44	166 Sqn
J/16550	F/O	PHILLIPS Samuel Alexander	13-06-44	514 Sqn	J/25123	F/O	PRESTON Stuart Marvin	13-05-44	431 Sqn
J/23210	F/O	PHILLIPS Walter	18-01-44	1659 HCU	J/90756	P/O	PRIAMO Joseph Lidio	23-04-44	431 Sqn
J/87756	P/O	PHILLIPS Winston Spencer Moyses	8-08-44	429 Sqn	R/182206	F/S	PRICE Charles Melville	31-01-44	97 Sqn
J/85584	P/O	PHINNEY Charles Garnet	26-03-44	426 Sqn	J/25375	F/O	PRICE David Mayson	14-10-44	115 Sqn
J/37732	F/O	PICARD Alfred Alexander	14-10-44	153 Sqn	J/86321	P/O	PRICE Donald Alexander	25-02-44	115 Sqn
R/140622	WO1	PICCIANO Raymond Daniel	6-11-44	214 Sqn	J/87218	P/O	PRICE Thomas Willard Percy	24-06-44	617 Sqn
R/180554	F/S	PICHE Joseph Laurence	30-01-44	622 Sqn	J/26855	F/O	PRICE Walter William	13-05-44	419 Sqn
J/91050	P/O	PICKERING David	24-04-44	425 Sqn	R/274918	Sgt	PRIDHAM Ernest James	15-11-44	1664 HCU
R/205794	F/S	PICKERING Robert Gardhum	29-08-44	50 Sqn	R/178786	Sgt	PRILL Berle Clinton	21-01-44	427 Sqn
J/29197	F/O	PIDCOCK Charles Trevor Leighton	15-10-44	425 Sqn	R/149547	Sgt	PRIME Gordon Oswald	11-08-44	24 OTU
K/225673	Sgt	PIDGEON George Walker	14-07-44	433 Sqn	J/88911	P/O	PRISKE Kenneth Wheatley	2-05-44	10 Sqn
R/174994	Sgt	PIERS Roy Spencer	24-05-44	20 OTU	J/86684	P/O	PRITCHARD Gordon Featherston	17-08-44	420 Sqn
J/89298	P/O	PIGEON John Jerome	2-08-44	425 Sqn	J/25974	F/O	PROBYN Dighton Walter	3-02-44	16 OTU
J/40651	F/O	PIKE Lawrence Ellwin	20-11-44	1656 HCU	J/27269	F/O	PROCTOR Leonard Douglas	22-03-44	408 Sqn
J/27735	F/O	PIKE Robert Eric Bowman	2-11-44	77 Sqn	J/22627	F/O	PRONGER Gordon Bentley	22-01-44	51 Sqn
J/21569	F/O	PIPER John Ralph	20-02-44	419 Sqn	J/90354	P/O	PROSOFSKY Alfred Wilfred	29-07-44	415 Sqn
J/86656	P/O	PIPRELL Gordon Leslie	30-08-44	101 Sqn	J/86197	P/O	PROSSER Leslie Thomas	16-02-44	426 Sqn
J/86151	F/O	PITKIN Edmund Francis	2-08-44	425 Sqn	R/214121	Sgt	PROTEAU Medrie Peter	21-02-44	23 OTU
J/43279	F/O	PITTMAN John Benjamin	2-12-44	433 Sqn	J/27843	F/O	PROUD Elmer Reginald	27-01-44	408 Sqn
R/194287	Sgt	PITTS Robert Michael	2-07-44	1667 HCU	J/95157	P/O	PROUDFOOT David Herbert	15-10-44	431 Sqn
R/96696	WO1	PLANTE Jean Marie Charles	23-06-44	1666 HCU	J/27626	P/O	PROUDFOOT William Wallace	13-06-44	427 Sqn
J/18616	F/O	PLATANA DFC Daniel Dominique	15-07-44	156 Sqn	J/19063	P/O	PROUDLOCK Thomas Harold	26-03-44	426 Sqn
J/90071	P/O	PLECAN Frank George	29-07-44	427 Sqn	R/220221	F/S	PROULX Richard Godfrey	29-07-44	622 Sqn
J/9694	F/L	PLEDGER DFC Thomas Oswald	13-06-44	408 Sqn	J/93111	P/O	PROUSE Victor Eugene	6-12-44	434 Sqn
J/18073	F/O	PLUNKETT Leonard Stanley	30-08-44	428 Sqn	R/202987	F/S	PRUNKLE Robert	4-12-44	619 Sqn
J/88707	P/O	PLUNKETT William [USA]	20-02-44	408 Sqn	J/89119	P/O	PUGH Lawrence John	15-03-44	77 Sqn
R/163007	Sgt	POCOCK Douglas Layne	22-01-44	432 Sqn	J/88342	P/O	PULHAM Donald Walter	22-03-44	425 Sqn
J/86307	P/O	POCOCK William Francis	1-07-44	626 Sqn	J/19506	P/O	PURMAL Vincent Robert	3-01-44	156 Sqn
R/133538	WO2	POE Robert David [United Kingdom]	20-01-44	1653 HCU	J/15990	P/O	PURNEY Elvin Curtis	28-05-44	550 Sqn
J/41700	P/O	POGSON William Henry	31-12-44	626 Sqn	R/217006	F/S	PURVIS Thomas Andrew	30-08-44	103 Sqn
J/35541	F/O	POLE Douglas Campbell	23-10-44	429 Sqn	R/225354	Sgt	PYCHE Harvey Ellsworth	22-10-44	1659 HCU
J/28873	P/O	POLE Ross Norman	13-06-44	419 Sqn	J/26350	F/O	QUANSTROM William	10-04-44	12 Sqn
J/91136	P/O	POLLOCK Albert Lyle	24-06-44	12 Sqn	J/27920	P/O	QUEEN Stanley James	6-07-44	424 Sqn
J/38253	F/O	POLLOCK John Robert	25-11-44	427 Sqn	R/179363	F/S	QUINN Francis Patrick Morgan	27-04-44	103 Sqn
R/250815	Sgt	POLLON Joseph Raymond	28-05-44	30 OTU	J/87110	P/O	QUINN Gerald Edgar	17-06-44	405 Sqn
R/159089	WO2	POLOWY Vincent Ronald	7-02-44	427 Sqn	J/88694	P/O	QUINN Harold Edward	10-04-44	57 Sqn
J/18921	P/O	POLSON Ronald Duncan	20-01-44	426 Sqn	J/19888	P/O	QUINN Joseph Dennis	19-04-44	419 Sqn
J/28798	F/O	POMEROY Elwood Cameron	29-07-44	405 Sqn	J/21394	F/O	QUIRT John Harry	4-11-44	101 Sqn
J/28355	F/O	POND Hubert William	28-04-44	434 Sqn	J/38241	F/O	RABKIN Hyman	2-11-44	415 Sqn
J/89375	P/O	POOL William Harry	21-07-44	622 Sqn	J/28696	F/O	RABOVSKY Moses	28-05-44	429 Sqn
J/36085	F/O	POPE Henry Milton	27-11-44	115 Sqn	J/26614	F/O	RABY William Keith	27-04-44	78 Sqn
J/28866	F/O	POPE William Alexander	2-05-44	1659 HCU	J/23119	F/O	RADCLIFFE Edward Ernest	24-07-44	582 Sqn
J/25808	F/L	PORTER John Edward	25-08-44	101 Sqn	R/184322	Sgt	RADCLIFFE Kenneth Lloyd	25-03-44	44 Sqn
J/89470	P/O	PORTER Roy Stanley	26-03-44	425 Sqn	J/17895	P/O	RAE Donald Arthur	14-01-44	432 Sqn
J/86838	P/O	PORTER Russel Lyle	15-06-44	433 Sqn	J/88120	P/O	RAE George Arthur	8-07-44	49 Sqn
R/283140	Sgt	POST Eric James	17-10-44	24 OTU	J/85912	P/O	RAE Harold Oliver	25-06-44	9 Sqn
J/91133	P/O	POTHIER DFC Bourneuf Freeman	7-05-44	405 Sqn	J/26452	F/O	RAFTERY Frederick Stephen [USA]	25-10-44	428 Sqn
J/23136	F/O	POTTER John Foster	11-04-44	550 Sqn	R/155420	Sgt	RAHN Robert Henry	31-01-44	1664 HCU
R/82734	WO1	POTTER John Milton	27-04-44	408 Sqn	R/127923	WO2	RAIKE John	16-09-44	405 Sqn
J/28194	F/O	POTTS Joseph Reginald	12-09-44	619 Sqn	R/58461	Sgt	RAINE Harold Thomas	15-02-44	419 Sqn
J/90954	F/O	POULOS Paul	29-07-44	425 Sqn	J/95176	P/O	RAMEY Lyman Phillip	21-11-44	433 Sqn
J/37012	F/O	POUND John Russell	6-09-44	1667 HCU	J/90346	P/O	RAMMAGE Albert John	19-07-44	49 Sqn
J/19169	F/L	POWDRILL DFC Ross	8-06-44	166 Sqn	J/12973	F/L	RAMSAY DFC David	28-04-44	405 Sqn
J/90765	P/O	POWELL Chester Owen	25-08-44	101 Sqn	J/24028	F/O	RAMSAY Jack McAllister	20-01-44	429 Sqn
R/208276	Sgt	POWELL James Lee [USA]	17-10-44	1664 HCU	J/22060	P/O	RAMSAY Kenneth Grant	18-03-44	76 Sqn
J/90053	P/O	POWER James Roderique	29-07-44	424 Sqn	R/208112	Sgt	RANKIN Jack Raymond	4-05-44	103 Sqn
J/86124	P/O	POWER Paul Joseph	2-02-44	432 Sqn	J/18141	F/O	RANSOM Glen Irvin	20-01-44	83 Sqn
R/133214	WO2	POWLEY David Alexander	14-01-44	9 Sqn	J/90916	P/O	RATHWELL Robert William	31-03-44	432 Sqn
R/167080	WO2	PRATLETT Oliver John Lancaster	15-07-44	103 Sqn	J/28242	P/O	RATNER Harry	25-05-44	427 Sqn
J/86893	P/O	PRATT Richard William	28-04-44	431 Sqn	J/17552	F/O	RAWBONE Walter Mansell	23-03-44	22 OTU
J/37535	F/O	PRAWDZIK Charles John	13-10-44	415 Sqn	R/180997	Sgt	RAYMOND Jean Paul	29-01-44	431 Sqn
J/18833	F/O	PREECE Charles James	23-11-44	1692 Flt	J/90353	P/O	REASON George Campbell	29-07-44	415 Sqn
J/94374	P/O	PREECE Gordon Lewis	31-03-44	101 Sqn	J/35091	F/O	REAUME Louis Joseph	2-11-44	408 Sqn

Service No	Rank	Name	Date	Unit
R/187678	Sgt	REAUME Robert Francis Charles [USA]	10-04-44	24 OTU
J/35732	F/O	REDDEN Clyde George	14-10-44	115 Sqn
R/159999	F/S	REDGRAVE Charles Derek [USA]	2-01-44	463 Sqn
J/28213	F/O	REDMONDS Alfred Samuel	25-04-44	420 Sqn
R/222193	Sgt	REDSHAW Donald Andrew Harvey	22-06-44	9 Sqn
J/95461	P/O	REEB John Couzens	30-08-44	115 Sqn
R/159120	WO2	REED Charles Leroy	18-03-44	76 Sqn
J/28669	F/O	REED Kenneth	17-10-44	19 OTU
J/85809	P/O	REED Raymond Alexander	5-08-44	425 Sqn
R/178831	Sgt	REED Victor Earl	20-02-44	429 Sqn
J/25591	F/O	REED William Reginald	22-01-44	433 Sqn
J/29274	F/O	REGIMBAL Wilfred Henry	2-11-44	415 Sqn
J/21821	F/O	REHKOPF Walter William	23-05-44	408 Sqn
J/36936	F/O	REID Allen James	4-12-44	166 Sqn
J/22367	F/O	REID Arthur Edward	8-02-44	138 Sqn
R/183902	F/S	REID Earl William	2-10-44	1664 HCU
J/14021	F/O	REID Earle Kerr	31-03-44	432 Sqn
J/28851	F/O	REID Harry	30-07-44	106 Sqn
R/157645	F/S	REID Herbert Spencer	6-01-44	467 Sqn
J/26681	F/O	REID Hewitt Harold Robinson	29-07-44	100 Sqn
J/41668	F/O	REID James Kennedy	31-08-44	22 OTU
J/40469	F/O	REID John	5-12-44	428 Sqn
J/22672	F/O	REID Malcolm John	20-02-44	83 Sqn
J/89732	P/O	REID William Ferguson	22-05-44	75 Sqn
J/24232	F/O	REID William Ian Fossen	16-03-44	408 Sqn
J/86455	F/L	REIF Arndt Walther [USA]	23-12-44	582 Sqn
J/20359	S/L	REILANDER Aloysius Valentine	15-02-44	424 Sqn
J/85674	F/O	REMBER Raymond Alexander [USA]	24-07-44	582 Sqn
R/171252	F/S	REMILLARD Joseph Lauret Roland	17-12-44	156 Sqn
R/194658	Sgt	REMOLE Douglas William	20-02-44	630 Sqn
J/11436	F/O	REMPEL Walter Earl	12-02-44	419 Sqn
J/27499	F/O	RENAUD George Kenneth	29-07-44	415 Sqn
J/25372	F/O	RENAUD Joseph Alphonse Leon Louis	24-03-44	425 Sqn
J/86739	P/O	RENAUD Joseph Gerard Maurice	3-06-44	405 Sqn
J/25818	F/O	RENNIE Robert Edward	6-11-44	50 Sqn
R/169236	WO2	RENNIE Ross Burton	12-09-44	576 Sqn
R/166835	F/S	RENNIE William Wilson	5-07-44	44 Sqn
J/91048	P/O	RENNING John James	23-04-44	424 Sqn
J/85040	P/O	RETTER Alan Joseph	16-06-44	405 Sqn
J/89876	P/O	REVELL Philip Charles	15-08-44	428 Sqn
J/89892	P/O	REY Francis Lawrence	25-06-44	9 Sqn
R/203113	Sgt	REYNOLDS Albert Chalmers	24-07-44	1666 HCU
J/93115	P/O	REYNOLDS Hartley Ernest	21-11-44	426 Sqn
R/161588	WO2	REYNOLDS John Albert	4-05-44	625 Sqn
R/280970	Sgt	RHEAUME Joseph Lawrence	7-12-44	24 OTU
J/92189	P/O	RHEUBOTTOM Alva Edison	4-11-44	640 Sqn
R/196199	F/S	RHEUBOTTOM James	25-07-44	300 Sqn
J/95464	P/O	RHIND John Campbell	29-12-44	419 Sqn
R/129126	WO2	RHOADES Ernest Albert	23-04-44	7 Sqn
J/93786	P/O	RHODES Kenneth Earl	21-07-44	514 Sqn
J/94110	P/O	RHUDE Ernest Ashley	18-12-44	158 Sqn
J/18089	F/O	RIACH Douglas Athol	20-02-44	78 Sqn
R/156946	WO2	RICCI Adolphe Joseph	13-06-44	158 Sqn
R/156762	WO2	RICE Alan Norman	31-03-44	101 Sqn
R/154916	F/S	RICHARD Clarence Edwin	11-04-44	49 Sqn
R/99395	Sgt	RICHARD Joseph Pierre Fernand	20-02-44	427 Sqn
J/19978	P/O	RICHARDS James Leonard	1-03-44	76 Sqn
J/28875	F/O	RICHARDS William Samuel	3-08-44	166 Sqn
R/153656	F/S	RICHARDSON David Ballantine	25-05-44	420 Sqn
J/89919	P/O	RICHARDSON Ernest James	28-05-44	12 Sqn
J/17320	F/O	RICHARDSON DFM Henry Holmes	14-04-44	5 LFS
J/21670	P/O	RICHTER Gordon William McKay	20-02-44	408 Sqn
J/90755	P/O	RICKERT Arthur Edward	22-03-44	408 Sqn
J/28219	F/O	RIDDELL John	8-02-44	18 OTU
R/259938	Sgt	RIDDOCH George	22-10-44	1659 HCU
R/172357	WO2	RIDDOCH Robert Alexander	25-06-44	44 Sqn
J/14577	F/O	RIDGERS DFC Cyril Frederick	26-02-44	408 Sqn
J/85631	P/O	RIDLEY Robert Burns	28-04-44	166 Sqn
J/12737	F/L	RIEGER Herbert William	6-06-44	97 Sqn
R/109302	Sgt	RIGDEN Stanley James	28-04-44	419 Sqn
R/148524	WO2	RIGGS Lewis	31-01-44	1664 HCU
J/35063	F/O	RILEY Virgel Lee	15-10-44	424 Sqn
J/40201	P/O	RINAHAN James Molloy	23-08-44	24 OTU
J/90077	P/O	RINGER Jack Junior	9-08-44	427 Sqn
J/85789	P/O	RITCHIE Charles Alexander	16-03-44	420 Sqn
J/23721	F/O	RITCHIE James Leigh	4-05-44	582 Sqn
J/25867	F/O	RITCHIE John Samuel	13-06-44	78 Sqn
J/90667	P/O	RITCHIE Wenford Maxwell	6-10-44	433 Sqn
J/89099	P/O	RIVERS Eric Thomas	15-10-44	7 Sqn
J/90063	P/O	ROACH Fred	13-05-44	426 Sqn
J/88496	P/O	ROACH Joseph Charles	8-05-44	49 Sqn
J/23756	F/O	ROACH Richard John	24-03-44	102 Sqn
J/86596	P/O	ROACH Sherman Lewis	20-02-44	408 Sqn
J/36862	F/O	ROBERTS Bryn Evans	14-10-44	166 Sqn
J/85903	P/O	ROBERTS Charles Anthony	13-08-44	83 Sqn
C/91052	P/O	ROBERTS Cyril Edmund	16-06-44	405 Sqn
J/25206	P/O	ROBERTS George Albert	4-03-44	138 Sqn
J/90060	P/O	ROBERTS James Victor	25-03-44	427 Sqn
J/4566	F/L	ROBERTS Warren Ainsley	30-01-44	405 Sqn
J/89911	P/O	ROBERTSHAW Russell William	30-01-44	622 Sqn
R/182689	F/S	ROBERTSON Clifford Conrad	2-11-44	153 Sqn
J/29156	P/O	ROBERTSON David Brownlee	16-12-44	115 Sqn
J/90352	P/O	ROBERTSON Walter Dennis	29-07-44	415 Sqn
J/20244	F/L	ROBERTSON Wilbert James	21-11-44	78 Sqn
J/91090	P/O	ROBINEAU Gilbert Euclide Rheal	26-02-44	432 Sqn
J/92149	P/O	ROBINSON Dallas Rex	25-02-44	115 Sqn
J/22748	F/O	ROBINSON Donald Alfred	24-03-44	433 Sqn
J/23353	P/O	ROBINSON George	10-04-44	12 Sqn
J/90245	P/O	ROBINSON Herbert Grant	17-06-44	431 Sqn
J/21989	F/O	ROBINSON James Freeman	28-05-44	420 Sqn
J/22460	F/O	ROBINSON Leroy Edward	31-03-44	426 Sqn
J/90311	P/O	ROBINSON Robert William	29-07-44	433 Sqn
J/36475	F/O	ROBITAILLE Edgar Albert	23-09-44	1664 HCU
J/95463	P/O	ROBSON Arthur Edward	21-11-44	433 Sqn
J/86588	P/O	ROBSON Donald Matthews	25-05-44	419 Sqn
J/25800	F/O	ROCHE Paul Martin	29-07-44	550 Sqn
R/215087	F/S	RODD Alan	11-06-44	90 Sqn
R/186316	F/S	RODGERS Donald James	12-10-44	166 Sqn
J/89733	P/O	RODGERS Herbert Henry	28-05-44	432 Sqn
R/207263	Sgt	RODGERS William Kenneth	25-01-44	16 OTU
R/148374	WO2	RODRIGUE Joseph Jean Paul Adrien	26-02-44	90 Sqn
J/93741	P/O	ROE Arthur Emerson [USA]	5-07-44	419 Sqn
J/16508	F/L	ROE George Reginald Burdick	25-06-44	149 Sqn
J/22911	F/O	ROGERS Bartlett Leadbetter	24-03-44	625 Sqn
J/89773	P/O	ROGERS Harold Thompson	25-06-44	50 Sqn
J/86134	P/O	ROGERS Sidney John	26-02-44	102 Sqn
J/85696	P/O	ROGERS Thomas Aubrey	29-06-44	426 Sqn
J/24589	F/O	ROGNAN Everett Raymond	27-04-44	408 Sqn
R/164800	Sgt	ROLLO Ross Campbell Andrew	19-03-44	1667 Sqn
J/19174	P/O	ROLPH Robert Harold	8-06-44	408 Sqn
J/27683	P/O	ROMULD Harold Magnus	17-06-44	425 Sqn
J/95100	P/O	RONAHAN John Menzies	23-04-44	149 Sqn
J/19511	P/O	ROOD Walter Everitt	15-02-44	434 Sqn
J/89473	P/O	ROSE Charles Edward	22-05-44	514 Sqn
J/88913	P/O	ROSE Clifford William	19-04-44	640 Sqn
R/157415	F/S	ROSE Donald Irwin	29-01-44	434 Sqn
J/85352	P/O	ROSE Harold Kenty	8-05-44	106 Sqn
J/36919	F/O	ROSE Robert Henry Montgomery	2-11-44	419 Sqn
J/44604	P/O	ROSEN Arthur	9-11-44	82 OTU
J/28758	F/O	ROSEN Walter Bigelow Tower [USA]	18-08-44	158 Sqn
C/89022	F/O	ROSKI Antonio George	17-08-44	420 Sqn
J/87240	P/O	ROSS Carman Vincent	28-05-44	429 Sqn

Service No.	Rank	Name	Date	Sqn
J/90046	P/O	ROSS Wallace Milton	11-05-44	50 Sqn
J/26796	F/O	ROSS William [USA]	26-08-44	101 Sqn
J/40029	F/O	ROSS William Stewart	30-08-44	86 OTU
R/135105	WO1	ROST William Francis	31-03-44	433 Sqn
J/36353	F/O	ROTH Robert Tait	12-12-44	195 Sqn
R/194573	F/S	ROUND Harold Geoffrey	11-08-44	24 OTU
R/188196	Sgt	ROWE Bruce Sherwin	29-01-44	431 Sqn
J/41261	F/O	ROWE John George McCaffery	30-11-44	82 OTU
J/86433	P/O	ROWELL Lloyd George	20-02-44	431 Sqn
J/40054	F/O	ROWLEY Adelbert Bateman	21-11-44	408 Sqn
J/92422	P/O	ROY Duncan McKenzie	20-11-44	22 OTU
J/92359	F/O	ROY Joseph Alphonse Paul Emile	24-09-44	429 Sqn
J/95441	F/O	RUHL Leslie John	2-11-44	428 Sqn
J/21210	F/O	RUMBLE Robert Mons	16-02-44	619 Sqn
J/87797	P/O	RUNNING Gilmer Arnold	5-11-44	424 Sqn
R/149338	WO2	RUPPEL Iverson Frederick	30-01-44	100 Sqn
J/86765	F/O	RUSH Edward James	31-03-44	9 Sqn
J/26291	F/O	RUSHFORTH William John Henry	17-06-44	102 Sqn
R/178903	Sgt	RUSHTON Nicholas Clayton	16-05-44	12 OTU
J/21724	F/O	RUSSELL Byron Allen	21-01-44	433 Sqn
J/90451	F/O	RUSSELL Ernest Albert	6-10-44	49 Sqn
J/29521	F/O	RUSSELL James Balfour	27-08-44	166 Sqn
J/18912	F/L	RUSSELL CGM Joseph Vincent	21-02-44	15 Sqn
J/86605	P/O	RUSSELL William Francis	25-03-44	433 Sqn
J/87872	P/O	RUTHERFORD Bruce Alexander Mackenzie	22-06-44	44 Sqn
R/181154	F/S	RUTZKI John	27-04-44	44 Sqn
J/21669	F/O	RYAN Donal Thomas	29-07-44	408 Sqn
J/90272	P/O	RYAN Gerald Ernest	30-09-44	426 Sqn
J/89250	P/O	RYAN Thomas Mitchell	18-04-44	433 Sqn
K/251459	F/S	RYE George	11-11-44	207 Sqn
J/25931	F/O	RYERSE Donald Arthur	31-08-44	103 Sqn
R/148282	F/S	RYNSKI Joseph Barney	22-12-44	405 Sqn
J/88898	P/O	SABINE Eugene Preston	25-05-44	192 Sqn
J/29415	P/O	SAGER Harry	13-06-44	78 Sqn
J/14787	P/O	SALABA Alexander Jerry	2-01-44	405 Sqn
J/9929	S/L	SALE DSO* DFC Douglas Julian	20-03-44	35 Sqn
J/25513	F/O	SALOMAA Ero Albaunus	6-07-44	582 Sqn
J/85454	P/O	SALTZBERRY Russell Arthur	23-04-44	405 Sqn
J/90290	P/O	SAMMON Douglas Wilfred	8-06-44	420 Sqn
J/94395	P/O	SAMSON Charles Nott	21-07-44	514 Sqn
J/92425	P/O	SAMUEL Allan Gilchrist	2-11-44	428 Sqn
R/220073	Sgt	SANDER Raymond Joseph	26-08-44	83 OTU
J/35040	F/O	SANDERS William Harold	15-10-44	431 Sqn
J/9534	F/L	SANDERSON Earl Albert	14-01-44	405 Sqn
R/176469	Sgt	SANDERSON Frank Gordon	20-01-44	419 Sqn
J/86545	F/O	SANDERSON George Benjamin	26-05-44	5 LFS
J/19659	P/O	SANDERSON Robert Louis	10-02-44	199 Sqn
J/88290	P/O	SANTO John Alexander	1-08-44	429 Sqn
J/89247	P/O	SAPRUNOFF Samuel	31-03-44	432 Sqn
R/166832	F/S	SARGENT William Earl	31-03-44	578 Sqn
R/163670	WO2	SARUK DFM Michael Alexander	23-05-44	576 Sqn
R/2129	Sgt	SAVAGE Emery	2-01-44	82 OTU
J/88165	P/O	SAVARD Joseph Georges Marcel	17-08-44	433 Sqn
R/284298	Sgt	SAVARD Joseph Ludger Norman	5-12-44	22 OTU
J/92471	P/O	SAVOIE Joseph William	1-11-44	425 Sqn
R/212173	F/S	SAWRY Michael	13-08-44	428 Sqn
J/25351	F/O	SCANLAN Wilfred George	17-09-44	115 Sqn
J/35883	F/O	SCHAEFER Robert Harry	4-12-44	619 Sqn
J/221219	F/S	SCHAFER Jacob	27-08-44	166 Sqn
J/213524	F/S	SCHAFF Leonard	14-10-44	166 Sqn
R/169831	F/S	SCHIEDEL Kenneth Edwin	27-01-44	467 Sqn
R/125729	WO2	SCHIMMENS Roy Frederick	10-04-44	24 OTU
J/86203	P/O	SCHIOLER Thomas Lorne	24-03-44	78 Sqn
J/90886	P/O	SCHLIEVERT Roy Cecil	23-10-44	419 Sqn
J/12768	P/O	SCHLITT Gordon Henry	30-01-44	22 OTU
J/86390	P/O	SCHMIDT Kenneth Lloyd	9-05-44	426 Sqn
R/213416	Sgt	SCHNAUFER Ralph Robert Henry	16-11-44	166 Sqn
R/166151	F/S	SCHOENTHALER Arthur Leopold	5-01-44	431 Sqn
J/89018	F/O	SCHOPP Harold Harrison [USA]	17-12-44	153 Sqn
R/111904	WO1	SCHRYER Joseph Albert Roland	8-08-44	419 Sqn
J/17658	F/O	SCHULTZ Arthur Bennett	30-01-44	405 Sqn
J/86922	P/O	SCHULTZ Gerhard Edgar Herbert	28-04-44	101 Sqn
J/86762	P/O	SCHWARTZ Meyer Edsel	24-02-44	405 Sqn
J/92368	P/O	SCHWERDFAGER James Elliot	25-10-44	431 Sqn
R/150897	WO2	SCHWERDFEGER Glenwood Allan	4-05-44	582 Sqn
J/19588	P/O	SCOBIE Benjamin Cyrus	28-05-44	427 Sqn
R/210634	Sgt	SCOTT Clarence Elgy	22-06-44	106 Sqn
R/149654	WO2	SCOTT Donald John	20-05-44	44 Sqn
J/14730	F/O	SCOTT George	17-08-44	433 Sqn
R/171123	F/S	SCOTT George Henry	27-01-44	408 Sqn
R/210098	F/S	SCOTT Jack Kyle	23-09-44	166 Sqn
R/123197	WO2	SCOTT John Ernest	3-01-44	432 Sqn
R/161591	WO2	SCOTT Lloyd George	16-03-44	76 Sqn
J/91113	P/O	SCOTT Raymond David	6-10-44	49 Sqn
J/93090	P/O	SCOTT Robert Burns	10-10-44	426 Sqn
J/182724	Sgt	SCOTT Thomas Fairfax	28-05-44	1659 HCU
J/86420	P/O	SCOTT Walter Hugh	23-05-44	106 Sqn
J/29485	F/O	SCOTT William Earl	23-05-44	429 Sqn
C/24753	F/O	SCOTT AFM William Francis	18-12-44	22 OTU
J/91095	P/O	SCULLY John Joseph	22-06-44	630 Sqn
J/40067	P/O	SCUTT Leonard Allan	23-06-44	1666 HCU
J/28965	P/O	SEABROOK Malcolm Thomas	2-05-44	1659 HCU
R/170739	F/S	SEALY Albert Edward	28-01-44	199 Sqn
J/14814	F/O	SEARS Earl Kitchener	22-03-44	426 Sqn
J/95162	P/O	SEARSON John Ellard	25-07-44	419 Sqn
J/89841	P/O	SEBESTYEN Denis	1-07-44	12 Sqn
R/153098	Sgt	SECKER Bruce Walter	27-09-44	Croft
J/94384	P/O	SEEDHOUSE Harold Charles	23-04-44	433 Sqn
J/90143	P/O	SEHLIN Donald Leslie	31-03-44	50 Sqn
J/23155	F/O	SELMAN Robert Gilroy	20-01-44	78 Sqn
J/85536	P/O	SENECAL Joseph Hector Gaeten	15-03-44	429 Sqn
J/88887	P/O	SERVICE Clyde James	6-10-44	106 Sqn
J/86301	P/O	SERVISS Dudley Thomas	4-05-44	405 Sqn
R/159475	WO2	SETTER Douglas James	2-05-44	10 Sqn
J/95477	P/O	SEYMOUR James Rodger	21-11-44	433 Sqn
J/23740	F/O	SEYMOUR John Henry	22-01-44	433 Sqn
R/201617	LAC	SEYMOUR Joseph Martin	15-09-44	62 Base
J/20419	F/O	SHANK George Albert William	5-01-44	431 Sqn
J/86809	P/O	SHANKS Jack Laverne	17-06-44	434 Sqn
J/23708	F/O	SHANNON Arthur Melvin	4-05-44	101 Sqn
J/29581	P/O	SHANNON George Roland Gillies	17-06-44	426 Sqn
J/18167	F/O	SHANNON DFM Robert Alfred	31-03-44	427 Sqn
J/91118	P/O	SHANTZ Ira Walter	4-12-44	619 Sqn
J/23351	F/O	SHAPIRO Martin	28-05-44	550 Sqn
J/37536	F/O	SHARP Andrew	8-11-44	158 Sqn
R/180338	WO2	SHARP Ronald	15-03-44	51 Sqn
J/21834	F/O	SHARPE George Edward	2-01-44	61 Sqn
R/101913	WO2	SHARPE Joseph Harold	18-01-44	1659 HCU
J/88915	P/O	SHAW Charles Hugh	10-05-44	106 Sqn
J/86367	P/O	SHAW Ernest Anson	11-07-44	408 Sqn
J/7896	F/L	SHAW Thomas Robert	28-01-44	426 Sqn
J/86608	P/O	SHEAHAN John Joseph Harold	31-03-44	425 Sqn
J/25872	F/O	SHEARSTONE William Joseph	18-08-44	630 Sqn
R/172051	F/S	SHEEHAN Edward Fanahan	28-04-44	51 Sqn
J/12823	F/O	SHEEN Robert Jordan	13-07-44	415 Sqn
J/89184	P/O	SHEPHERD Henry Ian	23-09-44	106 Sqn
J/29417	P/O	SHEPHERD Henry Lewis	22-12-44	189 Sqn
C/19904	P/O	SHEPHERD John Edward	4-05-44	405 Sqn
J/18196	F/O	SHERMAN Harold Maxwell	26-02-44	419 Sqn
R/144206	WO2	SHERMAN Murray	22-06-44	207 Sqn
J/17360	F/O	SHERMAN Stephen George Cockrane	10-05-44	97 Sqn
J/35038	F/O	SHERRILL John Frederick Leddra	29-07-44	434 Sqn
J/26644	F/O	SHERRILL Thomas Russell [USA]	23-05-44	408 Sqn
J/37006	F/L	SHERRY James Anthony	31-12-44	166 Sqn

R/211938	Sgt	SHERVEN Vernon Thomes	1-06-44	1667 HCU
R/99421	F/S	SHERWOOD Clyde Allison	27-01-44	432 Sqn
J/21455	F/O	SHEWAN David Allan	3-01-44	57 Sqn
J/915	F/L	SHEWFELT Harold Angus	5-12-44	428 Sqn
R/164713	F/S	SHIELDS Gordon James Bayne	10-04-44	PFNTU
R/146505	F/S	SHIELDS Kenneth James	20-12-44	419 Sqn
R/166344	Sgt	SHIELDS Robert William	14-02-44	22 OTU
J/38422	F/O	SHIELLS Robert Howard	2-12-44	433 Sqn
J/14201	F/O	SHIRLEY Alfred Wilson	26-02-44	427 Sqn
R/144198	WO2	SHOENER Kenneth Frank	31-03-44	427 Sqn
J/26539	F/O	SHOLTE Gordon Edwin	29-07-44	50 Sqn
R/170878	F/S	SHOOBRIDGE Donald	5-07-44	576 Sqn
J/91067	P/O	SHORT Clarence William Farraday	30-11-44	625 Sqn
J/88755	P/O	SHORT James Theodore	7-10-44	426 Sqn
J/23712	F/O	SHORTLIFFE Hance Logan	24-03-44	626 Sqn
J/92352	P/O	SHORTT John Patrick	25-07-44	419 Sqn
J/88968	P/O	SHUSTER Joesph Edward	19-07-44	9 Sqn
J/40095	P/O	SHWAIKOSKI John	11-08-44	24 OTU
R/209199	Sgt	SHYKOFF Joseph David	24-09-44	85 OTU
J/27697	F/O	SIDDONS Moody Albert	16-03-44	408 Sqn
J/87992	P/O	SIDEBOTTOM George Elswood	29-07-44	431 Sqn
J/19846	P/O	SIEBEN Joseph George	2-02-44	432 Sqn
J/92125	P/O	SIEMINS Archie Harry	22-06-44	630 Sqn
J/95156	P/O	SIGAL Harold	14-10-44	419 Sqn
J/19620	P/O	SIGURDSON Johann	29-02-44	1666 HCU
J/22679	F/O	SILTALA Torsti	29-01-44	429 Sqn
R/151355	F/S	SILVER Samuel Lewis	25-05-44	101 Sqn
J/22205	F/O	SIM Dennis MacDonald	27-01-44	408 Sqn
J/86165	P/O	SIMARD Arthur Gerald Sylvain	16-03-44	426 Sqn
J/89268	P/O	SIMM Stephen	26-08-44	207 Sqn
J/89960	P/O	SIMMONS Alfred Montague	25-06-44	44 Sqn
J/90758	P/O	SIMMONS Harold Edwin	4-05-44	420 Sqn
R/173565	Sgt	SIMMONS Raymond Frank	11-07-44	1666 HCU
R/166685	Sgt	SIMMS John	3-03-44	1666 HCU
J/90293	P/O	SIMONATO Enrico	13-06-44	427 Sqn
R/178580	F/S	SIMONSON Percy Hardy	26-03-44	49 Sqn
J/19182	F/O	SIMONSON Roy Edward	16-06-44	22 OTU
J/91097	P/O	SIMPSON Robert Alexander	21-07-44	101 Sqn
R/198631	F/S	SIMPSON Robert Neil	23-05-44	207 Sqn
R/208935	F/S	SIMS George Robert	15-07-44	576 Sqn
J/90392	P/O	SINCLAIR Alexander Gunn	5-07-44	424 Sqn
J/38263	P/O	SINCLAIR Andrew Ian	24-02-44	1664 HCU
R/76842	F/S	SINCLAIR David	20-02-44	35 Sqn
J/91094	P/O	SINCLAIR George Edward	12-05-44	427 Sqn
R/219174	F/S	SINCLAIR Robert John	13-08-44	166 Sqn
J/89843	P/O	SINGER Jacob Harry	16-07-44	44 Sqn
J/86913	P/O	SIRLUCK Robert	1-03-44	76 Sqn
R/131523	WO2	SIROVYAK John	22-01-44	640 Sqn
R/275016	Sgt	SKEBO Basil Andrew	24-09-44	24 OTU
R/188577	Sgt	SKEBO Patrick Sylvester	20-02-44	625 Sqn
J/90562	P/O	SKINGLE Douglas David	8-06-44	408 Sqn
J/25693	F/O	SLATER Harry	17-08-44	428 Sqn
J/86169	F/O	SLEETH Robert Lorne	13-09-44	158 Sqn
J/86376	P/O	SLEIGHER Joseph Simon	18-03-44	434 Sqn
J/20416	F/O	SLOAN William Russell	21-01-44	434 Sqn
R/165429	WO2	SMALLEY Ronald Whitehead	24-07-44	582 Sqn
J/43567	F/O	SMALLWOOD Jack Alfred	30-11-44	82 OTU
R/287355	Sgt	SMART John Christopher	18-12-44	22 OTU
R/204325	Sgt	SMIRL Glendon Arthur	14-04-44	77 Sqn
J/86299	P/O	SMITH Alfred	27-01-44	408 Sqn
J/24727	F/O	SMITH Allan Gorrie	28-05-44	427 Sqn
R/171824	WO2	SMITH Arthur Roy	8-06-44	138 Sqn
J/11053	F/L	SMITH Bert Howard	16-09-44	608 Sqn
J/8371	S/L	SMITH DFC Charles Woodward	27-01-44	408 Sqn
J/89806	P/O	SMITH Charles Worth	12-05-44	626 Sqn
R/150932	Sgt	SMITH Desmond Roderick	23-10-44	625 Sqn
R/180643	Sgt	SMITH Donald Murray	23-03-44	26 OTU
R/189692	Sgt	SMITH Earl	20-01-44	102 Sqn
J/12704	F/O	SMITH Edward Walter	14-01-44	156 Sqn
R/137513	F/S	SMITH Elliott Russell	28-10-44	419 Sqn
J/23545	F/O	SMITH Elwood Oscar	26-08-44	83 OTU
J/95175	P/O	SMITH Eric	4-11-44	626 Sqn
R/114479	F/S	SMITH Eric George	16-06-44	405 Sqn
J/18707	F/L	SMITH King's Commendation for Valuable Service in the Air Ernest Sutton	17-06-44	419 Sqn
R/175155	Sgt	SMITH Frederick Curtis	10-04-44	24 OTU
J/95481	P/O	SMITH George Edward	7-12-44	419 Sqn
J/21564	F/L	SMITH George John	1-05-44	405 Sqn
J/21556	F/O	SMITH Gerald Alfred [USA]	20-04-44	428 Sqn
J/29977	F/O	SMITH Grant Lyman	11-07-44	408 Sqn
J/89897	P/O	SMITH Harold Alexander	24-07-44	625 Sqn
J/19595	P/O	SMITH Harold Ingram	13-05-44	419 Sqn
J/24995	F/O	SMITH Howard Wallace	22-05-44	630 Sqn
J/90368	P/O	SMITH Jack Ogilvie	1-07-44	626 Sqn
J/22369	P/O	SMITH James Alvin	21-07-44	158 Sqn
J/95482	P/O	SMITH James Duncan	18-12-44	227 Sqn
J/18558	P/O	SMITH James Henry	15-04-44	1664 HCU
J/88301	P/O	SMITH John	29-07-44	431 Sqn
J/89042	P/O	SMITH Kenneth	20-02-44	408 Sqn
J/25520	P/O	SMITH Lawrence Lindsay	27-04-44	12 Sqn
J/35016	F/O	SMITH Leonard Joseph	29-05-44	82 OTU
C/18975	P/O	SMITH Lloyd Henry	31-03-44	427 Sqn
R/267154	Sgt	SMITH Neil Lauretz	16-11-44	166 Sqn
R/197664	Sgt	SMITH Norman	21-01-44	427 Sqn
C/89362	P/O	SMITH Norman Alfred	15-10-44	424 Sqn
J/88153	P/O	SMITH Phillip Seagar	25-05-44	419 Sqn
J/87021	P/O	SMITH Raymond Michael	8-06-44	622 Sqn
R/168261	F/S	SMITH Richard Nathaniel	27-08-44	166 Sqn
J/87649	P/O	SMITH Richmond Wesley	24-04-44	425 Sqn
J/86658	P/O	SMITH Ronald Ward	11-09-44	408 Sqn
R/167419	F/S	SMITH Roy	2-10-44	1664 HCU
J/89610	P/O	SMITH Roy Stanley	13-05-44	419 Sqn
J/90919	P/O	SMITH Royal Joseph	10-05-44	106 Sqn
J/85722	P/O	SMITH Sydney Emmington Fern Higgs	21-07-44	101 Sqn
R/184327	Sgt	SMITH Sydney James	24-01-44	428 Sqn
R/178906	F/S	SMITH Walter Perry	28-06-44	90 Sqn
J/27489	F/O	SMITH Wilfred James	29-07-44	100 Sqn
R/188673	Sgt	SMITH William Frederick	7-06-44	9 Sqn
J/27574	F/O	SMITH William Reginald	13-08-44	166 Sqn
J/18361	F/L	SMITH DFC William Robert	26-02-44	408 Sqn
R/169663	Sgt	SMOKE Milton Ray	20-02-44	429 Sqn
R/190191	F/S	SMYTHE James Ethelred	28-04-44	138 Sqn
J/17725	F/O	SNEDDON DFM James Allan	14-01-44	514 Sqn
J/90078	P/O	SNELL Dennis Edward	17-08-44	431 Sqn
J/89073	P/O	SNIDER Lloyd	2-08-44	425 Sqn
J/86562	P/O	SNOW Croix de Guerre avec Palme Grenfell William	28-04-44	434 Sqn
R/191177	Sgt	SOBESKI Victor	13-09-44	1658 HCU
J/90388	F/O	SODERSTROM Clarence Vernon	17-06-44	434 Sqn
J/13272	F/O	SOEDER William Ernest Paul	31-03-44	427 Sqn
R/150594	Sgt	SOLLIE John Berge	29-06-44	22 OTU
J/15190	F/O	SOLMUNDSSON Kjartan Ari	28-01-44	426 Sqn
J/24022	F/O	SOMERS Bruce Allan	22-06-44	207 Sqn
J/23585	F/O	SOMMERVILLE Alexander Lindsay	16-02-44	640 Sqn
J/23299	F/O	SONSHINE Murray	20-02-44	431 Sqn
J/86393	P/O	SOOTHERAN Arthur George	9-06-44	426 Sqn
J/23424	F/L	SOPER Sinclair Joseph Roberts	28-04-44	15 Sqn
J/88258	P/O	SOREL William Gerald	29-07-44	431 Sqn
J/36937	F/O	SORRENTI Vincent Andrew	29-12-44	419 Sqn
J/15900	F/L	SOUAILLARD Joseph Jules Henri Oliver	14-01-44	405 Sqn
R/185297	Sgt	SOUTHWICK William Lewis	7-08-44	1664 HCU
R/175943	F/S	SPACKMAN Harry Weston	20-01-44	158 Sqn
R/155929	Sgt	SPARKES Douglas Albert George	30-08-44	428 Sqn
J/23128	F/O	SPEARIN James Arnold	29-07-44	426 Sqn

ID	Rank	Name	Date	Sqn
J/86564	P/O	SPEARMAN Gordon Douglas	7-05-44	405 Sqn
J/26649	F/O	SPECTOR Joseph	22-05-44	100 Sqn
J/27831	F/O	SPEIRS George Herbert	6-12-44	432 Sqn
J/12262	F/L	SPELLER Donald Wesley	15-10-44	432 Sqn
R/188291	F/S	SPENCE David Jerome	17-11-44	24 OTU
J/18693	P/O	SPENCER Charles Corey Van Dusen	14-01-44	408 Sqn
R/270670	Sgt	SPENCER Gordon Leonard	17-10-44	1664 HCU
R/146367	F/S	SPENCER Stanley Derek	22-05-44	166 Sqn
J/89950	P/O	SPENSLEY Leonard	22-05-44	630 Sqn
J/92572	P/O	SPEVAK Jack	25-07-44	419 Sqn
J/16300	F/O	SPEYER Lloyd George	21-01-44	405 Sqn
R/210945	Sgt	SPINKS Albert Howard	29-05-44	82 OTU
R/183116	F/S	SPINKS Willis Eugene	22-06-44	44 Sqn
J/11590	F/L	SPOFFORD George Lewis	21-07-44	101 Sqn
J/17534	F/O	SPOONER Courtney Le Roy	21-01-44	84 OTU
J/28934	F/O	SPRAGGETT James Edward	13-08-44	428 Sqn
J/92433	F/O	SPRINGSTEIN Norman Ray	28-12-44	419 Sqn
J/24060	F/O	SPROTT John Coles	17-08-44	433 Sqn
R/225100	F/S	SQUIBB Harold Edward [USA]	13-08-44	166 Sqn
J/22846	F/O	SRIGLEY Joseph Ralph Gordon	17-08-44	428 Sqn
R/158503	F/S	STAINTON Arthur John	31-03-44	427 Sqn
J/90288	P/O	STAINTON William Charles	28-05-44	420 Sqn
R/178828	Sgt	STANLEY Ross Harvey	21-01-44	102 Sqn
R/144014	WO2	STANLEY Russell Henry Alvin	29-04-44	434 Sqn
J/35924	F/O	STAPLES Donald Anderson	2-11-44	408 Sqn
J/23460	F/O	STAPLETON John Wilkins	6-07-44	582 Sqn
J/85641	F/L	STARK DFC George Douglas	2-08-44	425 Sqn
R/198952	Sgt	STARNES Arley Carlisle	23-03-44	1664 HCU
J/89254	P/O	STARRUP Benjamin Victor	11-05-44	424 Sqn
J/92357	P/O	STEAR Victor	26-08-44	419 Sqn
J/92037	P/O	STECYK John Michael	1-07-44	625 Sqn
J/22138	F/L	STEEL-DAVIES George Everett	21-08-44	415 Sqn
J/25442	F/O	STEEVES Harold Birch	15-03-44	427 Sqn
J/19151	F/O	STEIN Arthur George	29-07-44	415 Sqn
J/36296	F/O	STEPHEN Charles Edward	28-06-44	22 OTU
J/4544	F/L	STEPHEN John James	20-02-44	429 Sqn
R/160280	Sgt	STEPHENS John Melville	3-02-44	28 OTU
J/28690	F/O	STEPHENS Wilbert	3-08-44	61 Sqn
J/86797	P/O	STEPHENSON Norman David Lesley	28-05-44	427 Sqn
R/95620	WO1	STEPHENSON Sidney Gordon	21-01-44	434 Sqn
J/85923	P/O	STERN Max	27-08-44	97 Sqn
J/5306	F/L	STERNS DFC William Meredith	20-02-44	156 Sqn
J/92919	P/O	STEVENS David Jason	21-11-44	426 Sqn
R/207875	Sgt	STEVENS Frank Charles	28-05-44	1659 HCU
J/206869	Sgt	STEVENS James Joseph Ursan	13-06-44	28 OTU
J/89945	F/O	STEVENS William George	27-04-44	106 Sqn
J/90301	P/O	STEVENS William Richard	5-07-44	408 Sqn
J/26657	F/O	STEVENSON Donald Gerald	4-08-44	424 Sqn
R/124239	WO2	STEVENSON George Edward	26-02-44	431 Sqn
J/88349	P/O	STEVENSON James Morton [USA]	7-06-44	9 Sqn
R/171883	WO2	STEVENSON Leslie Howard	27-08-44	576 Sqn
R/51668	F/S	STEWARDSON Clarence Cecil	13-10-44	1657 HCU
J/88141	P/O	STEWART Courtney Raymond	16-08-44	433 Sqn
J/19066	P/O	STEWART Howard Murray	16-02-44	432 Sqn
J/92122	P/O	STEWART James Bruce	30-01-44	207 Sqn
J/87408	P/O	STEWART James Gordon	24-02-44	1664 HCU
R/161156	WO2	STEWART Neil Macintyre	20-02-44	428 Sqn
J/15486	S/L	STEWART William Benjamin	13-06-44	408 Sqn
C/86790	P/O	STEWART William McGill	25-05-44	429 Sqn
J/29573	F/O	STIENSTRA Arthur	17-08-44	57 Sqn
J/18139	F/O	STILES Ernest Blair	3-01-44	83 Sqn
R/121112	WO2	STILES William Alfred	29-04-44	433 Sqn
R/282955	Sgt	STOCK Harry Arthur	17-11-44	24 OTU
J/24298	F/L	STOCKDALE George Edward	17-06-44	576 Sqn
J/92026	P/O	STOCKTON Andrew Hunter	15-02-44	550 Sqn
R/205581	Sgt	STOKES John Ridley	13-09-44	101 Sqn
R/205656	F/S	STONE Geoffrey William	8-11-44	158 Sqn
R/205766	Sgt	STONE William Reginald	3-02-44	28 OTU
R/180231	Sgt	STONEHAM Albert Louis	22-04-44	1660 HCU
J/36925	F/O	STONEMAN John Ross	12-10-44	166 Sqn
R/186431	F/S	STONER Melvin Harold	28-06-44	106 Sqn
R/130559	WO1	STORBAKKEN Reuben Alexander	27-04-44	83 Sqn
J/38262	F/O	STOREY Charles Theodore	11-09-44	408 Sqn
J/9863	S/L	STRACHAN DFC William Watson	16-02-44	432 Sqn
J/86763	P/O	STRAIN John Edward	25-02-44	460 Sqn
J/29978	F/O	STRATFORD Frederick	6-12-44	227 Sqn
J/95478	P/O	STREICH Willard Ainsley	30-11-44	429 Sqn
J/37031	F/O	STRICKLAND George John	17-10-44	1664 HCU
R/146997	WO2	STRINGER George Edward	26-02-44	90 Sqn
J/21814	P/O	STRIOWSKI Albert George	17-06-44	102 Sqn
J/92009	P/O	STROM Carl Walter	24-03-44	57 Sqn
J/90387	P/O	STROUD Claire Douglas	25-05-44	192 Sqn
J/9481	F/L	STROUT Alfred Carman	29-08-44	582 Sqn
J/18402	F/O	STUART Robert Claire	16-02-44	432 Sqn
R/270450	Sgt	STUBBS Norman Richard	20-11-44	1656 HCU
R/200124	F/S	STUBELT Robert Ford	8-05-44	106 Sqn
J/85870	P/O	STURMY William John Deblois	18-04-44	433 Sqn
J/95476	P/O	STUTTLE Norman Edward	6-11-44	432 Sqn
J/37528	F/O	SUCHAROV Mortimer Samuel	2-12-44	428 Sqn
J/17136	F/O	SUDDICK DFC William Edward	2-01-44	101 Sqn
J/15131	S/L	SUGGITT DFC William Reid	15-02-44	617 Sqn
J/29382	F/O	SULLIVAN Stafford John	25-07-44	50 Sqn
J/92698	P/O	SULZ Henry	4-11-44	626 Sqn
J/89358	P/O	SUMMERHAYES John Wilson	13-05-44	426 Sqn
J/46038	F/O	SUNSTRUM Alexander Lorne	17-10-44	19 OTU
J/89305	P/O	SURLES Charles Pittman [USA]	17-08-44	420 Sqn
J/89452	P/O	SURRIDGE Ernest Gordon	30-03-44	419 Sqn
R/196444	F/S	SUTHERLAND Allan Cameron [USA]	8-07-44	207 Sqn
R/60829	WO2	SUTHERLAND John [USA]	22-04-44	76 Sqn
R/189515	F/S	SUTHERLAND Joseph Arthur William	25-07-44	420 Sqn
R/177954	F/S	SUTHERLAND Roger Joseph	17-12-44	692 Sqn
J/90355	P/O	SUTHERLAND Ross Edwin	3-08-44	61 Sqn
J/92270	P/O	SUTHERLAND William Fraser	16-03-44	514 Sqn
R/161424	F/S	SUTHERS Harold	29-01-44	463 Sqn
J/90148	P/O	SUTTON Cyril Bertie	4-08-44	424 Sqn
R/83961	Sgt	SWAIN Samuel Jackson	21-01-44	433 Sqn
J/87036	P/O	SWAN John Kerr	13-06-44	434 Sqn
J/28221	P/O	SWANSON John Edward	30-08-44	101 Sqn
J/87024	P/O	SWARTZ Stanley John	5-07-44	428 Sqn
J/86402	P/O	SWINTON Thomas Ross	20-02-44	77 Sqn
J/25057	F/O	SWINTON William Auld	15-08-44	207 Sqn
J/26111	F/O	SYKES Leonard Taylor [USA]	5-07-44	424 Sqn
R/194099	Sgt	SYKES Peter Frederick James	6-01-44	12 Sqn
J/86398	P/O	SYKES Robert Frederick	15-02-44	102 Sqn
J/85382	P/O	SYLVAH Claude Michael	9-05-44	405 Sqn
J/87672	P/O	SYME Lorston Boss	8-08-44	429 Sqn
J/28570	P/O	SYMES George Jeffrey	1-11-44	106 Sqn
J/19357	P/O	SYMONS Francis Robert	3-01-44	426 Sqn
J/25119	F/O	SZYMANSKI Chester	22-06-44	57 Sqn
J/27196	F/O	TABOR John Francis Edward	17-06-44	426 Sqn
J/86108	F/O	TAILLON Adrian Frederick	19-07-44	425 Sqn
R/55608	Sgt	TAILLON Joseph Alphonse Gaston	20-02-44	427 Sqn
J/92452	F/O	TAIT Cecil Ralph	28-12-44	419 Sqn
J/19727	P/O	TANDY Frederick Arthur Ernest	13-06-44	434 Sqn
J/90291	P/O	TANUCK Gordon Stanley	8-06-44	420 Sqn
J/86430	P/O	TARBET Robert	29-01-44	419 Sqn
J/88729	P/O	TARPLEY Leslie Alfred	29-07-44	426 Sqn
J/93803	P/O	TARZWELL Herbert Chester	29-12-44	419 Sqn
R/106320	WO1	TASS Jack	15-05-44	82 OTU
R/173802	F/S	TATAI Stephen	21-02-44	630 Sqn
J/87587	P/O	TATE Donald Elgin	25-05-44	103 Sqn
R/257974	Sgt	TAYLOR Beverly Thomas	15-10-44	1664 HCU
R/160156	WO2	TAYLOR Charles William	2-01-44	550 Sqn
J/191622	F/S	TAYLOR Donald Allan	22-06-44	44 Sqn

ID	Rank	Name	Date	Unit
J/85317	P/O	TAYLOR DFM Ernest Alfred	19-08-44	10 Sqn
J/86732	F/O	TAYLOR Gerald McLaughlin	13-08-44	61 Sqn
J/92342	P/O	TAYLOR Glen William	17-06-44	419 Sqn
J/86442	P/O	TAYLOR Glenford Herbert	18-04-44	433 Sqn
R/168071	F/S	TAYLOR James Alvin	8-02-44	138 Sqn
J/10787	F/L	TAYLOR John Roy	31-03-44	425 Sqn
R/203228	Sgt	TAYLOR Richard John	13-06-44	28 OTU
J/21888	F/O	TAYLOR Robert Clifton	15-02-44	622 Sqn
J/24251	F/O	TAYLOR Thomas Wessel	13-05-44	426 Sqn
J/89913	P/O	TAYLOR William	15-03-44	408 Sqn
J/92135	P/O	TAZUK John Edward [USA]	6-10-44	433 Sqn
J/23404	F/O	TEASDALE Thomas Leo Whigham	25-03-44	166 Sqn
J/90302	P/O	TEES Bruce Edwin	14-07-44	433 Sqn
J/40019	P/O	TEES William Alan	4-07-44	24 OTU
J/36306	F/O	TERRIS George Thompson Gilbert	6-11-44	50 Sqn
J/14747	F/O	TESKEY John Dargavel	27-01-44	408 Sqn
J/23910	F/O	TETRAULT Joseph Octave Arthur Remi	23-05-44	425 Sqn
J/39172	F/O	TETROE Charles Wilfred	24-10-44	1659 HCU
J/87995	P/O	THAINE Francis Bruce	29-07-44	428 Sqn
J/11784	F/L	THATCHER William	14-01-44	408 Sqn
J/21300	P/O	THERIAULT Henri Paul	22-02-44	218 Sqn
J/35009	F/O	THERREAULT Jules Napoleon Robert	14-10-44	419 Sqn
J/90043	P/O	THIBEDEAU Roy Frederick	31-03-44	50 Sqn
J/19621	P/O	THICKE Douglas Andrew	18-03-44	434 Sqn
R/176973	F/S	THISTLE Frank Eleazer	4-10-44	82 OTU
J/10874	F/L	THISTLE Lawrence Bruce	13-06-44	427 Sqn
R/54324	WO2	THOM William Craig	29-01-44	77 Sqn
J/88633	P/O	THOMAS Arthur Evans Cosdett	28-06-44	106 Sqn
J/87559	P/O	THOMAS Douglas Osborne	13-05-44	640 Sqn
J/18090	F/O	THOMAS DFM Edwin Horton	14-01-44	514 Sqn
J/86485	P/O	THOMAS Robert	14-05-44	433 Sqn
J/85408	P/O	THOMPSON Arthur Cameron	29-01-44	431 Sqn
J/86074	P/O	THOMPSON Carlton Stewart [USA]	13-06-44	15 Sqn
J/29765	F/O	THOMPSON Charles Bruce	1-09-44	138 Sqn
J/88046	P/O	THOMSON Clifford Arnold	30-07-44	115 Sqn
R/197505	Sgt	THOMPSON Gilbert Frank Allerton	22-03-44	408 Sqn
R/70308	WO2	THOMPSON Harold Bruce	15-03-44	51 Sqn
J/35267	P/O	THOMPSON John Allen	14-07-44	24 OTU
J/28977	F/O	THOMPSON John William	27-09-44	619 Sqn
J/85435	P/O	THOMPSON Robert Henderson	20-01-44	158 Sqn
J/87372	P/O	THOMPSON Roderick John	24-03-44	207 Sqn
J/86841	P/O	THOMPSON Russell Bennett	3-06-44	158 Sqn
J/25699	F/O	THOMPSON Thomas Wellwood	29-06-44	76 Sqn
R/162116	F/S	THOMPSON William Colin	4-01-44	1658 HCU
J/88089	P/O	THOMPSON Willis Henry	4-05-44	460 Sqn
J/92623	P/O	THOMSON Alexander Sinclair	30-11-44	429 Sqn
J/90356	P/O	THOMSON Harold David	3-08-44	61 Sqn
J/90921	P/O	THOMSON James Sydney	12-05-44	432 Sqn
J/17443	F/O	THOMSON Richard Keith	31-03-44	76 Sqn
J/88701	P/O	THOMSON Thomas Allan	28-01-44	426 Sqn
J/19631	P/O	THORNTON Jack Hardy	31-03-44	207 Sqn
J/87162	P/O	THORPE Gordon Ralston	31-03-44	207 Sqn
J/25068	F/O	THRASHER Arthur Ross	18-04-44	433 Sqn
R/224882	F/S	THYRET Harry Ray	4-12-44	166 Sqn
J/92476	P/O	TIERNEY Thomas Bernard	4-10-44	419 Sqn
J/88771	P/O	TILLMANN William Gerard	25-03-44	424 Sqn
J/22697	P/O	TILT Francis Gorman	8-06-44	420 Sqn
J/29095	F/O	TILTON Arthur Andrew	16-05-44	26 OTU
J/21857	F/O	TIMMINS Wilbert Harry	14-01-44	408 Sqn
J/20618	F/O	TINDALL Charles Edward	22-03-44	425 Sqn
J/23964	F/O	TINKER Edmund Thomas	21-03-44	619 Sqn
J/26318	F/O	TINLINE John Evan	25-04-44	424 Sqn
J/26726	F/O	TIPLADY Charles William Eric	28-04-44	166 Sqn
J/28523	F/O	TITE DFC Joseph	22-12-44	405 Sqn
J/38329	F/O	TITLEMAN Daniel	16-06-44	22 OTU
R/271259	Sgt	TITT Donald Fraser	22-10-44	1659 HCU
R/113498	WO2	TOAL Gordon William Chester	21-01-44	427 Sqn
R/131283	WO2	TOBIN William Benedict	21-01-44	419 Sqn
R/90026	WO2	TOBIN William Robert	20-02-44	427 Sqn
J/87145	P/O	TODD Elvin George	13-06-44	408 Sqn
J/27271	F/O	TODD Frank Gilmour	12-10-44	432 Sqn
J/87363	P/O	TODHUNTER Charles Clarke	30-08-44	434 Sqn
J/27116	F/O	TOKAR Paul William	29-06-44	22 OTU
J/94224	P/O	TOLE Harold Keith	18-04-44	433 Sqn
J/87550	P/O	TOLMIE John Andrews	17-08-44	433 Sqn
J/90650	P/O	TOMLIN Douglas	25-04-44	635 Sqn
J/89352	P/O	TOMLINSON Walter Harold	6-07-44	424 Sqn
C/95173	P/O	TONERI Leonard Edwin	25-10-44	428 Sqn
J/95500	P/O	TONKIN Donald Clifford	24-12-44	408 Sqn
J/86167	P/O	TOPPING Frederick Wills	31-03-44	78 Sqn
J/14576	F/O	TOPPINGS Irving John	31-03-44	156 Sqn
R/160418	F/S	TORBET George Dudgeon	31-03-44	78 Sqn
R/213609	F/S	TOTH Leslie Wilfred	24-11-44	419 Sqn
J/25935	F/O	TOWNSEND Elwood Albert	29-07-44	405 Sqn
J/93539	P/O	TOWSLEY Leslie Robert	22-05-44	550 Sqn
J/19980	P/O	TRACEY John Chalmers	25-03-44	425 Sqn
J/22429	F/O	TRANMER William Thomas	30-01-44	207 Sqn
J/28343	F/O	TRANTER Roy Hudson	6-06-44	426 Sqn
J/23604	F/O	TRAVERS Charles [USA]	21-01-44	207 Sqn
R/159268	WO2	TREMBLAY Alfred Arthur Joseph	25-05-44	576 Sqn
J/25701	F/O	TREWIN Bertram Alfonso	18-04-44	158 Sqn
J/10801	F/L	TRICKETT Douglas Herbert	25-07-44	420 Sqn
J/92914	P/O	TROTT Donald Alexander	4-10-44	419 Sqn
J/87046	P/O	TRUDEAU Zenon Romeo	25-04-44	424 Sqn
J/89446	P/O	TRUDEL Roland Joseph	2-03-44	425 Sqn
J/25122	F/O	TRUEMAN Harry George	31-01-44	1660 HCU
J/88730	P/O	TRUSCOTT Harold Edmund	29-07-44	408 Sqn
J/87770	P/O	TRUSCOTT James Robert	5-07-44	49 Sqn
J/40009	F/O	TUCKER Joseph William	30-08-44	19 OTU
J/89456	P/O	TUCKER Kenneth David	28-04-44	419 Sqn
R/155964	F/S	TUFTS Harry William Robert	17-06-44	1660 HCU
R/252875	F/S	TURACHEK John Martin	30-08-44	90 Sqn
J/37152	P/O	TURNER Claude Sydney [USA]	24-03-44	425 Sqn
J/87128	P/O	TURNER Thomas Duncan	17-06-44	434 Sqn
J/95438	P/O	TUURI Albert William	28-07-44	101 Sqn
J/89394	P/O	TWETER Lloyd Allan	23-10-44	625 Sqn
J/88703	P/O	TWIGGE Gerald Andrew	29-01-44	10 Sqn
J/13758	F/L	TYNDALE Lorne Vincent	29-08-44	582 Sqn
J/23724	F/O	UNDERHILL Earl John	24-03-44	166 Sqn
J/90308	P/O	UNGER John	29-07-44	420 Sqn
J/87613	P/O	UNRUH Victor Allison	18-07-44	427 Sqn
J/16129	F/L	UNTERSEHER Emil	16-06-44	22 OTU
J/89809	P/O	UPPER Bedford Philip	21-07-44	158 Sqn
R/208306	F/S	URQUHART David	1-07-44	101 Sqn
J/86471	P/O	URQUHART James Arthur	29-07-44	428 Sqn
J/28220	F/O	URQUHART Kenneth Robertson	19-07-44	138 Sqn
J/23464	F/O	UYEN William	31-03-44	78 Sqn
J/93105	P/O	UZELMAN Peter	23-12-44	582 Sqn
J/23744	P/O	VAGG Robert Arthur James	12-02-44	12 OTU
J/90964	P/O	VALDE Victor Lewis	2-11-44	415 Sqn
J/21433	F/L	VALK John Chester	17-08-44	433 Sqn
J/89262	P/O	VANCE Warren William	29-07-44	425 Sqn
R/187653	Sgt	VANCOUGHNETT William Earl	19-03-44	578 Sqn
J/39016	F/O	VANDEKINDER Marcel Edward	6-09-44	1667 HCU
C/87883	P/O	VANDERVEEN Hugh Ledgerwood	29-07-44	425 Sqn
J/18998	F/O	VANDER DASSON DFM William Lorne	12-05-44	103 Sqn
J/92209	P/O	VANDETTE Roy Emmit	6-12-44	640 Sqn
J/89739	P/O	VANNIER Joseph Jacques Rodolphe	13-07-44	415 Sqn
J/28580	F/O	VAN ALSTYNE Philip Nairn Thompson		424 Sqn
J/89465	P/O	VAN BLARCOM Eugene Clifford	30-08-44	50 Sqn
J/88587	P/O	VAN DROOGENBROECK Francois Adrien Jean	26-07-44	429 Sqn

J/25706	F/O	VAN FLEET Ralph Douglas	31-03-44	640 Sqn	J/22590	F/O	WARWICK Vincent Maurice	22-01-44	427 Sqn
J/88845	P/O	VAN HORNE Lawrence Ross	12-09-44	106 Sqn	J/86885	P/O	WARYWODA Peter	23-03-44	9 Sqn
J/85605	P/O	VAN SLYKE Allan Ross	24-03-44	158 Sqn	J/94448	P/O	WASHOOK Michael	13-10-44	415 Sqn
R/221063	Sgt	VAN-EVERY George Hiram	23-07-44	83 OTU	R/193982	Sgt	WASSERMAN Zahleck	4-10-44	82 OTU
J/27694	F/O	VASILOFF Stephen Ambrose	13-08-44	429 Sqn	C/90376	P/O	WATERS Mervin Hugh	2-08-44	425 Sqn
J/90070	P/O	VATCHER Richard Robert	29-07-44	426 Sqn	J/87475	P/O	WATERSTON Ervin Gordon	20-02-44	10 Sqn
R/176665	F/S	VAUGHAN John Gilmore	31-03-44	78 Sqn	J/87826	P/O	WATSON Frederick Stubbs	29-07-44	425 Sqn
J/85634	P/O	VENBER Nick	1-05-44	420 Sqn	J/20076	F/L	WATSON MiD James Andrew	28-04-44	622 Sqn
R/198411	F/S	VENNING Owen Earle	27-11-44	189 Sqn	R/214200	Sgt	WATSON Kenneth Allan	6-09-44	1667 HCU
R/265583	Sgt	VEREGIN Howard Peter	23-08-44	20 OTU	J/38782	F/O	WATSON Lloyd George	30-11-44	429 Sqn
C/86760	P/O	VERNON Stanley James	20-02-44	431 Sqn	J/86806	P/O	WATSON Waldron Worthing	19-07-44	425 Sqn
J/19099	F/O	VIAU Raymond Gerald	6-07-44	424 Sqn	J/39281	F/O	WATSON William Douglas	23-07-44	83 OTU
J/96518	WO2	VIDAL Joseph Wilfrid Henri	7-02-44	427 Sqn	J/89063	P/O	WATT Alick	15-08-44	207 Sqn
J/159546	Sgt	VIGNEAULT Joseph Philorome Ambroise			R/222387	Sgt	WATT James	13-09-44	101 Sqn
			23-09-44	1664 HCU	J/89106	P/O	WATTERS James Francis	30-01-44	433 Sqn
J/85758	P/O	VIGOR Edmund Arthur	28-04-44	434 Sqn	J/20177	F/O	WATTERSON David Douglas	25-04-44	420 Sqn
R/199834	Sgt	VILLENEUVE Jules Robert Rene	20-11-44	22 OTU	J/25939	F/O	WATTS Frederick Hurbert	18-08-44	576 Sqn
J/86473	P/O	VINCENT DFC Gordon Kenneth Vimy			J/10777	F/L	WAY Wilfred Howard	7-06-44	103 Sqn
			28-07-44	425 Sqn	J/29371	F/O	WAYCHUK Walter Simeon	11-07-44	408 Sqn
R/197679	F/S	VINCENT Peter Horace Gordon	25-04-44	192 Sqn	R/154885	WO2	WAYE Wendell Clifford [USA]	30-06-44	51 Sqn
J/90950	P/O	VINETT Gerard Frederick	28-05-44	427 Sqn	J/24143	P/O	WEARY Frederick Percy Ogilvie	17-07-44	23 OTU
J/88202	P/O	VIPOND Blair Everett	4-07-44	12 Sqn	J/18150	F/O	WEATHERALL DFM Robert Lorne	20-05-44	7 Sqn
J/38130	P/O	VIPOND George Graham	2-05-44	429 Sqn	R/130225	WO2	WEATHERBY Charles Lewis	11-04-44	78 Sqn
J/95480	P/O	VIRAG James Emil	5-12-44	428 Sqn	J/19918	P/O	WEAVER Glen Mason	4-05-44	405 Sqn
J/7905	F/L	VIRTUE James Denholm	21-07-44	405 Sqn	R/180232	Sgt	WEBB Edward Charles	20-02-44	428 Sqn
J/87751	P/O	VIVIAN Jack Kenneth	16-06-44	405 Sqn	R/114846	WO1	WEBB Edward Victor	25-04-44	420 Sqn
J/28974	F/O	VLASSIE Nickolas	27-04-44	619 Sqn	J/5122	F/L	WEBB Stuart Douglas	10-11-44	608 Sqn
J/87663	P/O	VORNBROCK Wilfred Ferdinand	23-04-44	424 Sqn	J/38164	F/O	WEBBER Joseph Alexander	13-05-44	419 Sqn
J/86403	P/O	WADE Reginald Herbert	20-02-44	408 Sqn	J/21610	F/O	WEBLEY Leslie Charles Edgar	9-05-44	431 Sqn
J/87659	P/O	WAITE Allan Halford	21-02-44	425 Sqn	J/27175	P/O	WEBSTER Robert James	2-05-44	429 Sqn
R/273518	Sgt	WAKEFIELD John	20-10-44	1666 HCU	R/221579	Sgt	WEDIN Albert Ormond [USA]	8-05-44	83 OTU
J/93804	P/O	WAKELY Leo Paul	29-12-44	419 Sqn	J/95498	P/O	WEEDON James Frederick Gladstone	1-11-44	426 Sqn
J/86982	P/O	WAKELY Wilfred George	28-05-44	424 Sqn	J/92325	P/O	WEEKS Douglas Francis Christian	19-04-44	419 Sqn
R/216087	Sgt	WALDRON Weston Ross	4-02-44	82 OTU	J/86890	P/O	WEIR Ivan Arnold	24-04-44	102 Sqn
J/18652	F/O	WALKER AFM Bruce Douglas	8-08-44	419 Sqn	R/152759	F/S	WEIR Robert Norman	22-01-44	427 Sqn
J/86320	F/O	WALKER Donald Edward	26-10-44	166 Sqn	C/1651	F/L	WEIS Joseph William	8-06-44	408 Sqn
J/23729	F/O	WALKER George Sharpe	22-01-44	640 Sqn	J/35610	F/O	WEISS Gordon Thomas	4-11-44	101 Sqn
J/28784	F/O	WALKER Wallace	24-09-44	97 Sqn	J/27563	F/O	WELCH Gordon George	17-06-44	101 Sqn
J/91147	P/O	WALL Adolph Le Roy	9-10-44	76 Sqn	J/86424	P/O	WELLER Ronald Duncan	4-05-44	626 Sqn
J/18044	F/O	WALL Charles Douglas	3-01-44	83 Sqn	R/288516	Sgt	WELLS Stewart Willis	13-10-44	24 OTU
J/41664	F/O	WALL Walter Douglas	17-10-44	19 OTU	J/90955	P/O	WELSH Bernard Eugene	29-07-44	425 Sqn
J/27564	F/L	WALLACE Alfred Jerry	1-09-44	138 Sqn	J/87795	P/O	WELSH Lawrence Albert	21-11-44	78 Sqn
R/167989	Sgt	WALLACE Clarence Burdett	8-01-44	100 Sqn	J/24663	F/O	WENGER John	8-07-44	9 Sqn
J/23362	F/S	WALLACE Hugh Alexander	15-04-44	1664 HCU	J/6144	F/L	WERNHAM MiD James Chrystall	30-03-44	405 Sqn
J/28258	F/O	WALLACE John Douglas	29-04-44	434 Sqn	J/92539	P/O	WERT Clarence Martin	21-11-44	429 Sqn
J/35764	F/O	WALLACE William Matthew	14-07-44	433 Sqn	J/91060	P/O	WEST Albert Edward	29-07-44	57 Sqn
J/89460	P/O	WALLBANK Donald	15-06-44	433 Sqn	J/9142	S/L	WEST Robert George	23-06-44	76 Sqn
J/27582	P/O	WALLD Robert Albin	16-03-44	1664 HCU	R/162723	LAC	WESTCOTT Frederick Gregory	9-04-44	434 Sqn
J/35107	F/O	WALLINGFORD Kenneth Donald	6-12-44	635 Sqn	R/134419	F/S	WESTERGARD Ralph William	8-06-44	138 Sqn
J/92126	P/O	WALTON Richard John	22-06-44	630 Sqn	J/29785	F/O	WESTLAKE John Mitchell	18-04-44	428 Sqn
R/157319	WO2	WALTON Roy Harold	21-01-44	419 Sqn	R/197685	Sgt	WESTLEY Harold David	29-01-44	12 OTU
J/92960	P/O	WARBURTON John	25-11-44	427 Sqn	J/90025	P/O	WETTLAUFER Norman Harold	1-07-44	12 Sqn
J/92137	P/O	WARD Donald McLeod William	14-10-44	434 Sqn	J/88677	P/O	WEYERS James William	5-07-44	57 Sqn
J/26481	F/O	WARD Earl Woodrow	11-01-44	17 OTU	R/93150	WO1	WHALE Lloyd Leslie	16-02-44	420 Sqn
R/191520	F/S	WARD Gordon Lewis	25-02-44	115 Sqn	J/88871	P/O	WHALEN Vernon George	20-02-44	426 Sqn
R/183842	Sgt	WARDELL Leo Thompson	26-02-44	431 Sqn	R/118123	WO2	WHEELER James Arnold	20-02-44	57 Sqn
R/23122	P/O	WARKENTIN John Howard	24-03-44	429 Sqn	J/19486	P/O	WHEELER John Walter	15-02-44	434 Sqn
R/206109	F/S	WARLL Harold Peter	28-06-44	44 Sqn	R/197965	Sgt	WHEELER Maurice William	30-03-44	419 Sqn
J/39032	P/O	WARNE Rudolph Filmore	8-06-44	1666 HCU	J/91004	P/O	WHINFIELD George Ambrose Franklin		
J/92195	P/O	WARNOCK George Robert	4-05-44	460 Sqn				15-10-44	1664 HCU
J/22470	P/O	WARREN Arthur Louis	26-02-44	419 Sqn	J/25983	F/O	WHITBY Richard Reginald Frederick 'Ricky'		
J/17093	F/O	WARREN DFM Earle Freeman	7-05-44	156 Sqn				17-06-44	3 LFS
J/93781	P/O	WARREN Gordon	28-12-44	576 Sqn	R/194021	F/S	WHITE Bertram Louis	12-10-44	1657 HCU
J/18913	P/O	WARREN Reginald Lloyd	20-02-44	427 Sqn	R/77630	Sgt	WHITE Captain Clayton	13-06-44	419 Sqn
J/26703	P/O	WARREN Robert John Branch	26-07-44	103 Sqn	R/53218	F/S	WHITE Douglas George	2-11-44	166 Sqn
J/25041	F/O	WARREN Roy Edward	11-06-44	434 Sqn	R/200964	Sgt	WHITE Earl Douglas	18-07-44	115 Sqn
J/92111	P/O	WARREN-DARLEY George Henry	24-11-44	419 Sqn	J/22288	F/O	WHITE George Albert	8-07-44	9 Sqn
R/210363	Sgt	WARNE George Leonard	7-12-44	24 OTU	152	WO1	WHITE Godfrey Phillip	27-01-44	15 Sqn

ID	Rank	Name	Date	Sqn
R/193905	F/S	WHITE James Walker	4-05-44	50 Sqn
J/17506	F/O	WHITE DFM Robert John	31-03-44	427 Sqn
R/221536	Sgt	WHITE William Richard	9-07-44	622 Sqn
J/28941	F/O	WHITEHEAD William Anderson	15-10-44	207 Sqn
J/38243	F/O	WHITLEY Robert Newton	22-10-44	1659 HCU
J/87973	P/O	WHITSON Robert Daniel	29-07-44	408 Sqn
R/250965	Sgt	WHITTAKER John	12-05-44	15 Sqn
J/88716	P/O	WHITTAKER John Arthur	18-04-44	427 Sqn
R/198207	Sgt	WHITTINGSTALL Calvin George	22-10-44	1659 HCU
J/90316	P/O	WHYTE Gordon Edward	15-08-44	428 Sqn
J/19977	P/O	WICK Stanley Arthur	24-03-44	429 Sqn
J/21632	F/O	WICKENS Herbert Asquith	16-06-44	405 Sqn
R/191640	F/S	WICKHAM Walter Robert	15-10-44	1664 HCU
R/180285	Sgt	WICKS Philip Francis	29-01-44	434 Sqn
J/37806	F/O	WIDDESS Edward Henry	24-05-44	20 OTU
J/89966	P/O	WIGLEY Charles Victor Ross	13-08-44	77 Sqn
R/74336	Cpl	WILCOX Leonard Russell	24-04-44	425 Sqn
R/191982	F/S	WILDE Alan Raymond	13-10-44	24 OTU
R/151070	WO2	WILDFONG Gordon Walter	16-03-44	100 Sqn
J/27908	F/O	WILDING DFC John Archibald [USA]	9-09-44	426 Sqn
J/86917	P/O	WILKINSON Thomas Edward	24-03-44	76 Sqn
R/71274	F/S	WILLIAMS Arthur Raymond	14-01-44	408 Sqn
R/160076	WO2	WILLIAMS Elmer Fasken	4-12-44	166 Sqn
J/22780	F/O	WILLIAMS Erle Keith	25-02-44	619 Sqn
R/119950	WO2	WILLIAMS Gordon Ivan	31-01-44	97 Sqn
R/106082	F/S	WILLIAMS James Henry	6-08-44	50 Sqn
C/90374	P/O	WILLIAMS Joseph Edward	18-07-44	431 Sqn
J/85857	P/O	WILLIAMS Leslie Llewellyn	1-06-44	1667 HCU
J/88424	P/O	WILLIAMSON Albert John	19-07-44	207 Sqn
J/87864	P/O	WILLIAMSON John Sherwood	5-10-44	427 Sqn
J/89218	P/O	WILLIS Albert Anthony Joseph	3-09-44	426 Sqn
J/23367	F/O	WILLIS Gordon Keith	8-05-44	44 Sqn
J/89059	P/O	WILLSON David Gordon	18-07-44	427 Sqn
R/145481	F/S	WILLSON John Campbell [USA]	22-06-44	44 Sqn
J/39140	F/O	WILLISON Raymond Phillip	9-11-44	82 OTU
R/176589	F/S	WILLISTON Albert	21-01-44	514 Sqn
R/168352	Sgt	WILLMEK Frank	12-12-44	1664 HCU
R/209089	Sgt	WILLMOTT David Millar	13-06-44	90 Sqn
J/23777	S/L	WILMOT DFC* Brian Edmund	21-08-44	415 Sqn
J/95499	P/O	WILMOT Earl Duncan	9-11-44	625 Sqn
J/27994	F/O	WILSHER Frederick Harold	29-12-44	405 Sqn
J/86626	P/O	WILSON Donald Frederick	5-07-44	433 Sqn
J/92645	P/O	WILSON Edmond Kenneth	21-11-44	408 Sqn
J/91188	P/O	WILSON Erwin Curtis	16-10-44	207 Sqn
J/88025	P/O	WILSON Gordon Alexander	25-05-44	424 Sqn
J/37726	F/O	WILSON Gordon Douglas	18-12-44	432 Sqn
J/86677	F/O	WILSON Harold Earl	27-07-44	630 Sqn
J/89778	P/O	WILSON Harold Kenneth	25-05-44	424 Sqn
J/25855	F/O	WILSON Harry James [USA]	19-07-44	619 Sqn
J/95261	P/O	WILSON Harry William	13-06-44	408 Sqn
J/86417	P/O	WILSON Herbert Clarke	20-04-44	420 Sqn
J/23525	F/O	WILSON Hugh Ross	27-01-44	408 Sqn
J/90298	P/O	WILSON Jack	29-06-44	424 Sqn
R/64989	Sgt	WILSON James Archibald	21-01-44	419 Sqn
R/139291	WO2	WILSON James Archibald	22-01-44	433 Sqn
J/16948	F/O	WILSON James Henry	31-03-44	429 Sqn
J/92571	P/O	WILSON John	28-04-44	431 Sqn
J/18939	P/O	WILSON Kenneth Carl	21-01-44	405 Sqn
J/15458	F/L	WILSON Murray Gray	8-08-44	419 Sqn
J/89886	P/O	WILSON Norman Andison	25-05-44	424 Sqn
R/162866	WO2	WILSON Raymond Hathaway	31-03-44	51 Sqn
R/153559	WO1	WILSON Robert John	29-06-44	102 Sqn
J/86121	P/O	WILSON Robert Perry	27-01-44	432 Sqn
J/25378	F/O	WILSON Russel Nelson	13-06-44	419 Sqn
J/92343	F/O	WILSON Sidney Albert	17-06-44	434 Sqn
J/25025	F/O	WILSON Thomas Abercromby	6-12-44	429 Sqn
J/12709	F/O	WILSON Thomas Ferguson	10-04-44	635 Sqn
J/39036	F/O	WILSON Thomas Harvey	8-06-44	1666 HCU
R/155694	WO2	WILSON Thomas Orval	20-02-44	640 Sqn
J/37822	F/O	WILSON Victor Henry	25-10-44	115 Sqn
J/20701	F/O	WILSON William Harold	9-05-44	431 Sqn
R/155803	F/S	WILSON William Routledge	14-01-44	1656 HCU
J/12971	F/O	WILSON William Shelton	20-02-44	78 Sqn
J/192018	Sgt	WILT Francis Elvin	29-02-44	1666 HCU
J/87719	P/O	WILTSE Thomas Earl	21-08-44	415 Sqn
J/93659	P/O	WINDER John Shaw	17-06-44	101 Sqn
J/90300	P/O	WINDER William Henry	5-07-44	433 Sqn
J/88512	P/O	WINDSOR William Frederick	29-07-44	431 Sqn
J/8840	F/L	WINN Elmer Stanley	20-02-44	408 Sqn
J/88893	P/O	WINSTANLEY Thomas Sudworth	4-05-44	460 Sqn
R/164238	F/S	WINTERMUTE Harry A.	5-10-44	1666 HCU
J/92602	P/O	WINTERS Charles Hugh	18-03-44	115 Sqn
R/187610	Sgt	WIPER Murray Lyle	14-01-44	408 Sqn
J/26320	F/O	WISTOW George Leonard	11-08-44	12 Sqn
J/24276	F/O	WITTMACK Frederick	26-07-44	432 Sqn
J/90949	P/O	WIWSIANSKI Michael	23-05-44	432 Sqn
J/88324	P/O	WOELFLE Carlton Henry	21-07-44	101 Sqn
J/87092	P/O	WOLF Wilfred Lawrence	2-02-44	432 Sqn
J/35510	F/O	WOLFE John Joseph	15-10-44	408 Sqn
R/167285	F/S	WOLOWIEC Joseph Michael	17-05-44	1661 HCU
C/1771	F/L	WOOD Donald Zachary Taylor	14-10-44	434 Sqn
R/118348	Sgt	WOOD Edward Francis	2-08-44	158 Sqn
J/85582	P/O	WOOD Frederick Charles	24-03-44	578 Sqn
J/86392	P/O	WOOD William Edward	13-06-44	434 Sqn
J/23953	F/O	WOODALL William Thomas	22-05-44	57 Sqn
J/86325	P/O	WOODARD Thomas Harold	12-04-44	432 Sqn
R/251532	Sgt	WOODFORD Claude Calvin Warren	13-10-44	24 OTU
C/21286	F/O	WOODLEY Charles David	8-06-44	15 Sqn
R/130601	LAC	WOODMAN William Daniel Holloway	8-08-44	433 Sqn
J/19650	P/O	WOODROW William Edwin	28-04-44	431 Sqn
J/86372	P/O	WOODS Earle Deachman	8-06-44	78 Sqn
R/96024	Sgt	WOODS Raymond Craig	7-02-44	19 OTU
R/103923	WO1	WOODS Roderick Fred	29-01-44	51 Sqn
J/9115	F/L	WOODWARD John Adair	27-09-44	432 Sqn
J/28532	F/O	WOOLAVER Allison Stewart	4-07-44	24 OTU
J/86900	F/O	WOOLF De Voe	26-12-44	76 Sqn
J/26712	F/O	WOOLGAR William Francis	6-09-44	1667 HCU
J/90754	P/O	WOOLHETHER Spencer Elwood	22-03-44	408 Sqn
J/23297	F/O	WOOLVERTON Alan Whamond	20-02-44	428 Sqn
J/29687	F/O	WRENSHALL Bernard Hartley	8-08-44	15 Sqn
J/88789	P/O	WRIGHT Andrew Roy	21-11-44	75 Sqn
J/86212	P/O	WRIGHT Archibald John Stuart	3-06-44	158 Sqn
J/91173	P/O	WRIGHT Charles Thomas	24-06-44	12 Sqn
R/203453	Sgt	WRIGHT Dennis	26-05-44	5 LFS
J/85531	P/O	WRIGHT Harold Grover	22-03-44	426 Sqn
J/37736	F/O	WRIGHT Harry	25-10-44	428 Sqn
J/24794	F/O	WRIGHT Howard Clouston	29-07-44	427 Sqn
J/89895	P/O	WRIGHT James	8-07-44	9 Sqn
J/26422	F/O	WRIGHT John Edgar	4-03-44	138 Sqn
J/28272	F/O	WRIGHT Owen	23-05-44	103 Sqn
J/89217	P/O	WRIGHT William Baker	3-09-44	426 Sqn
J/86486	P/O	WRIGHT DFC William Henry	24-10-44	18 OTU
J/88779	P/O	WRIGHT William John Louis	1-08-44	429 Sqn
J/88632	P/O	WRIGLEY Gordon Paul	25-10-44	431 Sqn
J/85314	P/O	WRY Lawrence Alvin	16-03-44	514 Sqn
J/24960	F/O	WUNSCH Vernon Frederick	25-06-44	149 Sqn
J/26695	F/O	WYCKOFF Charles Beverly	23-05-44	24 OTU
J/25814	P/O	WYLLIE John Frederick	13-06-44	78 Sqn
R/187127	WO2	WYNNYK William Peter	4-12-44	166 Sqn
J/10397	F/L	WYSE George Percival	9-08-44	427 Sqn
R/256200	Sgt	YACKO John Frederick	23-08-44	20 OTU
J/90047	P/O	YARRINGTON Alvin Edward	13-05-44	431 Sqn
J/24789	F/O	YARUSH Fred	21-11-44	420 Sqn
J/90292	P/O	YATES John Francis Edward	8-06-44	420 Sqn
R/256193	F/S	YATES Prince Edward Gooderham	12-12-44	103 Sqn

J/95439	P/O	YATES Tom	27-08-44	115 Sqn
R/128270	WO1	YAWORSKI Adolf Edward	25-03-44	427 Sqn
J/85960	P/O	YELLAND James Joseph	20-02-44	166 Sqn
J/43864	F/O	YELLIN Benny	15-10-44	101 Sqn
J/88648	P/O	YEO Lorne Edgar	16-03-44	426 Sqn
J/90371	P/O	YEOMANS Joseph Trevor	14-07-44	77 Sqn
R/207939	F/S	YERDON Harold Robert Joseph	25-10-44	431 Sqn
R/128730	WO2	YOUNG Alastair James	25-03-44	427 Sqn
J/20962	F/O	YOUNG Albert Edward	28-04-44	434 Sqn
R/204280	F/S	YOUNG Clarence	31-12-44	166 Sqn
J/21880	F/O	YOUNG Harold James	21-04-44	57 Sqn
J/27272	F/O	YOUNG Henry Kenneth	16-03-44	426 Sqn
R/134821	Sgt	YOUNG James Osborne	23-04-44	429 Sqn
J/89253	P/O	YOUNG Joseph Philip	23-05-44	408 Sqn
J/87873	P/O	YOUNG Samuel	22-06-44	44 Sqn
J/42722	F/O	YOUNG Thomas McLaren	9-11-44	82 OTU
J/87328	P/O	YOUNG William Harold	1-05-44	420 Sqn
R/193650	F/S	YOUNGS William Alonzo	18-07-44	431 Sqn
J/89867	P/O	YOUNIE William Alexander	3-06-44	158 Sqn
J/22621	F/O	YOWNEY Myron	20-02-44	61 Sqn
J/7977	F/L	YUNKER Bernard	5-07-44	433 Sqn
J/95475	P/O	YUNSKO Walter	1-11-44	424 Sqn
R/85341	F/S	ZACHARIAS Henry Jacob	22-01-44	424 Sqn
J/95483	P/O	ZADOROZNY Stanley Ernest	18-12-44	432 Sqn
C/88488	P/O	ZAREIKIN Joseph M. [USA]	5-10-44	433 Sqn
J/15532	F/L	ZAVITZ Jack	29-07-44	420 Sqn
R/124095	Sgt	ZAYETS Peter	29-02-44	1666 HCU
J/42332	F/O	ZBURA George John	2-11-44	415 Sqn
J/86889	P/O	ZBYTNUIK Tony	18-04-44	428 Sqn
J/89947	P/O	ZEGARCHUK James Eugene	25-04-44	115 Sqn
R/186556	Sgt	ZIMMER Ronald	2-01-44	405 Sqn
J/43636	F/O	ZIMRING Bernard	4-11-44	101 Sqn
J/35036	F/O	ZORATTI Victor	11-07-44	1666 HCU
J/27319	F/O	ZUBIC Frank Joseph	2-01-44	101 Sqn
J/17205	F/O	ZULAUF DFM Franklin Roy	31-03-44	427 Sqn
J/90297	P/O	ZULINOV Vladimir	25-06-44	50 Sqn
J/28684	F/O	ZYWINA John	1-06-44	138 Sqn

Note

No.415 (Swordfish) Squadron officially transferred from Coastal Command to Bomber Command on the 12th July, coming under operational control of No.6 (Royal Canadian Air Force) Group. But before all the squadron was in place at East Moor, the Manston detachment was called upon on the evening of the 13th to mount an anti-E-boat patrol off the Dutch coast. One of the crews assigned to this task was captained by F/O Sheen and, subsequently, he took off in his Wellington XIII MF494 and set course for the patrol area. From this sortie nothing further was heard and the entire crew are now commemorated on the Runnymede Memorial and on this Roll. Also perpetuated on this Memorial are the names of P/O Leach and F/O Mennie who failed to return to Manston from an anti-shipping patrol flown on the 21st in Albacore I X9281. Despite an exhaustive search over the English Channel only the aircraft's dinghy was found.

The double blows of dread news that had been visited on so many Canadian families throughout 1943 continued into the New Year and before the year faded into history the Bernyk brothers, Victor a pilot and Michael a navigator, had been lost on operations, both being 21 years of age at the time of their deaths in April and December respectively. In the case of the 21 year old Grant brothers, Alexander and Robert (although of the same age, it is not reported that they were twins) from Montreal, barely a month separated the despatch of telegrams to their next of kin informing them that they were missing from air operations. Such terrible news must surely have tested the faith of their father who was a Minister of the Church. I suspect that George Coathump may have completed a tour of operations and was, therefore, a screened pilot instructor when he lost his life while posted to No.22 Operational Training Unit. Consequently, although aware that his younger sibling, Clifford, had failed to return some two months earlier, it is highly unlikely that he would have known for certain that Clifford had not survived. Not so 22-year-old Alan Durnin, for when he took off for Hamburg in late July, it was with the knowledge that his younger sibling, Graham, had died in an instant when his 426 (Thunderbird) Squadron Halifax exploded over Norfolk while outbound on the eve of D-Day to attack a coastal defence battery near Trouville. For his father and mother, Howard and Marcia Durnin of Hamilton, Ontario, still grieving over the death of Graham, notification that Alan was now missing would come as added weight to their immense sadness.

From the two Mara brothers to perish in the service of Bomber Command, Stanley, the youngest at 20, was first to fall with his decorated elder brother, 24-year-old Neil going down over Belgium in February 1945, following a midair collision; in the case of the Marcellus boys it was the reverse with Francis, age 26, dying with his entire crew when their Halifax broke up in the air near York, while 19-year-old Douglas, aware that the brother he looked up to with such pride was dead, disappeared without trace while raiding Osnabruck in December. In mentioning ages, with the accent on youth aircrew over the age of 30 (and certainly by 1944) were regarded as senior figures, thus for two brothers in their 30s to be killed on bombing operations was unusual. But this proved to be the case in respect of Bruce and Oscar Morrision who died over Germany in that desperate period known as the Battle of Berlin and it is in Germany's capital city that both are now at peace.

For Arthur and Pearl Burston, parents of Frank and Glen, and their sons respective wives Irene and Ella, the 5th July, 1944, ended as the most awful day of their lives for it was on this date that an 82 Operational Training Unit Wellington in which both boys were flying came down near Honiton in Devon with fatal consequences for its entire crew (see Volume 7, page 302 for further information). Any hopes that Martin and Hanna Skebo of Wilno, Ontario, may have harboured that their two young sons would be back in Canada to celebrate their coming of age were cruelly dashed in the space of seven months. Their eldest boy, 20-year-old Patrick, failed to return from Leipzig in the February, while Basil, just 19, disappeared without trace from a training sortie in late September.

From an all Lancaster force of 412 aircraft ordered to attack the Opel works at Russelsheim in late August, 17 failed to complete the round trip. Navigating one of the two 90 Squadron crews missing was F/O Francis Good, probably unaware that in the bomber stream was his brother, F/O Harold Good, guiding a 626 Squadron crew to the target. Neither made it back; another double tragedy falling on the same day that forever was etched in the minds of their loving parents each time the calander was turned to the 26th day of that high summer month. From White Rock, British Columbia, Maurice and Wallace Granbois enlisted together, Maurice to train as a wireless operator, while Wallace took a faster track to becoming operational, arriving on 514 Squadron as an air gunner. Commissioned when posted missing from a spring raid on Dusseldorf, he is buried in the Recihswald Forest War Cemetery, close to Maurice who failed to make it home in February of the following year. Similarly, resting near one another in Harrogate (Stonefall) Cemetery are the pilot brothers, Harold and Lloyd Hannah of Moose Jaw, Saskatchewan. Lloyd had been first to die when his Lancaster crashed soon after taking off for a visit to Duisburg, six members of his crew managing to parachute to safety before the final impact. Three weeks later, Harold found himself over Dusseldorf and while flying through the flak barrage splinters from a near burst pierced the cockpit, wounding him in the neck and back. In considerable distress, he was helped from his seat by the air bomber (F/L Martin) who then proceeded to bring the badly-damaged bomber home to a crash-landing which all survived. Sadly, however, Harold's wounds proved mortal and he died in late January 1945.

Although some months separated the enlistment of the Normandeau brothers, Alphonse and Paul, both trained as wireless operators and both died before reaching an operational squadron. Alphonse was killed in mid-March 1944, when his Halifax crashed on a training sortie, while Paul was at the Operational Training Unit stage of his training when, while staying at the *Knights of Columbus Club** in London's Leinster Terrace, he fell through a sky light and sustained injuries from which he never recovered. Alphonse now rests at Harrogate while his younger sibling is buried at Brookwood.

In the notes appended at the end of the Royal Air Force section, I remark upon the death of an airman who but for his terrible misfortune to be injured when landing by parachute might well have evaded capture, as did the rest of his crew. Henri Dube's death in November has certain parallels though in his case he survived for over six months after his 425 Squadron Halifax was shot down during operations to Karlsruhe in the April following which three of the seven were captured and four, including Dube, avoided the searches of the Germans. As to how Henri met his fate, I cannot be certain.

A high proportion of the non-operational deaths amongst air and ground staff came about through road traffic accidents and, usually, concern only one person. However, when F/O Leo Di Marco, a pilot serving with 429 (Bison) Squadron, collided with a milk truck at Annan, Dunbartonshire, the resultant crash not only took his life but that of his wife, who was riding pillion. It is highly probable that she came from Middlesbrough for it is in the town's Linthorpe Cemetery that her husband now rests. Unfortunately, his marital status is not indicated and there are no details reported as to the name of his young bride (I am quite confident in my own mind that in regard to Leo's age of 21 the marriage was quite recent to their all too early and sad demise).

P/O McRae, who is buried in Brookwood Military Cemetery, is erroneously recorded as belonging to 5 Squadron. Between various Record Office papers, there is a discrepancy regarding Sgt Matkin's unit; I show him as being posted to No.1666 Heavy Conversion Unit, while *They Shall Grow Not Old* places him with No.12 Operational Training Unit. His death was the result of a road traffic accident when he was struck by a taxi in the Bayswater Road, London. Discrepancies also arise in respect of WO2 Leslie Stevenson. Oliver Clutton-Brock's listing of prisoners of war reports WO2 Stevenson's death at Stalag-Luft VII (Bankau) on the date given in this section. Allison/Hayward, meanwhile, give the 28th of March, 1945, adding the rider that he was shot by one of the camp guards after leaving a barrack block during an alert. The matter is further confused by his entry in the Commonwealth War Graves Commission Runnymede Memorial register which reports his presumed death as the 27th August, 1944, the date on which his Lancaster came down during a raid on the port of Kiel. Canadian documents (that would have been consulted by Allison/Hayward) indicate that he was buried at Kreuzberg near Breslau.

Finally, although there is no indication of a relationship, it will be noted that John Leonard Nixon and John William Nixon, both of Toronto, must have stood next to each other at attestation as their service numbers are consecutive.

* The Knights of Columbus are a Catholic fraternity for men.

ROYAL NEW ZEALAND AIR FORCE
personnel

NZ429911	F/S	ADAMS James Main	20-09-44	622 Sqn
NZ424402	F/O	ADAMS Thomas Gordon Huie	20-11-44	514 Sqn
NZ428826	P/O	AGNEW Charles	22-11-44	630 Sqn
NZ39075	P/O	AITKEN John Milford	10-05-44	619 Sqn
NZ429078	F/S	AITKEN William Murray	20-04-44	1657 HCU
NZ402839	S/L	ALLPORT DFC Valentine	26-03-44	1655 MTU
NZ429128	F/S	ANDERSEN Kenneth Peder Christian	4-11-44	75 Sqn
NZ427173	F/S	ANDERSON Hector Hugh Watson	31-03-44	49 Sqn
NZ421344	F/O	ANDERSON John Graham	16-11-44	207 Sqn
NZ42354	P/O	ARMSTRONG Cecil Ernest	23-05-44	75 Sqn
NZ401368	F/L	ARMSTRONG DFM MiD Charles Anthony	12-06-44	139 Sqn
NZ427084	F/S	ARMSTRONG Ernest Robert	16-11-44	214 Sqn
NZ42996	P/O	ARMSTRONG John Walter	11-04-44	103 Sqn
NZ427492	F/S	ASHWORTH Colin James	16-11-44	214 Sqn
NZ4310154	F/S	ATKINSON Leslie Noel	24-02-44	51 Sqn
NZ429072	F/S	BAILEY Robert	23-04-44	75 Sqn
NZ415814	F/L	BAIN DFC David Percy	25-03-44	7 Sqn
NZ421345	P/O	BARKER Richard Stockdale	26-08-44	75 Sqn
NZ401749	W/C	BARRON DSO* DFC DFM James Fraser	20-05-44	7 Sqn
NZ426158	F/S	BARTON James Henry	12-05-44	626 Sqn
NZ424788	F/S	BATESON Benjamin William	25-06-44	75 Sqn
NZ402463	F/L	BENEFIELD DFC Clifton Francis	25-04-44	9 Sqn
NZ424963	F/O	BENNINGTON Ian Campbell	5-05-44	7 Sqn
NZ421007	P/O	BENSON Charles Selwyn	20-02-44	15 Sqn
NZ402533	F/S	BERGIN Joseph Stanley	21-01-44	15 Sqn
NZ421495	F/S	BETLEY Roland Desmond Ernest	16-06-44	75 Sqn
NZ427945	F/S	BIGGAR John Matthew	12-09-44	75 Sqn
NZ428180	P/O	BILLENS Hewitt Elliot	23-04-44	149 Sqn
NZ425976	P/O	BLACKMORE Davy George	22-05-44	622 Sqn
NZ415739	P/O	BLACKWELL Frank Sylvester	14-01-44	115 Sqn
NZ421846	F/S	BLACKWOOD Henry William Arthur	4-01-44	11 OTU
NZ405365	F/O	BLAIKIE DFM Ian Armstrong	5-08-44	161 Sqn
NZ429027	F/O	BLAKE Eric George	4-05-44	44 Sqn
NZ421496	P/O	BLANCE Ian Edward	29-07-44	75 Sqn
NZ422098	P/O	BONISCH Lester Lascelles	11-06-44	75 Sqn
NZ422251	F/O	BOOCOCK Walter	13-07-44	550 Sqn
NZ416966	P/O	BOSWELL-KITCHING Jack Lambert	14-01-44	115 Sqn
NZ421011	F/S	BOWLING Colin Baxter	13-04-44	90 Sqn
NZ422047	P/O	BOYCE Trevor Wilmot	13-06-44	166 Sqn
NZ428303	F/S	BOYD William James Victor	12-09-44	75 Sqn
NZ4215727	F/O	BRADSHAW Robert Ranui	4-10-44	550 Sqn
NZ415075	F/O	BRAITHWAITE Frederick Arthur	14-01-44	115 Sqn
NZ413020	F/O	BRENNAN Leonard James	26-09-44	692 Sqn
NZ412419	F/S	BREWER Eric Clive	28-03-44	161 Sqn
NZ413374	F/L	BROWN George	6-08-44	51 Sqn
NZ425444	F/S	BROWN Russell Howard	22-05-44	75 Sqn
NZ4212639	F/O	BROWNE Grant Wallace	24-12-44	622 Sqn
NZ42367	P/O	BRUHNS Harold Henry	24-02-44	75 Sqn
NZ425737	F/S	BRUNTON William Edward	19-10-44	57 Sqn
NZ421840	F/L	BUCHANAN David Graham	18-12-44	207 Sqn
NZ4212641	F/S	BURGESS Neil Conway	19-10-44	1651 HCU
NZ417016	P/O	BURKE Edgar Lawrence	23-05-44	75 Sqn
NZ414560	F/O	BURTT Henry John	21-07-44	75 Sqn
NZ421672	F/S	BUTLER Laurie Licence	24-02-44	75 Sqn
NZ427479	F/O	CAHIR James Gordon	27-08-44	57 Sqn
NZ415289	F/O	CALLAN Neville John	25-03-44	97 Sqn
NZ427185	F/O	CALLOW Horace	21-07-44	75 Sqn
NZ422364	F/S	CALMAN Lawrence Gordon	28-10-44	90 Sqn
NZ426213	F/O	CAMPBELL Ian Melville	23-09-44	61 Sqn
NZ411347	F/S	CARSON DFM Adrian Leslie Bernard	5-05-44	7 Sqn
NZ42828	F/S	CATO Raymond Leonard	31-03-44	101 Sqn
NZ425233	F/S	CHILD George	19-10-44	1651 HCU
NZ414863	P/O	CHILDS DFC Jack Leslie	15-03-44	463 Sqn
NZ4215731	F/S	CHING William Michael	4-12-44	57 Sqn
NZ425027	F/O	CHRISTENSEN Gavin Keith Henry	27-08-44	57 Sqn
NZ413551	F/L	CHRISTIANSEN John Horace	14-01-44	115 Sqn
NZ415076	F/O	CLARK Joseph Norman	16-11-44	207 Sqn
NZ4213388	F/O	CLARKE Francis Royden	23-11-44	1660 HCU
NZ422690	F/S	CLIFT John Edgar	2-05-44	7 Sqn
NZ4310148	F/S	CLIMO Frederick Walter Percival	29-07-44	75 Sqn
NZ416419	P/O	COLLENDER Ronald Gordon	12-09-44	514 Sqn
NZ42708	F/S	COOK Peter Jackson	16-06-44	75 Sqn
NZ421142	F/S	COOK Stephen Astley	28-05-44	75 Sqn
NZ42373	W/O	COOKE Wilfred Harold	24-06-44	622 Sqn
NZ422653	F/S	COOMBRIDGE Trevor Walter	27-12-44	75 Sqn
NZ426165	F/O	COPLAND James Ross	16-11-44	625 Sqn
NZ425978	F/S	COSGROVE Michael William	23-06-44	76 Sqn
NZ424430	F/S	COUCHMAN Leonard Neil	11-04-44	158 Sqn
NZ421358	F/S	COULTER Arthur Lawson	4-01-44	11 OTU
NZ417028	F/S	COURT James Ross	26-08-44	90 Sqn
NZ412658	F/O	COX John Grant	25-03-44	61 Sqn

Service No.	Rank	Name	Date	Sqn
NZ402168	F/L	CRAIG DFC James Fraser	15-03-44	550 Sqn
NZ416861	F/O	CRAMPTON Harold Thomas	11-08-44	514 Sqn
NZ422079	F/S	CROFT Lawrence Furby	29-10-44	582 Sqn
NZ427019	F/O	CULPAN Noel Somervell	17-12-44	57 Sqn
NZ424059	F/S	CUTHBERT Ross Walter	5-10-44	115 Sqn
NZ425562	F/O	DALE James Atkinson	25-08-44	75 Sqn
NZ428085	P/O	DALE Thomas Wilson	17-06-44	199 Sqn
NZ422057	F/O	DAVIDSON Neil Douglas	21-07-44	75 Sqn
NZ4310149	W/O	DAVIES George Albert	29-09-44	11 OTU
NZ422938	F/S	DE LANEY Douglas Howard	20-04-44	1657 HCU
NZ411866	F/O	DILLON Michael Frederick [India]	11-04-44	103 Sqn
NZ421929	F/O	DODDS Gordon Harry	10-12-44	139 Sqn
NZ422267	F/S	DONAGHY Thomas Rodgers	11-06-44	75 Sqn
NZ422269	F/O	DONNELLEY Norman Wilfred	19-07-44	619 Sqn
NZ413304	F/O	DRAWBRIDGE Herbert John	21-04-44	97 Sqn
NZ422070	F/O	DRUMMOND Kenneth	16-03-44	514 Sqn
NZ415522	W/O	DUDDING Keat	25-07-44	75 Sqn
NZ413046	F/S	DUFFY John Laurence	25-03-44	115 Sqn
NZ427967	F/S	DURIE Thomas Kerr	21-07-44	514 Sqn
NZ392026	F/O	ECKHOLD Morris Charles	13-07-44	550 Sqn
NZ39003	F/L	EDDY MBE Charlie [Australia]	19-04-44	115 Sqn
NZ425973	P/O	EDE DFC Raymond Benjamin	26-08-44	7 Sqn
NZ421364	F/O	ELLIOT Thomas Isaac	21-11-44	75 Sqn
NZ426883	P/O	ELVIN William	12-08-44	75 Sqn
NZ41400	F/O	ENTWISTLE Ian William	13-06-44	115 Sqn
NZ425140	F/S	FALKINER Philip	30-07-44	75 Sqn
NZ423939	F/S	FALLOON Henry Reid	23-04-44	582 Sqn
NZ404170	P/O	FARQUHARSON Charles Frederick	30-01-44	115 Sqn
NZ414971	F/L	FAUVEL Spencer Francis	28-05-44	75 Sqn
NZ425391	F/S	FERGUSSON Allister Archibald	22-05-44	75 Sqn
NZ417203	W/O	FIRTH Raymond	26-08-44	75 Sqn
NZ426196	F/S	FITNESS Gordon William	20-09-44	622 Sqn
NZ424777	F/S	FITZGERALD John	30-08-44	75 Sqn
NZ422382	F/O	FLEMING James Allan	25-08-44	75 Sqn
NZ42675	F/S	FLETCHER Andrew Crawford	21-07-44	75 Sqn
NZ421503	F/O	FLOOD George Ross	22-11-44	630 Sqn
NZ416105	F/S	FOSTER Charles Grierson	31-03-44	550 Sqn
NZ421931	F/O	FOWLER George Henry	25-02-44	149 Sqn
NZ42389	P/O	FRAMPTON Allan Stanley	18-03-44	115 Sqn
NZ41158	F/S	FRANCIS Donald Victor Roy	15-03-44	11 OTU
NZ404681	W/O	FRANKLIN George Rubin	21-06-44	15 Sqn
NZ402991	F/O	FRANKLIN DFC Kenneth Gordon	28-04-44	156 Sqn
NZ412421	F/O	FULKER DFC Leslie	12-09-44	158 Sqn
NZ639074	F/L	FUNNELL John Lucian	21-04-44	15 Sqn
NZ428189	F/S	FUREY Rex Patrick	19-10-44	1651 HCU
NZ416476	F/O	GALL DFC John	1-06-44	161 Sqn
NZ426364	F/S	GALLAGHER James Stanley	14-01-44	514 Sqn
NZ427481	P/O	GALLETLY Alan Russell	5-10-44	75 Sqn
NZ422277	F/O	GALLOWAY Keith Alexander	22-06-44	619 Sqn
NZ421698	F/S	GARBUTT James Robin	15-02-44	622 Sqn
NZ415277	F/S	GARDINER Trevor Lloyd	28-04-44	11 OTU
NZ416038	F/S	GARDNER George Edward John	8-06-44	622 Sqn
NZ429029	F/O	GILBERT Gerald Harman	15-03-44	11 OTU
NZ425836	F/S	GILES John Patrick Arthur	12-09-44	75 Sqn
NZ42324	W/O	GILLAN Gottfred Lyall	21-07-44	75 Sqn
NZ425394	Sgt	GILMORE Rae	6-05-44	11 OTU
NZ412224	S/L	GILMOUR DFC MiD Brian Montgomery	25-04-44	9 Sqn
NZ421847	F/S	GOLD John	20-04-44	1657 HCU
NZ424451	P/O	GOODYEAR Edmond Jack	16-06-44	61 Sqn
NZ414873	F/S	GOOLD Arthur Frederick	15-03-44	11 OTU
NZ421968	F/O	GOULDEN David Allan	10-05-44	550 Sqn
NZ424453	F/O	GOVER Cedric Charles William	12-06-44	101 Sqn
NZ421272	F/S	GOWER Kenneth Wilfred	28-05-44	75 Sqn
NZ413407	F/O	GRAHAM Ian Dundee	19-10-44	186 Sqn
NZ405253	F/O	GRANT Donald Irving	19-07-44	619 Sqn
NZ421969	F/S	GRANT Reginald Halsey	22-05-44	7 Sqn
NZ426170	F/O	GRAY Hugh Graham	26-03-44	192 Sqn
NZ424456	F/O	GREEN George Arthur	5-10-44	626 Sqn
NZ421702	F/O	GREEN William John	11-04-44	625 Sqn
NZ416479	F/O	GREEN DFC William Raeburn	19-07-44	49 Sqn
NZ428786	P/O	GUDGEON John Bernard	12-09-44	75 Sqn
NZ411397	S/L	GUNN MiD Garth Reginald	21-09-44	75 Sqn
NZ426239	F/S	HADFIELD Graham Stanley	14-03-44	75 Sqn
NZ426041	F/O	HADLEY Wilson Orchard	12-09-44	75 Sqn
NZ42395	F/L	HALE Lawrence Eastmure	16-06-44	75 Sqn
NZ415575	F/S	HAMILTON Albert Carl	20-02-44	78 Sqn
NZ424979	F/S	HAMILTON Gordon Eden	22-03-44	7 Sqn
NZ422392	F/S	HANNAH Allen James	21-01-44	7 Sqn
NZ421276	F/O	HARRINGTON Allan George	28-05-44	582 Sqn
NZ428112	P/O	HARRIS Donald Keith	5-11-44	10 Sqn
NZ416482	F/L	HARRIS Willis Mark	15-02-44	15 Sqn
NZ42189	F/S	HARRISON Colin Arthur	3-02-44	84 OTU
NZ412686	W/O	HARVEY John Reginald	26-08-44	12 OTU
NZ405487	F/O	HARVEY DFM William Leonard	14-01-44	514 Sqn
NZ411892	F/O	HAY DFC Balfour Richard John	27-07-44	139 Sqn
NZ421710	F/S	HAYWARD Arthur Hardie	3-01-44	156 Sqn
NZ429047	F/O	HAZARD Whelan Fallon	12-08-44	75 Sqn
NZ422658	P/O	HEATHCOTE George Dudley	21-04-44	15 Sqn
NZ411508	S/L	HEGMAN DSO DFC John Alfred	15-02-44	7 Sqn
NZ426126	F/S	HENDERSON Colin Selkirk	25-09-44	199 Sqn
NZ421713	F/O	HENDERSON Hugh William	5-03-44	75 Sqn
NZ427204	F/S	HENDERSON Matthew Roland	28-04-44	75 Sqn
NZ39918	S/L	HENEY DSO Harold Wright	28-05-44	582 Sqn
NZ422282	F/O	HERRON Robert Weir	28-04-44	75 Sqn
NZ425571	F/S	HEWETT Norman Horace	5-04-44	11 OTU
NZ426886	F/S	HICKFORD Leonard Charles	21-07-44	75 Sqn
NZ411405	F/L	HICKS Harold George	30-01-44	115 Sqn
NZ421918	F/S	HILL Kenneth Arthur	22-01-44	1662 HCU
NZ421053	F/O	HOLDER Donald Fraser	27-08-44	115 Sqn
NZ427210	P/O	HOLLAND Mervyn Charles	19-07-44	49 Sqn
NZ412882	F/O	HOSIE Bruce James	7-10-44	617 Sqn
NZ421511	F/S	HOUGHTON Eric George	25-07-44	15 Sqn
NZ424469	F/S	HOWARD Edward John Francis	4-11-44	75 Sqn
NZ428819	P/O	HOWELL Edward	21-07-44	75 Sqn
NZ41150	F/S	HUDSON John Gordon	23-04-44	514 Sqn
NZ422403	F/O	HUGHES Wyvern Frederick	20-02-44	166 Sqn
NZ42579	P/O	HULME James Evan McKenzie	30-07-44	102 Sqn
NZ416862	F/O	HUTCHINSON Mervyn Gillard	31-03-44	101 Sqn
NZ415971	F/L	HYNES Brian Maurice [Hong Kong]	28-10-44	115 Sqn
NZ42196	F/S	INGRAM William Ritchie	23-11-44	630 Sqn
NZ414632	F/L	IRWIN DFC William Alexander	24-06-44	7 Sqn
NZ428122	F/S	JACOBS Thomas George	18-12-44	3 LFS
NZ422067	F/S	JAMIESON George Chowen	14-03-44	11 OTU
NZ415636	F/S	JAMIESON Laurence Seymour	1-06-44	15 Sqn
NZ426998	P/O	JARRATT Lester Paul	30-07-44	102 Sqn
NZ429888	F/S	JENKINS Frederick Francis Arthur	29-07-44	75 Sqn
NZ424982	F/L	JOBLIN DFC George Russell	29-07-44	630 Sqn
NZ416502	F/O	JOHNSON DFC Samuel Graham	20-01-44	1653 HCU
NZ426320	F/O	JOHNSTON Haig Douglas	12-08-44	75 Sqn
NZ429344	F/O	JOHNSTONE Douglas Scott	8-06-44	138 Sqn
NZ421061	F/L	JOHNSTONE Robert Nicol	25-02-44	149 Sqn
NZ421707	P/O	JONES Arthur Stanley	5-03-44	75 Sqn
NZ403606	F/L	JONES DFC Twice MiD Frank Colwyn	15-02-44	7 Sqn
NZ425576	F/O	JONES Kenneth Walton	22-06-44	49 Sqn
NZ425611	F/O	JONES Roy King	21-07-44	75 Sqn
NZ42299	F/S	KAY Alan Lister	22-05-44	75 Sqn
NZ416005	F/S	KEITH David Robinson Neill	22-06-44	106 Sqn
NZ417215	F/S	KELL Lancelot [United Kingdom]	14-01-44	514 Sqn
NZ417067	F/O	KENNEDY Arthur Alexander	12-12-44	195 Sqn
NZ415328	F/L	KENNEDY George Mervyn	7-06-44	83 Sqn
NZ421811	P/O	KEWLEY William Edward	27-04-44	44 Sqn
NZ422660	P/O	KILLNER Walter Henry	14-10-44	428 Sqn
NZ405287	F/L	KNOBLOCK Douglas Lawrence	27-08-44	35 Sqn

NZ421514	Sgt	LAIRD Leonard Ernest		28-04-44	11 OTU	NZ424063	F/O	OXENHAM Charles Bryce	25-08-44	218 Sqn
NZ42300	F/L	LAMB Ronald David		28-05-44	582 Sqn	NZ426142	F/S	O'BRIEN Brian	1-06-44	115 Sqn
NZ425579	P/O	LAMBERT Maurice		17-06-44	103 Sqn	NZ426153	F/S	O'CALLAGHAN Jack	4-01-44	11 OTU
NZ421728	P/O	LAMMAS Manson		23-04-44	75 Sqn	NZ425403	F/S	O'CALLAGHAN Porauamati	27-08-44	57 Sqn
NZ428001	P/O	LAWRIE John		13-08-44	514 Sqn	NZ415221	F/L	O'CONNOR Kevin Bernard	4-03-44	199 Sqn
NZ412240	F/O	LEIGH Robert Eric		10-02-44	109 Sqn	NZ415710	F/O	O'DRISCOLL John Daniel	8-07-44	467 Sqn
NZ416831	F/L	LEVY Ross Victor 'Allan'		19-10-44	161 Sqn	NZ422999	F/O	PAGE Trevor Gerrick	19-07-44	100 Sqn
NZ391011	W/O	LISSETTE Leslie Harry		4-05-44	207 Sqn	NZ425467	F/S	PARKINSON Cyril Robert	31-03-44	101 Sqn
NZ426087	F/S	LISTER Albert Henry		18-03-44	1657 HCU	NZ427719	F/S	PARTRIDGE Alexander George	1-06-44	115 Sqn
NZ427215	F/O	LOCHHEAD Jack Lesney		13-06-44	166 Sqn	NZ424509	P/O	PATERSON Graham Warren	9-08-44	138 Sqn
NZ426052	F/S	LONGLEY Geoffrey Ernest		23-04-44	149 Sqn	NZ413467	F/L	PATRICK James Victor	5-07-44	9 Sqn
NZ42990	F/O	LUKEY Francis Henry Clark		28-05-44	75 Sqn	NZ422046	P/O	PATTERSON Eric John	9-03-44	1667 HCU
NZ414310	F/S	LUXTON David Newbury		25-03-44	7 Sqn	NZ421525	P/O	PATTERSON George Vernon Bentley		
NZ417219	F/O	MacDONALD William Hamish		20-05-44	7 Sqn				8-08-44	630 Sqn
NZ421829	F/O	MACKAY Kenneth McIndoe		21-07-44	75 Sqn	NZ41525	W/O	PAUL Thomas Keith	4-01-44	11 OTU
NZ421742	P/O	MARRIOTT DFM Colin Rupert		12-05-44	626 Sqn	NZ426917	F/S	PAYNE Douglas Beardsley	23-05-44	75 Sqn
NZ437320	P/O	MARSH Robert Joseph		5-12-44	11 OTU	NZ417232	F/S	PEEVERS Thomas Alexander	2-05-44	75 Sqn
NZ415637	F/S	MARSHALL Eric William Elliott		23-05-44	75 Sqn	NZ414335	F/L	PENFOLD DFC Colin Frederick	23-04-44	640 Sqn
NZ417082	F/L	MARTYN Leslie Arthur		21-11-44	75 Sqn	NZ416154	F/S	PENMAN Alexander Mitchell	21-10-44	75 Sqn
NZ421307	F/S	MASON James Rooker		28-05-44	75 Sqn	NZ425591	F/S	PEPPER Douglas Reid	25-07-44	622 Sqn
NZ415771	F/S	MASON Paul Eugene		14-01-44	514 Sqn	NZ428925	P/O	PERRY Lyndon Clifford	30-07-44	75 Sqn
NZ412714	F/O	MATHESON DFM Archibald Allisdair				NZ415223	F/O	PHILLIPS Simon	13-06-44	15 Sqn
				11-07-44	692 Sqn	NZ402894	F/O	POHE MiD Porokru Patapu	31-03-44	51 Sqn
NZ425122	P/O	MATHESON Kenneth Duncan		31-03-44	7 Sqn	NZ421143	F/S	POTTS Thomas Christopher	25-07-44	75 Sqn
NZ426055	P/O	MATHIAS Vincent William		30-11-44	578 Sqn	NZ427909	F/O	PRITCHARD Howard Edward	20-09-44	622 Sqn
NZ425586	F/S	McCALLUM Eric Donald		24-03-44	15 Sqn	NZ4210077	F/S	QUINN Eric James	21-07-44	75 Sqn
NZ39061	F/L	McCONNELL DFC Alexander Donovan				NZ2171	S/L	RABONE DFC Paul Wattling	24-07-44	23 Sqn
				17-06-44	550 Sqn	NZ423420	F/S	RAE Stanley Allan	13-06-44	78 Sqn
NZ429183	F/S	McCORMACK Terence Francis		16-11-44	214 Sqn	NZ414340	F/L	RALPH DFM James Clarence	3-01-44	156 Sqn
NZ421981	F/O	McFARLANE John Duncan King		19-10-44	186 Sqn	NZ414677	F/L	RAY Arthur Lyall	24-07-44	1660 HCU
NZ412709	F/L	McGREGOR Raymond		31-12-44	138 Sqn	NZ425012	F/S	REDWOOD Gerard Henry	21-07-44	75 Sqn
NZ428982	F/S	McILRAITH William Simpson		21-07-44	514 Sqn	NZ424547	P/O	RIDDLE Bertram Challis	31-03-44	207 Sqn
NZ411915	F/O	McINTOSH James Alexander		30-11-44	75 Sqn	NZ426058	F/S	RIDDLE Henry Robert	30-07-44	102 Sqn
NZ427217	F/S	McKENZIE John Murdoch Thomas		11-06-44	75 Sqn	NZ39579	F/L	ROBINSON Maldon Ulisse	31-03-44	50 Sqn
NZ422299	F/O	McLACHLAN Alastair McRae		1-06-44	115 Sqn	NZ413219	F/S	ROCHE Gerald Brian	21-07-44	75 Sqn
NZ415266	F/O	McLACHLAN Euan Wilfred		28-04-44	75 Sqn	NZ428770	F/O	RODGERS Alan Oswald	15-07-44	166 Sqn
NZ422972	F/S	McLAUGHLIN Alexander		16-11-44	214 Sqn	NZ42341	P/O	ROSS Francis Robert	28-05-44	582 Sqn
		[United Kingdom]				NZ415496	P/O	ROUND Heathcote George	27-08-44	1661 HCU
NZ422420	P/O	McLEAN Lamont Weir		21-07-44	514 Sqn	NZ414567	F/O	ROWBERRY Geoffrey Warren	14-03-44	75 Sqn
NZ415216	F/O	McRAE James Kenneth		25-07-44	75 Sqn	NZ416543	P/O	RULE John Edward	30-01-44	156 Sqn
NZ414319	P/O	MEE George James		27-04-44	57 Sqn	NZ424524	F/O	RUSSELL Alfred Gordon	27-08-44	57 Sqn
NZ416518	F/O	MEE DFC John Milward		25-03-44	7 Sqn	NZ41362	S/L	SACHTLER Euan Wilfred	2-05-44	75 Sqn
NZ42349	F/S	MELVILLE Robert James Ian		5-03-44	75 Sqn	NZ415369	F/O	SAGE Ernest Vernon	10-05-44	550 Sqn
NZ421746	P/O	MILES Haddon Shaw		27-12-44	75 Sqn	NZ428796	F/L	SANDERS Frederick George	16-11-44	15 Sqn
NZ427220	F/S	MILLER James Stuart		11-06-44	75 Sqn	NZ428259	F/S	SCOTT Alistair Henry	4-11-44	75 Sqn
NZ427508	F/S	MILN Montague John		23-09-44	61 Sqn	NZ421105	Sgt	SCOTT Francis Alexander Jack	28-05-44	75 Sqn
NZ28017	F/S	MILNE Bruce		25-06-44	75 Sqn	NZ428797	F/O	SCOTT John Harold	4-11-44	75 Sqn
NZ415551	W/O	MOOSMAN Milton Cecil		31-03-44	426 Sqn	NZ427066	P/O	SEARELL Lewis Paul	9-08-44	138 Sqn
NZ417228	F/O	MORGAN Kenneth Frederick		8-08-44	161 Sqn	NZ421993	P/O	SEWELL Francis Sylvester	8-06-44	622 Sqn
NZ421389	F/S	MORGAN Robert Carhampton		30-11-44	75 Sqn	NZ415721	F/L	SHEARER James Maxwell	7-05-44	576 Sqn
NZ426106	F/S	MOSLEY Stuart Edwin		5-10-44	75 Sqn	NZ424529	F/O	SHIRLEY William Lawrence	23-09-44	582 Sqn
NZ427090	F/S	MOWAT Colin James		5-04-44	11 OTU	NZ421538	P/O	SIDDALL Peter Charles	31-08-44	550 Sqn
NZ416967	F/S	MUIR Stewart Donald		16-06-44	7 Sqn	NZ425212	F/S	SIMPSON Alfred Alexander	21-07-44	75 Sqn
NZ428793	P/O	MULCAHY Cyril Desmond		12-08-44	75 Sqn	NZ416804	F/S	SINCLAIR George Andrew	25-07-44	622 Sqn
NZ404134	F/S	MULLALLY James Aloysius		23-03-44	426 Sqn	NZ42504	F/L	SMAILL DFC William Bagley	27-08-44	7 Sqn
NZ40776	F/L	MUNRO MiD Lindsay Will		3-01-44	83 Sqn	NZ414691	F/L	SMITH DFC MiD John Baird	10-05-44	97 Sqn
NZ415820	F/O	MURRAY Henry James		19-04-44	75 Sqn	NZ416022	W/O	SMITH Keith Alfred	28-04-44	75 Sqn
NZ405801	F/L	MYERS John William Anthony		19-07-44	75 Sqn	NZ425179	F/S	SMITH Keith Emmett	21-07-44	75 Sqn
NZ42117	P/O	NAIRNE Colin George		30-07-44	75 Sqn	NZ416587	P/O	SMITH Llewellyn Selwyn	31-03-44	514 Sqn
NZ40423	F/L	NEILSON DFC James Gillespie		20-01-44	1657 HCU	NZ411048	F/O	SOUTHWARD Keith	6-10-44	75 Sqn
NZ42336	F/S	NEILSON Kenneth McGregor		15-02-44	622 Sqn	NZ2213651	F/S	STACK John Matthew	19-10-44	1651 HCU
NZ416144	F/S	NEWEY George Roy		12-09-44	158 Sqn	NZ424531	P/O	STAFFORD Alan Gregory	10-05-44	9 Sqn
NZ415354	P/O	NEWMAN Rex		17-06-44	3 LFS	NZ421784	F/S	STAFFORD Keith Varndell	12-09-44	514 Sqn
NZ4210960	F/S	NEWMAN Ronald Wynne		30-11-44	75 Sqn	NZ424533	F/O	STEEL Malcolm Joseph	26-08-44	101 Sqn
NZ413227	F/S	NORTON William George		26-08-44	75 Sqn	NZ429216	F/O	STEVENSON Charles	16-11-44	15 Sqn
NZ427224	F/S	ODGERS Richard John		12-09-44	50 Sqn	NZ40990	F/L	STEWART MiD David Cameron	13-05-44	635 Sqn
NZ422310	P/O	ORCHISTON Kenneth Watson		18-03-44	630 Sqn	NZ414913	W/O	STIRLING Eric John Walter	8-07-44	50 Sqn
NZ422090	F/O	OVEREND Norman Rupert		12-09-44	15 Sqn	NZ421403	F/L	STOKES Noel Alfred Deal	29-07-44	75 Sqn

431

NZ425298	F/S	STONE Arthur Thompson	21-07-44	514 Sqn
NZ413725	F/O	STRANG Clement Russell	27-06-44	692 Sqn
NZ404472	F/L	ST. JOHN Anthony Garwyth	30-10-44	627 Sqn
NZ425182	F/S	SYVERSTON John David	31-07-44	100 Sqn
NZ41962	F/L	TAYLOR Charles Joseph	27-08-44	12 Sqn
NZ421295	F/O	TAYLOR Jack	8-08-44	106 Sqn
NZ404965	F/O	TAYLOR Mervyn James	26-02-44	1655 MTU
NZ422333	P/O	THOMPSON Paul	24-03-44	619 Sqn
NZ4211036	F/S	THOMSON Edward Leonard	12-08-44	75 Sqn
NZ416552	F/O	THOMSON Edward Nigel Jeffreys	23-03-44	17 OTU
NZ425776	F/O	THOMSON Jack Stewart	21-04-44	619 Sqn
NZ412612	F/O	THORNTON Robert Jack	11-09-44	514 Sqn
NZ421338	F/S	TODD Alan Walter	30-01-44	115 Sqn
NZ411795	F/L	TODD Cecil	5-05-44	7 Sqn
NZ39287	P/O	TONES John Robert	31-07-44	100 Sqn
NZ416672	W/O	TOOHEY Edward Wallace	16-06-44	75 Sqn
NZ415041	F/S	TOWNROW Leonard Arthur	24-04-44	100 Sqn
NZ415207	W/O	TOWNSEND Edgar Thomas	3-01-44	103 Sqn
NZ417297	W/O	TREWAVAS Nash James	22-03-44	103 Sqn
NZ421298	F/S	TUNNICLIFFE Vernon Grant	25-02-44	149 Sqn
NZ41556	P/O	TVRDEICH Ivan	24-03-44	15 Sqn
NZ42819	F/O	TWIDLE Douglas George	30-08-44	630 Sqn
NZ429046	F/S	VAUGHAN Douglas William	23-04-44	75 Sqn
NZ415208	F/O	VEITCH Reginald Clive	12-12-44	12 Sqn
NZ425805	F/S	VERCOE Peter Newman	25-07-44	622 Sqn
NZ421945	F/O	WAIN DFC John Herbert	2-05-44	7 Sqn
NZ42344	P/O	WALDRON Charles Keith	14-01-44	115 Sqn
NZ413326	P/O	WALLIS Bernard Forfar	23-04-44	582 Sqn
NZ404106	F/O	WALTERS DFC Jack William	20-05-44	7 Sqn
NZ42698	F/L	WARD John	31-10-44	90 Sqn
NZ422004	F/S	WARING Roy Stanley	14-06-44	11 OTU
NZ404978	S/L	WATSON DFC Raymond Johnson	5-03-44	75 Sqn
NZ428918	F/S	WATSON Walter Davis	30-08-44	75 Sqn
NZ415046	F/O	WATT Peter Sydney	2-01-44	207 Sqn
NZ421800	P/O	WATT Wilfred Arthur	12-05-44	630 Sqn
NZ404008	W/C	WATTS DSO DFC MiD Stephen Delancy	11-07-44	692 Sqn
NZ426183	F/S	WESTON Godfrey Randal	20-04-44	1657 HCU
NZ428800	F/O	WHITEHOUSE Keith Owen	25-07-44	75 Sqn
NZ42488	P/O	WHITTINGTON Harold	21-07-44	75 Sqn
NZ425213	P/O	WHITTLESTON Ronald Joffre	17-06-44	199 Sqn
NZ415397	F/L	WILKIE DFC Hugh Charles	18-04-44	1657 HCU
NZ41386	W/O	WILLIAMS DFM James Lionel Tupuae	26-08-44	83 Sqn
NZ429932	P/O	WILLIS Harry Richard	4-01-44	11 OTU
NZ421803	P/O	WILLIS William Jarvis	22-05-44	75 Sqn
NZ416582	P/O	WINDSOR DFM Bernard William	22-05-44	514 Sqn
NZ417140	F/O	WOOD Russell	22-06-44	44 Sqn
NZ412301	P/O	WOODHEAD Donald Bruce	19-08-44	16 OTU
NZ425510	F/S	WORTH Jim	21-07-44	75 Sqn
NZ417144	F/O	WRIGHT Claude Henry	14-01-44	115 Sqn
NZ426209	F/S	WRIGHT John Herbert	12-08-44	75 Sqn
NZ421134	F/O	YOUNG Eric Walter	13-08-44	83 Sqn
NZ425313	F/S	YOUNG Peter Dawbarn	19-10-44	1651 HCU

Note

P/O Kewley is commemorated in *They Shall Grow Not Old* (the Royal Canadian Air Force Roll) but there is no hint in his biography that his origins lay in Canada.

Although it may appear invidious on my part to single out certain persons for mention in these footnotes (space permitting, I would have presented the Roll in the form of a short biography for every airman and airwoman who lost their lives in the service of Bomber Command), there are entries that catch the eye and, in my opinion, warrant a few words of comment. For example, by one of those many quirks of fate two screened pilots, each decorated with a DFC and who had flown their tour of operations with 218 Squadron, died on the same day while instructing at separate Stirling heavy conversion units; namely F/L Gillespie Neilson with 26 sorties to his credit and P/O Samuel Johnson rested after flying 23 operational missions.

And Errol Martyn also observes that S/L Hegman understated his age by 12 years in order to qualify, in 1941, for pilot training! At the time of his death, flying pathfinder operations, he was on his 73rd sortie, 14 of these being to Berlin, while F/S Leslie Atkinson achieved the unique distinction in serving with three branches of the armed forces; the New Zealand Expeditionary Force (he arrived in the United Kingdom as a soldier); the Royal Air Force from October 1941, and then two years later transferring to his country's air force and in which he lost his life while flying his 16th operation. Fate dealt a cruel blow to W/O George Davis for as a Merchant Seaman he survived the sinking of his vessel before losing his life in the aftermath of a flying training accident (see Volume 7 and page 318 for further details).

To close these notes, 1944 witnessed the passing of many highly skilled New Zealanders (S/L Hegman mentioned above being just one of the many with a string of operations recorded in their Flying Log Books), the most decorated being W/C James Fraser Barron DSO and First Bar, DFC and DFM. In his all too short life of 23 years he managed to log an impressive 1,264 flying hours and come so close to flying 80 operational missions, failing to return on his 79th from what was probably regarded as a reasonably cushy target, the railway yards at Le Mans. As the 'Master Bomber' for this particular operation, he knew that his task would expose his aircraft and crew to the dangers of flak but there is some confusion as to how this resolute pilot and crew met their end. Captured German papers state that Barron's Lancaster fell to anti-aircraft fire but some credence must be afforded to the possibility of a mid-air collision after the wing commander elected to descend below cloud in order to join his deputy (S/L John Dennis DSO DFC perpetuated in the Royal Air Force section).

POLISH AIR FORCE
personnel

P.2482	P/O	ANDRUSZKIEWICZ Kazimierz	13-06-44	300 Sqn
P.705472	Sgt	BABIACKI Stanislaw	11-11-44	1662 HCU
P.793747	F/S	BADOWSKI Zygmunt	24-06-44	300 Sqn
P.2251	F/O	BAKUN Waclaw	13-06-44	300 Sqn
P.704838	Sgt	BARZDO Rajmund	13-06-44	300 Sqn
P.2097	F/O	BERGNER Mieczyslaw Jozef	23-05-44	300 Sqn
P.780153	Sgt	BLADOWSKI Feliks Stanislaw	13-06-44	300 Sqn
P.782542	Sgt	BOGUSZ Kazimierz	1-07-44	300 Sqn
P.794816	F/S	BOKROS Jan	13-06-44	300 Sqn
P.2527	F/O	BREGMAN Jerzy Jozef	19-07-44	300 Sqn
P.784014	Sgt	BUJNOWSKI Stanislaw	14-08-44	300 Sqn
P.793205	Sgt	BUKOWSKI Jozef	1-07-44	300 Sqn
P.2197	F/O	BURKIEWICZ Henryk Marian	13-06-44	300 Sqn
P.709544	F/S	BYCHOWSKI Jan Ryszard	22-05-44	300 Sqn
P.792743	Sgt	CENT Walerian	30-08-44	300 Sqn
P.784982	Sgt	CHABROWSKI Stanislaw Antoni	23-05-44	300 Sqn
P.704065	Sgt	CHMIELOWIEC Andrzej	13-07-44	18 OTU
P.2400	P/O	CWOJDZINSKI Boleslaw Michal	1-07-44	300 Sqn
P.2579	P/O	CZABANSKI Stanislaw	14-08-44	300 Sqn
P.794365	Sgt	CZYZYK Henryk Tadeusz	26-07-44	300 Sqn
P.780992	F/S	DANIELUK Jan	26-07-44	300 Sqn
P.704993	Sgt	DODA Wladyslaw	13-07-44	18 OTU
P.704723	Sgt	DUCHACZEK Jan	28-05-44	300 Sqn
P.704196	F/S	DUDZIAK Janusz	25-04-44	300 Sqn
P.1083	F/O	FEDORENKO Aleksander	25-04-44	300 Sqn
P.2485	P/O	FEIL Isaak Jozef	13-06-44	300 Sqn
P.783291	F/S	FUDALI Wladyslaw	1-07-44	300 Sqn
P.2404	F/O	GALAT Kazimierz	26-07-44	300 Sqn
P.784745	W/O	GAWLOWSKI Leon	13-07-44	18 OTU
P.782730	F/S	GOLEC Michal	13-06-44	300 Sqn
P.706050	Sgt	GRABOWSKI Stanislaw	14-08-44	300 Sqn
P.2406	F/O	GROBLICKI Andrzej Jakub	24-06-44	300 Sqn
P.2653	P/O	GRUBSKI Wieslaw	1-08-44	18 OTU
P.794849	Sgt	GRUDZINSKI Bogdan	24-07-44	300 Sqn

P.703718	Sgt	GRZESIAK Zygmunt		21-02-44	300 Sqn	P.705430	Sgt	PAWLOWSKI Piotr	20-05-44	18 OTU
P.706599	Sgt	GUTOWSKI Mieczyslaw		1-08-44	18 OTU	P.0740	F/O	PAWLUK Kazimierz	31-03-44	305 Sqn
P.2408	F/O	HAHN Mieczyslaw		13-06-44	300 Sqn	P.783189	W/O	PERUN Jozef	14-10-44	300 Sqn
P.2410	P/O	HORWACKI Eugeniusz		24-07-44	300 Sqn	P.794958	Sgt	PITKA Ferdinand	21-02-44	300 Sqn
P.704258	Sgt	HRYNIEWIECKI Stanislaw Tadeusz		13-07-44	18 OTU	P.706546	Sgt	PIWODA Franciszek	11-11-44	1662 HCU
P.0983	F/O	INGLING Zdzislaw		7-03-44	1662 HCU	P.794959	Sgt	PLONCZYNSKI Witold	21-02-44	300 Sqn
P.704596	F/S	JAGIELLO Jan		25-04-44	300 Sqn	P.784557	F/S	POGODZINSKI Edmund	25-04-44	300 Sqn
P.780009	F/S	JAGIELLO Wladyslaw		26-08-44	300 Sqn	P.782374	Sgt	POPOWICZ Tadeusz	24-06-44	300 Sqn
P.706780	Sgt	JAGUSZCZAK Stanislaw		21-11-44	1662 HCU	P.784462	Sgt	POROWSKI Edward	13-06-44	300 Sqn
P.794451	F/S	JANICKI Fryderyk		19-07-44	300 Sqn	P.2152	F/O	PRETKIEWICZ Marian Waclaw	30-08-44	300 Sqn
P.704437	Sgt	JANKOWIAK Kazimierz		23-05-44	300 Sqn	P.793556	F/S	PRUSS Wladyslaw	25-04-44	300 Sqn
P.706902	Sgt	JANKOWSKI Antoni Jozef		1-08-44	18 OTU	P.704017	Sgt	RADONSKI Jan Sylweriusz	21-11-44	1662 HCU
P.783084	Sgt	JANKOWSKI Bernard		28-05-44	300 Sqn	P.703028	F/S	RATAJCZAK Ignacy	19-07-44	300 Sqn
P.2250	F/O	JARNICKI Henryk Juliusz		8-03-44	300 Sqn	P.1999	F/L	REBINSKI Longin	14-08-44	300 Sqn
P.2264	F/O	JASINSKI Wladyslaw Marian		25-04-44	300 Sqn	P.793887	F/S	REMBECKI Franciszek	13-06-44	300 Sqn
P.2412	F/O	JOZEFOWICZ Eugeniusz Stanislaw		13-06-44	300 Sqn	P.1818	F/L	ROZANSKI Jerzy Wladyslaw	13-06-44	300 Sqn
P.706472	Sgt	JURKA Stanislaw		21-11-44	1662 HCU	P.703225	Sgt	ROZYCKI Zenon	25-04-44	300 Sqn
P.792027	F/S	KABACINSKI Wladyslaw		21-02-44	300 Sqn	P.792655	F/S	RUCINSKI Witold Waclaw	21-11-44	1662 HCU
P.781380	Sgt	KABULSKI Jan		26-07-44	300 Sqn	P.794048	F/S	RUTKIEWICZ Jozef Jan	30-08-44	300 Sqn
P.794494	F/S	KARALUN Wladyslaw		25-04-44	300 Sqn	P.780062	Sgt	RYBINSKI Czeslaw	23-05-44	300 Sqn
P.704610	F/S	KARDASIEWICZ Zdzislaw		30-08-44	300 Sqn	P.704796	F/S	RYMASZEWSKI Stanislaw	24-07-44	300 Sqn
P.0109	F/L	KIEWNARSKI Antoni Wladyslaw		31-03-44	305 Sqn	P.704227	F/S	RZETELNY Jan	11-11-44	1662 HCU
P.1989	F/O	KISIELEWICZ Jerzy Szymon		21-11-44	1662 HCU	P.793177	W/O	SARACHMAN Stanislaw	14-10-44	300 Sqn
P.706635	Sgt	KLEPACKI Lucjan		13-07-44	18 OTU	P.2253	P/O	SOKOLOWSKI Jozef	20-03-44	300 Sqn
P.704558	F/S	KLUCHA Lucjan Jozef		15-06-44	300 Sqn	P.782318	F/S	STANIEWSKI Jozef	24-06-44	300 Sqn
P.0243	F/L	KOLANOWSKI Wlodzimierz Adam		31-03-44	301 Sqn	P.703164	Sgt	STANKIEWICZ Alfons Olgierd	21-02-44	300 Sqn
P.704006	Sgt	KOROL Sergiusz		1-08-44	18 OTU	P.794733	F/S	STEC Wladyslaw	24-06-44	300 Sqn
P.780477	F/S	KOSZNIK Edmund		24-06-44	300 Sqn	P.793774	F/S	STOLOWSKI Jan	30-08-44	300 Sqn
P.794211	Sgt	KOT Boleslaw		7-03-44	300 Sqn	P.783132	W/O	STYSIAK Stefan	19-07-44	300 Sqn
P.780049	Sgt	KOZANECKI Kazimierz Feliks		23-05-44	300 Sqn	P.793195	Sgt	SUMIGA Jan Ernest	13-06-44	300 Sqn
P.780879	F/S	KOZIOLEK Jerzy Kazimierz		28-05-44	300 Sqn	P.703444	F/S	SWIECICKI-STECKI Stanislaw	14-10-44	300 Sqn
P.704718	Sgt	KOZLOWSKI Mieczyslaw		11-11-44	1662 HCU	P.2429	F/O	SWINIARSKI Henryk	14-10-44	300 Sqn
P.705020	Sgt	KRUSZCZAK Franciszek		21-11-44	1662 HCU	P.782001	Sgt	SZELIGA Mieczyslaw Gustaw	13-06-44	300 Sqn
P.703157	F/S	KRYSIAK Karol		25-04-44	300 Sqn	P.780364	F/S	SZYCHOWSKI Stanislaw	19-07-44	300 Sqn
P.705419	Sgt	KRZESINSKI Tadeusz		1-08-44	18 OTU	P.2263	F/L	SZYMANSKI Wladyslaw	28-05-44	300 Sqn
P.706495	Sgt	KULAGOWSKI Piotr		17-10-44	18 OTU	P.2330	P/O	TAPP William Wisdom	28-05-44	300 Sqn
P.0819	S/L	KUROWSKI Ludwik Jozef		25-04-44	300 Sqn	P.0375	F/O	TOBOLSKI Pawel Wilhelm	2-04-44	301 Sqn
P.703925	Sgt	LASKO Zbigniew		1-08-44	18 OTU	P.780750	W/O	TOMIEC Jozef	24-07-44	300 Sqn
P.703050	Sgt	LECHNICKI Klemens Felicjan		1-07-44	300 Sqn	P.0853	F/L	TRAWINSKI Henryk	14-08-44	300 Sqn
P.2280	F/O	LENARTOWICZ Kazimierz		8-03-44	300 Sqn	P.704024	F/S	WALECKI Jozef Zygmunt	25-04-44	300 Sqn
P.795154	Sgt	LEPPERT Wladyslaw Bronislaw		13-06-44	300 Sqn	P.784189	F/S	WIJTYK Michal Wlodzimierz	25-04-44	300 Sqn
P.704444	Sgt	LESZKOWICZ Antoni		22-05-44	300 Sqn	P.792294	Sgt	WINKIEL Leon	23-05-44	300 Sqn
P.706290	Sgt	LEWICKI Marian		13-07-44	18 OTU	P.2796	P/O	WISNIOWSKI Michal Egidiusz	11-11-44	1662 HCU
P.782035	Sgt	LISKIEWICZ Gustaw		8-03-44	300 Sqn	P.1780	F/S	WOCH Zbigniew Antoni	25-04-44	300 Sqn
P.703473	Sgt	LOKSZA Aleksander		8-03-44	300 Sqn	P.782600	F/S	WODO Kazimierz	25-04-44	300 Sqn
P.703158	Sgt	MACHULAK Boleslaw		8-03-44	300 Sqn	P.705050	Sgt	WOJTULEWICZ Franciszek	14-08-44	300 Sqn
P.780896	F/S	MACIEJEWSKI Ludwik		28-05-44	300 Sqn	P.704824	F/S	WROBLEWSKI Marian	13-06-44	300 Sqn
P.781538	W/O	MADEJOWSKI Andrzej		24-06-44	300 Sqn	P.783237	F/S	ZATLOUKAL Jan Stefan Tadeusz	24-07-44	300 Sqn
P.784157	F/S	MADRACKI Jan		30-08-44	300 Sqn	P.2248	F/O	ZIEMBINSKI Zygmunt	1-07-44	300 Sqn
P.703117	Sgt	MALECKI Ignacy		1-07-44	300 Sqn	P.793879	W/O	ZOLTANSKI Jozef	19-07-44	300 Sqn
P.2852	P/O	MALKOWSKI Jan Tadeusz Jozef		21-11-44	1662 HCU	P.2535	P/O	ZYWICKI Juliusz Jan	23-02-44	18 OTU
P.703439	F/S	MAMAK Stanislaw Jozef		19-07-44	300 Sqn					
P.780277	Sgt	MANEK Stefan		11-11-44	1662 HCU					
P.780079	F/S	MARONA Czeslaw		14-10-44	300 Sqn					
P.794716	F/S	MIGASZEWSKI Zbigniew		14-08-44	300 Sqn					
P.704218	Sgt	MILEWSKI Leszek		11-11-44	1662 HCU					
P.704821	Sgt	MISZTURAK Stanislaw		13-06-44	300 Sqn					
P.0913	F/L	MONDSCHEIN Jerzy Tomasz		25-03-44	304 Sqn					
P.780604	Sgt	MYSZOR Marian		28-05-44	300 Sqn					
P.703889	Sgt	NAWRATIL Kazimierz		23-05-44	300 Sqn					
P.2320	F/O	OSIKA Witold		28-05-44	300 Sqn					
P.0445	F/L	OSTASZEWSKI Stanislaw		19-07-44	300 Sqn					
P.794545	F/S	OSTROWSKI Antoni		24-07-44	300 Sqn					
P.2119	F/L	OSTROWSKI Mieczyslaw		24-07-44	300 Sqn					
P.0266	F/S	OSUCHOWSKI Zbigniew		14-10-44	300 Sqn					
P.704493	Sgt	PACULA Albin		13-06-44	300 Sqn					
P.794835	F/S	PAGIELLO Albrecht		26-07-44	300 Sqn					
P.780953	Sgt	PAWLIK Jozef		20-05-44	18 OTU					

Note

P/O Sokolowski was originally an army cadet, transferring at his own request to the air force and training as an air bomber. He is reported to have died in hospital and is buried at Brookwood. Sgt Klucha, the sole survivor from F/O Burkiewicz's crew, evaded capture for two days but was apprehended and murdered by a German civilian in Radevormwald, east of Remscheid.

FREE FRENCH AIR FORCE
personnel

628	Sgt	ACEZAT Louis Georges	7-08-44	347 Sqn
C15566	SLt	ADNET Andre Simon Joseph	6-12-44	347 Sqn
1027	Lt	ALLEGRE Paul Marius Marie [Morocco]	3-09-44	347 Sqn
C142	Cpl	ANDREU Jean-Baptiste [Algeria]	28-12-44	347 Sqn

ID	Rank	Name	Date	Unit
C11503	Cpl	ANTONIO Paul [Algeria]	28-12-44	347 Sqn
C5317	S/C	BAILLON Louis Desrie Henri	24-12-44	347 Sqn
000801	Lt	BALAS Chevalier de Legion d'Honneur Antoine Louis Marie	7-08-44	347 Sqn
000725	Capt	BARON Robert Louis Joseph	4-11-44	346 Sqn
291	S/C	BEAUVOIT MM Croix de Guerre Norbert Leon	4-11-44	346 Sqn
321	Capt	BERAUD Chevalier de Legion d'Honneur Joseph Alphonse	4-11-44	346 Sqn
000306	Lt	BERTHET Georges Henri [Morocco]	11-09-44	347 Sqn
C3010	S/C	BIAGGI MM Croix de Guerre Dominique Francois	10-09-44	346 Sqn
51338	S/C	BILLOT MM Marcel Emile Charles	21-03-44	20 OTU
001061	Lt	BLOT Raoul [Algeria]	26-05-44	20 OTU
66	Sgt	BOURELY MM Croix de Guerre Louis Paul Marie	4-11-44	346 Sqn
23	Sgt	BOUTILLIER MM Croix de Guerre Andre Marie Georges	21-11-44	346 Sqn
81036	A/C	BRIGALAND MM Croix de Guerre Roger Marcel	23-10-44	346 Sqn
633	Sgt	BRUNEAU MM Marcel Louis [Algeria]	21-03-44	20 OTU
1013	S/C	CARDONA MM Roger Edouard Gaetan [Algeria]	21-03-44	20 OTU
37437	A/C	CHABROUD Jean Antoine [Morocco]	4-11-44	346 Sqn
00812	Lt	CHAPRON Gerrard Maurice Henri	6-07-44	347 Sqn
9554	Adj	CHARAUDEAU Rene Louis	6-07-44	347 Sqn
001457	Adj	CHARLIER Andre	6-07-44	347 Sqn
40424	SLt	CHOURGNOZ Leon Armand Isidore	20-05-44	1663 HCU
000939	Lt	CONDE Henri Georges [Morocco]	2-11-44	346 Sqn
C14406	Cpl	CONSENTINO Gabriel Adrien Hubert [Tunisia]	28-12-44	347 Sqn
1014	S/C	CORMIER Charles Georges	4-11-44	346 Sqn
81054	S/C	COUPEAU Marcel Louis	10-09-44	346 Sqn
4052	Sgt	CROLAS Marcel Joseph Marie	8-11-44	1663 HCU
C3911	Adj	CUSIN Andre Maurice	13-07-44	347 Sqn
1057	Lt	DABADIE Chevalier de Legion d'Honneur Alphonse Maurice Henri	4-11-44	346 Sqn
000005	Cdr	DAGAN Noel Andre	4-11-44	FFAF HQ
1363	Sgt	DELPECH Pierre Fernand	8-11-44	1663 HCU
C15488	Sgt	DESRUMEAUX Jacques Jules Henri	7-08-44	347 Sqn
459	Sgt	DIDIERLAURENT Edouard Paul	8-11-44	1663 HCU
30002	Capt	D'HAUTECOURT Henri Joseph Bunderoet	9-06-44	141 Sqn
015175	Adj	ECHARDT Paul Alphonse	6-07-44	347 Sqn
15615	Sgt	EVEN Yves Jean Elie	24-12-44	347 Sqn
C3229	S/C	EYRAUD Julien	11-09-44	347 Sqn
5542	SLt	FAUGES Louis Andre Felix [Algeria]	21-11-44	346 Sqn
475	Sgt	FERNANDEZ Gabriel Havier	23-10-44	346 Sqn
53962	S/C	FINALE Wilson Georges	10-09-44	346 Sqn
164	Sgt	FISCHBACH Jean Lucien	26-05-44	20 OTU
C4251	Adj	FLAMENT Georges Henri	7-08-44	347 Sqn
231	Adj	FLECK Andre [Morocco]	21-11-44	346 Sqn
87843	SLt	FOURNIER Pierre Francois	23-10-44	346 Sqn
29412	Capt	GAUBERT Jean Louis	13-07-44	346 Sqn
003887	Lt	GAUTHERET Pierre Louis Eugene	24-12-44	347 Sqn
C16121	Cpl	GIMENEZ Fernand [Morocco]	28-12-44	347 Sqn
R467	Sgt	GODARD Pierre Georges Henri	7-07-44	347 Sqn
7199	Sgt	GODEFROY Jean Armedee	21-11-44	346 Sqn
C407	Cpl	GOMEZ Seraphin Antonio [Algeria]	28-12-44	347 Sqn
C2502	Adj	GRAINER Henri Fernand	24-12-44	347 Sqn
33782	Capt	GUILLOCHEAU Louis Robert	10-09-44	346 Sqn
1010	Adj	GUISE MM Raymond Eugene	4-11-44	346 Sqn
000335	Capt	HILAIRE Alain Georges Leopold [Morocco]	11-09-44	347 Sqn
000181	Lt	HYENNE Auguste Marie	54-11-44	346 Sqn
C11512	Cpl	JEANNELLE Georges	28-12-44	347 Sqn
C15471	S/C	JENGER MM Rodolphe Camille [Tunisia]	11-09-44	347 Sqn
8848	A/C	KIPFERLE Jules Joseph [Algeria]	10-09-44	346 Sqn
35162	Lt	KOCHER Charles Emile	9-06-44	141 Sqn
275	A/C	LAFFONT Francois Jean	21-11-44	346 Sqn
C3777	S/C	LAHERRERE-SOUIVIRRA Jean Baptiste	4-11-44	346 Sqn
003992	SLt	LAMBERT Jean Gustave Adolphe [Algeria]	4-11-44	346 Sqn
001105	Lt	LEECOMTE Luglien [Algeria]	21-03-44	20 OTU
1024	S/C	LELONG Henri	4-11-44	346 Sqn
8397	Sgt	LEMOUSER Marc Theophile Marie	20-05-44	1663 HCU
000807	Lt	LEROY Jacques Andre Georges	24-12-44	347 Sqn
221	Sgt	LHMOND Gabriel	10-09-44	346 Sqn
145	S/C	LIMACHER Roger Lucien	4-11-44	346 Sqn
37237	Capt	LOEW Claude Jean-Jacques	21-11-44	346 Sqn
5312	A/C	MABILLE Lucien Charles Louis [Morocco]	2-11-44	346 Sqn
C3936	A/C	MADAULE Jean Marius [Morocco]	11-09-44	347 Sqn
C13484	Adj	MARCHI Paul Pierre	20-05-44	1663 HCU
30972	Sgt	MAROUX Alexandre P.	8-11-44	1663 HCU
38017	Sgt	MARTIN Henri Louis Alphonse [Algeria]	4-11-44	346 Sqn
R2402	Cpl	MAUPETIT Rene	28-12-44	347 Sqn
343	S/C	MAXERAT Louis Rene Alexandre [Morocco]	4-11-44	346 Sqn
15475	S/C	MEYER Henri Joseph	2-11-44	346 Sqn
C5323	A/C	MEYER Jean Henri Charles	7-08-44	347 Sqn
C15469	A/C	MILLET Leonce Norbert	7-08-44	347 Sqn
C4735	Sgt	MOREAU MM Pierre Armand	3-09-44	347 Sqn
1693	Sgt	NOYEZ Jean Baptiste Alexandre	8-11-44	1663 HCU
430	Sgt	OLIVE Henri Leon [Morocco]	4-11-44	346 Sqn
000453	Lt	PASQUIER Raymond Marie Jean	13-07-44	346 Sqn
000804	Lt	PATURLE Pierre Maris	11-09-44	347 Sqn
001056	Lt	PELISSIER Marcel Adolphe [Algeria]	23-10-44	346 Sqn
001280	Capt	PERSON DFC Jean Francois Marie	6-12-44	347 Sqn
969	SLt	PETIOT Emile	13-07-44	346 Sqn
324	SLt	PETIT Andre Robert	2-11-44	346 Sqn
3018	Sgt	PINNELLI Laurent	8-11-44	1663 HCU
003195	SLt	PONTON A. [Morocco]	26-05-44	20 OTU
6483A	SLt	POTHUAU Alfred Henri	4-11-44	346 Sqn
1006	Lt	RAFFIN Pierre Henri Eugene	4-11-44	346 Sqn
2069	Sgt	REYNAL Jean Laurent Charles Marie	4-11-44	346 Sqn
001408	Capt	RICHARD Rene [Morocco]	26-05-44	20 OTU
35780	S/C	ROCA Guy Ulysse Alfort [Algeria]	4-11-44	346 Sqn
1018	S/C	ROIRON Robert Jean	23-10-44	346 Sqn
C4300	A/C	ROUILLAY Henri Rene [Morocco]	3-09-44	347 Sqn
37966	Sgt	SAYTOUR Francois Marius	2-11-44	346 Sqn
834	Sgt	SERRA Rene Pierre	13-07-44	346 Sqn
001097	Cmdt	SIMON Jean Joseph [Morocco]	23-10-44	346 Sqn
C05319	A/C	SIRE Andre David Cermand	7-08-44	347 Sqn
C13226	SLt	SOUILLAD Rene August Joseph	3-09-44	347 Sqn
C8272	Cpl	STALENG Lucien Honore Baptiste	28-12-44	347 Sqn
89	A/C	THIERY MM Georges Eugene [Morocco]	21-11-44	346 Sqn
927	SLt	TOIRON Justin Ehenne	8-11-44	1663 HCU
C1391	Sgt	TOURNON Jerome Jacques Armand	8-11-44	1663 HCU
101090	Lt	VANDENABELLE Paul Andre [Tunisia]	21-03-44	20 OTU
C15565	SLt	VARLET Gilbert Charles	6-07-44	347 Sqn
37973	S/C	VEGA MM Emmanuel Marcel [Algeria]	4-11-44	346 Sqn
2380	S/C	VERDIER Camille Philippe Justin	13-07-44	346 Sqn
4083	Lt	VIAL Robert Marius Louis	8-11-44	1663 HCU
37987	S/C	VIELLE Edmond	23-10-44	346 Sqn
003886	SLt	VIEULES Chevalier de Legion d'Honneur Jean	6-07-44	347 Sqn
C4150	A/C	VIGNERON Joseph Guy [Morocco]	4-11-44	346 Sqn
20	A/C	VIGNOLLES Charles Jacques Joseph	20-05-44	1663 HCU
003057	Lt	VLES Jean Claude	4-11-44	346 Sqn
1009	A/C	VOGEL Roger Louis Joseph	13-07-44	346 Sqn

C15478	Sgt	WITZMANN Henri Jean Christian [Morocco]	3-09-44	347 Sqn
00456	Lt	ZEILLER Pierre Jean Rene Michel Marie	23-10-44	346 Sqn

Note
The service number, rank, surname and Christian names shown in this section have been taken from the casualty card raised in respect of the individual. As will be observed, these differ in places from the information reported on the loss cards and subsequently used in Volume 5. These remarks apply equally with the Free French Air Force section published in the previous part (7) and that that follows (9). Where details of next of kin have been shown, I have attempted to determine if the airman concerned came from what in the Second World War were still French possessions, thus some entries have been suitably annotated. However, I am certain that due to the absence of information concerning relatives, a full picture has not been reported and the same may be true in respect of the awards.

ROYAL NORWEGIAN AIR FORCE
personnel

1077	2Lt	ANUNDSKAAS Tor	21-01-44	76 Sqn
5782	Sgt	BJOROY Haakon Granli	17-12-44	57 Sqn
5535	Sgt	EVENSEN Herolf John Ernst	5-06-44	97 Sqn
1126	Capt	EVENSEN Nils Christian	17-12-44	57 Sqn
82	F/S	FLAATEN Othmar Larsen	28-10-44	35 Sqn
838	F/S	GULLIKSEN Walter	17-12-44	57 Sqn
5561	Sgt	HAAGENSEN Finn	28-10-44	35 Sqn
1783	Capt	HAUSVIK Svein Johannes	28-10-44	35 Sqn
1205	Lt	JESPERSEN Finn Yarde	5-06-44	97 Sqn
5255	Capt	JOHNSEN Finn	30-03-44	156 Sqn
1492	Sgt	KARSMANN Rolf	30-03-44	156 Sqn
1611	Sgt	LINDAHL Rolf	23-08-44	83 OTU
1960	Sgt	MAGNUS Knut Baade	5-06-44	97 Sqn
1770	Lt	MOE Tycho Didrik Castberg	5-06-44	97 Sqn
1747	Sgt	MUNSTER Christian Andreas	5-06-44	97 Sqn
1745	Sgt	PEDERSEN Kaare	5-06-44	97 Sqn
5637	Sgt	UTNE Rolf	18-07-44	460 Sqn

Note
Apart from six, 2Lt Anundskaas, Sgt Bjoroy, Capt Evensen, F/S Gulliksen, Sgt Lindahl and Sgt Utne, all died with squadrons concerned with target marking.

SOUTH AFRICAN AIR FORCE
personnel

328419V	Lt	BECKER Philip August	4-12-44	57 Sqn
79229V	Lt	BEGBIE James Errol	2-11-44	102 Sqn
1359	Lt	FRANKLIN Peter Blundell	24-08-44	1666 HCU
103929V	Capt	HIRSCHFELD Geoffrey William	4-12-44	44 Sqn
206162V	Capt	THOMPSON Ronald Carby	17-09-44	102 Sqn
328523V	2Lt	WHITCHER Hermanus Abrance	17-05-44	29 OTU

WOMEN's AUXILIARY AIR FORCE
personnel

445195	LACW	BAILEY Dorothy Frances Joan	13-05-44	692 Sqn
450345	LACW	BOULTER Sadie Bell	10-10-44	22 OTU
2023868	LACW	CHURCHILL Joan	22-03-44	Upwood
476737	ACW1	DAVIES Ellen Phyllis	28-02-44	100 Group
2112312	ACW1	ELDON Ella Esterina	11-04-44	5 Group
2007259	LACW	LAMBERT Elsie Caroline	4-01-44	Marston Moor
438396	ACW1	MATTHEWS Evelyn	2-11-44	5 Group
2069400	LACW	PEACH Gwendoline	26-02-44	105 Sqn
472395	ACW1	WHITELEY Dorothy	4-01-44	199 Sqn

Note
The death of LACW Bailey was the second tragedy to strike her family in a little under a year for on the 26th of May 1943, her brother Sgt Sydney Arthur James Bailey, serving as an air gunner with 12 Squadron, failed to return from operations to Dusseldorf. Thus, most unusually, a brother and a sister had died in the service of Bomber Command.

Attached personnel
ROYAL AIR FORCE

624348	LAC	BOND Alfred Charles (serving with 5013 Airfield Construction Sqn)	26-02-44	
982036	LAC	CLAY John (serving with 9035 Servicing Echelon)	20-04-44	
1424625	LAC	DAY Wilfred Francis (serving with 2807 Sqn RAF Regt)	6-11-44	
1775218	LAC	FOSTER Arthur William (serving with 2731 Sqn RAF Regt)	22-12-44	
1520724	LAC	HAMER Herbert (serving with 2807 Sqn RAF Regt)	6-11-44	
536850	Cpl	HART Donald Alfred (serving with 9007 Servicing Echelon)	10-04-44	
1138209	LAC	McIVER Frederick Charles (serving with 2746 Sqn RAF Regt)	18-06-44	
1864961	AC2	WARNE Robert George (serving with 5013 Airfield Construction Sqn)	19-03-44	
1306483	F/S	WHITE Richard (serving with 2841 Sqn RAF Regt)	1-02-44	
1252914	Sgt	WILLIAMS William Charles (serving with 2841 Sqn RAF Regt)	3-02-44	

ROYAL CANADIAN AIR FORCE

R/58864	Sgt	LAW James (serving with 9408 Servicing Echelon)	27-06-44	

UNITED STATES ARMY AIR FORCE

O-886258	1Lt	BOYLE E. F.	23-04-44	431 Sqn
10601604	T/S	BROWN PH Norman H. H.	20-02-44	408 Sqn
10601585	T/S	CHIDESTER PH Stanley H.	25-03-44	576 Sqn
T-190832	F/O	DE BARDELEBEN PH Willis	2-01-44	207 Sqn
O-886262	1Lt	DOWDEN AM** PH Max E. (serving with the Royal Canadian Air Force)	22-05-44	625 Sqn
O-886185	1Lt	FARMAN PH John M.	27-04-44	431 Sqn
O-886289	1Lt	EVANS AM* Cameron O.	7-06-44	78 Sqn
O-886275	2Lt	FORDHAM Ernest N.	16-05-44	419 Sqn
10601564	T/S	GILE PH Ray J.	24-02-44	420 Sqn
–	F/L	GROVE R. M.	23-01-44	1679 HCFlt
10602608	T/S	HANNON H. J.	21-02-44	9 Sqn
O-886146	2Lt	HAUZENBERGER AM** PH Alfred	28-07-44	408 Sqn
10601403	T/S	HAYWOOD PH Jack E.	3-01-44	156 Sqn
10601048	T/S	JONES AM PH* Ereil	3-01-44	101 Sqn
10601615	T/S	KEISOW J.	25-07-44	630 Sqn
–	F/O	KRAUSE P. J.	24-04-44	425 Sqn
10601569	T/S	MARTIN AM PH Albert E.	22-06-44	44 Sqn
–	T/S	McINTYRE W. S.	4-03-44	20 OTU
O-886295	Lt	McROBERTS F. M.	7-12-44	429 Sqn
T-223116	F/O	McQUISTON C.	25-05-44	51 Sqn
10601618	M/S	MITCHELL W. W.	29-01-44	166 Sqn
O-886200	1Lt	PENNER S. W.	25-02-44	12 Sqn

T-223113	F/O	RAMSDELL PH Charles H.	15-06-44	433 Sqn	
o-886242	1Lt	RORKE Albert L.	16-02-44	432 Sqn	
T-223123	F/O	SARVIS AM* Robert J.	25-07-44	576 Sqn	
T-223129	F/O	SHEARER W. G.	25-07-44	166 Sqn	
O-886116	1Lt	SHOVE F. S.	27-04-44	408 Sqn	
O-886141	1Lt	SMITH DFC AM*** PH John K.	9-05-44	426 Sqn	
O-886173	1Lt	SOLOMON PH Frank B.	2-01-44	207 Sqn	
10601625	T/S	STEDMAN PH Ben H.	20-01-44	97 Sqn	
O-886270	1Lt	STEVENS R. E.	12-05-44	427 Sqn	
O-886273	1Lt	VAN HORN C. J.	7-06-44	83 Sqn	
–	T/S	WATKINS P.	15-04-44	1664 HCU	
–	1Lt	WEBER C. A.	5-02-44	115 Sqn	
T-223135	F/O	WHITE PH Larry	9-05-44	405 Sqn	
T-223105	F/O	WILKES AM* PH John E.	10-04-44	9 Sqn	

WOMEN'S AUXILIARY AIR FORCE

2112273	LACW	FEARON Dorothy	29-09-44	
		(serving with 9635 Servicing Echeleon)		

Postscript

Identified within this section are service numbers which tell us a great deal about the person so mentioned; reasonably familiar, particularly in the earlier parts of the Roll are those of the Royal Air Force Volunteer Reserve called up under the terms of the Military Training Act of July 1939, while others within the Royal Air Force section have numbers which specifically identify the area from which they enlisted and, where appropriate, I have annotated these with a suitable abbreviation following their Christian names. However, this section includes an airman (Sgt Herbert William Jennings) who commenced his service life in the army until he was transferred circa May 1937 into the Royal Air Force Regiment as an instructor. Not surprisingly, when he was killed in September 1944, he was flying as an air gunner.

The year also witnessed the deaths of five holders of the Victoria Cross, including the much-decorated W/C Guy Penrose Gibson famed, and honoured, for his leadership of 617 Squadron and in particular his outstanding courage during the attack on the Mohne Dam (in his book, *Enemy Coast Ahead* Gibson refers to this as the Mohne Lake) in May 1943. The circumstances surrounding his death on the 19th of September, 1944, and that of his navigator S/L James Brown Warwick DFC, has been the subject of much speculation but for what it is worth I consider his undue familiarity with the Mosquito may have been a contributory factor.

Less well known outside of air force circles are the deaths of F/O Cyril Joe Barton, the only Halifax pilot to be awarded the Victoria Cross, S/L Ian Willoughby Bazalgette, S/L Robert Anthony Maurice Palmer, both pathfinder pilots of extraordinary ability and P/O Andrew Charles Mynarski of the Royal Canadian Air Force. Of the last named, an air gunner, his award was only made possible by the witness of F/O Gordon Brophy, a fellow Canadian, and whose life Andrew Mynarski strove to save. The occasion was a low-level raid on the 12th/13th of June, 1944, targetting the marshalling yards at Cambrai in northern France during which their Lancaster was attacked by a night-fighter and set on fire. Such was the extent of the damage caused, plus the fierceness of the blaze in the fuselage which was spreading rapidly into the wing section, that the pilot, F/O Arthur de Breyne, had little hesitation in ordering his crew to bale out. However, during the attack F/O Brophy's rear turret was rendered almost inoperable and in order to make good his exit he had to resort to the slow process of manually winding his turret into a position from which he could escape and it was at this stage that his situation became totally impossible when the winding handle snapped.

Meanwhile, Mynarski had clambered down from his mid-upper turret and was about to make his way forward when he glanced back and in the light of the flames realised Brophy was trapped. Without any hesitation he made his way through the fire, a fire that was gaining in intensity by the second, and desperately tried to shift the jammed rear turret. By this time his flying clothing was well alight but this not deter the young Canadian who continued to exert all his physical strength in what was now rapidly becoming an horrific ordeal for both airmen. Time seemed to freeze as Gordon Brophy implored his colleague to leave him and save his own life and it was only then that Andrew Mynarski retreated through the flames but before baling out he turned, stood to attention and saluted the rear gunner whom he thought was now surely going to die. Moments later, eyewitnesses on the ground saw a fiery streak plummet earthwards before its progress was momentarily slowed by the deploying of a parachute. When found, P/O Andrew Charles Mynarski, though still alive, was beyond all human aid.

But what of his friend, F/O Gordon Brophy? By a miracle he not only survived the final impact which scattered blazing sections of the Lancaster in all directions but managed to evade capture, as did three other members of the crew including Arthur de Breyne. Thus, along with the testimonies of other members of the crew (two were picked up by the Germans and made prisoner) the outstanding courage of P/O Mynarski was richly acknowledged on the 11th of October, 1946, by the posthumous award of the Victoria Cross. Within Bomber Command he was the sole Canadian to be so honoured.

As recorded above, P/O Barton was the only Halifax pilot in Bomber Command to receive the nation's ultimate accolade for bravery and it was his actions of selfless endeavour to save the lives of his crew, regardless of the danger in which he was placing himself, that led to his award being promulgated on the 27th of June, 1944, nearly three months after his death from the terrible injuries received when his aircraft crashed near Ryehope Colliery in Co. Durham. A man of strong faith, it is reported* that in his last minutes of life and at a time when he was barely conscious the few words that he was able to whisper were those of concern for the well being of his crew.

Although the establishment of Path Finder Force had taken place two years previously, it was not until 1944 that two of its pilots would be honoured, posthumously, with the Victoria Cross. Both had already received decorations in recognition of their skill and resolute courage while conducting bombing operations, S/L Bazalgette gaining a DFC during his tour of operations with 115 Squadron which he completed in August, 1943. Then followed a tour as a flight commander with 20 OTU at Lossiemouth before he returned to operations in the late spring of 1944, being posted to Downham Market and joining 635 Squadron. By mid-June, he was being selected for the important role of deputy master bomber, the marshalling yards at Cambrai being the first target where he would assume command of the operation in the event of anything happening to the master bomber. Such was his ability in these matters that by late July, he was filling the position of master bomber though on the day of his tragic death he was flying in support of the two crews assigned to lead the raid on a V1 storage depot at Trossy St. Maximim. As was quite usual for raids on such relatively small targets, the total number of bombers allocated was well under a hundred and it was to be their misfortune to encounter fierce opposition in the form of exceptionally accurate ground fire which seriously damaged the master bomber's Lancaster and seconds later accounted for his deputy (please refer to page 369 of Volume 5 for details) as he entered the target area. Bazalgette's aircraft, too, was hit and it was only through his skill and determination to save his crew that he was able to release his markers and remove his crippled bomber from the cauldron of bursting flak shells. In those few moments of high drama his air bomber, F/L Ivan Alderwin Hibbert DFC was so dangerously wounded that despite immediate medical attention from the crew he would not be able to save himself by parachuting; furthermore, his Australian mid-upper air gunner, F/S Vernon Victor Russell Leeder, was near unconscious due to smoke inhalation. Their situation was critical and growing more perilous with each passing second. Thus, S/L Bazalgette gave his crew their last order; bale out. Four did so and though at this stage Bazalgette could easily have followed he chose, instead, to remain with the Lancaster and try to pull off an emergency landing in the hope of saving the lives of his two incapacitated companions. In his heart he must have known that he would need a miracle to succeed for both starboard engines were wrecked and the wing burnt and scarred in numerous places.

Somehow, and according to eyewitnesses on the ground, S/L Ian Willoughby Bazalgette DFC came close to achieving this miracle for he set his machine down in a field with near faultless precision but within seconds of doing so a massive explosion rent the air and the three airmen on board passed into eternity. From reports given by the four survivors, all of whom evaded capture, it seems likely that a good deal of petrol and hydraulic fluid was slopping about in the fuselage and it would only need the smallest of sparks to ignite this volatile mixture.

The second path finder pilot to gain a Victoria Cross for his actions in 1944, S/L Robert Anthony Maurice Palmer, had begun his association with bombing operations during the winter of 1940-1941, initially with 75 Squadron before completing his first tour with 149 Squadron. He, too, then spent time on instructional duties at 20 OTU, but unlike S/L Bazalgette's period of screening, Palmer's went on and on and despite repeated requests to return to operational duty it seemed as though Palmer was destined to finish the war as a flying instructor. And this might well have been the case had he not gained the sympathetic ear of his flight commander, the aforementioned Ian Bazalgette! However, it has to be a matter of conjecture as to whether his flight commander's recommendations played a part in his being posted away from Lossiemouth but by January 1944, Robert Palmer was flying Mosquitoes with 109 Squadron. Such was the frequency of operations that within six months he was coming to the end of his second tour and being anxious not to be returned to instructional duties he asked if he might continue in his present post. To his delight his application was accepted and by early December 1944 he had chalked up an impressive tally of 100 operational sorties, gaining a DFC and first bar in the process. Although a seasoned Mosquito pilot, Palmer was also familiar with the Lancaster and it was in such an aircraft, borrowed from 582 Squadron, that he took off from Little Staunton at 10.27 hours on the 23rd of December 1944, for what was to be his 111th and final mission.

His task was to lead a small force of Lancasters and Mosquitoes, all drawn from path finder units, to attack the marshalling yards at Cologne-Gremberg. Three formations were employed, each formation led by an *Oboe*-fitted Lancaster with similarly equipped Mosquitoes acting as back up. Palmer's position was at the head of the leading formation but soon after settling into their respective boxes, tragedy struck when two Lancasters, both from 35 Squadron, collided at 10,000 feet over the South Foreland and fell into the sea, not one airman surviving. Worse was to follow for when the now depleted force began their approach to the aiming point, the bombers found themselves not over the forecast 10/10 cloud but in clear skies. Soon the sky was thick with predicted flak which was proving to be extremely accurate and in those last few crucial seconds when it was so important for the master bomber to hold his position, Robert Palmer's aircraft was bracketed by a profusion of shell bursts which left two engines on fire and out of action and the entire fuselage section filled with choking smoke. Those who were following the master bomber could only wonder at his courage in refusing to take evasive action and thereby give himself and his crew a chance to bale out. Then, almost in the same moment that his markers arched onto the aiming below the Lancaster dropped from the sky streaming flames and trailing in its wake a single parachute beneath which was suspended F/S R. K. Yeulatt RCAF, the tail gunner, who soon was to experience what was fast becoming the dubious haven of a prisoner of war camp.

And the drama of the day was not yet over, for fighters were now appearing on the scene, their pilots showing scant regard for the profusion of ground fire. The 109 Squadron Mosquito that was backing Palmer up was clinically despatched, neither member of crew surviving, and this success was quickly followed by the shooting down of three more Lancasters, all from 582 Squadron, while a fourth aircraft from the squadron was so badly shot about that its crew, having regained the Allied lines, wisely abandoned their crippled machine. In the aftermath of this last action two, W/O A. A. L. Andersen and F/S J. G. Watson, both Australians were decorated with the DFC and DFM respectively, their awards being *Gazetted* on the 23rd of February, 1945.

As recounted in my introduction to this section, the end of 1944 witnessed Bomber Command operating at the peak of its efficiency and in the last four full months of the bombing campaign still to come the tempo of operations and the weight of attack continued almost unabated. For the unfortunate civilian population of Germany, the nightmare of night and day raiding had to be endured with the knowledge that the once halcyon days of success by their armed forces were over and it would now be only a matter of time before their country was occupied. For those whose geographical misfortune placed them in the path of the advancing Soviet armies this stark fact struck an additional dread fear into their hearts for they knew that little mercy would be shown by the conquering hordes from the east.

To close this section it is appropriate to mention the terrible atrocities of late March and early April 1944, when 50 of the Allied officers recaptured following the *Great Escape* from Stalag-Luft III were murdered by the Gestapo on the direct order of Adolf Hitler. Some had behind the wire since the earliest days of the war; the instigator of the breakout, South African born S/L Roger Bushell, a Spitfire pilot had been shot down over Dunkirk in May 1940.

* As recorded by Sgt 'Timber' Wood, P/O Barton's mid-upper air gunner and set out in his account of what took place during their fateful visit to Nuremberg on the night of the 30th/31st of March, 1944, and subsequently published in Hugh Cawdron's magnificent tribute to 578 Squadron, *'Based at Burn'*.

Part 9

Bomber Command Roll of Honour – 1945

Five full long weary years of war, years that had driven the warring factions to the utmost of their endeavours and now with the arrival of a New Year only the most fanatical of Hitler's followers remained resolute in their belief in the promised victory. Within the Allied camp was the knowledge that the end was, finally, in sight. Even so the mind-numbing effects of total war had sapped the strength of many and strong resolve was still a requisite to ensure there were no more stumbles like the recent German offensive through the Ardennes to hinder the final victory. For the airmen of Bomber Command who survived the misfortune of being shot down, these last few months of the bombing campaign were marked with great danger. Even before the turn of the year the bureaucracy necessary for the functioning of the German state was fast breaking down and with this deterioration came serious lapses in the procedures set down for the treatment of prisoners of war. Thus, from late 1944 onwards examples of mistreatment of captured airmen increased markedly and in more than a few cases summary executions were carried out, usually on the instructions of local officials and, on occasions, by the officials themselves. However, it must also be said that acts of great humanity towards downed airmen were also enacted by a now beleaguered population, often at considerable risk to the individual concerned. Furthermore, with the Soviet armies' advance from the east gaining in momentum, the German High Command issued orders for the abandonment of the prisoner-of-war camps that soon would be in Russian hands. The conditions in which these orders were implemented were near chaotic and in some instances the airmen had barely thirty minutes in which to gather together their meagre possessions and head out into the snow with their guards shuffling along beside them. Some years ago I was privileged to be allowed to read the diary of one such Royal Air Force airman who was involved in this mass exodus towards the west and it was immediately obvious from the outset, in early January 1945, that in order to survive the bitter winter conditions friend and foe alike would have to dredge up their own reserve of fortitude and courage in order to come through this ordeal. One entry, made quite early in the march, illustrates the stark facts of what faced each individual concerned when one of the guards, an elderly non-commissioned officer, collapsed with sheer fatigue and, as is wont in these situations, his section of the column came to a halt. Within a few minutes an officer appeared on the scene demanding to know the reason for the delay. The pitiful pleas from the guard, still lying where he fell, to be allowed a few minutes to recover fell on deaf ears and to the horror of the airmen in the immediate vicinity it became all too apparent that the officer was giving the guard a terrible ultimatum; he either got up and resumed his duties or he would be shot and as the poor fellow was quite unable to comply he was summarily executed and another guard was ordered to get the column on the move. This salutary lesson in their captors' interpretation of survival was, I am certain, not lost on any of the prisoners who witnessed this atrocity.

The hardships endured during this long march towards the west culminated, for one very large group of airmen and soldiers, in a tragedy not entirely of German making when Allied fighter pilots mistook their column, estimated at around 12,000 in number, and commenced to strafe. It is believed that seven fighters, identified as Typhoons, attacked before the eighth pilot realised that an awful mistake had been made and managed to stop his companions from running in for a second time. By this time at least 42 prisoners, many of them Bomber Command personnel who had survived the trauma of falling to either flak or fighter and the debilitating years of captivity that followed, lay dead (see Volume 6, page 210 for their identifies and further details pertaining to this tragic accident).

And so the final months of the war were played out against a background of stunning military actions on the ground and with Bomber Command and their American counterparts pounding away both by day and night in support. Much controversy has grown up in the postwar years concerning this phase of the bombing campaign but it has to be remembered that all operations were sanctioned by the chiefs of staff and their political masters. To his everlasting credit Sir Arthur Harris, who remained at the helm until total victory was achieved, never flinched or sought excuse for the actions that he deemed were necessary for his Command to play its part in defeating Nazism and the evil that such a culture would, had it been successful, have imposed on the whole of Europe.

ROYAL AIR FORCE,
ROYAL AIR FORCE (AUXILIARY AIR FORCE)
ROYAL AIR FORCE (VOLUNTEER RESERVE)
personnel

145660	F/L	ABBOTT Frederick Joseph	8-03-45	189 Sqn
1581934	F/S	ABBS Ronald Charles	26-02-45	12 Sqn
620836	W/O	ABRAMS Sidney Edward	7-01-45	103 Sqn
1407092	F/S	ACKERMAN George William	21-03-45	57 Sqn
2220646	Sgt	ACKLAND Peter	17-03-45	630 Sqn
1001091	F/S	ADAM DFM David Doig	5-03-45	635 Sqn
150225	F/O	ADAM Treless James Stewart [Australia]	14-01-45	128 Sqn
149989	F/O	ADAMS Albert Edward	4-04-45	115 Sqn
189035	P/O	ADAMS DFC Alexander James	21-02-45	166 Sqn
2218925	Sgt	ADAMS Andrew Mill	25-06-45	199 Sqn
1795799	F/S	AHERNE John Burke	22-03-45	97 Sqn
1596266	Sgt	AINSLEY Alan	21-02-45	158 Sqn
184307	F/O	AINSWORTH Kenneth William	21-03-45	61 Sqn
3030232	AC2	AITKEN Hunter Mason	2-03-45	57 Sqn
164761	F/O	AKENHEAD Thomas Skilbeck	7-03-45	625 Sqn
80126	F/L	ALBERTSON AFC Albert Ian [Rhodesia]	2-03-45	PFNTU
1399114	F/S	ALDER Kenneth Charles Robert	2-02-45	189 Sqn
179997	F/L	ALDHOUS MiD Bernard Joseph	9-03-45	90 Sqn
1492353	Sgt	ALDRED Bernard George	5-01-45	100 Sqn
651629	Sgt	ALDRIDGE John Edward	19-03-45	103 Sqn

127894	F/L	ALEXANDRA George Peter	3-02-45	170 Sqn	102137	F/L	BAKER Ronald	1-02-45	627 Sqn
1810280	F/S	ALFRED Joseph McKenzie [Trinidad]	26-02-45	75 Sqn	1322461	F/S	BALDWIN Ronald William Benjamin	5-01-45	61 Sqn
1365515	Sgt	ALLAN Andrew	5-01-45	51 Sqn	171305	F/O	BALL DFM Desmond Arthur John William		
1807338	Sgt	ALLAN Henry Gordon	2-04-45	1651 HCU				21-02-45	83 Sqn
1568345	F/S	ALLAN James	16-03-45	44 Sqn	1321859	W/O	BALL Ronald James	9-02-45	138 Sqn
183538	F/O	ALLAN Kenneth Cecil	24-02-45	214 Sqn	1592037	Sgt	BALLINGER George	4-04-45	186 Sqn
1896397	Sgt	ALLEN Clifford Bertram	3-09-45	26 OTU	710349	Sgt	BALLOCH Albert [Rhodesia]	3-02-45	44 Sqn
1399040	F/S	ALLEN Donald Charles	28-01-45	218 Sqn	1874899	F/S	BALLS Terence Arthur	14-01-45	1661 HCU
179320	F/L	ALLEN Eric Sidney	13-02-45	550 Sqn	1399979	F/S	BANGS Eric Cecil	21-02-45	156 Sqn
2223139	Sgt	ALLEN Harold John	5-04-45	576 Sqn	1899297	Sgt	BANKS Robert Charles	2-03-45	207 Sqn
1588012	F/S	ALLEN John Alban	30-07-45	166 Sqn	2221107	Sgt	BANNER William Taylor	9-02-45	214 Sqn
1602947	F/S	ALLEN Stuart Rufus	23-02-45	101 Sqn	1866838	Sgt	BANNISTER Douglas Patrick	14-02-45	576 Sqn
41978	F/L	ALLIES William Donald	23-03-45	214 Sqn	36022	W/C	BANNISTER William Geoffrey	2-02-45	90 Sqn
1798198	F/S	ALLINGHAM William George	19-03-45	640 Sqn	1455475	W/O	BARDSLEY Eric	19-04-45	576 Sqn
2209293	Sgt	ALLMAN Jack	1-02-45	166 Sqn	1853062	Sgt	BARFOOT Eric Edward	6-04-45	26 OTU
1574022	Sgt	ALLSEBROOK Percy John	14-07-45	626 Sqn	179071	F/O	BARKER Reginald	5-01-45	100 Sqn
1578224	W/O	AMOS Alwyn	21-03-45	75 Sqn	1193636	Sgt	BARLOW Dennis John 'Blackie'	5-04-45	166 Sqn
1897548	Sgt	ANDERSON Clifford Ronald	21-02-45	166 Sqn	198280	P/O	BARLOW George	3-07-45	166 Sqn
195050	P/O	ANDERSON John Alexander	19-03-45	77 Sqn	1802589	F/S	BARLOW Philip Tyers	3-03-45	463 Sqn
1321148	Sgt	ANDERSON John Clarke	4-04-45	192 Sqn	53823	F/O	BARNETT Edwin Alfred	21-03-45	617 Sqn
1098277	W/O	ANDERSON DFM Sydney Ross	12-01-45	617 Sqn	1059973	F/S	BARNFIELD Harry	4-03-45	214 Sqn
1603084	F/S	ANDREWS Denis William	15-01-45	578 Sqn	1113965	F/S	BARR Andrew Coulter	8-04-45	35 Sqn
2206065	Sgt	ANDREWS Eric George	26-02-45	12 Sqn	190947	F/O	BARR Derek Singleton	21-03-45	75 Sqn
1826084	Sgt	ANDREWS James Mark	10-04-45	415 Sqn	1796037	Sgt	BARR Ernest Henry Mackenzie	6-01-45	158 Sqn
3005078	F/S	ANDREWS Victor Henry	14-03-45	51 Sqn	851307	Sgt	BARRADELL Edward Bertram	28-01-45	218 Sqn
1676376	Sgt	ANNIS Leslie	16-03-45	51 Sqn	937633	W/O	BARRATT Reginald Harry	4-06-45	9 Sqn
174549	F/O	ANSCOMB Robert Joseph	2-03-45	57 Sqn	1798959	F/S	BARRETT Michael	19-03-45	640 Sqn
150291	F/O	ANSDELL Nicholas Agnew	4-03-45	12 Sqn	130337	F/L	BARRITT DFC John	21-02-45	166 Sqn
198616	P/O	ANSELL Gerald	8-02-45	50 Sqn	580820	W/O	BARRY George Donald	25-04-45	35 Sqn
1144814	F/S	ANTCLIFFE Kenneth	31-03-45	156 Sqn	1898551	Sgt	BARTHOLOMEW William Brian	8-01-45	619 Sqn
1826667	Sgt	ANTHONY David	17-03-45	550 Sqn	3050089	Sgt	BARTLETT Charles Henry	9-03-45	625 Sqn
1891334	Sgt	APLIN Donald Percy	8-02-45	57 Sqn	67566	F/L	BARTLETT Ronald William	8-02-45	61 Sqn
182177	P/O	APPLEYARD DFM Robert	8-03-45	195 Sqn	917435	F/S	BARTLETT William Kenvyn Jack	14-04-45	186 Sqn
1809956	Sgt	ARMITAGE Peter Spackman	2-03-45	622 Sqn	1587047	F/S	BARTON Edwin Charles	14-01-45	1661 HCU
1590063	Sgt	ARMITAGE Stanley	19-03-45	103 Sqn	2226081	Sgt	BARTON James	6-03-45	50 Sqn
1567638	F/S	ARMSTRONG Alexander	22-03-45	51 Sqn	42296	F/L	BASAN Lawrence Wallace	15-02-45	157 Sqn
1615683	F/S	ARMSTRONG George Henry	15-03-45	106 Sqn	1819449	Sgt	BASSETT Charles David	1-01-45	115 Sqn
1816600	F/S	ARTUS Alan Geoffrey	25-04-45	76 Sqn	184678	F/O	BASTICK Richard Stanley	21-02-45	576 Sqn
1816623	F/S	ASHFORD William	8-03-45	189 Sqn	1819553	Sgt	BATES Colin Frank	5-01-45	7 Sqn
1023844	Sgt	ASHTON Jack	3-02-45	10 Sqn	174301	F/L	BATES Derrick George	8-02-45	83 Sqn
3010619	Sgt	ASHUN Kenneth Cromwell	20-03-45	57 Sqn	1594894	Sgt	BATES Douglas	3-03-45	463 Sqn
1685149	F/S	ASHWORTH Terence	8-03-45	635 Sqn	189351	P/O	BATES Edward Percy	1-01-45	9 Sqn
1505117	Sgt	ASKEW Wilfred Robert	14-01-45	17 OTU	111258	S/L	BATES DFC Peter Anthony	7-02-45	141 Sqn
1055862	Sgt	ATKINS Clarence Leslie	8-01-45	49 Sqn	101055	F/L	BATTEN DFC Charles	24-09-45	16 OTU
1894040	F/S	ATKINS Ronald Frederick	8-06-45	11 OTU	544413	F/S	BATTEN Henry Thomas	23-02-45	138 Sqn
1594808	Sgt	ATKINSON Denis	12-01-45	77 Sqn	1545932	F/S	BATTERSBY Ronald Charles	15-01-45	61 Sqn
1591782	F/S	ATKINSON John Joffre	16-01-45	51 Sqn	1584485	F/S	BAULDIE David	19-04-45	76 Sqn
1065550	F/S	ATTERBY Edward	14-03-45	189 Sqn	117670	F/L	BAUM Dennis Jacob	4-03-45	1651 HCU
3031942	Sgt	AUSTEN Walter Gordon	7-03-45	170 Sqn	183825	F/O	BAUSH Charles William	8-03-45	57 Sqn
54938	F/O	AUSTIN George Jeffery	14-03-45	189 Sqn	1850413	F/S	BAXTER Denis George	21-02-45	578 Sqn
174610	F/O	AUSTIN Lewis Walter Castle	8-03-45	582 Sqn	1302773	Sgt	BAXTER Edward	1-02-45	622 Sqn
177980	F/L	AYLIEFF DFC James Martin	8-03-45	35 Sqn	1892188	Sgt	BAY Dennis William Sydney	6-03-45	50 Sqn
161085	F/O	AYRES DFC Kenneth Albert	13-03-45	153 Sqn	1322835	F/S	BEADLE Donald Joshua	2-05-45	169 Sqn
188891	F/O	AYRES Norman Siddall	21-03-45	223 Sqn	1868744	Sgt	BEALES Ronald	8-03-45	576 Sqn
1586864	Sgt	BACKWAY Henry George	4-01-45	103 Sqn	3040397	Sgt	BEAN Walter	21-02-45	578 Sqn
2215964	F/S	BADGER Colin Reginald	22-02-45	626 Sqn	3006185	Sgt	BEARD John Lawrence	14-03-45	75 Sqn
1897210	Sgt	BAILEY Reginald Leslie	31-03-45	429 Sqn	1594634	Sgt	BEARDSMORE Joseph David	7-01-45	462 Sqn
1877588	Sgt	BAILEY Roy Charles	29-01-45	3 LFS	1616954	Sgt	BEARE Royston John	15-06-45	15 Sqn
189698	F/O	BAILEY William James	6-03-45	153 Sqn	1063934	F/S	BEATON Alexander Collie	5-04-45	571 Sqn
189455	P/O	BAINBRIDGE William	5-01-45	10 Sqn	179980	F/O	BEATON DSO Donald	9-05-45	514 Sqn
2210627	Sgt	BAKER Albert Richard	4-04-45	186 Sqn	1826580	Sgt	BEAUCHAMP Arthur William	16-03-45	44 Sqn
152546	F/L	BAKER Denis George	3-10-45	1668 HCU	1276054	LAC	BEAZER Herbert William	3-02-45	Feltwell
3050406	Sgt	BAKER Eric Gordon	7-01-45	462 Sqn	1482487	Sgt	BECKETT Robert John	16-01-45	101 Sqn
49319	P/O	BAKER Frank Ernest	12-03-45	106 Sqn	1684458	F/S	BEDFORD Harold	14-03-45	106 Sqn
1582205	Sgt	BAKER Frederick Arthur	12-04-45	1654 HCU	185065	F/O	BELL George	21-03-45	617 Sqn
1862003	Sgt	BAKER John Clare	25-02-45	429 Sqn	151474	F/O	BELL Kenneth Thomas	2-02-45	51 Sqn
1867772	Sgt	BAKER John David	17-03-45	630 Sqn	143283	F/L	BELL Matthew William	15-03-45	227 Sqn
1603771	F/S	BAKER Neville Percy	7-03-45	171 Sqn	1389006	F/S	BELL Sydney Philip	14-07-45	626 Sqn

439

Number	Rank	Name	Date	Sqn
165156	F/O	BELL Thomas	3-10-45	1668 HCU
1377548	W/O	BELLAMY James Edward	21-03-45	223 Sqn
1684437	F/S	BELLWOOD Lawrence	22-04-45	218 Sqn
177135	F/L	BELOT DFC Denis	7-03-45	12 Sqn
1586544	F/S	BELSHAW Reginald Peter	8-03-45	576 Sqn
1596002	Sgt	BEMROSE Ernest Edward	3-02-45	90 Sqn
172049	F/O	BENDIX DFC Jack Lindsay	13-07-45	97 Sqn
77777	W/C	BENJAMIN DFC* Eric Arthur	20-02-45	627 Sqn
1893800	Sgt	BENNETT Arthur	3-04-45	625 Sqn
109072	S/L	BENNETT DFC Cyril Victor	13-01-45	515 Sqn
1025303	W/O	BENNETT Harold Whitney	25-02-45	1660 HCU
190245	F/O	BENNETT DFC Harry	4-03-45	214 Sqn
2211401	Sgt	BENNETT James Edward	19-02-45	90 Sqn
2214378	Sgt	BENNETT Kenneth	1-01-45	218 Sqn
1335173	F/S	BENNETT Robert Sidney	7-01-45	170 Sqn
189802	P/O	BENNETT William Gerald	7-02-45	158 Sqn
1897888	Sgt	BENSON Frank Norman	4-03-45	189 Sqn
1565145	F/S	BENSON Thomas Laidlaw	8-03-45	61 Sqn
3005762	Sgt	BENTLEY John Henry	22-03-45	431 Sqn
1873484	F/S	BENTLEY Ronald William	5-01-45	35 Sqn
1867172	Sgt	BENTON Jack Ernest	2-01-45	100 Sqn
169506	F/O	BERGER DFM Herbert Otto	16-01-45	100 Sqn
122344	F/L	BERRISFORD DFC* Norman Chesworth	24-03-45	139 Sqn
1800664	F/S	BERRY Albert James	14-02-45	10 Sqn
1802847	Sgt	BERRY William	17-03-45	550 Sqn
1601599	W/O	BERTLIN John Anthony Roden	11-01-45	20 OTU
1608602	Sgt	BEST Gerald Richard	14-01-45	1654 HCU
1868236	Sgt	BETTS Alfred Francis	8-10-45	166 Sqn
612515	Sgt	BETTS Douglas George	1-02-45	627 Sqn
1579109	F/S	BIBBY William Victor	21-02-45	576 Sqn
189576	P/O	BICKERTON John William	8-01-45	103 Sqn
1585155	F/S	BICKNELL Kenneth John Albert	5-01-45	77 Sqn
1802233	F/S	BICKNELL Terence James	1-03-45	153 Sqn
49334	F/L	BIDDER MiD Donald Vincent	19-02-45	PFNTU
172044	F/O	BIDDLECOMBE Charles William George	5-04-45	12 Sqn
159528	F/O	BIGGAR Donald Charlton	7-03-45	171 Sqn
1399771	F/S	BIGNELL Jack Cecil Robert	14-02-45	77 Sqn
1595492	Sgt	BILLARD Charles Edward	3-03-45	463 Sqn
2205644	Sgt	BILLINGTON Leslie Ernest	4-03-45	214 Sqn
1580691	F/S	BINCH Victor Hugh	4-03-45	227 Sqn
120950	F/L	BINGHAM DFC Kenneth Richard	8-02-45	44 Sqn
1575035	Sgt	BIRCH Harry	4-03-45	44 Sqn
2225274	Sgt	BIRD John Lambert	14-03-45	51 Sqn
1671448	F/S	BIRKETT William Norman	19-03-45	102 Sqn
56497	P/O	BIRKS Frederick William	10-04-45	78 Sqn
1823774	Sgt	BIRRELL Ian Ashley	5-04-45	153 Sqn
136451	F/L	BIRTWISTLE Norman	31-05-45	1660 HCU
1291345	F/S	BISHOP Henry Edward	17-01-45	514 Sqn
1862792	F/S	BISHOP Henry William	14-03-45	207 Sqn
1594570	Sgt	BLACK Robert	8-03-45	576 Sqn
162193	F/O	BLACKBOURN Geoffrey Robert Percival	1-01-45	100 Sqn
2204969	Sgt	BLACKSHAW Arthur Trevor	2-02-45	514 Sqn
1620678	F/S	BLACKSHAW George William	17-03-45	103 Sqn
125998	F/L	BLAIR John Coulter	10-03-45	16 OTU
54690	F/O	BLAKE Arthur Samuel	5-04-45	153 Sqn
1307324	Sgt	BLAKE Philip	21-03-45	578 Sqn
1621031	F/S	BLAKEY Harry Vernon	10-04-45	170 Sqn
1395787	F/S	BLAY Leslie Edward Harcourt	4-01-45	1652 HCU
1523986	Sgt	BLIGH Arthur	5-03-45	1662 HCU
650927	W/O	BLISS Harry	30-03-45	218 Sqn
191791	P/O	BLUNSTONE Frank	9-03-45	578 Sqn
1250558	F/S	BLYTH William	4-02-45	12 Sqn
3041131	Sgt	BLYTHE Benjamin	9-04-45	463 Sqn
1586951	F/S	BOAKES Edward James	15-01-45	61 Sqn
154328	F/O	BOBBY Cyril Roy	17-02-45	10 Sqn
104534	S/L	BODDINGTON DFC* Robert Anthony	14-02-45	635 Sqn
1894525	Sgt	BODDY Geoffrey Archer	30-10-45	1653 HCU
2213860	AC1	BODDY John	2-04-45	50 Sqn
1695305	Sgt	BODEN George Rex	1-01-45	630 Sqn
2206444	F/S	BOLLAND DFM George Eric	21-02-45	405 Sqn
184364	F/O	BOLTER Alec John	8-01-45	49 Sqn
190987	P/O	BOLTON Thomas Owen	8-02-45	49 Sqn
1800967	W/O	BOLTON William Frederick	3-05-45	199 Sqn
124151	F/L	BONAKIS Basil Demetrius	7-01-45	169 Sqn
551269	W/O	BOND Ivor Hexter	8-03-45	101 Sqn
581434	W/O	BONE William Andrew Irving	19-04-45	76 Sqn
1615924	Sgt	BOOKER Raymond Stanley Royden	15-02-45	115 Sqn
1594445	Sgt	BOOTH Colin	1-01-45	9 Sqn
148926	F/O	BOOTH Joseph Donald	1-01-45	115 Sqn
3031200	Sgt	BOOTH Sidney Dominic	21-03-45	419 Sqn
1594342	Sgt	BOOTHMAN Arthur	22-03-45	44 Sqn
2203135	Sgt	BORLAND Robert James	6-04-45	26 OTU
1079870	F/S	BOTTERILL DFM Harry	14-02-45	635 Sqn
190518	P/O	BOTTING John Charles	2-02-45	149 Sqn
1686053	Sgt	BOULDING Harry	4-02-45	12 Sqn
1604051	Sgt	BOULTON Arthur William Thomas	5-01-45	51 Sqn
1588184	Sgt	BOWDEN Harry	2-02-45	619 Sqn
1458696	Sgt	BOWDEN Stanley Jarvis	3-02-45	44 Sqn
1313633	F/S	BOWEN William Gerwyn	5-01-45	51 Sqn
1896336	Sgt	BOWERS Cecil Stanley	2-02-45	149 Sqn
953737	W/O	BOYDELL Eric	21-02-45	76 Sqn
184181	F/L	BOYLE John	8-02-45	50 Sqn
1626845	Sgt	BOYSON Geoffrey Arthur Taylor	5-01-45	189 Sqn
1881699	Sgt	BOZEAT Joseph Edward	19-02-45	90 Sqn
190658	P/O	BRADBURY Derek Arthur	7-03-45	578 Sqn
1623077	F/S	BRADLEY Arthur Andrew	3-05-45	199 Sqn
752204	F/S	BRADSHAW Ernest William	4-03-45	10 Sqn
1600770	F/S	BRAGG Alfred Leonard	14-02-45	186 Sqn
1893070	Sgt	BRAGG Samuel Arthur	26-02-45	12 Sqn
1684863	F/S	BRAIN Gordon	22-03-45	150 Sqn
1812034	F/S	BRAITHWAITE Charles Roberts William	22-03-45	214 Sqn
2206798	F/S	BRAND Walter	12-01-45	9 Sqn
187774	P/O	BRANSGROVE William Edward	5-01-45	10 Sqn
133370	F/L	BRAUND John Prower	15-02-45	77 Sqn
133362	F/L	BRAUND Marwood Paul	12-01-45	77 Sqn
1853723	F/S	BRAY William Thomas	22-03-45	97 Sqn
1853258	Sgt	BRAZIER John Bryan Russell	20-06-45	1660 HCU
1324079	F/S	BREACH Reginald George Andrew	15-03-45	207 Sqn
2202497	Sgt	BREAKS Raymond	29-01-45	156 Sqn
163592	F/O	BREAKWELL Raymond	21-03-45	61 Sqn
190865	P/O	BREARE John Barrie	1-02-45	101 Sqn
1596812	Sgt	BRENNAN Martin	1-01-45	75 Sqn
2225454	Sgt	BRICKELL Harold	14-04-45	186 Sqn
153982	F/O	BRICKMAN Frederick John	1-03-45	103 Sqn
1817057	F/S	BRIDDON William	4-03-45	214 Sqn
1685598	Sgt	BRIERLEY Albert	6-04-45	26 OTU
1580472	Sgt	BRIGGS Arthur Geoffrey	15-01-45	578 Sqn
1672935	F/S	BRIGGS Herbert Henry	5-03-45	102 Sqn
1892880	F/S	BRITTAIN John Goodworth	9-05-45	514 Sqn
1543556	F/S	BROCKBANK Samuel	1-01-45	83 Sqn
1869379	Sgt	BROCKHURST Eric David Thornton	21-03-45	223 Sqn
114154	W/C	BROGAN DFC MiD Michael Andrew	5-03-45	161 Sqn
1593536	Sgt	BROOK George Elliott	3-02-45	189 Sqn
1181084	Sgt	BROOKE Horace	22-03-45	460 Sqn
172486	F/L	BROOKER DFC* Bernard Chapman	11-03-45	156 Sqn
546637	Sgt	BROOKES Frederick	10-04-45	462 Sqn
1591223	F/S	BROOKS Cyril	5-04-45	12 Sqn
157077	F/L	BROOKS William Ernest	3-05-45	199 Sqn
1475525	W/O	BROTCHIE David B.	23-03-45	239 Sqn
658085	W/O	BROWN DFM Alexander	3-02-45	156 Sqn
746717	W/O	BROWN Arnold	20-04-45	107 Sqn

Service No	Rank	Name	Date	Sqn
915868	Sgt	BROWN Arthur Herbert	2-01-45	19 OTU
1874886	Sgt	BROWN Douglas Frederick	16-03-45	44 Sqn
51809	F/L	BROWN Edward George	16-03-45	170 Sqn
1595671	Sgt	BROWN George William	3-01-45	622 Sqn
1559298	F/S	BROWN James	24-03-45	158 Sqn
3040078	Sgt	BROWN John George	3-02-45	90 Sqn
46024	F/L	BROWN Philip	22-02-45	578 Sqn
2225786	Sgt	BROWN Philip John	12-03-45	460 Sqn
614115	W/O	BROWN Reginald Alfred	22-04-45	78 Sqn
2225158	Sgt	BROWN Robert Steedman	6-03-45	103 Sqn
1595165	Sgt	BROWN Ronald	5-01-45	619 Sqn
1086989	F/S	BROWN DFM Roy Styan	2-01-45	166 Sqn
124364	F/O	BROWN Thomas Dryburgh	1-02-45	166 Sqn
1804538	Sgt	BROWNE Derek John	6-03-45	207 Sqn
1256422	F/S	BROWNE Edmund William	16-03-45	61 Sqn
1897240	Sgt	BROWNE Patrick Joseph Vincent	12-01-45	5 LFS
1581820	Sgt	BROWNETT Henry John	15-03-45	550 Sqn
1601746	F/S	BRUNTON Anthony Martin	23-02-45	192 Sqn
137302	F/L	BRYAN Clifford Bagnell	15-01-45	85 Sqn
1317321	F/S	BRYANT Desmond	21-02-45	223 Sqn
1824646	Sgt	BRYCE Joseph	8-03-45	619 Sqn
1670036	F/S	BRYSON James	17-01-45	514 Sqn
1337316	F/S	BUCKLAND Peter George	9-02-45	214 Sqn
171366	F/O	BUCKLAND Ronald George	16-03-45	166 Sqn
1690398	Sgt	BUCKLEY John Thomas	4-04-45	115 Sqn
1796164	Sgt	BULGER Alan Patrick [Eire]	5-02-45	1654 HCU
1816650	F/S	BULL Albert Edward	10-04-45	44 Sqn
1394093	25gt	BULL James Henry	2-02-45	460 Sqn
1274943	F/S	BULLOCK Douglas Albert	5-01-45	10 Sqn
171614	F/L	BUNING Jan Johannes [Holland]	3-02-45	90 Sqn
1584121	Sgt	BUNN Anthony Hylton	21-03-45	463 Sqn
182353	P/O	BUNN Sidney John	6-01-45	51 Sqn
1118147	Sgt	BUNYAN William	9-02-45	214 Sqn
1880298	Sgt	BURBIDGE William Laurence	7-03-45	12 Sqn
1875571	Sgt	BURCH Geoffrey Harry	8-03-45	103 Sqn
1591356	Sgt	BURDALL James William	25-04-45	76 Sqn
145766	F/O	BURGOYNE GM Henry	3-01-45	166 Sqn
1251125	Sgt	BURN Dennis Gilbert	15-01-45	1668 HCU
1274214	LAC	BURNELL Benjamin	24-02-45	61 Sqn
2209624	F/S	BURNS Albert	7-03-45	576 Sqn
1629942	F/S	BURNS George Brodie	8-03-45	576 Sqn
191136	P/O	BURNS James Gerald [Eire]	4-04-45	78 Sqn
3022679	Sgt	BURNS William	5-02-45	1654 HCU
1867170	Sgt	BURRIDGE Colin Frederick Peter	21-02-45	49 Sqn
2203724	Sgt	BURROWS Harry	21-02-45	576 Sqn
51119	F/L	BURROWS Noel	9-02-45	192 Sqn
113354	F/L	BURROWS Noel Alfred	19-03-45	550 Sqn
3040594	Sgt	BURT Andrew Sweeting	5-03-45	207 Sqn
1872241	F/S	BURTON Harold James	21-02-45	153 Sqn
642138	F/S	BURTON Walter Matthew	5-01-45	51 Sqn
54204	F/O	BUSHELL Peter Douglas	7-04-45	83 Sqn
1617032	Sgt	BUSK Jack	2-01-45	19 OTU
1881458	F/S	BUTCHER Alfred Frank	8-01-45	49 Sqn
1605645	Sgt	BUTCHER Kenneth Hardy	5-04-45	166 Sqn
132607	F/L	BUTCHER DFC Leonard Arthur	28-01-45	16 OTU
1868746	Sgt	BUTLER Cecil Arthur	4-02-45	35 Sqn
1807758	Sgt	BUTLER Charles Edward	3-07-45	166 Sqn
1596394	F/S	BUTLER Cyril	4-02-45	12 Sqn
1149758	W/O	BUTTERWORTH James	10-01-45	20 OTU
1851287	Sgt	BUTTRUM-GARDINER Edward Percival	1-01-45	218 Sqn
188508	P/O	BYRNE John Riley	13-02-45	550 Sqn
179139	F/O	CADMAN DFC William Guy	7-02-45	141 Sqn
1591098	F/S	CAIRNS Joseph Davison	21-03-45	223 Sqn
1822619	Sgt	CAIRNS William Fordyce	12-01-45	5 LFS
154318	F/O	CALDERBANK William Frederick	20-03-45	57 Sqn
1624820	F/S	CALLAGHAN Harry	4-03-45	467 Sqn
2226286	Sgt	CALLAGHAN Michael Augustine	2-03-45	12 Sqn
177705	F/O	CALLUM Charles David	10-02-45	1667 HCU
1814318	Sgt	CALVERLEY Ivor John	21-05-45	100 Sqn
1514795	F/S	CALVERT Alan Hodgson	6-01-45	10 Sqn
186773	F/O	CAMERON David Peacock Robertson	20-05-45	20 OTU
3031383	Sgt	CAMERON Stanley Laidler	9-02-45	630 Sqn
153621	F/O	CAMERON Walter Stanley	2-01-45	100 Sqn
1820283	Sgt	CAMPBELL Roderick	4-03-45	1654 HCU
190300	P/O	CAMPBELL Samuel Stevenson	21-04-45	608 Sqn
1147957	F/S	CAMPEY Walter	31-03-45	692 Sqn
1578842	F/S	CAMPIN Kenneth Charles	10-01-45	20 OTU
2220467	Sgt	CANDY Roy Percy	7-01-45	103 Sqn
50217	F/L	CANE DFM Maurice John Thomas	13-04-45	571 Sqn
1795481	Sgt	CANNING William [Eire]	8-03-45	101 Sqn
1339403	Sgt	CANNOCK Lionel Eric	27-02-45	76 Sqn
1801327	F/S	CANNON Percival George	8-02-45	97 Sqn
1898171	Sgt	CARD Arthur	5-04-45	1652 HCU
195101	P/O	CARLEY Henry Joseph	8-03-45	192 Sqn
157180	F/O	CARLTON Howard Francis John	19-02-45	90 Sqn
1635254	LAC	CARR Frank	23-04-45	5 Group
1455177	F/S	CARR Peter Norman	14-02-45	161 Sqn
1590301	Sgt	CARR Thomas Edward	16-01-45	166 Sqn
1155863	F/S	CARR Thomas Stanley	21-02-45	156 Sqn
1683518	F/S	CARR Wilfrid Gordon	4-04-45	115 Sqn
1816917	Sgt	CARROTT Robert James	9-02-45	214 Sqn
1827680	Sgt	CARSON Alexander	15-02-45	630 Sqn
165049	F/O	CARSS Edward Boon	15-04-45	1667 HCU
1594696	Sgt	CARTER Donovan Yukin	12-03-45	106 Sqn
2221973	Sgt	CARTER Francis Edward	12-03-45	103 Sqn
189794	P/O	CARTER Leslie	8-03-45	578 Sqn
1301950	Sgt	CARTER Stanley Stewart	5-01-45	77 Sqn
1853102	F/S	CARTHEW William John	10-02-45	138 Sqn
187561	P/O	CARTHY DFC Sydney John	27-02-45	20 OTU
2226063	Sgt	CARTMELL Joseph Milburn	2-03-45	12 Sqn
1489925	F/S	CARTWRIGHT Gordon	14-03-45	57 Sqn
1801137	F/S	CARVELL John Frederick	23-02-45	192 Sqn
1594757	Sgt	CASTLE Herbert	14-03-45	106 Sqn
201308	P/O	CASTLE Ivor	13-12-45	26 OTU
53904	F/O	CATTERALL DFC Robert	2-05-45	169 Sqn
165666	F/O	CAWTHORP Roy Thomas	8-03-45	101 Sqn
185912	P/O	CEELEY Arthur Frederick	19-03-45	571 Sqn
1396938	F/S	CHALLIS Keith Leonard	17-03-45	576 Sqn
1565986	F/S	CHALMERS Henry Edward	2-03-45	75 Sqn
1693936	Sgt	CHAMBERS Francis Thomas	3-05-45	199 Sqn
191689	P/O	CHAMBERS John William	11-04-45	619 Sqn
1594677	Sgt	CHANDLER Thomas Herbert	29-01-45	408 Sqn
1628448	F/S	CHAPMAN Alan Osborn	29-09-45	550 Sqn
1877173	Sgt	CHAPMAN Arthur George	23-02-45	166 Sqn
150056	F/L	CHAPMAN Harry	7-03-45	625 Sqn
164041	F/O	CHAPMAN John Austin Charles	4-03-45	1654 HCU
2202909	Sgt	CHAPMAN Kenneth	12-04-45	1654 HCU
1576762	F/S	CHAPMAN CGM Leslie	1-02-45	61 Sqn
122930	F/L	CHAPMAN Reginald Clifford	8-03-45	35 Sqn
2214054	F/S	CHAPMAN Stanley	21-03-45	50 Sqn
1653100	Sgt	CHARLES David Arthur	11-03-45	463 Sqn
1665264	Sgt	CHARLES Walter James	16-03-45	12 Sqn
1512529	F/S	CHARLTON James Ferguson	8-03-45	189 Sqn
1897453	Sgt	CHATTERS William Albert Alfred	4-03-45	467 Sqn
161264	F/O	CHAUNDY DFM George Raymond Peter	15-01-45	692 Sqn
1320692	W/O	CHEESE Alfred Charles	6-01-45	171 Sqn
162260	F/O	CHEESEMAN Harold Norman	14-02-45	576 Sqn
1582776	F/S	CHELL Lional Hawkins	3-02-45	10 Sqn
1591797	F/S	CHESHIRE Kenneth George	9-02-45	192 Sqn
633841	F/S	CHESNUTT Cyril	8-03-45	49 Sqn
191835	P/O	CHETWYND-STAPYLTON Edward Miles	9-02-45	186 Sqn
1892895	Sgt	CHIDWICK Jeffrey James	2-02-45	9 Sqn

Service No	Rank	Name	Date	Unit
1184666	LAC	CHOPE Norman John	15-06-45	Bircham Newton
188188	F/O	CHOPPING Stanley George	14-03-45	51 Sqn
2205721	F/S	CHRISTIE Paul Anthony	7-01-45	622 Sqn
1801646	Sgt	CHURCH Cecil Arthur Jeffery	22-03-45	15 Sqn
2203996	Sgt	CHURCHILL Thomas	23-03-45	101 Sqn
1596784	Sgt	CLAPPERTON Kenneth William	22-03-45	207 Sqn
1605772	Sgt	CLAPTON Gerald Frederick Arthur	5-02-45	1669 HCU
163920	F/O	CLARK Anthony William	23-02-45	192 Sqn
941485	Sgt	CLARK Arthur Charles	5-01-45	103 Sqn
182483	F/O	CLARK Cecil Philip	3-02-45	156 Sqn
160772	F/L	CLARK Gerald Arthur	8-04-45	BCIS
163521	F/O	CLARK Phillip Charles Headley	1-03-45	153 Sqn
1388242	Sgt	CLARK Roy Stanley	22-04-45	75 Sqn
1811271	Sgt	CLARK Victor James	1-01-45	75 Sqn
619362	Sgt	CLARK William Andrew Alcwyn	5-02-45	1654 HCU
154941	F/O	CLARKE Frank	5-03-45	514 Sqn
3010578	Sgt	CLARKE George Allen	17-03-45	625 Sqn
1868276	Sgt	CLARKE Guy Archer	16-03-45	12 Sqn
151151	F/L	CLARKE DFC Michael Terence	16-04-45	617 Sqn
169486	F/O	CLARKE Norman	5-03-45	161 Sqn
3031556	Sgt	CLARKE Ronald Frederick	5-04-45	626 Sqn
129345	F/L	CLAY Thomas	20-06-45	1660 HCU
901682	W/O	CLAYDEN Douglas Jobson	19-04-45	405 Sqn
1398534	F/S	CLEARY William Laurence	6-01-45	207 Sqn
1396078	F/S	CLEMENTS John Anthony	2-02-45	44 Sqn
553446	W/O	CLEMENTSON William Sandison	4-03-45	192 Sqn
157176	F/O	CLIFFE Frank Gerald	16-03-45	170 Sqn
1582530	F/S	CLIFTON Alfred John	23-03-45	101 Sqn
190041	F/O	CLUER Roger	9-04-45	49 Sqn
1595187	Sgt	CLYDE Alexander Thomas	6-01-45	158 Sqn
183812	F/O	COAD Jack Ian	5-01-45	189 Sqn
1622241	F/S	COATES Jack	21-02-45	576 Sqn
1592713	F/S	COATES Lionel David Ian	5-01-45	10 Sqn
121906	F/L	COBB DFM Harry	8-04-45	35 Sqn
1603090	Sgt	COBDEN Walter Theophilus George	6-03-45	207 Sqn
157435	F/O	COCKAYNE Arthur Clarence	16-01-45	23 Sqn
67707	S/L	COCKBAIN DFC Stephen Legh	14-01-45	1661 HCU
185326	F/O	COCKCROFT Arthur Clarence	22-04-45	153 Sqn
1890967	F/S	COCOZZA Raphael Michael	14-03-45	57 Sqn
1062192	F/S	COFFEY John Bracken	5-04-45	153 Sqn
1597554	Sgt	COLQUHOUN William Love	21-02-45	158 Sqn
1621978	F/S	COLE Cecil	11-03-45	153 Sqn
1445279	W/O	COLE Edward Cyril	28-05-45	17 OTU
153057	F/O	COLE Ernest William	4-08-45	5 Group
2202552	F/S	COLE George	23-02-45	138 Sqn
1684124	F/S	COLES James	28-01-45	153 Sqn
578541	F/S	COLES Raymond George	1-02-45	166 Sqn
130650	F/L	COLLEY Noel Sidney Caesar	2-01-45	467 Sqn
1551018	F/S	COLLIER Thomas Phillips	3-04-45	625 Sqn
1880273	Sgt	COLLIN Henry Oswald	21-03-45	207 Sqn
87454	S/L	COLLINSON DFC Kenneth Lloyd	21-02-45	166 Sqn
1681850	Sgt	COLQUHOUN Douglas	15-03-45	432 Sqn
1234159	Sgt	CONNELL Leslie Franklin	12-01-45	77 Sqn
625341	W/O	CONNER Frederick Ronald	7-09-45	106 Sqn
2219046	Sgt	CONNING Robert Harold	23-02-45	150 Sqn
1881462	Sgt	CONROY Daniel	16-01-45	101 Sqn
1807509	F/S	COOK David Frederick	4-03-45	189 Sqn
1054100	Sgt	COOK Herbert	1-01-45	571 Sqn
1891492	Sgt	COOK Leslie Frederick	29-01-45	3 LFS
176417	F/O	COOK Norman Edward	8-04-45	1653 HCU
1893896	F/S	COOK Robert Bertram Roy	15-04-45	1667 HCU
1245900	Sgt	COOK Samuel	5-01-45	103 Sqn
196146	P/O	COOKE Douglas Marvin	6-03-45	432 Sqn
1813019	Sgt	COOKE Leonard Alexander	5-04-45	1652 HCU
3051677	Sgt	COOKE Leonard James	1-01-45	75 Sqn
182730	F/O	COOKE Michael John Hedley	15-03-45	207 Sqn
1604557	Sgt	COOLEY Peter	22-03-45	15 Sqn
1617503	Sgt	COOLEY William George	2-04-45	1651 HCU
160156	F/O	COOMBES Clifford	21-02-45	83 Sqn
1573835	Sgt	COONEY Thomas	5-03-45	102 Sqn
187004	P/O	COOPER Charles John	16-03-45	100 Sqn
154093	F/L	COOPER David Norman Anthony	21-02-45	625 Sqn
916151	W/O	COOPER Norman	22-03-45	214 Sqn
1604766	F/S	COOPER Norman	8-03-45	57 Sqn
1685251	Sgt	COOPER Ronald William Riverston	12-01-45	9 Sqn
1577019	F/S	COOPER William Joseph	12-03-45	106 Sqn
1893709	Sgt	COPE George Arthur	22-03-45	15 Sqn
41152	S/L	CORBET DFC Walter Henry	7-05-45	PFNTU
178520	F/O	COREWYN William George	15-01-45	61 Sqn
1398282	F/S	CORNELL Bryant Thomas	18-01-45	75 Sqn
1176517	Sgt	CORNISH William George	14-02-45	161 Sqn
2210978	Sgt	CORNWALL James Alex	20-03-45	7 Sqn
158704	F/L	CORNWALLIS Peter Brownell	27-02-45	138 Sqn
1538889	Sgt	CORY John Edwin	27-02-45	138 Sqn
1903525	Sgt	COTTER Thomas Anthony	15-04-45	138 Sqn
1815603	Sgt	COTTERELL Peter Samuel	6-01-45	158 Sqn
1604230	F/S	COTTERILL Thomas Henry	12-05-45	1651 HCU
1238674	F/S	COTTON Frederick William	8-02-45	83 Sqn
1581247	F/S	COTTON Percy	7-03-45	12 Sqn
152725	F/O	COULTON Harry	4-02-45	35 Sqn
1880701	Sgt	COURT Jack	8-01-45	49 Sqn
184760	P/O	COUZENS Robert Henry	5-01-45	429 Sqn
195714	F/O	COWAN George Hamilton	15-06-45	630 Sqn
178046	F/L	COWDEN DFC John Duncan Forbes	14-02-45	635 Sqn
3040693	Sgt	COWELL Frederick	2-02-45	78 Sqn
187512	F/L	COWLEY Norman Coatner	27-02-45	186 Sqn
171681	F/O	COX Albert	16-01-45	158 Sqn
515112	F/S	COX Cecil Edward	4-03-45	640 Sqn
3050655	Sgt	COX Derrick	13-03-45	153 Sqn
179313	F/L	COX Geoffrey	6-01-45	171 Sqn
1583336	F/S	COX Henry Francis	4-03-45	1654 HCU
157042	F/L	COX DFC Leslie Arnold	31-03-45	156 Sqn
1815413	Sgt	COX Norman McDonald	22-03-45	207 Sqn
49800	F/L	COX Ronald Edwin	4-04-45	78 Sqn
1680404	F/S	CRADDOCK Sydney	11-03-45	153 Sqn
3021187	Sgt	CRAIG John Desmond	1-02-45	166 Sqn
145700	F/L	CRAIK DFC James Fraser	14-02-45	635 Sqn
1872283	F/S	CRAMPIN Alan Joseph	1-03-45	103 Sqn
163535	F/O	CRAWFORD James	21-02-45	626 Sqn
187721	F/O	CRAWFORD Richard St. John Trevor	22-05-45	26 OTU
1684977	Sgt	CRAWHALL Stanley Joseph	5-04-45	1667 HCU
190372	P/O	CRESSWELL Frederick Allan	19-02-45	90 Sqn
1684278	F/S	CRITCHLEY Denis James	24-02-45	462 Sqn
2235590	Sgt	CRITTENDEN Arthur John	29-01-45	3 LFS
183376	F/O	CROFT Kenneth Norman Joseph	3-05-45	199 Sqn
1570260	Sgt	CROLL Alexander Harvey	7-02-45	77 Sqn
1894786	Sgt	CROLLIE Richard George	18-02-45	420 Sqn
1398447	F/S	CROOKES Charles	14-04-45	186 Sqn
1534727	F/S	CROSS DFM George	6-03-45	35 Sqn
1395339	Sgt	CROSS John William	21-03-45	97 Sqn
1892412	F/S	CROSSMAN Thomas James	7-03-45	625 Sqn
1566946	F/S	CROUCHER Henry	8-01-45	12 Sqn
1585464	F/S	CROUCHER John Harold	17-03-45	630 Sqn
3040754	Sgt	CROWE Donald McBean	9-02-45	186 Sqn
1315733	Sgt	CRUMP Reginald George	13-02-45	550 Sqn
647200	F/S	CRUTCHFIELD Edward Arthur	15-04-45	1661 HCU
141282	F/L	CRYER Jaques Edward 'Ted'	15-03-45	214 Sqn
1439614	F/S	CULLEN Charles Leslie	23-01-45	153 Sqn
1853122	Sgt	CUMBERWORTH Provis	30-10-45	1653 HCU
177853	F/L	CUMMING Raymond Stanley	15-02-45	78 Sqn
1881269	Sgt	CUMMINS William	22-03-45	166 Sqn
150242	F/L	CUNLIFFE Robert	15-02-45	625 Sqn
149252	F/O	CUNNINGHAM Wilfred James	22-03-45	214 Sqn
630648	F/S	CURRIE David Porter	15-06-45	630 Sqn
1800502	F/S	CURRIGAN Stanley William Guy	1-01-45	9 Sqn

Service No	Rank	Name	Date	Sqn/Unit
1826346	Sgt	CUTHILL Frederick John	17-04-45	156 Sqn
1016932	Sgt	DACEY George	5-01-45	158 Sqn
1671699	F/S	DAINTITH DFM Clifford	7-03-45	12 Sqn
1622283	F/S	DALBY William Edwin	22-02-45	50 Sqn
1594366	Sgt	DALE William Denis	21-03-45	214 Sqn
190366	P/O	DALY John	5-01-45	408 Sqn
2210620	Sgt	DANDY Gerald Edward	2-03-45	57 Sqn
1399655	F/S	DANE George Alfred	19-03-45	149 Sqn
1413547	F/S	DANIEL William Anthony	5-01-45	10 Sqn
3031902	Sgt	DANKS Ian Duncan Brodie	4-01-45	1652 HCU
56691	P/O	DARBY DFM Albert	12-04-45	1654 HCU
1816533	Sgt	DARBY Cecil Benham	10-02-45	1667 HCU
1481728	Sgt	DARBYSHIRE Herbert	16-03-45	49 Sqn
138046	F/O	DARKE Kenneth Charles	7-01-45	106 Sqn
1399727	Sgt	DARLING Albert William	4-03-45	1651 HCU
1676154	F/S	DARNEY Thomas Brown	16-01-45	186 Sqn
1902840	Sgt	DARRAGH Thomas Foster	22-02-45	218 Sqn
191980	P/O	DAVENPORT Robert Edward	5-03-45	10 Sqn
1381573	Sgt	DAVEY Charles Kenneth	8-02-45	57 Sqn
1393755	F/S	DAVEY Desmond	17-01-45	640 Sqn
196062	F/O	DAVEY Joseph	3-10-45	1668 HCU
1583729	Sgt	DAVID Jack Norman	19-03-45	460 Sqn
1837005	Sgt	DAVID Trevor Ephraim	24-02-45	462 Sqn
81393	F/L	DAVIDSON James Stuart	14-02-45	635 Sqn
1205745	F/S	DAVIDSON Vincent Campbell	17-03-45	550 Sqn
1589151	F/S	DAVIES Alan	17-03-45	103 Sqn
1869380	Sgt	DAVIES Anthony John Maxwell	21-03-45	61 Sqn
162865	F/O	DAVIES Charles	31-05-45	1660 HCU
177181	F/O	DAVIES David Clifford	4-03-45	1651 HCU
1600464	Sgt	DAVIES Dennis Howell	22-03-45	44 Sqn
1898051	Sgt	DAVIES George	5-04-45	626 Sqn
174052	F/O	DAVIES Gerald Mayella	22-03-45	218 Sqn
2219321	Sgt	DAVIES Herbert George	15-02-45	630 Sqn
1543191	Sgt	DAVIES John	15-02-45	189 Sqn
2211499	Sgt	DAVIES John	14-03-45	57 Sqn
1089959	LAC	DAVIES John Harold	23-04-45	Fulbeck
133640	F/L	DAVIES John Outram	2-02-45	189 Sqn
1514786	F/S	DAVIES John Samuel	14-03-45	51 Sqn
2205993	Sgt	DAVIES Leslie	15-02-45	115 Sqn
1653083	Sgt	DAVIES Reynold	14-01-45	17 OTU
162484	F/O	DAVIS Basil Owen	6-02-45	571 Sqn
1591071	Sgt	DAVIS Eric	2-03-45	57 Sqn
1814561	F/S	DAVIS John Clement	24-03-45	150 Sqn
196719	P/O	DAVIS Lawrence Fortnam	15-02-45	424 Sqn
658071	F/S	DAVIS Noel	30-04-45	635 Sqn
1816775	Sgt	DAVY Alan Churchill	4-03-45	1654 HCU
1375306	W/O	DAVY Frederick Edwin Thomas	6-01-45	171 Sqn
148397	F/L	DAWES DFC Jack Evelyn	3-04-45	139 Sqn
1811370	F/S	DAWES Walter Richard	5-01-45	50 Sqn
1864404	F/S	DAWSON William Frederick George	16-03-45	170 Sqn
1899663	Sgt	DAY Edmund Kenneth	16-03-45	625 Sqn
1581324	F/S	DAY Eric John	16-03-45	61 Sqn
190483	F/O	DAY James	5-04-45	166 Sqn
1684012	F/S	DAY John Gilbert	24-03-45	550 Sqn
2213761	Sgt	DAY Peter	7-01-45	170 Sqn
164090	F/O	DAY Peter John	9-02-45	15 Sqn
42559	F/L	DAY DFC Robert Ogilvie [South Africa]	24-03-45	139 Sqn
126999	S/L	DEAN William Erin Millar	3-01-45	622 Sqn
1608026	Sgt	DEAN William Thomas	22-03-45	460 Sqn
195696	P/O	DEBARR Frederick Henry	22-03-45	227 Sqn
1876612	Sgt	DEBONNAIRE Donald William	16-03-45	12 Sqn
1881358	F/S	DEE William John	22-03-45	15 Sqn
125748	F/O	DEFRAIGNE Charles Albert Henri Francois [Belgium]	24-03-45	166 Sqn
1683581	Sgt	DELAHUNTY Martin	2-02-45	640 Sqn
1814844	F/S	DELAVELEYE C. A. [Belgium]	7-03-45	550 Sqn
154385	F/O	DELIEU Albert William	23-02-45	150 Sqn
1699824	Sgt	DELLER Edwin	6-01-45	207 Sqn
1588726	Sgt	DENBIGH Arnold	6-03-45	582 Sqn
1566359	F/S	DENNISON Alexander Beveridge	13-02-45	550 Sqn
3041986	Sgt	DENT John Joseph Emerson	4-03-45	158 Sqn
1579338	F/S	DERRINGTON Howard Edmund	17-01-45	10 Sqn
1901902	Sgt	DEVELIN Robert Charles [Eire]	26-05-45	17 OTU
2210113	F/S	DEVER William Kenneth	2-04-45	29 OTU
1851905	Sgt	DEVERELL Anthony John	7-03-45	61 Sqn
1826573	Sgt	DEVLIN James	2-03-45	460 Sqn
1881244	Sgt	DEVLIN Richard	17-01-45	15 Sqn
1892018	F/S	DEW Thomas George William	15-03-45	49 Sqn
1837028	Sgt	DEWDNEY Charles James	21-03-45	207 Sqn
185127	P/O	DE BIJ Henri Mari	14-02-45	640 Sqn
605691	Sgt	DIAS Vivian Peter [British Guiana]	20-04-45	19 OTU
2220841	Sgt	DICKEN John Radford	10-04-45	630 Sqn
1583075	F/S	DICKENSON Gordon Leonard	6-03-45	207 Sqn
1451857	F/S	DICKINSON George Charles	9-02-45	15 Sqn
131121	F/L	DIEMER MiD Arthur Colin	11-03-45	156 Sqn
1040621	W/O	DIFFLEY James Hugh	2-01-45	19 OTU
'221828'	Sgt	DINNEN Robert Louis [Eire]	5-03-45	420 Sqn
139616	F/L	DISNEY Philip Allan	22-03-45	23 Sqn
1672038	Sgt	DIXON Arthur Thomas	21-02-45	626 Sqn
177009	F/O	DIXON Donald	30-03-45	635 Sqn
2207089	F/S	DIXON Eric	21-03-45	158 Sqn
1463894	Sgt	DIXON Jack	6-03-45	153 Sqn
1596554	Sgt	DIXON Thomas	7-03-45	170 Sqn
1009063	Cpl	DIXON Thomas Stanley	17-04-45	5 Group
1272566	Sgt	DOBSON Alan Thomas	9-02-45	15 Sqn
1590215	Sgt	DOBSON Ernest	9-02-45	214 Sqn
177257	F/L	DOBSON Reginald Frederick	23-02-45	103 Sqn
1821642	F/S	DOGGART Thomas Watters	7-03-45	44 Sqn
1899005	Sgt	DOGGETT Philip Leslie	15-04-45	1661 HCU
102594	F/L	DOHERTY DFC Robert Aubrey Alexander	23-02-45	608 Sqn
2218443	Sgt	DOLAN Stephen Joseph	5-01-45	15 Sqn
1826350	Sgt	DOLAN William	22-03-45	50 Sqn
81348	S/L	DON DFC Ralph Stidston	22-01-45	142 Sqn
1589606	Sgt	DONALDSON John	12-01-45	77 Sqn
154889	F/O	DONNER Roderick William	22-03-45	626 Sqn
178567	F/O	DONOHUE DFC John Richard Charles	14-02-45	635 Sqn
144626	F/O	DORAN Patrick Bryan	7-02-45	692 Sqn
3030826	Sgt	DOREY Dennis Archibald	2-02-45	50 Sqn
1603829	F/S	DORMER John Francis	28-01-45	153 Sqn
190886	F/O	DOUBLE Roy Franklin	31-05-45	1660 HCU
1815285	Sgt	DOUGLAS Clifford Bennett	26-02-45	12 Sqn
198108	P/O	DOUGLAS Gordon	25-06-45	50 Sqn
1373345	Sgt	DOUGLAS John	15-01-45	61 Sqn
2216269	Sgt	DOVASTON Leslie	15-03-45	405 Sqn
41266	S/L	DOW DFC Thomas Roy Asquith [Canada]	4-04-45	139 Sqn
1822334	Sgt	DOWNIE John	10-01-45	20 OTU
174041	F/O	DOYLE James	3-07-45	166 Sqn
163160	F/O	DRAKE Arthur Reginald Sheriff	21-03-45	163 Sqn
55096	F/O	DRAKE Bernard William	4-03-45	1653 HCU
149531	F/L	DRANE DFC Peter James	15-01-45	139 Sqn
175939	F/O	DRAPER Eric George	17-04-45	171 Sqn
1049545	F/S	DRAPER James	6-01-45	10 Sqn
1804021	Sgt	DRAWBRIDGE Henry William Nevil	5-02-45	1669 HCU
1903277	Sgt	DRENNAN Thomas Edward [Eire]	4-03-45	467 Sqn
55242	F/O	DRON William	8-02-45	49 Sqn
1353162	LAC	DRYDEN Douglas Fletcher	18-05-45	30 OTU
1826957	F/O	DRYSDALE William	5-03-45	207 Sqn
570597	Sgt	DUBOIS John	2-01-45	100 Sqn
1530936	F/S	DUCKWORTH Derek Dinshaw	8-03-45	218 Sqn
118147	F/L	DUKE DFM Eric Cecil	2-01-45	405 Sqn
2210530	Sgt	DUKE John Lawrence	28-02-45	75 Sqn
172456	F/O	DUKELOW Robert Burnaby Alexander	1-02-45	100 Sqn

443

Service #	Rank	Name	Date	Sqn
157337	F/L	DUNCAN George Robert Peebles	28-01-45	105 Sqn
1826025	Sgt	DUNCAN John	28-05-45	17 OTU
42957	W/C	DUNHAM DFC Peter Francis	19-02-45	90 Sqn
1596304	Sgt	DUNKERLEY Henry Hall	22-03-45	460 Sqn
1625326	Sgt	DUNKLEY Robert Frederick Stanley	5-04-45	166 Sqn
153256	F/O	DUNLOP Robert Duncan	7-01-45	106 Sqn
1798048	Sgt	DUNLOP Thomas Norman	8-03-45	57 Sqn
1141391	Sgt	DUNN Leslie William	16-03-45	170 Sqn
1515917	Sgt	DUNNE Thomas Rathband [Eire]	5-01-45	189 Sqn
1608367	Sgt	DUNSTONE Frank Victor James	8-02-45	57 Sqn
1602131	F/S	DUNTHORNE Derrick William	25-02-45	1660 HCU
1606092	Sgt	DUNVILLE Joseph Charlton	5-01-45	189 Sqn
1053444	W/O	DURNAN Hamilton	22-04-45	77 Sqn
1882568	Sgt	DURSTON Kenneth George	16-03-45	576 Sqn
154376	F/O	DUTFIELD Herbert Charles	16-01-45	186 Sqn
1623460	F/S	DUTTON Kenneth Lister	22-04-45	153 Sqn
1625445	F/S	DYER Jack	5-06-45	149 Sqn
2221046	F/S	DYKE James	19-03-45	77 Sqn
993035	F/S	DYSON Frank	17-04-45	171 Sqn
196262	P/O	D'ARCY John [Eire]	15-03-45	207 Sqn
141706	F/L	EAMES DFC Kenneth Horace	5-04-45	626 Sqn
1649851	Sgt	EARL Peter Richard	15-01-45	61 Sqn
1891740	F/S	EASTCOTT Dennis William	23-02-45	166 Sqn
177625	F/O	EASTWELL Frederick Stanley	2-03-45	51 Sqn
1768114	F/S	EASTWOOD Jack	13-07-45	97 Sqn
1615600	F/S	EBBAGE Francis Henry	14-03-45	75 Sqn
1901246	Sgt	EBBS Cecil Alexander	5-03-45	170 Sqn
2225711	Sgt	ECKFORD Robert Ivor Peter	15-02-45	115 Sqn
2203360	F/S	EDDLESTON Maurice Clive	14-02-45	77 Sqn
1880840	Sgt	EDE Sidney William	14-02-45	640 Sqn
178511	F/O	EDEN George Mason	20-06-45	1660 HCU
137170	F/L	EDEN Victor Geoffrey	31-05-45	1660 HCU
1817893	Sgt	EDGE William Frederick George	3-07-45	166 Sqn
2222026	Sgt	EDGE William Henry	5-03-45	207 Sqn
182690	F/O	EDMONDS Leslie Frederick	5-02-45	419 Sqn
1673394	F/S	EDMONDSON Joseph Philip	16-03-45	100 Sqn
1391039	F/S	EDWARDS Alfred Henry	3-02-45	90 Sqn
1699626	F/S	EDWARDS Bernard	2-02-45	189 Sqn
1214188	Sgt	EDWARDS Cyril	16-03-45	170 Sqn
1322520	W/O	EDWARDS Ernest James	14-01-45	630 Sqn
1800886	Sgt	EDWARDS Ernest Reginald	21-02-45	150 Sqn
1049072	Sgt	EDWARDS Frederick George	21-02-45	227 Sqn
1459369	Sgt	EDWARDS Gordon Charles	14-01-45	17 OTU
190988	P/O	EDWARDS Peter Thomas	15-03-45	227 Sqn
3050372	Sgt	EDWARDS Reginald Francis	18-02-45	626 Sqn
1852213	Sgt	EDWARDS Vernon Albert	9-02-45	61 Sqn
195404	P/O	EDWARDS William James	19-03-45	77 Sqn
1317671	F/S	EGAN Desmond Richard	16-03-45	626 Sqn
2220647	Sgt	EGAN James Brian	18-04-45	12 OTU
82543	F/L	EICHLER Bohuslav [Czechoslovakia]	5-01-45	142 Sqn
1891920	Sgt	ELCOME William Frederick Henry	11-03-45	463 Sqn
173049	F/O	ELKINGTON George Frank	22-04-45	49 Sqn
1530166	Sgt	ELLARBY Jack	16-03-45	1662 HCU
64297	F/L	ELLIOTT Alec	5-04-45	158 Sqn
1672286	F/S	ELLIOTT Frank Shackleton	5-04-45	100 Sqn
172726	F/O	ELLIOTT DFM Frank William	6-03-45	103 Sqn
1607037	F/S	ELLIOTT George Henry	14-03-45	51 Sqn
1591992	Sgt	ELLIOTT Leslie	17-03-45	550 Sqn
2218869	Sgt	ELLIOTT Thomas Tiffin	6-03-45	10 Sqn
183959	F/O	ELLIS Ernest Lewis	23-02-45	166 Sqn
111257	F/L	ELLIS Gabriel Hitch	20-03-45	85 Sqn
1395466	F/S	ELLIS Herbert William	5-04-45	7 Sqn
1817434	Sgt	ELLIS Peter Norman	14-02-45	161 Sqn
153237	F/O	ELLIS Thomas Oscar Eldred	2-02-45	189 Sqn
54542	F/O	ELLWOOD DFM MiD Mowbray	12-01-45	617 Sqn
1868141	Sgt	ELSON John Frederick	7-01-45	106 Sqn
1898571	Sgt	EMERSON George Ernest	19-03-45	102 Sqn
126587	F/L	ENDERBY DFC Patrick	4-04-45	105 Sqn
116884	F/L	ENDERSBY Jack Stuart	4-04-45	139 Sqn
997434	F/S	ENGLISH Robert	5-01-45	102 Sqn
1365096	W/O	ERSKINE William	16-04-45	11 OTU
190973	P/O	ETHERIDGE Nigel Paul	27-02-45	186 Sqn
2209136	Sgt	ETHERINGTON Kenneth Joseph	21-02-45	626 Sqn
2227596	Sgt	ETHERTON Randal Roy	1-02-45	101 Sqn
1422223	Sgt	EVANS BEM Albert John	12-01-45	5 LFS
1816433	F/S	EVANS Eric Leslie	3-02-45	189 Sqn
1602244	Sgt	EVANS Eric Walter	8-01-45	103 Sqn
2210219	Sgt	EVANS Harry	14-02-45	420 Sqn
124672	F/L	EVANS John Vernon	5-03-45	109 Sqn
1584222	F/S	EVANS Leonard William	22-04-45	49 Sqn
1339158	W/O	EVANS Reginald Gordon	25-04-45	426 Sqn
1652888	F/S	EVANS Richard Roy	20-03-45	7 Sqn
1671641	Sgt	EVANS Robert	22-01-45	153 Sqn
196117	P/O	EVANS William George	5-04-45	186 Sqn
19018	G/C	EVANS-EVANS DFC Anthony Caron	21-02-45	83 Sqn
1897192	Sgt	EVE John	17-03-45	576 Sqn
155223	S/L	EVERETT DFC** Daniel Bulmer	8-03-45	35 Sqn
190482	P/O	EVERS Gilbert Davey	28-01-45	218 Sqn
154904	F/O	EWIN Edward Henry	8-03-45	1658 HCU
1883514	Sgt	EWINGTON Edward George	3-04-45	625 Sqn
163714	F/O	EYLES Cyril Edward	8-03-45	619 Sqn
176684	F/O	EYNON Basil Walter	8-03-45	619 Sqn
191841	P/O	FAIRCLOUGH Ronald	15-03-45	207 Sqn
1678338	Sgt	FALLOWS James Levi	15-02-45	189 Sqn
107517	F/L	FARDELL Ashley Stanley John	10-03-45	16 OTU
1303911	F/S	FARLIE Charles David Craven	6-01-45	171 Sqn
1333628	W/O	FARMER Harry Lawrence	17-03-45	550 Sqn
1825746	Sgt	FARQUHAR James John	12-01-45	424 Sqn
1591148	Sgt	FARRAR Dennis William	2-02-45	51 Sqn
3005547	Sgt	FARROW Edward Anthony Jack	4-03-45	158 Sqn
1339259	F/S	FARROW James Robert	8-02-45	83 Sqn
1185167	Sgt	FAULKNER Douglas Alexander	25-04-45	431 Sqn
1624993	Sgt	FAULKNER Joseph	21-02-45	76 Sqn
1245828	F/S	FAYERS Ronald Charles	2-01-45	19 OTU
1594868	F/S	FEARNLEY Fred	5-03-45	10 Sqn
1798942	Sgt	FEATHERSTONE Thomas	17-01-45	640 Sqn
611641	W/O	FELL David	7-01-45	103 Sqn
1809630	F/S	FELTON DFM Henry William	16-04-45	617 Sqn
1580371	F/S	FELTON Norman Lewis Garfield	9-04-45	50 Sqn
3000547	Sgt	FENNER Raymond Charles	29-01-45	51 Sqn
55911	F/O	FENWICK DFC Charles	13-12-45	26 OTU
1850790	F/S	FENWICK John Edward Willoughby	1-01-45	115 Sqn
1824947	Sgt	FENWICK Stanley Reeves	6-01-45	171 Sqn
39868	S/L	FENWICK Victor Jack [Canada]	4-03-45	169 Sqn
989177	F/S	FERGUSON Harold	28-01-45	153 Sqn
1473577	F/S	FERGUSON John Joseph	23-03-45	239 Sqn
1056421	F/S	FERME Alexander Wightman	7-03-45	171 Sqn
83246	S/L	FEW DFC AFC Eric Stanley	21-04-45	608 Sqn
1390891	F/S	FIELD Peter Harold	4-03-45	10 Sqn
1285488	Sgt	FIELD William	15-03-45	550 Sqn
2206034	F/S	FIELDER Charles Kenneth	2-03-45	640 Sqn
1602338	W/O	FIELDER William Ewart	27-02-45	20 OTU
2219056	Sgt	FIELDING Denis Smith	22-03-45	150 Sqn
1583588	F/S	FILARATOFF Volek Edward	15-02-45	189 Sqn
1877705	Sgt	FINCH Cecil Harry	4-03-45	10 Sqn
1865655	Sgt	FINCH Edward	17-03-45	153 Sqn
191796	P/O	FINLAYSON Donald Dennis	8-02-45	44 Sqn
3020199	Sgt	FINLAYSON James	9-02-45	186 Sqn
1314004	F/S	FINLAYSON John Kennedy	17-03-45	153 Sqn
2225471	Sgt	FINNERTY Austin	16-03-45	49 Sqn
176001	F/O	FINNIGAN David Percy Maeers	9-02-45	192 Sqn
143764	F/L	FITCH DFC GM William Cross	21-02-45	83 Sqn
1902688	Sgt	FITZPATRICK John [Eire]	7-03-45	61 Sqn
1901178	Sgt	FITZPATRICK Patrick [Eire]	5-04-45	166 Sqn
1604231	F/S	FIVASH John Edward	11-07-45	10 OTU
1304368	W/O	FLACK Arthur George	15-02-45	166 Sqn

1581726	F/S	FLATTERY Frederick John	2-02-45	460 Sqn	1853287	Sgt	GAPPER Phillip	21-05-45	100 Sqn
1578541	F/S	FLAXMAN George	8-01-45	12 Sqn	172025	F/O	GARDNER John Vincent	16-03-45	166 Sqn
1670353	F/S	FLEET Samuel	1-02-45	61 Sqn	1815298	F/S	GARFIELD Lawrence William	14-07-45	626 Sqn
1549302	F/S	FLETCHER Edward Walter	28-01-45	153 Sqn	138682	F/L	GARFORTH Norman	26-01-45	578 Sqn
2212829	Sgt	FLETCHER Ernest Henry	2-02-45	78 Sqn	1587181	F/S	GARLAND Ronald Stanley	7-01-45	169 Sqn
1595386	Sgt	FLETCHER George	14-01-45	106 Sqn	1805125	F/S	GARRETT Maurice John Clive	22-04-45	49 Sqn
1595397	Sgt	FLETCHER George Henry	5-04-45	626 Sqn	1516668	Sgt	GASCOIGNE Thomas William	18-02-45	626 Sqn
1804162	F/S	FLINDALL Gerald Arthur	2-04-45	1651 HCU	1868804	F/S	GASCOYNE John Patrick	21-02-45	49 Sqn
1869316	Sgt	FLITT George Walter	2-03-45	207 Sqn	1449054	Sgt	GASH Arthur David	6-02-45	1653 HCU
165071	F/O	FLUTTER Robert Cyril	1-02-45	166 Sqn	1345057	W/O	GAVIN Keith Alexander Cameron Munro		
158001	F/O	FLYNN DFM William Gerrard	8-04-45	466 Sqn				3-05-45	199 Sqn
1319950	W/O	FORBES Donald	8-03-45	57 Sqn	2235544	Sgt	GEDGE Walter George	7-03-45	189 Sqn
1513573	Sgt	FORBES Walter	7-02-45	77 Sqn	1796593	Sgt	GEORGE David Burrows	22-01-45	153 Sqn
2209689	Sgt	FORD Charles Stuart	22-02-45	195 Sqn	1850477	Sgt	GEORGE William Alfred	4-01-45	10 OTU
1869393	Sgt	FORD Dennis Samuel	14-01-45	106 Sqn	1709173	Sgt	GEORGE William Arla	2-02-45	460 Sqn
1851367	Sgt	FORD Edward	9-04-45	50 Sqn	533767	Sgt	GERAN John William	24-03-45	550 Sqn
1535240	Sgt	FORD William Henry	4-03-45	1653 HCU	1656358	Sgt	GIBB Douglas James George	27-02-45	186 Sqn
173302	F/O	FORD William Wallace	16-04-45	11 OTU	1825597	Sgt	GIBB James Moffat	4-02-45	12 Sqn
654454	Sgt	FORREST Gavin Browning	1-07-45	150 Sqn	187911	F/O	GIBB William J. A.	9-04-45	61 Sqn
1591075	Sgt	FORREST John Grindle	14-01-45	460 Sqn	173411	F/O	GIBBINS Eric William	11-03-45	153 Sqn
1589967	Sgt	FORSTER Sidney	4-03-45	1664 HCU	1625259	Sgt	GIBBONS Bernard	9-04-45	630 Sqn
195659	P/O	FORSYTH James Greig	8-03-45	425 Sqn	1335091	F/S	GIBBS Eric William	16-03-45	61 Sqn
1107399	AC1	FORSYTH William	12-02-45	100 Sqn	1338451	F/S	GIBBS John Arthur	19-04-45	578 Sqn
1682638	Sgt	FORTIN Michael Kenneth	8-03-45	10 Sqn	142044	F/O	GIBBS MiD Ronald Alexander	3-02-45	10 Sqn
952987	W/O	FOSTER Charles Edward	7-02-45	77 Sqn	1596086	F/S	GIBSON Gordon	25-04-45	76 Sqn
126036	F/L	FOWLER DFC Leslie Gordon	15-03-45	214 Sqn	29136	S/L	GIBSON AFC Montgomery Vincent	8-03-45	101 Sqn
2221839	Sgt	FOX Alvin Clarke	3-03-45	207 Sqn	1891436	Sgt	GIBSON Thomas	25-03-45	166 Sqn
1394187	F/S	FOX Frank Albert	2-02-45	189 Sqn	1673230	Sgt	GIBSON Thomas Aidan	2-02-45	640 Sqn
1853226	Sgt	FOX William Henry	17-03-45	103 Sqn	3007622	Sgt	GIBSON William	3-07-45	166 Sqn
190367	P/O	FOY Charles	9-03-45	90 Sqn	1800407	F/S	GIBSON William Peter	21-05-45	300 Sqn
1899438	Sgt	FRAMPTON John Thomas	2-01-45	150 Sqn	1804542	F/S	GILBERT Charles Henry	14-01-45	1654 HCU
1880497	Sgt	FRANCIS Ernest Noel James	28-01-45	218 Sqn	627389	Sgt	GILBERT Dennis William	4-03-45	1653 HCU
1605533	Sgt	FRANKAL Bertram Max	8-04-45	466 Sqn	1602863	F/S	GILBERT Joseph Henry	2-01-45	166 Sqn
1851045	Sgt	FRANKLIN Alfred John	11-07-45	10 OTU	1900007	Sgt	GILBERT Robert Cecil	7-03-45	49 Sqn
1892117	Sgt	FRANKLIN Stanley James William Paul			195070	P/O	GILBERT Stanley Alan	7-03-45	578 Sqn
			5-01-45	102 Sqn	1514811	Sgt	GILES Eric Herbert	17-01-45	10 Sqn
1566905	F/S	FRASER Frederick	1-05-45	157 Sqn	3020559	Sgt	GILES Ian	6-03-45	426 Sqn
1566603	F/S	FRASER James Gibson	19-03-45	102 Sqn	1322210	F/S	GILES Stanley Frederick	5-03-45	207 Sqn
1604876	F/S	FREAKES Kenneth	15-02-45	115 Sqn	1626440	Sgt	GILFILLAN George Ross	14-02-45	103 Sqn
176265	F/O	FREEDMAN Harry Harold	17-01-45	15 Sqn	1114239	W/O	GILL Albert Townend	4-04-45	550 Sqn
2218746	Sgt	FREEMAN Ernest Albert	5-01-45	463 Sqn	155097	F/O	GILL DFC Croix de Guerre Kenneth	21-03-45	617 Sqn
1818935	Sgt	FREEMAN Harry Raymond	7-02-45	1662 HCU	2221490	Sgt	GILLEN Eamonn	5-01-45	100 Sqn
168800	F/L	FRENCH Kenneth Herbert	3-02-45	156 Sqn	1672004	Sgt	GILLESPIE Colin Campbell Frew	13-12-45	26 OTU
3030186	F/S	FRESHWATER Norman Ernest	5-01-45	10 Sqn	1235994	F/S	GINNO Leslie	2-02-45	467 Sqn
1678403	Sgt	FROGGATT Peter John	15-04-45	1661 HCU	777859	W/O	GLASSE Basil Henry [Rhodesia]	9-03-45	150 Sqn
145903	F/O	FROST Arthur	15-03-45	77 Sqn	158304	F/O	GLENVILLE Patrick	21-02-45	189 Sqn
169864	F/S	FROST DFM Harold	17-03-45	214 Sqn	1877439	F/S	GODDARD John Henry	5-01-45	50 Sqn
1647508	Sgt	FROST Harry	4-03-45	1654 HCU	1853495	Sgt	GODDARD Mervyn John Frederick Poole		
1474488	Sgt	FROST William Arthur	23-02-45	158 Sqn				3-02-45	90 Sqn
2235922	Sgt	FRY Arthur George	8-03-45	103 Sqn	1315463	F/S	GODDARD Ronald	30-03-45	635 Sqn
2218389	Sgt	FRYER John Lionel	7-02-45	12 Sqn	1895244	Sgt	GODDARD Victor Leslie	14-01-45	17 OTU
152276	F/O	FULLER Harry William	7-03-45	170 Sqn	179878	F/O	GOLDEN DFC Bert William	21-02-45	35 Sqn
1804431	Sgt	FULLER James Roe	2-02-45	44 Sqn	1826652	Sgt	GOLDSBURY Robert	31-03-45	156 Sqn
1802396	F/S	FULLER Martin Victor	4-04-45	550 Sqn	2235812	Sgt	GOLDSTEIN Jacob	16-03-45	166 Sqn
1324463	F/S	FULLER Wilfred Henry Charles	7-03-45	170 Sqn	1893883	Sgt	GOLDTHORNE Roy Charles Thomas	14-07-45	626 Sqn
176263	F/O	FULLER William Ernest	17-01-45	15 Sqn	165287	F/O	GOLDTHORPE Kenneth Russell	8-02-45	169 Sqn
1102518	Sgt	FULLWOOD Thomas Henry	9-02-45	619 Sqn	1808623	Sgt	GOOD Leslie George	14-01-45	26 OTU
183229	F/O	FURBER Donald William Henry	26-05-45	17 OTU	1803943	Sgt	GOODALL Alan Keith	23-02-45	192 Sqn
2201064	Sgt	FYTTON Robert Wade	21-03-45	227 Sqn	1587016	F/S	GOODBODY William John	8-03-45	635 Sqn
169640	F/O	GABBOTT DFM Walter	14-02-45	635 Sqn	1607158	Sgt	GOODENOUGH Frederick William Reece		
745360	W/O	GAGE John	19-04-45	99 Sqn				10-04-45	170 Sqn
1344926	W/O	GALBRAITH Daniel	16-01-45	102 Sqn	156058	F/O	GOODMAN DFM Stanley William	16-01-45	1653 HCU
146092	F/O	GALE Robert Michael	8-04-45	466 Sqn	1593711	Sgt	GOODWIN William John	15-03-45	582 Sqn
1592676	Sgt	GALLAGHER John	7-02-45	102 Sqn	1825828	Sgt	GORDON Alastair Stewart	5-01-45	100 Sqn
751913	W/O	GALLEY DFM John George	14-01-45	223 Sqn	2235366	Sgt	GORDON Norman Charles	1-02-45	101 Sqn
1399272	F/S	GALLOWAY Roy Thomas	7-03-45	61 Sqn	1605275	F/S	GORDON Ronald	21-03-45	463 Sqn
179290	F/L	GALLOWAY Somerville Russell	8-02-45	49 Sqn	1851679	Sgt	GORE Gerald	8-04-45	1653 HCU
2206781	F/S	GAMBLE Wilfred Sidney	16-01-45	186 Sqn	1021154	Sgt	GORE James	6-01-45	158 Sqn

Service No	Rank	Name	Date	Unit
52164	F/O	GORNALL DFC Leonard John	27-02-45	138 Sqn
1895350	F/S	GOSLING Denis	29-09-45	550 Sqn
702097	F/S	GOTHARD William Thomas	10-02-45	189 Sqn
1807770	Sgt	GOUGH Bernard Terence	11-03-45	153 Sqn
165295	F/O	GOULD Douglas Richard	20-02-45	1669 HCU
177586	F/O	GOULD John Charles	6-03-45	582 Sqn
1825511	Sgt	GOURLAY William	20-04-45	19 OTU
2209126	LAC	GRADY Francis	8-07-45	BCIS
1596167	Sgt	GRAHAM Alan	21-02-45	460 Sqn
135006	F/L	GRAHAM William Forster	21-03-45	619 Sqn
1653781	Sgt	GRANT Alfred Henry	5-01-45	7 Sqn
1803754	Sgt	GRANT Arthur Gordon	18-04-45	12 OTU
1532005	Sgt	GRANT Christopher Ignatius	21-02-45	432 Sqn
1811697	F/S	GRANT Frank William	21-02-45	158 Sqn
1822786	Sgt	GRANT James	11-07-45	10 OTU
1822048	Sgt	GRANT John	17-03-45	103 Sqn
190010	P/O	GRANT Percy	1-01-45	9 Sqn
1877215	Sgt	GRAPES Richard Thomas	4-03-45	192 Sqn
1621464	Sgt	GRAVES Percival Stanley	7-01-45	619 Sqn
1431510	LAC	GRAVES MiD Thomas Brian	9-02-45	83 Sqn
1565369	F/S	GRAY Alexander	2-02-45	640 Sqn
1384393	W/O	GRAY Eric Edward	5-03-45	161 Sqn
1595698	Sgt	GRAY John Edmund Arthur	17-04-45	462 Sqn
187810	F/O	GRAYSHAW John	14-02-45	10 Sqn
1898335	Sgt	GREATHEAD Kenneth George	14-02-45	576 Sqn
621821	W/O	GREEN Edward Arthur	21-04-45	218 Sqn
1623913	F/S	GREEN Geoffrey George	21-03-45	463 Sqn
191494	P/O	GREEN John Alexander	6-03-45	103 Sqn
135922	F/L	GREEN Leslie	20-06-45	1660 HCU
183823	F/O	GREEN Peter Isaac	21-02-45	227 Sqn
109054	S/L	GREEN DFC* Robert Joseph George	15-01-45	139 Sqn
2221048	Sgt	GREENFIELD Kennth Howard	17-03-45	630 Sqn
3041725	Sgt	GREENHOUGH Arthur William	23-03-45	101 Sqn
1594801	F/S	GREENWOOD Desmond	3-05-45	199 Sqn
1593603	F/S	GREENWOOD Geoffrey Terence	8-04-45	9 Sqn
1596752	Sgt	GREGORY Charles Henry	19-03-45	103 Sqn
2212876	Sgt	GREGORY John	9-02-45	15 Sqn
547263	W/O	GREGORY William Snowden	30-03-45	44 Sqn
1868476	Sgt	GREVETT Charles Edward	2-04-45	29 OTU
1524673	LAC	GRIFFIN John	28-04-45	Fulbeck
1880251	Sgt	GRIFFIN John Dennis	16-01-45	12 Sqn
159139	F/O	GRIFFITH Edward Owen	5-04-45	153 Sqn
2210474	Sgt	GRIFFITHS Albert Henry	16-01-45	10 Sqn
859551	F/S	GRIFFITHS Arthur John	28-05-45	17 OTU
24037	G/C	GRIFFITHS DFC MC [Czechoslovakia] John Francis	9-05-45	3 Group
1580829	F/S	GRIFFITHS Leslie Douglas	12-01-45	617 Sqn
1293125	F/S	GRIGGS Bertram Frederick	8-04-45	BCIS
1670596	F/S	GRIME James Douglas	22-03-45	207 Sqn
1852991	Sgt	GRIMSDELL Geoffrey Roy	19-03-45	102 Sqn
195380	P/O	GRIMSTONE DFM Arthur Reginald	14-03-45	85 Sqn
1826405	Sgt	GRINDLAY James	22-02-45	578 Sqn
1284873	F/S	GROOM George Jabez Arthur	1-01-45	83 Sqn
187136	P/O	GROUNDWATER Melvin Douglas	3-02-45	576 Sqn
195679	P/O	GRUNDY Eric	21-02-45	207 Sqn
1892367	Sgt	GRUNDY Kenneth	12-03-45	460 Sqn
49628	F/L	GRYNKIEWICZ Henryk Boleslaw	16-03-45	61 Sqn
1895420	Sgt	GULLICK Reginald William	28-01-45	428 Sqn
3020994	Sgt	GUNN Donald	4-04-45	550 Sqn
1804820	Sgt	GUNN John Sidney	14-01-45	26 OTU
1721922	Sgt	GUNN Richard Francis	22-03-45	51 Sqn
1898913	Sgt	GUNNER Ernest	14-04-45	186 Sqn
1587777	F/S	GUSCOTT Ronald Thomas Claud	17-03-45	166 Sqn
1819148	Sgt	GUY John Humphries	16-01-45	100 Sqn
847206	F/S	GWALTER Gordon Edward	16-03-45	61 Sqn
1804699	F/S	HADDER Leslie Arnold	4-03-45	214 Sqn
1491704	F/S	HADDON William John	9-04-45	61 Sqn
1616720	F/S	HADLAND Douglas Farrant	4-02-45	35 Sqn
1850564	F/S	HADLOW Desmond Hendry	6-03-45	576 Sqn
1624201	F/S	HAGYARD Eric Holberry	4-04-45	550 Sqn
3032082	F/S	HAINES Edward	21-02-45	166 Sqn
1321011	W/O	HAINSWORTH DFM Ronald William	7-03-45	405 Sqn
1808291	F/S	HALE Francis Michael	14-04-45	186 Sqn
179530	F/O	HALE Harold Bertram	21-02-45	223 Sqn
137293	F/L	HALEY MM Victor George	19-02-45	PFNTU
2200662	Sgt	HALL Ambrose William	15-01-45	625 Sqn
168650	F/O	HALL Bernard	17-05-45	630 Sqn
138412	F/L	HALL Colin George	21-03-45	189 Sqn
657207	F/S	HALL Cyril Thomas	14-03-45	189 Sqn
149916	F/O	HALL Gordon Albert	17-03-45	214 Sqn
1515150	F/S	HALL John	1-02-45	166 Sqn
1869558	Sgt	HALL John Derek	14-02-45	186 Sqn
850060	Sgt	HALL Joseph William	9-02-45	15 Sqn
1623632	Sgt	HALL Stanley Arthur	3-02-45	14 OTU
171332	F/L	HALLETT DFC Edward William	2-09-45	227 Sqn
154684	F/O	HALLOWELL Joseph Gordon	3-04-45	626 Sqn
2222007	Sgt	HALLS Vivian Montague Bailey	5-01-45	35 Sqn
174685	F/O	HAMILTON DFC Charles Blackley	13-04-45	85 Sqn
1568370	Sgt	HAMILTON Ramsay	25-03-45	408 Sqn
2209047	Sgt	HAMMOND Joseph Geoffrey	2-01-45	150 Sqn
1802061	Sgt	HAMMOND Walter William	2-02-45	50 Sqn
1898547	Sgt	HANCE Charles James	7-03-45	44 Sqn
1108260	Sgt	HANCOCK Gordon	21-02-45	550 Sqn
1568462	Sgt	HANLON John	22-03-45	166 Sqn
3000420	Sgt	HARAGAN William Maurice	9-02-45	138 Sqn
187235	F/O	HARALAMBIDES DFC S. C. [Cyprus]	5-04-45	7 Sqn
1603593	F/S	HARCOURT James Georges William	30-03-45	635 Sqn
1601210	F/S	HARDING Herbert George	12-03-45	106 Sqn
997847	F/S	HARDING James	5-01-45	102 Sqn
196875	P/O	HARDMAN MiD Ian	12-04-45	1654 HCU
948660	Sgt	HARDWICK Harry	6-01-45	51 Sqn
1895484	Sgt	HARDY Hubert William John	8-02-45	49 Sqn
1581827	F/S	HARES DFM Frank	4-03-45	214 Sqn
3034035	Sgt	HARFORD Richard Joseph	10-04-45	170 Sqn
1595729	Sgt	HARGREAVES Geoffrey	2-01-45	150 Sqn
189806	P/O	HARGREAVES Philip Joseph	8-03-45	578 Sqn
1593024	Sgt	HARKNESS Leslie	21-02-45	463 Sqn
1867365	F/S	HARLAND Richard	3-01-45	622 Sqn
798646	W/O	HARNETT Neil Willoughby [Newfoundland]	4-01-45	10 OTU
1583408	F/S	HARPER Harold Keith	24-04-45	218 Sqn
1620623	F/S	HARPER Leonard Stanley	21-02-45	189 Sqn
187961	P/O	HARRIS Alfred Charles	15-03-45	431 Sqn
154392	F/O	HARRIS Douglas John	4-03-45	158 Sqn
1851820	F/S	HARRIS Francis Harold James	21-02-45	166 Sqn
1852682	Sgt	HARRIS Gilbert John	16-01-45	12 Sqn
186470	P/O	HARRIS MiD James Carnegie	2-02-45	428 Sqn
1651299	Sgt	HARRIS Kenneth	14-01-45	1661 HCU
1582570	Sgt	HARRIS Peter William	5-02-45	14 OTU
1256507	Sgt	HARRIS Stanley Roy	4-02-45	12 Sqn
1585791	F/S	HARRISON Alfred Cecil	21-02-45	166 Sqn
2221713	Sgt	HARRISON Edward	18-02-45	626 Sqn
154682	F/O	HARRISON Howard Geoffrey	4-03-45	189 Sqn
1458627	F/S	HARRISON-BROADLEY Geoffrey	24-02-45	462 Sqn
150483	F/O	HARROP Eric	3-02-45	50 Sqn
186871	P/O	HARROP DFC Sidney James	18-03-45	85 Sqn
170221	F/L	HARROW William Duncan	6-01-45	10 Sqn
1800267	Sgt	HART Donald Underwood	7-03-45	170 Sqn
1880123	Sgt	HART Wallace Frederick	1-02-45	100 Sqn
1596168	Sgt	HARTLEY Horace	4-04-45	550 Sqn
172730	F/O	HARTMAN John Montague	21-02-45	161 Sqn
1880568	Sgt	HARTOP Robert	14-01-45	223 Sqn
1580971	F/S	HARTSHORN Joseph Reginald	1-02-45	100 Sqn
1344795	Sgt	HARVEY Forbes Minty	8-03-45	635 Sqn
1596012	Sgt	HARVEY William	2-02-45	514 Sqn
56419	P/O	HASLAM Gerald Stalker	16-01-45	186 Sqn

1464401	F/S	HASLER Bertie Ronald	23-02-45	138 Sqn	1897585	Sgt	HIGGINSON George Wilfred	1-02-45	101 Sqn
1568510	Sgt	HASSAN James Ramsay	2-02-45	50 Sqn	1684920	F/S	HILDER William Leslie	17-03-45	166 Sqn
1685876	Sgt	HASTINGS William	21-02-45	150 Sqn	160743	F/O	HILL Edgar Charles	15-02-45	166 Sqn
186516	F/O	HATCHER Paul Herbert	22-02-45	50 Sqn	3051022	Sgt	HILL Lawrence Abraham	10-04-45	170 Sqn
1894125	Sgt	HATHAWAY Arthur William	16-03-45	12 Sqn	162187	F/O	HILL Raymond Campbell	21-02-45	576 Sqn
1082053	F/S	HATHAWAY Maurice Ernest	9-02-45	15 Sqn	1894210	Sgt	HILL Thomas Leonard	21-03-45	50 Sqn
2220970	F/S	HATTON DFM George William	5-03-45	635 Sqn	1683935	F/S	HILL William Roland	6-01-45	635 Sqn
1091631	LAC	HATTON James Henry 'Harry'	10-03-45	Swannington	1606528	Sgt	HILLIER Clifford Frederick	4-01-45	103 Sqn
2223136	Sgt	HATTON Thomas Henry	15-02-45	625 Sqn	1338017	F/S	HILLIER William John	18-01-45	12 OTU
189795	P/O	HAUBER David	13-01-45	51 Sqn	1602644	F/S	HILLMAN Geoffrey Hugh	1-02-45	101 Sqn
185863	F/O	HAVELL William James [Canada]	8-03-45	103 Sqn	195458	F/L	HINES Bernard John	23-02-45	97 Sqn
1595485	Sgt	HAW Kenneth Robert	12-03-45	106 Sqn	1679250	F/S	HIRD Kenneth	5-06-45	149 Sqn
746982	W/O	HAWKINS Gordon Cyril George 'Todd'			74678	F/L	HIRONS DFC Arthur Walter	19-03-45	515 Sqn
			19-04-45	107 Sqn	1510732	F/S	HOBSON Arthur	7-01-45	630 Sqn
159994	F/O	HAWKINS Peter	21-03-45	61 Sqn	1320197	F/S	HODDER Harold Bert	5-01-45	189 Sqn
1593269	F/S	HAY Ian A.	7-03-45	61 Sqn	1899122	Sgt	HODDER John Walter	1-02-45	101 Sqn
1897966	Sgt	HAYES Dennis William	15-02-45	625 Sqn	516781	Sgt	HODGE George Edward William	6-02-45	1653 HCU
572871	F/S	HAYES Harold	25-02-45	1660 HCU	131036	F/L	HODGE Lionel Arthur Sydney	10-04-45	622 Sqn
1165935	F/S	HAYES Harry Thomas	8-03-45	578 Sqn	1588674	F/S	HODGES Stanley Gordon	19-02-45	1669 HCU
185432	F/O	HAYES Michael Dermot	4-04-45	550 Sqn	191940	P/O	HOGG Archibald Cecil	21-02-45	432 Sqn
3001529	Sgt	HAYLOCK Frank Robert	16-03-45	49 Sqn	2220626	Sgt	HOGG Christopher George	5-03-45	514 Sqn
1671853	F/S	HAYWARD Ralph Eugene	6-03-45	460 Sqn	1829950	Sgt	HOGG George	22-02-45	218 Sqn
		[Newfoundland]			1569216	Sgt	HOGGETT Stanley	8-02-45	50 Sqn
2210748	Sgt	HAZELBY Cyril Roland	5-03-45	428 Sqn	160621	F/O	HOLDER DFC Alfred Samuel John	3-05-45	199 Sqn
1623968	Sgt	HAZELDEN John Gordon	15-01-45	1668 HCU	1685217	Sgt	HOLDING Jack	3-02-45	550 Sqn
170210	F/O	HAZELL DFC Herbert William	15-01-45	625 Sqn	189857	P/O	HOLDITCH Robert William	17-01-45	1654 HCU
1867797	F/S	HEAD Dennis	13-03-45	153 Sqn			[New Zealand]		
1615776	F/S	HEADY John Joseph O'Brien	14-02-45	153 Sqn	1322482	F/S	HOLE Clifford Frederick John	14-03-45	57 Sqn
1300369	Sgt	HEALY Patrick James	4-03-45	214 Sqn	1111958	F/S	HOLLAND Eric	28-01-45	218 Sqn
54273	R/O	HEAP DFM Richard Eric	6-03-45	10 Sqn	195246	P/O	HOLLAND DFM Leslie George	6-03-45	35 Sqn
164617	F/O	HEATH Alfred Gordon 'Freddie'	4-03-45	12 Sqn	1817846	Sgt	HOLLIDAY Edgar Maurice	14-02-45	186 Sqn
148768	F/O	HEATH Alfred Laurence	16-04-45	617 Sqn	187891	P/O	HOLLINGS Richard Charles	6-01-45	10 Sqn
171190	F/O	HEATH DFM John Ettock	20-02-45	627 Sqn	1132602	F/S	HOLLINGWORTH James	16-01-45	11 OTU
1378655	W/O	HEATHMAN Charles Walter	19-04-45	214 Sqn	942590	Sgt	HOLLOWAY Denis Albert	7-01-45	630 Sqn
954030	W/O	HEEL Rowland	21-02-45	463 Sqn	1812795	Sgt	HOLLOWAY James	24-02-45	462 Sqn
1594663	Sgt	HEELEY Dennis	6-03-45	514 Sqn	195238	P/O	HOLMES George Peter	18-02-45	626 Sqn
163723	F/O	HEGAN Francis Joseph	15-02-45	115 Sqn	172938	F/O	HOLMES John Scrafton	21-03-45	189 Sqn
179888	F/O	HEGGARTY John	10-04-45	424 Sqn	1604724	Sgt	HOLMES Kenneth John	16-03-45	625 Sqn
1594806	Sgt	HELSTRIP Thomas	17-03-45	467 Sqn	1622827	F/S	HOLMES Reginald George	4-03-45	192 Sqn
3000858	Sgt	HEMMANT Eric Charles	1-02-45	100 Sqn	1676657	Sgt	HOLMES Roy	5-02-45	1669 HCU
1671712	F/S	HENDERSON Arthur	2-03-45	207 Sqn	178869	F/O	HOOD Gerald	21-03-45	100 Sqn
190545	F/O	HENDERSON Hugh	8-03-45	189 Sqn	154910	F/O	HOOK Edwin Frank	4-04-45	49 Sqn
1592009	F/S	HENDERSON James	21-03-45	57 Sqn	1589206	Sgt	HOOLEY Norman	11-07-45	10 OTU
164059	F/O	HENDERSON John	3-02-45	14 OTU	157579	F/O	HOOPER Joseph	5-03-45	1658 HCU
1564276	F/S	HENDERSON Robert	29-09-45	550 Sqn	2210185	F/S	HOPE Arthur Christian	16-04-45	11 OTU
187897	F/O	HENNESSY Basil Francis	22-03-45	44 Sqn	3051225	Sgt	HOPE Dennis William	12-04-45	1654 HCU
1596561	Sgt	HENSHAW Leonard	21-03-45	50 Sqn	628938	F/S	HOPKINS Alistar Gordon	17-01-45	10 Sqn
1877101	Sgt	HENSON Donald Henry	8-03-45	189 Sqn	1894541	Sgt	HOPPER Peter Charles	21-03-45	50 Sqn
1525610	F/S	HEPPENSTALL Robert Dennis	3-02-45	50 Sqn	162070	F/O	HOPWOOD John	10-04-45	630 Sqn
1800459	F/S	HERBERT Reginald Ernest	4-01-45	1652 HCU	1453403	F/S	HORNE Kenneth Alexander	21-03-45	189 Sqn
1038772	F/S	HERON Francis Wheater	27-02-45	76 Sqn	153841	F/O	HORSAMAN Granville	15-04-45	138 Sqn
1339463	F/S	HERON Frederick Henry	7-03-45	189 Sqn	68786	S/L	HORSLEY AFC Hugh Wilkinson	1-02-45	61 Sqn
1591235	Sgt	HERON Thomas William	21-02-45	150 Sqn	1853371	Sgt	HORTON Reginald John	26-01-45	578 Sqn
1585649	Sgt	HERRIDGE Cyril Bernard	4-01-45	1652 HCU	652139	F/S	HOSKINS John Stanley	1-01-45	75 Sqn
1898574	Sgt	HERRING Stanley William	9-02-45	61 Sqn	149594	F/O	HOUGHTON William	11-04-45	163 Sqn
1826680	Sgt	HETHERINGTON Rodney	24-02-45	462 Sqn	1586441	F/S	HOULDEY Robert Henry	4-03-45	158 Sqn
154823	F/O	HEWETT Alec Thomas	12-01-45	77 Sqn	1424247	F/S	HOUSE Terence Cornelius	26-01-45	578 Sqn
188618	P/O	HEWITT Kenneth Arthur John	16-04-45	617 Sqn	184910	P/O	HOVELL David Johnston	14-03-45	51 Sqn
1864292	F/S	HEWITT Peter Derrick	7-02-45	102 Sqn	1582382	F/S	HOWARD Eric Leslie	15-03-45	50 Sqn
1809777	Sgt	HEYWOOD William Frederick	2-03-45	622 Sqn	1898834	Sgt	HOWARD James	6-03-45	153 Sqn
151844	F/O	HIBBERT DFC Nowell Percy	29-01-45	156 Sqn	807287	Sgt	HOWARTH John	2-02-45	189 Sqn
1852888	Sgt	HICK Edwin George	19-03-45	102 Sqn	1866651	Sgt	HOWDLE Dennis George	2-02-45	467 Sqn
1230658	F/S	HICKEY James Stanley	17-02-45	103 Sqn	1836945	Sgt	HOWE Maurice Mathew	7-03-45	189 Sqn
1595141	Sgt	HICKS Norman	8-03-45	218 Sqn	1034631	W/O	HOWE Ralph Sidney	15-03-45	195 Sqn
1398604	F/S	HIGGINS Albert Edward	17-03-45	550 Sqn	1837105	Sgt	HOWELL Frederick John	21-02-45	150 Sqn
196841	P/O	HIGGINS Clarence Victor	8-04-45	9 Sqn	185230	P/O	HOWELL DFC John George	10-04-45	16 OTU
1519237	LAC	HIGGINS Claude Henry	24-02-45	61 Sqn	3001158	Sgt	HOWELL Norman Reeve	5-01-45	7 Sqn
1497198	F/S	HIGGINS William	4-04-45	153 Sqn	55640	F/O	HOWELL Thomas Henry	24-03-45	166 Sqn

1580197	F/S	HOWITT Wilfred Geoffrey	9-04-45	61 Sqn		1271724	Sgt	JEFFERY Roy	17-03-45	630 Sqn
949392	W/O	HOWSON William Johnson	3-02-45	550 Sqn		1397240	F/S	JEFFERY William Edward Arthur	16-03-45	576 Sqn
1898789	Sgt	HUBBARD George Alan	14-02-45	77 Sqn		1337545	F/S	JEFFREY Mervyn Ronald	16-03-45	100 Sqn
128891	F/L	HUCKLE DFC Alan William	19-03-45	640 Sqn		3030656	Sgt	JEFFRIES Waltger Thomas	2-02-45	460 Sqn
154277	F/O	HUDSON Roy Albert	9-02-45	619 Sqn		179570	F/O	JEFFS Alfred Edward	8-04-45	9 Sqn
189608	P/O	HUGHES Augustus Michael Burnand	8-02-45	83 Sqn		161812	F/O	JELLEY DFC Charles Frederick	6-01-45	635 Sqn
1881602	Sgt	HUGHES Derek William	18-02-45	626 Sqn		1866002	F/S	JENKINS Ernest Eric	18-02-45	626 Sqn
1873494	F/S	HUGHES Donald John	18-03-45	49 Sqn		1394968	F/S	JENKINS Roy Maurice	4-02-45	35 Sqn
1899158	Sgt	HUGHES Frederick Walter	14-03-45	101 Sqn		51300	F/L	JENKINS MiD Stanley Sackville	17-01-45	640 Sqn
2206716	Sgt	HUGHES James	25-04-45	408 Sqn		2219122	Sgt	JENKINS Thomas Edward	22-03-45	15 Sqn
53446	F/O	HUGHES Robert Emrys	17-03-45	550 Sqn		162373	F/O	JENKINS Walter Jack	3-02-45	186 Sqn
153136	F/O	HUGHESDON Percy Gerald	1-02-45	100 Sqn		1580231	Sgt	JENKINS William Howard Roger	10-04-45	630 Sqn
1870376	F/S	HULL Dennis Frank	9-04-45	49 Sqn		1826262	F/S	JENKINSON DFM Peter Raeburn	28-01-45	153 Sqn
2221119	Sgt	HULL Leslie	21-02-45	576 Sqn		1605649	Sgt	JENNINGS Ernest Walter	6-04-45	26 OTU
153478	F/O	HULL Owen Percy	12-01-45	9 Sqn		195710	P/O	JEROME Eric Stanley	5-03-45	426 Sqn
1410959	F/S	HULLAND John Edward	20-04-45	622 Sqn		1605504	F/S	JESSUP Sydney Charles	3-09-45	26 OTU
1595696	F/S	HUMAN Frederick	2-02-45	460 Sqn		1337264	Sgt	JEWISS Walter James	19-03-45	103 Sqn
1881628	Sgt	HUME Frank	22-03-45	166 Sqn		1805899	Sgt	JOEL Leonard Henry	31-03-45	156 Sqn
1614870	F/S	HUMPHREY Alfred George	14-01-45	17 OTU		1837104	Sgt	JOHNS Alfred Ivor	5-01-45	102 Sqn
1586576	Sgt	HUMPHREY James William	14-01-45	1654 HCU		1423534	F/S	JOHNS David Lewis	16-01-45	51 Sqn
119119	F/L	HUNT Eric Geoffrey	3-02-45	186 Sqn		61984	F/L	JOHNSON MiD Allan Edward	4-02-45	35 Sqn
154281	F/O	HUNT Harold Arnold	7-03-45	61 Sqn		1595131	F/O	JOHNSON Arrol	5-01-45	619 Sqn
1893291	Sgt	HUNT Kenneth Edward	25-03-45	166 Sqn		133387	F/L	JOHNSON Douglas Norman	3-07-45	627 Sqn
165396	F/O	HUNTER Alexander	4-03-45	12 Sqn		3050454	F/S	JOHNSON Geoffrey Ralph	13-04-45	158 Sqn
191511	P/O	HUNTER William John	22-02-45	578 Sqn		50002	F/L	JOHNSON DFC* Gerard Stansfield	8-02-45	97 Sqn
184168	F/O	HURLEY John Albert	5-03-45	102 Sqn		1874143	F/S	JOHNSON Henry Alfred	2-04-45	1651 HCU
1892474	Sgt	HURLEY Ronald	14-03-45	101 Sqn		1573913	Sgt	JOHNSON James	14-02-45	463 Sqn
161995	F/L	HURRELL Herbert George	21-02-45	10 Sqn		164489	F/O	JOHNSON John	1-03-45	166 Sqn
1588410	Sgt	HURST Herbert Kitchener	26-03-45	463 Sqn		1594492	Sgt	JOHNSON Joseph	22-03-45	207 Sqn
1717816	Sgt	HUSBAND Malcolm John	24-02-45	462 Sqn		1873157	F/S	JOHNSON Royce	7-03-45	170 Sqn
1595239	Sgt	HUTCHINSON Ronald	16-01-45	420 Sqn		3225021	Sgt	JOHNSTON Henry Corry	5-01-45	7 Sqn
154615	F/O	HUTTLESTONE George Henry	20-03-45	7 Sqn		1826329	Sgt	JOHNSTON John McAllister	1-02-45	101 Sqn
177385	F/O	HUYGENS Peter Lawrence	3-09-45	26 OTU		196324	P/O	JOHNSTON John Swanson	4-04-45	78 Sqn
157307	F/O	INGHAM Richard John	21-02-45	578 Sqn		1897886	Sgt	JOHNSTONE William Alexander Milne		
1507972	F/S	INSLEY Howard	5-01-45	619 Sqn					7-03-45	61 Sqn
1600302	F/S	IRELAND Eric Kenneth	17-03-45	619 Sqn		197085	P/O	JOLLY Clifford	24-04-45	218 Sqn
2202044	F/S	IRONMONGER Leonard Richard	1-02-45	101 Sqn		1168635	Sgt	JONES Alan	5-01-45	50 Sqn
1570883	F/S	ISLEY Derek Arnold	29-09-45	550 Sqn		47423	F/L	JONES DFC Alan Edgar	23-01-45	153 Sqn
1624266	Sgt	IVETT Philip Frederick	15-03-45	49 Sqn		178636	F/O	JONES DFM Allan Milton	24-02-45	214 Sqn
1592815	Sgt	JACKSON Bernard	5-01-45	10 Sqn		1614174	F/S	JONES Anthony William	9-04-45	50 Sqn
1620321	F/S	JACKSON Darrell	5-01-45	50 Sqn		1607193	F/S	JONES Clifford Arthur	28-08-45	11 OTU
160940	F/O	JACKSON Derek	4-02-45	16 OTU		1621640	F/S	JONES Clifford Thomas	17-04-45	171 Sqn
171791	F/L	JACKSON Fred	11-04-45	619 Sqn		1404691	Sgt	JONES David Daniel	1-01-45	630 Sqn
3040028	Sgt	JACKSON James Frederick	17-03-45	103 Sqn		1624612	F/S	JONES Derek Branston	17-03-45	625 Sqn
1676676	Sgt	JACKSON Peter Frederick Chester	9-04-45	49 Sqn		1320065	F/S	JONES Frank	2-01-45	150 Sqn
1853612	F/S	JACKSON Reginald John Harris	8-02-45	83 Sqn		3025053	Sgt	JONES Frederick George	21-02-45	550 Sqn
1827115	Sgt	JACKSON William Ralston	29-01-45	3 LFS		1324221	W/O	JONES Harold Bowen	25-02-45	1660 HCU
158225	F/O	JACOB Herbert Robert Spencer	22-04-45	218 Sqn		2218793	F/S	JONES Henry	1-01-45	83 Sqn
2225077	Sgt	JAMES Andrew	1-02-45	550 Sqn		1604702	Sgt	JONES Henry William	28-04-45	1653 HCU
1801848	F/S	JAMES Anthony Langford	2-02-45	189 Sqn		2206216	Sgt	JONES Ivor	17-03-45	550 Sqn
154377	F/O	JAMES Bernard Rees	7-02-45	102 Sqn		1837136	Sgt	JONES John Cuthbert	20-09-45	49 Sqn
1399544	Sgt	JAMES George Reginald	14-02-45	576 Sqn		1653028	F/S	JONES John Lewis	16-03-45	61 Sqn
1684956	F/S	JAMES John Charles	14-04-45	186 Sqn		1800039	F/S	JONES John Thomas	18-02-45	626 Sqn
1852456	Sgt	JAMES Michael Guy Burnett	6-04-45	26 OTU		1316189	F/S	JONES Joseph Henry	1-01-45	630 Sqn
1583124	F/S	JAMES Sidney Joseph	15-01-45	61 Sqn		1837130	F/S	JONES Leonard	5-06-45	149 Sqn
1869987	Sgt	JAMES Sydney Strettle	23-01-45	153 Sqn		1589280	F/S	JONES Maldwyn	8-02-45	44 Sqn
941154	Sgt	JAMES William Leslie	3-03-45	153 Sqn		153077	F/O	JONES Mervyn Peter	21-05-45	100 Sqn
1086218	Sgt	JAMES Willie Joshua	8-02-45	44 Sqn		176235	F/O	JONES DFC Owen Meredith Clement	28-01-45	153 Sqn
183019	F/O	JAMIESON John	17-04-45	156 Sqn		1808439	Sgt	JONES Peter Richard	8-02-45	50 Sqn
1522705	F/S	JAQUES Ronald Thornley	18-04-45	640 Sqn		1432441	W/O	JONES Robert	5-01-45	102 Sqn
33060	S/L	JARAND Arthur Henry	16-01-45	102 Sqn		1811322	Sgt	JONES Robert Alan Derek	22-03-45	214 Sqn
3010499	Sgt	JARMAN Thomas Handley	4-03-45	44 Sqn		189793	P/O	JONES Robert Edward	7-02-45	158 Sqn
1864299	F/S	JARVIS Alan Aubrey	10-04-45	170 Sqn		1673055	Sgt	JONES Robert Oswald	15-03-45	102 Sqn
3032389	Sgt	JARVIS Ernest Cornelius	23-02-45	550 Sqn		1256275	F/S	JONES Stanley Llewellyn	24-02-45	214 Sqn
172618	F/O	JASPER Thomas William	19-04-45	1692 Flt		158807	F/O	JONES Terence Cyril	16-01-45	420 Sqn
150147	F/L	JEFF Royston Donald	19-03-45	102 Sqn		933543	Cpl	JONES Thomas George Albert	13-07-45	5 Group
3030814	Sgt	JEFFERIES Peter Raymond	2-02-45	640 Sqn		1583280	Sgt	JONES Thomas John	22-03-45	227 Sqn
3035068	Sgt	JEFFERY Leslie John	1-03-45	166 Sqn		2210635	Sgt	JONES Trevor Robert	11-04-45	196 Sqn

Service No	Rank	Name	Date	Sqn
1045917	Sgt	JONES Victor	16-03-45	166 Sqn
146013	F/L	JONES DFC William Anwyl	6-03-45	109 Sqn
185500	P/O	JONES William Thomas	11-03-45	434 Sqn
1860588	Sgt	JORDAN Frank Ernest	6-04-45	26 OTU
1150197	F/S	JORDAN John Frederick	14-02-45	9 Sqn
1609235	Sgt	JUDD Jack Edward	2-02-45	44 Sqn
1803447	F/S	JUDGE Richard Bruce	16-03-45	44 Sqn
1566852	Sgt	KANE Patrick	7-03-45	170 Sqn
1548867	F/S	KAY Kingston	22-03-45	44 Sqn
78866	W/C	KAY DFC Leslie Herbert	2-02-45	149 Sqn
1897002	Sgt	KEAL Walter Bernard	7-02-45	77 Sqn
1314473	F/S	KEAR Ronald	1-01-45	83 Sqn
1874510	Sgt	KEEBLE Gordon Walter Edmund	3-04-45	626 Sqn
1809996	Sgt	KEEL Royston Elvin	1-01-45	218 Sqn
1899507	Sgt	KEELING Eric Durnham	5-02-45	1669 HCU
1826847	Sgt	KEENLEYSIDE William Scott	17-03-45	153 Sqn
1457806	F/S	KEIGHTLEY Robert Wilfred	7-01-45	619 Sqn
632921	Sgt	KELLEGHER Patrick Bernard	10-02-45	1667 HCU
1796693	Sgt	KELLEHER John Barry Mortimer	16-01-45	153 Sqn
1243202	F/S	KELLER Roland Jervis	5-01-45	169 Sqn
1867927	Sgt	KELLY Brian William	11-07-45	10 OTU
1583495	F/S	KELLY Edmund	5-04-45	103 Sqn
1131202	Sgt	KELLY Lawrence Gerard	1-01-45	9 Sqn
1682304	F/S	KELLY Thomas	8-03-45	635 Sqn
2206561	F/S	KELLY William	7-01-45	622 Sqn
1615828	Sgt	KEMP Kenneth Golder	21-02-45	158 Sqn
1676293	Sgt	KENDALL Francis Alderson	14-01-45	106 Sqn
1567340	F/S	KENDALL John Henry	21-02-45	223 Sqn
135033	F/L	KENDRICK George Alfred	12-01-45	617 Sqn
1817877	Sgt	KENNEDY John	6-01-45	207 Sqn
160043	F/O	KENNEDY Patrick William	10-04-45	44 Sqn
2208930	Sgt	KENNEDY William John	4-10-45	103 Sqn
1624620	F/S	KENNY John William	21-02-45	158 Sqn
924966	LAC	KENT George Bracebridge	28-09-45	5 Group
612923	Sgt	KENVIN Gwilym John Arthur	16-03-45	625 Sqn
148842	F/O	KERR DFM Brian Francis	22-03-45	214 Sqn
185226	F/O	KERR Holman Gordon Stanley	5-03-45	514 Sqn
1801030	F/S	KERR John Langley	23-02-45	192 Sqn
627549	Sgt	KERR Robert	7-03-45	550 Sqn
191000	P/O	KERR Thomas Macdonald	19-03-45	77 Sqn
701962	W/O	KERSHAW Frank Beckett	11-01-45	20 OTU
2209971	Sgt	KEWELL John Stanley	2-02-45	51 Sqn
1807467	F/S	KIDD Dennis William	11-03-45	156 Sqn
152873	F/O	KIDD George William Adriaan	8-02-45	49 Sqn
1800584	F/S	KIFF Alan Edward Sidney	9-02-45	405 Sqn
189049	F/O	KING Derek Norman	6-03-45	50 Sqn
164615	F/O	KING Harold Sydney John	10-02-45	1667 HCU
1585195	F/S	KING Henry Frank	16-01-45	466 Sqn
1595205	Sgt	KING Henry Joseph	4-01-45	1652 HCU
1242133	Sgt	KING Hugh Borthwick	22-02-45	626 Sqn
1335881	Sgt	KING John Paynter	16-01-45	1653 HCU
612231	F/S	KING John Robert	9-04-45	61 Sqn
42612	S/L	KING Leonard Frank Douglas	19-03-45	105 Sqn
187081	P/O	KING Roylance Sydney	8-04-45	466 Sqn
1897641	Sgt	KINGDOM Melvin Francis	1-03-45	153 Sqn
1097768	Sgt	KINGDON Sidney James	15-04-45	1667 HCU
1809598	Sgt	KINGHAM Peter Ronald James	8-06-45	11 OTU
1605950	Sgt	KIRBY Dennis Frank	14-01-45	50 Sqn
1606854	Sgt	KIRBY James Burton	5-03-45	420 Sqn
164706	F/O	KIRKBY Thomas Hugh Burton	7-03-45	61 Sqn
1001793	Sgt	KIRKCALDY Alexander	19-03-45	405 Sqn
1600924	F/S	KIRSCHNER Ainsley Rupert	3-07-45	166 Sqn
1812555	Sgt	KIRSH Henry William	8-01-45	467 Sqn
1678631	F/S	KITCHING Peter	21-03-45	61 Sqn
1853632	Sgt	KNAPMAN Leslie David	7-01-45	106 Sqn
1613421	F/S	KNIGHT James William	14-02-45	9 Sqn
1271238	F/S	KNIGHT Reginald Leslie Thomas	2-04-45	1651 HCU
1864685	Sgt	KNIGHT Ronald James	16-01-45	158 Sqn
195713	P/O	KNIGHT William	16-04-45	617 Sqn
1395508	F/S	KNIGHTBRIDGE Henry John	3-02-45	576 Sqn
1894692	F/S	KNOWLER George Vaughan	17-04-45	171 Sqn
3040961	Sgt	KNOWLES George Alfred	18-04-45	640 Sqn
163717	F/O	LACEY Arthur Norman	3-03-45	207 Sqn
160577	F/O	LACEY Robert Joseph	15-01-45	626 Sqn
123989	F/L	LAFFEY Thomas Victor	3-08-45	571 Sqn
128616	F/L	LAGESSE DFC Marie Joseph Marc [Mauritius]	10-01-45	128 Sqn
1588408	Sgt	LAIDLAW Adrian Gordon Stewart	5-04-45	166 Sqn
1532375	F/S	LAING Joseph William	15-03-45	207 Sqn
1183934	Sgt	LAKE George Russell	17-01-45	15 Sqn
1591298	Sgt	LAMBERT James Bernard	10-05-45	1651 HCU
1861818	F/S	LAMBERT Victor Walter	7-03-45	619 Sqn
1850986	Sgt	LANCASTER Francis Mervyn	21-03-45	61 Sqn
1810413	Sgt	LANE Peter Anthony	5-01-45	106 Sqn
1488857	Sgt	LANE William	21-03-45	61 Sqn
1819493	Sgt	LANE William Edmund	3-01-45	166 Sqn
2216243	Sgt	LANGFORD Norman	2-04-45	29 OTU
153296	F/O	LANGMEAD Geoffrey	2-02-45	189 Sqn
1043747	Sgt	LANGTON Fred Seddon	21-02-45	50 Sqn
1338252	F/S	LARCOMBE Stephen	15-04-45	138 Sqn
144444	F/O	LASCELLES DFM John Henry	3-02-45	156 Sqn
172776	F/O	LAST Charles Frank	27-02-45	20 OTU
3034709	Sgt	LAUENER Geoffrey Charles Henri	8-06-45	11 OTU
1578136	F/S	LAUTHER John Dennis	8-02-45	83 Sqn
43640	S/L	LAVERACK Kenneth Graham	25-03-45	166 Sqn
1621232	F/S	LAW Albert Arthur	5-01-45	100 Sqn
150650	F/O	LAW Donald Forbes	3-03-45	1651 HCU
1811071	F/S	LAW John Henry	4-03-45	640 Sqn
1835883	Sgt	LAWRENCE Gordon Neville	28-08-45	11 OTU
1586885	F/S	LAWRENCE Victor Jasper	22-03-45	150 Sqn
82728	W/C	LAWSON DSO* DFC Kenneth John	2-01-45	405 Sqn
2222713	Sgt	LAWTON Thomas Arnold	21-03-45	207 Sqn
1565563	F/S	LAWTON William Ellemore	19-04-45	76 Sqn
185864	P/O	LEACH Alan	5-01-45	51 Sqn
1602533	F/S	LEACH Patrick George	30-06-45	150 Sqn
3033640	Sgt	LEAHY Frederick Douglas	2-03-45	57 Sqn
1593355	Sgt	LEATHER Ernest	8-01-45	626 Sqn
1231015	F/S	LEAVERS Robert Leslie	8-03-45	103 Sqn
1622893	F/S	LEE Arthur	1-01-45	75 Sqn
1260515	F/S	LEE Frank William	16-01-45	466 Sqn
1582434	F/S	LEE George Alfred	7-03-45	625 Sqn
2204668	Sgt	LEE Thomas William	22-04-45	218 Sqn
645301	Sgt	LEEKE George Charles	16-03-45	49 Sqn
2218806	Sgt	LEES Norman	3-01-45	467 Sqn
189171	F/O	LEES William Spears	30-10-45	1653 HCU
1579463	F/S	LEESE Eric	1-01-45	630 Sqn
1897035	Sgt	LEFORTE Raymond Leslie	15-02-45	77 Sqn
144177	F/O	LEGGE Kenneth Charles Seymour	6-02-45	571 Sqn
1533770	LAC	LEIGH John	1-07-45	Wyton
1323194	F/S	LEIGH John Arthur	4-03-45	157 Sqn
1804526	Sgt	LEIGH Ronald	3-03-45	1651 HCU
157930	F/O	LEISK Colin Murray	3-03-45	207 Sqn
1824951	Sgt	LENNIE David Strang	8-02-45	97 Sqn
1826768	Sgt	LENNON James Miller	7-02-45	102 Sqn
1622714	Sgt	LENTON Thomas Leslie	16-01-45	186 Sqn
187224	F/O	LESLIE John Balloch	2-02-45	189 Sqn
1818761	Sgt	LESTER Gordon	3-03-45	576 Sqn
1812830	Sgt	LETCHFORD Thomas Luther	7-01-45	619 Sqn
910656	F/S	LETTS George Albert	23-02-45	138 Sqn
1322361	F/S	LEVEY Jack	8-03-45	635 Sqn
1337965	F/S	LEWIS David Gerald	2-03-45	622 Sqn
1582193	F/S	LEWIS John Roger	3-05-45	199 Sqn
147932	F/O	LEWIS John William	15-03-45	582 Sqn
1601794	F/S	LEWIS Robert Lea	18-02-45	626 Sqn
1398953	Sgt	LEWIS Ronald Keith Mortimer	8-01-45	30 OTU
1042987	F/S	LEWIS Ronald Samuel	23-02-45	150 Sqn

Service No	Rank	Name	Date	Sqn
1607234	Sgt	LEWIS William Charles	8-04-45	9 Sqn
154353	F/L	LEWSLEY Alfred James	4-04-45	78 Sqn
1323200	F/S	LEYLAND Michael	3-01-45	166 Sqn
191458	P/O	LINDLEY Keith Robert Hewson	26-02-45	12 Sqn
1444528	F/S	LINTOTT Herbert John	8-10-45	166 Sqn
1826016	Sgt	LIPP Peter	9-04-45	49 Sqn
1595712	Sgt	LISHMAN Archibald Rowan	18-04-45	640 Sqn
1649530	Sgt	LISTER Colin John Hill	8-06-45	11 OTU
1593725	Sgt	LISTER Robert	14-04-45	463 Sqn
1802092	F/S	LITTLE Derek Arthur	12-03-45	460 Sqn
1603630	Sgt	LITTLE Geoffrey Owen	21-03-45	463 Sqn
1893906	F/S	LITTLE Herbert Thomas	1-01-45	83 Sqn
2204311	Sgt	LITTLEMORE John	14-01-45	1661 HCU
49551	F/L	LIVERSIDGE George Alexander	10-02-45	1667 HCU
1135648	F/S	LIVICK John Edward	1-03-45	153 Sqn
155465	F/L	LIVINGSTONE DFC James Keith	1-02-45	467 Sqn
1832526	Sgt	LLOYD Cyril	4-01-45	103 Sqn
1865030	Sgt	LLOYD David Robert	8-03-45	619 Sqn
183459	F/O	LOCKE Graham Edward	3-02-45	189 Sqn
1162477	Sgt	LOCKETT Arthur	8-03-45	61 Sqn
154080	F/O	LOCOCK John Stanley Edward	1-02-45	50 Sqn
164707	F/O	LODGE Howard Johnson	15-03-45	153 Sqn
1823610	Sgt	LOGAN John Faucet	16-03-45	625 Sqn
1569774	Sgt	LOGIE George	6-01-45	142 Sqn
1079993	Sgt	LOMAX Herbert Cecil	15-03-45	50 Sqn
1624594	Sgt	LONG Bernard Charles	1-02-45	166 Sqn
1595982	Sgt	LONGSTAFF Charles Albert	14-03-45	75 Sqn
1622238	F/S	LONGWORTH Bob	14-02-45	640 Sqn
1487790	F/S	LONSDALE Gilbert Hugh	8-02-45	83 Sqn
1865658	Sgt	LOOK John Edward	2-02-45	50 Sqn
981732	Cpl	LOOKER James	22-01-45	1694 Flt
955266	W/O	LORD John	22-04-45	405 Sqn
154636	F/O	LORD William Winston	2-03-45	207 Sqn
623752	W/O	LOSH George Albert	19-04-45	102 Sqn
1606968	F/S	LOTH Joseph	3-05-45	199 Sqn
1818319	Sgt	LOWE Stanley William	25-03-45	415 Sqn
570626	W/O	LOWMAN Hugh Percival	19-04-45	1652 CU
1580552	Sgt	LOWNDES George Edward	3-02-45	186 Sqn
56625	F/O	LOWTHER Ernest James	15-02-45	625 Sqn
179534	F/O	LUCAS Harold Leslie	18-04-45	626 Sqn
1621055	F/S	LUCAS Leonard Reginald Johnstone	4-03-45	157 Sqn
1796949	Sgt	LUCEY Denis [Eire]	17-03-45	550 Sqn
1814168	Sgt	LUCK Robert Frank	20-02-45	1669 HCU
133373	F/L	LUGER Derek Eustace Arthur	29-05-45	550 Sqn
1592685	Sgt	LUKE Ernest	1-02-45	166 Sqn
1482190	F/S	LUNN Daniel	1-01-45	692 Sqn
1590635	Sgt	LUPTON John Thomas	21-02-45	207 Sqn
1813498	Sgt	LUXFORD Donald Frederick	2-02-45	90 Sqn
650438	Sgt	LYNCH John George	25-02-45	462 Sqn
1897853	Sgt	LYNN Edward Robson	17-05-45	1659 HCU
187095	P/O	LYNN DFC DFM Thomas	25-04-45	109 Sqn
2203534	Sgt	LYONS Joseph	22-03-45	44 Sqn
1568081	F/S	MacFARLANE James	3-01-45	622 Sqn
1823400	Sgt	MacGOWAN Robert	3-02-45	50 Sqn
547776	Sgt	MacLENNAN George Alexander	9-04-45	49 Sqn
1137803	W/O	MacPHEE Ian Malcolm	22-03-45	692 Sqn
153257	F/O	MACAULAY Hugh	22-04-45	49 Sqn
1567916	F/S	MACDONALD Alick John	16-03-45	460 Sqn
1589139	F/S	MACE Jack	7-01-45	170 Sqn
1894129	Sgt	MACFARLANE Alistair George Ross	6-02-45	1656 HCU
648811	F/S	MACKAY David John	1-02-45	101 Sqn
197183	P/O	MACKAY William Henry Vesey [Eire]	3-05-45	199 Sqn
188715	P/O	MACKENZIE Colin Downie	6-01-45	635 Sqn
1898393	Sgt	MACKENZIE Ernest	23-02-45	550 Sqn
1571947	Sgt	MACKIE John	6-02-45	1656 HCU
1567034	Sgt	MACLEAN Malcolm Fraser	8-01-45	30 OTU
40549	S/L	MACLEOD-SELKIRK Ian	14-04-45	101 Sqn
1823304	Sgt	MACPHERSON John	17-03-45	619 Sqn
1365066	F/S	MADDEN Charles	4-04-45	153 Sqn
51271	F/O	MADDOCKS Jack	14-01-45	571 Sqn
151614	F/O	MADEN Ronald	6-01-45	171 Sqn
1269063	W/O	MAGENIS Leslie Stewart	3-03-45	150 Sqn
1565120	F/S	MAGINLEY George Albert	13-02-45	550 Sqn
976750	W/O	MAHONEY Frederick	5-03-45	161 Sqn
1800604	F/S	MAHONEY John	7-03-45	170 Sqn
2209740	F/S	MAIDEN Royden Charles	8-10-45	166 Sqn
1880668	F/S	MAIDMENT George Edward	2-02-45	44 Sqn
1352703	Sgt	MAIRS Hamilton	18-04-45	12 OTU
2200210	F/S	MALCOLM George	6-01-45	61 Sqn
1897168	Sgt	MALCOLM John	9-02-45	15 Sqn
1591890	Sgt	MALKIN Peter Harry	3-02-45	170 Sqn
1808885	F/S	MALLORY William Rous	16-01-45	1653 HCU
1607329	F/S	MALTBY James	8-02-45	50 Sqn
1586368	Sgt	MANN Cyril Reuben Clifford	15-01-45	1668 HCU
1547351	F/S	MANN Harold	22-02-45	578 Sqn
1392155	Sgt	MANN Jack	15-01-45	431 Sqn
1810780	Sgt	MANN James	28-05-45	17 OTU
3000422	Sgt	MANNING Bernard Charles	9-04-45	49 Sqn
1604373	F/S	MARCHANT Charles Edward	4-04-45	115 Sqn
1803444	Sgt	MARDEN Alan Thomas Alfred	2-02-45	50 Sqn
701338	Sgt	MARETT Robert Alfred	8-01-45	103 Sqn
188495	P/O	MARLOW Edgar Hope	31-03-45	156 Sqn
3021911	Sgt	MARNOCH Jonathan G.	8-02-45	12 Sqn
1324141	W/O	MARRABLE Allan John	23-02-45	97 Sqn
1622221	F/S	MARRINAN John	22-03-45	166 Sqn
1593487	Sgt	MARRIOTT Richard	14-02-45	463 Sqn
182843	P/O	MARRITT DFM William Arthur	16-01-45	1653 HCU
1880671	F/S	MARSDEN Dennis	21-03-45	223 Sqn
1589746	Sgt	MARSDEN William	5-03-45	514 Sqn
157200	F/L	MARSH James Henry	16-01-45	12 Sqn
159890	F/O	MARSH Sidney	21-02-45	83 Sqn
188409	F/O	MARSHALL Allan John	16-01-45	10 Sqn
1337884	Sgt	MARSHALL Harry Alfred	16-01-45	405 Sqn
1597160	Sgt	MARSHALL Lewis	21-03-45	227 Sqn
1564879	F/S	MARSHALL William Henry McDonald	1-01-45	630 Sqn
1581323	F/S	MARSTON Kenneth Richard	6-03-45	576 Sqn
1160427	Sgt	MARTIN Arthur	21-02-45	153 Sqn
187049	P/O	MARTIN Basil	8-02-45	50 Sqn
1861750	Sgt	MARTIN Clifford Stanley	3-02-45	14 OTU
1813197	Sgt	MARTIN Edwin Horace John	15-04-45	1667 HCU
1324045	F/S	MARTIN Frederick George James	21-02-45	576 Sqn
1006035	Sgt	MARTIN George A.	28-04-45	1661 HCU
1595881	Sgt	MARTIN Jasper	29-01-45	5 LFS
175854	F/O	MARTIN DFC Robert Leslie	31-03-45	156 Sqn
1358095	W/O	MARTIN William Robert	22-05-45	26 OTU
154600	F/O	MASHEDER James Auton	12-01-45	77 Sqn
1469853	F/S	MASLIN Edwin Joseph	24-02-45	462 Sqn
1568576	Sgt	MASON Charles Spencer	8-03-45	576 Sqn
143659	F/O	MASON Frank Arthur	14-01-45	223 Sqn
1682434	LAC	MASTERMAN Leonard	22-04-45	Fulbeck
1813298	Sgt	MATHIAS John Lawrence	6-02-45	90 Sqn
1853269	F/S	MATON Stanley John James	7-03-45	619 Sqn
1585927	F/S	MATSUMOTO Gerald	21-03-45	207 Sqn
1897604	F/S	MATTHEWS Alfred Francis	8-03-45	101 Sqn
153043	F/O	MATTHEWS Aubrey Glyndwr	20-04-45	19 OTU
1187985	Sgt	MATTHEWS Cecil Allen	3-02-45	170 Sqn
155552	F/O	MATTHEWS DFM John Stuart	28-05-45	138 Sqn
1602108	Sgt	MATTHEWS Martin Frederick	22-03-45	15 Sqn
196950	P/O	MATTHEWS Reginald Raymond	29-09-45	550 Sqn
1597703	Sgt	MATTHEWS Sidney	17-03-45	550 Sqn
142217	F/L	MATTHEWS DFC Sidney Clayden	17-03-45	214 Sqn
1851647	Sgt	MAUNDER Frederick George	2-02-45	514 Sqn
1894889	F/S	MAWBY Cecil George Walter	20-05-45	20 OTU
1591495	Sgt	MAWSON Louis Donald Anthony	6-01-45	415 Sqn
1605742	Sgt	MAY William Ernest	7-03-45	576 Sqn

Number	Rank	Name	Date	Unit
175561	F/O	MAYERS Bernard	11-04-45	103 Sqn
3010669	Sgt	MAYERS Derrick Howard	14-02-45	161 Sqn
3020850	Sgt	MAYES Duncan Kennedy Watson	15-02-45	630 Sqn
1801363	F/S	MAYNARD Sidney James Samuel	1-01-45	83 Sqn
1804244	F/S	MAYO Norman George	8-03-45	103 Sqn
1037806	Sgt	McAFEE John	3-02-45	419 Sqn
1090496	F/S	McBURNEY Colin	10-04-45	44 Sqn
171070	F/O	McCABE Thomas M.	31-03-45	156 Sqn
1057952	Sgt	McCABREY William	28-01-45	405 Sqn
1343393	F/S	McCAFFRAY Thomas	4-03-45	12 Sqn
190166	P/O	McCALLUM Joseph Lawton	17-01-45	640 Sqn
190699	P/O	McCARTHY Eric Joseph Frank	21-02-45	49 Sqn
1394837	F/S	McCAULEY Denis Alphonsus	21-02-45	50 Sqn
1520473	F/S	McCHRYSTAL Gerard	7-03-45	61 Sqn
1592648	Sgt	McCLEMENTS Harry	20-03-45	7 Sqn
1584122	F/S	McCLEMONT Patrick Douglas	8-10-45	166 Sqn
1681945	F/S	McCLYMONT Hugh McClure	7-03-45	214 Sqn
1432236	F/S	McCORMACK Robert William	4-03-45	189 Sqn
638686	F/S	McCREADIE John	15-02-45	166 Sqn
195471	P/O	McDONALD Ashley Alexander	21-02-45	432 Sqn
1798275	Sgt	McDOWELL John Ritchie	16-01-45	101 Sqn
994024	W/O	McFARLANE James	22-03-45	214 Sqn
1324949	F/S	McFARLANE John George Fossett	18-03-45	622 Sqn
1572467	Sgt	McGARVIE Robert	17-04-45	462 Sqn
642488	F/S	McGLONE Anthony	17-01-45	514 Sqn
179064	F/O	McGONIGLE Frederick Desmond	16-01-45	101 Sqn
1901671	Sgt	McGOWAN Patrick [Eire]	18-04-45	12 OTU
976183	W/O	McGREGOR DFM Douglas Scott	3-03-45	153 Sqn
1670598	Sgt	McGUIRE Laurence Felix	5-04-45	166 Sqn
138688	F/L	McHARDY DFC George Lowson Smith	28-01-45	105 Sqn
3020834	Sgt	McINTOSH James Kerr Murdoch	3-04-45	625 Sqn
1573475	F/S	McIVOR Alexander	1-02-45	166 Sqn
196057	P/O	McKAIG Samuel	19-03-45	640 Sqn
1564926	F/S	McKAY Andrew John	15-02-45	189 Sqn
150574	F/O	McKAY Denis	3-02-45	14 OTU
176945	F/O	McKELLAR Alexander Farley	12-01-45	617 Sqn
1111489	W/O	McKENNA Maurice George	28-04-45	156 Sqn
1825949	Sgt	McKENZIE Donald Gordon	10-02-45	1666 HCU
872318	LAC	McKIE Thomas	24-04-45	Fulbeck
73003	S/L	McLAREN DFC Robert Duncan [Canada]	27-02-45	1409 Flt
1048611	Sgt	McLEAN William	7-01-45	626 Sqn
1577073	F/S	McLENAGHAN Eric Charles	16-01-45	153 Sqn
182488	F/O	McLEOD William	21-02-45	463 Sqn
1037338	Sgt	McLOUGHLIN Thomas Samuel	8-01-45	30 OTU
1806217	Sgt	McMANUS George William	26-02-45	75 Sqn
1880264	Sgt	McMARTH William	8-03-45	61 Sqn
1821038	F/S	McMILLAN Campbell McIntosh	8-04-45	9 Sqn
1565939	F/S	McMINN Reginald John	12-03-45	153 Sqn
939832	F/S	McMURRUGH Alfred	9-05-45	514 Sqn
1798690	Sgt	McNAMARA Nicholas	17-01-45	582 Sqn
3021606	Sgt	McNICOL Neil	16-03-45	12 Sqn
1826326	Sgt	McNIVEN Peter	5-04-45	186 Sqn
161717	F/O	McOWAN DFM Bruce John	3-10-45	1668 HCU
129934	F/L	McQUEEN Alastair Norman Leigh	9-02-45	15 Sqn
641994	W/O	McRAE William	8-03-45	622 Sqn
153938	F/O	McSHANE James Vincent	8-03-45	218 Sqn
3022917	Sgt	McSKIMMING Andrew	3-02-45	170 Sqn
1597236	Sgt	McWILLIAMS Francis	24-03-45	156 Sqn
172517	F/O	MEAD Lawrence George	3-01-45	622 Sqn
170457	F/O	MEADE Victor Francis Dobell	17-05-45	630 Sqn
412215	Sgt	MEADOWS Leonard Tom	8-01-45	30 OTU
185171	F/O	MEARNS John Ross	24-03-45	166 Sqn
1395032	F/S	MEARS John Ronald	21-02-45	7 Sqn
3022129	Sgt	MEECHAN William Boyd	6-03-45	153 Sqn
1579588	F/S	MEEKINGS Albert Edward	6-01-45	171 Sqn
1356894	Sgt	MEEKISON Frederick	5-01-45	77 Sqn
1813406	Sgt	MELLOR John	27-02-45	20 OTU
1817697	Sgt	MELLOR William	4-03-45	12 Sqn
1225149	LAC	MELLOWS Samuel	23-04-45	Fulbeck
159575	F/O	MEPHAM DFC William James	1-07-45	16 OTU
2218573	Sgt	MERCER Albert	29-01-45	5 LFS
154929	F/O	MERCER Gordon Ernest	9-02-45	138 Sqn
1893245	Sgt	MERCER Laurence John	31-03-45	431 Sqn
1323182	W/O	MERRALL Peter Alfred	1-05-45	157 Sqn
2211987	Sgt	MERRICK William Frank	17-01-45	640 Sqn
1522918	F/S	MERROW Victor Douglas	1-02-45	61 Sqn
1814404	Sgt	METZGER Harold	10-02-45	1667 HCU
1837286	Sgt	MICHAEL Vernon Ivor	5-01-45	90 Sqn
1297762	F/S	MICHAELS Arthur	17-03-45	630 Sqn
1254118	F/S	MIDDLETON John Wilfred	4-03-45	158 Sqn
1852348	F/S	MIDLANE Alan Leslie	15-03-45	51 Sqn
1567899	F/S	MILBURN John Wilson	28-01-45	153 Sqn
1894484	Sgt	MILES Leslie Edward	14-01-45	462 Sqn
55408	F/O	MILLAR Kenneth Charles	4-03-45	1651 HCU
1397989	F/S	MILLER Charles Edward	21-02-45	166 Sqn
1809260	F/S	MILLER Donald Fraser	21-03-45	214 Sqn
55237	F/O	MILLER Herbert Victor	3-03-45	207 Sqn
168689	F/L	MILLER DFM Robert	21-03-45	189 Sqn
131087	F/L	MILLER Stanley Edward	7-03-45	61 Sqn
873380	Sgt	MILLER Thomas	7-01-45	170 Sqn
1817207	Sgt	MILLICHAMP Denis Harold	26-04-45	50 Sqn
118465	S/L	MILLS Anthony Alan Frank	1-01-45	115 Sqn
157178	F/O	MILLS John Robert Moffatt	21-02-45	578 Sqn
1146367	Sgt	MILLS Laurence Dorning	21-03-45	61 Sqn
1051697	Sgt	MILNER Charles Luther	1-03-45	166 Sqn
1586947	Sgt	MILTON Frank	14-03-45	101 Sqn
1893981	F/S	MINNS Henry	5-04-45	7 Sqn
195029	P/O	MITCHAM William Abrum	5-04-45	626 Sqn
1521434	F/S	MITCHELL Donald Stafford	17-01-45	640 Sqn
1865449	Sgt	MITCHELL Frederick William	24-03-45	166 Sqn
1822506	Sgt	MITCHELL Jack	16-03-45	100 Sqn
1675573	Sgt	MITCHELL John	11-03-45	153 Sqn
1587814	F/S	MITCHELL Kenneth Albert Lawrence	31-03-45	156 Sqn
1897195	Sgt	MITCHELL Robert Frederick George	16-03-45	44 Sqn
1592400	Sgt	MITCHESON Robert Dixon	6-02-45	192 Sqn
1583378	Sgt	MOBBERLEY Eric Desmond	8-02-45	50 Sqn
1861942	Sgt	MOHUM James Stanley	8-03-45	635 Sqn
1078979	F/S	MOLYNEUX Alfred James	13-07-45	97 Sqn
179014	F/O	MONEYPENNY Ronald Frank	21-03-45	189 Sqn
1051821	F/S	MONTAGUE James	9-02-45	630 Sqn
1802239	F/S	MONTAGUE James Wilfred	21-05-45	100 Sqn
1826559	Sgt	MONTGOMERY Peter Ralston	7-03-45	576 Sqn
1817442	Sgt	MOONEY John Francis Arthur	21-02-45	576 Sqn
53786	F/O	MOONEY DFM Laurence	3-02-45	156 Sqn
1318107	LAC	MMOR Peter	8-05-45	Fulbeck
1685098	Sgt	MOORE Alan	2-02-45	90 Sqn
798812	Sgt	MOORE Alexander [Newfoundland]	22-03-45	150 Sqn
163606	F/O	MOORE Arthur Desmond	5-04-45	626 Sqn
573817	F/S	MOORE John Maurice	12-04-45	157 Sqn
1805235	Sgt	MOORE Kenneth Redfern	1-02-45	101 Sqn
1258843	Sgt	MOORE Lawrence	21-02-45	189 Sqn
164872	F/O	MOORE Leonard	23-02-45	608 Sqn
1685692	Sgt	MOORE Maurice	5-02-45	1654 HCU
1898052	Sgt	MOORE Peter Edward William	5-03-45	1663 HCU
911578	F/S	MOORE Richard Ernest	22-03-45	166 Sqn
1587862	F/S	MOORE Ronald Victor	4-04-45	635 Sqn
190352	P/O	MOORE Stanley Harrison	5-01-45	425 Sqn
1836726	F/S	MOORE Trevor Bryn	4-04-45	49 Sqn
49811	F/L	MOORE Wilfred Aubrey	5-01-45	16 OTU
163519	F/O	MOORE William Sidney John	7-03-45	170 Sqn
620750	Sgt	MORETON Arthur Pugh	9-04-45	61 Sqn
1801046	F/S	MORGAN George Alfred Cyril	23-02-45	192 Sqn
148475	F/O	MORGAN DFC John Reginald Dalton	5-04-45	142 Sqn
338722	F/S	MORGAN Leslie Gilbert	6-01-45	158 Sqn

1832989	Sgt	MORGAN Peter	5-01-45	102 Sqn		956435	LAC	NEWNHAM Leslie Aubrey	26-02-45	Wyton
1581491	F/S	MORLEY Eric Andrew	5-01-45	619 Sqn		906779	Sgt	NEWTON Roy Barrett	2-02-45	460 Sqn
1134042	F/S	MORONEY Denis	23-02-45	97 Sqn		1670779	Sgt	NICHOL John	14-03-45	75 Sqn
1801769	F/S	MORRIS Anthony	28-01-45	218 Sqn		1602153	F/S	NICHOLAS Ronald Ernest	14-02-45	77 Sqn
3040748	Sgt	MORRIS Donald	13-03-45	103 Sqn		746205	Sgt	NICHOLL Bruce Henry	21-03-45	75 Sqn
164354	F/O	MORRIS Edward John Stanley	6-03-45	153 Sqn		191358	P/O	NICHOLLS Frederick Thomas James	2-02-45	189 Sqn
1586397	F/S	MORRIS Eric	9-02-45	186 Sqn		115343	F/L	NICHOLLS DFC Geoffrey Amos	3-04-45	139 Sqn
197384	P/O	MORRIS Frederick Anthony	24-04-45	218 Sqn		1176177	Sgt	NICHOLLS John Thomas	16-03-45	12 Sqn
154529	F/O	MORRIS Gordon	5-03-45	207 Sqn		1318567	W/O	NICHOLLS Peter Maurice	24-04-45	218 Sqn
3000365	Sgt	MORRIS Peter Henry	28-01-45	428 Sqn		1990583	Sgt	NICHOLSON Alwyn	5-04-45	166 Sqn
3020201	Sgt	MORRIS Robert	15-03-45	405 Sqn		347984	W/O	NICHOLSON Charles	20-08-45	207 Sqn
1569430	Sgt	MORRISON Donald	3-04-45	625 Sqn		185768	P/O	NICHOLSON Francis Joseph	5-01-45	429 Sqn
1573091	Sgt	MORRISON Duncan	4-01-45	1652 HCU		2209105	Sgt	NICHOLSON John	25-04-45	76 Sqn
179386	F/L	MORRISON George Alexander James	31-03-45	156 Sqn		1684306	F/S	NICKLIN Arthur Bernard	5-01-45	15 Sqn
1559833	LAC	MORRISON John	2-03-45	207 Sqn		2235169	Sgt	NIELSEN Harold [Chile]	6-02-45	1653 HCU
1395952	W/O	MORRISON Richard Muir	11-07-45	10 OTU		1583975	F/S	NIGHTINGALE Norman William	2-02-45	514 Sqn
190400	P/O	MORRISON Thomas Frederick	21-02-45	158 Sqn		1836904	Sgt	NILES Ronald Frederick	3-02-45	170 Sqn
1596898	Sgt	MORTIMER David	23-02-45	101 Sqn		1106573	LAC	NOBLE Arthur	27-04-45	Snaith
1431168	W/O	MORTIMER Kenneth	19-04-45	514 Sqn		1890587	Sgt	NOLAN Richard	23-02-45	103 Sqn
157903	F/O	MORTIS Edward James	2-02-45	619 Sqn		190028	P/O	NOONAN George Bernard	5-01-45	425 Sqn
1893187	Sgt	MOUNT William Ernest Charles	16-01-45	466 Sqn		124330	F/L	NOREM Max Raymond	6-03-45	103 Sqn
1621552	F/S	MOUNTAIN Charles Denis	7-01-45	635 Sqn		1380254	W/O	NORMAN Arthur Jack	21-02-45	463 Sqn
195682	P/O	MOUSLEY Kenneth Charles	8-04-45	9 Sqn		2221343	Sgt	NORMAN Edward William	25-04-45	619 Sqn
1898825	Sgt	MOWL Kenneth Leslie	7-03-45	61 Sqn		154646	F/O	NORTON Arthur Joseph	8-02-45	97 Sqn
1685751	Sgt	MOWBRAY William	5-03-45	1658 HCU		1609939	Sgt	NORTON Henry Kenneth	2-02-45	626 Sqn
153794	F/O	MOYES Robert	10-01-45	20 OTU		188499	F/O	NYE Robert George	3-02-45	550 Sqn
1806639	Sgt	MOYLE James Frederick	3-02-45	550 Sqn		191818	P/O	OAK Albert Alfred	21-02-45	207 Sqn
752418	F/S	MUDDIMAN Arthur Alfred	16-01-45	51 Sqn		1868430	Sgt	OATES Neville Walter	15-02-45	166 Sqn
1390409	F/S	MUGGERIDGE Derrick William	7-02-45	77 Sqn		189950	P/O	OBERNECK Jean Charles [Belgium]	8-03-45	189 Sqn
186969	P/O	MUIR Cyril John Wilson	4-03-45	158 Sqn		629786	Sgt	OCKERBY Horace John	14-02-45	9 Sqn
1538890	W/O	MUIR DFM John	6-04-45	26 OTU		172043	F/O	ODDY Kenneth William	1-02-45	76 Sqn
1821246	Sgt	MUIR William Cook	2-01-45	100 Sqn		1897358	Sgt	OGDEN John Oliver Edward	3-10-45	1653 HCU
1378953	Sgt	MULDOWNEY DFM John Edward	2-01-45	19 OTU		1595990	F/O	OGILVIE Matthew	24-02-45	462 Sqn
132984	F/L	MULLAN DFC George Patrick	1-01-45	128 Sqn		1866584	Sgt	OLD Oliver	15-01-45	626 Sqn
128129	S/L	MULLER Melville Max Victor Lewis	8-04-45	35 Sqn		650144	W/O	OLDFIELD Stanley	11-03-45	156 Sqn
1389826	F/S	MUMFORD Mowbray Samuel George	14-03-45	51 Sqn		1893257	Sgt	OLIFF Alfred Ernest	6-02-45	1653 HCU
1566757	F/S	MUNRO Murray Swanson	10-04-45	630 Sqn		1523074	F/S	OLLERTON Raymond	15-04-45	1667 HCU
1600419	F/S	MURDOCH Anthony Frederick	7-01-45	619 Sqn		1615942	Sgt	OLSON Edward Peter Paul	10-04-45	44 Sqn
3045067	AC2	MURES Ronald Albert	9-02-45	Coningsby		2221412	Sgt	ORMSHAW William James	2-03-45	622 Sqn
1515909	Sgt	MURPHY John	14-02-45	186 Sqn		150425	F/O	ORR George Davidson	17-01-45	514 Sqn
1898019	Sgt	MURRAY George	15-03-45	582 Sqn		1825841	Sgt	ORR Thomas	12-03-45	433 Sqn
949532	Cpl	MURRAY John Douglas Haig	2-01-45	35 Sqn		153497	F/O	ORRY Gerald Francis	15-03-45	227 Sqn
173508	F/O	MURRAY-SHIRREFF James Edward	13-02-45	550 Sqn		56456	P/O	OSBOURN Harold	27-02-45	76 Sqn
153175	F/O	MUSCHAMP John Edward George	22-02-45	218 Sqn		146614	F/O	OSLER Thomas	5-01-45	427 Sqn
1593362	Sgt	MUSGRAVE Maurice	2-04-45	29 OTU		1851912	Sgt	OSMOND William	2-02-45	51 Sqn
1397280	F/S	MUST Reginald Sidney	17-01-45	10 Sqn		1802652	Sgt	OTTAWAY Douglas Alan	10-01-45	17 OTU
154260	F/O	MYERS Douglas Vernon	8-03-45	218 Sqn		154243	F/O	OUTTERSON George Alexander	2-04-45	1651 HCU
125980	F/L	NAIRN George Douglas Tolley	1-01-45	692 Sqn		1614940	F/S	OVERETT Alfred Clifford	5-01-45	77 Sqn
55254	F/O	NASH Thomas James Michael	1-05-45	157 Sqn		146350	F/O	OWEN Ivor Glyn	16-01-45	578 Sqn
190629	P/O	NAVIN James Michael	21-03-45	189 Sqn		1880977	Sgt	OWEN Roland	16-03-45	626 Sqn
162617	F/O	NAYLOR Francis James	10-04-45	83 Sqn		1398553	Sgt	O'BRIEN Anthony Aloysius	11-01-45	20 OTU
1358579	F/S	NEAL Roy	4-04-45	153 Sqn		69497	S/L	O'BRIEN DFC Michael William	22-03-45	23 Sqn
1896808	Sgt	NEALE Peter	5-01-45	51 Sqn		164488	F/O	O'CALLAGHAN Michael Arthur	15-02-45	166 Sqn
1100968	F/S	NEALE Raymond	4-02-45	35 Sqn		154742	F/O	O'CONNOR Henry John	3-02-45	576 Sqn
1386352	F/S	NEALE Reginald Frederick	11-03-45	463 Sqn		1795363	Sgt	O'DONNELL James	1-02-45	101 Sqn
165147	F/O	NEALE Thomas	8-04-45	1653 HCU		183649	F/O	O'DONNELL Ronald James	17-05-45	630 Sqn
1804382	Sgt	NEAVES Leslie Bertie	21-03-45	463 Sqn		1901574	Sgt	O'GORMAN Thomas	22-01-45	153 Sqn
1595970	Sgt	NEEDHAM Graham	3-02-45	426 Sqn		183181	F/L	O'HALLORAN Thomas Anthony	4-04-45	115 Sqn
2203200	Sgt	NELSON Peter Smith	23-03-45	101 Sqn		1396631	Sgt	O'KEEFE Daniel Patrick	8-03-45	49 Sqn
1564192	F/S	NESBIT Robert	8-04-45	227 Sqn		1799783	F/S	O'LOUGHLIN Mortimer	21-03-45	57 Sqn
1587443	F/S	NESBIT-BELL Frederick Albert Cecil	10-02-45	460 Sqn		982124	Sgt	O'MARAH Thomas Leslie	22-03-45	227 Sqn
190971	P/O	NEVENS John Joseph	15-03-45	153 Sqn		163844	F/O	O'REGAN Brian John	3-02-45	170 Sqn
1673392	F/S	NEWBIGGING John Power	9-04-45	50 Sqn		163610	F/O	O'REILLY Francis William	17-04-45	156 Sqn
1591945	Sgt	NEWBY Arthur Ronald	9-02-45	630 Sqn		1217980	Sgt	O'SHEA Francis Crohane Joseph	21-02-45	207 Sqn
1684756	F/S	NEWBY Joseph	21-02-45	49 Sqn		533494	Sgt	O'SULLIVAN DSM Daniel	7-03-45	576 Sqn
1603523	F/S	NEWLING Henry John	1-01-45	10 Sqn		1799564	Sgt	O'SULLIVAN Michael [Eire]	15-01-45	1659 HCU
162659	F/O	NEWMAN Kenneth	16-05-45	101 Sqn		179426	F/O	PADDICK Ernest George	8-02-45	214 Sqn
1816804	Sgt	NEWMAN Peter	22-03-45	214 Sqn		657555	W/O	PADDICK Sidney Robert	15-04-45	169 Sqn

Service No	Rank	Name	Date	Sqn
1837441	Sgt	PADMORE Frederick Augustus	21-05-45	100 Sqn
552485	F/S	PAGE Leslie Alfred	19-02-45	90 Sqn
1602672	Sgt	PAGE Richard Henry	5-03-45	1662 HCU
1333464	F/S	PAIGE Eric	5-06-45	149 Sqn
179271	F/O	PALEY George Henry	8-03-45	576 Sqn
1594310	Sgt	PALLISTER Frank	21-02-45	189 Sqn
190381	P/O	PALMER Charles Dixon	9-03-45	90 Sqn
1178429	Sgt	PALMER Charles Henry	7-01-45	103 Sqn
80048	S/L	PALMER Colin Murray [Rhodesia]	21-03-45	619 Sqn
2221381	F/S	PALMER Cyril Willie	23-02-45	97 Sqn
1603797	F/S	PALMER Frederick Russell	8-03-45	578 Sqn
1592609	Sgt	PANNETT Jack	1-02-45	50 Sqn
2225575	Sgt	PAPE Frederick James	14-04-45	186 Sqn
1002042	F/S	PAPPLE Frederick	5-01-45	550 Sqn
1579368	Sgt	PARBERY Donald George	4-04-45	49 Sqn
2220654	Sgt	PARDOE Anthony Arthur	27-02-45	20 OTU
170480	F/O	PARHAM William Phillips	3-02-45	10 Sqn
190279	P/O	PARKER Alvin Kenneth	16-01-45	420 Sqn
1850978	Sgt	PARKER Anthony Keith	23-02-45	103 Sqn
3041583	Sgt	PARKER Charles Dennis	14-01-45	26 OTU
3040675	Sgt	PARKER Donald	21-03-45	214 Sqn
1583688	F/S	PARKER Harry William	8-03-45	578 Sqn
157633	F/O	PARKER DFC William Stephenson	14-03-45	195 Sqn
1652685	Sgt	PARKHOUSE Evan Emlyn	5-01-45	15 Sqn
1580983	F/S	PARKIN Jim	8-04-45	10 Sqn
1623792	F/S	PARKIN Kennet	22-02-45	50 Sqn
2222307	Sgt	PARKINS Frederick	23-02-45	192 Sqn
1456507	F/S	PARKINSON Eric	2-03-45	460 Sqn
570544	W/O	PARR DFM Frederick	3-03-45	156 Sqn
1005807	LAC	PARR George	19-01-45	1653 HCU
1874893	Sgt	PARRETT Eric Stuart	8-01-45	30 OTU
1801881	Sgt	PARRISH Kenneth James	16-03-45	1664 HCU
3000991	Sgt	PARRY Robert Owen	4-03-45	12 Sqn
1196230	F/S	PARSONS Desmond John	5-01-45	77 Sqn
185301	F/L	PARSONS Eric George	14-03-45	75 Sqn
188557	P/O	PARSONS Peter John	17-03-45	153 Sqn
1025607	Sgt	PARSONS William Alfred	10-04-45	622 Sqn
2205050	Sgt	PASCOE Vincent	9-02-45	619 Sqn
1038029	Sgt	PASQUILL Norman	16-01-45	1653 HCU
2223018	Sgt	PASS Walter Patrick	15-02-45	625 Sqn
1812236	Sgt	PATCH Bernard John	11-03-45	463 Sqn
1825557	Sgt	PATERSON Harold Alexander	9-04-45	61 Sqn
1682300	F/S	PATERSON James	16-03-45	166 Sqn
1673073	Sgt	PATTERSON George Eric	6-01-45	207 Sqn
129483	F/L	PATTERSON DFC William Alan Clarke	8-04-45	466 Sqn
1571657	Sgt	PATTISON John Jackson	30-07-45	166 Sqn
54309	F/O	PATTISON Martin Henry	4-04-45	78 Sqn
163583	F/O	PAWSEY Thomas	25-02-45	462 Sqn
161730	F/O	PAYNE Alfred Migal	5-03-45	109 Sqn
1589407	Sgt	PAYNE Herbert	4-03-45	44 Sqn
190649	P/O	PEACE John Montgomery	1-03-45	103 Sqn
3010345	Sgt	PEACH Harold	21-02-45	576 Sqn
191087	P/O	PEACH John Eric	27-02-45	186 Sqn
1593715	Sgt	PEARCE Robert Alan Clark	19-03-45	77 Sqn
185421	P/O	PEARCE William George	21-02-45	625 Sqn
179178	F/O	PEARSON DFC Arthur Owen	31-05-45	1660 HCU
1697821	Sgt	PEARSON Frank	14-01-45	195 Sqn
1577370	W/O	PEARSON George Henry	2-01-45	166 Sqn
178069	F/L	PEARTON Charles	7-01-45	103 Sqn
1615706	Sgt	PECKETT Leslie	1-01-45	218 Sqn
1851763	Sgt	PECKHAM John Henry	29-09-45	550 Sqn
547928	Sgt	PECKHAM Nelson	8-03-45	61 Sqn
154573	F/O	PEDERSEN Niels Peter William	3-02-45	170 Sqn
1127353	W/O	PEEL Harry Siddell	23-02-45	50 Sqn
1895058	Sgt	PEGRAM Stewart John Alfred	24-02-45	462 Sqn
658300	F/S	PEILL Joseph Henry	5-01-45	50 Sqn
619581	Sgt	PEMBLE Douglas Howard	5-01-45	158 Sqn
3051692	Sgt	PENDLETON Leonard	19-03-45	103 Sqn
184794	P/O	PEPWORTH DFM Stanley Arthur	27-02-45	138 Sqn
1263001	F/S	PERCIVAL DFM Edward Arthur	17-03-45	214 Sqn
184289	F/O	PERKINS Robert George	9-04-45	49 Sqn
2223326	Sgt	PERKINS Walter	21-03-45	214 Sqn
56599	P/O	PERRING Charles Thomas William	11-04-45	619 Sqn
157335	F/O	PERRY Hugh Ernest James	21-02-45	578 Sqn
1823741	Sgt	PERRY John	2-01-45	166 Sqn
191460	P/O	PERRY Trevor John	21-02-45	189 Sqn
154799	F/O	PERRY William Neilson	7-02-45	218 Sqn
1087217	F/S	PETCH John William	22-04-45	49 Sqn
185214	P/O	PETHARD William Thomas	7-01-45	635 Sqn
1892292	Sgt	PETTMAN Albert Harry	14-02-45	103 Sqn
150236	F/L	PHELPS George Richard	1-03-45	166 Sqn
185299	F/O	PHILCOX Ian Hamilton Stuart	22-03-45	150 Sqn
1827202	Sgt	PHILIP William Smith	9-04-45	463 Sqn
1376114	F/S	PHILLIPS Albert Leonard	3-02-45	14 OTU
1897422	Sgt	PHILLIPS Bernard John	1-01-45	630 Sqn
1583109	F/S	PHILLIPS Dennis Harold	7-02-45	12 Sqn
1564419	F/S	PHILLIPS James	14-01-45	571 Sqn
1684876	Sgt	PHILPOT Dennis J.	22-04-45	153 Sqn
151758	F/O	PHILPOTT Cuthbert Lawson	14-02-45	9 Sqn
1684789	F/S	PHINN William	14-03-45	75 Sqn
1533083	Sgt	PICKERING John Moore	5-01-45	77 Sqn
1122361	Sgt	PICKERING William Edward	21-02-45	7 Sqn
164197	F/O	PICKERSGILL Maurice Desmond	4-01-45	103 Sqn
191702	P/O	PICKUP James	7-03-45	44 Sqn
1836107	F/S	PICTON John O. S.	7-03-45	189 Sqn
171882	F/O	PIDGEON Albert Henry John	8-03-45	35 Sqn
174945	F/O	PIERCE John Walton	4-03-45	169 Sqn
3033009	Sgt	PIKE William Raymond	10-01-45	17 OTU
183091	F/O	PILE DFM Kenneth Laurence	11-03-45	156 Sqn
190896	P/O	PILLING Frank	5-04-45	166 Sqn
1625985	F/S	PIMM Stanley Albert	30-03-45	635 Sqn
1852125	Sgt	PINSENT John Henry	7-01-45	170 Sqn
3030989	Sgt	PIPER Harry Robert	21-02-45	227 Sqn
163608	F/O	PITMAN Raymond Clifford	14-03-45	101 Sqn
1897011	Sgt	PITT Albert Stanley	9-02-45	186 Sqn
190669	F/O	PLANE Leonard	1-07-45	150 Sqn
1581191	F/S	PLANT Clifford	9-04-45	61 Sqn
3010599	Sgt	PLANT John Percival	5-03-45	170 Sqn
1824870	F/S	PLASTOW Henry Jacob	14-07-45	626 Sqn
3011828	Sgt	PLATT Thomas	4-03-45	1651 HCU
196398	P/O	PLUMB Donald Ivan	17-03-45	630 Sqn
138135	F/L	POLDEN Albert Frank West	7-03-45	189 Sqn
137230	F/L	POLGREAN William Henry	7-03-45	578 Sqn
195660	P/O	POLLARD John	12-01-45	424 Sqn
1865782	F/S	POLLARD Thomas William James	24-02-45	214 Sqn
124182	F/L	POLLOCK Edward Alexander [Chile]	1-02-45	166 Sqn
189069	P/O	PONTING Frederick Lewis John	17-04-45	156 Sqn
1325152	W/O	POOL Reginald Henry Alfred	3-05-45	199 Sqn
655599	W/O	POOLE DFM Francis John	1-01-45	83 Sqn
162285	F/O	POOLE Raymond	4-02-45	128 Sqn
44404	S/L	POOLEY DFC MiD Henry Richard	20-06-45	1660 HCU
605619	Sgt	POON-TIP Allan Percy	5-04-45	166 Sqn
1587647	F/S	POORE Donald Frank	22-04-45	153 Sqn
127878	F/L	POPE DFC Anthony Colin	31-03-45	156 Sqn
2220967	Sgt	POPE Enoch Edward	16-01-45	102 Sqn
1049025	F/S	POPE George Alfred	5-01-45	35 Sqn
151802	F/O	POPPLEWELL Ernest Malcolm	16-01-45	51 Sqn
197940	P/O	PORTEOUS James Cunningham	1-05-45	157 Sqn
1318075	W/O	PORTER Arthur Haydn	19-04-45	35 Sqn
1685119	Sgt	PORTER Herbert Walter	3-02-45	576 Sqn
1824774	F/S	PORTER James	15-06-45	630 Sqn
1103569	Sgt	PORTER James Henry	5-03-45	625 Sqn
153892	F/O	PORTER Kenneth Stanley [Channel Islands]	2-02-45	189 Sqn
3006161	Sgt	PORTER William Frank	16-01-45	1653 HCU
1385470	W/O	PORTWAY John Charles	8-06-45	608 Sqn

Service No.	Rank	Name	Date	Unit
53824	F/O	POSSEE DFC William Frank	14-03-45	227 Sqn
1204842	W/O	POSTON William	2-02-45	51 Sqn
1623636	F/S	POTTER Reginald	8-03-45	576 Sqn
2210442	Sgt	POTTER Wilfred George	2-02-45	460 Sqn
960474	Sgt	POTTS Ernest John	2-01-45	9 Sqn
183583	F/O	POTTS DFC Kenneth	5-01-45	35 Sqn
1831282	Sgt	POULSON Ronald	2-01-45	100 Sqn
1809356	F/O	POWELL Arthur Royston	6-01-45	57 Sqn
176370	F/L	POWELL Gordon Oswald	7-03-45	578 Sqn
1659641	Sgt	POWELL Jack	16-01-45	466 Sqn
103039	S/L	POWELL DFC John Leonard	16-04-45	617 Sqn
176193	F/O	POWELL Kenneth George	7-03-45	170 Sqn
1602783	F/S	POWELL Walter Ronald	15-02-45	189 Sqn
2220555	Sgt	POWER Stephen	9-03-45	90 Sqn
39601	W/C	POWLEY DFC AFC Francis Sidney [Canada]	4-04-45	153 Sqn
36925	Sgt	PRADES Henry Jacques Andre [France]	29-10-45	347 Sqn
1685992	Sgt	PRECIEUX Lois Octave [Mauritius]	7-01-45	550 Sqn
1582098	F/S	PRESCOTT Noel Gordon	8-01-45	12 Sqn
1833038	Sgt	PRESTON Charles Edwin	8-03-45	101 Sqn
1826725	Sgt	PRESTON George	14-02-45	115 Sqn
1813264	F/S	PRESTON Leslie Walter	11-05-45	427 Sqn
1080471	W/O	PRESTON Robert Edward	10-04-45	75 Sqn
1048598	LAC	PRICE Arnold	17-04-45	5 Group
1509811	W/O	PRICE Fred Thomas	30-04-45	625 Sqn
1899494	Sgt	PRICE Reginald Benjamin	4-01-45	11 OTU
1652787	Sgt	PRICE Ronald Watkin	7-01-45	619 Sqn
2209960	Sgt	PRICE Stanley John	15-02-45	640 Sqn
1191010	F/S	PRICHARD MiD Graham Arthur Rodney	4-03-45	467 Sqn
2218849	Sgt	PRIDDING James Barrie	6-03-45	640 Sqn
201082	P/O	PRINCE John Coleman	30-10-45	1653 HCU
1367312	F/S	PRINGLE Alexander	14-03-45	101 Sqn
188982	P/O	PRINGLE James William John	15-01-45	578 Sqn
3031571	Sgt	PRITCHARD Alfred Richard	5-01-45	51 Sqn
1566612	F/S	PROBERT William	18-04-45	640 Sqn
154321	F/O	PROUDLEY Robert Edward	15-02-45	630 Sqn
1437760	Sgt	PRUST Harold	9-04-45	49 Sqn
143665	F/L	PUDSEY DFM Twice MiD Kenneth	5-04-45	142 Sqn
1852074	Sgt	PULFORD Oliver James	14-01-45	625 Sqn
1896217	Sgt	PULHAM John Daniel	20-04-45	19 OTU
1319801	F/S	PULHAM Joseph William Charles	10-05-45	83 Sqn
1283964	Sgt	PULLAN Walter James	4-03-45	1651 HCU
1606932	Sgt	PUNNETT Edward Lionel	23-03-45	214 Sqn
1578843	F/S	PURVEY Harold Arthur	14-01-45	11 OTU
575245	W/O	PYKE Henry John	1-02-45	61 Sqn
1376695	F/S	QUADRY Marcel Louis [France]	28-04-45	11 OTU
1581305	F/S	QUINEY Ronald Albert	14-01-45	106 Sqn
1349659	AC2	QUINN William	5-06-45	149 Sqn
914247	F/S	QUINTON Albert Reginald	17-03-45	153 Sqn
1853452	Sgt	RABBETTS Gordon Leonard	17-05-45	630 Sqn
1804931	Sgt	RABIN Alfred Jack	22-01-45	153 Sqn
2219105	Sgt	RAFFERTY Charles Quinn	14-03-45	57 Sqn
710264	F/S	RAINSFORD Anthony [Rhodesia]	22-03-45	97 Sqn
1811907	Sgt	RALPH Gerald John Price	6-03-45	582 Sqn
1867776	Sgt	RALPH Jack Edward	6-02-45	1656 HCU
934263	W/O	RALPH Robert Edward	14-01-45	223 Sqn
190702	P/O	RALPH William Edward Charles	19-03-45	640 Sqn
2205987	F/S	RAMSAY Eric	14-03-45	75 Sqn
1869021	F/S	RAMSAY John Richard Alexander	2-02-45	619 Sqn
1482867	Sgt	RAMSBOTTOM Alan	20-03-45	57 Sqn
130989	F/L	RANALOW Patrick Baring Oates	10-04-45	35 Sqn
1676495	F/S	RANDALL Leslie	8-02-45	49 Sqn
134673	F/L	RANDON Joseph Charles	21-03-45	617 Sqn
1591174	Sgt	RATCLIFFE Walter Milton	16-03-45	61 Sqn
126889	F/L	RAW Leonard Charles	21-03-45	619 Sqn
166236	F/O	RAWLINSON Edward	20-04-45	19 OTU
2218660	F/S	RAWLINSON James	15-01-45	1668 HCU
809198	Sgt	RAWNSLEY Herbert Henry	28-05-45	17 OTU
162911	F/L	RAY John	23-02-45	97 Sqn
190958	F/O	RAY Maurice Edward Michael	2-03-45	622 Sqn
1047297	Sgt	RAYMENT Ronald Charles	16-03-45	170 Sqn
1595648	Sgt	RAYNER Albert Kemp	6-03-45	424 Sqn
1186489	W/O	READ Albert George Charles	19-04-45	76 Sqn
173774	F/O	READ DFC Basil Anthony	10-01-45	20 OTU
182747	F/O	REAKS Peter William	1-01-45	9 Sqn
177845	F/O	REDFERN DFC Ernest Cyril	12-01-45	9 Sqn
121366	F/L	REDFERN Thomas William	26-01-45	85 Sqn
1425147	W/O	REDFORD Arnold Evans	21-03-45	223 Sqn
1596594	Sgt	REDMILE George Edward William	2-01-45	150 Sqn
1381101	W/O	REDMOND George Clement	18-03-45	85 Sqn
1672621	F/S	REDMOND Robert	16-01-45	12 Sqn
1007113	W/O	REED Laurence	22-03-45	166 Sqn
1582745	F/S	REED Norman George	5-04-45	626 Sqn
591740	F/S	REES Kenneth Vincent	6-03-45	10 Sqn
1890497	Sgt	REEVES Derek James	23-02-45	103 Sqn
1566894	F/S	REID Douglas Finne	24-03-45	550 Sqn
1826182	Sgt	REID Richard Wallace	20-04-45	622 Sqn
1600606	Sgt	REIDY William Patrick	20-03-45	85 Sqn
2222184	Sgt	REILLY Andrew	6-03-45	514 Sqn
1590580	Sgt	RELTON Kenneth	8-03-45	578 Sqn
1587030	F/S	RENDLE Norman Drayton	11-07-45	10 OTU
173905	F/O	RENTON Francis Swan	5-01-45	550 Sqn
1805022	F/S	REX Edward Albert	2-02-45	619 Sqn
1211144	F/S	REYNOLDS Frederick	15-06-45	630 Sqn
1649222	Sgt	REYNOLDS William Graham	14-04-45	35 Sqn
1623310	F/S	RHODEN Kenneth	6-05-45	169 Sqn
174596	F/O	RHODES Ernest Herbert	15-01-45	578 Sqn
171812	F/O	RHODES Jack	1-03-45	153 Sqn
1623206	F/S	RHODES Jonah	15-06-45	630 Sqn
1867355	Sgt	RICE Denis Sidney	28-08-45	11 OTU
55924	P/O	RICE John Summerfield	15-02-45	78 Sqn
176192	F/O	RICH Leslie John	1-03-45	166 Sqn
1590458	Sgt	RICHARDS Donald Ernest	13-12-45	26 OTU
1836954	Sgt	RICHARDS Howell	22-03-45	44 Sqn
1603064	F/S	RICHARDS Jack William	17-03-45	166 Sqn
2218582	Sgt	RICHARDS Ralph	23-02-45	166 Sqn
1398924	Sgt	RICHARDS Reginald Charles	2-01-45	153 Sqn
1339173	F/S	RICHARDS Terence William	6-01-45	51 Sqn
1591870	Sgt	RICHARDSON Herbert	17-01-45	640 Sqn
1590550	Sgt	RICHARDSON Raymond	2-03-45	207 Sqn
1590833	Sgt	RICHARDSON Richard	15-01-45	61 Sqn
1563926	F/S	RICHARDSON Stanley	21-02-45	158 Sqn
1460401	F/S	RICHES Frederick Henry	14-02-45	640 Sqn
187301	F/O	RICKARD Ronald Arthur	20-05-45	20 OTU
617244	Sgt	RICKEARD Robert	8-01-45	12 Sqn
1386411	Sgt	RICKETTS Bernard Conrad	16-03-45	170 Sqn
173082	F/O	RICKETTS DFM Frederick James	21-03-45	619 Sqn
149967	F/L	RIDGEWELL Frederick Harold	25-02-45	462 Sqn
1591283	Sgt	RIDSDALE John Reuben	14-02-45	640 Sqn
1894783	Sgt	RILEY Patrick Joseph	3-02-45	14 OTU
55628	F/O	RITCHIE James	15-02-45	77 Sqn
1894110	F/S	ROBBINS Norman Reginald	4-10-45	103 Sqn
136689	F/L	ROBBINS Victor Stanley	20-04-45	622 Sqn
186931	F/O	ROBERTS Donald Michael	14-04-45	186 Sqn
1593519	Sgt	ROBERTS James William	19-07-45	1654 HCU
1210132	F/S	ROBERTS Lewis George	12-01-45	9 Sqn
1698482	Sgt	ROBERTS Ronald	25-04-45	426 Sqn
176984	F/O	ROBERTS William Edward	14-04-45	186 Sqn
1592154	F/S	ROBERTSHAW Thomas	7-01-45	635 Sqn
168782	F/O	ROBERTSON Gordon Angus	21-02-45	7 Sqn
1450835	Sgt	ROBERTSON Jack	14-01-45	12 Sqn
139238	F/L	ROBERTSON DFM John	11-03-45	156 Sqn
2206328	Sgt	ROBINSON Alan Kenneth	8-03-45	195 Sqn
3041016	Sgt	ROBINSON Basil	14-02-45	77 Sqn
2209776	F/S	ROBINSON Charles Albert	7-01-45	170 Sqn

Service No	Rank	Name	Date	Sqn
1593754	Sgt	ROBINSON David	22-03-45	460 Sqn
1474345	Sgt	ROBINSON Eric Raymond	7-03-45	550 Sqn
191444	P/O	ROBINSON Fred Vesey	2-02-45	78 Sqn
1595325	F/S	ROBINSON Geoffrey	24-02-45	462 Sqn
117514	F/L	ROBINSON DFM Kenneth	2-03-45	640 Sqn
946987	F/S	ROBINSON Leslie	8-04-45	9 Sqn
1894397	Sgt	ROBINSON Stanley Edward	30-03-45	635 Sqn
158124	F/O	ROBINSON Thomas Broadley	8-04-45	35 Sqn
1601365	F/S	ROBSON Bruce	6-03-45	10 Sqn
52699	F/O	ROBSON Clifford Allan	11-03-45	156 Sqn
165269	F/O	ROBSON James William	2-04-45	515 Sqn
121950	F/L	ROBSON DFC John Henry	15-01-45	139 Sqn
1602074	F/S	ROBSON Richard William	15-03-45	582 Sqn
165624	F/O	ROCHE Leonard	30-07-45	166 Sqn
160639	F/O	RODGER Donald	22-02-45	626 Sqn
1333583	F/S	RODWELL Deryck Grenville	8-02-45	50 Sqn
1585725	F/S	RODWELL Peter Henry	2-01-45	150 Sqn
1813968	W/O	ROE CGM DFM Victor Arthur	6-03-45	35 Sqn
2218611	Sgt	ROGAN William Henry	4-03-45	44 Sqn
150123	F/L	ROGERS Christopher Alan	4-03-45	158 Sqn
926635	LAC	ROGERS MiD James William	22-04-45	Fulbeck
1333583	F/S	RODWELL Deryck Grenville		
1588200	Sgt	ROLLINS Harold	11-03-45	463 Sqn
644506	Sgt	ROLLS George Edward	25-02-45	462 Sqn
168834	F/O	ROSS Henry	1-01-45	571 Sqn
154224	F/O	ROSS John	3-02-45	186 Sqn
134762	F/L	ROUSE Stanley Thomas	15-03-45	227 Sqn
1436507	F/S	ROWAN James Patrick	8-03-45	189 Sqn
1810260	Sgt	ROWSON Derrick John	6-04-45	26 OTU
638962	F/S	ROY James	8-03-45	103 Sqn
3006069	Sgt	RUSHWORTH Frank Alfred	14-02-45	103 Sqn
138894	F/L	RUSSELL DFC Clifford Owen	8-03-45	35 Sqn
161392	F/O	RUSSELL Geoffrey Lomax	2-01-45	150 Sqn
3040015	Sgt	RUSSELL Harry Gilbert	30-07-45	166 Sqn
1580401	F/S	RUSSELL John Leonard	3-02-45	50 Sqn
1597233	Sgt	RUSSELL Norman	6-03-45	50 Sqn
1801287	F/S	RUSSELL Richard Raven	4-03-45	44 Sqn
1606323	Sgt	RUSSELL Robert Cunningham	14-04-45	186 Sqn
1809231	Sgt	RUSSELL Ronald Edward	15-02-45	77 Sqn
162051	F/O	RUSSELL Wilfred Wood	7-02-45	102 Sqn
1595461	Sgt	RUTHERFORD George Fewster	12-01-45	77 Sqn
1899341	Sgt	RUTT Horace David	21-02-45	626 Sqn
1869776	Sgt	SADLER Charles Frank	4-04-45	153 Sqn
1882066	Sgt	SAFFILL Frederick Henry	26-02-45	75 Sqn
1566413	F/S	SAGE Gilbert Ferguson	21-02-45	7 Sqn
179595	F/O	SAGER Vincent Garstang	5-01-45	50 Sqn
2222106	Sgt	SALISBURY William Arthur	5-03-45	431 Sqn
130069	F/L	SALT Francis Charles	3-02-45	156 Sqn
155198	F/O	SALVONI DFC Raymond Terence	14-01-45	35 Sqn
1523568	Sgt	SAMUELS John Joseph	3-03-45	207 Sqn
1896933	Sgt	SANDAY George Arthur Edgar	25-03-45	462 Sqn
1589903	Sgt	SANDERSON Gerald	15-03-45	115 Sqn
1685244	Sgt	SANDERSON John Scaife	7-01-45	462 Sqn
1621826	Sgt	SANDERSON John Thomas	7-01-45	49 Sqn
1583772	Sgt	SANSOME Harry	1-01-45	75 Sqn
1474901	Sgt	SARGENT Henry Alfred	21-02-45	576 Sqn
150614	F/O	SASSOON Richard Joseph	10-04-45	630 Sqn
154588	F/O	SAUNDERS Charles Henry	21-03-45	61 Sqn
2205043	Sgt	SAUNDERS Clervaux Francis Morley	30-07-45	166 Sqn
153755	F/O	SAVAGE Bertram Arthur	15-04-45	1667 HCU
962804	Sgt	SAYERS Albert John	2-03-45	625 Sqn
131547	S/L	SAYERS AFC MiD John Bertram	25-02-45	1660 HCU
1590809	Sgt	SCAIFE Noel Frank	22-03-45	150 Sqn
1274307	F/S	SCARFF Albert George	5-01-45	158 Sqn
1567699	Sgt	SCOTT Alastair Wingate	3-04-45	626 Sqn
1567205	Sgt	SCOTT Alexander Sherriffs	1-02-45	166 Sqn
184179	F/O	SCOTT James Neil	7-01-45	106 Sqn
1591065	F/S	SCOTT John	3-03-45	467 Sqn
1399603	F/S	SCOTT Norman Stanley	7-01-45	462 Sqn
169005	F/L	SCOTT Peter	8-03-45	195 Sqn
1804436	Sgt	SCOTT Peter Louis Wyndham	21-02-45	7 Sqn
162469	F/O	SCOTT Stanley Owen	6-03-45	35 Sqn
1569472	Sgt	SCOTT Thomas	1-01-45	9 Sqn
1050587	Sgt	SCOTT Walter Bonnyman	7-02-45	102 Sqn
2221348	Sgt	SCOTT William John Ryland	8-02-45	61 Sqn
1593364	Sgt	SCOTT William Percy	5-01-45	550 Sqn
1860660	LAC	SCRASE Henry Keith	9-07-45	32 Base
1591560	Sgt	SCROWTHER Ronald	8-03-45	218 Sqn
1602122	F/S	SCULL Lionel Frank Frederick	8-03-45	83 Sqn
1077176	Sgt	SCURR Charles	3-02-45	100 Sqn
942139	Sgt	SEABRIDGE William Henry	3-02-45	10 Sqn
1862444	Sgt	SEAGER Roy Norman	23-02-45	192 Sqn
1577517	F/S	SEARBY William Stacey	1-04-45	57 Sqn
115349	F/L	SEARLES DFC Stanley Oliver	24-03-45	139 Sqn
171387	F/O	SEARS Jack Etherington	6-01-45	61 Sqn
1852400	Sgt	SEDGLEY Richard Henry	12-01-45	5 LFS
188180	F/O	SEEAR Ernest Frank	16-03-45	625 Sqn
2225607	Sgt	SEECKTS Walter	6-03-45	103 Sqn
1836500	Sgt	SEIGNOT Herbert Philip Claude	16-03-45	170 Sqn
1896760	Sgt	SELF Frederick Edward	17-03-45	550 Sqn
1685867	F/S	SELIGMANN Edouard Zadoc	8-10-45	166 Sqn
188352	P/O	SELLERS Stanley	15-01-45	625 Sqn
1811719	Sgt	SEMPLE William James Robert	5-04-45	1652 HCU
164465	F/O	SEYMOUR Alexander Sidney	10-04-45	622 Sqn
1851223	Sgt	SEYMOUR Raymond Ernest George	25-06-45	199 Sqn
1586237	Sgt	SHABOE Frederick George Arthur	5-02-45	1654 HCU
1835745	Sgt	SHAFER Ronald Frederick Douglas	4-03-45	12 Sqn
1608322	Sgt	SHAIEL-GOSLING Laurence Herbert	7-03-45	12 Sqn
87419	F/L	SHANNON DFC John Edward	1-02-45	166 Sqn
1867637	Sgt	SHARE Peter	2-01-45	100 Sqn
189071	F/O	SHARMAN Arthur	23-02-45	138 Sqn
155069	F/O	SHARMAN DFC Harold Owen	5-03-45	161 Sqn
1803380	F/S	SHARP Medley Benjamin	5-01-45	35 Sqn
917319	F/S	SHARPE Norman Eric Armour	9-02-45	630 Sqn
1811658	Sgt	SHAW Harold	11-03-45	463 Sqn
1802925	F/S	SHAW Joseph George	29-01-45	156 Sqn
177413	F/L	SHAW Kenneth	8-03-45	578 Sqn
958767	Sgt	SHAW Stanley	4-03-45	1654 HCU
1721515	Sgt	SHAW William	5-01-45	102 Sqn
1566269	Sgt	SHEARER John	22-02-45	50 Sqn
1897280	Sgt	SHEARRON James Frederick	14-03-45	57 Sqn
651465	Sgt	SHEAVILLS Ernest	4-04-45	115 Sqn
1491267	Sgt	SHELDON George Joshua	3-04-45	625 Sqn
153642	F/O	SHENTON Malcolm Jack	15-01-45	625 Sqn
50528	F/L	SHEPHARD Wilfred Herbert	16-03-45	44 Sqn
2221357	Sgt	SHEPHERD John Graham	6-01-45	207 Sqn
3025425	Sgt	SHEPPARD Donald Howard	8-03-45	195 Sqn
124546	F/L	SHEPPARD DFC Francis Edward	2-04-45	1651 HCU
1563203	F/S	SHERIDAN James Harvey	1-01-45	102 Sqn
514220	F/S	SHERRIFF DFM Arthur Albert	1-02-45	61 Sqn
1777165	Sgt	SHIELD Jonathan	8-02-45	97 Sqn
196126	P/O	SHIELD William Leonard	11-03-45	153 Sqn
187832	P/O	SHIRLEY James Frederick	5-01-45	102 Sqn
1604391	F/S	SHORT James Edward	10-04-45	44 Sqn
157422	F/O	SHORTTLE DFM Joseph Malpass	24-02-45	214 Sqn
1898606	Sgt	SIBLEY Cyril William	21-02-45	158 Sqn
1629469	Sgt	SIDE Ronald Harold Howard	6-02-45	1656 HCU
179585	F/O	SIDWELL DFC Kenneth Frederick	30-10-45	1653 HCU
183797	F/O	SIFTON Charles Robin	5-01-45	10 Sqn
165408	F/O	SIGNEY Henry	20-06-45	1660 HCU
1817848	Sgt	SILLS John Alfred	17-05-45	630 Sqn
1835887	Sgt	SILLS Myrddin	23-02-45	158 Sqn
923431	W/O	SILVEY Samuel Ernest	21-03-45	223 Sqn
1584983	Sgt	SIMMONDS George Herbert	4-04-45	49 Sqn
1397591	F/S	SIMMONS Alfred George	14-03-45	77 Sqn
1238641	Sgt	SIMPSON Albert	23-01-45	153 Sqn
3020020	Sgt	SIMPSON Walter	6-03-45	153 Sqn

Service No	Rank	Name	Date	Sqn/Unit
3025318	Sgt	SIMS John Nugent	25-04-45	431 Sqn
1394295	F/S	SIMS Leslie George	4-04-45	153 Sqn
3011705	Sgt	SIMS Leslie John	4-02-45	433 Sqn
1880755	Sgt	SIMS William Edward	6-01-45	218 Sqn
1365238	F/S	SINCLAIR Alexander	5-01-45	16 OTU
1802884	Sgt	SINCLAIR Francis Frederick	4-04-45	49 Sqn
1677297	Sgt	SINCLAIR James	8-03-45	61 Sqn
168775	F/O	SINCLAIR DFC John Mackie	21-02-45	166 Sqn
637117	Sgt	SINCLAIR John McDonald	23-02-45	97 Sqn
178092	F/O	SINCLAIR DFM Stafford Henry George	22-03-45	214 Sqn
153740	F/L	SINDALL Hereward Robert	6-01-45	635 Sqn
153833	F/O	SINFIELD DFC David Forster	21-02-45	156 Sqn
1438945	F/S	SINKINSON Eric William	23-02-45	138 Sqn
1549547	Sgt	SLATER Joshua Alderdice	23-02-45	101 Sqn
1589551	Sgt	SLATER Thomas	8-03-45	218 Sqn
1682293	F/S	SLAUGHTER Edward Crone	8-02-45	57 Sqn
3040416	Sgt	SLEEP Donald	8-01-45	103 Sqn
1826936	Sgt	SLIMAN Allan Melrose	14-04-45	75 Sqn
187565	P/O	SLINGSBY Harold Edwin	3-02-45	15 Sqn
137392	F/O	SLOGROVE Edward Arthur	15-02-45	115 Sqn
2219167	Sgt	SMAILS Eric	6-02-45	1656 HCU
2220737	Sgt	SMALL Billy Geoffrey Hicks	18-06-45	1663 HCU
1197077	Sgt	SMALLEY Herbert John	16-01-45	12 Sqn
170228	F/O	SMALLWOODS Ronald William	7-02-45	102 Sqn
1587792	Sgt	SMART Eric George Wason	29-01-45	3 LFS
1872063	F/S	SMEE Alan	9-03-45	90 Sqn
1594052	F/S	SMITH Albert Edward	2-04-45	189 Sqn
171702	F/O	SMITH DFC Charles Clifford	5-01-45	102 Sqn
184688	P/O	SMITH Charles Morrison	8-02-45	1658 HCU
150233	F/L	SMITH David Alexander	8-03-45	189 Sqn
2215998	F/S	SMITH Douglas Ellwood	17-04-45	156 Sqn
2221148	Sgt	SMITH Edward Thomas	13-02-45	550 Sqn
1896414	Sgt	SMITH Frank	1-02-45	101 Sqn
2222272	Sgt	SMITH Frederic	25-04-45	431 Sqn
68790	S/L	SMITH George Miller	6-03-45	109 Sqn
175274	F/O	SMITH Hulbert Abram	20-04-45	622 Sqn
1608781	Sgt	SMITH Ian Philip Hendry	4-01-45	11 OTU
1524154	Sgt	SMITH John Arthur William	4-03-45	1651 HCU
124796	F/L	SMITH John Benjamin Joseph	8-02-45	169 Sqn
1607430	F/S	SMITH John Clement	7-03-45	44 Sqn
190286	P/O	SMITH John Dorrian	5-01-45	427 Sqn
164200	F/O	SMITH John Duncan	21-03-45	207 Sqn
1588018	Sgt	SMITH John T.	5-03-45	102 Sqn
1114835	Sgt	SMITH Joseph Gerard	8-03-45	103 Sqn
1881097	Sgt	SMITH Kenneth John Boucher	7-03-45	550 Sqn
165669	F/L	SMITH Kenneth Samuel	6-03-45	35 Sqn
160198	F/O	SMITH Leonard Sidney	15-03-45	227 Sqn
1320175	F/S	SMITH Leslie Norman	28-08-45	11 OTU
1676114	Sgt	SMITH Newton	3-09-45	26 OTU
1608868	Sgt	SMITH Reginald Henry 'Reggie'	17-05-45	630 Sqn
170400	F/L	SMITH Robert Arthur	13-01-45	515 Sqn
3001167	Sgt	SMITH Ronald Sedgeley	4-04-45	550 Sqn
1622514	Sgt	SMITH Ronald Victor	4-03-45	467 Sqn
1603454	F/S	SMITH Ronald William Henry	17-03-45	467 Sqn
1395145	Sgt	SMITH Roy Peter	19-03-45	405 Sqn
1397906	F/S	SMITH Sidney	5-03-45	514 Sqn
1338304	F/S	SMITH Stanley	1-07-45	150 Sqn
173785	F/L	SMITH Thomas Cecil Birdwood	21-02-45	170 Sqn
1596679	Sgt	SMITH Thomas Cuthbert	3-02-45	10 Sqn
196338	P/O	SMITH Victor Patrick	9-04-45	61 Sqn
1576922	F/S	SMITH Wilfred Ernest	15-06-45	630 Sqn
190551	P/O	SMITH William Reveler	8-02-45	102 Sqn
1893583	Sgt	SMITHER Horace	16-03-45	625 Sqn
2221603	Sgt	SNAPE Rupert Desmond	16-03-45	44 Sqn
1823545	Sgt	SNEDDON James	27-02-45	186 Sqn
1462497	F/S	SNELLING Arthur William	21-03-45	61 Sqn
912579	Sgt	SOANES Robert Charles	7-01-45	622 Sqn
1867019	Sgt	SOLOMON Maurice Abraham	6-01-45	10 Sqn
1589666	Sgt	SOMERS John Vidal	14-04-45	186 Sqn
195069	P/O	SORRELL George Lionel	15-02-45	432 Sqn
2247417	Sgt	SORRELL Ronald Frank	3-02-45	14 OTU
1583954	Sgt	SOUDEN Charles William	6-02-45	1653 HCU
195242	P/O	SOUTH Ronald	9-03-45	90 Sqn
1813035	Sgt	SOUTHWARD Vincent Reginald Woodburn	17-05-45	630 Sqn
179187	F/O	SOWERBUTTS Richard Christopher	3-02-45	576 Sqn
1117648	LAC	SPARK William Christie	5-06-45	149 Sqn
1867038	Sgt	SPARKE James Alfred	3-02-45	186 Sqn
1218696	F/S	SPARKES William Joseph	14-03-45	514 Sqn
1595558	Sgt	SPENCER Eric	23-02-45	192 Sqn
937528	F/S	SPENCER George	17-01-45	514 Sqn
1589200	Sgt	SPERLING Royston	17-04-45	171 Sqn
115523	F/L	SPIERS Donald Seymour	22-04-45	218 Sqn
1607371	F/S	SPRATT William Sidney	5-01-45	51 Sqn
1803345	F/S	SPROSTON Hugh Raymond	4-04-45	49 Sqn
3030598	Sgt	SQUIRE Jack	1-02-45	101 Sqn
1895797	Sgt	SQUIRE Leslie	8-04-45	10 Sqn
1603578	Sgt	STAFFORD Alfred Ronald	6-03-45	50 Sqn
178375	F/O	STAGG Bernard Eric Stanley	5-04-45	626 Sqn
1239912	Sgt	STAGG Stuart Harry Campbell	3-04-45	29 OTU
1594910	Sgt	STAINTHORPE Harrison	3-02-45	186 Sqn
1335462	W/O	STANDING Ernest Edwin	23-02-45	103 Sqn
1893767	Sgt	STANES Dennis Bernard Neil	25-04-45	76 Sqn
1866386	Sgt	STANLEY James Frederick John	8-04-45	1653 HCU
1622882	F/S	STAPLES Edward Voster	14-04-45	103 Sqn
1801787	F/S	STAPLES Jack Sidney	5-01-45	51 Sqn
1456888	P/O	STAUBER Norman Henry	22-03-45	97 Sqn
1149349	F/S	STAZAKER James William	8-02-45	83 Sqn
1147965	F/S	STEAD Frank Ronald	15-03-45	207 Sqn
186187	P/O	STEAINSTREET Arthur	16-03-45	170 Sqn
1800692	F/S	STEAN George Dennis	15-02-45	640 Sqn
1339232	F/S	STEEDEN Arthur Douglas	7-01-45	622 Sqn
1818104	Sgt	STEEL Richard George	4-10-45	103 Sqn
186771	P/O	STEELE Edward Arthur	15-01-45	578 Sqn
561898	W/O	STEELE Frederick James William	14-04-45	214 Sqn
1890024	Sgt	STEELE Maurice Henry	9-04-45	78 Sqn
1590355	Sgt	STENNETT Raymond	1-02-45	166 Sqn
104586	F/L	STEPHEN Andrew Douglas	6-03-45	10 Sqn
1588197	Sgt	STEPHEN Edward Scott	8-06-45	608 Sqn
2204309	Sgt	STEPHENS Geoffrey Arthur	23-02-45	101 Sqn
1398405	F/S	STEPHENS Hugh Francis	8-01-45	103 Sqn
164130	F/O	STEPHENS Richard Walter	15-03-45	550 Sqn
628873	Sgt	STEPHENS Samuel James	21-02-45	101 Sqn
1590766	Sgt	STEPHENS William	9-02-45	186 Sqn
1802383	F/S	STEPHENSON George Forster Constable	15-03-45	227 Sqn
1390537	F/S	STERMAN Benjamin	5-01-45	550 Sqn
1522881	F/S	STEVENS Douglas Campbell	16-03-45	100 Sqn
189431	P/O	STEVENS Eric George	5-01-45	51 Sqn
1573426	Sgt	STEVENSON John	31-01-45	19 OTU
122098	F/L	STEWART Alastair Mackichan	11-03-45	156 Sqn
1673061	F/S	STEWART Dryden	21-03-45	75 Sqn
746477	W/O	STEWART John	7-02-45	77 Sqn
175167	F/O	STEWART John Andrew Sorley	16-01-45	158 Sqn
1826779	Sgt	STEWART Thomas Fraser	3-01-45	166 Sqn
1522711	Sgt	STILL Kenneth Ross	6-03-45	50 Sqn
1875441	Sgt	STIMPSON Peter	11-01-45	20 OTU
1673227	F/S	STOBART Maurice Wilfred	6-01-45	61 Sqn
1523168	F/S	STOBBS John	24-03-45	550 Sqn
1587275	F/S	STOCKER Clifford Isaac	21-03-45	75 Sqn
1804761	F/S	STOCKER Kenneth Frank	4-03-45	640 Sqn
2223471	Sgt	STOKES Harold Victor	15-04-45	138 Sqn
545602	F/S	STONE Eric John Dalton	26-02-45	12 Sqn
188993	P/O	STONE Frank Samuel	21-02-45	460 Sqn
958686	F/S	STONE John Leslie	8-03-45	57 Sqn

1592667	F/S	STOREY Albert	17-04-45	171 Sqn
190000	P/O	STOTT Harry Kenneth	17-03-45	103 Sqn
1097284	W/O	STOTT DFM Norman	21-03-45	189 Sqn
184023	F/O	STRACHAN Alexander Canning	15-02-45	189 Sqn
1568148	Sgt	STREATFIELD Alan	4-03-45	460 Sqn
1809414	Sgt	STREATFIELD Ronald Ernest	3-02-45	576 Sqn
527668	F/S	STRONG DFM William Samuel Henry	15-02-45	640 Sqn
1397017	F/S	STROUD DFM Frank William	20-02-45	44 Sqn
163582	F/O	STUART Arthur White	23-02-45	101 Sqn
1559208	Sgt	STUART Charles	3-02-45	550 Sqn
1591022	F/S	STUART Sidney	7-03-45	171 Sqn
1865453	Sgt	STUART-RITSON John Henry	7-03-45	550 Sqn
1800054	Sgt	STURROCK John Alexander McKenzie	15-01-45	692 Sqn
1259898	F/S	ST. LEDGER Albert Christopher	9-02-45	619 Sqn
538944	F/S	SULLIVAN Albert Victor 'Bert'	22-03-45	692 Sqn
1336564	F/S	SULLIVAN Ronald Joseph	3-07-45	166 Sqn
187480	F/O	SUMMERS George	31-05-45	1660 HCU
1851198	F/S	SUMMERS Gordon	8-02-45	83 Sqn
1869349	Sgt	SUMPTER Peter Allan	16-01-45	186 Sqn
1606202	F/S	SURMAN Kenneth	1-01-45	166 Sqn
1603505	Sgt	SURTEES Robert	16-03-45	170 Sqn
1397821	F/S	SUTHERLAND Vincent Joseph	19-03-45	102 Sqn
1183093	F/S	SUTTON Eric Thomas	25-04-45	76 Sqn
1474543	Sgt	SUTTON Kenneth William Thomas	6-01-45	158 Sqn
1898320	Sgt	SWAFFER Robert Leslie	21-02-45	576 Sqn
1822601	Sgt	SWAIN James	14-02-45	77 Sqn
1323649	F/S	SWAIN Richard John Frederick	1-02-45	101 Sqn
172347	F/O	SWALE DFC Kenneth	15-01-45	139 Sqn
1596538	Sgt	SWAN Robert	2-02-45	90 Sqn
1895002	Sgt	SWAN William Henry	14-02-45	103 Sqn
930413	F/S	SWEET John Vempley	26-01-45	578 Sqn
1398175	F/S	SWEETMAN Peter Charles [USA]	12-03-45	460 Sqn
1867568	Sgt	SWIFT David Walter Edward	17-03-45	576 Sqn
1623219	F/S	SWINGLER Derrick	21-03-45	50 Sqn
2220411	Sgt	SWINGLER Neville Charles	10-01-45	20 OTU
1626149	Sgt	SYKES Ernest Edward	18-04-45	408 Sqn
195926	P/O	SYMES Walter Thomas	5-03-45	426 Sqn
1853705	F/S	SYMONDS Gordon John	8-04-45	9 Sqn
1883370	Sgt	SYMONDS John	17-03-45	576 Sqn
1606560	F/S	TABOR Geoffrey Leonard Vyvyan	21-02-45	576 Sqn
179588	F/L	TAIT Ralph Roland	16-01-45	186 Sqn
638924	F/S	TAKLE Richard James	21-02-45	83 Sqn
3050821	Sgt	TALBOT James Alfred Arthur	19-06-45	103 Sqn
642289	F/S	TANDY William Stanley Horace	8-03-45	61 Sqn
1891873	Sgt	TANNEN Leslie Marcus	5-02-45	1669 HCU
165428	F/O	TARDIF Maurice Ernest Philip	11-07-45	10 OTU
1571479	Sgt	TARLTON Jack David Jules Lucien [Belgium]	2-01-45	166 Sqn
1605916	Sgt	TARR Leslie John	14-01-45	11 OTU
1890136	Sgt	TASKER Harold William	5-03-45	10 Sqn
3012866	Sgt	TATE Francis Joseph	16-01-45	12 Sqn
188539	P/O	TATHAM Kenneth Roy	27-02-45	20 OTU
154090	F/O	TAYLOR Albert Kenneth	4-04-45	78 Sqn
2255216	Sgt	TAYLOR Alexander William 'Sandy'	4-03-45	1651 HCU
1670564	F/S	TAYLOR Dennis	23-02-45	166 Sqn
189687	F/L	TAYLOR Geoffrey	4-10-45	103 Sqn
53495	F/O	TAYLOR George Laurence	6-03-45	103 Sqn
159879	F/L	TAYLOR DFC Herbert Frederick (served as BENSON H.)	31-03-45	156 Sqn
3011426	Sgt	TAYLOR Howard	14-01-45	9 Sqn
1336991	F/S	TAYLOR Jack Hugh	13-03-45	150 Sqn
1596665	Sgt	TAYLOR John Edward	17-03-45	576 Sqn
1869191	Sgt	TAYLOR John Edward	20-03-45	7 Sqn
197974	F/O	TAYLOR John Francis William	21-02-45	427 Sqn
1818668	Sgt	TAYLOR Malcolm Ernest	7-02-45	77 Sqn
3045039	Sgt	TAYLOR Michael Arthur	28-08-45	11 OTU
1580857	F/S	TAYLOR Ralph	21-03-45	61 Sqn
1590841	Sgt	TAYLOR Roy	2-01-45	153 Sqn
1459586	F/S	TAYLOR Samuel George	10-04-45	622 Sqn
1897176	Sgt	TAYLOR William Charles	13-03-45	153 Sqn
1809870	Sgt	TEANBY Thomas Edward	14-02-45	640 Sqn
553937	F/S	TEGGART Hugh Henry	1-02-45	166 Sqn
1825587	F/S	TELFER George Crooks	16-01-45	102 Sqn
1628710	F/S	TENNANT Humphrey Brown	27-02-45	76 Sqn
1580082	F/S	TERRY Hubert Joseph	4-03-45	44 Sqn
1823486	Sgt	TERRY Kenneth Edward	20-06-45	1660 HCU
1881084	Sgt	TERRY Robert Thomas	1-03-45	166 Sqn
186232	P/O	THAIN Maurice Joseph	14-02-45	9 Sqn
1160188	Sgt	THIRKETTLE George Horace	2-01-45	1050 Sqn
56400	P/O	THOMAS Arthur Glyndwyr	4-03-45	12 Sqn
132619	P/O	THOMAS Edward Ainsley	1-01-45	630 Sqn
1549455	F/S	THOMAS Gerald Basil	4-02-45	35 Sqn
1317034	F/S	THOMAS Glyn James	6-03-45	50 Sqn
161024	F/O	THOMAS Henry Albert	15-03-45	227 Sqn
605706	Sgt	THOMAS Herbert Percival [Jamaica]	5-03-45	514 Sqn
1652570	F/S	THOMAS Leslie	7-03-45	170 Sqn
1897685	F/S	THOMAS Richard Ward	6-01-45	10 Sqn
1592730	F/S	THOMAS Willy	8-04-45	9 Sqn
187130	P/O	THOMPSON Edward Henry	1-02-45	433 Sqn
1370700	F/S	THOMPSON VC George	23-01-45	9 Sqn
3050918	Sgt	THOMPSON Jack	30-05-45	90 Sqn
3040793	Sgt	THOMPSON James	4-03-45	1653 HCU
1059098	Sgt	THOMPSON John	14-01-45	26 OTU
1458564	F/S	THOMPSON John Ernest	8-03-45	57 Sqn
184972	P/O	THOMPSON John Swinnerton	15-02-45	78 Sqn
2210578	Sgt	THOMPSON Norman	14-01-45	1654 HCU
172099	F/O	THOMPSON DFC Paul Edward	4-03-45	189 Sqn
174908	F/O	THOMPSON Robert Fraser	18-05-45	30 OTU
1076295	F/S	THOMPSON Victor Arnold	6-04-45	26 OTU
182757	F/O	THOMSON Alexander Stuart	1-03-45	103 Sqn
1825993	Sgt	THOMSON George Edward	5-04-45	153 Sqn
710263	F/S	THOMSON Reginald Hamilton [Rhodesia]	14-01-45	106 Sqn
3020215	Sgt	THOMSON Robert	22-02-45	626 Sqn
339807	F/S	THORBURN Joseph Bonaventure [Newfoundland]	5-01-45	169 Sqn
1323695	Sgt	THORLEY George Thomas	7-03-45	576 Sqn
1801024	F/S	THORN Ernest Stanley	8-02-45	83 Sqn
190589	P/O	THORNBER Jacob	7-03-45	578 Sqn
184358	F/O	THORNE Peter	21-02-45	153 Sqn
1324224	W/O	THORNE MiD Peter Selwyn Courtney	2-02-45	102 Sqn
2225156	Sgt	THORNLEY John	16-01-45	10 Sqn
116637	F/L	THORNTON Edward Ross	5-03-45	170 Sqn
1521062	Sgt	THORNTON William Christopher [Eire]	7-03-45	44 Sqn
2207095	Sgt	THORP Arthur	9-04-45	408 Sqn
1393293	F/S	THORPE Roland Henry Albert	10-04-45	170 Sqn
1604281	F/S	THURSTON Eric Edward	10-01-45	20 OTU
1896557	F/S	THURSTON Walter Alfred James	10-04-45	433 Sqn
184159	P/O	TILBY Edward George	12-01-45	617 Sqn
1853257	F/S	TILEY Donald Henry George	2-03-45	640 Sqn
2210904	Sgt	TILLEY Robert Edward	5-06-45	149 Sqn
1805475	Sgt	TIMMS Bernard Arthur John	13-12-45	26 OTU
546494	Sgt	TIMMS Douglas James Joseph	2-01-45	100 Sqn
168666	F/O	TIMMS John Eric	11-06-45	162 Sqn
466711	F/O	TIMPERLEY Eric	14-02-45	161 Sqn
2205513	Sgt	TINSLEY Norman	1-02-45	550 Sqn
1673062	F/S	TODD Richard	5-03-45	608 Sqn
1683242	F/S	TOES Geoffrey Chapman	9-02-45	138 Sqn
195231	P/O	TOGWELL William Albert	5-03-45	426 Sqn
1580478	F/S	TOMKINS Ernest William Sydney	17-01-45	10 Sqn
1053192	LAC	TOMLINSON Samuel	13-06-45	Graveley
2221581	Sgt	TOMLINSON Thomas	16-03-45	170 Sqn
63848	S/L	TONG DFC Twice MiD Ronald Frederick Leonard	10-01-45	128 Sqn

2221300	Sgt	TONGUE Leslie	28-01-45	424 Sqn
116056	F/L	TOOTAL John Stuart	24-02-45	462 Sqn
2220183	Sgt	TOOTELL Ronald Edgar	9-02-45	149 Sqn
1852943	Sgt	TOPHAM Vivian Claude	7-01-45	462 Sqn
1799465	Sgt	TORNEY Thomas	21-03-45	61 Sqn
191781	F/O	TOTTLE Peter	5-06-45	149 Sqn
123616	F/L	TOUGH Douglas Pollock	19-03-45	105 Sqn
195111	P/O	TOWELL Richard William	24-02-45	214 Sqn
1361335	W/O	TOWNS DFC John	28-01-45	218 Sqn
1816861	Sgt	TOWSON Leslie Bland	19-03-45	550 Sqn
196992	P/O	TOY John	14-03-45	101 Sqn
638898	Sgt	TRAFFORD Reuben Victor	23-01-45	153 Sqn
130716	F/L	TRAIL George	14-01-45	223 Sqn
1398770	F/S	TRAYLEN Gordon Robert	7-01-45	622 Sqn
1576216	F/S	TREADWELL William John	3-02-45	189 Sqn
3032284	Sgt	TREBBLE Richard James	30-10-45	1653 HCU
60800	F/L	TREBY MiD Thomas	24-03-45	139 Sqn
187451	P/O	TRESIDDER Stanley Albert William	15-02-45	78 Sqn
164331	F/O	TRICE Walter John	3-03-45	1651 HCU
169063	F/L	TRICKS DFM Herbert	14-01-45	11 OTU
1474794	F/S	TROMP William Henry	1-03-45	103 Sqn
1594186	Sgt	TROTT Ernest Cecil Matthew	7-03-45	12 Sqn
189197	P/O	TROTTER Arthur Charles	22-03-45	460 Sqn
1540203	F/S	TROWSDALE Lawrence	24-02-45	415 Sqn
1852712	Sgt	TUCKER Evan Albert Ernest	9-02-45	192 Sqn
3040778	Sgt	TUNSTALL John Tengate	7-01-45	550 Sqn
1533387	W/O	TURNBULL Geoffrey Edgar	7-04-45	103 Sqn
1594612	Sgt	TURNER George	14-02-45	103 Sqn
1813672	F/S	TURNER James Henry William	2-03-45	640 Sqn
160755	F/O	TURNER Leonard Carlisle	5-04-45	153 Sqn
1594283	F/S	TURNER Philip	2-02-45	619 Sqn
1409692	LAC	TURNER Ronald	16-05-45	Witchford
1815060	Sgt	TURNER Stanley	11-06-45	162 Sqn
1159069	F/S	TURNER William James Cruse	7-03-45	44 Sqn
1681108	F/S	TWIGG Leonard Eric	23-02-45	239 Sqn
1868384	Sgt	TWIN Ronald Harold	6-03-45	576 Sqn
1415838	W/O	TYLER Morris John Edward	5-01-45	102 Sqn
1607381	Sgt	TYRRELL Leslie Frederick	8-03-45	101 Sqn
1009395	Sgt	UNDERHILL Francis Walter	18-02-45	626 Sqn
150656	F/O	UNDERWOOD Hubert Gregory	7-03-45	61 Sqn
145864	F/O	UNDERWOOD DFC William Harry Thomas	15-03-45	582 Sqn
164722	F/L	USHER DFC Kenneth	5-03-45	635 Sqn
3050447	Sgt	USHER Thomas Wilfred Henry	9-02-45	214 Sqn
101470	F/L	VALE MiD Eric Stanley	27-03-45	692 Sqn
1555433	F/S	VALENTINE George Baird	3-04-45	625 Sqn
190755	F/L	VAN AMSTERDAM DFC Vliegerkruis Andre Anton Johannes [Holland]	27-03-45	139 Sqn
1894282	Sgt	VAN NOEY Bernard Peter	22-05-45	26 OTU
1132434	Sgt	VAUDREY Harold	3-03-45	1651 HCU
164720	F/L	VENNING DFC David Lotan	5-03-45	635 Sqn
1587088	F/S	VENTON Maxwell	4-03-45	467 Sqn
163864	F/O	VICKERY John Leslie	8-04-45	35 Sqn
1595297	F/S	VIDAMOUR Harold John [Channel Islands]	14-02-45	77 Sqn
169518	F/O	VINALL DFM Twice MiD James William	17-03-45	214 Sqn
1604859	F/S	VINCENT Roger John	10-01-45	20 OTU
1445012	Sgt	VINCENT Thomas Richard William	8-01-45	30 OTU
1604526	F/S	VINE Henry William	21-02-45	576 Sqn
3025347	Sgt	VOLLER Peter Hadrian	5-02-45	1669 HCU
1850003	Sgt	VOWLER Leonard Jack	21-03-45	223 Sqn
1593397	Sgt	WADE Clifton	8-01-45	30 OTU
179945	F/L	WADHAM DFC Barry Simpson Herridge	5-04-45	7 Sqn
1899394	Sgt	WAGER Donald	5-03-45	170 Sqn
1627794	Sgt	WAGER Sydney Derrick	17-03-45	153 Sqn
1415543	F/S	WAITE Wilfred Arthur	1-01-45	10 Sqn
1853724	Sgt	WAKEFIELD Frederick William	15-02-45	166 Sqn
188294	F/O	WAKELING Albert Harry	6-03-45	207 Sqn
1817320	Sgt	WALKER Arthur Hall	4-03-45	12 Sqn
576851	F/S	WALKER Cyril Ivan	22-04-45	49 Sqn
1876300	F/S	WALKER Ernest Arthur	9-04-45	50 Sqn
1852227	F/S	WALKER Frederick Joseph	6-01-45	10 Sqn
187958	P/O	WALKER DFC George William	5-01-45	420 Sqn
156104	F/O	WALKER Ian George	1-01-45	239 Sqn
2205787	Sgt	WALKER John Keith	8-01-45	166 Sqn
2209766	Sgt	WALKER Stanley Hubert	21-03-45	463 Sqn
1623780	Sgt	WALKER Thomas Ellwood	8-01-45	49 Sqn
1824013	Sgt	WALKER Walter	16-03-45	576 Sqn
1800217	F/S	WALL Frederick Albert	6-03-45	514 Sqn
1614026	F/S	WALL Guy Reginald	9-04-45	49 Sqn
339706	F/S	WALLACE James Stewart	13-02-45	West Raynham
1716464	F/S	WALLER Leslie Bernard	8-02-45	50 Sqn
154752	F/O	WALLER Walter Dennis	5-03-45	1658 HCU
189401	F/O	WALLEY Neil	18-11-45	50 Sqn
159851	F/O	WALLS Bertram James	2-04-45	1651 HCU
52309	F/L	WALSH Leslie Victor	4-01-45	150 Sqn
1866667	F/S	WALTER William	12-01-45	617 Sqn
159465	F/O	WALTERS Raymond Leslie	11-07-45	10 OTU
1578741	F/S	WALTON Geoffrey	15-01-45	1659 HCU
1819769	Sgt	WALTON Stanley Charles	10-04-45	630 Sqn
1853234	Sgt	WARBEY Arthur Frank	4-03-45	1654 HCU
162829	F/L	WARD Edwin	19-03-45	77 Sqn
1866600	Sgt	WARD Frederick William	5-03-45	1662 HCU
1596140	Sgt	WARD Harold Edward	14-02-45	576 Sqn
1567245	F/S	WARD Walter Graham	30-04-45	428 Sqn
1475510	LAC	WARDLE Wilfred Herbert	5-06-45	149 Sqn
1895579	Sgt	WARES Alastair James Dallas	8-03-45	635 Sqn
1883315	Sgt	WARMAN Herbert Albert	5-03-45	1662 HCU
1622428	F/S	WARNE Ronald	4-03-45	1651 HCU
1399495	F/S	WARR William Barclay	3-02-45	514 Sqn
165534	F/O	WARREN Christopher Paul Wyeth	8-04-45	9 Sqn
162041	F/O	WARREN George Clarence	16-03-45	626 Sqn
1803653	F/S	WARRINGTON Peter John	9-04-45	49 Sqn
154741	F/O	WARWICK Reginald	2-01-45	100 Sqn
1419043	F/S	WATERS Cyril John	2-03-45	57 Sqn
'222048'	Sgt	WATERS Jack	19-02-45	1669 HCU
1293879	W/O	WATERSON Leonard Robert	13-12-45	26 OTU
1837061	Sgt	WATKINS Cyril Harry	14-03-45	207 Sqn
1522119	Sgt	WATKINS Harold Lionel	17-01-45	10 Sqn
152875	F/O	WATKINS Joseph Ridley	1-01-45	239 Sqn
3010677	Sgt	WATKINS Ronald Leslie	5-01-45	158 Sqn
1341027	Sgt	WATSON Andrew Maitland	18-02-45	626 Sqn
1596995	Sgt	WATSON Dennis Sydney	15-02-45	77 Sqn
159930	F/O	WATSON DFM Frank Taylor	2-01-45	105 Sqn
110889	S/L	WATSON DFC Fred	6-03-45	35 Sqn
169863	P/O	WATSON DFM Frederick John	5-03-45	161 Sqn
134317	W/C	WATSON DFM George	21-02-45	161 Sqn
1555045	F/S	WATSON Harold Munro	21-02-45	7 Sqn
174282	F/O	WATSON James	16-04-45	617 Sqn
1566050	F/S	WATSON James Hendry	7-01-45	635 Sqn
1430420	F/S	WATSON Neville	21-02-45	578 Sqn
1595208	Sgt	WATSON William John	6-03-45	514 Sqn
623703	W/O	WATSON William Philip Jeffery [New Zealand]	19-04-45	44 Sqn
1372528	F/S	WATT Christopher James Taggart	22-02-45	578 Sqn
1567734	F/S	WATT James	2-02-45	44 Sqn
1579768	F/S	WATT Robert	14-01-45	9 Sqn
155790	F/L	WATT William Wallace	23-02-45	101 Sqn
1892463	Sgt	WATTS Cyril William	2-03-45	57 Sqn
1810517	Sgt	WATTS George Stanley	22-05-45	26 OTU
186920	P/O	WAY DFC Cyril William	16-01-45	420 Sqn
1302052	Sgt	WAY William 'Billy'	25-06-45	199 Sqn
1624124	F/S	WEAVER Donald George	21-02-45	578 Sqn

Service No	Rank	Name	Date	Unit
159140	F/O	WEBB Donnart George	1-03-45	153 Sqn
1187233	F/S	WEBB Douglas William	9-02-45	192 Sqn
1816523	Sgt	WEBB Ernest William	14-02-45	576 Sqn
1813422	Sgt	WEBB George Leonard	2-02-45	9 Sqn
1034331	F/S	WEBB John	17-02-45	51 Sqn
2235550	Sgt	WEBB Sidney James	3-03-45	1651 HCU
2221373	F/S	WEBBER John	18-02-45	626 Sqn
1032389	F/S	WEBLEY William Cecil	3-02-45	186 Sqn
1685818	Sgt	WEBSTER Francis William	23-02-45	138 Sqn
173076	F/O	WEBSTER Robert Christie	8-04-45	35 Sqn
1672314	F/S	WEBSTER William Forrester	1-03-45	166 Sqn
184374	P/O	WEIGHT Christopher Joseph	4-01-45	103 Sqn
1622251	F/S	WEIGHTMAN William Edmund	6-09-45	576 Sqn
2218761	Sgt	WEIR Alex Philip	31-03-45	635 Sqn
155190	F/O	WELLER DFC Reginald Martin	8-03-45	35 Sqn
1389461	F/S	WELLINGTON Raymond	9-02-45	186 Sqn
1805639	F/S	WELLS Raymond Cecil Stanley	15-03-45	227 Sqn
133927	F/L	WELLSTEAD DFC DFM Leo Charles Raymond	1-01-45	128 Sqn
1601851	F/S	WELLSTEAD Sidney Albert	21-02-45	578 Sqn
1837071	Sgt	WELSH Charles Gallagher	14-03-45	462 Sqn
1597250	Sgt	WELSH Stanley	14-01-45	626 Sqn
1606174	Sgt	WELSH Walter Edward	4-03-45	466 Sqn
1894709	Sgt	WENHAM John Arthur	4-01-45	11 OTU
2205575	Sgt	WERRILL Roy	17-01-45	514 Sqn
1474264	F/S	WEST Arnold	22-03-45	207 Sqn
1247383	Sgt	WEST Edward Thomas	11-03-45	153 Sqn
195545	P/O	WEST MiD Robert William	21-03-45	75 Sqn
1398165	F/S	WESTACOTT Geoffrey Ernest Richard	9-04-45	50 Sqn
1806456	Sgt	WESTOBY Trevor John Hunter	12-04-45	157 Sqn
1579909	F/O	WESTON DFC David Walter	21-02-45	101 Sqn
1404936	Sgt	WHAITES Henry Charles	14-04-45	186 Sqn
1587289	F/S	WHALLEY George Benjamin	14-04-45	186 Sqn
2213579	F/S	WHEADON Sydney John	19-04-45	425 Sqn
2210765	Sgt	WHELDON John Neville	2-01-45	19 OTU
1473592	F/S	WHITAMS Anthony Ephraim	8-02-45	50 Sqn
178540	F/O	WHITBREAD William Ellis Leslie	17-01-45	10 Sqn
1167224	Sgt	WHITE Frederick Thomas	14-01-45	12 Sqn
1852873	Sgt	WHITE Graham Howard	22-03-45	227 Sqn
1590596	F/S	WHITE Guy Anthony	22-03-45	44 Sqn
175283	F/O	WHITE Kenneth	3-10-45	1668 HCU
1593734	F/S	WHITE Kenneth	8-03-45	189 Sqn
1166191	W/O	WHITE Maurice Charles	15-03-45	214 Sqn
1654216	Sgt	WHITEFOOT Derrick	2-03-45	57 Sqn
1511705	F/S	WHITEHEAD Wilfrid	17-03-45	103 Sqn
2201639	F/S	WHITEHOUSE Donald Stuart	8-03-45	57 Sqn
1801096	F/S	WHITEING Albert Edward	19-03-45	103 Sqn
1777435	Sgt	WHITELAW James Dixon	5-04-45	166 Sqn
1625037	Sgt	WHITELEY Harry	2-02-45	50 Sqn
2209367	Sgt	WHITFIELD Bernard	14-02-45	640 Sqn
646741	W/O	WHITFIELD Frederick	5-03-45	102 Sqn
1430889	F/S	WHITMORE John Rigby	5-01-45	51 Sqn
2201893	Sgt	WHITTAKER Edwin Eric	21-02-45	223 Sqn
1805467	Sgt	WHITTENBURY John	18-04-45	640 Sqn
178853	F/O	WHITTER DFM James	15-01-45	578 Sqn
1595362	F/S	WHYBROW Renison	6-01-45	635 Sqn
1881251	Sgt	WHYLES Horace Edwin	21-02-45	10 Sqn
53481	F/L	WHYMARK DSO DFC John Percy	4-10-45	103 Sqn
1399865	Sgt	WHYTE Arthur Hugh [Canada]	8-03-45	103 Sqn
1571971	Sgt	WHYTE John Chaplin	3-02-45	189 Sqn
1866506	Sgt	WICKS William Henry	14-02-45	153 Sqn
188324	P/O	WIDDICOMBE George Edward	4-01-45	103 Sqn
1399743	F/S	WIDDOWS Desmond Henry	1-02-45	101 Sqn
1881231	F/S	WIDDOWSON Alan Charles	21-03-45	158 Sqn
185673	P/O	WIGGINS Alexander Anderson	7-01-45	635 Sqn
1877431	Sgt	WIGGINS Ronald Rodney	8-02-45	49 Sqn
1387434	F/S	WIGHT Ronald Willi	16-03-45	170 Sqn
179769	F/O	WIGLEY DFC Henry Thomas	5-03-45	161 Sqn
591822	F/S	WILCOX Thomas Frederick	17-01-45	514 Sqn
1145716	LAC	WILD Robert Henry	29-03-45	35 Sqn
195935	F/O	WILDMAN Stanley David	14-06-45	218 Sqn
1899093	Sgt	WILKIE Eric Charles	17-03-45	166 Sqn
1801112	F/S	WILKINS Leonard Richard	17-01-45	15 Sqn
1454207	F/S	WILKINS Ronald Ernest	9-04-45	49 Sqn
1684373	F/S	WILKINSON Edward Wareham	22-03-45	227 Sqn
1596299	Sgt	WILKINSON George	2-03-45	207 Sqn
910004	F/S	WILKINSON John Ernest	9-04-45	49 Sqn
149065	F/O	WILKINSON Robert	17-03-45	103 Sqn
3020028	Sgt	WILKINSON William Middlemiss	23-02-45	192 Sqn
2221374	Sgt	WILLER Gordon Oliver	15-03-45	582 Sqn
2220828	Sgt	WILLERTON George Ronald	23-04-45	218 Sqn
1323497	F/S	WILLIAMS David Hamilton	5-01-45	15 Sqn
151596	F/L	WILLIAMS DFC Derek Gordon	2-01-45	139 Sqn
1591420	Sgt	WILLIAMS Donald	15-02-45	625 Sqn
924670	F/S	WILLIAMS Douglas Percy	6-05-45	169 Sqn
3010661	Sgt	WILLIAMS Griffith	14-03-45	51 Sqn
1416530	F/S	WILLIAMS DFM Gwilym	5-03-45	635 Sqn
2218948	Sgt	WILLIAMS Gwynne	7-01-45	103 Sqn
60770	F/L	WILLIAMS Henry Arthur Wellington	2-02-45	90 Sqn
1613184	F/S	WILLIAMS Henry Ronald	24-04-45	218 Sqn
2210913	F/S	WILLIAMS Idris	15-02-45	78 Sqn
1141627	F/S	WILLIAMS James William	16-03-45	626 Sqn
1605235	Sgt	WILLIAMS John Peter	31-03-45	156 Sqn
1836168	Sgt	WILLIAMS John Rodd	24-03-45	158 Sqn
1591275	F/S	WILLIAMS John Walter	12-01-45	9 Sqn
553298	Sgt	WILLIAMS Leo	15-03-45	153 Sqn
1897783	Sgt	WILLIAMS Leslie Alexander	5-01-45	61 Sqn
1852734	Sgt	WILLIAMS Owen Oliver	3-10-45	1668 HCU
1322617	F/S	WILLIAMS Peter Charles	19-03-45	515 Sqn
2212840	Sgt	WILLIAMS Robert John	15-01-45	419 Sqn
1499900	Sgt	WILLIAMS Stanley	11-07-45	10 OTU
164241	F/O	WILLIAMS Vincent Rees Macdonald	15-04-45	138 Sqn
187109	P/O	WILLIAMS William John Raymond	15-01-45	578 Sqn
1656359	Sgt	WILLICOMBE Haydn Raymond	3-01-45	622 Sqn
171573	F/O	WILLIS Geoffrey Lionel	30-07-45	166 Sqn
1604003	F/S	WILLIS Leslie Robert	6-04-45	170 Sqn
1053228	F/S	WILLIS Sydney	1-02-45	166 Sqn
1593340	F/S	WILSON Douglas	3-05-45	199 Sqn
3041268	Sgt	WILSON Eric	17-04-45	156 Sqn
1806521	Sgt	WILSON Eric Gordon	16-03-45	625 Sqn
1081717	LAC	WILSON Henry George	24-02-45	61 Sqn
1822188	Sgt	WILSON James	21-02-45	408 Sqn
1803275	Sgt	WILSON John	16-01-45	102 Sqn
1592933	Sgt	WILSON John Alexander	1-02-45	100 Sqn
1499366	F/S	WILSON John Kevin	8-02-45	57 Sqn
1894557	Sgt	WILSON Ray Venables Snell	6-01-45	51 Sqn
1597046	Sgt	WILSON Robert	13-03-45	153 Sqn
1558504	F/S	WILSON Robert MacLennan	30-03-45	635 Sqn
1796601	Sgt	WILSON William John	2-02-45	44 Sqn
1818452	Sgt	WINCH Dennis	12-01-45	9 Sqn
64893	F/L	WINDER Arthur Joseph	5-04-45	153 Sqn
53989	F/O	WINDER Kenneth William	22-01-45	153 Sqn
1601854	F/S	WINDUS Edward	17-04-45	462 Sqn
545011	W/O	WINGROVE Ralph Charles	8-04-45	1653 HCU
1821317	Sgt	WINNING Hector	21-02-45	207 Sqn
116985	F/L	WINNING Theodore Norman Gerald	17-02-45	51 Sqn
1868423	Sgt	WINSTANLEY Roger Francis	3-02-45	460 Sqn
1897367	Sgt	WINSTONE Randolph Edward Alexander	23-02-45	101 Sqn
2235862	Sgt	WISEMAN Peter Charles	21-03-45	619 Sqn
147583	S/L	WISHART DSO DFC* William Geoffrey	21-02-45	83 Sqn
1486959	Sgt	WITHRINGTON Richard Percival	21-05-45	27 OTU
161762	F/O	WITT Arthur Frederick	26-01-45	85 Sqn

Service No	Rank	Name	Date	Unit
102582	F/L	WIX DFC Douglas Louis	6-04-45	26 OTU
190918	P/O	WOFFENDEN Harry	16-03-45	12 Sqn
605581	Sgt	WONG Crafton Dudley [Jamaica]	4-01-45	10 OTU
154602	F/O	WOOD Arthur	14-02-45	77 Sqn
1048622	F/S	WOOD Dennis	14-02-45	186 Sqn
1812267	Sgt	WOOD Donald Frederick	16-03-45	576 Sqn
1107638	F/S	WOOD Frank	22-04-45	153 Sqn
146077	F/O	WOOD George Thomas	5-04-45	12 Sqn
115716	F/L	WOOD Henry [Rhodesia]	15-01-45	85 Sqn
1604157	F/S	WOOD James Raymond	29-01-45	156 Sqn
946040	Sgt	WOODARDS Harold	23-03-45	101 Sqn
2208205	Sgt	WOODBURN Kenneth	8-03-45	195 Sqn
1323440	F/S	WOODCHERRY John Frederick	5-04-45	12 Sqn
52114	F/L	WOODGER Frank Richard	24-02-45	214 Sqn
1625419	Sgt	WOODHEAD Colin	10-02-45	1667 HCU
160244	P/O	WOODHOUSE Geoffrey Clayton Rance	10-04-45	44 Sqn
907425	F/S	WOODHOUSE James	22-02-45	50 Sqn
1881002	Sgt	WOODS Brian Frederick	9-02-45	192 Sqn
1398131	Sgt	WOODS Charles William	8-01-45	30 OTU
1323707	Sgt	WOODS Leslie Raymond	11-01-45	20 OTU
186846	P/O	WOOLSTENHULME Harold	31-03-45	156 Sqn
160210	F/O	WORRALL Charles	2-02-45	44 Sqn
165703	F/O	WOTHERSPOON John	10-04-45	170 Sqn
3050042	Sgt	WRIGHT Derek Joseph	3-09-45	26 OTU
1897971	Sgt	WRIGHT Frank	4-04-45	49 Sqn
1398277	Sgt	WRIGHT Frank Eric	15-02-45	189 Sqn
178378	F/O	WRIGHT Graham Douglas	14-01-45	1654 HCU
195518	F/O	WRIGHT Harry	7-02-45	77 Sqn
1623547	F/S	WRIGHT Jack Adams	6-03-45	103 Sqn
1581990	Sgt	WRIGHT John Selby	8-01-45	30 OTU
176661	F/O	WRIGHT Ronald William	13-07-45	97 Sqn
1536328	F/S	WYATT John	7-03-45	171 Sqn
1607018	F/S	WYATT Paul Cochrane	5-06-45	149 Sqn
1322384	F/S	WYNN Ronald	21-02-45	223 Sqn
1892537	F/S	YANAL Peter Yoshihide	7-03-45	424 Sqn
1456112	F/S	YATES Edward Peter	15-02-45	78 Sqn
2221696	Sgt	YEARSLEY John Hubert	5-01-45	51 Sqn
196095	P/O	YEOMAN Ernest Yule	24-03-45	158 Sqn
1892052	F/S	YEOMANS William G.	23-03-45	101 Sqn
168774	F/O	YEULETT George Victor Rice	16-01-45	158 Sqn
163626	F/O	YOUNG Alexander Macdonald	14-01-45	50 Sqn
1284848	W/O	YOUNG Douglas Alexander Taylor	15-04-45	169 Sqn
1790121	Sgt	YOUNG John	6-03-45	460 Sqn
1591823	Sgt	YOUNG Leon	9-02-45	630 Sqn
164438	F/O	YOUNG Peter Newman	3-03-45	1651 HCU
185679	F/O	YOUNG Roland Robert John	14-02-45	576 Sqn
154575	F/O	YOUNG William	5-04-45	626 Sqn
163591	F/O	YOUNG William	5-01-45	15 Sqn
1615004	F/S	YOUNGMAN Peter William	8-10-45	166 Sqn
184182	F/O	YTHIER Pierre Aime Gerard [Mauritius]	23-02-45	150 Sqn

Note

Amongst the 42 prisoners of war who were killed, or died from their wounds, when their column was straffed by Allied fighters near the village of Gresse (see Volume 6 and appendix 10 for further details of this tragedy) was W/O William Philip Jeffery Watson whom Errol Martyn notes as being born in England, emigrated with his parents to New Zealand in 1926 and later joined the Royal New Zealand Artillery before returning to the United Kingdom in 1938, to join the regular air force. He had been a prisoner of war since the 22nd of April, 1940, after being shot down while flying with 44 Squadron (see Volume 1, page 40). Appendix 3 will show the names of airmen, from Bomber Command, who died while in captivity.

The circumstances in which the seven airmen with 'Fulbeck' given as their unit died are described on page 168 of Volume 8.

ROYAL AUSTRALIAN AIR FORCE personnel

Service No	Rank	Name	Date	Unit
428516	F/S	ALLAMBY Walter Vernon Wilfred	3-01-45	467 Sqn
431483	F/S	ALLEN Keith Stanley Franz	5-01-45	29 OTU
428596	W/O	ARNEY Harold James	21-03-45	97 Sqn
434611	F/S	ARNOLD Vincent James	16-03-45	12 Sqn
421143	F/O	ASTILL Alan Edwin [New Zealand]	14-01-45	462 Sqn
439556	F/S	ATKINSON Bruce Albert	17-01-45	29 OTU
433081	F/S	AYRE George Francis	15-01-45	692 Sqn
62186	F/O	BACON Lindsay Page	20-03-45	7 Sqn
423037	F/S	BACON Sydney Raymond	4-04-45	186 Sqn
417779	W/O	BAGSHAW Graham Morris	15-04-45	138 Sqn
424578	P/O	BAILEY Robert Owen	1-02-45	463 Sqn
417440	W/O	BAINSFATHER Ralph McPherson	7-03-45	49 Sqn
427182	F/O	BALL Alfred Desmond John	10-04-45	462 Sqn
425917	F/S	BARBELER Gerard Sydney	16-03-45	12 Sqn
9242	F/S	BARBER Raymond Franklin Lindsay	16-03-45	12 Sqn
437207	F/S	BARNDEN Leo Ronald	14-01-45	460 Sqn
417794	F/S	BARNETT Ross Frederick	6-03-45	582 Sqn
435012	F/S	BARRETT Allen Bernard	2-02-45	463 Sqn
428116	F/S	BARRETT Layton Challander	6-02-45	1656 HCU
422922	F/O	BARRETT Lindon Frederick Beves	16-01-45	466 Sqn
437109	F/O	BARROW Bruce Ernest	14-03-45	106 Sqn
424283	W/O	BATEUP John Edwin	22-01-45	153 Sqn
409653	F/O	BAUDINETTE Ivan Sydney	5-03-45	460 Sqn
429910	F/O	BAULDERSTONE Thomas Henry	9-04-45	463 Sqn
432092	F/S	BAYLEY Lindsay Arthur	8-04-45	9 Sqn
430920	F/S	BEAN Frederick Jack	2-02-45	467 Sqn
408434	F/O	BECK DFC James Arthur Gordon	4-04-45	186 Sqn
427427	F/O	BEESON John Leslie	7-02-45	158 Sqn
436327	F/O	BENNETT Richard Stewart	21-03-45	463 Sqn
432937	F/S	BENNETT Wilfred Stuart	5-04-45	1667 HCU
17354	F/O	BERRIMAN Vincent Gerald	9-04-45	50 Sqn
431194	F/S	BINDER Kenneth William	16-03-45	460 Sqn
431012	F/S	BIRD Norman Brian	3-02-45	460 Sqn
427892	F/O	BIRT Peter Norham	29-01-45	460 Sqn
424956	F/S	BOUTCHER William Edward	14-01-45	50 Sqn
435772	F/S	BOWMAN Anthony Ellis	9-04-45	630 Sqn
419026	F/L	BOYD Robert Douglas	1-02-45	101 Sqn
435276	F/S	BRADDOCK Bryant	21-02-45	460 Sqn
436381	F/S	BRADY John	1-02-45	100 Sqn
416165	F/O	BROOK DFC Kenneth Richard	4-03-45	1651 HCU
437490	F/O	BROWN Gordon Scott	3-02-45	460 Sqn
428620	F/S	BROWN Kenneth Thomas	2-03-45	625 Sqn
437400	F/O	BROWN Sidney Arthur	5-01-45	463 Sqn
430436	P/O	BROWNE Geoffrey Seymour	19-03-45	460 Sqn
423075	F/S	BROWNE Maxwell	5-01-45	189 Sqn
431195	F/S	BRUCKNER Maxwell Bright	8-01-45	467 Sqn
433799	F/S	BRUNSKILL Anthony George Stewart	8-04-45	21 OTU
418625	F/L	BRYANT John Derrick	12-03-45	460 Sqn
428753	P/O	BUCKMAN Patrick John	4-03-45	227 Sqn
430011	F/S	BULL Lawrence Joseph	21-03-45	97 Sqn
422402	P/O	BURCHER William Edward	7-01-45	103 Sqn
423053	P/O	BURGESS George Leonard	12-03-45	460 Sqn
426303	F/L	BURKE Ernest Patrick	16-01-45	166 Sqn
439540	F/S	BURTON Herbert Eric	9-04-45	630 Sqn
436142	F/S	BUTT Warren Henry	14-01-45	106 Sqn
421157	F/L	BUTTON Lyle Ewart	2-02-45	149 Sqn
428103	F/S	CAHILL Clyde McCartney	4-03-45	467 Sqn
433892	F/S	CALLAGHAN William Desmond	7-03-45	170 Sqn
69541	F/O	CALLAS Manoel	13-03-45	23 Sqn
434868	F/O	CAMERON Charles Jackson	3-03-45	467 Sqn
425118	F/L	CAMERON Gordon Oliver	8-02-45	83 Sqn
409507	W/O	CAMERON Royston Richard	22-03-45	207 Sqn
429070	F/O	CAMPBELL Herbert Thomas	21-02-45	460 Sqn
427063	P/O	CAMPBELL Victor Robert	21-03-45	57 Sqn
427436	F/S	CANN Leonard William	5-01-45	29 OTU

Number	Rank	Name	Date	Sqn
424964	W/O	CANTWELL Richard Power	15-03-45	582 Sqn
432936	F/S	CARLON Patrick John Paul	24-02-45	462 Sqn
410450	P/O	CARTER James Marshall	16-01-45	102 Sqn
435334	F/S	CARTER Phillip John	2-02-45	467 Sqn
432482	F/S	CASEY Allan James	14-01-45	128 Sqn
437495	F/O	CASSIDY Clyde Allen	5-01-45	106 Sqn
434240	W/O	CASTOR Ernest John	5-04-45	1667 HCU
417049	F/L	CAWTHORNE DFC Philip Edward	4-04-45	635 Sqn
431488	F/S	CHALMERS Murray Alexander	21-05-45	100 Sqn
432755	F/S	CHEATLE Raey Hilton	8-02-45	97 Sqn
437046	F/S	CHENOWETH Eric	31-03-45	635 Sqn
435185	F/S	CLARK Kevin George	31-03-45	635 Sqn
427294	F/L	CLARKE DFC Robert Mayo	7-01-45	635 Sqn
430159	F/S	CLARKE Trevor Turner	6-03-45	460 Sqn
434620	F/O	CLEGG Bernard Maxwell	21-02-45	460 Sqn
5870	F/O	COBERN Charles Alan	20-03-45	57 Sqn
429178	F/S	COLEMAN Maxwell John	13-02-45	463 Sqn
419981	W/O	COLLINS Laurence	16-01-45	101 Sqn
432486	F/S	CONLEY Graham Richard	2-03-45	622 Sqn
413154	F/L	CONN DFC Francis Leslie	1-02-45	100 Sqn
418227	F/O	COOK Kenneth Alan	14-01-45	9 Sqn
426544	W/O	COSSART James Bowes	14-03-45	106 Sqn
430103	F/S	COSTER John Stewart	21-03-45	97 Sqn
418813	F/L	COTTMAN John Dennis	21-03-45	97 Sqn
416549	F/O	CRAIG DFC William Gordon	8-04-45	BCIS
421576	F/O	CRISFORD Raymond Gavin	15-03-45	157 Sqn
419521	F/O	CRONE John Henry	17-01-45	15 Sqn
437401	F/S	CROSS Ronald Frank	2-02-45	467 Sqn
436545	F/S	CRYER Alan	4-03-45	12 Sqn
433250	F/S	CUNNINGHAM William Alexander	2-02-45	460 Sqn
432953	P/O	CURTIN Leo Patrick	23-02-45	103 Sqn
437403	F/S	DAVEY Robert Eric	4-03-45	460 Sqn
400365	F/L	DAVIES Gordon Alwood Tregaskis	29-05-45	460 Sqn
437781	F/S	DAVIS George Edward	4-03-45	12 Sqn
431092	F/S	DAY John Alfred	28-03-45	627 Sqn
432545	F/S	DELANEY Colin	31-03-45	635 Sqn
432360	W/O	DENT Ian Wilshire	25-06-45	199 Sqn
432404	F/S	DEVALL Bruce Thomas	17-01-45	29 OTU
423449	P/O	de VIS Selwyn George	19-03-45	77 Sqn
437120	F/S	DE GARIS William Sowden	5-03-45	207 Sqn
425834	W/O	DICKSON Andrew Stanley	4-04-45	153 Sqn
428968	F/S	DIXON Gregory Wills	4-03-45	466 Sqn
430736	F/S	DOCKERY Graeme Mark	10-02-45	460 Sqn
423676	F/O	DONALD James Richard	6-01-45	635 Sqn
434967	F/S	DONALD John Neal	5-04-45	1652 HCU
403564	W/C	DOUGLAS DFC AFC John Keith	8-02-45	467 Sqn
434453	F/O	DOWNES Thomas Neville	2-03-45	625 Sqn
418648	F/O	DOWNING Jeffrey John	10-02-45	460 Sqn
424391	F/S	DUNBAR Geoffrey James	3-01-45	467 Sqn
13488	F/S	DUNCAN William Francis	24-02-45	462 Sqn
419166	F/O	DUNLOP Norman Kenneth	7-01-45	170 Sqn
429652	F/O	DUNN Victor	3-02-45	460 Sqn
422148	F/L	DUNNE DFC John Joseph	14-02-45	9 Sqn
432498	F/S	EASTON Donald Murray	21-03-45	61 Sqn
430960	F/S	EATON Robert James	2-03-45	PFNTU
424717	F/S	EGGINS Robert Bruce	4-03-45	467 Sqn
427234	F/S	ELLIOT Burton Hampton	2-02-45	467 Sqn
432217	F/S	ELLIOTT Osric Brownrigg	3-03-45	463 Sqn
426221	F/O	ELY Vivian Clive	24-02-45	462 Sqn
430484	F/S	EMONSON Richard	3-01-45	467 Sqn
417354	F/O	ESSEX Adrian West	19-03-45	103 Sqn
427898	F/O	EVANS David Henry Robert	6-02-45	1653 HCU
419168	F/O	EVANS Harold Thomas	5-04-45	7 Sqn
436113	F/S	EVANS Neil Vernon	10-04-45	462 Sqn
19183	F/S	EVANS Thomas	5-04-45	1667 HCU
427311	F/S	EVERATT Frank Edgar	2-02-45	467 Sqn
434454	P/O	EVERETT Norman Wade	2-02-45	460 Sqn
419988	F/O	FAIRBAIRN DFC Charles Ridley	1-02-45	50 Sqn
417951	F/S	FARREN Frederick Stanley	7-03-45	61 Sqn
427079	F/O	FELGATE DFC Ian Lindsay	16-01-45	12 Sqn
429281	F/O	FERNLEY-STOTT Norman Charles	13-02-45	463 Sqn
425630	F/S	FINCHAM Charles Leslie	5-01-45	463 Sqn
429454	F/O	FISCHER Arthur Benjamin	4-04-45	49 Sqn
424293	F/O	FITZHARDINGE Allen Berkeley	1-02-45	50 Sqn
410475	P/O	FITZHENRY Stanley Herbert	2-01-45	405 Sqn
420554	F/O	FLETCHER Alan Noel	23-02-45	103 Sqn
428679	F/O	FLOCKHART Colin Kelvin	7-01-45	619 Sqn
434629	F/S	FOGARTY Kevin Gregory	15-02-45	630 Sqn
414219	W/C	FORBES DSO DFC William Alexander	21-02-45	463 Sqn
432779	F/S	FORD Clarence Frederick	5-04-45	1652 HCU
421587	F/O	FORREST MiD Russell Richard Napier	8-04-45	460 Sqn
430653	F/S	FORRESTER William	9-04-45	630 Sqn
434183	F/S	FOSTER Cecil Reginald Henry	17-04-45	462 Sqn
442340	F/S	FOWLER George Swan Murray	9-02-45	214 Sqn
29904	F/S	FOY Walter William	2-03-45	625 Sqn
417704	F/S	FRANCIS Eoin Samuel	6-01-45	622 Sqn
409532	F/O	FRANK Murray	10-04-45	462 Sqn
427782	W/O	FRANKLIN Harold Kendall	18-04-45	640 Sqn
424752	F/S	FRENCH Richard York	10-02-45	138 Sqn
428286	F/S	FROST William Gordon	21-02-45	576 Sqn
421198	W/O	FULLER Sydney Robert	14-01-45	462 Sqn
434180	F/S	GERRARD John Michael	2-03-45	460 Sqn
415639	F/O	GIBBERD DFC James Ernest	25-02-45	1660 HCU
417360	W/O	GILL Robert Douglas	18-02-45	626 Sqn
439630	F/S	GILLESPIE Anthony Edward	8-03-45	163 Sqn
430372	F/S	GLOURY John Danckert	8-01-45	467 Sqn
405307	W/O	GORDON Henry Vincent	2-03-45	460 Sqn
433522	F/S	GOULD Francis Edwin	21-02-45	463 Sqn
436496	F/S	GRAEBNER Everard Charles	8-04-45	21 OTU
431562	F/S	GRANT Llewellyn William	19-03-45	460 Sqn
417746	F/O	GRAY Dean	5-01-45	619 Sqn
434588	P/O	GRAYSON James Edward	5-04-45	1667 HCU
414674	F/L	GREENFIELD DFC Albert Paulton	9-04-45	61 Sqn
424584	P/O	GREENWOOD Bruce Frederick	22-03-45	51 Sqn
435168	F/S	GRICE John William	1-03-45	103 Sqn
435186	F/S	GRIFFIN James Noel	24-03-45	150 Sqn
417578	F/O	GRIVELL Robert Garfield	1-01-45	218 Sqn
409694	F/L	HALKYARD DFC Ralph Callister	5-04-45	7 Sqn
53477	Sgt	HALL Lionel Leslie	6-03-45	10 Sqn
425647	W/O	HALL Norman Joseph	24-02-45	462 Sqn
427322	P/O	HALLIDAY George Alan	9-04-45	466 Sqn
25661	F/S	HAMILTON John William	15-04-45	1667 HCU
433507	F/S	HAMILTON Reginald William	14-01-45	460 Sqn
429799	F/S	HARDY Ronald	3-02-45	514 Sqn
12694	W/O	HARRISON Charles Henry	8-04-45	21 OTU
428697	F/O	HART Clifford Seymour	24-02-45	103 Sqn
429458	P/O	HART Rochester Warren Lee	16-01-45	101 Sqn
429952	F/S	HAYES Douglas Lionel	5-04-45	1667 HCU
409303	F/O	HEDLEY Vernon James	16-03-45	460 Sqn
409918	F/L	HEITMANN Alan Walter	15-01-45	128 Sqn
423730	W/O	HEMSWORTH Ellis Wilby	6-03-45	582 Sqn
434787	F/S	HENDREN Keith Robert	1-02-45	101 Sqn
410980	P/O	HENDY Geoffrey Kenneth	7-01-45	635 Sqn
419001	F/O	HERING John Hubert	24-02-45	462 Sqn
29468	F/S	HESKETH Harold Thomas	8-02-45	619 Sqn
434527	F/S	HILL James William	9-04-45	463 Sqn
437854	F/S	HODGE Charles John	5-04-45	103 Sqn
414031	F/O	HOLE Lincoln	5-04-45	103 Sqn
418276	F/O	HOLLAWAY Kenneth George	18-02-45	626 Sqn
429054	F/L	HOLMES Jeffrey Howard	2-03-45	460 Sqn
405792	S/L	HOLMES DFC John Cecil	6-03-45	460 Sqn
429960	F/S	HORSTMANN Ronald Leslie	4-03-45	12 Sqn
419044	F/L	HOWELLS DFC Francis John	3-03-45	463 Sqn
435918	F/S	HOWLETT Fredrick James	9-04-45	630 Sqn
408440	F/O	HUDSPETH Donald George	5-03-45	460 Sqn
433107	F/S	HUGHES John Childe	5-04-45	1652 HCU

Service No	Rank	Name	Date	Squadron
409708	F/S	HULME William Henry	24-03-45	158 Sqn
410895	P/O	HUTCHESON Harold Joseph	7-01-45	103 Sqn
428774	W/O	HUTCHINGS Kelvin	14-01-45	460 Sqn
429570	W/O	HYDE James	16-03-45	12 Sqn
432191	F/O	INKSTER James Magnus	2-02-45	467 Sqn
432517	F/S	INNES Auburn Clyde	8-03-45	189 Sqn
428714	F/S	IRVING Colin Howe	16-03-45	12 Sqn
433727	F/S	ISAAC Mervyn George	14-01-45	462 Sqn
424866	F/S	ISLES James Love	16-03-45	467 Sqn
417195	F/O	JACKSON Frank Martin	11-04-45	619 Sqn
429965	F/O	JAMES William Charles	14-02-45	186 Sqn
415988	P/O	JARDINE Cyrus	21-03-45	57 Sqn
430123	F/S	JEFFREY Sidney Alexander	5-04-45	103 Sqn
17332	F/L	JENYNS Robert Lance	24-04-45	218 Sqn
428009	F/O	JETSON Ernest Thomas	7-03-45	44 Sqn
433171	P/O	JOHNSON Carl Edwin	14-07-45	460 Sqn
425806	W/O	JOHNSON John	2-02-45	463 Sqn
437965	F/S	JOHNSON Roger Robert	4-03-45	466 Sqn
427098	F/O	JOHNSTON James Malcolmson	4-03-45	227 Sqn
429286	W/O	JUDD William Bruce	21-03-45	207 Sqn
435564	F/S	JURD Milton Keith	16-03-45	460 Sqn
436038	F/S	KEAST Dixon Ross	5-02-45	1654 HCU
430174	F/S	KEE Kevin Anthony	24-03-45	150 Sqn
415429	F/O	KEHOE Desmond Noel	24-02-45	462 Sqn
426438	F/O	KELLY William Desmond	2-02-45	189 Sqn
423754	F/S	KEMP Francis Henry Ross	5-01-45	90 Sqn
434528	F/S	KERRIGAN Michael John	22-03-45	9 Sqn
421913	P/O	KILLEN John Gordon Treatt	3-02-45	100 Sqn
433109	F/S	KILPATRICK George	24-04-45	218 Sqn
437422	F/S	KILSBY Maxwell Bentley	5-04-45	1667 HCU
436330	F/S	KING Kenneth John	2-02-45	467 Sqn
432819	F/S	KIRKPATRICK Peter Leeton	8-02-45	57 Sqn
416863	W/O	KNIGHT Albert Ernest William	14-02-45	463 Sqn
429582	F/S	KREFTER John Julius	6-01-45	158 Sqn
432823	P/O	LANGHAM Keith Oswald	4-02-45	12 Sqn
416685	W/C	LANGLOIS DFC Eric Le Page	3-03-45	467 Sqn
419881	F/L	LAWSON Edward McMaster	2-03-45	207 Sqn
429153	P/O	LEVY Allan Neil	21-03-45	50 Sqn
422590	F/O	LEWIS Arthur	31-03-45	635 Sqn
19892	F/O	LEWIS Raymond Allan	21-03-45	207 Sqn
415946	P/O	LIND Gilbert Owen Hugh	21-03-45	57 Sqn
429235	F/S	LOCK Robert Henry	15-02-45	640 Sqn
433115	F/S	LOCKE Reginald Kingsley	14-03-45	106 Sqn
429708	F/S	LONDON Alexander Edmund	5-03-45	149 Sqn
435171	P/O	LONG Gordon David	1-01-45	115 Sqn
423514	F/S	LOVETT Angus Thomas Jellicoe	7-03-45	49 Sqn
429710	P/O	LUTZ Alfred Edward	4-03-45	1654 HCU
437622	F/S	LYONS Robert John	2-02-45	463 Sqn
428879	F/S	MacKNIGHT Bruce Cowper	14-01-45	9 Sqn
434641	F/S	MacLEAN John Erskine Brown	14-01-45	9 Sqn
414311	F/L	MACLEAN DFC Malcolm Hamilton Murray	5-03-45	608 Sqn
426633	F/S	MADDEN Patrick Joseph	4-03-45	467 Sqn
419193	F/O	MAGUIRE John	2-02-45	460 Sqn
417657	F/O	MALONEY Robert Lenard	16-01-45	578 Sqn
433733	F/S	MANGNALL Charles Richard	5-01-45	106 Sqn
429052	F/S	MANNELL Leslie Gordon Marshall	7-01-45	462 Sqn
432335	P/O	MANTON Paul Blake	4-03-45	640 Sqn
423801	W/O	MARGULES Maxwell Ernest	17-02-45	467 Sqn
423803	W/O	MARSHALL DFC Laurence William	20-03-45	1653 HCU
424640	F/O	MARTIN Robert	9-04-45	630 Sqn
432681	F/S	MASTERS Robert Lockyer	24-03-45	150 Sqn
424614	F/O	MATHIESON Milton Alexander	8-01-45	103 Sqn
429820	W/O	MAY Donald Bernard	2-02-45	460 Sqn
412167	W/O	MAYNE Elwyn Oswald Thomas	6-03-45	460 Sqn
429475	W/O	McBRYDE George Thomas	19-03-45	460 Sqn
428340	F/S	McDONELL Jack James Lewis	22-01-45	153 Sqn
435018	F/S	McGINN Keith Charles	8-03-45	103 Sqn
429239	P/O	McGRATH Angus Albert	24-02-45	103 Sqn
428401	F/S	McGUIGAN John Harrie	8-04-45	49 Sqn
426234	F/O	McINTOSH Donald Robert	14-01-45	106 Sqn
431183	F/S	McKASKILL Raymond Kevin	3-02-45	100 Sqn
432540	P/O	McKENNA Gordon Charles	3-02-45	156 Sqn
40520	F/S	McKENZIE Raymond Murdoch	9-02-45	61 Sqn
424442	W/O	McLELLAN Donald Campbell	4-03-45	1653 HCU
428577	P/O	McLEOD Bruce Maxwell Edward	4-04-45	78 Sqn
424791	P/O	McMANUS Terence Bellew	13-02-45	463 Sqn
412647	W/O	McNALLY John Joseph	5-03-45	170 Sqn
427919	F/S	McNAMARA Maurice James	14-01-45	9 Sqn
426422	F/S	McNAMEE William Andrew	8-01-45	467 Sqn
409062	F/O	McNULTY Neville Milne	28-02-45	128 Sqn
424778	S/L	MERRYFULL MBE Charles Joseph	8-07-45	199 Sqn
420232	P/O	MILLER Bruce English	15-03-45	157 Sqn
421750	W/O	MILLER Frederick Charles	7-01-45	49 Sqn
429723	P/O	MILLER Richard Albert George	10-02-45	460 Sqn
418292	F/O	MILNE Jack	5-01-45	463 Sqn
437435	F/S	MILNE Maxwell William	5-01-45	29 OTU
423814	W/O	MINETT Stanley James	14-01-45	462 Sqn
434731	P/O	MIROW Ronald Joseph	13-04-45	571 Sqn
442280	F/S	MITCHELL Ronald Walter	8-01-45	30 OTU
415345	F/L	MITCHELL William Hewitt Power	23-02-45	192 Sqn
429096	F/O	MOON Maxwell Walter	6-02-45	1653 HCU
412815	F/L	MORGAN DFM Thomas Ernest Victor	5-03-45	460 SQN
423161	F/O	MORRIS Philip Henry	24-03-45	150 Sqn
432534	F/O	MOSES George	17-03-45	467 Sqn
415265	W/O	MOSS Alexander Edward	19-03-45	460 Sqn
419732	W/O	MUMMERY Geoffrey Douglas	7-03-45	61 Sqn
7122	P/O	MUNRO Kelvin Gordon	7-03-45	35 Sqn
432022	P/O	MURRAY Aubrey George	21-03-45	97 Sqn
428162	F/O	MURRAY Lawrie Edmund	2-03-45	625 Sqn
432398	P/O	MYERSON Philip	29-01-45	408 Sqn
419332	P/O	NANSCAWEN John Barrie	8-02-45	467 Sqn
429615	W/O	NEILL William Arthur	16-03-45	12 Sqn
433277	F/O	NERNEY Kenneth Roy	6-01-45	158 Sqn
438300	F/S	NEWCOMBE John William	8-04-45	21 OTU
436058	F/O	NEWTON Frederick John	22-03-45	15 Sqn
429257	P/O	NICHOLS Leslie Joyhn	7-02-45	158 Sqn
37050	P/O	NICKLESS Harry Samuel	3-02-45	90 Sqn
426979	F/O	NICOL Alexander Hunter	14-01-45	50 Sqn
2678	P/O	NIELSON Searn Wrist	7-03-45	550 Sqn
439781	F/S	NOLAN Colin John	5-01-45	29 OTU
417595	W/O	ODGERS Lindsay Joseph	4-03-45	214 Sqn
427542	W/O	OLIVER Ernest Ronald William	24-02-45	462 Sqn
429124	F/O	OLIVER Richard Kay	2-02-45	463 Sqn
434001	F/O	OLSEN Allan	5-03-45	514 Sqn
419136	P/O	ORCHARD Norman Henry	11-03-45	463 Sqn
422251	F/L	ORDELL DFC Robin	3-02-45	100 Sqn
424538	F/O	OSBORNE Ian Ronald	3-02-45	100 Sqn
423174	F/S	O'BRIEN George John Patrick	12-03-45	106 Sqn
426796	F/S	O'DONOHUE Patrick Francis	6-03-45	514 Sqn
433473	F/S	O'HARA Douglas Glen	28-01-45	460 Sqn
425048	F/O	O'NEILL Benjamin Francis	2-03-45	640 Sqn
434330	F/S	O'REILLY Roy Thomas	17-01-45	29 OTU
424676	F/S	PAINE William Thomas	2-02-45	467 Sqn
428261	F/L	PALLING Aubrey Robert	21-03-45	57 Sqn
437202	F/S	PALMER David Charles	7-03-45	170 Sqn
415820	F/O	PALMER Geoffrey Robert	14-01-45	223 Sqn
426148	F/O	PARADISE John Edwin	22-03-45	51 Sqn
428877	F/S	PARRY Morgan James	16-03-45	460 Sqn
432425	F/S	PATERSON Dallas Joseph	23-02-45	192 Sqn
433130	F/S	PATON John Charles	9-03-45	90 Sqn
409437	F/O	PATTEN DFC Evan Charles	3-03-45	467 Sqn
419969	F/S	PATTINSON Norman David	16-01-45	1653 HCU
423007	F/O	PAULINE Claude Desmond	14-03-45	57 Sqn
8309	F/O	PEACE Eric Ralph	14-01-45	27 OTU
428480	P/O	PEARCE Allan Harry	2-02-45	467 Sqn

Service No	Rank	Name	Date	Sqn
432969	F/S	PEARCE Stanley David	5-04-45	103 Sqn
419970	F/O	PEARCE William Norman Roy	5-03-45	227 Sqn
426237	F/O	PEDERSEN Lawrence Roy	21-02-45	463 Sqn
432010	F/O	PEREZ Miguel Louis	6-01-45	207 Sqn
433167	F/S	PETERS Neville Edward	31-03-45	635 Sqn
432970	F/S	PETERSON Bernard Bruce	20-01-45	460 Sqn
437562	F/S	PETSCHEL Victor Edward	21-03-45	97 Sqn
436480	F/O	PITTS Warren Henry	21-03-45	227 Sqn
8651	F/S	PLANTE Robert Erskine	6-02-45	1656 HCU
424606	P/O	POLLARD Clifford Thomas	8-01-45	103 Sqn
437951	F/S	POPE Rhodric Leslie	10-02-45	460 Sqn
433742	F/S	PORTER Harvey James	13-03-45	103 Sqn
435625	F/S	PORTER Leonard John	8-01-45	30 OTU
422982	F/O	POWELL Vernon Douglas	5-01-45	106 Sqn
429832	F/S	PRIDMORE Walter Noel	4-03-45	12 Sqn
424635	F/S	PRINCE John Francis	5-01-45	463 Sqn
421047	F/L	PRITCHARD Jack Ivan	3-01-45	467 Sqn
431468	F/S	PROUSE James William	16-03-45	460 Sqn
415916	F/O	PUGH Harold Kenneth	18-04-45	640 Sqn
10046	P/O	QUILL William Keeran	5-01-45	102 Sqn
430318	W/O	QUINN Kevin Bernard	14-07-45	460 Sqn
414827	F/S	QUINN Roderick Philip	17-01-45	29 OTU
427742	F/S	RANKIN George Worland	2-03-45	460 Sqn
423892	F/L	RATE Allan John	24-02-45	462 Sqn
434011	F/S	RAY Frederick Charles Henry	5-03-45	466 Sqn
421050	F/O	REID DFC Alan Frank	3-03-45	467 Sqn
429266	W/O	REID Thomas	4-04-45	635 Sqn
424306	F/S	REYNOLDS Keith Kevin	3-02-45	100 Sqn
433648	F/S	RHODES Robert Craven	16-03-45	625 Sqn
412697	F/O	RICHARDSON Colin Robert Moore	9-04-45	630 Sqn
416787	F/L	RICHARDSON Jack McPherson	28-01-45	16 OTU
428189	F/S	RICHARDSON Russell Vernon	4-03-45	467 Sqn
428413	P/O	RIMMINGTON Dugald Geoffrey	14-02-45	103 Sqn
426468	P/O	RIORDAN Lex Maitland	17-01-45	15 Sqn
432632	F/S	ROBERTS Bruce Thomas	5-01-45	106 Sqn
422885	F/O	ROBINSON Alton Neil Goulburn	2-02-45	467 Sqn
435913	F/S	ROBINSON Anthony Gatward	10-02-45	460 Sqn
427484	F/S	ROBINSON Cavan Beadon	21-02-45	576 Sqn
55854	F/S	ROGERS Roy John	14-07-45	460 Sqn
417761	P/O	ROHRLACH Mervin Walter	7-01-45	462 Sqn
424322	F/O	ROLLS Patrick Morley [New Zealand]	16-03-45	625 Sqn
124764	F/S	ROLSTON Archibald George	12-04-45	1654 HCU
18839	F/S	ROSS Ian Stewart	12-01-45	617 Sqn
417519	F/S	RUGLESS George Ifould	5-01-45	15 Sqn
419142	F/S	RYAN John Francis	17-03-45	576 Sqn
428364	F/O	RYAN John Joseph Francis	4-03-45	44 Sqn
431186	F/S	SAULWICK Laurence Julius	8-01-45	467 Sqn
423179	F/S	SAUNDERS Cyril William	14-02-45	161 Sqn
435180	F/S	SAVAGE Douglas Irvine	5-01-45	29 OTU
428798	W/O	SAVILLE Gordon Reginald	4-04-45	115 Sqn
436950	F/S	SCHODDE Rex Crespin	19-03-45	460 Sqn
205850	F/O	SCOTT Andrew Hawkins	5-01-45	106 Sqn
434029	F/S	SERVOS Stephanos	8-01-45	467 Sqn
435489	F/S	SHANNON Evan Frederick	5-03-45	103 Sqn
432885	F/S	SHARP Jack Wallace	12-04-45	1654 HCU
428602	F/O	SHELTON Allan Percy William	4-03-45	466 Sqn
434808	P/O	SHEPLEY John Robert	21-02-45	578 Sqn
428367	W/O	SIMPSON William Alfred	5-01-45	463 Sqn
424609	F/S	SIMPSON William Thomas	16-01-45	466 Sqn
425979	P/O	SISLEY Noel Henry	2-02-45	640 Sqn
424471	W/O	SMITH Barry Sydney	1-02-45	50 Sqn
428057	F/S	SMITH Brian Patten	12-04-45	1654 HCU
429268	F/S	SMITH Eric Alfred	7-01-45	619 Sqn
442286	F/S	SMITH Murray Arthur	24-02-45	462 Sqn
432893	F/S	STACEY Jack	19-03-45	460 Sqn
422817	F/O	STANTON John Edward	26-02-45	138 Sqn
429834	F/O	STARK Roussel William Galloway	7-03-45	49 Sqn
435689	F/S	STEGMAN Lance Anthony	11-04-45	163 Sqn
410113	P/O	STUART Henry Montgomery Stanbrook	8-02-45	467 Sqn
409280	F/O	SUFFREN DFC Charles Edward	16-02-45	460 Sqn
432903	F/S	SUMMERSON Edward Thomas	1-02-45	101 Sqn
433169	F/S	SUMNER Edward Thomas	21-02-45	463 Sqn
422989	F/O	SWALES John Frederick	21-03-45	61 Sqn
427410	F/O	SWARBRICK Phillip	14-01-45	462 Sqn
430403	F/O	SWIFT Sydney Clifton	21-02-45	460 Sqn
424572	W/O	SYMONDS Leslie James	5-01-45	619 Sqn
430788	F/S	TAIT John Mickle	10-04-45	462 Sqn
432034	F/O	TANNER Norman William Neville	5-04-45	1652 HCU
437369	F/S	TARRANT Cecil James	16-03-45	625 Sqn
437172	F/O	TASKER Brian Stanley	9-02-45	61 Sqn
432346	W/O	TAYLOR Ronald Reginald	10-04-45	462 Sqn
434523	F/S	TAYLOR William Albert	2-02-45	463 Sqn
435192	F/S	TEAGUE John William	16-03-45	625 Sqn
424312	F/L	TERPENING DFC Robert Patrick	28-04-45	582 Sqn
432286	W/O	TERRAS Colin Hill	3-03-45	467 Sqn
429069	F/S	THOMAS Allen Benjamin	15-01-45	1668 HCU
410180	F/O	THOMAS Edwin William	17-03-45	467 Sqn
435357	F/S	THOMAS John Raymond	8-04-45	21 OTU
429081	F/O	THOMPSON Ivan Lindsay Vinall	15-01-45	1668 HCU
436777	F/S	THOMSON Trevor Andrew	2-03-45	460 Sqn
428373	P/O	TINSLEY John Herbert	7-03-45	12 Sqn
432388	F/S	TISDELL Errol Dallas	17-04-45	462 Sqn
417533	W/O	TORR Glen	6-03-45	582 Sqn
29856	W/O	TOVEY Brian Douglas	26-02-45	138 Sqn
413453	F/L	TROPMAN DFC Francis William Gordon	22-02-45	35 Sqn
433793	F/S	TROWBRIDGE Bruce Milton	7-03-45	550 Sqn
434431	P/O	TRUNK Victor Joseph	24-02-45	462 Sqn
428001	F/S	TRUSKETT Terence George	4-03-45	1653 HCU
417766	F/S	TUCKER Lawrence Stanley	10-02-45	138 Sqn
428833	P/O	VALERY Julien Francis	5-01-45	102 Sqn
437300	F/O	VALLENTINE Vivian Lawrence	5-04-45	103 Sqn
427364	F/S	VICKERS John Keith	8-04-45	21 OTU
427963	W/O	WALES Peter Henry	2-02-45	149 Sqn
436305	F/S	WALKER Alexander Beck	4-03-45	467 Sqn
423014	P/O	WALKER Gerald Duncan	14-01-45	460 Sqn
430231	F/O	WALKER John Stennett	7-03-45	170 Sqn
432686	F/O	WALLWORK Albert	15-02-45	630 Sqn
434485	F/S	WALTER Percy William Keith	5-01-45	106 Sqn
435468	F/S	WALTERS Charles Frederick	5-01-45	463 Sqn
426931	F/O	WALTERS John Llewellyn	4-02-45	12 Sqn
428814	F/O	WARD Rowland Telford	3-03-45	467 Sqn
418895	F/O	WATKIN Frank Edwin	2-03-45	640 Sqn
434547	F/S	WATSON Cleveland Charles	3-01-45	467 Sqn
417914	F/O	WATSON Dugald John	9-04-45	466 Sqn
424485	P/O	WATSON DFM John Grylls	28-04-45	582 Sqn
27178	F/O	WATTS DFC Reginald Gordon	2-04-45	29 OTU
413460	F/L	WAUGH Alexander William	11-03-45	692 Sqn
434068	W/O	WEBER Bertram Forbes	2-02-45	467 Sqn
424929	F/O	WEBER Keith	15-02-45	640 Sqn
35027	F/S	WEDD Clifton Warwick Frank	12-04-45	1654 HCU
427274	F/S	WEST Ian Albert	5-02-45	1669 HCU
419718	F/S	WESTON Alexander Harold	4-03-45	12 Sqn
431465	F/S	WHITE Robert John	17-01-45	29 OTU
424394	F/O	WIGGINS George Colin	14-02-45	161 Sqn
429034	F/S	WILKINS Frank Herbert	3-02-45	460 Sqn
436323	F/L	WILLIAMS Bernard Mathew	5-03-45	149 Sqn
427218	F/S	WILLIAMS Herbert John	8-01-45	467 Sqn
427597	F/S	WILSON Alexander	5-03-45	1662 HCU
432348	F/S	WILSON Bruce Thomas Talbot	13-02-45	463 Sqn
418769	F/S	WILSON Henry Leslie	14-01-45	50 Sqn
410405	P/O	WILSON Jack Murray Clyde	5-01-45	100 Sqn
403167	F/O	WILSON Lionel Adolphus	5-01-45	51 Sqn
433749	F/S	WILSON Sidney Gordon	28-01-45	460 Sqn
432928	F/S	WINTON Edward Robert	14-01-45	460 Sqn

424253	F/O	WOLFSON Harold Harry	2-03-45	640 Sqn		J/95123	P/O	ASHDOWN Edward Thomas	5-04-45	424 Sqn
426850	W/O	WOOD Albert Ernest	5-03-45	207 Sqn		J/39320	F/O	ASHDOWN Walter Ross	6-03-45	428 Sqn
410777	F/L	WOOD James Knox	4-02-45	128 Sqn		J/95411	P/O	ATCHISON John Melford	5-03-45	424 Sqn
410826	F/O	WOOLSTENCROFT Bernard Selby	8-04-45	9 Sqn		J/35829	P/O	ATKINSON John Leslie	5-03-45	426 Sqn
430728	F/S	WRIGHT Thomas Edward Harold	3-01-45	467 Sqn		J/95207	P/O	AUNE Clifford Norman	5-01-45	102 Sqn
429072	F/S	YORKSTON Ian Bailey	4-03-45	1653 HCU		J/40693	F/O	BAILEY Douglas James	16-01-45	12 Sqn
428488	F/S	YOUNG Robert John	3-02-45	189 Sqn		J/35708	F/O	BAILY Norman Godwin	29-01-45	408 Sqn
						R/191011	WO2	BAIRD Nelson George	7-03-45	408 Sqn
						J/39575	F/O	BAKER Douglas George	25-04-45	431 Sqn
						R/278667	Sgt	BAKER Ned	2-01-45	166 Sqn
						R/198093	WO2	BAKER Ralph Murray	19-03-45	405 Sqn
						J/93228	P/O	BALL Harold Lester	21-02-45	76 Sqn
						J/42447	F/O	BALL Joseph Dixon	15-03-45	434 Sqn
						R/260678	F/S	BANKS Alexander	19-03-45	425 Sqn
						J/95239	P/O	BARKER Malcolm Melly	16-03-45	12 Sqn
						J/40897	F/O	BARLOW Garnet Mack Bernard	14-02-45	431 Sqn
						J/16953	F/L	BARLOW John Preston	5-02-45	419 Sqn
						K/267555	F/S	BARNES Gordon John Lunney	15-02-45	429 Sqn
						J/41180	F/O	BARNES John Benjamin	24-03-45	550 Sqn
						J/40084	F/O	BATEMAN Donald William	23-02-45	158 Sqn
						J/94502	P/O	BATTLER Ralph Oscar	5-03-45	420 Sqn
						J/95240	P/O	BAXTER Leonard Earl	21-02-45	227 Sqn
						J/95237	P/O	BEACH Earl Victor	7-03-45	419 Sqn
						J/42250	F/O	BEATON Herbert John	5-03-45	431 Sqn
						J/94216	P/O	BEAUDRY Joseph Emile Roland	5-03-45	425 Sqn
						R/148844	F/S	BEAUMONT Lawrence Herbert	3-02-45	44 Sqn
						J/40392	F/O	BECK Albert John	21-02-45	626 Sqn
						R/177118	LAC	BEDARD Joseph Donat Marcel	16-04-45	432 Sqn
						R/274955	F/S	BEDELL Lyle Eugene	16-03-45	100 Sqn
						J/26674	P/O	BELCHER Leonard Ralph	6-01-45	415 Sqn
						J/95238	P/O	BELLAMY John Alwin	7-03-45	424 Sqn
						R/90886	F/S	BELLANTINO Dominico	7-03-45	424 Sqn
						J/27009	F/L	BENSON Ivor Bruce	25-02-45	429 Sqn
						J/40216	F/O	BENVILLE Lawrence John	5-01-45	408 Sqn
						J/23034	F/L	BERRY DFC Douglas Elliott	2-02-45	428 Sqn
						R/186388	F/S	BERRYMAN Stuart	30-04-45	428 Sqn
						J/95425	P/O	BIGGERSTAFF Richard Alan	5-03-45	426 Sqn
						R/202976	Sgt	BISHOP Edward Archibald	5-01-45	82 OTU
						J/92591	P/O	BISHOP DFC Hubert George	11-03-45	431 Sqn
						J/37721	F/O	BISHOP Stanley Buckland Stewart	3-02-45	90 Sqn
						J/35935	F/O	BLADES John Wilfred	28-01-45	428 Sqn
						J/88570	F/L	BLAIN Norman Philip	2-02-45	189 Sqn
						J/29884	F/O	BLANEY Laurence Allen	21-02-45	419 Sqn
						J/36313	F/O	BLEICH James Arthur	21-02-45	432 Sqn
						J/3467	S/L	BLENKINSOP DFC Croix de Guerre [Belgium] Edward Weyman	23-01-45	405 Sqn
						J/35755	F/O	BLOCH Harry	2-02-45	432 Sqn
						R/89500	F/S	BOARDMAN Leonard	4-03-45	1664 HCU
						J/93435	P/O	BODDY Howard Bruce	15-03-45	207 Sqn
						R/166028	WO1	BOMBY John	8-04-45	463 Sqn
						J/42472	F/O	BONTER Stewart Millen	15-03-45	432 Sqn
						J/41510	F/O	BOOTH Wyman Alexander	14-01-45	1666 HCU
						R/281134	F/S	BOOTY Cameron Harrison	22-04-45	153 Sqn
						J/9468	F/L	BORRETT William Fleming [USA]	16-01-45	415 Sqn
						R/255759	F/S	BOSTWICK Stanley Edward [USA]	15-02-45	429 Sqn
						J/24483	F/O	BOUCHER Rodolphe Joseph Lorenzo	27-02-45	76 Sqn
						J/85059	F/O	BOULTON Clive Arkoll	15-03-45	405 Sqn
						J/37559	F/O	BOWES Donald Stuart Maxwell	31-03-45	419 Sqn
						R/64172	Sgt	BOWMAN Edward Max	28-01-45	1664 HCU
						J/94382	F/O	BOYCE Ernest Bertin	2-03-45	622 Sqn
						J/46747	F/O	BOYD Allan Bernard	25-04-45	408 Sqn
						J/35891	F/O	BOYLE Bernard Francis	7-03-45	44 Sqn
						J/40730	F/O	BOYLE Clair Patrick	2-02-45	622 Sqn
						J/93961	P/O	BRADLEY Allan George	3-02-45	426 Sqn
						J/95208	P/O	BRADLEY Frank William	7-01-45	550 Sqn
						J/95245	P/O	BRAMBLEBY James Edwin	25-04-45	408 Sqn
						J/14007	F/L	BRAND Lorne William	5-01-45	420 Sqn

Note

With the war in Europe at an end, the repatriation of Royal Australian Air Force personnel serving in the United Kingdom proceeded with a degree of urgency and the Main Force bomber squadrons witnessed a rapid exodus of their Australian compatriots in the direction of the Personnel and Despatch Holding Centres to await shipment to their homeland. In total, the Royal Australian Air Force had contributed thirteen squadrons to the air war over Europe, and of this figure no less than eight had been associated with Bomber Command, some albeit but briefly, though four had stayed the course and in doing so had suffered quite considerable casualties, particularly 460 Squadron whose long service as a part of No.1 Group resulted in the setting of many records as Martin Middlebrook and Chris Everitt show in their summing up of the *Bomber Command War Diaries*, not least of which is the belief that no other squadron in Bomber Command dropped a higher bomb tonnage than '460'.

It is further noted, in respect of entries in this section, that F/O Rolston's service number suggests he may have been commissioned into the Royal Air Force (Volunteer Reserve). However, both the Commonwealth War Graves Commission data base and that for the Royal Australian Air Force, Roll of Honour section, shows him to be a serving member of the Royal Australian Air Force.

ROYAL CANADIAN AIR FORCE
personnel

J/95424	P/O	ABRAMS Robert William	6-03-45	576 Sqn
J/95443	P/O	ADAM Joseph Paul Hector	19-03-45	405 Sqn
J/36193	F/O	ADAMS John Charles	5-01-45	550 Sqn
J/42482	F/O	ADAMS Victor Robert	14-01-45	1666 HCU
J/6390	F/L	ADILMAN Bernard Mortimer	6-01-45	431 Sqn
J/37732	F/O	ADRAIN Robert Ross Anderson	8-04-45	463 Sqn
J/13051	F/L	ALDWORTH Frank Carter	15-02-45	424 Sqn
R/217734	F/S	ALGAR William Edwin	28-05-45	22 OTU
J/19255	F/O	ALLAN DFC George Ingram	22-01-45	142 Sqn
J/36317	F/O	ALLAN James	7-01-45	405 Sqn
R/266823	F/S	ALLAN Joseph William	7-03-45	424 Sqn
J/95213	P/O	ALLEN Alfred George	7-03-45	408 Sqn
R/221836	F/S	ALM Edwin Richard	25-02-45	427 Sqn
J/38392	F/O	ALTY Frederick Roy	31-03-45	431 Sqn
R/1454121	LAC	AMLIN Edsel Edward	3-05-45	Middleton St. George
J/42093	P/O	AMOS Lloyd Hilbourne	25-04-45	431 Sqn
J/95243	P/O	ANDERSON George	31-03-45	415 Sqn
J/92728	P/O	ANDERSON Mark Sylvester Harold	5-03-45	425 Sqn
C/95210	P/O	ANDERSON Nels Peter Helin	21-02-45	408 Sqn
J/36360	F/O	ANDERSON Peter Gordon	21-02-45	50 Sqn
J/16379	F/L	ANDERSON DFC Peter Murray	11-04-45	207 Sqn
J/41164	F/O	ANDERSON William Smith	14-02-45	420 Sqn
J/94671	P/O	ARCAND Joseph Jules Rodrigue	15-03-45	425 Sqn
J/93870	F/O	ARCHER William Edward	12-01-45	424 Sqn
J/39017	F/O	ARLOTTE Sidney George	3-02-45	426 Sqn
J/17036	F/L	ARMITT John	14-02-45	405 Sqn
J/43497	F/O	ARMOUR Jack Karl	16-01-45	101 Sqn
R/291562	Sgt	ARMSTRONG Arthur Ronald	17-05-45	1659 HCU
J/95127	P/O	ARMSTRONG Curwood Neville	5-04-45	424 Sqn
J/42241	F/O	ARMSTRONG David Malcolm	19-03-45	420 Sqn
J/5707	S/L	ARMSTRONG John David	7-03-45	128 Sqn
J/41627	F/O	ARMSTRONG Leonard Wilson	15-03-45	434 Sqn
J/40427	F/O	ARMSTRONG Oswald Walter	3-02-45	44 Sqn

J/95241	P/O	BRANSTON Leonard Frank	25-03-45	426 Sqn		R/207938	F/S	CLARK Donald Kenneth	14-01-45	223 Sqn
J/94854	P/O	BREDIN Mark Webster	15-03-45	419 Sqn		J/89818	F/O	CLARK Earl William	5-03-45	420 Sqn
J/38776	F/O	BREIR Harry Patrick	6-01-45	415 Sqn		J/90197	P/O	CLARK Harold Luther	28-01-45	428 Sqn
J/95242	P/O	BRENNAN Lawrence William	25-03-45	415 Sqn		J/37879	F/O	CLARK John Harvey	8-01-45	626 Sqn
R/212339	F/S	BREWER Morley Junior	27-02-45	429 Sqn		J/37640	F/O	CLARKE Charles John	7-01-45	550 Sqn
R/252616	F/S	BRIDGER Roger Thomas	20-04-45	1660 HCU		J/95223	P/O	CLARKE James Thomas [USA]	5-01-45	415 Sqn
J/38744	F/O	BRODIE Warren Argo	3-02-45	153 Sqn		J/25795	F/O	CARSON Owen Munro Wolvenden	8-01-45	1546 Flt
J/43608	F/O	BROOKS Wilfred Henry	23-03-45	101 Sqn		R/186020	F/S	CLEMENTS Hugh	1-01-45	218 Sqn
R/214565	F/S	BROWN Douglas Harold	7-01-45	405 Sqn		J/36136	F/O	CLIFFORD Anthony Arthur	18-05-45	408 Sqn
J/94898	P/O	BROWN Francis Norman	5-01-45	429 Sqn		R/279050	F/S	CLINE Verle Edmond [USA]	28-04-45	1653 HCU
R/220677	F/S	BROWN James Pirie	1-02-45	166 Sqn		J/15742	F/L	CLOTHIER John George	6-03-45	432 Sqn
J/95211	P/O	BROWN Raymon Clifford	24-02-45	415 Sqn		R/221212	F/S	COCKERHAM Lester	3-04-45	626 Sqn
J/40082	F/O	BROWN Robert Allan	17-04-45	171 Sqn		J/95234	P/O	COFILED Clarence Leonard	25-03-45	408 Sqn
J/94899	P/O	BROWN Walter Gordon	16-03-45	12 Sqn		J/39957	F/O	COLLINS James Thomas	7-02-45	12 Sqn
R/263269	F/S	BRUCE Robert Henry	5-04-45	24 OTU		C/95228	P/O	COLLINSON Leslie John	29-01-45	408 Sqn
J/94900	P/O	BRUGGEMAN Joseph Aloysius	16-01-45	405 Sqn		J/29388	F/O	COMBAZ Alfred Joseph	21-02-45	578 Sqn
J/40347	F/O	BRYDON Wilbert Alexander	5-03-45	170 Sqn		J/95141	F/O	CONLEY Walter Fred	5-11-45	429 Sqn
J/17456	F/L	BUCHANAN DFC Douglas John Alexander				J/18850	F/L	CONNOLLY Earl Wellington	14-02-45	405 Sqn
			5-02-45	419 Sqn		J/21847	F/L	CONNORS Frank Earl	16-03-45	1664 HCU
J/95232	P/O	BUCHANAN John Gilbert Ross	25-02-45	429 Sqn		J/29214	F/L	CONSTABLE William Mackie	23-02-45	170 Sqn
J/38727	F/O	BUCKMASTER John	7-03-45	550 Sqn		K/270515	F/S	COOK William Henry	3-02-45	550 Sqn
R/270474	F/S	BULLOCK Marquis Roland	4-03-45	189 Sqn		R/271065	F/S	COOKE John Leo	3-04-45	626 Sqn
J/91169	P/O	BULLOCK Veral Clarence	3-01-45	622 Sqn		R/269387	F/S	COOKSON William Remington	23-02-45	158 Sqn
J/95235	P/O	BURNS Melvin John 'Mel'	10-04-45	415 Sqn		J/92482	P/O	COOMBS Francis Alma	1-02-45	166 Sqn
J/42161	F/O	BURROWS Bernard Arthur	25-03-45	408 Sqn		J/95426	P/O	COONES Maxwell Warren	5-03-45	426 Sqn
J/95224	P/O	BUTLER Norman Arthur	6-01-45	415 Sqn		J/92339	P/O	COOPER Edgar Harvey	1-01-45	9 Sqn
J/38675	F/O	BUTTERWORTH Robert Stuart [USA]	19-03-45	405 Sqn		R/292666	Sgt	COOPER Edward James	1-03-45	24 OTU
						J/18182	F/O	COPELAND Thomas Donovan	11-03-45	434 Sqn
R/123964	WO2	BUTTREY John William	4-03-45	1664 HCU		J/88248	F/L	CORBETT DFC William David	8-03-45	425 Sqn
J/88732	F/O	BYERS Clyde Willis	16-01-45	153 Sqn		J/35810	F/O	COUTTS Harold Alexander	7-03-45	171 Sqn
J/38389	F/O	CAHOON Grant Alder	9-02-45	426 Sqn		J/12812	F/L	COWIE James Hector	9-02-45	15 Sqn
R/281867	F/O	CALDWELL Andrew Glen	6-03-45	429 Sqn		J/90034	P/O	COWIE Robert James [USA]	1-02-45	76 Sqn
R/271098	F/S	CALEY George Frederick	4-03-45	189 Sqn		J/29093	F/O	COYLE John William	3-03-45	20 OTU
R/188822	WO2	CAMERON Michael Cecil	18-05-45	408 Sqn		J/94267	F/O	COYNE DFC Edward Kenneth	5-04-45	7 Sqn
R/268487	F/S	CAMPBELL Donald Fletcher	7-01-45	103 Sqn		J/38252	F/O	CRAIB George Richard Robert Henry		
J/94333	F/O	CAMPBELL James Duncan	9-02-45	426 Sqn					15-01-45	431 Sqn
J/94275	P/O	CAMPBELL Roy	21-02-45	50 Sqn		J/95231	P/O	CRAIGIE Charles Cleghorn Brockie	24-02-45	415 Sqn
R/197245	F/S	CAMPBELL Thomas George	23-02-45	192 Sqn				[USA]		
J/39018	F/O	CAMPBELL Thomas Marnoch	5-03-45	426 Sqn		J/12954	S/L	CRAWFORD DFC Nathan	2-01-45	405 Sqn
J/21450	F/L	CAMPBELL William Gavin	30-04-45	428 Sqn		J/35134	F/O	CRESWELL George Elliott	21-02-45	432 Sqn
R/54631	F/S	CAMPEAU Joseph Lucien Almasse	31-03-45	429 Sqn		J/17170	S/L	CREW DFC Basil Glynn	5-01-45	427 Sqn
J/95225	P/O	CAMPTON Albert Spencer Blair	7-01-45	576 Sqn		J/88362	F/O	CROSSWELL Percy Bruce	14-04-45	429 Sqn
J/88306	F/O	CARLETON DFM Edmund Bruce	15-03-45	419 Sqn		J/41283	F/O	CROUCHER Lionel Charles	21-03-45	419 Sqn
J/94257	F/O	CARNEGIE Robert Campbell	12-01-45	424 Sqn		R/124020	WO1	CROW Robert King	16-01-45	153 Sqn
J/91150	P/O	CAROLAN Arthur Grattan	16-01-45	434 Sqn		J/43017	F/O	CRUICKSHANK John Duncan	25-04-45	431 Sqn
J/93886	P/O	CARRUTHERS Harold Allen	12-01-45	424 Sqn		J/92246	F/L	CULL Albert James	18-04-45	408 Sqn
J/40896	F/O	CARSON Sidney Thomas	27-02-45	429 Sqn		J/29601	F/O	CUMMER Franklin Howard [USA]	28-01-45	405 Sqn
J/94203	P/O	CARTER Hilton Mackay	21-03-45	214 Sqn		J/95226	P/O	CUNLIFFE Benjamin Robert	16-01-45	405 Sqn
R/188387	F/S	CARTER John Hunter	28-01-45	428 Sqn		J/42217	F/O	CUNNINGHAM John Charles	9-04-45	408 Sqn
R/183314	F/S	CARYI Charles Joseph Anthony	14-02-45	153 Sqn		J/95236	P/O	CURZON Dennis Rupert Humphrey	25-04-45	426 Sqn
J/43953	F/O	CASEY John Joseph	31-03-45	431 Sqn		R/257639	F/S	CUTHBERTSON Hugh	1-03-45	153 Sqn
J/38805	F/O	CASH Alfred Valentine [USA]	5-03-45	424 Sqn		R/279178	F/S	CYBULSKIE Adolph Joseph	14-02-45	427 Sqn
J/37805	F/O	CASHER Frederick Einar	24-04-45	429 Sqn		J/40809	F/O	DARLINGTON William	4-03-45	192 Sqn
R/279088	F/S	CHAPMAN Kenneth Frank	22-04-45	153 Sqn		J/37816	F/O	DART Henry Raymond	21-02-45	625 Sqn
J/38421	F/O	CHAPMAN William Merton	16-01-45	100 Sqn		J/92736	P/O	DAUGHTERS George David	7-03-45	408 Sqn
R/268734	LAC	CHARBONNEAU Regis Fernand	16-04-45	432 Sqn		J/41839	F/O	DAUPHINEE George Alfred Osborn	16-03-45	100 Sqn
R/274376	F/S	CHARLEBOIS Gordon Phillip	20-04-45	1660 HCU		C/190	W/C	DAVENPORT Ralph Frederick	11-03-45	431 Sqn
J/14047	F/L	CHARLTON Ross Conger	15-02-45	429 Sqn		J/93583	P/O	DAVEY Hugh Augustine [USA]	21-02-45	434 Sqn
J/40447	F/O	CHARRON Ronald Edward Oscar	5-03-45	425 Sqn		R/224874	F/S	DAVEY Jim Boyce	21-02-45	207 Sqn
J/94103	F/O	CHATFIELD Russell Edmund	28-01-45	424 Sqn		J/95227	P/O	DAVIDSON John McIntosh	16-01-45	426 Sqn
R/207284	F/S	CHAUVIN Joseph Leon Alfred	14-01-45	425 Sqn		R/203153	F/S	DAVIES Paul Wright	7-03-45	424 Sqn
R/180951	WO2	CHEVRIER Lawrence Theodore	4-03-45	1664 HCU		J/90989	P/O	DAVIS Ernest Leroy	16-01-45	102 Sqn
J/93829	P/O	CHISAMORE Joseph Alexander	3-02-45	426 Sqn		J/35097	F/O	DAVIS George Henry	15-03-45	431 Sqn
J/90196	P/O	CHITTIM Richard Hugh	2-01-45	166 Sqn		J/21582	P/O	DAYMOND Keith William	16-03-45	12 Sqn
J/23790	F/O	CHOBANIUK Nicholas	14-01-45	26 OTU		J/39871	F/O	DENNIS William Lewis	16-01-45	420 Sqn
J/36231	F/O	CHRISTIE Harry Dean	12-01-45	424 Sqn		J/44151	F/O	DENNISON Patrick Blake	31-03-45	431 Sqn
J/41488	F/O	CHRISTIE DFC* Herbert George	10-02-45	1666 HCU		J/89658	F/O	DESBIENS Jean Jacques Adrien Leonidas		
R/281050	F/S	CHURMS James William	5-04-45	626 Sqn					5-03-45	425 Sqn

ID	Rank	Name	Date	Unit
R/275670	F/S	DEWAR Walter William	6-03-45	576 Sqn
J/44346	F/O	DEWART Douglas Lyle	31-01-45	19 OTU
J/29166	F/O	DE MARCO Wilfred Tarquinas	25-04-45	619 Sqn
J/41610	F/O	DE WITT William Norton	6-03-45	419 Sqn
J/94525	P/O	DICKIE Gordon Douglas	5-04-45	24 OTU
R/190510	WO2	DICKSON John Arthur	21-02-45	625 Sqn
J/95230	P/O	DICKSON Walter Sydney	21-02-45	431 Sqn
J/93872	P/O	DOBBS Fernand Walter	12-01-45	424 Sqn
R/280274	F/S	DOHERTY William Joseph	21-02-45	166 Sqn
J/47071	F/O	DONALD Douglas Nugent [USA]	21-03-45	214 Sqn
J/94186	P/O	DOREY Albert	31-03-45	431 Sqn
J/89833	F/O	DORRELL Jack Wilfred [USA]	22-03-45	431 Sqn
J/12642	F/L	DOTTEN Frank Edmond	17-03-45	576 Sqn
R/106758	WO1	DOUGLAS Robert Gordon	19-04-45	419 Sqn
J/41672	F/O	DOWNWARD Alan Quilliam	3-02-45	514 Sqn
J/94756	P/O	DOYLE Gordon James	28-01-45	424 Sqn
J/27155	F/O	DRAPER Thomas Maynard	8-03-45	195 Sqn
J/41523	F/O	DUBEAU Robert Joseph	14-01-45	425 Sqn
R/262929	F/S	DUFRESNE Edward Charles	3-02-45	44 Sqn
J/35871	F/L	DUGGAN DFC John Philip	22-03-45	431 Sqn
R/170586	WO1	DUNCAN John William	28-05-45	22 OTU
J/95314	P/O	DUNCAN Robert Allison	9-04-45	408 Sqn
J/95525	P/O	DUNNIGAN William John	18-04-45	420 Sqn
J/95294	P/O	DUNPHY Hugh Ashley	5-01-45	102 Sqn
R/195383	F/S	DURLING Maurice Vaughn [USA]	2-01-45	153 Sqn
J/95296	P/O	DURNAN Grant	8-01-45	12 Sqn
J/93925	P/O	D'AVRIL Henri Jean Maurice Joseph	5-03-45	425 Sqn
R/170413	LAC	EASTER Reginald	15-05-45	Croft
R/201129	F/S	EBERLE Arthur Jason	2-01-45	153 Sqn
J/13417	F/L	EDWARDS Albert Gordon	15-03-45	431 Sqn
J/24653	F/L	ELCOATE William Robert	5-01-45	550 Sqn
J/87437	F/O	ELGIE Stewart Wallace	6-01-45	415 Sqn
J/93854	P/O	ELLINGSON John Philip	1-02-45	76 Sqn
J/95312	P/O	ELLIOTT Charles Alvin	21-03-45	419 Sqn
J/93762	P/O	ELLIOTT Herbert William	17-04-45	156 Sqn
R/201090	F/S	ELLIOTT Verne Douglas	8-01-45	166 Sqn
R/153918	Cpl	ELLIS William John	5-11-45	429 Sqn
J/22783	F/L	ELY Arthur Blevyn	25-04-45	408 Sqn
J/11482	F/L	EMERSON Ivor [USA]	5-03-45	426 Sqn
R/189328	F/S	EMERSON John Alexander	29-01-45	5 LFS
J/27037	F/L	EMMET Barry Desmond	25-04-45	431 Sqn
J/93863	P/O	ENGLISH Peter Frederick	3-02-45	419 Sqn
J/94406	P/O	EPOCH Jerome Aquinius	5-03-45	420 Sqn
J/36225	F/O	ESSENBURG Edwin	21-02-45	427 Sqn
J/85788	F/O	EVANS Allan Llewellyn	28-01-45	426 Sqn
J/17548	F/O	EVANS Earle Robert	15-03-45	428 Sqn
J/35885	F/L	EVANS Ronald Sylvester	10-04-45	415 Sqn
R/185896	F/S	EVENS Arthur Leslie	14-01-45	223 Sqn
J/95536	P/O	EVERS Orval Clare	9-05-45	514 Sqn
J/36627	F/O	EXEL Gordon Wynne	5-03-45	103 Sqn
J/37818	F/O	FADDEN Norval Gregory	16-01-45	434 Sqn
J/39529	F/O	FARRELL James Paul	13-03-45	433 Sqn
J/38025	F/O	FARROW Thomas Edison	17-03-45	619 Sqn
J/94221	F/O	FEDORCHUK Wolodemir	15-02-45	429 Sqn
J/42732	F/O	FEHRMAN David Arthur	18-05-45	408 Sqn
J/41496	F/O	FELDHANS Henry Johns	5-01-45	431 Sqn
J/40052	F/O	FENNELL Robert Edward	5-03-45	426 Sqn
J/45367	F/O	FENSKE Kenneth Gordon	1-02-45	101 Sqn
J/39923	F/O	FERGUSON Lawrence William	16-01-45	12 Sqn
J/15681	F/L	FERN Raymond John	11-03-45	434 Sqn
J/43561	F/O	FERNANDEZ Edward Earl	5-01-45	82 OTU
J/95301	P/O	FERNQUIST Virgil John	1-02-45	170 Sqn
J/94144	F/O	FETHERSTON George Howard	9-02-45	426 Sqn
R/190659	F/S	FETHERSTON William Henry	17-03-45	103 Sqn
R/265850	Sgt	FIELD Walter Harry George	14-01-45	1666 HCU
R/98998	WO2	FIELD William Ross	25-02-45	429 Sqn
R/278513	F/S	FIELDER John Edward	4-03-45	1664 HCU
J/89282	P/O	FIELDING George Frederick	1-06-45	433 Sqn
J/38445	F/O	FIFE Mervyn George	12-01-45	424 Sqn
R/220117	F/S	FILIPCHUK Sidney	28-01-45	428 Sqn
J/40410	F/O	FIRTH Murray Norman	21-02-45	77 Sqn
R/275323	F/S	FISHER Frederick George	27-02-45	429 Sqn
R/116477	WO2	FISHER Hugh Alexander	8-04-45	9 Sqn
J/40786	F/O	FISHER Richard Herbert	31-03-45	429 Sqn
J/41106	F/O	FISHER Warren James Keating	3-02-45	514 Sqn
R/264756	Sgt	FITZGIBBON Joseph Francis	29-01-45	5 LFS
J/29160	F/O	FLACK Leslie	6-03-45	514 Sqn
J/40057	F/O	FLEMING Vincent Bernard	25-02-45	429 Sqn
J/18971	F/O	FLEMING Wallace	28-01-45	424 Sqn
J/92541	P/O	FLETCHER Robert Cecil	31-03-45	156 Sqn
J/37711	F/O	FLORIPE Raoul Alberto Orozco [USA]	18-02-45	420 Sqn
R/109414	F/S	FOISY Leopold Orie	21-02-45	427 Sqn
J/41166	F/O	FOLEY Thomas Lynn	7-03-45	424 Sqn
J/89704	P/O	FORD Everett Morrison	14-02-45	427 Sqn
J/92183	P/O	FORSYTHE Edward Bruce	23-03-45	425 Sqn
J/95302	P/O	FOSTEY Allan Martin	9-02-45	405 Sqn
J/95324	P/O	FOURNIER Alphonse Marcel	15-03-45	425 Sqn
J/13989	F/L	FOWLIE John Mackintosh	16-03-45	1664 HCU
R/126002	WO1	FOX Vincent Albert	19-04-45	7 Sqn
J/45349	F/O	FRAME Daniel	22-03-45	428 Sqn
R/196942	F/S	FRANK Michael	16-01-45	153 Sqn
J/95308	P/O	FRASER Charles William	11-03-45	431 Sqn
J/85875	F/L	FREEMAN James Harold	29-01-45	156 Sqn
J/19042	F/O	FRENCH Raymond Alfred	14-02-45	405 Sqn
R/192965	WO2	FRY Thomas William	9-04-45	78 Sqn
R/183745	WO2	FULCHER Roy Everett	2-02-45	189 Sqn
J/94503	P/O	GABA William	5-03-45	420 Sqn
J/95295	P/O	GABRIEL Thomas Alfred	5-01-45	429 Sqn
J/93359	P/O	GALBRAITH Donald Irwin	15-03-45	405 Sqn
J/13694	F/L	GALBRAITH Roger Harrop	16-01-45	426 Sqn
R/274861	F/S	GALLAGHER Harold	14-02-45	427 Sqn
J/95305	P/O	GALLAGHER James	24-02-45	415 Sqn
J/11351	F/L	GALLIVAN Thomas Edward	3-02-45	44 Sqn
J/42505	F/O	GANT Maurice George	27-03-45	571 Sqn
R/179735	F/S	GARDINER John	21-02-45	207 Sqn
J/95311	P/O	GARNET Alan William	17-03-45	576 Sqn
J/10741	S/L	GARRETT Eric Thomas	5-03-45	426 Sqn
J/19068	F/O	GARRIOCK Henry Lloyd	15-03-45	419 Sqn
J/95293	P/O	GAUTHIER Lucien Andrew Joseph	7-01-45	550 Sqn
J/19058	F/O	GEEVES DFC Gerald Edward	2-01-45	405 Sqn
J/40435	F/O	GELL George William	10-04-45	622 Sqn
J/94402	P/O	GIBB James Stanley Marks	17-03-45	576 Sqn
J/95299	P/O	GIBBONS James David	16-01-45	100 Sqn
J/17248	F/O	GIBBS Jack Arthur	5-02-45	419 Sqn
R/205426	F/S	GIDILEVICH Fred Theodore	28-05-45	22 OTU
R/192634	F/S	GILLENDER Hunter	12-03-45	106 Sqn
J/87190	F/O	GILLETTE Orwin Rene	17-05-45	1659 HCU
J/86774	F/O	GILLISSIE William Gerald	6-01-45	431 Sqn
J/37870	F/O	GILMORE William James [USA]	21-02-45	408 Sqn
J/41544	F/O	GINGRAS Joseph Robert Real	14-01-45	425 Sqn
J/39988	F/O	GLADISH John Joseph	31-03-45	419 Sqn
J/95300	P/O	GLASS William James	16-01-45	12 Sqn
J/27927	F/O	GODDARD Robert Samuel	5-03-45	635 Sqn
R/281969	F/S	GONROSKI Philip Felix	6-03-45	429 Sqn
R/225325	Sgt	GOODWIN Lawrence Frederick Bransby [United Kingdom]	14-01-45	1666 HCU
J/86055	F/O	GORDON Fred Merrill	14-02-45	405 Sqn
R/203035	F/S	GOVE Keith Innes	28-01-45	1664 HCU
J/18627	F/O	GRAHAM Donald Curry	15-03-45	428 Sqn
12168A	F/S	GRAHAM James	16-03-45	1664 HCU
R/106461	F/S	GRAHAME John Howard James	16-03-45	1664 HCU
R/181811	WO2	GRANBOIS Maurice Emerson	21-02-45	207 Sqn
J/95304	P/O	GRANKA Bernard	14-02-45	431 Sqn
J/29142	F/O	GRANT Miles Carson	12-01-45	424 Sqn
R/223012	F/S	GRAY William Alexander	14-01-45	223 Sqn

ID	Rank	Name	Date	Sqn
J/95313	P/O	GREEN Robert John	31-03-45	434 Sqn
R/186454	WO2	GREEN William Monroe Leckie	10-04-45	622 Sqn
R/219812	F/S	GREENSTEIN Meyer	7-01-45	103 Sqn
J/87391	F/O	GREGOIRE DFC Leo Joseph Robert	3-03-45	153 Sqn
J/29194	F/O	GRIER Gordon Keith	9-02-45	415 Sqn
J/92644	P/O	GRIFFEY Kenneth William	4-03-45	1664 HCU
J/38819	F/O	GRIFFIN Michael Francis	5-03-45	103 Sqn
J/89832	F/O	GRISDALE Robert James	10-04-45	433 Sqn
J/95306	P/O	GUNDERSON Roald Benjamin	5-03-45	426 Sqn
J/19115	F/O	GUNNING Wilbert Arnold [USA]	22-04-45	427 Sqn
J/36930	F/O	GUREVITCH Cecil	15-01-45	431 Sqn
J/36854	F/O	GUTENSOHN Karl Gerhard	14-01-45	12 Sqn
J/94241	F/O	GUTHRIE George Scott	15-02-45	424 Sqn
J/95307	P/O	GUTTORMSON Hinrik	5-03-45	431 Sqn
J/24946	F/L	GUY Norman William	28-04-45	1653 HCU
J/95297	P/O	GYNANE John	8-01-45	12 Sqn
J/10986	F/L	HADLEY James Frederick	22-03-45	428 Sqn
R/211936	F/S	HAGERTY Stuart Samuel	27-02-45	138 Sqn
J/38360	F/O	HALIBURTON Gilbert Paul	31-03-45	434 Sqn
J/36977	F/O	HALL Clifford Wesley	23-02-45	158 Sqn
J/43949	F/O	HALL Paul John	5-03-45	425 Sqn
J/41163	F/O	HALSALL Gerald Lee	21-02-45	101 Sqn
J/36270	F/O	HALSTEAD Vernon Harvey	15-01-45	626 Sqn
R/278833	F/S	HALVORSON Clarence Julius	18-05-45	408 Sqn
J/20884	F/L	HAMIL Ross Curtis	15-03-45	428 Sqn
K/280563	F/S	HAMILTON Gerald Burton	22-01-45	153 Sqn
J/91199	P/O	HAMMOND Kenneth Morris	2-02-45	428 Sqn
J/88499	F/O	HANBIDGE Robert Donald Keith	8-01-45	12 Sqn
J/45540	F/O	HANDLEY Albert Harry	28-05-45	22 OTU
J/94848	P/O	HANLEY John Edwin	6-03-45	419 Sqn
J/95277	P/O	HANNA Donald	21-02-45	419 Sqn
J/40086	F/O	HANNA William Edward	25-04-45	431 Sqn
J/28186	F/O	HANNAH Croix de Guerre [France] Harold Allan	27-01-45	405 Sqn
R/203699	F/S	HARDING Oliver	21-02-45	625 Sqn
J/17193	F/L	HARRIS MiD Glenn Royal	6-03-45	432 Sqn
J/95280	P/O	HARRIS Howard Roger	5-03-45	431 Sqn
J/37989	F/O	HARRIS Robert Douglas	7-03-45	550 Sqn
J/40430	F/O	HARTOG Martin	31-03-45	431 Sqn
J/95281	P/O	HARVEY Leslie Wallace	7-03-45	550 Sqn
J/93509	P/O	HARVEY Ronald Erwin 'Ronnie'	16-01-45	420 Sqn
J/95276	P/O	HARYETT William Henry	2-02-45	432 Sqn
J/85451	F/L	HAW Robert Roy	15-03-45	431 Sqn
J/40463	F/O	HAWTHORNE Austin Arthur	22-04-45	163 Sqn
J/38394	F/O	HAY DSO Colin Maxwell	6-03-45	432 Sqn
J/88980	F/O	HAY George	5-01-45	429 Sqn
J/48077	F/O	HAY Glen James	11-05-45	24 OTU
J/39167	F/O	HAY Stanley Arthur	14-02-45	420 Sqn
J/3489	S/L	HAYES Edwin Alfred	6-03-45	432 Sqn
J/40061	F/O	HAYES Ernest	19-03-45	405 Sqn
R/61318	LAC	HEALY Roger Casement	18-02-45	62 Base
R/279247	Sgt	HEARD Alvin Walter	10-02-45	1666 HCU
J/40804	F/O	HECTOR Donal Kevin Joseph	11-03-45	431 Sqn
R/272476	F/S	HELLEKSON Leslie Claude	18-05-45	408 Sqn
J/95278	P/O	HENDERSON Douglas Anderson	21-02-45	427 Sqn
J/95282	P/O	HENDERSON Harry Leonard	7-03-45	214 Sqn
J/95547	P/O	HENDERSON William	14-04-45	419 Sqn
J/39288	F/O	HENNESSEY Hugh Richard John	16-03-45	419 Sqn
R/135181	WO2	HENRICHON Paul Edouard Adolphe	25-04-45	431 Sqn
J/95274	P/O	HENRY Frank	29-01-45	408 Sqn
J/45167	F/O	HEROUX Joseph Arthur Rosaire Gaetan	8-04-45	1659 HCU
C/10436	F/O	HESS Geoffrey Winslow [USA]	14-03-45	101 Sqn
R/278686	F/S	HIATT Lewis Ullysees Malcolm	25-04-45	431 Sqn
J/95285	P/O	HICKS Earl William	25-04-45	426 Sqn
J/92455	P/O	HICKSON John William	8-03-45	425 Sqn
J/40778	F/O	HILCHEY Ray Bertram	9-05-45	514 Sqn
J/38109	F/L	HILL David Walter	21-02-45	166 Sqn
J/35912	F/O	HILL Farley Cecil	18-04-45	408 Sqn
R/254854	Sgt	HILLIS Kenneth Millard	14-01-45	425 Sqn
J/94672	P/O	HINCH Lloyd George	19-03-45	425 Sqn
J/95284	P/O	HIRAK Joseph Michael	10-04-45	433 Sqn
J/95273	P/O	HISETTE Andre Jean Jules	16-01-45	51 Sqn
R/104233	F/S	HOCKLEY Herbert Henry	23-02-45	429 Sqn
J/95309	P/O	HODGE Daniel William	13-03-45	433 Sqn
J/38227	F/O	HODGSON Richard William	3-02-45	419 Sqn
J/93936	P/O	HOFFMAN Louis Edward	21-02-45	431 Sqn
J/92655	P/O	HOGAN Frank Edward	2-02-45	428 Sqn
J/40429	F/O	HOGGARD Gordon Albert	23-02-45	158 Sqn
R/254557	F/S	HOLLIDAY David Andrew	15-03-45	405 Sqn
J/45933	F/O	HOLLINGER Gregory Joseph	6-03-45	419 Sqn
J/95333	P/O	HOLMES Angus Wharing	14-03-45	50 Sqn
R/257034	F/S	HOLOWATY William	18-06-45	425 Sqn
R/187913	WO2	HOOKER Edwin Milton	31-03-45	429 Sqn
R/180743	WO2	HORNE Millard Henderson	7-01-45	103 Sqn
J/95283	P/O	HORNE Robert Ernest	15-03-45	431 Sqn
R/259913	F/S	HOSKINS Donald Dunk	2-01-45	153 Sqn
J/95275	P/O	HOUSE Brooks Earl	29-01-45	408 Sqn
J/94145	F/O	HOUSTON Clifford Elmer	9-02-45	426 Sqn
J/95257	P/O	HOVEY Vernon Earl	25-04-45	408 Sqn
J/37847	F/O	HOWALD Carl Herbert	4-02-45	433 Sqn
J/8790	F/L	HOWARD DFC James Paul Ogilvie	2-01-45	139 Sqn
J/46333	F/O	HOWARD William Morrison	31-01-45	19 OTU
J/95122	P/O	HOWES Charles Keith	5-04-45	424 Sqn
R/183291	F/S	HUDSON Claude Harold	12-01-45	424 Sqn
J/39279	F/O	HUMBERSTONE George Arthur	8-01-45	166 Sqn
J/44325	F/O	HUNT Wesley McDonald	5-04-45	24 OTU
J/94317	P/O	HUNTER Alvin George	21-02-45	432 Sqn
J/89092	P/O	HURST Neil Arbuthnot	4-02-45	433 Sqn
R/169558	WO2	HUTCHINS Donald Ross	8-01-45	626 Sqn
J/39872	F/O	HUTCHISON Alick Matheson	5-03-45	426 Sqn
J/95349	P/O	HYDE John William	5-03-45	425 Sqn
J/19131	F/O	HYDE Philip	28-01-45	426 Sqn
J/39503	F/O	HYLAND George Albert [USA]	31-03-45	415 Sqn
R/219755	F/S	INMAN John Ward	24-03-45	166 Sqn
J/37050	F/O	IRELAND Robert Addison [USA]	16-01-45	420 Sqn
J/26516	F/O	IRVINE Harry Charles	6-01-45	415 Sqn
R/174852	F/S	IRVING Frederick Cleveland	16-01-45	153 Sqn
J/40904	F/O	IRWIN Frederick Hansell [USA]	19-03-45	425 Sqn
R/283124	Sgt	ISABELLE Joseph Rene (served as MORIN)	28-05-45	22 OTU
C/18115	F/L	JAMES Leslie Kerry	6-01-45	431 Sqn
J/36138	F/O	JENSEN Arne Paul	9-04-45	408 Sqn
R/182696	F/S	JOHNS Irvine Lawrence	26-01-45	578 Sqn
R/277737	F/S	JOHNSON Clifford Theadore	22-03-45	166 Sqn
J/42264	F/O	JOHNSON Donald Hugh	5-04-45	626 Sqn
R/274586	F/S	JOHNSON Donald Wilfred	3-02-45	44 Sqn
J/40077	F/O	JOHNSON Robert Oliver	31-03-45	419 Sqn
R/121883	WO1	JOHNSON William Andrew	14-03-45	227 Sqn
R/134935	F/S	JOHNSON William Harvey	16-03-45	100 Sqn
R/276317	F/S	JOHNSTON Alexander	3-03-45	207 Sqn
C/89128	F/O	JOHNSTON Crawford Lee	29-01-45	408 Sqn
J/45931	F/O	JOHNSTON Jack Dennison	17-03-45	619 Sqn
J/95522	P/O	JOHNSTON Norman Hubert	25-04-45	619 Sqn
R/221221	F/S	JOHNSTONE Ross John Hugh	23-02-45	170 Sqn
J/95345	P/O	JOLICOEUR Fernand Leo	28-01-45	428 Sqn
R/218186	F/S	JONES Arthur Henry	16-03-45	1664 HCU
J/95346	P/O	JONES Arthur Malcolm	2-02-45	432 Sqn
J/88066	P/O	JONES Cyril John	7-03-45	550 Sqn
J/95537	P/O	JONES Gregory James	14-04-45	419 Sqn
J/45644	F/O	JONES Harold Alfred	17-05-45	1659 HCU
J/95350	P/O	JONES Jack Macdonald	25-03-45	415 Sqn
J/40037	F/O	JONES Lloyd Ingram	14-02-45	408 Sqn
J/93361	P/O	JONES Richard Barrow	15-03-45	405 Sqn
J/95347	P/O	JONES William Harvey	24-02-45	415 Sqn

ID	Rank	Name	Date	Sqn
J/93366	P/O	JOSLIN Kenneth Ross	8-01-45	626 Sqn
J/92691	F/O	KAECHELE Emmet Solomon	5-03-45	420 Sqn
J/94419	P/O	KASTNER Joseph John Michael	5-03-45	420 Sqn
C/85909	F/O	KAUCHARIK Joseph Anthony	14-02-45	405 Sqn
J/95377	P/O	KAVIZA Joseph Frank	29-01-45	156 Sqn
C/888	S/L	KAY Harry Leslie [USA]	28-01-45	428 Sqn
R/142448	F/S	KAY John Henry	30-04-45	428 Sqn
R/211187	F/S	KEARNEY Robert Emmett	21-02-45	166 Sqn
J/16490	F/L	KEARNS William Robert	5-02-45	419 Sqn
J/93166	P/O	KEATING Joseph Arthur	3-02-45	428 Sqn
J/92436	P/O	KELLY Ivan Wesley	31-03-45	156 Sqn
C/85137	F/O	KELWAY Connaught	5-01-45	427 Sqn
J/42491	F/O	KEMP Dennis Stuart	15-02-45	166 Sqn
J/93156	P/O	KENNEDY George Alexander	13-03-45	433 Sqn
J/47772	P/O	KENNY Jack [USA]	1-02-45	101 Sqn
J/89858	F/O	KERLUK William	16-01-45	12 Sqn
J/40366	F/O	KERR Bertram Clarence	16-03-45	12 Sqn
J/94215	P/O	KETCHEN John Barton	22-03-45	431 Sqn
J/18584	F/L	KIEHL BAUCH Aaron	16-01-45	434 Sqn
J/94849	P/O	KING Jack Alexander Stewart	6-03-45	419 Sqn
J/28299	F/O	KINGDON Robert Verdun	21-03-45	214 Sqn
R/250856	WO2	KINNEY Irvine James	4-04-45	635 Sqn
J/11038	F/L	KIRKPATRICK John Gillespie	5-03-45	426 Sqn
J/39890	F/O	KLATMAN Joseph	14-01-45	1666 HCU
R/105664	Sgt	KLEM John	7-03-45	424 Sqn
R/275494	F/S	KLEMENTOSKI Walter John	21-03-45	550 Sqn
J/16251	F/L	KNIGHTS DFC John Kingsley	14-02-45	405 Sqn
J/89848	P/O	KOPP John Walter	21-02-45	431 Sqn
J/94601	P/O	KOSSATZ Thomas Carle	15-03-45	434 Sqn
J/24167	F/L	KROEKER Walter	5-04-45	12 Sqn
J/95378	P/O	KUBIN John Richard	21-02-45	424 Sqn
R/253892	F/S	LAFERRIERE Joseph Claude Raul Andre	8-04-45	1659 HCU
J/26398	F/L	LAFFOLEY John Gifford Laurence	4-03-45	10 Sqn
J/94146	P/O	LAING James Christopher	9-02-45	426 Sqn
J/26053	F/L	LAING MiD Leslie Norman	15-03-45	405 Sqn
J/95374	P/O	LAMARRE Joseph Yves Jean Claude	6-01-45	425 Sqn
C/93898	P/O	LAMPHEAR Norman Robert [USA]	15-02-45	640 Sqn
J/43946	F/O	LANG Wallace Ewing	5-11-45	429 Sqn
J/9688	F/L	LARGE George Russell	16-04-45	408 Sqn
J/95382	P/O	LARSON John Alexander Henry	5-03-45	426 Sqn
J/17438	F/O	LATREMOUILLE Joe Richard	11-03-45	434 Sqn
R/202904	F/S	LAUT George Weston	7-03-45	424 Sqn
R/214612	WO2	LAWLEY Thomas Daniel	30-04-45	428 Sqn
J/43739	F/O	LAWRENCE Thomas Selborne	7-03-45	424 Sqn
J/95383	P/O	LAWTON Darwin Cameron	15-03-45	432 Sqn
J/42183	F/O	LAY William Robert	25-03-45	408 Sqn
J/94158	P/O	LECKY Clarence Reginald	11-03-45	431 Sqn
R/56113	WO1	LEDOUX Joseph Henri Roger Robert	31-03-45	429 Sqn
J/42216	F/O	LEE Jim Gen	23-03-45	101 Sqn
J/93959	P/O	LEEMING John	3-02-45	50 Sqn
J/94850	P/O	LEET Finely Ralph	6-03-45	419 Sqn
R/175258	LAC	LEFEVRE Allan William	21-06-45	433 Sqn
J/24304	F/O	LEITHEAD Frank Taylor	5-01-45	408 Sqn
J/94407	P/O	LEROUX Adrian Steve	6-03-45	429 Sqn
C/3879	F/L	LESESNE Charles [USA]	31-03-45	425 Sqn
J/24469	F/O	LESLIE William Alexander	1-03-45	24 OTU
J/40105	F/O	LEWIS Thomas Stewart	31-03-45	415 Sqn
J/37352	F/O	LE JAMBE Gilbert Newton Joseph	19-03-45	425 Sqn
R/203283	F/S	LE LIEVER Donald Elmer	23-02-45	170 Sqn
J/95386	P/O	LINDSAY Egan	24-03-45	550 Sqn
J/40040	F/O	LINEY Gerald Joseph	28-01-45	428 Sqn
J/27079	F/L	LING Frank James	14-03-45	50 Sqn
J/95376	P/O	LININGTON Donald Edwin	16-01-45	12 Sqn
J/94527	P/O	LINSTEAD John Blair	5-03-45	426 Sqn
J/41724	F/O	LITTLE Ralph Robert [USA]	23-03-45	101 Sqn
J/40372	F/O	LITTLE Thomas Bruce	29-01-45	408 Sqn
J/95258	P/O	LIVERMORE Carl Herman	25-04-45	76 Sqn
J/12206	F/L	LIVING Charles Henry	21-02-45	576 Sqn
J/95389	P/O	LIVINGSTON Gordon Archie	14-04-45	419 Sqn
J/42728	F/O	LLOYD George Henry	4-03-45	1664 HCU
J/42249	F/O	LOFT Charles Robert	14-04-45	419 Sqn
R/265925	Sgt	LONG Michael La Verne	14-01-45	1666 HCU
J/47170	F/O	LONG William James	17-05-45	1669 HCU
J/95388	P/O	LORENZ Douglas Leander	10-04-45	415 Sqn
J/92380	P/O	LOTHIAN Thomas James [Bahamas]	12-02-45	622 Sqn
J/40492	F/O	LOUGHEED Ralph James	7-01-45	103 Sqn
J/38242	F/O	LOUIE Quan Jil	16-01-45	420 Sqn
J/29556	F/O	LOWE Arthur Robert [USA]	5-03-45	425 Sqn
J/94582	P/O	LUXTON Eric Laurence	4-04-45	115 Sqn
R/201189	Sgt	LYNCH James Laurids	5-03-45	425 Sqn
J/41812	F/O	MABEE Keith Wearning	16-03-45	12 Sqn
R/252286	F/S	MacDONALD Charles Campbell	5-04-45	24 OTU
J/95362	P/O	MacDONALD Colin Bruce	5-03-45	431 Sqn
K/264905	F/S	MacDONALD James Livingston	8-02-45	619 Sqn
J/42188	F/O	MacDONALD Lorne Albert	14-02-45	153 Sqn
R/283114	Sgt	MacDONNELL Angus John	15-01-45	1659 HCU
J/94554	P/O	MacDOUGALL John Neil	5-03-45	426 Sqn
J/87425	F/O	MacFARLANE John Alexander	9-04-45	61 Sqn
R/217048	F/S	MacKAY John Garwood	8-01-45	166 Sqn
R/203166	F/S	MacKENZIE Hugh Munro	29-01-45	5 LFS
J/95385	P/O	MacKENZIE John	22-03-45	428 Sqn
R/65193	WO1	MacKENZIE Warren Ellwood	19-04-45	419 Sqn
J/35422	F/O	MacLEOD Malcolm Alexander	15-01-45	431 Sqn
J/39387	F/O	MacMILLAN Hubert Joseph	7-02-45	12 Sqn
J/13273	F/L	MacNABB Donald Scott	24-02-45	429 Sqn
C/27955	F/O	MacNEILL Bevan Terrill	7-03-45	419 Sqn
R/224743	F/S	MacNICOLL Robert Campbell	21-02-45	207 Sqn
J/95375	P/O	MACDONELL Charles Beverly	15-01-45	431 Sqn
J/88245	F/O	MACKIE DFC Alexander Morton	12-01-45	424 Sqn
J/94615	P/O	MACKIE Angus	27-02-45	429 Sqn
J/95390	P/O	MACLAREN Colin Charles	14-04-45	419 Sqn
J/95550	P/O	MACLENNAN Bruce	31-03-45	419 Sqn
C/12525	F/L	MACONACHIE James Roy Alexander	28-02-45	128 Sqn
J/95544	P/O	MAGEE James Thomas Joseph	6-03-45	576 Sqn
J/38058	F/O	MAGRATH Douglas Arthur	14-02-45	431 Sqn
J/20939	F/L	MAGUIRE Edward Stidston	21-02-45	432 Sqn
J/20876	F/L	MAGUIRE John Goodwin	21-02-45	432 Sqn
J/35749	F/O	MAHLER Laurence Herman	9-02-45	405 Sqn
J/95545	P/O	MAHR Rudolph Walter	8-03-45	101 Sqn
J/38216	F/O	MALLEN William Brown	21-02-45	76 Sqn
J/29566	F/O	MALONEY DFC William Patrick	21-02-45	625 Sqn
J/93797	F/O	MALTBY William Thomas	4-03-45	76 Sqn
J/93612	F/O	MALYON William John	16-03-45	12 Sqn
J/44304	F/O	MANNING Frederick John	28-03-45	692 Sqn
J/16120	F/L	MARA DFC Neil Duncan	4-02-45	433 Sqn
J/85813	F/O	MARCHANT John Phillip	25-03-45	408 Sqn
R/190707	WO2	MARK Clarence Robert Irwin	25-04-45	431 Sqn
R/266317	F/S	MARSH Francis Joseph	15-03-45	405 Sqn
J/88129	F/O	MARTIN Bernhard William	3-02-45	419 Sqn
J/88491	F/O	MARTIN Maurice James	9-02-45	405 Sqn
J/91116	P/O	MARTIN William David	16-01-45	434 Sqn
R/100717	Cpl	MASON Charles Richard	22-01-45	1692 Flt
J/45935	F/O	MATHESON William Henry	10-02-45	1666 HCU
J/90601	P/O	MATHISON Earl Donald	1-01-45	115 Sqn
J/37099	F/O	MATKIN Merlin Leigh	17-01-45	514 Sqn
R/202907	LAC	MATTSON Vernon Gilbert	13-02-45	1659 HCU
J/95402	P/O	MATUSZEWSKI George	31-03-45	419 Sqn
J/37824	F/O	McALLISTER Vincent Paul	8-03-45	425 Sqn
J/92212	F/O	McARTHUR William John	7-01-45	103 Sqn
K/271305	F/S	McAULAY Donald Joseph	7-01-45	103 Sqn
J/22700	F/L	McBRIDE Charles Wylie	17-03-45	619 Sqn
J/93280	P/O	McBRINN Patrick Joseph	1-02-45	76 Sqn
J/89343	P/O	McCALLUM Robert John	15-02-45	429 Sqn

ID	Rank	Name	Date	Sqn
J/94463	P/O	McCARTHY Benedict Joseph	5-03-45	426 Sqn
R/287915	Sgt	McCASKILL Richard Llewellyn	5-04-45	24 OTU
J/36312	F/O	McCAULEY Gordon Theodore	21-02-45	578 Sqn
J/95360	P/O	McCLARTY Edward John	21-02-45	432 Sqn
R/208972	F/S	McCLELLAND Wilfred Glenn	7-01-45	576 Sqn
J/41476	F/O	McCOLLUM Jack Ross	25-03-45	415 Sqn
J/95357	P/O	McCORMICK James Francis	16-01-45	420 Sqn
R/143248	WO2	McCOY Kenneth Lloyd Douglas [USA]	3-03-45	153 Sqn
J/40900		McCREA James Alexander	15-01-45	1659 HCU
J/25218	F/L	McCUTCHEON DFC Elvet Baxter	16-01-45	420 Sqn
J/37891	F/O	McDONALD John Alexander Francis	3-02-45	419 Sqn
R/145804	WO1	McDONALD John Swan	19-03-45	218 Sqn
R/278922	F/S	McDONALD Richard Albert	18-04-45	420 Sqn
J/95387	F/O	McDONALD Wesley Ernest	24-03-45	550 Sqn
J/39266	F/O	McELHONE John Joseph [USA]	14-02-45	431 Sqn
J/94252	P/O	McFAYDEN Donald Alexander	22-02-45	50 Sqn
J/95354	P/O	McFEE John Curwood	5-01-45	50 Sqn
J/40652	P/O	McGREGOR Duncan Pearson	15-01-45	1659 HCU
J/95355	P/O	McINNES Colin Harvey	5-01-45	432 Sqn
J/86652	F/O	McINTYRE Hubert Bates	9-02-45	405 Sqn
C/94955	P/O	McIVOR Kenneth Bruce	18-05-45	408 Sqn
J/95356	P/O	McKAY Alexander Grant	15-01-45	419 Sqn
J/28933	F/O	McKAY Donald Gordon	16-01-45	405 Sqn
J/38401	F/O	McKAY Murray Roy	9-04-45	49 Sqn
J/37716	F/O	McKEE Terrance Velleau	17-01-45	214 Sqn
J/95380	P/O	McKEOWN Kenneth Creighton	21-02-45	77 Sqn
J/38407	F/O	McLEAN George Daryll	22-03-45	431 Sqn
J/26306	F/O	McLEAN John Kenneth	8-01-45	166 Sqn
J/35287	F/O	McLEAN William Eugene	2-02-45	514 Sqn
C/95381	F/O	McLEOD Alan John	21-02-45	427 Sqn
J/94365	P/O	McLEOD Harold Dick	5-03-45	426 Sqn
J/42059	F/O	McLEOD John Clair	5-01-45	82 OTU
J/95353	P/O	McLEOD John William	1-01-45	115 Sqn
J/39929	F/O	McLEOD William Gordon	10-04-45	433 Sqn
J/95363	P/O	McMANUS Rupert George	7-03-45	408 Sqn
J/95358	P/O	McMASTER Malcolm Stalker	16-01-45	100 Sqn
J/35127	F/O	McMILLAN Colin William	21-02-45	432 Sqn
J/35716	F/O	McMILLAN Donald James	1-02-45	433 Sqn
J/35722	F/L	McMORRAN Albert Elmore	11-04-45	619 Sqn
J/36260	F/L	McMORRAN George Melvin Stark	8-03-45	619 Sqn
J/90038	P/O	McMULLEN William Stuart	13-01-45	428 Sqn
R/253156	F/S	McMURCHY Kenneth Cameron	15-02-45	424 Sqn
R/67119	Sgt	McMURDO John William	14-01-45	26 OTU
R/252422	F/S	McNEIL James Joseph	21-02-45	76 Sqn
J/92166	P/O	McNIE Donald Cameron	2-02-45	619 Sqn
J/29733	F/L	McPHEE Joseph Noel	15-03-45	49 Sqn
J/28958	F/L	McQUILLAN Murray Robert	23-02-45	97 Sqn
J/85341	F/O	McQUITTY Thomas	6-01-45	431 Sqn
J/89146	F/O	McSHANE John Thomas	1-02-45	433 Sqn
R/164145	WO1	McVICAR Glenn Duncan	1-03-45	24 OTU
7729	Sgt	McWHINNEY Albert Richard	3-02-45	514 Sqn
J/44158	F/O	MEDYNSKI Lorne	14-02-45	431 Sqn
J/29614	F/O	MELBOURNE Wilfred Laurier	4-02-45	433 Sqn
R/205716	F/S	MELLON Ralph Jackson	25-04-45	431 Sqn
J/18414	F/L	MELLSTROM DFC Melborn Leslie	10-04-45	405 Sqn
J/93949	P/O	MENDENHALL Wells Gibb	21-02-45	432 Sqn
R/223545	F/S	MERRIMAN Cyril Clinton	15-01-45	626 Sqn
J/38224	F/O	METCALFE Thomas	19-02-45	90 Sqn
J/24761	F/L	METIVIER Harry Alfred	31-03-45	419 Sqn
J/95395	P/O	MIELL Harold Edward	7-01-45	550 Sqn
J/27560	P/O	MILLAR Robert William	21-03-45	419 Sqn
J/88574	P/O	MILLER Allan Bernard	16-01-45	405 Sqn
J/42233	P/O	MILLER Donald Mitchell	18-04-45	408 Sqn
J/93406	P/O	MILLER Francis John	15-03-45	405 Sqn
J/94348	P/O	MILLER Kenneth Alexander	15-02-45	424 Sqn
J/94338	P/O	MILLER William Gordon	5-03-45	426 Sqn
J/95401	P/O	MILLMAN Robert Bruce	14-03-45	50 Sqn
J/6675	F/L	MILLS Clement Robert	14-02-45	153 Sqn
J/43411	F/O	MILLS Murray Allison	5-01-45	35 Sqn
J/95399	P/O	MINGUET Albert Emile	5-03-45	425 Sqn
R/263463	F/S	MINO Harold	17-03-45	619 Sqn
J/93003	P/O	MISON Charles Donald	6-01-45	171 Sqn
J/20407	F/L	MITCHELL DFC Charles George	8-03-45	35 Sqn
J/44683	F/O	MITCHELL Ewing Francis Willys	5-04-45	24 OTU
J/95457	P/O	MITCHELL Reginald Leroy	7-03-45	419 Sqn
J/25071		MODELAND Clarence Edward	5-04-45	12 Sqn
J/95452	P/O	MOGRIDGE Parker Reginald	16-01-45	415 Sqn
J/23484	F/L	MOIR Corson Stewart	21-02-45	432 Sqn
R/117982	LAC	MONGRAIN Joseph Armand Jean Marie	20-07-45	62 Base
R/208136	F/S	MONTGOMERY George Franklin	18-04-45	420 Sqn
J/38975	F/O	MOONEY Frank William	15-01-45	1659 HCU
R/274063	Sgt	MORGAN William Joseph	2-01-45	166 Sqn
J/37326	F/O	MORIN Joseph Lucien Viateur	15-03-45	431 Sqn
J/94355	P/O	MORIN Joseph Robert	8-03-45	425 Sqn
J/95458	P/O	MORPHY Earl Edward	31-03-45	419 Sqn
J/95454	P/O	MORRISON Alfred Hector	3-02-45	514 Sqn
J/38317	F/O	MORRISON Colin Ross Milne	25-04-45	76 Sqn
J/89791	P/O	MORTLEY Jack Clarence	29-01-45	408 Sqn
J/95543	P/O	MOYLE Joseph Francis Edward	8-02-45	619 Sqn
J/29516	F/L	MUNRO DFC Lorne Earle	31-03-45	156 Sqn
R/68046	Sgt	MURPHY Leroy Francis Joseph	18-04-45	420 Sqn
J/36314	F/O	MURRAY DFC Thomas Robertson	15-01-45	626 Sqn
J/39365	F/O	MYERS Frank Macgregor	5-03-45	426 Sqn
J/93930	P/O	NAULT Joseph Paul	6-03-45	429 Sqn
R/202923	F/S	NEAL Harold Allan	21-02-45	166 Sqn
J/40421	F/O	NEIL David Llewellyn	18-02-45	420 Sqn
J.95455	P/O	NEIL Edric Stephen	21-02-45	153 Sqn
J/42662	F/O	NEILSON Donald Maurice	18-04-45	420 Sqn
J/95459	P/O	NEILSON James Andrew	31-03-45	415 Sqn
J/39876	F/O	NELSON Thomas Joseph	4-03-45	189 Sqn
J/93892	P/O	NETZKE James Samuel	12-01-45	424 Sqn
R/290688	F/S	NEWMAN Davey William	18-04-45	420 Sqn
J/95456	P/O	NEWMAN Francis Edwin	21-02-45	431 Sqn
J/87580	F/O	NEWTON Clifford Sinclair [USA]	1-01-45	9 Sqn
J/17196	F/L	NEWTON Raymond William	15-03-45	428 Sqn
J/89450	F/O	NICHOLLS William Frederick	13-01-45	426 Sqn
R/162418	LAC	NICHOLSON Ronald Kenneth	17-06-45	1666 HCU
J/18427	F/O	NICKERSON Frederick John	6-01-45	431 Sqn
J/39314	F/O	NICOL William Frederick 'Bill' [USA]	17-03-45	576 Sqn
J/94159	P/O	NICOLLS Robert James	28-01-45	424 Sqn
J/94369	F/O	NIELSEN Marius Bendt	6-03-45	432 Sqn
J/41139	F/O	NIGHTINGALE William Edwin [United Kingdom]	8-03-45	103 Sqn
J/95453	P/O	NISBET Robert Albert	3-02-45	419 Sqn
J/95451	P/O	NOBLE George Adrian	20-01-45	420 Sqn
J/38343	F/O	NOVAK Henry Eugene	16-01-45	405 Sqn
J/40103	F/O	OAKES William Hugh	5-03-45	420 Sqn
J/43026	F/O	OLSON Donald Brant	14-02-45	405 Sqn
J/21973	F/L	ORDIN Carl Joseph	2-02-45	428 Sqn
J/39972	F/O	ORNSTEIN Morley	23-03-45	101 Sqn
J/94381	P/O	ORSER Gilbert Melbourne	6-03-45	432 Sqn
J/43415	F/O	OUROM Richard Knut	28-04-45	1653 HCU
J/95259	P/O	OUTERSON Joseph Lawrie 'Scrappy'	25-04-45	76 Sqn
J/29718	F/O	O'BRIEN John Anthony	29-01-45	408 Sqn
J/45422	F/O	O'BRYAN William Ernest Hugh	19-03-45	571 Sqn
R/212801	F/S	O'CONNOR George Dalton	31-01-45	19 OTU
J/89205	P/O	O'KANE Thomas Leslie	18-02-45	420 Sqn
J/35019	F/O	O'NEILL Thomas Joseph	22-02-45	626 Sqn
R/267626	F/S	O'REILLY Richard Joseph	16-03-45	100 Sqn
R/120092	F/S	O'ROURKE Edward John	3-04-45	626 Sqn
J/35525	F/O	PALANEK Anthony Joseph	21-03-45	419 Sqn
J/47443	F/O	PALLECK John Patrick Francis	8-06-45	24 OTU
J/95469	P/O	PANASUK Paul	19-03-45	425 Sqn

Service #	Rank	Name	Date	Squadron
J/94160	P/O	PARENT Leonard John	8-03-45	425 Sqn
J/36081	F/O	PARKER Kenneth George	5-03-45	426 Sqn
J/13600	F/L	PARKHURST Keith Edwin	15-03-45	405 Sqn
J/95585	P/O	PARKS Rowland Ira	17-03-45	103 Sqn
J/94893	P/O	PARRISH Charles William	16-03-45	419 Sqn
J/90535	P/O	PARTRIDGE William John Desmond	16-01-45	420 Sqn
J/41525	F/O	PASCAL Stephen	24-03-45	166 Sqn
U/190354	F/S	PATERSON Franklyn Hayward	21-02-45	170 Sqn
J/90015	P/O	PATRY Joseph Victor Leopold Andre	15-03-45	425 Sqn
J/27526	F/O	PATTERSON Wilfred Nicholson	21-02-45	626 Sqn
J/87362	F/O	PATZER Edwin Frederick	21-02-45	432 Sqn
J/95472	P/O	PAUL Robert Andrew	25-03-45	415 Sqn
J/95397	P/O	PAXTON James Gordon	2-03-45	408 Sqn
J/5549	F/L	PAYNE Harold Leslie	16-01-45	405 Sqn
J/89673	P/O	PEAK John Frederick	14-02-45	427 Sqn
J/35687	P/O	PEAKER George Ernest	19-03-45	405 Sqn
J/42664	P/O	PEARSON James Charles	16-03-45	1664 HCU
J/95473	P/O	PEDEN Gordon James	31-03-45	415 Sqn
J/95470	P/O	PELLANT James Walter	21-03-45	214 Sqn
J/94603	P/O	PELLETIER Joseph Louis Gaston	5-03-45	425 Sqn
J/93611	P/O	PENNINGTON John	21-02-45	76 Sqn
J/95518	P/O	PENNY Leo Joseph	16-01-45	420 Sqn
R/215508	F/S	PERRAULT Ernest Francis	19-03-45	405 Sqn
J/45525	F/O	PETERS Nicholas	7-03-45	214 Sqn
R/255048	LAC	PETLEY Ralph Edgar	6-08-45	76 Base
C/95400	P/O	PETTIFOR Arthur Clifford	11-03-45	431 Sqn
J/94363	P/O	PEVERLEY Edward James	17-03-45	576 Sqn
J/17869	F/O	PHELAN Terrence Benedict	21-02-45	207 Sqn
R/276302	F/S	PHILLIPS Gorden James	3-03-45	207 Sqn
J/93349	P/O	PHILLIPS Wilfred James	21-02-45	76 Sqn
J/92868	P/O	PICHE Jean Adolphe Fernand	5-01-45	425 Sqn
R/253010	F/S	PIERCY Reginald Frank	25-02-45	429 Sqn
J/92192	P/O	PIERSON Roy	1-02-45	433 Sqn
J/95468	P/O	PIERSON Thomas Clyde	13-03-45	433 Sqn
R/125451	WO1	PIXLEY Asa Nelson	18-04-45	408 Sqn
J/41513	P/O	PLANTE Arthur Vincent	13-03-45	433 Sqn
J/92187	P/O	PLAYTER Ross Alexander	3-02-45	428 Sqn
R/193831	F/S	POGSON Charles Herman	2-01-45	153 Sqn
J/39383	P/O	POKRYFKA Paul	24-02-45	415 Sqn
J/16530	F/L	POOL DFC George Robert	6-01-45	431 Sqn
J/94844	P/O	POOLE Norman Roland	6-03-45	419 Sqn
J/86081	P/O	PORRITT William Howard	16-04-45	432 Sqn
R/159132	WO1	POTVIN Joseph Adrian Leo	8-04-45	1659 HCU
R/190262	F/S	POUGNET James Maurice	9-04-45	78 Sqn
R/281135	F/S	PRESTON Arthur Wallace	15-03-45	153 Sqn
J/40515	F/O	PRIDHAM Kenneth Mark	10-02-45	1666 HCU
J/94371	P/O	PRINCE Henry Nixon	6-03-45	429 Sqn
R/164403	WO1	PYATT Robert Stanley	22-02-45	626 Sqn
J/25448	F/L	QUIGLEY Frederick Thomas	16-01-45	100 Sqn
J/38291	F/O	QUINN Donald Swallow	17-03-45	576 Sqn
R/166920	F/S	QUINN Robert Andrew	7-01-45	405 Sqn
J/93942	P/O	QUINN Thomas Phillip	29-01-45	408 Sqn
R/211384	F/S	RABINER Joseph	31-03-45	692 Sqn
R/221847	F/S	RAE John MacCauley	28-01-45	405 Sqn
J/95546	P/O	RAE Leslie Elmer	16-03-45	12 Sqn
R/152927	F/S	RAHKOLA Wayne John	8-01-45	626 Sqn
J/24809	F/O	RAINFORD Keith Willard	15-02-45	429 Sqn
J/41538	P/O	RAMSAY John	25-04-45	76 Sqn
R/87930	WO1	RAMSDEN Samuel Smart	22-04-45	97 Sqn
J/27234	F/S	RAMSEY Colin John Pope	21-02-45	158 Sqn
R/168095	WO2	RATHBONE Richard Barlow	29-01-45	5 LFS
J/40731	F/O	RATHWELL Douglas Gordon	31-03-45	434 Sqn
R/160471	WO2	RAU Orville Jack	15-03-45	431 Sqn
J/94588	P/O	REA John	31-03-45	419 Sqn
J/38761	F/O	REANEY Elias Eldon	15-02-45	424 Sqn
J/26340	F/O	RECH Edward Werner	14-01-45	12 Sqn
J/43105	F/O	REEDER Arthur Joseph	5-01-45	35 Sqn
J/89185	F/O	REID Daniel Clifford	2-01-45	153 Sqn
J/41869	F/O	REID Harold William	5-04-45	626 Sqn
R/190328	F/S	REID John Henry	29-01-45	5 LFS
J/35563	F/O	REID Sidney James	4-03-45	189 Sqn
J/38869	F/O	REID Stanley Arthur	5-03-45	431 Sqn
J/94243	P/O	REILLY Charles Thomas	12-01-45	424 Sqn
J/36568	F/O	REITLO Clifford Lester	6-03-45	419 Sqn
J/93258	P/O	REPSYS Peter Paul	15-03-45	431 Sqn
R/274514	F/S	REYNOLDS William Cyril Jeffrey	17-03-45	166 Sqn
J/37836	F/O	RHIND Edward	5-01-45	415 Sqn
R/252612	F/S	RICHARDS Edward Gordon Coke	15-03-45	49 Sqn
R/218495	F/S	RIGGS Leonard Earl	3-01-45	166 Sqn
J/26610	F/O	RILEY Norman Geoffrey	8-01-45	1546 Flt
C/95465	P/O	RINDER James Armitage	5-01-45	415 Sqn
J/93591	P/O	RINGROSE Dennis Joseph	6-03-45	432 Sqn
J/40335	F/O	RINK Wendelin	11-03-45	431 Sqn
J/5118	F/L	ROBB Peter Franklin	23-02-45	429 Sqn
J/93460	P/O	ROBERTS Charles James	6-03-45	10 Sqn
J/95323	P/O	ROBERTS David William	10-04-45	433 Sqn
R/263475	F/S	ROBERTS Wesley Grenfell	23-02-45	158 Sqn
J/95467	P/O	ROBERTSON Gordon Edwin	14-02-45	431 Sqn
J/45658	P/O	ROBILLARD Lou Jean	5-01-45	82 OTU
J/40915	F/O	ROBINSON Donald William Burroughs	7-03-45	424 Sqn
J/39006	F/O	ROBINSON Graeme Alastair	15-03-45	49 Sqn
J/40685	F/O	ROBINSON John Thomas	2-02-45	432 Sqn
J/95524	P/O	ROBINSON Stewart James Olson	5-04-45	424 Sqn
R/290092	F/S	ROBITAILLE Francis Clesphas Martial	20-04-45	1660 HCU
R/223493	Sgt	ROBSON Albert Russel	15-01-45	1659 HCU
R/151349	F/S	ROCHESTER John Lorne	1-03-45	103 Sqn
J/39294	F/O	ROCHFORD Joseph	5-04-45	424 Sqn
R/210007	F/S	ROLLER Ray Calvin	16-01-45	100 Sqn
R/261128	F/S	ROOT Clayton Edward	22-03-45	431 Sqn
J/92419	P/O	ROSE John Thomas	14-02-45	9 Sqn
J/8165	F/L	ROSS Donald Alexander	5-03-45	424 Sqn
J/43876	P/O	ROSS Donald Fraser	18-04-45	420 Sqn
J/41679	F/O	ROSS John Douglas Carlisle	25-04-45	426 Sqn
R/197407	F/S	ROSS John William	28-01-45	428 Sqn
J/93595	P/O	ROSS-ROSS Peter Donald	4-03-45	227 Sqn
R/274046	F/S	ROSU Sam	7-03-45	424 Sqn
J/35290	F/O	ROUSE Charles James	6-03-45	576 Sqn
J/41979	F/O	ROUTHIER Joseph Louis Philippe	8-04-45	1659 HCU
J/93926	P/O	ROUTLEY William Arthur	21-03-45	214 Sqn
J/16574	F/L	ROWE DFC Alfred George	11-03-45	434 Sqn
J/94670	P/O	ROY Joseph Donat Fernand Eugene	5-03-45	425 Sqn
R/207469	F/S	ROY Joseph Jules Pierre Raymond	25-04-45	431 Sqn
J/86214	P/O	ROY Vernon Shillington	14-02-45	427 Sqn
J/16411	F/L	RUBIN DFC Hector Bernard	21-03-45	419 Sqn
J/95474	P/O	RUDE Gordon Justine	31-03-45	415 Sqn
J/95466	P/O	RUMBALL Harold Marland	15-03-45	419 Sqn
J/93851	P/O	RUNDLE Sidney Gordon	28-01-45	426 Sqn
J/95488	P/O	RUSSELL David George	2-02-45	460 Sqn
J/38684	F/O	RUSSELL John Arnold	21-02-45	576 Sqn
J/94268	P/O	RUSSELL Lewis Alexander	24-02-45	415 Sqn
J/37745	F/O	RUTLAND Bruce Wells	14-03-45	50 Sqn
J/95260	P/O	RUTTER Albert Leroy	25-04-45	408 Sqn
R/201885	F/S	SABINE John Ernest	3-03-45	153 Sqn
J/22024	F/L	SALES James Ernest	5-01-45	432 Sqn
J/29724	F/L	SANDERSON Donald McWilliam	21-02-45	408 Sqn
J/14905	F/L	SANDERSON Mardyth Wesley [USA]	6-03-45	429 Sqn
R/181716	WO2	SANDOMIRSKY Marvin Max	3-03-45	153 Sqn
J/27612	F/O	SASLOVE Edward Lewis	7-01-45	576 Sqn
R/269079	F/S	SAUNDERCOOK Roland James	17-03-45	576 Sqn
R/193951	F/S	SAVAGE Edwin Robert	28-01-45	405 Sqn
J/35005	F/O	SAVARD Joseph Lionel Misael Raymond	5-01-45	429 Sqn
R/126096	LAC	SAVOIE Alyre	15-10-45	Leeming

ID	Rank	Name	Date	Unit
R/202506	Sgt	SAVY Joseph Aloysius	15-01-45	1659 HCU
J/88010	F/O	SAXE Samuel Leo	8-03-45	103 Sqn
J/13449	F/L	SCHEELAR Andrew Frank [USA]	5-01-45	408 Sqn
J/93071	P/O	SCHWARTZ Moses	15-02-45	78 Sqn
R/187219	F/S	SCORAH Alden Norman	14-02-45	427 Sqn
J/43783	F/O	SCOTT Frank	1-03-45	24 OTU
J/18994	F/O	SCOTT Gibson	11-03-45	434 Sqn
J/92782	P/O	SCOTT Norman Lester William	7-01-45	405 Sqn
J/41118	F/O	SCOTT Richard McDiarmid	27-02-45	429 Sqn
J/95497	P/O	SCOTT Thomas Delmer	3-04-45	432 Sqn
J/36516	F/O	SEABY Francis Edward	5-03-45	424 Sqn
J/95252	P/O	SEELEY Francis Gerald	10-04-45	433 Sqn
R/171212	F/S	SEGUIN Joseph Louis Paul	5-03-45	425 Sqn
J/42214	P/O	SEMENIUK William	5-04-45	626 Sqn
J/46101	F/O	SERGEANT Matthew Frederick Easton	5-04-45	626 Sqn
J/42248	F/O	SHANTZ Frederick Weber	25-03-45	408 Sqn
J/38730	F/O	SHATZKY Michael	8-03-45	101 Sqn
J/38729	F/O	SHAW George Guelph	16-01-45	434 Sqn
J/95490	P/O	SHEERAN Brian Terence	4-02-45	433 Sqn
J/38734	F/O	SHEPHARD George Harry Percival	21-02-45	625 Sqn
J/95492	P/O	SHERMAN Donald Edison	21-02-45	408 Sqn
K/263945	F/S	SHILLIDAY Robert Charles	16-01-45	153 Sqn
J/39342	F/O	SHIREY John William	16-01-45	426 Sqn
J/40907	F/O	SHORT William Edward	7-03-45	419 Sqn
J/93527	P/O	SICOTTE Joseph Georges Louis Raymond	8-04-45	1659 HCU
J/93945	P/O	SIEWERT Robert Lloyd	29-01-45	408 Sqn
J/94220	P/O	SILLS Earl Albert Henry	14-02-45	420 Sqn
J/95489	P/O	SILVER Robert George Earl	2-02-45	432 Sqn
R/125326	WO2	SIMARD Jean Jacques Marcel	14-01-45	425 Sqn
J/93466	P/O	SIMONIN Bernard Gerard	5-01-45	425 Sqn
J/95493	P/O	SIMPSON Robert John	21-02-45	49 Sqn
J/37506	F/O	SINDEN John Charles	14-02-45	420 Sqn
R/264550	F/S	SKINNER John Hedley	5-03-45	1662 HCU
R/123313	F/S	SLACK Kenneth Earl Clifford	9-05-45	433 Sqn
J/93609	P/O	SLAUENWHITE Lester Leon	25-04-45	76 Sqn
J/37723	F/O	SLAUGHTER Murray Charles	25-04-45	76 Sqn
J/41191	F/O	SLOCUM Arthur Gordon	15-02-45	625 Sqn
J/41413	F/O	SMALL George Henry	15-03-45	153 Sqn
J/25766	F/L	SMALLEY Robert Cecil	8-02-45	97 Sqn
J/35778	F/O	SMITH Donald George	17-03-45	405 Sqn
J/95487	P/O	SMITH Gerald Albert	28-01-45	405 Sqn
J/40650	F/O	SMITH Matthew Arnold	22-01-45	153 Sqn
J/95486	P/O	SMITH Norman Lawrence Lavek	16-01-45	405 Sqn
J/38711	F/O	SMITH Reginald Bertram	21-02-45	408 Sqn
J/87951	F/O	SMITH Robert George	5-03-45	420 Sqn
J/36983	F/O	SMITH MiD Robert Marshall	7-01-45	626 Sqn
J/95491	P/O	SMITH Vernon Beverley	15-02-45	424 Sqn
J/22913	F/L	SMITH William Dalton	5-04-45	12 Sqn
K/251009	LAC	SMITH William Herbert	4-04-45	63 Base
J/44733	F/L	SNETSINGER Arnold Joseph	10-02-45	1666 HCU
J/93048	P/O	SOLLIE Roald Frederick	5-03-45	420 Sqn
J/10995	F/L	SOMERVILLE John Hogarth	7-02-45	12 Sqn
J/94593	P/O	SOMMERVILLE William Muir	31-03-45	419 Sqn
J/35275	F/O	SOPER Walter Young James	8-01-45	166 Sqn
J/94334	F/O	SOUTHCOTT Ward Rex	21-02-45	50 Sqn
J/95495	P/O	SOWTER Roy Tyldesley	23-02-45	550 Sqn
J/86068	F/L	SPANKIE DFC Edward	1-02-45	166 Sqn
J/28709	F/L	SPARLING Leslie Garwood	7-01-45	405 Sqn
J/39399	F/O	SPENCE Donald William	7-01-45	419 Sqn
J/37483	F/O	SPENCER George Douglas Melbourne	15-01-45	419 Sqn
J/43502	F/O	SPICE Donald Angus	31-01-45	19 OTU
J/35536	F/O	SPLATT Lawrence William	7-01-45	405 Sqn
J/39881	F/O	SPRY Lorne Mortimore	10-04-45	415 Sqn
J/39910	F/O	STANDFIELD Donald Arthur	7-03-45	424 Sqn
J/42259	F/O	STANLEY James Kent	25-04-45	408 Sqn
J/42702	F/O	STANZEL Ross Samuel	14-02-45	153 Sqn
R/283110	Sgt	STAVENOW Leonard Charles	15-01-45	1659 HCU
J/86776	F/O	STAVES Arthur Wiebert	6-01-45	431 Sqn
R/79565	Cpl	STENHOUSE Robert Craig	18-03-45	62 Base
J/87987	F/L	STEPHARNOFF Arthur Lloyd	17-03-45	103 Sqn
J/40767	F/O	STEPHENS Donald Edward	3-02-45	514 Sqn
J/95484	P/O	STEVENS Elwood Leroy	5-01-45	102 Sqn
R/126276	F/S	STEVENS Gordon Brassett	14-04-45	22 OTU
J/41771	F/O	STEVENS Maurice Frederick	28-01-45	1664 HCU
J/92546	P/O	STEVENS Robert Slade	1-01-45	9 Sqn
R/88151	Sgt	STEVENSON John	8-04-45	1659 HCU
J/38861	F/O	STEWART DFC Jack Ormsby	15-03-45	434 Sqn
J/38395	F/O	STILLINGER Roy Edward	5-03-45	426 Sqn
J/17618	F/O	STILLINGS John Earl [USA]	8-04-45	1659 HCU
J/21558	F/L	STINGLE Robert John	25-04-45	431 Sqn
R/272834	F/S	STINSON Arnold Emerson	5-11-45	429 Sqn
J/8418	S/L	STINSON DFC Harold Keith	1-02-45	433 Sqn
J/35146	F/O	STOCK Morley Bernard	18-02-45	420 Sqn
J/92566	P/O	STONE Thomas Allen	9-02-45	405 Sqn
J/91014	P/O	STRAND William Russell	6-03-45	429 Sqn
J/95496	P/O	STREET John	2-03-45	408 Sqn
J/27997	F/O	STROH Kenneth Albert	8-01-45	626 Sqn
J/38301	F/O	STROSBERG Maurice	6-01-45	415 Sqn
J/95494	P/O	STUART Ralph Raymond	21-02-45	427 Sqn
J/42042	F/O	STYLES Jack Morris	3-02-45	426 Sqn
J/92757	P/O	ST. PIERRE Armand Leon Joseph	9-02-45	405 Sqn
J/15785	F/L	SUMMERS Arthur Benson	9-02-45	1695 Flt
J/95519	P/O	SUTHERLAND Alexander	15-03-45	419 Sqn
J/40338	F/O	SUTTAK James Emil	31-03-45	415 Sqn
J/93610	P/O	SWEET Ronald Ignatius	25-04-45	76 Sqn
R/135291	F/S	SWIHURA Andrew Anthony [USA]	21-02-45	207 Sqn
R/251797	Sgt	SWITZER John Ross	9-04-45	10 Sqn
R/278581	F/S	TAERUM Lorne Clifford	3-02-45	550 Sqn
J/40794	F/O	TAFLER Sydney Alexander	21-02-45	166 Sqn
J/39632	F/O	TAIT Earl Douglas	10-02-45	1666 HCU
J/95506	P/O	TAIT Ivan Francis	15-03-45	550 Sqn
J/35641	F/O	TALOCKA Joseph Peter	3-02-45	426 Sqn
J/42734	F/O	TAYLOR Arthur McLellan	9-04-45	408 Sqn
J/95507	P/O	TAYLOR DFC Robert	15-03-45	153 Sqn
J/27874	F/L	TEDFORD George Osborne	15-01-45	419 Sqn
J/95513	P/O	TEEVIN Russell Donald	10-04-45	415 Sqn
J/95510	P/O	TEMPLE Arthur John Guy	19-03-45	425 Sqn
J/27926	F/O	TERREAU Jean Paul Herbert	8-01-45	626 Sqn
J/95517	P/O	TESKEY Stanley James	25-04-45	426 Sqn
J/36319	F/O	THOMAS Kenneth George	7-03-45	171 Sqn
J/93899	P/O	THOMPSON Brian Sibbald	21-02-45	625 Sqn
J/38084	F/O	THOMPSON John Willard	21-02-45	223 Sqn
J/95523	P/O	THOMPSON Ralph Lindsay	14-03-45	50 Sqn
J/27160	F/O	THOMPSON Raymond Franklin	15-03-45	49 Sqn
R/189567	Sgt	THOMS Albert Cyril	1-03-45	24 OTU
J/90323	P/O	THOMSON Charles Sinclair	15-01-45	419 Sqn
C/20733	F/L	THOMSON George Homer	2-02-45	432 Sqn
J/94843	P/O	THOMSON Stuart McLean	5-04-45	429 Sqn
J/92417	P/O	THORNDYCRAFT Leonard Alfred	4-03-45	10 Sqn
J/27139	F/O	THORNE Robert Aubrey	15-02-45	429 Sqn
J/40556	P/O	THOROLDSON William Eric	23-03-45	101 Sqn
J/11980	F/L	THURLOW Jack Alvin	5-03-45	199 Sqn
J/41470	F/O	TILLEY Lloyd	17-03-45	619 Sqn
J/42181	F/O	TODD James	31-03-45	419 Sqn
J/95531	P/O	TOMS Robert Macpherson	9-05-45	514 Sqn
R/290172	F/S	TORBETT Angus Francis Wilson	17-05-45	1659 HCU
R/208304	WO2	TRAIN John	2-02-45	90 Sqn
J/46264	F/O	TRAVIS John Donald	28-04-45	1653 HCU
J/95501	P/O	TREMBLAY Jacques Joseph Maxine	5-01-45	429 Sqn
J/91026	P/O	TRENT Frederick Bernard	22-03-45	431 Sqn
J/38726	F/O	TROUT Robert Burns	17-02-45	420 Sqn
R/201388	F/S	TRYMBULAK Brony	17-05-45	1659 HCU
J/95511	P/O	TULK Hayward Selby	31-03-45	419 Sqn

J/95526	P/O	TUPLIN James Chester	25-04-45	426 Sqn
R/92602	WO1	TURNER Alan Frederick	5-03-45	102 Sqn
R/189991	WO2	TURNER Allan Frederick David	10-04-45	44 Sqn
C/93182	P/O	TURNER Dougal	16-01-45	434 Sqn
J/94478	P/O	TURNER Raymond Hilton	5-03-45	426 Sqn
J/38394	F/O	TURNER Walter Brian	28-01-45	405 Sqn
R/286646	F/S	TWEEDY John Lester	30-04-45	428 Sqn
J/37832	F/O	TYRRELL Arnold Jeffers	4-02-45	433 Sqn
J/42694	F/O	VALE William Richard	16-03-45	100 Sqn
R/268571	F/S	VALIQUETTE Joseph Claude	8-04-45	1659 HCU
J/95502	P/O	VALLIER Roy Ronald	2-02-45	432 Sqn
J/93812	P/O	VANDENBERGH John Wilton	5-01-45	420 Sqn
J/95514	P/O	VARDY Albert Edward	14-04-45	428 Sqn
J/37102	P/O	VATNE Norman Roger	15-01-45	419 Sqn
J/39916	F/O	VEITCH Laurence Edward	10-04-45	415 Sqn
J/95485	P/O	VERI Daniel	7-01-45	405 Sqn
J/94949	P/O	VICKERY Clifford Howard	16-03-45	419 Sqn
R/293614	Sgt	VINCENT Thomas Alexander	17-05-45	1659 HCU
J/38424	F/O	WADE Donald Allen	6-03-45	428 Sqn
J/95503	P/O	WAGNER William Wallace	21-02-45	408 Sqn
J/86364	F/O	WALFORD Clarence	2-02-45	428 Sqn
J/93724	P/O	WALKER Andrew Morrison Orr	15-01-45	626 Sqn
R/212817	WO2	WALKER Gordon Victor	25-04-45	619 Sqn
J/95512	P/O	WALKER James Dickson	9-04-45	408 Sqn
J/89880	P/O	WALLACE John Mackay	21-02-45	427 Sqn
J/28593	F/O	WALLIS Richard Macmillan	29-01-45	408 Sqn
J/38040	F/O	WALSH John Wallace Richard	14-01-45	425 Sqn
J/35832	F/L	WALTON William Archibald	19-03-45	640 Sqn
J/93038	P/O	WARE George Napier	8-03-45	425 Sqn
J/35230	P/O	WATSON David	29-01-45	156 Sqn
J/27864	F/L	WATSON Ernest William	16-01-45	420 Sqn
J/41735	F/O	WATSON Joseph William	5-04-45	424 Sqn
J/89387	F/L	WATT Alastair Clarence	17-03-45	103 Sqn
J/37111	F/O	WATTS Humphrey Stanley	5-03-45	426 Sqn
R/223796	F/S	WATTS William Charles	28-01-45	1664 HCU
J/94149	P/O	WAY William Albert	5-03-45	426 Sqn
J/40482	F/O	WEAVER Howard McElroy	5-03-45	424 Sqn
J/37739	F/O	WEBB Roger Jack	2-02-45	189 Sqn
J/38676	F/O	WEBB William	16-01-45	420 Sqn
J/94336	F/O	WEBBER William Waldemar	3-03-45	153 Sqn
J/40810	F/O	WEBER Wilfred Earl	5-03-45	170 Sqn
J/35507	F/O	WEBSTER Lester	21-02-45	427 Sqn
R/151294	WO2	WEBSTER Lindsay Wilkie	5-03-45	10 Sqn
R/208118	F/S	WEGENAST William Alexander	14-01-45	1666 HCU
R/183956	F/S	WEICKER Carl Heinrich	16-03-45	100 Sqn
J/36881	F/O	WELK John Gordon	16-01-45	420 Sqn
R/196558	F/S	WELLS Albert Eldon	8-01-45	166 Sqn
R/99738	WO1	WESTON Richard Verdun	2-01-45	166 Sqn
J/24034	F/L	WEY Edward George	3-03-45	426 Sqn
J/95516	P/O	WHITE Charles Henry	18-04-45	408 Sqn
J/94602	P/O	WHITE William George Stanley	15-03-45	434 Sqn
J/95508	P/O	WHITEHEAD John Alfred	15-03-45	434 Sqn
J/40432	F/O	WHITEHOUSE Kenneth Frank	27-02-45	429 Sqn
J/88009	F/O	WHITTON William George	5-02-45	433 Sqn
J/21439	F/L	WHYTE Stuart Paul	16-01-45	12 Sqn
J/42207	F/O	WHYTE William Edward	7-03-45	128 Sqn
J/95515	P/O	WIGHTMAN Edgar Ross	14-04-45	419 Sqn
C/988	W/C	WILLIAMS AFC Edwin Mountford	28-01-45	424 Sqn
R/284723	Sgt	WILLIAMS James Roy	28-04-45	1653 HCU
J/46275	F/O	WILLIAMS Robert Edward	20-04-45	19 OTU
J/95255	P/O	WILLIAMS Roland Wesley	18-04-45	408 Sqn
J/13366	F/L	WILLIAMSON Bruce Arthur	11-04-45	619 Sqn
R/201968	F/S	WILSON Donald Roger	28-04-45	1653 HCU
R/256657	Sgt	WILSON Edward Arthur	31-01-45	19 OTU
J/95505	P/O	WILSON James Howard	13-03-45	433 Sqn
R/130331	WO1	WILSON John Howard	14-02-45	153 Sqn
J/94673	P/O	WILSON John Shaw	19-03-45	425 Sqn
R/197780	WO2	WILSON Robert George	21-03-45	214 Sqn
J/95504	P/O	WILSON Ross Thomas	7-03-45	419 Sqn
J/94667	P/O	WILSON Wilfred Charles	7-02-45	12 Sqn
J/92521	P/O	WILSON William Thomas	16-01-45	434 Sqn
J/41386	F/O	WINCOTT Donald William	14-04-45	419 Sqn
J/94668	P/O	WOOD George Arthur [USA]	7-02-45	12 Sqn
J/95256	P/O	WOOD Hugh Raymond	18-04-45	408 Sqn
R/176382	F/S	WOOD Ronald Mark	21-02-45	223 Sqn
J/38720	F/O	WORT Hardy Edward	15-03-45	405 Sqn
J/95509	P/O	WOTHERSPOON Albert Edward	17-03-45	103 Sqn
R/287664	F/S	WRIGHT Edward James	30-04-45	428 Sqn
R/180139	WO2	WRYNN Frederick Charles	3-02-45	50 Sqn
J/37531	F/O	YOUNG Roy Aubry	6-03-45	514 Sqn
J/40890	F/O	ZIERLER Isaac Buck	10-04-45	433 Sqn
J/39003	F/O	ZUBACK George Adam	22-03-45	431 Sqn

Note

Likewise, the Canadian airmen were preparing to return home, taking with them their aircraft from the Lancaster-equipped squadrons. Since early 1943, the majority of the Royal Canadian Air Force squadrons assigned to Bomber Command had been administered by their own operational Group headquarters, namely No.6 (RCAF) Group lodged near Knaresborough at Allerton Park Castle. With the war in Europe over but hostilities continuing in the Pacific, plans were made for eight Lancaster formations to become part of the proposed Tiger Force and by mid-June all had departed the United Kingdom. Thus, with Group headquarters disbanding at the end of August, a quartet of units, namely 424, 427, 429 and 433 Squadrons came under the wing of No.1 Group, though for '424' and '433' this arrangement ended with their disbandment on the 15th of October, 1945, leaving '427' and '429'to soldier on until they, too, laid down their number plates on the 31st of May, 1946, by which time Bomber Command had become a mere shadow of its peak wartime potential. In respect of part of these observations, the death of P/O Fielding on the 1st June is noteworthy in that having survived 18 months as a prisoner of war (he had been captured in the aftermath of the Schweinfurt raid in February 1944) he died soon after his return to Canada, though his documents indicate he was still on the strength of 433 Squadron which at the time was still based in Yorkshire at Skipton-on-Swale. George Fielding is buried in British Columbia at Nanaimo Cemetery.

In Volume 8, page 130, I describe the loss of F/L Laing's aircraft, noting that after bailing out the pilot (Laing) landed in a tree and on releasing his parachute harness fell some thirty feet to the ground, fracturing both legs and dying as a result of his injuries. His biography in *They Shall Grow Not Old* is at odds with my summary, suggesting instead that he initially evaded capture but on being caught was handed over to the Gestapo who murdered him on the 19th (March), four days after being shot down. However, his entry in the Commonwealth War Graves Commission register for Hannover War Cemetery shows his death as occurring on the 15th, thus lending part credence to what I report in Volume 8.

Concerning the two McMorran brothers Albert and George, commemorated in this section, both died a mere month apart while serving with 619 Squadron. Albert, the younger at 25, had joined his country's air force just ahead of 28-year-old George and was the first to be commissioned. Both were pilots and each had attained the rank of flight lieutenant at the time of their deaths. Albert McMorran went down over Germany on the 11th April, a month after brother George had been posted missing from a visit to an oil refining plant at Harburg.

From Portage La Prairie, Manitoba, Donald and Murray McKay graduated from their initial flying training as air bombers, Donald eventually undertaking pathfinder duties with 405 Squadron while his younger sibling joined 49 Squadron. Neither lived to taste the sweet success of victory; Donald failing to return in mid-January, while Murray went down on almost the final hurdle of the bombing campaign with the course of war having less than a month to run.

Omitted from Volume 8, through an oversight on my part, is the loss on the 8th of January, 1945, of Oxford I LW903 from No.1546 Beam Approach Training Flight which flew into the ground 3 miles north-east of *'Chapgate'* (sic), Yorkshire, killing all three crew members, two of which were Canadians and whose names are now commemorated in this section. It is further reported that the Oxford was in transit at the time of the accident, having taken off from its base at Faldingworth with the intention of flying to an airfield used by No.18 (Pilots) Advanced Flying Unit, but encounterd inclement weather which was a contributory factor in the cause of the crash. The following the day, the 9th, No.1546 Flight disbanded.

ROYAL NEW ZEALAND AIR FORCE
personnel

NZ4212786	F/O	ADLAM Reginald George David	6-03-45	153 Sqn
NZ429286	P/O	AITCHISON Richard Justin	1-01-45	75 Sqn
NZ2350	F/O	ANDERSON Richard Bruce [United Kingdom]	6-01-45	61 Sqn
NZ425686	F/L	ARNOLD William Reginald	2-02-45	51 Sqn
NZ429740	P/O	ASHWORTH Frank Martin	22-03-45	227 Sqn
NZ42999	F/O	BAKER DFC Colin Roy	16-04-45	11 OTU
NZ4215788	F/S	BELL Raymond James McLean	5-04-45	166 Sqn
NZ42287	W/O	BENNETT Lionel John	9-02-45	214 Sqn
NZ4213790	F/S	BLACK Peter Noble	9-03-45	619 Sqn
NZ414376	F/L	BLEWETT Terence Douglas	17-01-45	75 Sqn
NZ428226	F/S	BOLGER Alexander Gordon	4-01-45	11 OTU
NZ429139	F/O	BROWN Alfred Errol	21-03-45	75 Sqn
NZ4312163	F/S	BURT Colin William	16-04-45	11 OTU
NZ429992	P/O	BUTLER Brian Leonard	9-02-45	192 Sqn
NZ425688	F/S	CARRODUS Ralph Franklin	26-04-45	50 Sqn
NZ428080	F/O	CHILDS Charles Phillip Dent	19-04-45	141 Sqn
NZ427187	F/L	CHING Alan Harold	8-08-45	571 Sqn
NZ4213790	F/S	CLARK Robert John	1-02-45	101 Sqn
NZ411565	W/O	CLARKE Alfred Bruce	5-04-45	571 Sqn
NZ425828	F/O	CONNOP Donald	15-01-45	578 Sqn
NZ416818	W/O	CRAWFORD John	4-03-45	189 Sqn
NZ427261	F/L	CURRIE John	8-04-45	10 Sqn
NZ427103	F/S	DAVIS Mervyn Desmond Sylvester	17-03-45	166 Sqn
NZ428087	W/O	DAWSON Ronald Gordon	19-04-45	141 Sqn
NZ4216679	F/O	DICKSON Douglas James	16-04-45	11 OTU
NZ411069	W/O	DIX MiD Francis Herbert	24-02-45	214 Sqn
NZ428784	F/O	DRIVER Leslie Keith	3-04-45	626 Sqn
NZ425241	P/O	DUNLOP Guy Rerenui	12-01-45	5 LFS
NZ425740	F/S	EVANS Cedric John	26-04-45	50 Sqn
NZ4211910	F/O	FERGUSON Robert Nicholas	9-03-45	619 Sqn
NZ427400	F/S	FERNYHOUGH Samuel	16-04-45	11 OTU
NZ428060	F/O	FRIEDRICH Louis Thomas	5-01-45	7 Sqn
NZ426079	W/O	GALLAGHER Cyril John	21-02-45	189 Sqn
NZ422384	F/S	GARDENER Charles Edward	4-03-45	1651 HCU
NZ414563	W/O	GRUBB James Harold	2-02-45	189 Sqn
NZ414614	F/L	GUMBLEY DFM Bernard Alexander	21-03-45	617 Sqn
NZ426171	F/O	GUTZEWITZ James Leslie	2-02-45	78 Sqn
NZ4211783	F/S	HAGLUND Francis Charles	4-01-45	10 OTU
NZ425790	F/S	HILL Peter John	12-01-45	5 LFS
NZ4210019	F/S	HITCHINS Eric Douglas	16-04-45	11 OTU
NZ421510	F/O	HODGSON Gilbert Ian	5-01-45	51 Sqn
NZ425610	F/O	HOGG Bruce Allan	4-01-45	10 OTU
NZ429923	F/O	HOLLOWAY Edgar John	21-03-45	75 Sqn
NZ40940	W/O	HOPE Lawrence Beresford Hamilton	19-04-45	75 Sqn
NZ422402	F/L	HORE DFC Marcel Launcelot	6-04-45	26 OTU
NZ413419	F/O	HUDSON AFC Gordon David	27-03-45	571 Sqn
NZ421372	F/L	HUNT Maurice Leonard	18-03-45	227 Sqn
NZ41590	F/O	HUTSON Leslie James	3-02-45	156 Sqn
NZ432207	F/S	IRELAND Bertram Leslie	14-01-45	11 OTU
NZ428121	F/O	JACKSON Keith	6-01-45	103 Sqn
NZ425476	W/O	JENKINS Bryce Desmond	5-01-45	7 Sqn
NZ416501	F/L	JENNINGS Peter Sinclair	17-04-45	171 Sqn
NZ4212723	F/O	KELLY DFC Keith Leslie	23-08-45	16 OTU
NZ2064	F/O	KINGSBURY Allan Albert	8-06-45	11 OTU

NZ422292	F/O	KNIGHT Robert Baines	9-02-45	630 Sqn
NZ427518	F/S	LAMONT John	9-02-45	630 Sqn
NZ414547	W/O	LLOYD Thomas Donald	29-01-45	3 LFS
NZ428130	P/O	LOCKYER Alfred Churchill	17-03-45	550 Sqn
NZ425580	F/S	LOVERIDGE Ian James	26-04-45	50 Sqn
NZ413442	F/L	MacKENZIE Kenneth James	8-03-45	218 Sqn
NZ426054	F/L	MANGOS Kenneth	8-02-45	44 Sqn
NZ414909	F/O	MARIA Hector Copeland	6-03-45	10 Sqn
NZ428141	F/S	MATTHEWS George Thomas	16-04-45	11 OTU
NZ425582	F/S	McGINN James Martin Manning [United Kingdom]	1-02-45	101 Sqn
NZ415706	F/L	McGREAL John Trevor	25-04-45	109 Sqn
NZ427046	F/S	McLENNAN Donald Wilford	4-01-45	11 OTU
NZ425211	F/S	MILLAR Jeffery Alexander	16-04-45	11 OTU
NZ42840	F/S	MOORE Robert Guthrie	5-01-45	7 Sqn
NZ413881	F/O	MORGAN John Perenara	15-01-45	692 Sqn
NZ40984	W/C	NEWTON DFC MiD Raymond John	1-01-45	75 Sqn
NZ413463	F/O	NICHOLLS AM [USA] John Austin Perress	16-04-45	11 OTU
NZ4213810	F/S	OAKEY Arthur Leslie Archibald	21-03-45	75 Sqn
NZ427313	F/S	OLDS Frederick Rossini	9-02-45	214 Sqn
NZ415778	F/O	PARLATO DFC Sidney Frederick	11-03-45	1690 Flt
NZ403024	F/O	PENTELOW Phillip James	6-03-45	35 Sqn
NZ42451	F/L	PLUMMER DFC Jack	21-03-45	75 Sqn
NZ424519	F/O	PROCTOR DFC George Mansell	23-08-45	16 OTU
NZ428253	F/S	REDPATH John Powell	4-01-45	11 OTU
NZ424260	F/S	REECE Michael	4-01-45	11 OTU
NZ422318	F/O	ROBERTSON James Peter	9-02-45	214 Sqn
NZ429205	F/O	ROBINSON Robert Bruce	29-01-45	3 LFS
NZ4213333	F/S	ROY Eric Alexander	17-03-45	166 Sqn
NZ421536	F/O	SCOTT Bruce Frederic	20-04-45	622 Sqn
NZ428984	F/O	SCOTT Russell James	21-03-45	75 Sqn
NZ4213940	F/S	SHAW Norman Steventon	14-01-45	11 OTU
NZ428798	F/O	SMITH Edward Percival	21-02-45	49 Sqn
NZ4211731	F/O	SPARKES Cecil Paul	9-03-45	619 Sqn
NZ411466	F/L	SPINLEY DFM MiD Maurice	3-02-45	156 Sqn
NZ4212868	F/S	STAPLES Richard Ludgvan	12-01-45	5 LFS
NZ421540	P/O	STERLING Joseph Darcy Keith	1-01-45	115 Sqn
NZ421849	F/L	STEWART George	7-03-45	214 Sqn
NZ429052	F/S	SWAP Morgan	17-03-45	153 Sqn
NZ428165	F/O	TARRANT Thomas Stephen Archer	2-02-45	50 Sqn
NZ421792	F/L	TAYLOR DFC Owen Patrick Fewster	30-04-45	97 Sqn
NZ4214136	P/O	TEMPERTON Evan Claude	3-02-45	15 Sqn
NZ425771	W/O	TENNANT Philip Athol	20-03-45	7 Sqn
NZ428168	F/O	THORPE Noel Humphrey	26-02-45	75 Sqn
NZ4215760	F/S	THWAITE Thomas Richard	26-04-45	50 Sqn
NZ427351	F/O	WALLACE Russell Francis	15-03-45	550 Sqn
NZ429439	F/S	WALTON Matthew Henry	4-01-45	10 OTU
NZ415804	F/L	WEATHERLEY Verrell	2-01-45	100 Sqn
NZ427822	F/L	WERNER Roland Leslie	22-03-45	207 Sqn
NZ426232	F/L	WHITECHURCH Edward Kimpton	22-03-45	227 Sqn
NZ426234	F/O	WILSON John Stanley	17-01-45	75 Sqn
NZ427358	F/S	WILSON Robert Bruce	4-03-45	1651 HCU
NZ429389	P/O	WINSTONE John William	7-03-45	214 Sqn
NZ425811	F/S	WOOD James Haswell	21-03-45	75 Sqn
NZ39301	F/L	YANOVICH Ivan Thomas	6-01-45	635 Sqn
NZ4213418	F/S	YATES John Melville	8-03-45	1651 HCU
NZ4213970	F/S	YOUNG Roderick Alan	4-01-45	1652 HCU

Note

The commitment of the Royal New Zealand Air Force to the war in Europe and in particular its long association with Bomber Command cannot be overstated. Of the the three major Commonwealth air forces to operate from the United Kingdom, the RNZAF was the smallest but what the force lacked in numbers it more than compensated for by an unflagging display of outstanding determination to be involved at all levels of air operations and readers of this Roll will observe that it was airmen from the Royal New Zealand Air Force (as opposed to the many New Zealanders serving with the Royal Air Force) that were the first of the Commonwealth forces to be commemorated. The last of their number to fall on an operational flight occurred on New Zealand's (and Australia's) national day of remembrance, namely ANZAC Day, the 25th of April, for it was the early hours of the 25th that F/L McCreal's 109 Squadron Mosquito crashed in Belgium (see Volume 8 and page 169 for details).

Mention has been made many times of Errol Martyn's outstanding work in commemorating the deaths of all New Zealand airmen but in closing this section I draw readers attention to Max Lambert's overall view of the night bombing campaign as seen from a Royal New Zealand Air Force prospective. Titled *Night after Night* it is a most worthy tribute.

POLISH AIR FORCE
personnel

P.703020	F/S	ANTOSZCZYSZYN Michal	5-11-45	300 Sqn
P.2732	P/O	BABIARZ Jozef	2-03-45	300 Sqn
P.780229	W/O	BANYS Jan	2-01-45	300 Sqn
P.2626	F/O	BARCIKOWSKI Jozef	23-02-45	300 Sqn
P.2721	F/O	BRANSZTED Jan	3-02-45	300 Sqn
P.704989	F/S	CHETNICKI Stefan	2-03-45	300 Sqn
P.706446	AC2	CHURCHAL Mieczyslaw	26-03-45	300 Sqn
P.706851	Sgt	CWENAR Stanislaw	2-03-45	300 Sqn
P.706584	F/S	CYMBALA Kazimierz	28-01-45	300 Sqn
P.706719	Sgt	DROZDOWICZ Romuald	2-01-45	300 Sqn
P.780727	Sgt	FILEK Jacek	2-03-45	300 Sqn
P.2648	F/L	FILIPEK Adam	23-02-45	300 Sqn
P.705000	F/S	FILIPIAK Boleslaw	2-03-45	300 Sqn
P.705003	F/S	GOLD Waclaw	9-04-45	300 Sqn
P.706613	Sgt	GOLDOWSKI Lucjan Stanislaw	13-02-45	300 Sqn
P.784105	F/S	HEINE Walenty Marian	2-01-45	300 Sqn
P.705005	F/S	HOROBIOWSKI Jan Roman	2-03-45	300 Sqn
P.704208	Sgt	JAMELINIEC Aleksander	13-02-45	300 Sqn
P.1093	S/L	JANAS Brunon Benedykt	2-01-45	300 Sqn
P.705695	Sgt	JUREWICZ Feliks	3-02-45	300 Sqn
P.705446	Sgt	KACZMARZ Antoni	13-02-45	300 Sqn
P.2575	F/L	KAPCIUK Zdzislaw	3-02-45	300 Sqn
P.1940	F/L	KIRKILEWICZ Mikolaj	2-03-45	300 Sqn
P.76636	F/L	KONARZEWSKI Jan	21-02-45	300 Sqn
P.705573	F/S	KOWALSKI Czeslaw	23-02-45	300 Sqn
P.794858	Sgt	KRASINSKI Stefan Piotr	9-04-45	300 Sqn
P.2905	P/O	KUCHARSKI Stefan Paul	9-04-45	300 Sqn
P.706482	Sgt	KULIK Mikolaj	2-03-45	300 Sqn
P.704443	Sgt	KULIKOWSKI Edmund	2-03-45	300 Sqn
P.705022	F/S	LISAK Rudolf	23-02-45	300 Sqn
P.2792	P/O	MAGIEROWSKI Ferdinand	23-02-45	300 Sqn
P.2722	P/O	MATUSZEWSKI Franciszek	16-01-45	300 Sqn
P.704308	Sgt	MODRANY Stanislaw	21-02-45	300 Sqn
P.2150	F/O	MODRO Zygmunt	3-02-45	300 Sqn
P.782865	Sgt	MROZEK Jozef	23-02-45	300 Sqn
P.705668	Sgt	MROZINSKI Jozef	2-03-45	300 Sqn
P.792387	W/O	MYKIETYN Marian	13-02-45	300 Sqn
P.2226	F/O	NIESZKODNY Adam Boleslaw	2-03-45	300 Sqn
P.704013	F/S	NIZINSKI Boleslaw	13-02-45	300 Sqn
P.794948	F/S	NOWAK Bernard	5-11-45	300 Sqn
P.704316	F/S	OGORZAL Mieczyslaw Franciszek	13-02-45	300 Sqn
P.704450	Sgt	OMIOTEK Wiktor	2-01-45	300 Sqn
P.706726	Sgt	PAROL Jozef	9-04-45	300 Sqn
P.2377	P/O	PASZKOWSKI Romuald Andrzej	28-01-45	300 Sqn
P.706646	F/S	PIETRZAK Zdzislaw	5-11-45	300 Sqn
P.794471	Sgt	PIOTROWSKI Mikolaj	16-01-45	300 Sqn
P.781228	W/O	PLACZEK Jozef	13-02-45	300 Sqn
P.704322	Sgt	REDER Roman	3-02-45	300 Sqn
P.1770	S/L	RUDAKOWSKI Henryk Anatoliusz	9-04-45	300 Sqn
P.793281	F/S	SKIBINSKI Piotr	5-11-45	300 Sqn
P.706697	Sgt	SMOCZKIEWICZ Antoni	16-01-45	300 Sqn
P.709547	F/S	STEBNICKI Jerzy	9-04-45	300 Sqn
P.706549	F/S	STOKARSKI Jerzy	23-02-45	300 Sqn
P.704962	F/S	SZUMSKI Wladyslaw	5-11-45	300 Sqn
P.704046	Sgt	SZYMANSKI Edward	2-03-45	300 Sqn
P.706817	Sgt	SZYMANSKI Zygmunt	9-04-45	300 Sqn
P.706704	Sgt	TRZEPIOTA Sabin	23-02-45	300 Sqn
P.704745	F/S	WARCHOLEK Bronislaw Wilhelm	5-11-45	300 Sqn
P.793480	Sgt	WIECKOWSKI Norbert	2-03-45	300 Sqn
P.780026	Sgt	WILK Bronislaw	3-02-45	300 Sqn
P.781108	Sgt	WRUS Maksymilian	2-01-45	300 Sqn
P.0847	F/L	WYGANOWSKI Wladyslaw	2-03-45	300 Sqn
P.0845	F/L	ZAREBSKI Zbigniew Edward	28-01-45	300 Sqn
P.2830	P/O	ZIEGENHIRTE Mieczyslaw Ludwik	23-02-45	300 Sqn
P.705532	Sgt	ZIELINSKI Stefan	2-01-45	300 Sqn

Note

By May 1945, those gallant Poles had sacrificed so much that it had become necessary to restrict their contribution to the bombing campaign to a single squadron, namely No.300 (Masovian) Squadron and since the high summer of 1944, even this unit had to lean on the ready support of non-Polish aircrew. Of the three other Polish squadrons that had operated with No.1 Group, it is appropriate to repeat that No.301 (Pomeranian) Squadron* disbanded in April 1943, its personnel being dispersed amongst 138, 300 and 305 Squadrons; No.304 (Silesian) Squadron was hived off to Coastal Command as a General Reconnaissance unit in May 1942, while No.305 (Ziemia Wielkopolska) Squadron left Bomber Command in September 1943, for the near equally dangerous role of flying daylight operations with the 2nd Tactical Air Force.

* On the 7th of November, 1944, No.1586 (Polish) (Special Duties) Flight operating from Brindisi, Italy, was re-numbered No.301 Squadron.

FREE FRENCH AIR FORCE
personnel

856	Adj	ACQUAVIVA MM Jean Andre [Corsica]	22-02-45	346 Sqn
940	S/C	ARRACHEQUESNE Rene Antoine	24-02-45	1663 HCU
08912	SLt	AULEN Jean Georges Maurice	7-02-45	347 Sqn
92	S/C	BAGOT MM Jean-Marie	7-02-45	347 Sqn
802	Sgt	BARDE MM Etienne Francoise	21-02-45	346 Sqn
152	S/C	BARITEAU MM Albert Arthus Emile	25-04-45	347 Sqn
4176	SLt	BAYLE Pierre Albert	21-02-45	346 Sqn
C3236	S/C	BERDEAUX MM Henri Andre [Algeria]	7-02-45	347 Sqn
936	S/C	BLASSIEAUX MM Roger Emile	24-02-45	1663 HCU
C13112	Sgt	BORDELAIS MM Croix de Guerre Roger Emile Victor [Morocco]	7-02-45	347 Sqn
37367	Sgt	BORDIER MM Maurice Jules Augusto [Algeria]	7-02-45	347 Sqn
785	Sgt	BOURREAU MM Croix de Guerre Guy Jean	21-02-45	346 Sqn
000718	Capt	BRACHET Chevalier de Legion d'Honneur Croix de Guerre Robert	13-01-45	347 Sqn
000082	Capt	BREARD Chevalier de Legion d'Honneur Croix de Guerre Raoul [Algeria]	21-02-45	346 Sqn
000912	Capt	BRESSON Chevalier de Legion d'Honneur Croix de Guerre Joseph Francois	16-01-45	347 Sqn
951	Sgt	BRULET MM Croix de Guerre Georges Alain Adrian [Tunisia]	15-03-45	346 Sqn
000685	Capt	BRUNET Clement Bertrand	14-03-45	347 Sqn
003984	SLt	CAPDEVILLE Pierre Jean Eugene	18-03-45	346 Sqn
37435	Adj	CHABRES Henri	15-03-45	347 Sqn
36484	Sgt	CHARPENTIER James Robert	16-03-45	346 Sqn
814	Lt	CHEMIN Antoine Lacharie	16-03-45	347 Sqn
36290	Capt	CHEVALIER Raymond Julien Adolphe	15-03-45	347 Sqn

572	Sgt	CHIERICI Paul	21-02-45	346 Sqn
C3634	S/C	DARGENTON Pierre Albert	16-01-45	347 Sqn
4160	Lt	DEDIEU Joseph Louis Antoine	24-02-45	1663 HCU
37481	S/C	DELAUZUN Maurice Aime [Algeria]	14-03-45	347 Sqn
003052	Lt	DEPLUS Jacques Philippe	16-03-45	346 Sqn
36718	S/C	DUFRENOY Francois Louis Marie	16-03-45	346 Sqn
351	SLt	DUGNAT Benoit Georges	21-02-45	346 Sqn
37474	S/C	DUSSAUT Alfred Auguste	18-03-45	346 Sqn
1368	Sgt	ESQUILAT Andre Marie Vincent	21-02-45	346 Sqn
1369	Sgt	FARNIER Roland Lucien [Algeria]	5-03-45	346 Sqn
004194	SLt	FAUCHET Gaston Jean Marie Alexandre	14-03-45	347 Sqn
004074	SLt	FAUVET Jacques Marcel [Morocco]	22-02-45	346 Sqn
654	Sgt	FERRERO Pierre Albert	25-04-45	347 Sqn
004093	SLt	FONTEIX Abel	5-03-45	346 Sqn
2106	Sgt	GIRAUDON Bernard Georges Rene	14-03-45	347 Sqn
19911	Lt	GONTHIER Andre Francois	18-03-45	346 Sqn
1375	Sgt	GORRIAS Jean Joseph [Algeria]	5-03-45	346 Sqn
466	Adj	GRIBOUVA Jean Eugene	16-03-45	346 Sqn
3943	SLt	GRIMAUD Jacques Andre Pierre [Morocco]	24-02-45	1663 HCU
944	Sgt	HAUTCOEUR Francois Marcel	15-03-45	346 Sqn
	Capt	HAUTCOEUR Pierre Jacques Georges	25-04-45	347 Sqn
976	Sgt	HELLMUTH Louis Roger [Algeria]	19-03-45	346 Sqn
453	Sgt	HOUDELOT MM Fernand Charles	5-03-45	346 Sqn
000937	Capt	JACQUOT Julien Jean Emile [Morocco]	25-04-45	347 Ssqn
003325	Lt	JOUMAS Chevalier de Legion d'Honneur Edouard Georges Marious Octave	21-02-45	346 Sqn
C3830	Adj	JOUZIER Edmond Jean	13-01-45	347 Sqn
2661	S/C	LACAZE Gabriel Amie	16-03-45	346 Sqn
004198	Lt	LAMONTAGNE Henri Eugene	15-03-45	346 Sqn
002494	Capt	LAUCOU Pierre Jean Gaston	4-03-45	347 Sqn
2113	Sgt	LAURENT Marcel Elie	24-02-45	1663 HCU
30917	Sgt	LECLERCQ MM Jacques Philippe	2-01-45	347 Sqn
30968	Sgt	LEDUC MM Gerard Guy	25-04-45	347 Sqn
600	S/C	LEMAIRE Jean	21-02-45	346 Sqn
1035	Sgt	LEROY Jean Nicholas	5-03-45	346 Sqn
945	Sgt	LE MASSON Pierre	4-03-45	347 Sqn
979	Sgt	LE MITHOUARD Paul Marie Joseph [Morocco]	7-02-45	347 Sqn
30665	Lt	LIGNON Edmond	13-03-45	23 Sqn
35006	Sgt	LOURDAUX Louis Georges Uvide Antoine	15-03-45	346 Sqn
1042	Sgt	LUGARO Pierre [Algeria]	14-03-45	347 Sqn
C15486	S/C	MALTERRE Robert Paul	13-01-45	347 Sqn
00819	Capt	MARIN Xavier Yves [Tunisia]	16-01-45	347 Sqn
1386	Sgt	MARTROU Louis Charles	21-02-45	346 Sqn
1576	Sgt	MEAU Pierre [Algeria]	6-01-45	347 Sqn
23	Sgt	MENNETRET Marcel Eugene Charles Emile [Morocco]	25-04-45	347 Sqn
257	SLt	MERCIER Roger Louis [Algeria]	25-04-45	347 Sqn
465	Sgt	MILLER Jean Eugene Toinet [Morocco]	14-03-45	347 Sqn
3361	Cmdt	OSTRE Georges Camille	15-03-45	347 Sqn
79	S/C	PATRIS Guy Marie Charles	18-03-45	346 Sqn
3775	S/C	PATRY Raymond Gaston	7-02-45	347 Sqn
03014	Capt	PELLIOT Bernard Louis Henri	7-02-45	347 Sqn
003739	Lt	PETUS Charles Marcel Bernard [Algeria]	23-01-45	347 Sqn
9778	Sgt	PIOLBOUT Roger Pierre Jean Louis	16-01-45	347 Sqn
1682	Adj	PORTESSEAU Louis Leon Jean	14-03-45	347 Sqn
1423	Sgt	RAMOND Rene Maurius Eugene	15-03-45	347 Sqn
002344	SLt	ROGNANT Cozentin Pierre Marie [Algeria]	7-02-45	347 Sqn
04120	SLt	ROQUE Georges Hippolyte Victor [Algeria]	24-02-45	1663 HCU
36493	Sgt	ROUGIER Louis Fernand	24-02-45	1663 HCU
003819	Lt	ROUVEL Jean Andre	5-03-45	346 Sqn
448	SLt	SCHILLING Maurice Joseph	5-03-45	346 Sqn
02562	Adj	SOUCILLE Pierre Jean Marie	21-02-45	346 Sqn
992	Sgt	ST. JEVIN Victor Jean [Algeria]	18-03-45	346 Sqn
1675	Sgt	TARTARIN Maxime Gabriel Georges	16-03-45	346 Sqn
00479	SLt	TERRIEN Jean Marie Bernard Louis	4-03-45	347 Sqn
1677	Sgt	TOUZART Pierre Louis Leon	16-03-45	346 Sqn
C1438	Sgt	TRIBERT Roland Gilbert	23-01-45	347 Sqn
1524	SLt	TROLLARD Paul-Julien [Algeria]	14-03-45	347 Sqn
4052	SLt	VEZOLLE Jean Henri Francois [Algeria]	5-01-45	347 Sqn
C5348	Adj	VILLENEUVE Andre Marius	16-01-45	347 Sqn
15573	A/C	VUILLEMOT Gabriel Louis Joseph [Tunisia]	16-01-45	347 Sqn
1071	Sgt	ZAVATTERO Lucien	22-02-45	346 Sqn

Note

Since the summer of 1944, the two Free French Air Force Halifax equipped squadrons had made a significant contribution to the bombing campaign, operating under the aegis of No.4 Group. In October 1945, however, and still equipped with Halifaxes, '346' and '347' were released from Royal Air Force control and with their aircraft gifted to the French government returned to France, both units officially departing from Elvington on the 20th.

ROYAL NORWEGIAN AIR FORCE
personnel

5734	Lt	BREIVIK Per	7-05-45	PFNTU
	2Lt	DIETRICHSON G.	20-04-45	622 Sqn

Note

Some documents show Lt Breivik's Christian name in the manner shown above, while others suggest he had been Christened with three names in the order of P. E. R.

SOUTH AFRICAN AIR FORCE
personnel

205959V	Capt	HEIDEN Ronald W. Frederick	5-01-45	102 Sqn
1105V	Lt	LACEY G. R.	15-02-45	630 Sqn
31794V	Lt	McGREGOR Charles William	8-02-45	97 Sqn
6101V	Maj	SWALES VC Edwin 'Ted'	23-02-45	582 Sqn
328470V	Lt	van HEERDEN Emile Johann	2-04-45	515 Sqn

WOMEN'S AUXILIARY AIR FORCE
personnel

2138184	ACW2	AUCKLAND Amelia Wright 'Milly'	23-09-45	100 Group
2142041	LACW	CHURCH Dorothy	13-12-45	8 Group
459756	ACW1	FRASER Christina Mitchell	22-04-45	
2120646	ACW1	HARRIS Glenys Doreen	24-09-45	16 OTU

Note

LACW Church died just two days before the disbandment of No.8 Group headquarters. She is buried in her home county of Kent at Canterbury Cemetery.

Attached personnel

ROYAL AIR FORCE

1074468	AC2	BRENCHLEY George Henry (serving with 5015 Airfield Construction Sqn)	22-04-45	
1115037	LAC	DIXON William (serving with 5002 Airfield Construction Sqn)	1-08-45	

1215156	Sgt	HAMMOND Cyril Leslie	22-04-45	
		(serving with 5015 Airfield Construction Sqn)		
1136875	LAC	HANCOX Haydn Spencer	22-05-45	
		(serving with 5015 Airfield Construction Sqn)		
1359297	LAC	HARRISON James John	10-03-45	
		(serving with 2763 Sqn RAF Regt)		
999520	LAC	LIGHTFOOT James	5-02-45	
		(serving with 9171 Servicing Echelon)		
1523870	F/S	MAYES Cecil Raymond	28-04-45	
		(serving with 5025 Airfield Construction Sqn)		
1853366	LAC	PLUMTREE Frank	22-04-45	
		(serving with 5015 Airfield Construction Sqn)		
1635925	LAC	SHAW Edwin	22-04-45	
		(serving with 5015 Airfield Construction Sqn)		
1158919	LAC	TAYLOR James	6-06-45	
		(serving with 5024 Airfield Construction Sqn)		
129065	F/L	WIMPENNY BSc AMICE Geoffrey	22-04-45	
		(serving with 5015 Airfield Construction Sqn)		
1296173	AC1	WILLIAMS Augustus John	13-06-45	53 RU
1861841	LAC	WRIGHT William	22-04-45	
		(serving with 5015 Airfield Construction Sqn)		

Note

Please refer to page 168 of Volume 8, for an account of the tragic accident that killed at least seven members of No.5015 Airfield Construction Squadron.

FLEET AIR ARM

–	Lt(A) ADDISON-SCOTT William George	1-07-45
	(detached from HMS *Goldcrest*)	

Note

Lt(A) Addison-Scott had been attached to 16 Operational Training Unit Upper Heyford and lost his life during a Mosquito demonstration flight (see Volume 7, page 344 for details).

Postscript

And so we come to the final postscript concerning those who lost their lives between the 3rd of September, 1939, and the 2nd of September, 1945, the date on which the Second World War officially ended, though in respect of servicemen and women named in the cemetery registers, published by the Commonwealth War Graves Commission, entries continue until the 31st of December, 1947. Thus, also included in this section are the names of airmen who lost their lives in air or ground accidents, or through illness, from the 3rd of September through to the end of the year.

The cost of six years of all-out total war fought by Bomber Command had been grievous in the extreme with over 57,000 airmen dead, a sacrifice that mere statistics cannot hope to assuage the grief and suffering of the families and friends of those who never lived to see the peace, and to the eternal disgrace of the politicians of the time (and here England's revered, and rightly so, Winston Churchill must be held to account) the survivors of the bombing campaign never received the recognition that they truly deserved. Popular belief suggests that Bomber Command's war following the Normandy invasion was little more than a swan song. Nothing could be further from the truth, for despite the gradual decline in interference from the enemy throughout the last winter of the war, the Luftwaffe were still able to inflict quite serious casualties with confirmed night fighter claims running into double figures on no less than sixteen occasions in the first three months of 1945, while in April, the last full month of bombing operations 23 Lancasters, two Halifaxes and 10 Mosquitoes are believed to have been shot down by the Luftwaffe's air arm. To illustrate these grim statistics even further, Allied air force burials in the concentration cemetery at Durnbach total 2,580 and of this awful figure many were as a direct result of air operations in the last four months of the bombing campaign.

Of the awards gained by the deceased in this section, all are worthy of note but the limitations of space decree that only a handful can be expanded upon. G/C Griffiths, a Canadian from Niagara Falls in the State of Ontario but serving with the Royal Air Force, whose death occurred practically before the ink on the surrender documents was dry, gained the first of his two decorations for his part in the disastrous reconnaissance by No.3 Group Wellingtons towards Wilhelmshaven in December 1939 (see Volume 1, pages 25 to 27), his entry in the *London Gazette* issued on the 2nd of January, 1941, reading:

'During December, 1939, in spite of adverse weather and strong opposition by anti-aircraft guns and enemy fighters, this officer led his squadron of 12 aircraft, and carried out a successful reconnaissance over strong naval enemy forces. The determination with which he pressed home this reconnaissance enabled him to bring back information of vital importance. In the course of this operation his formation accounted for no less than 5 enemy aircraft. By his personal example and thoroughness, he has been largely instrumental in maintaining his unit's high efficiency.'

A year later, the King granted unrestricted permission for the wearing of Czechoslovak Military Cross of 1939 and the Czechoslovak Medal for Gallantry to 8 officers, G/C Griffiths being a recipient of the Military Cross.

And, of course, it would be most remiss of me not to mention the names of the two recipients of the Victoria Cross who lost their lives in the last few months of the war. Both were posthumous and I can do no better than quote from their respective citations, the first being published in The *London Gazette* for F/S George Thompson, serving with 9 Squadron, and which appeared a month after he died from his terrible burns:

'This airman was the wireless operator in a Lancaster aircraft which attacked the Dortmund-Ems Canal in daylight on the 1st January, 1945.

'The bombs had just been released when a heavy shell hit the aircraft in front of the mid-upper turret. Fire broke out and dense smoke filled the fuselage. The nose of the aircraft was then hit and an inrush of air, clearing the smoke, revealed a scene of utter devastation. Most of the Perspex screen of the nose compartment had been shot away, gaping holes had been torn in the canopy above the pilot's head, the inter-communication wiring was severed, and there was a large hole in the floor of the aircraft. Bedding and other equipment were badly damaged or alight; one engine was on fire.

'Flight Sergeant Thompson saw that the gunner (Sgt E. J. Potts) was unconscious in the blazing mid-upper turret. Without hesitation he went down the fuselage into the fire and the exploding ammunition. He pulled the gunner from his turret and, edging his way round the hole in the floor, carried him away from the flames. With his bare hands, he extinguished the gunner's burning clothing. He himself sustained serious burns on his face, hand and legs.

'Flight Sergeant Thompson then noticed that the rear gun turret was also on fire. Despite his own severe injuries he moved painfully to the rear of the fuselage where he found the rear gunner (Sgt J. T. Price) with his clothing alight, overcome by flames and fumes. A second time Flight Sergeant Thompson braved the flames. With great difficulty he extricated the helpless gunner and carried him clear. Again, he used his bare hands, already burnt, to beat out the flames on a comrade's clothing.

'Flight Sergeant Thompson, by now almost exhausted, felt that his duty was yet not done. He must report the fate of the crew to the captain (F/O R. F. H. Denton RNZAF). He made the perilous journey back through the burning fuselage, clinging to the sides with his burnt hands to get across the hole in the floor. The flow of cold air caused him intense pain and frost-bite developed. So pitiful was his condition that his captain failed to recognise him. Still, his only concern was for the two gunners he had left in the rear of the aircraft. He was given such attention as was possible until a crash-landing was made some forty minutes later. When the aircraft was hit, Flight Sergeant Thompson might have devoted his efforts to quelling the fire and so have contributed to his own safety. He preferred to go through the fire to succour his comrades. He knew that he would then be in no position to hear or heed any order which might be given to abandon aircraft. He hazarded his own life in order to save the lives of others. Young in years and experience, his actions were those of a veteran.

'Three weeks later Flight Sergeant Thompson died of his injuries. One of the gunners (Sgt Potts) unfortunately died, but the other owes his life to the superb gallantry of Flight Sergeant Thompson, whose signal courage and self-sacrificing will ever be an inspiration to the Service.'

Further details, including the names of the entire crew, are reported on page 14 and 24 of Volume 8, while from a personal recollection I can recall seeing, as a trainee ground wireless operator at RAF Compton Bassett in the spring of 1955, an oil painting of F/S George Thompson VC hanging in the airmen's dining hall.

The second Victoria Cross won in 1945 was gained by a South African Air Force officer and path finder, Captain (subsequently Major) Edwin Swales from Durban. Again, it is the words in the citation that capture the intensity of the action displayed by this courageous bomber pilot:

'Captain Swales was the "master bomber" of a force of aircraft which attacked Pforzheim on the night of February 23rd, 1945. As "master bomber", he had the task of locating the target area with precision and of giving aiming instructions to the main force of bombers following in his wake.

'Soon after he had reached the target area he was engaged by an enemy fighter and one of his engines was put out of action. His rear guns failed. His crippled aircraft was an easy prey to further attacks. Unperturbed, he carried on with his allotted task; clearly and precisely he issued aiming instructions to the main force.

Meanwhile the enemy fighter closed the range and fired again. A second engine of Captain Swales' aircraft was put out of action. Almost defenceless, he stayed over the target area issuing his aiming instructions until he was satisfied that the attack had achieved its purpose.

'It is now known that the attack was one of the most concentrated and successful of the war.

'Captain Swales did not, however, regard his mission as completed. His aircraft was damaged. Its speed had been so much reduced that it could only with difficulty be kept in the air. The blind-flying instruments were no longer working. Determined at all costs to prevent his aircraft and crew from falling into enemy hands, he set course for home. After an hour he flew into thin-layered cloud. He kept his course by skilful flying between the layers, but later heavy cloud and turbulent air conditions were met. The aircraft, by now over friendly territory, became more and more difficult to control; it was losing height steadily. Realising that the situation was desperate Captain Swales ordered his crew to bale out. Time was very short and it required all his exertions to keep the aircraft steady while each of his crew moved in turn to the escape hatch and parachuted to safety. Hardly had the last crew-member jumped when the aircraft plunged to earth. Captain Swales was found dead at the controls.

'Intrepid in the attack, courageous in the face of danger, he did his duty to the last, giving his life that his comrades might live.'

Edwin Swales, as Chaz Bowyer so richly writes in his classic book *For Valour, The Air VCs*, was no stranger to the hazards of pathfinder duties, having commenced his tour of operations with 582 Squadron in July 1944. By the time of his death, due recognition of his dedication and commitment to duty had been acknowledged by the award of a Distinguished Flying Cross, *Gazetted* on the 23rd of February, the date on which he took off from Little Staughton for the last time.

In conclusion, readers of the eight volumes published in this series will realise that although I have covered losses from the training establishments up to the end of 1947, details pertaining to squadron casualties ceased with the ending of the war on the 2nd of September, 1945. As will already be realised, squadron personnel who perished between this date and the end of the year are included in this section, while parts 10 and 11 will name those who died in the first two years of peace.

Part 10

Bomber Command Roll of Honour – 1946

With the dawn of the first post-war New Year, Bomber Command was beginning to adjust to a peacetime role that saw it much reduced in size, and with this slimming down in numbers its operational potential was going into reverse. The most immediate indication of this 'slimming down' process is reflected by the closing down of four Group headquarters; 5, 6(RCAF), 8 and 100 Groups were all disbanded by the close of 1945 (No.4 Group had been transferred lock, stock and barrel to Transport Command on the 8th of May, 1945), leaving control of the Command's squadrons in the capable hands of No.1 Group and No.3 Group staffs.

In the last four months of 1945, all the specialist Mosquito squadrons that had served No.100 Group so well were either stood down or transferred to Fighter Command and with the pending disbandment of No.8 Group the need for a strong Light Night Striking Force was no longer a priority. Thus, another potent force of light-bomber squadrons were either disbanded or reduced in strength leaving the Main Force units that had survived the cull equipped with Lancasters.

From a cursory study of squadron diaries, most of the year was spent treading water while waiting to receive the Avro Lincoln, a type which, with the urgency of war no longer a factor, would take several years to complete before the Lancaster was retired as the Command's main heavy bomber. Lincoln service trials had been conducted by 44 Squadron in 1945, and in the August of that year, 57 Squadron received three aircraft for the same purpose but disposed of their holding a few months into the New Year, both squadrons continuing to use the Lancaster as their main type throughout the trials period. However, a start was made with deliveries beginning in May 1946, to 61 Squadron at Waddington and 100 Squadron, now domicile at Lindholme, and by the end of the year eight more squadrons were getting used to operating the latest product to leave the Avro factory.

Notwithstanding the reduced flying details, accidents continued to take their toll in lives throughout 1946, with those effecting the training establishments being covered in previous volumes. The first serious crash involving a squadron aircraft occurred on the 8th of January, when a Polish crew from 300 Squadron encountered failing visibility and due to an unserviceable radio the pilot decided to let down through the murk in an attempt to pinpoint his position. In doing so the Lancaster I NG269 struck some trees near Normanby* in Lincolnshire killing four of the seven-man crew.

And weather was to be a factor in every fatal accident involving squadron aircraft in 1946, all but one of these tragic events being telescoped into a period of just two months. Three days after the loss of the Lancaster, F/O John Harris flying a Spitfire V AD413 belonging to 1687 Bomber (Defence) Training Flight crashed heavily near Howden, while later in the month a combination of poor visibility, a low fuel state and the approaching dusk led to a 109 Squadron Mosquito XVI MM121 being abandoned over the Lincolnshire countryside. The pilot survived but his navigator, F/L Harvey, was not so fortunate. There are no details appended as to next of kin against his entry in the register for Cambridge City Cemetery leading me to suspect he was afforded a service burial.

February was to prove a very grim month. On the 1st, and while trying to establish their position, a 12 Squadron Lancaster III NE140 got into difficulties after entering cloud and in the attempted recovery broke up and fell to the ground near Beeby. Several documents report Beeby as in Lincolnshire, but the only location that I can trace with that name lies a few miles east-north-east of Leicester. Six bodies were recovered from debris; F/O Blummer, the pilot, and the air bomber, F/S Chessum, were buried at Binbrook from whence they had taken off on their ill-fated flight, while their four companions were claimed by their next of kin.

Then, on the 4th, a second 300 Squadron aircraft crashed in the vicinity of Aylestone Lane in Wigston Magna, south of Leicester. Contemporary reports say that over a 100 houses were damaged to varying degrees but, miraculously, no civilians were injured. Sadly, for the crew which was captained by their commanding officer, W/C Romuald Sulinski DSO, DFC, all perished. Thus, within the time frame of a month, 10 service funerals needed to be conducted at Newark Cemetery. The subsequent enquiry into this terrible accident concluded that the Lancaster had been struck by lightning and was on fire before it hurtled into the ground.

The County of Leicestershire was to be the scene for the next fatal squadron crash, this one featuring the loss of one of the Command's new Lincoln bombers. By a quirk of chance the Lincoln, which was being tested by a 57 Squadron crew, came down near the village of Queniborough, a mere 4 miles or so north-north-west from where the 12 Squadron Lancaster had fallen on the 1st. Their aircraft, a Mk.II carrying the serial RF385, had been built by the Armstrong Whitworth facility at Bagington and a superb air-to-air photograph of this Lincoln adorns the rear cover of Air-Britain's *Royal Air Force Aircraft PA100 – RZ999*.

The next day, six airmen from 115 Squadron were killed when their Lancaster III PB373 exploded in flight, its wreckage being scattered across fields near Leamington Spa. Eyewitnesses report the bomber, which was on an air test at the time with F/L Cantrell at the controls, spinning down from a considerable height (the g forces undoubtedly trapping its crew) before disintegrating at approximately 1,000 feet with fatal consequences for all those on board.

It was not until the 2nd of December that the next fatal accident involving a squadron happened. On this day, F/O Wareing and his navigator F/S Colbourne had taken off from Coningsby on a cross-country detail that would take them over the north Devon coast. Once again it was the weather that led to their deaths, for having entered cloud both engines of the Mosquito XVI PF573 began to splutter, and icing put paid to the efficiency of the carburettors. Out of control and on fire, the Mosquito came down on a golf course near the seaside resort of Ilfracombe.

* There are two villages in Lincolnshire with the name 'Normanby', one lies mid-distance between Gainsborough and Market Rasen while the second is in the north of the county above Scunthorpe. However, with 300 Squadron's base being at Faldingworth, I much suspect the crash occurred in the locality of the first named.

ROYAL AIR FORCE, AUXILIARY AIR FORCE and ROYAL AIR FORCE (VOLUNTEER RESERVE) personnel

1824865	F/S	ADAMS James	1-02-46	12 Sqn
154518	F/L	BERRY Frederick Reginald	21-02-46	115 Sqn
1812758	Sgt	BLAIKLEY Anthony Frederick Barnard	18-03-46	1653 HCU
191600	F/O	BLUMER Michael Francis	1-02-46	12 Sqn
1893897	Sgt	BONE Anthony	18-03-46	1653 HCU
1585056	Sgt	BRUNNING Norman Charles	18-01-46	17 OTU
3033600	Sgt	BUTLER Alfred Frederick	18-01-46	17 OTU
166725	F/O	BUTTON Geoffrey Sydney	18-01-46	17 OTU
153835	F/L	CANTRELL John Douglas	21-02-46	115 Sqn
1424441	F/S	CHESSUM Kenneth Stanley	1-02-46	12 Sqn
1605097	W/O	CLARK Derek Alfred	28-11-46	16 OTU
1850283	F/S	COLBOURNE Donald	2-12-46	139 Sqn
562039	F/S	COLLINGS Herman George	10-01-46	105 Sqn
3025459	Sgt	CRABB Lawson Terence	18-01-46	17 OTU
1593585	F/S	CRISP Maxwell Robert 'Max'	22-02-46	106 Sqn
1819939	F/S	CRUTCHLEY Dennis William	21-02-46	115 Sqn
1827224	F/S	DANSKY Robert	20-02-46	57 Sqn
1588838	F/S	DEXTER Frank Keighley	18-03-46	1653 HCU
1814207	F/S	DUNN Robert	6-09-46	21 OTU
57541	F/O	FERDINANDO Derrick James	6-09-46	21 OTU
1445082	F/S	FORBES James Burden	1-02-46	12 Sqn
1012192	LAC	FOXCROFT Thomas Francis	6-05-46	100 Sqn
1443627	LAC	GOODHAND Sidney Charles	31-01-46	100 Sqn
1520954	F/S	GORRIE Alexander Henderson	28-03-46	149 Sqn
569351	Sgt	GRAHAM Antony	6-10-46	57 Sqn
1567881	F/S	GRANT Sydney Bond	20-02-46	57 Sqn
152857	F/L	GRATTON Kenneth Gordon John	6-09-46	21 OTU
1869682	Sgt	GREATRIX William Bernard	6-09-46	21 OTU
177913	F/O	HARRIS DFC John	11-01-46	1687 Flt
161583	F/L	HARVEY Arthur Anthony	28-01-46	109 Sqn
150654	F/L	HORTON Michael Geoffrey	20-02-46	57 Sqn
37355	W/C	HULL DFC George Laurence Bazett [South Africa]	17-05-46	16 OTU
1681295	W/O	JOHNSON Robert Thomas	31-01-46	57 Sqn
2221568	F/S	KANE Harry Kenneth	15-01-46	35 Sqn
572774	F/S	KINNAIR William Spence	18-01-46	17 OTU
200736	F/O	LAMB DFM Jack Desmond	4-10-46	97 Sqn
1678598	F/S	LOW Sidney Caesar	1-02-46	12 Sqn
170467	F/L	MacLUCAS Malcolm Henry Graham	28-11-46	16 OTU
1829721	F/S	MARTIN Charles Munro	15-11-46	625 Sqn
191084	F/L	McGARRY John	12-07-46	3 Group
1410814	F/S	NEWMAN Maurice John	21-02-46	115 Sqn
1392418	W/O	NUTTING Reginald Thomas	18-03-46	1653 HCU
1737531	F/S	PAYNE Donald Frederick	21-02-46	115 Sqn
171788	F/L	PETTIT DFC Charles Henry	22-05-46	35 Sqn
170631	P/O	PURNELL Frederick Percy Edward	13-03-46	156 Sqn
185845	F/O	REES Evan Donald	20-02-46	57 Sqn
1876156	F/S	REEVE Russell Mouatt	20-02-46	57 Sqn
3032798	Sgt	ROBINSON Denis Eric	6-09-46	21 OTU
1850694	F/S	ROSSITER Alexander John	18-03-46	1653 HCU
124692	F/L	SMITH Anthony Matthew	23-03-46	582 Sqn
1811928	F/S	STEDMAN Ronald	21-02-46	115 Sqn
1604005	W/O	STONE Kenneth William	1-02-46	12 Sqn
1837524	F/S	THOMAS Albert Leo	3-07-46	44 Sqn
1818932	F/S	THOMAS Alfred Albert Willis	18-03-46	1653 HCU
3010632	F/S	URION Herbert	28-04-46	57 Sqn
3051950	Sgt	VALLER Thomas Edward	18-03-46	1653 HCU
57561	F/O	WAREING Edmund George Hanson	2-12-46	139 Sqn
1522610	W/O	WELLS George Arnold	20-02-46	57 Sqn
186942	F/O	WILDIN Leonard Albert	2-09-46	1660 HCU
1514962	W/O	YORK DFM Arthur John Alfred	20-02-46	57 Sqn

Note
Of the 60 airmen who died during the year, four appear in their respective cemetery registers with squadron details appended for units that had disbanded by the time of their passing. Nevertheless, each deserves to be commemorated for it is possible that their final illness can be identified with their operational service. W/O York's Distinguished Flying Medal had been *Gazetted* exactly one year previous to the day, his well merited award being gained while flying with 619 Squadron.

POLISH AIR FORCE
personnel

P.2506	F/O	BRODZIKOWSKI Witold Jan	8-01-46	300 Sqn
P.793023	W/O	BRZEZINSKI Waclaw	4-02-46	300 Sqn
P.2516	F/O	JEDRZEJCZYK Wladyslaw Ryszard	4-02-46	300 Sqn
P.704802	F/S	KORDYS Stanislaw	8-01-46	300 Sqn
P.783490	F/S	MIKULA Feliks	4-02-46	300 Sqn
P.792391	F/S	ROBASZEWSKI Wladyslaw	8-01-46	300 Sqn
P.782342	W/O	ROZGA Roman	8-01-46	300 Sqn
P.2930	F/O	SULGUT Czeslaw Kazimierz	4-02-46	300 Sqn
P.76647	W/C	SULINSKI DSO DFC Romuald	4-02-46	300 Sqn
P.794532	W/O	SZWANDT Michal	4-02-46	300 Sqn

Note
The circumstances of W/C Sulinski's death are reported in the introduction to this section. In addition to his British decorations, Colin Cummings reports on page 59 of his book *Final Landings* that he had been honoured with three Polish awards; Silver Cross of the Order of Military Virtue Class V, Bronze Cross of Merit and the Cross of Valour, the latter being bestowed upon him on four occasions. It is also reported that W/C Sulinski had completed several tours of operational flying with bomber squadrons and in addition had flown Special Operations Executive missions with 138 Squadron.

WOMEN'S AUXILIARY AIR FORCE (POLISH)
personnel

P.2793340	ACW2	GRYGLEWICZ Maria	30-03-46	300 Sqn
P.2792152	ACW1	KULINSKA Anastazja	6-07-46	300 Sqn

Part 11

Bomber Command Roll of Honour – 1947

The decline in the fortunes of Bomber Command continued throughout 1947, a year in which the last of the Operational Training Units and Heavy Conversion Units were disbanded, to be replaced by two Operational Conversion Units, namely '230' which formed at Lindholme with an establishment of 16 Lancasters and 3 Mosquitoes, and '231' which came into existence on the same day, the 15th of March, at Coningsby and taking over the role previously performed by No.16 Operational Training Unit. Both units came under the administrative wing of No.1 Group.

The situation regarding the heavy bomber squadrons remained fairly stable. The programme of Lancaster replacement with the Lincoln continued, though a measure of the lack of urgency in this direction is reflected in the tact that eight of the 22 heavy bomber squadrons would enter 1948, still equipped with the faithful 'Lanc'. Of the squadrons themselves, the Command was now served with units that had been the mainstay of the expansionist years of the late 1930s, the sole exception being 617 Squadron.

Two light-bomber squadrons equipped with Mosquito XVIs remained; 109 Squadron and 139 Squadron, both formations being based at Coningsby, though '139' had been detached to East Kirkby from the August, remaining there until February 1948.

Thankfully, 1947 also witnessed a decline in flying accidents and deaths in respect of all airmen in the year totalled 28, this figure including the sole Polish Air Force casualty, LAC Jozef Rabiej at Wyton on the 17th of July. The first fatal accident, coming on the 23rd of May, involved a Lincoln II RF365 from 61 Squadron which crashed heavily on approach to Waddington. Weather conditions are described as poor, it was night, and despite the fact that the pilot was in communication with ground controllers, on being advised that his aircraft was an estimated 150 feet above the glide slope an attempt to correct the situation resulted in the bomber descending too rapidly. After striking the ground a fire broke out and the Lincoln was destroyed, two lives being lost.

Four months later and a far more serious accident occurred; again it was a Lincoln (a Mk. II RE373), this one from 97 Squadron and it is thought that structural failure overtook the crew while flying in cloud. Whatever the cause, eight lives were lost; seven from the squadron and one, F/L Havard from 617 Squadron. Colin Cummings (for again I am drawing heavily on his book *Final Landings*) describes him as a navigator but acting as an air bomber for the flight in question.

The last two fatal crashes in the year are identified as a Mosquito XVI PF597 from 231 Operational Conversion Unit which came down, at night, near East Kirkby on the 10th of October, and a 35 Squadron Lancaster I TW647 (borrowed by a 115 Squadron crew) lost a month later following a midair collision between Norwich and Great Yarmouth with a Fighter Command Hornet I PX284 flown by P1 David McCandlish Steedman. Two Hornet squadrons, 19 Squadron (from which the ill-fated Hornet came) and 65 Squadron operating out of Church Fenton

and Linton-on-Ouse respectively, were participating in the fighter affiliation exercise, their pilots having been briefed not to close on the bomber formation beyond a range of 200 yards. In the heat of the moment, P1 Steedman delayed his break after attacking from the port quarter, passed beneath his target, which was the last Lancaster in the formation, and pulled up steeply into the path of F/O Clarke's Lancaster. The force of the impact was such that both aircraft began to break up, giving little chance for survival but, by a miracle, F/O Clarke was able to parachute and thus became the sole survivor. It had been a tragic accident of the first magnitude.

Readers of this section may possibly be perplexed at the rank identities reported. Certainly, it is a subject that I am not able to give a definitive reason but at face value it seems that those responsible for the administration of the air force decided on a rank structure that reflected a perceived degree of competence of the holder. However, I can only think that the system was proved to be either too complicated or unpopular (perhaps a mixture of both strands of opinion) and a reversion to ranks that were understood by all and sundry was reintroduced.

ROYAL AIR FORCE,
AUXILIARY AIR FORCE and
ROYAL AIR FORCE (VOLUNTEER RESERVE)
personnel

2206054	GII	ALLAN Geoffrey Alderson	11-11-47	115 Sqn
527043	EII	ALLISON William	24-09-47	97 Sqn
1893990	PII	BECKER Stanley Victor 'Stan'	10-10-47	231 OCU
3101262	AC2	BIGGINS Barry	23-05-47	61 Sqn
184118	F/O	CHANDLER Dennis Raymond James	30-04-47	218 Sqn
163572	F/L	COOK John George	24-09-47	97 Sqn
2263628	AC1	CUMMINGS Denis Frederick George	24-09-47	97 Sqn
1656102	NII	EDWARDS David Alvin Lloyd	11-11-47	115 Sqn
1295723	SII	EMERY Aleck Charles Richard [Canada]	11-11-47	115 Sqn
202511	F/O	FLOWER John Thomas	17-10-47	90 Sqn
166966	F/O	GILLESPIE William Henry	11-11-47	115 Sqn
1820826	PIV	GUEST Jack Anthony	24-09-47	97 Sqn
652918	F/S	HANNAH VC John	7-06-47	83 Sqn
163917	F/L	HAVARD Ronald Vernon	24-09-47	617 Sqn
1258752	AC1	HILLIER Harry Leonard	2-04-47	97 Sqn
1864065	NII	HINES Ronald Ernest Travers	23-05-47	61 Sqn
1903632	GII	MOORE John	11-11-47	115 Sqn
2204312	GII	RENSHAW William	28-07-47	207 Sqn
53733	F/L	SCATCHARD Harold Owen	11-11-47	115 Sqn
2326148	AC2	SHARP Kenneth	31-10-47	9 Sqn
1866055	GII	TRUNDLE Roy Andrew	24-09-47	97 Sqn
3000506	NIV	TUSTIN Roy Frederick	10-10-47	231 OCU
2218676	SII	WATTLEWORTH Albert	24-09-47	97 Sqn
926800	PI	WHITLOCK Stanley Frederick	24-09-47	97 Sqn
3031017	GII	WOODS Vincent Orville	24-09-47	97 Sqn
343939	W/O	WOOLLEY DFC Albert Edward	5-01-47	44 Sqn

Note
Commemorated in this section is John Hannah VC, perhaps one of the best remembered Victoria Cross holders of the Second World War. John Hannah gained his award in the most hazardous of circumstances when in September 1940, during an attack on the port of Antwerp by Hampdens of 83 Squadron his aircraft, captained by P/O Connor, was repeatedly hit by ground fire which in the final moments of the attack set fire to the rear fuselage. To gain an insight as to what happened in those near unbelivable minutes that followed I can only recommend a study is made of the account written by Chaz Bowyer in his book *For Valour The Air VCs* and from which I have drawn so much in the preparation of this Roll. Here it suffices for me to say that John Hannah, the aircraft's wireless operator (he had also qualified as an air gunner) displayed courage of a degree that belied not only his youth, for he was still two months short of his 19th birthday, but his operational experience as well, having arrived at Scampton as recently as the 11th of August. As Chaz Bowyer reports, the young aircrewman was terribly burnt about the face and hands as a consequence of his actions in fighting the blaze and, ultimately, providing his skipper with the means of bringing his aircraft back to base (not only had he (Hannah) saved the Hampden, he also assisted Connor in completing the return journey after the navigator and air gunner had been forced by the inferno to bale out from the sorely damaged bomber). Recognition for their valour came on 1st of October, with promulgation in *The London Gazette* of the award of the Victoria Cross to Sgt (as he then was) Hannah and a richly-deserved Distinguished Flying Cross to P/O Connor (commemorated in Part 4). Very sadly, the rigours that had been imposed on his young body were to prove fatal; by 1942 he had contracted tuberculosis and this led to a medical discharge from the service he so loved, his departure to civilian life being effective on the 10th December, 1942. John Hannah was the youngest airman to gain his country's highest honour and when he died on the 9th June, 1947, he left a widow and three young daughters. He is buried in Leicestershire at Birstall (St. James) Churchyard, his being one of the three service graves in the churchyard.

In the years since his death his Victoria Cross, presented on permanent loan by his widow, Janet, has been held first by 83 Squadron and on the disbandment of '83', station headquarters Scampton. However, in the 1990s Scampton underwent a period of inactivity and the site was placed under *Care and Maintenance* at which time the Cross was sent to the Royal Air Force Museum at Hendon where it is now displayed, along with John's silver cigarette case, in the Bomber Command Hall. Additionally, five items of his flying clothing are now with the museum, though presently these are being held in their storage facility at Stafford*.

Lastly, at Scampton's St. John the Baptist churchyard, where a total of 71 airmen (14 from 83 Squadron) now lie, a hybrid rose bush raised by E. W. Shaw of Willoughton, flowers in memory of John Hannah VC, airman extraordinaire.

* I am most grateful to Mervyn Hallam, Curator of Royal Air Force Scampton Museum, and Andy Simpson, Curator of Aircraft at Royal Air Force Museum Hendon, for details concerning the movement of John Hannah's Victoria Cross following the temporary closure of Scampton.

POLISH AIR FORCE
personnel

P.703810 LAC RABIEJ Jozef		17-07-47	Wyton

Attached personnel

ROYAL AIR FORCE

84961 S/L HUMPHREYS DFC Peter Harry		11-11-47	12 Group

Note
S/L Humphreys had been attached from 12 Group headquarters at Newton to accompany the 115 Squadron crew as an observer, presumably to observe the fighter tactics employed by the Hornet squadrons. Between May and November 1943, he had commanded 92 Squadron, then equipped with a mixture of Spitfire Vs and IXs, taking over his squadron in Tunisia before proceeding to Malta and participating in the invasion of Italy, gaining a Distinguished Flying Cross in the process. The citation, as Gazetted on the 1st of October, 1943, reading, 'This officer has commanded his squadron since May, 1943, and has led it with great skill and determination. During this period the squadron has destroyed at least 8 enemy aircraft, and Squadron Leader Humphrey has destroyed 2 of these, assisted in the destruction of another and damaged 4 more. This officer is a resourceful pilot whose example has been a great inspiration to others.'

Prior to being posted to the Middle East theatre of operations, Humphreys had fought in the *Battle of Britain* with 152 Squadron. In the immediate post war years, and having reverted to his substantive rank of flight lieutenant, he gained a permanent commission in the General Duties branch, details of this being promulgated by the Air Ministry on the 2nd of April, 1946, showing his seniority back-dated to the 1st of September, 1945.

Postscript
At the end of the previous part (1946), I chose not to write a postscript but with this being the last section of the Roll, I feel it incumbent on me to make a few observations. Only the most indifferent of people will fail to acknowledge the debt that our country, even to this day, owes to the men and women who served Bomber Command so loyally and often with scant recognition outside of the community of their squadron or unit. And I make no apology for repeating a passage from the postscript to Part 9 (1945) where I write in reference to the over 57,000 casualties suffered, *'mere statistics cannot hope to assuage the grief and suffering of families and friends of those who never lived to see the peace and to the eternal disgrace of politicians of the time ... the survivors of the bombing campaign never received the recognition that they truly deserved.'*

As an example of the awful despair that followed the arrival of the official telegram informing parents or wives that their loved ones had failed to return, followed by the numbing wait (which sometimes lasted for months) for further news to arrive, news that so often crushed the last remaining hopes that somehow their son or husband had survived, I can report on the experiences of a family in the village where I lived throughout the war years. In 1943, this family received news that their son was missing from operations and though in due course of time came a letter confirming his death in action, neither the mother or the father could bring themselves to accept that their eldest boy would never return and resume life on the family farm. Consequently, Kenneth's (and for the sake of family privacy I cannot reveal his surname) younger siblings never knew what happened to him and it was not until the 1980s that I was able to provide them with details of his operational flying and, through the great kindness of the late Hans de Haan, photographs of his headstone in the Dutch cemetery where he is now at peace.

Now, with the survivors from that great conflict of over 60 years ago in the late autumn of their lives, I salute them and end as I began in my introduction, with a verse from one of the greatest of all hymns, the hymn (attributed to Lyra Davidica [1708] and others) that is sung with such joy on Easter Sunday:

Jesus Christ Is Risen Today.

But the pains that He endured, Alleluia!

Our salvation have procured, Alleluia!

Now above the sky He's King, Alleluia!

Where the angels ever sing, Alleluia!

Royal Air Force
BOMBER COMMAND LOSSES

Appendices

Appendix 1

A Table of Casualty Statistics

In my introduction, I quote a figure of *'over 57,000'* names commemorated in this Roll of Honour; it is now necessary to be much more precise and explain in some detail the reasoning and methods used in garnering the statistics that follow. In recent years various figures have been bandied about as to how many airmen, and airwomen, died while serving with Bomber Command, the general consensus of opinion settling on *'55,500'*. The first question now must be; from where did this figure originate? Turning to the quite invaluable work of Martin Middlebrook and Chris Everitt in compiling their epic Bomber Command War Diaries and in particular to their analysis of the operational statistics for the period 3rd September, 1939 to 7th-8th May, 1945, the breakdown of aircrew casualties are shown as, and I now quote precisely from what is reported on page 708 of the diaries:

'The Air Ministry was able to compile the following figures up to 31 May 1947:

'Killed in action or died while prisoners of war	47,268
'Killed in flying or ground accidents	8,195
'Killed in ground-battle action	37
'Total fatal casualties to aircrew	**55,500**
'Prisoners of war, including many wounded	9,838
'Wounded in aircraft which returned from operations	4,200
'Wounded in flying or ground accidents in U. K.	4,203
'Total wounded, other than prisoners of war	**8,403**
'Total aircrew casualties	**73,741**

In a footnote, Martin states that the analysis here given was sent to him by letter from the Air Historical Branch, 25th June, 1969, and Appendix 41 of the British Official History, Volume IV, pp. 440-44.

On page 711, the authors show a breakdown of aircrew casualties by nationality, and omitting the percentage totals, these are given as:

Royal Air Force	38,462
Royal Canadian Air Force	9,919
Royal Australian Air Force	4,050
Royal New Zealand Air Force	1,679
Polish Air Force	929
Other Allied Air Forces	473
South African Air Force	34
Other Dominions	27

These figures come to 55,573 and the authors point out that the discrepancy between the *'55,500'* reported from the Air Ministry and the *'55,573'* arrived at from a breakdown of deaths by air force can be explained by the inclusion in the latter of 73 airmen who died from natural causes. Furthermore, the authors indicate that 91 airwomen (Women's Auxiliary Air Force) died on duty.

My analysis will differ from what has been reported in these opening statements; my database of names for inclusion in the Roll has been built up from a close inspection of the cemetery registers produced by the Commonwealth War Graves Commission, followed by an examination of other published works and which I credit in my introduction. Furthermore, in keeping with the Commonwealth War Graves Commission practice of reporting all service deaths up to the end of 1947, my Roll incorporates the names of all Bomber Command personnel that I have been able to identify who lost their lives up to the 31st December, 1947.

Casualties from the air forces concerned will be self explanatory, as should the method employed of reporting deaths from amongst attached personnel. And, what I believe to be a first, these sombre (such an adjective is needed to emphasise what follows) statistics are being broken down on a yearly basis, thus illustrating that as the bombing campaign increased in intensity, so the losses to aircrew rose significantly, despite ever-improving aircraft and aids to combat the scourge of the German night defences and in particular, what evolved by the middle years of the war as a formidable night fighter force.

What is significant are the increases that I am able to show in the table below, even when allowing for casualties incurred during 1946 and 1947, and for those who lost their lives while on attachment to other Commands and overseas theatres of operations. To take the Air Ministry reported figure of *'1,679'* in respect of the Royal New Zealand Air Force, my trawl of Errol Martyn's two volumes results in a total of *'1,703'* (1,699 up to the end of the war in Europe and four in the period twixt the 7th-8th May, and the surrender in the Far East). Likewise, deaths regarding Royal Canadian Air Force servicemen are up by 264, the Australians by 39 and the Polish Air Force by 48. But by far the largest increase is in Royal Air Force losses which are up over the 'official' figure by a margin of 1,330. I have not, however, been able to find the 91 Women's Auxiliary Air Force casualties, reported by Martin Middlebrook and Chris Everett, my figure of 41 (which includes two airwomen from the Polish Air Force) falling short by a difference of 50, and the South African Air Force by 22; and it is certain I have not been able to name every airman from the ground staff who died on duty with Bomber Command. Thus, my figure of 57,205, staggering though it is, cannot be taken as a definitive total.

The table is given overleaf.

Casualty Statistics

	1939	1940	1941	1942	1943	1944	1945	1946	1947	Total
Royal Air Force	319	2,656	4,471	6,174	11,493	11,734	2,871	60	26	39,804
Royal Australian Air Force			127	613	1,082	1,790	477			4,089
Royal Canadian Air Force			470	1,724	2,920	3,961	1,108			10,183
Royal New Zealand Air Force		31	181	531	452	398	110			1,703
Polish Air Force		20	178	354	196	153	65	10	1	977
Free French Air Force			1		4	121	92			218
Royal Indian Air Force			3							3
Royal Norwegian Air Force					15	17	2			34
South African Air Force					1	6	5			12
Women's Auxiliary Air Force			1	10	15	9	4	2		41
Attached personnel										
Royal Air Force	2			13	4	10	13		1	43
Royal Canadian Air Force						1				1
Royal New Zealand Air Force				2						2
Fleet Air Arm		7	1		3		1			12
United States Army Air Force				2	10	20	36			68
Women's Auxiliary Air Force						1				1
Army				8	2					10
Civilian				2	2					4
Total	**321**	**2,714**	**5,435**	**9,441**	**16,209**	**18,237**	**4,748**	**72**	**28**	**57,205**

Appendix 2

A Table of Personnel Statistics

This table reports the casualties sustained by airmen serving with Allied air forces, other than their own (principally the Royal Air Force, Commonwealth and Dominion air forces and the United States Army Air Force); it also includes enlistments from overseas locations (identified in the majority of cases by their service numbers) or whose entry in service documents suggests an association with the country shown, in the Roll, after their Christian names.

Royal Air Force	1939	1940	1941	1942	1943	1944	1945	1946	1947	Total
Amirante Islands						1				1
Argentina			1	7	7	3				18
Australia	7	25	14	9	14	12	1			82
Bahamas					1					1
Barbados			1	1	1					3
Bechuanaland						1				1
Belgium				1	5	9	4			19
Bermuda					1					1
Brazil			1	3	5	2				11
British Guiana					1	2	1			4
British Honduras					2				2	
Canada	11	70	58	59	47	53	6		1	305
Ceylon			1	1	2	1				5
Channel Islands		1	5	2	6	4	2			20
Chile			1	1	3	1	2			8
Cuba		1			1					2
Cyprus					2		1			3
Czechoslovakia		21	53	60		1	1			136
Denmark					1	1				2
Eire	2	55	29	24	55	57	15			237
Egypt					1					1
Far East			2	2	1					5
Fiji		1			1					2
France			1	3	2		2			8
Gibraltar			1							1
Grenada				1	2					3
Guatemala					1					1
Holland				2	2	4	2			10
Hong Kong						1				1
India	1				1	7				9
Iraq						1				1
Jamaica		1		3	3	3	2			12
Kenya		1	1	1	1	3				7
Luxembourg				1	1					2
Malaya						2				2
Mauritius				1	2	2	2			7
Mexico						1				1
Middle East			2	2	3					7
Newfoundland			1	35	11	9	4			60
New Guinea		1								1
New Zealand	7	56	24	23	18	9	2			139
Nigeria						1				1
Palestine					1					1
Paraguay						1				1
Peru						1				1
Poland				1						1
Portugal				1		1				2
Rhodesia		1	37	70	41	32	7			188
Seychelles				1						1
Soviet Union						1				1
South Africa	1	8	23	27	13	12	1	1		86
Spain					1					1
St. Lucia					2					2
Swaziland		1								1
Switzerland						1				1
Tanganyika				1	1					2
Trinidad				1	6	3	1			11
United States of America			1	10	16	14	1			42
Uruguay				1	1	2				4
Yugoslavia					1					1
Total	29	243	259	353	285	261	57	1	1	1,489

Royal Australian Air Force	1939	1940	1941	1942	1943	1944	1945	1946	1947	Total
Canada				1	2					3
Eire					1	2				3
New Guinea				1		1				2
New Ireland				1						1
New Zealand			2	1	1	7	1			12
United Kingdom			1	2	1	2				6
Total			3	6	5	12	1			27

Royal Canadian Air Force	1939	1940	1941	1942	1943	1944	1945	1946	1947	Total
Argentina			3	4	2	1				10
Australia						1				1
Bahamas				1			1			2
Brazil					1					1
British Guiana					2	1				3
Channel Islands						1				1
China				1						1
Cuba				1						1
Denmark						1				1
Dominican Republic					1					1
Eire					1	1				2
Guatemala						1				1
Hawaii						1				1
Jamaica			2	1		1				4
New Zealand				1						1
Poland			1							1
South Africa				1	1					2
St. Kitts					1					1
St. Lucia					1					1
Switzerland					1	1				2
Trinidad				1	3	1				5
United Kingdom			6	9	10	6	2			33
United States of America			25	125	154	122	36			462
Total			37	145	178	139	39			538

Royal New Zealand Air Force	1939	1940	1941	1942	1943	1944	1945	1946	1947	Total
Australia				3		1				4
Canada				1						1
Eire				1	2					3
Hong Kong						1				1
India						1				1
South Africa				1						1
United Kingdom				9	3	2	2			16
Total				15	5	5	2			27
OVERALL TOTAL	29	243	299	519	473	417	99	1	1	2,080

Note

It is striking how many American citizens served with the bomber arm of Allied air forces prior to their country's entry into the conflict and following the Japanese attack in December 1941, on Pearl Harbor, the number that elected to remain with the air force of their first choice. It should also be borne in mind that the 503 names identified may not be the true total as there are many entries in the registers produced by the Commonwealth War Graves Commission devoid of next of kin detail. However, I believe the figure of 462 in respect of the Royal Canadian Air Force to be reasonably accurate, 462 names having been traced through entries in the aforementioned registers and a trawl of the biographies reported in *They Shall Grow Not Old*.

Also, worthy of recognition is the contribution from airmen whose home was in the Republic of Ireland. Regarding their involvement with Bomber Command, most joined the ranks of the Royal Air Force (many arriving in the final years of peace and thus served as regulars), but as the table above shows, Irishmen from the south served with distinction in all three of the principal Commonwealth air forces and by the end of 1945, at least 245 had laid down their lives. And it is very important to remember that throughout the Second World War, and beyond, men from the Republic who joined the British armed forces were not allowed to wear their uniform when going home on leave or take any documentation which would identify them as such, leading to the suggestion that within that part of Ireland led by a government based in Dublin they and their families were looked upon with a degree at best with indifference and at worst with hostility.

Appendix 3

Airmen Who Died in Captivity

In the first appendix of his book *Footprints on the Sands of Time* (referred to often in the context of the Roll), Oliver Clutton-Brock identifies 10,999 Bomber Command airmen who became prisoners of war; some for the duration and a handful for just a matter of days. This huge total exceeds the figures, reported in italics, in Appendix 1 by 1,167 names.

Taking Oliver's work as my guiding light, and even though their names are reported in the appropriate sections of the Roll, I will now record the names of those who lost their lives while in captivity, either through natural causes or at the hands of their captors or as in the case of those who perished on the 19th April, 1945, by the tragic case of their prisoner of war column being mistaken by Royal Air Force Typhoon pilots for enemy troops.

The list, however, is restricted to airmen who spent years, or many months, as a prisoner and who had passed through the German administrative system at Dulag Luft near Frankfurt before being taken to a prison camp. Also included are those who evaded capture for a considerable period of time and then had the terrible misfortune to fall into the hands of the Gestapo who exacted the ultimate punishment in revenge or had them incarcerated in concentration camps where at least one died either from the common combination of malnutrition and disease. Others listed and which fall outside of the parameters here mentioned can be identified by my remarks.

In a departure from the alphabetical recording in the Roll of Honour pages I am presenting the names in chronological order of capture. The data in the colums following their squadron/unit identity show their prisoner of war number, N/K being appended where this information is not known and, in a few cases, 'None'. The last column records the date on which they died, brief remarks pertaining to the circumstances of their death, followed by cemetery or memorial details.

ROYAL AIR FORCE

39024	F/L	CASEY Michael James	16-10-39	57 Sqn	24	31-03-44 *Great Escape*; murdered. Buried Poznan Old Garrison Cemetery.
623703	W/O	WATSON William Philip Jeffery [New Zealand]	21-04-40	44 Sqn	13064	19-04-45 Killed in Typhoon attack. Buried Berlin 1939-1945 War Cemetery.
625503	W/O	TOWNSEND-COLES MiD Roland Brainerd	10-05-40	18 Sqn	N/K	15-07-44 Escaped from Heydekrug on 3-04-44 but was recaptured and murdered by the Gestapo at Tilsit, possibly in 05-44. Runnymede Memorial, panel 215.*
580641	Sgt	CORRIGAN Eugene Patrick [Eire]	23-05-40	61 Sqn	N/K	2-03-41 Died of peritonitis. Buried Berlin 1939-1945 War Cemetery.
41035	F/L	LEWIS Jack Maurice	6-07-40	102 Sqn	N/K	18-08-43 Struck by a train and fatally injured. Buried Poznan Old Garrison Cemetery.
746982	W/O	HAWKINS Gordon Cyril George	10-07-40	107 Sqn	131	19-04-45 Killed in Typhoon attack. Buried Berlin 1939-1945 War Cemetery.
42020	F/L	PALMER John Harold Tearl	11-07-40	82 Sqn	N/K	6-12-42 Died, possibly from natural causes. Buried Berlin 1939-1945 War Cemetery.
631689	W/O	GRIMSON MiD George John William	14-07-40	37 Sqn	134	14-04-44 Very likely to have been murdered after escaping from Heydekrug. Runnymede Memorial, panel 213.
42113	F/L	EDWARDS Robert Howard	28-07-40	142 Sqn	161	26-09-42 Shot while attempting to escape from Posen. Buried Poznan Old Garrison Cemetery.
37658	F/L	SWAIN Cyril Douglas	28-11-40	105 Sqn	388	31-03-44 *Great Escape*; murdered. Buried Poznan Old Garrison Cemetery.
745360	W/O	GAGE John	4-12-40	99 Sqn	430	19-04-45 Killed in Typhoon attack. Buried Berlin 1939-1945 War Cemetery.
42745	F/L	EVANS MiD Brian Herbert [Australia]	6-12-40	49 Sqn	456	31-03-44 *Great Escape*; murdered. Buried Poznan Old Garrison Cemetery.
742749	Sgt	SHAW John Cecil	6-12-40	49 Sqn	N/K	4-01-42 Killed during attempt to escape from Barth. Buried Berlin 1939-1945 War Cemetery.

561898	W/O	STEELE Frederick James William	7-12-40	214 Sqn	448	19-04-45 Killed in Typhoon attck. Buried Berlin 1939-1945 War Cemetery.
746717	W/O	BROWN Arnold	10-12-40	107 Sqn	422	20-04-45 Died in Boisenburg Hospital from wounds inflicted the previous day by the Typhoon attack. Buried Berlin 1939-1945 War Cemetery.
44177	F/L	HUMPHREYS Edgar Spottiswoode	19-12-40	107 Sqn	406	31-08-44 *Great Escape*; murdered. Buried Poznan Old Garrison Cemetery.
82532	F/L	VALENTA Arnost [Czechoslovkia]	6-02-41	311 Sqn	415	31-03-44 *Great Escape*; murdered. Buried Poznan Old Garrison Cemetery.
903056	Sgt	VAN KLAVEREN William Edward	12-03-41	102 Sqn	N/K	4-05-41 Died of diphtheria, Buried Berlin 1939-1945 War Cemetery.
89375	F/L	LONG James Leslie Robert	27-03-41	9 Sqn	522	13-04-44 *Great Escape*; murdered. Buried Poznan Old Garrison Cemetery.
937633	W/O	BARRATT Reginald Harry	9-06-41	9 Sqn	18299	4-06-45 Disappeared in post-war Hungary after escaping, probably from a working party, having exchanged identities with Rifleman G. S. Godden. Runnymede Memorial, panel 269.
970467	W/O	LEWIS Ernest Philip	27-06-41	10 Sqn	N/K	1-08-44 Escaped from Heydekrug on 25-03-44, only to be recaptured 07-44 and subsequently murdered by shooting. Buried Malbork Commonwealth War Cemetery.
580820	W/O	BARRY George Donald	8-07-41	35 Sqn	39259	25-04-45 Died in captivity. Buried Hanover War Cemetery.
46462	F/L	LEIGH Thomas Barker [Australia]	5-08-41	76 Sqn	63	31-03-44 *Great Escape*; murdered. Buried Poznan Old Garrison Cemetery.
581434	W/O	BONE William Andrew Irving	12-08-41	76 Sqn	143	19-04-45 Killed in Typhoon attack. Buried Berlin 1939-1945 War Cemetery.
903068	Sgt	CALVERT MiD Harrold Phillip [Canada]	16-08-41	10 Sqn	119	20-05-42 Involved in a mass escape May 1942, but recaptured and shot by civil Police at Dresden. Buried Berlin 1939-1945 War Cemetery.
84938	F/O	ROBINSON Thomas Myles	16-08-41	106 Sqn	N/K	10-10-41 Died, possibly from natural causes. Buried Hanover War Cemetery.
73022	F/L	WALENN Twice Mid Gilbert William	10-09-41	25 OTU	3776	29-03-44 *Great Escape*; murdered. Buried Poznan Old Garrison Cemetery.
920054	Sgt	REID Jeffrey Walter	17-09-41	75 Sqn	N/K	29-12-41 Killed at Teschen while in the act of removing fence boarding to help heat his prison hut. Buried Cracow Military Cemetery.
901682	W/O	CLAYDEN Douglas Jobson	19-09-41	405 Sqn	9669	19-04-45 Killed in Typhoon attack. Buried Berlin 1939-1945 War Cemetery.
955266	W/O	LORD John	19-09-41	405 Sqn	9659	22-04-45 Died from wounds received from Typhoon attack on 19-04-45. Buried Berlin 1939-1945 War Cemetery.
1378655	W/O	HEATHMAN Charles Walter	12-10-41	214 Sqn	24384	19-04-45 Killed in Typhoon attack. Buried Berlin 1939-1945 War Cemetery.
39103	S/L	KIRBY-GREEN Thomas Gresham	16-10-41	40 Sqn	652	29-03-44 *Great Escape*; murdered. Buried Poznan Old Garrison Cemetery.
43932	F/L	BULL DFC Leslie George	5-11-41	109 Sqn	667	29-03-44 *Great Escape*; murdered. Buried Poznan Old Garrison Cemetery.
45148	F/L	GRISMAN William Jack	5-11-41	109 Sqn	N/K	6-04-44 *Great Escape*; murdered. Buried Poznan Old Garrison Cemetery.
39305	S/L	CROSS DFC Ian Kingston Pembroke	12-02-42	103 Sqn	2	30-03-44 *Great Escape*; murdered. Buried Poznan Old Garrison Cemetery.
62324	F/O	LOVEGROVE Peter Anthony	8-04-42	83 Sqn	778	12-11-42 Died, possibly from natural causes. Buried Poznan Old Garrison Cemetery.
944044	W/O	STEPHEN Raymond Thomas	25-04-42	15 Sqn	184	29-07-44 Struck by lightning at Kopernikus. Buried Poznan Old Garrison Cemetery.

1053444	W/O	DURNAN Hamilton	26-04-42	77 Sqn	231	22-04-45 Possibly killed during a Mosquito attack in the area of his camp. Buried Berlin 1939-1945 War Cemetery.
106173	F/L	WILLIAMS MiD John Francis	27-04-42	107 Sqn	216*	6-04-44 *Great Escape*; murdered. Buried Poznan Old Garrison Cemetery.
1061420	W/O	CALLANDER DFM Edward	6-05-42	115 Sqn	38	7-03-44 Escaped from Heydekrug but was recaptured and executed. Runnymede Memorial, panel 213.
570626	W/O	LOWMAN Hugh Percival	30-05-42	1652 CU	431	19-04-45 Killed in Typhoon attack. Buried Berlin 1939-1945 War Cemetery.
1111489	W/O	McKENNA Maurice George	1-06-42	156 Sqn	512	28-04-45 Died from wounds caused by Typhoon attack on 19-04-45. Buried Berlin 1939-1945 War Cemetery.
614115	W/O	BROWN Reginald Alfred	25-06-42	78 Sqn	311	22-04-45 Possibly killed during a Mosquito attack in the area of his camp. Runnymede Memorial, panel 269.
623752	W/O	LOSH George Albert	25-06-42	102 Sqn	335	19-04-45 Killed in Typhoon attack. Buried Berlin 1939-1945 War Cemetery.
109488	F/L	THOMPSON Anthony William	31-07-42	24 OTU	N/K	5-07-44 Murdered at Graudenz. Buried Malbork Commonwealth War Cemetery.
778694	W/O	LEO Arthur John Owen [Rhodesia]	18-08-42	35 Sqn	N/K	20-08-44 Killed by an air attack while away from camp, probably Teschen, on a working party. Buried Cracow Military Cemetery.
777859	W/O	GLASSE Basil Henry [Rhodesia]	24-08-42	150 Sqn	27141	9-03-45 Died whilst being forced marched from Lamsdorf. Runnymede Memorial, panel 269.
1269062	W/O	MAGENIS Leslie Stewart	24-08-42	150 Sqn	27032	3-03-45 Died on forced march from Lamsdorf, weakened by dysentery. Buried Berlin 1939-1945 War Cemetery.
550013	F/S	COOK Alan Ronald	28-08-42	101 Sqn	N/K	19-06-43 Killed after escaping from a working party near Teschen. Buried Cracow Military Cemetery.
646741	W/O	WHITFIELD Frederick	8-09-42	102 Sqn	27049	5-03-45 Died, possibly from natural causes, at Lamsdorf. Buried Berlin 1939-1945 War Cemetery.
547263	W/O	GREGORY William Snowden	23-09-42	44 Sqn	27132	30-03-45 Died, possibly from natural causes, at Lamsdorf. Buried Hanover War Cemetery.
107520	F/L	STOWER John Gifford	16-11-42	142 Sqn	836	31-03-44 *Great Escape*; murdered. Buried Poznan Old Garrison Cemetery.
1080471	W/O	PRESTON Robert Edward	2-12-42	75 Sqn	946	10-04-45 Died, possibly from natural causes, at Barth. Buried Berlin 1939-1945 War Cemetery.
1323051	Sgt	HULSE Arthur Leslie	20-02-43	158 Sqn	N/K	10-02-44 Died, possibly from natural causes. Buried Berlin 1939-1945 War Cemetery.
1127353	W/O	PEEL Harry Siddell	25-02-43	50 Sqn	27581	23-02-45 Died from natural causes at Bad Lausick, south-east of Leipzig. Buried Berlin 1939-1945 War Cemetery.
658309	F/S	POLAND Robert George	12-03-43	76 Sqn	N/K	19-01-44 Died, possibly from natural causes, at Cracow. Buried Cracow Military Cemetery.
123026	F/L	STREET Denys Oliver	29-03-43	207 Sqn	992	6-04-44 *Great Escape*; murdered. Buried Berlin 1939-1945 War Cemetery.*
1186489	W/O	READ Albert George Charles	16-04-43	76 Sqn	1029	19-04-45 Killed in Typhoon attack. Buried Berlin 1939-1945 War Cemetery.
130452	F/O	STEWART MiD Robert Campbell	26-04-43	77 Sqn	N/K	31-03-44 *Great Escape*; murdered. Buried Poznan Old Garrison Cemetery.
650927	W/O	BLISS Harry	28-04-43	218 Sqn	1119	30-03-45 Died at Fallingbostel. Buried Becklingen War Cemetery.
1318075	W/O	PORTER Arthur Haydn	27-05-43	35 Sqn	44	19-04-45 Killed in Typhoon attack. Runnymede Memorial, panel 269.
1324224	W/O	THORNE MiD Peter Selwyn Courtney	27-07-43	102 Sqn	222444	2-02-45 Escaped from Muhlberg (Elbe) and managed to get as far as Holland where on 1-11-44 he was recaptured. Fatally injured, or shot, after jumping from a train taking him to Germany. Buried in Holland at Doetinchem (Loolaan) General Cemetery.*

610918	F/S	JONES DFM James Ellis	9-08-43	35 Sqn	N/K	2-04-44 Died from gun shot wounds inflicted on 28-03-44 at Muhlberg (Elbe). Buried Berlin 1939-1945 War Cemetery.
917722	Sgt	SMITH Charles Arthur	27-09-43	75 Sqn	N/K	8-04-44 Died, possibly from natural causes. Buried Berlin 1939-1945 War Cemetery.
1533387	W/O	TURNBULL Geoffrey Edgar	20-12-43	103 Sqn	N/K	7-04-45 Died, possibly from natural causes, at Muhlberg (Elbe). Buried Berlin 1939-1945 War Cemetery.
1455475	W/O	BARDSLEY Eric	20-01-44	576 Sqn	1093	19-04-45 Killed in Typhoon attack. Buried Berlin 1939-1945 War Cemetery.
1367884	F/S	McCULLOCH William	21-01-44	35 Sqn	N/K	7-03-44 Died, possibly from natural causes; camp details not known. Buried Berlin 1939-1945 War Cemetery.
1431168	W/O	MORTIMER Kenneth	30-01-44	514 Sqn	1094	19-04-45 Killed in Typhoon attack. Buried Berlin 1939-1945 War Cemetery.
1315456	F/S	CHANT Leslie	19-02-44	35 Sqn	N/K	2-12-44 Died of a coronary, possibly while being held at Fallingbostel. Buried Becklingen War Cemetery.
1509811	W/O	PRICE Fred Thomas	19-02-44	625 Sqn	1615	30-04-45 Died from wounds inflicted in Typhoon attack. Buried Berlin 1939-1945 War Cemetery.
2213579	F/S	WHEADON Sydney John	25-02-44	425 Sqn	2121	19-04-45 Killed in Typhoon attack. Buried Berlin 1939-1945 War Cemetery.
1813264	F/S	PRESTON Leslie Walter	18-03-44	427 Sqn	N/K	11-05-45 Died from peritonitis following abdominal surgery at Barth. Buried Berlin 1939-1945 War Cemetery.
1565563	F/S	LAWTON William Ellemore	24-03-44	76 Sqn	3263	19-04-45 Killed in Typhoon attack. Buried Berlin 1939-1945 War Cemetery.
1852348	F/S	MIDLANE Alan Leslie	24-03-44	51 Sqn	N/K	15-03-45 Died whilst undergoing surgical procedures. Buried Berlin 1939-1945 War Cemetery.
1584485	F/S	BAULDIE David	30-03-44	76 Sqn	3429	19-04-45 Killed in Typhoon attack. Buried Berlin 1939-1945 War Cemetery.
1338451	F/S	GIBBS John Arthur	22-04-44	578 Sqn	3566	19-04-45 Killed in Typhoon attack. Buried Berlin 1939-1945 War Cemetery.
1457196	Sgt	HALE Charles Thiepval	22-05-44	77 Sqn	None	22-06-44 Died in France. Cause and camp (if any) not known but indicated to have been a prisoner of war.
152583	F/O	HEMMENS Philip Derek	9-06-44	49 Sqn	N/K	18-10-44 Died while incarcerated in Buchenwald concentration camp. Runnymede Memorial, panel 206.
1400819	F/S	INGRAM Kenneth Herschel Callender	21-06-44	50 Sqn	None	2-10-44 Murdered in Holland by, most likely, the Gestapo. Buried Apeldoorn (Ugchellen-Heidehof) General Cemetery.
149550	F/L	WALKER DFC MiD Ronald Arthur	21-06-44	83 Sqn	None	9-07-44 Murdered at Tilburg, Holland, probably by the Gestapo. Runnymede Memorial, panel 203.
178869	F/O	HOOD Gerald	12-08-44	100 Sqn	None	21-03-45 Murdered in Holland by the Gestapo. Buried Almelo General Cemetery.
3050458	F/S	JOHNSON Geoffrey Ralph	25-10-44	158 Sqn	1111	13-04-45 Killed while trying to escape from Luckenwalde. Buried Berlin 1939-1945 War Cemetery.
154910	F/O	HOOK Edwin Frank	21-02-45	49 Sqn	N/K	4-04-45 Killed near Feucht during an Allied bombing raid. Buried Durnbach War Cemetery.
1604003	F/S	WILLIS Leslie Robert	21-02-45	170 Sqn	N/K	6-04-45 Died from wounds in a Dutch hospital near Steenwijk. Buried Steenwijkerwold (Kallenkote) General Cemetery.

* F/L Street is believed to be the only officer from the *Great Escape* to be buried outside of Poland.
* Oliver-Clutton Brock describes W/O Thorne's bid for freedom in *Footprints on the Sands of Time* pages 92-94, while the last days of W/O Townsend-Cole's life are recorded on pages 103-105.
* '216' shown in respect of F/L Williams is an educated guess. Oliver (Clutton-Brock) was not able to establish his prisoner of war identity but with the knowledge of his date of capture and the allocation of numbers at the time, particularly in regard to his surname, the number here reported would fit.

ROYAL AUSTRALIAN AIR FORCE

405001	Sgt	WYLLIE MiD Maxwell Joseph Andrew	2-07-42	460 Sqn	24985	22-04-43 Escaped from a work camp but was apprehended and fatally wounded by gunshots near Kressendorf. Buried Cracow Military Cemetery. Australian War Memorial, panel 108.*
409280	F/O	SUFFREN DFC Charles Edward	9-04-44	460 Sqn	None	16-02-45 Died from injuries; left hip broken in two place. Buried Durnbach War Cemetery. Australian War Memorial, panel 108.
421543	F/O	NOTT Jack Stewart	16-06-44	77 Sqn	None	9-07-44 Murdered. Runnymede Memorial, panel 257. Australian War Memorial, panel 128.
434528	F/S	KERRIGAN Michael John	14-01-45	9 Sqn	N/K	22-03-45 Died, possibly from natural causes. Buried Berlin 1939-1945 War Cemetery. Australian War Memorial, panel 125.

* See pages 30-33 of *Footprints on the Sands of Time* for further details concerning this atrocity.

ROYAL CANADIAN AIR FORCE

R/63605	Sgt	ROBERTSON Harry Malcolm	3-07-41	99 Sqn	N/K	30-04-42 Shot 29-04-42 while attempting to escape from Sagan; died from wounds. Buried Poznan Old Garrison Cemetery.
J/5312	F/L	McGILL George Edward	10-01-42	103 Sqn	1431	31-03-44 *Great Escape*; murdered. Buried Poznan Old Garrison Cemetery.
J/6144	F/L	WERNHAM MiD James Chrystall	8-06-42	405 Sqn	564	30-03-44 *Great Escape*; murdered. Buried Poznan Old Garrison Cemetery.
C/1631	F/L	LANGFORD MiD Patrick Wilson	28-07-42	16 OTU	710	31-03-44 *Great Escape*; murdered. Buried Poznan Old Garrison Cemetery.
J/10177	F/L	KIDDER MiD Gordon Arthur	13-10-42	150 Sqn	42822	29-03-44 *Great Escape*; murdered. Buried Poznan Old Garrison Cemetery.
R/92602	WO1	TURNER Alan Frederick	27-01-43	102 Sqn	27384	5-03-45 Died, possibly from natural causes, at Lamsdorf. Runnymede Memorial, panel 281.
R/126002	WO1	FOX Vincent Albert	9-03-43	7 Sqn	994	19-04-45 Killed in Typhoon attack. Buried Berlin 1939-1945 War Cemetery.
R/106758	WO1	DOUGLAS Robert Gordon	28-03-43	419 Sqn	897	19-04-45 Killed in Typhoon attack. Buried Berlin 1939-1945 War Cemetery.
R/87712	WO1	PERRY Keith Oliver	3-04-43	405 Sqn	N/K	23-08-43 Died, possibly from natural causes. Runnymede Memorial, panel 179.
J/9688	F/L	LARGE George Russell	12-06-43	408 Sqn	1502	16-04-45 Reported to have died whilst undergoing abdominal surgery in a Hamburg hospital. Buried Adegem Canadian War Cemetery.
R/145804	WO1	McDONALD John Swan	21-06-43	218 Sqn	204	19-03-45 Died at Fallingbostel. Buried Becklingen War Cemetery.
R/125451	WO1	PIXLEY Asa Nelson	9-07-43	408 Sqn	423	18-04-45 Died following admittance to hospital in Hamburg. Buried Hamburg Cemetery.
R/87930	WO1	RAMSDEN Samuel Smart	10-08-43	97 Sqn	1332	22-04-45 Killed in Mosquito attack near Barth. Buried in France at Choloy War Cemetery.
R/118348	Sgt	WOOD Edward Francis	23-08-43	158 Sqn	N/K	2-08-44 Died from natural causes at Muhlberg (Elbe). Buried Berlin 1939-1945 War Cemetery.
R/113624	WO1	MALLORY Herbert David	27-08-43	434 Sqn	222739	30-04-44 Struck from behind and killed by a Ju 88 making an ultra low pass over the exercise yard at Muhlberg (Elbe). Buried Berlin 1939-1945 War Cemetery.
J/11590	F/L	SPOFFORD George Lewis	26-11-43	101 Sqn	N/K	21-07-44 Died, possibly from natural causes, at Barth. Buried Berlin 1939-1945 War Cemetery.
R/65193	WO1	MacKENZIE Warren Ellwood	20-01-44	419 Sqn	874	19-04-45 Killed in Typhoon attack. Buried Berlin 1939-1945 War Cemetery.

J/9929	S/L	SALE DSO* DFC Douglas Julian	19-02-44	35 Sqn	None	20-03-44 Believed to have died from wounds, though not confirmed. Buried in France at Choloy War Cemetery.
J/89450	F/O	NICHOLLLS William Frederick	15-03-44	426 Sqn	2987	13-01-45 Died from tuberculosis at Gross Tychow. Runnymede Memorial, panel 279.
J/24034	F/L	WEY Edward George	30-03-44	426 Sqn	4117	31-03-45 Died from natural causes at Barth. Buried Berlin 1939-1945 War Cemetery.
J/88362	F/O	CROSSWELL Percy Bruce	22-04-44	429 Sqn	655	14-04-45 Shot while trying to escape from Luckenwalde on 13-04-45. Runnymede Memorial, panel 279.
J/3467	S/L	BLENKINSOP DFC Croix de Guerre [Belgium] Edward Weyman	27-04-44	405 Sqn	None	23-01-45 Joined the Belgian Resistance but, subsequently, captured and subjected to life in a forced labour camp. Incarcerated in Belsen concentration camp where he died from tuberculosis. Runnymede Memorial, panel 278.
J/24656	F/O	CLEMENT James McVicar	11-06-44	405 Sqn	None	9-08-44 Almost certain to have evaded capture before being caught and murdered in the vicinity of Tours, France. Buried St. Symphorten New Communal Cemetery, Indre-et-Loire.
J/28855	F/O	CARTER MiD Roy Edward	16-06-44	431 Sqn	None	9-07-44 Almost certain to have evaded capture, only to be caught at Tilburg, Holland, and murdered by the Gestapo. Runnymede Memorial, panel 245.
J/19162	F/O	BIRNIE Hugh Waldie	28-06-44	426 Sqn	None	22-08-44 Almost certain to have evaded capture, only to be murdered when apprehended. Runnymede Memorial, panel 245.
J/19863	F/O	JAMIESON Donald Sinclair	28-06-44	426 Sqn	None	22-08-44 From the same aircraft as F/O Birnie and suffered the same fate. Runnymede Memorial, panel 246.
R/223820	Sgt	DALGLISH William Logan	18-07-44	138 Sqn	None	6-08-44 Possibly evaded capture for a short period of time. Taken into military custody and murdered by being thrown over a cliff by a member of the Wehrmacht. Buried Beny-sur-Mer Canadian War Cemetery.
J/87265	P/O	HUGHES-GAMES Norman Edward	31-07-44	57 Sqn	7479	28-09-44 Died of Meningitis at Stalag Luft III at Sagan. Buried Poznan Old Garrison Cemetery.
R/171883	WO2	STEVENSON Leslie Howard	26-08-44	576 Sqn	757	27-12-44 Shot by a guard and fatally wounded at Barth. Runnymede Memorial, panel 255.
R/123313	F/S	SLACK Kenneth Earl Clifford	21-11-44	433 Sqn	1302	9-05-45 Drowned in the Elbe while attempting to save the life of his German guard. Runnymede Memorial, panel 282.

ROYAL NEW ZEALAND AIR FORCE

NZ40940	W/O	HOPE Lawrence Beresford Hamilton	8-11-41	75 Sqn	24510	19-04-45 Killed in Typhoon attack. Buried Berlin 1939-1945 War Cemetery.
NZ415041	F/S	TOWNROW Leonard Arthur	27-05-43	100 Sqn	None	24-04-44 Died from injuries in a Luftwaffe hospital nearly a year after being shot down on a raid to Essen. Buried in Holland at Leeuwarden Northern General Cemetery.
NZ402894	F/L	POHE MiD Poroku Patapu	22-09-43	51 Sqn	2433	31-03-44 *Great Escape*; murdered. Buried Poznan Old Garrison Cemetery.
NZ421792	F/L	TAYLOR DFC Owen Patrick Fewster	21-03-45	97 Sqn	N/K	Died from his spinal injuries at Sandbostel, south of Bremervorde. Buried Hanover War Cemetery.

POLISH AIR FORCE

P.781046	Sgt	CHRZANOWSKI Gustaw	7-11-41	300 Sqn	None	15-06-42 Died in hospital at Nice, France, while being treated for tuberculosis. Buried Caucada Cemetery, Military Section, Nice.
P.0243	F/L	KOLANOWSKI Wladzimierz Adam	7-11-41	301 Sqn	678	31-03-44 *Great Escape*; murdered. Buried Poznan Old Garrison Cemetery.
P.0913	F/L	MONDSCHEIN Jerzy Tomasz	7-11-41	304 Sqn	680	25-03-44 *Great Escape*; murdered. Buried Poznan Old Garrison Cemetery.
P.0740	F/O	PAWLUK Kazimierz	28-03-42	305 Sqn	23	31-03-44 *Great Escape*; murdered. Buried Poznan Old Garrison Cemetery.
P.781417	Sgt	RAJPOLD Czeslaw	25-06-42	18 OTU	N/K	26-08-43 Died; circumstances not known. Buried Berlin 1939-1945 War Cemetery.
P.0375	F/O	TOBOLSKI Pawel Wilhelm	25-06-42	301 Sqn	300	2-04-44 *Great Escape*; murdered. Buried Poznan Old Garrison Cemetery.
P.0109	F/L	KIEWNARSKI Antoni Wladyslaw	27-08-42	305 Sqn	42801	31-03-44 *Great Escape*; murdered. Buried Poznan Old Garrison Cemetery.
P.792624	Sgt	SKONIECZNY Jozef	25-11-42	300 Sqn	None	6-02-43 Sustained very serious burns. Believed to have suffered a massive heart attack, collapsed and died.

Note
Although thanked many times, due credit for supplying the cause of non-*Great Escape* deaths and burial details here shown goes to Betty Clements.

Each time an airman escaped from his prison camp the effect on the German military machine and the civil authorities was, generally, out of all proportion to the event itself. Considerable resources were tied down as searches were conducted and, of course, the longer the escapee managed to avoid being caught so the chance of a successful home run increased. These chances of success were always thin and everyone who went over the wire, tunnelled beneath it or employed some other ingenious means to make a bid for freedom were all too aware of the harsh penalties that might be imposed upon them if, and as so often happened, they were apprehended. For the most determined who wished to break free of the bonds of captivity, the consequences of dire punishment proved no barrier and, it has to be acknowledged, for the majority whose escape ended in capture the worst that happened to them was a spell in solitary confinement or to use the parlance of the time, a visit to the cooler. Nevertheless, as this appendix shows, many paid the ultimate price for having the audacity to put two fingers up at German authority and run for home, most being victims of frightful revenge meted out to 50 of the 76 Allied officers who tunnelled their way out of Stalag Luft III in March 1944 in what is now referred to as the *Great Escape*. As will be seen, 26 of the 50 had been shot down while flying with Bomber Command.

Postscript
At the eleventh hour Oliver Clutton-Brock has kindly alerted me to the fact that F/S Gordon Washbourne RAAF, who is commemorated in Part 8, survived when his 115 Lancaster was shot down on 7th-8th June 1944 (see the last entry on page 262 of Volume 5) and along with Sgt J E Parkinson was picked up by the French Resistance and taken to a house at Chatenay-Malabry in the south-west outskirts of Paris. Sgt Parkinson remained here for a few days but F/S Washbourne, along with some armed members of the Resistance, left for Paris on or about 9 June only to be apprehended. As is recorded in Volume 5, F/S Washbourne has no known grave. Although his passing does not fall within the strict parameters of this appendix, his death (and I am certain there were others) is a terrible reminder of the awful consequences that could befall any airman that had the misfortune to be picked up while trying to evade capture.

Sources and Bibliography

Principal Sources & Works Consulted

Air Historical Branch:
Casualty Indices

Commonwealth War Graves Commission:
Cemetery & Memorial registers, & website

Australian War Memorial Roll of Honour

The London Gazette:
Various Supplements

They Shall Grow Not Old: Les Allison & Harry Hayward; Commonwealth Air Training Plan Museum, 1991

For Your Tomorrow, Volume 1 1915-1942: Errol W. Martyn; Volplane Press, 1998
For Your Tomorrow, Volume 2 1943-1998: Errol W. Martyn; Volplane Press, 1999

Ksiega Lotnikow Polskich, Poleglych Zmarlych Izaginionych 1939-1946: Olgierd Cumft & Hubert Kazimierz Kujawa; Wydawnictwo Ministerstwa Obrony Narodowej, 1989

Memorial Books of No.1 & 5 Groups: Bomber Command, 1950
Memorial Books of No.2, 3, 8 & 100 Groups: Bomber Command, 1955

Footprints on the Sands of Time – RAF Bomber Command Prisoners of War in Germany 1939-1945: Oliver Clutton-Brock, Grub Street, 2003

Secondary Works Consulted

Angry Skies Across The Vale: Brian Kedward; Kedward, 2003
Avro Lancaster Roll of Honour 1942: Doug Cutherbertson, Cutherbertson, 2007
Based at Burn Mk II: Hugh Cawdron, Cawdron, 2001

Bomber Squadrons of the RAF and their Aircraft: Philip Moyes; Macdonald, 1964
Final Landings A Summary of RAF Aircraft and Combat Losses 1946-1949: Colin Cummings, Nimbus Publishing
For Valour The Air VCs: Chaz Bowyer; William Kimber, 1978
Lest We Forget – Bishopshalt School: Don Morgan; private publication
Lest We Forget – Ruislip, Northwood, Eastcote: Don Morgan; private publication
Night after Night – New Zealanders in Bomber Command: Max Lambert; Harper Collins (New Zealand) Ltd, 2005
Pilgrimages of Grace – A History of Croft Aerodrome: A. A. B. Todd; Todd, 1993
Royal Air Force Flying Training and Support Units: Ray Sturtivant; John Hamlin & James J. Halley; Air-Britain (Historians), 1997
Some of The Many – 77 Squadron 1939-1945, Roll of Honour: Roy Walker; Hollies Publications, 1995
Sparkhill Commercial School – Roll of Honour 1939-1945: Eric E. Rowley & Colin Lees; private publication
Sweeping The Skies – A History of No. 40 Squadron, RFC & RAF, 1916-56: David Gunby; The Pentland Press, 1995
Swift and Sure – Eighty Years of No. 51 Squadron: Keith S. Ford; Compaid Graphics, 1997
The Airmen of St. John's Beck Row – Roll of Honour; Peter & Maureen Wilson; Wilson, 1987
The Bomber Command War Diaries An Operational Reference Book 1939-1945: Martin Middlebrook & Chris Everitt Viking, 1985
The Squadrons of the Royal Air Force & Commonwealth 1918 - 1988: J. J. Halley, Air-Britain (Historians), 1988
The Story of RAF Edgehill, Locally Known as Shenington Aerodrome: Eric G. Kaye; Kaye, 1990
We Will Remember Them – 149 Squadron & 622 Squadron Roll of Honour 1939-1945: Peter & Maureen Wilson; Wilson, 1993
Wings Over York – The History of Ruffoth Airfield: Brian Mennell, Mennell, 2002
467 & 463 Squadrons RAAF: Frank Slack & Raymond Glynne-Owen; Slack/Owen

– *Further titles from Midland* –

RAF FIGHTER COMMAND LOSSES OF THE SECOND WORLD WAR
Norman Franks

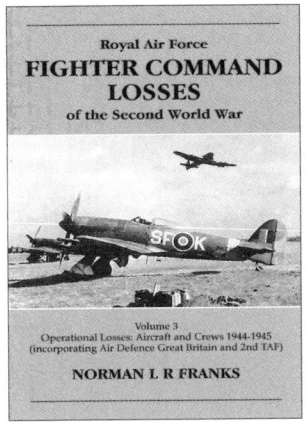

ROYAL AIR FORCE BOMBER COMMAND LOSSES of the SECOND WORLD WAR
W R Chorley

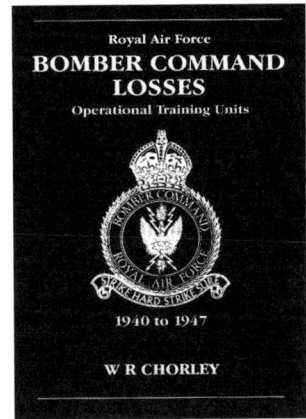

We hope you enjoyed this book . . .

Midland Publishing titles are edited and designed by an experienced and enthusiastic team of specialists.

Further titles are in preparation and we always welcome ideas from authors or readers for books they would like to see published.

In addition, our associate company, Midland Counties Publications, offers an exceptionally wide range of aviation, military, naval and transport books and DVDs for sale by mail-order around the world.

For a copy of the appropriate catalogue, or to order further copies of this book, and any of the titles mentioned on this or the following page, please write, telephone, fax or e-mail to:

Ian Allan Publishing
4 Watling Drive,
Hinckley, Leics,
LE10 3EY,
England
Tel: (+44) 01455 254 450
Fax: (+44) 01455 233 737
e-mail: midlandbooks@compuserve.com
www.ianallanpublishing.com

Following the Battle of France and the retreat through Dunkirk, Britain stood alone awaiting the inevitable onslaught from Germany. At the forefront of the UK's defence was Fighter Command and it was their Hurricanes, Spitfires, Blenheims and Defiants that became the world-famed 'Few' that managed to repulse the Luftwaffe in 'The Battle of Britain' during the summer of 1940.

Germany's failure to overcome the RAF and the decision to attack Russia, allowed Britain to consolidate, rebuild, go on the offensive, and after D-day, battle across Europe to the bitter end.

Between 1939-45 Fighter Command, ADGB and 2nd TAF lost over 5,000 aircrew. This work examines on a day-to-day basis the sacrifices made by these men during the desperate years of the war. The reasons and circumstances for the losses are given as crucial campaigns are enacted.

Available in 234 x 156mm sbk format:

Volume 1: 1939-41
Details 1,000 aircraft losses; 168pp
40 b/w pics 1 85780 286 1 **£12.99**

Volume 2: 1942-43
Details 1,800+ aircraft losses; 156pp
53 b/w pics 1 85780 075 3 **£12.95**

Volume 3: 1944-45
Details c.2,450 acft losses; 200pp
83 b/w pics 1 85780 093 1 **£14.95**

This highly acclaimed series identifies, on a day-by-day basis, the individual aircraft, crews and circumstances of each of the 10,000+ aircraft lost in the European Theatre of operations during the Second World War.

Appendices include loss totals by squadron and aircraft type each year; Group loss totals; Squadron bases, bomber OTU losses by unit and type, PoWs, escapers and evaders and the like.

Available in 234 x 156mm sbk format:

Volume 1: 1939-1940
160pp 0 904597 85 7 **£12.99**

Volume 2: 1941
224pp 0 904597 87 3 **£14.99**

Volume 3: 1942
318pp 0 904597 89 X **£16.99**

Volume 4: 1943
496pp 0 904597 90 3 **£18.99**

Volume 5: 1944
576pp 0 904597 91 1 **£23.99**

Volume 6: 1945
224pp 0 904597 92 X **£14.99**

Volume 7: OTUs 1940-1947
384pp 1 85780 132 6 **£18.99**

Volume 8: HCUs 1940-1947
272pp 1 85780 1563 **£16.99**

– *Further titles from Midland* –

BRITISH SECRET PROJECTS
Tony Buttler

A huge number of projects have been drawn by British companies over the last 50 years, but with few turned into hardware, little has been published about these fascinating 'might-have-beens'. This series makes extensive use of previously unpublished primary source material, much recently declassified. It gives an insight into a secret world where the public had little idea of what was going on, while at the same time presenting a coherent nationwide picture of military aircraft development and evolution. Each book includes many illustrations plus specially commissioned renditions of 'might-have-been' types in contemporary markings.

Available in 282 x 213mm hbk format:

Volume 1:
Jet Fighters since 1950
176pp, 130 b/w photos, 140 dwgs, 8pp of colour. 1 85780 095 8 **£24.95**

Volume 2:
Jet Bombers since 1949
224pp, 160 b/w photos, 3-view dwgs, 9pp of colour. 1 85780 130 X **£24.99**

Volume 3:
Fighters & Bombers 1935-1950
240pp, 228 b/w photos, c192 dwgs, 6pp of colour. 1 85780 179 2 **£29.99**

FARNBOROUGH: 100 YEARS OF BRITISH AVIATION
Peter J Cooper

Home to the famous biennial Farnborough Air Show, this Hampshire town has had a pivotal role in the history of British aviation from 1905 when flying first commenced there.

In 1908 His Majesty's Balloon Factory was set up. This was replaced by the Royal Aviation Factory, later renamed the Royal Aeronautical Establishment to differentiate it from the Royal Air Force. The RAE rapidly expanded and was the scene of many significant developments in British aviation for many decades. After the Second World War it played host to a considerable variety of aircraft, including a number of Axis types captured during the war. Farnborough's role as a development base continued after the war, although the name 'RAE' was to disappear when this part of Britain's defence establishment was reorganised. This led to the creation of DERA which was later partially privatised as QinetiQ. This is a fully illustrated history of Farnborough from 1905 onwards. It portrays in words and over 400 illustrations the airfield and the aircraft associated with it. In the course of his research, the author has unearthed a large number of previously unpublished images which appear in the book.

Hbk, 282 x 213 mm, 208 pages
173 colour, 200 b/w photos
1 85780 239 X **£24.99**

RAF COASTAL COMMAND LOSSES Volume 1
Aircraft and Crew Losses 1939-1941
Ross McNeill

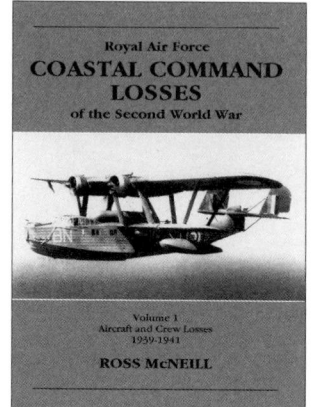

When war broke out in September 1939, the UK's armed forces were ill-prepared. RAF Coastal Command was little more than a reconnaissance force, with less than 300 aircraft (only 170 being operational) with which to combat the menace of the German cruisers, U-boats and magnetic mines that posed a real threat to Britain's very existence.

The invasion of Norway and the low countries, the need to provide 'weather' flights, photo-recce and air-sea rescue from Iceland to the Azores, almost stretched resources to breaking point, but improvements in armament, aircraft, training and U-boat detecting methods began to turn things around, and eventually closed the 'Atlantic Gap'. These were costly times for Coastal Command, by the end of 1941 its constituent units had lost 1,006 aircraft and suffered 2,026 fatal casualties.

This book records the losses on a day-by-day basis, listing the units, crews, aircraft types and service serial numbers, unit code letters, and circumstances behind each loss, where known. Appendices include summaries of losses by type, group and squadron, as well as details of unit bases, PoWs, escapers, evaders, and internees.

Sbk, 234 x 156 mm, 208 pages
32 b/w photographs
1 85780 128 8 **£16.99**